A Compendium of
the War of the Rebellion

Volume I

A Compendium of the War of the Rebellion

by
Frederick H. Dyer

With a New Introduction by
Bell Irvin Wiley

Volume I

NUMBER AND ORGANIZATION OF
THE ARMIES OF THE UNITED STATES

NEW YORK • THOMAS YOSELOFF • LONDON

Special Contents of This Edition
© 1959 by Sagamore Press, Inc.

Thomas Yoseloff, *Publisher*
11 East 36th Street
New York 16, N. Y.

Thomas Yoseloff Ltd.
123 New Bond Street
London W 1, England

Library of Congress Catalog Card Number: 59-12963

Printed in the United States of America

INTRODUCTION

HE DES MOINES *Register and Leader* of April 26, 1908 described Frederick H. Dyer's then forthcoming *Compendium of the War of the Rebellion* as "the most monumental war record ever undertaken and successfully completed by a single individual." Ten months later, on the eve of the book's publication, the Cedar Rapids *Republican* of February 14, 1909 stated: "Nothing of the kind has ever before been attempted. The records of the British War office show nothing of this character in the way of a compendium of the deeds of valor wrought by their soldiers; nor has the French government a work of similar character." These comments have the tone of journalistic fanfare but actually they are statements based on fact. And they are as valid now as they were fifty years ago. "Dyer's *Compendium*," as this book has come to be known by Civil War specialists, is truly unique. It is outstanding from the standpoints of organization, scope, comprehensiveness and richness in detail. It is unquestionably the most valuable Civil War reference work compiled by one author.

One of the most impressive characteristics of the work is its massiveness. The original manuscript consisted of 4,025 typed sheets. The printed version ran to 1,796 large pages (nine by twelve inches), most of which were filled with two columns of small, closely set type. The single volume of the original edition, bound in morocco and pebbled cloth, was about the size of the average unabridged dictionary, and weighed ten pounds.

The original edition consisted of 4,500 copies and was printed and bound for Dyer by the Torch Press of Cedar Rapids, Iowa. The price was ten dollars. A news story released shortly before publication stated that 1,032 reams of paper and 675 pounds of ink were required for the printing and that in the binding 6,770 feet of leather and 750 yards of cloth were used. It is not surprising that this notice, published in a Cedar Rapids paper, closed with the proud observation: "The making up of a book of this size and magnitude. . . has been a tremendous . . . [undertaking]. It is a great honor to the city to be able to say that a volume of this kind was done within its limits."

The book comprehends only the Union forces but it contains much information bearing on the Confederacy. It consists of three major parts and a comprehensive index of forty-five pages. Part I, numbering 578 pages, treats of numbers and organization. This section begins with a summary of enlistments and losses, originally prepared in the Adjutant General's office in 1885. Dyer does not adjust the total of 2,778,304 enlistments shown in this table to eliminate repeaters as does William F. Fox in *Regimental Losses in the Civil War*. Nor does his figure for aggregate losses (359,258) take cognizance of additional deaths compiled by the Adjutant General after 1885 and noted in *Battles and Leaders of the Civil War*, IV, 797, which raised the aggregate of Federal losses to 360,222.

The second section of Part I gives all the national cemeteries and their location. The third section is a list, arranged by states, of 2,494 regiments, 126 battalions, and 939 batteries and independent companies. This is represented as a complete list, but as one reviewer noted, it omits a few units the service of which is mentioned in the *Official Records*, including the First Colorado Cavalry (militia), the First East Florida and the First State Capital Guards of Kentucky. Moreover, some units which served under two different designations are counted twice, and a few are included which failed to complete their organization and never became a part of the Union Army.

The fourth section of Part I lists the nine hundred Federal regiments that lost fifty or more men in combat. These regiments are grouped by states and the losses of each are given in terms of killed and mortally wounded. This tabulation shows that the First Maine Heavy Artillery, with 423 killed or mortally wounded, had the heaviest combat losses of any Union regiment, and that the Fifth New Hampshire topped infantry regiments with an aggregate of 295 deaths from hostile action. Among other infantry regiments experiencing unusually heavy battle fatalities, and the aggregate for each in killed and mortally wounded were: Fifth New Hampshire, 295; Eighty-third Pennsylvania, 282; Seventh Wisconsin, 281; Fifth Michigan, 263; Twentieth Massachusetts, 260; Sixty-ninth New York, 259; Twenty-eighth Massachusetts, 250; One Hundred and Fifth Pennsylvania, 245; Fifteenth New Jersey, 240; and Forty-ninth Ohio, 202. The Negro regiment which suffered the most battle deaths was the Seventy-ninth United States Colored Infantry, whose losses in killed and mortally wounded aggregated 188.

Other sections of Part I include an alphabetical list of some 7,800 persons who headed brigades and larger organizations, along with the commands held by each, and a regimental index which lists by state all cavalry, artillery and infantry regiments, and for each gives the date of organization, higher headquarters to which it was assigned, and date on which it was mustered out of Federal service. The information contained in these indexes is repeated in the longer regimental histories given in Part III. Dyer probably justified the duplication on the ground that many users would want only a few basic facts about a regiment's service while others would desire a detailed summary.

The final and much the longest section of Part I is a remarkably full tabulation of army organizations. Here are listed all the departments, armies, corps, divisions and brigades on the Union side, along with the assignments, components and commanders.

Part II of the *Compendium*, covering 413 pages, is a record of Civil War engagements and losses, arranged both chronologically and by state. Events listed aggregate 10,455 and are classified as actions, affairs, assaults, battles, campaigns, captures, combats, engagements, expeditions, occupations, operations, raids, reconnaissances, scouts and sieges. Obviously some duplication results from this arrangement, as for example when a battle and the campaign or expedition of which it is a part each is listed as a separate event. Elimination of duplication would probably reduce the total number of events to about 8,700, which is the number listed in the *Index to Battles, Campaigns, Etc.* issued by the War Department in connection with the *Official Records.* The bulk of Part II (332 out of 413 pages) consists of a chronological listing of events by state, which gives the date, the character of the action, the place and the Federal units involved.

Part III, consisting of 759 pages, bears the heading "Regimental Histories," but the sketches, running to more than 3,550, include battalions, batteries and separate companies as well as regiments. The length of these histories ranges from a few lines in the instance of short term units, such as the Fourteenth Regiment Missouri Home Guard Infantry to a full page or more for organizations having extended and varied service, such as the Second Illinois Cavalry and the First Ohio Cavalry Regiments. As a general rule the history tells where the unit was organized, when it was mustered into Federal service, the higher headquarters to which it was assigned, areas in which it served, actions in which it participated, changes in its designation and status, date that it was mustered out, and the number of officers and men who died from battle causes and from disease.

The information contained in Part III was laboriously gleaned from hundreds of scattered sources. Archivists, librarians and historians have been spared countless hours of research by referring to it. The usefulness and value of Part III is so great that no other justification would have been needed for republication of the *Compendium* than to make these unit histories available to the many persons who have the Civil War as a field of special interest. It is regrettable that unit histories have not been similarly compiled for the Confederate side.

The author of this stupendous work was an unusual person. Pension records in the National Archives show that Dyer was born July 2, 1849 at Greenville, Connecticut. His parents died during his childhood. In July, 1863, shortly after his fourteenth birthday, Dyer and a companion ran away from school to join the army. The companion "changed his mind at the last moment," but Dyer was determined to become a soldier. As a safeguard against return to school, he assumed the last name of his fellow fugitive, and to overcome the barrier against the recruiting of minors without the consent of parents or guardians, he persuaded the companion's aunt to sign papers consenting to his enlistment. As a result of this maneuvering, "Frederick H. Metzger" was signed up for three years as a drummer boy in Company H Seventh Connecticut Infantry Regiment at Hartford, Connecticut on July 25, 1863, by Lieutenant John Thompson, who was temporarily at home on recruiting service. Two days later Surgeon Isaac D. Porter, after examining the recruit's ears, eyes, nose, chest and other critical parts, and after obtaining negative responses to such questions as: "Have you ever been sick?" "Have you ever had fits?" "Are you subject to piles?" "Are you in the habit of drinking?" and "Have you ever had the horrors?" certified his physical soundness and sent him on his way rejoicing. A short time later "Metzger," along with other recruits, joined the Seventh Connecticut, a unit which had been in existence since September, 1861, at Morris Island, South Carolina.

Records in the National Archives and the unit history contained in the *Compendium* show that the Seventh Connecticut performed miscellaneous services along the coast of South Carolina and Florida from August, 1863, until April, 1864. It participated in the capture of Forts Wagner and Gregg on Morris Island September 7, 1863 and in the Battle of Olustee (or Ocean Pond), Florida, February 20, 1864.

The regiment was transferred to Virginia in April, 1864, where it took part in Butler's unsuccessful campaign against Petersburg and Richmond. It participated in the fights at Drewry's Bluff, May 14-16 and Bermuda Hundred, June 14. In December, 1863, the Seventh Connecticut swapped its muzzle-loading Enfield rifles for seven-shot Spencer carbines, and thus became one of the few infantry regiments of the Civil War to be equipped with this new and terribly effective weapon. After the engagement at Bermuda Hundred a member of the regiment wrote his homefolk: "The Rebs made 3 charges on us but we stood up to the rack with our seven shooters . . . and piled the Rebs in heaps in front of us. . . . The Rebs hate our guns they call them the Yanks 7 Devils they say the Yankeys stand up there with their G. D. coffy mills wind em up in the morning, run all day shoot a thousand times . . . they are a good rifel."

The Seventh Connecticut moved to the north side of the James River late in September where it participated in the battles of Chaffin's Farm, Darbytown Road and other minor engagements. On November 2 the regiment was sent to New York "to suppress any riot that might occur at the [presidential] election . . . but as every thing went off quietly," the unit returned to Virginia on November 17. It took part in the successful assault on Fort Fisher, January 15, 1865, and the capture of Wilmington, February 22. The regiment remained on duty in the Wilmington-Goldsboro area until summer and was mustered out of the service at New Haven, Connecticut, on July 20, 1865. During the war 11 of its officers and 157 enlisted men were killed or mortally wounded and 4 officers and 192 enlisted men died of disease, making an aggregate loss of 364.

Little is known of Dyer's personal war experience beyond the meager information provided by the service record of "Frederick H. Metzger" in the National Archives. In 1913 Dyer wrote the Commissioner of Pensions that he was "never absent for a day" during his two years in the army. If he referred to abscence without leave, his claim is sustained by his service record, which shows him present throughout his service save for one short leave at St. Helena Island, South Carolina, in the fall of 1863. The company muster roll for July and August, 1864, shows that he was charged with $1.57 for two haversacks and a canteen, which he probably had lost. He reimbursed the government for the amount due. Like most soldiers, he was chronically in debt to the sutler, the Civil War prototype of the post exchange. In August, 1864, he owed $4.00. At the end of each of the next three bi-monthly pay periods his indebtedness was $2.00, and at the time he was mustered out of the service it was $20.00. The sutler had no occasion for concern, since the amounts due him were regularly deducted from his debtors' wages on payday.

On December 18, 1864, Dyer applied for a furlough, citing as a basis for his request his desire to visit a sister in New London, Connecticut, his "only near relative . . . [who is now] very sick and is not expected to recover." The fate of the sister, who is not mentioned in any other available records, is not known, but Dyer's application, though approved by the commanders of his company, regiment, brigade, division and corps, was turned down by Edwin O. Ord, Commanding General, Department of the James, on December 21.

In his indorsement of the request for leave, the Commander of the Second Brigade, First Division, Twenty-fourth Corps, stated: "Metzger is a good lad and may be trusted," and there is nothing in Dyer's record to suggest that he was anything but a solid character and a dutiful soldier.

When he returned to civilian life, Dyer resumed the use of his real name. In 1884, he wrote the Adjutant General, explaining the circumstances of of his enlistment and requesting that the records be "so amended or altered as to show the fact that Fred H. Dyer is the Fred H. Metzger who served in the 7th Conn." The Adjutant General replied that the records could not be changed, but that on receipt of affidavits proving that Frederick H. Dyer and Frederick H. Metzger were one and the same person, this evidence would be placed on file in his office.

Dyer apparently neglected to send in the required evidence. But twenty-seven years later, in August, 1911, when he applied for a pension he was required to submit an affidavit showing that he and the Frederick H. Metzger who served as musician in the Seventh Connecticut were identical. William H. Pierpont of New Haven, formerly a captain in the Seventh Connecticut and after the war an intimate associate of Dyer, stated on oath that he knew the pension applicant and the drummer boy to be the same person. The pension was granted, but not until the applicant had presented detailed information about his background, his family and his post-war activities. Dyer's case affords a striking example of the historical value of Civil War pension records.

After discharge from the army, Dyer attended Russell Military Institute and Hopkins Grammar School in New Haven. When he was eighteen he became a "commercial traveler," a vocation which he followed for about fourteen years. During this period he resided successively in New York, Philadelphia, Pittsburgh and Washington, Pennsylvania. While residing at Washington, Pennsylvania he and H. Frank Ward organized the firm of "Dyer and Ward—Printers, Stationers and Binders" and operated this business from 1881 to 1885. Dyer then moved to Detroit, where he lived until 1901. He resided in Brooklyn during the period 1901-1903 and then moved to Cleveland. His family remained in Cleveland until May, 1906, when they moved to Pittsburgh. Dyer established a separate residence in Des Moines, Iowa in 1903 or 1904 to begin intensive work on the *Compendium*. He remained in Des Moines until 1912, though he presumably made occasional visits to his family during this period. Letterheads used during the Des Moines sojourn bear the designation "The Dyer Publishing Company" but this firm seems to have been no more than the office in which Dyer wrote and promoted the *Compendium*.

In 1912 Dyer moved with his family to Boston, Massachusetts. He died in that city on September 21, 1917, in his sixty-eighth year of "coronary sclerosis" and was buried in Mount Hope Cemetery.

He was survived by Georgia Dickerson Dyer, aged 69, whom he married on January 6, 1875 in Bridgeville, Delaware. To this union seven children were born. All but three of the children died in infancy and only one, Thelma, born April 21, 1889, outlived the father. In 1915, Thelma was residing in Pittsburgh; nothing is known of her subsequent career. After Dyer's death, his widow moved to Wilkinsburg, Pennsylvania. She died there October 27, 1941.

A few months before the publication of the *Compendium* a newspaper reporter described Dyer as "fat, round and jolly," and possessed of "an inexhaustible fund of cheerfulness and good nature." When applying for a pension in 1911, Dyer specified his height as 5 feet, 6 inches; weight, 228; complexion, fair; eyes, blue; and hair, brown. Photographs taken about the time the *Compendium* was published reveal a portly figure, with a well-shaped head, round face and luxuriant mustache. Dyer must have been a personable man, for he held numerous positions in patriotic societies and for a time was Commander of the Pennsylvania Department of the Grand Army of the Republic.

Preparation of the *Compendium* extended over a period of about forty years. Shortly after Dyer joined the Grand Army of the Republic in 1867, his friends and associates began to call on him for information about the units in which they had served. Soon he began collecting data about Civil War engagements and organizations for various patriotic societies. His work as a commercial traveler brought him into contact with many ex-soldiers, veterans' organizations and state officials, and he apparently used these connections to build up his store of facts and figures. He became something of a "walking encyclopedia." A Des Moines journalist who interviewed him in the spring of 1908 stated: "It used to be a favorite trick of his to stand up in an audience of 500 or 1,000 old soldiers and challenge any man to name a regiment whose record of service he could not give. In his work he made the personal acquaintance of practically every important military man in the country, and he has had correspondence upon statistical and other matters with hundreds of them."

The evolution of the idea of writing a book and the manner in which the project developed were explained thus by Dyer himself in 1908:

"I hadn't been at this work very long before the idea struck me that a record of the officers of the war would be of value, giving their service, commands, battles, and so on, and in connection with my statistical work [for individuals and patriotic societies] I began to collect material for such a complete record. . . .

"The deeper I got into the thing the more I became convinced that someone ought to go still further and prepare a record of all the regiments and other organizations engaged in the war. Without any particular thought that I would ever get together such a compendium, I began to accumulate material along this line also. . . . [Later] I concluded that the compendium, if one was ever prepared, ought to be absolutely complete, and give all the information extant about all the campaigns, battles, actions, skirmishes, etc. of the war. Again, without any definite idea that I would ever undertake the compilation of such a volume, I accumulated still more material as I visited different capitals and dug into the various records of the war, state and national.

"I used to meet prominent military men who would tell me that I ought to get my material into book form. General Sherman told me that such a compendium would be invaluable and ought to be published; so did other authorities on military matters. . . .

"And so, after years of this sort of thing, this indefinite idea of a complete compendium became definite . . . and I put down in black and white a plan for working it out. I submitted this to many men of judgment until I felt that I had it absolutely perfect.

"Well, I was up against the doing of it at last, and then I hesitated.

"There were so many reasons why I should not go on—the time necessary, the expense, the enoromous amount of work involved. I had to make my living and I couldn't see my way altogether clear. . . . I suppose I was in this position for several years, not entirely inactive, for I kept on gathering more facts and figures and classifying them.

"Five years ago I put aside all ifs and ands and went at it. I brought my boxes and trunks and bags of material to Des Moines and waded into them.

"Well, here's my pile of manuscript—thousands of sheets, millions of words, involving the examination of 10,000,000 names and dates, every line of it prepared by myself without the aid of a secretary or even a stenographer. I hope that it is worth the while."

In this statement Dyer was not very specific about the sources consulted in preparing the *Compendium*. He apparently made little if any use of the records on file in the War Department at Washington. When a Kansas librarian wrote the Adjutant General in April, 1908, asking about the authenticity of Dyer's forthcoming book, she was informed that "nothing whatever is known in the War Department concerning the publication." This reply was based on an inquiry circulated among persons of many years' service in the War Department, including Joseph W. Kirkley, who was the principal civilian employed in the publication of the Army's *Official Records*

After the conclusion of hostilities, the War Department turned over to the Northern states muster rolls and other records bearing on the service of their troops, and Dyer seems to have made considerable use of materials on file in the state capitals, as well as the rosters and other publications issued by the state adjutant generals. He drew heavily on the *Official Records of the Union and Confederate Armies*, as well as sundry miscellaneous compilations issued by the War Department while his work was in preparation. These included *Chronological List of Battles, Engagements, Skirmishes, During the Rebellion of 1861* and *The War of the Rebellions Official Records of the Union and Confederate Armies, Series I, Index to Battles, Campaigns.*

Works such as *Battles and Leaders of the Civil War* and Frank Moore's *Rebellion Record* probably yielded much information. The many unit histories issued during the forty years following the war were another source of information. But these did not exist for many units, and some that were available left much to be desired in both accuracy and comprehensiveness. Much of the information contained in the "Regimental Histories" section of the *Compendium* appears to have been gleaned from unpublished sources.

How reliable is the *Compendium*? In attempting to answer this important question it should be stated first that no work which treats of such "facts" as the time when a person became an officer and the periods of his various commands, the date on which a unit was organized or disbanded, and the number of deaths resulting from a given battle, can be absolutely accurate. Determination of these "facts" involves not only judicious use of sources but also requires exercise of arbitrary judgments. Does a person become an officer when he is commissioned, when he takes the oath of office, when he reports for duty or when he is confirmed by the Senate? Does a regiment come into being when it is mustered in as a state organization or when it enters the Federal service? Is a man who dies from battle injuries a year after they were incurred to be included among the mortally wounded of the engagement in which he was wounded? These are some of the problems which enter into the compilation of military "facts."

Dyer put an enormous amount of time and effort into the preparation of the *Compendium*. According to the Des Moines *Register and Leader* of April 26, 1908: "He stuck to his work with a dogged determination that meant a sort of heroism that not many understand. For five years he kept at his desk leaving it only to eat a little and to sleep a little. He was at it before breakfast, he kept at it until after midnight. He isolated himself in his room for weeks at a stretch. . . . Seven times he went over his list of battles to make sure that nothing had been omitted and that no mistakes had been made in dates, that the list of killed had been properly reported and each time this revision took him seven months."

The Cedar Rapids *Daily Republican* of June 11, 1908, reported: "For the last five years . . . in a single room, surrounded by his desks and tables, his piles of papers and the ever convenient typewriter, he has labored continuously, knowing little difference between night and day and between Saturday and Sunday. He has been seated conveniently near to his bed, which was located in close proximity to his chair. Aside from a few hours each week, which it was absolutely essential that he should have in the open air for health's sake, he has toiled unceasingly."

The *Compendium* obviously was the work of a dedicated man, and the sense of mission that motivated the author was conducive to accuracy in its preparation. Another influence working to the same end was Dyer's realization that the book would be carefully examined by veterans who had first-hand knowledge of the content and who would be quick to call him to task for errors. Finally, the book was a commercial venture in which the author had a tremendous stake, and to sell, it had to win the confidence of a large group of informed and critical readers.

The *Compendium* was well received when it made its first appearance. One past commander-in-chief of the Grand Army of the Republic rated it as next in historical importance to the *Official Records* and praised it for "accuracy, system and completeness," while another stated: "I have tested it by an examination of Regimental records in which I am particularly interested and it is complete, compact and correct." Colonel Oran Perry of Indiana wrote Dyer: "While Adjutant General of this state I purchased for office use your *Compendium*. It has never been equalled and never will be surpassed. . . . I had occasion to follow the wanderings of my old regiment, the 69th Indiana, and was surprised at the accuracy with which the story was told." One of the most impressive tributes came from Colonel George W. Crosley, Historian of the Iowa Adjutant General's Department "I have, perhaps, had occasion to give the work more thorough examination than any one who has not been engaged in the compilation of military history . . . [as] I have for some years been engaged in the preparation of a work entitled *Roster and Record of Iowa Soldiers in the War of the Rebellion*. . . . I have availed myself of every source of official information in order to make the work as complete and comprehensive as possible. I can therefore have a better appreciation of the immense amount of labor you have devoted to the preparation of your *Compendium*. I regard it as far and away the most valuable work of its kind: . . Very many of the statistics which it contains cannot be found elsewhere. No general reader of history who desires the most accurate information obtainable should be without it."

The anonymous authority who reviewed the *Compendium* in the *American Historical Review* of July, 1910, pointed out some omissions and repetitions, and cited a few instances in which he considered the statistics of Fox and Phisterer to be more valid than those of Dyer. But, he concluded: "These comparisons serve to show rather the comprehensiveness of the book under review than to point out defects which will in any important particular mislead the student who uses its great array of facts. The work is a valuable addition to the literature of the Civil War."

The *Compendium* has weathered well the test of time. Archivists, librarians and historians who have had occasion to refer to it to any considerable extent have found it highly useful and generally reliable.

Soon after the *Compendium* was completed, a newspaper man who had recently visited the author in his study wrote: "He says that when he dies he doesn't care for a monument. He doesn't need it. His book will stand for his life long after the crumbling [of] any marble that might be raised for him." Republication of the *Compendium,* fifty years after its first appearance, in a more durable binding, a more wieldly form and a larger edition should do much to perpetuate the memory of Dyer and his magnificent achievement. Perhaps as the Civil War Centennial activities get under way throughout the country some historically minded organization in Connecticut, Iowa or the nation's capital will consider it appropriate to erect and dedicate a marble monument to this truly remarkable man who professed no interest in such memorials. If he were still alive he would doubtless be pleased by the well-deserved tribute.

During the presentation of this introduction I have received the kindly assistance of many people. I am particularly indebted to William J. Petersen, Superintendent of the State Historical Society of Iowa; Mildred E. Wilson, Librarian of the Iowa State Department of Archives and History; Mrs. M. C. Wheelwright of Des Moines; the Honorable Fred Schwengel, Iowa Congressman and fellow member of the President's Civil War Centennial Commission; Clyde C. Walton, Director, Illinois State Historical Library; and Milton E. Lord and Bradford M. Hill of the Boston Public Library. I am under very special obligation to members of the staff of the National Archives, and particularly to Dr. Dallas Irvine, who went to great trouble in digging out pertinent materials and who gave me the benefit of his abundant knowledge of Civil War records in my effort to determine the method of Dyer's research and the general quality of his work.

BELL IRVIN WILEY

Emory University
July 1, 1959

FOREWORD

HIS BOOK is the result of many years study and tabulation of the Official records of the War of the Rebellion, supplemented by authentic information from all reliable and available sources. Every book or work treating of that great struggle, has been studied and compared. State records, reports of the Adjutants General of the several States, Registers, Regimental Histories, and all reports and documents issued by the United States government or State Military Bureaus, have been carefully examined and matter there found collated, and after verification, added to the work. There has been a dearth of official information regarding certain statistics and data of great interest and value to both the participant in that great struggle and to the student who wishes details in connected form. The Official Records of the War, a monumental collection, is wonderfully deficient in many particulars, and is practically impossible to use except by a specialist. Its arrangement is such that only those familiar with it from the beginning are able to use it with benefit. Its many series, its various departments, its incomprehensible indices and its continued reference to one or more books in dealing with any subject, are beyond the average reader's ability to grasp. To remedy this for the one seeking information, to gather all relating to each subject, whether of statistics or events, into a connected and complete whole, to digest the voluminous history of the war, has been the object of the compiler.

The work is divided into three parts: Part I—Being devoted to vital and various statistics of value and interest, and to the formation of the various Armies and Departments of the war, the troops assigned to and serving with each, and their various Commanders from beginning to end.

Part II—Records the various Campaigns, Battles, Engagements, Skirmishes, and the important events and operations, showing Union troops engaged in each event, and losses sustained, where such was officially reported. This part is arranged first, alphabetically as a whole, then alphabetically and chronologically by States, thus making it easy to find any particular event.

Part III—Presents a concise history of every Regiment, Battalion, Battery or other organization mustered in by the several States and Territories, and by the United States. This part is arranged by States alphabetically, the troops of each State in numerical order beginning with Cavalry, following with Artillery, Heavy and Light, Engineers, Sharpshooters and Infantry.

Those who have furnished valuable information for this compilation are so many as to preclude special mention by name, but to them all my heartfelt acknowledgements are herewith extended, and the result is dedicated to the memory of all my Comrades, fallen or surviving, who participated in the events here recorded.

DES MOINES, IOWA.   FREDERICK H. DYER.

TABLE OF CONTENTS

PART I

Number and Organization of the Armies of the United States

      ***For fuller details see Index to Departments before Eastern and Western Departments and Armies.

PART II

Chronological Record of the Campaigns, Battles, Engagements, Actions, Combats, Sieges, Skirmishes, Etc., in the United States, 1861 to 1865

PART III

REGIMENTAL HISTORIES

Illustrations and Maps

A section of illustrations and maps appears in Volume II after page 696.

PART I.

---

*Number and Organization of the Armies
of the United States*

Summary of Troops Furnished by the Several States and Territories During the War of the Rebellion

STATES AND TERRITORIES.	White Troops.	Sailors and Marines.	Colored Troops.	Indian Nations.	Aggregate.	Total Deaths, All Causes.
Alabama	2,578	......	......	.....	2,578	345
Arkansas	8,289	......	......	.....	8,289	1,713
California	15,725	......	......	.....	15,725	573
Colorado	4,903	......	......	.....	4,903	323
Connecticut	51,937	2,163	1,784	.....	55,864	5,354
Dakota	206	......	......	.....	206	6
Delaware	11,236	94	954	.....	12,284	882
District of Columbia	11,912	1,353	3,269	.....	16,534	290
Florida	1,290	......	......	.....	1,990	215
Georgia	......	......	......	.....	......	15
Illinois	255,057	2,224	1,811	.....	259,092	34,834
Indiana	193,748	1,078	1,537	.....	196,363	26,672
Iowa	75,797	5	440	.....	76,242	13,001
Kansas	18,069	......	2,080	.....	20,149	2,630
Kentucky	51,743	314	23,703	.....	75,760	10,774
Louisiana	5,224	......	......	.....	5,224	945
Maine	64,973	5,030	104	.....	70,107	9,398
Maryland	33,995	3,925	8,718	.....	46,638	2,982
Massachusetts	122,781	19,983	2,966	.....	146,730	13,942
Michigan	85,479	498	1,387	.....	87,364	14,753
Minnesota	23,913	3	104	.....	24,020	2,584
Mississippi	545	......	......	.....	545	78
Missouri	100,616	151	8,344	.....	109,111	13,885
Nebraska	3,157	......	......	.....	3,157	239
Nevada	1,080	......	......	.....	1,080	33
New Hampshire	32,930	882	125	.....	33,937	4,882
New Jersey	67,500	8,129	1,185	.....	76,814	5,754
New Mexico	6,561	......	......	.....	6,561	277
New York	409,561	35,164	4,125	.....	448,850	46,534
North Carolina	3,156	......	......	.....	3,156	360
Ohio	304,814	3,274	5,092	.....	313,180	35,475
Oregon	1,810	......	......	.....	1,810	45
Pennsylvania	315,017	14,307	8,612	.....	337,936	33,183
Rhode Island	19,521	1,878	1,837	.....	23,236	1,321
Tennessee	31,092	......	......	.....	31,092	8,777
Texas	1,965	......	......	.....	1,965	141
Vermont	32,549	619	120	.....	33,288	5,224
Virginia	......	......	......	.....	......	42
Washington Territory	964	......	......	.....	964	22
West Virginia	31,872	133	196	.....	32,068	4,017
Wisconsin	91,029	......	165	.....	91,327	12,301
Indian Nations	......	......	......	3,530	3,530	1,018
Regular Army	......	......	......	.....	......	5,798
Colored Troops	......	......	*99,337	.....	99,337	**36,847
Veteran Volunteers	......	......	......	.....	......	106
U. S. Volunteers***	......	......	......	.....	......	243
U. S. Sharpshooters and Engineers	......	......	......	.....	......	552
Veteran Reserves	......	......	......	.....	......	1,672
Generals and Staff	......	......	......	.....	......	239
Miscellaneous—Bands, etc	......	......	......	.....	......	232
	2,494,592	101,207	178,975	3,530	2,778,304	359,528

*Colored Troops recruited in the Southern States. **Includes all the deaths in the 178,975 Colored Troops.
***Ex-Confederate Soldiers.

Eighty-six thousand seven hundred and twenty-four drafted men paid commutation and were exempted from service.

Summary of Losses During the War of the Rebellion

STATES AND TERRITORIES.	Killed and Mortally Wounded.	Died of Disease.	Died as Prisoners of War.	Deaths from Accident, etc.	Deaths, All Causes Except Battle.	Total Deaths.
Alabama	50	228	22	5	40	345
Arkansas	305	1,254	8	25	121	1,713
California	108	344	.....	62	59	573
Colorado	153	120	.....	25	25	323
Connecticut	1,947	2,542	526	101	238	5,354
Dakota	2	4	.....	.....	.....	6
Delaware	383	356	75	21	47	882
District of Columbia	41	150	44	10	45	290
Florida	18	189	.....	.....	8	215
Georgia	.....	13	.....	.....	2	15
Illinois	9,884	21,065	1,721	1,028	1,126	34,834
Indiana	7,243	16,663	1,152	791	853	26,672
Iowa	3,540	8,498	515	227	221	13,001
Kansas	737	1,638	36	104	115	2,630
Kentucky	2,478	6,383	860	454	599	10,774
Louisiana	214	624	15	36	56	945
Maine	3,184	5,257	541	118	298	9,393
Maryland	909	1,160	647	98	168	2,982
Massachusetts	6,115	5,530	1,483	257	557	13,942
Michigan	4,448	8,269	1,268	339	429	14,753
Minnesota	626	1,677	159	43	79	2,584
Mississippi	3	66	.....	1	8	78
Missouri	3,317	9,243	225	487	613	13,885
Nebraska	35	159	1	23	21	239
Nevada	2	29	.....	1	1	33
New Hampshire	1,903	2,427	294	76	182	4,882
New Jersey	2,578	2,415	419	134	208	5,754
New Mexico	73	144	.....	19	41	277
New York	19,085	19,835	4,710	914	1,990	46,534
North Carolina	43	216	49	3	49	360
Ohio	11,588	19,365	2,356	1,168	998	35,475
Oregon	11	21	.....	7	6	46
Pennsylvania	15,265	11,782	4,119	636	1,381	33,183
Rhode Island	460	648	84	69	60	1,321
Tennessee	744	4,086	1,150	375	422	6,777
Texas	12	101	1	6	21	141
Vermont	1,809	2,597	486	70	262	5,224
Virginia	10	16	13	2	1	42
Washington	.....	12	.....	5	5	22
West Virginia	1,247	1,878	617	150	125	4,017
Wisconsin	3,802	7,464	604	212	219	12,301
Indian Nations	107	775	.....	10	126	1,018
Regular Army	2,283	2,552	540	197	116	5,798
Colored Troops	2,894	29,658	98	576	3,621	36,847
Veteran Volunteers	1	82	.....	14	9	106
U. S. Volunteers*	12	202	.....	11	18	243
U. S. Sharpshooters	263	247	25	6	11	552
Veteran Reserves	27	1,424	.....	131	90	1,672
Generals and Staffs	85	142	1	10	1	239
Miscellaneous—Bands, etc.	16	200	2	1	13	232
	110,070	199,720	24,866	9,058	15,814	359,528

*Ex-Confederates.

A STATISTICAL EXHIBIT

Of Deaths in the United States Army During the Late War, as Shown by the Records of the Adjutant General's Office.

STATES, ETC.	Killed in Action		Died of Wounds Received in Action		Died of Disease		Accidental Deaths Except Drowned		Drowned		Murdered		Killed after Capture		Committed Suicide		Executed by U.S. Military Authorities	Executed by Enemy		Died from Sunstroke		Other Known Causes		Causes Not Stated		TOTAL		AGGREGATE
	Officers	Men	Officers	Men	Officers	Men	Officers	Men	Officers	Men	Officers	Men	Officers	Men	Officers	Men	Men	Officers	Men	Officers	Men	Officers	Men	Officers	Men	Officers	Men	
Alabama																												
Non-prisoners	3	16	1	28	1	227	1	4																	28	6	303	309
Prisoners				2		22																	2		10		36	36
Total Alabama	3	16	1	30	1	249	1	4															2		38	6	339	345
Arkansas																												
Non-prisoners	9	225	5	63	12	1,242	1	22		2	1	23					2						22		54	28	1,655	1,683
Prisoners				3		8													13				1		5		30	30
Total Arkansas	9	225	5	66	12	1,250	1	22		2	1	23					2		13				23		59	28	1,685	1,713
California																												
Non-prisoners	4	69	2	33	8	336	1	23	1	37	1	9			3	5	4					1	20		16	21	552	573
Prisoners																												
Total California	4	69	2	33	8	336	1	23	1	37	1	9			3	5	4					1	20		16	21	552	573
Colorado																												
Non-prisoners	4	114	2	35	3	117		14		10		2					2				1		9		9	9	313	322
Prisoners																									1		1	1
Total Colorado	4	114	2	35	3	117		14		10		2					2				1		9		10	9	314	323
Connecticut																												
Non-prisoners	81	1,021	56	751	57	2,485	2	45	1	53		3			2	10	24				9	1	27	1	92	201	4,520	4,721
Prisoners			2	36	1	525																	7		62	3	630	633
Total Connecticut	81	1,021	58	787	58	3,010	2	45	1	53		3			2	10	24				9	1	34	1	154	204	5,150	5,354
Dakota																												
Non-prisoners		2				4																					6	6
Prisoners																												
Total Dakota		2				4																					6	6
Delaware																												
Non-prisoners	18	189	11	165	10	346		17	1	3		3				1	1						11		29	40	766	806
Prisoners						75																		1		76	76
Total Delaware	18	189	11	165	10	421		17	1	3		3				1	1						11		30	40	842	882
District of Columbia																												
Non-prisoners	3	25	1	10	5	145		8		2						4							6		20	9	221	230
Prisoners				2		44																			14		60	60
Total Dist. Columbia	3	25	1	12	5	189		8		2						4							6		34	9	281	290

A STATISTICAL EXHIBIT

Of Deaths in the United States Army During the Late War, as Shown by the Records of the Adjutant General's Office—Continued.

STATES, ETC.	Killed in Action		Died of Wounds Received in Action		Died of Disease		Accidental Deaths Except Drowned		Drowned		Murdered		Killed after Capture		Committed Suicide		Executed by U.S. Military Authorities	Executed by Enemy		Died from Sunstroke		Other Known Causes		Causes Not Stated		TOTAL		AGGREGATE
	Officers	Men	Officers	Men	Officers	Men	Officers	Men	Officers	Men	Officers	Men	Officers	Men	Officers	Men	Men	Officers	Men	Officers	Men	Officers	Men	Officers	Men	Officers	Men	
Florida																												
Non-prisoners		8			2	187															1				5	2	211	213
Prisoners																			2								2	2
Total Florida		8			2	187													2		1				5	2	213	215
Georgia																												
Non-prisoners						13																			2		15	15
Prisoners																												
Total Georgia						13																			2		15	15
Illinois																												
Non-prisoners	339	5,535	205	3,666	307	20,758	18	452	20	536	4	41				33	7				13	4	120	6	822	903	31,983	32,886
Prisoners			7	142	3	1,718		1		1	1		2	16							7		7		50	12	1,936	1,948
Total Illinois	339	5,535	212	3,808	310	22,476	18	453	20	537	4	41	2	16		33	7				13	4	127	6	872	915	33,919	34,834
Indiana																												
Non-prisoners	244	4,028	151	2,733	204	16,429	8	296	9	478	1	20			1	10	8				18	2	74	1	248	621	24,742	25,363
Prisoners			5	82	9	1,143							3	4					1		2		2	2	56	19	1,290	1,309
Total Indiana	244	4,028	156	2,815	213	17,572	8	296	9	478	1	20	3	4	1	10	8		1		20	2	76	3	704	640	26,032	26,672
Iowa																												
Non-prisoners	119	1,946	71	1,254	100	8,398	3	114	1	108		5				8					12	2	44	1	109	297	11,998	12,295
Prisoners			11	139	7	508			1			3		3					3			1	4	1	28	21	685	706
Total Iowa	119	1,946	82	1,393	107	8,906	3	114	2	108		5		3		8			3		12	3	48	2	137	318	12,683	13,001
Kansas																												
Non-prisoners	24	494	7	181	27	1,611	2	66		36	1	14		11	1	3	4		2		1	3	24		53	64	2,480	2,544
Prisoners			2	29		36					1		1										1	1	5	2	84	86
Total Kansas	24	494	9	210	27	1,647	2	66		36	2	14	1	11	1	3	4		2		1	3	25		58	66	2,564	2,630
Kentucky																												
Non-prisoners	95	1,390	39	901	120	6,263	1	219	6	228					1	7	12				2	6	154		296	268	9,486	9,754
Prisoners				53	1	859							1	1					2				8	1	94	3	1,017	1,020
Total Kentucky	95	1,390	39	954	121	7,122	1	219	6	228			1	1	1	7	12		2		2	6	162	1	390	271	10,503	10,774
Louisiana																												
Non-prisoners	4	125	5	80	3	621		12		24						1	1				5		19		29	12	917	929
Prisoners						15																			1		16	16
Total Louisiana	4	125	5	80	3	636		12		24						1	1				5		19		30	12	933	945

	C1	C2	C3	C4	C5	C6	C7	C8	C9	C10	C11	C12	C13	C14	C15	C16	C17	C18	C19	C20	C21	C22	C23	C24	C25	C26
Maine Non-prisoners	115	1,658	86	1,291	59	5,198	1	55	3	59	1	12				5	5		15		5	2	162	267	8,465	8,732
Prisoners			4	30		541													1		12		78	4	662	666
Total Maine	115	1,658	90	1,321	59	5,739	1	55	3	59	1	12				5	5		16		17	2	240	271	9,127	9,398
Maryland Non-prisoners	33	494	15	351	18	1,142	9	58	1	39	1	7				4	10		1	3	38		45	71	2,189	2,260
Prisoners				16	7	640															7		51	7	715	722
Total Maryland	33	494	15	367	25	1,782	9	58	1	39	1	7				4	10		1	3	45		96	78	2,904	2,982
Massachusetts Non-prisoners	248	3,457	117	2,174	60	5,470	9	119	1	128	1	8				8	13		14	2	60		190	437	11,641	12,078
Prisoners			3	116	6	1,477													3	1	35		224	9	1,855	1,864
Total Massachusetts	248	3,457	120	2,290	66	6,947	9	119	1	128	1	8				8	13		17	3	95		414	446	13,496	13,942
Michigan Non-prisoners	156	2,642	65	1,478	75	8,194	7	121	2	211		8				10	2	1	7		44		270	307	12,987	13,294
Prisoners			8	99	3	1,265							2								26		55	12	1,447	1,459
Total Michigan	156	2,642	73	1,577	78	9,459	7	121	2	211		8	2			10	2	1	7		70		325	319	14,434	14,753
Minnesota Non-prisoners	21	373	11	209	26	1,651	1	18	2	22	3	1				3			1	1	16		36	62	2,330	2,392
Prisoners				12		159															2		18	1	191	192
Total Minnesota	21	373	11	221	26	1,810	1	18	2	22	3	1				3			1	1	18		54	63	2,521	2,584
Mississippi Non-prisoners				3		66		1										1			4		3		78	78
Prisoners																										
Total Mississippi				3		66		1										1			4		3		78	78
Missouri Non-prisoners	102	2,089	66	1,040	118	9,125	10	178	7	292	3	39	2	3		27	6		7	4	111		325	314	13,239	13,553
Prisoners				20		225							9								4		71	3	329	332
Total Missouri	102	2,089	66	1,060	118	9,350	10	178	7	292	3	39	9	3		27	6		7	4	115		396	317	13,568	13,885
Nebraska Non-prisoners	1	29		5	2	157		15		8	6	6			1						2		12	3	234	237
Prisoners						1																		2	2	2
Total Nebraska	1	29		5	2	158		15		8	6	6			1						2		12	3	236	239
Nevada Non-prisoners		2				29				1											1				33	33
Prisoners																										
Total Nevada		2				29				1											1				33	33
New Hampshire Non-prisoners	84	990	43	754	37	2,390	1	33		42		4				2	17		8		13		95	166	4,348	4,514
Prisoners	2			32		294								1							5		37		368	368
Total New Hampshire	86	990	43	786	37	2,684	1	33		42		4		1		2	17		8		18		132	166	4,716	4,882

A STATISTICAL EXHIBIT

Of Deaths in the United States Army During the Late War, as Shown by the Records of the Adjutant General's Office—Continued.

STATE, ETC.	Killed in Action		Died of Wounds Received in Action		Died of Disease		Accidental Deaths Except Drowned		Drowned		Murdered		Killed after Capture		Committed Suicide		Executed by U.S. Military Author'ies	Executed by Enemy		Died from Sun-stroke		Other Known Causes		Causes Not Stated		TOTAL		AGGREGATE
	Officers	Men	Officers	Men	Officers	Men	Officers	Men	Officers	Men	Officers	Men	Officers	Men	Officers	Men	Men	Officers	Men	Officers	Men	Officers	Men	Officers	Men	Officers	Men	
New Jersey Non-prisoners	114	1,550	33	828	27	2,388	2	57	4	71	1	1				6	9				6	1	38		97	181	5,051	5,232
Prisoners			5	48	1	418																1	8	1	40	8	514	522
Total New Jersey	114	1,550	38	876	28	2,806	2	57	4	71	1	1				6	9				6	2	46	1	137	189	5,565	5,754
New Mexico Non-prisoners	3	54			5	139	2	10			1	12				4	3						7	2	12	13	264	277
Prisoners																												
Total New Mexico	3	54			5	139	2	10			1	12				4	3						7	2	12	13	264	277
New York Non-prisoners	772	11,329	351	6,314	329	19,506	19	480	6	407	3	31		2	3	66	35				54	4	240	3	1,036	1,490	39,498	40,988
Prisoners			20	299	16	4,694		2		2								1			3	3	118		388	40	5,506	5,546
Total New York	772	11,329	371	6,613	345	24,200	19	482	6	407	3	31		2	3	66	35	1			57	7	358	3	1,424	1,530	45,004	46,534
North Carolina Non-prisoners	4	25		13	4	212		2				4		1									4		21	8	282	290
Prisoners				1		49													15		1			1	3	1	69	70
Total North Carolina	4	25		14	4	261		2				4		1					15		1		4		24	9	351	360
Ohio Non-prisoners	402	6,433	228	4,303	262	19,103	17	366	14	767	3	20		13	4	30	6		9		23	1	108		674	931	31,833	32,764
Prisoners			11	211	12	2,344	1			3											1		9	2	95	26	2,685	2,711
Total Ohio	402	6,433	239	4,514	274	21,447	18	366	14	770	3	20		13	4	30	6		9		24	1	117	2	769	957	34,518	35,475
Oregon Non-prisoners	1	9				21		3		4		1					1						4		1	1	44	45
Prisoners																												
Total Oregon	1	9				21		3		4		1					1						4		1	1	44	45
Pennsylvania Non-prisoners	608	8,743	268	5,284	181	11,601	8	345	7	274	3	14				34	23			1	23	3	103		900	1,076	27,344	28,420
Prisoners			8	354	7	4,112	1			1		4									3		17		256	16	4,747	4,763
Total Pennsylvania	608	8,743	276	5,638	188	15,713	9	345	7	275	3	18				34	23			1	26	3	120		1,156	1,092	32,091	33,183
Rhode Island Non-prisoners	18	278	10	148	16	632		31		38		1				1	2			1	2		5		35	45	1,173	1,218
Prisoners				6		84																	3		10		103	103
Total Rhode Island	18	278	10	154	16	716		31		38		1				1	2			1	2		8		45	45	1,276	1,321

	1	2	3	4	5	6	7	8	9	10	11	12	13	14	15	16	17	18	19	20	21	22
Tennessee Non-prisoners	25	16	240	44	4,042	2	65	2	305	24		3			1	7	63	1	214	97	5,398	5,495
Prisoners			22		1,150		1								3		4		99	2	1,280	1,282
Total Tennessee	25	16	262	44	5,192	2	66	2	305	24		3			4	7	67	1	313	99	6,678	6,777
Texas Non-prisoners	8		4	1	100		3		3	1							5		6	1	132	133
Prisoners					1												5		2		8	8
Total Texas	8		4	1	101		3		3	1							10		8	1	140	141
Vermont Non-prisoners	997	33	676	31	2,566	2	36		32	3		9	4		7	1	11		115	133	4,456	4,589
Prisoners		1	38	1	485									8	4	1	10		87	3	632	635
Total Vermont	997	34	714	32	3,051	2	36		32	3		9	4	8	11	2	21		202	136	5,088	5,224
Virginia Non-prisoners	4		6		16		2		2	1									1	2	29	29
Prisoners					13																13	13
Total Virginia	4		6		29		2		2	1				8					1	2	42	42
Washington Territory Non-prisoners					10	3	3		2	1											20	22
Total Washington Ter.					10	3	3		2	1											20	22
West Virginia Non-prisoners	717	18	412	20	1,858		94		56	7		5	2		1	1	29	3	59	101	3,239	3,340
Prisoners		2	37		617												1		19	2	675	677
Total West Virginia	717	20	449	20	2,475		94		56	7		5	2		1	1	30	3	78	103	3,914	4,017
Wisconsin Non-prisoners	2,270	71	1,270	101	7,363	3	109		100	6	1	14	1	1	10	2	20		134	293	11,297	11,590
Prisoners		5	71	4	600												5		26	9	702	711
Total Wisconsin	2,270	76	1,341	105	7,963	3	109		100	6	1	14	1	1	10	2	25		160	302	11,999	12,301
Indian Nations Non-prisoners	82	1	20	18	757	2	3		7	11	1						2		110	23	993	1,016
Prisoners																			1		2	2
Total Indian Nations	82	1	20	18	757	2	3		7	11	1						2		111	23	995	1,018
Veteran Reserve Corps Non-prisoners	1		26	26	1,398		79		50	13		11	1		5		47		11	30	1,642	1,672
Total V. R. C.	1		26	26	1,398		79		50	13		11	1		5		47		11	30	1,642	1,672
U. S. Veteran Volunteers, Hancock Corps Non-prisoners	1	3	1	3	79		8		6	1	1	1			1		5			4	102	106
Total U. S. Vet. Vols.	1	3	1	3	79		8		6	1	1	1			1		5			4	102	106

A STATISTICAL EXHIBIT

Of Deaths in the United States Army During the Late War, as Shown by the Records of the Adjutant General's Office—Concluded.

STATES, ETC.	Killed in Action		Died of Wounds Rec'd in Action		Died of Disease		Accidental Deaths Except Drowned		Drowned		Murdered		Killed after Capture		Committed Suicide		Executed by U.S. Military Author'ies	Executed by Enemy		Died from Sunstroke		Other Known Causes		Causes Not Stated		TOTAL		AGGREGATE
	Officers	Men	Officers	Men	Officers	Men	Officers	Men	Officers	Men	Officers	Men	Officers	Men	Officers	Men	Men	Officers	Men	Officers	Men	Officers	Men	Officers	Men	Officers	Men	
U.S. Vol. Engineers and Sharpshooters																												
Non-prisoners	9	158	5	91	3	244		5		1						1							2		8	17	510	527
Prisoners						25																					25	25
Total U.S. Vol. E, etc	9	158	5	91	3	269		5		1						1							2		8	17	535	552
U.S. Volunteer Infantry																												
Non-prisoners		6	1	5	2	200		6		5		5				1	2					1	5		4	4	239	243
Prisoners																												
Total U.S. V. Infy.		6	1	5	2	200		6		5		5				1	2					1	5		4	4	239	243
General and General Staff Officers, U.S. Volunteers																												
Non-prisoners	50		33		142		4		6													1				236		236
Prisoners			2		1																					3		3
Total Gen. Staff, etc.	50		35		143		4		6													1				239		239
U.S. Colored Troops																												
Non-prisoners	100	1,615	43	1,102	137	29,521	14	266	6	288	8	98			2	11	25				32	5	73	2	3,181	317	36,239	36,556
Prisoners				34	1	97		1					4	21				1					8	1	122	7	284	291
Total U.S. C. Troops	100	1,615	43	1,136	138	29,618	14	267	6	289	8	98	4	21	2	11	25	1			32	5	81	3	3,303	324	36,523	36,847
Miscellaneous U.S. Vols. (Brigade Bands, etc.)																												
Non-prisoners		13		3		200		2																	12		230	230
Prisoners						2																					2	2
Total Miscellaneous		13		3		202		2																	12		232	232
Regular Army																												
Non-prisoners	85	1,262	56	838	104	2,448	1	103		89	1	15			2	25	6			2	7	1	61	2	84	254	4,938	5,192
Prisoners			3	39	3	537								1									1		22	6	600	606
Total Regular Army	85	1,262	59	877	107	2,985	1	103		89	1	15		1	2	25	6			2	7	1	62	2	106	260	5,538	5,798
Recapitulation																												
Total Non-prisoners	4,142	62,916	2,124	38,816	2,712	197,008	140	3,967	105	4,882	37	483			26	365	267			5	288	55	1,660	19	10,063	9,365	320,665	330,030
Total Prisoners			99	1,973	83	24,783	2	5	1			6	14	90				4	60		20	7	312	9	2,030	219	29,279	29,498
Grand Aggregate	4,142	62,916	2,223	40,789	2,795	221,791	142	3,972	106	4,882	37	489	14	90	26	365	267	4	60	5	308	62	1,972	28	12,093	9,584	349,944	359,528

National Cemeteries and Their Location

STATE.	LOCATION.	KNOWN.	UNKNOWN.	TOTAL.
Alabama.....................	Mobile......	746	113	877
Arkansas....................	Fayetteville.....	438	776	1,214
	Fort Smith......	741	1,150	1,891
	Little Rock.....	3,303	2,354	5,657
California..................	San Francisco....	291	11	302
District of Columbia...........	Battla Ground.....	43	....	43
	Soldier's Home......	5,398	288	5,686
Florida.....................	Barrancas.....	843	711	1,554
	St. Augustine......	1,470	....	1,470
Georgia.....................	Andersonville.....	12,779	923	13,702
	Marietta......	7,195	2,963	10,158
Illinois....................	Camp Butler.....	1,008	354	1,362
	Mound City.....	2,473	2,762	5,235
	Rock Island.....	288	20	308
	Quincy......	167	55	222
Indiana....................	Crown Hill.....	680	32	712
	New Albany.....	2,152	676	2,828
Indian Territory..............	Fort Gibson.....	233	2,212	2,445
Iowa.......................	Keokuk.....	624	33	657
Kansas.....................	Fort Leavenworth.....	1,161	1,060	2,221
	Fort Scott.....	469	161	590
Kentucky...................	Cava Hill.....	3,354	583	3,937
	Camp Nelson.....	2,455	1,189	3,644
	Danville.....	1,175	153	1,328
	Lebanon.....	592	277	869
	Lexington.....	840	112	952
	Mill Springs.....	346	366	712
Louisiana...................	Alexandria.....	520	789	1,309
	Baton Rouge.....	2,485	532	3,017
	Chalmette.....	6,863	5,734	12,597
	Port Hudson.....	588	3,239	3,827
Maryland...................	Antietam.....	2,855	1,829	4,684
	Annapolis.....	2,288	204	2,492
	Loudon Park.....	1,900	208	2,108
Mexico.....................	Mexico City.....	386	760	1,136
Mississippi..................	Corinth.....	1,782	3,937	5,719
	Natchez.....	308	2,780	3,088
	Vicksburg.....	3,899	12,716	16,615
Montana....................	Custer Battlefield.....	261	....	261
Missouri....................	Jefferson Barracks.....	8,717	2,906	11,623
	Jefferson City.....	475	334	809
	Springfield.....	874	734	1,608
Nebraska...................	Fort McPherson.....	258	293	551
New Jersey..................	Finn's Point.....	106	2,539	2,645
	Beverly.....	157	7	164
New York...................	Cypress Hills, Brooklyn.....	4,438	366	4,804
	Woodlawn, Elmira.....	3,068	7	3,075
North Carolina..............	New Berne.....	2,185	1,091	3,276
	Raleigh.....	626	571	1,197
	Salisbury.....	97	12,035	12,132
	Wilmington.....	713	1,577	2,290
Pennsylvania................	Gettysburg.....	1,974	1,611	3,585
	Philadelphia.....	1,969	223	2,192
South Carolina..............	Beaufort.....	4,758	4,513	9,271
	Florence.....	206	2,799	3,005
Tennessee...................	Chattanooga.....	8,038	4,963	13,001
	Fort Donelson.....	158	511	669
	Knoxville.....	2,109	1,046	3,115
	Memphis.....	5,163	8,818	13,981
	Nashville.....	11,832	4,701	16,533
	Shiloh.....	1,234	2,362	3,596
	Stone River.....	3,811	2,334	6,145
Texas......................	Brownsville.....	1,443	1,379	2,822
	San Antonio.....	707	225	932
Virginia....................	Alexandria.....	3,401	123	3,524
	Arlington.....	11,905	4,349	16,254
	Ball's Bluff.....	1	24	25
	City Point.....	3,719	1,439	5,158
	Cold Harbor.....	672	1,286	1,958
	Culpeper.....	456	912	1,368
	Danville.....	1,175	153	1,328
	Fort Harrison.....	242	573	817
	Fredericksburg.....	2,488	12,785	15,273
	Glendale.....	236	961	1,197

National Cemeteries and Their Location—Concluded

State.	Location.	Known.	Unknown.	Total.
	Hampton....................	5,531	493	6,024
	Poplar Grove, Petersburg.........	2,198	4,001	6,199
	Seven Pines................	150	1,220	1,370
	Staunton...................	234	523	757
	Winchester..................	2,098	2,382	4,480
	Yorktown...................	748	1,435	2,183
West Virginia..................	Grafton....................	634	620	1,252
Totals**............	....	17,397	148,833	325,230

**Including 9,300 Confederates, mostly buried at Camp Butler, Ill., Cypress Hills, N. Y., Finn's Point, N. J., Fort Smith, Ark., Hampton, Va., Jefferson City, Mo., and Woodlawn Elmira, N. Y.

THIRD COLUMN   "Totals Known"

READ   **176,397**

Instead of   17,397

A Complete List of Regiments, Battalions, Batteries, Independent Companies, Etc., Arranged by States Alphabetically.

Abbreviations used.—Regt. for Regiment. Batt'n for Battalion, Co. for Company, Cav. for Cavalry, Arty. for Artillery, Infy. for Infantry, Batty. for Battery, H. A. for Heavy Artillery, L. A. for Light Artillery, Indpt. for Independent, S. M. for State Militia, N. G. for National Guard. Prov'l for Provisional, E. M. for Enrolled Militia, H. G. for Home Guard, A. D. for African Descent or Colored, U. S. C. T. for United States Colored Troops, etc.

ALABAMA

1st Regt. Cav.
1st Regt. Heavy Arty. A. D.
1st Regt. Infy. A. D.
2nd Regt. Infy. A. D.
3rd Regt. Infy. A. D
4th Regt. Infy. A. D.
 Total organizations, 6.

ARKANSAS

1st Regt. Cav.
2nd Regt. Cav.
3rd Regt. Cav.
4th Regt. Cav.
1st Batty. Light Arty.
1st Batty. L. A.—A. D.
1st Regt. Infy.
1st Batt'n Infy.
1st Regt. Infy. A. D.
2nd Regt. Infy.
2nd Regt. Infy. A. D.
3rd Regt. Infy.
3rd Regt. Infy. A. D.
4th Regt. Infy.
4th Regt. Infy. A. D.
5th Regt. Infy. A. D.
6th Regt. Infy. A. D.
 Total organizations, 17.

CALIFORNIA

1st Regt. Cav.
1st Batt'n Cav.
2nd Regt. Cav.
1st Regt. Infy.
1st Batt'n Mountaineers.
2nd Regt. Infy.
3rd Regt. Infy.
4th Regt. Infy.
5th Regt. Infy.
6th Regt. Infy.
7th Regt. Infy.
8th Regt. Infy.
 Total organizations, 12.

COLORADO

1st Regt. Cav.
2nd Regt. Cav.
3rd Regt. Cav.
McLain's Batty. L. A.
1st Regt. Infy.
2nd Regt. Infy.
3rd Regt. Infy.
Denver City Guard.
 Total organizations, 8.

CONNECTICUT

1st Regt. Cav.
1st Regt. Heavy Arty.
2nd Regt. Heavy Arty.
1st Batty. Light Arty.
2nd Batty. Light Arty.
3rd Batty. Light Arty.
1st Regt. Infy. 3-Mos.
2nd Regt. Infy. 3-Mos.
3rd Regt. Infy. 3-Mos.
4th Regt. Infy.
5th Regt. Infy.
6th Regt. Infy.
7th Regt. Infy.
8th Regt. Infy.
9th Regt. Infy.
10th Regt. Infy.
11th Regt. Infy.
12th Regt. Infy.
13th Regt. Infy.
14th Regt. Infy.
15th Regt. Infy.
16th Regt. Infy.
17th Regt. Infy.
18th Regt. Infy.
19th Regt. Infy.
20th Regt. Infy.
21st Regt. Infy.
22nd Regt. Infy.
23rd Regt. Infy.
24th Regt. Infy.
25th Regt. Infy.
26th Regt. Infy.
27th Regt. Infy.
28th Regt. Infy.
29th Regt. Infy. A. D.
30th Regt. Infy. A. D.
 Total organizations, 36.

DAKOTA TERRITORY

1st Batt'n Cav.
 Total organizations, 1.

DELAWARE

1st Regt. Cav.
Mulligan's Cav. Co.
Ahl's Heavy Arty. Co.
Nield's Batty. Light Arty.
1st Regt. Infy. 3-Mos.
1st Regt. Infy. 3-Yrs.
2nd Regt. Infy.
3rd Regt. Infy.
4th Regt. Infy.
5th Regt. Infy.
6th Regt. Infy.
7th Regt. Infy.
8th Regt. Infy.
9th Regt. Infy.
Sterling's Co. Infy.
 Total organizations, 15.

DIST. OF COLUMBIA

1st Regt. Cav.
Owens' Militia Cav. Co.
1st Regt. Infy.
2nd Regt. Infy.
2nd Batt'n Infy.
3rd Batt'n Infy.
5th Batt'n Infy.
8th Batt'n Infy.
Boyd's Militia Co. Infy.
Callan's Mil. Co. Infy.
Carrington's Mil. Co. Infy.
Clarke's Militia Co. Infy.
Cross' Mil. Co. Infy.
Degges' Mil. Co. Infy.
Elder's Mil. Co. Infy.
Ferguson's Mil. Co. Infy.
Fletcher's Mil. Co. Infy.
Foxwell's Mil. Co. Infy.
Gebhardt's Mil. Co. Infy.
Goddard's Mil. Co. Infy.
Grinnell's Mil. Co. Infy.
Kelly's Mil. Co. Infy.
King's Mil. Co. Infy.
Knight's Mil. Co. Infy.
Kyrzanowski's Mil. Co.
Loeffler's Mil. Co. Infy.
Mark's Mil. Co. Infy.
Miller's Mil. Co. Infy.
Morgan's Mil. Co. Infy.
Morrison's Mil. Co. Infy.
McBlair's Mil. Co. Infy.
McClelland's Mil. Co.
McDermott's Mil. Co.
McKim's Mil. Co. Infy.
Nally's Mil. Co. Infy.
Powell's Mil. Co. Infy.
Rodier's Mil. Co. Infy.
Rutherford's Mil. Co.
Smead's Mil. Co. Infy.
Thistleton's Mil. Co.
Williams' Mil. Co. Infy.
 Total organizations, 41.

FLORIDA

1st Regt. Cav.
2nd Regt. Cav.
 Total organizations, 2.

GEORGIA

1st Batt'n Infy.
 Total organizations, 1.

ILLINOIS

1st Regt. Cav.
2nd Regt. Cav.
3rd Regt. Cav.
4th Regt. Cav.
5th Regt. Cav.
6th Regt. Cav.
7th Regt. Cav.
8th Regt. Cav.
9th Regt. Cav.
10th Regt. Cav.
11th Regt. Cav.
12th Regt. Cav.
13th Regt. Cav.
14th Regt. Cav.
15th Regt. Cav.
16th Reg. Cav.
17th Regt. Cav.
Stewart's Cav. Batt'n.
Thielman's Cav. Batt'n.
Barker's Dragoons.
Carmichael's Cav. Co.
Dollins' Cav. Co.
Ford's Cav. Co.
Gilbert's Cav. Co.
Hutchin's Cav. Co.
Jenk's Cav. Co.
Kane County Cav. Co.
Marx's Cav. Co.
McClellan's Dragoons.
McClernand's Body Guard.
Naughton's Dragoons.
O'Harnett's Cav. Co.
Schambeck's Cav. Co.
Sherer's Cav. Co.
Smith's Cav. Co.
Stewart's Cav. Co.

Thielman's Cav. Co.
Batty. A. 1st Light Arty.
Batty. B. 1st Light Arty.
Batty. C. 1st Light Arty.
Batty. D. 1st Light Arty.
Batty. E. 1st Light Arty.
Batty. F. 1st Light Arty.
Batty. G. 1st Light Arty.
Batty. H. 1st Light Arty.
Batty. I. 1st Light Arty.
Batty. K. 1st Light Arty.
Batty. L. 1st Light Arty.
Batty. M. 1st Light Arty.
Batty. A. 2nd Light Arty.
Batty. B. 2nd Light Arty.
Batty. C. 2nd Light Arty.
Batty. D. 2nd Light Arty.
Batty. E. 2nd Light Arty.
Batty. F. 2nd Light Arty.
Batty. G. 2nd Light Arty.
Batty. H. 2nd Light Arty.
Batty. I. 2nd Light Arty.
Batty. K. 2nd Light Arty.
Batty. L. 2nd Light Arty.
Batty. M. 2nd Light Arty.
Bridges' Indpt. Batty. L. A.
Board of Trade Indpt. Batty.
Busteed's Indpt. Batty. L. A.
Chapman's Indpt. Batty. L. A.
Chicago Board Trade Batty.
Chicago Mercantile Batty.
Cogswell's Indpt. Batty. L. A.
Colvin's Indpt. Batty. L. A.
Cooley's Batty. L. A. See Chicago
    Mercantile.
Elgin Batty. Light Arty.
Renwick's Indpt. Batty. L. A. See El-
    gin Batty.
Smith's Indpt. Batty. L. A.
Springfield Indpt. Batty.
Stokes' Indpt. Batty. See Board
    Trade Batty.
Vaughan's Indpt. Batty. L. A. See
    Springfield Batty.
7th Regt. Infy. (3-Mos.)
7th Regt. Infy. (3-Yrs.)
8th Regt. Infy. (3-Mos.)
8th Regt. Infy. (3-Yrs.)
9th Regt. Infy. (3-Mos.)
9th Regt. Infy. (3-Yrs.)
10th Regt. Infy. (3-Mos.)
10th Regt. Infy. (3-Yrs.)
11th Regt. Infy. (3-Mos.)
11th Regt. Infy. (3-Yrs.)
12th Regt. Infy. (3-Mos.)
12th Regt. Infy. (3-Yrs.)
13th Regt. Infy.
14th Regt. Infy.
15th Regt. Infy.
16th Regt. Infy.
17th Regt. Infy.
18th Regt. Infy.
19th Regt. Infy.
20th Regt. Infy.
21st Regt. Infy.
22nd Regt. Infy.
23rd Regt. Infy.
24th Regt. Infy.
25th Regt. Infy.
26th Regt. Infy.
27th Regt. Infy.
28th Regt. Infy.
29th Regt. Infy.
30th Regt. Infy.
31st Regt. Infy.
32nd Regt. Infy.
33rd Regt. Infy.
34th Regt. Infy.
35th Regt. Infy.

36th Regt. Infy.
37th Regt. Infy.
38th Regt. Infy.
39th Regt. Infy.
40th Regt. Infy.
41st Regt. Infy.
42nd Regt. Infy.
43rd Regt. Infy.
44th Regt. Infy.
45th Regt. Infy.
46th Regt. Infy.
47th Regt. Infy.
48th Regt. Infy.
49th Regt. Infy.
50th Regt. Infy.
51st Regt. Infy.
52nd Regt. Infy.
53rd Regt. Infy.
54th Regt. Infy.
55th Regt. Infy.
56th Regt. Infy.
57th Regt. Infy.
58th Regt. Infy.
59th Regt. Infy.
60th Regt. Infy.
61st Regt. Infy.
62nd Regt. Infy.
63rd Regt. Infy.
64th Regt. Infy.
65th Regt. Infy.
66th Regt. Infy.
67th Regt. Infy.
68th Regt. Infy.
69th Regt. Infy.
70th Regt. Infy.
71st Regt. Infy.
72nd Regt. Infy.
73rd Regt. Infy.
74th Regt. Infy.
75th Regt. Infy.
76th Regt. Infy.
77th Regt. Infy.
78th Regt. Infy.
79th Regt. Infy.
80th Regt. Infy.
81st Regt. Infy.
82nd Regt. Infy.
83rd Regt. Infy.
84th Regt. Infy.
85th Regt. Infy.
86th Regt. Infy.
87th Regt. Infy.
88th Regt. Infy.
89th Regt. Infy.
90th Regt. Infy.
91st Regt. Infy.
92nd Regt. Infy.
93rd Regt. Infy.
94th Regt. Infy.
95th Regt. Infy.
96th Regt. Infy.
97th Regt. Infy.
98th Regt. Infy.
99th Regt. Infy.
100th Regt. Infy.
101st Regt. Infy.
102nd Regt. Infy.
103rd Regt. Infy.
104th Regt. Infy.
105th Regt. Infy.
106th Regt. Infy.
107th Regt. Infy.
108th Regt. Infy.
109th Regt. Infy.
110th Regt. Infy.
111th Regt. Infy.
112th Regt. Infy.
113th Regt. Infy.
114th Regt. Infy.

115th Regt. Infy.
116th Regt. Infy.
117th Regt. Infy.
118th Regt. Infy.
119th Regt. Infy.
120th Regt. Infy.
121st Regt. Infy.
122nd Regt. Infy.
123rd Regt. Infy.
124th Regt. Infy.
125th Regt. Infy.
126th Regt. Infy.
127th Regt. Infy.
128th Regt. Infy.
129th Regt. Infy.
130th Regt. Infy.
131st Regt. Infy.
132nd Regt. Infy.
133rd Regt. Infy.
134th Regt. Infy.
135th Regt. Infy.
136th Regt. Infy.
137th Regt. Infy.
138th Regt. Infy.
139th Regt. Infy.
140th Regt. Infy.
141st Regt. Infy.
142nd Regt. Infy.
143rd Regt. Infy.
144th Regt. Infy.
145th Regt. Infy.
146th Regt. Infy.
147th Regt. Infy.
148th Regt. Infy.
149th Regt. Infy.
150th Regt. Infy.
151st Regt. Infy.
152nd Regt. Infy.
153rd Regt. Infy.
154th Regt. Infy.
155th Regt. Infy.
156th Regt. Infy.
Chicago Light Arty. Co.
Chicago Zouaves—Co. A.
Chicago Zouaves—Co. B.
Chicago Light Infy. Co.
Cairo Sandwich Co.
Lockport Arty. Co.
Lincoln Rifles.
Light Arty. Co.
Houghtaling's Ottawa Co.
Sturgis Rifles.
Turner Union Cadets.
    Total organizations, 239.

INDIANA

1st Regt. Cav. (28th.)
2nd Regt. Cav. (41st)
3rd Regt. Cav. (45th)
4th Regt. Cav. (77th)
5th Regt. Cav. (90th)
6th Regt. Cav. (71st)
7th Regt. Cav. (119th)
8th Regt. Cav. (69th)
9th Regt. Cav. (121st)
10th Regt. Cav. (125th)
11th Regt. Cav. (126th)
12th Regt. Cav. (127th)
13th Regt. Cav. (131st)
Bracken's Cav. Co.
Stewart's Cav. Co.
Indpt. Co. Scouts.
1st Regt. Heavy Arty.
1st Batty. Light Arty.
2nd Batty. Light Arty.
3rd Batty. Light Arty.
4th Batty. Light Arty.
5th Batty. Light Arty.
6th Batty. Light Arty.

7th Batty. Light Arty.
8th Batty. Light Arty.
9th Batty. Light Arty.
10th Batty. Light Arty.
11th Batty. Light Arty.
12th Batty. Light Arty.
13th Batty. Light Arty.
14th Batty. Light Arty.
15th Batty. Light Arty.
16th Batty. Light Arty.
17th Batty. Light Arty.
18th Batty. Light Arty.
19th Batty. Light Arty.
20th Batty. Light Arty.
21st Batty. Light Arty.
22nd Batty. Light Arty.
23rd Batty. Light Arty.
24th Batty. Light Arty.
25th Batty. Light Arty.
Wilder's Batty. L. A.
6th Regt. Infy. (3-Mos.)
6th Regt. Infy. (3-Yrs.)
7th Regt. Infy. (3-Mos.)
7th Regt. Infy. (3-Yrs.)
8th Regt. Infy. (3-Mos.)
8th Regt. Infy. (3-Yrs.)
9th Regt. Infy. (3-Mos.)
9th Regt. Infy. (3-Yrs.)
10th Regt. Infy. (3-Mos.)
10th Regt. Infy. (3-Yrs.)
11th Regt. Infy. (3-Mos.)
11th Regt. Infy. (3-Yrs.)
12th Regt. Infy. (1-Year)
12th Regt. Infy. (3-Yrs.)
13th Regt. Infy.
14th Regt. Infy.
15th Regt. Infy.
16th Regt. Infy. (1-Year)
16th Regt. Infy. (3-Yrs.)
17th Regt. Infy.
18th Regt. Infy.
19th Regt. Infy.
20th Regt. Infy.
21st Regt. Infy.
22nd Regt. Infy.
23rd Regt. Infy.
24th Regt. Infy.
25th Regt. Infy.
26th Regt. Infy.
27th Regt. Infy.
28th Regt. Infy.
28th Regt. (1-Cav.)
28th Regt. Colored Infy.
29th Regt. Infy.
30th Regt. Infy.
31st Regt. Infy.
32nd Regt. Infy.
33rd Regt. Infy.
34th Regt. Infy.
35th Regt. Infy.
36th Regt. Infy.
37th Regt. Infy.
38th Regt. Infy.
39th Regt. Infy.
40th Regt. Infy.
41st Regt. (2nd Cav.)
42nd Regt. Infy.
43rd Regt. Infy.
44th Regt. Infy.
45th Regt. (3rd Cav.)
46th Regt. Infy.
47th Regt. Infy.
48th Regt. Infy.
49th Regt. Infy.
50th Regt. Infy.
51st Regt. Infy.
52nd Regt. Infy.
53rd Regt. Infy.
54th Regt. Infy. (3-Mos.)

54th Regt. Infy. (3-Yrs.)
55th Regt. Infy.
56th Regt. Infy.
57th Regt. Infy.
58th Regt. Infy.
59th Regt. Infy.
60th Regt. Infy.
61st Regt. Infy.
62nd Regt. Infy.
63rd Regt. Infy.
64th Regt. Infy.
65th Regt. Infy.
66th Regt. Infy.
67th Regt. Infy.
68th Regt. Infy.
69th Regt. Infy.
70th Regt. Infy.
71st Regt. Infy.
72nd Regt. Infy.
73rd Regt. Infy.
74th Regt. Infy.
75th Regt. Infy.
76th Regt. Infy.
77th Regt. (4th Cav.)
78th Regt. Infy.
79th Regt. Infy.
80th Regt. Infy.
81st Regt. Infy.
82nd Regt. Infy.
83rd Regt. Infy.
84th Regt. Infy.
85th Regt. Infy.
86th Regt. Infy.
87th Regt. Infy.
88th Regt. Infy.
89th Regt. Infy.
90th Regt. (5th Cav.)
91st Regt. Infy.
92nd Regt. Infy.
93rd Regt. Infy.
94th Regt. Infy.
95th Regt. Infy.
96th Regt. Infy.
97th Regt. Infy.
98th Regt. Infy.
99th Regt. Infy.
100th Regt. Infy.
101st Regt. Infy.
102nd Regt. Infy.
103rd Regt. Infy.
104th Regt. Infy.
105th Regt. Infy.
106th Regt. Infy.
107th Regt. Infy.
108th Regt. Infy.
109th Regt. Infy.
110th Regt. Infy.
111th Regt. Infy.
112th Regt. Infy.
113th Regt. Infy.
114th Regt. Infy.
115th Regt. Infy.
116th Regt. Infy.
117th Regt. Infy.
118th Regt. Infy.
119th Regt. (7th Cav.)
120th Regt. Infy.
121st Regt. (9th Cav.)
122nd Regt. Infy.
123rd Regt. Infy.
124th Regt. Infy.
125th Reg. (10th Cav.)
126th Regt. (11th Cav.)
127th Regt. (12th Cav.)
128th Regt. Infy.
129th Regt. Infy.
130th Regt. Infy.
131st Regt. (13th Cav.)
132nd Regt. Infy.

133rd Regt. Infy.
134th Regt. Infy.
135th Regt. Infy.
136th Regt. Infy.
137th Regt. Infy.
138th Regt. Infy.
139th Regt. Infy.
140th Regt. Infy.
141st Regt. Infy.
142nd Regt. Infy.
143rd Regt. Infy.
144th Regt. Infy.
145th Regt. Infy.
146th Regt. Infy.
147th Regt. Infy.
148th Regt. Infy.
149th Regt. Infy.
150th Regt. Infy.
151st Regt. Infy.
152nd Regt. Infy.
153rd Regt. Infy.
154th Regt. Infy.
155th Regt. Infy.
156th Regt. Infy.
157th Regt. Infy.
158th Regt. Infy.
Total organizations, 195.

IOWA

1st Regt. Cav.
2nd Regt. Cav.
3rd Regt. Cav.
4th Regt. Cav.
5th Regt. Cav.
6th Regt. Cav.
7th Regt. Cav.
8th Regt. Cav.
9th Regt. Cav.
1st Indpt. Batty. L. A.
2nd Indpt. Batt. L. A.
3rd Indpt. Batty. L. A.
4th Indpt. Batty. L. A.
1st Regt. Infy.
1st Regt. Colored Infy.
2nd Regt. Infy.
3rd Regt. Infy.
4th Regt. Infy.
5th Regt. Infy.
6th Regt. Infy.
7th Regt. Infy.
8th Regt. Infy.
9th Regt. Infy.
10th Regt. Infy.
11th Regt. Infy.
12th Regt. Infy.
13th Regt. Infy.
14th Regt. Infy.
15th Regt. Infy.
16th Regt. Infy.
17th Regt. Infy.
18th Regt. Infy.
19th Regt. Infy.
20th Regt. Infy.
21st Regt. Infy.
22nd Regt. Infy.
23rd Regt. Infy.
24th Regt. Infy.
25th Regt. Infy.
26th Regt. Infy.
27th Regt. Infy.
28th Regt. Infy.
29th Regt. Infy.
30th Regt. Infy.
31st Regt. Infy.
32nd Regt. Infy.
33rd Regt. Infy.
34th Regt. Infy.
35th Regt. Infy.
36th Regt. Infy.

37th Regt. Infy.
38th Regt. Infy.
39th Regt. Infy.
40th Regt. Infy.
41st Regt. Infy.
42nd Regt. Infy.
43rd Regt. Infy.
44th Regt. Infy.
45th Regt. Infy.
46th Regt. Infy.
47th Regt. Infy.
48th Regt. Infy.
49th Regt. Infy.
50th Regt. Infy.
Total organizations, 64.

KANSAS

2nd Regt. Cav.
5th Regt. Cav.
6th Regt. Cav.
7th Regt. Cav.
9th Regt. Cav.
11th Regt. Cav.
14th Regt. Cav.
15th Regt. Cav.
16th Reg. Cav.
1st Indpt. Batty. L. A.
2nd Indpt. Batty. L. A.
3rd Indpt. Batty. L. A.
Armstrong's Militia Batty.
Hopkins' Batty. L. A.
Updyke's Militia Batty.
Stever's Batty. L. A.
Zisch's Militia Batty.
1st Regt. Infy.
1st Regt. Colored Infy.
1st Regt. Militia Infy.
2nd Regt. Infy.
2nd Regt. Colored Infy.
2nd Regt. Militia Infy.
3rd Regt. Infy.
3rd Regt. Militia Infy.
4th Regt. Infy.
4th Regt. Militia Infy.
5th Regt. Infy.
5th Regt. Militia Infy.
6th Regt. Militia Infy.
7th Regt. Militia Infy.
8th Regt. Infy.
8th Regt. Militia Infy.
9th Regt. Militia Infy.
10th Regt. Infy.
10th Regt. Militia Infy.
11th Regt. Infy.
11th Regt. Militia Infy.
12th Regt. Infy.
12th Regt. Militia Infy.
13th Regt. Infy.
13th Regt. Militia Infy.
14th Regt. Militia Infy.
15th Regt. Militia Infy.
16th Regt. Militia Infy.
17th Regt. Infy.
17th Regt. Militia Infy.
18th Regt. Militia Infy.
19th Regt. Militia Infy.
20th Regt. Militia Infy.
21st Regt. Militia Infy.
22nd Regt. Militia Infy.
Leavenworth Col'd Militia.
Leavenworth State Guard.
Total organizations, 54.

KENTUCKY

1st Regt. Cav.
2nd Reg. Cav.
3rd Regt. Cav.
4th Regt. Cav.
5th Regt. Cav.

6th Regt. Cav.
7th Regt. Cav.
8th Regt. Cav.
9th Regt. Cav.
10th Regt. Cav.
11th Regt. Cav.
12th Regt. Cav.
13th Regt. Cav.
14th Regt. Cav.
15th Regt. Cav.
16th Regt. Cav.
17th Regt. Cav.
Munday's Cav. Batt'n.
Batty. A. Light Arty.
Batty. B. Light Arty.
Batty. C. Light Arty.
Batty. D. Light Arty.
Batty. E. Light Arty.
Simmond's Batty. L. A.
Patterson's Co. Engineers.
1st Regt. Infy.
2nd Regt. Infy.
3rd Regt. Infy.
4th Regt. Infy.
5th Regt. Infy.
6th Regt. Infy.
7th Regt. Infy.
8th Regt. Infy.
9th Regt. Infy.
10th Regt. Infy.
11th Regt. Infy.
12th Regt. Infy.
13th Regt. Infy.
14th Regt. Infy.
15th Regt. Infy.
16th Regt. Infy.
17th Regt. Infy.
18th Regt. Infy.
19th Regt. Infy.
20th Regt. Infy.
21st Regt. Infy.
22nd Regt. Infy.
23rd Regt. Infy.
24th Regt. Infy.
25th Regt. Infy.
26th Regt. Infy.
27th Regt. Infy.
28th Regt. Infy.
29th Regt. Infy.
30th Regt. Infy.
31st Regt. Infy.
32nd Regt. Infy.
33rd Regt. Infy.
34th Regt. Infy.
35th Regt. Infy.
36th Regt. Infy.
37th Regt. Infy.
38th Regt. Infy.
39th Regt. Infy.
40th Regt. Infy.
41st Regt. Infy.
42nd Regt. Infy.
43rd Regt. Infy.
44th Regt. Infy.
45th Regt. Infy.
46th Regt. Infy.
47th Regt. Infy.
48th Regt. Infy.
49th Regt. Infy.
50th Regt. Infy.
51st Regt. Infy.
52nd Reg. Infy.
53rd Regt. Infy.
54th Regt. Infy.
55th Regt. Infy.
Total organizations, 80.

LOUISIANA

1st Regt. Cav.
2nd Regt. Cav.

1st Reg. Heavy Arty. A. D.
1st Batty. L. A.—A. D.
2nd Batty. L. A.—A. D.
3rd Batty. L. A.—A. D.
1st Regt. Infy.
1st Regt. New Orleans Infy.
2nd Regt. Infy.
2nd Regt. N. O. Infy.
1st Regt. Native Guard Infy.
2nd Regt. Native Guard Infy.
3rd Regt. Native Guard Infy.
4th Regt. Native Guard Infy.
5th Regt. Infy. A. D.
6th Regt. Infy. A. D.
7th Regt Infy. A. D. (60 dys.)
7th Regt. Infy. A. D.
8th Regt. Infy. A. D.
9th Regt. Infy. A. D. (Old)
9th Regt. Infy. A. D. (New)
10th Regt. Infy. A. D.
11th Regt. Infy. A. D.
12th Regt. Infy. A. D.
Total organizations, 24.

MAINE

1st Regt. Cav.
2nd Reg. Cav.
1st Regt. Heavy Arty.
1st Indpt. Batty. L. A.
2nd Indpt. Batty. L. A.
3rd Indpt. Batty. L. A.
4th Indpt. Batty. L. A.
5th Indpt. Batty. L. A.
6th Indpt. Batty. L. A.
7th Indpt. Batty. L. A.
1st Batt'n Sharpshooters.
Co. D. 2nd U. S. S. S.
1st Regt. Infy.
1st Batt'n Infy.
1st Regt. Infy. (Veteran)
2nd Regt. Infy.
3rd Regt. Infy.
4th Regt. Infy.
5th Regt. Infy.
6th Regt. Infy.
7th Regt. Infy.
8th Regt. Infy.
9th Regt. Infy.
10th Regt. Infy.
11th Regt. Infy.
12th Regt. Infy.
13th Regt. Infy.
14th Regt. Infy.
15th Regt. Infy.
16th Regt. Infy.
17th Regt. Infy.
18th Regt. Infy.
19th Regt. Infy.
20th Regt. Infy.
21st Regt. Infy.
22nd Regt. Infy.
23rd Regt. Infy.
24th Regt. Infy.
25th Regt. Infy.
26th Regt. Infy.
27th Regt. Infy.
28th Regt. Infy.
29th Regt. Infy.
30th Regt. Infy.
31st Regt. Infy.
32nd Regt. Infy.
1st Co. Coast Guard.
2nd Co. Coast Guard.
3rd Co. Coast Guard.
4th Co. Coast Guard.
5th Co. Coast Guard.
6th Co. Coast Guard.
7th Co. Coast Guard.
Total organizations, 53.

MARYLAND

1st Regt. Cav.
1st Regt. Pot. Home Brig. Cav.
2nd Regt. Cav.
3rd Regt. Cav.
Purnell Legion Batt'n Cav.
Smith's Cav. Company.
Batty. A. Light Arty.
Batty. A. Light Arty (2nd)
Batty. B. Light Arty.
Batty. B. Light Arty. (2nd)
Batty. D. Light Arty.
Baltimore Batty. Light Arty.
1st Regt. Heavy Arty.
1st Regt. Infy.
1st Regt. Pot. Home Brig. Infy.
1st Regt. Eastern Shore Infy.
2nd Regt. Infy.
2nd Regt. Pot. Home Brig. Infy.
2nd Regt. Eastern Shore Infy.
3rd Regt. Infy.
3rd Regt. Pot. Home Brig. Infy.
4th Regt. Infy.
4th Regt. Pot. Home Brig. Infy.
5th Regt. Infy.
6th Regt. Infy.
7th Regt. Infy.
8th Regt. Infy.
9th Regt. Infy.
10th Regt. Infy.
11th Regt. Infy.
12th Regt. Infy.
13th Regt. Infy.
Purnell Legion Infy.
Balto. Light Guard.
Patapsco Guard.
    Total organizations, 35.

MASSACHUSETTS

1st Regt. Cav.
2nd Regt. Cav.
2nd Batt'n Cav.
3rd Regt. Cav.
4th Regt. Cav.
5th Regt. Cav. (Colored)
Devens' Cav. Batt'n.
Indpt. Cav. Batt'n.
1st Regt. Heavy Arty.
1st Batt'n Heavy Arty.
2nd Regt. Heavy Arty.
3rd Regt. Heavy Arty.
4th Regt. Heavy Arty.
1st Co. Unass'd H. A.
2nd Co. Unass'd H. A.
3rd Co. Unass'd H. A.
4th Co. Unass'd H. A.
5th Co. Unass'd H. A.
6th Co. Unass'd H. A.
7th Co. Unass'd H. A.
8th Co. Unass'd H. A.
9th Co. Unass'd H. A.
10th Co. Unass'd H. A.
11th Co. Unass'd H. A.
12th Co. Unass'd H. A.
13th Co. Unass'd H. A.
14th Co. Unass'd H. A.
15th Co. Unass'd H. A.
16th Co. Unass'd H. A.
17th Co. Unass'd H. A.
18th Co. Unass'd H. A.
19th Co. Unass'd H. A.
20th Co. Unass'd H. A.
21st Co. Unass'd H. A.
22nd Co. Unass'd H. A.
23rd Co. Unass'd H. A.
24th Co. Unass'd H. A.
25th Co. Unass'd H. A.
26th Co. Unass'd H. A.
27th Co. Unass'd H. A.
28th Co. Unass'd H. A.
29th Co. Unass'd H. A.
30th Co. Unass'd H. A.
Cook's Batty. Light Arty.
1st Batty. Light Arty.
2nd Batty. Light Arty.
3rd Batty. Light Arty.
4th Batty. Light Arty.
5th Batty. Light Arty.
6th Batty. Light Arty.
7th Batty. Light Arty.
8th Batty. Light Arty.
9th Batty. Light Arty.
10th Batty. Light Arty.
11th Batty. Light Arty.
11th Batty. Light Arty. Reorg.
12th Batty. Light Arty.
13th Batty. Light Arty.
14th Batty. Light Arty.
15th Batty. Light Arty.
16th Batty. Light Arty.
1st Co. Sharpshooters.
2nd Co. Sharpshooters.
1st Batt'n Infy.
1st Regt. Infy.
2nd Regt. Infy.
3rd Regt. Infy. (3-Mos.)
3rd Regt. Infy. (9-Mos.)
3rd Batt'n Rifles.
4th Regt. Infy. (3-Mos.)
4th Regt. Infy. (9-Mos.)
4th Batt'n Infy.
5th Regt. Infy. (3-Mos.)
5th Regt. Infy. (9-Mos.)
5th Regt. Infy. (100 Days)
6th Regt. Infy. (3-Mos.)
6th Regt. Infy. (9-Mos.)
6th Regt. Infy. (100 Days)
7th Regt. Infy.
8th Regt. Infy. (3-Mos.)
8th Regt. Infy. (9-Mos.)
8th Regt. Infy. (100 Days)
9th Regt. Infy.
10th Regt. Infy.
11th Regt. Infy.
12th Regt. Infy.
13th Regt. Infy.
14th Regt. Infy.
15th Regt. Infy.
16th Regt. Infy.
17th Regt. Infy.
18th Regt. Infy.
19th Regt. Infy.
20th Regt. Infy.
21st Regt. Infy.
22nd Regt. Infy.
23rd Regt. Infy.
24th Regt. Infy.
25th Regt. Infy.
26th Regt. Infy.
27th Regt. Infy.
28th Regt. Infy.
29th Regt. Infy.
30th Regt. Infy.
31st Regt. Infy.
32nd Regt. Infy.
33rd Regt. Infy.
34th Regt. Infy.
35th Regt. Infy.
36th Regt. Infy.
37th Regt. Infy.
38th Regt. Infy.
39th Regt. Infy.
40th Regt. Infy.
41st Regt. Infy.
42nd Regt. Infy.
42nd Regt. Militia Infy. (100 Days)
43rd Regt. Infy.
44th Regt. Infy.
45th Regt. Infy.
46th Regt. Infy.
47th Regt. Infy.
48th Regt. Infy.
49th Regt. Infy.
50th Regt. Infy.
51st Regt. Infy.
52nd Regt. Infy.
53rd Regt. Infy.
54th Regt. Infy. (Colored)
55th Regt. Infy. (Colored)
56th Regt. Infy.
57th Regt. Infy.
58th Regt. Infy.
59th Regt. Infy.
60th Regt. Infy.
61st Regt. Infy.
62nd Regt. Infy.
1st Co. Mass. Infy.
2nd Co. Mass. Infy.
3rd Co. Mass. Infy.
4th Co. Mass. Infy.
5th Co. Mass. Infy.
6th Co. Mass. Infy.
7th Co. Mass. Infy.
8th Co. Mass. Infy.
9th Co. Mass. Infy.
10th Co. Mass. Infy.
11th Co. Mass. Infy.
12th Co. Mass. Infy.
13th Co. Mass. Infy.
15th Co. Mass. Infy.
16th Co. Mass. Infy.
17th Co. Mass. Infy.
18th Co. Mass. Infy.
19th Co. Mass. Infy.
20th Co. Mass. Infy.
21st Co. Mass. Infy.
22nd Co. Mass. Infy.
23rd Co. Mass. Infy.
24th Co. Mass. Infy.
25th Co. Mass. Infy.
26th Co. Mass. Infy.
Boston Cadets.
Salem Cadets.
    Total organizations, 165.

MICHIGAN

1st Regt. Cav.
2nd Regt. Cav.
3rd Regt. Cav.
4th Regt. Cav.
5th Regt. Cav.
6th Regt. Cav.
7th Regt. Cav.
8th Regt. Cav.
9th Regt. Cav.
10th Regt. Cav.
11th Regt. Cav.
1st U. S. Lancers.
Chandler Horse Guard.
6th Regt. Heavy Arty.
Batty. A. 1st Light Arty.
Batty. B. 1st Light Arty.
Batty. C. 1st Light Arty.
Batty. D. 1st Light Arty.
Batty. E. 1st Light Arty.
Batty. F. 1st Light Arty.
Batty. G. 1st Light Arty.
Batty. H. 1st Light Arty.
Batty. I. 1st Light Arty.
Batty. K. 1st Light Arty.
Batty. L. 1st Light Arty.
Batty. M. 1st Light Arty.
13th Indpt. Batty. L. A.
14th Indpt. Batty. L. A.
1st Regt. Engineers.
Howland's Co. Engineers.
1st Regt. Sharpshooters.

Co. C. 1st U. S. S. S.
Co. I. 1st U. S. S. S.
Co. K. 1st U. S. S. S.
Co. B. 2nd U. S. S. S.
Brady's Co. S. S.
Dygert's Co. S. S.
Hall's Batt'n S. S.
Jardine's Co. S. S.
1st Regt. Infy (3-Mos.)
1st Regt. Infy. (3-Yrs.)
1st Regt. Infy. (Colored)
2nd Regt. Infy.
3rd Regt. Infy.
3rd Regt. Infy.—Reorg.
4th Regt. Infy.
4th Regt. Infy.—Reorg.
5th Regt. Infy.
6th Regt. Infy.
7th Regt. Infy.
8th Regt. Infy.
9th Regt. Infy.
10th Regt. Infy.
11th Regt. Infy.
11th Regt. Infy.—Reorg.
12th Regt. Infy.
13th Regt. Infy.
14th Regt. Infy.
15th Regt. Infy.
16th Regt. Infy.
17th Regt. Infy.
18th Regt. Infy.
19th Regt. Infy.
20th Regt. Infy.
21st Regt. Infy.
22nd Regt. Infy.
23rd Regt. Infy.
24th Regt. Infy.
25th Regt. Infy.
26th Regt. Infy.
27th Regt. Infy.
28th Regt. Infy.
29th Regt. Infy.
30th Regt. Infy.
Provost Guard Company.
Stanton Guard.
    Total organizations, 76.

MINNESOTA

1st Regt. Cav.
2nd Regt. Cav.
Brackett's Cav. Batt'n.
Hatch's Cav. Batt'n.
1st Regt. Heavy Arty.
1st Indpt. Batty. Light Arty.
2nd Indpt. Batty. Light Arty.
3rd Indpt. Batty. Light Arty.
1st Co. Sharpshooters.
2nd Co. Sharpshooters.
1st Regt. Infy.
2nd Regt. Infy.
3rd Regt. Infy.
4th Regt. Infy.
5th Regt. Infy.
6th Regt. Infy.
7th Regt. Infy.
8th Regt. Infy.
9th Regt. Infy.
10th Regt. Infy.
11th Regt. Infy.
    Total organizations, 21.

MISSOURI

1st Regt. Cav.
1st Regt. S. M. Cav.
1st Batt'n S. M. Cav.
1st Batt'n Cav. Miss. Marine Brigade.
1st Batt'n E. M. Cav.
2nd Regt. Cav.
2nd Regt. S. M. Cav.

2nd Batt'n S. M. Cav.
3rd Regt. Cav.
3rd Regt. S. M. Cav. (Old)
3rd Regt. S. M. Cav. (New)
4th Regt. Cav.
4th Regt. S. M. Cav.
5th Regt. Cav.
5th Regt. S. M. Cav. (Old)
5th Regt. S. M. Cav. (New)
6th Regt. Cav.
6th Regt. S. M. Cav.
7th Regt. Cav.
7th Regt. S. M. Cav.
8th Regt. Cav.
8th Regt. S. M. Cav.
9th Cav.
9th Regt. S. M. Cav.
10th Regt. Cav.
10th Regt. S. M. Cav.
11th Regt. Cav.
11th Regt. S. M. Cav.
12th Regt. Cav.
12th Regt. S. M. Cav.
13th Regt. Cav.
13th Regt. S. M. Cav.
14th Regt. Cav.
14th Regt. S. M. Cav.
15th Regt. Cav.
16th Regt. Cav.
Benton Hussars Cav. Batt'n.
Berry's Cav. Batt'n.
Bishop's Cav. Batt'n.
Black Hawk Cav. Batt'n.
Booneville S. M. Cav. Batt'n.
Bowen's Cav. Batt'n.
Cass Co. H. G. Cav. Batt'n.
Co. A. Cav. 1st U. S. R. C.
Fremont's Body Guard.
Fremont Hussars.
Fremont Rangers.
Hawkins' Cav. Co.
Hollan Horse Cav. Batt'n.
Irish Dragoons Cav. Co.
Loring's Cav. Co.
McFadden's S. M. Cav. Co.
Mountain Rangers Cav. Co.
Osage Rifles Mounted Co.
Schofields' Hussars.
Soboleski's Cav. Co.
Stewart's Cav. Batt'n.
White's Cav. Batt'n.
Backoff's Batt'n L. A.
Cavender's Batt'n L. A.
1st Batty. S. M. L. A.
1st Regt. Light Arty.
Batty. A. 1st L. A.
Batty. B. 1st L. A.
Batty. C. 1st L. A.
Batty. D. 1st L. A.
Batty. E. 1st L. A.
Batty. F. 1st L. A.
Batty. G. 1st L. A.
Batty. H. 1st L. A.
Batty. I. 1st L. A.
Batty. K. 1st L. A.
Batty. L. 1st L. A.
Batty. M. 1st L. A.
2nd Regt. Light Arty.
Batty. A. 2nd L. A.
Batty. B. 2nd L. A.
Batty. C. 2nd L. A.
Batty. D. 2nd L. A.
Batty. E. 2nd L. A.
Batty. F. 2nd L. A.
Batty. G. 2nd L. A.
Batty. H. 2nd L. A.
Batty. I. 2nd L. A.
Batty. K. 2nd L. A.
Batty. L. 2nd L. A.

Batty. M. 2nd L. A.
Buell's Batty. L. A.
Graesseles Batty. L. A.
Johnson's S. M. Batty. L. A.
Joyce's Batty. L. A.
Knipsel's Batty. L. A.
Kowald's Batty. L. A.
Landgraeber's Batty. L. A.
Lindsay's Batty. L. A.
Lovejoy's Batty. L. A.
McClanahan's Batty. L. A.
Mann's Batty. L. A.
Pfenninghausen's Batty.
Schofield's Batty, A. L. A.
Schwartz's Batty. L. A.
Walling's Batty. M. M. B.
Waschman's Batty. L. A.
Welfley's Batty. L. A.
Bissell's Engr. Regt.
1st Regt. Engrs.
Balz's Co. Sappers and Miners.
Gerster's Co. Pioneers.
Smith's Co. Telegraph Corps.
Wolster's Co. Sappers-Miners.
Birge's Regt. Sharpshooters.
Holman's Batt'n S. S.
1st Batt'n M. M. B. Infy.
1st Batt'n S. M. Infy.
1st Batt'n E. M. Infy.
1st Batt'n St. Louis City Gd.
1st Regt. Infy. (3-Mos.)
1st Regt. U. S. R. C. Infy. (3-Mos.)
1st Regt. U. S. R. C. Infy. (3-Yrs.)
1st Regt. Northeast Infy.
1st Regt. S. M. Infy.
1st Regt. E. M. Infy.
1st Regt. Prov'l E. M. Infy.
1st Regt. Colored Infy.
1st Regt. St. L. City Guard.
2nd Batt'n S. M. Infy.
2nd Batt'n St. L. City Guard.
2nd Batt'n St. L. City Gd. Colored.
2nd Regt. Infy. (3-Mos.)
2nd Regt. Infy. (3-Yrs.)
2nd Regt. U. S. R. C. Infy. (3-Mos.)
2nd Regt. U. S. R. C. Infy. (3-Yrs.)
2nd Regt. Northeast Infy.
2nd Regt. E. M. Infy.
2nd Regt. Prov'l E. M. Infy.
2nd Regt. Infy. Colored.
2nd Regt. St. L. City Guard.
3rd Batt'n S. M. Infy.
3rd Batt'n St. L. City Guard.
3rd Regt. Infy. (3-Mos.)
3rd Regt. Infy. (3-Yrs.)
3rd Regt. U. S. R. C. Infy. (3-Mos.)
3rd Regt. U. S. R. C. Infy. (3-Yrs.)
3rd Regt. E. M. Infy.
3rd Regt. Prov'l E. M. Infy.
3rd Regt. Colored Infy.
3rd Regt. St. L. City Guard.
4th Batt'n S. M. Infy.
4th Regt. Infy. (3-Mos.)
4th Regt. Infy. (3-Yrs.)
4th U. S. R. C. Infy. (3-Mos.)
4th U. S. R. C. Infy. (3-Yrs.)
4th Regt. E. M. Infy.
4th Regt. Prov'l E. M. Infy.
4th Regt. Colored Infy.
4th Regt. St. L. City Guard.
5th Regt. Infy. (3-Mos.)
5th Regt. Infy. (3-Yrs.)
5th U. S. R. C. Infy. (3-Mos.)
5th U. S. R. C. Infy. (3-Yrs.)
5th Regt. S. M. Infy.
5th Regt. E. M. Infy.
5th Regt. Prov'l E. M. Infy.
5th Regt. St. L. City Guard.
6th Batt'n S. M. Infy.

6th Regt. Infy.
6th Regt. E. M. Infy.
6th Regt. Prov'l E. M. Infy.
7th Battalion S. M. Infy.
7th Regt. Infy.
7th Regt. E. M. Infy.
7th Regt. Prov'l E. M. Infy.
8th Regt. Infy.
8th Regt. E. M. Infy.
8th Regt. Prov'l E. M. Infy.
9th Regt. Infy.
9th Regt. E. M. Infy.
9th Regt. Prov'l E. M. Infy.
10th Regt. Infy.
10th Regt. E. M. Infy.
10th Regt. Prov'l E. M. Infy.
11th Regt. Infy.
11th Regt. E. M. Infy.
11th Regt. Prov'l E. M. Infy.
12th Regt. Infy.
13th Regt. Infy.
13th Regt. E. M. Infy.
14th Regt. Infy.
14th Regt. H. G. Infy.
15th Regt. Infy.
15th Regt. H. G. Infy.
16th Regt. Infy.
17th Regt. Infy.
18th Regt. Infy.
19th Regt. Infy.
20th Regt. Infy.
21st Regt. Infy.
22nd Regt. Infy.
23rd Regt. Infy.
24th Regt. Infy.
25th Regt. Infy.
25th Reg. E. M. Infy.
26th Regt. Infy.
26th Regt. E. M. Infy.
27th Regt. Infy.
27th Regt. Mounted Infy.
27th Regt. E. M. Infy.
28th Regt. Infy.
28th Regt. E. M. Infy.
29th Regt. Infy.
29th Regt. E. M. Infy.
30th Regt. Infy.
30th Regt. E. M. Infy.
30th Regt. Prov'l E. M. Infy.
31st Regt. Infy.
31st Regt. E. M. Infy.
31st Regt. Prov'l E. M. Infy.
32nd Regt. Infy.
32nd Regt. E. M. Infy.
33rd Regt. Infy.
33rd Regt. E. M. Infy.
33rd Regt. Prov'l E. M. Infy.
34th Regt. Infy.
34th Reg. E. M. Infy.
35th Regt. Infy.
35th Regt. E. M. Infy.
35th Regt. Prov'l E. M. Infy.
36th Regt. Infy.
36th Regt. E. M. Infy.
37th Regt. Infy.
37th Regt. E. M. Infy.
38th Regt. Infy.
38th Regt. E. M. Infy.
39th Regt. Infy.
39th Regt. E. M. Infy.
40th Regt. Infy.
40th Regt. E. M. Infy.
41st Regt. Infy.
41st Regt. E. M. Infy.
42nd Regt. Infy.
42nd Regt. E. M. Infy.
42nd Prov'l E. M. Infy.
43rd Regt. Infy.
43rd Regt. E. M. Infy.

44th Regt. Infy.
44th Regt. Prov'l E. M. Infy.
45th Regt. Infy.
45th Regt. E. M. Infy.
46th Regt. Infy.
46th Regt. E. M. Infy.
47th Regt. Infy.
47th Regt. E. M. Infy.
48th Regt. Infy.
48th Regt. E. M. Infy.
49th Regt. Infy.
49th Regt. E. M. Infy.
50th Regt. Infy.
50th Regt. E. M. Infy.
51st Regt. Infy.
51st Regt. E. M. Infy.
51st Regt. Prov'l E. M. Infy.
52nd Regt. Infy.
52nd Regt. E. M. Infy.
53rd Regt. Infy.
53rd Regt. E. M. Infy.
53rd Regt. Prov'l E. M. Infy.
54th Regt. Infy.
54th Regt. E. M. Infy.
55th Regt. Infy.
55th Regt. E. M. Infy.
56th Regt. Infy.
56th Regt. E. M. Infy.
57th Regt. Infy.
57th Regt. Prov'l E. M. Infy.
58th Regt. Infy.
59th Regt. E. M. Infy.
60th Regt. E. M. Infy.
61st Regt. E. M. Infy.
61st Regt. Prov'l E. M. Infy.
62nd Regt. E. M. Infy.
63rd Regt. E. M. Infy.
64th Regt. E. M. Infy.
65th Regt. E. M. Infy.
66th Regt. E. M. Infy.
66th Regt. E. M. Infy.
66th Regt. Prov'l E. M. Infy.
67th Regt. E. M. Infy.
67th Regt. Prov'l E. M. Infy.
68th Regt. E. M. Infy.
68th Regt. Prov'l E. M. Infy.
70th Regt. E. M. Infy.
71st Regt. E. M. Infy.
72nd Regt. E. M. Infy.
72nd Regt. Prov'l E. M. Infy.
73rd Regt. E. M. Infy.
74th Regt. E. M. Infy.
74th Regt. Prov'l E. M. Infy.
75th Regt. E. M. Infy.
76th Regt. E. M. Infy.
77th Regt. E. M. Infy.
78th Regt. E. M. Infy.
79th Regt. E. M. Infy.
80th Regt. E. M. Infy.
80th Regt. Prov'l E. M. Infy.
81st Regt. Prov'l E. M. Infy.
82nd Regt. E. M. Infy.
85th Regt. E. M. Infy.
86th Regt. E. M. Infy.
87th Regt. Prov'l E. M. Infy.
88th Regt. E. M. Infy.
89th Regt. E. M. Infy.
Bayle's Indpt. Co. Infy.
Benton Cadets, Co. Infy.
Dietrich's Indpt. Co. Infy.
Gasconade Co. Batt'n R. C. Infy.
Krekel's Batt'n R. C. Infy.
Nagel's Co. R. C. Infy.
Osterhaus Batt'n Infy.
Peabody's Batt'n R. C. Infy.
Phelp's Indpt. Regt. Infy.
Van Horn's Batt'n R. C. Infy.
Albree's Batt'n S. M. Infy.
Cox's Batt'n S. M. Infy.

Cranor's Regt. S. M. Infy.
Dallmeyer's Regt. S. M. Infy.
Fagg's Regt. S. M. Infy.
Grundy Co. Batt'n S. M. Infy.
Harrison Co. Batt'n S. M. Infy.
James' Battalion S. M. Infy.
Joseph's Batt'n S. M. Infy.
Kimball's Regt. S. M. Infy.
Mercer Co. Batt'n S. M. Infy.
Simpson's Regt. S. M. Infy.
Richardson's Regt. S. M. Infy.
Thompson's Batt'n S. M. Infy.
Ward's Co. S. M. Infy.
Washington Co. Bn. S. M. Infy.
Adair Co. H. G. Co. Infy.
Adair Co. H. G. Co. Infy.
Allen's Citizens Corps.
Benton Co. H. G. Regt. Infy.
Booneville Batt'n H. G. Infy.
Brookfield H. G. Infy.
Caldwell Co. H. G. Co. Infy.
Cape Girardeau Batt'n H. G.
Carondelet Co. H. G. Co. Infy.
Cass Co. H. G. Regt. Infy.
Clinton Co. H. G. Co. Infy.
Clinton Co. H. G. Co. Infy.
Cole Co. H. G. Regt. Infy.
Dallas Co. H. G. Reegt. Infy.
DeKalb Co. H. G. Regt. Infy.
DeSoto Co. H. G. Co. Infy.
Douglass Co. H. G. Co. Infy.
Franklin Co. H. G. Batt'n Infy.
Fremont Rangers, H. G. (5 Cos.)
Gasconade Co. H. G. Batt'n Infy.
Gentry Co. H. G. Regt. Infy.
Green Co. H. G. Co. Infy.
Green and Christian Cos. H. G. Co.
        Infy.
Harrison Co. H. G. Regt. Infy.
Jefferson City H. G. Batt'n.
Johnson Co. H. G. Regt. Infy.
King's Co. R. R. Guard.
Knox Co. H. G. Regt. Infy.
Lawrence Co. H. G. Regt. Infy.
Lewis Co. H. G. Co. Infy.
Lexington Co. H. G. Co. Infy.
Livingston Co. H. G. Co. Infy.
Marion Co. H. G. Batt'n Infy.
Moniteau Co. H. G. Co. Infy.
Nodaway Co. H. G. Regt. Infy.
Osage Co. H. G. Batt'n Infy.
Osage Co. H. G. Regt. and
        Hickory Co. Batt'n H. G. Infy.
Ozark Co. H. G. Regt. Infy.
Pacific H. G. Batt'n Infy.
Pettis Co. H. G. Regt. Infy.
Phelps Co. H. G. Co. Infy.
Phelps Co. H. G. Co. Infy.
Pike Co. H. G. Regt. Infy.
Pilot Knob H. G. Co. Infy.
Polk Co. H. G. Regt. Infy.
Potosi Co H. G. Regt. Infy.
Putnam Co. H. G. (2 Cos.)
Sibley Point H. G. Co. Infy.
St. Charles Co. H. G. Batt'n.
Scott Co. H. G. Batt'n Infy.
Stonas H. G. Co. Infy.
Stone Prairie H. G. Co. Infy.
Stone Co. H. G. Regt. Infy.
Shawneetown H. G. Co. Infy.
Sullivan Co. H. G. (2 Cos.)
Shelby Co. H. G. Co. Infy.
Webster Co. H. G. Regt. Infy.
Andrews Co. Militia.
Audrian Co. Militia.
Bates Co. Militia.
Bogard Citizen Guard.
Bollinger Co. Militia.
Boone Co. Militia.

Bridges No. Mo. R. R. Militia.
Buchanan Co. E. M.
Buchanan Co. Union Guard.
Calhoun Citizen Guard.
Callaway Co. E. M.
Callaway Co. Militia.
Camden Co. Militia.
Cape Girardeau Co. Militia.
Carroll Co. Militia.
Chariton Co. Militia.
Clay Co. E. M.
Clay Co. Militia.
Clinton Co. E. M.
Cooper and Moniteau Cos. Militia.
Cooper Co. Militia.
Dallas Co. Militia.
DeKalb Co. Militia.
Howard Co. Militia.
Jackson Co. Militia.
Jasper Co. Militia.
Johnson Co. Militia.
Lafayette County Militia.
Lawrence Co. Militia.
Linn Co. Militia.
Livingston Co. Militia.
Merias Co. Militia.
Mississippi Co. E. M.
Mississippi Co. Militia.
Morgan Co. Militia.
Newman's Prov'l E. M.
Osage and Marias Cos. Mil.
Osage Co. Militia.
Pacific R. R. Militia.
Perry Co. Militia.
Pettis Co. Militia.
Pike Co. E. M.
Ray Co. Militia.
Rolla Battalion Citizen Gd.
St. Clair Co. Militia.
Saline Co. Militia.
Scott Co. E. M.
S. W. Branch Pacific R. R. Mil.
Stone Co. Militia.
Tanney Co. Militia.
Warren Co. Militia.
Washington Co. Militia.
Wright Co. Militia.
Total organizations, 447.

MISSISSIPPI

1st Regt. Cav. A. D.
1st Regt. Mounted Rifles.
1st Regt. Heavy Arty. A. D.
2nd Regt. Heavy Arty. A. D.
1st Regt. Infy. A. D.
2nd Regt. Infy. A. D.
3rd Regt. Infy. A. D.
4th Regt. Infy. A. D.
5th Regt. Infy. A. D.
6th Regt. Infy. A. D.
    Total organizations, 10

NEBRASKA

1st Regt. Cav.
1st Batt'n Cav.
2nd Regt. Cav.
1st Regt. Infy.
Omaha Scouts.
Pawnee Scouts.
    Total organizations, 6.

NEVADA

1st Batt'n Cav.
1st Batt'n Infy.
    Total organizations, 2.

NEW HAMPSHIRE

1st Regt. Cav.
2nd Regt. Cav.

1st Regt. Heavy Arty.
1st Co. Heavy Arty.
2nd Co. Heavy Arty.
Tarbell's Co. Militia H. A.
1st Battery Light Arty.
1st Co. Sharpshooters.
2nd Co. Sharpshooters.
3rd Co. Sharpshooters.
1st Regt. Infy.
2nd Regt. Infy.
3rd Regt. Infy.
4th Regt. Infy.
5th Regt. Infy.
6th Regt. Infy.
7th Regt. Infy.
8th Regt. Infy.
9th Regt. Infy.
10th Regt. Infy.
11th Regt. Infy.
12th Regt. Infy.
13th Regt. Infy.
14th Regt. Infy.
15th Regt. Infy.
16th Regt. Infy.
17th Regt. Infy.
18th Regt. Infy.
Chandler's Militia Co.
Houghton's Militia Co.
Litchfield's Militia Co.
    Total organizations, 31.

NEW JERSEY

1st Regt. Cav. (16th.)
2nd Regt. Cav. (32nd.)
3rd Regt. Cav. (37th.)
1st Batty. Light Arty.
2nd Batty. Light Arty.
3rd Batty. Light Arty.
4th Batty. Light Arty.
5th Batty. Light Arty.
1st Regt. Infy. (3-Mos.)
1st Regt. Infy. (3-Yrs.)
2nd Regt. Infy. (3-Mos.)
2nd Regt. Infy. (3-yrs.)
3rd Regt. Infy. (3-Mos.)
3rd Regt. Infy. (3-Yrs.)
4th Regt. Infy. (3-Mos.)
4th Regt. Infy. (3-Yrs.)
5th Regt. Infy.
6th Regt. Infy.
7th Regt. Infy.
8th Regt. Infy.
9th Regt. Infy.
10th Regt. Infy.
11th Regt. Infy.
12th Regt. Infy.
13th Regt. Infy.
14th Regt. Infy.
15th Regt. Infy.
16th Regiment—(1st Cav.)
17th Regt. Infy.
18th Regt. Infy.
19th Regt. Infy.
20th Regt. Infy.
21st Regt. Infy.
22nd Regt. Infy.
23rd Regt. Infy.
24th Regt. Infy.
25th Regt. Infy.
26th Regt. Infy.
27th Regt. Infy.
28th Regt. Infy.
29th Regt. Infy.
30th Regt. Infy.
31st Regt. Infy.
32nd Regiment—(2nd Cav.)
33rd Regt. Infy.
34th Regt. Infy.
35th Regt. Infy.

36th Regt. Infy.
37th Regiment—(3rd Cav.)
38th Regt. Infy.
39th Regt. Infy.
40th Regt. Infy.
    Total organizations, 49.

NEW MEXICO

1st Regt. Cav.
1st Batt'n Cav. and Infy.
Graydon's Cav. Co.
Graydon's Cav. Co. Reorg.
Haspell's Cav. Co.
Mink's Cav. Co.
Vidal's Cav. Co.
1st Regt. Infy.
1st Regt. Infy. Reorg.
1st Regt. Militia Infy.
2nd Regt. Militia Infy.
3rd Regt. Militia Infy.
4th Regt. Militia Infy.
5th Regt. Militia Infy.
Perea's Battalion Militia.
Alarid's Militia Co. Infy.
Gonzales Militia Co. Infy.
Moras Militia Co. Infy.
Tafolla's Militia Co. Infy.
    Total organizations, 19.

NEW YORK

1st Regt. Cav.
1st Regt. Veteran Cav.
1st Regt. Prov'l Cav.
1st Regt. Mounted Rifles.
1st Regt. Dragoons.
2nd Regt. Cav.
2nd Regt. Veteran Cav.
2nd Mounted Rifles.
2nd Regt. Prov'l Cav.
3rd Regt. Cav.
3rd Regt. Prov'l Cav.
4th Regt. Cav.
4th Regt. Prov'l Cav.
5th Regt. Cav.
6th Regt. Cav.
7th Regt. Cav. (1st M. R.)
7th Regt. Cav. (Black Hawk)
8th Regt. Cav.
9th Regt. Cav.
10th Regt. Cav.
11th Regt. Cav.
12th Regt. Cav.
13th Regt. Cav.
14th Regt. Cav.
15th Regt. Cav.
16th Regt. Cav.
17th Regt. Cav.
18th Regt. Cav.
19th Regt. Cav. (1st Dragoons)
20th Regt. Cav.
21st Regt. Cav.
22nd Regt. Cav.
23rd Battalion Cav.
24th Regt. Cav.
25th Regt. Cav.
26th Regt. Cav.
Devens' Cav. Co.
Oneida Cav. Co.
Sauers' Cav. Co.
2nd Regt. Heavy Arty.
2nd Batt'n Heavy Arty.
4th Regt. Heavy Arty.
4th Regt. N. G. Heavy Arty.
4th Batt'n Heavy Arty.
5th Regt. Heavy Arty.
5th Batt'n Heavy Arty.
6th Regt. Heavy Arty.
6th Batt'n Heavy Arty.
7th Regt. Heavy Arty.

7th Batt'n Heavy Arty.
8th Regt. Heavy Arty.
9th Regt. Heavy Arty.
10th Regt. Heavy Arty.
11th Regt. Heavy Arty.
12th Regt. Heavy Arty.
13th Regt. Heavy Arty.
13th Regt. S. M. Heavy Arty.
14 Regt. Heavy Arty.
15 Regt. Heavy Arty.
16th Regt. Heavy Arty.
Anthon's Batt'n L. A.
Rocket Batt'n Light Arty.
1st Batt'n Light Arty.
1st Batt'n Light Arty. N. G.
1st Batt'n Marine Arty.
2nd Batt'n Light Arty.
Batty. A. 1st Regt. L. A.
Batty. B. 1st Regt. L. A.
Batty. C. 1st Regt. L. A.
Batty. D. 1st Regt. L. A.
Batty. E. 1st Regt. L. A.
Batty. F. 1st Regt. L. A.
Batty. G. 1st Regt. L. A.
Batty. H. 1st Regt. L. A.
Batty. I. 1st Regt. L. A.
Batty. K. 1st Regt. L. A.
Batty. L. 1st Regt. L. A.
Batty. M. 1st Regt. L. A.
Batty. L. 2nd Regt. L. A.
Batty. A. 3rd Regt. L. A.
Batty. B. 3rd Regt. L. A.
Batty. C. 3rd Regt. L. A.
Batty. D. 3rd Regt. L. A.
Batty. E. 3rd Regt. L. A.
Batty. F. 3rd Regt. L. A.
Batty. G. 3rd Regt. L. A.
Batty. H. 3rd Regt. L. A.
Batty. I. 3rd Regt. L. A.
Batty. K. 3rd Regt. L. A.
Batty. L. 3rd Regt. L. A.
Batty. M. 3rd Regt. L. A.
1st Indpt. Batty. L. A.
2nd Indpt. Batty. L. A.
3rd Indpt. Batty. L. A.
4th Indpt. Batty. L. A.
5th Indpt. Batty. L. A.
6th Indpt. Batty. L. A.
7th Indpt. Batty. L. A.
8th Indpt. Batty. L. A.
9th Indpt. Batty. L. A.
10th Indpt. Batty. L. A.
11th Indpt. Batty. L. A.
12th Indpt. Batty. L. A.
13th Indpt. Batty. L. A.
14th Indpt. Batty. L. A.
15th Indpt. Batty. L. A.
16th Indpt. Batty. L. A.
17th Indpt. Batty. L. A.
18th Indpt. Batty. L. A.
19th Indpt. Batty. L. A.
20th Indpt. Batty. L. A.
21st Indpt. Batty. L. A.
22nd. Indpt. Batty. L. A.
23rd Indpt. Batty. L. A.
24th Indpt. Batty. L. A.
25th Indpt. Batty. L. A.
26th Indpt. Batty. L. A.
27th Indpt. Batty. L. A.
28th Indpt. Batty. L. A.
29th Indpt. Batty. L. A.
30th Indpt. Batty. L. A.
31st Indpt. Batty. L. A.
32nd Indpt. Batty. L. A.
33rd Indpt. Batty. L. A.
34th Indpt. Batty. L. A.
35th Indpt. Batty. L. A.
36th Indpt. Batty. L. A.
Allee's Indpt. Batty. L. A.

Bookwood's Batty. L. A.
Fish's Batty. L. A.
Goodwin's S. M. Batty. L. A.
Varian's Batty. L. A.
1st Regt. Engineers.
2nd Regt. Engineers.
15th Regt. Engineers.
50th Regt. Engineers.
1st Batt'n Sharpshooters.
Co. A. 1st U. S. Sharpshooters.
Co. B. 1st U. S. Sharpshooters.
Co. D. 1st U. S. Sharpshooters.
Co. H. 1st U. S. Sharpshooters.
1st Regt. Infy.
2nd Regt. S. M. Infy. (82nd.)
3rd Regt. Infy.
4th Regt. Infy.
4th Regt. N. G. Infy.
5th Regt. Infy (3-Mos.)
5th Regt. Infy.
5th Regt. N. G. Infy.
5th Regt. Veteran Infy.
6th Regt. Infy. (3-Mos.)
6th Regt. Infy.
6th Regt. N. G. Infy.
7th Regt. Infy.
7th Regt. S. M. Infy.
7th Regt. Veteran Infy.
8th Regt. S. M. Infy.
8th Regt. Infy.
8th Regt. N. G. Infy.
9th Regt. Infy.
9th Regt. Veteran Infy.
10th Regt. Infy.
10th Regt. N. G. Infy.
11th Regt. Infy.
11th Regt. N. G. Infy.
12th Regt. Infy. (3-Mos.)
12th Regt. Infy.
12th Regt. N. G. Infy.
13th Regt. Infy. (3-Mos.)
13th Regt. Infy.
13th Regt. N. G. Infy.
14th Regt. Infy.
14th Regt. S. M. Infy. (84th.)
15th Regt. Infy.
15th Regt. N. G. Infy.
16th Regt. Infy.
17th Regt. Infy.
17th Regt. Veteran Infy.
17th Regt. N. G. Infy.
18th Regt. Infy.
18th Regt. N. G. Infy.
19th Regt. Infy.
19th Regt. N. G. Infy.
20th Regt. Infy. (3-Mos.)
20th Regt. Infy.
20th Regt. S. M. Infy. (80th.)
20th Regt. Veteran Infy.
21st Regt. Infy.
21st Regt. N. G. Infy.
22nd Regt. Infy.
22nd Regt. N. G. Infy.
23rd Regt. Infy.
23rd N. G. Infy.
24th Regt. Infy. (3-Mos.)
24th Regt. Infy.
25th Regt. Infy. (3-Mos.)
25th Regt. Infy.
25th Regt. N. G. Infy.
26th Regt. Infy.
27th Regt. Infy.
28th Regt. Infy. (3-Mos.)
28th Regt. Infy.
28th Regt. N. G. Infy.
28th Regt. Infy.
29th Regt. Veteran Infy.
30th Regt. Infy.

31st Regt. Infy.
31st Regt. Veteran Infy.
32nd Regt. Infy.
33rd Regt. Infy.
34th Regt. Infy.
35th Regt. Infy.
36th Regt. Infy.
37th Regt. Infy.
37th Regt. Veteran Infy.
37th Regt. N. G. Infy.
38th Regt. Infy.
38th Regt. Veteran Infy.
39th Regt. Infy.
40th Regt. Infy.
41st Regt. Infy.
42nd Regt. Infy.
43rd Regt. Infy.
44th Regt. Infy.
45th Regt. Infy.
46th Regt. Infy.
47th Regt. Infy.
47th Regt. N. G. Infy.
48th Regt. Infy.
49 Regt. Infy.
50th Regt. Infy.
50th Regt. N. G. Infy.
51st Regt. Infy.
52nd Regt. Infy.
52nd Regt. N. G. Infy.
53rd Regt. Infy.
53rd Regt. Infy. Reorg.
54th Regt. Infy.
54th Regt. N. G. Infy.
55th Regt. Infy.
55th Regt. N. G. Infy.
56th Regt. Infy.
56th Regt. N. G. Infy.
57th Regt. Infy.
58th Regt. Infy.
58th Regt. N. G. Infy.
59th Regt. Infy.
60th Regt. Infy.
61st Regt. Infy.
62nd Regt. Infy.
63rd Regt. Infy.
64th Regt. Infy.
65th Regt. Infy.
65th Regt. N. G. Infy.
66th Regt. Infy.
67th Regt. Infy.
67th Regt. N. G. Infy.
68th Regt. Infy.
68th Regt. N. G. Infy.
69th Regt. S. M. Infy.
69th Regt. Infy.
69th Regt. N. G. Infy.
70th Regt. Infy.
71st Regt. Infy.
71st Regt. S. M. Infy.
71st Regt. N. G. Infy.
72nd Regt. Infy.
73rd Regt. Infy.
74th Regt. Infy.
74th Regt. N. G. Infy.
75th Regt. Infy.
76th Regt. Infy.
77th Regt. Infy.
77th Regt. N. G. Infy.
78th Regt. Infy.
79th Regt. Infy.
80th Regt. Infy. (20th S. M.)
81st Regt. Infy.
82nd Regt. Infy. (2nd S. M.)
83rd Regt. Infy.
84th Regt. Infy. (14th S. M.)
84th Regt. N. G. Infy.
85th Regt. Infy.
86th Regt. Infy.
87th Regt. Infy.

88th Regt. Infy.
89th Regt. Infy.
90th Regt. Infy.
91st Regt. Infy.
92nd Regt. Infy.
93rd Regt. Infy.
93rd Regt. N. G. Infy.
94th Regt. Infy.
95th Regt. Infy.
96th Regt. Infy.
97th Regt. Infy.
98th Regt. Infy.
98th Regt. N. G. Infy.
99th Regt. Infy.
99th Regt. N. G. Infy.
100th Regt. Infy.
101st Regt. Infy.
102nd Regt. Infy.
102nd Regt. N. G. Infy.
103rd Regt. Infy.
104th Regt. Infy.
105th Regt. Infy.
106th Regt. Infy.
107th Regt. Infy.
108th Regt. Infy.
109th Regt. Infy.
110th Regt. Infy.
111th Regt. Infy.
112th Regt. Infy.
113th Regt. Infy.
114th Regt. Infy.
115th Regt. Infy.
116th Regt. Infy.
117th Regt. Infy.
108th Regt. Infy.
119th Regt. Infy.
120th Regt. Infy.
121st Regt. Infy.
122nd Regt. Infy.
123rd Regt. Infy.
124th Regt. Infy.
125th Regt. Infy.
126th Regt. Infy.
127th Regt. Infy.
128th Regt. Infy.
129th Regt. Infy.
130th Regt. Infy.
131st Regt. Infy.
132nd Regt. Infy.
133rd Regt. Infy.
134th Regt. Infy.
135th Regt. Infy.
136th Regt. Infy.
137th Regt. Infy.
138th Regt. Infy.
139th Regt. Infy.
140th Regt. Infy.
141st Regt. Infy.
142nd Regt. Infy.
143rd Regt. Infy.
144th Regt. Infy.
145th Regt. Infy.
146th Regt. Infy.
147th Regt. Infy.
148th Regt. Infy.
149th Regt. Infy.
150th Regt. Infy.
151st Regt. Infy.
152nd Regt. Infy.
153rd Regt. Infy.
154th Regt. Infy.
155th Regt. Infy.
156th Regt. Infy.
157th Regt. Infy.
158th Regt. Infy.
159th Regt. Infy.
160th Regt. Infy.
161st Regt. Infy.
162nd Regt. Infy.

163rd Regt. Infy.
164th Regt. Infy.
165th Regt. Infy.
166th Regt. Infy.
167th Regt. Infy.
168th Regt. Infy.
169th Regt. Infy.
170th Regt. Infy.
171st Regt. Infy.
172nd Regt. Infy.
173rd Regt. Infy.
174th Regt. Infy.
175th Regt. Infy.
176th Regt. Infy.
177th Regt. Infy.
178th Regt. Infy.
179th Regt. Infy.
180th Regt. Infy.
181st Regt. Infy.
182nd Regt. Infy.
183rd Regt. Infy.
184th Regt. Infy.
185th Regt. Infy.
186th Regt. Infy.
187th Regt. Infy.
188th Regt. Infy.
189th Regt. Infy.
190th Regt. Infy.
191st Regt. Infy.
192nd Regt. Infy.
193rd Regt. Infy.
194th Regt. Infy.
Indpt. Batt'n Enfans Perdu.
Total organizations, 393.

NORTH CAROLINA

1st Regt. Heavy Arty. A. D.
1st Regt. Infy.
1st Regt. Infy. A. D.
2nd Regt. Infy.
2nd Regt. Mounted Infy.
2nd Regt. Infy. A. D.
3rd Regt. Mounted Infy.
3rd Regt. Infy. A. D.
Total organizations, 8.

OHIO

1st Regt. Cav.
2nd Regt. Cav.
3rd Regt. Cav.
4th Regt. Cav.
5th Regt. Cav.
6th Regt. Cav.
7th Regt. Cav.
8th Regt. Cav.
9th Regt. Cav.
10th Regt. Cav.
11th Regt. Cav.
12th Regt. Cav.
13th Regt. Cav.
1st Batt'n Cav.
2nd Batt'n Cav.
4th Batt'n Cav.
5th Batt'n Cav.
McLaughin's Cav. Batt'n.
Burdsall's Cav. Co.
George's Cav Co.
Harlan Light Cav.
Ironton Cav. Co.
Union Light Guard.
3rd Indpt. Cav. Co.
4th Indpt. Cav. Co.
5th Indpt. Cav. Co.
6th Indpt. Cav. Co.
7th Indpt. Cav. Co.
1st Regt. Heavy Arty.
2nd Regt. Heavy Arty.
Barnett's Arty.
Cotter's Batty. L. A.

Paulson's Batty. L. A.
Williams Batty. L. A.
Batty. A. 1st Regt. L. A.
Batty. B. 1st Regt. L. A.
Batty. C. 1st Regt. L. A.
Batty. D. 1st Regt. L. A.
Batty. E. 1st Regt. L. A.
Batty. F. 1st Regt. L. A.
Batty. G. 1st Regt. L. A.
Batty. H. 1st Regt. L. A.
Batty. I. 1st Regt. L. A.
Batty. K. 1st Regt. L. A.
Batty. L. 1st Regt. L. A.
Batty. M. 1st Regt. L. A.
1st Indpt. Batty. L. A.
2nd Indpt. Batty. L. A.
2nd Indpt. Batty. N. G. L. A.
3rd Indpt. Batty. L. A.
4th Indpt. Batty. L. A.
5th Indpt. Batty. L. A.
6th Indpt. Batty. L. A.
7th Indpt. Batty. L. A.
8th Indpt. Batty. L. A.
8th Indpt. Batty. N. G. L. A.
9th Indpt. Batty. L. A.
10th Indpt. Batty. L. A.
11th Indpt. Batty. L. A.
12th Indpt. Batty. L. A.
13th Indpt. Batty. L. A.
14th Indpt. Batty. L. A.
15th Indpt. Batty. L. A.
16th Indpt. Batty. L. A.
17th Indpt. Batty. L. A.
18th Indpt. Batty. L. A.
19th Indpt. Batty. L. A.
20th Indpt. Batty. L. A.
21st Indpt. Batty. L. A.
22nd Indpt. Batty. L. A.
23rd Indpt. Batty. L. A.
24th Indpt. Batty. L. A.
25th Indpt. Batty. L. A.
26th Indpt. Batty. L. A.
1st Batt'n Sharpshooters.
1st Co. Sharpshooters.
2nd Co. Sharpshooters.
3rd Co. Sharpshooters.
4th Co. Sharpshooters.
5th Co. Sharpshooters.
6th Co. Sharpshooters.
7th Co. Sharpshooters.
8th Co. Sharpshooters.
9th Co. Sharpshooters.
10th Co. Sharpshooters.
1st Regt. Infy. (3-Mos.)
1st Regt. Infy. (3-Yrs.)
2nd Regt. Infy. (3-Mos.)
2nd Regt. Infy. (3-Yrs.)
3rd Regt. Infy. (3-Mos.)
3rd Regt. Infy. (3-Yrs.)
4th Regt. Infy. (3-Mos.)
4th Regt. Infy. (3-Yrs.)
5th Regt. Infy. (3-Mos.)
5th Regt. Infy. (3-Yrs.)
6th Regt. Infy. (3-Mos.)
6th Regt. Infy. (3-Yrs.)
7th Regt. Infy. (3-Mos.)
7th Regt. Infy. (3-Yrs.)
8th Regt. Infy. (3-Mos.)
8th Regt. Infy. (3-Yrs.)
9th Regt. Infy. (3-Mos.)
9th Regt. Infy. (3-Yrs.)
10th Regt. Infy. (3-Mos.)
10th Regt. Infy. (3-Yrs.)
11th Regt. Infy. (3-Mos.)
11th Regt. Infy. (3-Yrs.)
12th Regt. Infy. (3-Mos.)
12th Regt. Infy. (3-Yrs.)
13th Regt. Infy. (3-Mos.)
13th Regt. Infy. (3-Yrs.)

14th Regt. Infy. (3-Mos.)
14th Regt. Infy. (3-Yrs.)
15th Regt. Infy. (3-Mos.)
15th Regt. Infy. (3-Yrs.)
16th Regt. Infy. (3-Mos.)
16th Regt. Infy. (3-Yrs.)
17th Regt. Infy. (3-Mos.)
17th Regt. Infy. (3-Yrs.)
18th Regt. Infy. (3-Mos.)
18th Regt. Infy. (3-Yrs.)
18th Regt. Infy. (Veteran)
19th Regt. Infy. (3-Mos.)
19th Regt. Infy. (3-Yrs.)
20th Regt. Infy. (3-Mos.)
20th Regt. Infy. (3-Yrs.)
21st Regt. Infy. (3-Mos.)
21st Regt. Infy. (3-Yrs.)
22nd Regt. Infy. (3-Mos.)
22nd Regt. Infy. (3-Yrs.)
23rd Regt. Infy.
24th Regt. Infy.
25th Regt. Infy.
26th Regt. Infy.
27th Regt. Infy.
28th Regt. Infy.
29th Regt. Infy.
30th Regt. Infy.
31st Regt. Infy.
32nd Regt. Infy.
33rd Regt. Infy.
34th Regt. Infy.
35th Regt. Infy.
36th Regt. Infy.
37th Regt. Infy.
38th Regt. Infy.
39th Regt. Infy.
40th Regt. Infy.
41st Regt. Infy.
42nd Regt. Infy.
43rd Regt. Infy.
44th Regt. Infy.
45th Regt. Infy.
46th Regt. Infy.
47th Regt. Infy.
48th Regt. Infy.
48th Batt'n Infy.
49th Regt. Infy.
50th Regt. Infy.
51st Regt. Infy.
52nd Regt. Infy.
53rd Regt. Infy.
54th Regt. Infy.
55th Regt. Infy.
56th Regt. Infy.
57th Regt. Infy.
58th Regt. Infy.
59th Regt. Infy.
60th Regt. Infy.
60th Regt. Infy. Reorg.
61st Regt. Infy.
62nd Regt. Infy.
63rd Regt. Infy.
64th Regt. Infy.
65th Regt. Infy.
66th Regt. Infy.
67th Regt. Infy.
68th Regt. Infy.
69th Regt. Infy.
70th Regt. Infy.
71st Regt. Infy.
72nd Regt. Infy.
73rd Regt. Infy.
74th Regt. Infy.
75th Regt. Infy.
76th Regt. Infy.
77th Regt. Infy.
78th Regt. Infy.
79th Regt. Infy.
80th Regt. Infy.

81st Regt. Infy.
82nd Regt. Infy.
83rd Regt. Infy.
84th Regt. Infy.
85th Regt. Infy.
86th Regt. Infy.
86th Regt. Infy. Reorg.
87th Regt. Infy.
88th Regt. Infy.
89th Regt. Infy.
90th Regt. Infy.
91st Regt. Infy.
92nd Regt. Infy.
93rd Regt. Infy.
94th Regt. Infy.
95th Regt. Infy.
96th Regt. Infy.
97th Regt. Infy.
98th Regt. Infy.
99th Regt. Infy.
100th Regt. Infy.
101st Regt. Infy.
102nd Regt. Infy.
103rd Regt. Infy.
104th Regt. Infy.
105th Regt. Infy.
106th Regt. Infy.
107th Regt. Infy.
108th Regt. Infy.
109th Regt. Infy.
110th Regt. Infy.
111th Regt. Infy.
112th Regt. Infy.
113th Regt. Infy.
114th Regt. Infy.
115th Regt. Infy.
116th Regt. Infy.
117th Regt. Infy.
118th Regt. Infy.
119th Regt. Infy.
120th Regt. Infy.
121st Regt. Infy.
122nd Regt. Infy.
123rd Regt. Infy.
124th Regt. Infy.
125th Regt. Infy.
126th Regt. Infy.
127th Regt. Infy.
128th Regt. Infy.
129th Regt. Infy.
130th Regt. Infy.
131st Regt. Infy.
132nd Regt. Infy.
133rd Regt. Infy.
134th Regt. Infy.
135th Regt. Infy.
136th Regt. Infy.
137th Regt. Infy.
138th Regt. Infy.
139th Regt. Infy.
140th Regt. Infy.
141st Regt. Infy.
142nd Regt. Infy.
143rd Regt. Infy.
144th Regt. Infy.
145th Regt. Infy.
146th Regt. Infy.
147th Regt. Infy.
148th Regt. Infy.
149th Regt. Infy.
150th Regt. Infy.
151st Regt. Infy.
152nd Regt. Infy.
153rd Regt. Infy.
154th Regt. Infy.
155th Regt. Infy.
156th Regt. Infy.
157th Regt. Infy.
158th Regt. Infy.

159th Regt. Infy.
160th Regt. Infy.
161st Regt. Infy.
162nd Regt. Infy.
163rd Regt. Infy.
164th Regt. Infy.
165th Regt. Infy.
166th Regt. Infy.
167th Regt. Infy.
168th Regt. Infy.
169th Regt. Infy.
170th Regt. Infy.
171st Regt. Infy.
172nd Regt. Infy.
173rd Regt. Infy.
174th Regt. Infy.
175th Regt. Infy.
176th Regt. Infy.
177th Regt. Infy.
178th Regt. Infy.
179th Regt. Infy.
180th Regt. Infy.
181st Regt. Infy.
182nd Regt. Infy.
183rd Regt. Infy.
184th Regt. Infy.
185th Regt. Infy.
186th Regt. Infy.
187th Regt. Infy.
188th Regt. Infy.
189th Regt. Infy.
190th Regt. Infy.
191st Regt. Infy.
192nd Regt. Infy.
193rd Regt. Infy.
194th Regt. Infy.
195th Regt. Infy.
196th Regt. Infy.
197th Regt. Infy.
198th Regt. Infy.
Hoffman's Batt'n Infy.
Baird's Indpt. Co. Infy.
Dennison Guard Infy.
Departmental Corps.
Trumbull Guard.
Wallace Guard.
 Total organizations, 315.

OREGON

1st Regt. Cav.
1st Regt. Infy.
 Total organizations, 2.

PENNSYLVANIA

1st Regt. Cav. (43rd).
1st Regt. Prov'l Cav.
2nd Regt. Cav. (59th).
2nd Regt. Prov'l Cav.
3rd Regt. Cav. (60th).
3rd Regt. Prov'l Cav.
4th Regt. Cav. (64th).
5th Regt. Cav. (65th).
6th Regt. Cav. (70th).
7th Regt. Cav. (80th).
8th Regt. Cav. (89th).
9th Regt. Cav. (92nd).
10th Regt. Cav.
11th Regt. Cav. (108th).
12th Regt. Cav. (113th).
13th Regt. Cav. (117th).
14th Regt. Cav. (139th).
15th Regt. Cav. (160th).
16th Regt. Cav. (161st).
17th Regt. Cav. (162nd).
18th Regt. Cav. (163rd).
19th Regt. Cav. (180th).
20th Regt. Cav. (6-Mos.)
20th Regt. Cav. (181st).
21st Regt. Cav. (6-Mos.)

21st Regt. Cav. (182nd).
22nd Regt. Cav. (6-Mos.)
22nd Regt. Cav. (185).
Indpt. Batt'n Cav.
Ringgold Batt'n Cav.
Anderson Troop Cav.
Bell's Co. Militia Cav.
Brown's Co. Militia Cav.
Comley's Co. Militia Cav.
Dick's Co. Militia Cav.
Hammill's Co. Militia Cav.
Hebble's Co. Cav.
Jones' Co. Militia Cav.
Lafayette Co. Cav.
Lambert's Co. Cav.
Morehead's Co. Cav.
Murray's Co. Cav.
Myers' Co. Cav.
Negley's Body Guard.
Phila. City Troop.
Reading City Guard.
Ringgold Co. Cav.
Sanno's Co. Cav.
Stroud's Co. Cav.
Union Cav. Co.
Warren's Cav. Co.
Washington Co. Cav. Co.
Weaver's Cav. Co.
2nd Regt. Heavy Arty. (112th).
2nd Regt. Heavy Arty. Prov'l.
3rd Regt. Heavy Arty. (152nd).
5th Regt. Heavy Arty. (205th).
6th Regt. Heavy Arty. (212th).
1st Marine Batt'n H. A.
Robert's Batt'n H. A.
Commonwealth Co. H. A.
Ermentrout's Co. Militia H. A.
Jones' Co. Heavy Arty.
Schooley's Co. Heavy Arty.
Batty. A. 1st Regt. L. A.
Batty. B. 1st Regt. L. A.
Batty. C. 1st Regt. L. A.
Batty. D. 1st Regt. L. A.
Batty. E. 1st Regt. L. A.
Batty. F. 1st Regt. L. A.
Batty. G. 1st Regt. L. A.
Batty. H. 1st Regt. L. A.
Batty. I. 1st Regt. L. A.
Indpt. Batty. A. Light Arty.
Indpt. Batty. B. Light Arty.
Indpt. Batty. C. Light Arty.
Indpt. Batty. D. Light Arty.
Indpt. Batty. E. Light Arty.
Indpt. Batty. F. Light Arty.
Indpt. Batty. G. Light Arty.
Indpt. Batty. H. Light Arty.
Indpt. Batty. I. Light Arty.
Knap's 1st Batt'n L. A.
Guss' Batty. Militia L. A.
Hasting's Batty. L. A.
Keystone Batty. L. A.
Keystone Batty. L. A. 2nd.
Knap's Militia Batty. L. A.
Landis' Phila. Batty. L. A.
Millin's Militia Batty. L. A.
Nevin's Batty. L. A.
Tyler's Park Batty. L. A.
Ullman's Batty. L. A.
Woodward's Batty. L. A.
Wrigley's Engineer Co.
Indpt. Co. Sharpshooters.
1st Regt. Infy. (3-Mos.)
1st Regt. Infy Reserves.
1st Regt. Rifles. (13th Res.).
1st Regt. Militia Infy.
1st Batt'n Infy. (6-Mos.)
1st Batt'n Infy. (100-Days)
2nd Regt. Infy. (3-Mos.)
2nd Regt. Infy. Reserves.

2nd Regt. Militia Infy.
2nd Batt'n Infy.
3rd Regt. Infy. (3-Mos.)
3rd Regt. Infy. Reserves.
3rd Regt. Militia Infy.
3rd Batt'n Infy.
4th Regt. Infy. (3-Mos.)
4th Regt. Infy. Reserves.
4th Regt. Militia Infy.
5th Regt. Infy. (3-Mos.)
5th Regt. Infy. Reserves.
5th Regt. Militia Infy.
6th Regt. Infy. (3-Mos.)
6th Regt. Infy. Reserves.
6th Regt. Militia Infy.
7th Regt. Infy. (3-Mos.)
7th Regt. Infy. Reserves.
7th Regt. Militia Infy.
8th Regt. Infy. (3-Mos.)
8th Regt. Infy. Reserves.
8th Regt. Militia Infy.
9th Regt. Infy. (3-Mos.)
9th Regt. Infy. Reserves.
9th Regt. Militia Infy.
10th Regt. Infy. (3-Mos.)
10th Regt. Infy. Reserves.
11th Regt. Infy. (3-Mos.)
11th Regt. Infy. (3-Yrs.)
11th Regt. Infy. Reserves.
11th Regt. Militia Infy.
12th Regt. Infy. (3-Mos.)
12th Regt. Infy. Reserves.
12th Regt. Militia Infy.
13th Regt. Infy. (3-Mos.)
13th Regt. Infy. Reserves.
13th Regt. Militia Infy.
14th Regt. Infy. (3-Mos.)
14th Regt. Reserves. (1-Cav.)
14th Regt. Militia Infy.
15th Regt. Infy. (3-Mos.)
15th Regt. Reserves. (1-L. A.)
15th Regt. Militia Infy.
16th Regt. Infy. (3-Mos.)
16th Regt. Militia Infy.
17th Regt. Infy. (3-Mos.)
17th Regt. Militia Infy.
18th Regt. Infy. (3-Mos.)
18th Regt. Militia Infy.
19th Regt. Infy. (3-Mos.)
19th Regt. Militia Infy.
20th Regt. Infy. (3-Mos.)
20th Militia Infy.
20th Regt. Emergency.
21st Regt. Infy. (3-Mos.)
21st Regt. Militia Infy.
22nd Regt. Infy. (3-Mos.)
22nd Regt. Militia Infy.
23rd Regt. Infy. (3-Mos.)
23rd Regt. Infy. (3-Yrs.)
23rd Regt. Militia Infy.
24th Regt. Infy. (3-Mos.)
24th Regt. Militia Infy.
25th Regt. Infy. (3-Mos.)
25th Regt. Militia Infy.
26th Regt. Infy
26th Regt. Emergency.
27th Regt. Infy.
27th Regt. Emergency.
28th Regt. Infy.
28th Regt. Emergency.
29th Regt. Infy.
29th Regt. Emergency.
30th Regt. Infy. (see 66)
30th Regt. Infy. (1st Res.)
30th Regt. Emergency.
31st Regt. Infy. (see 82)
31st Regt. Infy. (2nd Res.)
31st Regt. Emergency.
32nd Regt. Infy. (see 99)

32nd Regt. Infy. (3rd Res.)
32nd Regt. Militia Infy.
33rd Regt. Infy. (see 62)
33rd Regt. Infy. (4th Res.)
33rd Regt. Militia Infy.
34th Regt. Infy. (5th Res.)
34th Regt. Militia Infy.
35th Regt. Infy. (see 74)
35th Regt. Infy. (8th Res.)
35th Regt. Militia Infy.
36th Regt. Infy. (see 81)
36th Regt. Infy. (7th Res.)
36th Regt. Militia Infy.
37th Regt. Infy. (8th Res.)
37th Regt. Militia Infy.
38th Regt. Infy. (9th Res.)
38th Regt. Militia Infy.
39th Regt. Infy. (10th Res.)
39th Regt. Militia Infy.
40th Regt. Infy. (see 75)
40th Regt. Infy. (11th Res.)
40th Regt. Militia Infy.
41st Regt. Infy. (12th Res.)
41st Regt. Militia Infy.
42nd Regt. (13th Res.—1st Rifles.)
42nd Regt. Militia Infy.
43rd Regt. (14th Res.—1st Cav.)
43rd Regt. Militia Infy.
44th Regt. (15th Res.—1st L. A.)
44th Regt. Militia Infy.
45th Regt. Infy.
45th Regt. Militia Infy.
46th Regt. Infy.
46th Regt. Militia Infy.
47th Regt. Infy.
47th Regt. Militia Infy.
48th Regt. Infy.
48th Regt. Militia Infy.
49th Regt. Infy.
49th Regt. Militia Infy.
50th Regt. Infy.
50th Regt. Militia Infy.
51st Regt. Infy.
51st Regt. Militia Infy.
52nd Regt. Infy.
52nd Regt. Militia Infy.
53rd Regt. Infy.
53rd Regt. Militia Infy.
54th Regt. Infy.
54th Regt. Militia Infy.
55th Regt. Infy.
55th Regt. Militia Iufy.
56th Regt. Infy.
56th Regt. Militia Infy.
57th Regt. Infy.
57th Regt. Militia Infy.
58th Regt. Infy.
58th Regt. Militia Infy.
59th Regiment (2nd Cav.)
59th Regt. Militia Infy.
60th Regiment. (3rd Cav.)
60th Regt. Militia Infy.
61st Regt. Infy.
62nd Regt. Infy.
63rd Regt. Infy.
64th Regiment. (4th Cav.)
65th Regiment. (5th Cav.)
66th Regt. Infy.
67th Regt. Infy.
68th Regt. Infy.
69th Regt. Infy.
70th Regiment. (6th Cav.)
71st Regt. Infy.
72nd Regt. Infy.
73rd Regt. Infy.
74th Regt. Infy.
75th Regt. Infy.
76th Regt. Infy.
77th Regt. Infy.

78th Regt. Infy.
79th Regt. Infy.
80th Regiment. (7th Cav.)
81st Regt. Infy.
82nd Regt. Infy.
83rd Regt. Infy.
84th Regt. Infy.
85th Regt. Infy.
86th Regt. Infy.
87th Regt. Infy.
88th Regt. Infy.
89th Regiment. (8th Cav.)
90th Regt. Infy.
91st Regt. Infy.
92nd Regiment. (9th Cav.)
93rd Regt. Infy.
94th Regt. Infy.
95th Regt. Infy.
96th Regt. Infy.
97th Regt. Infy.
98th Regt. Infy.
99th Regt. Infy.
100th Regt. Infy.
101st Regt. Infy.
102nd Regt. Infy.
103rd Regt. Infy.
104th Regt. Infy.
105th Regt. Infy.
106th Regt. Infy.
107th Regt. Infy.
108th Regiment. (11th Cav.)
109th Regt. Infy.
110th Regt. Infy.
111th Regt. Infy.
112th Regiment. (2nd H. A.)
113th Regiment. (12th Cav.)
114th Regt. Infy.
115th Regt. Infy.
116th Regt. Infy.
117th Regiment. (13th Cav.)
118th Regt. Infy.
119th Regt. Infy.
120th Regt. Infy.
121st Regt. Infy.
122nd Regt. Infy.
123rd Regt. Infy.
124th Regt. Infy.
125th Regt. Infy.
126th Regt. Infy.
127th Regt. Infy.
128th Regt. Infy.
129th Regt. Infy.
130th Regt. Infy.
131st Regt. Infy.
132nd Regt. Infy.
133rd Regt. Infy.
134th Regt. Infy.
135th Regt. Infy.
136th Regt. Infy.
137th Regt. Infy.
138th Regt. Infy.
139th Regt. Infy.
140th Regt. Infy.
141st Regt. Infy.
142nd Regt. Infy.
143rd Regt. Infy.
144th Regt. Infy.
145th Regt. Infy.
146th Regt. Infy.
147th Regt. Infy.
148th Regt. Infy.
149th Regt. Infy.
150th Regt. Infy.
151st Regt. Infy.
152nd Regiment. (3rd H. A.)
153rd Regt. Infy.
154th Regt. Infy.
155th Regt. Infy.
156th Regt. Infy.

157th Regt. Infy.
158th Regt. Infy.
159th Regiment. (14th Cav.)
160th Regiment. (15th Cav.)
161st Regiment. (16th Cav.)
162th Regiment. (17th Cav.)
163rd Regiment. (18th Cav.)
164th Regt. Infy.
165th Regt. Infy.
166th Regt. Infy.
167th Regt. Infy.
168th Regt. Infy.
169th Regt. Infy.
170th Regt. Infy.
171st Regt. Infy.
172nd Regt. Infy.
173rd Regt. Infy.
174th Regt. Infy.
175th Regt. Infy.
176th Regt. Infy.
177th Regt. Infy.
178th Regt. Infy.
179th Regt. Infy.
180th Regiment. (19 Cav.)
181st Regiment. (20th Cav.)
182nd Regiment. (21st Cav.)
183rd Regt. Infy.
184th Regt. Infy.
185th Regiment. (22nd Cav.)
186th Regt. Infy.
187th Regt. Infy.
188th Regt. Infy.
189th Regt. Infy.
190th Regt. Infy.
191st Regt. Infy.
192nd Regt. Infy.
193rd Regt. Infy.
194th Regt. Infy.
195th Regt. Infy.
196th Regt. Infy.
197th Regt. Infy.
198th Regt. Infy.
199th Regt. Infy.
200th Regt. Infy.
201st Regt. Infy.
202nd Regt. Infy.
203rd Regt. Infy.
204th Regiment. (5th H. A.)
205th Regt. Infy.
206th Regt. Infy.
207th Regt. Infy.
208th Regt. Infy.
209th Regt. Infy.
210th Regt. Infy.
211th Regt. Infy.
212th Regiment. (6th H. A.)
213th Regt. Infy.
214th Regt. Infy.
215th Regt. Infy.
Indpt. Batt'n Militia Infy.
Litzinger's Bn. Mil. Infy.
Lininger's Bn. Mil. Infy.
McKeag's Batt'n Mil. Infy.
Zell's Batt'n Mil. Infy.
Baldwin's Co. Mil. Infy.
Beale's Co. Mil. Infy.
Campbell's Co. Mil. Infy.
Carson's Co. Mil. Infy.
Collis' Indpt. Co. Infy.
Departmental Corps.
Gorman's Co. Mil. Infy.
Green's Co. Mil. Infy.
Griffith's Co. Infy.
Guthrie's Co. Mil. Infy.
Helmboldt's Co. Mil. Infy.
Hubbell's Co. Mil. Infy.
Huff's Co. Mil. Infy.
James' Indpt. Co. Infy.
Jones' Indpt. Co. Infy.

Luther's Co. Mil. Infy.
McKnight's Co. Mil. Infy.
Mann's Co. Mil. Infy.
Mitchell's Co. Mil. Infy.
Rich's Co. Mil. Infy.
Roberts' Co. Mil. Infy.
Spear's Co. Mil. Infy.
Stephens' Co. Mil. Infy.
Tanner's Co. Infy.
Zouaves de Afrique.
   Total organizations, 383.

RHODE ISLAND

1st Regt. Cav.
2nd Regt. Cav.
3rd Regt. Cav.
7th Squadron Cav.
Batty. A. 3rd H. A.
Batty. B. 3rd H. A.
Batty. C. 3rd H. A.
Batty. D. 3rd H. A.
Batty. E. 3rd H. A.
Batty. F. 3rd H. A.
Batty. G. 3rd H. A.
Batty. H. 3rd H. A.
Batty. I. 3rd H. A.
Batty. K. 3rd H. A.
Batty. L. 3rd H. A.
Batty. M. 3rd H. A.
5th Regt. Heavy Arty.
14th Regt. Heavy Arty. A. D.
Batty. A. 1st Regt. L. A.
Batty. B. 1st Regt. L. A.
Batty. C. 1st Regt. L. A.
Batty. D. 1st Regt. L. A.
Batty. E. 1st Regt. L. A.
Batty. F. 1st Regt. L. A.
Batty. G. 1st Regt. L. A.
Batty. H. 1st Regt. L. A.
1st Batty. Light Arty.
10th Batty. Light Arty.
1st Regt. Infy.
2nd Regt. Infy.
3rd Regt. Infy.
4th Regt. Infy.
5th Regt. Infy.
6th Regt. Infy.
7th Regt. Infy.
8th Regt. Infy.
9th Regt. Infy.
10th Regt. Infy.
11th Regt. Infy.
12th Regt. Infy.
Indpt. Co. Hospital Guards.
   Total organizations, 41.

SOUTH CAROLINA

1st Regt. Infy. A. D.
2nd Regt. Infy. A. D.
3rd Regt. Infy. A. D.
4th Regt. Infy. A. D.
5th Regt. Infy. A. D.
   Total organizations, 5.

TENNESSEE

1st Regt. Cav.
1st Middle Tenn. Cav. (5-Cav.)
1st West Tenn. Cav. (6-Cav.)
2nd Regt. Cav.
2nd West. Tenn. Cav. (7-Cav.)
3rd Regt. Cav.
4th Regt. Cav.
5th East Tenn. Cav. (8-Cav.)
5th Regt. Cav.
6th Regt. Cav.
7th Regt. Cav.
8th Regt. Cav.
9th Regt. Cav.
10th Regt. Cav.

11th Regt. Cav.
12th Regt. Cav.
13th Regt. Cav.
14th Regt. Cav.
Bradford's Batt'n Cav.
Tenn. and Ala. Vidette Cav.
1st Regt. Heavy Arty. A. D.
2nd Regt. Heavy Arty. A. D.
Batty. A. Light Arty.
Batty. B. Light Arty.
Batty. C. Light Arty.
Batty. D. Light Arty.
Batty. E. Light Arty.
Batty. F. Light Arty.
Batty. G. Light Arty.
Batty. K. Light Arty.
Memphis Batty. L. A. A. D.
1st Regt. Infy.
1st Regt. Infy. A. D.
1st Regt. Mounted Infy.
1st Regt. E. M. Infy.
2nd Regt. Infy.
2nd Regt. Infy. A. D.
2nd Regt. Mounted Infy.
2nd Regt. E. M. Infy.
3rd Regt. Infy.
3rd Regt. Mounted Infy.
3rd Regt. E. M. Infy.
4th Regt. Infy.
4th Regt. Mounted Infy.
4th Regt. E. M. Infy.
5th Regt. Infy.
5th Regt. Mounted Infy.
6th Regt. Infy.
6th Regt. Mounted Infy.
7th Regt. Infy.
7th Regt. Mounted Infy.
8th Regt. Infy.
8th Regt. Mounted Infy.
9th Regt. Infy.
10th Regt. Infy.
Nashville Union Guards.
  Total organizations, 56.

TEXAS

1st Regt. Cav.
2nd Regt. Cav.
2nd Batt'n Cav.
Partizan Rangers.
  Total organizations, 4.

VERMONT

1st Regt. Cav.
1st Regt. Heavy Arty.
1st Co. Heavy Arty.
1st Batty. Light Arty.
2nd Batty. Light Arty.
3rd Batty. Light Arty.
Co. F. 1st U. S. S. S.
Co. E. 2nd U. S. S. S.
Co. H. 2nd U. S. S. S.
1st Regt. Infy.
2nd Regt. Infy.
3rd Regt. Infy.
4th Regt. Infy.
5th Regt. Infy.
6th Regt. Infy.
7th Regt. Infy.
8th Regt. Infy.
9th Regt. Infy.
10th Regt. Infy.
11th Regt. Infy.
12th Regt. Infy.
13th Regt. Infy.
14th Regt. Infy.
15th Regt. Infy.
16th Regt. Infy.
17th Regt. Infy.
18th Regt. Infy.
  Total organizations, 27.

VIRGINIA

Indpt. Batt'n Loudon Rangers,
  Total organizations, 1.

WASHINGTON

1st Regt. Infy.
  Total organizations, 1.

WEST VIRGINIA

1st Regt. Cav.
2nd Regt. Cav.
3rd Regt. Cav.
4th Regt. Cav.
5th Regt. Cav.
6th Regt. Cav.
7th Regt. Cav.
Batty. A. Light Arty.
Batty. B. Light Arty.
Batty. C. Light Arty.
Batty. D. Light Arty.
Batty. E. Light Arty.
Batty. F. Light Arty.
Batty. G. Light Arty.
Batty. H. Light Arty.
1st Regt. Infy. (3-Mos.)
1st Regt. Infy. (3-Yrs.)
1st Regt. Veteran Infy.
2nd Regt. Infy.
2nd Regt. Veteran Infy.
3rd Regt. Infy.
4th Regt. Infy.
5th Regt. Infy.
6th Regt. Infy.
7th Regt. Infy.
8th Regt. Infy.
9th Regt. Infy.
10th Regt. Infy.
11th Regt. Infy.
12th Regt. Infy.
13th Regt. Infy.
14th Regt. Infy.
15th Regt. Infy.
16th Regt. Infy.
17th Regt. Infy.
Indpt. Batt'n Infy.
1st Co. Loyal Virginians.
  Total organizations, 37.

WISCONSIN

1st Regt. Cav.
2nd Regt. Cav.
3rd Regt. Cav.
4th Regt. Cav.
1st Regt. Heavy Arty.
1st Indpt. Batty. L. A.
2nd Indpt. Batty. L. A.
3rd Indpt. Batty. L. A.
4th Indpt. Batty. L. A.
5th Indpt. Batty. L. A.
6th Indpt. Batty. L. A.
7th Indpt. Batty. L. A.
8th Indpt. Batty. L. A.
9th Indpt. Batty. L. A.
10th Indpt. Batty. L. A.
11th Indpt. Batty. L. A.
12th Indpt. Batty. L. A.
13th Indpt. Batty. L. A.
Co. G. 1st U. S. S. S.
1st Regt. Infy. (3-Mos.)
1st Regt. Infy.
2nd Regt. Infy.
3rd Regt. Infy.
4th Regt. Infy.
5th Regt. Infy.
6th Regt. Infy.
7th Regt. Infy.

8th Regt. Infy.
9th Regt. Infy.
10th Regt. Infy.
11th Regt. Infy.
12th Regt. Infy.
13th Regt. Infy.
14th Regt. Infy.
15th Regt. Infy.
16th Regt. Infy.
17th Regt. Infy.
18th Regt. Infy.
19th Regt. Infy.
20th Regt. Infy.
21st Regt. Infy.
22nd Regt. Infy.
23rd Regt. Infy.
24th Regt. Infy.
25th Regt. Infy.
26th Regt. Infy.
27th Regt. Infy.
28th Regt. Infy.
29th Regt. Infy.
30th Regt. Infy.
31st Regt. Infy.
32nd Regt. Infy.
33rd Regt. Infy.
34th Regt. Infy.
35th Regt. Infy.
36th Regt. Infy.
37th Regt. Infy.
38th Regt. Infy.
39th Regt. Infy.
40th Regt. Infy.
41st Regt. Infy.
42nd Regt. Infy.
43rd Regt. Infy.
44th Regt. Infy.
45th Regt. Infy.
46th Regt. Infy.
47th Regt. Infy.
48th Regt. Infy.
49th Regt. Infy.
50th Regt. Infy.
51st Regt. Infy.
52nd Regt. Infy.
53rd Regt. Infy.
  Total organizations, 73.

U. S. REGULAR ARMY

1st Regt. Cav.
2nd Regt. Cav.
3rd Regt. Cav.
4th Regt. Cav.
5th Regt. Cav.
6th Regt. Cav.
Batty. A. 1st Arty.
Batty. B. 1st Arty.
Batty. C. 1st Arty.
Batty. D. 1st Arty.
Batty. E. 1st Arty.
Batty. F. 1st Arty.
Batty. G. 1st Arty.
Batty. H. 1st Arty.
Batty. I. 1st Arty.
Batty. K. 1st Arty.
Batty. L. 1st Arty.
Batty. M. 1st Arty.
Batty. A. 2nd Arty.
Batty. B. 2nd Arty.
Batty. C. 2nd Arty.
Batty. D. 2nd Arty.
Batty. E. 2nd Arty.
Batty. F. 2nd Arty.
Batty. G. 2nd Arty.
Batty. H. 2nd Arty.
Batty. I. 2nd Arty.
Batty. K. 2nd Arty.
Batty. L. 2nd Arty.
Batty. M. 2nd Arty.

Batty. A. 3rd Arty.
Batty. B. 3rd Arty.
Batty. C. 3rd Arty.
Batty. D. 3rd Arty.
Batty. E. 3rd Arty.
Batty. F. 3rd Arty.
Batty. G. 3rd Arty.
Batty. H. 3rd Arty.
Batty. I. 3rd Arty.
Batty. K. 3rd Arty.
Batty. L. 3rd Arty.
Batty. M. 3rd Arty.
Batty. A. 4th Arty.
Batty. B. 4th Arty.
Batty. C. 4th Arty.
Batty. D. 4th Arty.
Batty. E. 4th Arty.
Batty. F. 4th Arty.
Batty. G. 4th Arty.
Batty. H. 4th Arty.
Batty. I. 4th Arty.
Batty. K. 4th Arty.
Batty. L. 4th Arty.
Batty. M. 4th Arty.
Batty. A. 5th Arty.
Batty. B. 5th Arty.
Batty. C. 5th Arty.
Batty. D. 5th Arty.
Batty. E. 5th Arty.
Batty. F. 5th Arty.
Batty. G. 5th Arty.
Batty. H. 5th Arty.
Batty. I. 5th Arty.
Batty. K. 5th Arty.
Batty. L. 5th Arty.
Batty. M. 5th Arty.
1st Batt'n Engineers.
1st Regt. Infy.
2nd Regt. Infy.
3rd Regt. Infy.
4th Regt. Infy.
5th Regt. Infy.
6th Regt. Infy.
7th Regt. Infy.
8th Regt. Infy.
9th Regt. Infy.
10th Regt. Infy.
11th Regt. Infy.
12th Regt. Infy.
13th Regt. Infy.
14th Regt. Infy.
15th Regt. Infy.
16th Regt. Infy.
17th Regt. Infy.
18th Regt. Infy.
19th Regt. Infy.
  Total organizations, 86.

U. S. VOLUNTEERS

1st Regt. Sharpshooters.
2nd Regt. Sharpshooters.
1st Co. Pontoneers.
1st Regt. Infy.
2nd Regt. Infy.
3rd Regt. Infy.
4th Regt. Infy.
5th Regt. Infy.
6th Regt. Infy.
1st Indpt. Co. Infy.
  Total organizations, 10.

U. S. VETERAN VOLS.

1st Regt. Engineers.
1st Regt. Infy.
2nd Regt. Infy.
3rd Regt. Infy.
4th Regt. Infy.
5th Regt. Infy.
6th Regt. Infy.

7th Regt. Infy.
8th Regt. Infy.
9th Regt. Infy.
  Total organizations, 10.

CORPS DE AFRIQUE

1st Regt. Cav.
1st Regt. Heavy Arty.
1st Regt. Engineers.
2nd Regt. Engineers.
3rd Regt. Engineers.
4th Regt. Engineers.
5th Regt. Engineers.
1st Regt. Infy.
2nd Regt. Infy.
3rd Regt. Infy.
4th Regt. Infy.
5th Regt. Infy.
6th Regt. Infy.
7th Regt. Infy.
8th Regt. Infy.
9th Regt. Infy.
10th Regt. Infy.
11th Regt. Infy.
12th Regt. Infy.
13th Regt. Infy.
14th Regt. Infy.
15th Regt. Infy.
16th Regt. Infy.
17th Regt. Infy.
18th Regt. Infy.
19th Regt. Infy.
20th Regt. Infy.
22nd Regt. Infy.
25th Regt. Infy.
26th Regt. Infy.
  Total organizations, 30.

U. S. COLORED TROOPS

1st Regt. Cav.
2nd Regt. Cav.
3rd Regt. Cav.
4th Regt. Cav.
5th Regt. Cav.
6th Regt. Cav.
1st Regt. Heavy Arty.
3rd Regt. Heavy Arty.
4th Regt. Heavy Arty.
5th Regt. Heavy Arty.
6th Regt. Heavy Arty.
7th Regt. Heavy Arty.
8th Regt. Heavy Arty.
9th Regt. Heavy Arty.
10th Regt. Heavy Arty.
11th Regt. Heavy Arty.
12th Regt. Heavy Arty.
13th Regt. Heavy Arty.
14th Regt. Heavy Arty.
Batty. A. 2nd Regt. L. A.
Batty. B. 2nd Regt. L. A.
Batty. C. 2nd Regt. L. A.
Batty. D. 2nd Regt. L. A.
Batty. E. 2nd Regt. L. A.
Batty. F. 2nd Regt. L. A.
Batty. G. 2nd Regt. L. A.
Batty. H. 2nd Regt. L. A.
Batty. I. 2nd Regt. L. A.
Indpt. Batty. Light Arty.
1st Regt. Infy.
2nd Regt. Infy.
3rd Regt. Infy.
4th Regt. Infy.
5th Regt. Infy.
6th Regt. Infy.
7th Regt. Infy.
8th Regt. Infy.
9th Regt. Infy.
10th Regt. Infy.
11th Regt. Infy (Old).

11th Regt. Infy (New).
12th Regt. Infy.
13th Regt. Infy.
14th Regt. Infy.
15th Regt. Infy.
16th Regt. Infy.
17th Regt. Infy.
18th Regt. Infy.
19th Regt. Infy.
20th Regt. Infy.
21st Regt. Infy.
22nd Regt. Infy.
23rd Regt. Infy.
24th Regt. Infy.
25th Regt. Infy.
26th Regt. Infy.
27th Regt. Infy.
28th Regt. Infy.
29th Regt. Infy.
30th Regt. Infy.
31st Regt. Infy.
32nd Regt. Infy.
33rd Regt. Infy.
34th Regt. Infy.
35th Regt. Infy.
36th Regt. Infy.
37th Regt. Infy.
38th Regt. Infy.
39th Regt. Infy.
40th Regt. Infy.
41st Regt. Infy.
42nd Regt. Infy.
43rd Regt. Infy.
44th Regt. Infy.
45th Regt. Infy.
46th Regt. Infy.
47th Regt. Infy.
48th Regt. Infy.
49th Regt. Infy.
50th Regt. Infy.
51st Regt. Infy.
52nd Regt. Infy.
53rd Regt. Infy.
54th Regt. Infy.
55th Regt. Infy.
56th Regt. Infy.
57th Regt. Infy.
58th Regt. Infy.
59th Regt. Infy.
60th Regt. Infy.
61st Regt. Infy.
62nd Regt. Infy.
63rd Regt. Infy.
64th Regt. Infy.
65th Regt. Infy.
66th Regt. Infy.
67th Regt. Infy.
68th Regt. Infy.
69th Regt. Infy.
70th Regt. Infy.
71st Regt. Infy.
72nd Regt. Infy.
73rd Regt. Infy.
74th Regt. Infy.
75th Regt. Infy.
76th Regt. Infy.
77th Regt. Infy.
78th Regt. Infy.
79th Regt. Infy. (Old).
79th Regt. Infy. (New).
80th Regt. Infy.
81st Regt. Infy.
82nd Regt. Infy.
83rd Regt. Infy. (Old).
83rd Regt. Infy. (New).
84th Regt. Infy.
85th Regt. Infy.
86th Regt. Infy.
87th Regt. Infy. (Old).

87th Regt. Infy. (New).
88th Regt. Infy. (Old).
88th Regt. Infy. (New).
89th Regt. Infy.
90th Regt. Infy.
91st Regt. Infy.
92nd Regt. Infy.
93rd Regt. Infy.
94th Regt. Infy.
95th Regt. Infy.
96th Regt. Infy.
97th Regt. Infy.
98th Regt. Infy.
99th Regt. Infy.
100th Regt. Infy.
101st Regt. Infy.
102nd Regt. Infy.
103rd Regt. Infy.
104th Regt. Infy.
105th Regt. Infy.
106th Regt. Infy.
107th Regt. Infy.
108th Regt. Infy.
109th Regt. Infy.
110th Regt. Infy.
111th Regt. Infy.
112th Regt. Infy.
113th Regt. Infy. (Old).
113th Regt. Infy. (New).
114th Regt. Infy.
115th Regt. Infy.
116th Regt. Infy.
117th Regt. Infy.
118th Regt. Infy.
119th Regt. Infy.
120th Regt. Infy.
121st Regt. Infy.
122nd Regt. Infy.
123rd Regt. Infy.
124th Regt. Infy.
125th Regt. Infy.
127th Regt. Infy.
128th Regt. Infy.
135th Regt. Infy.
136th Regt. Infy.
137th Regt. Infy.
138th Regt. Infy.
    Total organizations, 186.

U. S. VOLS.—INDIAN TROOPS

1st Regt. Indian Home Gd.
2nd Regt. Indian Home Gd.
3rd Regt. Indian Home Gd.
4th Regt. Indian Home Gd.
    Total organizations, 4.

U. S. VETERAN RESERVE CORPS

1st Regiment.
2nd Regiment.
3rd Regiment.
4th Regiment.
5th Regiment.
6th Regiment.
7th Regiment.
8th Regiment.
9th Regiment.
10th Regiment.
11th Regiment.
12th Regiment.
13th Regiment.
14th Regiment.
15th Regiment.
16th Regiment.
17th Regiment.
18th Regiment.
19th Regiment.
20th Regiment.
21st Regiment.
22nd Regiment.

23rd Regiment.
24th Regiment.
187th Co. 1st Batt'n.
238th Co. 1st Batt'n.
239th Co. 1st Batt'n.
243rd Co. 1st Batt'n.
244th Co. 1st Batt'n.
245th Co. 1st Batt'n.
246th Co. 1st Batt'n.
1st Co. 2nd Batt'n.
2nd Co. 2nd Batt'n.
3rd Co. 2nd Batt'n.
4th Co. 2nd Batt'n.
5th Co. 2nd Batt'n.
6th Co. 2nd Batt'n.
7th Co. 2nd Batt'n.
8th Co. 2nd Batt'n.
9th Co. 2nd Batt'n.
10th Co. 2nd Batt'n.
11th Co. 2nd Batt'n.
12th Co. 2nd Batt'n.
13th Co. 2nd Batt'n.
14th Co. 2nd Batt'n.
15th Co. 2nd Batt'n.
16th Co. 2nd Batt'n.
17th Co. 2nd Batt'n.
18th Co. 2nd Batt'n.
19th Co. 2nd Batt'n.
20th Co. 2nd Batt'n.
21st Co. 2nd Batt'n.
22nd Co. 2nd Batt'n.
23rd Co. 2nd Batt'n.
24th Co. 2nd Batt'n.
25th Co. 2nd Batt'n.
26th Co. 2nd Batt'n.
27th Co. 2nd Batt'n.
28th Co. 2nd Batt'n.
29th Co. 2nd Batt'n.
30th Co. 2nd Batt'n.
31st Co. 2nd Batt'n.
32nd Co. 2nd Batt'n.
33rd Co. 2nd Batt'n.
34th Co. 2nd Batt'n.
35th Co. 2nd Batt'n.
36th Co. 2nd Batt'n.
37th Co. 2nd Batt'n.
38th Co. 2nd Batt'n.
39th Co. 2nd Batt'n.
40th Co. 2nd Batt'n.
41st Co. 2nd Batt'n.
42nd Co. 2nd Batt'n.
43rd Co. 2nd Batt'n.
44th Co. 2nd Batt'n.
45th Co. 2nd Batt'n.
46th Co. 2nd Batt'n.
47th Co. 2nd Batt'n.
48th Co. 2nd Batt'n.
49th Co. 2nd Batt'n.
50th Co. 2nd Batt'n.
51st Co. 2nd Batt'n.
52nd Co. 2nd Batt'n.
53rd Co. 2nd Batt'n.
54th Co. 2nd Batt'n.
55th Co. 2nd Batt'n.
56th Co. 2nd Batt'n.
57th Co. 2nd Batt'n.
58th Co. 2nd Batt'n.
59th Co. 2nd Batt'n.
60th Co. 2nd Batt'n.
61st Co. 2nd Batt'n.
62nd Co. 2nd Batt'n.
63rd Co. 2nd Batt'n.
64th Co. 2nd Batt'n.
65th Co. 2nd Batt'n.
66th Co. 2nd Batt'n.
67th Co. 2nd Batt'n.
68th Co. 2nd Batt'n.
69th Co. 2nd Batt'n.
70th Co. 2nd Batt'n.

71st Co. 2nd Batt'n.
72nd Co. 2nd Batt'n.
73rd Co. 2nd Batt'n.
74th Co. 2nd Batt'n.
75th Co. 2nd Batt'n.
76th Co. 2nd Batt'n.
77th Co. 2nd Batt'n.
78th Co. 2nd Batt'n.
79th Co. 2nd Batt'n.
80th Co. 2nd Batt'n.
81st Co. 2nd Batt'n.
82nd Co. 2nd Batt'n.
83rd Co. 2nd Batt'n.
84th Co. 2nd Batt'n.
85th Co. 2nd Batt'n.
86th Co. 2nd Batt'n.
87th Co. 2nd Batt'n.
88th Co. 2nd Batt'n.
89th Co. 2nd Batt'n.
90th Co. 2nd Batt'n.
91st Co. 2nd Batt'n.
92nd Co. 2nd Batt'n.
93rd Co. 2nd Batt'n.
94th Co. 2nd Batt'n.
95th Co. 2nd Batt'n.
96th Co. 2nd Batt'n.
97th Co. 2nd Batt'n.
98th Co. 2nd Batt'n.
99th Co. 2nd Batt'n.
100th Co. 2nd Batt'n.
101st Co. 2nd Batt'n.
102nd Co. 2nd Batt'n.
103rd Co. 2nd Batt'n.
104th Co. 2nd Batt'n.
105th Co. 2nd Batt'n.
106th Co. 2nd Batt'n.
107th Co. 2nd Batt'n.
108th Co. 2nd Batt'n.
109th Co. 2nd Batt'n.
110th Co. 2nd Batt'n.
111th Co. 2nd Batt'n.
112th Co. 2nd Batt'n.
113th Co. 2nd Batt'n.
114th Co. 2nd Batt'n.
115th Co. 2nd Batt'n.
116th Co. 2nd Batt'n.
117th Co. 2nd Batt'n.
118th Co. 2nd Batt'n.
119th Co. 2nd Batt'n.
120th Co. 2nd Batt'n.
121st Co. 2nd Batt'n.
122nd Co. 2nd Batt'n.
123rd Co. 2nd Batt'n.
124th Co. 2nd Batt'n.
125th Co. 2nd Batt'n.
126th Co. 2nd Batt'n.
127th Co. 2nd Batt'n.
128th Co. 2nd Batt'n.
129th Co. 2nd Batt'n.
130th Co. 2nd Batt'n.
131st Co. 2nd Batt'n.
132nd Co. 2nd Batt'n.
133rd Co. 2nd Batt'n.
134th Co. 2nd Batt'n.
135th Co. 2nd Batt'n.
136th Co. 2nd Batt'n.
137th Co. 2nd Batt'n.
138th Co. 2nd Batt'n.
139th Co. 2nd Batt'n.
140th Co. 2nd Batt'n.
141st Co. 2nd Batt'n.
142nd Co. 2nd Batt'n.
143rd Co. 2nd Batt'n.
144th Co. 2nd Batt'n.
145th Co. 2nd Batt'n.
146th Co. 2nd Batt'n.
147th Co. 2nd Batt'n.
148th Co. 2nd Batt'n.
149th Co. 2nd Batt'n.

150th Co. 2nd Batt'n.	161st Co. 2nd Batt'n.	172nd Co. 2nd Batt'n.
151st Co. 2nd Batt'n.	162nd Co. 2nd Batt'n.	173rd Co. 2nd Batt'n.
152nd Co. 2nd Batt'n.	163rd Co. 2nd Batt'n.	174th Co. 2nd Batt'n.
153rd Co. 2nd Batt'n.	164th Co. 2nd Batt'n.	1st Indpt. Company.
154th Co. 2nd Batt'n.	165th Co. 2nd Batt'n.	2nd Indpt. Company.
155th Co. 2nd Batt'n.	166th Co. 2nd Batt'n.	3rd Indpt. Company.
156th Co. 2nd Batt'n.	167th Co. 2nd Batt'n.	4th Indpt. Company.
157th Co. 2nd Batt'n.	168th Co. 2nd Batt'n.	5th Indpt. Company.
158th Co. 2nd Batt'n.	169th Co. 2nd Batt'n.	6th Indpt. Company.
159th Co. 2nd Batt'n.	170th Co. 2nd Batt'n.	7th Indpt. Company.
160th Co. 2nd Batt'n.	171st Co. 2nd Batt'n.	Total organizations, 212.

A Summary by States of the Organizations of All Arms Furnished by Each.

ALABAMA—
Cavalry, 1 Regt.
Heavy Arty., 1 Regt.
Infantry, 4 Regts.
Total, 6.

ARKANSAS—
Cavalry, 4 Regts.
Light Arty., 2 Battys.
Infantry, 10 Regts.; 1 Batt'n.
Total, 17.

CALIFORNIA—
Cavalry, 2 Regts.; 1 Batt'n.
Infantry, 8 Regts.; 1 Batt'n.
Total, 12.

COLORADO—
Cavalry, 3 Regts.
Light Arty., 1 Batty.
Infantry, 3 Regts.; 1 Co.
Total, 8.

CONNECTICUT—
Cavalry, 1 Regt.
Heavy Arty., 2 Regts.
Light Arty., 3 Battys.
Infantry, 30 Regts.
Total, 36.

DAKOTA TERRITORY—
Cavalry, 1 Batt'n.
Total, 1.

DELAWARE—
Cavalry, 1 Regt.; 1 Co.
Heavy Arty., 1 Co.
Light Arty., 1 Batty.
Infantry, 10 Regts.; 1 Co.
Total, 15.

DIST. COLUMBIA—
Cavalry, 1 Regt.; 1 Co.
Infantry, 2 Regts.; 4 Batt'ns; 33 Cos.
Total, 41.

FLORIDA—
Cavalry, 2 Regts.
Total, 2.

GEORGIA—
Infantry, 1 Batt'n.
Total, 1.

ILLINOIS—
Cavalry, 17 Regts.; 3 Batt'ns; 17 Cos.
Light Arty., 35 Battys.
Infantry, 156 Regts.; 11 Cos.
Total, 239.

INDIANA—
Cavalry, 13 Regts.; 3 Cos.
Heavy Arty., 1 Regt.
Light Arty., 26 Battys.
Infantry, 152 Regts.
Total, 195.

IOWA—
Cavalry, 9 Regts.
Light Arty., 4 Battys.
Infantry, 51 Regts.
Total, 64.

KANSAS—
Cavalry, 9 Regts.
Light Arty., 8 Battys.
Infantry, 35 Regts.; 2 Cos.
Total, 54.

KENTUCKY—
Cavalry, 17 Regts.; 1 Batt'n.
Light Arty., 6 Battys.
Engrs., 1 Co.
Infantry, 55 Regts.
Total, 80.

LOUISIANA—
Cavalry, 2 Regts.
Heavy Arty., 1 Regt.
Light Arty., 3 Battys.
Infantry, 18 Regts.
Total, 24.

MAINE—
Cavalry, 2 Regts.
Heavy Arty., 1 Regt.
Light Arty., 7 Battys.
S. S., 1 Batt'n; 1 Co.
Infantry, 33 Regts.; 1 Batt'n; 7 Cos.
Total, 53.

MARYLAND—
Cavalry, 4 Regts.; 1 Batt'n; 1 Co.
Heavy Arty., 1 Regt.
Light Arty., 6 Battys.
Infantry, 20 Regts.; 2 Cos.
Total, 35.

MASSACHUSETTS—
Cavalry, 5 Regts.; 3 Batt'ns.
Heavy Arty., 4 Regts.; 1 Batt'n; 30 Cos.
Light Arty., 18 Battys.
S. S., 2 Cos.
Infantry, 71 Regts.; 3 Batt'ns; 28 Un-att. Cos.
Total, 165.

MICHIGAN—
Cavalry, 11 Regts.; 2 Cos.
Heavy Arty., 1 Regt.
Light Arty., 14 Battys.
Engrs., 1 Regt.; 1 Co.
S. S., 1 Regt.; 8 Cos.
Infantry, 35 Regts.; 2 Cos.
Total, 76.

MINNESOTA—
Cavalry, 2 Regts.; 2 Batt'ns.
Heavy Arty., 1 Regt.
Light Arty., 3 Battys.
S. S., 2 Cos.
Infantry, 11 Regts.
Total, 21.

MISSOURI—
Cavalry, 32 Regts.; 16 Batt'ns; 10 Cos.
Light Arty., 2 Batt'ns; 39 Battys.
Engrs., 2 Regts.; 4 Cos.
S. S., 1 Regt.; 1 Batt'n.
Infantry, 266 Regts.; 40 Batt'ns; 34 Cos.
Total, 447.

MISSISSIPPI—
Cavalry, 2 Regts.
Heavy Arty., 2 Regts.
Infantry, 6 Regts.
Total, 10.

NEBRASKA—
Cavalry, 2 Regts.; 1 Batt'n; 2 Cos.
Total, 6.

NEVADA—
Cavalry, 1 Batt'n.
Infantry, 1 Batt'n.
Total, 2.

NEW HAMPSHIRE—
Cavalry, 2 Regts.
Heavy Arty., 1 Regt.; 1 Co.
Light Arty., 1 Batty.
S. S., 3 Cos.
Infantry, 18 Regts.; 3 Cos.
Total, 29.

NEW JERSEY—
Cavalry, 3 Regts.
Light Arty., 5 Battys.
Infantry, 4 Regts.
Total, 49.

NEW MEXICO—
Cavalry, 1 Regt.; 1 Batt'n; 5 Cos.
Infantry, 7 Regts.; 5 Cos.
Total, 19.

NEW YORK—
Cavalry, 32 Regts.; 1 Batt'n; 3 Cos.
Heavy Arty., 26 Regts.; 5 Batt'ns.
Light Arty., 6 Batt'ns; 66 Battys.
Engrs., 4 Regts.
S. S., 1 Regt.; 1 Batt'n; 4 Cos.
Infantry, 254 Regts.; 1 Batt'n.
Total, 393.

NORTH CAROLINA—
Heavy Arty., 1 Regt.
Infantry, 7 Regts.
Total, 8.

OHIO—
Cavalry, 13 Regts.; 5 Batt'ns; 10 Cos.
Heavy Arty., 2 Regts.
Light Arty., 42 Battys.
S. S., 10 Cos.
Infantry, 227 Regts.; 1 Batt'n; 5 Cos.
Total, 315.

OREGON—
Cavalry, 1 Regt.
Infantry, 1 Regt.
Total, 2.

PENNSYLVANIA—
Cavalry, 28 Regts.; 3 Batt'ns; 22 Cos.
Heavy Arty., 5 Regts.; 2 Batt'ns.; 3 Cos.
Light Arty., 1 Batt'n; 29 Battys.
Engrs., 1 Co.
S. S., 1 Co.
Infantry, 258 Regts.; 5 Batt'ns, 25 Cos.
Total, 383.

RHODE ISLAND—
Cavalry, 3 Regts.; 1 Batt'n.
Heavy Arty., 3 Regts.
Light Arty., 10 Battys.
Infantry, 12 Regts.; 1 Co.
Total, 30.

SOUTH CAROLINA—
Infantry, 5 Regts.
Total, 5.

TENNESSEE—
Cavalry, 20 Regts.; 1 Batt'n.
Heavy Arty., 2 Regts.
Light Arty., 9 Battys.
Infantry, 23 Regts.; 1 Co.
Total, 56.

TEXAS—
Cavalry, 2 Regts.; 2 Batt'ns.
Total, 4.

VERMONT—
Cavalry, 1 Regt.
Heavy Arty., 1 Regt.; 1 Co.
Light Arty., 3 Battys.
Sharpshooters, 3 Cos.
Infantry, 18 Regts.
Total, 27.

VIRGINIA—
Cavalry, 1 Batt'n.
Total, 1.

WASHINGTON TER.—
Infantry, 1 Batt'n.
Total, 1.

WEST VIRGINIA—
Cavalry, 7 Regts.
Light Arty., 8 Battys.
Infantry, 20 Regts.; 1 Batt'n; 1 Co.
Total, 37.

WISCONSIN—
Cavalry, 4 Regts.
Heavy Arty., 1 Regt.
Light Arty., 13 Battys.
S. S., 1 Co.
Infantry, 54 Regts.
Total, 73.

U. S. REGULAR ARMY—
Cavalry, 6 Regts.
Artillery, 60 Battys.
Engineers, 1 Batt'n.
Infantry, 19 Regts.
Total, 86.

U. S. VOLUNTEERS—
Sharpshooters, 2 Regts.
Pontoneers, 1 Co.
Infantry, 6 Regts.; 1 Co.
Total, 10.

U. S. VETERAN VOLUNTEERS—
Engineers, 1 Regt.
Infantry, 9 Regts.
Total, 10.

CORPS DE AFRIQUE—
Cavalry, 1 Regt.
Heavy Arty., 1 Regt.
Engineers, 5 Regts.
Infantry, 22 Regts.
Total, 29.

U. S. COLORED TROOPS—
Cavalry, 6 Regts.
Heavy Arty., 13 Regts.
Light Arty., 10 Battys.
Infantry, 137 Regts.
Total, 167.

U. S. VOLS. INDIAN TROOPS—
Infantry, 4 Regts.
Total, 4.

U. S. VETERAN RESERVE CORPS—
Infantry, 24 Regts.; 188 Cos.
Total, 212.

RECAPITULATION—
Cavalry, Regts., 272; Batt'ns, 45; Cos., 78.
Heavy Arty., Regts., 61; Batt'ns, 8; Cos., 36.
Light Arty., Batt'ns, 9; *Battys., 432.
Engineers, Regts., 13; Batt'ns, 1; Cos., 7.
Sharp-S., Regts., 4; Batt'ns, 3; Cos., 35.
Infantry, Regts., 2,144; Batt'ns, 60; Cos., 351.
Total, 3,559 organizations.

*Includes the Battys. of all Light Arty. Regts., their service for the most part being as separate organizations.

Tabular Statement of Organizations in the Service of the United States During the Rebellion

State or Territory.	Cavalry. Regiments	Cavalry. Battalions	Cavalry. Companies	Heavy Arty. Regiments	Heavy Arty. Battalions	Heavy Arty. Companies	Light Arty. Regiments	Light Arty. Battalions	Light Arty. Batteries	Engineers. Regiments	Engineers. Battalions	Engineers. Companies	S.-S. Regiments	S.-S. Battalions	S.-S. Companies	Infantry. Regiments	Infantry. Battalions	Infantry. Companies	Totals
Alabama	1			1												4			6
Arkansas	4								2							10	1		17
California	2	1														8	1		12
Colorado	3								1							3		1	8
Connecticut	1			2					3							30			36
Dakota		1																	1
Delaware	1		1			1			1							10		1	15
District of Columbia	1		1													2	4	33	41
Florida	2																		2
Georgia																	1		1
Illinois	17	3	17						35							156		11	239
Indiana	13		3	1					26							152			195
Iowa	9								4							51			64
Kansas	9								8							35		2	54
Kentucky	17	1							6			1				55			80
Louisiana	2			1					3							18			24
Maine	2			1					7					1	1	33	1	7	53
Maryland	4	1	1	1					6							20		2	35
Massachusetts	5	3		4	1	30			18						2	71	3	27	164
Michigan	11		2	1					14	1		1	1		8	35		2	76
Minnesota	2	2		1					3						2	11			21
Missouri	32	16	10					2	39	2		4	1	1		266	40	34	447
Mississippi	2			2												6			10
Nebraska	2	1	2													1			6
Nevada		1															1		2
New Hampshire	2		1	1		1			1						3	18		3	30
New Jersey	3								5							41			49
New Mexico	1	1	5													7		5	19
New York	32	1	3	16	5			6	66	4				1	4	254	1		393
North Carolina				1												7			8
Ohio	13	5	10	2					42						10	227	1	5	315
Oregon	1															1			2
Pennsylvania	28	3	22	5	2	3		1	29			1			1	258	5	25	383
Rhode Island	3	1		3					10							12		1	30
South Carolina																5			5
Tennessee	20	1		2					9							23		1	56
Texas	2	2																	4
Vermont	1			1		1			3						3	18			27
Virginia		1																	1
Washington																1			1
West Virginia	7								8							20	1	1	37
Wisconsin	4			1					13						1	54			73
Regular Army	6								60		1					19			86
U.S. Volunteers													2			6		2	10
U.S. Veteran Vols										1						9			10
C. de A	1			1						5						22			29
U.S. Colored Troops	6			13					10							137			166
Indian Troops																4			4
V. R. C																24		188	212
Totals	272	45	78	61	8	36		9	432	13	1	7	4	3	35	2,144	60	351	3,559

A List of Regiments That Lost Fifty or More in Killed and Mortally Wounded.

Regiments	Officers	Men	Total	Regiments	Officers	Men	Total
1st Connecticut H. A.	2	49	51	59th Illinois	4	105	109
2nd Connecticut H. A.	12	242	254	64th Illinois	6	103	109
5th Connecticut	6	104	110	66th Illinois	6	73	79
6th Connecticut	8	99	107	72nd Illinois	7	79	86
7th Connecticut	11	157	168	73rd Illinois	5	109	114
8th Connecticut	8	112	120	74th Illinois	5	78	83
10th Connecticut	13	109	122	75th Illinois	3	94	97
11th Connecticut	8	149	148	76th Illinois	1	51	52
12th Connecticut	6	65	70	77th Illinois	2	66	68
14th Connecticut	17	188	205	78th Illinois	9	95	104
16th Connecticut	6	76	82	79th Illinois	4	81	85
17th Connecticut	5	48	53	80th Illinois	6	52	58
18th Connecticut	4	67	71	81st Illinois	8	66	74
20th Connecticut	4	76	80	82nd Illinois	4	98	102
21st Connecticut	5	55	60	84th Illinois	4	120	124
26th Connecticut	4	51	55	85th Illinois	4	86	90
				86th Illinois	3	73	76
1st Delaware	12	146	158	88th Illinois	5	98	103
2nd Delaware	6	93	99	89th Illinois	12	121	133
3rd Delaware	7	46	53	90th Illinois	2	58	60
4th Delaware	4	80	84	92nd Illinois	1	51	52
				93rd Illinois	4	147	151
2nd Illinois Cav.	8	50	58	95th Illinois	7	77	84
6th Illinois Cav.	5	60	65	96th Illinois	5	111	116
7th Illinois Cav.	5	59	64	99th Illinois	4	47	51
8th Illinois Cav.	7	68	75	100th Illinois	7	73	80
7th Illinois	8	81	89	101st Illinois	3	47	50
8th Illinois	6	160	166	102nd Illinois	..	51	51
9th Illinois	5	211	216	103rd Illinois	8	87	95
10th Illinois	2	48	50	104th Illinois	6	110	116
11th Illinois	7	179	186	105th Illinois	2	49	51
12th Illinois	5	143	148	111th Illinois	7	75	82
13th Illinois	6	61	67	112th Illinois	4	76	80
14th Illinois	..	62	62	115th Illinois	6	58	64
15th Illinois	6	81	87	116th Illinois	7	49	56
16th Illinois	3	54	57	123rd Illinois	3	82	85
17th Illinois	3	71	74	125th Illinois	9	88	97
18th Illinois	6	99	105	129th Illinois	..	50	50
19th Illinois	4	60	64				
20th Illinois	7	132	139	3rd Indiana Cav.	1	62	63
21st Illinois	6	124	130	6th Indiana Cav.	4	66	70
22nd Illinois	2	145	147	8th Indiana Cav.	9	138	147
23rd Illinois	4	50	54	1st Indiana H. A.	7	60	67
24th Illinois	3	86	89	6th Indiana	9	116	125
25th Illinois	3	80	83	7th Indiana	8	108	116
26th Illinois	2	88	90	8th Indiana	7	80	87
27th Illinois	7	96	103	9th Indiana	11	120	131
28th Illinois	9	97	106	10th Indiana	3	64	67
29th Illinois	5	70	75	11th Indiana	1	114	115
30th Illinois	10	115	125	12th Indiana	8	92	100
31st Illinois	9	166	175	13th Indiana	3	104	107
32nd Illinois	8	90	98	14th Indiana	11	139	150
33rd Illinois	2	56	58	15th Indiana	4	103	107
34th Illinois	11	129	140	16th Indiana	3	82	85
35th Illinois	7	91	98	17th Indiana	3	90	93
36th Illinois	11	193	204	18th Indiana	5	68	73
37th Illinois	4	60	64	19th Indiana	5	194	199
38th Illinois	7	107	114	20th Indiana	15	186	201
39th Illinois	12	129	141	22nd Indiana	14	139	153
40th Illinois	6	119	125	23rd Indiana	4	68	72
41st Illinois	8	107	115	24th Indiana	8	80	88
42nd Illinois	13	168	181	25th Indiana	7	81	88
43rd Illinois	8	75	83	26th Indiana	..	96	96
44th Illinois	6	129	135	27th Indiana	10	159	169
45th Illinois	9	76	85	29th Indiana	4	56	60
46th Illinois	7	74	81	30th Indiana	4	133	137
47th Illinois	5	58	63	31st Indiana	5	115	120
48th Illinois	10	113	123	32nd Indiana	7	164	171
49th Illinois	7	72	79	33rd Indiana	4	112	116
50th Illinois	2	60	62	35th Indiana	5	82	87
51st Illinois	9	106	115	36th Indiana	11	102	113
52nd Illinois	2	59	61	37th Indiana	5	80	85
53rd Illinois	8	80	88	38th Indiana	9	147	156
55th Illinois	9	148	157	40th Indiana	5	143	148
57th Illinois	3	65	68	42nd Indiana	5	108	113
58th Illinois	8	75	83	44th Indiana	4	76	80

Regiments	Officers	Men	Total
46th Indiana	4	66	70
47th Indiana	2	80	82
48th Indiana	..	88	88
50th Indiana	3	54	57
51st Indiana	1	55	56
53rd Indiana	9	98	107
57th Indiana	6	97	103
58th Indiana	4	60	64
63rd Indiana	3	53	56
66th Indiana	3	62	65
67th Indiana	1	52	53
69th Indiana	3	77	80
70th Indiana	2	96	98
73rd Indiana	3	47	50
74th Indiana	5	86	91
79th Indiana	3	50	53
80th Indiana	6	64	70
81st Indiana	4	52	56
82nd Indiana	3	65	68
83rd Indiana	5	56	61
84th Indiana	5	82	87
86th Indiana	2	70	72
87th Indiana	10	81	91
88th Indiana	9	55	64
89th Indiana	6	55	61
97th Indiana	3	51	54
100th Indiana	2	56	58
101st Indiana	3	51	54
123rd Indiana	4	47	51
1st Iowa Cav.	2	56	58
2nd Iowa Cav.	1	59	60
3rd Iowa Cav.	5	79	84
4th Iowa Cav.	4	51	55
5th Iowa Cav.	7	58	65
2nd Iowa	12	108	120
3rd Iowa	8	119	127
4th Iowa	6	109	115
5th Iowa	9	108	117
6th Iowa	8	144	152
7th Iowa	7	134	141
8th Iowa	4	98	102
9th Iowa	12	142	154
10th Iowa	6	95	101
11th Iowa	5	86	91
12th Iowa	4	76	80
13th Iowa	5	114	119
14th Iowa	5	59	64
15th Iowa	8	118	126
16th Iowa	7	94	101
17th Iowa	5	66	71
19th Iowa	6	86	92
21st Iowa	4	77	81
22nd Iowa	6	108	114
23rd Iowa	6	69	75
24th Iowa	9	119	128
25th Iowa	2	63	65
26th Iowa	6	70	76
28th Iowa	6	76	82
30th Iowa	8	65	73
32nd Iowa	6	101	107
33rd Iowa	3	65	68
36th Iowa	1	64	65
39th Iowa	6	58	64
2nd Kansas Cav.	2	62	64
6th Kansas Cav.	4	81	85
7th Kansas Cav.	3	55	58
9th Kansas Cav.	1	52	53
11th Kansas Cav.	..	61	61
14th Kansas Cav.	2	51	53
1st Kansas	7	120	127
8th Kansas	3	94	97
1st Kentucky Cav.	5	56	61
2nd Kentucky Cav.	5	51	56
1st Kentucky	..	60	60
2nd Kentucky	3	74	77
3rd Kentucky	6	103	109
4th Kentucky	1	118	119
5th Kentucky	8	149	157
6th Kentucky	10	105	115
8th Kentucky	4	56	60
9th Kentucky	8	96	104
10th Kentucky	2	70	72
13th Kentucky	8	50	58
14th Kentucky	5	49	54
15th Kentucky	9	128	137
16th Kentucky	2	50	52
17th Kentucky	7	128	135
18th Kentucky	5	85	90
21st Kentucky	3	57	60
22nd Kentucky	3	48	51
23rd Kentucky	5	84	89
1st Maine Cav.	15	159	174
1st Maine H. A.	23	400	423
2nd Maine	4	65	69
3rd Maine	10	124	134
4th Maine	14	156	170
5th Maine	8	99	107
6th Maine	12	141	153
7th Maine	15	113	128
8th Maine	6	128	134
9th Maine	10	172	182
10th Maine	8	74	82
11th Maine	7	115	122
12th Maine	3	49	52
14th Maine	5	81	86
16th Maine	9	172	181
17th Maine	12	195	207
19th Maine	3	189	192
20th Maine	9	138	147
31st Maine	18	165	183
32nd Maine	4	81	85
1st Maryland Cav.	3	65	68
1st Maryland	8	110	118
2nd Maryland	5	84	89
3rd Maryland	8	83	91
5th Maryland	1	63	64
6th Maryland	8	120	128
7th Maryland	1	78	79
8th Maryland	3	54	57
1st Massachusetts Cav.	6	93	99
2nd Massachusetts Cav.	8	82	90
3rd Massachusetts Cav.	5	101	106
1st Massachusetts H. A.	9	232	241
1st Massachusetts	8	134	142
2nd Massachusetts	14	176	190
7th Massachusetts	4	76	80
9th Massachusetts	15	194	209
10th Massachusetts	10	124	134
11th Massachusetts	11	153	164
12th Massachusetts	18	175	193
13th Massachusetts	4	117	121
15th Massachusetts	14	227	241
16th Massachusetts	16	134	150
18th Massachusetts	9	114	123
19th Massachusetts	14	147	161
20th Massachusetts	17	243	260
21st Massachusetts	11	148	159
22nd Massachusetts	9	207	216
23rd Massachusetts	4	80	84
24th Massachusetts	7	90	97
25th Massachusetts	7	154	161
26th Massachusetts	3	61	64
27th Massachusetts	4	165	169
28th Massachusetts	15	235	250
29th Massachusetts	4	53	57
30th Massachusetts	4	57	61
31st Massachusetts	..	52	52
32nd Massachusetts	5	139	144
33rd Massachusetts	7	104	111
34th Massachusetts	7	128	135

Regiments	Officers	Men	Total
35th Massachusetts	10	138	148
36th Massachusetts	6	105	111
37th Massachusetts	4	165	169
38th Massachusetts	4	73	77
39th Massachusetts	5	91	96
40th Massachusetts	5	67	72
54th Massachusetts	5	104	109
55th Massachusetts	3	64	67
56th Massachusetts	6	120	126
57th Massachusetts	10	191	201
58th Massachusetts	10	129	139
59th Massachusetts	7	83	90
1st Michigan Cav.	14	150	164
2nd Michigan Cav.	4	70	74
4th Michigan Cav.	3	48	51
5th Michigan Cav.	6	135	141
6th Michigan Cav.	7	128	135
7th Michigan Cav.	4	81	85
1st Michigan S. S.	6	131	137
1st Michigan	15	172	187
2nd Michigan	11	214	225
3rd Michigan	4	154	158
4th Michigan	12	177	189
5th Michigan	16	247	263
6th Michigan	2	76	78
7th Michigan	11	197	208
8th Michigan	11	212	223
10th Michigan	7	95	102
11th Michigan	5	107	112
12th Michigan	1	52	53
13th Michigan	4	68	72
14th Michigan	1	58	59
15th Michigan	3	60	63
16th Michigan	12	235	247
17th Michigan	7	128	135
19th Michigan	7	88	95
20th Michigan	13	111	124
21st Michigan	3	80	83
22nd Michigan	3	86	89
23rd Michigan	3	70	73
24th Michigan	12	177	189
26th Michigan	3	115	118
27th Michigan	10	215	225
1st Minnesota	10	177	187
2nd Minnesota	2	91	93
4th Minnesota	3	58	61
5th Minnesota	4	86	90
1st Missouri Cav.	2	51	53
2nd Missouri Cav.	3	53	56
4th Missouri Cav.	4	56	60
7th Missouri Cav.	4	55	59
10th Missouri Cav.	2	52	54
1st Missouri S. M. Cav.	2	71	73
3rd Missouri S. M. Cav.	4	57	61
6th Missouri S. M. Cav.	2	48	50
7th Missouri S. M. Cav.	4	56	60
8th Missouri S. M. Cav.	3	77	80
2nd Bn. Missouri S. M. Cav.	3	48	51
1st Missouri L. A.	4	177	181
2nd Missouri	6	85	91
3rd Missouri	3	89	92
6th Missouri	4	80	84
7th Missouri	4	52	56
8th Missouri	3	78	81
10th Missouri	3	98	101
11th Missouri	6	98	104
12th Missouri	10	102	112
15th Missouri	8	107	115
17th Missouri	6	62	68
18th Missouri	6	75	81
21st Missouri	2	68	70
23rd Missouri	2	57	59
25th Missouri	6	51	57
26th Missouri	6	112	118
29th Missouri	7	68	75
31st Missouri	4	51	55

Regiments	Officers	Men	Total
33rd Missouri	4	52	56
39th Missouri	2	130	132
44th Missouri	4	61	65
2nd New Hampshire	15	163	178
3rd New Hampshire	12	186	198
4th New Hampshire	4	93	97
5th New Hampshire	18	277	295
6th New Hampshire	10	177	187
7th New Hampshire	15	169	174
8th New Hampshire	8	94	102
9th New Hampshire	10	145	155
10th New Hampshire	8	58	66
11th New Hampshire	5	140	145
12th New Hampshire	11	170	181
13th New Hampshire	5	84	89
14th New Hampshire	8	63	71
1st New Jersey Cav.	12	116	128
2nd New Jersey Cav.	3	48	51
3rd New Jersey Cav.	3	47	50
1st New Jersey	9	144	153
2nd New Jersey	7	89	96
3rd New Jersey	9	148	157
4th New Jersey	5	156	161
5th New Jersey	12	126	138
6th New Jersey	3	124	127
7th New Jersey	11	126	137
8th New Jersey	9	167	176
9th New Jersey	7	89	96
10th New Jersey	2	91	93
11th New Jersey	11	131	142
12th New Jersey	9	168	177
13th New Jersey	3	71	74
14th New Jersey	8	139	147
15th New Jersey	8	232	240
28th New Jersey		51	51
33rd New Jersey	6	72	78
2nd New York Cav.	9	112	121
4th New York Cav.	5	52	57
5th New York Cav.	8	93	101
6th New York Cav.	9	67	76
8th New York Cav.	14	91	105
9th New York Cav.	6	84	90
10th New York Cav.	9	93	102
19th New York Cav.	4	126	130
21st New York Cav.	3	63	66
24th New York Cav.	7	107	114
1st New York Veteran Cav.	4	56	60
2nd New York M. R.	8	94	102
1st New York Arty.	6	93	99
2nd New York H. A.	10	204	214
4th New York H. A.	8	108	116
5th New York H. A.		90	90
6th New York H. A.	6	130	136
7th New York H. A.	14	277	291
8th New York H. A.	19	342	361
9th New York H. A.	6	198	204
14th New York H. A.	6	220	226
15th New York H. A.	8	142	150
1st New York		79	79
4th New York	2	62	64
5th New York	6	171	177
5th New York Veteran	8	91	99
7th New York	14	88	102
7th New York Veteran	3	52	55
8th New York		90	90
9th New York	2	69	71
10th New York	6	106	112
11th New York	3	48	51
12th New York	3	61	64
13th New York	4	67	71
14th New York	4	56	60
16th New York	5	106	111
17th New York	2	51	53
20th New York	8	53	61
21st New York	2	74	76
22nd New York	11	62	73

Regiments	Officers	Men	Total	Regiments	Officers	Men	Total
24th New York	6	82	88	120th New York	11	140	151
25th New York	7	54	61	121st New York	14	212	226
26th New York	5	101	106	122nd New York	6	85	91
27th New York	2	72	74	123rd New York	6	66	72
28th New York	2	66	68	124th New York	11	137	148
30th New York	6	72	78	125th New York	15	112	127
31st New York	6	62	68	126th New York	16	137	153
34th New York	3	90	93	128th New York	2	58	60
37th New York	5	69	74	131st New York	2	82	84
38th New York	3	72	75	134th New York	5	86	91
39th New York	8	107	115	136th New York	2	71	73
40th New York	10	228	238	137th New York	6	121	127
41st New York	1	69	70	139th New York	5	66	71
42nd New York	11	141	152	140th New York	8	141	149
43rd New York	13	110	123	141st New York	4	71	75
44th New York	4	178	182	142nd New York	3	126	129
45th New York	3	48	51	146th New York	7	126	133
46th New York	8	96	104	147th New York	9	154	163
47th New York	7	70	77	148th New York	4	112	116
48th New York	18	218	236	149th New York	4	129	133
49th New York	15	126	141	150th New York	2	49	51
51st New York	9	193	202	151st New York	5	101	106
52nd New York	14	139	153	152nd New York	3	66	69
56th New York	1	63	64	154th New York	2	81	83
57th New York	8	95	103	155th New York	9	105	114
59th New York	14	129	143	156th New York	4	56	60
60th New York	3	64	67	157th New York	7	87	94
61st New York	16	177	193	158th New York	2	49	51
62nd New York	3	85	88	159th New York	10	74	84
63rd New York	15	141	156	160th New York	6	53	59
64th New York	13	160	173	161st New York	1	55	56
65th New York	5	112	117	162nd New York	8	58	66
66th New York	9	88	97	164th New York	10	106	116
67th New York	5	96	101	169th New York	10	147	157
69th New York	13	246	259	170th New York	10	119	129
70th New York	9	181	190	179th New York	7	61	68
71st New York	5	83	88	182nd New York	8	65	73
72nd New York	11	150	161	185th New York	3	53	56
73rd New York	18	138	156				
74th New York	8	122	130	1st Ohio Cav.	6	45	51
75th New York	4	91	95	2nd Ohio Cav.	7	76	83
76th New York	12	161	173	3rd Ohio Cav.	1	58	59
77th New York	9	87	96	4th Ohio Cav.	5	50	55
78th New York	3	55	58	6th Ohio Cav.	5	52	57
79th New York	3	116	119	8th Ohio Cav.	3	53	56
80th New York	8	120	128	12th Ohio Cav.	..	50	50
81st New York	13	139	142	13th Ohio Cav.	4	61	65
82nd New York	10	171	181	1st Ohio	5	116	121
83rd New York	9	147	156	2nd Ohio	9	96	105
84th New York	8	154	162	3rd Ohio	4	87	91
86th New York	13	159	172	4th Ohio	8	95	103
88th New York	15	136	151	5th Ohio	9	137	146
89th New York	6	89	95	6th Ohio	4	82	86
90th New York	2	58	60	7th Ohio	10	174	184
91st New York	3	110	113	8th Ohio	8	124	132
92nd New York	1	67	68	9th Ohio	6	85	91
93rd New York	6	120	126	10th Ohio	3	86	89
94th New York	5	105	110	11th Ohio	4	50	54
95th New York	5	114	119	12th Ohio	3	93	96
96th New York	9	59	68	13th Ohio	8	109	117
97th New York	12	169	181	14th Ohio	5	141	146
98th New York	4	95	99	15th Ohio	7	172	179
100th New York	12	182	194	16th Ohio	2	63	65
102nd New York	7	66	73	17th Ohio	6	71	77
103rd New York	5	61	66	18th Ohio	4	72	76
104th New York	5	81	86	19th Ohio	7	104	111
105th New York	2	48	50	20th Ohio	2	87	89
106th New York	10	127	137	21st Ohio	6	166	172
107th New York	4	87	91	23rd Ohio	5	154	159
108th New York	9	95	104	24th Ohio	6	62	68
109th New York	5	160	165	25th Ohio	7	151	158
111th New York	10	210	220	26th Ohio	6	116	122
112th New York	9	122	131	27th Ohio	6	80	86
114th New York	9	112	121	28th Ohio	2	66	68
115th New York	7	128	135	29th Ohio	6	114	120
116th New York	5	91	96	30th Ohio	9	119	128
117th New York	7	123	130	31st Ohio	2	77	79
118th New York	6	93	99	32nd Ohio	5	99	104
119th New York	6	66	72	33rd Ohio	7	130	137

Regiments	Officers	Men	Total
34th Ohio	10	120	130
35th Ohio	5	75	80
36th Ohio	4	136	140
37th Ohio	9	102	111
38th Ohio	8	132	140
39th Ohio	2	62	64
40th Ohio	6	96	102
41st Ohio	8	168	176
42nd Ohio	1	58	59
43rd Ohio	4	61	65
45th Ohio	5	58	63
46th Ohio	10	124	134
47th Ohio	2	80	82
48th Ohio	3	54	57
49th Ohio	14	188	202
50th Ohio	6	70	76
51st Ohio	4	108	112
52nd Ohio	7	94	101
53rd Ohio	4	76	80
54th Ohio	4	83	87
55th Ohio	7	136	143
56th Ohio	3	55	58
57th Ohio	4	77	81
58th Ohio	3	85	88
60th Ohio	3	110	113
61st Ohio	7	68	75
62nd Ohio	11	102	113
63rd Ohio	2	91	93
64th Ohio	6	108	114
65th Ohio	8	114	122
66th Ohio	5	96	101
67th Ohio	11	131	142
68th Ohio	2	48	50
69th Ohio	5	84	89
70th Ohio	5	70	75
71st Ohio	3	66	69
72nd Ohio	4	56	60
73rd Ohio	4	167	171
74th Ohio	2	51	53
75th Ohio	4	110	114
76th Ohio	9	82	91
77th Ohio	2	68	70
78th Ohio	2	71	73
79th Ohio	..	54	54
80th Ohio	4	48	52
81st Ohio	4	58	62
82nd Ohio	16	122	138
83rd Ohio	4	52	56
89th Ohio	3	47	50
90th Ohio	5	77	82
91st Ohio	3	60	63
92nd Ohio	4	47	51
93rd Ohio	4	106	110
94th Ohio	2	52	54
95th Ohio	1	58	59
97th Ohio	1	92	93
98th Ohio	10	110	120
99th Ohio	4	80	84
100th Ohio	3	90	93
101st Ohio	9	86	95
105th Ohio	3	104	107
107th Ohio	3	54	57
110th Ohio	10	117	127
111th Ohio	2	52	54
113th Ohio	9	110	119
116th Ohio	4	90	94
118th Ohio	1	55	56
121st Ohio	9	92	101
122nd Ohio	7	86	93
123rd Ohio	1	90	91
124th Ohio	7	78	85
125th Ohio	7	104	111
126th Ohio	9	143	152
1st Pennsylvania Cav.	9	87	96
2nd Pennsylvania Cav.	6	52	58
4th Pennsylvania Cav.	9	89	98
5th Pennsylvania Cav.	1	76	77
6th Pennsylvania Cav.	7	71	78

Regiments	Officers	Men	Total
7th Pennsylvania Cav.	8	94	102
8th Pennsylvania Cav.	5	55	60
9th Pennsylvania Cav.	6	66	72
11th Pennsylvania Cav.	11	108	119
13th Pennsylvania Cav.	3	67	70
14th Pennsylvania Cav.	2	97	99
16th Pennsylvania Cav.	5	100	105
17th Pennsylvania Cav.	6	98	104
18th Pennsylvania Cav.	5	55	60
21st Pennsylvania Cav.	4	80	84
2nd Pennsylvania H. A.	5	221	226
1st Pennsylvania Reserves	6	102	108
2nd Pennsylvania Reserves	4	73	77
3rd Pennsylvania Reserves	3	69	72
4th Pennsylvania Reserves	2	76	78
5th Pennsylvania Reserves	14	127	141
6th Pennsylvania Reserves	3	107	110
7th Pennsylvania Reserves	3	80	83
8th Pennsylvania Reserves	5	153	158
9th Pennsylvania Reserves	6	131	137
10th Pennsylvania Reserves	7	153	160
11th Pennsylvania Reserves	11	185	196
12th Pennsylvania Reserves	1	110	111
13th Pennsylvania Reserves	11	151	162
11th Pennsylvania	12	224	236
23rd Pennsylvania	5	110	115
26th Pennsylvania	6	143	149
27th Pennsylvania	5	67	72
28th Pennsylvania	6	151	157
29th Pennsylvania	3	99	102
45th Pennsylvania	13	214	227
46th Pennsylvania	14	165	179
47th Pennsylvania	5	112	117
48th Pennsylvania	11	145	156
49th Pennsylvania	9	184	193
50th Pennsylvania	8	156	164
51st Pennsylvania	12	165	177
53rd Pennsylvania	5	195	200
54th Pennsylvania	5	108	113
55th Pennsylvania	7	201	208
56th Pennsylvania	7	111	118
57th Pennsylvania	12	149	161
58th Pennsylvania	6	68	74
61st Pennsylvania	19	218	237
62nd Pennsylvania	17	152	169
63rd Pennsylvania	17	169	186
67th Pennsylvania	2	77	79
68th Pennsylvania	10	61	71
69th Pennsylvania	12	166	178
71st Pennsylvania	14	147	161
72nd Pennsylvania	11	182	193
73rd Pennsylvania	5	98	103
74th Pennsylvania	2	54	56
75th Pennsylvania	6	46	52
76th Pennsylvania	9	161	170
77th Pennsylvania	5	60	65
78th Pennsylvania	2	68	70
79th Pennsylvania	4	118	122
81st Pennsylvania	18	190	208
82nd Pennsylvania	5	106	111
83rd Pennsylvania	11	271	282
84th Pennsylvania	6	119	125
85th Pennsylvania	7	90	97
87th Pennsylvania	10	80	90
88th Pennsylvania	8	101	109
90th Pennsylvania	5	98	103
91st Pennsylvania	6	110	116
93rd Pennsylvania	11	161	172
95th Pennsylvania	11	171	182
96th Pennsylvania	6	126	132
97th Pennsylvania	6	130	136
98th Pennsylvania	9	112	121
99th Pennsylvania	9	113	122
100th Pennsylvania	16	208	224
102nd Pennsylvania	10	171	181
103rd Pennsylvania	3	50	53
104th Pennsylvania	2	68	70
105th Pennsylvania	14	231	245
106th Pennsylvania	9	95	104

Regiments	Officers	Men	Total
107th Pennsylvania	2	106	108
109th Pennsylvania	3	61	64
110th Pennsylvania	7	111	118
111th Pennsylvania	7	138	145
114th Pennsylvania	7	66	73
116th Pennsylvania	8	137	145
118th Pennsylvania	9	132	141
119th Pennsylvania	9	132	141
121st Pennsylvania	5	104	109
125th Pennsylvania	2	48	50
130th Pennsylvania	4	56	60
132nd Pennsylvania	3	70	73
138th Pennsylvania	6	90	96
139th Pennsylvania	10	135	145
140th Pennsylvania	10	188	198
141st Pennsylvania	6	161	167
142nd Pennsylvania	7	148	155
143rd Pennsylvania	8	143	151
145th Pennsylvania	18	187	205
147th Pennsylvania	7	71	78
148th Pennsylvania	12	198	210
149th Pennsylvania	4	160	164
150th Pennsylvania	4	108	112
151st Pennsylvania	2	67	69
155th Pennsylvania	5	137	142
183rd Pennsylvania	4	92	96
184th Pennsylvania	3	110	113
187th Pennsylvania	..	66	66
188th Pennsylvania	10	114	124
198th Pennsylvania	6	67	73
203rd Pennsylvania	4	70	74
207th Pennsylvania	3	51	54
2nd Rhode Island	9	111	120
4th Rhode Island	5	68	73
7th Rhode Island	5	85	90
1st Tennessee Cav.	4	56	60
5th Tennessee Cav.	1	68	69
3rd Tennessee	3	54	57
8th Tennessee	2	48	50
1st Vermont Cav.	10	124	134
1st Vermont H. A.	10	154	164
2nd Vermont	6	218	224
3rd Vermont	5	201	206
4th Vermont	12	150	162
5th Vermont	11	202	213
6th Vermont	12	191	203
8th Vermont	4	115	119
10th Vermont	9	140	149
17th Vermont	14	133	147
1st West Virginia Cav.	10	71	81
2nd West Virginia Cav.	4	77	81
5th West Virginia Cav.	3	68	71
6th West Virginia Cav.	5	56	61
1st West Virginia	3	51	54
4th West Virginia	3	80	83
5th West Virginia	4	57	61
7th West Virginia	9	133	142
9th West Virginia	3	96	99
10th West Virginia	2	93	95
11th West Virginia	4	63	67
12th West Virginia	3	56	59
13th West Virginia	4	57	61
14th West Virginia	7	81	88
15th West Virginia	3	50	53

Regiments	Officers	Men	Total
1st Wisconsin Cav.	6	67	73
3rd Wisconsin Cav.	3	61	64
1st Wisconsin	6	151	157
2nd Wisconsin	10	228	238
3rd Wisconsin	9	158	167
4th Wisconsin	11	106	117
5th Wisconsin	15	180	195
6th Wisconsin	16	228	244
7th Wisconsin	10	271	281
8th Wisconsin	6	53	59
9th Wisconsin	..	77	77
10th Wisconsin	5	91	96
11th Wisconsin	6	80	86
12th Wisconsin	3	93	96
14th Wisconsin	6	116	122
15th Wisconsin	8	86	92
16th Wisconsin	6	141	147
18th Wisconsin	4	52	56
20th Wisconsin	5	100	105
21st Wisconsin	5	117	122
22nd Wisconsin	2	75	77
24th Wisconsin	8	103	111
25th Wisconsin	3	48	51
26th Wisconsin	12	176	188
29th Wisconsin	1	76	77
36th Wisconsin	7	150	157
37th Wisconsin	7	149	156
38th Wisconsin	1	56	57
1st United States Cav.	9	73	82
2nd United States Cav.	5	73	78
4th United States Cav.	3	59	62
5th United States Cav.	7	60	67
6th United States Cav.	2	50	52
1st United States Arty.	6	75	81
2nd United States Arty.	5	50	55
4th United States Arty.	6	87	93
5th United States Arty.	7	87	94
2nd United States	8	88	96
4th United States	2	58	60
7th United States	2	50	52
10th United States	3	83	86
11th United States	8	117	125
12th United States	8	118	126
13th United States	3	55	58
14th United States	8	158	166
15th United States	3	131	134
16th United States	7	92	99
17th United States	9	92	101
18th United States	9	209	218
19th United States	3	55	58
1st United States Vols., S. S.	10	143	153
2nd United States Vols., S. S.	8	117	125
5th United States Colored H. A.	4	124	128
1st United States Colored	4	67	71
4th United States Colored	3	102	105
5th United States Colored	4	77	81
6th United States Colored	8	79	87
7th United States Colored	1	84	85
8th United States Colored	4	115	119
13th United States Colored	4	86	90
19th United States Colored	3	47	50
22nd United States Colored	2	70	72
23rd United States Colored	4	82	86
31st United States Colored	3	48	51
35th United States Colored	4	49	53
43rd United States Colored	3	48	51
49th United States Colored	3	59	62
79th United States Colored	5	183	188

Alphabetical Index to Commanders of the Various Military Divisions, Departments, Armies, Army Corps, Divisions, Brigades, Etc.

Name	Brigade	Division, District, Etc.	Corps	Army or Dept.
Abbott, H. L.	Fourth,	Def. South Potomac,	Twenty-second,	Washington, D. C.
	Third,	Def. South Potomac,	Twenty-second,	Washington, D. C.
	Second,	Def. South Potomac,	Twenty-second,	Washington, D. C.
Abbott, J. C.	Second,	First,	Tenth,	Va. and N. C.
	Second,	First,	Twenty-fourth,	Dept. Va.
	Abbott's,		Terry's Prov'l,	Dept. N. C.
	Second,	First,	Tenth,	North Carolina.
	Abbott's Detchd.,		Tenth,	North Carolina.
Abercrombie, J. C.	Third,	Fourth,	Seventeenth,	Tennessee.
Abercrombie, J. J.	Sixth,	Second,		Pennsylvania.
	Second,			Shenandoah.
	Second,	Banks',		Potomac.
	Second,	First,	Banks' Fifth,	Potomac.
	Second,	First,		Shenandoah.
	Second,	Second,	Third,	Potomac.
	Second,	First,	Fourth,	Potomac.
		First,	Fourth,	Potomac.
		Abercrombie's,	Washington, D. C.,	Potomac.
		Abercrombie's,	Twenty-second,	Washington, D. C.
Abert, W. S.	Second,	Def. North Potomac,	Twenty-second,	Washington, D. C.
Acker, J. S.	Second,	Cavalry Division,	Twenty-third,	Ohio.
	Mounted,	Cavalry Division,	Twenty-third,	Ohio.
Adams, C. W.	Second,	Frontier,	Seventh,	Arkansas.
	First,	Frontier,	Seventh,	Arkansas.
Adams, R. N.	Second,	Second,	Sixteenth,	Tennessee.
	Second,	Fourth,	Fifteenth,	Tennessee.
Adams, S. C.	First,	First Cavalry,	Twenty-third,	Ohio.
Albright, Charles	Third,	Third,	Second,	Potomac.
Alcott, J. H.	Second,	Third,	Nineteenth,	Gulf.
Alden, A.	Third,	Second,	Tenth,	North Carolina.
Alexander, C. M.	First,	King's,	Twenty-second,	Washington, D. C.
		King's,	Twenty-second,	Washington, D. C.
Alexander, F. N.	Second,	1st Div. Dist. Kentucky,	Twenty-third,	Ohio.
Alexander, J. I.	First,	Seventh,	Sixteenth,	Tennessee.
	First,	Seventh,	Seventeenth,	Tennessee.
	First,	Second,	Seventeenth,	Tennessee.
	First,	Third,	Fifteenth,	Tennessee.
	Second,	Fourth,	Cavalry,	Mil. Div. Miss.
Alexander, J. M.	First Colored,	Dist. Memphis, 5th Div.	Sixteenth,	Tennessee.
Alford, S. M.	First,	Second,	Seventh,	Virginia.
	First,	Getty's, Dist. Norfolk,		Va. and N. C.
	Second,	North End Folly Island,	Tenth,	South.
	Second,	Vodges',	Tenth,	South.
	Second,	Gordon's, Folly Island,	Tenth,	South.
		Second,	Tenth,	Va. and N. C.
	First,	Second,	Tenth,	Va. and N. C.
Alger, R. A.	Second,	Third,	Cavalry,	Potomac.
Allabach, P. H.	Second,	Third,	Fifth,	Potomac.
Allard, T. B.	First,	Second,	Ninth,	Ohio.
Allcock, T.	Fourth,	Def. South Potomac,	Twenty-second,	Washington, D. C.
	First,	Def. North Potomac,	Twenty-second,	Washington, D. C.
Allen, B.	First,	Sixth,		Army Tenn.
Allen, D. B.	First,	Second,	Eleventh,	Cumberland.
Allen, J. A. P.	Second,	Def. North Potomac,	Twenty-second,	Washington, D. C.
Allen, J. D.		Dist. Southwest Mo.		Missouri.
Allen, Thos. S.	Third,	First,	Sixth,	Potomac.
	Third,	First,	Sixth,	Army Shen.
Ames, A.	Second,	First,	Eleventh,	Potomac.
		First,	Eleventh,	Potomac.
	Second,	South End Folly Island,	Tenth,	South.
	Second,	Forces Folly Island,	Tenth,	South.
		Forces Folly Island,	Tenth,	South.
		First Dist. Florida,	Tenth,	South.
		Third,	Tenth,	Va. and N. C.
	Third,	Third,	Eighteenth,	Potomac.
		Third,	Eighteenth,	Potomac.
	Third,	Second,	Eighteenth,	Potomac.
		Second,	Tenth,	Va. and N. C.
		Second,	Eighteenth,	Va. and N. C.
		First,	Tenth,	Va. and N. C.
			Tenth,	Va. and N. C.
		Second,	Twenty-fourth,	Va. and N. C.
		Ames,	Terry's Prov'l,	North Carolina.
		Second,	Tenth,	North Carolina.
			Tenth,	North Carolina.

Name	Brigade	Division, District, Etc.	Corps	Army or Dept.
Ames, J. W.	Second,	Third,	Eighteenth,	Va. and N. C.
	Third,	Third,	Eighteenth,	Va. and N. C.
	Second,	First,	Twenty-fifth,	Va. and N. C.
	Second,	Third,	Twenty-fifth,	Va. and N. C.
		District Wilmington, N. C.,		North Carolina.
Ammen, Jacob	Tenth,			Army Ohio.
	Tenth,	Fourth,		Army Ohio.
		Fourth,		Army Ohio.
		Fourth,	Twenty-third,	Ohio.
Amory, T. J. C.	First,	First,		North Carolina.
	Amory's,			North Carolina.
	First,	First,	Eighteenth,	North Carolina.
		First,	Eighteenth,	North Carolina.
		District Beaufort, N. C.,	Eighteenth,	North Carolina.
		Sub. Dist. Beaufort, N. C.,		Va. and N. C.
		Defences New Berne, N. C.,		Va. and N. C.
Anderson, Dan'l.	Third,	Second, Arkansas Exp.,		Tennessee.
	Third,	First (Cavalry),	Seventh,	Arkansas.
Anderson, N. L.	Second,	Third,	Fourth,	Cumberland.
Anderson, Robt.				Kentucky.
				Cumberland.
Anderson, Robt.	Third,	Third,	Third,	Army of Va.
	Third,	Third,	First,	Potomac.
Andress, J. F.	First,	Second,	Cavalry,	Mil. Div. Miss.
Andrews, C. C.	Second,	Second,	Seventh,	Arkansas.
		Second,	Seventh,	Arkansas.
	Third,		Reserve,	Gulf.
		Second,	Reserve,	Gulf.
		Second,	Thirteenth,	Gulf.
Andrews, E. B.	Second,	Kanawha,		West Va.
Andrews, G. L.	Second,	Second,	Fifth,	Potomac.
		Defences New Orleans,		Gulf.
	First,	Third,	Nineteenth,	Gulf.
		Second,	Nineteenth,	Gulf.
		District Port Hudson,	Nineteenth,	Gulf.
			Corps de Afrique,	Gulf.
		Dist. Baton Rouge and Port Hudson, La.,		Gulf.
Andrews, Geo. L.	Second,	First,	Twelfth,	Potomac.
	Fourth,	First,	Twelfth,	Potomac.
Andrews, J. W.	Third,	Third,	Second,	Potomac.
Anthony, D. C.	First,	Second,	Sixteenth,	Tennessee.
Appleton, J. F.	Ullman's,	U. S. Colored Troops, Port Hudson, La.,		Gulf.
	Second,	First, Corps de Afrique,		Gulf.
Arden, G. DeP.	Second,	Kitching's Prov'l,		Army Shen.
Armstrong, J. B.	Second,	Third,	Tenth,	Va. and N. C.
Armstrong, S. C.	Second,	Third,	Tenth,	Va. and N. C.
Armstrong, S. C.	Second,	Second,	Twenty-fifth,	Texas.
Arnold, L. G.		Dist. Pensacola, Fla.,		South.
		District West Fla.,		Gulf.
Arnold, R.		Cavalry Division,		Gulf.
Asboth, A.	Fifth,	Southwest Mo.,		Missouri.
		Second, Army S. W. Mo.,		Missouri.
		Fifth, Army Miss.,		Missouri.
		District Columbus, Ky.,	Sixteenth,	Tennessee.
		6th Div. Dist. Columbus,	Sixteenth,	Tennessee.
		Dist. West Florida,		Gulf.
Atkins, S. D.	First,	First,	Reserve,	Cumberland.
	Third,	Second,	Cavalry,	Cumberland.
	Third,	Third,	Cavalry,	Cumberland.
	Second,	Third,	Cavalry,	Mil. Dist. Miss.
Augur, C. C.	First,	McDowell's,		Potomac.
	First,	Third,	First,	Potomac.
	First,	King's,		Rappahannock.
	First,	First,	Third,	Army of Va.
		U. S. Forces Bat. Rouge, La.,	Nineteenth,	Gulf.
		First,	Nineteenth,	Gulf.
			Twenty-second,	Washington, D. C.
				Washington, D. C.
Austin, J.	Third,	Second,	Twelfth,	Potomac.
Averill, W. W.	First,	Cavalry,		Potomac.
	Cavalry,	Centre Grand Division,		Potomac.
		Second,	Cavalry,	Potomac.
	4th Separate,		Eighth,	Middle.
	4th Separate,			West Virginia.
		Fourth,		West Virginia.
		Second Cavalry,		West Virginia.

Name	Brigade	Division, District, Etc.	Corps	Army or Dept.
Ayres, R. B.	First,	First,	Fifth,	Potomac.
	Fourth,	First,	Fifth,	Potomac.
	First,	Second,	Fifth,	Potomac.
		Second,	Fifth,	Potomac.
Babcock, A. J.	Second,	First,		Army Tenn.
Bacon, Geo. A.	Third,	First Cavalry,	Sixteenth,	Tennessee.
Bailey, B. P.	First,	Third,	Third,	Potomac.
Bailey, G. W. K.	First,	First,	Thirteenth,	Gulf.
Bailey, Jos.	Engineer,		Nineteenth,	Gulf.
		Dist. West Fla.,		Gulf.
		Dist. Baton Rouge, La.,		Gulf.
		Cavalry Division,		Gulf.
	Engineer,			Mil. Div. W. Miss.
	Second,	Second Cavalry,		Gulf.
Bailey, W. P.	Fourth,	First,	Second,	Potomac.
Baird, A.	Twenty-seventh,	Seventh,		Ohio.
	Fourth,	Cumberland,		Ohio.
		Baird's,		Army Ky.
		Baird's,		Cumberland.
		First,	Reserve,	Cumberland.
		First,	Fourteenth,	Cumberland.
		Third,	Fourteenth,	Cumberland.
Baird, J. P.	Second,	First,	Eleventh,	Cumberland.
Baker, C.	First,	Second Cavalry,	Thirteenth,	Tennessee.
	First,	Third (Cavalry),	Dist. Eastern Ark.,	Missouri.
Baker, E. D.	Third,	Stone's,		Potomac.
Baker, James	First,	Second,		Army Tenn.
Baker, J. B.	Second,	Second,	Second,	Potomac.
Baldwin, P. P.	Third,	Second, Right Wing,	Fourteenth,	Cumberland.
	Third,	Second,	Twentieth,	Cumberland.
Baldwin, S. D.	Third,	Second,		Army Tenn.
Ball, W. H.	Second,	Third,	Sixth,	Army Shen.
Ballier, J. F.	First,	Second,	Sixth,	Potomac.
	Third,	Third,	Sixth,	Potomac.
	Wheaton's,			West Virginia.
Banbury, J.	Third,	Second,	Seventeenth,	Tennessee.
	Third,	Third,	Fifteenth,	Tennessee.
Bane, M. M.	Third,	District Corinth,	Thirteenth,	Tennessee.
	Third,	Dist. Corinth, Left Wing,	Sixteenth,	Tennessee.
	Third,	Second,	Sixteenth,	Tennessee.
Banks, N. P.		Banks',		Annapolis.
				Shenandoah.
				Potomac.
			Fifth,	Potomac.
				Shenandoah.
			Second,	Army of Va.
		Mil. Dist. of Washington,		Potomac.
			Nineteenth,	Gulf.
				Gulf.
Barlow, F. C.	Second,	Second,	Eleventh,	Potomac.
		First,	Eleventh,	Potomac.
		First,	Second,	Potomac.
		Second,	Second,	Potomac.
			Second,	Potomac.
Barnes, Chas.	Second,	Def. South Potomac,	Twenty-second,	Washington, D. C.
Barnes, James,	First,	First,	Fifth,	Potomac.
		First,	Fifth,	Potomac.
		Norfolk and Portsmouth,		Va. and N. C.
		Dist. St. Marys,		Va. and N. C.
Barnes, Jos. H.	Second,	First,	Ninth,	Potomac.
	First,	First,	Ninth,	Potomac.
	Third,	First,	Ninth,	Potomac.
Barnes, M.	Second,	First,	Twenty-first,	Cumberland.
Barnes, S. M.	Third,	Third,	Twenty-first,	Cumberland.
	Second,	First,	Fourth,	Cumberland.
Barney, A. M.	First,	Second,	Tenth,	Va. and N. C.
	First,	Second,	Tenth,	North Carolina.
Barney, V. G.	Second,	Third,	Twenty-fourth,	Va. and N. C.
Barnum, H. A.	Third.	Second,	Twentieth,	Cumberland.
Barrett, T. H.	Prov'l,	U. S. C. T. Dist. Morganza,		Gulf.
	Second,	U. S. C. T. Dist. Morganza.		Gulf.
	Second,	Second,	Twenty-fifth,	Texas.
		Second,	Twenty-fifth,	Texas.
	Third,	First,	Twenty-fifth,	Texas.
	Second,	Second,	Twenty-fifth,	Texas.
Barrett, W. W.	Second,	Third,	Twentieth,	Cumberland.
Barron, G. McL.	Third,	Def. South Potomac,	Twenty-second,	Washington.
Barry, H. W.	First,	Second,	Twenty-fifth,	Texas.

Name	Brigade	Division, District, Etc.	Corps	Army or Dept.
Barry, W. F.		Arty. Camp, Dist. Wash.,		Potomac.
		Light Arty., Depot,	Twenty-second,	Washington, D. C.
Barter, R. F.	First,	First,	Twenty-third,	Ohio.
	Fourth,	Third,	Twenty-third,	Ohio.
Bartholomew, O. A.	First,	Second,	Twenty-fifth,	Virginia.
Bartleson, F. A.	First,	First,	Twenty-first,	Cumberland.
Bartlett, J. J.	Second,	First,	Sixth,	Potomac.
		Third,	Sixth,	Potomac.
	Third,	First,	Fifth,	Potomac.
		First,	Fifth,	Potomac.
		Second,	Ninth,	Potomac.
Bartlett, W. C.	First,	Fourth,	Twenty-third,	Ohio.
	First,	Fourth, Dist. East Tenn.,		Cumberland.
Bartlett, W. F.	First,	First,	Ninth,	Potomac.
		First,	Ninth,	Potomac.
Barton, W. B.	Barton's,	Dist. Hilton Head, S. C.,	Tenth,	South.
	Barton's,	Hilton Head District,	Tenth,	South.
		Dist. Hilton Head, S. C.,	Tenth,	South.
	Barton's,	Florida Expedition,	Tenth,	South.
	Barton's,	Ames, Dist. Florida,	Tenth,	South.
	Second,	Second,	Tenth,	Va. and N. C.
	First,	Third,	Eighteenth,	Potomac.
Bassett, C. J.	First,	First, C. de A., U. S. C. T.,		Gulf.
Bassett, I. C.	Third,	First,	Sixth,	Potomac.
	Third,	First,	Sixth,	Army Shen.
Bassford, A.	Separate Cav.	Dist. Baton Rouge, La.		Gulf.
	Second Separate,	Cavalry Brigade,		Gulf.
Bates, D.	First,	Third,	Ninth,	Potomac.
	First,	First,	Twenty-fifth,	Va. and N. C.
	First,	Third,	Twenty-fifth,	Va. and N. C.
	First,	Paine's,	Terry's Prov'l,	North Carolina.
	First,	Third,	Tenth,	North Carolina.
		Third,	Tenth,	North Carolina.
Bates, Jas. L.	Second,	Second,	Fifth,	Potomac.
	Second,	Third,	Fifth,	Potomac.
Baxter, D. W. C.	Second,	Second,	Second,	Potomac.
	First,	Second,	Second,	Potomac.
		Second,	Second,	Potomac.
Baxter, H.	Second,	Second,	First,	Potomac.
		Second,	First,	Potomac.
	Second,	Second,	Fifth,	Potomac.
		Second,	Fifth,	Potomac.
Baxter, H.	Second,	Third,	Fifth,	Potomac.
Bayard, Geo. D.	Cavalry,			Mountains.
	Cavalry,		Third,	Army of Va.
	Cavalry,	Left Grand Division,		Potomac.
Bayley, T. M.	Second,	First,	Twenty-fifth,	Virginia.
	First,	First,	Twenty-fifth,	Texas.
Beach, B.	Third,	Fourth,	Seventeenth,	Tennessee.
Beach, Francis	Second,	Gettys., Norfolk and Ports.,		Va. and N. C.
Beadle, W. H. H.	Third,	Def. South Potomac,	Twenty-second,	Washington, D. C.
Beal, L. W.	Second,	Second,	Seventh,	Arkansas.
Beale, Geo. L.	Second,	First,	Nineteenth,	Gulf.
	First,	First,	Nineteenth,	Gulf.
	First,	First,	Nineteenth,	Army Shen.
	First,	First, Provisional,		Army Shen.
	First,	Dwight's,	Twenty-second,	Washington, D. C.
Beardsley, John	Cavalry,		First,	Army Virginia.
Beatty, J.	Second,	First, Centre,	Fourteenth,	Cumberland.
	Second,	First,	Fourteenth,	Cumberland.
	First,	Second,	Fourteenth,	Cumberland.
	Second,	Second,	Fourteenth,	Cumberland.
Beatty, S.	Eleventh,	Fifth,		Army Ohio.
	Eleventh,	Fifth,	Second,	Army Ohio.
	First,	Third, Left Wing,	Fourteenth,	Cumberland.
		Third, Left Wing,	Fourteenth,	Cumberland.
	First,	Third,	Twenty-first,	Cumberland.
		Third,	Twenty-first,	Cumberland.
	Third,	Third,	Fourth,	Cumberland.
	Second,	Third,	Fourth,	Cumberland.
		Third,	Fourth,	Texas.
Beaver, Jas. A.	First,	First,	Second,	Potomac.
Beaver, Jas. A.	Third,	First,	Second,	Potomac.
	Fourth,	First,	Second,	Potomac.
Beckwith, E. G.		Def. New Orleans, La.,	Nineteenth,	Gulf.
	Fourth,		Nineteenth,	Gulf.
Beecher, Jas. C.	Third, African,	Forces North End Folly Is.,	Tenth,	South.
	Third,	Vodges,	Tenth,	South.

Name	Brigade	Division, District, Etc.	Corps	Army or Dept.
Belknap, J. S.	First,	Fourth,	Eighteenth,	North Carolina.
Belknap, W. W.	Third,	Fourth,	Seventeenth,	Tennessee.
		Fourth,	Seventeenth,	Tennessee.
			Seventeenth,	Tennessee.
Bell, Louis	First,	Third,	Tenth,	Va. and N. C.
	Second,	Third,	Eighteenth,	Potomac.
	Third,	Third,	Tenth,	Va. and N. C.
	Third,	Second,	Twenty-fourth,	Va. and N. C.
	Third,	Ames,	Terry's Prov'l,	North Carolina.
Bendix, John E.	Third,	Third,	Second,	Potomac.
Benedict, Lewis	First,	Third,	Nineteenth,	Gulf.
	Third,	First,	Nineteenth,	Gulf.
Benham, H. W.	Benham's,	Army of Occupation,		West Virginia.
Bennett, J. E.	Third,	First,	Fourth,	Cumberland.
Bennett, T. W.	Third,	First,	Thirteenth,	Gulf.
	Second,	Third,	Nineteenth,	Gulf.
Benteen, F. W.		2d Cav. Dist. W. Tenn.,		Tennessee.
Benton, T. H.	Second,	Third, Arkansas Expedition,		Tennessee.
	Second,	Second,	Seventh,	Arkansas.
Benton, W. P.		First, Army S. E. Mo.		Missouri.
	First,	Fourteenth,	Thirteenth,	Tennessee.
	First,	First,	Thirteenth,	Tennessee.
		First,	Thirteenth,	Gulf.
	Second,	Second,	Thirteenth,	Gulf.
			Thirteenth,	Gulf.
		Dist. Baton Rouge, La.,		Gulf.
		Third,	Reserve,	Gulf.
		Third,	Thirteenth,	Gulf.
Bentzoni, C.		Dist. Eastern Arkansas,	Seventh,	Arkansas.
Berdan, H.	Second,	Third,	Third,	Potomac.
	Third,	Third,	Third,	Potomac.
	Second,	First,	Third,	Potomac.
Berry, H. G.	Third,	Third,	Third,	Potomac.
	Third,	First,	Third,	Potomac.
	Second,		Third,	Potomac.
Berry, W. W.	Third,	Second,	Twentieth,	Cumberland.
Berthoud, Alex. F.	Third,	First,	First,	Potomac.
Bertram, Henry	First,	Third, Army Frontier,		Missouri.
	Second,	Second,	Thirteenth,	Gulf.
	Bertram's,	U. S. Forces Mobile Bay,		Gulf.
		U. S. Forces Mobile Bay,		Gulf.
	First,	Second,	Thirteenth,	Gulf.
Beveridge, J. L.		District St. Louis, Mo.		Missouri.
		District Central Mo.,		Missouri.
Biddle, Chapman	First,	Third,	First,	Potomac.
Biddle, Geo. H.	Second,	First,	First,	Potomac.
Biddle, Jas.		Second,	Cavalry,	Ohio.
	First,	Cavalry,	Twenty-third,	Ohio.
	Second,	Sixth,	Cavalry,	Mil. Div. Miss.
Bidwell, D. D.	Third,	Second,	Sixth,	Potomac.
	Third,	Second,	Sixth,	Army Shen.
Bintliff, Jas.	First,	First,	Ninth,	Potomac.
	Third,	First,	Ninth,	Potomac.
Birge, H. W.	Third,	Fourth,	Nineteenth,	Gulf.
	First,	Fourth,	Nineteenth,	Gulf.
		Dist. La Fourche, La.,	Nineteenth,	Gulf.
		Dist. Baton Rouge, La.,	Nineteenth,	Gulf.
	Second,	Second,	Nineteenth,	Gulf.
	First,	Second,	Nineteenth,	Gulf.
	First,	Second,	Nineteenth,	Army Shen.
		Second,	Nineteenth,	Army Shen.
	First,	Grover's,		South.
		Grover's,		South.
		First,	Tenth,	North Carolina.
		District Savannah, Ga.		South.
Birney, D. B.	Second,	Heintzelman's,		Potomac.
	Second,	Third,	Third,	Potomac.
	Second,	First,	Third,	Potomac.
		First,	Third,	Potomac.
			Third,	Potomac.
		Third,	Second,	Potomac.
			Second,	Potomac.
			Tenth,	Va. and N. C.
				Va. and N. C.
Birney, William		District Florida,		South.
		District Hilton Head,		South.
	First,	Third,	Tenth,	Va. and N. C.
		Third,	Tenth,	Va. and N. C.

Name	Brigade	Division, District, Etc.	Corps	Army or Dept.
		Second,	Twenty-fifth,	Virginia.
Black, J. C.	First,	Second,	Thirteenth,	Gulf.
	Third,	Second,	Reserve,	Gulf.
	Third,	Second,	Thirteenth,	Gulf.
Blackman, A. M.	Third,	Third,	Tenth,	Va. and N. C.
Blair, F. P., Jr.	First,	Eleventh,	Thirteenth,	Tennessee.
	First,	4th, Yazoo Expedition,		Tennessee.
	First,	First,	Fifteenth,	Tennessee.
		Second,	Fifteenth,	Tennessee.
			Fifteenth,	Tennessee.
			Seventeenth,	Tennessee.
Blake, G. A. H.	Blake's	Cavalry Reserve,		Potomac.
Blake, J. W.	Second,	Second,	Fourth,	Cumberland.
Blaisdell, W.	First,	Second,	Third,	Potomac.
	Fourth,	Second,	Second,	Potomac.
Blanchard, J. W.	Third,	First,	Nineteenth,	Gulf.
Blanden, L.	Second,	Third, Det'mt Army, Tenn.,		Cumberland.
Blenker, Louis	First,	Fifth, Army N. E. Va.,		Potomac.
	Blenker's,	Division Potomac,		Potomac.
		Blenker's,		Potomac.
		Blenker's,	Second,	Potomac.
		Blenker's,		Mountains.
Bliss, Z. R.	First,	Second,	Ninth,	Ohio.
		Second,	Ninth,	Ohio.
Bliss, Z. R.	First,	Second,	Ninth,	Potomac.
Blood, J. H.	First,	Second,	Fifteenth,	Tennessee.
Bloodgood, E.	Second,	Third,	Twentieth,	Cumberland.
Blunt, Asa P.	Second,	Casey's, Mil. Dist. Wash.,		Potomac.
	Second,	Casey's,	Twenty-second,	Washington, D. C.
Blunt, J. G.		First, Army Frontier,		Missouri.
		District Frontier,		Missouri.
		Dist. Upper Arkansas,		Kansas.
		Dist. South Kansas.		Kansas.
				Kansas.
Bohlen, Henry	Third,	Blenker's,		Potomac.
	Third,	Blenker's,	Second,	Potomac.
	Third,	Blenker's,		Mountains.
	First,	Third,	First,	Army of Va.
Bollinger, H. C.	Second,	Penna. Reserves,	Twenty-second,	Washington, D. C.
Bond, E. S.	Second,	First,	Cavalry,	Ohio.
	Second,	Fourth,	Twenty-third,	Ohio.
Bond, J. R.	Second,	Second,	Twenty-third,	Ohio.
Boomer, G. B.	Third,	Seventh, Left Wing,	Thirteenth,	Tennessee.
	Third,	Seventh,	Sixteenth,	Tennessee.
	Third,	Seventh,	Seventeenth,	Tennessee.
Bossert, H. M.	Third,	First,	First,	Potomac.
Bouck, G.	Second,	Sixth, Left Wing,	Thirteenth,	Tennessee.
	First,	Third,	Fifteenth,	Tennessee.
Boughton, Edw.	First,	U. S. C. T. Memphis, Tenn.,		Tennessee.
Boughton, H.	First,	Third,	Eleventh,	Cumberland.
	Third,	First,	Twentieth,	Cumberland.
	Third,	First, Dist. Beaufort N. C.		North Carolina.
Bowen, S. K.	Third,	First,	Eighteenth,	Va. and N. C.
Bowen, T. M.	Third,	District Frontier,		Missouri.
	Third,	District Frontier,	Seventh,	Arkansas.
	First,	First,	Seventh,	Arkansas.
Bowerman, R. N.	Third,	Second,	Fifth,	Potomac.
	Second,	Second,	Fifth,	Potomac.
Bowman, H.	First,	First,	Ninth,	Ohio.
	First,	First,	Ninth,	Tennessee.
	Third,	First,	Ninth,	Potomac.
Bowman, S. M.	Second,	Third,	Third,	Potomac.
		District Delaware,	Eighth,	Middle.
Boyd, S. H.		Second, Army S. E. Mo.		Missouri.
Boyd, W. H.	Cavalry,	First,		West Virginia.
Boyle, J. T.	Eleventh,			Army Ohio.
	Eleventh,	First,		Army Ohio.
	Eleventh,	Fifth,		Army Ohio.
		District Louisville, Ky.		Ohio.
		District West Ky.,		Ohio.
Brackett, A. G.	Second,	First Cavalry,	Sixteenth,	Tennessee.
Bradley, L. P.	Third,	Third, Right Wing,	Fourteenth,	Cumberland.
	Third,	Third,	Twentieth,	Cumberland.
	Third,	Second,	Fourth,	Cumberland.
Bradley, L. W.	Fourth,	First,	Second,	Potomac.
Brady, Jas.	Second,	Def. South Potomac,	Twenty-second,	Washington, D. C.
	Third,	Def. South Potomac,	Twenty-second,	Washington, D. C.

Name	Brigade	Division, District, Etc.	Corps	Army or Dept.
Bragg, E. S.	Third,	Third,	Fifth,	Potomac.
	First,	Third,	Fifth,	Potomac.
	First,	Fourth,	Fifth,	Potomac.
	Third,	Fourth,	Fifth,	Potomac.
Brannan, J. M.		Dist. Key West, Fla.,		South.
		Dist. Beaufort, S. C.,		South.
		U. S. Forces, Beauf't, S. C.,	Tenth,	South.
			Tenth,	South.
				South.
		First,	Twenty-first,	Cumberland.
		Third,	Fourteenth,	Cumberland.
Brannon, J. F.	First,	Second,	Ninth,	Potomac.
Branson, D.	Second,	First,	Twenty-fifth,	Texas.
Brawner, M. H.	First,	Cavalry,	Seventh,	Arkansas.
	Separate,	Dismounted Cavalry,	Seventh,	Arkansas.
Brayman, M.	First,	Third,	Sixteenth,	Tennessee.
		Post Natchez, Dist. Vicks.,		Tennessee.
		District Cairo,		Tennessee.
Brewster, Wm. R.	Second,	Second,	Third,	Potomac.
	Second,	Fourth,	Second,	Potomac.
	Fourth,	Third,	Second,	Potomac.
Briggs, E.	First,	First,	Fifteenth,	Tennessee.
Briggs, H. S.	First,	First,	Fourth,	Potomac.
	3rd Separate,		Eighth,	Middle.
		First,	First,	Potomac.
Brigham, J. H.	Second,	First,	Fourteenth,	Cumberland.
Bringhurst, T. H.	First,	Third,	Thirteenth,	Gulf.
		Third,	Thirteenth,	Gulf.
Briscoe, J. C.	First,	First,	Tenth,	Va. and N. C.
	First,	First,	Twenty-fourth,	Va. and N. C.
	Second Indpt.		Twenty-fourth,	Virginia.
Broady, K. O.	Fourth,	First,	Second,	Potomac.
	First,	First,	Second,	Potomac.
Brooke, J. R.	Third,	First,	Second,	Potomac.
	Third,	Second,	Second,	Potomac.
	Fourth,	First,	Second,	Potomac.
		Second Prov'l,		Army Shen.
Brooks, W. T. H.	First,	W. F. Smith's,		Potomac.
	Second,	Second,	Fourth,	Potomac.
	Second,	Second,	Sixth,	Potomac.
		First,	Sixth,	Potomac.
		First,	Eighteenth,	Va. and N. C.
			Tenth,	Va. and N. C.
				Monongahela.
Broughton, H.	First,	Third,	Eleventh,	Cumberland.
Brown, A. H.	Second,	Fourth,	Thirteenth,	Gulf.
	Third,	Third,	Nineteenth,	Gulf.
Brown, E. B.		Dist. Southwest Mo.,		Missouri.
		Dist. Central Mo.,		Missouri.
Brown, E. E.		Dist. Rolla,		Missouri.
		Dist. Central Mo.,		Missouri.
Brown, H. L.	Third,	First,	Second,	Potomac.
		First,	Second,	Potomac.
	Fourth,	First,	Second,	Potomac.
Brown, H. W.	First,	First,	Sixth,	Potomac.
Brown, J. M.	Second,	First, Dist. Kentucky,	Twenty-third,	Ohio.
	Fourth,	First, Dist. Kentucky,	Twenty-third,	Ohio.
Brown, L. B.	First,	Second,	Fifth,	Potomac.
Brown, L. G.	Second,	Second,	Twenty-fifth,	Texas.
Brown, N. W.		U. S. Forces, Hilton Head,	Tenth,	South.
Brown, P. P.	Second,	First,	Eleventh,	Potomac.
		Dist. Hilton Head, S. C.,		South.
Brown, R. H.	First,	Fifth,	Cavalry,	Mil. Div. Miss.
Brown, S. B.	First,	First, Dist. Kentucky,	Twenty-third,	Ohio.
	Second,	Cavalry, Dist. East Tenn.,		Cumberland.
Browne, W. H.	Second,	Third,	Sixth,	Potomac.
	Second,	Veteran Reserve Corps,	Twenty-second,	Washington.
Brownlow, J. P.	First,	First,	Cavalry,	Cumberland.
Bruce, S. D.	Twenty-second,			Army Ohio.
	Twenty-second,	Fourth,		Army Ohio.
	First,	Third,	Reserve,	Cumberland.
	First,	Second, Dist. Kentucky,	Twenty-third,	Ohio.
Bruen, L. B.	First,	Second,	Fifth,	Potomac.
Bryant, G. E.	Third,	Fourth,	Sixteenth,	Tennessee.
	First,	Third,	Seventeenth,	Tennessee.
Bryant, T. M., Jr.	First,	Third,	Cavalry,	Potomac.
	Second,	Third,	Cavalry,	Potomac.
Bryner, J.	First,	Fifth,		Army Miss.

Name	Brigade	Division, District, Etc.	Corps	Army or Dept.
Buchanan, R. C.	First,	Second,	Fifth,	Potomac.
Buck, S. L.	First,	First,	Sixth,	Potomac.
Buckingham, P. B.	Third,	Third,	Twentieth,	Cumberland.
Buckley, H. M.	Fourth,	Second,	First,	Army Ohio.
Buckland, R. P.	Fourth,	Fifth,		Army Tennessee.
Buckland, R. P.	Fifth,	Dist. Memphis,	Thirteenth,	Tennessee.
	Third,	First, Dist. Memphis, R. W.,	Thirteenth,	Tennessee.
	Third,	Eighth,	Sixteenth,	Tennessee.
	First,	Third,	Fifteenth,	Tennessee.
		Third,	Fifteenth,	Tennessee.
	First,	First,	Sixteenth,	Tennessee.
		Dist. Memphis, Fifth Div.,	Sixteenth,	Tennessee.
Buell, C.	Provisional,	Abercrombie's,	Mil. Dist. Wash.,	Potomac.
Buell, D. C.		Buell's,		Potomac.
				Army Ohio.
				Ohio.
Buell, G. P.	First,	First, Left Wing,	Fourteenth,	Cumberland.
	Pioneer,			Cumberland.
	First,	First,	Twenty-first,	Cumberland.
	Second,	First,	Fourteenth,	Cumberland.
		First,	Fourteenth,	Cumberland.
Buford, John	Cavalry,		Second,	Army of Va.
	Cavalry,			Potomac.
	Reserve,	First,	Cavalry,	Potomac.
		First,	Cavalry,	Potomac.
Buford, N. B.	Flotilla,			Army Miss.
	First,	Third,		Army Miss.
	Second,	Third,		Army Miss.
		Dist. Eastern Arkansas,	Sixteenth,	Tennessee.
		Dist. Eastern Arkansas,	Seventh,	Arkansas.
Bull, J. M.	Third,	Third,	Second,	Potomac.
Burbank, S.	First,	Second,	Fifth,	Potomac.
	Second,	Second,	Fifth,	Potomac.
Burbridge, S. G.	First,	First, Army of Kentucky,		Ohio.
		First, Army of Kentucky,		Ohio.
	First,	Tenth,	Thirteenth,	Tennessee.
	First,	First, Yazoo Expedition,		Tennessee.
	First,	Fourth,	Thirteenth,	Gulf.
		Fourth,	Thirteenth,	Gulf.
		Dist. Kentucky, Fifth Div.,	Twenty-third,	Ohio.
Burgh, Henry B.	Third,	First Cavalry,	Sixteenth,	Tennessee.
Burke, D. F.	Second,	First,	Second,	Potomac.
Burke, John	Second,	First,	Second,	Potomac.
Burke, J. W.	Reserve,			Cumberland.
Burke, P. E.	Second,	Second,	Sixteenth,	Tennessee.
Burling, G. C.	Third,	Second,	Third,	Potomac.
Burnham, H.	Light,		Sixth,	Potomac.
	Third,	First,	Sixth,	Potomac.
	Second,	First,	Eighteenth,	Va. and N. C.
		First,	Eighteenth,	Va. and N. C.
Burns, W. W.	Third,	Stone's,		Potomac.
	Second,	Second,	Second,	Potomac.
		First,	Ninth,	Potomac.
Burnside, A. E.	Second,	Second,		Army N. E. Va.
			Expeditionary,	North Carolina.
				North Carolina.
			Ninth,	Potomac.
				Army Potomac.
				Dept. Potomac.
				Dept. Ohio.
				Army Ohio.
Burr, A. L.	Second,	First,	Fifth,	Potomac.
Buschbeck, A.	First,	First,	First,	Army of Va.
	First,	Second,	Eleventh,	Potomac.
		Second,	Eleventh,	Potomac.
	First,	Second,	Eleventh,	Cumberland.
		Second,	Eleventh,	Cumberland.
	Second,	Second,	Twentieth,	Cumberland.
Bussey, Cyrus	Second,	Third, Cavalry, E. Ark.,		Missouri.
	Second,	Second, Cavalry,	Thirteeenth,	Tennessee.
		Second, Cavalry,	Thirteeenth,	Tennessee.
	Second,	Cavalry, Dist. Eastern Ark.,	Sixteenth,	Tennessee.
		Cavalry, Dist. Eastern Ark.,	Sixteenth,	Tennessee.
	Cavalry,	Herron's,		Tennessee.
	First,	First, Cavalry, Ark. Exp.,		Tennessee.
		First, Cavalry, Ark. Exp.,		Tennessee.
	Third,	First,	Seventh,	Arkansas.
		First,	Seventh,	Arkansas.
		Third,	Seventh,	Arkansas.

Name	Brigade	Division. District, Etc.	Corps	Army or Dept.
Busteed, R.	Indpt.,		Seventh,	Virginia.
Butler, B. F.				Annapolis.
				Virginia.
				New England.
				Gulf.
			Nineteenth,	Gulf.
				Va. and N. C.
			Eighteenth,	Va. and N. C.
				Army James.
Butler, T. H.	Second,	Second,	Cavalry,	Ohio.
	First,	Cavalry,	Twenty-third,	Ohio.
	Second,	Cavalry,	Twenty-third,	Ohio.
	First,	Sixth,	Cavalry,	Mil. Div. Miss.
Butterfield, D.	Eighth,	Third,		Pennsylvania.
	Third,	Fitz John Porter's,		Potomac.
	Third,	First,	Third,	Potomac.
	Third,	First,	Fifth,	Potomac.
		First,	Fifth,	Potomac.
			Fifth,	Potomac.
		Third,	Twentieth,	Cumberland.
Buttrick, E. L.	Second,	Dist. Memphis, West Tenn.,		Tennessee.
Byington, C.	Third,	First,	Ninth,	Ohio.
Byrd, R. K.	First,	First,	Twenty-third,	Ohio.
		First,	Twenty-third,	Ohio.
	First,	Fourth,	Twenty-third,	Ohio.
	Third,	Third,	Twenty-third,	Ohio.
Byrnes, R.	Second,	First,	Second,	Potomac.
Cadwallader, G.				Annapolis.
				Pennsylvania.
		First,		Pennsylvania.
Cahill, T. W.		Def. New Orleans, La.,	Nineteenth,	Gulf.
	Second,	Second,	Nineteenth,	Gulf.
	Second,	Fourth,	Nineteenth,	Gulf.
Cake, H. L.	Second,	First,	Sixth,	Potomac.
Caldwell, H. C.	Reserve Cavalry,	Army S. E. Mo.,		Missouri.
Caldwell, J. C.	First,	First,	Second,	Potomac.
		First,	Second,	Potomac.
			Second,	Potomac.
Caldwell, W. W.	Thirty-second,	Ninth,		Army Ohio.
	Thirty-second,	Ninth,	Third,	Army Ohio.
	Third,	First,	Twentieth,	Cumberland.
Cameron, Dan'l	Second,	Third,	Twenty-third,	Ohio.
	First,	Fourth,	Twenty-third,	Ohio.
Cameron, R. A.	First,	Third,	Thirteenth,	Gulf.
		Third,	Thirteenth,	Gulf.
		Dist. LaFourche,		Gulf.
Campbell, A. P.	First,	First,	Cavalry,	Cumberland.
Campbell, E. L.	First,	First,	Sixth,	Potomac.
	First,	First,	Sixth,	Army Shen.
Campbell, F.	Third,	Third,	Seventeenth,	Tennessee.
Campbell, J. B.	Second,	Def. Bermuda Hundred,		Va. and N. C.
Campbell, J. M.	Fourth,	First,	Eighth,	Middle.
	Campbell's,			West Virginia.
	Third,	First,		West Virginia.
	First,	Second,		West Virginia.
	Third,	Second Infantry,		New Mexico.
Canby, E. R. S.				Mil. Div. W. Miss.
				Dept. Gulf.
Candy, C.	First,	Second,	Second,	Army of Va.
Candy, Chas.	First,	Second,	Twelfth,	Potomac.
	First,	Second,	Twelfth,	Cumberland.
		Second,	Twelfth,	Cumberland.
		Second,	Twentieth,	Cumberland.
	First,	Second,		West Virginia.
Capehart, Henry	Second,	Second Cavalry,		Army Shen.
	Third,	Third,	Cavalry,	Potomac.
	Third,	Third,	Cavalry,	Ohio.
Capron, H.	Second,	Second,	Cavalry,	Ohio.
	First,	Cavalry,	Twenty-third,	Ohio.
	Third,	Cavalry,	Twenty-third,	Ohio.
	Dism'td,	Cavalry,	Twenty-third,	Ohio.
		Cavalry,	Twenty-third,	Ohio.
	Third,	Cav. Dist. Ky. Fifth Div.,	Twenty-third,	Mil. Div. Miss.
	First,	Sixth,	Cavalry,	Potomac.
Carle, James	Third,	Third,	Fifth,	Army Miss.
Carlin, W. P.	Second,	Fourth,		Army Ohio.
	Thirty-first,	Ninth,		Army Ohio.
	Thirty-first,	Ninth,	Third,	Cumberland.
	Second,	First, Right Wing,	Fourteenth,	

Name	Brigade	Division, District, Etc.	Corps	Army or Dept.
	Second,	First,	Twentieth,	Cumberland.
	First,	First,	Fourteenth,	Cumberland.
		First,	Fourteenth,	Cumberland.
		Second Infantry,		West Virginia.
Carleton, J. H.				New Mexico.
Carlton, C. H.		Dist. West Ky.,		Kentucky.
		Post Chattanooga, Tenn.,		Cumberland.
	Second,	1st Sep. Div. Dist. Etowah,		Cumberland.
Carman, E. A.	Third,	First,	Twelfth,	Potomac.
	Second,	First,	Twentieth,	Cumberland.
Carr, E. A.	Third,	Army Southwest Mo.,		Missouri.
		Fourth, Army S. W. Mo.,		Missouri.
		Second, Dist. Eastern Ark.,		Missouri.
		Army S. W. Mo. Dist. E. Ark.,		Mo. and Tenn.
		District St. Louis, Mo.,		Missouri.
		Second, Army S. E. Mo.,		Missouri.
		Fourteenth,	Thirteenth,	Tennessee.
		Second, Ark. Expedition,		Tennessee.
		Left Wing,	Sixteeenth,	Tennessee.
		Second,	Seventh,	Arkansas.
		First Cavalry,	Seventh,	Arkansas.
		Dist. Little Rock, Ark.,	Seventh,	Arkansas.
		Third,	Sixteenth,	Gulf.
Carr, H. M.	Twenty-first,			Army Ohio.
Carr, J. B.	Third,	Second,	Third,	Potomac.
	First,	Second,	Third,	Potomac.
		Second,	Third,	Potomac.
		Third,	Third,	Potomac.
		Fourth,	Second,	Potomac.
		Third,	Eighteenth,	Va. and N. C.
		First,	Eighteenth,	Va. and N. C.
Carroll, S. S.	Fourth,	Shields',		Rappahannock,
	Fourth,	Second,	Third,	Army of Va.
	Second,	Whipple's, Mil. Dist. Wash.		Potomac.
	Second,	Third,	Third,	Potomac.
	Third,	Second,	Second,	Potomac.
	First,	Third,	Second,	Potomac.
		Fourth Prov'l,		West Virginia.
				West Virginia.
Carruth, S.	Second,	Second,	Ninth,	Ohio.
	Second,	Second,	Ninth,	Potomac.
	First,	First,	Ninth,	Potomac.
	First,	Second,	Ninth,	Potomac.
Carskadden, D.	Second,	First,	Fifteenth,	Tennessee.
Carter, J. P. T.	First,	First,	Twenty-third,	Ohio.
	Third,	Fourth,	Twenty-third,	Ohio.
Carter, S. P.	Twelfth,			Army Ohio.
	Twelfth,	First,		Army Ohio.
	Twenty-fourth,	Seventh,		Army Ohio.
	First,	Dist. Central Ky.,		Ohio.
	First,	First,	Twenty-third,	Ohio.
		First,	Twenty-third,	Ohio.
		Fourth,	Twenty-third,	Ohio.
		Second, Dist. Beaufort,		North Carolina.
		Div. Dist. Beaufort,		North Carolina.
		Third,	Twenty-third,	North Carolina.
			Twenty-third,	North Carolina.
Carver, L. D.	Second,	First,	Third,	Potomac.
Case, H.	First,	Third,	Twentieth,	Cumberland.
Casement, J. S.	Second,	Third,	Twenty-third,	Ohio.
	Second,	Third,	Twenty-third,	North Carolina.
Casey, Silas	Prov'l,	Division of the Potomac,		Potomac.
		Casey's,		Potomac.
		Third,	Fourth,	Potomac.
		Second,	Fourth,	Potomac.
	Prov'l,	Mil. Dist. Washington,		Potomac.
		Casey's, Mil. Dist. Wash.		Potomac.
		Casey's,	Twenty-second,	Washington.
Catherwood, E. C.		Dist. Rolla, Mo.,		Missouri.
Catterson, R. F.	Second,	First,	Fifteenth,	Tennessee.
Chamberlain, J. I.	Third,	First,	Fifth,	Potomac.
	First,	First,	Fifth,	Potomac.
		First,	Fifth,	Potomac.
Chamberlin, A. G.	African,	Norfolk and Portsmouth,		Va. and N. C.
	First,	Third,	Eighteenth,	Va. and N. C.
	Third,	Third,	Tenth,	North Carolina.
Chambers, A.	Third,	Sixth,	Seventeenth,	Tennessee.
		Sixth,	Seventeenth,	Tennessee.

Name	Brigade	Division, District, Etc.	Corps	Army or Dept.
	Third,	First,	Seventeenth,	Tennessee.
		First,	Seventeenth,	Cumberland.
Champion, T. E.	First,	First,	Reserve,	Cumberland.
	Second,	First,	Fourth,	Gulf.
Chapin, E. P.	First,	First,	Nineteenth,	Tennessee.
Chapin, M. W.	Thirty-eighth,	Twelfth,		Army Ohio.
Chaplin, D.	Third,	Third,	Second,	Potomac.
	Second,	Third,	Second,	Potomac.
Chapman, C. W.	Second,	Third,	Fourteenth,	Cumberland.
Chapman, Geo. H.	First,	First,	Cavalry,	Potomac.
	Second,	Third,	Cavalry,	Potomac.
	Second,	Third,	Cavalry,	Shenandoah.
		Second Cavalry,		West Virginia.
	First,	Third,	Cavalry,	Shenandoah.
		Third,	Cavalry,	Shenandoah.
Chapman, Wm.	Second,	Second,	Fifth,	Potomac.
Chatfield, J. L.	First,	First,		South.
		District Beaufort, S. C.	Tenth,	South.
		Dist. Hilton Head, S. C.	Tenth,	South.
Chetlain, A. L.		Dist. Memphis West Tenn.		Tennessee.
Christ, B. C.	Second,	First,	Ninth,	Potomac.
		First,	Ninth,	Potomac.
	First,	First,	Ninth,	Potomac.
	Second,	First,	Ninth,	Ohio.
	Third,	Second,	Ninth,	Ohio.
	Third,	Second,	Ninth,	Tennessee.
	First,	Third,	Ninth,	Potomac.
	Second,	Third,	Ninth,	Potomac.
Christian, W. H.	Second,	Second,	Third,	Army of Va.
	Second,	Second,	First,	Potomac.
Chrysler, M. H.	Fourth,	Cavalry,	Nineteenth,	Gulf.
	First,	Lucas' Cavalry, West, Fla.		Gulf.
	Third,	First,	Cavalry,	Gulf.
Church, Geo. E.	Second,	First,	Fourth,	Potomac.
Clapp, D. E.	Second,	Third,	Eighteenth,	Va. and N. C.
Clark, G.	Third,	First,	Sixth,	Army Shen.
Clark, G. W.	Second,	Fourth,	Thirteenth,	Gulf.
Clark, J. G.	First,	Second, Army Frontier,		Missouri.
		Second, Army Frontier,		Missouri.
	First,	Second,	Thirteenth,	Gulf.
Clark, J. C.	Second,	Second, U. S. C. T.		Gulf.
Clark, J. B.	Second,	Third,	Fifth,	Potomac.
Clark, T. S.	First,	Second,	Nineteenth,	Gulf.
Clark, W. T.	First,	Third,	Fifteenth,	Tennessee.
	Second,	Fourth,	Fifteenth,	Tennessee.
		Third,	Twenty-fifth,	Texas.
Classon, P. J.	Second,	First, Dist. Beaufort, N. C.		North Carolina.
	First,	Div. Dist. Beaufort, N. C.		North Carolina.
Clayton, Powell	Second,	Cavalry, Dist. Eastern Ark.,		Tennessee.
	Cavalry,	Thirteenth,	Thirteenth,	Tennessee.
	Cavalry,	Arkansas Expedition,	Sixteenth,	Tennessee.
	Indpt. Cavalry,		Seventh,	Arkansas.
	Separate,	Dismounted Cavalry,	Seventh,	Arkansas.
		Post Pine Bluff,	Seventh,	Arkansas.
Clift, W. J.	Second,	Fourth,	Cavalry,	Cumberland.
	Second,	Fourth,	Cavalry,	Mil. Div. Miss.
Cloud, W. F.	Third,			Kansas.
	Second,	First, Army Frontier,		Missouri.
		Dist. Southwest Mo.,		Missouri.
Cluserett, A.	Advance,			Mountains.
	Second,	Second,	Eighth,	Middle.
Coan, W. B.	Second,	Second,	Tenth,	Va. and N. C.
		Second,	Tenth,	Va. and N. C.
	Second,	Second,	Twenty-fourth,	Va. and N. C.
	Second,	Ames,	Terry's Prov'l,	North Carolina.
Coates, B. F.	Second,	Second, Infantry,		West Virginia.
	Second,	First, Infantry,		West Virginia.
Coates, J. H.	Second,	First,	Seventeenth,	Tennessee.
Cobb, A.	First,	Second,	Sixth,	Potomac.
	Third,	1st Sub. Dist. Middle Tenn.		Cumberland.
Cobb, J. C.	First,	Third, U. S. C. T.		Gulf.
	Prov'l,		Thirteenth,	Gulf.
	Engineer,		Thirteenth,	Gulf.
Cobham, G. A., Jr.	Second,	Second,	Twelfth,	Potomac.
	Second,	Second,	Twelfth,	Cumberland.
	Third,	Second,	Twentieth,	Cumberland.
Coburn, John.	Twenty-seventh,	Seventh,		Army Ohio.
	First,	Second, Army Kentucky,		Ohio.

Name	Brigade	Division, District, Etc.	Corps	Army or Dept.
	Second,	Baird's, Army Kentucky,		Cumberland.
	Third,	First,	Reserve,	Cumberland.
	Unattached,			Cumberland.
	Coburn's,	Murfreesborough, Tenn.		Cumberland.
	Second,	First,	Eleventh,	Cumberland.
	Second,	Third,	Twentieth,	Cumberland.
Cochrane, John	Third,	First,	Fourth,	Potomac.
	Third,	Third,	Sixth,	Potomac.
	First,	Third,	Sixth,	Potomac.
Cochran, J. J.	First,	Third, Army Kentucky,		Ohio.
	First,	Baird's, Army Ky.,		Cumberland.
Cockerill, J. R.	Third,	Dist. Memphis,	Thirteenth,	Tennessee.
	Second,	First, Dist. Memphis, R. W.	Thirteenth,	Tennessee.
	Second,	First,	Seventeenth,	Tennessee.
	Second,	First,	Sixteenth,	Tennessee.
	Third,	First,	Sixteenth,	Tennessee.
	Third,	Fourth,	Fifteenth,	Tennessee.
Coggswell, Wm.	Third,	Third,	Twentieth,	Cumberland.
Coggswell, M.	Artillery,	Def. South Potomac,	Twenty-second,	Washington.
Cole, G. W.	Cavalry,		Twenty-fifth,	Virginia.
	Third,	Third,	Twenty-fifth,	Texas.
		Third,	Twenty-fifth,	Texas.
Coleman, D. C.	First,	Second,	Fifteenth,	Tennessee.
Collier, F. H.	Third,	Third,	Sixth,	Potomac.
Collins, M. N.	Second,	Second,	Ninth,	Ohio.
Collis, C. H. T.	First,	First,	Third,	Potomac.
	Indpt.,		Ninth,	Potomac.
Colvin, J. A.	Second,	Second,	Twenty-fourth,	Va. and N. C.
	Second,	Ames,	Terry's Provl.,	North Carolina.
Connell, J. M.	First,	Third, Centre,	Fourteenth,	Cumberland.
	First,	Third,	Fourteenth,	Cumberland.
Connor, Selden	First,	Second,	Second,	Potomac.
Conrad, J.	Second,	Second,	Fourth,	Cumberland.
	Third,	Second,	Fourth,	Cumberland.
		Second,	Fourth.	Cumberland.
Conyngham, J. S.	First,	Second,	Twenty-third,	North Carolina.
Cook, John	Fourth,	Dist. Cairo,		Missouri.
	Third,	Second, Dist. Cairo,		Missouri.
	Third,	Second,		Army Tenn.
Cook, R. E.	Third,	Third,		West Virginia.
	Second,	Third, Infantry,		West Virginia.
Cooke, P. St. G.		Cavalry, Reserve,		Potomac.
		District Baton Rouge, La.,		Gulf.
Coon, D. E.	Second,	First Cavalry, West Tenn.,		Tennessee.
	Second,	Fifth,	Cavalry,	Mil. Div. Miss.
Coons, John	First,	Third,	Second,	Potomac.
	Third,	Third,	Second,	Potomac.
Cooper, James	First,	Siegel's,		Shenandoah.
	First,	Second,	Second,	Army of Va.
		Second,	Second,	Army of Va.
Cooper, J. A.	Third,	Third,	Twenty-third,	Ohio.
	Third,	Third,	Twelfth,	Cumberland.
	First,	Second,	Twenty-third,	Ohio.
		Second,	Twenty-third,	Ohio.
	First,	Second,	Twenty-third,	North Carolina.
		Second,	Twenty-third,	North Carolina.
Copeland, J. T.	Provisional,	Casey's, Mil. Dist. Wash.,		Potomac.
	First,	Cavalry,	Twenty-second,	Washington.
Coppinger, J. J.	Second,	Third,	Cavalry,	Army Shen.
Corcoran, M.	Corcoran's,			Virginia.
	Corcoran's,	Div. at Suffolk Va.,	Seventh,	Virginia.
		Division at Suffolk,	Seventh,	Virginia.
		First,	Seventh,	Virginia.
	First,	King's,	Twenty-second,	Washington.
		King's,	Twenty-second,	Washington.
Cornyn, F. M.	Cavalry,	Left Wing,	Sixteenth,	Tennessee.
	Third,	First, Cavalry,	Sixteenth,	Tennessee.
Corning, J. W.	Third,	Second,	Sixth,	Potomac.
Corse, J. M.	Fourth,	Fourth,	Fifteenth,	Tennessee.
	Second,	Fourth,	Fifteenth,	Tennessee.
		Second,	Sixteenth,	Tennessee.
		Fourth,	Fifteenth,	Tennessee.
Cosgrove, S.	Third,	First,	Twelfth,	Potomac.
Coster, C. R.	First,	Second,	Eleventh,	Potomac.
Couch, D. N.	Couch's,	Division of the Potomac,		Potomac.
	First,	Buell's (Keyes'),		Potomac.
		First,	Fourth,	Potomac.
		Third,	Sixth,	Potomac.

Name	Brigade	Division, District, Etc.	Corps	Army or Dept.
			Second,	Potomac.
				Susquehanna.
		Second,	Twenty-third,	Ohio.
		Second,	Twenty-third,	North Carolina
Coulter, R.	Third,	Second,	First,	Potomac.
	First,	Second,	First,	Potomac.
	Second,	Second,	Fifth,	Potomac.
		Second,	Fifth,	Potomac.
	Second,	Third,	Fifth,	Potomac.
	Third,	Third,	Fifth,	Potomac.
Cowan, J.	Second,	Second,	Thirteenth,	Gulf.
	First,	Fourth,	Thirteenth,	Gulf.
Cowdin, R.	First,	Abercrombie's, Mil. Dist.,	Washington,	Potomac.
	Second,	Abercrombie's,	Twenty-second,	Washington.
Cowles, D. S.	First,	Second,	Nineteenth,	Gulf.
Cox, J. D.	Kanawha,			West Va.
		Kanawha,		West Virginia.
		Kanawha,		Mountains.
		Kanawha,	Ninth,	Potomac.
			Ninth,	Potomac.
		Third,	Twenty-third,	Ohio.
			Twenty-third,	Ohio.
			Twenty-third,	North Carolina.
			Provisional,	North Carolina.
				North Carolina.
Cox, R. C.	Second,	Third,	Ninth,	Potomac.
Crabb, B.	Second,	Third, Army Frontier,		Missouri.
Craig, C. A.	Second,	Third,	Second,	Potomac.
Craig, James		District Nebraska,		Kansas.
Crandal, F. M.	First,	First, U. S. C. T. Dist. W. Fla.,		Gulf.
Crandall, L.	Consolidated,	First,	Second,	Potomac.
	Third,	Third,	Second,	Potomac.
Crane, A. B.	Second,	Third,	Twentieth,	Cumberland.
Crane, O. J.	First,	Second,	Twelfth,	Potomac.
Cranor, J.	Third,	Kanawha,		West Virginia.
		District Eastern Ky.,		Ohio.
Crawford, S. W.	First,	First,		Shenandoah.
	First,	First,	Second,	Army of Va.
		First,	Second,	Army of Va.
	First,	First,	Twelfth,	Potomac.
		Third,	Fifth,	Potomac.
	Second,	Fifth,	Potomac.
			Fifth,	Potomac.
Crebs, J. M.	Third,	Cavalry,		Gulf.
	1st, Sep. Cav.,			Gulf.
Creighton, W. R.	First,	Second,	Twelfth,	Potomac.
				Cumb.
Crittenden, E. W.	First,	Second,	Cavalry,	Ohio.
Crittenden, T. L.		Fifth,		Army Ohio.
			Second,	Army Ohio.
		Left Wing,	Fourteenth,	Cumberland.
			Twenty-first,	Cumberland.
		First,	Ninth,	Potomac.
Crittenden, T. T.	Third,	First,	Twentieth,	Cumberland.
Crocker, J. S.	Second,	Third,	Second,	Potomac.
Crocker, M. M.	First,	First,		Army Tenn.
	Third,	Sixth,		Army Tenn.
	Third,	Sixth, Dist. Corinth,		Army Tenn.
	Third,	Sixth,	Thirteenth,	Tennessee.
	Third,	Sixth,	Sixteenth,	Tennessee.
	Third,	Sixth,	Seventeenth,	Tennessee.
		Seventh,	Seventeenth,	Tennessee.
		Fourth,	Thirteenth,	Tennessee.
		Fourth,	Seventeenth,	Tennessee.
Crook, Geo.	Third,	Kanawha,		West Virginia.
		Kanawha,		West Virginia.
	Crook's,	Granger's Army Ky.,		Cumberland.
	Third,	Fourth,	Fourteenth,	Cumberland.
		Second,	Cavalry,	Cumberland.
		Third,		West Virginia.
		First, Infantry,		West Virginia.
				West Virginia.
		Second,	Cavalry,	Potomac.
			Cavalry,	Potomac.
Crooks, Wm.		Dist. Eastern Ark.,	Seventh,	Arkansas.
Cross, .E. E.	First,	First,	Second,	Potomac.
Cross, Nelson	Fourth,	First,	Sixth,	Potomac.
Cross, Wm.	First, East Tenn.	Second,	Twenty-third,	Ohio.
	Third,	Third,	Twelfth,	Cumberland.

Name	Brigade	Division, District, Etc.	Corps	Army or Dept.
Crowninshield, C.	Third, Reserve,	First,	Cavalry,	Army Shen.
		First,	Cavalry,	Army Shen.
Croxton, J. T.	First,	First,	Cavalry,	Cumberland.
	First,	First,	Cavalry,	Mil. Div. Miss.
Cruft, Chas.	First,	Third, Mil. Dist. Cario,		Missouri.
	Thirteenth,			Army Ohio.
	Thirteenth,	Fifth,		Army Ohio.
	Third,	Fourth,		Army Tenn.
	Second,	Army of Kentucky,		Ohio.
	Twenty-second,	Fourth,	Second,	Army Ohio.
	First,	Second, Left Wing	Fourteenth,	Cumberland.
	First,	Second,	Twenty-first,	Cumberland.
		Second,	Twenty-first,	Cumberland.
	First,	First,	Fourth,	Cumberland.
		First,	Fourth,	Cumberland.
		Second, Separate, Etowah,		Cumberland.
		Prov'l, Dist. Etowah,		Cumberland.
	First,	Dist. East Tenn.		Cumberland.
		Fourth, Dist. East Tenn.		Cumberland.
Cullen, E. M.	First,	First,	Eighteenth,	Va. and N. C.
	Second,	First,	Eighteenth,	Va. and N. C.
	Third,	First,	Eighteenth,	Va. and N. C.
	First,	Third,	Twenty-fourth,	Virginia.
Cummings, G. W.	Second,	Fourth,		Army Miss.
Cummings, H. J. B.	Third,	Second,	Sixteenth,	Tennessee.
Cummins, R. P.	Second,	Third,	First,	Potomac.
		Third,	First,	Potomac.
Currie, L. D. H.	Third,	First,	Nineteenth,	Gulf.
	Third,	First,	Nineteenth,	Army Shen.
Curry, W. L.	Second,	Second,	Second,	Potomac.
Curtin, J. I.	First,	Second,	Ninth,	Potomac.
		Third,	Ninth,	Potomac.
Curtis, J. F.	Second,	Dist. Etowah,		Cumberland.
	Second,	2nd Separate, Dist. Etowah,		Cumberland.
Curtis, N. M.	First,	Second,	Tenth,	Va. and N. C.
	Second,	Third,	Eighteenth,	Va. and N. C.
	First,	Second,	Twenty-fourth,	Va. and N. C.
	First,	Ames,	Terry's Prov'l,	North Carolina.
Curtis, S. R.		Army Southwest Mo.,		Missouri.
				Kansas.
				Missouri.
				Northwest.
Curtis, Wm. B.	Second,	First Infantry,		West Virginia.
	Second,	Independent,	Twenty-fourth,	Virginia.
Custer, Geo. A.	Second,	Third,	Cavalry,	Potomac.
	First,	First,	Cavalry,	Potomac.
	First,	First,	Cavalry,	Army Shen.
		Second Cavalry,		West Virginia.
		Third,	Cavalry,	Army Shen.
		Third,	Cavalry,	Potomac.
Cutcheon, B. M.	Second,	First,	Ninth,	Potomac.
Cutler, L.	Third,	Third,	First,	Potomac.
	Third,	King's,		Rappahannock.
	Fourth,	First,	First,	Potomac.
	Second,	First,	First,	Potomac.
		First,	First,	Potomac.
	First,	Fourth,	Fifth,	Potomac.
		Fourth,	Fifth,	Potomac.
Daggett, R.	First,	Second,	Twenty-fourth,	Va. and N. C.
	First,	Ames,	Terry's Prov'l,	North Carolina.
	First,	Second,	Tenth,	North Carolina.
	Second,	Second,	Tenth,	North Carolina.
Dana, E. L.	First,	Third,	First,	Potomac.
	Second,	Third,	Second,	Potomac.
Dana, N. J. T.	Second,	Stone's,		Potomac.
	Third,	Second,	Second,	Potomac.
		Second,	Thirteenth,	Gulf.
		First,	Thirteenth,	Gulf.
			Thirteenth,	Gulf.
		Dist. Vicksburg Miss.,		Tennessee.
			Sixteenth,	Tennessee.
				Mississippi.
Dandy, G. B.	Second,	Morris Island, S. C.,	Tenth,	South.
	Third,	First,	Tenth,	Va. and N. C.
	Third,	First,	Twenty-fourth,	Virginia.
	Second,	First,	Twenty-fourth,	Virginia.
Davidson, F. M.	Second,	Sixth,	Cavalry,	Mil. Div. Miss.
Davidson, J. H.	Second,	Third,	Twenty-fifth,	Texas.

Name	Brigade	Division, District, Etc.	Corps	Army or Dept.
Davidson, J. W.	Second,	W. F. Smith's,		Potomac.
	Third,	Second,	Fourth,	Potomac.
Davidson, J. W.	Third,	Second,	Sixth,	Potomac.
		Dist. St. Louis, Mo.,		Missouri.
		Dist. Southeast Mo.,		Missouri.
		Army Southeast Mo.,		Missouri.
		First Cavalry, S. E. Mo.,		Missouri.
		First Cavalry, Ark. Exp.,		Tennessee.
		Post Natchez, Dist. Vicks.,		Mississippi.
Davies, H. E.	First,	Third,	Cavalry,	Potomac.
	First,	Second,	Cavalry,	Potomac.
		Second,	Cavalry,	Potomac.
Davies, T. A.	Second,	Fifth,		Northeast Va.
Davies, T. A.		First,		Army Tenn.
		Second,		Army Tenn.
		Second, Dist. Corinth,		Tennessee.
		District Miss.		Tennessee.
		District Columbus,	Thirteenth,	Tennessee.
		District Columbus,	Sixteenth,	Tennessee.
		District Rolla,		Missouri.
		District North Kansas,		Kansas.
Davis, B. F.	Fifth,	Cavalry,		Potomac.
	First,	First,	Cavalry,	Potomac.
		First,	Cavalry,	Potomac.
Davis, E. J.	Fourth,	Cavalry,	Nineteenth,	Gulf.
	Separate Cav.			Gulf.
		Dist. Morganza,		Gulf.
	Cavalry.	Dist. Baton Rouge,		Gulf.
		Dist. Baton Rouge,		Gulf.
Davis, E. P.	First,	First,	Nineteenth,	Army Shen.
	Second,	First,	Nineteenth,	Army Shen.
	Second,	First, Provisional,		Army Shen.
Davis, H.	Second,	Cavalry, West Tenn.		Tennessee.
Davis, Jeff. C.		Third, Army Southwest Mo.,		Missouri.
		Fourth, Army Miss.		Mississippi.
		First, Right Wing,	Fourteenth,	Cumberland.
		First,	Twentieth,	Cumberland.
		Second,	Fourteenth,	Cumberland.
			Fourteenth,	Cumberland.
Davis, T. H.	Second,	Third,	Second,	Potomac.
Davis, W. R.		Dist. North Kansas,		Kansas.
Davis, W. W. H.	Second,	Second,	Eighteenth,	North Carolina.
	Second,	First, St. Helena Island,	Tenth,	South.
		U. S. Forces, Beaufort S. C.,	Tenth,	South.
		Forces, Port Royal Island,	Tenth,	South.
	Second,	Terry's First,	Tenth,	South.
	Davis',	Folly Island S. C.,	Tenth,	South.
		U. S. Forces Folly Island,	Tenth,	South.
	Fifth,	Morris Island, S. C.,	Tenth,	South.
	Second,	Morris Island, S. C.,	Tenth,	South.
		U. S. Forces Morris Island,	Tenth,	South.
		Dist. Hilton Head, S. C.,		South.
Dawson, S. K.	Third,	First,	Fourteenth,	Cumberland.
Day, H.	First,	Second,	Fifth,	Potomac.
Day, H. M.	Second,	Second,	Thirteenth,	Gulf.
	Second,	Third,	Thirteenth,	Gulf.
	Second,	Third,	Reserve,	Gulf.
Day, L.	First,	First,	Eighteenth,	North Carolina.
Day, N. W.	Second,	Second,	Nineteenth,	Army Shen.
	Second,	Second, Dist. Savannah, Ga.,		South.
	Third,	First,	Tenth,	North Carolina.
Dean, B. D.	Third,	Third,	Fifteenth,	Tennessee.
DeCourcey, J. F.	Twenty-sixth,	Seventh,		Army Ohio.
	Fourth,	Cumberland, Dist. W. Va.,		Ohio.
	Third,	Ninth, Left Wing,	Thirteenth,	Tennessee.
	Third,	Third, Yazoo Expedition,		Tennessee.
	Third,	Ninth,	Thirteenth,	Tennessee.
	Second,	Ninth,	Thirteenth,	Tennessee.
DeForrest, J. J.	First,	Second, St. Helena Island,	Tenth,	South.
	First,	First,	Eighteenth,	Va. and N. C.
DeForrest, O.	Third,	Cavalry,	Twenty-second,	Washington.
DeGroat, C. H.	Third,	First,	Seventeenth,	Tennessee.
Deimling, F. C.	Second,	Second,	Seventeenth,	Tennessee.
Deitzler, G. W.	First,	Sixth,	Thirteenth,	Tennessee.
	First,	Sixth,	Sixteenth,	Tennessee.
	First,	Sixth,	Seventeenth,	Tennessee.
DeLacy, Wm.	Second,	Second,	Second,	Potomac.
Dengler, A.	First,	First,	Seventh,	Arkansas.

Name	Brigade	Division, District, Etc.	Corps	Army or Dept.
Denison, A. W.	Second,	Second,	Fifth,	Potomac.
	Third,	Second,	Fifth,	Potomac.
Dennett, G. M.	First,	First,	Twenty-fifth,	Texas.
Dennis, E. S.	Second,	Third,	Seventeenth,	Tennessee.
		Dist. Northeast La.,		Tennessee.
		First,	Fifteenth,	Tennessee.
		First,	Seventeenth,	Tennessee.
		Second,	Nineteenth,	Gulf.
	Second,	Reserve,		Gulf.
	Second,	First,	Reserve,	Gulf.
	Second,	First,	Thirteenth,	Gulf.
		First,	Thirteenth,	Gulf.
Denver, J. W.	Third,	Fifth,		Army Tenn.
	Second,	Fifth, Dist. Memphis, Tenn.		Tennessee.
	Second,	Fifth, Dist. Memphis, Tenn.	Thirteenth,	Tennessee.
		First, Dist. Memphis, Tenn.	Thirteenth,	Tennessee.
		First,	Seventeenth,	Tennessee.
		First,	Sixteenth,	Tennessee.
DeRussy, G. A.		Def. South of the Potomac,	Twenty-second,	Washington,
DeTrobriand, R.	Second,	First,	Third,	Potomac.
	Third,	First,	Third,	Potomac.
	First,	Third,	Second,	Potomac.
		Third,	Second,	Potomac.
Devens, Chas., Jr.	First,	First,	Fourth,	Potomac.
	First,	Third,	Sixth,	Potomac.
	Second,	Third,	Sixth,	Potomac.
		Third,	Sixth,	Potomac.
		First,	Eleventh,	Potomac.
	Third,	First,	Eighteenth,	Va. and N. C.
		Third,	Eighteenth,	Va. and N. C.
		First,	Eighteenth,	Va. and N. C.
		Third,	Twenty-fourth,	Virginia.
			Twenty-fourth,	Virginia.
Deven, T. C.	Second,	Pleasanton's Cavalry,		Potomac.
	Second,	First,	Cavalry,	Potomac.
		First,	Cavalry,	Potomac.
Devereux, A. F.	Second,	Second,	Second,	Potomac.
Devol, H. F.	First,	Second Infantry,		West Virginia.
DeWitt, D. P.	Second,	Second,	Second,	Army of Va.
DiCesnola, L. P.	First,	Second,	Cavalry,	Potomac.
	Second,	First,	Cavalry,	Army Shen.
Dick, G. F.	Second,	Third,	Twenty-first,	Cumberland.
	Third,	Third,	Fourth,	Cumberland.
Dickerman, W. A.	Second,	Fourth,	Fifteenth,	Tennessee.
Dickey, T. L.		Cavalry,	Thirteenth,	Tennessee.
		Cavalry,	Sixteenth,	Tennessee.
Dickey, W. H.	First,	C. de A. U. S. C. T.		Gulf.
	Second,	Dist. Morganza, La.,		Gulf.
		Dist. Morganza, La.,		Gulf.
Dieckmann, J.	Fourth,	Def. South of the Potomac,	Twenty-second,	Washington.
Dill, D. J.	Second,	Second, Dist. Kentucky,	Twenty-third,	Ohio.
Dillard, W. Y.	First,	Fourth,	Twenty-third,	Ohio.
Dilworth, C. J.	Third,	Second,	Fourteenth,	Cumberland.
	Second,	Dist. Etowah,		Cumberland.
Diven, C. W.	First,	Third,	Ninth,	Potomac.
Dix, John A.				Annapolis.
				Pennsylvania.
Dix, John A.				Middle.
				Virginia.
			Seventh,	Virginia.
				East.
Doan, T.	Second,	Third,	Fourteenth,	Cumberland.
Dobbs, C. J.	First,	Second, Dist. Florida,	Tenth,	South.
Dodge, G. M.	First,	Army Southwest Mo.,		Missouri.
	First,	Fourth, Army, S. W. Mo.,		Missouri.
		District Mississippi,		Tennessee.
		Fourth, Dist. Jackson,		Tennessee.
		Fourth, Dist. Jackson,	Thirteenth,	Tennessee.
		Dist. Corinth,	Thirteenth,	Tennessee.
		Dist. Corinth,	Seventeenth,	Tennessee.
		Dist. Corinth,	Sixteenth,	Tennessee.
		Second,	Sixteenth,	Tennessee.
		Left Wing,	Sixteenth,	Tennessee.
				Missouri.
Dodge, J. B.	Third,	Second, Right Wing,	Fourteenth,	Cumberland.
	Second,	Second,	Twentieth,	Cumberland.
Donnelly, D.	First,	Banks',		Potomac.
	First,	First,	Fifth,	Potomac.
	First,	First,		Shenandoah.

Name	Brigade	Division, District, Etc.	Corps	Army or Dept.
Donohoe, M. T.	Second,	First,	Eighteenth,	Va. and N. C.
	Second,	Third,	Twenty-fourth,	Virginia.
Doolittle, C. C.	Third,	First, Army of Ky.		Ohio.
	Third,	Dist. Central Ky.,		Ohio.
	Third,	Second,	Reserve,	Cumberland.
	First,	Third,	Twenty-third,	Ohio.
	First,	Third,	Fourth,	Cumberland.
Doran, J. L.	First,	Sixth,		Army Tenn.
Dornblaser, B.	Second,	Fourth,	Sixteenth,	Tennessee.
	Second,	Fourth,	Seventeenth,	Tennessee.
	Second,	First,	Seventeenth,	Tennessee.
	First,	Second,	Nineteenth,	Gulf.
	Second,	First,	Thirteenth,	Gulf.
Dorr, J. B.	First,	First,	Cavalry,	Cumberland.
Doubleday, A.	Separate,			Rappahannock.
	Second,	First,	Third,	Army of Va.
		First,	Third,	Army of Va.
	Second,	First,	First,	Potomac.
		Third,	First,	Potomac.
		First,		Potomac.
Doubleday, U.	Second,	Third,	Tenth,	Va. and N. C.
	Second,	Second,	Twenty-fifth	Va. and N. C.
Douty, C.	First,	Third,	Cavalry,	Potomac.
Dow, Neal		Dist. West Florida,		Gulf.
	First,	Second,	Nineteenth,	Gulf.
Drake, F. M.	First,	Second,	Seventh,	Arkansas.
Drake, J. C.	First,	North End, Folly Island,	Tenth,	South.
	First,	Second, Dist. Florida,	Tenth,	South.
		Second, Dist. Florida,	Tenth,	South.
	Second,	Third,	Tenth,	Va. and N. C.
	Second,	Third,	Eighteenth,	Potomac.
Draper, A. G.		Dist. St. Marys,	Eighteenth,	Va. and N. C.
		Dist. St. Marys,	Twenty-second,	Washington.
	Second,	Third,	Eighteenth,	Va. and N. C.
		Third,	Eighteenth,	Va. and N. C.
	First,	Third,	Twenty-fifth,	Va. and N. C.
	First,	First,	Twenty-fifth,	Va. and N. C.
	First,	First,	Twenty-fifth,	Texas.
		First,	Twenty-fifth,	Virginia.
		Third,	Twenty-fifth,	Texas.
Drew, C. W.		First, U. S. C. T.		Gulf.
		Second, U. S. C. T.		Gulf.
	Third,	First, U. S. C. T. Dist. W. Fla.		Gulf.
Drish, J. F.	Second,	Third,	Sixteenth,	Tennessee.
DuBois, J. V.	Third,	Second,		Army Tennessee.
Dudley, N. A. M.	Third,	First,	Nineteenth,	Gulf.
	First,	First,	Nineteenth,	Gulf.
	Fourth,	Cavalry,	Nineteenth,	Gulf.
	First,	Cavalry,	Nineteenth,	Gulf.
	Third,	First,	Nineteenth,	Army Shen.
	First,	First,	Nineteenth,	Army Shen.
	Second,	1st, Sub. Dist. Middle, Tenn.,		Cumberland.
Duff, L. B.	Second,	Third,	Second,	Potomac.
Duffie, A. N.	First,	Second,	Cavalry,	Potomac.
		Second,	Cavalry,	Potomac.
	Third,	Third,		West Virginia.
	First,	Second, Cavalry,		West Virginia.
		First, Cavalry,		West Virginia.
Duffield, W. W.	Twenty-third,			Army Ohio.
Dumont, E.	Seventeenth,			Army Ohio.
	Seventeenth,	Third,		Army Ohio.
		Twelfth,		Army Ohio.
		Fifth, Centre,	Fourteenth,	Cumberland.
Duncan, S. A.	Second,	U. S. Forces, Yorktown, Va.,		Va. and N. C.
	Second,	Hinks', U. S. C. T.	Eighteenth,	Va. and N. C.
	Second,	Third,	Eighteenth,	Va. and N. C.
	Third,	Third,	Eighteenth,	Va. and N. C.
		Third,	Eighteenth,	Va. and N. C.
	Second,	First,	Twenty-fifth,	Va. and N. C.
	Second,	Third,	Twenty-fifth,	Va. and N. C.
	Second,	Paine's,	Terry's Prov'l,	North Carolina.
	Second,	Third,	Tenth,	North Carolina.
Dunham, C. L.	Second,	Dist. Jackson,	Sixteenth,	Tennessee.
Duryea, A.	First,	Ord's,		Rappahannock.
	Second,	Ord's,		Rappahannock.
	First,	Second,	Third,	Army of Va.
	First,	Second,	First,	Potomac.
Duryea, R.	Howell's,	Dist. Hilton Head, S. C.,	Tenth,	South.
Duryea, R. C.	Second,	First,	Second,	Potomac.

Name	Brigade	Division, District, Etc.	Corps	Army or Dept.
Dushane, N. T.	Third,	Third,	First,	Potomac.
	Second,	Third,	First,	Potomac.
		Third,	First,	Potomac.
	Third,	Second,	Fifth,	Potomac.
	Second,	Second,	Fifth,	Potomac.
Dustin, D.	Second,	Third,	Twentieth,	Cumberland.
		Third,	Twentieth,	Cumberland.
Dutton, A. H.	Third,	Third,	Ninth,	Potomac.
	Third,	Second,	Seventh,	Virginia.
	Heckman's,	Newport News, Va.,		Va. and N. C.
	Third,	First,	Eighteenth,	Va. and N. C.
Duval, I. H.		Second, Infantry,		West Virginia.
		First, Infantry,		West Virginia.
Dwight, C. C.	Third,	First,	Nineteenth,	Gulf.
Dwight, Wm.	First,	Fourth,	Nineteenth,	Gulf.
		Second,	Nineteenth,	Gulf.
		Third,	Nineteenth,	Gulf.
	First,	First,	Nineteenth,	Gulf.
		First,	Nineteenth,	Gulf.
		First,	Nineteenth,	Army Shen.
		Dwight's,	Twenty-second,	Washington.
Dye, Wm. McE.	Second,	Second, Army Frontier,		Missouri.
	First,	Second,	Thirteenth,	Gulf.
	Second,	Second,	Thirteenth,	Gulf.
	First,	U. S. Forces, Texas,		Gulf.
	Guppy's,	U. S. Forces, Mobile Bay,		Gulf.
	First,	Third,	Nineteenth,	Gulf.
	Fourth,		Reserve,	Gulf.
Dyer, I.		Dist. West Fla.,	Nineteenth,	Gulf.
Eaton, C. G.	First,	First, Det'mt Army Tenn.,		Cumberland.
Eckley, E. R.	Second,	Third, Army Miss.,		Mississippi.
	Second,	Seventh, Left Wing,	Thirteenth,	Tennessee.
	Second,	Seventh,	Sixteenth,	Tennessee.
	Second,	Seventh,	Seventeenth,	Tennessee.
Eckman, C. W.	First,	Second,	Sixth,	Potomac.
Eddy, Edward	Second,	Second,	Tenth,	Va. and N. C.
Eddy, Norman	First,	Seventh,	Sixteenth,	Tennessee.
	First,	Seventh,	Seventeenth,	Tennessee.
Edgerton, A. J.	Second,	First, C. de A. U. S. C. T.,		Gulf.
Edie, J. R.	Second,	First,	Fourteenth,	Cumberland.
Edmonds, J. C.	Third,	First,	Fifth,	Potomac.
Edwards, John	Second,	Dist. Frontier,		Missouri.
	Second,	Dist. Frontier,	Seventh,	Arkansas.
	First,	Dist. Frontier,	Seventh,	Arkansas.
		Dist. Frontier,	Seventh,	Arkansas.
	First,	Third,	Seventh,	Arkansas.
	Second,	Second,	Seventh,	Arkansas.
Edwards, Oliver	Fourth,	Second,	Sixth,	Potomac.
	Third,	First,	Sixth,	Army Shen.
		First,	Sixth,	Army Shen.
	Third,	First,	Sixth,	Potomac.
Egan, T. W.	First,	First,	Third,	Potomac.
	Third,	First,	Third,	Potomac.
	First,	Third,	Second,	Potomac.
	First,	Second,	Second,	Potomac.
		Second,	Second,	Potomac.
		Third Provisional,		Army Shen.
Egbert, G. T.	Fourth,	First,	Second,	Potomac.
Ege, Peter	Second,	Second,	Fourteenth,	Cumberland.
Eggleston, B. B.	Second,	Second,	Cavalry,	Cumberland.
	Second,	Second,	Cavalry,	Mil. Div. Miss.
Elliott, W. L.	Second,	Cavalry, Army Miss.		Missouri.
		Cavalry, Army Miss.		Mississippi.
	First,	Second,	Eighth,	Middle.
		Elliott's,	Eighth,	Middle.
		Third,	Third,	Potomac.
		First,	Cavalry,	Cumberland.
			Cavalry,	Cumberland.
		Second,	Fourth,	Cumberland.
				Northwest.
Ellis, A. Van H.	First,	Third,	Third,	Potomac.
Ellis, T. G.	Third,	Second,	Second,	Potomac.
Ellmaker, P. C.	Third,	First,	Sixth,	Potomac.
Ely, R.	Second,	First,	Ninth,	Potomac.
Ely, W. G.	Second,	First Infantry,		West Virginia.
Emerson, F.	First,	Fourth,	Thirteenth,	Gulf.
Emerson, Wm.	First,	Third,	Sixth,	Army Shen.
Emory, W. H.	Emory's,	Cavalry, Reserve,		Potomac.
	First,	Second,	Fourth,	Potomac.

Name	Brigade	Division, District, Etc.	Corps	Army or Dept.
	Emory's,			Middle.
		Emory's,	Nineteenth,	Gulf.
		Third,	Nineteenth,	Gulf.
		Defenses New Orleans, La.,	Nineteenth,	Gulf.
		Fourth,	Nineteenth,	Gulf.
		First,	Nineteenth,	Gulf.
			Nineteenth,	Gulf.
			Nineteenth,	Army Shen.
				West Virginia.
Engleman, A.	First,	Third,	Sixteenth,	Tennessee.
	First,	Kimball's Provisional,	Sixteenth,	Tennessee.
	First,	Kimball's, Dist. E. Ark.,	Sixteenth,	Tennessee.
	Second,	Second, Arkansas, Exp.,	Sixteenth,	Tennessee.
		Second, Arkansas, Exp.,	Sixteenth,	Tennessee.
	Second,	Second,	Seventh,	Arkansas.
	Third,	Third,	Seventh,	Arkansas.
	Second,	First,	Seventh,	Arkansas.
		First,	Seventh,	Arkansas.
Ent, W. H.	First,	Third,	Fifth,	Potomac.
Enyart, D. A.	First,	Second,	Twenty-first,	Cumberland.
	First,	First,	Fourth,	Cumberland.
Eppstein, J.		District Rolla, Mo.,		Missouri.
Erdelmeyer, F.	First,	Second,	Twentieth,	Cumberland.
Erskine, A.	First,	Cavalry,	Seventh,	Arkansas.
Este, G. P.	Third,	Third,	Fourteenth,	Cumberland.
		Third,	Fourteenth,	Cumberland.
Eustis, H. L.	Second,	Third,	Sixth,	Potomac.
		Second,	Sixth,	Potomac.
	Fourth,	Second,	Sixth,	Potomac.
	Third,	First,	Sixth,	Potomac.
Evans, A. W.	Third,	Cavalry,		Va. and N. C.
Evans, G. W.	First,	Second,	Fourteenth,	Cumberland.
Evans, J. C.	First,	First,	Fourth,	Cumberland.
Everett, Chas.	First,	Cavalry,		Gulf.
Ewing, H.	Third,	Second,	Fifteenth,	Tennessee.
		First,	Sixteenth,	Tennessee.
		Fourth,	Fifteenth,	Tennessee.
		Second, Dist. Ky.,	Twenty-third,	Ohio.
		Second,		Kentucky.
Ewing, Thos., Jr.		First, Army Frontier,		Missouri.
		Dist. Border,		Missouri.
		Dist. St. Louis,		Missouri.
		Dist. Rolla,		Missouri.
Fair, A. B.	Second,	Second,	Nineteenth,	Gulf.
Fairchild, C.	First,	Third,	Seventeenth,	Tennessee.
Fairchild, H. S.	First,	Third,	Ninth,	Potomac.
	First,	Second,	Seventh,	Virginia.
	Second,	North End Folly Island,	Tenth,	South.
	Second,	Third,	Eighteenth,	Va. and N. C.
	Fourth,	First,	Twenty-fourth,	Virginia.
	First,	First,	Twenty-fourth,	Virginia.
	Second,	First,	Twenty-fourth,	Virginia.
Fairleigh, T. B.	First,	Second, Dist. Kentucky,	Twenty-third,	Ohio.
Farnsworth, A.	Fourth,	Second,		South.
	Fourth,	Def. South Potomac,	Twenty-second,	Washington.
Farnsworth, E. J.	First,	Third,	Cavalry,	Potomac.
Farnsworth, J. F.	First,	Pleasanton's Cavalry,		Potomac.
	Second,	Cavalry,		Potomac.
Farnum J. E.	Second,	Second,	Third,	Potomac.
Farr, A. B.	First,	Second,	Nineteenth,	Gulf.
	Second,	Second,	Nineteenth,	Gulf.
	Second,	Third,	Nineteenth,	Gulf.
Farrar, B. G.	First,	First,	Fifteenth,	Tennessee.
Faulkner, J. K.	Third,	First,	Cavalry,	Cumberland.
Faulkner, L. B.	Third,	Third,	Twentieth,	Cumberland.
Fearing, H.	Second,	Third,	Nineteenth,	Gulf.
		Third,	Nineteenth,	Gulf.
Fearing, R. D.	Second,	Third,	Fourteenth,	Cumberland.
Feeney, Wm.	Fuller's,	Second, Left Wing,	Sixteenth,	Tennessee.
Fenton, W. M.	First,	Second,		South.
	First,	First,	Ninth,	Potomac.
	Second,	First,	Ninth,	Potomac.
		First,	Ninth,	Potomac.
Ferrero, Edw.	Second,	Second,		North Carolina.
	Second,	Second,	Ninth,	Potomac.
		Second,	Ninth,	Potomac.
	Second,	Second,	Ninth,	Ohio.
	Second,	Second,	Ninth,	Tennessee.
		First,	Ninth,	Ohio.

Name	Brigade	Division, District, Etc.	Corps	Army or Dept.
		First,	Ninth,	Potomac.
		Fourth,	Ninth,	Potomac.
		Third,	Ninth,	Potomac.
		Defenses Bermuda Hundred,		Va. and N. C.
Ferris, S. P.	First,	Third,	Nineteenth,	Gulf.
Ferry, O. S.	Second,	Shields',		Rappahannock.
	Third,	Second,	Fourth,	Potomac.
	Ferry's,	Division at Suffolk, Va.,	Seventh,	Virginia.
		Third,	Eighteenth,	North Carolina.
Ferry, O. S.		Second, St. Helena Island,	Tenth,	South.
		First, St. Helena Island,	Tenth,	South.
		Forces Seabrook Island,	Tenth,	South.
		Third,	Tenth,	Va. and N. C.
Fessenden, F.	First,	Casey's,	Twenty-second,	Washington,
	First,	Abercrombie's,	Twenty-second,	Washington,
	Third,	First,	Nineteenth,	Gulf.
	First,	Second Infantry,		West Virginia.
		First Infantry,		West Virginia.
Fessenden, J. D.	Second,	First,	Nineteenth,	Army Shen.
	Third,	First,	Nineteenth,	Army Shen.
	Third,	First, Provisional,		Army Shen.
Fisher, B. W.	Third,	Third,	First,	Potomac.
	Third,	Third,	Fifth,	Potomac.
	Third,	Penna. Reserve,	Twenty-second,	Washington,
Fiske, C. B.		Thirteenth,	Thirteenth,	Tennessee.
	Second,	Thirteenth,	Thirteenth,	Tennessee.
		Southeastern Missouri,		Missouri.
		Northern Missouri,		Missouri.
		St. Louis, Mo.,		Missouri.
Fitch, M. H.	Second,	First,	Fourteenth,	Cumberland.
Fitzhugh, C. L.	Second,	First,	Cavalry,	Potomac.
	Second,	First,	Cavalry,	Army Shen.
Fitz Simons, C. F.	Cavalry	First,		West Virginia.
Fletcher, F.	First,	First,	Fifteenth,	Tennessee.
Flory, A. M.	First,	Third,	Thirteenth,	Gulf.
Floyd-Jones, D. L.	Second,	Second,	Fifth,	Potomac.
Flynn, J.	First,	Second,	Twentieth,	Cumberland.
Fonda, J. G.	First,	Cavalry,		Gulf.
	Second,	Cavalry,		Gulf.
	Cavalry,	Dist. Baton Rouge, La.,		Gulf.
		Dist. Baton Rouge, La.,		Gulf.
Force, M. F.	Second,	Third,	Seventeenth,	Tennessee.
	First,	Third,	Seventeenth,	Tennessee.
		Third,	Seventeenth,	Tennessee.
		First,	Seventeenth,	Tennessee.
Ford, J. H.		Dist. Upper Arkansas,		Kansas.
Forest, O. D.	First,	Third,	Cavalry,	Potomac.
Forsythe, J. W.	Twentieth,			Army Ohio.
	Twentieth,	Sixth,		Army Ohio.
Foster, G. P.	Second,	Second,	Sixth,	Army Shen.
Foster, J. G.	First,	North Carolina Exp.,		
		First,		North Carolina.
				North Carolina.
			Eighteenth,	North Carolina.
		Forces St. Helena Island,	Tenth,	South.
				Va. and N. C.
				Ohio.
				South.
Foster, J. W.	Second,	Fourth,	Twenty-third,	Ohio.
Foster, R. S.	Foster's,	Div. at Suffolk, Va.,	Seventh,	Virginia.
	Second,	First,	Seventh,	Virginia.
	First,	North End Folly Island,	Tenth,	South.
		Forces North End Folly Is.,	Tenth,	South.
		Vodges, Dist. Florida,	Tenth,	South.
	First,	Second, Dist. Florida,	Tenth,	South.
		Second, Dist. Florida,	Tenth,	South.
		First,	Tenth,	Va. and N. C.
	Third,	First,	Tenth,	Va. and N. C.
		Second,	Tenth,	Va. and N. C.
		First,	Twenty-fourth,	Virginia.
Foster, S. A.	First,	Thirteenth,	Thirteenth,	Tennessee.
Fowler, A.	Third,	Fourth,	Fifteenth,	Tennessee.
	Third,	Second,	Fifteenth,	Tennessee.
Fowler, E. B.	First,	First,	First,	Potomac.
	Second,	First,	First,	Potomac.
	Second,	Fourth,	Fifth,	Potomac.
Fox, C. H.	First,	Sixth, Dist. Columbus,	Sixteenth,	Tennessee.
	First,	Third,	Eleventh,	Cumberland.

Name	Brigade	Division, District, Etc.	Corps	Army or Dept.
Frank, Paul	Third,	First,	Second,	Potomac.
		First,	Second,	Potomac.
Franklin, E.	First,	Third,	Third,	Potomac.
Franklin, F. E.	Third,	Scammon's,		West Virginia.
Franklin, Wm. B.	First,	Third,		Army N. E. Va.
	Franklin's,			Div. Potomac.
		Franklin's,		Potomac.
		First,	First,	Potomac.
		First,		Rappahannock.
			Sixth,	Potomac.
			Nineteenth,	Gulf.
Fraser, John	First,	First,	Second,	Potomac.
	Second,	Second,	Second,	Potomac.
	Third,	First,	Second,	Potomac.
	Fourth,	First,	Second,	Potomac.
Frazer, J. L.		U. S. Forces, Hilton Head,	Tenth,	South.
French, W. B.	Third,	Second,	Sixth,	Army Shen.
French, W. H.	Third,	Sumner's,		Potomac.
	Third,	First,	Second,	Potomac.
		Third,	Second,	Potomac.
		French's Command,	Eighth,	Middle.
			Third,	Potomac.
Fremont, J. C.				Western.
				Mountains.
			First,	Army of Va.
Frisbie, H. N.	First,	First, Corps de Afrique,		Gulf.
	First,	U. S. C. T. Morganza, La.,		Gulf.
Fry, S. S.	Second,	First,		Army Ohio.
	First,	Third,		Army Ohio.
	Second,	First,	Third,	Army Ohio.
		First, North Central Ky.,	Twenty-third,	Ohio.
Fuller, H. W.		Dist. Morganza, La.,		Gulf.
Fuller, J. W.	First,	Second,		Army Miss.
	First,	Eighth, Left Wing,	Thirteenth,	Tennessee.
	First,	Eighth,	Sixteenth,	Tennessee.
	Fuller's,	Second, Left Wing,	Sixteenth,	Tennessee.
	Fourth,	Second, Dist. Corinth,	Sixteenth,	Tennessee.
	Third,	Fifth, Dist. Memphis,	Sixteenth,	Tennessee.
	First,	Fourth,	Sixteenth,	Tennessee.
		Fourth,	Sixteenth,	Tennessee.
	First,	First,	Seventeenth,	Tennessee.
		First,	Seventeenth,	Tennessee.
Funk, A.	Third,	Third,	Second,	Potomac.
	Third,	First,	Second,	Potomac.
Funcke, O.	First,	Cavalry, Dist. West Tenn.,		Tennessee.
	Third,	Cavalry, Dist. West Tenn.,		Tennessee.
Fyffe, E. P.	First,	First,	Twenty-first,	Cumberland.
Fyffe, J. P.	Second,	Third,	Twenty-first,	Cumberland.
Gallagher, M. F.	Third,	First,	First,	Potomac.
Gallagher, T. F.	Third,	Third,	Third,	Army Va.
	Third,	Third,	First,	Potomac.
Gallup, G. W.		First, Eastern Ky.,	Twenty-third,	Ohio.
	First,	First, Dist. Ky., Fifth,	Twenty-third,	Ohio.
	First,	Second,	Twenty-third,	Ohio.
Gamble, Wm.	First,	Pleasanton's Cavalry,		Potomac.
	First,	First,	Cavalry,	Potomac.
Gansevoort, H. S.	Indpt. Cavalry,		Twenty-second,	Washington.
	First,	Second,	Cavalry,	Potomac.
Garfield, J. A.	Eighteenth,			Army Ohio.
	Twentieth,	Sixth,		Army Ohio.
Garrard, Israel	First,	Second,	Cavalry,	Ohio.
		Second,	Cavalry,	Ohio.
	First,	First,	Cavalry,	Ohio.
	First,	Cavalry, Dist. Ky., Fifth,	Twenty-third,	Ohio.
		Cavalry,	Twenty-third,	Ohio.
	Second,	Fourth,	Cavalry,	Mil. Div. Miss.
Garrard, Kenner	Third,	Second,	Fifth,	Potomac.
		Second,	Cavalry,	Cumberland.
		Second,	Cavalry,	Mil. Div. Miss.
		2nd, Detachm't, Army Tenn.		Cumberland.
		Second,	Sixteenth,	Gulf.
Garrard, T. T.	First,	Ninth,	Thirteenth,	Tennessee.
		Forces Somerset, Ky., First,	Twenty-third,	Ohio.
Garrett, John A.	Second,	First,	Seventh,	Arkansas.
	First,	First,	Seventh,	Arkansas.
	First,	Third,	Seventh,	Arkansas.
		Dist. South Kansas,		Kansas.
Gault, J. W.	First,	Third,	Twenty-third,	Ohio.

Name	Brigade	Division, District, Etc.	Corps	Army or Dept.
Gavin, James	Second,	First,	First,	Potomac.
Gay, E.	Third,	Cavalry,		Army Ohio.
Geary, J. W.	Separate,			Rappahannock.
	Second,	First,	Second,	Army of Va.
	First,	Second,	Second,	Army of Va.
		Second,	Twelfth,	Potomac.
		Second,	Twelfth,	Cumberland.
		Second,	Twentieth,	Cumberland.
Geddes, J. L.	Third,	Third,	Fifteenth,	Tennessee.
	Third,	First,	Sixteenth,	Tennessee.
	Third,	Third,	Sixteenth,	Gulf.
Geiger, W. F.	Second,	Third, Army Frontier,		Missouri.
		Third, Army Frontier,		Missouri.
	First,	First Cavalry, Ark. Exp.,	Sixteenth,	Tennessee.
	Second,	First Cavalry,	Seventh,	Arkansas.
	Third,	Second,	Seventh,	Arkansas.
	Third,	Cavalry,	Seventh,	Arkansas.
	Second,	Cavalry,	Seventh,	Arkansas.
	Separate,	(Dismounted Cavalry),	Seventh,	Arkansas.
George, James	Second,	Third,	Fourteenth,	Cumberland.
Getty, Geo. W.		Third,	Ninth,	Potomac.
		Second,	Seventh,	Virginia.
			Seventh,	Virginia.
				Virginia.
		Forces Norfolk and Ports,		Va. and N. C.
		Second,	Sixth,	Potomac.
		Second,	Sixth,	Army Shen.
			Sixth,	Army Shen.
			Sixth,	Potomac.
Gibbon, John	Fourth,	First,	Third,	Army of Va.
	Fourth,	First,	First,	Potomac.
		Second,	First,	Potomac.
		Second,	Second,	Potomac.
			Second,	Potomac.
			Eighteenth,	Va. and N. C.
			Twenty-fourth,	Virginia.
Gibbs, A.	Second Prov'l,	Div. at Suffolk, Va.,	Seventh,	Virginia.
	Reserve,	First,	Cavalry,	Potomac.
	Third, Reserve,	First,	Cavalry,	Army Shen.
		First,	Cavalry,	Army Shen.
Gibson, A. A.	First,	Def. South Potomac,	Twenty-second,	Washington.
	First,	Def. North Potomac,	Twenty-second,	Washington.
	Third,	Second,	Eighteenth,	Va. and N. C.
Gibson, H. G.	Second,	Fourth,	Twenty-third,	Ohio.
Gibson, Thos.	First,	Second Cavalry,		West Virginia.
Gibson, W. H.	Sixth,	Second,		Army Ohio.
	Sixth,	Second,	First,	Army Ohio.
	First,	Second, Right Wing,	Fourteenth,	Cumberland.
	First,	Second,	Twentieth,	Cumberland.
		Second,	Twentieth,	Cumberland.
	First,	Third,	Fourth,	Cumberland.
Giddings, G. K.	First,	Second,	Fifth,	Potomac.
Gilbert, C. C.		Tenth,	First,	Army Ohio.
			Third,	Army Ohio.
Gilbert, H. C.	Third,	First,	Reserve,	Cumberland.
Gilbert, J. I.	Third,	Third,	Sixteenth,	Tennessee.
	Gilbert's,	5th, Dist. Memphis,	Sixteenth,	Tennessee.
	Second,	Third,	Sixteenth,	Tennessee.
	Second,	2nd, Detm't Army Tenn.,		Cumberland.
	Second,	Second,	Sixteenth,	Gulf.
Gilbert, S. A.	Second,	Second, Army Kentucky,		Ohio.
	First,	District Central Ky.,		Ohio.
	Second,	First,	Twenty-third,	Ohio.
	Second,	Fourth,	Twenty-third,	Ohio.
	First,	Third,	Twenty-third,	Ohio.
Gile, G. W.	First,	Veteran Reserve Corps,	Twenty-second,	Washington.
Gillem, A. C.		Fourth,	Cavalry,	Cumberland.
		Cavalry, Dist. East Tenn.,		Cumberland.
Gillfillian, Jas.		4th, Sub. Dist. Middle Tenn.,		Cumberland.
Gillmore, Q. A.		Second, Army Kentucky,		Ohio.
		Dist. Central Kentucky,		Ohio.
			Tenth,	South.
				South.
			Tenth,	Va. and N. C.
Given, J.	Second,	Third,	Twenty-fifth,	Texas.
Given, Josiah	Third,	First,	Fourteenth,	Cumberland.
Glasgow, S. L.	Second,	First,	Thirteenth,	Gulf.
	First,	Third,	Nineteenth,	Gulf.

Name	Brigade	Division, District, Etc.	Corps	Army or Dept.
	First,	Second,	Reserve,	Gulf.
	First,	Second,	Thirteenth,	Gulf.
Gleason, N.	Second,	Third,	Fourteenth,	Cumberland.
Glenny, Wm.	Fourth,	First,	Second,	Potomac.
Glover, J. M.		District Rolla, Mo.,		Missouri.
	Second,	First Cav., Army S. E. Mo.,		Missouri.
	Second,	First Cavalry, Ark. Exp.,		Tennessee.
Goff, N., Jr.	Third,	Third,	Tenth,	North Carolina.
Good, T. H.		Dist. Beaufort, S. C.,	Tenth,	South.
		Dist. Port Royal Island,	Tenth,	South.
		District Beaufort, S. C.,		South.
Gooding, M.	First,	Fourth,		Army Miss.
	Thirtieth,	Ninth,		Army Ohio.
	Thirtieth,	Ninth,	Third,	Army Ohio.
Gooding, O. P.	Third,	Third,	Nineteenth,	Gulf.
	Second,	First,	Nineteenth,	Gulf.
	Fifth,	Cavalry,		Gulf.
	First,	Cavalry,		Gulf.
		Cavalry,		Gulf.
Goodrich, L.	Second,	Second, U. S. C. T.,		Gulf.
Goodrich, W. B.	Third,	Second,	Twelfth,	Potomac.
Gordon, Geo. H.	First,	Banks,		Potomac.
	Third,	Banks,		Potomac.
	Third,	First,	Bank's Fifth,	Potomac.
	Third,	First,		Shenandoah.
	Third,	First,	Second,	Army of Va.
	Third,	First,	Twelfth,	Potomac.
		First,	Twelfth,	Potomac.
		Second,	Fourth,	Virginia.
		First,	Eleventh,	Potomac.
		South End Folly Island,	Tenth,	South.
		Forces Folly Island, S. C.,	Tenth,	South.
		Dist. Florida,		South.
		U. S Forces Mobile Bay, Ala.,		Gulf.
Gorman, W. A.	First,	Stone's,		Potomac.
	First,	Second,	Second,	Potomac.
		Army Southwest Mo.,		Missouri.
		Dist. Eastern Arkansas,		Missouri.
		Dist. Eastern Arkansas,	Thirteenth,	Tennessee.
		Twelfth,	Thirteenth,	Tennessee.
Gould, J. P.	First,	First,	Ninth,	Potomac.
Gower, J. O.	First,	Third, Army Frontier,		Missouri.
		Third, Army Frontier,		Missouri.
Graham, C. K.	Second,	Second,	Third,	Potomac.
	Second,	First,	Third,	Potomac.
		Third,	Third,	Potomac.
	Naval,			Va. and N. C.
		Def. Bermuda Hundred, Va.,		Va. and N. C.
Graham, E. W.	Second,	Fourth,	Twenty-third,	Ohio.
Graham, H.	Second,	Grover's Div. Savannah, Ga.,		South.
	First,	First,	Tenth,	North Carolina.
Graham, L. P.	Graham's,			Potomac.
	Second,	Buell's (Key's),		Potomac.
	Second,	First,	Fourth,	Potomac.
Graham, S.	Second,	Third,		West Virginia.
	Second,	Second,		West Virginia.
Graham, S. A.	First Separate,		Eighth,	Middle Dept.
	Third Separate,		Eighth,	Middle Dept.
	Second,	Second,	Fifth,	Potomac.
Granger, Gordon		Cavalry,		Army Miss.
		Fifth,		Army Miss.
		Army of Kentucky,		Ohio.
		Dist. Central Kentucky,		Ohio.
			Reserve,	Cumberland.
			Fourth,	Cumberland.
		Dist. Southern Ala.,		Gulf.
			Reserve,	Gulf.
			Thirteenth,	Gulf.
Granger, G. F.	Third,	Second,	Twenty-fourth,	Va. and N. C.
	Third,	Ames,	Terry's Prov'l,	North Carolina.
	Third,	Second,	Tenth,	North Carolina.
Granger, R. S.		First,	Fourteenth,	Cumberland.
	Third,	First,	Fourteenth,	Cumberland.
		Third,	Reserve,	Cumberland.
		Dist. Nashville, Tenn.,		Cumberland.
		Post of Nashville, Tenn.,		Cumberland.
	First,	Dist. Nashville, Tenn.,		Cumberland.
	First,	Third,	Twelfth,	Cumberland.
		Dist. North Alabama,		Cumberland.

Name	Brigade	Division, District, Etc.	Corps	Army or Dept.
Grant, L. A.	Second,	Second,	Sixth,	Potomac.
	Second,	Second,	Sixth,	Army Shen.
		Second,	Sixth,	Army Shen.
Grant, U. S.		Dist. Southeast Mo.,		Missouri.
		Dist. West Tennessee,		Mississippi.
			Thirteenth,	Tennessee.
				Tennessee.
				Army Tenn.
				Mill. Div. Miss.
				Armies U. S.
Gravelly, J. J.		Dist. Southwest Missouri,		Missouri.
Graves, W. H.	First,	Third,	Sixteenth,	Tennessee.
	First,	Second, Arkansas Exp.,	Sixteenth,	Tennessee.
	Third,	Second, Arkansas Exp.,	Sixteenth,	Tennessee.
	Third,	Second,	Seventh,	Arkansas.
	First,	Second,	Seventh,	Arkansas.
	First,	First,	Seventh,	Arkansas.
Gray, Geo.	Second,	Third,	Cavalry,	Potomac.
Gray, R. J.	Third,	Second,	Tenth,	Va. and N. C.
Greeley, E. S.	Third,	First,	Twenty-fourth,	Virginia.
Green, John	First,	First,	Ninth,	Potomac.
Greene, Geo. S.	Third,	First,		Shenandoah.
	Third,	Second,	Second,	Army of Va.
	Second,	Second,	Second,	Army of Va.
		Second,	Second,	Army of Va.
	Third,	Second,	Twelfth,	Potomac.
		Second,	Twelfth,	Potomac.
	Third,	Second,	Twelfth,	Cumberland.
	Third,	Third,	Fourteenth,	Cumberland.
Greene, W. A.	Second,	Second,	Nineteenth,	Gulf.
Greenfield, A. J.	Second,	First Cavalry,		West Virginia.
Gregg, D. McM.	Second,	Cavalry,		Potomac.
	Second,	Pleasanton's Cavalry.		Potomac.
	Gregg's Cav.,	Left Grand Division,		Potomac.
		Third,	Cavalry,	Potomac.
		Second,	Cavalry,	Potomac.
			Cavalry,	Potomac.
Gregg, John I.	Second,	Second,	Cavalry,	Potomac.
	Third,	Second,	Cavalry,	Potomac.
		Second,	Cavalry,	Potomac.
Gregg, L.	Cavalry,	Post Little Rock, Ark.,	Seventh,	Arkansas.
Gregory, E. M.	First,	Third,	Fifth,	Potomac.
		Third,	Fifth,	Potomac.
	Third,	Second,	Fifth,	Potomac.
	First,	Second,	Fifth,	Potomac.
	Second,	First,	Fifth,	Potomac.
Gresham, W. Q.	Third,	Fourth,	Seventeenth,	Tennessee.
		Fourth,	Seventeenth,	Tennessee.
Greusel, N.	Second,	First, Army Southwest Mo.,		Missouri.
	First,	Fifth,		Army Miss.
	Thirty-seventh,	Eleventh,		Army Ohio.
	Thirty-seventh,	Eleventh,	Third,	Army Ohio.
	Second,	Second, Right Wing,	Fourteenth,	Cumberland.
	First,	Third,	Twentieth,	Cumberland.
Grider, B. C.	First,	Third, Left Wing,	Fourteenth,	Cumberland.
	First,	Third,	Twenty-first,	Cumberland.
Grider, J. H.	Second,	Second, Dist. Ky.,	Twenty-third,	Ohio.
Grier, D. P.	Second,	Tenth,	Thirteenth,	Tennessee.
	Second,	Fourth,	Thirteenth,	Gulf.
	First,	Fourth,	Thirteenth,	Gulf.
	First,	Third,	Reserve,	Gulf.
	First,	Third,	Thirteenth,	Gulf.
		Third,	Thirteenth,	Tennessee.
Grierson, B. H.	Grierson's Cav.,	Right Wing,	Thirteenth,	Tennessee.
	Grierson's Cav.,		Nineteenth,	Gulf.
	First,	First Cavalry,	Sixteenth,	Tennessee.
		First Cavalry,	Sixteenth,	Tennessee.
		West Tennessee,	Cavalry,	Tennessee.
		Cavalry, West Tenn.		Tennessee.
		Fourth,	Cavalry,	Mil. Div. Miss.
			Cavalry,	Mil. Div. W. Miss.
Griffin, Chas.	Second,	First,	Fifth,	Potomac.
		First,	Fifth,	Potomac.
			Fifth,	Potomac.
Griffin, S. G.	First,	Second,	Ninth,	Potomac.
	First,	Second,	Ninth,	Ohio.
	First,	Second,	Ninth,	Tennessee.
		Second,	Ninth,	Ohio.

Name	Brigade	Division, District, Etc.	Corps	Army or Dept.
	Second,	Second,	Ninth,	Potomac.
		Second,	Ninth,	Potomac.
Grimshaw, A. H.	First,	King's,	Twenty-second,	Washington.
	Third,	Second,	Fifth,	Potomac.
Grindley, J.	First,	Second,	Fifth,	Potomac.
Groesbeck, John	First,	First,		Army Miss.
	First,	Second,		Army Miss.
Grose, Wm.	Tenth,	Fourth,		Army Ohio.
	Nineteenth,	Fourth,		Army Ohio.
	Tenth,	Fourth,	Second,	Army Ohio.
	Third,	Second, Left Wing,	Fourteenth,	Cumberland.
	Third,	Second,	Twenty-first,	Cumberland.
	Third,	First,	Fourth,	Cumberland.
		First,	Fourth,	Cumberland.
	Second,	Second,	Fourth,	Cumberland.
Grosvenor, C. H.		Post Chattanooga, Tenn.,		Cumberland.
	Third,	Prov'l Division,	Dist. Etowah,	Cumberland.
	Second,	District Etowah,		Cumberland.
Grover, Cuvier	First,	Second,	Third,	Potomac.
	Grover's,	Mil. Dist. Washington,		Potomac.
		Grover's, Baton Rouge, La.,		Gulf.
		Fourth,	Nineteenth,	Gulf.
		Third,	Nineteenth,	Gulf.
		Second,	Nineteenth,	Gulf.
		Second,	Nineteenth,	Army Shen.
			Nineteenth,	Army Shen.
		Grover's. Dist. Savannah, Ga.,		South.
		Dist. Savannah, Ga.,		South.
Grummond, G. W.	First,	Second,	Fourteenth,	Cumberland.
Grower, W. T. C.	Third,	Fourth,	Sixteenth,	Tennessee.
Guernsey, W. B.		Dist. Beaufort, S. C.,		South.
Guiney, P. R.	Second,	First,	Fifth,	Potomac.
Guion, G. M.	Second,	Second,	Eighteenth,	Va. and N. C.
	First,	Second,	Eighteenth,	Va. and N. C.
Guitar, O.		District Northern Mo.,		Missouri.
		District Rolla,		Rolla.
Guppy, J. A.	Guppy's,	Mobile Bay, Ala.,		Gulf.
Guppy, J. G.	Third,	Second,	Nineteenth,	Gulf.
Gurney, Wm.	Third,	Abercrombie's, Mil. Dist.,	Washington,	Potomac.
	Third,	Abercrombie's,	Twenty-second,	Washington.
		Gurney's,	Seventh,	Virginia.
	First,	Second,	Fourth,	Virginia.
	First,	South End Folly Island,	Tenth,	South.
		Northern Dist. Morris I.,		South.
Guss, H. R.		Seabrook Island, S. C.,	Tenth,	South.
	First,	Morris Island, S. C.,	Tenth,	South.
	First,	Third,	Tenth,	Va. and N. C.
	Third,	Third,	Eighteenth,	Va. and N. C.
Gwyn, J.	Third,	Second,	Fifth,	Potomac.
		Second,	Fifth,	Potomac.
	Third,	First,	Fifth,	Potomac.
	First,	First,	Fifth,	Potomac.
Hackleman, P. A.	First,	Second,		Army Tenn.
	First,	Second, Dist. Corinth,		Army Tenn.
Hall, A. S.	Thirty-third.	Tenth,	First,	Army Ohio.
Hall, A. S.	First,	Fifth, Centre,	Fourteenth,	Cumberland.
	Second,	Fifth,	Fourteenth,	Cumberland.
	Second,	Fourth,	Fourteenth,	Cumberland.
Hall, Cyrus	Second,	Fourth, Right Wing,	Thirteenth.	Tennessee.
	Second,	Fourth,	Seventeenth,	Tennessee.
	Second,	Fourth,	Sixteenth,	Tennessee.
	Second,	Fourth,	Thirteenth.	Tennessee.
	Second,	Fourth,	Seventeenth.	Tennessee.
Hall, C. K.	First,	Third,	Sixth,	Potomac.
Hall, Geo. B.	Second,	Second.	Third,	Potomac.
Hall, H. H.	Fourth,	Def. South Potomac.	Twenty-second,	Washington.
Hall, J. A.		Light Arty. Depot.	Twenty-second,	Washington.
Hall, M. S.	First.	Fourth,		West Virginia.
	Third,	Independent,	Twenty-fourth,	Virginia.
Hall, N. J.	Third.	Second,	Second,	Potomac.
Hall, R. M.	First.	First,	Twenty-fifth.	Texas.
	Second,	First,	Twenty-fifth.	Texas.
Hall, Wm.	Third,	Sixth,	Seventeenth.	Tennessee.
		Sixth,	Seventeenth.	Tennessee.
	Third,	First,	Seventeenth.	Tennessee.
	Third,	Fourth,	Seventeenth.	Tennessee.
		Fourth,	Seventeenth.	Tennessee.
Hall, W. P.		Dist. Northern Missouri.		Missouri.

Name	Brigade	Division, District, Etc.	Corps	Army or Dept.
Halleck, H. W.				Missouri.
				Mississippi.
				Armies U. S.
				Virginia.
				Mil. Div. James.
Hallowell, E. N.	Third,	Sixth,	Seventeenth,	Tennessee.
Hamblin, J. E.	First,	Third,	Sixth,	Potomac.
	Second,	First,	Sixth,	Potomac.
	Second,	First,	Sixth,	Army Shen.
	Fourth,	First,	Sixth,	Army Shen.
	Third,	First,	Sixth,	Potomac.
Hambright, H. A.	Third,	First Centre,	Fourteenth,	Cumberland.
	Third,	First,	Fourteenth,	Cumberland.
	First,	First,	Fourteenth,	Cumberland.
	Second,	First,	Fourteenth,	Cumberland.
Hamlin, C.	Second,	First, Corps de Afrique,		Gulf.
		Dist. Port Hudson, La.,		Gulf.
		First, Corps de Afrique,		Gulf.
		Third, U. S. C. T.,		Gulf.
Hamilton, Chas.		Dist. Key West, Fla.,		Gulf.
Hamilton, C. S.	Third,	Banks' Div.,		Potomac.
		Third,	Third,	Potomac.
		Third,		Army Miss.
		District Corinth, Miss.,		Tennessee.
		District Corinth, Miss.,	Thirteenth,	Tennessee.
		Left Wing,	Thirteenth,	Tennessee.
		Left Wing,	Sixteenth,	Tennessee.
			Sixteenth,	Tennessee.
		Dist. West Tennessee,		Tennessee.
Hamilton, S.		First,		Army Miss.
		Second,		Army Miss.
		Third,		Army Miss.
Hamilton, W. D.	Mounted,	Cavalry,	Twenty-third,	Ohio.
Hammond, J. H.	First,	Second, Dist. Kentucky,	Twenty-third,	Ohio.
	First,	Seventh,	Cavalry,	Mil. Div. Miss.
		Seventh,	Cavalry,	Mil. Div. Miss.
Hancock, W. S.	Third,	W. F. Smith's,		Potomac.
	First,	Second,	Fourth,	Potomac.
	First,	Second,	Sixth,	Potomac.
		First,	Second,	Potomac.
		Second,		Potomac.
			First, Veteran,	Potomac.
				West Virginia.
				Middle Mil. Div.
Hanson, C. S.	Third,	First, Dist. Kentucky,	Twenty-third,	Ohio.
Hapeman, D.	First,	First,	Fourteenth,	Cumberland.
Hardin, M. D.	Third,	Third,	First,	Potomac.
	Third,	Third,	Fifth,	Potomac.
	First,	Third,	Fifth,	Potomac.
		Defenses North Potomac,	Twenty-second,	Washington.
Harding, C., Jr.		Dist. Northern Mo.,		Missouri.
	First,	Second, Army S. E. Mo.,		Missouri.
		Second, Army S. E. Mo.,		Missouri.
		District Central Mo.,		Missouri.
Harding, O. P.	Second,	Second,	Twenty-fourth,	Virginia.
	Second,	Ames,	Terry's Prov'l,	North Carolina.
Hare, A. M.	First,	First,		Army Tennessee.
Harker, C. G.	Twentieth,	Sixth,		Army Ohio.
	Twentieth,	Sixth,	Second,	Army Ohio.
	Third,	First, Left Wing,	Fourteenth,	Cumberland.
	Third,	First,	Twenty-first,	Cumberland.
	Third,	Second,	Fourth,	Cumberland.
Harlan, J. M.	Second,	First,	Third,	Army Ohio.
	Second,	Third, Centre,	Fourteenth,	Cumberland.
	Second,	Third,	Fourteenth,	Cumberland.
Harland, Edward	Second,	Third,	Ninth,	Potomac.
	Second,	Second,	Seventh,	Virginia.
	Second,	Getty's, Norfolk and Ports.,		Va. and N. C.
		Sub-Dist. Pamlico, N. C.,		Va. and N. C.
		Defenses New Berne, N. C.,		Va. and N. C.
		Sub-Dist. New Berne, N. C.,		Va. and N. C.
		First, Dist. Beaufort, N. C.,		North Carolina.
Harmon, O. F.	Third,	Second,	Fourteenth,	Cumberland.
Harney, W. S.				Dept. West.
Harriman, S.	First,	First,	Ninth,	Tennessee.
Harriman, W.	Second,	Second,	Ninth,	Potomac.
	Second,	Second,	Ninth,	Ohio.
Harris, A. L.	Second,	First,	Eleventh,	Potomac

Name	Brigade	Division, District, Etc.	Corps	Army or Dept.
Harris, C. L.	First,	First, Army S. E. Missouri,		Missouri.
	Second,	Fourteenth,	Thirteenth,	Tennessee.
	Second,	First,	Thirteenth,	Gulf.
	Third,	Second,	Sixteenth,	Gulf.
Harris, L. A.	Ninth,	Third,		Army Ohio.
	Ninth,	Third,	First,	Army Ohio.
Harris, T. M.	First,	Third,		West Virginia.
	Third,	First Infantry,		West Virginia.
		First Infantry,		West Virginia.
	Third,	Independent Div.,	Twenty-fourth,	Virginia.
		Independent Div.,	Twenty-fourth,	Virginia.
	First Indpt.,		Twenty-fourth,	Virginia.
Harrison, Benj.	Second,	Third,	Reserve,	Cumberland.
	First,	First,	Eleventh,	Cumberland.
	First,	Third,	Twentieth,	Cumberland.
	First,	Provisional,		Cumberland.
Harrow, Wm.	First,	Second,	Second,	Potomac.
		Second,	Second,	Potomac.
		Fourth,	Fifth,	Potomac.
Hart, F. D.	First,	Kitchings' Prov'l,		Army Shen.
Hart, J. S.	Second,	Third,	Twenty-third,	Ohio.
Hart, S. C.	Third,	Defenses South Potomac,	Twenty-second,	Washington.
Hart, T. D.	Second,	Forces Morris Island, S. C.,	Tenth,	South.
Hartranft, J. F.	Second,	Second,	Ninth,	Potomac.
		Second,	Ninth,	Ohio.
	First,	Third,	Ninth,	Potomac.
	Second,	First,	Ninth,	Potomac.
		First,	Ninth,	Potomac.
	First,	First,	Ninth,	Potomac.
	Provisional,		Ninth,	Potomac.
		Third,	Ninth,	Potomac.
Hartshorne, W. R.	Third,	Third,	Fifth,	Potomac.
Hartsuff, G. L.	Second,	First,		Shenandoah.
	Third,	Ord's,		Rappahannock.
	Third,	Second,	Third,	Army of Va.
	Third,	Second,	First,	Potomac.
			Twenty-third,	Ohio.
		Def. Bermuda Hundred, Va.,		Va. and N. C.
Hartwell, C. C.	Third,	Third, U. S. C. T.,		Gulf.
Hascall, M. S.	Fifteenth,			Army Ohio.
	Fifteenth,	Fourth,		Army Ohio.
	Fifteenth,	Sixth,		Army Ohio.
	Fifteenth,	Sixth,	Second,	Army Ohio.
	First,	First, Left Wing,	Fourteenth,	Cumberland.
		First, Left Wing,	Fourteenth,	Cumberland.
	First,	First,	Twenty-first,	Cumberland.
	Second,	Third,	Twenty-third,	Ohio.
	Second,	Second,	Twenty-third,	Ohio.
		Second,	Twenty-third,	Ohio.
		Third,	Twenty-third,	Ohio.
Haskell, F. A.	First,	Second,	Second,	Potomac.
Haskell, L. F.	Second,	Second,	Twenty-fifth,	Texas.
Haskins, J. A.		Def. North Potomac,	Mil. Dist. Wash.,	Potomac.
		Defenses Washington,		Potomac.
		Defenses North Potomac,	Twenty-second,	Washington.
Hastings, John	Fourth,	First,	Second,	Potomac.
Hatch, Edward	First,	Cavalry,		Army Miss.
	Second,	Cavalry, Right Wing,	Thirteenth,	Tennessee.
	Second,	First,	Sixteenth,	Tennessee.
	Third, ·	First,	Sixteenth,	Tennessee.
		First,	Sixteenth,	Tennessee.
		First,	Cavalry, W. Tenn.,	Tennessee.
		Fifth,	Cavalry,	Mil. Div. Miss.
Hatch, J. P.	Cavalry,		Banks' Fifth,	Potomac.
	Cavalry,			Shenandoah.
	Cavalry,		Second,	Army of Va.
	First,	First,	Third.	Army of Va.
		First,	Third,	Army of Va.
	First,	First,	First,	Potomac.
		First,	First,	Potomac.
		Dist. of Florida,		South.
				South.
		District Hilton Head, S. C.,		South.
		District Florida,		South.
		Morris Island, S. C.,		South.
		Coast Division,		South.
Hawkins, J. P.		1st Div. U. S. C. T. Dist.		
		Vicks.,		Tennessee.

Name	Brigade	Division, District, Etc.	Corps	Army or Dept.
		Fourth,	Sixteenth,	Tennessee.
		1st Div. U. S. C. T. West Fla.,		Gulf.
Hawkins, P. B.	Fourteenth,	Fifth,	Second,	Army Ohio.
Hawkins, R. C.	Fourth,			North Carolina.
	First,	Third,	Ninth,	Potomac.
	First,	Second,	Seventh,	Virginia.
Hawley, C. G.	First,	Fourth, Dist. East Tenn.,		Cumberland.
Hawley, J. R.	Third,	Morris Island, S. C.,	Tenth,	South.
		U. S. Forces St. Helena I.,	Tenth,	South.
	Second,	First, Dist. Florida,	Tenth,	South.
	Third,	First,	Tenth,	Va. and N. C.
	Second,	First,	Tenth,	Va. and N. C.
		Third,	Tenth,	Va. and N. C.
	Second,	First,	Twenty-fourth,	Virginia.
		First,	Twenty-fourth,	Virginia.
		District Wilmington, N. C.,	Tenth,	North Carolina.
Hawley, Wm.	Second,	First,	Twentieth,	Cumberland.
Hay, Geo.	Second,	Second,	Eighth,	Middle Dept.
Hayes, J.	First,	First,	Fifth,	Potomac.
	Third,	First,	Fifth,	Potomac.
	First,	Second,	Fifth,	Potomac.
Hayes, R. B.	First,	Third,	Eighth,	Middle Dept.
	First,	Scammon's,		West Virginia.
	First,	Third,		West Virginia.
	First,	First Infantry,		West Virginia.
		First Infantry,		West Virginia.
	First,	Second Infantry,		West Virginia.
		Second Infantry,		West Virginia.
Hayman, S. B.	First,	First,	Third,	Potomac.
	Third,	First,	Third,	Potomac.
Haynie, I. N.	First,	Third,	Seventeenth,	Tennessee.
Hays, Alex.	Third,	Abercrombie's,	Twenty-second,	Washington.
	Third,	Casey's,	Twenty-second,	Washington.
	Second,	Third,	Second,	Potomac.
		Third,	Second,	Potomac.
Hays, Wm.	Second,	Third,	Second,	Potomac.
		Second,	Second,	Potomac.
			Second,	Potomac.
Hays, W. H.	Second,	Third,	Fourteenth,	Cumberland.
	Third,	Third,	Fourteenth,	Cumberland.
Hayward, W. H.	First,	Defenses North Potomac,	Twenty-second,	Washington.
	Second,	Defenses North Potomac,	Twenty-second,	Washington.
Hazen, W. B.	Nineteenth,			Army Ohio.
	Nineteenth,	Fourth,		Army Ohio.
	Nineteenth,	Fourth,	Second,	Army Ohio.
	Second,	Second, Left Wing,	Fourteenth,	Cumberland.
	Second,	Second,	Twenty-first,	Cumberland.
	Second,	Third,	Fourth,	Cumberland.
		Second,	Fifteenth,	Tennessee.
			Fifteenth,	Tennessee.
Heath, F. E.	First,	Second,	Second,	Potomac.
Heath, T. T.	First,	First Cavalry,	Sixteenth,	Tennessee.
	Third,	Third,	Cavalry,	Mil. Div. Miss.
Heath, W. H.	Third,	1st, Detchm't Army Tenn.,		Cumberland.
	Third,	First,	Sixteenth,	Gulf.
Hecker, F.	First,	Third,	Eleventh,	Potomac.
	First,	Third,	Eleventh,	Cumberland,
	Third,	Third,	Eleventh,	Cumberland.
Heckman, C. A.	First,	Third,		North Carolina.
	Heckman's,			North Carolina.
	First,	Second,	Eighteenth,	North Carolina.
		Second,	Eighteenth,	North Carolina.
	First,	First, St. Helena Island,	Tenth,	South.
		Second, St. Helena Island,	Tenth,	South.
		District Beaufort, N. C.,	Eighteenth,	North Carolina.
		Sub-Dist. Beaufort, N. C.,	Eighteenth,	North Carolina.
		Defenses New Berne, N. C.,		Va. and N. C.
		Newport News, Va.,		Va. and N. C.
		Getty's, Norfolk and Ports,		Va. and N. C.
	First,	Second,	Eighteenth,	Va. and N. C.
		Second,	Eighteenth,	Va. and N. C.
			Eighteenth,	Va. and N. C.
		Third,	Twenty-fifth,	Virginia.
			Twenty-fifth,	Virginia.
Heg, H. C.	Second,	First,	Twentieth,	Cumberland.
	Third,	First,	Twentieth,	Cumberland.
Heine, Wm.	Second,	Forces Folly Island, S. C.,	Tenth,	South.
	Third,	Defenses South Potomac,	Twenty-second,	Washington.

Name	Brigade	Division, District, Etc.	Corps	Army or Dept.
	First,	Kitching's Provisional,		Army Shen.
		Kitching's Provisional,		Army Shen.
	First,	Defen. Bermuda Hundred,		Va. and N. C.
Heintzelman, S. P.		Third,		Army N. E. Va.
	Heintzelman's,			Div. Potomac.
		Heintzelman's,		Army Potomac.
			Third,	Potomac.
		Military Dist. Washington,		Potomac.
			Twenty-second,	Washington.
				Washington.
				Northern Dept.
Henderson, T. J.	Second,	First,	Cavalry,	Ohio.
	Third,	Third,	Twenty-third,	Ohio.
	Third,	Third,	Twenty-third,	North Carolina.
Henry, Guy V.	Light Brig.,	District Florida,	Tenth,	South.
	First,	Second,	Tenth,	Va. and N. C.
	Third,	First,	Eighteenth,	Va. and N. C.
	Third,	Third,	Twenty-fourth,	Virginia.
Hepburn, W. P.	Second,	First Cavalry,	Sixteenth,	Tennessee.
Herrick, T. P.	First,	First Cavalry,	Sixteenth,	Tennessee.
	First,	First Cavalry, West Tenn.,		Tennessee.
Herron, F. J.		Third, Army Frontier,		Missouri.
		Army Frontier,		Missouri.
		Herron's,	Thirteenth,	Tennessee.
		Second,	Thirteenth,	Tennessee.
		Second,	Thirteenth,	Gulf.
		U. S. Forces Texas,		Gulf.
		District Port Hudson,		Gulf.
Hibbetts, J. B.	First,	Fourth,	Seventeenth,	Tennessee.
Hickenlooper, A.	Third,	Fourth,	Seventeenth,	Tennessee.
Hicks, S. G.	First,	Fifth,		Army Tenn.
	Second,	First,	Sixteenth,	Tennessee.
	Second,	Fourth,	Fifteenth,	Tennessee.
Higgins, J.	Second,	First, Cavalry,		West Virginia.
Hildebrand, J.	Third,	Fifth,		Army Tenn.
Hill, S. G.	Third,	1st, Detachm't Army Tenn.,		Cumberland.
	Third,	First,	Sixteenth,	Tennessee.
Hills, C. W.	Hills',	Army Occupation,		West Virginia.
Hinks, E. W.		Hinks, U. S. C. T.,		Va. and N. C.
		Third,	Eighteenth,	Va. and N. C.
Hobart, H. C.	First,	First,	Fourteenth,	Cumberland.
Hobson, E. H.	Second,	Third,	Twenty-third,	Ohio.
	Second,	Fourth,	Twenty-third,	Ohio.
		S. Cent. Ky., 1st Div.,	Twenty-third,	Ohio.
		Dist. S. W. Ky., 1st Div.,	Twenty-third,	Ohio.
		Dist. Ky., Fifth Div.,	Twenty-third,	Ohio.
		First, Dist. Kentucky,	Twenty-third,	Ohio.
	First,	First, Dist. Kentucky,	Twenty-third,	Ohio.
		First,		Kentucky.
Hobson, W. E.	First,	Second,	Twenty-third,	Ohio.
	Second,	Second,	Twenty-third,	Ohio.
Hodge, J.	Colored,	U. S. Forces Texas,		Gulf.
Hoffman, J. W.	Second,	First,	Third,	Army of Va.
	Second,	First,	First,	Potomac.
	Second,	Fourth,	Fifth,	Potomac.
	Third,	Second,	Fifth,	Potomac.
	Third,	Third,	Fifth,	Potomac.
Hoge, G. B.	Second,	Fifth, Dist. Memphis,	Sixteenth,	Tennessee.
	First,	Dist. of Memphis, W. Tenn.,		Tennessee.
Hoge, Geo. W.	Third,	Second,	Twenty-third,	North Carolina.
Holbrook, C. L.	First,	First,	Eighteenth,	Va. and N. C.
Holbrook, W. C.		District West Florida,		Gulf.
Holliday, J. W.	Third,	Independent,	Twenty-fourth,	Virginia.
Holman, J. H.	African,	Forces Norfolk and Ports,		Va. and N. C.
	First,	Third,	Eighteenth,	Va. and N. C.
		Third,	Eighteenth,	Va. and N. C.
	Third,	Third,	Twenty-fifth,	Virginia.
	Third,	Paine's,	Terry's Prov'l,	North Carolina.
	Second,	Third,	Tenth,	North Carolina.
Holmes, S. A.	Second,	Third,		Army Tenn.
	Second,	Seventh,	Seventeenth,	Tennessee.
	Second,	Third,	Sixteenth,	Tennessee.
Hooker, Jos.	Hooker's,			Potomac.
		Hooker's,		Potomac.
		Second,	Third,	Potomac.
			Third,	Army of Va.
			First,	Potomac.
			Fifth,	Potomac.

Name	Brigade	Division, District, Etc.	Corps	Army or Dept.
				Army of Potomac.
				Dept. Potomac.
			11th, and 12th,	Cumberland.
			Twentieth,	Cumberland.
				Northern Dept.
Horn, J. W.	Second,	Third,	Third,	Potomac.
Hoskins, W. A.	Second,	Left Wing Forces,	Twenty-third,	Ohio.
Hotchkiss, C. T.	First,	Third,	Fourth,	Cumberland.
Hotchkiss, M. V.	Second,	Fourth,	Thirteenth,	Gulf.
Hovey, A. P.		2nd Dist. Eastern Ark.,		Missouri.
	First,	Twelfth,	Thirteenth,	Tennessee.
		Twelfth,	Thirteenth,	Tennessee.
		Fourth,	Sixteenth,	Tennessee.
		First,	Twenty-third,	Ohio.
Hovey, C. E.	First,	2nd, Dist. Eastern Ark.,		Missouri.
	Second,	Eleventh,	Thirteenth,	Tennessee.
	Second,	Fourth, Yazoo Expedition,		Tennessee.
	Second,	First,	Fifteenth,	Tennessee.
Howerd, O. O.	Third,	Third,		Army N. E. Va.
	Howard's,			Div. Potomac.
	First,	Sumner's,		Potomac.
	First,	First,	Second,	Potomac.
	Second,	Second,	Second,	Potomac.
		Second,	Second,	Potomac.
			Second,	Potomac.
			Eleventh,	Potomac.
			Eleventh,	Cumberland.
			Fourth,	Cumberland.
				Army Tenn.
				Dept. Tenn.
Howe, A. P.	Third,	First,	Fourth,	Potomac.
	Second,	First,	Fourth,	Potomac.
	Second,	Third,	Sixth,	Potomac.
	Third,	Third,	Sixth,	Potomac.
		Second,	Sixth,	Potomac.
		Light Arty. Camp,	Twenty-second,	Washington.
		Reserve Division,		West Virginia.
Howe, J. H.	Second,	Dist. Memphis, Fifth Div.,	Sixteenth,	Tennessee.
	Second,	Fourth,	Sixteenth,	Tennessee.
	Third,	Fourth,	Sixteenth,	Tennessee.
Howell, J. B.	Second,	Third,	Eighteenth,	North Carolina.
	Second,	Second,	Eighteenth,	North Carolina.
	Second,	Second, St. Helena Island,	Tenth,	South.
	Second,	Forces Folly Island, S. C.,	Tenth,	South.
	Second,	Forces Morris Island, S. C.,	Tenth,	South.
	Third,	South End Folly Island,	Tenth,	South.
	Howell's,	Hilton Head S. C. Dist.,	Tenth,	South.
		Hilton Head District,	Tenth,	South.
	First,	First,	Tenth,	Va. and N. C.
		First,	Tenth,	Va. and N. C.
		Third,	Tenth,	Va. and N. C.
Howland, H. N.	Second,	Second,	Cavalry,	Mil. Div. Miss.
Hoyt, H. M.	Second,	Forces Morris Island, S. C.,	Tenth,	South.
Hubbard, J.	Second,	Defenses South Potomac,	Twenty-second,	Washington.
	Second,	First,	Sixth,	Potomac.
Hubbard, L. F.	Second,	Third,	Fifteenth,	Tennessee.
	Second,	First,	Sixteenth,	Tennessee.
	Second,	First, Detachm't Army Tenn.,		Cumberland.
	Third,	First, Detachm't Army Tenn.,		Cumberland.
	Second,	First,	Sixteenth,	Gulf.
Hudnutt, J. O.	First,	Second,	Thirteenth,	Gulf.
Hudson, H. W.	First,	Second,	Second,	Potomac.
Hudson, J. G.	Second,	First,	Seventh,	Arkansas.
Huey, P.	Second,	Second,	Cavalry,	Potomac.
Hufty, B.	First,	First,	Sixth,	Army Shen.
Hughston, R. H.	Hughston's,	Gurney's,	Seventh,	Virginia.
Hull, J. C.	Second,	First,	Fifth,	Potomac.
Humphrey, T. W.	Second,	First,	Seventeenth,	Tennessee.
Humphrey, Wm.	Third,	First,	Ninth,	Ohio.
	Second,	Third,	Ninth,	Potomac.
	Second,	First,	Ninth,	Potomac.
Humphreys, A. A.		Third,	Fifth,	Potomac.
			Fifth,	Potomac.
		Second,	Third,	Potomac.
			Second,	Potomac.
Hunsdon, Chas.	Second,	Second,	Sixth,	Potomac.
Hunt, L. C.	First,	First,		North Carolina.
	First,	Fourth,	Eighteenth,	North Carolina.

Name	Brigade	Division, District, Etc.	Corps	Army or Dept.
Hunter, David		Second,		Army N. E. Va.
	Hunter's,			Div. Potomac.
				Western Dept.
				Kansas.
				South.
			Tenth,	South.
				West. Va.
Hunter, M. C.	First,	Third,	Fourteenth,	Cumberland.
Hurlbut, F. J.	Third,	Second,	Sixteenth,	Tennessee.
	Third,	Fourth,	Fifteenth,	Tennessee.
Hurlbut, S. A.		Fourth,		Army Tenn.
		Fourth, Dist. Memphis,		Tennessee.
		Fourth, Dist. Jackson,		Tennessee.
		District Jackson,	Thirteenth,	Tennessee.
		District Memphis,	Thirteenth,	Tennessee.
			Sixteenth,	Tennessee.
				Gulf.
Hurst, F.	Second,	First Cavalry,	Sixteenth,	Tennessee.
Hurt, J. S.	Second,	Third,	Twenty-third,	Ohio.
Huston, Daniel, Jr.	First,	Second, Army Frontier,		Missouri.
		Second, Army Frontier,		Missouri.
Hutchinson, F. S.	Third,	Second,	Fifteenth,	Tennessee.
Hyde, T. W.	Third,	Second,	Sixth,	Army Shen.
	Third,	Second,	Sixth,	Potomac.
Ingraham, T.	First,	Third,	Nineteenth,	Gulf.
Innes, C. H.	First,	First,	Fourth,	Potomac.
Ireland, D.	Third,	Second,	Twelfth,	Cumberland.
		Second,	Twelfth,	Cumberland.
	Third,	Second,	Twentieth,	Cumberland.
Irwin, W. S.	Second,	Defenses South Potomac,	Twenty-second,	Washington.
	Third,	Defenses South Potomac,	Twenty-second,	Washington.
Isaminger, J.	First,	Seventh,	Seventeenth,	Tennessee.
Jackson, C. F.	Third,	Third,	Third,	Army of Va.
	Third,	Third,	First,	Potomac.
	Third,	Third,	Fifth,	Potomac.
Jackson, E. P.	First,	First,	Seventeenth,	Tennessee.
Jackson, G. W.	Second,	Left Wing Forces,	Twenty-third,	Ohio.
	First,	Seventh,	Cavalry,	Mil. Div. Miss.
Jackson, J. S.		Tenth,		Army Ohio.
		Tenth,	First,	Army Ohio.
Jackson, N. J.	Second,	First,	Twelfth,	Potomac.
	Second,	Second,	Twelfth,	Potomac.
		First,	Twentieth,	Cumberland.
Jackson, R. H.		Second,	Twenty-fifth,	Virginia.
Jackson, S. M.	First,	Third,	Fifth,	Potomac.
Jacobi, A.	First,	First,	Seventh,	Arkansas.
Jacques, J. F.	First,	Second,	Fourth,	Cumberland.
Jameson, C. D.	Third,	Heintzelman's,		Potomac.
	First,	Third,	Third,	Potomac.
Jameson, Wm.	Third,	Third,	Second,	Potomac.
Janeway, H. H.	First,	Second,	Cavalry,	Potomac.
Jelleff, B.	Second	Second,	Twelfth,	Cumberland.
Jenkins, D. T.	Third,	Second,	Fifth,	Potomac.
Jenkins, J. W.	Second,	First,	Fifteenth,	Tennessee.
Jennings, W. H.	First,	Second,	Cavalry,	Cumberland.
Jennison, S. P.	First,	2nd, Detachm't Army Tenn.,		Cumberland.
Jewett, A. B.	Independent,		Twenty-second,	Washington.
Johnson, A. K.	Third,	Fourth, Right Wing,	Thirteenth,	Tennessee.
	Third,	Fourth,	Sixteenth,	Tennessee.
	Third,	Fourth,	Thirteenth,	Tennessee.
	Third,	Fourth,	Seventeenth,	Tennessee.
Johnson, C. A.	First,	Fourth,	Sixteenth,	Tennessee.
Johnson, D. D.	Second,	Second Infantry,		West Virginia.
Johnson, G. M. L.	Second,	Seventh,	Cavalry,	Mil. Div. Miss.
	Second,	First,	Cavalry,	Gulf.
Johnson, J. M.	First,	Third,	Seventh,	Arkansas.
Johnson, Lewis	First Colored,	Dist. Etowah,		Cumberland.
	Second,	District East Tenn.,		Cumberland.
Johnson, N. J.	Third,	Second,	Twenty-fourth,	Virginia.
	Third,	Ames,	Terry's Prov'l,	North Carolina.
Johnson, R. C.	Second,	Third,	Second,	Potomac.
Johnson, R. W.	Third,	McCook's Command,		Army Ohio.
	Sixth,			Army Ohio.
	Sixth,	Second,		Army Ohio.
		Second,	First,	Cumberland.
		Second, Right Wing,	Fourteenth,	Cumberland.
		Second,	Twentieth,	Cumberland.

Name	Brigade	Division, District, Etc.	Corps	Army or Dept.
		First,	Fourteenth,	Cumberland.
			Fourteenth,	Cumberland.
			Cavalry,	Cumberland.
		Sixth,	Cavalry,	Mil. Div. Miss.
		2nd Sub-Dist. Middle Tenn.,		Cumberland.
Johnston, R.	Third,	Cavalry,	Twenty-second,	Washington.
Jones, F. A.	First,	Second,	Twentieth,	Cumberland.
	Second,	Third,	Cavalry,	Cumberland.
Jones, J. G.	Fourteenth,			Army Ohio.
	Seventeenth,	Third,	First,	Army Ohio.
	Second,	Third, Centre,	Fourteenth,	Cumberland.
Jones, P. H.	First,	Second,	Eleventh,	Cumberland.
	Second,	Second,	Twentieth,	Cumberland.
Jones, Simeon	Second,	Third, U. S. C. T.,		Gulf.
Jones, S. B.	Ullman's,	Corps de Afrique,		Gulf.
	Second,	Second, Corps de Afrique,		Gulf.
Jones, Toland	First,	Second,	Fifteenth,	Tennessee.
	Second,	Second,	Fifteenth,	Tennessee.
Jones, W. S.	Second,	Second,	Fifteenth,	Tennessee.
	Third,	Fourth,	Fifteenth,	Tennessee.
Jordan, T. J.	First,	Third,	Cavalry,	Cumberland.
	First,	Third,	Cavalry,	Mil. Div. Miss.
Jourdan, J.	Second,	Fifth,	Eighteenth,	North Carolina.
	Jourdan's,		Eighteenth,	North Carolina.
		Sub-Dist. Beaufort, N. C.,		Va. and N. C.
	First,	Second,	Eighteenth,	Va. and N. C.
	Fourth,	First,	Twenty-fourth,	Virginia.
Judah, H. M.		First,		Army Tenn.
		Third,	Twenty-third,	Ohio.
		Second,	Twenty-third,	Ohio.
	First,	Second Separate, Etowah,		Cumberland.
	Second,	Separate, Dist. Etowah,		Cumberland.
Judd, H. B.		District Delaware,		Middle Dept.
Judson, W. R.	First,	First, Army Frontier,		Missouri.
		District Frontier,	Seventh,	Arkansas.
	Third,	District Frontier,	Seventh,	Arkansas.
	Second,	District Frontier,	Seventh,	Arkansas.
Judy, J. W.	Third,	Eighth,	Sixteenth,	Tennessee.
Kammerling, G.	Second,	Third,	Fourteenth,	Cumberland.
Kane, Thos. L.	Second,	First,	Twelfth,	Potomac.
	Second,	Second,	Twelfth,	Potomac.
Kappner, I. G.	Second Infantry,	Dist. West Tenn.,		Tennessee.
Karge, Jos.	First,	First, Cavalry,	Sixteenth,	Tennessee.
	First,	Second, West Tenn.,	Cavalry,	Tennessee.
	Second,	Fourth,	Cavalry,	Mil. Div. Miss.
	First,	First,	Cavalry,	Gulf.
	Second,	First,	Cavalry,	Gulf.
Kautz, A. V.	Cavalry,	Dist. Central Ky.,		Ohio.
	Third,	First,	Twenty-third,	Ohio.
		Cavalry,		Va. and N. C.
		First,	Twenty-fifth,	Virginia.
Kearny, Ph.	Kearny's,			Div. Potomac.
	First,	Franklin's,		Potomac.
	First,	First,	First,	Potomac.
	First,	First,		Rappahannock.
		Third,	Third,	Potomac.
		First,	Third,	Potomac.
Keifer, J. W.	Second,	Third,	Third,	Potomac.
	Second,	Third,	Sixth,	Potomac.
	Second,	Third,	Sixth,	Army Shen.
		Third,	Sixth,	Army Shen.
Keigwin, J.	First,	Ninth,	Thirteenth,	Tennessee.
	Second,	First,	Thirteenth,	Tennessee.
	Second,	First,	Thirteenth,	Gulf.
	Third,	First,	Thirteenth,	Gulf.
Keim, W. H.		Second,		Pennsylvania.
		Casey's,		Potomac.
	Second,	Third,	Fourth,	Potomac.
Kellogg, J. A.	First,	Third,	Fifth,	Potomac.
Kellogg, J. H.	Second,	First,	Cavalry,	Potomac.
Kellogg, W. P.	First,	Cavalry,		Army Miss.
Kelly, B. F.	Kelly's,	Army of Occupation,		West Virginia.
		Railroad District,		West Virginia.
		Railroad Division,		West Virginia.
		Railroad District,		Mountains.
		Railroad District,	Eighth,	Middle Dept.
		Def. Upper Potomac,	Eighth,	Middle Dept.

Name	Brigade	Division, District, Etc.	Corps	Army or Dept.
		First,	Eighth,	Middle Dept.
				West Virginia.
		Reserve, Harper's Ferry,		West Virginia.
Kelly, P.	Second,	First,	Second,	Potomac.
Kendrick, F. A.	First,	District Morganza, La.,		Gulf.
Kenly, J. R.	Maryland,	Def. Upper Potomac.	Eighth,	Middle Dept.
	First,	First,	Eighth,	Middle Dept.
	Kenly's,	French's Command,	Eighth,	Middle Dept.
		Third,	First,	Potomac.
		District Delaware,	Eighth,	Middle Dept.
		Third Separate,	Eighth,	Middle Dept.
	Kenly's,	Reserve Div.,		West Virginia.
	Kenly's,		Sixth,	Army Shen.
		Dist. Dela. and E. Shore,	Eighth,	Middle Dept.
	First Separate,		Eighth,	Middle Dept.
		Dist. Eastern Shore,	Eighth,	Middle Dept.
Kennett, John		Cavalry,		Army Ohio.
Kent, L.	Third,	First,	Reserve,	Gulf.
	Third,	First,	Thirteenth,	Gulf.
Kerwin, M.	Second,	Second,	Cavalry,	Potomac.
	Third,	Third,	Cavalry,	Mil. Div. Miss.
Keys, E. D.	First,	First,		Army N. E. Va.
	Keys',			Div. Potomac.
	Keys',	McDowell's,		Potomac.
		Keys',		Potomac.
			Fourth,	Potomac.
		Yorktown, Va.	Seventh,	Potomac.
		Div. at Suffolk, Va.,	Seventh,	Potomac.
Keilmansiegge, E.	Second,	Third,	Cavalry,	Potomac.
Kidd, J. H.	First,	First,	Cavalry,	Army Shen.
Kilpatrick, J.	First,	Third,	Cavalry,	Potomac.
	Second,	Second,	Cavalry,	Potomac.
		Third,	Cavalry,	Potomac.
		Third,	Cavalry,	Cumberland.
		Third,	Cavalry,	Mil. Div. Miss.
Kimball, N.	First,	Landers',		Potomac.
		Landers',		Potomac.
	First,	Second,	Banks' Fifth,	Potomac.
		Second,	Banks' Fifth,	Potomac.
	First,	Second,		Shenandoah.
	First,	Shields',		Rappahannock.
	Kimball's,		Second,	Potomac.
	First,	Third,	Second,	Potomac.
		Third,	Sixteenth,	Tennessee.
		Kimball's Prov'l,	Sixteenth,	Tennessee.
		Kimball's, Dist. E. Ark.,	Sixteenth,	Tennessee.
		Second, Arkansas Exp.,	Sixteenth,	Tennessee.
		Third, Arkansas Exp.,	Sixteenth,	Tennessee.
		Second,	Seventh,	Arkansas.
	First,	Second,	Fourth,	Cumberland.
		First,	Fourth,	Cumberland.
Kimball, Wm. K.	Second,	Fourth,	Nineteenth,	Gulf.
Kimberly, R. L.	Second,	Third,	Fourth,	Cumberland.
King, E. A.	Second,	Fourth,	Fourteenth,	Cumberland.
King, J. H.	Second,	First,	Fourteenth,	Cumberland.
	Third,	First,	Fourteenth,	Cumberland.
		First,	Fourteenth,	Cumberland.
	Regular,	Chattanooga, Tenn.,		Cumberland.
	First,	First, Separate, Etowah,		Cumberland.
King, Rufus,	Third,	McDowell's,		Potomac.
		King's, Third,	First,	Potomac.
		King's,		Rappahannock.
		First,	Third,	Army of Va.
		First,	First,	Potomac.
	Independent,		Seventh,	Virginia.
	Independent,		Fourth,	Virginia.
		First,	Fourth,	Virginia.
		King's,	Twenty-second,	Washington.
King, R. H.	Third,	Third,	Cavalry,	Cumberland.
King, W. S.	Third,	Defenses South Potomac,	Twenty-second,	Washington.
Kinney, P.	Second,	Second, Dist. Eastern Ark.,		Missouri.
Kinney, P.	Second,	Twelfth,	Thirteenth,	Tennessee.
Kinney, T. J.	Fourth,	Dist. Memphis, Fifth,	Sixteenth,	Tennessee.
	First,	Third,	Sixteenth,	Tennessee.
	Third,	First, Det'mt, Army Tenn.,		Cumberland.
Kinsey, W. B.	Third,	First,	Thirteenth,	Gulf.
Kirby, I. M.	First,	First,	Fourth,	Cumberland.

Name	Brigade	Division, District, Etc.	Corps	Army or Dept.
Kirk, E. N.	Fifth,	Second,		Army Ohio.
	Fifth,	Second,	First,	Army Ohio.
	Second,	Second, Right Wing,	Fourteenth,	Cumberland.
Kitching, J. H.	First,	Defenses North Potomac,	Twenty-second,	Washington.
	Independent,		Fifth,	Potomac.
	Third,	Second,	Fifth,	Potomac.
		Provisional,	Sixth,	Army Shen.
Kittredge, C. W.	First,	Thirteenth,	Thirteenth,	Tennessee.
	First,	Thirteenth,	Sixteenth,	Tennessee.
	First,	Third, Arkansas Exp.,		Tennessee.
Kleckner, Chas.	Third,	First,	Fourth,	Cumberland.
Klein, Robt.	First,	Third,	Cavalry,	Cumberland.
Kneffler, F.	First,	Third,	Twenty-first,	Cumberland.
	Third,	Third,	Fourth,	Cumberland.
Knipe, J. F.	First,	First,	Second,	Army of Va.
	First,	First,	Twelfth,	Potomac.
	First,	First,	Twelfth,	Cumberland.
		First,	Twelfth,	Cumberland.
	First,	First,	Twentieth,	Cumberland.
		First,	Twentieth,	Cumberland.
		Seventh,	Cavalry,	Mil. Div. Miss.
		First,	Cavalry,	Gulf.
	First,	Second,	Cavalry,	Gulf.
	Second,	First,	Cavalry,	Gulf.
Knowles, O. B.	Third,	Second,	Cavalry,	Potomac.
Kockersperger, C.	Second,	Second,	Second,	Potomac.
Koltes, J. A.	First,	Second,	First,	Army of Va.
Krez, C.	Third,	Third,	Reserve,	Gulf.
	Third,	Third,	Thirteenth,	Gulf.
Kreutzer, Wm.	First,	Third,	Twenty-fourth,	Virginia.
Krzyanowski, W.	Second,	Third,	First,	Army of Va.
	Second,	Third,	Eleventh,	Potomac.
	Second,	Third,	Eleventh,	Cumberland.
	Third,	Def. Nash. and Chatta. R. R.,		Cumberland.
Laiboldt, B.	Second,	Fifth,		Army Miss.
	Thirty-fifth,	Eleventh,		Army Ohio.
	Thirty-fifth,	Eleventh,	Third,	Army Ohio.
	Second,	Third, Right Wing,	Fourteenth,	Cumberland.
	Second,	Third,	Twentieth,	Cumberland.
Laflin, B.	First,	Second,	Second,	Potomac.
LaGrange, O. H.	Second,	First,	Cavalry,	Cumberland.
	Second,	First,	Cavalry,	Mil. Div. Miss.
Lamson, H. P.	Second,	First,	Cavalry,	Cumberland.
	Second,	First,	Cavalry,	Mil. Div. Miss.
Lander, F. W.	Second,	Stone's,		Potomac.
		Lander's,		West Virginia.
Landran, W. J.	Second,	First, Army Kentucky,		Ohio.
	Second,	Tenth, Left Wing,	Thirteenth,	Tennessee.
	Second,	First, Yazoo Expedition,		Tennessee.
	Second,	Tenth,	Thirteenth,	Tennessee.
	Second,	Fourth,	Thirteenth,	Gulf.
	First,	Fourth,	Thirteenth,	Gulf.
		Fourth,	Thirteenth,	Gulf.
	Second,	Cavalry,		Gulf.
Lane, J. C.	Second,	Second,	Twelfth,	Potomac.
Lane, J. Q.	Second,	Second,	Fourth,	Cumberland.
Langley, J. W.	Third,	Second,	Fourteenth,	Cumberland.
Lansing, H. S.	Third,	First,	Fifth,	Potomac.
Lauman, J. G.	Fourth,	Second, Mil. Dist. Cairo,		Missouri.
	First,	Second,		Army Tenn.
	Third,	Fourth,		Army Tenn.
	First,	Fourth,		Army Tenn.
		Fourth,		Army Tenn.
	First,	Fourth, Dist. Memphis,		Tennessee.
	Reserve,	Dist. Memphis,	Thirteenth,	Tennessee.
		Fourth, Right Wing,	Thirteenth,	Tennessee.
		Fourth,	Sixteenth,	Tennessee.
Lawler, A. J.	Second,	First,	Second,	Potomac.
Lawler, M. K.		Post Jackson,		Tennessee.
	First,	Dist. Jackson, Left Wing,	Sixteenth,	Tennessee.
	Second,	Third,	Sixteenth,	Tennessee.
	Second,	Fourteenth,	Thirteenth,	Tennessee.
		Fourth,	Thirteenth,	Gulf.
	Third,	First,	Thirteenth,	Gulf.
		First,	Thirteenth,	Gulf.
	Second,	First,	Thirteenth,	Gulf.
		First,	Thirteenth,	Gulf.
			Nineteenth,	Gulf.

Name	Brigade	Division, District, Etc.	Corps	Army or Dept.
		District Baton Rouge, La.,		Gulf.
		District Morganza, La.,		Gulf.
	First,		Reserve,	Gulf.
	First,	First,	Reserve,	Gulf.
Lazelle, H. M.	Indpt. Cavalry,		Twenty-second,	Washington.
Leaman, J. A.	Third,	First,	Seventh,	Arkansas.
Leasure, D.	Third,	First,	Ninth,	Potomac.
	Third,	First,	Ninth,	Ohio.
	Third,	First,	Ninth,	Tennessee.
	Second,	First,	Ninth,	Potomac.
		First,	Ninth,	Potomac.
Ledlie, J. H.	Artillery,		Eighteenth,	North Carolina.
	Artillery,	Defenses New Berne, N. C.,		North Carolina.
	First,	First,	Ninth,	Potomac.
		First,	Ninth,	Potomac.
Lee, A. L.	Second,	Cavalry,		Army Miss.
	First,	Cavalry, Left Wing,	Sixteenth,	Tennessee.
	Second,	Cavalry,	Sixteenth,	Tennessee.
	First,	Ninth,	Thirteenth,	Tennessee.
		Twelfth,	Thirteenth,	Tennessee.
		Third,	Thirteenth,	Tennessee.
		Third,	Thirteenth,	Gulf.
	First,	Third,	Nineteenth,	Gulf.
		Cavalry,		Gulf.
Lee, F. L.	Lee's Indpt.,	District New Berne, N. C.,		North Carolina.
Lee, H. C.	Third,	First,		North Carolina.
	Lee's,			North Carolina.
	Second,	First,	Eighteenth,	North Carolina.
	Second,	Getty's, Norfolk etc., Va.,		Va. and N. C.
Lee, H. T.	Third,	Defenses South Potomac,	Twenty-second,	Washington.
Lee, J. C.	Second,	First,	Eleventh,	Potomac.
	First,	Defenses South Potomac,	Twenty-second,	Washington.
Lee, W. R.	Third,	Second,	Second,	Potomac.
Le Favour, H. L.	Third,	Second,	Reserve,	Cumberland.
	Reserve,			Cumberland.
	Third,	Second, Separate, Etowah,		Cumberland.
Leggett, M. D.	Second,	Third, Right Wing,	Thirteenth,	Tennessee.
	First,	Third,	Seventeenth,	Tennessee.
	Second,	Third,	Seventeenth,	Tennessee.
		Third,	Seventeenth,	Tennessee.
			Seventeenth,	Tennessee.
Lehman, T. F.		Fourth,	Eighteenth,	North Carolina.
	First,	Dist. Albemarle, N. C.,		Dept. N. C.
		Sub. District Albermarle,		Va. and N. C.
		Roanoke Island, N. C.,		North Carolina.
Lemert, W. C.	Third,	Second,	Ninth,	Ohio.
Leonard, John	Second,	Second,	Third,	Potomac.
Leonard, S. H.	Third,	Second,	First,	Potomac.
	First,	Second,	First,	Potomac.
		Second,	First,	Potomac.
	First,	Second,	Fifth,	Potomac.
Lester, H. C.	Twenty-third,			Army Ohio.
Lewis, Geo. W.	First,	Cavalry,		Va. and N. C.
Lewis, J. M.	Second,	Thirteenth,	Thirteenth,	Tennessee.
	Second,	Third, Arkansas Exp.,		Tennessee.
	Second,	Third,	Seventh,	Arkansas.
Lightburn, J. A. J.	Fourth,	District Kanawha,		Mountains.
		District Kanawha,		Mountains.
		District Kanawha,		Ohio.
	Second,	Second,	Fifteenth,	Tennessee.
		Second,	Fifteenth,	Tennessee.
		Second Infantry,		West Virginia.
Limberg, G. T.	Thirty-ninth,	Twelfth,		Army Ohio.
Lincoln, W. S.	First,	Independent,	Twenty-fourth,	Virginia.
Lindsey, D. W.	Third,	Cumberland, Dist. W. Va.,		Ohio.
	Second,	Ninth, Left Wing,	Thirteenth,	Tennessee.
	Second,	Third, Yazoo Expedition,		Tennessee.
	Second,	Ninth,	Thirteenth,	Tennessee.
	Fourth,	First,	Thirteenth,	Tennessee.
	Fourth,	First,	Thirteenth,	Gulf.
Linton, J. P.	Second,	Third,		West Virginia.
Littell, J. S.	Second,	Second,	Tenth,	North Carolina.
		Second,	Tenth,	North Carolina.
Littlefield, M. S.	Third, African,	North End Folly Island,	Tenth,	South.
	Third,	First, Dist. Florida,	Tenth,	South.
		Dist. Hilton Head, S. C.,		South.
Livingston, R. R.	Second,	Second, Army S. E. Mo.,		Missouri.
		Dist. Northeastern Ark.,	Seventh,	Arkansas.

Name	Brigade	Division, District, Etc.	Corps	Army or Dept.
Loan, Benj.		District Northern Mo.,		Missouri.
		District Central Mo.,		Missouri.
Lockman, J. T.	Second,	Third,	Eleventh,	Cumberland.
	Second,	Second,	Twentieth,	Cumberland.
Lockwood, H. H.		Dist. Eastern Shore,	Eighth,	Middle Dept.
			Eighth,	Middle Dept.
	1st Separate,		Eighth,	Middle Dept.
	Lockwood's,	French's Command.	Eighth,	
	Second,	First,	Twelfth,	Potomac.
		Maryland Heights Div.,		West Virginia.
	3rd Separate,		Eighth,	Middle Dept.
		Second,	Fifth,	Potomac.
			Eighth,	Middle Dept.
				Middle Dept.
Logan, J.	Second,	Fourth,	Seventeenth,	Tennessee.
Logan, John A.	First,	First,		Army Tenn.
	First,	First, Dist. Jackson,		Army Tenn.
		District Jackson,		Army Tenn.
		Third, Right Wing	Thirteenth,	Tennessee.
		Third,	Seventeenth,	Tennessee.
			Fifteenth,	Tennessee.
				Army Tenn.
				Tennessee.
Long, C. H.	First,	Defenses North Potomac,	Twenty-second,	Washington.
Long, Eli	Second,	Second,	Cavalry,	Cumberland.
		Second,	Cavalry,	Mil. Div. Miss.
Longanecker, J. C.	Fourth,	First,		Pennsylvania.
Loomis, J. M.	Second,	Fifth, Army Miss.		Missouri.
	Second,	Eighth, Left Wing,	Thirteenth,	Tennessee.
	First,	First,	Sixteenth,	Tennessee.
	First,	Fourth,	Fifteenth,	Tennessee.
Lord, N. B.	Cavalry,	Getty's, Norfolk Va., Etc.,		Va. and N. C.
	First,	Cavalry,		Va. and N. C.
Love, Geo. M.	First,	First,	Nineteenth,	Gulf.
	Third,	First,	Nineteenth,	Gulf.
	First,	First,	Nineteenth,	Army Shen.
Love, S. P.	Second,	Second, Dist. Kentucky,	Twenty-third,	Ohio.
	Third,	First,	Cavalry,	Ohio.
	First,	Third,	Twenty-third,	Ohio.
Lovell, Chas. S.	Second,	Second,	Fifth,	Potomac.
Lowe, W. W.	Third,	Second,	Cavalry,	Cumberland.
	First,	Second,	Cavalry,	Cumberland.
	First,	Third,	Cavalry,	Cumberland.
		Third,	Cavalry,	Cumberland.
	Second,	Sixth,	Cavalry,	Mil. Div. Miss.
Lowell, C. R. Jr.	Indpt. Cavalry,		Twenty-second,	Washington.
	Reserve,	First,	Cavalry,	Army Shen.
	3rd, Reserve,	First,	Cavalry,	Army Shen.
Lucas, T. J.	First,	Fourth,	Thirteenth,	Gulf.
	First,	Cavalry,		Gulf.
		Lucas' Cavalry, West Fla.,		Gulf.
	Separate Cav.,	Dist. West Florida,		Gulf.
	Third,	First,	Cavalry,	Gulf.
Lum, C. M.	First,	Fourth,	Fourteenth,	Cumberland.
	First,	Second,	Fourteenth,	Cumberland.
Lyle, P.	Second,	Second,	First,	Potomac.
	First,	Second,	First,	Potomac.
	First,	Second,	Fifth,	Potomac.
	Fourth,	Fourth,	Fifth,	Potomac.
	First,	Third,	Fifth,	Potomac.
Lynch, J. C.	First,	First,	Second,	Potomac.
Lynch, W. F.	First,	Third, Detachment,	Sixteenth,	Gulf.
Lynde, E.	Third,	District Frontier,	Seventh,	Arkansas.
Lyon, Nath'l				Dept. West.
Lyon, W. P.	First,	Third,	Reserve,	Cumberland.
Lytle, W. H.	Seventeenth,	Third,		Army Ohio.
	Seventeenth,	Third,	First,	Army Ohio.
	First,	Third,	Twentieth,	Cumberland.
Macauley, D.	First,	Third,	Thirteenth,	Gulf.
	Third,	Second,	Nineteenth,	Army Shen.
	2nd Separate,		Eighth,	Middle Dept.
MacDonald, C. R.	Second,	Second,	Tenth,	North Carolina.
MacDougall, C. D.	Third,	First,	Second,	Potomac.
	Consolidated,	First,	Second,	Potomac.
MacGregor, J. D.	Third,	Third,	Second,	Potomac.
MacKenzie, R. S.	Second,	First,	Sixth,	Potomac.
	Second,	First,	Sixth,	Army Shen.
Mackey, C. H.	First,	First,	Seventh,	Arkansas.

Name	Brigade	Division, District, Etc.	Corps	Army or Dept.
Macy, G. N.	First,	Second,	Second,	Potomac.
	Consolidated,	First,	Second,	Potomac.
	Third,	First,	Second,	Potomac.
	First,	First,	Second,	Potomac.
		First,	Second,	Potomac.
Madill, H. J.	First,	First,	Third,	Potomac.
	First,	Third,	Second,	Potomac.
	Second,	Third,	Second,	Potomac.
	Third,	First,	Second,	Potomac.
Mahan, J. R.	First,	Left Wing Forces,	Twenty-third,	Ohio.
Majilton, A. L.	Second,	Third,	First,	Potomac.
	Second,	Third,	Fifth,	Potomac.
Mallon, J. E.	Third,	Second,	Second,	Potomac.
Malloy, A. G.	Second,	First,	Seventeenth,	Tennessee.
	Third,	Third,	Seventeenth,	Tennessee.
	First,	Second, District Beaufort,		North Carolina.
Malmsborg, A.	Second,	Second,	Fifteenth,	Tennessee.
Malmsborg, C.	Second,	Fifth,		Army Tenn.
Maltby, J. A.	Third,	Third,	Seventeenth,	Tennessee.
		Third,	Seventeenth,	Tennessee.
	Maltby's,	District Vicksburg, Miss.,		Tennessee.
Mann, A.	First,	Third,	Seventeenth,	Tennessee.
Mansfield, J. F. K.				Washington.
		Division at Suffolk, Va.,	Seventh,	Virginia.
			Twelfth,	Potomac.
Manson, M. D.	Second,			Army Ohio.
	Second,	First,		Army Ohio.
	Twenty-second,	Fourth,		Army Ohio.
	First,	Army Kentucky,		Ohio.
	First,	Third,	Twenty-third,	Ohio.
	Second,	Third,	Twenty-third,	Ohio.
		Second,	Twenty-third,	Ohio.
			Twenty-third,	Ohio.
Manter, F. H.	First,	First,	Fifteenth,	Tennessee.
Marble, J. M. C.	First,	Defenses North Potomac,	Twenty-second,	Washington.
	Second,	Defenses North Potomac,	Twenty-second,	Washington.
Marsh, C. C.	Second,	First,		Army Tenn.
	Third,	First, Dist. Jackson,		Army Tenn.
	First,	Third, Right Wing,	Thirteenth,	Tennessee.
	First,	Third,	Seventeenth,	Tennessee.
Marshall, E. G.	Provisional,	First,	Ninth,	Potomac.
	Third,	First,	Ninth,	Potomac.
	Second,	First,	Ninth,	Potomac.
	First,	Defenses North Potomac,	Twenty-second,	Washington.
Marshall, J. W.	Third,	Third,	Second,	Potomac.
Marshall, W. R.	Third,	First, Det'mt Army Tenn.,		Cumberland.
	Third,	First,	Sixteenth,	Gulf.
Marston, G.	First,	Third,	Tenth,	Va. and N. C.
	First,	First,	Eighteenth,	Va. and N. C.
		First,	Eighteenth,	Va. and N. C.
		District St. Marys,		Va. and N. C.
Martin, J. A.	Third,	First,	Twentieth,	Cumberland.
	First,	Third,	Fourth,	Cumberland.
Martin, J. S.	First,	Second,	Fifteenth,	Tennessee.
	Second,	Second,	Fifteenth,	Tennessee.
Martin, R.	First,	Fourth,	Fifteenth,	Tennessee.
Martindale, E.	Provisional,	Third,	Eighteenth,	Va. and N. C.
	Second,	Third,	Twenty-fifth,	Virginia.
	Third,	Second,	Twenty-fifth,	Virginia.
Martindale, J. H.	Second,	Fitz, John Porter's,		Potomac.
	First,	First,	Third,	Potomac.
	First,	First,	Fifth,	Potomac.
		Military Dist., Washington,	Twenty-second,	Washington.
		Second,	Eighteenth,	Va. and N. C.
			Eighteenth,	Va. and N. C.
Mason, E. C.	Third,	Second,	Sixth,	Potomac.
Mason, E. C.	Second,	Fourth,	Twentieth,	Cumberland.
	First,	District Nashville, Tenn.,		Cumberland.
Mason, J. S.	First,	Third,	Second,	Potomac.
Mattheson, R.	Third,	First,	Sixth,	Potomac.
Matthews, J. A.	First,	Third,	Ninth,	Potomac.
	Second,	Third,	Ninth,	Potomac.
Matthews, Stanley	Twenty-third,			Army Ohio.
	Twenty-third,			Army Ohio.
	Twenty-third,	Fifth,		Army Ohio.
	Third,	Third, Left Wing,	Second,	Fourteenth,	Cumberland.
	Third,	Third,	Twenty-first,	Cumberland.

Name	Brigade	Division, District, Etc.	Corps	Army or Dept.
Matthies, C. L.	Third,	Seventh,	Sixteenth,	Tennessee.
	Third,	Seventh,	Seventeenth,	Tennessee.
	Second,	Seventh,	Seventeenth,	Tennessee.
	Third,	Second,	Seventeenth,	Tennessee.
	Third,	Third,	Fifteenth,	Tennessee.
Mattson, H.	First,	Second,	Seventh,	Arkansas.
Maulsby, W. P.	Second,	Maryland Heights Div.		West Virginia.
	Second,	First,		West Virginia.
Maxwell, C.		Dist. Southwest Ky., 1st Div.	Twenty-third,	Ohio.
	Second,	Second, Dist. Kentucky,	Twenty-third,	Ohio.
McAllister, R.	First,	Second,	Third,	Potomac.
	First,	Fourth,	Second,	Potomac.
	Second,	Third,	Second,	Potomac.
	Third,	Third,	Second,	Potomac.
McArthur, John	First,	Second, Mil. Dist. Cairo,		Missouri.
	Second,	Second,		Army Tenn.
		Second,		Army Tenn.
	First,	Sixth,		Army Tenn.
		Sixth,		Army Tenn.
		Sixth, Left Wing,	Thirteenth,	Tennessee.
		Sixth,	Sixteenth,	Tennessee.
		Sixth,	Seventeenth,	Tennessee.
		First,	Seventeenth,	Tennessee.
		First,	Sixteenth,	Tennessee.
		Post Vicksburg, Miss.,		Tennessee.
		First, Det'mt Army Tenn.,		Cumberland.
		First,	Sixteenth,	Gulf.
McCall, Geo. A.		McCall's		Potomac.
		Second,	First,	Potomac.
		Third,	Fifth,	Potomac.
McCall, W. H. H.	First,	Third,	Ninth,	Potomac.
McCalmont, A. B.	First,	Third,	First,	Potomac.
	First,	Third,	Ninth,	Potomac.
McCandless, W.	First,	Third,	First,	Potomac.
	First,	Third,	Fifth,	Potomac.
	First,	Penna. Reserve,	Twenty-second,	Washington.
		Third,	Fifth,	Potomac.
McCaslin, M.	First,	Second,		West Virginia.
McChesney, J. M.		District Pamlico, N. C.,		Va. and N. C.
		Sub-Dist. Pamlico, N. C.,		Va. and N. C.
McClellan, G. B.		Army of Occupation W. Va.,		Ohio.
				Ohio.
		Division of the Potomac,		Potomac.
		Army of the Potomac,		Potomac.
				Potomac.
				Armies U. S.
McClellan, J. S.	Thirty-second,	Ninth,	Third,	Army Ohio.
	Third,	First, Right Wing,	Fourteenth,	Cumberland.
McClernand, J. A.	First,	Mil. District Cairo,		Missouri.
		First, Mil. Dist. Cairo,		Missouri.
		First, Dist. West Tenn.		Army Tenn.
		First. District Jackson,		Army Tenn.
		District Jackson,		Tennessee.
			Thirteenth,	Tennessee.
			Thirteenth,	Gulf.
McClure, J. D.	Second,	First,	Sixteenth,	Tennessee.
	Second,	First,	Sixteenth,	Gulf.
McClure, W. M.	Provisional,	Defenses Bermuda Hundred,		Va. and N. C.
McConnell, H. K.	Second,	Third,	Fourth,	Cumberland.
McCook, A. G.	First,	First,	Fourteenth,	Cumberland.
McCook, A. McD.		Division at Nolin, Ky.,		Army Ohio.
		Second,		Army Ohio.
			First,	Army Ohio.
		Right Wing,	Fourteenth,	Cumberland.
			Twentieth,	Cumberland.
		District Eastern Ark.,	Seventh,	Arkansas.
McCook, Daniel	Thirty-sixth,	Eleventh,		Army Ohio.
	Thirty-sixth,	Eleventh,	Third,	Army Ohio.
	Second,	Fourth, Centre,	Fourteenth,	Cumberland.
	Second,	Fourth,	Fourteenth,	Cumberland.
	Second,	Second,	Reserve,	Cumberland.
	Third,	Second,	Fourteenth,	Cumberland.
McCook, E. M.	First,	Cavalry,		Army Ohio.
	Second,	First,	Cavalry,	Cumberland.
		First,	Cavalry,	Cumberland.
		First,	Cavalry,	Mil. Div. Miss.
McCook, R. L.	McCook's,	Army of Occupation W. Va.,		Ohio.
	Second,	Kanawha,		Western Va.

Name	Brigade	Division, District, Etc.	Corps	Army or Dept.
	Third,			Army Ohio.
	Third,	First,		Army Ohio.
McCoy, T. F.	First,	Second,	First,	Potomac.
	First,	Third,	Fifth,	Potomac.
McCown, J. B.	First,	Third,	Fifteenth,	Tennessee.
McCrillis, L. F.	First,	First Cavalry,	Sixteenth,	Tennessee.
	Second,	First Cavalry,	Sixteenth,	Tennessee.
	Third,	First Cavalry,	Sixteenth,	Tennessee.
McDougall, A. L.	First,	First,	Twelfth,	Potomac.
McDowell, H. T.	First,	Fourth,	Sixteenth,	Tennessee.
	First,	First,	Seventeenth,	Tennessee.
McDowell, Irwin				Army N. E. Va.
		McDowell's,		Potomac.
			First,	Potomac.
				Rappahannock,
			Third,	Army of Va.
				Pacific.
McDowell, John A.	First,	Fifth,		Army Tenn.
	Second,	Fifth,		Army Tenn.
	Second,	Fifth, Dist. Memphis,		Army Tenn.
	First,	First, Right Wing,	Thirteenth,	Tennessee.
	Second,	First,	Sixteenth,	Tennessee.
		First,	Sixteenth,	Tennessee.
	First,	First,	Seventeenth,	Tennessee.
		First,	Seventeenth,	Tennessee.
McFadden, R. H.	Second,	Fourth,	Seventeenth,	Tennessee.
McGee, J. E.	Consolidated,	First,	Second,	Potomac.
McGinnis, G. F.	Third,	Second, Dist. Eastern Ark.,		Missouri.
	First,	Twelfth,	Thirteenth,	Tennessee.
	Third,	Twelfth,	Thirteenth,	Tennessee.
	First,	Third,	Thirteenth,	Gulf.
		Third,	Thirteenth,	Gulf.
	Third,	Third,	Nineteenth,	Gulf.
		Third,	Nineteenth,	Gulf.
		Second,	Nineteenth,	Gulf.
		U. S. Forces, Mouth White River,		Gulf.
	Third,		Reserve,	Gulf.
McGroarty, S. J.	First,	Third,	Eleventh,	Cumberland.
	Third,	Third,	Eleventh,	Cumberland.
		Third,	Eleventh,	Cumberland.
McIntosh, J. B.	First,	Second,	Cavalry,	Potomac.
	Second,	Second,	Cavalry,	Potomac.
		Cavalry,	Twenty-second,	Washington.
	First,	Third,	Cavalry,	Potomac.
	First,	Third,	Cavalry,	Army Shen.
McIvor, J. P.	First,	King's,	Twenty-second,	Washington.
	Second,	King's,	Twenty-second,	Washington.
	Fourth,	Second,	Second,	Potomac.
	Second,	Second,	Second,	Potomac.
		Second,	Second,	Potomac.
McKeag, G. W.	1st Infantry,	District West Tenn.,		Tennessee.
McKean, T. J.		Sixth,		Army Tenn.
		Sixth, Dist. Corinth,		Army Tenn.
		Fourth, Right Wing,	Thirteenth,	Tennessee.
		District West Florida,		Gulf.
		District Morganza, La.,		Gulf.
		Dist. Southwest Mo.,		Missouri.
		Dist. Northern Mo.,		Missouri.
		Dist. South Kansas,		Kansas.
		Dist. Nebraska,		Kansas.
McKeen, H. B.	First,	First,	Second,	Potomac.
	First,	Second,	Second,	Potomac.
McKendrie, A.	Reserve,	First,	Cavalry,	Army Shen.
McKibben, D. B.	First,	Dist. Pamlico, N. C.,	Eighteenth,	Va. and N. C.
McKibben, G. H.	First,	Defenses Bermuda Hundred,		Va. and N. C.
McLaughlin, J. A.	First,	First,	Reserve,	Gulf.
	First,	First,	Thirteenth,	Gulf.
		First,	Thirteenth,	Gulf.
McLaughlin, N. B.	Third,	First,	Ninth,	Potomac.
		First,	Ninth,	Potomac.
McLean, N. C.	Second,	First,	First,	Army of Va.
	Second,	First,	Eleventh,	Potomac.
		First,	Eleventh,	Potomac.
		First, District Kentucky,	Twenty-third,	Ohio.
	First,	Second,	Twenty-third,	Ohio.
	Third,	Third,	Twenty-third,	Ohio.
	Third,	Second,	Twenty-third,	North Carolina.
		Second,	Twenty-third,	North Carolina.

Name	Brigade	Division, District, Etc.	Corps	Army or Dept.
McLean, W. E.	First,	Thirteenth,	Thirteenth,	Tennessee.
	First,	Thirteenth,	Sixteenth,	Tennessee.
	First,	Thirteenth, Dist. E. Ark.,	Sixteenth,	Tennessee.
	First,	Second, Arkansas Exp.,	Sixteenth,	Tennessee.
		Second, Arkansas Exp.,	Sixteenth,	Tennessee.
	First,	Third,	Seventh,	Arkansas.
	Second,	Third,	Seventh,	Arkansas.
McMacken, W. E.	First,	First,	Fourth,	Cumberland.
McMahon, A.	Third,	First,	Fourteenth,	Cumberland.
McMillan, Jas.	Second,	First,	Nineteenth,	Army Shen.
		First,	Nineteenth,	Army Shen.
		First Independent,		West Virginia.
McMillan, J. W.	Second,	Third,	Nineteenth,	Gulf.
		Third,	Nineteenth,	Gulf.
	Second,	First,	Nineteenth,	Gulf.
	Second,	First,	Nineteenth,	Army Shen.
		First,	Nineteenth,	Army Shen.
		First Provisional,		Army Shen.
McMillan, W. L.	First,	Third,	Fifteenth,	Tennessee.
	First,	First,	Sixteenth,	Tennessee.
	First,	First, Det'mt Army Tenn.,		Cumberland.
	First,	First,	Sixteenth,	Gulf.
McNary, W. H.	First,	Second,	Eighteenth,	Va. and N. C.
McNulta, John	First,	Second,	Thirteenth,	Gulf.
	Second,	Second,	Thirteenth,	Gulf.
	Second,	U. S. Forces, Texas,		Gulf.
McNulta, J. J.	Second,	Third, Army Frontier,		Missouri.
McNeil, John		Dist. Northern Mo.,		Missouri.
		Dist. Southwest Mo.,		Missouri.
		Dist. Rolla, Mo.,		Missouri.
		Dist. LaFourche, La.,		Gulf.
		Dist. Port Hudson, La.,		Gulf.
		Dist. Central, Mo.,		Missouri.
McPherson, J. B.	Engineer,			Army Tenn.
		Right Wing,	Thirteenth,	Tennessee.
			Seventeenth,	Tennessee.
				Army Tenn.
				Tennessee.
McQuade, Jas.	Second.	First,	Fifth,	Potomac.
McQuiston, J. C.	Fourth,	Second,	Twenty-third,	Ohio.
	Second,	First,	Twenty-third,	Ohio.
	Second,	First,	Provisional,	North Carolina.
	Second,	First,	Twenty-third,	North Carolina.
McReynolds, A. T.	Fourth,	Cavalry,		Potomac.
	Third,	Second,	Eighth,	Middle Dept.
		Martinsburg, Va.,	Eighth,	Middle Dept,
Meade, Geo. G.	Second,	McCall's,		Potomac.
	Second,	Second,	First,	Potomac.
	Second,	Second,		Rappahannock.
		Second,		Rappahannock.
	Second,	Third,	Fifth,	Potomac.
	First,	Third,	Third,	Army of Va.
		Third,	First,	Potomac.
			First,	Potomac.
			Fifth,	Potomac.
				Army Potomac.
				Potomac.
Meagher, T. F.	Second,	Sumner's,		Potomac.
	Second,	First,	Second,	Potomac.
Meek, B. D.	Fourth,	First Cavalry,	Sixteenth,	Tennessee.
Mehringer, J.	First,	Fourth,	Twenty-third,	Ohio.
	Third,	Second,	Twenty-third,	Ohio.
	Third,	Second,	Twenty-third,	North Carolina.
Mehringer, J.	Second,	Second,	Twenty-third,	North Carolina.
Meredith, S.	Fourth,	First,	First,	Potomac.
		First,	First,	Potomac.
	First,	First,	First,	Potomac.
		Dist. West Kentucky,		Ohio.
		Dist. West Kentucky,		Kentucky.
Merriam, J.	Second,	Second,	Sixteenth,	Gulf.
Merrill, Lewis		District St. Louis, Mo.,		Missouri.
	First,	First Cavalry, Army S. E. M		Missouri.
	First,	First Cavalry, Ark. Exp.,		Tennessee.
	Second,	First Cavalry, Ark. Exp.		Tennessee.
Merrill, S.	Second,	First,	Thirteenth,	Gulf.
Merriman, W. S.	Second,	Second,	Sixteenth,	Tennessee.
	Second,	Fourth,	Fifteenth,	Tennessee.
Merritt, R. B.	Third,	First,	Nineteenth,	Gulf.
	Second,	Second,	Nineteenth,	Gulf.

Name	Brigade	Division, District, Etc.	Corps	Army or Dept.
Merritt, Wesley	Reserve,	First,	Cavalry,	Potomac.
		First,	Cavalry,	Potomac.
		First,	Cavalry,	Army Shen.
			Cavalry,	Army Shen.
			Cavalry,	Potomac.
Mersey, A.	Second,	Second,		Army Tenn.
	Second,	Second, Dist. Corinth,		Army Tenn.
	Second,	District Corinth,	Thirteenth,	Tennessee.
	Second,	District Corinth,	Seventeenth,	Tennessee.
	Second,	District Corinth,	Sixteenth,	Tennessee.
		Left Wing,	Sixteenth,	Tennessee.
	Second,	Second,	Sixteenth,	Tennessee.
		Second,	Sixteenth,	Tennessee.
Meservey, C. C.	Fourth,	Defenses South Potomac,	Twenty-second,	Washington.
Metcalf, E.		U. S. Forces Hilton Head S. C.,	Tenth,	South.
Miles, D.	Third,	First,	Fourteenth,	Cumberland.
Miles, D. S.	Fourth,	First,		Pennsylvania.
		Fifth,		Army N. E. Va.
	Railroad,			Middle Dept.
	Railroad,		Eighth,	Middle Dept.
Miles, N. A.	First,	First,	Second,	Potomac.
		First,	Second,	Potomac.
			Second,	Potomac.
Miller, A. O.	Fortieth,	Twelfth,		Army Ohio.
	Second,	Fifth, Centre,	Fourteenth,	Cumberland.
	First,	Fourth,	Fourteenth,	Cumberland.
	Third,	Second,	Cavalry,	Cumberland.
	First,	Second,	Cavalry,	Mil. Div. Miss.
	Third,	Second,	Cavalry,	Mil. Div. Miss.
Miller, H.	Second,	Defenses North Potomac,	Twenty-second,	Washington.
Miller, J. F.	7th Indpt.,			Army Ohio.
	Seventh,	Eighth,		Army Ohio.
	Third,	Second, Centre,	Fourteenth,	Cumberland.
	Third,	Second,	Fourteenth,	Cumberland.
		Post Nashville, Tenn.,		Cumberland.
Miller, J. K.	Third,	Fourth,	Cavalry,	Cumberland.
	Third,	Fourth,	Cavalry,	Mil. Div. Miss.
	Third,	Cavalry, Dist. East Tenn.,		Cumberland.
Miller, J. R.	Third,	First,	Sixth,	Potomac.
Miller, Madison	Second,	Sixth,		Army Tenn.
	Third,	Second,	Sixteenth,	Tennessee.
Miller, Silas	First,	Third,	Twentieth,	Cumberland.
Mills, J. K.	First,	Sixth, Dist. Columbus,	Sixteenth,	Tennessee.
	Second,	Third,	Sixteenth,	Tennessee.
Millroy, R. H.	Milroy's,	Cheat Mountain Dist.,		Mountains.
		Cheat Mountain Dist.,		Mountains.
	Independent,		First,	Army of Va.
		Milroy's, Upper Potomac	Eighth,	Middle Dept.
		Winchester, Va.,	Eighth,	Middle Dept.
		Second,	Eighth,	Middle Dept.
		Defenses Nash. and Chatta.Railroad,		Cumberland.
		1st Sub-Div., Middle Tenn.,		Cumberland.
Milward, H. K.	First,	Third,	Fourteenth,	Cumberland.
	Third,	Third,	Fourteenth,	Cumberland.
Mindel, G. W.	Second,	First,	Ninth,	Potomac.
	First,	Second,	Eleventh,	Cumberland.
	First,	Second,	Twentieth,	Cumberland.
	Second,	Second,	Twentieth,	Cumberland.
Miner, G. G.	First,	Second,	Cavalry,	Ohio.
Minty, R. H. G.	First,	Cavalry,		Cumberland.
	First,	First,	Cavalry,	Cumberland.
	First,	Second,	Cavalry,	Cumberland.
	Second,	Second,	Cavalry,	Mil. Div. Miss.
		Second,	Cavalry,	Mil. Div. Miss.
Mintzer, W. M.	Third,	First,	Second,	Potomac.
	Fourth,	First,	Second,	Potomac.
Mitchell, G. M.	Third,	Second,	Seventh,	Arkansas.
Mitchell, J. G.	Second,	First,	Reserve,	Cumberland.
	Second,	Second,	Fourteenth,	Cumberland.
	Second,	Provisional,		Cumberland.
Mitchell, O. M.				Ohio.
		Third,		Army Ohio.
				South.
			Tenth,	South.
Mitchell, R. B.	First,	Fourth,		Army Miss.
		Fourth,		Army Miss.
		Ninth,		Army Ohio.
		Ninth,	Third,	Army Ohio.
		First, Right Wing,	Fourteenth,	Cumberland.

Name	Brigade	Division, District, Etc.	Corps	Army or Dept.
		Fourth, Centre,	Fourteenth,	Cumberland.
		First,	Cavalry,	Cumberland.
			Cavalry,	Cumberland.
		District North Kansas,		Kansas.
		District Nebraska,		Kansas.
Mix, E.	First,	Sixth,	Cavalry,	Mil. Div. Miss.
Mix, S. H.	Cavalry,	Defenses New Berne,		North Carolina.
	First,	Cavalry,		Va. and N. C.
Mizner, J. K.	First, .	Cavalry,		Army Miss.
		Cavalry,		Army Miss.
	Cavalry,	Dist. Jackson, Left Wing,	Sixteenth,	Tennessee.
	Cavalry,	Third,	Sixteenth,	Tennessee.
	First,	First Cavalry,	Sixteenth,	Tennessee.
	Fourth,	Cavalry,	Seventh,	Arkansas.
	First,	Cavalry,	Seventh,	Arkansas.
Molineaux, E. L.	First,	Fourth,	Nineteenth,	Gulf.
	Third,	Fourth,	Nineteenth,	Gulf.
	Second,	Second,	Nineteenth,	Gulf.
	Second,	Second,	Nineteenth,	Army Shen.
	Second,	Grover's, Dist. Savannah, Ga.,		South.
Montgomery, Jas.	Third,	First, Morris Island, S. C.,	Tenth,	South.
	Fourth,	Morris Island, S. C.,	Tenth,	South.
	Third,	Morris Island, S. C.,	Tenth,	South.
	Montgomery's,	Hilton Head District,	Tenth,	South.
	Third,	Second Dist. Florida,	Tenth,	South.
Montgomery, M.	Third,	Kimball's, Provisional,	Sixteenth,	Tennessee.
	Third,	Kimball's, Dist. E. Ark.,	Sixteenth,	Tennessee.
		District Eastern Arkansas,	Sixteenth,	Tennessee.
	First,	Fourth,	Sixteenth,	Tennessee.
	Second,	First,	Seventeenth,	Tennessee.
Moon, J. C.	First,	First,	Twenty-fifth,	Texas.
	Second,	First,	Twenty-fifth,	Texas.
Moor, A.	Second,	District Kanawha,		West Virginia.
	First,	Fourth,		West Virginia.
	First,	First, Infantry,		West Virginia.
Moore, A. S.	First,	Second, Cavalry,		West Virginia.
Moore, David	Fourth,	District Memphis, Fifth,	Sixteenth,	Tennessee.
	First,	Third,	Sixteenth,	Tennessee.
	First,	Second, Det'mt Army Tenn.,		Cumberland.
		Second, Det'mt Army Tenn.,		Cumberland.
Moore, F. W.	First,	Second, Army Kentucky,		Ohio.
	First,	Fourth,	Thirteenth,	Gulf.
		Fourth,	Thirteenth,	Gulf.
	Third,	Third,	Nineteenth,	Gulf.
	Third,	Second,	Thirteenth,	Gulf.
Moore, J. B.	First,	Provisional,	Seventeenth,	Gulf.
	First,	Third, Det'mt Army Tenn.		Cumberland.
		Third, Det'mt Army Tenn.		Cumberland.
	First,	Third,	Sixteenth,	Gulf.
		Third,	Sixteenth,	Gulf.
Moore, J. H.	Second,	First,	Fourth,	Cumberland.
Moore, M. F.	Second,	Second,	Fourteenth,	Cumberland.
	Second,	First,	Fourteenth,	Cumberland.
	Third,	First,	Fourteenth,	Cumberland.
Moore, O. H.	First,	Second,	Twenty-third,	Ohio.
	First,	Second,	Twenty-third,	North Carolina.
	Second,	Second,	Twenty-third,	North Carolina.
		Second,	Twenty-third,	North Carolina.
Moore, R. M.	Third,	Third,	Sixteenth,	Tennessee.
	Third,	Third, Det'mt Army Tenn.		Cumberland.
	Third,	Second,	Sixteenth,	Gulf.
Moore, S. A.	Third,	Second,	Second,	Potomac.
Moore, W. P.	Cavalry,	District Baton Rouge, La.,		Gulf.
Morehead, T. G.	First,	Second,	Second,	Potomac.
	Third,	Second,	Second,	Potomac.
	Second,	Second,	Second,	Potomac.
Morgan, E. D.				New York.
Morgan, G. W.		Seventh,		Army Ohio.
		Cumberland, Dist. W. Va.,		Ohio.
		Ninth, Right Wing,	Thirteenth,	Tennessee.
		Third, Yazoo Expedition,		Tennessee.
		Ninth,	Thirteenth,	Tennessee.
Morgan, J. D.	Fourth,	First, Mil. Dist. Cairo,		Missouri.
	Second,	First,		Army Miss.
		First,		Army Miss.
	First,	Fourth,		Army Miss.
	Second,	Thirteenth,		Army Ohio.
	First,	Fourth, Centre,	Fourteenth,	Cumberland.
		Fourth,	Fourteenth,	Cumberland.

Name	Brigade	Division, District, Etc.	Corps	Army or Dept.
		Second,	Reserve,	Cumberland.
	First,	Second,	Fourteenth,	Cumberland.
		Second,	Fourteenth,	Cumberland.
Morgan, Jos. S.	First,	Fourth,	Nineteenth,	Gulf.
Morgan, Thos. J.	1st Colored,	District Etowah,		Cumberland.
Morgan, W. H.	Second,	Dist. Memphis, Fifth,	Sixteenth,	Tennessee.
	Third,	First Cavalry,	Sixteenth,	Tennessee.
Morrell, Geo. W.	First,	Fitz, John Porter's,		Potomac.
	Second,	First,	Third,	Potomac.
		First,	Fifth,	Potomac.
Morrell, Jos.		District Rolla, Mo.,		Missouri.
Morrill, John	First,	Fourth,	Sixteenth,	Tennessee.
Morris, Dwight	Third,	Third,	Second,	Potomac.
Morris, L. O.	Second,	Def. North Potomac,	Mil. Dist. Wash.,	Potomac.
	Second,	Defenses North Potomac,	Twenty-second,	Washington.
	Fourth,	First,	Second,	Potomac.
Morris, O. H.	Third,	First,	Second,	Potomac.
	Fourth,	First,	Second,	Potomac.
Morris, T. A.	Indiana,.	Army of Occupation,		West Virginia.
Morris, W. H.	Second,	First,	Eighth,	Middle Dept.
	First,	Third,	Third,	Potomac.
	First,	Third,	Sixth,	Potomac.
Morris, W. W.	2nd Separate,		Eighth,	Middle Dept.
		Defenses Baltimore, Md.,	Eighth,	Middle Dept.
			Eighth,	Middle Dept.
Morrison, A. B.	First,	Second,	Seventh,	Arkansas.
Morrison, D.	First,	First,	Ninth,	Potomac.
	First,	First,	Ninth,	Ohio.
Morrow, H. A.	First,	First,	First,	Potomac.
	First,	Third,	Fifth,	Potomac.
	Third,	Third,	Fifth,	Potomac.
Morton, St. Clair	Pioneer,			Cumberland.
Morton, Thos.	Second,	Second,		Army Tenn.
Mott, Gershom	Third,	Second,	Third,	Potomac.
	First,	Fourth,	Second,	Potomac.
		Fourth,	Second,	Potomac.
		Third,	Second,	Potomac.
			Second,	Potomac.
Mott, S. R.	Second,	Fourth,	Twenty-third,	Ohio.
	Second,	First,	Twenty-third,	Ohio.
	First,	Second,	Twenty-third,	Ohio.
	First,	Second,	Fifteenth,	Tennessee.
Moulton, O.		Sub. District Pamlico, N. C.,		Va. and N. C.
Mower, J. A.	Second,	Second,		Army Miss.
	Second,	Eighth,	Sixteenth,	Tennessee.
	Second,	Third,	Fifteenth,	Tennessee.
	Second,	First,	Sixteenth,	Tennessee.
		First,	Seventeenth,	Tennessee.
			Seventeenth,	Tennessee.
		First, Det'mt Army Tenn.,		Cumberland.
		Third, Det'mt Army Tenn.,		Cumberland.
			Twentieth,	Army Georgia.
			Thirteenth,	Gulf.
Mudd, J. J.	Cavalry,			Gulf.
	Second,	Cavalry,		
Muhleck, G. A.	First,	Second,	First,	Army of Va.
	First,	Second,	Eleventh,	Potomac.
Mulholland, St. C. A.	Fourth,	First,	Second,	Potomac.
Mulcahy, Thos.	First,	First,	Eighteenth,	Va. and N. C.
Mulligan, J. A.	Fifth,	First,	Eighth,	Middle Dept.
	Mulligan's,	First,		West Virginia.
		Second,		West Virginia.
		Third,		West Virginia.
Murphy, J. K.	Third,	First,	Twelfth,	Potomac.
Murphy, M.	Third,	First,	Seventh,	Virginia.
	First,	King's,	Twenty-second,	Washington.
	Second,	King's,	Twenty-second,	Washington.
	Fourth,	Second,	Second,	Potomac.
	Second,	Second,	Second,	Potomac.
Murphy, R. C.	Second,	Second,		Army Miss.
Murray, C. D.	First,	Dist. Memphis, Fifth,	Sixteenth,	Tennessee.
	First,	Third,	Sixteenth,	Tennessee.
Murray, E. H.	Third,	Third,	Cavalry,	Cumberland.
		Third,	Cavalry,	Cumberland.
	First,	Third,	Cavalry,	Mil. Div. Miss.
	Third,	Third,	Cavalry,	Mil. Div. Miss.
Nagle, Jas.	First,	Second,		North Carolina.
	First,	Second,	Ninth,	Potomac.
	First,	Second,	Ninth,	Ohio.

Name	Brigade	Division, District, Etc.	Corps	Army or Dept.
Naglee, H. M.	First,	Casey's,		Potomac.
	First,	Third,	Fourth,	Potomac.
	First,	Second,	Fourth,	Potomac.
	Naglee's,			North Carolina.
		Second,	Eighteenth,	North Carolina.
		First, St. Helena Island,	Tenth,	South.
		Forces St. Helena Island,	Tenth,	South.
			Seventh,	Virginia.
		District Virginia,		Va. and N. C.
Neely, G. W.	Detached,	Dist. Northeast La.,		Tennessee.
Neafie, A.	Third,	Second,	Nineteenth,	Army Shen.
Negley, J. S.	Fifth,	Second,		Pennsylvania.
	Fourth,	McCook's,		Army Ohio.
	Seventh,			Army Ohio.
	Seventh,	Second,		Army Ohio.
Negley, J. S.	7th Indpt.,			Army Ohio.
		Eighth,		Army Ohio.
		Second, Centre,	Fourteenth,	Cumberland.
		Second,	Fourteenth,	Cumberland.
Neibling, J. M.	Third,	First,	Fourteenth,	Cumberland.
Neill, T. H.	Third,	Second,	Sixth,	Potomac.
		Second,	Sixth,	Potomac.
Nelson, Wm.		Fourth,		Army Ohio.
		Army of Kentucky,		Ohio.
Nevin, D. J.	Third,	Third,	Sixth,	Potomac.
Newberry, W. C.	Second,	Third,	Ninth,	Potomac.
	Second,	First,	Ninth,	Potomac.
	First,	Second,	Cavalry,	Potomac.
Newton, John	Third,	Franklin's,		Army Potomac.
	Third,	First,	First,	Potomac.
	Third,	First,		Rappahannock.
	Third,	First,	Sixth,	Potomac.
		First,	Sixth,	Potomac.
		Third,	Sixth,	Potomac.
			First,	Potomac.
		Second,	Fourth,	Cumberland.
		District Key West, Fla.,		Gulf.
Nichols, G. F.	First,	Third,	Twenty-fourth,	Virginia.
Nichols, G. S.	Second,	First,	Cavalry,	Potomac.
	Second,	First,	Cavalry,	Army Shen.
Nickerson, F. S.	Third,	Second,	Nineteenth,	Gulf.
	First,	Second,	Nineteenth,	Gulf.
		Second,	Nineteenth,	Gulf.
	First,	Third,	Nineteenth,	Gulf.
		Third,	Nineteenth,	Gulf.
Noble, W. H.	Second,	First,	Eleventh,	Potomac.
	Second,	South End Folly Island,	Tenth,	South.
	Second,	Forces Folly Island, S. C.,	Tenth,	South.
	First,	First, District Florida,	Tenth,	South.
	4th Separate,	District Florida,		South.
Nodine, R. H.	First,	Third,	Fourth,	Cumberland.
Northcott, R. S.	First,	First, Infantry,		West Virginia.
Noyes, E. J.	Cavalry,	U. S. Forces Texas,		Gulf.
Nugent, Robt.	Second,	First,	Second,	Potomac.
Oberteuffer, J. H.	Third,	Defenses North Potomac,	Twenty-second,	Washington.
O'Brien, T.	First,	Second,	Second,	Potomac.
	Second,	Second,	Second,	Potomac.
O'Dowd, John	Third,	Second,	Twenty-third,	Ohio.
Oglesby, R. J.	Second,	Mil. Dist. Cairo,		Missouri.
	First,	First, Mil. Dist. Cairo,		Missouri.
	First,	First,		Army Tenn.
	Third,	First,		Army Tenn.
	Second,	Second,		Army Tenn.
	Second,	Second, District Corinth,		Tennessee.
		Left Wing,	Sixteenth,	Tennessee.
Olcott, E.	Second,	First,	Sixth,	Army Shen.
Oley, J. H.	Third,	Fourth,		West Virginia.
	First,	Second Cavalry,		West Virginia.
	Third,	Second Cavalry,		West Virginia.
	1st Separate,	District Kanawha,		West Virginia.
Oliver, J. M.	First,	Sixth,		Army Tenn.
	Second,	Sixth,		Army Tenn.
	Second,	Fourth,	Fifteenth,	Tennessee.
	Third,	Fourth,	Fifteenth,	Tennessee.
	First,	Fourth,	Fifteenth,	Tennessee.
	Third,	Second,	Fifteenth,	Tennessee.
		Second,	Fifteenth,	Tennessee.
Olmstead, W. A.	First,	Second,	Second,	Potomac.

Name	Brigade	Division, District, Etc.	Corps	Army or Dept.
Opdyke, E.	First,	Second,	Fourth,	Cumberland.
		Second,	Fourth,	Cumberland.
Ord, E. O. C.	Third,	McCall's,		Potomac.
	Third,	Second,	First,	Potomac.
	Third,	Second,		Rappahannock.
		Ord's,		Rappahannock.
		Second,		Army Tenn.
		Second, District Corinth,		Army Tenn.
		District Jackson,		Army Tenn.
			Thirteenth,	Tennessee.
			Thirteenth,	Gulf.
			Eighteenth,	Va. and N. C.
			Twenty-fourth,	Virginia.
				Virginia.
Orff, H.	First,	Third,	Thirteenth,	Gulf.
Orme, W. W.	Second,	Third, Army Frontier,		Missouri.
	Second,	Herron's,	Thirteenth,	Tennessee.
	Second,	Second,	Thirteenth,	Gulf.
O'Rorke, P. H.	Third,	Second,	Fifth,	Potomac.
Orr, J. M.	First,	First,	Twenty-third,	Ohio.
	First,	First,	Provisional Corps,	North Carolina.
	First,	First,	Twenty-third,	North Carolina.
Osband, E. D.	Cavalry,	District Vicksburg, Miss.,		Tennessee.
	Third,	Cavalry, West Tenn.,		Tennessee.
		Cavalry, West Tenn.,		Tennessee.
Osborn, F. A.	Third,	Second,	Tenth,	Va. and N. C.
Osborn, T. O.	Third,	Second, St. Helena Island,	Tenth,	South.
	Second,	Morris Island, S. C.,	Tenth,	South.
	First,	Third,	Eighteenth,	Va. and N. C.
	First,	First,	Twenty-fourth,	Virginia.
	First,	First,	Twenty-fourth,	Virginia.
Osterhaus, P. J.	Second,	Army Southwest Mo.,		Missouri.
	First,	First, Army Southwest Mo.,		Missouri.
		Third, Army S. W. Mo.,		Missouri.
		Dist. Eastern Ark.,		Missouri.
	First,	First, Dist. Eastern Ark.,		Tennessee.
		Ninth,	Thirteenth,	Tennessee.
		First,	Fifteenth,	Tennessee.
			Fifteenth,	Tennessee.
Otis, E. S.	First,	Second,	Fifth,	Potomac.
Owen, J. T.	Third,	Third,	Second,	Potomac.
		Third,	Second,	Potomac.
	Second,	Second,	Second,	Potomac.
		Second,	Second,	Potomac.
Owen, R.	First,	Tenth,	Thirteenth,	Tennessee.
	First,	Fourth,	Thirteenth,	Gulf.
Ozborn, L.	Second,	District Jackson,		Army Tenn.
Packer, W. W.	First,	First,	Twentieth,	Cumberland.
Paine, C. I.	Third,	Cavalry,		Gulf.
Paine, C. J.	First,	First,	Nineteenth,	Gulf.
		Third,	Eighteenth,	Va. and N. C.
		First,	Twenty-fifth,	Virginia.
		Third,	Twenty-fifth,	Virginia.
		Paine's,	Terry's Prov'l,	North Carolina.
		Third,	Tenth,	North Carolina.
Paine, E. A.	Third,	First, Mil. Dist. Cairo,		Missouri.
		Fourth,		Army Miss.
		First,		Army Miss.
		District W. Kentucky.		Ohio.
Paine, H. E.	Second,	Third,	Nineteenth,	Gulf.
Palmer, I. N.	Third,	Casey's,		Potomac.
	Third,	Third,	Fourth,	Potomac.
	First,	First,	Fourth,	Potomac.
			Eighteenth,	North Carolina.
				North Carolina.
		Defenses New Berne, N. C.		Va. and N. C.
		Dist. North Carolina,		Va. and N. C.
		Sub. Dist. New Berne,		North Carolina.
Palmer, I. N.		Sub. Dist. Beaufort, N. C.,		North Carolina.
		First, Beaufort, N. C.,		North Carolina.
Palmer, J. M.		Second,		Army Miss.
		Third,		Army Miss.
	First,	First,		Army Miss.
		First,		Army Miss.
		Thirteenth,		Army Ohio.
		Second, Left Wing,	Fourteenth,	Cumberland.
		Second,	Twenty-first,	Cumberland.
			Twenty-first,	Cumberland.

Name	Brigade	Division, District, Etc.	Corps	Army or Dept.
		First,	Fourth,	Cumberland.
			Fourteenth,	Cumberland.
Palmer, O. H.	Second,	Third,	Second,	Potomac.
Palmer, W. J.	Third,	Sixth,	Cavalry,	Mil. Div. Miss.
	First,	Cavalry, Dist. East. Tenn.		Cumberland.
Pardee, A. Jr.	First,	Second,	Twelfth,	Cumberland.
	First,	Second,	Twentieth,	Cumberland.
Parke, J. G.	Third,	N. Carolina Exp.		
		Third,		North Carolina.
		Third,	Ninth,	Potomac.
		Third,	Ninth,	Ohio.
			Ninth,	Ohio.
			Ninth,	Tennessee.
			Ninth,	Potomac.
				Army Potomac.
		District Alexandria,	Twenty-second,	Washington.
			Twenty-second,	Washington.
Parker, F. W.	Third,	Second,	Tenth,	Va. and N. C.
	First,	Second,	Tenth,	North Carolina.
Parker, J. R.	Second,	Fourth,	Thirteenth,	Gulf.
Parker, T. J.	First,	First,	Second,	Potomac.
Parrish, C. S.	Second,	First,	Twenty-third,	Ohio.
	Fourth,	Second,	Twenty-third,	Ohio.
Parrott, E. A.	Third,	Second,	Twentieth,	Cumberland.
Patrick, J. H.	First,	Second,	Twelfth,	Potomac.
Patrick, M. R.	Second,	McDowell's,		Potomac.
	Second,	Third,	First,	Potomac.
	Second,	King's,		Rappahannock.
	Third,	First,	Third,	Army of Va.
	Third,	First,	First,	Potomac.
		Provost Guard,		Army Potomac.
Patrick, M. T.	First,	Third,	Cavalry,	Cumberland.
Patterson, F. E.	Third,	Second,	Third,	Potomac.
Patterson, J. N.	Third,	First,	Eighteenth,	Va. and N. C.
	Second,	Third,	Twenty-fourth,	Virginia.
Patterson, M. L.	Third,	Fourth,	Twenty-third,	Ohio.
Patterson, Robt.				Pennsylvania.
Patterson, Thos.	First,	Third, Army S. W. Mo.,		Missouri.
Paul, G. R.	Third,	First,	First,	Potomac.
	First,	Second,	First,	Potomac.
		First,	First,	Potomac.
Payne, O. H.	Second,	First,	Twenty-first,	Cumberland.
	Second,	Third,	Fourth,	Cumberland.
Peabody, E.	First,	Sixth,		Army Tenn.
Pearce, J. S.	Second,	Second,	Fourteenth,	Cumberland.
Pearson, A. L.	First,	First,	Fifth,	Potomac.
	Third,	First,	Fifth,	Potomac.
Pease, P.	Third,	Third,	Sixteenth,	Tennessee.
Pease, W. R.	Third,	Def. N. Potomac,	Mil. Dist. Wash.,	Potomac.
	Third,	Defenses N. Potomac,	Twenty-second,	Washington.
	First,	Second,	Seventh,	Virginia.
Peck, J. J.	Third,	Buell (Keys),		Potomac.
	Third,	First,	Fourth,	Potomac.
		Second,	Fourth,	Potomac.
		Div. at Suffolk, Va.,	Seventh,	Virginia.
		Dist. N. Carolina,		Va. and N. C.
Pennington, A. C.	First,	Third,	Cavalry,	Potomac.
	First,	Third,	Cavalry,	Army Shen.
Pennypacker, C. D.	First,	Fourth,	Twenty-third,	Ohio.
	Third,	First,	Cavalry,	Ohio.
		First,	Cavalry,	Ohio.
Pennypacker, G.	Second,	Second,	Tenth,	Va. and N. C.
	Second,	Second,	Twenty-fourth,	Virginia.
	Second,	Ames,	Terry's Prov'l,	North Carolina.
Penrose, Wm. H.	First,	First,	Sixth,	Potomac.
	First,	First,	Sixth,	Army Shen.
Perczel, N.	Second,	Second,		Army Miss.
	Second,	Third,		Army Miss.
Perkins, J. G.	First,	First,	Twenty-fifth,	Texas.
	Third,	First,	Twenty-fifth,	Texas.
		First,	Twenty-fifth,	Texas.
Phelps, C. E.	Second,	Third,	First,	Potomac.
	Third,	Second,	Fifth,	Potomac.
Phelps, E. H.	Third,	Third,	Fourteenth,	Cumberland.
Phelps, J. E.	First,	Cavalry, West Tenn.,		Tennessee.
	Second,	Cavalry, West Tenn.,		Tennessee.
		Cavalry, West Tenn.,		Tennessee.
Phelps, J. W.		Ship Island Expedition,		
	First,			Gulf.

Name	Brigade	Division, District, Etc.	Corps	Army or Dept.
Phelps, Walter, Jr.	First,	First,	First,	Potomac.
Phillips, J. F.		Dist. Central Mo.,		Missouri.
Phillips, J. J.	Second,	Second,	Sixteenth,	Tennessee.
Phillips, W. A.	First,	District Frontier,		Missouri.
	Third,	First, Army Frontier,		Missouri.
	First,	District Frontier,	Seventh,	Arkansas.
	Indian,	District Frontier,	Seventh,	Arkansas.
	Third,	Third,	Seventh,	Arkansas.
	Indian,	Dist. South Kansas,		Kansas.
Piatt, A. S.	Piatt's,	Whipple's Mil. Dist. Wash.		Potomac.
	First,	Third,	Third,	Potomac.
Pickett, J.		Sub. Dist. Pamlico, N. C.,		Va. and N. C.
Pierce, B. R.	Second,	First,	Third,	Potomac.
	First,	Second,	Second,	Potomac.
	Second,	Third,	Second,	Potomac.
Pierce, E. W.	Second,	First,	Ninth,	Potomac.
	Second,	First,	Ninth,	Ohio.
Pierce, F. E.	Second,	Third,	Second,	Potomac.
	First,	Second,	Second,	Potomac.
	Third,	Second,	Second,	Potomac.
Pierson, G. N.	Second,	First,	Eighteenth,	North Carolina
Piper, Alex.	Third,	Defenses S. Potomac,	Twenty-second,	Washington.
	Third,	Defenses N. Potomac,	Twenty-second,	Washington.
	First,	Second,	Eighteeenth,	Va. and N. C.
	Second,	Third,	Eighteeenth,	Va. and N. C
Pile, W. A.		Dist. Port Hudson, La.,		Gulf.
	First,	First, U. S. C. T., W. Fla.,		Gulf.
Pinckney, B.	First,	Third, Army Frontier,		Missouri.
Plaisted, H. M.	First,	Morris Island, S. C.,	Tenth,	South.
	Second,	First,	Tenth,	Va. and N. C.
	Third,	First,	Tenth,	Va. and N. C.
	Third,	First,	Twenty-fourth,	Virginia.
Pleasants, H.	First,	Second,	Ninth,	Potomac.
Pleasanton, A.	Second,	Cavalry,		Potomac.
		Cavalry,		Potomac.
		First,	Cavalry,	Potomac.
			Cavalry,	Potomac.
		Dist. St. Louis, Mo.,		Missouri.
		Dist. Central Mo.,		Missouri.
Plummer, J. B.		Fifth,		Army Miss.
	Second,	First,		Army Miss.
	Second,	Second,		Army Miss.
	First,	Third,		Army Miss.
		Third,		Army Miss.
Poe, O. M.	Third,	First,	Third,	Potomac.
	First,	First,	Ninth,	Potomac.
	First,	First	Ninth,	Ohio.
Pomutz, G.	Third,	Fourth,	Seventeenth,	Tennessee.
Pond, F. B.	First,	First,	Tenth,	Va. and N. C.
		Third,	Tenth,	Va. and N. C.
Pope, John				Army Miss.
				Army of Va.
				Northwest.
Porter, A.	First,	Second,		Army N. E. Va
		Provost Guard,		Potomac.
Porter, Burr	Second,	Abercrombie's,	Twenty-second,	Washington.
	Porter's,	Gurney's,	Seventh,	Virginia.
	Second,	Second,	Fourth,	Potomac.
Porter, F. J.		Porter's,		Potomac.
		First,	Third,	Potomac.
			Fifth,	Potomac.
Porter, Jas. R.	First,	Third,	First,	Potomac.
Porter, P. A.	2nd Separate		Eighth,	Middle Dept.
	Second,	Maryland Heights,		West Virginia..
Post, P. S.	First,	First Right Wing,	Fourteenth,	Cumberland.
	First,	First,	Twentieth,	Cumberland.
	Third,	First,	Fourth,	Cumberland.
	Second,	Third,	Fourth,	Cumberland.
		Third,	Fourth,	Cumberland.
Potter, Andrew	First,	Independent,	Twenty-fourth,	Virginia.
Potter, E. E.		U. S. Forces Norfolk and Portsmouth,		Va. and N. C.
	3rd Separate,	Dist. Hilton Head, S. C.,		South.
	2nd Separate,	Dist. Beaufort, S. C.,		South.
	First,	Coast Division,		South.
Potter, J. H.	Second,	Third,	Third,	Potomac.
	Second.	Third,	Twenty-fourth,	Virginia.
		Provisional,		Va. and N. C.

Name	Brigade	Division, District, Etc.	Corps	Army or Dept.
Potter, R. B.		Second,	Ninth,	Potomac.
		Second,	Ninth,	Ohio.
		Second,	Ninth,	Tenn.
			Ninth,	Ohio.
			Ninth,	Potomac.
Potts, B. F.	Second,	Third,	Seventeenth,	Tennessee.
	First,	Fourth,	Seventeenth,	Tennessee.
		Fourth,	Seventeenth,	Tennessee.
Powell, E. H.	Second,	Third,	Twenty-fifth,	Virginia.
Powell, W. H.	Third,	Second Cavalry,		West Virginia.
	Second,	Second Cavalry,		West Virginia.
		Second Cavalry,		West Virginia.
Powers, C. J.	Second,	Third,	Second,	Potomac.
Prather, A. W.	First,	First,	Twenty-third,	North Carolina.
Pratt, C. E.	First,	Second,	Sixth,	Potomac,
	Light,		Sixth,	Potomac,
Prentiss, B. M.		Sixth,		Army Tenn.
		District Eastern Ark.,		Tennessee.
		District Eastern Ark.,	Thirteenth,	Tennessee.
Preston, A. W.	Second,	Third,	Cavalry,	Potomac.
Price, Francis.	Third,	Third,	Second,	Potomac.
Price, R. B.	Cavalry,	Mil. Dist. Washington,		Potomac.
	Indpt. Cavalry,		Twenty-second,	Washington.
	Second,	Cavalry,	Twenty-second,	Washington.
Price, S. W.	Third,	Third, Left Wing,	Fourteenth,	Cumberland.
Prince, H.	Second,	Second,	Second,	Army of Va.
		Second,	Second,	Army of Va.
		District of Cairo,		Tennessee.
		Fifth,	Eighteenth,	North Carolina.
		District Pamlico, N. C.,		North Carolina.
		Second,	Third,	Potomac.
		Third,	Sixth,	Potomac.
		District Columbus,	Sixteenth,	Tennessee.
Pugh, I. C.	First,	Fourth,		Army Tenn.
	First,	Fourth, Right Wing,	Thirteenth,	Tennessee.
	First,	Fourth,	Seventeenth,	Tennessee.
	First,	Fourth,	Sixteenth,	Tennessee.
	First,	Fourth,	Thirteenth,	Tennessee.
	Second,	Fourth,	Seventeenth,	Tennessee.
Pulford, John	Second,	Third,	Second,	Potomac.
Purington, G. A.	First,	Third,	Cavalry,	Army Shen.
Putnam, H.	Third,	Seventh,	Seventeenth,	Tennessee.
Putnam, H. S.	First,	U. S. Forces Folly Island,	Tenth,	South.
Quinn, F.		Sixth,		Army Tenn.
Quinn, T.	Second,	First Cavalry,		West Virginia.
Quinby, I. F.		Sixth,		Army Tenn.
		Dist. Corinth, West Tenn.,		Army Tenn.
		Dist. Mississippi, W. Tenn.,		Tennessee.
		Third,		Army Miss.
		District Corinth,	Thirteenth,	Tennessee.
		Seventh, Left Wing,	Thirteenth,	Tennessee.
		Seventh,	Sixteenth,	Tennessee.
		Seventh,	Seventeenth,	Tennessee.
Raffen, A. W.	Second,	Second,	Fourteenth,	Cumberland.
Rafferty, Thos.	Second,	Second,	Third,	Potomac.
Ralston, L. W.	Second,	Second,	Twelfth,	Cumberland.
Raith, J.	Third,	First,		Tennessee.
Ramsey, John	Fourth,	Second,	Second,	Potomac.
	Fourth,	First,	Second,	Potomac.
	Third,	Third,	Second,	Potomac.
		First,	Second,	Potomac.
Rand, A. A.	Provisional,		Eighteenth,	Va. and N. C.
Randall, F. V.	Third,	Third,	First,	Potomac.
Ransom, T. E. G.		Left Wing,	Sixteenth,	Tennessee.
	Second,	Sixth,	Sixteenth,	Tennessee.
	Second,	Sixth,	Seventeenth,	Tennessee.
	Third,	Second,	Thirteenth,	Gulf.
		Fourth,	Thirteenth,	Gulf.
		Fourth,	Sixteenth,	Tennessee.
			Seventeenth,	Tennessee.
		First,	Seventeenth,	Tennessee.
Ratliff, R. W.	Fourth,	First, District Ky.,	Twenty-third,	Ohio.
Raulston, J. B.	First.	First,	Eighteenth,	Va. and N. C.
	First,	Third,	Twenty-fourth,	Virginia.
Raulston, W. C.	Second,	Third,	Ninth,	Potomac.
Raum, G. B.	Second,	Seventh,	Seventeenth,	Tennessee.
	Second,	Second,	Seventeenth,	Tennessee.
	Second,	Third,	Fifteenth,	Tennessee.

Name	Brigade	Division, District, Etc.	Corps	Army or Dept.
Ray, D. M.	Second,	First,	Cavalry,	Cumberland.
Raynor, W. H.	Second,	Third,	Thirteenth,	Gulf.
Reardon, J. S.	Third,	First,		Army Tenn.
Redfield, J. H.	First,	Cavalry,		Gulf.
Reed, J. H.	Separate,	Dismounted Cavalry,	Seventh,	Arkansas.
Reed, W. P.	Reed's,	Baird's, Army Ky.,		Cumberland.
	Second,	First,	Reserve,	Cumberland.
Reeve, F. A.	First,	Third,	Twenty-third,	Ohio.
Reid, H. T.	Third,	Sixth, District Corinth,		Army Tenn.
		District Corinth,		Tennessee.
		District Corinth,	Thirteenth	Tennessee.
	First,	Sixth,	Seventeenth,	Tennessee.
Reilly, J. W.	Second,	First,	Twenty-third,	Ohio.
	First,	Third,	Twenty-third,	Ohio.
		Third,	Twenty-third,	North Carolina.
Reno, J. L.	Second,	North Carolina Exp.,		
		Second,		North Carolina.
		Second,	Ninth,	Potomac.
			Ninth,	Potomac.
Revere, J. W.	Second,	Second,	Third,	Potomac.
	Third,	Second,	Third,	Potomac.
Revere, W. H., Jr.	First,	Third,	Tenth,	North Carolina.
Reynolds, J. F.	First,	McCall's,		Potomac.
	First,	Second,	First,	Potomac.
	First,	McCall's,		Rappahannock.
	First,	Third,	Fifth,	Potomac.
		Third,	Third,	Army of Va.
			First,	Potomac.
Reynolds, J. J.		Cheat Mountain District,		West Va.
		Fifth, Centre,	Fourteenth,	Cumberland.
		Fifth,	Fourteenth,	Cumberland.
		Fourth,	Fourteenth,	Cumberland.
		Fourth,	Nineteenth,	Gulf.
			Nineteenth,	Gulf.
		District Morganza,		Gulf.
			Reserve,	Gulf.
			Seventh,	Arkansas.
				Arkansas.
Rhodes, F. L.	Fourth,	District Jackson,		Tennessee.
Rice, A. V.	Third,	Second,	Fifteenth,	Tennessee.
Rice, E. W.	First,	Second,	Sixteenth,	Tennessee.
		Second,	Sixteenth,	Tennessee.
	First,	Fourth,	Fifteenth,	Tennessee.
Rice, J. C.	Second,	First,	First,	Potomac.
		First,	First,	Potomac.
	Third,	First,	Fifth,	Potomac.
	Second,	Fourth,	Fifth,	Potomac.
Rice, R. H.	First,	Third,	Twenty-fourth,	Virginia.
Rice, S. A.	Second,	Thirteenth,	Thirteenth,	Tennessee.
	Second,	Thirteenth,	Sixteenth,	Tennessee.
	Second,	Third, Arkansas Exp.,		Tennessee.
		Third, Arkansas Exp.,		Tennessee.
	First,	Third,	Seventh,	Arkansas.
	Second,	Third,	Seventh,	Arkansas.
Richardson, I. B.	Fourth,	First,		Army N. E. Va.
	Richardson's,			Div. Potomac.
	First,	Heintzelman's,		Potomac.
		First,	Second,	Potomac.
Richardson, J. P.	Third,	Second,	Nineteenth,	Army Shen.
	Second,	Grover's Dist. Savannah,		South.
Richardson, R. M.	Second,	First Cavalry,		West Virginia.
Richmond, J.	Third,	District Jackson,	Sixteenth,	Tennessee.
	Second,	Third,	Sixteenth,	Tennessee.
	Second,	Kimball's Provisional,	Sixteenth,	Tennessee.
	Second,	Kimball's, Dist. East. Ark.,	Sixteenth,	Tennessee.
Richmond, N. P.	First,	Third,	Cavalry,	Potomac.
Rickards, Wm., Jr.	Third,	Second,	Twentieth,	Cumberland.
Ricketts, J. B.	First,	Ord's,		Rappahannock.
		Ord's,		Rappahannock.
		Second,	Third,	Army of Va.
			Third,	Army of Va.
		Second,	First,	Potomac.
	Third,		Sixth,	Potomac.
			Sixth,	Potomac.
	Third,		Sixth,	Army Shen.
			Sixth,	Army Shen.
Rigg, H. P.	First,	Second,	Second,	Potomac.

Name	Brigade	Division, District, Etc.	Corps	Army or Dept.
Rinaker, J. I.	Second,	Second,	Sixteenth,	Tennessee.
	First,	Second, Det'mt Army Tenn.,		Cumberland.
	First,	Second,	Sixteenth,	Gulf.
Ripley, E. H.	Second,	Second,	Eighteenth,	Va. and N. C.
	First,	Third,	Twenty-fourth,	Virginia.
Ritter, J. F.	Fourth,	Dist. Memphis, Fifth,	Sixteenth,	Tennessee.
	Reserve,	1st Cavalry, Ark. Exp.,		Tennessee.
	First,	First, Cavalry,	Seventh,	Arkansas.
	Third,	First,	Seventh,	Arkansas.
	Second,	Cavalry,	Seventh,	Arkansas.
Ritter, R.	First,	Third,	Thirteenth,	Gulf.
Roberts, B. S.		Third,	Eighth,	Middle Dept.
	Fourth Separate,		Eighth,	Middle Dept.
			Nineteenth,	Gulf.
		Cavalry,		Gulf.
		District West Tennessee,		Tennessee.
		Cavalry, Dist. West Tenn.,		Tennessee.
Roberts, C. W.	First,	First,	Fifth,	Potomac.
Roberts, G. W.	First,	First,		Army Miss.
	First,	Thirteenth,		Army Ohio.
	Third,	Third, Right Wing,	Fourteenth,	Cumberland.
Roberts, R. B.	First,	Third,	First,	Potomac.
	First,	Third,	Fifth,	Potomac.
Roberts, R. P.	Third,	First,	Second,	Potomac.
Roberts, S. H.	First,	Getty's Norfolk and Ports.,		Va. and N. C.
		District Currituck,		Va. and N. C.
	Third,	First,	Eighteenth,	Va. and N. C.
	Third,	Third,	Twenty-fourth,	Virginia.
Roberts, T. A.	Third,	First,	Third,	Potomac.
Robertson, W. B.	First,	Third,	Second,	Potomac.
Robinson, E. J.	Second,	Def. Nash. and Chatta. R. R.,		Cumberland.
Robinson, G. P.	Second,	First,	Ninth,	Potomac.
	Third,	First,	Ninth,	Potomac.
Robinson, H.	Third,	Cavalry,		Gulf.
Robinson, J. C.	Robinson's,			Virginia.
	Second,	Third,	Third,	Potomac.
	First,	Third,	Third,	Potomac.
	First,	First,	Third,	Potomac.
		Second,	First,	Potomac.
		Second,	Fifth,	Potomac.
Robinson, J. S.	First,	Third,	Eleventh,	Cumberland.
	Third,	First,	Twentieth,	Cumberland.
Robinson, M. S.	Second,	Fourth,	Fourteenth,	Cumberland.
Robinson, W. W.	First,	First,	First,	Potomac.
	Fourth,	First,	First,	Potomac.
	First,	Fourth,	Fifth,	Potomac.
Robinson, Z. B.	Second,	Third,	Eighteenth,	Va. and N. C.
Rodgers, R. S.	Third,	First,		West Virginia.
Rodgers, W. F.	Third,	First,	First,	Potomac.
Rodman, I. P.		Third,	Ninth,	Potomac.
Rogers, G. C.	Second,	Fourth,	Seventeenth,	Tennessee.
Root, A. R.	First,	Second,	First,	Potomac.
	Third,	Third,	Fifth,	Potomac.
Rose, T. E.	First,	First,	Fourth,	Cumberland.
	Second,	Second,	Twentieth,	Cumberland.
Rosecrans, W. S.	Rosecrans',	Army of Occupation,		West Virginia.
		Army of Occupation,		West Virginia.
				Western Va.
				Ohio.
				Mountains.
				Tennessee.
		District Corinth,		Army Miss.
				Army Cumberland.
				Cumberland.
			Fourteenth,	Cumberland.
				Missouri.
Ross, L. F.	Third,	First,		Army Tenn.
		First,		Army Tenn.
		Second, District Corinth,		Army Tenn.
		Eighth, Left Wing,	Thirteenth,	Tennessee.
		Thirteenth,	Thirteenth,	Tennessee.
Ross, S.	Second,	First,	Twelfth,	Potomac.
	First,	First,	Twelfth,	Potomac.
	First,	First,	Twelfth,	Cumberland.
	Second,	Third,	Twentieth,	Cumberland.
	Third,	Third,	Twentieth,	Cumberland.
Rousseau, L. H.	First,	McCook's,		Army Ohio.
	Fourth,			Army Ohio.
	Fourth,	Second,		Army Ohio.

Name	Brigade	Division, District, Etc.	Corps	Army or Dept.
		Third,	First,	Army 'Ohio.
		Third,		Army Ohio.
Rousseau, L. H.		First, Centre,	Fourteenth,	Cumberland.
		First,	Fourteenth,	Cumberland.
		Dist. Nashville, Tenn.,		Cumberland.
		Third,	Twelfth,	Cumberland.
		Fourth,	Twentieth,	Cumberland.
		Dist. Middle Tenn.,		Cumberland.
Rousseau, L. H.	Second,	Third,	Twenty-third,	North Carolina.
Rowe, D. W.	First,	Third,	Fifth,	Potomac.
Rowett, R.	Third,	Fourth,	Fifteenth,	Tennessee.
	Third,	Second,	Sixteenth,	Tennessee.
Rowley, T. A.	First,	Third,	First,	Potomac.
		Third,	First,	Potomac.
	Third,	Third,	Sixth,	Potomac.
Ruger, T. H.	First,	Second,	Twelfth,	Potomac.
	Third,	First,	Twelfth,	Potomac.
		First,	Twelfth,	Potomac.
	Third,	First,	Twelfth,	Cumberland.
	Second,	First,	Twentieth,	Cumberland.
		Second,	Twenty-third,	Ohio.
		First,	Twenty-third,	Ohio.
		First,	Twenty-third,	North Carolina.
		First,	Provisional,	North Carolina.
				North Carolina.
Rugg, H. P.	First,	Second,	Second,	Potomac.
Rumery, W. M.	Reserve,	First,	Cavalry,	Army Shen.
Runckle, B. P.	Second,	Dist. Central Ky.,		Ohio.
	Third,	Fourth,	Twenty-third,	Ohio.
Runyon, Theo.		Fourth (Reserve),		Army N. E. Va.
Rush, R. F.	Third,	Cavalry,		Potomac.
Rush, R. H.	First,	Veteran Reserve,	Twenty-second,	Washington.
Russell, C. S.	Second,	Fourth,	Ninth,	Potomac.
	Second,	Third,	Ninth,	Potomac.
	First,	Second,	Twenty-fifth,	Virginia.
	Third,	Second,	Twenty-fifth,	Virginia.
	Second,	First,	Twenty-fifth,	Virginia.
	Attached,	First,	Twenty-fifth,	Virginia.
	First,	Third,	Twenty-fifth,	Texas.
Russell, D. A.	Second,	Third,	Sixth,	Potomac.
	Third,	First,	Sixth,	Potomac.
		First,	Sixth,	Potomac.
		First,	Sixth,	Army Shen.
Rust, H., Jr.	Second,	Fourth,	Thirteenth,	Gulf.
	Second,	First,	Nineteenth,	Gulf.
Rust, J. D.	Second,	Third,	Tenth,	Va. and N. C.
Ryan, A. H.	Fourth,	Cavalry,	Seventh,	Arkansas.
Ryan, Geo.	Third,	Second,	Fifth,	Potomac.
Salm, Felix Prince	Second,	2nd Separate, Dist. Etowah,		Cumberland.
Salomon, C. E.	First,	First,	Seventh,	Arkansas.
	First,	Third,	Seventh,	Arkansas.
Salomon, F.	First,			Kansas.
	First,			Missouri.
		First, Army Frontier,		
		Dist. Eastern Ark.,	Thirteenth,	Tennessee.
	First,	Thirteenth,	Thirteenth,	Tennessee.
		Thirteenth,	Thirteenth,	Tennessee.
	First,	Dist. East. Arkansas,	Sixteenth,	Tennessee.
		Third, Arkansas Exp.,		Tennessee.
		Third,	Seventh,	Arkansas.
		First,	Seventh,	Arkansas.
Sanborn, J. B.	First,	Third,		Army Miss.
		Seventh,	Thirteenth,	Tennessee.
	First,	Seventh,	Seventeenth,	Tennessee.
		Seventh,	Seventeenth,	Tennessee.
		Dist. Southwest Mo.,		Missouri.
		Dist. Upper Arkansas,		Kansas.
Sanders, H. T.	Third,	First,	Eighteenth,	Va. and N. C.
Sanderson, T. W.	Second,	Third,	Cavalry,	Cumberland.
Sanderson, W. L.	First,	Fourth,	Seventeenth,	Tennessee.
Sanford, W. W.	Fourth,	First,	Sixteenth,	Tennessee.
	Fourth,	Fourth,	Fifteenth,	Tennessee.
Sanford, ——		Third,		Pennsylvania.
Sargent, Wm.	Third,	Second,	Fifth,	Potomac.
Saunders. W. P.		First,	Cavalry,	Ohio.
Sawtell, J. A.	Second,	Third,	Nineteenth,	Gulf.
Sawyer, E. B.	First,	Third,	Cavalry,	Potomac.
	Second,	Third,	Cavalry,	Potomac.

Name	Brigade	Division, District, Etc.	Corps	Arm- or Dept.
Saxton, Rufus		U. S. Forces Beaufort, S. C.,	Tenth,	South.
		Port Royal Island, S. C.,	Tenth,	South.
	1st Separate,	Northern District,		South.
	2nd Separate,	Dist. Beaufort, S. C.,		South.
Saylor, Thos.	Third,	1st Sub-Dist. Middle Tenn.,		Cumberland.
Scammon, E. P.	Scammon's,	Army of Occupation,		West. Virginia.
	First,	District Kanawha,		Mountains.
	Third,	Kanawha,		West Virginia.
	First,	Kanawha,		West Va.
		Third,	Eighth,	Middle Dept.
		Scammon's,		West Va.
		Third,		West Va.
	1st Separate,	Northern District,		South.
	3rd Separate,	Dist. Hilton Head, S. C.,		South.
	4th Separate,	District Florida,		South.
Schaeffer, F.	First,	2nd, Army Southwest Mo.,		Missouri.
	Thirty-fifth,	Eleventh,	Third,	Army Ohio.
	Second,	Third, Right Wing,	Fourteenth,	Cumberland.
Schall, E.	Second,	Second,	Ninth,	Potomac.
	Second,	Second,	Ninth,	Ohio.
Schall, J. W.	Third,	Third,	Third,	Potomac.
	First,	Third,	Sixth,	Potomac.
Schamberger, L.	Second,	Def. South Potomac,	Twenty-second,	Washington.
	Fourth,	Def. South Potomac,	Twenty-second,	Washington.
Schemmelfinnig, A.	First,	Third,	First,	Army of Va.
	First,	Third,	Eleventh,	Potomac.
	First,	First,	Eleventh,	Potomac.
		First,	Eleventh,	Potomac.
		Third,	Eleventh,	Potomac.
	First,	South End Folly Island,	Tenth,	South.
		South End Folly Island,	Tenth,	South.
		U. S. Forces Folly Island,	Tenth,	South.
		Northern District,	Tenth,	South.
	1st Separate.	Northern District,		South.
Schenck, R. C.	Second,	First,		Army N. E. Va.
	First,	Kanawha,		West Virginia.
		District Cumberland,		Mountains.
	Schenck's,			Mountains.
		First,	First,	Army of Va.
			First,	Army of Va.
			Eighth,	Middle Dept.
				Middle Dept.
Schirmer, L.	Second,	Def. South Potomac,	Twenty-second,	Washington.
	Fourth,	Def. South Potomac,	Twenty-second,	Washington.
Schlandecker, M.	Second,	Second,	Second,	Army of Va.
Schoepf, A.	First,			Army Ohio.
	First,	First,		Army Ohio.
		First,	Third,	Army Ohio.
Schofield, G. W.	Second,	Third,	Twenty-third,	North Carolina.
		Second,	Twenty-third,	North Carolina.
		First,	Twenty-third,	North Carolina.
Schofield, Hiram	Second,	U. S. C. T. Dist. Vicksburg,		Tennessee.
	Second,	Fourth,	Sixteenth,	Tennessee.
	Second,	First, U. S. C. T. West Fla.,		Gulf.
Schofield, J. M.		Dist. St. Louis, Mo.,		Missouri.
		Military Dist. Mo.,		Missouri.
		Dist. Southwest Mo.,		Missouri.
		Army Frontier,		Missouri.
		Third,	Fourteenth,	Cumberland.
				Missouri.
			Twenty-third,	Ohio.
Schofield, J. M.				Ohio.
			Twenty-third,	North Carolina.
				North Carolina.
Schoonmaker, J. M.	Second,	Fourth,		West Virginia.
	Second,	Second, Cavalry,		West Virginia.
	First,	Second, Cavalry,		West Virginia.
Schurz, Carl		Third,	First,	Army of Va.
		Third,	Eleventh,	Potomac.
			Eleventh,	Potomac.
		Third,	Eleventh,	Cumberland.
			Eleventh,	Cumberland.
Schwenck, S. K.	Second,	First,	Ninth,	Potomac.
Scott, D. D.	Third,	Third,	Seventeenth,	Tennessee.
Scott, G. W.	First,	First,	Second,	Potomac.
Scott, R. K.	Second,	Third,	Seventeenth,	Tennessee.
Scott, Winfield,				Armies U. S.

Name	Brigade	Division, District, Etc.	Corps	Army or Dept.
Scribner, B. F.	First,	Third, Centre,	Fourteenth,	Cumberland.
	First,	First,	Fourteenth,	Cumberland.
	Third,	First,	Fourteenth,	Cumberland.
Searing, Wm. M.	First,	First,	First,	Potomac.
Sears, F. A.	First,	Fourth,	Thirteenth,	Gulf.
Seaver, T. O.	Second,	Second,	Sixth,	Potomac.
Sedgewick, T. D.	Twenty-second,	Fourth,		Army Ohio.
	First,	Second,	Twenty-first,	Cumberland.
	First,	First,	Fourth,	Cumberland.
Sedgwick, John	Second,	Heintzelman's,		Potomac.
		Sedgwick's,		Potomac.
		Second,	Second,	Potomac.
			Second,	Potomac.
			Sixth,	Potomac.
			Ninth,	Potomac.
Sedgwick, T. D.	Second,	First,	Twenty-fifth,	Virginia.
Selfridge, J. L.	First,	First,	Twentieth,	Cumberland.
Sergeant, H. B.	First,	Second,	Cavalry,	Potomac.
Sergeant, Wm.	Third,	Second,	Fifth,	Potomac.
Seward, W. H.		Reserve,		West Virginia.
Sewell, F. D.	First,	Second,	Second,	Potomac.
Sewell, W. J.	Third,	Second,	Third,	Potomac.
Seymour, Truman	Third,	Second,		Rappahannock.
	Third,	Third,	Fifth,	Potomac.
		Third,	Fifth,	Potomac.
	Second,	Third,	Third,	Army of Va.
	First,	Third,	First,	Potomac.
		Forces, Port Royal Island,	Tenth,	South.
		U. S. Forces Beaufort, S. C.,	Tenth,	South.
		U. S. Forces Hilton Head,	Tenth,	South.
		Hilton Head District,	Tenth,	South.
		2nd, Morris Island, S. C.,	Tenth,	South.
		U. S. Forces Morris Island,	Tenth,	South.
		District Florida,	Tenth,	South.
	Second,	Third,	Sixth,	Potomac.
		Third,	Sixth,	Army Shen.
		Third,	Sixth,	Potomac.
	First,	Third,	Sixth,	Potomac.
Shackleford, J. M.	First,	Second,	Twenty-third,	Ohio.
	Third,	Fourth,	Twenty-third,	Ohio.
		Fourth,	Twenty-third,	Ohio.
Shaler, A.	First,	Third,	Sixth,	Potomac.
	Fourth,	First,	Sixth,	Potomac.
	Third,	Second,	Nineteenth,	Gulf.
		Second,	Seventh,	Arkansas.
Shane, John	Third,	Fourth,	Seventeenth,	Tennessee.
Shank, J. P. C.	First,	Cavalry, Dist. West Tenn.,		Tennessee.
Sharpe, Jacob		First,	Nineteenth,	Gulf.
	Second,	First,	Nineteenth,	Gulf.
	Third,	Second,	Nineteenth,	Gulf.
	Third,	Second,	Nineteenth,	Army Shen.
Shaw, Jas., Jr.	First,	Third,	Tenth,	Va. and N. C.
		Second,	Twenty-fifth,	Virginia.
	First,	Second,	Twenty-fifth,	Virginia.
Shaw, W. T.	Second,	Third.	Sixteenth,	Tennessee.
	Second,	Third, Detachment,	Sixteenth,	Gulf.
		Third,	Sixteenth,	Tennessee.
Shawa, A.	First,	Fifth,	Cavalry,	Mil. Div. Miss.
Sheldon, C. S.	First,	First,	Seventeenth,	Tennessee.
Sheldon, L. A.	First,	Ninth, Right Wing,	Thirteenth,	Tennessee.
	First,	Third, Yazoo Expedition,		Tennessee.
	Second,	Ninth,	Thirteenth,	Tennessee.
	Third,	First,	Thirteenth,	Gulf.
	Second,	First,	Thirteenth,	Gulf.
	First,	Third,	Nineteenth,	Gulf.
Shepard, I. F.		Dist. Northeast La.,		Tennessee.
	African,	Dist. Northeast La.,		Tennessee.
	First,	1st, U. S. C. T. Dist. Vicks.,		Tennessee.
Shepherd, O. L.	Fourth,	First, Centre,	Fourteenth,	Cumberland.
	Fourth,	First,	Fourteenth,	Cumberland.
Shepherd, R. B.	Third,	Def. North Potomac,	Twenty-second,	Washington.
	First,	Third,	Second,	Potomac.
Shepley, G. F.	Third,	New Orleans, La., Exp.,		
		Dist. Eastern Virginia,		Va. and N. C.
Sherburne, J. P.		Military Dist. Washington,		Potomac.
Sheridan, P. H.	Second,	Cavalry,		Army Miss.
		Eleventh,		Army Ohio.
		Eleventh,	Third,	Army Ohio.

Name	Brigade	Division, District, Etc.	Corps	Army or Dept.
		Third, Right Wing,	Fourteenth,	Cumberland.
		Third,	Twentieth,	Cumberland.
		Second,	Fourth,	Cumberland.
			Cavalry,	Potomac.
				Army Shen.
				Middle Mil. Div.
Sherman, F. T.	First,	Third,	Twentieth,	Cumberland.
	First,	Second,	Fourth,	Cumberland.
Sherman, T. W.		South Carolina Exp.,		
				South.
		Sixth,		Army Tenn.
		Sherman's, Carrollton, La.,	Nineteenth,	Gulf.
		Def. New Orleans, La.,	Nineteenth,	Gulf.
		Second,	Nineteenth,	Gulf.
Sherman, W. T.	Third,	First,		Army N. E. Va.
	Sherman's,			Div. Potomac.
				Cumberland.
		Dist. Southeast Mo.,		Missouri.
		Fifth,		Army Tenn.
		Fifth, District Memphis,		Army Tenn.
		District Memphis,	Thirteenth,	Tennessee.
		Yazoo Expedition,		Tennessee.
			Fifteenth,	Tennessee.
				Army Tenn.
				Tennessee.
				Mil. Div. Miss.
Sherrill, E.	Third,	Third,	Second,	Potomac.
Sherwine, Thos., Jr.	First,	First,	Fifth,	Potomac.
Shields, Jas.		Lander's,		Potomac.
		Second,	Banks' Fifth,	Potomac.
		Shields,		Shenandoah.
		Shields,		Rappahannock.
Shoemaker, M.	Third,	First,	Twenty-first,	Cumberland.
Shorey, S. G.	First,	Cavalry, West Tenn.,		Tennessee.
Showers, B. H.	Second,	Third,	Fourteenth,	Cumberland.
Shunk, D.	Second,	First, Army Southeast Mo.,		Missouri.
	First,	Fourteenth,	Thirteenth,	Tennessee.
	First,	First,	Thirteenth,	Gulf.
	Fourth,	Second,	Nineteenth,	Gulf.
	Fourth,	Second,	Nineteenth,	Army Shen.
Shurtliff, G. W.	Second,	Third,	Eighteenth,	Va. and N. C.
Siber, E.	Third,	Second,	Fifteenth,	Tennessee.
Sickel, H. G.		Third,	First,	Potomac.
	Second,	Penna. Reserve,	Twenty-second,	Washington.
	Third,	Penna. Reserve,	Twenty-second,	Washington.
	Second,	Penna. Res. Dist. Alex.	Twenty-second,	Washington.
	Third,	Second Infantry,		West Virginia.
	First,	First,	Fifth,	Potomac.
Sickles, D. E.	Second,	Hooker's,		Potomac.
	Second,	Second,	Third,	Potomac.
		Second.	Third,	Potomac.
			Third,	Potomac.
Sigel, A.		District Rolla, Mo.,		Missouri.
Sigel, Franz.	Fourth,	Army Southwest Mo.,		Missouri.
		First, Army S. W. Mo.,		Missouri.
		Sigel's,		Shenandoah.
			First,	Army of Va
			Eleventh,	Potomac.
		Reserve,		West Virginia.
				West Virginia.
Sigfried, J. K.	First,	Second,	Ninth,	Ohio.
		Second,	Ninth,	Ohio.
		Fourth,	Ninth,	Potomac.
Sill, J. W.	Ninth,			Army Ohio.
	Ninth,			Army Ohio.
	First,	Third, Right Wing,	Fourteenth,	Cumberland.
Simmons, S. G.	First,	Third,	Fifth,	Potomac.
Simonson, S. A.	First,	Independent,	Twenty-fourth,	Virginia.
Sinclair, W.	First,	Third,	First,	Potomac.
	First,	Third,	Fifth,	Potomac.
Sipes, W. E.	First,	Second,	Cavalry,	Cumberland.
Sirwell, Wm.	Third,	First,	Fourteenth,	Cumberland.
	Third,	Second,	Fourteenth,	Cumberland.
Slack, J. R.	First,	Second,		Army Miss.
	First,	Third,		Army Miss.
	First,	2nd, Dist. East Ark.,		Tennessee.
	First,	Twelfth,	Thirteenth,	Tennessee.
	Second,	Twelfth,	Thirteenth,	Tennessee.

Name	Brigade	Division, District, Etc.	Corps	Army or Dept.
	Second,	Third,	Thirteenth,	Tennessee.
	Second,	Third,	Thirteenth,	Gulf.
	First,	First,	Thirteenth,	Gulf.
	Second,	Second,	Nineteenth,	Gulf.
Slocum, H. W.	Second,	Franklin's,		Potomac.
	Second,	First,	First,	Potomac.
	Second,	First,		Rappahannock.
		First,	Sixth,	Potomac.
			Twelfth,	Cumberland.
		Dist. Vicksburg Miss.		Tennessee.
			Twentieth,	Cumberland.
				Army of Ga.
				Mississippi.
Slough, J. P.	Second,	Sigel's,		Shenandoah.
	Second,	Second,	Second,	Army of Va..
		Dist. Alexandria,	Mil. Dist. Wash.,	Potomac.
		Dist. Alexandria,	Twenty-second,	Washington.
Smith, A. A.		5th Sub Dist. Mid. Tenn.,		Cumberland.
Smith, A. J.		First, Army Kentucky,		Ohio.
		Tenth, Right Wing,	Thirteenth,	Tennessee.
		First, Yazoo Exp.,		Tennessee.
		Tenth,	Thirteenth,	Tennessee.
		Sixth, Dist. Columbus,	Sixteenth,	Tennessee.
		Third,	Sixteenth,	Tennessee.
		Right Wing,	Sixteenth,	Tennessee.
		Detch. 16th Corps,		Gulf.
		Detach. Army Tenn.		Cumberland.
			Sixteenth,	Gulf.
Smith, A. T.	Third,	2nd Separate, Dist. Etowah,		Cumberland.
Smith, B. F.	Third,	Third,	Third,	Potomac.
	Second,	Third,	Sixth,	Potomac.
	Second,	First,	Eighth,	Middle Dept.
		Martinsburg, Va.,	Eighth,	Middle Dept.
Smith, C. C.	Second,	Third,	Cavalry,	Cumberland.
Smith, C. F.				Washington.
		Mil. Dist. Cairo,		Missouri.
		Second,		Army Tenn.
Smith, C. H.	Second,	Second,	Cavalry,	Potomac.
	Third,	Second,	Cavalry,	Potomac.
		Second,	Cavalry,	Potomac.
Smith, F. C.	First,	Third,	Twentieth,	Cumberland.
Smith, G. A.	First,	2nd, Dist. Memphis, R. W.	Thirteenth,	Tennessee.
	First,	2nd, Yazoo Exp.,		Tennessee.
	First,	Second,	Fifteenth,	Tennessee.
		Second,	Fifteenth,	Tennessee.
		Fourth,	Seventeenth,	Tennessee.
		First,	Twenty-fifth,	Texas.
Smith, G. C.	First,	2nd, Army Kentucky,		Ohio.
		2nd, Army Kentucky,		Ohio.
Smith, James	Second,	First,	Nineteenth,	Gulf.
Smith, J. E.		Eighth,	Sixteenth,	Tennessee.
Smith, J. E.	First,	Third, Right Wing,	Thirteenth,	Tennessee.
	First,	Third,	Seventeenth,	Tennessee.
		Seventh,	Seventeenth,	Tennessee.
		Second,	Seventeenth,	Tennessee.
		Third,	Fifteenth,	Tennessee.
		Dist. W. Tennessee,		Tennessee.
Smith, J. K. K.	Second,	First,		Army Miss.
	First,	Second,		Army Miss.
Smith, M.	First,	First,	Fifteenth,	Tennessee.
		First,	Fifteenth,	Tennessee.
Smith, M. L.	Fifth,	Second, Dist. Cairo,		Missouri.
	First,	Third,		Army Tenn.
	First,	Fifth,		Army Tenn.
	First,	Fifth, Dist. Memphis,		Army Tenn.
	First,	District Memphis,	Thirteenth,	Tennessee.
		Second, Dist. Memphis,	Thirteenth,	Tennessee.
		Second, Yazoo Exp.,		Tennessee.
		Second,	Fifteenth,	Tennessee.
			Fifteenth,	Tennessee.
		Post Vicksburg, Miss.,		Tennessee.
Smith, Orland	Second,	Second,	Twelfth,	Potomac.
	Second,	Second,	Twelfth,	Cumberland.
Smith, P. C.	First,	Second,	Sixteenth,	Gulf.
Smith, R. F.	Second,	First,		Army Miss.
	First,	Fourth,	Fourteenth,	Cumberland.
		Fourth,	Fourteenth,	Cumberland.
	First,	Second,	Reserve,	Cumberland.

Name	Brigade	Division, District, Etc.	Corps	Army or Dept.
	First,	Second,	Fourteenth,	Cumberland.
Smith, R. P.	First,	Second,	Second,	Potomac.
	Second,	Second,	Second,	Potomac.
Smith, R. S.	First,	Second,	Fifth,	Potomac.
Smith, T. K.	Second,	Fifth,		Army Tenn.
	Second,	2nd, Yazoo Exp.,		Tennessee.
	Second,	Second,	Fifteenth,	Tennessee.
	Second,	First,	Seventeenth,	Tennessee.
	First,	Fourth,	Seventeenth,	Gulf.
		Provisional,	Seventeenth,	Cumberland.
		3rd, Det'mt Army Tenn.,		Div. Potomac.
Smith, Wm. F.	Smith's,			Potomac.
		Smith's,		Potomac.
		Second,	Fourth,	Potomac.
		Second,	Sixth,	Potomac.
			Sixth,	Potomac.
			Ninth,	Va. and N. C.
			Eighteenth,	Potomac.
Smith, W. F.	First,	Second,	Second,	Army Ohio.
Smith, W. S.	Seventeenth,	Third,		Army Ohio.
		Third,		Army Ohio.
		Fourth,		Army Ohio.
	Fourteenth,	Fifth,		Army Ohio.
		Fourth,	Second,	Cumberland.
		Second, Left Wing,	Fourteenth,	Tennessee.
		First,	Sixteenth,	Potomac.
Smyth, T. A.	Second,	Third,	Second,	Potomac.
	Second,	First,	Second,	Potomac.
	Third,	Second,	Second,	Potomac.
		Second,	Second,	Tennessee.
Smyth, Wm.	Third,	First,	Fifteenth,	Potomac.
Snyder, Jos.	First,	Third,	Second,	Potomac.
Soest, C.	First,	Second,	Eleventh,	Cumberland.
Spalding, Geo.	Second,	Fourth,	Cavalry,	Cumberland.
		Fourth,	Cavalry,	Mil. Div. Miss.
		Fourth,	Cavalry,	Missouri.
		Dist. N. Mo.,		Ohio.
Spaulding, B. J.	Third,	1st Dist. Kentucky,	Twenty-third,	North Carolina.
Spaulding, O. L.	Second,	Second,	Twenty-third,	Potomac.
Spear, Geo. C.		Light Division,	Sixth,	Va. and N. C.
Spear, S. P.	Cavalry,	U. S. Forces Yorktown, Va.		Va. and N. C.
	Second,	Cavalry,		Army Ohio.
Spears, J. G.	Twenty-fifth,	Seventh,		Ohio.
	First,	Cumberland Dist. W. Va.,	Fourteenth,	Cumberland.
	First,	Second, Centre,	Fourteenth,	Cumberland.
	First,	Second,		Ohio.
	East Tenn.,	Dist. Central Kentucky,	Reserve,	Cumberland.
	Third,	Third,		Cumberland.
	Spears',	Chattanooga, Tenn.,	Twelfth,	Cumberland.
	Third,	Third,	Twenty-third,	Ohio.
	First, East Tenn.	Second,	Cavalry,	Mil. Div. Miss.
Spencer, Geo. E.	Third,	Third,	Thirteenth,	Tennessee.
Spicely, W. T.	First,	Twelfth,	Thirteenth,	Tennessee.
	First,	Third,	Thirteenth,	Gulf.
	First,	Third,	Nineteenth,	Gulf.
	Second,	Third,	Reserve,	Gulf.
	Second,	Second,	Thirteenth,	Gulf.
	Second,	Second,	Seventh,	Virginia.
Spinola, F. R.	Independent,		Seventh,	Virginia.
	Spinola,	Division at Suffolk,	Eighteenth,	North Carolina.
	First,	Fifth,		North Carolina.
	First,	Dist. Pamlico, N. C.,		South.
		Beaufort, S. C.,	Tenth,	North Carolina.
Splaine, H.	Third,	Dist. Beaufort, N. C.,		South.
Spofford, W. P.	First,	U. S. Forces Morris Isl.,	Tenth,	Tennessee.
Spooner, B. J.	Second,	Second,	Fifteenth,	Tennessee.
Sprague, J. W.	Third,	5th, Dist. Memphis, Tenn.,	Sixteenth,	Tennessee.
	Second,	Fourth,	Sixteenth,	Tennessee.
	Second,	First,	Seventeenth,	Tennessee.
		First,	Seventeenth,	Tennessee.
Spurling, A. B.	Second,	Lee's Cavalry, W. Tenn.		Potomac.
Stagg, Peter	First,	First,	Cavalry,	Army Shen.
	First,	First,	Cavalry,	Army Shen.
		First,	Cavalry,	Potomac.
Stahel, J. H.	First,	Blenker's,		Potomac.
	First,	Blenker's,	Second,	Mountain.
	First,	Blenker's,		Army of Va.
	First,	First,	First,	

Name	Brigade	Division, District, Etc.	Corps	Army or Dept.
		First,	First,	Army of Va.
		First,	Eleventh,	Potomac.
			Eleventh,	Potomac.
		Cavalry,	Twenty-second,	Washington.
		First Cavalry,		West Virginia.
Stambaugh, F. S.	Fifth,	Second,		Army Ohio.
Stanley, D. S.		Second,		Army Miss.
		First,		Army Miss.
		Eighth, Left Wing,	Thirteenth,	Tennessee.
		Cavalry,		Cumberland.
			Cavalry,	Cumberland.
		First,	Fourth,	Cumberland.
			Fourth,	Cumberland.
Stanley, T. R.	Twenty-ninth,	Eighth,		Army Ohio.
	Second.	Second, Centre,	Fourteenth,	Cumberland.
	Second,	Second,	Fourteenth,	Cumberland.
	Engineer,			Cumberland.
		Post Chattanooga, Tenn.,		Cumberland.
	1st Separate,	Chattanooga, Tenn.,		Cumberland.
Stannard, Geo. J.	Second,	Abercrombie's,	Twenty-second,	Washington.
	Third,	Third,	First,	Potomac.
	First,	Second,	Eighteenth,	Va. and N. C.
		First,	Eighteenth,	Va. and N. C.
Stanton, D. F.	Second,	Second,	Fifth,	Potomac.
Stanton, J. F.	Second,	Second,	Eighth,	Middle Dept.
	Second,	Third,	Sixth,	Army Shen.
Starkweather, J. C.	Twenty-eighth,	Third,		Army Ohio.
	Twenty-eighth,	Third,	First,	Army Ohio.
	Third,	First, Centre,	Fourteenth,	Cumberland.
	Third,	First,	Fourteenth,	Cumberland.
	Second,	First,	Fourteenth,	Cumberland.
Starr, S. H.	Third,	Hooker's,		Potomac.
	Third,	Second,	Third,	Potomac.
	Reserve,	First,	Cavalry,	Potomac.
Starring, F. A.	First,	First,	Seventeenth,	Tennessee.
Stanton, J. F.	Second,	Third,	Sixth,	Army Shen.
Stearns, O. P.	First,	Third,	Ninth,	Potomac.
	Second,	Third,	Tenth,	North Carolina.
Stedman, G. A., Jr.	Second,	Second,	Eighteenth,	Va. and N. C.
Stedman, Wm.	First,	Second,	Cavalry,	Potomac.
Steedman, Jas. B.	Third,	First,	Third,	Army Ohio.
	Third,	Third, Center,	Fourteenth.	Cumberland.
	Third,	Third,	Fourteenth,	Cumberland.
	Second,	Third,	Fourteenth,	Cumberland.
		First,	Reserve.	Cumberland.
	First,	Second,	Fourth,	Cumberland.
		District Etowah,		Cumberland.
		Post Chattanooga, Tenn.,		Cumberland.
Steele, F.		First, Army S. W. Mo.,		Missouri.
		Army S. W. Mo.,		Missouri.
		Dist. S. W. Mo.,		Missouri.
		1st, S. E. Mo. Dist. E. Ark.,		Missouri.
		1st, Dist. E. Ark.,		Tennessee.
		Eleventh,	Thirteenth,	Tennessee.
		4th, Yazoo Exp.,		Tennessee.
		First,	Fifteenth,	Tennessee.
		Arkansas Exp.,		Tennessee.
			Seventh,	Arkansas.
				Arkansas.
		First,	Reserve,	Gulf.
		Dist. West. Florida,		Gulf.
Steere, W. H. P.	Third,	Second,	Seventh,	Virginia.
	Third,	Getty's Norfolk and Ports.,		Va. and N. C.
Steinrook, H. J.	Second,	Second,	Twelfth,	Potomac.
Stephens, Thomas	Third,	5th, Dist. Memphis,	Sixteenth,	Tennessee.
Sterl, O. W.	First,	Third,	Twenty-third,	Ohio.
	First,	Third,	Twenty-third,	North Carolina.
Stevens, A. F.	Third,	Third,	Ninth,	Ohio.
	First,	First,	Eighteenth,	Va. and N. C.
Stevens, I. I.	Second,	W. F. Smith's,		Potomac.
	Second,	South Carolina,	Expeditionary,	
		Second,		South.
		First,	Ninth,	Potomac.
Stevens, W. F.	Second,	Second,	Twelfth,	Cumberland.
Stevenson, J. D.	Fourth,	Third, Right Wing,	Thirteenth,	Tennessee.
	Third,	Third,	Seventeenth,	Tennessee.
		Third,	Seventeenth,	Tennessee.

Name	Brigade	Division, District, Etc.	Corps	Army or Dept.
		District Corinth,	Sixteenth,	Tennessee.
	First,	Third,		West Virginia.
		Reserve,		West Virginia.
				West Virginia.
Stevenson, M. L.	Second,	Second,	Seventh,	Arkansas.
Stevenson, T. G.	Second,	First,		North Carolina.
	Second,	Fourth,	Eighteenth,	North Carolina.
	First,	Second,	Eighteenth,	North Carolina.
	First,	First, St. Helena Island,	Tenth,	South.
		Second, St. Helena Island,	Tenth,	South.
	Stevenson's,	Seabrook Island, S. C.,	Tenth,	South.
	First,	First, Morris Island, S. C.,	Tenth,	South.
	Third,	Morris Island, S. C.,	Tenth,	South.
	First,	Morris Island, S. C.,	Tenth,	South.
		First,	Ninth,	Potomac.
Stewart, Jas., Jr.	First,	Second,	Eighteenth,	Va. and N. C.
		Sub-Dist. Beaufort, N. C.,		Va. and N. C.
		Sub-Dist. Beaufort, N. C.,		North Carolina.
	Second,	Division. Dist. Beaufort,		North Carolina.
		Third,	Twenty-third,	North Carolina.
Stewart, J. W.	Second,	First,	Cavalry,	Cumberland.
Stewart, R. R.	First,	Fifth,	Cavalry,	Mil. Div. Miss.
		Fifth,	Cavalry,	Mil. Div. Miss.
Stewart, W. S.	First,	Third,	Twenty-third,	North Carolina.
Stiles, I. N.	Third,	Third,	Twenty-third,	Ohio.
	First,	First,	Provisional,	North Carolina.
	First,	First,	Twenty-third,	North Carolina.
Stiles, J. W.	Third,	Banks',		Potomac.
	Third,	Second,	Third,	Army of Va.
Stockton, T. W. B.	Third,	First,	Fifth,	Potomac.
Stokes, W. B.	Third,	Third,	Twenty-third,	Ohio.
Stolbrand, C. J.	Second,	Fourth,	Seventeenth,	Tennessee.
Stone, C. P.	Seventh,	Third,		Pennsylvania.
	Third,			Shenandoah.
	Stone's,			Div. Potomac.
		Stone's,		Potomac.
	First,	Second,	Fifth,	Potomac.
Stone, G. A.	Second,	First,	Fifteenth,	Tennessee.
	Third,	First,	Fifteenth,	Tennessee.
Stone, Roy	Second,	Third,	First,	Potomac.
	Third,	Fourth,	Fifth,	Potomac.
Stone, W. M.		District Rolla, Mo.,		Missouri.
	Second,	First,	Thirteenth,	Tennessee.
	Second,	First,	Thirteenth,	Gulf.
Stoneman, Geo.		Cavalry, Reserve,		Potomac.
		Cavalry Command,		Potomac.
		Cavalry,		Potomac.
		First,	Second,	Potomac.
		First,	Third,	Potomac.
			Third,	Potomac.
			Cavalry,	Potomac.
		Cavalry,	Twenty-third,	Ohio.
			Twenty-third,	Ohio.
				Ohio.
		Dist. East Tennessee,		Cumberland.
Stoughton, E. H.	Second,	Casey's,		Potomac.
	Second,	Casey's,	Twenty-second,	Washington.
	Third,	First,	Sixth,	Potomac.
Stoughton, W. L.	Second,	First,	Fourteenth,	Cumberland.
	Second,	Second,	Fourteenth,	Cumberland.
Stout, Alex. M.	Third,	Third,	Fourth,	Cumberland.
Strawbridge, D. C.		U. S. Forces Hilton Head,	Tenth,	South.
Streight, A. D.	Provisional,		Fourteenth,	Cumberland.
	First,	Third,	Fourth,	Cumberland.
Strickland, S. A.	Thirty-fourth,	Tenth,	First,	Army Ohio.
	Third,	Fourth,	Twenty-third,	Ohio.
	Third,	Second,	Twenty-third,	Ohio.
	Third,	Second,	Twenty-third,	North Carolina.
Strong, Geo. C.		Forces St. Helena Island,	Tenth,	South.
	Second,	2nd, Morris Island, S. C.,	Tenth,	South.
Strong, W. K.		District St. Louis, Mo.,		Missouri.
		District Cairo,		Tennessee.
Stuart, D.	Second,	Fifth,		Army Tenn.
	Fourth,	District Memphis,	Thirteenth,	Tennessee.
	Second,	2nd, Dist. Memphis, R. W.,	Thirteenth,	Tennessee.
	Second,	2nd, Yazoo Expedition,		Tennessee.
		2nd, Yazoo Expedition,		Tennessee.
		Second,	Fifteenth,	Tennessee.

Name	Brigade	Division, District, Etc.	Corps	Army or Dept.
Sturgis, S. D.	Sturgis',	Mil. Dist. Washington,		Potomac.
		Sturgis', Division, Mil. Dist.,	Washington,	Potomac.
		Second,	Ninth,	Potomac.
		Second,	Ninth,	Ohio.
		District Central Ky.		Ohio.
			Cavalry,	Ohio.
		First,	Twenty-third,	Ohio.
Sudsburg, J. M.	Second,	First,	Ninth,	Potomac.
	Second,	Second,	Twelfth,	Potomac.
Sullivan, J. C.	Second,	Landers',		West Virginia.
	Second,	Second,	Banks Fifth,	Potomac.
	Second,	Second,		Shenandoah.
	Second,	Third,		Army Miss.
		District Jackson,		Tennessee.
		Dist. Jackson, Left Wing,	Thirteenth,	Tennessee.
		Maryland Heights,		West Virginia.
		First,		West Virginia.
		First Infantry,		West Virginia.
	1st Separate,	Dist. Kanawha,		West Virginia.
Sullivan, T.	First,	First,	Third,	Army of Va.
Sully, A.	First,	Second,	Second,	Potomac.
		Third,	Second,	Potomac.
Suman, I. C. B.	Second,	First,	Fourth,	Cumberland.
Sumner, E. V.				Pacific.
		Sumner's,		Potomac.
			Second,	Potomac.
Sumner, E. V.	Third,	Cavalry,		Va. and N. C.
Swain, E. D.	Second,	Second,	Fourth,	Cumberland.
Swayne, P. T.	Second,	1st, Army Kentucky,		Ohio.
	Second,	3rd, Army Kentucky,		Ohio.
	Second,	First,	Twenty-third,	Ohio.
	Fourth,	Second,	Twenty-third,	Ohio.
Swayne, Wagar	Third,	Fourth,	Sixteenth,	Tennessee.
	Second,	First,	Seventeenth,	Tennessee.
Sweeney, T. W.	Third,	2nd, Dist. Corinth,		Tennessee.
	First,	2nd, Dist. Corinth,		Tennessee.
	First,	District Corinth,	Thirteenth,	Tennessee.
	First,	District Corinth,	Sixteenth,	Tennessee.
	First,	District Corinth,	Seventeenth,	Tennessee.
	First,	Second,	Sixteenth,	Tennessee.
		Second,	Sixteenth,	Tennessee.
Sweitzer, J. B.	Second,	First,	Fifth,	Potomac.
		First,	Fifth,	Potomac.
Sykes, Geo.	Regular Infy.,			Potomac.
		Reg. Infy. Reserve,		Potomac.
		Second,	Fifth,	Potomac.
			Fifth,	Potomac.
		Dist. S. Kansas,		Kansas.
Tait, Jas. A.	Third,	Second,	Second,	Army of Va.
	Second,	Second,	Second,	Army of Va.
Talley, W. C.	First,	Third,	Fifth,	Potomac.
Tannatt, T. R.	First,	Defenses S. Potomac,	Twenty-second,	Washington.
	Second,	Defenses S. Potomac,	Twenty-second,	Washington.
	Artillery,	Defenses S. Potomac,	Twenty-second,	Washington.
		Defenses S. Potomac,	Twenty-second,	Washington.
	Second,	Third,	Second,	Potomac.
Taylor, M. C.	First,	First,	Fourteenth,	Cumberland.
Taylor, G. W.	First,	First,	Sixth,	Potomac.
Taylor, J. E.	Second,	First,	Fourth,	Cumberland.
Taylor, J. P.	First,	Second,	Cavalry,	Potomac.
		Second,	Cavalry,	Potomac.
Taylor, J. P.	Second,	Third,	Cavalry,	Potomac.
Taylor, Nelson	Second,	Second,	Third,	Potomac.
	Third,	Second,	First,	Potomac.
		Second,	First,	Potomac.
Taylor, R. F.	First,	Second,	Sixth,	Potomac.
Taylor, R. F.	First,	First, Cavalry,		West Virginia.
	Second,	First, Cavalry,		West Virginia.
Telford, W. H.	Second,	First,	Ninth,	Potomac.
Terrell, W. R.	Thirty-third,	Tenth,		Army Ohio.
	Thirty-third,	Tenth,	First,	Army Ohio.
Terry, A. H.		Forces Hilton Head, S. C.,	Tenth,	South.
		First, Morris Island, S. C.,	Tenth,	South.
		Forces Morris Island, S. C.,	Tenth,	South.
		Northern District,	Tenth,	South.
		First,	Tenth,	Va. and N. C.
			Tenth,	Va. and N. C.
		First,	Twenty-fourth,	Virginia.
			Twenty-fourth,	Virginia.

Name	Brigade	Division, District, Etc.	Corps	Army or Dept.
			Provisional,	North Carolina.
			Tenth,	North Carolina.
				Virginia.
Terry, H. D.	Terry's,	Division at Suffolk,	Seventh,	Virginia.
	First,	First,	Seventh,	Virginia.
		Third,	Sixth,	Potomac.
Thayer, J. M.	Third,	Third, Mil. Dist., Cairo,		Missouri.
	Second,	Third,		Army Tenn.
	Second,	First, Dist. Eastern Ark.,		Tennessee.
	Third,	Eleventh,	Thirteenth,	Tennessee.
	Third,	Fourth, Yazoo Expedition,		Tennessee.
	Third,	First,	Fifteenth,	Tennessee.
		First,	Fifteenth,	Tennessee.
		District Frontier,	Seventh,	Arkansas.
		District Eastern Ark.,	Seventh,	Arkansas.
Thayer, Wm.	Second,	Third,	Cavalry,	Cumberland.
	Second,	Third,	Cavalry,	Mil. Div. Miss.
Thoburn, Jos.	Second,	Second,		West Virginia.
	Second,	First, Infantry,		West Virginia.
		First, Infantry,		West Virginia.
Thomas, Geo. H.	First,	First,		Pennsylvania.
	First,			Shenandoah.
	First,	Banks,		Potomac.
		Camp Dick Robinson, Ky.,		Army Ohio.
		First,		Army Ohio.
		Second in command,		Army Ohio.
		Centre.	Fourteenth,	Cumberland.
			Fourteenth,	Cumberland.
				Army Cumb'd.
				Cumberland.
Thomas, H. G.	Second,	Defenses North Potomac,	Twenty-second,	Washington.
	Second,	Fourth,	Ninth,	Potomac.
	Second,	Third,	Ninth,	Potomac.
	Third,	Third,	Twenty-fifth,	Virginia.
	Third,	First,	Twenty-fifth,	Virginia.
Thomas, M. T.	Third,	First,	Twenty-third,	Ohio.
	Third,	First,	Provisional,	North Carolina.
	Third,	First,	Twenty-third,	North Carolina.
		First,	Twenty-third,	North Carolina.
Thomas, Stephen	Second,	First,	Nineteenth,	Gulf.
	Second,	First,	Nineteenth,	Army Shen.
Thompson, C. R.	Second, Colored,	District Etowah,		Cumberland.
		Third, Sub-Dist. Middle Tenn		Cumberland.
Thompson, J. L.	Second,	Third,	Cavalry,	Army Shen.
Thompson, Wm.	Second,	Cavalry,	Seventh,	Arkansas.
Thomson, Wm.	Second,	Cavalry, West Tenn.,		Tennessee.
Thornburg, D. G.	First,	Fourth,	Cavalry,	Cumberland.
	First,	Fourth,	Cavalry,	Mil. Div. Miss.
Thrall, Homer	Second,	Second,	Seventh,	Arkansas.
Throop, W. A.	First,	First,	Fifth,	Potomac.
Tibbits, W. B.	First,	First, Cavalry,		West Virginia.
	First,	Second, Cavalry,		West Virginia.
	Second,	Second, Cavalry,		West Virginia.
		Second, Cavalry,		West Virginia.
Tidball, J. C.	Third,	Defenses South Potomac,	Twenty-second,	Washington.
	Fourth,	Defenses South Potomac,	Twenty-second,	Washington.
Tidball, W. L.	Third,	Second,	Second,	Potomac.
Tilghman, B. C.	Second,	Second, Dist. Florida,	Tenth,	South.
	4th Separate,	District Florida,		South.
Tillson, John	First,	Second,	Reserve,	Cumberland.
	Third,	Fourth,	Sixteenth,	Tennessee.
	Third,	First,	Seventeenth,	Tennessee.
Tillson, Davis	Second,	Fourth,	Twenty-third,	Ohio.
		Fourth,	Twenty-third,	Ohio.
		Fourth, Dist. East Tenn.,		Cumberland.
		District East Tennessee,		Cumberland.
Tilton, W. S.	First,	First,	Fifth,	Potomac.
Tippin, A. H.	First,	First,	Third.	Potomac.
Titus, H. B.	First,	Second,	Ninth.	Potomac.
	Second,	Second,	Ninth.	Potomac.
Titus, S.	First,	Third,	Sixth,	Potomac.
Todd, J. B. S.		Sixth,		Army Tenn.
Toland, John T.	Third,	Scammon's,		West Virginia.
Tomlinson, A. A.	First,	Third,		West Virginia.
Torbert, A. T. A.	First,	First,	Sixth,	Potomac.
		First,	Sixth,	Potomac.
		First,	Cavalry,	Potomac.
			Cavalry,	Potomac.

Name	Brigade	Division, District, Etc.	Corps	Army or Dept.
			Cavalry,	Army Shen.
				Army Shen.
Torrey, W. H.	Second,	First,	Cavalry,	Cumberland.
Totten, James		Second, Army Frontier,		Missouri.
		District Central Mo.,		Missouri.
Tourtelotte, J. E.	Second,	Third,	Fifteenth,	Tennessee.
Tower, Z. B.	Second,	Ord's,		Rappahannock,
	Second,	Third,	Third,	Army of Va.
	Second,	Second,	Third,	Potomac.
Town, C. H.	Second,	Third,	Cavalry,	Potomac.
Town, G. W.	Third,	First,	Sixth,	Potomac.
Tracy, A. S.	Second,	Second,	Sixth,	Potomac.
	Second,	Second,	Sixth,	Army Shen.
Travers, G. W.	Second,	Third,	Ninth,	Potomac.
Trowbridge, L. S	First,	Cavalry, Dist. East Tenn.,		Cumberland.
True, C. J.	First,	First, Dist. Kentucky,	Twenty-third,	Ohio.
	Second,	First, Dist. Kentucky,	Twenty-third,	Ohio.
True, J. M.	Third,	Third,	Sixteenth,	Tennessee.
	True's,	Third, Arkansas Exp.,		Tennessee.
	Third,	Second,	Seventh,	Arkansas.
	Second,	Second,	Seventh,	Arkansas.
True, L. C.	Second,	Second,	Seventh,	Arkansas.
Truex, Wm. S.	First,	Third,	Sixth,	Army Shen.
Trumbull, M. M.	Cavalry,	Post Little Rock, Ark.,	Seventh,	Arkansas.
Tucker, James	Third,	First,	Twenty-third,	North Carolina.
Tupper, N. W.	First,	Second,	Fifteenth,	Tennessee.
Turchin, J. P.	Eighth,			Army Ohio.
	Eighth,			Army Ohio.
	Third,	Fourth,	Fourteenth,	Cumberland.
		Second,	Cavalry,	Cumberland.
	First,	Third,	Fourteenth,	Cumberland.
Turner, C.	Third,	Third,	Sixteenth,	Gulf.
Turner, J. W.		Second,	Tenth,	Va. and N. C.
		Independent,	Twenty-fourth,	Virginia.
			Twenty-fourth,	Virginia.
Turner, T. J.	First,	Fourth,		Army Tenn.
Tuttle, J. M.	First,	Second,		Army Tenn.
		Second,		Army Tenn.
	First,	Second, District Corinth,		Army Tenn.
		District Cairo,		Tennessee.
Tuttle, J. M.		Third,	Fifteenth,	Tennessee.
		First,	Sixteenth,	Tennessee.
		Post Natchez, Dist. Vicks.,		Tennessee.
Tyler, Daniel		First,		Army N. E. Va.
		First,		Army Miss.
		District Delaware,	Eighth,	Middle Dept.
Tyler, E. B.	Third,	Landers',		West Virginia.
	Third,	Second,	Banks, Fifth,	Potomac.
	Third,	Second,		Shenandoah.
	Third,	Shields',		Rappahannock.
	First,	Third,	Fifth,	Potomac.
		Defenses Baltimore, Md.,	Eighth,	Middle Dept.
			Eighth,	Middle Dept.
	3rd Separate,		Eighth,	Middle Dept.
	1st Separate,		Eighth,	Middle Dept.
Tyler, R. O.	Artillery,	Dist. Alexandria,	Mil. Dist. Wash.,	Potomac.
	Artillery,	Defenses Alexandria,	Twenty-second,	Washington.
		Defenses South Potomac,	Twenty-second,	Washington.
		King's,	Twenty-second,	Washington.
		Heavy Artillery,	Second,	Potomac.
	Fourth,	Second,	Second,	Potomac.
Tyndale, H.	First,	Second,	Twelfth,	Potomac.
	First,	Third,	Eleventh,	Potomac.
	First,	Third,	Eleventh,	Cumberland.
		Third,	Eleventh,	Cumberland.
	Third,	First,	Twentieth,	Cumberland.
	First,	First,	Fourth,	Cumberland.
Ullman, D.	Second,	Second,	Second,	Army of Va.
	Ullman's,	U. S. C. T. Port Hudson, La.		Gulf.
		First, Corps de Afrique,		Gulf.
		District Port Hudson, La.,		Gulf.
		Corps de Afrique, U. S. C. T.		Gulf.
		District Morganza, La.,		Gulf.
Upham, C. L.	Second,	Second, Dist. Beaufort, N. C.,		North Carolina.
Upton, Emory,	Second,	First,	Sixth,	Potomac.
	Second,	First,	Sixth,	Army Shen.
		First,	Sixth,	Army Shen.

Name	Brigade	Division, District, Etc.	Corps	Army or Dept.
		Fourth,	Cavalry,	Mil. Div. Miss.
	Cavalry,	Dist. East Tennessee,		Cumberland.
Utley, W. L.	Third,	First,	Reserve,	Cumberland.
Vail, J. G.	First,	Second,	Cavalry,	Mil. Div. Miss.
Van Arnsburg, G.	First,	First,	Eleventh,	Potomac.
	First,	Third,	Eleventh,	Potomac.
	First,	Third,	Eleventh,	Cumberland.
	First,	First,	Eleventh,	Cumberland.
Van Buren, T. B.	Second,	Second,	Second,	Army of Va.
	Second,	Second,	Twelfth,	Potomac.
Vance, J. W.	Second,	Second, Army Kentucky,		Ohio.
	Second,	Fourth,	Thirteenth,	Gulf.
Van Cleve, H. P.	Fourteenth,	Fifth,		Army Ohio.
		Fifth,	Second,	Army Ohio.
	Third,	Second, Left Wing,	Fourteenth,	Cumberland.
		Third,	Twenty-first,	Cumberland.
	Second,	District Nashville, Tenn.,		Cumberland.
	Second,	Third,	Twelfth,	Cumberland.
		Post Murfreesboro, Tenn.,		Cumberland.
	First,	Def. Nash. and Chatta. R. R.,		Cumberland.
	First,	1st, Sub-Dist. Middle, Tenn.,		Cumberland.
Van Derveer, F.	Third,	First,		Army Ohio.
	Third,	Third,	Fourteenth,	Cumberland.
	Second,	Third,	Fourteenth,	Cumberland.
	Second,	Second,	Fourteenth,	Cumberland.
Vandever, Wm.	Second,	Fourth, Army Southwest Mo.,		Missouri.
		Second, Army Frontier,		Missouri.
	First,	Ninth,	Thirteenth,	Tennessee.
	First,	Herron's,	Thirteenth,	Tennessee.
	First,	Second,	Thirteenth,	Tennessee.
	First,	Second,	Thirteenth,	Gulf.
	Third,	Second,	Sixteenth,	Tennessee.
	First,	Second,	Fourteenth,	Cumberland.
		Second,	Fourteenth,	Cumberland.
Van Valkenburg, J.	First,	First,	Third,	Potomac.
Van Voorhees, K. L.	Third,	Second,	Twelfth,	Cumberland.
Van Zant, J.	First,	Fourth,	Nineteenth,	Gulf.
	Second,	Fourth,	Nineteenth,	Gulf.
Veatch, J. C.	Second,	Fourth,		Army Tenn.
	Second,	Fourth, Dist. Jackson,		Tennessee.
		Fourth, Dist. Memphis, Tenn.,	Thirteenth,	Tennessee.
		District Memphis, Tenn.,	Sixteenth,	Tennessee.
		Fifth, Dist. Memphis,	Sixteenth,	Tennessee.
		Fourth,	Sixteenth,	Tennessee.
		First,	Reserve,	Gulf.
		First,	Thirteenth,	Gulf.
Viele, E. L.	First,	South Carolina,	Expeditionary,	
	Viele's,			Virginia.
	Viele's,	Norfolk, Va.,	Seventh,	Virginia.
Vincent, Strong	Third,	First,	Fifth,	Potomac.
Vinton, F. L.	Third,	Second,	Sixth,	Potomac.
Vodges, Israel		Forces North End Folly I.	Tenth,	South.
	First,	Second, Morris Island,	Tenth,	South.
		Forces Folly Island,	Tenth,	South.
		Second, Dist. Florida,	Tenth,	South.
	4th, Separate,	District Florida,		South.
		Norfolk and Portsmouth, Va		Va. and N. C.
Von Gilsa, L.	First,	First,	Eleventh,	Potomac.
	First,	Folly Island, S. C.,	Tenth,	South.
		South End Folly Island,	Tenth,	South.
Von Schack, G.	First,	First,	Second,	Potomac.
	Third,	First,	Second,	Potomac.
Von Steinwehr, A.	Second,	Blenker's,		Potomac.
	Second,	Blenker's,	Second,	Potomac.
	Second,	Blenker's,		Mountain.
		Second,	First,	Army of Va.
		Second,	Eleventh,	Potomac.
			Eleventh,	Potomac.
		Second,	Eleventh,	Cumberland.
			Eleventh,	Cumberland.
Von Vegesack, E.	Third,	Second,	Sixth,	Potomac.
Voris, A. C.	First,	First,	Tenth,	Va. and N. C.
	First,	Third,	Tenth,	Va. and N. C.
		First,	Tenth,	Va. and N. C.
	First,	First,	Twenty-fourth,	Virginia.
Wadsworth, J. S.	Second,	McDowell's,		Potomac.
	Second,	Third,	First,	Potomac.

Name	Brigade	Division, District, Etc.	Corps	Army or Dept.
		Military Dist. Washington,		Potomac.
		First,	First,	Potomac.
			First,	Fotomac.
		Fourth,	Fifth,	Potomac.
Wagner, G. D.	Twenty-first,	Sixth,		Army Ohio.
	Twenty-first,	Sixth,	Second,	Army Ohio.
	Second,	First, Left Wing,	Fourteenth,	Cumberland.
	Second,	First,	Twenty-first,	Cumberland.
		First,	Twenty-first,	Cumberland.
	Second,	Second,	Fourth,	Cumberland.
		Second,	Fourth,	Cumberland.
		District St. Louis, Mo.,		Missouri.
Wainwright, W. P.	Second,	First,	First,	Potomac.
Walcutt, C. C.	First,	First,	Sixteenth,	Tennessee.
	Second,	Fourth,	Fifteenth,	Tennessee.
	Second,	First,	Fifteenth,	Tennessee.
		First,	Fourteenth,	Cumberland.
Walker, E.	Second,	First,	Third,	Potomac.
	Second,	Third,	Second,	Potomac.
Walker, M. B.	First,	First,	Third,	Army Ohio.
	First,	Third, Centre,	Fourteenth,	Cumberland.
	First,	Third,	Fourteenth,	Cumberland.
Wallace, Lew		Third, Mil. Dist. Cairo,		Missouri.
		Third,		Army Tenn.
			Eighth,	Middle Dept.
				Middle Dept.
Wallace, Wm.	First,	Second, Right Wing,	Fourteenth,	Cumberland.
	First,	Second,	Twentieth,	Cumberland.
Wallace, W. H. L.	Third,	Military District Cairo,		Missouri.
	Second,	First, Mil. Dist. Cairo,		Missouri.
	Second,	First,		Army Tenn.
		Second,		Army Tenn.
Walworth, E. L.	Third,	Second,	Tenth,	Va. and N. C.
Walworth, N. H.	Third,	Third,	Twentieth,	Cumberland.
Wangelin, H.	Second,	First,	Fifteenth,	Tennessee.
	Third,	First,	Fifteenth,	Tennessee.
Ward, G. H.	First,	Second,	Second,	Potomac.
Ward, H. C.	Third,	Second,	Twenty-fifth,	Virginia.
	Third,	Second,	Twenty-fifth,	Texas.
Ward, J. E.	Second,	Third,	Twenty-fourth,	Virginia.
Ward, J. H. H.	Second,	Third,		Army N. E. Va.
	Second,	First,	Third,	Potomac.
		First,	Third,	Potomac.
	First,	Third,	Second,	Potomac.
Ward, L. M.	Second,	Provisional,	Seventeenth,	Gulf.
	First,	Third, Det'mt Army Tenn.,		Cumberland.
	First,	Third,	Sixteenth,	Gulf.
	Second,	Third,	Sixteenth,	Gulf.
Ward, W. T.	Sixteenth,			Army Ohio.
	Ward's,	Twelfth,		Army Ohio.
	Ward's,	Gallatin, Tenn.,		Cumberland.
	Second,	Third,	Reserve,	Cumberland.
	Ward's,	District Nashville, Tenn.,		Cumberland.
		First,	Eleventh,	Cumberland.
	First,	Third,	Twentieth,	Cumberland.
		Third,	Twentieth,	Cumberland.
Wardrop, D. W.	Reserve,	Division at Suffolk, Va.,	Seventh,	Virginia.
	Independent,		Seventh,	Virginia.
Waring, Geo. E. Jr.	Cavalry,	Army Southeast Mo.,		Missouri.
	First,	Sixth, Dist. Columbus,	Sixteenth,	Tennessee.
	Waring's,	First, Cavalry,	Sixteenth,	Tennessee.
	First,	First, Cavalry,	Sixteenth,	Tennessee.
		First, Cavalry,	Sixteenth,	Tennessee.
Warner, J. M.	First,	Defenses North Potomac,	Twenty-second,	Washington.
	First,	Second,	Sixth,	Potomac.
	First,	Second,	Sixth,	Army Shen.
	Second,	Second,	Sixth,	Army Shen.
Warren, F. H.	Second,	Second, Army Southeast Mo.,		Missouri.
	First,	First,	Thirteenth,	Gulf.
		First,	Thirteenth,	Gulf.
		District Baton Rouge, La.,		Gulf.
		U. S. Forces Texas,		Gulf.
Warren, G. K.	Third,	Second,	Fifth,	Potomac.
		Second,	Fifth,	Potomac.
			Second,	Potomac.
			Fifth,	Potomac.
		District Vicksburg, Miss.,		Mississippi.
				Mississippi.

Name	Brigade	Division, District, Etc.	Corps	Army or Dept.
Washburn, H. D.	First,	Fourteenth,	Thirteenth,	Tennessee.
	First,	First,	Thirteenth,	Gulf.
	First,	Second,	Nineteenth,	Army Shen.
	Fourth,	Second,	Nineteenth,	Army Shen.
	First,	Grover's, Dist. Savannah,		South.
	Third,	Grover's, Dist. Savannah,		South.
Washburne, C. C.		District Eastern Ark.,		Tennessee.
		Third, Cavalry, Dist. E. Ark.,		Tennessee.
		Second, Cavalry,	Thirteenth,	Tennessee.
		First Cavalry,	Sixteenth,	Tennessee.
		Ninth,	Thirteenth,	Tennessee.
		First,	Thirteenth,	Tennessee.
			Thirteenth,	Tennessee.
		First,	Thirteenth,	Gulf.
			Thirteenth,	Gulf.
		District West Tennessee,		Tennessee.
Wass, A. D.	Third,	Second,	Second,	Potomac.
Waters, L. H.	Third,	Second,	Twenty-first,	Cumberland.
	Third,	First,	Fourth,	Cumberland.
Watkins, L. D.	Third,	First,	Cavalry,	Cumberland.
	Third,	First,	Cavalry,	Mil. Div. Miss.
Wattles, S. H.	Indian,	District Frontier,	Seventh,	Arkansas.
Weaver, J. B.	First,	Second,	Sixteenth,	Tennessee.
Webb, A. S.	First,	Second,	Second,	Potomac.
	Second,	Second,	Second,	Potomac.
		Second,	Second,	Potomac.
Weber, Max	Weber's,			Virginia.
	Weber's,	Division at Suffolk, Va.,	Seventh,	Virginia.
Weber, Max	Third,	Third,	Second,	Potomac.
		Reserve,		West Virginia.
Webster, Geo.	Thirty-fourth,	Tenth,		Army Ohio.
	Thirty-fourth,	Tenth,	First,	Army Ohio.
Weddle, J.	Second,	Second Infantry,		West Virginia.
Weed, S. W.	Third,	Second,	Fifth,	Potomac.
Weeks, H. A.	Third,	First,	Fifth,	Potomac.
Weer, Wm.	Second,			Kansas.
		First, Army Frontier,		Missouri.
Weitzel, Godfrey	Reserve,		Nineteenth,	Gulf.
	Second,	First,	Nineteenth,	Gulf.
		First,	Nineteenth,	Gulf.
		Second,	Eighteenth,	Va. and N. C.
			Eighteenth,	Va. and N. C.
			Twenty-fifth,	Virginia.
Welch, N. E.	Third,	First,	Fifth,	Potomac.
Weld, S. M.	First,	First,	Ninth,	Potomac.
	Second,	Second,	Ninth,	Potomac.
Welling, J.	Third,	Defenses North Potomac.	Twenty-second,	Washington.
Wells, G. D.	Second,	Defenses South Potomac.	Twenty-second,	Washington.
	First,	Maryland Heights,		West Virginia.
	First,	First,		West Virginia.
	First,	First Infantry,		West Virginia.
Wells, H. H.		District Alexandria, Va.,	Twenty-second,	Washington.
Wells, M.	Third,	First Infantry,		West Virginia.
Wells, Oliver	First,	Fifth,	Cavalry,	Mil. Div. Miss.
	First,	First, Dist. West Tenn.,	Cavalry,	Tennessee.
Wells, Wm.	Second,	Third,	Cavalry,	Army Shen.
	Second,	Third,	Cavalry,	Potomac.
		Third,	Cavalry,	Potomac.
			Cavalry,	Potomac.
	1st Separate,		Twenty-second,	Washington.
Welsh, Thos.	Second,	First,		South.
	Second,	First,	Ninth,	Potomac.
	Third,	First,	Ninth,	Potomac.
		First,	Ninth,	Ohio.
		First,	Ninth,	Tennessee.
Wessells, H. W.	Second,	First,	Fourth,	Potomac.
	Second,	Second,	Fourth,	Potomac.
	Wessells',		Seventh,	Virginia.
	Wessells',	Division at Suffolk, Va.,	Seventh,	Virginia.
		First,		North Carolina.
		Fourth,	Eighteenth,	North Carolina.
		District Albermarle, N. C.,		Va. and N. C.
		Sub-Dis. Albermarle, Dist. N. C.,		Va. and N. C.
Wessells, L. W.	Second,	Defenses South Potomac,	Twenty-second,	Washington.
West, G. W.	Third,	First,	Third,	Potomac.
	Second,	Third,	Second,	Potomac.
	First,	Third,	Second,	Potomac.
	First,	Second,	Second,	Potomac.

Name	Brigade	Division, District, Etc.	Corps	Army or Dept.
West, H. R.	First,	First,	Twenty-fourth,	Virginia.
West, J. R.		Second,	Seventh,	Arkansas.
		Cavalry,	Seventh,	Arkansas.
	First,	First,	Cavalry,	Gulf.
		Second,	Cavalry,	Gulf.
West, R. M.	Advance,		Fourth,	Potomac.
	Advance,		Seventh,	Virginia.
	First,	Yorktown, Va.,		Va. and N. C.
		U. S. Forces, Yorktown, Va.,		Va. and N. C.
	First,	Cavalry,		Va. and N. C.
		Cavalry,		Va. and N. C.
Wever, C. R.	Second,	Seventh,	Seventeenth,	Tennessee.
	Second,	Second,	Seventeenth,	Tennessee.
	Second,	Third,	Fifteenth,	Tennessee.
Wheaton, Frank	Third,	Third,	Sixth,	Potomac.
		Third,	Sixth,	Potomac.
	First,	Second,	Sixth,	Potomac.
		Second,	Sixth,	Potomac.
	First,	Second.	Sixth,	Army Shen.
		First,	Sixth,	Army Shen.
		First,	Sixth,	Potomac.
Wheelock, Chas.	Third,	Second,	First,	Potomac.
	Second,	Second,	First,	Potomac.
	Second,	Third,	Fifth,	Potomac.
Whipple, A. W.	Whipple's,	Military Dist. Washington,		Potomac.
		Whipple's, Mil. Dist. Wash.,		Potomac.
		Third,	Third,	Potomac.
Whistler, J. N. G.	First,	Defenses South Potomac,	Twenty-second,	Washington.
Whittaker, W. C.	First,	First,	Reserve,	Cumberland.
		First,	Reserve,	Cumberland.
	Second,	First,	Fourth,	Cumberland.
		First,	Fourth,	Cumberland.
White, C. B.	Second,	Third,	Eighth,	Middle Dept.
	Second,	Scammon's,		West Virginia.
	Second,	Third,		West Virginia.
	Second,	Second Infantry,		West Virginia.
White, Frank	First,	Second,	Cavalry,	Mil. Div. Miss.
White, Julius	Second,	Third, Army Southwest Mo.,		Missouri.
	White's,	Harper's Ferry,		Army of Va.
	First,	Fourth,	Twenty-third,	Ohio.
		Fourth,	Twenty-third,	Ohio.
		Second,	Twenty-third,	Ohio.
		First,	Ninth,	Potomac.
White, Rich'd	First,	Third,	Tenth,	Va. and N. C.
White, T. J.	First,	Third,	Twenty-fifth,	Virginia.
Whiting, Chas. J.	First,	Cavalry,		Potomac.
	Reserve,	First,	Cavalry,	Potomac.
Whiting, H.	Second,	Second,	Sixth,	Potomac.
Whittlesey, Chas.	Third,	Third,		Army Tenn.
Wickersham, D.		Second, Army Frontier,		Missouri.
Wiedrich, M.	First,	Second,	Fifth,	Potomac.
Wilcox, A. T.	Second,	Third,	Twenty-third,	North Carolina.
Wild, E. A.	African,	North End Folly Island,	Tenth,	South.
		U. S. Forces Norfolk, Va.,		Va. and N. C.
	Second, African,	Norfolk, Va.,		Va. and N. C.
	First,	Hinks, U. S. C. T.		Va. and N. C.
		Third,	Twenty-fifth,	Virginia.
	Second,	First,	Twenty-fifth,	Virginia.
		First,	Twenty-fifth,	Virginia.
Wilder, J. T.	First,	Fifth,	Fourteenth,	Cumberland.
	Wilder's Mt'd,			Cumberland.
	First,	Fourth.	Fourteenth,	Cumberland.
	Third,	Second,	Cavalry,	Cumberland.
Wildes, T. F.	First,	First Infantry,		West Virginia.
	First,	Independent,	Twenty-fourth,	Virginia.
Wiles, G. F.	Second,	Third,	Seventeenth,	Tennessee.
Wiley, B. L.	First,	Cavalry Dist. Eastern Ark.		Tennessee.
Wilhelm, T.	Second,	Defences South Potomac,	Twenty-second,	Washington.
Wilkin, Alex.	Second,	First,	Sixteenth,	Tennessee.
	Second,	First,	Sixteenth,	Gulf.
Wilkinson, N.	Sixth,	First,	Eighth,	Middle Dept.
	Wilkinson's,			West Virginia.
	Third,	Second,		West Virginia.
	First,	Second Infantry,		West Virginia.
Willard, G. L.	Third,	Abercrombie's,	Twenty-second,	Washington.
	Third,	Third,	Second,	Potomac.
Willcox, O. B.	Second,	Third,		Army N. E. Va.
		First,	Ninth,	Potomac.

Name	Brigade	Division, District, Etc.	Corps	Army or Dept.
			Ninth,	Potomac.
		First,	Ninth,	Ohio.
			Ninth,	Ohio.
		District Central Ky.,		Ohio.
		Left Wing Forces,		Ohio.
		Second,	Ninth,	Ohio.
		Third,	Ninth,	Potomac.
		Mil. District Washington,	Twenty-second,	Washington.
Willett, J. M.	First,	Second,	Second,	Potomac.
	Second,	Second,	Second,	Potomac.
Williams, A. S.	Third,	First,		Pennsylvania.
	First,	Banks,		Potomac.
		First,	Banks, Fifth,	Potomac.
		First,		Shenandoah.
		First,	Second,	Army of Va.
			Second,	Army of Va.
		First,	Twelfth,	Potomac.
			Twelfth,	Potomac.
		First,	Twelfth,	Cumberland.
			Twelfth,	Cumberland.
		First,	Twentieth,	Cumberland.
			Twentieth,	Cumberland.
Williams, John	Second,	Third,	Second,	Potomac.
Williams, J. M.	Colored,		Seventh,	Arkansas
	Second,	District Frontier,	Seventh,	Arkansas
	Second,	First,	Seventh,	Arkansas
Williams, N. G.	First,	Fourth,		Army Tenn.
Williams, Robt.	First,	Fourth,	Fifteenth,	Tennessee.
Williams, Robert	Third,	Second,		South.
		Dist. Hilton Head, S. C.,		South.
Williams, Thos.	Fourth,	North Carolina,	Expeditionary,	
	Second,	New Orleans La. Exp.,		
Williamson, J. A.	Third,	First,	Fifteenth,	Tennessee.
	Second,	First,	Fifteenth,	Tennessee.
		District St. Louis, Mo.,		Missouri.
Willich, A.	Sixth,	Second,		Army Ohio.
	First,	Second, Right Wing,	Fourteenth,	Cumberland.
	First,	Second,	Twentieth,	Cumberland.
		Second,	Twentieth,	Cumberland.
		Third,	Fourth,	Cumberland.
	First,	Third,	Fourth,	Cumberland.
Wilson, J. H.		Third,	Cavalry,	Potomac.
		Third,	Cavalry,	Army Shen.
			Cavalry,	Mil. Div. Miss.
Wilson, J. M.		Dist. Delaware & Eastern Shore,	Eighth,	Middle Dept.
Wilson, Wm.	First,	First,	Second,	Potomac.
Wilson, Wm.	Consolidated,	First,	Second,	Potomac.
Wilson, Wm.	First,	Fourth,	Nineteenth,	Gulf.
Winslow, E. F.	Cavalry,	Third,	Fifteenth,	Tennessee.
	Cavalry,		Seventeenth,	Tennessee.
	Second,	First Cavalry,	Sixteenth,	Tennessee.
	Second,	Cavalry, West Tenn.,		Tennessee.
	Second,	Second, West Tenn.,	Cavalry,	Tennessee.
	First,	Fourth,	Cavalry,	Mil. Div. Miss.
Winthrop, F.	First,	Second,	Fifth,	Potomac.
		Third,	Fifth,	Potomac.
Wisewell, M. N.		Mil. Dist. Washington,	Twenty-second,	Washington.
	First,	Veteran Reserve,	Twenty-second,	Washington.
Wistar, I. J.	Reserve,	Division at Suffolk, Va.,	Seventh,	Virginia.
	Independent,		Seventh,	Virginia.
		U. S. Forces Yorktown, Va.,		Va. and N. C.
	Second,	Second,	Eighteenth,	Va. and N. C.
		Second,	Eighteenth,	Va. and N. C.
Wistar, L.	First,	Third,	First,	Potomac.
Withington, W. H.	First,	First,	Ninth,	Potomac.
Wolfe, E. H.	Third,	Third,	Sixteenth,	Tennessee.
	Third,	Second, Det'mt Army Tenn.,		Cumberland.
Wood, E. P.	Third,	First,		Army Tenn.
Wood, G. A.	Second,	First,	Twenty-first,	Cumberland.
Wood, J.	Third,	Memphis, Tenn., Dist. W. Tenn.,		Tennessee.
Wood, John,	Second,	Second,	Eleventh,	Cumberland.
	Third,	Third,	Twentieth,	Cumberland.
Wood, Oliver	Fourth,	Dist. Jackson, Left Wing,	Sixteenth,	Tennessee.
	Second,	Second, Arkansas Exp.,	Sixteenth,	Tennessee.
	Second,	Second,	Seventh,	Arkansas.
Wood, Thos. J.	Second,	McCook's Command,		Army Ohio.
	Fifth,			Army Ohio.

Name	Brigade	Division, District, Etc.	Corps	Army or Dept.
	Fifth,	Second,		Army Ohio.
		Sixth,		Army Ohio.
		Sixth,	Second,	Army Ohio.
		First, Left Wing,	Fourteenth,	Cumberland.
		First,	Twenty-first,	Cumberland.
			Twenty-first,	Cumberland.
		Third,	Fourth,	Cumberland.
			Fourth,	Cumberland.
Woodall, D.	Third,	Second,	Second,	Potomac.
Woodbury, D. P.		District Key West and Tortugas, Fla.,		Gulf.
Woodman, E. W.	Second,	Dist. West Florida,		Gulf.
	Third,	Dist. West Florida,		Gulf.
Woodruff, W. E.	Third,	First, Right Wing,	Fourteenth,	Cumberland.
Woods, C. R.	First,	First,	Fifteenth,	Tennessee.
	Second,	First,	Fifteenth,	Tennessee.
		First,	Fifteenth,	Tennessee.
		Third,	Seventeenth,	Tennessee.
Woods, J. J.	Third,	Third,	Fifteenth,	Tennessee.
	Third,	First,	Sixteenth,	Tennessee.
		First,	Sixteenth,	Tennessee.
Woods, W. B.	First,	First,	Fifteenth,	Tennessee.
Woodward, W. W.	Third,	Second,	Twenty-fifth,	Virginia.
	Third,	Second,	Twenty-fifth,	Texas.
Wool, John E.				Virginia.
				Middle Dept.
			Eighth,	Middle Dept.
				East.
Woolford, F.	Independent Cav.,		Twenty-third,	Ohio.
	Indpt. Cavalry,	Fourth,	Twenty-third,	Ohio.
	First,	First,	Cavalry,	Ohio.
		First,	Cavalry,	Ohio.
Worcester, G. S.	First,	Defenses North Potomac,	Twenty-second,	Washington.
	Third,	Defenses North Potomac,	Twenty-second,	Washington.
Worden, A.	Third,	Third,	Seventeenth,	Tennessee.
Worthington, W. H.	First,	Second,		Army Miss.
	Second,	Second,		Army Miss.
Wright, Dexter	First,	Casey's, Mil. Dist. Wash.,		Potomac.
Wright, E.	Second,	Third,	Tenth,	Va. and N. C.
	First,	Third,	Eighteenth,	Va. and N. C.
	Second,	Third,	Eighteenth,	Va. and N. C.
	Third,	First,	Twenty-fifth,	Virginia.
	Third,	Third,	Twenty-fifth,	Virginia.
	Third,	Paine's,	Terry's Prov'l,	North Carolina.
Wright, Geo.				Pacific.
Wright, H. G.	Third,	South Carolina,	Expeditionary,	
		First,		South.
		District West Kentucky,		Ohio.
				Ohio.
			Twenty-third,	Ohio.
		First,	Sixth,	Potomac.
			Sixth,	Potomac.
			Sixth,	Army Shen.
				Army Shen.
Wright, J. S.	Third,	First,	Seventeenth,	Tennessee.
Wyndham, Percy	Second,	Third,	Cavalry,	Potomac.
Wynkoop, G. C.	Second,	Second,		Pennsylvania.
	Second,	First Cavalry,		West Virginia.
		First Cavalry,		West Virginia.
Yates, Henry	Third,	Second,	Seventh,	Arkansas.
Yeoman, S. B.	Third,	First,	Twenty-fifth,	Virginia.
Young, J. M.	First,	Third,	Cavalry,	Cumberland.
Young, S. B. M.	Second,	Second,	Cavalry,	Potomac.
Young, V. E.	First,	Fourth,	Sixteenth,	Tennessee.
Zabriskie, A.	First,	Defenses Newberne, N. C.,	Eighteenth,	North Carolina.
Zahm, Lewis	Second,	Cavalry,		Army Ohio.
Zook, S. K.	Third,	First,	Second,	Potomac.
		First,	Second,	Potomac.
Zulavski, L. L.	First,	District West Florida,		Gulf.
	First,	First, U. S. C. T. West Fla.,		Gulf.
	Second,	First, U. S. C. T. West Fla.,		Gulf.

Regimental Index

ALABAMA

1st REGIMENT CAVALRY.—Org. at Huntsville, Ala., and Memphis, Tenn., Oct., 1862. Jany., 1863, Cavalry Brigade, Dist. Corinth, 16 Corps, Dept. Tenn. March, 1863, Cav. Brig., Dist. Corinth, 2 Div., 16 Corps. June, 1863, 3 Brig., 1 Div. 16 Corps. Aug., 1863, 1 Brig., 1 Div. Cav., 16 Corps. April, 1864, Cavalry, 4 Div., 16 Corps. May, 1864, Headqrs. 16 Corps. Sept., 1864, Unatt., 15 Corps. Nov., 1864, Unatt., Kilpatrick's 3 Div., Cav. Corps, Mil. Div. Miss. Jany., 1865, 2 Brig., 3 Div., Cav. Corps, Mil. Div. Miss. June, 1865, Dist. North Ala., Dept. Cumb'd. Mustered out Oct. 20, 1865.

1st REGIMENT SIEGE ARTILLERY, AFRICAN DESCENT.—Org. at Lagrange, Lafayette and Memphis, Tenn., June 20, 1863. June, 1863, Unatt., Dist. Corinth, 2 Div., 16 Corps, Dept. Tenn. Nov., 1863, Post Corinth, 2 Div., 16 Corps. Jany., 1864, Fort Pickering, Dist. Memphis, 5 Div., 16 Corps. Designation changed to 7th U. S. Colored Heavy Arty., April 26, 1864.

1st REGIMENT COLORED INFANTRY.—Org. at Corinth, Miss.. May 21, 1863. May, 1863, Unatt., Dist. Corinth, 2 Div., 16 Corps, Dept. Tenn. Nov., 1863, Post Corinth, Miss., 2 Div., 16 Corps. Jany., 1864, 1st Colored Brig., Dist. Memphis, Tenn., 5 Div., 16 Corps. Designation changed to 55th U. S. Colored Troops, March 11, 1864.

2nd REGIMENT COLORED INFANTRY.—Org. at Pulaski, Tenn., Nov. 20, 1863. Nov., 1863, Unatt., Dist. Corinth, 2 Div., 16 Corps, Dept. Tenn. Jany., 1864, Garrison Pulaski, Tenn., Dept. Tenn. Designation changed to 110th U. S. Colored Troops, June 25, 1864.

3rd REGIMENT COLORED INFANTRY.—Org. at Pulaski, Tenn., Jany. 13, 1864. Jany., 1864, Garrison Pulaski, Tenn. Designation changed to 111th U. S. Colored Troops, June 25, 1864.

4th REGIMENT COLORED INFANTRY.—Org. at Decatur, Ala., March 31, 1864. March, 1864, Garrison Pulaski, Tenn. Designation changed to 106th U. S. Colored Troops, May 16, 1864.

ARKANSAS

1st REGIMENT CAVALRY.—Org. at Springfield, Mo., June 10, 1862. June, 1862, Dist. S. W. Mo., Dept. Mo. Oct., 1862, 1 Brig., 3 Div., Army Frontier, Dept. Mo. Dec., 1862, Unatt., Army Frontier, Dept. Mo. June, 1863, Dist. S. W. Mo., Dept. Mo. June, 1864, 3 Brig., Frontier Div., 7 Corps, Dept. Ark. Feby., 1865, 2 Brig., 3 Div., 7 Corps, Dept. Ark. Feby., 1865, 1 Brig., 3 Div., 7 Corps, Dept. Ark. Mustered out Aug. 22, 1865.

2nd REGIMENT CAVALRY.—Org. at Springfield and Pilot Knob, Mo., July, 1862. July, 1862, Dist. S. W. Mo., Dept. Mo. July, 1862, Helena, Ark., Dist. Eastern Ark., Dept. Mo. Dec., 1862, 2 Brig., 3 Cav. Div., Dist. Eastern Ark., Dept. Tenn. Jany., 1863, 2 Brig., 2 Cav. Div., 13 Corps, Dept. Tenn. April, 1863, 2 Brig., Cav. Div., Dist. Eastern Ark., Dept. Tenn. May, 1863, Dist. S. W. Mo., Dept. Mo. Dec., 1864, Dist. West. Tenn., Dept. Tenn. Feby., 1865, 1 Brig., Cav. Div., Dist. West Tenn. Mustered out Aug. 20, 1865.

3rd REGIMENT CAVALRY.—Org. at Little Rock, Ark., Feby.. 1864. Feby., 1864, Little Rock, Ark., 7 Corps, Dept. Ark. May, 1864, 3 Brig., 2 Div., 7 Corps, Dept. Ark. Sept., 1864, 4 Brig., Cav. Div., 7 Corps. Feby., 1865, Post Lewisburg, Ark. Mustered out June 30, 1865.

4th REGIMENT CAVALRY.—Org. at large Dec., 1863. Dec., 1863, Post Little Rock, Ark., Dept. Ark. May, 1864, 2 Brig., Cav. Div., 7 Corps, Dept. Ark. Sept., 1864, 3 Brig., 1 Div., 7 Corps, Dept. Ark. Feby., 1865, Unassigned, 7 Corps, Dept. Ark. Feby., 1885, Cav. Brig., Post Little Rock, Ark. Mustered out June 30, 1865.

1st BATTERY LIGHT ARTILLERY.—Org. at Springfield, Mo., Aug. 31, 1863. Aug., 1863, Dist. S. W. Mo., Dept. Mo. March, 1864, 2 Brig., Dist. Frontier, 7 Corps, Dept. Ark. Feby., 1865, Arty., 3 Div., 7 Corps, Dept. Ark. Feby., 1865, 1 Brig., 3 Div., 7 Corps, Dept. Ark. Mustered out Aug. 10, 1865.

1st COLORED BATTERY LIGHT ARTILLERY.—Org.
at Pine Bluff, Ark., June 4, 1864. June, 1864, Post Pine Bluff, Ark., 7 Corps, Dept. Ark. Designation changed to Batty. "H," 2nd U. S. Colored Light Artillery, Dec. 13, 1864.

1st BATTALION INFANTRY.—Org. at Helena, Ark., July 20, 1862. July, 1862, District Eastern Ark., Dept. Mo. Mustered out Dec. 31, 1862.

1st REGIMENT INFANTRY.—Org. at Fayetteville, Ark., and mustered in March 25, 1863. March, 1863, Dist. S. W. Mo., Dept. Mo. Dec., 1863, 2 Brig., Dist. Frontier, Dept. Mo. Jany., 1864, 2 Brig., Frontier Div., 7 Corps, Dept. Ark. March, 1864, 1 Brig., Frontier Div., 7 Corps, Dept. Ark. Feby., 1865, 1 Brig., 3 Div., 7 Corps, Dept. Ark. Mustered out Aug. 10, 1865.

1st REGIMENT COLORED INFANTRY.—Org. at large May 1, 1863. May, 1863, Post Goodrich Landing, La., Dist. N. E. La., Dept. Tenn. Jany., 1864, 1st Colored Brig., Dist. Vicksburg, Miss., Dept. Tenn. Designation changed to 46th U. S. Colored Troops May 11, 1864.

2nd REGIMENT INFANTRY.—Org. at Springfield, Mo. and Fort Smith, Ark., Oct., 1862. Oct., 1862, Unatt., Dist. Frontier, Dept. Mo. Jany., 1864, Unatt., Dist. Frontier, 7 Corps, Dept. Ark. Jany., 1864, 2 Brig., Dist. Frontier, 7 Corps, Dept. Ark. May, 1864, 2 Brig., 2 Div., 7 Corps, Dept. Ark. Dec., 1864, 1 Brig., Frontier Div., 7 Corps, Dept. Ark. Feby., 1865, 1 Brig., 3 Div., 7 Corps, Dept. Ark. Mustered out Aug. 8, 1865.

2nd REGIMENT COLORED INFANTRY.—Org. in Arkansas at large Sept. 4, 1863. Sept., 1863, Dist. East. Ark., Dept. Ark. Jany., 1864, Dist. East. Ark., 7 Corps, Dept. Ark. Designation changed to 54th U. S. Colored Troops, March 11, 1864.

3rd REGIMENT INFANTRY.—Organization not completed.

3rd REGIMENT COLORED INFANTRY.—Org. at St. Louis, Mo., Aug. 12, 1863. Sept., 1863, Dist. East. Ark., Dept. Ark. Jany., 1864, Dist. East. Ark., 7 Corps, Dept. Ark. Designation changed to 56th U. S. Colored Troops March 11, 1864.

4th REGIMENT INFANTRY.—Org. at Fort Smith, Ark., Jany. to May, 1864. Jany., 1864, Dist. N. E. Ark., Dept. Ark. June, 1864, Fort Smith, Ark., Dist. Frontier, 7 Corps, Dept. Ark. Transferred to 2nd Arkansas Infantry Oct. 2, 1864.

4th REGIMENT COLORED INFANTRY.—Org. at Little Rock, Duvall's Bluff and Helena, Ark., Dec. 2, 1863. Jany., 1864, Dist. East. Ark., 7 Corps, Dept. Ark. Designation changed to 57th U. S. Colored Troops March 11, 1864.

5th REGIMENT COLORED INFANTRY.—(See 112th U. S. Colored Troops.)

6th REGIMENT COLORED INFANTRY.—(See 113th U. S. Colored Troops.)

CALIFORNIA

1st REGIMENT CAVALRY.—Org. in California at large Aug., 1861. Aug., 1861, Dept. Pacific. Jany., 1863, Dept. New Mexico. Mustered out Oct. 19, 1866.

1st BATTALION CAVALRY.—Org. in California at large March, 1863, to July, 1864. Duty in Dept. Pacific, Mustered out April 2, 1866.

2nd REGIMENT CAVALRY.—Org. at San Francisco, Cal., Sept. 5 to Oct. 18, 1861. Duty in Dept. Pacific. Mustered out July 12, 1866.

1st REGIMENT INFANTRY.—Org. in California at large Aug. to Oct., 1861. Duty in Dept. Pacific. Mustered out Oct. 21, 1866.

1st BATTALION MOUNTAINEERS.—Org. in California at large May 30, 1863, to March 16, 1864. Duty in Dept. Pacific. Mustered out June 14, 1865.

2nd REGIMENT INFANTRY.—Org. at San Francisco and at Carson City Sept. 2 to Dec. 30, 1861. Duty in Dept. Pacific. Mustered out July 2, 1866.

3rd REGIMENT INFANTRY.—Org. at Stockton and Benicia Barracks Sept. 15 to Dec. 3, 1861. Duty in Dept. Pacific. Mustered out July 26, 1866.

4th REGIMENT INFANTRY.—Org. at Sacramento, Placerville and Auburn Sept. and Oct., 1861. Duty in Dept. Pacific. Mustered out April 18, 1866.

5th REGIMENT INFANTRY.—Org. at various points Sept. to Nov., 1861. Duty in Dept. Pacific and Dept. New Mexico. Mustered out Nov. 27 to Dec. 14, 1864.

6th REGIMENT INFANTRY.—Org. at San Francisco Oct. 21, 1862. Duty in Dept. Pacific. Mustered out Oct. 25 to Dec. 20, 1865.

7th REGIMENT INFANTRY.—Org. at large Oct. to Dec., 1864. Duty in Dept. Pacific. Mustered out June 28, 1866.

8th REGIMENT INFANTRY.—Org. at large Nov., 1864. Duty in Dept. Pacific. Mustered out Oct. 24, 1865.

COLORADO TERRITORY

1st REGIMENT CAVALRY.—Org. Nov. 1, 1862, from 1st. Colo. Inf. Nov., 1862, Dist. Colo. July, 1864, Dist. Upper Ark. April, 1865 Dist. Plains. Mustered out Nov. 18, 1865.

2nd REGIMENT CAVALRY.—Org. Oct., 1863, by consolidation of 2nd and 3rd Colo. Infy. Oct., 1863, Dist. S. E. Mo., Dept. Mo. Dec., 1863, Dist. Cent. Mo., Dept. Mo. Dec., 1864, Dist. Upper Ark., Dept. Mo. Mustered out Sept. 23, 1865.

3rd REGIMENT CAVALRY.—Org. at Denver Aug. and Sept., 1864. Duty in Dist. Colo. Mustered out Dec. 31, 1864.

McLANE'S INDEPENDENT BATTERY LIGHT ARTILLERY.—Org. at Denver Dec. 15, 1862. Dec., 1862, Dist. Colo. July, 1864, Dist. Upper Ark. Dec., 1864, Dist. of South Kan. April, 1865, Dist. North Kan. Mustered out Aug. 31. 1865.

1st REGIMENT INFANTRY.—Org. at Denver and Camp Weld, Colo., Aug. 26 to Dec. 14, 1861. Duty in Dist. Colo. Designation changed to 1st Colorado Cavalry Nov. 1, 1862.

2nd REGIMENT INFANTRY.—Org. at Fort Garland, Central City, Fort Lyon and Denver, Dec., 1861. Dec., 1861, Dist. Colo. June, 1863, Dist. S. E. Mo., Dept. Mo. June, 1863, Dist. Frontier, Dept. Mo. July, 1863, Dist. Border, Dept. Mo. Dec., 1863, Dist. St. Louis, Mo., Dept. Mo. Consolidated with 3rd Colorado Infantry Oct., 1863, to form 2nd Colorado Cavalry.

3rd REGIMENT INFANTRY.—Org. at Denver and Camp Weld, Colo.. Sept., 1862. Sept., 1862, Dist. Colo. Feby., 1863, Dist. S. E. Mo., Dept. Mo. July, 1863, Reserve Cav. Brig., 1st Cav. Div., Dist. S. E. Mo., Dept. Mo. July, 1863, Dist. S. E. Mo., Dept. Mo. Consolidated with 2nd Colorado Infantry to form 2nd Colorado Cavalry Oct., 1863.

DENVER CITY HOME GUARD.—Org. at Denver Aug. to Oct., 1861. Duty in Dist. Colo. Mustered out April 1, 1862.

CONNECTICUT

1st REGIMENT CAVALRY.—Org. at West Meriden Nov. 2, 1861. Dec., 1861, Unatt. Dept. W. Va. April, 1862, R. R. Dist. Mt. Dept. April, 1862, Schenck's Brig., Mt. Dept. June. 1862, Cav. Brig., 1 Corps Army Va. Sept., 1862, Cav. Brig., 11 Corps Potomac. Jany., 1863, Def. Balto., Md., 8 Corps. Jany., 1863, 2nd Separate Brig., 8 Corps Middle Dept. (July, 1863, Lockwood's Md. Heights Div., Dept. W. Va., Det. Oct., 1863, Cav. Brig., 1 Div., Dept. W. Va., Det.) Jany., 1864, Cav. Reserve Balto., Md., 8 Corps. March, 1864, 1 Brig., 3 Div., Cav Corps, Potomac and Shenandoah. June, 1865, Cav. Brig., Dept. Wash. Mustered out Aug. 2, 1865.

1st REGIMENT HEAVY ARTILLERY.—Org. from 4th Infy. Jany. 2, 1862. Jany., 1862, Def. Washington, D. C. April, 1862, Siege Arty., Potomac. May, 1862, 3 Brig., 2 Div., 5 Corps, Potomac. July, 1862, Siege Arty. Army Potomac, Harrison's Landing, Va. Aug., 1862, Def. Alexandria, Va. (Oct., 1862, Res. Arty. Army Potomac, Cos. B. M. to Jany., 1864.) Feby., 1863, Arty. Def. Alexandria, Va., Tyler's, Div., 22 Corps. April, 1863, 2 Brig., DeRussy's Div., 22 Corps. Def. South Potomac. May, 1863, 3 Brig., DeRussy's Div., 22 Corps. Dec., 1863, 2 Brig., DeRussy's Div., 22 Corps. March, 1864, 4 Brig., DeRussy's Div., 22 Corps. May, 1864, Points of Rocks, Va., Dept. Va.

and N. C. June, 1864, Siege Arty., Dept. Va. and N. C. in the field, and Siege Arty. Army Potomac. May, 1865, Siege Arty., Dept. Va. July, 1865, 4 Brig., DeRussy's Div., Dept. Wash. Aug., 1865, 3 Brig., Dept. Wash. Mustered out Sept. 25, 1865.

2nd REGIMENT HEAVY ARTILLERY.—Org. from 19th Infy. Nov. 23, 1863. Nov., 1863, 2 Brig., DeRussy's Div., 22 Corps. Feby., 1864, 4 Brig., DeRussy's Div., 22 Corps. May, 1864, 2 Brig., 1 Div., 6 Corps, Potomac. Aug., 1864, 2 Brig., 1 Div., 6 Corps, Shenandoah. Dec., 1864, 2 Brig., 1 Div., 6 Corps, Potomac. June, 1865, 2 Brig., DeRussy's Div., 22 Corps. Mustered out Aug. 18, 1865.

1st BATTERY LIGHT ARTILLERY.—Org. at West Meriden and mustered in Oct. 26, 1861. Jany., 1862, Unatt. Sherman's S. C. Exp. Corps. April, 1862, 3 Brig., 2 Div., Dept. South. July, 1862, Dist. Beaufort, S. C., Dept. South. Sept., 1862, Dist. Beaufort, S. C., 10 Corps, Dept. South. July, 1863, Arty. Folly Island, S. C., 10 Corps. Jany., 1864, Folly Island, S. C., Northern Dist., 10 Corps. April, 1864, Arty., 1 Div., 10 Corps, Dept. Va. and N. C. Aug., 1864, Arty. Brig., 10 Corps. Dec., 1864, Arty. Brig. 25 Corps. Mustered out June 11, 1865.

2nd BATTERY LIGHT ARTILLERY.—Org. at Bridgeport Sept. 10, 1862. Oct., 1862, 2 Brig., Casey's Div., Def. Washington, D. C. Feby., 1863, 2 Brig., Casey's Div., 22 Corps. April, 1863, Arty. Abercrombie's Div., 22 Corps. June, 1863, 2 Vol. Brig., Arty. Res., Potomac. Aug., 1863, N. Y. City, Dept. East. Oct., 1863, Camp Barry, Washington, D. C., 22 Corps. Feby., 1864, Def. New Orleans, Dept. Gulf. June, 1864, Arty., 4 Div., 13 Corps, Dept. Gulf. June, 1864, Def. New Orleans. Aug., 1864, Arty. Res., Gulf. Aug., 1864, Unatt. Arty., 19 Corps, Gulf. Dec., 1864, Arty. Res., Reserve Corps Mil. Div., West Miss. Feby., 1865, Arty., 2 Div., Reserve Corps, M. D. W. M. Feby., 1865, Arty., 2 Div., 13 Corps, M. D. W. M. Mustered out Aug. 9, 1865.

3rd BATTERY LIGHT ARTILLERY.—Org. at New Haven Aug. to Oct., 1864. Nov., 1864, Def. City Point, Va. Dec., 1864, Siege Arty. Army James and Army Potomac. Mustered out June 23, 1865.

1st REGIMENT INFANTRY.—Org. at Hartford April 22, 1861. May, 1861, Mansfield's Command, Dept. Wash. June, 1861, Keyes Brig., Tyler's Div., McDowell's Army, N. E. Va. Mustered out July 31, 1861.

2nd REGIMENT INFANTRY.—Org. at New Haven May 7, 1861. May, 1861, Mansfield's Command, Dept. Wash., D. C. June, 1861, Keyes' Brig., Tyler's Div., McDowell's Army, N. E. Va. Mustered out Aug. 7, 1861.

3rd REGIMENT INFANTRY.—Org. at Hartford and mustered in May 14, 1861. May, 1861, Mansfield's Command, Dept. Wash., D. C. June, 1861, Keyes' Brig., Tyler's Div., McDowell's Army N. E. Va. Mustered out Aug. 12, 1861.

4th REGIMENT INFANTRY.—Org. at Hartford May 21, 1861. June, 1861, Abercrombie's 6 Brig., 2 Div., Dept. Penna. Aug., 1861, 2 Brig., Banks' Div., Potomac. Dec., 1861, Def. Washington. Designation changed to 1st Heavy Artillery January 2, 1862.

5th REGIMENT INFANTRY.—Org. at Hartford July 26, 1861. Aug., 1861, Geo. H. Thomas' Brig., Banks' Div., Shenandoah. Oct., 1861, Gordon's Brig., Banks' Div., Potomac. March, 1862, 1 Brig., 1 Div., Banks' 5 Corps. April, 1862, 1 Brig., 1 Div., Dept. Shenandoah. June, 1862, 1 Brig., 1 Div., 2 Corps, Army Va. Sept., 1862, 1 Brig., 1 Div., 12 Corps, Potomac. Oct., 1863, 1 Brig., 1 Div., 12 Corps, Cumb'd. April, 1864, 2 Brig., 3 Div., 20 Corps. April, 1864, 1 Brig., 1 Div., 20 Corps. June, 1865, 2 Brig., Bartlett's Div., 22 Corps. Mustered out July 19. 1865.

6th REGIMENT INFANTRY.—Org. at New Haven Sept. 12, 1861. Oct., 1861, Wright's 3 Brig., Sherman's S. C. Exp. Corps. April, 1862, 1 Brig., 1 Div., Dept. South. July, 1862, Dist. Beaufort, S. C., Dept. South. Sept., 1862, Dist. Beaufort, S. C., 10 Corps. March, 1863, Jacksonville. Fla., 10 Corps. April, 1863, Folly Island, S. C., 10 Corps. June, 1863, 2 Brig., U. S. Forces Folly Island, S. C., 10 Corps. July, 1863, 2 Brig., 2 Div., Morris Island, S. C., 10 Corps. July, 1863, 1 Brig., Morris Island, S. C., 10 Corps. Aug., 1863, Dist. Hilton Head, S. C., 10 Corps.

April, 1864, 3 Brig., 1 Div., 10 Corps, Dept. Va. and N. C., Army James. May, 1864, 2 Brig., 1 Div., 10 Corps. Dec., 1864, 2 Brig., 1 Div., 24 Corps. Jany., 1865, 2 Brig., 1 Div., Terry's Prov'l Corps, Dept. N. C. March, 1865, 2 Brig., 1 Div., 10 Corps, Ohio. April, 1865, Abbott's Det. Brig., 10 Corps. Mustered out Aug. 21, 1865.

7th REGIMENT INFANTRY.—Org. at New Haven Sept. 13, 1861. Oct., 1861, Wright's 3 Brig., Sherman's S. C. Exp. Corps. April, 1862, 1 Brig., 2 Div., Dept. South. July, 1862, Dist. Hilton Head, S. C., Dept. South. Sept., 1862, Dist. Beaufort, S. C., 10 Corps. Jany., 1863, Fernandina, Fla. April, 1863, Dist. Hilton Head, S. C., 10 Corps, Co.'s A, B, I, K, St. Augustine, Fla., Regt. (June, 1863, St. Helena Island, S. C., 10 Corps, Co.'s A, B, I, K. July, 1863, 2 Brig., Folly Island, S. C., 10 Corps, Co.'s A, B, I, K. July, 1863, 2 Brig., 2 Div., Morris Island, S. C., 10 Corps, Co.'s A, B, I, K. July, 1863, 1 Brig., Morris Island, 10 Corps, Co.'s A, B, I, K.) Aug., 1863, 3 Brig., Morris Island, S. C., 10 Corps. Oct., 1863, St. Helena Island, S. C., 10 Corps. Nov., 1863, 1 Brig., Morris Island, S. C., 10 Corps. Dec., 1863, St. Helena Island, S. C., 10 Corps. Feby., 1864, 2 Brig., Hawley's Brig., Dist. Fla. April, 1864, 3 Brig., 1 Div., 10 Corps, Dept. Va. and N. C., Army James. May, 1864, 2 Brig., 1 Div., 10 Corps. Dec., 1864, 2 Brig., 1 Div., 24 Corps. Jany., 1865, 2 Brig., 1 Div., Terry's Prov'l Corps, Dept. N. C. March, 1865, 2 Brig., 1 Div., 10 Corps, Dept. N. C., Army Ohio. April, 1865, Abbott's Det. Brig., 10 Corps. Mustered out July 20, 1865.

8th REGIMENT INFANTRY.—Org. at Hartford Sept. 21, 1861. Dec., 1861, Parke's 3 Brig., Burnside's N. C. Exp. Corps. April, 1862, 1 Brig., 3 Div., Dept. N. C. July, 1862, 2 Brig., 3 Div., 9 Corps, Potomac. April, 1863, 2 Brig., 2 Div., 7 Corps, Dept. Va. July, 1863, 2 Brig. Getty's Div., U. S. Forces Portsmouth, Va., Dept. Va. and N. C. Jany., 1864, Sub Dist. Albemarle, N. C., Dept. Va. and N. C. April 1864, 2 Brig., 1 Div., 18 Corps, Army James. Aug., 1864, Provost Guard 18 Corps. Dec., 1864, Provost Guard 24 Corps. Feby., 1865, 2 Brig., 3 Div., 24 Corps. July, 1865, 2nd Prov'l Brig., 24 Corps. Aug., 1865, Dept. Va. Mustered out Dec., 1865.

9th REGIMENT INFANTRY.—Org. at New Haven Sept. 26, 1861. Nov., 1861, Ship Island Expedition. March, 1862, 1 Brig., Dept. Gulf. Sept., 1862, Def. New Orleans, Gulf. Feby., 1863, 1 Brig., 3 Div., 19 Corps, Gulf. March, 1863, 2 Brig., 2 Div., 19 Corps. Aug., 1863, 2 Brig., 4 Div., 19 Corps. Feby., 1864, 1 Brig., 2 Div., 19 Corps. April, 1864, Dept. East. July, 1864, Bermuda Hundred, Va., 10 Corps. Aug., 1864, 1 Brig., 2 Div., 19 Corps Middle Mil. Div. Jany., 1865, Dist. Savannah, Dept. South, 1 Brig., Grover's Div. March, 1865, 1 Brig., 1 Div., 10 Corps, Army Ohio, Dept. N. C. May, 1865, Dist. Port Royal, Dept. South. Mustered out Aug. 3, 1865.

10th REGIMENT INFANTRY.—Org. at Hartford Oct. 22, 1861. Dec., 1861, Foster's 1 Brig., Burnside's N. C. Exp. Corps. April, 1862, 2 Brig., 1 Div., Dept. N. C. Jany., 1863, 2 Brig., 4 Div., 18 Corps, Dept. N. C. Feby., 1863, 2 Brig., 1 Div., 18 Corps, Dept. South. April, 1863, Stevenson's Brig., Seabrook Island, 10 Corps, Dept. South. July, 1863, 1 Brig., 1 Div., Morris Island, S. C., 10 Corps. July, 1863, 3 Brig., Morris Island, 10 Corps. Oct., 1863, St. Augustine, Fla. April, 1864, 2 Brig., 1 Div., 10 Corps, Dept. Va. and N. C., Army James. May, 1864, 3 Brig., 1 Div., 10 Corps. Dec., 1864, 3 Brig., 1 Div., 24 Corps. July, 1865, 2 Brig., 1 Div., 24 Corps. Mustered out Aug. 15, 1865.

11th REGIMENT INFANTRY.—Org. at Hartford Oct. 24 to Nov. 14, 1861. Dec., 1861, Williams' Brig., Burnside's N. C. Exp. Corps. April, 1862, 2 Brig., 2 Div., Dept. N. C. July, 1862, 2 Brig., 3 Div., 9 Corps, Potomac. April, 1863, 2 Brig., 2 Div., 7 Corps, Dept. Va. July, 1863, 2 Brig., Getty's Div., Portsmouth, Va., Dept. Va. and N. C. Oct., 1863, U. S. Forces Yorktown, Va. Jany., 1864, 1 Brig. U. S. Forces Yorktown, Va. April, 1864, 2 Brig., 2 Div., 18 Corps, Army James. Oct., 1864, Prov'l Div., Army James. Dec., 1864, 1 Brig., 3 Div., 24 Corps. July, 1865, 1st Indpt. Brig., 24 Corps. Aug., 1865, Dept. Va. Mustered out Dec. .., 1865.

12th REGIMENT INFANTRY.—Org. at Hartford Nov. 19 to Dec. 3, 1861. March, 1862, 1 Brig., Dept. Gulf. Oct., 1862, Weitzel's Reserve Brig., Dept. Gulf. Jany., 1863, 2 Brig., 1 Div., 19 Corps, Dept. Gulf. Aug., 1863, 3 Brig., 1 Div., 19 Corps. Feby., 1864, 2 Brig., 1 Div., 19 Corps. Aug., 1864, 2 Brig., 1 Div., 19 Corps, Middle Mil. Div. April, 1865, 2 Brig., 1 Prov'l Div., Army Shenandoah. April, 1865, 2 Brig., Dwight's Div., Dept. Wash. June, 1865, Dist. Savannah, Ga., Dept. South. Mustered out Aug. 12, 1865.

13th REGIMENT INFANTRY.—Org. at New Haven Nov. 25, 1861, to Jany. 7, 1862. March, 1862, 1 Brig., Dept. Gulf. Oct., 1862, Weitzel's Reserve Brig., Dept. Gulf. Dec., 1862, Grover's Div., Dept. Gulf. Jany., 1863, 3 Brig., 3 Div., 19 Corps, Dept. Gulf. Jany., 1863, 2 Brig., 4 Div., 19 Corps. March. 1863, 3 Brig., 4 Div., 19 Corps. Aug., 1863, 1 Brig., 4 Div., 19 Corps. Feby., 1864, 2 Brig., 2 Div., 19 Corps. Aug., 1864, 2 Brig., 2 Div., 19 Corps, Middle Mil. Div. Jany., 1865, 2 Brig., Grover's Div., Dist. Savannah. Ga., Dept. South. March, 1865, 1 Brig., 1 Div., 10 Corps, Army Ohio, Dept. N. C. April, 1865, Dist. Ga., Dept. South. Mustered out April 25, 1866.

14th REGIMENT INFANTRY.—Org. at Hartford Aug. 23, 1862. Aug., 1862, Whipple's Command Def. Washington. Sept., 1862, 2 Brig., 3 Div., 2 Corps, Potomac. March, 1864, 3 Brig., 2 Div., 2 Corps. Mustered out May 21, 1865.

15th REGIMENT INFANTRY.—Org. at New Haven Aug. 25, 1862. Aug., 1862, Casey's Prov'l Brig. Def. Washington. Oct., 1862, 1 Brig. Casey's Div., Def. Washington. Dec., 1862, 2 Brig., 3 Div., 9 Corps, Potomac. April, 1863, 2 Brig., 2 Div., 7 Corps, Dept. Va. July, 1863, 2 Brig., Getty's Div. U. S. Forces, Portsmouth, Va., Dept. Va. and N. C. Jany., 1864, Dist. Albemarle, N. C., Dept. Va. and N. C. Feby., 1864, Def. Newberne, N. C., Dept. Va. and N. C. Jany., 1865, Sub Dist. Newberne, Dept. N. C. March, 1865, 2 Brig., 2 Div., Dist. Beaufort, N. C., Dept. N. C. March, 1865, 1 Brig., 1 Div., Dist. Beaufort, Dept. N. C., Post of Kinston. N. C. Mustered out June 27, 1865.

16th REGIMENT INFANTRY.—Org. at Hartford Aug. 24, 1862. Sept., 1862, 2 Brig., 3 Div., 9 Corps, Potomac. April, 1863, 2 Brig., 2 Div., 7 Corps, Dept. Va. July, 1863, 2 Brig., Getty's Div. U. S. Forces, Portsmouth, Va., Dept. Va. and N. C. Jany., 1864, Dist. Albemarle, N. C., Dept. Va. and N. C. April, 1864, Def. Newberne, N. C., Dept. Va. and N. C. Jany., 1865, Roanoke Island, N. C., Dept. N. C. Mustered out June 24, 1865.

17th REGIMENT INFANTRY.—Org. at Bridgeport Aug. 28, 1862. Sept., 1862, Balto., Md., 8 Corps, Middle Dept. Oct., 1862, 2 Brig., 1 Div., 11 Corps, Potomac. Aug., 1863, 2 Brig., Gordon's Div. U. S. Forces, S. E. Folly Island, S. C., 10 Corps, Dept. South. Feby., 1864, 1 Brig., Ames Div., Dist. Fla., 10 Corps. April, 1864, Dist. Fla., Dept. South. Oct., 1864, 4 Separate Brig., Dept. South. Mustered out July 19, 1865.

18th REGIMENT INFANTRY.—Org. at Norwich Aug. 22, 1862. Aug., 1862, Def. Balto., Md., 8 Corps, Middle Dept. Jany., 1863, 2nd Separate Brig., 8 Corps. March, 1863, 2 Brig., 2 Div., 8 Corps. June, 1863, Unatt., Dept. Susquehanna. July, 1863, Unatt., Scammon's Div., Dept. W. Va. Dec., 1863, 3 Brig., 1 Div., Army W. Va. April, 1864, 1 Brig., 1 Div., W. Va. July, 1864, 2 Brig., 1 Infy. Div., W. Va. Oct., 1864, New Haven, Conn. Jany., 1865, 1 Brig., 3 Div., W. Va. April, 1865, 1 Brig., 2 Div., W. Va. Mustered out June 27, 1865.

19th REGIMENT INFANTRY.—Org. at Litchfield July 25 to Sept. 9, 1862. Sept., 1862, Slough's Brig., Dist. Alexandria, Va., Def. Washington. Jany., 1863, Tyler's Command Arty., Def. Alexandria, Va. Feby., 1863, Tyler's Command Arty., Def. Alexandria, 22 Corps. April, 1863, 2 Brig., DeRussy's Div., 22 Corps. Designation changed to 2nd Heavy Artillery Nov. 23, 1863.

20th REGIMENT INFANTRY.—Org. at New Haven Sept. 8, 1862. Oct., 1862, 2 Brig., 1 Div., 12 Corps, Potomac. May, 1863, 1 Brig., 1 Div., 12 Corps. Oct., 1863, 1 Brig., 1 Div., 12 Corps, Cumb'd. April, 1864, 1 Brig., 1 Div., 20 Corps. April, 1864, 2 Brig., 3 Div., 20 Corps. May, 1864, 3 Brig., 3 Div., 20 Corps. Mustered out June 13, 1865.

21st REGIMENT INFANTRY.—Org. at Norwich Sept. 5, 1862. Sept., 1862, 2 Brig., 3 Div., 9 Corps, Potomac.

Jany., 1863, 3 Brig., 3 Div., 9 Corps, Potomac. April, 1863, 3 Brig., 2 Div., 7 Corps, Dept. Va. July, 1863, 3 Brig., Getty's Div. U. S. Forces, Portsmouth, Va., Dept. Va. and N. C. Oct., 1863, Heckman's Brig., Newport News, Va., Dept. Va. and N. C. Feby., 1864, Def. Newberns, N. C., Dept. Va. and N. C. March, 1864, Sub Dist., Pamlico, N. C., Dept. Va. and N. C. May, 1864, 3 Brig., 1 Div., 18 Corps, Army James. Dec., 1864, 3 Brig., 3 Div., 24 Corps. Mustered out June 16, 1865.

22nd REGIMENT INFANTRY.—Org. at Hartford Sept. 20, 1862. Oct., 1862, 2 Brig., Abercrombie's Div., Def. Washington. Feby., 1863, 2 Brig., Abercrombie's Div., 22 Corps. April, 1863, 1 Brig., 3 Div., 7 Corps, Dept. Va. May, 1863, 2 Brig., 2 Div., 4 Corps, Dept. Va. Mustered out July 7, 1863.

23rd REGIMENT INFANTRY.—Org. at New Haven Nov. 14, 1862. Dec., 1862, Indpt. Command, Dept. Gulf. Jany., 1863, Def. New Orleans, Dept. Gulf. Mustered out Aug. 31, 1863.

24th REGIMENT INFANTRY.—Org. at Middletown and mustered in Nov. 18, 1862. Dec., 1862, Grover's Div., Dept. Gulf. Jany., 1863, 2 Brig., 4 Div., 19 Corps, Dept. Gulf. July, 1863, Def. New Orleans, Dept. Gulf. Mustered out Sept. 30, 1863.

25th REGIMENT INFANTRY.—Org. at Hartford and mustered in Nov. 11, 1862. Dec., 1862, Grover's Div., Dept. Gulf. Jany., 1863, 3 Brig., 4 Div., 19 Corps, Gulf. Mustered out Aug. 26, 1865.

26th REGIMENT INFANTRY.—Org. Norwich Nov. 10, 1862. Dec., 1862, Sherman's Div., Dept. Gulf. Jany., 1863, 1 Brig., 2 Div., 19 Corps, Gulf. Mustered out Aug. 17, 1863.

27th REGIMENT INFANTRY.—Org. at New Haven Oct., 1862. Oct., 1862, Def. Washington. Nov., 1862, 3 Brig., 1 Div., 2 Corps, Potomac. April, 1863, 4 Brig., 1 Div., 2 Corps. Mustered out July 27, 1863.

28th REGIMENT INFANTRY.—Org. New Haven Nov. 15, 1862. Dec., 1862, Dist. Pensacola, Fla., Dept. Gulf. May, 1863, 1 Brig., 3 Div., 19 Corps, Gulf. July, 1863, 2 Brig., 3 Div., 19 Corps. Mustered out Aug. 28, 1863.

29th REGIMENT INFANTRY.—(Colored.) Org. at Fair Haven and mustered in March 8, 1864. April, 1864, Dist. Beaufort, S. C., Dept. South. Aug., 1864, 1 Brig., 3 Div., 10 Corps, Dept. Va. and N. C., Army James. Oct., 1864, 2 Brig., 3 Div., 10 Corps. Nov., 1864, 1 Brig., 3 Div., 10 Corps. Dec., 1864, 2 Brig., 3 Div., 25 Corps. Jany., 1865, 2 Brig., 1 Div., 25 Corps. March, 1865, Dist. St. Mary's, 22 Corps. June, 1865, 2 Brig., 1 Div., 25 Corps, Dept. Texas. Mustered out Oct. 24, 1865.

30th REGIMENT INFANTRY.—(Colored.) Org. at Fair Haven. April, 1864, 2 Brig., 4 Div., 9 Corps, Potomac. Consolidated with 31st U. S. C. T. May 18, 1864.

DELAWARE

1st REGIMENT CAVALRY.—Org. at Wilmington Jany. 20, 1863. Feby., 1863, 1st Separate Brig., 8 Corps, Middle Dept. June, 1863. Cav. Res. Def. Balto., Md., 8 Corps, Middle Dept. Oct., 1863, 3d Separate Brig., 8 Corps, Middle Dept. Dec., 1863, Cav. Res. Def. Baltimo., 8 Corps. March, 1864, 3d Separate Brig., 8 Corps; May, 1864, 1 Brig., 1 Div., 6 Corps, Potomac. July, 1864, 1st Separate Brig., 8 Corps. Mustered out June 30, 1865.

MILLIGAN'S INDEPENDENT COMPANY CAVALRY. —Org. at Wilmington July 15, 1864. July, 1864, 3d Separate Brig., 8 Corps, Middle Dept. Mustered out Aug. 15, 1864.

AHL'S INDEPENDENT COMPANY HEAVY ARTILLERY.—Org. at Fort Delaware July 27, 1863. Garrison Fort Deleware. Mustered out July 25, 1865.

NIELD'S INDEPENDENT BATTERY LIGHT ARTILLERY.—Org. at Wilmington Aug. 30, 1862. Oct., 1862, Camp Barry, Def. Washington, D. C. Feby., 1863, Camp Barry, Def. Washington, 22 Corps. April, 1863, Unatt. Arty., 7 Corps, Dept. Va. June, 1863, Arty., 1 Div., 7 Corps, Dept. Va. July, 1863, Camp Barry, Def. Washington, 22 Corps. Aug., 1863, Dept. East. Oct., 1863, Camp Barry, Def. Washington, 22 Corps. Feby., 1864, Def. New Orleans, La., Dept. Gulf. July, 1864, Arty., 1 Div., 19 Corps, Gulf. July, 1864, Arty., 3 Div., 19 Corps, Gulf. Nov., 1864, Unass'd Arty., Res. Corps, Gulf. Dec., 1864, Arty., 2 Div., 7 Corps, Ark. Mustered out June 23, 1865.

1st REGIMENT INFANTRY.—(3 Months.) Org. at Wilmington May 22, 1861. May, 1861, Dix's Div., Baltimore, Md. Mustered out Aug. 30, 1861.

1st REGIMENT INFANTRY.—(3 Years.) Org. at Wilmington Sept. 10 to Oct. 19, 1861. Oct., 1861, Fort Monroe, Va., Dept. Va. May, 1862, 2 Brig., 1 Div., Dept. Va. July, 1862, Weber's Brig. Div. at Suffolk, Va., 7 Corps, Dept. Va. Sept., 1862, 3 Brig., 3 Div., 2 Corps, Potomac. May, 1863, 2 Brig., 3 Div., 2 Corps, Potomac. March, 1864, 3 Brig., 2 Div., 2 Corps, Potomac. Mustered out July 12, 1865.

2nd REGIMENT INFANTRY.—Org. at Wilmington June 12 to Oct. 7, 1861. Oct., 1861, Dix's Div., Balto., Md. June, 1862, 3 Brig., 1 Div., 2 Corps, Potomac. April, 1863, 4 Brig., 1 Div., 2 Corps, Potomac. June, 1864, 3 Brig., 2 Div., 2 Corps, Potomac. Mustered out July 1, 1864. Vets and Rcts to 1st. Del. Infy.

3rd REGIMENT INFANTRY.—Org. at Camden Dec. 30, 1861 to May 15, 1862. May, 1862, Slough's Brig., Def. Washington, D. C. May, 1862, Slough's 2 Brig., Sigel's Div., Dept. Shenandoah. June, 1862, 2 Brig., 2 Div., 2 Corps, Army Va. Aug., 1862, 3 Brig., 2 Div., 2 Corps, Army Va. Sept., 1862, 3 Brig., 2 Div., 12 Corps, Potomac. Oct., 1862, Def. Balto., Md., 8 Corps, Middle Dept. Jany., 1863, 3d Separate Brig., 8 Corps, Middle Dept. Oct., 1863, 1st Separate Brig., 8 Corps, Middle Dept. May, 1864, 2 Brig., 4 Div., 5 Corps, Potomac. Aug., 1864, 3 Brig, 2 Div., 5 Corps, Potomac. Mustered out June 3, 1865.

4th REGIMENT INFANTRY.—Org. at Wilmington June to Nov., 1862. Sept., 1862, Def. Balto., Md., 8 Corps, Middle Dept. Dec., 1862, Busteed's Indpt. Brig., 4 Corps, Dept. Va. May, 1863, King's Indpt. Brig., 4 Corps, Dept. Va. June, 1863, Unatt. 4 Corps, Dept. Va. July, 1863, Unass'd King's Div., 22 Corps. Jany., 1864, 1 Brig., Tyler's Div., 22 Corps. June, 1864, 2 Brig., 4 Div., 5 Corps, Potomac. Aug., 1864, 3 Brig., 2 Div., 5 Corps, Potomac. Mustered out June 3, 1865.

5th REGIMENT INFANTRY.—Org. at large Oct. 25 to Nov. 23, 1862. Dec., 1862, Unatt. Delaware, 8 Corps, Middle Dept. June, 1863, 2d Separate Brig., 8 Corps, Middle Dept. June, 1863, Fort Delaware, 8 Corps, Middle Dept. Mustered out Aug. 12, 1863.

6th REGIMENT INFANTRY.—Org. at large Oct. 25 to Dec. 18, 1862. Middle Dept., 8 Corps. Mustered out Sept. 5, 1863.

7th REGIMENT INFANTRY.—Org. at Wilmington July 12, 1864. Dist. Delaware, 8 Corps, Middle Dept. Mustered out Aug. 12, 1864.

8th REGIMENT INFANTRY.—Org. at Wilmington Oct., 1864. Oct., 1864, Dist. Del., 8 Corps, Middle Dept. Oct., 1864, Engineer Brig., Potomac. Dec., 1864, Provost Guard, Army Potomac. March, 1865, 3 Brig., 2 Div., 5 Corps, Potomac. Mustered out June 5, 1865.

9th REGIMENT INFANTRY.—Org. at Wilmington Sept., 1864. Sept., 1864, Dist. Del., 8 Corps, Middle Dept. Mustered out Jany. 23, 1865.

STERLING'S INDEPENDENT COMPANY INFANTRY.—Org. at Wilmington Aug. 30, 1864. Aug., 1864, Dist. Del., 8 Corps, Middle Dept. Mustered out July 17, 1865.

DAKOTA TERRITORY

1st CAVALRY BATTALION.—Org. Co. A at Yankton, D. T., April 1862; Co. B at Sioux City, Iowa, March 31, 1863. Attached to Dept. of the Northwest. Mustered out, Co. A, May 9, 1865; Co. B, Nov. 16, 1865.

DISTRICT OF COLUMBIA

1st REGIMENT CAVALRY.—Org. at Washington, D. C., June to Dec., 1863. Dec., 1863, Unass'd Dist. of Wash., 22 Corps. Jany., 1864, Cav. Brig. U. S. Forces, Yorktown, Va., Dept. Va. and N. C. April, 1864, 1 Brig., Kautz's Cav. Div., Army James, Dept. Va. and N. C. June, 1864, 2 Brig., Cav. Div., Dept. Va. and N. C. Jany., 1865, 2 Brig., Cav. Div., Dept. Va. Aug., 1865, Cav., Dept. Va. Mustered out Oct. 26, 1865.

OWENS' COMPANY MILITIA CAVALRY.—Org. at Washington April 26, 1861. Mustered out July 19, 1861.

1st REGIMENT INFANTRY.—Org. at Washington, D. C., July 23 to Oct. 25, 1861. Oct., 1861, Prov'l Brig., Casey's Div., Potomac. Nov., 1861, Robinson's Brig., Army Potomac. Dec., 1861, R. R. Guard, Bladensburg, Md. May, 1862, Miles' Command, Md. Heights. May, 1862, 2 Brig., Sigel's Div., Dept. Shenandoah. June, 1862, 2 Brig., 2 Div., 2 Corps, Army Va. Aug., 1862, 3 Brig., 2 Div., 2 Corps, Army Va. Sept., 1862, 3 Brig., 2 Div., 12 Corps, Potomac. Oct., 1862, Dist. Alexandria, Def. Washington. Feby., 1863, Slough's Brig., Def. Alexandria, 22 Corps. Consolidated with 2d D. C. Infy. Feby. 28, 1865.

2nd REGIMENT INFANTRY.—Org. at Washington Feby. 26, 1862. March, 1862, Wadsworth's Command, Def. Washington. Feby., 1863, Dist. Wash., 22 Corps. Jany., 1864, 1 Brig., Tyler's Div., 22 Corps. May, 1864, Dist. Alex., 22 Corps. June, 1864, Unatt. Haskin's Div., 22 Corps. Mustered out Sept. 12, 1865.

WILLIAMS' COMPANY MILITIA INFANTRY — Org. at Washington April 10, 1861. Mustered out July 10, 1861.

CARRINGTON'S COMPANY MILITIA INFANTRY.—Org. at Washington April 13, 1861. Mustered out July 10, 1861.

FLETCHER'S COMPANY MILITIA INFANTRY.—Org. at Washington April 24, 1861. Mustered out July 24, 1861.

M'CLELLAND'S COMPANY MILITIA INFANTRY.—Org. at Washington April 20, 1861. Mustered out July 20, 1861.

ELDER'S COMPANY MILITIA INFANTRY.—Org. at Washington April 20, 1861. Mustered out July 20, 1861.

SMEAD'S COMPANY MILITIA INFANTRY.—Org. at Washington April 15, 1861. Mustered out July 15, 1861.

M'BLAIRE'S COMPANY MILITIA INFANTRY.—Org. at Washington April 23, 1861. Mustered out July 23, 1861.

RODIER'S COMPANY MILITIA INFANTRY.—Org. at Washington April 13, 1861. Mustered out July 13, 1861.

POWELL'S COMPANY MILITIA INFANTRY.—Org. at Washington April 20, 1861. Mustered out July 17, 1861.

MORRISON'S COMPANY MILITIA INFANTRY.—Org. at Washington April 23, 1861. Mustered out July 16, 1861.

BOYD'S COMPANY MILITIA INFANTRY.—Org. at Washington April 18, 1861. Mustered out July 16, 1861.

GODDARD'S COMPANY MILITIA INFANTRY.—Org. at Washington April 17, 1861. Mustered out July 17, 1861.

MARK'S COMPANY MILITIA INFANTRY.—Org. at Washington April 17, 1861. Mustered out July 17, 1861.

MORGAN'S COMPANY MILITIA INFANTRY.—Org. at Washington April 17, 1861. Mustered out July 17, 1861.

NALLY'S COMPANY MILITIA INFANTRY.—Org. at Washington April 11, 1861. Mustered out July 11, 1861.

GRINNELL'S COMPANY MILITIA INFANTRY.—Org. at Washington April 22, 1861. Mustered out June 11, 1861.

THISTLETON'S COMPANY MILITIA INFANTRY.—Org. at Washington April 11, 1861. Mustered out July 11, 1861.

M'DERMOTT'S COMPANY MILITIA INFANTRY.—Org. at Washington April 18, 1861. Mustered out July 18, 1861.

M'KIM'S COMPANY MILITIA INFANTRY.—Org. at Washington April 11, 1861. Mustered out July 11, 1861.

FERGUSON'S COMPANY MILITIA INFANTRY—Org. at Washington April 22, 1861. Mustered out July 22, 1861.

GERHARDT'S COMPANY MILITIA INFANTRY.—Org. at Washington April 11, 1861. Mustered out July 11, 1861.

CROSS' COMPANY MILITIA INFANTRY.—Org. at Washington April 22, 1861. Mustered out July 15, 1861.

RUTHERFORD'S COMPANY MILITIA INFANTRY.—Org. at Washington April 11, 1861. Mustered out July 11, 1861.

MILLER'S COMPANY MILITIA INFANTRY.—Org. at Washington April 17, 1861. Mustered out July 17, 1861.

KING'S COMPANY MILITIA INFANTRY.—Org. at Washington April 15, 1861. Mustered out July 15, 1861.

KNIGHT'S COMPANY MILITIA INFANTRY.—Org. at Washington April 18, 1861. Mustered out July 18, 1861.

CALLAN'S COMPANY MILITIA INFANTRY.—Org. at Washington April 22, 1861. Mustered out July 22, 1861.

KYRZANOWSKY'S COMPANY MILITIA INFANTRY.—Org. at Washington April 22, 1861. Mustered out July 22, 1861.

LOEFFLER'S COMPANY MILITIA INFANTRY.—Org. at Washington April 11, 1861. Mustered out July 11, 1861.

LEGGE'S COMPANY MILITIA INFANTRY.—Org. at Washington April 17, 1861. Mustered out July 17, 1861.

CLARKE'S COMPANY MILITIA INFANTRY.—Org. at Washington April 24, 1861. Mustered out July 24, 1861.

KELLY'S COMPANY MILITIA INFANTRY.—Org. at Washington April 11, 1861. Mustered out July 11, 1861.

FOXWELL'S COMPANY MILITIA INFANTRY.—Org. at Washington April 15, 1861. Mustered out July 15, 1861.

FLORIDA

1st REGIMENT CAVALRY.—Org. at Barrancas, Fla., Dec., 1862, to Aug., 1864. Jany., 1863, Pensacola, Fla., Dist. West Fla., Dept. Gulf. Oct., 1864, 2 Brig., Dist. West Fla., Dept. Gulf. Jany., 1865, 3 Brig., Dist. West Fla., Dept. Gulf. March, 1865, 3 Brig., Lucas' Cav. Div., Steele's Command, Mil. Div., West Miss. April, 1865, Dist. West Fla. Mustered out Nov. 17, 1865.

2nd REGIMENT CAVALRY.—Org. at Cedar Keys and Key West, Fla., Dec., 1863, to June, 1864. Jany., 1864, Dist. Key West and Tortugas, Fla., Dept. Gulf. Mustered out Nov. 29, 1865.

GEORGIA

1st BATTALION INFANTRY.—Org. at Marietta, Ga., Oct. 31, 1864. Nov., 1864, Unatt., Dept. Cumb'd. March, 1865, 1 Brig., 2nd Separate Div., Dist. Etowah, Dept. Cumb'd. Mustered out July 19, 1865.

ILLINOIS

1st REGIMENT CAVALRY.—Co.'s A to G Org. at Alton, Ill., July 3, 1861, Co. H June 12, 1861. Co. I, July 9, 1861. Co. K., Dec. 9, 1861. July, 1861, Dept. Mo. (Co.'s A to G) mustered out July 14, 1862. Co.'s H and I, July, 1861, Mil. Dist., Cairo. Feby., 1862, 4 Brig., 1 Div., Mil. Dist., Cairo. March, 1862, Unatt., Army Miss. April, 1862, Cav. Div., Army Miss. June, 1862, Dist. Memphis. Mustered out July 15, 1862. Co. K, Jany., 1862, Army S. W. Mo. July, 1862, Dist. Eastern Ark., Dept. Mo. Oct., 1862, Army S. E. Mo. Mustered out Dec. 27, 1862.

2nd REGIMENT CAVALRY.—Org. Camp Butler, Ill., Aug. 12, 1861. Oct., 1861, Mil. Dist. Cairo. Feby., 1862, Unatt. Army Miss. (Co.'s G, H, I, & K.) April, 1862, to Nov., 1862, Dist. Columbus, Ky. (Co.'s A, F, G, H, I, K, M.) (Co.'s A and B, 1 Brig., 1 Div., Army Tenn. Feby. to March, 1862, 2 Div., Army Tenn., to July, 1862.) Cav. Dist., Jackson, Tenn. (Co.'s A, B, C, D), July to Nov., 1862. Nov. 1862, Cav., 4 Div., Right Wing 13 Corps, Tenn. Dec., 1862, 2 Brig., Cav. Div., 16 Corps, Tenn. March, 1863. Unatt., 13 Corps, Tenn. (detachment), Dist. Columbus, Ky., 16 Corps, Tenn., to May, 1863 (detachment), 4 Brig. Dist. Memphis, Tenn., 5 Div., 18 Corps, Tenn., to Aug., 1863 (detachment), Cav. Brig., 13 Corps, Dept. Gulf. Aug.-Sept., 1863 (7 Co.'s), 2 Brig. Cav. Div., Gulf, to Dec., 1863 (7 Co.'s), Dist. Columbus, Ky., 3 Div., 16 Corps, to Dec., 1863 (detachment). Waring's Cav. Brig., Cav. Div., 16 Corps, to Jany., 1864 (detachment), 3 Brig., Cav. Div., Gulf, Dec., 1863 to Jany., 1864 (7 Co.'s), 4 Brig., Cav. Div., Gulf, to June, 1864 (7 Co.'s), 1 Brig., 1 Cav. Div., 16 Corps, Tenn. Jany. to June, 1864 (detachment). Unatt. Def. New Orleans, La., Gulf, June to Aug., 1864 (7 Co.'s), 2 Brig., Cav. Div., Gulf, to Sept., 1864, 3 Brig., Cav. Div., Gulf, to Feby., 1865, separate Cav. Brig., Dist. West Fla., to March, 1865, 2 Brig., Cav. Div., Dist. West Fla., to April, 1865.

3 Brig., 1 Div., Cav. Corps, Mil. Div., West, Miss., to Nov., 1865. Mustered out Nov. 22, 1865.

3rd REGIMENT CAVALRY.—Org. at Camp Butler, Ill., Sept. 21, 1861. Oct., 1861, Dept. Mo. Jan., 1862, 3 Brig., Army S. W. Mo., Dept. Mo. Feby., 1862, 2 Brig., 4 Div., Army S. W. Mo. May, 1862, 2 Div., Army S. W. Mo. July, 1862, Dist. Eastern Ark., Dept. Mo. Dec., 1862, 3 Brig., Cav. Div., Dist. Eastern Ark. Dec., 1862, Unatt., Sherman's Yazoo Exp. Jany., 1863, Unatt., 13 Corps, Army Tenn. (Co.'s A, E, G, K, L and M), at Headqrs., Gen. McClernand and Osterhaus, to August, 1863 (Co.'s B, C, F, H and I), 2 Brig., 1 Cav. Div., 16 Corps, Tenn. March to June. 1863, 1 Brig., 1 Cav. Div., 16 Corps, to Aug., 1863, 1 Brig., 1 Div., 16 Corps, to Dec., 1863. (Co. D at headqurs., 15 Corps, to July, 1863, then with Arkansas Exp. to Dec., 1863). (Co.'s A, E, G, K, L and M). Cav. Brig., 13 Corps, Gulf, Aug.-Sept., 1863, 2 Brig., Cav. Div., Gulf, to Dec., 1863, then rejoined Regt. in Tenn. Dec., 1863, 1 Brig., 1 Cav. Div., 16 Corps, Tenn. April, 1864, 3 Brig., 1 Cav. Div., 16 Corps. June, 1864, 1 Brig., Cav. Div., Dist. West Tenn. July, 1864, 1 Brig., 1 Cav. Div., Dist. West Tenn. Nov., 1864, 1 Brig., 5 Div., Cav. Corps, Mil. Div. Miss. May, 1865, Dept. Northwest. Mustered out Oct. 10, 1865.

4th REGIMENT CAVALRY.—Org. at Ottawa, Ill., Sept. 26, 1861. Oct., 1861, Dist. Cairo. (Co. A detached as escort to Gen. U. S. Grant Nov., 1861, to Aug., 1863.) Feby., 1862, 2 Brig., 1 Div., Dist. Cairo and West Tenn. March, 1862, 2 Div., Army Tenn. (Co.'s E, F, G, H), 4 Div., Army Tenn. (Co.'s I, K, L, M), 1 Div., Army Tenn. (Co.'s A, B, C, D). April, 1862, 5 Div., Army Tenn. (Co.'s E, F, G, H, I, K, L, M.) July, 1862, 1 Div., Dist. Jackson, Tenn. (Co.'s A, B, C, D), 5 Div., Dist. Memphis, Tenn. (E, F, G, H, I, K, L, M.) Nov., 1862, Lee's 2 Brig., Cav. Div., 13 Corps, Tenn. Dec., 1862, Lee's Cav. Brig., 16 Corps, Tenn. March, 1863, 2 Brig., 1 Cav. Div., 16 Corps. May, 1863, 1 Brig., 1 Cav. Div., 16 Corps. Aug., 1863. Winslow's Cav. Brig., 15 Corps, and 17 Corps and Dist. of Vicksburg, Miss. Jany., 1864, Post Natchez, Miss., Dist. Vicksburg, Miss. Dec., 1864, 3 Brig., Cav. Div., Dist. West Tenn. June, 1865, 1 Brig., Cav. Div., West Tenn. Consolidated with 12th Illinois June 14, 1865.

5th REGIMENT CAVALRY.—Org. at Camp Butler, Ill., Aug. 31 to Dec. 30, 1861. Feby., 1862, Dept. Mo. March, 1862, Steele's Div., Army S. E. Mo. May, 1862, Army S. W. Mo. July, 1862, Dist. Eastern Ark., Dept. Mo. Dec., 1862, 1 Brig., 3 (Cav.) Div., Dist. Eastern Ark., Dept. Tenn. Jany., 1863, 1 Brig., 2 Cav. Div., 13 Corps, Tenn. April, 1863, 1 Brig., Cav. Div., Dist. Eastern Ark., Tenn. June, 1863, Cav. Herron's Div., 13 Corps, Tenn. Aug., 1863, Winslow's Cav. Brig., 15 Corps. Dec., 1863, Winslow's Cav. Brig., 17 Corps, to April, 1864, and Dist. Vicksburg, Miss. to Jany., 1865, 1 Brig., Cav. Div., Dist. West Tenn. June, 1865, Dept. Texas. Mustered out Oct., 27, 1865.

6th REGIMENT CAVALRY.—Org. at Camp Butler, Ill., Nov., 1861, to Jany., 1862. Nov., 1861, Dist. Cairo. Feby., 1862, Dist. Columbus, Ky. (7 Co.'s), and Dist. Memphis, Tenn. (5 Co.'s) from July, 1862. Nov., 1862, Dist. Memphis, Tenn., 13 Corps, Tenn. Dec., 1862, Grierson's 1 Brig., Cav. Div., 13 Corps, Tenn. Jany., 1863, 1 Brig., Cav. Div., 16 Corps, Tenn. March, 1863, 1 Brig., 1 Cav. Div., 16 Corps. May, 1863, Cav. Brig., 19 Corps, Gulf. June, 1863, 4 Brig., 1 Cav. Div., 16 Corps (detachment). Aug., 1863, 3 Brig., 1 Cav. Div., 16 Corps. Dec., 1863, 2 Brig., 1 Cav. Div., 16 Corps. April, 1864, 3 Brig., 1 Cav. Div., 16 Corps. July, 1864, 2 Brig., 1 Cav. Div., Dist. West Tenn. Nov., 1864, 2 Brig., 5 Div., Cav. Corps, Mil. Div. Miss. July, 1865, Dist. Alabama. Mustered out Nov. 5, 1865.

7th REGIMENT CAVALRY.—Org. at Camp Butler, Ill., Oct. 13, 1861. Oct., 1861, Dist. Cairo. Feby., 1862, 4 Brig., 1 Div., Dist. Cairo. March, 1862, Cav. Div., Army Miss. April, 1862, 1 Brig., Cav. Div., Army Miss. Nov., 1862, Cav. Right Wing, 13 Corps, Dept. Tenn. Dec., 1862, Griersen's 1 Cav. Brig., Cav. Div., 13 Corps, Tenn. Jany., 1863. 1 Brig., Cav. Div., 16 Corps, Tenn. March, 1863, 1 Brig., 1 Cav. Div., 16 Corps. May, 1863, Cav. Brig., 19 Corps, Gulf. June, 1863, 4 Brig., 1 Cav. Div., 16 Corps (detachment). Aug., 1863, 3 Brig., 1 Cav. Div., 16

Corps. Dec., 1863. 2 Brig., 1 Cav. Div., 16 Corps. April, 1864, 3 Brig., 1 Cav. Div., 16 Corps. July, 1864, 1 Brig., 1 Cav. Div., Dist. West. Penn. Nov., 1864, 1 Brig., 5 Div., Cav. Corps, Mil. Div., Miss. Nov., 1864, 2 Brig., 5 Div. Cav. Corps, M. D. M. July, 1865, Dist. Alabama. Mustered out Nov. 4, 1865.

8th REGIMENT CAVALRY.—Org. at St. Charles, Ill., Sept. 18, 1861. Dec., 1861, Sumner's Div., Army Potomac. March, 1862, Cav. 2 Corps Army Potomac. May, 1862, Stoneman's Light Brigade, Army Potomac. June, 1862, Averill's Cav. Brig., 5 Corps Army Potomac. July, 1862, 2 Brig., Stoneman's Cav. Div., Potomac. Sept., 1862, 1 Brig., Pleasanton's Cav. Div., Potomac. Feby., 1863, 1 Brig., 1 Div. Cav. Corps, Army Potomac. April, 1864, 2 Brig., 3 Div. Cav. Corps, Potomac (detachment). April, 1864, Unatt., Def. Washington, D. C., 22 Corps. Nov., 1864, 1st Separate Brig., 22 Corps, Dept. Washington. Mustered out July 17, 1865.

9th REGIMENT CAVALRY.—Org. at Camp Douglas, Chicago, Ill., Nov. 30, 1861. Feby., 1862, Steele's Div., Dist. S. E. Mo., Dept. Mo. May, 1862, Unatt. Cav., Army S. W. Mo., Dept. Mo. July, 1862, Dist. Eastern Ark., Dept. Mo. Dec., 1862, 2 Brig., 3 (Cav.) Div., Dist. Eastern Ark., Dept. Tenn. Jany., 1863, 2 Brig., 2 Cav. Div., 13 Corps Tenn. April, 1863, 2 Brig., 1 Cav. Div., 16 Corps, Tenn. June, 1863, 1 Brig., 1 Cav. Div., 16 Corps. Aug., 1863, 2 Brig., 1 Cav. Div., 16 Corps. April, 1864, 3 Brig., 1 Cav. Div., 16 Corps. June, 1864, 1 Brig., Cav. Div., Dist. West Tenn. July, 1864, 2 Brig., 1 Cav. Div., Dist. West Tenn. Nov., 1864, 2 Brig., 5 Div., Cav. Corps, Mil. Div. Miss. July, 1865, Dist. Alabama. Mustered out Oct. 31, 1865.

10th REGIMENT CAVALRY.—Org. at Camp Butler, Ill., Nov. 25, 1861. March, 1862, Dept. Mo. April, 1862, Dist. S. W. Mo., Dept. Mo. Oct., 1862, 1 Brig., 3 Div., Army Frontier, Dept. Mo. Dec., 1862, unatt., Army Frontier, Dept. Mo. Feby., 1863, 1 Brig., 2 Div., Army Frontier. May, 1863, 2 Brig., 1 Div., Dist. S. E. Mo., Dept. Mo. Aug., 1863, 2 Brig., 1 Cav. Div., Arkansas Expedition. Dec., 1863, 3 Brig., 1 Cav. Div., Army Ark. Jany., 1864, 3 Brig., 1 Cav. Div., 7 Corps, Ark. May, 1864, 3 Brig., 2 Div., 7 Corps, Ark. Sept., 1864, 3 Brig., Cav. Div., 7 Corps. Feby., 1865, 1 Brig., Cav. Div., 7 Corps. April, 1865, 1 Brig., 1 Cav. Div., Mil. Div. West Miss. May, 1865, 2 Brig., 2 Cav. Div., Mil. Div. West Miss. July, 1865, Dept. Texas. Mustered out Nov. 22, 1865. 1st. BATTALION, Cos. A, D, G, K.—June, 1862, Army S. W. Mo., Dept. Mo. July, 1862, Dist. Eastern Ark., Dept. Mo. Dec., 1862, 1 Brig., 2 Cav. Div., 13 Corps, Tenn. May, 1863, detached Brig., Dist. Northeast La. June, 1863, unatt., 13 Corps, Tenn., to July. Rejoined Regt. August 1, 1863.

11th REGIMENT CAVALRY.—Org. at Peoria, Ill., Dec. 20, 1861. April, 1862, 3 Div., Army Tenn. (1st Battalion), 6 Div., Army Tenn. (2nd and 3rd Battalions). July, 1862, Dist. Memphis, Tenn. (1st Battalion), Dist. Corinth, Miss. (2nd and 3rd Battalions). Sept., 1862, Dist. Jackson, Tenn. (Regt.) Nov., 1862, Cav. Brig., Dist. Jackson, Tenn. Left Wing 13 Corps, Tenn. Dec., 1862, Cav. Brig., Dist. Jackson, 16 Corps. March, 1863, Mizner's Cav. Brig., 3 Div., 16 Corps. June, 1863, 4 Brig., 1 Cav. Div., 16 Corps. Aug., 1863, Winslow's Cav. Brig., 15 Corps. Dec., 1863, Winslow's Cav. Brig., 17 Corps, and Dist. Vicksburg, Miss. Dec., 1864, 3 Brig., Cav. Div., Dist. West. Tenn. June, 1865, 1 Brig., Cav. Div., Dist. West. Tenn. Mustered out Sept. 30, 1865.

12th REGIMENT CAVALRY.—Org. at Camp Butler, Ill., Feby. 24, 1862. June, 1862, Martinsburg, W. Va., Dept. Va. Sept., 1862, 1 Brig., 2 Div., 12 Corps, Army Potomac. Oct., 1862, Defences Upper Potomac, Middle Dept. Feby., 1863, 2 Brig., 3 Div., Cav. Corps, Army Potomac. June, 1863, 1 Brig., 1 Div., Cav. Corps, Potomac. Nov., 1863, Chicago, Ill. Feby., 1864, Dist. St. Louis, Mo., Dept. Mo. April, 1864, 1 Brig., Cav. Div., Dept. Gulf. June, 1864, Dist. LaFourche, Dept. Gulf. Aug., 1864, 4 Brig., Cav. Div., Gulf. Aug., 1864, 3 Brig., Cav. Div., Gulf. Feby., 1865, 2 Brig., Cav. Div., Dist. West. Tenn. July, 1865, Dept. Texas. Mustered out May 29, 1866.

13th REGIMENT CAVALRY.—Org. at Camp Douglass, Ill., Oct., 30, 1861, to Feby. 20, 1862. Feby., 1862, Cav., Steele's Command, Dist. S. E. Mo. May, 1862, Dist. S. W. Mo., Dept. Mo. Oct., 1862, Cav. Brig., Dist. S. E. Mo. Feby., 1863, 1 Brig., 2 Div., Army S. E. Mo. March, 1863, Dist. S. E. Mo. July, 1863, Reserve Brig., 1 Cav. Div., Army S. E. Mo. Aug., 1863, Reserve Brig., 1 Cav. Div., Ark. Exp. Dec., 1863, Unatt., 2 Div., Army Ark. Jany., 1864, 1 Brig., 1 Cav. Div., 7 Corps, Ark. May, 1864, Clayton's Cav. Brig., 7 Corps. Sept., 1864, 1 Brig., Cav. Div., 7 Corps. Jany., 1865, Post Pine Bluff, Ark., 7 Corps. Mustered out Aug. 31, 1865.

14th REGIMENT CAVALRY.—Org. at Peoria, Ill., Jany. 7 to Feby. 6, 1863. April, 1863, 1 Brig., 3 Div., 23 Corps, Ohio. Aug., 1863, 2 Brig., 4 Div., 23 Corps. Oct., 1863, 4 Brig., 4 Div., 23 Corps. Nov., 1863, 2 Brig., 2 Cav. Div., Cav. Corps, Dept. Ohio. May, 1864, 3 Brig., Cav. Div., Dist. Ky., Dept. Ohio. June, 1864, 3 Brig., Cav. Div., 23 Corps. Aug., 1864, Dismounted Brig., Cav. Div., 23 Corps. Sept., 1864, 1 Brig., Cav. Div., 23 Corps. Nov., 1864, 1 Brig., 6 Div., Cav. Corps, Mil. Div. Miss. Dec., 1864, 2 Brig., 6 Div., Cav. Corps, Mil. Div. Miss. Dec, 1864, 1 Brig., 6 Div., Cav. Corps, Mil. Div. M. June, 1865, 2 Brig., 6 Div., Cav. Corps. Mustered out July 31, 1865.

15th REGIMENT CAVALRY.—Org. at Camp Butler, Ill., and in the field by consolidation of companies, Dec. 25, 1862. Jany., 1863, Dist. Columbus, Ky., 16 Corps, Tenn. March, 1863, Cav. Brig., Dist. Corinth, 16 Corps. June, 1863, 3 Brig., 1 Div., 16 Corps. Aug., 1863, Detached Brig., 1 Cav. Div., 16 Corps. Dec., 1863, Waring's Brig., Cav. Div., 16 Corps. Jany., 1864, Helena, Ark., Dist. Eastern Ark., 7 Corps, Dept. Ark. Consolidated with 10th Illinois Cavalry, Jany. 26, 1865.

16th REGIMENT CAVALRY.—Org. at Camp Butler, Ill., Jany. to April, 1863, and by assignment of companies in the field. Jany., 1863, 2 Div., 15 Corps, Tenn. (Thielman's Battalion). May, 1863, Headquarters 15 Corps (Thielman's Battalion). Oct., 1863, Knoxville, Tenn., Dept. Ohio. Nov., 1863, Cumberland Gap, Tenn., Left Wing Forces, Dept. Ohio. Jany., 1864, Dist. Clinch., Dept. Ohio. Feby., 1864, Camp Nelson, Ky., 23 Corps, Ohio. April, 1864, 3 Brig., 1 Div., Cav. Corps, Ohio. May, 1864, 1 Brig., Stoneman's Cav. Div., 23 Corps, Ohio. June, 1864, Detached, Cav. Brig., 3 Div., 23 Corps. Aug., 1864, Dismounted Cav. Brig., Cav. Div., 23 Corps. Sept., 1864, 1 Brig., Cav. Div., 23 Corps. Nov., 1864, 6 Div., Cav. Corps, Mil. Div. Miss. Mustered out Aug. 19, 1865. Company C., Schambeck's.—Jany., 1863, Kanawha Div., Dist. W. Va., Dept. Ohio. March, 1863, Averill's 4th Separate Brig., 8 Corps, Middle Dept. June, 1863, Averill's 4th Separate Brig., Dept. W. Va. Dec., 1863, 2 Brig., 4 Div., W. Va. April, 1864, Reserve Div., W. Va. Mustered out July 16, 1864.

17th REGIMENT CAVALRY.—Org. at St. Charles, Ill., Jany. 28, 1864. May, 1864, Dist. North Mo., Dept. Mo. (1st and 2nd Battalions), Alton, Ill. (3rd Battalion). Oct., 1864, Sanborn's Cav. Div., Dept. Mo. Nov., 1864, Dept. Mo. July, 1865, Dist. of the Plains, Dept. Mo. Mustered out Dec. 15, 1865.

STEWART'S CAVALRY BATTALION.—Org. by consolidation of Cav. Companies at Jackson, Tenn., July, 1862. July, 1862, Cav., Dist. Jackson, Tenn. Nov., 1862, Dist. Corinth, 13 Corps, Tenn. Assigned to 15th Regt. Illinois Cav., as Cos. A, B, C, D, E and F, Dec. 25, 1862.

THIELMAN'S CAVALRY BATTALION.—Org. at Smithland, Ky., Dec. 9, 1861, by consolidation of Thielman's, Marx's and Schambeck's Indpt. Cav. Companies. (Co. C, Schambeck, never served with the Battalion, being detached in West Va.) Nov., 1861, Dist. Paducah, Ky. March, 1862, 5 Div., Army Tenn. July, 1862, 5 Div., Dist. Memphis, Tenn. Nov., 1862, 3 Brig., Cav. Div., Right Wing 13 Corps, Dept. Tenn. Dec., 1862, Cav., 2 Div. Sherman's Yazoo Expedition. Jany., 1863, 2 Div., 15 Corps, Tenn. May, 1863, Headquarters 15 Corps, Tenn. Dec., 1863, Cumberland Gap, Tenn., Dept. Ohio. Joined 16th Illinois Cav. at Cumberland Gap, Tenn., Jany., 1864, to which it had been attached as Cos. A, B and C Jany., 1863.

BARKER'S DRAGOONS.—Org. at Chicago, Ill., April 19, 1861, at Cairo, Ill., and in West Va. as escort to Gen. McClellan. Mustered out Sept., 1861.

CARMICHAEL'S INDPT. CAVALRY COMPANY.—Org. as Cav. Co. B, 29th Ill. Infy., at Camp Butler, Ill., Aug. 19, 1861. Sept., 1861, Dist. Cairo. Feby., 1862, 1 Brig., 1 Div., Dist. West. Tenn., and Army Tenn. Assigned to Stewart's Ill. Cav. Battalion as Co. B, July, 1862.

DOLLINS' INDPT. CAVALRY COMPANY.—Org. at Cairo, Ill., with 31st Ill. Infy., Sept. 18, 1861. Sept., 1861, Dist. Cairo, Ill. Feby., 1862, 1 Brig., 1 Div., Dist. West. Tenn., and Army Tenn. Assigned to Stewart's Ill. Cav. Battalion as Co. C, July, 1863.

FORD'S INDPT. CAVALRY COMPANY.—Org. at Ottawa, Ill., with 53rd Ill. Infy., Jany. 1, 1862. Jany, 1862, Dept. Mo. March, 1862, Dist. Columbus, Ky. Assigned to Stewart's Indpt. Cav. Battalion, July, 1862.

GILBERT'S INDPT. CAVALRY COMPANY.—Org. at Geneva, Ill., with 52nd Ill. Infy., Oct. 25, 1861. Nov., 1861, Dept. Mo. March, 1862, 2 Div., Army Tenn. July, 1862, Dist. Jackson, Tenn. Assigned to 12th Ill. Cav. as Co. H, Aug., 1862, and to 15th Ill. Cav. as Co. G, Dec. 25, 1862.

HUTCHINS' INDPT. CAVALRY COMPANY.—Org. with 27th Ill. Infy., Aug. 10, 1861. Sept., 1861, Fort Holt, Ky. March, 1862, Dist. Columbus, Ky. Assigned to Stewart's Indpt. Cav. Battalion, July, 1862.

JENKS' INDPT. CAVALRY COMPANY.—Org. at Aurora, Ill., as Cav. Co. A, 36th Ill. Infy., Sept. 23, 1861. Oct., 1861, Dept. Mo. Jany., 1862, 2 Brig., Army S. W. Mo. March, 1862, 2 Brig., 1 Div., Army S. W. Mo. June, 1862, Cav. Div., Army Miss. Oct., 1862, 1 Brig., 2 Div., Army Miss. Nov., 1862, Dist. Corinth, Miss., 13 Corps, Dept. Tenn. Assigned to 15th Ill. Cav. as Co. I, Dec. 25, 1862.

DODSON'S KANE COUNTY INDPT. CAVALRY COMPANY.—Org. Sept. 1, 1861. Oct., 1861, Dept. Mo. May, 1862, 1 Div., Army S. W. Mo., Dept. Mo. July, 1862, Dist. Eastern Ark., Dept. Mo. Dec., 1862, 1 Brig., 3 (Cav.) Div., Dist. Eastern Ark., Dept. Tenn. Assigned to 15th Ill. Cav. as Co. H, Dec. 25, 1862.

MARK'S INDPT. CAVALRY COMPANY.—Org. Dec. 9, 1861, and assigned to Thielman's Indpt. Cav. Battalion as Co. B, Dec., 1861.

McCLELLAN'S DRAGOONS.—Org. at Chicago, Ill., Oct., 1861. Assigned to 12th Ill. Cav. as Cos. H and I, Feby., 1862, but served detached till Nov., 1863. Attached to Stoneman's Cav. Command, Army Potomac, to March, 1862; Blake's Brig. Cav. Res., Army Potomac, April, 1862; Headquarters Army Potomac, Nov. 1862; Provost Guard, Army Potomac, Feby., 1863; Headquarters 3rd and 2nd Divs., Cav. Corps, Army Potomac, to Nov., 1863, when joined Regiment.

McCLERNAND'S BODY GUARD.—Org. Jany. 21, to April 16, 1862. Assigned to 16th Ill. Cav. as Cos. I, K and L, April, 1862.

NAUGHTON'S IRISH DRAGOONS.—Org. at Jefferson City, Mo., Sept. 1, 1861, by authority of Gen. Fremont, to be attached to 23rd Ill. Infy. as a Cav. Company. Transferred to 3rd Mo. Cav. as Co. L, and to Curtis Horse, 5th Iowa Cav., as Co. L, Nov., 1861.

O'HARNETT'S INDPT. CAVALRY COMPANY.—Org. at Camp Butler with 30th Ill. Infy., Aug. 28, 1861. Sept., 1861, Dist. Cairo, Ill. Feby., 1862, 1 Brig., 1 Div., Dist. West. Tenn., and Army Tenn. Assigned to Stewart's Indpt. Cav. Battalion, July, 1862.

SCHAMBECK'S INDPT. CAVALRY COMPANY.—Org. at Chicago, Ill., July 8, 1861. Assigned to Thielman's Ill. Cav. Battalion as Co. C, Dec. 9, 1861, and to 16th Ill. Cav. as Co. C, Jany., 1863, but served detached entire term. July, 1861, 2 Brig., Army Occupation, West Va. Sept., 1861, McCook's Brig., Kanawha Dist., West Va. Oct., 1861, 2 Brig., Kanawha Dist., West Va. March, 1862, 4 Brig., Kanawha Div., Mt. Dept. Sept., 1862, 2 Brig., Kanawha Div., 9 Corps, Army Potomac. Oct., 1862, Kanawha Div., Dist. Kanawha, West Va., Dept. Ohio. March, 1863, 4 Separate Brig., 8 Corps, Middle Dept. June, 1863, 4 Separate Brig., West Va. Dec., 1863, 2

Brig., 4 Div., West Va. April, 1864, Reserve Div., West Va. Mustered out July 16, 1864.

SHERER'S INDPT. CAVALRY COMPANY.—Org. at Aurora, Ill., as Cav. Co. B, 36th Ill. Infy., Sept. 23, 1861. Sept., 1861, Dept. Mo. Jany., 1862, 2 Brig., Army S. W. Mo. March, 1862, 2 Brig., 1 Div., Army S. W. Mo. May, 1862, Cav., Army Miss. Sept., 1862, Cav., 9 Div., Army Ohio. Sept., 1862, 9 Div., 3 Corps, Army Ohio. Nov., 1862, Cav. Headquarters, Right Wing, Army Cumberland. Assigned to 15th Ill. Cav. as Co. K, Dec. 25, 1862.

STEWART'S INDPT. CAVALRY COMPANY.—Org. at Cape Girardeau, Mo., Aug. 10, 1861. Sept., 1861, Dist. Cairo. Feby., 1862, 1 Brig., 1 Div., Dist. West. Tenn., and Army Tenn. Assigned to Stewart's Indpt. Battalion as Co. A, July, 1862.

THIELMAN'S INDPT. CAVALRY COMPANY.—Org. at Chicago, Ill., July 2, 1861. Dist. Cairo and Paducah, Ky. Assigned to Thielman's Indpt. Battalion as Co. A, Dec. 9, 1861.

BATTERY A, 1st REGIMENT LIGHT ARTILLERY.—Org. at Cairo, Ill., July 16, 1861. July, 1861, Dist. Cairo. Feby., 1862, 1 Brig., 1 Div., Dist. Cairo. Feby., 1862, 3 Brig., 3 Div., Dist. Cairo. March, 1862, 2 Brig., 2 Div., Dist. West. Tenn. April, 1862, Arty., 3 Div., Army Tenn. July, 1862, Arty., 5 Div., Dist. Memphis, Tenn. Nov., 1862, Arty., 5 Div., Dist. Memphis, Tenn., 13 Corps, Dept. Tenn. Nov., 1862, Arty., 2 Div., Dist. Memphis, 13 Corps. Dec., 1862, Arty., 2 Div., Sherman's Yazoo Expedition. Jany., 1863, Arty., 2 Div., 15 Corps, Tenn. Nov., 1864, Garrison Arty., Nashville, Tenn., Dept. Cumberland. Dec., 1864, Arty. Reserve, Chattanooga, Tenn. Mustered out July 3, 1865.

BATTERY B, 1st REGIMENT LIGHT ARTILLERY.—Org. at Cairo, Ill., July 16, 1861. July, 1861, Dist. Cairo. Oct., 1861, 3 Brig., Dist. Cairo. Feby., 1862, 2 Brig., 1 Div., Dist. Cairo. Feby., 1862, Arty., 1 Div., Dist. West. Tenn., and Army Tenn. April, 1862, Arty., 5 Div., Army Tenn. July, 1862, Arty., 5 Div., Dist. Memphis, Tenn. Nov., 1862, Arty., 5 Div., Dist. Memphis, Right Wing 13 Corps, Tenn. Nov., 1862, Arty., 2 Div., Dist. Memphis, Tenn., 13 Corps. Dec., 1862, Arty., 2 Div. Sherman's Yazoo Expedition. Jany., 1863, Arty., 2 Div., 15 Corps, Tenn. Mustered out July 23, 1864. Battery reorganized March, 1865, by assignment of Bridge's Indpt. Battery. March, 1865, Garrison Arty., Nashville, Tenn., Dept. Cumberland. Mustered out July 6, 1865.

BATTERY C, 1st REGIMENT LIGHT ARTILLERY.—Org. at Ottawa, Ill., Oct. 31, 1861. Nov., 1861, Dist. Cairo. Feby., 1862, 4 Brig., 1 Div., Dist. Cairo. Feby., 1862, Arty. Div., Army Miss. April, 1862, Arty., 1 Div., Army Miss. Sept., 1862, Arty., 13 Div., Army Ohio. Nov., 1862, 3 Brig., 3 Div., Right Wing 14 Corps, Army Cumberland. Jany., 1863, Arty., 3 Div., 20 Corps, Army Cumberland. Oct., 1863, Arty., 1 Div., 14 Corps. July, 1864, Arty. Brig., 14 Corps. Mustered out June 12, 1865.

BATTERY D, 1st REGIMENT LIGHT ARTILLERY.—Org. at Cairo, Ill., and mustered in July 30, 1861. Nov., 1861, Dist. Cairo. Feby., 1862, 2 Brig., 1 Div., Dist Cairo. Feby., 1862, 3 Brig., 1 Div., Dist. West. Tenn. April, 1862, Arty., 1 Div., Army Tenn. July, 1862, Arty., 1 Div., Dist. Jackson, Tenn. Nov., 1862, Dist. Jackson, Tenn., 13 Corps. Nov., 1862, Arty., 3 Div., Right Wing 13 Corps, Tenn. Dec., 1862, Arty., 3 Div., 17 Corps. Nov., 1864, Arty. Reserve, Nashville, Tenn. March, 1865, 5th Sub-Dist. Middle Tenn. Mustered out July 28, 1865.

BATTERY E, 1st REGIMENT LIGHT ARTILLERY.—Org. at Chicago, Ill., Dec. 19, 1861. Feby., 1862, Dist. Cairo, Ill. March 1862, Arty., 5 Div., Army Tenn. July, 1862, Arty., 5 Div., Dist. Memphis, Tenn. Nov., 1862, 5 Div., Right Wing 13 Corps, Tenn. Nov., 1862, Arty., 1 Div., Dist. Memphis, 13 Corps. Dec., 1862, Arty., 8 Div., 16 Corps, Tenn. March, 1863, Arty., 3 Div., 15 Corps, Tenn. Dec., 1863, Arty., 1 Div., 16 Corps. June, 1864, Arty., Sturgis' Expedition. June, 1864, 1 Brig., 1 Div., 16 Corps. Dec., 1864, Arty., 1 Div. Detachment Army Tenn., Dept. Cumberland. Feby., 1865, Arty. Reserve, Chattanooga, Tenn., Dept. Cumberland. Mustered out July 1, 1865.

BATTERY F, 1st REGIMENT LIGHT ARTILLERY.—Org. at Camp Butler, Ill., Feby. 25, 1862. March, 1862, Dept. Mo. April, 1862, Arty., 3 Div., Army Tenn. July, 1862, Arty., 5 Div., Dist. Memphis, Tenn. Nov., 1862, Arty., 5 Div., Dist. Memphis, Tenn., Right Wing 13 Corps, Dept. Tenn. Nov., 1862, Arty., 1 Div., 13 Corps. Dec., 1862, Arty., 1 Div., 17 Corps. Jany., 1863, Arty., 1 Div., 16 Corps. July, 1863, Arty., 4 Div., 15 Corps. Nov., 1864, Arty. Reserve, Chattanooga, Tenn., Dept. Cumberland. Battery discontinued Feby. 22, 1865.

BATTERY G, 1st REGIMENT LIGHT ARTILLERY.—Org. at Cairo, Ill., Feby. 28, 1862. Feby., 1862, Dist. Cairo. March, 1862, Flotilla Brig., Army Miss. April, 1862, Arty. Div., Army Miss. July, 1862, Arty., Dist. Corinth, Miss. Nov., 1862, Arty., Dist. Corinth, Miss., 13 Corps, Tenn. Dec., 1862, Arty., Dist. Corinth, 17 Corps. Jany., 1863, Arty., Dist. Corinth, 16 Corps, Tenn. March, 1863, Arty., 2 Div., 16 Corps. Nov., 1863, Post Corinth, Miss., 16 Corps. Jany., 1864, Fort Pickering, Dist. Memphis, Tenn., 16 Corps. June, 1864, 1 Brig., Post Memphis, Dist. West. Tenn. Dec., 1864, Arty. Reserve, Dist. West. Tenn. Mustered out July 24, 1865.

BATTERY H, 1st REGIMENT LIGHT ARTILLERY.—Org. at Chicago, Ill., Feby. 20, 1862. Feby., 1862, St. Louis, Mo., Dept. Mo. April, 1862, Unassigned, Army Tenn. April, 1862, Arty., 5 Div., Army Tenn. July, 1862, Arty., 5 Div., Dist. Memphis, Right Wing 13 Corps, Tenn. Nov., 1862, Arty., 1 Div., Dist. Memphis, 13 Corps. Jany., 1863, Arty., 2 Div., 15 Corps, Tenn. Sept., 1864, Arty. Brig., 15 Corps. Mustered out June 14, 1865.

BATTERY I, 1st REGIMENT LIGHT ARTILLERY.—Org. at Chicago, Ill., Feby. 10, 1862. March, 1862, Benton Barracks, Mo., Dept. Mo. April, 1862, Unassigned, Army Tenn. May, 1862, Arty., 5 Div., Army Tenn. July, 1862, Arty., 5 Div., Dist. Memphis, Tenn. Nov., 1862, Arty., 5 Div., Dist. Memphis, Tenn., Right Wing 13 Corps, Dept. Tenn. Nov., 1862, Arty., 1 Div., Dist. Memphis, 13 Corps. Dec., 1862, Arty., 1 Div., 17 Corps. Jany., 1863, Arty., 1 Div., 16 Corps. July, 1863, Arty., 4 Div., 15 Corps. April, 1864, Arty. Reserve, Nashville, Tenn., Dept. Cumberland. Nov., 1864, Arty., 5 Div., Cav. Corps, Mil. Div. Miss. Mustered out July 26, 1865.

BATTERY K, 1st REGIMENT LIGHT ARTILLERY.—Org. at Shawneetown, Ill., Jany. 9, 1862. March, 1862, Cairo, Ill., Dist. Columbus, Ky. Nov., 1862, Dist. Columbus, Ky., 13 Corps, Tenn. Dec., 1862, Dist. Columbus, Ky., 16 Corps, Tenn. March, 1863, Dist. Columbus, Ky., 6 Div., 16 Corps, to Oct., 1863, 3 Brig., 1 Cav. Div., 16 Corps. Nov., 1863, 2 Brig., 1 Cav. Div., 16 Corps. June, 1864, 2 Brig., 1 Cav. Div., Dist. West. Tenn. Mustered out Dec. 10, 1864. (A section of Battery detached with Grierson's Cav. Brig., 13 Corps, Tenn., Nov., 1862, to March, 1863; 1 Brig., 1 Cav. Div., 16 Corps, to May, 1863; Cav. Brig., 19 Corps, Gulf, to July, 1863; 2 Brig., 1 Cav. Div., 16 Corps, Tenn., to Nov., 1863.)

BATTERY K, 1st REGIMENT LIGHT ARTILLERY.—Reorg. March, 1865, by assignment of Colvin's Indpt. Battery Light Arty. March, 1865, 2 Brig., 4 Div., Dist. East. Tenn., Dept. Cumberland. Mustered out July 15, 1865.

BATTERY L, 1st REGIMENT LIGHT ARTILLERY.—Org. at Chicago, Ill., Feby. 22, 1862. March, 1862, R. R. Dist., Mountain Dept., West Va. July, 1862, R. R. Dist., 8 Corps, Middle Dept. Sept., 1862, R. R. Dist., West Va., Dept. Ohio. Jany., 1863, New Creek Defences, Upper Potomac. 8 Corps. March, 1862, 5 Brig., 1 Div., 8 Corps. June, 1863, Mulligan's Brig., Scammon's Div., West Va. Dec., 1863, 2 Brig., 2 Div., West Va. April, 1864, Harper's Ferry, West Va., Reserve Div., West Va. Jany., 1865, Unatt., 3 Div., West Va. April, 1865, Unatt., 2 Div., West Va. Mustered out July 10, 1865.

BATTERY M, 1st REGIMENT LIGHT ARTILLERY.—Org. at Chicago, Ill., Aug. 12, 1862. Sept., 1862, Dist. Louisville, Ky., Dept. Ohio. Oct., 1862, 34 Brig., 10 Div., Army Ohio. Nov., 1862, 34 Brig., 10 Div., Dist. West. Ky., Dept. Ohio. Feby., 1863, Reed's Brig., Baird's Div., Army Ky., Dept. Cumberland. June, 1863, Arty., 1 Div., Reserve Corps, Cumberland. Oct., 1863, Arty., 2 Div., 4 Corps, Cumberland. July, 1864, Arty. Brig., 4 Corps. Oct., 1864, Unatt. Arty., Dept. Cumberland. Nov., 1864,

Garrison Arty., Cleveland, Tenn., Dept. Cumberland. Mustered out July 24, 1865.

BATTERY A, 2nd REGIMENT LIGHT ARTILLERY.— Org. at Peoria, Ill., Aug. 17, 1861. Aug., 1861, Dépt. Mo. Feby., 1862, 2 Brig., 3 Div., Army S. W. Mo., Dept. Mo. May, 1862, Arty., 3 Div., Army S. W. Mo. July, 1862, Dist. Eastern Ark., Dept. Mo. Jany., 1863, Arty., 12 Div., 13 Corps, Tenn. May, 1863, Arty., 14 Div., 13 Corps. July, 1863, 3 Brig., 1 Div., 13 Corps, Tenn. Aug., 1863, 3 Brig., 1 Div., 13 Corps, Gulf. Sept., 1863, Arty., 1 Div., 13 Corps, Gulf. June, 1864, Defences New Orleans, La. April, 1865, Dist. LaFourche, Dept. Gulf. Mustered out July 27, 1865.

BATTERY B, 2nd REGIMENT LIGHT ARTILLERY.— Org. at Springfield, Mo., June 20, 1861. July, 1861, Dept. Mo. April, 1862, Unatt. Arty., Army Tenn. May, 1862, Arty., 4 Div., Army Tenn. July, 1862, Arty, 1 Div., Dist. Jackson, Tenn. Nov., 1862, Arty., Dist. Jackson, Tenn., 13 Corps, Tenn. Dec., 1862, Dist. Corinth, 17 Corps, Tenn. Jany., 1863, Dist. Corinth, Miss., 16 Corps. March, 1863, Arty., 2 Div. 16 Corps. Nov., 1863, Post Corinth, 16 Corps. Jany., 1864, Fort Pickering, Memphis, Tenn., 16 Corps. April, 1864, Arty., 1 Div., 16 Corps. June, 1864, 2 Brig., Sturgis' Expedition. June, 1864, Fort Pickering, Memphis, Tenn., Dist West. Tenn. Mustered out July 15, 1865.

BATTERY C, 2nd REGIMENT LIGHT ARTILLERY.— Org. at Cairo, Ill., Aug. 5, 1861. Sept., 1861, Dept. Mo. March, 1862, Dist. Columbus, Ky. Nov., 1862, Dist. Columbus, Ky., 13 Corps, Tenn. Dec., 1862, Dist. Columbus, Ky., 16 Corps, Tenn., 6 Div., 16 Corps. June, 1863, 3 Div., Reserve Corps, Dept. Cumberland. Oct., 1863, Dist. Clarksville and Fort Donelson, Tenn., Dept. Cumberland. March, 1865, 5th Sub-Dist. Middle Tenn., Dept. Cumberland. Mustered out Aug. 3, 1865.

BATTERY D, 2nd REGIMENT LIGHT ARTILLERY.— Org. at Cairo, Ill., Dec. 17, 1861. Dec., 1861, Dist. Cairo. Feby., 1862, Arty., 3 Div., Dist Cairo. Feby., 1862, 1 Brig., 1 Div., Dist. West. Tenn. April, 1862. Arty., 1 Div., Army Tenn. July, 1862, Arty., 1 Div., Dist. Jackson, Tenn. Nov., 1862, Arty., Dist. Jackson, Tenn., 13 Corps., Dept. Tenn. Dec., 1862, Dist. Jackson, Tenn., 16 Corps. Jany., 1863, Arty., 1 Div., 16 Corps, Tenn. May, 1863, 2 Brig., Dist. Memphis, Tenn., 5 Div., 16 Corps. Dec., 1863, 3 Brig., 1 Cav. Div., 16 Corps. Jany., 1864, Dist. Memphis, Tenn., 16 Corps. Jany., 1864, Arty., 4 Div., 16 Corps. March, 1864, Decatur, Ala., Dist. Northern Ala., Dept. Cumberland. Mustered out Nov. 21, 1864.

BATTERY E, 2nd REGIMENT LIGHT ARTILLERY.— Org. at St. Louis, Mo., as Schwartz's Mo. Battery, Aug. 20, 1861. Sept., 1861, Dist. Cairo. Oct., 1861, 1st Brig., Dist. Cairo. Feby., 1862, 1 Brig., 1 Div., Dist. Cairo. Feby., 1862, 3 Brig., 1 Div., Dist. West. Tenn. April, 1862, Arty., 1 Div., Army Tenn. July, 1862, 1 Div., Dist. Jackson, Tenn. Nov., 1862, Arty., 3 Div., 13 Corps, Tenn. Dec., 1862, Arty., 4 Div., 17 Corps, Tenn. Jany., 1863, Arty., 4 Div., 16 Corps. July, 1863, Arty., 3 Div., 13 Corps, Tenn. Aug., 1863, Arty., 3 Div., 13 Corps, Gulf. Nov., 1863, Plaquemine, Dist. Baton Rouge, Dept. Gulf. June, 1864, Defences New Orleans. Mustered out Sept. 29, 1864.

BATTERY F, 2nd REGIMENT LIGHT ARTILLERY.— Org. at Cape Girardeau, Mo., Dec. 11, 1861. Dec., 1861, Dist. Cairo. April, 1862, Unatt. Arty., Army Tenn. April, 1862, Arty., 6 Div., Army Tenn. July, 1862, Arty., 6 Div., Dist. Corinth, Miss. Nov., 1862, Arty., 3 Div., Right Wing 13 Corps, Tenn. Dec., 1862, Arty., 6 Div., 16 Corps. Jany., 1863, Arty., 6 Div., 17 Corps. Aug., 1863, Arty., 4 Div., 17 Corps. Nov., 1864, Arty. Reserve, Nashville, Tenn., Dept. Cumberland. March, 1865, 5th Sub-Dist., Dist. Middle Tenn., Dept. Cumberland. Mustered out July 27, 1865.

BATTERY G, 2nd REGIMENT LIGHT ARTILLERY.— Org. at Camp Butler, Ill., Dec. 31, 1861. Dec., 1861, Fort Holt, Ky., Dept. Mo. March, 1862, Dist. Columbus, Ky. Nov., 1862, Dist. Jackson, Tenn., 13 Corps, Dept. Tenn. Dec., 1862, Arty., 3 Div., 17 Corps. Jany., 1863, Dist. Columbus, Ky., 6 Div., 16 Corps. June, 1864, Arty., 3 Div., 16 Corps. Dec., 1864, 3 Brig., 2 Div. Detachment, Army Tenn., Dept. Cumberland. Feby., 1865, Arty., 2

Div., 16 Corps., Mil. Div. West. Miss. March, 1865, Arty. Brig., 16 Corps. Mustered out Sept. 4, 1865.

BATTERY H, 2nd REGIMENT LIGHT ARTILLERY.— Org. at Camp Butler, Ill., Dec. 31, 1861. Feby., 1862, Dist. Cairo. March, 1862, Dist. Columbus, Ky. Nov., 1862, Dist. Columbus, Ky., 13 Corps, Dept. Tenn. Jany., 1863, Dist. Columbus, Ky., 16 Corps. June, 1863, 3 Div., Reserve Corps, Dept. Cumberland. Oct., 1863, Posts Fort Donelson and Clarksville, Tenn., Dept. Cumberland. March, 1865, 5th Sub-Dist., Dist. Middle Tenn., Dept. Cumberland. Mustered out July 29, 1865.

BATTERY I, 2nd REGIMENT LIGHT ARTILLERY.— Org. at Camp Butler, Ill., Dec. 31, 1861. Feby., 1862, Flotilla Brig., Army Miss. April, 1862, Arty. Div., Army Miss. Sept., 1862, Arty., 11 Div., Army Ohio. Sept., 1862, Arty., 11 Div., 3 Corps, Army Ohio. Nov., 1862, Arty., 4 Div., Centre 14 Corps, Cumberland. Jany., 1863, Arty., 4 Div., 14 Corps. June, 1863, Arty., 2 Div., Reserve Corps, Cumberland. Oct., 1863, Arty., 2 Div., 14 Corps. Jany., 1864, Arty., 1 Div., 11 Corps. April, 1864, Arty., 2 Div., 14 Corps. July, 1864, Arty. Brig., 14 Corps. Mustered out June 14, 1865.

BATTERY K, 2nd REGIMENT LIGHT ARTILLERY.— Org. at Camp Butler, Ill., Dec. 31, 1861. Feby., 1862, Dist. Cairo. March, 1862, Dist. Columbus, Ky. Nov., 1862, Dist. Columbus, Ky., 13 Corps, Dept. Tenn. Nov., 1862, Arty., 4 Div., Right Wing 13 Corps, Tenn. Dec., 1862, Arty., 4 Div., 17 Corps. Jany., 1863, Arty., 4 Div., 16 Corps. July, 1863, Arty., 4 Div., 13 Corps. Aug., 1863, Arty., 4 Div., 17 Corps. April, 1864, Arty., 1 Div., 17 Corps. Sept., 1864, Arty., Post Vicksburg, Miss., Dist Vicksburg, Miss. Nov., 1864, Arty. Reserve, Dist. Vicksburg. Mustered out Aug. 9, 1865.

BATTERY L, 2nd REGIMENT LIGHT ARTILLERY.— Org. at Chicago, Ill., Feby. 28, 1862. March, 1862, Benton Barracks, Mo. April, 1862, Arty., 4 Div., Army Tenn. July, 1862, Arty., 4 Div., Dist. Memphis, Tenn. Sept., 1862, Arty., 4 Div., Dist. Jackson, Tenn. Nov., 1862, Arty., 4 Div., 13 Corps, Tenn. Dec., 1862, Arty., 3, Div., 17 Corps, Tenn. April, 1864, Arty., 1 Div., 17 Corps. Sept., 1864, Post Vicksburg, Miss., Dist. Vicksburg, Miss. Nov., 1864, Arty. Reserve, Dist. Vicksburg, Miss. Mustered out Aug. 9, 1865.

BATTERY M, 2nd REGIMENT LIGHT ARTILLERY.— Org. at Chicago, Ill., June 6, 1862. July, 1862, R. R. Brig., 8 Corps, Middle Dept. Captured at Harper's Ferry, West Va., Sept. 15, 1862. June, 1863, 1 Brig., 4 Div., 23 Corps, Dept. Ohio. Aug., 1863, 2 Brig., 3 Div., 23 Corps. Dec., 1863, Dist. North Central Ky., 1 Div., 23 Corps. Jany., 1864, Dist. S. W. Ky., 1 Div., 23 Corps. Broken up April 11, 1864.

BRIDGE'S INDPT. BATTERY LIGHT ARTILLERY.— Authorized Jany., 1863, and org. at Nashville, Tenn., Jany. 14, 1863, from Co. C, 19th Ill. Infy. Feby., 1863, Pioneer Brig., Dept. Cumberland. June, 1863, 1 Brig., 2 Div., 14 Corps. Oct., 1863, Arty., 3 Div., 4 Corps, Cumberland. July, 1864, Arty. Brig., 4 Corps. Nov., 1864, Reserve Arty., 4 Corps. Dec., 1864, Garrison Arty., Nashville, Tenn. Transferred to 1st Ill. Arty. as Battery B, Dec. 21, 1864.

BUSTEED'S INDPT. BATTERY LIGHT ARTILLERY. —Org. at Chicago, Ill., Oct. 1, 1861. Disbanded and transferred to 1st N. Y. Light Arty., November 9, 1861.

CHICAGO BOARD OF TRADE BATTERY LIGHT ARTILLERY.—Org. at Chicago, Ill., Aug. 1, 1862. Sept., 1862, Arty., Dumont's 12 Div., Army Ohio. Nov., 1862, Pioneer Brig., Army Cumberland. March, 1863, 2 Brig., 2 Div., Cav. Corps, Cumberland. Oct., 1864, Arty., 2 Div., Cav. Corps, Mil. Div. Miss. Mustered out June 30, 1865.

CHAPMAN'S PEORIA INDPT. BATTERY LIGHT ARTILLERY.—Org. from 14th Ill. Infy. and attached to that Regt. till Feby., 1862, when designated Battery B, 2nd Light Arty., which see.

CHICAGO MERCANTILE BATTERY LIGHT ARTILLERY.—Org. at Chicago, Ill., Aug. 29, 1862. Nov., 1862, Arty.. 5 Div., Dist. Memphis, Tenn., 13 Corps, Dept. Tenn. Nov., 1862, Arty., 2 Div., Dist. Memphis, Tenn., 13 Corps. Dec., 1862, Arty., 10 Div. R. W., 13 Corps. Dec., 1862, Arty., 1 Div. Sherman's Yazoo Expedition. Jany., 1863, Arty., 10 Div., 13 Corps, Tenn. Aug., 1863, Arty., 4 Div.,

13 Corps, Gulf. March, 1864, Arty., 1 Div., 13 Corps, Gulf. June, 1864, Defences New Orleans, La. July, 1864, Arty. Reserve, Gulf. Nov., 1864, Arty., Cav. Div., Gulf. May, 1865, Defences New Orleans. Mustered out July 10, 1865.

COGSWELL'S 1st INDPT. BATTERY LIGHT ARTILLERY.—Org. at Ottawa, Ill., as Co. A Arty., 53rd Ill. Infy., Nov. 12, 1861. Detached as a Battery March 17, 1862. March, 1862, St. Louis, Mo. April, 1862, Arty., 3 Div., Army Tenn. July, 1862, Arty., 5 Div., Dist. Memphis, Tenn. Nov., 1862, Arty., 5 Div., Dist. Memphis, Tenn., Right Wing 13 Corps, Dept. Tenn. Nov., 1862, Arty., 1 Div., Dist. Memphis, Tenn. Dec., 1862, Arty., 1 Div., 17 Corps. Jany., 1863, Arty., 1 Div., 16 Corps. July, 1863, Arty., 4 Div., 15 Corps. July, 1863, Arty., 7 Div., 17 Corps. Sept., 1863, Arty., 2 Div., 17 Corps. Dec., 1863, Arty., 3 Div., 15 Corps. April, 1864, Arty. Reserve, Nashville, Tenn., Dept. Cumberland. Dec., 1864, 1 Brig., 1 Div., Detachment Army Tenn., Dept. Cumberland. Feby., 1865, Arty. Brig., 16 Corps, Mil. Div. West. Miss. Mustered out Aug. 14, 1865.

COLVIN'S 7th INDPT. BATTERY LIGHT ARTILLERY.—Org. Oct. 6, 1863, from 107th Ill., 33rd Ky. and 22nd Ind. Battery. Oct., 1863, 4 Brig., 4 Div., 23 Corps, Ohio. Nov., 1863, Arty., 2 Cav. Div., Cav. Corps, Ohio. April, 1864, 2 Brig., 4 Div., 23 Corps. Feby., 1865, 2 Brig., 4 Div., Dist. East. Tenn., Dept. Cumberland. Assigned to 1st Ill. Light Arty. as Battery K, March 23, 1865.

COOLEY'S 4th INDPT. BATTERY LIGHT ARTILLERY.—See Chicago Mercantile Battery.

ELGIN INDPT. BATTERY LIGHT ARTILLERY.—See Renwick's 5th Indpt. Battery. Org. at Elgin, Ill., Nov. 15, 1862. Dec., 1862, Dist. Western Ky., Dept. Ohio. April, 1863, 1 Brig., 3 Div., 23 Corps, Ohio. Aug., 1863, 1 Brig., 2 Div., 23 Corps. April, 1864, 2 Brig., 4 Div., 23 Corps. Feby., 1865, 2 Brig., 4 Div., Dist. East. Tenn., Dept. Cumberland. April, 1865, Arty., 1 Div., 23 Corps, Dept. North Carolina. Mustered out July 18, 1865.

HENSHAW'S 6th INDPT. BATTERY LIGHT ARTILLERY.—Org. at Ottawa, Ill., Dec. 3, 1862. Jany., 1863, Dist. Western Ky., Dept. Ohio. April, 1863, 1 Brig., 3 Div., 23 Corps, Ohio. Aug., 1863, 2 Brig., 2 Div., 23 Corps. April, 1864, 3 Brig., 4 Div., 23 Corps. Oct., 1864, 2 Brig., 4 Div., 23 Corps. Feby., 1865, 2 Brig., 4 Div., 23 Corps, Dist. East. Tenn., Dept. Cumberland. Mustered out July 18, 1865.

SMITH'S BATTERY CHICAGO LIGHT ARTILLERY.—Entered State service for three months, April 17, 1861; duty in Dist. Cairo. Mustered out July 16, 1861. Became Battery A, 1st Ill. Light Arty.

SPRINGFIELD INDPT. BATTERY LIGHT ARTILLERY, VAUGHAN'S 3rd INDPT. BATTERY.—Org. at Springfield, Ill., Aug. 21, 1862. Nov., 1862, Arty., Dist. Jackson, Tenn., 13 Corps, Dept. Tenn. Dec., 1862, Post Bolivar, Dist. Jackson, 16 Corps. March, 1863, 1 Brig., 3 Div., 16 Corps. May, 1863, 3 Brig., 3 Div., 16 Corps. Aug., 1863, True's Brig., Arkansas Exp. Sept., 1863, Arty., 2 Div., Ark. Exp. Jany., 1864, Unatt. Arty., 2 Div., 7 Corps, Dept. Ark. April, 1864, Arty., 3 Div., 7 Corps. May, 1864, Arty., 1 Div., 7 Corps. Mustered out June 30, 1865.

STOKES' 2nd INDPT. BATTERY LIGHT ARTILLERY.—See Chicago Board of Trade Battery.

VAUGHAN'S 3rd INDPT. BATTERY LIGHT ARTILLERY.—See Springfield Battery Light Arty.

7th REGIMENT INFANTRY, 3 MONTHS.—Org. at Springfield, Ill., April 25, 1861. Attached to Dist. Cairo. Mustered out July 25, 1861.

7th REGIMENT INFANTRY, 3 YEARS.—Org. at Cairo, Ill., July 25, 1861. July, 1861, Dist. Cairo. Oct., 1861, 4 Brig., Dist. Cairo. Feby., 1862, 3 Brig., 2 Div., Dist. W. Tenn., and Army Tenn. July, 1862, 3 Brig., 2 Div., Dist. Corinth, Miss. Nov., 1862, 3 Brig., Dist. Corinth, 13 Corps, Dept. Tenn. Dec., 1862, 3 Brig., Dist. Corinth, 17 Corps. Jany., 1863, 3 Brig., Dist. Corinth, 16 Corps. March, 1863, 3 Brig., 2 Div., 16 Corps. Sept., 1864, 3 Brig., 4 Div., 15 Corps. **Mustered out July 9, 1865.**

8th REGIMENT INFANTRY, 3 MONTHS.—Org. at Springfield, Ill., April 25, 1861. Duty in Dist. Cairo. Mustered out July 25, 1861.

8th REGIMENT INFANTRY, 3 YEARS.—Org. at Cairo, Ill., July 25, 1861. October, 1861, 2 Brig., Dist. Cairo. Feby., 1862, 1 Brig., 1 Div., Dist. Cairo. Feby., 1862, 1 Brig., 1 Div., Dept. West. Tenn., and Army Tenn. July, 1862, 1 Brig., 1 Div., Dist. Jackson, Tenn., Sept., 1862, 4 Brig., 1 Div., Dist. Jackson. Nov., 1862, 4 Brig., 3 Div., Dist. Jackson, Right Wing 13 Corps, Dept. Tenn. Dec., 1862, 3 Brig., 3 Div., 17 Corps, Tenn. April, 1864, Maltby's Brig., Dist. Vicksburg, Miss. Aug., 1864, 1 Brig., 2 Div., 19 Corps, Gulf. Dec., 1864, 2 Brig., Reserve Corps, Mil. Div. West. Miss. Feby., 1865, 2 Brig., 1 Div., Reserve Corps, M. D. W. M. Feby., 1865, 2 Brig., 1 Div., 13 Corps, M. D. M. W. June, 1865, Dept. La. Mustered out May 4, 1866.

9th REGIMENT INFANTRY, 3 MONTHS.—Org. at Springfield, Ill., April 26, 1861. Duty in Dist. Cairo. Mustered out July 26, 1861.

9th REGIMENT INFANTRY, 3 YEARS.—Org. at Cairo, Ill., July 26, to Aug. 31, 1861. July 1861, Dist. Cairo. Sept., 1861, Dist. Paducah, Ky., Feby., 1862, 1 Brig., 2 Div., Dist. Cairo. Feby., 1862, 1 Brig., 2 Div., Dist. West Tenn., and Army Tenn. March, 1862, 2 Brig., 2 Div., Army Tenn. July, 1862, 2 Brig., 2 Div., Dist. Corinth, Miss. Sept., 1862, 3 Brig., 2 Div., Dist. Corinth, Miss. Oct., 1862, 2 Brig., 2 Div., Dist. Corinth, Miss. Nov., 1862, 2 Brig., Dist. Corinth, 13 Corps, Dept. Tenn. Dec., 1862, 2 Brig., Dist. Corinth, 17 Corps. Jany, 1863, 2 Brig., Dist. Corinth, 16 Corps. March, 1863, 2 Brig., 2 Div., 16 Corps. Sept., 1864, Unatt., 3 Div., Cav. Corps, Cumberland. Nov., 1864, Unatt., 3 Div., Cav. Corps, Mil. Div. Miss. Mustered out July 9, 1865.

10th REGIMENT INFANTRY, 3 MONTHS.—Org. at Springfield, Ill., April 29, 1861. Duty in Dist. Cairo. Mustered out July 29, 1861.

10th REGIMENT INFANTRY, 3 YEARS.—Org. at Cairo, Ill., July 29, 1861. July, 1861, Dist. Cairo. Oct., 1861, 1 Brig., Dist. Cairo. Feby., 1862, 4 Brig., 1 Div., Dist. Cairo. Feby., 1862, 1 Brig., 4 Div., Army Miss. April, 1862, 2 Brig., 1 Div., Army Miss. Sept., 1862, 2 Brig., 13 Div., Army Ohio. Nov., 1862, 1 Brig., 4 Div., Centre 14 Corps, Dept. Cumberland. Jany., 1863, 1 Brig., 4 Div., 14 Corps. June, 1863, 1 Brig., 2 Div., Reserve Corps, Cumberland. Oct., 1863, 1 Brig., 2 Div., 14 Corps. Aug., 1864, 3 Brig., 4 Div., 16 Corps, Tenn. Sept., 1864, 3 Brig., 1 Div., 17 Corps. Mustered out July 4, 1865.

11th REGIMENT INFANTRY, 3 MONTHS.—Org. at Springfield, Ill., April 30, 1861. Duty in Dist. Cairo. Mustered out July 30, 1861.

11th REGIMENT INFANTRY, 3 YEARS.—Org. at Cairo, Ill., July 30, 1861. July, 1861, Dist. Cairo. Oct., 1861, 3 Brig., Dist. Cairo. Feby., 1862, 2 Brig., 1 Div., Dist. Cairo. Feby., 1862, 2 Brig., 1 Div., Dist. West. Tenn., and Army Tenn. July, 1862, 2 Brig., 1 Div., Dist. Jackson, Tenn. Aug., 1862, Dist. Cairo, Ill. Nov., 1862, 2 Brig., 6 Div., Left Wing 13 Corps, Dept. Tenn. Dec., 1862, 2 Brig., 6 Div., 16 Corps. Jany., 1863, 2 Brig., 6 Div., 17 Corps. Sept., 1863, 2 Brig., 1 Div., 17 Corps. Aug., 1864, 1 Brig., 2 Div., 19 Corps, Dept. Gulf. Dec., 1864, 2 Brig., Reserve Corps, Mil. Div. West. Miss. Feby., 1865, 2 Brig., 1 Div., Reserve Corps, M. D. W. M. Feby., 1865, 2 Brig., 1 Div., 13 Corps, M. D. M. W. July, 1865, Dept. La. Mustered out July 14, 1865.

12th REGIMENT INFANTRY, 3 MONTHS.—Org. at Springfield, Ill., May 2, 1861. Duty in Dist. Cairo. Mustered out Aug. 1, 1861.

12th REGIMENT INFANTRY, 3 YEARS.—Org. at Cairo, Ill., Aug. 1, 1861. Aug., 1861, Dist. Cairo. Oct., 1861, 3 Brig., Dist. Cairo. Feby., 1862, 1 Brig., 2 Div., Dist. Cairo. Feby., 1862, 2 Brig., 2 Div., Dist. West. Tenn., and Army Tenn. July, 1862, 2 Brig., 2 Div., Dist. Corinth, Miss. Sept., 1862, 1 Brig., 2 Div., Dist. Corinth, Miss. Nov., 1862, 2 Brig., Dist. Corinth, Miss., 13 Corps, Dept. Tenn. Dec., 1862, 2 Brig., Dist. Corinth, 17 Corps. Jany., 1863, 2 Brig., Dist. Corinth, 16 Corps. March, 1863, 2 Brig., 2 Div., 16 Corps. Sept., 1864, 2 Brig., 4 Div., 15 Corps. April, 1865, 1 Brig., 1 Div., 15 Corps. Mustered out July 19, 1865.

13th REGIMENT INFANTRY.—Org. at Dixon, Ill., May 24, 1861. July, 1861, Fremont's Army, West. Oct., 1861, Dist. Rolla, Mo., Dept. Mo. Jany., 1862, Unatt., Army S. W. Mo., Dept. Mo. March, 1862, 1 Brig., 2 Div., Army S. W. Mo. July, 1862, Helena, Ark., Dist. Eastern Ark., Dept. Mo. Nov., 1862, 2 Brig., 2 Div., Dist. Eastern Ark., Dept. Tenn. Dec., 1862, 2 Brig., 11 Div., 13 Corps, Tenn. Dec., 1862, 1 Brig., 4 Div., Sherman's Yazoo Expedition. Jany., 1863, 1 Brig., 1 Div., 15 Corps, Tenn. April, 1864, Unassigned, 3 Div., 15 Corps. Mustered out June 18, 1864.

14th REGIMENT INFANTRY.—Org. at Jacksonville, Ill., May 25, 1861. July, 1861, Dept. Mo. Feby., 1862, 2 Brig., 4 Div., Dist. West. Tenn., and Army Tenn. July, 1862, 2 Brig., 4 Div., Dist. Memphis, Tenn. Sept., 1862, 2 Brig., 4 Div., Dist. Jackson, Tenn. Nov., 1862, 2 Brig., 4 Div., Right Wing 13 Corps, Dept. Tenn. Dec., 1862, 2 Brig., 4 Div., 17 Corps. Jany., 1863, 2 Brig., 4 Div., 16 Corps. July, 1863, 2 Brig., 4 Div., 13 Corps. Aug., 1863, 2 Brig., 4 Div., 17 Corps. Nov., 1864, 1 Brig., 4 Div., 17 Corps. April, 1865, 2 Brig., 4 Div., 17 Corps. June, 1865, Dept. Mo. Mustered out September 18, 1865.

15th REGIMENT INFANTRY.—Org. at Freeport, Ill., May 24, 1861. July, 1861, Dept. Mo. Feby., 1862, 1 Brig., 4 Div., Dist. West. Tenn. March, 1862, 2 Brig., 4 Div., Dist. West. Tenn., and Army Tenn. July, 1862, 2 Brig., 4 Div., Dist. Memphis, Tenn. Sept., 1862, 2 Brig., 4 Div., Dist. Jackson, Tenn. Nov., 1862, 2 Brig., 4 Div., 13 Corps, Dept. Tenn. Dec., 1862, 2 Brig., 4 Div., 17 Corps. Jany., 1863, 2 Brig., 4 Div., 16 Corps. July, 1863, 2 Brig., 4 Div., 13 Corps. Aug., 1863, 2 Brig., 4 Div., 17 Corps. Nov., 1864, 1 Brig., 4 Div., 17 Corps. April, 1865, 2 Brig., 4 Div., 17 Corps. June, 1865, Dept. Mo. Mustered out Sept. 16, 1865.

16th REGIMENT INFANTRY.—Org. at Quincy, Ill., May 24, 1861. June, 1861, Dept. Mo. Feby., 1862, 4 Brig., 1 Div., Dist. Cairo. Feby., 1862, 1 Brig., 4 Div., Army Miss. April, 1862, 2 Brig., 1 Div., Army Miss. Sept., 1862, 2 Brig., 13 Div., Army Ohio. Nov., 1862, 1 Brig., 4 Div., Centre 14 Corps, Army Cumberland. Jany., 1863, 1 Brig., 4 Div., 14 Corps. June, 1863, 1 Brig., 2 Div., Reserve Corps, Cumberland. Oct., 1863, 1 Brig., 2 Div., 14 Corps. Mustered out July 8, 1865.

17th REGIMENT INFANTRY.—Org. at Peoria, Ill., May 24, 1861. July, 1861, Dist. Cairo. Oct., 1861. 5 Brig., Dist. Cairo. Feby., 1862, 3 Brig., 1 Div., Dist. Cairo, Dist. West. Tenn. and Army Tenn. July 1862, 3 Brig., 1 Div., Dist. Jackson, Tenn. Sept., 1862, Unatt., Dist. Jackson. Nov., 1862, 4 Brig., 3 Div., Right Wing 13 Corps, Dept. Tenn. Nov., 1862, 1 Brig., 6 Div., 16 Corps. Jany., 1863, 1 Brig., 6 Div., 17 Corps. July, 1863, 3 Brig., 3 Div., 17 Corps. April, 1864. Maltby's Brig., Dist. Vicksburg. Mustered out June 4, 1864.

18th REGIMENT INFANTRY.—Org. at Aurora, Ill., May 28, 1861. July, 1861, Dist. Cairo. Oct., 1861, 1 Brig., Dist. Cairo. Feby., 1862, 1 Brig., 1 Div., Dist. Cairo. Feby., 1862, 2 Brig., 1 Div., Dist. West. Tenn. March, 1862, 1 Brig., 1 Div., Dist. West. Tenn., and Army Tenn. July, 1862, 1 Brig., 1 Div., Dist. Jackson, Tenn. Sept., 1862, 2 Brig., 1 Div., Dist. Jackson. Nov., 1862, Dist. Jackson, 13 Corps, Dept. Tenn. Dec., 1862, 1 Brig., Dist. Jackson, 16 Corps. March, 1863, 2 Brig., 3 Div., 16 Corps. May, 1863, 2 Brig., Kimball's Provisional Div., 16 Corps. July, 1863, 2 Brig., Kimball's Div., Dist. Eastern Ark. Aug., 1863, 1 Brig., 2 Div., Arkansas Exp. Nov., 1863, 3 Brig., 2 Div., Army Ark. Jany., 1864, 3 Brig., 2 Div., 7 Corps, Dept. Ark. April, 1864, Post Pine Bluff, Ark., 7 Corps. May, 1864, 1 Brig., 2 Div., 7 Corps. Jany., 1865, Pontooneers, 7 Corps. May, 1865, 1 Brig., 1 Div., 7 Corps. Aug., 1865, Dept. Ark. Mustered out Dec. 16, 1865.

19th REGIMENT INFANTRY.—Org. at Chicago, Ill., June 4, 1861. July, 1861, Dept. Mo. Sept., 1861, Dept. Ky., Elizabethtown, Ky., Dept. Cumberland. Nov., 1861, 8 Brig., Army Ohio. Dec., 1861, 8 Brig., 3 Div., Army Ohio. July, 1862, Unatt., R. R. Guard, Army Ohio. Sept., 1862, 29 Brig., 8 Div., Army Ohio. Nov., 1862, 2 Brig., 2 Div., Centre 14 Corps, Army Cumberland. Jany., 1863, 2 Brig., 2 Div., 14 Corps. Oct., 1863, 2 Brig., 1 Div., 14 Corps. Oct., 1863, 1 Brig., 3 Div., 14 Corps. Mustered out July 9, 1864.

20th REGIMENT INFANTRY.—Org. at Joliet, Ill., June 13, 1861. July, 1861, Dist. Cairo. Oct., 1861, Bird's Point, Mo., Unatt. Feby., 1862, 2 Brig., 1 Div., Dist. Cairo. Feby., 1862, 2 Brig., 1 Div., Dist. West. Tenn., and Army Tenn. July, 1862, 2 Brig., 1 Div., Dist. Jackson, Tenn. Nov., 1862, 1 Brig., 3 Div., Right Wing 13 Corps, Dept. Tenn. Dec., 1862, 1 Brig., 3 Div., 17 Corps, Tenn. Mustered out July 16, 1865.

21st REGIMENT INFANTRY.—Org. at Mattoon, Ill., June 28, 1861. July, 1861, Dept. Mo. March, 1862, Steele's Command, Dist. S. E. Mo. May, 1862, 2 Brig., 4 Div., Army Miss. Sept., 1862, 31 Brig., 9 Div., Army Ohio. Sept., 1862, 31 Brig., 9 Div., 3 Corps, Army Ohio. Nov., 1862, 2 Brig., 1 Div., Right Wing 14 Corps, Dept. Cumberland. Jany., 1863, 2 Brig., 1 Div., 20 Corps, Cumberland. Oct., 1863, 1 Brig., 1 Div., 4 Corps, Cumberland. June, 1865, 2 Brig., 1 Div., 4 Corps. Aug., 1865, Dept. Texas. Mustered out December 16, 1865.

22nd REGIMENT INFANTRY.—Org. at Belleville, Ill., June 25, 1861. July, 1861, Dist. Cairo. Oct., 1861, 2 Brig., Dist. Cairo. Feby., 1862, 4 Brig., 1 Div., Dist. Cairo. Feby., 1862, 2 Brig., 4 Div., Army Miss. April, 1862, 1 Brig., 1 Div., Army Miss. Sept., 1862, 1 Brig., 13 Div., Army Ohio. Nov., 1862, 3 Brig., 3 Div., Right Wing 14 Corps, Dept. Cumberland. Jany., 1863, 3 Brig., 3 Div., 20 Corps, Cumberland. Oct., 1863, 3 Brig., 2 Div., 4 Corps, Cumberland. Mustered out July 7, 1864.

23rd REGIMENT INFANTRY.—Org. at Chicago, Ill., June 15, 1861. July, 1861, Dept. Mo. June, 1862, Harper's Ferry and New Creek, West Va., R. R. Dist., Mt. Dept. July, 1862, R. R. Dist., Middle Dept., 8 Corps. Sept., 1862, R. R. Dist., West Va. Jany., 1863, New Creek Defences, Upper Potomac, 8 Corps, Middle Dept. March, 1863, 5 Brig., 1 Div., 8 Corps. June, 1863, Mulligan's Brig., Scammon's Div., West Va. Dec., 1863, 2 Brig., 2 Div., West Va. April, 1864, Kelly's Command, Reserve Div., West Va. July, 1864, 1 Brig., 3 Infy. Div., West Va. July, 1864, 3 Brig., 1 Div., West Va. Dec., 1864, 2 Brig., Indpt. Div., 24 Corps, Army James. June, 1865, 1 Brig., Indpt. Div., 24 Corps. Mustered out July 24, 1865.

24th REGIMENT INFANTRY.—Org. at Chicago, Ill., July 8, 1861. July, 1861, Dept. Mo. Sept., 1861, Thomas' Command, Dept. Ohio. Nov., 1861, 8 Brig., Army Ohio. Dec., 1861, 8 Brig., 3 Div., Army Ohio. July, 1862, Unatt., R. R. Guard, Dept. Ohio. Sept., 1862, 28 Brig., 3 Div., Army Ohio. Sept., 1862, 28 Brig., 3 Div., 1 Corps, Army Ohio. Nov., 1862, 3 Brig., 1 Div., Centre 14 Corps, Dept. Cumberland. Jany., 1863, 3 Brig., 1 Div., 14 Corps, Cumberland. April, 1863, 2 Brig., 1 Div., 14 Corps. Oct., 1863, 3 Brig., 1 Div., 14 Corps. May, 1864. 1 Brig., 3 Div., 14 Corps. Mustered out Aug. 6, 1864.

25th REGIMENT INFANTRY.—Org. at St. Louis, Mo., Aug. 4, 1861. Aug., 1861, Dept. Mo. Jany., 1862, 4 Brig., Army S. W. Mo., Dept. Mo. March, 1862, 1 Brig., 1 Div., Army S. W. Mo. June, 1862, 1 Brig., 4 Div., Army Miss. Sept., 1862, 32 Brig., 9 Div., Army Ohio. Sept., 1862, 32 Brig., 9 Div., 3 Corps, Army Ohio. Nov., 1862, 3 Brig., 1 Div., Right Wing 14 Corps, Dept. Cumberland. Jany., 1863, 3 Brig., 1 Div., 20 Corps, Cumberland. Oct., 1863, 1 Brig., 3 Div., 4 Corps. Mustered out September 5, 1864.

26th REGIMENT INFANTRY.—Org. at Quincy, Ill., Aug. 31, 1861. Sept., 1861, Dept. Mo. March, 1862, 2 Brig., 5 Div., Army Miss. April, 1862, 1 Brig., 3 Div., Army Miss. April, 1862, 2 Brig., 2 Div., Army Miss. Nov., 1862, 2 Brig., 8 Div., Left Wing 13 Corps, Dept. Tenn. Dec., 1862, 2 Brig., 8 Div., 16 Corps, Tenn. Dec., 1862, 2 Brig., 1 Div., 17 Corps. Jany., 1863, 2 Brig., 1 Div., 16 Corps. March, 1863, 1 Brig., 1 Div., 16 Corps. July, 1863, 1 Brig., 4 Div., 15 Corps. Aug., 1864, 2 Brig., 4 Div., 15 Corps. Sept., 1864, 2 Brig., 1 Div., 15 Corps. Mustered out July 20, 1865.

27th REGIMENT INFANTRY.—Org. at Camp Butler, Ill. Aug. 10, 1861. Sept., 1861, Dist. Cairo. Feby., 1862, 1 Brig., 1 Div., Dist. Cairo. Feby., 1862, Flotilla Brig., Army Miss. April, 1862, 1 Brig., 1 Div., Army Miss. Sept., 1862, 1 Brig., 13 Div., Army Ohio. Nov., 1862, 3

Brig., 3 Div., Right Wing 14 Corps, Cumberland. Jany., 1863, 3 Brig., 3 Div., 20 Corps, Cumberland. Oct., 1864, 3 Brig., 2 Div., 4 Corps. Mustered out Sept. 20, 1864.

28th REGIMENT INFANTRY.—Org. at Camp Butler, Ill., Aug. 15, 1861. Aug., 1861, Dist. Cairo. Oct., 1861, 4 Brig., Dist. Cairo. Feby., 1862, 1 Brig., 4 Div., Dist. Cairo. Feby., 1862, 1 Brig., 4 Div., Dist. West. Tenn., and Army Tenn. July, 1862, 1 Brig., 4 Div., Dist. Memphis, Tenn. Sept., 1862, 1 Brig., 4 Div., Dist. Jackson, Tenn. Nov., 1862, 3 Brig., 4 Div., Right Wing 13 Corps, Dept. Tenn. Dec., 1862, 3 Brig., 4 Div., 17 Corps. Jany., 1863, 3 Brig., 4 Div., 16 Corps. July 1863, 3 Brig., 4 Div., 13 Corps. Aug., 1863, 3 Brig., 4 Div., 17 Corps. Aug., 1863, Post Natchez, Miss., Dist. Vicksburg, Miss. Oct., 1864, 3 Brig., 2 Div., 19 Corps, Gulf. Dec., 1864, 1 Brig, Reserve Corps, Mil. Div. West. Miss. Feby., 1865, 1 Brig., 3 Div., Reserve Corps, M. D. W. M. Feby., 1865, 1 Brig., 3 Div., 13 Corps, M. D. W. M. July, 1865, Dept. Texas. Mustered out March 15, 1866.

29th REGIMENT INFANTRY.—Org. at Camp Butler, Ill., Aug. 19, 1861. Sept., 1861, Dist. Cairo. Oct., 1861, 1 Brig., Dist. Cairo. Feby., 1862, 1 Brig., 1 Div., Dist. Cairo. Feby., 1862, 1 Brig., 1 Div., Dist. West. Tenn. March, 1862, 3 Brig., 1 Div., Army Tenn. July, 1862, 3 Brig., 1 Div., Dist. Jackson, Tenn. Sept., 1862, 2 Brig., 1 Div., Dist. Jackson, Tenn. Nov., 1862, Dist. Jackson, 13 Corps, Dept. Tenn. Dec., 1862, 1 Brig., Dist. Jackson, 13 Corps. Dec., 1862. Prisoners of War, Dec., 1862, Benton Barracks, Mo. July, 1863, 1 Brig., 3 Div., 17 Corps. Dec., 1863, Post Natchez, Miss., Dist. Vicksburg, Miss. Oct., 1864, Paducah, Ky., Nov., 1864, Memphis, Tenn., Dist. West Tenn. Jany., 1865, 1 Brig., Reserve Corps, Mil. Div. West. Miss. Feby., 1865, 3 Brig., 1 Div., Reserve Corps, M. D. W. M. Feby., 1865, 3 Brig., 1 Div., 13 Corps, M. D. W. M. July, 1865, Dept. Texas. Mustered out Nov. 28, 1865.

30th REGIMENT INFANTRY.—Org. at Camp Butler, Ill., Aug. 28, 1861. Sept., 1861, Dist. Cairo. Oct., 1861, 1 Brig., Dist. Cairo. Feby., 1862, 1 Brig., 1 Div., Dist. Cairo. Feby., 1862, 1 Brig., 1 Div., Dist. West. Tenn., and Army Tenn. July, 1862, 1 Brig., 1 Div., Dist. Jackson, Tenn. Sept., 1862, 3 Brig., 1 Div., Dist. Jackson, Tenn. Nov., 1862, 1 Brig., 3 Div., Right Wing 13 Corps, Dept. Tenn. Dec., 1862, 2 Brig., 3 Div., Right Wing 13 Corps. Dec., 1862, 2 Brig., 3 Div., 17 Corps. Dec., 1863, 3 Brig., 3 Div., 17 Corps. April, 1864, 1 Brig., 3 Div., 17 Corps. April, 1865, 1 Brig., 4 Div., 17 Corps. Mustered out July 16, 1865.

31st REGIMENT INFANTRY.—Org. at Jacksonville, Ill. Mustered in at Cairo, Ill., Sept. 18, 1861. Sept., 1861, Dist. Cairo. Oct., 1861, 1 Brig., Dist. Cairo. Feby., 1862, 1 Brig., 1 Div., Dist. Cairo. Feby., 1862, 1 Brig., 1 Div., Dist. West. Tenn., and Army Tenn. July, 1862, 1 Brig., 1 Div., Dist. Jackson, Tenn. Sept., 1862, 2 Brig., 1 Div., Dist. Jackson, Tenn. Nov., 1862, 1 Brig., 3 Div., Right Wing 13 Corps, Dept. Tenn. Dec., 1862, 1 Brig., 3 Div., 17 Corps. April, 1865, 2 Brig., 4 Div., 17 Corps. Mustered out July 19, 1865.

32nd REGIMENT INFANTRY.—Org. at Camp Butler, Ill., Dec. 31, 1861. Jany., 1862, Dist. Cairo. Feby., 1862, 4 Brig., 1 Div., Dist. Cairo. Feby., 1862, 1 Brig., 4 Div., Dist. West. Tenn., and Army Tenn. July, 1862, 1 Brig., 4 Div., Dist. Memphis, Tenn. Sept., 1862, 1 Brig., 4 Div., Dist. Jackson, Tenn. Nov., 1862, 3 Brig., 4 Div., Right Wing 13 Corps, Dept. Tenn. Dec., 1862, 3 Brig, 4 Div., 17 Corps. Jany., 1863, 3 Brig., 4 Div., 16 Corps. July, 1863, 3 Brig., 4 Div., 13 Corps. Aug., 1863, 3 Brig., 4 Div., 17 Corps. April, 1864, 1 Brig., 4 Div., 17 Corps. Nov., 1864, 3 Brig., 4 Div., 17 Corps. April, 1865, 2 Brig., 4 Div., 17 Corps. July, 1865, Dept. Mo. Mustered out Sept. 16, 1865.

33rd REGIMENT INFANTRY.—Org. at Camp Butler, Ill., Sept. 3, 1861. September, 1861, Dept. Mo. March, 1862, 2 Brig., Steele's Army S. E. Mo. May, 1862, 1 Div., Army S. W. Mo., Dept. Mo. July, 1862, 1 Div., Dist. Eastern Ark., Dept. Mo. Nov., 1862, 1 Brig., 1 Div., Army S. E. Mo., Dept. Mo. March, 1863, 1 Brig., 14 Div., 13 Corps, Dept. Tenn. July, 1863, 1 Brig., 1 Div., 13 Corps, Dept. Tenn. Aug., 1863, 1 Brig., 1 Div., 13 Corps, Gulf. June, 1864, Dist. LaFourche, La., Dept. Gulf. Feby., 1865, 1

Brig., 1 Div., 13 Corps, Mil. Div. West. Miss. June, 1865, Dept. Miss. Mustered out Nov. 24, 1865.

34th REGIMENT INFANTRY.—Org. at Camp Butler, Ill., Sept. 7, 1861. Oct., 1861, Johnson's 3 Brig., McCook's Div., Nolin, Ky., Dept. Ohio. Nov., 1861, 5 Brig., Army Ohio. Dec., 1861, 5 Brig., 2 Div., Army Ohio. Sept., 1862, 5 Brig., 2 Div., 1 Corps, Army Ohio. Nov., 1862, 2 Brig., 2 Div., Right Wing 14 Corps, Cumberland. Jany., 1863, 2 Brig., 2 Div., 20 Corps, Cumberland. Oct., 1863, Unatt., Dept. Cumberland. Nov., 1863, 2 Brig., 2 Div., 14 Corps. Mustered out July 12, 1865.

35th REGIMENT INFANTRY.—Org. at Decatur, Ill., and mustered in at St. Louis, Mo., Aug. 28, 1861. Sept., 1861, Dept. Mo. Jany., 1862, 1 Brig., Army S. W. Mo., Dept. Mo. March, 1862, 1 Brig., 4 Div., Army S. W. Mo. June, 1862, 1 Brig., 4 Div., Army Miss. Sept., 1862, 32 Brig., 9 Div., Army Ohio. Sept., 1862, 32 Brig., 9 Div., 3 Corps, Army Ohio. Nov., 1862, 3 Brig., 1 Div., Right Wing 14 Corps, Cumberland. Jany., 1863, 3 Brig., 1 Div., 20 Corps, Cumberland. Oct., 1863, 1 Brig., 3 Div., 4 Corps. Mustered out Sept. 27, 1864.

36th REGIMENT INFANTRY.—Org. at Aurora, Ill., Sept. 23, 1861. Sept., 1861, Dept. Mo. Jany., 1862, 2 Brig., Army S. W. Mo., Dept. Mo. March, 1862, 2 Brig., 1 Div., Army S. W. Mo. June, 1862, 1 Brig., 5 Div., Army Miss. Sept., 1862, 37 Brig., 11 Div., Army Ohio. Sept., 1862, 37 Brig., 11 Div., 3 Corps, Army Ohio. Nov., 1862, 1 Brig., 3 Div., Right Wing 14 Corps, Cumberland. Jany., 1863, 1 Brig., 3 Div., 20 Corps, Cumberland. Oct., 1863, 1 Brig., 2 Div., 4 Corps. Aug., 1865, Dept. Texas. Mustered out Sept. 23, 1865.

37th REGIMENT INFANTRY.—Org. at Chicago, Ill., Sept. 18, 1861. Sept., 1861, Dept. Mo. Feby., 1862, 2 Brig., 3 Div., Army S. W. Mo., Dept. Mo. May, 1862, Cassville, Mo., Dist. S. W. Mo. Sept., 1862, 2 Brig., 2 Div., Army Frontier, Dept. Mo. June, 1863, 1 Brig., Herron's Div., 13 Corps, Tenn. July, 1863, 1 Brig., 2 Div., 13 Corps, Tenn. Aug., 1863, 1 Brig., 2 Div., 13 Corps, Gulf. June, 1864, 1 Brig., 3 Div., 19 Corps, Gulf. Dec., 1864, 4 Brig., Reserve Corps, Gulf. Feby., 1865, 3 Brig., 2 Div., Reserve Corps, Mil. Div. West. Miss. Feby., 1865, 3 Brig., 2 Div., 13 Corps. July, 1865, Dept. Texas. Mustered out May 15, 1866.

38th REGIMENT INFANTRY.—Org. at Camp Butler, Ill., Aug. 15, 1861. Sept., 1861, Dept. Mo. March, 1862, 1 Brig., Steele's Command, Army S. E. Mo., Dept. Mo. June, 1862, 2 Brig., 4 Div., Army Miss. Sept., 1862, 31 Brig., 9 Div., Army Ohio. Sept., 1862, 31 Brig., 9 Div., 3 Corps, Army Ohio. Nov., 1862, 2 Brig., 1 Div., Right Wing 14 Corps, Cumberland. Jany., 1863, 2 Brig., 1 Div., 20 Corps, Cumberland. Oct., 1863, 1 Brig., 1 Div., 4 Corps. June, 1865, 2 Brig., 1 Div., 4 Corps. Aug., 1865, Dept. Texas. Mustered out March 20, 1866.

39th REGIMENT INFANTRY.—Org. at Chicago, Ill., Oct. 11, 1861. Nov., 1861, R. R. Guard, Dept. West Va. Jany., 1862, 1 Brig., Landers' Div., Army Potomac. March, 1862, 2 Brig., Shields' 2 Div., Banks' 5 Corps. April, 1862, 2 Brig., Shields' Div., Dept. Shenandoah. May, 1862, 2 Brig., Shields' Div., Dept. Rappahannock. July, 1862, 3 Brig., 2 Div., 4 Corps, Army Potomac. Sept., 1862, Ferry's Brig., Div. at Suffolk, Va., 7 Corps, Dept. Va. Dec., 1862, 1 Brig., 2 Div., 18 Corps, Dept. N. C. Feby., 1863, 3 Brig., 2 Div., 18 Corps, Dept. South. April, 1863, U. S. Forces, Folly Island, S. C., 10 Corps, Dept. South. June, 1863, 2 Brig., Folly Island, S. C., 10 Corps. June, 1863, 1 Brig., Folly Island, S. C., 10 Corps. July, 1863, 1 Brig., 2 Div., Morris Island, S. C., 10 Corps. July, 1863, 1 Brig., Morris Island, S. C., 10 Corps. Oct., 1863, Howell's Brig., Gordon's Div., Folly Island, S. C., 10 Corps. Dec., 1863, Dist. Hilton Head, S. C., 10 Corps. April, 1864, 1 Brig., 1 Div., 10 Corps, Army James, Dept. Va. and N. C. Dec., 1864, 1 Brig., 1 Div., 24 Corps. Aug., 1865, Norfolk, Va., Dist. Eastern Va., Dept. Va. Mustered out Dec. 6, 1865.

40th REGIMENT INFANTRY.—Org. at Springfield, Ill., Aug. 10, 1861. Sept., 1861, Dist. Paducah, Ky. March, 1862, 1 Brig., 5 Div., Army Tenn. May, 1862, 2 Brig., 5 Div., Army Tenn. July, 1862, 2 Brig., 5 Div., Dist. Memphis, Tenn. Nov., 1862, 2 Brig., 5 Div., Dist. Memphis, Tenn., 13 Corps, Dept. Tenn. Nov., 1862, 1 Brig., 1 Div.,

Dist. Memphis, Tenn., 13 Corps. Dec., 1862, 1 Brig., 1 Div., 17 Corps. Jany., 1863, 1 Brig., 1 Div., 16 Corps. March, 1863, 2 Brig., 1 Div., 16 Corps. July, 1863, 2 Brig., 4 Div., 15 Corps. Sept., 1864, 2 Brig., 1 Div., 15 Corps. Mustered out July 24, 1865.

41st REGIMENT INFANTRY.—Org. at Decatur, Ill., Aug. 5, 1861. Aug., 1861, Dist. Cairo. Oct., 1861, Unatt., Dist. Cairo. Dec., 1861, 1 Brig., 2 Div., Dist. Cairo. Feby., 1862, 1 Brig., 4 Div., Dist. West. Tenn., and Army Tenn. July, 1862, 1 Brig., 4 Div., Dist. Memphis, Tenn. Sept., 1862, 1 Brig., 4 Div., Dist. Jackson, Tenn. Nov., 1862, 1 Brig., 4 Div., Right Wing 13 Corps. Dec., 1862, 1 Brig., 4 Div., 17 Corps. Jany., 1863, 1 Brig., 4 Div., 16 Corps. July, 1863, 1 Brig., 4 Div., 13 Corps. Aug., 1863, 1 Brig., 4 Div., 17 Corps. March, 1864, 1 Provisional Div., 17 Corps, Gulf (Non-Vets.). June, 1864, 4 Brig., 1 Div., 16 Corps, Tenn. (Non-Vets.). July, 1864, 2 Brig., 4 Div., 17 Corps (Veterans). Nov., 1864, 1 Brig., 4 Div., 17 Corps. Consolidated with 53rd Ill. Infy. Dec. 23, 1864.

42nd REGIMENT INFANTRY.—Org. at Chicago, Ill., July 22, 1861. Oct., 1861, Dept. Mo. Feby., 1862, Flotilla Brig., Army Miss. April, 1862, 1 Brig., 1 Div., Army Miss. Sept., 1862, 1 Brig., 13 Div., Army Ohio. Nov., 1862, 3 Brig., 3 Div., Right Wing 14 Corps, Cumberland. Jany., 1863, 3 Brig., 3 Div., 20 Corps, Cumberland. Oct., 1863, 3 Brig., 2 Div., 4 Corps. June, 1865, 2 Brig., 2 Div., 4 Corps. Aug., 1865, Dept. Texas. Mustered out Dec. 16, 1865.

43rd REGIMENT INFANTRY.—Org. at Camp Butler, Ill., Oct. 12, 1861. Oct., 1861, Dept. Mo. Feby., 1862, 3 Brig., 1 Div., Dist. Cairo. Feby., 1862, 3 Brig., 1 Div, Dist. West. Tenn., and Army Tenn. July, 1862, 3 Brig., 1 Div., Dist. Jackson, Tenn. Sept., 1862, Unatt., Dist. Jackson, Tenn. Nov., 1862, Post Bolivar, Dist. Jackson, 13 Corps, Tenn. Dec., 1862, Post Bolivar, Dist. Jackson, 16 Corps. March, 1863, 1 Brig., 3 Div., 16 Corps. May, 1863, 1 Brig., Kimball's Provisional Div., 16 Corps. July, 1863, 1 Brig., Kimball's Provisional Div., Dist. Eastern Ark. Aug., 1863, 1 Brig., 2 Div., Ark. Exp. Nov., 1863, 2 Brig., 2 Div., Army Ark. Jany., 1864, 2 Brig., 2 Div., 7 Corps, Dept. Ark. March, 1864, 3 Brig., 3 Div., 7 Corps. May, 1864, Garrison Little Rock, Ark. Jany., 1865, 1 Brig., 1 Div., 7 Corps. Mustered out Nov. 30, 1865.

44th REGIMENT INFANTRY.—Org. at Chicago, Ill., Sept. 13, 1861. Sept., 1861, Dept. Mo. Jany., 1862, 4 Brig., Army S. W. Mo., Dept. Mo. Feby., 1862, 1 Brig., 1 Div., Army S. W. Mo. June, 1862, 1 Brig., 5 Div., Army Miss. Sept., 1862, 35 Brig., 11 Div., Army Ohio. Sept., 1862, 35 Brig., 11 Div., 3 Corps, Army Ohio. Nov., 1862, 2 Brig., 3 Div., Right Wing 14 Corps, Cumberland. Jany., 1863, 2 Brig., 3 Div., 20 Corps, Cumberland. Oct., 1863, 1 Brig., 2 Div., 4 Corps. Aug., 1865, Dept. Texas. Mustered out Sept. 25, 1865.

45th REGIMENT INFANTRY.—Org. at Galena, Ill., and mustered in at Camp Douglass, Ill., Dec. 25, 1861. Jany., 1862, Dist. Cairo. Feby., 1862, 2 Brig., 1 Div., Dist. Cairo. Feby., 1862, 2 Brig., 1 Div., Dist. West. Tenn., and Army Tenn. July, 1862, 2 Brig., 1 Div., Dist. Jackson, Tenn. Sept., 1862, 3 Brig., 1 Div., Dist. Jackson, Tenn. Nov., 1862, 1 Brig., 3 Div., Right Wing 13 Corps, Tenn. Dec., 1862, 1 Brig., 3 Div., 17 Corps. Mustered out July 12, 1865.

46th REGIMENT INFANTRY.—Org. at Camp Butler, Ill., Dec. 28, 1861. Feby., 1862, 2 Brig., 3 Div., Dist. Cairo. Feby., 1862, 2 Brig., 4 Div., Dist. West. Tenn., and Army Tenn. July, 1862, 2 Brig., 4 Div., Dist. Memphis, Tenn. Sept., 1862, 2 Brig., 4 Div., Dist. Jackson, Tenn. Nov., 1862, 2 Brig., 4 Div., Right Wing 13 Corps, Tenn. Dec., 1862, 2 Brig., 4 Div., 17 Corps. Jany., 1863, 2 Brig., 4 Div., 16 Corps. July, 1863, 2 Brig., 4 Div., 13 Corps. Aug., 1863, 2 Brig., 4 Div., 17 Corps. April, 1864, 2 Brig., 1 Div., 17 Corps. Aug., 1864, 1 Brig., 2 Div., 19 Corps, Gulf. Dec., 1864, 2 Brig., Reserve Corps, Mil. Div. West. Miss. Feby., 1865, 2 Brig., 1 Div., Reserve Corps, M. D. W. M. Feby., 1865, 2 Brig., 1 Div., 13 Corps, M. D. W. M. June, 1865, Dept. La. Mustered out Jany. 20, 1866.

47th REGIMENT INFANTRY.—Org. at Peoria, Ill., Aug. 16, 1861. Sept., 1861, Dept. Mo. Feby., 1862, 2 Brig., 2 Div., Army Miss. March, 1862, 1 Brig., 5 Div., Army Miss. April, 1862, 1 Brig., 3 Div., Army Miss. April, 1862, 2 Brig., 2 Div., Army Miss. Nov., 1862, 2 Brig., 8 Div., Left Wing 13 Corps, Tenn. Dec., 1862, 2 Brig., 8 Div., 16 Corps. April, 1863, 2 Brig., 3 Div., 15 Corps. Dec., 1863, 2 Brig., 1 Div., 16 Corps. March, 1864, 2 Brig., 1 Div., 16 Corps, Gulf. Nov., 1864, Chicago and Camp Butler, Ill. Dec., 1864, 2 Brig., 2 Div., Dist. Ky. Jany., 1865, 2 Brig., 1 Div., Detachment Army Tenn., Dept. Cumberland. Feby., 1865, 2 Brig., 1 Div., 16 Corps, Mil. Div. West. Miss. Aug., 1865, Dist. Ala., Gulf. Mustered out Jany. 21, 1866.

48th REGIMENT INFANTRY.—Org. at Camp Butler, Ill., Sept., 1861. Nov., 1861, Dist. Cairo. Feby., 1862, 2 Brig., 1 Div., Dist. Cairo. March, 1862, 2 Brig., 1 Div., Dist. West. Tenn., and Army Tenn. July, 1862, 2 Brig., 1 Div., Dist. Jackson, Tenn. Sept., 1862, Unatt., Bethel, Dist. Jackson, Tenn. Nov., 1862, Post Bethel, Dist. Jackson, Tenn., 13 Corps, Tenn. Dec., 1862, Post Bethel, Dist. Jackson, 16 Corps. March, 1863, 4 Brig., 1 Div., 16 Corps. July, 1863, 4 Brig., 4 Div., 15 Corps. Sept., 1863, 3 Brig., 4 Div., 15 Corps. Aug., 1864, 1 Brig., 4 Div., 15 Corps. Sept., 1864, 3 Brig., 2 Div., 15 Corps. Mustered out Aug. 15, 1865.

49th REGIMENT INFANTRY.—Org. at Camp Butler, Ill., Dec. 31, 1861. Nov., 1861, Dist. Cairo. Feby., 1862, 3 Brig, 1 Div., Dist. Cairo. Feby., 1862, 3 Brig., 1 Div., Dist. West. Tenn., and Army Tenn. July, 1862, 3 Brig., 1 Div., Dist. Jackson, Tenn. Sept., 1862, Unatt., Dist. Jackson, Tenn. Nov., 1862, Post Bethel, Dist. Jackson, Tenn., 13 Corps, Dept. Tenn. Dec., 1862, Post Bethel, Dist. Jackson, 16 Corps. March, 1863, 4 Brig., 1 Div., 16 Corps. May, 1863, 4 Brig., Dist. Memphis, Tenn., 5 Div., 16 Corps. July, 1863, 3 Brig., 3 Div., 16 Corps. Aug., 1863, True's Brig., Ark. Exp. Nov., 1863, Gilbert's Brig., Dist. Memphis, Tenn., 5 Div., 16 Corps. Jany., 1864, 3 Brig., 3 Div., 16 Corps. March, 1864, 3 Brig., 3 Div., 16 Corps, Gulf. June, 1864, 3 Brig., 3 Div., 16 Corps, Tenn. Nov., 1864, 3 Brig., 2 Div., Detachment Army Tenn., Dept. Cumberland. Dec., 1864, Garrison Paducah, Ky., Dept. Ky. Mustered out Sept. 5, 1865.

50th REGIMENT INFANTRY.—Org. at Quincy, Ill., Sept. 12, 1861. Oct., 1861, Dept. Mo. Feby., 1862, 3 Brig., 2 Div., Dist. Cairo. Feby., 1862, 3 Brig., 2 Div., Dist. West. Tenn., and Army Tenn. July, 1862, 3 Brig., 2 Div., Dist. Corinth, Miss. Nov., 1862, 3 Brig., Dist. Corinth, 13 Corps, Tenn. Dec., 1862, 3 Brig., Dist. Corinth, Miss., 17 Corps. Jany., 1863, 3 Brig., Dist. Corinth, 16 Corps. March, 1863, 3 Brig., 2 Div., 16 Corps. Sept., 1864, 3 Brig., 4 Div., 15 Corps. Mustered out July 13, 1865.

51st REGIMENT INFANTRY.—Org. at Camp Douglass, Ill., Dec. 24, 1861. Feby., 1862, 2 Brig., 4 Div., Army Miss. April, 1862, 1 Brig., 1 Div., Army Miss. Sept., 1862, 1 Brig., 13 Div., Army Ohio. Nov., 1862, 3 Brig., 3 Div., Right Wing 14 Corps, Army Cumb'd. Jany., 1863, 3 Brig., 3 Div., 20 Corps, Cumb'd. Oct., 1863, 3 Brig., 2 Div., 4 Corps. June, 1865, 2 Brig., 2 Div., 4 Corps. Aug., 1865, Dept. Texas. Mustered out Sept. 25, 1865.

52nd REGIMENT INFANTRY.—Org. at Geneva, Nov. 19, 1861. Nov., 1861, Dept. Mo. Feby., 1862, 3 Brig., 2 Div., Dist. Cairo. Feby., 1862, 3 Brig., 1 Div., Dist. West. Tenn. March, 1862, 2 Brig., 4 Div., Dist. West Tenn. March, 1862, 3 Brig., 2 Div., Army Tenn. July, 1862, 3 Brig., 2 Div., Dist. Corinth, Miss. Sept., 1862, 1 Brig., 2 Div., Dist. Corinth, Miss. Nov., 1862, 3 Brig., Dist. Corinth, 13 Corps, Dept. Tenn. Dec., 1862, 1 Brig., Dist. Corinth, 17 Corps. Jany., 1863, 1 Brig., Dist. Corinth, 16 Corps. March, 1863, 1 Brig., 2 Div., 16 Corps. Sept., 1864, 1 Brig., 4 Div., 15 Corps. Mustered out July 5, 1865.

53rd REGIMENT INFANTRY.—Org. at Ottawa and Chicago, Ill., Jany., 1862. April, 1862, 1 Brig., 4 Div., Army Tenn. July, 1862, 1 Brig., 4 Div., Dist. Memphis, Tenn. Sept., 1862, 1 Brig., 4 Div., Dist. Jackson, Tenn. Nov., 1862, 1 Brig., 4 Div., Right Wing 13 Corps, Tenn. Dec., 1862, 1 Brig., 4 Div., 17 Corps. Jany., 1863, 1 Brig., 4 Div., 16 Corps. July, 1863, 1 Brig., 4 Div., 13 Corps. Aug., 1863, 1 Brig., 4 Div., 17 Corps. April, 1864, 2 Brig.,

4 Div., 17 Corps. July, 1864, 1 Brig., 4 Div., 17 Corps. Mustered out July 22, 1865.

54th REGIMENT INFANTRY.—Org. at Anna, Ill., Feby. 18. 1862. Feby., 1862, Dist. Cairo. March, 1862, Dist. Columbus, Ky. Sept., 1862, Dist. Jackson, Tenn. Nov., 1862, Unatt., Dist. Jackson, Tenn., 13 Corps, Tenn. Dec., 1862, Unatt., Dist. Jackson, Tenn. Jany., 1863. 1 Brig., Dist. Jackson, Tenn., 16 Corps. March, 1863, 2 Brig., 3 Div., 16 Corps. May, 1863, 2 Brig., Kimball's Prov'l Div., 16 Corps. July, 1863, 2 Brig., Kimball's Prov'l Div., Dist. Eastern Ark. Aug., 1863, 1 Brig., 2 Div., Ark. Exp. Nov., 1863, 3 Brig., 2 Div., Army Ark. Jany., 1864, 3 Brig., 2 Div., 7 Corps, Dept. Ark. May, 1864, 1 Brig., 2 Div., 7 Corps. Aug., 1865, Dept. Ark. Mustered out Oct. 18, 1865.

55th REGIMENT INFANTRY.—Org. at Camp Douglass, Ill., Oct. 31, 1861. Nov., 1861, St. Louis, Mo. Jany., 1862, Dist. Paducah, Ky. March, 1862, 2 Brig., 5 Div., Army Tenn. May, 1862, 1 Brig., 5 Div., Army Tenn. July, 1862, 1 Brig., 5 Div., Dist. Memphis; Tenn. Nov., 1862, 4 Brig., 5 Div., Dist. Memphis, Tenn., Right Wing 13 Corps, Dept. Tenn. Dec., 1862, 2 Brig., 2 Div., Dist. Memphis, 13 Corps. Dec., 1862, 2 Brig., 2 Div., Sherman's Yazoo Exp. Jany., 1863, 2 Brig., 2 Div., 15 Corps, Army Tenn. Sept., 1863, 1 Brig., 2 Div., 15 Corps. Mustered out Aug. 14, 1865.

56th REGIMENT INFANTRY.—Org. at Shawneetown, Ill., Feb. 27, 1862. Feby., 1862, Dist. Paducah, Ky. April, 1862, 2 Brig., 3 Div., Army Miss. Nov., 1862, 2 Brig., 7 Div., Left Wing 13 Corps, Dept. Tenn. Dec., 1862, 2 Brig., 7 Div., 16 Corps. Jany., 1863, 2 Brig., 7 Div., 17 Corps. Sept., 1863, 2 Brig., 2 Div., 17 Corps. Dec., 1863, 2 Brig., 3 Div., 15 Corps. April, 1865, 2 Brig., 1 Div., 15 Corps. Mustered out Aug. 12, 1865.

57th REGIMENT INFANTRY.—Org. at Camp Douglass, Ill., Dec. 26, 1861. Feby., 1862, 2 Brig., 3 Div., Dist. Cairo. Feby., 1862, 3 Brig., 2 Div., Dist. West Tenn. and Army Tenn. July, 1862, 3 Brig., 2 Div., Dist. Corinth, Miss. Nov., 1862, 3 Brig., Dist. Corinth, Miss., 13 Corps, Dept. Tenn. Dec., 1862, 3 Brig., Dist. Corinth, 17 Corps. Jany., 1863, 3 Brig., Dist. Corinth, 16 Corps. March, 1863, 3 Brig., 2 Div., 16 Corps. Sept., 1864, 3 Brig., 4 Div., 15 Corps. Mustered out July 7, 1865.

58th REGIMENT INFANTRY.—Org. at Camp Douglass, Ill., Dec. 11, 1861. Feby., 1862, 2 Brig., 3 Div., Dist. Cairo. Feby., 1862, 3 Brig., 2 Div., Dist. West Tenn., and Army Tenn. May, 1862, Union Brig. 1st Brig., 2 Div., Army Tenn. July, 1862, 1 Brig., 2 Div., Dist. Corinth, Miss. Nov., 1862, 1 Brig., Dist. Corinth, Miss., 13 Corps, Dept. Tenn. Dec., 1862, Springfield, Ill. June, 1863, Dist. Columbus, Ky., 6 Div., 16 Corps, Tenn. Jany., 1864, 1 Brig., 3 Div., 16 Corps. March, 1864, 1 Brig., 3 Div., 16 Corps, Gulf. June, 1864, 1 Brig., 3 Div., 16 Corps, Tenn. Nov., 1864, 2 Brig., 3 Div., 16 Corps. Dec., 1864, 2 Brig., 2 Div., Detachment Army Tenn., Dept. Cumb'd. Feby., 1865, 2 Brig., 2 Div., 16 Corps, Mil. Div., West Miss. Aug., 1865, Dist, Ala. Mustered out April 15, 1866.

59th REGIMENT INFANTRY.—Org. at St. Louis, Mo., as 9th Missouri Infantry, Sept. 18, 1861. Sept., 1861, Kelton's Brig., Pope's Div., Army West. Nov., 1861, Dept. Mo. Designated 59th Illinois Infy. Feby. 12, 1862. Feby., 1862, 2 Brig., 3 Div., Army S. W. Mo., Dept. Mo. June, 1862, 1 Brig., 4 Div., Army Miss. Sept., 1862, 30 Brig., 9 Div., Army Ohio. Sept., 1862, 30 Brig., 9 Div., 3 Corps, Army Ohio. Nov., 1862, 1 Brig., 1 Div., Right Wing 14 Corps Army Cumb'd. Jany., 1863, 1 Brig., 1 Div., 20 Corps, Cumb'd. Oct., 1863, 2 Brig., 1 Div., 4 Corps. Oct., 1863, 3 Brig., 1 Div., 4 Corps. May, 1864, 2 Brig., 1 Div., 4 Corps. Aug., 1864, 3 Brig., 1 Div., 4 Corps. Aug., 1864, 2 Brig., 3 Div., 4 Corps. Aug., 1865, Dept. Texas. Mustered out Dec. 8, 1865.

60th REGIMENT INFANTRY.—Org. at Anna, Ill., Feby. 17, 1862. Feby., 1862, Dist. Cairo. March, 1862, 2 Brig., 1 Div., Army Miss. Sept., 1862, 2 Brig., 13 Div., Army Ohio. Nov., 1862, 1 Brig., 4 Div., Centre 14 Corps, Cumb'd. Jany., 1863, 1 Brig., 4 Div., 14 Corps. June, 1863, 1 Brig., 2 Div., Reserve Corps Cumb'd. Oct., 1863, 1 Brig., 2 Div., 14 Corps. Mustered out July 31, 1865.

61st REGIMENT INFANTRY.—Org. at Carrollton, Ill., Feby. 5, 1862. Feby., 1862, St. Louis, Mo. March, 1862,

2 Brig., 6 Div., Army Tenn. April, 1862, 1 Brig., 3 Div., Army Tenn. July, 1862, 3 Brig., 1 Div., Dist. Jackson, Tenn. Sept., 1862, Unatt., Dist. Jackson, Tenn. Nov., 1862, Post Bolivar, Tenn., Dist. Jackson, Tenn., 13 Corps, Dept. Tenn. Dec., 1862, Post Bolivar, Dist. Jackson, 16 Corps. March, 1863, 1 Brig., 3 Div., 16 Corps. May, 1863, 1 Brig., Kimball's Prov'l Div., 16 Corps. July, 1863, 1 Brig., Kimball's Prov'l Div., Dist. Eastern Ark. Aug., 1863, 1 Brig., 2 Div., Ark. Exp. Nov., 1863, 3 Brig., 2 Div., Army Ark. Jany., 1864, 3 Brig., 2 Div., 7 Corps, Dept. Ark. May, 1864, 1 Brig., 2 Div., 7 Corps. Oct., 1864, Dept. Mo. Nov., 1864, 1 Brig., Def. Nashville and Chatta. R. R., Dept. Cumb'd. Feby., 1865 Unatt., 4 Div., 20 Corps, Cumb'd. March, 1865, 2nd Sub Dist., Dist. Middle Tenn., Dept. Cumb'd. Mustered out Sept. 8, 1865.

62nd REGIMENT INFANTRY.—Org. at Anna, Ill., April 10, 1862. April, 1862, Dist. Columbus, Ky., Dist. West Tenn. Sept., 1862, Dist. Jackson, Tenn. Nov., 1862, Dist. Jackson, Tenn., 13 Corps, Dept. Tenn. Dec., 1862, 1 Brig., Dist. Jackson, Tenn., 16 Corps. March, 1863, 3 Brig., 3 Div., 16 Corps. Aug., 1863, True's Brig., Ark. Exp. Jany., 1864, Unatt., 2 Div., 7 Corps. May, 1864, 2 Brig., 2 Div., 7 Corps. July, 1865, Fort Gibson, C. N. Dept. Ark. Mustered out March 6, 1866.

63rd REGIMENT INFANTRY.—Org. Anna, Ill., Dec., 1861, mustered in April 10, 1862. April, 1862, Dist. Cairo. Sept., 1862. 4 Brig., 1 Div., Dist. Jackson, Tenn. Nov., 1862, 4 Brig., 3 Div., Right Wing 13 Corps, Dept. Tenn. Dec., 1862, 3 Brig., 3 Div., 17 Corps. Jany., 1863, Dist. Memphis, Tenn., 16 Corps. March, 1863, 4 Brig., Dist. Memphis, Tenn., 5 Div., 16 Corps. May, 1863, Detached Brig., Dist. N. E. Louisiana. June, 1863, 2 Brig., 6 Div., 17 Corps. July, 1863, 1 Brig., 7 Div., 17 Corps. Sept., 1863, 1 Brig., 2 Div., 17 Corps. Dec., 1863, 1 Brig., 3 Div., 15 Corps. April, 1865, 2 Brig., 4 Div., 15 Corps. Mustered out July 13, 1865.

64th REGIMENT INFANTRY.—Org. at Camp Butler, Ill., Dec., 1861. March, 1862, Unass'd Sharpshooters, Army Miss. April, 1862, 2 Brig., 1 Div., Army Miss. May, 1862, Unatt., Army Miss. Nov., 1862, Unatt., Dist. Corinth, 13 Corps, Dept. Tenn. Dec., 1862, Unatt., Dist. Corinth, 17 Corps. Jany., 1863, Unatt., Dist. Corinth, 16 Corps. March, 1863, Unatt., 2 Div., 16 Corps. Nov., 1863, Fuller's Brig., 2 Div., 16 Corps. March, 1864, 1 Brig., 4 Div., 16 Corps. Sept., 1864, 1 Brig., 1 Div., 17 Corps. Mustered out July 11, 1865.

65th REGIMENT INFANTRY.—Org. at Chicago, Ill., May 1, 1862. May, 1862., Martinsburg, W. Va., R. R. Dist., Mountain Dept. July, 1862, R. R. Dist., 8 Corps, Middle Dept. Sept., 1862, Prisoners of War. Oct., 1862, Camp Douglass, Ill. April, 1863, Dist. Central Ky., Dept. Ohio. May, 1863, 1 Brig., 4 Div., 23 Corps, Dept. Ohio. Aug., 1863, 2 Brig., 3 Div., 23 Corps, Ohio, to Feby., 1865, and Dept. North Carolina to July, 1865. Mustered out July 13, 1865.

66th REGIMENT INFANTRY.—"Birge's Sharpshooters." Org. as 14th Mo. Infy. at St. Louis, Mo. Sept.-Oct., 1861. Mustered in Nov. 23, 1861. Dec., 1861, Dept. Mo. Feby., 1862, 1 Brig., 2 Div., Dist. West Tenn. Feby., 1862, 4 Brig., 2 Div., West Tenn. March, 1862, 2 Brig., 2 Div., Army Tenn. July, 1862, 2 Brig., 2 Div., Dist. Corinth, Miss. Nov., 1862, Unatt., Dist. Corinth, 13 Corps, Dept. Tenn. Designation of Regiment changed to 66th Illinois Infy. Nov. 20, 1862. Dec., 1862, Unatt., Dist. Corinth, 17 Corps. Jany., 1862, Unatt., Dist. Corinth, 16 Corps. March, 1863, Unatt., 2 Div., 16 Corps. Nov., 1863, 2 Brig., 2 Div., 16 Corps. Sept., 1864, 2 Brig., 4 Div., 15 Corps. April, 1865, 3 Brig., 1 Div., 15 Corps. Mustered out July 7, 1865.

67th REGIMENT INFANTRY.—Org. Camp Douglass, Ill., June 13, 1862. Duty at Camp Douglass, Ill. Mustered out Oct. 6, 1862.

68th REGIMENT INFANTRY.—Org. at Camp Butler, Ill., June 16, 1862. July, 1862, Def. Washington, D. C. Aug., 1862, Provost at Alexandria, Va., Def. Washington. Mustered out Sept. 26, 1862.

69th REGIMENT INFANTRY.—Org. at Camp Douglass, Ill., June 14, 1862. Duty at Camp Douglass, Ill. Mustered out Oct. 23, 1862.

70th REGIMENT INFANTRY.—Org. at Camp Butler, Ill., July 4, 1862. Duty at Camp Butler, Ill. Mustered out Oct. 29, 1862.

71st REGIMENT INFANTRY.—Org. at Camp Douglass, Ill. Aug., 1862, Dist. Columbus, Ky., Dist. West Tenn. Mustered out Oct. 29, 1862.

72nd REGIMENT INFANTRY.—Org. Chicago, Ill., Aug. 23, 1862. Aug., 1862, Dist. Cairo. Sept., 1862, Dist. Columbus, Ky., Dept. Tenn. Nov., 1862, 1 Brig., 7 Div., Left Wing 13 Corps, Dept. Tenn. Dec., 1862, 1 Brig., 7 Div., 16 Corps. Jany., 1863, 1 Brig., 7 Div., 17 Corps. May, 1863, 2 Brig., 6 Div., 17 Corps. Sept., 1863, 1 Brig., 1 Div., 17 Corps. Nov., 1864, Unass'd, 23 Corps, Army Ohio. Dec., 1864, 1 Brig., 3 Div., Detachment Army Tenn., Dept. Cumb'd. Feby., 1865, 1 Brig., 3 Div., 16 Corps, Mil. Div. West Miss. Mustered out Aug. 6, 1865.

73rd REGIMENT INFANTRY.—Org. at Camp Butler, Ill., Aug. 21, 1862. Sept. 1862, 35 Brig., 11 Div., Army Ohio. Oct., 1862, 35 Brig., 11 Div., 3 Corps, Army Ohio. Nov., 1862, 2 Brig., 3 Div., Right Wing 14 Corps, Cumb'd. Jany., 1863, 2 Brig., 3 Div., 20 Corps, Cumb'd. Oct., 1863, 1 Brig., 2 Div., 4 Corps. Mustered out June 12, 1865.

74th REGIMENT INFANTRY.—Org. at Rockford, Ill., Sept. 4, 1862. Sept., 1862, 30 Brig., 9 Div., Army Ohio. Oct., 1862, 30 Brig., 9 Div., 3 Corps, Army Ohio. Nov., 1862, 1 Brig., 1 Div., Right Wing 14 Corps, Cumb'd. Jany., 1863, 1 Brig., 1 Div., 20 Corps, Cumb'd. Oct., 1863, 1 Brig., 2 Div., 4 Corps. Mustered out June 10, 1865.

75th REGIMENT INFANTRY.—Org. at Dixon, Ill., Sept. 2, 1862. Sept., 1862, 30th Brig., 9 Div., Army Ohio. Oct., 1862, 30 Brig., 9 Div., 3 Corps, Army Ohio. Nov., 1862, 1 Brig., 1 Div., Right Wing 14 Corps, Cumb'd. Jany., 1863, 1 Brig., 1 Div., 20 Corps, Cumb'd. Oct., 1863, 3 Brig., 1 Div., 4 Corps. Mustered out June 12, 1865.

76th REGIMENT INFANTRY.—Org. at Kankakee, Ill., Aug. 22, 1862. Sept., 1862, Dist. Columbus, Ky. Oct., 1862, 2 Brig., 4 Div., Dist. Jackson, Tenn. Nov., 1862, 2 Brig., 4 Div., Right Wing 13 Corps, Dept. Tenn. Dec., 1862, 2 Brig., 4 Div., 17 Corps. Jany., 1863, 2 Brig., 4 Div., 16 Corps. July, 1863, 2 Brig., 4 Div., 13 Corps. Aug., 1863, 2 Brig., 4 Div., 17 Corps. April, 1864, 2 Brig., 1 Div., 17 Corps. Aug., 1864, 1 Brig., 2 Div., 19 Corps, Gulf. Dec., 1864, 2 Brig., Reserve Corps, Mil. Div. West Miss. Feby., 1865, 2 Brig., 2 Div., Reserve Corps, M. D. W. M. Feby., 1865, 2 Brig., 2 Div., 13 Corps, M. D. W. M. Mustered out July 22, 1865.

77th REGIMENT INFANTRY.—Org. at Peoria, Ill., Sept. 3, 1862. Oct., 1862, 3 Div., Army Ky., Dept. Ohio. Oct., 1862, 2 Brig., 1 Div., Army Ky., Dept. Ohio. Nov., 1862, 2 Brig., 10 Div., 13 Corps, Dept. Tenn., 2 Brig., 1 Div., Sherman's Yazoo Exp. Jany., 1863, 2 Brig., 10 Div., 13 Corps. Aug., 1863, 2 Brig., 4 Div., 13 Corps, Gulf. Jany., 1864, 1 Brig., 4 Div., 13 Corps. June, 1864, Def. New Orleans, La. June, 1864, 3 Brig., 3 Div., 19 Corps, Gulf. Oct., 1864, Def. New Orleans. Feby., 1865, 1 Brig., 3 Div., Reserve Corps, Mil. Div. West Miss. Feby., 1865, 1 Brig., 3 Div., 13 Corps, M. D. W. M. Mustered out July 10, 1865.

78th REGIMENT INFANTRY.—Org. at Quincy, Ill., Sept. 1, 1862. Sept., 1862, 39th Brig., 12 Div., Army Ohio. Nov., 1862, R. R. Guard, Dept. Ohio. Nov., 1862, Dist. West Ky., Dept. Ohio. Feby., 1863, Reed's Brig., Baird's Div., Army Ky., Dept. Cumb'd. June, 1863, 2 Brig., 1 Div., Reserve Corps, Dept. Cumb'd. Oct., 1863, 2 Brig., 2 Div., 14 Corps. Mustered out June 7, 1865.

79th REGIMENT INFANTRY.—Org. at Mattoon, Ill., Aug. 28, 1862. Sept., 1862, 3 Brig., Cruft's Div., Army Ky., to Sept. 13, 1862, 4 Brig., 2 Div., Army Ohio. Oct., 1862, 5 Brig., 2 Div., 1 Corps, Army Ohio. Nov., 1862, 2 Brig., 2 Div., Right Wing 14 Corps, Cumb'd. Jany., 1863, 2 Brig., 2 Div., 20 Corps, Cumb'd. Oct., 1863, 3 Brig., 2 Div., 4 Corps. Mustered out June 12, 1865.

80th REGIMENT INFANTRY.—Org. at Centralia, Ill., Aug. 25, 1862. Sept., 1862, 33 Brig., 10 Div., Army Ohio. Oct., 1862, 33 Brig., 10 Div., 1 Corps, Army Ohio. Nov., 1862, 1 Brig., 5 Div., Centre 14 Corps. Jany., 1863, 1 Brig., 5 Div., 14 Corps. April, 1863, Streight's Prov'l Brig., Dept. Cumb'd. June, 1863, 2 Brig., 4 Div., 14 Corps. Oct., 1863, 3 Brig., 3 Div., 11 Corps. Dec., 1863, 3 Brig., 1 Div., 4 Corps. Mustered out June 10, 1865.

81st REGIMENT INFANTRY.—Org. at Anna, Ill., Aug. 26, 1862. Sept., 1862, Dist. Columbus, Ky., Dept. Tenn. Nov., 1862, 1 Brig., 3 Div., Right Wing 13 Corps, Dept. Tenn. Dec., 1862, 4 Brig., 3 Div., Right Wing, 13 Corps. Dec., 1862, 3 Brig., 3 Div., 17 Corps. March, 1864, 2 Brig. Prov'l Div., 17 Corps, Dept. Gulf (non-veterans). June, 1864, Detached Brig., 17 Corps (non-veterans). June, 1864, 2 Brig., Sturgis' Exp. (non-veterans), 4 Brig., 1 Div., 16 Corps. June to Dec., 1864 (non-veterans), 3 Brig., 3 Div., 17 Corps. April to Dec., 1864 (veterans). Dec., 1864, 2 Brig., 3 Div., Detachment Army Tenn., Dept. Cumb'd. Feby., 1865, 3 Brig., 3 Div., 16 Corps, Mil. Div. West Miss. Mustered out Aug. 5, 1865.

82nd REGIMENT INFANTRY.—Org. at Springfield, Ill., Sept. 26, 1862. Nov., 1862, 1 Brig., 3 Div., 11 Corps, Army Potomac. Oct., 1863, 3 Brig., 3 Div., 11 Corps, Army Cumb'd. April, 1864, 3 Brig., 1 Div., 20 Corps, Cumb'd. Mustered out June 9, 1865.

83rd REGIMENT INFANTRY.—Org. at Monmouth, Ill., Aug. 21, 1862. Sept., 1862, Dist. Columbus, Ky., Garrison Forts Henry and Heiman, Tenn. Nov., 1862, Dist. Columbus, Ky., 13 Corps, Dept. Tenn. Dec., 1862, Dist. Columbus, Ky., 16 Corps. June, 1863, 1 Brig., 3 Div., Reserve Corps, Dept. Cumb'd. Oct., 1863, Garrison Clarksville, Tenn., Dept. Cumb'd. April, 1864, Unass'd, 4 Div., 20 Corps, Cumb'd. March, 1865, 5th Sub Dist., Dist. Middle Tenn., Dept. Cumb'd. Mustered out June 26, 1865.

84th REGIMENT INFANTRY.—Org. at Quincy, Ill., Sept. 1, 1862. Oct., 1862, 10 Brig., 4 Div., 2 Corps, Army Ohio. Nov., 1862, 3 Brig., 2 Div., Left Wing 14 Corps, Cumb'd. Jany., 1863, 3 Brig., 2 Div., 21 Corps, Cumb'd. Oct., 1863, 3 Brig., 1 Div., 4 Corps. May, 1865, 2 Brig., 1 Div., 4 Corps. Mustered out June 8, 1865.

85th REGIMENT INFANTRY.—Org. at Peoria, Ill., Aug. 27, 1862. Sept., 1862, 36 Brig., 11 Div., Army Ohio. Oct., 1862, 36 Brig., 11 Div., 3 Corps, Army Ohio. Nov., 1862, 2 Brig., 4 Div., Centre 14 Corps, Cumb'd. Jany., 1863, 2 Brig., 4 Div., 14 Corps. June, 1863, 2 Brig., 2 Div., Reserve Corps, Cumb'd. Oct., 1864, 3 Brig., 2 Div., 14 Corps. Mustered out June 5, 1865.

86th REGIMENT INFANTRY.—Org. at Peoria, Ill., Aug. 27, 1862. Sept., 1862, 36 Brig., 11 Div., Army Ohio. Oct., 1862, 36 Brig., 11 Div., 3 Corps, Army Ohio. Nov., 1862, 2 Brig., 4 Div., Centre 14 Corps, Cumb'd. Jany., 1863, 2 Brig., 4 Div., 14 Corps. June, 1863, 2 Brig., 2 Div., Reserve Corps, Cumb'd. Oct., 1863, 3 Brig., 2 Div., 14 Corps. Mustered out June 6, 1865.

87th REGIMENT INFANTRY.—Org. at Shawneetown, Ill., Oct. 3, 1862. Jany., 1863, Dist. Memphis, Tenn., 16 Corps, Dept. Tenn. March, 1863, 3 Brig., Dist. Memphis, 5 Div., 16 Corps. June, 1863, 2 Brig., 12 Div., 13 Corps, Army Tenn. July, 1863, 2 Brig., 3 Div., 13 Corps. Aug., 1863, 2 Brig., 3 Div., 13 Corps, Gulf. Sept., 1863, Unatt. Cav. Div., Gulf. Nov., 1863, 1 Brig., Cav. Div., Gulf. Jany., 1864, 3 Brig., Cav. Div., Gulf. July, 1864, Cav. Brig., 19 Corps, Gulf. Dec., 1864, Cav. Brig., Reserve Corps, Mil. Div. West Miss. Feby., 1865, Cav. Dist. East. Ark., 7 Corps, Dept. Ark. Mustered out June 16, 1865.

88th REGIMENT INFANTRY.—Org. at Chicago, Sept. 4, 1862. Sept., 1862, 37 Brig., 11 Div., Army Ohio. Oct., 1862, 37 Brig., 11 Div., 3 Corps, Army Ohio. Nov., 1862, 1 Brig., 3 Div., Right Wing 14 Corps, Cumb'd. Jany., 1863, 1 Brig., 3 Div., 20 Corps, Cumb'd. Oct., 1863, 1 Brig., 2 Div., 4 Corps. Mustered out June 9, 1865.

89th REGIMENT INFANTRY.—Org. at Chicago, Ill., Aug. 27, 1862. Sept., 1862, 6 Brig., 2 Div., 1 Corps, Army Ohio. Nov., 1862, 1 Brig., 2 Div., Right Wing 14 Corps, Cumb'd. Jany., 1863, 1 Brig., 2 Div., 20 Corps, Cumb'd. Oct., 1863, 1 Brig., 3 Div., 4 Corps. Mustered out June 10, 1865.

90th REGIMENT INFANTRY.—Org. at Chicago, Ill., Sept. 7, 1862. Nov., 1862. R. R. Guard, 13 Corps, Dept. Tenn. Jany., 1863, 2 Brig., 1 Div., 16 Corps, Tenn. March, 1863, 1 Brig., 1 Div., 16 Corps. July, 1863, 1 Brig., 4 Div., 15 Corps. Sept., 1864, 3 Brig., 2 Div., 15 Corps. Mustered out June 6, 1865.

91st REGIMENT INFANTRY.—Org. at Camp Butler, Ill., Sept. 8, 1862. Oct., 1862, Unass'd, Dept. Ohio, R. R. Guard Louisville and Nashville R. R. Dec., 1862, Prisoners of War. Feby., 1863, Dist. St. Louis, Mo. July, 1863, 2 Brig., Herron's Div., 13 Corps, Dept. Tenn. July, 1863, 2 Brig., 2 Div., 13 Corps. Aug., 1863, 2 Brig., 2 Div., 13 Corps, Gulf. Oct., 1863, 1 Brig., 2 Div., 13 Corps, Gulf. June, 1864, 1 Brig., U. S. Forces, Texas. Aug., 1864, Garrison Brazos Santiago, Tex. Dec., 1864, Def. New Orleans, La. Feby., 1865, 2 Brig., 3 Div., 13 Corps, Mil. Div. West Miss. Mustered out July 12, 1865.

92nd REGIMENT INFANTRY.—Org. at Rockford, Ill., Sept. 4, 1862. Oct., 1862, 2 Brig., 3 Div., Army Ky., Dept. Ohio. Feby., 1863, 2 Brig., Baird's Div., Army Ky., Dept. Cumb'd. June, 1863, 1 Brig., 1 Div., Reserve Corps. July, 1863, 1 Brig., 4 Div., 14 Corps. Oct., 1863, Wilder's Mounted Inty. Brig., Cumb'd. Dec., 1863, 3 Brig., 2 Div., Cav. Corps, Cumb'd. April, 1864, 3 Brig., 3 Cav. Div., Cav. Corps, Cumb'd. Oct., 1864, 3 Brig., 3 Div., Cav. Corps, Mil. Div. Miss. Nov., 1864, 2 Brig., 3 Div., Cav. Corps, M. D. M. Mustered out June 21, 1865.

93rd REGIMENT INFANTRY.—Org. at Chicago, Oct. 13, 1862. Nov., 1862, 5 Brig., 5 Div., Dist. Memphis, 13 Corps, Dept. Tenn. Nov., 1862, 3 Brig., 1 Div., Dist. Memphis, Tenn., 13 Corps. Dec., 1862, 3 Brig., 7 Div., 16 Corps. Jany., 1863, 3 Brig., 7 Div., 17 Corps. Sept., 1863, 3 Brig., 2 Div., 17 Corps. Dec., 1863, 3 Brig., 3 Div., 15 Corps. Aug., 1864, 1 Brig., 3 Div., 15 Corps. April, 1865, 1 Brig., 1 Div., 15 Corps. Mustered out June 23, 1865.

94th REGIMENT INFANTRY.—Org. at Bloomington, Ill., Aug. 20, 1862. Sept., 1862, 2 Brig., 3 Div., Army Frontier, Dept. Mo. June, 1863, 2 Brig., Herron's Div., 13 Corps, Tenn. July, 1863, 2 Brig., 2 Div., 13 Corps, Tenn. Aug., 1863, 2 Brig., 2 Div., 13 Corps, Gulf. June, 1864, U. S. Forces Brownsville, Tex. Aug., 1864, U. S. Forces Mobile Bay, Dept. Gulf. Dec., 1864, Dist. Southern Ala., Dept. Gulf. Feby., 1865, 1 Brig., 2 Div., Reserve Corps, Mil. Div. West Miss. Feby., 1865, 1 Brig., 2 Div., 13 Corps, M. D. W. M. Mustered out July 17, 1865.

95th REGIMENT INFANTRY.—Org. at Rockford, Ill., Sept. 4, 1862. Nov., 1862, 1 Brig., 6 Div., Left Wing 13 Corps, Tenn. Dec., 1862, 1 Brig., 6 Div., 16 Corps. Jany., 1863, 1 Brig., 6 Div., 17 Corps. May, 1863, 2 Brig., 6 Div., 17 Corps. Sept., 1863, 2 Brig., 1 Div., 17 Corps. March, 1864, 2 Brig., Prov'l Div., 17 Corps, Gulf (non-veterans). June, 1864 2 Brig., Sturgis' Exp. (non-veterans). June, 1864, Detached Brig., 17 Corps (non-veterans), 4 Brig., 1 Div., 16 Corps (non-veterans) to Dec., 1864, 3 Brig., 3 Div., 17 Corps (veterans). April to Dec., 1864. 2 Brig., 3 Div., Detachment Army Tenn., Dept. Cumb'd. Feby., 1865, 3 Brig., 3 Div., 16 Corps, Mil. Div. West Miss. Mustered out Aug. 17, 1865.

96th REGIMENT INFANTRY.—Org. at Rockford, Ill., Sept. 6, 1862. Oct., 1862, 2 Brig., 3 Div., Army Ky., Dept. Ohio. Feby., 1863, 2 Brig., Baird's Div., Army Ky., Dept. Cumb'd. June, 1863, 1 Brig., 1 Div., Reserve Corps, Cumb'd. Oct., 1863, 3 Brig., 1 Div., 4 Corps. Oct., 1863, 2 Brig., 1 Div., 4 Corps. Mustered out June 10, 1865.

97th REGIMENT INFANTRY.—Org. at Camp Butler, Ill., Sept. 16, 1862. Oct., 1862, 2 Brig., 1 Div., Army Ky., Dept. Ohio. Nov., 1862, 2 Brig., 10 Div., 13 Corps, Tenn. Dec., 1862, 2 Brig., 1 Div., Sherman's Yazoo Exp. Jany., 1863, 2 Brig., 10 Div., 13 Corps. Aug., 1863, 2 Brig., 4 Div., 13 Corps, Gulf. Dec., 1863, 2 Brig., 4 Div., 19 Corps, Gulf. Feby., 1864, 2 Brig., 4 Div., 13 Corps. June, 1864, 2 Brig., 3 Div., 19 Corps, Gulf. Dec., 1864, Dist. Southern Ala., Gulf. Dec., 1864, 3 Brig., Reserve Corps, Mil. Div. West Miss. Feby., 1865, 2 Brig., 2 Div. Reserve Corps, M. D. W. M., 2 Brig., 2 Div., 13 Corps, M. D. W. M. Mustered out July 27, 1865.

98th REGIMENT INFANTRY.—Org. at Centralia, Ill., Sept. 3, 1862. Sept., 1862, 10 Brig., 12 Div., Army Ohio. Nov., 1862, 2 Brig., 5 Div., Centre 14 Corps, Cumb'd. Jany., 1863, 2 Brig., 5 Div., 14 Corps. June, 1863, 1 Brig., 4 Div., 14 Corps. Oct., 1863, Wilder's Mounted Infy. Brig., Cumb'd. Nov., 1863, 3 Brig., 2 Div., Cav. Corps, Cumb'd. Nov., 1863, 2 Brig., 2 Div., Cav. Corps, Cumb'd. Dec., 1863, 3 Brig., 2 Div., Cav. Corps, Cumb'd. Oct., 1864, 3 Brig., 2 Div., Cav. Corps. M. D. M. Nov., 1864,

1 Brig., 2 Div., Cav. Corps, Mil. Div. Miss. Mustered out June 27, 1865.

99th REGIMENT INFANTRY.—Org. at Florence, Ill., Aug. 23, 1862. Sept., 1862, Dist. Rolla, Dept. Mo. Nov., 1862, 1 Brig., 1 Div., Dist. Southeast Mo., Dept. Mo. March, 1863, 1 Brig., 14 Div., 13 Corps. July, 1863, 1 Brig., 1 Div., 13 Corps, Tenn. Aug., 1863, 1 Brig., 1 Div., 13 Corps, Gulf. June, 1864, Dist. LaFourche, Dept. Gulf. Aug., 1864, 2 Brig., 2 Div., 19 Corps, Gulf. Dec., 1864, 1 Brig., Reserve Corps, Mil. Div. West Miss. Feby., 1865, 1 Brig., 1 Div., Reserve Corps, M. D. W. M., 1 Brig., 1 Div., 13 Corps, M. D. W. M. Mustered out July 31, 1865.

100th REGIMENT INFANTRY.—Org. at Joliet, Ill., Aug. 30, 1862. Sept., 1862, 1 Brig., 2 Div., Army Ky., Dept. Ohio. Sept., 1862, 15 Brig., 6 Div., 2 Corps, Army Ohio. Nov., 1862, 1 Brig., 1 Div., Left Wing 14 Corps, Cumb'd. Jany., 1863, 1 Brig., 1 Div., 21 Corps, Cumb'd. Oct., 1863, 2 Brig., 2 Div., 4 Corps. Mustered out June 12, 1865.

101st REGIMENT INFANTRY.—Org. at Jacksonville, Ill., Sept. 2, 1862. Oct., 1862, Dist. Cairo. Dept., Tenn. Nov., 1862, 2 Brig., 4 Div., Right Wing 13 Corps, Tenn. Dec., 1862, 2 Brig., 4 Div., 17 Corps. Jany., 1863, 2 Brig., 4 Div., 16 Corps. Jany., 1863, Dist. Memphis, Tenn., 16 Corps. March, 1863, Ram Fleet, Miss., Squadron. June, 1863, Dist. Columbus, Ky., 6 Div., 16 Corps. July, 1863, 1 Brig., 6 Div., 16 Corps. Oct., 1863, 1 Brig., 3 Div., 11 Corps, Cumb'd. April, 1864, 3 Brig., 1 Div., 20 Corps, Cumb'd. Mustered out June 7, 1865.

102nd REGIMENT INFANTRY.—Org. at Knoxville, Ill., Sept. 1, 1862. Oct., 1862, Ward's Brig., Dumont's 12 Div., Army Ohio. Nov., 1862, Ward's Brig., Post Gallatin, Tenn., Dept. Cumb'd. June, 1863, 2 Brig., 3 Div., Reserve Corps, Cumb'd. Aug., 1863, Ward's Brig., Post Nashville, Tenn., Cumb'd. Jany., 1864, 1 Brig., 1 Div., 11 Corps, Cumb'd. April, 1864, 1 Brig., 3 Div., 20 Corps, Cumb'd. Mustered out June 6, 1865.

103rd REGIMENT INFANTRY.—Org. at Peoria, Ill., Oct. 2, 1862. Nov., 1862, 1 Brig., 4 Div., Right Wing 13 Corps, Tenn. Dec., 1862, 2 Brig., Dist. Jackson, Tenn., 16 Corps. March, 1863, 2 Brig., 1 Div., 16 Corps. July, 1863, 2 Brig., 4 Div., 15 Corps. Sept., 1864, 2 Brig., 1 Div., 15 Corps. Mustered out June 21, 1865.

104th REGIMENT INFANTRY.—Org. at Ottawa, Ill., Aug. 27, 1862. Sept., 1862, 39 Brig., 12 Div., Army Ohio. Nov., 1862, Dist. West Ky., Dept. Ohio. Dec., 1862, Prisoners of War. June, 1863, 1 Brig., 2 Div., 14 Corps. Oct., 1863, 1 Brig., 1 Div., 14 Corps. Mustered out June 6, 1865.

105th REGIMENT INFANTRY.—Org. at Dixon, Ill., Sept. 2, 1862. Oct., 1862, Ward's Brig., Dumont's 12 Div., Army Ohio. Nov., 1862, Ward's Brig., Post Gallatin, Tenn., Dept. Cumb'd. June, 1863, 2 Brig., 3 Div., Reserve Corps, Cumb'd. Aug., 1863, Ward's Brig., Post Nashville, Tenn., Cumb'd. Jany., 1864, 1 Brig., 1 Div., 11 Corps, Cumb'd. April, 1864, 1 Brig., 3 Div., 20 Corps. Mustered out June 7, 1865.

106th REGIMENT INFANTRY.—Org. at Lincoln, Sept. 18, 1862. Nov., 1862, Dist. Jackson, Tenn., Left Wing 13 Corps, Tenn. Dec., 1862, 4 Brig., Dist. Jackson, 16 Corps. March, 1863, 1 Brig., 3 Div., 16 Corps. May, 1863, 1 Brig., Kimball's Prov'l Div., 16 Corps. July, 1863, 1 Brig., Kimball's Prov'l Div., Dist. East. Ark. Aug., 1863, 1 Brig., 2 Div., Army Ark. Nov., 1863, 3 Brig., 2 Div., Army Ark. Jany., 1864, 3 Brig., 2 Div., 7 Corps, Dept. Ark. May, 1864, 2 Brig., 2 Div., 7 Corps. Mustered out July 12, 1865.

107th REGIMENT INFANTRY.—Org. at Camp Butler, Ill., Sept. 4, 1862. Oct., 1862, R. R. Guard Louisville and Nashville R. R., Dept. Ohio. Nov., 1862, Dist. West. Ky., Dept. Ohio. June, 1863, 1 Brig., 3 Div., 23 Corps, Dept. Ohio. Aug., 1863, 2 Brig., 2 Div., 23 Corps. Feby., 1865, 2 Brig., 2 Div., 23 Corps, Army Ohio, to Feby., 1865, and Dept. North Carolina to June, 1865. Mustered out June 21, 1865.

108th REGIMENT INFANTRY.—Org. at Peoria, Ill., Aug. 28, 1862. Oct., 1862, 2 Brig., 1 Div., Army Ky., Dept. Ohio. Nov., 1862, 2 Brig., 10 Div., 13 Corps, Tenn. Dec., 1862, 2 Brig., 1 Div., Sherman's Yazoo Exp. Jany., 1863, 2 Brig., 10 Div., 13 Corps, Tenn. May, 1863, Detached Brig., Dist. N. E. Louisiana. Aug., 1863, 1 Brig., 2 Div., 16 Corps. Nov., 1863, Post Corinth, Miss., 2 Div., 16 Corps. Jany., 1864, 2 Brig., Dist. Memphis, Tenn., 5 Div., 16 Corps. June, 1864, 2 Brig., Sturgis' Exp. June, 1864, 1 Brig., Post Memphis, Dist. West Tenn. Feby., 1865, 3 Brig., 3 Div., 16 Corps, Mil. Div. West Miss. Mustered out Aug. 5, 1865.

109th REGIMENT INFANTRY.—Org. at Anna, Ill., Sept. 11, 1862. Nov., 1862, Dist. Jackson, Tenn., 13 Corps, Tenn. Dec., 1862, Dist. Jackson, Tenn., 16 Corps. Jany., 1863, Dist. Memphis, Tenn., 16 Corps. Consolidated with 11th Illinois Infantry, April 10, 1863.

110th REGIMENT INFANTRY.—Org. at Anna, Ill., Sept. 11, 1862. Oct., 1862, 19 Brig., 4 Div., 2 Corps, Army Ohio. Nov., 1862, 2 Brig., 2 Div., Left Wing 14 Corps, Cumb'd., 2 Brig., 2 Div., 21 Corps, Cumb'd. May, 1863, Unatt., 21 Corps. Oct., 1863, 3 Brig., 2 Div., 14 Corps. Mustered out June 5, 1865.

111th REGIMENT INFANTRY.—Org. at Salem, Ill., Sept. 18, 1862. Nov., 1862, Dist. Columbus, Ky., 13 Corps, Dept. Tenn. Dec., 1862, Dist. Columbus, Ky., 16 Corps. Nov., 1863, 2 Brig., 2 Div., 16 Corps. March, 1864, 1 Brig., 2 Div., 15 Corps. Aug., 1864, 2 Brig., 2 Div., 15 Corps. Mustered out June 7, 1865.

112th REGIMENT INFANTRY.—Org. at Peoria, Ill., Sept. 20, 1862. Oct., 1862, 1 Brig., 2 Div., Army Ky., Dept. Ohio. Jany., 1863, 3 Brig., Dist. Central Ky., Dept. Ohio. April, 1863, 2 Brig., Dist. Central Ky., Dept. Ohio. June, 1863, 1 Brig., 1 Div., 23 Corps, Dept. Ohio. Aug., 1863, 1 Brig., 4 Div., 23 Corps. Oct., 1863, 2 Brig., 4 Div., 23 Corps. Nov., 1863, 2 Brig., 1 Div., Cav. Corps, Dept. Ohio. May, 1864, 1 Brig., 3 Div., 23 Corps. Aug., 1864, 3 Brig., 3 Div., 23 Corps. Army Ohio to Feby., 1865, and Dept. North Carolina to June, 1865. Mustered out June 20, 1865.

113th REGIMENT INFANTRY.—Org. at Chicago, Ill., Oct. 1, 1862. Nov., 1862, 1 Brig., Dist. Memphis, Tenn., Right Wing 13 Corps, Tenn. Nov., 1862, 1 Brig., 2 Div., Dist. Memphis, Tenn., 13 Corps. Dec., 1862, 1 Brig., 2 Div., Sherman's Yazoo Exp. Jany., 1863, 1 Brig., 2 Div., 15 Corps, Tenn. Aug., 1863, 3 Brig., 2 Div., 16 Corps. Nov., 1863, Post Corinth, Miss., 2 Div., 16 Corps. Jany., 1864, 2 Brig., Dist. Memphis, 16 Corps. June, 1864, 2 Brig., Sturgis' Exp. June, 1864, 1 Brig., Post Memphis, Tenn., Dist. West Tenn. Feby., 1865, Unass'd, Post Memphis Dist., West Tenn. Mustered out June 20, 1865.

114th REGIMENT INFANTRY.—Org. at Camp Butler, Ill., Sept. 18, 1862. Nov., 1862, 5 Brig., 5 Div., Dist. Memphis, Tenn., 13 Corps, Tenn. Nov., 1862, 3 Brig., 1 Div., 13 Corps, Tenn. Dec., 1862, 3 Brig., 8 Div., 16 Corps. April, 1863, 1 Brig., 3 Div., 15 Corps. Dec., 1863, 1 Brig., 1 Div., 16 Corps. June, 1864, 1 Brig., Sturgis' Exp. June, 1864, 1 Brig., 1 Div., 16 Corps. Dec., 1864, 1 Brig., 1 Div., Detachment Army Tenn., Dept. Cumb'd. Feby., 1865, Pontoneer's 16 Corps, Mil. Div. West Miss. Mustered out Aug. 3, 1865.

115th REGIMENT INFANTRY.—Org. at Camp Butler, Ill., Sept. 13, 1862. Oct., 1862, 2 Brig., 3 Div., Army Ky. Feby., 1863, 2 Brig., Baird's Div., Army Ky., Dept. Cumb'd. June, 1863, 1 Brig., 1 Div., Reserve Corps, Cumb'd. Oct., 1863, 1 Brig., 2 Div., 4 Corps. Oct., 1863, 2 Brig., 1 Div., 4 Corps. Mustered out June 11, 1865.

116th REGIMENT INFANTRY.—Org. at Decatur, Ill., Sept. 30, 1862. Nov., 1862, 4 Brig., 5 Div., Dist. Memphis, 13 Corps, Dept. Tenn. Nov., 1862, 2 Brig., 2 Div., Dist. Memphis, 13 Corps. Dec., 1862, 1 Brig., 2 Div., Sherman's Yazoo Exp. Jany., 1863, 1 Brig., 2 Div., 15 Corps, Tenn. Mustered out June 7, 1865.

117th REGIMENT INFANTRY.—Org. at Camp Butler, Ill., Sept. 19, 1862. Nov., 1862, Reserve Brig., Dist. Memphis, Tenn., Right Wing 13 Corps, Dept. Tenn. Jany., 1863, Dist. Memphis, 16 Corps. March, 1863, 1 Brig., 5 Div., 16 Corps. Jany., 1864, 3 Brig., 3 Div., 16 Corps. March, 1864, 3 Brig., 3 Div., 16 Corps, Gulf. June, 1864, 3 Brig., 3 Div., 16 Corps, Tenn. Dec., 1864, 3 Brig., 2 Div., Detachment Army Tenn., Dept. Cumb'd. Feby., 1865, 2 Brig., 2 Div., 16 Corps, Mil. Div. West Miss. Mustered out Aug. 5, 1865.

118th REGIMENT INFANTRY.—Org. at Camp Butler, Ill., Nov. 7, 1862. Dec., 1862, 1 Brig., 9 Div., Right Wing

13 Corps, Dept. Tenn., 1 Brig., 3 Div., Sherman's Yazoo Exp. Jany., 1863, 1 Brig., 9 Div., 13 Corps, Tenn. July, 1863, 3 Brig., 1 Div., 13 Corps. Aug., 1863, 3 Brig., 1 Div., 13 Corps, Gulf. Sept., 1863, 1 Brig., Cav. Div., Gulf. Nov., 1863, 2 Brig., Cav. Div., Gulf. July, 1864, 1 Brig., Cav. Div., Gulf. Sept., 1864, 2 Brig., Cav. Div., Gulf. Feby., 1865, Cav. Brig., Dist. Baton Rouge, La. July, 1865, Dept. Texas. Mustered out Oct. 1, 1865.

119th REGIMENT INFANTRY.—Org. at Quincy, Ill., Oct. 7, 1862. Nov., 1862, Dist. Jackson, Tenn., 13 Corps, Tenn. Dec., 1862, Dist. Columbus, Ky., 16 Corps. Jany., 1863, 3 Brig., Dist. Jackson, Tenn., 16 Corps. March, 1863, 4 Brig., 1 Div., 16 Corps. May, 1863, 4 Brig., Dist. Memphis, Tenn., 5 Div., 16 Corps. Jany., 1864, 1 Brig., 3 Div., 16 Corps. March, 1864, 1 Brig., 3 Div., 16 Corps, Gulf. June, 1864, 1 Brig., 3 Div., 16 Corps, Tenn. Dec., 1864, 1 Brig., 2 Div., Detachment, Army Tenn., Dept. Cumb'd. Feby., 1865, 1 Brig., 2 Div., 16 Corps, Mil. Div. West Miss. Mustered out Aug. 26, 1865.

120th REGIMENT INFANTRY.—Org. at Camp Butler, Ill., Oct. 28, 1862. Nov., 1862, 1 Brig., Dist. Memphis, 13 Corps, Tenn. Nov., 1862, 1 Brig., 2 Div., Dist. Memphis, Tenn., 13 Corps. Dec., 1862, Dist. Memphis, Tenn., 16 Corps. March, 1863, 2 Brig., Dist. Memphis, 5 Div., 16 Corps. May, 1863, Detached Brig., Dist. N. E. La. Aug., 1863, 3 Brig., 2 Div., 16 Corps. Dec., 1863, Post Corinth, Miss., 2 Div., 16 Corps. Jany., 1864, 2 Brig., Dist. Memphis, Tenn., 16 Corps. June, 1864, 2 Brig., Sturgis' Exp. June, 1864, 1 Brig., Post Memphis, Tenn., Dist. West Tenn. Feby., 1865, Unass'd, Post Memphis, Dist. West Tenn. June, 1865, 1 Infy. Brig., Dist. West Tenn. Mustered out Sept. 10, 1865.

121st REGIMENT INFANTRY.—Failed to complete organization.

122nd REGIMENT INFANTRY.—Org. at Carlinsville, Ill., Sept. 4, 1862. Nov., 1862, Dist. Jackson, Tenn., 13 Corps, Tenn. Jany., 1863, 4 Brig., Dist. Jackson, Tenn., 16 Corps. Feby., 1863, 2 Brig., Dist. Corinth, 16 Corps. March, 1863, 2 Brig., 2 Div., 16 Corps. Dec., 1863, Dist. Columbus, Ky., 6 Div., 16 Corps. June, 1864, 2 Brig., 3 Div., 16 Corps. Nov., 1864, 1 Brig., 3 Div., 16 Corps. Dec., 1864, 1 Brig., 2 Div., Detachment Army Tenn., Dept. Cumb'd. Feby., 1865, 1 Brig., 2 Div., Mil. Div. West Miss. Mustered out July 15, 1865.

123rd REGIMENT INFANTRY.—Org. at Mattoon, Ill., Sept. 6, 1862. Sept., 1862, 33 Brig., 10 Div., Army Ohio. Oct., 1862, 33 Brig., 10 Div., 1 Corps, Army Ohio. Nov., 1862, 1 Brig., 5 Div., Centre 14 Corps. Jany., 1863, 1 Brig., 5 Div., 14 Corps. June, 1863, 1 Brig., 4 Div., 14 Corps. Oct., 1863, Wilder's Brigade, Mounted Infy., Cumb'd. Dec., 1863, 3 Brig., 2 Div., Cav. Corps, Cumb'd. Nov., 1864, 3 Brig., 2 Div., Cav. Corps, Mil. Div. Miss. Mustered out June 27, 1865.

124th REGIMENT INFANTRY.—Org. at Camp Butler, Ill., Sept. 10, 1862. Nov., 1862, 1 Brig., 3 Div., Right Wing 13 Corps, Dept. Tenn. Dec., 1862, 1 Brig., 3 Div., 17 Corps, Tenn. April, 1864, Maltby's Brig., Dist. Vicksburg, Miss. Oct., 1864, 1 Brig., 2 Div., 19 Corps, Gulf. Oct., 1864 Maltby's Brig., Dist. Vicksburg, Miss. Feby., 1865, 3 Brig., 3 Div., 16 Corps, Mil. Div. West Miss. Mustered out Aug. 15, 1865.

125th REGIMENT INFANTRY.—Org. at Danville, Ill., Sept. 3, 1862. Sept., 1862, 36 Brig., 11 Div., Army Ohio. Oct., 1862, 36 Brig., 11 Div., 3 Corps, Army Ohio. Nov., 1862, 2 Brig., 4 Div., Centre 14 Corps. Jany., 1863, 2 Brig., 4 Div., 14 Corps. June, 1863, 2 Brig., 2 Div., Reserve Corps, Cumb'd. Oct., 1863, 3 Brig., 2 Div., 14 Corps. Mustered out June 9, 1865.

126th REGIMENT INFANTRY.—Org. at Alton, Ill., Sept. 4, 1862. Nov., 1864, Dist. Jackson, Tenn., 13 Corps, Dept. Tenn. Dec., 1862, 3 Brig., Dist. Jackson, Tenn., 16 Corps. March, 1863, 2 Brig., 3 Div., 16 Corps. May, 1863, 2 Brig., Kimball's Prov'l Div., 16 Corps, 2 Brig., Kimball's Prov'l Div., Dist. East. Ark. Aug., 1863, 2 Brig., 2 Div., Ark. Exp. Jany., 1864, 2 Brig., 2 Div., 7 Corps. March, 1864, 3 Brig., 3 Div., 7 Corps. Feby., 1865, Unatt., Mouth White River, Dept. Ark. Mustered out July 12, 1865.

127th REGIMENT INFANTRY.—Org. at Camp Douglass, Chicago, Ill., and mustered in Sept. 6, 1862. Nov.,

1862, 4 Brig., 5 Div., Dist. Memphis, Tenn., 13 Corps, Tenn. Nov., 1862, 2 Brig., 2 Div., Dist. Memphis, Tenn., 13 Corps. Dec., 1862, 2 Brig., 2 Div., Sherman's Yazoo Exp. Jany., 1863, 2 Brig., 2 Div., 15 Corps, Tenn. Sept., 1863, 1 Brig., 2 Div., 15 Corps. Mustered out June 17, 1865.

128th REGIMENT INFANTRY.—Org. at Camp Butler, Ill., Nov. 4, 1862. Nov., 1862, Dist. Columbus, Ky., 13 Corps, Dept. Tenn. Dec., 1862, Dist. Columbus, Ky., 16 Corps. Disbanded April 1, 1863, for want of discipline, by order Gen. Grant.

129th REGIMENT INFANTRY.—Org. Pontiac, Ill., Sept. 8, 1862. Sept., 1862, 38th Brig., 12 Div., Army Ohio. Nov., 1862, Bowling Green, Ky., Dist. Western Ky., Dept. Ohio. June, 1863, 2 Brig., 3 Div., Reserve Corps, Cumb'd. June, 1863, Garrison Gallatin, Tenn., Dept. Cumb'd. Aug., 1863, Ward's Brig., Dist. Nashville, Tenn., Dept. Cumb'd. Jany., 1864, 1 Brig., 1 Div., 11 Corps. April, 1864, 1 Brig., 3 Div., 20 Corps, Army Cumb'd. Mustered out June 8, 1865.

130th REGIMENT INFANTRY.—Org. at Camp Butler, Ill., Oct. 25, 1862. Nov., 1862, Reserve Brig., Dist. Memphis, Tenn., 13 Corps, Dept. Tenn. Dec., 1862, Dist. Memphis, Tenn., 16 Corps. March, 1863, 2 Brig., 10 Div., 13 Corps, Tenn. July, 1863, 2 Brig., 4 Div., 13 Corps, Gulf. June, 1864, 3 Brig., 3 Div., 19 Corps, Gulf. Oct., 1864, Def. New Orleans, La. Jany., 1865, Consolidated with 77th Illinois Infantry, Jany. 25, 1865. Revived June 23, 1865, 1 Brig., 3 Div., 13 Corps, Mil. Div. West Miss. Mustered out Aug. 25, 1865.

131st REGIMENT INFANTRY.—Org. at Fort Massac, Ill., Nov. 13, 1862. Dec., 1862, 2 Brig., 10 Div., Right Wing, 13 Corps, Dept. Tenn. Dec., 1862, 2 Brig., 1 Div., Sherman's Yazoo Exp. Jany., 1863, 2 Brig., 10 Div., 13 Corps, Tenn. March, 1863, Dist. Memphis, Tenn., 5 Div., 16 Corps. May, 1863, Detached Brig., Dist. N. E. Louisiana. July, 1863, Paducah, Ky., Dist. Columbus, Ky., 6 Div., 16 Corps. Oct., 1863, 1 Brig., 3 Div., 17 Corps. Consolidated with 29th Illinois Infantry, November 14, 1863.

132nd REGIMENT INFANTRY.—Org. at Chicago, Ill., June 1, 1864. June, 1864, Dist. Columbus, Ky., Dept. Tenn. Aug., 1864, Dist. Columbus, Ky., Dept. Ohio. Mustered out Oct. 17, 1864.

133rd REGIMENT INFANTRY.—Org. at Camp Butler, Ill., May 31, 1864. Prison Guard at Rock Island, Ill. Mustered out Sept. 24, 1864.

134th REGIMENT INFANTRY.—Org. at Chicago, Ill., May 31, 1864. June, 1864, Dist. Columbus, Ky., Dept. Tenn. Aug., 1864, Dist. Columbus, Ky., Dept. Ohio. Mustered out Oct. 25, 1864.

135th REGIMENT INFANTRY.—Org. at Mattoon, Ill., June 6, 1864. R. R. Guard in Dept. Mo. Mustered out Sept. 28, 1864.

136th REGIMENT INFANTRY.—Org. at Centralia, Ill., June 1, 1864. June, 1864, Dist. Columbus, Ky., Dept. Tenn. Aug., 1864, Dist. Columbus, Ky., Dept. Ohio. Sept., 1864, St. Louis, Mo., Dept. Mo. Mustered out Oct. 30, 1864.

137th REGIMENT INFANTRY.—Org. at Quincy, Ill., June 5, 1864. June, 1864, 3 Brig., Post Memphis, Tenn., Dist. West Tenn. Mustered out Sept. 4, 1864.

138th REGIMENT INFANTRY.—Org. at Quincy, Ill., June 21, 1864. June, 1864, Garrison at Fort Leavenworth, Kan., Dist. North Kansas. Mustered out Oct. 14, 1864.

139th REGIMENT INFANTRY.—Org. at Peoria, Ill., June 1, 1864. June, 1864, Dist. Columbus, Ky., Dept. Tenn., Garrison, Cairo, Ill. Sept., 1864, St. Louis, Mo., Dept. Mo., Mustered out Oct. 25, 1864.

140th REGIMENT INFANTRY.—Org. at Camp Butler, Ill., June 18, 1864. June, 1864, 3 Brig., Dist. Memphis, Tenn. Dist. West Tenn. Mustered out Oct. 29, 1864.

141st REGIMENT INFANTRY.—Org. at Elgin, Ill., June 16, 1864. June, 1864, Dist. Columbus, Ky., Dept. Tenn. Mustered out Oct. 10, 1864.

142nd REGIMENT INFANTRY.—Org. at Freeport, Ill., June 18, 1864. June, 1864, 3 Brig., Dist. Memphis, Tenn., Dist. West Tenn. Mustered out Oct. 27, 1864.

143rd REGIMENT INFANTRY.—Org. at Mattoon, June 11, 1864. June, 1864, 3 Brig., Post Memphis, Dist. West Tenn., July, 1864. Dist. East Ark., Dept. Ark. Garrison Helena, Ark. Mustered out Sept. 26, 1864.

144th REGIMENT INFANTRY.—Org. at Alton, Ill., Oct. 21, 1864. Dist. St. Louis, Dept. Mo. Mustered out July 14, 1865.

145th REGIMENT INFANTRY.—Org. at Camp Butler, Ill., June 9, 1864. June, 1864. Dist. St. Louis, Mo., Dept. Mo. Mustered out Sept. 23, 1864.

146th REGIMENT INFANTRY.—Org. at Camp Butler, Ill., Sept. 18, 1864. Guard duty in Illinois. Mustered out July 5, 1865.

147th REGIMENT INFANTRY.—Org. at Chicago, Ill., Feby. 18, 1865. March, 1865, 1 Brig., 2 Separate Div., Dist. Etowah, Dept. Cumb'd. July, 1865, Dept. Georgia. Mustered out Jany. 20, 1866.

148th REGIMENT INFANTRY.—Org. at Camp Butler, Ill., Feby. 21, 1865. March, 1865, 1 Brig., Def. Nashville and Chattanooga R. R., Dept. Cumb'd. April, 1865, 2 Brig., 1st Sub Dist., Dist. Middle Tenn. June, 1865, 3 Brig., 1st Sub Dist., Dist. Middle Tenn. Mustered out Sept. 5, 1865.

149th REGIMENT INFANTRY.—Org. at Camp Butler, Ill., Feby. 11, 1865. March, 1865, 2nd Brig., 2nd Separate Div., Dist. Etowah, Dept. Cumb'd. July, 1865, Dept. Georgia. Mustered out Jany. 27, 1866.

150th REGIMENT INFANTRY.—Org. at Camp Butler, Ill., Feby. 14, 1865. March, 1865, 2 Brig., 2nd Separate Div., Dist. Etowah, Dept. Cumb'd. July, 1865, Dept. Georgia. Mustered out Jany. 16, 1866.

151st REGIMENT INFANTRY.—Org. at Quincy, Ill., Feby. 23, 1865. March, 1865, 1st Brig., 2nd Separate Div., Dist. Etowah, Dept. Cumb'd. July, 1865, Dept. Georgia. Mustered out Jany. 24, 1866.

152nd REGIMENT INFANTRY.—Org. at Camp Butler, Ill., Feby. 18, 1865. March, 1865, 2 Brig., Def. Nashville and Chattanooga R. R., Dept. Cumb'd. April, 1865, 2nd Brig., 1st Sub Dist., Dist. Middle Tenn., Dept. Cumb'd. July, 1865, 1st Infy. Brig., Dist. West Tenn. Mustered out Sept. 9, 1865.

153rd REGIMENT INFANTRY.—Org. at Camp Fry, Ill., Feby. 27, 1865. March, 1865, 2nd Brig., Nashville and Chattanooga R. R., Dept. Cumb'd. April, 1865, 2nd Brig., 1st Sub Dist., Dist. Middle Tenn., Dept. Cumb'd. July, 1865, 1st Infy. Brig., Dist. West Tenn. Mustered out Sept. 15, 1865.

154th REGIMENT INFANTRY.—Org. at Camp Butler, Ill., Feby. 21, 1865. March, 1865, 1 Brig., Def. Nashville and Chattanooga R. R., Dept. Cumb'd. April, 1865, 1 Brig., 1 Sub Dist., Middle Tenn. Dept. Cumb'd. Mustered out Sept. 18, 1865.

155th REGIMENT INFANTRY.—Org. at Camp Butler, Ill., Feby. 28, 1865. March, 1865, 2 Brig., Def. Nashville and Chattanooga R. R., Dept. Cumb'd. April, 1865, 2 Brig., 1 Sub Dist., Middle Tenn., Dept. Cumb'd. Mustered out Sept. 4, 1865.

156th REGIMENT INFANTRY.—Org. Feby. 16, 1865. April, 1865, 3 Brig., 2 Separate Div., Dist. Etowah, Dept. Cumb'd. Mustered out Sept. 20, 1865.

FIRST TROOPS IN SERVICE—ON EXPEDITION TO CAIRO, ILL.:

Chicago Light Artillery Company, Org. April 21, 1861. Mustered out May 2, 1861.

Lockport Artillery Company, Org. April 22, 1861. Mustered out July 31, 1861.

Chicago Zouaves, Company A, Org. April 19, 1861. Mustered out May 3, 1861.

Chicago Zouaves, Company B, Org. April 15, 1861. Mustered out April 29, 1861.

Chicago Light Infantry Company, Org. April 19, 1861. Mustered out May 3, 1861.

Turner Union Cadets, Org. April 15, 1861. Mustered out April 29, 1861.

Lincoln Rifles, Org. April 15, 1861. Mustered out April 29, 1861.

Light Artillery Company, Org. April 21, 1861. Mustered out April 29, 1861.

Houghtailing's Ottawa Company, Org. April 18, 1861. Co. F, 10th Ill. Infy., 3 months.

Cairo Sandwich Company, Org. April 19, 1861, Co. C, 10th Ill. Inf., 3 months.

STURGIS RIFLES.—Org. at Chicago, Ill., May 6, 1861, June, 1861, Headquarters Dept. West Va. Aug., 1861, Headquarters Army Potomac. Mustered out Nov. 25, 1862.

INDIANA

1st REGIMENT CAVALRY.—(28th VOLS.). Org. at Evansville, Aug. 20, 1861. Sept., 1861, Dept. Mo. Feby., 1862, Dist. S. E. Mo., Dept. Mo. May, 1862, 1 Div., Army S. W. Mo. July, 1862, Dist. East. Ark., Dept. Mo. Dec., 1862, 1 Brig., 3 (Cav.) Div., Dist. East. Ark., Dept. Tenn. Jany., 1863, 1 Brig., 2 Cav. Div., 13 Corps, Dept. Tenn. April, 1863, 1 Brig., Cav. Div., Dist. East. Ark., 13 Corps, Tenn. May, 1863, 2 Brig., Cav. Div., Dist. East. Ark. June, 1863, Clayton's Indpt. Cav. Brig., Dist. East. Ark. July, 1863, Clayton's Cav. Brig., 13 Div., 16 Corps, Tenn. Aug., 1863, Clayton's Cav. Brig., Ark. Exp. Jany., 1864, Clayton's Cav. Brig., 7 Corps, Dept. Ark. Sept., 1864, 1 Brig., Cav. Div., 7 Corps, Ark. Feby., 1865, Mouth of White River, Ark. (Co. C. Jany., 1863, 12 Div., 13 Corps, Tenn. Aug., 1863, Cav. Brig., 13 Corps, Gulf. Sept., 1863, 2 Brig., Cav. Div., Gulf. Nov., 1863, 3 Brig., Cav. Div., Gulf. Dec., 1863, Unatt. Cav., Dept. Gulf. June, 1864, Def. New Orleans. July, 1864, Pine Bluff, Ark.) (Co.'s I and K, see Stewart's and Bracken's Cav. Co.'s) Mustered out May 31, 1865.

2nd REGIMENT CAVALRY.—(41st VOLS.) Org. at Indianapolis, Sept. 20, 1861. Dec., 1861, Cav. 4 Div., Army Ohio. June, 1862, Cav. Brig., Army Ohio. Sept., 1862, 1 Brig., Cav. Div., Army Ohio. Nov., 1862, 1 Brig., Cav. Div., Cumb'd. Jany., 1863, 2 Brig., 1 Cav. Div., Cumb'd. Oct., 1864, 2 Brig., 1 Div., Wilson's Cav. Corps, Mil. Div., Miss. Mustered out July 22, 1865.

3rd REGIMENT CAVALRY.—(45th VOLS.). Right Wing, Co.'s A, B, C, D, E and F. Org. at Madison, Aug. 22, 1861. Oct., 1861, Hooker's Div., Potomac. March, 1862, Lower Md. Middle Dept. May, 1862, Geary's Indpt. Brig., Dept. Rappahannock. June, 1862, Shield's Div., Dept. Rappahannock. July, 1862, Farnsworth's 2 Brig., Pleasanton's Cav. Div., Potomac. Nov., 1862, 2 Brig., Cav. Div., Potomac. Feby., 1863, 1 Brig., 1 Div., Cav. Corps, Potomac. April, 1864, 2 Brig., 3 Div., Cav. Corps, Potomac, and Army Shenandoah, Middle Mil. Div. Mustered out Aug. 2, 1865.

LEFT WING.—Co.'s G, H, I, K. Org. at Madison, Oct. 1, 1861. (Co. L Org. Oct., 1862, and M Org. Dec. 11, 1862.) Dec., 1861, 1 Div., Army Ohio, Co. G, 2 Div., Army Ohio, Co. H, 4 Div., Army Ohio, Co.'s K and I. June, 1862, Cav. Brig., Army Ohio. Sept., 1862, Cav., 1 Corps, Army Ohio. Nov., 1862, Cav., Right Wing 14 Corps, Cumb'd. Jany., 1863, 1 Brig., 2 Cav. Div., Cumb'd. April, 1864, 1 Brig., Kilpatrick's 3 Cav. Div., Cumb'd. Nov., 1864, 2 Brig., 3 Div., Wilson's Cav. Corps, Mil. Div. Miss. Transferred to 8th Indiana Cav., Dec., 1864.

4th REGIMENT CAVALRY.—(77th VOLS.). Org. at Indianapolis, Aug., 1862. Sept., 1862, Unatt., Army Ky., Dept. Ohio. Nov., 1862, Dist. West. Ky., Dept. Ohio. March, 1863, 2 Brig., 1 Cav. Div., Cumb'd. Oct., 1864, 2 Brig., 1 Div. Wilson's Cav. Corps, Mil. Div. Miss. (Co. C. at Headqrs. A. J. Smith, Oct., 1862, to Aug., 1863. Cav. Brig., 13 Corps, Gulf, to Sept., 1863. 2 Brig., Cav. Div., Gulf, to Nov., 1863. 3 Brig., Cav. Div., Gulf, to Jany., 1864. 1 Brig., Cav. Div., Gulf, to June, 1864.) Mustered out June 29, 1865.

5th REGIMENT CAVALRY.—(90th VOLS.). Org. at Indianapolis Aug. 22 to Oct. 30, 1862. Oct., 1862, Indiana. Feby., 1863, Dist. West. Ky., Dept. Ohio. June, 1863, 1 Brig., 3 Div., 23 Corps, Ohio. Aug., 1863, 2 Brig., 4 Div., 23 Corps, Ohio. Oct., 1863, 4 Brig., 4 Div., 23 Corps, Ohio. Nov., 1863, 2 Brig., 2 Cav. Div., Ohio. May, 1864, 1 Brig., Cav. Div., 23 Corps, Ohio. July, 1864, 2 Brig., Cav. Div., 23 Corps, Ohio. Aug., 1864, Dismounted Brig., Cav. Div., 23 Corps, Ohio. Sept., 1864, 1 Brig., Cav. Div., 23 Corps, Ohio. Sept., 1864, Dist. Louisville, Ky., Dept. Ohio. Nov., 1864, 1 Brig., 6 Div., Wilson's Cav. Corps, Mil. Div. Miss. Dec., 1864, 2 Brig., 6 Div., Cav. Corps, Mil. Div. Miss. Mustered out June 16, 1865.

6th REGIMENT CAVALRY.—(71st VOLS.). Org. at Indianapolis from 71st Ind. Infy., Feby. 23, 1863. Aug., 1863, Lexington, Ky., 1 Div., 23 Corps, Ohio. Sept., 1863, Willcox's Div., Left Wing Forces, 23 Corps, Ohio, Cumberland Gap. Jany., 1864, Dist. Clinch., Dept. Ohio. April, 1864, 2 Brig., 1 Div., Cav. Corps Ohio. May, 1864, 1 Brig., Cav. Div., 23 Corps, Ohio. July, 1864, 2 Brig., Cav. Div., 23 Corps, Ohio. Aug., 1864, Dismounted Brig., Cav. Div., 23 Corps, Ohio. Nov., 1864, 2 Brig., 6 Div. Wilson's Cav. Corps, Mil. Div. Miss. June, 1865, Dist. Middle Tenn., Dept. Cumb'd. Mustered out Sept. 15, 1865.

7th REGIMENT CAVALRY.—(119th VOLS.). Org. at Indianapolis Aug. 24 to Sept. 19, 1863. Dec., 1863, Dist. Columbus, 6 Div., 16 Corps, Tenn. Dec., 1863, Waring's Cav. Brig., 16 Corps, Tenn. Jany., 1864, 1 Brig., 1 Cav. Div., 16 Corps, Tenn. June, 1864, 1 Brig., 1 Cav. Div., Dist. West. Tenn. July, 1864, 1 Brig., 2 Cav. Div., Dist. West. Tenn. Nov., 1864, 2 Brig., 4 Div., Wilson's Cav. Corps, Mil. Div. Miss. Dec., 1864, 1 Brig., Cav. Div., Dist. West. Tenn. June, 1865, Dept. Texas. Mustered out Feby. 18, 1866.

8th REGIMENT CAVALRY.—Org. from 39th Ind. Infy., Oct. 15, 1863. Oct., 1863, 1 Brig., 2 Cav. Div., Cumberland. April, 1864, 2 Brig., Kilpatrick's 3 Cav. Div., Cumberland. Oct., 1864, 2 Brig., 3 Div., Wilson's Cav. Corps, Mil. Div. Miss. Nov., 1864, 1 Brig., 3 Div., Cav. Corps, M. D. M. Mustered out July 20, 1865.

9th REGIMENT CAVALRY.—(121st VOLS.). Org. at Indianapolis Dec. 7, 1863, to March 29, 1864. May, Dist. Northern Ala., Dept. Cumberland. Nov., 1864, 1 Brig., 7 Div., Wilson's Cav. Corps, Mil. Div. Miss. March, 1865, Dept. Miss. Mustered out Aug. 22, 1865.

10th REGIMENT CAVALRY.—(125th VOLS.). Org. at Columbus, Vincennes, Terre Haute, New Albany and Indianapolis, Dec. 30, 1863, to April 30, 1864. May, 1864, Dist. Northern Ala., Dept. Cumberland. Nov., 1864, 1 Brig., 7 Div., Wilson's Cav. Corps, Mil. Div. Miss. March, 1865, 2 Brig., 1 Cav. Div., Mil. Div. West. Miss., Dept. Gulf. May, 1865, 3 Brig., 1 Cav. Div. West. Miss. June, 1865, Dist. Vicksburg, Miss., Dept. Miss. Mustered out Aug. 31, 1865.

11th REGIMENT CAVALRY.—(126th VOLS.). Org. at Lafayette, Kokomo and Indianapolis Nov. 10, 1863, to April 2, 1864. May, 1864, Dist. Northern Ala., Dept. Cumberland. Nov., 1864, 1 Brig., 5 Div., Wilson's Cav. Corps, Mil. Div. Miss. May, 1865, Dept. Mo. July, 1865, Dist. Kansas, Dept. Mo. Mustered out Sept. 19, 1865.

12th REGIMENT CAVALRY.—(127th VOLS.). Org. at Kendallville Dec. 10, 1863, to April 28, 1864. May, 1864, Dist. Northern Ala., Dept. Cumberland. Sept., 1864, Tullahoma, Def. Nash. & Chatt. R. R., Dept. Cumberland. Nov., 1864, 2 Brig., 7 Div., Wilson's Cav. Corps, Mil. Div. Miss. Feby., 1865, 1 Brig., 1 Cav. Div., Mil. Div. West. Miss. April, 1865, 2 Brig., Cav. Div., Gulf. May, 1865, Dept. Miss. Mustered out Nov. 18, 1865.

13th REGIMENT CAVALRY.—(131st VOLS.). Org. at Indianapolis, Kokomo and New Albany Dec. 23, 1863, to April 29, 1864. May, 1864, Dist. Northern Ala., Dept. Cumberland. Nov., 1864, 2 Brig., 7 Div., Wilson's Cav. Corps, Mil. Div. Miss. Feby., 1865, 2 Brig., 1 Cav. Div., Mil. Div. West. Miss. May, 1865, Dept. Miss. Mustered out Nov. 18, 1865.

STEWART'S INDPT. CAVALRY COMPANY.—Org. at Indianapolis July 4, 1861. Assigned to 1st Ind. Cav. as Co. I Aug. 20, 1861. July, 1861, Escort to Gen. Rosecrans, Dept. West Va. Oct., 1861, R. R. Dist., West Va. March, 1862, R. R. Dist., Dept. Mts. March, 1862, Headqrs. Dept. Mts. June, 1862, Headqrs. 1 Corps, Army Va. Sept., 1862, Headqrs. 11 Corps, Potomac. Sept., 1863, Headqrs. Army Potomac. Mustered out May 31, 1865.

BRACKEN'S INDPT. CAVALRY COMPANY.—Org. at Indianapolis July 9, 1861. Assigned to 1st Ind. Cav. as Co. K Aug. 20, 1861. July, 1861, Escort to Gen. Rosecrans, Dept. West Va. Oct., 1861, R. R. Dist., West Va. March, 1862, R. R. Dist., Dept. Mts. March, 1862, Headqrs. Dept. Mts. June, 1862, Headqrs. 1 Corps, Army Va. Sept., 1862, Headqrs. 11 Corps, Potomac. Sept., 1863, Headqrs. Army Potomac. Mustered out May 31, 1865.

INDPT. COMPANY MOUNTED SCOUTS.—Org. at Leavenworth, Kans., Aug. 13, 1863. Mustered out April 23, 1864.

1st REGIMENT HEAVY ARTILLERY.—Org. from 21st Regt. Ind. Infy., Feby., 1863. Feby., 1863, Arty., 1 Div., 19 Corps, Gulf. Aug., 1863, Dist. Baton Rouge, La., Gulf. June, 1864, Unatt., 19 Corps, Gulf, and Dept. Gulf. Mustered out Jany. 10, 1866.

1st INDPT. BATTERY LIGHT ARTILLERY.—Org. at Indianapolis Aug. 16, 1861. Sept., 1861, Army of the West, Dept. Mo. Jany., 1862, 1 Brig., 3 Div., Army S. W. Mo., Dept. Mo. May, 1862, Arty., 1 Div., Army S. W. Mo., Dept. Mo. July, 1862, Dist. Eastern Ark., Dept. Mo. Oct., 1862, 2 Brig., 1 Div., Dist. S. E. Mo., Dept. Mo. March, 1863, Arty., 14 Div., 13 Corps, Tenn. July, 1863, Arty., 1 Div., 13 Corps, Tenn. Aug., 1863, Arty., 1 Div., 13 Corps, Gulf. Sept., 1863, Dist. LaFourche, Dept. Gulf. Feby., 1864, Arty., 1 Div., 13 Corps, Gulf. March, 1864, Arty., 4 Div., 13 Corps, Gulf. July, 1864, Arty. Res., Gulf. Feby., 1865, Arty. Brig., 16 Corps, Mil. Div. West. Miss. Mustered out Aug. 22, 1865.

2nd INDPT. BATTERY LIGHT ARTILLERY.—Org. at Indianapolis Aug. 9, 1861. Sept., 1861, Army West, Dept. Mo. Nov., 1861, Dist. Fort Scott, Dept. Kans. Aug., 1862, 3 Brig., Dept. Kans. Oct., 1862, 3 Brig., 1 Div., Army Frontier, Dept. Mo. Jany., 1863, Springfield, Mo., Dept. Mo. July, 1863, Dist. Frontier, Dept. Mo. Dec., 1863, 2 Brig., Dist. Frontier, Dept. Mo. Jany., 1864, 2 Brig., Dist. Frontier, 7 Corps, Ark. March, 1864, 1 Brig., Frontier Div., 7 Corps, Ark. Sept., 1864, Indianapolis, Ind. Oct., 1864, Post and Dist. of Nashville, Tenn., Dept. Cumberland. Feby., 1865, Garrison Arty., Murfreesboro, Tenn., Dept. Cumberland. Mustered out July 3, 1865.

3rd INDPT. BATTERY LIGHT ARTILLERY.—Org. at Indianapolis Aug. 24, 1861. Sept., 1861, Army West, Dept. Mo. Feby., 1862, Jefferson City, Mo., Dept. Mo. March, 1862, Central Dist. Mo., Dept. Mo. Feby., 1863, Dist. S. W. Mo., Dept. Mo. June, 1863, Dist. Rolla, Mo., Dept. Mo. July, 1863, Dist. St. Louis, Mo., Dept. Mo. Jany., 1864, Arty., 3 Div., 16 Corps, Tenn. March, 1864, Arty., 3 Div., 16 Corps, Detachment Army Tenn., Dept. Gulf. June, 1864, Arty., 3 Div., 16 Corps, Tenn. Dec., 1864, 2 Brig., 2 Div., Detachment Army Tenn., Dept. Cumberland. Feby., 1865, Arty., 1 Div., 16 Corps, Mil. Div. West. Miss. March, 1865, Arty. Brig., 16 Corps, M. D. W. M. Mustered out Aug. 21, 1865.

4th INDPT. BATTERY LIGHT ARTILLERY.—Org. at Indianapolis Sept. 30, 1861. Oct., 1861, Unatt., Army Ohio. June, 1862, Arty. Res., Army Ohio. July, 1862, 7th Indpt. Brig., Army Ohio. Aug., 1862, 28 Brig., 3 Div., Army Ohio. Sept., 1862, 28 Brig., 3 Div., 1 Corps, Army Ohio. Nov., 1862, 1 Brig., 3 Div., Right Wing 14 Corps, Dept. Cumberland. Jany., 1863, Arty., 3 Div., 20 Corps, Cumberland. Oct., 1863, Arty., 1 Div., 14 Corps, Cumberland. Oct., 1863, 2 Div., Arty. Res., Cumberland. Nov., 1863, Garrison Arty., Chattanooga, Tenn., Dept. Cumberland. Battery reorganized Oct., 1864. Oct., 1864, Garrison Arty., Nashville, Tenn., Dept. Cumberland. March, 1865, 1 Brig., 1 Sub-Dist., Dist. Middle Tenn., Dept. Cumberland. Mustered out July 1, 1865.

5th INDPT. BATTERY LIGHT ARTILLERY.—Org. at Indianapolis Nov. 22, 1861. Dec., 1861, Arty., 3 Div., Army Ohio. Sept., 1862, 9 Brig., 3 Div., 1 Corps, Army Ohio. Nov., 1862, 3 Brig., 2 Div., Right Wing 14 Corps, Cumberland. Jany., 1863, Arty., 2 Div., 20 Corps, Cumberland. Oct., 1863, Arty., 1 Div., 4 Corps, Cumberland. July, 1864, Arty. Brig., 4 Corps, Cumberland. Sept., 1864, Garrison Arty., Chattanooga, Tenn., Dept. Cumberland. Mustered out Nov. 26, 1864.

6th INDPT. BATTERY LIGHT ARTILLERY.—Org. at Indianapolis Sept. 7, 1861. Dec., 1861, Dist. Paducah, Ky. March, 1862, Arty., 5 Div., Army Tenn. July, 1862, Arty., 5 Div., Dist. Memphis, Tenn., Dept. Tenn. Nov., 1862, Arty., 1 Div., Right Wing 13 Corps, Dept. Tenn. Dec., 1862, Arty., 1 Div., 17 Corps, Tenn. Jany., 1863, Arty., 1 Div., 16 Corps, Tenn. July, 1863, Arty., 3 Div., 15 Corps, Tenn. Dec., 1863, Arty., 1 Div., 16 Corps, Tenn. June, 1864, 1 Brig., Sturgis' Exp. June, 1864, Arty., 1 Div., 16 Corps, Tenn. Nov., 1864, 1 Brig., Post and Det.,

Memphis, Tenn., Dist. West. Tenn. Dec., 1864, Arty. Res., Dist. West. Tenn. Mustered out July 22, 1865.

7th INDPT. BATTERY LIGHT ARTILLERY.—Org. at Indianapolis Dec. 2, 1861. Jany., 1862, Arty., 4 Div., Army Ohio. June, 1862, Arty., 1 Div., Army Ohio. Sept., 1862, Arty., 5 Div., 2 Corps, Army Ohio. Nov., 1862, Arty., 3 Div., Left Wing 14 Corps, Cumberland. Jany., 1863, Arty., 3 Div., 21 Corps, Cumberland. Oct., 1863, Arty., 3 Div., 14 Corps, Cumberland. July, 1864, Arty. Brig., 14 Corps, Cumberland. Oct., 1864, Garrison Arty., Chattanooga, Tenn., Dept. Cumberland. April, 1865, 2 Brig., 4 Div., Dist. East. Tenn., Dept. Cumberland. Mustered out July 20, 1865.

8th INDPT. BATTERY LIGHT ARTILLERY.—Org. at Indianapolis Dec. 13, 1861. Jany., 1862, Arty., 4 Div., Army Ohio. March, 1862, Arty., 6 Div., Army Ohio. Sept., 1862, 15 Brig., 6 Div., 2 Corps, Army Ohio. Nov., 1862, 1 Brig., 1 Div., Left Wing 14 Corps, Cumberland. Jany., 1863, Arty., 1 Div., 21 Corps, Cumberland. Oct., 1863, 2 Div., Arty. Res., Cumberland. Nov., 1863, Garrison Arty., Chattanooga, Tenn., Dept. Cumberland. Mustered out Jany. 25, 1865.

9th INDPT. BATTERY LIGHT ARTILLERY.—Org. at Indianapolis Dec. 20, 1861. Reorg. at Cairo, Ill., Feby. 25, 1862. April, 1862, Arty., 3 Div., Army Tenn. July, 1862, Arty., 1 Div., Dist. Jackson, Dept. Tenn. Sept., 1862, Arty., 4 Div., Dist. Jackson, Dept. Tenn. Nov., 1862, Arty., 4 Div., Right Wing 13 Corps, Dept. Tenn. Dec., 1862, Arty., 4 Div., 17 Corps, Tenn. Jany., 1863, Arty., 4 Div., 16 Corps, Tenn. March, 1863, Arty., Dist. Columbus, 6 Div., 16 Corps, Tenn. July, 1863, 1 Brig., Dist. Columbus, 6 Div., 16 Corps, Tenn. Jany., 1864, Arty., 3 Div., 16 Corps, Tenn. March, 1864, Arty., 3 Div., 16 Corps, Det. Army Tenn., Dept. Gulf. June, 1864, Arty., 3 Div., 16 Corps, Tenn. Dec., 1864, 1 Brig., 2 Div., Det. Army Tenn., Dept. Cumberland. Jany., 1865, Indiana. March, 1865, Camp Butler, Ill. Mustered out June 26, 1865.

10th INDPT. BATTERY LIGHT ARTILLERY.—Org. at Indianapolis Jany. 25, 1862. Jany., 1862, Arty., 4 Div., Army Ohio. June, 1862, Res. Arty., Army Ohio. July, 1862, Arty., 6 Div., Army Ohio. Sept., 1862, 21 Brig., 6 Div., 2 Corps, Army Ohio. Nov., 1862, 2 Brig., 1 Div., Left Wing 14 Corps, Cumberland. Jany., 1863, Arty., 1 Div., 21 Corps, Cumberland. Oct., 1863, Arty., 2 Div., 4 Corps, Cumberland. March, 1864, Garrison Arty., Chattanooga, Tenn., Dept. Cumberland. April, 1864, Unatt. Arty., Dept. Cumberland. Aug., 1864, Dist. North. Ala., Dept. Cumberland. Mustered out July 10, 1865.

11th INDPT. BATTERY LIGHT ARTILLERY.—Org. at Indianapolis Dec. 17, 1861. Jany., 1862, Unatt., Army Ohio. June, 1862, Res. Arty., Army Ohio. Sept., 1862, Post. and Def. Nashville, Tenn. Nov., 1862, Res. Arty., Centre 14 Corps, Cumberland. Jany., 1863, Garrison Arty., Dist. Nashville, Dept. Cumberland. June, 1863, Arty., 3 Div., 20 Corps, Cumberland. Oct., 1863, 2 Div., Arty. Res., Cumberland. Nov., 1863, Garrison Arty., Chattanooga, Tenn. May, 1864, Siege Arty., Army Cumberland. Oct., 1864, Garrison Arty., Chattanooga, Tenn. Consolidated with 18th Ind. Battery, Nov. 21, 1864.

12th INDPT. BATTERY LIGHT ARTILLERY.—Org. at Indianapolis and Jeffersonville, Jany. 25, 1862. Jany., 1862, Unatt., Army Ohio. June, 1862, Res. Arty., Army Ohio. Sept., 1862, Post. and Def. Nashville, Tenn., Ohio and Cumberland. Mustered out July 7, 1865.

13th INDPT. BATTERY LIGHT ARTILLERY.—Org. at Indianapolis Feby. 22, 1862. Feby., 1862, Unassigned, Ky., Army Ohio. Sept., 1862, Arty., 12 Div., Army Ohio. Nov., 1862, Ward's Brig., Post Gallatin, Dept. Cumberland. June, 1863, Garrison Arty., Gallatin, Tenn., Dept. Cumberland. Jany., 1865, Garrison Arty., Chattanooga, Tenn., Cumberland. Mustered out July 10, 1865.

14th INDPT. BATTERY LIGHT ARTILLERY.—Org. at Indianapolis March 24, 1862. April, 1862, Arty., 1 Div., Army Tenn. July, 1862, Arty., 1 Div., Dist. Jackson, Dept. Tenn. Nov., 1862, Arty., Dist. Jackson, 13 Corps, Dept. Tenn. Dec., 1862, Arty., Dist. Jackson, 16 Corps, Tenn. March, 1863, Arty., 3 Div., 16 Corps, Tenn. June, 1863, Arty., Dist. Corinth, 2 Div., 16 Corps, Tenn. Nov., 1863, Post Corinth, 2 Div., 16 Corps, Tenn. Jany., 1864,

Arty., 3 Div., 16 Corps, Tenn. June, 1864, Unatt. Arty., Dist. West. Tenn. Dec., 1864, Arty., 3 Div., Det. Army Tenn., Dept. Cumberland. Feby., 1865, Arty., 3 Div., 16 Corps, Mil. Div. West. Miss. March, 1865, Arty. Brig., 16 Corps, M. D. W. M. Mustered out Sept. 1, 1865.

15th INDPT. BATTERY LIGHT ARTILLERY.—Org. at Indianapolis July 5, 1862. July, 1862, D'Utassy's Brig., White's Div., Army Va. Sept., 1862, Miles' Command, Harper's Ferry, West Va. Sept., 1862, Camp Douglass, Ill., and Indianapolis, Ind. April, 1863, Dist. Central Ky., Dept. Ohio. June, 1863, 2 Brig., 4 Div., 23 Corps, Ohio. July, 1863, 2 Brig., 1 Div., 23 Corps, Ohio. Aug., 1863, 1 Brig., 4 Div., 23 Corps, Ohio. Oct., 1863, 2 Brig., 4 Div., 23 Corps, Ohio. Nov., 1863, 2 Brig., 1 Cav. Div., Ohio. Dec., 1863, Arty., 2 Div., 9 Corps, Ohio. April, 1864, Arty., 3 Div., 23 Corps, Ohio. Dec., 1864, Arty., 2 Div., 23 Corps, Ohio. Feby., 1865, Arty., 2 Div., 23 Corps, Dept. N. C. Mustered out June 30, 1865.

16th INDPT. BATTERY LIGHT ARTILLERY.—Org. at Indianapolis March 24, 1862. May, 1862, Mil. Dist. Washington, D. C. June, 1862, Arty., 2 Corps, Army Va. Sept., 1862, Arty., 2 Div., 12 Corps, Potomac. Oct., 1862, Arty., 2 Brig., Def. North Potomac, Def. Washington, D. C. Feby., 1863, Fort Washington, Def. Washington, North Potomac, 22 Corps. May, 1864, 2 Brig., DeRussy's Div., 22 Corps. July, 1864, 3 Brig., DeRussy's Div., 22 Corps. Dec., 1864, 1 Brig., DeRussy's Div., 22 Corps. Mustered out July 5, 1865.

17th INDPT. BATTERY LIGHT ARTILLERY.—Org. at Indianapolis May 20, 1862. July, 1862, Def. Baltimore, Md., 8 Corps, Middle Dept. Jany., 1863, Def. Upper Potomac, 8 Corps. March, 1863, 1 Brig., 1 Div., 8 Corps. June, 1863, Md. Brig., French's Div., 8 Corps. July, 1863, 2 Brig., Md. Heights Div., West Va. July, 1863, 1 Brig., Md. Heights Div., West Va. Dec., 1863, 1 Brig., 1 Div., West Va. Jany., 1864, Wheaton's Brig., 1 Div., West Va. April, 1864, Res. Div., Harper's Ferry, West Va. Aug., 1864, Res. Arty., 19 Corps, Middle Mil. Div. Oct., 1864, Garrison Arty., Frederick City and Winchester, Va., M. M. D. Dec., 1864, Arty. Brig., 19 Corps, Army Shenandoah. March, 1865, Arty. Res., Army Shenandoah. Mustered out July 8, 1865.

18th INDPT. BATTERY LIGHT ARTILLERY.—Org. at Indianapolis Aug. 20, 1862. Sept., 1862, Arty., 12 Div., Army Ohio. Nov., 1862, Arty., 5 Div., Centre 14 Corps, Cumberland. Jany., 1863, Arty., 5 Div., 14 Corps, Cumberland. June, 1863, Arty., 4 Div., 14 Corps, Cumberland. June, 1863, Arty., Wilder's Mounted Brig., Cumberland. Nov., 1863, 3 Brig., 2 Cav. Div., Cumberland. Jany., 1864, Arty., 1 Cav. Div., Cumberland. Oct., 1864, Arty., 1 Div., Wilson's Cav. Corps, Mil. Div. Miss. Mustered out June 30, 1865.

19th INDPT. BATTERY LIGHT ARTILLERY.—Org. at Indianapolis Aug. 5, 1862. Sept., 1862, 34 Brig., 10 Div., Army Ohio. Oct., 1862, 34 Brig., 10 Div., 1 Corps, Army Ohio. Nov., 1862, Arty., 5 Div., Centre 14 Corps, Cumberland. Jany., 1863, Arty., 5 Div., 14 Corps, Cumberland. June, 1863, Arty., 4 Div., 14 Corps, Cumberland. Oct., 1863, Arty., 3 Div., 14 Corps, Cumberland. July, 1864, Arty. Brig., 14 Corps, Cumberland. Mustered out June 10, 1865.

20th INDPT. BATTERY LIGHT ARTILLERY.—Org. at Indianapolis Sept. 19, 1862. Dec., 1862, Dist. Western Ky., Dept. Ohio. May, 1863, Post and Dist. Nashville, Tenn., Dept. Cumberland. Jany., 1864, Arty., 1 Div., 11 Corps, Cumberland. April, 1864, Unatt., 4 Div., 20 Corps, Cumberland. July, 1864, Arty. Brig., 14 Corps, Cumberland. Nov., 1864, Arty., Provisional Div., Dist. Etowah, Dept. Cumberland. Jany., 1865, Garrison Arty., Chattanooga, Tenn., Cumberland. Mustered out June 10, 1865.

21st INDPT. BATTERY LIGHT ARTILLERY.—Org. at Indianapolis Sept. 9, 1862. Sept., 1862, Arty., 2 Div., Army Ky., Dept. Ohio. Oct., 1862, Unassigned, Army Ky., Dept. Ohio. Dec., 1862, Arty., 3 Div., Army Ky., Dept. Ohio. Feby., 1863, Crook's Brig., Baird's Div., Army Ky., Dept. Cumberland. June, 1863, Arty., 4 Div., 14 Corps, Cumberland. Oct., 1863, 2 Div., Arty. Res., Cumberland. March, 1864, Garrison Arty., Columbia, Dept. Cumberland. Nov., 1864, Garrison Arty., Nashville, Tenn., Cum-

berland. March, 1865, 2nd Sub-Dist., Dist. Middle Tenn., Dept. Cumberland. Mustered out June 26, 1865.

22nd INDPT. BATTERY LIGHT ARTILLERY.—Org. at Indianapolis Dec. 15, 1862. March, 1863, Unassigned, Army Ky., Dept. Ohio. June, 1863, 1 Brig., 2 Div., 23 Corps, Ohio. Aug., 1863, Russellsville, Ky., 1 Div., 23 Corps, Ohio. Dec., 1863, Dist. S. W. Ky., 1 Div., 23 Corps, Ohio. April, 1864, Camp Burnside, Ky., Dist. Ky., Dept. Ohio. June, 1864, Arty., 2 Div., 23 Corps, Ohio. Nov., 1864, Garrison Arty., Nashville, Tenn., Dept. Cumberland. Dec., 1864, Arty., 1 Div., 23 Corps, Ohio. Feby., 1865, Arty., 1 Div., 23 Corps, Dept. N. C. April, 1865, Arty., 1 Div., 10 Corps, Ohio, Dept. N. C. Mustered out July 7, 1865.

23rd INDPT. BATTERY LIGHT ARTILLERY.—Org. at Indianapolis Nov. 8, 1862. Nov., 1862, Indianapolis, Ind. July, 1863, Dist. Louisville, Ky., Dept. Ohio. Sept., 1863, Arty., Willcox's Div., Left Wing Forces 23 Corps, Ohio. Oct., 1863, 1 Brig., Willcox's Div., 23 Corps, Ohio. Jany., 1864, Dist. Clinch, Dept. Ohio. April, 1864, Arty., 1 Div., 23 Corps, Ohio. Aug., 1864, Arty., 3 Div., 23 Corps, Ohio. Feby., 1865, Arty., 3 Div., 23 Corps, Dept. N. C. Mustered out July 2, 1865.

24th INDPT. BATTERY LIGHT ARTILLERY.—Org. at Indianapolis Nov. 29, 1862. March, 1863, Dist. Western Ky., Dept. Ohio. June, 1863, 2 Brig., 3 Div., 23 Corps, Ohio. Aug., 1863, 2 Brig., 4 Div., 23 Corps, Ohio. Oct., 1863, Arty. Res., 23 Corps, Ohio. April, 1864, Arty., 1 Div., 23 Corps, Ohio. July, 1864, Arty., Cav. Div., 23 Corps, Ohio. Aug., 1864, Arty., 2 Div., 23 Corps, Ohio. Oct., 1864, Garrison Arty., Nashville, Tenn., Dept. Cumberland. Jany., 1865, Garrison Arty., Louisville, Ky. Mustered out Aug. 3, 1865.

25th INDPT. BATTERY LIGHT ARTILLERY.—Org. at Indianapolis Sept. 4 to Nov. 28, 1864. Dec., 1864, Arty. Brig., 4 Corps, Dept. Cumberland. Feby., 1865, Unatt. Arty., Dept. Cumberland. March, 1865, Garrison Arty., Decatur, Ala., Dept. Cumberland. Mustered out July 20, 1865.

26th INDPT. BATTERY LIGHT ARTILLERY ("WILDER'S" or "RIGBY'S INDPT. BATTERY").—Org. at Indianapolis June 12, 1861, as Co. A, 17th Ind. Infy. July, 1861, Reynolds, Cheat Mt. Dist., West Va. Nov., 1861, Milroy's Command, Cheat Mt., West Va. March, 1862, Milroy's Cheat Mt. Brig., Dept. Mts. June, 1862, Milroy's Indpt. Brig., 1 Corps, Army Va. July, 1862, Piatt's Brig., Winchester, Va. Aug., 1862, Trimble's Brig., White's Div., Winchester, Va. Sept., 1862, Miles' Command, Harper's Ferry, West Va. Captured Sept. 15, 1862. Oct., 1862, Camp Douglass, Ill., and Indianapolis, Ind. March, 1863, Central Dist. Ky., Dept. Ohio. June, 1863, 2 Brig., 1 Div., 23 Corps, Ohio. July, 1863, 2 Brig., 4 Div., 23 Corps, Ohio. Aug., 1863, Res. Arty., 23 Corps, Ohio. Oct., 1863, 2 Brig., 3 Div., 23 Corps, Ohio. April, 1864, 2 Brig., 4 Div., 23 Corps, Ohio. Feby., 1865, 2 Brig., 4 Div., Dist. East. Tenn., Dept. Cumberland. March, 1865, 1 Brig., 4 Div., Dist. East. Tenn., Dept. Cumberland. Mustered out July 19, 1865.

6th REGIMENT INFANTRY (3 MONTHS).—Org. at Indianapolis April 22-27, 1861. June, 1861, Kelly's Command, West Va. July, 1861, Morris' Brig., West Va. Mustered out Aug. 2, 1861.

6th REGIMENT INFANTRY (3 YEARS).—Org. at Madison Sept., 1861. Oct., 1861, 1 Brig., McCook's Div., at Nolin, Ky. Nov., 1861, 4 Brig., Army Ohio. Dec., 1861, 4 Brig., 2 Div., Army Ohio. Sept., 1862, 4 Brig., 2 Div., 1 Corps, Army Ohio. Nov., 1862, 3 Brig., 2 Div., Right Wing 14 Corps, Cumberland. Jany., 1863, 3 Brig., 2 Div., 20 Corps, Cumberland. Oct., 1863, 2 Brig., 3 Div., 4 Corps, Cumberland. Mustered out Sept. 22, 1864.

7th REGIMENT INFANTRY (3 MONTHS).—Org. at Indianapolis April 21-27, 1861. June, 1861, Kelly's Command, West Va. July, 1861, Morris' Brig., West Va. Mustered out Aug. 2, 1861.

7th REGIMENT INFANTRY (3 YEARS).—Org. at Indianapolis Sept. 13, 1861. Oct., 1861, Cheat Mt. Dist., West Va. Jany., 1862, 3 Brig., Lander's Div., Potomac. March, 1862, 3 Brig., Shields' 2 Div., Banks' 5 Corps. April, 1862, 3 Brig., Shields' Div., Dept. Shenandoah. May, 1862, 4 Brig., Shields' Div., Dept. Rappahannock.

June, 1862, 4 Brig., 2 Div., 3 Corps, Army Va. Sept., 1862, 2 Brig., 1 Div., 3 Corps, Army Va. Sept., 1862, 2 Brig., 1 Div., 1 Corps, Potomac. March, 1864, 2 Brig., 4 Div., 5 Corps, Potomac. April, 1864, 1 Brig., 4 Div., 5 Corps, Potomac. Aug., 1864, 3 Brig., 3 Div., 5 Corps, Potomac. Mustered out Sept. 20, 1864.

8th REGIMENT INFANTRY (3 MONTHS).—Org. at Indianapolis April 21-27, 1861. June, 1861, Rosecrans' Brig., Army West Va. Mustered out Aug. 6, 1861.

8th REGIMENT INFANTRY (3 YEARS).—Org. at Indianapolis Aug. 20 to Sept. 5, 1861. Sept., 1861, Army West, Dept. Mo. Jany., 1862, 1 Brig., 3 Div., Army S. W. Mo., Dept. Mo. May, 1862, 1 Div., Army S. W. Mo., Dept. Mo. July, 1862, Dist. Eastern Ark., Dept. Mo. Oct., 1862, 2 Brig., 1 Div., Dist. S. E. Mo., Dept. Mo. March, 1863, 1 Brig., 14 Div., 13 Corps, Tenn. July, 1863, 1 Brig., 1 Div., 13 Corps, Tenn. Aug., 1863, 1 Brig., 1 Div., 13 Corps, Gulf. June, 1864, Dist. LaFourche, Dept. Gulf. Aug., 1864, 3 Brig., 2 Div., 19 Corps, Middle Mil. Div. Aug., 1864, 4 Brig., 2 Div., 19 Corps, M. M. D. Dec., 1864, 1 Brig., 2 Div., 19 Corps, Army Shenandoah. Jany., 1865, 1 Brig., Grover's Div., Dist. Savannah, Ga., Dept. South. Mustered out Aug. 28, 1865.

9th REGIMENT INFANTRY (3 MONTHS).—Org. at Indianapolis April 22-27, 1861. June, 1861, Kelly's Command, West Va. July, 1861, Morris' Brig., West Va. Mustered out July 29, 1861.

9th REGIMENT INFANTRY (3 YEARS).—Org. at Laporte Sept. 5, 1861. Sept., 1861, Cheat Mt. Dist., West Va. March, 1862, 19 Brig., 4 Div., Army Ohio. Sept., 1862, 19 Brig., 4 Div., 2 Corps, Army Ohio. Nov., 1862, 2 Brig., 2 Div., Left Wing 14 Corps, Cumberland. Jany., 1863, 2 Brig., 2 Div., 21 Corps, Cumberland. Oct., 1863, 3 Brig., 1 Div., 4 Corps, Cumberland. June, 1865, 2 Brig., 1 Div., 4 Corps, Cumberland. Aug., 1865, Dept. Texas. Mustered out Sept. 28, 1865.

10th REGIMENT INFANTRY (3 MONTHS).—Org. at Indianapolis April 22-25, 1861. June, 1861, Rosecrans' Brig., Army West Va. Mustered out Aug. 6, 1861.

10th REGIMENT INFANTRY (3 YEARS).—Org. at Indianapolis Sept. 18, 1861. Oct., 1861, Bardstown, Ky., Thomas' Command, Army Ohio. Nov., 1861, 2 Brig., Army Ohio. Dec., 1861, 2 Brig., 1 Div., Army Ohio. Sept., 1862, 2 Brig., 1 Div., 3 Corps, Army Ohio. Nov., 1862, 2 Brig., 3 Div., Centre 14 Corps, Cumberland. Jany., 1863, 2 Brig., 3 Div., 14 Corps, Cumberland. Oct., 1863, 3 Brig., 3 Div., 14 Corps, Cumberland. Dec., 1863, Garrison Chattanooga, Tenn., Cumberland. April, 1864, 3 Brig., 3 Div., 14 Corps, Cumberland. Mustered out Sept. 19, 1864.

11th REGIMENT INFANTRY (3 MONTHS).—Org. at Indianapolis April 21-25, 1861. June, 1861, Unassigned, Dept. West Va. July, 1861, Patterson's Army. Mustered out Aug. 4, 1861.

11th REGIMENT INFANTRY (3 YEARS).—Org. at Indianapolis Aug. 31, 1861. Sept., 1861, Dist. Paducah, Ky., Dept. Mo. Feby., 1862, 5 Brig., 2 Div., Army Tenn. Feby., 1862, 1 Brig., 3 Div., Army Tenn. July, 1862, Helena, Ark., Dist. Eastern Ark., Dept. Mo. Dec., 1862, 3 Brig., 2 Div., Dist. Eastern Ark., Dept. Tenn. Jany., 1863, 3 Brig., 12 Div., 13 Corps, Tenn. Feby., 1863, 1 Brig., 12 Div., 13 Corps, Tenn. July, 1863, 1 Brig., 3 Div., 13 Corps, Tenn. Aug., 1863, 1 Brig., 3 Div., 13 Corps, Gulf. June, 1864, 2 Brig., 2 Div., 19 Corps, Gulf. Aug., 1864, 2 Brig., 2 Div., 19 Corps, Army Shenandoah, Middle Mil. Div. Jany., 1865, 2nd Separate Brig., 8 Corps, Middle Dept. Mustered out July 26, 1865.

12th REGIMENT INFANTRY (1 YEAR).—Org. at Indianapolis May, 1861. July, 1861, Abercrombie's Brig., Dept. Shenandoah. Oct., 1861, Abercrombie's Brig., Banks' Div., Potomac. March, 1862, 2 Brig., 1 Div., Banks' 5 Corps. April, 1862, 2 Brig., 1 Div., Dept. Shenandoah. Mustered out May 16, 1862.

12th REGIMENT INFANTRY (3 YEARS).—Org. at Indianapolis May 27 to Aug. 17, 1862. Aug., 1862, Cruft's Brig., Richmond, Ky., Army Ky., Dept. Ohio. Sept., 1862, Indianapolis, Ind. Nov., 1862, 2 Brig., Dist. Memphis, 13 Corps, Tenn. Nov., 1862, 1 Brig., 1 Div., Dist. Memphis, 13 Corps, Tenn. Dec., 1862, 1 Brig., 1 Div., 17 Corps, Tenn. Jany., 1863, 1 Brig., 1 Div., 16 Corps, Tenn.

July, 1863, 1 Brig., 4 Div., 15 Corps, Tenn., Sept., 1864, 1 Brig., 1 Div., 15 Corps, Tenn. Mustered out June 8, 1865.

13th REGIMENT INFANTRY.—Org. at Indianapolis June 19, 1861. June, 1861, Rosecrans' Brig., West Va. July, 1861, 1 Brig., Army Occupation, West Va. Sept., 1861, Reynolds' Cheat Mt. Brig., West Va. Nov., 1861, Milroy's Command, Cheat Mt. Dist., West Va. Jany., 1862, 2 Brig., Lander's Div., West Va. March, 1862, 2 Brig., Shields' 2 Div., Banks' 5 Corps. April, 1862, 2 Brig., Shields' Div., Dept. Shenandoah. May, 1862, 2 Brig., Shields' Div., Dept. Rappahannock. July, 1862, Ferry's 2 Brig., 2 Div., 4 Corps, Potomac. Sept., 1862, Ferry's Brig., Div. at Suffolk, Va., 7 Corps, Dept. Va. Sept., 1862, Foster's Provisional Brig., Div. at Suffolk, 7 Corps. April, 1863, 2 Brig., 1 Div., 7 Corps. July, 1863, 1 Brig., Vodges' Div., Folly Island, S. C., 10 Corps, Dept. South. Jany., 1864, 1 Brig., Vodges' Div., Folly Island, Northern Dist., Dept. South. Feby., 1864, 1 Brig., Vodges' Div., Dist. Fla., Dept. South. April, 1864, 2 Brig., 3 Div., 10 Corps, Army James, Dept. Va. and N. C. May, 1864, 2 Brig., 3 Div., 18 Corps. June, 1864, 3 Brig., 2 Div., 10 Corps. Dec., 1864, 3 Brig., 2 Div., 24 Corps. Jany., 1865, 3 Brig., 2 Div., Terry's Provisional Corps, Dept. N. C. March, 1865, 3 Brig., 2 Div., 10 Corps, Army Ohio, Dept. N. C. Mustered out Sept. 5, 1865.

14th REGIMENT INFANTRY.—Org. at Terre Haute June 7, 1861. July, 1861, 1 Brig., Army Occupation, West Va. Sept., 1861, Reynolds' Cheat Mt. Dist., West Va. Dec., 1861, 1 Brig., Lander's Div., West Va. March, 1862, 1 Brig., Shields' 2 Div., Banks' 5 Corps. April, 1862, 1 Brig., Shields' Div., Dept. Shenandoah. May, 1862, 1 Brig., Shields' Div., Dept. Rappahannock. June, 1862, Kimball's Indpt. Brig., 2 Corps, Potomac. Sept., 1862, 1 Brig., 3 Div., 2 Corps, Potomac. March, 1864, 3 Brig., 2 Div., 2 Corps, Potomac. Mustered out June 16, 1864.

15th REGIMENT INFANTRY.—Org. at Lafayette June 14, 1861. July, 1861, 1 Brig., Army Occupation, West Va. Sept., 1861, Reynolds' Command, Cheat Mt. Dist., West Va. Nov., 1861, 15 Brig., Army Ohio. Dec., 1861, 15 Brig., 4 Div., Army Ohio. March, 1862, 15 Brig., 8 Div., Army Ohio. March, 1862, 21 Brig., 6 Div., Army Ohio. Sept., 1862, 21 Brig., 6 Div., 2 Corps, Army Ohio. Nov., 1862, 2 Brig., 1 Div., Left Wing 14 Corps, Cumberland. Jany., 1863, 2 Brig., 1 Div., 21 Corps, Cumberland. Oct., 1863, 2 Brig., 2 Div., 4 Corps, Cumberland. Feby., 1864, Garrison at Chattanooga, Tenn., Dept. Cumberland. Mustered out June 25, 1864.

16th REGIMENT INFANTRY (1 YEAR).—Org. at Richmond May, 1861. July, 1861, Abercrombie's Brig., Dept. Shenandoah. Oct., 1861, Abercrombie's Brig., Banks' Div., Potomac. March, 1862, 2 Brig., 1 Div., Banks' 5 Corps. April, 1862, 2 Brig., 1 Div., Dept. Shenandoah. Mustered out May 23, 1862.

16th REGIMENT INFANTRY (3 YEARS).—Org. at Indianapolis May 27 to Aug. 19, 1862. Aug., 1862, Manson's Brig., Richmond, Ky., Army Ky. Nov., 1862, 1 Brig., 10 Div., Right Wing 13 Corps, Dept. Tenn. Dec., 1862, 1 Brig., 1 Div., Sherman's Yazoo Exp. Jany., 1863, 1 Brig., 10 Div., 13 Corps, Tenn. July, 1863, 1 Brig., 4 Div., 13 Corps, Tenn. Aug., 1863, 1 Brig., 4 Div., 13 Corps, Gulf. Sept., 1863, Unatt., Cav. Div., Gulf. Nov., 1863, 1 Brig., Cav. Div., Gulf. June, 1864, 4 Brig., Cav. Div., Gulf. Aug., 1864, Dist. LaFourche, Dept. Gulf. Mustered out June 30, 1865.

17th REGIMENT INFANTRY.—Org. at Indianapolis June 12, 1861. Aug., 1861, Unatt., Dist. Kanawha, West Va. Sept., 1861, Cheat Mt. Dist., West Va. Nov., 1861, 15 Brig., Army Ohio. Jany., 1862, 15 Brig., 4 Div., Army Ohio. Jany., 1862, 15 Brig., 6 Div., Army Ohio. Sept., 1862, 15 Brig., 6 Div., 2 Corps, Army Ohio. Nov., 1862, 1 Brig., 1 Div., Left Wing 14 Corps, Cumberland. Dec., 1862, 2 Brig., 5 Div., Centre 14 Corps, Cumberland. Jany., 1863, 2 Brig., 5 Div., 14 Corps, Cumberland. June, 1863, 1 Brig., 4 Div., 14 Corps, Cumberland. Oct., 1863, Wilder's Mounted Brig., Cumberland. Nov., 1863, 3 Brig., 2 Cav. Div., Cumberland. Nov., 1863, 2 Brig., 2 Cav. Div., Cumberland. Nov., 1863, 3 Brig., 2 Cav. Div., Cumberland. Oct., 1864, 1 Brig., 2 Div., Wilson's Cav. Corps, Mil. Div. Miss. Mustered out Aug. 8, 1865.

18th REGIMENT INFANTRY.—Org. at Indianapolis Aug. 16, 1861. Sept., 1861, Army West., Dept. Mo. Jany., 1862, 1 Brig., 3 Div., Army S. W. Mo., Dept. Mo. May, 1862, 1 Div., Army S. W. Mo., Dept. Mo. July, 1862, Dist. Eastern Ark., Dept. Mo. Oct., 1862, 2 Brig., 1 Div., Dist. S. E. Mo., Dept. Mo. March, 1863, 1 Brig., 14 Div., 13 Corps, Tenn. July, 1863, 1 Brig., 1 Div., 13 Corps, Tenn. Aug., 1863, 1 Brig., 1 Div., 13 Corps, Gulf. June, 1864, 3 Brig., 2 Div., 19 Corps, Gulf. Aug., 1864, 3 Brig., 2 Div., 19 Corps, Army Shenandoah, Middle Mil. Div. Aug., 1864, 4 Brig., 2 Div., 19 Corps, M. M. D. Dec., 1864, 1 Brig., 2 Div., 19 Corps. Jany., 1865, 1 Brig., Grover's Div., Dist. Savannah, Ga., Dept. South. Mustered out Aug. 28, 1865.

19th REGIMENT INFANTRY.—Org. at Indianapolis July 29, 1861. Aug., 1861, 3 Brig., McDowell's Div., Potomac. March, 1862, 1 Brig., King's 3 Div., 1 Corps, Potomac. April, 1862, 3 Brig., King's Div., Dept. Rappahannock. June, 1862, 4 Brig., 1 Div., 3 Corps, Army Va. Sept., 1862, 4 Brig., 1 Div., 1 Corps, Potomac. June, 1863, 1 Brig., 1 Div., 1 Corps, Potomac. March, 1864, 1 Brig., 4 Div., 5 Corps, Potomac. Aug., 1864, 3 Brig., 3 Div., 5 Corps, Potomac. Sept., 1864, 1 Brig., 3 Div., 5 Corps, Potomac. Consolidated with 20th Ind. Infy., Oct. 19, 1864.

20th REGIMENT INFANTRY.—Org. at Lafayette July 22, 1861. Aug., 1861, Baltimore, Md., Dix's Div. Sept., 1861, Hatteras Inlet, N. C., Dept. Va. Nov., 1861, Fortress Monroe, Va., Dept. Va. May, 1862, Robinson's Brig., Dept. Va. June, 1862, 1 Brig., 3 Div., 3 Corps, Potomac. Aug., 1862, 1 Brig., 1 Div., 3 Corps, Potomac. March, 1863, 2 Brig., 1 Div., 3 Corps, Potomac. March, 1864, 1 Brig., 3 Div., 2 Corps, Potomac. Mustered out July 12, 1865.

21st REGIMENT INFANTRY.—Org. at Indianapolis July 24, 1861. Aug., 1861, Dix's Div., Baltimore, Md. Feby., 1862, Butler's New Orleans Exp. March, 1862, 2 Brig., Dept. Gulf. Oct., 1862, Indpt. Command, Dept. Gulf. Jany., 1863, Unatt., 1 Div., 19 Corps, Gulf. Designation changed to 1st Ind. Heavy Arty., Feby., 1863.

22nd REGIMENT INFANTRY.—Org. at Madison Aug. 15, 1861. Sept., 1861, Army West, Dept. Mo. Jany., 1862, 1 Brig., 3 Div., Army S. W. Mo., Dept. Mo. May, 1862, 1 Brig., 4 Div., Army Miss. Sept., 1862, 30 Brig., 9 Div., Army Ohio. Sept., 1862, 30 Brig., 9 Div., 3 Corps, Army Ohio. Nov., 1862, 1 Brig., 1 Div., Right Wing 14 Corps, Cumberland. Jany., 1863, 1 Brig., 1 Div., 20 Corps, Cumberland. Oct., 1863, 2 Brig., 1 Div., 4 Corps, Cumberland. Oct., 1863, 1 Brig., 2 Div., 4 Corps, Cumberland. Jany., 1864, 3 Brig., 2 Div., 14 Corps, Cumberland. Mustered out July 24, 1865.

23rd REGIMENT INFANTRY.—Org. at New Albany, July 29, 1861. Aug., 1861, Dist. Paducah, Dept. Mo. Feby., 1862, 3 Brig., 3 Div., Army Tenn. March, 1862, 2 Brig., 3 Div., Army Tenn. July, 1862, Unatt., Dist. Jackson, Dept. Tenn. Nov., 1862, 2 Brig., 3 Div., Left Wing 13 Corps, Dept. Tenn. Dec., 1862, 1 Brig., 3 Div., Left Wing 13 Corps, Tenn. Dec., 1862, 1 Brig., 3 Div., 17 Corps, Tenn. Jany., 1864, 3 Brig., 4 Div., 17 Corps, Tenn. April, 1864, 1 Brig., 4 Div., 17 Corps, Tenn. Mustered out July 23, 1865.

24th REGIMENT INFANTRY.—Org. at Vincennes July 31, 1861. Aug., 1861., Army West, Dept. Mo. Feby., 1862, 1 Brig., 3 Div., Army Tenn. July, 1862, Helena, Ark., Dist. Eastern Ark., Dept. Mo. Nov., 1862, 3 Brig., 2 Div., Dist. Eastern Ark., Dept. Tenn. Jany., 1863, 3 Brig., 12 Div., 13 Corps, Tenn. Feby., 1863, 1 Brig., 12 Div., 13 Corps, Tenn. July, 1863, 1 Brig., 3 Div., 13 Corps, Tenn. Aug., 1863, 1 Brig., 3 Div., 13 Corps, Gulf. June, 1864, Bailey's Engr. Brig., Gulf. Aug., 1864, 2 Brig., 3 Div., 19 Corps, Gulf. Dec., 1864, 3 Brig., Res. Corps, Mil. Div. West. Miss. Feby., 1865, 2 Brig., 2 Div., Res. Corps, M. D. W. M. Feby., 1865, 2 Brig., 2 Div., 13 Corps, M. D. W. M. July, 1865, Dept. Texas. Mustered out Nov. 15, 1865.

25th REGIMENT INFANTRY.—Org. at Evansville Aug. 19, 1861. Sept., 1861, Army West, Dept. Mo. Dec., 1861, St. Louis, Mo. Feby., 1862, 3 Brig., 1 Div., Mil. Dist. Cairo. Feby., 1862, 4 Brig., 2 Div., Mil. Dist. Cairo. Feby., 1862, 2 Brig., 4 Div., Army Tenn. July, 1862, 2 Brig., 4 Div., Dist. Memphis, Tenn., Dept. Tenn. Sept., 1862, 2 Brig.,

4 Div., Dist. Jackson, Dept. Tenn. Nov., 1862, 3 Brig., 4 Div., Right Wing 13 Corps, Dept. Tenn. Dec., 1862, 3 Brig., 4 Div., 17 Corps, Tenn. Jany., 1863, Dist. Memphis, Tenn., 16 Corps, Tenn. March, 1863, 2 Brig., Dist. Memphis, 5 Div., 16 Corps, Tenn. Dec., 1863, 3 Brig., Cav. Div., 16 Corps, Tenn. Jany., 1864, 2 Brig., 4 Div., 16 Corps, Tenn. March, 1864, 3 Brig., 4 Div., 16 Corps, Tenn. Sept., 1864, 3 Brig., 1 Div., 17 Corps, Tenn. Mustered out July 17, 1865.

26th REGIMENT INFANTRY.—Org. at Indianapolis Aug. 30, 1861. Sept., 1861, Army West, Dept. Mo. Jany., 1862, Sedalia, Mo., Dept. Mo. June, 1862, Dist. S. W. Mo., Dept. Mo. Oct., 1862, 1 Brig., 2 Div., Army Frontier, Dept. Mo. June, 1863, 1 Brig., Herron's Div., 13 Corps, Tenn. July, 1863, 1 Brig., 2 Div., 13 Corps, Tenn. Aug., 1863, 1 Brig., 2 Div., 13 Corps, Gulf. June, 1864, Dist. LaFourche, Gulf. Feby., 1865, 1 Brig., 1 Div., 16 Corps, Mil. Div. West. Miss. Aug., 1865, Dept. Miss. Mustered out Jany. 15, 1866.

27th REGIMENT INFANTRY.—Org. at Indianapolis Sept. 12, 1861. Sept., 1861, Stiles' Brig., Banks' Div., Potomac. March, 1862, 3 Brig., 1 Div., Banks' 5 Corps. April, 1862, 3 Brig., 1 Div., Dept. Shenandoah. June, 1862, 3 Brig., 1 Div., 2 Corps, Army Va. Sept., 1862, 3 Brig., 1 Div., 12 Corps, Potomac. Oct., 1863, 3 Brig., 1 Div., 12 Corps, Cumberland. April, 1864, 2 Brig., 1 Div., 20 Corps, Cumberland. Mustered out Nov. 4, 1864.

28th REGIMENT.—(See 1st REGIMENT CAVALRY.)

29th REGIMENT INFANTRY.—Org. at Laporte Aug. 27, 1861. Oct., 1861, Wood's 2 Brig., McCook's Div., Nolin, Ky., Army Ohio. Nov., 1861, 5 Brig., Army Ohio. Dec., 1861, 5 Brig., 2 Div., Army Ohio. Sept., 1862, 5 Brig., 2 Div., 1 Corps, Army Ohio. Nov., 1862, 2 Brig., 2 Div., Right Wing 14 Corps, Cumberland. Jany., 1863, 2 Brig., 2 Div., 20 Corps, Cumberland. Oct., 1863, 1 Brig., 1 Div., 4 Corps, Cumberland. April, 1864, 1st Separate Brig., Garrison Chattanooga, Tenn., Dept. Cumberland. Jany., 1865, 2 Brig., 1st Separate Div., Dist. Etowah, Dept. Cumberland. May, 1865, 2 Brig., 2nd Separate Div., Dist. Etowah, Dept. Cumberland, and Dept. Ga. Mustered out Dec. 2, 1865.

30th REGIMENT INFANTRY.—Org. at Fort Wayne Sept. 24, 1861. Oct., 1861, Wood's 2 Brig., McCook's Div., at Nolin, Ky., Army Ohio. Nov., 1861, 5 Brig., Army Ohio. Dec., 1861, 5 Brig., 2 Div., Army Ohio. Sept., 1862, 5 Brig., 2 Div., 1 Corps, Army Ohio. Nov., 1862, 2 Brig., 2 Div., Right Wing 14 Corps, Cumberland. Jany., 1863, 2 Brig., 2 Div., 20 Corps, Cumberland. Oct., 1863, 3 Brig., 1 Div., 4 Corps, Cumberland. June, 1865, 2 Brig., 1 Div., 4 Corps, Cumberland. Aug., 1865, Dept. Texas. Mustered out Nov. 25, 1865.

31st REGIMENT INFANTRY.—Org. at Terre Haute Sept. 20, 1861. Oct., 1861, Owensburg, Ky. Nov., 1861, 13 Brig., Army Ohio. Dec., 1861, 13 Brig., 5 Div., Army Ohio. Feby., 1862, 1 Brig., 3 Div., Army Tenn. March, 1862, 3 Brig., 4 Div., Army Tenn. April, 1862, 22 Brig., 4 Div., Army Ohio. Sept., 1862, 22 Brig., 4 Div., 2 Corps, Army Ohio. Nov., 1862, 1 Brig., 2 Div., Left Wing 14 Corps, Cumberland. Jany., 1863, 1 Brig., 2 Div., 21 Corps, Cumberland. Oct., 1863, 1 Brig., 1 Div., 4 Corps, Cumberland. Aug., 1865, Dept. Texas. Mustered out Dec. 8, 1865.

32nd REGIMENT INFANTRY.—Org. at Indianapolis Aug. 24, 1861. Oct., 1861, Johnson's Brig., McCook's Div., Nolin, Ky., Army Ohio. Nov., 1861, 6 Brig., Army Ohio. Dec., 1861, 6 Brig., 2 Div., Army Ohio. Sept., 1862, 6 Brig., 2 Div., 1 Corps, Army Ohio. Nov., 1862, 1 Brig., 2 Div., Right Wing 14 Corps, Cumberland. Jany., 1863, 1 Brig., 2 Div., 20 Corps, Cumberland. Oct., 1863, 1 Brig., 3 Div., 4 Corps, Cumberland. Oct., 1864, Post Chattanooga, Tenn., Cumberland. Nov., 1864, 2 Brig., 1st Separate Div., Dist. Etowah, Dept. Cumberland. June, 1865, 1 Brig., 3 Div., 4 Corps, Cumberland. Aug., 1865, Dept. Texas. Mustered out Dec. 4, 1865.

33rd REGIMENT INFANTRY.—Org. at Indianapolis Sept. 16, 1861. Oct., 1861, Crab Orchard, Ky., Thomas' Command, Army Ohio. Nov., 1861, 1 Brig., Army Ohio. Dec., 1861, 1 Brig., 1 Div., Army Ohio. Feby., 1862, 27 Brig., 7 Div., Army Ohio. Oct., 1862, 1 Brig., 3 Div., Army Ky., Dept. Ohio. Feby., 1863, Coburn's Brig.,

Baird's Div., Army Ky., Dept. Cumberland. June, 1863, 3 Brig., 1 Div., Res. Corps, Cumberland. Oct., 1863, Coburn's Brig., Unatt., Post Murfreesboro, Tenn., Dept. Cumberland. Jany., 1864, 2 Brig., 1 Div., 11 Corps, Cumberland. April, 1864, 2 Brig., 3 Div., 20 Corps, Cumberland. Mustered out July 21, 1865.

34th REGIMENT INFANTRY.—Org. at Anderson Sept. 16, 1861. Oct., 1861, Jeffersonville, Ind. Nov., 1861, 10 Brig., Army Ohio. Dec., 1861, 10 Brig., 4 Div., Army Ohio. Feby., 1862, 1 Brig., 2 Div., Army Miss. April, 1862, 1 Brig., 3 Div., Army Miss., Garrison New Madrid. July, 1862, Helena, Ark., Dist. Eastern Ark., Dept. Mo. Nov., 1862, 3 Brig., 2 Div., Dist. Eastern Ark., Dept. Tenn. Jany., 1863, 3 Brig., 12 Div., 13 Corps, Tenn. Feby., 1863, 1 Brig., 12 Div., 13 Corps, Tenn. July, 1863, 1 Brig., 3 Div., 13 Corps, Tenn. Aug., 1863, 1 Brig., 3 Div., 13 Corps, Gulf. March, 1864, Def. New Orleans. Dec., 1864, Brazos, Santiago, U. S. Forces, Texas. June, 1865, Dept. Texas. Mustered out Feby. 3, 1866.

35th REGIMENT INFANTRY.—Org. at Indianapolis Dec. 11, 1861. March, 1862. Negley's 7 Indpt. Brig., Army Ohio. July, 1862, 23 Indpt. Brig., Army Ohio. Sept., 1862, 23 Brig., 5 Div., 2 Corps, Army Ohio. Nov., 1862, 3 Brig., 3 Div., Left Wing 14 Corps, Cumberland. Jany., 1863, 3 Brig., 3 Div., 21 Corps, Cumberland. Oct., 1863, 2 Brig., 1 Div., 4 Corps, Cumberland. Mustered out Sept. 30, 1865.

36th REGIMENT INFANTRY.—Org. at Richmond Sept. 16, 1861. Oct., 1861, Jeffersonville, Ind. Nov., 1861, 10 Brig., Army Ohio. Dec., 1861, 10 Brig., 4 Div., Army Ohio. Sept., 1862, 10 Brig., 4 Div., 2 Corps, Army Ohio. Nov., 1862, 3 Brig., 2 Div., Left Wing 14 Corps, Cumberland. Jany., 1863, 3 Brig., 2 Div., 21 Corps, Cumberland. Oct., 1863, 3 Brig., 1 Div., 4 Corps, Cumberland. June, 1865, 2 Brig., 1 Div., 4 Corps, Cumberland. Consolidated with 30th Ind. Infy., July 12, 1865.

37th REGIMENT INFANTRY.—Org. at Lawrenceburg Sept. 16, 1861. Oct., 1861, Mouth Salt River, Ky., Thomas' Command, Army Ohio. Nov., 1861, 8 Brig., Army Ohio. Dec., 1861, 8 Brig., 3 Div., Army Ohio. July, 1862, Unatt., Army Ohio, R. R. Guard. Sept., 1862, 7 Brig., 8 Div., Army Ohio. Nov., 1862, 3 Brig., 2 Div., Centre 14 Corps, Cumberland. Jany., 1863, 3 Brig., 2 Div., 14 Corps, Cumberland. Oct., 1863, 3 Brig., 1 Div., 14 Corps, Cumberland. Oct., 1864, 3 Brig., 2 Div., 14 Corps, Cumberland. Mustered out July 25, 1865.

38th REGIMENT INFANTRY.—Org. at New Albany Sept. 18, 1861. Oct., 1861, Wood's Brig., McCook's Command, Nolin, Ky., Army Ohio. Nov., 1861, 7 Brig., Army Ohio. Dec., 1861, 7 Brig., 2 Div., Army Ohio. March, 1862, 7 Indpt. Brig., Army Ohio. July, 1862, 9 Brig., 3 Div., Army Ohio. Sept., 1862, 9 Brig., 3 Div., 1 Corps, Army Ohio. Nov., 1862, 1 Brig., 1 Div., Centre 14 Corps, Cumberland. Jany., 1863, 1 Brig., 1 Div., 14 Corps, Cumberland. April, 1864, 3 Brig., 1 Div., 14 Corps, Cumberland. June, 1865, 1 Brig., 1 Div., 14 Corps. Mustered out July 15, 1865.

39th REGIMENT INFANTRY.—Org. at Indianapolis Aug. 29, 1861. Oct., 1861, Wood's Brig., McCook's Command, Nolin, Ky., Army Ohio. Nov., 1861, 6 Brig., Army Ohio. Dec., 1861, 6 Brig., 2 Div., Army Ohio. Sept., 1862, 6 Brig., 2 Div., 1 Corps, Army Ohio. Nov., 1862, 1 Brig., 2 Div., Right Wing 14 Corps, Cumberland. Jany., 1863, 1 Brig., 2 Div., 20 Corps, Cumberland. April, 1863, Unassigned, Cav. Corps, Cumberland. Designation changed to 8th Ind. Cav., Oct. 15, 1863.

40th REGIMENT INFANTRY.—Org. at Lafayette and Indianapolis Dec. 30, 1861. Jany., 1862, 21 Brig., Army Ohio. Jany., 1862, 21 Brig., 6 Div., Army Ohio. Sept., 1862, 21 Brig., 6 Div., 2 Corps, Army Ohio. Nov., 1862, 2 Brig., 1 Div., Left Wing 14 Corps, Cumberland. Jany., 1863, 2 Brig., 1 Div., 21 Corps, Cumberland. Oct., 1863, 2 Brig., 2 Div., 4 Corps, Cumberland. June, 1865, 1 Brig., 2 Div., 4 Corps, Cumberland. Aug., 1865, Dept. Texas. Mustered out Dec. 21, 1865.

41st REGIMENT.—(See 2nd REGIMENT CAVALRY.)

42nd REGIMENT INFANTRY.—Org. at Evansville Oct. 9, 1861. Nov., 1861, 14 Brig., Army Ohio. Dec., 1861, 14 Brig., 5 Div., Army Ohio. April, 1862, 17 Brig., 3 Div., Army Ohio. Sept., 1862, 17 Brig., 3 Div., 1 Corps,

Army Ohio. Nov., 1862, 2 Brig., 1 Div., Centre 14 Corps, Cumberland. Jany., 1863, 2 Brig., 1 Div., 14 Corps, Cumberland. April, 1863, 1 Brig., 2 Div., 14 Corps. Oct., 1863, 1 Brig., 1 Div., 14 Corps, Cumberland. Mustered out July 21, 1865.

43rd REGIMENT INFANTRY.—Org. at Terre Haute Sept. 27, 1861. Nov., 1861, 14 Brig., Army Ohio. Dec., 1861, 14 Brig., 5 Div., Army Ohio. Feby., 1862, 1 Brig., 2 Div., Army Miss. April, 1862, 2 Brig., 3 Div., Army Miss. July, 1862, Helena, Ark., Dist. Eastern Ark., Dept. Mo. Dec., 1862, 1 Brig., 2 Div., Dist. Eastern Ark., Dept. Tenn. Jany., 1863, 1 Brig., 12 Div., 13 Corps, Tenn. Feby., 1863, 1 Brig., 13 Div., 13 Corps, Tenn. July, 1863, 1 Brig., 13 Div., 16 Corps, Ark. Exp. Aug., 1863, 1 Brig., 3 Div., Ark. Exp. Jany., 1864, 1 Brig., 3 Div., 7 Corps, Dept. Ark. April, 1864, 2 Brig., 3 Div., 7 Corps, Ark. May, 1864, 2 Brig., 1 Div., 7 Corps, Ark. July, 1864, Camp Morton, Ind. Mustered out June 14, 1865.

44th REGIMENT INFANTRY.—Org. at Fort Wayne Nov. 22, 1861. Nov., 1861, 13 Brig., Army Ohio. Dec., 1861, 13 Brig., 5 Div., Army Ohio. Feby., 1862, 1 Brig., 3 Div., Army Tenn. March, 1862, 3 Brig., 4 Div., Army Tenn. April, 1862, 14 Brig., 5 Div., Army Ohio. Sept., 1862, 14 Brig., 5 Div., 2 Corps, Army Ohio. Nov., 1862, 2 Brig., 3 Div., Left Wing 14 Corps, Cumberland. Jany., 1863, 2 Brig., 3 Div., 21 Corps, Cumberland. Oct., 1863, 3 Brig., 3 Div., 4 Corps, Cumberland. Nov., 1863, Post Chattanooga, Tenn., Dept. Cumberland. April, 1864, 1st Separate Brig., Post Chattanooga, Tenn., Dept. Cumberland. Jany., 1865, 2 Brig., 1st Separate Div., Dist. Etowah, Dept. Cumberland. May, 1865, 2 Brig., 4 Div., Dist. East. Tenn., Dept. Cumberland. Mustered out Sept. 14, 1865.

45th REGIMENT.—(See 3rd REGIMENT CAVALRY.)

46th REGIMENT INFANTRY.—Org. at Logansport Nov. 1 to Dec. 2, 1861. Jany., 1862, 19 Brig., Army Ohio. Jany., 1862, 19 Brig., 4 Div., Army Ohio. Feby., 1862, 1 Brig., 2 Div., Army Miss. April, 1862, 2 Brig., 3 Div., Army Miss. July, 1862, Helena, Ark., Dist. Eastern Ark., Dept. Mo. Dec., 1862, 1 Brig., 2 Div., Dist. Eastern Ark., Dept. Tenn. Jany., 1863, 1 Brig., 12 Div., 13 Corps, Tenn. Feby., 1863, 1 Brig., 13 Div., 13 Corps, Tenn. March, 1863, 1 Brig., 12 Div., 13 Corps, Tenn. July, 1863, 1 Brig., 3 Div., 13 Corps, Tenn. Aug., 1863, 1 Brig., 3 Div., 13 Corps, Gulf. July, 1864, 4 Brig., 1 Div., Dist. Ky., Dept. Ohio. Dec., 1864, Garrison Lexington, Ky., Dist. Ky., Dept. Ohio. Mustered out Sept. 4, 1865.

47th REGIMENT INFANTRY.—Org. at Indianapolis Nov. 2 to Dec. 13, 1861. Jany., 1862, 19 Brig., Army Ohio. Jany., 1862, 19 Brig., 4 Div., Army Ohio. Feby., 1862, 1 Brig., 2 Div., Army Miss. April, 1862, 2 Brig., 3 Div., Army Miss. July, 1862, Helena, Ark., Dist. Eastern Ark., Dept. Mo. Dec., 1862, 1 Brig., 2 Div., Dist. Eastern Ark., Dept. Tenn. Jany., 1863, 1 Brig., 12 Div., 13 Corps, Tenn. Feby., 1863, 1 Brig., 13 Div., 13 Corps, Tenn. March, 1863, 2 Brig., 12 Div., 13 Corps, Tenn. July, 1863, 2 Brig., 3 Div., 13 Corps, Tenn. Aug., 1863, 2 Brig., 3 Div., 13 Corps, Gulf. June, 1864, Dist. LaFourche, Gulf. July, 1864, 2 Brig., 2 Div., 19 Corps, Gulf. Dec., 1864, 1 Brig., Res. Corps, Mil. Div. West. Miss. Feby., 1865, 1 Brig., 1 Div., Res. Corps, M. D. W. M. Feby., 1865, 1 Brig., 1 Div., 13 Corps, M. D. W. M. May, 1865, Dept. La. Mustered out Oct. 23, 1865.

48th REGIMENT INFANTRY.—Org. at Goshen Dec. 5, 1861, to Jany. 28, 1862. Feby., 1862, Dist. Paducah, Ky. May, 1862, 2 Brig., 3 Div., Army Miss. May, 1862, 1 Brig., 3 Div., Army Miss. Nov., 1862, 1 Brig., 7 Div., Left Wing 13 Corps, Dept. Tenn. Dec., 1862, 1 Brig., 7 Div., 16 Corps, Tenn. Jany., 1863, 1 Brig., 7 Div., 17 Corps, Tenn. Sept., 1863, 1 Brig., 2 Div., 17 Corps, Tenn. Dec., 1863, 1 Brig., 3 Div., 15 Corps, Tenn. April, 1865, 2 Brig., 4 Div., 15 Corps, Tenn. Mustered out July 15, 1865.

49th REGIMENT INFANTRY.—Org. at Jeffersonville Nov. 21, 1861. Dec., 1861, 12 Brig., 1 Div., Army Ohio. March, 1862, 24 Brig., 7 Div., Army Ohio. Oct., 1862, 3 Brig., Cumberland Div., Dist. West Va., Dept. Ohio. Nov., 1862, 2 Brig., 9 Div., Right Wing 13 Corps, Tenn. Dec., 1862, 2 Brig., 3 Div., Sherman's Yazoo Exp. Jany., 1863, 2 Brig., 9 Div., 13 Corps, Tenn. Feby, 1863, 1 Brig., 9

Div., 13 Corps, Tenn. July, 1863, 3 Brig., 1 Div., 13 Corps, Tenn. Aug., 1863, 3 Brig., 1 Div., 13 Corps, Gulf. March, 1864. 2 Brig., 1 Div., 13 Corps, Gulf. July, 1864, 4 Brig., 1 Div., Dist. Ky. Mustered out Sept. 13, 1865.

50th REGIMENT INFANTRY.—Org. at Seymour Sept. 12, 1861. Jany., 1862, 15 Brig., 4 Div., Army Ohio. June, 1862, Unassigned, R. R. Guard, Army Ohio. Sept., 1862, Captured at Munfordsville, Ky., Oct., 1862, Dist. Louisville, Ky., Dept. Ohio. Nov., 1862, Dist. Jackson, Tenn., 13 Corps, Dept. Tenn. Dec., 1862, 2 Brig., Dist. Jackson, 16 Corps, Tenn. March, 1863, 3 Brig., 3 Div., 16 Corps, Tenn. Aug., 1863, True's Brig., Ark. Exp. Jany., 1864, Unassigned, 2 Div., 7 Corps, Ark. April, 1864, 1 Brig., 3 Div., 7 Corps, Ark. May, 1864, 1 Brig., 1 Div., 7 Corps, Ark. Feby., 1865, 2 Brig., 3 Div., 13 Corps, Mil. Div. West. Miss. April, 1865, 3 Brig., 2 Div., 16 Corps, M. D. W. M. Consolidated with 52nd Ind. Infy., May 26, 1865.

51st REGIMENT INFANTRY.—Org. at Indianapolis Dec. 14, 1861. Jany., 1862, 20 Brig., Army Ohio. Jany., 1862, 20 Brig., 6 Div., Army Ohio. Sept., 1862, 20 Brig., 6 Div., 2 Corps, Army Ohio. Nov., 1862, 3 Brig., 1 Div., Left Wing 14 Corps, Cumberland. Jany., 1863, 3 Brig., 1 Div., 21 Corps, Cumberland. April, 1863, Straight's Provisional Brig., Dept. Cumberland. May, 1863, Captured. Prisoners of war. Dec., 1863, Post Chattanooga, Tenn., Dept. Cumberland. April, 1864, 1st Separate Brig., Chattanooga, Tenn., Dept. Cumberland. Sept., 1864, 2 Brig., 2 Div., 4 Corps, Cumberland. Nov., 1864, 1 Brig., 3 Div., 4 Corps, Cumberland. Aug., 1865, Dept. Texas. Mustered out Dec. 13, 1865.

52nd REGIMENT INFANTRY.—Org. at Rushville and Indianapolis Feby., 1, 1862. Feby., 1862, 1 Brig., 3 Div., Army Tenn. March, 1862, Garrison Forts Henry and Heiman, Tenn. April, 1862, 1 Brig., 4 Div., Army Tenn. May, 1862, 2 Brig., 4 Div., Army Tenn. July, 1862, 2 Brig., 4 Div., Dist. Memphis, Tenn., Dept. Tenn. Sept., 1862, Garrison Fort Pillow, Tenn. Nov., 1862, Dist. Columbus, 13 Corps, Dept. Tenn. Jany., 1863, Dist. Columbus, 6 Div., 16 Corps, Tenn. Jany., 1864, 3 Brig., 3 Div., 16 Corps, Tenn. Dec., 1864, 3 Brig., 2 Div., Detachment Army Tenn., Dept. Cumberland. Feby., 1865, 3 Brig., 2 Div., 16 Corps, Mil. Div. West. Miss. Mustered out Sept. 10, 1865.

53rd REGIMENT INFANTRY.—Org. at New Albany and Indianapolis Feby. 19 to March 6, 1862. March, 1862, 2 Brig., 4 Div., Army Tenn. July, 1862, 2 Brig., 4 Div., Dist. Memphis, Tenn., Dept. Tenn. Sept., 1862, 2 Brig., 4 Div., Dist. Jackson, Dept. Tenn. Nov., 1862, 3 Brig., 4 Div., Dist. Jackson, 13 Corps, Tenn. Dec., 1862, 3 Brig., 4 Div., 17 Corps, Tenn. Jany., 1863, 3 Brig., 4 Div., 16 Corps, Tenn. July, 1863, 3 Brig., 4 Div., 13 Corps, Tenn. Aug., 1863, 3 Brig., 4 Div., 17 Corps, Tenn. May, 1864, 1 Brig., 4 Div., 17 Corps, Tenn. Mustered out July 21, 1865.

54th REGIMENT INFANTRY.—Org. at Indianapolis for three months, May 30 to June 10, 1862. Duty at Camp Morton, Ind. Mustered out Oct. 4, 1862.

54th REGIMENT INFANTRY (1 YEAR).—Org. at Indianapolis Oct. and Nov., 1862. Dec., 1862, 3 Brig., 9 Div., Right Wing 13 Corps, Dept. Tenn. Dec., 1862, 3 Brig., 3 Div., Sherman's Yazoo Exp. Jany., 1863, 3 Brig., 9 Div., 13 Corps, Tenn. Feby., 1863, 2 Brig., 9 Div., 13 Corps, Tenn. July, 1863, 4 Brig., 1 Div., 13 Corps, Tenn. Aug., 1863, 4 Brig., 1 Div., 13 Corps, Gulf. Sept., 1863, 3 Brig., 1 Div., 13 Corps, Gulf. Mustered out Dec. 8, 1863.

55th REGIMENT INFANTRY.—Org. for three months at Indianapolis June 16, 1862. June, 1862, Camp Morton, Ind. Aug., 1862, Manson's Brig., Dist. Central Ky. Mustered out Sept. 6 to Oct. 21, 1862.

56th REGIMENT INFANTRY.—(Failed to complete organization.)

57th REGIMENT INFANTRY.—Org. at Indianapolis and Richmond Nov. 18, 1861. Jany., 1862, 21 Brig., Army Ohio. Jany., 1862, 21 Brig., 6 Div., Army Ohio. Sept., 1862, 21 Brig., 6 Div., 2 Corps, Army Ohio. Nov., 1862, 2 Brig., 1 Div., Left Wing 14 Corps, Cumberland. Jany., 1863, 2 Brig., 1 Div., 21 Corps, Cumberland. Oct., 1863, 2 Brig., 2 Div., 4 Corps, Cumberland. June, 1865, 1 Brig., 2 Div., 4 Corps, Cumberland. Aug., 1865, Dept. Texas. Mustered out Dec. 14, 1865.

58th REGIMENT INFANTRY.—Org. at Princeton and Indianapolis Nov. 12 to Dec. 22, 1861. Jany., 1862, 21 Brig., Army Ohio. March, 1862, 15 Brig., 6 Div., Army Ohio. Sept., 1862, 15 Brig., 6 Div., 2 Corps, Army Ohio. Nov., 1862, 1 Brig., 1 Div., Left Wing 14 Corps, Cumberland. Jany., 1863, 1 Brig., 1 Div., 21 Corps, Cumberland. Oct., 1863, 2 Brig., 2 Div., 4 Corps, Cumberland. April, 1864, Unatt., Pontooneers, Dept. Cumberland and Army Ga. Mustered out July 25, 1865.

59th REGIMENT INFANTRY.—Org. at Gosport and Indianapolis Feby. 11, 1862. Feby., 1862, 1 Brig., 2 Div., Army Miss. April, 1862, 2 Brig., 3 Div., Army Miss. April, 1862, 1 Brig., 3 Div., Army Miss. Nov., 1862, 1 Brig., 7 Div., Left Wing 13 Corps, Dept. Tenn. Dec., 1862, 1 Brig., 7 Div., 16 Corps, Tenn. Jany., 1863, 1 Brig., 7 Div., 17 Corps, Tenn. Sept., 1863, 1 Brig., 3 Div., 17 Corps, Tenn. Dec., 1863, 1 Brig., 3 Div., 15 Corps, Tenn. April, 1865, 2 Brig., 4 Div., 15 Corps, Tenn. Mustered out July 17, 1865.

60th REGIMENT INFANTRY.—Org. at Evansville and Indianapolis Feby. 19 to March 21, 1862. March, 1862, Camp Morton, Ind., June, 1862, Garrison Munfordsville, Ky. Captured Sept., 1862. Nov., 1862, 1 Brig., 10 Div., Right Wing 13 Corps, Dept. Tenn. Dec., 1862, 1 Brig., 1 Div., Sherman's Yazoo Exp. Jany., 1863, 1 Brig., 10 Div., 13 Corps, Tenn. Aug., 1863, 1 Brig., 4 Div., 13 Corps, Gulf. June, 1864, Dist. LaFourche, Dept. Gulf. Dec., 1864, Dist. Southern Ala., Dept. Gulf. Feby., 1865, 1 Brig., 2 Div., Res. Corps, Mil. Div. West. Miss. Feby., 1865, 1 Brig., 2 Div., 13 Corps, M. D. W. M. Mustered out March 11, 1865.

61st REGIMENT INFANTRY.—(Failed to complete organization.)

62nd REGIMENT INFANTRY.—(Failed to complete organization.)

63rd REGIMENT INFANTRY.—Org. at Lafayette Feby. 21, 1862. Feby., 1862, Prison Guard, Camp Morton, Ind. May, 1862, Sturgis' Brig., Def. Washington, D. C. Aug., 1862, Piatt's Brig., Potomac. Oct., 1862, Indianapolis, Ind. Dec., 1862, R. R. Guard, Dist. Western Ky., Dept. Ohio. June, 1863, Unatt., 2 Div., 23 Corps, Ohio. Aug., 1863, New Haven, Ky., 1 Div., 23 Corps, Ohio. Oct., 1863, Dist. S. C. Ky., 1 Div., 23 Corps, Ohio. Jany., 1864, Dist. S. W. Ky., 1 Div., 23 Corps, Ohio. April, 1864, 1 Brig., 3 Div., 23 Corps, Ohio. April, 1864, 2 Brig., 3 Div., 23 Corps, Ohio. Aug., 1864, 3 Brig., 3 Div., 23 Corps, Ohio. Feby., 1865, 3 Brig., 3 Div., 23 Corps, Dept. N. C. Mustered out June 21, 1865.

64th REGIMENT INFANTRY.—(Org. not completed. Intended to be organized as 1st Regt. L. Arty.)

65th REGIMENT INFANTRY.—Org. at Princeton Aug. 18 to Sept. 10, 1862. Unassigned, Dist. West. Ky., Dept. Ohio. June, 1863, 1 Brig., 2 Div., 23 Corps, Ohio. Aug., 1863, 2 Brig., 4 Div., 23 Corps, Ohio. Oct., 1863, 4 Brig., 4 Div., 23 Corps, Ohio. Nov., 1863, 2 Brig., 2 Cav. Div., Ohio. April, 1864, 2 Brig., 3 Div., 23 Corps, Ohio. Feby., 1865, 2 Brig., 3 Div., 23 Corps, Dept. N. C. Mustered out June 22, 1865.

66th REGIMENT INFANTRY.—Org. at New Albany Aug. 19, 1862. Aug., 1862, Cruft's Brig., 2 Div., Army Ky. Captured Aug. 30, 1862. Dec., 1862, 1 Brig., Dist. Corinth, 13 Corps, Dept. Tenn. Dec., 1862, 1 Brig., Dist. Corinth, 17 Corps, Tenn. Jany., 1863, 1 Brig., Dist. Corinth, 16 Corps, Tenn. March, 1863, 1 Brig., 2 Div., 16 Corps, Tenn. Sept., 1864, 1 Brig., 4 Div., 15 Corps, Tenn. Mustered out June 3, 1865.

67th REGIMENT INFANTRY.—Org. at Madison Aug. 20, 1862. Sept., 1862, 1 Brig., 2 Div., Army Ky., Dept. Ohio. Captured Munfordsville, Ky., Sept. 17, 1862. Nov., 1862, 1 Brig., 10 Div., Right Wing 13 Corps, Tenn. Dec., 1862, 1 Brig., 1 Div., Sherman's Yazoo Exp. Jany., 1863, 1 Brig., 10 Div., 13 Corps, Tenn. Aug., 1863, 1 Brig., 4 Div., 13 Corps. Gulf. June, 1864, 3 Brig., 3 Div., 19 Corps, Gulf. Dec., 1864, 3 Brig., Res. Corps, Mil. Div. West. Miss. Consolidated with 24th Ind. Infy., Dec. 21, 1864.

68th REGIMENT INFANTRY.—Org. at Indianapolis Aug. 19, 1862. Aug., 1862, 1 Brig., 2 Div., Army Ky.,

Dept. Ohio. Sept., 1862, Captured at Munfordsville, Ky. Jany., 1863, 2 Brig., 4 Div., 14 Corps, Cumberland. Oct., 1863, 2 Brig., 3 Div., 14 Corps, Cumberland. Oct., 1863, 1 Brig., 3 Div., 4 Corps, Cumberland. April, 1864, Garrison at Chattanooga, Tenn., Dept. Cumberland. Nov., 1864, 2 Brig., 1st Separate Div., Dist. Etowah, Dept. Cumberland. Mustered out June 20, 1865.

69th REGIMENT INFANTRY.—Org. at Richmond Aug. 19, 1862. Aug., 1862, Manson's 1 Brig., Army Ky., Dept. Ohio. Captured at Richmond, Ky., Aug. 30, 1862. Nov., 1862, 1 Brig., 9 Div., Right Wing 13 Corps, Dept. Tenn. Dec., 1863, 1 Brig., 3 Div., Sherman's Yazoo Exp. Jany., 1863, 1 Brig., 9 Div., 13 Corps, Tenn. July, 1863, 3 Brig., 1 Div., 13 Corps, Tenn. Aug., 1863, 3 Brig., 1 Div., 13 Corps, Gulf. March, 1864, 2 Brig., 1 Div., 13 Corps, Gulf. June, 1864, 2 Brig., 3 Div., 19 Corps, Gulf. Dec., 1864, Dist. Southern Ala., Dept. Gulf. Dec., 1864, 3 Brig., Res. Corps, Mil. Div. West. Miss. Feby., 1865, 2 Brig., 2 Div., Res. Corps, M. D. W. M. Feby., 1865, 2 Brig., 2 Div., 13 Corps, M. D. W. M. Mustered out July 5, 1865.

70th REGIMENT INFANTRY.—Org. at Indianapolis July 22 to Aug. 8, 1862. Sept., 1862, Dist. Louisville, Ky., Dept. Ohio. Nov., 1862, Ward's Brig., Dumont's Div. (12) Army Ohio and Cumberland. Dec., 1862, Ward's Brig., Post Gallatin, Tenn., Dept. Cumberland. June, 1863, 2 Brig., 3 Div., Res. Corps, Cumberland. Oct., 1863, Ward's Brig., Post and Dist. Nashville, Tenn., Dept. Cumberland. Jany., 1864, 1 Brig., 1 Div., 11 Corps, Cumberland. April, 1864, 1 Brig., 3 Div., 20 Corps, Cumberland. Mustered out June 8, 1865.

71st REGIMENT INFANTRY.—Org. at Terre Haute July 21 to Aug. 26, 1862. Aug., 1862, Manson's 1 Brig., Richmond, Ky. Captured Aug. 30, 1862. Dec., 1862, Dist. Ky., Dept. Ohio. Captured Dec. 28, 1862, at Muldraugh's Hill, Ky. Designation changed to 6th Regt. Cav., Feby. 23, 1863.

72nd REGIMENT INFANTRY.—Org. at Lafayette Aug. 16, 1862. Sept., 1862, 40 Brig., 12 Div., Army Ohio. Nov., 1862, 2 Brig., 5 Div., Centre 14 Corps, Cumberland. Jany., 1863, 2 Brig., 5 Div., 14 Corps, Cumberland. June, 1863, 1 Brig., 4 Div., 14 Corps, Cumberland. Oct., 1863, Wilder's Mounted Infy. Brig., Cav. Corps, Cumberland. Dec., 1863, 3 Brig., 2 Cav. Div., Cumberland. Jany., 1864, 3 Brig., Grierson's Cav. Div., 16 Corps, Tenn. March, 1864, 3 Brig., 2 Cav. Div., Cumberland. Oct., 1864, 1 Brig., 2 Div., Wilson's Cav. Corps, Mil. Div. Miss. Mustered out June 26, 1865.

73rd REGIMENT INFANTRY.—Org. at South Bend Aug. 16, 1862. Sept., 1862, 20 Brig., 6 Div., Army Ohio. Sept., 1862, 20 Brig., 6 Div., 2 Corps, Army Ohio. Nov., 1862, 3 Brig., 1 Div., Left Wing 14 Corps, Cumberland. Jany., 1863, 3 Brig., 1 Div., 21 Corps, Cumberland. April, 1863, Streight's Provisional Brig., Cumberland. Captured May 3, 1863. Dec., 1863, Post and Dist. Nashville, Dept. Cumberland. Jany., 1864, 1 Brig., Dist. Nashville, Dept. Cumberland. Jany., 1864, 1 Brig., Rousseau's 3 Div., 12 Corps, Cumberland. April, 1864, 1 Brig., 4 Div., 20 Corps, Cumberland. March, 1865, Dist. Northern Ala., Dept. Cumberland. Mustered out July 1, 1865.

74th REGIMENT INFANTRY.—Org. at Fort Wayne Aug. 21, 1862. Sept., 1862, 2 Brig., 1 Div., Army Ohio. Sept., 1862, 2 Brig., 1 Div., 3 Corps, Army Ohio. Nov., 1862, 2 Brig., 3 Div., Centre 14 Corps, Cumberland. Jany., 1863, 2 Brig., 3 Div., 14 Corps, Cumberland. Oct., 1863, 3 Brig., 3 Div., 14 Corps, Cumberland. Mustered out June 9, 1865.

75th REGIMENT INFANTRY.—Org. at Wabash Aug. 19, 1862. Sept., 1862, 40 Brig., 12 Div., Army Ohio. Nov., 1862, 2 Brig., 5 Div., Centre 14 Corps, Cumberland. Jany., 1863, 2 Brig., 5 Div., 14 Corps, Cumberland. June, 1863, 2 Brig., 4 Div., 14 Corps, Cumberland. Oct., 1863, 2 Brig., 3 Div., 14 Corps, Cumberland. Mustered out June 8, 1865.

76th REGIMENT INFANTRY.—Org. at Indianapolis July 20, 1862. Mustered out Aug. 20, 1862.

77th REGIMENT.—(See 4th REGIMENT CAVALRY.)

78th REGIMENT INFANTRY.—Org. at Indianapolis Aug. 5, 1862. Mustered out Oct. 3, 1862.

79th REGIMENT INFANTRY.—Org. at Indianapolis Aug. 20 to Sept. 2, 1862. Sept., 1862, 11 Brig., 5 Div., Army Ohio. Sept., 1862, 11 Brig., 5 Div., 2 Corps, Army Ohio. Nov., 1862, 1 Brig., 3 Div., Left Wing, 14 Corps, Cumberland. Jany., 1863, 1 Brig., 3 Div., 21 Corps, Cumberland. Oct., 1863, 3 Brig., 3 Div., 4 Corps, Cumberland. Mustered out June 7, 1865.

80th REGIMENT INFANTRY.—Org. at Princeton and Indianapolis Sept. 8, 1862. Sept., 1862, 34 Brig., 10 Div., Army Ohio. Sept., 1862, 34 Brig., 10 Div., 1 Corps, Army Ohio. Nov., 1862, Dist. Western Ky., Dept. Ohio. June, 1863, 2 Brig., 3 Div., 23 Corps, Ohio. Aug., 1863, 1 Brig., 2 Div., 23 Corps, Ohio. June, 1864, 2 Brig., 2 Div., 23 Corps, Ohio. Feby., 1865, 2 Brig., 2 Div., 23 Corps, Dept. N. C. Mustered out June 22, 1865.

81st REGIMENT INFANTRY.—Org. at New Albany Aug. 29, 1862. Sept., 1862, 32 Brig., 9 Div., Army Ohio. Sept., 1862, 32 Brig., 9 Div., 3 Corps, Army Ohio. Nov., 1862, 3 Brig., 1 Div., Right Wing, Army Cumberland. Jany., 1863, 3 Brig., 1 Div., 20 Corps, Cumberland. March, 1863, 2 Brig., 1 Div., 20 Corps, Cumberland. Oct., 1863, 1 Brig., 1 Div., 4 Corps, Cumberland. Mustered out June 13, 1865.

82nd REGIMENT INFANTRY.—Org. at Indianapolis and Camp Emerson Aug. 30, 1862. Sept., 1862, 1 Brig., 1 Div., Army Ohio. Sept., 1862, 1 Brig., 1 Div., 3 Corps, Army Ohio. Nov., 1862, 1 Brig., 3 Div., Centre 14 Corps, Cumberland. Jany., 1863, 1 Brig., 3 Div., 14 Corps, Cumberland. Mustered out June 9, 1865.

83rd REGIMENT INFANTRY.—Org. at Lawrenceburg Sept. 4 to Nov. 5, 1862. Nov., 1862, 4 Brig., 5 Div., Dist. Memphis, Tenn., 13 Corps, Dept. Tenn. Nov., 1862, 2 Brig., 2 Div., Dist. Memphis, Tenn., 13 Corps, Dept. Tenn. Dec., 1862, 2 Brig., 2 Div., Sherman's Yazoo Exp. Jany., 1863, 2 Brig., 2 Div., 15 Corps, Tenn. Mustered out June 3, 1865.

84th REGIMENT INFANTRY.—Org. at Richmond and Indianapolis Sept. 3, 1862. Sept., 1862, Covington, Ky., Dept. Ohio. Oct., 1862, 3 Brig., Kanawha Div., West Va., Dept. Ohio. Nov., 1862, Dist. Eastern Ky., Dept. Ohio. Feby., 1863, 2 Brig., Baird's 3 Div., Army Ky., Dept. Ohio. Feby., 1863, Baird's Div., Franklin, Tenn., Dept. Cumberland. June, 1863, 1 Brig., 1 Div., Reserve Corps, Dept. Cumberland. Oct., 1863, 2 Brig., 1 Div., 4 Corps, Cumberland. Aug., 1864, 3 Brig., 1 Div., 4 Corps, Cumberland. Mustered out June 14, 1865.

85th REGIMENT INFANTRY.—Org. at Terre Haute Sept. 2, 1862. Sept., 1862, 1 Brig., 2 Div., Army Ky., Dept. Ohio. Oct., 1862, 1 Brig., 3 Div., Army Ky., Dept. Ohio. Feby., 1863, Coburn's Brig., Baird's Div., Army Ky., Dept. Cumberland. June, 1863, 3 Brig., 1 Div., Res. Corps, Cumberland. Oct., 1863, Coburn's Unatt. Brig., Dept. Cumberland. Dec., 1863, Coburn's Brig., Post Murfreesboro, Tenn., Dept. Cumberland. Jany., 1864, 2 Brig., 1 Div., 11 Corps, Cumberland. April, 1864, 2 Brig., 3 Div., 20 Corps, Cumberland. Mustered out June 12, 1865.

86th REGIMENT INFANTRY.—Org. at Lafayette Sept. 4, 1862. Sept., 1862, 14 Brig., 5 Div., Army Ohio. Sept., 1862, 14 Brig., 5 Div., 2 Corps, Army Ohio. Nov., 1862, 2 Brig., 3 Div., Left Wing 14 Corps, Cumberland. Jany., 1863, 2 Brig., 3 Div., 21 Corps, Cumberland. Oct., 1863, 3 Brig., 3 Div., 4 Corps, Cumberland. Mustered out June 6, 1865.

87th REGIMENT INFANTRY.—Org. at South Bend Aug. 31, 1862. Sept., 1862, 3 Brig., 1 Div., Army Ohio. Sept., 1862, 3 Brig., 1 Div., 3 Corps, Army Ohio. Nov., 1862, 3 Brig., 3 Div., Centre 14 Corps Cumberland. Jany., 1863, 3 Brig., 3 Div., 14 Corps, Cumberland. Oct., 1863, 2 Brig., 3 Div., 14 Corps, Cumberland. Mustered out June 10, 1865.

88th REGIMENT INFANTRY.—Org. at Fort Wayne Aug. 29, 1862. Sept., 1862, 17 Brig., 3 Div., Army Ohio. Sept., 1862, 17 Brig., 3 Div., 1 Corps, Army Ohio. Nov., 1862, 2 Brig., 1 Div., Centre 14 Corps, Cumberland. Jany., 1863, 2 Brig., 1 Div., 14 Corps, Cumberland. April, 1863, 1 Brig., 2 Div., 14 Corps, Cumberland. Oct., 1863, 1 Brig., 1 Div., 14 Corps, Cumberland. Mustered out June 7, 1865.

89th REGIMENT INFANTRY.—Org. at Indianapolis Aug. 28, 1862. Sept., 1862, Munfordsville, Ky., Dept.

Ohio. Captured Sept., 17, 1862. Oct., 1862, Indianapolis, Ind. Jany., 1863, Dist. Memphis, Tenn., 16 Corps, Tenn. March, 1863, 1 Brig., Dist. Memphis, Tenn., 5 Div., 16 Corps, Tenn. Jany., 1864, 1 Brig., 3 Div., 16 Corps, Tenn. March, 1864, 1 Brig., 3 Div., 16 Corps, Detachment Army Tenn., Dept. Gulf. June, 1863, 1 Brig., 3 Div., 16 Corps, Dept. Tenn. Dec., 1863, 1 Brig., 2 Div., Detachment Army Tenn., Dept. Cumberland. Feby., 1865, 1 Brig., 2 Div., 16 Corps, Mil. Div. West. Miss. Mustered out July 19, 1865.

90th REGIMENT.—(See 5th REGIMENT CAVALRY.)

91st REGIMENT INFANTRY.—Org. at Evansville Oct. 1, 1862. Dec., 1862, Dist. Western Ky., Dept. Ohio. June, 1863, 1 Brig., 2 Div., 23 Corps, Ohio. Aug., 1863, Russellville, Ky., 1 Div., 23 Corps, Ohio. Oct., 1863, Dist. S. W. Ky., Dept. Ohio. Oct., 1863, Dist. Somerset, Ky., 1 Div., 23 Corps, Ohio. Jany., 1864, Dist. Clinch, Dept. Ohio. April, 1864, 1 Brig., 4 Div., 23 Corps, Ohio. June, 1864, 1 Brig., 2 Div., 23 Corps, Ohio. Aug., 1864, 3 Brig., 2 Div., 23 Corps, Ohio. Feby., 1865, 3 Brig., 2 Div., 23 Corps, Dept. N. C. Mustered out June 28, 1865.

92nd REGIMENT INFANTRY.—(Failed to complete organization.)

93rd REGIMENT INFANTRY.—Org. at Madison, Indianapolis and New Albany, Aug. 15 to Oct. 31, 1862. Nov., 1862, 5 Brig., Dist. Memphis, Tenn., 13 Corps, Dept. Tenn. Nov., 1862, 3 Brig., 1 Div., Dist. Memphis, 13 Corps, Tenn. Dec., 1862, 3 Brig., 8 Div., 16 Corps, Tenn. April, 1863, 1 Brig., 3 Div., 15 Corps, Tenn. Dec., 1863, 1 Brig., 1 Div., 16 Corps, Tenn. Dec., 1864, 1 Brig., 1 Div., Detachment Army Tenn., Dept. Cumberland. Feby., 1865, 1 Brig., 1 Div., 16 Corps, Mil. Div. West. Miss. Mustered out Aug. 10, 1865.

94th REGIMENT INFANTRY.—(Failed to complete organization.)

95th REGIMENT INFANTRY.—(Failed to complete organization.)

96th REGIMENT INFANTRY.—(Failed to complete organization.)

97th REGIMENT INFANTRY.—Org. at Terre Haute Sept. 20, 1862. Oct., 1862, Dist. Louisville, Ky., Dept. Ohio. Nov., 1862, 3 Brig., Dist. Memphis, Tenn., 13 Corps, Tenn. Nov., 1862, 2 Brig., 1 Div., Dist. Memphis, 13 Corps, Tenn. Dec., 1862, 2 Brig., 1 Div., 17 Corps, Tenn. Jany., 1863, 2 Brig., 1 Div., 16 Corps, Tenn. March, 1863, 3 Brig., 1 Div., 16 Corps, Tenn. July, 1863, 3 Brig., 4 Div., 15 Corps, Tenn. April, 1864, 2 Brig., 4 Div., 15 Corps, Tenn. Aug., 1864, 2 Brig., 1 Div., 15 Corps, Tenn. Mustered out June 9, 1865.

98th REGIMENT INFANTRY.—(Failed to complete organization.)

99th REGIMENT INFANTRY.—Org. at South Bend Oct. 21, 1862. Oct., 1862, Dist. Louisville, Ky., Dept. Ohio. Nov., 1862, 3 Brig., Dist. Memphis, Tenn., 13 Corps, Dept. Tenn. Nov., 1862, 2 Brig., 1 Div., Dist. Memphis, 13 Corps, Tenn., Dec., 1862, 2 Brig., 1 Div., 17 Corps, Tenn. Jany., 1863, 2 Brig., 1 Div., 16 Corps, Tenn., March, 1863, 3 Brig., 1 Div., 16 Corps, Tenn. July, 1863, 3 Brig., 4 Div., 15 Corps, Tenn. Aug., 1864, 1 Brig., 4 Div., 15 Corps, Tenn. Sept., 1864, 3 Brig., 2 Div., 15 Corps, Tenn. Mustered out June 5, 1865.

100th REGIMENT INFANTRY.—Org. at Fort Wayne Sept. 10, 1862. Nov., 1862, 2 Brig., Dist. Memphis, Tenn., 13 Corps, Dept. Tenn. Nov., 1862, 1 Brig., 1 Div., Dist. Memphis, 13 Corps, Dept. Tenn. Dec., 1862, 1 Brig., 1 Div., 17 Corps, Tenn. Jany., 1863, 1 Brig., 1 Div., 16 Corps, Tenn. July, 1863, 1 Brig., 4 Div., 15 Corps, Tenn. Aug., 1864, 2 Brig., 4 Div., 15 Corps, Tenn. Sept., 1864, 2 Brig., 1 Div., 15 Corps, Tenn. Mustered out June 8, 1865.

101st REGIMENT INFANTRY.—Org. at Wabash Sept., 1862. Sept., 1862, 33 Brig., 10 Div., Army Ohio. Sept., 1862, 33 Brig., 10 Div., 1 Corps, Army Ohio. Nov., 1862, 2 Brig., 5 Div., Centre 14 Corps Cumberland. Jany., 1863, 1 Brig., 5 Div., 14 Corps, Cumberland. June, 1863, 2 Brig., 4 Div., 14 Corps, Cumberland. Oct., 1863, 2 Brig., 3 Div., 14 Corps, Cumberland. June, 1865, 1 Brig., 3 Div., 14 Corps, Cumberland. Mustered out June 24, 1865.

102nd, 103rd, 104th, 105th, 106th, 107th, 108th, 109th, 110th, 111th, 112th, 113th and 114th REGIMENTS IN-

FANTRY.—Org. for Morgan Raid July 10, 1863. Mustered out July 16-18, 1863.

115th REGIMENT INFANTRY.—Org. at Indianapolis Aug. 13, 1863. Sept., 1863, Mahan's 1 Brig., Willcox's Div., Left Wing Forces 23 Corps, Dept. Ohio. Mustered out Feby. 25, 1864.

116th REGIMENT INFANTRY.—Org. at Lafayette Aug. 17, 1863. Sept., 1863, Mahan's 1 Brig., Willcox's Div., Left Wing Forces 23 Corps, Dept. Ohio. Oct., 1863, 2 Brig., Willcox's Div., Left Wing Forces, Dept. Ohio. Jany., 1864, Dist. Clinch, Dept. Ohio. Mustered out Feby. 29 to March 2, 1864.

117th REGIMENT INFANTRY.—Org. at Indianapolis Sept. 17, 1863. Sept., 1863, Mahan's 1 Brig., Willcox's Left Wing Forces, 23 Corps, Dept. Ohio. Dec., 1863, 1 Brig., 3 Div., 23 Corps, Ohio. Jany., 1864, Dist. Clinch, Dept. Ohio. Mustered out Feby. 23-27, 1864.

118th REGIMENT INFANTRY.—Org. at Wabash July and Aug., 1863. Sept., 1863, Mahan's 1 Brig., Willcox's Left Wing Forces, 23 Corps, Dept. Ohio. Oct., 1863, 2 Brig., Willcox's Left Wing Forces, Dept. Ohio. Jany., 1864, Dist. Clinch, Dept. Ohio. Mustered out March 1-4, 1864.

119th REGIMENT.—(See 7th REGIMENT CAVALRY.)

120th REGIMENT INFANTRY.—Org. at Columbus Dec., 1863, to March, 1864. April, 1864, 1 Brig., 1 Div., 23 Corps, Ohio. June, 1864, 4 Brig., 3 Div., 23 Corps, Ohio. Aug., 1864, 3 Brig., 3 Div., 23 Corps, Ohio. Dec., 1864, 1 Brig., 1 Div., 23 Corps, Ohio. Feby., 1865, 1 Brig., 1 Div., 23 Corps, Dept. N. C. Aug., 1865, Dept. N. C. Mustered out Jany. 8, 1866.

121st REGIMENT.—(See 9th REGIMENT CAVALRY.)

122nd REGIMENT INFANTRY.—(Failed to complete organization.)

123rd REGIMENT INFANTRY.—Org. at Greensburg, Terre Haute and Indianapolis, Dec. 25, 1863, to March 7, 1864. April, 1864, 2 Brig., 1 Div., 23 Corps, Ohio. June, 1864, 4 Brig., 2 Div., 23 Corps, Ohio. Aug., 1864, 3 Brig., 2 Div., 23 Corps, Ohio. Dec., 1864, 2 Brig., 1 Div., 23 Corps, Ohio. Feby., 1865, 2 Brig., 1 Div., 23 Corps, Dept. N. C. Mustered out Aug. 25, 1865.

124th REGIMENT INFANTRY.—Org. at Richmond, Terre Haute and Indianapolis, Nov., 1863, to March, 1864. April, 1864, 1 Brig., 1 Div., 23 Corps, Ohio. June, 1864, 4 Brig., 3 Div., 23 Corps, Ohio. Aug., 1864, 2 Brig., 3 Div., 23 Corps, Ohio. Dec., 1864, 1 Brig., 1 Div., 23 Corps, Ohio. Feby., 1865, 1 Brig., 1 Div., 23 Corps, Dept. N. C. Mustered out Aug. 31, 1865.

125th REGIMENT.—(See 10th REGIMENT CAVALRY.)
126th REGIMENT.—(See 11th REGIMENT CAVALRY.)
127th REGIMENT.—(See 12th REGIMENT CAVALRY.)

128th REGIMENT INFANTRY.—Org. at Michigan City Dec. 15, 1863, to March 7, 1864. April, 1864, 1 Brig., 1 Div., 23 Corps, Ohio. June, 1864, 4 Brig., 3 Div., 23 Corps, Ohio. Aug., 1864, 3 Brig., 3 Div., 23 Corps, Ohio. Dec., 1864, 1 Brig., 1 Div., 23 Corps, Ohio. Feby., 1865, 1 Brig., 1 Div., 23 Corps, Dept. N. C. Aug., 1865, Dept. N. C. Mustered out April 10, 1866.

129th REGIMENT INFANTRY.—Org. at Kendallsville and Michigan City, Dec. 16, 1863, to March 1, 1864. April, 1864, 2 Brig., 1 Div., 23 Corps, Ohio. June, 1864, 4 Brig., 2 Div., 23 Corps, Ohio. Aug., 1864, 2 Brig., 2 Div., 23 Corps, Ohio. Dec., 1864, 2 Brig., 1 Div., 23 Corps, Ohio. Feby., 1865, 2 Brig., 1 Div., 23 Corps, Dept. N. C. Mustered out Aug. 29, 1865.

130th REGIMENT INFANTRY.—Org. at Kokomo, Dec., 1863, to March, 1864. April, 1864, 2 Brig., 1 Div., 23 Corps, Ohio. June, 1864, 4 Brig., 2 Div., 23 Corps, Ohio. Aug., 1864, 1 Brig., 2 Div., 23 Corps, Ohio. Dec., 1864, 2 Brig., 1 Div., 23 Corps, Ohio. Feby., 1865, 2 Brig., 1 Div., 23 Corps, Dept. N. C. Aug., 1865, Dept. N. C. Mustered out Dec. 2, 1865.

131st REGIMENT INFANTRY.—See 13th Regiment Cavalry.

132nd REGIMENT INFANTRY.—Org. at Indianapolis, May 18, 1864. May, 1864, R. R. Guard, Dept. Cumb'd. Mustered out Sept. 7, 1864.

133rd REGIMENT INFANTRY.—Org. at Indianapolis, May 17, 1864. June, 1864, Post Bridgeport, Ala., R. R. Guard, Dept. Cumb'd. Mustered out Sept. 5, 1864.

134th REGIMENT INFANTRY.—Org. at Indianapolis, May 24, 1864. June, 1864, R. R. Guard, Dept. Cumb'd. Mustered out Sept. 2, 1864.

135th REGIMENT INFANTRY.—Org. at Indianapolis, May 23, 1864. June, 1864, R. R. Guard, Dept. Cumb'd. Mustered out Sept. 29, 1864.

136th REGIMENT INFANTRY.—Org. at Indianapolis, May 21, 1864. June, 1864, R. R. Guard, Dept. Cumb'd. Mustered out Sept. 2, 1864.

137th REGIMENT INFANTRY.—Org. at Indianapolis, May 26, 1864. June, 1864, R. R. Guard, Dept. Cumb'd. Mustered out Sept. 21, 1864.

138th REGIMENT INFANTRY.—Org. at Indianapolis, May 27, 1864. June, 1864, R. R. Guard, Dept. Cumb'd. Mustered out Sept. 22, 1864.

139th REGIMENT INFANTRY.—Org. at Indianapolis, June 5, 1864. June, 1864, R. R. Guard, Dept. Cumb'd. Mustered out Sept. 29, 1864.

140th REGIMENT INFANTRY.—Org. at Indianapolis, Oct. 24, 1864. Nov., 1864, 1 Brig., Def. Nash. & Chatta. R. R., Dept. Cumb'd. Jany., 1865, 3 Brig., 3 Div., 23 Corps, Ohio. Feby., 1865, 3 Brig., 3 Div., 23 Corps, Dept. N. C. Mustered out July 11. 1865.

141st REGIMENT INFANTRY.—(Failed to complete organization.)

142nd REGIMENT INFANTRY.—Org. at Indianapolis, Sept. 13 to Nov. 18, 1864. Nov., 1864, 2 Brig., 4 Div., 20 Corps, Dept. Cumb'd. March, 1865, Garrison Nashville, Tenn., Dept. Cumb'd. Mustered out July 14, 1865.

143rd REGIMENT INFANTRY.—Org. at Indianapolis, Feby. 21, 1865. March, 1865, 1 Brig., 1st Sub. Dist., Dist. Middle Tenn., Dept. Cumb'd. Mustered out Oct. 17, 1865.

144th REGIMENT INFANTRY.—Org. at Indianapolis, March 6, 1865. March, 1865, 1 Brig., 2 Prov'l Div., Army Shenandoah. Mustered out Aug. 5, 1865.

145th REGIMENT INFANTRY.—Org. at Indianapolis, Feby., 1865. March, 1865, 1 Brig., 2d Separate Div., Dist. Etowah, Dept. Cumb'd. July, 1865, Dept. Ga. Mustered out Jany. 21, 1866.

146th REGIMENT INFANTRY.—Org. at Indianapolis, Feby. and March, 1865. March, 1865, 1 Brig., 2 Prov'l Div., Army Shenandoah. Mustered out Aug. 31, 1865.

147th REGIMENT INFANTRY.—Org. at Indianapolis, Jany. to March, 1865. March, 1865, 1 Brig., 3 Prov'l Div., Army Shenandoah. Mustered out Aug. 4, 1865.

148th REGIMENT INFANTRY.—Org. at Indianapolis, Feby. 25, 1865. March, 1865, 2nd Sub Dist., Dist. Middle Tenn. Dept. Cumb'd. Mustered out Sept. 5, 1865.

149th REGIMENT INFANTRY.—Org. at Indianapolis, Feby., 1865. Feby., 1865, Dist. Northern Ala., Dept. Cumb'd. Mustered out Sept. 25, 1865.

150th REGIMENT INFANTRY.—Org. at Indianapolis, Feby., 1865. March, 1865, 1 Brig., 2 Prov'l Div., Army Shenandoah. Mustered out Aug. 6, 1865.

151st REGIMENT INFANTRY.—Org. at Indianapolis, Jany. to March, 1865. March, 1865, 2 Brig., Def. Nash. & Chatta. R. R., Dept. Cumb'd. April, 1865, 2 Brig., 1st Sub Dist., Dist. Middle Tenn., Dept. Cumb'd. June, 1865, Nashville, Tenn. Mustered out Sept. 19, 1865.

152nd REGIMENT INFANTRY.—Org. at Indianapolis, Feby. and March, 1865. March, 1865, 1 Brig., 3 Prov'l Div., Army Shenandoah. Mustered out Aug. 30, 1865.

153rd REGIMENT INFANTRY.—Org. at Wabash, Feby., 1865. March, 1865, Dept. Ky. Mustered out Sept. 4, 1865.

154th REGIMENT INFANTRY.—Org. at Indianapolis, April, 1865. May, 1865, Dept. W. Va. Mustered out Aug. 4, 1865.

155th REGIMENT INFANTRY.—Org. at Indianapolis, April, 1865. April, 1865, Prov'l Brig., 3 Div., 9 Corps. May, 1865, Dover, Del., Middle Dept. Mustered out Aug. 4, 1865.

156th REGIMENT INFANTRY.—Org. at Indianapolis, April, 1865. April, 1865, Dept. W. Va. Mustered out Aug. 4, 1865.

157th and 158th REGIMENTS INFANTRY.—(Failed to complete organization.)

BASSETT'S INDEPENDENT COMPANY INFANTRY. —Org. at Indianapolis, July 18, 1862. Mustered out Aug. 26, 1862.

KEASBY'S INDEPENDENT COMPANY INFANTRY. —Org. at Indianapolis, July 17, 1862. Mustered out Aug. 26, 1862.

BROWN'S INDEPENDENT COMPANY INFANTRY. —Org. at Indianapolis, July 16, 1862. Mustered out Aug. 26, 1862.

MONROE'S INDEPENDENT COMPANY INFANTRY. —Org. at Indianapolis, July 26, 1862. Mustered out Aug. 26, 1862.

PATTON'S INDEPENDENT COMPANY INFANTRY. —Org. at Indianapolis, July 25, 1862. Mustered out Aug. 26, 1862.

SMITH'S INDEPENDENT COMPANY INFANTRY.— Org. at Chicago, Ill., April 17, 1861. Mustered out July 16, 1861.

IOWA

1st REGIMENT CAVALRY.—Org. at Davenport, Ia., Aug.-Sept., 1861. Oct., 1861, Fremont's Army West and Dept. Mo. March, 1862, Dist. Central Mo., Dept. Mo. Oct., 1862, 2 Brig., 3 Div., Army Frontier, Dept. Mo. Nov., 1862, 1 Brig., 3 Div., Army Frontier. June, 1863, 2 Brig., 1 Cav. Div., Army Southeast Mo. Aug., 1863, 2 Brig., Davidson's 1st Cav. Div., Ark. Exp. Jany., 1864, 3 Brig., 1 Cav. Div., 7 Corps, Dept. Ark. Sept., 1864, 2 Brig., Cav. Div., 7 Corps, Dept. Ark. (Veterans in Dept. Mo. June to Dec., 1864.) Feby., 1865, 1 Brig., Cav. Div., 7 Corps. Feby., 1865, 2 Brig., Cav. Div., Dist. West Tenn. June, 1865, Dept. Gulf. Aug., 1865, Dept. Texas. Mustered out Feby. 15, 1866.

2nd REGIMENT CAVALRY.—Org. at Davenport, Ia., Aug.-Sept., 1861. Dec., 1861, Dept. Mo. March, 1862, Unass'd, Army Miss. April, 1862, 2 Brig., Cav. Div., Army Miss. June, 1862, Cav., 5 Div., Army Miss. Sept., 1862, 2 Brig., Cav. Div., Army Miss. Nov., 1862, Grierson's Cav. Brig., Left Wing 13 Corps, Dept. Tenn. Dec., 1862, 1 Brig., Cav. Div., 16 Corps, Tenn. March, 1863 (Dist. Memphis, Tenn., 16 Corps. Jany. to March, 1863, 6 Co.'s.), 1 Brig., 1 Cav. Div., 16 Corps. May, 1863, 2 Brig., 1 Cav. Div., 16 Corps. Aug., 1863, 3 Brig., 1 Cav. Div., Div. 16 Corps. Dec., 1863, 2 Brig., 1 Cav. Div., 16 Corps. July, 1864, 2 Brig., 1 Cav. Div., Dist. West Tenn. Nov. 1864, 2 Brig., 5 Div., Cav. Corps, Mil. Div. Miss. June, 1865, Dept. Miss. Mustered out Sept. 19, 1865.

3rd REGIMENT CAVALRY.—Org. at Keokuk, Ia., Aug. 30-Sept. 14, 1861. Nov., 1861, Benton Barracks, Mo. Feby., 1862, Curtis' Army Southwest Mo., Dept. Mo. May, 1862, 3 Brig., 1 Div., Army Southwest Mo. July, 1862, Dist. East. Ark., Dept. Mo. Oct., 1862, 3 Brig, 4 Div., Dist. East. Ark. Dec., 1862, 2 Brig., Cav. Div., Dist. East. Ark., Dept. Tenn. Jany., 1863, 2 Brig., 2 Cav. Div., 13 Corps, Dept. Tenn. April, 1863, 2 Brig., Cav. Div., Dist. East. Ark., Dept. Tenn. June, 1863, Bussy's Cav. Brig., Herron's Div., 13 Corps, Tenn. Aug., 1863, Reserve Cav. Brig., Army Ark. Jany., 1864, 1 Brig., 1 Div., 7 Corps, Dept. Ark. May, 1864, 3 Brig., 1 Div., 7 Corps, Ark. (detachment), 2 Brig., 1 Cav. Div., 16 Corps, Tenn. (Veterans.) June, 1864, 2 Brig., Cav. Div., Sturgis' Exp. (Veterans.) June, 1864, 2 Brig., 2 Cav. Div., Dist. West Tenn. (Veterans.) Sept., 1864, 2 Brig., Cav. Div., 7 Corps, Ark. (detachment). Nov., 1864, 1 Brig., 4 Div., Wilson's Cav. Corps, Mil. Div. Miss. Dec., 1864, 2 Brig., Cav. Div., Dist. West Tenn. (detachment). Feby., 1865, 1 Brig., 4 Div., Cav. Corps, Mil. Div. Miss. (regiment). June, 1865, Dist. Georgia. Mustered out Aug. 9, 1865.

Companies E, F, G and H served detached, Dec., 1861, to Aug., 1863. Dec., 1861, Unatt., Dept. Mo. Feby., 1862, Dist. North Mo., Dept. Mo. Aug., 1862, Dist Southwest Mo., Dept. Mo. Nov., 1862, Cav. Brig., Dist. Southeast, Mo. June, 1863, Reserve Cav. Brig, Army Southeast Mo. Aug., 1863, Reserve Brig., 1 Cav. Div., Ark. Exp. Rejoined Regiment at Little Rock, Ark., Oct. 1, 1863.

4th REGIMENT CAVALRY.—Org. at Camp Harlan, Mt. Pleasant, Ia., Nov. 23, 1861, to Jany. 1, 1862. March, 1862, Unatt., Army Southwest Mo., Dept. Mo. May, 1862, 2 Div., Army Southwest Mo. July, 1862, Dist. East. Ark., Dept. Mo. Dec., 1862, 2 Brig., 1 Cav. Div., Dist. East. Ark., Dept. Tenn. Jany., 1863, 2 Brig., 2 Cav. Div., 13 Corps, Tenn. May, 1863, Unatt., 15 Corps,

Tenn. Aug., 1863, Winslow's Cav. Brig., 15 Corps. Dec., 1863, Winslow's Cav. Brig., 17 Corps. April, 1864, 2 Brig., 1 Cav. Div., 16 Corps. July, 1864, 2 Brig., 2 Div. Cav. Corps, Dist. West Tenn. Nov., 1864, 1 Brig., 4 Div., Cav. Corps, Mil. Div. Miss. Dec., 1864, 2 Brig., Cav. Div., Dist. West Tenn. Feby., 1865, 1 Brig., 4 Div., Cav. Corps, Mil. Div. Miss. June, 1865, Dept. Georgia. Mustered out Aug. 10, 1865.

5th REGIMENT CAVALRY.—Org. at Curtis' Horse by order Gen. Fremont, by consolidation of Companies from Iowa, Minnesota, Nebraska and Missouri, Oct. to Dec., 1861. Nov., 1861, Benton Barracks, Mo., Dept. Mo. Feby., 1862, Garrison Forts Henry and Heiman and Donelson, Tenn. Dist. Columbus, Ky. Nov., 1862, Dist. Columbus, Ky., 13 Corps, Dept. Tenn. Dec., 1862, Dist. Columbus, Ky., 16 Corps. June, 1863, 1 Brig., 2 Div., Cav. Corps, Army Cumb'd. Aug., 1863, 3 Brig., 2 Div., Cav. Corps, Cumb'd. Nov., 1863, 1 Brig., 2 Div., Cav. Corps, Cumb'd. April, 1864, 1 Brig., 3 Div., Cav. Corps, Cumb'd. Nov., 1864, 2 Brig., 6 Div., Cav. Corps, Mil. Div. Miss. Dec., 1864, 1 Brig., 6 Div., Cav. Corps, M. D. M. Dec., 1864, 2 Brig., 6 Div., M. D. M. Feby., 1865, 2 Brig., 4 Div., Cav. Corps, M. D. M. Mustered out Aug. 11, 1865.

6th REGIMENT CAVALRY.—Org. at Davenport, Ia., Jany. 31 to March 5, 1863. Service in Dist. of the Plains, Mustered out Oct. 17, 1865.

7th REGIMENT CAVALRY.—Org. at Davenport, Ia., April 27-July 13, 1863. Service in Dist. of the Plains. Mustered out June 22, 1866.

8th REGIMENT CAVALRY.—Org. at Davenport, Ia., Sept. 30, 1863. Nov., 1863, Def. Nashville and Northwestern R. R., Dept. Cumb'd. March, 1864, 1 Brig., 1 Div., Cav. Corps, Cumb'd. Nov., 1864, 1 Brig., 1 Div., Wilson's Cav. Corps, Mil. Div. Miss. June, 1865, Dept. Georgia. Mustered out Aug. 13, 1865.

9th REGIMENT CAVALRY.—Org. at Davenport, Ia., Nov. 30, 1863. Dec., 1863, Dist. St. Louis, Mo., Dept. Mo. April, 1864, 3 (Cav.) Brig., 2 Div., 7 Corps, Dept. Ark. Sept., 1864. 3 Brig., Cav. Div., 7 Corps, Dept. Ark. Feby., 1865, Cav. Brig., Post Little Rock, Ark., 1 Div., 7 Corps. Aug., 1865, Dept. Ark. Mustered out March 23, 1866.

1st INDEPENDENT BATTERY LIGHT ARTILLERY. Org. at Burlington, Ia., Aug. 17, 1861. Dec., 1861, 1 Brig., Dist. Southwest Mo., Dept. Mo. Feby., 1862, 1 Brig., 4 Div., Army Southwest Mo. May, 1862, Arty., 2 Div., Army Southwest Mo. July, 1862, Dist. East. Ark., Dept. Mo. Dec., 1862, 3 Brig., 11 Div., Right Wing 13 Corps, Dept. Tenn. Dec., 1862, 3 Brig., 4 Div., Sherman's Yazoo Exp. Jany., 1863, Arty., 1 Div., 15 Corps, Tenn. April, 1864, Arty., 4 Div., 15 Corps. Sept., 1864, Arty., 1 Div., 15 Corps. Nov., 1864, Arty. Reserve, Nashville, Tenn., Dept. Cumb'd. Mustered out July 5, 1865.

2nd INDEPENDENT BATTERY LIGHT ARTILLERY. —Org. in Iowa at large, and mustered in at Council Bluffs, Ia., Aug. 18, 1861. Oct., 1861, Dist. St. Louis, Mo., Dept. Mo. March, 1862, Arty. Div., Army Miss. April, 1862, Arty., 3 Div., Army Miss. April, 1862, Arty., 2 Div., Army Miss. Oct., 1862, Arty., Dist. Corinth, Miss. Nov., 1862, Arty., 2 Brig., 8 Div., 13 Corps, Dept. Tenn. Dec., 1862, Arty., 2 Brig., 8 Div., 16 Corps. April, 1863, Arty., 3 Div., 15 Corps. Dec., 1863, Arty., 1 Div., 16 Corps. Dec., 1864, Arty., 2 Brig., 1 Div., Detachment Army Tenn., Dept. Cumb'd. Feby., 1865, Arty., 1 Div., 16 Corps, Mil. Div. West Miss. March, 1865, Arty. Brig., 16 Corps. Mustered out Aug. 7, 1865.

3rd INDEPENDENT BATTERY LIGHT ARTILLERY. —Org. at Dubuque, Ia., Sept. 24, 1861. Oct., 1861, Dept. Mo. Jany., 1862, Unatt., Army Southwest Mo., Dept. Mo. Feby., 1862, 2 Brig., 4 Div., Army Southwest Mo. May, 1862, Arty., 2 Div., Army Southwest Mo. July, 1862, Arty., Dist. East. Ark., Dept. Mo., and Dept. Tenn. Jany., 1863, Arty., 13 Div., 13 Corps, Dept. Tenn. July, 1863, Arty., 13 Div., 16 Corps. Aug., 1863, Arty., 3 Div., Ark. Exp. Jany., 1864, Arty., 3 Div., 7 Corps, Dept. Ark. May, 1864, Arty., 1 Div., 7 Corps, Dept. Ark. Aug., 1865, Dept. Ark. Mustered out Oct. 23, 1865.

4th INDEPENDENT BATTERY LIGHT ARTILLERY. —Org. at Davenport, Ia., Nov. 23, 1863. Attached to Dept. Northwest to Feby., 1864. Def. New Orleans, La.,

Dept. Gulf, to June, 1864. Dist. LaFourche, Dept. Gulf, to July, 1865. Mustered out July 14, 1865.

1st REGIMENT INFANTRY, 3 MONTHS.—Org. at Keokuk, Ia., May 14, 1861. June, 1861, Lyon's Army of the West. Mustered out Aug. 21, 1861.

1st REGIMENT COLORED INFANTRY.—Org. at Keokuk, Ia., and St. Louis, Mo., Oct. 11 to Dec. 4, 1863. Dec., 1863, Dist. East. Ark., Dept. Ark. Jany., 1864, Dist. East. Ark., 7 Corps, Dept. Ark. Designation changed to 60th U. S. C. T. March 11, 1864, which see.

2nd REGIMENT INFANTRY.—Org. at Keokuk, Ia., May 27, 1861. June, 1861, Dept. Mo. Oct., 1861, 3 Brig., Dist. Cairo. Oct., 1861, Dist. St. Louis, Mo., Dept. Mo. Feby., 1862, 4 Brig., 2 Div., Dist. Cairo. Feby., 1862, 1 Brig., 2 Div., Dist. West Tenn. and Army Tenn. July, 1862, 1 Brig., 2 Div., Dist. Corinth, Miss. Sept., 1862, 3 Brig., 2 Div., Dist. Corinth. Oct., 1862, 2 Brig., 2 Div., Dist. Corinth. Nov., 1862, 1 Brig., 2 Div., Dist. Corinth, Miss., 13 Corps, Dept. Tenn. Dec., 1862, 1 Brig., Dist. Corinth, 17 Corps. Jany., 1863, 1 Brig., Dist. Corinth, 16 Corps. March, 1863, 1 Brig., 2 Div., 16 Corps. Sept., 1864, 1 Brig., 4 Div., 15 Corps. Mustered out July 12, 1865.

3rd REGIMENT INFANTRY.—Org. at Keokuk, Ia., June 8, 1861. July, 1861, Dept. Mo. March, 1862, 1 Brig., 4 Div., Army Tenn. July, 1862, 1 Brig., 4 Div., Dist. Memphis, Tenn. Sept., 1862, 1 Brig., 4 Div., Dist. Jackson, Tenn. Nov., 1862, 1 Brig., 4 Div., Right Wing 13 Corps, Dept. Tenn. Dec., 1862, 1 Brig., 4 Div., 17 Corps. Jany., 1863, 1 Brig., 4 Div., 16 Corps. July, 1863, 1 Brig., 4 Div., 13 Corps. Aug., 1863, 1 Brig., 4 Div., 17 Corps. March, 1864 (1 Brig., Prov'l Div., 17 Corps, Gulf, non-veterans), 1 Brig., 4 Div., 17 Corps (veterans). Veterans consolidated to a Battalion of 3 Co.'s, July, 1864, and transferred to 2nd Iowa Infy. as Co.'s A, F and I, Nov. 4, 1864.

4th REGIMENT INFANTRY.—Org. at Council Bluffs, Ia., Aug. 8, 1861. Aug., 1861, Dept. Mo. Dec., 1861, 1 Brig., Army Southwest Mo., Dept. Mo. Feby., 1862, 1 Brig., 4 Div., Army Southwest Mo., Dept. Mo. May, 1862, 2 Div., Army Southwest Mo. July, 1862, Dist. East. Ark., Dept. Mo. Nov., 1862, 2 Brig., 2 Div., Dist. East. Ark. Dec., 1862, 3 Brig., 11 Div., Right Wing 13 Corps, Dept. Tenn. Dec., 1862, 3 Brig., 4 Div., Sherman's Yazoo Exp. Jany., 1863, 3 Brig., 1 Div., 15 Corps, Tenn. Sept., 1863, 2 Brig., 1 Div., 15 Corps. Sept., 1864, 3 Brig., 1 Div., 15 Corps. Mustered out July 24, 1865.

5th REGIMENT INFANTRY.—Org. at Burlington, Ia., July 15, 1861. Aug., 1861, Fremont's Army West and Dept. Mo. March, 1862, 1 Brig., 2 Div., Army Miss. April, 1862, 2 Brig., 3 Div., Army Miss. April, 1862, 1 Brig., 3 Div., Army Miss. Nov., 1862, 3 Brig., 7 Div., Left Wing 13 Corps, Dept. Tenn. Dec., 1862, 3 Brig., 7 Div., 16 Corps. Jany., 1863, 3 Brig., 7 Div., 17 Corps. Sept., 1863, 3 Brig., 2 Div., 17 Corps. Dec., 1863, 3 Brig., 3 Div., 15 Corps. Consolidated with 5th Iowa Cavalry Sept. 1, 1864.

6th REGIMENT INFANTRY.—Org. at Burlington, Ia., July 17, 1861. Aug., 1861, Dept. Mo. March, 1862, 1 Brig., 5 Div., Army Tenn. May, 1862, 2 Brig., 5 Div., Army Tenn. July, 1862, 2 Brig., 5 Div., Dist. Memphis, Tenn. Nov., 1862, 2 Brig., 5 Div., Dist. Memphis, Tenn., 13 Corps, Dept. Tenn. Nov., 1862, 1 Brig., 1 Div., Dist. Memphis, Tenn., 13 Corps. Dec., 1862, 1 Brig., 1 Div., 17 Corps. Jany., 1863, 1 Brig., 1 Div., 16 Corps. March, 1863, 2 Brig., 1 Div., 16 Corps. May, 1863, 4 Brig., 1 Div., 16 Corps. July, 1863, 4 Brig., 4 Div., 15 Corps. Sept., 1863, 2 Brig., 4 Div., 15 Corps. Sept., 1864, 2 Brig., 1 Div., 15 Corps. Mustered out July 21, 1865.

7th REGIMENT INFANTRY.—Org. at Burlington, Ia., July 24 to Aug. 4, 1861. Sept., 1861, Dist. Cairo. Feby., 1862, 4 Brig., 2 Div., Dist. Cairo. Feby., 1862, 1 Brig., 2 Div., Dist. West Tenn. and Army Tenn. July, 1862, 1 Brig., 2 Div., Dist. Corinth, Miss. Sept., 1862, 3 Brig., 2 Div., Dist. Corinth. Oct., 1862, 2 Brig., 2 Div., Dist. Corinth. Nov., 1862, 1 Brig., Dist. Corinth, 13 Corps. Dept. Tenn. Dec., 1862, 1 Brig., Dist. Corinth, 17 Corps. Jany., 1863, 1 Brig., Dist. Corinth, 16 Corps. March, 1863, 1 Brig., 2 Div., 16 Corps. Sept., 1864, 1 Brig., 4 Div., 15 Corps. Mustered out July 12, 1865.

8th REGIMENT INFANTRY.—Org. at Davenport, Ia., Aug.-Sept., 1861. Oct., 1861, Dept. Mo. March, 1862, 3 Brig., 2nd Div., Army Tenn. April, 1862, 1 Brig., 2 Div., Army Tenn. July, 1862, 1 Brig., 2 Div., Dist. Corinth, Miss. Nov., 1862, 1 Brig., Dist. Corinth, 13 Corps, Dept. Tenn. Dec., 1862, Davenport, Ia. Jany., 1863, Dist. St. Louis, Mo., Dept. Mo. April, 1863, 3 Brig., 3 Div., 15 Corps, Tenn. Dec., 1863, 3 Brig., 1 Div., 16 Corps. June, 1864, Unass'd, Memphis, Tenn., Dist. West Tenn. Feby., 1865, 3 Brig., 3 Div., 16 Corps, Mil. Div. West Miss. Aug., 1865, Dist. Ala. Mustered out April 20, 1866.

9th REGIMENT INFANTRY.—Org. at Dubuque, Ia., Sept. 24, 1861. Oct., 1861, Dept. Mo. Jany., 1862, Un-att., Army Southwest Mo., Dept. Mo. Feby., 1862, 2 Brig., 4 Div., Army Southwest Mo. July, 1862, Dist. East. Ark., Dept. Mo. Dec., 1862, 3 Brig., 1 Div., Dist. East. Ark., Dept. Tenn. Dec., 1862, 3 Brig., 11 Div., Right Wing, 13 Corps, Dept. Tenn. Dec., 1862, 3 Brig., 4 Div., Sherman's Yazoo Exp. Jany., 1863, 3 Brig., 1 Div., 15 Corps. Sept., 1863, 2 Brig., 1 Div., 15 Corps. Sept., 1864, 3 Brig., 1 Div., 15 Corps. Mustered out July 18, 1865.

10th REGIMENT INFANTRY.—Org. at Iowa City and Montezuma, Ia., Sept. 6 to Oct. 26, 1861. Oct., 1861, Dist. Cairo. Oct., 1861, 5 Brig., Dist. Cairo. Feby., 1862, 4 Brig., 1 Div., Dist. Cairo. Feby., 1862, 2 Brig., 2 Div., Army Miss. April, 1862, 2 Brig., 3 Div., Army Miss. April, 1862, 1 Brig., 3 Div., Army Miss. May, 1862, 2 Brig., 3 Div., Army Miss. Nov., 1862, 3 Brig., 7 Div., Left Wing 13 Corps, Dept. Tenn. Dec., 1862, 3 Brig., 7 Div., 16 Corps. Jany., 1863, 3 Brig, 7 Div., 17 Corps. Sept., 1863, 3 Brig., 2 Div., 17 Corps. Dec., 1863, 3 Brig., 3 Div., 15 Corps. Aug., 1864, 2 Brig., 3 Div., 15 Corps. April, 1865, 1 Brig., 2 Div., 15 Corps. Mustered out Aug. 15, 1865.

11th REGIMENT INFANTRY.—Org. at Davenport, Ia., Sept. 28 to Oct. 18, 1861. Nov., 1861, Dept. Mo. March, 1862, 1 Brig., 1 Div., Army Tenn. April, 1862, 3 Brig., 6 Div., Army Tenn. July, 1862, 3 Brig., 6 Div., Dist. Corinth, Miss. Nov., 1862, 3 Brig., 6 Div., Left Wing 13 Corps, Dept. Tenn. Dec., 1862, 3 Brig., 6 Div., 16 Corps. Jany., 1863, 3 Brig., 6 Div., 17 Corps. Sept., 1863, 3 Brig., 1 Div., 17 Corps. April, 1864, 3 Brig., 4 Div., 17 Corps. Mustered out July 15, 1865.

12th REGIMENT INFANTRY.—Org. at Dubuque, Ia., Nov. 25, 1861. Dec., 1861, Dist. Cairo. Feby., 1862, 1 Brig., 2 Div., Dist. West Tenn. and Army Tenn. July, 1862, 1 Brig., 2 Div., Dist. Corinth, Miss. Nov., 1862, 1 Brig., Dist. Corinth, 13 Corps, Dept. Tenn. Dec., 1862, Davenport, Ia. Jany., 1863, Dist. St. Louis, Mo., Dept. Mo. April, 1863, 3 Brig., 3 Div., 15 Corps, Tenn. Dec., 1863, 3 Brig., 1 Div., 16 Corps. Dec., 1864, 3 Brig., 1 Div., Detachment Army Tenn., Dept. Cumb'd. Feby., 1865, 3 Brig., 1 Div., 16 Corps, Mil. Div. West Miss. Aug., 1865, Dist., Ala. Mustered out Jany. 20, 1866.

13th REGIMENT INFANTRY.—Org. at Davenport, Ia., Oct. 18 to Nov. 2, 1861. Nov., 1861, Dept. Mo. Feby., 1862, 1 Brig., 1 Div., Army Tenn. April, 1862, 3 Brig., 6 Div., Army Tenn. July, 1862, 3 Brig., 6 Div., Dist. Corinth, Miss. Nov., 1862, 3 Brig., 6 Div., Left Wing 13 Corps, Dept. Tenn. Dec., 1862, 3 Brig., 6 Div., 16 Corps. Jany., 1863, 3 Brig., 6 Div., 17 Corps. Sept., 1863, 3 Brig., 1 Div., 17 Corps. April, 1864, 3 Brig., 4 Div., 17 Corps. Mustered out July 21, 1865.

14th REGIMENT INFANTRY.—Org. at Davenport, Ia., Nov. 6, 1861. Dec., 1861, Dept. Mo. Feby., 1862, 4 Brig., 2 Div., Dist. Cairo. Feby., 1862, 1 Brig., 2 Div., Dist. West Tenn. and Army Tenn. July, 1862, Union Brig., 2 Div., Dist. Corinth, Miss. Nov., 1862, 1 Brig., 2 Div., Dist. Corinth, 13 Corps, Dept. Tenn. Dec., 1862, Davenport, Ia. Jany., 1863, Dist. St. Louis, Mo., Dept. Mo. April, 1863, Cairo, Ill., Dist. Columbus, Ky., 6 Div., 16 Corps, Tenn. Jany., 1864, 2 Brig., 3 Div., 16 Corps, Tenn. Nov., 1864, Springfield, Ill. Old members mustered out Nov. 2, 1864. Veterans and Recruits, Aug. 8, 1865.

15th REGIMENT INFANTRY.—Org. at Keokuk, Ia., Feby. 22, 1862. March, 1862, 3 Brig., 6 Div., Army Tenn. July, 1862, 3 Brig., 6 Div., Dist. Corinth, Miss. Nov., 1862, 3 Brig., 6 Div., Left Wing 13 Corps, Dept. Tenn. Dec., 1862, 3 Brig., 6 Div., 16 Corps. Jany., 1863, 3 Brig., 6 Div., 17 Corps. Sept., 1863, 3 Brig., 1 Div., 17 Corps.

April, 1864, 3 Brig., 4 Div., 17 Corps. Mustered out July 24, 1865.

16th REGIMENT INFANTRY.—Org. in Iowa at large, Dec. 10, 1861, to March, 1862. April, 1862, 2 Brig., 6 Div., Army Tenn. April, 1862, 3 Brig., 6 Div., Army Tenn. July, 1862, 3 Brig., 6 Div., Dist. Corinth, Miss. Nov., 1862, 3 Brig., 6 Div., Left Wing 13 Corps, Dept. Tenn. Dec., 1862, 3 Brig., 6 Div., 16 Corps. Jany., 1863, 3 Brig., 6 Div., 17 Corps. Sept., 1863, 3 Brig., 1 Div., 17 Corps. April, 1864, 3 Brig., 4 Div., 17 Corps. Mustered out July 19, 1865.

17th REGIMENT INFANTRY.—Org. at Keokuk, Ia., March 21-April 16, 1862. April, 1862, Dept. Mo. May, 1862, 2 Brig., 3 Div., Army Miss. Nov., 1862, 2 Brig., 7 Div., Left Wing 13 Corps, Dept. Tenn. Dec., 1862, 2 Brig., 7 Div., 16 Corps. Jany., 1863, 2 Brig., 7 Div., 17 Corps. Sept., 1863, 2 Brig., 2 Div., 17 Corps. Dec., 1863, 2 Brig., 3 Div., 15 Corps. April, 1865, 3 Brig., 2 Div., 15 Corps. Mustered out July 25, 1865.

18th REGIMENT INFANTRY.—Org. at Clinton, Ia., Aug. 6, 1862. Aug., 1862, Dist. Southwest Mo., Dept. Mo. Oct., 1862, 1 Brig., 2 Div., Army Frontier, Dept. Mo. June, 1863, Dist. Southwest Mo., Dept. Mo. Oct., 1863, Dist. Frontier, Dept. Mo. Dec., 1863, 2 Brig., Dist. Frontier, Dept. Mo. Jany., 1864, 2 Brig., Dist. Frontier, 7 Corps, Dept. Ark. March, 1864, 1 Brig., Dist. Frontier, 7 Corps. Jany., 1865, 1 Brig., 3 Div., 7 Corps. Mustered out July 20, 1865.

19th REGIMENT INFANTRY.—Org. at Keokuk, Ia., Aug. 25, 1862. Sept., 1862, Dist. Southwest Mo., Dept. Mo. Oct., 1862, 2 Brig., 3 Div., Army Frontier, Dept. Mo. June, 1863, 2 Brig., Herron's Div., 13 Corps, Dept. Tenn. July, 1863, 2 Brig., 2 Div., 13 Corps. Aug., 1863, 2 Brig., 2 Div., 13 Corps, Dept. Gulf. June, 1864, U. S. Forces, Texas. Aug., 1864, Dist. West Florida, Dept. Gulf. Dec., 1864, Dist. Southern Ala., Dept. Gulf. Feby., 1865, 1 Brig., 2 Div., 13 Corps, Mil. Div., West Miss. Mustered out July 10, 1865.

20th REGIMENT INFANTRY.—Org. Clinton, Ia., Aug. 25, 1862. Sept., 1862, Dist. Southwest Mo., Dept. Mo. Oct., 1862, 2 Brig., 2 Div., Army Frontier, Dept. Mo. June, 1863, 1 Brig., Herron's Div., 13 Corps, Dept. Tenn. July, 1863, 1 Brig., 2 Div., 13 Corps. Aug., 1863, 1 Brig., 2 Div., 13 Corps, Gulf. Oct., 1863, 2 Brig., 2 Div., 13 Corps, Gulf. Jany., 1864, 2 Brig., 4 Div., 13 Corps. Feby., 1864, 2 Brig., 2 Div., 13 Corps. June, 1864, 1 Brig., U. S. Forces, Texas. Aug., 1864, U. S. Forces, Mobile Bay. Sept., 1864, 1 Brig., 3 Div., 19 Corps, Gulf. Dec., 1864, 4 Brig., Reserve Corps, Mil. Div. West Miss. Feby., 1865, 3 Brig., 2 Div., Reserve Corps, M. D. W. M. Feby., 1865, 3 Brig., 2 Div., 13 Corps. Mustered out July 8, 1865.

21st REGIMENT INFANTRY.—Org. at Dubuque, Ia., Aug., 1862. Sept., 1862, Dist. St. Louis and Rolla, Mo., Dept. Mo. Oct., 1862, Warren's Brig., Dist. Southeast Mo., Dept. Mo. Jany., 1863, 2 Brig., 2 Div., Army Southeast Mo., Dept. Mo. March, 1863, 2 Brig., 14 Div., 13 Corps, Dept. Tenn. July, 1863, 2 Brig., 1 Div., 13 Corps. Aug., 1863, 2 Brig., 1 Div., 13 Corps, Gulf. March, 1864, 1 Brig., 1 Div., 13 Corps. June, 1864, Dist. LaFourche, Dept. Gulf. Aug., 1864, 2 Brig., 2 Div., 19 Corps, Gulf. Dec., 1864, 1 Brig., Reserve Corps, Mil. Div. West Miss. Feby., 1865, 1 Brig., 1 Div., Reserve Corps, M. D. W. M. Feby., 1865, 1 Brig., 1 Div., 13 Corps. Mustered out July 15, 1865.

22nd REGIMENT INFANTRY.—Org. at Iowa City, Ia., Sept. 9, 1862. Oct., 1862, Dist. St. Louis and Rolla, Mo. Feby., 1863, 2 Brig., 2 Div., Army Southeast Mo., Dept. Mo. March, 1863, 2 Brig., 14 Div., 13 Corps, Tenn. July, 1863, 2 Brig., 1 Div., 13 Corps. Aug., 1863, 2 Brig., 1 Div., 13 Corps, Gulf. March, 1864, 1 Brig., 1 Div., 13 Corps, Gulf. June, 1864, Def. New Orleans, La. Aug., 1864, 2 Brig., 2 Div., 19 Corps, Gulf. July, 1864, 2 Brig., 2 Div., 19 Corps, Army Shenandoah, Middle Mil. Div. Jany., 1865, 2 Brig., Grover's Div., Dist. Savannah, Ga., Dept. South. March, 1865, 1 Brig., 1 Div., 10 Corps, Dept. North Carolina. April, 1865, Dist. Savannah, Ga., Dept. South. Mustered out July 25, 1865.

23rd REGIMENT INFANTRY.—Org. at Des Moines, Ia., Sept. 19, 1862. Sept., 1862, Dept. Mo. Feby., 1863, 2 Brig., 2 Div., Army Southeast Mo., Dept. Mo. March,

1863, 2 Brig., 14 Div., 13 Corps, Tenn. July, 1863, 2 Brig., 1 Div., 13 Corps. Aug., 1863, 2 Brig., 1 Div., 13 Corps, Gulf. March, 1864, 1 Brig., 1 Div., 13 Corps, Gulf. June, 1864, 1 Brig., 3 Div., 19 Corps, Gulf. Dec., 1864, 4 Brig., Reserve Corps, Mil. Div. West Miss. Feby., 1865, 1 Brig., 2 Div., Reserve Corps, M. D. W. M. Feby., 1865, 1 Brig., 2 Div., 13 Corps, M. D. W. M. Mustered out July 26, 1865.

24th REGIMENT INFANTRY.—Org. at Muscantine, Ia., Sept. 18, 1862. Nov., 1862, Dist. East. Ark., Dept. Mo. Dec., 1862, 3 Brig., 1 Div., Dist. East Ark., Dept. Tenn. Dec., 1862, 2 Brig., 2 Div., Dist. East. Ark., Dept. Tenn. Jany., 1863, 2 Brig., 13 Div., 13 Corps, Tenn. Feby., 1863, 2 Brig., 12 Div., 13 Corps. July, 1863, 2 Brig., 3 Div., 13 Corps. Aug., 1863, 2 Brig., 3 Div., 13 Corps, Gulf. June, 1864, Dist. LaFourche, La., Gulf. July, 1864, 3 Brig., 2 Div., 19 Corps, Army Shenandoah, Middle Mil. Div. Aug., 1864, 4 Brig., 2 Div., 19 Corps. Dec., 1864, 3 Brig., 2 Div., 19 Corps. Jany., 1865, 3 Brig., Grover's Div., Dist. Savannah, Ga., Dept. South. March, 1865, 1 Brig., 1 Div., 10 Corps, Dept. North Carolina. April, 1865, Dist. Savannah, Ga., Dept. South. Mustered out July 17, 1865.

25th REGIMENT INFANTRY.—Org. at Mount Pleasant, Ia., Sept. 27, 1862. Oct., 1862, Dist. East. Ark., Dept. Mo. Dec., 1862, 3 Brig., 1 Div., Dist. East. Ark., Dept. Tenn. Dec., 1862, 2 Brig., 11 Div., Right Wing 13 Corps, Dept. Tenn. Dec., 1862, 2 Brig., 4 Div., Sherman's Yazoo Exp. Jany., 1863, 2 Brig., 1 Div., 15 Corps, Tenn. Dec., 1863, 3 Brig., 1 Div., 15 Corps. April, 1864, 2 Brig., 1 Div., 15 Corps. Sept., 1864, 3 Brig., 1 Div., 15 Corps. Mustered out June 6, 1865.

26th REGIMENT INFANTRY.—Org. at Clinton, Ia., Sept. 30, 1862. Oct., 1862, Dist. East. Ark., Dept. Mo. Dec., 1862, 2 Brig., 1 Div., Dist. East. Ark., Dept. Tenn. Dec., 1862, 3 Brig., 11 Div., Right Wing 13 Corps, Tenn. Dec., 1862, 3 Brig., 4 Div., Sherman's Yazoo Exp. Jany., 1863, 3 Brig., 1 Div., 15 Corps, Tenn. Sept., 1863, 2 Brig., 1 Div., 15 Corps. Dec., 1863, 1 Brig., 1 Div., 15 Corps. April, 1865, 3 Brig., 1 Div., 15 corps. Mustered out June 6, 1865.

27th REGIMENT INFANTRY.—Org. at Dubuque, Ia., Oct. 3, 1862. Oct., 1862, Dept. Northwest. Nov., 1862, Dist. Memphis, Right Wing 13 Corps, Tenn. Dec., 1862, Dist. Jackson, Tenn., 16 Corps, Tenn. March, 1863, 3 Brig., 3 Div., 16 Corps. Aug., 1863, True's Brig., Ark. Exp. Nov., 1863, Gilbert's Brig., Dist. Memphis, Tenn., 5 Div., 16 Corps. Jany., 1864, 2 Brig., 3 Div., 16 Corps. Dec., 1864, 2 Brig., 2 Div., Detachment Army Tenn., Dept. Cumb'd. Feby., 1865, 2 Brig., 2 Div., 16 Corps, Mil. Div. West Miss. Mustered out Aug. 8, 1865.

28th REGIMENT INFANTRY.—Org. at Iowa City, Ia., Oct. 10, 1862. Nov., 1862, 2 Brig., 1 Div., Dist. East. Ark., Dept. Mo. Dec., 1862, 2 Brig., 2 Div., Dist. East. Ark., Dept. Tenn. Jany., 1863, 2 Brig., 12 Div., 13 Corps, Tenn. July, 1863, 2 Brig., 3 Div., 13 Corps. Aug., 1863, 2 Brig., 3 Div., 13 Corps, Gulf. June, 1864, Dist. La-Fourche, Dept. Gulf. July, 1864, 3 Brig., 2 Div., 19 Corps, Gulf, and Army Shenandoah, Middle Mil. Div. Aug., 1864, 4 Brig., 2 Div., 19 Corps. Dec., 1864, 2 Brig., 2 Div., 19 Corps. Jany., 1865, 2 Brig., Grover's Div., Dist. Savannah, Ga., Dept. South. March, 1865, 1 Brig., 1 Div., 10 Corps, Dept. North Carolina. April, 1865, Dist. Savannah, Ga., Dept. South. Mustered out July 31, 1865.

29th REGIMENT INFANTRY.—Org. at Camp Dodge, Council Bluffs, Ia., Dec. 1, 1862. Dec., 1862, Dist. St. Louis, Mo., Dept. Mo. Jany., 1863, 2 Brig., 13 Div., 13 Corps, Tenn. July, 1863, 2 Brig., 13 Div., 16 Corps. Aug., 1863, 2 Brig., 3 Div., Ark. Exp. Jany., 1864, 2 Brig., 3 Div., 7 Corps, Dept. Ark. March, 1864, 1 Brig., 3 Div., 7 Corps. May, 1864, 1 Brig., 1 Div., 7 Corps. Nov., 1864, 2 Brig., 2 Div., 7 Corps. Feby., 1865, 2 Brig., 3 Div., Reserve Corps, Mil. Div. West Miss. Feby., 1865, 2 Brig., 3 Div., 13 Corps. July, 1865, Dept. Texas. Mustered out Aug. 10, 1865.

30th REGIMENT INFANTRY.—Org. at Keokuk, Ia., Sept. 20, 1862. Oct., 1862, Dist. East. Ark., Dept. Mo. Dec., 1862, 2 Brig., 1 Div., Dist. East. Ark., Dept. Tenn. Dec., 1862, 3 Brig., 11 Div., Right Wing 13 Corps, Dept. Tenn. Dec., 1864, 3 Brig., 4 Div., Sherman's Yazoo Exp.

Jany., 1863, 3 Brig., 1 Div., 15 Corps. Sept., 1863, 2 Brig., 1 Div., 15 Corps. Dec., 1863, 1 Brig., 1 Div., 15 Corps. Sept., 1864, 3 Brig., 1 Div., 15 Corps. Mustered out June 5, 1865.

31st REGIMENT INFANTRY.—Org. at Davenport, Ia., Oct. 13, 1862. Dec., 1862, 3 Brig., 1 Div., Dist. East. Ark., Dept. Tenn. Dec., 1862, 2 Brig., 11 Div., Right Wing 13 Corps, Tenn. Dec., 1862, 2 Brig., 4 Div., Sherman's Yazoo Exp. Jany., 1863, 2 Brig., 1 Div., 15 Corps, Tenn. Sept., 1864, 3 Brig., 1 Div., 15 Corps. Mustered out June 27, 1865.

32nd REGIMENT INFANTRY.—Org. at Dubuque, Ia., Oct. 6, 1862. Nov., 1862, Dept. Mo. Dec., 1862, Dist. Columbus, Ky., 6 Div., 16 Corps, Dept. Tenn. Jany., 1864, 2 Brig., 3 Div., 16 Corps. Dec., 1864, 2 Brig., 2 Div., Detach. Army Tenn., Dept. Cumb'd. Feby., 1865, 2 Brig., 2 Div., 16 Corps, Mil. Div. West Miss. Co.'s A, D, F, G, detached from Regiment Nov., 1862, to Jany., 1864. Nov., 1862, Dist. Southeast Mo., Dept. Mo. July, 1863, Reserve Cav. Brig., Army Southeast Mo., Dept. Mo. Aug., 1863, Reserve Cav. Brig., 1 Cav. Div., Dist. Southeast Mo. Aug., 1863, Reserve Brig., 1 Cav. Div., Ark. Exp. Dec., 1863, 1 Brig., 1 Cav. Div., Army Ark. Regiment mustered out Aug. 24, 1865.

33rd REGIMENT INFANTRY.—Org. at Oskaloosa, Ia., Oct., 4, 1862. Nov., 1862, Dept. Mo. Jany., 1863, 1 Brig., 13 Div., 13 Corps, Tenn. July, 1863, 2 Brig., 13 Div., 16 Corps, Dist. East. Ark. Aug., 1863, 2 Brig., 3 Div., Ark, Exp. Jany., 1864, 2 Brig., 3 Div., 7 Corps, Dept. Ark. March, 1864, 1 Brig., 3 Div., 7 Corps. May, 1864, 1 Brig., 1 Div., 7 Corps. Feby., 1865, 3 Brig., 3 Div., Reserve Corps, Mil. Div. West Miss. Feby., 1865, 3 Brig., 3 Div., 13 Corps. Mustered out July 17, 1865.

34th REGIMENT INFANTRY.—Org. at Burlington, Ia., Oct. 15, 1862. Dec., 1862, 2 Brig., 1 Div., Dist. East. Ark., Dept. Tenn. Dec., 1862, 3 Brig., 11 Div., Right Wing 13 Corps, Tenn. Dec., 1864, 3 Brig., 4 Div., Sherman's Yazoo Exp. Jany., 1863, 3 Brig., 1 Div., 15 Corps, Tenn. April, 1863, Dist. St. Louis, Mo., Dept. Mo. Garrison, Pilot Knob, Mo. June, 1863, 1 Brig., Herron's Div., 13 Corps, Tenn. July, 1863, 1 Brig., 2 Div., 13 Corps. Aug., 1863, 1 Brig., 2 Div., 13 Corps, Gulf. Dec., 1863, 3 Brig., 2 Div., 13 Corps. Jany., 1864, 2 Brig., 4 Div., 13 Corps. March, 1864, 2 Brig., 1 Div., 13 Corps. April, 1864, 2 Brig., 4 Div., 13 Corps. June, 1864, Def. New Orleans. Aug., 1864, 2 Brig., 3 Div., 19 Corps, Gulf. Dec., 1864, 3 Brig., Reserve Corps, Mil. Div. West Miss. Feby., 1865, 3 Brig., 2 Div., Reserve Corps, M. D. W. M. Feby., 1865, 3 Brig., 2 Div., 13 Corps, M. D. W. M. Mustered out Aug. 15, 1865.

35th REGIMENT INFANTRY.—Org. at Muscatine, Ia., Sept. 18, 1862. Nov., 1862, Dist. Columbus, Ky., 13 Corps, Dept. Tenn. Dec., 1862, Dist. Columbus, Ky., 16 Corps. March, 1863, Dist. Columbus, Ky., 6 Div., 16 Corps. April, 1863, 3 Brig., 3 Div., 15 Corps. Dec., 1863, 3 Brig., 1 Div., 16 Corps. Dec., 1864, 3 Brig., 1 Div., Detach. Army Tenn., Dept. Cumb'd. Feby., 1865, 3 Brig., 1 Div., 16 Corps, Mil. Div. West Miss. Mustered out Aug. 10, 1865.

36th REGIMENT INFANTRY.—Org. at Keokuk, Ia., Oct. 4, 1862. Jany., 1863, 1 Brig., 13 Div., 13 Corps, Tenn. Feby., 1863, 2 Brig., 13 Div., 13 Corps. July, 1863, 2 Brig., 13 Div., 16 Corps, Dist. East. Ark. Aug., 1863, 1 Brig., 13 Div., 16 Corps. Aug., 1863, 1 Brig., 3 Div., Ark. Exp. Jany., 1864, 1 Brig., 3 Div., 7 Corps, Dept. Ark. March, 1864, 2 Brig., 3 Div., 7 Corps. May, 1864, 2 Brig., 1 Div., 7 Corps. Feby., 1865, 1 Brig., 1 Div., 7 Corps. March, 1865, 1 Brig., 2 Div., 7 Curps. Mustered out Aug. 24, 1865.

37th REGIMENT INFANTRY.—Org. at Muscatine, Ia., Dec. 15, 1862. Jany., 1863, Dist. St. Louis, Mo., Dept. Mo., July, 1863, Alton, Ill. Jany., 1864, Rock Island, Ill. June, 1864, Memphis, Tenn. Dist. West Tenn. Aug., 1864, Indianapolis, Ind., Cincinnati, Columbus and Gallipolis, Ohio. Mustered out May 24, 1865.

38th REGIMENT INFANTRY.—Org. at Dubuque, Ia., Dec. 4, 1862. Dec., 1862, Dist. Columbus, Ky., 16 Corps, Tenn. June, 1863, 1 Brig., Herron's Div., 13 Corps, Tenn. July, 1863, 1 Brig., 2 Div., 13 Corps. Aug., 1863, 1 Brig., 2 Div., 13 Corps, Gulf. June, 1864, 1 Brig., U. S. Forces,

Texas. Aug., 1864, U. S. Forces, Mobile Bay. Oct., 1864, Dist. LaFourche, Dept. Gulf. Consolidated with 34th Iowa Infantry, Dec. 12, 1864.

39th REGIMENT INFANTRY.—Org. at Des Moines and Davenport, Ia., Nov. 24, 1862. Dec., 1862, 3 Brig., Dist. Corinth, 17 Corps. Jany., 1863, 3 Brig., Dist. Corinth, 16 Corps. March, 1863, 3 Brig., 2 Div., 16 Corps. Sept., 1864, 3 Brig., 4 Div., 15 Corps. Mustered out Aug. 2, 1865.

40th REGIMENT INFANTRY.—Org. at Iowa City, Ia., Nov. 15, 1862. Dec., 1862, Dist. Columbus, Ky., 16 Corps, Tenn. June, 1863, 3 Brig., Kimball's Prov'l Div., 16 Corps. July, 1863, 3 Brig., Prov'l Div., Dist. East. Ark. Aug., 1863, 2 Brig., 2 Div., Ark. Exp. Jany., 1864, 2 Brig., 2 Div., 7 Corps, Dept. Ark. March, 1864, 3 Brig., 3 Div., 7 Corps. May, 1864, 2 Brig., 1 Div., 7 Corps. Feby., 1865, 1 Brig., 1 Div., 7 Corps. Feby., 1865, 1 Brig., 3 Div., 7 Corps. Mustered out June 5, 1865.

41st REGIMENT INFANTRY.—Org. as Co.'s A, B and C, 14th Iowa Infy., Oct. 1861, Detached by order Gen. Fremont, and on special duty in Dakota Territory, to April, 1863. Permanently detached from 14th Iowa, Sept. 18, 1862, and designated 41st Iowa Battalion Infy. Transferred to 7th Iowa Cav. as Co.'s K, L and M.

42nd REGIMENT INFANTRY.—Failed to complete organization.

43rd REGIMENT INFANTRY.—Failed to complete organization.

44th REGIMENT INFANTRY.—Org. at Davenport, Ia., June 1, 1864. R. R. Guard, Dept. Tenn. Mustered out Sept. 15, 1864.

45th REGIMENT INFANTRY.—Org. at Keokuk, Ia., May 25, 1864. R. R. Guard in Tenn. Mustered out Sept. 16, 1864.

46th REGIMENT INFANTRY.—Org. at Davenport, Ia., June 10, 1864. 2 Brig., Dist. Memphis, Tenn., Dist. West. Tenn. Mustered out Sept. 23, 1864.

47th REGIMENT INFANTRY.—Org. at Davenport, Ia., June 4, 1864. Dist. East. Ark., 7 Corps, Dept. Ark. Mustered out Sept. 28, 1864.

48th REGIMENT INFANTRY.—Org. at Davenport, Ia., July 13, 1864. Prison Guard at Rock Island, Ill. Mustered out Oct. 10, 1864.

KANSAS

2nd REGIMENT CAVALRY.—Org. at Kansas City, Kan., as 12th Kansas Infy. At Fort Leavenworth, Kan., designation changed to 9th Kansas Infy., Feby. 4, 1862, and to 2nd Cav., March 5, 1862. Nov., 1861, Dept. Kan. Aug., 1862, 3 Brig., Dept. Kan. Oct., 1862, 2 Brig., 1 Div., Army Frontier, Dept. Mo. Feby., 1863, Dist. Southwest Mo., Dept. Mo. Dec., 1863, Dist. Frontier, Dept. Mo. Jany., 1864, 2 Brig., Dist. Frontier, 7 Corps, Dept. Ark. March, 1864, 1 Brig., Dist. Frontier, 7 Corps. April, 1864, 3 Brig., Dist. Frontier, 7 Corps. Jany., 1865, 2 Brig., 3 Div., 7 Corps. Feby., 1865, Unatt., 7 Corps. Mustered out Aug. 17, 1865.

5th REGIMENT CAVALRY.—Org. at Leavenworth City, Kan., July 12, 1861, to Jany. 22, 1862. Nov., 1861, Unatt., Dept. Kan. June, 1862, Unatt., Army Southwest Mo., Dept. Mo. July, 1862, Dist. East. Ark., Dept. Mo. Dec., 1862, 2 Brig., 3 Cav., Div., Dist. East. Ark., Dept. Tenn. Jany., 1863, 2 Brig., 2 Cav. Div., 13 Corps, Dept. Tenn. April, 1863, 2 Brig., Cav. Div., Dist. East. Ark., Dept. Tenn. June, 1863, Clayton's Indpt. Cav. Brig., Dist. East. Ark., Dept. Tenn. Aug., 1863, Clayton's Indpt. Cav. Brig., Ark. Exp. Jany., 1864, Pine Bluff, Ark., 7 Corps, Dept. Ark. Sept., 1864, 1 Brig., Cav. Div., 7 Corps, Dept. Ark. Feby., 1865, Post. St. Charles, Ark., Unass'n, 7 Corps, Dept. Ark. Non-veterans mustered out Co.'s A to H, Aug. 11 to Dec. 8, 1864, Co.'s I and K mustered out June 22, 1865. Co.'s L and M consolidated with 15th Kansas Cav., Aug. 22, 1865.

6th REGIMENT CAVALRY.—Org. at Fort Scott, Kan., July, 1861. Nov., 1861, Unatt., Dept. Kan. Aug., 1862, 2 Brig., Dept. Kan. Oct., 1862, 2 Brig., 1 Div., Army Frontier, Dept. Mo. Feby., 1863, 1 Brig., 1 Div., Army Frontier. June, 1863, Dist. Frontier, Dept. Mo. Jany., 1864, Unatt., Dist. Frontier, 7 Corps, Dept. Ark. March,

1864, 3 Brig., Dist. Frontier, 7 Corps. Jany., 1865, 2 Brig., 3 Div., 7 Corps. Feby., 1865, 1 Brig., 2 Div., 7 Corps. Mustered out Aug. 27, 1865.

7th REGIMENT CAVALRY.—Org. at Fort Leavenworth, Kan., Oct. 28, 1861. Nov., 1861, Unatt., Dept. Kan. June, 1862, 5 Div., Army Miss. Sept., 1862, 2 Brig., Cav. Div., Army Miss. Nov., 1862, 1 Brig., Cav. Div., 13 Corps, Dept. Tenn. Dec., 1862, 2 Brig., Cav. Div., 16 Corps, Tenn. March, 1863, Cav. Brig., Dist. Corinth, 2 Div., 16 Corps. June, 1863, 3 Brig., 1 Cav. Div., 16 Corps. Aug., 1863, 1 Brig., 1 Cav. Div., 16 Corps. Feby., 1864, Unatt., 1 Cav. Div., 16 Corps. June, 1864, 1 Brig., 1 Cav. Div., 16 Corps. Dist. West Tenn. Sept., 1864, Dist. St. Louis, Mo., Dept. Mo. July, 1865, Dept. Kan. Mustered out Sept. 29, 1865.

9th REGIMENT CAVALRY.—Org. at Fort Leavenworth, Kan., Oct. 24, 1861, to April 25, 1862, by consolidation of Indp't Battalions, Squadrons and Detachments originally formed for other Regiments. Nov., 1861, Unass'n, Dept. Kan. Aug., 1862, 1 Brig., Dept. Kan. Oct., 1862, 1 Brig., 1 Div., Army Frontier, Dept. Mo. June, 1863, Dist. Frontier, Dept. Mo. July, 1863, Dist. Border Dept. Mo. Jany., 1864, Dept. Kan. May, 1864, 3 Brig., Dist. Frontier, 7 Corps, Dept. Ark. Sept., 1864, 4 Brig., Cav. Div., 7 Corps. Jany., 1865, 2 Brig., 3 Div., 7 Corps. Feby., 1865, Unass'd, 2 Div., 7 Corps. Mustered out July 17, 1865.

11th REGIMENT CAVALRY.—Org. at Camp Lyon, near Fort Leavenworth, Kan., Aug. 29-Sept. 14, 1862, as 11th Kansas Infy. Designation changed to 11th Cav., April, 1863. Oct., 1862, 1 Brig., 1 Div., Army Frontier, Dept. Mo. Feby., 1863, Dist. Rolla, Dept. Mo. April, 1863, Dist. Kan., Dept. Mo. June, 1863, Dist. Rolla, Mo., Dept. Mo. July, 1863, Dist. Border, Dept. Mo. Jany., 1864, Dept. Kan. June, 1864, Dist. South Kan., Dept. Kan. Feby., 1865, Dist. Upper Ark. March, 1865, 2 Brig., 2 Div., 7 Corps, Dept. Ark. April, 1865, Dist. Plains, Dept. Mo. Mustered out Sept. 26, 1865.

14th REGIMENT CAVALRY.—Org. at Fort Scott and Leavenworth, Kan., as a Battalion of 4 Co.'s, as escort to Gen. Blunt. Regiment org. at Fort Scott, Kan., Nov., 1862. April, 1863, Dist. Frontier, Dept. Mo. Jany. 1864, Unatt., Dist. Frontier, 7 Corps, Dept. Ark. March, 1864, 3 Brig., Dist. Frontier, 7 Corps. Jany., 1865, 2 Brig., 3 Div., 7 Corps. Feby., 1865, Unatt., 7 Corps, Pine Bluff, Ark. Mustered out June 25, 1865.

15th REGIMENT CAVALRY.—Org. at Leavenworth, Kan., Sept. and Oct., 1863. Oct., 1863, Dist. Border, Dept. Mo. Jany., 1864, Dept. Kan. June, 1864, Dist. South Kan. April, 1865, Dist. North Kan. Mustered out Oct. 19, 1865. Co. H mustered out Dec. 7, 1865.

16th REGIMENT CAVALRY.—Org. at Leavenworth City, Kan., Nov., 1863, to May, 1864. Jany., 1864, Dept. Kan. June, 1864, Dist. North Kan. April, 1865, Dist. Plains, Dept. Mo. Mustered out Dec. 16, 1865.

1st BATTERY LIGHT ARTILLERY.—Org. at Mound City, July 24, 1861. Nov., 1861, Unass'd, Dept. Kan. Aug., 1862, 2 Brig., Dept. Kan. Oct., 1862, 1 Brig., 1 Div., Army Frontier, Dept. Mo. Feby., 1863, Dist. Southwest Mo., Dept. Mo. June, 1863, Dist. Rolla, Mo., Dept. Mo. June, 1863, Dist., Columbus, Ky., 6 Div., 16 Corps, Dept. Tenn. Nov., 1863, Def. Nashville and Northwestern R. R., Dept. Cumb'd. Nov., 1864, 2 Colored Brig., Dist. Etowah, Dept. Cumb'd. Jany., 1865, Arty., Dist. Nashville, Tenn., Dept. Cumb'd. Mustered out July 17, 1865.

2nd BATTERY LIGHT ARTILLERY.—Org. at Fort Scott, Kan., Sept. 10, 1862. Sept., 1862, Dept. Kan. Sept., 1862, 1 Brig., Dept. Kan. Oct., 1862, 2 Brig., 1 Div., Army Frontier, Dept. Mo. (1 Section), Fort Scott, Dept. Kan. Feby., 1863, 2 Brig., 1 Div., Army Frontier, Dept. Mo. Feby., 1863, Dist. Southwest Mo., Dept. Mo. June, 1863, Dist. Frontier, Dept. Mo. Jany., 1864, Unatt., Dist. Frontier, 7 Corps, Dept. Ark. May, 1864, 1 Brig., Dist. Frontier, 7 Corps. Feby., 1865, 1 Brig., 3 Div., 7 Corps. Mustered out Aug. 11, 1865.

3rd BATTERY LIGHT ARTILLERY.—Org. as Co. B, 2nd Kansas Cav., Dec. 9, 1861. Org. as a Battery with guns captured at Old Fort Wayne, and designated as Hopkins' Battery, Oct. 27, 1862. Designated 3rd Battery, Oct. 1, 1863. Oct., 1862, 3 Brig., 1 Div., Army Frontier,

Dept. Mo. Feby., 1863, 1863, Dept. Mo. Feby., 1863, Dist. Northern Ark., Dept. Mo. June, 1863, Dist. Frontier, Dept. Mo. Dec., 1863, 3 Brig., Dist. Frontier, Dept. Mo. Jany., 1864, 3 Brig., Dist. Frontier, 7 Corps, Dept. Ark. Mustered out Jany. 18, 1865. Veterans and Recruits to 2nd Kansas Battery.

ARMSTRONG'S BATTERY LIGHT ARTILLERY.—Attached to 1st Kansas Colored Infy.

HOPKINS' BATTERY LIGHT ARTILLERY.—Attached to 2nd Kansas Cavalry. (See 3rd Kansas Battery.)

OPDYKE'S BATTERY LIGHT ARTILLERY.—Attached to 9th Kansas Cavalry.

STOVER'S BATTERY LIGHT ARTILLERY.—Attached to 2nd Kansas Cavalry.

ZISCH'S MILITIA BATTERY LIGHT ARTILLERY.—Duty at Fort Leavenworth, Kan., Oct., 1864.

1st REGIMENT INFANTRY.—Org. at Camp Lincoln, Fort Leavenworth, Kan., May 20-June 3, 1861. July, 1861, Deitzler's Brig., Lyon's Army West, Aug., 1861, Dept. Mo., Nov., 1861, Dept. Kan. June, 1862, Dist. Columbus, Ky., Dept. Tenn. Sept., 1862, 1 Brig., 6 Div., Dist. Corinth, Miss. Nov., 1862, 1 Brig., 6 Div., Left Wing 13 Corps. Dept. Tenn. Dec., 1862, 1 Brig., 6 Div., 16 Corps. Jany., 1863, 1 Brig., 6 Div., 17 Corps. July, 1863, Dist. Vicksburg, Miss. Sept., 1863, 1 Brig., 1 Div., 17 Corps. Aug., 1864, Unatt., 2 Div., 19 Corps, Dept. Gulf. Dec., 1864, Dist. East. Ark., 7 Corps, Dept. Ark. Jany., 1865, Headqrs. 7 Corps, Dept. Ark. Mustered out Aug. 30, 1865.

1st REGIMENT COLORED INFANTRY.—Org. at Fort Scott, Kan., as a Battalion, Jany. 13, 1863. Jany., 1863, Dept. Kan. June, 1863, Dist Frontier, Dept. Mo. Jany., 1864, Unatt., Dist. Frontier, 7 Corps, Dept. Ark. March, 1864, 2 Brig., Dist. Frontier, 7 Corps. Designation changed to 79th U. S. C. T. (new). Dec. 13, 1864.

1st REGIMENT MILITIA INFANTRY.—Called into service Oct. 9, 1864, to repel Price's invasion; disbanded Oct. 29, 1864.

2nd REGIMENT INFANTRY.—3 MONTHS. Org. at Lawrence, Kan., May, 1861. Mustered in at Kansas City, June 20, 1861. July, 1861, Deitzler's Brig., Lyon's Army of the West. Aug., 1861, Dept. Mo. Mustered out Oct. 31, 1861.

2nd REGIMENT COLORED INFANTRY.—Org. at Fort Scott and Fort Leavenworth, Kan., Aug. 11 to Oct. 17, 1863. Oct., 1863, Dist. Frontier, Dept. Mo. Jany., 1864, Unatt., Dist. Frontier, 7 Corps, Dept. Ark. March, 1864, 2 Brig., Dist. Frontier, 7 Corps. Designation changed to 83rd U. S. C. T. (new), Dec. 13, 1864, which see.

2nd REGIMENT MILITIA INFANTRY.—Called into service Oct. 9, 1864, to repel Price's invasion. Disbanded Oct. 29, 1864.

3rd REGIMENT INFANTRY.—Org. not completed. Consolidated with 4th Kansas Infy. to form 10th Kansas Infy., April 3, 1862.

3rd REGIMENT MILITIA INFANTRY.—Called into service Oct. 9, 1864, to repel Price's invasion. Disbanded Oct. 29, 1864.

4th REGIMENT INFANTRY.—Org. not completed. Consolidated with 3rd Kansas Infy. to form 10th Kansas Infy., April 3, 1862.

4th REGIMENT MILITIA INFANTRY.—Called into service Oct. 9, 1864, to repel Price's invasion. Disbanded Oct. 29, 1864.

5th REGIMENT INFANTRY.—2 Co.'s Org. at Fort Scott, Kan. Attached to Lane's Kansas Brig. Discontinued Oct., 1861, and merged into other organizations.

5th REGIMENT MILITIA INFANTRY.—Called into service Oct. 9, 1864, to repel Price's invasion. Discontinued Oct. 29, 1864.

6th REGIMENT MILITIA INFANTRY.—Called into service Oct. 9, 1864, to repel Price's invasion. Discontinued Oct. 29, 1864.

7th REGIMENT MILITIA INFANTRY.—Called into service Oct. 9, 1864, to repel Price's invasion. Disbanded Oct. 29, 1864.

8th REGIMENT INFANTRY.—Org. Aug., 1861, for service in the State. Nov., 1861, Unatt., Dept. Kansas. June, 1862, 2 Brig., 4 Div., Army Miss. (Co.'s B, F, H, I, K). July, 1862, 1 Brig., 4 Div., Army Miss. Sept., 1862, 32 Brig., 9 Div., Army Ohio. Oct., 1862, 32 Brig., 9 Div., 3 Corps, Army Ohio. Nov., 1862, 3 Brig., 1 Div., Right Wing 14 Corps., Cumb'd. Jany., 1863, 3 Brig., 1 Div., 20 Corps, Cumb'd, and Post Nashville, Tenn., Dept. Cumb'd. Co.'s A, C, D, F, Attached to Dist. Kans., to Feby., 1863, then joined Regiment at Nashville, Tenn. Feby. 22, 1863. Co. G joined March 29, 1863. Oct., 1863, 1 Brig., 3 Div., 4 Corps, Dept. Cumb'd. Aug., 1865, Dept. Texas. Mustered out Nov. 29, 1865. Discharged at Fort Leavenworth, Kan., Jany. 9, 1866.

8th REGIMENT MILITIA INFANTRY.—Called into service Oct. 9, 1864, to repel Price's invasion. Disbanded Oct. 29, 1864.

9th REGIMENT MILITIA INFANTRY.—Called into service Oct. 9, 1864. to repel Price's invasion. Disbanded Oct. 29, 1864.

10th REGIMENT INFANTRY.—Org. at Paola, Kan., by consolidation of 3rd and 4th Kansas Infy., April 3, 1862. April, 1862, Unass'd, Dept. Kan. Aug., 1862, 2 Brig., Dept. Kan. Oct., 1862, 2 Brig., 1 Div., Army Frontier, Dept. Mo. Feby., 1863, Dist. Rolla, Mo., Dept. Mo. June, 1863, Dist. St. Louis, Mo., Dept. Mo. Aug., 1863, Dist. Kan., Dept. Mo. Jany., 1864, Alton, Ill. Aug., 1864. Dist. St. Louis, Mo., Dept. Mo. Nov., 1864, Nashville, Tenn., Dept. Cumb'd. Dec., 1864, 2 Brig., 2 Div., Detach. Army Tenn., Dept. Cumb'd. Feby., 1865, 2 Brig., 2 Div., 16 Corps, Mil. Div. West Miss. Mustered out Aug. 30, 1865.

10th REGIMENT MILITIA INFANTRY.—Called into service Oct. 9, 1864, to repel Price's invasion. Disbanded Oct. 29, 1864.

11th REGIMENT INFANTRY.—Org. at Camp Lyon, near Fort Leavenworth, Kan., Aug. 29-Sept. 14, 1862. Oct., 1862, 1 Brig., 1 Div., Army Frontier, Dept. Mo. Feby., 1863, Dist. Rolla, Dept. Mo. April, 1863, Dist. Kan., Dept. Mo. Designation changed to 11th Kansas Cav. April, 1863, which see.

11th REGIMENT MILITIA INFANTRY.—Called into service Oct. 9, 1864, to repel Price's invasion. Disbanded Oct. 29, 1864.

12th REGIMENT INFANTRY.—Org. at Paola, Kan., Sept., 1862. Sept., 1862, Unass'd, Dept. Kan. June, 1863, Unatt., Dist. Frontier, Dept. Mo. Jany., 1864, Unatt., Dist. Frontier, 7 Corps, Dept. Ark. March, 1864, 2 Brig., Dist. Frontier, 7 Corps. May, 1864, 1 Brig., Dist. Frontier, 7 Corps. Feby., 1865, 1 Brig., 3 Div., 7 Corps. Feby., 1865, 1 Brig., 1 Div., 7 Corps. Mustered out June 3, 1865.

12th REGIMENT MILITIA INFANTRY.—Called into service Oct. 9, 1864, to repel Price's invasion. Disbanded Oct. 29, 1864.

13th REGIMENT INFANTRY.—Org. at Atchison, Kan., Sept. 20, 1862. Oct., 1862, 2 Brig., 1 Div., Army Frontier, Dept. Mo. Feby., 1863, Dist. Southwest Mo., Dept. Mo. June, 1863, Dist. Frontier, Dept. Mo. Dec., 1863, 3 Brig., Dist. Frontier, Dept. Mo. Jany., 1864, 3 Brig., Dist. Frontier, 7 Corps, Dept. Ark. Feby., 1865, 1 Brig., 3 Div., 7 Corps. Feby., 1865, 1 Brig., 2 Div., 7 Corps. Feby., 1865, 1 Brig., 1 Div., 7 Corps. Mustered out June 3, 1865.

13th REGIMENT MILITIA INFANTRY.—Called into service Oct. 9, 1864, to repel Price's invasion. Disbanded Oct. 29, 1864.

14th REGIMENT MILITIA INFANTRY.—Called into service Oct. 9, 1864, to repel Price's invasion. Disbanded Oct. 29, 1864.

15th REGIMENT MILITIA INFANTRY.—Called into service Oct. 9, 1864, to repel Price's invasion. Disbanded Oct. 29, 1864.

16th REGIMENT MILITIA INFANTRY.—Called into service Oct. 9, 1864, to repel Price's invasion. Disbanded Oct. 29, 1864.

17th REGIMENT INFANTRY.—Org. at Fort Leavenworth, Kan., July 28, 1864. Duty in Dist. North Kan. Mustered out Nov. 16, 1864.

17th REGIMENT MILITIA INFANTRY.—Called into service Oct. 9, 1864, to repel Price's invasion. Disbanded Oct. 29, 1864.

18th REGIMENT MILITIA INFANTRY.—Called into service Oct. 9, 1864, to repel Price's invasion. Disbanded Oct. 29, 1864.

19th REGIMENT MILITIA INFANTRY.—Called into service Oct. 9, 1864, to repel Price's invasion. Disbanded Oct. 29, 1864.

20th REGIMENT MILITIA INFANTRY.—Called into service Oct. 9, 1864, to repel Price's invasion. Disbanded Oct. 29, 1864.

21st REGIMENT MILITIA INFANTRY.—Called into service Oct. 9, 1864, to repel Price's invasion. Disbanded Oct. 29, 1864.

22nd REGIMENT MILITIA INFANTRY.—Called into service Oct. 29, 1864, to repel Price's invasion. Disbanded Oct. 29, 1864.

LEAVENWORTH COLORED MILITIA' INFANTRY.—Called into service Oct. 9, 1864. Disbanded Oct. 29, 1864.

LEAVENWORTH STATE GUARD.—Called into service Oct. 9, 1864. Disbanded Oct. 29, 1864.

KENTUCKY

1st REGIMENT CAVALRY.—Org. at Liberty, Burkesville and Monticello, Ky., Oct. 28, 1861. Oct., 1861, Thomas' Command, Camp Dick Robinson, Ky. Dec., 1861, 1 Div., Army Ohio. (5 Co.'s Garfield's 18 Brig., Army Ohio, Dec., 1861, to March, 1862.) March, 1862, Unatt., Army Ohio. Sept., 1862. 1 Brig., Cav. Div., Army Ohio. Nov., 1862, Post Gallatin, Tenn., Dept. Cumb'd. April, 1863, Dist. Central Ky., Dept. Ohio. June, 1863, 1 Brig., 1 Div., 23 Corps, Army Ohio. Aug., 1863, Indpt. Cav. Brig., 23 Corps. Nov., 1863, 1 Brig., 1 Div., Cav. Corps, Dept. Ohio. May, 1864, Indpt. Cav. Brig., 23 Corps. Aug., 1864, 4 Brig., 1 Div., Dist. Ky., Dept. Ohio. Dec. 1864, Mil. Dist. Ky., and Dept. Ky. Mustered out Sept. 20, 1865.

2nd REGIMENT CAVALRY.—Org. at Muldraugh's Hill, Ky., Sept. 9, 1861, to Feby. 13, 1862. Oct., 1861, Rousseau's Brig., McCook's Command, at Nolin, Ky. Dec., 1861, 2 Div., Army Ohio. Sept., 1862, Unatt. Cav., 1 Corps, Army Ohio. Nov., 1862, Cav., 1 Div., Centre 14 Corps, Cumb'd. Jany., 1863, 2 Brig., 2 Div., Cav. Corps, Cumb'd. April, 1864, 2 Brig., 3 Div., Cav. Corps, Cumb'd. Oct., 1864, 2 Brig., 3 Div., Cav. Corps, Mil. Div. Miss. Nov., 1864, 1 Brig., 3 Div., Cav. Corps, Mil. Div. Miss. Mustered out July 27, 1865.

3rd REGIMENT CAVALRY.—Org. in Calhoun and Clay Cos., Ky., Dec. 13, 1861. Dec., 1861, Cav., 5 Div., Army Ohio. June, 1862, Cav. Brig., Army Ohio. Sept., 1862, 1 Brig., Cav. Div., Army Ohio. Nov., 1862, 1 Brig., Cav. Div., Cumb'd. Jany., 1863, 1 Brig., 1 Div., Cav. Corps, Cumb'd. March, 1863, Dist. West Ky., Dept. Ohio. June, 1863, 1 Brig., 2 Div., 23 Corps, Ohio. Aug., 1863, Unatt., Hopkinsville, Ky., 1 Div., 23 Corps. Oct., 1863, Dist. South Central Ky., 1 Div., 23 Corps. Nov., 1863, Dist. Nashville, Tenn., Dept. Cumb'd. April, 1864, 3 Brig., 3 Div., Cav. Corps, Cumb'd. Oct., 1864, 1 Brig., 3 Div., Cav. Corps, Mil. Div. Miss. Mustered out July 15, 1865.

4th REGIMENT CAVALRY.—Org. at Louisville, Ky., Dec. 24, 1861. March, 1862, Unatt. Cav., Army Ohio. Sept., 1862, 1 Brig., Cav. Div., Army Ohio. Oct., 1862, Dist. Louisville, Ky., Dept. Ohio. Nov., 1862, Dist. West Ky., Dept. Ohio. Jany., 1863, 1 Brig., 1 Div., Cav. Corps, Cumb'd. July, 1863, 3 Brig., 1 Div., Cav. Corps, Cumb'd. Nov., 1864, 3 Brig., 1 Div., Cav. Corps, Mil. Div. Miss. Jany., 1865, 2 Brig., 1 Div., Cav. Corps, M. D. M. Mustered out Aug. 21, 1865.

5th REGIMENT CAVALRY.—Org. at Columbus, Ky., Dec., 1861, to Feby., 1862, and mustered in at Gallatin, Tenn., March 31, 1862. March, 1862, Unatt. Cav., Army Ohio. Sept., 1862, 2 Brig., Cav. Div., Army Ohio. Nov., 1862, Cav., 4 Div., Centre 14 Corps, Cumb'd. Jany., 1863, 2 Brig., 1 Div., Cav. Corps, Cumb'd. April, 1863, Dist. Central Ky., Dept. Ohio. June, 1863, 2 Brig., 4 Div., 23 Corps, Dept. Ohio. July, 1863, 3 Brig., 1 Div., Cav. Corps, Cumb'd. April, 1864, 3 Brig., 3 Div., Cav. Corps, Cumb'd. Oct., 1864, 3 Brig., 3 Div., Cav. Corps, Mil. Div. Miss. Nov., 1864, 1 Brig., 3 Div., Cav. Corps, M. D. M. Jany., 1865, 3 Brig., 3 Div., Cav. Corps, M. D. M. Mustered out May 3, 1865.

6th REGIMENT CAVALRY.—Org. in Central Ky., July to Oct., 1862. (Munday's 1st Battalion assigned as Co.'s A, B, C, D and E.) Aug., 1862, Cav., Army of Ky., Dept. Ohio. Oct., 1862, Unatt., Louisville, Ky., Dept. Ohio. Nov., 1862, Unatt., Army Ky. and Dist. Central Ky., Dept. Ohio. Jany., 1863, 1 Brig., 1 Div., Cav. Corps, Cumb'd. July, 1863, 3 Brig., 1 Div., Cav. Corps, Cumb'd. Nov., 1864, 3 Brig., 1 Div., Cav. Corps, Mil. Div. Miss. Jany., 1865, 1 Brig., 1 Div., Cav. Corps, M. D. M. Mustered out Sept. 6, 1865.

7th REGIMENT CAVALRY.—Org. at large, Ky. Mustered in at Paris, Ky., Aug. 16, 1862. Aug., 1862, Unassigned, Army Ky., Dept. Ohio. Nov., 1862, Dist. Central Ky., Dept. Ohio. March, 1863, 1 Brig., 1 Div., Cav. Corps, Cumberland. July, 1863, 3 Brig., 1 Div., Cav. Corps, Cumberland. Nov., 1864, 3 Brig., 1 Div., Cav. Corps, Mil. Div. Miss. Jany., 1865, 2 Brig., 1 Div., Cav. Corps, M. D. M. Mustered out July 10, 1865.

8th REGIMENT CAVALRY.—Org. at Russellsville, Ky., Aug. 13, 1862. Aug., 1862, Dist. Louisville, Dept. Ohio. Nov., 1862, Unatt., Bowling Green, Ky., Dist. West. Ky., Dept. Ohio. June, 1863, 1 Brig., 2 Div., 23 Corps, Ohio. Aug., 1863, Unass'd, Bowling Green, Ky., 1 Div., 23 Corps. Mustered out Sept. 23, 1863.

9th REGIMENT CAVALRY.—Org. at Emminence, Ky., Aug. 22, 1862. Sept., 1862, 3 Brig., Cav. Div., Army Ohio. Nov., 1862, Dist. Western Ky., Dept. Ohio. June, 1863, 2 Brig., 3 Div., 23 Corps, Ohio. Aug., 1863, Emminence, Ky., 1 Div., 23 Corps. Mustered out Sept. 11, 1863.

10th REGIMENT CAVALRY.—Org. at Covington, Lexington and Crab Orchard, Ky., Sept. 8 to Nov. 11, 1862. Oct., 1862, Cav., 1 Div., Army Ky., Dept. Ohio. Nov., 1862, Unatt., Army Ky., Dept. Ohio (2nd Battalion, attached to Dist. East. Ky., Dept. Ohio, to June, 1863, and 1 Brig., 4 Div., 23 Corps, Ohio, to Aug., 1863). Nov., 1862, Dist. Central Ky., Dept. Ohio. April, 1863, 2 Brig., Dist. Central Ky., Dept. Ohio. June, 1863, 2 Brig., 4 Div., 23 Corps, Ohio. July, 1863, 2 Brig., 1 Div., 23 Corps. Aug., 1863, Mt. Sterling, Ky., 1 Div., 23 Corps. Mustered out Sept. 17, 1863.

11th REGIMENT CAVALRY.—Co.'s A, C, D and E org. at Harrodsburg, Ky., July, 1862. Regt. org. at Louisville, Ky., Sept. 26, 1862. Nov., 1862, Dist. Western Ky., Dept. Ohio. June, 1863, 2 Brig., 3 Div., 23 Corps, Ohio. Aug., 1863, Indpt. Cav. Brig., 23 Corps, Ohio. Nov., 1863, 1 Brig., 1 Div., Cav. Corps, Ohio. April, 1864, 3 Brig., Cav. Div., Dist. Ky., Dept. Ohio. June, 1864, Indpt. Cav. Brig., Cav. Div., 23 Corps, Ohio. Sept., 1864, Mil. Dist. Ky., Dept. Ohio. March, 1865, 2 Brig., Cav. Div., Dist. East. Tenn., Dept. Cumberland. Mustered out July 17, 1865.

12th REGIMENT CAVALRY.—Org. at Caseyville and Owensboro, Ky., Nov. 17, 1862. Dec., 1862, Dist. Western Ky., Dept. Ohio. June, 1863, 2 Brig., 3 Div., 23 Corps, Ohio. Aug., 1863, Indpt. Cav. Brig., 23 Corps. Nov., 1863, 1 Brig., 1 Div., Cav. Corps, Dept. Ohio. April, 1864, 3 Brig., Cav. Div., Dist. Ky., Dept. Ohio. May, 1864, 1 Brig., Cav. Div., 23 Corps, Ohio. June, 1864, Detached, Cav. Brig., 3 Div., 23 Corps. Aug., 1864, Dismounted Brig., Cav. Div., 23 Corps. Sept., 1864, 1 Brig., Cav. Div., 23 Corps. Sept., 1864, Dist. Louisville, Ky., Dept. Ohio. Nov., 1864, 2 Brig., 4 Div., 23 Corps. March, 1865, 2 Brig., Cav. Div., Dist. East. Tenn., Dept. Cumberland. July, 1865, Cav. Brig., Dist. East. Tenn. Mustered out Aug. 23, 1865.

13th REGIMENT CAVALRY.—Org. at Columbia Dec. 22, 1863. Dec., 1863, Dist. South Central Ky., 1 Div., 23 Corps, Ohio. Jany., 1864, Dist. S. W. Ky., Dept. Ohio. April, 1864, 2 Brig., 1 Div., Dist. Ky., 23 Corps. July, 1864, 1 Brig., 1 Div., Dist. Ky., 23 Corps. Mustered out Jany. 10, 1865.

14th REGIMENT CAVALRY.—Org. at Mt. Sterling and Irvin, Ky., Aug. 21, 1862, to Feby. 13, 1863. Nov., 1862, Dist. Central Ky., Dept. Ohio. June, 1863, 2 Brig., 4 Div., 23 Corps, Ohio. July, 1863, 2 Brig., 1 Div., 23 Corps. Aug., 1863, Dist. North Central Ky., 1 Div., 23 Corps. Jany., 1864, Dist. S. W. Ky., Dept. Ohio. Mustered out March 24, 1864.

15th REGIMENT CAVALRY.—Org. at Owensboro, Ky., Oct., 1862. Oct., 1862, Dist. Columbus, Ky., 13 Corps, Tenn. Jany., 1863, Dist. Columbus, Ky., 16 Corps. Aug., 1863, Detached Brig., Dist. Columbus, Ky., 6 Div., 16 Corps. Mustered out Oct. 29, 1863.

16th REGIMENT CAVALRY.—Org. at Paducah, Ky., Sept., 1863, Attached to 2 Brig., 2 Div., Cav. Corps, Dept. Ohio. May, 1864, 1 Cav. Brig., Dist. Ky., 5 Div., 23 Corps. Consolidated with 12th Ky. Cav., Oct. 15, 1864.

17th REGIMENT CAVALRY.—Org. at Russellville, Ky., April 25, 1865. Dept. Ky. Mustered out Sept. 20, 1865.

MUNDAY'S 1st BATTALION CAVALRY.—Org. at Lexington, Ky., Dec., 1861, to Jany., 1862. Attached to 12 Brig., Army Ohio. Feby., 1862, 7 Div., Army Ohio. Assigned to 6th Ky. Cav., Oct., 1862, as Co.'s A, B, C, D and E. See 6th Cav.

BATTERY A LIGHT ARTILLERY.—Org. at Camp Muldraugh's Hill, Ky., from Louisville Legion, Sept. 27, 1861. Oct., 1861, Rousseau's Brig., McCook's Command, Army Ohio. Dec., 1861, Arty., 2 Div., Army Ohio. Aug., 1862, 28 Brig., 3 Div., Army Ohio. Oct., 1862, Arty., 3 Div., 1 Corps, Army Ohio. Nov., 1862, 3 Brig., 1 Div., Centre 14 Corps, Cumberland. Jany., 1863, Arty., 1 Div., 14 Corps. Oct., 1863, Unassigned, Army Cumberland. Dec., 1863, Post Murfreesboro, Tenn., Dept. Cumberland. March, 1864, 2 Div., Arty. Res., Cumberland. Nov., 1864, Arty. Brig., 4 Corps. Aug., 1865, Dept. Texas. Mustered out Nov. 15, 1865.

BATTERY B LIGHT ARTILLERY.—Org. at Camp Dick Robinson, Ky., Oct. 8, 1861. Oct., 1861, Thomas' Command, Camp Dick Robinson, Ky., Dept. Ohio. Dec., 1861, Arty., 1 Div., Army Ohio. March, 1862, Unatt., Army Ohio. March, 1862, 23 Indpt. Brig., Army Ohio. Sept., 1862, Arty., 8 Div., Army Ohio. Nov., 1862, Arty., 2 Div., Centre 14 Corps, Cumberland. Jany., 1863, Arty., 2 Div., 14 Corps. Oct., 1863, Unatt., Army Cumberland. Dec., 1863, Arty. Brig., 12 Corps, Cumberland. April, 1864, Unatt., Dept. Cumberland. Aug., 1864, Def. Nashville & Chattanooga R. R., Dept. Cumberland. Oct., 1864, Arty. Brig., 4 Corps, Cumberland. Mustered out Nov. 16, 1864.

BATTERY C LIGHT ARTILLERY.—Commenced organizing at Lebanon, Ky., May, 1863. Captured July 3, 1863. Reorganized at Louisville Sept. 10, 1863. Sept., 1863, Dist. Louisville, Ky., 1 Div., 23 Corps, Dept. Ohio. Oct., 1863, Dist. South Central Ky., Dept. Ohio. Jany., 1864, Dist. S. W. Ky., Dept. Ohio. April, 1864, 3 Brig., 1 Div., Dist. Ky., 5 Div., 23 Corps. Dec., 1864, Mt. Sterling, Ky., Dist. Ky. Feby., 1865, Little Rock, Ark., 7 Corps, Dept. Ark. Mustered out July 26, 1865.

BATTERY D LIGHT ARTILLERY.—Not organized.

BATTERY E LIGHT ARTILLERY.—Org. at Camp Nelson, Ky., Oct. to Dec., 1863. Oct., 1863, Dist. North Central Ky., 1 Div., 23 Corps, Dept. Ohio. Nov., 1863, Dist. Somerset, Ky., 1 Div., 23 Corps. Jany., 1864, Dist. S. W. Ky., Dept. Ohio. April, 1864, 4 Brig., 1 Div., Dist. Ky., 5 Div., 23 Corps. Dec., 1864, Garrison Lexington, Mil. Dist. Ky. and Dept. Ky. Mustered out Aug. 1, 1865.

SIMMONDS' BATTERY LIGHT ARTILLERY.—Org. at Pendleton, Ohio, from Co. E, 1st Ky. Infy., June 3, 1861. Permanently detached Jany., 1862. Jany., 1862, Dist. Kanawha, Dept. West Va. March, 1862, 2 Brig., Kanawha Div., West Va. Sept., 1862, 2 Brig., Kanawha Div., 9 Corps, Army Potomac. Oct., 1862, Dist. Kanawha, West Va., Dept. Ohio. March, 1863, 1 Brig., 3 Div., 8 Corps, Middle Dept. June, 1863, 1 Brig., Scammon's Div., West Va. Dec., 1863, 3 Brig., 3 Div., West Va. April, 1864, Arty., 2 Infy. Div., West Va. July, 1864, Res. Div., Harper's Ferry, West Va. April, 1865, 2 Brig., 1 Infy. Div., West Va. Mustered out July 20, 1865.

PATTERSON'S INDPT. COMPANY ENGINEERS.— Org. at Camp Haskins, Ky., Oct., 1861. Oct., 1861, Unatt., Army Ohio. March, 1862, Engrs., 7 Div., Army Ohio. Oct., 1862, Cumberland Div., Dist. West Va., Dept. Ohio. Nov., 1862, 9 Div., Right Wing 13 Corps, Dept. Tenn. Dec., 1862, Unatt., Sherman's Yazoo Exp. Jany., 1863, Unatt., 9 Div., 13 Corps, Army Tenn. July, 1863, Unatt., 13 Corps, Tenn. Aug., 1863, Unatt., 13 Corps, Dept. Gulf.

Oct., 1863, Unatt., 13 Corps, Texas. July, 1864, Engr. Brig., Gulf. Mustered out Jany. 22, 1865.

1st REGIMENT INFANTRY.—First org. at Pendleton, Ohio, for three months, April and May, 1861. Reorganized by Ky. for three years, June, 1861. July, 1861, Kanawha Brig., West Va. Oct., 1861, Thomas' Command, Camp Dick Robinson, Ky. Nov., 1861, 11 Brig., Army Ohio. Jany., 1862, 22 Brig., Army Ohio. Feby., 1862, 22 Brig., 4 Div., Army Ohio. Sept., 1862, 22 Brig., 4 Div., 2 Corps, Army Ohio. Nov., 1862, 1 Brig., 2 Div., Left Wing, 14 Corps, Army Cumberland. Jany., 1863, 1 Brig., 2 Div., 21 Corps, Cumb'd. Oct., 1863, 1 Brig., 1 Div., 4 Corps. Mustered out June 18, 1864.

2nd REGIMENT INFANTRY.—Org. at Pendleton, Ohio, May-June, 1861. July, 1861, Kanawha Brig., West Va. Oct., 1861, Dist. Kanawha, West Va. Jany., 1862, 22 Brig., Army Ohio. Feby., 1862, 22 Brig., 4 Div., Army Ohio. Sept., 1862, 22 Brig., 4 Div., 2 Corps, Army Ohio. Nov., 1862, 1 Brig., 2 Div., Left Wing 14 Corps, Cumberland. Jany., 1863, 1 Brig., 2 Div., 21 Corps. Oct., 1863, 1 Brig., 1 Div., 4 Corps. Mustered out June 19, 1864.

3rd REGIMENT INFANTRY.—Org. at Camp Dick Robinson, Ky., Oct. 8, 1861. Oct., 1861, Thomas' Command, Dept. Ohio. Nov., 1861, Unatt., London, Dept. Ohio. March, 1862, 15 Brig., 4 Div., Army Ohio. March, 1862, 15 Brig., 6 Div., Army Ohio. Sept., 1862, 15 Brig., 6 Div., 2 Corps, Army Ohio. Nov., 1862, 1 Brig., 1 Div., Left Wing 14 Corps, Cumberland. Jany., 1863, 1 Brig., 1 Div., 21 Corps, Cumberland. April, 1863, 3 Brig., 1 Div., 21 Corps. Oct., 1863, 3 Brig., 2 Div., 4 Corps. Mustered out Jany. 10, 1865.

4th REGIMENT INFANTRY.—Org. at Camp Dick Robinson, Ky., Oct. 9, 1861. Oct., 1861, Thomas' Command, Dept. Ohio. Nov., 1861, 2 Brig., Army Ohio. Dec., 1861, 2 Brig., 1 Div., Army Ohio. Sept., 1862, 2 Brig., 1 Div., 3 Corps, Army Ohio. Nov., 1862, 2 Brig., 3 Div., Centre 14 Corps, Cumberland. Jany., 1863, 2 Brig., 3 Div., 14 Corps. Oct., 1863, 3 Brig., 3 Div., 14 Corps. June, 1864, 1 Brig., 1 Div., Cav. Corps, Cumberland. Nov., 1864, 1 Brig., 1 Div., Cav. Corps, Mil. Div. Miss. Mustered out Aug. 17, 1865.

5th REGIMENT INFANTRY ("Louisville Legion").— Org. at Camp Joe Holt, Ky., Sept. 9, 1861. Oct., 1861, Rousseau's 1 Brig., McCook's Command, at Nolin, Ky. Nov., 1861, 4 Brig., Army Ohio. Dec., 1861, 4 Brig., 2 Div., Army Ohio. Sept., 1862, 4 Brig., 2 Div., 1 Corps, Army Ohio. Nov., 1862, 3 Brig., 2 Div., Right Wing 14 Corps, Cumberland. Jany., 1863, 3 Brig., 2 Div., 20 Corps, Cumberland. Oct., 1863, 2 Brig., 3 Div., 4 Corps. July, 1864, Unatt., 4 Div., 20 Corps, Cumberland. Mustered out Sept. 14, 1864.

6th REGIMENT INFANTRY.—Org. at Sigel, Muldraugh's Hill and Shepherdsville, Ky., Sept. 9, 1861. Oct., 1861, Rousseau's 1 Brig., McCook's Command, at Nolin, Ky. Nov., 1861, 12 Brig., Army Ohio. Dec., 1861, 12 Brig., 1 Div., Army Ohio. Jany., 1862, 19 Brig., 4 Div., Army Ohio. Sept., 1862, 19 Brig., 4 Div., 2 Corps, Army Ohio. Nov., 1862, 2 Brig., 2 Div., Left Wing 14 Corps, Cumberland. Jany., 1863, 2 Brig., 2 Div., 21 Corps, Cumberland. Oct., 1863, 2 Brig., 3 Div., 4 Corps. Aug., 1864, 1 Brig., Defenses Nashville & Chattanooga R. R. Sept., 1864, Unatt., 4 Div., 20 Corps, Cumberland. Mustered out Jany. 2, 1865.

7th REGIMENT INFANTRY ("One of the first recruited in State. Old 3rd.").—Org. at Camp Dick Robinson, Ky., Sept. 22, 1861. Oct., 1861, Thomas' Command, Dept. Ohio. Jany., 1862, 12 Brig., 1 Div., Army Ohio. March, 1862, 24 Brig., 7 Div., Army Ohio. Oct., 1862, 3 Brig., Cumberland Div., Dist. West Va., Dept. Ohio. Nov., 1862, 2 Brig., 9 Div., Right Wing 13 Corps, Dept. Tenn. Dec., 1862, 2 Brig., 3 Div., Sherman's Yazoo Exp. Jany., 1863, 2 Brig., 9 Div., 13 Corps, Tenn. Feby., 1863, 1 Brig., 9 Div., 13 Corps. July, 1863, 1 Brig., 3 Div., 13 Corps. Aug., 1863, 3 Brig., 1 Div., 13 Corps, Gulf. Nov., 1863, Plaquemine, La., Dept. Gulf. March, 1864, 2 Brig., 1 Div., 13 Corps. June, 1864, 1 Brig., 3 Div., 19 Corps, Gulf. Dec., 1864, Dist. Baton Rouge, La., Dept. Gulf. April, 1865, Provisional Brig., Dist. Baton Rouge, La., and Dept. Gulf. Mustered out March 11, 1866.

8th REGIMENT INFANTRY.—Org. at Estill Springs and Lebanon, Ky., Oct., 1861. Oct., 1861, Thomas' Command, Dept. Ohio. Jany., 1862, 16 Brig., Army Ohio. Feby., 1862, 23 Indpt. Brig., Army Ohio. Sept., 1862, 23 Brig., 5 Div., Army Ohio. Sept., 1862, 23 Brig., 5 Div., 2 Corps, Army Ohio. Nov., 1862, 3 Brig., 3 Div., Left Wing 14 Corps, Cumberland. Jany., 1863, 3 Brig., 3 Div., 21 Corps. Oct., 1863, 2 Brig., 1 Div., 4 Corps. April, 1864, 1st Separate Brig., Post Chattanooga, Tenn. Nov., 1864, 2 Brig., Dist. Etowah, Dept. Cumberland. Mustered out Feby., 1865.

9th REGIMENT INFANTRY.—Org. at Camp Boyle, Adair Co., Ky., Nov. 20, 1861. Nov., 1861, Thomas' Command, Army Ohio. Nov., 1861, 11 Brig., Army Ohio. Dec., 1861, 11 Brig., 1 Div., Army Ohio. March, 1862, 11 Brig., 5 Div., Army Ohio. Sept., 1862, 11 Brig., 5 Div., 2 Corps, Army Ohio. Nov., 1862, 1 Brig., 3 Div., Left Wing 14 Corps, Cumberland. Jany., 1863, 1 Brig., 3 Div., 21 Corps, Cumberland. Oct., 1863, 3 Brig., 3 Div., 4 Corps. Mustered out Dec. 15, 1864.

10th REGIMENT INFANTRY.—Org. at Lebanon, Ky., Nov. 21, 1861. Nov., 1861, 2 Brig., Army Ohio. Dec., 1861, 2 Brig., 1 Div., Army Ohio. Sept., 1862, 2 Brig., 1 Div., 3 Corps, Army Ohio. Nov., 1862, 2 Brig., 3 Div., Centre 14 Corps, Cumberland. Jany., 1863, 2 Brig., 3 Div., 14 Corps. Oct., 1863, 3 Brig., 3 Div., 14 Corps. Mustered out Dec. 6, 1864.

11th REGIMENT INFANTRY.—Org. at Camp Calhoun, Ky., Dec. 9, 1861. Nov., 1861, -4 Brig., Army Ohio, Dec., 1861, 14 Brig., 5 Div., Army Ohio. Sept., 1862, 14 Brig., 5 Div., 2 Corps, Army Ohio. Nov., 1862, 1 Brig., 3 Div., Left Wing 14 Corps, Cumberland. Jany., 1863, 1 Brig., 3 Div., 21 Corps. April, 1863, Dist. Western Ky., Dept. Ohio. June, 1863, 3 Brig., 3 Div., 23 Corps, Dept. Ohio. Aug., 1863, Unatt., Bowling Green, Ky., 1 Div., 23 Corps. Oct., 1863, 1 Brig., 4 Div., 23 Corps. Nov., 1863, 3 Brig., 1 Div., Cav. Corps, Dept. Ohio. April, 1864, 3 Brig., 4 Div., 23 Corps. June, 1864, 3 Brig., 3 Div., 23 Corps. Aug., 1864, 1 Brig., 3 Div., 23 Corps. Mustered out Dec. 16, 1864.

12th REGIMENT INFANTRY.—Org. at Camp Dick Robinson and Clio, Ky., Sept., 1861, to Jany., 1862. Oct., 1861, Camp Dick Robinson, Ky. Nov., 1861, 1 Brig., Army Ohio. Dec., 1861, 1 Brig., 1 Div., Army Ohio. Sept., 1862, 1 Brig., 1 Div., 3 Corps, Army Ohio. Nov., 1862, 1 Brig., 3 Div., Centre 14 Corps, Cumberland. Dec., 1862, Dist. Western Ky., Dept. Ohio. June, 1863, 1 Brig., 2 Div., 23 Corps. Aug., 1863, 1 Brig., 3 Div., 23 Corps. Dec., 1863, Camp Burnside, Ky. Dec., 1863, 2 Brig., Left Wing Forces, 23 Corps. June, 1864, 3 Brig., 3 Div., 23 Corps. Aug., 1864, 1 Brig., 3 Div., 23 Corps, Army Ohio, to Feby., 1865, and Dept. N. C. to July, 1865. Mustered out July 11, 1865.

13th REGIMENT INFANTRY.—Org. at Camp Hobson, near Greensburg, Ky., and mustered in at Green River Dec. 10, 1861. Nov., 1861, 16 Brig., Army Ohio. Dec., 1861, 11 Brig., 1 Div., Army Ohio. March, 1862, 11 Brig., 5 Div., Army Ohio. Sept., 1862, 11 Brig., 5 Div., 2 Corps, Army Ohio. Nov., 1862, 1 Brig., 3 Div., Left Wing 14 Corps, Cumberland. Dec., 1862, Dist. Western Ky., Dept. Ohio. June, 1863, 2 Brig., 3 Div., 23 Corps, Dept. Ohio. Aug., 1863, 2 Brig., 2 Div., 23 Corps. April, 1864, 1 Brig., 2 Div., 23 Corps. June, 1864, 2 Brig., 2 Div., 23 Corps. Mustered out Jany. 12, 1865.

14th REGIMENT INFANTRY.—Org. at Camp Wallace, Lawrence Co., Ky., Dec. 10, 1861. Dec., 1861, 18 Brig., Army Ohio. March, 1862, 27 Brig., 7 Div., Army Ohio. Oct., 1862, 2 Brig., 3 Div., Army Ky., Dept. Ohio. Feby., 1863, Dist. Eastern Ky., Dept. Ohio. June, 1863, 1 Brig., 4 Div., 23 Corps, Ohio. Sept., 1863, Louisa, Ky., Dist. Eastern Ky., 1 Div., 23 Corps. April, 1864, 1 Brig., 1 Div., Dist. Ky., 5 Div., 23 Corps. May, 1864, 3 Brig., 2 Div., 23 Corps. Aug., 1864, 1 Brig., 2 Div., 23 Corps. Dec., 1864, 1 Div., Mil. Dist. and Dept. Ky. Mustered out Sept. 15, 1865.

15th REGIMENT INFANTRY.—Org. at New Haven, Ky., Dec. 14, 1861. Nov., 1861, 16 Brig., Army Ohio. Dec., 1861, 17 Brig., Army Ohio. Jany., 1862, 17 Brig., 3 Div., Army Ohio. Sept., 1862, 17 Brig., 3 Div., 1 Corps, Army Ohio. Nov., 1862, 2 Brig., 1 Div., Centre 14 Corps, Cumberland. Jany., 1863, 2 Brig., 1 Div., 14 Corps. April, 1863, 1 Brig., 2 Div., 14 Corps. Oct., 1863, 1 Brig., 1 Div., 14 Corps. Nov., 1863, Post Chattanooga, Tenn. April, 1864, 1 Brig., 1 Div., 14 Corps. Mustered out Jany. 14, 1865.

16th REGIMENT INFANTRY.—Org. at Camp Kenton, Ky., Jany. 27, 1862. Jany., 1862, 18 Brig., Army Ohio. March, 1862, Unatt., Army Ohio. Nov., 1862, Dist. Western Ky., Dept. Ohio. June, 1863, 2 Brig., 3 Div., 23 Corps. Aug., 1863, 1 Brig., 2 Div., 23 Corps. April, 1864, 1 Brig., 3 Div., 23 Corps. March, 1865, 1 Brig., 3 Div., 23 Corps, Dept. N. C. Mustered out July 15, 1865.

17th REGIMENT INFANTRY.—Org. at Hartford and Calhoun, Ky., Sept. to Dec., 1861. Nov., 1861, 13 Brig., Army Ohio. Dec., 1861, 13 Brig., 5 Div., Army Ohio. Feby., 1862, 1 Brig., 3 Div., Army Tenn. March, 1862, 3 Brig., 4 Div., Army Tenn. April, 1862, 10 Brig., 4 Div., Army Ohio. July, 1862, 9 Brig., 3 Div., Army Ohio. Sept., 1862, Dist. Western Ky., Dept. Ohio. Nov., 1862, Post Clarksville, Tenn., Dept. Cumberland. March, 1863, 1 Brig., 3 Div., 21 Corps, Cumberland. Oct., 1863, 3 Brig., 3 Div., 4 Corps. Mustered out Jany. 23, 1865.

18th REGIMENT INFANTRY.—Org. at large, Ky., Feby. 8, 1862. Feby., 1862, Unatt., Army Ohio. Aug., 1862, Cruft's Brig., Richmond, Ky., Army Ky. Sept., 1862, 1 Brig., 2 Div., Army Ky., Dept. Ohio. Oct., 1862, Unatt., Army Ky., Dept. Ohio. Dec., 1862, 1 Brig., 2 Div., Army Ky., Dept. Ohio. Feby., 1863, Cruft's Brig., Baird's Div., Army Ky., Dept. Cumberland. June, 1863, 3 Brig., 4 Div., 14 Corps, Cumberland. Oct., 1863, 3 Brig., 3 Div., 14 Corps. June, 1865, 1 Brig., 3 Div., 14 Corps. Mustered out July 18, 1865.

19th REGIMENT INFANTRY.—Org. at Camp Harwood, Ky., Jany. 2, 1862. Jany., 1862, 20 Brig., Army Ohio. Feby., 1862, 20 Brig., 6 Div., Army Ohio. March, 1862, 27 Brig., 7 Div., Army Ohio. Oct., 1862, 2 Brig., 1 Div., Army Ky., Dept. Ohio. Nov., 1862, 2 Brig., 10 Div., Right Wing 13 Corps, Dept. Tenn. Dec., 1862, 2 Brig., 1 Div., Sherman's Yazoo Exp. Jany., 1863, 2 Brig., 10 Div., 13 Corps, Tenn. Aug., 1863, 2 Brig., 4 Div., 13 Corps, Gulf. March, 1864, 1 Brig., 4 Div., 13 Corps. June, 1864, Def. New Orleans. June, 1864, Dist. Baton Rouge, La., Dept. Gulf. Mustered out Jany. 26, 1865.

20th REGIMENT INFANTRY.—Org. at Lexington, Camp Dick Robinson and Smithland, Ky., and mustered in Jany. 6, 1862. Jany., 1862, 22 Brig., Army Ohio. Feby., 1862, 22 Brig., 4 Div., Army Ohio. Sept., 1862, 22 Brig., 4 Div., 2 Corps, Army Ohio. Nov., 1862, 1 Brig., 2 Div., Left Wing 14 Corps, Cumb'd. Dec., 1862, Dist. Western Ky., Dept. Ohio. June, 1863, Unassigned, 2 Div., 23 Corps, Dept. Ohio. Aug., 1863, Dist. Louisville, Ky., 1 Div., 23 Corps. April, 1864, 2 Brig., 2 Div., Dist. Ky., 5 Div., 23 Corps. May, 1864, 3 Brig., 2 Div., 23 Corps. Dec., 1864, Unatt., Dist. Ky., Dept. Ohio. Mustered out Jany. 17, 1865.

21st REGIMENT INFANTRY.—Org. at Camps Hobson and Ward, Ky., Dec. 31, 1861. Dec., 1861, 11 Brig., 1 Div., Army Ohio. March, 1862, 11 Brig., 5 Div., Army Ohio. June, 1862, 7 Indpt. Brig., Army Ohio. July, 1862, 23 Indpt. Brig., Army Ohio. Aug., 1862, 23 Brig., 5 Div., Army Ohio. Sept., 1862, 23 Brig., 5 Div., 2 Corps, Army Ohio. Nov., 1862, 3 Brig., 3 Div., Left Wing 14 Corps, Cumb'd. Jany., 1863, 3 Brig., 3 Div., 21 Corps, Cumb'd. Oct., 1863, Unatt., Army Cumb'd. Jany., 1864, 2 Brig., 1 Div., 4 Corps. June, 1865, 1 Brig., 1 Div., 4 Corps. Aug., 1865, Dept. Texas. Mustered out Dec. 9, 1865.

22nd REGIMENT INFANTRY.—Org. at Louisa, Ky., Jany. 20, 1862. Jany., 1862, 18 Brig., Army Ohio. March, 1862, 26 Brig., 7 Div., Army Ohio. Oct., 1862, 4 Brig., Cumb'd Div., Dist. West Va., Dept. Ohio. Nov., 1862, 3 Brig., 9 Div., Right Wing 13 Corps, Dept. Tenn. Dec., 1862, 3 Brig., 3 Div., Sherman's Yazoo Exp. Jany., 1863, 3 Brig., 3 Div., 13 Corps, Tenn. Feby., 1863, 2 Brig., 9 Div., 13 Corps. July, 1863, 4 Brig., 1 Div., 13 Corps. Aug., 1863, 4 Brig., 1 Div., 13 Corps, Dept. Gulf. Sept., 1863, 3 Brig., 1 Div., 13 Corps. Nov., 1863, Plaquemine, La., Dist. Baton Rouge, La., Dept. Gulf. March, 1864, 2 Brig., 1 Div., 13 Corps. June, 1864, 2 Brig., 3 Div., 19 Corps, Gulf. Mustered out Jany. 20, 1865.

23rd REGIMENT INFANTRY.—Org. at Camp King, Lexington, Ky., Jany. 2, 1862. Jany., 1862, Dist. Ky., Dept. Ohio. March, 1862, 23 Indpt. Brig., Army Ohio. July, 1862, 10 Brig., 4 Div., Army Ohio. Sept., 1862, 10 Brig., 4 Div., 2 Corps, Army Ohio. Nov., 1862, 3 Brig., 2 Div., Left Wing 14 Corps, Cumb'd. Jany., 1863, 3 Brig., 2 Div., 21 Corps, Cumb'd. Oct., 1863, 2 Brig., 3 Div., 4 Corps. Aug., 1864, 2 Brig., 1 Div., 4 Corps. June, 1865, 1 Brig., 1 Div., 4 Corps. Aug., 1865, Dept. Texas. Mustered out Dec. 27, 1865.

24th REGIMENT INFANTRY.—Org. at Lexington, Ky., Dec. 21, 1861. Jany., 1862, 21 Brig., Army Ohio. Jany., 1862, 21 Brig., 6 Div., Army Ohio. Sept., 1862, 21 Brig., 6 Div., 2 Corps, Army Ohio. Nov., 1862, 2 Brig., 1 Div., Left Wing 14 Corps, Cumb'd. Dec., 1862, 2 Brig., 2 Div., Army Ky., Dept. Ohio. Jany., 1863, 1 Brig., Dist. Central Ky., Dept. Ohio. June, 1863, 2 Brig., 1 Div., 23 Corps. July, 1863, 2 Brig., 4 Div., 23 Corps. Aug., 1863, 2 Brig., 3 Div., 23 Corps. Dec., 1864, Louisa, Ky., Mil. Dist. Ky. Mustered out Jany. 31, 1865.

25th REGIMENT INFANTRY.—Org. at Calhoun, Ky., Jany. 1, 1862. Nov., 1861, 13 Brig., Army Ohio. Dec., 1861, 13 Brig., 5 Div., Army Ohio. Feby., 1862, 1 Brig., 3 Div., Army Tenn. March, 1862, 3 Brig., 4 Div., Army Tenn. Consolidated with 17th Ky. Infy., April 13, 1862.

26th REGIMENT INFANTRY.—Org. at Owensboro, Ky., July to Nov., 1861, and mustered in at Nashville, Tenn., March 5, 1862. Nov., 1861, 14 Brig., Army Ohio. Dec., 1861, 14 Brig., 5 Div., Army Ohio. Sept., 1862, 14 Brig., 5 Div., 2 Corps, Army Ohio. Nov., 1862, 2 Brig., 3 Div., Left Wing 14 Corps, Cumb'd. Nov., 1862, Dist. Western Ky., Dept. Ohio. June, 1863, Unatt., 2 Div., 23 Corps, Ohio. Aug., 1863, Unatt., Bowling Green, Ky., 1 Div., 23 Corps. Oct., 1863, Dist. S. W. Ky., 1 Div., 23 Corps. April, 1864, 2 Brig., 2 Div., Dist. Ky., 5 Div., 23 Corps. Dec., 1864, 1 Brig., 2 Div., 23 Corps, Dept. Ohio, to Feby., 1865, and Dept. N. C. to July. Mustered out July 10, 1865.

27th REGIMENT INFANTRY.—Org. at Rochester, Ky., Dec. 16, 1861, to March 21, 1862. March, 1862, 19 Brig., 4 Div., Army Ohio. Sept., 1862, 19 Brig., 4 Div., 2 Corps, Army Ohio. Nov., 1862, 2 Brig., 2 Div., Left Wing 14 Corps, Cumb'd. Nov., 1862, Dist. West. Ky., Dept. Ohio. June, 1863, Unatt., 2 Div., 23 Corps, Dept. Ohio. Aug., 1863, Unatt., Munfordsville, Ky., 1 Div., 23 Corps. Oct., 1863, 1 Brig., 4 Div., 23 Corps. Nov., 1863, 3 Brig., 1 Div., Cav. Corps, Dept. Ohio. April, 1864, 3 Brig., 4 Div., 23 Corps. June, 1864, 3 Brig., 2 Div., 23 Corps. Dec., 1864, Unatt., Dist. Ky., Dept. Ohio. Feby., 1865, 2 Div., Dept. Ky. Mustered out March 29, 1865.

28th REGIMENT INFANTRY.—Org. at Louisville and New Haven, Ky., Oct. 10, 1861, to May 9, 1862. Jany., 1862, 16 Brig., Army Ohio. Feby., 1862, 23 Indpt. Brig., Army Ohio. Aug., 1862, Dumont's Indpt. Brig., Army Ohio. Oct., 1862, Dist. Louisville, Ky., Dept. Ohio. Nov., 1862, Clarksville Dist., Western Ky., Dept. Ohio. June, 1863, 1 Brig., 3 Div., Res. Corps, Cumb'd. Oct., 1863, Unatt., Dept. Cumb'd. April, 1864, 1 Brig., 2 Div., 4 Corps. May, 1864, 2 Brig., 2 Div., 4 Corps. Aug., 1865, Dept. Texas. Mustered out Dec. 14, 1865.

29th REGIMENT INFANTRY.—(Failed to complete organization.)

30th REGIMENT INFANTRY.—Org. at Somerset and Frankfort, Ky., Feby. to April, 1864. April, 1864, 4 Brig., 1 Div., Dist. Ky., 5 Div., 23 Corps, Dept. Ohio. Aug., 1864, 2 Brig., 1 Div., Dist. Ky., Dept. Ohio. Mustered out April 18, 1865.

31st REGIMENT INFANTRY.—(Failed to complete organization.)

32nd REGIMENT INFANTRY.—Org. at Frankfort and Camp Burnside, Ky., Aug., 1862. Sept., 1862, Dist. West. Ky., Dept. Ohio. April, 1863, 2 Brig., Dist. Central Ky., Dept. Ohio. June, 1863, 1 Brig., 1 Div., 23 Corps, Dept. Ohio. Mustered out Aug. 12, 1863.

33rd REGIMENT INFANTRY.—Org. at Munfordsville, Ky., Sept. 13, 1862. Oct., 1862, Dist. Western Ky., Dept. Ohio. April, 1863, 2 Brig., Dist. Central Ky., Dept. Ohio. June, 1863, Unatt., Munfordsville, Ky., 1 Div., 23 Corps, Dept. Ohio. Aug., 1863, Unatt., 2 Div., 23 Corps. Oct., 1863, Dist. South Central Ky., Dept. Ohio, 1 Div., 23

Corps. Jany., 1864, Dist. S. W. Ky., Dept. Ohio. Mustered out by consolidation with 26th Ky. Infy., April 1, 1864.

34th REGIMENT INFANTRY.—Org. at Louisville, Ky., Oct. 3, 1862. Oct., 1862, Dist. Western Ky., Dept. Ohio. June, 1863, Unatt., Bowling Green, Ky., 2 Div., 23 Corps, Dept. Ohio. Aug., 1863, Unatt., Bowling Green, Ky., 1 Div., 23 Corps. Oct., 1863, Dist. South Central Ky., 1 Div., 23 Corps. Oct., 1863, Left Wing Forces, Cumb'd Gap, 23 Corps. Jany., 1864, Dist. Clinch, Dept. Ohio. April, 1864, 1 Brig., 4 Div., 23 Corps. Dec., 1864, 2 Brig., 4 Div., 23 Corps. Jany., 1865, 1 Brig., 4 Div., 23 Corps. Feby., 1865, 1 Brig., 4 Div., Dist. East. Tenn., Dept. Cumb'd. March, 1865, 2 Brig., 4 Div., Dist. East. Tenn., Cumb'd. Mustered out June 24, 1865.

35th REGIMENT INFANTRY.—Org. at Owensboro, Ky., Sept. 26, 1863, and mustered in Oct. 20, 1863. Oct., 1863, Dist. S. W. Ky., Dept. Ohio. April, 1864, 2 Brig., 2 Div., Dist. Ky., 5 Div., 23 Corps, Dept. Ohio. July, 1864, 1 Brig., 1 Div., Dist. Ky., 5 Div., 23 Corps. Mustered out Dec. 29, 1864.

36th REGIMENT INFANTRY.—(Failed to complete organization.)

37th REGIMENT INFANTRY.—Org. at Glasgow Sept. 17 to Dec. 22, 1863. Oct., 1863, Dist. South Central Ky., 1 Div., 23 Corps, Dept. Ohio. Jany., 1864, Dist. S. W. Ky., 1 Div., 23 Corps. April, 1864, 3 Brig., 1 Div., Dist. Ky., 5 Div., 23 Corps. Mustered out Dec. 29, 1864.

38th REGIMENT INFANTRY.—(Failed to complete organization.)

39th REGIMENT INFANTRY.—Org. at Peach Orchard, Ky., Nov. 18, 1862, and mustered in Feby. 16, 1863. Dec., 1862, Dist. Eastern Ky., Dept. Ohio. June, 1863, 1 Brig., 4 Div., 23 Corps, Dept. Ohio. Aug., 1863, Dist. Eastern Ky., 1 Div., 23 Corps. April, 1864, 1 Brig., 1 Div., Dist. Ky., 5 Div., 23 Corps. July, 1864, 3 Brig., 1 Div., Dist. Ky., Dept. Ohio. Dec., 1864, Louisa, Ky., Dist. and Dept. Ky. Mustered out Sept. 15, 1865.

40th REGIMENT INFANTRY.—Org. at Grayson and Falmouth, Ky., July 30, 1863. Aug., 1863, Dist. North Central Ky., 1 Div., 23 Corps, Dept. Ohio. April, 1864, 1 Brig., 2 Div., Dist. Ky., 5 Div., 23 Corps, Dept. Ohio. July, 1864, 1 Brig., 1 Div., Dist. Ky., Dept. Ohio. Mustered out Dec. 30, 1864.

41st REGIMENT INFANTRY.—(Failed to complete organization.)

42nd REGIMENT INFANTRY.—(Failed to complete organization.)

43rd REGIMENT INFANTRY.—(Failed to complete organization.)

44th REGIMENT INFANTRY.—(Failed to complete organization.)

45th REGIMENT INFANTRY.—Org. in Ky. at large, Oct. 10, 1863. Oct., 1863, Dist. North Central Ky., 1 Div., 23 Corps, Dept. Ohio. Jany., 1864, Dist. S. W. Ky., 1 Div., 23 Corps, Dept. Ohio. April, 1864, 4 Brig., 1 Div., Dist. Ky., 5 Div., 23 Corps. July, 1864, 2 Brig., 1 Div., Dist. Ky., Dept. Ohio. Jany., 1865, Unatt., Dist. Ky., Dept. Ohio. Mustered out Feby. 14, 1865.

46th REGIMENT INFANTRY.—(Failed to complete organization.)

47th REGIMENT INFANTRY.—Org. at Irvine and Camp Nelson, Ky., Oct. 5, 1863, to Jany., 1864. Oct., 1863, Dist. North Central Ky., 1 Div., 23 Corps, Dept. Ohio. Jany., 1864, Dist. S. W. Ky., 1 Div., 23 Corps, Dept. Ohio. April, 1864, 4 Brig., 1 Div., Dist. Ky., 5 Div., 23 Corps, Dept. Ohio. July, 1864, Camp Nelson, Ky., Dist. Ky., and Dept. Ky. Mustered out April 12, 1865.

48th REGIMENT INFANTRY.—Org. at Princeton, Ky., Oct. 26, 1863. Nov., 1863, Dist. S. W. Ky., 1 Div., 23 Corps, Dept. Ohio. April, 1864, 1 Brig., 2 Div., Dist. Ky., 5 Div., 23 Corps, Dept. Ohio. Mustered out Dec. 19, 1864.

49th REGIMENT INFANTRY.—Org. at Camp Nelson, Ky., Sept. 19, 1863. Sept., 1863, Dist. Somerset, Ky., 1 Div., 23 Corps, Dept. Ohio. Jany., 1864, Dist. S. W. Ky., Dept. Ohio. April, 1864, 4 Brig., 1 Div., Dist. Ky., 5 Div., 23 Corps, Dept. Ohio. July, 1864, Camp Nelson, Ky., Dept. Ohio. Mustered out Dec. 26, 1864.

50th REGIMENT INFANTRY.—(Failed to complete organization.)

51st REGIMENT INFANTRY.—(Failed to complete organization.)

52nd REGIMENT INFANTRY.—Org. at Franklin and Scottsville, Ky., Oct. 16, 1863, to March 3, 1864. Nov., 1863, 3 Brig., 1 Div., Dist. Ky., Dept. Ohio. July, 1864, 2 Brig., 2 Div., Dist. Ky., Dept. Ohio. Oct., 1864, 1 Brig., 2 Div., Dist. Ky., 5 Div., 23 Corps. Mustered out Jany. 17, 1865.

53rd REGIMENT INFANTRY.—Org. at Covington, Ky., Sept., 1864. Attached to Mil. Dist. and Dept. Ky. Mustered out Sept. 17, 1865.

54th REGIMENT INFANTRY.—Org. at New Castle, Ky., Sept., 1864. Attached to Mil. Dist. and Dept. Ky. Mustered out Sept. 1, 1865.

55th REGIMENT INFANTRY.—Org. at Covington, Ky., Nov., 1864. Attached to Mil. Dist. and Dept. Ky. Mustered out Sept. 19, 1865.

LOUISIANA

1st REGIMENT CAVALRY.—Org. at New Orleans, La., Aug., 1862. Sept., 1862, Weitzel's Res. Brig., Dept. Gulf. Jany., 1863, Unassigned, 1 Div., 19 Corps, Gulf. May, 1863, Cav. Command, 19 Corps. Aug., 1863, Def. New Orleans. Sept., 1863, 1 Brig., Cav. Div., Gulf. Jany., 1864, 3 Brig., Cav. Div., Gulf. July, 1864, Morganza, La. Aug., 1864, Cav. Brig., 19 Corps, Gulf. Dec., 1864, Separate Cav. Brig., Res. Corps, Mil. Div. West. Miss. Feby., 1865, Separate Cav. Brig., Dist. West. Fla. March, 1865, 1 Brig., Lucas' Cav. Div., Steele's Command, M. D. W. M. April, 1865, 3 Brig., 1 Div., Cav. Corps, Gulf. July, 1865, Dept. Gulf. Mustered out Dec. 18, 1865.

2nd REGIMENT CAVALRY.—Org. at New Orleans Nov. 25, 1863, as 3rd La. Infy. Nov., 1863, Def. New Orleans, Dept. Gulf. Consolidated with 1st Cav., Sept. 7, 1864.

1st REGIMENT HEAVY ARTILLERY (AFRICAN DESCENT).—Org. at New Orleans, La., Nov. 29, 1862. Dec., 1862, Def. New Orleans, La., Dept. Gulf. Designation changed to 1st Corps de Afrique, Heavy Arty., Nov. 19, 1863, which see.

1st BATTERY LIGHT ARTILLERY (AFRICAN DESCENT).—Org. at Hebron's Plantation, Miss., Nov. 6, 1863. Jany., 1864, 1 Brig., U. S. C. T., Dist. Vicksburg, Miss., Dept. Tenn. April, 1864, Post Goodrich Landing, Dist. Vicksburg, Miss. Designation changed to Battery C, 3rd U. S. Colored Light Arty., April 26, 1864, which see.

2nd BATTERY LIGHT ARTILLERY (AFRICAN DESCENT).—Org. at Black River Bridge, Miss., Dec. 21, 1863. Jany., 1864, Post Vicksburg, Miss., Dist. Vicksburg. March, 1864, Post Goodrich Landing, Dist. Vicksburg, Miss. Designation changed to Battery D, 3rd U. S. Colored Light Arty., April 26, 1864, which see.

3rd BATTERY LIGHT ARTILLERY (AFRICAN DESCENT).—Org. at Helena, Ark., Dec. 1, 1863. Jany., 1864, Dist. Eastern Ark., 7 Corps, Dept. Ark. Designation changed to Battery E, 3rd U. S. Colored Light Arty., April 26, 1864, which see.

1st REGIMENT INFANTRY.—Org. at New Orleans, La., July 30, 1862. Sept., 1862, Weitzel's Res. Brig., Dept. Gulf. Jany., 1863, 1 Brig., 1 Div., 19 Corps, Gulf. March, 1863, 1 Brig., 4 Div., 19 Corps. Aug., 1863, 2 Brig., 4 Div., 19 Corps. Oct., 1863, Dist. LaFourche, La., Gulf. Feby., 1864, 2 Brig., 2 Div., 19 Corps. June, 1864, Dist. LaFourche, La., Dept. Gulf. Aug., 1864, 2 Brig., 2 Div., 19 Corps, Gulf. Nov., 1864, Dist. LaFourche, Gulf. Mustered out July 12, 1865.

1st REGIMENT NEW ORLEANS INFANTRY.—Org. at New Orleans, La., March 6, 1864. March, 1864, Def. New Orleans, La., Dept. Gulf. April, 1865, Dist. LaFourche and Dept. Gulf. Mustered out May, 1866.

2nd REGIMENT INFANTRY.—Org. at New Orleans, La., Sept. 29, 1862. Dec., 1862, Grover's Div., Dept. Gulf. Jany., 1863, 3 Brig., 1 Div., 19 Corps, Dept. Gulf. May, 1863, 1 Brig., 1 Div., 19 Corps. July, 1863, Dist. Baton Rouge, La., Gulf. Sept., 1863, Unatt., Cav. Div., Dept. Gulf. Nov., 1863, 3 Brig., Cav. Div., Gulf. Jany., 1864, 1 Brig., Cav. Div., Gulf. Aug., 1864, Post Port Hudson, La. Sept., 1864, Dist. Baton Rouge, La., Gulf. April,

1865, Prov'l Brig., Dist. Baton Rouge, Dept. Gulf. Mustered out Sept. 11, 1865.

2nd REGIMENT NEW ORLEANS INFANTRY.—Failed to complete organization and transferred to 1st Regt. New Orleans Infy.

1st REGIMENT NATIVE GUARD, INFANTRY.—Org. at New Orleans, La., Sept. 27, 1862. Sept., 1862, Def. New Orleans, La., Dept. Gulf. Dec., 1862, Indpt. Command, Dept. Gulf. Jany., 1863, Unatt., 1 Div., 19 Corps, Dept. Gulf. Designation changed to 1st Corps de Afrique Infy., June 6, 1863, which see.

2nd REGIMENT NATIVE GUARD, INFANTRY.—Org. at New Orleans, La., Oct. 19, 1862. Oct., 1862, Def. New Orleans. La., Dept. Gulf. Dec., 1862, Indpt. Command, Dept. Gulf. Jany., 1863, Def. New Orleans, Dept. Gulf. Designation changed to 2nd Corps de Afrique Infy., June 6, 1863, which see.

3rd REGIMENT NATIVE GUARD, INFANTRY.—Org. at New Orleans, La., Nov. 24, 1862. Dec., 1862, Indpt. Command, Dept. Gulf. Jany., 1863, Unatt., 1 Div., 19 Corps, Gulf. Designation changed to 3rd Corps de Afrique Infy., June 6, 1863, which see.

4th REGIMENT NATIVE GUARD, INFANTRY.—Org. at New Orleans, La., Feby. 10, 1863. Feby., 1863, Unatt., 1 Div., 19 Corps, Dept. Gulf. Designation changed to 4th Corps de Afrique Infy., June 6, 1863, which see.

5th REGIMENT INFANTRY (AFRICAN DESCENT).—(Organization not completed.)

6th REGIMENT INFANTRY (AFRICAN DESCENT).—Org. at New Orleans, La., July 4, 1863. Mustered out Aug. 13, 1863.

7th REGIMENT INFANTRY (AFRICAN DESCENT).—Org. at New Orleans, La., July 10, 1863. Mustered out Aug. 6, 1863.

7th REGIMENT INFANTRY (AFRICAN DESCENT).—Org. at Memphis, Tenn., Holly Springs, Miss., and Island No. 10, Mo., Dec. 1, 1863. Jany., 1864, Dist. Vicksburg, Miss. March, 1864, Unatt., 1 Div., U. S. C. T., Dist. Vicksburg. Designation changed to 64th U. S. C. T., March 11, 1864.

8th REGIMENT INFANTRY (AFRICAN DESCENT).—Org. at Lake Providence, La., May 5, 1863. May, 1863, African Brig., Dist. N. E. La. July, 1863, Post Vicksburg, Miss., Dist. Vicksburg, Miss. March, 1864, 2 Brig., 1 Div., U. S. C. T., Dist. Vicksburg, Miss. Designation changed to 47th U. S. C. T., March 11, 1864.

9th REGIMENT INFANTRY (AFRICAN DESCENT).—Org. at Memphis, Tenn., and Vicksburg, Miss., Nov. 19, 1863. Nov., 1863, Dist. Memphis, Tenn., 5 Div., 16 Corps, Dept. Tenn. March, 1864, Post Natchez, Miss., Dist. Vicksburg, Miss. Designation changed to 63rd U. S. C. T., March 11, 1864.

10th REGIMENT INFANTRY (AFRICAN DESCENT).—Org. at Lake Providence and Goodrich Landing, La., May to Aug., 1863. May, 1863, Post Goodrich Landing, Dist. N. E. La., Dept. Tenn. Jany., 1864, 1 Brig., U. S. C. T., Dist. Vicksburg, Miss. Designation changed to 48th U. S. C. T., March 11, 1864.

11th REGIMENT INFANTRY (AFRICAN DESCENT).—Org. at Milliken's Bend, La., May 22 to Aug. 22, 1863. May, 1863, African Brig., Dist. N. E. La., Dept. Tenn. July, 1863, Post Goodrich Landing, Dist. Vicksburg, Miss., Dept. Tenn. Jany., 1864, 1 Brig., U. S. C. T., Dist. Vicksburg. Dept. Tenn. Designation changed to 49th U. S. C. T., March 11, 1864.

12th REGIMENT INFANTRY (AFRICAN DESCENT).—Org. at Vicksburg, Miss., May to July, 1863. May, 1863, African Brig., Dist. N. E. La. July, 1863, Post Vicksburg, Miss., Dist. Vicksburg. Designation changed to 50th U. S. C. T., March 11, 1864.

MAINE

1st REGIMENT CAVALRY.—Org. at Augusta, Me., Nov. 5, 1861. March, 1862, Miles' R. R. Brig., Potomac. March, 1862, Cav. Brig., Banks' 5 Corps, and Dept. Shenandoah (Co.'s A, B, E, H, M(. April, 1862, Cav., McDowell's, Dept. Rappahannock (Co.'s C, D, F, G, I, K, L). May, 1862, Bayard's Cav. Brig., Dept. Rappahannock (Co.'s C, D, F, G, I, K, L). June, 1862, Bayard's Cav. Brig., 3

Corps, Army Va. (Regt.). Sept., 1862, Bayard's Brig., Cav. Div., Army Potomac. Jany., 1863, 1 Brig., 3 Div., Cav. Div., Army Potomac. June, 1863, 3 Brig., 2 Div., Cav. Corps, Potomac. Aug., 1863, 2 Brig., 2 Div., Cav. Corps, Potomac. Oct., 1864, 3 Brig., 2 Div., Cav. Corps, Potomac. May, 1865, Dept. Va. Mustered out Aug. 1, 1865.

2nd REGIMENT CAVALRY.—Org. at Augusta, Me., Nov. 30, 1863, to Jany. 2, 1864. April, 1864, Dist. La-Fourche, Dept. Gulf. July, 1864, Pensacola, Fla., Dist. West. Fla., Dept. Gulf. Oct., 1864, 2 Brig., Dist. West. Fla. Jany., 1865, 3 Brig., Dist. West Fla. March, 1865, 2 Brig., Lucas' Cav. Div., Steele's Command, Mil. Div. West. Miss. April, 1865, Dist. West. Fla., Dept. Gulf. Mustered out Dec. 6, 1865.

1st REGIMENT HEAVY ARTILLERY.—Org. Jany. 6, 1863, from 18th Infy. Jany., 1863, 2 Brig., Def. North Potomac, Dept. Washington. Feby., 1863, 2 Brig., Has-kins' Div., 22 Corps, Def. North Potomac. May, 1864, Tyler's Heavy Arty. Div., 2 Corps, Potomac. May, 1864, 2 Brig., 4 Div., 2 Corps, Potomac. July, 1864, 2 Brig., 3 Div., 2 Corps, Potomac. June, 1865, 3 Brig., Haskins' Div., 22 Corps. Mustered out Sept. 11, 1865.

1st INDPT. BATTERY LIGHT ARTILLERY.—Org. at Portland, Me., Dec. 18, 1861. Feby., 1862, Butler's New Orleans Exp. March, 1862, 3 Brig., Dept. Gulf. Oct., 1862, Weitzel's Res. Brig., Dept. Gulf. Jany., 1863, Arty., 1 Div., 19 Corps, Gulf. Jany., 1864, Arty., 2 Div., 19 Corps, Gulf. April, 1864, Camp Barry, 22 Corps, Def. Washington, D. C. May, 1864, 1 Brig., DeRussy's Div., 22 Corps. July, 1864, Arty., 2 Div., 19 Corps, Shenandoah. Dec., 1864, Arty. Brig., 19 Corps, Shenandoah. Feby., 1865, Arty. Res., Shenandoah. Mustered out July 15, 1865.

2nd INDPT. BATTERY LIGHT ARTILLERY.—Org. at Augusta, Me., Nov. 30, 1861. Dec., 1861, Augusta, Me. March, 1862, Fort Preble, Me. April, 1862, Arty., 2 Div., Dept. Rappahannock. June, 1862, Arty., 2 Div., 3 Corps, Army Va. June, 1862, Unatt., Pontoneers, 3 Corps, Army Va. Sept., 1862, Arty., 2 Div., 1 Corps, Potomac. June, 1863, Arty. Brig., 1 Corps, Potomac. Nov., 1863, Camp Barry, Def. Washington, 22 Corps. April, 1864, Arty., 1 Div., 9 Corps, Potomac. July, 1864, Arty. Brig., 9 Corps, Potomac. Sept., 1864, Arty. Res., Potomac, Def. City Point, Va. Mustered out June 16, 1865.

3rd INDPT. BATTERY LIGHT ARTILLERY.—Org. at Augusta, Me., Dec. 11, 1861. April, 1862, Pontoneers, Dept. Rappahannock. June, 1862, Pontoneers, 3 Corps, Army Va. Sept., 1862, 1 Brig., Haskins' Div., Dept. Washington. Feby., 1863, 1 Brig., Haskins' Div., 22 Corps. Transferred to 1st Me. H. A. as Co. M, March 28, 1863. Reorg. Feby., 1864. Feby., 1864, Camp Barry, Def. Washington, 22 Corps. July, 1864, Arty., 3 Div., 9 Corps, Potomac. Aug., 1864, Arty. Res., Potomac. Mustered out June 17, 1865.

4th INDPT. BATTERY LIGHT ARTILLERY.—Org. at Augusta, Me., Dec. 21, 1861. April, 1862, Def. Washington. June, 1862, Arty., 2 Div., 2 Corps, Army Va. Sept., 1862, Arty., 2 Div., 12 Corps, Potomac. Oct., 1862, Def. Upper Potomac, 8 Corps, Middle Dept. March, 1863, 2 Brig., 1 Div., 8 Corps. June, 1863, French's Div., 8 Corps. July, 1863, Arty. Brig., 3 Corps, Potomac. March, 1864, Arty. Brig., 6 Corps, Potomac. Aug., 1864, Arty. Res., Potomac. Dec., 1864, Arty. Brig., 6 Corps, Potomac. March, 1865, Arty. Res., Potomac. Mustered out June 17, 1865.

5th BATTERY LIGHT ARTILLERY.—Org. at Augusta, Me., Dec. 4, 1861. April, 1862, Mil. Dist. Washington, D. C. May, 1862, Arty., 2 Div., Dept. Rappahannock. June, 1862, Arty., 2 Div., 3 Corps, Army Va. Sept., 1862, Arty., 2 Div., 1 Corps, Potomac. June, 1863, Arty. Brig., 1 Corps, Potomac. March, 1864, 2 Brig., Arty. Res., Potomac. April, 1864, Arty. Brig., 5 Corps, Potomac. June, 1864, Arty. Brig., 6 Corps, Potomac and Shenandoah. Dec., 1864, Arty. Brig., 19 Corps, Shenandoah. March, 1865, Arty. Res., Army Shenandoah. Mustered out June 6, 1865.

6th INDPT. BATTERY LIGHT ARTILLERY.—Org. at Augusta, Me., and mustered in Jany. 1, 1862. April, 1862, Whipple's Command, Def. Washington, D. C. June, 1862, Arty., 2 Div., 2 Corps, Army Va. Aug., 1862, Arty.,

3 Div., 3 Corps, Potomac. Aug., 1862, Arty., 1 Div., 3 Corps, Potomac. Sept., 1862, Arty., 2 Div., 12 Corps, Potomac. May, 1863, 1 Vol. Brig., Arty. Res., Potomac. June, 1863, 4 Vol. Brig., Arty., Res. July, 1863, 1 Vol. Brig., Arty. Res. Dec., 1863, 2 Vol. Brig., Arty. Res., Potomac. April, 1864, Arty. Brig., 2 Corps, Potomac. March, 1865, Arty. Res., Potomac. Mustered out June 7, 1865.

7th INDPT. BATTERY LIGHT ARTILLERY.—Org. at Augusta, Me., Dec. 30, 1863. Feby., 1864, Camp Barry, Def. Washington, D. C., 22 Corps. April, 1864, Arty., 3 Div., 9 Corps, Potomac. July, 1864, Arty. Brig., 9 Corps, Potomac. Mustered out June 21, 1865.

1st BATTALION SHARPSHOOTERS.—Org. at Augusta, Me., Oct. 27 to Dec. 29, 1864. Nov., 1864, Engr. Brig., City Point, Dept. Va. and N. C. Jany., 1865, 3 Brig., 1 Div., 5 Corps, Potomac. Mustered out June 21, 1865.

1st REGIMENT INFANTRY.—Org. at Portland and mustered in April 28, 1861, for three months. June, 1861, Def. Washington, D. C. Mustered out Aug. 5, 1861.

1st REGIMENT VETERAN INFANTRY.—Org. at Charlestown, Va., by consolidation of the veterans and recruits of the 5th, 6th and 7th Me. Infy., Aug., 1864. Aug., 1864, 3 Brig., 2 Div., 6 Corps, Army Shenandoah. Dec., 1864, 3 Brig., 2 Div., 6 Corps, Potomac. Mustered out June 28, 1865.

1st BATTALION INFANTRY.—Org. at Augusta and Portland, Me., Feby. and March, 1865, from the 21st, 24th, 25th and 26th Unassigned Co.'s. March, 1865, 2 Brig., Dwight's Div., Dept. Washington. June, 1865, Dwight's Div., Dept. South. July, 1865, 4 Sub-Dist., S. C., Dept. South. Aug., 1865, 3 Sub-Dist., Dept. South. Mustered out April 5, 1866.

2nd REGIMENT INFANTRY.—Org. at Bangor, Me., and mustered in May 28, 1861. June, 1861, Keyes' Brig., Tyler's Div., McDowell's Army, N. E. Va. Aug., 1861, Fort Corcoran, Def. Washington, D. C. Oct., 1861, Martindale's Brig., Porter's Div., Potomac. March, 1862, 1 Brig., 1 Div., 3 Corps, Potomac. May, 1862, 1 Brig., 1 Div., 5 Corps, Potomac. Mustered out June 9, 1863.

3rd REGIMENT INFANTRY.—Org. at Augusta and mustered in June 4, 1861. June, 1861, Howard's Brig., Heintzelman's Div., McDowell's Army, N. E. Va. Aug., 1861, Howard's Brig., Div. Potomac. Oct., 1861, Sedgwick's Brig., Heintzelman's Div., Potomac. March, 1862, 2 Brig., 3 Div., 3 Corps, Potomac. Aug., 1862, 2 Brig., 1 Div., 3 Corps, Potomac. March, 1864, 1 Brig., 3 Div., 2 Corps, Potomac. Mustered out June 28, 1864.

4th REGIMENT INFANTRY.—Org. at Rockland and mustered in June 15, 1861. June, 1861, Howard's Brig., Heintzelman's Div., McDowell's Army, N. E. Va. Aug., 1861, Howard's Brig., Div. Potomac. Oct., 1861, Sedgwick's Brig., Heintzelman's Div., Potomac. March, 1862, 2 Brig., 3 Div., 3 Corps, Potomac. Aug., 1862, 2 Brig., 1 Div., 3 Corps, Potomac. March, 1864, 2 Brig., 3 Div., 2 Corps, Potomac. May, 1864, 1 Brig., 3 Div., 2 Corps, Potomac. Mustered out July 19, 1864.

5th REGIMENT INFANTRY.—Org. at Portland, Me., and mustered in June 24, 1861. June, 1861, Howard's Brig., Heintzelman's Div., McDowell's Army, N. E. Va. Aug., 1861, Heintzelman's Brig., Div. Potomac. Oct., 1861, Slocum's Brig., Franklin's Div., Potomac. March, 1862, 2 Brig., 1 Div., 1 Corps, Potomac. April, 1862, 2 Brig., 1 Div., Dept. Rappahannock. May, 1862, 2 Brig., 1 Div., 6 Corps, Potomac. Mustered out July 27, 1864.

6th REGIMENT INFANTRY.—Org. at Portland, Me., and mustered in July 15, 1861. Aug., 1861, W. F. Smith's Brig., Div. Potomac. Oct., 1861, Stevens' Brig., Smith's Div., Potomac. March, 1862, 1 Brig., 2 Div., 4 Corps, Potomac. May, 1862, 1 Brig., 2 Div., 6 Corps, Potomac. Jany., 1863, Light Div., 6 Corps, Potomac. May, 1863, 3 Brig., 1 Div., 6 Corps, Potomac. July, 1864, 3 Brig., 1 Div., 6 Corps, Shenandoah. Mustered out Aug. 15, 1864.

7th REGIMENT INFANTRY.—Org. at Augusta, Me., and mustered in Aug. 21, 1861. Aug., 1861, Dix's Div., Baltimore, Md. Oct., 1861, Stevens' Brig., Smith's Div., Potomac. March, 1862, 3 Brig., 2 Div., 4 Corps, Potomac. May, 1862, 3 Brig., 2 Div., 6 Corps, Potomac, to Aug.,

1864, and Army Shenandoah to Sept., 1864. Mustered out Sept. 5, 1864.

8th REGIMENT INFANTRY.—Org. at Augusta, Me., and mustered in Sept. 7, 1861. Oct., 1861, Viele's 1 Brig., Sherman's S. C. Exp. April, 1862, Dist. Beaufort, Dept. South. Sept., 1862, U. S. Forces, Port Royal Island, S. C., 10 Corps, Dept. South. April, 1863, Dist. Hilton Head, S. C., 10 Corps. Nov., 1863, Dist. Beaufort, S. C., 10 Corps. April, 1864, 2 Brig., 3 Div., 10 Corps, Dept. Va. and N. C. May, 1864, 1 Brig., 3 Div., 10 Corps. May, 1864, 2 Brig., 2 Div., 18 Corps. Dec., 1864, 4 Brig., 1 Div., 24 Corps. May, 1865, 2 Brig., 1 Div., 24 Corps. Aug., 1865, Dept. Va. Mustered out Jany. 18, 1866.

9th REGIMENT INFANTRY.—Org. at Augusta, Me., and mustered in Sept. 22, 1861. Oct., 1861, Wright's 3 Brig., Sherman's S. C. Exp. Feby., 1862, Fernandina, Fla., Dept. South. Jany., 1863, Dist. Hilton Head, S. C., 10 Corps, Dept. South. June, 1863, St. Helena Island, S. C., 10 Corps. July, 1863, 2 Brig., Folly Island, S. C., 10 Corps. July, 1863, 2 Brig., 2 Div., Morris Island, S. C., 10 Corps. Aug., 1863, 1 Brig., Morris Island, S. C., 10 Corps. Jany., 1864, Morris Island, Northern Dist., 10 Corps. April, 1864, 1 Brig., 3 Div., 10 Corps, Dept. Va. and N. C. May, 1864, 2 Brig., 3 Div., 18 Corps. June, 1864, 3 Brig., 2 Div., 10 Corps. Dec., 1864, 3 Brig., 2 Div., 24 Corps. Jany., 1865, 3 . Brig., 2 Div., Terry's Prov'l Corps, Dept. N. C. March, 1865, 3 Brig., 2 Div., 10 Corps, Dept. N. C. Mustered out July 13, 1865.

10th REGIMENT INFANTRY.—Org. at Portland, Me., and mustered in Oct. 4, 1861. Oct., 1861, Dix's Command, Baltimore, Md. Nov., 1861, R. R. Brig., Potomac. April, 1862, 1 Brig., Williams' Div., Dept. Shenandoah. June, 1862, 1 Brig., 1 Div., 2 Corps, Army Va. Sept., 1862, 1 Brig., 1 Div., 12 Corps, Potomac. April, 1863, Headqrs. 12 Corps, Potomac and Cumb'd. Transferred to 29th Me., Nov. 1, 1863.

11th REGIMENT INFANTRY.—Org. at Augusta and mustered in Nov. 12, 1861. Nov., 1861, Davis' Prov'l Brig., Potomac. Nov., 1861, 1 Brig., Casey's Div., Potomac. March, 1862, 1 Brig., 3 Div., 4 Corps, Potomac. June, 1862, 1 Brig., 2 Div., 4 Corps, Potomac. Dec., 1862, Naglee's Brig., Dept. N. C. Jany., 1863, 2 Brig., 2 Div., 18 Corps, Dept. N. C. Feby., 1863, 1 Brig., 2 Div., 18 Corps, Dept. South. April, 1863, Dist. Beaufort, S. C., 10 Corps, Dept. South. June, 1863, Fernandina, Fla., Dept. South. Oct., 1863, 1 Brig., Morris Island, S. C., 10 Corps. April, 1864, 2 Brig., 1 Div., 10 Corps, Dept. Va. and N. C. May, 1864, 3 Brig., 1 Div., 10 Corps, Army James. Dec., 1864, 3 Brig., 1 Div., 24 Corps. July, 1865, 2 Brig., 1 Div., 24 Corps. Aug., 1865, Dept. Va. Mustered out Feby. 2. 1866.

12th REGIMENT INFANTRY.—Org. at Portland, Me., and mustered in Nov. 6, 1861. Dec., 1861, Ship Island Exp. March, 1862, 3 Brig., Dept. Gulf. Nov., 1862, Grover's Div., Dept. Gulf. Jany., 1863, 2 Brig., 4 Div., 19 Corps, Gulf. July, 1863, Def. New Orleans, La., Gulf. Aug., 1863, 2 Brig., 4 Div., 19 Corps, Gulf. Feby., 1864, 1 Brig., 2 Div., 19 Corps, Gulf. Aug., 1864, 1 Brig., 2 Div., 19 Corps, Shenandoah. March, 1865, 1 Brig., Grover's Div., Dist. Savannah, Ga., Dept. South, and 1 Brig., 1 Div., 10 Corps, Dept. N. C. July, 1865, Dist. Savannah, Ga., Dept. · South. Mustered out April 18, 1866.

13th REGIMENT INFANTRY.—Org. at Augusta, Me., and mustered in Dec. 13, 1861. Nov., 1861, Butler's New Orleans Exp. March, 1862, 3 Brig., Dept. Gulf. July, 1862, Indpt. Command, Dept. Gulf. Dec., 1862, Def. New Orleans, Gulf. Aug., 1863, 2 Brig., 4 Div., 19 Corps, Gulf. Oct., 1863, 2 Brig., 2 Div., 13 Corps, Gulf. Dec., 1863, 3 Brig., 2 Div., 13 Corps, Gulf. Jany., 1864, 2 Brig., 4 Div., 13 Corps, Gulf. Feby., 1864, 2 Brig., 1 Div., 19 Corps, Gulf. Aug., 1864, 2 Brig., 1 Div., 19 Corps, Shenandoah. Sept., 1864, Res. Div., West Va. Mustered out Jany. 5, 1865.

14th REGIMENT INFANTRY.—Org. at Augusta, Me., and mustered in Dec. 31, 1861. Jany., 1862, Butler's New Orleans Exp. March, 1862, 3 Brig., Dept. Gulf. Nov., 1862, Sherman's Div., Gulf. Jany., 1863, 3 Brig., 2 Div., 19 Corps, Gulf. July, 1863, 1 Brig., 3 Div., 19 Corps, Gulf. Sept., 1863, 2 Brig., 3 Div., 19 Corps, Gulf. Feby.,

1864, 1 Brig., 2 Div., 19 Corps, Gulf. Aug., 1864, 1 Brig., 2 Div., 19 Corps, Shenandoah. Jany., 1865, 1 Brig., Grover's Div., Dist. Savannah, Ga., Dept. South. March, 1865, 1 Brig., 1 Div., 10 Corps, Dept. N. C. April, 1865, Dept. South. Mustered out Aug. 28, 1865.

15th REGIMENT INFANTRY.—Org. at Augusta and mustered in Jany. 23, 1862. Jany., 1862, Butler's New Orleans Exp. March, 1862, 3 Brig., Dept. Gulf. Sept., 1862, Dist. West. Fla., Dept. Gulf. July, 1863, Def. New Orleans, Gulf. Aug., 1863, 2 Brig., 4 Div., 19 Corps, Gulf. Oct., 1863, Unatt., 2 Div., 13 Corps, Gulf. Dec., 1863, 3 Brig., 2 Div., 13 Corps, Gulf. Jany., 1864, 2 Brig., 4 Div., 13 Corps, Gulf. Feby., 1864, 2 Brig., 1 Div., 19 Corps, Gulf. Aug., 1864, 2 Brig., 1 Div., 19 Corps, Shenandoah. Sept., 1864, Res. Div., West Va. Jany., 1865, 1 Brig., 1 Div., 19 Corps, Shenandoah. Feby., 1865, 2 Brig., 1 Div., Prov'l, Shenandoah. April, 1865, 2 Brig., 1 Div., Def. Washington, 22 Corps. June, 1865, 3 Sep. Brig., Dist. S. C., Dept. South. Mustered out July 5, 1866.

16th REGIMENT INFANTRY.—Org. at Augusta and mustered in Aug. 14, 1862. Aug., 1862, Whipple's Command, Def. Washington, D. C. Sept., 1862, 3 Brig., 2 Div., 1 Corps, Potomac. Nov., 1862, 1 Brig., 2 Div., 1 Corps, Potomac. March, 1864, 1 Brig., 2 Div., 5 Corps, Potomac. June, 1864, 1 Brig., 3 Div., 5 Corps, Potomac. Sept., 1864, 2 Brig., 3 Div., 5 Corps, Potomac. Mustered out June 5, 1865.

17th REGIMENT INFANTRY.—Org. at Camp King, Cape Elizabeth, Me., and mustered in Aug. 18, 1862. Aug., 1862, Def. Washington, North Potomac. Oct., 1862, 3 Brig., 1 Div., 3 Corps, Potomac. March, 1864, 2 Brig., 3 Div., 2 Corps, Potomac. June, 1864, 1 Brig., 3 Div., 2 Corps, Potomac. March, 1865, 2 Brig., 3 Div., 2 Corps, Potomac. Mustered out June 4, 1865.

18th REGIMENT INFANTRY.—Org. at Bangor and mustered in Aug. 21, 1862. Aug., 1862, Def. Washington, D. C., North Potomac. Oct., 1862, 2 Brig., Def. North Potomac, Def. Washington, D. C. Designation changed to 1st Heavy Arty., Jany. 6, 1863.

19th REGIMENT INFANTRY.—Org. at Bangor, Me., and mustered in Aug. 25, 1862. Aug., 1862, Def. Washington, D. C., North Potomac. Oct., 1862, 1 Brig., 2 Div., 2 Corps, Potomac. Mustered out May 31, 1865.

20th REGIMENT INFANTRY.—Org. at Portland, Me., and mustered in Aug. 29, 1862. Sept., 1862, 1 Brig., 1 Div., 5 Corps, Potomac. Sept., 1862, 3 Brig., 1 Div., 5 Corps, Potomac. Mustered out July 16, 1865.

21st REGIMENT INFANTRY.—Org. at Augusta, Me., and mustered in Oct. 14, 1862. Oct., 1862, New York, Dept. East. Feby., 1863, 1 Brig., 1 Div., 19 Corps, Dept. Gulf. Mustered out Aug. 25, 1863.

22nd REGIMENT INFANTRY.—Org. at Bangor and mustered in Oct. 10, 1862. Oct., 1862, 3 Brig., Casey's Div., Def. Washington, D. C. Dec., 1862, Grover's Div., Dept. Gulf. Jany., 1863, 1 Brig., 4 Div., 19 Corps, Gulf. Mustered out Aug. 14, 1863.

23rd REGIMENT INFANTRY.—Org. at Portland and mustered in Sept. 29, 1862. Oct., 1862, Grover's Brig., Def. Washington, D. C. Feby., 1863, Jewett's Brig., 22 Corps, Def. Washington, D. C. June, 1863, Slough's Brig., Dist. Alexandria, 22 Corps. Mustered out July 15, 1863.

24th REGIMENT INFANTRY.—Org. at Augusta and mustered in Oct. 16, 1862. Oct., 1862, N. Y., Dept. East. Feby., 1863, 3 Brig., 2 Div., 19 Corps, Gulf. Mustered out Aug. 25, 1863.

25th REGIMENT INFANTRY.—Org. at Portland and mustered in Sept. 29, 1862. Oct., 1862, 3 Brig., Casey's Div., Def. Washington, D. C. Dec., 1862, 1 Brig., Casey's Div., Def. Washington, D. C. Feby., 1863, 1 Brig., Casey's Div., 22 Corps. April, 1863, 1 Brig., Abercrombie's Div., 22 Corps. Mustered out July 10, 1863.

26th REGIMENT INFANTRY.—Org. at Bangor and mustered in Oct. 11, 1862. Oct., 1862, 3 Brig., Casey's Div., Def. Washington, D. C. Dec., 1862, Grover's Div., Dept. Gulf. Jany., 1863, 3 Brig., 4 Div., 19 Corps, Gulf. Mustered out Aug. 17, 1863.

27th REGIMENT INFANTRY.—Org. at Portland and mustered in Sept. 30, 1862. Oct., 1862, 3 Brig., Casey's Div., Def. Washington, D. C. Dec., 1862, 1 Brig., Casey's

Div., Def. Washington, D. C. Feby., 1863, 1 Brig., Casey's Div., 22 Corps. April, 1863, 1 Brig., Abercrombie's Div., 22 Corps. Mustered out July 17, 1863.

28th REGIMENT INFANTRY.—Org. at Augusta and mustered in Oct. 18, 1862. Oct., 1862, N. Y., Dept. East. Jany., 1863, 2 Brig., 2 Div., 19 Corps, Gulf. May, 1863, 3 Brig., 2 Div., 19 Corps, Gulf. Mustered out Aug. 31, 1863.

29th REGIMENT INFANTRY.—Org. at Augusta and mustered in Dec. 17, 1863. Feby., 1864, 2 Brig., 1 Div., 19 Corps, Gulf. March, 1864, 1 Brig., 1 Div., 19 Corps, Gulf. Aug., 1864, 1 Brig., 1 Div., 19 Corps, Shenandoah. Feby., 1865, 1 Brig., 1 Prov'l Div., Shenandoah. April, 1865, Dept. Washington, D. C. June, 1865, Dist. S. C., Dept. South. Mustered out June 21, 1866.

30th REGIMENT INFANTRY.—Org. and mustered in Jany. 8, 1864. Feby., 1864, 3 Brig., 1 Div., 19 Corps, Gulf. Aug., 1864, 3 Brig., 1 Div., 19 Corps, Shenandoah. Dec., 1864, Garrison Winchester, Va., Army Shenandoah. March, 1865, 3 Brig., 1 Div., Prov'l Army, Shenandoah. April, 1865, Dept. Washington, 22 Corps. Mustered out Aug. 20, 1865.

31st REGIMENT INFANTRY.—Org. at Augusta March 1 to April 29, 1864. April, 1864, 2 Brig., 2 Div., 9 Corps, Potomac. Mustered out July 15, 1865.

32nd REGIMENT INFANTRY.—Org. at Augusta March 3 to May 6, 1864. April, 1864, 2 Brig., 2 Div., 9 Corps, Potomac. Consolidated with 31st Me., Dec. 12, 1864.

CO. A COAST GUARD INFANTRY.—Mustered in at Belfast March 18, 1864. March, 1865, Fort Washington, Def. Washington, 22 Corps. Mustered out June 1, 1865.

CO. B COAST GUARD INFANTRY.—Mustered in at Augusta April 27, 1864. May, 1864, Fort Foote, Def. North Potomac, 22 Corps. Mustered out June 24, 1865.

CO. C COAST GUARD INFANTRY.—Mustered in at Eastport May 16, 1864. Mustered out Sept. 6, 1865.

CO. D COAST GUARD INFANTRY.—Mustered in at Augusta Jany. 6, 1865. Mustered out Sept. 6, 1865.

CO. E COAST GUARD INFANTRY.—Mustered in at Augusta Jany. 7, 1865. Mustered out July 7, 1865.

CO. F COAST GUARD INFANTRY.—Mustered in at Augusta Jany. 6, 1865. Mustered out July 6, 1865.

1st UNASSIGNED COMPANY.—Assigned to 29th Infy.
2nd UNASSIGNED COMPANY.—Assigned to 16th Infy.
3rd UNASSIGNED COMPANY.—Assigned to 9th Infy.
4th UNASSIGNED COMPANY.—Assigned to 31st Infy.
5th UNASSIGNED COMPANY.—Assigned to 19th Infy.
6th UNASSIGNED COMPANY.—Assigned to 31st Infy.
7th UNASSIGNED COMPANY.—Org. at Augusta Oct. 25, 1864. Mustered out July 6, 1865.
8th UNASSIGNED COMPANY.—Assigned to 11th Infy.
9th UNASSIGNED COMPANY.—Assigned to 20th Infy.
10th UNASSIGNED COMPANY.—Assigned to 12th Infy.
11th UNASSIGNED COMPANY.—Assigned to 12th Infy.
12th UNASSIGNED COMPANY.—Assigned to 12th Infy.
13th UNASSIGNED COMPANY.—Assigned to 14th Infy.
14th UNASSIGNED COMPANY.
15th UNASSIGNED COMPANY.—Assigned to 12th Infy.
16th UNASSIGNED COMPANY.—Assigned to 12th Infy.
17th UNASSIGNED COMPANY.—Assigned to 14th Infy.
18th UNASSIGNED COMPANY.—Assigned to 12th Infy.
19th UNASSIGNED COMPANY.—Org. at Augusta March 25, 1865. Mustered out May 23, 1865.
20th UNASSIGNED COMPANY.—Assigned to 14th Infy.
21st UNASSIGNED COMPANY.—Assigned to 1st Battalion Infy.
22nd UNASSIGNED COMPANY.—Assigned to 14th Infy.
23rd UNASSIGNED COMPANY.—Assigned to 14th Infy.

24th UNASSIGNED COMPANY.—Assigned to 1st Battalion Infy.
25th UNASSIGNED COMPANY.—Assigned to 1st Battalion Infy.
26th UNASSIGNED COMPANY.—Assigned to 1st Battalion Infy.
27th UNASSIGNED COMPANY.—Not mustered.
28th UNASSIGNED COMPANY.—Not mustered.
29th UNASSIGNED COMPANY.—Org. at Augusta April 26, 1865. Mustered out May 19, 1865.
30th UNASSIGNED COMPANY.—Org. at Augusta April 18, 1865. Mustered out May 19, 1865.

MARYLAND

1st REGIMENT CAVALRY.—Org. at Baltimore and Williamsport, Md., Pittsburg, Pa., and Washington, D. C., Aug., 1861, to June, 1862. Jany., 1862, Balto., Md., Dix's Div., Middle Dept. April, 1862, Hatch's Cav. Brig., Dept. Shenandoah. June, 1862, Hatch's Cav. Brig., 2 Corps, Army Va. Sept., 1862, Cav. Brig., 11 Corps, Potomac. Feby., 1863, Def. Upper Potomac, 8 Corps, Middle Dept. Feby., 1863, 2 Brig., 3 Div., Cav. Corps, Potomac. June, 1863, 1 Brig., 2 Div., Cav. Corps, Potomac. Oct., 1863, Provost Marshal Gen'l's Command, Army Potomac. March, 1864, 3 Separate Brig., 8 Corps, Middle Dept. June, 1864, 3 Brig., 1 Div., 10 Corps, Army James, Dept. Va. & N. C. Oct., 1864, 3 Brig., Cav. Div., Dept. Va. and N. C. Jany., 1865, 3 Brig., Cav. Div., Dept. Va. March, 1865, 2 Brig., Cav. Div., Dept. Va. April, 1865, Cav. Brig., Dept. Va. Mustered out Aug. 8, 1865.

1st REGIMENT, POTOMAC HOME BRIGADE, CAVALRY.—Org. at Frederick, Md., Aug. 10 to Nov. 27, 1861, as Cole's Battalion Md. Cav. Aug., 1861, Unatt., Dept. West Va. Jany., 1862, Cav. Landers' Div., Potomac. March, 1862, Hatch's Cav. Brig., Banks' 5 Corps. April, 1862, Hatch's Cav. Brig., Dept. Shenandoah. May, 1862, R. R. Brig., Middle Dept. Sept., 1862, Cav., 12 Corps, Potomac. Nov., 1862, Def. Upper Potomac, 8 Corps, Middle Dept. March, 1863, 3 Brig., 1 Div., 8 Corps. July, 1863, 2 Brig., Md. Heights Div., West Va. Dec., 1863, Cav. Brig., 1 Div., West Va. April, 1864, 1 Brig., 1 Cav. Div., West Va. Aug., 1864, 3 Brig., 1 Div., Cav. Corps, Middle Mil. Div. Oct., 1864, Res. Div., Harper's Ferry, West Va. Jany., 1865, 3 Brig., 3 Div., West Va. Feby., 1865, 1 Brig., 2 Div., West Va. Mustered out June 28, 1865.

2nd REGIMENT CAVALRY.—Org. at Annapolis and Balto. July 1 to Aug. 12, 1863. At Balto., Md., 8 Corps, Middle Dept. Mustered out Jany. 6 to Feby. 26, 1864.

3rd REGIMENT CAVALRY.—Org. at Balto., Md., Aug. 8, 1863 to Jany. 9, 1864. Aug., 1863, Cav. Res., 8 Corps, Balto., Md., Middle Dept. Jany., 1864, Def. New Orleans, La., Dept. Gulf. March, 1864, Dist. LaFourche, Dept. Gulf. June, 1864, Dist. Morganza, Dept. Gulf. Aug., 1864, 3 Brig., 3 Div., 19 Corps, Gulf. Oct., 1864, U. S. Forces, Mobile Bay, Dept. Gulf. Dec., 1864, Dist. Southern Ala., Mil. Dist. West. Miss. May, 1865, 1 Brig., 2 Div., Cav. Corps, West. Miss., Dept. Gulf. June, 1865, Dept. Miss. Mustered out Sept. 7, 1865.

PURNELL LEGION CAVALRY.—Org. Co.'s A and B at Pikesville, Md., Sept. to Nov., 1861; Co. C at Balto., Md., Sept., 1862.

Co. A.—Nov., 1861. Dix's Div., Balto., Md. July, 1862, Def. Balto., 8 Corps, Middle Dept. July, 1862, Dist. Eastern Shore, Md., 8 Corps. Jany., 1863, 1 Separate Brig., 8 Corps. June, 1863, Lockwood's Brig., 8 Corps. July, 1863, Dist. Eastern Shore, 8 Corps. Mustered out July 28, 1865.

Co. B.—Nov., 1861, Dix's Div., Balto., Md. July, 1862, Annapolis, Md., 8 Corps, Middle Dept. June, 1863, Def. Balto., Md., 8 Corps. Oct., 1863, 3 Separate Brig., 8 Corps. Dec., 1863, 1 Separate Brig., 8 Corps. Jany., 1864, Annapolis, Md., 8 Corps. May, 1864, 2 Brig., 2 Div., 5 Corps, Potomac. Mustered out Oct. 26, 1864.

Co. C.—Sept., 1862, Def. Balto., Md., 8 Corps, Middle Dept. Jany., 1863, 2 Separate Brig., 8 Corps. Feby., 1863, 1 Separate Brig., 8 Corps. June, 1863, 3 Separate Brig., 8 Corps. Aug., 1863, Dist. Delaware, 8 Corps. May, 1864, 2 Brig., 2 Div., 5 Corps, Potomac. Mustered out Oct. 26, 1864.

SMITH'S INDPT. COMPANY CAVALRY.—Org. at Snow Hill. Md., Oct. 15, 1862. Sept., 1862, Def. Balto., Md., 8 Corps, Middle Dept. Oct., 1862, Dist. Eastern Shore, Md., 8 Corps. Jany., 1863, 1 Separate Brig., 8 Corps. June, 1863, Unatt., Eastern Shore, Md., 8 Corps. March, 1864, 3 Separate Brig., 8 Corps. Oct., 1864, 1 Separate Brig., 8 Corps. Mustered out June 30, 1865.

BATTERY A LIGHT ARTILLERY.—Org. at Balto. and Pikesville Aug. and Sept., 1861. Sept., 1861, Arty., Dix's Div., Middle Dept. May, 1862, 4 Brig., Arty. Res., 5 Corps, Potomac. Sept., 1862, Arty., 1 Div., 6 Corps, Potomac. May, 1863, 4 Vol. Brig., Arty. Res., Potomac. July, 1863, 3 Vol. Brig., Arty. Res., Potomac. Oct., 1863, Arty. Brig., 1 Corps, Potomac. March, 1864, Camp Barry, Def. Washington, 22 Corps. May, 1864, 1 Brig., DeRussy's Div., 22 Corps. July, 1864, Res. Div., Dept. West Va., Harper's Ferry, West Va. Jany., 1865, 3 Brig., 3 Div., West Va. Consolidated with Battery B, March 11, 1865.

BATTERY A JUNIOR LIGHT ARTILLERY.—Org. at Balto., Md., for 6 months, July 14, 1863. July, 1863, Def. Balto., Md., 8 Corps, Middle Dept. Oct., 1863, 3 Separate Brig., 8 Corps. Dec., 1863, Arty. Res., Balto., Md., 8 Corps. Mustered out Jany. 19, 1864.

BATTERY B LIGHT ARTILLERY.—Org. at Balto. and Pikesville Sept. and Oct., 1861. Oct., 1861, Dix's Div., Balto., Md., Middle Dept. May, 1862, 4 Brig., Arty. Res., 5 Corps, Potomac. Sept., 1862, Arty., 2 Div., 6 Corps, Potomac. Jany., 1863, Provost Guard, Army Potomac. May, 1863, Unatt., Arty. Res., Potomac. June, 1863, Camp Barry, Def. Washington, 22 Corps. Aug., 1863, 2 Brig., Md. Heights Div., West Va. Dec., 1863, 2 Brig., 1 Div., West Va. April, 1864, Arty., 1 Div., West Va. May, 1864, Arty. Brig., Dept. West Va. July, 1864, Harper's Ferry, West Va., Res. Div., West Va. April, 1865, 2 Brig., 1 Div., West Va. Mustered out July 3, 1865.

BATTERY B JUNIOR LIGHT ARTILLERY.—Org. at Balto. for 6 months, July 14, 1863. July, 1863, Def. Balto., 8 Corps, Middle Dept. Oct., 1863, 3 Separate Brig., 8 Corps. Dec., 1863, Arty. Res., Balto., Md., 8 Corps. Mustered out Jany. 16, 1864.

BATTERY D LIGHT ARTILLERY.—Org. at Balto. Feby. 29, 1864. March, 1864, 3 Separate Brig., 8 Corps, Middle Dept. June, 1864, 3 Brig., DeRussy's Div., 22 Corps. Aug., 1864, 4 Brig., DeRussy's Div., 22 Corps. Oct., 1864, 3 Brig., DeRussy's Div., 22 Corps. Feby., 1865, 1 Brig., DeRussy's Div., 22 Corps. Mustered out June 24, 1865.

BALTIMORE BATTERY LIGHT ARTILLERY.—Org. at Balto. Aug. 18, 1862. Aug., 1862, Def. Balto., Md., 8 Corps, Middle Dept. Sept., 1862, Md. Brig., Williamsport, Md., Def. Upper Potomac, 8 Corps. Jany., 1863, Def. Upper Potomac, 8 Corps. March, 1863, 3 Brig., 2 Div., 8 Corps. June, 1863, French's Div., 8 Corps. July, 1863, Def. Balto., 8 Corps. Oct., 1863, 3 Separate Brig., 8 Corps. Dec., 1863, Arty. Res., 8 Corps. July, 1864, Dist. Harper's Ferry, West Va., Res. Div., Dept. West Va. Jany., 1865, Camp Barry, Def. Washington, 22 Corps. Mustered out June 17, 1865.

1st REGIMENT INFANTRY.—Org. at Balto. May, 1861. June, 1861, Def. Upper Potomac, Dept. Shenandoah. Aug., 1861, Dix's Div., Balto., Md. Oct., 1861, Gordon's Brig., Banks' Div., Potomac. March, 1862, 1 Brig., 1 Div., Banks' 5 Corps. April, 1862, 1 Brig., 1 Div., Dept. Shenandoah. June, 1862, Balto., Md., Middle Dept. Sept., 1862, Md. Brig., Def. Upper Potomac, 8 Corps. March, 1863, 1 Brig., 1 Div., 8 Corps. June, 1863, Md. Brig., French's Div., 8 Corps. July, 1863, 3 Brig., 3 Div., 1 Corps, Potomac. Dec., 1863, 2 Brig., 3 Div., 1 Corps, Potomac. March, 1864, 3 Brig., 2 Div., 5 Corps, Potomac. June, 1864, 2 Brig., 2 Div., 5 Corps, Potomac. Mustered out July 2, 1865.

1st REGIMENT, POTOMAC HOME BRIGADE, INFANTRY.—Org. at Frederick Aug. 15 to Dec. 13, 1861. Jany., 1862, Unatt., Banks' Div., Potomac. March, 1862, Unassigned, Banks' 5 Corps, and Dept. Shenandoah. May, 1862, R. R. Brig., Middle Dept. July, 1862, R. R. Brig., 8 Corps, Middle Dept. Sept., 1862, Annapolis, Md., 8 Corps. March, 1863, 1 Separate Brig., 8 Corps. June, 1863, Lockwood's Brig., 8 Corps. July, 1863, 2 Brig., 1 Div., 12 Corps, Potomac. July, 1863, 2 Brig., Md. Heights

Div., West Va. Dec., 1863, 2 Brig., 1 Div., West Va. April, 1864, Harper's Ferry, West Va., Res. Div., Dept. West Va. Jany., 1865, 3 Brig., 3 Div., West Va. Designated 13th Md. Infy., April 8, 1865.

1st REGIMENT EASTERN SHORE INFANTRY.—Org. at Cambridge Sept., 1861. Oct., 1861, Dix's Div., Balto., Md. Nov., 1861, Eastern Shore, Md., and Va., Middle Dept. July. 1862, Dist. Eastern Shore, 8 Corps, Middle Dept. Jany., 1863, 1 Separate Brig., 8 Corps. June, 1863, Lockwood's Brig., 8 Corps. July, 1863, 2 Brig., 1 Div., 12 Corps, Potomac. July, 1863, 2 Brig., Md. Heights Div., West Va. Oct., 1863, 1 Separate Brig., 8 Corps. March, 1864, 3 Separate Brig., 8 Corps. June, 1864, 1 Separate Brig., 8 Corps. Sept., 1864, Res. Div., Dept. West Va. Consolidated with 11th Md. Infy., Feby. 23, 1865.

2nd REGIMENT INFANTRY.—Org. at Balto., Md., June to Sept. 1861. Sept., 1861, Dix's Div., Balto., Md. April, 1862, 1 Brig., 2 Div., Dept. N. C. July, 1862, 1 Brig., 2 Div., 9 Corps, Potomac. April, 1863, 1 Brig., 2 Div., 9 Corps, Ohio. June, 1863, Unassigned, 1 Div., 23 Corps, Ohio. Oct., 1863, 1 Brig., 2 Div., 9 Corps, Ohio. Jany., 1864, 2 Brig., 2 Div., 9 Corps, Ohio. April, 1864, 2 Brig., 3 Div., 9 Corps, Potomac. June, 1864, 2 Brig., 2 Div., 9 Corps, Potomac. Mustered out July 17, 1865.

2nd REGIMENT, POTOMAC HOME BRIGADE, INFANTRY.—Org. at Cumberland Aug. 27 to Oct. 31, 1861. Oct., 1861, R. R. Dist. West Va. March, 1862, Dist. Cumb'd, Md., Dept. Mts. April, 1862, R. R. Dist., Dept. Mts. July, 1862, R. R. Dist., 8 Corps, Middle Dept. Sept., 1862, R. R. Dist., West Va. Jany., 1863, Def. Upper Potomac, 8 Corps. March, 1863, 5 Brig., 1 Div., 8 Corps. June, 1863, Mulligan's Brig., Scammon's Div., West Va. Dec., 1863, 2 Brig., 2 Div., West Va. April, 1864, Kelly's Command, Res. Div., West Va. April, 1865, 2 Brig., 1 Div., West Va. (Co. F, Cav. Jany., 1863, Martinsburg, West Va., 8 Corps. March, 1863, 3 Brig., 1 Div., 8 Corps. June, 1863, 1 Brig., Md. Heights Div., West Va. Dec., 1863, Cav. Brig., 1 Div., West Va.) Mustered out May 29, 1865.

2nd REGIMENT EASTERN SHORE INFANTRY.—Org. at Charlestown Oct. 2 to Dec. 28, 1861. Oct., 1861, Dix's Div., Balto., Md. March, 1862, Eastern Shore, Md. and Va., Middle Dept. July, 1862, Dist. Eastern Shore, 8 Corps. Jany., 1863, 1 Separate Brig., 8 Corps. June, 1863, Lockwood's Brig., 8 Corps. July, 1863, 2 Brig., 1 Div., 12 Corps, Potomac. July, 1863, 2 Brig., Lockwood's Md. Heights Div., West Va. Dec., 1863, 2 Brig., 1 Div., West Va. April, 1864, 1 Brig., 1 Infy. Div., West Va. July, 1864, 2 Brig., 1 Infy. Div., West Va. Oct., 1864, Dist. Harper's Ferry, West Va., Res. Div., West Va. Consolidated with 1st E. S. Regt., Jany. 23, 1865.

3rd REGIMENT INFANTRY.—Org. at Balto. and Williamsport June 18, 1861, to Feby. 17, 1862. Feby., 1862, Dix's Div., Balto., Md. May, 1862, 1 Brig., Sigel's Div., Dept. Shenandoah. June, 1862, 1 Brig., 2 Div., 2 Corps, Army Va. Aug., 1862, 2 Brig., 2 Div., 2 Corps, Army Va. Sept., 1862, 2 Brig., 2 Div., 12 Corps, Potomac. Oct., 1862, 2 Brig., 1 Div., 12 Corps, Potomac. May, 1863, 1 Brig., 1 Div., 12 Corps, Potomac. Oct., 1863, 1 Brig., 1 Div., 12 Corps, Cumb'd. April, 1864, 2 Brig., 1 Div., 9 Corps, Potomac. June, 1864, 1 Brig., 1 Div., 9 Corps, Potomac. July, 1864, 2 Brig., 1 Div., 9 Corps, Potomac. Sept., 1864, 3 Brig., 1 Div., 9 Corps, Potomac. Mustered out July 31, 1865.

3rd REGIMENT, POTOMAC HOME BRIGADE, INFANTRY.—Org. at Balto., Cumb'd and Hagerstown, Oct. 31, 1861, to May 20, 1862. Nov., 1861, R. R. Dist., West Va. Jany., 1862, Landers' Div., Potomac. March, 1862, R. R. Dist., Dept. Mts. July, 1862, R. R. Brig., 8 Corps, Middle Dept. Sept., 1862, Harper's Ferry, West Va. Sept., 1862, Annapolis, Md., 8 Corps. July, 1863, 3 Separate Brig., 8 Corps. Oct., 1863, 1 Separate Brig., 8 Corps. July, 1864, Kenly's Indpt. Brig., 6 Corps, Army Shenandoah. Aug., 1864, Kenly's Brig., Res. Div., Dept. West Va. Oct., 1864, Kelly's Command, Res. Div., West Va. April, 1865, 1 Brig., 1 Div., West Va. Mustered out May 29, 1865.

4th REGIMENT INFANTRY.—Org. at Balto. July and Aug., 1862. Sept., 1862, Md. Brig., Def. Upper Potomac,

8 Corps, Middle Dept. March, 1863, 1 Brig., 1 Div., 8 Corps. June, 1863, Md. Brig., French's Div., 8 Corps. July, 1863, 3 Brig., 3 Div., 1 Corps, Potomac. Dec., 1863, 2 Brig., 3 Div., 1 Corps, Potomac. March, 1864, 3 Brig., 2 Div., 5 Corps, Potomac. June, 1864, 2 Brig., 2 Div., 5 Corps. Potomac. Mustered out May 31, 1865.

4th REGIMENT, POTOMAC HOME BRIGADE, INFANTRY.—Org. not completed. 3 Co.'s org. for guard duty on the B. & O. R. R. between Martinsburg and Harper's Ferry, West Va. Consolidated with 3rd Regt., P. H. B., Infy., Aug. 11, 1862.

5th REGIMENT INFANTRY.—Org. at Balto., Sept., 1861. Sept., 1861, Dix's Div., Balto., Md. March, 1862, Fort Monroe, Va., Dept. Va. July, 1862, Weber's Brig. Div. at Suffolk, Va., 7 Corps, Dept. Va. Sept., 1862, 3 Brig., 3 Div., 2 Corps, Potomac. Dec., 1862, Point of Rocks, Md., Def. Upper Potomac, 8 Corps. March, 1863, 2 Brig., 1 Div., 8 Corps. July, 1863, Def. Balto., 8 Corps. Jany., 1864, Dist. Del., 8 Corps. June, 1864, 3 Brig., 2 Div., 18 Corps, Army James, Dept. Va. and N. C. Aug., 1864, 2 Brig., 1 Div., 18 Corps. Dec., 1864, 2 Brig., 3 Div., 24 Corps. July, 1865, 2d Indpt. Brig., 24 Corps. Mustered out Sept. 1, 1865.

6th REGIMENT INFANTRY.—Org. at Balto., Aug. 12 to Sept. 8, 1862. Sept., 1862, Md. Brig., Def. Upper Potomac, 8 Corps, Middle Dept. March, 1863, 3 Brig., 2 Div., 8 Corps. June, 1863, Md. Brig., French's Command, 8 Corps. July, 1863, 2 Brig., 3 Div., 3 Corps, Potomac. March, 1864, 2 Brig., 3 Div., 6 Corps, Potomac, and Army Shenandoah, Middle Mil. Div. Mustered out June 20, 1865.

7th REGIMENT INFANTRY.—Org. at Balto., Aug. and Sept., 1862. Sept., 1862, Md. Brig., Def. Upper Potomac, 8 Corps, Middle Dept. March, 1863, 1 Brig., 1 Div., 8 Corps. June, 1863, Md. Brig., French's Command, 8 Corps. July, 1863, 3 Brig., 3 Div., 1 Corps, Potomac. Dec., 1863, 2 Brig., 3 Div., 1 Corps, Potomac. March, 1864, 3 Brig., 2 Div., 5 Corps, Potomac. June, 1864, 2 Brig., 2 Div., 5 Corps, Potomac. Mustered out May 31, 1865.

8th REGIMENT INFANTRY.—Org. at Balto., Aug., 1862. Sept., 1862, Md. Brig., Def. Upper Potomac, 8 Corps, Middle Dept. March, 1863, 1 Brig., 1 Div., 8 Corps. June, 1863, Md. Brig., French's Command, 8 Corps. July, 1863, 3 Brig., 3 Div., 1 Corps, Potomac. Dec., 1863, 2 Brig., 3 Div., 1 Corps, Potomac. March, 1864, 3 Brig., 2 Div., 5 Corps, Potomac. June, 1864, 2 Brig., 2 Div., 5 Corps, Potomac. Mustered out May 31, 1865.

9th REGIMENT INFANTRY.—Org. at Balto., June and July, 1863. July, 1863, 2 Brig., Md. Heights, Div., W. Va. July, 1863, 1 Brig., Md. Heights Div., W. Va. Dec., 1863, 1 Brig., 1 Div., W. Va. Mustered out Feby. 24, 1864.

10th REGIMENT INFANTRY.—Org. at Balto., June and July, 1863. July, 1863, 2 Brig., Md. Heights Div., W. Va. July, 1863, 1 Brig., Md. Heights Div., W. Va. Dec., 1863, 1 Brig., 1 Div., W. Va. Jany., 1864, 2d Separate Brig., 8 Corps. Mustered out Jany. 29, 1864.

11th REGIMENT INFANTRY.—Org. for 100 days at Balto., June 16, 1864. June, 1864, 3d Separate Brig., 8 Corps, Middle Dept. July, 1864, 1st Separate Brig., 8 Corps. Mustered out Oct. 1, 1864.

11th REGIMENT INFANTRY.—Re-organized for 1 year at Balto., Monrovia and Relay House, Md. Sept. to Dec., 1864. Sept., 1864, 1st Separate Brig., 8 Corps. Mustered out June 15, 1864.

12th REGIMENT INFANTRY.—Org. for 100 days at Balto., July 30, 1864. Aug., 1864, 1st Separate Brig., 8 Corps. Sept., 1864, Res. Div., W. Va. Mustered out Nov. 14, 1864.

13th REGIMENT INFANTRY.—Org. April 8, 1865, from 1st Md. P. H. B. Infy. April, 1865, 1 Brig., 2 Infy. Div., W. Va. Mustered out May 29, 1865.

PURNELL LEGION.—Org. at Salisbury and Pikesville, Oct. 31 to Dec., 31, 1861. Oct., 1861, Dix's Div., Balto., Md. March, 1862, Lockwood's Brig., Middle Dept. May, 1862, 2 Brig., Sigel's Div., Dept. Shenandoah. June, 1862, 2 Brig., 2 Div., 2 Corps. Army Va. Aug., 1862, 3 Brig., 2 Div., 2 Corps, Army Va. Sept., 1862, 3 Brig., 2 Div.,

12 Corps, Potomac. Oct., 1862, 2 Brig., 2 Div., 12 Corps, Potomac. Dec., 1862, Frederick, Md., 8 Corps, Middle Dept. Feby., 1863, 3d Separate Brig., 8 Corps. June, 1863, 1st Separate Brig., 8 Corps. June, 1864, 2 Brig., 2 Div., 5 Corps, Potomac. Mustered out Oct. 24, 1864.

BALTIMORE LIGHT INFANTRY.—(5 CO.'S.) Org. at Balto., Nov. and Dec., 1861. Dec., 1861, Dix's Div., Balto. Consolidated to 2 Co.'s and consolidated with 3d Md. Infy., May 24, 1862.

M'GOWAN'S INDEPENDENT COMPANY INFANTRY.—(PATAPSCO GUARDS). Org. at Ellicott's Mills, Sept. 25, 1861. Sept., 1861, Dix's Div., Balto., Md. March, 1862, R. R. Brig., Middle Dept. July, 1862, R. R. Brig., 8 Corps, Middle Dept. Sept., 1862, Unass'd, 8 Corps. Jany., 1863, 2d Separate Brig., 8 Corps. June, 1863, York, Pa., Dept. Susquehanna. Mustered out Aug. 17, 1865.

MASSACHUSETTS

1st REGIMENT CAVALRY.—Org. at Readville, Mass., Sept. 5 to Nov. 1, 1861. Jany., 1862, Unatt., Dept. South. April, 1862, 3 Brig., 2 Div., Dept. South. Sept., 1862, 2 Brig., Pleasanton's Cav. Div., Potomac (8 Co.'s). (4 Co.'s, I, K, L, M, remained in Dept. South, attached to Dist. Beaufort, 10 Corps, Dept. South, and designated Indpt. Battalion, Mass. Cav., Aug. 4, 1863). Oct., 1862, Averill's Cav. Brig., Potomac. Feby., 1863, 1 Brig., 2 Div., Cav. Corps, Potomac. March, 1865, City Point, Va., Army Potomac. April, 1865, Provost Guard, Potomac. May, 1865, Headqrs. Army Potomac. Co.'s C and D attached to Provost Guard, Army Potomac, from April, 1864. Regiment mustered out June 29, 1865.

BATTALION 2nd CAVALRY.—(3 Co.'s.) Org. at Lowell, Mass., Dec. 6 to Dec. 27, 1861. Jany., 1862, Butler's New Orleans Exp. March, 1862, Unatt., Dept. Gulf. Oct., 1862, Def. New Orleans (Co. C.), Sherman's Div., Dept. Gulf (Co. A.), Weitzel's Reserve Brig., Dept. Gulf. (Co. B.) Jany., 1863, 2 Div., 19 Corps, Dept. Gulf (Co. A), 1 Div., 19 Corps (Co. B). Co.'s assigned to 3rd Mass. Cav. as Co.'s L and M, July 22, 1863.

2nd REGIMENT CAVALRY.—Org. at Readville, Mass., and in California, Dec. 10, 1862, to June 20, 1863. Feby., 1863, Unatt., 4 Corps, Dept. Va. (Co.'s A, B, C, D, K) May, 1863, Casey's Prov'l Brig., 22 Corps (Co.'s E, F, G H, I, L, M). June, 1863, 1 Brig., 1 Div., 4 Corps (Co.'s A, B, C, D, K). July, 1863, King's Div., 22 Corps (Co.'s A, B, C, D, K). Sept., 1863, Cav. Brig., 22 Corps. Aug., 1864, 3 Brig., 1 Div., Cav. Corps, Army Shenandoah, Middle Mil. Div. Sept., 1864, 3 (Reserve) Brig., 1 Div., Cav. Corps, Army Shenandoah. March, 1865, 3 Brig., 1 Div., Cav. Corps, Potomac. Mustered out July 20, 1865.

3rd REGIMENT CAVALRY.—Org. from 41st Mass. Infy., June 17, 1863. June, 1863, 2 Brig., 4 Div, 19 Corps, Gulf. July, 1863, Def. New Orleans, Gulf. Aug., 1863, Cav., Dist. Port Hudson, La., Gulf. Oct., 1863, Unatt., Cav. Div., Gulf. Jany., 1864, 4 Brig., Cav. Div., Gulf. June, 1864, 2 Brig., 2 Div., 19 Corps, Gulf. July, 1864, 2 Brig., 2 Div., 19 Corps, Army Shenandoah. Feby., 1865, Reserve Cav. Brig., Shenandoah. June, 1865, Dept. Mo. Mustered out Sept. 28, 1865.

4th REGIMENT CAVALRY.—Org. at Readville, Mass., Dec. 26, 1863, to Feby. 8, 1864. Indpt. Battalion Mass. Cav., assigned Feby. 12, 1864, as 1st Battn. Feby., 1864, Light Brig., Dist. Fla., Dept. South (1st Battn.). April, 1864, Unatt. Cav., Dept. Va. and N. C., 10th, 18th, 24th and 25th Corps. Aug., 1865, Dept. Va. April, 1864, Dist. Hilton Head, S. C., Dept. South (2nd Battn.). June, 1864, Dist. Beaufort, Dept. South. Nov., 1864, Unatt., Coast Div., Dept. South. Jany., 1865, 1st Separate Brig., Northern Dist., Dept. South. March, 1865, 1st Separate Brig., Dist. Charleston, Dept. South. April, 1864, Dept. South (3d Battn.). May, 1864, Unatt. Cav., Dept. Va. and N. C., 10th, 18th, 24th and 25th Corps. June, 1865, Dept. Va. Regiment mustered out Nov. 14, 1865.

5th REGIMENT COLORED CAVALRY.—Org. at Readville, Mass., Jany. 9 to May 5, 1864. May, 1864, Unass'd, Hinck's Colored Div., 18 Corps. June, 1864, 1 Brig., 3 Div., 18 Corps. June, 1864, Point Lookout, Md. Dist. St. Mary's. March, 1865, Unatt., 25 Corps, Dept. Va. June, 1865, Dept. Texas. Mustered out Oct. 31, 1865.

INDEPENDENT BATTALION CAVALRY.—Org. Aug. 4, 1863, from Co.'s I, K, L and M, 1st Mass. Cav. Aug., 1863, Dist. Beaufort, S. C., 10 Corps, Dept. South. Feby., 1864, Light Brig., Dist. Fla., Dept. South. Ass'd to 4th Mass. Cav. as 1st Battalion, Feby. 12, 1864.

DEVEN'S BATTALION MOUNTED RIFLES.—Org. at Worcester, Mass., April 19, 1861. April, 1861, Def. of Baltimore, Md. Mustered out Aug. 3, 1861.

1st REGIMENT HEAVY ARTILLERY.—Org. from 14th Mass. Infy., Jany. 1, 1862. Jany., 1862, Wadsworth's Command, Def. Washington. May, 1862, Whipple's Brig., Def. Wash. Dec., 1862, Arty., Dist. Alexandria. Jany., 1863, Def. Upper Potomac, 8 Corps (Co's B, C, H, I). Feby., 1863, Arty., Dist. Alexandria, 22 Corps. March, 1863, 2 Brig., 1 Div., 8 Corps (Co's B, C, H, I). April, 1863, 1 Brig., DeRussy's Div., 22 Corps. June, 1863, Indpt. Brig., French's Div., 8 Corps (Co.'s B, C, H, I). July, 1863, Arty. Reserve, Potomac (Co.'s B, C, H, I). Aug., 1863, Unatt., Md. Heights Div., Dept. W. Va. (Co.'s B, C, H, I), to Dec., 1863. April, 1864, 2 Brig., Tyler's Heavy Arty. Div., Potomac. May, 1864, 2 Brig., 3 Div., 2 Corps, Potomac. May, 1865, Dept. Wash. Mustered out Aug. 16, 1865.

1st UNATTACHED COMPANY HEAVY ARTILLERY. —Org. Feby. 26, 1862. Assigned to 1st Battalion Mass. Heavy Arty. as Co. A, April, 1863.

1st BATTALION HEAVY ARTILLERY.—Org. April, 1863, from 1st, 2nd, 4th and 5th Unatt. Co.'s H, A, for garrison duty in Mass. Forts. Mustered out June 29, 1865.

2nd REGIMENT HEAVY ARTILLERY.—Org. at Readville and Boston, July 28 to Dec. 24, 1863. Jany., 1864, Def. Newberne, N. C., Dept. Va. and N. C. Jany., 1865, Dist. Newberne, Dept. N. C. March, 1865, 1 Brig., 1 Div., Dist. Beaufort, N. C., Dept. N. C. April, 1865, Post Kinston, N. C., Dept. N. C. Mustered out Sept. 15, 1865.

2nd UNATTACHED COMPANY HEAVY ARTILLERY. —Org. Nov. 3, 1862. Assigned to 1st Battalion Mass. H. A. as Co. B, April, 1863.

3rd REGIMENT HEAVY ARTILLERY.—Org. Aug., 1864, from 3d, 6th, 7th, 8th, 9th, 10th, 11th, 12th, 13th, 14th, 15th and 16th, Unatt. Co.'s Mass. Heavy Arty. Dec., 1864, 2 Brig., Hardin's Div., 22 Corps. (Co. I attached to Engr. Brig., Army James, from Aug., 1864, to May, 1865.) Mustered out Sept. 18, 1865.

3rd UNATTACHED COMPANY HEAVY ARTILLERY. Org Jany. 10, 1863, Garrison Forts in Boston Harbor. May, 1864, 2 Brig., DeRussy's Div., 22 Corps. July, 1864, 3 Brig., DeRussy's Div., 22 Corps. Dec., 1864, 1 Brig., DeRussy's Div., 22 Corps. Dec., 1864, 2 Brig., Hardin's Div., 22 Corps. Assigned to 3rd Mass. Heavy Arty. as Co. A, Aug., 1864.

4th REGIMENT HEAVY ARTILLERY.—Org. Aug., 1864, from 17th, 18th, 19th, 20th, 21st, 22nd, 23rd, 24th, 25th, 26th, 27th and 28th Unatt. Co.'s Mass. H. A. Dec., 1864, 2 Brig., Hardin's Div., 22 Corps. Mustered out June 17, 1865.

4th UNATTACHED COMPANY HEAVY ARTILLERY. Org. April 22, 1863, Garrison Forts in Boston Harbor. Assigned to 1st Battalion, Mass. Heavy Arty., April, 1863, as Co. C.

5th UNATTACHED COMPANY HEAVY ARTILLERY. Org. June 6, 1863. Assigned to 1st Battalion, Mass H. A., as Co. D. April, 1863.

6th UNATTACHED COMPANY HEAVY ARTILLERY. Org. May 9, 1863. Garrison Forts in Boston Harbor. May, 1864, 3 Brig., Hardin's Div., 22 Corps. Assigned to 3rd Mass. H. A., Aug., 1864.

7th UNATTACHED COMPANY HEAVY ARTILLERY. Org. Aug. 14, 1863. May, 1864, 3 Brig., Hardin's Div., 22 Corps. Assigned to 3rd Mass. Heavy Arty., Aug., 1864.

8th UNATTACHED COMPANY HEAVY ARTILLERY. Org. Aug. 14, 1863. May, 1864, 3 Brig., Hardin's Div., 22 Corps. Assigned to 3rd Mass. Heavy Arty., Aug., 1864.

9th UNATTACHED COMPANY HEAVY ARTILLERY. Org. Aug. 27, 1863. May, 1864, 3 Brig., Hardin's Div., 22 Corps. Assigned to 3rd Mass. Heavy Arty., Aug., 1864.

10th UNATTACHED COMPANY HEAVY ARTILLERY.—Org. Sept. 16, 1863. May, 1864, 3 Brig., Hardin's Div., 22 Corps. Assigned to 3d Mass. Heavy Arty., Aug., 1864.

11th UNATTACHED COMPANY HEAVY ARTILLERY.—Org. Oct. 20, 1863. May, 1864, 3 Brig., Hardin's Div., 22 Corps. Assigned to 3d Mass. Heavy Arty., Aug., 1864.

12th UNATTACHED COMPANY HEAVY ARTILLERY.—Org. Nov. 20, 1863. May, 1864, 3 Brig., Hardin's Div., 22 Corps. Assigned to 3d Mass. Heavy Arty., Aug., 1864.

13th UNATTACHED COMPANY HEAVY ARTILLERY.—Org. Feby. 10, 1864. Assigned to 3d Mass. Heavy Arty., Aug., 1864.

14th UNATTACHED COMPANY HEAVY ARTILLERY.—Org. May 12, 1864. June, 1864, 3 Brig., Hardin's Div., 22 Corps. Assigned to 3d Mass. Heavy Arty., Aug., 1864.

15th UNATTACHED COMPANY HEAVY ARTILLERY.—Org. May 20, 1864. May, 1864, 2 Brig., DeRussy's Div., 22 Corps. July, 1864, 1 Brig., DeRussy's Div., 22 Corps. Assigned to 3d Mass. Heavy Arty., Aug., 1864.

16th UNATTACHED COMPANY HEAVY ARTILLERY.—Org. Aug., 1864. Assigned to 3d Mass. Heavy Arty., Aug., 1864.

17th UNATTACHED COMPANY HEAVY ARTILLERY.—Org. Aug., 1864. Assigned to 4th Mass. Heavy Arty., Aug., 1864.

18th UNATTACHED COMPANY HEAVY ARTILLERY.—Org. Aug., 1864. Assigned to 4th Mass. Heavy Arty., Aug., 1864.

19th UNATTACHED COMPANY HEAVY ARTILLERY.—Org. Aug., 1864. Assigned to 4th Mass. Heavy Arty., Aug., 1864.

20th UNATTACHED COMPANY HEAVY ARTILLERY.—Org. Aug., 1864. Assigned to 4th Mass. Heavy Arty., Aug., 1864.

21st UNATTACHED COMPANY HEAVY ARTILLERY.—Org. Aug., 1864. Assigned to 4th Mass. Heavy Arty., Aug., 1864.

22nd UNATTACHED COMPANY HEAVY ARTILLERY.—Org. Aug., 1864. Assigned to 4th Mass. Heavy Arty., Aug., 1864.

23rd UNATTACHED COMPANY HEAVY ARTILLERY.—Org. Aug., 1864. Assigned to 4th Mass. Heavy Arty., Aug., 1864.

24th UNATTACHED COMPANY HEAVY ARTILLERY.—Org. Aug., 1864. Assigned to 4th Mass. Heavy Arty., Aug., 1864.

25th UNATTACHED COMPANY HEAVY ARTILLERY.—Org. Aug., 1864. Assigned to 4th Mass. Heavy Arty., Aug., 1864.

26th UNATTACHED COMPANY HEAVY ARTILLERY.—Org. Aug., 1864. Assigned to 4th Mass. Heavy Arty., Aug., 1864.

27th UNATTACHED COMPANY HEAVY ARTILLERY.—Org. Aug., 1864. Assigned to 4th Mass. Heavy Arty., Aug., 1864.

28th UNATTACHED COMPANY HEAVY ARTILLERY.—Org. Aug., 1864. Assigned to 4th Mass. Heavy Arty., Aug., 1864.

29th UNATTACHED COMPANY HEAVY ARTILLERY.—Org. Sept. 20, 1864. Oct., 1864, 1 Brig., DeRussy's Div., 22 Corps. Mustered out June 16, 1865.

30th UNATTACHED COMPANY HEAVY ARTILLERY.—Org. Sept. 1, 1864. Oct., 1864, 1 Brig., DeRussy's Div., 22 Corps. Mustered out June 16, 1865.

COOK'S BATTALION LIGHT ARTILLERY.—Org. at Relay House, Md., April 20, 1861. Mustered out Aug. 3, 1861.

1st BATTERY LIGHT ARTILLERY.—Org. at Camp Cameron, Aug. 27, 1861. Oct., 1861, Franklin's Div. Potomac. March, 1862, Arty., 1 Div., 1 Corps, Potomac. May, 1862, Arty., 1 Div., 6 Corps, Potomac. June, 1863, Arty. Brig., 6 Corps, Potomac. July, 1864, Arty., 1 Div., 6 Corps, Shenandoah. Sept., 1864, Arty. Brig., 6 Corps, Shenandoah. Mustered out Oct. 19, 1864.

2nd BATTERY LIGHT ARTILLERY.—Org. at Quincy and mustered in July 31, 1861. Aug., 1861, Dix's Command, Baltimore, Md. March, 1862, 2 Brig., Dept. Gulf. Nov., 1862, Grover's Div., Dept. Gulf. Jany., 1863, Arty.,

4 Div., 19 Corps, Dept. Gulf. Aug., 1863, Arty. Reserve, Dept. Gulf. Sept., 1863, Arty., Cav. Div., Dept. Gulf. Aug., 1864, Unatt. Arty., Dept. Gulf. Aug., 1864, Separate Cav. Brig., 19 Corps, Dept. Gulf. Dec., 1864, Unatt. Arty.. Reserve Corps, Mil. Div. West Miss. Feby., 1865, Lucas' Cav. Div., Steele's Command, M. D. W. M. April, 1865, 3 Brig., 1 Div., Cav. Corps, West Miss. June, 1865, Dept. Miss. Mustered out Aug. 11, 1865.

3rd BATTERY LIGHT ARTILLERY.—Org. at Boston, Sept. 5, 1861. Oct., 1861, Fitz John Porter's Div., Potomac. March, 1862, Arty., 1 Div., 3 Corps, Potomac. May, 1862, Arty., 1 Div., 5 Corps, Potomac. June, 1863, Arty. Brig., 5 Corps, Potomac. Mustered out Sept. 16, 1864.

4th BATTERY LIGHT ARTILLERY.—Org. at Lowell, Nov. 17, 1861. Dec., 1861, Ship Island, Miss., Exp. March, 1862, 1 Brig., Dept. Gulf. Oct., 1862, Indpt. Command, Dept. Gulf. Jany., 1863, Arty., 3 Div., 19 Corps, Dept. Gulf. Nov., 1863, Arty. Reserve, 19 Corps. Feby., 1864. Arty., 1 Div., 19 Corps. March, 1864, Def. New Orleans, Dept. Gulf. Dec., 1864, Unatt., Arty. Reserve Corps, Mil. Div. West Miss. Feby., 1865, Arty., 1 Div., Reserve Corps, M. D. W. M. March, 1865, Arty., 1 Div., 13 Corps, M. D. W. M. July, 1865, Dept. Texas. Mustered out Nov. 10, 1865.

5th BATTERY LIGHT ARTILLERY.—Org. at Lynnfield and Readville, and mustered in Dec. 10, 1861. Jany., 1862, Fitz John Porter's Div., Potomac. March, 1862, Arty., 1 Div., 3 Corps, Potomac. May, 1862, Arty., 1 Div., 5 Corps, Potomac. June, 1863, 1 Vol. Brig., Arty. Reserve, Potomac. July, 1863, Arty. Brig., 5 Corps, Potomac. Mustered out June 12, 1865.

6th BATTERY LIGHT ARTILLERY.—Org. at Lowell and mustered in Jany. 20, 1862. March, 1862, 2 Brig., Dept. Gulf. Oct., 1862, Weitzel's Reserve Brig., Dept. Gulf. Jany., 1863, Arty., 1 Div., 19 Corps, Dept. Gulf. Aug., 1863, Arty. Reserve, Dept. Gulf. Dec., 1863, Arty., 1 Div., 19 Corps. June, 1864, Reserve Arty., Def. New Orleans. Mustered out Aug. 7, 1865.

7th BATTERY LIGHT ARTILLERY.—Org. at Fortress Monroe, Va., from Richardson's Indpt. Infy. Co., March 17, 1862. March, 1862, Fortress Monroe, Va., Dept. Va. June, 1862, Newport News, Va., Dept. Va. July, 1862, Yorktown, Va. Oct., 1862, Arty. Div. at Suffolk, 7 Corps, Dept. Va. April, 1863, Arty., 1 Div., 7 Corps, Dept. Va. July, 1863, Camp Barry, Def. Washington, 22 Corps. Feby., 1864, Arty., 2 Div., 19 Corps, Dept. Gulf. Dec., 1864, Reserve Arty., Reserve Corps, Mil. Div. West Miss. Feby., 1865, Arty., 1 Div., Reserve Corps, M. D. W. M. Feby., 1865, Arty., 1 Div., 13 Corps, M. D. W. M. April, 1865, Arty., 1 Div., U. S. C. T., Dist. W. Fla. July, 1865, Dept. Texas. Mustered out Nov. 10, 1865.

8th BATTERY LIGHT ARTILLERY.—Org. at North Cambridge, June 24, 1862. July, 1862, Cook's Brig., Sturgis' Res. Corps, Def. Washington. Aug., 1862, Arty., 1 Div., 9 Corps, Potomac. Mustered out Nov. 29, 1862.

9th BATTERY LIGHT ARTILLERY.—Org. at Readville and mustered in Aug. 10, 1862. Sept., 1862, Abercrombie's Div., Def. Washington. Feby., 1863, 2 Brig., Abercrombie's Div., 22 Corps. May, 1863, Camp Barry, Def. Washington, 22 Corps. July, 1863, 1 Vol. Brig., Arty. Reserve, Potomac. Dec., 1863, 2 Vol. Brig., Arty. Reserve, Potomac. April, 1864, 3 Vol. Brig., Arty. Reserve, Potomac. May, 1864, Arty. Brig., 5 Corps, Potomac. Mustered out June 6, 1865.

10th BATTERY LIGHT ARTILLERY.—Org. at Lynnfield, and mustered in Sept. 9, 1862. Oct., 1862, Grover's Brig., Def. Washington. Feby., 1863, Jewett's Brig., 22 Corps. June, 1863, Arty. French's Div., 8 Corps. July, 1863, Arty. Brig., 3 Corps, Potomac. March, 1864, Arty. Brig., 2 Corps, Potomac. Mustered out June 14, 1865.

11th BATTERY LIGHT ARTILLERY.—Org. at Boston, and mustered in for 9 months Aug. 25, 1862. Nov., 1862, Arty., Casey's Div., Def. Washington, and 22 Corps. April, 1863, Arty., Abercrombie's Div., 22 Corps. Mustered out May 29, 1863.

11th BATTERY LIGHT ARTILLERY.—(REORGANIZED.) Org. at Readville, and mustered in Jany. 2, 1864. Feby., 1864, Def. Washington, 22 Corps. April, 1864, Arty., 2 Div., 9 Corps, Potomac. May, 1864, Arty. Brig.,

2 Corps, Temp'y. July, 1864, Arty. Brig., 9 Corps, Potomac. Aug., 1864, Arty. Brig., 5 Corps, Potomac, Temp'y. Mustered out June 16. 1865.

12th BATTERY LIGHT ARTILLERY.—Org. at Readville, Oct. 3 to Dec. 29, 1862. Feby., 1863, Arty., 1 Div., 19 Corps, Dept. Gulf.. July, 1863, Arty. Reserve, 19 Corps. Oct., 1863, Garrison Arty., Port Hudson, Dept. Gulf. Dec., 1863, Arty., 1 Div., Corps de Afrique, Dept. Gulf. March, 1864, Garrison Arty., Port Hudson, La., Dept. Gulf. Mustered out July 25, 1865.

13th BATTERY LIGHT ARTILLERY.—Org. at Readville, and mustered in Dec. 13, 1862. Jany., 1863, Def. New Orleans, Dept. Gulf. June, 1863, Arty., 4 Div., 19 Corps, Dept. Gulf. Aug., 1863, Def. New Orleans, Dept. Gulf. (Battery attached to 2d Mass. Batty., Sept., 1863, to Feby., 1864, to 6th Mass. Batty. to March, 1864, and to Batty. L, 1st U. S. Arty., to June, 1864.) June, 1864, Def. New Orleans. Mustered out July 28, 1865.

14th BATTERY LIGHT ARTILLERY.—Org. at Readville, and mustered in Feby. 27, 1864. April, 1864, Arty., 1 Div., 9 Corps, Potomac. Aug., 1864, Reserve Arty., Potomac. Oct., 1864, Duty with 2 Corps, Potomac. Jany., 1865, with Arty. Brig., 6 Corps, Potomac. March, 1865, with Arty. Brig., 9 Corps, Potomac. Mustered out June 16, 1865.

15th BATTERY LIGHT ARTILLERY.—Org. at Lowell and Fort Warren, and mustered in Feby. 17, 1863. April, 1863, Def. New Orleans, Dept. Gulf. July, 1864, Reserve Arty., Gulf. Feby., 1865, Arty., 2 Div. 13 Corps, Mil. Div. West Miss. Mustered out Aug. 4, 1865.

16th BATTERY LIGHT ARTILLERY.—Org. at Readville, and mustered in April 4, 1864. March, 1864, Camp Barry, Dept. Washington, 22 Corps. June, 1864, 2 Brig., DeRussy's Div., 22 Corps. July, 1864, Camp Barry, 22 Corps. Nov., 1864, 1st Separate Brig., 22 Corps. Mustered out July 13, 1865.

1st COMPANY SHARPSHOOTERS.—Org. at Lynnfield, and mustered in Sept. 2, 1861. Sept., 1861, Lander's Brig., Stone's Div., Potomac. Jany., 1862, Gorman's Brig., Sedgwick's Div., Potomac. March, 1862, 1 Brig., 2 Div., 2 Corps, Potomac. Mustered out Sept. 6, 1864.

2nd COMPANY SHARPSHOOTERS.—Org. at Lynnfield, and mustered in Sept. 3, 1861. Oct., 1861, Martindale's Brig., Porter's Div., Potomac. March, 1862, 1 Brig., 1 Div., 3 Corps, Potomac. May, 1862, 1 Brig., 1 Div., 5 Corps, Potomac. March, 1864, 2 Brig., 1 Div., 5 Corps, Potomac. Mustered out Oct. 17, 1864.

1st REGIMENT INFANTRY.—Org. at Boston, and mustered in May 23-27, 1861. June, 1861, Richardson's Brig., Tyler's Div., McDowell's Army N. E. Va. Aug., 1861, Hooker's Brig., Div. Potomac. Oct., 1861, 1 Brig., Hooker's Div., Army Potomac. March, 1862, 1 Brig., 2 Div., 3 Corps, Potomac. March, 1864, 1 Brig., 4 Div., 2 Corps, Potomac. Mustered out May 25, 1864.

1st BATTALION INFANTRY.—Org. at Fortress Monroe, Va., from 3-years' Co.'s. of 3d and 4th Regts., Mass. Militia Infy., July, 1861. July, 1861, Fortress Monroe, Camp Hamilton and Newport News, Va., Dept. Va. Transferred to 29th Mass. Infy., as Co.'s A, B, C, D, E, I and K, Dec. 13, 1861.

2nd REGIMENT INFANTRY.— Org. at West Roxbury and mustered in May 25, 1861. July, 1861, Abercrombie's Brig., Patterson's Army. July, 1861, Abercrombie's Brig., Banks' Div., Shenandoah. Aug., 1861, Gordon's Brig.. Banks' Div., Potomac. March, 1862, Gordon's 3 Brig., Williams' 1 Div., Banks' 5 Corps. April, 1862, 3 Brig., 1 Div., Dept. Shenandoah. June, 1862, 3 Brig., 1 Div., 2 Corps, Army Va. Sept., 1863, 3 Brig., 1 Div., 12 Corps, Potomac. Oct., 1863, 3 Brig., 1 Div., 12 Corps, Cumb'd. April, 1864, 2 Brig., 1 Div., 20 Corps. Mustered out July 11, 1865.

3rd REGIMENT MILITIA INFANTRY.—Org. at Fortress Monroe, Va., for three months, April 22, 1861. April, 1861, Fort Monroe and Camp Hamilton, Va. Mustered out July 22, 1861.

3rd REGIMENT MILITIA INFANTRY.—Org. at Lakeville for 9 months, Sept., 1862. Oct., 1862, 3 Brig., 1 Div., Dept. N. C. Dec., 1862, Heckman's Brig., Dept. N. C. Jany., 1863, 2 Brig., 5 Div., 18 Corps, Dept. N. C. April,

1863, Jourdan's Indpt. Brig., Def. Newberne, N. C. Mustered out June 26, 1863.

3rd BATTALION RIFLES.—Org. at Worcester, April, 1861. Mustered out Aug. 3, 1861.

4th REGIMENT MILITIA INFANTRY.—Org. at Fortress Monroe, Va., for three months, April 22, 1861. April, 1861, Dept. of Va. Mustered out July 22, 1861.

4th REGIMENT MILITIA INFANTRY.—Org. at Lakeville for nine months and mustered in Sept. 23, 1862. Feby., 1863, 1 Brig., 3 Div., 19 Corps, Dept. Gulf. Mustered out Aug. 28, 1863.

4th BATTALION MILITIA INFANTRY.—Org. at Boston, May 27, 1862. Mustered out May 31, 1862.

5th REGIMENT MILITIA INFANTRY.—Org. for three months, April 21, 1861. Mustered in at Washington, D. C., May 1, 1861. June, 1861, Franklin's Brig., Heintzelman's Div., McDowell's Army, N. E. Va. Mustered out Aug. 1, 1861.

5th REGIMENT MILITIA INFANTRY.—Org. at Wenham for nine months and Oct., 1862. Nov., 1862, 3 Brig., 1 Div., Dept. N. C. Dec., 1862, Lee's Brig., Dept. N. C. Jany., 1863, 2 Brig., 1 Div., 18 Corps, Dept. N. C. Mustered out July 2, 1863.

5th REGIMENT MILITIA·INFANTRY.—Org. at Readville for 100 days, July 18-26, 1864. July, 1864, Def. Balto., Md., 2nd Separate Brig., 8 Corps, Middle Dept. Mustered out Nov. 16, 1864.

6th REGIMENT MILITIA INFANTRY.—Org. April 15 and mustered in at Washington, D. C., for three months. April 22, 1861. Duty at Relay House and Balto., Md. Mustered out Aug. 2, 1861.

6th REGIMENT MILITIA INFANTRY.—Org. at Lowell for nine months, and mustered in Aug. 31, 1862. Sept., 1862. Foster's Prov'l Brig., Div. at Suffolk, 7 Corps, Dept. Va. April, 1863, 2 Brig., 1 Div., 7 Corps, Dept. Va. Mustered out June 3, 1863.

6th REGIMENT INFANTRY.—Org. at Readville for 100 days, July, 1864. July, 1864, 1 Brig., DeRussy's Div., 22 Corps. Aug., 1864, Fort Delaware Middle Dept. Mustered out Oct. 27, 1864.

7th REGIMENT INFANTRY.—Org. at Taunton and mustered in June 15, 1861. Aug., 1861, Couch's Brig., Div. Potomac. Oct., 1861, Couch's Brig., Buell's Div., Potomac. March, 1862, 1 Brig., 1 Div., 4 Corps, Potomac. Sept., 1862, 1 Brig., 3 Div., 6 Corps, Potomac. Oct., 1862, 2 Brig., 3 Div., 6 Corps, Potomac. Jany., 1864, 4 Brig., 2 Div., 6 Corps. Mustered out July 5, 1864.

8th REGIMENT MILITIA INFANTRY.—Org. at Boston for three months, April 16, 1861. April, 1861, Def. Washington and Relay House, Md. Mustered out Aug. 1, 1861.

8th REGIMENT MILITIA INFANTRY.—Org. at Wenham for nine months, Sept. 15 to Oct. 30, 1862. Nov., 1862, 2 Brig., 1 Div., Dept. N. C. Dec., 1862, Heckman's Brig., Dept. N. C. Jany., 1863, 2 Brig., 5 Div., 18 Corps, Dept. N. C. April, 1863, Jourdan's Indpt. Brig., Def. Newberne, N. C., Dept. N. C. Mustered out Aug. 7, 1863.

8th REGIMENT MILITIA INFANTRY.—Org. at Readville for 100 days, July, 1864. July, 1864, 3 Separate Brig., 8 Corps, Middle Dept. Mustered out Nov. 10, 1864.

9th REGIMENT INFANTRY.—Org. at Boston, June 11, 1861. June, 1861, Def. Washington. Aug., 1861, Sherman's Brig., Div. Potomac. Oct., 1861, Morrell's Brig., Porter's Div., Army Potomac. March, 1862, 2 Brig., 1 Div., 3 Corps, Potomac. May, 1862, 2 Brig., 1 Div., 5 Corps, Potomac. Mustered out June 21, 1864.

10th REGIMENT INFANTRY.—Org. at Springfield, June 21, 1861. Aug., 1861, Couch's Brig., Div., Potomac. Oct., 1861, Couch's Brig., Buell's Div., Potomac. March, 1862, 1 Brig., 1 Div., 4 Corps, Potomac. Sept., 1862, 1 Brig., 3 Div., 6 Corps, Potomac. Oct., 1862, 2 Brig., 3 Div., 6 Corps, Potomac. Jany., 1864, 4 Brig., 2 Div., 6 Corps, Potomac. Mustered out July 6, 1864.

11th REGIMENT INFANTRY.—Org. at Readville and mustered in June 13, 1861. June, 1861, Franklin's Brig., Heintzelman's Div., McDowell's Army, N. E. Va. Aug., 1861, Hooker's Brig., Div. Potomac. Oct., 1861, 1 Brig., Hooker's Div., Potomac. March, 1862, 1 Brig., 2 Div., 3 Corps, Potomac. March, 1864, 2 Brig., 4 Div., 2 Corps,

Potomac. May, 1864, 4 Brig., 3 Div., 2 Corps. June, 1864, 3 Brig., 3 Div., 2 Corps. Mustered out June 14, 1865.

12th REGIMENT INFANTRY.—Org. at Fort Warren, and mustered in June 26, 1861. Aug., 1861, Thomas' Brig., Dept. Shenandoah. Oct., 1861, Abercrombie's 2 Brig., Banks' Div., Potomac. March, 1862, 2 Brig., 1 Div., Banks' 5 Corps. May, 1862, 3 Brig., 2 Div., Dept. Rappahannock. June, 1862, 3 Brig., 2 Div., 3 Corps, Army Va. Sept., 1862, 3 Brig., 2 Div., 1 Corps, Potomac. Nov., 1862, 2 Brig., 2 Div., 1 Corps, Potomac. March, 1864, 2 Brig., 2 Div., 5 Corps. May, 1864, 2 Brig., 3 Div., 5 Corps. Mustered out July 8, 1864.

13th REGIMENT INFANTRY.—Org. at Fort Independence, June 16, 1861. Aug., 1861, Stile's Brig., Banks' Div., Potomac. Oct., 1861, Abercrombie's 2 Brig., Banks' Div., Potomac. March, 1862, 2 Brig., 1 Div., Banks' 5 Corps. May, 1862, 3 Brig., 2 Div., Dept. Rappahannock. June, 1862, 3 Brig., 2 Div., 3 Corps, Army Va. Sept., 1862, 3 Brig., 2 Div., 1 Corps, Potomac. May, 1863, 1 Brig., 2 Div., 1 Corps. March, 1864, 1 Brig., 2 Div., 5 Corps, Potomac. June, 1864, 1 Brig., 3 Div., 5 Corps. Mustered out Aug. 1, 1864.

14th REGIMENT INFANTRY.—Org. at Fort Warren and mustered in July 5, 1861. Aug., 1861, Sherman's Brig., Div. Potomac. Aug., 1861, Fort Albany, Def. Washington. Designation changed to 1st Mass. Heavy Arty., Jany. 1, 1862.

15th REGIMENT INFANTRY.—Org. at Worcester and mustered in June 12, 1861. Aug., 1861, Gorman's Brig., Stone's Div., Potomac. March, 1862, 1 Brig., 2 Div., 2 Corps, Potomac. Mustered out July 28, 1864.

16th REGIMENT INFANTRY.—Org. at Cambridge, June 29, 1861. Aug., 1861, Fort Monroe and Camp Hamilton, Va., Dept. Va. May, 1862, 1 Brig., 1 Div., Dept. Va. June, 1862, 1 Brig., 2 Div., 3 Corps, Potomac. March, 1864, 1 Brig., 4 Div., 2 Corps, Potomac. May, 1864, 3 Brig., 3 Div., 2 Corps. Mustered out July 27, 1864.

17th REGIMENT INFANTRY.—Org. at Lynnfield, July 22, 1861. Aug., 1861, Dix's Div., Baltimore, Md. March, 1862, 1 Brig., N. C. Exp. Corps. April, 1862, 1 Brig., 1 Div., Dept. N. C. Dec., 1862, Amory's Brig., Dept. N. C. Jany., 1863, 1 Brig., 1 Div., 18 Corps, Dept. N. C. July, 1863, Def. Newberne, Dept. Va. and N. C. July, 1864, Sub Dist. Beaufort, N. C., Dept. Va. and N. C. Jany., 1865, Sub Dist. Beaufort, Dept. N. C. March, 1865, 1 Brig., Div. at Beaufort, Dept. N. C. April, 1865, 3 Brig., 3 Div., 23 Corps, Dept. N. C. Mustered out July 11, 1865.

18th REGIMENT INFANTRY.—Org. at Readville and Boston, and mustered in Aug. 27, 1861. Aug., 1861, Fort Corcoran, Def. Washington. Oct., 1861, Martindale's Brig., Porter's Div., Potomac. March, 1862, 1 Brig., 1 Div., 3 Corps, Potomac. May, 1862, 1 Brig., 1 Div., 5 Corps, Potomac. March, 1864, 3 Brig., 1 Div., 5 Corps. Consolidated with 32nd Mass. Infy., Oct. 21, 1864.

19th REGIMENT INFANTRY.—Org. at Lynnfield, Aug. 28, 1861. Sept., 1861, Lander's Brig., Div. Potomac. Oct., 1861, Lander's Brig., Stone's Div., Potomac. March, 1862, 3 Brig., 2 Div., 2 Corps, Potomac. March, 1864, 1 Brig., 2 Div., 2 Corps. Mustered out June 30, 1865.

20th REGIMENT INFANTRY.—Org. at Readville, Aug. 29 to Sept. 4, 1861. Sept., 1861, Lander's Brig., Div. Potomac. Oct., 1861, Lander's Brig., Stone's Div., Potomac. March, 1862, 3 Brig., 2 Div., 2 Corps, Potomac. March, 1864, 1 Brig., 2 Div., 2 Corps. Mustered out July 16, 1865.

21st REGIMENT INFANTRY.—Org. at Worcester, July 19 to Aug. 19, 1861. Dec., 1861, Reno's Brig., Burnside's Exp. Corps. April, 1862, 2 Brig., 2 Div., Dept. N. C. July, 1862, 2 Brig., 2 Div., 9 Corps, Potomac. April, 1863, 2 Brig., 2 Div., 9 Corps, Ohio. June, 1863, Unass'd, 1 Div., 23 Corps, Ohio. Oct., 1863, 1 Brig., 2 Div., 9 Corps, Ohio. April, 1864, 2 Brig., 1 Div., 9 Corps, Potomac. June, 1864, 1 Brig., 1 Div., 9 Corps. Sept., 1864, 2 Brig., 1 Div., 9 Corps. Transferred to 36th Mass. Infy., Oct. 21, 1864.

22nd REGIMENT INFANTRY.—Org. at Lynnfield Sept. 4 to Oct. 6, 1861. Oct., 1861. Martindale's Brig., Porter's Div., Potomac. March, 1862, 1 Brig., 1 Div., 3 Corps,

Potomac. May, 1862, 1 Brig., 1 Div., 5 Corps, Potomac. March, 1864, 2 Brig., 1 Div., 5 Corps. Mustered out Oct. 17, 1864.

23rd REGIMENT INFANTRY.—Org. Sept. 28, 1861. Dec., 1861, Foster's 1 Brig., Burnside's Exp. Corps. April, 1862, 1 Brig., 1 Div., Dept. N. C. Dec., 1862, Heckman's Brig., Dept. N. C. Jany., 1863, 1 Brig., 2 Div., 18 Corps, Dept. N. C. Feby., 1863, 1 Brig., 1 Div., 18 Corps, Dept. South. April, 1863, Dist. Beaufort, N. C., Dept. N. C. July, 1863, Def. Newberne, Dept. Va. and N. C. Oct., 1863, Heckman's Brig., Newport News, Va., Dept. Va. and N. C. Jany., 1864, 3 Brig., U. S. Forces, Portsmouth, Va., Dept. Va. and N. C. April, 1864, 1 Brig., 2 Div., 18 Corps, Army James. Sept., 1864, Def. Newberne, N. C., Dept. Va. and N. C. Jany., 1865, Dist. Newberne, N. C., Dept. N. C. March, 1865, 1 Brig., 1 Div., Dist. Beaufort, Dept. N. C. March, 1865, Post Kinston, N. C., Dept. N. C. Mustered out June 25, 1865.

24th REGIMENT INFANTRY.—Org. at Readville, Sept. to Dec., 1861. Dec., 1861, Foster's 1 Brig., Burnside's Exp. Corps. April, 1862, 2 Brig., 1 Div., Dept. N. C. Jany., 1863, 2 Brig., 4 Div., 18 Corps, Dept. N. C. Feby., 1863, 2 Brig., 1 Div., 18 Corps, Dept. South. April, 1863, Stevenson's Brig., Seabrook Island, S. C., 10 Corps, Dept. South. July, 1863, 1 Brig., 1 Div., Morris Island, S. C., 10 Corps. July, 1863, 3 Brig., Morris Island, S. C., 10 Corps. Sept., 1863, St. Augustine, Fla., Dept. South. Feby., 1864, Jacksonville, Fla., Dept. South. Feby., 1864, 1 Brig., Vodge's Div., Dist. Fla. April, 1864, 2 Brig., 1 Div., 10 Corps, Army James, Dept. Va. and N. C. May, 1864, 3 Brig., 1 Div., 10 Corps. Dec., 1864, 3 Brig., 1 Div., 24 Corps. July, 1865, 2 Brig., 1 Div., 24 Corps. Aug., 1865, Dept. Va. Mustered out Jany. 20, 1866.

25th REGIMENT INFANTRY.—Org. at Worcester, Sept. 1 to Oct. 21, 1861. Dec., 1861, Foster's 1 Brig., Burnside's Exp. Corps. April, 1862, 1 Brig., 1 Div., Dept. N. C. Dec., 1862, Lee's Brig., Dept. N. C. Jany., 1863, 2 Brig., 1 Div., 18 Corps, Dept. N. C. June, 1863, 2 Brig., 1 Div., Def. Newberne, N. C. Aug., 1863, Dist. Pamlico, Dept. Va. and N. C. Sept., 1863, Def. Newberne, N. C., Dept. Va. and N. C. Oct., 1863, Heckman's Brig., Newport News, Va., Dept. Va. and N. C. Jany., 1864, Unatt., U. S. Forces, Portsmouth, Va., Dept. Va. and N. C. March, 1864, 2 Brig., U. S. Forces, Portsmouth, Va. April, 1864, 1 Brig., 2 Div., 18 Corps. Sept., 1864, Def. Newberne, N. C. March, 1865, 3 Brig., 2 Div., Dist. Beaufort, N. C., Dept. N. C. March, 1865, 2 Brig., Div., Dist. Beaufort, N. C., Dept. N. C. April, 1865, 3 Brig., 1 Div., 23 Corps, Dept. N. C. Mustered out July 28, 1865.

26th REGIMENT INFANTRY.—Org. at Cambridge, Aug. 28, 1861. Dec., 1861, Ship Island, Miss., Exp. March, 1862, 2 Brig., Dept. Gulf. Oct., 1862, Def. New Orleans, La. Jany., 1863, 2 Brig., 2 Div., 19 Corps, Dept. Gulf. July, 1863, 2 Brig., 3 Div., 19 Corps. Feby., 1864, 2 Brig., 2 Div., 19 Corps. June, 1864, 1 Brig., 2 Div., 19 Corps. July, 1864, 1 Brig., 2 Div., 19 Corps, Shenandoah. Jany., 1865, 2 Brig., 1 Div., 19 Corps. April, 1865, 2 Brig., 1 Prov'l Div., Shenandoah. April, 1865, 2 Brig., 1 Div., Def. Washington, D. C. June, 1865, Dept. South. Mustered out Aug. 26, 1865.

27th REGIMENT INFANTRY.—Org. at Springfield and mustered in Sept. 20, 1861. Dec., 1861, Foster's 1 Brig., Burnside's Exp. Corps. April, 1862, 2 Brig., 1 Div., Dept. N. C. July, 1862, 2 Brig., 1 Div., 9 Corps, Potomac. Aug., 1862, 1 Brig., 1 Div., Dept. N. C. Nov., 1862, 3 Brig., 1 Div., Dept. N. C. Dec., 1862, Lee's Brig., Dept. N. C. Jany., 1863, 2 Brig., 1 Div., 18 Corps, Dept. N. C. June, 1863, 2 Brig., 1 Div., Def. Newberne, Dept. N. C. Oct., 1863, Heckman's Brig., Newport News, Va., Dept. Va. and N. C. Jany., 1864, U. S. Forces, Portsmouth, Va. March, 1864, 2 Brig., U. S. Forces, Portsmouth, Va. April, 1864, 1 Brig., 2 Div., 18 Corps, Army James. Sept., 1864, Dist. Beaufort, N. C. Jany., 1865, Sub Dist. Newberne, Dept. N. C. March, 1865, 2 Brig., 2 Div., Dist. Beaufort, N. C., Dept. N. C. March, 1865, Dist. Newberne, Dept. N. C. Mustered out June 26, 1865.

28th REGIMENT INFANTRY.—Org. at Cambridge and Boston, Dec. 12, 1861. Feby., 1862, Unatt., Dept. South.

April, 1862, 1 Brig., 2 Div., Dept. South. July, 1862, 1 Brig., 1 Div., 9 Corps, Potomac. Sept., 1862, 2 Brig., 1 Div., 2 Corps, Potomac. June, 1864, 1 Brig., 1 Div., 2 Corps. Nov., 1864, 2 Brig., 1 Div., 2 Corps. Mustered out June 29, 1865.

29th REGIMENT INFANTRY.—Org. at Newport News, Va., from 1st Battalion, Mass. Infy., Dec. 13, 1861. Dec., 1861, Newport News, Va., Dept. Va. May, 1862, 1 Brig., 1 Div., Dept. Va. June, 1862, 2 Brig., 1 Div., 2 Corps, Potomac. Dec., 1862, 2 Brig., 1 Div., 9 Corps, Potomac. April, 1863, 2 Brig., 1 Div., 9 Corps, Ohio. June, 1863, 3 Brig., 2 Div., 9 Corps, Tenn. Aug., 1863, 2 Brig., 1 Div., 9 Corps, Ohio. May, 1864, 3 Brig., 1 Div., 5 Corps, Potomac. June, 1864, 2 Brig., 1 Div., 9 Corps, Potomac. July, 1864, 1 Brig., 1 Div., 9 Corps. Sept., 1864, 3 Brig., 1 Div., 9 Corps. Mustered out July 29, 1865.

30th REGIMENT INFANTRY.—Org. at Lowell, Dec. 31, 1861. Jany., 1862, Ship Island, Miss., Exp. March, 1862, 3 Brig., Dept. Gulf. Oct., 1862, Def. New Orleans, La. Jany., 1863, 3 Brig., 1 Div., 19 Corps, Dept. Gulf. Aug., 1863, 1 Brig., 1 Div., 19 Corps. July, 1864, 1 Brig., 1 Div., 19 Corps, Shenandoah. March, 1865, 1 Brig., 1 Prov'l Div., Shenandoah. April, 1865, Dept. Washington, D. C. June, 1865, Dist. S. C., Dept. South. Mustered out Dec. 1, 1865.

31st REGIMENT INFANTRY.—Org. at Pittsfield, Nov. 20, 1861, to Feby. 20, 1862. March, 1862, 2 Brig., Dept. Gulf. Oct., 1862, Sherman's Div., Dept. Gulf. Jany., 1863, 3 Brig., 3 Div., 19 Corps, Dept. Gulf. July, 1863, 2 Brig., 1 Div., 19 Corps. Dec., 1863, 4 Brig., Cav. Div., Gulf. June, 1864, Def. New Orleans. Sept., 1864, 1 Brig., Cav. Div., Gulf. Oct., 1864, Def. New Orleans. Feby., 1865, Separate Cav. Brig., Dist. West Fla. March, 1865, 1 Brig., Lucas' Cav. Div., Steele's Command, Mil. Div. West Miss. April, 1865, Dist. Mobile, Ala. Mustered out Sept. 30, 1865.

32nd REGIMENT INFANTRY.—Org. Nov. 25, 1861. Nov., 1861, Fort Warren, Boston Harbor. May, 1862, Def. Washington. July, 1862, 1 Brig., 1 Div., 5 Corps, Potomac. Sept., 1862, 2 Brig., 1 Div., 5 Corps. Oct., 1864, 3 Brig., 1 Div., 5 Corps. Mustered out June 29, 1865.

33rd REGIMENT INFANTRY.—Org. at Springfield, Aug. 6, 1862. Aug., 1862, Def. Washington. Oct., 1862, 2 Brig., 2 Div., 11 Corps, Potomac. Oct., 1863, 2 Brig., 2 Div., 11 Corps, Cumb'd. April, 1864, 3 Brig., 3 Div., 20 Corps. Mustered out June 11, 1865.

34th REGIMENT INFANTRY.—Org. at Worcester, Aug. 1, 1862. Aug., 1862, Def. Washington. Dec., 1862, Dist. Alexandria, Va. Feby., 1863, Tyler's Brig., Dist. Alexandria, 22 Corps. April, 1863, 2 Brig., DeRussy's Div., 22 Corps, Def. Washington, South of Potomac. June, 1863, Martindale's Command, Garrison Washington, 22 Corps. July, 1863, 1 Brig., Md. Heights Div., Dept. W. Va. Dec., 1863, 1 Brig., 1 Div., Dept. W. Va. Jany., 1864, Unatt., 1 Div., W. Va. April, 1864, 2 Brig., 1 Infy. Div., W. Va. June, 1864, 1 Brig., 1 Infy. Div., W. Va. Dec., 1864, 1 Brig., Indpt. Div., 24 Corps, Army James., Dept. Va. Mustered out June 16, 1865.

35th REGIMENT INFANTRY.—Org. at Worcester Aug. 1, 1862. Aug., 1862, Whipple's Command, Def. Washington. Sept., 1862, 2 Brig., 2 Div., 9 Corps, Potomac. April, 1863, 2 Brig., 2 Div., 9 Corps, Ohio. June, 1863, 2 Brig., 2 Div., 9 Corps, Tenn. Aug., 1863, 2 Brig., 2 Div., 9 Corps, Ohio. April, 1864, 1 Brig., 1 Div., 9 Corps, Potomac. May, 1864, Acting Engrs., 1 Div., 9 Corps, Potomac. July, 1864, 1 Brig., 1 Div., 9 Corps. Sept., 1864, 1 Brig., 2 Div., 9 Corps. Mustered out June 9, 1865.

36th REGIMENT INFANTRY.—Org. at Worcester and mustered in Aug. 30, 1862. Sept., 1862, 3 Brig., 1 Div., 9 Corps, Potomac. April, 1863, 1 Brig., 1 Div., 9 Corps, Ohio. June, 1863, 1 Brig., 1 Div., 9 Corps, Tenn. Aug., 1863, 1 Brig., 1 Div., 9 Corps, Ohio. April, 1864, 1 Brig., 2 Div., 9 Corps, Potomac. Mustered out June 8, 1865.

37th REGIMENT INFANTRY.—Org. at Pittsfield, Aug. 30, 1862. Sept., 1862, 2 Brig., 3 Div., 6 Corps, Potomac. March, 1864, 4 Brig., 2 Div., 6 Corps. July, 1864, 3 Brig., 1 Div., 6 Corps. Aug., 1864, 3 Brig., 1 Div., 6 Corps, Shenandoah. Dec., 1864, 3 Brig., 1 Div., 6 Corps, Potomac. Mustered out June 30, 1865.

38th REGIMENT INFANTRY.—Org. and mustered in Aug. 24, 1862. Aug., 1862, Def. Balto., Md., 8 Corps, Middle Dept. Jany., 1863, 3 Brig., 3 Div., 19 Corps, Dept. Gulf. Aug., 1863, 2 Brig., 1 Div., 19 Corps. Feby., 1864, 3 Brig., 2 Div., 19 Corps. July, 1864, 3 Brig., 2 Div., 19 Corps, Shenandoah. Jany., 1865, 3 Brig., Grover's Div., Dist. Savannah, Dept. South. March, 1865, 3 Brig., 1 Div., 10 Corps, Dept. N. C. April, 1865, Dist. Savannah, Dept. South. Mustered out June 30, 1865.

39th REGIMENT INFANTRY.—Org. at Lynnfield, Aug. 13 to Sept. 2, 1862. Oct., 1862, Grover's Brig., Dist. Washington, D. C. Feby., 1863, Jewett's Indpt. Brig., 22 Corps. May, 1863, Dist. Washington, 22 Corps. July, 1863, 1 Brig., 2 Div., 1 Corps, Potomac. March, 1864, 1 Brig., 2 Div., 5 Corps, Potomac. June, 1864, 1 Brig., 3 Div., 5 Corps. Sept., 1864, 2 Brig., 3 Div., 5 Corps. Mustered out June 1, 1865.

40th REGIMENT INFANTRY.—Org. at Lynnfield, Aug., 1862. Sept., 1862, 2 Brig., Abercrombie's Div., Def. Washington. Feby., 1863, 2 Brig., Abercrombie's Div., 22 Corps. April, 1863, 1 Brig., 3 Div., 7 Corps, Dept. Va. May, 1863, 2 Brig., 2 Div., 4 Corps, Dept. Va. July, 1863, 2 Brig., Gordon's Div., South End Folly Island, S. C., 10 Corps, Dept. South. Jany., 1864, 2 Brig., Gordon's Div., Folly Island, S. C., Northern Dist., Dept. South. Jany., 1864, 1 Brig., Hilton Head Dist., Dept. South. Feby., 1864, Light Brigade, Dist. Fla., Dept. South. April, 1864, 1 Brig., 2 Div., 10 Corps, Army James, Dept. Va. and N. C. May, 1864, 3 Brig., 1 Div., 18 Corps, Potomac. Dec., 1864, 3 Brig., 3 Div., 24 Corps. Mustered out June 16, 1865.

41st REGIMENT INFANTRY.—Org. at Lynnfield, Aug. 31 to Nov. 1, 1862. Dec., 1862, Grover's Div., Dept. Gulf. Jany., 1863, 2 Brig., 4 Div., 19 Corps, Gulf. Designation changed to 3rd Cavalry, June 17, 1863.

42nd REGIMENT INFANTRY.—Org. at Readville, Nov. 11, 1862. Dec., 1862, Sherman's Div., Dept. Gulf. Jany., 1863. 2 Brig., 2 Div., 19 Corps, Gulf. Mustered out Aug. 20, 1863.

43rd REGIMENT INFANTRY.—Org. at Readville, Sept. 12 to Oct. 23, 1862. Nov., 1862, 1 Brig., 1 Div., Dept. N. C. Dec., 1862, Amory's Brig., Dept. N. C. Jany., 1863, 1 Brig., 1 Div., 18 Corps, Dept. N. C. July, 1863, 1 Brig., Md. Heights Div., W. Va. Mustered out July 30, 1863.

44th REGIMENT INFANTRY.—Org. at Readville and mustered in Sept. 12, 1862. Nov., 1862, 2 Brig., 1 Div., Dept. N. C. Jany., 1863, 2 Brig., 4 Div., 18 Corps, Dept. N. C. May, 1863, Lee's Brig., Def. Newberne, N. C. Mustered out June 18, 1863.

45th REGIMENT INFANTRY.—Org. at Readville, Sept. 26 to Oct. 28, 1862. Nov., 1862, 1 Brig., 1 Div., Dept. N. C. Dec., 1862, Amory's Brig., Dept. N. C. Jany., 1863, 1 Brig., 1 Div., 18 Corps, Dept. N. C. Mustered out July 8, 1863.

46th REGIMENT INFANTRY.—Org. at Readville, Sept. 25 to Oct. 30, 1862. Nov., 1862, 3 Brig., 1 Div., Dept. N. C. Dec., 1862, Lee's Brig., Dept. N. C. Jany., 1863, 2 Brig., 1 Div., 18 Corps, Dept. N. C. June, 1863, 8 Corps, Middle Dept. Mustered out July 29, 1863.

47th REGIMENT INFANTRY.—Org. at Readville, Oct. 16, 1862. Jany., 1863, 2 Brig., 2 Div., 19 Corps, Gulf. Mustered out Sept. 1, 1863.

48th REGIMENT INFANTRY.—Org. at Wenham and mustered in Oct. 28, 1862. Feby., 1863, 1 Brig., 1 Div., 19 Corps, Gulf. Mustered out Sept. 3, 1863.

49th REGIMENT INFANTRY.—Org. at Pittsfield and mustered in Oct. 28, 1862. Feby., 1863, 1 Brig., 1 Div., 19 Corps, Gulf. Mustered out Sept. 1, 1863.

50th REGIMENT INFANTRY.—Org. at Boxford, Sept. 16 to Nov. 11, 1862. Jany., 1863, 3 Brig., 1 Div., 19 Corps, Gulf. Mustered out Aug. 24, 1863.

51st REGIMENT INFANTRY.—Org. at Worcester, Sept. 25 to Oct. 30, 1862. Nov., 1862, 1 Brig., 1 Div., Dept. N. C. Dec., 1862, Amory's Brig., Dept. N. C. Jany., 1863, 1 Brig., 1 Div., 18 Corps, Dept. N. C. June, 1863, 8 Corps, Middle Dept. Mustered out July 27, 1863.

52nd REGIMENT INFANTRY.—Org. at Greenfield, Oct., 1862. Dec., 1862, Grover's Div., Dept. Gulf. Jany., 1863, 2 Brig., 4 Div., 19 Corps, Gulf. Mustered out Aug. 14, 1863.

53rd REGIMENT INFANTRY.—Org. at Groton Junction, Oct. 17 to Nov. 6, 1862. Nov., 1862, New York, Dept. East. Jany. 1863, 3 Brig., 3 Div., 19 Corps, Gulf. Mustered out Sept. 2, 1863.

54th REGIMENT INFANTRY.—(COLORED). Org. at Readville and mustered in May 13, 1863. June, 1863, St. Helena Island, S. C., 10 Corps, Dept. South. July, 1863, 3 Brig., 1 Div., Morris Island, S. C., 10 Corps. July, 1863, 3 Brig., Morris Island, 10 Corps. Aug., 1863, 4 Brig., Morris Island, 10 Corps. Nov., 1863, 3 Brig., Morris Island, 10 Corps. Jany., 1864, Montgomery's Brig., Dist. Hilton Head, S. C., 10 Corps. Feby., 1864, Montgomery's Brig., Dist. Fla., Dept. South. Feby., 1864, 3 Brig., Ames' Div., Dist. Fla. April, 1864, Folly and Morris Islands, S. C., Northern Dist., Dept. South. Oct., 1864, 1st Separate Brig., Dept. South. Nov., 1864, 2 Brig., Coast Div., Dept. South. Feby., 1865, 1st Separate Brig., Northern Dist., Dept. South. March, 1865, 1st Separate Brig., Dist. Charleston, S. C., Dept. South. June, 1865, 3d Sub Dist., Dist. Charleston, Dept. S. C. Mustered out Aug. 20, 1865.

55th REGIMENT INFANTRY.—(COLORED). Org. at Readville and mustered in June 22, 1863. July, 1863, Wild's African Brigade, Vodge's Div., North End Folly Island, S. C., 10 Corps, Dept. South. Oct., 1863, 3 Brig., Vodge's Div., Folly Island, 10 Corps. Feby., 1864, 3 Brig., Ames Div., Dist. Fla., Dept. South. April, 1864, Dist. Folly and Morris Islands, Northern Dist., Dept. South. Oct., 1864, 1st Separate Brig., Dept. South. Nov., 1864, 2 Brig., Coast Div., Dept. South. Feby., 1865, 1st Separate Brig., Dept. South. March, 1865, 1st Separate Brig., Dist. Charleston, Dept. South. June, 1865, Dist. Charleston, S. C., Dept. S. C. Mustered out Aug. 29, 1865.

56th REGIMENT INFANTRY.—Org. at Readville, Dec. 26, 1863, to Feby. 24, 1864. April, 1864, 1 Brig., 1 Div., 9 Corps, Potomac. Sept., 1864, 2 Brig., 2 Div., 9 Corps. Mustered out July 12, 1865.

57th REGIMENT INFANTRY.—Org. at Worcester and Readville and mustered in April 6, 1864. April, 1864, 1 Brig., 1 Div., 9 Corps, Potomac. Sept., 1864, 3 Brig., 1 Div., 9 Corps. Mustered out July 30, 1865.

58th REGIMENT INFANTRY.—Org. at Readville, April 25, 1864. May, 1864, 1 Brig., 2 Div., 9 Corps, Potomac. Mustered out July 26, 1865.

59th REGIMENT INFANTRY.—Org. at Readville, Dec. 3, 1863, to April 20, 1864. May, 1864, 1 Brig., 1 Div., 9 Corps, Potomac. Sept., 1864, 3 Brig., 1 Div., 9 Corps. Mustered out by consolidation with 57th Mass. Infy., May 26, 1865.

60th REGIMENT INFANTRY.—Org. for 100 days, Aug. 1, 1864. Aug., 1864, Indianapolis, Ind. Mustered out Nov. 30, 1864.

61st REGIMENT INFANTRY.—Org. at Gallop's Island, Boston Harbor, Aug. to Oct., 1864. Oct., 1864, Benham's Engr. Brig., Dept. Va. and N. C. March, 1865, Indpt. Brig., 9 Corps, Potomac. April, 1865, 1 Brig., 2 Div., 5 Corps, Potomac. Mustered out July 16, 1865.

62nd REGIMENT INFANTRY.—Org. April, 1865, not completed. Mustered out May 5, 1865.

MICHIGAN

1st REGIMENT CAVALRY.—Org. at Detroit, Aug. 21 to Sept. 6, 1861. Oct., 1861, Cav. Brig., Army Potomac. Dec., 1861, Cav., Banks' Corps, Potomac. March, 1862, Cav., 1 Div., Banks' 5 Corps. April, 1862, Hatch's Cav. Brig., Dept. Shenandoah. June, 1862, Cav. Brig., 2 Corps, Army Va. Sept., 1862, Unass'd, Alexandria, Va. Sept., 1862, Price's Cav. Brig., Def. Washington, and 22 Corps. March, 1863, 2 Brig., Stahel's Cav. Div., 22 Corps. June, 1863, 1 Brig., Stahel's Cav. Div., 22 Corps. June, 1863, 2 Brig., 3 Div., Cav. Corps, Potomac. March, 1864, 1 Brig., 1 Div., Cav. Corps, Potomac, and Middle Mil. Div. May, 1865, Dept. Mo. Aug., 1865, Dist. of the Plains, Dept. Mo. Sept., 1865, Dist. Dakota, Dept. Mo. Dec., 1865, Dist. Utah, Dept. Mo. Mustered out March 25, 1866.

2nd REGIMENT CAVALRY.—Org. at Detroit, Oct., 1861. Nov., 1861, Jefferson Barracks, Mo. Feby., 1862,

Cav. Div., Army Miss. April, 1862, 2 Brig., Cav. Div., Army Miss. Sept., 1862, 2 Brig., Cav. Div., Army Ohio. Nov., 1862, Unatt., Dist. Central Ky., Dept. Ohio. March, 1863, 1 Brig., 1 Cav. Div., Cumb'd. June, 1864, Dist. Nashville, Tenn., Dept. Cumb'd. Oct., 1864, 1 Brig., 1 Div. Cav., Cumb'd. Nov., 1864, 1 Brig., 1 Div. Wilson's Cav. Corps, Mil. Div. Miss. Mustered out Aug. 17, 1865.

3rd REGIMENT CAVALRY.—Org. at Grand Rapids, Aug. 24 to Nov. 28, 1861. Dec., 1861, Benton Barracks, Mo. March, 1862, Cav. Div., Army Miss. April, 1862, 1 Brig., Cav. Div., Army Miss. June, 1862, 5 Div., Army Miss. Sept., 1862, 2 Brig., Cav. Div., Army Miss. Nov., 1862, 3 Brig., Cav. Div., 13 Corps, Dept. Tenn. Dec., 1862, Cav. Brig., Dist. Jackson, 16 Corps, Tenn. March, 1863, Mizner's Cav. Brig., 3 Div., 16 Corps, Tenn. June, 1863, 2 Brig., 1 Cav. Div., 16 Corps, Tenn. Aug., 1863, 1 Brig., 1 Div. Cav., 16 Corps, Tenn. Jany., 1864, Regt. Vereranize. March, 1864, St. Louis, Mo. May, 1864, 3 Brig., 2 Div., 7 Corps, Dept. Ark. Aug., 1864, 4 Brig., Cav. Div., 7 Corps, Ark. Feby., 1865, 1 Brig., Cav. Div., 7 Corps, Ark. April, 1865, 1 Brig., 1 Cav. Div., Mil. Div. West Miss. May, 1865, 2 Brig., 2 Div., Cav. Corps, West Miss. Aug., 1865, Dept. Texas. Mustered out Feby. 16, 1866.

4th REGIMENT CAVALRY.—Org. at Detroit, Aug. 28, 1862. Oct., 1862, 1 Brig., Cav. Div., Army Ohio. Nov., 1862, 1 Brig., Cav. Div., Cumb'd. Jany., 1863, 1 Brig., 2 Cav. Div., Cumb'd. Oct., 1863, 2 Brig., 2 Cav. Div., Cumb'd. Nov., 1863, 1 Brig., 2 Cav. Div., Cumb'd. Nov., 1864, 1 Brig., 2 Div., Wilson's Cav. Corps, Mil. Div. Miss. Nov., 1864, 2 Brig., 2 Div., Wilson's Cav. Corps, M. D. M. Mustered out July 1, 1865.

5th REGIMENT CAVALRY.—Org. at Detroit, Aug. 2 to Sept. 2, 1862. Dec., 1862, Prov'l Cav. Brig., Casey's Div., Dept. Washington. Feby., 1863, Prov'l Cav. Brig., Casey's Div., 22 Corps. March, 1863, 1 Brig., Stahel's Cav. Div., 22 Corps. June, 1863, 2 Brig., 3 Div., Cav. Corps, Potomac. March, 1864, 1 Brig., 1 Div., Cav. Corps, Potomac, and Middle Mil. Div. Mustered out June 23, 1865.

6th REGIMENT CAVALRY.—Org. at Grand Rapids, May 28 to Oct. 13, 1862. Dec., 1862, Prov'l Cav. Brig., Casey's Div., Dept. Washington. Feby., 1863, Prov'l Cav. Brig., Casey's Div., 22 Corps. March, 1863, 1 Brig., Stahel's Cav. Div., 22 Corps. June, 1863, 2 Brig., 3 Div., Cav. Corps, Potomac. March, 1864, 1 Brig., 1 Div., Cav. Corps, Potomac, and Middle Mil. Div. June, 1865, Dist. of the Plains, Dept. Mo. Sept., 1865, Dist. Dakota, Dept. Mo. Mustered out Nov. 24, 1865.

7th REGIMENT CAVALRY.—Org. at Grand Rapids, Oct., 1862, to June, 1863. Feby., 1863, Prov'l Brig., Casey's Div., 22 Corps. March, 1863, 1 Brig., Stahel's Cav. Div., 22 Corps. June, 1863, 2 Brig., 3 Div., Cav. Corps, Potomac. March, 1864, 1 Brig., 1 Div., Cav. Corps, Potomac, and Middle Mil. Div. June, 1865, Dist. of the Plains, Dept. Mo. Sept., 1865, Dist. Dakota, Dept. Mo. Mustered out Dec. 15, 1865.

8th REGIMENT CAVALRY.—Org. at Mt. Clements, Dec. 30, 1862, to May 2, 1863. June, 1863, 2 Brig., 4 Div., 23 Corps, Dept. Ohio. July, 1863, 2 Brig., 1 Div., 23 Corps, Ohio. Aug., 1863, 1 Brig., 4 Div., 23 Corps, Ohio. Oct., 1863, 2 Brig., 4 Div., 23 Corps, Ohio. Nov., 1863, 2 Brig., 1 Cav. Div., Ohio. May, 1864, 3 Brig., Cav. Div., Dist. Ky., Dept. Ohio. June, 1864, 3 Brig., Cav. Div., 23 Corps, Ohio. Nov., 1864, 1 Brig., 6 Div., Wilson's Cav. Corps, Mil. Div. Miss. June, 1865, Cav., Dist. West Tenn., Dept. Cumb'd. Mustered out Sept. 22, 1865.

9th REGIMENT CAVALRY.—Org. at Coldwater, Jany. 8 to May 19, 1863. May, 1863, 3 Brig., 1 Div., 23 Corps, Dept. Ohio. Aug., 1863, 3 Brig., 4 Div., 23 Corps, Ohio. Nov., 1863, 1 Brig., 2 Cav. Div., Ohio. May, 1864, 1 Brig., Cav. Div., Dist. Ky., Dept. Ohio. July, 1864, 1 Brig., Cav. Div., 23 Corps, Ohio. Aug., 1864, Mounted Brig., Cav. Div., 23 Corps, Ohio. Sept., 1864, 2 Brig., Cav. Div., 23 Corps, Ohio. Oct., 1864, 2 Brig., 3 Div., Wilson's Cav. Corps, Mil. Div. Miss. Nov., 1864, 2 Brig., Kilpatrick's Cav. Div., Army Ga. Mustered out July 21, 1865.

10th REGIMENT CAVALRY.—Org. at Grand Rapids, Sept. 18 to Nov. 23, 1863. Nov., 1863, Dist. North Central Ky., 1 Div., 23 Corps, Dept. Ohio. April, 1864, 2 Brig., 4 Div., 23 Corps, Dept. Ohio. Feby., 1865, 2 Brig., 4 Div., Dist. East Tenn., Dept. Cumb'd. March, 1865, 1 Brig., Cav. Div., Dist. East Tenn., Dept. Cumb'd. July, 1865, Cav. Brig., Dist. East Tenn., Dept. Cumb'd. Mustered out Nov. 11, 1865.

11th REGIMENT CAVALRY.—Org. at Kalamazoo and Detroit Oct. 7 to Dec. 10, 1863. Dec., 1863, Lexington, Ky., Dept. Ohio. April, 1864, 1 Brig., 1 Div., Dist. Ky., 5 Div., 23 Corps, Dept. Ohio. Aug., 1864, 4 Brig., 1 Div., Dist. Ky., Dept. Ohio. Feby., 1865, 2 Brig., Cav. Div., Dist. East Tenn., Dept. Cumb'd. June, 1865, Cav. Brig., Dist. East Tenn., Cumb'd. Consolidated with 8th Mich. Cav., July 20, 1865.

1st U. S. LANCERS.—Org. at Detroit, Saginaw and St. Johns Nov. 30, 1861, to Feby. 20, 1862. Mustered out March 20, 1862.

CHANDLER'S HORSE GUARDS.—Org. at Coldwater Sept. 19, 1861. Mustered out Nov. 22, 1861.

6th REGIMENT HEAVY ARTILLERY.—Org. July 28, 1863, from 6th Mich. Infy. July, 1863, 1 Brig., 2 Div., 19 Corps, Gulf. Aug., 1863, Dist. Port Hudson, La., Dept. Gulf. June, 1864, Bailey's Engr. Brig., Dept. Gulf. Aug., 1864, U. S. Forces, Mobile Bay, Dept. Gulf. Dec., 1864, Dist. Southern Ala., Dept. Gulf. Mustered out Aug. 20, 1865.

BATTERY A, 1st REGIMENT LIGHT ARTILLERY.—Org. at Detroit and Coldwater May 28, 1861. June, 1861, McCook's Brig., Army Occupation, West Va. Aug., 1861, Reynolds', Cheat Mt. Dist., West Va. Dec. 1861, Arty., 3 Div., Army Ohio. Sept., 1862, 17 Brig., 3 Div., 1 Corps, Army Ohio. Nov., 1862, 2 Brig., 1 Div., Centre 14 Corps, Cumb'd. Jany., 1863, Arty., 1 Div., 14 Corps, Cumb'd. Dec., 1863, Garrison Arty., Chattanooga, Tenn., Dept. Cumb'd. Mustered out July 12, 1865.

BATTERY B, 1st REGIMENT LIGHT ARTILLERY.—Org. at Detroit Sept. 10 to Dec. 14, 1861. March, 1862, Arty., 4 Div., Army Tenn. Captured April 6, 1862. Reorg. Dec., 1862. Jany., 1863, Dist. Corinth, 16 Corps, Dept. Tenn. March, 1863, Arty., Dist. Corinth, 2 Div., 16 Corps, Tenn. Sept., 1864, Arty. Brig., 15 Corps, Tenn. Mustered out June 14, 1865.

BATTERY C, 1st REGIMENT LIGHT ARTILLERY.—Org. at Grand Rapids Nov. 23 to Dec. 17, 1861. Feby., 1862, Arty. Div., Army Miss. April, 1862, Arty., 2 Div., Army Miss. Nov., 1862, 1 Brig., 8 Div., 13 Corps, Dept. Tenn. Dec., 1862, 1 Brig., 8 Div., 16 Corps, Tenn. March, 1863, 4 Brig., 2 Div., Dist. Corinth, 16 Corps. May, 1863, 3 Brig., Dist. Memphis, Tenn., 5 Div., 16 Corps, Tenn. Nov., 1863, Fuller's Brig., 2 Div., 16 Corps, Tenn. March, 1864, Arty., 4 Div., 16 Corps, Tenn. Sept., 1864, Arty., 1 Div., 17 Corps, Tenn. Nov., 1864, Arty. Brig., 17 Corps, Tenn. Mustered out June 22, 1865.

BATTERY D, 1st REGIMENT LIGHT ARTILLERY.—Org. at White Pigeon Sept. 17 to Dec. 7, 1861. Jany., 1862, Arty., 1 Div., Army Ohio. Sept., 1862, Arty., 1 Div., 3 Corps, Army Ohio. Nov., 1862, Arty., 3 Div., Centre 14 Corps, Cumb'd. Jany., 1863, Arty., 3 Div., 14 Corps, Cumb'd. Oct., 1863, 2 Div., Arty. Res., Cumb'd. March, 1864, Garrison Arty., Murfreesboro, Tenn., Dept. Cumb'd. July, 1864, 1 Brig., Def. Nash. & Chatta. R. R. Dept. Cumb'd. March, 1865, 1 Brig., 1st Sub-Dist., Dist. Middle Tenn., Dept. Cumb'd. Mustered out Aug. 3, 1865.

BATTERY E, 1st REGIMENT LIGHT ARTILLERY.—Org. at Grand Rapids, Albion and Marshall and mustered in Dec. 6, 1861. Dec., 1861, Arty., 5 Div., Army Ohio. June, 1862, Arty. Res., Army Ohio. Aug., 1862, Post Nashville, Tenn. June, 1863, 2 Brig., 3 Div., Res. Corps, Cumb'd. Oct., 1863, Garrison Arty., Nashville, Tenn. Dec., 1864, Arty. Brig., 4 Corps, Cumb'd. Feby., 1865, Unatt., Dist. North. Ala., Dept. Cumb'd. Mustered out July 30, 1865.

BATTERY F, 1st REGIMENT LIGHT ARTILLERY.—Org. at Detroit and Coldwater and mustered in Jany. 9, 1862. March, 1862, Garrison West Point, Ky., Dept. Ohio. June, 1862, Unatt., Dept. Ohio. Aug., 1862, Cruft's Brig., Richmond, Ky., Dept. Ohio. Sept., 1862, 2 Brig., 2 Div., Army Ky., Dept. Ohio. Oct., 1862, Dist. Louisville, Ky., Dept. Ohio. Dec., 1862, Bowling Green, Ky., Dist. West. Ky., Dept. Ohio. June, 1863, Unatt., 2 Div., 23 Corps, Ohio. Aug., 1863, Munfordsville, Ky., 1 Div., 23 Corps, Ohio. Aug., 1863, Dist. South Central Ky., 1 Div., 23 Corps, Ohio. Jany., 1864, Unatt., 2 Div., 23 Corps, Ohio. May, 1864, Arty., 2 Div., 23 Corps, Ohio. Nov., 1864, Dist. Nashville, Tenn. Dec., 1864, Arty., 1 Div., 23 Corps, Ohio. Feby., 1865, Arty., 1 Div., 23 Corps, Dept. N. C. April, 1865, Post Newberne, N. C., Dept. N. C. Mustered out July 1, 1865.

BATTERY G, 1st REGIMENT LIGHT ARTILLERY.— Org. at Kalamazoo and mustered in Jany. 17, 1862. March, 1862, Arty., 7 Div., Army Ohio. Oct., 1862, Arty., Cumb'd Div., Dist. West Va., Dept. Ohio. Nov., 1862, Arty., 9 Div., Right Wing 13 Corps, Dept. Tenn. Dec., 1862, Arty., 3 Div., Sherman's Yazoo Exp. Jany., 1863, Arty., 9 Div., 13 Corps, Tenn. July, 1863, Arty., 1 Div., 13 Corps, Tenn. Aug., 1863, Arty., 1 Div., 13 Corps, Gulf. June, 1864, Def. New Orleans, La. Aug., 1864, Arty. Res., Gulf. Oct., 1864, U. S. Forces, Mobile Bay, Dept. Gulf. Dec., 1864, Dist. Southern Ala., Dept. Gulf. Mustered out Aug. 6, 1865.

BATTERY H, 1st REGIMENT LIGHT ARTILLERY.— Org. at Monroe and mustered in March 6, 1862. March, 1862, Arty. Div., Army Miss. July, 1862, Dist. Columbus, Dept. Tenn. Nov., 1862, Arty., 3 Div., Right Wing 13 Corps, Dept. Tenn. Dec., 1862, Arty., 3 Div., 17 Corps, Tenn. Oct., 1864, Post Chattanooga, Tenn. Nov., 1864, Post Nashville, Tenn. Feby., 1865, Post Chattanooga, Tenn. Mustered out July 22, 1865.

BATTERY I, 1st REGIMENT LIGHT ARTILLERY.— Org. at Detroit Aug. 29, 1862. Oct., 1862, Camp Barry, Def. Washington. Feby., 1863, Price's Cav. Brig., 22 Corps. March, 1863, Arty., Stahel's Cav. Div., 22 Corps. June, 1863, 1 Brig., Horse Arty., Potomac. Aug., 1863, 2 Brig., Horse Arty., Potomac. Nov., 1863, Arty. Brig., 11 Corps, Cumb'd. March, 1864, Arty., 3 Div., 11 Corps, Cumb'd. April, 1864, Arty., 3 Div., 20 Corps, Cumb'd. July, 1864, Arty. Brig., 20 Corps. Oct., 1864, Unatt. Arty., Dept. Cumb'd. Nov., 1864, Res. Arty., Chattanooga, Tenn., Dept. Cumb'd. Mustered out July 14, 1865.

BATTERY K, 1st REGIMENT LIGHT ARTILLERY.— Org. at Grand Rapids Nov. 21, 1862, to Feby. 20, 1863. Feby., 1863, Camp Barry, Def. Washington, D. C., 22 Corps. April, 1863, 1 Brig., DeRussy's Div., 22 Corps. June, 1863, Camp Barry, 22 Corps. Nov., 1863, Arty. Brig., 11 Corps, Cumb'd. March, 1864, Garrison Arty., Chattanooga, Tenn., Dept. Cumb'd. March, 1865, 2 Brig., 4 Div., Dist. East. Tenn., Dept. Cumb'd. Mustered out July 22, 1865.

BATTERY L, 1st REGIMENT LIGHT ARTILLERY.— Org. at Coldwater and mustered in April 11, 1863. June, 1863, Arty., 3 Div., 23 Corps, Dept. Ohio. Sept., 1863, Willcox's Div., Cumb'd Gap, Left Wing Forces, 23 Corps, Ohio. Jany., 1864, Dist. Clinch, Dept. Ohio. April, 1864, 1 Brig., 4 Div., 23 Corps, Ohio. Aug., 1864, 2 Brig., 4 Div., 23 Corps, Ohio. Feby., 1865, 2 Brig., 4 Div., Dist. East. Tenn., Dept. Cumb'd. Mustered out Aug. 22, 1865.

BATTERY M, 1st REGIMENT LIGHT ARTILLERY.— Org. at Detroit, Mt. Clemens and Dearborn June 30, 1863. July, 1863, Indianapolis, Ind. Sept., 1863, Willcox's Div., 23 Corps, Left Wing Forces, Dept. Ohio. Jany., 1864, Dist. Clinch, Dept. Ohio. April, 1864, 1 Brig., 4 Div., 23 Corps, Ohio. Feby., 1865, 1 Brig., 4 Div., Dist. East. Tenn., Dept. Cumb'd. March, 1865, 2 Brig., 4 Div., Dist. East. Tenn., Dept. Cumb'd. Mustered out Aug. 1, 1865.

13th INDPT. BATTERY LIGHT ARTILLERY.— Org. at Grand Rapids Jany. 20, 1864. Feby., 1864, Camp Barry, Def. Washington, D. C., 22 Corps. May, 1864, 1 Brig., Hardin's Div., Def. North Potomac, 22 Corps. July, 1864, Fort Foote, Def. North Potomac, 22 Corps. Oct., 1864, 1 Brig., Hardin's Div., 22 Corps. Mustered out July 1, 1865.

14th INDPT. BATTERY LIGHT ARTILLERY.— Org. at Kalamazoo Jany. 5, 1864. Feby., 1864, Camp Barry, Def. Washington, D. C., 22 Corps. May, 1864, 1 Brig., Hardin's Div., Def. North Potomac, 22 Corps. Aug., 1864, 2 Brig., Hardin's Div., 22 Corps. Dec., 1864, 3 Brig., Hardin's Div., 22 Corps. Mustered out July 1, 1865.

HOWLAND'S COMPANY ENGINEERS.— Org. at Battle Creek Sept. 16, 1861. Mustered out Jany. 8, 1862.

1st REGIMENT ENGINEERS AND MECHANICS.— Org. at Detroit Dec. 11, 1861. Dec., 1861, Unatt., Army Ohio. June, 1862, Engr. Brig., Army Tenn. Sept., 1862, Unatt., Army Ohio. Nov., 1862, Unatt., Army and Dept. Cumb'd. Mustered out Sept. 22, 1865.

1st REGIMENT SHARPSHOOTERS.— Org. at Kalamazoo and Dearborn April 14 to Oct. 7, 1863. Aug., 1863, Camp Douglas, Chicago, Ill. March, 1864, 2 Brig., 3 Div., 9 Corps, Potomac. Sept., 1864, 2 Brig., 1 Div., 9 Corps, Potomac. Mustered out July 28, 1865.

HALL'S INDPT. BATTALION SHARPSHOOTERS.— Org. at Marshall Aug. 27 to Nov. 2, 1864. Attached to 16th Mich. Infy. and consolidated with that Regt., April 10, 1865.

BRADY'S INDPT. COMPANY SHARPSHOOTERS.— Org. at Detroit Feby. 3, 1862. Attached to 16th Mich. Infy., which see.

JARDINE'S INDPT. COMPANY SHARPSHOOTERS.— Org. at Saginaw May 3, 1864. Attached to 16th Mich. Infy., which see.

DYGERT'S INDPT. COMPANY SHARPSHOOTERS.— Org. Feby., 1862. Attached to 16th Mich. Infy., which see.

COMPANY SHARPSHOOTERS.— Org. Aug. 21, 1861. Attached to 1st U. S. S. S. as Co. C.

COMPANY SHARPSHOOTERS.— Org. March 4, 1862. Attached to 1st U. S. S. S. as Co. I.

COMPANY SHARPSHOOTERS.— Org. March 30, 1862. Attached to 1st U. S. S. S. as Co. K.

COMPANY SHARPSHOOTERS.— Org. Oct. 4, 1861. Attached to 2nd U. S. S. S. as Co. B.

1st REGIMENT INFANTRY (3 MONTHS).— Org. at Fort Wayne and Detroit May 1, 1861. June, 1861, Willcox's Brig., Heintzelman's Div., McDowell's Army, N. E. Va. Mustered out Aug. 7, 1861.

1st REGIMENT INFANTRY (3 YEARS).— Org. at Detroit and mustered in Sept. 16, 1861. Sept., 1861, 1 Brig., Hooker's Div., Potomac. Feby., 1862, R. R. Brig., Army Potomac. March, 1862, 1 Brig., 2 Div., 3 Corps, Potomac. March, 1862, Camp Hamilton, Va., Dept. Va. May, 1862, Robinson's Brig., Dept. Va. June, 1862, 1 Brig., 1 Div., 5 Corps, Potomac. March, 1864, 3 Brig., 1 Div., 5 Corps, Potomac. Mustered out July 9, 1865.

2nd REGIMENT INFANTRY.— Org. at Detroit May 25, 1861. June, 1861, Richardson's Brig., Tyler's Div., McDowell's Army, N. E. Va. Aug., 1861, Richardson's Brig., Div. Potomac. Oct., 1861, Richardson's Brig., Heintzelman's Div., Potomac. March, 1862, 3 Brig., 3 Div., 3 Corps, Potomac. Aug., 1862, 3 Brig., 1 Div., 3 Corps. Potomac. Nov., 1862, 1 Brig., 1 Div., 9 Corps, Potomac. April, 1863, 1 Brig., 1 Div., 9 Corps, Ohio. June, 1863, 3 Brig., 1 Div., 9 Corps, Tenn. Aug., 1863, 3 Brig., 1 Div., 9 Corps, Ohio. Jany., 1864, 2 Brig., 1 Div., 9 Corps, Ohio. April, 1864, 1 Brig., 3 Div., 9 Corps, Potomac. July, 1864, 2 Brig., 3 Div., 9 Corps. Sept., 1864, 2 Brig., 1 Div., 9 Corps, Potomac. Mustered out July 28, 1865.

3rd REGIMENT INFANTRY.— Org. at Grand Rapids June 10, 1861. June, 1861, Richardson's Brig., Tyler's Div., McDowell's Army, N. E. Va. Aug., 1861, Richardson's Brig., Div. Potomac. Oct., 1861, Richardson's Brig., Heintzelman's Div., Potomac. March, 1862, 3 Brig., 3 Div., 3 Corps, Potomac. Aug., 1862, 3 Brig., 1 Div., 3 Corps, Potomac. March, 1864, 2 Brig., 3 Div., 2 Corps, Potomac. Mustered out June 10, 1864. Vets. and recruits transferred to 5th Mich. Infy., June 13, 1864.

3rd REGIMENT INFANTRY (REORGANIZED).— Org. at Grand Rapids, Adrian and Pontiac Aug. 24 to Oct. 12, 1864. Oct., 1864, Dist. Northern Ala., Dept. Cumb'd. Nov., 1864, 1 Brig., Def. Nash. & Chatt. R. R., Dept. Cumb'd. Jany., 1865, 3 Brig., 3 Div., 4 Corps, Cumb'd. June, 1865, 2 Brig., 3 Div., 4 Corps, Cumb'd. Aug., 1865, Dept. Texas. Mustered out May 26, 1866.

4th REGIMENT INFANTRY.— Org. at Adrian June 20, 1861. June, 1861, Willcox's Brig., Heintzelman's Div., McDowell's Army, N. E. Va. Aug., 1861, Sherman's Brig., Div. Potomac. Oct., 1861, Morrell's Brig., Porter's Div., Potomac. March, 1862, 2 Brig., 1 Div., 3 Corps, Potomac. May, 1862, 2 Brig., 1 Div., 5 Corps, Potomac. Mustered out June 20 to July 18, 1864.

4th REGIMENT INFANTRY (REORGANIZED).—Org. at Adrian and Hudson Oct. 14, 1864. Oct., 1864, Dist. Northern Ala., Dept. Cumb'd. Nov., 1864, 1 Brig., Def. Nash. & Chatt. R. R., Dept. Cumb'd. Jany., 1865, 3 Brig., 3 Div., 4 Corps, Cumb'd. June, 1865, 2 Brig., 3 Div., 4 Corps. Aug., 1865, Dept. Texas. Mustered out May 26, 1866.

5th REGIMENT INFANTRY.—Org. at Detroit and mustered in Aug. 28, 1861. Oct., 1861, Richardson's Brig., Heintzelman's Div., Potomac. March, 1862, 3 Brig., 3 Div., 3 Corps, Potomac. Aug., 1862, 3 Brig., 1 Div., 3 Corps, Potomac. March, 1864, 2 Brig., 3 Div., 2 Corps, Potomac. Mustered out July 5, 1865.

6th REGIMENT INFANTRY.—Org. at Kalamazoo Aug. 20, 1861. Sept., 1861, Dix's Div., Balto., Md. Feby., 1862, Butler's New Orleans Exp. March, 1862, 2 Brig., Dept. Gulf. Nov., 1862, Sherman's Div., Dept. Gulf. Jany., 1863, 1 Brig., 2 Div., 19 Corps, Dept. Gulf. Designation changed to 6th Regt. Heavy Arty., July 28, 1863.

7th REGIMENT INFANTRY.—Org. at Monroe Aug. 22, 1861. Sept., 1861, Landers' Brig., Stone's (Sedgwick's) Div., Potomac. March, 1862, 3 Brig., 2 Div., 2 Corps, Potomac. Dec., 1863, 1 Brig., 2 Div., 2 Corps, Potomac. Mustered out July 5, 1865.

8th REGIMENT INFANTRY.—Org. at Detroit Aug. and Sept., 1861. Mustered in Sept. 23, 1861. Oct., 1861, Stevens' 2 Brig., Sherman's S. C. Exp. Corps. April, 1862, 1 Brig., 2 Div., Dept. South. July, 1862, 1 Brig., 1 Div., 9 Corps, Potomac. Sept., 1862, 2 Brig., 1 Div., 9 Corps, Potomac. Dec., 1862, 1 Brig., 1 Div., 9 Corps, Potomac. April, 1863, 1 Brig., 1 Div., 9 Corps, Ohio. June, 1863, 3 Brig., 1 Div., 9 Corps, Tenn. Aug., 1863, 1 Brig., 1 Div., 9 Corps, Ohio. April, 1864, 1 Brig., 3 Div., 9 Corps, Potomac. Sept., 1864, 1 Brig., 1 Div., 9 Corps, Potomac. April, 1865, 2 Brig., 1 Div., 9 Corps, Potomac. Mustered out July 30, 1865.

9th REGIMENT INFANTRY.—Org. at Detroit and mustered in Oct. 15, 1861. Oct., 1861, Thomas' Command, Dept. Cumb'd. Nov., 1861, 16 Brig., Army Ohio. March, 1862, 23 Indpt. Brig., Army Ohio. Nov., 1862, Headqrs. 14 Corps, Dept. Cumb'd. Feby., 1864, Headqrs. Dept. Cumb'd in the field. May, 1864, Res. Brig., Dept. Cumb'd. Oct., 1864, Headqrs. Dept. Cumb'd, Chattanooga, Tenn. June, 1865, Nashville, Tenn. Mustered out Sept. 15, 1865.

10th REGIMENT INFANTRY.—Org. at Flint and mustered in Feby. 6, 1862. April, 1862, 2 Brig., 1 Div., Army Miss. Sept., 1862, 2 Brig., 13 Div., Army Ohio. Nov., 1862, 1 Brig., 4 Div., Centre 14 Corps, Cumb'd. Jany., 1863, 1 Brig., 4 Div., 14 Corps, Cumb'd. June, 1863, 1 Brig., 2 Div., Res. Corps, Cumb'd. Oct., 1862, 2 Brig., 1 Div., 14 Corps, Cumb'd. Mustered out July 19, 1865.

11th REGIMENT INFANTRY.—Org. at White Pigeon Aug. 24 to Sept. 29, 1861. Dec., 1861, Unassigned, R. R. Guard, Army Ohio. Sept., 1862, 29 Brig., 8 Div., Army Ohio. Nov., 1862, 2 Brig., 2 Div., Centre 14 Corps, Cumb'd. Jany., 1863, 2 Brig., 2 Div., 14 Corps, Cumb'd. Oct., 1863, 2 Brig., 1 Div., 14 Corps, Cumb'd. Mustered out Sept. 30, 1864. Vets. and recruits transferred to 11th Regt. (Reorg.), April, 1865.

11th REGIMENT INFANTRY (REORGANIZED).—Org. at Jackson Jany. 4 to Feby. 26, 1865. April, 1865, 3 Brig., 2 Separate Div., Dist. Etowah, Dept. Cumb'd. July, 1865, 2 Brig., 4 Div., Dist. East. Tenn., Dept. Cumb'd. Mustered out Sept. 16, 1865.

12th REGIMENT INFANTRY.—Org. at Niles, Dowagiac and Buchanan Dec. 9, 1861, to March 1, 1862. March, 1862, 1 Brig., 6 Div., Army Tenn. April, 1862, 1 Brig., 1 Div., Tenn. July, 1862, 1 Brig., 1 Div., Dist. Jackson, Dept. Tenn. Nov., 1862, Unatt., Dist. Jackson, 13 Corps, Dept. Tenn. Dec., 1862, Post Bolivar, Dist. Jackson, 16 Corps, Tenn. March, 1863, 1 Brig., 3 Div., 16 Corps, Tenn. May, 1863, 1 Brig., Kimball's Prov'l Div., 16 Corps, Tenn. July, 1863, 1 Brig., Kimball's Prov'l Div., Dist. Eastern Ark. Aug., 1863, 1 Brig., 2 Div., Ark. Exp. Nov., 1863, 3 Brig., 2 Div., Ark. Exp. Jany., 1864, 3 Brig., 2 Div., 7 Corps, Dept. Ark. May, 1864, 1 Brig., 2 Div., 7 Corps, Ark. July, 1865, Dept. Ark. Mustered out **Feby. 15, 1866.**

13th REGIMENT INFANTRY.—Org. at Kalamazoo and mustered in Jany. 17, 1862. Jany., 1862, 15 Brig., 4 Div., Army Ohio. March, 1862, 20 Brig., 6 Div., Army Ohio. Sept., 1862, 20 Brig., 6 Div., 2 Corps, Ohio. Nov., 1862, 3 Brig., 1 Div., Left Wing 14 Corps, Cumb'd. Jany., 1863, 3 Brig., 1 Div., 21 Corps, Cumb'd. April, 1863, 1 Brig., 1 Div., 21 Corps, Cumb'd. Oct., 1863, 2 Brig., 2 Div., 4 Corps, Cumb'd. Nov., 1863, Engr. Brig., Cumb'd. Oct., 1864, 2 Brig., 1 Div., 14 Corps, Cumb'd. Mustered out July 25, 1865.

14th REGIMENT INFANTRY.—Org. at Ypsilanti and Detroit Jany. 7 to Feby. 18, 1862. April, 1862, 2 Brig., 1 Div., Army Miss. Sept., 1862, 2 Brig., 13 Div., Army Ohio. Nov., 1862, 1 Brig., 4 Div., Centre 14 Corps, Cumb'd. Jany., 1863, 1 Brig., 4 Div., 14 Corps, Cumb'd. June, 1863, 1 Brig., 2 Div., Res. Corps, Cumb'd. Oct., 1863, 1 Brig., 2 Div., 14 Corps, Cumb'd. Dec., 1863, Columbia, Tenn., Dept. Cumb'd. May, 1864, 1 Brig., 2 Div., 14 Corps, Cumb'd. Mustered out July 18, 1865.

15th REGIMENT INFANTRY.—Org. at Detroit, Monroe and Grand Rapids Oct. 16, 1861, to March 13, 1862. April, 1862, 2 Brig., 6 Div., Army Tenn. July, 1862, 2 Brig., 6 Div., Dist. Corinth, Dept. Tenn. Nov., 1862, 2 Brig., 6 Div., Left Wing 13 Corps, Dept. Tenn. Dec., 1862, Unatt., 1 Div., 17 Corps, Dept. Tenn. Jany., 1863, Unatt., 1 Div., 16 Corps, Tenn. June, 1863, 2 Brig., 1 Div., 16 Corps, Tenn. July, 1863, 2 Brig., 4 Div., 15 Corps, Tenn. Jany., 1864, Unatt., 4 Div., 15 Corps, Tenn. April, 1864, 3 Brig., 4 Div., 15 Corps, Tenn. Aug., 1864, 1 Brig., 4 Div., 15 Corps, Tenn. Sept., 1864, 3 Brig., 2 Div., 15 Corps. Mustered out Aug. 13, 1865.

16th REGIMENT INFANTRY ("STOCKTON'S INDPT. REGIMENT").—Org. at Plymouth and Detroit July, 1861. Sept., 1861, Butterfield's Brig., Porter's Div., Potomac. March, 1862, 3 Brig., 1 Div., 3 Corps, Potomac. May, 1862, 3 Brig., 1 Div., 5 Corps, Potomac. Mustered out July 18, 1865.

17th REGIMENT INFANTRY.—Org. at Detroit Aug. 8 to 22, 1862. Sept., 1862, 1 Brig., 1 Div., 9 Corps, Potomac. April, 1863, 1 Brig., 1 Div., 9 Corps, Ohio. June, 1863, 1 Brig., 1 Div., 9 Corps, Tenn. Aug., 1863, 3 Brig., 1 Div., 9 Corps, Ohio. Jany., 1864, 2 Brig., 1 Div., 9 Corps, Ohio. April, 1864, 1 Brig., 3 Div., 9 Corps, Potomac. May, 1864, Acting Engrs., 3 Div., 9 Corps, Potomac. Sept., 1864, Acting Engrs., 1 Div., 9 Corps, Potomac. April, 1865, 1 Brig., 1 Div., 9 Corps, Potomac. Mustered out June 3, 1865.

18th REGIMENT INFANTRY.—Org. at Hillsdale Aug. 26, 1862. Sept., 1862, 3 Brig., 1 Div., Army Ky., Dept. Ohio. Nov., 1862, 1 Brig., 2 Div., Army Ky., Dept. Ohio. Jany., 1863, 3 Brig., Dist. Central Ky., Dept. Ohio. April, 1863, Garrison Nashville, Tenn., Dept. Cumb'd. June, 1863, 3 Brig., 2 Div., Res. Corps, Dept. Cumb'd. Oct., 1863, Unatt., Dept. Cumb'd, Nashville, Tenn. Jany., 1864, 1 Brig., Dist. Nashville, Dept. Cumb'd. Jany., 1864, 1 Brig., Rousseau's 3 Div., 12 Corps, Cumb'd. April, 1864, 1 Brig., 4 Div., 20 Corps, Cumb'd. March, 1865, Dist. North. Ala., Dept. Cumb'd. Mustered out June 26, 1865.

19th REGIMENT INFANTRY.—Org. at Dowagiac and mustered in Sept. 5, 1862. Oct., 1862, 1 Brig., 3 Div., Army Ky., Dept. Ohio. Feby., 1863, Coburn's Brig., Baird's Div., Army Ky., Dept. Cumb'd. June, 1863, 3 Brig., 1 Div., Res. Corps, Cumb'd. Oct., 1863, Coburn's Unatt. Brig., Dept. Cumb'd. Dec., 1863, Post Murfreesboro, Tenn., Dept. Cumb'd. Jany., 1864, 2 Brig., 1 Div., 11 Corps, Cumb'd. April, 1864, 2 Brig., 3 Div., 20 Corps, Cumb'd. Mustered out June 10, 1865.

20th REGIMENT INFANTRY.—Org. at Jackson Aug. 15 to 19, 1862. Sept., 1862, 1 Brig., 1 Div., 9 Corps, Potomac. April, 1863, 1 Brig., 1 Div., 9 Corps, Ohio. June, 1863, 3 Brig., 1 Div., 9 Corps, Tenn. Aug., 1863, 3 Brig., 1 Div., 9 Corps, Ohio. Jany., 1864, 1 Brig., 1 Div., 9 Corps, Ohio. April, 1864, 2 Brig., 3 Div., 9 Corps, Potomac. Sept., 1864, 2 Brig., 1 Div., 9 Corps, Potomac. Mustered out May 30, 1865.

21st REGIMENT INFANTRY.—Org. at Grand Rapids Sept. 3, 1862. Sept., 1862, 37 Brig., 11 Div., Army Ohio. Sept., 1862, 37 Brig., 11 Div., 3 Corps, Army Ohio. Nov., 1862, 1 Brig., 3 Div., Right Wing 14 Corps, Cumb'd. Jany., 1863, 1 Brig., 3 Div., 20 Corps, Cumb'd. Oct.,

1863, 1 Brig., 2 Div., 4 Corps, Cumb'd. Nov., 1863, Engr. Brig., Dept. Cumb'd. Nov., 1864, 2 Brig., 1 Div., 14 Corps. Cumb'd. Mustered out June 8, 1865.

22nd REGIMENT INFANTRY.—Org. at Pontiac and mustered in Aug. 29, 1862. Sept., 1862, 3 Brig., 1 Div., Army Ky., Dept. Ohio. Nov., 1862, 1 Brig., 2 Div., Army Ky., Dept. Ohio. Jany., 1863, 3 Brig., Dist. Central Ky., Dept. Ohio. April, 1863, Dist. Nashville, Tenn., Dept. Cumb'd. June, 1863, 3 Brig., 2 Div., Res. Corps, Cumb'd. Sept., 1863, 1 Brig., 1 Div., Res. Corps, Cumb'd. Oct., 1863, 3 Brig., 2 Div., 14 Corps, Cumb'd. Nov., 1863, Engr. Brig., Dept. Cumb'd. May, 1864, Res. Brig., Dept. Cumb'd. April, 1865, 3 Brig., 2 Separate Div., Dist. Etowah, Dept. Cumb'd. Mustered out June 26, 1865.

23rd REGIMENT INFANTRY.—Org. at East Saginaw Sept. 11-13, 1862. Sept., 1862, 38 Brig., 12 Div., Army Ohio. Nov., 1862, Dist. West. Ky., Dept. Ohio. June, 1863, 1 Brig., 3 Div., 23 Corps, Dept. Ohio. Aug., 1863, 2 Brig., 2 Div., 23 Corps, Ohio. Feby., 1865, 2 Brig., 2 Div., 23 Corps, Dept. N. C. Mustered out June 28, 1865.

24th REGIMENT INFANTRY.—Org. at Detroit Aug. 13-15, 1862. Aug., 1862, Def. Washington, D. C. Oct., 1862, 1 Brig., 1 Div., 1 Corps, Potomac. Nov., 1862, 4 Brig., 1 Div., 1 Corps, Potomac. June, 1863, 1 Brig., 1 Div., 1 Corps, Potomac. March, 1864, 1 Brig., 4 Div., 5 Corps, Potomac. Aug., 1864, 3 Brig., 3 Div., 5 Corps, Potomac. Sept., 1864, 1 Brig., 3 Div., 5 Corps, Potomac. Feby., 1865, Springfield, Ill., Northern Dept. Mustered out June 30, 1865.

25th REGIMENT INFANTRY.—Org. at Kalamazoo Sept. 10-22, 1862. Oct., 1862, Dist. Louisville, Dept. Ohio. Dec., 1862, Dist. Western Ky., Dept. Ohio. June, 1863, Unatt., 2 Div., 23 Corps, Ohio. Aug., 1863, 1 Brig., 2 Div., 23 Corps, Ohio. Feby., 1865, 1 Brig., 2 Div., 23 Corps, Dept. N. C. Mustered out June 24, 1865.

26th REGIMENT INFANTRY.—Org. at Jackson Sept. 10 to Dec. 12, 1862. Dec., 1862, Dist. Alexandria, Def. Washington. Feby., 1863, Slough's Brig., Garrison Alex., 22 Corps. April, 1863, Ferry's 1 Brig., Corcoran's 1 Div., 7 Corps, Dept. Va. July, 1863, N. Y., Dept. East. Oct., 1863, 1 Brig., 1 Div., 2 Corps, Potomac. Mustered out June 4, 1865.

27th REGIMENT INFANTRY.—Org. at Port Huron, Ovid and Ypsilanti and mustered in April 10, 1863. April, 1863, 2 Brig., 1 Div., 9 Corps, Ohio. June, 1863, 1 Brig., 1 Div., 9 Corps, Tenn. Aug., 1863, 2 Brig., 1 Div., 9 Corps, Ohio. April, 1864, 1 Brig., 3 Div., 9 Corps, Potomac. Sept., 1864, 1 Brig., 1 Div., 9 Corps, Potomac. Mustered out July 26, 1865.

28th REGIMENT INFANTRY.—Org. at Kalamazoo and Marshall Aug. 17 to Oct. 17, 1864. Dec., 1864, Post Nashville, Tenn., Dept. Cumb'd. Jany., 1865, 2 Brig., 1 Div., 23 Corps, Ohio. Feby., 1865, 2 Brig., 1 Div., 23 Corps, Dept. N. C. April, 1865, Dist. Raleigh, N. C., Dept. N. C. Aug., 1865, Dist. Wilmington, N. C., Dept. N. C. Jany., 1866, Dist. Newberne, N. C. Mustered out June 5, 1866.

29th REGIMENT INFANTRY.—Org. at East Saginaw Oct. 3, 1864. Oct., 1864, Dist. North. Ala., Dept. Cumb'd. Nov., 1864, 1 Brig., Def. Nash. & Chatt. R. R., Dept. Cumb'd. Dec., 1864, 3 Brig., Def. Nash. & Chatt. R. R., Cumb'd. Feby., 1865, Unatt., 4 Div., 20 Corps, Cumb'd. March, 1865, 3 Brig., 1st Sub-Dist., Middle Tenn., Dept. Cumb'd. Mustered out Sept. 6, 1865.

30th REGIMENT INFANTRY.—Org. at Detroit Nov. 7, 1864, to Jany. 9, 1865, for duty in the State. Mustered out June 30, 1865.

STANTON GUARDS.—Org. at Detroit May 10, 1862. Mustered out Sept. 25, 1862.

INDPT. COMPANY PROVOST GUARD.—Org. at Detroit Jany. 3, 1863. Mustered out May 9, 1865.

MINNESOTA

1st REGIMENT CAVALRY.—Org. at St. Cloud, St. Peters and Fort Snelling, Minn., Oct. 9 to Dec. 30, 1862. Duty in Dept. N. W. Mustered out Dec. 7, 1865.

2nd REGIMENT CAVALRY.—Org. at Fort Snelling, Minn., Dec. 5, 1863, to Jany. 5, 1864. Duty in Dept. N. W. Mustered out May 4, 1866.

BRACKETT'S BATTALION CAVALRY.—Org. Feby. 25, 1864, from Co.'s G, I and K, 5th Iowa Cav. Duty in Dept. N. W. Mustered out June 1, 1866.

HATCH'S INDPT. BATTALION CAVALRY.—Org. at Fort Snelling and St. Paul July 25, 1863, to Sept. 1, 1864. Duty in Dept. N. W. Mustered out June 22, 1866.

1st REGIMENT HEAVY ARTILLERY.—Org. at St. Paul, Minn., and Rochester, Minn., Sept., 1864, to Feby., 1865. Garrison Post Chattanooga, Tenn., Dept. Cumb'd. Mustered out Sept. 27, 1865.

1st BATTERY LIGHT ARTILLERY.—Org. at Fort Snelling, Minn., Nov. 21, 1861. March, 1862, Buckland's Brig., Sherman's 5 Div., Army Tenn. April, 1862, 2 Brig., 6 Div., Army Tenn. July, 1862, Arty., 6 Div., Dist. Corinth, Miss. Nov., 1862, Arty., 6 Div., Left Wing 13 Corps, Dept. Tenn. Dec., 1862, Arty., 6 Div., 16 Corps. Jany., 1863, Arty., 6 Div., 17 Corps. Sept., 1863, Arty., 1 Div., 17 Corps. April, 1864, Arty., 4 Div., 17 Corps, Oct., 1864, Arty. Brig., 17 Corps. Mustered out July 1, 1865.

2nd BATTERY LIGHT ARTILLERY.—Org. at Fort Snelling March 21, 1862. April, 1862, Benton Barracks, Mo. May, 1862, Arty., 4 Div., Army Miss. Sept., 1862, 31 Brig., 9 Div., Army Ohio. Sept., 1862, 31 Brig., 9 Div., 3 Corps, Army Ohio. Nov., 1862, 2 Div., 1 Div., Right Wing 14 Corps, Cumb'd. Jany., 1863, Arty., 1 Div., 20 Corps, Cumb'd. Oct., 1863, Arty., 2 Div., 14 Corps. April, 1864, Unatt., Dept. Cumberland. Oct., 1864, Garrison Arty., Post Chattanooga, Tenn., Dept. Cumb'd. April, 1865, 2 Brig., 4 Div., Dist. East. Tenn., Dept. Cumb'd. Mustered out Aug. 16, 1865.

3rd BATTERY LIGHT ARTILLERY.—Org. at Fort Snelling, Minn., Feby. 2 to May 5, 1863. Duty in Dept. N. W. Mustered out Feby. 27, 1866.

1st COMPANY SHARPSHOOTERS.—Org. at Fort Snelling, Minn., Oct. 5, 1861. Assigned to 2nd U. S. Sharpshooters as Co. A, Feby. 10, 1862, which see.

2nd COMPANY SHARPSHOOTERS.—Org. at St. Paul, Minn., Nov. 23, 1861, to March 17, 1862. Mustered in March 20, 1862. Attached to 1st U. S. Sharpshooters as Co. I, which see.

1st REGIMENT INFANTRY.—Org. at Fort Snelling, Minn., and mustered in April 29, 1861. June, 1861, Franklin's Brig., Heintzelman's Div., McDowell's Army, N. E. Va. Aug., 1861, Stone's Brig., Div. Potomac. Oct., 1861, Gorman's Brig., Stone's (Sedgwick's) Div., Army Potomac. March, 1862, 1 Brig., 2 Div., 2 Corps, Army Potomac. Mustered out July 14, 1865.

2nd REGIMENT INFANTRY.—Org. at Fort Snelling, Minn., June 26 to Sept. 12, 1861. Oct., 1861, Thomas' Command, Army Ohio. Nov., 1861, 3 Brig., Army Ohio. Dec., 1861, 3 Brig., 1 Div., Army Ohio. Sept., 1862, 3 Brig., 1 Div., 3 Corps, Army Ohio. Nov., 1862, 3 Brig., 3 Div., Centre 14 Corps, Cumb'd. Jany., 1863, 3 Brig., 3 Div., 14 Corps. Oct., 1863, 2 Brig., 3 Div., 14 Corps. June, 1865, 1 Brig., 3 Div., 14 Corps. Mustered out July 11, 1865.

3rd REGIMENT INFANTRY.—Org. at Fort Snelling, Minn., Oct. 2 to Nov. 14, 1861. Nov., 1861, 16 Brig., Army Ohio. March, 1862, 23 Indpt. Brig., Army Ohio. July, 1862, Captured Murfreesboro, Tenn. Aug., 1862, Dept. N. W. Feby., 1863, Dist. Columbus, Ky., 6 Div. 16 Corps, Dept. Tenn. May, 1863, 3 Brig., Kimball's Prov'l Div., 16 Corps. July, 1863, 3 Brig., Kimball's Prov'l Div., Dist. Eastern Ark. Aug., 1863, 2 Brig., 2 Div., Army Ark. Nov., 1863, 3 Brig., 2 Div., Army Ark. Jany., 1864, 3 Brig., 2 Div., 7 Corps, Dept. Ark. May, 1864, 1 Brig., 2 Div., 7 Corps. Mustered out Sept. 2, 1865.

4th REGIMENT INFANTRY.—Org. at Fort Snelling, Minn., Oct. 4 to Dec. 23, 1861. May, 1862, 1 Brig., 3 Div., Army Miss. Nov., 1862, 1 Brig., 7 Div., Left Wing 13 Corps, Dept. Tenn. Dec., 1862, 1 Brig., 7 Div., 16 Corps. Jany., 1863, 1 Brig., 7 Div., 17 Corps. Sept., 1863, 1 Brig., 2 Div., 17 Corps. Dec., 1863, 1 Brig., 3 Div., 15 Corps. April, 1865, 1 Brig., 1 Div., 15 Corps. Mustered out July 19, 1865.

5th REGIMENT INFANTRY.—Org. at Fort Snelling, Minn., March 15 to April 30, 1862. May, 1862, 2 Brig., 2 Div., Army Miss. Nov., 1862, 2 Brig., 8 Div., Left Wing 13 Corps, Dept. Tenn. Dec., 1862, 2 Brig., 8 Div.,

16 Corps. April, 1863, 2 Brig., 3 Div., 15 Corps. Dec., 1863, 2 Brig., 1 Div., 16 Corps. Dec., 1864, 2 Brig., 1 Div., Detachment Army Tenn., Dept. Cumb'd. Feby., 1865, 2 Brig., 1 Div., 16 Corps, Mil. Div. West. Miss. July, 1865, Dist. Ala. Mustered out Sept. 6, 1865.

6th REGIMENT INFANTRY.—Org. at Camp Release and Fort Snelling, Minn., Sept. 29 to Nov. 20, 1862. Sept., 1862, Dept. N. W. June, 1864, Helena, Ark., Dist. Eastern Ark., 7 Corps, Dept. Ark. Nov., 1864, Dist. St. Louis, Mo., Dept. Mo. Feby., 1865, 2 Brig., 2 Div., 16 Corps, Mil. Div. West. Miss. Mustered out Aug. 19, 1865.

7th REGIMENT INFANTRY.—Org. at Camp Release and Fort Snelling, Minn., Aug. 16 to Oct. 30, 1862. Aug., 1862, Dept. N. W. Oct., 1863, Dist. St. Louis, Mo., Dept. Mo. April, 1864, Paducah, Ky. June, 1864, 3 Brig., 1 Div., 16 Corps, Dept. Tenn. Dec., 1864, 3 Brig., 1 Div., Detachment Army Tenn., Dept. Cumb'd. Feby., 1865, 3 Brig., 1 Div., 16 Corps, Mil. Div. West. Miss. Mustered out Aug. 16, 1865.

8th REGIMENT INFANTRY.—Org. at large in Minn. June 2 to Sept. 2, 1862. Sept., 1862, Dept. N. W. Oct., 1864, Dist. North. Ala., Dept. Cumb'd. Nov., 1864, 1 Brig., Def. Nash. & Chatt. R. R., Dept. Cumb'd. Dec., 1864, 3 Brig., 1 Div., 23 Corps, Army Ohio, to Feby., 1865, and Dept. N. C. to July, 1865. Mustered out July 10, 1865.

9th REGIMENT INFANTRY.—Org. at large in Minn. Aug. 15 to Oct. 31, 1862. Oct., 1862, Dept. N. W. Oct., 1863, Dept. Mo. June, 1864, 1 Brig., Sturgis' Exp. June, 1864, 2 Brig., 1 Div., 16 Corps, Dept. Tenn. Dec., 1864, 2 Brig., 1 Div., Detachment Army Tenn., Dept. Cumb'd. Feby., 1865, 2 Brig., 1 Div., 16 Corps, Mil. Div. West. Miss. Mustered out Aug. 24, 1865.

10th REGIMENT INFANTRY.—Org. at large in Minn. Aug. 12 to Nov. 15, 1862. Aug., 1862, Dept. N. W. Oct., 1863, Dist. St. Louis, Mo., Dept. Mo. April, 1864, Dist. Columbus, Ky., Dept. Tenn. June, 1864, 1 Brig., 1 Div., 16 Corps. Dec., 1864, 1 Brig., 1 Div., 16 Corps, Detachment Army Tenn., Dept. Cumb'd. Feby., 1865, 1 Brig., 1 Div., 16 Corps, Mil. Div. West. Miss. Mustered out Aug. 19, 1865.

11th REGIMENT INFANTRY.—Org. at Fort Snelling, Minn., Aug. and Sept., 1864. Oct., 1864, Post Gallatin. Tenn., Dept. Cumb'd. Nov., 1864, R. R. Guard, Louisv. & Nash. R. R., Dept. Cumb'd. March, 1865, 4th Sub-Dist., Dist. Middle Tenn., Dept. Cumb'd. Mustered out June 26, 1865.

MISSOURI

1st REGIMENT CAVALRY.—Org. at Jefferson Barracks, Mo., Sept. 6, 1861. Sept., 1861, Army West and Dept. Mo.

1st Battalion (Co.'s A, C, D, E).—Nov., 1861, Fort Leavenworth, Kan. May, 1862, Dist. S. W. Mo., Dept. Mo. Oct., 1862, 2 Brig., 2 Div., Army Frontier, Dept. Mo. Feby., 1863, 2 Brig., 3 Div., Army Frontier, Dept. Mo. June, 1863, 1 Brig., 1 Cav. Div., Army S. E. Mo., Dept. Mo. Aug., 1863, Res. Brig., 1 Cav. Div., Ark. Exp. Dec., 1863, 1 Brig., 1 Cav. Div., Army Ark. Jany., 1864, 1 Brig., 1 Cav. Div., 7 Corps, Dept. Ark. May, 1864, 3 Brig., 1 Div., 7 Corps. Sept., 1864, 2 Brig., Cav. Div., 7 Corps. March, 1865, Separate Brig., 7 Corps, to muster out.

2nd Battalion (Co.'s B, H, I and L).—Jany., 1862, 3 Brig., Army S. W. Mo., Dept. Mo. Feby., 1862, 2 Brig., 3 Div., Army S. W. Mo. April, 1862, Cassville, Mo., Dist. S. W. Mo., Dept. Mo. Oct., 1862, Unatt., 2 Div., Army Frontier, Dept. Mo., to Jany., 1863, then same as 1st Battalion.

3rd Battalion (Co.'s F, G, K, M).—Jany., 1862, 3 Brig., Army S. W. Mo., Dept. Mo. Feby., 1862, 2 Brig., 3 Div., Army S. W. Mo. May, 1862, 2 Div., Army S. W. Mo. July, 1862, Dist. Eastern Ark., Dept. Mo. Dec., 1862, 1 Brig., 3 (Cav.) Div., Dist. Eastern Ark., Dept. Tenn. Jany., 1863, Helena, Ark., Dist. Eastern Ark., 13 Corps, Tenn. Jany., 1863, Dist. Memphis, Tenn., 16 Corps. March, 1863, 4 Brig., Dist. Memphis, Tenn., 5 Div., 16 Corps. June, 1863, Dept. Mo. Dec., 1863, New Madrid, Mo., Dept. Mo., to Sept., 1864. (Co. F detached May 10, 1862, as escort to Headqrs. 4 Div., Army Miss. Sept., 1862, 9

Div., 3 Corps, Army Ohio. Nov., 1862, 1 Div., Right Wing 14 Corps, Cumb'd. Jany., 1863, 1 Div., 20 Corps, Cumb'd. Oct., 1863, Headqrs. Dept. Mo., to Sept., 1864.) Regt. consolidated to 7 Co.'s Sept. 10, 1864. Mustered out Sept. 1, 1865.

1st REGIMENT STATE MILITIA CAVALRY.—Org. at large in Mo. Feby. 3 to April 8, 1862. April, 1862, Dist. Central Mo., Dept. Mo. July, 1863, Dist. Border, Dept. Mo. Jany., 1864, Dist. Central Mo., Dept. Mo. Mustered out July 12, 1865.

1st BATTALION STATE MILITIA CAVALRY.—Org. at St. Charles, Mo., March 26, 1862. March, 1862, Dist. Central Mo., Dept. Mo. Broken up Nov. 11, 1862.

1st BATTALION CAVALRY, MISS. MARINE BRIGADE.—Org. at Benton Barracks, Mo., Jany. and Feby., 1863. Consolidated with 1st Infy., Miss. Marine Brig., Aug., 1864.

1st BATTALION ENROLLED MILITIA CAVALRY.—Called into service Sept. 25, 1864, to resist Price's invasion of Mo. Relieved from active service Oct. 31, 1864.

2nd REGIMENT CAVALRY ("MERRILL HORSE").—Org. at Benton Barracks, Mo., Sept. 3 to Dec. 11, 1861. Sept., 1861, Army West and Dept. Mo. Jany., 1862, Dist. N. E. Mo., Dept. Mo. June, 1863, 1 Brig., 1 Cav. Div., Army S. E. Mo., Dept. Mo. Aug., 1863, 1 Brig., 1 Cav. Div., Ark. Exp. Dec., 1863, 2 Brig., 1 Cav. Div., Army Ark. Jany., 1864, 2 Brig., 1 Cav. Div., 7 Corps, Dept. Ark. May, 1864, 3 Brig., 2 Div., 7 Corps. Sept., 1864, 3 Brig., Cav. Div., 7 Corps. Feby., 1865, 2 Brig., Cav. Div., Dist. West. Tenn. Mustered out Sept. 19, 1865.

2nd REGIMENT STATE MILITIA CAVALRY.—Org. in Mo. at large Dec., 1861, to April, 1862. Feby., 1862, Dist. North. Mo., Dept. Mo. March, 1863, Dist. St. Louis, Dept. Mo. June, 1863, Dist. S. E. Mo., Dept. Mo. July, 1863, Dist. St. Louis, Mo., Dept. Mo. Mustered out April 20, 1865.

2nd BATTALION STATE MILITIA CAVALRY.—Org. at Harrisville and Kansas City, Mo., March 17 to May 5, 1862. May, 1862, Dist. Central Mo., Dept. Mo. Mustered out March 31, 1863.

3rd REGIMENT CAVALRY.—Org. at Palmyra and St. Louis, Mo., Oct., 15, 1861, to March 6, 1862. March, 1862, Dist. Rolla, Dept. Mo. Dec., 1862, Cav. Brig., Army S. E. Mo., Dept. Mo. June, 1863, 2 Brig., 1 Cav. Div., Army S. E. Mo., Dept. Mo. Aug, 1863, 2 Brig., 1 Cav. Div., Ark. Exp. Dec., 1863, 3 Brig., 1 Cav. Div., Army Ark. Jany., 1864, 3 Brig., 1 Cav. Div., 7 Corps, Dept. Ark. Sept., 1864, 2 Brig., Cav. Div., 7 Corps. March, 1865, Separate Cav. Brig., 7 Corps. Mustered out June 14, 1865.

3rd REGIMENT STATE MILITIA CAVALRY (OLD).—Org. at Louisiana, Pike Co., May 5, 1862. June, 1862, Dist. S. W. Mo., Dept. Mo. Dec., 1862, Dist. Central Mo., Dept. Mo. Disbanded Feby. 4, 1863.

3rd REGIMENT STATE MILITIA CAVALRY (NEW).—Org. from 10th Mo. S. M. Cav. Regiment Feb. 2, 1863. March, 1863, Dist. St. Louis, Mo., Dept. Mo. June, 1863, Dist. S. E. Mo., Dept. Mo. July, 1863, Dist. St. Louis, Mo., Dept. Mo. Mustered out July 13, 1865.

4th REGIMENT CAVALRY.—Org. Feby., 1862, by consolidation of Fremont Hussars and 3 Co.'s Hollan Horse. Feby., 1862, 3 Brig., Army S. W. Mo., Dept. Mo. March, 1862, Cav., 2 Div., Army S. W. Mo., Dept. Mo. May, 1862, Cav., 3 Div., Army S. W. Mo., Dept. Mo. July, 1862, Dist. Eastern. Ark., Dept. Mo. Oct., 1862, Cav. Brig., Army S. E. Mo., Dept. Mo. April, 1863, Dist. Columbus, Ky., 6 Div., 16 Corps, Dept. Tenn. Dec., 1863, Waring's Detached Brig., Dist. Columbus, Ky. Jany., 1864, 1 Brig., 1 Cav. Div., 16 Corps. June, 1864, 1 Brig., Sturgis' Exp. June, 1864, 1 Brig., 2 Cav. Div., Dist. West. Tenn. Dec., 1864, 1 Brig., Cav. Div., Dist. West. Tenn. March, 1865, Unatt., Dept. Miss. May, 1865, 2 Brig., 2 Div., Cav. Corps, Mil. Div. West. Miss., and Dept. Texas. Mustered out Nov. 13, 1865.

4th REGIMENT STATE MILITIA CAVALRY.—Org. at St. Joseph, Mo., Jany. 28 to May 14, 1862. June, 1862, Dist. S. W. Mo., Dept. Mo. Dec., 1862, Dist. Central Mo., Dept. Mo. July, 1863, Dist. Border, Dept. Mo. Jany., 1864, Dist. Central Mo., Dept. Mo. Mustered out July 8, 1865.

5th REGIMENT CAVALRY.—Org. Feby. 14, 1862, by consolidation of Benton Hussars and 3 Co.'s Hollan Horse. Feby., 1862. Unatt., 2 Div., Army S. W. Mo., Dept. Mo. Oct., 1862, Cav., Army S. E. Mo., Dept. Mo. Consolidated with 4th Mo. Cav., Nov. 15, 1862.

5th REGIMENT STATE MILITIA CAVALRY (OLD). —Org. at St. Joseph, Mo., March-April, 1862. Attached to Dist. Central Mo., Dept. Mo., to Feby., 1863. Reorg. Feby. 2, 1863, from 13th Mo. S. M. Cav. Dist. Rolla to June, 1863. See 5th S. M. Cav. (New).

5th REGIMENT STATE MILITIA CAVALRY (NEW). —Org. Feby. 2, 1863, from 13th Mo. S. M. Cav. Feby., 1863, Dist. Rolla, Dept. Mo. June, 1863, Dist. Border, Dept. Mo. Oct., 1863, Dist. Rolla, Dept. Mo. Mustered out July 8, 1865.

6th REGIMENT CAVALRY.—Org. Feby. 14, 1862, by consolidation of Wright's, Woods' and Hawkins' Battalions Cav. Feby., 1862, Dist. S. W. Mo., Dept. Mo. July, 1862, Dist. Eastern Ark. Dec., 1862, 1 Brig., (3 Cav.) Div., Dist. Eastern Ark. (6 Co.'s.) Jany., 1863, 1 Brig., 2 Cav. Div., 13 Corps, Dept. Tenn. (6 Co.'s.) April, 1863, Headqrs. 13 Corps. (6 Co.'s.) Aug., 1863, Cav. Brig., 13 Corps. Gulf. (6 Co.'s). Nov., 1863, 3 Brig., Cav. Div., Gulf. (7 Co.'s). Jany., 1864, 1 Brig., Cav. Div., Gulf. (7 Co.'s.) Dec., 1864. Dist. South. Ala., Gulf. Feby., 1865, Separate Brig., Dist. Baton Rouge, La., Gulf. (7 Co.'s.) Feby., 1865, Cav. Brig., Dist. Baton Rouge, La. July, 1865, Dept. Texas. Mustered out Sept. 12, 1865. Co.'s A, D, E and L attached to Dist. S. W. Mo., Dept. Mo., to Oct., 1862; 2 Brig., 2 Div., Army Frontier, Dept. Mo., to June, 1863; Dist. S. E. Mo., Dept. Mo., to Oct., 1863; Dist. St. Louis, Mo., Dept. Mo., to muster out.

6th REGIMENT STATE MILITIA CAVALRY.—Org. at large in Mo. Feby. 27 to April 23, 1862. April, 1862, Dist. Central Mo., Dept. Mo. June, 1862, Dist. S. W. Mo., Dept. Mo. Dec., 1862, Dist. Central Mo., Dept. Mo. July, 1863, Dist. S. W. Mo., Dept. Mo. Oct., 1864, Dist. North. Mo., Dept. Mo. Feby., 1865, Dist. S. W. Mo., Dept. Mo Mustered out July 18, 1865

7th REGIMENT CAVALRY.—Org. Feby. 20, 1862, by consolidation of Black Hawk Cav. and Unatt. Co.'s. Feby., 1862, Dept. Kan. June, 1862, Dist. S. W. Mo., Dept. Mo. Oct., 1862, 1 Brig., 2 Div., Army Frontier, Dept. Mo. June, 1863, 1 Brig., 1 Cav. Div., Army S. E. Mo., Dept. Mo. Aug., 1863, 1 Brig., 1 Cav. Div., Ark. Exp. Jany., 1864, 1 Brig., 1 Cav. Div., 7 Corps, Dept. Ark. May, 1864, Clayton's Indpt. Cav. Brig., 7 Corps. Sept., 1864, 1 Brig., Cav. Div., 7 Corps. Feby., 1865, 2 Brig., Cav. Div., 7 Corps. Consolidated with 1st Mo. Cav., Feby. 22, 1865.

7th REGIMENT STATE MILITIA CAVALRY.—Org. at large in Mo. March-April, 1862. April, 1862, Unatt., Dept. Mo. Sept., 1862, Dist. S. W. Mo., Dept. Mo. Oct., 1862, Unatt., Army Frontier, Dept. Mo. June, 1863, Dist. Central Mo., Dept. Mo. Mustered out July 11, 1865.

8th REGIMENT CAVALRY.—Org. at Springfield, Mo., Aug. 6 to Sept. 15, 1862. Oct., 1862, 2 Brig., 3 Div., Army Frontier, Dept. Mo. June, 1863, 1 Brig., 1 Cav. Div., Army S. E. Mo., Dept. Mo. Aug., 1863, 1 Brig., 1 Cav. Div., Ark. Exp. Dec., 1863, 2 Brig., 1 Cav. Div., Army Ark. Jany., 1864, 1 Brig., 1 Cav. Div., 7 Corps, Dept. Ark. May, 1864, 3 Brig., 2 Div., 7 Corps. Sept., 1864, 3 Brig., Cav. Div., 7 Corps. Feby., 1865, 2 Brig., Cav. Div., 7 Corps. March, 1865, 1 Separate Cav. Brig., 7 Corps. Mustered out July 20, 1865.

8th REGIMENT STATE MILITIA CAVALRY.—Org. at Jefferson City, Bolivar, Warsaw and Linn Creek, Dec. 18, 1861, to May 6, 1862. May, 1862, Unatt., Dept. Mo. Sept., 1862, Dist. S. W. Mo., Dept. Mo. Mustered out July 17, 1865.

9th REGIMENT CAVALRY.—Org. Oct. 1862, by assignment of Bowen's Battalion and other bodies. Consolidated with 10th Cavalry and so designated Dec. 4, 1862, Co.'s G and H attached to 3rd Missouri Cavalry, Dec. 11, 1862.

9th REGIMENT STATE MILITIA CAVALRY.—Org. at large in Mo. Feby. 12, 1862, to Sept. 20, 1863. May, 1862, Dist. Rolla, Dept. Mo. Feby., 1863, Dist. North. Mo., Dept. Mo. Mustered out July 13, 1865.

10th REGIMENT CAVALRY.—Org. Oct., 1862, from 28th Mo. Infy. Oct., 1863, Dist. St. Louis, Mo., Dept. Mo. Jany., 1863, Dist. Memphis, Tenn., 16 Corps, Dept. Tenn. March, 1863, Cav. Brig., Dist. Corinth, 16 Corps. June, 1863, 3 Brig., 1 Cav. Div., 16 Corps. Aug., 1863, Cav. Brig., 15 Corps. Dec., 1863, Winslow's Cav. Brig., 17 Corps, and Dist. Vicksburg, Miss. April, 1864, 2 Brig., 1 Cav. Div., 16 Corps. June, 1864, 2 Brig., Cav. Div., Sturgis' Exp. June, 1864, 2 Brig., 1 Cav. Div., Dist. West. Tenn. Nov., 1864, 1 Brig., 4 Div., Cav. Corps, Mil. Div. Miss. Dec., 1864, 2 Brig., Cav. Div., Dist. West. Tenn. Feby., 1865, 1 Brig., 4 Div., Cav. Corps, Mil. Div. Miss. May, 1865, 2 Brig., 4 Div., Cav. Corps, M. D. M. Mustered out June 20, 1865.

10th REGIMENT STATE MILITIA CAVALRY.—Org. at Louisiana, Mo., May 5, 1862. May, 1862, Dist. St. Louis, Mo., Dept. Mo., and Dist. North. Mo., Dept. Mo. Designation changed to 3rd Mo. S. M. Cav., Feby. 2, 1863.

11th REGIMENT CAVALRY.—Org. at Benton Barracks and St. Joseph, Mo., March 28 to Dec. 11, 1863. April, 1863, Dist. St. Louis, Mo., Dept. Mo. Dec., 1863, Dist. S. W. Mo., Dept. Mo. Jany., 1864, Dist. N. E. Ark., 7 Corps, Dept. Ark. May, 1864, 3 Brig., 2 Div., 7 Corps. Sept., 1864, 3 Brig., Cav. Div., 7 Corps. Feby., 1865, 2 Brig., Cav. Div., 7 Corps. March, 1865, Separate Brig., Cav. Div., 7 Corps. Mustered out July 27, 1865.

11th REGIMENT STATE MILITIA CAVALRY.—Org. at large in Mo. Jany. 1 to April 20, 1862. Dist. North. Mo., Dept. Mo. Consolidated with 2nd Mo. S. M. Cav., Sept. 1, 1862.

12th REGIMENT CAVALRY.—Org. at St. Louis, Mo., Nov. 3, 1863, to March 23, 1864. March, 1864, Dist. St. Louis, Mo., Dept. Mo. July, 1864, 1 Brig., 1 Cav. Div., Dist. West. Tenn. Nov., 1864, 1 Brig., 5 Div., Cav. Corps, Mil. Div. Miss. May, 1865, Dept. Mo., Eastern Div., Powder River Exp. Mustered out April 9, 1866.

12th REGIMENT STATE MILITIA CAVALRY.—Org. in Mo. at large Dec. 5, 1861, to May 8, 1862. Dept. Mo. Broken up Feby. 4, 1863.

13th REGIMENT CAVALRY.—Org. Sept., 1864, to Feby., 1865, from Veterans of Mo. S. M. Regts. Attached to Dist. Rolla, Mo., and Dept. Mo. Mustered out July 3, 1866.

13th REGIMENT STATE MILITIA CAVALRY.—Org. May 19, 1862. Attached to Dist. Rolla, Dept. Mo. Designation changed to New 5th S. M. Cav., Feby. 2, 1863.

14th REGIMENT CAVALRY.—Org. at St. Louis and Springfield, Mo., Nov. 30, 1864, to May 13, 1865. Attached to Dist. St. Louis, Mo., Dept. Mo., to June, 1865; Dist. Plains, Dept. Mo., to Nov., 1865. Mustered out Nov. 17, 1865.

14th REGIMENT STATE MILITIA CAVALRY.—Org. at large in Mo. March to May, 1862. Attached to Dist. S. W. Mo., Dept. Mo. Disbanded March 3, 1863.

15th REGIMENT CAVALRY.—Org. Nov. 1, 1863, from 7th Enrolled Militia Mo. Infy. Attached to Dist. S. W. Mo., Dept. Mo., to April, 1865; Dist. North. Mo., Dept. Mo. Mustered out July 1, 1865.

16th REGIMENT CAVALRY.—Org. at Springfield, Mo., Nov. 1, 1863, from 6th Mo. Enrolled Militia Infy. Attached to Dist. S. W. Mo., Dept. Mo., to April, 1865; Dist. North. Mo. to July, 1865. Mustered out July 1, 1865.

BENTON HUSSARS CAVALRY BATTALION.—Org. at St. Louis, Mo., Sept. 18 to Dec., 23, 1861. Jany., 1862, 2 Div., Army S. W. Mo., Dept. Mo. Transferred to 5th Mo. Cav., Feby. 14, 1862.

BERRY'S CAVALRY BATTALION.—Org. in Upper Mo. June to Aug., 1861. Dept. Mo. Mustered out Feby. 1, 1862.

BISHOP'S CAVALRY BATTALION ("BLACK HAWK CAVALRY").—Org. at Henderson and LaClede, Mo., Nov. 14 to Dec. 31, 1861. Attached to Dist. N. E. Mo. Transferred to 7th Mo. Cav., Feby. 20, 1862.

BLACK HAWK CAVALRY BATTALION.—(See BISHOP'S CAVALRY BATTALION.)

BOONEVILLE STATE MILITIA CAVALRY BATTALION ("EPSTEIN'S").—Org. at Booneville March 24, 1862. Org. as 13th Mo. S. M. Cav., May 19, 1862. Attached to Dist. Rolla, Mo. Designation changed to 5th Mo. S. M. Cav., Feby. 2, 1863.

BOWEN'S CAVALRY BATTALION.—Org. at Rolla, Mo., July 10 to Oct. 10, 1861. Attached to Dept. Mo. to Jany., 1862. Unatt., Army S. W. Mo., Dept. Mo., and Dist. S. W. Mo., to Oct., 1862; 1 Brig., 3 Div., Army Frontier. Dept. Mo., to Jany., 1863. Transferred to 9th Mo. Cav., Oct. 1, 1862, and to 3rd Mo. Cav., Dec. 17, 1862.

CASS COUNTY HOME GUARD CAVALRY BAT-TALION.—Org. in Cass Co., Mo., June to Aug., 1861, for duty in Cass and adjoining counties and to protect bridges. Mustered out Feby. 28, 1862.

COMPANY A CAVALRY, 1st U. S. RESERVE CORPS.—Org. at St. Louis, Mo., May 16, 1861. Mustered out Aug. 18, 1861.

FREMONT'S BODY GUARD.—Org. at Cincinnati, Ohio, and St. Louis, Mo., Aug., 1861. Attached to Headqrs. Western Dept. Mustered out by order Secretary of War, Nov. 30, 1861.

FREMONT HUSSARS.—Org. at St. Louis, Mo., Sept., 1861. Attached to Army West to Nov., 1861; Unatt., Army S. W. Mo., Dept. Mo., to Feby., 1862. Transferred to 2nd Mo. Cav., Jany. 9, 1862, and to 4th Mo. Cav., Feby. 14, 1862.

FREMONT RANGERS.—Org. at Cape Girardeau, Mo., Aug., 1861. Mustered out Jany. 25, 1862.

HAWKINS' CAVALRY COMPANY.—Org. Sept., 1861. Assigned to 6th Mo. Cav., Feby. 14, 1862.

HOLLAN HORSE, U. S. RESERVE CORPS.—Org. at St. Louis and Warrenton, Mo., Oct. 14, 1861, to Feby. 1, 1862. Transferred to 4th and 5th Mo. Cav., Feby., 1862.

IRISH DRAGOONS ("NAUGHTON'S").—Org. at Jefferson City, Mo., Sept. 11, 1861. Assigned to 3rd Mo. Cav., as Co. L and to 5th Iowa Cav. ("Curtis Horse") as Co. L. Nov., 1861.

LORING'S CAVALRY COMPANY.

M'FADDEN'S STATE MILITIA CAVALRY COMPANY.

MOUNTAIN RANGERS (14th MISSOURI S. M. CAVALRY).

OSAGE RIFLES.—Org. at St. Louis, Mo., Nov. 1, 1861. Assigned to "Curtis Horse," 5th Iowa Cav., as Co. M, Dec., 1861.

SCHOFIELD'S HUSSARS (Co. I, 13th MISSOURI S. M. CAVALRY).

SOBOLESKI'S INDPT. COMPANY LANCERS.—Org. at Benton Barracks, Mo., Nov.-Dec., 1861. Mustered out Jany. 24, 1862.

STEWART'S CAVALRY BATTALION.—Org. at St. Louis, Mo., Sept. to Nov., 1861. Duty in Dist. S. E. Mo. Mustered out Feby. 2, 1862.

WHITE'S CAVALRY BATTALION (2nd MISSOURI S. M. CAVALRY).

BACKOFF'S BATTALION LIGHT ARTILLERY.—Org. at St. Louis, Mo., April 22 to May 18, 1861. July, 1861, 2 Brig., Lyons' Army West. Mustered out Aug. 26, 1861.

CAVENDER'S BATTALION LIGHT ARTILLERY.—(See BATTERRIES D, H and K, 1st MISSOURI LIGHT ARTILLERY.)

1st BATTERY STATE MILITIA LIGHT ARTILLERY ("WASCHMAN'S").—Org. at Independence, Mo., May 6, 1862. Attached to Dist. Central Mo., Dept. Mo. Disbanded Jany. 17, 1864.

1st REGIMENT LIGHT ARTILLERY.—Org. at St. Louis, Mo., Sept. 1, 1861, from 1st Mo. Infy.

BATTERY A, 1st REGIMENT LIGHT ARTILLERY.—Oct., 1861, Dept. Mo. March, 1862, Steele's Command, S. E. Mo., Dept. Mo. May, 1862, Arty., 1 Div., Army S. W. Mo., Dept. Mo. July, 1862, Dist. Eastern Ark., Dept. Mo. Oct., 1862, Dist. S. E. Mo., Dept. Mo. Jany., 1863, Arty., 13 Div., 13 Corps, Dept. Tenn. March, 1863, Arty., 12 Div., 13 Corps. July, 1863, Arty., 3 Div., 13 Corps. Aug., 1863, Arty., 3 Div., 13 Corps, Dept. Gulf. July, 1864, Arty. Res., Dept. Gulf. April, 1865, Hawkins' Colored Div., Mil. Div. West. Miss. June, 1865, Dept. Ala. Mustered out Aug. 23, 1865.

BATTERY B, 1st REGIMENT LIGHT ARTILLERY.—Oct., 1861, Dept. Mo. Jany., 1862, 2 Brig., Army S. W. Mo., Dept. Mo. Disbanded April, 1862. Battery reorg. Dec., 1862, by assignment of Welfley's Indpt. Battery Mo.

Light Arty. Dec., 1862, Arty., 2 Div., Army S. E. Mo., Dept. Mo. March, 1863, Dist. S. E. Mo., Dept. Mo. June, 1863, Arty., 2 Brig., Herron's Div., 13 Corps, Dept. Tenn. July, 1863, Arty., 2 Div., 13 Corps. Aug., 1863, Arty., 2 Div., 13 Corps, Gulf. June, 1864, U. S. Forces, Texas, Dept. Gulf. July, 1864, Def. New Orleans, La. Aug., 1864, Res. Arty., Dept. Gulf. Consolidated with Batteries A, F and G, 1st Mo. Arty., Sept. 13, 1864. See Battery A, 1st Mo. Arty.

BATTERY C, 1st REGIMENT LIGHT ARTILLERY.—Original Co. C, disbanded Sept., 1861. Reorg. by assignment of Mann's Indpt. Battery Mo. Light Arty., Aug., 1862. Aug., 1862, 4 Div., Dist. Memphis, Tenn. Sept., 1862, Arty., 4 Div., Dist. Jackson, Tenn. Nov., 1862, Arty., 4 Div., Left Wing 13 Corps, Dept. Tenn. Dec., 1862, 2 Brig., 6 Div., 16 Corps. Jany., 1863, 2 Brig., 6 Div., 17 Corps. Sept., 1863, Arty., 1 Div., 17 Corps. April, 1864, Arty., 4 Div., 17 Corps. Nov., 1864, Arty. Res., Nashville, Tenn., Dept. Cumb'd. Mustered out July 11, 1865.

BATTERY D, 1st REGIMENT LIGHT ARTILLERY.—Feby., 1862, 3 Brig., 2 Div., Dist. Cairo. Feby., 1862, 3 Brig., 2 Div., Dist. West. Tenn., and Army Tenn. April, 1862, Arty., 2 Div., Army Tenn. July, 1862, Arty., Dist. Corinth, Miss. Nov., 1862, Arty., Dist. Corinth, 13 Corps, Dept. Tenn. Dec., 1862, Arty., Dist. Corinth, 17 Corps. Jany., 1863, Arty., Dist. Corinth, 16 Corps. March, 1863, Arty., 2 Div., 16 Corps. Sept., 1863, Arty., 4 Div., 15 Corps. April, 1864, Arty. Res., Huntsville, Ala., Dept. Cumb'd. May, 1864, Arty., 3 Div., 15 Corps. Sept., 1864, Arty., Huntsville, Ala. Consolidated with Battery C, 1st Mo. Light Arty., April 11, 1865.

BATTERY E, 1st REGIMENT LIGHT ARTILLERY.—Oct., 1861, Fremont's Army West. Jany., 1862, Dist. Central Mo., Dept. Mo. June, 1862, Dist. S. W. Mo., Dept. Mo. Oct., 1862, 2 Brig., 3 Div., Army Frontier, Dept. Mo. June, 1863, 1 Brig., Herron's Div., 13 Corps, Dept. Tenn. July, 1863, Arty., 2 Div., 13 Corps. Aug., 1863, 1 Brig., 2 Div., 13 Corps, Dept. Gulf. Sept., 1863, Arty., 2 Div., 13 Corps. Mustered out June, 1864.

Battery reorg. Sept. 14, 1864, by the assignment of Segebarth's Battery, Penna. Light Arty. Sept., 1864, Arty., Post Vicksburg, Miss. Nov., 1864, Res. Arty., Dist. Vicksburg, Miss. Mustered out Jany. 1, 1865.

BATTERY F, 1st REGIMENT LIGHT ARTILLERY.—Oct., 1861, Fremont's Army West. Jany., 1862, Central Dist. Mo., Dept. Mo. June, 1862, Dist. S. W. Mo., Dept. Mo. Oct., 1862, 2 Brig., 2 Div., Army Frontier, Dept. Mo. June, 1863, 1 Brig., Herron's Div., 13 Corps, Dept. Tenn. July, 1863, Arty., 2 Div., 13 Corps. Aug., 1863, 1 Brig., 2 Div., 13 Corps, Dept. Gulf. Aug., 1863, Arty., 2 Div., 13 Corps. Feby., 1864, Arty., 4 Div., 13 Corps. June, 1864, Def. New Orleans, La., to Aug., 1864, Res. Arty., Dept. Gulf. Dec., 1864, Dist. Southern Ala. Feby., 1865, 1 Brig., 2 Div., 13 Corps, Mil. Div. West. Miss. Mustered out Aug. 11, 1865.

BATTERY G, 1st REGIMENT LIGHT ARTILLERY.—Oct., 1861, Fremont's Army West, and Dept. Mo. March, 1862, Arty., 3 Div., Army Miss. April, 1862, Arty., 1 Div., Army Miss. June, 1862, Arty., 5 Div., Army Miss. Sept., 1862, Arty., 11 Div., Army Ohio. Sept., 1862, Arty., 11 Div., 3 Corps, Army Ohio. Nov., 1862, 2 Brig., 3 Div., Right Wing 14 Corps, Cumb'd. Jany., 1863, Arty., 3 Div., 20 Corps, Cumb'd. Oct., 1863, Arty., 2 Div., 4 Corps. April, 1864, Garrison Arty., Chattanooga, Tenn., Dept. Cumb'd. Nov., 1864, 1 Brig., 1 Separate Div., Dist. Etowah, Dept. Cumb'd. Mustered out July 28, 1865.

BATTERY H, 1st REGIMENT LIGHT ARTILLERY.—Oct., 1861, Dept. Mo. Feby., 1862, 3 Brig., 2 Div., Dist. Cairo. March, 1862, 3 Brig., 2 Div., Dist. West. Tenn., and Army Tenn. April, 1862, Arty., 2 Div., Army Tenn. July, 1862, Arty., 2 Div., Dist. Corinth, Miss. Nov., 1862, Arty., Dist. Corinth, 13 Corps, Dept. Tenn. Dec., 1862, Arty., Dist. Corinth, 17 Corps. Jany., 1863, Arty., Dist. Corinth, 16 Corps. March, 1863, Arty., 2 Div., 16 Corps. Sept., 1864, Arty. Brig., 15 Corps. Mustered out June 16, 1865.

BATTERY I, 1st REGIMENT LIGHT ARTILLERY.—Original Co. disbanded Jany., 1862. Battery reorg. by assignment of Buell's Indpt. Battery Mo. Light Arty.,

Aug., 1862. Aug., 1862, Arty., Dist. Corinth, Miss. Nov., 1862, Arty., Dist. Corinth, Miss.. 13 Corps, Dept. Tenn. Dec., 1862, Arty., Dist. Corinth, 17 Corps. Jany., 1863, Arty., Dist. Corinth, 16 Corps. March, 1863, Arty., 2 Div., 16 Corps. May, 1864, Dist. Nashville, Tenn., Dept. Cumb'd. Mustered out June 30, 1865.

BATTERY K, 1st REGIMENT LIGHT ARTILLERY.—Oct., 1861, Dept. Mo. Feby., 1862, 3 Brig., 2 Div., Dist. Cairo. Feby., 1862, 3 Brig., 2 Div., Dist. West. Tenn. and Army Tenn. April, 1862, Arty., 2 Div., Army Tenn. July, 1862, Arty., 2 Div., Dist. Corinth, Miss. Nov., 1862, Arty., Dist. Corinth, Miss., 13 Corps, Dept. Tenn. Dec., 1862, Arty., Dist. Corinth, 17 Corps. Jany., 1863, Arty., Dist. Jackson, 16 Corps. March, 1863, Arty., 1 Div., 16 Corps. July, 1863, Arty., 13 Div., 16 Corps, Dist. Eastern Ark. Aug., 1863, Arty., 3 Div., Ark. Exp. Jany., 1864, Arty., 3 Div., 7 Corps, Dept. Ark. May, 1864, Arty., 2 Div., 7 Corps. Feby., 1865, Arty., 1 Div., 7 Corps. Mustered out Aug. 4, 1865.

BATTERY L, 1st REGIMENT LIGHT ARTILLERY.—Original Co., Duty at St. Louis, Mo., till Jany., 1862. Disbanded Jany., 1862. Battery reorg. by assignment of Battery A, Schofield's Mo. Light Arty., Oct., 1862. Oct., 1862, 1 Brig., 3 Div., Army Frontier, Dept. Mo. June, 1863, Dist. St. Louis, Mo., Dept. Mo. Dec., 1863, Dist. S. W. Mo., Dept. Mo. Jany., 1864, Dist. Central Mo., Dept. Mo. April, 1865, Dist. North. Mo., Dept. Mo. Mustered out July 20, 1865.

BATTERY M, 2nd REGIMENT LIGHT ARTILLERY.—Oct., 1861, Dept. Mo. March, 1862, Arty., 5 Div., Army Miss. April, 1862, Arty. Div., Army Miss. June, 1862, Arty., 1 Div., Army Miss. Sept., 1862, Arty., 3 Div., Army Miss. Nov., 1862, Arty., 7 Div., Left Wing 13 Corps, Dept. Tenn. Dec., 1862, Arty., 7 Div., 16 Corps. Jany., 1863, Arty., 7 Div., 17 Corps. Sept., 1863, Arty., 1 Div., 17 Corps. March, 1864, Arty., Prov'l Div., 17 Corps, Dept. Gulf. June, 1864, 4 Brig., 1 Div., 16 Corps. Sept., 1864, Arty. Res., Dist. West. Tenn. Mustered out July 25, 1865.

2nd REGIMENT LIGHT ARTILLERY.—Org. at St. Louis, Mo., as 1st Regt. Mo. Arty., U. S. Res. Corps, Sept. 16-Nov. 6, 1861. Designation changed to 2nd Mo. Light Arty., Nov. 20, 1861.

BATTERY A, 2nd REGIMENT LIGHT ARTILLERY.—Jany., 1862, Dist. St. Louis, Mo., Dept. Mo. Nov., 1862, Dist. Rolla, Dept. Mo. Feby., 1863, Dist. St. Louis, Mo., Dept. Mo. Reorg. Sept., 1863, from Batteries C and D. Sept., 1863, Dist. St. Louis, Mo., Dept. Mo. Dec., 1864, Arty., 3 Div., Detachment Army Tenn., Dept. Cumb'd. March, 1865, 3rd Sub-Dist., Dist. Middle Tenn., Dept. Cumb'd. June, 1865, Dist. St. Louis, Mo., Dept. Mo. Mustered out Aug. 24, 1865.

BATTERY B, 2nd REGIMENT LIGHT ARTILLERY.—Jany., 1862, Dist. St. Louis, Mo., Dept. Mo. June, 1864, Dist. Rolla, Dept. Mo. Oct., 1864, Dist. St. Louis, Mo., Dept. Mo. July, 1865, Dist. Plains, Dept. Mo. Mustered out Dec. 20, 1865.

BATTERY C, 2nd REGIMENT LIGHT ARTILLERY.—Jany., 1862, Dist. St. Louis, Mo., Dept. Mo. Sept., 1862, Dist. Rolla, Mo., Dept. Mo. Feby., 1863, Dist. St. Louis, Mo., Dept. Mo. Reorg. Sept., 1863, from Batteries I and H. Sept., 1863, Dist. St. Louis, Mo., Dept. Mo. Aug., 1864, Dist. North Mo., Dept. Mo. July, 1865, Dist. Plains, Dept. Mo. Mustered out Dec. 20, 1865.

BATTERY D, 2nd REGIMENT LIGHT ARTILLERY.—Jany., 1862, Dist. St. Louis, Mo., Dept. Mo. March, 1863, Dist. S. E. Mo., Dept. Mo. Aug., 1863, Arty., Ark. Exp. Reorg. Sept., 1863, from Batteries A, F, G and K. Sept., 1863, Dist. St. Louis, Mo., Dept. Mo. Jany., 1864, Arty., 1 Cav. Div., 7 Corps, Dept. Ark. May, 1864, Arty., 2 Div., 7 Corps. Feby., 1865, Mouth White River, Ark. Aug., 1865, Dept. Ark. Mustered out Nov. 21, 1865.

BATTERY E, 2nd REGIMENT LIGHT ARTILLERY.—Jany., 1862, Dist. St. Louis, Mo., Dept. Mo. Reorg. Sept., 1863, from Batteries F, L and M. Sept., 1863, Dist. St. Louis, Mo., Dept. Mo. Jany., 1864, Arty. 1 Cav. Div., 7 Corps, Dept. Ark. April, 1864, Arty., 3 Div., 7 Corps. May, 1864, Arty., 1 Div., 7 Corps. Aug., 1865, Dept. Ark. Mustered out Nov. 22, 1865.

BATTERY F, 2nd REGIMENT LIGHT ARTILLERY.—Jany., 1862, Dist. St. Louis, Mo., Dept. Mo. Sept., 1862, Dist. Rolla, Mo., Dept. Mo. Feby., 1863, Dist. St. Louis, Mo., Dept. Mo. Transferred to New Battery D, Sept., 1863. Reorg. Sept. 30, 1863, by assignment of Landgraeber's Battery Mo. Flying Arty. Sept., 1863, Arty., 1 Div., 15 Corps, Army Tenn. Nov., 1864, Arty. Res., Nashville, Tenn., Dept. Cumb'd. March, 1865, 3rd Sub-Dist., Dist. Middle Tenn., Dept. Cumb'd. June, 1865, Dist. St. Louis, Mo., Dept. Mo. Mustered out Aug. 25, 1865.

BATTERY G, 2nd REGIMENT LIGHT ARTILLERY.—Jany., 1862, Dist. St. Louis, Mo., Dept. Mo. Nov., 1862, Dist. Rolla, Mo., Dept. Mo. Feby., 1863, Dist. St. Louis, Mo., Dept. Mo. Transferred to Battery D Sept., 1863. Reorg. at St. Louis, Mo., Nov. 15, 1863. Nov., 1863, Dist. St. Louis, Mo., Dept. Mo. Aug., 1864, 1 Brig., Dist. Memphis, Tenn., Dist. West Tenn. Dec., 1864, Arty. Res., Dist. West Tenn. Mustered out Aug. 22, 1865.

BATTERY H, 2nd REGIMENT LIGHT ARTILLERY.—Jany., 1862, Dist. St. Louis, Mo. Transferred to Battery C, Sept., 1863. Reorg. at Springfield, Mo., Dec. 4, 1863. Dec., 1863, Dist. S. W. Mo., Dept. Mo. July, 1865, Dist. Plains, Dept. Mo. Mustered out Nov. 20, 1865.

BATTERY I, 2nd REGIMENT LIGHT ARTILLERY.—Jany., 1862, Dist. St. Louis, Mo., Dept. Mo. Transferred to Battery C, Sept., 1863. Reorg. at Springfield, Mo., Dec. 28, 1863. Dec., 1863, Dist. S. W. Mo., Dept. Mo. Dec., 1864. 3 Brig., 1 Div., Detachment Army Tenn., Dept. Cumb'd. March, 1865, 3rd Sub-Dist., Dist. Middle Tenn., Dept. Cumb'd. June, 1865, Dist. St. Louis, Mo., Dept. Mo. Mustered out Aug. 23, 1865.

BATTERY K, 2nd REGIMENT LIGHT ARTILLERY.—Jany., 1862, Dist. St. Louis, Mo., Dept. Mo. June, 1863, Arty., 1 Cav. Div., Army S. E. Mo., Dept. Mo. July, 1863, Res. Brig., 1 Cav., Div., Army S. E. Mo., Dept. Mo. Aug., 1863, Arty., 1 Cav. Div., Ark. Exp. Transferred to Battery D Sept., 1863. Reorg. at Springfield, Mo., Jany. 14, 1864. Jany., 1864, Dist. St. Louis, Mo., Dept. Mo. June, 1865, Dist. Plains, Dept. Mo. Mustered out Nov. 25, 1865.

BATTERY L, 2nd REGIMENT LIGHT ARTILLERY.—Jany., 1862, Dist. St. Louis, Mo., Dept. Mo. Sept., 1862, Dist. Rolla, Mo., Dept. Mo. Feby., 1863, Dist. St. Louis, Mo., Dept. Mo. Transferred to Battery E Sept., 1863. Reorg. at Sedalia, Mo., Jany. 20, 1864. Jany., 1864, Dist. St. Louis, Mo., and Dist. Central Mo. April, 1865, Dist. North Mo., Dept. Mo. July, 1865, Dist. Plains, Dept. Mo. Mustered out Nov. 25, 1865.

BATTERY M, 2nd REGIMENT LIGHT ARTILLERY.—Jany., 1862, Dist. St. Louis, Mo., Dept. Mo. Nov., 1862, Arty., 2 Div., Army S. E. Mo., Dept. Mo. March, 1863, Dist. S. E. Mo., Dept. Mo. June, 1863, 1 Cav. Div., Dist. S. E. Mo., Dept Mo. July, 1863, Res. Brig., 1 Cav. Div., Army S. E. Mo, Dept. Mo. Aug., 1863, Arty., 1 Cav. Div., Ark. Exp. Transferred to Co. E Sept., 1863. Reorg. at St. Louis, Mo., Feby. 15, 1864. Feby., 1864, Dist. St. Louis, Mo., Dept. Mo. June, 1865, Dist. Plains, Dept. Mo. Mustered out Dec. 20, 1865.

BUELL'S INDPT. BATTERY LIGHT ARTILLERY.—Org. at St. Louis, Mo., July 12, 1861. July, 1861, Dept. Mo. Feby., 1862, 1 Brig., 3 Div., Dist. West. Tenn. March, 1862, Arty., 3 Div., Army Tenn. April, 1862, Arty., 2 Div., Army Tenn. June, 1862, 2 Brig., 3 Div., Army Miss. Assigned to 1st Mo. Light Arty. as Battery 1, Aug., 1862, which see.

GRAESSELE'S INDPT. BATTERY LIGHT ARTILLERY.—(See KNISPEL'S BATTERY.)

JOHNSON'S STATE MILITIA BATTERY LIGHT ARTILLERY.—Attached to 1st Mo. S. M. Cav.

JOYCE'S BATTERY LIGHT ARTILLERY.—Attached to 10th Mo. Cav.

KNISPEL'S BATTERY LIGHT ARTILLERY.—Attached to 4th Mo. Cav.

KOWALD'S BATTERY LIGHT ARTILLERY.—Org. Aug., 1861, but not completed. Mustered out Dec. 14, 1861.

LANDGRAEBER'S BATTERY HORSE ARTILLERY.—Org. at St. Louis, Mo., Oct. 8, 1861. Oct., 1861, Dept. Mo. Jany., 1862, 5 Brig., Army S. W. Mo., Dept. Mo. March, 1862, Arty., 2 Div., Army S. W. Mo., Dept. Mo.

July, 1862, Arty., Dist. Eastern Ark., Dept. Mo. Dec., 1862, 2 Brig., 11 Div., Dept. Tenn. Dec., 1862, 2 Brig., 4 Div., Sherman's Yazoo Exp. Jany., 1863, Arty., 1 Div., 15 Corps, Army Tenn. Assigned to 2nd Mo. Light Arty. as Battery F, Sept. 30, 1863.

LINDSAY'S BATTERY LIGHT ARTILLERY.—Attached to 68th Enrolled Militia Mo. Infy.

LOVEJOY'S BATTERY LIGHT ARTILLERY.—Attached to 2nd Mo. Cav.

M'CLENAHAN'S BATTERY LIGHT ARTILLERY.—Attached to 2nd Mo. S. M. Cav.

MANN'S INDPT. BATTERY LIGHT ARTILLERY.—Org. at St. Louis, Mo., Nov. 4, 1861, to Feby. 14, 1862. Feby., 1862, 2 Brig., 4 Div., Dist. West. Tenn. March, 1862, Arty., 4 Div., Army Tenn. July, 1862, 2 Brig., 4 Div., Dist. Memphis, Tenn. Assigned to 1st Mo. Light Arty. as Battery C, Aug. 1862, which see.

PFENNINGHAUSSEN'S BATTERY LIGHT ARTILLERY.—(See LANDGRAEBER'S BATTERY.)

SCHOFIELD'S BATTERY A LIGHT ARTILLERY.—Org. at St. Louis, Mo., July 25, 1862. Attached to Dept. Mo. till Oct. Assigned to 1st Mo. Light Arty. as Battery L, Oct., 1862.

SCHWARTZ'S BATTERY LIGHT ARTILLERY.—Org. at St. Louis, Mo., Aug. 20, 1861. Sept., 1861, Dist. Cairo. Designation changed to Battery E, 2nd Ill. Light Arty., Feby. 1, 1862.

WALLING'S BATTERY MISSISSIPPI MARINE BRIGADE.—Org. at Phila., Pa., as Battery C, Segebarth's Penna. Artillery, Sept. 22 to Dec. 27, 1862. Duty on the Miss. River and at Vicksburg, Miss. Assigned to 1st Mo. Light Arty. as Battery E, Sept. 14, 1864.

WASCHMAN'S BATTERY LIGHT ARTILLERY.—(See 1st MISSOURI S. M. BATTERY.)

WELFLEY'S INDPT. BATTERY LIGHT ARTILLERY.—Org. at St. Louis, Mo., Sept. 25, 1861. Oct., 1861, Dept. Mo. Jany., 1862, Army S. W. Mo., Dept. Mo. March, 1862, Arty., 1 Div., Army S. W. Mo., Dept. Mo. May, 1862, Arty., 3 Div., Army S. W. Mo., Dept. Mo. July, 1862, Arty., Dist. Eastern Ark., Dept. Mo. Oct., 1862, Dist. S. E. Mo., Dept. Mo. Assigned to 1st Mo. Light Arty. as Battery B, Dec., 1862, which see.

BISSELL'S ENGINEER REGIMENT OF THE WEST.—Org. at St. Louis, Mo. July 10 to Oct. 31, 1861. Nov., 1861, Dept. Mo. March, 1862, Unatt., Army Miss. July, 1862, Dist. Columbus, Ky. Dec., 1862, Dist. Columbus, Ky., 13 Corps, Dept. Tenn. Jany., 1863, Unatt. Engrs., Dept. Tenn. Consolidated with 25th Mo. Infy. to form 1st Mo. Engrs., Feby. 17, 1864.

1st REGIMENT ENGINEERS.—Org. Feby. 17, 1864, by consolidation of Bissell's Engr. Regt. of the West and 25th Mo. Infy. Feby., 1864, Def. Nashville & Northwestern R. R., Dept. Cumb'd. April, 1864, Engrs., Sherman's Army, Mil. Div. Miss. Mustered out July 22, 1865.

BALZ'S COMPANY SAPPERS AND MINERS.—Org. at St. Louis, Mo., Sept. and Oct., 1861. Mustered out Feby. 19, 1862.

GERSTER'S INDPT. COMPANY PIONEERS.—Org. at St. Louis, Mo., Aug., 1861. Sept., 1861, Army West. and Dept. Mo., and Unatt., Dist. S. W. Mo., Dept. Mo., to Sept., 1862. Mustered out Sept., 1862.

SMITH'S INDPT. COMPANY TELEGRAPH CORPS.—Org. at St. Louis, Mo., Sept. 1, 1861. Mustered out Dec. 10, 1861.

WOLSTER'S INDPT. COMPANY SAPPERS AND MINERS.—Org. at St. Louis, Mo., May 10, 1861. Mustered out Sept. 1, 1861.

BIRGE'S REGIMENT WESTERN SHARPSHOOTERS.—Org. at Benton Barracks, Mo., Sept.-Oct., 1861. Mustered in as 14th Mo. Infy., Nov. 23, 1861, which see.

HOLMAN'S BATTALION SHARPSHOOTERS.

1st BATTALION MISSISSIPPI MARINE BRIGADE, INFANTRY.—Org. at St. Louis, Mo., Jany. 3 to April 4, 1863. Org. for duty in Western waters. Oct., 1863, Dist. N. E. La., Dept. Tenn. April, 1864, Dist. Vicksburg, Miss. Mustered out Feby. 1, 1865.

1st BATTALION STATE MILITIA INFANTRY.—Org. at St. Joseph, Mo., Sept. 19, 1861. Mustered out Feby., 1862.

1st BATTALION ENROLLED MILITIA INFANTRY.—Duty in 1st Mil. Dist., Mo.

1st BATTALION ST. LOUIS CITY GUARD.—Org. Sept. 25, 1864. Mustered out Oct. 31, 1864.

1st REGIMENT INFANTRY (3 MONTHS).—Org. at St. Louis, Mo., April 22, 1861. July, 1861, 3 Brig., Lyons' Army West. Designation of Regt. changed to 1st. Mo. Light Arty., Sept. 1, 1861.

1st REGIMENT U. S. RESERVE CORPS INFANTRY (3 MONTHS).—Org. at St. Louis, Mo., May 7, 1861. June, 1861, Lyons' Army West. Mustered out Aug. 20, 1861.

1st REGIMENT U. S. RESERVE CORPS INFANTRY (3 YEARS).—Org. at St. Louis, Mo., Sept. 3, 1861. Sept., 1861, 4 Div., Army West. and Dept. Mo. Feby., 1862, Dist. St. Louis, Mo., Dept. Mo. Mustered out Oct. 6, 1862.

1st REGIMENT NORTHEAST INFANTRY.—Org. at Athens, Mo., Oct. 25, 1861. Consolidated with 2nd Northeast Regt., Feby. 1, 1862.

1st REGIMENT STATE MILITIA INFANTRY.—Org. at St. Louis, Mo., May 13, 1862. Attached to Dist. St. Louis, Mo., Dept. Mo. Mustered out May, 1865.

1st REGIMENT ENROLLED MILITIA INFANTRY.—Called into service Sept. 25, 1864. Relieved Oct. 31, 1864.

1st REGIMENT PROVISIONAL ENROLLED MILITIA INFANTRY.—Called into service Feby. 3, 1863. Served 8th Mil. Dist.. Mo.

1st REGIMENT COLORED INFANTRY.—Org. at Benton Barracks, Mo., Dec. 7-14, 1863. Dec., 1863, Dist. St. Louis, Mo. Jany., 1864, Port Hudson, La. Designation changed to 62nd U. S. C. T., March 11, 1864, which see.

1st REGIMENT ST. LOUIS CITY GUARD INFANTRY.—Org. Sept. 25, 1864. Relieved Oct. 31, 1864.

2nd BATTALION STATE MILITIA INFANTRY.—Org. at Cameron, Mo., Sept. 11, 1861. Mustered out March 14, 1862.

2nd BATTALION ST. LOUIS CITY GUARD INFANTRY.—Org. Sept. 25, 1864. Relieved Oct. 31, 1864.

2nd BATTALION ST. LOUIS CITY GUARD COLORED INFANTRY.—Org. Sept. 25, 1864. Relieved Oct. 31, 1864.

2nd REGIMENT INFANTRY (3 MONTHS).—Org. at St. Louis, Mo., April 22, 1861. July, 1861, Lyons' Army West. Mustered out July 31, 1861.

2nd REGIMENT INFANTRY (3 YEARS).—Org. at St. Louis, Mo., Sept. 10, 1861. Nov., 1861, 5 Brig., Army S. W. Mo., Dept. Mo. Feby., 1862, 1 Brig., 2 Div., Army S. W. Mo., Dept. Mo. May, 1862, 2 Brig., 5 Div., Army Miss. Sept., 1862, 35 Brig., 11 Div., Army Ohio. Sept., 1862, 35 Brig., 11 Div., 3 Corps, Army Ohio. Nov., 1862, 2 Brig., 3 Div., Right Wing 14 Corps, Cumb'd. Jany., 1863, 2 Brig., 3 Div., 20 Corps, Cumb'd. Oct., 1863, 1 Brig., 2 Div., 4 Corps. May, 1864, Garrison Dalton, Ga. Mustered out Oct. 1, 1864.

2nd REGIMENT U. S. RESERVE CORPS INFANTRY (3 MONTHS).—Org. at St. Louis, Mo., May 7, 1861. Attached to Lyons' Army West. Mustered out Aug. 16, 1861.

2nd REGIMENT U. S. RESERVE CORPS INFANTRY (3 YEARS).—Org. at St. Louis, Mo., Aug. 23 to Sept. 20, 1861. Sept., 1861, Dist. St. Louis, Mo., Dept. Mo., Feby., 1862, 4 Div., Army S. W. Mo., Dept. Mo. May, 1862, 2 Div., Army Miss. June, 1862, 5 Div., Army Miss. Mustered out Sept. 3, 1862.

2nd REGIMENT NORTHEAST INFANTRY.—Org. July, 1861, Consolidated with 1st Northeast Regt. to form 21st Missouri Infy. Dec. 31, 1861.

2nd REGIMENT STATE MILITIA INFANTRY.

2nd REGIMENT ENROLLED MILITIA INFANTRY.—Called Sept. 25, 1864. Relieved Oct. 31, 1864.

2nd REGIMENT PROVISIONAL ENROLLED MILITIA INFANTRY.—Called Feby. 3, 1863. Served in 8th Mil. Dist. Mo.

2nd REGIMENT COLORED INFANTRY.—Org. at Benton Barracks, Mo., Dec. 18, 1863, to Jany. 16, 1864. Designation changed to 65th U. S. C. T., March 11, 1864, which see.

2nd REGIMENT ST. LOUIS CITY GUARD INFANTRY.—Called Sept. 25, 1864. Relieved Oct. 31, 1864.

3rd BATTALION STATE MILITIA INFANTRY.—Org. at St. Joe, Mo., Oct. 25, 1861. Mustered out Feby. 11, 1862.

3rd BATTALION ST. LOUIS CITY GUARD INFANTRY.—Called Sept. 25, 1864. Relieved Oct. 31, 1864.

3rd REGIMENT INFANTRY.—(3 MONTHS). Org. at St. Louis, Mo., April 22, 1861. July, 1861, Lyons' Army West. Mustered out Sept. 4, 1861.

3rd REGIMENT INFANTRY.—(3 YEARS). Org. at St. Louis, Mo., Sept. 3, 1861, to Jany. 13, 1862. Jany., 1862, 2 Brig., Army Southwest Mo., Dept. Mo. Feby., 1862, Unass'n, Army Southwest Mo., Dept. Mo. May, 1862, 3 Div., Army Southwest Mo., Dept. Mo. July, 1862, Dist. East. Ark., Dept. Mo. Dec., 1862, 1 Brig., 1 Div., Dist. East. Ark. Dec., 1862, 1 Brig., 11 Div., 13 Corps, Dept. Tenn. Dec., 1862, 2 Brig., 4 Div., Sherman's Yazoo Exp. Jany., 1863, 2 Brig., 1 Div., 15 Corps, Tenn. Sept., 1863, 1 Brig., 1 Div., 15 Corps. Dec., 1863, 3 Brig., 1 Div., 15 Corps. Mustered out Nov. 22, 1864.

3rd REGIMENT U. S. RESERVE CORPS.—(3 MONTHS). Org. at St. Louis, Mo., May 8, 1861. May, 1861, Lyons' Army of the West. Mustered out Aug. 18, 1861.

3rd REGIMENT U. S. RESERVE CORPS.—(3 YEARS). Org. at St. Louis, Mo., Aug.-Sept., 1861. Consolidated with Gasconade Battalion Jany. 18, 1862, to form 4th Mo. Infy., which see.

3rd REGIMENT ENROLLED MILITIA INFANTRY.—Called Sept. 25, 1864. Relieved Oct. 31, 1864.

3rd REGIMENT PROVISIONAL ENROLLED MILITIA INFANTRY.—Duty in Northwest Missouri.

3rd REGIMENT COLORED INFANTRY.—Org. at Benton Barracks, Mo. Designation changed to 67th U. S. C. T., March 11, 1864, which see.

3rd REGIMENT ST. LOUIS CITY GUARD INFANTRY.—Called Sept. 25, 1864. Relieved Oct. 31, 1864.

4th BATTALION STATE MILITIA INFANTRY.—Org. at Rockfort, Mo., Nov. 9, 1861. Mustered out Feby. 11, 1862.

4th REGIMENT INFANTRY.—(3 MONTHS). Org. at St. Louis, Mo., April 22, 1861. May, 1861, Dist. Cairo. Mustered out July 30, 1861.

4th REGIMENT INFANTRY.—(3 YEARS). Org. at St. Louis, Mo., by consolidation of Gasconade Battalion and 3rd U. S. Reserve Corps. Jany, 1862, Duty in Districts of Southwest Mo. and St. Louis, Mo. Mustered out Feby. 1, 1863.

4th REGIMENT U. S. RESERVE CORPS.—(3 MONTHS). Org. at St. Louis, Mo., May 8, 1861. May, 1861, Lyons' Army of the West. Mustered out Aug. 27, 1861.

4th REGIMENT U. S. RESERVE CORPS.—(3 YEARS). Org. at St. Louis, Mo., Sept., 1861. Dist. St. Louis. Mustered out Jany. 13, 1862.

4th REGIMENT ENROLLED MILITIA INFANTRY.—Called Sept. 25, 1864. Relieved Oct. 31, 1864.

4th REGIMENT PROVISIONAL ENROLLED MILITIA INFANTRY.—Placed on duty April 23, 1863. Duty in North Mo.

4th REGIMENT COLORED INFANTRY.—Org. at Benton Barracks, Mo. Designation changed to 68th U. S. C. T., March 11, 1864.

4th REGIMENT ST. LOUIS CITY GUARD INFANTRY.—Called Sept. 25, 1864. Relieved Oct. 31, 1864.

5th REGIMENT INFANTRY.—(3 MONTHS). Org. at St. Louis, Mo., May 13, 1861. July, 1861, Lyons' Army of the West. Mustered out Aug. 27, 1861.

5th REGIMENT INFANTRY.—(3 YEARS). Org. at St. Louis, Mo., March 18, 1862. Mustered out Nov. 22, 1862.

5th REGIMENT U. S. RESERVE CORPS INFANTRY.—(3 MONTHS). Org. at St. Louis, Mo., May 11, 1861. May, 1861, Lyons' Army of the West. Mustered out Aug. 31, 1861.

5th REGIMENT U. S. RESERVE CORPS INFANTRY.—(3 YEARS). Org. at St. Louis, Mo., Sept., 1861. Transferred to 5th Mo. Infy., March 18, 1862.

5th REGIMENT STATE MILITIA INFANTRY.—Org. at Louisiana, Mo., Sept., 1861. Mustered out Feby. 5, 1862.

5th REGIMENT ENROLLED MILITIA INFANTRY.—Called Sept. 25, 1864. Relieved Oct. 31, 1864.

5th REGIMENT PROVISIONAL ENROLLED MILITIA INFANTRY.—

5th REGIMENT ST. LOUIS CITY GUARD INFANTRY.—Called Sept. 25, 1864. Relieved Oct. 31, 1864.

6th BATTALION STATE MILITIA INFANTRY.—Org. at Bethany, Mo., Oct. 14, 1861. Mustered out March, 1862.

6th REGIMENT INFANTRY.—Org. at St. Louis, Mo., June 15-July 9, 1861. July, 1861, Pilot Knob, Mo. Sept. 1861, Fremont's Army of the West and Dept. Mo. April, 1862, 1 Brig., 5 Div., Army Tenn. July, 1862, 1 Brig., 5 Div., Dist. Memphis, Tenn. Nov., 1862, 1 Brig., 5 Div., Dist. Memphis, Right Wing 13 Corps, Dept. Tenn. Nov., 1862, 1 Brig., 2 Div., Right Wing 13 Corps. Dec., 1862, 1 Brig., 2 Div., Sherman's Yazoo Exp. Jany., 1863, 1 Brig., 2 Div., 15 Corps, Army Tenn. Mustered out Aug. 17, 1865.

6th REGIMENT ENROLLED MILITIA INFANTRY.—Called Sept. 25, 1864. Relieved Oct. 31, 1864.

6th REGIMENT PROVISIONAL ENROLLED MILITIA INFANTRY.—Duty at Springfield, Mo., and in the Dist. of Southwest Mo., Dept. Mo. Designated 16th Mo. Cav., Nov. 1, 1864.

7th BATTALION STATE MILITIA INFANTRY.—Org. at Gallatin, Mo., Oct. 5, 1861. Mustered out March 4, 1862.

7th REGIMENT INFANTRY.—Org. at St. Louis, Mo., June, 1861. June, 1861, Booneville, Mo. Sept., 1861, Fremont's Army of the West and Dept. Mo. Feby., 1862, Lexington, Mo., Dept. Mo. July, 1862, Unatt., Army Tenn. Sept., 1862, 4 Brig., 1 Div., Dist. Jackson, Tenn. Nov., 1862, 4 Brig., 3 Div., Left Wing 13 Corps, Dept. Tenn. Dec., 1862, 3 Brig., 3 Div., 17 Corps, Tenn. April, 1864, Maltby's Brig., Dist. Vicksburg, Miss. June, 1864, 1 Brig., Memphis, Tenn., Dist. West Tenn. Aug., 1864, 1 Brig., 2 Div., 19 Corps, Dept. Gulf. Consolidated with 11th Mo. Infy., Dec. 17, 1864.

7th REGIMENT ENROLLED MILITIA INFANTRY.—Called Sept. 25, 1864. Relieved Oct. 31, 1864.

7th REGIMENT PROVISIONAL ENROLLED MILITIA INFANTRY.—Duty in Dist. Southwest Mo., 1862, 1863, 1864. Designated 15th Mo. Cav., Nov. 1, 1864.

8th REGIMENT INFANTRY.—Org. at St. Louis, Mo., June 12 to Aug. 14, 1861. July, 1861, Cape Girardeau, Mo. Sept., 1862, Dist. Paducah, Ky. Feby., 1862, 5 Brig., 2 Div., Dist. Cairo. Feby., 1862, 1 Brig., 3 Div., Dist. West Tenn. and Army Tenn. May, 1862, 1 Brig., 5 Div., Army Tenn. July, 1862, 1 Brig., 5 Div., Dist. Memphis, Tenn. Nov., 1862, 1 Brig., 5 Div., Right Wing 13 Corps, Dept. Tenn. Nov., 1862, 1 Brig., 2 Div., Right Wing, 13 Corps. Dec., 1862, 1 Brig., 2 Div., Sherman's Yazoo Exp. Jany., 1863, 1 Brig., 2 Div., 15 Corps, Army Tenn. Mustered out Aug. 14, 1865.

8th REGIMENT ENROLLED MILITIA INFANTRY.—

8th REGIMENT PROVISIONAL ENROLLED MILITIA INFANTRY.—Duty in Dist. Southeast Mo., 1863. Mustered out Oct. 26, 1863.

9th REGIMENT INFANTRY.—Org. at St. Louis, Mo., July 6 to Sept 6, 1861. Sept., 1861, Kelton's Brig., Pope's Div., Fremont's Army of the West and Dept. Mo. Feby., 1862, 2 Brig., 3 Div., Army Southwest Mo., Dept. Mo. Transferred to Illinois as 59th Regt. Ill. Infy., Feby. 12, 1862, which see.

9th REGIMENT ENROLLED MILITIA INFANTRY.—

9th REGIMENT PROVISIONAL ENROLLED MILITIA INFANTRY.—Called for duty in 1863. Mustered out Nov., 1863.

10th REGIMENT INFANTRY.—Org. at St. Louis, Mo., Aug., 1861. Sept., 1861, Dept. Mo. May, 1862, 2 Brig., 3 Div., Army Miss. Nov., 1862, 2 Brig., 7 Div., Left Wing 13 Corps, Dept. Tenn. Dec., 1862, 2 Brig., 7 Div., 16 Corps. Jany., 1863, 2 Brig., 7 Div., 17 Corps. Sept., 1863, 2 Brig., 2 Div., 17 Corps. Dec., 1863, 2 Brig., 3 Div., 15 Corps. Mustered out Oct. 31, 1864.

10th ENROLLED MILITIA INFANTRY.—Called into service Sept. 25, 1864. Relieved Oct. 31, 1864.

10th PROVISIONAL ENROLLED MILITIA INFANTRY.—Called into service against Price, 1863.

11th REGIMENT INFANTRY.—Org. at St. Louis, Mo., Aug., 1861. Aug., 1861, Dist. Cairo. Feby., 1862, 2 Brig., 1 Div., Army Miss. March, 1862, 2 Brig., 5 Div., Army Miss. April, 1862, 1 Brig., 3 Div., Army Miss. April, 1862, 2 Brig., 2 Div., Army Miss. Nov., 1862, 2 Brig., 3 Div., Left Wing 13 Corps, Dept. Tenn. Dec., 1862, 2 Brig., 8 Div., 16 Corps. April, 1863, 2 Brig., 3 Div., 15 Corps. Dec., 1863, 2 Brig., 1 Div., 16 Corps. Dec., 1864, 2 Brig., 1 Div., Detach., Army Tenn., Dept. Cumb'd. Feby., 1865, 2 Brig., 1 Div., 16 Corps, Mil. Div. West Miss. Aug., 1865, Dept. Ala. Mustered out Jany. 15, 1866.

11th REGIMENT ENROLLED MILITIA INFANTRY.—Duty in Southwest Mo. Relieved from service Oct. 31, 1864.

11th REGIMENT PROVISIONAL ENROLLED MILITIA INFANTRY.—Duty at St. Louis, 1st Mil. Dist. Mo.

12th REGIMENT INFANTRY.—Org. at St. Louis, Mo., Aug., 1861. Sept., 1861, Fremont's Army of the West and Dept. Mo. Jany., 1862, 2 Brig., Army Southwest Mo., Dept. Mo. Feby., 1862, 2 Brig., 1 Div., Army Southwest Mo., Dept. Mo. May, 1862, 3 Div., Army Southwest Mo., Dept. Mo. July, 1862, Dist. East. Ark., Dept. Mo. Dec., 1862, 1 Brig., 1 Div., Dist. East. Ark. Dec., 1862, 1 Brig., 11 Div., Right Wing 13 Corps, Dept. Tenn. Dec., 1862, 2 Brig., 4 Div., Sherman's Yazoo Exp. Jany., 1863, 2 Brig., 1 Div., 15 Corps, Army Tenn. Sept., 1863, 1 Brig., 1 Div., 15 Corps. Dec., 1863, 2 Brig., 1 Div., 15 Corps. Mustered out Aug. 12 to Nov. 14, 1864. Veterans and recruits consolidated with detachments from 3rd and 17th Mo. Infy., and subsequently transferred to 15th Mo. Infy.

13th REGIMENT INFANTRY.—Org. at St. Louis, Mo., Aug. 9 to Nov. 5, 1861. Dec., 1861, Dept. Mo. Feby., 1862, 3 Brig., 2 Div., Dist. Cairo. Feby., 1862, 2 Brig., 2 Div., Dist. West Tenn. and Army Tenn. Transferred to Ohio as 22nd Ohio Infy., May 29, 1862, which see.

13th REGIMENT ENROLLED MILITIA INFANTRY.—Called into service Sept. 25, 1864. Relieved Oct. 31, 1864.

14th REGIMENT INFANTRY.—Org. at St. Louis, Mo., as Birge's Western Sharpshooters. Mustered in as 14th Infy., Nov. 23, 1861. Dec., 1861, Dept. Mo. Feby., 1862, 4 Brig., 2 Div., Dist. Cairo. Feby., 1862, 2 Brig., 2 Div., Dist. West Tenn. and Army Tenn. July, 1862, 2 Brig., 2 Div., Dist. Corinth, Miss. Nov., 1862, Unatt., 2 Div., Dist. Corinth, Miss., 13 Corps, Dept. Tenn. Dec., 1862, Unatt., Dist. Corinth, Miss., 16 Corps. Transferred to Illinois as 66th Ill. Infy., Jany. 26, 1863, which see.

14th REGIMENT HOME GUARD INFANTRY.—Org. at Lexington, Mo., Aug., 1861. Mustered out Oct. 19, 1861.

15th REGIMENT INFANTRY.—Org. at St. Louis, Mo., Aug.-Sept., 1861. Nov., 1861, Dept. Mo. Jany., 1862, 5 Brig., Army Southwest Mo., Dept. Mo. Feby., 1862, 1 Brig., 2 Div., Army Southwest Mo., Dept. Mo. June, 1862, 1 Brig., 5 Div., Army Miss. Sept., 1862, 35 Brig., 11 Div., Army Ohio. Sept., 1862, 35 Brig., 11 Div., 3 Corps, Army Ohio. Nov., 1862, 2 Brig., 3 Div., Right Wing 14 Corps, Cumb'd. Jany., 1863, 2 Brig., 3 Div., 20 Corps, Cumb'd. Oct., 1863, 1 Brig., 2 Div., 4 Corps. April, 1864, 3 Brig., 2 Div., 4 Corps. June, 1865, 2 Brig., 2 Div., 4 Corps. Aug., 1865, Dept. Texas. Mustered out Dec. 25, 1865.

15th REGIMENT HOME GUARD INFANTRY.—Org. in Polk County Mo., June, 1861. Mustered out Dec., 1861.

16th REGIMENT INFANTRY.—Failed to complete organization.

17th REGIMENT INFANTRY.—Org. at St. Louis, Mo., Aug., 1861. Sept., 1861, Fremont's Army of the West, and Dept. Mo. Jany., 1862, 2 Brig., Army Southwest Mo., Dept. Mo. March, 1862, 1 Brig., 1 Div., Army Southwest Mo., Dept. Mo. May, 1862, 3 Div., Army Southwest Mo., Dept. Mo. July, 1862, Dist. East. Ark., Dept. Mo. Dec., 1862, 1 Brig., 1 Div., Dist. East. Ark.

Dec., 1862, 1 Brig., 11 Div., Right Wing 13 Corps, Dept. Tenn. Dec., 1862, 2 Brig., 4 Div., Sherman's Yazoo Exp. Jany., 1863, 2 Brig., 1 Div., 15 Corps, Tenn. Sept., 1863, 1 Brig., 1 Div., 15 Corps. Dec., 1863, 3 Brig., 1 Div., 15 Corps. Mustered out Sept.-Oct., 1864. Veterans and Recruits to 15th Mo. Infy.

18th REGIMENT INFANTRY.—Org. at LaClede, Mo., July to Nov., 1861. Dist. St. Louis, Mo., Dept. Mo. March, 1862, 2 Brig., 6 Div., Army Tenn. July, 1862, 2 Brig., 6 Div., Dist. Corinth, Miss. Nov., 1862, 2 Brig., 6 Div., Left Wing 13 Corps, Dept. Tenn. Nov., 1862, 3 Brig., Dist. Corinth, 13 Corps. Dec., 1862, 3 Brig., Dist. Corinth, 17 Corps. Jany., 1863, 3 Brig., Dist. Corinth, 16 Corps. March, 1863, 3 Brig., 2 Div., 16 Corps. Nov., 1863, Fuller's Brig., 2 Div., 16 Corps. Jany., 1864, 3 Brig., 2 Div., 16 Corps. March, 1864, 1 Brig., 4 Div., 16 Corps. Sept., 1864, 1 Brig., 1 Div., 17 Corps. Mustered out July 18, 1865.

19th REGIMENT INFANTRY.—Failed to complete organization.

20th REGIMENT INFANTRY.—Failed to complete organization.

21st REGIMENT INFANTRY.—Org. Feby. 1, 1862, from 1st and 2nd Northeast Mo. Infy. March, 1862, 1 Brig., 6 Div., Army Tenn. July, 1862, 1 Brig., 6 Div., Dist. Corinth, Miss. Nov., 1862, 1 Brig., 6 Div., Left Wing 13 Corps, Dept. Tenn. Dec., 1862, Dist. Columbus, Ky., 16 Corps. May, 1863, 4 Brig., Dist. Memphis, Tenn., 5 Div., 16 Corps. Jany., 1864, 1 Brig., 3 Div., 16 Corps. Dec., 1864, 1 Brig., 2 Div., Detach. Army Tenn., Dept. Cumb'd. Feby., 1865, 1 Brig., 2 Div., 16 Corps, Mil. Div. West Miss. Aug., 1865, Dept. Ala. Mustered out April 19, 1866.

22nd REGIMENT INFANTRY.—Org. at large in Mo., Aug. to Dec., 1861. Dec., 1861, Dept. Mo. March, 1862, Unass'n, Army Miss. Disbanded April, 1862.

23rd REGIMENT INFANTRY.—Org. at large in Mo., Sept., 1861. Sept., 1861, Dept. Mo., Macon City and Chillicothe, Mo. March, 1862, St. Louis, Mo., Dept. Mo. April, 1862, Unass'n, 6 Div., Army Tenn. Captured April 6, 1862. June, 1862, St. Louis, Mo., Dept. Mo. June, 1863, Dist. Rolla, Mo., Dept. Mo. Dec., 1863, Unatt., Dist. Nashville, Tenn., Dept. Cumb'd. Jany., 1864, 2 Brig., Dist. Nashville, Tenn., Dept. Cumb'd. April, 1864, Unass'd, 4 Div., 20 Corps, Dept. Cumb'd. July, 1864, 1 Brig., 3 Div., 14 Corps, Cumb'd. Mustered out July 18, 1865.

24th REGIMENT INFANTRY.—Org. at large in Mo., Oct. 24 to Dec. 28, 1861. Jany., 1862, 1 Brig., Army Southwest Mo., Dept. Mo. Feby., 1862, Unass'n, Army Southwest Mo., Dept. Mo. July, 1862, Dist. East. Ark., Dept. Mo. Oct., 1862, 2 Brig., 2 Div., Dist. Southeast Mo., Dept. Mo. Feby., 1863, 1 Brig., 2 Div., Army Southeast Mo., Dept. Mo. March, 1863, Dist. Southeast Mo., Dept. Mo. June, 1863, Dist. Columbus, Ky., 6 Div., 16 Corps, Dept. Tenn. July, 1863, 1 Brig., Dist. Columbus, 6 Div., 16 Corps. Jany., 1864, 2 Brig., 3 Div., 16 Corps. Mustered out Oct., 1864, to Feby., 1865. Company E detached. May, 1862, 2 Brig., 3 Div., Army Miss. Nov., 1862, 2 Brig., 7 Div., Left Wing 13 Corps, Dept. Tenn. Dec., 1862, 2 Brig., 7 Div., 16 Corps. Jany., 1863, 2 Brig., 7 Div., 17 Corps. Sept., 1863, 2 Brig., 2 Div., 17 Corps. Dec., 1863, 2 Brig., 3 Div., 15 Corps. Companies F and K detached, and on duty in Dist. Southeast Mo. to July, 1863, Reserve Brig., 1 Cav. Div., Dist. Southeast Mo., Dept. Mo. Aug., 1863, Unatt., Cav. Div., Ark. Exp. Jany., 1864, Unatt., 1 Div., 7 Corps, Dept. Ark. Feby., 1864, 2 Brig., 3 Div., 16 Corps, Tenn.

25th REGIMENT INFANTRY.—Org. at 13th Mo. Infy., June, 1861. Designation changed to 25th Mo. Infy. Sept., 1861, Dept. Mo. March, 1862, 1 Brig., 6 Div., Army Tenn. July, 1862, 1 Brig., 6 Div., Dist. Corinth, Miss. Sept., 1862, 1 Brig., 2 Div., Dist. Southeast Mo., Dept. Mo. March, 1863, Dist. Northwest Mo., Dept. Mo. June, 1863, Garrison New Madrid, Dist. Columbus, 6 Div., 16 Corps, Dept. Tenn. Consolidated with Engr. Regt. of the West to form 1st Mo. Engrs., Feby., 17, 1864. (See 1st Engineers.)

25th REGIMENT ENROLLED MILITIA INFANTRY.—Duty in Northwestern Missouri.

26th REGIMENT INFANTRY.—Org. in Mo. at large, Sept. to Dec., 1861. Dec., 1861, Dept. Mo. Feby., 1862, 2 Brig., 2 Div., Army Miss. April, 1863, 1 Brig., 3 Div., Army Miss. Nov., 1862, 3 Brig., 7 Div., Left Wing 13 Corps, Dept. Tenn. Dec., 1862, 3 Brig., 7 Div., 16 Corps. Jany., 1863, 3 Brig., 7 Div., 17 Corps. Sept., 1863, 3 Brig., 2 Div., 17 Corps. Dec., 1863, 3 Brig., 3 Div., 15 Corps. Aug., 1864, 2 Brig., 3 Div., 15 Corps. April, 1865, 3 Brig., 2 Div., 15 Corps. Mustered out Aug. 13, 1865.

26th REGIMENT ENROLLED MILITIA INFANTRY. —Duty in Dist. Southwest Mo., Dept. Mo.

27th REGIMENT INFANTRY.—Org. at St. Louis, Mo., Sept. 2, 1862, to Jany. 8, 1863. Sept., 1862, Dist. St. Louis, Mo., Dept. Mo. Jany., 1863, Dist. Rolla, Mo., Dept. Mo. March, 1863, 1 Brig., 1 Div., 15 Corps, Army Tenn. Mustered out June 13, 1865. Co's F, G and I transferred to consolidated Battalion 31st and 32nd Mo. Infy.

27th REGIMENT MOUNTED INFANTRY.—Org. in Mo. at large May to Nov., 1861., Dept. Mo. Mustered out Jany. 27 to Feby. 28, 1862.

27th REGIMENT ENROLLED MILITIA INFANTRY. —Duty in North Mo.

28th REGIMENT INFANTRY.—Failed to complete organization.

28th REGIMENT ENROLLED MILITIA.—Called into service Sept. 25, 1864. Relieved Oct. 31, 1864.

29th REGIMENT INFANTRY.—Org. at Benton Barracks and St. Louis, Mo., July to Oct., 1862. Oct., 1862, Cape Girardeau, Mo., Dept. Mo. Dec., 1862, 1 Brig., 11 Div., Right Wing 13 Corps, Dept. Tenn. Dec., 1862, 1 Brig., 4 Div., Sherman's Yazoo Exp. Jany., 1863, 1 Brig., 1 Div., 15 Corps, Army Tenn. Dec., 1863, 2 Brig., 1 Div., 15 Corps. April, 1864, 3 Brig., 1 Div., 15 Corps. Sept., 1864, 1 Brig., 1 Div., 15 Corps. Nov., 1864, Unatt., 15 Corps. Mustered out June 12, 1865.

29th REGIMENT ENROLLED MILITIA INFANTRY. —Duty at Lancaster, Mo.

30th REGIMENT INFANTRY.—Org. at St. Louis, Mo., Sept.-Oct., 1862. Oct., 1862, Cape Girardeau, Mo., Dept. Mo. Dec., 1862, 1 Brig., 11 Div., Right Wing 13 Corps, Dept. Tenn. Dec., 1862, 1 Brig., 4 Div., Sherman's Yazoo Exp. Jany., 1863, 1 Brig., 1 Div., 15 Corps, Army Tenn. Aug., 1863, Dist. Natchez, Miss., Post Vidalia. April, 1864, 1 Brig., 1 Div., 17 Corps, Aug., 1864, 1 Brig., 2 Div., 19 Corps, Dept. Gulf. Dec., 1864, 2 Brig., Reserve Corps, Mil. Div. West Miss. Feby., 1865, 3 Brig., 1 Div., Reserve Corps, M. D. W. M. Feby., 1865, 3 Brig., 1 Div., 13 Corps, M. D. W. M. July, 1865, Dept. Texas. Mustered out Aug. 21, 1865.

30th REGIMENT ENROLLED MILITIA INFANTRY. —At Trenton, Grundy Co., Mo.

30th REGIMENT PROVISIONAL ENROLLED MILITIA INFANTRY.—Duty in 7th Mil. Dist. Mo.

31st REGIMENT INFANTRY.—Org. at St. Louis, Carondelet and Ironton, Mo., Aug. 11 to Oct. 7, 1862. Oct., 1862, Cape Girardeau, Mo., Dept. Mo. Dec., 1862, 1 Brig., 11 Div., Right Wing 13 Corps, Dept. Tenn. Dec., 1862, 1 Brig., 4 Div., Sherman's Yazoo Exp. Jany., 1863, 1 Brig., 1 Div., 15 Corps, Army Tenn. Dec., 1863, 2 Brig., 1 Div., 15 Corps. April, 1864, 3 Brig., 1 Div., 15 Corps. Sept., 1864, 1 Brig., 1 Div., 15 Corps. Consolidated with 32nd Mo. Infy., Nov. 12, 1864, as 31st and 32nd Consolidated Battalion. Mustered out July 18, 1865.

31st REGIMENT ENROLLED MILITIA INFANTRY.— Duty in 7th Mil. Dist., Mo.

31st PROVISIONAL ENROLLED MILITIA INFANTRY.—Duty at Albany, Mo.

32nd REGIMENT INFANTRY.—Org. at Benton Barracks, Mo., St. Louis, Mo., Oct. 18 to Dec. 8, 1862. Oct., 1862, Cape Girardeau, Mo., Dept. Mo. Dec., 1862, 1 Brig., 11 Div., Right Wing 13 Corps, Dept. Tenn. Dec., 1862, 1 Brig., 4 Div., Sherman's Yazoo Exp. Jany., 1863, 1 Brig., 1 Div., 15 Corps. Dec., 1863, 3 Brig., 1 Div., 15 Corps. Sept., 1864, 1 Brig., 1 Div., 15 Corps. Mustered out July 18, 1865.

32nd REGIMENT ENROLLED MILITIA INFANTRY. —At Hannibal, Mo.

33rd REGIMENT INFANTRY.—Org. at Benton Barracks, Mo., Aug. 29 to Sept. 5, 1862. Sept., 1862, Dist. St. Louis, Mo., Dept. Mo. Jany., 1863, 1 Brig., 13 Div., 13 Corps, Dept. Tenn. Feby., 1863, 2 Brig., 13 Div., 13 Corps. July, 1863, 2 Brig., 13 Div., 16 Corps. Aug., 1863, Garrison Helena, Ark., Army Ark. Jany., 1864, 1 Brig., 4 Div., 16 Corps, Dept. Tenn. March, 1864, 3 Brig., 1 Div., 16 Corps. Dec., 1864, 3 Brig., 1 Div. Detach. Army Tenn., Dept. Cumb'd. Feby., 1865, 3 Brig., 1 Div., 16 Corps, Mil. Div. West Miss. Mustered out Aug. 10, 1865.

33rd REGIMENT ENROLLED MILITIA INFANTRY. —Duty in 7th Mil. Dist., Dept. Mo.

33rd REGIMENT PROVISIONAL ENROLLED MILITIA INFANTRY.—Duty in North Mo.

34th REGIMENT INFANTRY.—Failed to complete organization.

34th REGIMENT ENROLLED MILITIA INFANTRY. —Called into service Sept. 25, 1864. Relieved from active service Oct. 30, 1864.

35th REGIMENT INFANTRY.—Org. at Benton Barracks, Mo., Dec. 3, 1862. Jany., 1863, 2 Brig., 12 Div., 13 Corps, Dept. Tenn. Feby., 1863, 2 Brig., 13 Div., 13 Corps. March, 1863, 1 Brig., 13 Div., 13 Corps. July, 1863, 2 Brig., 13 Div., 16 Corps, Ark. Aug., 1863, Garrison Helena, Ark., Dist. East. Ark. Jany., 1864, Helena, Ark., 7 Corps, Dept. Ark. Feby., 1865, 1 Brig., 1 Div., 7 Corps. Mustered out June 28, 1865.

35th REGIMENT ENROLLED MILITIA INFANTRY. —Called into service against Price, 1863.

35th PROVISIONAL ENROLLED MILITIA INFANTRY.—Duty in 8th Mil. Dist., Dept. Mo.

36th REGIMENT INFANTRY.—Failed to complete organization.

36th REGIMENT ENROLLED MILITIA INFANTRY.—

37th REGIMENT INFANTRY.—Failed to complete organization.

37th REGIMENT ENROLLED MILITIA INFANTRY. —Duty in 8th Mil. Dist., Dept. Mo.

38th REGIMENT INFANTRY.—Failed to complete organization.

38th REGIMENT ENROLLED MILITIA INFANTRY. —Duty in Ralls and Linn Counties, Mo., 1862-1864.

39th REGIMENT INFANTRY.—Org. at Hannibal, Mo., Aug. 18 to Sept. 30, 1864. Sept., 1864, Dist. St. Louis, Dept. Mo. Nov., 1864, Nashville, Tenn., Dept. Cumb'd. Dec., 1864, Dist. Ky., Dept. Ohio. Jany., 1865, Nashville, Tenn., Dept. Cumb'd. Jany., 1865, Dist. St. Louis, Mo., Dept. Mo. Mustered out July 19, 1865.

39th REGIMENT ENROLLED MILITIA INFANTRY. —Duty in Platte Co., ·Mo.

40th REGIMENT INFANTRY.—Org. at Benton Barracks, Mo., Aug. 11 to Sept. 8, 1864. Sept., 1864, Dist. St. Louis, Mo., Dept. Mo. Nov., 1864, Paducah, Ky. Nov., 1864, 3 Brig., 3 Div., 4 Corps, Dept. Cumb'd. Dec., 1864, 1 Brig., 3 Div., Detach., Army Tenn., Dept. Cumb'd. Feby., 1865, 1 Brig., 3 Div., 16 Corps, Mil. Div. West Miss. March, 1865, 2 Brig., 3 Div., 16 Corps. Mustered out Aug. 8, 1865.

40th REGIMENT ENROLLED MILITIA INFANTRY. —Duty in Dist. Central Mo., Dept. Mo.

41st REGIMENT INFANTRY.—Org. at Benton Barracks, Mo., Aug. and Sept., 1864. Sept., 1864, Garrison at St. Louis, Mo. Mustered out July 11, 1865.

41st REGIMENT ENROLLED MILITIA INFANTRY.—

42nd REGIMENT INFANTRY.—Org. at Macon, Mo., Sept., 1864. Sept., 1864, Dist. North Mo., Dept. Mo. Feby., 1865, Unatt., 4 Div., 20 Corps, Dept. Cumb'd. March, 1865, 2 Brig., Def. Nash. & Chatta. R. R. April, 1865, 2 Brig., 1st Sub Dist., Dist. Middle Tenn., Dept. Cumb'd. Mustered out June 28, 1865.

42nd REGIMENT ENROLLED MILITIA INFANTRY.—

42nd REGIMENT PROVISIONAL ENROLLED MILITIA INFANTRY.—Duty in Central Dist., Mo.

43rd REGIMENT INFANTRY.—Org. at St. Joe, Mo., Aug. and Sept., 1864. Sept., 1864, Dist. North Mo., Dept. Mo. April, 1865, Dist. Central Mo., Dept. Mo. Mustered out June 30, 1865.

43rd ENROLLED MILITIA INFANTRY.—Called into service against Shelby, 1863.

44th REGIMENT INFANTRY.—Org. at St. Joe, Mo., Aug. 22-Sept. 7, 1864. Sept., 1864, Dist. Rolla, Mo., Dept. Mo. Nov., 1864, Paducah, Ky., Dist. Ky., Dept. Ohio. Nov., 1864, Unatt., 23 Corps, Army Ohio. Dec., 1864, 2 Brig., 3 Div., Detach., Army Tenn., Dept. Cumb'd. Feby., 1865, 1 Brig., 3 Div., 16 Corps, Mil. Div. West Miss. Mustered out Aug. 15, 1865.

44th REGIMENT ENROLLED MILITIA INFANTRY.— 44th REGIMENT PROVISIONAL ENROLLED MILITIA INFANRY.—Duty in North Mo.

45th REGIMENT INFANTRY.—Org. at Sedalia, Warrensburg and Otterville, Mo., Aug. 10 to Sept. 17, 1864. Sept., 1864, Dist. St. Louis, Mo., Dept. Mo. Dec., 1864, 4 Div., 23 Corps, Dept. Ohio. Mustered out March 6, 1865.

45th REGIMENT ENROLLED MILITIA INFANTRY. —Duty in North Mo.

46th REGIMENT INFANTRY.—Org. at Springfield, Mo., Aug. to Nov., 1864. Dist. Southwest. Mo. Dept. Mo. March, 1865, 2 Brig., 1st Sub. Dist., Dist. Middle Tenn., Dept. Cumb'd. Mustered out May 20, 1865.

46th REGIMENT ENROLLED MILITIA INFANTRY. —Duty in 8th Mil. Dist., Mo.

47th REGIMENT INFANTRY.—Org. at Pilot Knob, Mo., Aug. 29-Sept. 11, 1864. Sept., 1864, Dist. Southeast Mo., Dept. Mo. Dec., 1864, Nashville, Tenn., and Pulaski, Tenn., Dept. Cumb'd. Mustered out March 30, 1865.

47th REGIMENT ENROLLED MILITIA INFANTRY. —Duty in North Mo.

48th REGIMENT INFANTRY.—Org. at St. Louis, Jefferson City and Rolla, Mo., Aug. 3 to Nov. 22, 1864. Sept., 1864, Dist. Rolla, Mo., Dept. Mo. Dec., 1864, R. R. Guard, Tenn. and Ala. R. R., Dept. Cumb'd. Feby., 1865, Camp Douglass, Ill. Mustered out June 29, 1865.

48th REGIMENT ENROLLED MILITIA INFANTRY. —Duty in Platte and Clinton Counties, Mo.

49th REGIMENT INFANTRY.—Org. at Warrenton, Mexico, Macon and St. Louis, Mo., Aug. 31, 1864, to Feby. 5, 1865. Jany., 1865, Dist. North Mo., Dept. Mo. Feby., 1865, 2 Brig., 3 Div., 16 Corps, Mil. Div. West Miss. Aug., 1865. Dept. Ala. Mustered out Dec. 20, 1865.

49th REGIMENT ENROLLED MILITIA INFANTRY. —Duty in North Mo.

50th REGIMENT INFANTRY.—Org. in Mo. at large, Sept. 11, 1864, to April 27, 1865, St. Louis Mo., Dept. Mo. Mustered out Aug. 11, 1865.

50th REGIMENT ENROLLED MILITIA INFANTRY. —Duty in 8th Mil. Dist. Mo. Relieved Jany. 5, 1865.

51st REGIMENT INFANTRY.—Org. at St. Joe, Mo., March 1 to April 14, 1865. Mustered out Aug. 31, 1865.

51st REGIMENT ENROLLED MILITIA INFANTRY. —Duty in 7th Mil. Dist. Mo.

51st REGIMENT PROVISIONAL ENROLLED MILITIA INFANTRY.—Duty in Ray and Carroll Counties, Mo.

52nd REGIMENT INFANTRY.—Failed to complete organization.

52nd REGIMENT ENROLLED MILITIA.—Called Sept. 25, 1864; Relieved Oct. 31, 1864.

53rd REGIMENT INFANTRY.—Failed to complete organization.

53rd REGIMENT ENROLLED MILITIA INFANTRY. —Duty in North Mo.

53rd PROVISIONAL ENROLLED MILITIA INFANTRY.—Duty in North Mo.

54th REGIMENT INFANTRY.—Failed to complete organization.

54th REGIMENT ENROLLED MILITIA INFANTRY. —Duty in Franklin Co. and operations against Price, 1862-1864.

55th REGIMENT INFANTRY.—Failed to complete organization.

55th REGIMENT ENROLLED MILITIA INFANTRY. —Duty in Franklin Co. and operations against Price.

56th REGIMENT INFANTRY.—Failed to complete organization.

56th REGIMENT ENROLLED MILITIA INFANTRY. —Operations against Marmaduke and Price, 1863-1864.

57th REGIMENT INFANTRY.—Failed to complete organization.

57th REGIMENT PROVISIONAL ENROLLED MILITIA INFANTRY.—Duty in 7th Mil. Dist. Mo.

58th REGIMENT INFANTRY.—Failed to complete organization.

59th REGIMENT ENROLLED MILITIA INFANTRY. —Duty in North Mo.; relieved Jany 5, 1865.

60th REGIMENT ENROLLED MILITIA INFANTRY. —Duty in Dist. Central Mo.

61st REGIMENT ENROLLED MILITIA INFANTRY. —Duty in Dist. North Mo.

61st REGIMENT PROVISIONAL ENROLLED MILITIA INFANTRY.--Duty in 8th Mil Dist., North Mo.

62nd REGIMENT ENROLLED MILITIA INFANTRY. —Duty in Linn County.

63rd REGIMENT ENROLLED MILITIA INFANTRY. Duty in 7th Mil. Dist. Mo.

64th REGIMENT ENROLLED MILITIA INFANTRY. Duty in 1st Mil. Dist., Mo.

65th REGIMENT ENROLLED MILITIA INFANTRY. —Duty in Dist. North Mo.

66th REGIMENT ENROLLED MILITIA INFANTRY. —Duty in 8th Mil. Dist. Mo.

66th REGIMENT PROVISIONAL ENROLLED MILITIA INFANTRY.—Duty in Dist. North Mo.

67th REGIMENT ENROLLED MILITIA INFANTRY. —Duty in Dist. North Mo.

67th REGIMENT PROVISIONAL ENROLLED MILITIA INFANTRY.—At Danville, Mo.

68th REGIMENT ENROLLED MILITIA INFANTRY.— 68th REGIMENT PROVISIONAL ENROLLED MILITIA NFANTRY.—Duty in 1st Mil. Dist. Mo.

69th REGIMENT ENROLLED MILITIA INFANTRY. —Duty in North Mo. Relieved Jany. 17, 1865.

69th REGIMENT PROVISIONAL ENROLLED MILITIA INFANTRY.—Duty in North Mo.

70th REGIMENT ENROLLED MILITIA INFANTRY. —Duty in Dist. North Mo.

71st REGIMENT ENROLLED MILITIA INFANTRY. —Duty in Ray County.

72nd REGIMENT ENROLLED MILITIA INFANTRY. —Duty in 4th Mil. Dist. Mo., Southwest Mo.

72nd REGIMENT PROVISIONAL ENROLLED MILITIA INFANTRY.—Duty at Springfield, Mo.

73rd REGIMENT ENROLLED MILITIA INFANTRY. —Duty in Dist. Southwest Mo.

74th REGIMENT ENROLLED MILITIA INFANTRY. —Duty in Dist. Southwest Mo.

74th REGIMENT PROVISIONAL ENROLLED MILITIA INFANTRY.—Duty at Sand Springs, Mo.

75th REGIMENT ENROLLED MILITIA INFANTRY. —Duty in 8th Mil. Dist. Mo.

76th REGIMENT ENROLLED MILITIA INFANTRY. —Duty in Southwest Mo. Relieved Feby. 28, 1865.

77th REGIMENT ENROLLED MILITIA INFANTRY.— 78th REGIMENT ENROLLED MILITIA INFANTRY. —Duty in 1st Mil. Dist. Mo.

79th REGIMENT ENROLLED MILITIA INFANTRY. —Duty in 1st Mil. Dist. Mo.

80th REGIMENT ENROLLED MILITIA INFANTRY. —Called into service Sept. 25, 1864. Relieved Oct. 31, 1864.

80th REGIMENT PROVISIONAL ENROLLED MILITIA INFANTRY.—Called into service Sept. 25, 1864. Relieved Oct. 21, 1864.

81st REGIMENT PROVISIONAL ENROLLED MILITIA INFANTRY.—Duty in 7th Mil. Dist. Mo.

82nd REGIMENT ENROLLED MILITIA INFANTRY. —Duty in Dist. North Mo.

82nd REGIMENT PROVISIONAL ENROLLED MILITIA INFANTRY.—Duty in Dist. North Mo.

85th REGIMENT ENROLLED MILITIA INFANTRY. —Called into service Sept. 25, 1864. Relieved Oct. 31, 1864.

86th REGIMENT ENROLLED MILITIA INFANTRY. —Duty in North Mo.

87th REGIMENT PROVISIONAL ENROLLED MILITIA INFANTRY.—Duty in 7th Mil. Dist. Mo.

88th REGIMENT ENROLLED MILITIA INFANTRY. —Duty in 7th Mil. Dist. Mo.

89th REGIMENT ENROLLED MILITIA INFANTRY. —Duty in 8th Mil. Dist. Mo.

BAYLES' INDEPENDENT COMPANY INFANTRY.—Org. at St. Louis, Mo., May 11, 1861. Mustered out Aug. 11, 1861.

BENTON CADETS INDEPENDENT COMPANY INFANTRY.—Org. at St. Louis, Mo., Sept.-Oct., 1861. Mustered out Jany. 8, 1862.

DIETRICH'S INDEPENDENT COMPANY RESERVE CORPS INFANTRY.—Org. at Manchester, Mo., Aug. 15, 1861. Mustered out Feby. 3, 1862.

GASCONADE COUNTY BATTALION RESERVE CORPS INFANTRY.—Org. June, 1861. Transferred to 4th Mo. Infy. Jany. 18, 1862.

KREKEL'S INDEPENDENT BATTALION RESERVE CORPS INFANTRY.—Org. at St. Charles, Mo., Aug., 1861. Mustered out Jany. 10, 1862.

NAGEL'S INDEPENDENT COMPANY RESERVE CORPS INFANTRY.—Org. at St. Louis, Mo., June 6, 1861. Mustered out Oct. 7, 1861.

OSTERHAUS' BATTALION INFANTRY.—Org. at St. Louis, Mo., April 23-May 3, 1861. Attached to Lyons' Army of the West. Mustered out Aug. 31, 1861. (See 2nd Mo. Infy., 3 Co's.).

PEABODY'S INDEPENDENT BATTALION RESERVE CORPS INFANTRY.—Org. at St. Joseph, Mo., May, 1861. Consolidated with Van Horn's Battalion to form 25th Mo. Infy., Dec., 1861.

PHELPS' INDEPENDENT REGIMENT INFANTRY.—Org. at Rolla, Mo., Sept. 22 to Dec. 27, 1861. Served Unatt., Army Southwest Mo., to Feby., 1862, 2 Brig., 4 Div., Army Southwest Mo., Dept. Mo. Mustered out May 13, 1862.

VAN HORN'S BATTALION RESERVE CORPS INFANTRY.—Org. at St. Louis, Mo., May 1, and mustered in at Kansas City, Mo., May 24, 1861. Transferred to 25th Mo. Infy. Dec., 1861.

ALBREE'S BATTALION STATE MILITIA INFANTRY.—See 1st Battalion S. M. Infy.

BURN'S BATTALION STATE MILITIA INFANTRY.—See 6th Battalion S. M. Infy.

COX'S BATTALION STATE MILITIA INFANTRY.—See 2nd Battalion S. M. Infy.

CRANOR'S REGIMENT STATE MILITIA INFANTRY.—Org. in Gentry County, Mo., Oct. 1, 1861. Duty in Northwest Mo. Mustered out Feby., 1862.

DALLMEYERS' REGIMENT STATE MILITIA INFANTRY.—Org. at Camp Matthews, Gasconade County, Mo., Sept. 14, 1861. Mustered out Feby., 1862.

FAGG'S REGIMENT STATE MILITIA INFANTRY.—See 5th Regiment State Militia Infy.

GRUNDY COUNTY BATTALION STATE MILITIA INFANTRY.—Org. at Trenton, Grundy County, Mo., Oct. 20, 1861. Mustered out March 4, 1862.

HARRISON COUNTY BATTALION STATE MILITIA INFANTRY.—See. 7th Battalion S. M. Infy.

JAMES' BATTALION STATE MILITIA INFANTRY.—Org. at Cameron, Mo., Oct. 2, 1861. Mustered out March 13, 1862.

JOSEPH'S BATTALION STATE MILITIA INFANTRY.—See 3rd Battalion S. M. Infy.

KIMBALL'S REGIMENT STATE MILITIA INFANTRY.—Org. at St. Joseph, Mo., Oct. 2, 1861. Duty in Northwest Mo. Mustered out April 2, 1862.

MERCER COUNTY BATTALION (CLARK'S) STATE MILITIA INFANTRY.—Org. at Utica, Mo., Sept. 19, 1861. Mustered out March 19, 1862.

RICHARDSON'S REGIMENT STATE MILITIA INFANTRY.—Org. Oct. 1, 1861. Mustered out Dec. 18, 1861.

SIMPSON'S REGIMENT STATE MILITIA INFANTRY.—Org. at Perryville, Mo., Oct. 10, 1861. Duty in Dist. Southeast Mo. Mustered out Feby. 25, 1862.

THOMPSON'S BATTALION STATE MILITIA INFANTRY.—See 4th Battalion S. M. Infy.

WARD'S COMPANY STATE MILITIA INFANTRY.—Duty in Dist. Central Mo.

WASHINGTON COUNTY BATTALION STATE MILITIA INFANTRY.—Org. at Potosi, Sept. 19, 1861. Duty in Dist. Southeast Mo. Mustered out Jany. 8, 1862.

ADAIR COUNTY HOME GUARD COMPANY INFANTRY, MOUNTED.—Formed May, 1861. Mustered out Oct., 1861.

ADAIR COUNTY HOME GUARD COMPANY INFANTRY.—Org. Aug., 1861. Mustered out Oct., 1861.

ALLEN'S CITIZENS' CORPS HOME GUARD COMPANY INFANTRY.—Org. June, 1861. Mustered out Sept., 1861.

BENTON COUNTY REGIMENT HOME GUARD INFANTRY.—Org. June 13, 1861. Mustered out Sept. 13, 1861.

BOONEVILLE BATTALION HOME GUARD INFANTRY.—Org. June, 1861. Mustered out Aug., 1861.

BROOKFIELD COMPANY HOME GUARD INFANTRY.—Org. at Brookfield, June, 1861. Mustered out Aug., 1861.

CALDWELL COUNTY COMPANY HOME GUARD INFANTRY.—Org. June, 1861. Mustered in to six months militia, Sept. 24, 1861.

CAPE GIRARDEAU BATTALION HOME GUARD INFANTRY.—Org. June, 1861. Mustered out Sept., 1861.

CARONDELET COUNTY COMPANY HOME GUARD INFANTRY.—Org. June, 1861. Mustered out Aug., 1861.

CASS COUNTY REGIMENT HOME GUARD INFANTRY.—Org. June, 1861. Mustered out Sept., 1861.

CLINTON COUNTY COMPANY HOME GUARD INFANTRY.—Org. June, 1861. Mustered out Nov., 1861.

CLINTON COUNTY COMPANY HOME GUARD INFANTRY.—Org. June, 1861. Mustered out Sept., 1861.

COLE COUNTY REGIMENT HOME GUARD INFANTRY.—Org. in Mo. at large June 11 to July 1, 1861. Disbanded Oct. 1, 1861.

DALLAS COUNTY REGIMENT HOME GUARD INFANTRY.—Org. June, 1861. Mustered out Aug., 1861.

DEKALB COUNTY REGIMENT HOME GUARD INFANTRY.—Org. June, 1861. Mustered out Sept., 1861.

DESOTO COUNTY COMPANY HOME GUARD INFANTRY.—Org. June, 1861. Mustered out Sept., 1861.

DOUGLASS COUNTY COMPANY HOME GUARD INFANTRY.—Org. at Springfield, Mo., July, 1861. Joined Phelps' Regt., Oct. 13, 1861.

FRANKLIN COUNTY BATTALION HOME GUARD INFANTRY.—Org. June, 1861. Mustered out Sept., 1861.

FREMONT RANGERS' HOME GUARD INFANTRY.—(5 CO'S.). Org. Aug., 1861. Mustered out Dec. 18, 1861.

GASCONADE COUNTY BATTALION, 2ND HOME GUARD INFANTRY.—Org. June, 1861. Mustered out Sept., 1861.

GREENE COUNTY COMPANY HOME GUARD INFANTRY.—Org. June, 1861. Mustered out Sept., 1861.

GENTRY COUNTY REGIMENT HOME GUARD INFANTRY.—Org. June, 1861. Mustered out Oct., 1861.

HARRISON COUNTY REGIMENT HOME GUARD INFANTRY.—Org. Sept. 3, 1861. Mustered out Sept. 23, 1861.

JEFFERSON CITY BATTALION HOME GUARD INFANTRY.—Org. June, 1861. Mustered out Aug., 1861.

JOHNSON COUNTY REGIMENT HOME GUARD INFANTRY.—Org. June, 1861. Mustered out Sept., 1861.

KING'S COMPANY E. R. GUARD.—Org. Sept. and Oct., 1861. Mustered out Jany. 23, 1861.

KNOX COUNTY REGIMENT HOME GUARD INFANTRY.—Org. July, 1861. Mustered out Oct., 1861.

LAWRENCE COUNTY REGIMENT HOME GUARD INFANTRY.—Org. May 25, 1861. Mustered out Aug. 10, 1861.

LEWIS COUNTY COMPANY HOME GUARD INFANTRY.—Org. June, 1861. Mustered out July 16, 1861.

LEXINGTON COUNTY COMPANY HOME GUARD INFANTRY.—Org. Aug. 12, 1861. Mustered out Oct. 22, 1861.

LIVINGSTON COUNTY COMPANY HOME GUARD INFANTRY.—Org. June, 1861. Mustered out Sept., 1861.

MARION COUNTY BATTALION HOME GUARD INFANTRY.—Org. July, 1861. Disbanded Sept., 1861.

MONITEAU COUNTY COMPANY HOME GUARD INFANTRY.—Org. June, 1861. Disbanded Aug., 1861.

NODAWAY COUNTY REGIMENT HOME GUARD INFANTRY.—Org. July, 1861. Mustered out Aug., 1861.

OSAGE COUNTY BATTALION HOME GUARD INFANTRY.—Org. May 27, 1861. Mustered out July 21, 1861.

OSAGE COUNTY REGIMENT AND HICKORY BATTALION HOME GUARD INFANTRY.—Org. June and July, 1861. Mustered out Dec., 1861.

OZARK COUNTY REGIMENT HOME GUARD INFANTRY.—Org. June, 1861. Mustered out Oct., 1861.

PACIFIC BATTALION (INKS) HOME GUARD INFANTRY.—Org. June, 1861. Mustered out Sept. 17, 1861.

PETTIS COUNTY REGIMENT HOME GUARD INFANTRY.—Org. June, 1861. Mustered out Aug., 1861.

PHILIPS COUNTY COMPANY HOME GUARD INFANTRY.—(MARIAS CO. INDPT. COMPANY). Org. June, 1861. Mustered out Sept., 1861.

PHILIPS COUNTY COMPANY HOME GUARD INFANTRY.—(BENNIGHT'S). Org. July, 1861. Mustered out Sept. 20, 1861.

PIKE COUNTY REGIMENT HOME GUARD INFANTRY.—Org. July, 1861. Mustered out Sept., 1861.

PILOT KNOB COMPANY HOME GUARD INFANTRY.—Org. June, 1861. Mustered out Oct., 1861.

POLK COUNTY REGIMENT HOME GUARD INFANTRY.—Org. June, 1861. Mustered out Dec., 1861.

POTOSI COUNTY REGIMENT HOME GUARD INFANTRY.—Org. July, 1861. Mustered out Sept., 1861.

PUTNAM COUNTY HOME GUARD INFANTRY.—(2 CO'S.). Org. Aug., 1861. Mustered out Oct., 1861.

SIBLEY POINT COMPANY HOME GUARD INFANTRY.—Org. June, 1861. Mustered out Sept., 1861.

ST. CHARLES COUNTY BATTALION HOME GUARD INFANTRY.—Org. July, 1861. Mustered out Aug., 1861.

SCOTT COUNTY BATTALION HOME GUARD INFANTRY.—Org. May, 1861. Mustered out Aug., 1861.

STONAS' INDPT. COMPANY OZARK COUNTY HOME GUARD INFANTRY.—Org. July, 1861. Mustered out Oct., 1861.

STONE PRAIRIE (BARRY CO.) COMPANY HOME GUARD INFANTRY.—Org. June, 1861. Mustered out Aug., 1861.

STONE COUNTY REGIMENT HOME GUARD INFANTRY.—Org. June 5, 1861. Mustered out July 9, 1861.

SHAWNEETOWN (PUTNAM CO.) COMPANY HOME GUARD INFANTRY.—Org. July, 1861. Mustered out Sept., 1861.

SULLIVAN COUNTY HOME GUARD INFANTRY.—Org. June, 1861. Mustered out Sept., 1861.

SHELBY COUNTY COMPANY HOME GUARD INFANTRY.—Org. July 22, 1861. Mustered out Sept., 1861.

WEBSTER COUNTY REGIMENT HOME GUARD INFANTRY.—Org. July, 1861. Mustered out Aug. 18, 1861.

MILITIA ORGANIZATIONS.

ANDREWS COUNTY MILITIA.
AUDRAIN COUNTY MILITIA.
BATES COUNTY MILITIA.
BOGARD CITIZENS' GUARD.
BOLLINGER COUNTY MILITIA.
BOONE COUNTY MILITIA.
BRIDGES' NORTH MISSOURI R. R. MILITIA.
BUCHANAN COUNTY MILITIA.
BUCHANAN COUNTY UNION GUARD.
CALHOUN CITIZENS' CORPS.
GALLOWAY COUNTY MILITIA.
GALLOWAY COUNTY ENROLLED MILITIA.
CAMDEN COUNTY MILITIA.
CAPE GIRARDEAU COUNTY MILITIA.
CARROLL COUNTY MILITIA.
CHARITON COUNTY MILITIA.
CLAY COUNTY MILITIA.
CLAY COUNTY ENROLLED MILITIA.
CLINTON COUNTY ENROLLED MILITIA.
COOPER AND MONITEAU COUNTY MILITIA.
COOPER COUNTY MILITIA.
DALLAS COUNTY MILITIA.
DEKALB COUNTY MILITIA.
HOWARD COUNTY MILITIA.
JACKSON COUNTY MILITIA.
JASPER COUNTY MILITIA.
JOHNSON COUNTY MILITIA.
LAFAYETTE COUNTY MILITIA.
LAWRENCE COUNTY MILITIA.
LINN COUNTY MILITIA.

LIVINGSTON COUNTY MILITIA.
MARIES COUNTY MILITIA.
MISSISSIPPI COUNTY ENROLLED MILITIA.
MISSISSIPPI COUNTY MILITIA.
MORGAN COUNTY MILITIA.
NEWMAN'S PROV'L ENROLLED MILITIA.
OSAGE AND MARIAS COUNTY MILITIA.
OSAGE COUNTY MILITIA.
PACIFIC R. R. MILITIA.
PERRY COUNTY MILITIA.
PETTIS COUNTY MILITIA.
PIKE COUNTY ENROLLED MILITIA.
RAY COUNTY MILITIA.
ROLLA BATTALION CITIZENS' GUARD.
ST. CLAIR COUNTY MILITIA.
SALINE COUNTY MILITIA.
SCOTT COUNTY ENROLLED MILITIA.
SOUTHWEST BRANCH PACIFIC R. R. MILITIA.
STONE COUNTY MILITIA.
TANNEY COUNTY MILITIA.
WARREN COUNTY MILITIA.
WASHINGTON COUNTY MILITIA.
WRIGHT COUNTY MILITIA.

MISSISSIPPI

1st REGIMENT COLORED CAVALRY.—Org. at Vicksburg, Miss., Oct. 9, 1863. Oct., 1863, Post Goodrich Landing, Dist. Northeast La., Dept. Tenn. Jany., 1864, 1 Brig., U. S. C. T., Dist. Vicksburg, Miss. Designation changed to 3rd U. S. C. Cav., March 11, 1864, which see.

1st REGIMENT MOUNTED RIFLES.—Org. at Memphis, Tenn., March, 1864. March, 1864, Dist. Memphis, Tenn., 16 Corps, Dept. Tenn. June, 1864, 1 Brig., Cav. Div., Dist. West Tenn. July, 1864, 1 Brig., 2 Cav. Div., Dist. West Tenn. Dec., 1864, 1 Brig., Cav. Div., Dist. West Tenn. Mustered out June 26, 1865.

1st REGIMENT HEAVY ARTILLERY, AFRICAN DESCENT.—Org. at Vicksburg, Miss., Aug. 7, 1863. Aug., 1863, Post Vicksburg, Miss., Dist. Northeast La., Dept. Tenn. March, 1864, Unass'd, 1 Div., U. S. C. T., Dist. Vicksburg, Dept. Tenn. Designation changed to 5th U. S. C. Heavy Arty., April 26, 1864, which see.

2nd REGIMENT COLORED HEAVY ARTILLERY, AFRICAN DESCENT.—Org. at Natchez, Miss., Sept. 12, 1863. Sept., 1863, Post Natchez, Miss., Dist. Northeast La., Dept. Tenn. Jany., 1864, Post Vicksburg, Miss. March, 1864, Post Natchez, Miss. Designation changed to 6th U. S. Heavy Arty., April 26, 1864, which see.

1st REGIMENT INFANTRY, AFRICAN DESCENT.—Org. at Milliken's Bend, La., and Vicksburg, Miss., May 16, 1863. May, 1863, African Brig., Dist. Northeast La., Dept. Tenn. July, 1863, Post Vicksburg, Miss. March, 1864, Post Goodrich Landing, Dist. Vicksburg, Miss. Designation changed to 51st U. S. C. T., March 11, 1864, which see.

2nd REGIMENT INFANTRY, AFRICAN DESCENT.—Org. at Vicksburg, Miss., July 27, 1863. July, 1863, Post Vicksburg, Miss., Dist. Vicksburg, Dept. Tenn. Designation changed to 52nd U. S. C. T. March 11, 1864, which see.

3rd REGIMENT INFANTRY, AFRICAN DESCENT.—Org. at Warrenton, Miss., May 19, 1863. May, 1863, African Brig., Dist. Northeast La., Dept. Tenn. July, 1863, Post Goodrich Landing, Dist. Vicksburg, Miss., Dept. Tenn. Jany., 1864, 1 Brig., U. S. C. T., Dist. Vicksburg, Miss. Designation changed to 53rd U. S. C. T., March 11, 1864, which see.

4th REGIMENT INFANTRY, AFRICAN DESCENT.—Org. at Vicksburg, Miss., Dec. 11, 1863. Jany., 1864, Post Vicksburg, Miss., Dist. Vicksburg, Miss., Dept. Tenn. March, 1864, Post Goodrich Landing, Dist. Vicksburg, Miss. Designation changed to 66th U. S. C. T. March 11, 1864.

5th REGIMENT INFANTRY, AFRICAN DESCENT.—Failed to complete organization.

6th REGIMENT INFANTRY, AFRICAN DESCENT.—Org. at Natchez, Miss., Aug. 27, 1863. Aug., 1863, Post Natchez, Miss., Dist. Vicksburg, Miss., Dept. Tenn. Jany., 1864, Post Vicksburg, Miss. March, 1864, Dist. Natchez, Miss. Designation changed to 58th U. S. C. T., March 11, 1864.

NEBRASKA

1st REGIMENT CAVALRY.—Org. from 1st Nebraska Infy., Oct. 11, 1863. Oct., 1863, Dist. Southeast Mo., Dept. Mo. Nov., 1863, Dist. Northeast Ark., Dept. Mo. Jany., 1864, Dist. Northeast Ark., 7 Corps, Dept. Ark. May, 1864, 3 Brig., 2 Div., 7 Corps, Dept. Ark. Sept., 1864, 4 Brig., Cav. Div., 7 Corps. Oct., 1864, Dist. Nebraska. Designated 1st Nebraska Veteran Cav., July 10, 1865. Mustered out July 1, 1866.

1st BATTALION CAVALRY.—Org at Omaha, Jany. to Aug., 1864. Attached to Dist. Neb. Consolidated with 1st Vet. Cav., July 10, 1865.

2nd REGIMENT CAVALRY.—Org. at Omaha, Oct. 23, 1862. Attached to Dist. Neb. Mustered out Dec. 23, 1863.

1st REGIMENT INFANTRY.—Org. at Omaha, Neb., June 11 to July 21, 1861. Aug., 1861, Dept. Mo. Feby., 1862, 3 Brig., 3 Div., Dist. Cairo. Feby., 1862, 2 Brig., 3 Div., Dist. West Tenn. and Army Tenn. July, 1862, Helena, Ark., Dist. East. Ark., Dept. Mo. Oct., 1862, 2 Brig., 2 Div., Army Southeast Mo., Dept. Mo. March, 1863, Dist. Southeast Mo., Dept. Mo. Designation changed to 1st Neb. Cav., Oct. 11, 1863, which see.

INDEPENDENT COMPANY OMAHA SCOUTS.—Org. at Omaha, May 3, 1865. Attached to Dist. Neb. Mustered out July 16, 1866.

INDEPENDENT COMPANY PAWNEE SCOUTS.—Org. at Columbus, Neb., Jany. 13, 1865. Attached to Dist. Neb. Mustered out April 1, 1866.

NEVADA

1st BATTALION CAVALRY.—Org. at Fort Churchill, June 22, 1863. Attached to Dept. of the Pacific. Mustered out July 21, 1866.

1st BATTALION INFANTRY.—Org. at Fort Churchill, Dec. 24, 1863. Attached to Dept. of the Pacific. Mustered out Dec. 23, 1865.

NEW HAMPSHIRE

1st REGIMENT CAVALRY.—Org. Jany. 7, 1864, from N. H. Battalion 1st R. I. Cav. April, 1864, Cav. Div., 22 Corps. May, 1864, 2 Brig., 3 Div., Cav. Corps, Potomac (5 Co's.). July, 1864, Cav. Brig., Def. Washington, 22 Corps. Aug., 1864, 1 Brig., 3 Div., Cav. Corps, Shenandoah (5 Co's.). Feby., 1865, Cav., Dept. Shenandoah (5 Co's.). Mustered out July 15, 1865.

2nd REGIMENT CAVALRY.—Org. Dec., 1863, from 8th Infy. Dec., 1863, 4 Brig., Cav. Div., Gulf. July, 1864, Def. New Orleans, Gulf. Sept., 1864, Post Natchez, La., Dist. Vicksburg, Dept. Miss. Jany., 1865, Post Videlia, La. March, 1865, Post Natchez, La. Mustered out Oct. 29, 1865.

1st REGIMENT HEAVY ARTILLERY.—Org. at Concord, July 22, 1863, to Oct., 17, 1864. May, 1864, 2 Brig., Haskin's Div., North Pot., 22 Corps (Co. A). May, 1864, 3 Brig., Haskin's Div., North Pot., 22 Corps (Co. B). July, 1864, 1 Brig., Hardin's Div., 22 Corps (Co. A). Aug., 1864, 2 Brig., Haskin's Div., 22 Corps (Co. A). Oct., 1864, 3 Brig., DeRussy's Div., 22 Corps (Co's C, D, E, F, G, H, I, K, L). Nov., 1864, Portsmouth, N. H. (Co. A). Dec., 1864, 1 Brig., Hardin's Div., 22 Corps (Regt.). Feby., 1865, Portsmouth, N. H. (Co. B). Mustered out Sept. 11, 1865.

1st INDEPENDENT BATTERY, LIGHT ARTILLERY.—Org. at Manchester and mustered in Sept. 21, 1861. Nov., 1861, McDowell's Div., Potomac. March, 1862, Arty., 3 Div., 1 Corps, Potomac. April, 1862, Arty., King's Div., Dept. Rappahannock. June, 1862, Arty., 1 Div., 3 Corps, Army Va. Sept., 1862, Arty., 1 Div., 1 Corps, Potomac. May, 1863, 3 Vol. Brig., Arty. Reserve, Potomac. Oct., 1863, Arty. Brig., 3 Corps, Potomac. April, 1864, Arty. Brig., 2 Corps, Potomac. Mustered out June 9, 1865.

1st COMPANY SHARPSHOOTERS.—Org. and mustered in Sept. 9, 1861. Assigned to 1st. U. S. S. S. as Co. E. (See 1st U. S. S. S.) Mustered out Sept. 8, 1864.

2nd COMPANY SHARPSHOOTERS.—Org. and mustered in Nov. 28, 1861. Assigned to 2d U. S. S. S. as Co. F. (See 2d U. S. S. S.)

3rd COMPANY SHARPSHOOTERS.—Org. and mustered in Dec. 10, 1861. Assigned to 2d U. S. S. S. as Co. G. (See 2nd U. S. S. S.)

1st REGIMENT INFANTRY.—Org. at Concord and mustered in May 1, 1861, for three months. June, 1861, Stone's Rockville Exp. July, 1861, Stone's 7 Brig., Patterson's Army. July, 1861, 3 Brig., Banks' Div., Shenandoah. Mustered out Aug. 9, 1861.

2nd REGIMENT INFANTRY.—Org. at Portsmouth, May 31 to June 8, 1861. June, 1861, Burnside's Brig., Hunter's Div., McDowell's Army N. E. Va. Aug., 1861, Hooker's Brig. Div., Potomac. Oct., 1861, 1 Brig., Hooker's Brig. Div., Potomac. March, 1862, 1 Brig., 2 Div., 3 Corps, Potomac. Feby., 1863, New Hampshire. June, 1863, 3 Brig., 2 Div., 3 Corps, Potomac. July, 1863, Point Lookout, Md., Dist. St. Mary's. April, 1864, 2 Brig., 2 Div., 18 Corps, Dept. Va. and N. C. June, 1864, Provost Guard, 18 Corps. Aug., 1864, 1 Brig., 1 Div., 18 Corps. Oct., 1864, 3 Brig., 1 Div., 18 Corps. Dec., 1864, 3 Brig., 3 Div., 24 Corps. Aug., 1865, Dept. Va. Mustered out Dec. 19, 1865.

3rd REGIMENT INFANTRY.—Org. at Concord and mustered in Aug. 23, 1861. Oct., 1861, 1 Brig., Sherman's S. C. Exp. April, 1862, 3 Brig., 2 Div., Dept. South. July, 1862, Dist. Hilton Head, Dept. South. Sept., 1862, Dist. Hilton Head, S. C., 10 Corps. April, 1863, Guss Brig., Seabrook Island, S. C., 10 Corps. June, 1863, St. Helena Island. July, 1863, 2 Brig., Folly Island, S. C., 10 Corps. July, 1863, 2 Brig., 2 Div., Morris Island, 10 Corps. Aug., 1863, 1 Brig., Morris Island, 10 Corps. April, 1864, Light Brig., Dist. Fla., Dept. South. April, 1864, 3 Brig., 1 Div., 10 Corps, Dept. Va. and N. C. May, 1864, 2 Brig., 1 Div., 10 Corps. Dec., 1864, 2 Brig., 1 Div., 24 Corps. Jany., 1865, 2 Brig., 1 Div., Terry's Prov'l Corps, Dept. N. C. March, 1865, 2 Brig., 1 Div., 10 Corps, Dept. N. C. April, 1865, Abbott's Detached Brig., 10 Corps, Dept. N. C. Mustered out July 25, 1865.

4th REGIMENT INFANTRY.—Org. at Manchester and mustered in Sept. 18, 1861. Oct., 1861, Wright's 3 Brig., Sherman's S. C. Exp. Feby., 1862, St. Augustine, Fla., Dept. South. Sept., 1862, Dist. Beaufort, S. C., 10 Corps. April, 1863, U. S. Forces, Folly Island S. C., 10 Corps. June, 1863, 1 Brig., Folly Island, 10 Corps. July, 1863, 1 Brig., 1 Div., Morris Island, S. C., 10 Corps. July, 1863, 1 Brig., Morris Island, 10 Corps. Jany., 1864, Dist. Beaufort, S. C., 10 Corps. Feby., 1864, Foster's 1 Brig., Vodge's Div., Dist. Fla. April, 1864, 1 Brig., 3 Div., 10 Corps, Dept. Va. and N. C. May, 1864, 3 Brig., 3 Div., 18 Corps. June, 1864, 3 Brig., 2 Div., 10 Corps. Dec., 1864, 3 Brig., 2 Div., 24 Corps. Jany., 1865, 3 Brig., 2 Div., Terry's Prov'l Corps, Dept. N. C. March, 1865, 3 Brig., 2 Div., 10 Corps, Dept. N. C. Mustered out Aug. 23, 1865.

5th REGIMENT INFANTRY.—Org. at Concord and mustered in Oct. 22, 1861. Oct., 1861, Howard's Brig., Sumner's Div., Potomac. March, 1862, 1 Brig., 1 Div., 2 Corps, Potomac. July, 1863, Dept. East. Nov., 1863, Point Lookout, Md. May, 1864, 1 Brig., 1 Div., 2 Corps, Potomac. Mustered out July 17, 1865.

6th REGIMENT INFANTRY.—Org. at Keene and mustered in Nov. 27, 1861. Dec., 1861, Williams' 4 Brig., Burnside's Exp. Corps. April, 1862, 4 Brig., Dept. N. C. July, 1862, 1 Brig., 2 Div., 9 Corps, Potomac. April, 1863, 1 Brig., 2 Div., 9 Corps, Army Ohio. June, 1863, 1 Brig., 2 Div., 9 Corps, Army Tenn. Aug., 1863, 1 Brig., 2 Div., 9 Corps, Ohio. Sept., 1863, Dist. N. C., Ky., 1 Div., 23 Corps, Ohio. Feby., 1864, 1 Brig., 2 Div., 9 Corps, Ohio. April, 1864, 2 Brig., 2 Div., 9 Corps, Army Potomac. Mustered out July 17, 1865.

7th REGIMENT INFANTRY.—Org. at Manchester and mustered in Dec 13, 1861. Feby., 1862, Brannan's Command, Dist. Fla. June, 1862, Dist. Beaufort, S. C., Dept. South. Sept., 1862, St. Augustine, Fla., Dept. South. May, 1863, Fernandina, Fla. June, 1863, 1 Brig., Folly Island, S. C., 10 Corps. July, 1863, 1 Brig., 2 Div., Morris Island, 10 Corps. July, 1863, 3 Brig., Morris Island, S. C., 10 Corps. Nov., 1863, 1 Brig., Morris Island, 10 Corps. Dec., 1863, St. Helena Island, S. C., 10 Corps. Feby., 1864, Hawley's Brig., Dist. Fla. Feby., 1864, 2 Brig., Ames Div., Dist. Fla. April, 1864, 3 Brig., 1 Div.,

10 Corps, Dept. Va. and N. C. May, 1864, 2 Brig., 1 Div., 10 Corps. Dec., 1864, 2 Brig., 1 Div., 24 Corps. Jany., 1865, 2 Brig., 1 Div., Terry's Prov'l Corps, Dept. N. C. March, 1865, 2 Brig., 1 Div., 10 Corps, Dept. N. C. April, 1865, Abbott's Detached Brig., 10 Corps. Mustered out July 17, 1865.

8th REGIMENT INFANTRY.—Org. at Manchester and mustered in Dec. 23, 1861. Feby., 1862, Butler's New Orleans Exp. March, 1862, 1 Brig., Dept. Gulf. Nov., 1862, Indpt. Command, Dept. Gulf. Jany., 1863, 1 Brig., 3 Div., 19 Corps, Gulf. Jany., 1863, 2 Brig., 3 Div., 19 Corps, Gulf. Designation changed to 2d Cav., Dec., 1863.

9th REGIMENT INFANTRY.—Org. at Concord and mustered in Aug. 15, 1862. Aug., 1862, Whipple's Command, Def. Washington, D. C. Sept., 1862, 1 Brig., 2 Div., 9 Corps, Potomac. April, 1863, 1 Brig., 2 Div., 9 Corps, Army Ohio. June, 1863, 1 Brig., 2 Div., 9 Corps, Army Tenn. Aug., 1863, 1 Brig., 2 Div., 9 Corps, Ohio. Sept., 1863, Dist. N. C., Ky., 1 Div., 23 Corps, Ohio. Feby., 1864, 1 Brig., 2 Div., 9 Corps, Potomac. April, 1864, 2 Brig., 2 Div., 9 Corps, Potomac. Mustered out June 10, 1865.

10th REGIMENT INFANTRY.—Org. at Manchester and mustered in Sept. 4, 1862. Oct., 1862, 1 Brig., 3 Div., 9 Corps, Potomac. April, 1863, 1 Brig., 2 Div., 7 Corps, Dept. Va. July, 1863, 3 Brig., Getty's Div., Portsmouth, Va., Dept. Va. and N. C. April, 1864, 2 Brig., 1 Div., 18 Corps. Dec., 1864, 2 Brig., 3 Div., 24 Corps. Mustered out June 21, 1865.

11th REGIMENT INFANTRY.—Org. at Concord and mustered in Sept. 2, 1862. Sept., 1862, Casey's Div., Def. Washington. Oct., 1862, 2 Brig., 2 Div., 9 Corps, Potomac. April, 1863, 2 Brig., 2 Div., 9 Corps, Army Ohio. June, 1863, 2 Brig., 2 Div., 9 Corps, Army Tenn. Aug., 1863, 2 Brig., 2 Div., 9 Corps, Ohio. April, 1864, 2 Brig., 2 Div., 9 Corps, Potomac. Mustered out June 4, 1865.

12th REGIMENT INFANTRY.—Org. at Concord and mustered in Sept. 10, 1862. Sept., 1862, Whipple's Command, Def. Washington, D. C. Nov., 1862, 2 Brig., 3 Div., 3 Corps, Potomac. June, 1863, 1 Brig., 2 Div., 3 Corps, Potomac. July, 1863, Point Lookout, Md., Dist. St. Mary's. April, 1864, 2 Brig., 2 Div., 18 Corps, Dept. Va. and N. C. Oct., 1864, Prov'l Div., Dept. Va. and N. C. Dec., 1864, 2 Brig., 3 Div., 24 Corps. Mustered out June 21, 1865.

13th REGIMENT INFANTRY.—Org. at Concord and mustered in Sept. 20, 1862. Oct., 1862, 1 Brig., Casey's Div., Def. Washington, D. C. Dec., 1862, 1 Brig., 3 Div., 9 Corps, Potomac. Feby., 1863, 3 Brig., 3 Div., 9 Corps, Potomac. April, 1863, 3 Brig., 2 Div., 7 Corps, Dept. Va. July, 1863, 3 Brig., Getty's Div., Portsmouth, Va., Dept. Va. and N. C. April, 1864, 2 Brig., 1 Div., 18 Corps, Dept. Va. and N. C. July, 1864, 1 Brig., 1 Div., 18 Corps. Dec., 1864, 1 Brig., 3 Div., 24 Corps. Mustered out June 22, 1865.

14th REGIMENT INFANTRY.—Org. at Concord and mustered in Sept. 24, 1862. Oct., 1862, Grover's Brig., Def. Washington, D. C. Feby., 1863, Jewett's Indpt. Brig., 22 Corps. May, 1863, Dist. Washington, 22 Corps. March, 1864, Def. New Orleans, Dept. Gulf. June, 1864, 1 Brig., 2 Div., 19 Corps, Gulf. Aug., 1864, 1 Brig., 2 Div., 19 Corps, Shenandoah. Jany., 1865, 1 Brig., Grover's Div., Dist. Savannah, Dept. South. June, 1865, Dept. South. Mustered out July 8, 1865.

15th REGIMENT INFANTRY.—Org. at Concord and mustered in Nov. 12, 1862. Dec., 1862, Sherman's Div., Dept. Gulf. Jany., 1863, 1 Brig., 2 Div., 19 Corps, Gulf. July, 1863, 2 Brig., 3 Div., 19 Corps, Gulf. Mustered out Aug. 13, 1863.

16th REGIMENT INFANTRY.—Org. at Concord and mustered in Oct. 24, 1862. Dec., 1862, Sherman's Div., Gulf. Jany., 1863, 3 Brig., 3 Div., 19 Corps, Gulf. Jany., 1863, 1 Brig., 3 Div., 19 Corps, Gulf. May, 1863, 1 Brig., 2 Div., 19 Corps, Gulf. Mustered out Aug. 20, 1863.

17th REGIMENT INFANTRY.—Org. commenced Nov. 19, 1862. Not completed. 2 Co.'s transferred to 2nd.

18th REGIMENT INFANTRY.—Org. at Concord. Mustered in Sept. 13, 1864. Sept., 1864, Benham's Engr. Brig., Army James. Dec., 1864, Clough's Prov'l Brig.,

---

Ferrero's Div., Def. Bermuda Hundred, Va. March, 1865, 3 Brig., 1 Div., 9 Corps, Potomac. May, 1865, Garrison Washington, D. C. Mustered out July 29, 1865.

NEW JERSEY

1st REGIMENT CAVALRY (16th VOLS.).—Org. at Trenton Aug. 14, 1861. Oct., 1861, Heintzelman's Div., Potomac. March, 1862, Wadsworth's Command, Mil. Dist. Washington. May, 1862, Bayard's Cav. Brig., Dept. Rappahannock. June, 1862, Bayard's Cav. Brig., 3 Corps, Army Va. Sept., 1862, Def. Washington, Bayard's Cav. Brig., Cav. Div., Potomac. Feby., 1863, 2 Brig., 3 Div., Cav. Corps, Potomac. June, 1863, 1 Brig., 1 Div., Cav. Corps, Potomac. May, 1865, 1 Brig., 1 Div., Cav. Corps, Dept. Washington. Mustered out July 24, 1865.

2nd REGIMENT CAVALRY (32nd VOLS.).—Org. at Trenton Aug. 15, 1863. Oct., 1863, Stoneman's Cav. Div., Def. Washington, 22 Corps. Dec., 1863, Dist. Columbus, Ky., 6 Div., 16 Corps, Dept. Tenn. Dec., 1863, Waring's Cav. Brig., 16 Corps, Tenn. Jany., 1864, 1 Brig., 1 Div., Cav. Corps, 16 Corps, Tenn. June, 1864, 1 Brig., Cav. Div., Dist. West. Tenn., Dept. Tenn. July, 1864, 1 Brig., 2 Div., Cav. Corps, Dist. West. Tenn., Dept. Tenn. Nov., 1864, 2 Brig., 4 Div., Cav. Corps, Mil. Div. Miss. Dec., 1864, 1 Brig., Cav. Div., Dist. West. Tenn. Feby., 1865, 1 Brig., 1 Div. Cav., Mil. Div. West. Miss. April, 1865, 2 Brig., 1 Div., Cav. Corps, Gulf. May, 1865, Dept. Miss. Mustered out Nov. 1, 1865.

3rd REGIMENT CAVALRY (39th VOLS.).—Org. at Trenton Jany. 22, 1864. April, 1864, Cav., 9 Corps, Potomac. May, 1864, 1 Brig., 3 Div., Cav. Corps, Potomac, and Middle Mil. Div. Mustered out Aug. 1, 1865.

1st BATTERY A LIGHT ARTILLERY.—Org. at Hoboken Aug. 12, 1861. Aug., 1861, Kearney's Brig. Div., Potomac. Oct., 1861, Arty., Franklin's Div., Potomac. March, 1862, Arty., 1 Div., 1 Corps, Potomac. April, 1862, Arty., 1 Div., Dept. Rappahannock. May, 1862, Arty., 1 Div., 6 Corps, Potomac. May, 1863, Arty. Brig., 6 Corps, Potomac. June, 1863, 4 Vol. Brig., Arty. Res., Potomac. Oct., 1863, 3 Vol. Brig., Arty. Res., Potomac. March, 1864, 2 Vol. Brig., Arty. Res., Potomac. May, 1864, Arty. Brig., 6 Corps, Potomac. July, 1864, Arty. Res., Potomac. Dec., 1864, Arty. Brig., 6 Corps, Potomac. Mustered out June 22, 1865.

2nd BATTERY B LIGHT ARTILLERY.—Org. at Trenton Sept. 3, 1861. Oct., 1861, Hamilton's Div., Def. Washington. March, 1862, Arty., 3 Div., 3 Corps, Potomac. June, 1862, Arty. Res., 3 Corps, Potomac. Aug., 1862, Arty., 2 Div., 3 Corps, Potomac. Jany., 1863, Arty., 1 Div., 3 Corps, Potomac. May, 1863, Arty. Brig., 3 Corps, Potomac. March, 1864, 2 Vol. Brig., Arty. Res., Potomac. May, 1864, Arty. Brig., 2 Corps, Potomac Mustered out June 16, 1865.

3rd BATTERY C LIGHT ARTILLERY.—Org. at Trenton Sept. 11, 1863. Sept., 1863, Barry's Arty. Command, Def. Washington, 22 Corps. May, 1864, Arty., Abercrombie's Command, Potomac. June, 1864, Arty. Brig., 2 Corps, Potomac. Sept., 1864, Arty. Res., Potomac. Mustered out June 19, 1865.

4th BATTERY D LIGHT ARTILLERY.—Org. at Trenton Sept. 11, 1863. Sept., 1863, Barry's Arty. Command, Def. Washington, 22 Corps. April, 1864, Arty., 2 Div., 10 Corps, Army James, Dept. Va. and N. C. May, 1864, Unatt. Arty., 10 Corps. June, 1864, Arty., 2 Div., 10 Corps. Aug., 1864, Arty. Brig., 10 Corps. Dec., 1864, Arty. Brig., Brig., 25 Corps. Mustered out June 17, 1865.

5th BATTERY E LIGHT ARTILLERY.—Org. at Trenton Sept. 8, 1863. Sept., 1863, Barry's Arty. Command, Def. Washington, 22 Corps. April, 1864, Arty., 1 Div., 10 Corps, Army James, Dept. Va. and N. C. Aug., 1864, Arty. Brig., 10 Corps. Dec., 1864, Arty. Brig., 25 Corps. Mustered out June 12, 1865.

1st REGIMENT INFANTRY (3 MONTHS).—Org. at Trenton April 30, 1861. May, 1861, Runyon's N. J. Brig., Def. Washington. June, 1861, 1 Brig., Runyon's Res. Div., McDowell's Army, N. E. Va. Mustered out July 31, 1861.

1st REGIMENT INFANTRY (3 YEARS).—Org. at Trenton May 31, 1861. June, 1861, 2 Brig., Runyon's

Res. Div., McDowell's Army, N. E. Va. Aug., 1861, Kearney's Brig., Div. Potomac. Oct., 1861, Kearney's Brig., Franklin's Div., Potomac. March, 1862, 1 Brig., 1 Div., 1 Corps, Potomac. April, 1862, 1 Brig., 1 Div., Dept. Rappahannock. May, 1862, 1 Brig., 1 Div., 6 Corps, Potomac. Mustered out June 23, 1864.

1st VETERAN BATTALION INFANTRY.—Org. Dec., 1864. Dec., 1864, 1 Brig., 1 Div., 6 Corps, Potomac. Mustered out June 29, 1865.

2nd REGIMENT INFANTRY (3 MONTHS).—Org. at Trenton April 26, 1861. May, 1861, Runyon's N. J. Brig., Def. Washington. June, 1861, 1 Brig., Runyon's Res. Div., McDowell's Army, N. E. Va. Mustered out July 31, 1861.

2nd REGIMENT INFANTRY (3 YEARS).—Org. at Trenton May 27, 1861. June, 1861, 2 Brig., Runyon's Res. Div., McDowell's Army, N. E. Va. Aug., 1861, Kearney's Brig., Div. Potomac. Oct., 1861, Kearney's Brig., Franklin's Div., Potomac. March, 1862, 1 Brig., 1 Div., 1 Corps, Potomac. April, 1862, 1 Brig., 1 Div., Dept. Rappahannock. May, 1862, 1 Brig., 1 Div., 6 Corps, Potomac. Mustered out June 21, 1864.

2nd REGIMENT VETERAN INFANTRY.—Org. at Trenton April 15, 1865. April, 1865, 1 Brig., 1 Div., 6 Corps, Potomac. Mustered out July 11, 1865.

3rd REGIMENT INFANTRY (3 MONTHS).—Org. at Trenton April 27, 1861. May, 1861, Runyon's N. J. Brig., Def. Washington. June, 1861, 1 Brig., Runyon's Res. Div., McDowell's Army, N. E. Va. Mustered out July 31, 1861.

3rd REGIMENT INFANTRY (3 YEARS).—Org. at Trenton May 25, 1861. June, 1861, 2 Brig., Runyon's Res. Div., McDowell's Army, N. E. Va. Aug., 1861, Kearney's Brig., Div. Potomac. Oct., 1861, Kearney's Brig., Franklin's Div., Potomac. March, 1862, 1 Brig., 1 Div., 1 Corps, Potomac. April, 1862, 1 Brig., 1 Div., Dept. Rappahannock. May, 1862, 1 Brig., 1 Div., 6 Corps, Potomac. Mustered out June 23, 1864.

3rd VETERAN BATTALION INFANTRY.—Org. at Burke's Station, Va., near Petersburg, Va., Dec. 17, 1864. Dec., 1864, 1 Brig., 1 Div., 6 Corps, Potomac. Mustered out June 29, 1865.

4th REGIMENT INFANTRY (3 MONTHS).—Org. at Trenton April 25, 1861. May, 1861, Runyon's N. J. Brig., Def. Washington. June, 1861, 1 Brig., Runyon's Res. Div., McDowell's Army, N. E. Va. Mustered out July 31, 1861.

4th REGIMENT INFANTRY (3 YEARS).—Org. at Trenton Aug. 9, 1861. Aug., 1861, Kearney's Brig., Div. Potomac. Oct., 1861, Kearney's Brig., Franklin's Div., Potomac. March, 1862, 1 Brig., 1 Div., 1 Corps, Potomac. April, 1862, 1 Brig., 1 Div., Dept. Rappahannock. May, 1862, 1 Brig., 1 Div., 6 Corps, Potomac. July, 1864, 1 Brig., 1 Div., 6 Corps, Middle Mil. Div. Dec., 1864, 1 Brig., 1 Div., 6 Corps, Potomac. Mustered out July 9, 1865.

5th REGIMENT INFANTRY.—Org. at Trenton Aug. 17, 1861. Sept., 1861, Casey's Prov'l Brig., Div. Potomac. Oct., 1861, 3 Brig., Hooker's Div., Potomac. March, 1862, 3 Div., 2 Div., 3 Corps, Potomac. March, 1864, 1 Brig., 4 Div., 2 Corps, Potomac. May, 1864, 3 Brig., 3 Div., 2 Corps, Potomac. Mustered out by transfer to 7th N. J., Nov. 6, 1864.

6th REGIMENT INFANTRY.—Org. at Trenton Aug. 24, 1861. Sept., 1861, Casey's Prov'l Brig., Div. Potomac. Oct., 1861, 3 Brig., Hooker's Div., Potomac. March, 1862, 3 Brig., 2 Div., 3 Corps, Potomac. March, 1864, 1 Brig., 4 Div., 2 Corps, Potomac. May, 1864, 3 Brig., 3 Div., 2 Corps, Potomac. Mustered out Sept. 7, 1864. Vets. and recruits to 8th N. J. Infy.

7th REGIMENT INFANTRY.—Org. at Trenton Aug. 27, 1861. Sept., 1861, Casey's Prov'l Brig., Div. Potomac. Oct., 1861, 3 Brig., Hooker's Div., Potomac. March, 1862, 3 Brig., 2 Div., 3 Corps, Potomac. March, 1864, 1 Brig., 4 Div., 2 Corps, Potomac. May, 1864, 3 Brig., 3 Div., 2 Corps, Potomac. Mustered out July 17, 1865.

8th REGIMENT INFANTRY.—Org. at Trenton Aug. 22 to Sept. 14, 1861. Sept., 1861, Casey's Prov'l Brig., Div. Potomac. Oct., 1861, 3 Brig., Hooker's Div., Poto-

mac. March, 1862, 3 Brig., 2 Div., 3 Corps, Potomac. March, 1864, 1 Brig., 4 Div., 2 Corps, Potomac. May, 1862, 3 Brig., 3 Div., 2 Corps, Potomac. Mustered out July 17, 1865.

9th REGIMENT INFANTRY.—Org. at Trenton Sept. 13 to Oct. 15, 1861. Nov., 1861, 3 Brig., Casey's Div., Potomac. Jany., 1862, 2 Brig., Burnside's N. C. Exp. Corps. April, 1862, 1 Brig., 3 Div., Dept. N. C. July, 1862, 2 Brig., 1 Div., Dept. N. C. Dec., 1862, Heckman's Brig., Dept. N. C. Jany., 1863, 1 Brig., 2 Div., 18 Corps, Dept. N. C. Feby., 1863, 1 Brig., 1 Div., 18 Corps, Dept. South. April, 1863, Dist. Beaufort, N. C., 18 Corps, Dept. N. C. June, 1863, Jourdan's Indpt. Brig., Dept. N. C. July, 1863, Dist. Beaufort, N. C. Oct., 1863, Heckman's Command, Newport News, Va., Dept. Va. and N. C. Jany., 1864, 3 Brig., Heckman's Div., Portsmouth, Va., Dept. Va. and N. C. March, 1864, 2 Brig., Portsmouth, Va., Dept. Va. and N. C. April, 1864, 1 Brig., 2 Div., 18 Corps, Army James. Sept., 1864, Dist. Beaufort, N. C., Dept. Va. and N. C. Jany., 1865, Sub-Dist. Beaufort, N. C., Dept. N. C. Feby., 1865, 1 Brig., 1 Div., Dist. Beaufort, N. C., Dept. N. C. March, 1865, 2 Brig., Div. Dist. Beaufort, N. C. April, 1865, 2 Brig., 3 Div., 23 Corps, Dept. N. C. Mustered out July 12, 1865.

10th REGIMENT INFANTRY.—Org. at Beverly Oct. 9, 1861. Dec., 1861, Wadsworth's Command, Def. Washington, and 22 Corps. April, 1863, 3 Brig., 1 Div., 7 Corps, Dept. Va. July, 1863, Phila., Pa., Dept. Susquehanna. Sept., 1863, Pottsville, Pa., Dept. Susquehanna. Nov., 1863, Sub-Dist. Carbon, Dept. Susquehanna. April, 1864, 1 Brig., 1 Div., 6 Corps, Potomac, and Army Shenandoah, Middle Mil. Div. Mustered out July 1, 1865.

11th REGIMENT INFANTRY.—Org. at Trenton Aug. 15, 1862. Sept., 1862, Whipple's Command, Def. Washington. Nov., 1862, 1 Brig., 2 Div., 3 Corps, Potomac. March, 1864, 1 Brig., 4 Div., 2 Corps, Potomac. May, 1864, 3 Brig., 3 Div., 2 Corps. Mustered out July 5, 1865.

12th REGIMENT INFANTRY.—Org. at Woodbury Sept. 4, 1862. Sept., 1862, Unatt., Balto., Md., 8 Corps, Middle Dept. Dec., 1862, 2 Brig., 3 Div., 2 Corps, Potomac. March, 1864, 3 Brig., 2 Div., 2 Corps, Potomac. Mustered out July 15, 1865.

13th REGIMENT INFANTRY.—Org. at Newark Aug. 25, 1862. Sept., 1862, 3 Brig., 2 Div., Banks' 2 Corps, Army Va. Sept., 1862, 3 Brig., 1 Div., 12 Corps, Potomac. Oct., 1863, 3 Brig., 1 Div., 12 Corps, Cumb'd. April, 1864, 2 Brig., 1 Div., 20 Corps, Cumb'd. Mustered out June 8, 1865.

14th REGIMENT INFANTRY.—Org. at Freehold Aug. 26, 1862. Sept., 1862, Def. Balto., Md., 8 Corps, Middle Dept. Jany., 1863, 3 Separate Brig., 8 Corps. June, 1863, 3 Prov'l Brig., French's Div., 8 Corps. July, 1863, 1 Brig., 3 Div., 3 Corps, Potomac. March, 1864, 1 Brig., 3 Div., 6 Corps, Potomac, and Army Shenandoah, Middle Mil. Div. Mustered out June 18, 1865.

15th REGIMENT INFANTRY.—Org. at Camp Fair Oaks Aug. 25, 1862. Aug., 1862, Def. Washington, D. C. Oct., 1862, 1 Brig., 1 Div., 6 Corps, Potomac, and Army Shenandoah, Middle Mil. Div. Mustered out June 22, 1865.

16th REGIMENT.—(See 1st REGIMENT CAVALRY.)

17th REGIMENT INFANTRY.—(Failed to complete organization.)

18th REGIMENT INFANTRY.—(Failed to complete organization.)

19th REGIMENT INFANTRY.—(Failed to complete organization.)

20th REGIMENT INFANTRY.—(Failed to complete organization.)

21st REGIMENT INFANTRY.—Org. at Trenton Sept. 22, 1862. Sept., 1862, 3 Brig., 2 Div., 6 Corps, Potomac. Mustered out June 19, 1863.

22nd REGIMENT INFANTRY.—Org. at Trenton Sept. 22, 1862. Sept., 1862, Dist. Washington, D. C. Oct., 1862, Prov'l Brig., Casey's Div., Def. Washington. Dec., 1862, Patrick's Command, Provost Guard, Army Potomac. Jany., 1863, 3 Brig., 1 Div., 1 Corps, Potomac. Mustered out June 27, 1863.

23rd REGIMENT INFANTRY.—Org. at Beverly Sept. 13, 1862. Sept., 1862, 1 Brig., 1 Div., 6 Corps, Potomac. Mustered out June 27, 1863.

24th REGIMENT INFANTRY.—Org. at Beverly Sept. 16, 1862. Sept., 1862, Dist. Washington, D. C. Oct., 1862, Prov'l Brig., Casey's Div., Def. Washington. Dec., 1862, 1 Brig., 3 Div., 2 Corps, Potomac. Mustered out June 29, 1863.

25th REGIMENT INFANTRY.—Org. at Beverly Sept. 18, 1862. Oct., 1862, 2 Brig., Casey's Div., Dept. Washington, D. C. Dec., 1862, 1 Brig., 3 Div., 9 Corps, Potomac. Feby., 1863, 3 Brig., 3 Div., 9 Corps, Potomac. April, 1863, 3 Brig., 2 Div., 7 Corps, Dept. Va. Mustered out June 20, 1863.

26th REGIMENT INFANTRY.—Org. at Camp Frelinghausen Sept. 18, 1862. Oct., 1862, 2 Brig., 2 Div., 6 Corps, Potomac. Mustered out June 27, 1863.

27th REGIMENT INFANTRY.—Org. at Camp Frelinghausen Sept. 19, 1862. Oct., 1862, 2 Brig., Casey's Div., Def. Washington. Dec., 1862, 2 Brig., 1 Div., 9 Corps, Potomac. Mustered out July 2, 1863.

28th REGIMENT INFANTRY.—Org. at Freehold Sept. 22, 1862. Oct., 1862, Prov'l Brig., Casey's Div., Def. Washington. Dec., 1862, 1 Brig., 3 Div., 2 Corps, Potomac. Mustered out July 6, 1863.

29th REGIMENT INFANTRY.—Org. at Freehold Sept. 22, 1862. Sept., 1862, Dist. Washington, D. C. Oct., 1862, Prov'l Brig., Casey's Div., Def. Washington. Dec., 1862, Patrick's Command, Provost Guard, Army Potomac. Dec., 1862, 3 Brig., 1 Div., 1 Corps, Potomac. Mustered out July 6, 1863.

30th REGIMENT INFANTRY.—Org. at Camp Kearney Sept. 17, 1862. Sept., 1862, Dist. Washington, D. C. Oct., 1862, Prov'l Brig., Casey's Div., Def. Washington, D. C. Dec., 1862, Patrick's Command, Provost Guard, Army Potomac. Dec., 1862, 3 Brig., 1 Div., 1 Corps, Potomac. Mustered out June 27, 1863.

31st REGIMENT INFANTRY.—Org. at Camp Kearney Sept. 17, 1862. Sept., 1862, Dist. Washington, D. C. Oct., 1862, Prov'l Brig., Casey's Div., Def. Washington. Dec., 1862, Patrick's Command, Provost Guard, Army Potomac. Dec., 1862, 3 Brig., 1 Div., 1 Corps, Potomac. Mustered out June 24, 1863.

32nd REGIMENT.—(See 2nd REGIMENT CAVALRY.)

33rd REGIMENT INFANTRY.—Org. at Newark Aug. 29, 1863. Sept., 1863, 1 Brig., 2 Div., 11 Corps, Potomac. Oct., 1863, 1 Brig., 2 Div., 11 Corps, Cumb'd. April, 1864, 2 Brig., 2 Div., 20 Corps, Cumb'd. Mustered out July 17, 1865.

34th REGIMENT INFANTRY.—Org. at Trenton Sept. 2, 1863, to Nov. 9, 1863. Dec., 1863, Dist. Columbus, Ky., 6 Div., 16 Corps, Tenn. Aug., 1864, Dist. Paducah, Ky., Dept. Ohio. Feby., 1865, 3 Brig., 2 Div., 16 Corps, Mil. Div. West. Miss. Aug., 1865, Dist. Ala., Dept. Gulf. Mustered out April 10, 1866.

35th REGIMENT INFANTRY.—Org. at Flemmington Sept. 15, 1863. Oct., 1863, Prov'l Brig., Casey's Div., 22 Corps, Def. Washington. Nov., 1863, Dist. Columbus, Ky., 6 Div., 16 Corps, Tenn. Jany., 1864, 1 Brig., 4 Div., 16 Corps, Tenn. March, 1864, 2 Brig., 4 Div., 16 Corps, Tenn. Sept., 1864, 2 Brig., 1 Div., 17 Corps, Tenn. Mustered out July 20, 1865.

36th REGIMENT.—(See 3rd REGIMENT CAVALRY.)

37th REGIMENT INFANTRY.—Org. at Trenton June 23, 1864. July, 1864, Unatt., 10 Corps, Army James, Dept. Va. and N. C. Mustered out Oct. 1, 1864.

38th REGIMENT INFANTRY.—Org. at Trenton Sept. 23, 1864. Sept., 1864, Separate Brig., Army James, Dept. Va. and N. C. Garrison duty at Fort Powhatan. Mustered out June 30, 1865.

39th REGIMENT INFANTRY.—Org. at Newark Oct. 3, 1864. Oct., 1864, Benham's Engr. Brig., City Point, Va. Oct., 1864, 1 Brig., 2 Div., 9 Corps, Potomac. Mustered out June 17, 1865.

40th REGIMENT INFANTRY.—Org. at Trenton Feby. 2, 1865. Feby., 1865, 1 Brig., 1 Div., 6 Corps, Potomac. Mustered out July 13, 1865.

NEW MEXICO

1st REGIMENT CAVALRY.—Org. May 31, 1862, by consolidation of 1st, 2nd, 4th and 5th New Mexico Infy. Attached to Dept. New Mexico. Mustered out Sept. 30, 1866.

1st BATTALION CAVALRY AND INFANTRY.—Org. from 1st Cav., Aug. 31, 1866. Mustered out Nov. 23, 1867.

GRAYDON'S CAVALRY COMPANY.—Org. at Fort Craig Oct. 29, 1861. Mustered out Jany. 29, 1862.

GRAYDON'S CAVALRY COMPANY (REORGANIZED).—Org. at Fort Craig. Feby. 9, 1862. Mustered out April 29, 1862.

MINK'S CAVALRY COMPANY.—Org. at Santa Fe July 20, 1861. Mustered out Oct. 29, 1861.

HASPELL'S CAVALRY COMPANY.—Org. at Albuquerque July 23, 1861. Mustered out Oct. 30, 1861.

VILAL'S CAVALRY COMPANY.—Org. at Santa Fe July 12, 1861. Mustered out Oct. 12, 1861.

1st REGIMENT INFANTRY.—Org. at Fort Union and Santa Fe July 1 to Aug. 13, 1861. Mustered out May 31, 1862. Reorg. Oct. 1, 1863, Dept. New Mexico. Mustered out Nov. 7, 1866.

1st REGIMENT MILITIA INFANTRY.—Org. at large, New Mexico. Nov., 1861. Mustered out Feby., 1862.

2nd REGIMENT INFANTRY.—Org. at Santa Fe July-Aug., 1861. Mustered out May 31, 1862.

3rd REGIMENT INFANTRY.—Org. at Fort Union and Albuquerque Aug. 30 to Oct. 10, 1861. Mustered out March 20, 1862.

4th REGIMENT INFANTRY.—Org. Fort Union Sept., 1861. Mustered out May 31, 1862.

5th REGIMENT INFANTRY.—Org. at Albuquerque Nov., 1861. Mustered out May 31, 1861.

PEREA'S BATTALION MILITIA INFANTRY.—Org. at large, New Mexico, Nov.-Dec., 1861. Mustered out Feby. 28, 1862.

ALARID'S COMPANY MILITIA INFANTRY.—Org. at Santa Fe Dec. 10, 1861. Mustered out Feby. 28, 1862.

GONZALES' COMPANY MILITIA INFANTRY.—Org. at Fort Craig Nov. 23, 1861. Mustered out Feby., 1862.

MORA'S COMPANY MILITIA INFANTRY.—Org. at Mora Nov. 14, 1861. Mustered out Feby., 1862.

TAFFOLA'S COMPANY MILITIA INFANTRY.—Org. at Fort Craig Nov. 20, 1861. Mustered out Feby., 1862.

NEW YORK

1st REGIMENT "LINCOLN" CAVALRY.—Org. at New York July 16 to Aug. 31, 1861. July, 1861, Def. Washington and Alexandria. Oct., 1861, Franklin's and Heintzelman's Divs., Potomac. March, 1862, 1 Div., 1 Corps, Potomac. April, 1862, 1 Div., Dept. Rappahannock. May, 1862, Cav., 6 Corps, Potomac. July, 1862, 1 Cav. Brig., Potomac. Sept., 1862, 4 Brig., Cav. Div., Potomac. Oct., 1862, Averill's Cav. Command, 8 Corps, Middle Dept. Nov., 1862, 2 Brig., Def. Upper Potomac, 8 Corps. Jany., 1863, Milroy's Command, Winchester, Va. March, 1863, 1 Brig., 2 Div., 8 Corps. March, 1863, 3 Brig., 2 Div., 8 Corps. June, 1863, Pierce's Brig., Dept. Susquehanna. Aug., 1863, McReynold's Brig., Dept. W. Va. Nov., 1863, Cav. Brig., 1 Div., W. Va. April, 1864, 1 Brig., 1 Cav. Div., W. Va. June, 1864, 2 Brig., 1 Cav. Div., W. Va. July, 1864, 1 Brig., 1 Div. Cav., W. Va. Aug., 1864, 2 Brig., 2 Cav. Div., W. Va. Dec., 1864, 3 Brig., 3 Div., Cav. Corps, Middle Mil. Div., and Potomac. Mustered out June 27, 1865.

1st REGIMENT VETERAN CAVALRY.—Org. at Geneva July 31 to Nov. 19, 1863. Aug., 1863, Cav. Div., Def. Washington, 22 Corps. Feby., 1864, Cav. Brig., 1 Div., W. Va. April, 1864, 1 Brig., 1 Cav. Div., W. Va. July, 1864, 2 Brig., 1 Cav. Div., W. Va. Aug., 1864, 1 Brig., 1 Cav. Div., W. Va. Aug., 1864, Cumb'd, Md. Oct., 1864, 1 Separate Brig., Dist. Kanawha, W. Va. Mustered out July 20, 1865.

1st REGIMENT MOUNTED RIFLES (ALSO DESIGNATED 7th CAVALRY).—First two Co.'s org. at N. Y. City and mustered in at Fortress Monroe, Va., July 30, 1861. Other Co.'s org. at Newburg and N. Y. City, Sept. 18, 1861, to Aug., 1862. July, 1861, Fort Monroe, Va.,

Dept. Va. May, 1862, Unatt., Dept. Va. July, 1862, Unatt., Div. at Suffolk, 7 Corps, Dept. Va. April, 1863, Cav., 7 Corps, Dept. Va. July, 1863, Cav. Brig., U. S. Forces, Portsmouth, Va., Dept. Va. and N. C. Oct., 1863, U. S. Forces, Yorktown, Va., Dept. Va. and N. C. April, 1864, Unatt., Army James, Dept. Va. and N. C. July, 1864, Cav. Brig., Dept. Va. and N. C. Oct., 1864, 3 Brig., Kautz's Cav. Div., Dept. Va. and N. C. March, 1865, Headqrs. Dept. Va. April, 1865, Dist. East. Va., Dept. Va. Consolidated with 3d Cav. July 21, 1865.

1st REGIMENT DRAGOONS.—Org. Sept. 10, 1863, from 19th Cav., which see.

1st REGIMENT PROVISIONAL CAVALRY.—Org. June 17, 1865, by consolidation of the 10th and 24th Regts. Cav. Mustered out July 19, 1865.

2nd REGIMENT CAVALRY.—(HARRIS LIGHT). Org. Aug. 9 to Oct. 8, 1861. Oct., 1861, McDowell's Div., Potomac. March, 1862, King's 3 Div., 1 Corps, Potomac. April, 1862, King's Div., Dept. Rappahannock. June, 1862, Bayard's Cav. Brig., 3 Corps, Army Va. Sept., 1862, Bayard's Cav. Brig., Potomac (Co's A, D, I, K, 3 Div., 1 Corps, Potomac, to Oct., 1862). Dec., 1862, Gregg's Cav. Brig., Potomac. Feby., 1863, 1 Brig., 3 Div., Cav. Corps, Potomac. (May, 1863, Unatt., Yorktown, Va., 4 Corps, Dept. Va., Battn. June, 1863, 1 Brig., 1 Div., 4 Corps, Battn.), 2 Brig., 2 Div., Cav. Corps, Potomac Regt. (July, 1863, King's Div., 22 Corps, Battn.) Aug., 1863, 1 Brig., 3 Div., Cav. Corps, Potomac, and Middle Mil. Div. Mustered out June 5, 1865.

2nd REGIMENT VETERAN CAVALRY.—Org. at Saratoga Springs, and mustered in by Co's., Aug. 15 to Dec. 30, 1863. Aug., 1863, Cav. Div., Dept. Washington, 22 Corps. Feby., 1864, 5 Brig., Cav. Div., 19 Corps, Gulf. June, 1864, 4 Brig., Cav. Div., Gulf. Aug., 1864, Separate Cav. Brig., Gulf. Dec., 1864, Separate Cav. Brig., Reserve Corps, Mil. Div. West Miss. Feby., 1865, Separate Cav. Brig., Dist. West Fla., M. D. W. M. March, 1865, 1 Brig., Lucas Cav. Div., M. D. W. M. April, 1865, 3 Brig., 1 Div., Cav. Corps, West Miss. July, 1865, Dept. Ala. Mustered out Nov. 8, 1865.

2nd REGIMENT MOUNTED RIFLES.—Org. at Lockport and Buffalo, and mustered in by Co's. Oct. 31, 1863, to Feby. 13, 1864. March, 1864, Def. Washington, 22 Corps. May, 1864, Prov'l Brig., 1 Div., 9 Corps, Potomac. June, 1864, 3 Brig., 1 Div., 9 Corps. June, 1864, 1 Brig., 2 Div., 9 Corps. Sept., 1864, 2 Brig., 2 Div., 9 Corps. Nov., 1864, 3 Brig., 2 Div., Cav. Corps, Potomac. May, 1865, Dept. Va. Mustered out Aug. 10, 1865.

2nd REGIMENT PROVISIONAL CAVALRY.—Org. June 17, 1865, by consolidation of the 6th and 15th Regts. Cavalry. Mustered out Aug. 9, 1865.

3rd REGIMENT CAVALRY.—Org. in New York at large and mustered in at Washington, D. C., Sept. 9, 1861. Oct., 1861, Banks' Div. and Stone's Div., Potomac. March, 1862, Def. Washington. April, 1862, Unatt., Dept. N. C. Dec., 1862, Unatt., 18 Corps, Dept. N. C. May, 1863, Cav. Brig., 18 Corps. July, 1863, Def. Newberne, N. C., Dept. Va. and N. C. Oct., 1863, Heckman's Command, Newport News, Va., Dept. Va. and N. C. April, 1864, 1 Brig., Kautz's Cav. Div., Dept. Va. and N. C. Dec., 1864, Norfolk, Va., Dept. Va. Jany., 1865, Portsmouth, Va., Dept. Va. March, 1865, Suffolk, Va., Dept. Va. June, 1865, Norfolk, Va. Consolidated with 1st Mounted Rifles, July 21, 1865, to form 4th Prov'l Cav.

3rd REGIMENT PROVISIONAL CAVALRY.—Org. June 23, 1865, by consolidation of 13th and 16th Regts. Cavalry. Mustered out Sept. 21, 1865.

4th REGIMENT CAVALRY.—Org. at New York City, Aug. 10 to Nov. 15, 1861. Oct., 1861, Blenker's Div., Potomac. March, 1862, Blenker's 2 Div., 2 Corps, Potomac. April, 1862, Blenker's Div., Dept. Mts. May, 1862, Advance Brig., Mt. Dept. June, 1862, Buford's Cav. Brig., 1 Corps, Army Va. Sept., 1862, Cav. Brig., 11 Corps, Potomac. Feby., 1863, 1 Brig., 2 Div., Cav. Corps, Potomac. June, 1863, 2 Brig., 2 Div., Cav. Corps, Potomac. Aug., 1863, 2 Brig., 1 Div., Cav. Corps, Potomac, and Middle Mil. Div. Consolidated with 9th Cavalry, Feby. 27, 1865.

4th REGIMENT PROVISIONAL CAVALRY.—Org. July

21, 1865, by consolidation of 1st Mounted Rifles and 3rd Cavalry. Mustered out Nov. 29, 1865.

5th REGIMENT CAVALRY.—(1st IRA HARRIS GUARD).—Org. at New York City, and mustered in Aug. 15 to Oct. 31, 1861. Nov., 1861, Dix's Command, Balto., Md. March, 1862, Banks' 5 Corps. April, 1862, Hatch's Cav. Brig., Dept. Shenandoah. June, 1862, Hatch's Cav. Brig., 2 Corps, Army Va. Sept., 1862, Wyndham's Cav. Brig., Def. Washington. Feby., 1863, Price's Indpt. Cav. Brig., 22 Corps. April, 1863, 3 Brig., Stahel's Cav. Div., 22 Corps. June, 1863, 1 Brig., 3 Div., Cav. Corps, Potomac. Aug., 1864, 1 Brig., 3 Div., Cav. Corps, Middle Mil. Div. March, 1865, Cav. Brig., Army Shenandoah. Mustered out July 19, 1865.

6th REGIMENT CAVALRY.—Org. at New York City, Sept. 12 to Dec. 19, 1861. Dec., 1861, York, Pa. March, 1862, Wadsworth's Command, Mil. Dist. Washington. (Co's. D, K, with 2 Corps, Potomac. March, 1862, to July, 1863, Co's. F, H, with 4 Corps, Potomac. March, 1862, to Aug., 1863, and in Def. Washington, 22 Corps, to Oct., 1863.) Aug., 1862, Unatt. Cav., 9 Corps, Potomac. Dec., 1862, 2 Brig., Pleasanton's Cav. Div., Potomac. Feby., 1863, 2 Brig., 1 Div., Cav. Corps, Potomac, and Middle Mil. Div. Consolidated with 15th Cav., June 17, 1865, to form 2nd Prov'l Cavalry.

7th REGIMENT CAVALRY.—(See 1st Mounted Rifles).

8th REGIMENT CAVALRY.—Org. at Rochester, and mustered in Nov. 23, 1861. Dec., 1861, Cav. Brig., Potomac. March, 1862, Cav., Banks' 5 Corps. April, 1862, Hatch's Cav. Brig., Dept. Shenandoah. May, 1862, R. R. Brig., Middle Dept. July, 1862, R. R. Brig., 8 Corps, Middle Dept. Sept., 1862, 5 Brig., Pleasanton's Cav. Div., Potomac. Nov., 1862, 1 Brig., Pleasanton's Cav. Div., Potomac. Feby., 1863, 1 Brig., 1 Div., Cav. Corps, Potomac. March, 1864, 2 Brig., 3 Div., Cav. Corps, Potomac and Middle Mil. Div. Mustered out June 27, 1865.

9th REGIMENT CAVALRY.—Org. at Westfield and Albany, Sept. 9 to Nov. 19, 1861. Nov., 1861, Wadsworth's Command, Mil. Dist. Washington. March, 1862, Arty. Reserve, Potomac. May, 1862, Def. Washington. June, 1862, Cav. Brig., 1 Corps, Army Va. Sept., 1862, Cav. Brig., 11 Corps, Potomac. Feby., 1863, 1 Brig., 1 Div., Cav. Corps, Potomac. June, 1863, 2 Brig., 1 Div., Cav. Corps, Potomac, and Middle Mil. Div. Mustered out June 17, 1865.

10th REGIMENT CAVALRY.—Org. at Elmira, Sept. 27, 1861. Dec., 1861, Gettysburg, Pa. March, 1862, Def. Balto., Md. April, 1862, Mil. Dist. Washington. Aug., 1862, Bayard's Cav. Brig., 3 Corps, Army Va. Sept., 1862, Bayard's Cav. Brig., Potomac. Feby., 1863, 1 Brig., 3 Div., Cav. Corps, Potomac. June, 1863, 3 Brig., 2 Div., Cav. Corps, Potomac. Aug., 1863, 2 Brig., 2 Div., Cav. Corps, Potomac. May, 1864, 1 Brig., 2 Div., Cav. Corps, Potomac. Consolidated with 24th Cavalry, June 17, 1865, to form 1st Prov'l Cav.

11th REGIMENT CAVALRY.—Org. at New York City, Dec., 1861, to May, 1862. May, 1862, Wadsworth's Command, Mil. Dist. Washington. Feby., 1863, Mil. Dist. Washington, 22 Corps. March, 1864, Dist. LaFourche, Dept. Gulf. Aug., 1864, 2 Brig., Cav. Div., Gulf. Feby., 1865, 2 Brig., Cav. Div., Dist. West Tenn., Dept. Cumb'd. June, 1863, 1 Brig., Cav. Div., Dist. West Tenn. July, 1865, Dist. Memphis, Tenn. Mustered out Sept. 30, 1865.

12th REGIMENT CAVALRY.—Org. at New York City, Nov., 1862, to Sept., 1863. May, 1863, Cav. Brig., 18 Corps, Dept. N. C. July, 1863, Def. Newberne, N. C., Dept. Va. and N. C. Oct., 1863, Heckman's Command, Newport News, Va., Dept. Va. and N. C. Jany., 1864, Dist. Albemarle, N. C., Dept. Va. and N. C. Feby., 1864, Palmer's Brig., Peck's Div., Dept. Va. and N. C. Jany., 1865, Sub Dist. Newberne, Dept. N. C. March, 1865, Cav. Div., Dist. Beaufort, N. C., Dept. N. C. April, 1865, Kilpatrick's Cav. Div., Dept. N. C. Mustered out July 19, 1865.

13th REGIMENT CAVALRY.—Org. at Staten Island, June 20, 1863. June, 1863, Cav. Brig., 22 Corps. Dec., 1863, Tyler's Div., 22 Corps. Jany., 1864, 3 Brig., Tyler's Div., 22 Corps. May, 1864, Cav. Brig., 22 Corps. Nov.,

1864, 1st Separate Brig., 22 Corps. Consolidated with 16th Cav. to form 3rd Prov'l Cav., June 23, 1865.

14th REGIMENT CAVALRY.—Org. at New York City, Nov. 24, 1862, to July 18, 1863. March, 1863, Def. New Orleans, La., Dept. Gulf. May, 1863, Grierson's Cav. Div., Gulf. July, 1863, Def. New Orleans, Gulf. Sept., 1863, 1 Brig., Cav. Div., 19 Corps, Gulf. Nov., 1863, 3 Brig., Cav. Div., 19 Corps. Jany., 1864, 1 Brig., Cav. Div., 19 Corps. July, 1864, Dist. Baton Rouge, Gulf. Dec., 1864, Separate Cav. Brig., Dist. Baton Rouge, Gulf. Feby., 1865, Dist. Morganzia, Gulf. April, 1865, Def. New Orleans. May, 1865, 1 Brig., 2 Div., Cav. Corps, Mil. Dist. W. Miss. (Co. M at Pensacola, Fla., Dist. West Fla., Sept., 1863, to Feby., 1865.) Consolidated with 18th Cav., June 12, 1865.

15th REGIMENT CAVALRY.—Org. at Syracuse, Aug. 26, 1863, to Jany. 24, 1864. Sept., 1863, Def. Washington, 22 Corps. Jany., 1864, Cav. Brig., 1 Div., W. Va. April, 1864, 2 Brig., 1 Cav. Div., W. Va. June, 1864, 1 Brig., 1 Cav. Div., W. Va. July, 1864, 2 Brig., 1 Cav. Div., W. Va. Aug., 1864, Remount Camp Cumb'd, Md. Aug., 1864, 1 Brig., 1 Div. Cav., W. Va. Sept., 1864, 2 Brig., 3 Div., Cav. Corps, Middle Mil. Div. March, 1865, 2 Brig., 3 Div., Cav. Corps, Potomac. Consolidated with 6th Cav., June 17, 1865, to form 2nd Prov'l Cav.

16th REGIMENT CAVALRY.—Org. at Plattsburg, June 19, to Sept. 5, 1863. Aug., 1863, Cav. Brig., 22 Corps. Oct., 1863, DeRussy's Div., South Potomac, 22 Corps. Dec., 1863, 4 Brig., DeRussy's Div., 22 Corps. March, 1864, Cav. Brig., 22 Corps. Nov., 1864, 1st Separate Brig., 22 Corps. Consolidated with 13th Cav., June 23, 1865, to form 3rd Prov'l Cav.

17th REGIMENT CAVALRY.—(Failed to complete organization.)

18th REGIMENT CAVALRY.—Org. at New York, July 18, 1863, to Jany., 1864. Sept., 1863, Def. Washington, 22 Corps. Dec., 1863, Cav. Div., 22 Corps. March, 1864, 5 Brig., Cav. Div., Gulf. June, 1864, Dist. LaFourche, Dept. Gulf. Jany., 1865, Dist. Bonnet Carre, Southern Dist. La., Dept. Gulf. May, 1865, 1 Brig., 2 Cav. Div., Mil. Dist. W. Miss. Sept., 1865, Dept. Texas. Mustered out May 31, 1866.

19th REGIMENT CAVALRY.—(1st DRAGOONS). Org. Aug. 11, 1863, from 130th Inftry. Aug., 1863, Unatt., Cav. Corps, Potomac. Oct., 1863, Reserve Brig., 1 Div., Cav. Corps, Potomac, and Middle Mil. Div. Sept., 1864, 2 Brig., 1 Div., Cav. Corps, M. D. M. March, 1865, 2 Brig., 1 Div., Cav. Corps, Potomac. Mustered out June 30, 1865.

20th REGIMENT CAVALRY.—Org. at Sackett's Harbor, Sept. 3 to Sept. 23, 1863. Nov., 1863, U. S. Forces, Portsmouth, Va., Dept. Va. and N. C. Jany., 1864, Heckman's Div., 18 Corps. April, 1864, Def. Portsmouth, Va., Dept. Va. and N. C. May, 1864, Dist. East. Va., Dept. Va. and N. C. Dec., 1864, 1 Brig., Kautz's Cav. Div., Dept. Va. and N. C. April, 1865, Cav. Brig., Dept. Va. (Co. D with Separate Brig., Def. Bermuda Hundred, Va. Dec., 1864, to June, 1865, Co. F at Fort Powhattan, Separate Brig., Def. Bermuda Hundred, Va. Dec., 1864, to June, 1865, Co. G, with 1 Brig., Mackenzie's Cav. Div., Army James. March to June, 1865, Co. I, with Prov'l Div., Army James, March to June, 1865.) Mustered out July 31, 1865.

21st REGIMENT CAVALRY.—Org. at Troy, and mustered in by Co's. Aug. 28, 1863, to Jan., 1864. Sept., 1863, Def. Washington, 22 Corps. Jany., 1864, Cav. Brig., 1 Div., W. Va. April, 1864, 1 Brig., 1 Cav. Div., W. Va. Aug., 1864, Cumb'd, Md., W. Va. Aug., 1864, 2 Brig., 1 Cav. Div., W. Va. Nov., 1864, 1 Brig., 2 Div. Cav., W. Va. March, 1865, Tibbett's Command, Harper's Ferry, W. Va. May, 1865, Dept. Washington. June, 1865, Dept. Mo. Mustered out June 23 to Aug. 31, 1866.

22nd REGIMENT CAVALRY.—Org. at Rochester and mustered in by Co's. Dec. 20, 1863, to Feby. 23, 1864. March, 1864, Cav., 9 Corps, Potomac. April, 1864, 4 Div., 9 Corps, Potomac. May, 1864, 2 Brig., 3 Div., Cav. Corps, Potomac, and Middle Mil. Div., March, 1865, Cav. Brig., Army Shenandoah. Mustered out Aug. 1, 1865.

23rd REGIMENT CAVALRY.—Only two Co's. org. Jany. to May, 1863. May, 1863, Cav. Brig., 18 Corps, Dept. N. C. July, 1863, Def. Newberne, Dept. N. C. and Va. Oct., 1863, Sub Dist. Beaufort, N. C., Dept. Va. and N. C. Jany., 1865, Sub Dist. Newberne, Dept. N. C. Mustered out July 22, 1865.

24th REGIMENT CAVALRY.—Org. at Auburn, and mustered in by Co's. Dec. 28, 1863, to Jany. 26, 1864. Feby., 1864, Def. Washington, 22 Corps. April, 1864, Marshall's Prov'l Brigade, 1 Div., 9 Corps, Potomac. June, 1864, 3 Brig., 1 Div., 9 Corps, Potomac. June, 1864, 2 Brig., 3 Div., 9 Corps. Sept., 1864, 2 Brig., 1 Div., 9 Corps. Oct., 1864, 1 Brig., 2 Div., Cav. Corps, Potomac. Consolidated with 10th Cav., June 17, 1865, to form 1st Prov'l Cav.

25th REGIMENT CAVALRY.—Org. at Saratoga Springs and Hart's Island, N. Y. Mustered in by Co's. Feby. 20, to Oct. 20. 1864. April, 1864, Def. Washington, 22 Corps. June, 1864, Provost Guard, Army Potomac. July, 1864, Def. Washington, 22 Corps. Aug., 1864, 3 Brig., 1 Div., Cav. Corps, Middle Mil. Div. Sept., 1864, 1 Brig., 1 Div., Cav. Corps, Middle Mil. Div. Jany., 1865, Unatt., 2nd Infy. Div., W. Va. Mustered out June 27, 1865.

26th REGIMENT CAVALRY.—Org. at Plattsburg, Feby. 11, to Feby. 24, 1865. Service on borders of New York. Mustered out June 26 to July 7, 1865.

DEVIN'S COMPANY, 1st CAVALRY N. Y. S. M.—Org. for three months, and mustered in at Washington, D. C., July 14, 1861. Mustered out Oct. 23, 1861.

SAUERS' CO. C HUSSARS, 3rd CAVALRY N. Y. S. M.—Vol. for three months, July, 1861. Mustered out Nov. 2, 1861.

ONEIDA INDEPENDENT COMPANY CAVALRY.—Org. at Oneida, and mustered in Sept. 4, 1861. Sept., 1861, Stoneman's Cav. Command, Potomac. April, 1862, Headqrs. Army Potomac. Mustered out June 13, 1865.

2nd REGIMENT HEAVY ARTILLERY.—Org. at Staten Island, and mustered in by Co's., Sept. 18 to Dec. 12, 1861. Dec., 1861, Mil. Dist. Washington, D. C. May, 1862, Sturgis' Command, Mil. Dist. Washington. Jany., 1863, Arty. Def. Alexandria, Va. Feby., 1863, Arty. Def. Alexandria, 22 Corps. April, 1863, 1 Brig., DeRussy's Div., 22 Corps. April, 1864, 2 Brig., DeRussy's Div., 22 Corps. May, 1864, Tyler's Heavy Arty. Div., 2 Corps, Potomac. May. 1864, 1 Brig., 1 Div., 2 Corps, Potomac. June, 1865, 1 Brig., DeRussy's Div., 22 Corps. Mustered out Sept. 29, 1865.

4th REGIMENT HEAVY ARTILLERY.—Org. at New York, Nov., 1861, to Feby., 1862. Feby., 1862, Mil. Dist. Washington, D. C. May, 1862, Whipple's Command, Def. Washington. Oct., 1862, Abercrombie's Div., Def. Washington. Feby., 1863, Abercrombie's Div., 22 Corps. April, 1863, 1 Brig., DeRussy's Div., 22 Corps. May, 1863, 4 Brig., DeRussy's Div., 22 Corps. Dec., 1863, 3 Brig., DeRussy's Div., 22 Corps. March, 1864, Arty. Brig., 6 Corps, Potomac, Co's. C, D, L, M; Arty. Brig., 5 Corps, Potomac, Co's E, F, H, K; Arty. Brig., 2 Corps, Potomac, Co's. A, B, G, I. May 31, 1864, Arty. Brig., 2 Corps. June 25, 1864, Arty. Reserve, Potomac, 1 Brig., 3 Div., 2 Corps, Co's. C, D, L, M, to July 13, 1864. 2 Brig., 3 Div., 2 Corps, Co's. E, F, H, K, to July 13, 1864. Aug., 1864, Unatt., 1 Div., 2 Corps. Sept., 1864, 4 Brig., 1 Div., 2 Corps. March, 1865, 2 Brig., 1 Div., 2 Corps. June, 1865, 3 Brig., DeRussy's Div., 22 Corps. Aug., 1865, 2 Brig., Dept. Washington. (C with Arty. Brig., 2 Corps, Oct., 1864, to May, 1865. D with Arty. Brig., 2 Corps, July to Dec., 1864. L with Arty. Brig., 2 Corps, July, 1864, to March, 1865.) Mustered out Aug. 16, 1865.

4th REGIMENT NATIONAL GUARD HEAVY ARTILLERY.—Raised in New York, and mustered in at Harrisburg, Pa., June 20, 1863. Mustered out July 24, 1863.

5th REGIMENT HEAVY ARTILLERY.—Org. by consolidation of 1st and 2nd Jackson Heavy. March 6, 1862, 6th Battalion (3rd Battalion, Black River Heavy Arty.). Assigned Dec. 31, 1862. May, 1862, Def. Balto., Md., 8 Corps, Middle Dept. (Co's. A, F, at Harper's Ferry, Va., June to Sept., 1862.) Jany., 1863, 2nd Separate Brig., 8 Corps. (Co's. I, K, L, M, Dec., 1862, 3 Brig., Haskin's Div., North of the Potomac, Def. Washington. Feby., 1863,

3 Brig., Haskin's Div., 22 Corps. May, 1863, 1 Brig., De-Russy's Div., Def. Washington, South Potomac, 22 Corps. Nov., 1863, Reserve Div., Harper's Ferry, Va., Dept. W. Va., to Oct., 1864.) April, 1864, 1 Brig., 1 Div., W. Va. (1st Battalion). June, 1864, 1 Brig., 1 Div., W. Va. (2nd Battalion). July, 1864, Res. Div., Dist. Harper's Ferry, W. Va. Jany., 1865, 2 Brig., 3 Infy. Div., W. Va. April, 1865, 2 Brig., 2 Div., W. Va. Mustered out July 19, 1865.

6th REGIMENT HEAVY ARTILLERY.—Org. as 135th Infy. at Yonkers, and mustered in Sept. 2, 1862. Designated 6th H. A. Oct. 3, 1862. Sept., 1862, Def. Balto., Md., 8 Corps, Middle Dept. Jany., 1863, Def. Upper Potomac, 8 Corps. March, 1863, 2 Brig., 1 Div., 8 Corps. June, 1863, 3 Prov'l Brig., French's Div., 8 Corps. July, 1863, 1 Brig., 3 Div., 3 Corps, Potomac. Aug., 1863, Arty. Res., Potomac, and Ammunition Train Guard, Army Potomac. April, 1864, 1 Brig., Arty. Res., Potomac. May, 1864, Kitchen's Indpt. Brig., 5 Corps, Potomac. June, 1864, 3 Brig., 2 Div., 5 Corps. Aug., 1864, 1 Brig., Hardin's Div., 22 Corps. Sept., 1864, Kitching's Prov'l Div., Middle Mil. Div. Dec., 1864, Prov'l Div., Dept. Va. and N. C. Dec., 1864, 2 Brig., Prov'l Div., Army James. Jany., 1865, 2 Brig., Infy. Div., Def. Bermuda Hundred, Va. March, 1865, 2 Brig., Ferrero's Div., Dept. Va. May, 1865, Sub Dist. Roanoke Dist., Nottaway, Dept. Va. Mustered out Aug. 24, 1865.

7th REGIMENT HEAVY ARTILLERY.—Org. from 113th N. Y. Infy., Dec. 19, 1862. Dec., 1862, Def. North Potomac, Washington, D. C. Feby., 1863, 2 Brig., Haskin's Div., 22 Corps. May, 1864, Tyler's Heavy Arty. Div., 2 Corps, Potomac. May, 1864, 4 Brig., 1 Div., 2 Corps. Nov., 1864, 2 Brig., 1 Div., 2 Corps. Feby., 1865, Def. Balto., Md., 8 Corps, Middle Dept. Mustered out Aug. 1, 1865.

8th REGIMENT HEAVY ARTILLERY.—Org. from 129th N. Y. Infy., Oct. 19, 1862. Oct., 1862, Def. Balto., Md., 8 Corps, Middle Dept. Jany., 1863, 2nd Separate Brig., 8 Corps. July, 1863, 2 Brig., Md. Heights Div., W. Va. July, 1863, 2nd Separate Brig., 8 Corps. May, 1864, Tyler's Heavy Arty. Div., 2 Corps, Potomac. May 29, 1864, 4 Brig., 2 Div., 2 Corps. June, 1864, 2 Brig., 2 Div., 2 Corps. Mustered out June 5, 1865.

9th REGIMENT HEAVY ARTILLERY.—Org. from 138th N. Y. Infy., Dec. 9, 1862. Dec., 1862, 2 Brig., Def. Washington, North Potomac. Feby., 1863, 2 Brig., Haskin's Div., 22 Corps. April, 1864, 3 Brig., Haskin's Div., 22 Corps. May, 1864, 2 Brig., 3 Div., 6 Corps, Potomac. (2nd Battalion detached with Arty. Brig., 3 Corps, Potomac, May 31 to June 10, 1864, with 1 Brig., Hardin's Div., 22 Corps, to Sept. 23, 1864, with Keim's Prov'l Brig., to Oct. 13, 1864.) Consolidated to 4 Co's. and transferred to 2nd Heavy Arty., June 27, 1865.

10th REGIMENT HEAVY ARTILLERY.—Org. by consolidation of 4th, 5th and 7th Battalions Black River Heavy Arty. at Sackett's Harbor, Sept. 11 to Dec. 22, 1862. Sept., 1862, 3 Brig., Haskin's Div., Def. Washington. Feby., 1863, 3 Brig., Haskin's Div., 22 Corps. March, 1864, 3 Brig., DeRussy's Div., 22 Corps. May, 1864, 2 Brig., 3 Div., 18 Corps, Dept. Va. and N. C. June, 1864, 1 Brig., 2 Div., 18 Corps. Aug., 1864, 1 Brig., DeRussy's Div., 22 Corps. Sept., 1864, 2 Brig., Kitching's Prov'l Div., Middle Mil. Div. Dec., 1864, 2 Brig., Prov'l Div., Def. Bermuda Hundred, Va., Dept. Va. and N. C. Jany., 1865, 2 Brig., Ferrero's Div., Army James. March, 1865, 2 Brig., Ferrero's Div., Dept. Va. June, 1865, Dist. Nottaway, Dept. Va. Mustered out June 27, 1865.

11th REGIMENT HEAVY ARTILLERY.—Only 4 Co's. organized, July, 1863. Transferred to 4th Heavy Arty., as 3d Battalion, July 25, 1863.

12th REGIMENT HEAVY ARTILLERY.—(Failed to complete organization.)

13th REGIMENT MILITIA HEAVY ARTILLERY.—Raised in New York and Org. at Suffolk, Va., May 28, 1862. Mustered out Sept. 28, 1862.

13th REGIMENT HEAVY ARTILLERY.—Org. at N. Y. and mustered in at Elmira by Co's. Aug. 4, 1863, to March 14, 1864. Oct., 1863, Def. Norfolk and Portsmouth, Va., Dept. Va. and N. C. (1st and 2nd Battalions). Naval Brigade, Dept. Va. and N. C. (3d Battalion). May, 1864,

3 Div., 18 Corps, Co's. A, H. Jany., 1865, Def. Bermuda Hundred, Va., Army James. Mustered out July 18, 1865.

14th REGIMENT HEAVY ARTILLERY.—Org at Rochester and mustered in by Co's. Aug. 29, 1863, to Jany. 17, 1864. Oct., 1863, Forts N. Y. Harbor. April, 1864, Marshall's Prov'l Brig., 1 Div., 9 Corps, Potomac. June, 1864, 3 Brig., 1 Div., 9 Corps. June, 1864, 2 Brig., 1 Div., 9 Corps. Sept., 1864, 3 Brig., 1 Div., 9 Corps. June, 1865, 1 Brig., Hardin's Div., 22 Corps. Mustered out Aug. 26, 1865.

15th REGIMENT HEAVY ARTILLERY.—Org. from 3rd Battalion, German Heavy Arty., Sept. 30, 1863. Sept., 1863, 2 Brig., DeRussy's Div., 22 Corps. Dec., 1863, 4 Brig., DeRussy's Div., 22 Corps. Feby., 1864, Arty. Res., Army Potomac. March, 1864, 1 Brig., Arty. Res., Potomac. May, 1864, Kitching's Indpt. Brig., 5 Corps, Potomac. June, 1864, 3 Brig., 2 Div., 5 Corps. Aug., 1864, 1 Brig., 2 Div., 5 Corps. May, 1865, 4 Brig., DeRussy's Div., 22 Corps. June, 1865, 1 Brig., DeRussy's Div., 22 Corps. (Co. F attached to Arty. Res., Potomac, June to Dec., 1864. Co. M attached to Arty. Brig., 5 Corps, Jany. to June, 1865.) Mustered out Aug. 22, 1865.

16th REGIMENT HEAVY ARTILLERY.—Org. in N. Y. State and mustered in by Co's. Sept. 28, 1863, to Feby. 2, 1864. Jany., 1864, Fort Monroe, Yorktown and Gloucester Point, Va., Dept. Va. and N. C. July, 1864, 1 Brig., 3 Div., 10 Corps, Army James. Co's. E, H, 2 Brig., 1 Div., 10 Corps, A, B, C, F, G, K, M. Dec., 1864, Separate Brig., Fort Pocohontas, Va. E, H, 2 Brig., 1 Div., 24 Corps, A, B, C, F, G, K, M. Jany., 1865, 2 Brig., 1 Div., Terry's Prov'l Corps, Dept. N. C., A, B, C, F, G, K, M. March, 1865, 2 Brig., 1 Div., 10 Corps, Army Ohio, Dept. N. C., A, B, C, F, G, K, M. July, 1865, 3 Brig., DeRussy's Div., 22 Corps. (Co. L attached to 2 Brig., 1 Div., 10 Corps, Oct. to Dec., 1864, then to Arty. Brig., 24 Corps, to July, 1865.) Regiment mustered out Aug. 21, 1865.

3rd BATTALION GERMAN HEAVY ARTILLERY.—Org. at N. Y. City Oct. 14 to Dec. 19, 1861. Dec., 1861, Def. Washington. March, 1862, Mil. Dist. Washington. May, 1862, Whipple's Command, Mil. Dist. Washington. Feby., 1863, 1 Brig., DeRussy's Div., 22 Corps. June, 1863, 2 Brig., DeRussy's Div., 22 Corps. Transferred to 15th Heavy Arty., Sept. 30, 1863.

4th BATTALION.—(1st BATTALION BLACK RIVER ARTY.) HEAVY ARTILLERY.—Org. at Sackett's Harbor and mustered in Sept. 18, 1862. Transferred to 10th Heavy Arty., Dec. 31, 1862.

5th BATTALION (2nd BATTALION BLACK RIVER ARTY.) HEAVY ARTILLERY.—Org. at Sackett's Harbor and mustered in Sept. 11, 1862. Sept., 1862, Def. Washington, North of Potomac. Oct., 1862, 3 Brig., Def. Washington, North of Potomac. Transferred to 10th Heavy Arty., Dec. 31, 1862.

6th BATTALION (3rd BATTALION BLACK RIVER ARTY.) HEAVY ARTILLERY.—Org. at Sackett's Harbor, Sept., 1862. Sept., 1862, Def. Washington, North of Potomac. Oct., 1862, 3 Brig., Def. Washington, North of Potomac. Transferred to 5th Heavy Arty., Dec. 31, 1862.

7th BATTALION (4th BATTALION BLACK RIVER ARTY.) HEAVY ARTILLERY.—Org. at Sackett's Harbor, Sept., 1862. Sept., 1862, Def. Washington, North of Potomac. Oct., 1862, 3 Brig., Def. Washington, North of Potomac. Transferred to 10th N. Y. Heavy Arty. as Co's. I, K, L, M, Dec. 31, 1862.

1st BATTALION LIGHT ARTILLERY, BATTERY A.—Org at New York City and mustered in Aug. 26, 1861. Oct., 1861, Arty. Res., Potomac. May, 1862, 3 Brig., Arty. Res., 5 Corps, Potomac. Sept., 1862, Arty. Res., 5 Corps. Dec., 1862, Arty. Res., Potomac. Designation changed to 29th N. Y. Indpt. Battery March 5, 1863.

1st BATTALION LIGHT ARTILLERY, BATTERY "B." —Org. at New York City and mustered in Aug. 12, 1861. Oct., 1861, Arty. Res., Potomac. May, 1862, 3 Brig., Arty. Res., 5 Corps, Potomac. Sept., 1862, Arty Res., 5 Corps. Dec., 1862, Arty Res., Potomac. Designation changed to 30th N. Y. Indpt. Battery, Light Arty., March 5, 1863.

1st BATTALION LIGHT ARTILLERY, BATTERY "C." —Org. at New York City Sept. 11, 1861. Oct., 1861, Arty. Res., Potomac. May, 1862, 3 Brig., Arty. Res., 5 Corps,

Potomac. Sept., 1862, Arty. Res., 5 Corps. Dec., 1862, Arty. Res., Potomac. Designation changed to 31st N. Y. Indpt. Battery, Light Arty., March 5, 1863.

1st BATTALION LIGHT ARTILLERY, BATTERY "D."—Org. at New York City Sept. 20, 1861. Oct., 1861, Arty. Res., Potomac. May, 1862, 3 Brig., Arty. Res., 5 Corps, Potomac. Sept., 1862, Arty. Res., 5 Corps. Dec., 1862. Arty. Res., Potomac. Designation changed to 32nd Indpt. Battery, N. Y. Light Arty., March 5, 1863.

1st BATTALION NATIONAL GUARD LIGHT ARTILLERY.—Org. for 100 days Aug. 2, 1864. Stationed at Elmira, N. Y. Mustered out Nov. 22, 1864.

1st MARINE ARTILLERY.—Naval Brig., Org. at New York City, and mustered in Nov. 12, 1861. April, 1862, Unatt., Newberne, N. C., Dept. N. C. Dec., 1862, Unatt., 18 Corps, Dept. N. C. Jany., 1863, Arty. Brig., 18 Corps. Disbanded March, 1863.

ANTHON'S BATTALION LIGHT ARTILLERY.—Org. not completed, the several Co's. consolidated and designated 20th and 28th N. Y. Indpt. Batteries, Light Arty.

"BARRY'S" ROCKET BATTALION.—Org. at Albany, N. Y., Dec. 6-7, 1861. Dec., 1861, Def. Washington. April, 1862, Newberne, N. C., Dept. N. C. Nov., 1862, Arty. Brig., Dept. N. C. Discontinued Nov. 1, 1862,. Co. A designated 23rd, and Co. B 24th Indpt. N. Y. Battys.

2nd BATTALION LIGHT ARTILLERY.—4 Co's. Org. at New York City and mustered in Dec. 9, 1861. Consolidated to two Co's. Dec. 21, 1861.

BATTERY "A."—Org. from orig. Co's. B and D, Dec. 21, 1861. Dec., 1861, Def. Washington. March, 1862, Arty., 1 Div., 2 Corps, Potomac. Broken up May, 1862, and sections assigned to Batty. C, 4th U. S. Arty., and to Battys. B and G, 1st N. Y. Arty.

BATTERY "B."—Org. from original Co's. A and C, Dec. 21, 1861. Dec., 1861, Def. Washington. March, 1862, Williams' 1 Div., Banks' 5 Corps. April, 1862, Doubleday's Brig., Dept. Rappahannock. June, 1862, Res. Arty., Army Va. Sept., 1862, Relay House, 8 Corps. Designated 15th N. Y. Indpt. Battery, Light Arty., Oct., 1862.

1st REGIMENT LIGHT ARTILLERY.—

BATTERY "A."—Org. at Utica and mustered in Sept. 12, 1861. Nov., 1861, Def. Washington. March, 1862, Arty., 3 Div., 4 Corps, Potomac. Guns captured May 31, 1862. Men transferred June 15, 1862, to Battys. D and H, 1st N. Y. Arty., and to 7th and 6th N. Y. Indpt. Battys. Battery reorganized at Utica Jany., 1864, Camp Barry, Def. Washington, and 22 Corps. June, 1863, Whipple's Brig., Sigel's Div., Dept. Susquehanna. Jany., 1864, Lehigh Dist., Dept. Susquehanna. May, 1864, Harrisburg, Pa., Dept. Susquehanna. Aug., 1864, Dist. Monongahelia, Dept. Susquehanna. Oct., 1864, Chambersburg, Pa., Dept. Susquehanna. Nov., 1864, Allegheny City, Pa., Dept. Susquehanna. Dec., 1864, Dist. Philadelphia, Dept. Susquehanna. Mustered out June 28, 1865.

BATTERY "B."—Org. at Elmira and mustered in Aug. 30, 1861. Nov., 1861, Sumner's Div., Potomac. March, 1862, Arty., 1 Div., 2 Corps, Potomac. May, 1863, Arty. Brig., 2 Corps. June, 1863, 1 Vol. Brig., Arty. Res., Potomac. July, 1863, Arty Brig., 2 Corps. July, 1863, 2 Vol. Brig., Arty. Res., Potomac. Dec., 1863, Arty. Res., Potomac. Jany., 1864, 1 Brig., Arty Res., Potomac. March, 1864, 3 Brig., Arty Res., Potomac. May, 1864, Arty. Brig., 5 Corps, Potomac. Mustered out June 18, 1865.

BATTERY "C."—Org. at Elmira and mustered in Sept. 6, 1861. Nov., 1861, Wadsworth's Command, Def. Washington. Sept., 1862, Arty., 3 Div., 5 Corps, Potomac. May, 1863, Arty Brig., 5th Corps, Potomac. April, 1864, 3 Brig., Arty. Res., Potomac. May, 1864, Arty. Brig., 5 Corps. March, 1865, Arty Res., Potomac. Mustered out June 17, 1865.

BATTERY "D."—Org. at Elmira and mustered in Sept. 6, 1861. Nov., 1861, Arty. Res., Potomac. March, 1862, Arty., 2 Div., 3 Corps, Potomac. July, 1863, Arty. Brig., 3 Corps. Dec., 1862, Arty., 1 Div., 9 Corps, Potomac. Feby., 1863, Arty., 2 Div., 3 Corps, Potomac. May, 1863, Arty. Brig., 3 Corps, Potomac. March, 1865, Arty. Brig., 5 Corps, Potomac. Mustered out June 16, 1865.

BATTERY "E."—Org. at Elmira and mustered in Sept. 13, 1861. Nov., 1861, Smith's Div., Potomac. March, 1862, Arty., 2 Div., 4 Corps, Potomac. May, 1862, Arty., 2 Div., 6 Corps, Potomac. June, 1863, Arty. Brig., 1 Corps, Potomac. March, 1864, Arty. Brig., 5 Corps, Potomac. March, 1865, Arty. Res., Potomac. April, 1865, Arty. Brig., 5 Corps. Mustered out June 6, 1865.

BATTERY "F."—Org. at Elmira and mustered in Sept. 14, 1861. Nov., 1861, Franklin's Div., Potomac. March, 1862, Arty., 1 Div., 1 Corps, Potomac. April, 1862, Arty., 1 Div., Dept. Rappahannock. May, 1862, Arty., 1 Div., 6 Corps, Potomac. June, 1862, Arty. Res., Yorktown, Va., 4 Corps. Dec., 1862, Res. Arty., Yorktown, Va., 7 Corps, Dept. Va. May, 1863, Unatt. Arty., 4 Corps, Dept. Va. July, 1863, Camp Barry, Def. Washington, 22 Corps. May, 1864, 2 Brig., DeRussy's Div., 22 Corps. July, 1864, 3 Brig., DeRussy's Div., 22 Corps. Dec., 1864, 1 Brig., DeRussy's Div., 22 Corps. Mustered out June 17, 1865.

BATTERY "G."—Org. at Elmira and mustered in Sept. 24, 1861. Nov., 1861, Sumner's Div., Potomac. March, 1862, Richardson's 1 Div., 2 Corps, Potomac. May, 1862, Unatt., Arty. Res., 5 Corps, Potomac. June, 1862, Res. Arty., 2 Corps. Nov., 1862, Arty., 3 Div., 2 Corps. May, 1863, 1 Vol. Brig., Arty Res., Potomac. June, 1863, 4 Vol. Brig., Arty. Res., Potomac. Aug., 1863, Arty. Brig., 2 Corps. Sept., 1864, Arty. Res., Potomac, attached to 2 Corps. Jany., 1865, Arty. Res., Potomac, attached to 9 Corps. Mustered out June 19, 1865.

BATTERY "H."—Org. at Elmira and mustered in Oct. 10, 1861. Nov., 1861, Casey's Div., Potomac. March, 1862, Arty., 3 Div., 4 Corps, Potomac. June, 1862, Res. Arty., 4 Corps, Gloucester Point and Yorktown, Va. Dec., 1862, Res. Arty., Yorktown, 7 Corps, Dept. Va. May, 1863, Res. Arty., 4 Corps, Dept. Va. July, 1863, Def. Washington, 22 Corps. Oct., 1863, Arty. Brig., 1 Corps, Potomac. March, 1864, Arty. Brig., 5 Corps, Potomac. Mustered out June 19, 1865.

BATTERY "I."—Org. at Buffalo Oct., 1861. Oct., 1861, Blenker's Div., Potomac. March, 1862, 3 Brig., Blenker's Div., 2 Corps, Potomac. April, 1862, 3 Brig., Blenker's Div., Dept. Mountains. June, 1862, Res. Arty., 1 Corps, Army Va. July, 1862, 2 Brig., 2 Div., 1 Corps, Army Va. Sept., 1862, Arty., 2 Div., 11 Corps, Potomac. May, 1863, Arty. Brig., 11 Corps, Potomac. Oct., 1863, Arty. Brig., 11 Corps, Cumb'd. Jany., 1864, Arty., 2 Div., 11 Corps, Cumb'd. April, 1864, Arty., 1 Div., 20 Corps. July, 1864, Arty. Brig., 20 Corps. Mustered out June 23, 1865.

BATTERY "K."—Org. at Elmira and mustered in Nov. 20, 1861. Nov., 1861, Def. Washington. April, 1862, R. R. Brig., Middle Dept. May, 1862, 2 Brig., Sigel's Div., Dept. Shenandoah. June, 1862, Arty., 2 Div., 2 Corps, Army Va. Sept., 1862, Arty., 2 Div., 12 Corps, Potomac. Oct., 1862, Arty., 1 Div., 12 Corps. Feby., 1863, Def. Washington, 22 Corps. April, 1863, Arty., 1 Div., 12 Corps, Potomac. May, 1863, 4 Vol. Brig., Arty. Res., Potomac. July, 1863, 3 Vol. Brig., Arty. Res., Potomac. March, 1864, 1 Brig., Arty. Res., Potomac. March, 1864, Camp Barry, Def. Washington, 22 Corps. May, 1864, 1 Brig., DeRussy's Div., 22 Corps. July, 1864, 2 Brig., DeRussy's Div., 22 Corps. Oct., 1864, 1 Brig., DeRussy's Div., 22 Corps. Mustered out June 20, 1865.

BATTERY "L."—Org. at Rochester, Sept., 1861. Mustered in at Elmira, Nov. 17, 1861. Nov., 1861, Def. Washington. Feby., 1862, Dix's Div., Balto., Md. May, 1862, 1 Brig., Sigel's Div., Dept. Shenandoah. June, 1862, Arty., 1 Div., 3 Corps, Army Va. Sept., 1862, Arty., 1 Div., 1 Corps, Potomac. May, 1863, Arty. Brig., 1 Corps, Potomac. March, 1864, Arty. Brig., 5 Corps, Potomac. March, 1865, Arty. Res., Potomac. April, 1865, Arty. Brig., 5 Corps. Mustered out June 17, 1865.

BATTERY "M."—Org. at Lockport and mustered in at Rochester Nov. 15, 1861. Nov., 1861, Arty., Banks' Div., Potomac. March, 1862, Arty., Williams' 1 Div., Banks' 5 Corps. April, 1862, Arty., 1 Div., Dept. Shenandoah. June, 1862, Arty., 1 Div., 2 Corps, Army Va. Sept., 1862, Arty., 1 Div., 12 Corps, Potomac. May, 1863, Arty. Brig., 12 Corps, Potomac. Oct., 1863, Arty. Brig., 12 Corps, Cumb'd. April, 1864, Arty., 1 Div., 20 Corps. July, 1864, Arty. Brig., 20 Corps. Mustered out June 23, 1865.

3rd REGIMENT HEAVY ARTILLERY.—Org. from 19th N. Y. Infy., Dec. 11, 1861.

BATTERY "A."—Org. from "A" 19th Infy. Dec., 1861, Def. Washington. March, 1862, Unatt., Dept. N. C. Dec., 1862, Arty. Brig., Dept. N. C. Jany., 1863, Arty. Brig., 18 Corps, Dept. N. C. Feby., 1863, Arty. Heckman's 2 Div., 18 Corps, Dept. South. April, 1863, Def. Newberne, N. C., Dept. N. C. Mustered out June 2, 1863.

Battery reorganized and mustered in Sept. 23, 1864. Sept., 1864, Dist. N. C., Dept. Va. and N. C. Jany., 1865, Dist. Beaufort, N. C., Dept. N. C. March, 1865, Carter's Div., Prov'l Corps, Dept. N. C. Mustered out July 3, 1865.

BATTERY "B."—Org. from "B," 19th Infy. Dec., 1861, Def. Washington. Consolidated with Battys C and E, Dec., 1861.

BATTERY "B."—2nd. Org. at New York and mustered in Dec. 19, 1861. Dec., 1861, Def. Washington, D. C. March, 1862, Unatt., Dept. N. C. Dec., 1862, Arty. Brig., Dept. N. C. Jany., 1863, Arty. Brig., 18 Corps, Dept. N. C. Feby., 1863, Arty. Brig., 18 Corps, Dept. South. April, 1863, Guss' Brig., Seabrook Island, S. C., 10 Corps, Dept. South. June, 1863, Stevenson's Brig., Seabrook Island, S. C., 10 Corps. July, 1863, Arty., 1 Div., 10 Corps, Morris Island, S. C. Dec., 1863, Dist. Folly Island, S. C., 10 Corps. Feby., 1864, Arty., Northern Dist., Dept. South. Oct., 1864, 1st Separate Brigade, Dept. South. Nov., 1864, Arty. Brig., Coast Div., Dept. South. Jany., 1865, 1st Separate Brig., Northern Dist., Dept. South. March, 1865, 1st Separate Brig., Dist. Charleston, Dept. South. Mustered out July 13, 1865.

BATTERY "C."—Org. from "C," 19th Infy. Dec., 1861, Def. Washington. March, 1862, Unatt., Dept. N. C. Dec., 1862, Arty. Brig., Dept. N. C. Jany., 1863, Arty. Brig., 18 Corps, Dept. N. C. May, 1863, Def. Newberne, N. C., Dept. N. C. Mustered out June 2, 1863.

BATTERY "C."—2nd, Org. and mustered in Aug. 31, 1863. Sept., 1863, Def. Newberne, N. C., Dept. Va. and N. C. May, 1864, Sub Dist. Beaufort, N. C., Dept. Va. and N. C. Jany., 1865, Sub Dist. Beaufort, N. C., Dept. N. C. March, 1865, Arty., 1 Div., Dist. Beaufort, Dept. N. C. April, 1865, Dist. Newberne, Dept. N. C. Mustered out July 14, 1865.

BATTERY "D."—Org. from "D," 19th Infy. Dec., 1861, Def. Washington. March, 1862, Unatt., Dept. N. C. Dec., 1862, Arty. Brig., Dept. N. C. Jany., 1863, Arty. Brig., 18 Corps, Dept. N. C. Feby., 1863, Arty. Heckman's 2 Div., 18 Corps, Dept. South. April, 1863, Def. Newberne, N. C., 18 Corps, Dept. N. C. Mustered out June 2, 1863.

BATTERY "D."—2nd, Org. at Syracuse Feby., 1864. Feby., 1864, Def. Newberne, N. C., Dept. Va. and N. C. Jany., 1865, Dist. Newberne, N. C., Dept. N. C. Feby., 1865, Arty., 1 Div., Dist. Beaufort, N. C., Dept. N. C. March, 1865, Arty. Div., Dist. Beaufort, N. C., Dept. N. C. April, 1865, Res. Arty., 23 Corps, Dept. N. C. Mustered out July 5, 1865.

BATTERY "E."—Org. from "E," 19th Infy. Dec., 1861, Def. Washington. March, 1862, Unatt., Dept. N. C. Dec., 1862, Arty. Brig., Dept. N. C. Jany., 1863, Arty. Brig., 18 Corps, Dept. N. C. May, 1863, Def. Newberne, N. C., Dept. N. C. April, 1864, U. S. Forces, Yorktown, Pa., Dept. Va. and N. C. May, 1864, Arty., 3 Div., 18 Corps. June, 1864, Arty. Brig., 18 Corps. June, 1864, Arty., 1 Div., 10 Corps. Aug., 1864, Arty. Brig., 10 Corps. Oct., 1864, Arty. Brig., 18 Corps. Dec., 1864, Arty. Brig., 24 Corps. Mustered out July 24, 1865.

BATTERY "F."—Org. as 10th N. Y. Indpt. Batty. at Syracuse, and mustered in Dec., 1861. Dec., 1861, Def. Washington. March, 1862, Unatt., Dept. N. C. Dec., 1862, Arty. Brig., Dept. N. C. Jany., 1863, Arty. Brig., 18 Corps, Dept. N. C. Feby., 1863, Arty., St. Helena Island, S. C., 18 Corps, Dept. South. April, 1863, U. S. Forces, Folly Island, S. C., 10 Corps. July, 1863, Arty. Morris Island, S. C., 10 Corps. Nov., 1863, Folly Island, S. C., 10 Corps. March, 1864, Dist. Beaufort, S. C., Dept. South. Sept., 1864, Dist. Fla., Dept. South. Nov., 1864, Arty. Brig., Coast Div., Dept. South. Jany., 1865, 1st Separate Brig., Northern Dist., Dept. South. March, 1865, 1st Separate Brig., Dist. Charleston, Dept. South. Mustered out July 24, 1865.

BATTERY "G."—Org. from "G," 19th Infy. Dec., 1861, Def. Washington. March, 1862, Unatt., Dept. N. C. Dec., 1862, Arty. Brig., Dept. N. C. Jany., 1863, Arty. Brig., 18 Corps, Dept. N. C. May, 1863, Def. Newberne, N. C., 18 Corps. Mustered out June 2, 1863.

BATTERY "G."—2nd, Org. Feby., 1864. Feby., 1864, Def. Newberne, N. C., Dept. Va. and N. C. Feby., 1865, Arty. Div., Dist. Beaufort, N. C., Dept. N. C. April, 1865, Arty. Res., 23 Corps, Dept. N. C. Mustered out July 7, 1865.

BATTERY "H."—Org. at Rome, Feby. 22, 1862. Feby., 1862, Def. Washington. March, 1862, Unatt., Dept. N. C. Dec., 1862, Arty. Brig., Dept. N. C. Jany., 1863, Arty. Brig., 18 Corps, Dept. N. C. May, 1863, Arty., Def. Newberne, N. C., 18 Corps. Oct., 1863, Heckman's Command, Newport News, Va., Dept. Va. and N. C. Jany., 1864, U. S. Forces, Portsmouth, Va., Dept. Va. and N. C. June, 1864, Arty. Brig., 18 Corps, Army James. Aug., 1864, Arty. Brig., 10 Corps, Army James. Oct., 1864, Arty. Brig., 18 Corps. Dec., 1864, Arty. Brig., 24 Corps. Mustered out June 24, 1865.

BATTERY "I."—Org. as "I," 19th Infy. Dec., 1861, Def. Washington. March, 1862, Unatt., Dept. N. C. Dec., 1862, Arty. Brig., Dept. N. C. Jany., 1863, Arty. Brig., 18 Corps, Dept. N. C. May, 1863, Def. Newberne, Dept. N. C. Aug., 1863, Def. Newberne, N. C., Dept. Va. and N. C. Feby., 1865, Res. Arty. Div., Dist. Beaufort, Dept. N. C. April, 1865, Res. Arty., 23 Corps, Dept. N. C. Mustered out July 8, 1865.

BATTERY "K."—Org. at Auburn and mustered in Dec. 20, 1861. Dec., 1861, Def. Washington. March, 1862, Unatt., Dept. N. C. Dec., 1862, Arty. Brig., Dept. N. C. Jany., 1863, Arty. Brig., 18 Corps, Dept. N. C. May, 1863, Def. Newberne, N. C., Dept. N. C. April, 1864, U. S. Forces, Yorktown, Va., Dept. Va. and N. C. May, 1864, Arty., 1 Div., 18 Corps, Army James. May, 1864, Arty., 3 Div., 18 Corps. June, 1864, Arty. Brig., 18 Corps. Dec., 1864, Arty. Brig., 24 Corps. Mustered out June 30, 1865.

BATTERY "L."—Org. March 5, 1865, from 24th N. Y. Indpt. Batty. March, 1865, Dept. N. C. Mustered out July 7, 1865.

BATTERY "M."—Org. Jany. 24, 1862, from Co. I, 76th N. Y. Infy. Feby, 1862, Def. Washington. March, 1862, Unatt., Dept. N. C. Dec., 1862, Arty. Brig., Dept. N. C. Jany., 1863, Arty. Brig., 18 Corps, Dept. N. C. May, 1863, Def. Newberne, N. C., 18 Corps. Oct., 1863, Heckman's Command, Newport News, Va., Dept. Va. and N. C. Dec., 1863, Arty. Brig., U. S. Forces, Portsmouth, Va., Dept. Va. and N. C. April, 1864, Arty., 1 Div., 18 Corps, Army James. June, 1864, Arty., 3 Div., 18 Corps. June, 1864, Arty. Brig., 18 Corps. Dec., 1864, Arty. Brig., 24 Corps. Musterel out June 26, 1865.

BOOKWOOD'S BATTERY LIGHT ARTILLERY.—Org. June, 1861, from detachments of 8th and 29th N. Y. Infy. July, 1861, Blenker's Brig., Miles' Div., McDowell's Army, N. E. Va. Reorganized at Washington, D. C., Aug. 16, 1861, and designated 2nd N. Y. Indpt. Battery, Light Arty., Dec. 7, 1861.

VARIAN'S BATTERY LIGHT ARTILLERY.—(State Militia). Org. from 1st Troop, Washington Grays, April 19, 1861. April, 1861, Def. Washington. June, 1861, Keyes' Brig., Tyler's Div., McDowell's Army, N. E. Va. Mustered out July 20, 1861.

1st INDEPENDENT BATTERY LIGHT ARTILLERY.— Org. at Auburn and mustered in Nov. 23, 1861. Dec., 1861, W. F. Smith's Div., Potomac. March, 1862, Arty., 2 Div., 4 Corps, Potomac. May, 1862, Arty., 2 Div., 6 Corps, Potomac. May, 1863, Arty. Brig., 6 Corps, Potomac. July, 1864, Arty., 2 Div., 6 Corps, Middle Mil. Div. Sept., 1864, Arty. Brig., 6 Corps, Middle Mil. Div. Dec., 1864, Arty. Brig., 6 Corps, Potomac. Mustered out June 23, 1865.

2nd INDEPENDENT BATTERY LIGHT ARTILLERY. —(Blenker's Battery). Org. at Washington, D. C., from Bookwood's Battery, Aug. 16, 1861. Aug., 1861, Blenker's Brig. Div., Potomac. Oct., 1861, Blenker's Brig., Hooker's Div., Potomac. Nov., 1861, Blenker's Div., Potomac. March, 1862, Blenker's 2 Div., 2 Corps, Potomac. April,

1862, Blenker's Div., Dept. Mts. June, 1862, 1 Brig., 1 Div., 1 Corps, Army Va. Sept., 1862, Arty., 1 Div., 11 Corps, Potomac. March, 1863, Res. Arty., 11 Corps, Potomac. May, 1863, Arty. Brig., 11 Corps. Mustered out June 6, 1863.

3rd INDEPENDENT BATTERY LIGHT ARTILLERY.
—Org. from Co. D, 82nd N. Y. Infy. (2nd State Militia). Dec. 7, 1861. Dec. 1861, W. F. Smith's Div., Potomac. March, 1862, Arty., 2 Div., 4 Corps, Potomac. May, 1862, Arty., 2 Div., 6 Corps, Potomac. Aug., 1862, Arty., 1 Div., 4 Corps, Potomac. Sept., 1862, Arty., 3 Div., 6 Corps. Nov., 1862, Arty., 2 Div., 6 Corps. Jany., 1863, Arty., Light Div., 6 Corps. May, 1863, Arty., 2 Div., 6 Corps. June, 1863, Arty. Brig., 6 Corps. July, 1864, Arty. Res., Potomac. Dec., 1864, Arty. Brig., 6 Corps. Mustered out June 24, 1865.

4th INDEPENDENT BATTERY LIGHT ARTILLERY.
—Org. from Arty. Co. L, Serrell's N. Y. Engineers, Dec. 7, 1861. Dec., 1861, Hooker's Div., Potomac. March, 1862, Arty., 2 Div., 3 Corps, Potomac. May, 1863, Arty. Brig., 3 Corps, Potomac. July, 1863, 1 Vol. Brig., Arty. Res., Potomac. July, 1863, Camp Barry, Def. Washington, 22 Corps. Sept., 1863, 1 Vol. Brig., Arty. Res., Potomac. Broken up Dec. 4, 1863.

5th INDEPENDENT BATTERY LIGHT ARTILLERY.
—Org. at New York City and mustered in Nov. 8, 1861. Nov., 1861, Arty. Res., Potomac. May, 1862, Unatt., Arty. Res., 5 Corps, Potomac. Sept., 1862, Res. Arty., 5 Corps, Potomac. Dec., 1862, Arty. Res., Potomac. May, 1863, 2 Vol. Brig., Arty. Res., Potomac. Nov., 1863, 1 Vol. Brig., Arty. Res., Potomac. March, 1864, 2 Brig., Arty. Res., Potomac. May, 1864, Arty. Brig., 5 Corps. May, 1864, 1 Brig., DeRussy's Div., 22 Corps. July, 1864, Arty. Brig., 6 Corps, Middle Mil. Div. Aug., 1864, Arty., 1 Div., 19 Corps, Middle Mil. Div. Dec., 1864, Arty. Brig., 19 Corps. Feby., 1865, Arty. Res., Army Shenandoah. April, 1865, Arty. Res., Dept. Washington. Mustered out July 6, 1865.

6th INDEPENDENT BATTERY LIGHT ARTILLERY.
—Org. from Arty. Co. K, 83rd N. Y. Infy. (9th **Militia**), Dec. 7, 1861. Dec., 1861, Arty., Stone's Div., Potomac. Dec., 1861, Arty., Hooker's Div., Army Potomac. March, 1862, Arty., 2 Div., 3 Corps, Potomac. June, 1862, Res. Arty., 3 Corps, Potomac. Dec., 1862, Arty. Res., Potomac. Feby., 1863, Arty., 1 Div., Cav. Corps, Potomac. May, 1863, 1 Brig., Horse Arty., Potomac, attached to 2 Div., Cav. Corps, Potomac, to March, 1864. March, 1864, Horse Arty. Res., Potomac. June, 1864, Def. Washington, 22 Corps. Sept., 1864, Horse Arty., Middle Mil. Div., 1 Div., Cav. Corps. Dec., 1864, Horse Arty. Res., Army Shenandoah. April, 1865, Horse Arty. Brig., 22 Corps. Mustered out July 8, 1865.

7th INDEPENDENT BATTERY LIGHT ARTILLERY.
—Org. from Arty. Co., 56th N. Y. Infy., Dec. 7, 1861. Dec., 1861, Casey's Div., Potomac. March, 1862, Arty., 3 Div., 4 Corps, Potomac. June, 1862, Arty., 2 Div., 4 Corps, Potomac. Sept., 1862, Arty., Norfolk and Portsmouth, Va., 7 Corps, Dept. Va. July, 1863, Norfolk, Va., Dept. Va. and N. C. March, 1864, U. S. Forces, Yorktown, Va., Dept. Va. and N. C. April, 1864, Arty., 2 Div., 18 Corps, Army James. June, 1864, Arty. Brig., 18 Corps. Dec., 1864, Arty Brig., 24 Corps. Jany., 1865, Ferrero's Infy. Dif., Def. Bermuda Hundred, Va. April, 1865, Arty. Brig., 24 Corps. Mustered out July 22, 1865.

8th INDEPENDENT BATTERY LIGHT ARTILLERY.
—Org. from Co. 56th N. Y. Infy., Dec. 7, 1861. Dec., 1861, Casey's Div., Potomac. March, 1862, Arty., 3 Div., 4 Corps, Potomac. June, 1862, Res. Arty., 4 Corps, Yorktown, Va. Dec., 1862, Arty., Yorktown, Va., 7 Corps, Dept. Va. May, 1863, Unatt. Arty., Yorktown, Va., 4 Corps. June, 1863, 1 Brig., 1 Div., 4 Corps. July, 1863, Arty. Res., Dept. Va. and N. C., Yorktown, Va. Jany., 1864, U. S. Forces, Portsmouth, Va., Dept. Va. and N. C. (1 section with Kautz's Cav. Div., Dept. Va. and N. C., May, 1864). Mustered out June 30, 1865.

9th INDEPENDENT BATTERY LIGHT ARTILLERY.
—Org. from Co. F, 41st N. Y. Infy., Dec. 7, 1861. Dec., 1861, Def. Washington. Feby., 1863, 2 Brig., Haskin's Div., Def. Washington, 22 Corps. April, 1864, 3 Brig., Haskin's Div., 22 Corps. Mustered out June 13, 1864.

10th INDEPENDENT BATTERY LIGHT ARTILLERY.
—Org. Nov. and Dec., 1861. Transferred to 3rd N. Y. Arty. as Co. F, Jany. 21, 1862. Batty. reorganized at N. Y. City, and mustered in April 9, 1862. April, 1862, Wadsworth's Command, Def. Washington. June, 1862, Arty., 2 Corps, Army Va. Sept., 1862, Arty., 2 Div., 12 Corps, Potomac. Nov., 1862, Arty., 3 Div., 3 Corps, Potomac. May, 1863, Arty. Brig., 3 Corps, Potomac. June, 1863, 1 Vol. Brig., Arty. Res., Potomac. July, 1863, Camp Barry, Def. Washington, 22 Corps. Transferred to 6th N. Y. Batty., June 21, 1864.

11th INDEPENDENT BATTERY LIGHT ARTILLERY.
—Org. at Albany and mustered in Jany. 8, 1862. Jany., 1862, Wadsworth's Command, Def. Washington. Aug., 1862, Whipple's Command, Def. Washington. Nov., 1862, Arty., 3 Div., 3 Corps, Potomac. May, 1863, Arty. Brig., 3 Corps, Potomac. May, 1863, 4 Vol. Brig., Arty. Res., Potomac (attached to Batty. "K," 1st N. Y. Arty., to Jany., 1864). Jany., 1864, 2 Brig., Arty. Res., Potomac. April, 1864, 3 Brig., Arty. Res., Potomac. May, 1864, Arty. Brig., 2 Corps, Potomac. May, 1865, Arty. Res., Potomac. Mustered out June 13, 1865.

12th INDEPENDENT BATTERY LIGHT ARTILLERY.
—Org. at Albany and mustered in Jany. 14, 1862. Jany., 1862, Wadsworth's Command, Def. Washington. Feby., 1863, Def. Washington, 22 Corps. July, 1863, Arty. Brig., 3 Corps, Potomac. March, 1864, 2 Brig., Arty. Res., Potomac. May, 1864, Arty Brig., 2 Corps, Potomac. Sept., 1864, Arty. Res., Potomac. Mustered out June 14, 1865.

13th INDEPENDENT BATTERY LIGHT ARTILLERY.
—Org. at New York City, and mustered in Oct. 15, 1861. Oct., 1861, Baker's Brig., Stone's Div., Potomac. Dec., 1861, Blenker's Div., Potomac. March, 1862, Blenker's 2 Div., 2 Corps, Potomac. April, 1862, 2 Brig., Blenker's Div., Dept. Mts. June, 1862, 2 Brig., 2 Div., 1 Corps, Army Va. July, 1862, Res. Arty., 1 Corps, Army Va. Sept., 1862, Arty., 1 Div., 11 Corps, Potomac. May, 1863, Arty. Brig., 11 Corps, Potomac. Oct., 1863, Arty. Brig., 11 Corps, Cumb'd. March, 1864, Arty., 3 Div., 11 Corps. April, 1864, Arty., 2 Div., 20 Corps. July, 1864, Arty. Brig., 20 Corps. Sept., 1864, Unatt. Arty., Dept. Cumb'd. Dec., 1864, Tullahoma, Def. Nash. & Chatta. R. R. March, 1865, 2 Brig., 1 Sub Dist. Middle Tenn., Dept. Cumb'd. Mustered out July 28, 1865.

14th INDEPENDENT BATTERY LIGHT ARTILLERY.
—Org. Oct., 1862, from Batty. "A," 2nd Battalion Arty. 1st section with Batty. "C," 4th U. S. Arty., Oct., 1862, to Jany., 1863, and with Batty. "G," 1st N. Y. Arty. to Sept., 1863. 2nd section with Batty. "G," 1st N. Y. Arty., Oct., 1862, to Sept., 1863. 3rd section with Batty. "B," 1st N. Y. Arty., Oct., 1862, to Sept., 1863. Transferred to Battys. B and G, 1st N. Y. Arty., Sept. 7, 1863.

15th INDEPENDENT BATTERY LIGHT ARTILLERY.
—Org. Oct., 1862, from Batty. "B," 2nd Battalion Arty. Oct., 1862, 8 Corps, Middle Dept. Jany., 1863, Arty. Res., Potomac. May, 1863, 2nd Vol. Brig., Arty Res., Potomac. July, 1863, 1 Vol. Brig., Arty. Res., Potomac. Sept., 1863, 3 Vol. Brig., Arty. Res., Potomac. Dec., 1863, 2 Brig., Arty. Res., Potomac. May, 1864, Arty. Brig., 5 Corps, Potomac. Dec., 1864, Def. Washington, 22 Corps. Dec., 1864, Res. Div., Dept. W. Va. Transferred to 32nd N. Y. Batty., Feby. 4, 1865.

16th INDEPENDENT BATTERY LIGHT ARTILLERY.
—Org. at Binghampton and mustered in at Washington, D. C., March 27, 1862. March, 1862, Def. Washington. Oct., 1862, Arty. Camp, Def. Washington. Feby., 1863, Arty. Camp, 22 Corps. April, 1863, Unatt., Suffolk, Va., 7 Corps, Dept. Va. April, 1863, Res. Brig., 3 Div., 7 Corps. June, 1863, Wistar's Indpt. Brig., 7 Corps. July, 1863, U. S. Forces, Yorktown, Va., Dept. Va. and N. C. Oct., 1863, Heckman's Command, Newport News, Va., Dept. Va. and N. C. June, 1864, Arty. Brig., 18 Corps, Army James. Aug., 1864, Arty. Brig., 10 Corps. Oct., 1864, Arty. Brig., 18 Corps. Dec., 1864, Arty. Brig., 24 Corps. Jany., 1865, Arty., 2 Div., Terry's Prov'l Corps, Dept. N. C. March, 1865, Arty., 2 Div., 10 Corps, Army Ohio., Dept. N. C. Mustered out July 6, 1865.

17th INDEPENDENT BATTERY LIGHT ARTILLERY.
—Org. at Lockport and mustered in Aug. 26, 1862. Aug., 1862, Mil. Dist. Washington. Oct., 1862, Abercrombie's Div. Def. Washington. Feby., 1863, Abercrombie's Div., 22 Corps. June, 1863, Camp Barry, Def. Washington, 22 Corps. July, 1863, King's Div., 22 Corps. March, 1864, Camp Barry, 22 Corps. May, 1864, 2 Brig., DeRussy's Div., 22 Corps. July, 1864, Arty. Brig., 18 Corps, Army James. Dec., 1864, Arty. Brig., 24 Corps. Mustered out June 12, 1865.

18th INDEPENDENT BATTERY LIGHT ARTILLERY.
—Org. at Rochester and mustered in Sept. 13, 1862. Dec., 1862, Sherman's Div., Dept. Gulf. Jany., 1863, Arty., 2 Div., 19 Corps, Gulf. May, 1863, Arty., 1 Div., 19 Corps, Gulf. Aug., 1863, Def. New Orleans. Dec., 1863, Dist. Baton Rouge, Dept. Gulf. Feby., 1865, Siege Arty., Mil. Div. W. Miss. Mustered out July 20, 1865.

19th INDEPENDENT BATTERY LIGHT ARTILLERY.
—Org. at Lockport and mustered in at Elmira, Oct. 27, 1862. Oct., 1862, Def. Washington, 22 Corps. April, 1863, Unatt., Suffolk, Va., 7 Corps, Dept. Va. June, 1863, Arty., 1 Div., 7 Corps, Dept. Va. July, 1863, Camp Barry, Def. Washington, 22 Corps. March, 1864, Arty., 2 Div., 9 Corps, Potomac. July, 1864, Arty. Brig., 9 Corps, Potomac. Mustered out June 13, 1865.

20th INDEPENDENT BATTERY LIGHT ARTILLERY.
—Org. at New York City, Dec. 27, 1862. Jany., 1863, Garrison Forts in N. Y. Harbor, Dept. East. Mustered out July 31, 1865.

21st INDEPENDENT BATTERY LIGHT ARTILLERY.
—Org. at Oswego and mustered in at New York City, Dec. 12, 1862. Jany., 1863, Def. New Orleans, Dept. Gulf. May, 1863, Arty., 2 Div., 19 Corps, Gulf. July, 1863, Garrison Port Hudson, La., Gulf. July, 1864, Res. Arty., Gulf. Feby., 1865, Arty., 3 Div., Res. Corps, Mil. Div. West Miss. March, 1865, Arty., 3 Div., 13 Corps, M. D. W. M. Mustered out Sept. 8, 1865.

22nd INDPT. BATTERY LIGHT ARTILLERY.—Org. at Lockport and mustered in at Elmira, Oct. 28, 1862. Nov., 1862, Mil. Dist. Washington. Dec., 1862, 2 Brig., Def. North Potomac, Def. Washington. Assigned to 9th N. Y. H. A. as Co. M, Feby. 5, 1863.

23rd INDPT. BATTERY LIGHT ARTILLERY.—Org. from Battery A, Rocket Battalion, Nov. 1, 1862. Confirmed Feby. 11, 1863. Feby., 1863, Arty. Brig., 18 Corps, Dept. N. C. May, 1863, Dist. Pamlico, Dept. N. C. Feby., 1864, Def. Newberne, Dept. Va. and N. C. Feby., 1865, Dist. Beaufort, N. C., Dept. N. C. April, 1865, Kilpatrick's Cav. Div., Dept. N. C. Mustered out July 14, 1865.

24th INDPT. BATTERY LIGHT ARTILLERY.—Org. from Battery B, Rocket Battalion, Nov. 1, 1862. Confirmed Feby. 11, 1863. Feby., 1863, Arty. Brig., 18 Corps, Dept. N. C. May, 1863, Dist. Albemarle, Dept. N. C. Jany., 1864, Dist. Plymouth, N. C., Dept. Va. and N. C. Transferred to 3rd N. Y. Arty. as Battery L, March 8, 1865.

25th INDPT. BATTERY LIGHT ARTILLERY.—Org. at Lockport and mustered in Dec. 12, 1862. Jany., 1863, Def. New Orleans, Dept. Gulf. July, 1863, Arty. Res., Gulf. Aug., 1863, Arty., 4 Div., 19 Corps, Gulf. Dec., 1863, Arty. Res., Gulf. Feby., 1864, Arty., 1 Div., 19 Corps, Gulf. May, 1864, Def. New Orleans. June, 1864, Dist. LaFourche, Gulf. Dec., 1864, Southern Dist. La., Dept. Gulf. Mustered out Aug. 1, 1865.

26th INDPT. BATTERY LIGHT ARTILLERY.—Org. at Rochester, N. Y. Jany., 1863, Def. New Orleans, Dept. Gulf. June, 1863, Arty. Res., Gulf. Aug., 1863, Arty., 4 Div., 19 Corps, Gulf. Oct., 1863, Dist. LaFourche, Gulf. Feby., 1864, Arty., 2 Div., 19 Corps. Aug., 1864, Arty., 2 Div., 19 Corps, Gulf. Dec., 1864, Arty., Res. Corps, Mil. Div. West. Miss. Feby., 1865, Arty., 3 Div., Res. Corps, M. D. W. M. March, 1865, Arty., 3 Div., 13 Corps, M. D. W. M. July, 1865, Dept. Ala. Mustered out Aug. 12, 1865.

27th INDPT. BATTERY LIGHT ARTILLERY.—Org. at Buffalo and mustered in Dec. 17, 1862. Dec., 1862, Mil. Dist. Washington. Feby., 1863, Mil. Dist. Washington, 22 Corps. July, 1863, Phila., Pa., Dept. Susquehanna. Jany., 1864, Camp Barry, Def. Washington, 22 Corps. April,

1864, Res. Arty., 9 Corps, Potomac. June, 1864, Arty., 1 Div., 9 Corps. July, 1864, Arty. Brig., 9 Corps. Mustered out June 22, 1865.

28th INDPT. BATTERY LIGHT ARTILLERY.—Org. at Fort Schuyler, N. Y., and mustered in Dec. 27, 1862. Dec., 1862, Garrison at Fort Schuyler, N. Y. Harbor, Dept. East. Mustered out July 31, 1865.

29th INDPT. BATTERY LIGHT ARTILLERY—Org. from Battery A, 1st Battalion Light Arty., March 16, 1863. March, 1863, Arty. Res., Potomac. May, 1863, 2 Vol. Brig., Arty. Res., Potomac. (Attached to 32nd Indpt. Battery, July, 1863, to Aug., 1864.) Consolidated with 32nd N. Y. Indpt. Battery, Aug. 15, 1864.

30th INDPT. BATTERY LIGHT ARTILLERY.—Org. from Battery B, 1st Battalion Light Arty., March 16, 1863. March, 1863, Arty. Res., Potomac. May, 1863, 2 Vol. Brig., Arty. Res., Potomac. July, 1863, 1 Div., Dept. Susquehanna. Aug., 1863, Arty., Martinsburg, Va. Dec., 1863, Arty., 1 Div., W. Va. May, 1864, Arty. Brig., W. Va. July, 1864, Arty. Res. Div., Harper's Ferry, W. Va. Jany., 1865, Camp Barry, Washington, D. C., 22 Corps. Mustered out June 23, 1865.

31st INDPT. BATTERY LIGHT ARTILLERY.—Org. from Battery C, 1st Battalion Light Arty., March 16, 1863. March, 1863, Arty. Res., Potomac. May, 1863, 2 Vol. Brig., Arty. Res., Potomac. July, 1863, Harper's Ferry, W. Va., Dept. W. Va. (Attached to 30th N. Y. Indpt. Battery, Jany. to Oct., 1864.) Transferred to 30th N. Y. Indpt. Battery, Oct. 25, 1864.

32nd INDPT. BATTERY LIGHT ARTILLERY.—Org. from Battery D, 1st Battalion Light Arty., March 16, 1863. March, 1863, Arty. Res., Potomac. May, 1863, 2 Vol. Brig., Arty. Res., Potomac. June, 1863, Camp Barry, Washington, D. C., 22 Corps. July, 1863, 2 Brig., Md. Heights Div., Dept. W. Va. Sept., 1863, 2 Brig., 1 Div., W. Va. Dec., 1863, Arty., 1 Div., W. Va. April, 1864, Res. Div., Dept W. Va. Dec, 1864, Arty., 3 Div., W. Va. Jany., 1865, 1 Brig, 2 Infy. Div., W. Va. March, 1865, 1 Brig., 1 Infy. Div., W. Va. Mustered out July 14, 1865.

33rd INDPT. BATTERY LIGHT ARTILLERY.—Org. at Buffalo and mustered in at Elmira, Sept. 4, 1863. Sept., 1863, Camp Barry, Washington, D. C., 22 Corps. Feby., 1864, U. S. Forces, Yorktown, Va., Dept. Va. and N. C. April, 1864, Arty., 3 Div., 19 Corps, Army James, Dept. Va. and N. C. May, 1864, Unatt. Arty., 10 Corps. June, 1864, Arty., 3 Div., 10 Corps. Aug., 1864, Arty. Brig., 10 Corps. Oct., 1864, Separate Brig., Dept. Va. and N. C., Garrison Arty., Fort Pocohontas, on James River. Jany., 1865, Ferrero's Div., Def. Bermuda Hundred, Va. April, 1865, Dept. Va. Mustered out June 25, 1865.

34th INDPT. BATTERY LIGHT ARTILLERY.—Org. as Co. L, 2nd Heavy. Arty., and mustered in Nov. 28, 1861. Dec., 1861, Def. Washington. (Detached from Regt. March, 1862.) March, 1862, Sturgis' Brig., Def. Washington. June, 1862, 2 Brig., 3 Div., 1 Corps, Army Va. Sept., 1862, Arty., 1 Div., 9 Corps, Potomac. Oct., 1862, Arty., 2 Div., 9 Corps, Potomac. Dec., 1862, Arty., 3 Div., 9 Corps, Potomac. Feby., 1863, Arty., 2 Div., 9 Corps, Potomac. April, 1863, Arty., 2 Div., 9 Corps, Ohio. June, 1863, Arty., 2 Div., 9 Corps, Tenn. Aug., 1863, Arty., 2 Div., 9 Corps, Ohio. Sept., 1863, Arty., 1 Div., 9 Corps, Ohio. April, 1864, Arty., 3 Div., 9 Corps, Potomac. July, 1864, Arty. Brig., 9 Corps, Potomac. Mustered out June 21, 1865.

35th INDPT. BATTERY LIGHT ARTILLERY.—(Organization not completed.)

36th INDPT. BATTERY LIGHT ARTILLERY.—(Organization not completed.)

1st REGIMENT ENGINEERS ("SERRELL'S ENGINEERS").—Org. at N. Y. City and mustered in Oct. 11, 1861. Oct., 1861, Unatt., Sherman's S. C. Exp. Corps. April, 1862, Dist. Hilton Head, S. C., Dept. South. Sept., 1862, Dist. Hilton, Head, S. C., 10 Corps, Dept. South. April, 1864, Engrs., 10 Corps, Dept. Va. and N. C. May, 1864, Engr. Brig., Army James, Dept. Va. and N. C. (Co.'s A, C, G and I in Dept. South, April, 1864, to June, 1865.) Mustered out June 30, 1865.

2nd REGIMENT ENGINEERS.—(Organization not completed. Men enlisted transferred to 15th N. Y. Engrs., Oct. 9, 1863.)

15th REGIMENT ENGINEERS.—Org. from 15th N. Y. Infy., Oct. 25, 1861. Nov., 1861, Engr. Brig., Army Potomac. Mustered out June 13, 1865.

50th REGIMENT ENGINEERS.—Org. from 50th N. Y. Infy., Oct. 22, 1861. Oct., 1861, Def. Washington and Alexandria. March, 1862, Engr. Brig., Army Potomac. Mustered out June 19, 1865.

1st U. S. SHARPSHOOTERS.—(Co.'s A, D and H org. at Albany, N. Y., Co. B at N. Y., and mustered in at Washington, D. C., Nov. 29, 1861.) See 1st U. S. Sharpshooters. Co. A mustered out Aug. 14, 1864; Co. D, Aug. 28, 1864. Transferred to 2nd U. S. Sharpshooters, Dec. 31, 1864.

6th COMPANY SHARPSHOOTERS.—Org. at Rochester, Sept. 13, 1862. Assigned to 1st Battalion Sharpshooters, Jany., 1863.

7th COMPANY SHARPSHOOTERS.—Org. at Jamestown, Sept. 12, 1862. Assigned to 1st Battalion Sharpshooters, Jany., 1863.

8th COMPANY SHARPSHOOTERS.—Org. at Staten Island, Jany., 1863. Assigned to 1st Battalion Sharpshooters, Jany., 1863.

9th COMPANY SHARPSHOOTERS.—Org. at Staten Island, Jany., 1863. Assigned to 1st Battalion Sharpshooters, Jany., 1863. (Org. for 9 months.)

1st BATTALION SHARPSHOOTERS.—Org. from 6th, 7th, 8th and 9th Co.'s Sharpshooters Jany., 1863. Feby., 1863, Gibbs' 2 Prov'l Brig., Div. at Suffolk, Va., 7 Corps, Dept. Va. April, 1863, 1 Brig., 1 Div., 7 Corps, Dept. Va. July, 1863, 1 Brig., 1 Div., 1 Corps, Potomac. March, 1864, 1 Brig., 4 Div., 5 Corps, Potomac. Aug., 1864, 3 Brig., 3 Div., 5 Corps. Sept., 1864, 1 Brig., 3 Div., 5 Corps. Mustered out, Co.'s A, B and C, July 19, 1865; Co. D, Aug. 3, 1863.

1st REGIMENT INFANTRY.—Org. at N. Y. City and mustered in May 14, 1861. May, 1861, Fort Monroe and Camp Hamilton, Va., Dept. Va. July, 1861, Newport News, Va., Dept. Va. May, 1862, 1 Brig., 1 Div., Dept. Va. June, 1862, 3 Brig., 3 Div., 3 Corps, Potomac. Aug., 1862, 2 Brig., 1 Div., 3 Corps, Potomac. Sept., 1862, 3 Brig., 1 Div., 3 Corps. Mustered out May 25, 1863.

2nd REGIMENT INFANTRY ("TROY REGIMENT").—Org. at Troy and mustered in May 14, 1861. May, 1861, Fort Monroe and Camp Hamilton, Va., Dept. Va. July, 1861, Newport News, Va., Dept. Va. May, 1862, 1 Brig., 1 Div., Dept. Va. June, 1862, 3 Brig., 2 Div., 3 Corps, Potomac. Mustered out May 26, 1863.

2nd REGIMENT STATE MILITIA INFANTRY.—(See 82nd N. Y. Infy.)

3rd REGIMENT INFANTRY.—Org. at Albany and mustered in May 14, 1861. June, 1861, Fort Monroe and Camp Hamilton, Va., Dept. Va. July, 1861, Dix's Command, Balto., Md. June, 1862, Newport News, Va., Dept. Va. July, 1862, Weber's Brig., Div. at Suffolk, Va., 7 Corps, Dept. Va. Sept., 1862, Fort Monroe, Va., Dept. Va. April, 1863, Suffolk, Va., 1 Div., 7 Corps, Dept. Va. July, 1863, Alvord's Brig., Vodges' Div., N. E. Folly Island, S. C., 10 Corps, Dept. South. Jany., 1864, 2 Brig., Vodges' Div., Northern Dist., Dept. South. Feby., 1864, 2 Brig., Gordon's Div., Northern Dist., Dept. South. April, 1864, 1 Brig., 2 Div., 10 Corps, Army James, Dept. Va. and N. C. May, 1864, 3 Brig., 3 Div., 18 Corps. June, 1864, 1 Brig., 2 Div., 10 Corps. Dec., 1864, 1 Brig., 2 Div., 24 Corps. Jany., 1865, 1 Brig., 2 Div., Terry's Prov'l Corps, Dept. N. C. March, 1865, 1 Brig., 2 Div., 10 Corps, Army Ohio, Dept. N. C. Mustered out Aug. 28, 1865.

4th REGIMENT INFANTRY ("SCOTT LIFE GUARD").—Org. at N. Y. City and mustered in May 2 to 9, 1861. June, 1861, Newport News, Va., Dept. Va. July, 1861, Dix's Command, Balto., Md. June, 1862, Weber's Brig. Div. at Suffolk, Va., 7 Corps, Dept. Va. Sept., 1862, 3 Brig., 3 Div., 2 Corps, Potomac. Mustered out May 25, 1863.

4th REGIMENT NATIONAL GUARD INFANTRY.—Org. for 30 days, June 18, 1863. June, 1863, Dept. Susquehanna. Mustered out July 24, 1863.

5th REGIMENT INFANTRY (3 MONTHS).—Org. at N. Y. and mustered in April 19, 1861. April, 1861, Annapolis, Md. May, 1861, Def. Washington. July, 1861, Butterfield's Brig., Sandford's Div., Patterson's Army. July, 1861, 3 Brig., Banks' Div., Dept. Shenandoah. Mustered out Aug. 7, 1861.

5th REGIMENT INFANTRY ("DURYEA'S ZOUAVES").—Org. at N. Y. City and mustered in May 9, 1861. June, 1861, Newport News, Va., Dept. Va. July, 1861, Dix's Command, Balto., Md. March, 1862, Sykes' Regular Infy. Res., Potomac. May, 1862, 3 Brig., 2 Div., 5 Corps, Potomac. Mustered out May 14, 1863.

5th REGIMENT NATIONAL GUARD INFANTRY.—Org. for 30 days, June, 1863. June, 1863, Yates' Brig., Davies' Div., Dept. Susquehanna. Mustered out July 22, 1863.

5th REGIMENT VETERAN INFANTRY.—Org. at N. Y. City, Oct. 14, 1863. Oct., 1863, Garrison Alexandria, Va., 22 Corps. May, 1864, 1 Brig., 1 Div., 5 Corps, Potomac. June, 1864, 1 Brig., 2 Div., 5 Corps. June, 1865, Hart's Island, N. Y. Mustered out Aug. 21, 1865.

6th REGIMENT INFANTRY (3 MONTHS).—Org. April 19, 1861. April, 1861, Annapolis, Md. May, 1861, Def. Washington. Mustered out July 31, 1861.

6th REGIMENT INFANTRY ("WILSON'S ZOUAVES").—Org. at N. Y. City, April 30 to May 25, 1861. June, 1861, Santa Rosa Island, Fla. May, 1862, Pensacola, Fla., Dist. W. Fla., Dept. South. Dec., 1862, Grover's Div., Dept. Gulf. Jany., 1863, 1 Brig., 4 Div., 19 Corps, Gulf. Mustered out June 25, 1863.

6th REGIMENT NATIONAL GUARD INFANTRY.—Org. for 30 days, June 22, 1863. June, 1863, 2 Separate Brig., 8 Corps, Balto., Md., Middle Dept. Mustered out July 22, 1863.

7th REGIMENT STATE MILITIA INFANTRY.—Org. under special call of the President, April 17, 1861. April, 1861, Def. Washington, D. C. Mustered out June 3, 1861.

7th REGIMENT INFANTRY.—Org. at N. Y. City, April 23, 1861. April, 1861, Newport News, Va., Dept. Va. May, 1862, 1 Brig., 1 Div., 2 Corps, Potomac. Mustered out May 8, 1863.

7th REGIMENT STATE MILITIA INFANTRY.—Reorg. for 3 months, May 25, 1862. May, 1862, Dix's Command, Middle Dept. July, 1862, 8 Corps, Middle Dept. Mustered out Sept. 5, 1862.

7th REGIMENT STATE MILITIA INFANTRY.—Reorg. for 30 days, June 16, 1863. June, 1863, Morris' Brig., 8 Corps, Middle Dept. July, 1863, 3 Brig., 3 Div., 3 Corps, Potomac. Mustered out July 20, 1863.

7th REGIMENT VETERAN INFANTRY.—Org. at Hart's Island, N. Y. Harbor, March 29 to Aug. 9, 1864. May, 1864, Co.'s A and B Attached to 52nd N. Y. Infy., 3 Brig., 1 Div., 2 Corps, Potomac. June, 1864, Consolidated Brig., 1 Div., 2 Corps, Potomac. Nov., 1864, 3 Brig., 1 Div., 2 Corps. June, 1865, Hart's Island, N. Y. Harbor. Mustered out Aug. 4, 1865.

8th REGIMENT INFANTRY, MILITIA ("WASHINGTON GRAYS").—Org. for 3 months, April, 1861. Mustered in at Washington, D. C., April 26, 1861. April, 1861, Def. Washington, D. C. June, 1861, Porter's Brig., Hunter's Div., McDowell's Army, N. E. Va. Mustered out Aug. 2, 1861.

8th REGIMENT INFANTRY ("1st GERMAN RIFLES").—Org. at N. Y. City and mustered in April 23, 1861. June, 1861, Blenker's Brig., Miles' Div., McDowell's Army, N. E. Va. Aug., 1861, Blenker's Brig., Div. Potomac. Oct., 1861, Stahel's Brig., Blenker's Div., Potomac. March, 1862, 1 Brig., Blenker's 2 Div., 2 Corps, Potomac. April, 1862, 1 Brig., Blenker's Div., Dept. Mts. June, 1862, 1 Brig., 1 Div., 1 Corps, Army Va. Sept., 1862, 1 Brig., 1 Div., 11 Corps, Potomac. Mustered out April 23, 1863.

8th REGIMENT NATIONAL GUARD INFANTRY.—Org. for 3 months, May 29, 1862. June, 1862, Def. Washington, D. C. Mustered out Sept. 9, 1862.

9th REGIMENT INFANTRY ("HAWKINS' ZOUAVES").—Org. at N. Y. City and mustered in May 4,

1861. June, 1861, Newport News, Va., Dept. Va. Jany., 1862, Parkes' 3 Brig., Burnside's N. C. Exp. Corps. April, 1862, 4 Brig., Dept. N. C. July, 1862, 1 Brig., 3 Div., 9 Corps, Potomac. April, 1863, 1 Brig., 2 Div., 7 Corps, Dept. Va. Mustered out May 20, 1863.

9th REGIMENT VETERAN INFANTRY.—(Organization not completed. Men enlisted transferred to 17th N. Y. Veteran Infy., Oct. 14, 1863.)

10th REGIMENT INFANTRY ("NATIONAL GUARD ZOUAVES").—Org. at N. Y. City, April 27 to May 2, 1861. June, 1861, Fort Monroe and Camp Hamilton, Va., Dept. Va. May, 1862, 1 Brig., 1 Div., Dept. Va. June, 1862, 3 Brig., 2 Div., 5 Corps, Potomac. Sept., 1862, 3 Brig., 3 Div., 2 Corps, Potomac. May, 1863, 2 Brig., 3 Div., 2 Corps. March, 1864, 3 Brig., 2 Div., 2 Corps. Mustered out June 30, 1865.

11th REGIMENT INFANTRY ("1st N. Y. FIRE ZOUAVES," "ELLSWORTH'S ZOUAVES").—Org. at N. Y. City and mustered in May 7, 1861. June, 1861, Willcox's Brig., Heintzelman's Div., McDowell's Army, N. E. Va. Aug., 1861, New York. Oct., 1861, Newport News, Va., Dept. Va. May, 1862, New York. Mustered out June 2, 1862.

11th REGIMENT NATIONAL GUARD INFANTRY.—Org. for 3 months, May 28, 1862. June, 1862, 2 Brig., Sigel's Div., Dept. Shenandoah. June, 1862, Harper's Ferry, Va. Mustered out Sept. 16, 1862.

11th REGIMENT NATIONAL GUARD INFANTRY.—Org. for 30 days, June 18, 1863. June, 1863, 4 Brig., 1 Div., Dept. Susquehanna. Mustered out July 20, 1863.

12th REGIMENT INFANTRY.—Org. for 3 months, April 21, 1861. May, 1861, Mansfield's Command, Def. Washington. June, 1861, 8 Brig., 3 Div., Patterson's Army, Shenandoah. Mustered out Aug. 5, 1861.

12th REGIMENT INFANTRY ("ONONDAGA REGIMENT," "INDEPENDENCE GUARD").—Org. at Elmira and mustered in May 8, 1861. June, 1861, Richardson's Brig., Tyler's Div., McDowell's Army, N. E. Va. Aug., 1861, Richardson's Brig., Div. Potomac. Oct., 1861, Wadsworth's Brig., McDowell's Div., Potomac. March, 1862, Butterfield's 3 Brig., Porter's 1 Div., 3 Corps, Potomac. May, 1862, 3 Brig., 1 Div., 5 Corps, Potomac. May, 1863, Headqrs. 5 Corps, Potomac. Transferred to 5th N. Y. Veteran Infy., June 2, 1864.

12th REGIMENT NATIONAL GUARD INFANTRY.—Org. for 3 months and mustered in May 31, 1862. June, 1862, R. R. Brig., 8 Corps, Middle Dept. Sept., 1862, R. R. Brig., Dept. W. Va. Mustered out Oct. 12, 1862.

12th REGIMENT NATIONAL GUARD INFANTRY.—Org. for 30 days, June 18, 1863. June, 1863, 1 Brig., Dana's Div., Dept. Susquehanna. Mustered out July 20, 1863.

13th REGIMENT INFANTRY.—Org. for 3 months, April 23, 1861. April, 1861, Annapolis, Md. June, 1861, Balto., Md. Mustered out Aug. 6, 1861.

13th REGIMENT INFANTRY ("ROCHESTER REGIMENT").—Org. at Rochester and mustered in April 25, 1861. June, 1861, Sherman's Brig., Tyler's Div., McDowell's Army, N. E. Va. Aug., 1861, Fort Corcoran, Def. Washington. Oct., 1861, Martindale's Brig., Porter's Div., Potomac. March, 1862, 1 Brig., 1 Div., 3 Corps, Potomac. May, 1862, 1 Brig., 1 Div., 5 Corps, Potomac. Transferred to 140th N. Y. Infy., June 23, 1863.

13th REGIMENT NATIONAL GUARD INFANTRY.—Org. for 3 months, May 30, 1862. June, 1862, Dix's Div., Balto., Md., Middle Dept. July, 1862, Weber's Brig. Div. at Suffolk, Va., Dept. Va. Mustered out Sept. 28, 1862.

13th REGIMENT NATIONAL GUARD INFANTRY.—Org. for 30 days, June 20, 1863. June, 1863, 2 Brig., 1 Div., Dept. Susquehanna. Mustered out July 20, 1863.

14th REGIMENT INFANTRY ("1st ONEÏDA CO. REGIMENT").—Org. at Albany, May 24, 1861. June, 1861, Porter's Brig., Hunter's Div., McDowell's Army, N. E. Va. Aug., 1861, W. T. Sherman's Brig., Div. Potomac. Oct., 1861, Morrell's Brig., Porter's Div., Potomac. March, 1862, 2 Brig., 1 Div., 3 Corps, Potomac. May, 1862, 2 Brig., 1 Div., 5 Corps, Potomac. Mustered out May 24, 1863.

14th REGIMENT STATE MILITIA INFANTRY.—(14th BROOKLYN).—See 84th N. Y. Infy.

15th REGIMENT INFANTRY.—Org. at N. Y. City and mustered in June 17, 1861. June, 1861, Def. Washington. Aug., 1861, Franklin's Brig., Div. Potomac. Sept., 1861, Newton's Brig., Div. Potomac. Designated 15th Engrs., Oct. 25, 1861.

15th REGIMENT NATIONAL GUARD INFANTRY.—Org. for 30 days, June 6, 1864. Duty in N. Y. Harbor. Mustered out July 7, 1864.

16th REGIMENT INFANTRY.—Org. at Albany and mustered in May 15, 1861. June, 1861, Davies' Brig., Miles' Div., McDowell's Army, N. E. Va. Aug., 1861, Heintzelman's Brig., Div. Potomac. Oct., 1861, Slocum's Brig., Franklin's Div., Potomac. March, 1862, 2 Brig., 1 Div., 1 Corps, Potomac. April, 1862, 2 Brig., 1 Div., Dept. Rappahannock. May, 1862, 2 Brig., 1 Div., 6 Corps, Potomac. Mustered out May 22, 1863.

17th REGIMENT INFANTRY ("WESTCHESTER CHASSEURS").—Org. at N. Y. City and mustered in May 20, 1861. June, 1861, Mansfield's Command, Def. Washington. Aug., 1861, Garrison Fort Ellsworth, Def. Washington. Oct., 1861, Butterfield's Brig., Porter's Div., Potomac. March, 1862, 3 Brig., 1 Div., 3 Corps, Potomac. May, 1863, 3 Brig., 1 Div., 5 Corps, Potomac. Mustered out June 2, 1863.

17th REGIMENT VETERAN INFANTRY.—Org. at Staten Island, June 13 to Oct. 17, 1863. Oct., 1863, Def. Washington. Nov., 1863, Dist. Columbus, Ky., 6 Div., 16 Corps, Tenn. Jany., 1864, 2 Brig., 4 Div., 16 Corps, Tenn. March, 1864, 3 Brig., 4 Div., 16 Corps, Tenn., Decatur, Ala., Dist. Northern Ala., Dept. Tenn. Aug., 1864, 1 Brig., 2 Div., 14 Corps, Cumb'd. Mustered out July 13, 1865.

17th REGIMENT NATIONAL GUARD INFANTRY.—Org. for 30 days, July 3, 1863. July, 1863, 2 Separate Brig., 8 Corps, Middle Dept. Mustered out Aug. 13, 1863.

18th REGIMENT INFANTRY.—Org. at Albany and mustered in May 17, 1861. June, 1861, Davies' Brig., Miles' Div., McDowell's Army, N. E. Va. Aug., 1861, Franklin's Brig., Div. Potomac. Oct., 1861, Newton's Brig., Franklin's Div., Potomac. March, 1862, 3 Brig., 1 Div., 1 Corps, Potomac. April, 1862, 3 Brig., 1 Div., Dept. Rappahannock. May, 1862, 3 Brig., 1 Div., 6 Corps, Potomac. Mustered out May 28, 1863.

18th REGIMENT NATIONAL GUARD INFANTRY.—Org. for 30 days, July 3, 1863. July, 1863, 2 Separate Brig., 8 Corps, Middle Dept. Mustered out Aug. 15, 1863.

19th REGIMENT INFANTRY ("SEWARD INFANTRY").—Org. at Elmira and mustered in May 22, 1861. June, 1861, Dept. Washington, D. C. July, 1861, Butterfield's Brig., Sandford's Div., Patterson's Army, Shenandoah. July, 1861, 1 Brig., Banks' Div., Shenandoah. Aug., 1861, Gordon's Brig., Banks' Div., Potomac. Designation changed to 3rd N. Y. Arty., Dec. 11, 1861.

19th REGIMENT NATIONAL GUARD INFANTRY.—Org. for 3 months, May 26, 1862. June, 1862, Balto., Md., 8 Corps, Middle Dept. Mustered out Sept. 6, 1862.

20th REGIMENT INFANTRY.—Org. for 3 months, April 23, 1861. May, 1861, Annapolis and Balto., Md. Mustered out Aug. 2, 1861.

20th REGIMENT INFANTRY ("UNITED TURNER REGIMENT").—Org. at N. Y. City and mustered in May 6, 1861. June, 1861, Fort Monroe and Camp Hamilton, Va. May, 1862, 2 Brig., 1 Div., Dept. Va. June, 1862, 3 Brig., 2 Div., 6 Corps, Potomac. Mustered out June 1, 1863.

20th REGIMENT VETERAN INFANTRY.—(Organization not completed. Men enlisted transferred to 16th N. Y. Cav., Oct. 14, 1863.)

21st REGIMENT INFANTRY ("1st BUFFALO REGIMENT").—Org. at Buffalo and mustered in May 8, 1861. June, 1861, Mansfield's Command, Def. Washington. Oct., 1861, Wadsworth's Brig., McDowell's Div., Potomac. March, 1862, 2 Brig., 3 Div., 1 Corps, Potomac. April, 1862, 2 Brig., King's Div., Dept. Rappahannock. June, 1862, 3 Brig., 1 Div., 3 Corps, Army Va. Sept., 1862, 3 Brig., 1 Div., 1 Corps, Potomac. Jany., 1863, Provost Guard, Army Potomac. Mustered out May 18, 1863.

21st REGIMENT NATIONAL GUARD INFANTRY.— Org. for 30 days, June 22, 1863. June, 1863, Harrisburg, Pa. Mustered out Aug. 6, 1863.

22nd REGIMENT INFANTRY ("NORTHERN N. Y. REGIMENT").—Org. at Troy and mustered in May 6, 1861. July, 1861, Def. Washington. Aug., 1861, Keyes' Brig., Div. Potomac. Oct., 1861, Keyes' Brig., McDowell's Div., Potomac. March, 1862, 1 Brig., 3 Div., 1 Corps, Potomac. April, 1862, 1 Brig., King's Div., Dept. Rappahannock. June, 1862, 1 Brig., 1 Div., 3 Corps, Army Va. Sept., 1862, 1 Brig., 1 Div., 1 Corps, Potomac. Mustered out June 19, 1863.

22nd REGIMENT NATIONAL GUARD INFANTRY.— Org. for 3 months, May 28, 1862. June, 1862, Balto., Md., 8 Corps, Middle Dept. Mustered out Sept. 5. 1862.

22nd REGIMENT NATIONAL GUARD INFANTRY.— Org. for 30 days, June 18, 1863. June, 1863, 4 Brig., 1 Div., Dept. Susquehanna. July, 1863, 3 Brig., 2 Div., 6 Corps, Potomac. Mustered out July 24, 1863.

23rd REGIMENT INFANTRY ("SOUTHERN TIER REGIMENT").—Org. at Elmira, May 10, 1861. Aug., 1861, Hunter's Brig., Div. Potomac. Oct., 1861, Wadsworth's Brig., McDowell's Div., Potomac. March, 1862, 2 Brig., 3 Div., 1 Corps, Potomac. April, 1862, 2 Brig., King's Div., Dept. Rappahannock. June, 1862, 3 Brig., 1 Div., 3 Corps, Army Va. Sept., 1862, 3 Brig., 1 Div., 1 Corps, Potomac. Jany., 1863, Provost Guard, Army Potomac. Mustered out May 22, 1863.

23rd REGIMENT NATIONAL GUARD INFANTRY.— Org. for 30 days, June 16, 1863. June, 1863, 3 Brig., 1 Div., Dept. Susquehanna. Mustered out July 22, 1863.

24th REGIMENT INFANTRY ("OSWEGO COUNTY REGIMENT").—Org. at Elmira and mustered in July 2, 1861. Aug., 1861, Keyes' Brig., Div. Potomac. Oct., 1861, Keyes' Brig., McDowell's Div., Potomac. Jany., 1862, Augur's Brig., McDowell's Div., Potomac. March, 1862, 1 Brig., 3 Div., 1 Corps, Potomac. April, 1862, 1 Brig., King's Div., Dept. Rappahannock. June, 1862, 1 Brig., 1 Div., 3 Corps, Army Va. Sept., 1862, 1 Brig., 1 Div., 1 Corps, Potomac. Mustered out May 29, 1863.

25th REGIMENT INFANTRY.—Org. for 3 months, April 22, 1861. April, 1861, Mansfield's Command, Mil. Dist. Washington. Mustered out Aug. 4, 1861.

25th REGIMENT INFANTRY ("UNION RANGERS"). —Org. at N. Y. City, May 11, 1861. Mustered in June 26, 1861. July, 1861, McCunn's Brig., Army N. E. Va. Aug., 1861, Hunter's Brig., Div. Potomac. Oct., 1861, Butterfield's Brig., Porter's Div., Potomac. March, 1862, 1 Brig., 1 Div., 3 Corps, Potomac. May, 1862, 1 Brig., 1 Div., 5 Corps, Potomac. Mustered out July 10, 1863.

25th REGIMENT NATIONAL GUARD INFANTRY.— Org. for 3 months, May 31, 1862. July, 1862, Webber's Brig., Div. at Suffolk, Va., 7 Corps, Dept. Va. Mustered out Sept. 8, 1862.

26th REGIMENT INFANTRY ("2nd ONEIDA REGIMENT").—Org. at Elmira and mustered in May 21, 1861. June, 1861, McCunn's Brig., Army N. E. Va. Aug., 1861, Heintzelman's Brig., Div. Potomac. Oct., 1861, Slocum's Brig., Franklin's Div., Potomac. Nov., 1861, Wadsworth's Command. Def. Washington. May, 1862, 1 Brig., 2 Div., Dept. Rappahannock. June, 1862, 2 Brig., 2 Div., 3 Corps, Army Va. Sept., 1862, 2 Brig., 2 Div., 1 Corps, Potomac. Mustered out May 28, 1863.

27th REGIMENT INFANTRY ("UNION REGIMENT"). —Org. at Elmira, May 21, 1861. July, 1861, Porter's Brig., Hunter's Div., McDowell's Army, N. E. Va. Aug., 1861, Heintzelman's Brig., Div. Potomac. Oct., 1861, Slocum's Brig., Franklin's Div., Potomac. March, 1862, 2 Brig., 1 Div, 1 Corps, Potomac. April, 1862, 2 Brig., 1 Div., Dept. Rappahannock. May, 1862, 2 Brig., 1 Div., 6 Corps, Potomac. Mustered out May 31, 1863.

28th REGIMENT INFANTRY.—Org. for 3 months, April 23, 1861. April, 1861, Def. Washington, D. C. Mustered out Aug. 5, 1861.

28th REGIMENT INFANTRY ("SCOTT LIFE GUARDS").—Org. at Albany and mustered in May 22, 1861. June, 1861, Mansfield's Command, Def. Washington. July, 1861, Butterfield's Brig., Keim's Div., Patterson's Army, Shenandoah. July, 1861, 1 Brig., Banks' Div.,

Shenandoah. Oct., 1861, Gordon's Brig., Banks' Div., Potomac. March, 1862, 1 Brig., 1 Div., Banks' 5 Corps. April, 1862, 1 Brig., 1 Div., Dept. Shenandoah. June, 1862, 1 Brig., 1 Div., 2 Corps, Army Va. Sept., 1862, 1 Brig., 1 Div., 12 Corps, Potomac. Mustered out June 2, 1863.

28th REGIMENT NATIONAL GUARD INFANTRY.— Org. for 30 days, June 20, 1863. June, 1863, 2 Brig., 1 Div., Dept. Susquehanna. Mustered out July 23, 1863.

28th REGIMENT NATIONAL GUARD INFANTRY.— Org. for 100 days, Sept. 2, 1864. Duty in N. Y. Mustered out Nov. 13, 1864.

29th REGIMENT INFANTRY ("ASTOR RIFLES," "1st GERMAN INFANTRY").—Org. at N. Y. City and mustered in June 6, 1861. June, 1861, Blenker's Brig., Miles' Div., McDowell's Army, N. E. Va. Aug., 1861, Blenker's Brig., Div. Potomac. Oct., 1861, Blenker's Brig., Hooker's Div., Potomac. Nov., 1861, 2 Brig., Blenker's Div., Potomac. March, 1862, 2 Brig., Blenker's 2 Div., 2 Corps, Potomac. April, 1862, 2 Brig., Blenker's Div., Dept. Mts. June, 1862, 1 Brig., 2 Div., 1 Corps, Army Va. Sept., 1862, 1 Brig., 2 Div., 11 Corps, Potomac. Mustered out June 20, 1863.

29th REGIMENT VETERAN INFANTRY.—(Failed to complete organization. Men enlisted transferred to 13th N. Y. Heavy Arty., Oct. 14, 1863.)

30th REGIMENT INFANTRY.—Org. at Troy and mustered in June 1, 1861. June, 1861, Def. Washington. Aug., 1861, Keyes' Brig., Div. Potomac. Oct., 1861, Keyes' Brig., McDowell's Div., Potomac. March, 1862, 1 Brig., 3 Div., 1 Corps, Potomac. April, 1862, 1 Brig., King's Div., Dept. Rappahannock. June, 1862, 1 Brig., 1 Div., 3 Corps, Army Va. Sept., 1862, 1 Brig., 1 Div., 1 Corps, Potomac. Mustered out June 18, 1863.

31st REGIMENT INFANTRY ("BAXTER'S LIGHT GUARD," "MONTEZUMA REGIMENT").—Org. at N. Y. City and mustered in May 14, 1861. June, 1861, Davies' Brig., Miles' Div., McDowell's Army, N. E. Va. Aug., 1861, Franklin's Brig., Div. Potomac. Oct., 1861, Newton's Brig., Franklin's Div., Potomac. March, 1862, 3 Brig., 1 Div., 1 Corps, Potomac. April, 1862, 3 Brig., 1 Div., Dept. Rappahannock. May, 1862, 3 Brig., 1 Div., 6 Corps, Potomac. Feby., 1863, Light Div., 6 Corps, Potomac. May, 1863, 2 Brig., 1 Div., 6 Corps, Potomac. Mustered out June 4, 1863.

31st REGIMENT VETERAN INFANTRY.—(Failed to complete organization. Men enlisted transferred to 5th N. Y. Veteran Infy., Oct. 14, 1863.)

32nd REGIMENT INFANTRY ("1st CALIFORNIA REGIMENT").—Org. at Staten Island and mustered in May 31, 1861. June, 1861, Davies' Brig., Miles' Div., McDowell's Army, N. E. Va. Aug., 1861, Franklin's Brig., Div. Potomac. Oct., 1861, Newton's Brig., Franklin's Div., Potomac. March, 1862, 3 Brig., 1 Div., 1 Corps, Potomac. April, 1862, 3 Brig., 1 Div., Dept. Rappahannock. May, 1862, 3 Brig., 1 Div., 6 Corps, Potomac. Mustered out June 9, 1863.

33rd REGIMENT INFANTRY ("ONTARIO REGIMENT").—Org. at Elmira and mustered in July 3, 1861. Aug., 1861, W. F. Smith's Brig., Div. Potomac. Oct., 1861, 2 Brig., Smith's Div., Potomac. March, 1862, 3 Brig., 2 Div., 4 Corps, Potomac. May, 1862, 3 Brig., 2 Div., 6 Corps. Jany., 1863, 1 Brig., 2 Div., 6 Corps. March, 1863, 3 Brig., 1 Div., 6 Corps. Mustered out June 30, 1863.

34th REGIMENT INFANTRY ("HERKIMER REGIMENT").—Org. at Albany and mustered in June 15, 1861. Aug., 1861, Stone's Brig., Div. Potomac. Oct., 1861, Gorman's Brig., Stone's (Sedgwick's) Div., Potomac. March, 1862, 1 Brig., 2 Div., 2 Corps, Potomac. Mustered out June 30, 1863.

35th REGIMENT INFANTRY ("JEFFERSON CO. REGIMENT").—Org. at Elmira and mustered in June 11, 1861. Aug., 1861, Hunter's Brig., Div. Potomac. Oct., 1861, Wadsworth's Brig., McDowell's Div., Potomac. March, 1862, 2 Brig., 3 Div., 1 Corps, Potomac. April, 1862, 2 Brig., King's Div., Dept. Rappahannock. June, 1862, 3 Brig., 1 Div., 3 Corps, Army Va. Sept., 1862, 3 Brig., 1 Div., 1 Corps, Potomac. Jany., 1863, Patrick's Command, Provost Guard, Potomac. Mustered out June 5, 1863.

36th REGIMENT INFANTRY ("WASHINGTON VOLS.").—Org. at N. Y. City and mustered in June 17, 1861. Aug., 1861, Couch's Brig., Div. Potomac. Oct., 1861, Couch's Brig., Buell's Div., Potomac. March, 1862, 1 Brig., 1 Div., 4 Corps, Potomac. Sept., 1862, 1 Brig., 3 Div., 6 Corps, Potomac. Oct., 1862, 2 Brig., 3 Div., 6 Corps, Potomac. Mustered out July 13, 1863.

37th REGIMENT INFANTRY ("IRISH RIFLES").—Org. at N. Y. City and mustered in June 7, 1861. June, 1861, Def. Washington. Aug., 1861, Hunter's Brig., Div. Potomac. Oct., 1861, Richardson's Brig., Heintzelman's Div., Potomac. March, 1862, 3 Brig., 3 Div., 3 Corps, Potomac. Aug., 1862, 3 Brig., 1 Div., 3 Corps, Potomac. (Co.'s H and I at Fort Washington and in Dist. Washington, Oct., 1861, to April, 1862.) Mustered out June 22, 1863.

37th REGIMENT NATIONAL GUARD INFANTRY.—Org. for 3 months, May 29, 1862. June, 1862, 8 Corps, Middle Dept. Mustered out Sept. 2, 1862.

37th REGIMENT NATIONAL GUARD INFANTRY.—Org. for 30 days June 18, 1863. June, 1863, 4 Brig., 1 Div., Dept. Susquehanna. Mustered out July 22, 1863.

37th REGIMENT NATIONAL GUARD INFANTRY.—Org. for 30 days, May 6, 1864. Duty in N. Y. Harbor. Mustered out June 6, 1864.

38th REGIMENT INFANTRY ("2nd SCOTT LIFE GUARD").—Org. at N. Y. City and mustered in June 3, 1861. June, 1861, Willcox's Brig., Heintzelman's Div., McDowell's Army, N. E. Va. Aug., 1861, Howard's Brig., Div. Potomac. Oct., 1861, Sedgwick's Brig., Heintzelman's Div., Potomac. March, 1862, 2 Brig., 3 Div., 3 Corps, Potomac. Aug., 1862, 2 Brig., 1 Div., 3 Corps, Potomac. Mustered out June 22, 1863.

38th REGIMENT VETERAN INFANTRY.—(Failed to complete organization. Men enlisted transferred to 5th N. Y. Veteran Infy., Oct. 14, 1863.)

39th REGIMENT INFANTRY ("GARIBALDI GUARD").—Org. at N. Y. City and mustered in at Washington, D. C., June 6, 1861. June, 1861, Blenker's Brig., Miles' Div., McDowell's Army, N. E. Va. Aug., 1861, Blenker's Brig., Div. Potomac. Oct., 1861, Blenker's Brig., Hooker's Div., Potomac. Nov., 1861, Stahel's 1 Brig., Blenker's Div., Potomac. March, 1862, 1 Brig., Blenker's 2 Div., 2 Corps, Potomac. April, 1862, 1 Brig., Blenker's Div., Dept. Mts. July, 1862, White's Brig., Winchester, Va., Army Va. Sept., 1862, Miles' Command, Harper's Ferry, Va. Sept., 1862, Camp Douglas, Ill. Dec., 1862, 3 Brig., Casey's Div., Dept. Washington. Feby., 1863, 3 Brig., Casey's Div., 22 Corps. April, 1863, 3 Brig., Abercrombie's Div., 22 Corps. June, 1863, 3 Brig., 3 Div., 2 Corps, Potomac. March, 1864, 3 Brig., 1 Div., 2 Corps, Potomac. June, 1864, Consolidated Brig., 1 Div., 2 Corps. Nov., 1864, 3 Brig., 1 Div., 2 Corps. Mustered out July 1, 1865.

40th REGIMENT INFANTRY ("MOZART REGIMENT," "CONSTITUTION GUARD").—Org. at Yonkers, June 27, 1861. July, 1861, Def. Washington. Aug., 1861, Howard's Brig., Div. Potomac. Oct., 1862, Sedgwick's Brig., Heintzelman's Div., Potomac. March, 1862, 2 Brig., 3 Div., 3 Corps, Potomac. Aug., 1862, 2 Brig., 1 Div., 3 Corps, Potomac. May, 1863, 3 Brig., 1 Div., 3 Corps. March, 1864, 1 Brig., 3 Div., 2 Corps, Potomac. Mustered out June 27, 1865.

41st REGIMENT INFANTRY ("DEKALB REGIMENT," "YAGER REGIMENT").—Org. at Yorkville and mustered in June 6, 1861. July, 1861, 2 Brig., Runyon's Res. Div., McDowell's Army, N. E. Va. Aug., 1861, W. T. Sherman's Brig., Div. Potomac. Oct., 1861, Martindale's Brig., Porter's Div., Potomac. Nov., 1861, Unassigned, Blenker's Div., Potomac. March, 1862, Unassigned, Blenker's 2 Div., 2 Corps, Potomac. April, 1862, Unassigned, Blenker's Div., Dept. Mts. June, 1862, 1 Brig., 1 Div., 1 Corps, Army Va. Sept., 1862, 1 Brig., 1 Div., 11 Corps, Potomac. Aug., 1863, 1 Brig., Gordon's Div., Folly Island, S. C., 10 Corps, Dept. South. April, 1864, Folly Island, Northern Dist., Dept. South. Aug., 1864, 1 Brig., Hardin's Div., 22 Corps. Sept., 1862, 2 Brig., Kitching's Prov'l Div., Army Shenandoah. Dec., 1864, 1 Brig., Fer-

rero's Div., Def. Bermuda Hundred, Va., Dept. Va. Aug., 1865, Dept. Va. Mustered out Dec. 9, 1865.

42nd REGIMENT INFANTRY ("TAMMANY REGIMENT," "JACKSON GUARD").—Org. at Great Neck and mustered in June 22, 1861. July, 1861, Def. Washington. Aug., 1861, Stone's Brig., Div. Potomac. Oct., 1861, Gorman's Brig., Stone's (Sedgwick's) Div., Potomac. Jany., 1862, Burns' Brig., Sedgwick's Div., Potomac. March, 1862, 3 Brig., 2 Div., 2 Corps, Potomac. March, 1864, 1 Brig., 2 Div., 2 Corps, Potomac. Mustered out July 13, 1864.

43rd REGIMENT INFANTRY ("ALBANY AND YATES RIFLES").—Org. at Albany, Aug. and Sept., 1861. Oct., 1861, Hancock's Brig., W. F. Smith's Div., Potomac. March, 1862, 1 Brig., 2 Div., 4 Corps, Potomac. May, 1862, 1 Brig., 2 Div., 6 Corps, Potomac. Feby., 1863, Light Div., 6 Corps, Potomac. May, 1863, 3 Brig., 2 Div., 6 Corps. July, 1864, 3 Brig., 2 Div., 6 Corps, Middle Mil. Div. Dec., 1864, 3 Brig., 2 Div., 6 Corps, Potomac. Mustered out June 27, 1865.

44th REGIMENT INFANTRY ("PEOPLE'S ELLSWORTH REGIMENT").—Org. at Albany and mustered in Aug. 30, 1861. Oct., 1861, Butterfield's Brig., Porter's Div., Potomac. March, 1862, 3 Brig., 1 Div., 3 Corps, Potomac. May, 1862, 3 Brig., 1 Div., 5 Corps, Potomac. Mustered out Oct. 11, 1864.

45th REGIMENT INFANTRY ("5th GERMAN RIFLES").—Org. at N. Y. City and mustered in Sept. 9, 1861. Oct., 1861, Stahel's Brig., Blenker's Div., Potomac. March, 1862, Stahel's 1 Brig., Blenker's 2 Div., 2 Corps, Potomac. April, 1862, 1 Brig., Blenker's Div., Dept. Mts. June, 1862, 1 Brig., 1 Div., 1 Corps, Army Va. Sept., 1862, 1 Brig., 1 Div., 1 Corps, Potomac. May, 1863, 1 Brig., 3 Div., 11 Corps, Potomac. Oct., 1863, 1 Brig., 3 Div., 11 Corps, Cumb'd. April, 1864, 3 Brig., 1 Div., 20 Corps. July, 1864, Unassigned, 4 Div., 20 Corps. Nov., 1864, 2 Brig., 4 Div., 20 Corps. March, 1865, 1 Brig., 1 Div., Dist. Nashville, Dept. Cumb'd. Consolidated with 58th N. Y. Infy., June 30, 1865.

46th REGIMENT INFANTRY ("FREMONT RIFLES").—Org. at N. Y. City and mustered in by Co.'s July 29 to Sept. 16, 1861. Nov., 1861, Viele's 1 Brig., Sherman's S. C. Exp. Corps. April, 1862, 2 Brig., 2 Div., Dept. South. July, 1862, 2 Brig., 1 Div., 9 Corps, Potomac. April, 1863, 2 Brig., 1 Div., 9 Corps, Ohio. June, 1863, 3 Brig., 2 Div., 9 Corps, Tenn. Aug., 1863, 2 Brig., 1 Div., 9 Corps, Ohio. May, 1864, 2 Brig., 4 Div., 5 Corps, Potomac. June, 1864, 2 Brig., 3 Div., 9 Corps, Potomac. Sept., 1864, 2 Brig., 1 Div., 9 Corps, Potomac. Mustered out July 28, 1865.

47th REGIMENT INFANTRY ("WASHINGTON GREYS").—Org. at N. Y. City and mustered in Sept. 14, 1861. Nov., 1861, Viele's 1 Brig., Sherman's S. C. Exp. Corps. April, 1862, 2 Brig., 2 Div., Dept. South. July, 1862, Dist. Hilton Head, S. C., 10 Corps, Dept. South. April, 1863, Ossabaw Sound, Ga., Dept. South. July, 1863, Folly Island, S. C., 10 Corps. Aug., 1863, 5 Brig., Morris Island, S. C., 10 Corps. Oct., 1863, Unatt., Folly Island, S. C., 10 Corps. Nov., 1863, Dist. Hilton Head, S. C. Dec., 1863, Barton's Brig., Dist. Hilton Head, S. C., 10 Corps. Feby., 1864, Barton's Brig., Dist. Fla. Feby., 1864, Barton's Brig., Ames' Div., Dist. Fla. April, 1864, 2 Brig., 2 Div., 10 Corps, Army James, Dept. Va. and N. C. May, 1864, 1 Brig., 3 Div., 18 Corps. June, 1864, 2 Brig., 2 Div., 10 Corps. Dec., 1864, 2 Brig., 2 Div., 24 Corps. Jany., 1865, 2 Brig., 2 Div., Terry's Prov'l Corps, Dept. N. C. March, 1865, 2 Brig., 2 Div., 10 Corps, Army Ohio, Dept. N. C. Mustered out Aug. 30, 1865.

47th REGIMENT NATIONAL GUARD INFANTRY.—Org. for 3 months, May 27, 1862. June, 1862, Balto., Md., 8 Corps, Middle Dept. Mustered out Sept. 1, 1862.

47th REGIMENT NATIONAL GUARD INFANTRY.—Org. for 30 days, June 17, 1863. June, 1863, 1 Brig., DeRussy's Div., Def. Washington, South Potomac, 22 Corps. July, 1863, 3 Brig., DeRussy's Div., 22 Corps. Mustered out July 23, 1863.

48th REGIMENT INFANTRY ("CONTINENTAL GUARD," "PERRY'S SAINTS").—Org. at Brooklyn, Sept. 10, 1861. Nov., 1861, Viele's 1 Brig., Sherman's S. C.

Exp. Corps. April, 1862, Fort Pulaski, Ga., Dept. South. Sept., 1862, Fort Pulaski, Ga., Dist. Hilton Head, S. C., 10 Corps, Dept. South. May, 1863, St. Helena Island, S C., 10 Corps. July, 1863, 2 Brig., Folly Island, S. C., 10 Corps. July, 1863, 2 Brig., 2 Div., Morris Island, S. C., 10 Corps. Aug., 1863, St. Augustine, Fla. Nov., 1863, Dist. Hilton Head, S. C., 10 Corps. Dec., 1863, Barton's Brig., Dist. Hilton Head, S. C., 10 Corps. Feby., 1864, Barton's Brig., Dist. Fla. Feby., 1864, Barton's Brig., Ames' Div., Dist. Fla. April, 1864, 2 Brig., 2 Div., 10 Corps, Army James, Dept. Va. and N. C. May, 1864, 1 Brig., 3 Div., 18 Corps. June, 1864, 2 Brig., 2 Div., 10 Corps. Dec., 1864, 2 Brig., 2 Div., 24 Corps. Jany., 1865, 2 Brig., 2 Div., Terry's Prov'l Corps, Dept. N. C. March, 1865, 2 Brig., 2 Div., 10 Corps, Army Ohio, Dept. N. C. July, 1865, Dept. N. C. Mustered out Sept. 1, 1865.

49th REGIMENT INFANTRY.—Org. at Buffalo and mustered in Sept. 18, 1861. Oct., 1861, Stevens' Brig., W. F. Smith's Div., Potomac. March, 1862, 3 Brig., 2 Div., 4 Corps, Potomac. May, 1862, 3 Brig., 2 Div., 6 Corps, Potomac. July, 1864, 3 Brig., 2 Div., 6 Corps, Middle Mil. Div. Dec., 1864, 3 Brig., 2 Div., 6 Corps, Potomac. Mustered out June 27, 1865.

50th REGIMENT INFANTRY.—Org. at Elmira, Sept. 18, 1861. Oct., 1861, 3 Brig, Porter's Div., Potomac. Designation changed to 50th N. Y. Engrs., Oct. 22, 1861.

50th REGIMENT NATIONAL GUARD INFANTRY.—Org. for 3 months, Aug. 27, 1864. Duty at Elmira, N. Y. Mustered out Dec. 3, 1864.

51st REGIMENT INFANTRY ("SHEPARD RIFLES").—Org. at N. Y. City, July 27 to Oct. 23, 1861. Oct., 1861, Reno's 2 Brig., Burnside's N. C. Exp. Corps. April, 1862, 2 Brig., 2 Div., Dept. N. C. July, 1862, 2 Brig., 2 Div., 9 Corps, Potomac. April, 1863, 2 Brig., 2 Div., 9 Corps, Ohio. June, 1863, 2 Brig., 2 Div., 9 Corps, Tenn. Aug., 1863, Dist. Somerset, Ky., 1 Div., 23 Corps, Ohio. Oct., 1863, Dist. N. C., Ky., 1 Div., 23 Corps. Jany., 1864, 2 Brig., 2 Div., 9 Corps, Ohio. May, 1864, Acting Engrs., 2 Div., 9 Corps, Potomac. July, 1864, 1 Brig., 2 Div., 9 Corps, Potomac. Mustered out July 25, 1865.

52nd REGIMENT INFANTRY ("GERMAN RANGERS," "SIGEL RIFLES").—Org. at N. Y. City, Oct. 11, 1861. Oct., 1861, French's Brig., Sumner's Div., Potomac. March, 1862, 3 Brig., 1 Div., 2 Corps, Potomac. June, 1864, Consolidated Brig., 1 Div., 2 Corps. Nov., 1864, 3 Brig., 1 Div., 2 Corps. Mustered out July 25, 1865.

52nd REGIMENT NATIONAL GUARD INFANTRY.—Org. for 30 days, June 19, 1863. June, 1863, 3 Brig., 1 Div., Dept. Susquehanna. Mustered out July 15, 1863.

53rd REGIMENT INFANTRY ("D'EPINEUEL'S ZOUAVES").—Org. at N. Y. City, Aug. 27 to Nov. 15, 1861. Nov., 1861, Parkes' 3 Brig., Burnside's N. C. Exp. Corps. Mustered out March 21, 1862.

54th REGIMENT INFANTRY.—Org. at Hudson, Sept. 5 to Oct. 16, 1861. Nov., 1861, Prov'l Brig., Casey's Div., Potomac. Dec., 1861, Steinwehr's Brig., Blenker's Div., Potomac. March, 1862, 2 Brig., Blenker's 2 Div., 2 Corps, Potomac. April, 1862, 2 Brig., Blenker's Div., Dept. Mts. June, 1862, 2 Brig., 3 Div., 1 Corps, Army Va. Sept., 1862, 2 Brig., 3 Div., 11 Corps, Potomac. Nov., 1862, 1 Brig., 1 Div., 11 Corps, Potomac. Aug., 1863, 1 Brig., Gordon's Div., Folly Island, S. C., 10 Corps, Dept. South. April, 1864, Folly Island, S. C., Northern Dist., Dept. South. Oct., 1864, Morris Island, S. C., 1 Separate Brig., Dept. South. July, 1865, 3 Sub-Dist., Dept. South. Aug., 1865, Dept. South. Mustered out April 14, 1866.

55th REGIMENT INFANTRY ("GARDE DE LAFAYETTE").—Org. at N. Y. City and mustered in Aug. 28, 1861. Oct., 1861, Peck's Brig., Buell's Div., Potomac. March, 1862, 3 Brig., 1 Div., 4 Corps, Potomac. July, 1862, 2 Brig., 1 Div., 4 Corps. Sept., 1862, 3 Brig., 1 Div., 3 Corps, Potomac. Nov., 1862, 2 Brig., 1 Div., 3 Corps, Potomac. Consolidated with 38th N. Y. Infy., Dec. 21, 1862.

55th REGIMENT NATIONAL GUARD INFANTRY.—Org. for 30 days, June 24, 1863. June, 1863, 2 Separate Brig., 8 Corps, Middle Dept. Mustered out July 27, 1863.

56th REGIMENT INFANTRY ("10th LEGION").—Org. at Newburg and mustered in Oct. 28, 1861. Nov., 1861, 1 Brig., Casey's Div., Potomac. March, 1862, 1 Brig., 3 Div., 4 Corps, Potomac. June, 1862, 1 Brig., 2 Div., 4 Corps, Potomac. Dec., 1862, Naglee's Brig., Dept. N. C. Jany., 1863, 2 Brig., 3 Div., 18 Corps, Dept. N. C. Feby., 1863, 2 Brig., 2 Div., 18 Corps, Dept. South. April, 1863, Stevenson's Brig., Seabrook Island, S. C., 10 Corps, Dept. South. July, 1863, 2 Brig., 1 Div., Morris Island, S. C., 10 Corps. July, 1863, Davis' Brig., Folly Island, S. C., 10 Corps. Aug., 1863, Dist. Beaufort, S. C., 10 Corps. April, 1864, Dist. Beaufort, S. C., Dept. South. Sept., 1864, Morris Island, S. C., Northern Dist., Dept. South. Nov., 1864, 1 Brig., Coast Div., Dept. South. Jany., 1865, 1 Separate Brig., Morris Island, S. C., Dept. South. March, 1865, 4 Separate Brig., Dept. South. July, 1865, 2 Sub-Dist., Dist. Western S. C., Dept. South. Mustered out Oct. 17, 1865.

56th REGIMENT NATIONAL GUARD INFANTRY.—Org. for 30 days, June 18, 1863. June, 1863, 3 Brig., 1 Div., Dept. Susquehanna. Mustered out July 24, 1863.

56th REGIMENT NATIONAL GUARD INFANTRY.—Org. for 100 days, Aug. 2, 1864. Duty at Elmira, N. Y. Mustered out Nov. 6, 1864.

57th REGIMENT INFANTRY ("NATIONAL GUARD RIFLES").—Org. at N. Y. City, Aug. 12 to Nov. 19, 1861. Nov., 1861, French's Brig., Sumner's Div., Potomac. March, 1862, 3 Brig., 1 Div., 2 Corps, Potomac. June, 1864, Consolidated Brig., 1 Div., 2 Corps, Potomac. Mustered out July 14 to Oct. 15, 1864.

58th REGIMENT INFANTRY ("POLISH LEGION").—Org. at N. Y. City, Aug. 31 to Nov. 21, 1861. Nov., 1861, Bohlan's Brig., Blenker's Div., Potomac. March, 1862, 2 Brig., Blenker's 2 Div., 2 Corps, Potomac. April, 1862, 2 Brig., Blenker's Div., Dept. Mts. June, 1862, 2 Brig., 3 Div., 1 Corps, Army Va. Sept., 1862, 2 Brig., 3 Div., 11 Corps, Potomac. Oct., 1863, 2 Brig., 3 Div., 11 Corps, Cumb'd. April, 1864, Unatt., 4 Div., 20 Corps. July, 1864, 3 Brig., Def. Nashv. & Chatta. R. R., Dept. Cumb'd. Feby., 1865, Unatt., 4 Div., 20 Corps, Stevenson, Ala., Dist. N. Ala., Dept. Cumb'd. July, 1865, Dist. Nashville, Tenn., Cumb'd. Mustered out Oct. 1, 1865.

58th REGIMENT NATIONAL GUARD INFANTRY.—Org. for 100 days, Aug. 27, 1864. Duty at Elmira, N. Y. Mustered out Dec. 3, 1864.

59th REGIMENT INFANTRY.—Org. at N. Y. City, July 1 to Nov. 23, 1861. Nov., 1861, Wadsworth's Command, Def. Washington. Jany., 1862, 2 Brig., Casey's Div., Potomac. March, 1862, Def. Washington. May, 1862, Sturgis' Brig., Def. Washington. July, 1862, 3 Brig., 2 Div., 2 Corps, Potomac. March, 1864, 1 Brig., 2 Div., 2 Corps, Potomac. Mustered out June 30, 1865.

60th REGIMENT INFANTRY ("ST. LAWRENCE REGIMENT").—Org. at Ogdensburg and mustered in Oct. 30, 1861. Nov., 1861, Dix's Div., Balto., Md. March, 1862, R. R. Brig., Army Potomac. June, 1862, 2 Brig., Sigel's Div., Dept. Shenandoah. June, 1862, 2 Brig., 2 Div., 2 Corps, Army Va. Aug., 1862, 3 Brig., 2 Div., 2 Corps, Army Va. Sept., 1862, 3 Brig., 2 Div., 12 Corps, Potomac. Oct., 1862, 2 Brig., 2 Div., 12 Corps, Potomac. May, 1863, 3 Brig., 2 Div., 12 Corps, Potomac. Oct., 1863, 3 Brig., 2 Div., 12 Corps, Cumb'd. April, 1864, 3 Brig., 2 Div., 20 Corps. Mustered out June 17, 1865.

61st REGIMENT INFANTRY ("ASTOR REGIMENT," "1st REGIMENT CLINTON GUARD").—Org. at N. Y. City, Nov. 21, 1861. Nov., 1861, Howard's Brig., Sumner's Div., Potomac. March, 1862, 1 Brig., 1 Div., 2 Corps, Potomac. Mustered out July 14, 1865.

62nd REGIMENT INFANTRY ("ANDERSON ZOUAVES").—Org. at N. Y. City and mustered in June 30, 1861. Aug., 1861, Def. Washington. Oct., 1861, Peck's Brig., Buell's Div., Potomac. March, 1862, 3 Brig., 1 Div., 4 Corps, Potomac. July, 1862, 2 Brig., 1 Div., 4 Corps, Potomac. Sept., 1862, 2 Brig., 3 Div., 6 Corps, Potomac. Oct., 1862, 3 Brig., 3 Div., 6 Corps, Potomac. Jany., 1864, Wheaton's Brig., Dept. W. Va. March, 1864, 1 Brig., 2 Div., 6 Corps, Potomac. July, 1864, 1 Brig., 2 Div., 6 Corps, Middle Mil. Div. Dec., 1864, 1 Brig., 2 Div., 6 Corps, Potomac. July, 1865, Fort Schuyler, N. Y. Mustered out Aug. 30, 1865.

63rd REGIMENT INFANTRY ("INDPT. IRISH REGIMENT," "3rd REGIMENT IRISH BRIGADE").—Org. at

N. Y. City, Aug. 7 to Nov. 4, 1861. Nov., 1861, Meagher's Brig., Sumner's Div., Potomac. March, 1862, 2 Brig., 1 Div., 2 Corps, Potomac. June, 1864, Consolidated Brig., 1 Div., 2 Corps, Potomac. Nov., 1864, 2 Brig., 1 Div., 2 Corps. Mustered out June 30, 1865.

64th REGIMENT INFANTRY ("CATTARAUGUS REGIMENT").—Org. at Elmira, Sept. 10 to Dec. 10, 1861. Dec., 1861, Casey's Prov'l Div. Jany., 1862, Howard's Brig., Sumner's Div., Potomac. March, 1862, 1 Brig., 1 Div., 2 Corps, Potomac. June, 1862, 3 Brig., 1 Div., 2 Corps, Potomac. Aug., 1862, 1 Brig., 1 Div., 2 Corps, Potomac. April, 1863, 4 Brig., 1 Div., 2 Corps, Potomac. Mustered out July 14, 1865.

65th REGIMENT INFANTRY ("1st U. S. CHASSEURS").—Org. at Willett's Point, N. Y., Sept., 1861. Sept., 1861, Def. Washington. Oct., 1861, Graham's Brig., Buell's Div., Potomac. March, 1862, 2 Brig., 1 Div., 4 Corps, Potomac. July, 1862, 3 Brig., 1 Div., 4 Corps, Potomac. Sept., 1862, 2 Brig., 3 Div., 6 Corps, Potomac. Oct., 1862, 1 Brig., 3 Div., 6 Corps, Potomac. April, 1864, 4 Brig., 1 Div., 6 Corps, Potomac. July, 1864, 2 Brig., 1 Div., 6 Corps, Middle Mil. Div. Dec., 1864, 2 Brig., 1 Div., 6 Corps, Potomac. Mustered out July 17, 1865.

65th REGIMENT NATIONAL GUARD INFANTRY.—Org. for 30 days, June 19, 1863. June, 1863, Dept. Susquehanna. Mustered out July 30, 1863.

66th REGIMENT INFANTRY ("GOVERNOR'S GUARD").—Org. at N. Y. City and mustered in Nov. 4, 1861. Nov., 1861, Graham's Brig., Buell's Div., Potomac. Jany., 1862, French's Brig., Sumner's Div., Potomac. March, 1862, 3 Brig., 1 Div., 2 Corps, Potomac. March, 1864, 4 Brig., 1 Div., 2 Corps, Potomac. May, 1865, Fort Richmond, N. Y. Harbor. Mustered out Aug. 30, 1865.

67th REGIMENT INFANTRY ("1st LONG ISLAND").—Org. at Brooklyn, June 24, 1861. Aug., 1861, Graham's Brig., Div. Potomac. Oct., 1861, Graham's Brig., Buell's Div., Potomac. March, 1862, 2 Brig., 1 Div., 4 Corps, Potomac. July, 1862, 3 Brig., 1 Div., 4 Corps, Potomac. Sept., 1862, 2 Brig., 3 Div., 6 Corps, Potomac. Oct., 1862, 1 Brig., 3 Div., 6 Corps, Potomac. April, 1864, 4 Brig., 1 Div., 6 Corps, Potomac. July, 1864, 2 Brig., 1 Div., 6 Corps, Middle Mil. Div. Consolidated with 65th N. Y. Infy., Sept. 1, 1864.

67th REGIMENT NATIONAL GUARD INFANTRY.—Org. for 30 days, June 25, 1863. June, 1863, Dept. Susquehanna. Mustered out Aug. 3, 1863.

68th REGIMENT INFANTRY ("CAMERON RIFLES," "2nd GERMAN RIFLES").—Org. at N. Y. City, Aug. 1, 1861. Aug., 1861, Blenker's Brig., Div. Potomac. Oct., 1861, Blenker's Brig., Hooker's Div., Potomac. Nov., 1861, Steinwehr's 2 Brig., Blenker's Div., Potomac. March, 1862, 2 Brig., Blenker's 2 Div., 2 Corps, Potomac. April, 1862, 2 Brig., Blenker's Div., Dept. Mts. June, 1862, 1 Brig., 2 Div., 1 Corps, Army Va. July, 1862, 2 Brig., 3 Div., 1 Corps, Army Va. Sept., 1862, 2 Brig., 3 Div., 11 Corps, Potomac. Oct., 1862, 1 Brig., 3 Div., 11 Corps, Potomac. May, 1863, 1 Brig., 1 Div., 11 Corps, Potomac. July, 1863, 2 Brig., 2 Div., 11 Corps, Potomac. Oct., 1863, 3 Brig., 3 Div., 11 Corps, Cumb'd. April, 1864, Unatt., 4 Div., 20 Corps. July, 1864, 3 Brig., Def. Nashv. & Chatta. R. R., Dept. Cumb'd. Dec., 1864, Unassigned, Dist. Etowah, Dept. Cumb'd. March, 1865, 2 Brig., 2 Separate Div., Dist. Etowah, Dept. Cumb'd. July, 1865, Dist. Allatoona, Ga. Nov., 1865, Dist. Savannah, Ga. Mustered out Nov. 30, 1865.

68th REGIMENT NATIONAL GUARD INFANTRY.—Org. for 30 days, June 22, 1863. June, 1863, 5 Brig., 1 Div., Dept. Susquehanna. Mustered out July 25, 1863.

69th REGIMENT STATE MILITIA INFANTRY.—Org. for 3 months, April 23, 1861. May, 1861, Def. Washington, D. C. June, 1861, Sherman's Brig., Tyler's Div., McDowell's Army, N. E. Va. Mustered out Aug. 3, 1861.

69th REGIMENT INFANTRY ("1st REGIMENT IRISH BRIGADE").—Org. at N. Y. and mustered in Nov. 18, 1861. Nov., 1861, Meagher's Brig., Sumner's Div., Potomac. March, 1862, 2 Brig., 1 Div., 2 Corps, Potomac. June, 1864, Consolidated Brig., 1 Div., 2 Corps, Potomac. Nov., 1864, 2 Brig., 1 Div., 2 Corps, Potomac. Mustered out June 30, 1865.

69th REGIMENT NATIONAL GUARD INFANTRY.—Org. for 3 months, May 26, 1862. June, 1862, Def. Washington. Mustered out Sept. 3, 1862.

69th REGIMENT NATIONAL GUARD INFANTRY.—Org. for 30 days, June 22, 1863. June, 1863, 2 Separate Brig., 8 Corps, Middle Dept. Mustered out July 25, 1863.

69th REGIMENT NATIONAL GUARD INFANTRY.—Org. for 3 months, July 6, 1864. Duty in N. Y. Harbor. Mustered out Oct. 6, 1864.

70th REGIMENT INFANTRY ("1st REGIMENT EXCELSIOR BRIGADE").—Org. at Staten Island and mustered in June 20, 1861. Sept., 1861, Sickles' Brig., Div. Potomac. Oct., 1861, Sickles' Brig., Hooker's Div., Potomac. March, 1862, 2 Brig., 2 Div., 3 Corps, Potomac. March, 1864, 2 Brig., 4 Div., 2 Corps, Potomac. May, 1864, 4 Brig., 3 Div., 2 Corps. Mustered out July 7, 1864.

71st REGIMENT MILITIA INFANTRY.—Org. for 3 months, April 10, 1861. April, 1861, Mansfield's Command, Def. Washington. June, 1861, Burnside's Brig., Hunter's Div., McDowell's Army, N. E. Va. Mustered out July 31, 1861.

71st REGIMENT INFANTRY ("2nd REGIMENT EXCELSIOR BRIGADE").—Org. at Staten Island, N. Y., June, 1861. Sept., 1861, Sickles' Brig., Div. Potomac. Oct., 1861, Sickles' Brig., Hookers' Div., Potomac. March, 1862, 2 Brig., 2 Div., 3 Corps, Potomac. March, 1864, 2 Brig., 4 Div., 2 Corps, Potomac. May, 1864, 4 Brig., 3 Div., 2 Corps. Mustered out July 30, 1864.

71st REGIMENT NATIONAL GUARD INFANTRY.—Org. for 3 months, May 12, 1862. May, 1862, Sturgis' Command, Def. Washington. Mustered out Sept. 2, 1862.

71st REGIMENT NATIONAL GUARD INFANTRY.—Org. for 30 days, June 17, 1863. June, 1863, 1 Brig., 1 Div., Dept. Susquehanna. Mustered out July 22, 1863.

72nd REGIMENT INFANTRY ("3rd REGIMENT EXCELSIOR BRIGADE").—Org. at Staten Island, N. Y. Sept., 1861, Sickles' Brig., Div. Potomac. Oct., 1861, Sickles' Brig., Hooker's Div., Potomac. March, 1862, 2 Brig., 2 Div., 3 Corps, Potomac. March, 1864, 2 Brig., 4 Div. 2 Corps, Potomac. May, 1864, 4 Brig., 3 Div., 2 Corps, Potomac. Mustered out June 20 to Oct. 31, 1864.

73rd REGIMENT INFANTRY ("4th REGIMENT EXCELSIOR BRIGADE").—Org. at Staten Island, N. Y. Sept., 1861, Sickles' Brig., Div. Potomac. Oct., 1861, Sickles' Brig., Hooker's Div., Potomac. March, 1862, 2 Brig., 2 Div., 3 Corps, Potomac. March, 1864, 2 Brig., 4 Div., 2 Corps, Potomac. May, 1864, 4 Brig., 3 Div., 2 Corps. July, 1864, 1 Brig., 3 Div., 2 Corps. Mustered out June 29, 1865.

74th REGIMENT INFANTRY ("5th REGIMENT EXCELSIOR BRIGADE").—Sept., 1861, Sickles' Brig., Div. Potomac. Oct., 1861, Sickles' Brig., Hooker's Div., Potomac. March, 1862, 2 Brig., 2 Div., 3 Corps, Potomac. March, 1864, 2 Brig., 4 Div., 2 Corps, Potomac. May, 1864, 4 Brig., 3 Div., 2 Corps, Potomac. July, 1864, 1 Brig., 3 Div., 2 Corps. Mustered out June 19 to Aug. 3, 1864.

75th REGIMENT INFANTRY ("2nd AUBURN").—Org. at Auburn and mustered in Nov. 26, 1861. Dec., 1861, Santa Rosa Island, Fla., Dept. Fla. Feby., 1862, Dist. Santa Rosa Island, Dept. Gulf. March, 1862, Western Dist. Fla., Dept. South. Aug., 1862, Pensacola, Fla., Dist. W. Fla., Dept. Gulf. Sept., 1862, Weitzel's Res. Brig., Dept. Gulf. Jany., 1863, 2 Brig, 1 Div., 19 Corps, Gulf. July, 1863, 3 Brig., 1 Div., 19 Corps, Gulf. Oct., 1863, Unassigned, Cav. Div., 19 Corps, Gulf. Dec., 1863, 1 Brig., Cav. Div., Gulf. June, 1864, 1 Brig., 2 Div., 19 Corps, Gulf. Aug., 1864, 1 Brig., 2 Div., 19 Corps, Middle Mil. Div. Jany., 1865, 1 Brig., Grover's Div., Dist. Savannah, Dept. South. June, 1865, Dept. South. Mustered out Aug. 23, 1865.

76th REGIMENT INFANTRY ("COURTLAND CO. REGIMENT").—Org. at Courtland and Albany and mustered in Jany. 16, 1862. Jany., 1862, 3 Brig., Casey's Div., Potomac. March, 1862, Wadsworth's Command, Mil. Dist. Washington. May, 1862, Doubleday's Brig., Dept. Rappahannock. June, 1862, 2 Brig., 1 Div., 3 Corps, Army Va. Sept., 1862, 2 Brig., 1 Div., 1 Corps, Potomac. Jany., 1864, 1 Brig., 1 Div., 1 Corps, Potomac. March, 1864, 2 Brig., 1 Div., 1 Corps, Potomac. March, 1864, 2 Brig.,

4 Div., 5 Corps, Potomac. Aug., 1864, 3 Brig., 2 Div., 5 Corps, Potomac. Sept., 1864, 3 Brig., 3 Div., 5 Corps, Potomac. Mustered out July 1, 1864, to Jany. 1, 1865.

77th REGIMENT INFANTRY ("BEMIS HEIGHTS REGIMENT").—Org. at Saratoga and mustered in Nov. 23, 1861. Nov., 1861, 3 Brig., Casey's Div., Potomac. March, 1862, 3 Brig., 2 Div., 4 Corps, Potomac. May, 1862, 3 Brig., 2 Div., 6 Corps, Potomac. July, 1864, 3 Brig., 2 Div., 6 Corps, Middle Mil. Div. Dec., 1864, 3 Brig., 2 Div., 6 Corps, Potomac. Mustered out June 27, 1865.

77th REGIMENT NATIONAL GUARD INFANTRY.—Org. for 100 days, Aug. 2, 1864. Duty at Elmira, N. Y. Mustered out Nov. 19, 1864.

78th REGIMENT INFANTRY ("1st REGIMENT EAGLE BRIGADE," "CAMERON HIGHLANDERS").—Org. at N. Y. City and mustered in Jany. to April, 1862. April, 1862, 2 Brig., Sigel's Div., Dept. Shenandoah. June, 1862, 2 Brig., 2 Div., 2 Corps, Army Va. Aug., 1862, 3 Brig., 2 Div., 2 Corps, Army Va. Sept., 1862, 3 Brig., 2 Div., 12 Corps, Potomac. Oct., 1863, 3 Brig., 2 Div., 12 Corps, Cumb'd. April, 1864, 3 Brig., 2 Div., 20 Corps. Consolidated with 102nd N. Y. Infy., July 2, 1864.

79th REGIMENT INFANTRY ("HIGHLANDERS").—Org. at N. Y. and mustered in May 29, 1861. June, 1861, Sherman's Brig., Tyler's Div., McDowell's Army, N. E. Va. Aug., 1861, W. F. Smith's Brig., Div. Potomac. Oct., 1861, Stevens' Brig., W. F. Smith's Div., Potomac. Nov., 1861, Stevens' 2 Brig., Sherman's S. C. Exp. Corps. April, 1862, 2 Brig., 2 Div., Dept. South. July, 1862, 2 Brig., 1 Div., 9 Corps, Potomac. Sept., 1862, 1 Brig., 1 Div., 9 Corps, Potomac. April, 1863, 1 Brig., 1 Div., 9 Corps, Ohio. June, 1863, 3 Brig., 1 Div., 9 Corps, Tenn. Aug., 1863, 1 Brig., 1 Div., 9 Corps, Ohio. April, 1864, 2 Brig., 3 Div., 9 Corps, Potomac. Sept., 1864, 1 Brig., 1 Div., 9 Corps, Potomac. Oct., 1864, Provost Guard, 9 Corps, Potomac. Mustered out July 14, 1865.

80th REGIMENT INFANTRY ("ULSTER GUARD," "2nd STATE MILITIA").—Org. at Kingston, Sept. 20 to Oct. 20, 1861. Nov., 1861, Wadsworth's Brig., McDowell's Div., Potomac. March, 1862, 2 Brig., 3 Div., 1 Corps, Potomac. April, 1862, 2 Brig., King's Div., Dept. Rappahannock. June, 1862, 3 Brig., 1 Div., 3 Corps, Army Va. Sept., 1862, 3 Brig., 1 Div., 1 Corps, Potomac. Jany., 1863, Patrick's Command, Provost Guard, Army Potomac. June, 1863, 1 Brig., 3 Div., 1 Corps, Potomac. July, 1863, Provost Guard, Potomac. June, 1864, City Point, Va., Provost Guard, Headqrs. Army Potomac. March, 1865, Indpt. Brig., 9 Corps, Potomac. April, 1865, Richmond, Va., Dept. Va. Nov., 1865, Norfolk and Portsmouth, Va., Dept. Va. Mustered out Jany. 29, 1866.

81st REGIMENT INFANTRY ("OSWEGO REGIMENT," "MOHAWK RANGERS").—Org. at Albany, Dec. 20, 1861, to Feby. 20, 1862. March, 1862, 3 Brig., 3 Div., 4 Corps, Potomac. June, 1862, 2 Brig., 2 Div., 4 Corps, Potomac. June, 1862, 1 Brig., 2 Div., 4 Corps, Potomac. Dec., 1862, Naglee's Brig., Dept. N. C. Jany., 1863, 1 Brig., 2 Div., 18 Corps, Dept. N. C. Feby., 1863, 1 Brig., 1 Div., 18 Corps, Dept. South. April, 1863, Dist. Beaufort, N. C., 18 Corps, Dept. N. C. Oct., 1863, Heckman's Command, Newport News, Va., Dept. Va. and N. C. Jany., 1864, Dist. Currituck, Dept. Va. and N. C. March, 1864, 1 Brig., Heckman's Div., Dept. Va. and N. C. April, 1864, 1 Brig., 1 Div., 18 Corps, Army James. Dec., 1864, 1 Brig., 3 Div., 24 Corps. July, 1865, 1 Indpt. Brig., 24 Corps, Dept. Va. Mustered out Aug. 31, 1865.

82nd REGIMENT INFANTRY ("2nd N. Y. STATE MILITIA").—Org. May 8, 1861. Mustered in at Washington, D. C., May 28, 1861. June, 1861, Schenck's Brig., Tyler's Div., McDowell's Army, N. E. Va. Aug., 1861, Stone's Brig., Div., Potomac. Oct., 1861, Gorman's Brig., Stone's (Sedgwick's) Div., Potomac. March, 1862, 1 Brig., 2 Div., 2 Corps, Potomac. Mustered out June 25, 1864.

83rd REGIMENT INFANTRY ("9th N. Y. STATE MILITIA," "CITY GUARD").—Org. at N. Y. and mustered in at Washington, D. C., June 8, 1861. June, 1861, Stone's Command, Shenandoah. July, 1861, Stone's Brig., Patterson's Army, Shenandoah. Oct., 1861, Stiles' Brig.,

Banks' Div., Potomac. March, 1862, Abercrombie's 2 Brig., Williams' 1 Div., Banks' 5 Corps. April, 1862, 2 Brig., 1 Div., Dept. Shenandoah. May, 1862, 3 Brig., 2 Div., Dept. Rappahannock. June, 1862, 3 Brig., 2 Div., 3 Corps, Army Va. Sept., 1862, 3 Brig., 2 Div., 1 Corps, Potomac. May, 1863, 2 Brig., 2 Div., 1 Corps, Potomac. March, 1864, 2 Brig., 2 Div., 5 Corps, Potomac. May 9-30, 1864, 2 Brig., 3 Div., 5 Corps, Potomac. Mustered out June 23, 1864.

84th REGIMENT INFANTRY ("14th BROOKLYN").—Org. at Brooklyn and mustered in at Washington May 23, 1861. May, 1861, Mansfield's Command, Dept. Washington. June, 1861, Porter's Brig., Hunter's Div., McDowell's Army, N. E. Va. Aug., 1861, Keyes' Brig., Div. Potomac. Oct., 1861, Keyes' Brig., McDowell's Div., Potomac. March, 1862, 1 Brig., 3 Div., 1 Corps, Potomac. April, 1862, 1 Brig., King's Div., Dept. Rappahannock. June, 1862, 1 Brig., 1 Div., 3 Corps, Army Va. Sept., 1862, 1 Brig., 1 Div., 1 Corps, Potomac. June, 1863, 2 Brig., 1 Div., 1 Corps, Potomac. March, 1864, 2 Brig., 4 Div., 5 Corps, Potomac. Mustered out June 14, 1864.

84th REGIMENT NATIONAL GUARD INFANTRY.—Org. for 30 days, July 3, 1863. July, 1863, Balto., Md., 8 Corps, Middle Dept. Mustered out Aug. 4, 1863.

84th REGIMENT NATIONAL GUARD INFANTRY.—Org. for 100 days, July 12, 1864. July, 1864, 1 Brig., DeRussy's Div., 22 Corps, Def. Washington, and Winchester, Va. Mustered out Oct. 29, 1864.

85th REGIMENT INFANTRY.—Org. at Elmira and mustered in Dec. 2, 1861. Dec., 1861, 3 Brig., Casey's Div., Potomac. March, 1862, 3 Brig., 3 Div., 4 Corps, Potomac. June, 1862, 2 Brig., 2 Div., 4 Corps, Potomac. Sept., 1862, Wessell's Brig., Div. at Suffolk, Va., 7 Corps, Dept. Va. Dec., 1862, 1 Brig., 1 Div., Dept. N. C. Jany., 1863, 1 Brig., 4 Div., 18 Corps, Dept. N. C. May, 1863, Dist. Albemarle, Dept. N. C. Aug., 1863, Sub-Dist. Albemarle, Dept. Va. and N. C. April, 1864, Sub-Dist. Albemarle, Dist. N. C., Dept. Va. and N. C. Feby., 1865, 1 Brig., 2 Div., Dist. Beaufort, N. C., Dept. N. C. March, 1865, 2 Brig., Div. Dist. Beaufort, N. C., Dept. N. C. April, 1865, Unatt., 23 Corps, Dept. N. C. Mustered out June 27, 1865.

86th REGIMENT INFANTRY ("STEUBEN RANGERS").—Org. at Elmira and mustered in Nov. 20, 1861. Nov., 1861, Def. Washington. March, 1862, Wadsworth's Command, Mil. Dist. Washington. Aug., 1862, Piatt's Brig., Whipple's Div., Mil. Dist. Washington. Sept., 1862, 1 Brig., 3 Div., 3 Corps, Potomac. June, 1863, 2 Brig., 1 Div., 3 Corps, Potomac. March, 1864, 1 Brig., 3 Div., 2 Corps, Potomac. Mustered out June 27, 1865.

87th REGIMENT INFANTRY ("13th BROOKLYN").—Org. at Brooklyn and mustered in Nov. 20, 1861. Nov., 1861, 3 Brig., Casey's Div., Potomac. March, 1862, 1 Brig., 3 Div., 3 Corps, Potomac. Aug., 1862, 1 Brig., 1 Div., 3 Corps, Potomac. Consolidated with 40th N. Y., Sept. 6, 1862.

88th REGIMENT INFANTRY ("MEAGHER'S OWN," "5th REGIMENT IRISH BRIGADE").—Org. at Fort Schuyler, N. Y. Dec., 1861, Meagher's Brig., Sumner's Div., Potomac. March, 1862, 2 Brig., 1 Div., 2 Corps, Potomac. June, 1864, Consolidated Brig., 1 Div., 2 Corps, Potomac. Nov., 1864, 2 Brig., 1 Div., 2 Corps, Potomac. Mustered out June 30, 1865.

89th REGIMENT INFANTRY ("DICKINSON GUARD").—Org. at Elmira and mustered in Dec. 4, 1861. Dec., 1861, Prov'l Brig., Casey's Div., Potomac. Dec., 1861, Williams' Brig., Burnside's N. C. Exp. Corps. April, 1862, 4 Brig., Dept. N. C. July, 1863, 1 Brig., 3 Div., 9 Corps, Potomac. April, 1863, 1 Brig., 2 Div., 7 Corps, Dept. Va. July, 1863, Alvord's Brig., Vodge's Div., N. E. Folly Island, S. C., 10 Corps, Dept. South. Jany., 1864, 2 Brig., Folly Island, S. C., Northern Dist. Dept. South. Feby., 1864, 2 Brig., Gordon's Div., Northern Dist., Dept. South. April, 1864, 1 Brig., 2 Div., 10 Corps, Army James, Dept. Va. and N. C. May, 1864, 1 Brig., 2 Div., 18 Corps. June, 1864, 3 Brig., 2 Div., 18 Corps. Dec., 1864, 4 Brig., 1 Div., 24 Corps. May, 1865, 3 Brig., 1 Div., 24 Corps. June, 1865, 2 Brig., 1 Div., 24 Corps. Mustered out Aug. 3, 1865.

90th REGIMENT INFANTRY.—Org. by consolidation of the McClellan Chasseurs and the McClellan Rifles, Nov. and Dec., 1861, at N. Y. City. Jany., 1862, Brannan's Fla. Exp. March, 1862, Dist. Key West, Dept. South. Aug., 1862, Dist. Key West, Fla., Dept. Gulf. Nov., 1862, Dist. Beaufort, S. C., 10 Corps, Dept. South. March, 1863, Key West, Fla., Dept. Gulf. April, 1863, 1 Brig., 4 Div., 19 Corps, Dept. Gulf. Feby., 1864, 2 Brig., 2 Div., 19 Corps, Gulf. July, 1864, 1 Brig., 1 Div., 19 Corps, Middle Mil. Div. March, 1865, 1 Brig., 1 Prov'l Div., Army Shenandoah. April, 1865, 1 Brig., Dwight's Div., Dept. Washington, D. C. June, 1865, 1 Brig., Dwight's Div., Dept. South. July, 1865, 3 Brig., 1 Div., Dept. Ga. Jany., 1866, Dept. Ga. Mustered out Feby. 9, 1866.

91st REGIMENT INFANTRY ("ALBANY REGIMENT").—Org. at Albany, Sept. to Dec., 1861. Jany., 1862, Pensacola, Fla., Brannan's Command, Dist. Fla. March, 1862, Dist. Key West, Fla., Dist. West. Fla., Dept. South. Aug., 1862, Dist. West. Fla., Dept. Gulf. Jany., 1863, 1 Brig., 3 Div., 19 Corps, Gulf. Jany., 1863, 2 Brig., 4 Div., 19 Corps, Gulf. March, 1863, 1 Brig., 4 Div., 19 Corps, Gulf. July, 1863, Garrison Fort Jackson, Def. New Orleans. Oct., 1864, Balto., Md., 8 Corps, Middle Dept. Feby., 1865, 1 Brig., 3 Div., 5 Corps, Potomac. June, 1865, 3 Brig., 3 Div., 5 Corps. Mustered out July 3, 1865.

92nd REGIMENT INFANTRY.—Org. at Potsdam and mustered in Jany. 1, 1862. March, 1862, 3 Brig., 3 Div., 4 Corps, Potomac. June, 1862, 2 Brig., 3 Div., 4 Corps, Potomac. Sept., 1862, Wessell's Brig., Div. at Suffolk, Va., 7 Corps, Dept. Va. Dec., 1862, 1 Brig., 1 Div., Dept. N. C. Jany., 1863, 1 Brig., 4 Div., 18 Corps, Dept. N. C. May, 1863, Lee's Brig., Def. Newberne, Dept. N. C. Aug., 1863, Sub-Dist. Albemarle, N. C., Dept. Va. and N. C. April, 1864, Palmer's Brig., Peck's Div., 18 Corps, Dept. Va. and N. C. April, 1864, 3 Brig., 1 Div., 18 Corps. Oct., 1864, 2 Brig., 1 Div., 18 Corps. Consolidated with 96th N. Y. Infy., Dec. 1, 1864.

93rd REGIMENT INFANTRY ("MORGAN RIFLES"). —Org. at Albany, Oct., 1861, to Jany., 1862. March, 1862, 3 Brig., 3 Div., 4 Corps, Potomac. May, 1862, Provost Guard, Army Potomac. April, 1864, 3 Brig., 3 Div., 2 Corps, Potomac. Mustered out June 29, 1865.

93rd REGIMENT NATIONAL GUARD INFANTRY.— Org. for 100 days, July 20, 1864. Mustered out Nov. 1, 1864.

94th REGIMENT INFANTRY ("BELLE JEFFERSON RIFLES").—Org. at Sackett's Harbor and mustered in March 10, 1862. March, 1862, Wadsworth's Command, Def. Washington. May, 1862, 1 Brig., 2 Div., Dept. Rappahannock. June, 1862, 2 Brig., 2 Div., 3 Corps, Army Va. Sept., 1862, 2 Brig., 2 Div., 1 Corps, Potomac. Dec., 1862, 1 Brig., 2 Div., 1 Corps, Potomac. May, 1863, Provost Guard, Army Potomac. June, 1863, 1 Brig., 2 Div., 1 Corps, Potomac. Dec., 1863, Dist. Annapolis, Md., 8 Corps, Middle Dept. May, 1864, 2 Brig., 2 Div., 5 Corps, Potomac. May 30, 1864, 1 Brig., 2 Div., 5 Corps. June 6, 1864, 1 Brig., 3 Div., 5 Corps. June 11, 1864, 2 Brig., 3 Div., 5 Corps. Sept., 1864, 3 Brig., 3 Div., 5 Corps. Oct., 1864, 2 Brig., 3 Div., 5 Corps. Nov., 1864, 3 Brig., 3 Div., 5 Corps. Mustered out July 18, 1865.

95th REGIMENT INFANTRY ("WARREN RIFLES"). —Org. at N. Y. City, Nov., 1861, to March, 1862. March, 1862, Wadsworth's Command, Def. Washington. May, 1862, Doubleday's Brig., Dept. Rappahannock. June, 1862, 2 Brig., 1 Div., 3 Corps, Army Va. Sept., 1862, 2 Brig., 1 Div., 1 Corps, Potomac. March, 1864, 2 Brig., 4 Div., 5 Corps, Potomac. Aug., 1864, 3 Brig., 2 Div., 5 Corps, Potomac. Sept., 1864, 3 Brig., 3 Div., 5 Corps, Potomac. Mustered out July 16, 1865.

96th REGIMENT INFANTRY ("M'COMB'S PLATTSBURG REGIMENT").—Org. at Plattsburg, Feby. 20 to March 7, 1862. March, 1862, 3 Brig., 3 Div., 4 Corps, Potomac. June, 1862, 2 Brig., 2 Div., 4 Corps, Potomac. Sept., 1862, Wessell's Brig., Div. at Suffolk, Va., 7 Corps, Dept. Va. Dec., 1862, 1 Brig., 1 Div., Dept. N. C. Jany., 1863, 1 Brig., 4 Div., 18 Corps, Dept. N. C. May, 1863, Dist. Albemarle, Dept. N. C. Oct., 1863, Heckman's Command, Newport News, Va., Dept. Va. and N. C. Dec.,

1863, Dist. Currituck, Dept. Va. and N. C. March, 1864, 1 Brig., Heckman's Div., 18 Corps, Army James, Dept. Va. and N. C. April, 1864, 1 Brig., 1 Div., 18 Corps. July, 1864, 2 Brig., 1 Div., 18 Corps. Dec., 1864, 2 Brig., 3 Div., 24 Corps. June, 1865, 1 Brig., 3 Div., 24 Corps. July, 1865, 1 Indpt. Brig., 24 Corps. Aug., 1865, Dept. Va. Mustered out Feby. 6, 1866.

97th REGIMENT INFANTRY. ("CONKLING RIFLES.")—Org. at Boonville and mustered in Feby. 18, 1862. March, 1862, Wadsworth's Command, Def. Washington. May, 1862, 2 Brig., 2 Div., Dept. Rappahannock. June, 1862, 1 Brig., 2 Div., 3 Corps, Army Va. Sept., 1862, 1 Brig., 2 Div., 1 Corps, Potomac. Dec., 1862, 1 Brig., 2 Div., 1 Corps, Potomac. May, 1863, 2 Brig., 2 Div., 1 Corps, Potomac. March, 1864, 2 Brig., 2 Div., 5 Corps, Potomac. May, 1864, 2 Brig., 3 Div., 5 Corps, Potomac. Mustered out July 18, 1865.

98th REGIMENT INFANTRY. ("MALONE AND LYON REGIMENT.")—Org. Jany. 25 to Feby. 8, 1862. March, 1862, 3 Brig., 3 Div., 4 Corps, Potomac. June, 1862, 2 Brig., 2 Div., 4 Corps, Potomac. July, 1862, 1 Brig., 2 Div., 4 Corps, Potomac. Dec., 1862, Naglee's Brig., Dept. N. C. Jany., 1863, 1 Brig., 2 Div., 18 Corps, Dept. N. C. Feby., 1863, 1 Brig., 1 Div., 18 Corps, Dept. South. April, 1863, Dist. Beaufort, N. C., Dept. N. C. Oct., 1863, Heckman's Command, Newport News, Va., Dept. Va. and N. C. Jany., 1864, Dist. Currituck, Dept. Va. and N. C. March, 1864, 1 Brig., Heckman's Div., 18 Corps, Army James, Dept. Va. and N. C. April, 1864, 1 Brig., 1 Div., 18 Corps. Dec., 1864, 1 Brig., 3 Div., 24 Corps. June, 1865, 2 Brig., 3 Div., 24 Corps. July, 1865, 2nd Indpt. Brig., 24 Corps. Mustered out Aug. 31, 1865.

99th REGIMENT NATIONAL GUARD INFANTRY.— Org. for 100 days, Aug. 10, 1864. Duty at Elmira, N. Y. Mustered out Dec. 22, 1864.

99th REGIMENT INFANTRY ("UNION COAST GUARD.")—Org. at New York City May 28, 1861. May, 1861, Fort Monroe and Camp Hamilton, Va., Dept. Va. May, 1862, 3 Brig., 1 Div., Dept. Va. July, 1862, Norfolk, Va., 7 Corps, Dept. Va. Feby., 1863, Terry's Prov'l Brig. Div. at Suffolk, Va., 7 Corps. April, 1863, Reserve Brig., 7 Corps. July, 1863, U. S. Forces, Yorktown, Va., Dept. Va. and N. C. Oct., 1863, Newberne, N. C., Dept. Va. and N. C. Jany., 1865, Sub Dist. Newberne, N. C., Dept N. C. Mustered out July 15, 1865.

99th REGIMENT NATIONAL GUARD INFANTRY.— Org. for 100 days Aug. 2, 1864. Duty at Elmira, N. Y. Mustered out Nov. 9, 1864.

100th REGIMENT INFANTRY. ("2nd EAGLE REGIMENT.")—Org. at Buffalo Jany., 1862. March, 1862, 1 Brig., 3 Div., 4 Corps, Potomac. June, 1862, 1 Brig., 2 Div., 4 Corps, Potomac. Dec., 1862, Naglee's Brig., Dept. N. C. Jany., 1863, 2 Brig., 2 Div., 18 Corps, Dept. N. C. Feby., 1863, 1 Brig., 2 Div., 18 Corps, Dept. South. April, 1863, Folly Island, S. C., 10 Corps, Dept. South. June, 1863, 2 Brig., Folly Island, S. C., 10 Corps. July, 1863, 1 Brig., Folly Island, S. C., 10 Corps. July, 1863, 2 Brig., 1 Div., Morris Island, S. C., 10 Corps. Aug., 1863, 3 Brig., Morris Island, S. C., 10 Corps. Nov., 1863, 2 Brig., Morris Island, S. C., 10 Corps. Jany., 1864, 2 Brig., Morris Island, S. C., Northern Dist., 10 Corps. April, 1864, 2 Brig., 1 Div., 10 Corps, Army James, Dept. Va. and N. C. May, 1864, 3 Brig., 1 Div., 10 Corps. Dec., 1864, 3 Brig., 1 Div., 24 Corps. July, 1865, 2 Brig., 1 Div., 24 Corps. Mustered out Aug. 28, 1865.

101st REGIMENT INFANTRY. ("UNION REGIMENT.")—Org. at Hancock Sept. 2, 1861. March, 1862, Wadsworth's Command, Def. Washington. May, 1862, Whipple's Brig., Def. Washington. June, 1862, 2 Brig., 3 Div., 3 Corps, Potomac. Aug., 1862, 2 Brig., 1 Div., 3 Corps, Potomac. Transferred to 37th N. Y. Infy. Dec. 24, 1862.

102nd REGIMENT INFANTRY. ("VAN BUREN LIGHT INFANTRY.")—Org. at New York City, March, 1862, Wadsworth's Command, Def. Washington. May, 1862, Cooper's 1 Brig., Sigel's Div., Dept. Shenandoah. June, 1862, 1 Brig., 2 Div., 2 Corps, Army Va. Aug., 1862, 2 Brig., 2 Div., 2 Corps, Army Va. Sept., 1862, 2

Brig., 2 Div., 12 Corps, Potomac. Oct., 1862, 3 Brig., 2 Div., 12 Corps, Potomac. Oct., 1863, 3 Brig., 2 Div., 12 Corps, Cumb'd. April, 1864, 3 Brig., 2 Div., 20 Corps. Mustered out July 21, 1865.

102nd REGIMENT NATIONAL GUARD REGIMENT. —Org. for 100 days, Aug. 6, 1864. Duty at Elmira, N. Y. Mustered out Nov. 13, 1864.

103rd REGIMENT INFANTRY. ("SEWARD INFANTRY.")—Org. at New York City, Nov., 1861, to March, 1862. March, 1862, Norfolk, Va., Dept. Va. April, 1862, 1 Brig., 2 Div., Dept. Va. July, 1862, 1 Brig., 3 Div., 9 Corps, Potomac. April, 1863, 1 Brig., 2 Div., 7 Corps, Dept. Va. July, 1863, Alvord's Brig., Vodge's Div., Folly Island, S. C., 10 Corps, Dept. South. Jany., 1864, 2 Brig., Folly Island, S. C., Northern Dist., 10 Corps. April, 1864, Folly Island, Northern Dist., Dept. South. Aug., 1864, 3 Brig., DeRussy's Div., Def. Washington, 22 Corps. Sept., 1864, 1 Brig., Kitching's Prov'l Div., Army Shenandoah. Dec., 1864, 1 Brig., Prov'l Div., Dept. Va. and N. C. March, 1865, 1 Brig., Infy., Dept. Va. May, 1865, Dept. Va. Mustered out Dec. 7, 1865.

104th REGIMENT INFANTRY. ("WADSWORTH GUARDS," "LIVINGSTON CO. REGIMENT.")—Org. at Geneseo, Oct., 1861, to March, 1862. March, 1862, Wadsworth's Command, Def. Washington. May, 1862, 2 Brig., 2 Div., Dept. Rappahannock. June, 1862, 1 Brig., 2 Div., 3 Corps, Army Va. Sept., 1862, 1 Brig., 2 Div., 1 Corps, Potomac. March, 1864, 1 Brig., 2 Div., 5 Corps, Potomac. June, 1864, 1 Brig., 3 Div., 5 Corps, Potomac. Aug., 1864, 2 Brig., 3 Div., 5 Corps, Potomac. Sept., 1864, Provost Guard, 5 Corps, Potomac. May, 1865, 2 Brig., 3 Div., 5 Corps, Potomac. Mustered out July 17, 1865.

105th REGIMENT INFANTRY. ("LEROY REGIMENT.")—Org. at LeRoy, March 28, 1862. April, 1862, Duryea's Brig., Mil. Dist. Wash. May, 1862, 2 Brig., 2 Div., Dept. Rappahannock. June, 1863, 1 Brig., 2 Div., 3 Corps, Army Va. Sept., 1862, 1 Brig., 2 Div., 1 Corps, Potomac. Mustered out by transfer to 94th New York Infy., March 17, 1863.

106th REGIMENT INFANTRY. ("ST. LAWRENCE CO. REGIMENT.")—Org. at Ogdensburg and mustered in Aug. 27, 1862. Aug., 1862, R. R. Dist., 8 Corps, Middle Dept. Sept., 1862, R. R. Dist, Dept. W. Va. Jany., 1863, Martinsburg, W. Va., 8 Corps. March, 1863, 3 Brig., 1 Div., 8 Corps. June, 1863, Elliott's Command, 8 Corps. July, 1863, 3 Brig., 3 Div., 3 Corps, Potomac. March, 1864, 1 Brig., 3 Div., 6 Corps, Potomac. Aug., 1864, 1 Brig., 3 Div., 6 Corps, Middle Mil. Div. Dec., 1864, 1 Brig., 3 Div., 6 Corps, Potomac. Mustered out June 27, 1865.

107th REGIMENT INFANTRY. ("CAMPBELL GUARD.")—Org. at Elmira and mustered in Aug. 13, 1862. Aug., 1862, Whipple's Command, Def. Washington. Sept., 1862, 3 Brig., 1 Div., 12 Corps, Potomac. Oct., 1863, 3 Brig., 1 Div., 12 Corps, Cumb'd. April, 1864, 2 Brig., 1 Div., 20 Corps. Mustered out June 5, 1865.

108th REGIMENT INFANTRY. ("ROCHESTER REGIMENT.")—Org. at Rochester and mustered in Aug. 18, 1862. Aug., 1862, Whipple's Command, Def. Washington. Sept., 1862, 2 Brig., 3 Div., 2 Corps, Potomac. March, 1864, 3 Brig., 2 Div., 2 Corps, Potomac. Mustered out May 28, 1865.

109th REGIMENT INFANTRY.—Org. at Binghampton and mustered in Aug. 27, 1862. Aug., 1862, Def. Balto., Md., 8 Corps, Middle Dept. Oct., 1862, Def. Washington. March, 1863, R. R. Guard, 22 Corps. June, 1864, 1 Brig., 3 Div., 9 Corps, Potomac. Sept., 1864, 1 Brig., 1 Div., 9 Corps, Potomac. Mustered out June 4, 1865.

110th REGIMENT INFANTRY.—Org. at Oswego and mustered in Aug. 27, 1862. Aug., 1862, Def. Balto., Md., 8 Corps, Middle Dept. Oct., 1862, Emery's Brig., 8 Corps. Nov., 1862, Emery's Brig., New Orleans Exp. Dec., 1862, Sherman's Div., Dept. Gulf. Jany., 1863, 3 Brig., 3 Div., 19 Corps, Gulf. Feby., 1863, 1 Brig., 3 Div., 19 Corps, Gulf. Feby., 1864, Key West, Fla., Dist. West Fla., Dept. Gulf. Mustered out Aug. 28, 1865.

111th REGIMENT INFANTRY.—Org. at Auburn and mustered in Aug. 20, 1862. Aug., 1862, Miles' Command, Harper's Ferry, W. Va. Sept., 1862, Camp Douglass, Ill. Dec., 1862, Wadsworth's Command, Def. Washington. Feby., 1863, 3 Brig., Casey's Div., 22 Corps. April, 1863, 3 Brig., Abercrombie's Div., 22 Corps. June, 1863, 3 Brig., 3 Div., 2 Corps, Potomac. March., 1864, 3 Brig., 1 Div., 2 Corps, Potomac. June, 1864, Consolidated Brig., 1 Div., 2 Corps. Nov., 1864, 3 Brig., 1 Div., 2 Corps. Mustered out June 3, 1865.

112th REGIMENT INFANTRY. ("CHATAUQUA REGIMENT.")—Org. at Jamestown, Sept. 11, 1862. Sept., 1862, Foster's Prov'l Brig., Div. at Suffolk, Va., 7 Corps, Dept. Va. Dec., 1862, Gibbs' Prov'l Brig., Div. at Suffolk, 7 Corps. April, 1863, 2 Brig., 1 Div., 7 Corps, Dept. Va. July, 1863, Foster's Brig., Vodge's Div., Folly Island, S. C., 10 Corps, Dept. South. Feby., 1864, 2 Brig., Vodge's Div., Dist. Fla. April, 1864, 2 Brig., 3 Div., 10 Corps, Army James, Dept. Va. and N. C. May, 1864, 2 Brig., 3 Div., 18 Corps. June, 1864, 1 Brig., 2 Div., 10 Corps. Dec., 1864, 1 Brig., 2 Div., 24 Corps. Jany., 1865, 1 Brig., 2 Div., Terry's Prov'l Corps, Dept. N. C. March, 1865, 1 Brig., 2 Div., 10 Corps, Army Ohio, Dept. N. C. Mustered out June 13, 1865.

113th REGIMENT INFANTRY.—Org. Aug. 18, 1862. Sept., 1862, Def. Washington. Designation changed to 7th N. Y. Heavy Arty., Dec. 19, 1862.

114th REGIMENT INFANTRY.—Org. at Norwich and mustered in Sept. 3, 1862. Sept., 1862, Emery's Brig., Def. Balto., Md., 8 Corps, Middle Dept. Nov., 1862, Emery's Brig., Banks' La. Exp. Dec., 1862, Sherman's Div., Dept. Gulf. Jany., 1863, 1 Brig., 3 Div., 19 Corps, Dept. Gulf. Feby., 1863, 2 Brig., 1 Div., 19 Corps, Gulf. July, 1863, 3 Brig., 1 Div., 19 Corps, Gulf. Feby., 1864, 1 Brig., 1 Div., 19 Corps, Gulf. July, 1864, 1 Brig., 1 Div., 19 Corps, Middle Mil. Div. March, 1865, 1 Brig., 1 Prov'l Div., Army Shenandoah. April, 1865, 1 Brig., Dwight's Div., Dept. Washington. Mustered out June 8, 1865.

115th REGIMENT INFANTRY. ("IRON-HEARTED REGIMENT.")—Org. at Fonda and mustered in Aug. 26, 1862. Sept., 1862, Miles' Command, Harper's Ferry, W. Va., R. R. Brig., 8 Corps. Sept., 1862, Camp Douglas, Ill. Dec., 1862, 3 Brig., Casey's Div., Def. Washington. Dec., 1862, Busteed's Indpt. Brig., 7 Corps, Dept. Va. Jany., 1863, Dist. Hilton Head, S. C., 10 Corps, Dept. South. June, 1863, Dist. Beaufort, S. C., 10 Corps. Dec., 1863, Dist. Hilton Head, S. C., 10 Corps. Jany., 1864, Barton's Brig., Dist. Hilton Head, S. C., 10 Corps. Feby., 1864, Barton's Brig., Dist. Fla. Feby., 1864, Barton's Brig., Ames' Div., Dist. Fla. April, 1864, 2 Brig., 2 Div., 10 Corps, Army James, Dept. Va. and N. C. May, 1864, 1 Brig., 3 Div., 18 Corps. June, 1864, 2 Brig., 2 Div., 10 Corps. July, 1864, 3 Brig., 2 Div., 10 Corps. Dec., 1864, 3 Brig., 2 Div., 24 Corps. Jany., 1865, 3 Brig., 2 Div., Terry's Prov'l Corps, Dept. N. C. March, 1865, 3 Brig., 2 Div., 10 Corps, Army Ohio, Dept. N. C. Mustered out June 17, 1865.

116th REGIMENT INFANTRY.—Org. at Buffalo, Aug. 30 to Sept. 3, 1862. Sept., 1862, Emery's Brig., Balto., Md., 8 Corps, Middle Dept. Nov., 1862, Emery's Brig., Banks' La. Exp. Dec., 1862, Sherman's Div., Dept. Gulf. Jany., 1863, 1 Brig., 3 Div., 19 Corps, Gulf. Feby., 1863, 1 Brig., 1 Div., 19 Corps, Gulf. July, 1864, 1 Brig., 1 Div., 19 Corps, Middle Mil. Div. March, 1865, 1 Brig., 1 Prov'l Div., Army Shenandoah. April, 1865, 1 Brig., Dwight's Div., Dept. Washington. Mustered out June 21, 1865.

117th REGIMENT INFANTRY. ("4th ONEIDA REGIMENT.")—Org. at Oneida and mustered in Aug. 8, 1862. Aug., 1862, Def. Washington, North of Potomac. Oct., 1862, 2nd and 3rd Brig., Haskin's Div., Def. Washington. Feby., 1863, 2nd and 3rd Brig., Haskin's Div., 22 Corps. April, 1863, 1 Brig., 2 Div., 7 Corps, Dept. Va. July, 1863, Alvord's Brig., Vodge's Div., Folly Island, S. C., 10 Corps, Dept. South. Feby., 1864, 2 Brig., Folly Island, Northern Dist., Dept. South. April, 1864, 1 Brig., 2 Div., 10 corps, Army James, Dept. Va. and N. C. May, 1864, 3 Brig., 3 Div., 18 Corps. June, 1864, 1 Brig., 2 Div., 10 Corps. Dec., 1864, 1 Brig., 2 Div., 24 Corps. Jany., 1865, 1 Brig., 2 Div., Terry's Prov'l Corps, Dept. N. C. March,

1865, 1 Brig., 2 Div., 10 Corps, Army Ohio, Dept. N. C. Mustered out June 8, 1865.

118th REGIMENT INFANTRY. ("ADIRONDACK REGIMENT.")—Org. at Plattsburg and mustered in Aug. 27, 1862. Sept., 1862, Prov'l Brig., Abercrombie's Div., Def. Washington. Feby., 1863, Dist. Washington, 22 Corps. April, 1863, Reserve Brig., 3 Div., 7 Corps, Dept. Va. July, 1863, U. S. Forces, Yorktown, Va., Dept. Va. and N. C. Oct., 1863, Heckman's Command, Newport News, Va., Dept. Va. and N. C. Jany., 1864, 1 Brig., U. S. Forces, Yorktown, Dept. Va. and N. C. Feby., 1864, Unatt., Yorktown, Va. April, 1864, 2 Brig., 1 Div., 18 Corps. Dec., 1864, 2 Brig., 3 Div., 24 Corps. Mustered out June 13, 1865.

119th REGIMENT INFANTRY.—Org. at New York City and mustered in Sept. 4, 1862. Sept., 1862, 2 Brig., 3 Div., 11 Corps, Potomac. Oct., 1863, 2 Brig., 3 Div., 11 Corps, Cumb'd. April, 1864, 2 Brig., 2 Div., 20 Corps. Mustered out June 7, 1865.

120th REGIMENT INFANTRY. ("ULSTER REGIMENT," "WASHINGTON GUARD.")—Org. at Kingston and mustered in Aug. 22, 1862. Aug., 1862, Whipple's Brig., Def. Washington. Oct., 1862, 1 Brig., 2 Div., 3 Corps, Potomac. Dec., 1862, 2 Brig., 2 Div., 3 Corps, Potomac. March, 1864, 2 Brig., 4 Div., 2 Corps, Potomac. May, 1864, 4 Brig., 3 Div., 2 Corps. July, 1864, 3 Brig., 3 Div., 2 Corps. Mustered out June 3, 1865.

121st REGIMENT INFANTRY. ("OTSEGO AND HERKIMER REGIMENT.")—Org. at Herkimer and mustered in Aug. 13, 1862. Sept., 1862, 2 Brig., 1 Div., 6 Corps, Potomac. Aug., 1864, 2 Brig., 1 Div., 6 Corps, Middle Mil. Div. Dec., 1864, 2 Brig., 1 Div., 6 Corps, Potomac. Mustered out June 25, 1865.

122nd REGIMENT INFANTRY. ("ONONDAGAS.")— Org. at Syracuse and mustered in Aug. 28, 1862. Sept., 1862, 3 Brig., 1 Div., 4 Corps, Potomac. Sept., 1862, 2 Brig., 3 Div., 6 Corps, Potomac. Oct., 1862, 1 Brig., 3 Div., 6 Corps, Potomac. Jany., 1864, Johnson's Island, Ohio. March, 1864, 4 Brig., 1 Div., 6 Corps, Potomac. July, 1864, 3 Brig., 2 Div., 6 Corps, Middle Mil. Div. Dec., 1864, 3 Brig., 2 Div., 6 Corps, Potomac. Mustered out June 23, 1865.

123rd REGIMENT INFANTRY. ("WASHINGTON CO. REGIMENT.")—Org. at Salem and mustered in Sept. 4, 1862. Sept., 1862, 2 Brig., 1 Div., 12 Corps, Potomac. May, 1863, 1 Brig., 1 Div., 12 Corps. Oct., 1863, 1 Brig., 1 Div., 12 Corps, Cumb'd. April, 1864, 1 Brig., 1 Div., 20 Corps. Mustered out June 8, 1865.

124th REGIMENT INFANTRY. ("AMERICAN GUARD," "ORANGE BLOSSOMS.")—Org. at Goshen and mustered in Sept. 5, 1862. Sept., 1862, Piatt's Brig., Whipple's Div., 3 Corps, Potomac. Oct., 1862, 1 Brig., 3 Div., 3 Corps, Potomac. June, 1863, 2 Brig., 1 Div., 3 Corps, Potomac. Feby., 1863, 3 Brig., Casey's Div., 22 Corps. March, 1864, 1 Brig., 3 Div., 2 Corps, Potomac. Mustered out June 3, 1865.

125th REGIMENT INFANTRY.—Org. at Troy and mustered in Aug. 29, 1862. Sept., 1862, Miles' Command, Harper's Ferry, W. Va. Sept., 1862, Camp Douglass, Ill. Dec., 1862, 3 Brig., Casey's Div., Def. Washington. Feby., 1863, 3 Brig., Abercrombie's Div., 22 Corps. June, 1863, 3 Brig., 3 Div., 2 Corps, Potomac. March, 1864, 3 Brig., 1 Div., 2 Corps, Potomac. June, 1864, Consolidated Brig., 1 Div., 2 Corps, Potomac. Nov., 1864, 3 Brig., 1 Div., 2 Corps, Potomac. Mustered out June 5, 1865.

126th REGIMENT INFANTRY.—Org. at Geneva and mustered in Aug. 22, 1862. Aug., 1862, Miles' Command, Harper's Ferry, W. Va. Sept., 1862, Camp Douglass, Ill. Dec., 1862, 3 Brig., Casey's Div., Def. Washington. Feby., 1863, 3 Brig., Casey's Div., 22 Corps. April, 1863, 3 Brig., Abercrombie's Div., 22 Corps. June, 1863, 3 Brig., 3 Div., 2 Corps, Potomac. March, 1864, 3 Brig., 1 Div., 2 Corps, Potomac. June, 1864, Consolidated Brig., 1 Div., 2 Corps, Potomac. Nov., 1864, 3 Brig., 1 Div., 2 Corps, Potomac. Mustered out June 3, 1865.

127th REGIMENT INFANTRY. ("NATIONAL VOLUNTEERS.")—Org. at Staten Island and mustered in Sept. 8, 1862. Oct., 1862, 2 Brig., 1 Div., 12 Corps, Po-

tomac. Oct., 1862, 4 Brig., 1 Div., 12 Corps, Potomac. Oct., 1862, 3 Brig., Abercrombie's Div., Def. Washington, and 22 Corps. April, 1863, 2 Brig., 3 Div., 7 Corps, Dept. Va. July, 1863, 1 Brig., 1 Div., 11 Corps, Potomac. Aug., 1863, 1 Brig., Gordon's Div., Folly Island, S. C., 10 Corps, Dept. South. Jany., 1864, 1 Brig., Folly Island, S. C., Northern Dist., Dept. South. April, 1864, Morris Island, S. C. Northern Dist., Dept. South. Oct., 1864, Dist. Beaufort, S. C., 2nd Separate Brig., Dept. South. Nov., 1864, 1 Brig., Coast Div., Dept. South. Jany., 1865, 1st Separate Brig., Northern Dist., Dept. South. March, 1865, 1st Separate Brig., Dist. Charleston, S. C., Dept. South. Mustered out June 30, 1865.

128th REGIMENT INFANTRY.—Org. at Hudson and mustered in Sept. 4, 1862. Sept., 1862, Def. Balto., Md., 8 Corps, Middle Dept. Dec., 1862, Sherman's Div., Dept. Gulf. Jany., 1863, 1 Brig., 2 Div., 19 Corps, Gulf. July, 1863, 2 Brig., 1 Div., 19 Corps, Gulf. Feby., 1864, 3 Brig., 2 Div., 19 Corps, Gulf. July, 1864, 3 Brig., 2 Div., 19 Corps, Middle Mil. Div. Jany., 1865, 3 Brig., Grover's Div., Dist. Savannah, Ga., Dept. South. March, 1865, 3 Brig., 1 Div., 10 Corps, Army Ohio, Dept. N. C. April, 1865, Dist. Savannah, Ga., Dist. South. Mustered out July 12, 1865.

129th REGIMENT INFANTRY.—Org. at Lockport and mustered in Aug. 22, 1862. Aug., 1862, Balto., Md., 8 Corps, Middle Dept. Designation changed to 8th N. Y. Heavy Arty., Oct. 3, 1862.

130th REGIMENT INFANTRY.—Org. at Portage and mustered in Sept. 2, 1862. Sept., 1862, Foster's Prov'l Brig., Div. at Suffolk, Va., 7 Corps, Dept. Va. Dec., 1862, Gibbs' Prov'l Brig., Div. Suffolk, 7 Corps. April, 1863, 1 Brig., 1 Div., 7 Corps, Dept. Va. July, 1863, Def. Washington, 22 Corps. July, 1863, Provost Guard, Army Potomac. Designation changed to 19th N. Y. Cav., Aug. 11, 1863.

131st REGIMENT INFANTRY. ("1st REGIMENT METROPOLITAN GUARD.")—Org. at New York City and mustered in Sept. 6, 1862. Sept., 1862, Annapolis, Md., 8 Corps, Middle Dept. Dec., 1862, Grover's Div., Dept. Gulf. Jany., 1863, 1 Brig., 4 Div., 19 Corps, Gulf. Feby., 1864, 2 Brig., 2 Div., 19 Corps, Gulf. July, 1864, 2 Brig., 2 Div., 19 Corps, Middle Mil. Div. Jany., 1865, 2 Brig., Grover's Div., Dist. Savannah, Ga., Dept. South. March, 1865, 1 Brig., 1 Div., 10 Corps, Army Ohio, Dept. N. C. April, 1865, Dist. Savannah, Ga., Dept. South. Mustered out July 26, 1865.

132nd REGIMENT INFANTRY. ("2nd REGIMENT EMPIRE BRIGADE.")—Org. at New York City and mustered in at Washington, D. C., Oct. 4, 1862. Oct., 1862, Spinola's Brig., Div. at Suffolk, Va., 7 Corps, Dept. Va. Jany. 1863, 1 Brig., 5 Div., 18 Corps, Dept. N. C. March, 1863, 2 Brig., 5 Div., 18 Corps, Dept. N. C. July, 1863, Unatt., Def. Newberne, Dept. Va. and N. C. Jany., 1864, Palmer's Brig., Peck's Div., 18 Corps, Dept. Va. and N. C. April, 1864, Sub Dist. Newberne, N. C., Dept. Va. and N. C. Feby., 1865, 2 Brig., 1 Div., Dist. Beaufort, N. C., Dept. N. C. March, 1865, 1 Brig., Div., Dist. Beaufort, N. C., Dept. N. C. April, 1865, 1 Brig., 2 Div., 23 Corps, Army Ohio, Dept. N. C. Mustered out June 29, 1865.

133rd REGIMENT INFANTRY. ("2nd METROPOLITAN GUARD.")—Org. at New York City and mustered in Sept. 24, 1862. Oct., 1862, Abercrombie's Div., Def. Washington. Nov., 1862, Grover's Brig., Banks' La. Exp. Dec., 1862, Grover's Div., Dept. Gulf. Jany., 1863, 2 Brig., 3 Div., 19 Corps, Gulf. Oct., 1863, Def. New Orleans. April, 1864, 1 Brig., 2 Div., 19 Corps, Gulf. June, 1864, 3 Brig., 1 Div., 19 Corps, Gulf. Aug., 1864, 3 Brig., 1 Div., 19 Corps, Middle Mil. Div. March, 1865, 3 Brig., 1st Prov'l Div., Army Shenandoah. April, 1865, 3 Brig., Dwight's Div., Dept. Washington. Mustered out June 6, 1865.

134th REGIMENT INFANTRY.—Org. at Schoarie and mustered in Sept. 22, 1862. Sept., 1862, 2 Brig., 2 Div., 11 Corps, Potomac. May, 1863, 1 Brig., 2 Div., 11 Corps, Potomac. Oct., 1863, 1 Brig., 2 Div., 11 Corps, Cumb'd. April, 1864, 2 Brig., 2 Div., 20 Corps. Mustered out June 10, 1865.

135th REGIMENT INFANTRY. ("ANTHONY WAYNE GUARD.")—Org. at Yonkers and mustered in Sept. 2, 1862. Sept., 1862, Balto., Md., 8 Corps, Middle Dept. Designation changed to 6th N. Y. Heavy Arty., Oct. 3, 1862.

136th REGIMENT INFANTRY. ("IRON CLADS.")—Org. at Portage and mustered in Sept. 25, 1862. Oct., 1862, 1 Brig., 3 Div., 11 Corps, Potomac. Nov., 1862, 2 Brig., 2 Div., 11 Corps, Potomac. Oct., 1863, 2 Brig., 2 Div., 11 Corps, Cumb'd. April, 1864, 3 Brig., 3 Div., 20 Corps. Mustered out June 13, 1865.

137th REGIMENT INFANTRY.—Org. at Binghampton and mustered in Sept. 25, 1862. Oct., 1862, 2 Brig., 1 Div., 12 Corps, Potomac. Oct., 1862, 4 Brig., 1 Div., 12 Corps, Potomac. Oct., 1862, 3 Brig., 2 Div., 12 Corps, Potomac. Oct., 1863, 3 Brig., 2 Div., 12 Corps, Cumb'd. April, 1864, 3 Brig., 2 Div., 20 Corps. Mustered out June 9, 1865.

138th REGIMENT INFANTRY. ("2nd AUBURN.")—Org. at Auburn and mustered in Sept. 8, 1862. Oct., 1862, 2 Brig., 1 Div., 12 Corps, Potomac. Oct., 1862, 4 Brig., 1 Div., 12 Corps, Potomac. Oct., 1862, 2 Brig., Def. Washington, D. C., North Potomac. Designation changed to 9th N. Y. Heavy Arty., Dec. 9, 1862.

139th REGIMENT INFANTRY.—Org. at Brooklyn and mustered in Sept. 9, 1862. Sept., 1862, Camp Hamilton, Va., Dept. Va. Dec., 1862, Busteed's Indpt. Brig., 7 Corps, Dept. Va. April, 1863, West's Brig., 7 Corps, Dept. Va. May, 1863, West's Advance Brig., 4 Corps, Dept. Va. July, 1863, Wistar's Brig., U. S. Forces, Yorktown, Va., Dept. Va. and N. C. Jany., 1864, 1 Brig., U. S. Forces, Yorktown, Va., Dept. Va. and N. C. Feby., 1864, Dist. Currituck, Dept. Va. and N. C. March, 1864, Heckman's Div., Portsmouth, Va., 18 Corps. April, 1864, 1 Brig., 1 Div., 18 Corps, Army James. Dec., 1864, 1 Brig., 3 Div., 24 Corps. Mustered out June 19, 1865.

140th REGIMENT INFANTRY. ("MONROE CO. REGIMENT." "ROCHESTER RACE HORSES.")—Org. at Rochester and mustered in Sept. 13, 1862. Oct., 1862, 2 Brig., 2 Div., 12 Corps, Potomac. Nov., 1862, 3 Brig., 2 Div., 5 Corps, Potomac. March, 1864, 4 Brig., 1 Div., 5 Corps, Potomac. April, 1864, 1 Brig., 1 Div., 5 Corps, Potomac. June, 1864, 1 Brig., 2 Div., 5 Corps, Potomac. Mustered out June 3, 1865.

141st REGIMENT INFANTRY.—Org. at Elmira and mustered in Sept. 11, 1862. Sept., 1862, Unatt., 8 Corps, Middle Dept. Oct., 1862, 2 Brig., Abercrombie's Div., Def. Washington. Feby., 1863, 2 Brig., Abercrombie's Div., 22 Corps. April, 1863, 1 Brig., 3 Div., 7 Corps, Dept. Va. May, 1863, 2 Brig., 2 Div., 4 Corps, Dept. Va. July, 1863, 2 Brig., 3 Div., 11 Corps, Potomac. Oct., 1863, 2 Brig., 3 Div., 11 Corps, Cumb'd. April, 1864, 1 Brig., 1 Div., 20 Corps. Mustered out June 8, 1865.

142nd REGIMENT INFANTRY. ("ST. LAWRENCE CO. REGIMENT.")—Org. at Ogdensburg and mustered in Sept. 29, 1862. Oct., 1862, 3 Brig., Abercrombie's Div., Def. Washington. Feby., 1863, 2 Brig., Abercrombie's Div., 22 Corps. April, 1863, 2 Brig., 3 Div., 7 Corps, Dept. Va. May, 1863, 1 Brig., 2 Div., 4 Corps, Dept. Va. July, 1863, 1 Brig., 1 Div., 11 Corps, Potomac. Aug., 1863, 1 Brig., Gordon's Div., Folly Island, S. C., 10 Corps, Dept. South. Jany., 1864, 1 Brig., Gordon's Div., Morris Island, S. C., Northern Dist., 10 Corps. April, 1864, 1 Brig., 2 Div., 10 Corps, Army James, Dept. Va. and N. C. May, 1864, 3 Brig., 3 Div., 18 Corps. June, 1864, 1 Brig., 2 Div., 10 Corps. Dec., 1864, 1 Brig., 2 Div., 24 Corps. Jany., 1865, 1 Brig., 2 Div., Terry's Prov'l Corps, Dept. N. C. March, 1865, 1 Brig., 2 Div., 10 Corps, Army Ohio, Dept. N. C. Mustered out June 7, 1865.

143rd REGIMENT INFANTRY. ("SULLIVAN CO. REGIMENT.")—Org. at Monticello and mustered in Oct. 8, 1862. Oct., 1862, 3 Brig., Abercrombie's Div., Def. Washington. Feby., 1863, 3 Brig., Abercrombie's Div., 22 Corps. April, 1863, 2 Brig., 3 Div., 7 Corps, Dept. Va. May, 1863, 1 Brig., 2 Div., 4 Corps, Dept. Va. July, 1863, 1 Brig., 3 Div., 11 Corps, Potomac. Oct., 1863, 1 Brig., 3 Div., 11 Corps, Cumb'd. April, 1864, 3 Brig., 1 Div., 20 Corps. Mustered out July 20, 1865.

144th REGIMENT INFANTRY.—Org. at Delhi and mustered in Sept. 27, 1862. Oct., 1862, 3 Brig., Abercrombie's Div., Def. Washington. Feby., 1862, 3 Brig., Abercrombie's Div., 22 Corps. April, 1863, 2 Brig., 3 Div., 7 Corps, Dept. Va. May, 1863, 1 Brig., 2 Div., 4 Corps, Dept. Va. July, 1863, 2 Brig., 1 Div., 11 Corps, Potomac. Aug., 1863, 2 Brig., Gordon's Div., Folly Island, S. C., 10 Corps, Dept. South. Feby., 1864, 1 Brig., Ames' Div., Dist. Fla. April, 1864, Dist. Fla., Dept. South. June, 1864, Dist. Hilton Head, S. C., Dept. South. Oct., 1864, 3d Separate Brig., Dept. South. Nov., 1864, 1 Brig., Coast Div., Dept. South. Jany., 1865, 3d Separate Brig., Hilton Head, S. C., Dept. South. May, 1865, Port Royal, S. C., Dept. South. Mustered out June 25, 1865.

145th REGIMENT INFANTRY. ("STANTON LEGION.")—Org. at Staten Island and mustered in Sept. 11, 1862. Sept., 1862, 2 Brig., 1 Div., 12 Corps, Potomac. Oct., 1862, 2 Brig., 2 Div., 12 Corps, Potomac. May, 1863, 2 Brig., 1 Div., 12 Corps, Potomac. May, 1863, 1 Brig., 1 Div., 12 Corps, Potomac. Oct., 1863, 1 Brig., 1 Div., 12 Corps, Cumb'd. Regiment disbanded Dec. 9, 1863.

146th REGIMENT INFANTRY. ("5th ONEIDA." "HALLECK INFANTRY." "GARRARD'S TIGERS.")—Org. at Rome and mustered in Oct. 10, 1862. Oct., 1862, Casey's Div., Def. Washington. Nov., 1862, 3 Brig., 2 Div., 5 Corps, Potomac. March, 1864, 4 Brig., 1 Div., 5 Corps, Potomac. April, 1864, 1 Brig., 1 Div., 5 Corps, Potomac. June, 1864, 1 Brig., 2 Div., 5 Corps, Potomac. Mustered out July 16, 1865.

147th REGIMENT INFANTRY. ("OSWEGO REGIMENT.")—Org. at Oswego and mustered in Sept. 22, 1862. Sept., 1862, Def. Washington. Dec., 1862, Provost Guard, Army Potomac. Jany., 1863, 3 Brig., 1 Div., 1 Corps, Potomac. March, 1863, 2 Brig., 1 Div., 1 Corps, Potomac. March, 1864, 2 Brig., 4 Div., 5 Corps, Potomac. Aug., 1864, 3 Brig., 2 Div., 5 Corps. Sept., 1864, 3 Brig., 3 Div., 5 Corps. Mustered out June 7, 1865.

148th REGIMENT INFANTRY.—Org. at Geneva and mustered in Sept. 14, 1862. Sept., 1862, Viele's Command, Norfolk, Va., Dept. Va., 7 Corps. July, 1863, Norfolk, Va., Dept. Va. and N. C. Oct., 1863, Wistar's Brig., U. S. Forces, Yorktown, Va., Dept. Va. and N. C. April, 1864, 2 Brig., 2 Div., 18 Corps, Army James. Sept., 1864, 1 Brig., 2 Div., 18 Corps. Dec., 1864, 4 Brig., 1 Div., 24 Corps. May, 1865, 2 Brig., 1 Div., 24 Corps. Mustered out June 22, 1865.

149th REGIMENT INFANTRY. ("4th ONONDAGA.")—Org. at Syracuse and mustered in Sept. 18, 1862. Sept., 1862, 2 Brig., 1 Div., 12 Corps, Potomac. Oct., 1862, 4 Brig., 1 Div., 12 Corps, Potomac. Oct., 1862, 3 Brig., 2 Div., 12 Corps, Potomac. Oct., 1863, 3 Brig., 2 Div., 12 Corps, Cumb'd. April, 1864, 3 Brig., 2 Div., 20 Corps. Mustered out June 12, 1865.

150th REGIMENT INFANTRY. ("DUCHESS CO. REGIMENT.")—Org. at Poughkeepsie and mustered in Oct. 10, 1862. Oct., 1862, Balto., Md., 8 Corps, Middle Dept. Jany., 1863, 2d Separate Brig., 8 Corps. Feby., 1863, 3d Separate Brig., 8 Corps. July, 1863, 2 Brig., 1 Div., 12 Corps, Potomac. July, 1863, 3 Brig., 1 Div., 12 Corps, Potomac. Oct., 1863, 3 Brig., 1 Div., 12 Corps, Cumb'd. April, 1864, 2 Brig., 1 Div., 20 Corps. Mustered out June 8, 1865.

151st REGIMENT INFANTRY.—Org. at Lockport and mustered in Oct. 22, 1862. Oct., 1862, Def. Balto., Md., 8 Corps, Middle Dept. Jany., 1863, 3d Separate Brig., 8 Corps. June, 1863, 3 Prov'l Brig., French's Div., 8 Corps. July, 1863, 1 Brig., 3 Div., 3 Corps, Potomac. April, 1864, 1 Brig., 3 Div., 6 Corps, Potomac. July, 1864, 1 Brig., 3 Div., 6 Corps, Middle Mil. Div. Dec., 1864, 1 Brig., 3 Div., 6 Corps, Potomac. Mustered out June 26, 1865.

152nd REGIMENT INFANTRY.—Org. at Mohawk and mustered in Oct. 14, 1862. Oct., 1862, Prov'l Brig., Abercrombie's Div., Def. Washington. Feby., 1863, Dist. Washington, 22 Corps. April, 1863, 1 Brig., 1 Div., 7 Corps, Dept. Va. July, 1863, Dept. East, New York. Oct., 1863, 1 Brig., 2 Div., 2 Corps, Potomac. March, 1864, 2 Brig., 2 Div., 2 Corps, Potomac. June, 1864, 1

Brig., 2 Div., 2 Corps, Potomac. Mustered out June 13, 1865.

153rd REGIMENT INFANTRY.—Org. at Fonda and mustered in Oct. 17, 1862. Oct., 1862, Prov'l Brig., Abercrombie's Div., Def. Washington. Oct., 1862, Dist. Alex., Def. Washington. Feby., 1863, Dist. Alex., 22 Corps. Aug., 1863, Martindale's Command, Garrison of Washington, 22 Corps. Feby., 1864, 1 Brig., 1 Div., 19 Corps, Gulf. July, 1864, 1 Brig., 1 Div., Middle Mil. Div. March, 1865, 2 Brig., 1 Prov'l Div., Army Shenandoah. April, 1865, 2 Brig., Dwight's Div., Dept. Washington. June, 1865, Dist. Ga., Dept. South. Mustered out Oct. 2, 1865.

154th REGIMENT INFANTRY.—Org. at Jamestown and mustered in Sept. 24, 1862. Sept., 1862, 1 Brig., 2 Div., 11 Corps, Potomac. Oct., 1863, 1 Brig., 2 Div., 11 Corps, Cumb'd. April, 1864, 2 Brig., 2 Div., 20 Corps. Mustered out June 11, 1865.

155th REGIMENT INFANTRY.—Org. at New York City and mustered in Nov. 18, 1862. Nov., 1862, Newport News, Va., Dept. Va. Dec., 1862, Corcoran's Brig., Div. at Suffolk, 7 Corps, Dept. Va. April, 1863, 3 Brig., 1 Div., 7 Corps, Dept. Va. July, 1863, Corcoran's Brig., King's Div., Def. Washington, 22 Corps. Nov., 1863, 1 Brig., Corcoran's Div., 22 Corps. Dec., 1863, 2 Brig., Tyler's Div., 22 Corps. May, 1862, 4 Brig., 2 Div., 2 Corps, Potomac. June, 1864, 2 Brig., 2 Div., 2 Corps, Potomac. Mustered out July 15, 1865.

156th REGIMENT INFANTRY. ("THE MOUNTAIN LEGION.")—Org. at Kingston and mustered in Nov. 17, 1862. Dec., 1862, Sherman's Div., Dept. Gulf. Jany., 1863, 1 Brig., 3 Div., 19 Corps, Gulf. Jany., 1863, 3 Brig., 3 Div., 19 Corps, Gulf. July, 1863, 2 Brig., 1 Div., 19 Corps, Gulf. Feby., 1864, 3 Brig., 2 Div., 19 Corps, Gulf. July, 1864, 3 Brig., 2 Div., 19 Corps, Middle Mil. Div. Jany., 1865, 3 Brig., Grover's Div., Dist. Savannah, Ga., Dept. South. March, 1865, 3 Brig., 1 Div., 10 Corps, Army Ohio, Dept. N. C. April, 1865, Dept. Ga. Mustered out Oct. 23, 1865.

157th REGIMENT INFANTRY.—Org. at Hamilton and mustered in Sept. 19, 1862. Sept., 1862, 1 Brig., 3 Div., 11 Corps, Potomac. July, 1863, 2 Brig., 1 Div., 11 Corps, Potomac. Aug., 1863, 2 Brig., Gordon's Div., Folly Island, S. C., 10 Corps, Dept. South. Feby., 1864, 1 Brig., Ames' Div., Dist. Fla. April, 1864, Dist. Fla., Dept. South. June, 1864, Dist. Hilton Head, S. C., Dept. South. Oct., 1864, 3d Separate Brig., Dept. South. Nov., 1864, 1 Brig., Coast Div., Dept. South. Feby., 1865, 1st Separate Brig., Northern Dist., Dept. South. March, 1865, 1st Separate Brig., Dist. Charleston, Dept. South. Mustered out July 10, 1865.

158th REGIMENT INFANTRY. ("1st EMPIRE REGIMENT.")—Org. at Brooklyn and mustered in Nov. 10, 1862. Nov., 1862, Viele's Command, Norfolk, Va., Dept. Va. Dec., 1862, Spinola's Brig., Div. at Suffolk, Va., 7 Corps, Dept. Va. Jany., 1863, 2 Brig., 5 Div., 18 Corps, Dept. N. C. April, 1863, Jourdan's Indpt. Brig., Dept. N. C. July, 1863, Def. Newberne, N. C., Dept. N. C. Dec., 1863, Sub Dist. Beaufort, N. C., Dept. Va. and N. C. Aug., 1864, 1 Brig., 2 Div., 18 Corps. Dec., 1864, 4 Brig., 1 Div., 24 Corps. May, 1865, 2 Brig., 1 Div., 24 Corps. Mustered out June 30, 1865.

159th REGIMENT INFANTRY. ("2nd DUCHESS AND COLUMBIA REGIMENT.")—Org. at New York City and mustered in Nov. 1, 1862. Nov., 1862, Grover's Div., Gulf. Jany., 1863, 3 Brig., 4 Div., 19 Corps, Gulf. Aug., 1863, 1 Brig., 4 Div., 19 Corps, Gulf. Feby., 1864, 2 Brig., 2 Div., 19 Corps, Gulf. July, 1864, 2 Brig., 2 Div., 19 Corps, Middle Mil. Div. Jany., 1865, 2 Brig., Grover's Div., Dist. Savannah, Ga., Dept. South. March, 1865, 3 Brig., 1 Div., 10 Corps, Army Ohio, Dept. N. C. April, 1865, Dist. Savannah, Dept. South. July, 1865, Dist. Augusta, Dept. Ga. Mustered out Oct. 12, 1865.

160th REGIMENT INFANTRY.—Org. at Auburn and mustered in Nov. 21, 1862. Dec., 1862, Sherman's Div., Dept. Gulf. Jany., 1863, 2 Brig., 1 Div., 19 Corps, Gulf. July, 1863, 3 Brig., 1 Div., 19 Corps, Gulf. Feby., 1864, 2 Brig., 1 Div., 19 Corps, Gulf. June, 1864, 3 Brig., 1 Div., 19 Corps, Gulf. July, 1864, 3 Brig., 1 Div., 19 Corps, Middle Mil. Div. March, 1865, 3 Brig., 1 Prov'l

Div., Army Shenandoah. April, 1865, 3 Brig., Dwight's Div., Dept. Washington. June, 1865, 3 Brig., Dwight's Div., Dept. South. Mustered out Nov. 1, 1865.

161st REGIMENT INFANTRY.—Org. at Elmira Aug. to Oct., 1862. Dec., 1862, Grover's Div., Gulf. Jany., 1863, 3 Brig., 1 Div., 19 Corps, Gulf. Aug., 1863, 1 Brig., 1 Div., 19 Corps, Gulf. June, 1864, Bailey's Engr. Brig., Gulf. Aug., 1864, 3 Brig., 2 Div., 19 Corps, Gulf. Aug., 1864, Guppy's Brig., U. S. Forces, Mobile Bay. Dec., 1864, U. S. Forces, Res. Corps, Mouth of White River, Mil. Div. West Miss. Feby., 1865, 3 Brig., 1 Div., Res. Corps, M. D. W. M. Feby., 1865, 3 Brig., 1 Div., 13 Corps, M. D. W. M. May, 1865, Dist. W. Fla., Dept. Fla. July, 1865, Sub Dist., Key West Dist., Middle Fla., Dept. Fla. Mustered out Nov. 12, 1865.

162nd REGIMENT INFANTRY. ("3rd METROPOLITAN GUARD.")—Org. at New York, Aug. 22 to Oct. 18, 1862. Oct., 1862, Abercrombie's Div., Def. Washington. Dec., 1862, Sherman's Div., Gulf. Jany., 1863, 3 Brig., 3 Div., 19 Corps, Gulf. March, 1863, 1 Brig., 3 Div., 19 Corps, Gulf. May, 1863, 1 Brig., 2 Div., 19 Corps, Gulf. Aug., 1863, 1 Brig., 3 Div., 19 Corps, Gulf. Feby., 1864, 3 Brig., 1 Div., 19 Corps, Gulf. July, 1864, 3 Brig., 1 Div., 19 Corps, Middle Mil. Div. March, 1865, 3 Brig., 1 Prov'l Div., Army Shenandoah. April, 1865, 3 Brig., Dwight's Div., Dept. Washington. June, 1865, Dept. Ga. Mustered out Oct. 13, 1865.

163rd REGIMENT INFANTRY. ("3rd EMPIRE REGIMENT.")—Org. at New York City and mustered in Oct. 10, 1862. Oct., 1862, Carroll's 2 Brig., Whipple's Div., Def. Washington. Nov., 1862, 2 Brig., 3 Div., 3 Corps, Potomac. Transferred to 73rd N. Y. Infy., Jany. 20, 1863.

164th REGIMENT INFANTRY. ("CORCORAN GUARD.")—Org. at New York City, Sept. and Oct., 1862. Nov., 1862, Newport News, Va., Dept. Va. Dec., 1862, Corcoran's Brig., Div. at Suffolk, Va., 7 Corps, Dept. Va. April, 1863, 3 Brig., 1 Div., 7 Corps. July, 1863, Corcoran's Brig., King's Div., 22 Corps. Nov., 1863, 1 Brig., Corcoran's Div., 22 Corps. Dec., 1863, 2 Brig., Tyler's Div., 22 Corps. May, 1864, 4 Brig., 2 Div., 2 Corps, Potomac. June, 1864, 2 Brig., 2 Div., 2 Corps, Potomac. Mustered out July 15, 1865.

165th REGIMENT INFANTRY.—Org. at New York City, Nov., 1862. Dec., 1862, Indpt. Command, Dept. Gulf. Jany., 1863, 3 Brig., 2 Div., 19 Corps, Gulf. July, 1863, 1 Brig., 3 Div., 19 Corps, Gulf. Feby., 1864, 3 Brig., 1 Div., 19 Corps, Gulf. July, 1864. 3 Brig., 1 Div., 19 Corps, Middle Mil. Div. March, 1865, 3 Brig., 1 Prov'l Div., Army Shenandoah. April, 1865, 3 Brig., Dwight's Div., Dept. Washington. June, 1865, 3 Brig., Dwight's Div., Dept. South. Mustered out Sept. 1, 1865.

166th REGIMENT INFANTRY.—(Failed to complete organization.)

167th REGIMENT INFANTRY.—(Failed to complete organization.)

168th REGIMENT INFANTRY. ("19th MILITIA.")—Org. at Newburg and mustered in Feby. 11, 1863. Feby., 1863, Busteed's Indpt. Brig., 4 Corps, Dept. Va. April, 1863, King's Indpt. Brig., 4 Corps, Dept. Va. June, 1863, 3 Brig., 1 Div., 4 Corps, Dept. Va. July, 1863, 2 Brig., 2 Div., 11 Corps, Potomac. Oct., 1863, 2 Brig., 2 Div., 11 Corps, Cumb'd. Mustered out Oct. 31, 1863.

169th REGIMENT INFANTRY.—Org. at New York City and Troy, Sept. 25 to Oct. 6, 1862. Oct., 1862, Prov'l Brig., Abercrombie's Div., Def. Washington. Feby., 1863, Mil. Dist. Washington, 22 Corps. April, 1863, Foster's 2 Brig., Corcoran's 1 Div., 7 Corps, Dept. Va. July, 1863, Foster's Brig., Vodge's Div., Folly Island, S. C., 10 Corps, Dept. South. Feby., 1864, 1 Brig., Vodge's Div., Dist. Fla. April, 1864, 2 Brig., 3 Div., 10 Corps, Army James, Dept. Va. and N. C. May, 1864, 2 Brig., 3 Div., 18 Corps. June, 1864, 3 Brig., 2 Div., 10 Corps. Dec., 1864, 3 Brig., 2 Div., 24 Corps. Jany., 1865, 3 Brig., 2 Div., Terry's Prov'l Corps, Dept. N. C. March, 1865, 3 Brig., 2 Div., 10 Corps, Army Ohio, Dept. N. C. Mustered out July 19, 1865.

170th REGIMENT INFANTRY. ("4th CORCORAN LEGION.")—Org. at New York City and mustered in at Staten Island, Oct. 7, 1862. Nov., 1862, Newport

News, Va., Dept. Va. Dec., 1862, Corcoran's Brig., Div. at Suffolk, Va., 7 Corps, Dept. Va. April, 1863, 3 Brig., 1 Div., 7 Corps, Dept. Va. July, 1863, Corcoran's Brig., King's Div., 22 Corps. Nov., 1863, 1 Brig., Corcoran's Div., 22 Corps. Dec., 1863, 2 Brig., Tyler's Div., 22 Corps. May, 1864, 4 Brig., 2 Div., 2 Corps, Potomac. June, 1864, 2 Brig., 2 Div., 2 Corps, Potomac. Mustered out July 15, 1865.

171st REGIMENT INFANTRY.—(Failed to complete organization.)

172nd REGIMENT INFANTRY.—(Failed to complete organization.)

173rd REGIMENT INFANTRY. ("4th NATIONAL GUARD.")—Org. at Brooklyn, Oct. and Nov., 1862. Dec., 1862, Grover's Div., Dept. Gulf. Jany., 1863, 2 Brig., 3 Div., 19 Corps, Gulf. Sept., 1863, 1 Brig., 3 Div., 19 Corps, Gulf. Feby., 1864, 1 Brig., 1 Div., 19 Corps. March, 1864, 3 Brig., 1 Div., 19 Corps, Gulf. July, 1864, 3 Brig., 1 Div., 19 Corps, Middle Mil. Div. March, 1865, 2 Brig., 1 Prov'l Div., Army Shenandoah. April, 1865, 3 Brig., Dwight's Div., Dept. Washington. July, 1865, Sub Dist. Ogeechee, Dist. Savannah, Dept. South. Mustered out Oct. 18, 1865.

174th REGIMENT INFANTRY. ("5th METROPOLITAN GUARD.")—Org. at New York City and mustered in Nov. 12, 1862. Dec., 1862, Grover's Div., Dept. Gulf. Jany., 1863, 2 Brig., 1 Div., 19 Corps, Gulf. Jany., 1863, 3 Brig., 1 Div., 19 Corps, Gulf. Aug., 1863, 1 Brig., 1 Div., 19 Corps, Gulf. Consolidated with 162nd N. Y. Infy., Feby. 17, 1864.

175th REGIMENT INFANTRY.—Org. in New York at large, Sept. and Oct., 1862. Nov., 1862, Suffolk, Va., Dept. Va. Jany., 1863, 3 Brig., 3 Div., 19 Corps, Gulf. May, 1863, 3 Brig., 2 Div., 19 Corps, Gulf. Aug., 1863, 2 Brig., 1 Div., 19 Corps, Gulf. Feby., 1864, 3 Brig., 2 Div., 19 Corps, Gulf. July, 1864, 3 Brig., 2 Div., 19 Corps, Middle Mil. Div. Jany., 1865, 3 Brig., Grover's Div., Dist. Savannah, Dept. South. March, 1865, 3 Brig., 1 Div., 10 Corps, Army Ohio, Dept. N. C. April, 1865, Dist. Savannah, Dept. South. July, 1865, Dist. Ga., Dept. South. Mustered out Nov. 29, 1865.

176th REGIMENT INFANTRY. ("IRONSIDES.")— Org. at New York Nov. 20, 1862, to Jany. 10, 1863. Jany., 1863, Def. New Orleans, La. Feby., 1864, 1 Brig., 2 Div., 19 Corps, Gulf. June, 1864, 3 Brig., 2 Div., 19 Corps, Gulf. July, 1864, 3 Brig., 2 Div., 19 Corps, Middle Mil. Div. Jany., 1865, 3 Brig., Grover's Div., Dist. Savannah, Ga., Dept. South. March, 1865, 3 Brig., 1 Div., 10 Corps, Army Ohio, Dept. N. C. April, 1865, Dist. Savannah, Dept. South. July, 1865, Dist. Ga., Dept. South. Mustered out April 27, 1866.

177th REGIMENT INFANTRY. ("10th NATIONAL GUARD.")—Org. at Albany and mustered in Nov. 21, 1862. Jany., 1863, 3 Brig., 2 Div., 19 Corps, Gulf. July, 1863, 1 Brig., 3 Div., 19 Corps, Gulf. Mustered out Sept. 10, 1863.

178th REGIMENT INFANTRY.—Org. at Staten Island June 18, 1863. June, 1863, 3 Brig., DeRussy's Div., 22 Corps. July, 1863, Provost Guard, Washington, D. C., 22 Corps. Nov., 1863, Dist. Columbus, Ky., 6 Div., 16 Corps Tenn. Jany., 1864, 3 Brig., 3 Div., 16 Corps, Tenn. March, 1864, 3 Brig., 3 Div., 16 Corps, Det. Army Tenn., Dept. Gulf. Dec., 1864, 3 Brig., 2 Div., Det. Army Tenn., Dept. Cumb'd. Feby., 1865, 2 Brig., 3 Div., 16 Corps, Mil. Div. West Miss. Aug., 1865, Dist. Ala., Dept. Gulf. Mustered out April 20, 1866.

179th REGIMENT INFANTRY.—Org. at Elmira and mustered in by Co's. April 5 to Sept. 15, 1864. May, 1864, Def. Washington, 22 Corps. June, 1864, 2 Brig., 1 Div. 9 Corps, Potomac. June, 1864, 1 Brig., 1 Div., 9 Corps, Potomac. July, 1864, 2 Brig., 1 Div., 9 Corps, Potomac. Sept., 1864, 2 Brig., 2 Div., 9 Corps, Potomac. Mustered out June 8, 1865.

180th REGIMENT INFANTRY.—(Failed to complete organization.)

181st REGIMENT INFANTRY.—(Failed to complete organization.)

182nd REGIMENT INFANTRY. ("69th NEW YORK NATIONAL GUARD ARTILLERY.")—Org. at New York City, Nov., 1862. Nov., 1862, Newport News, Va.,

Dept. Va. Dec., 1862, Corcoran's Brig., Div. at Suffolk, Va., 7 Corps, Dept. Va. April, 1863, 3 Brig., 1 Div., 7 Corps, Dept. Va. July, 1863, Corcoran's Brig., King's Div., 22 Corps. Nov., 1863, 1 Brig., Corcoran's Div., 22 Corps. Dec., 1863, 2 Brig., Tyler's Div., 22 Corps. May, 1864, 4 Brig., 2 Div., 2 Corps, Potomac. June, 1864, 2 Brig., 2 Div., 2 Corps, Potomac. Mustered out July 11, 1865.

183rd REGIMENT INFANTRY.—Failed to complete organization.)

184th REGIMENT INFANTRY.—Org. at Oswego and mustered in at Elmira, Sept. 12, 1864. Sept., 1864, Def. Bermuda Hundred, Va., Dept. Va. and N. C. Sept., 1864, 1 Brig., 3 Div., 6 Corps, Potomac. (Co's. A, B, D, F). Dec., 1864, Separate Brig., Army James. Mustered out June 29, 1865.

185th REGIMENT INFANTRY.—Org. at Syracuse and mustered in Sept. 19, 1864. Sept., 1864, 1 Brig., 1 Div., 5 Corps, Potomac. Mustered out May 30, 1865.

186th REGIMENT INFANTRY.—Org. at Sackett's Harbor and mustered in Aug. and Sept., 1864. Sept., 1864, 2 Brig., 2 Div., 9 Corps, Potomac. Mustered out June 2, 1865.

187th REGIMENT INFANTRY.—Org. at Buffalo and mustered in Oct. 13, 1864. Oct., 1864, 2 Brig., 1 Div., 5 Corps, Potomac. Mustered out July 1, 1865.

188th REGIMENT INFANTRY.—Org. at Rochester and mustered in Oct. 4-22, 1864. Oct., 1864, 2 Brig., 1 Div., 5 Corps, Potomac. Mustered out July 1, 1865.

189th REGIMENT INFANTRY.—Org. at Elmira, Oct. 3, 1864. Oct., 1864, 2 Brig., 1 Div., 5 Corps, Potomac. Mustered out June 1, 1865.

190th REGIMENT INFANTRY.—(Failed to complete organization.)

191st REGIMENT INFANTRY.—(Failed to complete organization.)

192nd REGIMENT INFANTRY.—Org. at Albany and mustered in by Co's. March 13 to April 8, 1865. April, 1865, 3 Brig., 3 Prov'l Div., Army Shenandoah. Mustered out Aug. 28, 1865.

193rd REGIMENT INFANTRY.—Org. at Albany and mustered in by Co's. March 6 to April 9, 1865. April, 1865, 3 Brig., 3 Prov'l Div., Army Shenandoah. Mustered out Jany. 28, 1866.

194th REGIMENT INFANTRY.—Org. at Elmira and mustered in March 29 to April 27, 1865. Mustered out May 3 to May 10, 1865.

INDEPENDENT BATTALION. ("ENFAN'S PERDU.") —Org. at New York April to June, 1862. April, 1862, Unatt., Yorktown, Va., 4 Corps, Potomac. July, 1862, 1 Brig., 2 Div., 4 Corps, Potomac. Dec., 1862, Naglee's Brig., Dept. N. C. Jany., 1863, 2 Brig., 2 Div., 18 Corps, Dept. N. C. Feby., 1863, 1 Brig., 2 Div., 18 Corps, Dept. South. April, 1863, Dist. Beaufort, S. C., 10 Corps. June, 1863, St. Helena Island, S. C., 10 Corps. July, 1863, 1 Brig., Folly Island, S. C., 10 Corps. July, 1863, 1 Brig., 2 Div., Morris Island, S. C., 10 Corps. July, 1863, 2 Brig., Morris Island, N. C., 10 Corps. Aug., 1863, Davis' Brig., Folly Island, S. C., 10 Corps. Aug., 1863, 5 Brig., Morris Island, S. C., 10 Corps. Nov., 1863, 2 Brig., Morris Island, S. C., 10 Corps. Dec., 1863, Dist. Hilton Head, S. C., 10 Corps. Transferred to 47th N. Y. Infy., Jany. 30, 1864.

NORTH CAROLINA

1st REGIMENT HEAVY ARTILLERY, AFRICAN DESCENT.—Org. at New Berne and Morehead City, N. C., March, 1864. March, 1864, Dist. New Berne, N. C., Dept. Va. and N. C. Designation changed to 14th U. S. Colored Heavy Artilly March 17, 1864, which see.

1st REGIMENT INFANTRY.—Org. June 27, 1862. July, 1862, Unatt., Dept. N. C. Dec., 1862, Unatt., 18 Corps, Dept. N. C. Jany., 1863, Unatt., 5 Div., 18 Corps, July, 1863, Dist. Pamlico, Dept. Va. and N. C. April, 1864, Sub Dist., Beaufort, N. C., Dept. Va. and N. C. Jany., 1865, Sub Dist. New Berne, N. C., Dept. N. C. Mustered out June 27, 1865.

1st REGIMENT INFANTRY, AFRICAN DESCENT.— Org. at New Berne, N. C., and Portsmouth, Va., June 30,

1863. Aug., 1863, Wild's African Brigade, U. S. Forces, Folly Island, S. C., 10 Corps, Dept. South. Dec., 1863, 3rd Brig., Vodge's Div., Folly Island, S. C. Designation changed to 35th U. S. C. T., Feby. 9, 1864, which see.

2nd REGIMENT INFANTRY.—Org. at Newberne, N. C., Nov., 1863. Nov., 1863, Def. of Newberne, N. C., Dept. Va. and N. C. Jany., 1865, Sub Dist., Newberne, N. C., Dept. N. C. Consolidated with 1st North Carolina Infy., Feby. 27, 1865.

2nd REGIMENT MOUNTED INFANTRY.—Org. at Knoxville, Tenn., Oct., 1863. Oct., 1863, 1 Brig., Willcox's Div., Left Wing forces Dept. Ohio. Jany., 1864, Dist. Clinch, Dept. Ohio. April, 1864, 1 Brig., 4 Div., 23 Corps. Ohio. Feby., 1865, 1 Brig., 4 Div., Dist. East Tenn., Dept. Cumb'd. Mustered out Aug. 16, 1865.

2nd REGIMENT INFANTRY, AFRICAN DESCENT.— Org. at Portsmouth, Va., Oct. 28, 1863. Dec., 1863, Wild's African Brig., Dept. Va. and N. C. Designation changed to 36th U. S. C. T., Feby. 8, 1864, which see.

3rd REGIMENT MOUNTED INFANTRY.—Org. at Knoxville, Tenn., June, 1864. July, 1864, 2 Brig., 4 Div., 23 Corps, Dept. Ohio. Feby., 1865, 2 Brig., 4 Div., Dist. East Tenn., Dept. Cumb'd. Mustered out Aug. 8, 1865.

3rd REGIMENT INFANTRY, AFRICAN DESCENT.— Org. at Norfolk, Va., Jany. 30, 1864. Designation changed to 37th U. S. C. T., Feby. 8, 1864, which see.

OHIO

1st REGIMENTAL CAVALRY.—Org. at Camp Chase, Aug. 17 to Oct. 30, 1861. Nov., 1861, 1 Div., Army Ohio (May, 1862, Unatt., 5 Div., Army Ohio, Co's F, I, K, L, M). Oct., 1862, Zahm's 2 Brig., Cav. Div., Army Ohio (Oct., 1862, Unatt., 2 Corps, Army Ohio, Co's. F, I, K, L, M). Nov., 1862, 2 Brig., Cav. Div., Cumb'd. Jany., 1863, 2 Brig., 1 Div., Cav., Cumb'd. March, 1863, 2 Brig., 2 Cav. Div., Cumb'd. Oct., 1864, 2 Brig., 2 Div., Wilson's Cav. Corps, Mil. Div. Miss. Feby., 1865, 2 Brig., 4 Div., Cav. Corps, Mil. Div. Miss. May, 1865, 1 Brig., 4 Div. Cav. Corps, M. D. M. Mustered out Sept. 26, 1865. (Co's. A and C, Sept., 1861, Army Occupation W. Va. Oct., 1861, Cheat Mt. Dist., W. Va. Jany., 1862, Landers' Div., Potomac. March, 1862, Shields' Div., Banks' 5 Corps, Dept. Shenandoah. May, 1862, Shields' Div., Dept. Rappahannock. June, 1862, Headqrs. 2 Corps, Army Va. Sept., 1862, Price's Cav. Brig., Def. Washington. March, 1863, 2 Brig., Stahel's Cav. Div., 22 Corps. June, 1863, Headqrs. 3 Div., Cav. Corps, Potomac. Dec., 1863, Def. Washington, 22 Corps. Rejoined regiment Jany., 1864.)

2nd REGIMENT CAVALRY.—Org. at Cleveland, Aug. to Oct., 1861. Feby., 1862, Doubleday's Brig., Dept. Mo. June, 1862, Fort Scott, Kan., Dept. Kan. Aug., 1862, Solomon's Brig., Dept. Kan. Oct., 1862, 1 Brig., 1 Div., Army Frontier. Dec., 1862, Columbus, Ohio. April, 1863, 1 Cav. Brig., Dist. Central Ky., Dept. Ohio. June, 1863, 3 Brig., 1 Div., 23 Corps, Ohio. Aug., 1863, 3 Brig., 4 Div., 23 Corps, Ohio. Nov., 1863, 1 Brig., 2 Div., Cav. Corps, Ohio. Feby., 1864, Columbus, Ohio. April, 1864, Cav., 9 Corps, Potomac. May 24, 1864, 1 Brig., 3 Div., Cav. Corps, Potomac, and Middle Mil. Div. June, 1865, Dept. Mo. Mustered out Oct. 12, 1865.

3rd REGIMENT CAVALRY.—Org. at Camp Worcester, Sept. 4 to Dec. 11, 1861. Jany., 1862, Camp Dennison, Ohio. Feby., 1862, Jeffersonville, Ind. March, 1862, 6 Div., Army Ohio. June, 1862, Cav. Brig., Army Ohio. Sept., 1862, 2 Brig., Cav. Div., Army Ohio. Nov., 1862, 2 Brig., Cav. Div., Cumb'd. Jany., 1863, 2 Brig., 1 Cav. Div., Cumb'd. March, 1863, 2 Brig., 2 Cav. Div., Cumb'd. Oct., 1864, 2 Brig., 2 Div., Wilson's Cav. Corps, Mil. Div. Miss. Mustered out Aug. 4, 1865.

4th REGIMENT CAVALRY.—Org. at Cincinnati, Lima, St. Mary's and Camp Dennison, Nov., 1861. Dec., 1861, 3 Div., Army Ohio. Oct., 1862, 2 Brig., Cav. Div., Army Ohio. Nov., 1862, 2 Brig., Cav. Div., Cumb'd. Jany., 1863, 2 Brig., 1 Cav. Div., Cumb'd. March, 1863, 2 Brig., 2 Cav. Div., Cumb'd. Oct., 1864, 2 Brig., 2 Div., Wilson's Cav. Corps, Mil. Div. Miss. Mustered out July 15, 1865.

5th REGIMENT CAVALRY.—Org. at Camp Dick Corwin, Oct. 23 to Nov. 14, 1861. Nov., 1861, Camp Dennison, Ohio. March, 1862, Dist. Paducah, Ky. March, 1862, Sherman's 5 Div., Tenn. April, 1862, 4 Div., Tenn. (1st and 2nd Battalions), 2 Div., Tenn. (3d Battalion). July, 1862, 4 Div., Dist. Memphis, Dept. Tenn. (1st and 2nd Battns.), Unatt., Dist. Corinth, Dept. Tenn. (3rd Battn.). Sept., 1862, Dist. Jackson, Dept. Tenn. (1st and 2nd Battns.). Nov., 1862, Dist. Jackson, 13 Corps, Dept. Tenn. (1st and 8nd Battns.), Dist. Corinth, Dept. Tenn., 13 Corps (3rd Battn.). Dec., 1862, 2 Brig., Cav. Div., 13 Corps, Dept. Tenn. (1st and 2nd Battns.), Dist. Corinth, 16 Corps, Dept. Tenn. (3rd Battn.). March, 1863, 2 Brig., 1 Cav. Div., 16 Corps (1st and 2nd Battns.), Cav. Brig., 2 Div., 16 Corps, Tenn. (3rd Battn.). March, 1863, 3 Brig., 5 Div., Dist. Memphis, 16 Corps, Tenn. (1st and 2nd Battns.). May, 1863, 4 Brig., 5 Div., Dist. Memphis, 16 Corps, Tenn. (1st and 2nd Battns.). June, 1863, 3 Brig., 1 Cav. Div., 16 Corps, Tenn. (3rd Battn.). Aug., 1863, 1 Brig., 1 Div., 16 Corps, Tenn. (Regt.). Oct., 1863, Unatt., 15 Corps, Tenn. April, 1864, Cav., 3 Div., 15 Corps, Tenn. Oct., 1864, 2 Brig., Kilpatrick's 3 Cav. Div., M. D. Miss. Jany., 1865, 3 Brig., 3 Cav. Div., M. D. Miss. June, 1865, Dept. N. C. Mustered out Oct. 30, 1865.

6th REGIMENT CAVALRY.—Org. at Warren, Ohio, Oct. 7, 1861. May, 1862, Cav. Mountain Dept. June, 1862, 2 Brig., 2 Div., 1 Corps, Army Va. July, 1862, Cav. Brig., 1 Corps, Army Va. Sept., 1862, Cav. Brig., 11 Corps, Potomac. Feby., 1863, 1 Brig., 2 Div., Cav. Corps, Potomac. June, 1863, 2 Brig., 2 Div., Cav. Corps, Potomac. Aug., 1863, 1 Brig., 2 Div., Cav. Corps, Potomac. Oct., 1864, 3 Brig., 2 Div., Cav. Corps, Potomac. May, 1865, Dept. Va. Mustered out Aug. 7, 1865.

7th REGIMENT CAVALRY.—Org. at Ripley, Oct., 1862. Nov., 1862, Dist. Central Ky., Dept. Ohio. Jany., 1863, 2 Brig., Dist. Central Ky., Dept. Ohio. April, 1863, 1 Cav. Brig., Dist. Central Ky., Dept. Ohio. June, 1863, 3 Brig., 1 Div., 23 Corps, Ohio. Aug., 1863, 3 Brig., 4 Div., 23 Corps, Ohio. Nov., 1863, 1 Brig., 2 Div., Cav. Corps, Ohio. May, 1864, 1 Brig., Cav. Div., Dist. Ky., 5 Div., 23 Corps, Ohio. July, 1864, 1 Brig., Cav. Div., 23 Corps, Ohio. Aug., 1864, Mounted Brig., Cav. Div., 23 Corps, Ohio. Sept., 1864, 2 Brig., Cav. Div., 23 Corps, Ohio. Nov., 1864, 2 Brig., 6 Div., Cav. Corps, Mil. Div. Miss. Dec., 1864, 1 Brig., 6 Div., Cav. Corps, M. D. M. Feby., 1865, 2 Brig., 4 Div., Wilson's Cav. Corps, Mil. Div. Miss. Mustered out July 4, 1865.

8th REGIMENT CAVALRY.—Org. Jany., 1864, from 44th Regt. Ohio Infy. Jany., 1864, Camp Dennison, Ohio. May, 1864, 1 Brig., 2 Cav. Div., W. Va. (Detachment at Beverly, W. Va., July, 1864, to Dec., 1864.) Dec., 1864, Reserve Div., W. Va., Beverly and Clarksburg, W. Va. April, 1865, 1 Brig., 1 Div., W. Va. Mustered out July 30, 1865.

9th REGIMENT CAVALRY.—Org. at Zanesville and Camp Dennison, Ohio, Oct. to Dec., 1862. May, 1863, 2 Brig., 1 Div., 23 Corps, Ohio (1st Battalion). July, 1863, 2 Brig., 4 Div., 23 Corps, Ohio (1st Battn.). Oct., 1863, 4 Brig., 4 Div., 23 Corps, Ohio. Nov., 1863, 2 Brig., 2 Div., Cav. Corps, Ohio (1st Battn.). March, 1864, Athens, Florence and Decatur, Ala., Dist. North Ala., Dept. Cumb'd. (Regt.). Aug., 1864, Mounted Brig., Garrard's Cav. Div., 23 Corps, Ohio. Sept., 1864, 2 Brig., Cav. Div., 23 Corps, Ohio. Oct., 1864, 2 Brig., Kilpatrick's 3 Cav. Div., Cav. Corps, Mil. Div. Miss. June, 1865, Dept. N. C. Mustered out Aug. 2, 1865.

10th REGIMENT CAVALRY.—Org. at Camp Chase and Cleveland, Oct., 1862, to Feby., 1863. March, 1863, 2 Brig., 2 Div., Cav. Corps, Cumb'd. Aug., 1863, 3 Brig., 2 Cav. Div., Cumb'd. Nov., 1863, 2 Brig., 2 Cav. Div., Cumb'd. April, 1864, 2 Brig., Kilpatrick's 3 Cav. Div., Cumb'd. Oct., 1864, 2 Brig., 3 Div., Cav. Corps, Mil. Div. Miss. June, 1865, Dept. N. C. Mustered out July 24, 1865.

11th REGIMENT CAVALRY.—Org. from 1st Battalion Ohio Cav. and a Battalion org. at Camps Dennison and Chase, June 26 to July 31, 1863. Attached to Dist. Plains, Dept. Kans., and Dept. Mo. Mustered out April 1, 1865 (1st Battalion), and July 14, 1866 (Regt.).

12th REGIMENT CAVALRY.—Org. at Camp Cleveland, Oct. to Dec., 1863. April, 1864, 2 Brig., 5 Div., 23 Corps, Dist. Ky., Dept. Ohio. July, 1864, 4 Brig., 1 Div., Dist. Ky., Dept. Ohio. Feby., 1865, 1 Brig., Cav. Div., Dist. East. Tenn., Dept. Cumb'd. July, 1865, Cav. Brig., Dist. East. Tenn. Mustered out Nov. 14, 1865.

13th REGIMENT CAVALRY.—Org. May 5, 1864, by consolidation of 4th and 5th Indpt. Battalions. May, 1864, Def. Washington, 22 Corps. June, 1864, 1 Brig., 3 Div., 9 Corps, Potomac. Aug., 1864, 1 Brig., 1 Corps, 9 Corps, Potomac. Dec., 1864, 3 Brig., 2 Div., Cav. Corps, Potomac. May, 1865, Sub-Dist. Appomattox, Dist. Nottaway, Dept. Va. Mustered out Aug. 10, 1865.

McLAUGHLIN'S SQUADRON CAVALRY.—Org. at Mansfield, Oct. and Nov., 1861. Dec., 1861, 18 Brig., Army Ohio. March, 1862, Dist. Eastern Ky., Dept. Ohio. July, 1862, 3 Brig., Kanawha Dist., W. Va. Nov., 1862, Dist. Eastern Ky., Dept. Ohio. June, 1863, 1 Brig., 4 Div., 23 Corps, Ohio. Sept., 1863, Headqrs. 23 Corps, Ohio. April, 1864, 3 Brig., 2 Div., Dist. Ky., 5 Div., 23 Corps, Dept. Ohio. June, 1864, 3 Brig., Cav. Div., 23 Corps, Ohio. Aug., 1864, Mounted Brig., Cav. Div., 23 Corps. Sept., 1864, 2 Brig., Cav. Div., 23 Corps. Oct., 1864, 2 Brig., Kilpatrick's 3 Div., Cav. Corps, Mil. Div. Miss. Consolidated with 5th Ohio Cav., July 28, 1865.

1st BATTALION CAVALRY.—Org. Feby., 1862, from 6th Ohio. Cav. Attached to Dist. Plains, Dept. Kans., and Dept. Mo. Transferred to 11th Ohio Cav., July, 1863.

2nd BATTALION CAVALRY.—Org. at Columbus and mustered in (1st Co.) Aug. 6, 1864, and (2nd Co.) Oct. 16, 1864. Mustered out (1st Co.) Oct. 15, 1864, and (2nd Co.) Dec. 16, 1864.

4th INDPT. BATTALION CAVALRY.—Org. at Cincinnati, Aug. 3 to Sept. 20, 1863. Mustered out Feby. 15 to March 14, 1864.

5th INDPT. BATTALION CAVALRY.—Org. at Columbus, July 9 to Sept. 2, 1863. Mustered out Feby. 15, 1864.

BURDSALL'S INDPT. CAVALRY COMPANY.—Org. at Carthage, June 5, 1861. June, 1861, Rosecrans' Brig., Army Occupation, W. Va. July, 1861, 1 Brig., Army Occupation, W. Va. Mustered out Aug. 23, 1861.

GEORGE'S INDPT. CAVALRY COMPANY.—Org. at Gallipolis, July 2, 1861. July, 1861, Cox's Kanawha Brig., W. Va. Mustered out Sept. 19, 1861.

3rd INDPT. CAVALRY COMPANY.—Org. at Camp Chase, July 4, 1861. July, 1861, Cox's Kanawha Brig., Army Occupation, W. Va. Oct., 1861, Dist. Kanawha, Dept. W. Va. March, 1862, Kanawha Div., Mt. Dept. Sept., 1862, Kanawha Div., 9 Corps, Potomac. Oct., 1862, Kanawha Div., Dist. W. Va., Dept. Ohio. March, 1863, 4 Separate Brig., 8 Corps, Middle Dept. June, 1863, Averill's 4 Separate Brig., Dept. W. Va. Dec., 1863, 2 Brig., 4 Div., W. Va. April, 1864, Kelly's Command, Res. Div., W. Va. April, 1865, 2 Brig., 1 Infy. Div., W. Va. Mustered out May 22, 1865.

4th INDPT. CAVALRY COMPANY.—Org. at Georgetown, July 9, 1861. Aug., 1861, Dept. Mo. Sept., 1861, Army West, Dept. Mo. Feby., 1862, Halleck's Headqrs., St. Louis, Mo., Dept. Mo. April, 1862, Headqrs. Dept. Miss. July, 1862, Dist. Jackson, Dept. Tenn. Sept., 1862, 4 Brig., Dist. Jackson, Dept. Tenn. Dec., 1862, Headqrs. 17 Corps, Army Tenn. April, 1864, Headqrs. Army Tenn. July, 1864, Headqrs. 17 Corps, Army Tenn. Mustered out May 28, 1865.

HARLAN LIGHT CAVALRY.—Org. at Camp Chase, Aug. 31, 1861. Attached to 11th Pa. Cav. as Co. M, Sept., 1861.

6th INDPT. CAVALRY COMPANY.—Org. at Camp Dennison, Aug. and Sept., 1861. Assigned to 3rd N. Y. Cav., Nov., 1861, as Co. L.

UNION LIGHT GUARD.—Org. at Columbus, Dec. 17, 1863. Body Guard to President Lincoln, Def. Washington, 22 Corps. Mustered out Sept. 9, 1865.

1st REGIMENT HEAVY ARTILLERY.—Org. from 117th Regt. Ohio. Infy., May 2, 1863. May, 1863, Covington, Ky., Dept. Ohio. Aug., 1863, Dist. North Central Ky., Dept. Ohio. April, 1864, 2 Brig., 4 Div., 23 Corps,

Ohio. Feby., 1865, 1 Brig., 4 Div., Dist. East. Tenn., Dept. Cumb'd. Mustered out July 25, 1865.

2nd REGIMENT HEAVY ARTILLERY.—Org. at Camp Dennison, Ohio, and Covington, Ky., June to Sept., 1863. Sept., 1863, Dist. Ky., Dept. Ohio. May, 1864, Cleveland, Tenn., Dept. Ohio. Oct., 1864, 2 Brig., 4 Div., 23 Corps, Ohio. Feby., 1865, 2 Brig., 4 Div., Dist. East. Tenn., Dept. Cumb'd. March. 1865, 1 Brig., 4 Div., Dist. East. Tenn., Dept. Cumb'd. Mustered out Aug. 23, 1865.

1st REGIMENT LIGHT ARTILLERY.—Co.'s A, B, C, D, E and F Org. at Columbus, Ohio, for 3 months, April 22, 1861. May, 1861, Army W. Va. Mustered out July 27, 1861.

1st REGIMENT LIGHT ARTILLERY (3 YEARS).

BATTERY A.—Org. at Camp Chase, Sept. 6, 1861. Oct., 1861, Camp Nevin, Ky., Thomas' Command, Army Ohio. Nov., 1861, Negley's Brig., McCook's Command, at Nolin, Ky. Dec., 1861. 6 Brig., 2 Div., Army Ohio. Sept., 1862, Arty., 2 Div., 1 Corps, Army Ohio. Nov., 1862, 1 Brig., 2 Div., Right Wing 14 Corps, Cumb'd. Jany., 1863, Arty., 2 Div., 20 Corps, Cumb'd. Oct., 1863, 1 Div., Arty. Res., Cumb'd. March, 1864, 2 Div., Arty. Res., Cumb'd. April, 1864, Arty., 2 Div., 4 Corps, Cumb'd. July, 1864, Arty. Brig., 4 Corps, Cumb'd. Nov., 1864, Dist. Nashville, Dept. Cumb'd. March, 1865, 4th Sub-Dist., Middle Tenn., Dept. Cumb'd. Mustered out July 31, 1865.

BATTERY B.—Org. at Cincinnati and mustered in Oct. 8, 1861. Oct., 1861, Camp Dick Robinson, Ky. Dec., 1861, Arty., 1 Div., Army Ohio. March, 1862, 7 Indpt. Brig., Army Ohio. July, 1862, Arty., 4 Div., Army Ohio. Sept., 1862, 22 Brig., 4 Div., 2 Corps, Army Ohio. Nov., 1862, Arty., 2 Div., Left Wing 14 Corps, Cumb'd. Jany., 1863, Arty., 2 Div., 21 Corps, Cumb'd. Oct., 1863, 1 Div., Arty. Res., Cumb'd. March, 1864, Arty., 2 Div., 12 Corps, Cumb'd. April, 1864, Garrison Arty., Bridgeport, Ala., Dept. Cumb'd. Mustered out July 22, 1865.

BATTERY C.—Org. at Cincinnati and mustered in Sept. 9, 1861. Oct., 1861, Camp Dick Robinson, Ky. Dec., 1861, Arty., 1 Div., Army Ohio. Sept., 1862, Arty., 1 Div., 3 Corps, Ohio. Nov., 1862, Arty., 3 Div., Centre 14 Corps, Cumb'd. Jany., 1863, Arty., 3 Div., 14 Corps, Cumb'd. Oct., 1863, 1 Div., Arty. Res., Cumb'd. March, 1864, Arty., 2 Div., 11 Corps, Cumb'd. April, 1864, Arty., 3 Div., 20 Corps. July, 1864, Arty. Brig., 20 Corps. Mustered out June 15, 1865.

BATTERY D.—Org. at Cincinnati and mustered in Oct. 17, 1861. Oct., 1861, Nelson's Command, Mt. Sterling, Ky. Dec., 1861, Arty., 2 Div., Army Ohio. Feby., 1862, Arty., 4 Div., Army Ohio. Sept., 1862, Captured at Munfordsville, Ky. Oct., 1862, 33 Brig., 10 Div., 1 Corps, Army Ohio. (Section.) Nov., 1862, 2 Brig., Cav. Div., Cumb'd. (Section.) Dec., 1862, Arty., 1 Cav. Div., Cumb'd. (Section.) March, 1863, Arty., 2 Div. Cav., Cumb'd. (Section, to Dec., 1863.) Battery at Columbus, Ohio, Jany. to April, 1863. April, 1863, 2 Brig., 1 Div., 23 Corps, Ohio. July, 1863, 1 Brig., 4 Div., 23 Corps, Ohio. Aug., 1863, 1 Brig., 3 Div., 23 Corps, Ohio. April, 1864, Arty., 3 Div., 23 Corps, Ohio. Feby., 1865, Arty., 3 Div., 23 Corps, Dept. N. C. Mustered out July 15, 1865.

BATTERY E.—Org. at Camp Dennison and mustered in Oct. 7, 1861. Dec., 1861, Arty., 3 Div., Army Ohio. Sept., 1862, Arty., 2 Div., 1 Corps, Army Ohio. Nov., 1862, 2 Brig., 2 Div., Right Wing 14 Corps, Cumb'd. Jany., 1863, Post Nashville, Tenn., Dept. Cumb'd. June, 1863, Arty., 2 Div., Res. Corps, Cumb'd. Oct., 1863, Unassigned, Dept. Cumb'd. Nov., 1863, 1 Div., Arty. Res., Cumb'd. Dec., 1863, Garrison Arty. at Bridgeport, Ala., Dept. Cumb'd. July, 1864, 2 Div., Arty. Res., Cumb'd. Nov., 1864, Garrison Arty., Nashville, Tenn., Dept. Cumb'd. Mustered out July 10, 1865.

BATTERY F.—Org. at Camp Dennison and mustered in Dec. 2, 1861. Dec., 1861, Arty., 4 Div., Army Ohio. Feby., 1862, Arty., 6 Div., Army Ohio. July, 1862, Arty., 4 Div., Ohio. Sept., 1862, 19 Brig., 4 Div., 2 Corps, Army Ohio. Nov., 1862, Arty., 2 Div., Left Wing 14 Corps, Cumb'd. Jany., 1863, Arty., 2 Div., 21 Corps, Cumb'd. Oct., 1863, Arty., 1 Div., Arty. Res., Cumb'd. March, 1864, 2 Div., Arty. Res., Cumb'd. March, 1864, Garrison Arty., Decatur,

Ala., Dist. Northern Ala., Dept. Cumb'd. Mustered out July 22, 1865.

BATTERY G.—Org. at Camp Dennison and mustered in Dec. 17, 1861. March, 1862, Arty., 5 Div., Army Ohio. June, 1862, Arty. Res., Army Ohio. Sept., 1862, Arty., 8 Div., Army Ohio. Nov., 1862, Arty., 2 Div., Centre 14 Corps, Cumb'd. Jany., 1863, Arty., 2 Div., 14 Corps, Cumb'd. Oct., 1863, 1 Div., Arty. Res., Cumb'd. March, 1864, 2 Div., Arty. Res., Cumb'd. Aug., 1864, Unatt. Arty., Dept. Cumb'd. Oct., 1864, Arty., Post Chattanooga, Tenn., Dept. Cumb'd. Nov., 1864, Arty. Brig., 4 Corps, Cumb'd. Mustered out Aug. 31, 1865.

BATTERY H.—Org. at Camp Dennison and mustered in Nov. 7, 1861. Jany., 1861, Arty., Lander's Div., Potomac. March, 1862, Arty., Shields' 2 Div., Banks' 5 Corps. April, 1862, Arty., Shields' Div., Dept. Shenandoah. May, 1862, Arty., Shields' Div., Dept. Rappahannock. June, 1862, Alexandria, Va., Def. Washington. Oct., 1862, Arty., 3 Div., 3 Corps, Potomac. May, 1863, 1 Vol. Brig., Arty. Res., Potomac. June, 1863, 3 Vol. Brig., Arty. Res., Potomac. Aug., 1863, 4 Vol. Brig., Arty. Res., Potomac. Oct., 1863, Arty. Brig., 2 Corps, Potomac. Dec., 1863, Arty Res., Potomac. Feby., 1864, 2 Vol. Brig., Arty. Res., Potomac. April, 1864, 3 Vol. Brig., Arty. Res., Potomac. May, 1864, Arty. Brig., 6 Corps, Potomac. July, 1864, Arty. Res., Potomac. Dec., 1864, Arty Brig., 6 Corps, Potomac. March, 1865, Arty. Res., Potomac. Mustered out June 17, 1865.

BATTERY I.—Org. at Camp Dennison and mustered in Dec. 3, 1861. Feby., 1862, Milroy's Command, Cheat Mt. Dist., W. Va. April, 1862, Milroy's Indpt. Brig., Dept. Mts. June, 1862, Unatt., 3 Div., 1 Corps, Army Va. Sept., 1862, Arty., 3 Div., 11 Corps, Potomac. May, 1863, Arty. Brig., 11 Corps, Potomac. Oct., 1863, Arty. Brig., 11 Corps, Cumb'd. Nov., 1863, Arty., 2 Div., 4 Corps, Cumb'd. Dec., 1863, Garrison Arty., Chattanooga, Tenn., Dept. Cumb'd. April, 1864, Arty., 1 Div., 14 Corps, Cumb'd. July, 1864, Arty. Brig., 14 Corps, Cumb'd. Sept., 1864, Garrison Arty., Chattanooga, Tenn. March, 1865, 2 Separate Div., Dist. Etowah, Dept. Cumb'd. Mustered out July 24, 1865.

BATTERY K.—Org. at Cleveland, Marietta and Camp Dennison, Sept. 1 to Dec. 28, 1861. Dec., 1861, Cheat Mt. Dist., W. Va. March, 1862, Cheat Mt. Dist., Dept. Mts. June, 1862, 2 Brig., 1 Div., 1 Corps, Army Va. Sept., 1862, Arty., 1 Div., 11 Corps, Potomac. March, 1863, Res. Arty., 11 Corps, Potomac. May, 1863, Arty. Brig., 11 Corps, Potomac. Oct., 1863, Arty. Brig., 11 Corps, Cumb'd. Dec., 1863, Garrison Arty., Bridgeport, Ala., Dept. Cumb'd. April, 1864, Unatt. Arty., Dept. Cumb'd. May, 1864, Stevenson, Ala., Dist. North. Ala., Dept. Cumb'd. Oct., 1864, 3 Brig., Def. Nashv. & Chatt. R. R., Dept. Cumb'd. March, 1865, Post Stevenson, Ala., Dept. Cumb'd. Mustered out July 4, 1865.

BATTERY I.—Org. at Camp Dennison, Oct. 8, 1861, to Jany. 20, 1862. Jany., 1862, Lander's Div., Potomac. March, 1862, Arty., Shields' 2 Div., Banks' 5 Corps. April, 1862, Arty., Shields' Div., Dept. Shenandoah. May, 1862, Arty., Shields' Div., Dept. Rappahannock. June, 1862, Alexandria, Va., Def. Washington. Sept., 1862, Arty., 3 Div., 5 Corps, Potomac. Oct., 1862, Arty., 2 Div., 5 Corps, Potomac. May, 1863, Arty. Brig., 5 Corps, Potomac. April, 1864, Camp Barry, Def. Washington, 22 Corps. May, 1864, 2 Brig., Hardin's Div., 22 Corps. July, 1864, Arty., 1 Div., 19 Corps, Middle Mil. Div. Aug., 1864, Res. Div., Dept. W. Va. Sept., 1864, Arty. Brig., Dept. W. Va. Jany., 1865, 1 Separate Brig., 3 Div., W. Va. April, 1865, Arty., 2 Div., W. Va. Mustered out July 4, 1865.

BATTERY M.—Org. at Camp Dennison, Dec. 3, 1861. Dec., 1861, Bacon Creek, Ky. Feby., 1862, Arty. Res., Army Ohio. Sept., 1862, Arty., 8 Div., Army Ohio. Nov., 1862, Arty., 2 Div., Centre 14 Corps, Cumb'd. Jany., 1863, Arty., 2 Div., 14 Corps, Cumb'd. Oct., 1863, 1 Div., Arty. Res., Cumb'd. March, 1864, 2 Div., Arty. Res., Cumb'd. July, 1864, Arty. Brig., 4 Corps, Cumb'd. Oct., 1864, Garrison Arty., Chattanooga, Tenn., Dept. Cumb'd. Consolidated with Battery 1, 1st Ohio L. A., April 11, 1865.

COTTER'S INDPT. BATTERY LIGHT ARTILLERY.—Org. at Cleveland, April 25, 1861. Mustered in at Camp Chase, Ohio, July 1, 1861. July, 1861, Cox's Kanawha Brig., W. Va. Mustered out Sept. 3, 1861.

WILLIAMS' INDPT. BATTERY LIGHT ARTILLERY.—Org. at Canton, June 25, 1861. Mustered in at Camp Chase, Ohio, June 28, 1861. July, 1861, Cox's Kanawha Brig., W. Va. Mustered out Nov. 6, 1861.

1st INDPT. BATTERY LIGHT ARTILLERY.—Org. at Columbus, Aug. 6, 1861. Aug., 1861, Cox's Brig., Dist. Kanawha, W. Va. Sept., 1861, Benham's Brig., Dist. Kanawha, W. Va. Oct., 1861, 1 Brig., Dist. Kanawha, W. Va. March, 1862, 1 Brig., Kanawha Div., Dept. Mts. Sept., 1862, 1 Brig., Kanawha Div., 9 Corps, Potomac. Oct., 1862, 3 Brig., Kanawha Div., Dist. W. Va., Dept. Ohio. March, 1863, 2 Brig., 3 Div., 8 Corps, Middle Dept. June, 1863, 2 Brig., Scammon's Div., W. Va. Dec., 1863, 2 Brig., 3 Div., W. Va. April, 1864, Arty., 2 Infy. Div., W. Va. July, 1864, Arty. Brig., W. Va. Aug., 1864, Arty., Res. Div., Dist. Harper's Ferry, W. Va. April, 1865, 3 Brig., Hardin's Div., Def. Washington, 22 Corps. Mustered out June 26, 1865.

2nd INDPT. BATTERY LIGHT ARTILLERY.—Org. at Camp Chase, Aug. 7, 1861. Aug., 1861, Jefferson City, Mo. Oct., 1861, Army West, Dept. Mo. Jany., 1862, 5 Brig., Army S. W. Mo., Dept. Mo. March, 1862, Arty., 2 Div., Army S. W. Mo. May, 1862, Arty., 3 Div., Army S. W. Mo. July, 1862, Dist. Eastern Ark., Dept. Mo. Jany., 1863, Arty., 12 Div., 13 Corps, Dept. Tenn. July, 1863, Arty., 3 Div., 13 Corps, Dept. Tenn., and Dept. Gulf. Nov., 1863, Placquemine, Dist. Baton Rouge, Gulf. March, 1864, Arty., 3 Div., 13 Corps, Gulf. June, 1864, Def. New Orleans, Gulf. Aug., 1864, Res. Arty., Gulf. Feby., 1865, Post Ship Island, Dept. Gulf. Mustered out Aug. 10, 1865.

2nd NATIONAL GUARD BATTERY LIGHT ARTILLERY.—Org. at Cleveland for 60 days, Oct. 17, 1864. Mustered out Dec. 22, 1864.

3rd INDPT. BATTERY LIGHT ARTILLERY.—Org. at Canton, Minerva and Massillon, Nov. 9, 1861, to March 15, 1862. March, 1862, Arty., 6 Div., Army Tenn. July, 1862, Arty., 6 Div., Dist. Corinth, Miss., Dept. Tenn. Nov., 1862, Arty., 3 Div., Left Wing 13 Corps, Dept. Tenn. Dec., 1862, Arty., 3 Div., 17 Corps, Tenn. Nov., 1864, Arty. Res., Nashville, Tenn., Dept. Cumb'd. March, 1865, Garrison Fort Donelson, Tenn., 5th Sub-Dist., Dist. Middle Tenn., Dept. Cumb'd. Mustered out July 31, 1865.

4th INDPT. BATTERY LIGHT ARTILLERY.—Org. at Cincinnati, Aug. 17, 1861. Sept., 1861, Army West, Dept. Mo. Feby., 1862, Arty., 1 Div., Army S. W. Mo. May, 1862, Arty., 3 Div., Army S. W. Mo., Dept. Mo. July, 1862, Dist. Eastern Ark., Dept. Mo. Nov., 1862, 2 Brig., 11 Div., Right Wing 13 Corps, Dept. Tenn. Dec., 1862, 2 Brig., 4 Div., Sherman's Yazoo Exp., Dept. Tenn. Jany., 1863, Arty., 1 Div., 15 Corps, Army Tenn. Nov., 1864, Arty. Res., Nashville, Tenn., Dept. Cumb'd. Consolidated with 10th Ohio Battery L. A., March 19, 1865.

5th INDPT. BATTERY LIGHT ARTILLERY.—Org. at St. Louis, Mo., under authority of Gen. Fremont, Aug. 31, 1861. Mustered in at St. Louis, Mo., Sept. 22, 1861. Oct., 1861, Jefferson City, Dept. Mo. March, 1862, Arty., 6 Div., Army Tenn. July, 1862, Arty., 6 Div., Dist. Corinth, Miss., Dept. Tenn. Nov., 1862, Arty., 6 Div., Left Wing 13 Corps, Dept. Tenn. Dec., 1862, Arty., 4 Div., 17 Corps, Army Tenn. Jany., 1863, Arty., 4 Div., 16 Corps, Tenn. July, 1863, Arty., 13 Div., 16 Corps, Tenn. Aug., 1863, Arty., 3 Div., Ark. Exp. Nov., 1863, 3 Brig., 2 Div., Ark. Exp. Jany., 1864, 3 Brig., 2 Div., 7 Corps, Ark. May, 1864, Arty., 2 Div., 7 Corps, Ark. Oct., 1864, Arty., 1 Div., 7 Corps, Ark. Mustered out July 31, 1865.

6th INDPT. BATTERY LIGHT ARTILLERY.—Org. at Mansfield, Dec. 10, 1861. Jany., 1862, Arty., 5 Div., Army Ohio. March, 1862, Arty. Res., Army Ohio. June, 1862, Arty., 6 Div., Army Ohio. Sept., 1862, 20 Brig., 6 Div., 2 Corps, Army Ohio. Nov., 1862, 3 Brig., 1 Div., Left Wing 14 Corps, Cumb'd. Jany., 1863, Arty., 1 Div., 21 Corps, Cumb'd. Oct., 1863, Arty., 3 Div., 4 Corps, Cumb'd. July, 1864, Arty. Brig., 4 Corps, Cumb'd. June, 1865, Dept. La. Mustered out Sept. 1, 1865.

7th INDPT. BATTERY LIGHT ARTILLERY.—Org. at Camp Dennison, Jany. 1, 1862. April, 1862, Arty., 5

Div., Army Tenn. June, 1862, Arty., 4 Div., Dist. Memphis, Tenn., Dept. Tenn. Sept., 1862, Arty., 4 Div., Dist. Jackson, Tenn., Dept. Tenn. Nov., 1862, Arty., 4 Div., Right Wing 13 Corps, Dept. Tenn. Dec., 1862, Arty, 4 Div., 17 Corps, Tenn. Jany., 1863, Arty., 4 Div., 16 Corps, Tenn. July, 1863, Arty., 4 Div., 13 Corps, Tenn. Aug., 1863, Arty., 4 Div., 17 Corps, Tenn. April, 1864, Arty., 1 Div., 17 Corps, Tenn. Sept., 1864, Arty., Post. Vicksburg, Miss., Dist. Vicksburg. Nov., 1864, Arty. Res., Dist. Vicksburg. Mustered out Aug. 11, 1865.

8th INDPT. BATTERY LIGHT ARTILLERY.—Org. at Camp Dennison, March 11, 1862. April, 1862, Unatt. Arty., Army Tenn. April, 1862, Arty., 5 Div., Army Tenn. April, 1862, Arty., 3 Div., Army Tenn. July, 1862, Arty., 5 Div., Dist. Memphis, Tenn., Dept. Tenn. Nov., 1862, Arty., 2 Div., Dist. Memphis, Tenn., Right Wing 13 Corps, Dept. Tenn. Dec., 1862, Arty., 2 Div., Sherman's Yazoo Exp. Jany., 1863, Arty., 2 Div., 15 Corps, Army Tenn. Sept., 1863, Arty., 1 Div., 17 Corps, Dept. Tenn. April, 1864, Maltby's Brig., Dist. Vicksburg, Dept. Tenn. Nov., 1864, Arty. Res., Dist. Vicksburg, Miss. Mustered out Aug. 7, 1865.

8th NATIONAL GUARD BATTERY LIGHT ARTILLERY.—Org. at Johnson's Island, Ohio, Aug. 15, 1864. Mustered out Oct. 17, 1864.

8th INDPT. BATTERY LIGHT ARTILLERY.—Org. at Cleveland for 4 months, Dec. 19, 1864. On duty at Johnson's Island, Ohio. Mustered out April 19, 1865.

9th INDPT. BATTERY LIGHT ARTILLERY.—Org. at Camp Wood, Oct. 11, 1861. Jany., 1862, Arty., 12 Brig., 1 Div., Army Ohio. March, 1862, 24 Brig., 7 Div., Army Ohio. Oct., 1862, Unatt., Army Ky., Dept. Ohio. Dec., 1862, Arty., 3 Div., Army Ky., Dept. Ohio. Feby., 1863, Coburn's Brig., Baird's Div., Army Ky., Dept. Cumb'd. June, 1863, Arty., 1 Div., Res. Corps, Cumb'd. Oct., 1863, Coburn's Unatt. Brig., Dept. Cumb'd. Dec., 1863, Arty., 1 Div., 12 Corps, Cumb'd. April, 1864, Unassigned, 4 Div., 20 Corps, Cumb'd. July, 1864, 3 Brig., Def. Nashv. & Chatt. R. R., Dept. Cumb'd. Dec., 1864, Garrison Arty., Bridgeport, Ala., Dept. Cumb'd. Mustered out July 25, 1865.

10th INDPT. BATTERY LIGHT ARTILLERY.—Org. at Camp Dennison, March 3, 1862. April, 1862, Arty., 6 Div., Army Tenn. July, 1862, Arty., 6 Div., Dist. Corinth, Tenn. Nov., 1862, 6 Div., Left Wing 13 Corps, Dept. Tenn. Dec., 1862, 3 Brig., 6 Div., 16 Corps, Tenn. Jany., 1863, 3 Brig., 6 Div., 17 Corps, Army Tenn. Sept., 1863, Arty., 1 Div., 17 Corps, Tenn. April, 1864, Arty., 4 Div., 17 Corps, Tenn. April, 1864, Arty., 3 Div., 17 Corps, Tenn. Nov., 1864, Arty. Res., Nashville, Tenn., Dept. Cumb'd. Feby., 1865, 2 Brig., 4 Div., Dist. East. Tenn., Dept. Cumb'd. Mustered out July 17, 1865.

11th INDPT. BATTERY LIGHT ARTILLERY.—Org. at St. Louis, Mo., Oct. 27, 1861. Nov., 1861, Army West, Dept. Mo. March, 1862, Arty., 2 Div., Army Miss., Dept. Mo. April, 1862, Arty., 3 Div., Army Miss. Nov., 1862, Arty., 7 Div., Left Wing 13 Corps, Dept. Tenn. Dec., 1862, Arty., 7 Div., 16 Corps, Tenn. Jany., 1863, Arty., 7 Div., 17 Corps, Tenn. July, 1863, Kimball's Div., Ark. Exp. Aug., 1863, 2 Brig., 2 Div., Ark. Exp. Jany., 1864, Arty., 2 Div., 7 Corps, Dept. Ark. May, 1864, Garrison Pine Bluff, Ark., 2 Div., 7 Corps, Dept. Ark. Mustered out Nov. 5, 1864.

12th INDPT. BATTERY LIGHT ARTILLERY.—Org. March 17, 1862, from Co. D, 25th Ohio Infy. March, 1862, Milroy's Command, Cheat Mt. Dist., Dept. Mts. June, 1862, Milroy's Indpt. Brig., 1 Corps, Army Va. Sept., 1862, Arty., 2 Div., 11 Corps, Potomac. Jany., 1863, Provost Guard, Army Potomac. May, 1863, Unatt., Arty. Res., Potomac. June, 1863, Camp Barry, Def. Washington, 22 Corps. Sept., 1863, Arty. Brig., 11 Corps, Potomac. Oct., 1863, Arty. Brig., 11 Corps, Cumb'd. Dec., 1863, 2 Div., Arty. Res., Dept. Cumb'd. April, 1864, Garrison Arty., Murfreesboro, Tenn., Dept. Cumb'd. July, 1864, 1 Brig., Def. Nashv. & Chatt. R. R., Dept. Cumb'd. Mustered out July 10, 1865.

13th INDPT. BATTERY LIGHT ARTILLERY.—(Only one Section org. and mustered in Feby. 15, 1862. March, 1862, Arty., 4 Div., Army Tenn. Discontinued April 20, 1862, and men transferred to other Batteries.)

14th INDPT. BATTERY LIGHT ARTILLERY.—Org. at Cleveland, Sept. 10, 1861. Feby., 1862, 1 Brig., 4 Div., Army Tenn. April, 1862, Arty., 1 Div., Army Tenn. July, 1862, Arty., 1 Div., Dist. Jackson, Tenn., Dept. Tenn. Nov., 1862, Arty., Dist. Jackson, Tenn., 13 Corps, Dept. Tenn. Dec., 1862, Arty., Dist. Jackson, Tenn., 16 Corps, Dept. Tenn. March, 1863, Arty., 3 Div., 16 Corps, Tenn. June, 1863, Dist. Corinth, Miss., 2 Div., 16 Corps, Tenn. Jany., 1864, Arty., 4 Div., 16 Corps, Tenn. Sept., 1864, Arty., 1 Div., 17 Corps, Tenn. Nov., 1864, Arty., Post Nashville, Tenn., Cumb'd. Nov., 1864, Arty., 7 Div., Wilson's Cav. Corps, Mil. Div. Miss. Feby., 1865, Arty., 1 Cav. Div., Gulf. June, 1865, Dept. Miss. Mustered out Aug. 9, 1865.

15th INDPT. BATTERY LIGHT ARTILLERY.—Org. at Camp Dennison, Feby. 1, 1862. April, 1862, Arty., 4 Div., Army Tenn. July, 1862, 4 Div., Dist. Memphis, Tenn., Dept. Tenn. Sept., 1862, 4 Div., Dist. Jackson, Tenn., Dept. Tenn. Nov., 1862, 4 Div., Right Wing 13 Corps, Dept. Tenn. Dec., 1862, Arty., 4 Div., 17 Corps, Tenn. Jany., 1863, Arty., 4 Div., 16 Corps, Tenn. July, 1863, Arty., 4 Div., 13 Corps, Tenn. Aug., 1863, Arty., 4 Div., 17 Corps, Tenn. Nov., 1864, Arty. Brig., 17 Corps, Tenn. Mustered out June 20, 1865.

16th INDPT. BATTERY LIGHT ARTILLERY.—Org. at Springfield, Aug. 20, 1861. Sept., 1861, Dept. Mo. March, 1862, 1 Div., Dist. S. E. Mo., Dept. Mo. May, 1862, Arty., 1 Div., Army Southwest, Dept. Mo. July, 1862, Dist. Eastern Ark., Dept. Mo. Jany., 1863, Arty., 12 Div., 13 Corps, Dept. Tenn. July, 1863, Arty., 3 Div., 13 Corps, Dept. Tenn. Aug., 1863, Arty., 3 Div., 13 Corps, Dept. Gulf. Jany., 1864, Arty., 1 Div., 13 Corps, Gulf. June, 1864, Def. New Orleans, La., Dept. Gulf. Aug., 1864, Arty. Res., Gulf. Mustered out Aug. 2, 1865.

17th INDPT. BATTERY LIGHT ARTILLERY.—Org. at Dayton, Aug. 21, 1862. Sept., 1862, Arty., 1 Div., Army Ky., Dept. Ohio. Oct., 1862, Unatt., Army Ky., Lexington, Ky., Dept. Ohio. Nov., 1862, Arty., 10 Div., Right Wing 13 Corps, Dept. Tenn. Dec., 1862, Arty., 1 Div., Sherman's Yazoo Exp. Jany., 1863, Arty., 10 Div., 13 Corps, Army Tenn. Aug., 1863, 2 Brig., 4 Div., 13 Corps, Gulf. June, 1864, Def. New Orleans, La., Gulf. Aug., 1864, U. S. Forces, Mobile Bay, Dept. Gulf. Sept., 1864, Unatt. Arty., 19 Corps, Gulf. Dec., 1864, Unatt. Arty., Res. Corps, Mil. Div. West. Miss. Feby., 1865, Arty. Brig., 16 Corps, M. D. W. M. Mustered out Aug. 16, 1865.

18th INDPT. BATTERY LIGHT ARTILLERY.—Org. at Camp Portsmouth and mustered in Sept. 13, 1862. Oct., 1862, Arty., 2 Div., Army Ky., Dept. Ohio. Feby., 1863, 2 Brig., Baird's Div., Army Ky., Dept. Cumb'd. June, 1863, Arty., 1 Div., Res. Corps, Dept. Cumb'd. Oct., 1863, 1 Div., Arty. Res., Cumb'd. March, 1864, 2 Div., Arty. Res., Cumb'd. Dec., 1864, Unassigned, Dist. Etowah, Dept. Cumb'd. Jany., 1865, Post Chattanooga, Tenn., Cumb'd. Mustered out June 29, 1865.

19th INDPT. BATTERY LIGHT ARTILLERY.—Org. at Cleveland, Sept. 10, 1862. Oct., 1862, Unatt., Army Ky., Dept. Ohio. Dec., 1862, Arty., 2 Div., Army Ky., Dept. Ohio. Jany., 1863, Dist. Central Ky., Dept. Ohio. June, 1863, 2 Brig., 4 Div., 23 Corps, Ohio. July, 1863, 2 Brig., 1 Div., 23 Corps, Ohio. Aug., 1863, Res. Arty., 23 Corps, Ohio. Jany., 1864, 1 Brig., 3 Div., 23 Corps, Ohio. April, 1864, Arty., 2 Div., 23 Corps, Ohio. Feby., 1865, Arty., 2 Div., 23 Corps, Dept. N. C. Mustered out July 17, 1865.

20th INDPT. BATTERY LIGHT ARTILLERY.—Org. at Camp Taylor, Cleveland, Oct. 29, 1862. Feby., 1863, Arty., 2 Div., 20 Corps, Cumb'd. Oct., 1863, 1 Div., Arty. Res., Cumb'd. Nov., 1863, Arty., 3 Div., 4 Corps, Cumb'd. Dec., 1863, Garrison Arty., Chattanooga, Tenn., Dept. Cumb'd. Nov., 1864, Garrison Arty., Nashville, Tenn., Dept. Cumb'd. Feby., 1865, Garrison Arty., Chattanooga, Tenn., Cumb'd. Mustered out July 13, 1865.

21st INDPT. BATTERY LIGHT ARTILLERY.—Org. at Camp Dennison, April 29, 1863. Sept., 1863, Willcox's Left Wing Forces, 9 Corps, Dept. Ohio. Oct., 1863, 2 Brig., Left Wing Forces, Dept. Ohio. Jany., 1864, Dist. Clinch, Dept. Ohio. April, 1864, 2 Brig., 4 Div., 23 Corps, Ohio. Feby., 1865, 2 Brig., 4 Div., Dist. East. Tenn., Dept. Cumb'd. Mustered out July 21, 1865.

22nd INDPT. BATTERY LIGHT ARTILLERY.—Org. at Camp Chase, July 14, 1863. Sept., 1863, Unatt., Cumb'd Gap, Willcox's Command, 9 Corps, Dept. Ohio. Jany., 1864, Dist. Clinch, Dept. Ohio. April, 1864, 1 Brig., 4 Div., 23 Corps, Ohio. Aug., 1864, 2 Brig., 4 Div., 23 Corps, Ohio. Feby., 1865, 2 Brig., 4 Div., Dist. East. Tenn., Dept. Cumb'd. Mustered out July 13, 1865.

23rd INDPT. BATTERY LIGHT ARTILLERY.—(See Simmons' Ky. Battery.)

24th INDPT. BATTERY LIGHT ARTILLERY.—Org. at Camp Dennison, Aug. 4, 1863. Aug., 1863, Camp at Johnson's Island, Ohio. Aug., 1864, Camp Douglass, Ill. Mustered out June 24, 1865.

25th INDPT. BATTERY LIGHT ARTILLERY.—Org. Feby. 17, 1863, from 2nd Ohio Cav.; first detached, Aug., 1862. Oct., 1862, 1 Brig., 1 Div., Army Frontier. June, 1863, Arty., Cav. Div., Dist. S. E. Mo., Dept. Mo. Aug., 1863, Arty., 1 Cav. Div., Ark. Exp. Jany., 1864, Columbus, Ohio. April, 1864, Arty., 3 Div., 7 Corps, Ark. May, 1864, Arty., 1 Div., 7 Corps, Ark. Feby., 1865, Arty., Cav. Div., 7 Corps, Ark. July, 1865, Garrison Arty., Little Rock, Ark. Mustered out Dec. 12, 1865.

26th INDPT. BATTERY LIGHT ARTILLERY.—Org. July 20, 1862, from Co. F, 32nd Ohio Infy. July, 1862, Garrison Winchester, Va. Sept., 1862, Miles' Command, Harper's Ferry, Va. Captured Sept. 15, 1862. Rejoined 32nd Ohio Infy. at Memphis, Tenn. Again detached with captured Battery, May 16, 1863. May, 1863, Arty., 3 Div., 17 Corps, Tenn. Rejoined 32nd Ohio Infy., Aug., 1863. Dec. 22, 1863, Designated 26th Ohio Battery. March, 1864, Maltby's Brig., Dist. Vicksburg, Miss., Dept. Tenn. Dec., 1864, Post Natchez, Dist. Vicksburg, Miss. June, 1865, Dept. Texas. Mustered out Sept. 2, 1865.

PAULSEN'S INDPT. BATTERY LIGHT ARTILLERY.— Org. at Columbus, Sept. 2, 1862. Mustered out Sept. 22, 1862.

1st INDPT. COMPANY SHARPSHOOTERS.—Org. at Dayton, Sept. and Oct., 1861. Attached to Birge's Western S. S., 14th Mo. Infy. and later 66th Ill. Infy., as Co. G.

2nd INDPT. COMPANY SHARPSHOOTERS.—Org. at Findlay, Sept. and Oct., 1861. Attached to Birge's Western Sharpshooters, later 14th Mo. Infy. and 66th Ill. Infy. as Co. H.

3rd INDPT. COMPANY SHARPSHOOTERS.—Org. at Lima, March and April, 1862. Attached to Birge's Western Sharpshooters, later 14th Mo. Infy. and 66th Ill. Infy., as Co. K.

4th INDPT. COMPANY SHARPSHOOTERS.—Org. at Goshen and Camp Dennison and mustered in Sept. 29, 1862. Attached to 79th Ohio Infy. as Co. K.

5th INDPT. COMPANY SHARPSHOOTERS.—Org. at Camp Cleveland, Feby. 25, 1863. March, 1863, at Headqrs. Dept. Cumb'd. Gen. Rosecrans to Nov., 1863, and Gen. Thomas to muster out. Mustered out July 19, 1865.

6th INDPT. COMPANY SHARPSHOOTERS.—Org. at Camp Cleveland, Dec. 30, 1862. At Headqrs. Dept. Cumb'd. Gen. Rosecrans to Nov., 1863, and Gen. Thomas to muster out. Mustered out July 19, 1865.

7th INDPT. COMPANY SHARPSHOOTERS.—Org. at Camp Cleveland, Jany. 27, 1863. At Headqrs. Dept. Cumb'd. Gen. Rosecrans to Nov., 1863, and Gen. Thomas to muster out. Mustered out July 28, 1865.

8th INDPT. COMPANY SHARPSHOOTERS.—Org. at Camp Dennison, March 9, 1863. March, 1863, Headqrs. Dept. Cumb'd, to Nov., 1863, Gen. Rosecrans; Headqrs. Dept. Cumb'd, to May 1864, Gen. Thomas, and at Headqrs. Mil. Div. Miss., to muster out, Gen. Sherman. Mustered out July 19, 1865.

9th INDPT. COMPANY SHARPSHOOTERS.—Org. Feby. 26, 1864. Attached to 60th Ohio Infy. as Co. G.

10th INDPT. COMPANY SHARPSHOOTERS.—Org. April, 1, 1864. Attached to 60th Ohio Infy. as Co. H.

1st REGIMENT INFANTRY (3 MONTHS).—Org. at large, April 14 to April 29, 1861. June, 1861, Schenck's 1 Brig., Tyler's 1 Div., McDowell's Army, N. E. Va. Mustered out Aug. 2, 1861.

1st REGIMENT INFANTRY (3 YEARS).—Org. at Dayton, Aug. 5 to Oct. 30, 1861. Nov., 1861, 4 Brig., Army Ohio. Dec., 1861, 4 Brig., 2 Div., Army Ohio. Sept., 1862, 4 Brig., 2 Div., 1 Corps, Army Ohio. Nov., 1862, 3 Brig., 2 Div., Right Wing 14 Corps, Cumb'd. Jany., 1863, 3 Brig., 2 Div., 20 Corps, Cumb'd. Oct., 1863, 2 Brig., 3 Div., 4 Corps, Cumb'd. Mustered out Sept. 24, 1864.

2nd REGIMENT INFANTRY (3 MONTHS).—Org. at Columbus, April 17, 1861. June, 1861, Schenck's 1 Brig., Tyler's 1 Div., McDowell's Army, N. E. Va. Mustered out Aug. 9, 1861.

2nd REGIMENT INFANTRY (3 YEARS).—Org. at Camp Dennison, July 17 to Sept. 20, 1861. Oct., 1861, 9 Brig., Army Ohio. Dec., 1861, 9 Brig., 3 Div., Army Ohio. Sept., 1862, 9 Brig., 3 Div., 1 Corps, Army Ohio. Nov., 1862, 1 Brig., 1 Div.. Centre 14 Corps, Cumb'd. Jany., 1863, 1 Brig., 1 Div., 14 Corps, Cumb'd. June, 1864, Headqrs. 14 Corps, Cumb'd. Mustered out Oct. 10, 1864.

3rd REGIMENT INFANTRY (3 MONTHS).—Org. at Camp Jackson, April 27, 1861. July, 1861, 1 Brig., Army Occupation, W. Va. Mustered out July 24, 1861.

3rd REGIMENT INFANTRY (3 YEARS).—Org. at Camp Dennison, June, 1861. July, 1861, 1 Brig., Army Occupation, W. Va. Sept., 1861, Reynolds' Command, Cheat. Mt., W. Va. Nov., 1861, 17 Brig., Army Ohio. Dec., 1861, 17 Brig., 3 Div., Army Ohio. Sept., 1862, 17 Brig., 3 Div., 1 Corps, Army Ohio. Nov., 1862, 2 Brig., 1 Div., Centre 14 Corps, Cumb'd. Jany., 1863, 2 Brig., 1 Div., 14 Corps, Cumb'd. April, 1863, Streight's Prov'l Brig., Army Cumb'd. Aug., 1863, Unatt., Army Cumb'd. Nov., 1863, 2 Brig., 2 Div., 14 Corps, Cumb'd. April, 1864, Garrison at Chattanooga, Tenn. Mustered out June 21, 1864.

4th REGIMENT INFANTRY (3 MONTHS).—Org. at Camp Jackson, April 25, 1861. July, 1861, 3 Brig., Army Occupation, W. Va. Mustered out July 24, 1861.

4th REGIMENT INFANTRY (3 YEARS).—Org. at Camp Dennison, June, 1861. June, 1861, McCook's Advance Brig., W. Va. July, 1861, 3 Brig., Army Occupation, W. Va. Nov., 1861, Kelly's Command, W. Va. Jany., 1862, 2 Brig., Lander's Div., Potomac. March, 1862, 1 Brig., Shields' 2 Div., Banks' 5 Corps. May, 1862, Kimball's Indpt. Brig., Dept. Rappahannock. July, 1862, Kimball's Indpt. Brig., 2 Corps, Potomac. Sept., 1862, 1 Brig., 3 Div., 2 Corps, Potomac. March, 1864, 3 Brig., 2 Div., 2 Corps, Potomac. Mustered out July 12, 1865.

5th REGIMENT INFANTRY (3 MONTHS).—Org. at Camp Harrison, Cincinnati, May 9, 1861. July, 1861, Unatt., Army W. Va. Mustered out July 24, 1861.

5th REGIMENT INFANTRY (3 YEARS)—Org. at Camp Dennison, June 21, 1861. July, 1861, Unatt., Army W. Va. Aug., 1861, Kelly's Command, W. Va. Jany., 1862, 2 Brig., Lander's Div., Potomac. March, 1862, 2 Brig., Shields' 2 Div., Banks' 5 Corps. April, 1862, 2 Brig., Shields' Div., Dept. Shenandoah. May, 1862, 3 Brig., Shields' Div., Dept. Rappahannock. June, 1862, 2 Brig., 1 Div., 2 Corps, Army Va. Aug., 1862, 1 Brig., 2 Div., 2 Corps, Army Va. Sept., 1862, 1 Brig., 2 Div., 12 Corps. Potomac. Oct., 1863, 1 Brig., 2 Div., 12 Corps, Cumb'd. April, 1864, 1 Brig., 2 Div., 20 Corps. Mustered out July 26, 1865.

6th REGIMENT INFANTRY (3 MONTHS).—Org. at Camp Harrison, Cincinnati, May 12, 1861. July, 1861, 1 Brig., Army Occupation, W. Va. Mustered out July 24, 1861.

6th REGIMENT INFANTRY (3 YEARS).—Org. at Camp Dennison, June, 1861. July, 1861, 1 Brig., Army Occupation, W. Va. Sept., 1861, Reynolds' Command, Cheat Mt., W. Va. Nov., 1861, 10 Brig., Army Ohio. Dec., 1861, 10 Brig., 4 Div., Army Ohio. Sept., 1862, 10 Brig., 4 Div., 2 Corps, Army Ohio. Nov., 1862, 3 Brig., 2 Div., Left Wing 14 Corps, Cumb'd. Jany., 1863, 3 Brig., 2 Div., 21 Corps, Cumb'd. Oct., 1863, 2 Brig., 3 Div., 4 Corps, Cumb'd. Mustered out June 23, 1864.

7th REGIMENT INFANTRY (3 MONTHS).—Org. at Cleveland, April 22-25, 1861. July, 1861, Army Occupation, W. Va. Mustered out July 24, 1861.

7th REGIMENT INFANTRY (3 YEARS).—Org. at Cleveland and Camp Dennison, June, 1861. July, 1861,

Unatt., Army Occupation, W. Va. Sept., 1861, Kelly's Command, W. Va. Jany., 1862, 3 Brig., Lander's Div., Potomac. March, 1862, 3 Brig., Shields' 2 Div., Banks' 5 Corps. April, 1862, 3 Brig., Shields' Div., Dept. Shenandoah. May, 1862, 3 Brig., Shields' Div., Dept. Rappahannock. June, 1862, 2 Brig., 1 Div., 2 Corps, Army Va. Aug., 1862, 1 Brig., 2 Div., 2 Corps, Army Va. Sept., 1862, 1 Brig., 2 Div., 12 Corps, Potomac. Oct., 1863, 1 Brig., 2 Div., 12 Corps, Cumb'd. April, 1864, 1 Brig., 2 Div., 20 Corps. Mustered out July 6, 1864.

8th REGIMENT INFANTRY (3 MONTHS).—Org. at Cleveland, April 18 to May 4, 1861. July, 1861, 3 Brig., Army Occupation, W. Va. Mustered out July 24, 1861.

8th REGIMENT INFANTRY (3 YEARS).—Org. at Camp Dennison, June, 1861. July, 1861, Hill's Brig., Army Occupation, W. Va. July, 1861, 3 Brig., Army Occupation, W. Va. Jany., 1862, Lander's Div., Potomac. March, 1862, 1 Brig., Shields' Div., Banks' 5 Corps. May, 1862, Kimball's Indpt. Brig., Dept. Rappahannock. July, 1862, Kimball's Indpt. Brig., 2 Corps, Potomac. Sept., 1862, 1 Brig., 3 Div., 2 Corps, Potomac. March, 1864, 3 Brig., 2 Div., 2 Corps, Potomac. Mustered out July 13, 1864.

9th REGIMENT INFANTRY (3 MONTHS).—Org. at Camp Harrison, Cincinnati, May 8, 1861. June, 1861, McCook's Advance Brig., W. Va. July, 1861, 3 Brig., Army Occupation, W. Va. Mustered out Aug. 4, 1861.

9th REGIMENT INFANTRY (3 YEARS).—Org. at Camp Dennison. May 27 to June 13, 1861. Aug., 1861, 3 Brig., Army Occupation, W. Va. Aug., 1861, 2 Brig., Kanawha Div., W. Va. Nov., 1861, 3 Brig., Army Ohio. Dec., 1861, 3 Brig., 1 Div., Army Ohio. Sept., 1862, 3 Brig., 1 Div., 3 Corps, Army Ohio. Nov., 1862, 3 Brig., 3 Div., Centre 14 Corps, Cumb'd. Jany., 1863, 3 Brig., 3 Div., 14 Corps, Cumb'd. Oct., 1863, 2 Brig., 3 Div., 14 Corps, Cumb'd. Mustered out June 7, 1864.

10th REGIMENT INFANTRY (3 MONTHS).—Org. at Cincinnati, May 1-12, 1861. July, 1861, Rosecrans' Brig., W. Va. Mustered out Aug. 21, 1861.

10th REGIMENT INFANTRY (3 YEARS).—Org. at Camp Dennison, June 4, 1861. June, 1861, Rosecrans' Brig., W. Va. July, 1861, 2 Brig., Army Occupation, W. Va. Sept., 1861, Benham's Brig., Kanawha Div., W. Va. Oct., 1861, 1 Brig., Kanawha Div., W. Va. Nov., 1861, 17 Brig., Army Ohio. Dec., 1861, 17 Brig., 3 Div., Army Ohio. Sept., 1862, 17 Brig., 3 Div., 1 Corps, Army Ohio. Nov., 1862, 2 Brig., 1 Div., Centre 14 Corps, Cumb'd. Jany., 1863, 2 Brig., 1 Div., 14 Corps, Cumb'd. Jany., 1863, Headqrs. Provost Guard, Dept. Cumb'd. Mustered out June 3, 1864.

11th REGIMENT INFANTRY (3 MONTHS).—Org. at Camp Dennison, April 18-26, 1861. July, 1861, Cox's Kanawha Brig., W. Va. Mustered out July 20, 1861.

11th REGIMENT INFANTRY (3 YEARS).—Org. at Camp Dennison, June 20, 1861. July, 1861, Cox's Kanawha Brig., W. Va. Oct., 1861, 2 Brig., Dist. Kanawha, W. Va. March, 1862, 3 Brig., Kanawha Div., Dept. Mts. May, 1862, 2 Brig., Kanawha Div., Dept. Mts. Sept., 1862, 2 Brig., Kanawha Div., 9 Corps, Potomac. Oct., 1862, 2 Brig., Kanawha Div., Dist. W. Va., Dept. Ohio. Feby., 1863, Crook's Brig., Baird's Div., Army Ky., Dept. Cumb'd. June, 1863, 3 Brig., 4 Div., 14 Corps, Cumb'd. Oct., 1863, 1 Brig., 3 Div., 14 Corps, Cumb'd. Mustered out June 11, 1865.

12th REGIMENT INFANTRY (3 MONTHS).—Org. at Columbus, April and May, 1861. July, 1861, 4 Brig., Army Occupation, W. Va. Mustered out July 25, 1861.

12th REGIMENT INFANTRY (3 YEARS).—Org. at Camp Dennison, June 28, 1861. July, 1861, Cox's Kanawha Brig., W. Va. Sept., 1861, Benham's Brig., Dist. Kanawha, W. Va. Oct., 1861, 1 Brig., Dist. Kanawha, W. Va. March, 1862, 1 Brig., Kanawha Div., W. Va., Dept. Mts. Sept., 1862, 1 Brig., Kanawha Div., 9 Corps, Potomac. Oct., 1862, 1 Brig., Kanawha Div., Dist. W. Va., Dept. Ohio. March, 1863, 2 Brig., 3 Div., 8 Corps, Middle Dept. June, 1863, 2 Brig., Scammon's Div., W. Va. Dec., 1863, 2 Brig., 3 Div., W. Va. April, 1864, 2 Brig., 2 Infy. Div., W. Va. Mustered out July 11, 1864.

13th REGIMENT INFANTRY (3 MONTHS).—Org. at Columbus, April 20-May 7, 1861. July, 1861, 2 Brig., Army Occupation, W. Va. Mustered out Aug. 14 to Aug. 25, 1861.

13th REGIMENT INFANTRY (3 YEARS).—Org. at Camp Dennison, June 12 to June 26, 1861. Aug., 1861, 2 Brig., Army Occupation, W. Va. Sept., 1861, Benham's Brig., Dist. Kanawha, W. Va. Oct., 1861, 1 Brig., Kanawha Div., W. Va. Nov., 1861, 17 Brig., Army Ohio. Dec., 1861, 17 Brig., 3 Div., Army Ohio. April, 1862, 14 Brig., 5 Div., Army Ohio. Sept., 1862, 14 Brig., 5 Div., 2 Corps, Army Ohio. Nov., 1862, 2 Brig., 3 Div., Left Wing 14 Corps, Cumb'd. Jany., 1863, 2 Brig., 3 Div., 21 Corps, Cumb'd. Oct., 1863, 3 Brig., 3 Div., 4 Corps, Cumb'd. June, 1865, 2 Brig., 3 Div., 4 Corps, Cumb'd. Aug., 1865, Dept. Texas. Mustered out Dec. 5, 1865.

14th REGIMENT INFANTRY (3 MONTHS).—Org. at Toledo, April 25, 1861. May, 1861, Kelly's Command, W. Va. June, 1861, Morris' Brig., Army Occupation, W. Va. Mustered out Aug. 13, 1861.

14th REGIMENT INFANTRY (3 YEARS).—Org. at Toledo, Aug. 14 to Sept. 5, 1861. Oct., 1861, Camp Dick Robinson, Ky. Nov., 1861, 2 Brig., Army Ohio. Dec., 1861, 2 Brig., 1 Div., Army Ohio. Sept., 1862, 2 Brig., 1 Div., 3 Corps, Army Ohio. Nov., 1862, 2 Brig., 3 Div., Centre 14 Corps, Cumb'd. Jany., 1863, 2 Brig., 3 Div., 14 Corps, Cumb'd. Oct., 1863, 3 Brig., 3 Div., 14 Corps, Cumb'd. Mustered out July 11, 1865.

15th REGIMENT INFANTRY (3 MONTHS).—Org. at Columbus, April 27, 1861. May, 1861, Army W. Va. June, 1861, Hill's Brig., Army Occupation, W. Va. Mustered out Aug. 27-31, 1861.

15th REGIMENT INFANTRY (3 YEARS).—Org. at Mansfield, Sept., 1861. Nov., 1861, McCook's Command at Nolin, Ky. Nov., 1861, 6 Brig., Army Ohio. Dec., 1861, 6 Brig., 2 Div., Army Ohio. Sept., 1862, 6 Brig., 2 Div., 1 Corps, Army Ohio. Nov., 1862, 1 Brig., 2 Div., Right Wing 14 Corps, Cumb'd. Jany., 1863, 1 Brig., 2 Div., 20 Corps, Cumb'd. Oct., 1863, 1 Brig., 3 Div., 4 Corps, Cumb'd. Aug., 1865, Dept. Texas. Mustered out Nov. 21, 1865.

16th REGIMENT INFANTRY (3 MONTHS).—Org. at Columbus May 3, 1861. May, 1861, Kelly's Command, W. Va. July, 1861. Hill's Brig., Army Occupation, W. Va. Mustered out Aug. 18, 1861.

16th REGIMENT INFANTRY (3 YEARS).—Org. at Camp Chase, Wooster and Zanesville, Sept. 23 to Dec. 2, 1861. Jany., 1862, 12 Brig., Army Ohio. March, 1862, 26 Brig., 7 Div., Army Ohio. Oct., 1862, 4 Brig., Cumb'd Div., Dist. W. Va., Dept. Ohio. Nov., 1862, 3 Brig., 9 Div., Right Wing 13 Corps, Dept. Tenn. Dec., 1862, 3 Brig., 3 Div., Sherman's Yazoo Exp. Jany., 1863, 3 Brig., 9 Div., 13 Corps, Tenn. Feby., 1863, 2 Brig., 9 Div., 13 Corps, Tenn. July, 1863, 4 Brig., 1 Div., 13 Corps, Tenn. Aug., 1863, 4 Brig., 1 Div., 13 Corps, Gulf. Sept., 1863, 3 Brig., 1 Div., 13 Corps, Gulf. March, 1864, 2 Brig., 1 Div., 13 Corps, Gulf. June, 1864, 2 Brig., 3 Div., 19 Corps, Gulf. Mustered out Oct. 31, 1864.

17th REGIMENT INFANTRY (3 MONTHS).—Org. at Lancaster, April 20, 1861. June, 1861, Rosecrans' Brig., W. Va. July, 1861, 2 Brig., Army Occupation, W. Va. Mustered out Aug. 15, 1861.

17th REGIMENT INFANTRY (3 YEARS).—Org. at Camp Dennison, Aug. 30, 1861. Oct., 1861, Camp Dick Robinson, Ky. Nov., 1861, 1 Brig., Army Ohio. Dec., 1861, 1 Brig., 1 Div., Army Ohio. Sept., 1862, 1 Brig., 1 Div., 3 Corps, Army Ohio. Nov., 1862, 1 Brig., 3 Div., Centre 14 Corps, Cumb'd. Jany., 1863, 1 Brig., 3 Div., 14 Corps, Cumb'd. Mustered out July 16, 1865.

18th REGIMENT INFANTRY (3 MONTHS).—Org. in Ohio at large, April 17 to May 29, 1861. June, 1861, Cox's Kanawha Brig., W. Va. Mustered out Aug. 28, 1861.

18th REGIMENT INFANTRY (3 YEARS).—Org. at Athens, Aug. 16 to Sept. 28, 1861. Nov., 1861, 8 Brig., Army Ohio. Dec., 1861, 8 Brig., 3 Div., Army Ohio. July, 1862, Unatt., R. R. Guard, Army Ohio. Sept., 1862, 29 Brig., 8 Div., Army Ohio. Nov., 1862, 2 Brig., 2 Div., Centre 14 Corps, Cumb'd. Jany., 1863, 2 Brig., 2 Div., 14 Corps, Cumb'd. Oct., 1863, 2 Brig., 1 Div., 14 Corps, Cumb'd. Nov., 1863, Engr. Brig., Dept. Cumb'd. Mustered out Nov. 9, 1864.

18th REGIMENT VETERAN INFANTRY.—Org. Oct., 1864, by consolidation of the Veterans and Recruits of 1st, 2nd, 18th, 24th and 35th Ohio Infy. Oct., 1864, Post Chattanooga, Tenn., Dept. Cumb'd. Nov., 1864, 2 Brig., 1 Separate Div., Dist. Etowah, Dept. Cumb'd. July, 1865, Dist. Augusta, Ga., Dept. Cumb'd. Mustered out Oct. 9, 1865.

19th REGIMENT INFANTRY (3 MONTHS).—Org. at Columbus, April and May, 1861. June, 1861, Cox's Kanawha Brig. W. Va. Mustered out Aug. 26-31, 1861.

19th REGIMENT INFANTRY (3 YEARS).—Org. at Alliance, Sept. 25, 1861. Oct., 1861, Thomas' Command, Army Ohio. Nov., 1861, 11 Brig., Army Ohio. Dec., 1861, 11 Brig., 1 Div., Army Ohio. March, 1862, 11 Brig., 5 Div., Army Ohio. Sept., 1862, 11 Brig., 5 Div., 2 Corps, Army Ohio. Nov., 1862, 1 Brig., 3 Div., Left Wing 14 Corps, Cumb'd. Jany., 1863, 1 Brig., 3 Div., 21 Corps, Cumb'd. Oct., 1863, 3 Brig., 3 Div., 4 Corps, Cumb'd. June, 1865, 2 Brig., 3 Div., 4 Corps, Cumb'd. Aug., 1865, Dept. Texas. Mustered out Oct. 24, 1865.

20th REGIMENT INFANTRY (3 MONTHS).—Org. at Columbus, April and May, 1861. June, 1861, Kelly's Command, W. Va. Mustered out Aug. 18-29, 1861.

20th REGIMENT INFANTRY (3 YEARS).—Org. at Columbus, Aug. 19 to Sept. 21, 1861. Feby., 1862, 3 Brig., 3 Div., Army Tenn. May, 1862, 2 Brig., 3 Div., Army Tenn. July, 1862, Unatt., Dist. Jackson, Dept. Tenn. Nov., 1862, 2 Brig., 3 Div., Right Wing 13 Corps, Dept. Tenn. Dec., 1862, 2 Brig., 3 Div., 17 Corps, Army Tenn. Mustered out July 15, 1865.

21st REGIMENT INFANTRY (3 MONTHS).—Org. at Cleveland, April 27, 1861. July, 1861, Cox's Kanawha Brig., W. Va. Mustered out Aug. 12, 1861.

21st REGIMENT INFANTRY (3 YEARS).—Org. at Findlay, Sept. 19, 1861. Oct., 1861, Thomas' Command, Army Ohio. Nov., 1861, 9 Brig., Army Ohio. Dec., 1861, 9 Brig., 3 Div., Army Ohio. July, 1862, 7 Indpt. Brig., Army Ohio. Sept., 1862, 7 Brig., 8 Div., Army Ohio. Nov., 1862, 3 Brig., 2 Div., Centre 14 Corps, Cumb'd. Jany., 1863, 3 Brig., 2 Div., 14 Corps, Cumb'd. Oct., 1863, 3 Brig., 1 Div., 14 Corps, Cumb'd. June, 1865, 1 Brig., 1 Div., 14 Corps. Mustered out July 25, 1865.

22nd REGIMENT INFANTRY (3 MONTHS).—Org. at Columbus, April and May, 1861. July, 1861, Cox's Kanawha Brig., W. Va. Mustered out Aug. 19, 1861.

22nd REGIMENT INFANTRY (3 YEARS).—Org. from 13th Mo. Infy., July 7, 1862. July, 1862, 2 Brig., 2 Div., Army Tenn. July, 1862, 2 Brig., 2 Div., Dist. Corinth, Dept. Tenn. Sept., 1862, 1 Brig., 2 Div., Dist. Corinth, Dept. Tenn. Oct., 1862, 2 Brig., 2 Div., Dist. Corinth, Dept. Tenn. Nov., 1862, 2 Brig., Dist. Corinth, 13 Corps, Dept. Tenn. Dec., 1862, 2 Brig., Dist. Corinth, 17 Corps, Army Tenn. Dec., 1862, 4 Brig., Dist. Jackson, 16 Corps, Tenn. March, 1863, 2 Brig., 3 Div., 16 Corps, Tenn. May, 1863, Kimball's Prov'l Div., 16 Corps, Tenn. July, 1863, 2 Brig., Kimball's Div., Dist. Eastern Ark. Aug., 1863, 2 Brig., 2 Div., Ark. Exp. Jany., 1864, 2 Brig., 2 Div., 7 Corps, Ark. March, 1864, 3 Brig., 3 Div., 7 Corps, Ark. May, 1864, 2 Brig., 2 Div., 7 Corps, Ark. Feby., 1865, 1 Brig., 3 Div., 7 Corps, Ark. Mustered out Aug. 28, 1865.

23rd REGIMENT INFANTRY.—Org. at Columbus and mustered in June 11, 1861. Aug., 1861, Cox's Kanawha Brig., W. Va. Sept., 1861, Scammon's Brig., Dist. Kanawha, W. Va. Oct., 1861, 3 Brig., Kanawha Div., W. Va. March, 1862, 1 Brig., Kanawha Div., Dept. Mts. Sept., 1862, 1 Brig., Kanawha Div., 9 Corps, Potomac. Oct., 1862, 1 Brig., Kanawha Div., Dist. W. Va., Dept. Ohio. March, 1863, 1 Brig., 3 Div., 8 Corps, Middle Dept. June, 1863, 1 Brig., Scammon's Div., W. Va. Dec., 1863, 1 Brig., 3 Div., W. Va. April, 1864, 1 Brig., 2 Infy. Div., W. Va. Jany., 1865, 1 Brig., 1 Infy. Div., W. Va. April, 1865, 1 Brig., 4 Prov'l Div., W. Va. Mustered out July 26, 1865.

24th REGIMENT INFANTRY.—Org. at Camps Chase and Jackson, May 29 to June 17, 1861. Aug., 1861, Cheat Mt. Brig., W. Va. Nov., 1861, 10 Brig., Army Ohio. Dec., 1861, 10 Brig., 4 Div., Army Ohio. Sept., 1862, 10 Brig., 4 Div., 2 Corps, Army Ohio. Nov., 1862, 3 Brig., 2 Div., Left Wing 14 Corps, Cumb'd. Jany., 1863, 3 Brig., 2 Div.,

21 Corps, Cumb'd. Oct., 1863, 3 Brig., 1 Div., 4 Corps, Cumb'd. April, 1864, 1 Separate Brig., Post Chattanooga, Tenn., Cumb'd. Mustered out June 17-24, 1864.

25th REGIMENT INFANTRY.—Org. at Columbus and mustered in June 28, 1861. Aug., 1861, Cheat Mt. Dist., W. Va. Nov., 1861, Milroy's Command, Cheat Mt. Dist., Dept. W. Va. April, 1862, Milroy's Brig., Dept. Mts. June, 1862, 2 Brig., 1 Div., 1 Corps, Army Va. Sept., 1862, 2 Brig., 1 Div., 11 Corps, Potomac. Aug., 1863, 2 Brig., Gordon's Div., Folly Island, S. C., 10 Corps, Dept. South. Jany., 1864, Dist. Hilton Head, S. C., 10 Corps. April, 1864, Dist. Hilton Head. S. C., Dept. South. Oct., 1864, 3 Separate Brig., Dept. South. Nov., 1864, 1 Brig., Coast Div., Dept. South. Feby., 1865, 3 Separate Brig., Dist. Hilton Head, S. C., Dept. South. March, 1865, 1 Separate Brig., Dist. Charleston, S. C., Dept. South. Aug., 1865, 4 Separate Brig., Dist. Western S. C., Dept. South. Jany., 1866, Dept. South. Mustered out June 16, 1866.

26th REGIMENT INFANTRY.—Org. at Columbus, June 8 to July 24, 1861. Aug., 1861, Cox's Kanawha Brig., W. Va. Oct., 1861, Dist. Kanawha, W. Va. Jany., 1862, 15 Brig., 4 Div., Army Ohio. March, 1862, 15 Brig., 6 Div., Army Ohio. Sept., 1862, 15 Brig., 6 Div., 2 Corps, Army Ohio. Nov., 1862, 1 Brig., 1 Div., Left Wing 14 Corps, Cumb'd. Jany., 1863, 1 Brig., 1 Div., 21 Corps, Cumb'd. Oct., 1863, 2 Brig., 2 Div., 4 Corps, Cumb'd. June, 1865, 1 Brig., 2 Div., 4 Corps, Cumb'd. Aug., 1865, Dept. Texas. Mustered out Oct. 21, 1865.

27th REGIMENT INFANTRY.—Org. at Camp Chase, July 15 to Aug. 18, 1861. Sept., 1861, Dept. Mo. Feby., 1862, 1 Brig., 1 Div., Army Miss. Dept. Mo. April, 1862, 1 Brig., 2 Div., Army Miss. Nov., 1862, 1 Brig., 8 Div., Left Wing 13 Corps, Dept. Tenn. Dec., 1862, 1 Brig., 8 Div., 16 Corps, Tenn. March, 1863, 4 Brig., Dist. Corinth, Miss., 2 Div., 16 Corps, Tenn. May, 1863, 3 Brig., Dist. Memphis, Tenn., 5 Div., 16 Corps, Tenn. Nov., 1863, Fuller's 4 Brig., 2 Div., 16 Corps, Tenn. March, 1864, 1 Brig., 4 Div., 16 Corps, Tenn. Sept., 1864, 1 Brig., 1 Div., 17 Corps, Tenn. Mustered out July 11, 1865.

28th REGIMENT INFANTRY.—Org. at Camp Dennison and mustered in July 6, 1861. Aug., 1861, 2 Brig., Army Occupation, W. Va. Oct., 1861, McCook's 2 Brig., Dist. Kanawha, W. Va. March, 1862, 2 Brig., Kanawha Div., Dept. Mts. Sept., 1862, 2 Brig., Kanawha Div., 9 Corps, Potomac. Oct., 1862, 2 Brig., Kanawha Div., Dist. W. Va., Dept. Ohio. March, 1863, 4 Separate Brig., 8 Corps, Middle Dept. June, 1863, Averill's 4 Separate Brig., W. Va. Dec., 1863, 1 Brig., 4 Div., W. Va. April, 1864, 1 Brig., 1 Infy. Div., W. Va. Mustered out June 23, 1864. Regt. Reorg. Sept., 1864, Res. Div., Dist. Harper's Ferry, W. Va. Nov., 1864, 1 Brig., 1 Infy. Div., W. Va. Mustered out July 13, 1865.

29th REGIMENT INFANTRY.—Org. at Jefferson, Aug., 1861. Jany., 1862, 3 Brig., Lander's Div., Potomac. March, 1862, 3 Brig., Shields' 2 Div., Banks' 5 Corps. April, 1862, 3 Brig., Shields' Div., Dept. Shenandoah. May, 1862, 3 Brig., Shields' Div., Dept. Rappahannock. June, 1862, 2 Brig., 1 Div., 2 Corps, Army Va. Aug., 1862, 1 Brig., 2 Div., 2 Corps, Army Va. Sept., 1862, 1 Brig., 2 Div., 12 Corps, Potomac. Oct., 1863, 1 Brig., 2 Div., 12 Corps, Cumb'd. April, 1864, 1 Brig., 2 Div., 20 Corps. Mustered out July 13, 1865.

30th REGIMENT INFANTRY.—Org. at Columbus, Aug. 28, 1861. Sept., 1861, Scammon's Brig., Dist. Kanawha, W. Va. Oct., 1861, 3 Brig., Dist. Kanawha. March, 1862, 1 Brig., Kanawha Div., Mt. Dept. Sept., 1862, 1 Brig., Kanawha Div., 9 Corps, Potomac. Oct., 1862, 1 Brig., Kanawha Div., Dist. W. Va., Dept. Ohio. Jany., 1863, 3 Brig., 2 Div., 15 Corps, Tenn. Oct., 1863, 2 Brig., 2 Div., 15 Corps, Tenn. Aug., 1864, 1 Brig., 2 Div., 15 Corps, Tenn. July, 1865, Dept. Ark. Mustered out Aug. 13, 1865.

31st REGIMENT INFANTRY.—Org. at Columbus, Aug. and Sept., 1861. Oct., 1861, Camp Dick Robinson, Ky., Army Ohio. Nov., 1861, 12 Brig., Army Ohio. Dec., 1861, 12 Brig., 1 Div., Army Ohio. Jany., 1862, 1 Brig., 1 Div., Army Ohio. Sept., 1862, 1 Brig., 1 Div., 3 Corps, Army Ohio. Nov., 1862, 1 Brig., 3 Div., Centre 14 Corps, Cumb'd.

Jany., 1863, 1 Brig., 3 Div., 14 Corps, Cumb'd. Mustered out July 20, 1865.

32nd REGIMENT INFANTRY.—Org. at Mansfield, Aug. 20 to Sept. 7, 1861. Sept., 1861, Kimball's Brig., Cheat. Mt. Dist., W. Va. Nov., 1861, Milroy's Brig., Reynolds' Command, Cheat Mt., W. Va. March, 1862, Milroy's Brig., Dept. Mts. April, 1862, Schenck's Brig., Dept. Mts. June, 1862, Piatt's 2 Brig., 1 Div., 1 Corps, Army Va. July, 1862, Piatt's Brig., White's Div., Winchester, Va. Sept., 1862, Miles' Command, Harper's Ferry, Va. Captured Sept. 15, 1862. Jany., 1863, 3 Brig., 3 Div., 17 Corps, Tenn. Dec., 1863, 2 Brig., 3 Div., 17 Corps, Tenn. July, 1864, 1 Brig., 4 Div., 17 Corps, Tenn. April, 1865, 2 Brig., 4 Div., 17 Corps, Tenn. Mustered out July 20, 1865.

33rd REGIMENT INFANTRY.—Org. at Portsmouth, Aug. 5 to Sept. 13, 1861. Oct., 1861, 9 Brig., Army Ohio. Dec., 1861, 9 Brig., 3 Div., Army Ohio. Sept., 1862, 9 Brig., 3 Div., 1 Corps, Army Ohio. Nov., 1862, 1 Brig., 1 Div., Centre 14 Corps, Cumb'd. Jany., 1863, 1 Brig., 1 Div., 14 Corps, Cumb'd. Mustered out July 12, 1865.

34th REGIMENT INFANTRY.—Org. at Camps Lucas and Dennison, July 27 to Sept. 14, 1861. Sept., 1861, Cox's Kanawha Brig., W. Va. Oct., 1861, Unatt., Kanawha Dist., W. Va. March, 1862, 2 Brig., Kanawha Div., Dept. Mts. Sept., 1862, Point Pleasant, Dist. Kanawha, Dist. W. Va., Dept. Ohio. March, 1863, 2 Brig., 3 Div., 8 Corps, Middle Dept. June, 1863, 2 Brig., Scammon's Div., W. Va. July, 1863, 3 Brig., Scammon's Div., W. Va. Dec., 1863, 3 Brig., 3 Div., W. Va. April, 1864, 1 Brig., 2 Cav. Div., W. Va. June, 1864, 3 Brig., 2 Cav. Div., W. Va. July, 1864, 2 Brig., 2 Infy. Div., W. Va. Jany., 1865, Unassigned, 1 Infy. Div., W. Va. Consolidated with 36th Ohio Infy., Feby. 24, 1865.

35th REGIMENT INFANTRY.—Org. at Hamilton, Aug. and Sept., 1861. Oct., 1861, R. R. Guard, Cynthiana, Ky., Army Ohio. Nov., 1861, 3 Brig., Army Ohio. Dec., 1861, 3 Brig., 1 Div., Army Ohio. Sept., 1862, 3 Brig., 1 Div., 3 Corps, Army Ohio. Nov., 1862, 3 Brig., 3 Div., Centre 14 Corps, Cumb'd. Jany., 1863, 3 Brig., 3 Div., 14 Corps, Cumb'd. Oct., 1863, 2 Brig., 3 Div., 14 Corps, Cumb'd. Mustered out Aug. 25 to Sept. 28, 1864.

36th REGIMENT INFANTRY.—Org. at Marietta, July 30 to Aug. 31, 1861. Sept., 1861, Cox's Kanawha Brig., W. Va. Oct., 1861, Dist. Kanawha, Dept. W. Va. March, 1862, 3 Brig., Kanawha Div., Dept. Mts. Sept., 1862, 2 Brig., Kanawha Div., 9 Corps, Potomac. Oct., 1862, 2 Brig., Kanawha Div., Dist. W. Va., Dept. Ohio. Feby., 1863, Crook's Brig., Baird's Div., Army Ky., Dept. Ohio, and Dept. Cumb'd. June, 1863, 3 Brig., 4 Div., 14 Corps, Cumb'd. Oct., 1863, 1 Brig., 3 Div., 14 Corps, Cumb'd. April, 1864, 1 Brig., 2 Infy. Div., W. Va. Jany., 1865, 1 Brig., 1 Infy. Div., W. Va. Mustered out July 27, 1865.

37th REGIMENT INFANTRY.—Org. at Camp Dennison, Ohio, and mustered in Oct. 2, 1861. Oct., 1861, Benham's Brig., Dist. Kanawha, Dept. W. Va. Oct., 1861, Dist. Kanawha, Dept. W. Va. March, 1862, 2 Brig., Kanawha Div., Dept. Mts. May, 1862, 2 Brig., Kanawha Div., W. Va. Aug., 1862, Dist. Kanawha, W. Va., Dept. Ohio. Dec., 1862, Ewing's Brig., Kanawha Div., W. Va., Dept. Ohio. Jany., 1863, 3 Brig., 2 Div., 15 Corps, Tenn. Oct., 1863, 2 Brig., 2 Div., 15 Corps, Tenn. Mustered out Aug. 7, 1865.

38th REGIMENT INFANTRY.—Org. at Defiance, July 24 to Sept. 1, 1861. Oct., 1861, 1 Brig., Army Ohio. Dec., 1861, 1 Brig., 1 Div., Army Ohio. Sept., 1862, 1 Brig., 1 Div., 3 Corps, Army Ohio. Nov., 1862, 1 Brig., 3 Div., Centre 14 Corps, Cumb'd. Jany., 1863, 1 Brig., 3 Div., 14 Corps, Cumb'd. Oct., 1863, 3 Brig., 3 Div., 14 Corps, Cumb'd. Mustered out July 12, 1865.

39th REGIMENT INFANTRY.—Org. at Camp Dennison, July 31 to Aug. 13, 1861. Sept., 1861, Dept. Mo. Feby., 1862, 1 Brig., 1 Div., Army Miss., Dept. Mo. April, 1862, 1 Brig., 2 Div., Army Miss. Nov., 1862, 1 Brig., 8 Div., Left Wing 13 Corps, Dept. Tenn. Dec., 1862, 1 Brig., 8 Div., 16 Corps, Tenn. March, 1863, 4 Brig., Dist. Corinth, Miss., 2 Div., 16 Corps, Tenn. May, 1863, 3 Brig., Dist. Memphis, Tenn., 5 Div., 16 Corps, Tenn. Nov., 1863, Fuller's Brig., 2 Div., 16 Corps, Tenn. Jany.,

1864, 1 Brig., 4 Div., 16 Corps, Tenn. Sept., 1864, 1 Brig., 1 Div., 17 Corps, Tenn. Mustered out July 9, 1865.

40th REGIMENT INFANTRY.—Org. at Columbus, Sept. to Nov., 1861. Dec., 1861, 18 Brig., Army Ohio. March, 1862, Unatt., Army Ohio. Aug., 1862, Dist. Eastern Ky., Dept. Ohio. Oct., 1862, Dist. Kanawha, W. Va., Dept. Ohio. Feby., 1863, 2 Brig., Baird's Div., Army Ky., Dept. Cumb'd. June, 1863, 1 Brig., 1 Div., Res. Corps, Cumb'd. Oct., 1863, 1 Brig., 2 Div., 4 Corps, Cumb'd. Oct., 1863, 2 Brig., 1 Div., 4 Corps, Cumb'd. Transferred to 51st Ohio Infy., Dec. 10, 1864.

41st REGIMENT INFANTRY.—Org. at Camp Wood, Aug. 26 to Oct. 29, 1861. Dec., 1861, 15 Brig., Army Ohio. Jany., 1862, 15 Brig., 4 Div., Army Ohio. Feby., 1862, 19 Brig., 4 Div., Army Ohio. Sept., 1862, 19 Brig., 4 Div., 2 Corps, Army Ohio. Nov., 1862, 2 Brig., 2 Div., Left Wing 14 Corps, Cumb'd. Jany., 1863, 2 Brig., 2 Div., 21 Corps, Cumb'd. Oct., 1863, 2 Brig., 3 Div., 4 Corps, Cumb'd. Aug., 1865, Dept. Texas. Mustered out Nov. 27, 1865.

42nd REGIMENT INFANTRY.—Org. at Camp Chase, Sept. to Nov., 1861. Nov., 1861, 18 Brig., Army Ohio. March, 1862, 26 Brig., 7 Div., Army Ohio. Oct., 1862, 4 Brig., Cumb'd Div., Dist. W. Va., Dept. Ohio. Nov., 1862, 3 Brig., 9 Div., Right Wing 13 Corps, Dept. Tenn. Dec., 1863, 3 Brig., 3 Div., Sherman's Yazoo Exp. Jany., 1863, 3 Brig., 9 Div., 13 Corps, Tenn. Feby., 1863, 2 Brig., 9 Div., 13 Corps, Tenn. July, 1863, 4 Brig., 1 Div., 13 Corps, Tenn. Aug., 1863, 4 Brig., 1 Div., 13 Corps, Gulf. Sept., 1863, 3 Brig., 1 Div., 13 Corps, Gulf. Nov., 1863, Plaquemine, Dist. Baton Rouge, La., Gulf. March, 1864, 2 Brig., 1 Div., 13 Corps, Gulf. June, 1864, 1 Brig., 3 Div., 19 Corps, Gulf. Mustered out Dec. 2, 1864.

43rd REGIMENT INFANTRY.—Org. at Mt. Vernon, Sept. 28, 1861, to Feby. 1, 1862. Feby., 1862, 1 Brig., 1 Div., Army Miss., Dept. Mo. March, 1862, 2 Brig., 1 Div., Army Miss. April, 1862, 1 Brig., 2 Div., Army Miss. Nov., 1862, 1 Brig., 8 Div., Left Wing 13 Corps, Dept. Tenn. Dec., 1862, 1 Brig., 8 Div., 16 Corps, Tenn. March, 1863, 4 Brig., Dist. Corinth, Miss., 2 Div., 16 Corps, Tenn. May, 1863, 3 Brig., Dist. Memphis, Tenn., 5 Div., 16 Corps, Tenn. Nov., 1863, Fuller's Brig., 2 Div., 16 Corps, Tenn. March, 1864, 2 Brig., 4 Div., 16 Corps, Tenn. Sept., 1864, 2 Brig., 1 Div., 17 Corps, Tenn. Mustered out July 13, 1865.

44th REGIMENT INFANTRY.—Org. at Springfield, Sept. 12 to Oct. 14, 1861. Oct., 1861, Benham's Brig., W. Va. Oct., 1861, 1 Brig., Kanawha Div., W. Va. March, 1862, 3 Brig., Kanawha Div., Dept. Mts. Sept., 1862, 2 Brig., 2 Div., Army Ky., Dept. Ohio. Jany., 1863, 1 Brig., Dist. Central Ky., Dept. Ohio. June, 1863, 2 Brig., 1 Div., 23 Corps, Ohio. July, 1863, 2 Brig., 4 Div., 23 Corps, Ohio. Aug., 1863, 1 Brig., 3 Div., 23 Corps, Ohio. Designation changed to 8th Ohio Cav., Jany., 1864.

45th REGIMENT INFANTRY.—Org. at Camp Chase, Aug. 19, 1862. Sept., 1862, 3 Div., Army Ky., Dept. Ohio. Oct., 1862, 1 Brig., 2 Div., Army Ky., Dept. Ohio. Jany., 1863, Dist. Central Ky., Dept. Ohio. June, 1863, 2 Brig., 1 Div., 23 Corps, Ohio. July, 1863, 2 Brig., 4 Div., 23 Corps, Ohio. Aug., 1863, 1 Brig., 4 Div., 23 Corps, Ohio. Oct., 1863, 2 Brig., 4 Div., 23 Corps, Ohio. Dec., 1863, 3 Brig., 1 Div., Cav. Corps, Ohio. April, 1864, 2 Brig., 2 Div., 23 Corps, Ohio. June, 1864, 1 Brig., 2 Div., 23 Corps, Ohio. June, 1864, 2 Brig., 1 Div., 4 Corps, Cumb'd. Mustered out June 12, 1865.

46th REGIMENT INFANTRY.—Org. at Worthington, Oct. 16, 1861, to Jany. 28, 1862. Feby., 1862, Dist. Paducah, Ky. March, 1862, 1 Brig., 5 Div., Tenn. May, 1862, 2 Brig., 5 Div., Tenn. July, 1862, 2 Brig., 5 Div., Dist. Memphis, Tenn., Dept. Tenn. Nov., 1862, 2 Brig., 5 Div., Right Wing 13 Corps, Dept. Tenn. Nov., 1862, 1 Brig., 1 Div., Dist. Memphis, Tenn., 13 Corps, Dept. Tenn. Dec., 1862, 1 Brig., 1 Div., 17 Corps, Tenn. Jany., 1863, 1 Brig., 1 Div., 16 Corps, Tenn. March, 1863, 2 Brig., 1 Div., 16 Corps, Tenn. July, 1863, 2 Brig., 4 Div., 15 Corps, Tenn. Sept., 1864, 2 Brig., 1 Div., 15 Corps, Tenn. Mustered out July 22, 1865.

47th REGIMENT INFANTRY.—Org. at Camp Dennison, Aug. 13, 1861. Sept., 1861, McCook's Brig., Kanawha

Dist., W. Va. Oct., 1861, 2 Brig., Kanawha Div., W. Va. March, 1862, 2 Brig., Kanawha Div., W. Va., Dept. Mts. May, 1862, 3 Brig., Kanawha Div., W. Va. Aug., 1862, Dist. Kanawha, Dist. W. Va., Dept. Ohio. Dec., 1862, Ewing's Brig., Kanawha Div., W. Va. Jany., 1863, 3 Brig., 2 Div., 15 Corps, Tenn. Oct., 1863, 2 Brig., 2 Div., 15 Corps, Tenn. Mustered out Aug. 11, 1865.

48th REGIMENT INFANTRY.—Org. at Camp Dennison, Sept. to Dec., 1861. Feby., 1862, Dist. Paducah, Ky. March, 1862, 4 Brig., 5 Div., Army Tenn. May, 1862, 3 Brig., 5 Div., Army Tenn. July, 1862, 3 Brig., 5 Div., Dist. Memphis, Tenn., Dept. Tenn. Nov., 1862, 3 Brig., 5 Div., Right Wing 13 Corps, Dept. Tenn. Nov., 1862, 2 Brig., 1 Div., Dist. Memphis, Right Wing 13 Corps, Dept. Tenn. Dec., 1862, 2 Brig., 1 Div., Sherman's Yazoo Exp. Jany., 1863, 2 Brig., 10 Div., 13 Corps, Tenn. Aug., 1863, 2 Brig., 4 Div., 13 Corps, Tenn., and Gulf. April, 1864, Captured. Nov., 1864, Def. New Orleans, La., Dept. Gulf. Dec., 1864, 3 Brig., Res. Corps, Mil. Div. West. Miss. Consolidated with 83rd Ohio Infy., Jany. 17, 1865.

48th BATTALION INFANTRY.—Org. July 24, 1865, by consolidation of the 83rd and 114th Ohio Infy. July, 1865, Dept. Texas. Mustered out May 9, 1866.

49th REGIMENT INFANTRY.—Org. at Tiffin, Aug. and Sept., 1861. Oct., 1861, Johnson's Brig., McCook's Div., at Nolin, Ky. Nov., 1861, 6 Brig., Army Ohio. Dec., 1861, 6 Brig., 2 Div., Army Ohio. Sept., 1862, 6 Brig., 2 Div., 1 Corps, Army Ohio. Nov., 1862, 1 Brig., 2 Div., Right Wing 14 Corps, Cumb'd. Jany., 1863, 1 Brig., 2 Div., 20 Corps, Cumb'd. Oct., 1863, 1 Brig., 3 Div., 4 Corps, Cumb'd. Aug., 1865, Dept. Texas. Mustered out Nov. 30, 1865.

50th REGIMENT INFANTRY.—Org. at Camp Dennison, Aug. 27, 1862. Sept., 1862, 34 Brig., 10 Div., Army Ohio. Sept., 1862, 34 Brig., 10 Div., 1 Corps, Army Ohio. Nov., 1862, Dist. West. Ky., Dept. Ohio. May, 1863, Unatt., 2 Div., 23 Corps, Ohio. Aug., 1863, Unatt., 1 Div., 23 Corps, Ohio. Sept., 1863, Dist. S. C. Ky., 1 Div., 23 Corps. April, 1864, 3 Brig., 4 Div., 23 Corps, Ohio. June, 1864, 3 Brig., 2 Div., 23 Corps, Ohio. Feby., 1865, 3 Brig., 2 Div., 23 Corps, Dept. N. C. Mustered out June 26, 1865.

51st REGIMENT INFANTRY.—Org. at Canal Dover, Sept. 17 to Oct. 26, 1861. Nov., 1861, 15 Brig., Army Ohio. Dec., 1861, 15 Brig., 4 Div., Army Ohio. March, 1862, Unatt., Nashville, Tenn. June, 1862, 10 Brig., 4 Div., Army Ohio. July, 1862, 23 Indpt. Brig., Army Ohio. Aug., 1862, 23 Brig., 5 Div., Army Ohio. Sept., 1862, 23 Brig., 5 Div., 2 Corps, Army Ohio. Nov., 1862, 3 Brig., 3 Div., Left Wing 14 Corps, Cumb'd. Jany., 1863, 3 Brig., 3 Div., 21 Corps, Cumb'd. Oct., 1863, 2 Brig., 1 Div., 4 Corps, Cumb'd. June, 1865, 1 Brig., 1 Div., 4 Corps, Cumb'd. Aug., 1865, Dept. Texas. Mustered out Oct. 3, 1865.

52nd REGIMENT INFANTRY.—Org. at Camp Dennison, Aug., 1862. Sept., 1862, 36 Brig., 11 Div., Army Ohio. Oct., 1862, 36 Brig., 11 Div., 3 Corps, Army Ohio. Nov., 1862, 2 Brig., 4 Div., Centre 14 Corps, Cumb'd. Jany., 1863, 2 Brig., 4 Div., 14 Corps, Cumb'd. June, 1863, 2 Brig., 2 Div., Res. Corps, Cumb'd. Oct., 1863, 3 Brig., 2 Div., 14 Corps, Cumb'd. Mustered out June 3, 1865.

53rd REGIMENT INFANTRY.—Org. at Jackson, Sept. 3, 1861, to Feby. 11, 1862. Feby., 1862, Dist. Paducah, Ky. March, 1862, 3 Brig., 5 Div., Army Tenn. July, 1862, 3 Brig., 5 Div., Dist. Memphis, Tenn., Dept. Tenn. Nov., 1862, 3 Brig., 5 Div., Right Wing 13 Corps, Dept. Tenn. Nov., 1862, 2 Brig., 1 Div., Dist. Memphis, Tenn., 13 Corps, Dept. Tenn. Dec., 1862, 2 Brig., 1 Div., 17 Corps, Tenn. Jany., 1863, 2 Brig., 1 Div., 16 Corps. March, 1863, 3 Brig., 1 Div., 16 Corps, Tenn. July, 1863, 3 Brig., 4 Div., 15 Corps, Tenn. May, 1864, 2 Brig., 2 Div., 15 Corps, Tenn. Mustered out Aug. 11, 1865.

54th REGIMENT INFANTRY.—Org. at Camp Dennison, Oct., 1861. Feby., 1862, Dist. Paducah, Ky. March, 1862, 2 Brig., 5 Div., Army Tenn. May, 1862, 1 Brig., 5 Div., Army Tenn. July, 1862, 1 Brig., 5 Div., Dist. Memphis, Tenn., Dept. Tenn. Nov., 1862, 1 Brig., 5 Div., Right Wing 13 Corps, Dept. Tenn. Nov., 1862, 1 Brig., 2 Div., Right Wing, Dist. Memphis, 13 Corps, Dept. Tenn. Dec., 1862, 2 Brig., 2 Div., Sherman's Yazoo Exp. Jany.,

1863, 2 Brig., 2 Div., 15 Corps, Tenn. Mustered out Aug. 15, 1865.

55th REGIMENT INFANTRY.—Org. at Norwalk, Sept. to Dec., 1861. Jany., 1862, R. R. Dist., W. Va. March, 1862, R. R. Dist., Dept. Mts. April, 1862, Schenck's Brig., Dept. Mts. June, 1862, 2 Brig., 1 Div., 1 Corps, Army Va. Sept., 1862, 2 Brig., 1 Div., 11 Corps, Potomac. May, 1863, 2 Brig., 2 Div., 11 Corps, Potomac. Oct., 1863, 2 Brig., 2 Div., 11 Corps, Cumb'd. April, 1864, 3 Brig., 3 Div., 20 Corps. Mustered out July 11, 1865.

56th REGIMENT INFANTRY.—Org. at Camp Morrow, Oct. to Dec., 1861. Feby., 1862, 3 Brig., 3 Div., Army Tenn. July, 1862, Dist. Eastern Ark., Helena, Ark. Nov., 1862, 2 Brig., 12 Div., Dist. Eastern Ark., Dept. Tenn. Jany., 1863, 2 Brig., 12 Div., 13 Corps, Tenn. July, 1863, 2 Brig., 3 Div., 13 Corps, Tenn. Aug., 1863, 2 Brig., 3 Div., 13 Corps, Gulf. June, 1864, Def. New Orleans, La., Gulf. Mustered out April 25, 1866.

57th REGIMENT INFANTRY.—Org. at Findlay, Sept. 16, 1861. Feby., 1862, Dist. Paducah, Ky. March, 1862, 3 Brig., 5 Div., Army Tenn. May, 1862, 1 Brig., 5 Div., Army Tenn. July, 1862, 1 Brig., 5 Div., Dist. Memphis, Tenn., Dept. Tenn. Nov., 1862, 4 Brig., 5 Div., Right Wing 13 Corps, Dept. Tenn. Nov., 1862, 2 Brig., 2 Div., Dist. Memphis, 13 Corps, Dept. Tenn. Dec., 1862, 2 Brig., 2 Div., Sherman's Yazoo Exp. Jany., 1863, 2 Brig., 2 Div., 15 Corps, Tenn. Sept., 1863, 1 Brig., 2 Div., 15 Corps, Tenn. Mustered out Aug. 14, 1865.

58th REGIMENT INFANTRY.—Org. at Camp Chase, Oct. 1, 1861, to Jany. 28, 1862. Feby., 1862, 3 Brig., 3 Div., Dist. Cairo. Feby., 1862, 2 Brig., 3 Div., Army Tenn. July, 1862, Helena, Ark., Dist. Eastern Ark. Nov., 1862, 1 Brig., 1 Div., Dist. Eastern Ark., Dept. Tenn. Dec., 1862, 1 Brig., 11 Div., Right Wing 13 Corps, Dept. Tenn. Dec., 1862, 1 Brig., 4 Div., Sherman's Yazoo Exp. Jany., 1863, 1 Brig., 1 Div., 15 Corps, Tenn. Feby., 1863, detached duty on Iron Clads, Miss. Squadron. Sept., 1863, 1 Brig., 1 Div., 17 Corps, Tenn. Sept., 1864, Post Vicksburg, Miss., Dist. Miss. Mustered out Sept. 10, 1865.

59th REGIMENT INFANTRY.—Org. at Ripley, Sept. 12, 1861. Oct., 1861, Olympian Springs, Ky., Dept. Ohio. Nov., 1861, 11 Brig., Army Ohio. Dec., 1861, 11 Brig., 1 Div., Army Ohio. March, 1862, 11 Brig., 5 Div., Army Ohio. Sept., 1862, 11 Brig., 5 Div., 2 Corps, Army Ohio. Nov., 1862, 2 Brig., 3 Div., Left Wing 14 Corps, Cumb'd. Jany., 1863, 2 Brig., 3 Div., 21 Corps, Cumb'd. Oct., 1863, 3 Brig., 3 Div., 4 Corps, Cumb'd. Sept., 1864, Unatt., 4 Div., 20 Corps, Cumb'd. Oct., 1864, Tullahoma, Def. Nashv. & Chatt. R. R., Cumb'd. Mustered out Oct. 31, 1864.

60th REGIMENT INFANTRY.—Org. at Gallipolis, Feby. 25, 1862. March, 1862, Unatt., Dist. Kanawha, W. Va., Dept. Mts. May, 1862, Cluserett's Advance Brig., Dept. Mts. June, 1862, Piatt's Brig., 1 Div., 1 Corps, Army Va. Sept., 1862, Miles' Command, Harper's Ferry, Va., R. R. Brig., 8 Corps. Mustered out Nov. 10, 1862.

60th REGIMENT INFANTRY.—Reorg. at Cleveland and Columbus, Feby. to April, 1864. April, 1864, 2 Brig., 3 Div., 9 Corps, Potomac. Sept., 1864, 2 Brig., 1 Div., 9 Corps, Potomac. Mustered out July 28, 1865.

61st REGIMENT INFANTRY.—Org. at Camp Chase, April 23, 1862. June, 1862, 1 Brig., 3 Div., 1 Corps, Army Va. Sept., 1862, 1 Brig., 3 Div., 11 Corps, Potomac. Oct., 1862, 2 Brig., 2 Div., 11 Corps, Potomac. Nov., 1862, 1 Brig., 3 Div., 11 Corps, Potomac. Oct., 1863, 1 Brig., 3 Div., 11 Corps, Cumb'd. April, 1864, 3 Brig., 1 Div., 20 Corps. Consolidated with 82nd Ohio Infy., March 31, 1865.

62nd REGIMENT INFANTRY.—Org. at Zanesville, McConnellsville and Somerton, Sept. 17 to Dec. 24, 1861. Jany., 1862, 2 Brig., Lander's Div., Potomac. March, 1862, 2 Brig., Shields' 2 Div., Banks' 5 Corps. April, 1862, 2 Brig., Shields' Div., Dept. Shenandoah. May, 1862, 2 Brig., Shields' Div., Dept. Rappahannock. July, 1862, 3 Brig., 2 Div., 4 Corps, Potomac. Sept., 1862, Ferry's Brig., Div. at Suffolk, Va., 7 Corps, Dept. Va. Jany., 1863, 1 Brig., 3 Div., 18 Corps, Dept. N. C. Feby., 1863, 3 Brig., 2 Div., 18 Corps, Dept. South. April, 1863, U. S. Forces, Folly

Island, S. C., 10 Corps, Dept. South. June, 1863, 1 Brig., Folly Island, S. C., 10 Corps. July, 1863, 1 Brig., 2 Div., Morris Island, S. C., 10 Corps. July, 1863, 2 Brig., Morris Island, S. C., 10 Corps. Oct., 1863, Howell's Brig., Gordon's Div., Folly Island, S. C., 10 Corps. Dec., 1863, Dist. Hilton Head, S. C., 10 Corps. April, 1864, 1 Brig., 1 Div., 10 Corps, Army James, Dept. Va. and N. C. Dec., 1864, 1 Brig., 1 Div., 24 Corps. Consolidated with 67th Ohio Infy., Sept. 1, 1865.

63rd REGIMENT INFANTRY.—Org. at Marietta, Aug., 1861, to Feby., 1862. Feby., 1862, 2 Brig., 1 Div., Army Miss. April, 1862, 1 Brig., 2 Div., Army Miss. Nov., 1862, 1 Brig., 8 Div., Left Wing, 13 Corps, Dept. Tenn. Dec., 1862, 1 Brig., 8 Div., 16 Corps, Tenn. March, 1863, 4 Brig., Dist. Corinth, Miss., 2 Div., 16 Corps, Tenn. May, 1863, 3 Brig., Dist. Memphis, Tenn., 5 Div., 16 Corps, Tenn. Nov., 1863. Fuller's Brig., 2 Div., 16 Corps, Tenn. March, 1864, 2 Brig., 4 Div., 16 Corps, Tenn. Sept., 1864, 2 Brig., 1 Div., 17 Corps. Mustered out July 8, 1865.

64th REGIMENT INFANTRY.—Org. at Camp Buckingham, Mansfield, Nov. 6 to Dec. 14, 1861. Jany., 1862, 20 Brig., Army Ohio. Jany., 1862, 20 Brig., 6 Div., Army Ohio. Sept., 1862, 20 Brig., 6 Div., 2 Corps, Army Ohio. Nov., 1862, 3 Brig., 1 Div., Left Wing 14 Corps, Cumb'd. Jany., 1863, 3 Brig., 1 Div., 21 Corps, Cumb'd. Oct., 1863, 3 Brig., 2 Div., 4 Corps. June, 1865, 2 Brig., 2 Div., 4 Corps, Cumb'd. Aug., 1865, Dept. Texas. Mustered out Dec. 3, 1865.

65th REGIMENT INFANTRY.—Org. at Mansfield, Oct. 3 to Nov. 14, 1861. Jany., 1862, 20 Brig., Army Ohio. Jany., 1862, 20 Brig., 6 Div., Army Ohio. Sept., 1862, 20 Brig., 6 Div., 2 Corps, Army Ohio. Nov., 1862, 3 Brig., 1 Div., Left Wing 14 Corps, Cumb'd. Jany., 1863, 3 Brig., 1 Div., 21 Corps, Cumb'd. Oct., 1863, 3 Brig., 2 Div., 4 Corps, Cumb'd. June, 1865, 2 Brig., 2 Div., 4 Corps, Cumb'd. Aug., 1865, Dept. Texas. Mustered out Nov. 30, 1865.

66th REGIMENT INFANTRY.—Org. at Camp McArthur, Urbana, Dec., 1861, to Jany., 1862. Jany., 1862, 2 Brig., Lander's Div., Potomac. March, 1862, 2 Brig., Shields' 2 Div., Banks' 5 Corps. April, 1862, 2 Brig., Shields' Div., Dept. Shenandoah. May, 1862, 2 Brig., Shields' Div., Dept. Rappahannock. June, 1862, 3 Brig., Shields' Div., Dept. Rappahannock. June, 1862, 2 Brig., 1 Div., 2 Corps, Army Va. Aug., 1862, 1 Brig., 2 Div., 2 Corps, Army Va. Sept., 1862, 1 Brig., 2 Div., 12 Corps, Potomac. Oct., 1863, 1 Brig., 2 Div., 12 Corps, Cumb'd. April, 1864, 1 Brig., 2 Div., 20 Corps. Mustered out July 15, 1865.

67th REGIMENT INFANTRY.—Org. in Ohio at large, Oct., 1861. to Jany., 1862. Jany., 1862, 1 Brig., Lander's Div., Potomac. March, 1862, 1 Brig., Shields' 2 Div., Banks' 5 Corps. April, 1862, 1 Brig., Shields' Div., Dept. Shenandoah. May, 1862, 1 Brig., Shields' Div., Dept. Rappahannock. May, 1862, 2 Brig., Shields' Div., Dept. Rappahannock. July, 1862, 3 Brig., 2 Div., 4 Corps, Potomac. Sept., 1862, Ferry's Brig., Div. at Suffolk, Va., 7 Corps, Dept. Va. Jany., 1863, 1 Brig., 3 Div., 18 Corps, Dept. N. C. Feby., 1863, 3 Brig., 2 Div., 18 Corps, Dept. South. April, 1863, U. S. Forces, Folly Island, S. C., 10 Corps, Dept. South. June, 1863, 1 Brig., Folly Island, S. C., 10 Corps. July, 1863, 1 Brig., 2 Div., Morris Island, S. C., 10 Corps. July, 1863, 2 Brig., Morris Island, S. C., 10 Corps. Oct., 1863, Howell's Brig., Gordon's Div., Folly Island, S. C., 10 Corps. Dec., 1863, Dist. Hilton Head, S. C., 10 Corps. April, 1864, 1 Brig., 1 Div., 10 Corps, Army James, Dept. Va. and N. C. Dec., 1864, 1 Brig., 1 Div., 24 Corps. Aug., 1865, Dept. Va. Mustered out Dec. 7, 1865.

68th REGIMENT INFANTRY.—Org. at Camp Latta, Napoleon, Oct. to Dec., 1861. Feby., 1862, 3 Brig., 3 Div., Dist. Cairo. Feby., 1862, 2 Brig., 3 Div., Army Tenn. May, 1862, 3 Brig., 3 Div., Army Tenn. July, 1862, Unatt., Dist. Jackson, Dept. Tenn. Nov., 1862, 2 Brig., 3 Div., Right Wing 13 Corps, Dept. Tenn. Dec., 1862, 2 Brig., 3 Div., 17 Corps, Army Tenn. Mustered out July 10, 1865.

69th REGIMENT INFANTRY.—Org. at Hamilton, Nov., 1861, to April, 1862. April, 1862, Unatt. Infy., Army Ohio, Nashville and Franklin, Tenn. Sept., 1862, 29 Brig., 8 Div., Army Ohio. Nov., 1862, 2 Brig., 2 Div., Centre 14 Corps, Cumb'd. Jany., 1863, 2 Brig., 2 Div., 14 Corps, Cumb'd. Oct., 1863, 2 Brig., 1 Div., 14 Corps, Cumb'd. Sept., 1864, 3 Brig., 1 Div., 14 Corps, Cumb'd. Nov., 1864, 2 Brig., 1 Div., 14 Corps, Cumb'd. Mustered out July 17, 1865.

70th REGIMENT INFANTRY.—Org. at West Union, Oct. 14, 1861. Feby., 1862, Dist. Paducah, Ky. March, 1862, 4 Brig., 5 Div., Army Tenn. May, 1862, 3 Brig., 5 Div., Army Tenn. July, 1862, 3 Brig., 5 Div., Dist. Memphis, Tenn., Dept. Tenn. Nov., 1862, 3 Brig., 5 Div., Dist. Memphis, Tenn., Right Wing 13 Corps, Dept. Tenn. Nov., 1862, 2 Brig., 1 Div., Dist. Memphis, 13 Corps, Dept. Tenn. Dec., 1862, 2 Brig., 1 Div., 17 Corps, Tenn. Jany., 1863, 2 Brig., 1 Div., 16 Corps, Tenn. March, 1863, 3 Brig., 1 Div., 16 Corps, Tenn. July, 1863, 3 Brig., 4 Div., 15 Corps, Tenn. Aug., 1864, 1 Brig., 4 Div., 15 Corps, Tenn. Sept., 1864, 3 Brig., 2 Div., 15 Corps, Tenn. Mustered out Aug. 14, 1865.

71st REGIMENT INFANTRY.—Org. at Camp Todd, Sept., 1861, to Jany., 1862. Feby., 1862, Dist. Paducah, Ky. March, 1862, 2 Brig., 5 Div., Army Tenn. April, 1862, Garrison Fort Donelson, Tenn. June, 1863, 1 Brig., 3 Div., Res. Corps, Cumb'd, Unatt., Garrison Fort Donelson and Clarksville, Tenn. Sept., 1863, Post Gallatin, Tenn., Dept. Cumb'd. April, 1864, Unassigned, 4 Div., 20 Corps, Cumb'd. Aug., 1864, 2 Brig., 3 Div., 4 Corps, Cumb'd. June, 1865, 1 Brig., 3 Div., 4 Corps, Cumb'd. Aug., 1865, Dept. Texas. Mustered out Nov. 30, 1865.

72nd REGIMENT INFANTRY.—Org. at Fremont, Oct., 1861, to Feby., 1862. Feby., 1862, Dist. Paducah, Ky. March, 1862, 4 Brig., 5 Div., Army Tenn. May, 1862, 3 Brig., 5 Div., Army Tenn. July, 1862, 3 Brig., 5 Div., Dist. Memphis, Tenn., Dept. Tenn. Nov., 1862, 5 Brig., 5 Div., Dist. Memphis, Right Wing 13 Corps, Dept. Tenn. Nov., 1862, 3 Brig., 1 Div., Dist. Memphis, 13 Corps, Dept. Tenn. Dec., 1862, 3 Brig., 8 Div., 16 Corps, Tenn. April, 1863, 1 Brig., 3 Div., 15 Corps, Tenn. Dec., 1863, 1 Brig., 1 Div., 16 Corps, Tenn. Dec., 1864, 1 Brig., 1 Div., Det. Army Tenn., Dept. Cumb'd. Feby., 1865, 1 Brig., 1 Div., 16 Corps, Mil. Dist. West. Miss. July, 1865, Dept. Miss. Mustered out Sept. 11, 1865.

73rd REGIMENT INFANTRY.—Org. at Chillicothe, Dec. 30, 1861. Jany., 1862, Cheat Mt. Dist., W. Va. March, 1862, Schenck's Brig., Dept. Mts. June, 1862, 2 Brig., 1 Div., 1 Corps, Army Va. Sept., 1862, 2 Brig., 1 Div., 11 Corps, Potomac. Oct., 1862, 2 Brig., 2 Div., 11 Corps, Potomac. Oct., 1863, 2 Brig., 2 Div., 11 Corps, Cumb'd. April, 1864, 3 Brig., 3 Div., 20 Corps, Cumb'd. Mustered out July 20, 1865.

74th REGIMENT INFANTRY.—Org. at Xenia, Oct. 5, 1861, to March 27, 1862. May, 1862, Dumont's Indpt. Brig., Army Ohio. June, 1862, Unatt., Army Ohio. Sept., 1862, 7 Brig., 8 Div., Army Ohio. Nov., 1862, 3 Brig., 2 Div., Centre 14 Corps, Cumb'd. Jany., 1863, 3 Brig., 2 Div., 14 Corps, Cumb'd. Oct., 1863, 3 Brig., 1 Div., 14 Corps, Cumb'd. June, 1865, 2 Brig., 1 Div., 14 Corps, Cumb'd. Mustered out July 10, 1865.

75th REGIMENT INFANTRY.—Org. at Camp McLean, Nov. 7, 1861, to Jany. 8, 1862. Jany., 1862, Milroy's Command, Cheat Mt. Dist., W. Va. March, 1862, Milroy's Brig., Dept. Mts. April, 1862, Schenck's Brig., Dept. Mts. June, 1862, 2 Brig., 1 Div., 1 Corps, Army Va. Sept., 1862, 2 Brig., 1 Div., 11 Corps, Potomac. July, 1863, 2 Brig., Gordon's Div., Folly Island, S. C., 10 Corps, Dept. South. Feby., 1864, 1 Brig., Ames' Div., Dist. Fla. April, 1864, Dist. Fla., Dept. South. Oct., 1864, 4 Separate Brig., Dept. South. Dec., 1864, 1 Brig., Coast Div., Dept. South. Dec., 1864, 3 Separate Brig., Dept. South. Jany., 1865, 4 Separate Brig., Dept. South. Mustered out July 27, 1865.

76th REGIMENT INFANTRY.—Org. at Camp Sherman, Oct. 5, 1861, to Feby. 3, 1862. Feby., 1862, 3 Brig., 3 Div., Dist. West. Tenn. Feby., 1862, 3 Brig., 3 Div., Army Tenn. July, 1862, Helena, Ark., Dist. Eastern Ark. Dec., 1862, 1 Brig., 1 Div., Dist. Eastern Ark., Dept. Tenn. Dec., 1862, 2 Brig., 11 Div., 13 Corps, Dept. Tenn. Dec., 1862, 1 Brig., 4 Div., Sherman's Yazoo Exp. Jany.,

1863, 2 Brig., 1 Div., 15 Corps, Tenn. Sept., 1863, 1 Brig., 1 Div., 15 Corps, Tenn. Mustered out July 15, 1865.

77th REGIMENT INFANTRY.—Org. at Marietta, Sept. 28, 1861, to Jany. 5, 1862. Feby., 1862, Dist. Paducah, Ky. March, 1862, 3 Brig., 5 Div., Army Tenn. May, 1862, 2 Brig., 5 Div., Army Tenn. July, 1862, 2 Brig., 5 Div., Dist. Memphis, Tenn., Dept. Tenn. Aug., 1862, Alton, Ill. Aug., 1863, 1 Brig., 3 Div., Ark. Exp. Jany., 1864, 1 Brig., 3 Div., 7 Corps, Ark. April, 1864, 2 Brig., 3 Div., 7 Corps, Ark. May, 1864, 2 Brig., 1 Div., 7 Corps, Ark. Feby., 1865, 3 Brig., 3 Div., 13 Corps, Mil. Div. West. Miss. June, 1865, Dept. Texas. Mustered out March 8, 1866.

78th REGIMENT INFANTRY.—Org. at Zanesville, Oct., 1861, to Jany., 1862. Feby., 1862, 2 Brig., 3 Div., Dist. West. Tenn. March, 1862, 3 Brig., 3 Div., Army Tenn. July, 1862, Unatt., Dist. Jackson, Tenn., Dept. Tenn. Nov., 1862, 2 Brig., 3 Div., Right Wing 13 Corps, Dept. Tenn. Dec., 1862, 2 Brig., 3 Div., 17 Corps, Tenn. Mustered out July 11, 1865.

79th REGIMENT INFANTRY.—Org. at Camp Dennison, Aug., 1862. Sept., 1862, Ward's Brig., 12 Div., Army Ohio. Nov., 1862, Ward's Brig., Post Gallatin, Tenn., Dept. Cumb'd. June, 1863, 2 Brig., 3 Div., Res. Corps, Cumb'd. Aug., 1863, Ward's Brig., Nashville, Tenn., Dept. Cumb'd. Jany., 1864, 1 Brig., 1 Div., 11 Corps, Cumb'd. April, 1864, 1 Brig., 3 Div., 20 Corps, Cumb'd. Mustered out June 9, 1865.

80th REGIMENT INFANTRY.—Org. at Canal Dover, Oct., 1861, to Jany., 1862. Feby., 1862, Dist. Paducah, Ky. April, 1862, 2 Brig., 3 Div., Army Miss. Nov., 1862, 2 Brig., 7 Div., Left Wing 13 Corps, Dept. Tenn. Dec., 1862, 2 Brig., 7 Div., 16 Corps, Tenn. Jany., 1863, 2 Brig., 7 Div., 17 Corps, Tenn. Sept., 1863, 2 Brig., 2 Div., 17 Corps, Tenn. Dec., 1863, 2 Brig., 3 Div., 15 Corps, Tenn. April, 1865, 1 Brig., 2 Div., 15 Corps, Tenn. Mustered out Aug. 13, 1865.

81st REGIMENT INFANTRY.—Org. in Ohio at large, Aug. and Sept., 1861. Sept., 1861, Dept. Mo. March, 1862, 2 Brig., 2 Div., Army Tenn. July, 1862, 2 Brig., 2 Div., Dist. Corinth, Miss., Dept. Tenn. Sept., 1862, 1 Brig., 2 Div., Dist. Corinth, Miss., Dept. Tenn. Nov., 1862, 2 Brig., Dist. Corinth, Miss., 13 Corps, Dept. Tenn. Dec., 1862, 2 Brig., Dist. Corinth, Miss., 17 Corps, Tenn. Jany., 1863, 2 Brig., Dist. Corinth, Miss., 16 Corps, Tenn. March, 1863, 2 Brig., 2 Div., 16 Corps, Tenn. Sept., 1864, 2 Brig., 4 Div., 15 Corps, Tenn. Mustered out July 13, 1865.

82nd REGIMENT INFANTRY.—Org. at Kenton, Oct. to Dec., 1861. Jany., 1862, Dist. Cumb'd, Md., Dept. W. Va. March, 1862, Cumb'd, Md., Dept. Mts. April, 1862, Schenck's Brig., Dept. Mts. June, 1862, Milroy's Indpt. Brig., 1 Corps, Army Va. Sept., 1862, Headqrs. 3 Div., 11 Corps, Potomac. Dec., 1862, Headqrs. 11 Corps, Potomac. May, 1863, 2 Brig., 3 Div., 11 Corps, Potomac. July, 1863, 1 Brig., 3 Div., 11 Corps, Potomac. Oct., 1863, 1 Brig., 3 Div., 11 Corps, Cumb'd. April, 1864, 3 Brig., 1 Div., 20 Corps, Cumb'd. Mustered out July 24, 1865.

83rd REGIMENT INFANTRY.—Org. at Camp Dennison, Aug. and Sept., 1862. Sept., 1862, 1 Brig., 2 Div., Army Ky., Dept. Ohio. Dec., 1862, 1 Brig., 10 Div., 13 Corps, Dept. Tenn. Dec., 1862, 1 Brig., 1 Div., Sherman's Yazoo Exp. Jany., 1863, 1 Brig., 10 Div., 13 Corps, Tenn. Aug., 1863, 1 Brig., 4 Div., 13 Corps, Gulf. Jany., 1864, 2 Brig., 3 Div., 13 Corps, Gulf. March, 1864, 1 Brig., 4 Div., 13 Corps, Gulf. June, 1864, 3 Brig., 3 Div., 19 Corps, Gulf. Dec., 1864, Post Natchez, Dist. Vicksburg, Miss. Jany., 1865, 3 Brig., Res. Corps, Mil. Div. West Miss. Feby., 1865, 3 Brig., 2 Div., Res. Corps, M. D. W. M. Feby., 1865, 3 Brig., 2 Div., 13 Corps, M. D. W. M. Mustered out July 24, 1865.

84th REGIMENT INFANTRY.—Org. at Camp Chase, May and June, 1862. June, 1862, R. R. Dist., Dept. Mts. July, 1862, R. R. Dist., 8 Corps, Middle Dept. Mustered out Oct. 14, 1862.

85th REGIMENT INFANTRY.—Org. at Camp Chase, May and June, 1862. Prison Guard at Camp Chase. Mustered out Sept. 27, 1862.

86th REGIMENT INFANTRY.—Org. at Camp Chase, June 10, 1862. June, 1862, R. R. Dist., Dept. Mts. July, 1862, R. R. Dist., 8 Corps, Middle Dept. Mustered out Sept. 25, 1862.

86th REGIMENT INFANTRY.—Reorganized for 6 months at Camp Cleveland, July 14, 1863. Sept., 1863, Willcox's Div., Left Wing Forces, 23 Corps, Dept. Ohio. Oct., 1863, 3 Brig., 2 Div., 9 Corps, Ohio. Jany., 1864, Dist. Clinch, Dept. Ohio. Mustered out Feby. 10, 1864.

87th REGIMENT INFANTRY.—Org. at Camp Chase, June 10, 1862. July, 1862, R. R. Brig., 8 Corps, Middle Dept., Miles' Command, Harper's Ferry, Va. Mustered out Oct. 4, 1862.

88th REGIMENT INFANTRY.—Org. at Camp Chase, June, 1862. At Camp Chase and Cincinnati, Ohio. Mustered out Sept. 26, 1862.

89th REGIMENT INFANTRY.—Org. at Camp Dennison, Aug. 26, 1862. Sept., 1862, Army Ky., Dept. Ohio. Oct., 1862, 2 Brig., Kanawha Div., W. Va., Dept. Ohio. Feby., 1863, Crook's Brig., Baird's Div., Army Ky., Dept. Cumb'd. June, 1863, 3 Brig., 4 Div., 14 Corps, Cumb'd. Sept., 1863, 1 Brig., 1 Div., Res. Corps, Cumb'd. Oct., 1863, 1 Brig., 3 Div., 14 Corps, Cumb'd. Mustered out June 7, 1865.

90th REGIMENT INFANTRY.—Org. at Camp Circlesville, Lancaster, Aug. 29, 1862. Sept., 1862, 22 Brig., 4 Div., Army Ohio. Sept., 1862, 22 Brig., 4 Div., 2 Corps, Army Ohio. Nov., 1862, 1 Brig., 2 Div., Left Wing 14 Corps, Cumb'd. Jany., 1863, 1 Brig., 2 Div., 21 Corps, Cumb'd. Oct., 1863, 1 Brig., 1 Div., 4 Corps, Cumb'd. Mustered out June 13, 1865.

91st REGIMENT INFANTRY.—Org. at Camp Ironton, Sept. 7, 1862. Sept., 1862, Point Pleasant, W. Va., Dist. Kanawha, Dept. Ohio. March, 1863, 2 Brig., 3 Div., 8 Corps, Middle Dept. June, 1863, 2 Brig., Scammon's Div., W. Va. Dec., 1863, 2 Brig., 3 Div., W. Va. April, 1864, 2 Brig., 2 Infy. Div., W. Va. Jany., 1865, 1 Brig., 3 Div., W. Va. April, 1865, 1 Brig., 4 Prov'l Div., W. Va. Mustered out June 24, 1865.

92nd REGIMENT INFANTRY.—Org. at Camp Marietta and Galipolis, Sept. 7-17, 1862. Oct., 1862, Dist. Kanawha, W. Va., Dept. Ohio. Dec., 1862, 2 Brig., Kanawha Div., W. Va. Feby., 1863, Crook's Brig., Baird's Div., Army Ky., Dept. Cumb'd. June, 1863, 3 Brig., 4 Div., 14 Corps, Cumb'd. Oct., 1863, 1 Brig., 3 Div., 14 Corps, Cumb'd. Mustered out June 10, 1865.

93rd REGIMENT INFANTRY.—Org. at Dayton, Aug. 20, 1862. Sept., 1862, Ward's Brig., 12 Div., Army Ohio. Sept., 1862, 4 Brig., 2 Div., 1 Corps, Army Ohio. Nov., 1862, 3 Brig., 2 Div., Right Wing 14 Corps, Cumb'd. Jany., 1863, 3 Brig., 2 Div., 20 Corps, Cumb'd. Oct., 1863, 2 Brig., 3 Div., 4 Corps, Cumb'd. Mustered out June 6, 1865.

94th REGIMENT INFANTRY.—Org. at Camp Piqua, Aug. 22, 1862. Sept., 1862, 9 Brig., 3 Div., 1 Corps, Army Ohio. Nov., 1862, 1 Brig., 1 Div., Centre 14 Corps, Cumb'd. Jany., 1863, 1 Brig., 1 Div., 14 Corps, Cumb'd. Mustered out June 5, 1865.

95th REGIMENT INFANTRY.—Org. at Camp Chase, Aug. 19, 1862. Aug., 1862, Cruft's Brig., Army Ky., Dept. Ohio. Captured Aug. 30, 1862. April, 1863, 1 Brig., 3 Div., 15 Corps, Tenn. Dec., 1863, 1 Brig., 1 Div., 16 Corps, Tenn. Dec., 1864, 1 Brig., 1 Div. Det., Army Tenn., Dept. Cumb'd. Feby., 1865, 1 Brig., 1 Div., 16 Corps, Mil. Div. West Miss. Mustered out Aug. 14, 1865.

96th REGIMENT INFANTRY.—Org. at Camp Delaware, Aug. 29, 1862. Sept., 1862, 2 Brig., 2 Div., Army Ky., Dept. Ohio. Oct., 1862, 1 Brig., 1 Div., Army Ky., Dept. Ohio. Nov., 1862, 1 Brig., 10 Div., Right Wing 13 Corps, Dept. Tenn. Dec., 1862, 1 Brig., 1 Div., Sherman's Yazoo Exp. Jany., 1863, 1 Brig., 10 Div., 13 Corps, Army Tenn. Aug., 1863, 1 Brig., 4 Div., 13 Corps, Tenn. and Gulf. March, 1864, 2 Brig., 4 Div. 13 Corps Gulf. June 1864, 3 Brig., 3 Div., 19 Corps, Gulf. Dec., 1864, U. S. Forces, mouth of White River, Res. Corps, Mil. Div. West Miss. Feby., 1865, 1 Brig., 3 Div., Res. Corps, Mil. Div. W. Miss. Feby., 1865, 1 Brig., 3 Div., 13 Corps, M. D. W. M. Mustered out July 7, 1865.

97th REGIMENT INFANTRY.—Org. at Zanesville, Sept. 1, 1862. Sept., 1862, 21 Brig., 6 Div., Army Ohio. Sept., 1862, 21 Brig., 6 Div., 2 Corps, Army Ohio. Nov., 1862, 2 Brig., 1 Div., Left Wing 14 Corps, Cumb'd. Jany., 1863, 2 Brig., 1 Div., 21 Corps, Cumb'd. Oct., 1863, 2 Brig., 2 Div., 4 Corps, Cumb'd. Mustered out June 10, 1865.

98th REGIMENT INFANTRY.—Org. at Steubenville, Aug. 20, 1862. Sept., 1862, 34 Brig., 10 Div., Army Ohio. Sept., 1862, 34 Brig., 10 Div., 1 Corps, Army Ohio. Nov., 1862, Dist. West Ky., Dept. Ohio. Feby., 1863, Reed's Brig., Baird's Div., Army Ky., Dept. Cumb'd June, 1863, 2 Brig., 1 Div., Res. Corps, Cumb'd. Oct., 1863, 2 Brig., 2 Div., 14 Corps, Cumb'd. Mustered out June 1, 1865.

99th REGIMENT INFANTRY.—Org. at Lima, Aug. 26, 1862. Sept., 1862, 23 Brig., 5 Div., Army Ohio. Sept., 1862, 23 Brig., 5 Div., 2 Corps, Army Ohio. Nov., 1862, 3 Brig., 3 Div., Left Wing 14 Corps, Cumb'd. Jany., 1863, 3 Brig., 3 Div., 21 Corps, Cumb'd. Oct., 1863, 2 Brig., 1 Div., 4 Corps, Cumb'd. June, 1864, 3 Brig., 1 Div., 23 Corps, Ohio. June, 1864, 4 Brig., 2 Div., 23 Corps, Ohio. Aug., 1864, 1 Brig., 2 Div., 23 Corps, Ohio. Consolidated with 50th Ohio Infy., Dec. 31, 1864.

100th REGIMENT INFANTRY.—Org. at Toledo, July to Sept., 1862. Sept., 1862, 2 Brig., 1 Div., Army Ky., Dept. Ohio. Oct., 1862, 2 Brig., 2 Div., Army Ky., Dept. Ohio. Jany., 1863, Dist. Central Ky., Dept. Ohio. June, 1863, 2 Brig., 1 Div., 23 Corps, Ohio. July, 1863, 2 Brig., 4 Div., 23 Corps, Ohio. Aug., 1863, 1 Brig., 3 Div., 23 Corps, Ohio. Feby., 1865, 1 Brig., 3 Div., 23 Corps, Dept. N. C. Mustered out June 20, 1865.

101st REGIMENT INFANTRY.—Org. at Monroeville, Aug. 30, 1862. Sept., 1862, 31 Brig., 9 Div., Army Ohio. Sept., 1862, 31 Brig., 9 Div., 3 Corps, Army Ohio. Nov., 1862, 2 Brig., 1 Div., Right Wing 14 Corps, Cumb'd. Jany., 1863, 2 Brig., 1 Div., 20 Corps, Cumb'd. Oct., 1863, 1 Brig., 1 Div., 4 Corps, Cumb'd. Mustered out June 12, 1865.

102nd REGIMENT INFANTRY.—Org. at Mansfield, Aug. 18, 1862. Sept., 1862, 38 Brig., 12 Div., Army Ohio. Nov., 1862, Dist. West. Ky., Dept. Ohio. Dec., 1862, Clarksville, Tenn., Dept. Cumb'd. June, 1863, 1 Brig., 3 Div., Res. Corps, Cumb'd. Oct., 1863, Unatt., Dist. Nashville, Tenn., Dept. Cumb'd. Jany., 1864, 1 Brig., Dist. Nashville, Dept. Cumb'd. Jany., 1864, 1 Brig., 3 Div., 12 Corps, Cumb'd. April, 1864, 1 Brig., 4 Div., 20 Corps, Cumb'd. April, 1865, Dist. North Ala., Dept. Cumb'd. Mustered out June 30, 1865.

103rd REGIMENT INFANTRY.—Org. at Cleveland, Aug., 1862. Sept., 1862, 2 Brig., 1 Div., Army Ky., Dept. Ohio, to Oct., 1862, 2 Brig., 2 Div., Army Ky., Dept. Ohio. to Jany., 1863, 1 Brig., Dist. Central Ky., Dept. Ohio. June, 1863, 1 Brig., 1 Div., 23 Corps, Dept. Ohio. Aug., 1863, 2 Brig., 3 Div., 23 Corps, Ohio. Feby., 1865, 2 Brig., 3 Div., 23 Corps, Dept. N. C. May, 1865, Dept. N. C. Mustered out June 12, 1865.

104th REGIMENT INFANTRY.—Org. at Massillon, Aug. 30, 1862. Sept., 1862, 2 Brig., 1 Div., Army Ky., Dept. Ohio. Nov., 1862, 2 Brig., 2 Div., Army Ky., Dept. Ohio. Jany., 1863, 1 Brig., Dist. Central Ky., Dept. Ohio. June, 1863, 2 Brig., 1 Div., 23 Corps, Ohio. July, 1863, 2 Brig., 4 Div., 23 Corps, Ohio. Aug., 1863, 1 Brig., 3 Div., 23 Corps, Ohio. Feby., 1865, 1 Brig., 3 Div., 23 Corps, Dept. N. C. Mustered out June 17, 1865.

105th REGIMENT INFANTRY.—Org. at Cleveland, Aug. 20, 1862. Sept., 1862, 33 Brig., 10 Div., Army Ohio. Sept., 1862, 33 Brig., 10 Div., 2 Corps, Army Ohio. Nov., 1862, 1 Brig., 5 Div., Centre 14 Corps, Cumb'd. Jany., 1863, 1 Brig., 5 Div., 14 Corps, Cumb'd. June, 1863, 2 Brig., 4 Div., 14 Corps, Cumb'd. Oct., 1863, 2 Brig., 3 Div., 14 Corps, Cumb'd. Mustered out June 3, 1865.

·106th REGIMENT INFANTRY.—Org. at Camp Dennison, Aug. 26, 1862. Sept., 1862, 39 Brig., 12 Div., Army Ohio. Nov., 1862, Dist. West. Ky., Dept. Ohio. Dec., 1862, Prisoners' War. March, 1862, Dist. West. Ky., Dept. Ohio. June, 1863, Post Gallatin, Tenn., Dept. Cumb'd. May, 1864, Unass'd, 4 Div., 20 Corps, Cumb'd. Garrison Bridgeport, Ala. July, 1864, 3 Brig., Def. Nash. & Chatta. R. R., Dept. Cumb'd. Feby., 1865, Stevenson, Ala., Dist.

Northern Ala., Dept. Cumb'd. Mustered out June 29, 1865.

107th REGIMENT INFANTRY.—Org. at Camp Cleveland, Sept. 9, 1862. Sept., 1862, Def. Cincinnati, Ohio, Dept. Ohio. Oct., 1862, 2 Brig., 3 Div., 11 Corps, Potomac. Dec., 1862, 2 Brig., 1 Div., 11 Corps, Potomac. July, 1863, 1 Brig., 1 Div., 11 Corps, Potomac. Aug., 1863, 1 Brig., Gordon's Div., Folly Island, S. C., 10 Corps, Dept. South. Jany., 1864, 2 Brig., Gordon's Div., Folly Island, S. C., Northern Dist., Dept. South. Feby., 1864, 1 Brig., Ames' Div., Dist. Fla., Dept. South. April, 1864, Dist. Fla., Dept. South. Oct., 1864, 4th Separate Brig., Dist. Fla., Dept. South. Nov., 1864, 1 Brig., Coast Div., Dept. South. Dec., 1864, 3d Separate Brig., Dept. South. Jany., 1865, 1st Separate Brig., Northern Dist., Dept. South. March, 1865, 1st Separate Brig., Dist. Charleston, Dept. South. Mustered out July 10, 1865.

108th REGIMENT INFANTRY.—Org. at Camp Dennison, Aug., 1862. Sept., 1862, 39 Brig., 12 Div., Army Ohio. Nov., 1862, Dist. West Ky., Dept. Ohio. Dec., 1862, Prisoners' War. March, 1863, Dist. Central Ky., Dept. Ohio. June, 1863, 3 Brig., 2 Div., Res. Corps, Cumb'd. Oct., 1863, Unass'd, Dept. Cumb'd. Dec., 1863, 2 Brig., 2 Div., 14 Corps, Cumb'd. Mustered out June 9, 1865.

109th REGIMENT INFANTRY.—(Failed to complete organization.)

110th REGIMENT INFANTRY.—Org. at Camp Piqua, Oct. 3, 1862. Nov., 1862, R. R. Div., Clarksburg, W. Va., Middle Dept. Jany., 1863, Milroy's Command, Winchester, Va., 8 Corps, Middle Dept. March, 1863, 1 Brig., 2 Div., 8 Corps, Middle Dept. June, 1863, 1 Brig., Elliott's Command, 8 Corps. July, 1863, 2 Brig., 3 Div., 3 Corps, Potomac. March, 1864, 2 Brig., 3 Div., 6 Corps, Army Potomac and Army Shenandoah, Middle Mil. Div. Mustered out June 25, 1865.

111th REGIMENT INFANTRY.—Org. at Toledo, Sept. 5, 1862. Sept., 1862, 38 Brig., 12 Div., Army Ohio. Nov., 1862, Dist. West. Ky., Dept. Ohio. May, 1863, 1 Brig., 3 Div., 23 Corps, Ohio. Aug., 1863, 2 Brig., 2 Div., 23 Corps, Ohio. Feby., 1865, 2 Brig., 2 Div., 23 Corps, Dept. N. C. Mustered out June 27, 1865.

112th REGIMENT INFANTRY.—(Failed to complete organization.)

113th REGIMENT INFANTRY.—Org. at Camp Chase and Zanesville, Oct. 10 to Dec. 12, 1862. Dec., 1862, Dist. West. Ky., Dept. Ohio. Feby., 1865, Reed's Brig., Baird's Div., Army Ky., Dept. Cumb'd. June, 1863, 2 Brig., 1 Div., Res. Corps, Cumb'd. Oct., 1863, 2 Brig., 2 Div., 14 Corps, Cumb'd. Mustered out July 6, 1865.

114th REGIMENT INFANTRY.—Org. at Camp Circlesville, Sept., 1862. Nov., 1862, 2 Brig., 9 Div., Right Wing 13 Corps, Dept. Tenn. Dec., 1862, 2 Brig., 3 Div. Sherman's Yazoo Exp. Jany., 1863, 2 Brig., 9 Div., 13 Corps, Tenn. July, 1863, 4 Brig., 1 Div., 13 Corps, Tenn. Aug., 1863, 4 Brig., 1 Div., 13 Corps, Gulf. Sept., 1863, 3 Brig., 1 Div., 13 Corps, Gulf. March, 1864, 2 Brig., 1 Div., 13 Corps, Gulf. June, 1864, 2 Brig., 3 Div., 19 Corps, Gulf. Dec., 1864, 3 Brig., 2 Div., Res. Corps, Mil. Div. W. Miss. Feby., 1865, 3 Brig., 2 Div., 13 Corps, M. D. W. M. Mustered out July 31, 1865.

115th REGIMENT INFANTRY.—Org. at Camp Massilon, Aug. and Sept., 1862. Sept., 1862, Cincinnati, O., Dept. Ohio. Oct., 1863, Post Murfreesboro, Tenn., Dept. Cumb'd. Jany., 1864, 2 Brig., 3 Div., 12 Corps, Cumb'd. April, 1864, Unass'd, 4 Div., 20 Corps, Cumb'd. July, 1864, 1 Brig., Def. Wash. and Chatta. R. R., Dept. Cumb'd. March, 1865, 1 Brig., 1 Sub Dist., Dist. Middle Tenn., Dept. Cumb'd. Mustered out June 22, 1865.

116th REGIMENT INFANTRY.—Org. at Marietta and Gallipolis, Sept. 18, 1862. Oct., 1862, R. R. Div., West Va. Jany., 1863, Romney, Va., Def. Upper Potomac, 8 Corps, Middle Dept. March, 1863, 1 Brig., 2 Div., 8 Corps, Middle Dept. June, 1863, 1 Brig., Elliott's Command, 8 Corps. July, 1863, 1 Brig., 1 Div., Dept. Susquehanna. July, 1863, McReynold's Command, Martinsburg, W. Va., Dept. W. Va. Dec., 1863, 3 Brig., 1 Div., W. Va. April, 1864, 1 Brig., 1 Infy. Div., W. Va. Dec., 1864,

1 Brig., Indpt. Div., 24 Corps, Army James. Mustered out June 14, 1865.

117th REGIMENT INFANTRY.—(See 1st Ohio Heavy Artillery.)

118th REGIMENT INFANTRY.—Org. at Cincinnati and Camp Mansfield, Sept., 1862. Sept., 1862, 2 Brig., 2 Div., Army Ky., Dept. Ohio. Nov., 1862, 1 Brig., 1 Div., Army Ky., Dept. Ohio. Nov., 1862, Dist. Central Ky., Dept. Ohio. June, 1863, 2 Brig., 4 Div., 23 Corps, Ohio. July, 1863, 2 Brig., 1 Div., 23 Corps, Ohio. Aug., 1863, 1 Brig., 2 Div., 23 Corps, Ohio. April, 1864, 2 Brig., 2 Div., 23 Corps, Ohio. Feby., 1865, 2 Brig., 2 Div., 23 Corps, Dept. N. C. Mustered out June 24, 1865.

119th REGIMENT INFANTRY.—(Failed to complete organization.)

120th REGIMENT INFANTRY.—Org. at Mansfield, Aug., 1862. Oct., 1862, Unatt., Army Ky., Dept. Ohio. Nov., 1862, 1 Brig., 9 Div., Right Wing 13 Corps, Dept. Tenn. Dec., 1862, 1 Brig., 3 Div., Sherman's Yazoo Exp. Jany., 1863, 1 Brig., 9 Div., 13 Corps, Tenn. July, 1863, 3 Brig., 1 Div., 13 Corps, Tenn. Aug., 1863, 3 Brig., 1 Div., 13 Corps, Gulf. Nov., 1863, Plaquemine, La., Dist. Baton Rogue, Gulf. March, 1864, 2 Brig., 1 Div., 13 Corps, Gulf. June, 1864, 2 Brig., 3 Div., 19 Corps, Gulf. Aug., 1864, 2 Brig., 2 Div., 19 Corps, Gulf. Consolidated with 114th Ohio Infy., Nov. 27, 1864.

121st REGIMENT INFANTRY.—Org. at Delaware, Sept. 11, 1862. Sept., 1862, 34 Brig., 10 Div., Army Ohio. Oct., 1862, 34 Brig., 10 Div., 1 Corps, Army Ohio. Nov., 1862, Dist. West. Ky., Dept. Ohio. Feby., 1863, Reed's Brig., Baird's Div., Army Ky., Dept. Cumb'd. June, 1863, 2 Brig., 1 Div., Res. Corps, Cumb'd. Oct., 1863, 2 Brig., 2 Div., 14 Corps, Cumb'd. Mustered out June 8, 1865.

122nd REGIMENT INFANTRY.—Org. at Zanesville, Sept. 30 to Oct. 8, 1862. Nov., 1862, R. R. Div., West Va. Jany., 1863, Milroy's Command, Winchester, Va., 8 Corps, Middle Dept. Feby., 1863, 1 Brig., 2 Div., 8 Corps. June, 1863, Elliott's Command, 8 Corps. July, 1863, 2 Brig., 3 Div., 3 Corps, Potomac. March, 1864, 2 Brig., 3 Div., 6 Corps, Potomac. July, 1864, 2 Brig., 3 Div., 6 Corps, Middle Mil. Div. Dec., 1864, 2 Brig., 3 Div., 6 Corps, Potomac. Mustered out June 26, 1865.

123rd REGIMENT INFANTRY.—Org. at Monroeville, Aug. to Oct., 1862. Nov., 1862, R. R. Div., West Va. Jany., 1863, Def. Upper Potomac, 8 Corps, Middle Dept. March, 1863, 1 Brig., 2 Div., 8 Corps. July, 1863, 1 Brig., 1 Div., Dept. Susquehanna. July, 1863, McReynold's Command, Martinsburg, W. Va. Dec., 1863, 3 Brig., 1 Div., W. Va. April, 1864, 1 Brig., 1 Infy. Div., W. Va. Dec., 1864, 1 Brig., Indpt. Div., 24 Corps, Army James. Mustered out June 12, 1865.

124th REGIMENT INFANTRY.—Org. at Cleveland, Aug. to Dec., 1862. Dec., 1862, Dist. West. Ky., Dept. Ohio. Feby., 1863, Franklin, Tenn., Dept. Cumb'd. June, 1863, 2 Brig., 2 Div., 21 Corps, Cumb'd. Oct., 1863, 2 Brig., 3 Div., 4 Corps, Cumb'd. Mustered out June 16, 1865.

125th REGIMENT INFANTRY.—Org. at Columbus and Cleveland, Sept. and Oct., 1862. Oct., 1862, Dist. West. Ky., Dept. Ohio. Feby., 1863, Franklin, Tenn., Dept. Cumb'd. June, 1863, 3 Brig., 1 Div., 21 Corps, Cumb'd. Oct., 1863, 3 Brig., 2 Div., 4 Corps, Cumb'd. Oct., 1864, 1 Brig., 2 Div., 4 Corps, Cumb'd. Mustered out Sept. 25, 1865.

126th REGIMENT INFANTRY.—Org. at Camp Steubenville, Sept. 4, 1862. Oct., 1862, R. R. Div., West Va. Jany., 1863, Martinsburg, W. Va., 8 Corps, Middle Dept. March, 1863, 3 Brig., 1 Div., 8 Corps. June, 1863, 3 Brig., French's Div., 8 Corps. July, 1863, 3 Brig., 3 Div., 3 Corps, Potomac. March, 1864, 2 Brig., 3 Div., 6 Corps, Potomac. Aug., 1864, 2 Brig., 3 Div., 6 Corps, Middle Mil. Div. Dec., 1864, 2 Brig., 3 Div., 6 Corps, Potomac. Mustered out June 25, 1865.

127th REGIMENT INFANTRY.—(See 5th U. S. C. T.)

128th REGIMENT INFANTRY.—Org. at Columbus and Johnson's Island, Dec., 1863, to Jany., 1864. Prison Guard at Johnson's Island, near Sandusky, Ohio. Mustered out July 17, 1865.

129th REGIMENT INFANTRY.—Org. at Cleveland, Aug. 10, 1863. Sept., 1863, Willcox's Left Wing Forces, 23 Corps, Dept. Ohio. Oct., 1863, 3 Brig., 2 Div., 9 Corps, Ohio. Jany., 1864, Dist. Clinch, Dept. Ohio. Mustered out March 10, 1864.

130th REGIMENT INFANTRY.—Org. at Sandusky and mustered in May 13, 1864. June, 1864, 2 Brig., 3 Div., 10 Corps, Army James. Mustered out Sept. 22, 1864.

131st REGIMENT INFANTRY.—Org. at Camp Chase, May 14, 1864. May, 1864, 2 Separate Brig., 8 Corps, Middle Dept. Mustered out Aug. 25, 1864.

132nd REGIMENT INFANTRY.—Org. at Camp Chase, May 15, 1864. June, 1864, 2 Brig., 3 Div., 10 Corps, Army James. Mustered out Sept. 10, 1864.

133rd REGIMENT INFANTRY.—Org. at Camp Chase, May 6, 1864. May, 1864, Res. Div., Dept. W. Va. June, 1864, 1 Brig., 3 Div., 10 Corps, Army James. Mustered out Aug. 20, 1864.

134th REGIMENT INFANTRY.—Org. at Camp Chase, May 6, 1864. June, 1864, 2 Brig., 3 Div., 10 Corps, Army James. Mustered out Aug. 31, 1864.

135th REGIMENT INFANTRY.—Org. at Camp Chase, May 11, 1864. May, 1864, R. R. Guard, Res. Div., W. Va. Mustered out Sept. 1, 1864.

136th REGIMENT INFANTRY.—Org. at Camp Chase, May 13, 1864. May, 1864, 2 Brig., DeRussy's Div., 22 Corps. July, 1864, 3 Brig., DeRussy's Div., 22 Corps. Mustered out Aug. 31, 1864.

137th REGIMENT INFANTRY.—Org. at Camp Dennison, May 10, 1864. May, 1864, Def. Balto., Md., 8 Corps, Middle Dept. Mustered out Aug. 19, 1864.

138th REGIMENT INFANTRY.—Org. at Camp Dennison, May 14, 1864. May, 1864, 1 Brig., DeRussy's Div., 22 Corps. June, 1864, 2 Brig., 3 Div., 10 Corps, Army James. Mustered out Sept. 1, 1864.

139th REGIMENT INFANTRY.—Org. at Camp Chase, May 15, 1864. May, 1864, Prison Guard, Point Lookout, Md. Mustered out Aug. 26, 1864.

140th REGIMENT INFANTRY.—Org. at Gallipolis, May 10, 1864. May, 1864, Garrison Charleston, W. Va., Res. Div., W. Va. Mustered out Sept. 3, 1864.

141st REGIMENT INFANTRY.—Org. at Gallipolis, May 14, 1864. May, 1864, Garrison Charleston, W. Va., Res. Div., W. Va. Mustered out Sept. 3, 1864.

142nd REGIMENT INFANTRY.—Org. at Camp Chase, May 13, 1864. May, 1864, 2 Brig., DeRussy's Div., 22 Corps. June, 1864, 2 Brig., 3 Div., 10 Corps, Army James. Mustered out Sept. 2, 1864.

143rd REGIMENT INFANTRY.—Org. at Camp Chase, May 12, 1864. May, 1864, 1 Brig., Haskin's Div., 22 Corps. June, 1864, 1 Brig., 3 Div., 10 Corps, Army James. Mustered out Sept. 13, 1864.

144th REGIMENT INFANTRY.—Org. at Camp Chase, May 11, 1864. May, 1864, Def. Balto., Md., and 1st Separate Brig., 8 Corps, Middle Dept. July, 1864, Kenly's Indpt. Brig., 8 Corps. Mustered out Aug. 31, 1864.

145th REGIMENT INFANTRY.—Org. at Camp Chase, May 12, 1864. May, 1864, 1 Brig., DeRussy's Div., 22 Corps. Mustered out Aug. 20, 1864.

146th REGIMENT INFANTRY.—Org. at Camp Dennison, May 12, 1864. May, 1864, Garrison Fayetteville, W. Va., Res. Div., W. Va. Mustered out Sept. 7, 1864.

147th REGIMENT INFANTRY.—Org. at Camp Dennison, May 16, 1864. May, 1864, 1 Brig., DeRussy's Div., 22 Corps. July, 1864, 2 Brig., DeRussy's Div., 22 Corps. Mustered out Aug. 30, 1864.

148th REGIMENT INFANTRY.—Org. at Marietta, May 17, 1864. May, 1864, Res. Div., W. Va. June, 1864, 1 Brig., 3 Div., 10 Corps, Army James. Mustered out Sept. 14, 1864.

149th REGIMENT INFANTRY.—Org. at Camp Dennison, May 8, 1864. May, 1864, Def. Balto., Md., 8 Corps, Middle Dept. July, 1864, 1st Separate Brig., 8 Corps. July, 1864, Kenly's Indpt. Brig., 8 Corps. Mustered out Aug. 30, 1864.

150th REGIMENT INFANTRY.—Org. at Cleveland, May 5, 1864. May, 1864, 1 Brig., Haskin's Div., 22

Corps. July, 1864, 2 Brig., Haskin's Div., 22 Corps. Mustered out Aug. 23, 1864.

151st REGIMENT INFANTRY.—Org. at Camp Chase, May 13, 1864. May, 1864, 2 Brig., Haskin's Div., 22 Corps. July, 1864, 1 Brig., Haskin's Div., 22 Corps. Mustered out Aug. 27, 1864.

152nd REGIMENT INFANTRY.—Org. at Camp Dennison, May 11, 1864. May, 1864, New Creek, W. Va., Dept. W. Va. June, 1864, R. R. Guard, Res. Div., W. Va. Mustered out Sept. 2, 1864.

153rd REGIMENT INFANTRY.—Org. at Camp Dennison, May 10, 1864. May, 1864, R. R. Guard, Res. Div., Dept. W. Va. Mustered out Sept. 9, 1864.

154th REGIMENT INFANTRY.—Org. at Camp Dennison, May 9, 1864. May, 1864, New Creek, W. Va., Res. Div., Dept. W. Va. Mustered out Sept. 1, 1864.

155th REGIMENT INFANTRY.—Org. at Camp Dennison, May 8, 1864. May, 1864. New Creek, W. Va., Res. Div., Dept. W. Va. June, 1864, Norfolk, Va., Dept. Va. and N. C. Mustered out Aug. 27, 1864.

156th REGIMENT INFANTRY.—Org. at Camp Dennison, May 15, 1864. May, 1864, Cincinnati, Ohio. July, 1864, Kelly's Command, Res. Div., Dept. W. Va. Mustered out Sept. 1, 1864.

157th REGIMENT INFANTRY.—Org. at Camp Chase, May 15, 1864. May, 1864, Def. Balto., Md., 8 Corps, Middle Dept. Mustered out Sept. 2, 1864.

158th REGIMENT INFANTRY.—Org. not completed.

159th REGIMENT INFANTRY.—Org. at Zanesville, May 9, 1864. May, 1864, Def. Balto., Md., 3d Separate Brig., 8 Corps, Middle Dept. Mustered out Aug. 24, 1864.

160th REGIMENT INFANTRY.—Org. at Zanesville, May 12, 1864. May, 1864, Res. Div., Dept. W. Va. Mustered out Sept. 7, 1864.

161st REGIMENT INFANTRY.—Org. at Camp Chase, May 9, 1864. May, 1864, Res. Div., Dept. W. Va. Mustered out Sept. 2, 1864.

162nd REGIMENT INFANTRY.—Org. at Camp Chase, May 20, 1864. June, 1864, Dist. Ky., Dept. Ohio. Mustered out Sept. 4, 1864.

163rd REGIMENT INFANTRY.—Org. at Camp Chase, May 12, 1864. May, 1864, 1 Brig., Haskin's Div., 22 Corps. June, 1864, 1 Brig., 3 Div., 10 Corps, Army James. Mustered out Sept. 10, 1864.

164th REGIMENT INFANTRY.—Org. at Camp Taylor, Cleveland, May 11, 1864. May, 1864, 1 Brig., DeRussy's Div., 22 Corps. Mustered out Aug. 27, 1864.

165th REGIMENT INFANTRY.—Org. at Camp Dennison, May 14, 1864. May, 1864, Johnson's Island, Ohio. June, 1864, Dist. Ky., Dept. Ohio. Aug., 1864, Cumb'd, Md. Mustered out Aug. 31, 1864.

166th REGIMENT INFANTRY.—Org. at Camp Cleveland, May 13, 1864. May, 1864, 2 Brig., DeRussy's Div., 22 Corps. July, 1864, 3 Brig., DeRussy's Div., 22 Corps. Mustered out Sept. 9, 1864.

167th REGIMENT INFANTRY.—Org. at Hamilton, May 14, 1864. May, 1864, Camp Piatt and Gauley Bridge, W. Va., Res. Div., Dept. W. Va. Mustered out Sept. 8, 1864.

168th REGIMENT INFANTRY.—Org at Camp Dennison, May 19, 1864. May, 1864, Dist. Ky., Dept. Ohio. Mustered out Sept. 8, 1864.

169th REGIMENT INFANTRY.—Org. at Camp Cleveland, May 13, 1864. May, 1864, 1 Brig., DeRussy's Div., 22 Corps. July, 1864, 2 Brig., DeRussy's Div., 22 Corps. Mustered out Sept. 4, 1864.

170th REGIMENT INFANTRY.—Org. at Bellaire, May 13, 1864. May, 1864, 2 Brig., Haskin's Div., 22 Corps. July, 1864, Res. Div., Dept. W. Va. Mustered out Sept. 10, 1864.

171st REGIMENT INFANTRY.—Org. at Sandusky, May 7, 1864. May, 1864, Dist. Ky., Dept. Ohio. Mustered out Aug. 20, 1864.

172nd REGIMENT INFANTRY.—Org. at Gallipolis, May 14, 1864. Duty at Gallipolis. Mustered out Sept. 3, 1864.

173rd REGIMENT INFANTRY.—Org. at Gallipolis, Sept., 1864. Sept., 1864, Post and Def. Nashville, Tenn.,

Dept. Cumb'd. March, 1865, 3d Sub Dist., Dist. Middle Tenn., Dept. Cumb'd. Mustered out June 26, 1865.

174th REGIMENT INFANTRY.—Org. at Camp Chase, Aug. 18 to Sept. 21, 1864. Oct., 1864, Dist. North Ala., Dept. Cumb'd. Dec., 1864, 3 Brig., 1 Div., 23 Corps, Ohio. Feby., 1865, 3 Brig., 1 Div., 23 Corps, Dept. N. C. Mustered out June 28, 1865.

175th REGIMENT INFANTRY.—Org. at Camp Dennison, Oct., 1864. Oct., 1864, Columbia, Tenn., Dept. Cumb'd. Nov., 1864, 3 Brig., 3 Div., 23 Corps, Ohio. Dec., 1864, Post Columbia, Tenn., Dept. Cumb'd. March, 1865, 2d Sub Dist., Dist. Middle Tenn., Dept. Cumb'd. Mustered out June 27, 1865.

176th REGIMENT INFANTRY.—Org. at Camp Chase, Aug. 10 to Sept. 21, 1864. Sept., 1864, Post and Def. Nashville, Tenn., Dept. Cumb'd. Dec., 1864, 2 Brig., 4 Div., 20 Corps, Cumb'd. March, 1865, Garrison Nashville, Tenn., Dept. Cumb'd. Mustered out June 14, 1865.

177th REGIMENT INFANTRY.—Org. at Camp Cleveland, Sept. and Oct., 1864. Oct., 1864, Tullahoma, Tenn., Def. Nash. & Chatta. R. R., Dept. Cumb'd. Jany., 1865, 2 Brig., 3 Div., 23 Corps, Ohio. Feby., 1865, 2 Brig., 3 Div., 23 Corps, Dept. N. C. Mustered out June 24, 1865.

178th REGIMENT INFANTRY.—Org. at Camp Chase, Sept. 26, 1864. Oct., 1864, Tullahoma, Tenn., Def. Nash. & Chatta. R. R., Dept. Cumb'd. Jany., 1865, 3 Brig., 1 Div., 23 Corps, Ohio. Feby., 1865, 3 Brig., 1 Div., 23 Corps, Dept. N. C. Mustered out June 29, 1865.

179th REGIMENT INFANTRY.—Org. at Camp Chase, Sept. 28, 1864. Oct., 1864, Post and Def. Nashville, Tenn., Dept. Cumb'd. Dec. 1864, 2 Brig., 4 Div., 20 Corps, Cumb'd. March, 1865, Garrison Nashville, Tenn., Dept. Cumb'd. Mustered out June 17, 1865.

180th REGIMENT INFANTRY.—Org. at Camp Chase, Sept. and Oct., 1864. Oct., 1864, 3 Brig., Def. Nash. & Chatta. R. R., Dept. Cumb'd. Jany., 1865, 1 Brig., 1 Div., 23 Corps, Ohio. Feby., 1865, 1 Brig., 1 Div., 23 Corps, Dept. N. C. Mustered out July 12, 1865.

181st REGIMENT INFANTRY.—Org. at Camp Dennison, Sept. 29 to Oct. 10, 1864. Oct., 1864, Dist. No. Ala., Dept. Cumb'd. Oct., 1864, 1 Brig., Def. Nash. & Chatta. R. R., Dept. Cumb'd. Jany., 1865, 3 Brig., 2 Div., 23 Corps, Ohio. Feby., 1865, 3 Brig., 2 Div., 23 Corps, Dept. N. C. Mustered out July 14, 1865.

182nd REGIMENT INFANTRY.—Org. at Camp Chase, Aug. 4 to Oct. 13, 1864. Nov., 1864, Post and Def. Nashville, Tenn., Dept. Cumb'd. Dec., 1864, 2 Brig., 4 Div., 20 Corps, Cumb'd. March, 1865, Garrison Nashville, Tenn. Mustered out July 7, 1865.

183rd REGIMENT INFANTRY.—Org. at Cincinnati and Sandusky, Sept. and Oct., 1864. Nov., 1864, 3 Brig., 2 Div., 23 Corps, Ohio. Feby., 1865, 3 Brig., 2 Div., 23 Corps, Dept. N. C. Mustered out July 17, 1865.

184th REGIMENT INFANTRY.—Org. at Camp Chase, Feby., 1865. March, 1865, Garrison Bridgeport, Ala. and Edgefield, Tenn:, Dept. Cumb'd. Mustered out Sept. 20, 1865.

185th REGIMENT INFANTRY.—Org. at Camp Chase, Feby. 25, 1865. Duty in Dept. Ky. Mustered out Sept. 26, 1865.

186th REGIMENT INFANTRY.—Org. at Camp Chase, Feby., 1865. March, 1865, 2 Brig., 2 Separate Div., Dist. Etowah, Dept. Cumb'd. May, 1865, 2 Brig., 1 Separate Div., Dist. Etowah, Dept. Cumb'd. July, 1865, 2 Brig., 4 Div., Dist. East Tenn., Dept. Cumb'd. Mustered out Sept. 13, 1865.

187th REGIMENT INFANTRY.—Org. at Camp Chase, March 2, 1865. March, 1865, 1 Brig., 2d Separate Div., Dist. Etowah, Dept. Cumb'd. Mustered out Jany. 20, 1866.

188th REGIMENT INFANTRY.—Org. at Camp Chase, March 2, 1865. March, 1865, 1 Brig., Def. Nash and Chatta. R. R., Dept. Cumb'd. April, 1865, 1 Brig., 1 Sub Dist., Dist. Middle Tenn., Dept. Cumb'd. Mustered out Sept. 21, 1865.

189th REGIMENT INFANTRY.—Org. at Camp Chase, Jany. to March, 1865. March, 1865, Dist. North Ala., Dept. Tenn. Mustered out Sept. 28, 1865.

190th REGIMENT INFANTRY.—(Failed to complete organization.)

191st REGIMENT INFANTRY.—Org. at Camp Chase, Jany. and Feby., 1865. March, 1865, 2 Brig., 2 Prov'l Div., Army Shenandoah. Mustered out Aug. 27, 1865.

192nd REGIMENT INFANTRY.—Org. at Camp Chase, March 9, 1865. March, 1865, 2 Brig., 2 Prov'l Div., Army Shenandoah. Mustered out Sept. 1, 1865.

193rd REGIMENT INFANTRY.—Org. at Camp Chase, March, 1865. March, 1865, 1 Brig., 3 Prov'l Div., Army Shenandoah. Mustered out Aug. 4, 1865.

194th REGIMENT INFANTRY.—Org. at Camp Chase, March, 1865. March, 1865, 1 Brig., 3 Prov'l Div., Army Shenandoah. April, 1865, Def. Washington, 22 Corps. Mustered out Oct. 24, 1865.

195th REGIMENT INFANTRY.—Org. at Camp Chase, March, 1865. March, 1865, 2 Brig., 2 Prov'l Div., Army Shenandoah. April, 1865, Alexandria, Va., 22 Corps. Mustered out Dec. 18, 1865.

196th REGIMENT INFANTRY.—Org. at Camp Chase, March 25, 1865. April, 1865, 2 Brig., 2 Prov'l Div., Army Shenandoah. July, 1865, Def. Balto., Md. Mustered out Sept. 11, 1865.

197th REGIMENT INFANTRY.—Org. at Camp Chase, March 28, 1865. April, 1865, Prov'l Div., 9 Corps. May, 1865, Dover, Del., 3d Separate Brig., 8 Corps. Mustered out July 31, 1865.

198th REGIMENT INFANTRY.—Org. at Camp Chase, April 17 to 27, 1865. Mustered out May 8, 1865.

HOFFMAN'S BATTALION INFANTRY.—Org. Dec., 1861, for Prison Guard duty at Johnson's Island, near Sandusky, Ohio. Transferred to 128th Ohio Infy., Jany. 5, 1864.

JONES' INDEPENDENT BATTALION INFANTRY.—Org. Sept. 25, 1861. Mustered out Jany. 9, 1862.

DENNISON GUARD.—Org. at Camp Dennison, May to Aug., 1862. Mustered out Jany. 24, 1863.

TRUMBULL GUARD.—Org. at Gallipolis, Nov. 9, 1862, River Guard. Mustered out July 1, 1865.

WALLACE GUARD.—Org. at Cincinnati, Sept. 2, 1862. Mustered out Oct. 4, 1862.

BARD'S INDEPENDENT COMPANY.—Org. at Cincinnati, Sept. 2, 1862. Mustered out Oct. 3, 1862.

DEPARTMENTAL CORPS.—Org. at Barnesville, Somerton and Hendrysburg, Dept. Monongahela, July 12 to 27, 1863. Mustered out Nov. 1, 1864.

OREGON

1st REGIMENT CAVALRY.—Org. at large, Nov. 21, 1861. Attached to the Dept. of the Pacific. Mustered out Nov. 20, 1866.

1st REGIMENT INFANTRY.—Org. at large, Nov. 11, 1864, to Jany. 2, 1865. Attached to Dept. of the Pacific. Mustered out July 19, 1867.

PENNSYLVANIA

1st REGIMENT CAVALRY.—(14th RESERVE CORPS, 44th VOLS.)—Org. at Harrisburg, Aug. 5 to Sept. 6, 1861. Oct., 1861, McCall's Div., Potomac. March, 1862, Cav., McCall's Div., 1 Corps, Potomac. April, 1862, Bayard's Cav. Brig., Dept. Rappahannock. June, 1862, Bayard's Cav. Brig., 3 Corps, Army Va. Sept., 1862, Bayard's Cav. Brig., Potomac. Oct., 1862, Bayard's Cav. Brig., Cav. Div., Potomac. Feby., 1863, 2 Brig., 3 Div., Cav. Corps, Potomac. June, 1863, 1 Brig., 2 Div., Cav. Corps. Potomac. Consolidated with 6th and 17th Pa. Cav. to form 2nd Prov'l Cav., June 17, 1865.

1st REGIMENT PROVISIONAL CAVALRY.—Org. June 17, 1865, by consolidation of 2nd and 20th Pa. Cav. Mustered out July 13, 1865.

1st BATALLION MILITIA CAVALRY.—Org. at Harrisburg, July 13, 1863. July, 1863, Dept. Susquehanna. Mustered out Aug. 21, 1863.

2nd REGIMENT CAVALRY.—(59th VOLS.). Org. at Phila. and Harrisburg, Sept., 1861, to April, 1862. April, 1862, Dix's Div., Def. Baltimo., Md. April, 1862, Sturgis' Command, Def. Washington, D. C. Aug., 1862, Buford's Cav. Brig., 2 Corps, Army Va. Sept., 1862, Price's Cav. Brig., Def. Washington, D. C. March, 1863, 2 Brig., Stahel's Cav. Div., 22 Corps, Def. Washington,

D. C. June, 1863, Provost Guard, Army Potomac. Dec., 1863, 2 Brig., 2 Div., Cav. Corps, Potomac. Feby., 1865, Provost Guard, Army Potomac. Consolidated with 20th Pa. Cav., June 17, 1865, to form 1st Prov'l Cav.

2nd REGIMENT PROVISIONAL CAVALRY.—Org. by consolidation of 1st, 6th and 17th Pa. Cav., June 17, 1865. Mustered out Aug. 7, 1865.

3rd REGIMENT CAVALRY.—(60th VOLS.) "Young's Ky. Light Cavalry." Org. at Phila., July and Aug., 1861. Oct., 1861, Porter's Div., Potomac. March, 1862, Cav., 3 Corps, Potomac. July, 1862, 1 Brig. Cav., Div. Potomac. Sept., 1862, 5 Brig., Pleasanton's Cav., Div. Potomac. Nov., 1862, Averill's Cav. Brig., Centre Grand Div. Potomac. Feby., 1863, 2 Brig., 2 Div., Cav. Corps, Potomac. June, 1863, 3 Brig., 2 Div., Cav. Corps, Potomac. March, 1864, Heador's Army, Potomac. Provost Marshal General's Command. Transferred to 5th Pa. Cav., May 8, 1865.

3rd REGIMENT PROVISIONAL CAVALRY.—Org. June 24, 1865, by consolidation of 18th and 22nd Pa. Cav. Mustered out Oct. 31, 1865.

4th REGIMENT CAVALRY.—(64th VOLS.) Org. at Harrisburg, Phila. and Pittsburg, Aug. to Oct., 1861. Dec., 1861, Def. Washington. May, 1862, McCall's Div., Dept. Rappahannock. June, 1862, McCall's Div., 5 Corps, Potomac. July, 1862, 1 Brig. Cav., Div. Potomac. Sept., 1862, 3 Brig., Pleasanton's Cav. Div., Potomac. Nov., 1862, Averill's Cav. Brig., Centre Grand Div. Potomac. Feby., 1863, 2 Brig., 2 Div., Cav. Corps, Potomac. June, 1863, 3 Brig., 2 Div., Cav. Corps, Potomac. Aug., 1863, 2 Brig., 2 Div., Cav. Corps., Potomac. Mustered out July 1, 1865.

5th REGIMENT CAVALRY.—(65th VOLS.). "Cameron Dragoons." Org. at Phila., July to Sept., 1861. Sept., 1861, Smith's Div., Def. Washington. May, 1862, Unatt., Yorktown, Va., 4 Corps, Potomac. Dec., 1862, Unatt., Yorktown, Va., 7 Corps, Dept. Va. April, 1863, West's Advance Brig., 7 Corps, Dept. Va. May, 1863, Advance Brig., 4 Corps. June, 1863, 2 Brig., 1 Div., 4 Corps. July, 1863, Wistar's Brig., Yorktown, Va., Dept. Va. and N. C. Dec., 1863, Cav. Brig., U. S. Forces, Portsmouth, Va., Dept. Va. and N. C. Dec., 1863, Dist. Currituck, Va., Dept. Va. and N. C. Jany., 1864, Heckman's Div., 18 Corps, Dept. Va. and N. C. April, 1864, 2 Brig., Cav. Div., Army James, Dept. Va. and N. C. June, 1864, 1 Brig., Kautz's Cav. Div., Dept. Va. and N. C. April, 1865, Cav. Brig., Dept. Va. June, 1865, Richmond, Va., Dist. Henrico, Dept. Va. Mustered out Aug. 1, 1865.

6th REGIMENT CAVALRY.—(70th VOLS.). "Rush's Lancers." Org. at Phila. and Reading, Aug. to Oct., 1861. Dec., 1861, Def. Washington, D. C. March, 1862, Emory's Brig., Cooke's Cav., Div. Potomac. April, 1862, Emory's Brig., Cav. Res., Potomac. July, 1862, 2 Brig., Cav. Div., Potomac. Sept., 1862, 3 Brig., Pleasanton's Cav. Div., Potomac. Nov., 1862, Heador's Left, Grand Div., Potomac. Feby., 1863, Res. Cav. Brig., Cav. Corps, Potomac. June, 1863, Res. Brig., 1 Div., Cav. Corps, Potomac. Aug., 1864, Reserve (3) Brig., 1 Div., Cav. Corps, Army Shenandoah, Middle Mil. Div. and Army Potomac. Consolidated with 1st and 17th Pa. Cav., June 17, 1865, to form 2d Prov'l Cav.

7th REGIMENT CAVALRY.—(80th VOLS.). Org. at Harrisburg, Sept. to Dec., 1861. Dec., 1861, Unatt., Army Ohio. March, 1862, Negley's 7th Indpt. Brig., Post Nashville, Army Ohio (Co's A, D, H, I). Dumont's Indpt. Brig., Post Nashville, Army Ohio (Co's C, E, F, K). Duffield's 23d Indpt. Brig., Army Ohio (Co's B, G, L, M). Sept., 1862, Cav., 8 Div., Army Ohio (Co's A, C, D, E, F, H, I, K). Unatt., Headqrs. Army Ohio (Co's B, G, L, M). Nov., 1862, 1 Brig., Cav. Div., Army Cumb'd. Jany., 1863, 1 Brig., 2 Div. Cav., Cumb'd. Oct., 1864, 2 Brig., 2 Div., Cav. Corps, Mil. Div. Miss. Mustered out Aug. 23, 1865.

8th REGIMENT CAVALRY.—(89th VOLS.). Org. at Phila., Aug. to Oct., 1861. Oct., 1861, F. J. Porter's Div., Potomac. March, 1862, Unatt., 4 Corps, Potomac. April, 1862, Blake's Brig., Cav. Command, Potomac. July, 1862, 2 Brig., Stoneman's Cav. Div., Potomac.

Sept., 1862, 2 Brig., Pleasanton's Cav. Div., Potomac. Feby., 1863, 2 Brig., 1 Div., Cav. Corps, Potomac. June, 1863, 2 Brig., 2 Div., Cav. Corps, Potomac. May, 1865, Dept. Va. Consolidated with 18th Pa. Cav., July 24, 1865.

9th REGIMENT CAVALRY.—(92nd VOLS.). Org. at Harrisburg, Oct. and Nov., 1861. Jany., 1862, Unatt., Cav., Army Ohio. Sept., 1862, 3 Brig., Cav. Div., Army Ohio. Nov., 1862, Dist. Louisville, Ky., Army Ky., Dept. Ohio. Dec., 1862, Dist. Central Ky., Dept. Ohio. March, 1863, 1 Brig., 1 Cav. Div., Cumb'd. May, 1864, Dist. Ky., Dept. Ohio. Sept., 1864, Dist. Middle Tenn., Dept. Cumb'd. Oct., 1864, 1 Brig., 3 Div., Cav. Corps, Cumb'd. Nov., 1864, 1 Brig., Kilpatrick's, 3 Div., Wilson's Cav. Corps, Mil. Div. Miss. July, 1865, 3 Brig., 3 Div., Cav., Dept. N. C. Mustered out July 18, 1865.

10th REGIMENT CAVALRY.—(Failed to complete organization.)

11th REGIMENT CAVALRY.—(108th VOLS.). "Harlan's Iowa Cavalry." Org. at Phila., Aug. to Oct., 1861. Oct., 1861, Def. Washington, D. C. Nov., 1861, Camp Hamilton, Va., Dept. Va. April, 1862, Unatt., Dept. Va. July, 1862, Unatt., Div. at Suffolk, Va., 7 Corps, Dept. Va. Aug., 1863, U. S. Forces, Portsmouth, Va., Dept. Va. and N. C. Oct., 1863, Cav. Brig., Portsmouth, Va., Dept. Va. and N. C. Jany., 1864, Cav. Brig., U. S. Forces, Yorktown, Va. April, 1864, 2 Brig., Cav. Div., Dept. Va. and N. C. June, 1865, Dept. Va. Mustered out Aug. 13, 1865.

12th REGIMENT CAVALRY.—(113th VOLS.). Org. at Phila., Dec., 1861, to April, 1862. April, 1862, Mil. Dist. Washington, D. C. Sept., 1862, 4 Brig., Pleasanton's Cav. Div., Potomac. Oct., 1862, Averill's Cav. Command, 8 Corps, Middle Dept. Nov., 1862, Def. Upper Potomac, 8 Corps. Feby., 1863, 1 Brig., 2 Div., 8 Corps. June, 1863, Pierce's Brig., Reynold's Command, Dept. Susquehanna. Aug., 1863, Reynold's Command, Martinsburg, W. Va., Dept. W. Va. Oct., 1863, 3 Brig., 1 Div., W. Va. April, 1864, Res. Div., Dept. W. Va. July, 1864, 1 Brig., 1 Cav. Div., W. Va. Aug., 1864, Res. Div., Harper's Ferry, W. Va. Jany., 1865, 3 Infy. Div., W. Va. April, 1865, Cav., Brig., Army Shenandoah. Mustered out July 20, 1865.

13th REGIMENT CAVALRY.—(117th VOLS.). Org. at Phila. and Harrisburg, Dec., 1861. April, 1862, Def. Baltimore, Md., Middle Dept. Sept., 1862, Upper Potomac, 8 Corps, Middle Dept. Jany., 1863, Elliott's Brig., Milroy's Command, Winchester, Va., 8 Corps. Feby., 1863, 1 Brig., 2 Div., 8 Corps. July, 1863, 3 Brig., 2 Div., Cav. Corps, Potomac. Aug., 1863, 2 Brig., 2 Div., Cav. Corps, Potomac. May 3-26, 1864, Cav., 9 Corps, Potomac. May 26, 1864, 2 Brig., 2 Div., Cav. Corps, Potomac. Feby., 1865, Terry's Prov'l Corps, Dept. N. C. March, 1865, 3 Brig., Kilpatrick's Cav. Div., Dept. N. C. Mustered out July 14, 1865.

14th REGIMENT CAVALRY.—(159th VOLS.). Org. at Phila. and Erie, Oct. and Nov., 1862. Dec., 1862, Def. Upper Potomac, 8 Corps, Middle Dept. March, 1863, 1 Brig., 1 Div., 8 Corps. March, 1863, 4th Separate Brig., 8 Corps. June, 1863, Averill's 4th Separate Brig., Dept. W. Va. Dec., 1863, 2 Brig., 4 Div., W. Va. April, 1864, 2 Brig., 2 Cav. Div., W. Va. June, 1864, 1 Brig., 2 Cav. Div., W. Va. Aug., 1864, 3 Brig., 1 Div., Cav. Corps, Middle Mil. Div. Aug., 1864, 1 Brig., 2 Cav. Div., W. Va. April, 1865, 1st Separate Brig., De Russy's Div., 22 Corps. Mustered out Aug. 24, 1865.

15th REGIMENT CAVALRY.—(160th Vols.). Org. at Harrisburg, Sept., 1862. Nov., 1862, Louisville, Ky., Dept. Ohio. Nov., 1862, Unatt., Nashville, Tenn., Army Cumb'd. Dec., 1862, Res. Cav., Cav. Div., Cumb'd. Jany., 1863, Unatt., Cav. Headqrs., Dept. Cumb'd. Oct., 1863, Unatt., Cav., Dept. Cumb'd. May, 1864, Post and Dist. Nashville, Tenn., Dept. Cumb'd. Aug., 1864, Unatt., Dept. Cumb'd. Jany., 1865, 3 Brig., 6 Div., Cav. Corps, Mil. Div. Miss. March, 1865, 1 Brig., Cav. Div., Dist. East Tenn. Mustered out July 18, 1865.

16th REGIMENT CAVALRY.—(161st VOLS.). Org. at Harrisburg, Sept. to Nov., 1862. Nov., 1862, Def. Washington, D. C. Jany., 1863, Averill's Cav. Brig.,

Potomac. Feby., 1863, 2 Brig, 2 Div., Cav. Corps, Potomac. June, 1863, 3 Brig., 2 Div., Cav. Corps, Potomac. Aug., 1863, 2 Brig., 2 Div., Cav. Corps, Potomac. Mustered out Aug. 11, 1865.

17th REGIMENT CAVALRY.—(162nd VOLS.). Org. at Harrisburg, Sept. to Nov., 1862. Nov., 1862, Cav. Brig., 11 Corps, Potomac. Feby., 1863, 2 Brig., 1 Div., Cav. Corps, Potomac. Aug., 1864, 2 Brig., 1 Div., Cav. Corps, Middle Mil. Div. March, 1865, 2 Brig., 1 Div., Cav. Corps, Potomac. Consolidated with 1st and 6th Pa. Cav., June 17, 1865, to form 2d Prov'l Cav.

18th REGIMENT CAVALRY.—(163rd VOLS.). Org. at Pittsburg and Harrisburg, Oct. to Dec., 1862. Dec., 1862, Price's Cav. Brig., Def. Washington, D. C. Feby., 1863, Price's Cav. Brig., 22 Corps. April, 1863, 3 Brig., Stahel's Cav. Div., 22 Corps. May, 1863, 2 Brig., Stahel's Cav. Div., 22 Corps. June, 1863, 1 Brig., 3 Div., Cav. Corps, Potomac, and Middle Mil. Div. Consolidated with 22d Penna. Cav., June 24, 1865, to form 3d Prov'l Cav.

19th REGIMENT CAVALRY.—(180th VOLS.). Org. at Phila., June to Oct., 1863. Dec., 1863, Dist. Columbus, Ky., 6 Div., 16 Corps, Dept. Tenn. Dec., 1863, Waring's Cav. Brig., 16 Corps, Tenn. Jany., 1864, 1 Brig., 1 Cav. Div., 16 Corps, Tenn. June, 1864, 1 Brig., Cav. Div., Dist. West Tenn., Dept. Tenn. July, 1864, 1 Brig., 2 Cav. Div., Dist. West Tenn. Nov., 1864, 2 Brig., 4 Div., Cav. Corps, Mil. Div. Miss. Nov., 1864, 1 Brig., 7 Div., Cav. Corps, Mil. Div. Miss. Feby., 1865, 2 Brig., 7 Div., Cav. Corps, Mil. Div. Miss. March, 1865, Cav. Brig., Dist. Baton Rouge, La., Dept. Gulf. Aug., 1865, Dept. La. Dec., 1865, Dept. Texas. Mustered out May 14, 1866.

20th REGIMENT CAVALRY.—Org. for 6 months at Harrisburg, June 23 to Aug. 1, 1863. July, 1863, Pierce's Brig., Dept. Susquehanna. Aug., 1863, Sir John's Run, Def. B. & O. R. R., Dept. W. Va. Sept., 1863, Campbell's Brig., Dept. W. Va. Nov., 1863, 1 Brig., 2 Div,, W. Va. Mustered out Jany. 25, 1864.

20th REGIMENT CAVALRY.—(181st VOLS.). Org. at Harrisburg and Phila., Feby., 1864. Feby., 1864, Cav. Brig., 1 Div., Dept. W. Va. April, 1864, 2 Brig., 1 Cav. Div., W. Va. Nov., 1864, 2 Brig., 1 Div., Cav. Corps, Middle Mil. Div. and Potomac. Consolidated with 2d Pa. Cav., June 17, 1865, to form 1st Prov'l Cav.

21st REGIMENT CAVALRY.—Org. for 6 months at Harrisburg, June 23 to Aug. 1, 1863. Aug., 1863, Unatt., Dept. W. Va. Dec., 1863, Cav. Brig., 1 Div., W. Va. Mustered out Feby. 20, 1864.

21st REGIMENT CAVALRY.—(182nd VOLS.). Org. at Harrisburg, Feby., 1864. May, 1864, Def. Washington, D. C., 22 Corps. June, 1864, 2 Brig., 1 Div., 5 Corps, Potomac. Sept., 1864, 1 Brig., 1 Div., 5 Corps, Potomac. Oct., 1864, 3 Brig., 2 Div., Cav. Corps, Potomac. March, 1865, 2 Brig., 2 Div., Cav. Corps, Potomac. Mustered out July 8, 1865.

22nd REGIMENT CAVALRY.—Org. for 6 months at Harrisburg, June and July, 1863. July, 1863, Dept. Susquehanna. Aug., 1863, Unatt., Dept. W. Va. Dec., 1863, Cav. Brig., 1 Div., West Va. Mustered out Feby. 5, 1864.

22nd REGIMENT CAVALRY.—(185th VOLS.). Org. at Chambersburg, Feby., 1864. Feby., 1864, Cav. Brig., 1 Div., W. Va. March, 1864, Cumb'd, Md., Res. Div., Dept. W. Va. April, 1864, 2 Brig., 1 Cav. Div., W. Va. (Detchmt.), Pleasant Valley, Md. (Dismtd. men). May, 1864, Camp Stoneman, 22 Corps (Dismtd. men). June, 1864, Kelly's Command, Res. Div., W. Va. (Dismtd. men). Aug., 1864, 3 Brig., 1 Div., Cav. Corps, Middle Mil. Div. Aug., 1864, 1 Brig., 2 Cav. Div., W Va. Dec. 1864, Res. Div., Dept. W. Va. April, 1865, 2 Brig., 1 Infy. Div., W. Va. Consolidated with 18th Pa. Cav., June 24, 1865, to form 3d Prov'l Cav.

RINGGOLD BATTALION CAVALRY.—Org. Sept., 1862. (Key's, Work's, Young's, Barr's and Cheserown's Cav. Co's.) Sept., 1862, R. R. Div., W. Va. Jany., 1863, Romney, W. Va., Def. Upper Potomac. March, 1863, 4 Brig., 1 Div., 8 Corps, Middle Dept. June, 1863, Campbell's Brig., Scammon's Div., W. Va. Dec., 1862, 2 Brig.,

2 Div., W. Va. Transferred to 22d Pa. Cav., Feb. 22, 1864.

KEY'S RINGGOLD CAVALRY COMPANY.—Org. at Washington, Pa., June 29, 1861. July, 1861, Army Occ., W. Va. Oct., 1861, Cheat Mt. Dist., W. Va. Jany., 1862, Lander's Div., Potomac. March, 1862, Hatch's Cav. Command, Banks' 5 Corps. April, 1862, R. R. Div., W. Va. July, 1862, R. R. Dist., 8 Corps, Middle Dept. Sept., 1862, R. R. Dist., W. Va. Jany., 1863, Romney, W. Va., Def. Upper Potomac, 8 Corps. March, 1863, 4 Brig., 1 Div., 8 Corps. June, 1863, Campbell's Brig., Scammon's Div., W. Va. Dec., 1863, 2 Brig., 2 Div., W. Va. Transferred to Ringgold Battalion Pa. Cav., Sept., 1862.

GREENFIELD'S WASHINGTON CAVALRY COMPANY.—Org. at Wheeling, W. Va., Aug. 19, 1861. Sept., 1861, Army Occupation, W. Va. Nov., 1861, R. R. Dist., W. Va. Jany., 1862, Lander's Div., Potomac. March, 1862, Hatch's Cav. Command, Banks' 5 Corps. April, 1862, R. R. Dist., Mt. Dept. July, 1862, R. R. Dist., 8 Corps, Middle Dept. Sept., 1862, R. R. Dist., W. Va. Jany., 1863, Springfield, W. Va., Def. Upper Potomac, 8 Corps. March, 1863, 4 Brig., 1 Div., 8 Corps. June, 1863, Campbell's Brig., Scammon's Div., W. Va. Dec., 1863, 3 Brig., 2 Div., W. Va. Transferred to Ringgold Battalion, Feby. 9, 1864.

SMITH'S LAFAYETTE CAVALRY COMPANY.—Org. at Wheeling, W. Va., Nov. 6, 1862. Dec., 1862, Def. Upper Potomac, 8 Corps, Middle Dept. March, 1863, 4 Brig., 1 Div., 8 Corps. June, 1863, Campbell's Brig., Scammon's Div., W. Va. Dec., 1863, 2 Brig., 2 Div., W. Va. Transferred to Ringgold Battalion, Feby. 9, 1864.

PHILADELPHIA CITY TROOP CAVALRY.—Org. at Phila., May 13, 1861. June, 1861, Geo. H. Thomas' Command, Patterson's Army Shenandoah. Mustered out Aug. 17, 1861.

PHILADELPHIA CITY TROOP CAVALRY.—Re-org. at Phila., June 16, 1863. June, 1863, Dept. Susquehanna. Mustered out July 31, 1863.

UNION CAVALRY COMPANY.—Org. at Allegheny, April 5, 1861. Attached to 1st Va. Union Cav. Transferred to 1st Md. Cav. as Co. G, Jany., 1862.

READING CITY TROOP CAVALRY.—Org. at Reading, July 30, 1861. Transferred to 1st Pa. Cav. as Co. L, Nov., 1861.

MOREHEAD CAVALRY COMPANY.—Org. at Allegheny, Aug. 19, 1861. Transferred to 1st Md. Cav. as Co. L, Jany., 1862.

ANDERSON TROOP CAVALRY.—Org. at Carlisle, Nov. 30, 1861. Dec., 1861, Unatt., Headqrs. Army Ohio. Nov., 1862, Unatt., Headqrs. Army Cumb'd. Mustered out March, 1863.

NEGLEY'S BODY GUARD.—Org. at Phila., Jany. 21, 1862. Mustered out Jany. 26, 1862.

BELL'S INDEPENDENT CAVALRY COMPANY.—Org. Oct., 1862. Transferred to 22d Pa. Cav., Feby. 22, 1864.

INDEPENDENT BATTALION VOLUNTEER CAVALRY.—Org. at Pittsburg, June and July, 1863. Mustered out Dec. 29, 1863.

STROUD'S INDEPENDENT CAVALRY COMPANY.—(R. R. Troops.) Org. at Phila., July 15, 1864. Mustered out Oct. 31, 1864.

SANNO'S INDEPENDENT CAVALRY COMPANY.—Org. at Harrisburg, July 15, 1864. Mustered out Oct. 29, 1864.

HIBBLE'S INDEPENDENT CAVALRY COMPANY.—Org. at Lancaster, July 19, 1864. Mustered out Oct. 29, 1864.

WARREN'S INDEPENDENT CAVALRY COMPANY.—Org. at Harrisburg, Aug. 17, 1864. Mustered out Nov. 30, 1864.

LAMBERT'S INDEPENDENT CAVALRY COMPANY.—Org. at Harrisburg, Aug. 12, 1864. Mustered out Nov. 25, 1864.

WEAVER'S INDEPENDENT CAVALRY COMPANY.—Org. at Chambersburg, Sept., 1864. Mustered out Aug. 4, 1865.

BELL'S INDEPENDENT COMPANY MILITIA CAVALRY.—Org. at Altoona, June 30, 1863. Mustered out Aug. 9, 1863.

DICK'S INDEPENDENT COMPANY MILITIA CAVALRY.—Org. at Pittsburg, July 9, 1863. Mustered out Oct. 5, 1863.

HAMMELL'S INDEPENDENT COMPANY MILITIA CAVALRY.—Org. at Phila., July 2, 1863. Mustered out Sept. 16, 1864.

MYER'S INDEPENDENT COMPANY MILITIA CAVALRY.—Org. at Harrisburg, June 20, 1863. Mustered out July 31, 1863.

COMLEY'S INDEPENDENT COMPANY MILITIA CAVALRY.—Org. at Harrisburg, July 19, 1863. Mustered out July 30, 1863.

JONES' INDEPENDENT COMPANY MILITIA CAVALRY.—Org. at Harrisburg, June 21, 1863. Mustered out Aug. 12, 1863.

BROWN'S INDEPENDENT COMPANY MILITIA CAVALRY.—Org. at Harrisburg, June 19, 1863. Mustered out Aug. 1, 1863.

MURRAY'S INDEPENDENT COMPANY MILITIA CAVALRY.—Org. at Harrisburg, June 18, 1863. Mustered out Aug. 11, 1863.

2nd REGIMENT HEAVY ARTILLERY.—(112th VOLS.). Org. at Phila., Feby. 8, 1862. Feby., 1862, Def. Washington, D. C. (Fort Delaware, Co's L and M, to Nov., 1862). March, 1862, Arty. Brig., Mil. Dist. Washington. Aug., 1862, Def. Washington, North Potomac. Oct., 1862, 1 Brig., Haskin's Div., Def. Washington, North Potomac. Feby., 1863, 1 Brig., Haskin's Div., 22 Corps. March, 1864, 1 Brig., DeRussy's Div., 22 Corps. June, 1864, 3 Brig., 2 Div., 18 Corps, Army James, Dept. Va. and N. C. Dec., 1864, Prov'l Brig., Def. Bermuda Hundred, Va., Army James, Dept. Va. and N. C. April, 1865, 1 Brig., Ferrero's Div., Dept. Va. May, 1865, Sub-Dist. Blackwater, Dist. Nottaway, Dept. Va. Mustered out Jany. 29, 1866.

2nd REGIMENT PROVISIONAL HEAVY ARTILLERY.—Org. April 20, 1864, from surplus men of 2nd Heavy Arty. May, 1864, Prov'l Brig., 1 Div., 9 Corps, Potomac. June, 1864, 3 Brig., 1 Div., 9 Corps, Potomac. June, 1864, 2 Brig., 1 Div., 9 Corps, Potomac. Disbanded Aug. 20, 1864, and returned to 2nd Regt. Heavy Arty.

3rd REGIMENT HEAVY ARTILLERY.—(152nd VOLS.). Org. Feby. 17, 1863, by consolidation of Robert's Battalion Heavy Arty. and Segebarth's Battalion Pa. Marine Arty. Feby., 1863, Camp Hamilton, Va., 7 Corps, Dept. Va. May, 1863, Fortress Monroe, Va., 7 Corps, Dept. Va. Aug., 1863, Fortress Monroe, Va., Dept. Va. and N. C. May, 1864, Dist. Eastern Va., Dept. Va. and N. C. June, 1865, Dist. Fortress Monroe, Dept. Va. (Co. H, Feby., 1863, Fort Delaware. March, 1863, 2nd Separate Brig., 8 Corps, Middle Dept. May, 1863, 3rd Separate Brig., 8 Corps. July, 1863, Def. Balto., Md., 8 Corps. Oct., 1863, 3rd Separate Brig., 8 Corps. Dec., 1863, Arty. Res., Balto., 8 Corps. March, 1864, 3rd Separate Brig., 8 Corps. July, 1864, 1 Separate Brig., 8 Corps.) Regt. mustered out Nov. 9, 1865.

5th REGIMENT HEAVY ARTILLERY.—(204th VOLS.). Org. at Pittsburg, Aug. and Sept., 1864. Oct., 1864, Dist. Alexandria, Def. Washington, 22 Corps. Nov., 1864, 1st Separate Brig., 22 Corps. Mustered out June 30, 1865.

6th REGIMENT HEAVY ARTILLERY.—(212th VOLS.). Org. at Pittsburg, Sept. 15, 1864. Oct., 1864, Dist. Alexandria, Def. Washington, 22 Corps. Nov., 1864, 2 Brig., De Russy's Div., 22 Corps. Mustered out June 12, 1865.

ROBERTS' BATTALION HEAVY ARTILLERY.—Org. at Harrisburg and Phila., Oct. 8 to Nov. 14, 1862. Transferred to 3rd Regt. Pa. Heavy Arty., Feby. 17, 1863.

SEGEBARTH'S BATTALION MARINE ARTILLERY.—Org. at Phila., Jany. 15, 1862, to Jany. 31, 1863. Feby., 1862, Fort Delaware, Middle Dept. Transferred to 3rd Pa. Heavy Arty., Feby. 17, 1863.

COMMONWEALTH INDEPENDENT COMPANY HEAVY ARTILLERY.—Org. at Phila., April 24, 1861.

Garrison at Fort Delaware. Mustered out Aug. 5, 1861.

WOODWARD'S INDEPENDENT COMPANY HEAVY ARTILLERY.—Org. at Phila., July 9, 1863. Mustered out Feby. 1, 1864.

TYLER'S INDEPENDENT COMPANY HEAVY ARTILLERY.—Org. at Pittsburg, June 16, 1863. June, 1863, Mulligan's Brig., Scammon's Div., W. Va. Dec., 1863, Arty., 1 Div., West Va. Mustered out July 28, 1864.

GUSS' INDEPENDENT COMPANY HEAVY ARTILLERY.—Org. at West Chester, July 1, 1863. Mustered out Aug. 24, 1863.

ERMENTROUT'S INDEPENDENT COMPANY HEAVY ARTILLERY.—Org. at Reading, July 3, 1863. Mustered out Aug. 26, 1863.

1st REGIMENT LIGHT ARTILLERY.—(15th RESERVE CORPS, 44th VOLS.). Org. at Phila., Aug. 5, 1861.

BATTERY A.—Org. at Phila., Aug. 5, 1861. Aug., 1861, McCall's Pa. Reserve Div., Potomac. March, 1862, Arty., 2 Div., 1 Corps, Potomac. April, 1862, Arty., McCall's Div., Dept. Rappahannock. June, 1862, Arty., 3 Div., 5 Corps, Potomac. Aug., 1862, Arty., 3 Div., 3 Corps, Army Va. Sept., 1862, Arty., 3 Div., 1 Corps, Potomac. Feby., 1863, Arty., 3 Div., 9 Corps, Potomac. April, 1863, Arty., 2 Div., 7 Corps, Dept. Va. July, 1863, Arty., Portsmouth, Va., Dept. Va. and N. C. Jany., 1864, Arty., Heckman's Div., 18 Corps, Dept. Va. and N. C. April, 1864, Arty., Def. Portsmouth, Va., Dept. Va. and N. C. May, 1864, Dist. Eastern Va., Dept. Va. and N. C. July, 1864, Unatt., Dept. Va. and N. C. Aug., 1864, Arty Brig., 10 Corps, Army James. Oct., 1864, Arty. Brig., 18 Corps. Dec., 1864, Arty. Brig., 24 Corps. Mustered out July 25, 1865.

BATTERY "B."—Org. at Phila., Aug. 5, 1861. Aug., 1861, McCall's Pa. Reserve Div., Potomac. March, 1862, Arty., 2 Div., 1 Corps, Potomac. April, 1862, Arty., McCall's Div., Dept. Rappahannock. June, 1862, Arty., 3 Div., 5 Corps, Potomac. Aug., 1862, Arty., 3 Div., 3 Corps, Army Va. Sept., 1862, Arty., 3 Div., 1 Corps, Potomac. May, 1863, Arty. Brig., 1 Corps, Potomac. March, 1864, Arty. Brig., 5 Corps, Potomac. March, 1865, Arty. Reserve, Potomac. Mustered out June 9, 1865.

BATTERY "C."—Org. at Phila., Aug. 5, 1861. Aug., 1861, Arty., Smith's Div., Potomac. March, 1862, Arty., 1 Div., 4 Corps, Potomac. Sept., 1862, Arty., 3 Div., 6 Corps, Potomac. May, 1863, Arty. Brig., 6 Corps, Potomac. June, 1863, Barry's Command, Def. Washington, 22 Corps. July, 1863, 1 Brig., Lockwood's Div., Dept. Susquehanna. Aug., 1863, Md. Heights Div., Dept. W. Va., Harper's Ferry, Va. Consolidated with Batty. "D," Oct. 23, 1863.

BATTERY "C" RE-ORGANIZED.—Dec., 1864. Jany., 1865, Unatt., 3rd Infy. Div., W. Va. April, 1865, 1 Brig., 2nd Infy. Div., W. Va. Mustered out June 29, 1865.

BATTERY "D."—Org. at Phila., Aug. 5, 1861. Aug., 1861, Def. Washington, D. C. Oct., 1861, Buell's Div., Potomac. March, 1862, Arty., 1 Div., 4 Corps, Potomac. Sept., 1862, Arty., 3 Div., 6 Corps, Potomac. May, 1863, Arty. Brig., 6 Corps, Potomac. June, 1863, Camp Barry, Def. Washington, 22 Corps. Aug., 1863, Unatt., Dept. W. Va. Dec., 1863, 1 Brig., 1 Div., Army W. Va. Jany., 1864, Wheaton's Brig., Dept. W. Va. April, 1864, Reserve Div., Dept. W. Va. Aug., 1864, Arty. Brig., W. Va. Jany., 1865, 1st Separate Brig., 3 Div., W. Va. April, 1865, Unatt., 2 Div., W. Va. May, 1865, 2 Brig., 2 Div., W. Va. Mustered out June 30, 1865.

BATTERY "E."—Org. at Phila., Aug. 5, 1861. Aug., 1861, Def. Washington, D. C. Oct., 1861, Smith's Div., Potomac. Nov., 1861, Buell's Div., Potomac. March, 1862, Arty., 1 Div., 4 Corps, Potomac. June, 1862, Res. Arty., 4 Corps, Potomac, Yorktown, Va. Dec., 1862, Unatt., Arty., 7 Corps, Dept. Va. May, 1863, Unatt., Arty., 4 Corps, Dept. Va. June, 1863, 2 Brig., 1 Div., 4 Corps, Dept. Va. July, 1863, U. S. Forces, Yorktown, Va., Dept. Va. and N. C. April, 1864, Def. Yorktown and Williamsburg, Dept. Va. and N. C. June, 1864, Unatt.,

Dept. Va. and N. C. July, 1864, Arty. Brig., 18 Corps. Aug., 1864, Arty. Brig., 10 Corps. Dec., 1864, Arty. Brig., 25 Corps. Mustered out July 20, 1865.

BATTERY "F."—Org. at Phila., Aug. 5, 1861. Aug., 1861, Def. Washington, D. C. Oct., 1861, Banks' Div., Potomac. March, 1862, Arty., Williams' 1 Div., Banks' 5 Corps. April, 1862, Arty., 1 Div., Dept. Shenandoah. May, 1862, Arty., 2 Div., Dept. Rappahannock. June, 1862, Arty., 2 Div., 3 Corps, Army Va. Sept., 1862, Arty., 2 Div., 1 Corps, Potomac. Jany., 1863, Arty., 3 Div., 1 Corps, Potomac. May, 1863, 3rd Vol. Brig. Arty. Res., Potomac. July, 1863, Arty. Brig., 2 Corps, Potomac. Sept., 1864, Arty. Res., Potomac, attached to 2 Corps, Potomac. Mustered out June 9, 1865.

BATTERY "G."—Org. at Phila., Aug. 5, 1861. Aug., 1861, Arty., McCall's Pa. Reserve Div., Potomac. March, 1862, Arty., 2 Div., 1 Corps, Potomac. April, 1862, Arty., McCall's 2 Div., Dept. Rappahannock. June, 1862, Arty., 3 Div., 5 Corps, Potomac. Aug., 1862, Arty., 3 Div., 3 Corps, Army Va. Sept., 1862, Arty., 3 Div., 1 Corps, Potomac. May, 1863, 3rd Vol. Brig., Arty. Res., Potomac. July, 1863, Arty. Brig., 2 Corps, Potomac. April, 1864. Camp Barry, Def. Washington, 22 Corps. May, 1864, 1 Brig., De Russy's Div., 22 Corps. July, 1864, Res. Div., Point of Rocks, Md., Dept. W. Va. Jany., 1865, Arty., 3 Infy. Div., W. Va. April, 1865, 3 Brig., Hardin's Div., 22 Corps. Mustered out June 29, 1865.

BATTERY "H."—Org. at Phila., Aug. 5, 1861. Aug., 1861, Def. Washington, D. C. Oct., 1861, Buell's Div., Potomac. March, 1862, Arty., 1 Div., 4 Corps, Potomac. July, 1862, Res. Arty., 4 Corps, Potomac, Yorktown, Va. Dec., 1862, Res. Arty., Yorktown, Va., 7 Corps, Dept. Va. May, 1863, Unatt., Arty., 4 Corps, Dept. Va. July, 1863, Camp Barry, Def. Washington, 22 Corps. May, 1864, 1 Brig., De Russy's Div., 22 Corps. Mustered out June 27, 1865.

BATTERY "I."—Org. March 2, 1865. March, 1865, De Russy's Div., Def. Washington, South Potomac, 22 Corps. Mustered out July 1, 1865.

INDEPENDENT BATTERY "A" LIGHT ARTILLERY.—Org. at Phila., Sept. 19, 1861. Garrison at Fort Delaware entire term. Mustered out June 30, 1865.

INDEPENDENT BATTERY "B" LIGHT ARTILLERY.—Org. at Erie and Chambersburg, Aug., 1861. Nov., 1861, Negley's Brig., McCook's Div., Army Ohio. Dec., 1861, Arty., 2 Div., Army Ohio. June, 1862, Arty., 5 Div., Army Ohio. Sept., 1862, Arty., 5 Div., 2 Corps, Army Ohio. Nov., 1862, Arty., 3 Div., Left Wing, 14 Corps, Cumb'd. Jany., 1863, Arty., 3 Div., 21 Corps, Cumb'd. Oct., 1863, Arty., 3 Div., 4 Corps, Cumb'd. April, 1864, Arty., 1 Div., 4 Corps, Cumb'd. July, 1864, Arty. Brig., 4 Corps, Cumb'd. Aug., 1865, Dept. Tex. Mustered out Oct. 12, 1865.

INDEPENDENT BATTERY "C" LIGHT ARTILLERY.—Org. at Pittsburg, Nov. 6, 1861. Dec., 1861, Def. Washington. May, 1862, Arty., 2 Div., Dept. Rappahannock. June, 1862, Arty., 2 Div., 3 Corps, Army Va. Sept., 1862, Arty., 2 Div., 1 Corps, Potomac. June, 1863, 1st Vol. Brig. Arty. Reserve, Potomac. Nov., 1863, Arty. Brig., 2 Corps, Potomac. March, 1864, Camp Barry, Def. Washington, 22 Corps. Mustered out June 30, 1865.

INDEPENDENT BATTERY "D" LIGHT ARTILLERY.—"Durell's." Org. at Doylestown, Sept. 24, 1861. Nov., 1861, McDowell's Div., Potomac. March, 1862, Arty., 3 Div., 1 Corps, Potomac. April, 1862, Arty., King's Div., Dept. Rappahannock. June, 1862, Arty., 1 Div., 3 Corps, Army Va. Aug., 1862, Arty., 2 Div., 9 Corps, Potomac. April, 1863, Arty., 2 Div., 9 Corps, Ohio. June, 1863, Arty., 1 Div., 9 Corps, Tenn. Aug., 1863, Arty., 2 Div., 9 Corps, Ohio. Aug., 1863, Covington, Ky., Dept. Ohio. April, 1864, Arty., 4 Div., 9 Corps, Potomac. July, 1864, Arty. Brig., 9 Corps, Potomac. Mustered out June 13, 1865.

INDEPENDENT BATTERY "E" LIGHT ARTILLERY.—"KNAPPS." Org. at Point of Rocks, Md., Sept., 1861, from 28th Pa. Infy. and Rcts. Sept., 1861, Arty., Smith's Div., Potomac. Jany., 1862, Arty., Banks' Div., Potomac. March, 1862, Geary's Separate Brig., Banks' 5 Corps. April, 1862, Geary's Separate Brig.,

Dept. Shenandoah. May, 1862, Geary's Separate Brig., Dept. Rappahannock. June, 1862, Arty., 2 Corps, Army Va. Sept., 1862, Arty., 2 Div., 12 Corps, Potomac. May, 1863, Arty. Brig., 12 Corps, Potomac. Oct., 1863, Arty. Brig., 12 Corps, Cumb'd. Dec., 1863, Arty., 2 Div., 12 Corps, Cumb'd. April, 1864, Arty., 2 Div., 20 Corps, Cumb'd. July, 1864, Arty. Brig., 20 Corps. Mustered out June 14, 1865.

INDEPENDENT BATTERY "F" LIGHT ARTILLERY.—"HAMPTONS." Org. at Williamsport, Dec. 7, 1861. Jany., 1862, Arty., Banks' Div., Potomac. March, 1862, Arty., 1 Div., Banks' 5 Corps. April, 1862, Arty., 1 Div., Dept. Shenandoah. June, 1862, Arty., 2 Corps, Army Va. Aug., 1862, 1 Brig., 3 Div., 1 Corps, Army Va. Sept., 1862, Arty., 2 Div., 12 Corps, Potomac. May, 1863, 4 Vol. Brig., Arty. Res., Potomac. (July) 1863, 1 Vol. Brig., Arty. Res., Potomac. Oct., 1863, Arty. Brig., 2 Corps, Potomac. March, 1864, Camp Barry, Def. Washington, 22 Corps. May, 1864, 2 Brig., De Russy's Div., 22 Corps. July, 1864, Harper's Ferry, Va., Res. Div., Dept. W. Va. Jany., 1865, 1st Separate Brig., 3 Div., W. Va. April, 1865, 3 Brig., Hardin's Div., 22 Corps. Mustered out June 26, 1865.

INDEPENDENT BATTERY "G" LIGHT ARTILLERY.—Org. at Harrisburg, Aug. 22, 1862. Garrison at Fort Delaware entire term. Mustered out June 15, 1865.

INDEPENDENT BATTERY "H" LIGHT ARTILLERY.—Org. at Pittsburg, Oct. 21, 1862. Oct., 1862, Camp Barry, Def. Washington. Feby., 1863, Camp Barry, Def. Washington, 22 Corps. April, 1863, Slough's Command, Dist. Alexandria, 22 Corps. Nov., 1864, Camp Barry, Def. Washington, 22 Corps. Mustered out June 18, 1865.

INDEPENDENT BATTERY "I" LIGHT ARTILLERY.—Org. at Harrisburg, Dec. 31, 1863, to Jany. 7, 1864. Feby., 1864, Camp Barry, Def. Washington, 22 Corps. May, 1864, 2 Brig., De Russy's Div., 22 Corps. July, 1864, 3 Brig., De Russy's Div., 22 Corps. Dec., 1864, 1 Brig., De Russy's Div., 22 Corps. Mustered out June 23, 1865.

KEYSTONE BATTERY LIGHT ARTILLERY.—Org. at Phila., Aug. 13, 1862. Aug., 1862, Casey's Prov'l Brig., Dist. Washington. Oct., 1862, Arty., Casey's Div., Def. Washington. Feby., 1863, Arty., Casey's Div., 22 Corps. April, 1863, Arty., Abercrombie's Div., 22 Corps. June, 1863, Camp Barry, 22 Corps. July, 1863, Arty. Brig., 3 Corps, Potomac. July, 1863, Md. Heights Div., Dept. W. Va. Mustered out Aug. 20, 1863.

INDEPENDENT BATTALION LIGHT ARTILLERY.—Org. at Pittsburg, May and June, 1864. June, 1864, 3 Brig., Hardin's Div., 22 Corps. June, 1864, 1 Brig., Hardin's Div., 22 Corps. Mustered out Sept. 6, 1864.

NEVIN'S INDEPENDENT BATTERY LIGHT ARTILLERY.—Org. at Harrisburg, June and July, 1863. June, 1863, Dept. Susquehanna. July, 1863, Phila., Pa. Nov., 1863, Dept. W. Va. Mustered out Jany. 7, 1864.

ULLMAN'S INDEPENDENT BATTERY LIGHT ARTILLERY.—Org. at Harrisburg, Feby. 14, 1862. Mustered out March 7, 1862.

HASTINGS' INDEPENDENT BATTERY LIGHT ARTILLERY.—Org. at Phila., July 12, 1864. Mustered out Oct. 25, 1864.

KNAP'S INDEPENDENT MILITIA BATTERY.—Org. at Pittsburg, June 27, 1863. Mustered out Aug. 15, 1863.

2nd KEYSTONE INDEPENDENT MILITIA BATTERY.—Org. at Phila., July 6, 1863. Mustered out Aug. 24, 1863.

MILLER'S INDEPENDENT MILITIA BATTERY.—Org. at Harrisburg, June 19, 1863. Mustered out July 25, 1863.

LANDIS' INDEPENDENT MILITIA BATTERY.—Org. at Phila., June 27, 1863. Mustered out July 30, 1863.

WRIGLEY'S INDEPENDENT ENGINEER COMPANY.—Org. at Phila., Aug. 9, 1862. Aug., 1862, Whipple's Command, Def. Washington, D. C. Oct., 1862, Engineers, Army Potomac. Nov., 1862, Harper's Ferry, Va., Dept. W. Va. March, 1863, 2 Brig., 3 Div., 8 Corps, Middle Dept. June, 1863, Unatt., Dept. W. Va. Dec.,

1863, Unatt., 1 Div., W. Va. April, 1864, Res. Div., Dept. W. Va. Mustered out June 20, 1865.

INDEPENDENT COMPANY SHARPSHOOTERS.—Org. June, 1861. Ass'd to 2nd U. S. Sharpshooters as Co. C.

M'LANE'S ERIE REGIMENT INFANTRY.—Org. at Erie, April 27, 1861. Mustered out July 20, 1861.

1st REGIMENT INFANTRY.—Org. for three months at Harrisburg, April 20, 1861. June, 1861, 2 Brig., 2 Div., Patterson's Army Shenandoah. Mustered out July 27, 1861.

1st BATTALION VOLUNTEER INFANTRY.—Org. at Harrisburg, June and July, 1863. Provost duty in Pa. Mustered out Jany. 9, 1864.

1st BATTALION VOLUNTEER INFANTRY.—Org. for 100 days at Phila., Pittsburg and Harrisburg, July, 1864. July, 1864, 1 Brig., De Russy's Div., 22 Corps. Mustered out Nov. 14, 1864.

1st RESERVE CORPS INFANTRY.—(See 30th Regt. Infy.)

2nd REGIMENT INFANTRY.—Org. for three months at Harrisburg, April 20, 1861. June, 1861, 2 Brig., 2 Div., Patterson's Army Shenandoah. Mustered out July 26, 1861.

2nd BATTALION VOLUNTEER INFANTRY.—Org. at Pittsburg, June and July, 1863. July, 1863, Dept. Susquehanna. Aug., 1863, Unatt., Dept. W. Va. Dec., 1863, 1 Brig., 2 Div., W. Va. Mustered out Jany. 21, 1864.

2nd RESERVE CORPS INFANTRY.—(See 31st Regt. Infy.)

3rd REGIMENT INFANTRY.—Org. for three months at Harrisburg, April 20, 1861. June, 1861, 2 Brig., 2 Div., Patterson's Army Shenandoah. Mustered out July 30, 1861.

3rd BATTALION VOLUNTEER INFANTRY.—Org. at Phila., June and July, 1863. Mustered out Jany. 29, 1864.

3rd RESERVE CORPS INFANTRY.—(See 32nd Regt. Infy.)

4th REGIMENT INFANTRY.—Org. for three months at Harrisburg, April 20, 1861. April, 1861, Def. Washington. June, 1861, Franklin's Brig., Heintzelman's Div., McDowell's Army N. E. Va. Mustered out July 27, 1861.

4th RESERVE CORPS INFANTRY.—(See 33rd Regt. Infy.)

5th REGIMENT INFANTRY.—Org. for three months at Harrisburg, April 20, 1861. April, 1861, Dept. Washington, D. C. Mustered out July 24, 1861.

5th RESERVE CORPS INFANTRY.—(See 34th Regt. Infy.)

6th REGIMENT INFANTRY.—Org. for three months at Harrisburg April 22, 1861. June, 1861, 1 Brig., 1 Div., Patterson, Army Shenandoah. Mustered out July 27, 1861.

6th RESERVE CORPS INFANTRY.—(See 35th REGIMENT INFANTRY.)

7th REGIMENT INFANTRY.—Org. for three months at Harrisburg April 23, 1861. June, 1861, 3 Brig., 1 Div., Patterson's Army Shenandoah. Mustered out July 29, 1861.

7th RESERVE CORPS INFANTRY.—(See 36th Regt. Infy.)

8th REGIMENT INFANTRY.—Org. for three months at Harrisburg April 23, 1861. June, 1861, 3 Brig., 1 Div., Patterson's Army Shenandoah. Mustered out July 29, 1861.

8th RESERVE CORPS INFANTRY.—(See 37th Regt. Infy.)

9th REGIMENT INFANTRY.—Org. for three months at Harrisburg April 24, 1861. June, 1861, 4 Brig., 1 Div., Patterson's Army Shenandoah. Mustered out July 29, 1861.

9th RESERVE CORPS INFANTRY.—(See 38th Regt. Infy.)

10th REGIMENT INFANTRY.—Org. for three months at Harrisburg April 26, 1861. June, 1861, 3 Brig., 1 Div., Patterson's Army Shenandoah. Mustered out July 31, 1861.

10th RESERVE CORPS INFANTRY.—(See 39th Regt. Infy.)

11th REGIMENT INFANTRY.—Org. for three months at Harrisburg April 26, 1861. June, 1861, 6 Brig., 2 Div., Patterson's Army Shenandoah. Mustered out Aug. 1, 1861.

11th REGIMENT INFANTRY (3 YEARS).—Org. at Westmoreland Co. and Harrisburg, Nov. 27, 1861. Nov.., 1861, Dix's Command, Middle Dept. Annapolis, Md. April, 1862, Wadsworth's Command, Def. Washington. May, 1862, 3 Brig., 2 Div., Dept. Rappahannock. June, 1862, 3 Brig., 2 Div., 3 Corps, Army Va. Sept., 1861, 3 Brig., 2 Div., 1 Corps, Potomac. May, 1863, 2 Brig., 2 Div., 1 Corps, Potomac. July 1, 1863, 1 Brig., 2 Div., 1 Corps, Potomac. July 18, 1863, 2 Brig., 2 Div., 1 Corps, Potomac. March, 1864, 2 Brig., 2 Div., 5 Corps, Potomac. May, 1864, 2 Brig., 3 Div., 5 Corps, Potomac. March, 1865, 3 Brig., 3 Div., 5 Corps, Potomac. Mustered out July 1, 1865.

11th RESERVE CORPS INFANTRY.—(See 40th Regt. Infy.)

12th REGIMENT INFANTRY.—Org. for three months at Harrisburg April 25, 1861. May, 1861, R. R. Guard Northern Central R. R. June, 1861, 3 Brig., 1 Div., Patterson's Army Shenandoah. Mustered out Aug. 5, 1861.

12th RESERVE CORPS INFANTRY.—(See 41st Regt. Infy.)

13th REGIMENT INFANTRY.—Org. for three months at Harrisburg April 25, 1861. June, 1861, 4 Brig., 1 Div., Patterson's Army Shenandoah. Mustered out Aug. 6, 1861.

13th RESERVE CORPS INFANTRY.—(See 42nd Regt. Infy.)

14th REGIMENT INFANTRY.—Org. for three months at Harrisburg April 30, 1861 June, 1861, 5 Brig., 2 Div., Patterson's Army Shenandoah. Mustered out Aug. 7, 1861.

14th RESERVE CORPS.—(See 1st Regt. Cav.)

15th REGIMENT INFANTRY.—Org. for three months at Harrisburg April 27, 1861. June, 1861, 5 Brig., 2 Div., Patterson's Army Shenandoah. Mustered out Aug. 8, 1861.

15th RESERVE CORPS.—(See 1st Regt. Light Arty.)

16th REGIMENT INFANTRY.—Org. at Harrisburg for three months May 3, 1861. June, 1861, 4 Brig., 1 Div., Patterson's Army Shenandoah. Mustered out July 30, 1861.

17th REGIMENT INFANTRY.—Org. for three months at Phila. April 25, 1861. June, 1861, 1 Brig., 1 Div., Patterson's Army Shenandoah. Mustered out Aug. 2, 1861.

18th REGIMENT INFANTRY.—Org. for three months at Phila. April 24, 1861. May, 1861, Balto., Md., Mustered out Aug. 6, 1861.

19th REGIMENT INFANTRY.—Org. for three months at Phila. April 27, 1861. May, 1861, Balto., Md. Mustered out Aug. 29, 1861.

20th REGIMENT INFANTRY.—Org. for three months at Phila. April 30, 1861. June, 1861, 3 Brig., 1 Div., Patterson's Army Shenandoah. Mustered out Aug. 6, 1861.

20th REGIMENT MILITIA INFANTRY.—Org. at Harrisburg June 17, 1863. June, 1863, Dept. Susquehanna. Mustered out Aug. 10, 1863.

21st REGIMENT INFANTRY.—Org. for three months at Harrisburg April 20, 1861. June, 1861, 1 Brig., 1 Div., Patterson's Army Shenandoah. Mustered out Aug. 9, 1861.

22nd REGIMENT INFANTRY.—Org. for three months at Phila. April 23, 1861. May, 1861, Balto., Md. Mustered out Aug. 7, 1861.

23rd REGIMENT INFANTRY.—Org. for three months at Phila. April 21, 1861. June, 1861, 1 Brig., 1 Div., Patterson's Army Shenandoah. Mustered out July 31, 1861.

23rd REGIMENT INFANTRY (3 YEARS).—Org. at Phila. Aug. 31, 1861. Sept., 1861, Def. Washington. Oct., 1861, Graham's Brig., Buell's Div., Potomac. March, 1862, 2 Brig., 1 Div., 4 Corps, Potomac. July, 1862, 3 Brig., 1 Div., 4 Corps, Potomac. Sept., 1862, 3

Brig., 3 Div., 6 Corps, Potomac. Oct., 1862, 1 Brig., 3 Div., 6 Corps, Potomac. Jany., 1864, Johnson's Island, Sandusky, Ohio. May, 1864, 4 Brig., 1 Div., 6 Corps, Potomac. July, 1864, 3 Brig., 1 Div., 6 Corps, Potomac and Shenandoah. Mustered out Sept. 8, 1864.

24th REGIMENT INFANTRY.—Org. for three months at Phila. May 8, 1861. June, 1861, 5 Brig., 2 Div., Patterson's Army. June, 1861, 2 Brig., 2 Div., Patterson's Army Shenandoah. Mustered out Aug. 10, 1861.

25th REGIMENT INFANTRY.—Org. for three months at Harrisburg April 18, 1861. April, 1861, Def. Washington, D. C.. June, 1861, 7 Brig., 3 Div., Patterson's Army Shenandoah. Mustered out Aug. 1, 1861.

26th REGIMENT INFANTRY.—Org. at Phila. May 27, 1861. June, 1861, Def. Washington, D. C. Aug. 1861, Hooker's Brig., Div. Potomac. Oct. 1861, 1 Brig. Hooker's Div., Potomac. March, 1862, 1 Brig., 2 Div., 3 Corps, Potomac. March, 1864, 1 Brig., 4 Div., 2 Corps, Potomac. Mustered out June 18, 1864.

26th REGIMENT MILITIA INFANTRY.—Org. at Harrisburg June 22, 1863. June, 1863, Dept. Susquehanna. Mustered out July 31, 1863.

27th REGIMENT INFANTRY.—Org. at Phila. May 31, 1861. June, 1861, Blenker's Brig., Miles' Div., McDowell's Army N. E. Va. Aug., 1861, Blenker's Brig., Div. Potomac. Oct., 1861, Blenker's Brig., Hooker's Div., Potomac. Nov., 1861, Stahel's Brig., Blenker's Div., Potomac. March, 1862, 1 Brig., Blenker's 2 Div., 2 Corps, Potomac. April, 1862, 1 Brig., Blenker's Div., Dept. Mts. June, 1862, 1 Brig., 1 Div., 1 Corps, Army Va. Sept., 1862, 1 Brig., 1 Div., 11 Corps, Potomac. Oct., 1862, 1 Brig., 2 Div., 11 Corps, Potomac. Oct., 1863, 1 Brig., 2 Div., 11 Corps, Cumb'd. April, 1864, 2 Brig., 2 Div., 20 Corps, Cumb'd. (Co. F. detached in Def. Washington and 22 Corps from Aug., 1862.) Mustered out June 11, 1864.

27th REGIMENT MILITIA INFANTRY.—Org. at Harrisburg June 22, 1863. June, 1863, Dept. Susquehanna. Mustered out July 31, 1863.

28th REGIMENT INFANTRY.—Org. at Phila. June 28, 1861. July, 1861, Thomas' Brig., Dept. Shenandoah. Aug., 1861, 1 Brig., Banks' Div., Dept. Shenandoah. March, 1862, 1 Brig., 1 Div., Banks' 5 Corps. March, 1862, Geary's Indpt. Command, Banks' 5 Corps. April, 1862, Geary's Indpt. Command, Dept. Shenandoah. May, 1862, Geary's Indpt. Command, Dept. Rappahannock. June, 1862, 2 Brig., 1 Div., 2 Corps, Army Va. Aug., 1862, 1 Brig., 2 Div., 2 Corps, Army Va. Sept., 1862, 1 Brig., 2 Div., 12 Corps, Potomac. Oct. 1863, 1 Brig., 2 Div., 12 Corps, Cumb'd. April, 1864, 1 Brig., 2 Div., 20 Corps, Cumb'd. June, 1865, 3 Brig., Bartlett's Div., 22 Corps. Mustered out July 18, 1865.

28th REGIMENT MILITIA INFANTRY.—Org. at Harrisburg June 23, 1863. June, 1863, Dept. Susquehanna. Mustered out July 28, 1863.

29th REGIMENT INFANTRY.—Org. at Phila. July 1, 1861. Aug., 1861, Gordon's Brig., Dept. Shenandoah. Aug., 1861, Stiles' 3 Brig., Banks' Div., Potomac. March, 1862, 3 Brig., 1 Div., Banks' 5 Corps. April, 1862, 3 Brig., 1 Div., Dept. Shenandoah. June, 1862, 3 Brig., 1 Div.

29th REGIMENT INFANTRY CONTINUED.—2 Corps, Army Va. Sept. 1862, 3 Brig., 1 Div., 12 Corps, Potomac. March, 1863, 2 Brig., 2 Div., 12 Corps, Potomac. Oct. 1863, 2 Brig., 2 Div., 12 Corps, Cum'd. April, 1864, 3 Brig., 2 Div., 20 Corps, Cum'd. Mustered out July 11, 1865.

29th REGIMENT MILITIA INFANTRY.—Org. at Harrisburg June 23, 1863. June, 1863, Dept. Susquehanna. Mustered out Aug. 1, 1863.

30th REGIMENT INFANTRY (1st RESERVES).— Org. at West Chester July 26, 1861. July, 1861, Dix's Command, Balto., Md. Sept., 1861, 1 Brig., McCall's Pa. Res. Div., Potomac. March, 1862, 1 Brig., 2 Div., 1 Corps, Potomac. April, 1862, 1 Brig., McCall's Div., Dept. Rappahannock. June, 1862, 1 Brig., 3 Div., 5 Corps, Potomac. Aug., 1862, 1 Brig., 3 Div., 3 Corps, Army Va. Sept., 1862, 1 Brig., 3 Div., 1 Corps, Potomac. Feby., 1863, 1 Brig., Pa. Res. Div., 22 Corps. June, 1863, 1 Brig., 3 Div., 5 Corps, Potomac. Mustered out June 13, 1864.

30th REGIMENT MILITIA INFANTRY.—Org. at Harrisburg June 25, 1863. June, 1863, Dept. Susquehanna. Mustered out July 29, 1863.

31st REGIMENT INFANTRY (2nd RESERVE CORPS).—Org. at Phila. July, 1861. Sept. 1861, 1 Brig., McCall's Pa. Res. Div., Potomac. March, 1862, 1 Brig., 2 Div., 1 Corps, Potomac. April, 1862, 1 Brig., McCall's Div., Dept. Rappahannock. June, 1862, 1 Brig., 3 Div., 5 Corps, Potomac. Aug. 1862, 1 Brig., 3 Div., 3 Corps, Army Va. Sept. 1862, 1 Brig., 3 Div., 1 Corps, Potomac. Feby., 1863, 1 Brig., Pa. Res. Div., 22 Corps. June, 1863, 1 Brig., 3 Div., 5 Corps, Potomac. Mustered out June 16, 1864.

31st REGIMENT MILITIA INFANTRY.—Org. at Harrisburg June 30, 1863. June, 1863, Dept. Susquehanna. Mustered out Aug. 8, 1863.

32nd REGIMENT INFANTRY (3rd RESERVE CORPS).—Org. at Phila. and Easton July 28, 1861. Aug. 1861, Def. Washington D. C. Sept., 1861, 2 Brig., McCall's Div. Pa. Res., Potomac. March, 1862, 2 Brig., 2 Div., 1 Corps, Potomac. April, 1862, 2 Brig., McCall's Div., Dept. Rappahannock. June, 1862, 2 Brig., 3 Div., 5 Corps, Potomac. Aug., 1862, 2 Brig., 3 Div., 3 Corps, Army Va. Sept., 1862, 2 Brig., 3 Div., 1 Corps, Potomac. Feby., 1863, 2 Brig., Pa. Res. Div., 22 Corps. April, 1863, Dist. Alexandria, 22 Corps. Jany., 1864, Dept. W. Va. April, 1864, 3 Brig., 2 Infy. Div., West Va. Mustered out June, 17, 1864.

32nd REGIMENT MILITIA INFANTRY.—Org. at Harrisburg June, 26, 1863. June, 1863, Dept. Susquehanna. Mustered out Aug., 1, 1863.

33rd REGIMENT INFANTRY (4th RESERVE CORPS).—Org. at Harrisburg July 17, 1861. Sept., 1861, 2 Brig., McCall's Pa. Res. Div., Potomac. March, 1862, 2 Brig., 2 Div., 1 Corps, Potomac. April, 1862, 2 Brig., McCall's Div., Dept. Rappahannock. June, 1862, 2 Brig., 3 Div., 5 Corps, Potomac. Aug., 1862, 2 Brig., 3 Div., 3 Corps, Army Va. Sept., 1862, 2 Brig., 3 Div., 1 Corps, Potomac. Feby., 1863, 2 Brig., Pa. Res. Div., 22 Corps, Jany., 1864, Dept. W. Va. April, 1864, 3 Brig., 3 Div., W. Va. Mustered out June 17, 1864.

33rd REGIMENT MILITIA INFANTRY.—Org. at Harrisburg June 28, 1863. June, 1863, Dept. Susquehanna. Mustered out Aug. 4, 1863.

34th REGIMENT INFANTRY (5th RESERVE CORPS).—Org. at Harrisburg Aug. 17, 1861. Sept., 1861, 1 Brig., McCall's Pa. Res. Div., Potomac. March, 1862, 1 Brig., 2 Div., 1 Corps, Potomac. April, 1862, 1 Brig., McCall's Div., Dept. Rappahannock. June, 1862, 1 Brig., 3 Div., 5 Corps, Potomac. Aug., 1862, 1 Brig., 3 Div., 3 Corps, Army Va. Sept., 1862, 1 Brig., 3 Div., 1 Corps, Potomac. Nov., 1862, 3 Brig., 3 Div., 1 Corps, Potomac. Feby., 1863, 3 Brig., Pa. Res. Div., 22 Corps. April, 1863, Dist. Alexandria, 22 Corps. June, 1863, 3 Brig., 3 Div., 5 Corps, Potomac. Mustered out June 13, 1864.

34th REGIMENT MILITIA INFANTRY.—Org. at Reading July 3, 1863. July, 1863, Dept. Susequehanna. Mustered out Aug. 10, 1863.

35th REGIMENT INFANTRY (6th RESERVE CORPS).—Org. at Harrisburg June, 1861. Aug., 1861, 3 Brig., McCall's Pa. Res. Div., Potomac. March, 1862, 3 Brig., 2 Div., 1 Corps, Potomac. April, 1862, 3 Brig., McCall's Div., Dept. Rappahannock. June, 1862, 3 Brig., 3 Div., 5 Corps, Potomac. July, 1862, 1 Brig., 3 Div., 5 Corps, Potomac. Aug., 1862, 1 Brig., 3 Div., 3 Corps, Army Va. Sept., 1862, 1 Brig., 3 Div., 1 Corps, Potomac. Feby., 1863, 1 Brig., Pa. Res. Div., 22 Corps. June, 1863, 1 Brig., 3 Div., 5 Corps, Potomac. Mustered out June 11, 1864.

35th REGIMENT MILITIA INFANTRY.—Org. at Harrisburg July 4, 1863. July, 1863, Dept. Susquehanna. Mustered out Aug. 7, 1863.

36th REGIMENT INFANTRY (7th RESERVE CORPS).—Org. at Camps Wayne and Curtin July 27, 1861. Sept., 1861, 2 Brig., McCall's Pa. Res. Div., Potomac. March, 1862, 2 Brig., 2 Div., 1 Corps, Potomac. April, 1862, 2 Brig., McCall's Div., Dept. Rappahannock. June, 1862, 2 Brig., 3 Div., 5 Corps, Potomac. Aug., 1862,

2 Brig., 3 Div., 3 Corps, Army Va. Sept., 1862, 2 Brig., 3 Div., 1 Corps, Potomac. Feby., 1863, 2 Brig., Pa. Res. Div., 22 Corps. April, 1863, Dist. Alexandria, 22 Corps. June, 1863, Def. Washington. April, 1864, 1 Brig., 3 Div., 5 Corps, Potomac. Mustered out June 16, 1864.

36th REGIMENT MILITIA INFANTRY.—Org. at Harrisburg July 4, 1863. July, 1863, Dept. Susquehanna. Mustered out Aug. 11, 1863.

37th REGIMENT INFANTRY (8th RESERVE CORPS).—Org. at Pittsburg, Clarion and Uniontown July 29, 1861. Sept., 1861, 1 Brig., McCall's Pa. Res. Div., Potomac. March, 1862, 1 Brig., 2 Div., 1 Corps, Potomac. April, 1862, 1 Brig., McCall's Div., Dept. Rappahannock. June, 1862, 2 Brig., McCall's Div., Dept. Rappahannock. June, 1862, 2 Brig., 3 Div., 5 Corps, Potomac. Aug., 1862, 2 Brig., 3 Div., 3 Corps, Army Va. Sept., 1862, 2 Brig., 3 Div., 1 Corps, Potomac. Feby., 1863, 2 Brig., Pa. Res. Div., 22 Corps. April, 1863, Dist. Alexandria, 22 Corps. April, 1864, 3 Brig., 3 Div., 5 Corps, Potomac. Mustered out May 24, 1864.

37th REGIMENT MILITIA INFANTRY.—Org. at Harrisburg, July 4, 1863. July, 1863, Dept. Susquehanna. Mustered out Aug. 3, 1863.

38th REGIMENT INFANTRY.—(9th RESERVE CORPS). Org. at Allegheny Co., July 27, 1861. Sept., 1861, 3 Brig., McCall's Pa. Res. Div., Potomac. March, 1862, 3 Brig., 2 Div., 1 Corps, Potomac. April, 1862, 3 Brig., McCall's Div., Dept. Rappahannock. June, 1862, 3 Brig., 3 Div., 5 Corps, Potomac. Aug., 1862, 3 Brig., 3 Div., 3 Corps, Army Va. Sept., 1862, 3 Brig., 3 Div., 1 Corps, Potomac. Feby., 1863, 3 Brig., Pa. Res. Div., 22 Corps. June, 1863, 3 Brig., 3 Div., 5 Corps, Potomac. Mustered out May 12, 1864.

38th REGIMENT MILITIA INFANTRY.—Org. at Reading, July 3, 1863. Mustered out Aug. 7, 1863.

39th REGIMENT INFANTRY.—(10th RESERVE CORPS). Org. at Harrisburg, July 21, 1861. Aug., 1861, Def. Washington. Sept., 1861, 3 Brig., McCall's Div. Pa. Res., Potomac. March, 1862, 3 Brig., 2 Div., 1 Corps, Potomac. April, 1862, 3 Brig., McCall's Div., Dept. Rappahannock. June, 1862, 3 Brig., 3 Div., 5 Corps, Potomac. Aug., 1862, 3 Brig., 3 Div., 3 Corps, Army Va. Sept., 1862, 3 Brig., 3 Div., 1 Corps, Potomac. Feby., 1863, 3 Brig., Pa. Res. Div., 22 Corps. June, 1863, 3 Brig., 3 Div., 5 Corps, Potomac. Mustered out June 11, 1864.

39th REGIMENT MILITIA INFANTRY.—Org. at Reading, July 4, 1863. Mustered out Aug. 2, 1863.

40th REGIMENT INFANTRY.—(11th RESERVE CORPS). Org. at Pittsburg, June, 1861. July, 1861, Def. Washington, D. C. Sept., 1861, 2 Brig., McCall's Pa. Res. Div., Potomac. March, 1862, 2 Brig., 2 Div., 1 Corps, Potomac. April, 1862, 2 Brig., McCall's Div., Dept. Rappahannock. June, 1862, 2 Brig., 3 Div., 5 Corps, Potomac. Aug., 1862, 3 Brig., 3 Div., 3 Corps, Army Va. Sept., 1862, 3 Brig., 3 Div., 1 Corps, Potomac. Feby., 1863, 3 Brig., Pa. Res. Div., 22 Corps. June, 1863, 3 Brig., 3 Div., 5 Corps, Potomac. Nov., 1863, 1 Brig., 3 Div., 5 Corps, Potomac. Mustered out June 13, 1864.

40th REGIMENT MILITIA INFANTRY.—Org. at Harrisburg, July 14, 1863. Mustered out Aug. 16, 1863.

41st REGIMENT INFANTRY.—(12th RESERVE CORPS). Org. at Harrisburg, Aug. 11, 1861. Sept., 1861, 3 Brig., McCall's Pa. Res. Div., Potomac. March, 1862, 3 Brig., 2 Div., 1 Corps, Potomac. April, 1862, 3 Brig., McCall's Div., Dept. Rappahannock. June, 1862, 3 Brig., 3 Div., 5 Corps, Potomac. Aug., 1862, 3 Brig., 3 Div., 3 Corps, Army Va. Sept., 1862, 3 Brig., 3 Div., 1 Corps, Potomac. Feby., 1863, 3 Brig., Pa. Res. Div., 22 Corps. June, 1863, 3 Brig., 3 Div., 5 Corps, Potomac. Mustered out June 11, 1864.

41st REGIMENT MILITIA INFANTRY.—Org. at Reading, July 5, 1863. Mustered out Aug. 4, 1863.

42nd REGIMENT INFANTRY.—(13th RESERVE CORPS). "1st Penna. Rifles." Org. at Harrisburg, June 21, 1861. Aug., 1861, Thomas' Brig., Banks' Div., Shenandoah. Oct., 1861, 2 Brig., McCall's Pa. Res. Div., Potomac. March, 1862, 1 Brig., 2 Div., 1 Corps, Potomac. April, 1862, 3 Brig., McCall's Div., Dept. Rappahannock. May, 1862, Bayard's Cav., Brig., Dept. Rappahannock (Co's C, G, H, I). June, 1862, 3 Brig.

3 Div., 5 Corps, Potomac, Unatt., Dept. Rappahannock Co's C, G, H, I). June, 1862, Unatt., 3 Corps, Army Va. Co's C, G, H, I). Aug., 1862, 3 Brig., 3 Div., 3 Corps, Army Va. Sept., 1862, 1 Brig., 3 Div., 1 Corps, Potomac. Feby., 1863, 1 Brig., Pa. Res. Div., 22 Corps. June, 1863, 1 Brig., 3 Div., 5 Corps, Potomac. Mustered out June 11, 1864.

42nd REGIMENT MILITIA INFANTRY.—Org. at Reading, July 6, 1863. Mustered out Aug. 11, 1863.

43rd REGIMENT.—(14th RESERVE CORPS). See 1st Regt. Cav.

43rd REGIMENT MILITIA INFANTRY.—Org. at Reading, July 6, 1863. Mustered out Aug. 13, 1863.

44th REGIMENT.—(15th RESERVE CORPS). See 1st Regt. Light Arty.

44th REGIMENT MILITIA INFANTRY.—Org. at Harrisburg, July 9, 1863. Mustered out Aug. 27, 1863.

45th REGIMENT INFANTRY.—Org. at Harrisburg, Oct. 21, 1861. Oct., 1861, Jameson's Brig., Heintzelman's Div., Potomac. Oct., 1861, Unatt., Sherman's S. C. Exp. Corps. April, 1862, 2 Brig., 1 Div., Dept. South. July, 1862, 2 Brig., 1 Div., 9 Corps, Potomac. Sept., 1862, 3 Brig., 1 Div., 9 Corps, Potomac. April, 1863, 3 Brig., 1 Div., 9 Corps, Ohio. June, 1863, 1 Brig., 1 Div., 9 Corps, Tenn. Aug., 1863, 1 Brig., 1 Div., 9 Corps, Ohio. April, 1864, 1 Brig., 2 Div., 9 Corps, Potomac. Mustered out July 17, 1865.

45th REGIMENT MILITIA INFANTRY.—Org. at Harrisburg, Aug. 13, 1863. Mustered out Aug. 29, 1863.

46th REGIMENT INFANTRY.—Org. at Harrisburg, Oct. 31, 1861. Nov., 1861, Gordon's Brig., Banks' Div., Potomac. March, 1862, 1 Brig., 1 Div., Banks' 5 Corps. April, 1862, 1 Brig., 1 Div., Dept. Shenandoah. June, 1862, 1 Brig., 1 Div., 2 Corps, Army Va. Sept., 1862, 1 Brig., 1 Div., 12 Corps, Potomac. Oct., 1863, 1 Brig., 1 Div., 12 Corps, Cumb'd. April, 1864, 1 Brig., 1 Div., 20 Corps, Cumb'd. Mustered out July 16, 1865.

46th REGIMENT MILITIA INFANTRY.—Org. at Huntingdon, July 8, 1863. Mustered out Aug. 18, 1863.

47th REGIMENT INFANTRY.—Org. at Harrisburg, Aug. and Sept., 1861. Oct., 1861, 3 Brig., W. F. Smith's Div., Potomac. Jany., 1862, Key West, Fla., Dept. South. June, 1862, Dist. Beaufort, S. C., Dept. South. Nov., 1862, Dist. Key West, Fla., Dept. Gulf. Feby., 1864, 2 Brig., 1 Div., 19 Corps, Gulf. July, 1864, 2 Brig., 1 Div., 19 Corps, Army Shenandoah. Middle Mil. Div. March, 1865, 2 Brig., 1 Prov'l Div., Army Shenandoah. April, 1865, 2 Brig., Dwight's Div., Dept. Washington. May, 1865, 3 Brig., Dwight's Div., Dept. South. June, 1865, 1st Sub Dist., Dept. S. C. July, 1865, 1st Separate Brig., Dept. South. Mustered out Dec. 25, 1865.

47th REGIMENT MILITIA INFANTRY.—Org. at Harrisburg, July 9, 1863. Mustered out Aug. 13, 1863.

48th REGIMENT INFANTRY.—Org. at Harrisburg, Oct. 1, 1861. Dec., 1861, Williams' Brig., Burnside's N. C. Exp. Corps. April, 1862, 1 Brig., 2 Div., Dept. N. C. July, 1862, 1 Brig., 2 Div., 9 Corps, Potomac. April, 1863, 1 Brig., 2 Div., 9 Corps, Ohio. June, 1863, Unass'd, 1 Div., 23 Corps, Ohio. Oct., 1863, 1 Brig., 2 Div., 9 Corps, Ohio. April, 1864, 1 Brig., 2 Div., 9 Corps, Potomac. Mustered out July 17, 1865.

48th REGIMENT MILITIA INFANTRY.—Org. at Reading, July 8, 1863. Mustered out Aug. 26, 1863.

49th REGIMENT INFANTRY.—Org. at Harrisburg and Lewistown, Sept., 1861. Oct., 1861, Hancock's Brig., Smith's Div., Potomac. March, 1862, 1 Brig., 2 Div., 4 Corps, Potomac. May, 1862, 1 Brig., 2 Div., 6 Corps. Feby., 1863, 3 Brig., 1 Div., 6 Corps, Potomac, and Army Shenandoah, Middle Mil. Div. Mustered out July 15, 1865.

49th REGIMENT MILITIA INFANTRY.—Org. at Harrisburg, July 14, 1863. Mustered out Sept. 2, 1863.

50th REGIMENT INFANTRY.—Org. at Harrisburg, Oct. 1, 1861. Oct., 1861, Steven's 2 Brig., Sherman's S. C. Exp. Corps. April, 1862, Dist. Beaufort, S. C., Dept. South. July, 1862, 1 Brig., 1 Div., 9 Corps, Potomac. Sept., 1862, 2 Brig., 1 Div., 9 Corps, Potomac. April, 1863, 2 Brig., 1 Div., 9 Corps, Ohio. June, 1863, 3 Brig., 2 Div., 9 Corps, Ohio. June, 1863, 3 Brig., 2 Div., 9 Corps, Tenn. Aug., 1863, 2 Brig., 1 Div., 9 Corps, Ohio.

April, 1864, 2 Brig., 3 Div., 9 Corps, Potomac. Sept., 1864, 2 Brig., 1 Div., 9 Corps, Potomac. Mustered out July 30, 1865.

50th REGIMENT MILITIA INFANTRY.—Org. at Harrisburg, July 11, 1863. Mustered out Aug. 15, 1863.

51st REGIMENT INFANTRY.—Org. at Harrisburg, Nov. 16, 1861. Dec., 1861, Reno's Brig., Burnside's N. C. Exp. Corps. April, 1862, 2 Brig., 2 Div., Dept. N. C. July, 1862, 2 Brig., 2 Div.,.9 Corps, Potomac. April, 1863, 2 Brig., 2 Div., 9 Corps, Ohio. June, 1863, 2 Brig., 2 Div., 9 Corps, Tenn. Aug., 1863, 2 Brig., 2 Div., 9 Corps, Ohio. April, 1864, 1 Brig., 3 Div., 9 Corps, Potomac. Sept., 1864, 1 Brig., 1 Div., 9 Corps, Potomac. Mustered out July 27, 1865.

52nd REGIMENT INFANTRY.—Org. at Harrisburg, Nov. 5, 1861. Nov., 1861, 1 Brig., Casey's Div., Potomac. March, 1862, 1 Brig., 3 Div., 4 Corps, Potomac. June, 1862, 1 Brig., 2 Div., 4 Corps, Potomac. Dec., 1862, Naglee's Brig., Dept. N. C. Jany., 1863, 2 Brig., 2 Div., 18 Corps, Dept. N. C. Feby., 1863, 2 Brig., 1 Div., 18 Corps, Dept. South. April, 1863, Dist. Beaufort, S. C., 10 Corps, Dept. South. July, 1863, 2 Brig., 1 Div., Morris Island, S. C., 10 Corps, Dept. South. July, 1863, Davis' Brig., Folly Island, S. C., 10 Corps. Aug., 1863, 1 Brig., Morris Island, S. C., 10 Corps. Nov., 1863, 2 Brig., Morris Island, S. C., 10 Corps. April, 1864, Dist. Hilton Head, S. C., Dept. South. June, 1864, Morris Island, Northern Dist., Dept. South. Oct., 1864, 1st Separate Brig., Dept. South. March, 1865, 1 Brig., 2 Div., 23 Corps, Army Ohio, Dept. N. C. Mustered out July 12, 1865.

52nd REGIMENT MILITIA INFANTRY.—Org. at Phila., July 9, 1863. Mustered out Sept. 1, 1863.

53rd REGIMENT INFANTRY.—Org. at Harrisburg, Nov. 7, 1861. Nov., 1861, French's Brig., Sumner's Div., Potomac. March, 1862, 3 Brig., 1 Div., 2 Corps, Potomac. April, 1863, 4 Brig., 1 Div., 2 Corps, Potomac. Mustered out June 30, 1865.

53rd REGIMENT MILITIA INFANTRY.—Org. at Reading, July 13, 1863. Mustered out Aug. 18, 1863.

54th REGIMENT INFANTRY.—Org. at Harrisburg, Feby. 27, 1862. Feby., 1862, Def. Washington. May, 1862, R. R. Brig., Middle Dept. July, 1862, R. R. Dist., 8 Corps, Middle Dept. Sept., 1862, R. R. Dist., W. Va. Jany., 1863, Def. Upper Potomac, 8 Corps, Middlle Dept. March, 1863, 4 Brig., 1 Div., 8 Corps. June, 1863, Campbell's Brig., Scammon's Div., W. Va. Dec., 1863, 1 Brig., 2 Div., W. Va. April, 1864, 2 Brig., 1 Infy. Div., W. Va. June, 1864, 3 Brig., 2 Infy. Div., W. Va. July, 1864, 2 Brig., 3 Div., W. Va. July, 1864, 3 Brig., 1 Div., W. Va. Dec., 1864, 2 Brig., Indpt. Div., 24 Corps, Army James. June, 1865, 1 Brig., Indpt. Div., 24 Corps. Mustered out July 15, 1865.

54th REGIMENT MILITIA INFANTRY.—Org. at Pittsburg, July 4, 1863. Mustered out Aug. 17, 1863.

55th REGIMENT INFANTRY.—Org. at Harrisburg, Dec. 4, 1861. Dec., 1861, Unatt., Sherman's S. C. Exp. Corps. Jany., 1862, 1 Brig., S. C. Exp. Corps. Feby., 1862, Edisto Island, S. C. July, 1862, Dist. Beaufort, S. C., Dept. South. April, 1864, 1 Brig., 3 Div., 10 Corps, Army James, Dept. Va. and N. C. May, 1864, 1 Brig., 2 Div., 18 Corps. Dec., 1864, 4 Brig., 1 Div., 24 Corps. May, 1865, 2 Brig., 1 Div., 24 Corps. Mustered out Aug. 30, 1865.

55th REGIMENT MILITIA INFANTRY.—Org. at Pittsburg, July 3, 1863. July, 1863, Wilkinson's Brig., Scammon's Div., W. Va. Mustered out July 18, 1863.

56th REGIMENT INFANTRY.—Org. at Harrisburg, March 7, 1862. March, 1862, Mil. Dist. Washington. May, 1862, Doubleday's Separate Brig., Dept. Rappahannock. June, 1862, 2 Brig., 1 Div., 3 Corps, Army Va. Sept., 1862, 2 Brig., 1 Div., 1 Corps, Potomac. March, 1864, 2 Brig., 4 Div., 5 Corps, Potomac. Aug., 1864, 3 Brig., 2 Div., 5 Corps, Potomac. Sept., 1864, 3 Brig., 3 Div., 5 Corps, Potomac. Mustered out July 1, 1865.

56th REGIMENT MILITIA INFANTRY.—Org. at Pittsburg, July 5, 1863. Mustered out Aug. 13, 1863.

57th REGIMENT INFANTRY.—Org. at Harrisburg, Dec. 14, 1861. Dec., 1861, Prov'l Brig. Casey's Div., Potomac. Feby., 1862, Jameson's Brig., Heintzelman's Div., Potomac. March, 1862, 1 Brig., 3 Div., 3 Corps, Potomac.

Aug., 1862, 2 Brig., 1 Div., 3 Corps, Potomac. March, 1863, 1 Brig., 1 Div., 3 Corps. March, 1864, 2 Brig., 3 Div., 2 Corps, Potomac. Mustered out June 29, 1865.

57th REGIMENT MILITIA INFANTRY.—Org. at Pittsburg, June 8, 1863. Mustered out Aug. 17, 1863.

58th REGIMENT INFANTRY.—Org. at Phila., Sept. 21, 1861, to March 1, 1862. March, 1862, Camp Hamilton, Va., Dept. Va. May, 1862, 3 Brig., 1 Div., Dept. Va. July, 1862, Viele's Command, Norfolk, Va., 7 Corps, Dept. Va. Oct., 1862, Foster's Prov'l Brig., Div. at Suffolk, 7 Corps, Dept. Va. Dec., 1862, Gibbs' Prov'l Brig., Div. at Suffolk, Va., 7 Corps. Jany., 1863, 2 Brig., 3 Div., 18 Corps, Dept. N. C. April, 1863, Jourdan's Indpt. Brig., Def. Newberne, N. C., 18 Corps. June, 1863, Dist. Pamlico, Dept. N. C. Aug., 1863, Sub Dist. Pamlico, Dist. N. C., Dept. Va. and N. C. May, 1864, 3 Brig., 1 Div., 18 Corps, Army James, Dept. Va. and N. C. Dec., 1864, 3 Brig., 3 Div., 24 Corps. June, 1865, 2 Brig., 3 Div., 24 Corps. July, 1865, 1 Indpt. Brig., 24 Corps. Aug., 1865, Dist. S. W. Va., Dept. Va. Sept., 1865, Dist. Cent. Va., Dept. Va. Mustered out Jany. 24, 1866.

58th REGIMENT MILITIA INFANTRY.—Org. at Pittsburg, July 10, 1863. Mustered out Aug. 15, 1863.

59th REGIMENT.—See 2nd Regt. Cav.

59th REGIMENT MILITIA INFANTRY.—Org. at Phila., July 9, 1863. Mustered out Sept. 9, 1863.

60th REGIMENT.—See 3rd Regt. Cav.

60th REGIMENT MILITIA INFANTRY.—Org. at Phila., July 20, 1863. Mustered out Sept. 8, 1863.

61st REGIMENT INFANTRY.—Org. at Pittsburg, Sept. 7, 1861. Oct., 1861, Jameson's Brig., Heintzelman's Div., Potomac. Feby., 1862, Graham's Brig., Buell's Div., Potomac. March, 1862, 2 Brig., 1 Div., 4 Corps, Potomac. July, 1862, 3 Brig., 1 Div., 4 Corps, Potomac. Sept., 1862, 2 Brig., 3 Div., 6 Corps, Potomac. Oct., 1862, 1 Brig., 3 Div., 6 Corps, Potomac. Feby., 1863, Light Div., 6 Corps, Potomac. May, 1863, 3 Brig., 2 Div., 6 Corps, Potomac. July, 1864, 3 Brig., 2 Div., 6 Corps, Army Shenandoah, Middle Mil. Div. Dec., 1864, 3 Brig., 2 Div., 6 Corps, Potomac. Mustered out June 28, 1865.

62nd REGIMENT INFANTRY.—Org. at Pittsburg, Aug. 31, 1861. Oct., 1861, Morrell's Brig., Porter's Div., Potomac. March, 1862, 2 Brig., 1 Div., 3 Corps, Potomac. May, 1862, 2 Brig., 1 Div., 5 Corps, Potomac. Mustered out July 13, 1865.

63rd REGIMENT INFANTRY.—Org. at Pittsburg, Aug. 1, 1861. Oct., 1861, Jameson's Brig., Heintzelman's Div., Potomac. March, 1862, 1 Brig., 3 Div., 3 Corps, Potomac. Aug., 1862, 1 Brig., 1 Div., 3 Corps, Potomac. March, 1864, 2 Brig., 3 Div., 2 Corps, Potomac. Mustered out Sept. 9, 1864.

64th REGIMENT.—See 4th Regt. Cav.

65th REGIMENT.—See 5th Regt. Cav.

66th REGIMENT INFANTRY.—Org. at Phila., July 8, 1861. Consolidated with 73rd and 99th Infy., Feby., 1862.

67th REGIMENT INFANTRY.—Org. at Phila., March 31, 1862. April, 1862, Dix's Command, Def. Balto., Md. July, 1862, Annapolis, Md., Def. Balto., Middle Dept. Jany., 1863, Def. Upper Potomac, 8 Corps, Middle Dept. March, 1863, 3 Brig., 2 Div., 8 Corps. June, 1863, Elliott's Command, 8 Corps. July, 1863, 3 Brig., 3 Div., 3 Corps, Potomac. March, 1864, 2 Brig., 3 Div., 6 Corps, Potomac. July, 1864, 2 Brig., 3 Div., 6 Corps, Army Shenandoah, Middle Mil. Div. Dec., 1864, 2 Brig., 3 Div., 6 Corps, Potomac. Mustered out July 17, 1865.

68th REGIMENT INFANTRY.—Org. at Phila., Aug. and Sept., 1862. Oct., 1862, 1 Brig., 1 Div., 3 Corps, Potomac. March, 1864, Provost Guard, Army Potomac. April, 1865, Collis' Brig., 9 Corps, Potomac. April, 1865, Hart's Island, N. Y. Harbor. Mustered out June 9, 1865.

69th REGIMENT INFANTRY.—Org. at Phila., Aug. 18, 1861. Oct., 1861, Baker's Brig., Stone's (Sedgwick's) Div., Potomac. March, 1862, 2 Brig., 2 Div., 2 Corps, Potomac. June, 1864, 3 Brig., 2 Div., 2 Corps, Potomac. Mustered out July 1, 1865.

70th REGIMENT.—See 6th Regt. Cav.

71st REGIMENT INFANTRY.—Org. at Phila., Aug. 18, 1861. Oct., 1861, Baker's Brig., Stone's (Sedgwick's)

Div. Potomac. March, 1862, 2 Brig., 2 Div., 2 Corps, Potomac. Mustered out July 2, 1864.

72nd REGIMENT INFANTRY.—Org. at Phila., Aug. 10, 1861. Oct., 1861, Baker's Brig., Stone's (Sedgwick's) Div., Potomac. March, 1862, 2 Brig., 2 Div., 2 Corps, Potomac. June, 1864, 3 Brig., 2 Div., 2 Corps, Potomac. Mustered out Aug. 24, 1864.

73rd REGIMENT INFANTRY.—Org. at Phila., Sept. 19, 1861. Oct., 1861, Blenker's Brig., Potomac. Nov., 1861, Steinwehr's 2 Brig., Blenker's Div., Potomac. March, 1862, 2 Brig., Blenker's 2 Div., 2 Corps, Potomac. April, 1862, 2 Brig., Blenker's Div., Dept. Mts. June, 1862, 1 Brig., 2 Div., 1 Corps, Army Va. Sept., 1862, 1 Brig., 2 Div., 11 Corps, Potomac. Oct., 1863, 1 Brig., 2 Div., 11 Corps, Cumb'd. April, 1864, 2 Brig., 2 Div., 20 Corps, Cumb'd. Mustered out July 14, 1865.

74th REGIMENT INFANTRY.—Org. at Pittsburg, Sept. 30, 1861. Oct., 1861, Blenker's Brig., Potomac. Nov., 1861, Bohlen's Brig., Blenker's Div., Potomac. March, 1862, 3 Brig., Blenker's 2 Div., 2 Corps, Potomac. April, 1862, 3 Brig., Blenker's Div., Dept. Mts. June, 1862, 1 Brig., 3 Div., 1 Corps, Army Va. Sept., 1862, 1 Brig., 3 Div., 11 Corps, Potomac. Nov., 1862, 1 Brig., 2 Div., 11 Corps, Potomac. July, 1863, 1 Brig., 1 Div., 11 Corps, Potomac. Aug., 1863, 1 Brig., Gordon's Div., Folly Island, S. C., 10 Corps, Dept. South. April, 1864, 1 Brig., Folly Island, S. C., Northern Dist., Dept. South. Aug., 1864, 2 Brig., DeRussy's Div., Def. Washington, 22 Corps. Oct., 1864, Res. Div., Dept. W. Va. Jany., 1865, 2 Brig., 2 Infy. Div., W. Va. Jany., 1865, 1 Brig., 1 Infy. Div., W. Va. May, 1865, Sub Dist. Clarksburg, W. Va., Dept. W. Va. Mustered out Aug. 29, 1865.

75th REGIMENT INFANTRY.—Org. at Phila., Sept. 28, 1861. Oct., 1861, Casey's Prov'l Div., Potomac. Nov., 1861, 3 Brig., Blenker's Div., Potomac. March, 1862, 3 Brig., Blenker's Div., 2 Corps, Potomac. April, 1862, 3 Brig., Blenker's Div., Dept. Mts. June, 1862, 2 Brig., 3 Div., 1 Corps, Army Va. Sept., 1862, 2 Brig., 3 Div., 11 Corps, Potomac. Oct., 1863, 3 Brig., 3 Div., 11 Corps, Cumb'd. April, 1864, Unatt., 4 Div., 20 Corps, Cumb'd. June, 1864, Unatt., Def. Nash. and Northwestern R. R., Cumb'd. Aug., 1864, Unatt., 4 Div., 20 Corps, Cumb'd. March, 1865, 1 Brig., 1st Sub Dist., Dist. Middle Tenn., Dept. Cumb'd. Mustered out Sept. 1, 1865.

76th REGIMENT INFANTRY.—Org. at Harrisburg, Oct. 18, 1861. Oct., 1861, Wright's 3 Brig., Sherman's S. C. Exp. Corps. April, 1862, 2 Brig., 1 Div., Dept. South. July, 1862, Dist. Hilton Head, S. C., Dept. South. Sept., 1862, U. S. Forces, Hilton Head, S. C., 10 Corps. April, 1863, Guss' Brig., Seabrook Island, S. C., 10 Corps. June, 1863, Dist. Hilton Head, S. C., 10 Corps. June, 1863, St. Helena Island, S. C., 10 Corps. July, 1863, 2 Brig., Folly Island, S. C., 10 Corps. July, 1863, 2 Brig., 2 Div., Morris Island, S. C., 10 Corps. July, 1863, 1 Brig., Morris Island, S. C., 10 Corps. Aug., 1863, Dist. Hilton Head, S. C., 10 Corps. April, 1864, 2 Brig., 2 Div., 10 Corps, Army James, Dept. Va. and N. C. May, 1864, 1 Brig., 3 Div., 18 Corps. June, 1864, 2 Brig., 2 Div., 10 Corps. Dec., 1864, 2 Brig., 2 Div., 24 Corps. Jany., 1865, 2 Brig., 2 Div., Terry's Prov'l Corps, Dept. N. C. March, 1865, 2 Brig., 2 Div., 10 Corps, Army Ohio, Dept. N. C. Mustered out July 18, 1865.

77th REGIMENT INFANTRY.—Org. at Pittsburg, Oct. 15, 1861. Oct., 1861, Negley's 4 Brig., McCook's Command, Army Ohio. Nov., 1861, 5 Brig., Army Ohio. Dec., 1861, 5 Brig., 2 Div., Army Ohio. Sept., 1862, 5 Brig., 2 Div., 1 Corps, Ohio. Nov., 1862, 2 Brig., 2 Div., Right Wing, 14 Corps, Cumb'd. Jany., 1863, 2 Brig., 2 Div., 20 Corps, Cumb'd. Oct., 1863, 3 Brig., 1 Div., 4 Corps, Cumb'd. June, 1865, 1 Brig., 1 Div., 4 Corps. Aug., 1865, Dept. Tex. Mustered out Dec. 6, 1865.

78th REGIMENT INFANTRY.—Org. at Pittsburg, Oct. 18, 1861. Oct., 1861, Negley's 4 Brig., McCook's Command, Army Ohio. Nov., 1861, 7 Brig., Army Ohio. Dec., 1862, 7 Brig., 2 Div., Ohio. March, 1862, Negley's 7 Indpt. Brig., Ohio. June, 1862, Unatt., Army Ohio. Sept., 1862, 7 Brig., 8 Div., Army Ohio. Nov., 1862, 3 Brig., 2 Div., Centre, 14 Corps, Cumb'd. Jany., 1863, 3 Brig., 2 Div., 14 Corps, Cumb'd. Oct., 1863, 3 Brig.,

1 Div., 14 Corps, Cumb'd. July, 1864, Unass'd, 4 Div., 20 Corps, Cumb'd. Oct., 1864, Garrison at Nashville, Tenn. Mustered out Sept. 11, 1865.

79th REGIMENT INFANTRY.—Org. at Lancaster, Sept. 19, 1861. Oct., 1861, Negley's 4 Brig., McCook's Command, Army Ohio. Nov., 1861, 7 Brig., Army Ohio. Dec., 1861, 7 Brig., 2 Div., Army Ohio. March, 1862, Negley's 7 Indpt. Brig., Army Ohio. July, 1862 Unatt., Army Ohio. Sept., 1862, 28 Brig., 3 Div., Army Ohio. Sept., 1862, 28 Brig., 3 Div., 1 Corps, Ohio. Nov., 1862, 3 Brig., 1 Div., Centre, 14 Corps, Cumb'd. Jany., 1863, 3 Brig., 1 Div., 14 Corps, Cumb'd. April, 1863, 2 Brig., 1 Div., 14 Corps, Cumb'd. Oct., 1863, 3 Brig., 1 Div., 14 Corps, Cumb'd. Mustered out Sept. 11, 1865.

80th REGIMENT.—See 7th Regt. Cav.

81st REGIMENT INFANTRY.—Org. at Phila., Oct. 31, 1861. Nov., 1861, Howard's Brig., Heintzelman's Div., Potomac. March, 1862, 1 Brig., 1 Div., 2 Corps, Potomac. Mustered out June 29, 1865.

82nd REGIMENT INFANTRY.—Org. at Phila. and Pittsburg, Aug., 1861. Oct., 1861, Graham's Brig., Buell's Div., Potomac. March, 1862, 2 Brig., 1 Div., 4 Corps, Potomac. July, 1862, 3 Brig., 1 Div., 4 Corps, Potomac. Sept., 1862, 3 Brig., 3 Div., 6 Corps, Potomac. Oct., 1862, 1 Brig., 3 Div., 6 Corps, Potomac. Jany., 1864, Johnson's Island, Sandusky, Ohio. May, 1864, 4 Brig., 1 Div., 6 Corps, Potomac. July, 1864, 3 Brig., 1 Div., 6 Corps, Potomac and Army Shenandoah, Middle Mil. Div. Mustered out July 13, 1865.

83rd REGIMENT INFANTRY.—Org. at Erie, Sept. 13, 1861. Oct., 1861, Butterfield's Brig., Porter's Div., Potomac. March, 1862, 3 Brig., 1 Div., 3 Corps, Potomac. May, 1862, 3 Brig., 1 Div., 5 Corps, Potomac. Mustered out June 28, 1865.

84th REGIMENT INFANTRY.—Org. at Harrisburg, Nov. 22, 1861. Jany., 1862, 1 Brig., Lander's Div., Potomac. March, 1862, 1 Brig., Shield's 2 Div., Banks' 5 Corps. April, 1862, 1 Brig., Shield's Div., Dept. Shenandoah. May, 1862, 4 Brig., Shield's Div., Dept. Rappahannock. June, 1862, 4 Brig., 2 Div., 3 Corps, Army Va. Sept., 1862, 2 Brig., 3 Div., 3 Corps, Potomac. June, 1863, 1 Brig., 2 Div., 3 Corps, Potomac. March, 1864, 2 Brig., 4 Div., 2 Corps. May, 1864, 4 Brig., 3 Div., 2 Corps, Potomac. July, 1864, 2 Brig., 3 Div., 2 Corps, Potomac. Consolidated with 57th Pa. Infy., Jany. 13, 1865.

85th REGIMENT INFANTRY.—Org. at Uniontown, Oct. 16 to Nov. 12, 1861. Dec., 1861, 2 Brig., Casey's Div., Potomac. March, 1862, 2 Brig., 3 Div., 4 Corps, Potomac. June, 1862, 2 Brig., 2 Div., 4 Corps, Potomac. Sept., 1862, Wessell's Brig., Div. at Suffolk, Va., 7 Corps, Dept. Va. Dec., 1862, 1 Brig., 1 Div., Dept. N. C. Jany., 1863, 2 Brig., 3 Div., 18 Corps, Dept. N. C. Feby., 1863, 2 Brig., 2 Div., 18 Corps, Dept. South. April, 1863, Folly Island, S. C., 10 Corps, Dept. South. June, 1863, 2 Brig., Folly Island, S. C., 10 Corps. July, 1863, 1 Brig., Folly Island, S. C., 10 Corps. July, 1863, 1 Brig., 2 Div., Morris Island, S. C., 10 Corps. Aug., 1863, 2 Brig., Morris Island, S. C., 10 Corps. Oct., 1863, Howell's Brig., Gordon's Div., Folly Island, S. C., 10 Corps. Dec., 1863, Dist. Hilton Head, S. C., 10 Corps. April, 1864, 1 Brig., 1 Div., 10 Corps, Army James, Dept. Va. and N. C. Mustered out Nov. 22, 1864.

86th REGIMENT INFANTRY.—(Failed to complete organization).

87th REGIMENT INFANTRY.—Org. at Yorktown, Pa., Sept. 1, to 25, 1861. Oct., 1861, Dix's Div., Balto. Md. July, 1862, R. R. Dist., Middle Dept. Sept., 1862, New Creek, W. Va., R. R. Div., 8 Corps, Middle Dept. Jany., 1863, Milroy's Command, Winchester, Va., 8 Corps, March, 1863, 2 Brig., 2 Div., 8 Corps. June, 1863, Elliott's Command, 8 Corps. June, 1863, Bloody Run, Pa., Dept. Susquehanna. July, 1863, 3 Brig., 3 Div., 3 Corps, Potomac. March, 1864, 1 Brig., 3 Div., 6 Corps, Potomac and Army Shenandoah, Middle Mil. Div. Mustered out June 29, 1865.

88th REGIMENT INFANTRY.—Org. at Phila., Sept., 1861. Oct., 1861, Def. Washington, D. C. May, 1862, 1 Brig., 2 Div., Dept. Rappahannock. June, 1862, 2 Brig., 2 Div., 3 Corps, Army Va. Sept., 1862, 2 Brig., 2 Div.,

1 Corps, Potomac. March, 1863, 3 Brig., 2 Div., 1 Corps, Potomac. May, 1863, 2 Brig., 2 Div., 1 Corps, Potomac. March, 1864, 2 Brig., 2 Div., 5 Corps, Potomac. May, 1864, 2 Brig., 3 Div., 5 Corps, Potomac. March, 1865, 3 Brig., 3 Div., 5 Corps, Potomac. Mustered out June 30, 1865.

89th REGIMENT.—See 8th Regt. Cav.

90th REGIMENT INFANTRY.—Org. at Phila., Oct. 1, 1861. Oct., 1861, Def. Washington, D. C. May, 1862, 1 Brig., 2 Div., Dept. Rappahannock. June, 1862, 2 Brig., 2 Div., 3 Corps, Army Va. Sept., 1862, 2 Brig., 2 Div., 1 Corps, Potomac. March, 1864, 2 Brig., 2 Div., 5 Corps, Potomac. May, 1864, 1 Brig., 2 Div., 5 Corps, Potomac. June, 1864, 1 Brig., 3 Div., 5 Corps, Potomac. Sept., 1864, 2 Brig., 3 Div., 5 Corps, Potomac. Consolidated with 11th Pa. Infy., Nov. 26, 1864.

91st REGIMENT INFANTRY.—Org. at Phila., Sept. 9 to Dec. 4, 1862. Jany., 1862, Def. Washington, D. C. Aug., 1862, 1 Brig., 3 Div., 5 Corps, Potomac. May, 1863, 3 Brig., 2 Div., 5 Corps, Potomac. March, 1864, 4 Brig., 1 Div., 5 Corps, Potomac. April, 1864, 1 Brig., 1 Div., 5 Corps, Potomac. June, 1864, 1 Brig., 2 Div., 5 Corps, Potomac. June, 1864, 2 Brig., 2 Div., 5 Corps, Potomac. July, 1864, 2 Brig., 1 Div., 5 Corps, Potomac. Dec., 1864, 3 Brig., 1 Div., 5 Corps, Potomac. March, 1865, 1 Brig., 3 Div., 5 Corps, Potomac. Mustered out July 10, 1865.

92nd REGIMENT.—See 9th Regt. Cav.

93rd REGIMENT INFANTRY.—Org. at Lebanon, Sept. 21 to Oct. 28, 1861. Oct., 1861, Peck's Brig., Couch's Div., Potomac. March, 1862, 3 Brig., 1 Div., 4 Corps, Potomac. July, 1862, 2 Brig., 1 Div., 4 Corps, Potomac. Sept., 1862, 2 Brig., 3 Div., 6 Corps, Potomac. Oct., 1862, 3 Brig., 3 Div., 6 Corps, Potomac. Jany., 1864, 1 Brig., 2 Div., 6 Corps, Potomac. July, 1864, 1 Brig., 2 Div., 6 Corps, Army Shenandoah, Middle Mil. Div. Dec., 1864, 1 Brig., 2 Div., 6 Corps, Potomac. Mustered out June 27, 1865.

94th REGIMENT INFANTRY.—(Failed to complete organization).

95th REGIMENT INFANTRY.—Org. at Phila., Aug. 23 to Oct. 16, 1861. Nov., 1861, Newton's Brig., Franklin's Div., Potomac. March, 1862, 3 Brig., 1 Div., 1 Corps, Potomac. April, 1862, 2 Brig., 1 Div., Dept. Rappahannock. May, 1862, 3 Brig., 1 Div., 6 Corps, Potomac. May, 1863, 2 Brig., 1 Div., 6 Corps, Potomac and Army Shenandoah, Middle Mil. Div. Mustered out July 17, 1865.

96th REGIMENT INFANTRY.—Org. at Pottsville, Sept. 9 to Oct. 30, 1861. Nov., 1861, Slocum's Brig., Franklin's Div., Potomac. March, 1862, 2 Brig., 1 Div., 1 Corps, Potomac. April, 1862, 2 Brig., 1 Div., Dept. Rappahannock. May, 1862, 2 Brig., 1 Div., 6 Corps, Potomac and Army Shenandoah, Middle Mil. Div. Mustered out Oct. 21, 1864.

97th REGIMENT INFANTRY.—Org. at West Chester, Aug. 22 to Oct. 28, 1861. Nov., 1861, Dept. Va. Dec., 1861, Wright's 3 Brig., Sherman's S. C. Exp. Corps. April, 1862, 1 Brig., 1 Div., Dept. South. July, 1862, Dist. Hilton Head, S. C., Dept. South. Sept., 1862, U. S. Forces, Hilton Head, S. C., 10 Corps, Dept. South. April, 1863, Stevenson's Brig., Seabrook Island, S. C., 10 Corps. July, 1863, 1 Brig., 1 Div., Morris Island, S. C., 10 Corps. July, 1863, 3 Brig., Morris Island, S. C., 10 Corps. Aug., 1863, 1 Brig., Morris Island, S. C., 10 Corps. Oct., 1863, Fernandina, Fla. April, 1864, 1 Brig., 3 Div., 10 Corps, Army James, Dept. Va. and N. C. May, 1864. 3 Brig., 3 Div., 18 Corps. June, 1864, 3 Brig., 2 Div., 10 Corps. Dec., 1864, 2 Brig., 2 Div., 24 Corps. Jany., 1865, 2 Brig., 2 Div., Terry's Prov'l Corps, Dept. N. C. March, 1865, 2 Brig., 2 Div., 10 Corps, Army Ohio, Dept. N. C. Mustered out Aug. 28, 1865.

98th REGIMENT INFANTRY.—Org. at Phila., Aug. 23 to Nov. 6, 1861. Nov., 1861, Peck's Brig., Buell's Div., Potomac. March, 1862, 3 Brig., 1 Div., 4 Corps, Potomac. July, 1862, 2 Brig., 1 Div., 4 Corps, Potomac. Sept., 1862, 2 Brig., 3 Div., 6 Corps, Potomac. Oct., 1862, 3 Brig., 3 Div., 6 Corps, Potomac. Jany., 1864, Wheaton's Brig., Dept. W. Va. March, 1864, 1 Brig., 2 Div., 6 Corps, Potomac. July, 1864, 1 Brig., 2 Div., 6 Corps, Army Shenandoah, Middle Mil. Div. Dec., 1864, 1 Brig., 2 Div., 6 Corps, Potomac. Mustered out June 29, 1865.

99th REGIMENT INFANTRY.—Org. at Phila. as 32nd, July 26, 1861, to Jany. 18, 1862. Sept., 1861, Def. Washington, D. C. Oct., 1861, Jameson's Brig., Heintzelman's Div., Potomac. Feby., 1862, Garrison at Washington, Mil. Dist. Washington. June, 1862, 3 Brig., 3 Div., 3 Corps, Potomac. Aug., 1862, 3 Brig., 1 Div., 3 Corps, Potomac. Dec., 1862, 2 Brig., 1 Div., 3 Corps, Potomac. Aug., 1863, 3 Brig., 1 Div., 3 Corps, Potomac. Oct., 1863, 2 Brig., 1 Div., 3 Corps, Potomac. March, 1864, 1 Brig., 3 Div., 2 Corps, Potomac. Mustered out July 1, 1865.

100th REGIMENT INFANTRY.—"ROUNDHEADS." Org. at Pittsburg, Aug. 31, 1861. Oct., 1861, Steven's 2 Brig., Sherman's S. C. Exp. Corps. April, 1862, 2 Brig., 2 Div., Dept. South. July, 1862, 2 Brig., 1 Div., 9 Corps, Potomac. Sept., 1862, 3 Brig., 1 Div., 9 Corps, Potomac. April, 1863, 3 Brig., 1 Div., 9 Corps, Ohio. June, 1863, 3 Brig., 1 Div., 9 Corps, Tenn. Aug., 1863, 3 Brig., 1 Div., 9 Corps, Ohio. Jany., 1864, 2 Brig., 1 Div., 9 Corps, Ohio and Potomac. June, 1864, 1 Brig., 1 Div., 9 Corps, Potomac. Sept., 1864, 3 Brig., 1 Div., 9 Corps, Potomac. Mustered out July 24, 1865.

101st REGIMENT INFANTRY.—Org. at Harrisburg, Nov. 21, 1861, to Feby. 24, 1862. March, 1862, 2 Brig., 3 Div., 4 Corps, Potomac. June, 1862, 2 Brig., 2 Div., 4 Corps, Potomac. Sept., 1862, Wessell's Brig., Div. at Suffolk, 7 Corps, Dept. Va. Dec., 1862, 1 Brig., 1 Div., Dept. N. C. Jany., 1863, 1 Brig., 4 Div., 18 Corps, Dept. N. C. May, 1863, Dist. Albemarle, Dept. N. C. Aug., 1863, Sub-Dist. Albemarle, Dist. N. C., Dept. Va. and N. C. Jany., 1865, Def. Roanoke Island, N. C., Dept. N. C. Mustered out June 25, 1865.

102nd REGIMENT INFANTRY.—Org. at Pittsburg, Aug., 1861. Oct., 1861, Peck's Brig., Buell's Div., Potomac. March, 1862, 3 Brig., 1 Div., 4 Corps, Potomac. July, 1862, 2 Brig., 1 Div., 4 Corps, Potomac. Sept., 1862, 2 Brig., 3 Div., 6 Corps, Potomac. Oct., 1862, 3 Brig., 3 Div., 6 Corps, Potomac. Jany., 1864, Wheaton's Brig., Dept. W. Va. March, 1864, 1 Brig., 2 Div., 6 Corps, Potomac. July, 1864, 1 Brig., 2 Div., 6 Corps, Army Shenandoah, Middle Mil. Div. Dec., 1864, 1 Brig., 2 Div., 6 Corps, Potomac. Mustered out June 28, 1865.

103rd REGIMENT INFANTRY.—Org. at Kittanning, Sept. 7, 1861, to Feby. 22, 1862. March, 1862, 2 Brig., 3 Div., 4 Corps, Potomac. June, 1862, 2 Brig., 2 Div., 4 Corps, Potomac. Sept., 1862, Wessell's Brig., Div. at Suffolk, 7 Corps, Dept. Va. Dec., 1862, 1 Brig., 1 Div., Dept. N. C. Jany., 1863, 1 Brig., 4 Div., 18 Corps, Dept. N. C. May, 1863, Dist. Albemarle, Dept. N. C. Aug., 1863, Sub-Dist. Albemarle, Dist. N. C., Dept. Va. and N. C. Jany., 1865, Dist. Albemarle, Dept. N. C. Mustered out June 25, 1865.

104th REGIMENT INFANTRY.—Org. at Doylestown, Sept. 20 to Oct. 16, 1861. Nov., 1861, 1 Brig., Casey's Div., Potomac. March, 1862, 1 Brig., 3 Div., 4 Corps, Potomac. June, 1862, 1 Brig., 2 Div., 4 Corps, Potomac. Dec., 1862, Naglee's Brig., Dept. N. C. Jany., 1863, 2 Brig., 2 Div., 18 Corps, Dept. N. C. Feby., 1863, 2 Brig., 1 Div., 18 Corps, Dept. South. April, 1863, Dist. Beaufort, S. C., 10 Corps, Dept. South. July, 1863, 2 Brig., 1 Div., Morris Island, S. C., 10 Corps. July, 1863, Davis' Brig., Folly Island, S. C., 10 Corps. Aug., 1863, 5 Brig., Morris Island, S. C., 10 Corps. Nov., 1863, 2 Brig., Morris Island, S. C., 10 Corps. April, 1864, Dist. Hilton Head, S. C., Dept. South. June, 1864, Morris Island, S. C., Northern Dist., Dept. South. Aug., 1864, Dist. Fla., Dept. South. Aug., 1864, 3 Brig., DeRussy's Div., 22 Corps, Def. Washington. Sept., 1864, 1 Brig., Kitching's Prov'l Div., Army Shenandoah. Dec., 1864, 1 Brig., Def. Bermuda Hundred, Va., Dept. Va. and N. C. April, 1865, Norfolk and Portsmouth, Dept. Va. Mustered out Aug. 25, 1865.

105th REGIMENT INFANTRY.—Org. at Pittsburg, Sept. 9 to Oct. 31, 1861. Oct., 1861, Jameson's Brig., Heintzelman's Div., Potomac. March, 1862, 1 Brig., 3 Div., 3 Corps, Potomac. Aug., 1862, 1 Brig., 1 Div., 3 Corps, Potomac. March, 1864, 2 Brig., 3 Div., 2 Corps, Potomac. Mustered out July 11, 1865.

106th REGIMENT INFANTRY.—Org. at Phila., Aug. 14 to Oct. 31, 1861. Oct., 1861, Baker's Brig., Stone's (Sedgwick's) Div., Potomac. March, 1862, 2 Brig., 2 Div., 2 Corps, Potomac. June, 1864, 3 Brig., 2 Div., 2 Corps, Potomac. Mustered out June 30, 1865.

107th REGIMENT INFANTRY.—Org. at Harrisburg, Feby. 20 to March 8, 1862. March, 1862, Def. Washington. April, 1862, 1 Brig., 2 Div., Dept. Rappahannock. June, 1862, 1 Brig., 2 Div., 3 Corps, Army Va. Sept., 1862, 1 Brig., 2 Div., 1 Corps, Potomac. March, 1864, 1 Brig., 2 Div., 5 Corps, Potomac. June, 1864, 1 Brig., 3 Div., 5 Corps, Potomac. Sept., 1864, 2 Brig., 3 Div., 5 Corps, Potomac. Feby., 1865, 3 Brig., 3 Div., 5 Corps, Potomac. Mustered out July 13, 1865.

108th REGIMENT.—See 11th Regt. Cav.

109th REGIMENT INFANTRY.—Org. at Phila., March to May, 1862. March, 1862, Def. Washington. May, 1862, 1 Brig., Sigel's Div., Dept. Shenandoah. June, 1862, 2 Brig., 2 Div., 2 Corps, Army Va. Sept., 1862, 2 Brig., 2 Div., 12 Corps, Potomac. Oct., 1862, 3 Brig., 2 Div., 12 Corps, Potomac. Jany., 1863, 2 Brig., 2 Div., 12 Corps, Potomac. Oct., 1863, 2 Brig., 2 Div., 12 Corps, Cumb'd. April, 1864, 2 Brig., 2 Div., 20 Corps, Cumb'd. Consolidated with 111th Pa. Infy., March 31, 1865.

110th REGIMENT INFANTRY.—Org. as 31st Infy. at Harrisburg, Huntingdon and Phila., Aug. 19, 1861. Jany., 1862, Tyler's Brig., Lander's Div., Potomac. March, 1862-3, 3 Brig., Shield's 2 Div., Banks' 5 Corps. April, 1862, 3 Brig., Shield's Div., Dept. Shenandoah. May, 1862, 4 Brig., Shield's Div., Dept. Rappahannock. June, 1862, 4 Brig., 2 Div., 3 Corps, Army Va. Sept., 1862, 2 Brig., 3 Div., 3 Corps, Potomac. June, 1863, 3 Brig., 1 Div., 3 Corps, Potomac. March, 1864, 1 Brig., 3 Div., 2 Corps, Potomac. Mustered out June 28, 1865.

111th REGIMENT INFANTRY.—Org. at Erie, Dec., 1861. March, 1862, Dix's Div., Balto., Md. May, 1862, Cooper's 1 Brig., Sigel's Div., Dept. Shenandoah. June, 1862, 1 Brig., 2 Div., 2 Corps, Army Va. Aug., 1862, 2 Brig., 2 Div., 2 Corps, Army Va. Sept., 1862, 2 Brig., 2 Div., 12 Corps, Potomac. Oct., 1862, 3 Brig., 2 Div., 12 Corps, Potomac. Jany., 1863, 2 Brig., 2 Div., 12 Corps, Potomac. Oct., 1863, 2 Brig., 2 Div., 12 Corps, Cumb'd. April, 1864, 3 Brig., 2 Div., 20 Corps, Cumb'd. Mustered out July 19, 1865.

112th REGIMENT.—See 2nd Regt. Heavy Arty.

113th REGIMENT.—See 12th Regt. Cav.

114th REGIMENT INFANTRY.—Org. Phila., Aug. 13 to Sept. 27, 1862. Oct., 1862, 1 Brig., 1 Div., 3 Corps, Potomac. March, 1864, Provost Guard, Headqrs. Army Potomac. April, 1865, Collis' Indpt. Brig., 9 Corps, Potomac. April, 1865, 1 Brig., 2 Div., 5 Corps, Potomac. Mustered out May 29, 1865.

115th REGIMENT INFANTRY.—Org. at Harrisburg and Phila., Jany. 28, 1862. Feby., 1862, Camden, N. J. July, 1862, 3 Brig., 2 Div., 3 Corps, Potomac. March, 1864, 1 Brig., 4 Div., 2 Corps, Potomac. May, 1864, 3 Brig., 3 Div., 2 Corps, Potomac. Consolidated with 110th Regt. Infy., June 24, 1864.

116th REGIMENT INFANTRY.—Org. at Phila., June 11 to Sept. 4, 1862. Oct., 1862, 2 Brig., 1 Div., 2 Corps, Potomac. June, 1864, 4 Brig., 1 Div., 2 Corps, Potomac. Mustered out July 14, 1865.

117th REGIMENT.—See 13th Regt. Cav.

118th REGIMENT INFANTRY.—Org. at Phila., Aug. 15 to Aug. 30, 1862. Sept., 1862, Def. Washington, D. C. Sept., 1862, 1 Brig., 1 Div., 5 Corps, Potomac. April, 1864, 3 Brig., 1 Div., 5 Corps, Potomac. Mustered out June 1, 1865.

119th REGIMENT INFANTRY.—Org. at Phila., Aug. 15 to Sept. 17, 1862. Sept., 1862, 1 Brig., 2 Div., 6 Corps, Potomac. Feby., 1863, 3 Brig., 1 Div., 6 Corps, Potomac. Aug., 1864, 3 Brig., 1 Div., 6 Corps, Army Shenandoah, Middle Mil. Div. Dec., 1864, 3 Brig., 1 Div., 6 Corps, Potomac. Mustered out June 19, 1865.

120th REGIMENT INFANTRY.—(Failed to complete organization.)

121st REGIMENT INFANTRY.—Org. at Phila., Aug. 22 to Sept. 5, 1862. Oct., 1862, 1 Brig., 3 Div., 1 Corps, Potomac. March, 1864, 3 Brig., 4 Div., 5 Corps, Potomac. June, 1864, 1 Brig., 1 Div., 5 Corps, Potomac. Sept., 1864, 3 Brig., 3 Div., 5 Corps, Potomac. Mustered out June 2, 1865.

122nd REGIMENT INFANTRY—Org. at Harrisburg, Aug. 11 to Sept. 10, 1862. Sept., 1862, Piatt's Brig., Def. Washington. Nov., 1862, 3 Brig., 3 Div., 3 Corps, Potomac. Mustered out May 16, 1863.

123rd REGIMENT INFANTRY.—Org. at Harrisburg, Aug., 1862. Sept., 1862, 2 Brig., 3 Div., 5 Corps, Potomac. Mustered out May 13, 1863.

124th REGIMENT INFANTRY.—Org. at Harrisburg, Aug., 1862. Aug., 1862, Whipple's Command, Def. Washington. Sept., 1862, 1 Brig., 1 Div., 12 Corps, Potomac. Nov., 1862, 2 Brig., 1 Div., 12 Corps, Potomac. March, 1863, 2 Brig., 2 Div., 12 Corps, Potomac. Mustered out May 16, 1863.

125th REGIMENT INFANTRY.—Org. at Harrisburg, Aug. and Sept., 1862. Aug., 1862, Whipple's Command, Def. Washington. Sept., 1862, 1 Brig., 1 Div., 12 Corps, Potomac. Nov., 1862, 2 Brig., 1 Div., 12 Corps, Potomac. March, 1863, 2 Brig., 2 Div., 12 Corps, Potomac. Mustered out May 18, 1863.

126th REGIMENT INFANTRY.—Org. at Harrisburg, Aug., 1862. Aug., 1862, Def. Washington, D. C. Sept., 1862, 1 Brig., 3 Div., 5 Corps, Potomac. Mustered out May 20, 1863.

127th REGIMENT INFANTRY.—Org. at Harrisburg, Aug., 1862. Aug., 1862, Whipple's Command, Def. Washington. Dec., 1862, 3 Brig., 2 Div., 2 Corps, Potomac. Mustered out May 29, 1863.

128th REGIMENT INFANTRY.—Org. at Harrisburg, Aug., 1862. Aug., 1862, Whipple's Command, Def. Washington. Sept., 1862, 1 Brig., 1 Div., 12 Corps, Potomac. Mustered out May 19, 1863.

129th REGIMENT INFANTRY.—Org. at Harrisburg, Aug., 1862. Aug., 1862, Whipple's Command, Def. Washington. Aug., 1862, 1 Brig., 3 Div., 5 Corps, Potomac. Mustered out May 18, 1863.

130th REGIMENT INFANTRY.—Org. at Harrisburg, Aug. 9-18, 1862. Aug., 1862, Whipple's Command, Def. Washington. Sept., 1862, 2 Brig., 3 Div., 2 Corps, Potomac. Mustered out May 21, 1863.

131st REGIMENT INFANTRY.—Org. at Harrisburg, Aug., 1862. Aug., 1862, Whipple's Command, Def. Washington. Sept., 1862, 2 Brig., 3 Div., 5 Corps, Potomac. Mustered out May 23, 1863.

132nd REGIMENT INFANTRY.—Org. at Harrisburg, Aug. 11-18, 1862. Aug., 1862, Whipple's Command, Def. Washington. Sept., 1862, 1 Brig., 3 Div., 2 Corps, Potomac. Dec., 1862, 2 Brig., 3 Div., 2 Corps, Potomac. Mustered out May 24, 1863.

133rd REGIMENT INFANTRY.—Org. at Harrisburg, Aug., 1862. Sept., 1862, 2 Brig., 3 Div., 5 Corps, Potomac. Mustered out May 26, 1863.

134th REGIMENT INFANTRY.—Org. at Harrisburg, Aug. 11-23, 1862. Aug., 1862, Def. Washington. Sept., 1862, 1 Brig., 3 Div., 5 Corps, Potomac. Mustered out May 26, 1863.

135th REGIMENT INFANTRY.—Org. at Harrisburg, Aug., 1862. Sept., 1862, Mil. Dist. Washington. Feby., 1863, 1 Brig., 3 Div., 1 Corps, Potomac. Mustered out May 24, 1863.

136th REGIMENT INFANTRY.—Org. at Harrisburg, Aug. 15-27, 1862. Aug., 1862, Def. Washington, North Potomac. Sept., 1862, 2 Brig., 2 Div., 1 Corps, Potomac. Mustered out May 29, 1863.

137th REGIMENT INFANTRY.—Org. at Harrisburg, Aug. 25, 1862. Sept., 1862, 1 Brig., 2 Div., 6 Corps, Potomac. Dec., 1862, Patrick's Command, Provost Guard, Potomac. Mustered out June 1, 1863.

138th REGIMENT INFANTRY.—Org. at Harrisburg, Aug. 16 to Sept. 12, 1862. Sept., 1862, Relay House, Def. Balto., 8 Corps, Middle Dept. Feby., 1863, 3rd Separate Brig., 8 Corps. June, 1863, Elliott's Command, 8 Corps. July, 1863, 2 Brig., 3 Div., 3 Corps, Potomac. March, 1864, 2 Brig., 3 Div., 6 Corps, Potomac. July,

1864, 2 Brig., 3 Div., 6 Corps, Army Shenandoah, Middle Mil. Div. Dec., 1864, 2 Brig., 3 Div., 6 Corps, Potomac. Mustered out June 23, 1865.

139th REGIMENT INFANTRY.—Org. at Pittsburg, Sept. 1, 1862. Sept., 1862, 2 Brig., 1 Div., 4 Corps, Potomac. Sept., 1862, 2 Brig., 3 Div., 6 Corps, Potomac. Oct., 1862, 3 Brig., 3 Div., 6 Corps, Potomac. Jany., 1864, Wheaton's Brig., Dept. W. Va. March, 1864, 1 Brig., 2 Div., 6 Corps, Potomac. July, 1864, 1 Brig., 2 Div., 6 Corps, Army Shenandoah, Middle Mil. Div. Dec., 1864, 1 Brig., 2 Div., 6 Corps, Potomac. Mustered out June 21, 1865.

140th REGIMENT INFANTRY.—Org. at Pittsburg and Harrisburg, Aug. and Sept., 1862. Sept., 1862, Parktown, Md., 8 Corps, Middle Dept. Dec., 1862, 3 Brig., 1 Div., 2 Corps, Potomac. Sept., 1863, 1 Brig., 1 Div., 2 Corps, Potomac. Mustered out May 31, 1865.

141st REGIMENT INFANTRY.—Org. at Harrisburg, Aug. 26 to Sept. 2, 1862. Sept., 1862, 1 Brig., 1 Div., 3 Corps, Potomac. March, 1864, 1 Brig., 3 Div., 2 Corps, Potomac. July, 1864, 2 Brig., 3 Div., 2 Corps, Potomac. Mustered out May 28, 1865.

142nd REGIMENT INFANTRY.—Org. at Harrisburg, Aug. and Sept., 1862. Oct., 1862, 2 Brig., 3 Div., 1 Corps, Potomac. Feby., 1863, 1 Brig., 3 Div., 1 Corps, Potomac. March, 1864, 3 Brig., 4 Div., 5 Corps, Potomac. June, 1864, 1 Brig., 1 Div., 5 Corps, Potomac. Sept., 1864, 3 Brig., 3 Div., 5 Corps, Potomac. Mustered out May 29, 1865.

143rd REGIMENT INFANTRY.—Org. at Harrisburg and Wilkesbarre Aug. 26 to Oct. 10, 1862. Aug., 1862, Def. Washington, North Potomac. Oct., 1862, 1 Brig., Def. Washington, North Potomac. Jany., 1863, 2 Brig., 3 Div., 1 Corps, Potomac. Dec., 1863, 1 Brig., 3 Div., 1 Corps, Potomac. March, 1864, 3 Brig., 4 Div., 5 Corps, Potomac. June, 1864, 1 Brig., 1 Div., 5 Corps, Potomac. Sept., 1864, 1 Brig., 3 Div., 5 Corps, Potomac. Feby., 1865, Hart's Island, N. Y. Harbor. Mustered out June 12, 1865.

144th REGIMENT INFANTRY.—(Failed to complete organization.)

145th REGIMENT INFANTRY.—Org. at Erie Aug. and Sept., 1862. Sept., 1862, 2 Brig., 1 Div., 2 Corps, Potomac. Oct., 1862, 1 Brig., 1 Div., 2 Corps, Potomac. April, 1863, 4 Brig., 1 Div., 2 Corps, Potomac. Mustered out May 31, 1865.

146th REGIMENT INFANTRY.—(Failed to complete organization.)

147th REGIMENT INFANTRY.—Org. at Harrisburg Sept. to Nov., 1862. Oct., 1862, 1 Brig., 2 Div., 12 Corps, Potomac. Oct., 1863, 1 Brig., 2 Div., 12 Corps, Cumb'd. April, 1864, 1 Brig., 2 Div., 20 Corps, Cumb'd. Mustered out July 15, 1865.

148th REGIMENT INFANTRY.—Org. at Harrisburg Oct. 8, 1862. Oct., 1862, Unatt., Def. Balto., Md., 8 Corps. Dec., 1862, 1 Brig., 1 Div., 2 Corps, Potomac. Sept., 1863, 3 Brig., 1 Div., 2 Corps, Potomac. March, 1864, 4 Brig., 1 Div., 2 Corps, Potomac. Mustered out June 1, 1865.

149th REGIMENT INFANTRY.—Org. at Harrisburg Aug., 1862. Oct., 1862, Def. Washington. Feby., 1863, 2 Brig., 3 Div., 1 Corps, Potomac. Dec., 1863, 1 Brig., 3 Div., 1 Corps, Potomac. March, 1864, 3 Brig., 4 Div., 5 Corps, Potomac. June, 1864, 1 Brig., 1 Div., 5 Corps, Potomac. Sept., 1864, 1 Brig., 3 Div., 5 Corps, Potomac. Mustered out June 24, 1865.

150th REGIMENT INFANTRY.—Org. at Phila. and Harrisburg Aug. and Sept., 1862. Oct., 1862, Def. Washington. Feby., 1863, 2 Brig., 3 Div., 1 Corps, Potomac. Dec., 1863,· 1 Brig., 3 Div., 1 Corps, Potomac. March, 1864, 3 Brig., 4 Div., 5 Corps, Potomac. June, 1864, 1 Brig., 1 Div., 5 Corps, Potomac. Sept., 1864, 1 Brig., 3 Div., 5 Corps, Potomac. Mustered out June 23, 1865.

151st REGIMENT INFANTRY.—Org. at Harrisburg Oct. 18 to Nov. 24, 1862. Dec., 1862, 3 Brig., Casey's Div., Def Washington. Feby., 1863, 1 Brig., 3 Div., 1 Corps, Potomac. Mustered out July 27, 1863.

152nd REGIMENT.—(See 3rd Regt. Heavy Arty.)

153rd REGIMENT INFANTRY.—Org. at Easton Sept., 1862. Nov., 1862, 1 Brig., 1 Div., 11 Corps, Potomac. Mustered out July 24, 1863.

154th REGIMENT INFANTRY.—Org. at Phila. Dec. 29, 1862, to Jany. 21, 1863. On Provost duty at Phila., Pa. Mustered out Sept. 29 to Oct. 21, 1863.

155th REGIMENT INFANTRY.—Org. at Harrisburg and Pittsburg Sept. 2-19, 1862. Sept., 1862, 2 Brig., 3 Div., 5 Corps, Potomac. May, 1863, 3 Brig., 2 Div., 5 Corps, Potomac. March, 1864, 4 Brig., 1 Div., 5 Corps, Potomac. April, 1864, 1 Brig., 1 Div., 5 Corps, Potomac, June, 1864, 1 Brig., 2 Div., 5 Corps, Potomac. June, 1864, 2 Brig., 2 Div., 5 Corps, Potomac. July, 1864, 2 Brig., 1 Div., 5 Corps, Potomac. Dec., 1864, 3 Brig., 1 Div., 5 Corps, Potomac. Mustered out June 2, 1865.

156th REGIMENT INFANTRY.—(Failed to organize.)

157th REGIMENT INFANTRY.—Org. at Phila. Oct., 1862, to Feby., 1863. Feby., 1863, Def Washington, 22 Corps. Dec., 1863, Unatt., Tyler's Div., 22 Corps. Jany., 1864, 1 Brig., Tyler's Div., 22 Corps. June, 1864, 2 Brig., 4 Div., 5 Corps, Potomac. Aug., 1864, 3 Brig., 2 Div., 5 Corps, Potomac. Transferred to 191st Pa. Infy., March 21, 1865.

158th REGIMENT INFANTRY.—Org. at Chambersburg Nov. 1, 1862. Dec., 1862, Spinola's Brig., Div. at Suffolk, Va., 7 Corps, Dept. Va. Jany., 1863, 1 Brig., 5 Div., 18 Corps, Dept. N. C. May, 1863, Dist. Pamlico, N. C., Dept. N. C. June, 1863, Spinola's Brig., 7 Corps, Dept. Va. July, 1863, Harper's Ferry, Va. Mustered out Aug. 12, 1865.

159th REGIMENT.—(See 14th Regt. Cav.)

160th REGIMENT.—(See 15th Regt. Cav.)

161st REGIMENT.—(See 16th Regt. Cav.)

162nd REGIMENT.—(See 17th Regt. Cav.)

163rd REGIMENT.—(See 18th Regt. Cav.)

164th REGIMENT.—(Failed to complete organization.)

165th REGIMENT INFANTRY.—Org. at Chambersburg and Gettysburg Nov. 25 to Dec. 5, 1862. Dec., 1862, Foster's Brig. Div. at Suffolk, Va., 7 Corps, Dept. Va. April, 1863, 2 Brig., 1 Div., 7 Corps, Dept. Va. Mustered out July 28, 1863.

166th REGIMENT INFANTRY.—Org. at York Oct. 24 to Dec. 8, 1862. Dec., 1862, Foster's Brig. Div. at Suffolk, 7 Corps, Dept. Va. April, 1863, 2 Brig., 1 Div., 7 Corps, Dept. Va. Mustered out July 28, 1863.

167th REGIMENT INFANTRY.—Org. at Reading Nov. 10 to Dec. 6, 1862. Dec., 1862, Foster's Brig. Div. at Suffolk, Va., 7 Corps, Dept. Va. April, 1863, 1 Brig., 1 Div., 7 Corps, Dept. Va. July, 1863, 1 Brig., 1 Div., 1 Corps, Potomac. Mustered out Aug. 12, 1863.

168th REGIMENT INFANTRY.—Org. at Pittsburg Oct. 16 to Dec. 1, 1862. Dec., 1862, Spinola's Brig. Div. at Suffolk, Va., 7 Corps, Dept. Va. Jany., 1863, 2 Brig., 5 Div., 18 Corps, Dept. N. C. May, 1863, Dist. Pamlico, Dept. N. C. June, 1863, Spinola's Brig., 7 Corps, Dept. Va. July, 1863, Harper's Ferry, W. Va. Mustered out July 25, 1863.

169th REGIMENT INFANTRY.—Org. at Pittsburg Oct. 16, 1862. Dec., 1862, Busteed's Indpt. Brig., 7 Corps, Dept. Va. April, 1863, King's Indpt. Brig., Yorktown, Va., 4 Corps. June, 1863, 1 Brig., 1 Div., 4 Corps. July, 1863, 1 Brig., 3 Div., 11 Corps, Potomac. Mustered out July 27, 1863.

170th REGIMENT INFANTRY.—(Failed to complete organization.)

171st REGIMENT INFANTRY.—Org. at Harrisburg Oct. and Nov., 1862. Dec., 1862, Spinola's Brig., Div. at Suffolk, Va., 7 Corps, Dept. Va. Jany., 1863, 1 Brig., 5 Div., 18 Corps, Dept. N. C. May, 1863, Dist. Pamlico, Dept. N. C. June, 1863, Spinola's Brig., 7 Corps, Dept. Va. July, 1863, Harper's Ferry, W. Va. Mustered out Aug. 8, 1863.

172nd REGIMENT INFANTRY.—Org. at Harrisburg Oct. 27, to Nov. 29, 1862. Dec., 1862, Unass'd. Yorktown, Va., 7 Corps, Dept. Va. April, 1863, West's Brig., 7 Corps, Dept. Va. May, 1863, West's Advance Brig., 4 Corps.

June, 1863, 3 Brig., 1 Div., 4 Corps. July, 1863, 1 Brig., 3 Div., 11 Corps, Potomac. Mustered out Aug. 1, 1863.

173rd REGIMENT INFANTRY.—Org. at Harrisburg Oct. and Nov., 1862. Dec., 1862, Norfolk, Va., 7 Corps, Dept. Va. July, 1863, 1 Brig., 2 Div., 11 Corps, Potomac. Mustered out Aug. 18, 1863.

174th REGIMENT INFANTRY.—Org. at Phila. Nov., 1862. Dec., 1862, Ferry's Brig., Div. at Suffolk, Va., 7 Corps, Dept. Va. Jany., 1863, 2 Brig., 3 Div., 18 Corps, Dept. N. C. Feby., 1863, 2 Brig., 2 Div., 18 Corps, Dept. South. Feby., 1863, Dist. Beaufort, S. C., 10 Corps, Dept. South. June, 1863, Dist. Hilton Head, S. C., Dept. South, 10 Corps. Mustered out Aug. 7, 1863.

175th REGIMENT INFANTRY.—Org. at Phila. Nov. 6, 1862. Dec., 1862, Gibb's Prov'l Brig., Div. at Suffolk, Va., 7 Corps, Dept. Va. Dec., 1862, Spinola's Brig., Div. at Suffolk, 7 Corps. Jany., 1863, 1 Brig., 5 Div., 18 Corps, Dept. N. C. May, 1863, Dist. Pamlico, Dept. N. C. June, 1863, 8 Corps, Middle Dept. July, 1863, 1 Brig., Md. Heights, Div. W. Va. Mustered out Aug. 7, 1863.

176th REGIMENT INFANTRY.—Org. at Phila. Nov. 3-11, 1862. Dec., 1862, Foster's Brig., Div. at Suffolk, Va., 7 Corps, Dept. Va. Dec., 1862, Ferry's Brig., Div. at Suffolk, 7 Corps. Jany., 1863, 1 Brig., 3 Div., 18 Corps, Dept. N. C. Feby., 1863, 3 Brig., 2 Div., 18 Corps, Dept. South. Feby., 1863, Dist. Beaufort, S. C., 10 Corps, Dept. South. June, 1863, Dist. Hilton Head, S. C., 10 Corps. Mustered out Aug. 19, 1863.

177th REGIMENT INFANTRY.—Org. at Harrisburg Dec. 12, 1862, to Jany. 8, 1863. Dec., 1862, Ferry's Prov'l Brig., Div. at Suffolk, 7 Corps, Dept. Va. March, 1863, Viele's Brig., Norfolk, Va., 7 Corps. July, 1863, 2 Brig., 2 Div., 12 Corps, Potomac. Mustered out Aug. 7, 1863.

178th REGIMENT INFANTRY.—Org. at Harrisburg Nov. 27, 1862. Dec., 1862, Busteed's Indpt. Brig., 7 Corps, Dept. Va. April, 1863, West's Indpt. Brig., 7 Corps. May, 1863, West's Advance Brig., 4 Corps. July, 1863, King's Div., 22 Corps. Mustered out Aug., 1863.

179th REGIMENT INFANTRY.—Org. at Phila. and Harrisburg Oct. 23, to Dec. 6, 1862. Dec., 1862, Busteed's Indpt. Brig., 7 Corps, Dept. Va. April, 1863, West's Indpt. Brig., 7 Corps. May, 1863, King's Indpt. Brig., 4 Corps. June, 1863, West's Advance Brig., 4 Corps. July, 1863, King's Div., 22 Corps. Mustered out July 27, 1863.

180th REGIMENT.—(See 19th REGIMENT CAVALRY.)

181st REGIMENT.—(See 20th REGIMENT CAVALRY.)

182nd REGIMENT.—(See 21st REGIMENT CAVALRY.)

183rd REGIMENT INFANTRY.—Org. at Phila. Dec. 24, 1863, to March 8, 1864. April, 1864, 1 Brig., 1 Div., 2 Corps, Potomac. March, 1865, 4 Brig., 1 Div., 2 Corps. Mustered out July 13, 1865.

184th REGIMENT INFANTRY.—Org. at Harrisburg May, 1864. May, 1864, 1 Brig., 2 Div., 2 Corps, Potomac. Mustered out July 14, 1865.

185th REGIMENT.—(See 22nd REGIMENT CAVALRY.)

186th REGIMENT INFANTRY.—Org. at Phila. Jany. 29 to May 31, 1864. Provost duty in Phila. Mustered out Aug. 15, 1865.

187th REGIMENT INFANTRY.—Org. at Phila. March 3, to May 4, 1864. May, 1864, 1 Brig., 1 Div., 5 Corps, Potomac. Sept., 1864, Phila., Pa. Mustered out Aug. 3, 1865.

188th REGIMENT INFANTRY.—Org. at Fort Monroe, Va., Dept. Va. & N. C. April 1, 1864, from surplus men of 3rd Pa. Heavy Arty. May, 1864, 3 Brig., 1 Div., 18 Corps, Army James, Dept. Va. & N. C. Dec., 1864, 3 Brig., 3 Div., 24 Corps. Aug. 1865, Dept. Va. Mustered out Dec., 14, 1865.

189th REGIMENT.—(Failed to complete organization.)

190th REGIMENT INFANTRY.—Org. in the field March and April, 1864, from Veterans and Recruits of the Reserve Corps. May, 1864, 3 Brig., 3 Div., 5 Corps,

Potomac. Aug., 1864, 1 Brig., 3 Div., 5 Corps, Potomac. Sept., 1864, 3 Brig., 2 Div., 5 Corps, Potomac. Mustered out June 28, 1865.

191st REGIMENT INFANTRY.—Org. in the field May 1864, from Veterans and Recruits of the 2nd, 5th, 6th, 8th, and 10th Res. Corps. May, 1864, 3 Brig., 3 Div., 5 Corps, Potomac. Aug., 1864, 1 Brig., 3 Div., 5 Corps, Potomac. Sept., 1864, 3 Brig., 2 Div., 5 Corps Potomac. Mustered out June 28, 1865.

192nd REGIMENT INFANTRY.—Org. at Harrisburg, July, 1864. July, 1864, Def. Balto., Md., 2 Separate Brig,. 5 Corps, Middle Dept. Aug., 1864, Gallipolis, Ohio, Northern Dept. Jany., 1865, Cincinnati, Ohio, Northern Dept. April, 1865, 2 Brig., 3 Div., Army Shenandoah. July, 1865, Sub-Dist. Harper's Ferry, W. A., Dept. W. Va. Mustered out Aug. 24, 1865.

193rd REGIMENT INFANTRY.—Org. at Pittsburg, July 19, 1864, for 100 days. July, 1864, 3 Separate Brig., 8 Corps, Middle Dept. Mustered out Nov. 19, 1864.

194th REGIMENT INFANTRY.—Org. at Harrisburg, July 17-24, 1864, for 100 days. July, 1864, 3 Separate Brig., 8 Corps, Middle Dept. Mustered out Nov. 6, 1864.

195th REGIMENT INFANTRY.—Org. at Harrisburg, July 24, 1864, for 100 days. July, 1864, 3 Separate Brig., 8 Corps, Middle Dept. Aug., 1864, 1 Separate Brig., 8 Corps. Mustered out Nov. 4, 1864.

195th REGIMENT INFANTRY.—Reorg. from 1st, 195th Infy. for 1 year, Oct. 3, 1864. Oct., 1864, Res. Div., W. Va. Jany., 1865, 1 Brig., 3 Infy. Div., W. Va. March, 1865, Cincinnati, Ohio, Northern Dept. April, 1865, 2 Brig., 3 Div., Army Shenandoah. July, 1865, Def. Washington, 22 Corps. Mustered out Jany. 31, 1866.

196th REGIMENT INFANTRY.—Org. at Phila. July 20, 1864, for 100 days. July, 1864, 3 Separate Brig., 8 Corps, Middle Dept. Aug., 1864, Camp Douglass, Ills. Mustered out Nov. 17, 1864.

197th REGIMENT INFANTRY.—Org. at Phila. July 22, 1864, for 100 days. July, 1864, 3 Separate Brig., 8 Corps, Middle Dept. Aug., 1864, Rock Island, Ills. Mustered out Nov. 11, 1864.

198th REGIMENT INFANTRY.—Org. at Phila. Sept. 2, to Oct. 27, 1864. Sept., 1864, 1 Brig., 1 Div., 5 Corps, Potomac. Mustered out June 4, 1865.

199th REGIMENT INFANTRY.—Org. at Phila. Sept. 2 to Nov. 30, 1864. Oct., 1864, 1 Brig., 1 Div., 10 Corps, Army James, Dept. Va. & N. C. Dec., 1864, 1 Brig., 1 Div., 24 Corps. Mustered out June 28, 1865.

200th REGIMENT INFANTRY.—Org. at Harrisburg, Aug. and Sept., 1864. Sept., 1864, Engineer Brig., Army Potomac. Oct., 1864, Prov'l Brig., Army James, Dept. Va. & N. C. Nov. 1864, Prov'l Brig., 9 Corps, Potomac. Dec., 1864, 1 Brig., 3 Div., 9 Corps, Potomac. Mustered out May 30, 1865.

201st REGIMENT INFANTRY.—Org. at Harrisburg, Aug. 24-29, 1864. Sept., 1864, Dept. Susquehanna. Oct., 1864, Dist. Alex. Def. Washington, 22 Corps. May, 1865, Fort Delaware. Mustered out June 21, 1865.

202nd REGIMENT INFANTRY.—Org. at Harrisburg, Aug. and Sept., 1864. Sept., 1864, Dept. Susquehanna. Oct., 1864, Dist. Alex. Def. Washington, 22 Corps. Nov., 1864, 1st Separate Brig., 22 Corps. May, 1865, Dept. Pa. Mustered out Aug. 3, 1865.

203rd REGIMENT INFANTRY.—Org. at Phila. and Harrisburg, Aug. and Sept., 1864. Sept., 1864, 2 Brig., 2 Div., 10 Corps, Army James, James Dept. Va. & N. C. Dec., 1864, 2 Brig., 2 Div., 24 Corps. Jany., 1865, 2 Brig., 2 Div., Terry's Prov'l Corps, Dept. N. C. March, 1865, 2 Brig., 2 Div., 10 Corps, Army Ohio, Dept. N. C. Mustered out June 22, 1865.

204th REGIMENT INFANTRY.—(See 5th Regt. Heavy Arty.)

205th REGIMENT INFANTRY.—Org. at Harrisburg, Aug. and Sept., 1864. Sept. 1864, Prov'l Brig., Def. Bermuda Hundred, Army James. Oct., 1864, Hartranf's Prov'l Brig., 9 Corps, Potomac. Dec., 1864, 2 Brig., 3 Div., 9 Corps, Potomac. Mustered out June 2, 1865.

206th REGIMENT INFANTRY.—Org. at Pittsburg, Sept., 1864. Sept., 1864, Prov'l Brig., Def. Bermuda Hundred, Va., Army James. Oct., 1864, 3 Brig.; 1 Div., 10 Corps. Dec., 1864, 3 Brig., 1 Div., 24 Corps. Mustered out June 26, 1865.

207th REGIMENT INFANTRY.—Org. at Harrisburg, Sept., 1864. Sept., 1864, Prov'l Div., Def. Bermuda Hundred, Va., Army James. Nov., 1864, Prov'l Brig., 9 Corps, Potomac. Dec., 1864, 2 Brig., 3 Div., 9 Corps, Potomac. Mustered out May 31, 1865.

208th REGIMENT INFANTRY.—Org. at Harrisburg, Aug. 16, to Sept. 13, 1864. Sept., 1864, Prov'l Brig., Def. Bermuda Hundred, Va., Army James. Nov., 1864, Prov'l Brig., 9 Corps, Potomac. Dec., 1864, 1 Brig., 3 Div., 9 Corps, Potomac. Mustered out June 1, 1865.

209th REGIMENT INFANTRY.—Org. at Harrisburg, Sept. 8-17, 1864. Sept., 1864, Prov'l Brig., Def. Bermuda Hundred, Va., Army James. Nov., 1864, Prov'l Brig., 9 Corps, Potomac. Dec., 1864 1 Brig., 3 Div., 9 Corps, Potomac. Mustered out May 21, 1865.

210th REGIMENT INFANTRY.—Org. at Harrisburg, Sept., 12-24, 1864. Oct., 1864, 3 Brig., 2 Div., 5 Corps, Potomac. Mustered out May 30, 1865.

211th REGIMENT INFANTRY.—Org. at Pittsburg, Sept., 1864. Sept., 1864, Prov'l Brig., Def. Bermuda Hundred, Va., Army James. Nov., 1864, Prov'l Brig., 9 Corps, Potomac. Dec., 1864, 2 Brig., 3 Div., 9 Corps, Potomac. Mustered out June 2, 1865.

212th REGIMENT.—(See 6th Regt. Heavy Arty.)

213th REGIMENT INFANTRY.—Org. at Phila. Feby. 4, to March 2, 1865. March, 1865, 5 Corps, Middle Dept. Mustered out Nov. 15, 1865.

214th REGIMENT INFANTRY.—Org. at Phila. March, 1865. April, 1865, 2 Brig., 3 Prov'l Div., Shenandoah. July, 1865, Def. Washington, 22 Corps. Mustered out March 21, 1866.

215th REGIMENT INFANTRY.—Org. at Phila., April, 1865. Duty in Delaware. Mustered out July 31, 1865.

COLLIS' INDEPENDENT COMPANY ZOUAVES DE AFRIQUE.—Org. at Phila., Aug. 17, 1861. Aug., 1861, Banks' Div., Shenandoah. Oct., 1861, Banks' Div., Potomac. March, 1862, Unatt., Banks' 5 Corps. March, 1862, Geary's Indpt. Brig., Shenandoah. April, 1862, 3 Brig., 1 Div., Dept. Shenandoah. June, 1862, Unatt., 2 Corps, Army Va. July, 1862, 3 Brig., 1 Div., 2 Corps, Army Va. Transferred to 114th Pa. Infy., Aug., 1862, as Co. A.

JAMES' COMPANY INFANTRY.—"WARREN COUNTY RIFLES." Org. at Warren, Aug. and Sept., 1862. Sept., 1862, Provost, Harrisburg, Pa. March, 1863, Provost, City Washington, 22 Corps. May, 1863, Provost, Alexandria, Va., 22 Corps. Mustered out July 20, 1865.

JONES' INDEPENDENT COMPANY INFANTRY.— Org. at Harrisburg, Oct. 2, 1862. Mustered out July 9, 1863.

GRIFFITH'S INDEPENDENT COMPANY INFANTRY.—Org. at Pittsburg, June and July, 1863. Mustered out Aug., 1863.

TANNER'S INDEPENDENT COMPANY INFANTRY. —Org. at Pittsburg, Aug. 30, 1864. Mustered out Dec. 10, 1864.

DEPARTMENTAL CORPS VOLUNTEER INFANTRY.—Org. in Dept. Monongahela, June 24 to Oct. 15, 1863. Mustered out July 21 to Nov. 1, 1864.

INDEPENDENT BATTALION MILITIA INFANTRY. —Org. at Huntingdon, July 18, 1863. Mustered out Aug. 8, 1863.

BALDWIN'S INDEPENDENT COMPANY MILITIA INFANTRY.—Org. at Garland, Aug. 9, 1862. Mustered out June 5, 1863.

GUTHRIE'S INDEPENDENT COMPANY MILITIA INFANTRY.—Org. at Pittsburg, Oct. 16, 1862. Mustered out July 23, 1863.

HUBBELL'S INDEPENDENT COMPANY MILITIA INFANTRY.—Org. at Phila., Nov. 14, 1862. Mustered out Aug. 15, 1863.

LUTHER'S INDEPENDENT COMPANY MILITIA INFANTRY.—Org. at Harrisburg, Oct., 1862, to Feby., 1863. Mustered out July, 1863.

HUFF'S INDEPENDENT COMPANY MILITIA INFANTRY.—Org. at Altoona, July 1, 1863. Mustered out Aug., 1863.

ROBERTS' INDEPENDENT COMPANY MILITIA INFANTRY.—Org. at West Chester, July 1, 1863. Mustered out July 8, 1863.

CAMPBELL'S INDEPENDENT COMPANY MILITIA INFANTRY.—Org. at Phila., July 2, 1863. Mustered out Sept. 16, 1863.

MITCHELL'S INDEPENDENT COMPANY MILITIA INFANTRY.—Org. at Harrisburg, July 18, 1863. Mustered out Sept. 2, 1863

HELMBOLD'S INDEPENDENT COMPANY MILITIA INFANTRY.—Org. at Harrisburg, July 18, 1863. Mustered out Sept. 7, 1863.

GREEN'S INDEPENDENT COMPANY MILITIA INFANTRY.—Org. at West Chester, July 6, 1863. Mustered out Sept. 3, 1863.

BEALE'S INDEPENDENT COMPANY MILITIA INFANTRY.—Org. at West Chester, July 6, 1863. Mustered out Sept. 4, 1863.

STEPHENS' INDEPENDENT COMPANY MILITIA INFANTRY.—Org. at Lancaster, July 2, 1863. Mustered out July 30, 1863.

RICH'S INDEPENDENT COMPANY MILITIA INFANTRY.—Org. at Phila., June 29, 1863. Mustered out July 8, 1863.

M'KNIGHT'S INDEPENDENT COMPANY MILITIA INFANTRY.—Org. at Phila., July 11, 1863. Mustered out Aug., 1863.

SPEAR'S INDEPENDENT COMPANY MILITIA INFANTRY.—Org. at Phila., June 17, 1863. Mustered out July 21, 1863.

GERMAN'S INDEPENDENT COMPANY MILITIA INFANTRY.—Org. at Phila., June 18, 1863. Mustered out July 23, 1863.

MANN'S INDEPENDENT COMPANY MILITIA INFANTRY.—Org. at Phila., June 17, 1863. Mustered out July 24, 1863.

RHODE ISLAND

1st REGIMENT CAVALRY.—Org. at Pawtucket, Dec. 14, 1861, to March 3, 1862. March, 1862, Stoneman's Cav. Command, Potomac. April, 1862, Hatch's Cav. Brig., Banks' 5 Corps, Dept. Shenandoah. May, 1862, Shield's Div., Dept. Rappahannock (3d Battalion), Geary's Command, Dept. Rappahannock (1 Battalion). June, 1862, Bayard's Cav. Brig., 3 Corps, Army Va. Sept., 1862, Stoneman's Corps of Observation. Dec., 1862, Averill's Cav. Brig., Centre Grand Div., Potomac. Feby., 1863, 1 Brig., 2 Div., Cav. Corps, Potomac. Jany., 1864, Cav. Brig., Camp Stoneman, 22 Corps. May, 1864, Abercrombie's Command, Belle Plains, Va. June, 1864, Res. Brig., 1 Cav. Div., Cav. Corps, Potomac. Aug., 1864, Headqrs. Cav. Corps, Army Shenandoah, Middle Mil. Div. Oct., 1864, 3 (Reserve) Brig., 1 Div., Cav. Corps, Army Shenandoah. March, 1865, Cav. Brig., Army Shenandoah. June, 1865, Cav. Brig., Middle Dept. Mustered out Aug. 3, 1865.

2nd REGIMENT CAVALRY.—Org. at Providence, Nov. 21, 1862. Jany., 1863, Unatt., 1 Div., 19 Corps, Dept. Gulf. July, 1863, Cav. Brig., 19 Corps. Transferred to 1st La. Cav., Aug. 24, 1864.

3rd REGIMENT CAVALRY.—Org. at Providence, Sept. 12, 1863. Jany., 1864, Def. New Orleans, Dept. Gulf. March, 1864, 5 Brig., Cav. Div., Dept. Gulf. June, 1864, Def. New Orleans. Oct., 1864, Dist LaFourche, Dept. Gulf. Mustered out Nov. 29, 1865.

7th SQUADRON CAVALRY.—Org. at Providence and mustered in June 24, 1862. June, 1862, Wadsworth's Command, Def. Washington, D. C. July, 1862, Sturgis, Command, Def. Washington, D. C. Aug., 1862, Winchester, Va. Sept., 1862, Miles' Command, Harper's Ferry, Va. Mustered out Sept. 26, 1862.

3rd REGIMENT HEAVY ARTILLERY.—Org. at Hilton Head, S. C., from 3rd R. I. Infy., Dec. 19, 1861. Co's L and M org. at Providence, March 17, 1862.

BATTERY "A."—Dec., 1861. Unatt., Sherman's S. C. Exp. Corps. April, 1862, 3 Brig., 1 Div., Dept. South. July, 1862, Dist. Hilton Head, S. C., Dept. South. Sept., 1862, Dist. Hilton Head, S. C., 10 Corps. Jany., 1863, Dist. Beaufort, S. C., 10 Corps. Nov., 1863, U. S. Forces, Morris Island, S. C., 10 Corps. Dec., 1863, Folly Island, S. C., 10 Corps. Jany., 1864, Dist. Hilton Head, S. C., 10 Corps. April, 1864, Dist. Fla., Dept. South. Oct., 1864, Dist. Beaufort, S. C., 2nd Separate Brig., Dept. South. Nov., 1864, Arty. Brig., Coast Div., Dept. South. Jany., 1865, Dist. Beaufort, S. C., Dept. South. May, 1865, Dept. S. C. Mustered out Aug. 27, 1865.

BATTERY "B."—Dec., 1861., Unatt., Sherman's S. C. Exp. Corps. April, 1862, 3 Brig., 1 Div., Dept. South. July, 1862, U. S. Forces. Hilton Head, S. C., Dept. South. Sept., 1862, Dist. Hilton Head, S. C., 10 Corps, Dept. South. July, 1863, Folly Island, S. C., 10 Corps. July, 1863, U. S. Forces, Morris Island, S. C., 10 Corps. April, 1864, Dist. Hilton Head, S. C., Dept. South. Oct., 1864, 1 Separate Brig., Northern Dist., Morris Island, S. C., Dept. South. Mustered out Aug. 27, 1865.

BATTERY "C."—Dec., 1862, Unatt., Sherman's S. C. Exp. Corps. April, 1862, 3 Brig., 1 Div., Dept. South. July, 1862, Dist. Hilton Head, S. C., Dept. South. Sept., 1862, Dist. Hilton Head, S. C., 10 Corps. Jany., 1863, U. S. Forces, Port Royal Island, S. C., 10 Corps. June, 1863, St. Helena Island, S. C., 10 Corps. June, 1863, 2 Brig., Folly Island, S. C., 10 Corps. July, 1863, U. S. Forces, Morris Island, S. C., 10 Corps. Oct., 1863, Gordon's Div., Folly Island, S. C., 10 Corps. Dec., 1863, Dist. Hilton Head, 10 Corps. Feby., 1864, Arty., Dist. Fla., Dept. South. April, 1864, Arty., 3 Div., 10 Corps, Dept. Va. and N. C. May, 1864, Unatt., Arty., 10 Corps. June, 1864, Arty., 1 Div., 10 Corps. Aug., 1864, Arty. Brig., 10 Corps. Dec., 1864, Arty. Brig., 25 Corps. Mustered out June 9, 1865.

BATTERY "D."—Dec., 1861, Unatt., Sherman's S. C. Exp. Corps. April, 1862, 3 Brig., 1 Div., Dept. South. July, 1862, Dist. Hilton Head, S. C., Dept. South. Sept., 1862, Dist. Hilton Head, S. C., 10 Corps. April, 1863, Folly Island, S. C., 10 Corps. July, 1863, Morris Island, S. C., 10 Corps. March, 1864, Fort Pulaski, Ga., Dist. Hilton Head, Dept. South. Oct., 1864, 1 Separate Brig., Morris Island, S. C., Northern Dist., Dept. South. Mustered out Aug. 27, 1865.

BATTERY "E."—Dec., 1861, Unatt., Sherman's S. C. Exp. Corps. April, 1862, 3 Brig., 1 Div., Dept. South. July, 1862, Dist. Hilton Head, S. C., Dept. South. Sept., 1862, Dist. Hilton Head, S. C., 10 Corps. Nov., 1863, Morris Island, S. C., 10 Corps. April, 1864, Morris Island, S. C., Northern Dist., Dept. South. Mustered out Oct. 4, 1864.

BATTERY "F."—Dec., 1861, Unatt., Sherman's S. C. Exp. Corps. April, 1862, 3 Brig., 1 Div., Dept. South. July, 1862, Dist. Hilton Head, S. C., Dept. South. Sept., 1862, Dist. Hilton Head, S. C., 10 Corps. Dec., 1863, Tybee Island, S. C., 10 Corps. April, 1864, Morris Island, S. C., Northern Dist., Dept. South. Mustered out Oct. 4, 1864.

BATTERY "G."—Dec., 1861, Unatt., Sherman's S. C. Exp. Corps. April, 1862, 3 Brig., 1 Div., Dept. South. May, 1862, Garrison Fort Pulaski, Ga., Dept. South, 10 Corps. April, 1864, Tybee Island, S. C., Dept. South. Mustered out Sept., 1864.

BATTERY "H."—Dec., 1861, Unatt., Sherman's S. C. Exp. Corps. April, 1862, 3 Brig., 1 Div., Dept. South. July, 1862, Dist. Hilton Head, S. C., Dept. South. Sept., 1862, Dist. Hilton Head, Dept. South, 10 Corps. April, 1864, Morris Island, S. C., Northern Dist., Dept. South. Mustered out Oct. 4, 1864.

BATTERY "I."—Dec., 1861, Unatt., Sherman's S. C. Exp. Corps. April, 1862, 3 Brig., 1 Div., Dept. South. July, 1862, Dist. Hilton Head, S. C., Dept. South. Sept., 1862, Dist. Hilton Head, Dept. South, 10 Corps. April, 1863, Folly Island, S. C., 10 Corps. July, 1863, Morris Island, S. C., 10 Corps. April, 1864, Morris Island, S. C., Northern Dist., Dept. South. Mustered out Oct. 4, 1864.

BATTERY "K."—Dec., 1861, Unatt., Sherman's S. C. Exp. Corps. April, 1862, 3 Brig., 1 Div., Dept. South. July, 1862, Dist. Hilton Head, S. C., Dept. South. Sept., 1862, Dist. Hilton Head, S. C., 10 Corps. Dec., 1863, Fort Pulaski, Ga., Dist. Hilton Head, S. C., 10 Corps, Dept. South. Mustered out Oct. 4, 1864.

BATTERY "L."—April, 1862, 2 Brig., 1 Div., Dept. South. July, 1862, Dist. Hilton Head, S. C., Dept. South. Sept., 1862, Dist. Hilton Head, S. C., 10 Corps. Dec., 1863, Fort Pulaski, Ga., Dist. Hilton Head, S. C., 10 Corps, Dept. South. Sept., 1864, Morris Island, S. C., 1 Separate Brig., Dept. South. Transferred to other Co's March 10, 1865.

BATTERY "M."—April, 1862, 3 Brig., 1 Div., Dept. South. July, 1862, Dist. Hilton Head, S. C., Dept. South. Sept., 1862, Dist. Hilton Head, S. C., 10 Corps. July, 1863, Folly Island, 10 Corps. July, 1863, Morris Island, S. C., 10 Corps. April, 1864, Morris Island, Northern Dist., Dept. South. Consolidated with other Co's March 10, 1865.

5th REGIMENT HEAVY ARTILLERY.—Org. July, 1863, from 5th Battalion R. I. Infy. July, 1863, Def. of Newberne, Dept. Va. and N. C. Jany., 1865, Sub Dist. Newberne, Dept. N. C. Mustered out June 26, 1865.

14th REGIMENT HEAVY ARTILLERY.—(COLORED). Org. at Providence, Aug. 28, 1863, to Jany. 25, 1864. Dec., 1863, Def. of New Orleans, Dept. Gulf (1 Battn.). Jany., 1864, Unatt., 13 Corps, Dept. Gulf (1 Battn.). Feby., 1864, Def. New Orleans, Dept. Gulf (2 Battn.). Designated 5th U. S. Colored Heavy Arty., April 4, 1864, and 11th U. S. Colored Heavy Arty., May 21, 1864.

1st BATTERY LIGHT ARTILLERY.—Org. at Providence, April, 1861, and mustered in at Washington, D. C., May 2, 1861. June, 1861, Hunter's Div., McDowell's Army, N. E. Va. June, 1861, Thomas' Brig., Patterson's Army. Mustered out Aug. 30, 1861.

BATTERY "A" 1st LIGHT ARTILLERY.—Org. at Providence and mustered in June 6, 1861. June, 1861, Burnside's Brig., Hunter's Div., McDowell's Army, N. E. Va. Aug., 1861, Dept. Shenandoah. Oct., 1861, Banks' Div., Army Potomac. March, 1862, Arty., 2 Div., 2 Corps, Army Potomac. June, 1863, Arty. Brig., 2 Corps, Potomac. Transferred to Batty. "B," Sept. 30, 1864.

BATTERY "B" 1st LIGHT ARTILLERY.—Org. at Providence and mustered in Aug. 13, 1861. Aug., 1861, Stone's Brig., Div. Potomac. Oct., 1861, Arty., Stone's (Sedgwick's) Div., Potomac. March, 1862, Arty., 2 Div., 2 Corps, Potomac. June, 1863, Arty. Brig., 2 Corps, Potomac. Mustered out June 13, 1865.

BATTERY "C" 1st LIGHT ARTILLERY.—Org. at Providence and mustered in Aug. 25, 1861. Sept., 1861, Porter's Div., Potomac. March, 1862, Arty., 1 Div., 3 Corps, Potomac. May, 1862, Arty., 1 Div., 5 Corps, Potomac. May, 1863, 3 Vol. Brig., Arty. Res., Potomac. June, 1863, Arty. Brig., 6 Corps, Potomac and Shenandoah. Nov., 1864, Camp Barry, 22 Corps. Consolidated with Battery "G," Dec. 22, 1864.

BATTERY "D" 1st LIGHT ARTILLERY.—Org. at Providence and mustered in Sept. 4, 1861. Oct., 1861, McDowell's Div., Potomac. March, 1862, Arty., 1 Div., 1 Corps, Potomac. April, 1862, Arty., 3 Div., Dept. Rappahannock. June, 1862, Arty., 3 Div., 3 Corps, Army Va. Sept., 1862, Arty., 1 Div., 1 Corps, Potomac. Oct., 1862, Arty., 1 Div., 9 Corps, Potomac. March, 1863, Arty., 2 Div., 9 Corps, Potomac. April, 1863, Arty., 2 Div., 9 Corps, Ohio. June, 1863, Unass'd, 1 Div., 23 Corps, Ohio. Aug., 1863, Arty. Res., 23 Corps, Ohio. Oct., 1863, Arty., 1 Div., 9 Corps, Ohio. April, 1864, Res. Arty., 9 Corps, Potomac. June, 1864, 1 Brig., Haskin's Div., Def. Washington, 22 Corps. Aug., 1864, Res. Arty., 19 Corps, Middle Mil. Dist. Dec., 1864, Arty. Brig., 19 Corps, Army Shenandoah. March, 1865, Arty. Res., Shenandoah. Mustered out July 17, 1865.

BATTERY "E" 1st LIGHT ARTILLERY.—Org. at Providence, Sept. 23, 1861. Oct., 1861, Heintzelman's Div., Potomac. March, 1862, Arty., 3 Div., 3 Corps, Potomac. Aug., 1862, Arty., 1 Div., 3 Corps, Potomac. June, 1863, Arty. Brig., 3 Corps. March, 1864, Arty. Brig., 6 Corps, Potomac. July, 1864, Arty. Res., Potomac. Dec., 1864, Arty. Brig., 6 Corps, Potomac. April, 1865, Arty. Res., Potomac. Mustered out June 14, 1865.

BATTERY "F," 1st LIGHT ARTILLERY.—Org. at Providence, Oct. 29, 1861. Dec., 1861, Unatt., Burnside's Exp. Corps. April, 1862, Unatt., Dept. N. C. Dec., 1862, Arty. Brig., Dept. N. C. Jany., 1863, Arty. Brig., 18 Corps, Dept. N. C. May, 1863, Def. Newberne, Dept. N. C. Nov., 1863, Dist. St. Mary's, Dept. W. Va. and N. C. Jany., 1864, U. S. Forces, Yorktown, Va., Dept. Va. and N. C. April, 1864, Arty., 2 Div., 18 Corps, Dept. Va. and N. C. June, 1864, Arty. Brig., 18 Corps. Dec., 1864, Arty. Brig., 24 Corps. Mustered out June 27, 1865.

BATTERY "G" 1st LIGHT ARTILLERY.—Org. at Providence, Dec., 1861. Dec., 1861, Arty., Sedgwick's Div., Potomac. March, 1862, Arty. Res., 2 Corps, Potomac. Oct., 1862, Arty., 3 Div., 2 Corps, Potomac. May, 1863, 4 Vol. Brig., Arty. Res., Potomac. July, 1863, Arty. Brig., 6 Corps, Potomac and Shenandoah. Nov., 1864, Camp Barry, 22 Corps. Dec., 1864, Arty. Brig., 6 Corps, Potomac. Mustered out June 24, 1865.

BATTERY "H" 1st LIGHT ARTILLERY.—Org. at Providence, Oct. 14, 1862. Oct., 1862, Camp Barry, Def. Washington, D. C. Oct., 1862, Stannard's 2 Brig., Casey's Div., Def. Washington. Feby., 1863, Arty., Casey's Div., 22 Corps. April, 1863, Arty., Abercrombie's Div., 22 Corps. May, 1863, 3 Brig., DeRussy's Div., 22 Corps. Nov., 1863, Camp Barry, 22 Corps. April, 1864, Arty., 1 Div., 9 Corps, Potomac. May, 1864, Res. Arty., 9 Corps, Potomac. June, 1864, 2 Brig., DeRussy's Div., 22 Corps. July, 1864, 1 Brig., DeRussy's Div., 22 Corps. Oct., 1864, City Point, Va., Dept. Va. and N. C. Dec., 1864, Arty. Res., Potomac. Mustered out June 28, 1865.

10th BATTERY LIGHT ARTILLERY.—Org. at Providence, May, 1862. May, 1862, Whipple's Command, Def. Washington, D. C. Mustered out Aug. 30, 1862.

1st REGIMENT INFANTRY.—Org. in R. I., April, 1861, and mustered in at Washington, D. C., May 2, 1861. June, 1861, Burnside's Brig., Hunter's Div., McDowell's Army of N. E. Va. Mustered out Aug. 2, 1861.

2nd REGIMENT INFANTRY.—Org. at Providence, June, 1861. June, 1861, Burnside's Brig., Hunter's Div., McDowell's Army of N. E. Va. Aug., 1861, Couch's Brig., Div. Potomac. Oct., 1861, Couch's Brig., Buell's Div., Potomac. March, 1862, 1 Brig., 1 Div., 4 Corps, Potomac. Sept., 1862, 1 Brig., 1 Div., 6 Corps, Potomac. Oct., 1862, 2 Brig., 3 Div., 6 Corps, Potomac. March, 1864, 4 Brig., 2 Div., 6 Corps. July, 1864, 3 Brig., 1 Div., 6 Corps, Potomac and Shenandoah. Mustered out July 13, 1865.

3rd REGIMENT INFANTRY.—Org. at Providence, Aug., 1861. Sept., 1861, Fort Hamilton, N. Y. Harbor. Nov., 1861, Unatt., Sherman's S. C. Exp. Corps. Designation changed to 3rd Heavy Arty., Dec. 19, 1861.

4th REGIMENT INFANTRY.—Org. at Providence and mustered in at Washington, D. C., Oct. 30, 1861. Nov., 1861, Casey's Prov'l Div., Potomac. Nov., 1861, Howard's Brig., Sumner's Div., Potomac. Dec., 1861, Parke's 3 Brig., Burnside's N. C. Exp. Corps. April, 1862, 1 Brig., 3 Div., Dept. N. C. July, 1862, 2 Brig., 3 Div., 9 Corps, Potomac. Jany., 1863, 3 Brig., 3 Div., 9 Corps, Potomac. April, 1863, 3 Brig., 2 Div., 7 Corps, Dept. Va. July, 1863, 3 Brig., Getty's Div., Portsmouth, Va., Dept. Va. and N. C. Jany., 1864, 3 Brig., Heckman's Div., Portsmouth, Va. March, 1864, Norfolk, Va. April, 1864, Point Lookout, Md. District, St. Mary's. July, 1864, 1 Brig., 2 Div., 9 Corps, Potomac. Mustered out Oct. 15, 1864.

5th REGIMENT INFANTRY.—Org. at Providence, Dec. 27, 1861. Dec., 1861, Parkes' 3 Brig., Burnside's N. C. Exp. Corps. April, 1862, 1 Brig., 3 Div., Dept. N. C. July, 1862, 2 Brig., 1 Div., Dept. N. C. Jany., 1863, 2 Brig., 4 Div., 18 Corps, Dept. N. C. May, 1863, Lee's Brig., Def. Newberne, Dept. N. C. Designation changed to 5th Heavy Arty., July, 1863.

6th REGIMENT INFANTRY.—(Failed to complete organization).

7th REGIMENT INFANTRY.—Org. at Providence, Sept. 4, 1862. Oct., 1862, 2 Brig., Casey's Div., Def. Washington, D. C. Oct., 1862, 1 Brig., 2 Div., 9 Corps, Potomac. April, 1863, 1 Brig., 2 Div., 9 Corps, Ohio. June, 1863, 1 Brig., 2 Div., 9 Corps, Tenn. Sept., 1863, Dist. N. C., Ky., 1 Div., 23 Corps, Ohio. April, 1864, 1

Brig., 2 Div., 9 Corps, Potomac. May, 1864, Acting Engrs., 2 Div., 9 Corps, Potomac. Jany., 1865, 1 Brig., 2 Div., 9 Corps, Potomac. Mustered out July 13, 1865.

8th REGIMENT INFANTRY.—(Failed to complete organization).

9th REGIMENT INFANTRY.—Org. at Providence, May 26, 1862. June, 1862, Sturgis' Brig., Def. Washington, D. C. Mustered out Sept. 2, 1862.

10th REGIMENT INFANTRY.—Org. at Providence, May 26, 1862. June, 1862, Sturgis' Brig., Def. Washington, D. C. Mustered out Sept. 1, 1862.

11th REGIMENT INFANTRY.—Org. at Providence and mustered in Oct. 1, 1862. Oct., 1862, Def. Washington, D. C. Dec., 1862, Dist. Alexandria, Def. Washington. Feby., 1863, Dist. Alexandria, Def. Washington, 22 Corps. April, 1863, 1 Brig., 1 Div., 7 Corps, Dept. Va. June, 1863, 2 Brig., 1 Div., 4 Corps, Dept. Va. Mustered out July 13, 1863.

12th REGIMENT INFANTRY.—Org. at Providence and mustered in Oct. 13, 1862. Oct., 1862, 1 Brig., Casey's Div., Def. Washington, D. C. Dec., 1862, 1 Brig., 2 Div., 9 Corps, Potomac. April, 1863, 1 Brig., 2 Div., 9 Corps, Ohio. May, 1863, 1 Brig., 1 Div., 23 Corps, Ohio. Mustered out July 29, 1863.

INDEPENDENT COMPANY HOSPITAL GUARDS.—Org. at Portsmouth Grove, Dec. 6, 1862. Mustered out Aug. 26, 1865.

SOUTH CAROLINA

1st REGIMENT INFANTRY.—(AFRICAN DESCENT). Org. at Beaufort, S. C., Jany. 31, 1863. Jany., 1863, Dist. Beaufort, S. C., 10 Corps, Dept. South. Jany., 1864, Barton's Brig., Dist. Hilton Head, S. C., 10 Corps. Designation changed to 33rd U. S. C. T., Feby. 8, 1864, which see.

2nd REGIMENT INFANTRY.—(AFRICAN DESCENT). Org. at Beaufort, S. C., and Hilton Head, S. C., May 22, 1863. May, 1863, Dists. of Hilton Head and Beaufort, S. C. July, 1863, 3 Brig., 1 Div., Morris Island, S. C., 10 Corps. July, 1863, 2 Brig., Morris Island, S. C., 10 Corps. Aug., 1863, 4 Brig., Morris Island, S. C., 10 Corps. Nov., 1863, 3 Brig., Morris Island, S. C., 10 Corps. Jany., 1864, Montgomery's Brig., Dist. Hilton Head, S. C., 10 Corps. Feby., 1864, 3 Brig., Vodge's Div., Dist. Fla. Designation changed to 34th U. S. C. T., Feby. 8, 1864, which see.

3rd REGIMENT INFANTRY.—(AFRICAN DESCENT). Org. at Hilton Head, S. C., June, 1863. June, 1863, Dist. of Hilton Head, S. C., 10 Corps, Dept. South. Jany., 1864, Barton's Brig., Dist. Hilton Head, S. C., 10 Corps. Feby., 1864, 3 Brig., Vodge's Div., Dist. Fla. Designation changed to 21st U. S. C. T. after consolidation with 4th S. C., March 14, 1864.

4th REGIMENT INFANTRY.—(AFRICAN DESCENT). Org. at Fernandina, Fla., July, 1863. July, 1863, Fernandina, Fla., Dept. South. Jan., 1864, Barton's Brig., Dist. Hilton Head, S. C., 10 Corps. Feby., 1864, 3 Brig., Vodge's Div., Dist. Fla., Dept. South. Consolidated with 3rd S. C. and designated 21st U. S. C. T,. March 14, 1864.

5th REGIMENT INFANTRY.—(AFRICAN DESCENT). (Failed to complete organization and transferred to 3rd and 4th South Carolina Infy.)

TENNESSEE

1st REGIMENT CAVALRY.—Org. at Camp Dennison, Ohio, Nov., 1862, from 4th Tenn. Infy. Dec., 1862, Res. Brig., Cav. Div., Cumberland. Jan., 1863, 1 Brig., 1 Div., Cav. Corps, Cumb'd. Nov., 1864, 1 Brig., 1 Div., Cav. Corps, Mil. Div. Miss. Jany., 1865, Dist. Middle Tenn., Dept. Cumb'd. Mustered out June, 1865.

1st MIDDLE TENNESSEE CAVALRY.—(See 5th Cav.).

1st WEST TENNESSEE CAVALRY.—(See 6th Cav.).

2nd REGIMENT CAVALRY.—Org. at Murfreesboro, Tenn., July, 1862. July, 1862, 7 Div., Army Ohio. Oct., 1862, Dist. West. Va., Dept. Ohio. Nov., 1862, Unatt., Cav. Div., 14 Corps, Army Cumb'd. Nov., 1862, Res. Cav. Brig., Cav. Div., Cumb'd. March, 1863, 2 Brig., 1 Cav. Div., Cav. Corps, Cumb'd. Jany., 1864, 3 Brig., Cav. Div., 16 Corps, Tenn. April, 1864, 1 Brig., 4 Div., Cav. Corps, Cumb'd. June, 1864, Dist. North Ala., Dept. Cumb'd. Oct., 1864, 1 Brig., 4 Div., Cav. Corps, Mil. Div. Miss. Nov., 1864, 1 Brig., 7 Div., Cav. Corps, Mil. Div. Miss. March, 1865, Dept. Miss. May, 1865, Dept. Cumb'd. Mustered out July 6, 1865.

2nd WEST TENNESSEE CAVALRY.—(See 7th Cav.).

3rd REGIMENT CAVALRY.—Org. at Murfreesboro and Nashville, Tenn., Jany 27, 1863. Nov., 1862, 4 Div., Centre, 14 Corps, Cumb'd. Jany., 1863, Post Nashville, Tenn., Dept. Cumb'd. June, 1863, 2 Brig., 1 Div., Cav. Corps, Cumb'd. Aug., 1863, Post Nashville, Tenn., Dept. Cumb'd. Jany., 1864, 3 Brig., Cav. Div., 16 Corps, Tenn. April, 1864, 1 Brig., 4 Div., Cav. Corps, Cumb'd. June, 1864, Dist. North Ala., Dept. Cumb'd. Oct., 1864, 1 Brig., 4 Div., Cav. Corps, Mil. Div. Miss. Nov., 1864, 2 Brig., 6 Div., Cav. Corps, Mil. Div. Miss. and Dist. Middle Tenn., Dept. Cumb'd. Mustered out Aug. 3, 1865.

4th REGIMENT CAVALRY.—Org. at Nashville, Tenn., Feby. 9, 1863. Feby., 1863, Post Nashville, Tenn., Dept. Cumb'd. Jany., 1864, 3 Brig., Cav. Div., 16 Corps, Tenn. April, 1864, 1 Brig., 4 Div., Cav. Corps, Cumb'd. June, 1864, Dists. of Nashville, Tenn., and North Ala., Dept. Cumb'd. Oct., 1864, 1 Brig., 4 Div., Cav. Corps, Mil. Div. Miss. Dec., 1864, 1 Brig., 7 Div., Cav. Corps, Mil. Div. Miss. Feby., 1865, 2 Brig., 7 Div., Cav. Corps, Mil. Div. Miss. Feby., 1865, 2 Brig., 1 Div., Cav. Corps, Mil. Div. West Miss. March, 1865, 1 Brig., 2 Cav. Div., West Miss. Mustered out July 12, 1865.

5th REGIMENT CAVALRY.—(1st MIDDLE TENN. CAVALRY). Org. at Murfreesboro, Nashville and Carthage, Tenn., July 15, 1862. July, 1862, Post Nashville, Tenn., Dept. Ohio. Nov., 1862, Res. Cavalry, Cav. Div., Cumb'd. Jany., 1863, Post Nashville Tenn., Cumb'd. June, 1863, Post Nashville, Tenn., Res. Corps, Cumb'd. June, 1863, 1 Brig., 2 Div., Cav. Corps, Cumb'd. Aug., 1863, 3 Brig., 2 Div., Cav. Corps, Cumb'd. Nov., 1863, 1 Brig., 2 Div., Cav. Corps, Cumb'd. April, 1864, 2 Brig., 4 Div., Cav. Corps, Mil. Div. Miss. Nov., 1864, 3 Brig., 6 Div., Cav. Corps, Mil. Div. Miss. Feby., 1865, Dist. Middle Tenn., Dept. Cumb'd. Mustered out Aug. 14, 1865.

5th REGIMENT EAST TENNESSEE CAVALRY.—Org. at Camp Nelson, Ky. (5 Co's) for 10th Tenn. Cav. June 30 to Aug. 14, 1863. June, 1863, Dist. Central Ky., Dept. Ohio. July, 1863, 3 Brig., 3 Div., 23 Corps, Dept. Ohio. July 1863, 2 Brig., 4 Div., 23 Corps. July, 1863, 2 Brig., 1 Div., 23 Corps. Assigned to 8th Tenn. Cav., Aug., 1863, which see.

6th REGIMENT CAVALRY.—(1st MIDDLE TENN. CAVALRY). Org. at Bethel, LaGrange, Bolivar, Trenton, etc., Tenn., Aug. 11, 1862. Aug., 1862, Dist. Jackson, Tenn., Dept. Tenn. Nov., 1862, Dist. Jackson, Tenn., 13 Corps, Dept. Tenn. Dec., 1862, Cav. Brig., Dist. Jackson, Tenn., 16 Corps. March, 1863, Cav. Brig., 3 Div., 16 Corps. June, 1863, 2 Brig., 1 Cav. Div., 16 Corps. Dec., 1863, 1 Brig., 1 Cav. Div., 16 Corps. June, 1864, Unass'd, Dist. West Tenn., Dept. Tenn. Nov., 1864, 2 Brig., 4 Div., Cav. Corps, Mil. Div. Miss. Dec., 1864, 2 Brig., 7 Div., Cav. Corps, Mil Div. Miss. Feby., 1865, 1 Brig., 6 Div., Cav. Corps, Mill. Div. Miss. and Dist. Middle Tenn. Mustered out July 26, 1865.

7th REGIMENT CAVALRY.—(2nd WEST TENN. CAVALRY). Org. at Jackson, Grand Junction and Trenton, Tenn., Aug. 28, 1862. Aug., 1862, Dist. Jackson, Tenn., Dept. Tenn. Nov., 1862, Dist. Jackson, Tenn., 13 Corps, Dept. Tenn. Dec., 1862, Cav. Brig., Dist. Jackson, 16 Corps. April, 1863, Unass'd, 1 Div., 16 Corps. June, 1863, 4 Brig., 1 Cav. Div., 16 Corps. Aug., 1863, Dist. Columbus, Ky., 6 Div., 16 Corps. Oct., 1863, Detached Cav. Brig., 16 Corps. Dec., 1863, Waring's Cav. Brig., 16 Corps. Jany., 1864, Dist. Columbus, Ky. Mustered out Aug. 9, 1865.

8th REGIMENT CAVALRY.—(5th EAST TENN CAVALRY). Org. Aug., 1863, by consolidation of 5 Co's org. at Camp Nelson, Ky., June 30 to Aug. 14, 1863, for 10th Tenn. Cav. and 7 Co's org. in Tenn. at large, for 5th East Tenn. Cav. Aug., 1863, 2 Brig., 4 Div., 23 Corps, Dept. Ohio. Oct., 1863, 4 Brig., 4 Div., 23 Corps. April, 1864, 3 Brig., 4 Div., Cav. Corps Cumb'd. Oct., 1864, 3 Brig., 4 Div., Cav. Corps, Mil. Div. Miss. Nov., 1864, Dist. East Tenn., Dept. Cumb'd. March, 1865, 3 Brig., Cav. Div., Dist. East Tenn. July, 1865, Cav. Brig., Dist. East Tenn. Mustered out Sept. 11, 1865.

9th REGIMENT CAVALRY.—Org. at Knoxville, Aug. 13, 1863. Sept., 1863, Dist. North Central Ky., Dept. Ohio. April, 1864, 3 Brig., 4 Div., Cav. Corps, Cumb'd. Oct., 1864, 3 Brig., 4 Div., Cav. Corps, Mil. Div. Miss. Nov., 1864, Dist. East Tenn., Dept. Cumb'd. March, 1865, 3 Brig., Cav. Div., Dist. East Tenn., Dept. Cumb'd. July, 1865, Cav. Brig., Dist. East Tenn. Mustered out Sept. 11, 1865.

10th REGIMENT CAVALRY.—Org. at Nashville, Tenn., Aug. 25, 1863. Sept., 1863, Dist. North Central Ky., Dept. Ohio. Jany., 1864, Def. Nashville and Northwestern R. R., Dept. Cumb'd. April, 1864, 2 Brig., 4 Div., Cav. Corps, Cumb'd. Oct., 1864, 2 Brig., 4 Div., Cav. Corps, Mil. Div. Miss. Nov., 1864, 1 Brig., 5 Div., Cav. Corps, Mil. Div. Miss. Feby., 1865, 1 Brig., 7 Div., Cav. Corps, Mil. Div. Miss. March, 1865, Dept. Miss. May, 1865, Dept. Cumb'd. Mustered out Aug. 1, 1865.

11th REGIMENT CAVALRY.—Org. at large, May to Oct., 1863. Aug., 1863, Willcox's Div. Left Wing Forces, 23 Corps, Dept. Ohio. Jany., 1864, Dist. Clinch, Dept. Ohio. April, 1864, 1 Brig., 4 Div., 23 Corps. Consolidated with 9th Tenn. Cav., Jan. 9, 1865.

12th REGIMENT CAVALRY.—Org. at Nashville, Tenn., Aug. 24, 1863. Aug., 1863, Dist. Nashville, Tenn., Dept. Cumb'd. Jany., 1864, Def. Nashville and Northwestern R. R., Dept. Cumb'd. April, 1864, 2 Brig., 4 Div., Cav. Corps, Cumb'd. Oct., 1864, 2 Brig., 4 Div., Cav. Corps, Mil. Div. Miss. Dec., 1864, 2 Brig., 5 Div., Cav. Corps, Mil. Div. Miss. Feby., 1865, 1 Brig., 5 Div., Cav. Corps. Mil. Div. Miss. May, 1865, Dept. Mo. Mustered out October 7, 1865.

13th REGIMENT CAVALRY.—Org. at Strawberry Plains, Nashville and Gallatin, Tenn., Oct., 1863. Oct., 1863, Dist. Columbus, Ky., 6 Div., 16 Corps, Dept. Tenn. Nov., 1863, Dist. North Central Ky., Dept. Ohio. Jany., 1864, Dist. Nashville, Tenn., Dept. Cumb'd. April, 1864, 3 Brig., 4 Div., Cav. Corps, Cumb'd. Oct., 1864, 3 Brig., 4 Div., Cav. Corps, Mil. Div. Miss. Nov., 1864, Dist. East Tenn., Dept. Cumb'd. March, 1865, 3 Brig., Cav. Div., Dist. East Tenn., Dept. Cumb'd. July, 1865, Cav. Brig., Dist. East Tenn. Mustered out Sept. 5, 1865.

14th REGIMENT CAVALRY.—(Failed to complete organization. Those enlisted on duty Def. Nashville and Northwestern R. R., Dept. Cumb'd.)

BRADFORD'S BATTALION CAVALRY.—Org. Dec., 1863, at Paducah, Ky., Dist. Cairo, Dept. Tenn., to Feby., 1864, at Fort Pillow, Tenn., to April, 1864. Consolidated to a Co., April, 1864, and assigned to 14th Tenn. Cav. as Co. A; then to 6th Tenn. Cav. as Co. E.

1st TENNESSEE AND ALABAMA VIDETTE CAVALRY.—Org. (Co's A, B, C, G and H) at Stevenson and Bridgeport, Ala., Sept. 10, 1863, to April 26, 1864, (Co's D, E, and F) at Tracy City and Nashville, Tenn., Dec. 9, 1863, to Feby. 24, 1864. Mustered out June 16, 1864.

1st REGIMENT HEAVY ARTILLERY.—(AFRICAN DESCENT). Org. at Memphis, Tenn., June, 1863. June, 1863, 1 Brig., 5 Div., Dist. Memphis, Tenn., 16 Corps, Dept. Tenn. April, 1864, designation changed to 3rd U. S. C. Heavy Arty., April 26, 1864, which see.

2nd REGIMENT HEAVY ARTILLERY.—(AFRICAN DESCENT). Org. at Columbus, Ky., June, 1863. June, 1863, Dist. Columbus, Ky., 6 Div., 16 Corps, Dept. Tenn. Designation changed to 4th U. S. Colored Heavy Arty., April 26, 1864, which see.

1st BATTALION LIGHT ARTILLERY.—Org. at Memphis, Nashville and Knoxville, Tenn., July 13, 1862, to Oct. 16, 1863.

BATTERY "A" LIGHT ARTILLERY.—Aug., 1862, Post Nashville, Tenn., Dept. Ohio. Nov., 1862, Post Clarksville, Tenn., Dist. Western Ky., Dept. Ohio. April,

1863, Post Clarksville, Dist. Central Ky., Dept. Ohio. June, 1863, 1 Brig., 1 Div., Res. Corps, Cumb'd. June, 1863, 1 Brig., 3 Div., Res. Corps, Cumb'd. Aug., 1863, 3 Brig., 3 Div., Res. Corps, Cumb'd. Aug., 1863, 3 Brig., 4 Div., 23 Corps, Ohio. Nov., 1863, 2 Div., Arty. Res., Cumb'd. March, 1864, Garrison, Decatur, Ala., Dist. Northern Ala., Dept. Cumb'd. April, 1864, Arty., 4 Div., Cav. Corps, Cumb'd. Oct., 1864, Arty., 6 Div., Cav. Corps, Mil. Div. Miss. March, 1865, Dist. Middle Tenn., Dept. Cumb'd. Mustered out July, 1865.

BATTERY "B" LIGHT ARTILLERY.—Dist. Ky., Dept. Ohio. Aug., 1863, Willcox's Div., Left Wing Forces, 23 Corps, Ohio. Jany., 1864, Dist. Clinch, Dept. Ohio. April, 1864, 1 Brig., 4 Div., 23 Corps, Ohio. Feby., 1865, 1 Brig., 4 Div., Dist. East Tenn., Dept. Cumb'd. March, 1865, 2 Brig., 4 Div., Dist. East Tenn. Mustered out July, 1865.

BATTERY "C" LIGHT ARTILLERY.—Att. to Def. Memphis, Tenn., Fort Pickering, 16 Corps, Dept. Tenn. March, 1864, Post and Dist. Nashville, Tenn., Dept. Cumb'd. March, 1865, Arty., 3rd Sub Dist., Dist. Middle Tenn. Mustered out July, 1865.

BATTERY "D" LIGHT ARTILLERY.—Att. to Post and Dist. Nashville, Tenn., to March, 1865, 3 Brig., 4 Div., Dist. East Tenn., Dept. Cumb'd. Mustered out July, 1865.

BATTERY "E" LIGHT ARTILLERY.—Att. to Dist. North Central Ky., 1 Div., 23 Corps, Dept. Ohio. Oct., 1863, to April, 1864, Dist. Nashville, Tenn., Dept. Cumb'd, to May, 1865, 1 Brig., 4 Div., Dist. East Tenn., Dept. Cumb'd. Mustered out July, 1865.

BATTERY "F" LIGHT ARTILLERY.—Att. to 1 Brig., 4 Div., 23 Corps, Dept. Ohio, and duty in Dist. East Tenn., entire term. Mustered out July, 1865.

BATTERY "G" LIGHT ARTILLERY.—Duty at Nashville and Bull's Gap, Tenn., entire term. Att. to Governor's Guard. Mustered out July, 1865.

BATTERY "K" LIGHT ARTILLERY.—Garrison duty at Knoxville, Tenn. Mustered out July, 1865.

MEMPHIS LIGHT BATTERY.—(AFRICAN DESCENT). Org. at Memphis, Tenn., Nov. 23, 1863, Dist. Memphis, Tenn., 5 Div., 16 Corps, Dept. Tenn. Jany., 1864, 1 Colored Brig., Dist. Memphis, Tenn., 16 Corps. Designation of Batty. changed to Batty. "F" 2nd U. S. Colored Light Arty., April 26, 1864, which see.

1st REGIMENT INFANTRY.—Org. at Camp Dick Robinson, Ky., Aug.-Sept., 1861. Oct., 1861, Thomas' Command, Dept. Ohio. Nov., 1861, 12 Brig., Army Ohio. Dec., 1861, 12 Brig., 1 Div., Army Ohio. Feby., 1862, 24 Brig., 7 Div., Army Ohio. Oct., 1862, 3 Brig., Cumb'd Div., Dist. West Va., Dept. Ohio. Nov., 1862, 1 Brig., 2 Div., Centre, 14 Corps, Cumb'd. Jany., 1863, 1 Brig., 2 Div., 14 Corps. April, 1863, Dist. Central Ky., Dept. Ohio. June, 1863, 1 Brig., 1 Div., 23 Corps, Army Ohio. Aug., 1863, 1 Brig., 4 Div., 23 Corps. Oct., 1863, 2 Brig., 4 Div., 23 Corps. Nov., 1863, 2 Brig., 1 Div., Cav. Corps, Dept. Ohio. April, 1864, 3 Brig., 4 Div., 23 Corps. May, 1864, 3 Brig., 3 Div., 23 Corps. Aug., 1864, 2 Brig., 4 Div., 23 Corps. Feby., 1865, 2 Brig., 4 Div., Dist. East Tenn., Cumb'd. Mustered out Aug. 8, 1865.

1st REGIMENT MOUNTED INFANTRY.—Org. at Nashville and Carthage, Tenn., Dec., 1863, to Nov., 1864. Att. to Dist. Middle Tenn., Dept. Cumb'd, to Feby., 1865, 1 Brig., 1st Sub Dist., Dist Middle Tenn. Mustered out July 22, 1865.

1st REGIMENT INFANTRY.—(AFRICAN DESCENT). Org. at LaGrange, Tenn., June 6, 1863, and mustered in June 27, 1863. June, 1863, Dist. Corinth, 2 Div., 16 Corps, Dept. Tenn. Nov., 1863, Post Corinth, Miss., 16 Corps. Jany., 1864, 1 Colored Brig., Dist. Memphis, Tenn., 5 Div., 16 Corps. Designation changed to 59th U. S. C. T., March 11, 1864, which see.

1st REGIMENT ENROLLED MILITIA INFANTRY.—Org. at Memphis, Tenn., for the defense of that city.

2nd REGIMENT INFANTRY.—Org. at Camp Dick Robinson and Somerset, Ky., Sept. 28, 1861. Oct., 1861, Thomas' Command, Army Ohio. Nov., 1861, 12 Brig., Army Ohio. Dec., 1861, 12 Brig., 1 Div., Army Ohio. Feby., 1862, 24 Brig., 7 Div., Army Ohio. Oct., 1862, 3 Brig., Cumb'd Div., Dist. W. Va., Dept. Ohio. Nov.,

1862, 1 Brig., 2 Div., Centre 14th Corps, Cumb'd. Jany., 1863, 1 Brig., 2 Div., 14 Corps. April, 1863, 2 Brig., Dist. Central Ky., Dept. Ohio. June, 1863, 1 Brig., 1 Div., 23 Corps, Army Ohio. Aug., 1863, 3 Brig., 4 Div., 23 Corps. Nov., 1863, 1 Brig., 2 Div., Cav. Corps, Dept. Ohio. April, 1864, 2 Brig., 4 Div., 23 Corps. Feby., 1865, 2 Brig., 4 Div., Dist. East Tenn., Cumb'd. Mustered out Aug. 3, 1865.

2nd REGIMENT MOUNTED INFANTRY.—Org. at Nashville, Clifton and Franklin, Tenn., Oct. 2, 1863, to April 10, 1864. Att. to Def. Nashville and Chattanooga R. R., Dept. Cumb'd, to March, 1865, 2 Brig., Dist. East Tenn., Cumb'd, to June, 1865. Mustered out June 27, 1865.

2nd REGIMENT INFANTRY.—(AFRICAN DESCENT). Org. at LaGrange, Tenn., June 30, 1863. June, 1863, 1 Brig., 2 Div., 16 Corps, Dept. Tenn. Nov., 1863, Post Corinth, Miss., 2 Div., 16 Corps. Jany., 1864, 1 Colored Brig., Dist. Memphis, Tenn., 5 Div., 16 Corps. Designation of Regt. changed to 61st U. S. C. T., March 11, 1864, which see.

2nd REGIMENT ENROLLED MILITIA.—Org. at Memphis, Tenn., for the protection of that city.

3rd REGIMENT INFANTRY.—Org. at Flat Lick, Ky., Dec., 1861, to Feby., 1862. Feby., 1862, 25 Brig., 7 Div., Army Ohio. Oct., 1862, 1 Brig., Cumb'd Div., Dist. West Va., Dept. Ohio. Nov., 1862, 1 Brig., 2 Div., Centre, 14 Corps, Cumb'd. Jany., 1863, 1 Brig., 2 Div., 14 Corps. April, 1863, Dist. Central Ky., Dept. Ohio. June, 1863, 3 Brig., 3 Div., 23 Corps, Dept. Ohio. Aug., 1863, 3 Brig., 3 Div., Res. Corps, Cumb'd. Oct., 1863, 2 Brig., 2 Div., 14 Corps. Nov., 1863, Spear's Brig., Chattanooga, Tenn. Dec., 1863, Spear's Tenn. Brig., 2 Div., 23 Corps, Dept. Ohio. Jany., 1864, 3 Brig., 3 Div., 12 Corps, Cumb'd. April, 1864, 1 Brig., 2 Div., 23 Corps. Mustered out Feby. 23, 1865.

3rd REGIMENT MOUNTED INFANTRY.—Org. at Loudon, Strawberry Plains and Knoxville, Tenn., July to Sept., 1864. Mustered out Nov. 30, 1864.

3rd REGIMENT ENROLLED MILITIA INFANTRY. —Org. at Memphis, Tenn., for the protection of that city.

4th REGIMENT INFANTRY.—Org. at Camp Garber, near Flat Lick, Ky., Nov., 1861, to March, 1862. March, 1862, 25 Brig., 7 Div., Army Ohio. Oct., 1862, 1 Brig., Cumb'd Div., Dist. W. Va., Dept. Ohio. Designation changed to 1st Tenn. Cav., Nov. 1, 1862, which see. Regt. re-org. at Nashville, Tenn., May, 1863. May, 1863, Dist. North Central Ky., 1 Div., 23 Corps, Ohio. Jany., 1864, 2 Brig., Dist. Nashville, Tenn., Cumb'd. Jany., 1864, 2 Brig., 3 Div., 12 Corps, Cumb'd. April, 1864, 3 Brig., 4 Div., 23 Corps, Ohio. Oct., 1864, 2 Brig., 4 Div., 23 Corps. Feby., 1865, 2 Brig., 4 Div., Dist. East Tenn., Cumb'd. March, 1865, 1 Brig., 4 Div., Dist. East Tenn. Mustered out Aug. 2, 1865.

4th REGIMENT MOUNTED INFANTRY.—Org. at large in Tenn., Sept. 1, 1864. Mustered out Aug. 25, 1865.

4th REGIMENT ENROLLED MILITIA INFANTRY. —Org. at Memphis, Tenn., for the protection of that city.

5th REGIMENT INFANTRY.—Org. at Barboursville, Ky., and Harrison, Tenn., Feby.-March, 1862. March, 1862, 25 Brig., 7 Div., Army Ohio. Oct., 1862, 1 Brig., Cumb'd Div., Dist. W. Va., Dept. Ohio. Nov., 1862, 1 Brig., 2 Div., Centre, 14 Corps, Cumb'd. Jany., 1863, 1 Brig., 2 Div., 14 Corps. April, 1863, Dist. Central Ky., Dept. Ohio. June, 1863, 3 Brig., 3 Div., 23 Corps, Ohio. Aug., 1863, 3 Brig., 3 Div., Res. Corps, Cumb'd. Oct., 1863, 2 Brig., 2 Div., 14 Corps. Nov., 1863, Spear's Tenn. Brig., Chattanooga, Tenn. Dec., 1863, Spear's Tenn. Brig., 2 Div., 23 Corps. Jany., 1864, 3 Brig., 3 Div., 12 Corps, Cumb'd. April, 1864, 2 Brig., 3 Div., 23 Corps. June, 1864, 3 Brig., 3 Div., 23 Corps. Dec., 1864, 2 Brig., 3 Div., 23 Corps. Jany., 1865, Post Nashville, Tenn. Feby., 1865, 2 Brig., 3 Div., 23 Corps, Dept. N. C. Mustered out June 30, 1865.

5th REGIMENT MOUNTED INFANTRY.—Org. at Cleveland, Nashville, Calhoun and Chattanooga, Tenn.,

Sept. 23, 1864. Att. to Dist. Etowah, Dept. Cumb'd. Mustered out July 17, 1865.

6th REGIMENT INFANTRY.—Org. at Boston and Williamsburg, Ky., April 18, 1862. April, 1862, 25 Brig., 7 Div., Army Ohio. Oct., 1862, 1 Brig., Cumb'd. Div., Dist. W. Va., Dept. Ohio. Nov., 1862, 1 Brig., 2 Div., Centre, 14 Corps, Cumb'd. Jany., 1863, 1 Brig., 2 Div., 14 Corps. April, 1863, Dist. Central Ky., Dept. Ohio. June, 1863, 3 Brig., 3 Div., 23 Corps, Ohio. Aug., 1863, 3 Brig., 3 Div., Res. Corps, Cumb'd. Oct., 1863, 2 Brig., 2 Div., 14 Corps. Nov., 1863, Spear's Tenn. Brig., Chattanooga, Tenn. Dec., 1863, Spear's Tenn. Brig., 2 Div., 23 Corps. Jany., 1864, 3 Brig., 3 Div., 12 Corps, Cumb'd. April, 1864, 1 Brig., 2 Div., 23 Corps. Feby., 1865, 1 Brig., 2 Div., 23 Corps, Dept. N. C. Mustered out April 2 to May 17, 1865.

6th REGIMENT MOUNTED INFANTRY.—Org. at Chattanooga, Tenn., Aug. 20, 1864. Att. to Dist. Etowah, Dept. Cumb'd. Feby., 1865, 1 Brig., 2 Separate Div., Dist. Etowah, Dept. Cumb'd. Mustered out June 30, 1865.

7th REGIMENT INFANTRY.—Org. in Tenn. at large, Aug. 10, 1862, to June 1, 1863. Att. to Dist. Jackson, Tenn., to Nov., 1862, Dist. Jackson, Tenn., 13 Corps, Dept. Tenn., to Dec., 1862, Dist. Jackson, Tenn., 3 Div., 16 Corps, to July, 1863. Mustered out July 31, 1863.

7th REGIMENT MOUNTED INFANTRY.—Org. at Athens and Nashville, Tenn., Aug., 1864. Att. to Dist. East Tenn., to March, 1865, 2 Brig., Dist. East Tenn., to July, 1865. Mustered out July 27, 1865.

8th REGIMENT INFANTRY.—Org. at Camp Dick Robinson and Camp Nelson, Ky., Nov. 11, 1862, to Aug. 11, 1863. Nov., 1862, Dist. Central Ky., Dept. Ohio. June, 1863, 2 Brig., 4 Div., 23 Corps, Dept. Ohio. July, 1863, 2 Brig., 1 Div., 23 Corps. Aug., 1863, 2 Brig., 3 Div., 23 Corps. Sept., 1863, 2 Brig., Left Wing Forces, 23 Corps. Jany., 1864, 1 Brig., 3 Div., 23 Corps. Feby., 1865, 1 Brig., 3 Div., 23 Corps, Dept. N. C. Mustered out June 30, 1865.

8th REGIMENT MOUNTED INFANTRY.—Org. at Nashville and Carthage, Tenn., Nov., 1864. Attached to Dist. Middle Tenn., Dept. Cumb'd. Feby., 1865, 4th Sub Dist., Dist. Middle Tenn., Dept. Cumb'd. Mustered out August 17, 1865.

9th REGIMENT.—(See 6th Regt. Cav.).

10th REGIMENT INFANTRY.—(1st MIDDLE TENN. INFANTRY). Org. at Nashville, Tenn., May to Aug., 1862. May, 1862, Post and Dist. Nashville, Tenn., Dept. Cumb'd. June, 1863, 3 Brig., 2 Div., Res. Corps, Cumb'd. Sept., 1863, Def. Nashville and Northwestern R. R. Jany., 1864, 1 Brig., Nashville, Tenn. Jany., 1864, 1 Brig., 3 Div., 12 Corps, Cumb'd. April, 1864, 1 Brig., 4 Div., 20 Corps, Cumb'd. April, 1865, 1 Brig., 4 Div., Dist. East Tenn. Mustered out June 23, 1865.

NASHVILLE UNION GUARDS.—Org. at Nashville, Sept., 1862, for post duty at Nashville. No reports on file.

TEXAS

1st REGIMENT CAVALRY.—Org. at New Orleans, La., Nov., 1862. Nov., 1862, Indpt. Command, Dept. Gulf. Jany., 1863, Def. New Orleans, La. May, 1863, Cav., 19 Corps, Dept. Gulf. July, 1863, Def. New Orleans, La. Oct., 1863, Unatt., Cav. 13 Corps, Gulf. June, 1864, Cav. Brig., U. S. Forces, Tex. June, 1864, Dist. Morganza, La., Gulf. Aug., 1864, Separate Cav. Brig., 19 Corps, Gulf. Nov., 1864, 2nd Separate Cav. Brig., 19 Corps, Gulf. Dec., 1864, Separate Cav. Brig., Res. Corps, Mil. Div. West Miss. Feby., 1865, Cav. Brig., Dist. Baton Rouge, La., Gulf. July, 1865, Dept. Tex. Mustered out Nov. 4, 1865.

2nd REGIMENT CAVALRY.—Org. at Brownsville, Tex., Oct. 15, 1863. Dec., 1863, Unatt., Cav., 13 Corps, Tex., Dept. Gulf. June, 1864, Cav. Brig., U. S. Forces, Tex. June, 1864, Dist. Morganza, La., Dept. Gulf. Aug., 1864, Separate Cav. Brig., 19 Corps, Gulf. Consolidated with 1st Tex. Cav., Sept. 10, 1864.

2nd BATTALION CAVALRY.—Org. at Brazos Santiago, Tex., March, 1865. Duty in Dept. Tex. Mustered out November 10, 1865.

INDEPENDENT COMPANY PARTISAN RANGERS. —Org. at Brownsville, Tex., Nov. 10, 1863. Duty in Tex. Mustered out July 21, 1864.

VERMONT

1st REGIMENT CAVALRY.—Org. at Burlington and mustered in Nov. 19, 1861. Dec., 1861, Annapolis, Md. Jany., 1862, Banks' 1 Div., Potomac. March, 1862, Hatch's Cav. Brig., Banks' 5 Corps, and Dept. Shenandoah. June, 1862, Cav. Brig., 2 Corps, Army Va. Sept., 1862, Price's Cav. Brig., Def. Washington and 22 Corps. March, 1863, 3 Brig., Stahel's Cav. Div., 22 Corps. June, 1863, 1 Brig., 3 Div., Cav. Corps, Potomac. Aug., 1863, 2 Brig., 3 Div., Cav. Corps, Potomac and Shenandoah, Middle Mil. Div. Mustered out Aug. 9, 1865.

1st REGIMENT HEAVY ARTILLERY.—Org. from 11th Vermont Infry., Dec. 10, 1862. Dec., 1862, 1 Brig., Haskin's Div., Def. Washington and 22 Corps. May, 1864, 2 Brig., 2 Div., 6 Corps, Potomac. Aug., 1864, 2 Brig., 2 Div., 6 Corps, Shenandoah, Middle Mil. Div. Dec., 1864, 2 Brig., 2 Div., 6 Corps, Potomac. June, 1865, Middle Dept., 8 Corps. Mustered out Aug. 25, 1865.

1st COMPANY HEAVY ARTILLERY.—Org. at Port Hudson, La., from surplus recruits of the 2nd Vt. Battery L. A. Garrison Port Hudson, La. Mustered out July 25, 1865.

1st INDEPENDENT BATTERY LIGHT ARTILLERY.—Org. at Brattleboro and mustered in Feby. 18, 1862. March, 1862, 1 Brig., Dept. Gulf. Sept., 1862, Arty., Sherman's Div., Dept. Gulf. Jany., 1863, Arty., 2 Div., 19 Corps, Gulf. July, 1863, Arty., 3 Div., 19 Corps, Gulf. Sept., 1863, Dist. LaFourche, Dept. Gulf. March, 1864, Arty., 1 Div., 19 Corps, Gulf. June, 1864, Dist. La Fourche, Gulf. Mustered out Aug. 10, 1864.

2nd INDEPENDENT BATTERY LIGHT ARTILLERY. Org. at Brandon and mustered in Dec. 24, 1861. March, 1862, 1 Brig., Dept. Gulf. Sept., 1862, Def. New Orleans, Gulf. Jany., 1863, Arty., 3 Div., 19 Corps, Gulf. July, 1863, Def. Port Hudson, La., Gulf. Sept., 1863, Arty., 2 Div., Corps D'Afrique, Gulf. Mustered out July 31, 1865.

3rd INDEPENDENT BATTERY LIGHT ARTILLERY.—Org. at Burlington and mustered in Jany. 1, 1864. Jany., 1864, Camp Barry, Def. Washington, 22 Corps. April, 1864, Arty., 4 Div., 9 Corps, Potomac. July, 1864, Arty. Brig., 9 Corps, Potomac. Aug., 1864, Arty. Res., Potomac. Sept., 1864, Arty. Res., Att. to 2 Corps, Potomac. Jany., 1865, Arty. Res., Att. to 6 Corps, Potomac. Mustered out June 15, 1865.

COMPANY F, FIRST UNITED STATES SHARPSHOOTERS.—Org. at West Randolph, Sept. 13, 1861. (See 1st U. S. S. S.)

COMPANY E SECOND UNITED STATES SHARPSHOOTERS.—Org. at West Randolph and mustered in Nov. 9, 1861. (See 2nd U. S. S. S.)

COMPANY H 2nd UNITED STATES SHARPSHOOTERS.—Org. at West Randolph and mustered in Nov. 9, 1861. (See 2nd U. S. S. S.)

1st REGIMENT INFANTRY.—Org. at Rutland and mustered in for three months, May 9, 1861. June, 1861, Fort Monroe and Camp Hamilton, Dept. Va. Mustered out Aug. 15, 1861.

2nd REGIMENT INFANTRY.—Org. at Burlington and mustered in June 20, 1861. June, 1861, Howard's Brig., Heintzelman's Div., McDowell's Army N. E. Va. Aug., 1861, W. F. Smith's Brig., Div. Potomac. Oct., 1861, Brook's Brig., Smith's Div., Potomac. March, 1862, 2 Brig., 2 Div., 4 Corps, Potomac. May, 1862, 2 Brig., 2 Div., 6 Corps, Potomac and Shenandoah, Middle Mil. Div. Mustered out July 15, 1865.

3rd REGIMENT INFANTRY.—Org. at St. Johnsbury and mustered in July 16, 1861. Aug., 1861, W. F. Smith's Brig. Div., Potomac. Oct., 1861, Brook's Brig., Smith's Div., Potomac. March, 1862, 2 Brig., 2 Div., 4 Corps, Potomac. May, 1862, 2 Brig., 2 Div., 6 Corps,

Potomac and Shenandoah, Middle Mil. Div. Mustered out July 11, 1865.

4th REGIMENT INFANTRY.—Org. at Brattleboro and mustered in Sept. 21, 1861. Oct., 1861, Brook's Brig., Smith's Div., Potomac. March, 1862, 2 Brig., 2 Div., 4 Corps, Potomac. May, 1862, 2 Brig., 2 Div., 6 Corps, Potomac and Shenandoah, Middle Mil. Div. Mustered out July 13, 1865.

5th REGIMENT INFANTRY.—Org. at St. Albans and mustered in Sept. 16, 1861. Oct., 1861, Brook's Brig., Smith's Div., Potomac. March, 1862, 2 Brig., 2 Div., 4 Corps, Potomac. May, 1862, 2 Brig., 2 Div., 6 Corps, Potomac and Shenandoah, Middle Mil. Div. Mustered out June 29, 1865.

6th REGIMENT INFANTRY.—Org. at Montpelier and mustered in Oct. 15, 1861. Oct., 1861, Brook's Brig., Smith's Div., Potomac. March, 1862, 2 Brig., 2 Div., 4 Corps, Potomac. May, 1862, 2 Brig., 2 Div., 6 Corps, Potomac and Shenandoah, Middle Mil. Div. Mustered out June 26, 1865.

7th REGIMENT INFANTRY.—Org. at Brattleboro and mustered in Feby. 12, 1862. March, 1862, 1 Brig., Dept. Gulf. Oct., 1862, Pensacola, Fla., Dist. W. Fla., Dept. Gulf. Oct., 1864, Def. New Orleans, Gulf. Feby., 1865, 2 Brig., 3 Div., Res. Corps, Mil. Div. West. Miss. Feby., 1865, 2 Brig., 3 Div., 13 Corps, Mil. Div. West Miss. July, 1865, Dept. Tex. Mustered out March 14, 1866.

8th REGIMENT INFANTRY.—Org. at Brattleboro and mustered in Feby. 18, 1862. March, 1862, 1 Brig., Dept. Gulf. Sept., 1862, Indpt. Command, Gulf. Dec., 1862, Weitzel's Res. Brig., Gulf. Jany., 1863, 2 Brig., 1 Div., 19 Corps, Gulf. Aug., 1863, 3 Brig., 1 Div., 19 Corps, Gulf. Feby., 1864, 2 Brig., 1 Div., 19 Corps, Gulf. Aug., 1864, 2 Brig., 1 Div., 19 Corps, Shenandoah. March. 1865, 2 Brig., 1 Prov'l Div., Shenandoah. April, 1865, 2 Brig., 1 Div., Def. Washington, 22 Corps. Mustered out June 28, 1865.

9th REGIMENT INFANTRY.—Org. at Brattleboro and mustered in July 9, 1862. July, 1862, Piatt's Brig., Winchester, Va. Sept., 1862, Miles' Command, Harper's Ferry, Va. Sept., 1862, Camp Douglass, Chicago, Ill. April, 1863, Wardrop's Res. Brig., 7 Corps, Dept. Va. June, 1863, Wistar's Indpt. Brig., 7 Corps. July, 1863, Yorktown, Va., Dept. Va. and N. C. Oct., 1863, Dist. Beaufort, N. C., Dept. Va. and N. C. July, 1864, Def. Newberne, N. C. Sept., 1864, 2 Brig., 2 Div., 18 Corps. Dec., 1864, 2 Brig., 3 Div., 24 Corps. July, 1865, 2nd Indpt. Brig., 24 Corps. Aug., 1865, Dept. Va. Mustered out Dec. 1, 1865.

10th REGIMENT INFANTRY.—Org. at Brattleboro and mustered in Sept. 1, 1862. Sept., 1862, Grover's Brig., Def. Washington. Feby., 1863, Jewett's Indpt. Brig., 22 Corps. June, 1863, French's Div., 8 Corps. July, 1863, 1 Brig., 3 Div., 3 Corps, Potomac. March, 1864, 1 Brig., 3 Div., 6 Corps, Potomac. Aug., 1864, 1 Brig., 3 Div., 6 Corps, Shenandoah. Dec., 1864, 1 Brig., 3 Div., 6 Corps, Potomac. Mustered out June 22, 1865.

11th REGIMENT INFANTRY.—Org. at Brattleboro and mustered in Sept. 1, 1862. Sept., 1862, Def. Washington, North Potomac. Oct., 1862, 1 Brig., Haskin's Div., Def. Washington, North Potomac. Designation changed to 1st Heavy Arty., Dec. 10, 1862.

12th REGIMENT INFANTRY.—Org. at Brattleboro, Oct. 4, 1862. Oct., 1862, 2 Brig., Abercrombie's Div., Def. Washington. Feby., 1863, 2 Brig., Casey's Div., 22 Corps. April, 1863, 2 Brig., Abercrombie's Div., 22 Corps. July, 1863, 3 Brig., 3 Div., 1 Corps, Potomac. Mustered out July 14, 1863.

13th REGIMENT INFANTRY.—Org. at Brattleboro, Oct. 12, 1862. Oct., 1862, 2 Brig., Abercrombie's Div., Def. Washington. Feby., 1863, 2 Brig., Casey's Div., 22 Corps. April, 1863, 2 Brig., Abercrombie's Div., 22 Corps. July, 1863, 3 Brig., 3 Div., 1 Corps, Potomac. Mustered out July 21, 1863.

14th REGIMENT INFANTRY.—Org. at Brattleboro, Oct. 21, 1862. Oct., 1862, 2 Brig., Abercrombie's Div., Def. Washington. Feby., 1863, 2 Brig., Casey's Div., 22 Corps. April, 1863, 2 Brig., Abercrombie's Div., 22

Corps. July, 1863, 3 Brig., 3 Div., 1 Corps, Potomac. Mustered out July 30, 1863.

15th REGIMENT INFANTRY.—Org. at Brattleboro, Oct. 22, 1862. Oct., 1862, 2 Brig., Abercrombie's Div., Def. Washington. Feby., 1863, 2 Brig., Casey's Div., 22 Corps. April, 1863, 2 Brig., Abercrombie's Div., 22 Corps. July, 1863, 3 Brig., 3 Div., 1 Corps, Potomac. Mustered out Aug. 5, 1863.

16th REGIMENT INFANTRY.—Org. at Brattleboro, Oct. 23, 1862. Oct., 1862, 2 Brig., Abercrombie's Div., Def. Washington. Feby., 1863, 2 Brig., Casey's Div., 22 Corps. April, 1863, 2 Brig., Abercrombie's Div., 22 Corps. July, 1863, 3 Brig., 3 Div., 1 Corps, Potomac. Mustered out Aug. 10, 1863.

17th REGIMENT INFANTRY.—Org. at Brattleboro, Jany. 5 to April 12, 1864. April, 1864, 2 Brig., 2 Div., 9 Corps, Potomac. Mustered out July 14, 1865.

VIRGINIA

MEANS' LOUDON RANGERS.—Org. at Waterford, Va., and Point of Rocks, Md., Co. A, June 20, 1862, Co. B, Jany. 26, 1864. Attached to Point of Rocks, Md., Middle Dept. June, 1862, R. R. Dist., 8 Corps, Middle Dept., to Sept., 1862; R. R. Dist., W. Va., to Jany., 1863; Point of Rocks, Md., 8 Corps, Middle Dept., to March, 1863; Unatt., 8 Corps, to May, 1863; 3rd Separate Brig., 8 Corps, to June, 1863; Lockwood's Command, 8 Corps, to July, 1863; 3rd Separate Brig., 8 Corps, to Aug., 1863; 2 Brig., Maryland Heights Div., Dept. W. Va., to Dec., 1863; Unatt., 1 Div., W. Va., to April, 1864; Res. Div., Dept. W. Va., to Jany., 1865; 3 Brig., 3 Div., W. Va., to April, 1865; Unatt., 2 Div., W. Va., to May, 1865. Mustered out at Bolivar, W. Va., May 31, 1865.

WASHINGTON

1st REGIMENT INFANTRY.—Org. at Fort Vancouver and Fort Steilacoom, Washington Ter. Mustered out Dec. 11, 1865.

WEST VIRGINIA

1st REGIMENT CAVALRY.—Org. at Wheeling, Clarksburg and Morgantown, July 10 to Nov. 25, 1861. Oct., 1861, Cheat Mt. Dist., West Va. Jany., 1862, Cav., Landers' Div., Potomac, 8 Co.'s. March, 1862, Shields' Div., Banks' 5 Corps, 8 Co.'s; Milroy's Brig., Dept. Mts., Co's C, E, L. May, 1862, Shields' Div., Dept. Rappahannock. May, 1862, Geary's Indpt. Brig., Dept. Rappahannock. May, 1862, Hatch's Cav. Brig., Dept. Shenandoah. June, 1862, Buford's Cav. Brig., 2 Corps, Army Va.; Milroy's Indpt. Brig., 1 Corps, Army Va., Co.'s C, E, L. Aug., 1862, Alexandria, Va., Unassigned, Def. Washington. Dec., 1862, Price's Cav. Brig., Def. Washington and 22 Corps. April, 1863, 3 Brig., Stahel's Cav. Div., 22 Corps. June, 1863, 1 Brig., 3 Div., Cav. Corps, Potomac. Dec., 1863, Unass'd, Dept. W. Va. March, 1864, 2 Brig., 2 Cav. Div., Dept. W. Va. May, 1864, 3 Brig., 2 Cav. Div., W. Va. July, 1864, 2 Brig., 2 Div., Cav. W. Va. Jany., 1865, 2 Brig., 2 Div., Cav. Corps, Middle Mil. Div. March, 1865, 3 Brig., 3 Div., Cav. Corps, Potomac. (Co. A, March, 1863, Averill's 4th Separate Brig., 8 Corps, Middle Dept. June, 1863, Averill's 4th Separate Brig., West Va. April, 1864, Kelly's Command, Res. Div., Dept. West Va. Dec., 1864 to April, 1865, 1 Brig., 1 Infy. Div., W. Va., to muster out.) (Co. K, Dec., 1862, Def. Upper Potomac, 8 Corps, Middle Dept. Jany., 1863, Milroy's Command, Winchester, Va., 8 Corps. March, 1863, 2 Brig., 2 Div., 8 Corps. July, 1863, Dept. Susquehanna. July, 1863, Martinsburg, W. Va. Dec., 1863, 1 Brig., 3 Div., W. Va. Rejoined Regt. Dec., 1863.) Regt. mustered out July 8, 1865.

2nd REGIMENT CAVALRY.—Org. at Parkersburg, Nov., 1861. Dec., 1861, Dist. Kanawha, Dept. W. Va. March, 1862, Unatt., Dist. Kanawha, W. Va. May, 1863, Unatt., Kanawha Div., W. Va. Sept., 1862, Unatt., Point Pleasant, Dist. Kanawha, Dept. Ohio. March, 1863, Unatt., 3 Div., 8 Corps, Middle Dept. June, 1863, Wilkinson's Brig., Scammon's Div., Dept. W. Va. July, 1863, 3 Brig., Scammon's Div., W. Va. Dec., 1863, 3 Brig., 3 Div., W. Va. March, 1864, 1 Brig., 2 Cav. Div.,

W. Va. May, 1864, 3 Brig., 2 Cav. Div., W. Va. July, 1864, 2 Brig., 2 Cav. Div., W. Va. Jany., 1865, 2 Brig., 2 Div., Cav. Corps, Middle Mil. Div. March, 1865, 3 Brig., 3 Div., Cav. Corps, Potomac. Mustered out June 30, 1865.

3rd REGIMENT CAVALRY.—Org. Dec., 1861. Dec., 1861, R. R. Dist., W. Va. March, 1862, R. R. Dist., Dept. Mts. May, 1862, Unatt., Mt. Dept. June, 1862, 2 Brig., 2 Div., 1 Corps, Army Va. (Co.'s A, C.) Sept., 1862, Dist. W. Va., Dept. Ohio. Heaqrs. 11 Corps, Potomac. (Co.'s A, C.) Dec., 1862, Headqrs. Grand Reserve Div., Potomac. (Co.'s A, C.) Jany., 1863, Milroy's Command, Winchester, Va., 8 Corps. (Co.'s D, E.) Feby., 1863, 2 Brig., 2 Div., 8 Corps, Middle Dept. (Co.'s D, E.), 4 Separate Brig., 8 Corps. (Co.'s F, H, I.) June, 1863, 4 Separate Brig., W. Va. (Co.'s F, H, I.). Bloody Run, Dept. Susquehanna, (Co.'s D, E.); Scammon's Div., Dept. W. Va. (1 Co.) July, 1863, McReynolds' Command, Martinsburg, W. Va. (Co.'s D, E.) Dec., 1863, 1 Brig., 3 Div., W. Va. (1 Co.); 2 Brig., 4 Div., W. Va. (3 Co.'s); 3 Brig., 3 Div., W. Va. (2 Co.'s). March, 1864, 3 Brig., 2 Cav. Div., W. Va. May, 1864, 2 Brig., 2 Cav. Div., W. Va. Jany., 1865, 3 Brig., 3 Div., Cav. Corps, Army Shenandoah. March, 1865, 3 Brig., 3 Div., Cav. Corps, Potomac. Mustered out June 30, 1865.

4th REGIMENT CAVALRY.—Org. at Parkersburg and Wheeling, July and Aug. 1863. Aug. 1863, Wilkinson's Brig., Dept. W. Va. Dec., 1863, 3 Brig., 2 Div., W. Va. April, 1864, Kelly's Com'd, Res. Div., W. Va. Mustered out June 23, 1864.

5th REGIMENT CAVALRY.—Org. Jany., 1864, from 2nd West Va. Mounted Infy. Jany., 1864, 3 Brig., 4 Div., Dept. W. Va. April, 1864, 3 Brig., 2 Div. Cav. Dept. W. Va. June, 1864, 2 Brig., 2 Cav. Div., W. Va. July, 1864, Kelly's Command, Res. Div., W. Va. Transferred to 6th W. Va. Cav., Dec. 14, 1864.

6th REGIMENT CAVALRY.—Org. Jany., 1864, from 3rd West Va. Mounted Infy. Jany., 1864, 3 Brig., 4 Div., Dept. West Va. April, 1864, Kelly's Command, Res. Div., West Va. Jany., 1865, Remount Camp, Pleasant Valley. April, 1865, Def. Washington, 22 Corps. June, 1865, Dist. of the Plains, Dept. Mo. Mustered out May 22, 1866.

7th REGIMENT CAVALRY.—Org. Jany. 26, 1864, from 8th West Va. Infy. Jany., 1864, 3 Brig., 4 Div., Dept. West Va. April, 1864, 3 Brig., 2 Cav. Div., W. Va. June, 1864, 2 Brig., 2 Div. Cav., W. Va. July, 1864, Kanawha Valley, W. Va., 1 Separate Brig., Dept. West Va. Mustered out Aug. 1, 1865.

INDEPENDENT BATTALION CAVALRY ("LOUDON RANGERS").—Org. at Waterford, Va., and Point of Rocks, Md., Co. A, June 20, 1862; Co. B, Jany. 26, 1864. June, 1862, Point of Rocks, Md., Middle Dept. July, 1862, Point of Rocks, Md., 8 Corps, Middle Dept. Sept., 1862, R. R. Dist., West Va. Jany., 1863, Point of Rocks, Md., 8 Corps. March, 1863, Unatt., 8 Corps, May, 1863, 3 Separate Brig., 8 Corps. June, 1863, Lockwood's Command, 8 Corps. July, 1863, 3 Separate Brig., 8 Corps. Aug., 1863, 2 Brig., Md. Heights Div., W. Va. Dec., 1863, Unatt., Dept. W. Va. April, 1864, Reserve Div., West Va. Jany., 1865, 3 Brig., 3 Div., West Va. April, 1865, Unatt., 2 Div., West Va. Mustered out May 31, 1865.

BATTERY "A" LIGHT ARTILLERY.—Org. at Wheeling, June 28, 1861. July, 1861, Unatt., Army Occupation, West Va. Sept., 1861, Reynolds, Cheat Mt. Dist., Dept. W. Va. Jany., 1862, Landers' Div., Potomac. March, 1862, Arty., Shields' 2 Div., Banks' 5 Corps. April, 1862, Arty., Shields' Div., Dept. Shenandoah. May, 1862, Arty., Shields' Div., Dept. Rappahannock. June, 1862, Mil. Dist., Washington. Feby., 1863, Camp Barry, Def. Washington, 22 Corps. July, 1863, Md. Heights Div., Dept. W. Va. Dec., 1863, 1 Brig., 1 Div., West Va. Dec., 1863, Wheaton's Brig., 1 Div., W. Va. April, 1864, Res. Div., West Va. Harper's Ferry, W. Va. Oct., 1864, 1 Separate Brig., Kanawha Valley, West Va. Mustered out July 27, 1865.

BATTERY "B" LIGHT ARTILLERY.—Org. at Ceredo, Oct. 1, 1861. Oct., 1861, Reynolds Cheat Mt. Dist., West Va. Jany., 1862, Landers' Div., Potomac. March, 1862, Arty., Shields' 2 Div., Banks' 5 Corps. April, 1862, Arty., Shields' Div., Dept. Shenandoah. May, 1862, Arty., Shields' Div., Dept. Rappahannock. June, 1862, Mil. Dist., Washington, D. C. Sept., 1862, R. R. Dist., West Va. Jany., 1863, Milroy's Command, Winchester, Va., 8 Corps, Middle Dept. Feby., 1863, 2 Brig., 2 Div., 8 Corps. May, 1863, 4 Separate Brig., 8 Corps. June, 1863, Averill's 4 Separate Brig., Dept. W. Va. Dec., 1863, 1 Brig., 4 Div., West Va. April, 1864, Arty., 1 Cav., Div. W. Va. Transferred to Battery "E" Feby. 13, 1865.

BATTERY "C" LIGHT ARTILLERY.—Org. at Wheeling, Jany. 25, 1862, to March, 30, 1862. April, 1862, Unatt., R. R. Dist., Dept. Mts. May, 1862, 1 Brig., Blenker's Div., Dept. Mts. June, 1862, Res. Arty., 1 Corps, Army Va. Sept., 1862, Arty., 3 Div., 11 Corps, Army Potomac. March, 1863, Res. Arty., 11 Corps, Potomac. May, 1863, 3 Vol. Brig., Arty. Res., Potomac. Aug., 1863, 4 Vol. Brig., Arty. Res., Potomac. Oct., 1863, 2 Brig., Arty. Res., Potomac. Nov., 1863, 1 Vol. Brig., Arty. Res., Potomac. March, 1864, Camp Barry, Def. Washington, 22 Corps. May, 1864, 2 Brig., De Russy's Div., 22 Corps. July, 1864, 4 Brig., DeRussy's Div., 22 Corps. Oct., 1864, 3 Brig., DeRussy's Div., 22 Corps. Dec., 1864, 1 Brig., DeRussy's Div., 22 Corps. Mustered out June 28, 1865.

BATTERY "D" LIGHT ARTILLERY.—Org. at Wheeling Aug. 20, 1862. Sept., 1862, R. R. Dist., Dist. W. Va., Dept. Ohio. Jany., 1863, Milroy's Command, Winchester, Va., 8 Corps, Middle Dept. Feby., 1863, 1 Brig., 2 Div., 8 Corps. June, 1863, 2 Brig., 2 Div., 8 Corps. June, 1863, Mulligan's Brig., Dept. W. Va. Dec., 1863, 2 Brig., 2 Div., West Va. March, 1864, 2 Infy. Div., West Va. May, 1864, Arty. Brig., West Va. Aug., 1864, Kelly's Command, Res Div., West Va. Aug., 1864, Wheeling, W. Va. Sept., 1864, Parkersburg, W. Va. April, 1865, 1 Brig., 1 Div., W. Va. Mustered out June 27, 1865.

BATTERY "E" LIGHT ARTILLERY.—Org. at Buckhannon, Sept. 13, 1862. Sept., 1862, R. R. Dist., Dist. W. Va., Dept. Ohio. Jany., 1863, Romney, W. Va., 8 Corps, Middle Dept. March, 1863, 4 Brig., 1 Div., 8 Corps. June, 1863, Campbell's Brig., Dept. W. Va. Dec., 1863, 1 Brig., 2 Div., W. Va. April, 1864, Kelly's Command, Res. Div., W. Va. July, 1864, Arty. Brig., West Va. July, 1864. Arty., 1 Cav. Div., W. Va. Oct., 1864, Arty. Dist., Harper's Ferry, W. Va. Jany., 1865, Camp Barry, Def. Washington, D. C., 22 Corps. Mustered out June 28, 1865.

BATTERY "F" LIGHT ARTILLERY.—Org. April 8, 1863, from Co. C, 6th W. Va. Infy. July, 1862, R. R. Dist., 8 Corps, Middle Dept. Sept., 1862, R. R. Div., Dist. W. Va., Dept. Ohio. Jany., 1863, Martinsburg, W. Va., 8 Corps, March, 1863, 3 Brig., 1 Div., 8 Corps. June, 1863, Arty., French's Command, 8 Corps. July, 1863, Camp Barry, Def. Washington, 22 Corps. Dec., 1863, 3 Brig., 2 Div., West Va. April, 1864, Kelly's Command, Res. Div., W. Va. July, 1864, Arty. Brig., West Va. Transferred to Battery "A" Sept. 14, 1864.

BATTERY "G" LIGHT ARTILLERY.—Org. May 26, 1863, from Co. G, 2nd West Va. Infy. April, 1862, Milroy's Brig., Dept. Mts. April, 1862, R. R. Dist., Dept. Mts. July, 1862, R. R. Dist., 8 Corps, Middle Dept. Sept., 1862, R. R. Dist., Dist. West Va., Dept. Ohio. Jany., 1863, Romney, W. Va., Def. Upper Potomac, 8 Corps. March, 1863, 4 Separate Brig., 8 Corps. June, 1863, Averill's 4 Separate Brig., West Va. Dec., 1863, 3 Brig., 4 Div., West Va. April, 1864, Res. Div., Dept. West Va. May, 1864, Arty., 2 Cav. Div., West Va. June, 1864, Arty. Brig., West Va. Mustered out June 22, 1864.

BATTERY "H" LIGHT ARTILLERY.—Org at Maryland Heights, Jany. 4, 1864. Jany., 1864, Heavy Arty., 1 Div., West. Va. April, 1864, Kelly's Command, Res. Div., West Va. Mustered out July 11, 1865.

1st REGIMENT INFANTRY (3 MONTHS).—Org. at Wheeling, May 15 to June 1, 1861. June, 1861, Kelly's Command, Army Occupation, West Va. July, 1861, 1 Brig., Army Occupation, W. Va. Mustered out Aug. 27, 1861.

1st REGIMENT INFANTRY (3 YEARS).—Org. at Wheeling, Sept. 25 to Nov. 14, 1861. Nov., 1861, R. R. Dist., W. Va. Jany., 1862, 3 Brig., Landers' Div., Potomac. March, 1862, 3 Brig., Shields' 2 Div., Banks' 5 Corps. April, 1862, 3 Brig., Shields' Div., Dept. Shenandoah. May, 1862, 3 Brig., Shields' Div., Dept. Rappahannock. June, 1862, 4 Brig., 2 Div., 3 Corps, Army Va. Sept., 1862, 2 Brig., Whipple's Div., Def. Washington. Oct., 1862, Wheeling, W. Va. Dec., 1862, Cumberland, Md. Dec., 1862, North Mt., Def. Upper Potomac, 8 Corps. March, 1863, 4 Brig., 1 Div., 8 Corps, Middle Dept. June, 1863, Campbell's Brig., Scammon's Div., Dept. West Va. Dec., 1863, 2 Brig., 2 Div., West Va. April, 1864, 2 Brig., 1 Infy. Div., West Va. Oct., 1864, Res. Div. Oct., 1864, Cumberland, Md. Consolidated with 4th W. Va. Infy., Dec. 10, 1864, to form 2nd W. Va. Veteran Infy.

1st REGIMENT VETERAN INFANTRY.—Org. Nov. 9, 1864, by consolidation of 5th and 9th W. Va. Infy. Nov., 1864, 1 Brig., 2 Infy. Div., West Va. Jany., 1865, 1 Brig., 1 Infy. Div., West Va. April, 1865, 1 Brig., 4 Prov'l Div., W. Va. Mustered out July 21, 1865.

2nd REGIMENT INFANTRY.—Org. at Wheeling, May 21 to July 21, 1861. July, 1861, 1 Brig., Army Occupation, West Va. Sept., 1861, Cheat Mt. Dist., W. Va. March, 1862, Cheat Mt. Dist., Dept. Mts. April, 1862, Milroy's Brig., Dept. Mts. June, 1862, Milroy's Indpt. Brig., 1 Corps, Army Va. Sept., 1862, Def. Washington, D. C. Oct., 1862, Beverly, W. Va., Dist. W. Va., Dept. Ohio. March, 1863, 4 Separate Brig., 8 Corps. June, 1863, Averill's 4 Separate Brig., Dept. West Va. Dec., 1863, 3 Brig., 4 Div., W. Va. Designated 5th W. Va. Cav., Jany., 1864.

2nd REGIMENT VETERAN INFANTRY.—Org. Dec. 21, 1864, by consolidation of 1st and 4th W. Va. Infy. Dec., 1864, Res. Div., West Va. April, 1865, 2 Brig., 1 Infy. Div., West Va. Mustered out July 16, 1865.

3rd REGIMENT INFANTRY.—Org at Wheeling, Clarksburg and Newburg, W. Va., June 5 to July 10, 1861. July, 1861, Unatt., West Va. Sept., 1861, Cheat Mt. Dist., W. Va. March, 1862, Cheat Mt. Dist., Dept. Mts. April, 1862, Milroy's Indpt. Brig., Dept. Mts. June, 1862, Milroy's Indpt. Brig., 1 Corps, Army Va. Sept., 1862, Def. Washington, D. C. Oct., 1862, Unatt., Dist. W. Va., Dept. Ohio. March, 1863, Averill's 4 Separate Brig., 8 Corps, Middle Dept. June, 1863, Averill's 4 Separate Brig., West Va. Dec., 1863, 3 Brig., 4 Div., West Va. Designated 6th West Va. Cav., Jany., 1864.

4th REGIMENT INFANTRY.—Org. at Mason City, Point Pleasant and Grafton, June 17 to Aug. 22, 1861. Aug., 1861, Unassigned, Dist. Kanawha, Dept. W. Va. March, 1862, 4 Brig., Kanawha Div., Dept. Mts., W. Va. Sept., 1862, Point Pleasant, Dist. Kanawha, W. Va., Dept. Ohio. Jany., 1863, 3 Brig., 2 Div., 15 Corps, Army Tenn. Oct., 1863, 2 Brig., 2 Div., 15 Corps, Tenn. May, 1864, 2 Brig., 1 Infy. Div., West Va. Consolidated with 1st West Va. Infy., Dec. 21, 1864, to form 2nd Veteran Infy.

5th REGIMENT INFANTRY.—Org. at Ceredo, Sept., 1861. Oct., 1861, Unatt., Dist. Kanawha, Dept. W. Va. March, 1862, Dist. Cumberland, Dept. Mts. April, 1862, Milroy's Indpt. Brig., Dept. Mts. June, 1862, Milroy's Indpt. Brig., 1 Corps, Army Va. Sept., 1862, Def. Washington, D. C. Oct., 1862, Dist. Kanawha, W. Va., Dept. Ohio. Jany., 1863, Unatt., Dist. Kanawha, West Va. March, 1863, 1 Brig., 3 Div., 8 Corps, Middle Dept. June, 1863, 1 Brig., Scammon's Div., West Va. Dec., 1863, 1 Brig., 3 Div., West Va. April, 1864, 1 Brig., 2 Infy. Div., West Va. Consolidated with 9th W. Va. Infy. Nov. 9, 1864, to form 1st Veteran Infy.

6th REGIMENT INFANTRY.—Org. at Grafton, Mannington, Cairo, Parkersburg and Wheeling, Aug. 13 to Dec. 26, 1861. Oct., 1861, R. R. Dist., W. Va. March, 1862, R. R. Dist., Dept. Mts. July, 1862, R. R. Dist., 8 Corps, Middle Dept. Sept., 1862, R. R. Div., West Va. Jany., 1863, Clarksburg, W. Va., 8 Corps, Middle Dept. March, 1863, 6 Brig., 1 Div., 8 Corps. June, 1863, Wilkinson's Brig., Scammon's Div., W. Va. Dec., 1863, 3 Brig., 2 Div., West Va. April, 1864, Kelly's

Command, Res. Div., West Va. April, 1865, 1 Brig., 1 Infy. Div., West Va. Mustered out June 10, 1865.

7th REGIMENT INFANTRY.—Org. at Portland, Cameron, Grafton, Wheeling, Morgantown and Greenland. July 16 to Dec. 3, 1861. Nov., 1861, R. R. Dist., West Va. Jany., 1862, 1 Brig., Landers' Div., Potomac. March, 1862, 1 Brig., Shields' Div., Banks' 5 Corps. April, 1862, 1 Brig., Shields' Div., Dept. Shenandoah. May, 1862, 1 Brig., Shields' Div., Dept. Rappahannock. July, 1862. Kimball's Indpt. Brig., 2 Corps, Potomac. Sept., 1862, 1 Brig., 3 Div., 2 Corps, Potomac. March, 1864, 3 Brig., 2 Div., 2 Corps, Potomac. Mustered out July 1, 1865.

8th REGIMENT INFANTRY.—Org. at Buffalo, Nov., 1861. Nov., 1861, Uassigned, Dist. Kanawha, W. Va. March, 1862, Unatt., Dist. Kanawha, W. Va., Dept. Mts. May, 1862, Cluserett's Advance Brig., Dept. Mts. June, 1862, Bohlen's Brig., 3 Div., 1 Corps, Army Va. Sept., 1862, Milroy's Indpt. Brig., Def. Washington. Oct., 1862, Point Pleasant, Dist. Kanawha, Dept. Ohio. March, 1863, Averill's 4 Separate Brig., 8 Corps, Middle Dept. June, 1863, Averill's 4 Separate Brig., Dept. West Va. Dec., 1863, 3 Brig., 4 Div., Dept. West Va. Designation changed to 7th West Va. Cav. Jany., 26, 1864.

9th REGIMENT INFANTRY.—Org. at large in W. Va. Nov. 28, 1861 to April 30, 1862. Dec., 1861, Unatt., Dist. Kanawha, W. Va. March, 1862, Dist. Kanawha, Dept. Mts. May, 1862, 4 Brig., Kanawha Div., Dept. Mts. Sept., 1862, Dist. Kanawha, Dept. Ohio. Jany., 1863, Milroy's Command, Winchester, Va., 8 Corps. Feby., 1863, 2 Brig., 2 Div., 8 Corps. June, 1863, 1 Brig., Scammon's Div., Dept. W. Va. Aug., 1863, 2 Brig., Scammon's Div., West Va. Dec., 1863, 2 Brig., 3 Div., W. Va. April, 1864, 2 Brig., 2 Infy., Div. W. Va. Consolidated with 5th W. Va. Infy. Nov. 9, 1864, to form 1st Veteran Infy.

10th REGIMENT INFANTRY.—Org. at large, March to May, 1862. March, 1862, Cheat Mt. Dist., Dept. Mts. May, 1862, R. R. Dist., Dept. Mts. July, 1862, R. R. Dist., 8 Corps, Middle Dept. Sept., 1862, R. R. Div., W. Va. Jany., 1863, Milroy's Command, Winchester, Va., 8 Corps. March, 1863, Averill's 4 Separate Brig., 8 Corps. June, 1863, Averill's 4 Separate Brig., Dept. West Va. Dec., 1863, 1 Brig., 4 Div., West Va. April, 1864, Kelly's Command, Res. Div., West Va. July, 1864, 3 Brig., 1 Infy., Div. W. Va. July, 1864, 1 Brig., 3 Div., W. Va. Dec., 1864, 3 Brig., Infy. Div., 24 Corps, Dept. Va. June, 1865, 2 Brig., Infy. Div., 24 Corps. Mustered out Aug. 9, 1865.

11th REGIMENT INFANTRY.—Org. at large, West Va. Oct., 1861. Oct., 1861, R. R. Dist., W. Va. March, 1862, R. R. Dist., Dept. Mts. July, 1862, R. R. Dist., 8 Corps, Middle Dept. Sept., 1862, R. R. Div., West Va. Jany., 1863, Parkersburg, W. Va. March, 1863, 6 Brig., 1 Div., 8 Corps. June, 1863, Wilkinson's Brig., Scammon's Div., W. Va. Dec., 1863, 3 Brig., 2 Div., W. Va. April, 1864, 3 Brig., 2 Infy. Div., W. Va. July, 1864, 2 Brig., 3, Infy. Div., W. Va. July, 1864, 3 Brig., 1 Div., W. Va. Dec., 1864, 3 Brig., Infy. Div., W. Va. Mustered out June 17, 1865.

12th REGIMENT INFANTRY.—Org. at Wheeling, Aug. 30, 1862. Aug., 1862, R. R. Dist., 8 Corps, Middle Dept. Jany., 1863, Milroy's Command, Winchester, Va., 8 Corps. Feby., 1863, 2 Brig., 2 Div., 8 Corps. June, 1863, 1 Brig., 1 Div., Dept. Susquehanna. July, 1863, McReynolds' Command, Martinsburg, W. Va. Dec., 1863, 1 Brig., 1 Div., W. Va. Jany., 1864, 1 Brig., 2 Div., West Va. April, 1864, 2 Brig., 1 Infy. Div., West Va. Dec., 1864, 2 Brig., Infy. Div., 24 Corps, Dept. Va. Mustered out June 16, 1865.

13th REGIMENT INFANTRY.—Org. at Mt. Pleasant and Barboursville, Oct., 1862. Oct., 1862, Point Pleasant, Dist. Kanawha, W. Va., Dept. Ohio. March, 1863, 1 Brig., 3 Div., 8 Corps, Middle Dept. June, 1863, 1 Brig., Scammon's Div., Dept. W. Va. Dec., 1863, 1 Brig., 3 Div., West Va. Jany., 1864, 1 Brig., 2 Div., W. Va. April, 1864, 1 Brig., 2 Infy. Div., W. Va. Jany., 1865, 1 Brig., 1 Infy. Div., W. Va. April, 1865, 1 Brig., 4 Prov'l Div., W. Va. Mustered out June 22, 1865.

14th REGIMENT INFANTRY.—Org. at Wheeling, Aug. 25, 1862. Sept., 1862, R. R. Div., West Va. Jany.,

1863, New Creek, W. Va., Def. Upper Potomac, 8 Corps, Middle Dept. March, 1863, 5 Brig., 1 Div., 8 Corps. June, 1863, Mulligan's Brig., Scammon's Div., Dept. W. Va. Dec., 1863, 2 Brig., 2 Div., West Va. April, 1864, 2 Brig., 2 Infy. Div., W. Va. Jany., 1865, 1 Brig., 2 Infy. Div., West Va. Mustered out June 28, 1865.

15th REGIMENT INFANTRY.—Org. at Wheeling, Aug. to Oct., 1862. Oct., 1862, R. R. Div., W. Va. Jany., 1863, Sir Johns Run, Def. Upper Potomac, 8 Corps, Middle Dept. March, 1863, 3 Brig., 1 Div., 8 Corps. June, 1863, Unatt., New Creek, W. Va., Dept. W. Va. Aug., 1863, Campbell's Brig., Scammon's Div., Dept. W. Va. Dec., 1863, 1 Brig., 2 Div., W. Va. April, 1864, 3 Brig., 2 Infy. Div., W. Va. April, 1864, 2 Brig., 3 Infy. Div., W. Va. July, 1864, 3 Brig., 1 Infy. Div., W. Va. Dec., 1864, 3 Brig., Infy. Div., 24 Corps, Dept. Va. Mustered out June 14, 1865.

16th REGIMENT INFANTRY.—Org. at Washington, D. C., Aug. and Sept., 1862. Oct., 1862, 2 Brig., Abercrombie's Div., Def. Washington. Feby., 1863, 2 Brig., Abercrombie's Div., 22 Corps. April, 1863, 2 Brig., DeRussy's Div., Def. Washington, South Potomac, 22 Corps. Mustered out June 10, 1863.

17th REGIMENT INFANTRY.—Org. at Wheeling, Sept. 26, 1864. Oct., 1864, Reserve Div., Dept. W. Va. April, 1865, 1 Brig., 1 Infy. Div., W. Va. Mustered out June 30, 1865.

INDEPENDENT BATTALION INFANTRY.—Org. at Wheeling, Oct. 1, 1862 to Jany. 9, 1863. Mustered out Co. B, April 23, 1864; Co. A, May 31, 1865.

1st INDEPENDENT COMPANY LOYAL VIRGINIANS.—Org. at Cobb's Island, June 30, 1864. Mustered out Dec. 1, 1865.

WISCONSIN

1st REGIMENT CAVALRY.—Org. at Ripon and Kenosha, Wis., Sept. 1, 1861 to Feby., 1862. April, 1862, Vandever's Brig., Dist. S. E. Mo., Dept. Mo. Oct., 1862, Cav. Brig., Dist. S. E. Mo., Dept. Mo. June, 1863, 2 Brig., 1 Cav. Div., Cumb'd. Oct., 1864, 2 Brig., 1 Div., Cav. Corps, Mil. Div. Miss. Mustered out July 19, 1865.

2nd REGIMENT CAVALRY.—Org. at Milwaukee, Wis., Dec. 30, 1861 to March 10, 1862. March, 1862, Benton Barracks, Mo. June, 1862, Steele's Army, S. W. Mo., Dept. Mo. July, 1862, Dist. E. Ark., Dept. Mo. Nov., 1862, 2 Brig., Cav. Div., Dist. E. Ark., Dept. Tenn. Jany., 1863, 2 Brig., 2 Cav. Div., 13 Corps, Tenn. Feby., 1863, 3 Brig., Dist. Memphis, 5 Div., 16 Corps, Tenn. June, 1863, Bussey's Cav. Brig., Herron's Div., 13 Corps, Tenn. Aug., 1863, Cav. Brig., 16 Corps, Tenn. Sept., 1863, 1 Div., 17 Corps, Tenn. Jany., 1864, Winslow's Cav. Brig., Dist. Vicksburg. Dec., 1864, 3 Brig., Cav. Div., Dist. West Tenn. July, 1865, 2 Brig., 2 Cav. Div., Mil. Div., Gulf. Nov., 1865. Dept. of Texas. First Battalion.—June, 1862, Dept. Missouri. Oct., 1863, 1 Brig., 3 Div., Army Frontier, Dept. Mo. June, 1863, Dist. Rolla, Dept. Mo. Sept., 1864, Dist. North Missouri, Dept. Mo. Regt. mustered out November 15, 1865.

3rd REGIMENT CAVALRY.—Org. at Janesville, Wis., November 30, 1861 to Jany. 31, 1862. March, 1862, Benton Barracks, Mo. May, 1862, Dept. of Kansas. Sept., 1862, Solomon's 1 Brig., Herron's 1 Div., Army Frontier., Dept. Mo. Nov., 1862, Cav. Command, Herron's Div., Army Frontier, Dept. Mo. June, 1863, Dist. Frontier, Dept. Mo. Dec., 1863, 3 Brig., Dist. Frontier. Jany., 1864, Unassigned, Dist. Frontier, 7 Corps, Dept. Ark. April, 1864, Unassigned, Little Rock, 7 Corps. Sept., 1864, 4 Brig., Cav. Div., 7 Corps. Feby., 1865, Cav. Brig., Post Little Rock, Ark., 7 Corps. April, 1865, Unassigned, 1 Div., 7 Corps. June, 1865, Dist. South Kansas, Dept. Mo. Mustered out September 8, 1865. Companies A, C, D, F, and M.—Oct., 1863, Dist. Border, Dept. Mo. Jany., 1864, Unassigned, Dept. Kansas. June, 1864, Dist. South Kansas. April, 1865, Dist. North Kansas. Mustered out, September 29, 1865. Co.'s G and L mustered out October 26, 1865.

4th REGIMENT CAVALRY.—Org. at Racine as 4th Infantry, July 2, 1861. July, 1861, Dix's Div., Baltimore,

Md. Feby., 1862, Williams' Brig., Butler's N. O. Exp. April. 1862, 2 Brig., Dept. Gulf. Dec., 1862, Grover's Div., Dept. Gulf. Jany., 1863, 2 Brig., 3 Div., 19 Corps, Gulf. July, 1863, Cav. Brig., 19 Corps. July, 1863, Dist. Baton Rouge, La., Gulf. (designation changed to 4th Cavalry, August 22, 1863.) Oct., 1863, Unatt., Cav. Div., Gulf. Jany., 1864, Dist. Baton Rouge, La., Gulf. June, 1864, 4 Brig. Cav. Div., Gulf. Aug., 1864, 2 Brig., Cav. Div., Gulf. Feby., 1865, Cav. Brig., Dist. Baton Rouge, La., Gulf. March, 1865, 1 Brig., 1 Cav. Div., Mil. Div., West Miss. April, 1865, 2 Brig., 1 Div., Cav. Corps, Gulf. May, 1865, 3 Brig., 1 Cav. Div., Gulf. July, 1865, Dept. Texas. Mustered out May 28, 1866.

1st REGIMENT HEAVY ARTILLERY.—Battery A org. as Co. K, 2nd Wis. Infy. Detached from Regt. Aug. 1861. Permanently detached as Battery A, Dec. 9, 1861. Dec., 1861, Mil. Dist., Washington. May, 1862, Whipple's Command, Mil. Dist., Washington. Feby., 1863, Def. Alexandria, 22 Corps. April, 1863, 3 Brig., DeRussy's Div., 22 Corps. Dec., 1863, 4 Brig., DeRussy's Div., 22 Corps. March, 1864, 3 Brig., DeRussy's Div., 22 Corps. May, 1864, 2 Brig., DeRussy's Div., 22 Corps. Mustered out August 18, 1865. Battery B.—Sept., 1863, Murfreesboro, Tenn., Dept. Cumb'd. Jany., 1864, Lexington, Ky. Mustered out August 30, 1865. Battery C.—Nov., 1863, 2 Div., Arty. Res., Dept. Cumb'd. Dec., 1863, Garrison Arty., Chattanooga, Tenn., Dept. Cumb'd. April, 1865, 3 Brig., 4 Div., Dist. East Tenn. Mustered out September 21, 1865. Battery D.—Mustered in November 7, 1863. Feby., 1864, Def. New Orleans, La., Gulf. July, 1864, Dist. LaFourche, La., Gulf. June, 1865, Def. of Washington, 22 Corps. Mustered out August 18, 1865. Companies E, F, G, H, I, K, L, and M., organized Sept. and Oct., 1864. Oct., 1864, 3 Brig., DeRussy's Div., 22 Corps. Dec., 1864, 4 Brig., DeRussy's Div., 22 Corps. Mustered out June 26, 1865.

1st BATTERY LIGHT ARTILLERY.—Org. at LaCrosse, Wis., Oct. 10, 1861. Jany., 1862, Louisville, Ky. April, 1862, Arty., 7 Div., Army Ohio. Oct., 1862, Cumberland Div., Dist. West Va., Dept. Ohio. Nov., 1862, Arty., 9 Div., R. W., 13 Corps, Tenn. Dec., 1862, Arty., 3 Div., Sherman's Yazoo Exp. Jany., 1863, Arty., 9 Div., 13 Corps, Tenn. July, 1863, 4 Brig., 1 Div., 13 Corps, Tenn. Aug., 1863, 4 Brig., 1 Div., 13 Corps, Gulf. Aug., 1863, Def. New Orleans, La., Gulf. Jany., 1864, Arty., 1 Div., 13 Corps, Gulf. June, 1864, Dist. Morganza, Gulf. Aug., 1864, Arty., Cav. Div., Gulf. Feby., 1865, Cav. Brig., Dist. Baton Rouge, La., Gulf. Mustered out July 18, 1865.

2nd BATTERY LIGHT ARTILLERY.—Org. at LaCrosse, Wis., Oct. 10, 1861. Jany., 1862, Fortress Monroe, Va., Dept. Va. July, 1862, Fortress Monroe, Va., 7 Corps, Dept. Va. Sept., 1862, Camp Hamilton, Va., 7 Corps, Va. Jany., 1863, Arty., Div. at Suffolk, 7 Corps. April, 1863, Arty., 1 Div., 7 Corps. June, 1863, 2 Brig., 1 Div., 4 Corps, Dept. Va. Aug., 1863, Arty., Yorktown, Va., Dept. Va., and N. C. Jany., 1864, Point Lookout, Md. Mustered out July 10, 1865.

3rd BATTERY LIGHT ARTILLERY.—Org. at Racine, Wis., Oct. 10, 1861. Jany., 1862, Louisville, Ky. March, 1862, Arty., 5 Div., Army Ohio. Sept., 1862, Arty., 5 Div., 2 Corps, Army Ohio. Nov., 1862, Arty., 3 Div., Left Wing 14 Corps, Cumb'd. Jany., 1863, Arty., 3 Div., 21 Corps, Cumb'd. Oct., 1863, 2 Div., Arty. Res., Cumb'd. March, 1864, Garrison Arty., Chattanooga, Tenn., Cumb'd. Mustered out July 20, 1865.

4th BATTERY LIGHT ARTILLERY.—Org. at Racine, Oct. 1, 1861. Jany., 1862, Fortress Monroe, Va., Dept. Va. Sept., 1862, Camp Hamilton, Va., 7 Corps, Dept. Va. Jany., 1863, Arty., Div. at Suffolk, Va., 7 Corps, Va. April, 1863, Arty., 1 Div., 7 Corps, Va. May, 1863, 2 Brig., 2 Div., 4 Corps, Va. July, 1863, Yorktown, Va., Dept. Va. and N. C. Dec., 1863, Arty. Brig., U. S. Forces, Norfolk and Portsmouth, Va. April, 1864, Arty., 1 Div., 18 Corps, Army James. June, 1864, Arty., Cav. Div., Army James. Mustered out July 3, 1865.

5th BATTERY LIGHT ARTILLERY.—Org. at Racine, Wis., Oct. 10, 1861. March, 1862, Arty. Div., Army Miss. May, 1862, Arty., 4 Div., Army Miss. Sept., 1862,

30 Brig., 9 Div., Army Ohio. Oct., 1862, 30 Brig., 9 Div., 3 Corps, Army Ohio. Nov., 1862, 1 Brig., 1 Div., Right Wing 14 Corps, Army Cumb'd. Jany., 1863, Arty., 1 Div., 20 Corps, Cumb'd. Oct., 1863, Arty., 2 Div., 14 Corps. July, 1864, Arty. Brig., 14 Corps. Mustered out June 6, 1865.

6th BATTERY LIGHT ARTILLERY.—Org. at Racine, Wis., Oct. 2, 1861. March, 1862, Arty. Div., Army Miss. Sept., 1862, Arty., 3 Div., Army Miss. Nov., 1862, Arty., 7 Div., Left Wing 13 Corps, Tenn. Dec., 1862, Arty., 7 Div., 16 Corps, Tenn. Jany., 1863, Arty., 7 Div., 17 Corps, Tenn. Sept., 1863, Arty., 2 Div., 17 Corps. Dec., 1863, Arty., 3 Div., 15 Corps. Nov., 1864, Garrison Arty., Nashville, Tenn. Feby., 1865, Arty. Res., Chattanooga, Tenn., Cumb'd. Mustered out July 3, 1865.

7th BATTERY LIGHT ARTILLERY.—Org. at Racine, Oct. 4, 1861. March, 1862, Arty. Div., Army Miss. July, 1862, Arty., Dist. Columbus, Ky., Tenn. Nov., 1862, Arty., Dist. Columbus, 13 Corps, Tenn. Dec., 1862, Arty., Dist. Jackson, Tenn., 16 Corps, Tenn. March, 1863, Arty., 3 Div., 16 Corps. July, 1863, 4 Brig., Dist. Memphis, Tenn., 5 Div., 16 Corps. Jany., 1864, Arty., Dist. Memphis, 16 Corps. June, 1864, 2 Brig., Cav. Div., Sturgis' Exp. June, 1864, 2 Brig., Memphis, Tenn., Dist. West Tenn. Sept., 1864, Unatt., Dist. Memphis, Dist. West Tenn. Dec., 1864, Unatt., Arty. Res., Dist. West Tenn. Mustered out July 20, 1865.

8th BATTERY LIGHT ARTILLERY.—Org. at Racine, Wis., Jany. 8, 1862. March, 1862, Benton Barracks, Mo. April, 1862, Dept. of Kansas. June, 1862, Arty., 4 Div., Army Miss. Aug., 1862, Arty., 2 Div., Army Miss. Sept., 1862, 32 Brig., 9 Div., Army Ohio. Sept., 1862, 32 Brig., 9 Div., 3 Corps, Army Ohio. Nov., 1862, 3 Brig., 1 Div., Right Wing 14 Corps, Cumb'd. Jany., 1863, Arty., 1 Div., 20 Corps, Cumb'd. Oct., 1863, 2 Div., Arty. Res., Cumb'd. April, 1864, Post Murfreesboro, Tenn., Cumb'd. July, 1864, 1 Brig., Def. Nashville and Chattanooga R. R., Cumb'd. March, 1865, 1 Brig., 1 Sub Dist., Dist. Middle Tenn., Cumb'd. Mustered out Aug. 10, 1865.

9th BATTERY LIGHT ARTILLERY.—Org. at Burlington, Wis., Jany. 27, 1862. Attached to Dept. of Kan. and Dept. of New Mex. and Dist. of Colo. Mustered out Sept. 30, 1865.

10th BATTERY LIGHT ARTILLERY.—Org. at New Lisbon, Wis., Feby. 10, 1862. March, 1862, Benton Barracks, Mo. May, 1862, Arty. Div., Army Miss. July, 1862, Arty., 1 Div., Army Miss. Sept., 1862, Arty., 13 Div., Army Ohio. Nov., 1862, Arty., 4 Div., Centre 14 Corps, Cumb'd. Jany., 1863, Arty., 4 Div., 14 Corps, Cumb'd. June, 1863, Arty., 2 Div., Res. Corps, Cumb'd. Oct., 1863, Unass'd, Dept. Cumb'd. Nov., 1863, 2 Div., Arty. Res., Cumb'd. April, 1864, Arty., Kilpatrick's 3 Cav. Div., Cumb'd. Nov., 1864, Arty., 3 Div., Cav. Corps, Mil. Div. Miss. Mustered out April 26, 1865.

11th BATTERY LIGHT ARTILLERY.—Org. at Madison, Wis., Feby. 22, 1862. Transferred to 1st Ill. Light Arty. as Batty. "L," Feby., 1862.

12th BATTERY LIGHT ARTILLERY.—Org. at St. Louis, Mo., Feby. and March, 1862. May, 1862, Arty. Div., Army Miss. Sept., 1862, Arty., 3 Div., Army Miss. Nov., 1862, Arty., 7 Div., Left Wing 13 Corps, Tenn. Dec., 1862, Arty., 7 Div., 16 Corps, Tenn. Jany., 1863, Arty., 7 Div., 17 Corps, Tenn. Sept., 1863, Arty., 2 Div., 17 Corps. Dec., 1863, Arty., 3 Div., 15 Corps. Sept., 1864, Arty. Brig., 15 Corps. Mustered out June 7, 1865.

13th BATTERY LIGHT ARTILLERY.—Org. at Milwaukee, Wis., Dec. 29, 1863. Feby., 1864, Dist. Baton Rouge, La., Dept. Gulf. Mustered out July 20, 1865.

COMPANY G 1st BERDAN SHARPSHOOTERS.—Org. at Camp Randall, Wis. (See 1st U. S. Sharpshooters.)

1st REGIMENT INFANTRY (3 MONTHS).—Org. at Milwaukee, Wis., April 27, 1861. June, 1861, Abercrombie's 6 Brig., Negley's 2 Div., Patterson's Army. Mustered out Aug. 21, 1861.

1st REGIMENT INFANTRY (3 YEARS).—Org. at Milwaukee, Wis., Oct. 19, 1861. Nov., 1861, 7 Brig., Army Ohio. Dec., 1861, 7 Brig., 2 Div., Army Ohio. Feby., 1862, 7 Indpt. Brig., Army Ohio. Aug., 1862, 28

Brig., 3 Div., Army Ohio. Sept., 1862, 28 Brig., 3 Div., 1 Corps, Army Ohio. Nov., 1862, 3 Brig., 1 Div., Centre 14 Corps, Cumb'd. Jany., 1863, 3 Brig., 1 Div., 14 Corps, Cumb'd. April, 1863, 2 Brig., 1 Div., 14 Corps. Oct., 1863, 3 Brig., 1 Div., 14 Corps. Mustered out Oct. 13, 1864.

2nd REGIMENT INFANTRY.—Org. at Madison, June 11, 1861. June, 1861, Sherman's Brig., Tyler's Div., McDowell's Army N. E. Va. Aug., 1861, Fort Corcoran Div., Potomac. Oct., 1861, King's Brig., McDowell's Div., Army Potomac. March, 1862, 3 Brig., 3 Div., 1 Corps, Army Potomac. April, 1862, 3 Brig., King's Div., Dept. Rappahannock. June, 1862, 4 Brig., 1 Div., 3 Corps, Army Va. Sept., 1862, 4 Brig., 1 Div., 1 Corps, Army Potomac. June, 1863, 1 Brig., 1 Div., 1 Corps. March, 1864, 1 Brig., 4 Div., 5 Corps. Aug., 1864, 3 Brig., 3 Div., 5 Corps. Sept., 1864, 1 Brig., 3 Div., 5 Corps. Consolidated with 6th Wis. Infy., Nov., 22, 1864.

3rd REGIMENT INFANTRY.—Org. at Fond du Lac, Wis., June 19, 1861. July, 1861, Hamilton's Brig., Patterson's Army. Oct., 1861, Stiles' Brig., Banks' Div., Army Potomac. March, 1862, 3 Brig., 1 Div., Banks' 5 Corps. April, 1862, 3 Brig., 1 Div., Dept. Shenandoah. June, 1862, 3 Brig., 1 Div., 2 Corps, Army Va. Sept. 1862, 3 Brig., 1 Div., 12 Corps, Army Potomac. Oct., 1863, 3 Brig., 1 Div., 12 Corps, Cumb'd. April, 1864, 2 Brig., 1 Div., 20 Corps, Cumb'd. Mustered out July 18, 1865.

4th REGIMENT INFANTRY.—Org. at Racine, Wis., July 2, 1861. (See 4th Regt. Cav.)

5th REGIMENT INFANTRY.—Org. at Madison, Wis., July 12, 1861. Aug., 1861, King's Brig., McDowell's Div., Army Potomac. Oct., 1861, Hancock's Brig., Smith's Div, Army Potomac. March, 1862, 1 Brig., 2 Div., 4 Corps, Army Potomac. May, 1862, 1 Brig., 2 Div., 6 Corps, Army Potomac. Feby., 1863, Light Div., 6 Corps. May, 1863, 3 Brig., 1 Div., 6 Corps. Jany., 1864, 3 Brig., 2 Div., 6 Corps. Feby., 1864, 3 Brig., 1 Div., 6 Corps. Aug., 1864, 3 Brig., 1 Div., 6 Corps, Army Shenandoah. Dec., 1864, 3 Brig., 1 Div., 6 Corps, Potomac. Mustered out July 11, 1865.

6th REGIMENT INFANTRY.—Org. at Madison, Wis., July 16, 1861. Aug., 1861, King's Brig., McDowell's Div., Army Potomac. March, 1862, 1 Brig., 3 Div., 1 Corps, Army Potomac. April, 1862, 3 Brig., King's Div., Dept. Rappahannock. June, 1862, 4 Brig., 1 Div., 3 Corps, Army Va. Sept., 1862, 4 Brig., 1 Div., 1 Corps, Army Potomac. June, 1863, 1 Brig., 1 Div., 1 Corps. March, 1864, 1 Brig., 4 Div., 5 Corps. Aug., 1864, 3 Brig., 3 Div., 5 Corps. Sept., 1864, 1 Brig., 3 Div., 5 Corps. Mustered out July 14, 1865.

7th REGIMENT INFANTRY.—Org. at Madison, Wis., Sept. 2, 1861. Sept., 1861, King's Brig., McDowell's Div., Army Potomac. March, 1862, 1 Brig., 3 Div., 1 Corps, Army Potomac. April, 1862, 3 Brig., King's Div., Dept. Rappahannock. June, 1862, 4 Brig., 1 Div., 3 Corps, Army Va. Sept., 1862, 4 Brig., 1 Div., 1 Corps, Army Potomac. June, 1863, 1 Brig., 1 Div., 1 Corps. March, 1864, 1 Brig., 4 Div., 5 Corps. Aug., 1864, 3 Brig., 3 Div., 5 Corps. Sept., 1864, 1 Brig., 3 Div., 5 Corps. Mustered out July 3, 1865.

8th REGIMENT INFANTRY.—Org. at Madison and mustered in Sept. 13, 1861. Oct., 1861, Dept. Missouri. Jany., 1862, 3 Brig., Dist. Cairo. March, 1862, 1 Brig., 5 Div., Army Miss. April, 1862, 1 Brig., 3 Div., Army Miss. April, 1862, 2 Brig., 2 Div., Army Miss. Nov., 1862, 2 Brig., 8 Div., Left Wing 13 Corps, Tenn. Dec., 1862, 2 Brig., 8 Div., 16 Corps, Tenn. April, 1863, 2 Brig., 3 Div., 15 Corps. Dec., 1863, 2 Brig., 1 Div., 16 Corps. March, 1864, 2 Brig., 1 Div., 16 Corps, Gulf. June, 1864, 2 Brig., 1 Div., 16 Corps, Tenn. Dec., 1864, 2 Brig., 1 Div., Det. Army Tenn., Dept. Cumb'd. Feby., 1865, 2 Brig., 1 Div., 16 Corps (new), Mil. Div. West Miss. Mustered out Sept. 5, 1865.

9th REGIMENT INFANTRY.—Org. at Milwaukee, Wis., Oct. 26, 1861. Jany., 1862, Dept. of Kan. Aug., 1862, 1 Brig., Dept. of Kan. Oct., 1862, 1 Brig., 1 Div., Army Frontier, Dept. Mo. June 1863, Dist. Rolla and Dist. St. Louis, Mo., Dept. Mo. Aug., 1863, 2 Brig., 3 Div., Ark. Exp. Jany., 1864, 2 Brig.,

3 Div., 7 Corps, Ark. March, 1864, 1 Brig., 3 Div., 7 Corps. May, 1864, 1 Brig., 1 Div., 7 Corps. Aug., 1865, Dept. of Ark. Mustered out Jany. 30, 1866.

10th REGIMENT INFANTRY.—Org. at Milwaukee, Wis., Oct. 14, 1861. Dec., 1861, 9 Brig., Army Ohio. Dec., 1861, 9 Brig., 3 Div., Army Ohio. Sept., 1862, 9 Brig., 3 Div., 1 Corps, Army Ohio. Nov., 1862, 1 Brig., 1 Div., Centre 14 Corps, Cumb'd. Jany., 1863, 1 Brig., 1 Div., 14 Corps, Cumb'd. Mustered out Oct. 25, 1864.

11th REGIMENT INFANTRY.—Org. at Madison, Wis., and mustered in Oct. 18, 1861. Nov., 1861, Dept. Mo. March, 1862, Dist. S. E. Mo., Dept. Mo. May, 1862, 1 Brig., 1 Div., Army S. W. Mo., Dept. Mo. July, 1862, Dist. Eastern Ark., Dept. Mo. Oct., 1862, 1 Brig., 1 Div., Dist. S. E. Mo., Dept. Mo. March, 1863, 2 Brig., 14 Div., 13 Corps, Tenn. July, 1863, 2 Brig., 1 Div., 13 Corps, Tenn. Aug., 1863, 2 Brig., 1 Div., 13 Corps, Gulf. May, 1864, Dist. LaFource, La., Gulf. Feby., 1865, 3 Brig., 2 Div., 16 Corps, Mil. Div. West Miss. Mustered out Sept. 4, 1865.

12th REGIMENT INFANTRY.—Org. at Madison, Wis., Oct. 18 to Dec. 13, 1861. Feby., 1862, Dept. of Kan. June, 1862, Dist. Columbus, Ky., Tenn. Oct., 1862, 3 Brig., 4 Div., Dist. Jackson, Tenn. Nov., 1862, 3 Brig., 4 Div., Right Wing 13 Corps, Tenn. Dec., 1862, 3 Brig., 4 Div., 17 Corps. Jany., 1863, 3 Brig., 4 Div., 16 Corps, Tenn. July, 1863, 3 Brig., 4 Div., 13 Corps, Tenn. Aug., 1863, 3 Brig., 4 Div., 17 Corps. July, 1864, 1 Brig., 3 Div., 17 Corps. Mustered out July 20, 1865.

13th REGIMENT INFANTRY.—Org. at Janesville, Wis., Oct. 17, 1861. Jany., 1862, Dept. of Kan. June, 1862, Dist. Columbus, Ky., Tenn. Aug., 1862, Garrison Forts Henry and Donelson, Tenn. June, 1863, 1 Brig., 3 Div., Res. Corps, Cumb'd. Oct., 1863, Post and Dist. Nashville, Tenn., Cumb'd. Jany., 1864, 1 Brig., Rousseau's 3 Div., 12 Corps, Cumb'd. April, 1864, 1 Brig., 4 Div., 20 Corps, Cumb'd. March, 1865, 3 Brig., 3 Div., 4 Corps, Cumb'd. Aug., 1865, Dept. Tex. Mustered out Nov. 24, 1865.

14th REGIMENT INFANTRY.—Org. at Fond du Lac, Wis., Jany. 30, 1862. March, 1862, Unatt., Army Tenn. May, 1862, 2 Brig., 5 Div., Tenn. May, 1862, Provost Guard, Pittsburg Landing, Tenn. Aug., 1862, 2 Brig., 6 Div., Dist. Corinth, Miss. Nov., 1862, 2 Brig., 6 Div., Left Wing 13 Corps, Tenn. Dec., 1862, 2 Brig., 6 Div., 16 Corps, Tenn. Jany., 1863, 2 Brig., 6 Div., 17 Corps. Sept., 1863, 2 Brig., 1 Div., 17 Corps. March, 1864, 2 Brig., Prov'l Div., 17 Corps, Gulf. June, 1864, Detached Brig., 17 Corps, and 4 Brig., 1 Div., 16 Corps. Aug., 1864, 1 Brig., 3 Div., 16 Corps. Dec., 1864, 1 Brig., 3 Div., Detachment Army Tenn., Dept. Cumb'd. Feby., 1865, 1 Brig., 3 Div., 16 Corps, Mil. Div. West Miss. March, 1865, 2 Brig., 3 Div., 16 Corps. Aug., 1865, Dist. Ala. (Veterans attached to 3 Brig., 3 Div., 17 Corps, April to Nov., 1864.) Mustered out Oct. 9, 1865.

15th REGIMENT INFANTRY.—Org. at Madison, Wis., Feby 14, 1862. March, 1862, Flotilla Brig., Army Miss. April, 1862, Garrison at Island No. 10. July, 1862, 2 Brig., 4 Div., Army Miss. Sept., 1862, 31 Brig., 9 Div., Army Ohio. Sept., 1862, 31 Brig., 9 Div., 3 Corps, Army Ohio. Nov., 1862, 2 Brig., 1 Div., Right Wing 14 Corps, Cumb'd, 2 Brig., 1 Div., 20 Corps, Cumb'd. March, 1863, 3 Brig., 1 Div., 20 Corps. Oct., 1863, 1 Brig., 3 Div., 4 Corps, Cumb'd. Nov., 1864, 2 Brig., 1 Separate Div., Dist. Etowah, Dept. Cumb'd. Mustered out Feby. 13, 1865.

16th REGIMENT INFANTRY.—Org. at Madison, Wis., Jany. 31, 1862. March, 1862, 1 Brig., 6 Div., Tenn. July, 1862, 1 Brig., 6 Div., Dist. Corinth, Miss. Nov., 1862, 1 Brig., 6 Div., Left Wing 13 Corps, Tenn. Dec., 1862, 1 Brig., 6 Div., 16 Corps. Jany., 1863, 1 Brig., 6 Div., 17 Corps, Tenn. Sept., 1863, 1 Brig., 1 Div., 17 Corps. April, 1864, 1 Brig., 3 Div., 17 Corps. Mustered out July 12, 1865.

17th REGIMENT INFANTRY.—Org. at Madison, Wis., March 15, 1862. April, 1862, 1 Brig., 6 Div., Tenn. July, 1862, 1 Brig., 6 Div., Dist. Corinth, Miss. Nov., 1862, 1 Brig., 6 Div., Left Wing 13 Corps, Tenn. Dec., 1862, 2 Brig., 6 Div., 16 Corps, Tenn. Jany., 1863, 2 Brig., 6 Div., 17 Corps. Sept., 1863, 2 Brig., 1 Div.,

17 Corps. April, 1864, 3 Brig., 3 Div., 17 Corps. Nov., 1864, 2 Brig., 3 Div., 17 Corps. Mustered out July 14, 1865.

18th REGIMENT INFANTRY.—Org. at Milwaukee, Wis., March 15, 1862. April, 1862, 2 Brig., 6 Div., Tenn. July, 1862, 2 Brig., 6 Div., Dist. of Corinth, Miss. Nov., 1862, 2 Brig., 6 Div., Left Wing 13 Corps, Tenn. Dec., 1862, 2 Brig., 6 Div., 16 Corps. Tenn. Jany., 1863, 2 Brig., 6 Div., 17 Corps. May, 1863, 1 Brig., 7 Div., 17 Corps. Sept., 1863, 1 Brig., 2.Div., 17 Corps. Dec., 1863, 1 Brig., 3 Div., 15 Corps. April, 1865, 2 Brig., 4 Div., 15 Corps. Non-veterans attached to 93rd Ill. Infy. Nov.-Dec., 1864. Veterans attached to 1 Brig., 1 Prov'l Div., Dept. Cumb'd, Dec., 1864. to Feby., 1865. Dist. of New Berne, N. C., to April, 1865.) Mustered out July 18, 1865.

19th REGIMENT INFANTRY.—Org. at Madison. Wis., April 30. 1862. June. 1862. Dist. Norfolk and Portsmouth, Va., 7 Corps, Dept. Va. April, 1863. Res. Brig., 3 Div., 7 Corps, Va. June, 1863. Wister's Indpt. Brig., 7 Corps. July, 1863. Yorktown, Va., Dept. Va. and N. C. Aug., 1863. Newport News. Va., Dept. of Va. and N. C. Oct., 1863. New Berne, N. C.. Dept. Va. and N. C. April, 1864, 3 Brig.. 1 Div.. 18 Corps, Army James. June, 1864, 2 Brig., 2 Div., 18 Corps. Aug., 1864. Norfolk. Va., Dept. Va. and N. C. Oct., 1864. 3 Brig., 2 Div.. 18 Corps. Dec., 1864. 1 Brig., 3 Div., 24 Corps. July. 1865, 1 Indpt. Brig., 24 Corps. Mustered out Aug. 9, 1865.

20th REGIMENT INFANTRY.—Org. at Madison, Wis., Aug. 23, 1862. Sept., 1862, 1 Brig., 3 Div., Army Frontier, Dept. Mo. June, 1863. 2 Brig.. Herron's Div.. 13 Corps, Tenn. Aug., 1863. 2 Brig., 2 Div.. 13 Corps. Gulf. June. 1864. U. S. Forces. Tex. Aug., 1864, U. S. Forces. Mobile Bay. Dec., 1864, Dist. Southern Ala.. Gulf. Feby., 1865, 1 Brig., 2 Div., Res. Corps. Mil. Div. West Miss. Feby.. 1865, 1 Brig.. 2 Div., 13 Corps, Mil. Div. West Miss. Mustered out July 14, 1865.

21st REGIMENT INFANTRY.—Org. at Oshkosh, Wis., Sept. 5, 1862. Sept., 1862, 28 Brig., 3 Div., Army Ohio. Sept., 1863, 23 Brig., 3 Div., 1 Corps, Army Ohio. Nov., 1862, 3 Brig., 1 Div., Centre 14 Corps, Cumb'd. Jany., 1863, 3 Brig., 1 Div., 14 Corps, Cumb'd. April, 1863, 2 Brig., 1 Div., 14 Corps. April, 1864, 1 Brig., 1 Div., 14 Corps. Mustered out June 8. 1865.

22nd REGIMENT INFANTRY.—Org. at Racine, Wis., Sept. 2. 1862. Sept., 1862, 2 Brig., 1 Div., Army Ky., Dept. Ohio. Nov., 1862, 1 Brig., 3 Div., Army Ky. Feby., 1863, Coburn's Brig.. Baird's Div., Army Ky., Dept. Cumb'd. June. 1863, 3 Brig., 1 Div., Res. Corps, Cumb'd. Oct., 1863, Coburn's Unatt. Brig., Cumb'd. Dec.. 1863, Post of Murfreesboro, Tenn.. Cumb'd. Jany., 1864. 2 Brig., 1 Div., 11 Corps, Cumb'd. April, 1864, 2 Brig., 3 Div., 20 Corps, Cumb'd. Mustered out June 12, 1865.

23rd REGIMENT INFANTRY.—Org. at Madison, Wis., Aug. 30, 1862. Sept. 1862. 2 Brig., 2 Div., Army Ky., Dept. Ohio. Oct., 1862, 1 Brig., 1 Div., Army Ky., Dept. Ohio. Nov., 1862, 1 Brig., 10 Div., Right Wing 13 Corps, Tenn. Dec., 1862, 1 Brig., 1 Div., Sherman's Yazoo Exp. Jany., 1863, 1 Brig., 10 Div., 13 Corps, Tenn. Aug., 1863, 1 Brig., 4 Div., 13 Corps, Gulf. June, 1864, Def. New Orleans, La. Aug., 1864, 3 Brig., 2 Div., 19 Corps, Gulf. Aug., 1864, Guppy's Brig., Mobile Bay. Oct., 1864, Dist. Eastern Ark., 7 Corps, Ark. Feby., 1865, 3 Brig., 1 Div., Res. Corps, Mil. Div. West Miss. Feby., 1865, 3 Brig., 1 Div., 13 Corps. Mustered out July 4, 1865.

24th REGIMENT INFANTRY.—Org. at Milwaukee, Wis., Aug. 15, 1862. Sept., 1862, 37 Brig., 11 Div., Army Ohio. Sept., 1862, 37 Brig., 11 Div., 3 Corps, Army Ohio. Nov:, 1862, 1 Brig., 3 Div., Right Wing 14 Corps, Cumb'd. Jany., 1863, 1 Brig., 3 Div., 20 Corps, Cumb'd. Oct., 1863, 1 Brig., 2 Div., 4 Corps, Cumb'd. Mustered out June 10, 1865.

25th REGIMENT INFANTRY.—Org. at LaCrosse, Wis., Sept. 14, 1862. Sept., 1862, Dept.. Northwest. Feby., 1863, Dist. Columbus, Ky., 6 Div., 16 Corps, Tenn. May, 1863, 3 Brig., Kimball's Prov'l Div., 16 Corps. July, 1863, 3 Brig., Kimball's Div., Dist. Eastern Ark. Aug., 1863, Helena, Ark., 2 Brig., 2 Div., Army of Ark. Jany., 1864, Dist. Eastern Ark., 7 Corps. Jany., 1864,

1 Brig., 4 Div., 16 Corps, Tenn. March, 1864, 2 Brig., 4 Div., 16 Corps. Sept., 1864, 2 Brig., 1 Div., 17 Corps. Mustered out June 7, 1865.

26th REGIMENT INFANTRY.—Org. at Milwaukee, Wis., Sept. 17, 1862. Oct.. 1862, 2 Brig., 3 Div., 11 Corps, Army Potomac. Oct., 1863, 2 Brig., 3 Div., 11 Corps, Cumb'd. April, 1864, 3 Brig., 3 Div., 20 Corps, Cumb'd. Mustered out June 17, 1865.

27th REGIMENT INFANTRY.—Org. at Milwaukee, Wis., March 7, 1863. March, 1863, Dist. Columbus, Ky., 6 Div., 16 Corps, Tenn. May, 1863, 3 Brig., Kimball's Prov'l Div., 16 Corps. July, 1863, 3 Brig., Kimball's Div., Dist. Eastern Ark. Aug., 1863. 2 Brig., 2 Div., Ark. Exp. Jany., 1864, 2 Brig., 2 Div., 7 Corps, Ark. April, 1864, 3 Brig., 3 Div., 7 Corps. May, 1864, 2 Brig., 1 Div., 7 Corps. Feby., 1865, 3 Brig., 3 Div., Res. Corps, Mil. Div. West Miss. Feby., 1865. 3 Brig., 3 Div., 13 Corps. Mustered out Aug. 29, 1865.

28th REGIMENT INFANTRY.—Org. at Milwaukee, Wis., Oct. 14, 1862. Jany., 1863, 2 Brig., 13 Div., 13 Corps, Tenn. March, 1863, 1 Brig., 13 Div., 13 Corps. July, 1863, 1 Brig., 13 Div., 16 Corps. Aug., 1863, 2 Brig., 3 Div., Ark. Exp. Jany.. 1864, 2 Brig., 3 Div., 7 Corps, Ark. April, 1864, Post Pine Bluff, Ark., 7 Corps. May, 1864, 1 Brig., 1 Div., 7 Corps. Feby., 1865, 3 Brig., 3 Div., Res. Corps, Mil Div. West Miss. Feby., 1865, 3 Brig., 3 Div., 13 Corps. June, 1865, Dept. Tex. Mustered out Aug. 23, 1865.

29th REGIMENT INFANTRY.—Org. at Madison, Wis., Sept. 27, 1862. Nov., 1862, 3 Brig., 12 Div., Dist. Eastern Ark., Dept. Tenn. Jany., 1863, 3 Brig., 12 Div., 13 Corps, Tenn. Feby., 1863, 1 Brig., 12 Div., 13 Corps. July, 1863, 1 Brig.. 3 Div., 13 Corps, Tenn. Aug., 1863, 1 Brig., 3 Div., 13 Corps, Gulf. June, 1864, Dist. La-Fourche, La., Dept. Gulf. Aug., 1864, 2 Brig., 2 Div., 19 Corps, Gulf. Dec., 1864, 1 Brig., Res. Corps, Mil. Div. West Miss. Feby., 1865, 1 Brig., 1 Div., Res. Corps, Mil. Div. West Miss. Feby., 1865, 1 Brig., 1 Div., 13 Corps, Mil. Div. West Miss. Mustered out June 22, 1865.

30th REGIMENT INFANTRY.—Org. at Madison, Wis., Oct. 21, 1862. Duty in Dept. Northwest and in Mil. Dist. and Dept. Ky. Mustered out Sept. 20, 1865.

31st REGIMENT INFANTRY.—Co's A to F, org. at Prairie du Chien, Wis., Oct. 9, 1862. Co's G, H, I, K, org. at Racine, Wis., Dec. 24, 1862. March, 1863, Dist. Columbus, Ky. 6 Div., 16 Corps, Tenn. Oct., 1863, Unatt., Dept. Cumb'd. Nov., 1863, Post Murfreesboro, Tenn., Dept. Cumb'd. Jany., 1864, 2 Brig., Rousseau's 3 Div., 12 Corps, Cumb'd. April, 1864. Unatt., 4 Div., 20 Corps, Cumb'd. July, 1864, 3 Brig., 1 Div., 20 Corps, Cumb'd. Mustered out July 8, 1865.

32nd REGIMENT INFANTRY.—Org. at Oshkosh, Wis., Sept. 25, 1862. Nov., 1862, 5 Brig., Dist. Memphis, Tenn., 13 Corps, Dept. Tenn. Nov., 1862, 3 Brig., 1 Div., Dist. Memphis, 13 Corps. Dec., 1862, 3 Brig., 8 Div., 16 Corps, Tenn. March, 1862, 2 Brig., Dist. Memphis, Tenn., 5 Div., 16 Corps. Dec., 1863, 3 Brig., 1 Cav. Div., 16 Corps. Jany., 1864, 2 Brig., 4 Div., 16 Corps. March, 1864, 3 Brig., 4 Div., 16 Corps. Sept., 1864, 3 Brig., 1 Div., 17 Corps. Mustered out June 12, 1865.

33rd REGIMENT INFANTRY.—Org. at Racine, Wis., Oct. 18, 1862. Nov., 1862, Res. Brig., 5 Div., Dist. Memphis, Tenn., 13 Corps, Dept. Tenn. Dec., 1862, 1 Brig., 4 Div., 17 Corps. Jany., 1863, 1 Brig., 4 Div., 16 Corps. July, 1863, 1 Brig., 4 Div., 13 Corps. Aug., 1863, 1 Brig., 4 Div., 17 Corps. March, 1864, 1 Brig., Prov'l Div., 17 Corps, Gulf. June, 1864, Detached Brig., 17 Corps, and 4 Brig., 1 Div., 16 Corps. Dec., 1864, 1 Brig., 3 Div., Detachment Army Tenn., Dept. Cumb'd. Feby., 1865, 1 Brig., 3 Div., 16 Corps, Mil. Div. West Miss. Mustered out Aug. 9, 1865.

34th REGIMENT INFANTRY.—Org. at Madison, Wis., Dec., 1862. Feby., 1863, Dist. Columbus, Ky., 6 Div., 16 Corps, Tenn., and Dist. of Memphis, Tenn., 5 Div., 16 Corps. Mustered out Sept. 8, 1863.

35th REGIMENT INFANTRY.—Org. at Milwaukee, Wis., Feby. 27, 1864. May, 1864, Dist. Port Hudson, La., Gulf. June, 1864, 1 Brig., 3 Div., 19 Corps, Gulf. Dec., 1864, 4 Brig., Res. Div., Gulf. Feby., 1865, 1 Brig.,

3 Div., Res. Corps, Mil. Div. West Miss. Feby., 1865, 1 Brig., 3 Div., 13 Corps. July, 1865, Dept. Tex. Mustered out March 15, 1866.

36th REGIMENT INFANTRY.—Org. at Madison, Wis., March 23, 1864. May, 1864, 1 Brig., 2 Div., 2 Corps, Army Potomac. Mustered out July 12, 1865.

37th REGIMENT INFANTRY.—Org. at Madison, Wis., April 9, 1864. May, 1864, Casey's Brig., 22 Corps. June, 1864, 1 Brig., 3 Div., 9 Corps, Army Potomac. Sept., 1864, 1 Brig., 1 Div., 9 Corps. Mustered out July 26, 1865.

38th REGIMENT INFANTRY.—Org. at Madison, Wis., April 15, 1864. May, 1864, Casey's Prov'l Brig., 22 Corps. June, 1864, 1 Brig., 3 Div., 9 Corps, Army Potomac. Sept., 1864, 1 Brig., 1 Div., 9 Corps. Mustered out July 26, 1865.

39th REGIMENT INFANTRY.—Org. at Milwaukee, June 3, 1864. June, 1864, 2 Brig., Dist. of Memphis, Tenn., Dist. West Tenn. Mustered out Sept. 22, 1864.

40th REGIMENT INFANTRY.—Org. at Madison, Wis., June 7, 1864. June, 1864, Post and Def. Memphis, Tenn., Dist. West Tenn. Mustered out Sept. 22, 1864.

41st REGIMENT INFANTRY.—Org. at Milwaukee, Wis., June 8, 1864. June, 1864, 2 Brig., Dist. Memphis, Tenn., Dist. West Tenn. Mustered out Sept. 24, 1864.

42nd REGIMENT INFANTRY.—Org. at Madison, Wis., Sept. 7, 1864. Sept., 1864, Post of Cairo, Ill. Mustered out June 20, 1864.

43rd REGIMENT INFANTRY.—Org. at Madison, Wis., Aug. 8-Sept. 30, 1864. Oct.. 1864, Nashville and Northwestern R. R., Dept. Cumb'd. Dec., 1864, 3 Brig., Def. Nashville and Northwestern R. R., Cumb'd. March, 1865, 3 Brig., 1 Sub Dist., Dist. Middle Tenn. Mustered out June 24, 1865.

44th REGIMENT INFANTRY.—Org. at Madison, Wis., Oct. 7, 1864. Nov., 1864, Post of Nashville, Tenn., Dept. Cumb'd. March, 1865, Paducah, Ky., Dept. Ky. Mustered out Aug. 28, 1865.

45th REGIMENT INFANTRY.—Org. at Madison, Wis., Nov. 8, 1864. Nov., 1864, Post of Nashville, Tenn., Dept. Cumb'd. Feby., 1865, 2 Brig., 4 Div., 20 Corps, Cumb'd. March, 1865, Post of Nashville, Tenn. Mustered out July 17, 1865.

46th REGIMENT INFANTRY.—Org. at Madison, Wis., March 2, 1865. March, 1865, 2 Brig., 1 Sub Dist., Dist. of Middle Tenn. Mustered out Sept. 27, 1865.

47th REGIMENT INFANTRY.—Org. at Madison, Wis., Feby. 27, 1865. March, 1865, 2 Brig., Def. Nashville and Chattanooga R. R., Dept. Cumb'd. April, 1865, 2 Brig., 1 Sub Dist., Dist. Middle Tenn. Mustered out Sept. 4, 1865.

48th REGIMENT INFANTRY.—Org. at Milwaukee, Wis., Feby.-March, 1865. March, 1865, Dept. Kan. Mustered out Dec. 30, 1865, to March 24, 1866.

49th REGIMENT INFANTRY.—Org. at Madison, Wis., Feby. 24-March 5, 1865. March, 1865, Dist. St. Louis, Mo., Dept. of Mo. Mustered out Nov. 8, 1865.

50th REGIMENT INFANTRY.—Org. at Madison, Wis., March-April, 1865. Dept. of Kan. Mustered out June 14, 1866.

51st REGIMENT INFANTRY.—Org. at Milwaukee, Wis., March 20-April 29, 1865. Dept. of Mo. Mustered out Aug. 16-30, 1865.

52nd REGIMENT INFANTRY.—Org. at Madison, Wis., April, 1865. Dept. of Mo. Mustered out July 28, 1865.

53rd REGIMENT INFANTRY.—Org. at Madison, Wis., March-April, 1865. Dept. Kan. Mustered out by transfer to 51st Wis. Infy., June 10, 1865.

UNITED STATES REGULAR ARMY

1st REGIMENT CAVALRY.—April, 1861, Dept. Pacific. Jany., 1862, Cooke's Cav. Res., Potomac. March, 1862, 2 Brig., Cav. Res., Potomac. July, 1862, Headqrs. Army Potomac. Feby., 1863, Res. Cav. Brig., 1 Div., Cav. Corps, Potomac. Aug., 1864, Res. (3) Brig., 1 Div., Cav. Corps, Army Shenandoah, Middle Mil. Div. Dec., 1864, Headqrs. Cav. Corps, Army Shenandoah. March, 1865, Res. (3) Brig., 1 Div., Cav. Corps, Potomac.

2nd REGIMENT CAVALRY.—June, 1861, Thomas' Brig., Patterson's Army Shenandoah. July, 1861, 1 Brig.,

Banks' Div., Shenandoah. Aug., 1861, Cav. Res., Potomac. March, 1862, Provost Guard, Army Potomac. Feby., 1863, Res. Cav. Brig., 1 Div., Cav. Corps, Potomac. Aug., 1864, Res. (3) Brig., 1 Div., Cav. Corps, Army Shenandoah, Middle Mil. Div. March, 1865, Cav. Brig., Army Shenandoah. Co. C, June, 1861, Lyon's Command, Dept. Mo. Sept., 1861. Dist. Paducah, Ky., Dept. Mo. Feby., 1862, 2 Div., Army Tenn. July, 1862. 2 Div., Dist. Corinth, Miss., Dept. Tenn. Nov., 1862, Dist. Corinth, 13 Corps, Dept. Tenn. Jany., 1863, Dist. Memphis, Tenn., escort to Gen. Grant. Joined Regt. at Falmouth, Va., May, 1863. Co. G, Oct., 1861, Dept. New Mex. Oct., 1862, Dept. Kans. Joined Regt. at Falmouth, Va., Jany., 1863. Co. I, Oct., 1861, Dept. New Mex. Oct., 1862, Dept. Kan. Joined Regt. at Falmouth, Va., Jany., 1863.

3rd REGIMENT CAVALRY.—April, 1861, Dept. New Mex. Sept., 1862, Jefferson Barracks, Mo.. Dept. Mo. Dec., 1862, Dist. Memphis, Tenn, 16 Corps, Dept. Tenn. March, 1863, Unatt., Dist. Memphis, Tenn., 16 Corps. May, 1863, 2 Brig., Dist. Memphis, 5 Div., 16 Corps. Oct., 1863, Unatt., 15 Corps, Tenn. March, 1864, St. Louis, Mo., Dept. Mo. May, 1864, Unatt., 7 Corps, Dept. Ark. Sept., 1864, 2 Brig., Cav. Div., 7 Corps, Ark. Feby., 1865, Cav. Little Rock, Ark., 7 Corps, Ark. July, 1865, Dept. Ark.

4th REGIMENT CAVALRY.—April, 1861, Dept. Kan. July, 1861, Heintzelman's Div.. McDowell's Army N. E. Va. (Co's A, E). July, 1861, Lyon's Army West (Co's D, I). Nov., 1861. Dept. Mo. (Co's B, C, D, L). Nov., 1861, Dist. Paducah, Ky.. Dept. Mo. (Co's D, I, K). Nov., 1861, Headqrs. Army Potomac (Co's A, E). Joined Regt. in Tenn., Nov., 1862. Feby.. 1862, McClernand's 1 Div., Army Tenn. March, 1862, Unass'd, Army Miss. (Co's B, C, D, L). April, 1862, Cav. Div., Army Miss. (Co's B, C, D, G, I, K). June, 1862, Headqrs. Army Ohio. Nov., 1862, Headqrs. Army Cumb'd. Jany., 1863, 1 Brig., 2 Cav. Div., Cumb'd. Oct., 1864, 1 Brig., 2 Div., Wilson's Cav. Corps, Mil. Div. Miss. Oct., 1864, Headqrs. Cav. Corps, Mil. Div. Miss.

5th REGIMENT CAVALRY.—Jany., 1862, Cooke's Cav. Res., Potomac. March, 1862, 1 Brig., Cooke's Cav. Res., Potomac. July, 1862, 1 Brig., Cav. Div., Potomac. Sept., 1862, 1 Brig., Pleasanton's Cav. Div., Potomac. Nov., 1862, Averill's Cav. Brig., Potomac. Feby., 1863, Res. Cav. Brig., 1 Div. Cav. Corps, Potomac. Aug., 1864, Res. (3) Brig., 1 Div., Cav. Corps, Army Shenandoah, Middle Mil. Div. March, 1865, 3 Brig., 1 Div., Cav. Corps, Potomac.

6th REGIMENT CAVALRY.—Org. at Pittsburg, Pa., Oct., 1861, Def. Washington, D. C. March, 1862, 1 Brig., Cooke's Cav. Res., Potomac. July, 1862, 2 Brig., Cav. Div. Potomac. Sept., 1862, 1 Brig., Pleasanton's Cav. Div., Potomac. Nov., 1862, 2 Brig., Pleasanton's Cav. Div., Potomac. Feby., 1863, Res. Cav. Brig., 1 Div., Cav. Corps, Potomac. Aug., 1864, Res. (3) Brig., 1 Div., Cav. Corps, Army Shenandoah, Middle Mil. Div. Oct., 1864, Headqrs. Cav. Corps, Mil. Div. Miss. March, 1865, 3 Brig., 1 Div., Cav. Corps, Potomac.

1st REGIMENT ARTILLERY.—

BATTERY "A."—April, 1861, Pensacola, Fla., Dept. South. Aug., 1862, Dist. West Fla., Dept. Gulf. Dec., 1862, Def. New Orleans, Dept. Gulf. Jany., 1863, Arty., 1 Div., 19 Corps, Gulf. Aug., 1863, Def. New Orleans, Dept. Gulf. Feby., 1864, Arty., 1 Div., 19 Corps, Gulf. Aug., 1864, Camp Barry, Def. Washington, D. C., 22 Corps. Dec., 1864, 1 Brig., DeRussy's Div., 22 Corps.

BATTERY "B."—Jany., 1861, Fort Taylor, Key West, Fla. June, 1862, Dist. Beaufort, S. C., Dept. South. Sept., 1862, U. S. Forces, Port Royal Island, S. C., 10 Corps, Dept. South. May, 1863, Dist. Hilton Head, S. C., 10 Corps. June, 1863, St. Helena Island, S. C., 10 Corps. July, 1863, Arty., 1 Div., Morris Island, S. C.. 10 Corps. Dec., 1863, Arty., Gordon's Div., Folly Island, S. C., 10 Corps. Feby., 1864, Light Brig., Dist. Fla. April, 1864, Arty., 2 Div., 10 Corps, Army James, Dept. Va. and N. C. May, 1864, Arty., 1 Div., 18 Corps. June, 1864, Arty. Brig., 18 Corps. Oct., 1864, Arty., Cav. Div., Dept. Va. and N. C. April, 1865, Arty. Brig., 24 Corps. Aug., 1865, Dept. Tex.

BATTERY "C."—April, 1861, Fortress Monroe, Va. Dec., 1861, Unatt., Burnside's Exp. Corps. April, 1862, Unatt., Dept. N. C. Dec., 1862, Arty. Brig., Dept. N. C. Jany., 1863, Arty. Brig., 18 Corps, Dept. N. C. Feby., 1863, Arty., 18 Corps, Dept. South. April, 1863, U. S. Forces, Hilton Head, S. C., 10 Corps, Dept. South. April, 1863, U. S. Forces, Folly Island, S. C., 10 Corps. July, 1863, U. S. Forces, Morris Island, S. C., 10 Corps. Aug., 1863, Sub Dist. Beaufort, N. C., Dept. Va. and N. C. July, 1864, consolidated with Batty. "D" 1st Arty., 2 Div., 10 Corps, Army James, Dept. Va. and N. C. Aug., 1864, Arty. Brig., 10 Corps. (Batty. detached from Batty. "D," Oct. 31, 1864.) Oct., 1864, Dept. East.

BATTERY "D."—July, 1861, Fort Washington, D. C. Nov., 1861, Fort Taylor, Fla. June, 1862, Dist. Beaufort, S. C., Dept. South. Sept., 1862, U. S. Forces, Port Royal Island, S. C., 10 Corps, Dept. South. April, 1864, Arty., 2 Div., 10 Corps, Army James, Dept. Va. and N. C. May, 1864, Unatt., Arty., 10 Corps. June, 1864, Arty., 2 Div., 10 Corps. Aug., 1864, Arty. Brig., 10 Corps. Dec., 1864. Arty. Brig., 25 Corps. May, 1865, Dept. Tex.

BATTERY "E."—June, 1861, Unass'd, Dept. Pa. July, 1861, 2 Brig., Dept. Shenandoah. Aug., 1861, Def. Washington, D. C. Oct., 1861, Hooker's Div., Potomac. March, 1862, Arty. Res., Potomac. May, 1862, 2 Brig., Arty. Res., 5 Corps. Sept., 1862, Arty., 2 Div., 5 Corps, Potomac. Oct., 1862, Arty., 3 Div., 5 Corps, Potomac. May, 1863, 2 Regular Brig., Arty. Res., Potomac. June, 1863, 2 Brig., Horse Arty., Potomac. June, 1864, 2 Brig., DeRussy's Div., 22 Corps, Def. Washington. July, 1864, 1 Brig., DeRussy's Div., 22 Corps.

BATTERY "F."—April, 1861, Dist. Pensacola, Dept. South. Aug., 1862, Dist. West Fla., Dept. Gulf. Dec., 1862, Def. New Orleans. Dept. Gulf. Jany., 1863, Arty., 3 Div., 19 Corps, Gulf. Nov., 1863, Arty., Cav. Div., Gulf. March, 1864. Arty., 2 Div., 19 Corps, Gulf. April, 1864, Arty., Cav. Div., 19 Corps, Gulf. July, 1864, Def. Washington, D. C., 22 Corps.

BATTERY "G."—June, 1861, Richardson's Brig., Tyler's Div., McDowell's Army N. E. Va. Aug., 1861, Richardson's Brig., Div. Potomac. Oct., 1861, Arty. Res., Potomac. (Temp'y attached to Battys. "E" and "K.") May, 1862, 2 Brig., Arty. Res., 5 Corps, Potomac. Sept., 1862, Arty., 2 Div., 5 Corps, Potomac. Oct., 1862, Arty., 3 Div., 5 Corps, Potomac. May, 1863, 2 Regular Brig., Arty. Res. Potomac. June, 1863, 2 Brig., Horse Arty., Potomac. June, 1864, 2 Brig., DeRussy's Div., Def. Washington. D. C., South Potomac, 22 Corps.

BATTERY "H."—April, 1861, Fort Sumpter, S. C. June, 1861, Patterson's Army Shenandoah. Aug., 1861, Arty. Res., Potomac. March, 1862, Arty., 2 Div., 3 Corps, Potomac. May, 1863, 1 Regular Brig., Arty. Res., Potomac. Oct., 1863, 3 Brig., Arty. Res., Potomac. Dec., 1863, 2 Brig., Arty. Res., Potomac. March, 1864, Camp Barry, Def. Washington. D. C., 22 Corps. (Consolidated with Batty. "I," April 20, 1864, 2 Brig., Horse Arty., Potomac, attached to 2 Div., Cav. Corps, Potomac.) May, 1865, Dept. Washington, D. C.

BATTERY "I."—June, 1861, Willcox's Brig., Heintzelman's Div., McDowell's Army N. E. Va. Aug., 1861, Stone's Brig., Div. Potomac. Oct., 1861, Arty., Stone's (Sedgwick's) Div., Potomac. March, 1862, Arty., 2 Div., 2 Corps, Potomac. Nov., 1862, Res. Arty., 2 Corps, Potomac. May, 1863. Arty. Brig., 2 Corps, Potomac. Nov., 1863, 2 Brig., Horse Arty., Potomac. May, 1865, Dept. Washington, D. C.

BATTERY "K."—April, 1861, Fort Taylor, Fla. Jany., 1862, Arty. Res., Potomac. May, 1862, 2 Brig., Arty. Res., 5 Corps. Potomac. Aug., 1862, Arty., 1 Div., 3 Corps, Potomac. Sept., 1862, Res. Arty., 5 Corps, Potomac. Dec., 1862, Arty. Res., Potomac. June, 1863, 2 Brig., Horse Arty., Potomac. June, 1864, Camp Barry, Def. Washington, D. C., 22 Corps. Aug., 1864, Horse Arty., Army Shenandoah, Middle Mil. Div. Dec., 1864, Horse Arty. Res., Army Shenandoah. April, 1865, Cav. Brig., Army Shenandoah.

BATTERY "L."—April, 1861, Dist. Pensacola, Fla., Dept. South. Aug., 1862, Dist. West Fla., Dept. Gulf. Dec., 1862, Grover's Div., Dept. Gulf. Jany., 1863, Arty.,

4 Div., 19 Corps, Gulf. Aug., 1863, Arty. Res., 19 Corps, Gulf. Jany., 1864, Arty., 1 Div., 19 Corps, Gulf. Aug., 1864, Def. Washington, D. C., 22 Corps, Horse Arty., Army Shenandoah, Middle Mil. Div. Dec., 1864, Horse Arty. Res., Army Shenandoah. April, 1865, Cav. Brig., Army Shenandoah.

BATTERY "M."—April, 1861, Fort Jefferson, Fla. June, 1862, Dist. Beaufort, S. C., Dept. South. Sept., 1862, U. S. Forces, Port Royal Island, S. C., 10 Corps, Dept. South. Nov., 1863, U. S. Forces, Hilton Head, S. C., 10 Corps. Feby., 1864, Arty., Dist. Fla. April, 1864, Arty., 1 Div., 10 Corps, Army James, Dept. Va. and N. C. May, 1864, Arty., 3 Div., 10 Corps. Aug., 1864, Arty. Brig., 10 Corps. Dec., 1864, Arty. Brig., 25 Corps. May, 1865, Dept. Tex.

2nd REGIMENT ARTILLERY.—

BATTERY "A."—June, 1861, Blenker's Brig., Miles' Div., McDowell's Army N. E. Va. Aug., 1861, Heintzelman's Brig., Div. Potomac. Oct., 1861, Blenker's Brig., Potomac. Oct., 1861, Arty. Res., Potomac. May, 1862, 1 Brig., Horse Arty., 5 Corps, Potomac. Sept., 1862, Arty., Cav. Div., Potomac. Feby., 1863, Arty., 2 Div., Cav. Corps, Potomac. June, 1863, 2 Brig., Horse Arty., Potomac. May, 1865, Dept. Washington, D. C.

BATTERY "B" (CONSOLIDATED WITH BATTERY "L").—Oct., 1861, Arty. Res., Potomac. May, 1862, 1 Brig., Horse Arty., Arty. Res., 5 Corps, Potomac. Sept., 1862, Arty., Cav. Div., Potomac. Nov., 1862, Averill's Cav. Brig., Right Grand Div., Potomac. Feby., 1863, Arty., 1 Div., Cav. Corps, Potomac. June, 1863, 1 Brig., Horse Arty., Potomac. Aug., 1864, Horse Arty., Army Shenandoah, Middle Mil. Div. Dec., 1864, Res. Horse Arty., Army Shenandoah. April, 1865, Horse Arty. Brig., 22 Corps.

BATTERY "C."—April, 1861, Dist. Pensacola, Fla. Aug., 1862, Dist. West Fla., Dept. Gulf. Sept., 1862, New Orleans, La., Dept. Gulf, to Dec., 1862, Grover's Div., Dept. Gulf. Jany., 1863, Arty., 4 Div., 19 Corps, Gulf. Dec., 1863, Dist. Baton Rouge, Dept. Gulf. Feby., 1864, Arty., 2 Div., 19 Corps, Gulf. July, 1864, Def. Washington, D. C., 22 Corps.

BATTERY "D."—June, 1861, Willcox's Brig., Heintzelman's Div., McDowell's Army N. E. Va. Aug., 1861, Kearny's Brig. Div., Potomac. Oct., 1861, Arty., Franklin's Div., Potomac. March, 1862, Arty., 1 Div., 1 Corps, Potomac. April, 1862, Arty., 1 Div., Dept. Rappahannock. May, 1862, Arty., 1 Div., 6 Corps, Potomac. May, 1863, Arty. Brig., 6 Corps, Potomac. July, 1863, 1 Brig., Horse Arty., Potomac. Aug., 1864, Horse Arty., Army Shenandoah, Middle Mil. Div. Dec., 1864, Res. Horse Arty., Army Shenandoah. April, 1865, Horse Arty., Def. Washington, 22 Corps.

BATTERY "E."—June, 1861, Schenck's Brig., Tyler's Div., McDowell's Army N. E. Va. Aug., 1861, Arty. Div., Potomac. Oct., 1861, Arty., Porter's Div., Potomac. March, 1862, Arty. Res., Potomac. May, 1862, 5 Brig., Arty. Res., 5 Corps, Potomac. Sept., 1862, Arty., 1 Div., 9 Corps, Potomac. Dec., 1862, Arty., 3 Div., 9 Corps, Potomac. Feby., 1863, Arty., 1 Div., 9 Corps, Potomac. April, 1863, Dist. Central Ky., Dept. Ohio. June, 1863, Arty. Res., 9 Corps, Ohio. Aug., 1863, Arty., 1 Div., 9 Corps, Ohio. April, 1864, Res. Arty., 9 Corps, Potomac. June, 1864, Camp Barry, Def. Washington, D. C., 22 Corps. Consolidated with Batty. "C" 2nd Arty., Aug. 24, 1864. Nov., 1864, 1 Separate Brig., 22 Corps.

BATTERY "F."—Oct., 1861, Dept. Mo. March, 1862, Arty. Div., Army Miss., Dept. Mo. April, 1862, Arty., 2 Div., Army Miss. Nov., 1862, Arty., 8 Div., Left Wing 13 Corps, Dept. Tenn. Dec., 1862, 1 Brig., 8 Div., 16 Corps, Tenn. March, 1863, Arty., 2 Div., Dist. Corinth, 16 Corps, Tenn. May, 1863, 3 Brig., Dist. Memphis, 5 Div., 16 Corps, Tenn. Nov., 1863, Fuller's Brig., 2 Div., 16 Corps, Tenn. Jany., 1864, Arty., 4 Div., 16 Corps, Tenn. Sept., 1864, Arty., 1 Div., 17 Corps, Tenn. Nov., 1864, Arty., Dist. Nashville, Tenn., Dept. Cumb'd.

BATTERY "G."—June, 1861, Davies' Brig., Miles' Div., McDowell's Army N. E. Va. Aug., 1861, Kearny's Brig., Div. Potomac. Oct., 1861, Arty., Franklin's Div., Potomac. Jany., 1862, Arty., Heintzelman's Div., Potomac. March, 1862, Arty., 3 Div., 3 Corps, Potomac.

Aug., 1862, Arty., 1 Div., 4 Corps, Potomac. Sept., 1862, Arty., 3 Div., 6 Corps, Potomac. May, 1863, Arty. Brig., 6 Corps, Potomac. Aug., 1863, 2 Brig., Horse Arty., Potomac. June, 1864, 1 Brig., DeRussy's Div., Def. Washington, South Potomac, 22 Corps.

BATTERYY "H."—April, 1861, Dist. Pensacola, Fla. Aug., 1862, Dist. West Fla., Dept. Gulf. May, 1864, Dept. East.

BATTERY "I."—April, 1861, Balto., Md. Oct., 1861, Dix's Div., Balto., Md., Middle Dept. July, 1862, Def. Balto., Md., 8 Corps, Middle Dept. Jany., 1863. 1 Separate Brig., 8 Corps. May, 1864, 2 Brig., Haskins, Div., Def. Washington, North Potomac. 22 Corps. July, 1864, 1 Brig., Hardin's Div., 22 Corps. Nov., 1864, Fort Foote, Def. North Potomac. 22 Corps. April, 1865, Dept. Cumb'd. June, 1865, Middle Dept.

BATTERY "K."—April, 1861, Dist. Pensacola, Fla. Aug., 1862, Dist. West Fla. Dept. Gulf. May, 1864, Def. Balto.. Md., 8 Corps, Middle Dept.

BATTERY "L."—June, 1861, Dept. Va., to Sept., 1861, Arty. Res., Potomac. May, 1862, 1 Brig., Horse Arty., Res. Arty., 5 Corps. Potomac. Sept., 1862, Arty.. Pleasanton's Cav. Div., Potomac. Nov., 1862, Averill's Cav. Brig., Right Grand Div., Potomac. Feby., 1863, Arty., 1 Div., Cav. Corps, Potomac. June, 1863, 1 Brig., Horse Arty., Potomac. Aug., 1864, Horse Arty., Army Shenandoah, Middle Mil. Div. Dec., 1864, Res. Horse Arty., Army Shenandoah. April, 1864, Horse Arty. Brig., 22 Corps.

BATTERY "M."—June, 1861, Richardson's Brig., Tyler's Div., McDowell's Army N. E. Va. Aug., 1861, Franklin's Brig. Div., Potomac. Oct., 1861, Franklin's Div., Potomac. March, 1862, Aty. Res., Potomac. May, 1862, 1 Brig., Horse Arty., Arty. Res., 5 Corps, Potomac. Sept., 1862, Arty., Cav. Div., Potomac. Feby., 1863. Reserve Cav. Brig., 1 Div., Cav. Corps, Potomac. June, 1863, 1 Brig., Horse Arty., Potomac. Aug., 1864, Horse Arty., Army Shenandoah, Middle Mil. Div. Dec., 1864, Res. Horse Arty., Army Shenandoah. April, 1865, Horse Arty. Brig., 22 Corps.

3rd REGIMENT ARTILLERY.—

BATTERY "A."—April, 1861, Dept. Pacific. Feby., 1862, Carlton's New Mex. Exp. July, 1862, Dept. New Mex.

BATTERY "B."—At San Francisco, Cal., Dept. Pacific.

BATTERY "C."—April, 1861, San Francisco, Cal., Dept. Pacific. Nov., 1861, Dept. East. March, 1862, Arty. Res., Potomac. (Attached to Batty "G.") May, 1862, 1 Brig., Horse Arty., Arty. Res., 5 Corps, Potomac. Sept., 1862, Arty., Cav. Div., Potomac. (Batty. "G" broken up Oct., 1862.) Nov., 1862, Bayard's Cav. Brig., Potomac. Feby., 1863, Arty. Res., Potomac. May, 1863, 2 Regular Brig., Arty. Res., Potomac. June, 1863, 2 Brig., Horse Arty., Potomac. (Attached to Batt'ys F and K, March, 1864.) Aug., 1864, Horse Arty., Army Shenandoah, Middle Mil. Div. Dec., 1864, Horse Arty. Res., Army Shenandoah. April, 1865, Horse Arty. Brig., 22 Corps.

BATTERY "D."—April, 1861, Fort Vancouver. Feby., 1862, San Francisco, Dept. Pacific.

BATTERY "E."—May, 1861, Def. Washington, D. C. June, 1861, Sherman's Brig., Tyler's Div., McDowell's Army N. E. Va. Aug., 1861, Sherman's Brig., Div. Potomac. Oct., 1861, Porter's Div., Potomac. Oct., 1861, Sherman's S. C. Expedition. April, 1862, 2 Brig., 1 Div., Dept. South. July, 1862, Dist. Hilton Head, S. C., Dept. South. Sept., 1862, U. S. Forces, Hilton Head, S. C., 10 Corps, Dept. South. June, 1863, U. S. Forces, Folly Island, S. C., 10 Corps. July, 1863, U. S. Forces, Morris Island, S. C., 10 Corps. Jany., 1864, Arty., Folly Island, S. C., Northern Dist., 10 Corps. Feby., 1864, Arty., Ames' Div., Dist. Fla., Dept. South. April, 1864, Arty., 3 Div., 10 Corps, Army James, Dept. Va. and N. C. May, 1864, Arty., 1 Div., 10 Corps. June, 1864, Arty., 2 Div., 10 Corps. Aug., 1864, Arty. Brig., 10 Corps. Dec., 1864, Arty. Brig., 25 Corps. Jany., 1865, Arty., 3 Div., Terry's Prov'l Corps, Dept. N. C. March, 1865, Arty., 3 Div., 10 Corps, Dept. N. C.

BATTERY "F" (Attached to Battery K.).—Oct., 1861, Arty. Res., Potomac. May, 1862, 5 Brig., Arty. Res., 5 Corps, Potomac. Sept., 1862, Arty., 1 Div., 3 Corps, Potomac. May, 1863, 1 Regular Brig., Arty. Res., Potomac. Nov., 1863, Arty. Brig., 5 Corps, Potomac. March, 1864, Arty. Res., Potomac. (Consolidated with Battery C, Feby., 1864.) April, 1864, 1 Brig., Horse Arty., Potomac. Aug., 1864, Horse Arty., Army Shenandoah, Middle Mil. Div. Dec., 1864, Res. Horse Arty., Army Shenandoah. April, 1865, Horse Arty. Brig., 22 Corps.

BATTERY "G."—April, 1862, Dept. Pacific. Nov., 1861, Dept. East. March, 1862, Arty. Res., Potomac. (Attached to Battery C.) May, 1862, 1 Brig., Horse Arty., Arty. Res., 5 Corps, Potomac. Sept., 1862, Arty., Cav. Div., Potomac. Broken up Oct., 1862. Reorganized April, 1864. April, 1864, Arty. Res., 9 Corps, Potomac. May, 1864, 3 Brig., Hardin's Div., Def. Washington, D. C., North Potomac, 22 Corps. July, 1864, 1 Brig., Hardin's Div., 22 Corps. Dec., 1864, Fort Foote, Def. Washington, North Potomac. 22 Corps. April, 1865, 2 Brig., Hardin's Div., 22 Corps.

BATTERY "H."—Dept. Pacific, Oct., 1861, Dept. East.
BATTERY "I."—Dept. Pacific, July, 1864, Dept. East.
BATTERY "K" (Attached to Battery F.).—Oct., 1861, Arty. Res., Potomac. May, 1862, 5 Brig., Arty. Res., 5 Corps, Potomac. Sept., 1862, Arty., 1 Div., 3 Corps, Potomac. May, 1863, 1 Regular Brig., Arty. Res., Potomac. Nov., 1863, Arty. Brig., 5 Corps, Potomac, Consolidated with Battery C, Feby., 1864.

BATTERY "L."—April, 1861, San Francisco, Cali., Dept. Pacific. Nov., 1861, Dept. East. March, 1862, Arty. Res., Potomac. May, 1862, Arty., 2 Div., 5 Corps, Potomac. Dec., 1862, Arty., 1 Div., 9 Corps, Potomac. April, 1863, Arty., 1 Div., 9 Corps, Ohio. June, 1863, Arty. Res., 9 Corps, Tenn. Aug., 1863, Arty., 1 Div., 9 Corps, Ohio. Oct., 1863, Arty., 2 Div., 9 Corps, Ohio. Jany., 1864, Arty., 1 Div., 9 Corps, Ohio. April, 1864, Res. Arty., 9 Corps, Potomac. June, 1864, Camp Barry, Def. Washington, 22 Corps. Feby., 1865, Dist. Alexandria, 22 Corps.

BATTERY "M."—April, 1861, San Francisco, Cali., Dept. Pacific. Nov., 1861, Dept. East. March, 1862, Arty. Res., Potomac. May, 1862, Arty., 2 Div., 5 Corps, Potomac. Dec., 1862, Arty., 1 Div., 9 Corps, Potomac. April, 1863, Arty., 1 Div., 9 Corps, Ohio. June, 1863, Arty. Res., 9 Corps, Tenn. Aug., 1863, Arty., 1 Div., 9 Corps, Ohio. Oct., 1863, Arty., 2 Div., 9 Corps, Ohio. Jany., 1864, Arty., 1 Div., 9 Corps, Ohio. April, 1864, Res. Arty., 9 Corps, Potomac. June, 1864, Camp Barry, Def. Washington, 22 Corps. Feby., 1865, Dist. Alexandria, 22 Corps.

4th REGIMENT ARTILLERY.—

BATTERY "A" (Consolidated with Battery C at Washington, D. C., Oct., 1861.) Nov., 1861, Arty., Sumner's Div., Potomac. March, 1862, Arty., 1 Div., 2 Corps, Potomac. Nov., 1862, Res. Arty., 2 Corps, Potomac. May, 1863, Arty. Brig., 2 Corps, Potomac. July, 1863, 1 Brig., Horse Arty., Potomac. June, 1864, 1 Brig., Hardin's Div., 22 Corps. July, 1864, Camp Barry, Def. Washington, D. C., 22 Corps.

BATTERY "B."—Oct., 1861, McDowell's Div., Potomac. March, 1862, Arty., 1 Div., 1 Corps, Potomac. April, 1862, Arty., 3 Div., Dept. Rappahannock. June, 1862, Arty., 1 Div., 3 Corps, Army Va. Sept., 1862, Arty., 1 Div., 1 Corps, Potomac. May, 1863, Arty. Brig., 1 Corps. March, 1864, Arty. Brig., 5 Corps, Potomac. May, 1865, Dept. Washington.

BATTERY "C" (Attached to Battery "A," 4 Arty., to Oct., 1862.) Nov., 1861, Sumner's Div., Potomac. March, 1862, Arty., 1 Div., 2 Corps, Potomac. May, 1863, 1 Regular Brig., Arty. Res., Potomac. Nov., 1863, Arty. Brig., 6 Corps, Potomac. March, 1864, Arty. Res., Potomac. Consolidated with Battery E, 4 Arty., April, 1864, 1 Brig., Horse Arty., Potomac. Aug., 1864, Horse Arty., Army Shenandoah, Middle Mil. Div. (Attached to 1 Div., Cav. Corps.) March, 1865, Horse Arty., Res. Army Shenandoah. (Attached to 3 Div., Cav Corps.) May, 1865, Horse Arty. Brig., 22 Corps.

BATTERY "D."—April, 1861, Fortress Monroe, Va., Dept. Va. July, 1862, Viele's Command, Norfolk, Va., 7 Corps, Dept. Va. April, 1863, Unatt., Arty., 7 Corps, Dept. Va. June, 1863, Arty., 1 Div., 7 Corps. Aug., 1863, U. S. Forces Norfolk and Portsmouth, Va., Dept. Va. and N. C. Dec., 1863, Arty. Brig., U. S. Forces Portsmouth and Norfolk, Va., Dept. Va. and N. C. April, 1864, Arty., 2 Div., 18 Corps. June, 1864, Arty., 2 Div., 10 Corps. Aug., 1864, Arty. Brig., 10 Corps. Dec., 1864, Arty. Brig., 25 Corps. May, 1865, Dept. Texas.

BATTERY "E."—Org. at Camp Monroe, Ohio. July, 1861, 2 Brig., Army Occupation, W. Va. Sept., 1861, Scammon's Brig., Dept. W. Va. Oct., 1861, Kelly's Command, R. R. Dist., W. Va. Jany., 1862. Arty., Landers' Div., W. Va. March, 1862, Arty., Shields' 2 Div., Banks' 5 Corps. April, 1862, Arty., Shields' Div., Shenandoah. May, 1862, Arty., Shields' Div., Dept. Rappahannock. June, 1862, Unatt., 3 Corps, Army Va. Sept., 1862, Arty., 2 Div., 9 Corps, Potomac. Feby., 1863, Reserve Brig., 1 Div., Cav. Corps, Potomac. May, 1863, 1 Brig., Horse Arty., Potomac. Aug., 1864, Horse Arty., Army Shenandoah, Middle Mil. Div. Dec., 1864, Arty., 1 Div., Cav. Corps, Army Shenandoah. March, 1865, 3 Brig., 1 Div., Cav. Corps, Potomac. May, 1865, Horse Arty. Brig., 22 Corps.

BATTERY "F."—April, 1861, Balto., Md. July, 1861, Stone's Brig., Patterson's Army, Shenandoah. July, 1861, Arty., Banks' Div., Shenandoah. Oct., 1861, Arty., Banks' Div., Potomac. March, 1862, Arty., 1 Div., Banks' 5 Corps. April, 1862, Arty., 1 Div., Dept. Shenandoah. June, 1862, Arty., 1 Div., 2 Corps, Army Va. Sept., 1862, Arty., 1 Div., 12 Corps, Potomac. May, 1863, Arty. Brig., 12 Corps, Potomac. Oct., 1863, Arty. Brig., 12 Corps, Cumb'd. March, 1864, 1 Div., Arty. Res., Cumb'd.

BATTERY "G."—Org. at Cincinnati, Ohio. July, 1861, 3 Brig., Army Occupation, W. Va. Sept., 1861, Cheat Mt. Dist., W. Va. Dec., 1861, Def. Washington, D. C. March, 1862, Arty. Res., Potomac. May, 1862, 2 Brig., Horse Arty., Arty. Res., 5 Corps, Potomac. Sept., 1862, Arty. Res., 5 Corps. Nov., 1862, Arty. Res., Potomac. May, 1863, 1 Regular Brig., Arty. Res., Potomac. June, 1863, Arty. Brig., 11 Corps, Potomac. Oct., 1863, Arty. Brig., 11 Corps, Cumb'd. Nov., 1863, Arty., 2 Div., 4 Corps, Cumb'd. March, 1864, 1 Div., Arty. Res., Cumb'd. Transferred to Battery I, 4 Arty., Oct., 1864. Reorganized, Feby., 1865. Feby., 1865, Camp Barry, Def. Washington, 22 Corps.

BATTERY "H."—Jany., 1862, Louisville, Ky. (United with Battery M, 4 Arty., Feby. 1862 to Jany., 1863.) Feby., 1862, Arty., 5 Div., Army Ohio. May, 1862, Arty., 4 Div., Army Ohio. Sept., 1862, 10 Brig., 4 Div., 2 Corps, Army Ohio. Nov., 1862, Arty., 2 Div., Left Wing, 14 Corps, Cumb'd. Jany., 1863, Arty., 2 Div., 21 Corps, Cumb'd. Oct., 1863, Arty., 1 Div., 4 Corps, Cumb'd. March, 1864, 1 Div., Arty. Res., Cumb'd. Transferred to Battery I. 4 Arty., Oct., 1864. Reorganied at Washington, D. C., Feby., 1865. Feby., 1865, Camp Barry, Def. Washington, 22 Corps.

BATTERY "I."—July, 1861, Unatt., Army Occupation, W. Va. Sept., 1861, 3 Brig., Kanawha Div., W. Va. Dec., 1861, Arty., 1 Div., Army Ohio. Sept., 1862, Arty., 1 Div., 3 Corps, Army Ohio. Nov., 1862, Arty., 1 Div., Centre 14 Corps, Cumb'd. Jany., 1863, Arty., 3 Div., 14 Corps, Cumb'd. April, 1864, Garrison Arty., Nashville, Tenn., Dept. Cumb'd. Oct., 1864, 1 Div., Arty. Res., Cumb'd. Nov., 1864, Arty., 6 Div., Cav. Corps, Mil. Div. Miss. Feby., 1865, Arty., 2 Div., Cav. Corps, M. D. M.

BATTERY "K."—Aug., 1861, Arty. Res., Potomac. June, 1862, Arty. Res., 3 Corps, Potomac. Aug., 1862, Arty., 2 Div., 3 Corps, Potomac. May, 1863, Arty. Brig., 3 Corps, Potomac. March, 1864, Arty. Brig., 2 Corps, Potomac. June, 1865, Dept. Washington, D. C.

BATTERY "L."—July, 1861, Fortress Monroe, Va., Dept. Va. July, 1862, Arty. Div. at Suffolk, Va., 7 Corps, Dept. Va. April, 1863, Unatt., Arty., 7 Corps, Dept. Va. June, 1863, Arty., 1 Div., 7 Corps, Dept. Va. Aug., 1863, U. S. Forces Norfolk and Portsmouth, Dept.

Va. and N. C. Dec., 1863, U. S. Forces Yorktown, Va., Dept. Va. and N. C. April, 1864, Arty., 1 Div., 18 Corps. June, 1864, Arty. Brig., 18 Corps. Dec., 1864, Arty. Brig., 24 Corps. Aug., 1865, Dept. Va.

BATTERY "M."—Jany., 1862, Louisville, Ky. (United with Battery H, 4 Arty., Feby. 1862 to Jany., 1863.) Feby., 1862, Arty., 5 Div., Army Ohio. May, 1862, Arty., 4 Div., Army Ohio. Sept., 1862, 10 Brig., 4 Div., 2 Corps, Army Ohio. Nov., 1862, Arty., 2 Div., Left Wing 14 Corps, Cumb'd. Jany., 1863, Arty., 2 Div., 21 Corps, Cumb'd. Oct., 1863, Arty., 1 Div., 4 Corps, Cumb'd. March, 1864, 1 Div., Arty. Res., Cumb'd. Oct., 1864, Croxton's Cav. Brig., Nov., 1864, Arty. Brig., 4 Corps. Feby., 1865, Garrison Arty., Bridgeport, Ala.

5th REGIMENT ARTILLERY.—

BATTERY "A."—Org. July, 1861. March, 1862, Arty. Res., Potomac. May, 1862, 2 Brig., Horse Arty., Arty. Res., 5 Corps, Potomac. Sept., 1862, Arty., 3 Div., 9 Corps, Potomac. April, 1863, Arty., 2 Div., 7 Corps, Dept. Va. July, 1863, U. S. Forces Portsmouth, Va., Dept. Va. & N. C. April, 1864, Arty., 1 Div., 18 Corps. June, 1864, Arty. Brig., 18 Corps. Dec., 1864, Arty. Brig., 24 Corps. May, 1865, Dept. Va.

BATTERY "B."—Org. Nov., 1862. Nov., 1862, Fort Hamilton, N. Y. Harbor. June, 1863, 1 Div., Dept. Susquehanna. July, 1863, Unatt., Dept. W. Va. Dec., 1863, 3 Brig., 2 Div., West Va. May, 1864, Arty. Brig., West Va. Dec., 1864, Reserve Div., W. Va. Jany., 1865, 1 Separate Brig., 3 Div., W. Va. April, 1865, Arty., 2 Div., W. Va. July, 1865, Dept. Washington, D. C.

BATTERY "C."—Org. Sept., 1861. Oct., 1861, Arty., McCall's Div., Potomac. March, 1862, Arty., 2 Div., 1 Corps, Potomac. April, 1862, Arty., 2 Div., Dept. Rappahannock. June, 1862, Arty., 3 Div., 5 Corps, Potomac. Aug., 1862, Arty., 3 Div., 3 Corps, Army Va. Sept., 1862, Arty., 3 Div., 1 Corps, Potomac. Feby., 1863, Arty., 2 Div., 1 Corps, Potomac. May, 1863, 1 Regular Brig., Arty. Res., Potomac. July, 1863, Camp Barry, Def. Washington, 22 Corps. Consolidated with Battery I, Nov., 1863, Arty. Brig., 2 Corps, Potomac. March, 1865, Arty. Reserve, Potomac.

BATTERY "D." ("WEST POINT BATTERY.")— Oct., 1861, Porter's Div., Potomac. March, 1862, Arty., 1 Div., 3 Corps, Potomac. May, 1862, Arty., 1 Div., 5 Corps, Potomac. May, 1863, Arty. Brig., 5 Corps, Potomac. Nov., 1863. Camp Barry, Def. Washington, 22 Corps. March, 1864, Arty. Brig., 5 Corps, Potomac. Consolidated with Batty. G, 5th Arty., Nov., 1864. June, 1865, Dept. Washington.

BATTERY "E."—Org. May, 1862. May, 1862, Fort Hamilton, N. Y., Harbor. June, 1863, Dept. Susquehanna. April, 1864, 3 Brig., Arty. Reserve, Potomac. May, 1864, Arty. Brig., 6 Corps, Potomac. July, 1864, Arty. Res., Potomac. Dec., 1864, Arty. Brig., 6 Corps, Potomac. June, 1865, Dept. Washington.

BATTERY "F."—Org. Sept., 1861. Oct., 1861, W. F. Smith's Div., Potomac. March, 1862, Arty., 2 Div., 4 Corps, Potomac. May, 1862, Arty., 2 Div., 6 Corps, Potomac. May, 1863, Arty. Brig., 6 Corps, Potomac. Dec., 1863, Camp Barry, Def. Washington, 22 Corps. July, 1864, Arty. Brig., 18 Corps, Dept. Va. and N. C. Dec., 1864, Arty. Brig., 24 Corps. May, 1865, Dept. Va.

BATTERY "G."—Org. June, 1862. June, 1862, Fort Hamilton, N. Y., Harbor. Dec., 1862, Def. New Orleans, Dept. Gulf. Jany., 1863, Arty., 2 Div., 19 Corps, Gulf. May, 1863, Arty., 1 Div., 19 Corps, Gulf. July, 1863, Garrison Arty., Port Hudson, La. Aug., 1863, Def. New Orleans, La. Feby., 1864, Arty., Cav. Div., Gulf. June, 1864, Dist. LaFourche, Dept. Gulf. Aug., 1864, U. S. Forces, Mobile Bay, Dept. Gulf. Oct., 1864, N. Y., Dept. East. Consolidated with Batty. D, 5th Arty., Nov., 1864.

BATTERY "H."—Org. Sept., 1861. Dec., 1861, Arty., 1 Div., Army Ohio. May, 1862, Arty., 4 Div., Army Ohio. Sept., 1862, Arty., 10 Brig., 4 Div., 2 Corps, Army Ohio. Nov., 1862, Arty., 2 Div., Left Wing 14 Corps, Cumb'd. Jany., 1863, Arty., 2 Div., 21 Corps, Cumb'd. Oct., 1863, Arty., 1 Div., 4 Corps, Cumb'd. March, 1864, 1 Div., Arty. Reserve, Dept. Cumb'd. Nov., 1864, Garrison Arty., Nashville, Tenn., Dept. Cumb'd. April, 1865, Dept. East.

BATTERY "I."—Org. Sept., 1861. March, 1862, Arty. Res., Potomac. May, 1862, Arty., 2 Div., 5 Corps, Potomac. May, 1863, Arty. Brig., 5 Corps, Potomac. July, 1863, Camp Barry, Def. Washington, 22 Corps. Consolidated with Batty. C, 5th Arty., Nov., 1863. Nov., 1863, Arty. Brig., 2 Corps, Potomac. March, 1865, Arty. Res., Potomac. June, 1865, Dept. Washington.

BATTERY "K."—Org. Sept., 1861. Oct., 1861, Provost Guard, Army Potomac. March, 1862, Arty. Res., Potomac. May, 1862, 2 Brig., Arty. Res., 5 Corps, Potomac. Sept., 1862, Arty., 2 Div., 5 Corps, Potomac. Oct., 1862, Arty. Res., Potomac. May, 1863, Arty. Brig., 12 Corps, Potomac. Sept., 1863, Arty. Brig., 12 Corps, Cumb'd. Oct., 1863, Arty., 2 Div., 12 Corps, Cumb'd. March, 1864, 1 Div., Arty Res., Cumb'd. Aug., 1864, Arty. Brig., 20 Corps, Cumb'd. Oct., 1864, Garrison Arty., Chattanooga, Tenn., Dept. Cumb'd.

BATTERY "L."—Org. Oct., 1862. Oct., 1862, Def. Balto., Md., 8 Corps, Middle Dept. Jany., 1863, 2d Separate Brig., 8 Corps. Feby., 1863, 3d Separate Brig., 8 Corps. March, 1863, 2 Brig., 2 Div., 8 Corps. June, 1863, 1 Brig., 2 Div., 8 Corps. July, 1863, 3d Separate Brig.. 8 Corps. Aug., 1863, Camp Barry, Def. Washington, 22 Corps. July, 1864, Arty., 2 Cav. Div., West Va. Nov., 1864, Horse Arty., Cav. Corps, Army Shenandoah, Middle Mil. Div. Dec., 1864, Reserve Horse Arty., Army Shenandoah. April, 1865, Cav. Div., Dept. Washington, 22 Corps.

BATTERY "M."—Org. Nov., 1861. March, 1862, Arty. Res., Potomac. June, 1862, Res. Arty., 4 Corps, Potomac. Dec., 1862, Res. Arty., Yorktown, Va., 7 Corps, Dept. Va. May, 1863, Unatt., Arty., 4 Corps, Yorktown, Va. July, 1863, Arty. Brig., 6 Corps, Potomac. July, 1864, Arty., 3 Div., 6 Corps, Army Shenandoah, Middle Mil. Div. Sept., 1864, Arty. Brig., 6 Corps, Army Shenandoah. Dec., 1864, Res. Div., Harper's Ferry, West Va. Jany., 1865, Camp. Barry, Def. Washington, D. C., 22 Corps.

1st ENGINEER BATTALION.—Engineer Brigade, Army Potomac, all through.

1st REGIMENT INFANTRY.—April, 1861, Dept. Mo. (Co.'s A, B, C, D, H, I). March, 1862, Unass'd, Army Miss., Dept. Mo. July, 1862, Post Corinth, Miss., Dept. Tenn. Nov., 1862, Unatt., Dist. Corinth, 13 Corps, Dept. Tenn. Dec., 1862, Unatt., Dist. Corinth, 17 Corps, Tenn. Jany., 1863, Dist. Corinth, 16 Corps, Tenn. March, 1863, 1 Brig., 14 Corps, Tenn. July, 1863, 1 Brig., 1 Div., 13 Corps, Tenn. Aug., 1863, Headqrs. 13 Corps, Dept. Gulf. Oct., 1863, Def. New Orleans, La. Feby., 1864, 2 Brig., 4 Div., 13 Corps, Gulf. March, 1864, Def. New Orleans, La. April, 1865, Dist. LaFourche, Dept. Gulf.

2nd REGIMENT INFANTRY.—March, 1862, Sykes' Regular Infy. Reserve Brig., Potomac. May, 1862, 2 Brig., 2 Div., 5 Corps, Potomac. July, 1863, 1 Brig., 2 Div., 5 Corps, Potomac. March, 1864, 4 Brig., 1 Div., 5 Corps, Potomac. April, 1864, 1 Brig., 1 Div., 5 Corps, Potomac. June, 1864, 1 Brig., 2 Div., 5 Corps, Potomac. June, 1864, Provost Guard, 2 Div., 5 Corps, Potomac. Oct.. 1864, Newport Barracks, Ky.

3rd REGIMENT INFANTRY.—June, 1861, Porter's Brig., Hunter's Div., McDowell's Army, N. E. Va. Aug., 1861, Porter's City Guard, Washington. March, 1862, Sykes' Regular Infy. Reserve Brig., Potomac. May, 1862, 1 Brig., 2 Div., 5 Corps, Potomac. Aug., 1863, Dept. East. Oct., 1864, Def. Washington, 22 Corps. Feby., 1865, Headqrs. Army Potomac. May, 1865, Dept. Washington.

4th REGIMENT INFANTRY.—April, 1861, Dept. Pacific. Oct., 1861, Def. Washington. March, 1862, Sykes' Regular Infy. Reserve Brig., Potomac. May, 1862, 1 Brig., 2 Div., 5 Corps, Potomac. Aug., 1863, Dept. East. April, 1864, 1 Brig., 1 Div., 9 Corps, Potomac. June, 1864, 1 Brig., 2 Div., 5 Corps, Potomac. June, 1864, City Point, Va., Headqrs. Army Potomac. May, 1865, Dept. Va.

5th REGIMENT INFANTRY.—Dept. New Mexico all through.

6th REGIMENT INFANTRY.—April, 1861, California. Dept. Pacific. Nov., 1861, Def. Washington, D. C. March, 1862, Sykes' Regular Infy. Reserve Brig., Potomac. May, 1862, 2 Brig., 2 Div., 5 Corps, Potomac. June, 1863, 1 Brig., 2 Div., 5 Corps, Potomac. Aug., 1863, Dept. East. May, 1865, Dist. Savannah, Ga., Dept. South.

7th REGIMENT INFANTRY.—April, 1861, Dept. New Mexico. Aug., 1861, Jefferson Barracks, Mo. Oct., 1862, 2 Brig., 2 Div., 5 Corps, Potomac. Aug., 1863, Dept. East.

8th REGIMENT INFANTRY.—April, 1861, Dept. Texas. Aug., 1861, City Guard, Def. Washington, D. C. March, 1862, Provost Guard, Army Potomac. May, 1862, 1 Brig., Sigel's Div., Dept. Shenandoah (Co's A, D.) June, 1862, 1 Brig., 2 Div., 2 Corps, Army Va. June, 1862, Headqrs. Army Va. (Co's A, D). Sept., 1862, 2 Brig., 2 Div., 12 Corps, Potomac (Co's A, D). Sept., 1862, Headqrs. Army Potomac. July, 1863, Dept. East. April, 1864, Provost Guard, 9 Corps, Potomac. Oct., 1864, 1 Brig., 2 Div., 5 Corps, Potomac. Nov., 1864, Balto., Md., 8 Corps, Middle Dept.

9th REGIMENT INFANTRY.—On duty at Posts near San Francisco, Cal., Dept. Pacific, Sept., 1861, to Nov., 1865.

10th REGIMENT INFANTRY.—Jany., 1862, Def. Washington. March, 1862, Sykes' Regular Infy. Reserve Brig., Potomac. May, 1862, 2 Brig., 2 Div., 5 Corps, Potomac. Aug., 1863, Dept. East. April, 1864, 1 Brig., 1 Div., 9 Corps, Potomac. June, 1864, 1 Brig., 2 Div., 5 Corps, Potomac. Oct., 1864, Headqrs. Army Potomac. Nov., 1864, Dept. East. April, 1865, Headqrs. Army Potomac. May, 1865, Dept. Washington, D. C., to Oct., 1865.

11th REGIMENT INFANTRY.—Org. at Fort Independence, Mass. Oct., 1861, Dix's Div., Middle Dept. March, 1862, Sykes' Regular Infy. Reserve Brig., Potomac. May, 1862, 2 Brig., 2 Div., 5 Corps, Potomac. Sept., 1863, 1 Brig., 2 Div., 5 Corps, Potomac. March, 1864, 4 Brig., 1 Div., 5 Corps, Potomac. April, 1864, 1 Brig., 1 Div., 5 Corps, Potomac. June, 1864, 1 Brig., 2 Div., 5 Corps, Potomac. Nov., 1864, Annapolis, Md., 8 Corps, Middle Dept. Jany., 1865, City Point, Va., Headqrs. Army Potomac. June, 1865, Dept. Va.

12th REGIMENT INFANTRY.—Org. at Fort Hamilton, N. Y., Harbor. March, 1862, Sykes' Regular Infy. Reserve Brig., Potomac. May, 1862, 1 Brig., 2 Div., 5 Corps, Potomac. Aug., 1863, Dept. East. Sept., 1863, 1 Brig., 2 Div., 5 Corps. March, 1864, 4 Brig., 1 Div., 5 Corps, Potomac. April, 1864, 1 Brig., 1 Div., 5 Corps, Potomac. June, 1864, 1 Brig., 2 Div., 5 Corps', Potomac. Nov., 1864, Dept. East.

13th REGIMENT INFANTRY.—Org. at Jefferson Barracks, Mo. Feby., 1862, Alton, Ill. Sept., 1862, Newport, Ky., Dept. Ohio. Nov., 1862, Dist. Memphis, Tenn., 13 Corps, Dept. Tenn. Dec., 1862, 1 Brig., 2 Div., Sherman's Yazoo Exp. Jany., 1863, 1 Brig., 2 Div., 15 Corps, Tenn. Jany., 1863, Headqrs. 15 Corps, Tenn. Sept., 1863, 1 Brig., 2 Div., 15 Corps, Tenn. Dec., 1863, Dist. Nashville, Tenn., Dept. Cumb'd. July, 1865, St. Louis, Mo.

14th REGIMENT INFANTRY.—Org. at Fort Trumbull, Conn. March, 1862, Sykes' Regular Infy. Reserve Brig., Potomac. May, 1862, 1 Brig., 2 Div., 5 Corps, Potomac. March, 1864, 4 Brig., 1 Div., 5 Corps. April, 1864, 1 Brig., 1 Div., 5 Corps, Potomac. June, 1864, 1 Brig., 2 Div., 5 Corps, Potomac. Nov., 1864, Dept. East. April, 1865, Provost Guard, Army Potomac. June, 1865, Dept. Va.

15th REGIMENT INFANTRY.—Org. at Wheeling, W. Va. Oct., 1861, Rousseau's Brig., McCook's Command, at Nolin, Ky., Army Ohio. Nov., 1861, 4 Brig., Army Ohio. Dec., 1861, 4 Brig., 2 Div., Army Ohio. Sept., 1862, 4 Brig., 2 Div., 1 Corps, Army Ohio. Nov., 1862, 3 Brig., 2 Div., Right Wing 14 Corps, Cumb'd. Dec., 1862, 4 Brig., 1 Div., Centre 14 Corps, Cumb'd. Jany., 1863, 4 Brig., 1 Div., 14 Corps, Cumb'd. April, 1863, 3 Brig.,

1 Div., 14 Corps, Cumb'd. Oct., 1863, 2 Brig., 1 Div., 14 Corps, Cumb'd. Sept., 1864, Regular Brig., Chattanooga, Tenn., Dept. Cumb'd. Nov., 1864, 1 Brig., 1st Separate Div., Dist. Etowah, Dept. Cumb'd.

16th REGIMENT INFANTRY.—Org. at Chicago, Ill. Nov., 1861, 3 Brig., Army Ohio. Dec., 1861, 4 Brig., 2 Div., Army Ohio. Sept., 1862, 4 Brig., 2 Div., 1 Corps, Army Ohio. Nov., 1862, 3 Brig., 2 Div., Right Wing 14 Corps, Dept. Cumb'd. Dec., 1862, 4 Brig., 1 Div., Centre 14 Corps, Cumb'd. Jany., 1863, 4 Brig., 1 Div., 14 Corps, Cumb'd. April, 1863, 3 Brig., 1 Div., 14 Corps, Cumb'd. Oct., 1863, 2 Brig., 1 Div., 14 Corps, Cumb'd. Sept., 1864, Regular Brig., Chattanooga, Tenn., Dept. Cumb'd. Nov., 1864, 1 Brig., 1st Separate Div., Dist. Etowah, Dept. Cumb'd.

17th REGIMENT INFANTRY.—Org. at Fort Preble, Me. March, 1862, Sykes' Regular Infy. Reserve Brig., Potomac. May, 1862, 2 Brig., 2 Div., 5 Corps, Potomac. Sept., 1863, 1 Brig., 2 Div., 5 Corps, Potomac. March, 1864, 4 Brig., 1 Div., 5 Corps, Potomac. April, 1864, 1 Brig., 1 Div., 5 Corps, Potomac. June, 1864, 1 Brig., 2 Div., 5 Corps, Potomac. Nov., 1864, Dept. East.

18th REGIMENT INFANTRY.—Org. at Columbus, Ohio. Oct., 1861, 3 Brig., Army Ohio. Dec., 1861, 3 Brig., 1 Div., Army Ohio. Sept., 1862, 3 Brig., 1 Div., 3 Corps, Army Ohio. Nov., 1862, 3 Brig., 3 Div., Centre 14 Corps, Cumb'd. Dec., 1862, 4 Brig., 1 Div., Centre 14 Corps, Cumb'd. Jany., 1863, 4 Brig., 1 Div., 14 Corps, Cumb'd. April, 1863, 3 Brig., 1 Div., 14 Corps, Cumb'd. Oct., 1863, 2 Brig., 1 Div., 14 Corps, Cumb'd. Sept., 1864, Regular Brig., Chattanooga, Tenn., Dept. Cumb'd. Nov., 1864, 1 Brig., 1st Separate Div., Dist. Etowah, Dept. Cumb'd.

19th REGIMENT INFANTRY.—Org. at Indianapolis, Ind. Oct., 1861, Rousseau's Brig., McCook's Command, Army, Ohio. Nov., 1861, 4 Brig., Army Ohio. Dec., 1861, 4 Brig., 2 Div., Army Ohio. Sept., 1862, 4 Brig., 2 Div., 1 Corps, Army Ohio. Nov., 1862, 3 Brig., 2 Div., Right Wing 14 Corps, Cumb'd. Dec., 1862, 4 Brig., 1 Div., Centre 14 Corps, Cumb'd. Jany., 1863, 4 Brig., 1 Div., 14 Corps, Cumb'd. April, 1863, 3 Brig., 1 Div., 14 Corps. Oct., 1863, 2 Brig., 1 Div., 14 Corps, Cumb'd. Sept., 1864, Regular Brig., Chattanooga, Tenn. Nov., 1864, 1 Brig., 1st Separate Div., Dist. Etowah, Dept. Cumb'd.

U. S. VOLUNTEERS

1st REGIMENT SHARPSHOOTERS.—Org. Co's A, B, D, H in New York, C, I, K in Mich., E in New Hampshire, F in Vermont, and G in Wisconsin, Aug., 1861, to April, 1862. Oct., 1861, Unass'd, Army Potomac and Martindale's Brig., Porter's Div., Potomac. March, 1862, Unass'd, 1 Div., 3 Corps, Potomac. May, 1862, 3 Brig., 1 Div., 5 Corps, Potomac. March, 1863, 3 Brig., 3 Div., 3 Corps, Potomac. June, 1863, 2 Brig., 1 Div., 3 Corps, Potomac. Sept., 1863, 3 Brig., 1 Div., 3 Corps, Potomac. March, 1864, 2 Brig., 3 Div., 2 Corps, Potomac. Mustered out Dec. 31, 1864. Vets and Recruits to 2nd Regiment S. S.

2nd REGIMENT SHARPSHOOTERS.—Org. Co. A in Minn., Oct. 5, 1861; B in Mich., Oct. 4, 1861; C in Penna., Oct., 1861; D in Maine, Nov. 2, 1861; E and H in Vermont, Nov. 9 and Dec. 31, 1861; F and G in New Hampshire, Nov. 26 and Dec. 12, 1861. Dec., 1861, Def. Washington. March, 1862, Augur's Brig., King's 1 Div., McDowell's 1 Corps, Potomac. April, 1862, 1 Brig., King's Div., Dept. Rappahannock. June, 1862, 1 Brig., 1 Div., 3 Corps, Army Va. Sept., 1862, 1 Brig., 1 Div., 1 Corps, Potomac. March, 1863, 3 Brig., 3 Div., 3 Corps, Potomac. June, 1863, 2 Brig., 1 Div., 3 Corps, Potomac. March, 1864, 1 Brig., 3 Div., 2 Corps, Potomac. Broken up Feby., 1865. Co. A to 1st Minn., B to 5th Mich., C to 105th Penna., D to 17th Me., E and H to 4th Vt., and F and G to 5th N. H.

1st REGIMENT INFANTRY.—Org. at Point Lookout, Md., Jany. 21 to April 22, 1864. Mustered out May 21, 1866.

2nd REGIMENT INFANTRY.—Org. at Rock Island, Ill., Oct., 1864. Mustered out Nov. 7, 1865.

3rd REGIMENT INFANTRY.—Org. at Rock Island, Ill., Oct., 1864. Mustered out Nov. 29, 1865.

4th REGIMENT INFANTRY.—Org. at Point Lookout, Md., Oct. 31, 1864. Mustered out July 2, 1866.

5th REGIMENT INFANTRY.—Org. at Alton and Camp Douglass, Ill., March to May, 1865. Mustered out Nov. 13, 1866.

6th REGIMENT INFANTRY.—Org. at Columbus, Ohio., Camp Morton, Ind., and Camp Douglass, Ill., April 2, 1865. Mustered out Nov. 3, 1866.

1st INDEPENDENT COMPANY.—Org. at Balto., Md., Oct. 5, 1863, as Co. G, 1st Conn. Cav. Designation changed to 1st Indpt. Company, April 5, 1865. Mustered out Nov. 16, 1865.

1st COMPANY PONTOONERS.—Org. at New Orleans, Feby. 28, 1865. Mustered out May 12, 1866.

U. S. VETERAN VOLUNTEERS

1st REGIMENT ENGINEERS.—Org. in Dept. Cumb'd from Pioneer Brig., Dept. Cumb'd, July 8, 1864. Engineer Brig., Dist. Cumb'd. Mustered out Sept. 26, 1865.

1st REGIMENT INFANTRY.—Org. at Washington Dec., 1864, to March, 1865. Jany., 1865, 1st Veteran Corps, Washington, D. C. March, 1865, 1 Brig., 1 Div., 1 Veteran Corps, Middle Mil. Div. April, 1865, 2 Brig., 4 Prov'l Div., Army Shenandoah. June, 1865, 2d Separate Brig., Middle Dept. July, 1865, Dist. Balto., Middle Dept. Mustered out July 21, 1866.

2nd REGIMENT INFANTRY.—Org. at Camp Stoneman, Jany. to March, 1865. March, 1865, 2 Brig., 1 Div., 1 Vet. Corps. June, 1865, Dist. N. Y. Mustered out Aug. 1, 1866.

3rd REGIMENT INFANTRY.—Org. at Camp Stoneman, Feby. to March, 1865. April, 1865, 2 Brig., 4 Prov'l Div., Army Shenandoah. June, 1865, Camp Butler, Ill. Mustered out July 20, 1866.

4th REGIMENT INFANTRY.—Org. at Camp Stoneman, Dec., 1864, to May, 1865. Mustered out Aug. 6, 1866.

5th REGIMENT INFANTRY.—Org. at Camp Stoneman, Jany. to April, 1865. Mustered out July 20, 1866.

6th REGIMENT INFANTRY.—Org. at Camp Stoneman, March-April, 1865. Mustered out July 27, 1866.

7th REGIMENT INFANTRY.—Org. at Camp Stoneman. Jany. 25 to April 14, 1865. April, 1865, 3 Brig., 1 Div., 1 Vet. Corps. July, 1865, Phila. Dist., Pa., Middle Dept. April, 1866, Schuylkill, Dist., Pa., Middle Dept. Mustered out July 23, 1866.

8th REGIMENT INFANTRY.—Org. at Camp Stoneman, Feby. to April, 1865. Mustered out July 28, 1866.

9th REGIMENT INFANTRY.—Org. at Camp Stoneman, March to June, 1865. Mustered out July 1, 1866.

CORPS DE AFRIQUE—U. S. COLORED VOLUNTEERS

1st REGIMENT CAVALRY.—Org. at New Orleans, La., Sept. 12, 1863. Sept., 1863, Def. New Orleans, La., Dept. Gulf. March, 1864, Dist. Port Hudson, Dept. Gulf. Designation changed to 4th U. S. Colored Cavalry April 4, 1864.

1st REGIMENT HEAVY ARTILLERY.—Org. at New Orleans, La., from 1st Louisiana Colored Heavy Arty., Nov. 19, 1863. Dec., 1863, Def. New Orleans, La., Dept. Gulf. Designation changed to 10th U. S. Colored Heavy Artillery, May 21, 1864.

1st REGIMENT ENGINEERS.—Org. at Camp Parapet, April 28, 1863. April, 1863, Unatt., 1st Div., 19 Corps, Gulf. Aug., 1863, Engineer Brig., Corps de Afrique, Gulf. Oct., 1863, Engineer Brig., 13 Corps, Dept. Gulf. Designation changed to 95th U. S. Colored Troops, April 4, 1864.

2nd REGIMENT ENGINEERS.—Org. at New Orleans, La., Aug. 15, 1863. Aug., 1863, Engineer Brig., Gulf. Oct., 1863, Unatt., 13 Corps, Texas, Dept. Gulf. March, 1864, Prov'l Brig., 13 Corps, Texas, Dept. Gulf. Designation changed to 96th U. S. Colored Troops, April 4, 1864.

3rd REGIMENT ENGINEERS.—Org. at New Orleans, La., Aug. 26, 1863. Aug., 1863, Engineer Brig., Dept. Gulf. Oct., 1863, Unatt., 13 Corps, Texas, Dept. Gulf. March, 1864, Prov'l Brig., 13 Corps, Texas, Dept. Gulf. Designation changed to 97th U. S. Colored Troops, April 4, 1864.

4th REGIMENT ENGINEERS.—Org. at New Orleans, La., Sept. 8, 1863. Sept., 1863, Engineer Brig., Dept. Gulf. Designation changed to 98th U. S. Colored Troops, April 4, 1864.

5th REGIMENT ENGINEERS.—Org. Feb. 10, 1864, from 15th Regt., Corps de Afrique. Feby., 1864, Engineer Brig., Dept. Gulf. Designation changed to 99th U. S. Colored Troops, April 4, 1864.

1st REGIMENT INFANTRY.—Org. June 6, 1863, from 1st Regt. Louisiana Native Guard. June, 1863, Def. New Orleans, La., Dept. Gulf. July, 1863, Port Hudson, La., Dept. Gulf. Dec., 1863, 1st Brig., 1 Div., Corps de Afrique, Dept. Gulf. Designation changed to 73rd U. S. Colored Troops, April 4, 1864.

2nd REGIMENT INFANTRY.—Org. June 6, 1863, from 2nd Regt., Louisiana Native Guard. June, 1863, Def. New Orleans, Dept. Gulf. Sept., 1863, 1st Brig., 1 Div. Corps de Afrique. Oct., 1863, Def. New Orleans, Dept. Gulf. Designation changed to 74th U. S. Colored Troops, April 4, 1864.

3rd REGIMENT INFANTRY.—Org. June 6, 1863, from 3rd Regt. Louisiana Native Guard. June, 1863, Unatt., 1 Div., 19 Corps, Dept. Gulf. July, 1863, Port Hudson, La., Dept. Gulf. Sept., 1863, 1 Brig., 1 Div., Corps de Afrique. Oct., 1863, Def. New Orleans, Dept. Gulf. Designation changed to 75th U. S. Colored Troops, April 4, 1864.

4th REGIMENT INFANTRY.—Org. June 6, 1863, from 4th Regt. Louisiana Native Guard. June, 1863, Unatt., 1 Div., 19 Corps. Dept. Gulf. July, 1863, Def. New Orleans, La., Dept. Gulf. Sept., 1863, 2 Brig., 1 Div., Corps de Afrique, Dept. Gulf. March, 1864, Garrison Port Hudson, La., Dept. Gulf. Designation changed to 76th U. S. Colored Troops, April 4, 1864.

5th REGIMENT INFANTRY.—Org. at Fort St. Phillip, Sept., 1863. Sept., 1863, 1 Brig., 2 Div., Corps de Afrique, Dept. Gulf. Dec., 1863, Def. New Orleans, Dept. Gulf. Jany., 1864, 1 Brig., 2 Div., Corps de Afrique. Designation changed to 77th U. S. Colored Troops, April 4, 1864.

6th REGIMENT INFANTRY.—Org. at Port Hudson, La., Sept. 4, 1863. Sept., 1863, Ullman's Brig., Corps de Afrique, Dept. Gulf. Sept., 1863, 2 Brig., 2 Div., Corps de Afrique, Dept. Gulf. March, 1864, Garrison Port Hudson, La., Dept. Gulf. Designation changed to 78th U. S. Colored Troops, April 4, 1864.

7th REGIMENT INFANTRY.—Org. at Port Hudson, La., Aug. 31, 1863. Sept., 1863, Ullman's Brig., Corps de Afrique, Dept. Gulf. Dec., 1863, 2 Brig., 1 Div., Corps de Afrique, Dept. Gulf. Designation changed to 79th U. S. Colored Troops, April 4, 1864.

8th REGIMENT INFANTRY.—Org. at Port Hudson, La., Sept. 1, 1863. Sept., 1863, Ullman's Brig., Corps de Afrique, Dept. Gulf. Dec., 1863, 2 Brig., 1 Div., Corps de Afrique, Dept. Gulf. March, 1864, Garrison at Port Hudson, La., Dept. Gulf. Designation changed to 80th U. S. Colored Troops, April 4, 1864.

9th REGIMENT INFANTRY.—Org. at Port Hudson, La., Sept. 2, 1863. Sept., 1863, Ullman's Brig., Corps de Afrique, Dept. Gulf. Dec., 1863, 2 Brig., 1 Div., Corps de Afrique, Dept. Gulf. March, 1864, Garrison at Port Hudson, La. Designation changed to 81st U. S. Colored Troops, April 4, 1864.

10th REGIMENT INFANTRY.—Org. at Port Hudson, La., Sept. 1, 1863. Sept., 1863, Ullman's Brig., Corps de Afrique, Dept. Gulf. Dec., 1863, 2 Brig., 1 Div., Corps de Afrique, Dept. Gulf. Designation changed to 82nd U. S. Colored Troops, April 4, 1864.

11th REGIMENT INFANTRY.—Org. at Port Hudson, La., Aug. 17, 1863. Aug., 1863, Port Hudson, La., Dept. Gulf. Dec., 1863, 1 Brig., 1 Div., Corps de Afrique, Dept. Gulf. Designation changed to 83rd U. S. Colored Troops, April 4, 1864.

12th REGIMENT INFANTRY.—Org. at Port Hudson, La., Sept. 24, 1863. Sept., 1863, Garrison Port Hudson, La. Dec., 1863, 1 Brig., 1 Div., Corps de Afrique, Dept. Gulf. Designation changed to 84th U. S. Colored Troops, April 4, 1864.

13th REGIMENT INFANTRY.—Org. at New Orleans, La., Sept., 1863. Sept., 1863, 1 Brig., 2 Div., Corps de Afrique, Dept. Gulf. Dec., 1863, Unatt., 13 Corps, Texas, Dept. Gulf. Designation changed to 85th U. S. Colored Troops, April 4, 1864.

14th REGIMENT INFANTRY.—Org. at New Orleans, La., Aug. 12, 1863. Aug., 1863, Def. New Orleans, La. Sept., 1863, 1 Brig., 2 Div., Corps de Afrique, Dept. Gulf. Oct., 1863, Dist. West Fla., Dept. Gulf. Designation changed to 86th U. S. Colored Troops, April 4, 1864.

15th REGIMENT INFANTRY.—Org. at New Orleans, La., Aug. 27, 1863. Sept., 1863, 1 Brig., 2 Div., Corps de Afrique, Dept. Gulf. Oct., 1863, Engr. Brig., Dept. Gulf. Designation changed to 5th Corps de Afrique Engrs., Feby. 10, 1864.

16th REGIMENT INFANTRY.—Org. at New Orleans, Oct. 8, 1863. Oct., 1863, 1 Brig., 2 Div., Corps de Afrique. Oct., 1863, Unatt., 2 Div., 13 Corps, Texas. Designation changed to 87th U. S. Colored Troops, April 4, 1864.

17th REGIMENT INFANTRY.—Org. at Port Hudson, La., Sept. 24, 1863. Oct., 1863, 2 Brig., 2 Div., Corps de Afrique, Dept. Gulf. Designation changed to 88th U. S. Colored Troops, April 4, 1864.

18th REGIMENT INFANTRY.—Org. at Port Hudson, La., Oct. 9, 1863. Oct., 1863, 2 Brig., 2 Div., Corps de Afrique, Dept. Gulf. Designation changed to 89th U. S. Colored Troops, April 4, 1864.

19th REGIMENT INFANTRY.—Org. at Madisonville, La., Feby. 11, 1864. Feby., 1864, Madisonville, La., Dept. Gulf. Designation changed to 90th U. S. Colored Troops, April 4, 1864.

20th REGIMENT INFANTRY.—Org. at Fort Pike, La., Sept. 1, 1863. Sept., 1863, Def. New Orleans. Designation changed to 91st U. S. Colored Troops, April 4, 1864.

22nd REGIMENT INFANTRY.—Org. at New Orleans, La., Sept. 30, 1863. Oct., 1863, Dist. LaFourche, Dept. Gulf. Feby., 1864, 2 Brig., 2 Div., Corps de Afrique, Dept. Gulf. March, 1864, 1 Brig., 1 Div., Corps de Afrique. Designation changed to 92nd U. S. Colored Troops, April 4, 1864.

25th REGIMENT INFANTRY.—Org. at New Iberia, Nov. 21, 1863. Dec., 1863, 1 Brig., 2 Div., Corps de Afrique, Dept. Gulf. March, 1864, Dist. LaFourche, Dept. Gulf. Designation changed to 93rd U. S. Colored Troops, April 4, 1864.

UNITED STATES COLORED TROOPS

1st REGIMENT CAVALRY.—Org. at Camp Hamilton, Va., Dec. 22, 1863. Dec., 1863, Fort Monroe, Va., Dept. Va. and N. C. April, 1864, Unatt., Williamsburg, Va., Dept. Va. and N. C. June, 1864, 1 Brig., 3 Div., 18 Corps, Army James. Aug., 1864, Def. Portsmouth, Va., Dist. Eastern Va. May, 1865, Cav. Brig., 25 Corps, Dept. Va., and Dept. Texas. Mustered out Feby. 4, 1866.

2nd REGIMENT CAVALRY.—Org. at Fortress Monroe, Va., Dec. 22, 1863. Dec., 1863, Fort Monroe, Va., Dept. Va. and N. C. April, 1864, Unatt., Williamsburg, Va., Dept. Va. and N. C. June, 1864, 2 Brig., 3 Div., 18 Corps, Army James. Aug., 1864, Unatt., 3 Div., 18 Corps. Dec., 1864, Unatt., 25 Corps. May, 1865, Cav. Brig., 25 Corps, Dept. Va., and Dept. Texas. Mustered out Feby. 12, 1866.

3rd REGIMENT CAVALRY.—Org. March 11, 1864, from 1st Miss. Cav., African Descent. March, 1864, 1 Brig., U. S. C. T., Dist. Vicksburg, Dept. Tenn. April, 1864, Winslow's Cav. Brig., Dist. Vicksburg. Dec., 1864, 3 Brig., Cav. Div., Dist. West. Tenn. Jany., 1865, Unatt. Cav., Dist. West. Tenn. June, 1865, 1 Brig., Cav. Div., Dist. West. Tenn. Mustered out Jany. 26, 1866.

4th REGIMENT CAVALRY.—Org. April 4, 1864, from 1 Corps de Afrique Cav. April, 1864, Def. New Orleans,

La., Dept. Gulf. Aug., 1864, Dist. Port Hudson, La., Gulf. Oct., 1864, 1 Brig., 2 Div., U. S. C. T., Dept. Gulf. Dec., 1864, Dist. Port Hudson, La., Gulf. July, 1865, Dept. Miss. Mustered out March 20, 1866.

5th REGIMENT CAVALRY.—Org. at Camp Nelson, Ky., Oct. 24, 1864. Oct., 1864, 1 Div., Dist. Ky., Dept. Ohio. Feby., 1865, Dist. Ky. and Dept. Ark. Mustered out March 20, 1866.

6th REGIMENT CAVALRY.—Org. at Camp Nelson, Ky., Oct. 24, 1864. Oct., 1864, 1 Div., Dist. Ky., Dept. Ohio. Feby., 1865, Mil. Dist. and Dept. Ky., and Dept. Ark. Mustered out April 15, 1866.

1st REGIMENT HEAVY ARTILLERY.—Org. at Knoxville, Tenn., Fey. 20, 1864. Fey., 1864, 2 Brig., 4 Div., 23 Corps, Dept. Ohio. Feby., 1865, 2 Brig., 4 Div., Dist. East. Tenn., Dept. Cumb'd. March, 1865, 1 Brig., 4 Div., Dist. East. Tenn. Mustered out March 31, 1866.

3rd REGIMENT HEAVY ARTILLERY.—Org. from 1st Tenn. Heavy Arty., African Descent. Designated 2nd U. S. Colored Heavy Arty., March 11, 1864, and 3rd U. S. Colored Heavy Arty., April 26, 1864. March, 1864, Dist. Memphis, Tenn., Dept. Tenn. June, 1864, Memphis, Tenn., Dist. West. Tenn. July, 1865, 2 Infy. Brig., Dist. West. Tenn. Sept., 1865, Dist. West. Tenn. Mustered out April 30, 1866.

4th REGIMENT HEAVY ARTILLERY.—Org. from 2nd Tenn. Heavy Arty., African Descent. Designation 3rd Heavy Arty., March 11, 1864, and 4th Heavy Arty., April 26, 1864. March, 1864, Dist. Columbus, Ky., 16 Corps, Dept. Tenn. Aug., 1864, Dist. Columbus, Ky., Dept. Ohio. June, 1865, Dept. Ark. Mustered out Feby. 25, 1866.

5th REGIMENT HEAVY ARTILLERY.—Org. from 1st Miss. Heavy Arty., African Descent. Designated 4th Heavy Arty., March 11, 1864, and 5th Heavy Arty., April 26, 1864. March, 1864, 2 Div., U. S. C. T., Dist. Vicksburg, Miss. Feby., 1865, Unatt., Post Vicksburg, Miss., Dept. Miss., and Dept. Gulf. Mustered out May 20, 1866.

6th REGIMENT HEAVY ARTILLERY.—Org. from 2nd Miss. Heavy Arty., African Descent. Designated 5th Heavy Arty., March 11, 1864, and 6th Heavy Arty., April 26, 1864. March, 1864, Post Natchez, Miss., Dist. Vicksburg, Miss., Dept. Tenn., and Dept. Miss. Feby., 1865, Post Natchez, Miss., Dept. Miss. April, 1865, Dept. Gulf. Mustered out May 13, 1866.

7th REGIMENT HEAVY ARTILLERY.—Org. from 1st Ala. Siege Arty., African Descent. Designated 6th Heavy Arty., March 11, 1864, and 7th Heavy Arty., April 26, 1864. March, 1864, Dist. Memphis, Tenn., 16 Corps, Dept. Tenn. June, 1864, Memphis, Tenn., Dist. West. Tenn. Designated 11th U. S. Colored Troops (New), Jany. 23, 1865.

8th REGIMENT HEAVY ARTILLERY.—Org. at Paducah Ky., April 26, 1864. April, 1864, Paducah, Ky., Dist. Columbus, Ky., 16 Corps, Dept. Tenn. Aug., 1864, Paducah, Ky., Dept. Ohio. Feby., 1865, Dept. Ky. Mustered out Feby. 10, 1866.

9th REGIMENT HEAVY ARTILLERY.—Org. at Clarksville and Nashville, Tenn., Oct. 8 to Nov. 1, 1864. Oct., 1864, Dist. Nashville, Tenn., Dept. Cumb'd. Broken up May 5, 1865.

10th REGIMENT HEAVY ARTILLERY.—Org. from 1 Corps de Afrique, Heavy Arty. Designated 7th Heavy Arty., April 4, 1864, and 10th Heavy Arty., May 21, 1864. April, 1864, Def. New Orleans, La., Dept. Gulf. Oct., 1864, 1 Brig., 3 Div., U. S. C. T., Gulf. Nov., 1864. Def. New Orleans, La., Dept. Gulf. Mustered out Feby. 22, 1867.

11th REGIMENT HEAVY ARTILLERY.—Org. from 14th Rhode Island Colored Heavy Arty. Designated 8th Heavy Arty., April 4, 1864, and 11th Heavy Arty., May 21, 1864. April, 1864, Def. New Orleans, La., Dept. Gulf. Mustered out Oct. 2, 1865.

12th REGIMENT HEAVY ARTILLERY.—Org. at Camp Nelson, Ky., July 15, 1864. July, 1864, 2 Brig., 1 Div., Dist. Ky., Dept. Ohio. Jany., 1865, Mil. Dist. Ky. and Dept. Ky. Mustered out April 24, 1866.

13th REGIMENT HEAVY ARTILLERY.—Org. at Camp Nelson, Ky., June 23, 1864. June, 1864, Mil. Dist.

Ky., Dept. Ohio, to Feby., 1865, Dept. Ky. Mustered out Nov. 18, 1865.

14th REGIMENT HEAVY ARTILLERY.—Org. from 1st N. C. Heavy Arty., African Descent, March 17, 1864. March, 1864, Def. Newberne, N. C., Dept. Va. and N. C. Jany., 1865, Sub-Dist. Newberne, N. C., and Sub-Dist. Beaufort, N. C., Dept. N. C. Mustered out Dec 11, 1865.

BATTERY "A," 2nd REGIMENT LIGHT ARTILLERY.—Org. at Nashville, Tenn., April 30, 1864. April, 1864, Post and Dist. Nashville, Tenn., Dept. Cumb'd. March, 1865, Dist. Middle Tenn. Mustered out Jany. 13, 1866.

BATTERY "B," 2nd REGIMENT LIGHT ARTILLERY.—Org. at Fort Monroe, Va., Jany. 8, 1864. Jany., 1864, Fort Monroe, Va., Dept. Va. and N. C. April, 1864, Arty., Hincks' Colored Div., 18 Corps, Army James. May, 1864, Rand's Prov'l Brig., 18 Corps. June, 1864, Arty. Brig., 18 Corps. June, 1864, Unatt. Arty., Dept. Va. and N. C. July, 1864, Def. Norfolk and Portsmouth, Va., Dept. Va. and N. C. May, 1865, Arty., 25 Corps, and Dept. Texas. Mustered out March 17, 1866.

BATTERY "C," 2nd REGIMENT LIGHT ARTILLERY.—Org. from 1st La. Battery, African Descent, April 26, 1864. Designated Battery "A," March 11, 1864, and Battery "C," April 26, 1864. March, 1864, Post Goodrich Landing, Dist. Vicksburg, Miss., Dept. Tenn. May, 1864, Post Vicksburg, Miss. July, 1864, Post Milliken's Bend, La., Dist. Vicksburg. Dec., 1864, Res. Arty. Post Vicksburg, Miss., Dept. Miss. Mustered out Dec. 28, 1865.

BATTERY "D," 2nd REGIMENT LIGHT ARTILLERY.—Org. from 2nd La. Battery, African Descent. Designated Battery "B," March 11, 1864, and Battery "D," April 26, 1864. March, 1864, Post Goodrich Landing, Dist. Vicksburg, Miss., Dept. Tenn. Dec., 1864, Res. Arty., Dist. Vicksburg, Dept. Miss. Mustered out Dec. 28, 1865.

BATTERY "E," 2nd REGIMENT LIGHT ARTILLERY.—Org. from 3rd La. Battery, African Descent. Designated Battery "C," March 11, 1864, and Battery "E," April 26, 1864. March, 1864, Dist. Eastern Ark., 7 Corps, Dept. Ark. Mustered out Sept. 26, 1865.

BATTERY "F," 2nd REGIMENT LIGHT ARTILLERY.—Org. from Memphis Light Battery, African Descent. Designated Battery "D," March 11, 1864, and Battery "F," April 26, 1864. March, 1864, 1 Colored Brig., Dist. Memphis, Tenn., 16 Corps, Dept. Tenn. June, 1864, 3 Brig., Sturgis' Exp. June, 1864, Post and Def. Memphis, Tenn., Dist. West. Tenn. Dec., 1864, Arty. Res., Dist. West. Tenn. April, 1865, Bridgeport, Ala., Dept. Cumb'd. July, 1865, 2 Infy. Brig., Dist. West. Tenn. Consolidated with 3rd U. S. C. H. A., Dec. 28, 1865.

BATTERY "G," 2nd REGIMENT LIGHT ARTILLERY.—Org. at Hilton Head, S. C., May 24, 1864. June, 1864, Dist. Hilton Head, S. C., Dept. South. Aug., 1864, Dist. Beaufort, S. C., Dept. South. Oct., 1864, 2 Separate Brig., Dept. South. June, 1865, Dept. South. Mustered out Aug. 12, 1865.

BATTERY "H," 2nd REGIMENT LIGHT ARTILLERY.—Org. from 1st Ark. Battery, African Descent, Dec. 13, 1864. Dec., 1864, Post Pine Bluff, Ark., 7 Corps, and Dept. Ark. Mustered out Sept. 15, 1865.

BATTERY "I," 2nd REGIMENT LIGHT ARTILLERY.—Org. at Memphis, Tenn., April 19, 1864. May, 1864, Dist. Memphis, 16 Corps, Dept. Tenn. June, 1864, Colored Brig., Memphis, Tenn., Dist. West. Tenn. Dec., 1864, Arty. Res., Dist. West. Tenn. April, 1865, Stevenson, Ala. July, 1865, Dept. Tenn. Mustered out Jany. 10, 1866.

INDEPENDENT BATTERY LIGHT ARTILLERY.—Org. at Leavenworth, Kans., Dec. 23, 1864. Attached to Dist. North Kans., Dept. Kans. Mustered out July 22, 1865.

1st REGIMENT INFANTRY.—Org. in Dist. Columbia, May 19 to June 30, 1863. July, 1863, U. S. Forces Norfolk and Portsmouth, Va., Dept. Va. and N. C. Oct., 1863, U. S. Forces Yorktown, Va., Dept. Va. and N. C.

April, 1864, 1 Brig., Hincks' Colored Div., 18 Corps, Army James. June, 1864. 1 Brig., 3 Div., 18 Corps. Dec., 1864, 1 Brig., 1 Div., 25 Corps. Dec., 1864, 1 Brig., 3 Div., 25 Corps. March, 1865, 1 Brig., 3 Div., 10 Corps, Dept. N. C. Aug., 1865, Dept. N. C. Mustered out Sept. 29, 1865.

2nd REGIMENT INFANTRY.—Org. at Arlington, Va., June 20 to Nov. 11, 1863. Dec., 1863, Def. New Orleans, La., Dept. Gulf. Feby., 1864, Dist. Key West, Fla., Dept. Gulf. July, 1865, Dept. Fla. Mustered out Jany. 5, 1866.

3rd REGIMENT INFANTRY.—Org. at Camp William Penn, near Phila., Pa., Aug. 3-10, 1863. Aug., 1863, 4 Brig., Morris Island, S. C., 10 Corps, Dept. South. Nov., 1863, 3 Brig., Morris Island, S. C., 10 Corps, Dept. South. Jany., 1864, Montgomery's Brig., Dist. Hilton Head, S. C., 10 Corps, Dept. South. Feby., 1864, 2 Brig., Vodge's Div., Dist. Fla., Dept. South. April, 1864, Dist. Fla., Dept. South. Oct., 1864, 4 Separate Brig., Dist. Fla., Dept. South. July, 1865, Dept. Fla. Mustered out Oct. 31, 1865.

4th REGIMENT INFANTRY.—Org. at Baltimore, Md., July 15 to Sept. 1, 1863. Oct., 1863, U. S. Forces Yorktown, Va., Dept. Va. and N. C. Jany., 1864, 2 Brig., U. S. Forces Yorktown, Va., Dept. Va. and N. C. April, 1864, 2 Brig., Hincks' Colored Div., 18 Corps, Army James. June, 1864, 2 Brig., 3 Div., 18 Corps. Dec., 1864, 2 Brig., 1 Div., 25 Corps. Jany., 1865, 2 Brig., 3 Div., 25 Corps. March, 1865, 2 Brig., 3 Div., 10 Corps, Dept. N. C. Aug., 1865, Dept. N. C. Mustered out May 4, 1866.

5th REGIMENT INFANTRY.—Org. at Camp Delaware, Ohio, Aug. 6, 1863, to Jany. 15, 1864. Nov., 1863, U. S. Forces Norfolk and Portsmouth, Va., Dept. Va. and N. C. Jany., 1864, 2 Brig., U. S. Forces Yorktown, Va., Dept. Va. and N. C. April, 1864, 2 Brig., Hincks' Colored Div., 18 Corps, Army James. June, 1864, 2 Brig., 3 Div., 18 Corps. Dec., 1864, 3 Brig., 1 Div., 25 Corps. Dec., 1864, 3 Brig., 3 Div., 25 Corps. March, 1865, 2 Brig., 3 Div., 10 Corps, Dept. N. C. Aug., 1865, Dept. N. C. Mustered out Sept. 20, 1865.

6th REGIMENT INFANTRY.—Org. at Camp William Penn, near Phila., Pa., July 28 to Sept. 12, 1863. Nov., 1863, U. S. Forces Yorktown, Va., Dept. Va. and N. C. Jany., 1864, 2 Brig., Hincks' Colored Div., 18 Corps, Army James. June, 1864, 2 Brig., 3 Div., 18 Corps. Aug., 1864, 3 Brig., 3 Div., 18 Corps. Dec., 1864, 2 Brig., 1 Div., 25 Corps. Dec., 1864, 2 Brig., 3 Div., 25 Corps. March, 1865, 3 Brig., 3 Div., 10 Corps, Dept. N. C. Aug., 1865, Dept. N. C. Mustered out Sept. 20, 1865.

7th REGIMENT INFANTRY.—Org. at Baltimore, Md., Sept. 26 to Nov. 12, 1863. Nov., 1863, Camp Benedict, Md. March, 1864, Jacksonville, Fla., Dist. Fla., Dept. South. July, 1864, Dist. Hilton Head, S. C., Dept. South. July, 1864, Jacksonville, Fla., Dist. Fla., Dept. South. Aug., 1864, 1 Brig., 3 Div., 10 Corps, Army James. Dec., 1864, 1 Brig., 2 Div., 25 Corps. Jany., 1866, Dept. Texas. Mustered out Nov. 16, 1866.

8th REGIMENT INFANTRY.—Org. at Camp William Penn, near Phila., Pa., Sept. 22 to Dec. 24, 1863. Jany., 1864, Howell's Brig., Dist. Hilton Head, S. C., Dept. South. Feby., 1864, Hawley's Brig., Seymour's Div., Dist. Fla., Dept. South. April, 1864, Dist. Fla., Dept. South. Aug., 1864, 1 Brig., 3 Div., 10 Corps, Army James. Dec., 1864, 2 Brig., 2 Div., 25 Corps. April, 1865, 1 Brig., 2 Div., 25 Corps, and Dept. Texas. Mustered out Nov. 10, 1865.

9th REGIMENT INFANTRY.—Org. at Camp Stanton, Md., Nov. 11-30, 1863. Nov., 1863, Camp Benedict, Md. March, 1864, Dist. Hilton Head, S. C., Dept. South. April, 1864, Dist. Beaufort, S. C., Dept. South. Aug., 1864, 1 Brig., 3 Div., 10 Corps, Army James. Dec., 1864, 2 Brig., 3 Div., 25 Corps. Jany., 1865, 2 Brig., 1 Div., 25 Corps, and Dept. Texas. Mustered out Nov. 26, 1866.

10th REGIMENT INFANTRY.—Org. in Va., Nov. 18, 1863. Dec., 1863, Drummondstown, Va., Dept. Va. and N. C. April, 1864, 1 Brig., Hincks' Colored Div., 18 Corps, Army James. June, 1864, 1 Brig., 3 Div., 18

Corps. July, 1864, Unatt., 18 Corps. Aug., 1864, 3 Brig., 3 Div., 18 Corps. Dec., 1864, 3 Brig., 3 Div., 25 Corps. Jany., 1865, 3 Brig., 1 Div., 25 Corps. Jany., 1865, Attached Brig., 1 Div., 25 Corps. June, 1865, Dept. Texas. Mustered out May 17, 1866.

11th REGIMENT INFANTRY (OLD).—Org. at Fort Smith, Ark., Dec. 19, 1863, to March 3, 1864. March, 1864, 2 Brig., Dist. Frontier, 7 Corps, Dept. Ark. Jany., 1865, Colored Brig., 7 Corps. Feby., 1865, 2 Brig., 1 Div., 7 Corps, Ark. Consolidated with 112th and 113th U. S. C. T., April 22, 1865, to form New 113th U. S. C. T.

11th REGIMENT INFANTRY (NEW).—Org. from 7th U. S. Colored Heavy Arty., Jany. 23, 1865. Jany., 1865, Post and Def. Memphis, Tenn., Dist. West. Tenn. July, 1865, 2 Infy. Brig., Dist. West. Tenn., and Dept. Tenn. Mustered out Jany. 12, 1866.

12th REGIMENT INFANTRY.—Org. in Tenn. at large, July 24 to Aug. 14, 1863. Oct., 1863, Def. Nashv. & N. W. R. R., Dept. Cumb'd. Dec., 1864, 2 Colored Brig., Dist. Etowah, Dept. Cumb'd. Jany., 1865, Def. Nashv. & N. W. R. R., Dist. Middle Tenn. May, 1865, 3rd Sub-Dist., Dist. Middle Tenn. Mustered out Jany. 16, 1866.

13th REGIMENT INFANTRY.—Org. at Nashville, Tenn., Nov. 19, 1863. Nov., 1863, Def. Nashv. & N. W. R. R., Dept. Cumb'd. Nov., 1864, 2 Colored Brig., Dist. Etowah, Dept. Cumb'd. Jany., 1865, Def. Nashv. & N. W. R. R., Dist. Middle Tenn., Dept. Cumb'd. May, 1865, 3rd Sub-Dist., Dist. Middle Tenn., Dept. Cumb'd. Mustered out Jany. 10, 1866.

14th REGIMENT INFANTRY.—Org. at Gallatin, Tenn., Nov. 16, 1863, to Jany. 8, 1864. Dec., 1863, Post Gallatin, Tenn. Jany., 1864, Post Chattanooga, Tenn., Dept. Cumb'd. Nov., 1864, Unatt., Dist. Etowah, Dept. Cumb'd. Dec., 1864, 1 Colored Brig., Dist. Etowah. May, 1865, Dist. East. Tenn. Aug., 1865, Dept. Tenn. and Dept. Ga. Mustered out March 26, 1866.

15th REGIMENT INFANTRY.—Org. at Nashville, Tenn., Dec. 2, 1863, to March 11, 1864. Jany., 1864, Post and Dist. Nashville, Tenn., Dept. Cumb'd. Aug., 1864, Post Springfield, Tenn., Dist. Nashville, Tenn., Dept. Cumb'd. March, 1865, 5th Sub-Dist., Dist. Middle Tenn., Dept. Cumb'd. Mustered out April 7, 1866.

16th REGIMENT INFANTRY.—Org. at Nashville, Tenn., Dec. 4, 1863, to Feby. 16, 1864. Feby., 1864, Post Chattanooga, Tenn., Dept. Cumb'd. Nov., 1864, Unatt., Dist. Etowah, Dept. Cumb'd. Dec., 1864, 1 Colored Brig., Dist. Etowah, Dept. Cumb'd. Jany., 1865, Unatt., Dist. Etowah. March, 1865, 1 Colored Brig., Dept. Cumb'd. April, 1865, 5th Sub-Dist., Dist. Middle Tenn. July, 1865, 2 Brig., 4 Div., Dist. East. Tenn. Mustered out April 30, 1866.

17th REGIMENT INFANTRY.—Org. at Nashville, Tenn., Dec. 12-21, 1863. Dec., 1863, Post Murfreesboro, Tenn., Dept. Cumb'd. April, 1864, Post and Dist. Nashville, Tenn., Dept. Cumb'd. Dec., 1864, 1 Colored Brig., Dist. Etowah, Dept. Cumb'd. Jany., 1865, Post and Dist. Nashville, Tenn., Dept. Cumb'd. Mustered out April 25, 1866.

18th REGIMENT INFANTRY.—Org. in Mo. at large, Feby. 1 to Sept. 28, 1864. Feby., 1864, Dist. St. Louis, Dept. Mo. Dec., 1864, Unassigned, Dist. Etowah, Dept. Cumb'd. Dec., 1864, 1 Colored Brig., Dist. Etowah, Dept. Cumb'd. Jany., 1865, Unassigned, Dist. Etowah, Dept. Cumb'd. March, 1865, 1 Colored Brig., Dept. Cumb'd. July, 1865, 2 Brig., 4 Div., Dist. East. Tenn., and Dept. Tenn. Mustered out Feby. 21, 1866.

19th REGIMENT INFANTRY.—Org. at Camp Stanton, Md., Dec. 25, 1863, to Jany. 16, 1864. April, 1864, 2 Brig., 4 Div., 9 Corps, Army Potomac. Sept., 1864, 2 Brig., 3 Div., 9 Corps. Dec., 1864, 3 Brig., 3 Div., 25 Corps. Jany., 1865, 3 Brig., 1 Div., 25 Corps. Jany., 1866., Dept. Texas. Mustered out Jany. 15, 1867.

20th REGIMENT INFANTRY.—Org. at Riker's Island, N. Y., Feby. 9, 1864. March, 1864, Def. New Orleans, La., Dept. Gulf. Dec., 1864, Dist. Southern Ala., Dept. Gulf. Feby., 1865, Def. New Orleans, La., Dept. Gulf. June, 1865, Dist. LaFourche, Dept. Gulf. Aug., 1865, Nashville, Tenn. Mustered out Oct. 7, 1865.

21st REGIMENT INFANTRY.—Org. from 3rd and 4th Regiments, S. C. Colored Infy., March 14, 1864. March, 1864, 3 Brig., Vodge's Div., Dist. Fla., Dept. South. April, 1864, Morris Island, S. C., Northern Dist., Dept. South. Oct., 1864, 1 Separate Brig., Dept. South. Feby., 1865, Garrison Charleston, S. C., Dept. South. Aug., 1865, Dept. South. Mustered out Oct. 7, 1866.

22nd REGIMENT INFANTRY.—Org. at Phila., Pa., Jany. 10-29, 1864. Jany., 1864, U. S. Forces Yorktown, Va., Dept. Va. and N. C. April, 1864, 1 Brig., Hincks' Colored Div., 18 Corps, Army James. June, 1864, 1 Brig., 3 Div., 18 Corps. June, 1864, 2 Brig., 3 Div., 18 Corps. Aug., 1864, 1 Brig., 3 Div., 18 Corps. Aug., 1864, 1 Brig., 3 Div., 10 Corps. Sept., 1864, 1 Brig., 3 Div., 18 Corps. Dec., 1864, 1 Brig., 3 Div., 25 Corps. Dec., 1864, 1 Brig., 1 Div., 25 Corps., and Dept. Texas. Mustered out Oct. 16, 1865.

23rd REGIMENT INFANTRY.—Org. at Camp Casey, Va., Nov. 23, 1863, to June 30, 1864. April, 1864, 2 Brig., 4 Div., 9 Corps, Army Potomac. Sept., 1864, 2 Brig., 3 Div., 9 Corps. Dec., 1864, 3 Brig., 3 Div., 25 Corps. Dec., 1864, 3 Brig., 1 Div., 25 Corps, and Dept. Texas. Mustered out Nov. 30, 1865.

24th REGIMENT INFANTRY.—Org. at Camp William Penn, near Phila., Pa., Jany. 30 to March 30, 1865. May, 1865, Def. Washington, D. C., 22 Corps. June, 1865, Point Lookout, Md. July, 1865, Sub-Dist. Roanoke, Va., Dept. Va. Mustered out Oct. 1, 1865.

25th REGIMENT INFANTRY.—Org. at Phila., Pa., Jany. 3 to Feby. 12, 1864. May, 1864, Def. New Orleans, La., Dept. Gulf. July, 1864, Dist. Pensacola, Fla., Dept. Gulf. Oct., 1864, 1 Brig., 3 Div., U. S. C. T., Dept. Gulf. Oct., 1864, 1 Brig., Dist. West Fla., Dept. Gulf. Jany., 1865, 3 Brig, 1 Div., U. S. C. T., Dist. West Fla. Feby., 1865, 1 Brig., 1 Div., U. S. C. T., Dist. West Fla. April, 1865, Unatt., Dist. West Fla. July, 1865, Dept. Fla. Mustered out Dec. 6, 1865.

26th REGIMENT INFANTRY.—Org. at Riker's Island, N. Y. Harbor, Feby. 27, 1864. April, 1864, Dist. Beaufort, S. C., Dept. South. Oct., 1864, 2 Separate Brig., Dept. South. Jany., 1865, 1 Separate Brig., Dept. South. Feby., 1865, 2 Separate Brig., Dept. South. June, 1865, Dept. South. Mustered out Aug. 28, 1865.

27th REGIMENT INFANTRY.—Org. at Camp Delaware, Ohio, Jany. 16, 1864. March, 1864, 1 Brig., 4 Div., 9 Corps, Army Potomac. Sept., 1864, 1 Brig., 3 Div., 9 Corps. Dec., 1864, 1 Brig., 1 Div., 25 Corps. Dec., 1864, 1 Brig., 3 Div., 25 Corps. Jany., 1865, 3 Brig., 3 Div., 25 Corps. March, 1865, 3 Brig., 3 Div., 10 Corps, Dept. N. C. July, 1865, Dept. N. C. Mustered out Sept. 21, 1865.

28th REGIMENT INFANTRY.—Org. at Indianapolis, Ind., Dec. 24, 1863, to March 31, 1864. April, 1864, Def. Washington, 22 Corps. June, 1864, White House, Va., Abercrombie's Command. July, 1864, 2 Brig., 4 Div., 9 Corps, Army Potomac. Sept., 1864, 2 Brig., 3 Div., 9 Corps. Dec., 1864, 3 Brig., 2 Div., 25 Corps. April, 1865, Attached Brig., 1 Div., 25 Corps. April, 1865, Dist. St. Marys, 22 Corps. May, 1865, Dept. Texas. Mustered out Nov. 8, 1865.

29th REGIMENT INFANTRY.—Org. at Quincy, Ill., April 24, 1864. May, 1864, Def. Washington, 22 Corps. June, 1864, White House, Va., Abercrombie's Command. July, 1864, 2 Brig., 4 Div., 9 Corps. Sept., 1863, 2 Brig., 3 Div., 9 Corps. Dec., 1864, 3 Brig., 2 Div., 25 Corps, and Dept. Texas. Mustered out Nov. 6, 1865.

30th REGIMENT INFANTRY.—Org. at Camp Stanton, Md., Feby. 12 to March 18, 1864. March, 1864, 1 Brig., 4 Div., 9 Corps, Army Potomac. Sept., 1864, 1 Brig., 3 Div., 9 Corps. Dec., 1864, 1 Brig., 1 Div., 25 Corps. Dec., 1864, 1 Brig., 3 Div., 25 Corps. March, 1865, 1 Brig., 3 Div., 10 Corps, Dept. N. C. July, 1865, Dept. N. C. Mustered out Dec. 10, 1865.

31st REGIMENT INFANTRY.—Org. at Hart's Island, N. Y., April 29, 1864. April, 1864, 2 Brig., 4 Div., 9 Corps, Army Potomac. Sept., 1864, 2 Brig., 3 Div., 9 Corps. Dec., 1864, 3 Brig., 2 Div., 25 Corps. June, 1865, Dept. Texas. Mustered out Nov. 7, 1865.

32nd REGIMENT INFANTRY.—Org. at Camp William Penn, Phila., Pa., Feby. 17 to March 7, 1864. May, 1864, Bailey's Brig., Dist. Hilton Head, S. C., Dept. South. June, 1864, Morris Island, S. C., Northern District, Dept. South. Oct., 1864, 3 Separate Brig., Dept. South. Nov., 1864, 2 Brig., Coast Div., Dept. South. Dec., 1864, 2 Separate Brig., Dept. South. June, 1865, Dept. of the South. Mustered out August 22, 1865.

33rd REGIMENT INFANTRY.—Org. Feby. 8, 1864, from 1st South Carolina Colored Infantry. Feby., 1864, U. S. Forces, Port Royal Island, S. C., 10 Corps, Dept. South. April, 1864, Dist. Beaufort, S. C., Dept. South. July, 1864, Folly Island, S. C., Northern Dist., Dept. South. Oct., 1864, 1 Separate Brigade, Dept. South. March, 1865, Dist. Savannah, Ga., Dept. of the South. June, 1865, Dept. South. Mustered out Jany. 31, 1866.

34th REGIMENT INFANTRY.—Org. Feby. 8, 1864, from 2nd South Carolina Colored Infantry. Feby., 1864, Montgomery's Brig., Dist. Fla., Dept. South. Feby., 1864, 3 Brig., Vodge's Div., Dist. Fla. April, 1864, Morris Island, S. C., Northern Dist., Dept. South. June, 1864, Dist. Beaufort, S. C., Dept. South. Aug., 1864, Dist. Florida, Dept. South. Oct., 1864, 4 Separate Brig., Dept. South. Nov., 1864, 1 Brig., Coast Div., Dept. South. Dec., 1864, 2 Brig., Coast Div., Dept. South. Jany., 1865, 4 Separate Brig., Dist. Fla., Dept. South, and Dept. Fla. Mustered out Feby. 28, 1866.

35th REGIMENT INFANTRY.—Org. Feby. 8, 1864, from 1st North Carolina Colored Infantry. Feby., 1864, Montgomery's Brig., Dist. Fla., Dept. South. Feby., 1864, 2 Brig., Vodge's Div., Dist. Fla., Dept. South. April, 1864, Dist. Fla., Dept. South. Oct., 1864, 4 Separate Brig., Dept. South. Nov., 1864, 2 Brig., Coast Div., Dept. South. Dec., 1864, 4 Separate Brig., Dept. South. March, 1865, 1 Separate Brig., Dept. South. Aug., 1865, Dept. South. Mustered out June 1, 1866.

36th REGIMENT INFANTRY.—Org. Feby. 8, 1864, from 2nd North Carolina Colored Infantry. Feby., 1864, U. S. Forces Norfolk and Portsmouth Va., Dept. Va. and N. C. April, 1864, Dist. St. Mary's, Dept. Va. and N. C. June, 1864, Unatt., Army James. Aug., 1864, 2 Brig., 3 Div., 18 Corps. Dec., 1864, 1 Brig., 3 Div., 25 Corps. Dec., 1864, 1 Brig., 1 Div., 25 Corps and Dept. Texas. Mustered out Oct. 28, 1866.

37th REGIMENT INFANTRY.—Org. Feby. 8, 1864, from 3rd North Carolina Colored Infantry. Feby., 1864, U. S. Forces Norfolk and Portsmouth, Va., Dept. Va. and N. C. April, 1864. 1 Brig., Hincks' Colored Div., 18 Corps, Army James. June, 1864, 1 Brig., 3 Div., 18 Corps. July, 1864, Unatt., Army James. Aug., 1864, 1 Brig., 3 Div., 18 Corps. Dec., 1864, 3 Brig., 3 Div., 25 Corps. Jany., 1865, 3 Brig., 3 Div., Terry's Prov'l Corps, Dept. N. C. March, 1865, 2 Brig., 3 Div., 10 Corps, Dept. N. C. Aug., 1865, Dept. North Carolina. Mustered out Feby. 11, 1867.

38th REGIMENT INFANTRY.—Org. in Virginia, Jany. 23, 1864. Feby., 1864, U. S. Forces Norfolk and Portsmouth, Va., Dept. Va. and N. C. June, 1864, Unatt., Dept. Va. and N. C. Aug., 1864, 2 Brig., 3 Div., 18 Corps, Army James. Dec., 1864, 1 Brig., 3 Div., 25 Corps. Dec., 1864, 1 Brig., 1 Div., 25 Corps and Dept. Texas. Mustered out Jany. 25, 1867.

39th REGIMENT INFANTRY.—Org. at Baltimore, Md., March 22-31, 1864. April, 1864, 1 Brig., 4 Div., 9 Corps, Army Potomac. Sept., 1864, 1 Brig., 3 Div., 9 Corps. Dec., 1864, 2 Brig., 1 Div., 25 Corps. Dec., 1864. 2 Brig., 3 Div., 25 Corps. Jany., 1865, 2 Brig., 3 Div., Terry's Prov'l Div., Dept. North Carolina. March, 1865, 2 Brig., 3 Div., 10 Corps, Dept. N. C. Aug., 1865, Dept. North Carolina. Mustered out December 4, 1865.

40th REGIMENT INFANTRY.—Org. at Nashville and Greenville, Tenn., Feby. 29, 1864. March, 1864, Def. Louisville and Nashville R. R., Dept. Cumb'd. June, 1864, Defenses Nashville and Northwestern R. R., Dept. Cumb'd. Dec., 1864, Def. Louisville and Nashville R. R., Dept. Cumb'd. April, 1865, 2 Brig., 4 Div., Dist. East Tenn. July, 1865, 1 Brig., 4 Div., Dist. East Tenn. Aug., 1865, Dept. Tennessee. Mustered out April 25, 1866.

41st REGIMENT INFANTRY.—Org. at Camp William Penn, Phila., Pa., Sept. 30 to Dec. 7, 1864. Oct., 1864, 1 Brig., 3 Div., 10 Corps, Army James. Dec., 1864, 2 Brig., 3 Div., 25 Corps. Jany., 1865, 2 Brig., 1 Div., 25 Corps. Jany., 1865, 2 Brig., 2 Div., 25 Corps and Dept. Texas. Mustered out Dec. 10, 1865.

42nd REGIMENT INFANTRY.—Org. at Chattanooga and Nashville, Tenn., April 20, 1864. April, 1864, Unatt., Chattanooga, Tenn., Dept. Cumb'd. Nov., 1864, Unatt., Dist. Etowah, Dept. Cumb'd. Dec., 1864, 1st Colored Brig., Dist. Etowah, Dept. Cumb'd. Jany., 1865, Unatt., Dist. Etowah, Dept. Cumb'd. March, 1865, 1st Colored Brig., Dept. Cumb'd. July, 1865, 2 Brig., 4 Div., Dist. East Tenn. July, 1865, Dept. of Georgia. Mustered out Jany. 31, 1866.

43rd REGIMENT INFANTRY.—Org. at Phila., Pa., March 12 to June 3, 1864. April, 1864, 1 Brig., 4 Div., 9 Corps, Army Potomac. Sept., 1864, 1 Brig., 3 Div., 9 Corps. Dec., 1865, 3 Brig., 3 Div., 25 Corps. Jany., 1865, 3 Brig., 1 Div., 25 Corps. Mustered out Oct. 20, 1865.

44th REGIMENT INFANTRY.—Org. at Chattanooga, Tenn., April 7, 1864. April, 1864, Unatt., Chattanooga, Tenn., Dept. Cumb'd. Nov., 1864, Unatt., Dist. Etowah, Dept. Cumb'd. Dec., 1864, 1st Colored Brig., Dist. Etowah, Dept. Cumb'd. Jany., 1865, Unatt., Dist. Etowah, Dept. Cumb'd. March, 1865, 1st Colored Brig., Dept. Cumb'd. July, 1865, 2 Brig., 4 Div., Dist. East Tenn. July, 1865, Dept. Georgia. Mustered out April 30, 1866.

45th REGIMENT INFANTRY.—Org. at Phila., Pa., June 13 to Aug. 19, 1864. July, 1864, Prov'l Brig., Casey's Div., 22 Corps. (4 Co.'s to March, 1865.) Sept., 1864, 2 Brig., 3 Div., 10 Corps. Dec., 1864, 2 Brig., 2 Div., 25 Corps and Dept. Texas. Mustered out Nov. 4, 1865.

46th REGIMENT INFANTRY.—Org. from 1st Arkansas Colored Infantry, May 11, 1864. May, 1864, Post Milliken's Bend, La., Dist. Vicksburg, Miss. Nov., 1864, 2 Brig., 1 Div., U. S. C. T., Dist. Vicksburg, Miss. Jany., 1865, 2 Brig., Post and defenses Memphis, Tenn., Dist. West Tenn. Feby., 1865, New Orleans, La., Dept. Gulf. May, 1865, Dept. Texas. Mustered out Jany. 30, 1866.

47th REGIMENT INFANTRY.—Org. March 11, 1864, from 8th Louisiana Colored Infantry. March, 1864, 2 Brig., 1 Div., U. S. C. T., Dist. Vicksburg, Miss. Oct., 1864, 2 Brig., 4 Div., 16 Corps. Nov., 1864, 2 Brig., 1 Div., U. S. C. T., Dist. Vicksburg, Miss. Feby., 1865, 2 Brig., 1 Div., U. S. C. T., Mil. Div. West Miss. June, 1865, Dept. Gulf. Mustered out January 5, 1866.

48th REGIMENT INFANTRY.—Org. March 11, 1864, from 10th Louisiana Colored Infantry. March, 1864, 1st Colored Brigade, Dist. Vicksburg, Miss. April, 1864, 1 Brig., 1 Div., U. S. C. T., Dist Vicksburg, Miss. Feby., 1865, 3 Brig., 1 Div., U. S. C. T., Mil. Div. West Miss. May, 1865, 1 Brig, 1 Div., U. S. C. T., Dist. West Fla. June, 1865, Dept. Gulf. Mustered out Jany. 4, 1866.

49th REGIMENT INFANTRY.—Org. March 11, 1864, from 11 Louisiana Colored Infantry. March, 1864, 1st Colored Brig., Dist. Vicksburg, Miss. April, 1864, 1 Brig., 1 Div., U. S. C. T., Dist. Vicksburg, Miss. April, 1864, 2 Brig., 1 Div., U. S. C. T., Dist. Vicksburg, Miss. Oct., 1864, 1 Brig., 4 Div., 16 Corps. Nov., 1864, 1 Brig., 1 Div., U. S. C. T., Dist. Vicksburg, Miss. June, 1865, Dept. Miss. Mustered out March 27, 1867.

50th REGIMENT INFANTRY.—Org. March 11, 1864, from 12th Louisiana Colored Infantry. March, 1864, 2 Brig., 1 Div., U. S. C. T., Dist. Vicksburg, Miss. Oct., 1864, 2 Brig., 4 Div., 16 Corps. Nov., 1864, 2 Brig., 1 Div., U. S. C. T., Dist. Vicksburg, Miss. Feby., 1865, 2 Brig., 1 Div., U. S. C. T., Mil. Div. West Miss. June, 1865, Dept. Gulf. Mustered out March 20, 1866.

51st REGIMENT INFANTRY.—Org. March 11, 1864, from 1st Mississippi Colored Infantry. March, 1864, Post Goodrich Landing, Dist. Vicksburg, Miss., Dept. Tenn. Dec., 1864, 1 Brig., 1 Div., U. S. C. T., Dist. Vicksburg, Miss. Feby., 1865, 2 Brig., 1 Div., U. S. C. T., Mil. Div. West Miss. June, 1865, Dept. Gulf. Mustered out June 16, 1866.

52nd REGIMENT INFANTRY.—Org. March 11, 1864, from 2nd Mississippi Colored Infantry. March, 1864, 2 Brig., 1 Div., U. S. C. T., Dist. Vicksburg, Miss., Dept. Tenn. Oct., 1864, 2 Brig., 4 Div., 16 Corps. Nov., 1864, 2 Brig., 1 Div., U. S. C. T., Dist Vicksburg, Miss. Feby., 1865, Maltby's Brig., Dist. Vicksburg, Miss., and Dept. Miss. Mustered out May 5, 1866.

53rd REGIMENT INFANTRY.—Org. March 11, 1864, from 3rd Mississippi Colored Infantry. March, 1864, 1 Brig., 1 Div., U. S. C. T., Dist. Vicksburg, Miss., Dept. Tenn. Oct., 1864, 1 Brig., 4 Div., 16 Corps. Nov., 1864, Dept. Arkansas. Feby., 1865, Dist. Vicksburg, Miss. and Dept. Miss. Mustered out March 8, 1866.

54th REGIMENT INFANTRY.—Org. March 11, 1864, from 2nd Arkansas Colored Infantry. March, 1864, 2 Brig., Dist. Frontier, 7 Corps, Ark. Jany., 1865, Colored Brig., 7 Corps, Ark. Feby., 1865, 2 Brig., 1 Div., 7 Corps, Ark. Aug., 1865, Dept. Ark. Mustered out Dec. 31, 1866.

55th REGIMENT INFANTRY.—Org. March 11, 1864, from 1st Alabama Colored Infantry. March, 1864, 1st Colored Brig., Dist. Memphis, Tenn., 16 Corps, Dept. Tenn. April, 1864, Fort Pickering, Post and Defenses, Memphis Dist., West Tenn. June, 1864, 3 Brig., Infantry Div., Sturgis' Expedition. June, 1864, 1st Colored Brig., Dist. Memphis, West Tenn. Jany., 1865, 2 Brig., Post and Defenses of Memphis, Tenn. Feby., 1865, 2 Brig., U. S. C. T., Morganza, La., Dept. Gulf. April, 1865, Dist. Port Hudson, La., Dept. Gulf. Mustered out December 31, 1865.

56th REGIMENT INFANTRY.—Org. March 11, 1864, from 3rd Ala. Colored Infy. March, 1864, Dist. Eastern Arkansas, 7 Corps, Dept. Ark. Aug., 1865, Dept. Ark. Mustered out Sept. 15, 1866.

57th REGIMENT INFANTRY.—Org. March 11, 1864, from 4th Ark. Colored Infy. March, 1864, Dist. Eastern Arkansas, 7 Corps, Dept. Ark. May, 1864, 1 Brig., 2 Div., 7 Corps, Dept. Ark. Jany., 1865, Colored Brig., 7 Corps, Ark. Feby., 1865, 2 Brig., 1 Div., 7 Corps. Aug., 1865, Dept. Arkansas. Mustered out December 13, 1866.

58th REGIMENT INFANTRY.—Org. March 11, 1864, from 6th Miss. Colored Infantry. March, 1864, Post Natchez, Miss., Dist. Vicksburg, Miss., Dept. Tenn. Feby., 1865, Post Natchez Dist., Vicksburg, Miss., Dept. Miss. April, 1865, Post Natchez, Dept. Gulf. Mustered out April 30, 1866.

59th REGIMENT INFANTRY.—Org. March 11, 1864, from 1st Tenn. Colored Infy. March, 1864, 1st Colored Brig., Dist. Memphis, Tenn., Dept. Tenn. June, 1864, 3 Brig., Infy. Div., Sturgis' Exp. June, 1864, 1st Colored Brigade, Dist. Memphis, Tenn., Dist. West Tenn. Feby., 1865, Fort Pickering, Defenses Memphis, Tenn., Dist. West Tenn. July, 1865, 2 Brig., Dist. West Tenn. Sept., 1865, Dept. Tennessee. Mustered out Jany. 31, 1866.

60th REGIMENT INFANTRY.—Org. March 11, 1864, from 1st Iowa Colored Infy. March, 1864, Dist. Eastern Arkansas, 7 Corps, Dept. Ark. April, 1865, 2 Brig., 1 Div., 7 Corps, Ark. Aug., 1865, Dept. Arkansas. Mustered out October 15, 1865.

61st REGIMENT INFANTRY.—Org. March 11, 1864, from 2nd Tenn. Colored Infy. March, 1864, Dist. Memphis, Tenn., 16 Corps, Dept. Tenn. June, 1864, 1 Colored Brig., Memphis, Tenn., Dist. West Tenn. Feby., 1865, 1 Brig., U. S. C. T., Morganza, La., Dept. Gulf. April, 1865, 1 Brig., 1 Div., U. S. C. T., Dist. West Fla. June, 1865, Dist. Alabama. Mustered out Dec. 30, 1865.

62nd REGIMENT INFANTRY.—Org. March 11, 1864, from 1st Mo. Colored Infy. March, 1864, Dept. Missouri. March, 1864, Dist. Baton Rouge, La., Dept. Gulf. June, 1864, Prov'l Brig., Dist. Morganza, La., Dept. Gulf. Sept., 1864, 2 Brig., 1 Div., U. S. C. T., Dist., Morganza, La., Dept. Gulf. Sept., 1864, Port Hudson, La., Dept. Gulf. Sept., 1864, Brazos, Santiago, Texas. Oct., 1864, 1 Brig., 2 Div., U. S. C. T., Gulf. Dec., 1864, Brazos, Santiago, Texas. June, 1865, Dept. Texas. Mustered out March 31, 1866.

63rd REGIMENT INFANTRY.—Org. March 11, 1864, from 9th La. Colored Infy. March, 1864, Post Natchez, Miss., Dist. Vicksburg, Miss. Feby., 1865, Sub Dist.

Vidalia, Dist. Natchez, Dept. Miss. Mustered out January 9, 1866.

64th REGIMENT INFANTRY.—Org. March 11, 1864, from 7th La. Colored Infy. March, 1864, Unatt., 1 Div., U. S. C. T., Dist. Vicksburg, Miss. May, 1864, Dist. Natchez, Miss., Dist. of Vicksburg, Miss. Sept., 1864, Davis Bend, Miss., Dist. Vicksburg, Miss. Dec., 1864, Unatt., 1 Div., U. S. C. T., Dist. Vicksburg, Miss. Feby., 1865, Post of Vicksburg, Miss. and Dept. of Miss. Mustered out March 13, 1866.

65th REGIMENT INFANTRY.—Org. March 11, 1864, from 2nd Mo. Colored Infy. March, 1864, Dept. Missouri. June, 1864, Prov'l Brig., Dist. Morganza, Dept. Gulf. Sept., 1864, 2 Brig., 1 Div., U. S. C. T., Morganza, La. Feby., 1865, 1 Brig., 1 Div., U. S. C. T., Morganza, La. May, 1865, Northern Dist. Louisiana, Dept. Gulf. Mustered out Jany. 8, 1867.

66th REGIMENT INFANTRY.—Org. March 11, 1864, from 4th Miss. Colored Infy. March, 1864, Post Goodrich Landing, Dist. Vicksburg, Miss. Feby., 1865, Little Rock, Ark., Unatt., 2 Div., 7 Corps, Dept. Ark. Feby., 1865, Unatt., Dist., Vicksburg, Miss. and Dept of Miss. Mustered out March 20, 1866.

67th REGIMENT INFANTRY.—Org. March 11, 1864, from 3rd Mo. Colored Infy. March, 1864, Dist. Port Hudson, La., Dept. Gulf. June, 1864, Prov'l Brig., Dist. Morganza, Dept. Gulf. Sept., 1864, 2 Brig., 1 Div., U. S. C. T., Dist. Morganza, La. Feby., 1865, 1 Brig., 1 Div., U. S. C. T., Dist. Morganza, Dept. Gulf. May, 1865, Northern Dist., Louisiana, Dept. Gulf. Mustered out by consolidation with 65th U. S. C. T., July 12, 1865.

68th REGIMENT INFANTRY.—Org. March 11, 1864, from 4th Mo. Colored Infy. March, 1864, Dist. Memphis, Tenn., 16 Corps, Dept. Tenn. June, 1864, 1 Colored Brig., Memphis, Tenn., Dist. West Tenn. Dec., 1864, Fort Pickering, Defenses Memphis, Tenn. Feby., 1865, 3 Brig., 1 Div., U. S. C. T., Mil. Div. West Miss. May, 1865, 1 Brig., 1 Div., U. S. C. T., Dist. West Fla. June, 1865, Dept Miss. Mustered out February 5, 1866.

69th REGIMENT INFANTRY.—Org. at Pine Bluff, Devall's Bluff and Helena, Ark and Memphis, Tenn., December 14, 1864 to March 17, 1865. Attached to these points Dept. Ark. and Dist. West Tenn. Discontinued September 20, 1865.

70th REGIMENT INFANTRY.—Org. at Natchez, Miss., April 23 to Oct. 1, 1864. April, 1864, Post Natchez, Miss., Dist. Vicksburg, Miss. June, 1865, Dept. Miss. Mustered out March 7, 1866.

71st REGIMENT INFANTRY.—Org. at Black River Bridge and Natchez, Miss. and Alexandria, La. March 3 to August 13, 1864. Attached to Dist. Natchez, Miss., Dist. Vicksburg, Miss. Consolidated with 70th Regiment Infy. Nov. 8, 1864.

72nd REGIMENT INFANTRY.—Org. at Covington, Ky. April, 18, 1865. Discontinued May 3, 1865.

73rd REGIMENT INFANTRY.—Org. April 4, 1864, from 1st Corps de Afrique Infantry. April, 1864, 1 Brig., 1 Div., Corps de Afrique, Dept. Gulf. March, 1865, 1 Brig., 1 Div., U. S. C. T., Dist. West Fla. May, 1865, 3 Brig., 1 Div., U. S. C. T., Dist. West Fla. July, 1865, Dept. Texas. Consolidated with 96th U. S. C. T., September 27, 1865.

74th REGIMENT INFANTRY.—Org. April 4, 1864, from 2nd Regt., Corps de Afrique Infy. April, 1864, Def. New Orleans, La., Dept. Gulf. Oct., 1864, 3 Brig., 3 Div., U. S. C. T., Gulf. Oct., 1864, Def. New Orleans, Gulf. Mustered out Oct. 11, 1865.

75th REGIMENT INFANTRY.—Org. April 4, 1864, from 3rd Corps de Afrique Infy. April, 1864, 1 Brig., 1 Div., U. S. C. T., Gulf. Feby., 1865, Dist. LaFourche, Gulf. July, 1865, Dept. Gulf. Mustered out Nov. 25, 1865.

76th REGIMENT INFANTRY.—Org. April 4, 1864, from 4th Corps de Afrique Infy. April, 1864, 2 Brig., 1 Div., U. S. C. T., Gulf. April, 1864, Post Port Hudson, La., Gulf. Oct., 1864, 1 Brig., 2 Div., U. S. C. T., Gulf. Feby., 1865, 3 Brig., 1 Div., U. S. C. T., Dist. West Fla. May, 1865, 1 Brig., Div., U. S. C. T., Dist. West Fla. June, 1865, Dept. Gulf. Mustered out Dec. 31, 1865.

77th REGIMENT INFANTRY.—Org. April 4, 1864, from 5th Corps de Afrique Infy. April, 1864, Def. New Orleans, La., Dept. Gulf. Oct., 1864, 3 Brig., 3 Div., U. S. C. T., Gulf. Oct., 1864, Def. New Orleans, La., Gulf. Consolidated with 10th U. S. C. Heavy Arty., Oct. 1, 1865.

78th REGIMENT INFANTRY.—Org. April 4, 1864, from 6th Corps de Afrique Infy. April, 1864, 2 Brig., 2 Div., Corps de Afrique, Gulf. July, 1864, 2 Brig., 1 Div., Corps de Afrique, Gulf. July, 1864, Garrison Port Hudson, La. Oct., 1864, 2 Brig., 2 Div., U. S. C. T., Gulf. Oct., 1864, Post Port Hudson, La., Gulf. April, 1865, Dist. LaFourche, La., Dept. Gulf. Mustered out Jany. 6, 1866.

79th REGIMENT INFANTRY (OLD).—Org. April 4, 1864, from 7th Corps de Afrique Infy. April, 1864, 2 Brig., 1 Div., Corps de Afrique, Gulf. June, 1864, 2 Brig., 2 Div., Corps de Afrique. Broken up July 28, 1864.

79th REGIMENT INFANTRY (NEW).—Org. Dec. 3, 1864, from 1st Kans. Colored Infy. Dec., 1864, 2 Brig., Dist. Frontier, 7 Corps, Dept. Ark. Jany., 1865, Colored Brig., 7 Corps, Ark. Feby., 1865, 2 Brig., 1 Div., 7 Corps, Ark. Aug., 1865, Dept. Ark. Mustered out Oct. 1, 1865.

80th REGIMENT INFANTRY.—Org. April 4, 1864, from 8th Corps de Afrique Infy. April, 1864, Garrison Port Hudson, La., Dept. Gulf. June, 1864, 2 Brig., 1 Div., Corps de Afrique, Gulf. July, 1864, Def. New Orleans, La., Gulf. Oct., 1864, 3 Brig., 3 Div., U. S. C. T., Gulf. Oct., 1864, Def. New Orleans, La., Dept. Gulf. Mustered out March 1, 1867.

81st REGIMENT INFANTRY.—Org. April 4, 1864, from 9th Corps de Afrique Infy. April, 1864, 2 Brig., 1 Div., Corps de Afrique, Gulf. July, 1864, Garrison Port Hudson, La. July, 1864, Engr. Brig., Dept. Gulf. Sept., 1864, 2 Brig., 2 Div., U. S. C. T., Gulf. Feby., 1865, Garrison Port Hudson, La. July, 1865, Dept. Gulf. Mustered out Nov. 30, 1866.

82nd REGIMENT INFANTRY.—Org. April 4, 1864, from 10th Regt., Corps de Afrique Infy. April, 1864, 2 Brig., 1 Div., Corps de Afrique, Gulf. July, 1864, Def. New Orleans, La. Aug., 1864, Pensacola, Fla., Dist. West Fla., Gulf. Oct., 1864, 1 Brig., 3 Div., U. S. C. T., Gulf. Oct., 1864, 1 Brig., Dist. West Fla., Gulf. Jany., 1865, 3 Brig., Dist. West Fla., Gulf. March, 1865, 1 Brig., 1 Div., U. S. C. T., Dist. West. Fla. May, 1865, Pensacola, Fla., Dist. West Fla. and Dept. Fla. Mustered out Sept. 10, 1866.

83rd REGIMENT INFANTRY. (OLD.)—Org. April 4, 1864, from 11th Corps de Afrique Infy. April, 1864, 1 Brig., 1 Div., Corps de Afrique, Gulf. June, 1864, Prov'l Brig., Morganza, La. Broken up July 28, 1864.

83rd REGIMENT INFANTRY. (NEW.)—Org. Dec. 13, 1864, from 2nd Kan. Colored Infy. Dec., 1864, 2 Brig., Dist. Frontier, 7 Corps, Ark. Jany., 1865, Colored Brig., 7 Corps, Ark. Feby., 1865, 2 Brig., 1 Div., 7 Corps, Ark. Aug., 1865, Dept. Ark. Mustered out Oct. 9, 1865.

84th REGIMENT INFANTRY.—Org. April 4, 1864, from 12th Corps de Afrique Infy. April, 1864, 1 Brig., 1 Div., Corps de Afrique, Gulf. Feby., 1865, 1 Brig., 1 Div., U. S. C. T., Dist. Morganza, Gulf. Feby., 1865, 2 Brig., 1 Div., U. S. C. T., Morganza, La. May, 1865, Northern Dist., Louisiana, Dept. Gulf. Mustered out March 14, 1866.

85th REGIMENT INFANTRY.—Org. April 4, 1864, from 13th Corps de Afrique Infy. April, 1864, Prov'l Brig., 13. Corps, Texas. Consolidated with 77th U. S. C. T., May 24, 1864.

86th REGIMENT INFANTRY.—Org. April 4, 1864, from 14th Corps de Afrique Infy. April, 1864, Dist. West Fla., Dept. Gulf. Oct., 1864, 1 Brig., 3 Div., U. S. C. T., Gulf. Nov., 1864, 1 Brig., Dist. West Fla., Gulf. Jany., 1865, 3 Brig., Dist. West Fla., Gulf. March, 1865, 1 Brig., 1 Div., U. S. C. T., Dist. West Fla. May, 1865, Pensacola, Fla., Dist. West Fla. July, 1865, Dept. Fla. Mustered out April 10, 1866.

87th REGIMENT INFANTRY. (OLD.)—Org. April 4, 1864, from 16th Corps de Afrique Infy. April, 1864, Unatt., 2 Div., 13 Corps, Texas, Dept. Gulf. June, 1864, Colored Brig., U. S. Forces, Texas. Aug., 1864, U. S. Forces, Texas. Consolidated with 95th U. S. C. T., Nov. 26, 1864, to form 87th U. S. C. T. (New).

87th REGIMENT INFANTRY. (NEW.)—Org. by consolidation of 87th Regt. (Old), and 95th U. S. C. T., Nov. 26, 1864. Attached to Dept. Texas. Consolidated with 34th U. S. C. T., Aug. 14, 1865.

88th REGIMENT INFANTRY. (OLD.)—Org. April 4, 1864, from 17th Corps de Afrique Infy. April, 1864, 2 Brig., 2 Div., Corps de Afrique, Gulf. Broken up July 28, 1864.

88th REGIMENT INFANTRY. (NEW.)—Org. at Memphis, Tenn., Feby. 20, 1865. Feby., 1865, Post and Def. Memphis, Tenn., Dist. West Tenn. July, 1865, 2nd Infy. Brig., Dist. West Tenn. Sept., 1865, Dept. Tenn. Consolidated with 3rd U. S. C. Heavy Arty., Dec. 16, 1865.

89th REGIMENT INFANTRY.—Org. April 4, 1864, from 18th Corps de Afrique Infy. April, 1864, 2 Brig., 2 Div., Corps de Afrique, Gulf. Broken up July 28, 1864.

90th REGIMENT INFANTRY.—Org. April 4, 1864, from 19th Corps de Afrique Infy. April, 1864, 2 Brig., 2 Div., Corps de Afrique, Gulf. Broken up July 28, 1864.

91st REGIMENT INFANTRY.—Org. April 4, 1864, from 20th Corps de Afrique Infy. April, 1864, 2 Brig., 2 Div., Corps de Afrique, Gulf. Broken up July 7, 1864.

92nd REGIMENT INFANTRY.—Org. April 4, 1864, from 22nd Corps de Afrique Infy. April, 1864, 1 Brig., 1 Div., Corps de Afrique, Gulf. Aug., 1864, 1 Brig., 1 Div., Corps de Afrique, Dist. Morganza, Gulf. Oct., 1864, 1 Brig., 1 Div., U. S. C. T., Gulf. Feby., 1865, 2 Brig., 2 Div., U. S. C. T., Morganza, Gulf. June, 1865, Northern Dist. Louisiana, Gulf. Mustered out Dec. 31, 1865.

93rd REGIMENT INFANTRY.—Org. April 4, 1864, from 26th Corps de Afrique Infy. April, 1864, Dist. LaFourche, Gulf. Oct., 1864, 2 Brig., 3 Div., U. S. C. T., Gulf. Oct., 1864, Dist. LaFourche, Gulf. Broken up June 23, 1865.

94th REGIMENT INFANTRY.—Failed to complete organization.

95th REGIMENT INFANTRY.—Org. April 4, 1864, from 1st Corps de Afrique Engrs. April, 1864, Engr. Brig., 13 Corps, Gulf. June, 1864, Colored Brig., U. S. Forces, Texas. Consolidated with 87th U. S. C. T. (Old), to form 87th U. S. C. T. (New), Nov. 26, 1864.

96th REGIMENT INFANTRY.—Org. from 2nd Corps de Afrique Engrs., April 4, 1864. April, 1864, Prov'l Brig., 13 Corps, Gulf. June, 1864, Engr. Brig., Gulf. Oct., 1864, U. S. Forces, Mobile Bay. Oct., 1864, 1 Brig., 3 Div., U. S. C. T., Gulf. Oct., 1864, U. S. Forces, Mobile Bay. Dec., 1864, Dist. Southern Ala., Gulf. March, 1865, Engr. Brig., 13 Corps, Mil. Div. West Miss. June, 1865, Unass'd, Dept. Gulf. Mustered out Jany. 29, 1866.

97th REGIMENT INFANTRY.—Org. April 4, 1864, from 3rd Corps de Afrique Engrs. April, 1864, Prov'l Brig., 13 Corps, Texas, Dept. Gulf. June, 1864, Engr. Brig., Gulf. Oct., 1864, U. S. Forces, Mobile Bay. Oct., 1864, 1 Brig., 3 Div., U. S. C. T., Gulf. Nov., 1864, 1 Brig., Dist. West Fla., Gulf. Jany., 1865, 3 Brig., Dist. West Fla. March, 1865, Engr. Brig., Mil. Div. West Miss. June, 1865, Unass'd, Dept. Gulf. Mustered out April 6, 1866.

98th REGIMENT INFANTRY.—Org. April 4, 1864, from 4th Corps de Afrique Engrs. April, 1864, Engr. Brig., Dept. Gulf. July, 1864, Def. New Orleans, La., Gulf. Oct., 1864, 2 Brig., 3 Div., U. S. C. T., Gulf. Oct., 1864, Dist. LaFourche, Dept. Gulf. Consolidated with 78th U. S. C. T., Aug. 26, 1865.

99th REGIMENT INFANTRY.—Org. April 4, 1864, from 5th Corps de Afrique Engrs. April, 1864, Engr. Brig., Dept. Gulf. Oct., 1864, 2 Brig., 1 Div., U. S. C. T., Gulf. Feby., 1865, Dist. Key West, Fla., Gulf. July, 1865, Dept. Fla. Mustered out April 23, 1866.

100th REGIMENT INFANTRY.—Org. in Kentucky at large, May 3 to June 1, 1864. June, 1864, Def. Nash. & Northwestern R. R., Dept. Cumb'd. Dec., 1864, 2nd Colored Brig., Dist. Etowah, Dept. Cumb'd. Jany., 1865, Def. Nash. & Northwestern R. R., Dept. Cumb'd. Mustered out Dec. 26, 1865.

101st REGIMENT INFANTRY.—Org. in Tennessee at large, Sept. 16, 1864. Oct., 1864, Def. Louisville & Nashville R. R., Dept. Cumb'd. March, 1865, Dept. Tenn. Mustered out Jany. 21, 1866.

102nd REGIMENT INFANTRY.—Org. May 23, 1864, from 1st Michigan Colored Infy. May, 1864, Dist. Beaufort, S. C., Dept. South. Aug., 1864, Dist. Fla., Dept. South. Oct., 1864, 2 Separate Brig., Dept. South. Nov., 1864, 2 Brig., Coast Div., Dept. South. Feby., 1865, 2 Separate Brig., Dept. South. March, 1865, 1 Separate Brig., Dept. South. June, 1865, Dept. South. Mustered out Sept. 30, 1865.

103rd REGIMENT INFANTRY.—Org. at Hilton Head, S. C., March 10, 1865. March, 1865, Dist. Savannah, Ga., Dept. South. June, 1865, Dept. South. Mustered out April 15-20, 1866.

104th REGIMENT INFANTRY.—Org. at Beaufort, S. C., April 28 to June 25, 1865., Dept. South. Mustered out Feby. 5, 1866.

105th REGIMENT INFANTRY.—Failed to complete organization.

106th REGIMENT INFANTRY.—Org. May 16, 1864, from 4th Ala. Colored Infy. May, 1864, Garrison Pulaski, Dist. North Ala., Dept. Cumb'd. Consolidated with 40th U. S. C. T., Nov. 7, 1865.

107th REGIMENT INFANTRY.—Org. at Louisville, Ky., May 3, 1864. May, 1864, Mil., Dist. Ky., Dept. Ohio. Oct., 1864, Prov'l Brig., 3 Div., 18 Corps, Army James. Dec., 1864, 3 Brig., 1 Div., 25 Corps. Dec., 1864, 3 Brig., 3 Div., 25 Corps. Jany., 1865, 1 Brig., 3 Div., 25 Corps. Jany., 1865, 1 Brig., 3 Div., Terry's Prov'l Corps, Dept. N. C. March, 1865, 1 Brig., 3 Div., 10 Corps, Dept. N. C. Aug., 1865, Dept. North Carolina. Mustered out Nov. 22, 1866.

108th REGIMENT INFANTRY.—Org. at Louisville, Ky., June 20, 1864. June, 1864, 1 Brig., 2 Div., Dist. Ky., 5 Div., 23 Corps, Dept. Ohio. Jany., 1865, Mil. Dist. Ky. and Dept. Ky. Mustered out March 21, 1866.

109th REGIMENT INFANTRY.—Org. at Louisville, Ky. June, 1864, 3 Brig., 1 Div., Dist. Ky., 5 Div., 23 Corps, Dept. Ohio. Oct., 1864, Martindale's Prov'l Brig., 18 Corps, Army James. Dec., 1864, 1 Brig., 2 Div., 25 Corps, and Dept. Texas. Mustered out Feby. 6, 1866.

110th REGIMENT INFANTRY.—Org. June 25, 1864, from 2nd Ala. Colored Infy. June, 1864, Garrison Pulaski, Tenn., Dist. North Ala., Dept. Cumb'd. Feby., 1865. Def. Nashville and Northwestern R. R., Dept. Cumb'd. March, 1865, 3rd Sub Dist., Middle Tenn., Dept. Cumb'd. July, 1865, Dept. Tenn. Mustered out Feby. 6, 1866.

111th REGIMENT INFANTRY.—Org. June 25, 1864, from 3rd Ala. Colored Infy. June, 1864, Garrison Pulaski, Tenn., Dist. North Ala., Dept. Cumb'd. Feby., 1865, Def. Nashville & Northwestern R. R., Dept. Cumb'd. March, 1865, 3rd Sub Dist., Middle Tenn. July, 1865, Dept. Tenn. Mustered out April 30, 1866.

112th REGIMENT INFANTRY.—Org. at Little Rock, Ark., April 23 to November 8, 1864. June, 1864, Unatt., 1 Div., 7 Corps, Dept. Ark. Jany., 1865, Colored Brig., 7 Corps, Ark. Feby., 1865, 2 Brig., 1 Div., 7 Corps. Transferred to 113th U. S. C. T. (New), April 1, 1865.

113th REGIMENT INFANTRY. (OLD.)—Org. June 25, 1864, from 6th Ark. Colored Infy. June, 1864, Unatt., 1 Div., 7 Corps, Dept. Ark. Jany., 1865, Colored Brig., 7 Corps, Ark. Feby., 1865, 2 Brig., 1 Div., 7 Corps, Ark. Consolidated with 11th (Old) and 112th U. S. C. T. to form New 113th U. S. C. T., April 1, 1865.

113th REGIMENT INFANTRY. (NEW.)—Org. April 1, 1865, by consolidation of 11th (Old), 112th and 113th (Old), U. S. C. T. April, 1865, 2 Brig., 1 Div., 7 Corps, Dept. Ark. Aug., 1865, Dept. Ark. Mustered out April 9, 1866.

114th REGIMENT INFANTRY.—Org. at Camp Nelson, Ky., July 4, 1864. Aug., 1864, Mil. Dist. Ky. Jany., 1865, 3 Brig., 1 Div., 25 Corps, Army James. April, 1865, 2 Brig., 1 Div., 25 Corps and Dept. Texas. Mustered out April 2, 1867.

115th REGIMENT INFANTRY.—Org. at Bowling Creek, Ky., July 15 to Oct. 21, 1864. Oct., 1864, 2 Brig., 2 Div., Dist. Ky., 5 Div., 23 Corps, Dept. Ohio. Jany., 1865, 1 Brig., 2 Div., 25 Corps, Army James. March, 1865, 2 Brig., 1 Div., 25 Corps, Dept. Texas. Mustered out Feby. 10, 1866.

116th REGIMENT INFANTRY.—Org. at Camp Nelson, Ky., June 6 to July 12, 1864. July, 1864, Mil. Dist. Ky., Dept. Ohio. Oct., 1864, Unatt., 10 Corps, Army James. Nov., 1864, 1 Brig., 3 Div., 10 Corps. Dec., 1864, 1 Brig., 2 Div., 25 Corps. April, 1865, 3 Brig., 2 Div., 25 Corps. Jany., 1866, Dept. Texas. Sept., 1866, Dept. Gulf. Mustered out Jany. 17, 1867.

117th REGIMENT INFANTRY.—Org. at Covington, Ky., July 18 to Sept. 27, 1864. Oct., 1864, Prov'l Brig., 3 Div., 18 Corps, Army James. Dec., 1864, 1 Brig., 2 Div., 25 Corps, Dept. Texas. Mustered out Aug. 10, 1867.

118th REGIMENT INFANTRY.—Org. at Balto., Md., Oct. 19, 1864. Oct., 1864, Prov'l Brig., 18 Corps, Army James. Dec., 1864, 1 Brig., 3 Div., 25 Corps. Dec., 1864, 1 Brig., 1 Div., 25 Corps, Dept. Texas. Mustered out Feby. 6, 1866.

119th REGIMENT INFANTRY.—Org. at Camp Nelson, Ky., Jany. 18 to May 16, 1865, Dept. Ky. Mustered out April 27, 1866.

120th REGIMENT INFANTRY.—Org. at Henderson, Ky., Nov., 1864. Attached to Dept. Ky. Mustered out by discontinuance June 21, 1865.

121st RERGIMENT INFANTRY.—Org. at Maysville, Ky., Oct. 8, 1864. Attached to Dept. Ky. Discontinued June 30, 1865.

122nd REGIMENT INFANTRY.—Org. at Louisville, Ky., Dec. 31, 1864. Jany., 1865, Unatt., 25 Corps, Army James. Dept. Texas. Mustered out Feby. 8, 1866.

123rd REGIMENT INFANTRY.—Org. at Louisville, Ky., Dec. 2, 1864. Attached to Dept. Ky. Mustered out Oct. 16, 1865.

124th REGIMENT INFANTRY.—Org. at Camp Nelson, Ky., Jany. 1 to April 27, 1865. Attached to Dept. Ky. Mustered out Oct. 24, 1865.

125th REGIMENT INFANTRY.—Org. at Louisville, Ky., Feby. 13 to June 2, 1865. Attached to Dept. Ky. Mustered out Dec. 20, 1867.

127th REGIMENT INFANTRY.—Org. at Phila., Pa., Aug. 23 to Sept. 10, 1864. Oct., 1864, 1 Brig., 3 Div., 10 Corps, Army James. Nov., 1864, 2 Brig., 3 Div., 10 Corps. Dec., 1864, 2 Brig., 2 Div., 25 Corps, Dept. Texas. Mustered out Oct. 20, 1865.

128th REGIMENT INFANTRY.—Org. at Hilton Head, S. C., April, 1865. Attached to Dept. South. Mustered out Oct. 10, 1866.

135th REGIMENT INFANTRY.—Org. at Goldsboro, N. C., March 28, 1865. Attached to Dept. North Carolina. Mustered out Oct. 23, 1865.

136th REGIMENT INFANTRY.—Org. at Atlanta, Ga., July 15, 1865. Attached to Dept. Georgia. Mustered out Jany. 4, 1866.

137th REGIMENT INFANTRY.—Org. at Selma, Ala., April 8, 1865. Mustered in at Macon, Ga., June 1, 1865. Attached to Dept. Georgia. Mustered out Jany. 15, 1866.

138th REGIMENT INFANTRY.—Org. at Atlanta, Ga., July 15, 1865. Attached to Dept. Georgia. Mustered out Jany. 6, 1866.

UNITED STATES VOLUNTEERS—INDIAN TROOPS

1st REGIMENT INDIAN HOME GUARD.—Org. at Leroy, Kan., May 22, 1862. May, 1862, Dept. Kan. Aug., 1862, 3 Brig., Dept. Kan. Oct., 1862, 3 Brig., 1 Div., Army Frontier. Feby., 1863, Dist. Northwest Ark., Dept. Mo. June, 1863, Dist. Frontier, Dept. Mo. Dec., 1863, 1 Brig., Dist. Frontier, Dept. Mo. Jany., 1864, 1 Brig., Dist. Frontier, 7 Corps, Dept. Ark. Feby., 1864, Indian Brig., Dist. Frontier, 7 Corps, Ark. Feby., 1865, 3 Brig., 3 Div., 7 Corps. Mustered out May 31, 1865.

2nd REGIMENT INDIAN HOME GUARD.—Org. at Big Creek and 5-Mile Creek, Kan., June 22 to July 18, 1862. June, 1862, Dept. Kan. Aug., 1862, 1 Brig., Dept. Kan. Oct., 1862, 3 Brig., 1 Div., Army Frontier. Feby., 1863, Dist. Northwest Ark., Dept. Mo. June, 1863, Dist. Frontier, Dept. Mo. Dec., 1863, 1 Brig., Dist. Frontier, Dept. Mo. Jany., 1864, 1 Brig., Dist. Frontier, 7 Corps, Ark. Feby., 1864, Indian Brig., Dist. Frontier, 7 Corps, Ark. Feby., 1865, 3 Brig., 3 Div., 7 Corps. Mustered out May 31, 1865.

3rd REGIMENT INDIAN HOME GUARD.—Org. at Big Creek and 5-Mile Creek, Kan., June 22 to July 18, 1862. June, 1862, Dept. Kan. Aug., 1862, 1 Brig., Dept. Kan. Oct., 1862, 3 Brig., 1 Div., Army Frontier. Feby., 1863, Dist. Northwest Ark., Dept. Mo. June, 1863, Dist. Frontier, Dept. Mo. Dec., 1863, 1 Brig., Dist. Frontier, Dept. Mo. Jany., 1864, 1 Brig., Dist. Frontier, 7 Corps, Ark. Feby., 1864, Indian Brig., Dist. Frontier, 7 Corps, Ark. Feby., 1865, 3 Brig., 3 Div., 7 Corps. Mustered out May 31, 1865.

4th REGIMENT INDIAN HOME GUARD.—Org. commenced but not completed. Men transferred to other organizations.

Military Divisions and Departments as Constituted During the War of the Rebellion, Their Boundaries and Commanderies

Commanding Armies of the United States

The President of the United States, Commander in Chief

Winfield Scott, Brevet Lieutenant General.	To November 6, 1861.
Geo. B. McClellan, Major General.	November 5, 1861, to March 11, 1862.
No General Commander from March 11 to July 11, 1862.	
H. W. Halleck, Major General.	July 11, 1862, to March 12, 1864.
Ulysses S. Grant, Lieutenant General.	March 12, 1864, to March 4, 1869.

DEPARTMENT OF THE WEST (in existence). Merged into Western Department July 3, 1861.

W. S. Harney, Brigadier General.	November 17, 1860, to May 31, 1861.
Nath'l Lyon, Brigadier General.	May 31, 1861, to July 3, 1861.

DEPARTMENT OF THE EAST (in existence). Abolished Aug. 17, 1861. Recreated Jany. 3, 1863.

John E. Wool, Major General.	To Aug. 17, 1861.
John E. Wool, Major General.	Jany. 12, 1863, to July 18, 1863.
John A. Dix, Major General.	July 18, 1863, to June 27, 1865.

DEPARTMENT OF FLORIDA (in existence). Merged into Department of the South, March 15, 1861.

Harvey Brown, Brevet Colonel U. S. A.	Apr. 13, 1861, to Feby. 22, 1862.
L. G. Arnold, Brigadier General.	Feby. 22, 1862, to Mch. 15, 1862.

DEPARTMENT OF THE PACIFIC (in existence).

E. V. Sumner, Brigadier General.	Apr. 25, 1861, to Oct. 20, 1861.
Geo. Wright, Colonel U. S. A.	Oct. 20, 1861, to July 1, 1864.
Irvin McDowell, Major General.	July 1, 1864, to June 27, 1865.

DEPARTMENT OF WASHINGTON.—Constituted April 9, 1861, to consist of District of Columbia to its original boundaries, and the State of Maryland as far as Bladensburg. Merged into Military Division of the Potomac July 25, 1861. Recreated Feby. 2, 1863.

C. F. Smith, Lieut. Colonel U. S. A.	Apr. 10, 1861, to Apr. 28, 1861.
J. K. F. Mansfield, Colonel U. S. A.	Apr. 28, 1861, to Mch. 15, 1862.
S. P. Heintzelman, Major General.	Feby. 7, 1863, to Oct. 14, 1863.
C. C. Augur, Major General.	Oct. 14, 1863, to June 27, 1865.

DEPARTMENT OF ANNAPOLIS.—Constituted April 27, 1861, to include the Counties for 20 miles each side of the Railroad from Annapolis to the City of Washington, as far as Bladensburg. Changed to Dept. of Maryland, July 19, 1861, and merged into Dept. of Pennsylvania, July 25, 1861.

B. F. Butler, Brigadier General.	Apr. 27, 1861, to May 15, 1861.
Geo. Cadwallader, Major General.	May 15, 1861, to June 11, 1861.
N. P. Banks, Major General.	June 11, 1861, to July 19, 1861.
John A. Dix, Major General.	July 19, 1861, to July 25, 1861.

DEPARTMENT OF PENNSYLVANIA.—Constituted April 27, 1861, to consist of Pennsylvania, Delaware, and all of Maryland not embraced in Departments of Annapolis and Washington. Merged into Department of the Potomac, Aug. 24, 1861. Recreated Dec. 1, 1864.

Robert Patterson, Major General.	Apr. 29, 1861, to July 25, 1861.
John A. Dix, Major General.	July 25, 1861, to Aug. 24, 1861.
Geo. Cadwallader, Major General.	Dec. 1, 1864, to June 27, 1865.

DEPARTMENT OF THE OHIO.—Constituted May 3, 1861, to consist of Ohio, Indiana, Illinois. Dept. extended to embrace West Virginia and Pennsylvania lying North of the Great Kanawha, North and West of the Greenbrier, etc. State of Missouri added to Department June 6, 1861. Illinois transferred to Western Dept. July 3, 1861. Boundaries changed Sept. 19, 1861, to consist of Ohio, Indiana, and so much of Kentucky as lies within 15 miles of Cincinnati, Ohio. State of Michigan added Nov. 9, 1861. Also Kentucky, East of Cumberland River. Merged into Mountain Department and Dept. of Mississippi March 11, 1862. Recreated Aug. 19, 1862, to consist of the States of Ohio, Michigan, Indiana, Illinois, Wisconsin, and Kentucky East of Tennessee River and including Cumberland Gap. Annexed to Department of the Cumberland Jany. 17, 1865.

Geo. B. McClellan, Major General.	May 13, 1861, to July 23, 1861.
W. S. Rosecrans, Brigadier General.	July 23, 1861, to Sept. 21, 1881.
O. M. Mitchell, Brigadier General.	Sept. 21, 1861, to Nov. 15, 1861.
D. C. Buell, Brigadier General.	Nov. 15, 1861, to Mch. 11, 1862.
H. G. Wright, Major General.	Aug. 25, 1862, to Mch. 25, 1863.
A. E. Burnside, Major General.	Mch. 25, 1863, to Dec. 11, 1863.
J. G. Foster, Major General.	Dec. 11, 1863, to Feby. 9, 1864.
J. M. Schofield, Major General.	Feby. 9, 1864, to Nov. 17, 1864.
Geo. Stoneman, Major General.	Nov. 17, 1864, to Jany. 17, 1865.

DEPARTMENT OF VIRGINIA.—Created May, 1861. Merged into Dept. of Virginia and North Carolina July 15, 1863. Recreated Jany. 31, 1865. (Also known as Army of the James from Jany. 31, 1865.)

B. F. Butler, Major General.	May 22, 1861, to Aug. 17, 1861.
John E. Wool, Major General.	Aug. 17, 1861, to June 17, 1862.
John A. Dix, Major General.	June 17, 1862, to July 15, 1863.
E. O. C. Ord, Major General.	Jany. 31, 1865, to May .., 1865.
A. H. Terry, Major General.	May .., 1865, to June 27, 1865.

DEPARTMENT OF NORTHEAST VIRGINIA.—Constituted May 27, 1861, to consist of that part of Virginia East of the Allegheny Mountains and North of James River, except Fort Monroe and 60 miles around the same. Merged into Department of the Potomac July 25, 1861.

Irvin McDowell, Major General.   May 27, 1861, to July 25, 1861.

DEPARTMENT OF KENTUCKY.—Created May 28, 1861, to consist of the State of Kentucky lying within 100 miles of the Ohio River. Merged into the Dept. of the Cumberland Aug. 15, 1861. Recreated Feby. 10, 1865.

Robert Anderson, Colonel U. S. A.   May 28, 1861, to Aug. 15, 1861.
J. M. Palmer, Major General.   Feby. 18, 1865, to June 27, 1865.

WESTERN DEPARTMENT.—Constituted July 3, 1861, to consist of the States of Illinois, and States and Territories West of the Mississippi River and on this side of the Rocky Mountains, including New Mexico. Merged into Department of Missouri and Kansas Nov. 9, 1861.

John C. Fremont, Major General.   July 25, 1861, to Nov. 2, 1861.
David Hunter, Major General.   Nov. 2, 1861, to Nov. 9, 1861.

DEPARTMENT OF THE SHENANDOAH.—Constituted July 19, 1861, to consist of the Valley of Virginia, Counties of Washington and Alleghany in Maryland, and such parts of Virginia as may be covered by the Army in its operations. Merged into the Department of the Potomac Aug. 17, 1861. Recreated April 4, 1862. Merged into Army of Virginia June 26, 1862.

N. P. Banks, Major General.   July 25, 1861, to Aug. 17, 1861.
N. P. Banks, Major General.   Apr. 4, 1862, to June 26, 1862.

MILITARY DISTRICT OF THE POTOMAC.—Constituted July 25, 1861, by consolidation of the Department of Washington and the Department of Northeast Virginia. Changed to Department or Army of the Potomac Aug. 15, 1861.

Geo. B. McClellan, Major General.   July 25, 1861, to Aug. 15, 1861.

DEPARTMENT, OR ARMY OF THE POTOMAC.—Created Aug. 15, 1861, from Military District of the Potomac.

Geo. B. McClellan, Major General.   Aug. 15, 1861, to Nov. 9, 1862.
A. E. Burnside, Major General.   Nov. 9, 1862, to Jany. 26, 1863.
Joseph Hooker, Major General.   Jany. 26, 1863, to June 28, 1863.
Geo. G. Meade, Major General.   June 28, 1863, to Dec. 30, 1864.
John G. Parke, Major General.   Dec. 30, 1864, to Jany. 11, 1865.
Geo. G. Meade, Major General.   Jany. 11, 1865, to June 27, 1865.

DEPARTMENT OF THE CUMBERLAND.—Constituted Aug. 15, 1861, to consist of the States of Kentucky and Tennessee. Merged into Departments of Missouri and Ohio Nov. 9, 1861. Recreated Oct. 24, 1862, to consist of Tennessee East of the Tennessee River, and such parts of Alabama and Georgia as may be taken possession of by United States forces.

Robert Anderson, Brigadier General.   Sept. 24, 1861, to Oct. 8, 1861.
W. T. Sherman, Brigadier General.   Oct. 8, 1861, to Nov. 9, 1861.
W. S. Rosecrans, Major General.   Oct. 30, 1862, to Oct. 20, 1863.
Geo. H. Thomas, Major General.   Oct. 20, 1863, to June 27, 1865.

DEPARTMENT OF NEW ENGLAND.—Created Oct. 1, 1861, consisting of the Six New England States. Discontinued Feby. 20, 1862.

B. F. Butler, Major General.   Oct. 1, 1861, to Feby. 20, 1862.

DEPARTMENT OF WESTERN VIRGINIA.—Organized Oct. 11, 1861, from Department of the Ohio. Merged into Mountain Department March 11, 1862.

W. S. Rosecrans, Brigadier General.   Oct. 11, 1861, to Mch. 11, 1862.

DEPARTMENT OF NEW YORK.—Organized Oct., 1861. Merged into Department of the East Jany. 3, 1863.

E. D. Morgan, Major General.   Oct. 26, 1861, to Jany. 3, 1863.

DEPARTMENT OF NEW MEXICO.—Created Nov. 9, 1861, to consist of the Territory of New Mexico.

W. W. Loring, Colonel U. S. A.   Mch. 23, 1861, to June 16, 1861.
E. R. S. Canby, Bvt. Lieut.-Col. U. S. A.   June 16, 1861, to June 22, 1861.
James H. Carleton, Brigadier General.   Sept. 18, 1862, to June 27, 1865.

DEPARTMENT OF KANSAS.—Created Nov. 9, 1861, to consist of the State of Kansas, the Indian Territory West of Arkansas, and the Territories of Nebraska, Colorado and Dakota. Merged into the Department of Mississippi March 11, 1862. Recreated May 2, 1862. Merged into the Department of Missouri, Sept. 19, 1862. Recreated Jany. 1, 1864. Merged into the Department of Missouri, Jany. 3, 1865.

David Hunter, Major General.   Nov. 20, 1861, to Mch. 11, 1862.
J. G. Blunt, Brigadier General.   May 5, 1862, to Sept. 19, 1862.
S. R. Curtis, Major General.   Jany. 16, 1864, to Jany. 30, 1865.

DEPARTMENT OF MISSOURI.—Created Nov. 9, 1861, to consist of the States of Missouri, Iowa, Minnesota, Wisconsin, Arkansas, and that portion of Kentucky West of the Cumberland River. Merged into Department of Mississippi March 11, 1862. Recreated Sept. 19, 1862, to consist of Missouri, Arkansas, Kansas, and bordering Indian Territory. Colorado and Nebraska Territories added Oct. 11, 1862.

H. W. Halleck, Major General.   Nov. 19, 1861, to Mch. 11, 1862.
S. R. Curtis, Major General.   Sept. 24, 1862, to May 24, 1863.
J. M. Schofield, Major General.   May 24, 1863, to Jany. 30, 1864.
W. S. Rosecrans, Major General.   Jany. 30, 1864, to Dec. 9, 1864.
G. M. Dodge, Major General.   Dec. 9, 1864, to June 27, 1865.

DEPARTMENT OF NORTH CAROLINA.—Created Jany. 7, 1862, to consist of the State of North Carolina. Merged into Department of Virginia and North Carolina July 15, 1863. Recreated Jany. 31, 1865.

A. E. Burnside, Brigadier General.   Jany. 13, 1862, to July 10, 1862.
J. G. Foster, Major General.   July 10, 1862, to July 15, 1863.
J. M. Schofield, Major General.   Jany. 31, 1865, to June 27, 1865.

DEPARTMENT OF KEY WEST.—Created Feby., 1862. Merged into Department of the South March 15, 1862.

J. M. Brannan, Brigadier General.	Feby. 21, 1862, to Mch. 15, 1862.

DEPARTMENT OF THE GULF.—Constituted Feby. 23, 1862. To comprise all of the Coast of the Gulf of Mexico West of Pensacola Harbor, and so much of Gulf States as may be occupied by U. S. forces. West Florida added Aug. 8, 1862.

B. F. Butler, Major General.	Mch. 20, 1862, to Dec. 17, 1862.
N. P. Banks, Major General.	Dec. 17, 1862, to Sept. 23, 1864.
S. A. Hurlbut, Major General.	Sept. 23, 1864, to Apr. 22, 1865.
N. P. Banks, Major General.	Apr. 22, 1865, to June 3, 1865.
E. R. S. Canby, Major General.	June 3, 1865, to June 27, 1865.

MOUNTAIN DEPARTMENT.—Created March 11, 1862, from Department of Western Virginia. Merged into Army of Virginia, June 26, 1862.

W. S. Rosecrans, Brigadier General.	Mch. 14, 1862, to Mch. 29, 1862.
J. C. Fremont, Major General.	Mch. 29, 1862, to June 26, 1862.

DEPARTMENT OF MISSISSIPPI.—Created March 15, 1862, from Departments of Missouri, Ohio and Kansas. Merged into Dept. of Missouri Sept. 19 1862. Recreated Nov. 28, 1864.

H. W. Halleck, Major General.	Mch. 13, 1862, to Sept. 19, 1862.
N. J. T. Dana, Major General.	Dec. 8, 1864, to May 14, 1865.
G. K. Warren, Major General.	May 14, 1865, to June 24, 1865.
H. W. Slocum, Major General.	June 24, 1865, to June 27, 1865.

DEPARTMENT OF THE SOUTH.—Created March 15, 1862. To consist of States of South Carolina, Georgia and Florida. Dept. of Key West added March 15, 1862. West Florida detached Aug. 8, 1862, and annexed to Dept. of the Gulf.

David Hunter, Major General.	Mch. 21, 1862, to Sept. 5, 1862.
J. M. Brannan, Brigadier General.	Sept. 5, 1862, to Sept. 17, 1862.
O. M. Mitchell, Major General.	Sept. 17, 1862, to Oct. 27, 1862.
J. M. Brannan, Brigadier General.	Oct. 27, 1862, to Jany. 20, 1863.
David Hunter, Major General.	Jany. 20, 1863, to June 12, 1863.
Q. A. Gilmore, Brigadier General.	June 12, 1863, to May 1, 1864.
J. P. Hatch, Brigadier General.	May 1, 1864, to May 26, 1864.
J. G. Foster, Major General.	May 26, 1864, to Feby. 9, 1865.
Q. A. Gillmore, Major General.	Feby. 9, 1865, to June 28, 1865.

MIDDLE DEPARTMENT.—Constituted March 22, 1862. To consist of States of New Jersey, Pennsylvania, Delaware, The Eastern Shore of Maryland and Virginia and the Counties of Cecil, Harford, Baltimore and Ann Arundel. Md.

John A. Dix, Major General.	Mch. 22, 1862, to June 9, 1862.
John E. Wool, Major General.	June 9, 1862, to Dec. 22, 1862.
R. C. Schenck, Major General.	Dec. 22, 1862, to Aug. 10, 1863.
W. W. Morris, Bvt. Brig. General.	Aug. 10, 1863, to Aug. 31, 1863.
R. C. Schenck, Major General.	Aug. 31, 1863, to Sept. 28, 1863.
E. B. Tyler, Brigadier General.	Sept. 28, 1863, to Oct. 10, 1863.
R. C. Schenck, Major General.	Oct. 10, 1863, to Dec. 5, 1863.
H. H. Lockwood, Brigadier General.	Dec. 5, 1863, to Mch. 22, 1864.
Lew Wallace, Major General.	Mch. 22, 1864, to Feby. 1, 1865.
W. W. Morris, Bvt. Brig. General.	Feby. 1, 1865, to Apr. 19, 1865.
Lew Wallace, Major General.	Apr. 19, 1865, to June 27, 1865.

DEPARTMENT OF THE RAPPAHANNOCK.—Constituted April 4, 1862, to consist of that portion of Virginia East of the Blue Ridge and West of the Potomac, and the Fredericksburg and Richmond, R. R. including the District of Columbia and the country between the Potomac and the Patuxent. Merged into the Army of Virginia June 26, 1862.

Irvin McDowell, Brigadier General.	Apr. 4, 1862, to June 26, 1862.

ARMY OF VIRGINIA.—Constituted June 26, 1862, to consist of the forces under Major General Fremont, Mountain Dept., Major General Banks, Dept. of the Shenandoah and Major General McDowell, Dept. of the Rappahannock, and including the forces at Washington, D. C., under Brigadier General Sturgis. Merged into Army of the Potomac Sept. 2, 1862.

John Pope, Major General.	June 26, 1862, to Sept. 2, 1862.

DEPARTMENT OF THE NORTHWEST.—Constituted Sept. 6, 1862, to consist of the States of Wisconsin, Iowa, Minnesota and Territories of Nebraska and Dakota.

John Pope, Major General.	Sept. 16, 1862, to Nov. 28, 1862.
W. L. Elliott, Brigadier General.	Nov. 28, 1862, to Feby. 18, 1863.
John Pope, Major General.	Feby. 13, 1863, to Feby. 13, 1865.
S. R. Curtis, Major General.	Feby. 13, 1865, to June 27, 1865.

DEPARTMENT AND ARMY OF THE TENNESSEE.—Created Oct. 16, 1862, to include Cairo, Fort Henry and Fort Donelson, Northern Mississippi and portions of Kentucky and Tennessee West of the Tennessee River.

U. S. Grant, Major General.	Oct. 25, 1862, to Oct. 24, 1863.
W. T. Sherman, Major General.	Oct. 24, 1863, to Mch. 26, 1864.
J. B. McPherson, Major General.	Mch. 26, 1864, to July 22, 1864.
John A. Logan, Major General.	July 22, 1864, to July 27, 1864.
O. O. Howard, Major General.	July 27, 1864, to May 19, 1865.
John A. Logan, Major General.	May 19, 1865, to Aug. 1, 1865.

DEPARTMENT OF THE MONONGAHELA.—Created June 9, 1863, to consist of that portion of Pennsylvania West of Johnstown and the Laurel Hill range of mountains, and the Counties of Hancock, Brooke and Ohio in the State of West Virginia, and Counties of Columbiana, Jefferson and Belmont in the State of Ohio. Merged into Dept. of the Susquehanna April 6, 1864.

W. T. H. Brooks, Major General.	June 11, 1863, to Apr. 6, 1864.

DEPARTMENT OF WEST VIRGINIA.—Formed June, 1863.

B. F. Kelly, Brigadier General.	June 28, 1863, to Mch. 10, 1864.
F. Sigel Major General.	Mch. 10, 1864, to May 21, 1864.
David Hunter, Major General.	May 21, 1864, to Aug. 9, 1864.
George Crook, Major General.	Aug. 9, 1864, to Feby. 22, 1865.
J. D. Stevenson, Brigadier General.	Feby. 22, 1865, to Feby. 28, 1865.
W. S. Hancock, Major General.	Feby. 28, 1865, to Mch. 1, 1865.
S. S. Carroll, Bvt. Major General.	Mch. 1, 1865, to Mch. 7, 1865.
W. S. Hancock, Major General.	Mch. 7, 1865, to Mch. 20, 1865.
Geo. Crook, Major General.	Mch. 20, 1865, to Mch. 22, 1865.
W. S. Hancock, Major General.	Mch. 22, 1865, to June 27, 1865.

DEPARTMENT OF THE SUSQUEHANNA.—Created June 9, 1863, to consist of that portion of Pennsylvania East of Johnstown and the Laurel Hill Range of Mountains. Changed to Dept. of Pennsylvania Dec. 1, 1864.

D. N. Couch, Major General.	June 11, 1863, to Dec. 1, 1864.

DEPARTMENT OF VIRGINIA AND NORTH CAROLINA.—(ARMY OF THE JAMES.) Created July 15, 1863, by consolidation of the Departments of Virginia and North Carolina. Organized into Army of the James April, 1864. Departments separated Jany. 31, 1865, under their respective names.

J. G. Foster, Major General.	July 18, 1863, to Nov. 11, 1863.
B. F. Butler, Major General.	Nov. 11, 1863, to Aug. 27, 1864.
E. O. C. Ord, Major General.	Aug. 27, 1864, to Sept. 7, 1864.
B. F. Butler, Major General.	Sept. 7, 1864, to Dec. 14, 1864.
E. O. C. Ord, Major General.	Dec. 14, 1864, to Dec. 24, 1864.
B. F. Butler, Major General.	Dec. 24, 1884, to Jany. 8, 1865.
E. O. C. Ord, Major General.	Jany. 8, 1865, to Jany. 31, 1865.

MILITARY DIVISION OF THE MISSISSIPPI.—Created Oct. 18, 1863. Composed of Department of the Ohio, Department of the Tennessee, Department of the Cumberland, and Arkansas. Department of Arkansas transferred to Military Division of West Mississippi May 7, 1864.

Ulysses S. Grant, Major General.	Oct. 18, 1863, to Mch. 18, 1864.
W. T. Sherman, Major General.	Mch. 18, 1864, to June 27, 1865.

NORTHERN DEPARTMENT.—Constituted Jany. 12, 1864, to consist of the States of Michigan, Ohio, Indiana and Illinois.

S. P. Heintzelman, Major General.	Jany. 20, 1864, to Oct. 1, 1864.
Joseph Hooker, Major General.	Oct. 1, 1864, to June 27, 1865.

DEPARTMENT OF ARKANSAS.—Created Jany. 6, 1864, to consist of Arkansas except Fort Smith. Fort Smith and Indian Territory added April 17, 1864. Embraced in Military Division West Mississippi May 7, 1864.

Frederick Steele, Major General.	Jany. 30, 1864, to Dec. 22, 1864.
J. J. Reynolds, Major General.	Dec. 22, 1864, to Aug. .., 1865.

MILITARY DIVISION OF WEST MISSISSIPPI.—Created May 7, 1864, to consist of the Department of Arkansas and Department of the Gulf. Arkansas transferred to Military Division of Missouri March 21, 1865. Discontinued May, 1865.

E. R. S. Canby, Major General.	May 11, 1864, to May, 1865.

MIDDLE MILITARY DIVISION.—Created Aug. 6, 1864.

P. H. Sheridan, Major General.	Aug. 6, 1864, to Feby. 27, 1865.
W. S. Hancock, Major General.	Feby. 27, 1864, to June 27, 1865.

ARMY OF GEORGIA.—Constituted March 28, 1865. To consist of the 14th and 20th Army Corps.

H. W. Slocum, Major General.	Mch. 28, 1865, to June 1, 1865.

MILITARY DIVISION OF THE JAMES.—Created April 19, 1865, to consist of the Dept. of Virginia, and such parts of North Carolina as are not occupied by the command of Gen. W. T. Sherman.

H. W. Halleck, Major General.	Apr. 19, 1865, to June 27, 1865.

Eastern Departments and Armies

Index to Eastern Departments and Armies

Department of Pennsylvania

Constituted April 27, 1861, to consist of Pennsylvania, Delaware, and all of Maryland, not embraced in the Departments of Annapolis and Washington. Merged into the Department of the Potomac Aug. 24, 1861.

COMMANDER.

Robert Patterson.......	Major General.....................	April, 27, 1861, to Aug. 24, 1861.

1st DIVISION.— COMMANDERS.

Geo. Cadwallader.......	Brigadier General..................	April 27, 1861, to July 25, 1861.
John A. Dix..........	Major General.....................	July 25, 1861, to Aug. 24, 1861.

1st BRIGADE, 1st DIVISION.— COMMANDER.

Geo. H. Thomas........	Col. 2d U. S. Cav.................	To July 25, 1861.

6th Penna. Infy......June, 1861	From New Organization...........	No change to Muster Out..........	July, 1861
17th Penna. Infy......June, 1861	From New Organization...........	No change to Muster Out..........	July, 1861
21st Penna. Infy......June, 1861	From New Organization...........	No change to Muster Out..........	July, 1861
23d Penna. Infy......June, 1861	From New Organization...........	No change to Muster Out..........	July, 1861
2d U. S. Cav..........June, 1861	From Carlisle Barracks, Pa........	To 1-Brig. Dept. Shenandoah.......	July, 1861
1st R. I. Batty. Arty......June, 1861	From Hunter's Div., N. E. Va......	To 1-Brig. Dept. Shenandoah.......	July, 1861

3d BRIGADE.— COMMANDER.

A. S. Wiliams........	Brigadier General..................	To July 25, 1861.

7th Penna. Infy........June, 1861	From New Organization...........	No change to Muster Out..........	July, 1861
8th Penna. Infy........June, 1861	From New Organization...........	No change to Muster Out..........	July, 1861
10th Penna. Infy........June, 1861	From New Organization...........	No change to Muster Out..........	July, 1861
12th Penna. Infy........June, 1861	From New Organization...........	No change to Muster Out..........	July, 1861

4th BRIGADE.— COMMANDERS.

J. C. Longenecker......	Col. U. S. A.....................	To July 2, 1861.
D. S. Miles..........	....	To July 25, 1861.

9th Penna. Infy........June, 1861	From New Organization...........	No change to Muster Out..........	July, 1861
13th Penna. Infy........June, 1861	From New Organization...........	No change to Muster Out..........	July, 1861
16th Penna. Infy........June, 1861	From New Organization...........	No change to Muster Out..........	July, 1861
2d & 3d U. S. Infy......June, 1861	From Regular Army..............	To Defences of Washington........	July, 1861

2d DIVISION.— COMMANDER.

W. H. Keim..........	Major General.....................	To July 25, 1861.

2d BRIGADE.— COMMANDER.

Geo. C. Wynkoop.......	Brigadier General..................	To July 25, 1861.

1st Penna. Infy........June, 1861	From New Organization...........	No change to Muster Out..........	July, 1861
2d Penna. Infy........June, 1861	From New Organization...........	No change to Muster Out..........	July, 1861
3d Penna. Infy........June, 1861	From New Organization...........	No change to Muster Out..........	July, 1861
24th Penna. Infy........June, 1861	From New Organization...........	To 5-Brig. Keim's 2-Div..........	June, 1861

5th BRIGADE.— COMMANDER.

J. S. Negley..........	Brigadier General................	

14th Penna. Infy........June, 1861	From New Organization...........	No change to Muster Out..........	July, 1861
15th Penna. Infy........June, 1861	From New Organization...........	No change to Muster Out..........	July, 1861
24th Penna. Infy........June, 1861	From 2-Brig. Keim's 2-Div........	No change to Muster Out..........	July, 1861

6th BRIGADE.— COMMANDER.

J. J. Abercrombie.......	Col. U. S. A.....................	

11th Penna. Infy........June, 1861	From New Organization...........	No change to Muster Out..........	July, 1861
1st Wisconsin Infy......June, 1861	From New Organization...........	No change to Muster Out..........	July, 1861
4th Conn. Infy........June, 1861	From New Organization...........	To 2-Brig. Banks' Dept. Shenandoah.	July, 1861
2d Mass. Infy..........June, 1861	From New Organization...........	To 2-Brig. Banks' Dept. Shenandoah.	July, 1861

3d DIVISION.— COMMANDER.

C. P. Sanford..........	Major General....................	

7th BRIGADE.— COMMANDER.

C. P. Stone............	Col. U. S. A....................	

1st New Hampshire Infy..July, 1861	From Stone's Rockville Expedition..	To 3-Brig. Banks' Dept. Shenandoah.	July, 1861
83d (9-S. M.) N. Y. Infy..July, 1861	From Stone's Rockville Expedition..	To 3-Brig. Banks' Dept. Shenandoah.	July, 1861
25th Penna. Infy........July, 1861	From Stone's Rockville Expedition..	No change to Muster Out..........	July, 1861
Dist. Columbia Vols......July, 1861	From Stone's Rockville Expedition..	Defences Washington..............	July, 1861
Batty. F. 4th U. S. Arty..July, 1861	From Carlisle, Pa.................	Banks' Dept. Shenandoah..........	July, 1861

8th BRIGADE.— COMMANDER.

Daniel Butterfield......	Col. 12th New York Infy............	To July 29, 1861.

5th New York Infy.......July, 1861	From Wash'g'n D. C. Dept. N. E. Va.	No change to Muster Out..........	July, 1861
12th New York Infy......July, 1861	From Wash'g'n D. C. Dept. N. E. Va.	No change to Muster Out..........	July, 1861
19th New York Infy......July, 1861	From Wash'g'n D. C. Dept. N. E. Va.	To 1-Brig. Banks' Dept. Shenandoah.	July, 1861
28th New York Infy......July, 1861	From Wash'g'n D. C. Dept. N. E. Va.	To 1-Brig. Banks' Dept. Shenandoah.	July, 1861

UNASSIGNED.—

11th Indiana Infy........July, 1861	From Cumberland, Md.............	No change to Muster Out..........	July, 1861

Department of Northeastern Virginia

Created May 28, 1861. Merged into Department of the Potomac Aug. 17, 1861.

IRVIN MC DOWELL, BRIGADIER GENERAL COMMANDING.

1st DIVISION.— COMMANDER.

Daniel Tyler..........	Brigadier General.................		

1st BRIGADE.— COMMANDER.

E. D. Keyes............	Col. U. S. A.......................		
2d Maine Infy...........June, 1861	From New Organization...........	To Fort Corcoran Dept. Potomac....	Aug., 1861
1st Connecticut Infy......June, 1861	From New Organization...........	No change to Muster Out..........	Aug., 1861
2d Connecticut Infy......June, 1861	From New Organization...........	No change to Muster Out..........	Aug., 1861
3d Connecticut Infy......June, 1861	From New Organization...........	No change to Muster Out..........	Aug., 1861
Varian's N. Y. Mil. Batty..June, 1861	From New Organization...........	No change to Muster Out..........	Aug., 1861

2d BRIGADE.— COMMANDER.

R. C. Schenck............	Brigadier General.................		
1st Ohio Infy............June, 1861	From New Organization...........	No change to Muster Out..........	Aug., 1861
2d Ohio Infy............June, 1861	From New Organization...........	No change to Muster Out..........	Aug., 1861
82d N. Y. (2d S. M.) Infy..June, 1861	From New Organization...........	To Stone's Brigade Div. Potomac...	Aug., 1861
Batty. E, 2d U. S. Arty..June, 1861	From Regular Army...............	To Dept. of Potomac..............	Aug., 1861

3d BRIGADE.— COMMANDER.

W. T. Sherman.........	Col. U. S. A.......................		
13th New York Infy......June, 1861	From New Organization...........	To Fort Corcoran Dept. Potomac....	Aug., 1861
69th New York Mil. Infy.June, 1861	From New Organization...........	No change to Muster Out..........	Aug., 1861
79th New York Infy......June, 1861	From New Organization...........	To W. F. Smith's Brig. Div. Potomac	Aug., 1861
2d Wisconsin Infy.......June, 1861	From New Organization...........	To Fort Corcoran Dept. Potomac....	Aug., 1861
Batty. E, 3d U. S. Arty..June, 1861	From Regular Army...............	To Dept. of the Potomac..........	Aug., 1861

4th BRIGADE.— COMMANDER.

I. B. Richardson.......	Col. 2d Michigan Infy.............		
1st Massachusetts Infy..June, 1861	From New Organization...........	To Hooker's Brig. Div. Potomac....	Aug., 1861
12th New York Infy......June, 1861	From New Organization...........	To Richardson's Brig. Div. Potomac.	Aug., 1861
2d Michigan Infy........June, 1861	From New Organization...........	To Richardson's Brig. Div. Potomac.	Aug., 1861
3d Michigan Infy........June, 1861	From New Organization...........	To Richardson's Brig. Div. Potomac.	Aug., 1861
Batty. G, 1st U. S. Arty..June, 1861	From Regular Army...............	To Richardson's Brig. Div. Potomac.	Aug., 1861
Batty. M, 2d U. S. Arty..June, 1861	From Regular Army...............	To Franklin's Brig. Div. Potomac...	Aug., 1861

2d DIVISION.— COMMANDER.

David Hunter..........	Colonel U. S. A....................	To July 21, 1861.	

1st BRIGADE.— COMMANDER.

Andrew Porter.........	Col. U. S. A.......................		
8th N. Y. (S. M.) Infy..June, 1861	From New Organization...........	No change to Muster Out..........	Aug., 1861
14th New York Infy..June, 1861	From New Organization...........	To Sherman's Brig. Div. Potomac.	Aug., 1861
84th N. Y. (14-Bkln.) Infy.June, 1861	From New Organization...........	To Keyes Brig. Div. Potomac....	Aug., 1861
27th New York Infy..June, 1861	From New Organization...........	To Heintzelman's Brig. Div. Pot'm'c	Aug., 1861
2d U. S. Infy. Cos. C. G..June, 1861	From Regular Army...............	To City Guard Washington.......	Aug., 1861
3d " Cos. B, D, G, H, K..June, 1861	From Regular Army...............	To City Guard Washington.......	Aug., 1861
8th U. S. Infy. Co. G...June, 1861	From Regular Army...............	To Provost Guard Div. Potomac....	Aug., 1861
1st U. S. Cav. Cos. A, E..June, 1861	From Regular Army...............	To Cav. Reserve Div. Potomac....	Aug., 1861
3d U. S. Cav. Cos. B,E,G,I.June, 1861	From Regular Army...............	To Cav. Reserve Div. Potomac....	Aug., 1861
2d U. S. Dragoons Co. K..June, 1861	From Regular Army...............	To Cav. Reserve Div. Potomac....	Aug., 1861
Batt'n U. S. Marines....June, 1861	From Regular Navy...............	To U. S. Navy...................	Aug., 1861

2d BRIGADE.— COMMANDER.

A. S. Burnside.........	Col. 1st Rhode Island Infy.		
2d New Hanmpshire Infy.June, 1861	From New Organization...........	To Hooker's Brigade Div. Potomac	Aug., 1861
1st Rhode Island Infy...June, 1861	From New Organization...........	No change to Muster Out..........	Aug., 1861
2d Rhode Island Infy...June, 1861	From New Organization...........	To Couch's Brig. Div. Potomac....	Aug., 1861
71st N. Y. S. M. Infy....June, 1861	From New Organization...........	No change to Muster Out..........	Aug., 1861
Batty. Arty. with 2d R. I.June, 1861	From New Organization...........	To Couch's Brig. Div. Potomac....	Aug., 1861
2-Howitzers with 71 N. Y.June, 1861	From New Organization...........	No change to Muster Out..........	Aug., 1861

3d DIVISION.— COMMANDER.

S. P. Heintzelman.....	Col. U. S. A.		

1st BRIGADE.— COMMANDER.

W. B. Franklin..........	Colonel U. S. A.		
5th Massachusetts Infy..June, 1861	From New Organization...........	No change to Muster Out..........	Aug., 1861
11th Massachusetts Infy.June, 1861	From New Organization...........	To Hooker's Brig. Div. Potomac....	Aug., 1861
1st Minnesota Infy......June, 1861	From New Organization...........	To Stone's Brig. Div. Potomac.....	Aug., 1861
Batty I, 1st U. S. Arty...June, 1861	From Regular Army...............	To Stone's Brig. Div. Potomac.....	Aug., 1861

2d BRIGADE.— COMMANDERS.

O. B. Willcox.........	Col. 1st Michigan Infy...........	To July 21, 1861.	
J. H. H. Ward........	Col. 38th New York Infy..........	To Aug., 1861.	
11th New York Infy.....June, 1861	From New Organization...........	To New York...................	Aug., 1861
38th New York Infy.....June, 1861	From New Organization...........	To Howard's Brig. Div. Potomac...	Aug., 1861
1st Michigan Infy.......June, 1861	From New Organization...........	No change to Muster Out..........	Aug., 1861
4th Michigan Infy.......June, 1861	From New Organization...........	To Sherman's Brig. Div. Potomac..	Aug., 1861
Batty D, 3d U. S. Arty...June, 1861	From Regular Army...............	To Kearney's Brig. Div. Potomac....	Aug., 1861

3d BRIGADE.— COMMANDER.

O. O. Howard..........	Col. 3d Maine Infy.		
3d Maine Infy..........June, 1861	From New Organization...........	To Howard's Brig. Div. Potomac...	Aug., 1861
4th Maine Infy..........June, 1861	From New Organization...........	To Howard's Brig. Div. Potomac...	Aug., 1861
5th Maine Infy..........June, 1861	From New Organization...........	To Heintzelman's Brig. Div. P't'm'c	Aug., 1861
2d Vermont Infy........June, 1861	From New Organization...........	To W. F. Smith's Brig. Div. Potom..	Aug., 1861

4th (RESERVE) DIVISION.—		COMMANDER.			
Theodore Runyon	Brigadier General.				

1st BRIGADE.—					
1st New Jersey (3-Mos.).June, 1861	From New Organization	No change to Muster Out	Aug.,	1861
2d New Jersey (3-Mos.)..June, 1861	From New Organization	No change to Muster Out	Aug.,	1861
3d New Jersey (3-Mos.).June, 1861	From New Organization	No change to Muster Out	Aug.,	1861
4th New Jersey (3-Mos.).June, 1861	From New Organization	No change to Muster Out	Aug.,	1861
2d BRIGADE.—				
1st New Jersey (3-Yrs.)..June, 1861	From New Organization	To Kearney's Brig. Div. Potomac..	Aug.,	1861
2d New Jersey (3-Yrs.)..June, 1861	From New Organization	To Kearney's Brig. Div. Potomac..	Aug.,	1861
3d New Jersey (3-Yrs.)..June, 1861	From New Organization	To Kearney's Brig. Div. Potomac..	Aug.,	1861
41st New York Infy.....June, 1861	From New Organization	To W. T. Sherman's Brig. Div. Pot.	Aug.,	1861

5th DIVISION.—		COMMANDER.			
D. S. Miles	Colonel U. S. A.				

1st BRIGADE.—		COMMANDER.			
Louis Blenker	Col. 8th New York Infy.				
8th New York Infy.....June, 1861	From New Organization	To Blenker's Brig. Div. Potomac...	Aug.,	1861
29th New York Infy.....June, 1861	From New Organization	To Blenker's Brig. Div. Potomac...	Aug.,	1861
39th New York Infy.....June, 1861	From New Organization	To Blenker's Brig. Div. Potomac...	Aug.,	1861
27th Pennsylvania Infy.June, 1861	From New Organization	To Blenker's Brig. Div. Potomac...	Aug.,	1861
Batty. A, 3d U. S. Arty..June, 1861	From Regular Army	To Heintzelman's Brig. Div. P't'm'c	Aug.,	1861
Bookwood's N. Y. Batty.June, 1861	From 8th and 29th New York Infy.	To 2d N. Y. Indpt. Batty. Blenker..	Aug.,	1861

2d BRIGADE.—		COMMANDER.			
Thomas A. Davies	Col. U. S. A.				
16th New York Infy....June, 1861	From New Organization	To Heintzelman's Brig. Div.˙ P't'm'c	Aug.,	1861
18th New York Infy....June, 1861	From New Organization	To Franklin's Brig. Div. Potomac..	Aug.,	1861
31st New York Infy....June, 1861	From New Organization	To Franklin's Brig. Div. Potomac..	Aug.,	1861
32d New York Infy.....June, 1861	From New Organization	To Franklin's Brig. Div. Potomac..	Aug.,	1861
Batty. G, 2d U. S. Arty...June, 1861	From Regular Army	To Kearney's Brig. Div. Potomac..	Aug.,	1861

Department of the Shenandoah

Constituted July 19, 1861, to consist of the Valley of Virginia, the Counties of Washington and Allegheny in Maryland, and such parts of Virginia as may be covered by the army in its operations. Discontinued Aug. 17, 1861, and merged into the Department of the Potomac.

COMMANDER.

N. P. Banks	Major General	July 25, 1861 to Aug. 17, 1861.	

1st BRIGADE.—		COMMANDER.			
Geo. H. Thomas	Col. 2d U. S Cav				
19th New York Infy.....July, 1861	From 8-Brig. 3-Div. Dept. Penna..	To Gordon's Brig. Banks' Div. Pot.	Aug.,	1861
28th New York Infy.....July, 1861	From 8-Brig. 3-Div. Dept. Penna..	To Gordon's Brig. Banks' Div. Pot.	Aug.,	1861
2d Penna. Infy.........July, 1861	From 2-Brig. 1-Div. Dept. Penna..	No change to Muster Out	Aug.,	1861
28th Penna. Infy.......July, 1861	From New Organization	To Gordon's Brig. Banks' Div. Pot.	Aug.,	1861
5th Conn. Infy.........July, 1861	From New Organization	To Gordon's Brig. Banks' Div. Pot.	Aug.,	1861
1st Rhode Island Batty..July, 1861	From 1-Brig. 1-Div. Dept. Penna..	No change to Muster Out	Aug.,	1861
2d U. S. Cavalry.......July, 1861	From 1-Brig. 1-Div. Dept. Penna..	To Defences of Washington	Aug.,	1861
Phila. Pa. City Troop....July, 1861	From 1-Brig. 1-Div. Dept. Penna..	No change to Muster Out	Aug.,	1861

2d BRIGADE.—		COMMANDER.			
J. J Abercrombie	Col. U S A	July 25, 1861, to Aug. 17, 1861.			
2d Mass. Infy..........July, 1861	From 6-Brig. 2-Div. Dept. Penna..	To Abercrombie's Brig. Banks' Div...	Aug.,	1861
12th Mass. Infy........July, 1861	From New Organization	To Abercrombie's Brig. Banks' Div...	Aug.,	1861
12th Indiana Infy......July, 1861	From New Organization	To Abercrombie's Brig. Banks' Div...	Aug.,	1861
16th Indiana Infy......July, 1861	From New Organization	To Abercrombie's Brig. Banks' Div...	Aug.,	1861
4th Conn. Infy.........July, 1861	From 6-Brig. 2-Div. Dept. Penna..	To Abercrombie's Brig. Banks' Div...	Aug.,	1861
Batty. E, 1st U. S. Arty..July, 1861	From Unass'd Dept Penna	To Defences of Washington D. C..	Aug.,	1861

3d BRIGADE.—		COMMANDERS.			
C. P. Stone	Col. U. S. A	July 25, 1862, to Aug. 8, 1862.			
J. W. Stiles	Col. 83d (9-S. M.) N. Y. Infy	Aug. 8, 1862, to Aug. 17, 1862.			
1st New Hampshire Infy.July, 1861	From 7-Brig. 3-Div. Dept. Penna..	No change to Muster Out	Aug.,	1861
83d (9-S. M.) N. Y. Infy.July, 1861	From 7-Brig. 3-Div. Dept. Penna..	To Stiles Brig. Banks' Div. Potomac	Aug.,	1861
3d Wisconsin Infy.....July, 1861	From New Organization	To Stiles Brig. Banks' Div. Potomac	Aug.,	1861
Batty. F, 4th U. S. Arty..July, 1861	From 7-Brig. 3-Div. Dept. Penna..	To Arty. Banks' Div. Potomac.....	Aug.,	1861

Department of the Potomac

(Better known as the Army of the Potomac.)

Created July 25, 1861, by the consolidation of the Department of Washington, and the Department of Northeastern Virginia. Discontinued June 28, 1865.

COMMANDERS.

Geo. B. McClellan	Major General	Aug. 20, 1861, to Nov. 9, 1862.	
A. E. Burnside	Major General	Nov. 9, 1862, to Jany. 26, 1863.	
Jos. Hooker	Major General	Jany. 26, 1863, to June 28, 1863.	
Geo. G. Meade	Major General	June 28, 1963, to Dec. 30, 1864.	
John G. Parke	Major General	Dec. 30, 1864, to Jany. 11, 1865.	
Geo. G. Meade	Major General	Jany. 11, 1865, to June 28, 1865.	

DIVISION OF THE POTOMAC.—Brigade Organization. Aug., 1861.

HUNTER'S BRIGADE.—

COMMANDER.				
David Hunter	Brigadier General.			
23d New York Infy	Aug., 1861	From New Organization	To Wadsworth's Brig. McDowell's D.	Oct., 1861
25th New York Infy	Aug., 1861	From Dept. of Washington	To Butterfield's Brig. Porter's Div.	Oct., 1861
35th New York Infy	Aug., 1861	From New Organization	To Wadsworth's Brig. McDowell's D.	Oct., 1861
37th New York Infy	Aug., 1861	From New Organization	To Richardson's B. Heintzelman's D.	Oct., 1861

HEINTZELMAN'S BRIGADE.—

COMMANDER.				
S. P. Heintzelman	Brigadier General.			
5th Maine Infy	Aug., 1861	From 3-Brig. 3-Div. N. E. Va.	To Slocum's Brig. Franklin's Div.	Oct., 1861
16th New York Infy	Aug., 1861	From 2-Brig. 5-Div. N. E Va.	To Slocum's Brig. Franklin's Div.	Oct., 1861
26th New York Infy	Aug., 1861	From New Organization	To Slocum's Brig. Franklin's Div.	Oct., 1861
27th New York Infy	Aug., 1861	From 1-Brig. 2-Div. N. E. Va.	To Slocum's Brig. Franklin's Div.	Oct., 1861
Batty. A, 2d U. S. Arty	Aug., 1861	From 1-Brig. 5-Div. N. E. Va.	To Blenker's Potomac	Oct., 1861

SHERMAN'S BRIGADE.—

COMMANDER.				
W. T. Sherman	Brigadier General.			
9th Massachusetts Infy	Aug., 1861	From New Organization	To Martindale's Brig. Porter's Div.	Oct., 1861
14th New York Infy	Aug., 1861	From 1-Brig. 2-Div. N. E. Va.	To Morrell's Brig. Porter's Div.	Oct., 1861
41st New York Infy	Aug., 1861	From 2-B. Runyon's 4-D. N. E. Va.	To Martindale's Brig. Porter's Div.	Oct., 1861
4th Michigan Infy	Aug., 1861	From 2-Brig. 3-Div. N. E. Va.	To Morrell's Brig. Porter's Div.	Oct., 1861
Batty. E, 3d U. S. Arty	Aug., 1861	From 3-Brig. 1-Div. N. E. Va.	To Arty. Porter's Div.	Oct., 1861
2d U. S. Cav. Co. I	Aug., 1861	From 1-Brig. 2-Div. N. E. Va.	To Provost Gd. Div. Potomac	Oct., 1861

KEARNEY'S BRIGADE.—

COMMANDER.				
Philip Kearney	Brigadier General.			
1st New Jersey Infy	Aug., 1861	From 2-B. Runyon's 4-D. N. E. Va.	To Kearney's Brig. Franklin's Div.	Oct., 1861
2d New Jersey Infy	Aug., 1861	From 2-B. Runyon's 4-D. N. E. Va.	To Kearney's Brig. Franklin's Div.	Oct., 1861
3d New Jersey Infy	Aug., 1861	From 2-B. Runyon's 4-D. N. E. Va.	To Kearney's Brig. Franklin's Div.	Oct., 1861
4th New Jersey Infy	Aug., 1861	From New Organization	To Kearney's Brig. Franklin's Div.	Oct., 1861
1st New Jersey Batty.	Aug., 1861	From New Organization	To Arty. Franklin's Div	Oct., 1861
Batty. D, 2d U. S. Arty.	Aug., 1861	From 2-Brig. 3-Div. N. E. Va.	To Arty. Franklin's Div	Oct., 1861
Batty. G, 2d U. S. Arty.	Aug., 1861	From 2-Brig. 5-Div. N. E. Va.	To Arty. Franklin's Div	Oct., 1861
2d U. S. Cavalry Co. G	Aug., 1861	From 1-Brig. 2-Div. N. E. Va.	To Provost Guard Div. Potomac.	Oct., 1861

HOOKER'S BRIGADE.—

COMMANDER.				
Jos. Hooker	Brigadier General.			
2d New Hampshire Infy	Aug., 1861	From 2-Brig. 2-Div. N. E. Va.	To 1-Brig. Hooker's Div	Oct., 1861
1st Massachusetts Infy	Aug., 1861	From 4-Brig. 1-Div. N. E. Va.	To 1-Brig. Hooker's Div	Oct., 1861
11th Massachusetts Infy	Aug., 1861	From 3-Brig. 3-Div. N. E. Va.	To 1-Brig. Hooker's Div	Oct., 1861
26th Pennsylvania Infy	Aug., 1861	From New Organization	To 1-Brig. Hooker's Div	Oct., 1861

KEYES' BRIGADE.—

COMMANDER.				
E. D. Keyes	Brigadier General.			
22d New York Infy	Aug., 1861	From New Organization	To Keyes' Brig. McDowell's Div.	Oct., 1861
24th New York Infy	Aug., 1861	From New Organization	To Keyes' Brig. McDowell's Div.	Oct., 1861
30th New York Infy	Aug., 1861	From New Organization	To Keyes' Brig. McDowell's Div.	Oct., 1861
84th N. Y. (14-S. M.)	Aug., 1861	From 1-Brig. 2-Div. Army N. E. Va.	To Keyes' Brig. McDowell's Div.	Oct., 1861

FRANKLIN'S BRIGADE.—

COMMANDER.				
W. B. Franklin	Brigadier General.			
15th New York Infy	Aug., 1861	From Dept. of Washington	To Newton's Brig. Franklin's Div.	Oct., 1861
18th New York Infy	Aug., 1861	From 2-Brig. 5-Div. N. E. Va.	To Newton's Brig. Franklin's Div.	Oct., 1861
31st New York Infy	Aug., 1861	From 2-Brig. 5-Div. N. E. Va.	To Newton's Brig. Franklin's Div.	Oct., 1861
32d New York Infy	Aug., 1861	From 2-Brig. 5-Div. N. E. Va.	To Newton's Brig. Franklin's Div.	Oct., 1861
Batty. M, 2d U. S. Arty.	Aug., 1861	From 2-Brig. 5-Div. N. E. Va.	To Newton's Brig. Franklin's Div.	Oct., 1861
1st N. Y. (Lincoln) Cav.	Aug., 1861	From New Organization	To Newton's Brig. Franklin's Div.	Oct., 1861

BLENKER'S BRIGADE.—

COMMANDER.				
Louis Blenker	Brigadier General.			
8th New York Infy	Aug., 1861	From 1-Brig. 5-Div. N. E. Va.	To Blenker's Brig. Hooker's Div.	Oct., 1861
29th New York Infy	Aug., 1861	From 1-Brig. 5-Div. N. E. Va.	To Blenker's Brig. Hooker's Div.	Oct., 1861
39th New York Infy	Aug., 1861	From 1-Brig. 5-Div. N. E. Va.	To Blenker's Brig. Hooker's Div.	Oct., 1861
27th Pennsylvania Infy	Aug., 1861	From 1-Brig. 5-Div. N. E. Va.	To Blenker's Brig. Hooker's Div.	Oct., 1861
2d N. Y. Indpt. Battery.	Aug., 1861	From 1-Brig. 5-Div. N. E. Va.	To Blenker's Brig. Hooker's Div.	Oct., 1861

RICHARDSON'S BRIGADE.—

COMMANDER.				
I. B. Richardson	Brigadier General.			
12th New York Infy	Aug., 1861	From 4-Brig. 1-Div. N. E. Va.	To Wadsworth's B. McDowell's Div.	Oct., 1861
2d Michigan Infy	Aug., 1861	From 4-Brig. 1-Div. N. E. Va.	To Wadsworth's B. McDowell's Div.	Oct., 1861
3d Michigan Infy	Aug., 1861	From 4-Brig. 1-Div. N. E. Va.	To Wadsworth's B. McDowell's Div.	Oct., 1861
Batty. G. 1st U. S. Arty.	Aug., 1861	From 4-Brig. 1-Div. N. E. Va.	To Wadsworth's B. McDowell's Div.	Oct., 1861

STONE'S BRIGADE.—

COMMANDER.				
C. P. Stone	Brigadier General.			
34th New York Infy	Aug., 1861	From New Organization	To Gorman's Brig. Stone's Div	Oct., 1861
42d New York Infy	Aug., 1861	From New Organization	To Gorman's Brig. Stone's Div	Oct., 1861
82d N. Y. (2d S. M.)	Aug., 1861	From 2-Brig. 1-Div. N. E. Va.	To Gorman's Brig. Stone's Div	Oct., 1861
1st Minnesota Infy	Aug., 1861	From 1-Brig. 3-Div. N. E. Va.	To Gorman's Brig. Stone's Div	Oct., 1861
Batty. I. 1st U. S. Arty.	Aug., 1861	From 1-Brig. 3-Div. N. E. Va.	To Arty. Stone's Div	Oct., 1861
Batty. H. 1st R. I. Arty.	Sept., 1861	From New Organization	To Arty. Stone's Div	Oct., 1861

SMITH'S BRIGADE.—

COMMANDER.				
W. F. Smith	Col. 3d Vermont Infy.			
2d Vermont Infy	Aug., 1861	From 3-Brig. 3-Div. N. E. Va.	To Brook's Brig. Smith's Div	Oct., 1861
3d Vermont Infy	Aug., 1861	From New Organization	To Brook's Brig. Smith's Div	Oct., 1861
6th Maine Infy	Aug., 1861	From New Organization	To Stevens' Brig. Smith's Div	Oct., 1861
33d New York Infy	Aug., 1861	From New Organization	To Stevens' Brig. Smith's Div	Oct., 1861
79th New York Infy	Aug., 1861	From 3-Brig. 1-Div. N. E. Va.	To Stevens' Brig. Smith's Div	Oct., 1861
3d N. Y. Indpt. Batty.	Aug., 1861	From 2-Brig. 1-Div. N. E. Va.	To Hancock's Brig. Smith's Div.	Oct., 1861
2d U. S. Cavalry, Co. H.	Aug., 1861	From 1-Brig. 2-Div. N. E. Va.	To Provost Guard Potomac	Oct., 1861

COUCH'S BRIGADE.—

	COMMANDER.				
D. N. Couch..........	Col. 7th Mass. Infy.				
7th Massachusetts Infy.Aug., 1861	From New Organization...........	To Couch's Brig. Buell's Div.......	Oct.,	1861
10th Massachusetts Infy.Aug., 1861	From New Organization...........	To Couch's Brig. Buell's Div.......	Oct.,	1861
2d Rhode Island Infy....Aug., 1861	From 2-Brig. 2-Div. N. E. Va......	To Couch's Brig. Buell's Div.......	Oct.,	1861
36th New York Infy....Aug., 1861	From New Organization...........	To Couch's Brig. Buell's Div.......	Oct.,	1861

HOWARD'S BRIGADE.—

	COMMANDER.				
O. O. Howard..........	Col. 3d Maine Infy.				
3d Maine Infy..........Aug., 1861	From 3-Brig. 3-Div. N. E. Va.....	To Sedgwick's B. Heintzelman's D.	Oct.,	1861
4th Maine Infy..........Aug., 1861	From 3-Brig. 3-Div. N. E. Va.....	To Sedgwick's B. Heintzelman's D.	Oct.,	1861
38th New York Infy......Aug., 1861	From 2-Brig. 3-Div. N. E. Va.....	To Sedgwick's B. Heintzelman's D.	Oct.,	1861
40th New York Infy......Aug., 1861	From New Organization...........	To Sedgwick's B. Heintzelman's D.	Oct.,	1861

GRAHAM'S BRIGADE.—

	COMMANDER.				
L. P. Graham.........	Brigadier General.				
23d Pennsylvania Infy...Sept., 1861	From New Organization...........	To Graham's Brig. Buell's Div.....	Oct.,	1861
31st (82d) Penna. Infy..Sept., 1861	From New Organization...........	To Graham's Brig. Buell's Div.....	Oct.,	1861
65th New York Infy.....Sept., 1861	From New Organization...........	To Graham's Brig. Buell's Div.....	Oct.,	1861
67th New York Infy.....Sept., 1861	From New Organization...........	To Graham's Brig. Buell's Div.....	Oct.,	1861
FORT CORCORAN.—				
2d Maine Infy..........Aug., 1861	From 1-Brig. 1-Div. N. E. Va......	To Martindale's Brig. Porter's Div..	Oct.,	1861
13th New York Infy.....Aug., 1861	From 3-Brig. 1-Div. N. E. Va......	To Martindale's Brig. Porter's Div..	Oct.,	1861
2d Wisconsin Infy.......Aug., 1861	From 3-Brig. 1-Div. N. E. Va......	To King's Brig. McDowell's Div...	Oct.,	1861
FORT RUNYAN.—				
21st New York Infy......Aug., 1861	From Unattached N. E. Va........	To Wadsworth's B. McDowell's Div.	Oct.,	1861
FORT ELLSWORTH.—				
17th New York Infy......Aug., 1861	From Unattached N. E. Va........	To Butterfield's B. Porter's Div....	Oct.,	1861

Army of the Potomac

As organized into Divisions Oct., 1861, to March, 1862.

BANKS' DIVISION.—Organized Aug. 17, 1861, by transfer from Dept. of the Shenandoah to Dept. of the Potomac.

COMMANDER.

N. P. Banks..........	Major General.....................	Aug. 17, 1861, to March 13, 1862.

1st BRIGADE.—

COMMANDERS.

Geo. H. Thomas.......	Col. 2d U. S. Cav.................	Aug. 17, 1861, to Aug. 28, 1861.		
Geo. H. Gordon.......	Col. 2d Mass. Infy...............	Aug. 28, 1861, to Oct. 18, 1861.		
A. S. Williams.........	Brigadier General................	Oct. 18, 1861, to March 13, 1862.		
D. Donnelly..........	Col. 28th New York Infy.........	March 13, 1862, to March 20, 1862.		
19th New York Infy......Aug., 1861	From 1-B. Banks' D. Shenandoah..	To reorganization as 3d N. Y. Arty.	Dec.,	1861
28th New York Infy......Aug., 1861	From 1-B. Banks' D. Shenandoah..	To 1-Brig. 1-Div. Banks' 5-C. Pot..	Mch.,	1862
5th Connecticut Infy.....Aug., 1861	From 1-B. Banks' D. Shenandoah..	To 1-Brig. 1-Div. Banks' 5-C. Pot..	Mch.,	1862
28th Pennsylvania Infy.Aug., 1861	From 1-B. Banks' D. Shenandoah..	To Geary's Indpt. Brig. 5-Corps Pot.	Mch.,	1862
2d Massachusetts Infy...Aug., 1861	From 2d B. Banks' Div. Shenandoah	To 3-Brig. Banks' Div. Pot........	Mch.,	1862
1st Maryland Infy.......Aug., 1861	From Dix's Div. Baltimore, Md.....	To 1-Brig. 1-Div. Banks' 5-C. Pot..	Mch.,	1862
46th Penna. Infy.........Nov., 1861	From New Organization..........	To 1-Brig. 1-Div. Banks' 5-C. Pot..	Mch.,	1862

2d BRIGADE.—

COMMANDER.

J. J. Abercrombie......	Brigadier General................	Aug. 17, 1861, to March 13, 1862.		
2d Massachusetts Infy...Aug., 1861	From 1-B. Banks' D. Shenandoah..	To 1-Brig. Banks' Div. Potomac...	Aug.,	1861
12th Massachusetts Infy.Aug., 1861	From 1-B. Banks' D. Shenandoah..	To 2-Brig. 1-Div. Banks' 5-C. Pot..	Mch.,	1862
12th Indiana Infy.......Aug., 1861	From 2-B. Banks' D. Shenandoah..	To 2-Brig. 1-Div. Banks' 5-C. Pot..	Mch.,	1862
16th Indiana Infy.......Aug., 1861	From 2-B. Banks' D. Shenandoah..	To 2-Brig. 1-Div. Banks' 5-C. Pot..	Mch.,	1862
30th Pennsylvania Infy...Oct., 1861	From New Organization..........	To con. with 73d and 99th Pa.....	Mch.,	1862
13th Massachusetts Infy.Oct., 1861	From 3-Brig. Banks' Div. Potomac.	To 2-Brig. 1-Div. Banks' 5-C. Pot..	Mch.,	1862
2d Massachusetts Infy....Mch., 1862	From 3-Brig. Banks' Div. Potomac.	To 2-Brig. 1-Div. Banks' 5-C. Pot..	Mch.,	1862

3d BRIGADE.—

COMMANDERS.

J. W. Stiles...........	Col. 83d New York Infy...........	Aug. 17, 1861, to Oct. 8, 1861.		
C. S. Hamilton.........	Brigadier General................	Oct. 8, 1861, to March 13, 1862.		
Geo. H. Gordon.......	Col. 2d Massachusetts Infy.......	March 13, 1862, to March 14, 1862.		
3d Wisconsin Infy.......Aug., 1861	From 3-B. Banks' D. Shenandoah..	To 3-B. 1-Div. Banks' 5-C. Pot....	Mch.,	1862
29th Pennsylvania Infy.Aug., 1861	From New Organization..........	To 3-B. 1-Div. Banks' 5-C. Pot....	Mch.,	1862
13th Massachusetts Infy.Aug., 1861	From New Organization..........	To 2-B. 1-Div. Banks' 5-Corps Pot..	Mch.,	1862
27th Indiana Infy.......Aug., 1861	From New Organization..........	To 3-B. 1-Div. Banks' 5-C. Pot....	Mch.,	1862
83d N. Y. (9th S.M) Infy.Aug., 1861	From 3-B. Banks' D. Shenandoah..	To 2-B. 1-Div. Banks' 5-Corps Pot.	Mch.,	1862
2d Massachusetts Infy...Mch., 1862	From 2-B. Banks' Div. Potomac...	To 3-Brig. 1-Div. Banks, 5-C. Pot.	Mch.,	1862
ARTILLERY.—				
Batty. A. 1st R. I. Arty...Aug., 1861	From New Organization..........	To Arty. 2-Div. 2-Corps Potomac..	Mch.,	1862
Indpt. Batty. F, Pa. Arty.Oct., 1861	From Defenses of Washington.....	To Arty. 1-Div. Banks' 5-C. Pot...	Mch.,	1862
Batty. F, 4th U. S. Arty..Oct., 1861	From Defenses of Washington.......	To Arty. 1-Div. Banks' 5-Corps Pot.	Mch.,	1862
Batty. M, 1st N. Y. Arty..Nov., 1861	From New Organization..........	To Arty. 1-Div. Banks' 5-Corps Pot.	Mch.,	1862
Batty. F, 1st Penna. Arty.Dec., 1861	From New Organization..........	To Arty. 1-Div. Banks' 5-Corps Pot.	Mch.,	1862
CAVALRY.—				
3d New York Cavalry....Sept., 1861	From New Organization..........	To Defenses of Washington.......	Mch.,	1862
1st Michigan Cavalry....Dec., 1861	From Cav. Brig. Potomac.........	To Hatch's Cav. Banks' 5-C. Pot...	Mch.,	1862
1st Vermont Cavalry....Jan., 1862	From Annapolis, Md..............	To Hatch's Cav. Banks' 5-C. Pot...	Mch.,	1862

McDOWELL'S DIVISION.

COMMANDER.

Irvin McDowell.........	Brigadier General.................	Oct. 3, 1861, to March 13, 1862.		

1st BRIGADE.—

COMMANDERS.

E. D. Keyes...........	Brigadier General................	Oct. 3, 1861, to Nov. 9, 1861.		
C. C. Augur...........	Brigadier General................	Nov. 9, 1861, to March 13, 1862.		
22d New Infy....Oct., 1861	From Keyes' Brig. Div. Potomac...	To 1-Brig. 3-Div. 1-Corps Potomac.	Mch.,	1862
24th New York Infy.....Oct., 1861	From Keyes' Brig. Div. Potomac...	To 1-Brig. 3-Div. 1-Corps Potomac.	Mch.,	1862
30th New York Infy.....Oct., 1861	From Keyes' Brig. Div. Potomac...	To 1-Brig. 3-Div. 1-Corps Potomac.	Mch.,	1862
34th N. Y. (14-Bklyn.)...Oct., 1861	From Keyes' Brig. Div. Potomac...	To 1-Brig. 3-Div. 1-Corps Potomac.	Mch.,	1862

2d BRIGADE.— COMMANDERS.

J. S. Wadsworth	Brigadier General	Oct. 3, 1861, to March 12, 1862.
M. R. Patrick	Brigadier General	March 12, 1862, to March 13, 1862.

12th New York Infy	Oct., 1861	From Richardson's B. D. Potomac..	To 3-Brig. Porter's Div. Potomac	Mch., 1862
21st New York Infy	Oct., 1861	From Fort Runyon Div. Potomac..	To 2-Brig. 3-Div. 1-Corps Potomac.	Mch., 1862
23d New York Infy	Oct., 1861	From Hunter's Brig. Div. Potomac.	To 2-Brig. 3-Div. 1-Corps Potomac.	Mch., 1862
35th New York Infy	Oct., 1861	From Hunter's Brig. Div. Potomac.	To 2-Brig. 3-Div. 1-Corps Potomac.	Mch., 1862
80th N. Y. (20-S. M.)	Oct., 1861	From New Organization	To 2-Brig. 3-Div. 1-Corps Potomac.	Mch., 1862

3d BRIGADE.— COMMANDER.

Rufus King	Brigadier General	Oct. 3, 1861, to March 13, 1862.

2d Wisconsin Infy	Oct., 1861	From Fort Corcoran Div. Potomac.	To 3-Brig. 1-Div. 1-Corps Pot	Mch., 1862
6th Wisconsin Infy	Oct., 1861	From New Organization	To 3-Brig. 1-Div. 1-Corps Pot	Mch., 1862
7th Wisconsin Infy	Oct., 1861	From New Organization	To 3-Brig. 1-Div. 1-Corps Pot	Mch., 1862
19th Indiana Infy	Oct., 1861	From New Organization	To 3-Brig. 1-Div. 1-Corps Pot	Mch., 1862
ARTILLERY.—				
Batty. G. 1st U. S. Arty	Oct., 1861	From Richardson's Brig. Div. Pot..	To Arty. Res. Pot. Att. to E. & K.	Feb., 1862
Batty. M. 2d U. S. Arty	Oct., 1861	From Franklin's Brig. Div. Pot	To Arty. Reserve Potomac	Mch., 1862
CAVALRY.—				
2d New York Cavalry	Oct., 1861	From New Organization	To 3-Div. 1-Corps Potomac	Mch., 1862

HEINTZELMAN'S DIVISION.— COMMANDER.

S. P. Heintzelman	Brigadier General	Oct. 3, 1861, to March 13, 1862.

1st BRIGADE.— COMMANDER.

I. B. Richardson	Brigadier General	Oct. 3, 1861, to March 13, 1862.

2d Michigan Infy	Oct., 1861	From Richardson's Brig. Div. Pot..	To 3-Brig. 3-Div. 3-Corps Pot	Mch., 1862
3d Michigan Infy	Oct., 1861	From Richardson's Brig. Div. Pot..	To 3-Brig. 3-Div. 3-Corps Pot	Mch., 1862
5th Michigan Infy	Oct., 1861	From New Organization	To 3-Brig. 3-Div. 3-Corps Pot	Mch., 1862
37th New York Infy	Oct., 1861	From Hunter's Brig. Div. Potomac.	To 3-Brig. 3-Div. 3-Corps Pot	Mch., 1862

2d BRIGADE.— COMMANDERS.

John Sedgwick	Brigadier General	Oct. 3, 1861, to Feb. 19, 1862.
D. B. Birney	Brigadier General	Feb. 19, 1862, to March 13, 1862.

3d Maine Infy	Oct., 1861	From Howard's Brig. Div. Potomac.	To 2-Brig. 3-Div. 3-Corps Pot	Mch., 1862
4th Maine Infy	Oct., 1861	From Howard's Brig. Div. Potomac.	To 2-Brig. 3-Div. 3-Corps Pot	Mch., 1862
38th New York Infy	Oct., 1861	From Howard's Brig. Div. Potomac.	To 2-Brig. 3-Div. 3-Corps Pot	Mch., 1862
40th New York Infy	Oct., 1861	From Howard's Brig. Div. Potomac.	To 2-Brig. 3-Div. 3-Corps Pot	Mch., 1862

3d BRIGADE.— COMMANDER.

C. D. Jameson	Brigadier General	Oct. 3, 1861, to March 13, 1862.

32d (99th) Penna. Infy	Oct., 1861	From New Organization	To Garrison at Washington	Feb., 1862
45th Penna. Infy	Oct., 1861	From New Organization	To Unatt. Sherman's S. C. Exp	Oct., 1861
57th Penna. Infy	Oct., 1861	From New Organization	To 1-Brig. 3-Div. 3-Corps Pot	Mch., 1862
61st Penna. Infy	Oct., 1861	From New Organization	To Graham's Brig. Buell's Div. Pot.	Feb., 1862
63d Penna. Infy	Oct., 1861	From New Organization	To 1-Brig. 3-Div. 3-Corps Pot	Mch., 1862
105th Penna. Infy	Oct., 1861	From New Organization	To 1-Brig. 3-Div. 3-Corps Pot	Mch., 1862
ARTILLERY.—				
Batty. G. 2d U. S. Arty	Oct., 1861	From Kearny's Brig. Div. Pot	To Arty. 3-Div. 3-Corps Potomac..	Mch., 1862
CAVALRY.—				
1st New Jersey Cavalry	Oct., 1861	From New Organization	To Defenses of Washington	Mch., 1862

PORTER'S DIVISION.— COMMANDER.

Fitz John Porter	Brigadier General	Oct. 3, 1861, to March 13, 1862.

1st BRIGADE.— COMMANDER.

G. W. Morrell	Brigadier General	Oct. 3, 1861, to March 13, 1862.

33d (62d) Penna. Infy	Oct., 1861	From New Organization	To 2-Brig. 1-Div. 3-Corps Pot	Mch., 1862
4th Michigan Infy	Oct., 1861	From Sherman's Brig. Div. Pot	To 2-Brig. 1-Div. 3-Corps Pot	Mch., 1862
9th Massachusetts Infy	Oct., 1861	From Sherman's Brig. Div. Pot	To 2-Brig. 1-Div. 3-Corps Pot	Mch., 1862
14th New York Infy	Oct., 1861	From Sherman's Brig. Div. Pot	To 2-Brig. 1-Div. 3-Corps Pot	Mch., 1862

2d BRIGADE.— COMMANDER.

J. H. Martindale	Brigadier General	Oct. 3, 1861, to March 13, 1862.

13th New York Infy	Oct., 1861	From Fort Corcoran Div. Potomac.	To 1-Brig. 1-Div. 3-Corps Pot	Mch., 1862
41st New York Infy	Oct., 1861	From Sherman's Brig. Div. Pot	To Blenker's Div. Potomac	Dec., 1861
2d Maine Infy	Oct., 1861	From Fort Corcoran Div. Potomac.	To 1-Brig. 1-Div. 3-Corps Pot	Mch., 1862
18th Massachusetts Infy	Oct., 1861	From New Organization	To 1-Brig. 1-Div. 3-Corps Pot	Mch., 1862
22d Massachusetts Infy	Oct., 1861	From New Organization	To 1-Brig. 1-Div. 3-Corps Pot	Mch., 1862

3d BRIGADE.— COMMANDER.

D. Butterfield	Brigadier General	Oct. 3, 1861, to March 13, 1862.

17th New York Infy	Oct., 1861	From Fort Ellsworth Div. Pot	To 3-Brig. 1-Div. 3-Corps Pot	Mch., 1862
25th New York Infy	Oct., 1861	From Hunter's Brig. Div. Potomac.	To 1-Brig. 1-Div. 3-Corps Pot	Mch., 1862
44th New York Infy	Oct., 1861	From New Organization	To 3-Brig. 1-Div. 3-Corps Pot	Mch., 1862
83d Pennsylvania Infy	Oct., 1861	From New Organization	To 3-Brig. 1-Div. 3-Corps Pot	Mch., 1862
16th Michigan Infy	Oct., 1861	From New Organization	To 3-Brig. 1-Div. 3-Corps Pot	Mch., 1862
12th New York Infy	Mch., 1862	From Wadsworth's B. McDowell's D.	To 3-Brig. 1-Div. 3-Corps Pot	Mch., 1862
ARTILLERY.—				
Batty. E, 2d U. S. Arty	Oct., 1862	From Unatt. Div. Potomac	To Arty. Reserve Potomac	Mch., 1862
Batty. E, 3d U. S. Arty	Oct., 1862	From Sherman's Brig. Div. Pot	To T. W. Sherman's S. C. Exp	Oct., 1862
3d Mass. Battery	Oct., 1862	From New Organization	To Arty. 1-Div. 3-Corps Potomac	Mch., 1862
5th Mass. Battery	Oct., 1862	From New Organization	To Arty. 1-Div. 3-Corps Potomac..	Mch., 1862
CAVALRY.—				
3d Pennsylvania Cav	Oct., 1861	From New Organization	To Unatt. 3-Corps Potomac	Mch., 1862
8th Pennsylvania Cav	Oct., 1861	From New Organization	To Unatt. 4-Corps Potomac	Mch., 1862

FRANKLIN'S DIVISION.— COMMANDER.

W. B. Franklin	Brigadier General	Oct. 3, 1861, to March 13, 1862.

1st BRIGADE.—   COMMANDER.

Philip Kearny........	Brigadier General......		Oct. 3, 1861, to March 13, 1862.	
1st New Jersey Infy.....Oct., 1861	From Kearny's Brig. Div. Pot....	To 1-Brig. 1-Div. 1-Corps Potomac.	Mch., 1862
2d New Jersey Infy......Oct., 1861	From Kearny's Brig. Div. Pot.....	To 1-Brig. 1-Div. 1-Corps Potomac.	Mch., 1862
3d New Jersey Infy......Oct., 1861	From Kearny's Brig. Div. Pot.....	To 1-Brig. 1-Div. 1-Corps Potomac.	Mch., 1862
4th New Jersey Infy......Oct., 1861	From Kearny's Brig. Div. Pot.....	To 1-Brig. 1-Div. 1-Corps Potomac.	Mch., 1862

2d BRIGADE.—   COMMANDER.

Henry W. Slocum......	Brigadier General..............	Oct. 3, 1861, to March 13, 1862.	
5th Maine Infy...........Oct., 1861	From Heintzelman's Brig. Div. Pot..	To 2-Brig. 1-Div. 1-Corps Pot....	Mch., 1862
16th New York Infy.....Oct., 1861	From Heintzelman's Brig. Div. Pot..	To 2-Brig. 1-Div. 1-Corps Pot....	Mch., 1862
26th New York Infy.....Oct., 1861	From Heintzelman's Brig. Div. Pot..	To Defenses of Washington.......	Nov., 1861
27th New York Infy.....Oct., 1861	From Heintzelman's Brig. Div. Pot..	To 2-Brig. 1-Div. 1-Corps Pot.....	Mch., 1862
96th Pennsylvania Infy..Oct., 1861	From New Organization..........	To 2-Brig. 1-Div. 1-Corps Pot.....	Mch., 1862

3d BRIGADE.—   COMMANDER.

John Newton..........	Brigadier General..............	Oct. 3, 1861, to March 13, 1862.	
15th New York Infy.....Oct., 1861	From Franklin's Brig. Div. Pot....	To Engineers ·Army Potomac......	Nov., 1862
18th New York Infy......Oct., 1861	From Franklin's Brig. Div. Pot....	To 3-Brig. 1-Div. 1-Corps Pot.....	Mch., 1862
31st New York Infy......Oct., 1861	From Franklin's Brig. Div. Pot....	To 3-Brig. 1-Div. 1-Corps Pot.....	Mch., 1862
32d New York Infy......Oct., 1861	From Franklin's Brig. Div. Pot....	To 3-Brig. 1-Div. 1-Corps Pot'....	Mch., 1862
95th Pennsylvania Infy..Oct., 1861	From New Organization..........	To 3-Brig. 1-Div. 1-Corps Pot.....	Mch., 1862
ARTILLERY.—			
Batty. A, 1st N. J. Arty..Oct., 1861	From Kearny's Brig. Div. Potomac.	To Arty. 1-Div. 1-Corps Potomac..	Mch., 1862
Batty. D, 2d U. S. Arty...Oct., 1861	From Kearny's Brig. Div. Potomac.	To Arty. 1-Div. 1-Corps Potomac..	Mch., 1862
Batty. G, 2d U. S. Arty...Oct., 1861	From Kearny's Brig. Div. Potomac.	To Arty. 3-Div. 3-Corps Potomac..	Mch., 1862
Batty. M, 2d U. S. Arty...Oct., 1861	From Franklin's Brig. Div. Pot....	To Arty. Reserve Potomac........	Mch., 1862
Batty. F, 1st N. Y. Arty...Oct., 1861	From New Organization..........	To Arty. 1-Div. 1-Corps Potomac..	Mch., 1862
CAVALRY.—			
1st N. Y. (Lincoln) Cav...Oct., 1861	From Franklin's Brig. Div. Pot....	To Unatt. Cav. 1-Corps Potomac..	Mch., 1862

STONE'S DIVISION.—   COMMANDERS.

C. P. Stone...........	Brigadier General..............	Oct. 3, 1861, to Feb. 18, 1862.
John Sedgwick........	Brigadier General..............	Feb. 19, 1862, to March 13, 1862.

1st BRIGADE.—   ·COMMANDER.

Willis A. Gorman.....	Brigadier General............,....	Oct. 3, 1861, to March 13, 1862.	
34th New York Infy......Oct., 1861	From Stone's Brig. Div. Potomac..	To 1-Brig. 2-Div. 2-Corps Pot....	Mch., 1862
42d New York Infy......Oct., 1861	From Stone's Brig. Div. Potomac..	To Dana's Brig. Stone's Div. Pot...	Jan., 1862
52d New York (2-S. M.)...Oct., 1861	From Stone's Brig. Div. Potomac..	To 1-Brig. 2-Div. 2-Corps Pot....	Mch., 1862
1st Minnesota Infy......Oct., 1861	From Stone's Brig. Div. Potomac..	To 1-Brig. 2-Div. 2-Corps Pot....	Mch., 1862
15th Massachusetts Infy..Oct., 1861	From New Organization..........	To 1-Brig. 2-Div. 2-Corps Pot....	Mch., 1862
(4-Co. Mass. S. S. attached.)			

2d BRIGADE.—   COMMANDERS.

F. W. Lander.........	Brigadier General..............	Oct. 3, 1861, to Oct. 29, 1861.	
N. J. T. Dana.........	Brigadier General..............	Oct. 20, 1861, to March 13, 1862.	
19th Massachusetts Infy.Oct., 1861	From Lander's Brig. Div. Potomac.	To 3-Brig. 2-Div. 2-Corps Potomac.	Mch., 1862
20th Massachusetts Infy..Oct., 1861	From Lander's Brig. Div. Potomac.	To 3-Brig. 2-Div. 2-Corps Potomac.	Mch., 1862
7th Michigan Infy......Oct., 1861	From New Organization..........	To 3-Brig. 2-Div. 2-Corps Pot....	Mch., 1862
42d New York Infy.......Jan., 1862	From Gorman's Brig. Stone's D. P.	To 3-Brig. 2-Div. 2-Corps Pot....	Mch., 1862

3d BRIGADE.—   COMMANDERS.

E. D. Baker...........	Col. 71st Penna. Infy..............	Oct. 3, 1861, to Oct. 22, 1861. Killed.	
W. W. Burns.........	Brigadier General..............	Oct. 22, 1861, to March 13, 1862.	
69th Pennsylvania Infy...Oct., 1861	From New Organization..........	To 2-Brig. 2-Div. 2-Corps Potomac.	Mch., 1862
71st Pennsylvania Infy...Oct., 1861	From New Organization..........	To 2-Brig. 2-Div. 2-Corps Potomac.	Mch., 1862
72d Pennsylvania Infy...Oct., 1861	From New Organization..........	To 2-Brig. 2-Div. 2-Corps Potomac.	Mch., 1862
106th Pennsylvania Infy.Oct., 1861	From New Organization..........	To 2-Brig. 2-Div. 2-Corps Potomac.	Mch., 1862
ARTILLERY.—			
Batty. B, 1st R. I. Arty...Oct., 1861	From Stone's Brig. Div. Potomac..	To Arty. 2-Div. 2-Corps Potomac..	Mch., 1862
6th N. Y. Indpt. Batty...Oct., 1861	From New Organization..........	To Hooker's Div. Potomac........	Dec., 1861
13th N. Y. Indpt. Batty...Oct., 1861	From New Organization..........	To Blenker's Div. Potomac.......	Dec., 1861
Batty. I, 1st U. S. Arty...Feb., 1862	From Stone's Brig. Div. Potomac..	To Arty. 2-Div. 2-Corps Potomac..	Mch., 1862
CAVALRY.—			
3d New York, 6-Cos......Oct., 1861	From New Organization..........	To Dept. North Carolina.........	Apr., 1862

BUELL'S DIVISION.   COMMANDERS.

D. C. Buell...........	Brigadier General..............	Oct. 3, 1861, to Nov. 9, 1861.
E. D. Keyes...........	Brigadier General..............	Nov. 9, 1861, to March 13, 1862.

1st BRIGADE.—   COMMANDER.

D. N. Couch..........	Brigadier General..............	Oct. 3, 1861, to March 13, 1862.	
2d Rhode Island Infy.....Oct., 1861	From Couch's Brig. Div. Potomac..	To 1-Brig. 1-Div. 4-Corps Pot....	Mch., 1862
7th Massachusetts Infy...Oct., 1861	From Couch's Brig. Div. Potomac.	To 1-Brig. 1-Div. 4-Corps Pot....	Mch., 1862
10th Massachusetts Infy..Oct., 1861	From Couch's Brig. Div. Potomac.	To 1-Brig. 1-Div. 4-Corps Pot....	Mch., 1862
36th New York Infy.....Oct., 1861	From Couch's Brig. Div. Potomac..	To 1-Brig. 1-Div. 4-Corps Pot....	Mch., 1862

2d BRIGADE.—   COMMANDER.

L. P. Graham..........	Brigadier General..............	Oct. 3, 1861, to March 13, 1862.	
23d Pennsylvania Infy...Oct., 1861	From Graham's Brig. Div. Potomac.	To 2-Brig. 1-Div. 4-Corps Potomac.	Mch., 1862
31st (82d) Penna. Infy...Oct., 1861	From Graham's Brig. Div. Potomac.	To 2-Brig. 1-Div. 4-Corps Potomac.	Mch., 1862
65th New York Infy......Oct., 1861	From Graham's Brig. Div. Potomac.	To 2-Brig. 1-Div. 4-Corps Potomac.	Mch., 1862
67th New York Infy......Oct., 1861	From Graham's Brig. Div. Potomac.	To 2-Brig. 1-Div. 4-Corps Potomac.	Mch., 1862
61st Pennsylvania Infy..Feb., 1862	From 3-Brig. Heintzelman's D. Pot.	To 2-Brig. 1-Div. 4-Corps Potomac.	Mch., 1862

3d BRIGADE.—   COMMANDER.

J. J. Peck............	Brigadier General..............	Oct. 3, 1861, to March 13, 1862.	
55th New York Infy......Oct., 1861	From New Organization..........	To 3-Brig. 1-Div. 4-Corps Pot.....	Mch., 1862
62d New York Infy......Oct., 1861	From New Organization..........	To 3-Brig. 1-Div. 4-Corps Pot.....	Mch., 1862
93d Pennsylvania Infy...Oct., 1861	From New Organization..........	To 3-Brig. 1-Div. 4-Corps Pot.....	Mch., 1862
98th Pennsylvania Infy...Oct., 1861	From New Organization..........	To 3-Brig. 1-Div. 4-Corps Pot.....	Mch., 1862
102d Pennsylvania Infy...Oct., 1861	From New Organization..........	To 3-Brig. 1-Div. 4-Corps Pot.....	Mch., 1862
ARTILLERY.—			
Batty. D, 1st Penna. Arty.Oct., 1861	From New Organization..........	To Arty. 1-Div. 4-Corps Potomac..	Mch., 1862
Batty. H, 1st Penna. Arty.Oct., 1861	From New Organization..........	To Arty. 1-Div. 4-Corps Potomac..	Mch., 1862

McCALL'S DIVISION.— COMMANDER.

Geo. A. McCall........	Brigadier General.................	Oct. 3, 1861, to March 13, 1862.

1st BRIGADE.— COMMANDER.

John F. Reynolds.....	Brigadier General.................	Oct. 3, 1861, to March 13, 1862.

1st Penna. Reserves......Oct., 1861	From New Organization..........	To 1-Brig. 2-Div. 1-Corps Potomac.	Mch., 1862
2d Penna. Reserves.......Oct., 1861	From New Organization..........	To 1-Brig. 2-Div. 1-Corps Potomac.	Mch., 1862
5th Penna. Reserves.....Oct., 1861	From New Organization..........	To 1-Brig. 2-Div. 1-Corps Potomac.	Mch., 1862
8th Penna. Reserves.....Oct., 1861	From New Organization..........	To 1-Brig. 2-Div. 1-Corps Potomac.	Mch., 1862

2d BRIGADE.— COMMANDER.

Geo. G. Meade........	Brigadier General.................	Oct. 3; 1861, to March 13, 1862.

3d Penna. Reserves.......Oct., 1861	From New Organization..........	To 2-Brig. 2-Div. 1-Corps Potomac.	Mch., 1862
4th Penna. Reserves.....Oct., 1861	From New Organization..........	To 2-Brig. 2-Div. 1-Corps Potomac.	Mch., 1862
7th Penna. Reserves.....Oct., 1861	From New Organization..........	To 2-Brig. 2-Div. 1-Corps Potomac.	Mch., 1862
11th Penna. Reserves....Oct., 1861	From New Organization..........	To 2-Brig. 2-Div. 1-Corps Potomac.	Mch., 1862
13th Pa. Reserves 1-Rifles.Oct., 1861	From New Organization..........	To 3-Brig. 2-Div. 1-Corps Potomac.	Mch., 1862

3d BRIGADE.— COMMANDER.

E. O. C. Ord..........	Brigadier General.................	Oct. 3, 1861, to March 13, 1862.

6th Penna. Reserves.....Oct., 1861	From New Organization..........	To 3-Brig. 2-Div. 1-Corps Potomac.	Mch., 1862
9th Penna. Reserves.....Oct., 1861	From New Organization..........	To 3-Brig. 2-Div. 1-Corps Potomac.	Mch., 1862
10th Penna. Reserves....Oct., 1861	From New Organization..........	To 3-Brig. 2-Div. 1-Corps Potomac.	Mch., 1862
12th Penna. Reserves....Oct., 1861	From New Organization..........	To 3-Brig. 2-Div. 1-Corps Potomac.	Mch., 1862
ARTILLERY.—			
Batty. A, 1st Pa. Arty....Oct., 1861	From New Organization..........	To Arty. 2-Div. 1-Corps Potomac..	Mch., 1862
Batty. B, 1st Pa. Arty....Oct., 1861	From New Organization..........	To Arty. 2-Div. 1-Corps Potomac..	Mch., 1862
Batty. C, 1st Pa. Arty....Oct., 1861	From New Organization..........	To Arty. 2-Div. 1-Corps Potomac..	Mch., 1862
Batty. C, 5th U. S. Arty...Oct., 1861	From New Organization..........	To Arty. 2-Div. 1-Corps Potomac..	Mch., 1862
CAVALRY.—			
1st Penna. Cavalry......Oct., 1861	From New Organization..........	To Cav. 2-Div. 1-Corps Potomac...	Mch., 1862

HOOKER'S DIVISION.— COMMANDER.

Joseph Hooker........	Brigadier General................	

1st BRIGADE.— COMMANDER.

H. M. Naglee..........	Brigadier General.................	Oct. 3, 1861, to March 13, 1862.

2d New Hampshire Infy..Oct., 1861	From Hooker's Brig. Div. Potomac.	To 1-Brig. 2-Div. 3-Corps Potomac.	Mch., 1862
1st Massachusetts Infy..Oct., 1861	From Hooker's Brig. Div. Potomac.	To 1-Brig. 2-Div. 3-Corps Potomac.	Mch., 1862
11th Massachusetts Infy..Oct., 1861	From Hooker's Brig. Div. Potomac.	To 1-Brig. 2-Div. 3-Corps Potomac.	Mch., 1862
26th Pennsylvania Infy..Oct., 1861	From Hooker's Brig. Div. Potomac.	To 1-Brig. 2-Div. 3-Corps Potomac.	Mch., 1862
1st Michigan Infy.......Oct., 1861	From New Organization..........	To 1-Brig. 2-Div. 3-Corps Potomac.	Mch., 1862

2d BRIGADE.— COMMANDER.

D. E. Sickles.........	Brigadier General.................	Oct. 3, 1861, to March 13, 1862

70th New York Infy.....Oct., 1861	From New Organization..........	To 2-Brig. 2-Div. 3-Corps Potomac.	Mch., 1862
71st New York Infy......Oct., 1861	From New Organization..........	To 2-Brig. 2-Div. 3-Corps Potomac.	Mch., 1862
72d New York Infy......Oct., 1861	From New Organization..........	To 2-Brig. 2-Div. 3-Corps Potomac.	Mch., 1862
73d New York Infy......Oct., 1861	From New Organization..........	To 2-Brig. 2-Div. 3-Corps Potomac.	Mch., 1862
74th New York Infy.....Oct., 1861	From New Organization..........	To 2-Brig. 2-Div. 3-Corps Potomac.	Mch., 1862

3d BRIGADE.— COMMANDERS.

Louis Blenker........	Brigadier General.................	Oct. 3, 1861, to Dec., 1861.
S. H. Starr............	Col. 5th New Jersey Infy.........	Dec., 1861, to March 13, 1862.

8th New York Infy......Oct., 1861	From Blenker's Brig. Div. Potomac	To 1-Brig. Blenker's Div. Potomac.	Dec., 1862
29th New York Infy......Oct., 1861	From Blenker's Brig. Div. Potomac	To 2-Brig. Blenker's Div. Potomac.	Dec., 1862
39th New York Infy......Oct., 1861	From Blenker's Brig. Div. Potomac	To 1-Brig. Blenker's Div. Potomac.	Dec., 1862
27th Pennsylvania Infy..Oct., 1861	From Blenker's Brig. Div. Potomac	To 1-Brig. Blenker's Div. Potomac.	Dec., 1862
2d N. Y. Indpt. Bty. Arty.Oct., 1861	From Blenker's Brig. Div. Potomac	To Arty. Blenker's Div. Potomac..	Dec., 1862
5th New Jersey Infy....Dec., 1861	From Casey's Prov'l. Div. Potomac.	To 3-Brig. 2-Div. 3-Corps Potomac.	Mch., 1862
6th New Jersey Infy......Dec., 1861	From Casey's Prov'l. Div. Potomac.	To 3-Brig. 2-Div. 3-Corps Potomac.	Mch., 1862
7th New Jersey Infy......Dec., 1861	From Casey's Prov'l. Div. Potomac.	To 3-Brig. 2-Div. 3-Corps Potomac.	Mch., 1862
8th New Jersey Infy......Dec., 1861	From Casey's Prov'l. Div. Potomac.	To 3-Brig. 2-Div. 3-Corps Potomac.	Mch., 1862
8th New York Batty......Dec., 1861	From Stone's Div. Potomac.......	To Arty 2-Div. 3-Corps Potomac...	Mch., 1862
4th N. Y. Indpt. Batty....Jan., 1862	From Defenses of Washington.....	To Arty 2-Div. 3-Corps Potomac...	Mch., 1862
ARTILLERY.—			
Batty. E, 1st U. S. Arty...Oct., 1861	From Dist. of Washington........	To Arty Reserve Potomac.........	Mch., 1862
CAVALRY.—			
3d Indiana Cavalry.......Oct., 1861	From New Organization..........	To Unatt. Lower Maryland........	Mch., 1862

SMITH'S DIVISION.— COMMANDER.

W. F. Smith...........	Brigadier General.................	Oct. 3, 1861, to March 13, 1862.

1st BRIGADE.— COMMANDER.

W. T. H. Brooks......	Brigadier General.................	Oct. 3, 1861, to March 13, 1862.

2d Vermont Infy........Oct., 1861	From W. F. Smith's Brig. Div. Pot.	To 2-Brig. 2-Div. 4-Corps Potomac.	Mch., 1862
3d Vermont Infy........Oct., 1861	From W. F. Smith's Brig. Div. Pot.	To 2-Brig. 2-Div. 4-Corps Potomac.	Mch., 1862
4th Vermont Infy........Oct., 1861	From New Organization..........	To 2-Brig. 2-Div. 4-Corps Potomac.	Mch., 1862
5th Vermont Infy........Oct., 1861	From New Organization..........	To 2-Brig. 2-Div. 4-Corps Potomac.	Mch., 1862
6th Vermont Infy........Oct., 1861	From New Organization..........	To 2-Brig. 2-Div. 4-Corps Potomac.	Mch., 1862

2d BRIGADE.— COMMANDERS.

I. I. Stevens..........	Brigadier General.................	Oct. 3, 1861, to Oct. 26, 1861.
J. W. Davidson........	Brigadier General.................	Oct. 26, 1861, to March 13, 1862.

6th Maine Infy.........Oct., 1861	From W. F. Smith's Brig. Div. Pot.	To 1-Brig. 2-Div. 4-Corps Potomac.	Mch., 1862
7th Maine Infy.........Oct., 1861	From Dix's Div. Baltimore, Md....	To 3-Brig. 2-Div. 4-Corps Potomac.	Mch., 1862
33d New York Infy......Oct., 1861	From W. F. Smith's Brig. Div. Pot.	To 3-Brig. 2-Div. 4-Corps Potomac.	Mch., 1862
49th New York Infy......Oct., 1861	From New Organization..........	To 3-Brig. 2-Div. 4-Corps Potomac.	Mch., 1862
79th New York Infy......Oct., 1861	From W. F. Smith's Brig. Div. Pot.	To T. W. Sherman's S. C. Exp.....	Oct., 1861
77th New York Infy......Dec., 1861	From New Organization..........	To 3-Brig. 2-Div. 4-Corps Potomac.	Mch., 1862

3d BRIGADE.—   COMMANDER.

W. S. Hancock	Brigadier General	Oct. 3, 1861, to March 13, 1862.	
43d New York Infy......Oct., 1861	From New Organization...........	To 1-Brig. 2-Div. 4-Corps Potomac.	Mch., 1862
47th Pennsylvania Infy...Oct., 1861	From New Organization...........	To Dept. of Florida..............	Jany., 1862
49th Pennsylvania Infy...Oct., 1861	From New Organization...........	To 1-Brig. 2-Div. 4-Corps Potomac.	Mch., 1862
5th Wisconsin Infy......Oct., 1861	From New Organization...........	To 1-Brig. 2-Div. 4-Corps Potomac.	Mch., 1862
1st U. S. Sharpshooters...Oct., 1861 (Cos. B and E.)	From New Organization...........	To 1-Div. 3-Corps Potomac.......	Mch., 1862
ARTILLERY.—			
3d N. Y. Indpt. Batty.....Oct., 1861	From W. F. Smith's Brig. Div. Pot.	To Arty. 2-Div. 4-Corps Potomac...	Mch., 1862
Batty. E, 1st Pa. Arty....Oct., 1861	From New Organization...........	To Arty. 1-Div. 4-Corps Potomac...	Mch., 1862
Batty. F, 5th U. S. Arty...Oct., 1861	From New Organization...........	To Arty. 2-Div. 4-Corps Potomac..	Mch., 1862

BLENKER'S DIVISION.—   COMMANDER.

Louis Blenker	Brigadier General	Dec., 1861, to March, 1862.	

1st BRIGADE.—   COMMANDER.

J. H. Stahel	Brigadier General	Dec., 1861, to March, 1862.	
8th New York Infy.......Dec., 1861	From Blenker's B. Hooker's D. Pot.	To 1-B. Blenker's Div. 2-Corps Pot.	Mch., 1862
39th New York Infy......Dec., 1861	From Blenker's Brig. Hooker's Div.	To 1-B. Blenker's Div. 2-Corps Pot.	Mch., 1862
45th New York Infy......Dec., 1861	From New Organization...........	To 1-B. Blenker's Div. 2-Corps Pot.	Mch., 1862
27th Pennsylvania Infy...Dec., 1861	From Blenker's Brig. Hooker's Div.	To 1-B. Blenker's Div. 2-Corps Pot.	Mch., 1862

2d BRIGADE.—   COMMANDER.

A. Von Steinwehr	Brigadier General	Dec., 1861, to March, 1862.	
29th New York Infy......Dec., 1861	From Blenker's Brig. Hooker's Div.	To 2-Brig. Blenker's Div. 2-Corps..	Mch., 1862
54th New York Infy......Dec., 1861	From Casey's Prov'l Brig. Pot.....	To 2-Brig. Blenker's Div. 2-Corps..	Mch., 1862
68th New York Infy......Dec., 1861	From Casey's Prov'l Brig. Pot.....	To 2-Brig. Blenker's Div. 2-Corps..	Mch., 1862
73d Pennsylvania Infy....Dec., 1861	From New Organization...........	To 2-Brig. Blenker's Div. 2-Corps..	Mch., 1862

3d BRIGADE.—   COMMANDER.

Henry Bohlen	Col. 75th Pennsylvania Infy.......	Dec., 1861, to March, 1862.	
58th New York Infy......Dec., 1861	From New Organization...........	To 3-Brig. Blenker's Div. 2-Corps..	Mch., 1862
35th (74th) Pa. Infy......Dec., 1861	From New Organization...........	To 3-Brig. Blenker's Div. 2-Corps..	Mch., 1862
40th (75th) Pa. Infy......Dec., 1861	From Casey's Prov'l Command Pot.	To 3-Brig. Blenker's Div. 2-Corps..	Mch., 1862
UNATTACHED.—			
41st New York Infy......Dec., 1861	From Martindale's Brig. Porter's D.	To Unattached Blenker's D. 2-Corps	Mch., 1862
2d N. Y. Indpt. Batty....Dec., 1861	From Blenker's Brig. Hooker's Div.	To Arty. Blenker's Div. 2-Corps....	Mch., 1862
13th N. Y. Indpt. Batty...Dec., 1861	From Burns' Brig. Stone's Div. Pot.	To Arty. Blenker's Div. 2-Corps....	Mch., 1862
4th New York Cavalry....Dec., 1861	From New Organization...........	To Unattached Blenker's D. 2-Corps	Mch., 1862

SUMNER'S DIVISION.—   COMMANDER.

E. V. Sumner	Brigadier General	Nov. 25, 1861, to March 13, 1862.	

1st BRIGADE.—   COMMANDER.

O. O. Howard	Brigadier General	Nov. 25, 1861, to March 13, 1862.	
5th New Hampshire Infy.Nov., 1861	From New Organization...........	To 1-Brig. 1-Div. 2-Corps Potomac.	Mch., 1862
4th Rhode Island Infy...Nov., 1861	From New Organization...........	To 3-Brig. Burnside Expedition....	Jany., 1862
61st New York Infy......Nov., 1861	From New Organization...........	To 1-Brig. 1-Div. 2-Corps Potomac.	Mch., 1862
81st Pennsylvania Infy...Nov., 1861	From New Organization...........	To 1-Brig. 1-Div. 2-Corps Potomac.	Mch., 1862
64th New York Infy.....Jany., 1862	From New Organization...........	To 1-Brig. 1-Div. 2-Corps Potomac.	Mch., 1862

2d BRIGADE.—   COMMANDER.

T. F. Meagher	Brigadier General	Nov. 25, 1861, to March 13, 1862.	
63d New York Infy......Nov., 1861	From New Organization...........	To 2-Brig. 1-Div. 2-Corps Potomac.	Mch., 1862
69th New York Infy......Nov., 1861	From New Organization...........	To 2-Brig. 1-Div. 2-Corps Potomac.	Mch., 1862
88th New York Infy......Nov., 1861	From New Organization...........	To 2-Brig. 1-Div. 2-Corps Potomac.	Mch., 1862

3d BRIGADE.—   COMMANDER.

W. H. French	Brigadier General	Nov. 25, 1861, to March 13, 1862.	
52d New York Infy......Nov., 1861	From New Organization...........	To 3- Brig. 1-Div. 2-Corps Potomac.	Mch., 1862
57th New York Infy......Nov., 1861	From New Organization...........	To 3- Brig. 1-Div. 2-Corps Potomac.	Mch., 1862
66th New York Infy......Nov., 1861	From New Organization...........	To 3- Brig. 1-Div. 2-Corps Potomac.	Mch., 1862
53d Pennsylvania Infy...Nov., 1861	From New Organization...........	To 3- Brig. 1-Div. 2-Corps Potomac.	Mch., 1862
ARTILLERY, SUMNER'S DIVISION.—			
Batty. B, 1st N. Y. Arty..Nov., 1861	From New Organization...........	To Arty. 1-Div. 2-Corps Potomac...	Mch., 1862
Batty. G, 1st N. Y. Arty..Nov., 1861	From New Organization...........	To Arty. 1-Div. 2-Corps Potomac...	Mch., 1862
Batty. A & C, 4th U. S...Nov., 1861	From New Organization...........	To Arty. 1-Div. 2-Corps Potomac...	Mch., 1862
CAVALRY.—			
8th Illinois Cavalry......Nov., 1861	From New Organization...........	To Cav. 5-Corps Potomac..........	Mch., 1862

CASEY'S PROVISIONAL BRIGADE.   COMMANDER.

Silas Casey	Brigadier General	Oct., 1861, to Jany., 1862.	
5th New Jersey Infy......Oct., 1861	From New Organization...........	To 3-Brig. Hooker's Div. Potomac..	Dec., 1861
6th New Jersey Infy......Oct., 1861	From New Organization...........	To 3-Brig. Hooker's Div. Potomac..	Dec., 1861
7th New Jersey Infy......Oct., 1861	From New Organization...........	To 3-Brig. Hooker's Div. Potomac..	Dec., 1861
8th New Jersey Infy......Oct., 1861	From New Organization...........	To 3-Brig. Hooker's Div. Potomac..	Dec., 1861
4th New Hampshire Infy..Oct., 1861	From New Organization...........	To Sherman's S. C. Expedition......	Oct., 1861
40th (75th) Pa. Infy......Oct., 1861	From New Organization...........	To 3-Brig. Blenker's Div. Potomac..	Dec., 1861
100th Penna. Infy........Oct., 1861	From New Organization...........	To Sherman's S. C. Expedition......	Oct., 1861
54th New York Infy......Oct., 1861	From New Organization...........	To 2-Brig. Blenker's Div. Potomac..	Dec., 1861
68th New York Infy......Oct., 1861	From New Organization...........	To 2-Brig. Blenker's Div. Potomac..	Dec., 1861
64th New York Infy......Dec., 1861	From New Organization...........	To 1-Brig. Sumner's Div. Potomac..	Dec., 1861

CASEY'S DIVISION.—   COMMANDER.

Silas Casey	Brigadier General	Dec., 1861, to March, 1862.	

1st BRIGADE.—   COMMANDER.

H. M. Naglee	Brigadier General	Dec., 1861, to Mch., 1862.	
56th New York Infy......Dec., 1861	From New Organization...........	To 1-Brig. 3-Div. 4-Corps Potomac.	Mch., 1862
52d Pennsylvania Infy....Dec., 1861	From New Organization...........	To 1-Brig. 3-Div. 4-Corps Potomac.	Mch., 1862
104th Penna. Infy.......Dec., 1861	From New Organization...........	To 1-Brig. 3-Div. 4-Corps Potomac.	Mch., 1862
11th Maine Infy.........Dec., 1861	From New Organization...........	To 1-Brig. 3-Div. 4-Corps Potomac.	Mch., 1862

2d BRIGADE.— COMMANDER.

W. H. Keim	Brigadier General	Dec., 1861, to March, 1862.	
59th New York Infy......Dec., 1861	From New Organization	To Defences of Washington........	Mch., 1862
86th New York Infy......Dec., 1861	From New Organization..........	To Defences of Washington........	Mch., 1862
85th Pennsylvania Infy...Dec., 1861	From New Organization..........	To 2-Brig. 3-Div. 4-Corps Potomac.	Mch., 1862

3d BRIGADE.— COMMANDER.

I. N. Palmer	Brigadier General	Dec., 1861, to March, 1862.	
9th New Jersey Infy......Dec., 1861	From New Organization..........	To 2-Brig. Burnside Expedition....	Dec., 1862
77th New York Infy......Dec., 1861	From New Organization..........	To 3-Brig. 2-Div. 4-Corps Potomac..	Mch., 1862
85th New York Infy......Dec., 1861	From New Organization..........	To 3-Brig. 3-Div. 4-Corps Potomac..	Mch., 1862
87th New York Infy......Dec., 1861	From New Organization..........	To 1-Brig. 3-Div. 3-Corps Potomac..	Mch., 1862
76th New York Infy......Dec., 1861	From New Organization..........	To Wadsworth's Command Wash'n	Mch., 1862
ARTILLERY.—			
Batty. A, 1st N. Y. Arty..Dec., 1861	From New Organization..	To Arty. 3-Div. 4-Corps Potomac...	Mch., 1862
Batty. H, 1st N. Y. Arty..Dec., 1861	From New Organization..	To Arty. 3-Div. 4-Corps Potomac.,..	Mch., 1862
7th N. Y. Indpt. Batty....Dec., 1861	From New Organization..	To Arty. 3-Div. 4-Corps Potomac...	Mch., 1862
8th N. Y. Indpt. Batty....Dec., 1861	From New Organization..	To Arty. 3-Div. 4-Corps Potomac...	Mch., 1862

PROVOST GUARD.— COMMANDER.

Andrew Porter	Col. 16th U. S. Infy	Oct. 3, 1861, to Mch., 1862.	
Sturgis Ills. Rifles........Oct., 1861	From Headqrs. Div. Potomac......	To Headqrs. Army Potomac......	Mch., 1862
1st U. S. Infy............Oct., 1861	From Regular Army...........	To Infantry Reserve Potomac......	Mch., 1862
2d U. S. Infy. Detachmt...Oct., 1861	From Regular Army...........	To Infantry Reserve Potomac......	Mch., 1862
3d U. S. Infy. Detachmt...Oct., 1861	From Regular Army...........	To Infantry Reserve Potomac......	Mch., 1862
8th U. S. Infy. Co. G.....Oct., 1861	From Regular Army...........	To Infantry Reserve Potomac......	Mch., 1862
4th U. S. Cav. Cos. A, E...Oct., 1861	From Regular Army...........	To Headqrs. Army Potomac......	Mch., 1862
Batty. K, 5th U. S. Arty...Oct., 1861	From New Organization........	To Arty. Reserve Potomac........	Mch., 1862
GARRISON ALEXANDRIA.—			
88th Pennsylvania Infy...Oct., 1861	From New Organization........	To Dist. Washington.............	Mch., 1862
FORT ALBANY.—			
14th Massachusetts Infy...Oct., 1861	From Defences of Washington.....	To Dist. Washington.............	Mch., 1862
FORT WASHINGTON.—			
37th New York Infy. H. I.Oct., 1861	From Hunter's Brig. Div. Potomac.	To Dist. Washington.............	Mch., 1862
Batty. D, 1st U. S. Arty...Oct., 1861	From Regular Army..............	To Fort Taylor, Fla.............	Nov., 1861

STONEMAN'S CAVALRY COMMAND.— COMMANDER.

Geo. Stoneman	Brigadier General.		
6th United States Cav....Oct., 1861	From Regular Army.............	To Cavalry Reserve Army Potomac	Jany., 1862
4th Penna. Cav..........Oct., 1861	From New Organization.........	To Wadsworth's Command Wash'n	Jany., 1862
11th Penna. Cav..........Oct., 1861	From New Organization.........	To Dept. of Virginia.............	Nov., 1861
Oneida, N. Y., Cav. Co.....Oct., 1861	From New Organization.........	To Headqrs. Army Potomac.......	Jany., 1862
Barker's Ills. Dragoons....Oct., 1861	From New Organization.........	To Cav. Reserve Potomac.........	Jany., 1862

CAVALRY RESERVE.— COMMANDER.

Philip St. George Cooke	Brigadier General.		
1st United States Cav....Jan., 1862	From Regular Army.............	To 2-Brig. Cav. Reserve Potomac..	Mch., 1862
2d United States Cav....Jan., 1862	From Regular Army.............	To Provost Guard Army Potomac...	Mch., 1862
4th U. S. Cav. (2 Cos.)....Jan., 1862	From Regular Army.............	To Headqrs. Army Potomac.......	Mch., 1862
5th United States Cav....Jan., 1862	From Regular Army.............	To 1-Brig. Cav. Reserve Potomac...	Mch., 1862
6th United States Cav....Jan., 1862	From Regular Army.............	To 1-Brig. Cav. Reserve Potomac...	Mch., 1862
6th Penna. Cavalry......Jan., 1862	From New Organization.........	To 1-Brig. Cav. Reserve Potomac...	Mch., 1862

DIX'S DIVISION, BALTIMORE, MD.— COMMANDER.

John A. Dix	Major General	July 25, 1861, to Mch. 22, 1862.	
3d New York Infy......July, 1861	From Camp Hamilton Dept. Va....	To Middle Department............	Mch., 1862
4th New York Infy......July, 1861	From Camp Hamilton Dept. Va....	To Middle Department............	Mch., 1862
5th New York Infy......July, 1861	From Newport News Dept. Va.....	To Sykes' Regular Infy. Div. Pot..	Mch., 1862
13th New York Infy......July, 1861	From Annapolis, Md.............	No change to Muster Out.........	Aug., 1861
20th N. Y. State Militia..July, 1861	From Annapolis, Md.............	No change to Muster Out.........	Aug., 1861
12th Penna. Infy.........July, 1861	From R. R. Guard..............	No change to Muster Out.........	Aug., 1861
18th Penna. Infy.........July, 1861	From Baltimore, Md.............	No change to Muster Out.........	Aug., 1861
19th Penna. Infy.........July, 1861	From Baltimore, Md.............	No change to Muster Out.........	Aug., 1861
22d Penna. Infy.........July, 1861	From Baltimore, Md.............	No change to Muster Out.........	Aug., 1861
1st Penna. Reserves......July, 1861	From New Organization.........	To Reynold's B. McCall's Div. Pot.	Oct., 1861
21st Indiana Infy.........July, 1861	From New Organization.........	To Ship Island, Miss., Dept. Gulf..	Feb., 1862
20th Indiana Infy........Aug., 1861	From New Organization.........	To Dept. of Virginia.............	Sept., 1861
1st Delaware Infy........Aug., 1861	From Baltimore, Md.............	No change to Muster Out.........	Aug., 1861
6th Michigan Infy.......Aug., 1861	From New Organization.........	To Butler's New Orleans Expedition	Feb., 1862
17th Mass. Infy.........Aug., 1861	From New Organization.........	To Foster's Brig. N. C. Expedition	Mch., 1862
7th Maine Infy..........Aug., 1861	From New Organization.........	To Davidson's Brig. Smith's Div. P.	Oct., 1861
87th Penna. Infy.........Aug., 1861	From New Organization.........	To Middle Department............	Mch., 1862
2d Maryland Infy........Aug., 1861	From New Organization.........	To Middle Department............	Mch., 1862
5th Maryland Infy........Aug., 1861	From New Organization.........	To Fort Monroe Dept. Va........	Mch., 1862
Patapsco, Md., Guard....Aug., 1861	From New Organization.........	To R. R. Brig. Middle Dept........	Mch., 1862
2d Delaware Infy........Aug., 1861	From New Organization.........	To Middle Department............	Mch., 1862
Purnell, Md., Legion.....Oct., 1861	From New Organization.........	To Eastern Shore Middle Dept.....	Mch., 1862
1st Maryland E. Shore....Oct., 1861	From New Organization.........	To Eastern Shore Middle Dept.....	Mch., 1862
2d Maryland E. Shore....Oct., 1861	From New Organization.........	To Eastern Shore Middle Dept.....	Mch., 1862
10th Maine Infy.........Oct., 1861	From New Organization.........	To R. R. Brig. Middle Dept........	Mch., 1862
11th Penna. Infy.........Nov., 1861	From New Organization.........	To Middle Department............	Mch., 1862
Balto., Md., Light Infy....Nov., 1861	From New Organization.........	To Middle Department............	Mch., 1862
60th New York Infy....Nov., 1861	From New Organization.........	To R. R. Brig. Middle Dept........	Mch., 1862
3d Maryland Infy........Feb., 1862	From New Organization.........	To Middle Department............	Mch., 1862
ARTILLERY.—			
Batty. I, 2d U. S. Arty....July, 1861	From Regular Army.............	To Middle Department............	Mch., 1862
Cook's Mass. Batty.......July, 1861	From New Organization.........	No change to Muster Out.........	Aug., 1861
2d Mass. Indpt. Batty....Aug., 1861	From New Organization.........	To Butler's New Orleans Expedition	Feb., 1862
Batty. A, Maryland Arty.Sept., 1861	From New Organization.........	To Middle Department............	Mch., 1862
Batty. B, Maryland Arty.Sept., 1861	From New Organization.........	To Middle Department............	Mch., 1862
Batty. L, 1st N. Y. Arty..Feb., 1862	From Defences of Washington.....	To Middle Department............	Mch., 1862
CAVALRY.—			
5th New York Cav......Nov., 1861	From New Organization.........	To Cav. Banks' 5-Corps Potomac...	Mch., 1862
Purnell, Md., Legion Cav.Nov., 1861	From New Organization.........	To Balto., Md., Middle Dept.......	Mch., 1862
1st Maryland Cav........Jan., 1862	From New Organization.........	To Balto., Md., Middle Dept.......	Mch., 1862
10th New York Cav......Mch., 1862	From Gettysburg, Pa............	To Balto., Md., Middle Dept.......	Mch., 1862

Army of the Potomac

As organized from March, 1862, to its discontinuance June 28, 1865.

At General Headquarters

GUARDS AND ORDERLIES.—
Oneida, N. Y., Indpt.

Cav. Co................Mch., 1862	From City Guard Washington, D. C.	No change to Muster Out.........	June, 1865
Sturgis, Ills., Rifles......Mch., 1862	From Provost Guard Washington..	No change to Muster Out.........	Nov., 1862
McClellan, Ill., Dragoons.Mch., 1862	From Stoneman's Cav. Comd. Pot..	To Provost Guard Potomac.......	Nov., 1862
4th U. S. Cav. (Cos. A, E).Mch., 1862	From Provost Guard Washington..	To Dept. of the Cumb'd............	Jan., 1863
1st U. S. Cavalry.......July, 1862	From 2-Brig. Cav. Res. Potomac..	To Res. Brig. 1-Div. Cav. Corps Pot.	Feb., 1863
4th U. S. Infy..........June, 1864	From 1-Brig. 1-Div. 9-Corps Pot..	To Dept. of Virginia...............	May, 1865

PROVOST GUARD.—   COMMANDERS.

Andrew Porter........	Col. 16th U. S. Infy................	Mch. 13, 1862, to Aug. 6, 1862.
W. H. Wood...........	Major 17th U. S. Infy..............	Aug. 6, 1862, to Sept. 12, 1862.
M. R. Patrick........	Brigadier General..................	Sept. 12, 1862, to ———

2d U. S. Cavalry.......Mch., 1862	From Dept. of Washington........	To Res. Brig. 1-Div. Cav. Corps Pot.	Feb., 1863
8th U. S. Infy.........Mch., 1862	From Dept. of Washington........	To Dept. of the East...........	July, 1862
17th U. S. Infy. Cos. A, E.Mch., 1862	From Dept. of Washington........	To 2-Brig. 2-Div. 5-Corps Potomac.	Apr., 1862
19th U. S. Infy. Cos. G, H.Mch., 1862	From Dept. of Washington........	To Dept. of the Cumb'd............	Nov., 1862
93d New York Infy.....May, 1862	From 3-Brig. 3-Div. 4-Corps Potom.	To 2-Brig. 3-Div. 2-Corps Potomac.	Apr., 1864
22d New Jersey Infy.....Dec., 1862	From Defences of Washington.....	To 3-Brig. 1-Div. 1-Corps Potomac.	Jan., 1863
29th New Jersey Infy....Dec., 1862	From Defences of Washington.....	To 3-Brig. 1-Div. 1-Corps Potomac.	Jan., 1863
30th New Jersey Infy....Dec., 1862	From Defences of Washington.....	To 3-Brig. 1-Div. 1-Corps Potomac.	Jan., 1863
31st New Jersey Infy....Dec., 1862	From Defences of Washington.....	To 3-Brig. 1-Div. 1-Corps Potomac.	Jan., 1863
9th New York Infy. Co. G.Dec., 1862	From Dept. of North Carolina......	No change to Muster Out.........	May, 1863
McClellan, Ills. Dragoons.Dec., 1862	From Headqrs. Guard Potomac....	Transferred to 12th Ills. Cav......	Feb., 1863
147th New York Infy.....Dec., 1862	From Defences of Washington.....	To 3-Brig. 1-Div. 1-Corps Potomac.	Jan., 1863
137th Penna. Infy.......Dec., 1862	From 1-Brig. 2-Div. 6-Corps Potom.	To 3-Brig. 1-Div. 1-Corps Potomac.	Jan., 1863
21st New York Infy......Jan., 1862	From 3-Brig. 1-Div. 1-Corps Potom.	No change to Muster Out.........	June, 1863
23d New York Infy......Jan., 1863	From 3-Brig. 1-Div. 1-Corps Potom.	No change to Muster Out.........	June, 1863
35th New York Infy......Jan., 1863	From 3-Brig. 1-Div. 1-Corps Potom.	No change to Muster Out.........	June, 1863
80th (20th S. M.) N. Y....Jan., 1863	From 3-Brig. 1-Div. 1-Corps Potom.	To 1-Brig. 3-Div. 1-Corps Potomac.	June, 1863
12th Ohio Indpt. Batty....Jan., 1863	From Defences of Washington.....	To Unatt. Arty. Reserve Potomac..	May, 1863
Batty. B, 1st Maryland A.Jan., 1863	From Defences of Washington.....	To Unatt. Arty. Reserve Potomac..	May, 1863
94th New York Infy.....May, 1863	From 1-Brig. 2-Div. 1-Corps Potom.	To 1-Brig. 2-Div. 1-Corps Potomac.	June, 1863
2d Penna. Cavalry.......June, 1863	From 2-B. Stahel's Cav. Div. 22-C.	To 2-Brig. 2-Div. Cav. Corps Potom.	July, 1863
80th New York Infy.....July, 1863	From 1-Brig. 3-Div. 1-Corps Pot..	To. Indpt. Brig. 9-Corps Potomac.	Mch., 1865
130th New York Infy....July, 1863	From 1-Brig. 1-Div. 7-Corps Va..	To Unatt. Cav. Corps Potomac....	Aug., 1863
1st Maryland Cavalry.....Oct., 1863	From 1-Brig. 2-Div. Cav. Corps Pot.	To 3-Sep. Brig. 8-Corps Middle Dept.	Feb., 1864
3d Penna. Cavalry.......Mch., 1864	From 1-Brig. 2-Div. Cav. Corps Pot.	Consolidated with 5th Pa. Cav....	May, 1865
114th Penna. Infy.......Mch., 1864	From 1-Brig. 1-Div. 3-Corps Pot..	To Collis' Indpt. Brig. 9-Corps Pot.	Mch., 1865
68th Pennsylvania Infy....Mch., 1864	From 1-Brig. 1-Div. 3-Corps Pot..	To Collis' Indpt. Brig. 9-Corps Pot.	Mch., 1865
1st Mass. Cav. Cos. C, D.April, 1864	From 1-Brig. 2-Div. Cav. Corps Pot.	No change to Muster Out.........	June, 1865
8th Delaware Infy.......Dec., 1864	From Engr. Brig. Potomac........	To 3-Brig. 2-Div. 5-Corps Potomac.	Mch., 1865
1st Mass. Cavalry.......Feb., 1865	From 1-Brig. 2-Div. Cav. Corps Pot.	No change to Muster Out.........	June, 1865
3d U. S. Infy...........Feb., 1865	From Defences of Washington.....	To. Dept. of Washington..........	June, 1865
11th U. S. Infy.........Feb., 1865	From Annapolis, Md..............	To. Dept. of Virginia..............	May, 1865
2d Penna. Cavalry.......Feb., 1865	From 2-Brig. 2-Div. Cav. Corps Pot.	No change to Muster Out.........	June, 1865
10th U. S. Infy.........Apr., 1865	From Buffalo, N. Y..............	To. Dept. of Washington..........	June, 1865
14th U. S. Infy.........Apr., 1865	From Annapolis, Md..............	To. Dept. of Virginia..............	June, 1865

ARTILLERY RESERVE.—

Batty. H, 1st U. S. Arty..Oct., 1861	From Defences of Washington.....	To Arty. 2-Div. 3-Corps Potomac..	Mch., 1862
Battys. K & G, 1st U. S...Oct., 1861	From Richardson's Brig. Div. Pot..	To 2-B. Arty. Reserve 5-Corps Pot.	May, 1862
Batty. A, 2d U. S. Arty....Oct., 1861	From Regular Army..............	To 1-Brig. Horse Arty. 5-Corps Pot.	May, 1862
Battys. B & L, 2d U. S....Oct., 1861	From Regular Army..............	To 1-Brig. Horse Arty. 5-Corps Pot.	May, 1862
Battys. F & K, 3d U. S....Oct., 1861	From Regular Army..............	To 5-Brig. Arty. Res. 5-Corps Pot.	May, 1862
Batty. K, 4th U. S. Arty...Oct., 1861	From Regular Army..............	To Arty. Reserve 3-Corps Pot.....	May, 1862
Batty. A, 5th U. S. Arty...Oct., 1861	From New Organization...........	To 2-Brig. Arty. Res. 5-Corps Pot...	May, 1862
By. A, 1st N. Y. Bn. Arty.Oct., 1861	From New Organization...........	To 3-Brig. Arty. Res. 5-Corps Pot..	May, 1862
By. B, 1st N. Y. Bn. Arty.Oct., 1861	From New Organization...........	To 3-Brig. Arty. Res. 5-Corps Pot..	May, 1862
By. C, 1st N. Y. Bn. Arty.Oct., 1861	From New Organization...........	To 3-Brig. Arty. Res. 5-Corps Pot..	May, 1862
By. D, 1st N. Y. Bn. Arty.Oct., 1861	From New Organization...........	To 3-Brig. Arty. Res. 5-Corps Pot..	May, 1862
5th N. Y. Indpt. Batty....Nov., 1861	From New Organization...........	To Unatt. Arty. Res. 5-Corps Pot..	May, 1862
Batty. E, 1st U. S. Arty...Mch., 1862	From Hooker's Div. Potomac......	To 2-Brig. Arty. Res. 5-Corps Pot..	May, 1862
Batty. E, 2d U. S. Arty....Mch., 1862	From. Porter's Div. Potomac......	To 5-Brig. Arty. Res. 5-Corps Pot..	May, 1862
Batty. M, 2d U. S. Arty....Mch., 1862	From McDowell's Div. Potomac....	To 1-Brig. Horse Arty. 5-Corps Pot.	May, 1862
Battys. C & G, 3d U. S...Mch., 1862	From Regular Army..............	To 1-Brig. Horse Arty. 5-Corps Pot.	May, 1862
Battys. L & M, 3d U. S..Mch., 1862	From Regular Army..............	To Arty 2-Div. 5-Corps Potomac..	May, 1862
Batty. G, 4th U. S. Arty...Mch., 1862	From Cheat. Mt. Dist., West Va....	To 2-Brig. Arty. Res. 5-Corps Pot..	May, 1862
Batty. I, 5th U. S. Arty...Mch., 1862	From New Organization...........	To Arty. 2-Div. 5-Corps Potomac..	May, 1862
Batty. K, 5th U. S. Arty...Mch., 1862	From Provost Guard Washington..	To 2-Brig. Arty. Res. 5-Corps Pot..	May, 1862
Batty. M, 5th U. S. Arty...Mch., 1862	From New Organization...........	To Res. Arty. 4-Corps Potomac....	May, 1862
Batty. K, 5th U. S. Arty...Oct., 1862	From Arty. 2-Div. 5-Corps Potomac	To Arty. Brig. 12-Corps Potomac..	May, 1863
Batty. K, 1st U. S. Arty...Dec., 1862	From Res. Arty. 5-Corps Potomac..	To 2-Regular Brig. Arty. Res. Pot.	May, 1863
Batty. A, 2d U. S. Arty...Dec., 1862	From Cav. Div. Potomac..........	To Averill's Cav. Brig. Potomac...	Jan., 1863
Batty. G, 4th U. S. Arty...Dec., 1862	From Res. Arty. 5-Corps Potomac..	To 1 Regular Brig. Arty. Res. Pot.	May, 1863
5th N. Y. Indpt. Batty....Dec., 1862	From Res. Arty. 5-Corps Potomac..	To 2-Vol. Brig. Arty. Res. Pot....	May, 1863
A, 1st N. Y. Battn. Arty..Dec., 1862	From Res. Arty. 5-Corps Potomac..	Designated 29th N. Y. Batty......	Mch., 1863
B, 1st N. Y. Battn. Arty..Dec., 1862	From Res. Arty. 5-Corps Potomac..	Designated 30th N. Y. Batty......	Mch., 1863
C, 1st N. Y. Battn. Arty..Dec., 1862	From Res. Arty. 5-Corps Potomac..	Designated 31st N. Y. Batty......	Mch., 1863
D, 1st N. Y. Battn. Arty..Dec., 1862	From Res. Arty. 5-Corps Potomac..	Designated 32d N. Y. Batty.......	Mch., 1863
6th N. Y. Indpt. Batty....Dec., 1862	From Arty. Res. 3-Corps Potomac..	To Arty 1-Div. Cav. Corps Potomac	Feb., 1863
15th N. Y. Indpt. Batty...Dec., 1862	From Defences Balto., Md., 8-Corps	To 2-Vol. Brig. Arty Res. Potomac	May, 1863
Battys. B & L, 2d U. S...Jan., 1863	From Averill's Cav. Brig. Potomac.	To Res. Brig. Cav. Corps Potomac..	May, 1863
Bs. B & M, 1st Conn. H. A.Feb., 1863	From Def. Washington 22-Corps...	To 2-Vol. Brig. Arty. Res. Potomac	May, 1863
Batty. C, 3d U. S. Arty...Feb., 1863	From Gregg's Cav. Brig. Potomac..	To 2-Regular Brig. Arty. Res. Pot.	May, 1863
Cos. B & M, 1st Conn. H. A.Mch., '64	From 1-Brig. Arty. Res. Potomac..	To DeRussy's Div. 22 Corps........	Apr., 1864
5th N. Y. Indpt. Batty....Mch., 1864	From 1-Brig. Arty. Res. Potomac..	To 2-Brig. Arty. Res. Potomac.....	Apr., 1864
11th N. Y. Indpt. Batty...Mch., 1864	From 2-Brig. Arty. Res. Potomac..	To 3-Brig. Arty. Res. Potomac.....	Apr., 1864
12th N. Y. Indpt. Batty...Mch., 1864	From Arty. Brig. 3-Corps Potomac.	To Arty. Brig. 2-Corps Potomac....	Apr., 1864
15th N. Y. Indpt. Batty...Mch., 1864	From 2-Brig. Arty. Res. Potomac..	To 2-Brig. Arty. Res. Potomac.....	Apr., 1864
Batty. B, 1st N. Y. Arty..Mch., 1864	From 1-Brig. Arty. Res. Potomac..	To 3-Brig. Arty. Res. Potomac.....	Apr., 1864
Batty. C, 1st N. Y. Arty..Mch., 1864	From Arty. Brig. 5-Corps Potomac.	To 3-Brig. Arty. Res. Potomac.....	Apr., 1864
Batty. A, 1st N. J. Arty...Mch., 1864	From 1-Brig. Arty. Res. Potomac..	To 2-Brig. Arty. Res. Potomac.....	Apr., 1864

Unit	Date	From	To	Date
Batty. B, 1st N. J. Arty.	Mch., 1864	From Arty. Brig. 3-Corps Potomac.	To 2-Brig. Arty. Res. Potomac.	Apr., 1864
1st New Hamp. Batty.	Mch., 1864	From Arty. Brig. 3-Corps Potomac.	To Arty Brig. 2-Corps Potomac.	Apr., 1864
Batty. H, 1st Ohio Arty.	Mch., 1864	From 2-Brig. Arty. Res. Potomac.	To 3-Brig. Arty. Res. Potomac.	Apr., 1864
5th Maine Indpt. Batty.	Mch., 1864	From Arty. Brig. 1-Corps Potomac.	To 2-Brig. Arty. Res. Potomac.	Apr., 1864
6th Maine Indpt. Batty.	Mch., 1864	From 2-Brig. Arty. Res. Potomac.	To Arty. Brig. 2-Corps Potomac.	Apr., 1864
9th Mass. Indpt. Batty.	Mch., 1864	From 2-Brig. Arty. Res. Potomac.	To 3-Brig. Arty. Res. Potomac.	Apr., 1864
Batty. H, 1st U. S.	Mch., 1864	From 2-Brig. Arty. Res. Potomac.	To Consol. with Batty I, 1st U. S.	Apr., 1864
Battys. F & K, 3d U. S.	Mch., 1864	From Arty. Brig. 5-Corps Potomac.	To Consol. with Batty. C, 3d U. S.	Apr., 1864
Batty. C, 4th U. S. Arty.	Mch., 1864	From Arty. Brig. 5-Corps Potomac.	To Consol. with Batty. E, 4th U. S.	Apr., 1864
15th N. Y. H'vy Ay. Co. F.	June, '64	From 3-Brig. 2-Div. 5-Corps Pot.	To 1-Brig. 2-Div. 5-Corps.	Dec., 1864
4th Maine Indpt. Batty.	July, 1864	From Arty. Brig. 6-Corps Potomac.	To Arty. Brig. 6-Corps Potomac.	Dec., 1864
Batty. A, 1st N. J. Arty.	July, 1864	From Arty. Brig. 6-Corps Potomac.	To Arty. Brig. 6-Corps Potomac.	Dec., 1864
3d N. Y. Indpt. Batty.	July, 1864	From Arty. Brig. 6-Corps Potomac.	To Arty. Brig. 6-Corps Potomac.	Dec., 1864
Batty. H, 1st Ohio Arty.	July, 1864	From Arty. Brig. 6-Corps Potomac.	To Arty. Brig. 6-Corps Potomac.	Dec., 1864
Batty. E, 1st R. I. Arty.	July, 1864	From Arty. Brig. 6-Corps Potomac.	To Arty. Brig. 6-Corps Potomac.	Dec., 1864
Batty. E, 5th U. S. Arty.	July, 1864	From Arty. Brig. 6-Corps Potomac.	To Arty. Brig. 6-Corps Potomac.	Dec., 1864
4th N. Y. Heavy Arty.	July, 1864	From 2d-5th and 6th Corps Pot.	To 1-Div. 2-Corps Potomac.	Aug., 1864
2d Maine Indpt. Batty.	Aug., 1864	From Arty. Brig. 9-Corps Pot.	No change to Muster Out.	May, 1865
3d Maine Indpt. Batty.	Aug., 1864	From Arty. Brig. 9-Corps Pot.	No change to Muster Out.	June, 1865
14th Mass. Indpt. Batty.	Aug., 1864	From Arty. Brig. 9-Corps Pot.	No change to Muster Out.	June, 1865
3d Vermont Indpt. Batty.	Aug., 1864	From Arty. Brig. 9-Corps Pot.	No change to Muster Out.	June, 1865
Battys. H and I, 1st U. S.	Aug., 1864	From Horse Arty. Potomac.	To 2-Div. Cav. Corps Potomac.	Oct., 1864
Batty. H, 1st R. I. Arty.	Dec., 1864	From Def. City Point Va.	To Arty. Brig. 6-Corps Potomac.	Jan., 1865
4th Maine Indpt. Batty.	Mch., 1865	From Arty. Brig. 6-Corps Potomac.	No change to Muster Out.	June, 1865
Battys. C and I, 5th U. S.	Mch., 1865	From Arty. Brig. 2-Corps Potomac.	To Dept. Washington.	June, 1865
6th Maine Indpt. Batty.	Mch., 1865	From Arty. Brig. 6-Corps Potomac.	No change to Muster Out.	June, 1865
5th Mass. Indpt. Batty.	Mch., 1865	From Arty. Brig. 5-Corps Potomac.	To Arty. Brig. 5-Corps Potomac.	Apr., 1865
9th Mass. Indpt. Batty.	Mch., 1865	From Arty. Brig. 2-Corps Potomac.	No change to Muster Out.	June, 1865
3d New Jersey Batty.	Mch., 1865	From Arty. Brig. 2-Corps Potomac.	No change to Muster Out.	June, 1865
Batty. C, 1st N. Y. Arty.	Mch., 1865	From Arty. Brig. 5-Corps Potomac.	To Arty. Brig. 5-Corps Potomac.	Apr., 1865
Batty. E, 1st N. Y. Arty.	Mch., 1865	From Arty. Brig. 5-Corps Potomac.	To Arty. Brig. 5-Corps Potomac.	Apr., 1865
Batty. G, 1st N. Y. Arty.	Mch., 1865	From Arty. Brig. 5-Corps Potomac.	No change to Muster Out.	June, 1865
Batty. L, 1st N. Y. Arty.	Mch., 1865	From Arty. Brig. 5-Corps.	To Arty. Brig. 5-Corps Potomac.	Apr., 1865
12th N. Y. Indpt. Batty.	Mch., 1865	From Arty. Brig. 2-Corps Potomac	To Arty. Brig. 2-Corps Potomac.	Apr., 1865
Batty. H, 1st Ohio Arty.	Mch., 1865	From Arty. Brig. 5-Corps Potomac.	No change to Muster Out.	June, 1865
Batty. B, 1st Penna. Arty.	Mch., 1865	From Arty. Brig. 5-Corps Potomac.	No change to Muster Out.	June, 1865
Batty. F, 1st Penna. Arty.	Mch., 1865	From Arty. Brig. 2-Corps Potomac.	No change to Muster Out.	June, 1865
Batty. E, 1st R. I. Arty.	Apr., 1865	From Arty. Brig. 6-Corps Potomac.	No change to Muster Out.	June, 1865
15th N. Y. Heavy Arty.	M.Apr., 1865	From Arty. Brig. 5-Corps Potomac.	To Def. of Washington 22-C.	May, 1865

1st BRIGADE HORSE ARTILLERY.—

Batty. I, 1st Michigan	June 1863	From Cav. Div. 22-Corps.	To 2-Brig. Horse Arty. Potomac.	Aug., 1863
6th N. Y. Indpt. Batty.	June, 1863	From 1-Div. Cav. Corps Potomac.	To Camp Barry 22-Corps.	June, 1864
Battys. E and L, 2d U. S.	June, 1863	From Res. Brig. Cav. Corps Pot.	To Res. Horse Arty. Army Shen.	Dec., 1864
Batty. M, 2d U. S. Arty.	June, 1863	From Res. Brig. Cav. Corps Pot.	To Arty. 3-Div. Cav. Corps Pot.	Dec., 1864
Batty. E, 4th U. S. Arty.	June, 1863	From Res. Brig. Cav. Corps Pot.	To Arty. 1-Div. Cav. Corps.	Dec., 1864
Batty. D, 2d U. S. Arty.	July, 1863	From Arty. Brig. 6-Corps Potomac.	To Res. Horse Arty Army Shen.	Dec., 1864
Batty. A, 4th U. S. Arty.	July, 1863	From Arty. Brig. 2-Corps Potomac.	To Def. of Washington 22-Corps.	June, 1864
6th N. Y. Indpt. Batty.	Sept., 1864	From Camp Barry 22-Corps.	To Res. Horse Arty. Army Shen.	Dec., 1864

2d BRIGADE HORSE ARTILLERY.—

Battys. E and G, 1st U. S.	June, 1863	From 2-Reg. Brig. Arty. Res. Pot.	To De Russy's Div. 22-Corps.	June, 1864
Batty. K, 1st U. S. Arty.	June, 1863	From 2-Reg. Brig. Arty. Res. Pot.	To Camp Barry 22-Corps.	June, 1864
Batty. A, 2d U. S. Arty.	June, 1863	From 2-Div. Cav. Corps Potomac.	To Dept. of Washington.	June, 1865
Batty. C, 3d U. S. Arty.	June, 1863	From 2-Reg. Brig Arty. Res. Pot.	To Battys. F and K, 3d U. S. Arty.	Mch., 1864
Batty. G, 2d U. S. Arty.	Aug., 1863	From Arty. Brig. 6-Corps Potomac.	To De Russy's Div. 22-Corps.	June, 1864
Batty. I, 1st Mich. Arty.	Aug., 1863	From 1-Brig. Horse Arty. Potomac.	To Arty. Brig. 11-Corps Cumb'd.	Oct., 1863
Batty. I, 1st U. S. Arty.	Nov., 1863	From Arty. Brig. 2-Corps Potomac.	To Dept. of Washington.	May, 1865
C, F and K, 3d U. S. Arty.	Apr., 1863	From Arty. Res. Potomac.	To Res. Horse Arty. Army Shen.	Dec., 1864

1st REGULAR BRIGADE, ARTILLERY RESERVE.—

Unit	Date	From	To	Date
Batty. B, 1st U. S. Arty.	May, 1863	From Arty. 2-Div. 3-Corps Potomac	To 3-Brig. Arty. Res. Potomac.	Oct., 1863
Battys. F and K, 3d U. S.	May, 1863	From Arty. 1-Div. 3-Corps Potomac	To Arty. Brig. 5-Corps Potomac.	Nov., 1863
Batty. C, 4th U. S Arty.	May, 1863	From Arty 1-Div 3-Corps Potomac	To Arty. Brig. 6-Corps Potomac.	Nov., 1863
Batty. G, 4th U. S. Arty.	May, 1863	From Arty Res. Potomac.	To Arty. Brig. 11-Corps Potomac.	June, 1863
Batty. C, 5th U. S. Arty.	May, 1863	From Arty. 2-Div. 1-Corps Potomac	To Consol. with I, 5th Arty.	July, 1863

2d REGULAR BRIGADE, ARTILLERY RESERVE.—

Unit	Date	From	To	Date
Battys. E and G, 1st U. S.	May, 1863	From Arty. 3-Div. 5-Corps Potomac	To 2-Brig. Horse Arty. Potomac.	June, 1863
Batty. K, 1st U. S. Arty.	May, 1863	From Arty. Res. Potomac.	To 2-Brig. Horse Arty. Potomac.	June, 1863
Batty. A, 2d U. S. Arty.	May, 1863	From Arty. 2-Div. Cav. Corps Pot.	To 2-Brig. Horse Arty. Potomac.	June, 1863
Batty. C, 3d U. S. Arty.	May, 1863	From Arty Res. Potomac.	To 2-Brig. Horse Arty. Potomac.	June, 1863

1st VOLUNTEER BRIGADE, ARTILLERY RESERVE.—

6th Maine Indpt. Batty.	May, 1863	From Arty. 2-Div. 12-Corps Pot.	To 4th Vol. Brig. Arty Res. Pot.	June, 1863
5th Mass. Indpt. Batty.	May, 1863	From Arty. 1-Div. 5-Corps Pot.	To Arty. Brig. 5-Corps Potomac.	July, 1863
Batty. B, 1st N. Y. Arty.	May, 1863	From Arty. 1-Div. 2-Corps Pot.	To Arty Brig. 2-Corps Potomac.	July, 1863
Batty. G, 1st N. Y. Arty.	May, 1863	From Arty. 3-Div. 2-Corps Pot.	To 4-Vol. Brig. Arty. Res. Pot.	June, 1863
10th N. Y. Indpt. Batty.	May, 1863	From Arty. 3-Div. 3-Corps Pot.	To Camp Barry 22-Corps.	July, 1863
Batty. H, 1st Ohio Arty.	May, 1863	From Arty. 3-Div. 3-Corps Pot.	To 3-Vol. Brig. Arty. Res. Potomac.	June, 1863
Indpt. Batty. C, Penna.	May, 1863	From Arty. 2-Div. 1-Corps Pot.	To Arty. Brig. 2-Corps Potomac.	Oct., 1863
Indpt. Batty. F, Penna.	July, 1863	From 4-Vol. Brig. Arty. Res. Pot.	To Arty. Brig. 2-Corps Potomac.	Oct., 1863
5th Mass. Indpt. Batty.	July, 1863	From Arty. Brig. 5-Corps Pot.	To Arty. Brig. 5-Corps Potomac.	Aug., 1863
9th Mass. Indpt. Batty.	July, 1863	From Abercrombie's Div. 22-Corps.	To 2-Brig. Arty. Res. Potomac.	Dec., 1863
4th N. Y. Indpt. Batty.	July, 1863	From Arty. Brig 3-Corps Pot.	To Camp Barry 22-Corps.	July, 1863
15th N. Y. Indpt. Batty.	July, 1863	From 2-Vol. Brig. Arty. Res. Pot.	To 4-Vol. Brig. Arty. Res. Pot.	Aug., 1863
6th Maine Indpt. Batty.	July, 1863	From 4-Vol. Brig. Arty. Res. Pot.	To 2-Brig. Arty. Res. Potomac.	Oct., 1863
Batty. A, 1st N. J. Arty.	July, 1863	From 4-Vol. Brig. Arty. Res. Pot.	To 3-Vol. Brig. Arty. Res. Potomac	Oct., 1863
4th N. Y. Indpt. Batty.	Sept., 1863	From Camp Barry 22-Corps.	Broken Up.	Dec., 1863
Batty. A, 1st N. J. Arty.	Nov., 1863	From 3-Vol. Brig. Arty. Res. Pot.	To Unatt. Arty. Res. Potomac.	Dec., 1863
1st Conn. H. A. Cos. B, M.	Nov., 1863	From 2-Vol. Brig. Arty. Res. Pot.	To Unatt. Arty. Res. Potomac.	Mch., 1864
Batty. B, 1st N. Y. Arty.	Nov., 1863	From 2-Vol. Brig. Arty. Res. Pot.	To Unatt. Arty. Res. Potomac.	Mch., 1864
5th N. Y. Indpt. Batty.	Nov., 1863	From 2-Vol. Brig. Arty. Res. Pot.	To Unatt. Arty. Res. Potomac.	Mch., 1864
Batty. C, 1st W. Va. Arty.	Nov., 1863	From 2-Vol. Brig. Arty. Res. Pot.	To Def. of Washington 22-Corps.	Mch., 1864
6th N. Y. Heavy Arty.	Apr., 1864	From Ammunition Train Guard Pot.	To Kitching's H. A. Brig. 5-Corps.	May, 1864
15th N. Y. Heavy Arty.	Apr., 1864	From Def. of Washington 22-Corps.	To Kitching's H. A. Brig. 5-Corps.	May, 1864

2d VOLUNTEER BRIGADE, ARTILLERY RESERVE.—

Unit	Date	From	To	Date
1st Conn. Heavy A. B. M.	May, 1863	From Arty. Res. Potomac.	To 1-Brig. Arty. Res. Potomac.	Nov., 1863
5th N. Y. Indpt. Batty.	May, 1863	From Arty. Res. Potomac.	To 1-Brig. Arty. Res. Potomac.	Nov., 1863
15th N. Y. Indpt. Batty.	May, 1863	From Arty. Res. Potomac.	To 1-Vol. Brig. Arty. Res. Potomac.	July, 1863
29th N. Y. Indpt. Batty.	May, 1863	From Arty. Res. Potomac.	Attached to 30th N. Y. Batty.	July, 1863
30th N. Y. Indpt. Batty.	May, 1863	From Arty. Res. Potomac.	To 1-Div. Dept. Susquehanna.	July, 1863

32d N. Y. Indpt. Batty...May, 1863	From Arty. Res. Potomac.........	To Camp Barry 22-Corps..........	July, 1863
2d Conn. Indpt. Batty...July, 1863	From Arty. 22-Corps............	To Dept. of the East.............	Aug., 1863
Batty. B, 1st N. Y. Arty..July, 1863	From Arty. Brig. 2-Corps Potomac.	To 1-Brig. Arty. Res. Potomac...	Dec., 1863
Batty. C, 1st W. Va. Arty.Oct., 1863	From 4-Vol. Brig. Arty. Res. Pot.	To 1-Brig. Arty. Res. Potomac...	Dec., 1863
6th Maine Indpt. Batty...Dec., 1863	From 1-Vol. Brig. Arty. Res. Pot..	To Arty. Brig. 2-Corps Potomac..	Apr., 1864
9th Mass. Indpt. Batty...Dec., 1863	From 1-Vol. Brig. Arty. Res. Pot..	To Unatt. Arty. Res. Potomac..	Mch., 1864
11th N. Y. Indpt. Batty..Dec., 1863	From 3-Vol. Brig. Arty. Res. Pot..	To Unatt. Arty. Res. Potomac..	Mch., 1864
15th N. Y. Indpt. Batty..Dec., 1863	From 3-Vol. Brig. Arty. Res. Pot..	To Unatt. Arty. Res. Potomac..	Mch., 1864
Batty. H, 1st Ohio Arty..Dec., 1863	From Arty. Brig. 2-Corps Pot....	To Unatt. Arty. Res. Potomac..	Mch., 1864
Batty. H, 1st U. S. Arty..Dec., 1863	From 3-Vol. Brig. Arty. Res. Pot..	To Unatt. Arty. Res. Potomac..	Mch., 1864
Batty. K, 1st N. Y. Arty..Dec., 1863	From 3-Vol. Brig. Arty. Res. Pot..	To Camp Barry 22-Corps..........	Mch., 1864
5th Maine Indpt. Batty..Apr., 1864	From Unatt. Arty. Res. Potomac	To Arty. Brig. 6-Corps Potomac..	May, 1864
Batty. A, 1st N. J. Arty..Apr., 1864	From Unatt. Arty. Res. Potomac	To Arty. Brig. 6-Corps Potomac..	May, 1864
Batty. B, 1st N. J. Arty..Apr., 1864	From Unatt. Arty. Res. Potomac	To Arty. Brig. 2-Corps Potomac...	May, 1864
5th N. Y. Indpt. Batty..Apr., 1864	From Unatt. Arty. Res. Potomac	To Arty. Brig. 5-Corps Potomac...	May, 1864
12th N. Y. Indpt. Batty..Apr., 1864	From Unatt. Arty. Res. Potomac	To Arty. Brig. 5-Corps Potomac...	May, 1864
15th N. Y. Indpt. Batty..Apr., 1864	From Unatt. Arty. Res. Potomac	To Arty. Brig. 5-Corps Potomac...	May, 1864

3d VOLUNTEER BRIGADE, ARTILLERY RESERVE.—

1st. N. H. Batty........May, 1863	From Arty. 1-Div. 1-Corps Pot...	To Arty. Brig. 3-Corps Potomac...	Dec., 1863
Batty. F, 1st Penna. Arty.May, 1863	From Arty. 2-Div. 1-Corps Pot...	To Arty. Brig. 2-Corps Potomac..	July, 1863
Batty. G, 1st Penna. Arty.May, 1863	From Arty. 3-Div. 1-Corps Pot...	To Arty. Brig. 2-Corps Potomac..	July, 1863
Batty. C, 1st R. I. Arty..May, 1863	From Arty. 1-Div. 5-Corps Pot...	To Arty. Brig. 6-Corps Potomac..	June, 1863
Batty. C, 1st W. Va. Arty.May, 1863	From Res. Arty. 11-Corps Pot.....	To 4-Vol. Brig. Arty. Res. Pot...	Aug., 1863
Batty. H, 1st Ohio Arty..June, 1863	From 1-Vol. Brig. Arty. Res. Pot.	To 4-Vol. Brig. Arty. Res. Pot...	Aug., 1863
Batty. A, 1st Md. Arty..July, 1863	From 4-Vol. Brig. Arty. Res. Pot.	To Arty. Brig. 1-Corps Potomac..	Dec., 1863
Batty. K, 1st N. Y. Arty.July, 1863	From 4-Vol. Brig. Arty. Res. Pot.	To 2-Brig. Arty. Res. Potomac..	Dec., 1863
11th N. Y. Indpt. Batty..July, 1863	From 4-Vol. Brig. Arty. Res. Pot.	To Arty. Brig. Arty. Res. Potomac..	Dec., 1863
Batty. A, 1st N. J. Arty..Oct., 1863	From 1-Vol. Brig. Arty. Res. Pot..	To 1-Brig. Arty. Res. Potomac..	Dec., 1863
15th N. Y. Indpt. Batty..Oct., 1863	From 4-Vol. Brig. Arty. Res. Pot?	To 2-Brig. Arty. Res. Potomac..	Dec., 1863
Batty. H, 1st U. S. Arty..Oct., 1863	From 1-Reg. Brig. Arty. Res. Pot.	To 2-Brig. Arty. Res. Potomac..	Dec., 1863
9th Mass. Indpt. Batty...Apr., 1864	From Unatt. Arty. Res. Potomac..	To Arty. Brig. 5-Corps Potomac..	May, 1864
Batty. B, 1st N. Y. Arty..Apr., 1864	From Unatt. Arty. Res. Potomac..	To Arty. Brig. 5-Corps Potomac..	May, 1864
Batty. C, 1st N. Y. Arty..Apr., 1864	From Unatt. Arty. Res. Potomac..	To Arty. Brig. 5-Corps Potomac..	May, 1864
11th N. Y. Indpt. Batty..Apr., 1864	From Unatt. Arty. Res. Potomac..	To Arty. Brig. 2-Corps Potomac..	May, 1864
Batty. H, 1st Ohio Arty.Apr., 1864	From Unatt. Arty. Res. Potomac..	To Arty. Brig. 6-Corps Potomac..	May, 1864
Batty. E, 5th U. S. Arty..Apr., 1864	From Dept. Susquehanna..........	To Arty. Brig. 6-Corps Potomac...	May, 1864

4th VOLUNTEER BRIGADE, ARTILLERY RESERVE.—

Batty. A, 1st Md. Arty...May, 1863	From Arty. 1-Div. 6-Corps Pot....	To 3-Brig. Arty. Res. Potomac....	July, 1863
Batty. K, 1st N. Y. Arty..May, 1863	From Arty. 1-Div. 12-Corps Pot...	To 3-Brig. Arty. Res. Potomac....	July, 1863
11th N. Y. Indpt. Batty..May, 1863	From Arty. 3-Div. 2-Corps.......	To 3-Brig. Arty. Res. Potomac....	July, 1863
Batty. G, 1st R. I. Arty..May, 1863	From Arty. 3-Div. 2-Corps Pot....	To Arty. Brig. 6-Corps Potomac..	July, 1863
6th Maine Indpt. Batty.June, 1863	From 1-Vol. Brig. Arty. Res. Pot..	To 1-Vol. Brig. Arty. Res. Potomac..	July, 1863
Batty. A, 1st N. J. Arty..June, 1863	From Arty. Brig. 6-Corps Pot....	To 1-Vol. Brig. Arty. Res. Potomac..	July, 1863
Batty. G, 1st N. Y. Arty..June, 1863	From 1-Vol. Brig. Arty. Res. Pot..	To 3-Vol. Brig. Arty. Res. Potomac..	July, 1863
Batty. H, 1st Ohio Arty.Aug., 1863	From 3-Vol. Brig. Arty. Res. Pot..	To Arty. Brig. 2-Corps Potomac...	Oct., 1863
Batty. C, 1st W. Va. Arty.Aug., 1863	From 3-Vol. Brig. Arty. Res. Pot..	To 2-Vol. Brig. Arty. Res. Potomac..	Oct., 1863
15th N. Y. Indpt. Batty..Aug., 1863	From 1-Vol. Brig. Arty. Res. Pot..	To 3-Vol. Brig. Arty. Res. Potomac..	Oct., 1863

UNATTACHED ARTILLERY RESERVE.—

Batty. B, 1st Md. Arty..May, 1863	From Patrick's Provost Guard Pot.	To Camp Barry 22-Corps..........	June, 1863
12th Ohio Indpt. Batty..May, 1863	From Patrick's Provost Guard Pot.	To Camp Barry 22-Corps..........	June, 1863
6th N. Y. Heavy Arty....July, 1863	From 3-Prov'l. Brig. French's Div.	To Ammunition Train Guard Pot..	Aug., 1863
4th N. J. Infy...........July, 1863	From 1-Brig. 1-Div. 6-Corps Pot..	To 1-Brig. 1-Div. 6-Corps Potomac.	July, 1863
32d Mass. Infy Co. C....July, 1863	From 2-Brig. 1-Div. 5-Corps Pot..	To 2-Brig. 1-Div. 5-Corps Pot...	July, 1863

SIEGE ARTILLERY.—

1st Conn. Heavy Arty...Mch., 1862	From Def. of Washington..........	To Def. of Washington...........	July, 1862
1st Conn. H. A. B. and M.Oct., 1862	From Def. of Washington..........	To 2-Vol. Brig. Arty. Res. Pot.....	May, 1863
1st Conn. Heavy Arty...Mch., 1865	From Dept. Va. and N. C.........	To Dept. of Virginia.............	May, 1865
3d Conn. Indpt. Batty..Mch., 1865	From Dept. Va. and N. C.........	To Dept. of Virginia.............	May, 1865

EINGINEER BRIGADE.—

15th N. Y. Engineers....Mch., 1862	From Unatt. Potomac.............	No change to Muster Out.........	June, 1865
50th N. Y. Engineers..Mch., 1862	From Unatt. Potomac.............	No change to Muster Out.........	June, 1865
Batt. U. S. Engineers..Mch., 1862	From Unatt. Potomac.............	To Dept. Washington............	June, 1865
8th Del. Infy............Oct., 1864	From New Organization..........	To Provost Guard Potomac.......	Dec., 1864
61st Mass. Infy........Oct., 1864	From New Organization..........	To Collis Indpt. Brig. 9-Corps Pot.	Mch., 1865
18th N. H. Infy........Oct., 1864	From New Organization..........	To Def. Bermuda Hundred........	Dec., 1864
1st Maine Sharpshooters.Dec., 1864	From New Organization..........	To 3-Brig. 1-Div. 5-Corps Pot....	Jan., 1865
Hall's Mich. S. S......Jan., 1865	From New Organization..........	To Consol. with 1st Mich. S. S...	Apr., 1865

CAVALRY RESERVE.—	**COMMANDER.**		
Philip St. Geo. Cooke..	Brigadier General................	March 13, 1861 to July 5, 1861.	
1st BRIGADE.—			
Col. Wm. H. Emery...			
5th U. S. Cav..........Mch., 1862	From Cav. Res. Potomac..........	To 1-Brig. Cav. Div. Potomac.....	July, 1862
6th U. S. Cav..........Mch., 1862	From Cav. Res. Potomac..........	To 1-Brig. Cav. Div. Potomac.....	July, 1862
6th Penna. Cav.........Mch., 1862	From Cav. Res. Potomac..........	To 2-Brig. Cav. Div. Potomac.....	July, 1862

2d BRIGADE.—	**COMMANDER.**		
Geo. A. H. Blake......	Colonel		
1st U. S. Cav..........Mch., 1862	From Cav. Res. Potomac..........	To Headquarters Army Potomac...	July, 1862
8th Penna. Cav.........Mch., 1862	From Unatt. 4-Corps Potomac......	To 2-Brig. Cav. Div. Potomac.....	July, 1862
Barker's Ills. Dragoons..Mch., 1862	From Cav. Res. Potomac..........	To Headquarters Army Potomac...	Apr., 1862

INFANTRY RESERVE.—	**COMMANDER.**		
George Sykes..........	Brigadier General................		
2d U. S. Infy..........Mch., 1862	From Regular Army..............	To 2-Brig. 2-Div. 5-Corps Pot.....	May, 1862
3d U. S. Infy..........Mch., 1862	From Regular Army..............	To 1-Brig. 2-Div. 5-Corps Pot.....	May, 1862
4th U. S. Infy..........Mch., 1862	From Regular Army..............	To 1-Brig. 2-Div. 5-Corps Pot.....	May, 1862
6th U. S. Infy..........Mch., 1862	From Regular Army..............	To 2-Brig. 2-Div. 5-Corps Pot.....	May, 1862
10th U. S. Infy..........Mch., 1862	From Regular Army..............	To 2-Brig. 2-Div. 5-Corps Pot.....	May, 1862
11th U. S. Infy..........Mch., 1862	From Regular Army..............	To 2-Brig. 2-Div. 5-Corps Pot.....	May, 1862
12th U. S. Infy..........Mch., 1862	From Regular Army..............	To 1-Brig. 2-Div. 5-Corps Pot.....	May, 1862
14th U. S. Infy..........Mch., 1862	From Regular Army..............	To 1-Brig. 2-Div. 5-Corps Pot.....	May, 1862
17th U. S. Infy..........Mch., 1862	From Regular Army..............	To 2-Brig. 2-Div. 5-Corps Pot.....	May, 1862
5th N. Y. Infy..........Mch., 1862	From Dix's Div. Baltimore, Md.....	To 3-Brig. 2-Div. 5-Corps Pot.....	May, 1862

First Army Corps

Created March 3, 1862. Announced March 13, 1862. Discontinued April 4, 1862, and merged into the Department of the Rappahannock.

COMMANDER.

Irvin McDowell........	Major General.....................	March 13, 1862, to April 4, 1862.

1st DIVISION.—   **COMMANDER.**

W. B. Franklin.......	Brigadier General..................	March 13, 1862, to April 4, 1862.

1st BRIGADE. 1st DIVISION.—   **COMMANDER.**

Philip Kearny.........	Brigadier General..................	March 13, 1862, to April 4, 1862.

Unit	From	To		
1st N. J. Infy............Mch., 1862	From Kearny's Brig. Franklin's D.	To 1-Brig. 1-Div. Dept. Rappahn'k.	Apr.,	1862
2d N. J. Infy............Mch., 1862	From Kearny's Brig. Franklin's D.	To 1-Brig. 1-Div. Dept. Rappahn'k.	Apr.,	1862
3d N. J. Infy............Mch., 1862	From Kearny's Brig. Franklin's D.	To 1-Brig. 1-Div. Dept. Rappahn'k.	Apr.,	1862
4th N. J. Infy............Mch., 1862	From Kearny's Brig. Franklin's D.	To 1-Brig. 1-Div. Dept. Rappahn'k.	Apr.,	1862

2d BRIGADE. 1st DIVISION.—   **COMMANDER.**

H. W. Slocum.........	Brigadier General..................	March 13, 1862, to April 4, 1862.

Unit	From	To		
16th N. Y. Infy..........Mch., 1862	From Slocum's Brig. Franklin's D.	To 2-Brig. 1-Div. Dept. Rappahn'k.	Apr.,	1862
27th N. Y. Infy..........Mch., 1862	From Slocum's Brig. Franklin's D.	To 2-Brig. 1-Div. Dept. Rappahn'k.	Apr.,	1862
5th Maine Infy..........Mch., 1862	From Slocum's Brig. Franklin's D.	To 2-Brig. 1-Div. Dept. Rappahn'k.	Apr.,	1862
96th Penna. Infy........Mch., 1862	From Slocum's Brig. Franklin's D.	To 2-Brig. 1-Div. Dept. Rappahn'k.	Apr.,	1862

3d BRIGADE. 1st DIVISION.—   **COMMANDER.**

John Newton..........	Brigadier General..................	March 13, 1862, to April 4, 1862.

Unit	From	To		
18th N. Y. Infy..........Mch., 1862	From Newton's Brig. Franklin's D.	To 3-Brig. 1-Div. Dept. Rapphn'k..	Apr.,	1862
31st N. Y. Infy..........Mch., 1862	From Newton's Brig. Franklin's D.	To 3-Brig. 1-Div. Dept. Rapphn'k..	Apr.,	1862
32d N. Y. Infy..........Mch., 1862	From Newton's Brig. Franklin's D.	To 3-Brig. 1-Div. Dept. Rapphn'k..	Apr.,	1862
95th Penna. Infy........Mch., 1862	From Newton's Brig. Franklin's D.	To 3-Brig. 1-Div. Dept. Rapphn'k..	Apr.,	1862

ARTILLERY—1st DIVISION.—

Batty. A, 1st Mass. Arty.Mch., 1862	From Arty. Franklin's Div........	To Arty. 1-Div. Dept. Rappahn'k..	Apr.,	1862
Batty. F, 1st N. Y. Arty.Mch., 1862	From Arty. Franklin's Div........	To Arty. 1-Div. Dept. Rappahn'k..	Apr.,	1862
Batty. A, 1st N. J. Arty.Mch., 1862	From Arty. Franklin's Div........	To Arty. 1-Div. Dept. Rappahn'k..	Apr.,	1862
Batty. D, 2d U. S. Arty.Mch., 1862	From Arty. Franklin's Div........	To Arty. 1-Div. Dept. Rappahn'k..	Apr.,	1862

2d DIVISION.—   **COMMANDER.**

Geo. A. McCall........	Brigadier General..................	March 13, 1862, to April 4, 1862.

1st BRIGADE.—   **COMMANDER.**

J. F. Reynolds........	Brigadier General..................	March 13, 1862, to April 4, 1862.

Unit	From	To		
1st Penna. Res..........Mch., 1862	From Reynolds' Brig. McCall's D...	To 1-Brig. 2-Div. Dept. Rappahn'k.	Apr.,	1862
2d Penna. Res..........Mch., 1862	From Reynolds' Brig. McCall's D...	To 1-Brig. 2-Div. Dept. Rappahn'k.	Apr.,	1862
5th Penna. Res..........Mch., 1862	From Reynolds' Brig. McCall's D...	To 1-Brig. 2-Div. Dept. Rappahn'k.	Apr.,	1862
8th Penna. Res..........Mch., 1862	From Reynolds' Brig. McCall's D...	To 1-Brig. 2-Div. Dept. Rappahn'k.	Apr.,	1862

2d BRIGADE.—   **COMMANDER.**

Geo. G. Meade.........	Brigadier General..................	March 13, 1862, to April 4, 1862.

Unit	From	To		
3d Penna. Res..........Mch., 1862	From Meade's Brig. McCall's Div.	To 2-Brig. 2-Div. Dept. Rappahn'n.	Apr.,	1862
4th Penna. Res..........Mch., 1862	From Meade's Brig. McCall's Div.	To 2-Brig. 2-Div. Dept. Rappahn'k.	Apr.,	1862
7th Penna. Res..........Mch., 1862	From Meade's Brig. McCall's Div.	To 2-Brig. 2-Div. Dept. Rappahn'k.	Apr.,	1862
11th Penna. Res..........Mch., 1862	From Meade's Brig. McCall's Div.	To 2-Brig. 2-Div. Dept. Rappahn'k.	Apr.,	1862

3d BRIGADE.—   **COMMANDER.**

E. O. C. Ord...........	Brigadier General..................	March 13, 1862, to April 4, 1862.

Unit	From	To		
6th Penna. Res..........Mch., 1862	From Ord's Brig. McCall's Div....	To 3-Brig. 2-Div. Dept. Rappahn'k.	Apr.,	1862
9th Penna. Res..........Mch., 1862	From Ord's Brig. McCall's Div....	To 3-Brig. 2-Div. Dept. Rappahn'k.	Apr.,	1862
10th Penna. Res..........Mch., 1862	From Ord's Brig. McCall's Div....	To 3-Brig. 2-Div. Dept. Rappahn'k.	Apr.,	1862
12th Penna. Res..........Mch., 1862	From Ord's Brig. McCall's Div....	To 3-Brig. 2-Div. Dept. Rappahn'k.	Apr.,	1862
1st Penna. Rifles........Mch., 1862	From Meade's Brig. McCall's Div.	To 3-Brig. 2-Div. Dept. Rappahn'k.	Apr.,	1862

ARTILLERY. 2d DIVISION.—

Batty. A, 1st Pa. Arty..Mch., 1862	From Arty. McCall's Div. Pot.....	To Arty. 2-Div. Dept. Rappahn'k.	Apr.,	1862
Batty. B, 1st Pa. Arty...Mch., 1862	From Arty. McCall's Div. Pot.....	To Arty. 2-Div. Dept. Rappahn'k.	Apr.,	1862
Batty. G, 1st Pa. Arty...Mch., 1862	From Arty. McCall's Div. Pot.....	To Arty. 2-Div. Dept. Rappahn'k.	Apr.,	1862
Batty. C, 5th U. S. Arty..Mch., 1862	From Arty. McCall's Div. Pot.....	To Arty. 2-Div. Dept. Rappahn'k.	Apr.,	1862

CAVALRY, 2d DIVISION.—

Unit	From	To		
1st Penna. Cav.........Mch., 1862	From Cav. McCall's Div. Potomac.	To McCall's Div. Dept. Rappahn'k.	Apr.,	1862

3d DIVISION.—   **COMMANDER.**

Rufus King...........	Brigadier General..................	March 13, 1862, to April 4, 1862.

1st BRIGADE.—   **COMMANDER.**

C. C. Augur...........	Brigadier General..................	March 13, 1862, to April 4, 1862.

Unit	From	To		
22d N. Y. Infy..........Mch., 1862	From Augur's Brig. McDowell's D.	To 1-Brig. 3-Div. Dept. Rappahn'k.	Apr.,	1862
24th N. Y. Infy..........Mch., 1862	From Augur's Brig. McDowell's D.	To 1-Brig. 3-Div. Dept. Rappahn'k.	Apr.,	1862
30th N. Y. Infy..........Mch., 1862	From Augur's Brig. McDowell's D.	To 1-Brig. 3-Div. Dept. Rappahn'k.	Apr.,	1862
84th N. Y. (14-Bklyn)..Mch., 1862	From Augur's Brig. McDowell's D.	To 1-Brig. 3-Div. Dept. Rappahn'k.	Apr.,	1862

2d BRIGADE.—   **COMMANDERS.**

J. S. Wadsworth......	Brigadier General..................	March 13, 1862, to March 17, 1862.
M. R. Patrick..........	Brigadier General..................	March 17, 1862, to April 4, 1862.

Unit	From	To		
21st N. Y. Infy..........Mch., 1862	From Patrick's Brig. McDowell's D.	To 2-Brig. 3-Div. Dept. Rappahn'k.	Apr.,	1862
23d N. Y. Infy..........Mch., 1862	From Patrick's Brig. McDowell's D.	To 2-Brig. 3-Div. Dept. Rappahn'k.	Apr.,	1862
35th N. Y. Infy..........Mch., 1862	From Patrick's Brig. McDowell's D.	To 2-Brig. 3-Div. Dept. Rappahn'k.	Apr.,	1862
80th (20-S. M.) N. Y....Mch., 1862	From Patrick's Brig. McDowell's D.	To 2-Brig. 3-Div. Dept. Rappahn'k.	Apr.,	1862

3d BRIGADE.—   **COMMANDER**

L. Cutler..............	Col. 6th Wis. Infy.............	March 13, 1862, to April 4, 1862.

Unit	From	To		
2d Wis. Infy..........Mch., 1862	From King's Brig. McDowell's Div.	To 3-Brig. 3-Div. Dept. Rappahn'k.	Apr.,	1862
6th Wis. Infy..........Mch., 1862	From King's Brig. McDowell's Div.	To 3-Brig. 3-Div. Dept. Rappahn'k.	Apr.,	1862
7th Wis. Infy..........Mch., 1862	From King's Brig. McDowell's Div.	To 3-Brig. 3-Div. Dept. Rappahn'k.	Apr.,	1862
19th Ind. Infy..........Mch., 1862	From King's Brig. McDowell's Div.	To 3-Brig. 3-Div. Dept. Rappahn'k.	Apr.,	1862

```
ARTILLERY, 3d DIVISION.—
1st N. H. Batty..........Mch., 1862|From Arty. McDowell's Div. Pot...|To Arty. 3-Div. Dept. Rappahn'k..|Apr., 1862
Batty. D, 1st R. I. Arty.Mch., 1862|From Arty. McDowell's Div. Pot...|To Arty. 3-Div. Dept. Rappahn'k..|Apr., 1862
Indpt. Batty. D, Penna..Mch., 1862|From Arty. McDowell's Div. Pot...|To Arty. 3-Div. Dept. Rappahn'k..|Apr., 1862
Batty. B, 4th U. S. Arty.Mch., 1862|From Arty. McDowell's Div. Pot...|To Arty. 3-Div. Dept. Rappahn'k..|Apr., 1862
CAVALRY.—
2d N. Y. Cav............Mch., 1862|From McDowell's Div. Potomac...|To 3-Div. Dept. Rappahannock.....|Apr., 1862
```

First Army Corps

Re-created Sept. 12, 1862, from 3d Army Corps, Army of Virginia. Discontinued March 24, 1864, and merged into the 5th Army Corps, Army of the Potomac.

COMMANDERS.

Jos. Hooker..........	Major General..................	Sept. 12, 1862, to Sept. 17, 1862.	
Geo. G. Meade........	Brigadier General..............	Sept. 17, 1862, to Sept. 29, 1862.	
J. F. Reynolds........	Brigadier General..............	Sept. 29, 1862, to Jan. 2, 1863.	
J. S. Wadsworth......	Brigadier General..............	Jan. 2, 1863, to Jan. 4, 1863.	
J. F. Reynolds........	Major General..................	Jan. 4, 1863, to March 1, 1863.	
J. S. Wadsworth......	Brigadier General..............	March 1, 1863, to March 9, 1863.	
J. F. Reynolds........	Major General..................	March 9, 1863. to July 1, 1863.	Killed.
A. Doubleday.........	Major General..................	July 1, 1863, to July 2, 1863.	
John Newton..........	Major General..................	July 2, 1863, to March 24, 1864.	

1st DIVISION.— COMMANDERS.

Rufus King...........	Brigadier General..............	Sept. 12, 1862, to Sept. 14, 1862.
J. P. Hatch..........	Brigadier General..............	Sept. 14, 1862.
A. Doubleday.........	Brigadier General..............	Sept. 14, 1862, to Dec. 22, 1862.
G. R. Paul...........	Brigadier General..............	Dec. 22, 1862, to Dec. 27, 1862.
J. S. Wadsworth......	Brigadier General..............	Dec. 27, 1862, to Jan. 2, 1863.
A. Doubleday.........	Brigadier General..............	Jan. 2, 1863, to Jan. 4, 1863.
J. S. Wadsworth......	Brigadier General..............	Jan. 4, 1863, to Feb. 27, 1863.
S. Meredith..........	Brigadier General..............	Feb. 27, 1863, to March 1, 1863.
G. R. Paul...........	Brigadier General..............	March 1, 1863, to March 9, 1863.
J. S. Wadsworth......	Brigadier General..............	March 9, 1863, to July 15, 1863.
L. Cutler............	Brigadier General..............	July 15, 1863, to Aug. 5, 1863.
H. S. Briggs.........	Brigadier General..............	Aug. 5, 1863, to Aug. 23, 1863.
John C. Rice.........	Brigadier General..............	Aug. 23, 1863, to Sept. 23, 1863.
L. Cutler............	Brigadier General..............	Sept. 23, 1863, to Nov. 13, 1863.
S. Meredith..........	Brigadier General..............	Nov. 13, 1863.
L. Cutler............	Brigadier General..............	Nov. 13, 1863, to Jan. 14, 1864.
J. C. Rice...........	Brigadier General..............	Jan. 14, 1864, to Feb. 10, 1864.
L. Cutler............	Brigadier General..............	Feb. 10, 1864, to March 20, 1864.
J. C. Rice...........	Brigadier General..............	March 20, 1864, to March 24, 1864.

1st BRIGADE, 1st DIVISION.— COMMANDERS.

J. P. Hatch..........	Brigadier General..............	Sept. 12, 1862, to Sept. 14, 1862.
Walter Phelps, Jr.....	Col. 22d N. Y. Infy...........	Sept. 14, 1862, to March 20, 1863.
W. M. Searing........	Col. 30th N. Y. Infy..........	March 20, 1863, to April 9, 1863.
Walter Phelps, Jr.....	Col. 22d N. Y. Infy..........	April 9, 1863, to May 30, 1863.
E. B. Fowler.........	Col. 84th N. Y. Infy..........	May 30, 1863, to June 16, 1863.
S. Meredith..........	Brigadier General..............	June 16, 1863, to July 2, 1863.
W. W. Robinson.......	Col. 7th Wis. Infy............	July 2, 1863, to Jan. 3, 1864.
H. A. Morrow.........	Col. 24th Mich. Infy..........	Jan. 3, 1864, to Feb. 28, 1864.
W. W. Robinson.......	Col. 7th Wis. Infy............	Feb. 28, 1864, to March 24, 1864.

```
22d N. Y. Infy..........Sept., 1862|From 1-Brig. 1-Div. 3-Corps A. Va.|No change to Muster Out..........|June, 1863
24th N. Y. Infy.........Sept., 1862|From 1-Brig. 1-Div. 3-Corps A. Va.|No change to Muster Out..........|May, 1862
30th N .Y. Infy.........Sept., 1862|From 1-Brig. 1-Div. 3-Corps A. Va.|No change to Muster Out..........|June, 1863
84th N. Y. Infy.:.......Sept., 1862|From 1-Brig. 1-Div. 3-Corps A. Va.|To 2-Brig. 1-Div. 1-Corps Pot....|June, 1863
24th Mich. Infy.........Sept., 1862|From New Organization..........|To 4-Brig. 1-Div. 1-Corps Pot....|Nov., 1862
2d U. S. Sharpshooters...Sept., 1862|From 1-Brig. 1-Div. 3-Corps Pot.|To 3-Brig. 3-Div. 3-Corps Pot....|Mch., 1863
Brigade reorganized by transfer of 4-Brig. 1-Div. 1-Corps June, 1863.
19th Ind. Infy.........June, 1863|From 4-Brig. 1-Div. 1-Corps Pot.|To 1-Brig. 4-Div. 5-Corps Pot....|Mch., 1864
24th Mich. Infy.........June, 1863|From 4-Brig. 1-Div. 1-Corps Pot.|To 1-Brig. 4-Div. 5-Corps Pot....|Mch., 1864
2d Wis. Infy...........June, 1863|From 4-Brig. 1-Div. 1-Corps Pot.|To 1-Brig. 4-Div. 5-Corps Pot....|Mch., 1864
6th Wis. Infy...........June, 1863|From 4-Brig. 1-Div. 1-Corps Pot.|To 1-Brig. 4-Div. 5-Corps Pot....|Mch., 1864
7th Wis. Infy..........June, 1863|From 4-Brig. 1-Div. 1-Corps Pot.|To 1-Brig. 4-Div. 5-Corps Pot....|Mch., 1864
1st N. Y. Bat. S. S.....July, 1863|From 1-Brig. 1-Div. 7-Corps Pot.|To 1-Brig. 4-Div. 5-Corps Pot....|Mch., 1864
167th Penna. Infy.......July, 1863|From 1-Brig. 1-Div. 7-Corps D. Va.|No change to Muster Out.........|Aug., 1863
76th N. Y. Infy.........Jan., 1864|From 2-Brig. 1-Div. 1-Corps Pot.|To 2-Brig. 1-Div. 1-Corps Pot....|Mch., 1864
```

2d BRIGADE.— COMMANDERS.

A. Doubleday.........	Brigadier General..............	Sept. 12, 1862, to Sept. 14, 1862.
W. P. Wainwright......	Col. 76th N. Y. Infy..........	Sept. 14, 1862, to Sept. 17, 1862.
J. W. Hoffman........	Lt.-Col. 56th Penna. Infy..........	Sept. 17, 1862, to Nov. 9, 1862.
W. P. Wainwright......	Col. 76th N. Y. Infy..........	Nov. 9, 1862, to Nov. 20, 1862.
James Gavin..........	Col. 7th Ind. Infy............	Nov. 20, 1862, to Dec. 22, 1862.
A. Doubleday.........	Brigadier General..............	Dec. 22, 1862, to Dec. 28, 1862.
Geo. H. Biddle........	Col. 95th N. Y. Infy..........	Dec. 28, 1862, to Jan. 4, 1863.
A. Doubleday.........	Brigadier General..............	Jan. 4, 1863, to Jan. 18, 1863.
James Gavin..........	Col. 7th Ind. Infy............	Jan. 18, 1863, to March 26, 1863.
L. Cutler............	Brigadier General..............	March 26, 1863, to July 15, 1863.
E. B. Fowler.........	Col. 84th N. Y. Infy..........	July 15, 1863, to Aug. 16, 1863.
Geo. H. Biddle........	Col. 95th N. Y. Infy..........	Aug. 16, 1863, to Sept. 23, 1863.
J. C. Rice...........	Brigadier General..............	Sept. 23, 1863, to Sept. 24, 1863.
E. B. Fowler.........	Col. 95th N. Y. Infy..........	Sept. 24, 1863, to Oct. 5, 1863.
J. C. Rice...........	Brigadier General..............	Oct. 5, 1863, to Jan. 14, 1864.
J. W. Hoffman........	Col. 56th Penna. Infy..........	Jan. 14, 1864, to Feb. 10, 1864.
J. C. Rice...........	Brigadier General..............	Feb. 10, 1864, to March 24, 1864.

```
7th Ind. Infy...........Sept., 1862|From 4-Brig. 2-Div. 3-Corps A. Va.|To 1-Brig. 4-Div. 5-Corps Pot.....|Mch., 1864
76th N. Y. Infy.........Sept., 1862|From 2-Brig. 1-Div. 3-Corps A. Va.|To 1-Brig. 1-Div. 1-Corps Pot.....|Jan., 1864
95th N. Y. Infy.........Sept., 1862|From 2-Brig. 1-Div. 3-Corps A. Va.|To 2-Brig. 4-Div. 5-Corps Pot.....|Mch., 1864
56th Penna. Infy........Sept., 1862|From 2-Brig. 1-Div. 3-Corps A. Va.|To 2-Brig. 4-Div. 5-Corps Pot.....|Mch., 1864
147th N. Y. Infy........Mch., 1863|From 3-Brig. 1-Div. 1-Corps Pot.|To 2-Brig. 4-Div. 5-Corps Pot.....|Mch., 1864
84th N. Y. Infy.........June, 1863|From 1-Brig. 1-Div. 1-Corps Pot.|To 2-Brig. 4-Div. 5-Corps Pot.....|Mch., 1864
76th N. Y. Infy.........Mch., 1864|From 1-Brig. 1-Div. 1-Corps Pot...|To 2-Brig. 4-Div. 5-Corps Pot.....|Mch., 1864
```

3d BRIGADE, 1st DIVISION.—

COMMANDERS.

M. R. Patrick	Brigadier General	Sept. 12, 1862, to Oct. 6, 1862.
W. F. Rogers	Col. 21st N. Y. Infy	Oct. 6, 1862, to Oct. 14, 1862.
G. R. Paul	Brigadier General	Oct. 14, 1862, to Feb. 17, 1863.
H. M. Bossart	Col. 137th Penna. Infy	Feb. 17, 1863, to March 9, 1863.
G. R. Paul	Brigadier General	March 9, 1863, to March 29, 1862.
A. T. Berthoud	Col. 31st N. Y. Infy	March 29, 1863, to April 20, 1863.
G. R. Paul	Brigadier General	April 20, 1863, to June 16, 1863.

Brigade Discontinued June 16, 1863.

21st N. Y. Infy	Sept., 1862	From 3-Brig. 1-Div. 3-Corps A. Va.	To Provost Guard Army Potomac..	Jan.,	1863
23d N. Y. Infy	Sept., 1862	From 3-Brig. 1-Div. 3-Corps A. Va.	To Provost Guard Army Potomac..	Jan.,	1863
35th N. Y. Infy	Sept., 1862	From 3-Brig. 1-Div. 3-Corps A. Va.	To Provost Guard Army Potomac..	Jan.,	1863
80th N. Y. Infy	Sept., 1862	From 3-Brig. 1-Div. 3-Corps A. Va.	To Provost Guard Army Potomac..	Jan.,	1863
147th N. Y. Infy	Jan., 1863	From Provost Guard Army Pot...	To 2-Brig. 1-Div. 1-Corps Pot..	Mch.,	1863
22d N. J. Infy	Jan., 1863	From Provost Guard Army Pot...	No change to Muster Out	June,	1863
29th N. J. Infy	Jan., 1863	From Provost Guard Army Pot...	No change to Muster Out	June,	1863
30th N. J. Infy	Jan., 1863	From Provost Guard Army Pot...	No change to Muster Out	June,	1863
31st N. J Infy	Jan., 1863	From Provost Guard Army Pot...	No change to Muster Out	June,	1863
137th Penna. Infy	Jan., 1863	From Provost Guard Army Pot...	No change to Muster Out	June,	1863

4th BRIGADE.—

COMMANDERS.

John Gibbon	Brigadier General	Sept. 12, 1862, to Nov. 6, 1862.
L. Cutler	Col. 6th Wis. Infy	Nov. 5, 1862, to Nov. 26, 1862.
S. Meredith	Brigadier General	Nov. 26, 1862, to Dec. 13, 1862.
W. W. Robinson	Col. 7th Wis. Infy	Dec. 13, 1862, to March 1, 1863.
S. Meredith	Brigadier General	March 1, 1863, to June 16, 1862.

Designation changed to 1-Brig. 1-Div. June 16, 1863.

2d Wis. Infy	Sept., 1862	From 4-Brig. 1-Div. 3-Corps A. Va.	To 1-Brig. 1-Div. 1-Corps Pot....	June,	1863
6th Wis. Infy	Sept., 1862	From 4-Brig. 1-Div. 3-Corps A. Va.	To 1-Brig. 1-Div. 1-Corps Pot....	June,	1863
7th Wis. Infy	Sept., 1862	From 4-Brig. 1-Div. 3-Corps A. Va.	To 1-Brig. 1-Div. 1-Corps Pot....	June,	1863
19th Ind. Infy	Sept., 1862	From 4-Brig. 1-Div. 3-Corps A. Va.	To 1-Brig. 1-Div. 1-Corps Pot....	June,	1863
24th Mich. Infy	Nov., 1862	From 1-Brig. 1-Div. 1-Corps Pot...	To 1-Brig. 1-Div. 1-Corps Pot....	June,	1863

ARTILLERY, 1st DIVISION.—

1st N. H. Batty	Sept., 1862	From Arty. 1-Div. 3-Corps A. Va.	To 3-Vol. Brig. Arty. Res. Pot...	May,	1863
Batty. D, 1st R. I. Arty	Sept., 1862	From Arty. 1-Div. 3-Corps A. Va.	To Arty. 2-Div. 9-Corps Potomac..	Oct.,	1862
Batty. L, 1st N. Y. Arty	Sept., 1862	From Arty. 1-Div. 3-Corps A. Va.	To Arty. Brigade 1-Corps Potomac.	May,	1863
Batty. B, 1st U. S. Arty	Sept., 1862	From Arty. 1-Div. 3-Corps A. Va.	To Arty. Brigade 1-Corps Potomac.	May,	1863

2d DIVISION.—

COMMANDERS.

J. B. Ricketts	Brigadier General	Sept. 12, 1862, to Oct. 4, 1862.
Nelson Taylor	Brigadier General	Oct. 4, 1862, to Nov. 5, 1862.
John Gibbon	Brigadier General	Nov. 5, 1862, to Dec. 13, 1862.
Nelson Taylor	Brigadier General	Dec. 13, 1862, to Dec. 30, 1862.
J. C. Robinson	Brigadier General	Dec. 30, 1862, to Mch. 24, 1864.
S. H. Leonard	Col. 13th Mass. Infy	Temp'y in Feby., 1863.

1st BRIGADE.—

COMMANDERS.

Abram Duryea	Brigadier General	Sept. 12, 1862, to Oct. 5, 1862.
T. F. McCoy	Col. 107th Penna. Infy	Oct. 5, 1862, to Nov. 15, 1862.
A. R. Root	Col. 94th N. Y. Infy	Nov. 15, 1862, to May 11, 1863.
T. F. McCoy	Col. 107th Penna. Infy	May 11, 1863, to May 21, 1863.
S. H. Leonard	Col. 13th Mass. Infy	May 21, 1863, to June 17, 1863.
G. R. Paul	Brigadier General	June 17, 1863, to July 1, 1863.
S. H. Leonard	Col. 13th Mass. Infy	July 1, 1863.
A. R. Root	Col. 94th N. Y. Infy	July 1, 1863.
Richard Coulter	Col. 11th Penna. Infy	July 1, 1863, to July 3, 1863.
Peter Lyle	Col. 90th Penna. Infy	July 3, 1863.
Richard Coulter	Col. 11th Penna. Infy	July 3, 1863, to July 5, 1863.
Peter Lyle	Col. 90th Penna. Infy	July 5, 1863, to Dec. 11, 1863.
T. F. McCoy	Col. 107th Penna. Infy	Dec. 11, 1863, to Jany. 31, 1864.
S. H. Leonard	Col. 13th Mass. Infy	Jany. 31, 1864, to Mch. 24, 1864.

97th N. Y. Infy	Sept., 1862	From 1-Brig. 2-Div. 3-Corps A'y Va.	To 3-Brig. 2-Div. 1-Corps Pot....	Dec.,	1862
104th N. Y. Infy	Sept., 1862	From 1-Brig. 2-Div. 3-Corps A'y Va.	To 1-Brig. 2-Div. 5-Corps Pot....	Mch.,	1864
105th N. Y. Infy	Sept., 1862	From 1-Brig. 2-Div. 3-Corps A'y Va.	To Consol. with 97th N. Y	Mch.,	1863
107th Penna. Infy	Sept., 1862	From 1-Brig. 2-Div. 3-Corps A'y Va.	To 1-Brig. 2-Div. 5-Corps Pot....	Mch.,	1864
16th Me. Infy	Nov., 1862	From 3-Brig. 2-Div. 1-Corps Pot.	To 1-Brig. 2-Div. 5-Corps Pot....	Mch.,	1864
94th N. Y. Infy	Dec., 1862	From 2-Brig. 2-Div. 1-Corps Pot.	To Prov. Guard Army Potomac	May,	1863
13th Mass. Infy	May, 1863	From 3-Brig. 2-Div. 1-Corps Pot.	To 1-Brig. 2-Div. 5-Corps Pot....	Mch.,	1864
94th N. Y. Infy	June, 1863	From Prov. Guard, Army Potomac.	To Dist. Annapolis 8-Corps	Dec.,	1863
11th Penna. Infy	July, 1863	From 2-Brig. 2-Div. 1-Corps Pot...	To 2-Brig. 2-Div. 1-Corps Pot....	July,	1863
39th Mass. Infy	July, 1863	From Dist. Wash., 22 Corps	To 1-Brig. 2-Div. 5-Corps Pot....	Mch.,	1864

2d BRIGADE, 2d DIVISION.—

COMMANDERS.

W. H. Christian	Col. 26th N. Y. Infy	Sept. 12, 1862, to Sept. 18, 1862.
Peter Lyle	Col. 90th Penna. Infy	Sept. 18, 1862, to April 21, 1863.
Henry Baxter	Brigadier General	April 21, 1863, to Dec. 31, 1863.
Chas. Wheelock	Col. 97th Penna. Infy	Dec. 31, 1863, to Feby. 2, 1864.
Henry Baxter	Brigadier General	Feby. 2, 1864, to Mch. 24, 1864.

26th N. Y. Infy	Sept., 1862	From 2-Brig. 2-Div. 3-Corps A'y Va.	No change to Muster Out	June,	1863
94th N. Y. Infy	Sept., 1862	From 2-Brig. 2-Div. 3-Corps A'y Va.	To 1-Brig. 2-Div. 1-Corps Pot....	Dec.,	1862
88th Penna. Infy	Sept., 1862	From 2-Brig. 2-Div. 3-Corps A'y Va.	To 3-Brig. 2-Div. 1-Corps Pot....	Mch.,	1863
90th Penna. Infy	Sept., 1862	From 2-Brig. 2-Div. 3-Corps A'y Va.	To 2-Brig. 2-Div. 5-Corps Pot....	Mch.,	1864
12th Mass. Infy	Nov., 1862	From 3-Brig. 2-Div. 1-Corps Pot.	To 2-Brig. 2-Div. 5-Corps Pot....	Mch.,	1864
136th Penna. Infy	Nov., 1862	From Def. Washington N. Pot.	No change to Muster Out	May,	1863
83rd N. Y. Infy	May, 1863	From 3-Brig. 2-Div. 1-Corps Pot...	To 2-Brig. 2-Div. 5-Corps Pot....	May,	1864
97th N. Y. Infy	May, 1863	From 3-Brig. 2-Div. 1-Corps Pot...	To 2-Brig. 2-Div. 5-Corps Pot....	May,	1864
11th Penna. Infy	May, 1863	From 3-Brig. 2-Div. 1-Corps Pot...	To 1-Brig. 2-Div. 1-Corps Pot....	July,	1863
88th Penna. Infy	July, 1863	From 3-Brig. 2-Div. 1-Corps Pot...	To 2-Brig. 2-Div. 5-Corps Pot....	Mch.,	1864
11th Penna. Infy	July, 1863	From 1-Brig. 2-Div. 1-Corps Pot...	To 2-Brig. 2-Div. 5-Corps Pot....	Mch.,	1864

3d BRIGADE, 1st DIVISION.—

COMMANDERS.

Geo. L. Hartsuff	Brigadier General	Sept. 12, 1862, to Sept. 17, 1862.
Richard Coulter	Col. 11th Penna. Infy	Sept. 17, 1862, to Oct. 4, 1862.
Nelson Taylor	Brigadier General	Oct. 4, 1862, to Dec. 13, 1862.
S. H. Leonard	Col. 13th Mass. Infy	Dec. 13, 1862, to Dec. 30, 1862.
Nelson Taylor	Brigadier General	Dec. 30, 1862, to Jany. 23, 1863.
S. H. Leonard	Col. 13th Mass. Infy	Jany. 23, 1863, to Feby. 17, 1863.

3d BRIGADE, 1st DIVISION.—Continued. COMMANDERS.

Chas. Wheelock	Col. 97th N. Y. Infy.............	Feby. 17, 1863, to Mch. 17, 1863.
Richard Coulter	Col. 11th Penna. Infy...........	Mch. 17, 1863, to Apr. 10, 1863.
S. H. Leonard.........	Col. 13th Mass. Infy...........	Apr. 10, 1863, to May 20, 1863.

Brigade discontinued May 20, 1863.

16th Me. Infy............Sept., 1862	From New Organization...........	To 1-Brig. 2-Div. 1-Corps Pot......	Nov., 1862
12th Mass. Infy........Sept., 1862	From 3-Brig. 2-Div. 3-Corps A'y Va.	To 2-Brig. 2-Div. 1-Corps Pot......	Dec., 1862
13th Mass. Infy........Sept., 1862	From 3-Brig. 2-Div. 3-Corps A'y Va.	To 1-Brig. 2-Div. 1-Corps Pot......	May, 1863
83rd (9-S. M.) N. Y. Infy.Sept., 1862	From 3-Brig. 2-Div. 3-Corps A'y Va.	To 2-Brig. 2-Div. 1-Corps Pot......	May, 1863
11th Penna. Infy.........Sept., 1862	From 3-Brig. 2-Div. 3-Corps A'y Va.	To 2-Brig. 2-Div. 1-Corps Pot......	May, 1863
97th N. Y. Infy..........Dec., 1862	From 1-Brig. 2-Div. 1-Corps Pot...	To 2-Brig. 2-Div. 1-Corps Pot......	May, 1863
88th Penna. Infy.........Mch., 1863	From 2-Brig. 2-Div. 1-Corps Pot...	To 2-Brig. 2-Div. 1-Corps Pot......	May, 1863

ARTILLERY, 2d DIVISION.—

Batty. F, 1st Penna. Arty.Sept., 1862	From Arty. 2-Div. 3-Corps A'y Va.	To Arty. 3-Div. 1-Corps Pot........	Jany., 1863
Ind. Batty. C, Penna. Arty.Sept., 1862	From Arty. 2-Div. 3-Corps A'y Va.	To 1-Vol. Brig. Arty. Res. Pot......	May, 1863
2d Me. Ind. Batty........Sept., 1862	From Arty. 2-Div. 3-Corps A'y Va.	To Arty. Brig. 1-Corps Pot........	May, 1863
5th Me. Ind. Batty.......Sept., 1862	From Arty. 2-Div. 3-Corps A'y Va.	To Arty. Brig. 1-Corps Pot........	May, 1863
Batty. C, 5th U. S. Arty..Feby., 1863	From Arty. 3-Div. 1-Corps Pot....	To 1st Reg. Brig. Arty. Res. Pot...	May, 1863

3d DIVISION.— COMMANDERS.

Geo. G. Meade........	Brigadier General	Sept. 12, 1862, to Sept. 17, 1862.
Truman Seymour	Brigadier General	Sept. 17, 1862, to Sept. 29, 1862.
Geo. G. Meade........	Brigadier General	Sept. 29, 1862, to Dec. 25, 1862.
H. G. Sickel...........	Col. 3d Penna. Reserves.......	Dec. 25, 1862, to Jany. 11, 1863.
J. R. Kenley...........	Brigadier General	Jany. 11, 1863, to Jany. 18, 1863.
A. Doubleday	Brigadier General	Jany. 18, 1863, to Feby. 3, 1863.
R. P. Cummings	Col. 142d Penna. Infy.........	Feby. 3, 1863, to Feby. 5, 1863.
A. Doubleday	Brigadier General	Feby. 5, 1863, to June 30, 1863.
T. A. Rowley..........	Brigadier General	June 30, 1863, to July 2, 1863.
A. Doubleday	Major General	July 2, 1863, to July 11, 1863.
J. R. Kenly...........	Brigadier General	July 11, 1863, to Mch. 24, 1864.

1st BRIGADE, 3d DIVISION.— COMMANDERS.

Truman Seymour	Brigadier General	Sept. 12, 1862, to Sept. 17, 1862.
R. B. Roberts.........	Col. 1st Penna. Reserves.......	Sept. 17, 1862, to Sept. 29, 1862.
Truman Seymour	Brigadier General	Sept. 29, 1862, to Nov. 14, 1862.
Wm. Sinclair	Col. 6th Penna. Reserves.......	Nov. 14, 1862, to Dec. 13, 1862.
W. McCandless	Col. 2d Penna. Reserves...........	Dec. 13, 1862, to Feby. 17, 1863.
Jas. R. Porter	Col. 135th Penna. Infy.........	Feby. 17, 1863, to Mch. 28, 1863.
T. A. Rowley..........	Brigadier General	Mch. 28, 1863, to June 30, 1863.
Chapman Biddle	Col. 121st Penna. Infy.........	June 30, 1863, to July 2, 1863.
T. A. Rowley..........	Brigadier General	July 2, 1863, to July 10, 1863.
Chapman Biddle	Col. 121st Penna. Infy.........	July 10, 1863, to Sept. 14, 1863.
A. B. McCalmont......	Lt.-Col. 142d Penna. Infy.......	Sept. 14, 1863, to Oct. 14, 1863.
Chapman Biddle	Col. 121st Penna. Infy.........	Oct. 14, 1863, to Dec. 28, 1863.
L. Wistar	Col. 150th Penna. Infy.........	Dec. 28, 1863, to Feby. 12, 1864.
E. L. Dana............	Col. 143d Penna. Infy.........	Feby. 12, 1864, to Mch. 24, 1864.

1st Penna. Reserves.....Sept., 1862	From 1-Brig. 3-Div. 3-Corps A'y Va.	To 1-Brig. Pa. Res. Div. 22 Corps..	Feb., 1863
2d Penna. Reserves.....Sept., 1862	From 1-Brig. 3-Div. 3-Corps A'y Va.	To 1-Brig. Pa. Res. Div. 22 Corps..	Feb., 1863
5th Penna. Reserves.....Sept., 1862	From 1-Brig. 3-Div. 3-Corps A'y Va.	To 3-Brig. 3-Div. 1-Corps Pot......	Nov., 1862
6th Penna. Reserves.....Sept., 1862	From 1-Brig. 3-Div. 3-Corps A'y Va.	To 1-Brig. Pa. Res. Div. 22 Corps..	Feb., 1863
13th Penna. Reserves.....Sept., 1862	From 1-Brig. 3-Div. 3-Corps A'y Va.	To 1-Brig. Pa. Res. Div. 22 Corps..	Feb., 1863
121st Penna. Infy........Oct., 1862	From New Organization...........	To 3-Brig. 4-Div. 5-Corps Pot......	Mch., 1864
135th Penna. Infy.......Feby., 1863	From Def. of Washington........	No change to Muster Out...........	May, 1863
142d Penna. Infy.......Feby., 1863	From 2-Brig. 3-Div. 1-Corps Pot...	To 3-Brig. 4-Div. 5-Corps Pot......	Mch., 1864
151st Penna. Infy.......Feby., 1863	From Def. of Washington........	No change to Muster Out...........	July, 1863
80th N. Y. Infy.........June, 1863	From Provost Guard Potomac......	To Provost Guard Potomac........	July, 1863
143d Penna. Infy.......Dec., 1863	From 2-Brig. 3-Div. 1-Corps Pot...	To 3-Brig. 4-Div. 5-Corps Pot......	Mch., 1864
149th Penna. Infy.......Dec., 1863	From 2-Brig. 3-Div. 1-Corps Pot...	To 3-Brig. 4-Div. 5-Corps Pot......	Mch., 1864
150th Penna. Infy.......Dec., 1863	From 2-Brig. 3-Div. 1-Corps Pot...	To 3-Brig. 4-Div. 5-Corps Pot......	Mch., 1864

2d BRIGADE.— COMMANDERS.

A. L. Majilton.........	Col. 4th Penna. Reserves...........	Sept. 12, 1862, to Dec. 27, 1862.
R. P. Cummings.......	Col. 142d Penna. Infy...........	Dec. 27, 1862, to Feby. 16, 1863.
Roy Stone	Brigadier General	Feby. 16, 1863, to July 1, 1863.
L. Wistar	Col. 150th Penna. Infy...........	July 1, 1863.
E. L. Dana............	Col. 143d Penna. Infy...........	July 1, 1863, to Aug. 22, 1863.
L. Wistar	Col. 150th Penna. Infy...........	Aug. 22, 1863, to Dec. 28, 1863.
Chas. E. Phelps.......	Col. 7th Md. Infy...............	Dec. 28, 1863, to Jany. 20, 1864.
N. T. Dushane........	Col. 1st Md. Infy...............	Jany. 20, 1864, to Mch. 24, 1864.

3d Penna. Reserves.....Sept., 1862	From 2-Brig. 3-Div. 3-Corps A'y Va.	To 2-Brig. Pa. Res. Div. 22-Corps...	Feb., 1863
4th Penna. Reserves.....Sept., 1862	From 2-Brig. 3-Div. 3-Corps A'y Va.	To 2-Brig. Pa. Res. Div. 22-Corps...	Feb., 1863
7th Penna. Reserves.....Sept., 1862	From 2-Brig. 3-Div. 3-Corps A'y Va.	To 2-Brig. Pa. Res. Div. 22-Corps...	Feb., 1863
8th Penna. Reserves.....Sept., 1862	From 2-Brig. 3-Div. 3-Corps A'y Va.	To 2-Brig. Pa. Res. Div. 22-Corps...	Feb., 1863
142d Penna. Infy........Oct., 1862	From New Organization...........	To 1-Brig. 3-Div. 1-Corps Pot......	Feb., 1863
143d Penna. Infy.......Feb., 1863	From Def. of Washington........	To 1-Brig. 3-Div. 1-Corps Pot......	Dec., 1863
149th Penna. Infy.......Feb., 1863	From Def. of Washington........	To 1-Brig. 3-Div. 1-Corps Pot......	Dec., 1863
150th Penna. Infy.......Feb., 1863	From Def. of Washington........	To 1-Brig. 3-Div. 1-Corps Pot......	Dec., 1863
Brigade consolidated with 1-Brig. Dec. 28, 1863. Reorg. by transfer of 3-Brig. 3-Div. Dec. 28, 1863.			
1st Md. Infy............Dec., 1863	From 3-Brig. 3-Div. 1-Corps Pot...	To 3-Brig. 2-Div. 5-Corps Pot......	Mch., 1864
4th Md. Infy............Dec., 1863	From 3-Brig. 3-Div. 1-Corps Pot...	To 3-Brig. 2-Div. 5-Corps Pot......	Mch., 1864
6th Md. Infy............Dec., 1863	From 3-Brig. 3-Div. 1-Corps Pot...	To 3-Brig. 2-Div. 5-Corps Pot......	Mch., 1864
8th Md. Infy............Dec., 1863	From 3-Brig. 3-Div. 1-Corps Pot...	To 3-Brig. 2-Div. 5-Corps Pot......	Mch., 1864

3d BRIGADE, 3d DIVISION.— COMMANDERS.

T. F. Gallagher........	Col. 11th Penna. Reserves........	Sept. 12, 1862, to Sept. 14, 1862.	
R. Anderson	Lt.-Col. 9th Penna. Reserves......	Sept. 14, 1862	
J. W. Fisher..........	Col. 5th Penna. Reserves.........	Sept. 14, 1862, to Oct. 2, 1862.	
C. F. Jackson........	Brigadier General	Oct. 2, 1862, to Dec. 13, 1862.	Killed.
J. W. Fisher.........	Col. 5th Penna. Reserves.........	Dec. 13, 1862, to Dec. 30, 1862.	
M. D. Hardin.........	Col. 12th Penna. Reserves.......	Dec. 30, 1862, to Jan. 10, 1863.	
J. W. Fisher.........	Col. 5th Penna. Reserves.........	Jan. 10, 1863, to Feb. 12, 1863.	

Brigade discontinued Feb. 12, 1863. Reorg. by assignment of Regiments June 25, 1863.

Geo. J. Stannard......	Brigadier General	June 25, 1863, to July 3, 1863.
F. V. Randall.........	Col. 13th Vt. Infy...............	July 3, 1863, to July 11, 1863.
N. T. Dushane........	Col. 1st Md. Infy...............	July 11, 1863, to Dec. 28, 1863.

Brigade discontinued Dec. 28, 1863. Designated 2-Brig. 3-Div. 1-Corps.

3d BRIGADE, 3d DIVISION.—Continued.

9th Penna. Reserves.....Sept., 1862	From 3-Brig. 3-Div. 3-Corps A'y Va..	To 3-Brig. Pa. Res. Div. 22-Corps...	Feb., 1863
10th Penna. Reserves.....Sept., 1862	From 3-Brig. 3-Div. 3-Corps A'y Va..	To 3-Brig. Pa. Res. Div. 22-Corps...	Feb., 1863
11th Penna. Reserves.....Sept., 1862	From 3-Brig. 3-Div. 3-Corps A'y Va..	To 3-Brig. Pa. Res. Div. 22-Corps...	Feb., 1863
12th Penna. Reserves.....Sept., 1862	From 3-Brig. 3-Div. 3-Corps A'y Va..	To 3-Brig. Pa. Res. Div. 22-Corps...	Feb., 1863
5th Penna. Reserves.....Nov., 1862	From 1-Brig. 3-Div. 1-Corps Pot...	To 3-Brig. Pa. Res. Div. 22-Corps...	Feb., 1863
12th Vt. Infy...........June, 1863	From 2-Br. Abercrombie's Div. 22-C.	No change to Muster Out..........	July, 1863
13th Vt. Infy...........June, 1863	From 2-Br. Abercrombie's Div. 22-C.	No change to Muster Out..........	July, 1863
14th Vt. Infy...........June, 1863	From 2-Br. Abercrombie's Div. 22-C.	No change to Muster Out..........	July, 1863
15th Vt. Infy...........June, 1863	From 2-Br. Abercrombie's Div. 22-C.	No change to Muster Out..........	July, 1863
16th Vt. Infy...........June, 1863	From 2-Br. Abercrombie's Div. 22-C.	No change to Muster Out..........	July, 1863
1st Md. Infy..........July, 1863	From Md. Brig. French's Div. 8-C..	To 2-Brig. 3-Div. 1-Corps Pot......	Dec., 1863
4th Md. Infy..........July, 1863	From Md. Brig. French's Div. 8-C..	To 2-Brig. 3-Div. 1-Corps Pot......	Dec., 1863
7th Md. Infy..........July, 1863	From Md. Brig. French's Div. 8-C..	To 2-Brig. 3-Div. 1-Corps Pot......	Dec., 1863
8th Md. Infy..........July, 1863	From Md. Brig. French's Div. 8-C..	To 2-Brig. 3-Div. 1-Corps Pot......	Dec., 1863

ARTILLERY, 3d DIVISION.—

Batty. A, 1st Pa. Arty...Sept., 1862	From Arty. 3-Div. 3-Corps A'y Va..	To Arty. 3-Div. 9-Corps Pot......	Feb., 1863
Batty. B, 1st Pa. Arty...Sept., 1862	From Arty. 3-Div. 3-Corps A'y Va..	To Arty. Brig. 1-Corps Pot........	May, 1863
Batty. G, 1st Pa. Arty...Sept., 1862	From Arty. 3-Div. 3-Corps A'y Va..	To 3-Vol. Brig. Arty. Res. Pot.....	May, 1863
Batty C, 5th U. S. Arty...Sept., 1862	From Arty. 3-Div. 3-Corps A'y Va..	To Arty. 2-Div. 1-Corps Pot......	Jan., 1863
Batty. F, 1st Pa. Arty....Jan., 1863	From Arty. 2-Div. 1-Corps Pot...	To 3-Vol. Brig. Arty. Res. Pot.....	May, 1863

ARTILLERY BRIGADE, 1st ARMY CORPS.—

2d Me. Ind. Batty.......May, 1863	From Arty. 2-Div. 1-Corps Pot...	To Camp Barry, Wash., 22 Corps...	Oct., 1863
5th Me. Ind. Batty......May, 1863	From Arty. 2-Div. 1-Corps Pot...	To 2-Brig. Arty. Res. Pot........	Mch., 1864
Batty. L, 1st N. Y. Arty...May, 1863	From Arty. 1-Div. 1-Corps Pot...	To Arty. Brig. 5-Corps Pot........	Mch., 1864
Batty. B, 1st Pa. Arty...May, 1863	From Arty. 3-Div. 1-Corps Pot...	To Arty. Brig. 5-Corps Pot........	Mch., 1864
Batty. B, 4th U. S. Arty...May, 1863	From Arty. 1-Div. 1-Corps Pot...	To Arty. Brig. 5-Corps Pot........	Mch., 1864
Batty. E, 1st N. Y. Arty...June, 1863	From Arty. 3-Div. 6-Corps Pot...	To Arty. Brig. 5-Corps Pot........	Mch., 1864
Batty. H, 1st N. Y. Arty...Oct., 1863	From Camp Barry, Wash., 22-Corps.	To Arty. Brig. 5-Corps Pot........	Mch., 1864
Batty. A, Md. Arty.......Oct., 1863	From 3-Vol. Brig. Arty. Res. Pot...	To Camp Barry, Wash., 22-Corps...	Mch., 1864

Second Army Corps

Created March 3, 1862, by the President of the United States. Announced March 13, 1862, in General Order No. 101, Army of the Potomac. Discontinued June 28, 1865.

CORPS COMMANDERS.

E. V. Sumner........	Major General	Mch. 13, 1862, to Oct. 7, 1862.	
D. N. Couch.........	Major General	Oct. 7, 1862, to Dec. 26, 1862.	
John Sedgwick	Major General	Dec. 26, 1862, to Jan. 26, 1863.	
O. O. Howard........	Major General	Jan. 26, 1863, to Feb. 5, 1863.	
D. N. Couch.........	Major General	Feb. 5, 1863, to May 22, 1863.	
W. S. Hancock.......	Major General	May 22, 1863, to July 1, 1863.	
John Gibbon	Brigadier General	July 1, 1863, to July 2, 1863.	
W. S. Hancock.......	Major General	July 2, 1863, to July 3, 1863.	
Wm. Hays	Brigadier General	July 3, 1863, to Aug. 16, 1863.	
G. K. Warren........	Major General	Aug. 16, 1863, to Aug. 26, 1863.	
J. C. Caldwell.......	Brigadier General	Aug. 26, 1863, to Sept. 2, 1863.	
G. K. Warren........	Major General	Sept. 2, 1863, to Dec. 16, 1863.	
J. C. Caldwell.......	Brigadier General	Dec. 16, 1863, to Dec. 29, 1863.	
G. K. Warren........	Major General	Dec. 29, 1863, to Jan. 9, 1864.	
J. C. Caldwell.......	Brigadier General	Jan. 9, 1864, to Jan. 15, 1864.	
G. K. Warren........	Major General	Jan. 15, 1864, to Mch. 24, 1864.	
W. S. Hancock.......	Major General	Mch. 24, 1864, to June 18, 1864.	
D. B. Birney........	Major General	June 18, 1864, to June 27, 1864.	
W. S. Hancock.......	Major General	June 27, 1864, to Nov. 26, 1864.	
A. A. Humphreys......	Major General	Nov. 26, 1864, to Feb. 15, 1865.	
Gershom Mott	Bvt. Major General.................	Feb. 15, 1865, to Feb. 17, 1865.	
N. A. Miles.........	Bvt. Major General.................	Feb. 17, 1865, to Feb. 25, 1865.	
A. A. Humphreys......	Major General	Feb. 25, 1865, to Apr. 22, 1865.	
F. C. Barlow.........	Bvt. Major General.................	Apr. 22, 1865, to May 5, 1865.	
A. A. Humphreys......	Major General	May 5, 1865, to June 9, 1865.	
Gershom Mott	Bvt. Major General.................	June 9, 1865, to June 20, 1865.	
A. A. Humphreys......	Major General	June 20, 1865, to June 28, 1865.	

1st DIVISION.— COMMANDERS.

I. B. Richardson......	Brigadier General	Mch. 13, 1862, to July 17, 1862.	
Geo. Stoneman	Brigadier General	July 17, 1862, to Aug. 15, 1862.	
I. B. Richardson......	Brigadier General	Aug. 15, 1862, to Sept. 17, 1862.	Mort. Wnd.
J. C. Caldwell.......	Brigadier General	Sept. 17, 1862.	
W. S. Hancock.......	Brigadier General	Sept. 17, 1862, to Jan. 24, 1863.	
S. K. Zook..........	Brigadier General	Jan. 24, 1863, to Feb. 20, 1863.	
W. S. Hancock.......	Brigadier General	Feb. 20, 1863, to May 22, 1863.	
J. C. Caldwell.......	Brigadier General	May 22, 1863, to Dec. 9, 1863.	
Paul Frank	Col. 52d N. Y. Infy.............	Dec. 9, 1863, to Jan. 9, 1864.	
H. L. Brown.........	Col. 145th N. Y. Infy...........	Jan. 9, 1864, to Jan. 15, 1864.	
J. C. Caldwell.......	Brigadier General	Jan. 15, 1864, to Mch. 24, 1864.	
Paul Frank	Col. 52d N. Y. Infy.............	Mch. 24, 1864, to Mch. 25, 1864.	
F. C. Barlow........	Brigadier General	Mch. 25, 1864, to July 29, 1864.	
N. A. Miles.........	Brigadier General	July 29, 1864, to Feb. 15, 1865.	
Geo. N. Macy........	Bvt. Brigadier General.............	Feb. 15, 1865, to Feb. 22, 1865.	
John Ramsey	Bvt. Brigadier General.............	Feb. 22, 1865, to Feb. 25, 1865.	
N. A. Miles.........	Bvt. Major General.................	Feb. 25, 1865, to May 20, 1865.	
John Ramsey	Bvt. Brigadier General.............	May 20, 1865, to June 28, 1865.	

1st BRIGADE, 1st DIVISION.— COMMANDERS.

O. O. Howard........	Brigadier General	Mch. 13, 1862, to June 1, 1862.	
Thos. J. Parker......	Col. 64th N. Y. Infy...........	June 1, 1862, to June 4, 1862.	
J. C. Caldwell.......	Brigadier General	June 4, 1862, to Dec. 13, 1862.	
G. Von Schack.......	Col. 7th N. Y. Infy............	Dec. 13, 1862, to Feb. 14, 1863.	
J. C. Caldwell.......	Brigadier General	Feb. 14, 1863, to May 22, 1863.	
E. E. Cross.........	Col. 5th N. H. Infy............	May 22, 1863, to July 2, 1863.	Killed.
H. B. McKean........	Col. 81st Penna. Infy...........	July 2, 1863, to July 4, 1863.	
N. A. Miles.........	Col. 61st N. Y. Infy...........	July 4, 1863, to July 19, 1863.	
James A. Beaver......	Col. 148th Penna. Infy..........	July 19, 1863, to July 28, 1863.	
N. A. Miles.........	Col. 61st N. Y. Infy...........	July 28, 1863, to Dec. 25, 1863.	

1st BRIGADE, 1st DIVISION.—Continued.   COMMANDERS.

H. B. McKean	Col. 81st Penna. Infy	Dec. 25, 1863, to Mch. 14, 1864.
K. O. Broady	Lt.-Col. 61st N. Y. Infy	Mch. 14, 1864, to Mch. 25, 1864.
N. A. Miles	Col. 61st N. Y. Infy	Mch. 25, 1864, to July 29, 1864.
J. C. Lynch	Col. 183d Penna. Infy	July 29, 1864, to Oct. 6, 1864.
Wm. Wilson	Col. 81st Penna. Infy	Oct. 6, 1864, to Oct. 27, 1864.
K. O. Broady	Col. 61st N. Y. Infy	Oct. 27, 1864, to Nov. 3, 1864.
Geo. N. Macy	Bvt. Brigadier General	Nov. 3, 1864, to Feb. 15, 1865.
G. W. Scott	Col. 61st N. Y. Infy	Feb. 15, 1865, to Mch. 17, 1865.
Geo. N. Macy	Bvt. Brigadier General	Mch. 17, 1865, to Apr. 17, 1865.
John Fraser	Col. 140th Penna. Infy	Apr. 17, 1865, to May 31, 1865.
G. W. Scott	Col. 61st N. Y. Infy	May 31, 1865, to June 20, 1865.
Wm. Wilson	Col. 81st Penna. Infy	June 20, 1865, to June 28, 1865.

5th N. H. Infy....Mch., 1862	From Howard's Brig. Sumner's Div.	To Dept. of the East.	July, 1863
61st N. Y. Infy....Mch., 1862	From Howard's Brig. Sumner's Div.	No change to Muster Out	July, 1865
64th N. Y. Infy....Mch., 1862	From Howard's Brig. Sumner's Div.	To 3-Brig. 1-Div. 2-Corps Pot	June, 1862
81st Penna. Infy....Mch., 1862	From Howard's Brig. Sumner's Div.	No change to Muster Out	June, 1865
7th N. Y. Infy....May, 1862	From Dept. of Va.	No change to Muster Out	May, 1863
64th N. Y. Infy....Aug., 1862	From 3-Brig. 1-Div. 2-Corps Pot	To 4-Brig. 1-Div. 2-Corps Pot	Apr., 1863
145th Penna. Infy....Oct., 1862	From 2-Brig. 1-Div. 2-Corps Pot	To 4-Brig. 1-Div. 2-Corps Pot	Apr., 1863
148th Penna. Infy....Dec., 1862	From New Organization	To 3-Brig. 1-Div. 2-Corps Pot	Dec., 1863
140th Penna. Infy....Sept., 1863	From 3-Brig. 1-Div. 2-Corps Pot	No change to Muster Out	May, 1865
26th Mich. Infy....Oct., 1863	From Dept. of the East	No change to Muster Out	June, 1865
183rd Penna. Infy....Apr., 1864	From New Organization	To 4-Brig. 1-Div. 2-Corps Pot	Mch., 1865
2d N. Y. Heavy Arty....May, 1864	From Tyler's H. A. Div. 2-C. Pot	To Dept. of Washington	May, 1865
28th Mass. Infy....June, 1864	From 2-Brig. 1-Div. 2-Corps Pot	To 2-Brig. 1-Div. 2-Corps Pot	Nov., 1864
5th N. H. Infy....June, 1864	From Point Lookout, Md.	No change to Muster Out	June, 1865
4th N. Y. Heavy Arty...Aug., 1864	From Arty. Res. Potomac	To 4-Brig. 1-Div. 2-Corps Pot	Sept., 1864

2d BRIGADE.—   COMMANDERS.

T. F. Meagher	Brigadier General	Mch. 13, 1862, to June 28, 1862.	
Robt. Nugent	Col. 69th N. Y. Infy	June 28, 1862, to June 29, 1862.	
T. F. Meagher	Brigadier General	June 29, 1862, to July 16, 1862.	
Robt. Nugent	Col. 69th N. Y. Infy	July 16, 1862, to Aug. 8, 1862.	
T. F. Meagher	Brigadier General	Aug. 8, 1862, to Sept. 17, 1862.	
John Burke	Col. 63d N. Y. Infy	Sept. 17, 1862, to Sept. 18, 1862.	
T. F. Meagher	Brigadier General	Sept. 18, 1862, to Dec. 20, 1862.	
P. Kelly	Col. 88th N. Y. Infy	Dec. 20, 1862, to Feb. 18, 1863.	
T. F. Meagher	Brigadier General	Feb. 18, 1863, to May 8, 1863.	
P. Kelly	Col. 88th N. Y. Infy	May 8, 1863, to Jan. 12, 1864.	
R. Byrnes	Col. 28th Mass. Infy	Jan. 12, 1864, to Feb. 14, 1864.	
A. J. Lawler	Major 28th Mass. Infy	Feb. 14, 1864, to Mch. 25, 1864.	
T. A. Smythe	Col. 1st Del. Infy	Mch. 25, 1864, to May 17, 1864.	
R. Byrnes	Col. 28th Mass. Infy	May 17, 1864, to June 3, 1864.	Mort. Wnd.
Pat'k Kelly	Col. 88th N. Y. Infy	June 3, 1864, to June 16, 1864.	Killed.
Rich'd Byrnes	Col. 28th Mass. Infy	June 16, 1864, to June 28, 1864.	

Brigade consolidated with 3d Brigade June 27, 1864, and designated Consolidated Brig. 1-Div. Reorganized Nov. 2, 1864.

D. F. Burke	Lt.-Col. 88th N. Y. Infy	Nov. 2, 1864, to Nov. 5, 1864.
Robt. Nugent	Col. 69th N. Y. Infy	Nov. 5, 1864, to Jan. 29, 1865.
R. C. Duryea	Col. 7th N. Y. Heavy Arty	Jan. 29, 1865, to Feb. 17, 1865.
Robert Nugent	Col. 69th N. Y. Infy	Feb. 17, 1865, to June 28, 1865.

63d N. Y. Infy....Mch., 1862	From Meagher's Brig. Sumner's Div.	To Consol. Brig. 1-Div. 2-Corps	June, 1864
69th N. Y. Infy....Mch., 1862	From Meagher's Brig. Sumner's Div.	To Consol. Brig. 1-Div. 2-Corps	June, 1864
88th N. Y. Infy....Mch., 1862	From Meagher's Brig. Sumner's Div.	To Consol. Brig. 1-Div. 2-Corps	June, 1864
29th Mass. Infy....June, 1862	From Dept. of Va.	To 2-Brig. 1-Div. 9-Corps Pot	Dec., 1862
145th Penna. Infy....Sept., 1862	From New Organization	To 1-Brig. 1-Div. 2-Corps Pot	Oct., 1862
116th Penna. Infy....Oct., 1862	From New Organization	To 4-Brig. 1-Div. 2-Corps Pot	June, 1864
28th Mass. Infy....Dec., 1862	From 1-Brig. 1-Div. 9-Corps Pot	To 1-Brig. 1-Div. 2-Corps Pot	June, 1864
63d N. Y. Infy....Nov., 1864	From Consol. Brig. 1-Div. 2-Corps	No change to Muster Out	June, 1865
69th N. Y. Infy....Nov., 1864	From Consol. Brig. 1-Div. 2-Corps	No change to Muster Out	June, 1865
88th N. Y. Infy....Nov., 1864	From Consol. Brig. 1-Div. 2-Corps	No change to Muster Out	June, 1865
28th Mass. Infy....Nov., 1864	From 1-Brig. 1-Div. 2-Corps Pot	No change to Muster Out	June, 1865
7th N. Y. Heavy Arty...Nov., 1864	From 4-Brig. 1-Div. 2-Corps Pot	To Baltimore, Md., 8-Corps	Feb., 1865
4th N. Y. Heavy Arty...Mch., 1865	From 4-Brig. 1-Div. 2-Corps Pot	To Dept. of Washington	June, 1865

3d BRIGADE, 1st DIVISION.—   COMMANDERS.

W. H. French	Brigadier General	Mch. 13, 1862, to July 20, 1862.	
J. R. Brooke	Col. 53d Penna. Infy	July 20, 1862, to Aug. 10, 1862.	
W. H. French	Brigadier General	Aug. 10, 1862, to Sept. 6, 1862.	
J. R. Brooke	Col. 53d Penna. Infy	Sept. 6, 1862, to Oct. 6, 1862.	
S. K. Zook	Col. 57th N. Y. Infy	Oct. 6, 1862, to Jan. 24, 1863.	
R. P. Roberts	Col. 140th Penna. Infy	Jan. 24, 1863, to Feb. 12, 1863.	
Paul Frank	Col. 52d N. Y. Infy	Feb. 12, 1863, to Mch. 24, 1863.	
S. K. Zook	Col. 57th N. Y. Infy	Mch. 24, 1863, to May 15, 1863.	
O. H. Morris	Col. 66th N. Y. Infy	May 15, 1863, to May 25, 1863.	
S. K. Zook	Col. 57th N. Y. Infy	May 25, 1863, to July 2, 1863.	Killed.
John Fraser	Lt.-Col. 140th Penna. Infy	July 2, 1863, to July 28, 1863.	
Paul Frank	Col. 52d N. Y. Infy	July 28, 1863, to Oct. 10, 1863.	
Jas. A. Beaver	Col. 148th N. Y. Infy	Oct. 10, 1863, to Dec. 12, 1863.	
Paul Frank	Col. 52d N. Y. Infy	Dec. 12, 1863, to Jan. 17, 1864.	
Jas. A. Beaver	Col. 148th Penna. Infy	Jan. 17, 1864, to Feb. 20, 1864.	
Paul Frank	Col. 52d N. Y. Infy	Feb. 20, 1864, to Mch. 20, 1864.	
A. Funk	Col. 39th N. Y. Infy	Mch. 20, 1864, to Mch. 25, 1864.	
Paul Frank	Col. 52d N. Y. Infy	Mch. 25, 1864, to May 10, 1864.	
H. L. Brown	Col. 145th N. Y. Infy	May 10, 1864, to May 12, 1864.	
C. D. McDougall	Col. 111th N. Y. Infy	May 10, 1864, to June 27, 1864.	

Brigade consolidated with 2d Brigade June 27, 1864, and designated Consolidated Brigade, 1st Division. Reorganized Nov. 2, 1864.

Geo. N. Macy	Bvt. Brig. General	No. 2, 1864, to Nov. 4, 1864.
C. D. McDougall	Col. 111th N. Y. Infy	Nov. 4, 1864, to Jan. 19, 1865.
H. J. Madill	Bvt. Brig. General	Jan. 19, 1865, to Jan. 28, 1865.
G. Von Schack	Col. 7th N. Y. Infy	Jan. 28, 1865, to Feb. 22, 1865.
Wm. M. Mintzer	Col. 53d Penna. Infy	Feb. 22, 1865, to Feb. 25, 1865.
H. J. Madill	Bvt. Brig. General	Feb. 25, 1865, to Apr. 2, 1865.
C. D. McDougall	Bvt. Brig. General	Apr. 2, 1865, to May 28, 1865.
A. Funk	Col. 39th N. Y. Infy	May 28, 1865, to June 28, 1865.

3d BRIGADE, 1st DIVISION.—Continued.

52d N. Y. Infy..........Mch., 1862	From French's Brig. Sumner's Div.	To Consol. Brig. 1-Div. 2-Corps....	June, 1864
57th N. Y. Infy..........Mch., 1862	From French's Brig. Sumner's Div.	To Consol. Brig. 1-Div. 2-Corps....	June, 1864
66th N. Y. Infy..........Mch., 1862	From French's Brig. Sumner's Div.	To 4-Brig. 1-Div. 2-Corps Pot......	Mch., 1864
53d Penna. Infy..........Mch., 1862	From French's Brig. Sumner's Div.	To 4-Brig. 1-Div. 2-Corps Pot..,,..	Apr., 1863
2d Del. Infy...........June, 1862	From Dix's Div., Baltimore, Md....	To 4-Brig. 1-Div. 2-Corps Pot......	Apr., 1863
64th N. Y. Infy........June, 1862	From 1-Brig. 1-Div. 2-Corps Pot...	To 3-Brig. 1-Div. 2-Corps Pot......	Aug., 1862
27th Conn. Infy........Nov., 1862	From Def. of Washington	To 4-Brig. 1-Div. 2-Corps Pot......	Apr., 1863
140th Penna. Infy.......Dec., 1862	From Middle Dept. 8-Corps.......	To 1-Brig. 1-Div. 2-Corps Pot......	Sept., 1863
148th Penna. Infy.......Sept., 1863	From 1-Brig. 1-Div. 2-Corps Pot...	To 4-Brig. 1-Div. 2-Corps Pot......	Mch., 1864
7th N. Y. Infy..........Mch., 1864	From Reorganization	To Consol. Brig. 1-Div. 2-Corps....	June, 1864
39th N. Y. Infy..........Mch., 1864	From 3-Brig. 3-Div. 2-Corps Pot...	To Consol. Brig. 1-Div. 2-Corps....	June, 1864
111th N. Y. Infy..........Mch., 1864	From 3-Brig. 3-Div. 2-Corps Pot...	To Consol. Brig. 1-Div. 2-Corps....	June, 1864
125th N. Y. Infy..........Mch., 1864	From 3-Brig. 3-Div. 2-Corps Pot...	To Consol. Brig. 1-Div. 2-Corps....	June, 1864
126th N. Y. Infy..........Mch., 1864	From 3-Brig. 3-Div. 2-Corps Pot...	To Consol. Brig. 1-Div. 2-Corps....	June, 1864
7th N. Y. Infy..........Nov., 1864	From Consol. Brig. 1-Div. 2-Corps..	Hart's Island, N. Y...............	June, 1865
39th N. Y. Infy..........Nov., 1864	From Consol. Brig. 1-Div. 2-Corps..	No change to Muster Out..........	June, 1865
52d N. Y. Infy..........Nov., 1864	From Consol. Brig. 1-Div. 2-Corps..	No change to Muster Out..........	June, 1865
111th N. Y. Infy..........Nov., 1864	From Consol. Brig. 1-Div. 2-Corps..	No change to Muster Out..........	June, 1865
125th N. Y. Infy..........Nov., 1864	From Consol. Brig. 1-Div. 2-Corps..	No change to Muster Out..........	June, 1865
126th N. Y. Infy..........Nov., 1864	From Consol. Brig. 1-Div. 2-Corps..	No change to Muster Out..........	June, 1865

4th BRIGADE, 1st DIVISION.—Organized Apr. 13, 1863.

COMMANDERS.

J. R. Brooke...........	Col. 53d Penna. Infy.............	Apr. 13, 1863, to May 20, 1863.	
W. P. Bailey..........	Col. 2d Delaware Infy............	May 20, 1863, to June 12, 1863.	
J. R. Brooke...........	Col. 53d Penna. Infy.............	June 12, 1863, to Aug. 29, 1863.	
J. A. Beaver..........	Col. 148th Penna. Infy...........	Aug. 29, 1863, to Sept. 20, 1863.	
J. R. Brooke...........	Col. 53d Penna. Infy.............	Sept. 20, 1863, to Dec. 29, 1863.	
W. P. Bailey..........	Col. 2d Delaware Infy............	Dec. 29, 1863, to Jan. 10, 1864.	
L. W. Bradley........	Major 64th New York Infy..........	Jan. 10, 1864, to Feb. 12, 1864.	
H. L. Brown..........	Col. 145th Penna. Infy...........	Feb. 12, 1864, to Mch. 25, 1864.	
J. R. Brooke...........	Col. 53d Penna. Infy.............	Mch. 25, 1864, to June 3, 1864.	
O. H. Morris..........	Col. 66th New York Infy...........	June 3, 1864.	Killed.
Lewis O. Morris.......	Col. 7th New York Heavy Arty.....	June 3, 1864, to June 4, 1864.	Killed.
J. A. Beaver..........	Col. 148th Penna. Infy...........	June 4, 1864, to June 16, 1864.	
John Hastings.........	Lt.-Col. 7th New York Heavy Arty...	June 16, 1864, to June 21, 1864.	
John Fraser...........	Col. 140th Penna. Infy...........	June 21, 1864, to June 22, 1864.	
John Hastings.........	Lt.-Col. 7th N. Y. Heavy Arty.....	June 22, 1864, to July 25, 1864.	
K. O. Broady..........	Lt.-Col. 61st N. Y. Infy..........	July 25, 1864, to Aug. 25, 1864.	
Wm. Glenny...........	Lt.-Col. 64th N. Y. Infy..........	Aug. 25, 1864, to Oct. 7, 1864.	
St. C. A. Mulholland....	Lt.-Col. 116th Pa. Infy..........	Oct. 7, 1864, to Dec. 30, 1864.	
Wm. Glenny...........	Col. 64th N. Y. Infy.............	Dec. 30, 1864, to Jan. 13, 1865.	
J. Ramsey............	Col. 8th N. J. Infy..............	Jan. 13, 1865, to Apr. 20, 1865.	
W. M. Mintzer........	Col. 53d Penna. Infy............	Apr. 20, 1865, to May 20, 1865.	
St. C. A. Mulholland....	Lt.-Col. 116th Pa. Infy..........	May 20, 1865, to June 3, 1865.	
G. T. Egbert..........	Col. 183d Penna. Infy...........	June 3, 1865, to June 28, 1865.	

27th Conn. Infy.........Apr., 1863	From 3-Brig. 1-Div. 2-Corps Pot....	No change to muster out.........	July, 1863
2d Del. Infy.........Apr., 1863	From 3-Brig. 1-Div. 2-Corps Pot....	To 3-Brig. 2-Div. 2-Corps Pot....	July, 1864
64th N. Y. Infy.........Apr., 1863	From 1-Brig. 1-Div. 2-Corps Pot...	No change to muster out.........	July, 1865
53d Penna. Infy.........Apr., 1863	From 3-Brig. 1-Div. 2-Corps Pot...	No change to muster out.........	June, 1865
145th Penna. Infy.........Apr., 1863	From 1-Brig| 1-Div. 2-Corps Pot...	No change to muster out.........	June, 1865
148th Penna. Infy.........Mch., 1864	From 3-Brig. 1-Div. 2-Corps Pot...	No change to muster out.........	June, 1865
66th N. Y. Infy.........Mch., 1864	From 3-Brig. 1-Div. 2-Corps Pot...	To N. Y.......................	May, 1865
7th N. Y. Heavy Arty.....May, 1864	From Tyler's Heavy Arty. Div. 2-C..	To 2-Brig. 1-Div. 2-Corps Pot....	Nov., 1864
116th Penna. Infy.......June, 1864	From 2-Brig. 1-Div. 2-Corps Pot...	No change to muster out.........	July, 1865
4th N. Y. Heavy Arty.....Sept., 1864	From Unatt. 1-Div. 2-Corps Pot....	To 2-Brig. 1-Div. 2-Corps Pot......	Mch., 1865
183d Penna. Infy.........Mch., 1865	From 1-Brig. 1-Div. 2-Corps Pot....	No change to muster out.........	July, 1865

**CONSOLIDATED BRIGADE.—Organized June 27, 1864, by consolidation of 2d and 3d Brigades, 1st Division, 2d Corps.
Discontinued Nov. 2, 1864.**

COMMANDERS.

C. D. McDougall.......	Col. 111th N. Y. Infy.............	June 27, 1864, to June 30, 1864.
L. Crandall...........	Col. 125th N. Y. Infy.............	June 30, 1864, to Aug. 29, 1864.
Wm. Wilson...........	Lt.-Col. 81st Penna. Infy.........	Aug. 29, 1864, to Sept. 12, 1864.
J. E. McGee...........	Col. 69th N. Y. Infy..............	Sept. 12, 1864, to Oct. 13, 1864.
Geo. N. Macy..........	Col. 20th Mass. Infy.............	Oct. 13, 1864, to Oct. 27, 1864.
C. D. McDougall.......	Col. 111th N. Y. Infy.............	Oct. 27, 1864, to Nov. 2, 1864.

7th N. Y. Infy..........June, 1864	From 3-Brig. 1-Div. 2-Corps Pot....	To 3-Brig. 1-Div. 2-Corps Pot....	Nov., 1864
39th N. Y. Infy..........June, 1864	From 3-Brig. 1-Div. 2-Corps Pot....	To 3-Brig. 1-Div. 2-Corps Pot....	Nov., 1864
52d N. Y. Infy..........June, 1864	From 3-Brig. 1-Div. 2-Corps Pot....	To 3-Brig. 1-Div. 2-Corps Pot....	Nov., 1864
57th N. Y. Infy..........June, 1864	From 3-Brig. 1-Div. 2-Corps Pot....	No change to muster out..........	Oct., 1864
63d N. Y. Infy..........June, 1864	From 2-Brig. 1-Div. 2-Corps Pot...	To 2-Brig. 1-Div. 2-Corps Pot....	Nov., 1864
69th N. Y. Infy..........June, 1864	From 2-Brig. 1-Div. 2-Corps Pot...	To 2-Brig. 1-Div. 2-Corps Pot....	Nov., 1864
88th N. Y. Infy..........June, 1864	From 2-Brig. 1-Div. 2-Corps Pot...	To 2-Brig. 1-Div. 2-Corps Pot....	Nov., 1864
111th N. Y. Infy..........June, 1864	From 3-Brig. 1-Div. 2-Corps Pot...	To 3-Brig. 1-Div. 2-Corps Pot....	Nov., 1864
125th N. Y. Infy..........June, 1864	From 3-Brig. 1-Div. 2-Corps Pot...	To 3-Brig. 1-Div. 2-Corps Pot....	Nov., 1864
126th N. Y. Infy..........June, 1864	From 3-Brig. 1-Div. 2-Corps Pot...	To 3-Brig. 1-Div. 2-Corps Pot....	Nov., 1864

ARTILLERY, 1st DIVISION.—

A. & C. 4th U. S. Arty...Mch., 1862	From Arty. Sumner's Div. Pot......	To Corps Reserve Arty............	Nov., 1862
Batty. B, 1st N. Y. Arty...Mch., 1862	From Arty. Sumner's Div. Pot......	To Arty. Brig. 2 Corps Pot........	May, 1863
Batty. G, 1st N. Y. Arty...Mch., 1862	From Arty. Sumner's Div. Pot......	To Corps Reserve Arty............	Nov., 1862
A, 2d Battn. N. Y. Arty...Mch., 1862	From Defenses of Washington.....	Broken up......................	May, 1862
Batty. C, 4th U. S. Arty...Nov., 1862	From Corps Reserve Arty.........	To 1 Regular Brig. Arty. Res. Pot..	May, 1863

2nd DIVISION.—   **COMMANDERS.**

John Sedgwick.........	Brigadier General..................	Mch. 13, 1862, to Sept. 17, 1862.
O. O. Howard.........	Brigadier General..................	Sept. 17, 1862, to Jan. 26, 1863.
J. T. Owen...........	Brigadier General..................	Jan. 26, 1863, to Feb. 7, 1863.
O. O. Howard.........	Major General.....................	Feby. 7, 1863, to Apr. 1, 1863.
J. T. Owen...........	Brigadier General..................	Apr. 1, 1863, to Apr. 11, 1863.
John Gibbon...........	Brigadier General..................	Apr. 11, 1863, to July 1, 1863.
William Harrow.......	Brigadier General..................	July 1, 1863, to July 2, 1863.
John Gibbon...........	Brigadier General..................	July 2, 1863, to July 4, 1863.
William Harrow.......	Brigadier General..................	July 4, 1863, to Aug. 15, 1863.
A. S. Webb...........	Brigadier General..................	Aug. 15, 1863, to Dec. 10, 1863.
DeWitt C. Baxter......	Col. 72d Penna. Infy.............	Dec. 10, 1863, to Dec. 21, 1863.
John Gibbon...........	Major General.....................	Dec. 21, 1863, to July 31, 1864.

2nd DIVISION.—Continued.   COMMANDERS.

T. A. Smythe	Col. 1st Del. Infy	July 31, 1864, to Aug. 22, 1864.
John Gibbon	Major General	Aug. 22, 1864, to Sept. 4, 1864.
T. W. Egan	Brigadier General	Sept. 4, 1864, to Sept. 25, 1864.
John Gibbon	Major General	Sept. 25, 1864, to Oct. 8, 1864.
T. W. Eagan	Brigadier General	Oct. 8, 1864, to Oct. 29, 1864.
John Gibbon	Major General	Oct. 29, 1864, to Dec. 23, 1864.
Thos. A. Smythe	Brigadier General	Dec. 23, 1864, to Feb. 25, 1865.
William Hays	Brigadier General	Feb. 25, 1865, to Apr. 6, 1865.
F. C. Barlow	Bvt. Major General	Apr. 6, 1865, to May 28, 1865.
J. P. McIvor	Col. 170th N. Y. Infy	May 28, 1865, to June 28, 1865.

1st BRIGADE, 2d DIVISION.—   COMMANDERS.

Willis A. Gorman	Brigadier General	Mch. 13, 1862, to Oct. 29, 1862.	
A. Sully	Brigadier General	Oct. 29, 1862, to Dec. 19, 1862.	
T. G. Morehead	Col. 106th Penna. Infy	Dec. 19, 1862, to Jan. 25, 1863.	
F. D. Sewell	Col. 19th Me. Infy	Jan. 25, 1863, to Feb. 7, 1863.	
G. H. Ward	Col. 15th Mass. Infy	Feb. 7, 1863, to Mch. 10, 1863.	
A. Sully	Brigadier General	Mch. 10, 1863, to May 1, 1863.	
H. W. Hudson	Col. 82d N. Y. Infy	May 1, 1863, to May 3, 1863.	
Byron Laflin	Col. 34th N. Y. Infy	May 3, 1863, to May 13, 1863.	
T. G. Morehead	Col. 106th Penna. Infy	May 13, 1863, to June 8, 1863.	
William Harrow	Brigadier General	June 8, 1863, to July 1, 1863.	
F. E. Heath	Col. 19th Me. Infy	July 1, 1863, to July 2, 1863.	
William Harrow	Brigadier General	July 2, 1863, to July 4, 1863.	
F. E. Heath	Col. 19th Me. Infy	July 4, 1863, to Aug. 28, 1863.	
DeWitt C. Baxter	Col. 72d Penna. Infy	Aug. 28, 1863, to Sept. 28, 1863.	
R. P. Smith	Col. 71st Penna. Infy	Sept. 28, 1863, to Oct. 6, 1863.	
F. E. Heath	Col. 19th Me. Infy	Oct. 6, 1863, to Oct. 22, 1863.	
DeWitt C. Baxter	Col. 72d Penna. Infy	Oct. 22, 1863, to Dec. 10, 1863.	
H. W. Hudson	Col. 82d N. Y. Infy	Dec. 10, 1863, to Jan. 2, 1864.	
DeWitt C. Baxter	Col. 72d Penna. Infy	Jan. 2, 1864, to Feb. 10, 1864.	
T. O'Brien	Major 152d N. Y. Infy	Feb. 10, 1864, to Feb. 27, 1864.	
Selden Connor	Col. 19th Me. Infy	Feb. 27, 1864, to Mch. 25, 1864.	
A. S. Webb	Brigadier General	Mch. 25, 1864, to May 12, 1864.	
H. B. McKean	Col. 81st Penna. Infy	May 12, 1864, to June 3, 1864.	
F. A. Haskell	Col. 36th Wis. Infy	June 3, 1864.	Killed.
B. R. Pierce	Brigadier General	June 3, 1864, to June 22, 1864.	Killed.
W. F. Smith	Major 1st Del. Infy	June 22, 1864, to June 27, 1864.	
F. E. Pierce	Lt.-Col. 59th N. Y. Infy	June 27, 1864, to Aug. 13, 1864.	
Geo. N. Macy	Col. 20th Mass. Infy	Aug. 13, 1864, to Aug. 14, 1864.	
H. P. Rugg	Lt.-Col. 59th N. Y. Infy	Aug. 14, 1864, to Aug. 27, 1864.	
T. W. Egan	Brigadier General	Aug. 27, 1864, to Sept. 4, 1864.	
H. P. Rugg	Lt.-Col. 59th N. Y. Infy	Sept. 4, 1864, to Sept. 25, 1864.	
T. W. Egan	Brigadier General	Sept. 25, 1864, to Nov. 15, 1864.	
J. M. Willetts	Col. 8th N. Y. Heavy Arty	Nov. 15, 1864, to Jan. 19, 1865.	
W. L. Olmstead	Col. 59th N. Y. Infy	Jan. 19, 1865, to Mch. 1, 1865.	
G. W. West	Col. 17th Me. Infy	Mch. 1, 1865, to Mch. 14, 1865.	
W. L. Olmstead	Col. 59th N. Y. Infy	Mch. 14, 1865, to June 28, 1865.	

1st Minn. Infy	Mch., 1862	From Gorman's B. to Sedgwick's D.	No change to muster out	June, 1865
(2d Co. S. S. Att.)				
15th Mass. Infy	Mch., 1862	From Gorman's B. to Sedgwick's D.	No change to muster out	June, 1864
(1st Co. S. S. Att.)				
34th N. Y. Infy	Mch., 1862	From Gorman's B. to Sedgwick's D.	No change to muster out	June, 1863
82d (20-S. M.) N. Y. Infy	Mch., 1862	From Gorman's B. to Sedgwick's D.	No change to muster out	May, 1865
19th Me. Infy	Oct., 1862	From Def. of Washington	No change to muster out	May, 1865
152d N. Y. Infy	Oct., 1863	From Dept. of the East	To 2-Brig. 2-Div. 2-Corps Pot	Mch., 1864
7th Mich. Infy	Mch., 1864	From 3-Brig. 2-Div. 2-Corps Pot	No change to muster out	June, 1865
42d N. Y. Infy	Mch., 1864	From 3-Brig. 2-Div. 2-Corps Pot	No change to muster out	July, 1864
59th N. Y. Infy	Mch., 1864	From 3-Brig. 2-Div. 2-Corps Pot	No change to muster out	June, 1865
19th Mass. Infy	Mch., 1864	From 3-Brig. 2-Div. 2-Corps Pot	No change to muster out	June, 1865
20th Mass. Infy	Mch., 1864	From 3-Brig. 2-Div. 2-Corps Pot	No change to muster out	July, 1865
184th Penna. Infy	June, 1864	New organization	No change to muster out	July, 1865
36th Wisconsin Infy	June, 1864	From New Organization	No change to Muster Out	June, 1865
152d N. Y. Infy	June, 1864	From 2-Brig. 2-Div. 2-Corps Pot	No change to Muster Out	June, 1865

2d BRIGADE, 2d DIVISION.—   COMMANDERS.

W. W. Burns	Brigadier General	Mch. 13, 1862, to July 10, 1862.
J. T. Owen	Col. 69th Penna. Infy	July 10, 1862, to July 30, 1862.
DeWitt C. Baxter	Col. 72d Penna. Infy	July 30, 1862, to Aug. 27, 1862.
O. O. Howard	Brigadier General	Aug. 27, 1862, to Sept. 17, 1862.
J. T. Owen	Col. 69th Penna. Infy	Sept. 17, 1862.
DeWitt C. Baxter	Col. 72d Penna. Infy	Sept. 17, 1862, to Oct. 10, 1862.
W. W. Burns	Brigadier General	Oct. 10, 1862, to Nov. 12, 1862.
J. T. Owen	Col. 69th Penna Infy	Nov. 12, 1862, to Jan. 26, 1863.
DeWitt C. Baxter	Col. 72d Penna. Infy	Jan. 26, 1863, to Feb. 7, 1863.
J. T. Owen	Brigadier General	Feb. 7, 1863, to Apr. 1, 1863.
DeWitt C. Baxter	Col. 72d Penna. Infy	Apr. 1, 1863, to Apr. 11, 1863.
J. T. Owen	Brigadier General	Apr. 11, 1863, to June 28, 1863.
A. S. Webb	Brigadier General	June 28, 1863, to Aug. 15, 1863.
W. L. Curry	Lt-Col. 106th Penna. Infy	Aug. 15, 1863, to Sept. 2, 1863.
DeWitt C. Baxter	Col. 72d Penna. Infy	Sept. 2, 1863, to Oct. 22, 1863.
A. F. Devereux	Col. 19th Mass. Infy	Oct. 22, 1863, to Jan. 8, 1864.
R. P. Smith	Col. 71st Penna. Infy	Jan. 8, 1864, to Mch. 18, 1864.
C. Kockersperger	Lt.-Col. 106th Penna. Infy	Mch. 18, 1864, to Mch. 26, 1864.
T. G. Morehead	Col. 106th Penna. Infy	Mch. 26, 1864, to Apr. 25, 1864.
J. T. Owen	Brigadier General	Apr. 25, 1864, to June 12, 1864.
John Fraser	Col. 140th Penna. Infy	June 12, 1864, to June 21, 1864.
Timothy O'Brien	Major 152d N. Y. Infy	June 21, 1864, to June 26, 1864.

Brigade broken up June 26, 1864, and assigned to the 1st and 3d Brigades. Reorganized by transfer of Regiments, June 27, 1864.

M. Murphy	Col. 69th N. Y. Infy	June 26, 1864, to Oct. 27. 1864.
J. M. Willetts	Col. 8th N. Y. Heavy Arty	Oct. 27, 1864, to Nov. 3, 1864.
J. P. McIvor	Col. 170th N. Y. Infy	Nov. 3, 1864, to Nov. 27, 1864.
M. Murphy	Col. 69th N. Y. Infy	Nov. 27, 1864, to Feb. 5, 1865.
J. P. McIvor	Col. 170th N. Y. Infy	Feb. 5, 1865, to May 28, 1865.
J. B. Baker	Col. 8th N. Y. Heavy Arty	May 28, 1865, to June 29, 1865.
William DeLacy	Lt.-Col. 164th N. Y. Infy	June 29, 1865, to July 1, 1865.

2d BRIGADE, 2d DIVISION.—Continued.

Regiment	Organized	From	To	Muster Out
69th Penna. Infy	Mch., 1862	From Burns' Brig. Sedgwick's Div.	To 3-Brig. 2-Div. 2-Corps Pot.	June, 1864
71st Penna. Infy	Mch., 1862	From Burns' Brig. Sedgwick's Div.	No change to Muster Out	June, 1864
72d Penna. Infy	Mch., 1862	From Burns' Brig. Sedgwick's Div.	To 3-Brig. 2-Div. 2-Corps Pot.	June, 1864
106th Penna. Infy	Mch., 1862	From Burns' Brig. Sedgwick's Div.	To 3-Brig. 2-Div. 2-Corps Pot.	June, 1864
152d N. Y. Infy	Mch., 1864	From 1-Brig. 2-Div. 2-Corps Pot.	To 1-Brig. 2-Div. 2-Corps Pot.	June, 1864
155th N. Y. Infy	June, 1864	From 4-Brig. 2-Div. 2-Corps Pot.	No change to Muster Out	July, 1865
164th N. Y. Infy	June, 1864	From 4-Brig. 2-Div. 2-Corps Pot.	No change to Muster Out	July, 1865
170th N. Y. Infy	June, 1864	From 4-Brig. 2-Div. 2-Corps Pot.	No change to Muster Out	July, 1865
182d (69th) N. Y. Infy	June, 1864	From 4-Brig. 2-Div. 2-Corps Pot.	No change to Muster Out	July, 1865
8th N. Y. Heavy Arty	June, 1864	From 4-Brig. 2-Div. 2-Corps Pot.	No change to Muster Out	June, 1865

3d BRIGADE, 2d DIVISION.—

COMMANDERS.

N. J. T. Dana	Brigadier General	March 13, 1862, to Aug. 5, 1862.	
W. L. Tidball	Col. 59th N. Y. Infy	Aug. 5, 1862, to Sept. 7, 1862.	
N. J. T. Dana	Brigadier General	Sept. 7, 1862, to Sept. 17, 1862.	
Norman J. Hall	Col. 7th Mich. Infy	Sept. 17, 1862 to Dec. 15, 1862.	
William R. Lee	Col. 20th Mass. Infy	Dec. 15, 1862 to Dec. 29, 1862.	
J. R. Brooke	Col. 53d Penna. Infy	Dec. 29, 1862, to Mch. 20, 1863.	
Norman J. Hall	Col. 7th Mich., Infy	Mch. 20, 1863, to July 18, 1863.	
J. E. Mallon	Col. 42d N. Y. Infy	July 18, 1863, to Oct. 15, 1863.	Killed.
A. D. Wass	Lt.-Col. 19th Mass. Infy	Oct. 15, 1863, to Oct. 19, 1863.	
T. G. Morehead	Col. 106th Penna. Infy	Oct. 19, 1863, to Mch. 25, 1864.	
S. S. Carroll	Col. 8th Ohio Infy	Mch. 25, 1864, to May 13, 1864.	
Theo. G. Ellis	Col. 14th Conn. Infy	May 13, 1864, to May 17, 1864.	
Thos. A. Smythe	Col. 1st Dela. Infy	May 17, 1864, to July 31, 1864.	
S. A. Moore	Lt.-Col. 14th Conn. Infy	July 31, 1864, to Aug. 14, 1864.	
F. E. Pierce	Lt.-Col. 108th N. Y. Infy	Aug. 14, 1864, to Aug. 23, 1864.	
Thos. A. Smythe	Col. 1st Dela. Infy	Aug. 23, 1864, to Nov. 5, 1864.	
S. A. Moore	Col. 14th Conn. Infy	Nov. 5, 1864, to Nov. 15, 1864.	
Thos. A. Smythe	Brigadier General	Nov. 15, 1864, to Dec. 22, 1864.	
F. E. Pierce	Lt.-Col. 108th N. Y. Infy	Dec. 22, 1864, to Feb. 10, 1865.	
Daniel Woodall	Col. 1st Dela. Infy	Feb. 10, 1865, to Feb. 28, 1865.	
Thos. A. Smythe	Brigadier General	Feb. 28, 1865, to Apr. 7, 1865.	Mort. Wnd.
Daniel Woodall	Col. 1st Dela. Infy	Apr. 7, 1865, to June 28, 1865.	

Regiment	Organized	From	To	Muster Out
19th Mass. Infy	Mch., 1862	From Dana's Brig. Sedgwick's Div.	To 1-Brig. 2-Div. 2-Corps Pot.	Mch., 1864
20th Mass. Infy	Mch., 1862	From Dana's Brig. Sedgwick's Div.	To 1-Brig. 2-Div. 2-Corps Pot.	Mch., 1864
7th Mich. Infy	Mch., 1862	From Dana's Brig. Sedgwick's Div.	To 1-Brig. 2-Div. 2-Corps Pot.	Mch., 1864
42d N. Y. Infy	Mch., 1862	From Dana's Brig. Sedgwick's Div.	To 1-Brig. 2-Div. 2-Corps Pot.	Mch., 1864
59th N. Y. Infy	July, 1862	From Sturgis' Brig. Def. Washington	To 1-Brig. 2-Div. 2-Corps Pot.	Mch., 1864
127th Penna. Infy	Dec., 1862	From Defences of Washington	No change to Muster Out	May, 1863
1st Dela. Infy	Mch., 1864	From 2-Brig. 3-Div. 2-Corps Pot.	No change to Muster Out	July, 1865
4th Ohio Infy	Mch., 1864	From 1-Brig. 3-Div. 2-Corps Pot.	No change to Muster Out	July, 1865
8th Ohio Infy	Mch., 1864	From 1-Brig. 3-Div. 2-Corps Pot.	No change to Muster Out	June, 1864
14th Conn. Infy	Mch., 1864	From 2-Brig. 3-Div. 2-Corps Pot.	No change to Muster Out	May, 1865
7th W. Va. Infy	Mch., 1864	From 1-Brig. 3-Div. 2-Corps Pot.	No change to Muster Out	June, 1865
14th Ind. Infy	Mch., 1864	From 1-Brig. 3-Div. 2-Corps Pot.	No change to Muster Out	June, 1864
12th N. J. Infy	Mch., 1864	From 2-Brig. 3-Div. 2-Corps Pot.	No change to Muster Out	July, 1865
10th N. Y. Infy	Mch., 1864	From 2-Brig. 3-Div. 2-Corps Pot.	No change to Muster Out	June, 1865
108th N. Y. Infy	Mch., 1864	From 2-Brig. 3-Div. 2-Corps Pot.	No change to Muster Out	May, 1865
69th Penna. Infy	June, 1864	From 2-Brig. 2-Div. 2-Corps Pot.	No change to Muster Out	June, 1865
72d Penna. Infy	June, 1864	From 2-Brig. 2-Div. 2-Corps Pot.	No change to Muster Out	Aug., 1864
106th Penna. Infy	June, 1864	From 2-Brig. 2-Div. 2-Corps Pot.	No change to Muster Out	June, 1865
2d Dela. Infy	July, 1864	From 4-Brig. 1-Div. 2-Corps Pot.	No change to Muster Out	Sept., 1864

4th BRIGADE, 2d DIVISION.—Organized May 9, 1864.

COMMANDERS.

M. Murphy	Col. 182d (69th) N. Y. Infy	May 9, 1864, to May 18, 1864.	
J. P. McIvor	Col. 170th N. Y. Infy	May 18, 1864, to May 29, 1864.	
R. O. Tyler	Brigadier General	May 29, 1864, to June 7, 1864.	
J. P. McIvor	Col. 170th N. Y. Infy	June 7, 1864, to June 17, 1864.	
John Ramsey	Col. 8th N. J. Infy	June 17, 1864, to June 20, 1864.	Killed.
William Blaisdell	Col. 11th Mass. Infy	June 20, 1864, to June 22, 1864.	
J. P. McIvor	Col. 170th N. Y. Infy	June 22, 1864, to June 26, 1864.	

Brigade discontinued and designated 2d Brig. 2d Div. 2d Corps, June 26, 1864.

Regiment	Organized	From	To	Muster Out
155th N. Y. Infy	May, 1864	From Tyler's Div. 22-Corps	To 2-Brig. 2-Div. 2-Corps Pot.	June, 1864
164th N. Y. Infy	May, 1864	From Tyler's Div. 22-Corps	To 2-Brig. 2-Div. 2-Corps Pot.	June, 1864
170th N. Y. Infy	May, 1864	From Tyler's Div. 22-Corps	To 2-Brig. 2-Div. 2-Corps Pot.	June, 1864
182d (69th) N. Y. Infy	May, 1864	From Tyler's Div. 22-Corps	To 2-Brig. 2-Div. 2-Corps Pot.	June, 1864
8th N. Y. Heavy Arty	May, 1864	From Tyler's Heavy Arty. Div. 2-C.	To 2-Brig. 2-Div. 2-Corps Pot.	June, 1864

ARTILLERY, 2d DIVISION.—

Battery	Organized	From	To	Muster Out
Batty. A. 1st D. I. Arty	Mch., 1862	From Bank's Div. Pot.	To Arty Brig. 2-Corps Pot.	May, 1863
Batty. B. 1st R. I. Arty	Mch., 1862	From Sedgwick's Div. Pot.	To Corps Arty. Reserve	May, 1862
Batty. G. 1st R. I. Arty	Mch., 1862	From Sedgwick's Div. Pot.	To Corps Arty. Reserve	June, 1862
Batty. I. 1st U. S. Arty	Mch., 1862	From Sedgwick's Div. Pot.	To Corps Arty. Reserve	Nov., 1862

3d DIVISION.—Organized Sept. 10, 1862.   COMMANDERS.

W. H. French	Brigadier General	Sept. 10, 1862, to Dec. 20, 1862.
A. Sully	Brigadier General	Dec. 20, 1862, to Jan. 10, 1863.
W. H. French	Major General	Jan. 10, 1863, to June 28, 1863.
Alex. Hays	Brigadier General	June 28, 1863, to Aug. 15, 1863.
J. T. Owen	Brigadier General	Aug. 15, 1863, to Sept. 6, 1863.
Alex. Hays	Brigadier General	Sept. 6, 1863, to Dec. 14, 1863.
J. T. Owen	Brigadier General	Dec. 14, 1863, to Jan. 4, 1864.
Alex. Hays	Brigadier General	Jan. 4, 1864, to Feb. 10, 1864.
J. T. Owen	Brigadier General	Feb. 10, 1864, to Mch. 25, 1864.
D. B. Birney	Major General	Mch. 25, 1864, to June 18, 1864.
Gershom Mott	Brigadier General	June 18, 1864, to June 27, 1864.
D. B. Birney	Major General	June 27, 1864, to July 23, 1864.
Gershom Mott	Brigadier General	July 23, 1864, to Oct. 8, 1864.
R. DeTrobriand	Brigadier General	Oct. 8, 1864, to Oct. 21, 1864.
Gershom Mott	Brigadier General	Oct. 21, 1864, to Feb. 15, 1865.
R. DeTrobriand	Brigadier General	Feb. 15, 1865, to Mch. 2, 1865.
Gershom Mott	Brigadier General	Mch. 2, 1865, to Apr. 6, 1865.
R. DeTrobriand	Brigadier General	Apr. 6, 1865, to May 16, 1865.
Gershom Mott	Bvt. Major General	May 16, 1865, to June 9, 1865.
R. DeTrobriand	Brigadier General	June 9, 1865, to June 20, 1865.
Gershom Mott	Bvt. Major General	June 20, 1865, to June 28, 1865.

1st BRIGADE, 3d DIVISION.—   COMMANDERS.

N. Kimball	Brigadier General	Sept. 10, 1862, to Dec. 13, 1862.	Wounded.
J. S. Mason	Brigadier General	Dec. 13, 1862.	
W. B. Robertson	Col. 24th N. J. Infy	Dec., 1862, to Feb., 1863.	
John Coons	Col. 14th Ind. Infy	Feb., 1863, to Mch., 1863.	
Jos. Snider	Col. 7th W. Va. Infy	Mch., 1863, to Apr., 1863.	
S. S. Carroll	Col. 8th Ohio Infy	Apr., 1863, to July, 1863.	
Jos. Snider	Col. 7th W. Va. Infy	July, 1863, to Sept. 7, 1863.	
S. S. Carroll	Col. 8th Ohio Infy	Sept. 7, 1863, to Mch. 24, 1864.	
T. W. Egan	Col. 40th N. Y. Infy	Mch. 24, 1864, to Apr. 20, 1864.	
J. H. H. Ward	Brigadier General	Apr. 20, 1864, to May 12, 1864.	
Thos. W. Egan	Col. 40th N. Y. Infy	May 12, 1864, to June 16, 1864.	
H. J. Madill	Col. 141st Penna. Infy	June 16, 1864, to July 12, 1864.	
R. DeTrobriand	Brigadier General	July 12, 1864, to Oct. 8, 1864.	
William R. Brewster	Col. 73d N. Y. Infy	Oct. 8, 1864, to Oct. 21, 1864.	
R. DeTrobriand	Brigadier General	Oct. 21, 1864, to Jan. 2, 1865.	
H. J. Madill	Bvt. Brig. General	Jan. 2, 1865, to Jan. 18, 1865.	
G. W. West	Bvt. Brig. General	Jan. 18, 1865, to Jan. 25, 1865.	
R. DeTrobriand	Brigadier General	Jan. 25, 1865, to Feb. 15, 1865.	
G. W. West	Bvt. Brig. General	Feb. 15, 1865, to Mch. 2, 1865.	
R. DeTrobriand	Brigadier General	Mch. 2, 1865, to Apr. 6, 1865.	
R. B. Shepherd	Col. 1st Me. Heavy Arty	Apr. 6, 1865, to May 16, 1865.	
R. DeTrobriand	Brigadier General	May 16, 1865, to June 28, 1865.	

7th W. Va. Infy ... Sept., 1862	From Kimball's In. Brig. 2-Corps Pot	To 3-Brig. 2-Div. 2-Corps Pot	Mch., 1864
4th Ohio Infy ... Sept., 1862	From Kimball's In. Brig. 2-Corps Pot	To 3-Brig. 2-Div. 2-Corps Pot	Mch., 1864
8th Ohio Infy ... Sept., 1862	From Kimball's In. Brig. 2-Corps Pot	To 3-Brig. 2-Div. 2-Corps Pot	Mch., 1864
14th Ind. Infy ... Sept., 1862	From Kimball's In. Brig. 2-Corps Pot	To 3-Brig. 2-Div. 2-Corps Pot	Mch., 1864
132d Penna. Infy ... Sept., 1862	From Whipple's Command, Wash	To 2-Brig. 3-Div. 2-Corps Pot	Nov., 1862
24th N. J. Infy ... Dec., 1862	From Def. of Washington	No change to Muster Out	June, 1863
28th N. J. Infy ... Dec., 1862	From Def. of Washington	No change to Muster Out	June, 1863
20th Ind. Infy ... Mch., 1864	From 2-Brig. 1-Div. 3-Corps Pot	No change to Muster Out	June, 1865
40th N. Y. Infy ... Mch., 1864	From 3-Brig. 1-Div. 3-Corps Pot	No change to Muster Out	June, 1865
86th N. Y. Infy ... Mch., 1864	From 2-Brig. 1-Div. 3-Corps Pot	No change to Muster Out	June, 1865
124th N. Y. Infy ... Mch., 1864	From 2-Brig. 1-Div. 3-Corps Pot	No change to Muster Out	June, 1865
99th Penna. Infy ... Mch., 1864	From 2-Brig. 1-Div. 3-Corps Pot	No change to Muster Out	June, 1865
110th Penna. Infy ... Mch., 1864	From 1-Brig. 1-Div. 3-Corps Pot	No change to Muster Out	June, 1865
141st Penna. Infy ... Mch., 1864	From 1-Brig. 1-Div. 3-Corps Pot	To 2-Brig. 3-Div. 2-Corps Pot	July, 1864
3d Me. Infy ... Mch., 1864	From 2-Brig. 1-Div. 3-Corps Pot	No change to Muster Out	June, 1864
2d U. S. Sharpshooters ... Mch., 1864	From 2-Brig. 1-Div. 3-Corps Pot	No change to Muster Out	Feb., 1865
4th Me. Infy ... May, 1864	From 2-Brig. 3-Div. 3-Corps Pot	No change to Muster Out	June, 1864
17th Me. Infy ... June, 1864	From 2-Brig. 3-Div. 2-Corps Pot	To 2-Brig. 3-Div. 2-Corps Pot	Jan., 1865
4th N. Y. H. A. 1st Battn. June, 1864	From Arty. Brig. 2-Corps Pot	Arty. Reserve Potomac	July, 1864
73rd N. Y. Infy ... July, 1864	From 4-Brig. 3-Div. 2-Corps Pot	No change to Muster Out	June, 1865
74th N. Y. Infy ... July, 1864	From 4-Brig. 3-Div. 2-Corps Pot	No change to Muster Out	Aug., 1864
1st Me. Heavy Arty ... July, 1864	From 3-Brig. 3-Div. 2-Corps Pot	Dept. of Washington	June, 1865

2d BRIGADE, 3d DIVISION.—   COMMANDERS.

Dwight Morris	Col. 14th Conn. Infy	Sept. 12, 1862, to Dec. 13, 1862.	
C. H. Palmer	Col. 108th N. Y. Infy	Dec. 13, 1862, to Dec. 20, 1862.	
R. C. Johnson	Col. 12th N. J. Infy	Dec. 20, 1862, to Jan. 24, 1863.	
Dwight Morris	Col. 14th Conn. Infy	Jany. 24, 1863, to Feb. 12, 1863.	
William Hays	Brig. General	Feb. 12, 1863, to May 3, 1863.	
Chas. J. Powers	Col. 108th N. Y. Infy	May 3, 1863, to May 16, 1863.	
T. A. Smythe	Col. 1st Del. Infy	May 16, 1863, to July 3, 1863.	
F. E. Pierce	Lt.-Col. 108th N. Y. Infy	July 3, 1863, to July 4, 1863.	
T. A. Smythe	Col. 1st Del. Infy	July 4, 1863, to Aug. 14, 1863.	
T. H. Davis	Lt.-Col. 12th N. J. Infy	Aug. 14, 1863, to Sept. 3, 1863.	
T. A. Smythe	Col. 1st Del. Infy	Sept. 3, 1863, to Dec. 28, 1863.	
Chas. J. Powers	Col. 108th N. Y. Infy	Dec. 28, 1863, to Feb. 13, 1864.	
T. A. Smythe	Col. 1st Del. Infy	Feb. 13, 1864, to Mch. 25, 1864.	
Alex. Hays	Brig. General	Mch. 25, 1864, to May 5, 1864.	Killed.
John S. Crocker	Col. 93d N. Y. Infy	May 5, 1864, to May 18, 1864.	
Elijah Walker	Col. 4th Me. Infy	May 18, 1864, to May 23, 1864.	
Byron R. Pierce	Col. 3d Mich. Infy	May 23, 1864, to May 29, 1864.	
Thos. R. Tannatt	Col. 1st Mass. Heavy Arty	May 29, 1864, to June 16, 1864.	
Levi B. Duff	Major 105th Penna. Infy	June 16, 1864.	
John Williams	Major	June 16, 1864.	
R. McAllister	Col. 11th N. J. Infy	June 16, 1864, to June 24, 1864.	
B. R. Pierce	Brig. General	June 24, 1864, to July 22, 1864.	
Daniel Chaplin	Col. 1st Me. Heavy Arty	July 22, 1864, to July 28, 1864.	
H. J. Madill	Col. 141st Penna. Infy	July 28, 1864, to Aug. 11, 1864.	
C. A. Craig	Col. 105th Penna. Infy	Aug. 11, 1864, to Aug. 16, 1864.	Killed.
John Pulford	Col. 5th Mich. Infy	Aug. 16, 1864, to Aug. 26, 1864.	
B. R. Pierce	Brig. General	Aug. 26, 1864, to Jan. 25, 1865.	
G. W. West	Col. 17th Me. Infy	Jan. 25, 1864, to Feb. 15, 1865.	
B. R. Pierce	Brig. General	Feb. 15, 1865, to June 28, 1865.	

14th Conn. Infy ... Sept., 1862	From New Organization	To 3-Brig. 2-Div. 2 Corps Pot	Mch., 1864
108th N. Y. Infy ... Sept., 1862	From Whipple's Com'd Washington	To 3-Brig. 2-Div. 2 Corps Pot	Mch., 1864
130th Penna. Infy ... Sept., 1862	From New Organization	No change to Muster Out	May, 1863
132nd Penna. Infy ... Nov., 1862	From 1-Brig. 3-Div. 2-Corps Pot	No change to Muster Out	May, 1863
12th N. J. Infy ... Dec., 1862	From Baltimore, Md., Middle Dept	To 3-Brig. 2-Div. 2 Corps Pot	Mch., 1864
10th N. Y. Infy ... May, 1863	From 3-Brig. 3-Div. 2-Corps Pot	To 3-Brig. 2-Div. 2 Corps Pot	Mch., 1864
1st Del. Infy ... May, 1863	From 3-Brig. 3-Div. 2 Corps Pot	To 3-Brig. 2-Div. 2-Corps Pot	Mch., 1864
4th Me. Infy ... Mch., 1864	From 2-Brig. 1-Div. 3-Corps Pot	To 1-Brig. 3-Div. 3-Corps Pot	May, 1864
17th Me. Infy ... Mch., 1864	From 2-Brig. 1-Div. 3-Corps Pot	To 1-Brig. 3-Div. 3-Corps Pot	June, 1864
3d Mich. Infy ... Mch., 1864	From 3-Brig. 1-Div. 3-Corps Pot	Transf'd to 5th Mich. Infy	June, 1864
5th Mich. Infy ... Mch., 1864	From 3-Brig. 1-Div. 3-Corps Pot	No change to Muster Out	June, 1865
57th Penna. Infy ... Mch., 1864	From 1-Brig. 1-Div. 3-Corps Pot	No change to Muster Out	June, 1865
63d Penna. Infy ... Mch., 1864	From 1-Brig. 1-Div. 3-Corps Pot	Transf'd to 105th Penna. Infy	Sept., 1864
105th Penna. Infy ... Mch., 1864	From 1-Brig. 1-Div. 3-Corps Pot	No change to Muster Out	June, 1865
1st U. S. Sharpshooters ... Mch., 1864	From 3-Brig. 1-Div. 3-Corps Pot	No change to Muster Out	Sept., 1864
93d N. Y. Infy ... Mch., 1864	From Provost Guard Pot	No change to Muster Out	June, 1865
1st Mass. Heavy Arty ... May, 1864	From Tyler's Heavy Arty. Div. 2-C	To Dept. of Washington	June, 1865
4th N. Y. H. A. 2d Battn. June, 1864	From Arty. Brig. 2-Corps Pot	To Arty. Reserve Potomac	July, 1864
84th Penna. Infy ... July, 1864	From 4-Brig. 3-Div. 2-Corps Pot	Consol. with 57th Penna	Jan., 1865
141st Penna. Infy ... July, 1864	From 1-Brig. 3-Div. 2-Corps Pot	No change to Muster Out	May, 1865
17th Me. Infy ... Jan., 1865	From 1-Brig. 3-Div. 2-Corps Pot	No change to Muster Out	June, 1865

3d BRIGADE, 3d DIVISION.— COMMANDERS.

Max Weber	Brig. General	Sept. 12, 1862, to Sept. 17, 1862.	
J. W. Andrews	Col. 1st Del. Infy	Sept. 17, 1862, to Dec. 13, 1862.	
Wm. Jameson	Lt.-Col. 4th N. Y. Infy	Dec. 13, 1862.	
J. W. Marshall	Lt.-Col. 10th N. Y. Infy	Dec. 13, 1862, to Jan. 5, 1863.	
J. D. McGregor	Col. 4th N. Y. Infy	Jan. 5, 1863, to Feb. 24, 1863.	
Chas. Albright	Col. 132d Penna. Infy	Feb. 24, 1863, to Mch. 16, 1863.	
John E. Bendix	Col. 4th N. Y. Infy	Mch. 16, 1863, to Apr. 27, 1863.	
J. D. McGregor	Col. 10th N. Y. Infy	Apr. 27, 1863, to May 2, 1863.	Killed.
Chas. Albright	Col. 132nd Penna. Infy	May 2, 1863, to May 23, 1863.	Killed.

Brigade discontinued May 23, 1863. Reorganized from Def. of Washington, 22 Corps, June 28, 1863.

G. L. Willard	Col. 125th N. Y. Infy	June 28, 1863, to July 2, 1863.	
E. Sherrill	Col. 126th N. Y. Infy	July 2, 1863, to July 3, 1863.	
J. M. Bull	Lt.-Col. 126th N. Y. Infy	July· 3, 1863, to July 17, 1863.	
J. Coons	Col. 14th Ind. Infy	July 17, 1863, to Aug. 15, 1863.	
J. T. Owen	Brigadier General	Aug. 15, 1863, to Dec. 14, 1863.	
L. Crandall	Col. 127th N. Y. Infy	Dec. 14, 1863, to Jan. 4, 1864.	
J. T. Owen	Brigadier General	Jan. 4, 1864, to Feb. 10, 1864.	
A. Funk	Col. 39th N. Y. Infy	Feb. 10, 1864, to Mch. 25, 1864.	

Brigade discontinued March 25, 1864. Reorganized May 13, 1864, from 1-Brig. 4-Div. 2-Corps.

Gershom Mott	Brigadier General	May 13, 1864, to June 18, 1864.	
Daniel Chaplin	Col. 1st Me. Heavy Arty	June 18, 1864, to June 27, 1864.	
Gershom Mott	Brigadier General	June 27, 1864, to July 23, 1864.	
R. McAllister	Col. 11th N. J. Infy	July 23, 1864, to Dec. 12, 1864.	
James Ramsey	Bvt. Brig. General	Dec. 12, 1864, to June 7, 1865.	
R. McAllister	Col. 11th N. J. Infy	Jan. 13, 1865, to June 7, 1865.	
Francis Price	Col. 7th N. J. Infy	June 7, 1865, to June 28, 1865.	

1st Del. Infy......Sept., 1862	From Suffolk, Va.; 7-Corps	To 2-Brig. 3-Div. 2-Corps Pot	May, 1863
5th Maryland Infy......Sept., 1862	From Suffolk, Va.; 7-Corps	To Milroy's Com'd 8 Corps	Dec., 1863
4th N. Y. Infy......Sept., 1862	From Suffolk, Va.; 7-Corps	No change to Muster Out	May, 1863
10th N. Y. Infy......Oct., 1862	From 3-Brig. 2-Div. 5-Corps Pot	To 2-Brig. 3-Div. 2-Corps Pot	May, 1863
132d Penna. Infy......Dec., 1862	From 2-Brig. 3-Div. 2-Corps Pot	No change to Muster Out	May, 1863
39th N. Y. Infy......June, 1863	From 3-Brig. Abercrombie's Div. 22-C	To 3-Brig. 1-Div. 2-Corps Pot	Mch., 1864
111th N. Y. Infy......June, 1863	From 3-Brig. Abercrombie's Div. 22-C	To 3-Brig. 1-Div. 2-Corps Pot	Mch., 1864
125th N. Y. Infy......June, 1863	From 3-Brig. Abercrombie's Div. 22-C	To 3-Brig. 1-Div. 2-Corps Pot	Mch., 1864
126th N. Y. Infy......June, 1863	From 3-Brig. Abercrombie's Div. 22-C	To 3-Brig. 1-Div. 2-Corps Pot	Mch., 1864
5th N. J. Infy......May, 1864	From 1-Brig. 4-Div. 2-Corps Pot	No change to Muster Out	Nov., 1864
6th N. J. Infy......May, 1864	From 1-Brig. 4-Div. 2-Corps Pot	No change to Muster Out	Sept., 1864
7th N. J. Infy......May, 1864	From 1-Brig. 4-Div. 2-Corps Pot	No change to Muster Out	June, 1865
8th N. J. Infy......May, 1864	From 1-Brig. 4-Div. 2-Corps Pot	No change to Muster Out	June, 1865
11th N. J. Infy......May, 1864	From 1-Brig. 4-Div. 2-Corps Pot	No change to Muster Out	June, 1865
115th Penna. Infy......May, 1864	From 1-Brig. 4-Div. 2-Corps Pot	Consol. with 110th Penna	June, 1864
16th Mass. Infy......May, 1864	From 1-Brig. 4-Div. 2-Corps Pot	No change to Muster Out	July, 1864
1st Me. Heavy Arty......May, 1864	From Tyler's Heavy Arty. Div. 2-C.	To 1-Brig. 3-Div. 2-Corps Pot	July, 1864
11th Mass. Infy......July, 1864	From 4-Brig. 3-Div. 2-Corps Pot	No change to Muster Out	June, 1865
120th N. Y. Infy......July, 1864	From 4-Brig. 3-Div. 2-Corps Pot	No change to Muster Out	June, 1865
72d N. Y. Infy......July, 1864	From 4-Brig. 3-Div. 2-Corps Pot	No change to Muster Out	Oct., 1864

4th BRIGADE, 3d DIVISION.—Organized May 13, 1864, from 2-Brig. 4-Div. 2-Corps. Discontinued July 3, 1864.

COMMANDER.

Wm. R. Brewster	Col. 73d N. Y. Infy	May 13, 1864, to July 3, 1864.	

11th Mass. Infy......May, 1864	From 2-Brig. 4-Div. 2-Corps Pot	To 3-Brig. 3-Div. 2-Corps Pot	July, 1864
70th N. Y. Infy......May, 1864	From 2-Brig. 4-Div. 2 Corps Pot	No change to Muster Out	July, 1864
71st N. Y. Infy......May, 1864	From 2-Brig. 4-Div. 2 Corps Pot	No change to Muster Out	July, 1864
72d N. Y. Infy......May, 1864	From 2-Brig. 4-Div. 2 Corps Pot	To 3-Brig. 3-Div. 2-Corps Pot	July, 1864
73d N. Y. Infy......May, 1864	From 2-Brig. 4-Div. 2 Corps Pot	To 1-Brig. 3-Div. 2-Corps Pot	July, 1864
74th N. Y. Infy......May, 1864	From 2-Brig. 4-Div. 2 Corps Pot	To 1-Brig. 3-Div. 2-Corps Pot	July, 1864
120th N. Y. Infy......May, 1864	From 2-Brig. 4-Div. 2 Corps Pot	To 3-Brig. 3-Div. 2-Corps Pot	July, 1864
84th Penna. Infy......May, 1864	From 2-Brig. 4-Div. 2 Corps Pot	To 2-Brig. 3-Div. 2-Corps Pot	July, 1864

ARTILLERY, 3d DIVISION.—

Batty. G, 1st N. Y. Arty..Sept., 1864	From Reserve Arty. 2-Corps Pot	To 1-Vol. Brig. Arty Reserve Pot	May, 1863
Batty. G, 1st R. I. Arty..Sept., 1864	From Reserve Arty. 2-Corps Pot	To 4-Vol. Brig. Arty. Reserve Pot	May, 1863

4th DIVISION.—Organized March 24, 1864, from 2d Div. 3-Corps. Consolidated with 3d Division May 13, 1864.

COMMANDERS.

J. B. Carr	Brigadier General	Mch. 25, 1864, to May 2, 1864.	
Gershom Mott	Brigadier General	May 2, 1864, to May 13, 1864.	

1st BRIGADE, 4th DIVISION.— COMMANDERS.

Gershom Mott	Brigadier General	Mch. 25, 1864, to May 2, 1864.	
Robert McAllister	Col. 11th N. J. Infy	May 2, 1864, to May 13, 1864.	

1st Mass Infy......Mch., 1864	From 1-Brig. 2-Div. 3-Corps Pot	No change to Muster Out	May, 1864
16th Mass. Infy......Mch., 1864	From 1-Brig. 2-Div. 3-Corps Pot	To 3-Brig. 3-Div. 2-Corps Pot	May, 1864
5th N. J. Infy......Mch., 1864	From 3-Brig. 2-Div. 3-Corps Pot	To 3-Brig. 3-Div. 2-Corps Pot	May, 1864
6th N. J. Infy......Mch., 1864	From 3-Brig. 2-Div. 3-Corps Pot	To 3-Brig. 3-Div. 2-Corps Pot	May, 1864
7th N. J. Infy......Mch., 1864	From 3-Brig. 2-Div. 3-Corps Pot	To 3-Brig. 3-Div. 2-Corps Pot	May, 1864
8th N. J. Infy......Mch., 1864	From 3-Brig. 2-Div. 3-Corps Pot	To 3-Brig. 3-Div. 2-Corps Pot	May, 1864
11th N. J. Infy......Mch., 1864	From 1-Brig. 2-Div. 3-Corps Pot	To 3-Brig. 3-Div. 2-Corps Pot	May, 1864
26th Penna. Infy......Mch., 1864	From 1-Brig. 2-Div. 3-Corps Pot	No change to Muster Out	May, 1864
115th Penna. Infy......Mch., 1864	From 3-Brig. 2-Div. 3-Corps Pot	To 3-Brig. 3-Div. 2-Corps Pot	May, 1864

2d BRIGADE, 4th DIVISION.— COMMANDER.

Wm. R. Brewster	Col. 73d N. Y. Infy	Mch. 25, 1864, to May 13, 1864.	

11th Mass. Infy......Mch., 1864	From 1-Brig. 2-Div. 3-Corps Pot	To 4-Brig. 3-Div. 2-Corps Pot	May, 1864
70th N. Y. Infy......Mch., 1864	From 2-Brig. 2-Div. 3-Corps Pot	To 4-Brig. 3-Div. 2-Corps Pot	May, 1864
71st N. Y. Infy......Mch., 1864	From 2-Brig. 2-Div. 3-Corps Pot	To 4-Brig. 3-Div. 2-Corps Pot	May, 1864
72d N. Y. Infy......Mch., 1864	From 2-Brig. 2-Div. 3-Corps Pot	To 4-Brig. 3-Div. 2-Corps Pot	May, 1864
73d N. Y. Infy......Mch., 1864	From 2-Brig. 2-Div. 3-Corps Pot	To 4-Brig. 3-Div. 2-Corps Pot	May, 1864
74th N. Y. Infy......Mch., 1864	From 2-Brig. 2-Div. 3-Corps Pot	To 4-Brig. 3-Div. 2-Corps Pot	May, 1864
120th N. Y. Infy......Mch., 1864	From 2-Brig. 2-Div. 3-Corps Pot	To 4-Brig. 3-Div. 2-Corps Pot	May, 1864
84th Penna. Infy......Mch., 1864	From 1-Brig. 2-Div. 3-Corps Pot	To 4-Brig. 3-Div. 2-Corps Pot	May, 1864

KIMBALL'S INDEPENDENT BRIGADE.—Joined Corps from Department of the Rappahannock, July 4, 1862. Designated 1st Brigade, 3d Division, Sept. 12, 1862.

COMMANDER.

Nathan Kimball........	Col. 14th Ind. Infy.................	July to Sept., 1862

14th Ind. Infy............July, 1862	From Kimball's Indpt. Brig., Rapp..	To 1-Brig. 3-Div. 2-Corps Pot......	Sept., 1862
4th Ohio Infy............July, 1862	From Kimball's Indpt. Brig. Rapp..	To 1-Brig. 3-Div. 2-Corps Pot......	Sept., 1862
8th Ohio Infy............July, 1862	From Kimball's Indpt. Brig. Rapp..	To 1-Brig. 3-Div. 2-Corps Pot......	Sept., 1862
7th West Va. Infy.......July, 1862	From Kimball's Indpt. Brig. Rapp..	To 1-Brig. 3-Div. 2-Corps Pot......	Sept., 1862

BLENKER'S DIVISION.—Transferred to the Department of the Mountains, March 31, 1862.

COMMANDER.

Louis Blenker..........	Brigadier General..................	

1st BRIGADE.—

COMMANDER.

Julius Stahel...........	Brigadier General..................	

8th N. Y. Infy...........Mch., 1862	From 1-Brig. Blenker's Div. Pot....	To 1-Brig. Blenker's Div. Mts......	Mch., 1862
39th N. Y. Infy..........Mch., 1862	From 1-Brig. Blenker's Div. Pot....	To 1-Brig. Blenker's Div. Mts......	Mch., 1862
45th N. Y. Infy..........Mch., 1862	From 1-Brig. Blenker's Div. Pot....	To 1-Brig. Blenker's Div. Mts......	Mch., 1862
27th Penna. Infy.........Mch., 1862	From 1-Brig. Blenker's Div. Pot....	To 1-Brig. Blenker's Div. Mts......	Mch., 1862

2nd BRIGADE.—

COMMANDER.

A. Von Steinwehr......	Brigadier General..................	

29th N. Y. Infy..........Mch., 1862	From 2-Brig. Blenker's Div. Pot....	To 2-Brig. Blenker's Div. Mts......	Mch., 1862
54th N. Y. Infy..........Mch., 1862	From 2-Brig. Blenker's Div. Pot....	To 2-Brig. Blenker's Div. Mts......	Mch., 1862
68th N. Y. Infy..........Mch., 1862	From 2-Brig. Blenker's Div. Pot....	To 2-Brig. Blenker's Div. Mts......	Mch., 1862
73d Penna. Infy..........Mch., 1862	From 2-Brig. Blenker's Div. Pot....	To 2-Brig. Blenker's Div. Mts......	Mch., 1862

3d BRIGADE.—

COMMANDER.

Henry Bohlen..........	Brigadier General..................	

58th N. Y. Infy..........Mch., 1862	From 3-Brig. Blenker's Div. Pot....	To 3-Brig. Blenker's Div. Mts......	Mch., 1862
25th (74th) Pa. Infy......Mch., 1862	From 3-Brig. Blenker's Div. Pot....	To 3-Brig. Blenker's Div. Mts......	Mch., 1862
40th (75th) Pa. Infy......Mch., 1862	From 3-Brig. Blenker's Div. Pot....	To 3-Brig. Blenker's Div. Mts......	Mch., 1862
UNATTACHED.—			
41st N. Y. Infy...........Mch., 1862	From Unatt. Blenker's Div. Pot....	To Unatt. Blenker's Div. Mts.......	Mch., 1862
2d N. Y. Ind. Batty. Arty.Mch., 1862	From Unatt. Blenker's Div. Pot....	To Unatt. Blenker's Div. Mts.......	Mch., 1862
13th N. Y. Ind. Batty. Arty.Mch., 1862	From Unatt. Blenker's Div. Pot....	To Unatt. Blenker's Div. Mts.......	Mch., 1862
4th N. Y. Cav............Mch., 1862	From Unatt. Blenker's Div. Pot....	To Unatt. Blenker's Div. Mts.......	Mch., 1862

TYLER'S HEAVY ARTILLERY DIVISION.—Joined May 18, 1864, from Def. of Washington, 22 Corps.

COMMANDER.

R. O. Tyler...........	Brigadier General..................	

1st Me. Heavy Arty.......May, 1864	From 2-Brig. Tyler's Div. 22 Corps.	To 3-Brig. 3-Div. 2-Corps Pot......	May, 1864
1st Mass. Heavy Arty......May, 1864	From 2-Brig. Tyler's Div. 22 Corps.	To 2-Brig. 3-Div. 2-Corps Pot......	May, 1864
2d N. Y. Heavy Arty......May, 1864	From 2-Brig. Tyler's Div. 22 Corps.	To 1-Brig. 1-Div. 2-Corps Pot......	May, 1864
7th N. Y. Heavy Arty.....May, 1864	From 2-Brig. Tyler's Div. 22 Corps.	To 4-Brig. 1-Div. 2-Corps Pot......	May, 1864
8th N. Y. Heavy Arty.....May, 1864	From 2-Brig. Tyler's Div. 22 Corps.	To 4-Brig. 2-Div. 2-Corps Pot......	May, 1864
CORPS ARTILLERY, RESERVE.—			
Batty. A, 1st R. I. Arty...May, 1862	From Arty. 2-Div. 2-Corps Pot.....	To Arty. Brig. 2-Corps Pot........	May, 1863
Batty. G, 1st R. I. Arty...May, 1862	From Arty. 3-Div. 2-Corps Pot.....	To Arty. 3-Div. 2-Corps Pot........	Sept., 1862
Batty. G, 1st N. Y. Arty...June, 1862	From Arty. 1-Div. 2-Corps Pot.....	To Arty. 3-Div. 2-Corps Pot........	Sept., 1862
Batty. I, 1st U. S. Arty...Nov., 1862	From Arty. 2-Div. 2-Corps Pot.....	To Arty. Brig. 2-Corps Pot........	May, 1863
Batty. A, 4th U. S. Arty...Nov., 1862	From Arty. 1-Div. 2-Corps Pot.....	To Arty. Brig. 2-Corps Pot........	May, 1863
ARTILLERY BRIGADE.—			
Batty. A, 1st R. I. Arty...May, 1862	From Arty. 2-Div. 2-Corps Pot.....	Consol. with Batty. B, 1-R. I......	Sept., 1864
Batty. B, 1st R. I. Arty...May, 1863	From Corps Arty. Reserve..........	No change to Muster Out.........	June, 1865
Batty. I, 1st U. S. Arty...May, 1863	From Arty. 2-Div. 2-Corps Pot.....	To 2-Brig. Horse Arty. Pot........	Nov., 1863
Batty. A, 4th U. S. Arty...May, 1863	From Arty. 1-Div. 2-Corps Pot.....	To 1-Brig. Horse Arty. Pot........	June, 1863
Batty. B, 1st N. Y. Arty...May, 1863	From Arty. 1-Div. 2-Corps Pot.....	To 1-Vol. Brig. Arty. Res. Pot.....	June, 1863
Batty. B, 1st N. Y. Arty...July, 1863	From 1-Vol. Brig. Arty. Res. Pot...	To 2-Vol. Brig. Arty. Res. Pot.....	July, 1863
Batty. G, 1st N. Y. Arty...Aug., 1863	From 4-Vol. Brig. Arty. Res. Pot...	To Arty. Reserve Potomac.........	Mch., 1865
Batty. F, 1st Pa. Arty...Aug., 1863	From 3-Vol. Brig. Arty. Res. Pot...	To Arty. Reserve Potomac.........	Sept., 1864
Batty. G, 1st Pa. Arty...Aug., 1863	From 3-Vol. Brig. Arty. Res. Pot...	To Camp Barry Wash. 22-Corps...	Mch., 1864
Batty. H, 1st Ohio Arty...Oct., 1863	From 4-Vol. Brig. Arty. Res. Pot...	To 2-Brig. Arty. Res. Pot........	Nov., 1863
Indpt. Batty. C, Pa. Arty...Oct., 1863	From 1-Vol. Brig. Arty. Res. Pot...	To Camp Barry Wash. 22-Corps...	Mch., 1864
Indpt. Batty. F, Pa. Arty...Oct., 1863	From 1-Vol. Brig. Arty. Res. Pot...	To Camp Barry Wash. 22-Corps...	Mch., 1864
Battys. C & I, 5th U. S...Oct., 1863	From Camp Barry. Wash., 22-C....	To Arty. Res. Pot.................	Mch., 1865
Batty. K, 4th U. S. Arty...Mch., 1864	From Arty. Brig. 3-Corps Pot.....	To Dept. of Washington..........	June, 1865
10th Mass. Indpt. Batty..Mch., 1864	From Arty. Brig. 3-Corps Pot.....	No change to Muster Out........	June, 1865
12th N. Y. Indpt. Batty...May, 1864	From 2-Brig. Arty. Reserve Pot....	To Arty. Res. Potomac...........	Mch., 1865
6th Me. Indpt. Batty.....Apr., 1864	From 2-Brig. Arty. Reserve Pot....	To Arty. Res. Potomac...........	Mch., 1865
1st N. H. Batty.........Apr., 1864	From Arty. Brig. 3-Corps Pot.....	No change to Muster Out........	June, 1865
4th N. Y. H. A. 3d Battn..Apr., 1864	From 3-Brig. DeRussy's Div. 22-C..	To 4-Brig. 1-Div. 2-Corps Pot.....	June, 1864
4th N Y. H. A., Co. D....May, 1864	From Arty. Brig. 5-Corps Pot.....	To 4-Brig. 1-Div. 2-Corps Pot.....	June, 1864
11th N. Y. Indpt. Batty...May, 1864	From 3-Brig. Arty. Res. Pot.......	No change to Muster Out........	June, 1865
Batty. B, 1st N. J. Arty...May, 1864	From 2-Brig. Arty. Reserve Pot....	No change to Muster Out........	June, 1865
4th N. Y. H. A., Co. L....July, 1864	From Arty. Brig. 6-Corps Pot.....	To Arty. Res. Pot...............	Mch., 1865
4th N. Y. H. A., Co. C....Sept., 1864	From Arty. Res. Pot..............	To Arty. Res. Pot...............	Mch., 1865
12th N. Y. Indpt. Batty...April, 1865	From Arty. Res. Pot..............	No change to Muster Out........	June, 1865

Third Army Corps

Created March 3, 1862, by order of the President of the U. S. Announced March 13, 1862, in General Order No. 101, Army of the Potomac. Broken up and discontinued March 24, 1864.

CORPS COMMANDERS.

S. P. Heintzelman......	Brigadier General..................	Mch. 13, 1862, to Oct. 30, 1862.
Geo. Stoneman.........	Brigadier General..................	Oct. 30, 1862, to Feb. 5, 1863.
D. E. Sickles...........	Major General....................	Feb. 5, 1863, to May 29, 1863.
D. B. Birney...........	Major General....................	May 29, 1863, to June 3, 1863.
D. E. Sickles...........	Major General....................	June 3, 1863, to July 2, 1863.
D. B. Birney...........	Major General....................	July 2, 1863, to July 7, 1863.
W. H. French...........	Major General....................	July 7, 1863, to Jan. 28, 1864.
D. B. Birney...........	Major General....................	Jan. 28, 1864, to Feb. 17, 1864.
W. H. French...........	Major General....................	Feb. 17, 1864, to Mch. 24, 1864.

1st DIVISION, 3d CORPS.— COMMANDERS.

Fitz John Porter	Brigadier General	Mch. 13, 1862, to May 18, 1862.	
Division transferred to 5th Provisional Corps May 18, 1862. Reorganized from 3d Div. 3d Corps, Aug. 5, 1862.			
Philip Kearny	Major General	Aug. 5, 1862, to Sept. 1, 1862.	Killed.
D. B. Birney	Brigadier General	Sept. 1, 1862, to Sept. 13, 1862.	
Geo. Stoneman	Brigadier General	Sept. 13, 1862, to Oct. 30, 1862.	
D. B. Birney	Major General	Oct. 30, 1862, to May 29, 1863.	
J. H. H. Ward	Brigadier General	May 29, 1863, to June 3, 1863.	
D. B. Birney	Major General	June 3, 1863, to July 2, 1863.	
J. H. H. Ward	Brigadier General	July 2, 1863, to July 7, 1863.	
D. B. Birney	Major General	July 7, 1863, to Jan. 28, 1864.	
J. H. H. Ward	Brigadier General	Jan. 28, 1864, to Feb. 17, 1864.	
D. B. Birney	Major General	Feb. 17, 1864, to Mch. 24, 1864.	

1st BRIGADE, 1st DIVISION.— COMMANDERS.

J. H. Martindale	Brigadier General	Mch. 13, 1862, to May 18, 1862.
J. C. Robinson	Brigadier General	Aug. 5, 1862, to Dec. 30, 1862.
S. B. Hayman	Col. 37th N. Y. Infy.	Dec. 30, 1862, to Feb. .., 1862.
J. Van Valkenburg	Col. 20th Ind. Infy.	Feb. .., 1863, to Feb. .., 1863.
C. H. T. Collis	Col. 114th Penna. Infy.	Feb. .., 1863, to March .., 1863.
C. K. Graham	Brigadier General	Mch. .., 1863, to May 14, 1863.
Thos. W. Egan	Col. 40th N. Y. Infy.	May 4, 1863, Temp'y.
H. J. Madill	Col. 141st Penna. Infy.	May 14, 1863, to May, 1863.
A. H. Tippin	Col. 68th N. Y. Infy.	May, 1863, to June, 1863.
C. K. Graham	Brigadier General	June, 1863, to July 2, 1863.
A. H. Tippin	Col. 68th N. Y. Infy.	July 2, 1863, to July 3, 1863.
H. J. Madill	Col. 141st Penna. Infy.	July 3, 1863, to Aug., 1863.
C. H. T. Collis	Col. 114th Penna. Infy.	Aug., 1863, to Mch. 24, 1864.

2d Me. Infy.	Mch., 1862	From Martindale's Brig. Porter's D.	To 1-Brig. 1-Div. 5-Corps Pot.	May, 1862
18th Mass. Infy.	Mch., 1862	From Martindale's Brig. Porter's D.	To 1-Brig. 1-Div. 5-Corps Pot.	May, 1862
(2d Co. S. S. Att.)				
22d Mass. Infy.	Mch., 1862	From Martindale's Brig. Porter's D.	To 1-Brig. 1-Div. 5-Corps Pot.	May, 1862
13th N. Y. Infy.	Mch., 1862	From Martindale's Brig. Porter's D.	To 1-Brig. 1-Div. 5-Corps Pot.	May, 1862
25th N. Y. Infy.	Mch., 1862	From Martindale's Brig. Porter's D.	To 1-Brig. 1-Div. 5-Corps Pot.	May, 1862
Brigade reorganized Aug. 5, 1862.		from 1-Brig. 3-Div.		
20th Ind. Infy.	Aug., 1862	From 1-Brig. 3-Div. 3-Corps Pot.	To 2-Brig. 1-Div. 3-Corps Pot.	Mch., 1863
63d Penna. Infy.	Aug., 1862	From 1-Brig. 3-Div. 3-Corps Pot.	To 3-Brig. 2-Div. 2-Corps Pot.	Mch., 1864
105th Penna. Infy.	Aug., 1862	From 1-Brig. 3-Div. 3-Corps Pot.	To 1-Brig. 3-Div. 2-Corps Pot.	Mch., 1864
87th N. Y. Infy.	Aug., 1862	From 1-Brig. 3-Div. 3-Corps Pot.	Consol with 40th N. Y.	Sept., 1862
141st Penna.	Sept., 1862	From New Organization	To 1-Brig. 3-Div. 2-Corps Pot.	Mch., 1864
68th Penna. Infy.	Oct., 1862	From New Organization	To Provost Guard Pot.	Mch., 1864
114th Penna. Infy.	Oct., 1862	From New Organization	To Provost Guard Pot.	Mch., 1864
57th Penna. Infy.	Mch., 1863	From 2-Brig. 1-Div. 3-Corps Pot.	To 2-Brig. 3-Div. 2-Corps Pot.	Mch., 1864

2d BRIGADE, 1st DIVISION.— COMMANDERS.

Geo. W. Morrell	Brigadier General	Mch. 13, 1862, to May 18, 1862.
D. B. Birney	Brigadier General	Aug. 5, 1862, to Sept. 1, 1862.
J. H. H. Ward	Col. 38th N. Y. Infy.	Sept. 1, 1862, to Sept. 13, 1862.
D. B. Birney	Brigadier General	Sept. 13, 1862, to Oct. 30, 1862.
J. H. H. Ward	Brigadier General	Oct. 30, 1862, to Jan. 26, 1863.
R. DeTrobriand	Col. 38th N. Y. Infy.	Jan. 26, 1863, to Feb. 15, 1863.
J. H. H. Ward	Brigadier General	Feb. 15, 1863, to Mch. 1863.
R. DeTrobriand	Col. 38th New York Infy.	Mch., 1863, to Apr., 1863.
J. H. H. Ward	Brigadier General	Apr., 1862, to May 29, 1863.
R. DeTrobriand	Col. 38th New York Infy.	May 29, 1863, to June 3, 1863.
J. H. H. Ward	Brigadier General	June 3, 1863, to July 2, 1863.
Hiram Berdan	Col. 1st U. S. Sharpshooters	July 2, 1863, to July 7, 1863.
J. H. H. Ward	Brigadier General	July 7, 1863, to Aug., 1863.
L. D Carver	Lt.-Col. 4th Maine Infy.	Aug., 1863, to Sept., 1863.
J. H. H. Ward	Brigadier General	Sept., 1863, to Dec. 29, 1863.
E. Walker	Col. 4th Maine Infy.	Dec. 29, 1863, to Jan. 17, 1864.
J. H. H. Ward	Brigadier General	Jan. 17, 1864, to Jan. 28, 1864.
E. Walker	Col. 4th Maine Infy.	Jan. 28, 1864, to Feb. 17, 1864.
J. H. H. Ward	Brigadier General	Feb. 17, 1864, to Mch. 24, 1864.

14th New York Infy.	Mch., 1862	From Morrell's Brig. Porter's Div.	To 2-Brig. 1-Div. 5-Corps Potomac.	May, 1862
4th Michigan Infy.	Mch., 1862	From Morrell's Brig. Porter's Div.	To 2-Brig. 1-Div. 5-Corps Potomac.	May, 1862
9th Mass. Infy.	Mch., 1862	From Morrell's Brig. Porter's Div.	To 2-Brig. 1-Div. 5-Corps Potomac.	May, 1862
62d Penna. Infy.	Mch., 1862	From Morrell's Brig. Porter's Div.	To 2-Brig. 1-Div. 5-Corps Potomac.	May, 1862
Brigade reorganized Aug. 5, 1862		from 2-Brig. 3-Div.		
3d Maine Infy.	Aug., 1862	From 2-Brig. 3-Div. 3-Corps Potom.	To 1-Brig. 3-Div. 2-Corps Potomac.	Mch., 1864
4th Maine Infy.	Aug., 1862	From 2-Brig. 3-Div. 3-Corps Potom.	To 3-Brig. 1-Div. 3-Corps Potomac.	Sept., 1863
1st New York Infy.	Aug., 1862	From 2-Brig. 3-Div. 3-Corps Potom.	No change to Muster Out.	June, 1863
38th New York Infy.	Aug., 1862	From 2-Brig. 3-Div. 3-Corps Potom.	To 3-Brig. 1-Div. 3-Corps Potomac.	May, 1863
40th New York Infy.	Aug., 1862	From 2-Brig. 3-Div. 3-Corps Potom.	To 3-Brig. 1-Div. 3-Corps Potomac.	Nov., 1862
101st New York Infy.	Aug., 1862	From 2-Brig. 3-Div. 3-Corps Potom.	To 1-Brig. 1-Div. 3-Corps Potomac.	Mch., 1863
57th Penna. Infy.	Aug., 1862	From 1-Brig. 3-Div. 3-Corps Potom.	Consolidated with 38th N. Y.	Dec., 1862
55th New York Infy.	Sept., 1862	From 3-Brig. 1-Div. 3-Corps Potom.	To 1-Brig. 3-Div. 2-Corps Potomac.	Mch., 1864
99th Penna. Infy.	Dec., 1863	From 3-Brig. 1-Div. 3-Corps Potom.	To 3-Brig. 1-Div. 2-Corps Potomac.	Mch., 1864
20th Indiana Infy.	Mch., 1863	From 1-Brig. 3-Div. 3-Corps Potom.	To 3-Brig. 1-Div. 3-Corps Potomac.	Sept., 1863
1st U. S. Sharpshooters	June, 1863	From 3-Brig. 1-Div. 3-Corps Potom.	To 3-Brig. 1-Div. 2-Corps Potomac.	Mch., 1864
2d U. S. Sharpshooters	June, 1863	From 3-Brig. 1-Div. 3-Corps Potom.	To 1-Brig. 3-Div. 2-Corps Potomac.	Mch., 1864
86th New York Infy.	June, 1863	From 3-Brig. 1-Div. 3-Corps Potom.	To 3-Brig. 1-Div. 2-Corps Potomac.	Mch., 1864
124th New York Infy.	June, 1863	From 1-Brig. 3-Div. 3-Corps Potom.	To 1-Brig. 3-Div. 2-Corps Potomac.	Mch., 1864

3d BRIGADE, 1st DIVISION.— COMMANDERS.

D. Butterfield	Brigadier General	March 13, 1862, to May 18, 1862.
O. M. Poe	Col. 2d Mich. Infy.	Aug. 5, 1862, to Sept., 1862.
H. G. Berry	Brigadier General	Sept. 1862, to Oct., 1862.
R. DeTrobriand	Col. 38th N. Y. Infy.	Oct., 1862, to Nov., 1862.
H. G. Berry	Brigadier General	Nov., 1862, to Jan., 1863.
T. A. Roberts	Col. 17th Maine Infy.	Jan., 1863, to Feb., 1863.
S. B. Hayman	Col. 37th N. Y. Infy.	Feb., 1863, to June 3, 1863.
R. DeTrobriand	Col. 35th N. Y. Infy.	June 3, 1863, to Nov. 22, 1863.

3d BRIGADE, 1st DIVISION.—Continued.   COMMANDERS.

Name	Rank	Dates
T. W. Egan	Col. 40th N. Y. Infy	Nov. 22, 1863, to Dec. 30, 1863.
B. R. Pierce	Col. 3d Mich. Infy	Dec. 30, 1863, to Jan., 1864.
G. W. West	Col. 17th Maine Infy	Jan., 1864, to Feb., 1864.
T. W. Egan	Col. 40th N. Y. Infy	Feb., 1864, to March 24, 1864.

12th N. Y. Infy	Mch., 1862	From Butterfield's Brig. Porter's D.	To 3-Brig. 1-Div. 5-CorpsPot	May,	1862
17th N. Y. Infy	Mch., 1862	From Butterfield's Brig. Porter's D.	To 3-Brig. 1-Div. 5-CorpsPot	May,	1862
44th N. Y. Infy	Mch., 1862	From Butterfield's Brig. Porter's D.	To 3-Brig. 1-Div. 5-CorpsPot	May,	1862
83d Penna. Infy	Mch., 1862	From Butterfield's Brig. Porter's D.	To 3-Brig. 1-Div. 5-CorpsPot	May,	1862
16th Mich. Infy	Mch., 1862	From Butterfield's Brig. Porter's D.	To 3-Brig. 1-Div. 5-CorpsPot	May,	1862
Brigade reorganized Aug. 5, 1862, from 3d Brig. 3d Division.					
2d Mich. Infy	Aug., 1862	From 3-Brig. 3-Div. 3-Corps Pot.	To 1-Brig. 1-Div. 9-Corps Pot	Nov.	1862
3d Mich. Infy	Aug., 1862	From 3-Brig. 3-Div. 3-Corps Pot.	To 2-Brig. 3-Div. 2-Corps Pot	Mch.,	1864
5th Mich. Infy	Aug., 1862	From 3-Brig. 3-Div. 3-Corps Pot.	To 2-Brig. 3-Div. 2-Corps Pot	Mch.,	1864
37th N. Y. Infy	Aug., 1862	From 3-Brig. 3-Div. 3-Corps Pot.	No change to Muster Out	June,	1863
99th Penna. Infy	Aug., 1862	From 3-Brig. 3-Div. 3-Corps Pot.	To 2-Brig. 1-Div. 3-Corps Pot	Dec.,	1862
1st N. Y. Infy	Sept., 1862	From 3-Brig. 3-Div. 3-Corps Pot.	No change to Muster Out	June,	1863
55th N. Y. Infy	Sept., 1862	From 2-Brig. 1-Div. 4-Corps Pot.	To 2-Brig. 1-Div. 3-Corps Pot	Nov.,	1862
17th Maine Infy	Oct., 1862	From Def. of Washington	To 2-Brig. 3-Div. 2-Corps Pot	Mch.,	1864
101st N. Y. Infy	Nov., 1862	From 2-Brig. 1-Div. 3-Corps Pot.	Consol. with 37th N. Y.	Dec.,	1862
40th N. Y. Infy	May, 1863	From 2-Brig. 1-Div. 3-Corps Pot.	To 1-Brig. 3-Div. 2-Corps Pot	Mch.,	1864
110th Penna. Infy	June, 1862	From 3-Brig. 2-Div. 3-Corps Pot.	To 1-Brig. 3-Div. 2-Corps Pot	Mch.,	1864
1st U. S. Sharpshooters	Sept., 1863	From 2-Brig. 1-Div. 3-Corps Pot.	To 2-Brig. 3-Div. 2-Corps Pot	Mch.,	1864

ARTILERY, 1st DIVISION.—

3d Mass. Indpt. Batty	Mch., 1862	From Porter's Div. Potomac	To Arty. 1-Div. 5-Corps Potomac	May,	1862
5th Mass. Indpt. Batty	Mch., 1862	From Porter's Div. Potomac	To Arty. 1-Div. 5-Corps Potomac	May,	1862
Batty. C, 1st R. I. Arty	Mch., 1862	From Porter's Div. Potomac	To Arty. 1-Div. 5-Corps Potomac	May,	1862
Batty. D, 5th U. S. Arty	Mch., 1862	From Porter's Div. Potomac	To Arty. 1-Div. 5-Corps Potomac	May,	1862
Batty. E, 1st R. I.	Aug., 1862	From Arty. 3-Div. 3-Corps Pot	To Arty. Brig. 3-Corps Potomac	May,	1863
6th Maine Indpt. Batty	Aug., 1862	From 2-Div. 2-Corps Army Va	To Arty. 2-Div. 12-Corps Potomac	Sept.,	1862
Batty. K, 1st U. S. Arty	Aug., 1862	From 2-Brig. Arty. Res. 5-Corps P.	To Arty. Res. 5-Corps Potomac	Sept.,	1862
Battys. F & K, 3d U. S.	Aug., 1862	From 5-Brig. Arty. Res. 5-Corps P.	To 1-Reg. Brig. Arty. Res. Pot	May,	1863
Batty. B, 1st N. J. Arty	Jan., 1863	From Arty 2-Div. 3-Corps Pot	To Arty. Brigade 3-Corps Potomac.	May,	1863

SHARPSHOOTERS.—

		From	To		
1st United States Div	Mch., 1862	From Porter's Div. Potomac	To Unatt. 1-Div. 5-Corps Pot	May,	1862

2d DIVISION.—

Name	Rank	Dates	
Joseph Hooker	Brigadier General	March 13, 1862, to Sept. 5, 1862.	
D. E. Sickles	Brigadier General	Sept. 5, 1862, to Jan. 12, 1863.	
J. B. Carr	Brigadier General	Jan. 12, 1863, to Feb. 8, 1863.	
H. G. Berry	Brigadier General	Feb. 8, 1863, to May 3, 1863.	Killed.
J. B. Carr	Brigadier General	May 3, 1863, to May 23, 1863.	
A. A. Humphrey	Major General	May 23, 1863, to July 9, 1863.	
J. B. Carr	Brigadier General	July 9, 1863, to July 10, 1863.	
Henry Prince	Brigadier General	July 10, 1863, to March 24, 1864.	

1st BRIGADE, 2d DIVISION.—   COMMANDERS.

Name	Rank	Dates
H. M. Naglee	Brigadier General	March 13, 1862, to April 27, 1862.
C. Grover	Brigadier General	April 27, 1862, to Sept. 16, 1862.
J. B Carr	Brigadier General	Sept. 16, 1862, to Jan. 12, 1863.
Wm. Blaisdell	Col. 11th Mass. Infy	Jan. 12, 1863, to Feb. 8, 1863.
J. B. Carr	Brigadier General	Feb. 8, 1863, to May 3, 1863.
Wm. Blaisdell	Col. 11th Mass. Infy	May 3, 1863, to May 23, 1863.
J. B. Carr	Brigadier General	May 23, 1863, to Oct. 5, 1863.
R. McAllister	Col. 11th N. J. Infy	Oct. 5, 1863 to Dec., 1863.
Wm. Blaisdell	Col. 11th Mass. Infy	Dec., 1864, to Mch. 24, 1864.

1st Michigan Infy	Mch., 1862	From 1-Brig. Hooker's Div. Potomac	To Dept. of Virginia	Mch.,	1862
1st Mass. Infy	Mch., 1862	From 1-Brig. Hooker's Div. Potomac	To 1-Brig. 4-Div. 2-Corps Potomac.	Mch.,	1864
11th Mass. Infy	Mch., 1862	From 1-Brig. Hooker's Div. Potomac	To 2-Brig. 4-Div. 2-Corps Potomac.	Mch.,	1864
2d New Hampshire Infy	Mch., 1862	From 1-Brig. Hooker's Div. Potomac	To New Hampshire	Feb.,	1863
26th Penna. Infy	Mch., 1862	From 1-Brig. Hooker's Div. Potomac	To 1-Brig. 4-Div. 2-Corps Potomac.	Mch.,	1864
16th Mass. Infy	June, 1862	From 1-Brig. 1-Div. Dept. of Va	To 1-Brig. 4-Div. 2-Corps Potomac.	Mch.,	1864
120th New York Infy	Oct., 1862	From Dept. of Washington	To 2-Brig. 2-Div. 3-Corps Potomac.	Dec.,	1862
11th New Jersey Infy	Nov., 1862	From Dept. of Washington	To 1-Brig. 4-Div. 2-Corps Potomac.	Mch.,	1864
84th Penna. Infy	June, 1863	From 2-Brig. 3-Div. 3-Corps Potom.	To 2-Brig. 4-Div. 2-Corps Potomac.	Mch.,	1864
12th New Hamp. Infy	June, 1863	From 2-Brig. 3-Div. 3-Corps Potom.	To Point Lookout, Md	July,	1863

2d BRIGADE, 2d DIVISION.—   COMMANDERS.

Name	Rank	Dates
Nelson Taylor	Col. 72d New York Infy	Mch. 13, 1862, to May 11, 1862.
J. J. Abercrombie	Brigadier General	May 11, 1862, to May 24, 1862.
D. E. Sickles	Brigadier General	May 24, 1862, to July 16, 1862.
Nelson Taylor	Col. 72d New York Infy	July 16, 1862, to Sept. 5, 1862.
Geo. B. Hall	Col. 71st New York Infy	Sept. 5, 1862, to Dec. 24, 1862.
J. W. Revere	Brigadier General	Dec. 24, 1862, to Feb., 1863.
J. E. Farnum	Lt.-Col. 70th N. Y. Infy	Feb., 1863, to Feb., 1863.
C. K. Graham	Brigadier General	Feb., 1863, to Mch., 1863.
J. W. Revere	Brigadier General	Mch., 1863, to May 3, 1863.
J. E. Farnum	Col. 70th New York Infy	May 3, 1863, to May, 1863.
W. R. Brewster	Col. 73d New York Infy	May, 1863, to July 11, 1863.
Thos. Rafferty	Major 71st New York Infy	July 11, 1863, to July 23, 1863.
J. E. Farnum	Col. 70th New York Infy	July 23, 1863, to July 24, 1863.
W. R. Brewster	Col. 73d New York Infy	July 24, 1863, to Aug. 10, 1863.
John Leonard	Lt.-Col. 72d N. Y. Infy	Aug. 10, 1863, to Jan., 1864.
W. R. Brewster	Col. 73d New York Infy	Jan., 1864, to Feb., 1864.
		Feb., 1864, to Mch. 24, 1864.

70th New York Infy	Mch., 1862	From Sickles' Brig. Hooker's Div.	To 2-Brig. 4-Div. 2-Corps Potomac.	Mch.,	1864
71st New York Infy	Mch., 1862	From Sickles' Brig. Hooker's Div.	To 2-Brig. 4-Div. 2-Corps Potomac.	Mch.,	1864
72d New York Infy	Mch., 1862	From Sickles' Brig. Hooker's Div.	To 2-Brig. 4-Div. 2-Corps Potomac.	Mch.,	1864
73d New York Infy	Mch., 1862	From Sickles' Brig. Hooker's Div.	To 2-Brig. 4-Div. 2-Corps Potomac.	Mch.,	1864
74th New York Infy	Mch., 1862	From Sickles' Brig. Hooker's Div.	To 2-Brig. 4-Div. 2-Corps Potomac.	Mch.,	1864
120th New York Infy	Dec., 1862	From 1-Brig. 2-Div. 3-Corps Potom.	To 2-Brig. 4-Div. 2-Corps Potomac.	Mch.,	1864

3d BRIGADE, 2d DIVISION.—   COMMANDERS.

Name	Rank	Dates
S. H. Starr	Col. 5th New Jersey Infy	Mch. 13, 1862, to May 3, 1862.
F. E. Patterson	Brigadier General	May 3, 1862, to May 31, 1862.
S. H. Starr	Col. 5th New Jersey Infy	May 31, 1862, to June 1, 1862.
J. B. Carr	Col. 2d New York Infy	June 1, 1862, to June 6, 1862.
F. E. Patterson	Brigadier General	June 6, 1862, to Nov. 22, 1862.

3d BRIGADE, 2d DIVISION.—Continued.   COMMANDERS.

J. W. Revere............	Col. 7th New Jersey Infy..........	Nov. 22, 1862, to Dec. 25, 1862.
Gershom Mott.........	Brigadier General...................	Dec. 25, 1862, to May 3, 1863.
W. J. Sewell............	Col. 5th New Jersey Infy..........	May 3, 1863, to June, 1863.
G. C. Burling..........	Col. 6th New Jersey Infy..........	June, 1863, to Aug. 29, 1863.
Gershom Mott.........	Brigadier General...................	Aug. 29, 1863, to Feb. 16, 1864.
G. C. Burling..........	Col. 6th New Jersey Infy..........	Feb. 16, 1864, to ————, 1864.
Gershom Mott.........	Brigadier General.................	————, 1864, to Mch. 24, 1864.

5th New Jersey Infy...Mch., 1862	From 3-Brig. Hooker's Div. Pot....	To 1-Brig. 4-Div. 2-Corps Potomac.	Mch.,	1864
6th New Jersey Infy...Mch., 1862	From 3-Brig. Hooker's Div. Pot....	To 1-Brig. 4-Div. 2-Corps Potomac.	Mch.,	1864
7th New Jersey Infy...Mch., 1862	From 3-Brig. Hooker's Div. Pot....	To 1-Brig. 4-Div. 2-Corps Potomac.	Mch.,	1864
8th New Jersey Infy...Mch., 1862	From 3-Brig. Hooker's Div. Pot....	To 1-Brig. 4-Div. 2-Corps Potomac.	Mch.,	1864
2d New York Infy......June, 1862	From Dept. of Virginia............	No change to Muster Out..........	May,	1863
115th Penna. Infy......July, 1862	From New Organization...........	To 1-Brig. 4-Div. 2-Corps Potomac.	Mch.,	1864
2d New Hampshire Infy..June, 1863	From New Hampshire.............	To Point Lookout, Md............	July,	1863
ARTILLERY, 2d DIVISION.—				
Batty. H, 1st U. S. Arty...Mch., 1862	From Arty. Reserve Potomac......	To 1-Regular Brig. Arty. Res. Pot.	May,	1863
4th N. Y. Indpt. Batty...Mch., 1862	From Arty. Hooker's Div. Potomac.	To Arty. Brigade 3-Corps Potomac.	May,	1863
6th N. Y. Indpt. Batty...Mch., 1862	From Arty. Hooker's Div. Potomac.	To Reserve Arty. 3-Corps Potomac.	June,	1862
Batty. D, 1st N. Y. Arty.Mch., 1862	From Arty. Reserve Potomac......	To Reserve Arty. 3-Corps Potomac.	June,	1862
Batty. B, 1st N. J. Arty..Aug., 1862	From Reserve Arty. 3-Corps Potom.	To Arty. 1-Div. 3-Corps Potomac.	Jan.,	1863
Batty. K, 4th U. S. Arty..Aug., 1862	From Reserve Arty. 3-Corps Potom.	To Arty. Brigade 3-Corps Potomac.	May,	1863
Batty. D, 1st N. Y. Arty..Feb., 1863	From Arty. 1-Div. 9-Corps Potomac	To Arty. Brigade 3-Corps Potomac.	May,	1863

3d DIVISION.—   COMMANDERS.

C. S. Hamilton........	Brigadier General...................	Mch. 13, 1862, to Apr. 30, 1862.	
Philip Kearny.........	Brigadier General...................	Apr. 30, 1862, to Aug. 5, 1862.	
Designation changed to 1st Division Aug. 5, 1862. Reorganized Nov. 8, 1862.			
A. W. Whipple.........	Brigadier General...................	Nov. 8, 1862, to May 3, 1863. Mort.	Wnd.
C. K. Graham..........	Brigadier General...................	May 3, 1863, to June 20, 1863.	
Discontinued June 20, 1863. Reorganized July 10, 1863.			
W. L. Elliott..........	Brigadier General...................	July 10, 1863, to Oct. 5, 1863.	
J. B. Carr.............	Brigadier General...................	Oct. 5, 1863, to Mch. 24, 1864.	
Division transferred to 6th Army Corps Mch. 24, 1864.			

1st BRIGADE, 3d DIVISION.—   COMMANDERS.

C. D. Jameson.........	Brigadier General...................	Mch. 13, 1862, to June 12, 1862.
J. C. Robinson.........	Brigadier General...................	June 12, 1862, to Aug. 5, 1862.
A. S. Piatt............	Brigadier General...................	Nov. 8, 1862, to Dec. 14, 1862.
E. Franklin...........	Col. 122d Penna. Infy...........	Dec. 14, 1862, to Dec. 17, 1862.
B. P. Bailey...........	Col. 86th New York Infy.........	Dec. 17, 1862, to Jan., 1863.
A. S. Piatt............	Brigadier General...................	Jan., 1863, to Feb., 1863.
B. P. Bailey...........	Col. 86th New York Infy.........	Feb., 1863, to Apr., 1863.
E. Franklin...........	Col. 122d Penna. Infy...........	Apr., 1863, to May, 1863.
A. Van H. Ellis........	Col. 124th New York Infy........	May, 1863, to June 20, 1863.
W. H. Morris..........	Brigadier General...................	July 10, 1863, to Mch 24, 1864.

57th Penna. Infy........Mch., 1862	From Jameson's B. Heintzelman's D.	To 2-Brig. 1-Div. 3-Corps Potomac	Aug.,	1862
63d Penna. Infy........Mch., 1862	From Jameson's B. Heintzelman's D.	To 1-Brig. 1-Div. 3-Corps Potomac.	Aug.,	1862
105th Penna. Infy......Mch., 1862	From Jameson's B. Heintzelman's D.	To 1-Brig. 1-Div. 3-Corps Potomac.	Aug.,	1862
87th New York Infy....Mch., 1862	From 3-Brig. Casey's Div. Potomac	To 1-Brig. 1-Div. 3-Corps Potomac.	Aug.,	1862
20th Indiana Infy......June, 1862	From Dept. of Virginia............	To 1-Brig. 1-Div. 3-Corps Potomac.	Aug.,	1862
86th New York Infy.....Nov., 1862	From Piatt's B. Dept. Washington.	To 2-Brig. 1-Div. 3-Corps Potomac.	June,	1863
124th New York Infy....Nov., 1862	From Piatt's B. Dept. Washington.	To 2-Brig. 1-Div. 3-Corps Potomac.	June,	1863
122d Penna. Infy.......Nov., 1862	From Piatt's B. Dept. Washington.	No change to Muster Out..........	May,	1863
151st New York Infy....July, 1863	From 3-Provl. B. French's Div. 8-C.	To 3-Div. 6-Corps Potomac.	Mch.,	1864
14th New Jersey Infy....July, 1863	From 3-Provl. B. French's Div. 8-C.	To 1-Brig. 3-Div. 6-Corps Potomac.	Mch.,	1864
10th Vermont Infy......July, 1863	From 3-Provl. B. French's Div. 8-C.	To 1-Brig. 3-Div. 6-Corps Potomac.	Mch.,	1864
6th N. Y. Heavy Arty...July, 1863	From 3-Provl. B. French's Div. 8-C.	To Unatt. Arty. Reserve Potomac..	Aug.,	1863

2d BRIGADE, 3d DIVISION.—   COMMANDERS.

D. B. Birney..........	Brigadier General...................	Mch. 13, 1862, to May 30, 1862.
J. H. H. Ward.........	Col. 38th New York Infy..........	May 30, 1862, to June 9, 1862.
J. C. Robinson.........	Brigadier General...................	June 9, 1862, to June 12, 1862.
D. B. Birney..........	Brigadier General...................	June 12, 1862, to Aug. 5, 1862.
S. S. Carroll..........	Col. 8th Ohio Infy................	Nov. 8, 1862, to Jan. 12, 1863.
J. H. Potter...........	Col. 12th New Hampshire Infy....	Jan. 12, 1863, to Feb. 19, 1863.
Hiram Berdan.........	Col. 1st U. S. Sharpshooters.......	Feb. 19, 1863, to Mch., 1863.
S. M. Bowman.........	Col. 84th Penna. Infy............	Mch., 1863, to June 20, 1863.
J. W. Keifer..........	Col. 110th Ohio Infy.............	July 10, 1863, to Aug. 14, 1863.
J. W. Horne...........	Col. 6th Maryland Infy...........	Aug. 14, 1863, to Sept. 14, 1863.
J. W. Keifer..........	Col. 110th Ohio Infy.............	Sept. 14, 1863, to Mch. 24, 1864.

38th New York Infy......Mch., 1862	From 2-Brig. Heintzelman's Div...	To 2-Brig. 1-Div. 3-Corps Potomac.	Aug.,	1862
40th New York Infy......Mch., 1862	From 2-Brig. Heintzelman's Div...	To 2-Brig. 1-Div. 3-Corps Potomac.	Aug.,	1862
3d Maine Infy..........Mch., 1862	From 2-Brig. Heintzelman's Div...	To 2-Brig. 1-Div. 3-Corps Potomac.	Aug.,	1862
4th Maine Infy.........Mch., 1862	From 2-Brig. Heintzelman's Div...	To 2-Brig. 1-Div. 3-Corps Potomac.	Aug.,	1862
101st New York Infy....June, 1862	From Whipple's Command Wash...	To 2-Brig. 1-Div. 3-Corps Potomac.	Aug.,	1862
12th New Hamp. Infy....Nov., 1862	From Whipple's Command Wash...	To 1-Brig. 2-Div. 3-Corps Potomac.	June,	1863
163d New York Infy......Nov., 1862	From 2-Brig. Whipple's Div. Wash.	Transferred to 73d New York.....	Jan.,	1863
1st West Va. Infy.......Nov., 1862	From 2-Brig. Whipple's Div. Wash.	To Dept. West Va...............	Nov.,	1862
84th Penna. Infy........Nov., 1862	From 2-Brig. Whipple's Div. Wash.	To 1-Brig. 2-Div. 3-Corps Potomac.	June,	1863
110th Penna. Infy.......Nov., 1862	From 2-Brig. Whipple's Div. Wash.	To 3-Brig. 1-Div. 3-Corps Potomac.	June,	1863
6th Maryland Infy......July, 1863	From 1-B. Elliott's Command 8-C.	To 2-Brig. 3-Div. 6-Corps Potomac.	Mch.,	1864
138th Penna. Infy.......July, 1863	From 1-B. Elliott's Command 8-C.	To 2-Brig. 3-Div. 6-Corps Potomac.	Mch.,	1864
110th Ohio Infy........July, 1863	From 1-B. Elliott's Command 8-C.	To 2-Brig. 3-Div. 6-Corps Potomac.	Mch.,	1864
122d Ohio Infy.........July, 1863	From 1-B. Elliott's Command 8-C.	To 2-Brig. 3-Div. 6-Corps Potomac.	Mch.,	1864

3d BRIGADE, 3d DIVISION.—   COMMANDERS.

H. G. Berry............	Brigadier General...................	Mch. 13, 1862, to Aug. 5, 1862.
Brigade reorganized March 13, 1863.		
Hiram Berdan.........	Col. 1st U. S. Sharpshooters.......	Mch. 13, 1863, to June 20, 1863.
B. F. Smith...........	Col. 126th Ohio Infy.............	July 10, 1863, to Aug. 28, 1863.
J. W. Schall...........	Col. 87th Penna. Infy............	Aug. 28, 1863, to Sept. 17, 1863.
B. F. Smith...........	Col. 126th Ohio Infy.............	Sept. 17, 1863, to Mch. 24, 1864.

2d Michigan Infy......Mch., 1862	Fr. Rich'rds'n's B. Heintzelm'n's D.	To 3-Brig. 1-Div. 3-Corps Potomac.	Aug.,	1862
3d Michigan Infy.......Mch., 1862	Fr. Rich'rds'n's B. Heintzelm'n's D.	To 3-Brig. 1-Div. 3-Corps Potomac.	Aug.,	1862
5th Michigan Infy......Mch., 1862	Fr. Rich'rds'n's B. Heintzelm'n's D.	To 3-Brig. 1-Div. 3-Corps Potomac.	Aug.,	1862
37th New York Infy.....Mch., 1862	Fr. Rich'rds'n's B. Heintzelm'n's D.	To 3-Brig. 1-Div. 3-Corps Potomac.	Aug.,	1862
1st New York Infy......June, 1862	From 1-Brig. 1-Div. Dept. Va......	To 3-Brig. 1-Div. 3-Corps Potomac.	Aug.,	1862
99th Penna. Infy........June, 1862	From Military Dist. Washington...	To 3-Brig. 1-Div. 3-Corps Potomac.	Aug.,	1862

3d BRIGADE, 3d DIVISION.—Continued.

1st U. S. Sharpshooters..Mch., 1863	From 1-Div. 5-Corps Potomac......	To 2-Brig. 1-Div. 3-Corps Potomac.	June, 1863
2d U. S. Sharpshooters...Mch., 1863	From 1-Brig. 1-Div. 1-Corps Potom.	To 2-Brig. 1-Div. 3-Corps Potomac.	June, 1863
106th New York Infy....July, 1863	From 3-Brig. French's Com'd 8-C..	To 1-Brig. 3-Div. 6-Corps Potomac.	Mch., 1864
67th Penna. Infy........July, 1863	From 1-Brig. Elliott's Com'd 8-C..	To 2-Brig. 3-Div. 6-Corps Potomac.	Mch., 1864
87th Penna. Infy........July, 1863	From Dept. Susquehanna..........	To 1-Brig. 3-Div. 6-Corps Potomac.	Mch., 1864
126th Ohio Infy.........July, 1863	From 3-Brig. French's Com'd 8-C..	To 2-Brig. 3-Div. 6-Corps Potomac.	Mch., 1864

ARTILLERY, 3d DIVISION.—

Batty. E, 1st R. I. Arty..Mch., 1862	From Hamilton's Div. Potomac....	To Arty 1-Div. 3-Corps Potomac...	July, 1862
Batty. B, 1st N. J. Arty..Mch., 1862	From Hamilton's Div. Potomac....	To Reserve Arty. 3-Corps Potomac.	June, 1862
Batty. G, 2d U. S. Arty..Mch., 1862	From Hamilton's Div. Potomac....	To Arty 1-Div. 4-Corps Potomac...	Aug., 1862
10th N. Y. Indpt. Batty...Nov., 1862	From Arty. 1-Div. 12-Corps Potom.	To Arty. Brigade 3-Corps Potomac.	May, 1863
11th N. Y. Indpt. Batty...Nov., 1862	From Whipple's Div. Wash., D. C..	To Arty. Brigade 3-Corps Potomac.	May, 1863
Batty. H, 1st Ohio Arty..Nov., 1862	From Whipple's Div. Wash., D. C..	To 1-Vol. Brig. Arty. Res. Potomac.	May, 1863

RESERVE ARTILLERY, 3d CORPS.—

Batty. D, 1st N. Y. Arty..June, 1862	From Arty 2-Div. 3-Corps Potomac	To Arty. 1-Div. 9-Corps Potomac...	Dec., 1862
6th N. Y. Indpt. Batty...June, 1862	From Arty 2-Div. 3-Corps Potomac	To Arty. Reserve Potomac........	Dec., 1862
Batty. B, 1st N. J. Arty..June, 1862	From Arty. 3-Div. 3-Corps Potomac	To Arty. 2-Div. 3-Corps Potomac..	Aug., 1862
Batty. K, 4th U. S. Arty..June, 1862	From Arty. Reserve Potomac......	To Arty. 2-Div. 3-Corps Potomac..	Aug., 1862

ARTILLERY BRIGADE, 3d CORPS.

Batty. E, 1st R. I. Arty..May, 1863	From Arty. 1-Div. 3-Corps Potomac	To Arty. Brigade 6-Corps Potomac.	Mch., 1864
Batty. E, 1st N. Y. Arty..May, 1863	From Arty. 2-Div. 3-Corps Potomac	To Arty. Brigade 5-Corps Potomac.	Mch., 1864
4th N. Y. Indpt. Batty...May, 1863	From Arty. 2-Div. 3-Corps Potomac	To 1-Vol. Brigade Arty. Res. Potom.	July, 1863
10th N. Y. Indpt. Batty...May, 1863	From Arty. 2-Div. 3-Corps Potomac	To 1-Vol. Brigade Arty. Res. Potom.	July, 1863
11th N. Y. Indpt. Batty...May, 1863	From Arty. 3-Div. 3-Corps Potomac	To 4-Vol. Brigade Arty. Res. Potom.	June, 1863
Batty. B, 1st N. J. Arty..May, 1863	From Arty. 1-Div. 3-Corps Potomac	To 2-Brigade Arty. Res. Potomac..	Mch., 1864
Batty. K, 4th U. S. Arty..May, 1863	From Arty. 2-Div. 3-Corps Potomac	To Arty. Brigade 2-Corps Potomac.	Mch., 1864
4th Maine Indpt. Batty..July, 1863	From Arty. French's Div. 8-Corps..	To Arty. Brigade 6-Corps Potomac.	Mch., 1864
10th Mass. Indpt. Batty..July, 1863	From Arty. French's Div. 8-Corps..	To Arty. Brigade 2-Corps Potomac.	Mch., 1864
12th N. Y. Indpt. Batty..July, 1863	From Arty. Camp Barry 22-Corps..	To 2-Brig. Arty. Res. Potomac.....	Mch., 1864
Keystone Penna. Batty...July, 1863	From Arty. Camp Barry 22-Corps..	No change to Muster Out..........	Aug., 1863
1st New Hampshire Batty.Oct., 1863	From 3-Vol. Brig. Arty. Res. Potom.	To Arty. Brigade 2-Corps Potomac.	Mch., 1864

Fourth Army Corps

Created March 3, 1862, by order of the President of the U. S. Announced March 13, 1862, in G. O. No. 101,
the Potomac. Discontinued Aug. 1, 1863.

CORPS COMMANDER.

E. D Keyes............	Brigadier General..................	March 13, 1862, to Aug. 1, 1863.

1st DIVISION, 4th CORPS.—   COMMANDERS.

D. N Couch..........	Brigadier General..................	Mch. 13, 1862, to July 12, 1862.
J. J. Abercrombie......	Brigadier General..................	July 12, 1862, to Aug. 12, 1862.
D. N Couch..........	Brigadier General..................	Aug. 12, 1862, to Sept. 26, 1862.
Division transferred to 6th Army Corps Sept. 26, 1862. Reorganized June 17, 1863.		
Rufus King..........	Brigadier General..................	June 17, 1863, to July 15, 1863.

1st BRIGADE, 1st DIVISION.—   COMMANDERS.

H. S. Briggs..........	Col. 10th Mass. Infy..............	Mch. 13, 1862, to May 1, 1862.
Chas. Devens, Jr.......	Brigadier General..................	May 1, 1862, to May 31, 1862.
C. H. Innes...........	Col. 36th New York Infy........	May 31, 1862, to June 7, 1862.
I. N. Palmer..........	Brigadier General..................	June 7, 1862, to July 26, 1862.
Chas. Devens, Jr.......	Brigadier General..................	July 26, 1862, to Sept. 26, 1862.
Hector Tyndale........	Brigadier General..................	June 17, 1863, to July 15, 1863.

2d Rhode Island Infy....Mch., 1862	From Briggs' Brig. Couch's Div...	To 2-Brig. 3-Div. 6-Corps Potomac.	Sept., 1862
7th Mass. Infy..........Mch., 1862	From Briggs' Brig. Couch's Div...	To 2-Brig. 3-Div. 6-Corps Potomac.	Sept., 1862
10th Mass. Infy.........Mch., 1862	From Briggs' Brig. Couch's Div...	To 2-Brig. 3-Div. 6-Corps Potomac.	Sept., 1862
36th New York Infy.....Mch., 1862	From Briggs' Brig. Couch's Div...	To 2-Brig. 3-Div. 6-Corps Potomac.	Sept., 1862
2d Mass. Cavalry.......June, 1863	From Unatt. Yorktown, Va., 7-Corps	To King's Div. 22-Corps Washington	July, 1863
(Cos. A, B, C, D, K.)			
2d N. Y. Cav. (Battalion).June, 1863	From Unatt. Yorktown, Va., 7-Corps	To King's Div. 22-Corps Washington	July, 1863
169th Penna. Infy.......June, 1863	From King's Indpt. Brig. 7-Corps..	To 1-Brig. 3-Div. 11-Corps Potomac	July, 1863
8th N. Y. Indpt. Batty....June, 1863	From Unatt. Yorktown 4-Corps....	To Arty. R. Yktn. Dept. Va. & N. C.	July, 1863

2d BRIGADE, 1st DIVISION.—   COMMANDERS.

L. P. Graham..........	Brigadier General..................	Mch. 13, 1862, to May 19, 1862.
H. W. Wessells........	Brigadier General..................	May 19, 1862, to May 24, 1862.
J. J. Abercrombie......	Brigadier General	May 24, 1862, to July 5, 1862.
Designation changed to 3d Brigade July 5, 1862.		
A. P. Howe...........	Brigadier General	July 5, 1862, to Sept. 26, 1862.
Geo. E. Church........	Col. 11th R. I. Infy..............	June 17, 1863, to July 15, 1863.

65th N. Y. Infy.........Mch., 1862	From Graham's Brig. Couch's Div..	To 3-Brig. 1-Div. 4-Corps Pot......	July, 1862
67th N. Y. Infy.........Mch., 1862	From Graham's Brig. Couch's Div..	To 3-Brig. 1-Div. 4-Corps Pot......	July, 1862
23d Penna. Infy.........Mch., 1862	From Graham's Brig. Couch's Div..	To 3-Brig. 1-Div. 4-Corps Pot......	July, 1862
61st Penna. Infy.........Mch., 1862	From Graham's Brig. Couch's Div..	To 3-Brig. 1-Div. 4-Corps Pot......	July, 1862
31st Penna. Infy.........Mch., 1862	From Graham's Brig. Couch's Div..	To 3-Brig. 1-Div. 4-Corps Pot......	July, 1862
(Designated 82d June, 1862.)			
55th N. Y. Infy........July, 1862	From 3-Brig. 1-Div. 4-Corps Pot....	To 2-Brig. 1-Div. 3-Corps Pot......	Sept., 1862
62d N. Y. Infy.........July, 1862	From 3-Brig. 1-Div. 4-Corps Pot....	To 3-Brig. 3-Div. 6-Corps Potomac.	Sept., 1862
93d Penna. Infy........July, 1862	From 3-Brig. 1-Div. 4-Corps Pot....	To 3-Brig. 3-Div. 6-Corps Potomac.	Sept., 1862
98th Penna. Infy........July, 1862	From 3-Brig. 1-Div. 4-Corps Pot....	To 3-Brig. 3-Div. 6-Corps Potomac.	Sept., 1862
102d Penna. Infy........July, 1862	From 3-Brig. 1-Div. 4-Corps Pot...	To 3-Brig. 3-Div. 6-Corps Potomac.	Sept., 1862
139th Penna. Infy.......Sept., 1862	From New Organization..........	To 3-Brig. 3-Div. 6-Corps Pot......	Sept., 1862
5th Penna. Cav. Det.....June, 1863	From Adv. Brig. Yorktown, 7-Corps.	To Yorktown, Va., Dept. Va. & N. C.	July, 1863
11th R. I. Infy.........June, 1863	From 1-Brig. 1-Div. 7-Corps Va....	No change to Muster Out.........	July, 1863
Batty. E, 1st Pa. Arty....June, 1863	From Res. Arty., Yorktown, 7-Corps.	To Yorktown, Va., Dept. Va. & N. C.	July, 1863
2d Wis. Indpt. Batty.....June, 1863	From Div. at Suffolk, 7 Corps Va...	To Yorktown, Va., Dept. Va. & N. C.	July, 1863

3d BRIGADE, 1st DIVISION.—   **COMMANDERS.**

J. J. Peck	Brigadier General	Mch. 13, 1862, to June 23, 1862.
A. P. Howe	Brigadier General	June 23, 1862, to July 5, 1862.

Designation changed to 2d Brigade July 5, 1862.

John Cochrane	Brigadier General	July 5, 1862, to Sept. 26, 1862.
Chas. Klecker	Col. 172d Penna. Infy	June 17, 1863, to July 8, 1863.

93d Penna. Infy	Mch., 1862	From Peck's Brig. Couch's Div. Pot.	To 2-Brig. 1-Div. 4-Corps Pot	July, 1862
98th Penna. Infy	Mch., 1862	From Peck's Brig. Couch's Div. Pot.	To 2-Brig. 1-Div. 4-Corps Pot	July, 1862
102d Penna. Infy	Mch., 1862	From Peck's Brig. Couch's Div. Pot.	To 2-Brig. 1-Div. 4-Corps Pot	July, 1862
55th N. Y. Infy	Mch., 1862	From Peck's Brig. Couch's Div. Pot.	To 2-Brig. 1-Div. 4-Corps Pot	July, 1862
62d N. Y. Infy	Mch., 1862	From Peck's Brig. Couch's Div. Pot.	To 2-Brig. 1-Div. 4-Corps Pot	July, 1862
65th N. Y. Infy	July, 1862	From 2-Brig. 1-Div. 4-Corps Pot	To 2-Brig. 3-Div. 6-Corps Pot	Sept. 1862
67th N. Y. Infy	July, 1862	From 2-Brig. 1-Div. 4-Corps Pot	To 2-Brig. 3-Div. 6-Corps Pot	Sept. 1862
23d Penna. Infy	July, 1862	From 2-Brig. 1-Div. 4-Corps Pot	To 2-Brig. 3-Div. 6-Corps Pot	Sept. 1862
61st Penna. Infy	July, 1862	From 2-Brig. 1-Div. 4-Corps Pot	To 2-Brig. 3-Div. 6-Corps Pot	Sept. 1862
82d Penna. Infy	July, 1862	From 2-Brig. 1-Div. 4-Corps Pot	To 2-Brig. 3-Div. 6-Corps Pot	Sept. 1862
122d N. Y. Infy	Sept., 1862	From New Organization	To 2-Brig. 2-Div. 11-Corps Pot	July, 1862
168th N. Y. Infy	June, 1863	From King's Indpt. Brig. 7-Corps Va.	To 1-Brig. 3-Div. 11-Corps Pot	July, 1863
172d Penna. Infy	June, 1863	From Advance Brig. 7-Corps Va.		
ARTILLERY, 1st DIVISION.—			
Batty. C, 1st Pa. Arty	Mch., 1862	From Def. of Washington	To Arty. 3-Div. 6-Corps Pot	Sept., 1862
Batty. D, 1st Pa. Arty	Mch., 1862	From Def. of Washington	To Arty. 3-Div. 6-Corps Pot	Sept., 1862
Batty. E, 1st Pa. Arty	Mch., 1862	From Arty. Couch's Div. Pot	To Res. Arty. 4-Corps Pot	June, 1862
Batty. H, 1st Pa. Arty	Mch., 1862	From Arty. Couch's Div. Pot	To Res. Arty. 4-Corps Pot	June, 1862
3d N. Y. Indpt. Batty	Aug., 1862	From Arty. 3-Div. 3-Corps Pot	To Arty. 3-Div. 6-Corps Pot	Sept., 1862
Batty. G, 2d U. S. Arty	Aug., 1862	From Arty 2-Div. 6-Corps Pot	To Arty. 2-Div. 6-Corps Pot	Sept., 1862

2d DIVISION.—   **COMMANDERS.**

W. F. Smith	Brigadier General	Mch. 13, 1862, to May 18, 1862.

Division transferred to 6th Prov'l Corps May 18, 1862. Reorganized June 6, 1862, from 3-Div. 4-Corps.

Silas Casey	Brigadier General	June 6, 1862, to June 24, 1862.
J. J. Peck	Brigadier General	June 24, 1862, to Sept. 26, 1862.

Division transferred to Dept. Va. Sept. 26, 1862. Reorganized May 4, 1863.

Geo. H. Gordon	Brigadier General	May 4, 1863, to July 15, 1863.

1st BRIGADE, 2d DIVISION.—   **COMMANDERS.**

W. S. Hancock	Brigadier General	Mch. 13, 1862, to May 18, 1862.
H. M. Naglee	Brigadier General	June 7, 1862, to July 6, 1862.
W. H. Emory	Brigadier General	July 6, 1862, to Aug. 10, 1862.
H. M. Naglee	Brigadier General	Aug. 10, 1862, to Sept. 26, 1862.
William Gurney	Col. 127th N. Y. Infy	May 4, 1863, to July 15, 1863.

6th Me. Infy	Mch., 1862	From Hancock's Brig. Smith's Div..	To 1-Brig. 2-Div. 6-Corps Pot	May, 1862
43d N. Y. Infy	Mch., 1862	From Hancock's Brig. Smith's Div..	To 1-Brig. 2-Div. 6-Corps Pot	May, 1862
49th Penna. Infy	Mch., 1862	From Hancock's Brig. Smith's Div..	To 1-Brig. 2-Div. 6-Corps Pot	May, 1862
5th Wis. Infy	Mch., 1862	From Hancock's Brig. Smith's Div..	To 1-Brig. 2-Div. 6-Corps Pot	May, 1862
11th Me. Infy	June, 1862	From 1-Brig. 3-Div. 4-Corps Pot	To Naglee's Brig. Dept. N. C..	Dec., 1862
56th N. Y. Infy	June, 1862	From 1-Brig. 3-Div. 4-Corps Pot	To Naglee's Brig. Dept. N. C..	Dec., 1862
81st N. Y. Infy	June, 1862	From 2-Brig. 2-Div. 4-Corps Pot	To Naglee's Brig. Dept. N. C..	Dec., 1862
98th N. Y. Infy	June, 1862	From 2-Brig. 2-Div. 4-Corps Pot	To Naglee's Brig. Dept. N. C..	Dec., 1862
100th N. Y. Infy	June, 1862	From 1-Brig. 3-Div. 4-Corps Pot	To Naglee's Brig. Dept. N. C..	Dec., 1862
52d Penna. Infy	June, 1862	From 1-Brig. 3-Div. 4-Corps Pot	To Naglee's Brig. Dept. N. C..	Dec., 1862
104th Penna. Infy	June, 1862	From Unatt. Yorktown, Va., 4-Corps.	To Naglee's Brig. Dept. N. C..	Dec., 1862
Indpt. N. Y. Battn	June, 1862	From Hughston's B. Gurney's D. 7-C.	To 1-Brig. 1-Div. 11-Corps Pot	July, 1863
127th N. Y. Infy	May, 1863	From Hughston's B. Gurney's D. 7-C.	To 1-Brig. 1-Div. 11-Corps Pot	July, 1863
142d N. Y. Infy	May, 1863	From Hughston's B. Gurney's D. 7-C.	To 1-Brig. 3-Div. 11-Corps Pot	July, 1863
143d N. Y. Infy	May, 1863	From Hughston's B. Gurney's D. 7-C.	To 2-Brig. 1-Div. 11-Corps Pot	July, 1863
144th N. Y. Infy	May, 1863	From Hughston's B. Gurney's D. 7-C.		

2d BRIGADE, 2d DIVISION.—   **COMMANDERS.**

W. T. H. Brooks	Brigadier General	Mch. 13, 1862, to May 18, 1862.
H. W. Wessells	Brigadier General	June 7, 1862, to Sept. 26, 1862.
Burr Porter	Col. 40th Mass. Infy	May 4, 1863, to July 15, 1863.

2d Vt. Infy	Mch., 1862	From Brooks' Brig. Smith's Div. Pot.	To 2-Brig. 2-Div. 6-Corps Pot	May, 1862
3d Vt. Infy	Mch., 1862	From Brooks' Brig. Smith's Div. Pot.	To 2-Brig. 2-Div. 6-Corps Pot	May, 1862
4th Vt. Infy	Mch., 1862	From Brooks' Brig. Smith's Div. Pot.	To 2-Brig. 2-Div. 6-Corps Pot	May, 1862
5th Vt. Infy	Mch., 1862	From Brooks' Brig. Smith's Div. Pot.	To 2-Brig. 2-Div. 6-Corps Pot	May, 1862
6th Vt. Infy	Mch., 1862	From Brooks' Brig. Smith's Div. Pot.	To 2-Brig. 2-Div. 6-Corps Pot	May, 1862
81st N. Y. Infy	June, 1862	From 3-Brig. 3-Div. 4-Corps Pot	To 1-Brig 2-Div. 4-Corps Pot	June, 1862
85th N. Y. Infy	June, 1862	From 3-Brig. 3-Div. 4-Corps Pot	To Wessell's B. Div. at Suffolk, 7-C.	Sept. 1862
92d N. Y. Infy	June, 1862	From 3-Brig. 3-Div. 4-Corps Pot	To Wessell's B. Div. at Suffolk, 7-C.	Sept. 1862
96th N. Y. Infy	June, 1862	From 2-Brig. 3-Div. 4-Corps Pot	To Wessell's B. Div. at Suffolk, 7-C.	Sept. 1862
98th N. Y. Infy	June, 1862	From 2-Brig. 3-Div. 4-Corps Pot	To 1-Brig. 2-Div. 4-Corps Pot	June, 1862
85th Penna. Infy	June, 1862	From 2-Brig. 3-Div. 4-Corps Pot	To Wessell's B. Div. Suffolk, 7-Corps.	Sept. 1862
101st Penna. Infy	June, 1862	From 2-Brig. 3-Div. 4-Corps Pot	To Wessell's B. Div. Suffolk, 7-Corps.	Sept. 1862
103d Penna. Infy	June, 1862	From 2-Brig. 3-Div. 4-Corps Pot	To Wessell's B. Div. Suffolk, 7-Corps.	Sept. 1862
22d Conn. Infy	May, 1863	From Porter's Br. Gurney's Div. 7-C.	No change to Muster Out	July, 1863
40th Mass. Infy	May, 1863	From Porter's Br. Gurney's Div. 7-C.	To 2-Brig. 1-Div. 11-Corps Pot	July, 1863
141st N. Y. Infy	May, 1863	From Porter's Br. Gurney's Div. 7-C.	To 2-Brig. 3-Div. 11-Corps Pot	July, 1863
4th Wis. Batty	May, 1863	From Arty. 7-Corps Dept. Va	Yorktown, Va., Dept. Va. & N. C.	July, 1863

3d BRIGADE, 2d DIVISION.—   **COMMANDERS.**

J. W. Davidson	Brigadier General	Mch. 13, 1862, to May 18, 1862.
O. S. Ferry	Brigadier General	July 5, 1862, to Sept. 26, 1862.

33d N. Y. Infy	Mch., 1862	From Davidson's Brig. Smith's Div..	To 3-Brig. 2-Div. 6-Corps Pot	May, 1862
49th N. Y. Infy	Mch., 1862	From Davidson's Brig. Smith's Div..	To 3-Brig. 2-Div. 6-Corps Pot	May, 1862
77th N. Y. Infy	Mch., 1862	From Davidson's Brig. Smith's Div..	To 3-Brig. 2-Div. 6-Corps Pot	May, 1862
7th Me. Infy	Mch., 186	From Davidson's Brig. Smith's Div..	To 3-Brig. 2-Div. 6-Corps Pot	May, 1862
39th Ill. Infy	July, 1862	From 2-Brig. Shields' Div. Rappa..	To Ferry's Brig. Div. Suffolk, 7-C.	Sept. 1862
13th Ind. Infy	July, 1862	From 2-Brig. Shields' Div. Rappa..	To Ferry's Brig. Div. Suffolk, 7-C.	Sept. 1862
62d Ohio Infy	July, 1862	From 2-Brig. Shields' Div. Rappa..	To Ferry's Brig. Div. Suffolk, 7-C.	Sept. 1862
67th Ohio Infy	July, 1862	From 2-Brig. Shields' Div. Rappa..	To Ferry's Brig. Div. Suffolk, 7-C.	Sept. 1862
ARTILLERY, 2d DIVISION.—			
Batty. E, 1st N. Y. Arty	Mch., 1862	From Arty. Smith's Div. Pot	To Arty. 2-Div. 6-Corps Pot	May, 1862
1st N. Y. Indpt. Batty	Mch., 1862	From Arty. Smith's Div. Pot	To Arty. 2-Div. 6-Corps Pot	May, 1862
3d N. Y. Indpt. Batty	Mch., 1862	From Arty. Smith's Div. Pot	To Arty. 2-Div. 6-Corps Pot	May, 1862
Batty. F, 5th U. S. Arty	Mch., 1862	From Arty. Smith's Div. Pot	To Arty. 2-Div. 6-Corps Pot	May, 1862
7th N. Y. Indpt. Batty	Mch., 1862	From Arty. 3-Div. 4-Corps Pot	To Norfolk and Portsmouth, 7-Corps.	Sept., 1862

3d DIVISION.— COMMANDER.

Silas Casey	Brigadier General	Mch. 13, 1862, to June 7, 1862.

Division discontinued June 7, 1862. Troops to 2-Div. 4-Corps.

1st BRIGADE, 3d DIVISION.— COMMANDER.

H. M. Naglee..........	Brigadier General	Apr. 27, 1862, to June 7, 1862.

52d Penna. Infy....Mch., 1862	From 1-Brig. Casey's Div. Pot......	To 1-Brig. 2-Div. 4-Corps Pot......	June, 1862
104th Penna. Infy......Mch., 1862	From 1-Brig. Casey's Div. Pot......	To 1-Brig. 2-Div. 4-Corps Pot......	June, 1862
56th N. Y. Infy......Mch., 1862	From 1-Brig. Casey's Div. Pot......	To 1-Brig. 2-Div. 4-Corps Pot......	June, 1862
11th Me. Infy........Mch., 1862	From 1-Brig. Casey's Div. Pot......	To 1-Brig. 2-Div. 4-Corps Pot......	June, 1862
100th N. Y. Infy....Mch., 1862	From New Organization............	To 1-Brig. 2-Div. 4-Corps Pot......	June, 1862

2d BRIGADE, 3d DIVISION.— COMMANDER.

William H. Keim.......	Brigadier General	Mch. 13, 1862, to June 7, 1862.

85th Penna. Infy......Mch., 1862	From 2-Brig. Casey's Div. Pot......	To 2-Brig. 2-Div. 4-Corps Pot......	June, 1862
101st Penna. Infy......Mch., 1862	From New Organization............	To 2-Brig. 2-Div. 4-Corps Pot......	June, 1862
103d Penna. Infy......Mch., 1862	From New Organization............	To 2-Brig. 2-Div. 4-Corps Pot......	June, 1862
96th N. Y. Infy......Mch., 1862	From New Organization............	To 2-Brig. 2-Div. 4-Corps Pot......	June, 1862

3d BRIGADE, 3d DIVISION.— COMMANDER.

I. N. Palmer..........	Brigadier General	Mch. 13, 1862, to June 7, 1862.

81st N. Y. Infy......Mch., 1862	From New Organization............	To 2-Brig. 2-Div. 4-Corps Pot......	June, 1862
85th N. Y. Infy......Mch., 1862	From 3-Brig. Casey's Div. Pot......	To 2-Brig. 2-Div. 4-Corps Pot......	June, 1862
92d N. Y. Infy......Mch., 1862	From New Organization............	To 2-Brig. 2-Div. 4-Corps Pot......	June, 1862
93d N. Y. Infy......Mch., 1862	From New Organization............	To Provost Guard Pot............	May, 1862
96th N. Y. Infy......Mch., 1862	From New Organization............	To 2-Brig. 2-Div. 4-Corps Pot......	June, 1862
98th N. Y. Infy......Mch., 1862	From New Organization............	To 2-Brig. 2-Div. 4-Corps Pot......	June, 1862

ARTILLERY, 3d DIVISION.—

Batty. A, 1st N. Y. Arty..Mch., 1862	From Arty. Casey's Div. Pot.......	Captured	May 31, '62
Batty. H, 1st N. Y. Arty..Mch., 1862	From Arty. Casey's Div. Pot.......	To Res. Arty. 4-Corps Pot.......	June, 1862
7th N. Y. Indpt. Batty....Mch., 1862	From Arty. Casey's Div. Pot.......	To Arty. 2-Div. 4-Corps Pot......	June, 1862
8th N. Y. Indpt. Batty....Mch., 1862	From Arty. Casey's Div. Pot.......	To Res. Arty. 4-Corps Pot.......	June, 1862

RESERVE ARTILLERY, 4th CORPS.—

Batty. F, 1st N. Y. Arty...June, 1862	From Arty. 1-Div. 6-Corps Pot......	To Res. Arty. Yorktown, Va., 7-C..	Dec., 1862
Batty. H, 1st N. Y. Arty...June, 1862	From Arty. 3-Div. 4-Corps Pot......	To Res. Arty. Yorktown, Va., 7-C..	Dec., 1862
8th N. Y. Indpt. Batty...June, 1862	From Arty. 3-Div. 4-Corps Pot......	To Res. Arty. Yorktown, Va., 7-C..	Dec., 1862
Batty. E, 1st Pa. Arty....June, 1862	From Arty. 1-Div. 4-Corps Pot......	To Res. Arty. Yorktown, Va., 7-C..	Dec., 1862
Batty. H, 1st Pa. Arty....June, 1862	From Arty. 1-Div. 4-Corps Pot......	To Res. Arty. Yorktown, Va., 7-C..	Dec., 1862
Batty. M, 5th U. S. Arty..June, 1862	From Arty. Res., Yorktown, Va.....	To Res. Arty. Yorktown, Va., 7-C..	Dec., 1862

KING'S INDPT. BRIGADE.—

4th Del. Infy............May, 1863	From King's Ind. Brig. 7-Corps Va.	To Unatt. 4 Corps...............	June, 1863
168th N. Y. Infy........May, 1863	From King's Ind. Brig. 7-Corps Va.	To 3-Brig. 1-Div. 4-Corps Pot......	June, 1863
169th Penna. Infy......May, 1863	From King's Ind. Brig. 7-Corps Va.	To 3-Brig. 1-Div. 4-Corps Pot......	June, 1863
179th Penna. Infy......May, 1863	From King's Ind. Brig. 7-Corps Va.	To West's Indpt. Brig. 4-Corps Pot.	June, 1863

WEST'S ADVANCE BRIGADE.— COMMANDER.

R. M. West............	Col. 1st Penna. Light Arty........	May 4, 1863, to July 15, 1863.

139th N. Y. Infy......May, 1863	From West's Adv. Brig. 7-Corps Va.	To U. S. Forces Yorkt'n, Va. & N. C..	July, 1863
172d Penna. Infy......May, 1863	From West's Adv. Brig. 7-Corps Va.	To Unatt. 4-Corps Pot............	May, 1863
178th Penna. Infy......May, 1863	From West's Adv. Brig. 7-Corps Va.	To 2-Brig. King's Div. 22-Corps...	July, 1863
5th Penna. Battn......May, 1863	From West's Adv. Brig. 7-Corps Va.	To U. S. Forces Yorkt'n, Va. & N. C..	July, 1863
6th N. Y. Cav. Battn.....May, 1863	From West's Adv. Brig. 7-Corps Va.	To Def. of Washington 22-Corps...	July, 1863
179th Penna. Infy......June, 1863	From King's Indpt. Brig. 4-Corps..	To 2-Brig. King's Div. 22-Corps....	July, 1863

UNATTACHED.—

172d Penna. Infy........May, 1863	From West's Adv. Brig. 4-Corps.....	To 3-Brig. 1-Div. 4-Corps..........	June, 1863
4th Del. Infy............June, 1863	From King's Indpt. Brig. 4-Corps...	To 1-Brig. King's Div. 22-Corps...	July, 1863
8th Penna. Cav..........Mch., 1862	From Porter's Div. Pot............	To 2-Brig. Cav. Res. Pot..........	Apr., 1862
2d Mass. Cav...........May, 1863	From Cav. Yorktown, 7-Corps......	To 1-Brig. 1-Div. 4-Corps.........	June, 1863
6th N. Y. Cav. A,B,C,D,K..May, 1863	From Cav. Yorktown, 7-Corps......	To West's Adv. Brig. 4-Corps......	May, 1863
Batty. F, 1st N. Y. Arty..May, 1863	From Unatt. Ar. Yorktown, Va., 7-C.	To Def. of Washington 22-Corps.....	July, 1863
Batty. H, 1st N. Y. Arty..May, 1863	From Unatt. Ar. Yorktown, Va., 7-C.	To Def. of Washington 22-Corps.....	July, 1863
8th N. Y. Indpt. Batty....May, 1863	From Unatt. Ar. Yorktown, Va., 7-C.	To 1-Brig. 1-Div. 4-Corps.........	June, 1863
Batty. E, 1st Pa. Arty....May, 1863	From Unatt. Ar. Yorktown, Va., 7-C.	To 2-Brig. 1-Div. 4-Corps.........	June, 1863
Batty. H, 1st Pa. Arty....May, 1863	From Unatt. Ar. Yorktown, Va., 7-C.	To Def. of Washington 22-Corps.....	July, 1863
Batty. M, 5th U. S. Arty..May, 1863	From Unatt. Ar. Yorktown, Va., 7-C.	To Arty. Brig. 6-Corps Pot.........	July, 1863

Fifth Army Corps

Created March 3, 1862, by order of the President of the U. S. Announced March 13, 1862, in General Order No. 101, Army Potomac. Discontinued April 4, 1862, and merged into the Department of the Shenandoah.

N. P. Banks...........	Major General	Mch. 13, 1862, to Apr. 4, 1862.

1st DIVISION.— COMMANDER.

A. S. Williams........	Brigadier General	Mch. 13, 1862, to Apr. 4, 1862.

1st BRIGADE, 1st DIVISION.— COMMANDER.

D. Donnelly	Col. 28th N. Y. Infy.............	Mch. 13, 1862, to Apr. 4, 1862.

5th Conn. Infy..........Mch., 1862	From 1-Brig. Banks' Div. Pot.......	To 1-Brig. 1-Div. Dept. Shenandoah.	Apr., 1862
28th N. Y. Infy..........Mch., 1862	From 1-Brig. Banks' Div. Pot.......	To 1-Brig. 1-Div. Dept. Shenandoah.	Apr., 1862
28th Penna. Infy........Mch., 1862	From 1-Brig. Banks' Div. Pot.......	To 1-Brig. 1-Div. Dept. Shenandoah.	Apr., 1862
46th Penna. Infy........Mch., 1862	From 1-Brig. Banks' Div. Pot.......	To 1-Brig. 1-Div. Dept. Shenandoah.	Apr., 1862
1st Md. Infy............Mch., 1862	From 1-Brig. Banks' Div. Pot.......	To 1-Brig. 1-Div. Dept. Shenandoah.	Apr., 1862

2d BRIGADE, 1st DIVISION.— COMMANDER.

J. J. Abercrombie	Brigadier General	Mch. 13, 1862, to Apr. 4, 1862.		
12th Mass. Infy....Mch., 1862	From 2-Brig. Banks' Div. Pot...	To 2-Brig. 1-Div. Dept. Shenandoah.	Apr.,	1862
13th Mass. Infy....Mch., 1862	From 2-Brig. Banks' Div. Pot...	To 2-Brig. 1-Div. Dept. Shenandoah.	Apr.,	1862
83d (9-S. M.) N. Y. Infy..Mch., 1862	From 2-Brig. Banks' Div. Pot...	To 2-Brig. 1-Div. Dept. Shenandoah.	Apr.,	1862
12th Ind. Infy....Mch., 1862	From 2-Brig. Banks' Div. Pot...	To 2-Brig. 1-Div. Dept. Shenandoah.	Apr.,	1862
16th Ind. Infy....Mch., 1862	From 2-Brig. Banks' Div. Pot...	To 2-Brig. 1-Div. Dept. Shenandoah.	Apr..	1862

3d BRIGADE, 1st DIVISION.— COMMANDER.

Geo. H. Gordon	Brigadier General	Mch. 13, 1862, to Apr. 4, 1862.		
2d Mass. Infy....Mch., 1862	From 3-Brig. Banks' Div. Pot...	To 3-Brig. 1-Div. Dept. Shenandoah.	Apr.,	1862
29th Penna. Infy....Mch., 1862	From 3-Brig. Banks' Div. Pot...	To 3-Brig. 1-Div. Dept. Shenandoah.	Apr.,	1862
27th Ind. Infy....Mch., 1862	From 3-Brig. Banks' Div. Pot...	To 3-Brig. 1-Div. Dept. Shenandoah.	Apr.,	1862
3d Wis. Infy....Mch., 1862	From 3-Brig. Banks' Div. Pot...	To 3-Brig. 1-Div. Dept. Shenandoah.	Apr.,	1862
ARTILLERY, 1st DIVISION.—				
Batty. M, 1st N. Y. Arty..Mch., 1862	From Arty. Banks' Div. Pot...	To Arty. 1-Div. Dept. Shenandoah..	Apr.,	1862
Batty. F, 1st Pa. Arty...Mch., 1862	From Arty. Banks' Div. Pot...	To Arty. 1-Div. Dept. Shenandoah..	Apr.,	1862
Indpt. Batty. F, Pa. Arty..Mch., 1862	From Arty. Banks' Div. Pot...	To Arty. 1-Div. Dept. Shenandoah..	Apr.,	1862
Batty. F, 4th U. S. Arty..Mch., 1862	From Arty. Banks' Div. Pot...	To Arty. 1-Div. Dept. Shenandoah..	Apr.,	1862

2d DIVISION.— COMMANDER.

James Shields	Brigadier General	Mch. 13, 1862. to Apr. 4, 1862.	

1st BRIGADE, 2d DIVISION.— COMMANDER.

Nathan Kimball	Col. 14th Ind. Infy	Mch. 13, 1862, to Apr. 4, 1862.		
84th Penna. Infy....Mch., 1862	From 1-Brig. Lander's Div. W. Va.	To 1-Brig. 2-Div. Dept. Shenandoah	Apr.,	1862
4th Ohio Infy....Mch., 1862	From 1-Brig. Lander's Div. W. Va.	To 1-Brig. 2-Div. Dept. Shenandoah	Apr.,	1862
8th Ohio Infy....Mch., 1862	From 1-Brig. Lander's Div. W. Va.	To 1-Brig. 2-Div. Dept. Shenandoah	Apr.,	1862
67th Ohio Infy....Mch., 1862	From 1-Brig. Lander's Div. W. Va.	To 1-Brig. 2-Div. Dept. Shenandoah	Apr.,	1862
14th Ind. Infy....Mch., 1862	From 1-Brig. Lander's Div. W. Va.	To 1-Brig. 2-Div. Dept. Shenandoah	Apr.,	1862
7th W. Va. Infy....Mch., 1862	From 1-Brig. Lander's Div. W. Va.	To 1-Brig. 2-Div. Dept. Shenandoah	Apr.,	1862

2d BRIGADE, 2d DIVISION.— COMMANDER.

J. C. Sullivan	Col. 13th Ind. Infy	Mch. 13, 1862, to Apr. 4, 1862.		
5th Ohio Infy....Mch., 1862	From 2-Brig. Lander's Div. W. Va.	To 2-Brig. 2-Div. Dept. Shenandoah	Apr.,	1862
62d Ohio Infy....Mch., 1862	From 2-Brig. Lander's Div. W. Va.	To 2-Brig. 2-Div. Dept. Shenandoah	Apr.,	1862
66th Ohio Infy....Mch., 1862	From 2-Brig. Lander's Div. W. Va.	To 2-Brig. 2-Div. Dept. Shenandoah	Apr.,	1862
13th Ind. Infy....Mch., 1862	From 2-Brig. Lander's Div. W. Va.	To 2-Brig. 2-Div. Dept. Shenandoah	Apr.,	1862
39th Ill. Infy....Mch., 1862	From 2-Brig. Lander's Div. W. Va.	To 2-Brig. 2-Div. Dept. Shenandoah	Apr.,	1862

3d BRIGADE, 2d DIVISION.— COMMANDER.

E. B. Tyler	Col. 7th Ohio Infy	Mch. 13, 1862, to Apr. 4, 1862.		
7th Ohio Infy....Mch., 1862	From 3-Brig. Lander's Div. W. Va.	To 3-Brig. 2-Div. Dept. Shenandoah	Apr.,	1862
29th Ohio Infy....Mch., 1862	From 3-Brig. Lander's Div. W. Va.	To 3-Brig. 2-Div. Dept. Shenandoah	Apr.,	1862
7th Ind. Infy....Mch., 1862	From 3-Brig. Lander's Div. W. Va.	To 3-Brig. 2-Div. Dept. Shenandoah	Apr.,	1862
1st W. Va. Infy....Mch., 1862	From 3-Brig. Lander's Div. W. Va.	To 3-Brig. 2-Div. Dept. Shenandoah	Apr.,	1862
110th Penna. Infy....Mch., 1862	From 3-Brig. Lander's Div. W. Va.	To 3-Brig. 2-Div. Dept. Shenandoah	Apr.,	1862
ARTILLERY 2d DIVISION.—				
Batty. A, 1st W. Va. Arty.Mch., 1862	From Arty. Lander's Div. W. Va.	To Arty. 2-Div. Dept. Shenandoah	Apr.,	1862
Batty. B, 1st W. Va. Arty.Mch., 1862	From Arty. Lander's Div. W. Va.	To Arty. 2-Div. Dept. Shenandoah	Apr.,	1862
Batty. H, 1st Ohio Arty..Mch., 1862	From Arty. Lander's Div. W. Va.	To Arty. 2-Div. Dept. Shenandoah	Apr.,	1862
Batty. L, 1st Ohio Arty..Mch., 1862	From Arty. Lander's Div. W. Va.	To Arty. 2-Div. Dept. Shenandoah	Apr.,	1862
Batty. E, 4th U. S. Arty..Mch., 1862	From Arty. Lander's Div. W. Va.	To Arty. 2-Div. Dept. Shenandoah	Apr.,	1862

CAVALRY COMMAND.— COMMANDER.

John P. Hatch	Brigadier General	Mch. 28, 1862, to Apr. 4, 1862.		
1st Me. Cav. (7 Cos.)	From New Organization	To Hatch's Cav. Dept. Shenandoah..	Apr.,	1862
1st Vt. Cav....Mch., 1862	From Banks' Div. Pot...	To Hatch's Cav. Dept. Shenandoah..	Apr.,	1862
1st Mich. Cav....Mch., 1862	From Banks' Div. Pot...	To Hatch's Cav. Dept. Shenandoah..	Apr.,	1862
1st R. I. Cav....Mch., 1862	From Banks' Div. Pot...	To Hatch's Cav. Dept. Shenandoah..	Apr.,	1862
5th N. Y. Cav....Mch., 1862	From Dix's Div. Baltimore, Md...	To Hatch's Cav. Dept. Shenandoah..	Apr.,	1862
8th N. Y. Cav....Mch., 1862	From Cav. Brig. Pot...	To Hatch's Cav. Dept. Shenandoah..	Apr.,	1862
1st Md. P. H. B. Cav....Mch., 1862	From Lander's Div. West Va...	To Hatch's Cav. Dept. Shenandoah..	Apr.,	1862
1st W. Va. Cav. Sqdn....Mch., 1862	From Lander's Div. West Va...	To Hatch's Cav. Dept. Shenandoah..	Apr.,	1862
1st Ohio Cav., Co.'s A, C.Mch., 1862	From Lander's Div. West Va...	To Hatch's Cav. Dept. Shenandoah..	Apr.,	1862
Ringgold Penna. Cav...Mch., 1862	From Lander's Div. West Va...	To Kelly's Command, R. R. Dist...	Apr.,	1862
Washington Co. (Pa.) Cav.Mch., 1862	From Lander's Div. West Va...	To Kelly's Command, R. R. Dist...	Apr.,	1862
UNATTACHED.—				
1st Md. P. H. B. Infy....Mch., 1862	From Railroad District...	To R. R. District, Middle Dept...	Mch.,	1862
4th Md. P. H. B. Infy....Mch., 1862	From Railroad District...	To R. R. District, Middle Dept...	Mch.,	1862

Fifth Army Corps

Re-created and organized provisionally May 18, 1862. Confirmed by War Department, 1862. Discontinued June 28, 1865.

CORPS COMMANDERS.

Fitz John Porter	Brigadier General	May 18, 1862, to Nov. 10, 1862.	
Joseph Hooker	Major General	Nov. 10, 1862, to Nov. 16, 1862.	
D. Butterfield	Brigadier General	Nov. 16, 1862, to Dec. 25, 1862.	
Geo. G. Meade	Major General	Dec. 25, 1862, to Jan. 26, 1863.	
Charles Griffin	Brigadier General	Jan. 26, 1863, to Feb. 1, 1863.	
George Sykes	Major General	Feb. 1, 1863, to Feb. 5, 1863.	
Geo. G. Meade	Major General	Feb. 5, 1863, to Feb. 16, 1863.	
Geo. Sykes	Major General	Feb. 16, 1863, to Feb. 23, 1863.	
A. A. Humphreys	Major General	Feb. 23, 1863, to Feb. 28, 1863.	
Geo. G. Meade	Major General	Feb. 28, 1863, to June 28, 1863.	
Geo. Sykes	Major General	June 28, 1863, to Oct. 7, 1863.	
S. W. Crawford	Brigadier General	Oct. 7, 1863, to Oct. 15, 1863.	
Geo. Sykes	Major General	Oct. 15, 1863, to Mch. 23, 1864.	
G. K. Warren	Major General	Mch. 23, 1864, to Jan. 2, 1865.	
S. W. Crawford	Bvt. Major General	Jan. 2, 1865, to Jan. 27, 1865.	
G. K. Warren	Major General	Jan. 27, 1865, to Apr. 1, 1865.	
Chas. Griffin	Major General	Apr. 1, 1865, to June 28, 1865.	

1st DIVISION.—   COMMANDERS.

G. W. Morrell	Brigadier General	May 18, 1862, to Oct. 30, 1862.
Chas. Griffin	Brigadier General	Oct. 30, 1862, to Nov. 1, 1862.
D. Butterfield	Brigadier General	Nov. 1, 1862, to Nov. 16, 1862.
Chas. Griffin	Brigadier General	Nov. 16, 1862, to Dec. 26, 1862.
James Barnes	Col. 18th Mass. Infy	Dec. 26, 1862, to Feb. 1, 1863.
Chas. Griffin	Brigadier General	Feb. 1, 1863, to May 5, 1863.
James Barnes	Brigadier General	May 5, 1863, to July 21, 1863.
Charles Griffin	Brigadier General	July 21, 1863, to Oct. 24, 1863.
J. B. Sweitzer	Col. 62d Penna. Infy	Oct. 24, 1863, to Nov. 6, 1863.
J. J. Bartlett	Brigadier General	Nov. 6, 1863, to Dec. 31, 1863.
J. B. Sweitzer	Col. 62d Penna. Infy	Dec. 31, 1863, to Feb. 3, 1864.
J. J. Bartlett	Brigadier General	Feb. 3, 1864, to Apr. 3, 1864.
Charles Griffin	Brigadier General	Apr. 3, 1864, to July 21, 1864.
J. J. Bartlett	Brigadier General	July 21, 1864, to Aug. 9, 1864.
Charles Griffin	Brigadier General	Aug. 9, 1864, to Dec. 24, 1864.
J. J. Bartlett	Brigadier General	Dec. 24, 1864, to Jan. 4, 1865.
Charles Griffin	Bvt. Major General	Jan. 4, 1865, to Apr. 1, 1865.
J. J. Bartlett	Brigadier General	Apr. 1, 1865, to Apr. 25, 1865.
J. L. Chamberlain	Brigadier General	Apr. 25, 1865, to June 28, 1865.

1st BRIGADE, 1st DIVISION.—   COMMANDERS.

J. H. Martindale	Brigadier General	May 18, 1862, to July 10, 1862.
James Barnes	Col. 18th Mass. Infy	July 10, 1862, to Dec. 26, 1862.
Chas. W. Roberts	Col. 2d Me. Infy	Temporarily in July.
C. A. Johnson	Col. 25th N. Y. Infy	Dec. 26, 1862, to Feb. 1, 1863.
James Barnes	Brigadier General	Feb. 1, 1863, to May 5, 1863.
W. S. Tilton	Col. 22d Mass. Infy	May 5, 1863, to Aug. 18, 1863.
James Barnes	Brigadier General	Aug. 18, 1863, to Sept. 21, 1863.
Thos. Sherwin, Jr	Lt.-Col. 22d Mass. Infy	Sept. 21, 1863, to Oct. 1, 1863.
J. Hayes	Col. 18th Mass. Infy	Oct. 1, 1863, to Nov. 19, 1863.
W. S. Tilton	Col. 22d Mass. Infy	Nov. 19, 1863, to Mch. 25, 1864.
R. B. Ayres	Brigadier General	Mch. 25, 1864, to June 5, 1864.
J. L. Chamberlain	Brigadier General	June 6, 1864, to June 18, 1864.
W. S. Tilton	Col. 22d Mass. Infy	June 18, 1864, to Aug. 22, 1864.
W. A. Throop	Lt.-Col. 1st Mich. Infy	Aug. 22, 1864, to Sept. 24, 1864.
H. G. Sickel	Col. 198th Penna. Infy	Sept. 24, 1864, to Nov. 7, 1864.
J. Gwyn	Col. 118th Penna. Infy	Nov. 7, 1864, to Nov. 19, 1864.
J. L. Chamberlain	Brigadier General	Nov. 19, 1864, to Jan. 5, 1865.
H. G. Sickel	Col. 198th Penna. Infy	Jan. 5, 1865, to Feb. 27, 1865.
J. L. Chamberlain	Brigadier General	Feb. 27, 1865, to Apr. 11, 1865.
A. L. Pierson	Bvt. Brig. General	Apr. 11, 1865, to June 28, 1865.

2d Me. Infy	May, 1862	From 1-Brig. 1-Div. 3-Corps Pot	No change to Muster Out	May, 1863
18th Mass. Infy	May, 1862	From 1-Brig. 1-Div. 3-Corps Pot	To 3-Brig. 1-Div. 5-Corps Pot	Mch., 1864
22d Mass. Infy	May, 1862	From 1-Brig. 1-Div. 3-Corps Pot	To 3-Brig. 1-Div. 5-Corps Pot	Mch., 1864
(2d Co. S. S. att.)				
13th N. Y. Infy	May, 1862	From 1-Brig. 1-Div. 3-Corps Pot	No change to Muster Out	June, 1863
25th N. Y. Infy	May, 1862	From 1-Brig. 1-Div. 3-Corps Pot	No change to Muster Out	June, 1863
1st Mich. Infy	June, 1862	From Dept. of Va	To 3-Brig. 1-Div. 5-Corps Pot	Mch., 1864
32d Mass. Infy	July, 1862	From Dept. of Washington, D. C	To 2-Brig. 1-Div. 5-Corps Pot	Aug., 1862
118th Penna. Infy	Sept., 1862	From Dept. of Washington, D. C	To 3-Brig. 1-Div. 5-Corps Pot	Mch., 1864
20th Me. Infy	Sept., 1862	From Dept. of Washington, D. C	To 3-Brig. 1-Div. 5-Corps Pot	Mch., 1864
Brigade discontinued Mch. 25, 1864.		Reorganized from 4-Brig. 1-Div. Apr. 1, 1864.		
140th N. Y. Infy	Apr., 1864	From 4-Brig. 1-Div. 5-Corps Pot	To 1-Brig. 2-Div. 5-Corps Pot	June, 1864
146th N. Y. Infy	Apr., 1864	From 4-Brig. 1-Div. 5-Corps Pot	To 1-Brig. 2-Div. 5-Corps Pot	June, 1864
91st Penna. Infy	Apr., 1864	From 4-Brig. 1-Div. 5-Corps Pot	To 1-Brig. 2-Div. 5-Corps Pot	June, 1864
155th Penna. Infy	Apr., 1864	From 4-Brig. 1-Div. 5-Corps Pot	To 1-Brig. 2-Div. 5-Corps Pot	June, 1864
2d U. S. Infy	Apr., 1864	From 4-Brig. 1-Div. 5-Corps Pot	To Provost Guard 2-Div. 5-Corps	June, 1864
11th U. S. Infy	Apr., 1864	From 4-Brig. 1-Div. 5-Corps Pot	To 1-Brig. 2-Div. 5-Corps Pot	June, 1864
12th U. S. Infy	Apr., 1864	From 4-Brig. 1-Div. 5-Corps Pot	To 1-Brig. 2-Div. 5-Corps Pot	June, 1864
14th U. S. Infy	Apr., 1864	From 4-Brig. 1-Div. 5-Corps Pot	To 1-Brig. 2-Div. 5-Corps Pot	June, 1864
17th U. S. Infy	Apr., 1864	From 4-Brig. 1-Div. 5-Corps Pot	To 1-Brig. 2-Div. 5-Corps Pot	June, 1864
Brigade discontinued June 5, 1864.		Reorganized June 6, 1864, from 3-Brig. 4-Div.		
121st Penna. Infy	June, 1864	From 3-Brig. 4-Div. 5-Corps Pot	To 3-Brig. 3-Div. 5-Corps Pot	Sept., 1864
142d Penna. Infy	June, 1864	From 3-Brig. 4-Div. 5-Corps Pot	To 3-Brig. 3-Div. 5-Corps Pot	Sept., 1864
143d Penna. Infy	June, 1864	From 3-Brig. 4-Div. 5-Corps Pot	To 1-Brig. 3-Div. 5-Corps Pot	Sept., 1864
149th Penna. Infy	June, 1864	From 3-Brig. 4-Div. 5-Corps Pot	To 1-Brig. 3-Div. 5-Corps Pot	Sept., 1864
150th Penna. Infy	June, 1864	From 3-Brig. 4-Div. 5-Corps Pot	To 1-Brig. 3-Div. 5-Corps Pot	Sept., 1864
187th Penna. Infy	June, 1864	From New Organization	To Philadelphia, Penna	Sept., 1864
185th N. Y. Infy	Sept., 1864	From New Organization	No change to Muster Out	May, 1865
198th Penna. Infy	Sept., 1864	From New Organization	No change to Muster Out	June, 1865
21st Penna. Cav. Dismtd	Sept., 1864	From 2-Brig. 1-Div. 5-Corps Pot	To 1-Brig. 2-Div. Cav. Corps Pot	Oct., 1864

2d BRIGADE, 1st DIVISION.—   COMMANDERS.

J. J. Abercrombie	Brigadier General	May 18, 1862, to June 26, 1862.
Charles Griffin	Brigadier General	June 26, 1862, to Oct. 30, 1862.
J. B. Sweitzer	Col. 62d Penna. Infy	Oct. 30, 1862, to Nov. 1, 1862.
Charles Griffin	Brigadier General	Nov. 1, 1862, to Nov. 16, 1862.
J. B. Sweitzer	Col. 62d Penna. Infy	Nov. 16, 1862, to Mch. 12, 1863.
James McQuade	Col. 14th N. Y. Infy	Mch. 12, 1863, to Apr. 12, 1863.
J. B. Sweitzer	Col. 62d Penna. Infy	Apr. 12, 1863, to Oct. 24, 1863.
P. R. Guiney	Col. 9th Mass. Infy	Oct. 24, 1863, to Nov. 16, 1863.
J. B. Sweitzer	Col. 62d Penna. Infy	Nov. 16, 1863, to Dec. 18, 1863.
J. C. Hull	Lt.-Col. 62d Penna. Infy	Dec. 18, 1863, to Jan. 10, 1864.
P. R. Guiney	Col. 9th Mass. Infy	Jan. 10, 1864, to Feb. 3, 1864.
J. B. Sweitzer	Col. 62d Penna. Infy	Feb. 3, 1864, to July 3, 1864.
E. M. Gregory	Col. 91st Penna. Infy	July 3, 1864, to Jan. 22, 1865.
A. L. Burr	Col. 189th N. Y. Infy	Jan. 22, 1865, to Feb. 25, 1865.
E. M. Gregory	Col. 91st Penna. Infy	Feb. 25, 1865, to June 28, 1865.

9th Mass. Infy	May, 1862	From 2-Brig. 1-Div. 3-Corps Pot	No change to Muster Out	June, 1864
14th N. Y. Infy	May, 1862	From 2-Brig. 1-Div. 3-Corps Pot	No change to Muster Out	May, 1864
62d Penna. Infy	May, 1862	From 2-Brig. 1-Div. 3-Corps Pot	No change to Muster Out	July, 1864
4th Mich. Infy	May, 1862	From 2-Brig. 1-Div. 3-Corps Pot	No change to Muster Out	July, 1864
32d Mass. Infy	Aug., 1862	From 1-Brig. 1-Div. 5-Corps Pot	To 3-Brig. 1-Div. 5-Corps Pot	Oct., 1864
22d Mass. Infy	Mch., 1864	From 1-Brig. 1-Div. 5-Corps Pot	No change to Muster Out	Oct., 1864
(2d Co. S. S. Att.)				
91st Penna. Infy	June, 1864	From 1-Brig. 2-Div. 5-Corps Pot	To 3-Brig. 1-Div. 5-Corps Pot	Nov., 1864
155th Penna. Infy	June, 1864	From 1-Brig. 2-Div. 5-Corps Pot	To 3-Brig. 1-Div. 5-Corps Pot	Nov., 1864
21st Penna. Cav. Dismdt	June, 1864	From New Organization	To 1-Brig. 1-Div. 5-Corps Pot	Sept., 1864

2d BRIGADE, 1st DIVISION.—Continued.

187th N. Y. Infy..........Oct., 1864	From New Organization............	No change to Muster Out.........	June, 1865
188th N. Y. Infy..........Oct., 1864	From New Organization............	No change to Muster Out.........	June, 1865
189th N. Y. Infy..........Oct., 1864	From New Organization............	No change to Muster Out.........	June, 1865

3d BRIGADE, 1st DIVISION.— COMMANDERS.

D. Butterfield	Brigadier General	May 18, 1862, to Aug. 30, 1862.	
H. S. Lansing.........	Col. 17th N. Y. Infy.............	Aug. 30, 1862.	
H. A. Weeks..........	Col. 12th N. Y. Infy.............	Aug. 30, 1862.	
J. C. Rice.............	Col. 44th N. Y. Infy.............	Aug. 30, 1862.	
H. S. Lansing.........	Col. 17th N. Y. Infy.............	Aug. 30, 1862, to Sept. 18, 1862.	
T. B. W. Stockton......	Col. 16th Mich. Infy.............	Sept. 18, 1862, to Dec. .., 1862.	
H. A. Weeks..........	Col. 12th N. Y. Infy.............	Dec. .., 1862, to Jan. .., 1863.	
T. B. W. Stockton......	Col. 16th Mich. Infy.............	Jan. .., 1863, to May 20, 1863.	
Strong Vincent	Col. 83d Penna. Infy.............	May 20, 1863, to July 2, 1863.	Killed.
J. C. Rice.............	Col. 44th N. Y. Infy.............	July 2, 1863, to Aug. 26, 1863.	
J. L. Chamberlain.....	Col. 20th Me. Infy...............	Aug. 26, 1863, to Nov. 19, 1863.	
J. Hayes	Col. 18th Mass. Infy.............	Nov. 19, 1863, to Apr. 3, 1864.	
J. J. Bartlett.........	Brigadier General	Apr. 3, 1864, to July 20, 1864.	
N. E. Welch..........	Col. 16th Mich. Infy.............	July 20, 1864, to Aug. 9, 1864.	
J. J. Bartlett.........	Brigadier General	Aug. 9, 1864, to Aug. 17, 1864.	
James Gwyn	Col. 118th Penna. Infy..........	Aug. 17, 1864, to Oct. 1, 1864.	
J. J. Bartlett.........	Brigadier General	Oct. 1, 1864, to Dec. 23, 1864.	
A. L. Pierson........	Col. 155th Penna. Infy..........	Dec. 23, 1864, to Jan. 6, 1865.	
J. J. Bartlett.........	Brigadier General	Jan. 6, 1865, to Jan. 27, 1865.	
A. L. Pierson........	Bvt. Brig. General	Jan. 27, 1865, to Mch. 7, 1865.	
J. J. Bartlett.........	Brigadier General	Mch. 7, 1865, to Apr. 1, 1865.	
A. L. Pierson........	Bvt. Brig. General	Apr. 1, 1865, to Apr. 10, 1865.	
J. J. Bartlett.........	Brigadier General	Apr. 10, 1865, to Apr. 25, 1865.	
J. L. Chamberlain.....	Brigadier General	Apr. 25, 1865, to June 29, 1865.	
J. C. Edmonds........	Col. 32d Mass. Infy.............	June 29, 1865.	
E. Spear	Col. 20th Me. Infy.............		

12th N. Y. Infy..........May, 1862	From 3-Brig. 1-Div. 3-Corps Pot....	No change to Muster Out.........	May, 1863
17th N. Y. Infy..........May, 1862	From 3-Brig. 1-Div. 3-Corps Pot....	No change to Muster Out.........	May, 1863
44th N. Y. Infy..........May, 1862	From 3-Brig. 1-Div. 3-Corps Pot....	No change to Muster Out.........	Oct., 1864
83d Penna. Infy..........May, 1862	From 3-Brig. 1-Div. 3-Corps Pot....	No change to Muster Out.........	June, 1865
16th Mich. Infy..........May, 1862	From 3-Brig. 1-Div. 3-Corps Pot....	No change to Muster Out.........	June, 1865
(Brady's S. S. Att.)			
20th Me. Infy..........Sept., 1862	From New Organization............	No change to Muster Out.........	June, 1865
18th Mass. Infy..........Mch., 1864	From 1-Brig. 1-Div. 5-Corps Pot....	No change to Muster Out.........	Oct., 1864
1st Mich. Infy..........Mch., 1864	From 1-Brig. 1-Div. 5-Corps Pot....	No change to Muster Out.........	June, 1865
118th Penna. Infy..........Mch., 1864	From 1-Brig. 1-Div. 5-Corps Pot....	No change to Muster Out.........	June, 1865
29th Mass. Infy..........May, 1864	From Veteran Furlough............	To 1-Brig. 1-Div. 9-Corps Pot.....	June, 1864
32d Mass. Infy..........Oct., 1864	From 2-Brig. 1-Div. 5-Corps Pot....	No change to Muster Out.........	June, 1865
91st Penna. Infy..........Nov., 1864	From 2-Brig. 2-Div. 5-Corps Pot....	To 1-Brig. 3-Div. 5-Corps Pot.....	Mch., 1865
155th Penna. Infy..........Nov., 1864	From 2-Brig. 2-Div. 5-Corps Pot....	No change to Muster Out.........	June, 1865
1st Me. Sharpshooters.....Jan., 1865	Engr. Brig. City Point, Pot..........	No change to Muster Out.........	June, 1865

4th BRIGADE, 1st DIVISION.—Organized by consolidation of 1st and 3d Brigades 2d Division Mch. 23, 1864. ued Apr., 1864, and designated 1-Brig. 1-Div. 5-Corps.

COMMANDER.

R. B. Ayres............	Brigadier General	Mch. 23, 1864, to Apr. .., 1864.	

2d U. S. Infy..........Mch., 1864	From 1-Brig. 2-Div. 5-Corps Pot....	To 1-Brig. 1-Div. 5-Corps Pot......	Apr., 1864
11th U. S. Infy..........Mch., 1864	From 1-Brig. 2-Div. 5-Corps Pot....	To 1-Brig. 1-Div. 5-Corps Pot......	Apr., 1864
12th U. S. Infy..........Mch., 1864	From 1-Brig. 2-Div. 5-Corps Pot....	To 1-Brig. 1-Div. 5-Corps Pot......	Apr., 1864
14th U. S. Infy..........Mch., 1864	From 1-Brig. 2-Div. 5-Corps Pot....	To 1-Brig. 1-Div. 5-Corps Pot......	Apr., 1864
17th U. S. Infy..........Mch., 1864	From 1-Brig. 2-Div. 5-Corps Pot....	To 1-Brig. 1-Div. 5-Corps Pot......	Apr., 1864
140th N. Y. Infy..........Mch., 1864	From 3-Brig. 2-Div. 5-Corps Pot....	To 1-Brig. 1-Div. 5-Corps Pot......	Apr., 1864
146th N. Y. Infy..........Mch., 1864	From 3-Brig. 2-Div. 5-Corps Pot....	To 1-Brig. 1-Div. 5-Corps Pot......	Apr., 1864
91st Penna. Infy..........Mch., 1864	From 3-Brig. 2-Div. 5-Corps Pot....	To 1-Brig. 1-Div. 5-Corps Pot......	Apr., 1864
155th Penna. Infy..........Mch., 1864	From 3-Brig. 2-Div. 5-Corps Pot....	To 1-Brig. 1-Div. 5-Corps Pot......	Apr., 1864

ARTILLERY, 1st DIVISION.—

3d Mass. Indpt Batty....May, 1862	From Arty. 1-Div. 3-Corps Pot......	To Arty. Brig. 5-Corps Pot........	May, 1863
5th Mass. Indpt. Batty...May, 1862	From Arty. 1-Div. 3-Corps Pot......	To 1-Vol. Brig. Arty. Res. Pot......	May, 1863
Batty. C, 1st R. I. Arty..May, 1862	From Arty. 1-Div. 3-Corps Pot......	To 3-Vol. Brig. Arty. Res. Pot......	May, 1863
Batty. D, 5th U. S. Arty..May, 1862	From Arty. 1-Div. 3-Corps Pot......	To Arty. Brig. 5-Corps Pot........	May, 1863

SHARPSHOOTERS.—

1st U. S.................May, 1862	From 1-Div. 3-Corps Pot...........	To 3-Brig. 3-Div. 3-Corps Pot......	Mch., 1863

2d DIVISION.— COMMANDERS.

George Sykes..........	Brigadier General...................	May 18, 1862, to Dec. 1862.	
G. K. Warren..........	Brigadier General...................	Dec., 1862, to Jan., 1863.	
George Sykes..........	Brigadier General...................	Jan., 1863, to June 28, 1863.	
R. B. Ayres..........	Brigadier General...................	June 28, 1863, to Mch. 24, 1864.	

Division reorganized Mch. 24, 1864., from 1st Army Corps. Discontinued June 5, 1864, and troops transferred to other Divisions. Reorganized June 6, 1864.

Henry Baxter..........	Brigadier General...................	Mch. 24, 1864, to Apr., 1864.	
J. C. Robinson.........	Brigadier General...................	Apr., 1864, to May 8, 1864.	
R. Coulter...........	Col. 11th Penna. Infy...........	May 8, 1864, to May 9, 1864.	
H. H. Lockwood.......	Brigadier General...................	May 9, 1864, to June 2, 1864.	
S. W. Crawford.......	Brigadier General...................	June 2, 1864, to June 5, 1864.	
R. B. Ayres..........	Brigadier General...................	June 6, 1864, to Dec. 22, 1864.	
James Gwyn..........	Bvt. Brig. General.................	Dec. 22, 1864, to Jan. 8, 1865.	
R. B. Ayres..........	Bvt. Major General.................	Jan. 8, 1865, to June 28, 1865.	

1st BRIGADE, 2d DIVISION.— COMMANDERS.

R. C. Buchanan........	Lt.-Col. 4th U. S. Infy.............	May 18, 1862, to Jan. 27, 1863.	
R. S. Smith...........	Major 12th U. S. Infy.............	Jan. 27, 1863, to Apr. 21, 1863.	
R. B. Ayres..........	Brigadier General.................	Apr. 21, 1863, to June 28, 1863.	
Hannibal Day........	Col. 6th U. S. Infy.............	June 28, 1863, to Aug. 22, 1863.	
G. K. Giddings.......	Major 14th U. S. Infy.............	Aug. 22, 1863, to Sept. 23, 1863.	
Sidney Burbank......	Col. 2d U. S. Infy.............	Sept. 23, 1863, to Jan., 1864.	
L. B. Brown..........	Major 12th U. S. Infy.............	Jan., 1864, to Mch. 23, 1864.	

Consolidated with 3d Brigade and Designated 4th Brig. 1-Div. 5th Corps. Reorganized March 24, 1864.

S. H. Leonard.........	Col. 13th Mass. Infy.............	Mch. 24, 1864, to May 6, 1864.	
Peter Lyle...........	Col. 90th Penna. Infy...........	May 6, 1864, to June 5, 1864.	

Brigade transferred to 1st Brig. 3d Div. 5th Corps June 5, 1864. Reorganized from 1st Brig. 1-Div. 5-Corps June 6, 1864.

1st BRIGADE, 2d DIVISION.—Continued. COMMANDERS.

R. B. Ayres.............	Brigadier General....................	June 6, 1864.
E. M. Gregory..........	Col. 91st Penna. Infy.............	June 6, 1864, to June 20, 1864.
Joseph Hayes..........	Brigadier General...............	June 20, 1864, to Aug. 19, 1864.
F. Winthrop...........	Col. 5th New York Infy...........	Aug. 19, 1864, to Aug. 21, 1864.
C. P. Stone.............	Col. 14th U. S. Infy.............	Aug. 21, 1864, to Sept. 10, 1864.
F. Winthrop...........	Col. 5th New York Infy.........	Sept. 10, 1864, to Sept. 30, 1864.
E. S. Otis..............	Lt.-Col. 140th New York Infy......	Sept. 30, 1864, to Oct. 1, 1864.
James Grindley........	Major 146th New York Infy........	Oct. 1, 1864, to Oct. 3, 1864.
F. Winthrop...........	Col. 5th New York Infy.........	Oct. 3, 1864, to Feb. 16, 1865.
M. Wiedrich...........	Lt.-Col. 15th N. Y. H. Arty.......	Feb. 16, 1865, to Mch. 12, 1865.
F. Winthrop...........	Col. 5th New York Infy..........	Mch. 12, 1865, to Apr. 1, 1865.
James Grindley........	Col. 146th New York Infy..........	Apr. 1, 1865, to Apr. 3, 1865.
Joseph Hayes..........	Brigadier General................	Apr. 3, 1865, to June 28, 1865.

3d United States Infy.....May, 1862	From Sykes' Infy. Res. Potomac...	To 4-Brig. 1-Div. 5-Corps Potomac.	Mch., 1864
4th United States Infy....May, 1862	From Sykes' Infy. Res. Potomac...	To Dept. East.....................	Aug., 1863
12th United States Infy...May, 1862	From Sykes' Infy. Res. Potomac...	To 4-Brig. 1-Div. 5-Corps Potomac.	Mch., 1864
14th United States Infy...May, 1862	From Sykes' Infy. Res. Potomac...	To 4-Brig. 1-Div. 5-Corps Potomac.	Mch., 1864
6th United States Infy...June, 1863	From 2-Brig. 2-Div. 5-Corps Potom.	To Dept. East.....................	Aug., 1863
2d United States Infy....July, 1863	From 2-Brig. 2-Div. 5-Corps Potom.	To 4-Brig. 2-Div. 5-Corps Potomac.	Mch., 1864
11th United States Infy..Sept., 1863	From 2-Brig. 2-Div. 5-Corps Potom.	To 4-Brig. 2-Div. 5-Corps Potomac.	Mch., 1864
17th United States Infy..Sept., 1863	From 2-Brig. 2-Div. 5-Corps Potom.	To 4-Brig. 2-Div. 5-Corps Potomac.	Mch., 1864
16th Maine Infy..........Mch., 1864	From 1-Brig. 2-Div. 1-Corps Potom.	To 1-Brig. 3-Div. 5-Corps Potomac.	June, 1864
13th Mass. Infy.........Mch., 1864	From 1-Brig. 2-Div. 1-Corps Potom.	To 1-Brig. 3-Div. 5-Corps Potomac.	June, 1864
39th Mass................Mch., 1864	From 1-Brig. 2-Div. 1-Corps Potom.	To 1-Brig. 3-Div. 5-Corps Potomac.	June, 1864
104th New York Infy....Mch., 1864	From 1-Brig. 2-Div. 1-Corps Potom.	To 1-Brig. 3-Div. 5-Corps Potomac.	June, 1864
107th Penna. Infy.......Mch., 1864	From 1-Brig. 2-Div. 1-Corps Potom.	To 1-Brig. 3-Div. 5-Corps Potomac.	June, 1864
90th Penna. Infy........May, 1864	From 2-Brig. 2-Div. 5-Corps Potom.	To 1-Brig. 3-Div. 5-Corps Potomac.	June, 1864
94th New York Infy.....May, 1864	From 2-Brig. 2-Div. 5-Corps Potom.	To 2-Brig. 3-Div. 5-Corps Potomac.	June, 1864
140th New York Infy....June, 1864	From 1-Brig. 1-Div. 5-Corps Potom.	No change to Muster Out..........	June, 1865
146th New York Infy....June, 1864	From 1-Brig. 1-Div. 5-Corps Potom.	No change to Muster Out..........	June, 1865
91st Penna. Infy.......June, 1864	From 1-Brig. 1-Div. 5-Corps Potom.	To 2-Brig. 2-Div. 5-Corps Potomac.	June, 1864
155th Penna. Infy......June, 1864	From 1-Brig. 1-Div. 5-Corps Potom.	To 2-Brig. 2-Div. 5-Corps Potomac.	June, 1864
2d United States Infy...June, 1864	From 1-Brig. 1-Div. 9-Corps Potom.	To Dept. East.....................	Nov., 1864
4th United States Infy..June, 1864	From 1-Brig. 1-Div. 9-Corps Potom.	To Headqrs. Army Potomac........	June, 1864
10th United States Infy..June, 1864	From 1-Brig. 1-Div. 9-Corps Potom.	To Headqrs. Army Potomac........	Oct., 1864
11th United States Infy..June, 1864	From 1-Brig. 1-Div. 5-Corps Pot..	To Dept. East.....................	Nov., 1864
12th United States Infy..June, 1864	From 1-Brig. 1-Div. 5-Corps Pot..	To Dept. East.....................	Nov., 1864
14th United States Infy..June, 1864	From 1-Brig. 1-Div. 5-Corps Pot..	To Dept. East.....................	Nov., 1864
17th United States Infy..June, 1864	From 1-Brig. 1-Div. 5-Corps Pot..	To Dept. East.....................	Oct., 1864
5th N. Y. Vet'n. Infy....June, 1864	From 1-Brig. 1-Div. 5-Corps Pot..	To Dept. East.....................	Apr., 1865
15th N. Y. Heavy Arty...Aug., 1864	From 3-Brig. 2-Div. 5-Corps Pot....	To Def. Washington 22-Corps.....	May, 1865
8th U. S. Infantry.......Oct., 1864	From Headquarters 9-Corps Pot....	To Dept. East.....................	Nov., 1864
61st Mass. Infy........Apr., 1865	From Indpt. Brigade 9-Corps Pot....	No change to Muster Out..........	June, 1865
114th Penna. Infy......Apr., 1865	From Headquarters Army Potomac.	No change to Muster Out..........	May, 1865

2d BRIGADE, 2d DIVISION.— COMMANDERS.

William Chapman.....	Lt.-Col. 3d U. S. Infy.............	May 18, 1862, to June 27, 1862.	
Chas. S. Lovell........	Major 10th U. S. Infy.............	June 27, 1862, to June 29, 1862.	
William Chapman.....	Lt.-Col. 3d U. S. Infy.............	June 29, 1862, to Oct., 1862.	
Chas. S. Lovell........	Major 10th U. S. Infy.............	Oct., 1862, to Nov., 1862.	
Geo. L. Andrews......	Major 17th U. S. Infy.............	Nov., 1862, to Dec. 14, 1862.	
Chas. S. Lovell........	Major 10th U. S. Infy.............	Dec. 14, 1862, to Jan., 1863.	
Geo. L. Andrews......	Major 17th U. S. Infy.............	Jan., 1863, to Feb., 1863.	
DeL. Floyd-Jones......	Major 11th U. S. Infy.............	Feb., 1863, to March, 1863.	
S. Burbank.............	Col. 2d U. S. Infy.............	March, 1863, to Sept. 23, 1863.	

Brigade discontinued Sept. 23, 1863. Reorganized March 23, 1864.

Richard Coulter........	Col. 11th Penna. Infy.............	March 23, 1863, to April, 1864.	
Henry Baxter..........	Brigadier General.............	Apr., 1863, to May 6, 1863.	
Richard Coulter........	Col. 11th Penna. Infy.............	May 6, 1864, to May 8, 1864.	
James L. Bates........	Col. 12th Mass. Infy.............	May 8, 1864, to May 9, 1864.	

Brigade temporarily disbanded May 9, to May 18, 1864. Transferred to 2d Brig. 3d Div. June 5, 1864, Reorganized from 3d Brig. 2d Div. June 6, 1864.

James L. Bates........	Col. 12th Mass. Infy.............	May 18, 1864, to June 5, 1864.	
N. T. Dushane........	Col. 1st Maryland Infy.............	June 6, 1864, to Aug. 21, 1864.	Killed.
S. A. Graham..........	Col. Purnell Md. Legion.............	Aug. 21, 1864, to Oct. 24, 1864.	
A. W. Dennison.......	Col. 8th Maryland Infy.............	Oct. 24, 1864, to Jan. 22, 1865.	
R. N. Bowerman.......	Col. 4th Maryland Infy.............	Jan. 22, 1865, to Feb. 14, 1865.	
A. W. Dennison.......	Col. 8th Md. Infy.............	Feb. 14, 1865, to March 31, 1865.	
R. N. Bowerman.......	Col. 4th Md. Infy.............	March 31, 1865, to April 1, 1865.	
D. L. Stanton.........	Col. 1st Md. Infy.............	April 1, 1865, to May 16, 1865.	
A. W. Dennison.......	Col. 8th Md. Infy..................	May 16, 1865, to June 28, 1865.	

2d United States Infy.....May, 1862	From Sykes' Infy. Res. Potomac..	To 1-Brig. 2-Div. 5-Corps Pot....	July, 1863
6th U. S. Infy..........May, 1862	From Sykes' Infy. Res. Potomac..	To Dept. East.....................	Aug., 1863
10th United States Infy...May, 1862	From Sykes' Infy. Res. Potomac..	To Dept. East.....................	Aug., 1863
11th United States Infy..May, 1862	From Sykes' Infy. Res. Potomac..	To 1-Brig. 2-Div. 5-Corps Pot....	Sept., 1863
17th United States Infy..May, 1862	From Sykes' Infy. Res. Potomac..	To 1-Brig. 2-Div. 5-Corps Pot....	Sept., 1863
7th United States Infy...Oct., 1862	From Jefferson Barracks, Mo.......	To Dept. East.....................	Aug., 1863
12th Mass. Infy.........Mch., 1864	From 2-Brig. 2-Div. 1-Corps Pot...	To 2-Brig. 3-Div. 5-Corps Pot....	June, 1864
83d (9-S. M.) N. Y. Infy.Mch., 1864	From 2-Brig. 2-Div. 1-Corps Pot...	To 2-Brig. 3-Div. 5-Corps Pot....	June, 1864
97th N. Y. Infy.........Mch., 1864	From 2-Brig. 2-Div. 1-Corps Pot...	To 2-Brig. 3-Div. 5-Corps Pot....	June, 1864
11th Penna. Infy........Mch., 1864	From 2-Brig. 2-Div. 1-Corps Pot...	To 2-Brig. 3-Div. 5-Corps Pot....	June, 1864
88th Penna. Infy........Mch., 1864	From 2-Brig. 2-Div. 1-Corps Pot...	To 2-Brig. 3-Div. 5-Corps Pot....	June, 1864
90th Penna. Infy........Mch., 1864	From 2-Brig. 2-Div. 1-Corps Pot...	To 1-Brig. 2-Div. 5-Corps Pot....	May, 1864
94th N. Y. Infy.........May, 1864	From Dist. Annapolis 8-Corps...	To 1-Brig. 2-Div. 5-Corps Pot....	May, 1864
1st Md. Infy............June, 1864	From 3-Brig. 2-Div. 5-Corps Pot....	No change to Muster Out..........	June, 1865
4th Md. Infy............June, 1864	From 3-Brig. 2-Div. 5-Corps Pot....	No change to Muster Out..........	May, 1865
7th Md. Infy............June, 1864	From 3-Brig. 2-Div. 5-Corps Pot....	No change to Muster Out..........	May, 1865
8th Md. Infy............June, 1864	From 3-Brig. 2-Div. 5-Corps Pot....	No change to Muster Out..........	May, 1865
Purnell Md. Legion......June, 1864	From 3-Brig. 2-Div. 5-Corps Pot....	No change to Muster Out..........	Oct., 1864
91st Penna. Infy.......June, 1864	From 1-Brig. 2-Div. 5-Corps Pot....	To 2-Brig. 1-Div. 5-Corps Pot....	June, 1864
155th Penna. Infy......June, 1864	From 1-Brig. 2-Div. 5-Corps Pot....	To 2-Brig. 1-Div. 5-Corps Pot....	June, 1864

3d BRIGADE, 2d DIVISION.— COMMANDERS.

G. K. Warren..........	Col. 5th N. Y. Infy.............	May 18, 1862, to Dec., 1862.	
P. H. O'Rorke.........	Col. 140th N. Y. Infy.............	Dec., 1862, to Jan., 1863.	
G. K. Warren..........	Brigadier General.............	Jan., 1863, to Feb. 5, 1863.	
P. H. O'Rorke.........	Col. 140th N. Y. Infy.............	Feb. 5, 1863, to June 3, 1863.	
S. W. Reed............	Brigadier General.............	June, 1863, to July 3, 1863.	Killed.
Kenner Garrard.......	Brigadier General................	July 3, 1863, to Dec. 7, 1863.	

3d BRIGADE, 2d DIVISION.—Continued.   COMMANDERS.

E. M. Gregory	Col. 91st Penna. Infy	Dec. 7, 1863, to Dec., 1863.
George Ryan	Col. 140th N. Y. Infy	Dec., 1863, to Jan., 1864.
D. T. Jenkins	Col. 146th N. Y. Infy	Jan., 1864, to Feb. 15, 1864.
George Ryan	Col. 140th N. Y. Infy	Feb. 15, 1864, to March 23, 1864.

Consolidated with 1st Brigade and designated 4th Brigade 1-Division March 23, 1864. Reorganized March 24, 1864, from 1st Army Corps. Designation changed to 2d Brigade 2-Division June 6, 1864. Reorganized June 6, 1864, from Kitching's Indpt. Brigade.

N. T. Dushane	Col. 1st Md. Infy	March 23, 1864, to Apr., 1864.
A. W. Dennison	Col. 8th Md. Infy	April, 1864, to May 8, 1864.
Charles E. Phelps	Col. 7th Md. Infy	May 8, 1864.
R. N. Bowerman	Col. 4th Md. Infy	May 8, 1864, to May 23, 1864.
N. T. Dushane	Col. 1st Md. Infy	May 23, 1864, to June 6, 1864.
J. H. Kitching	Col. 8th N. Y. Heavy Arty	June 6, 1864, to Aug. 21, 1864.

Brigade discontinued Aug. 21, 1864. Reorganized Aug. 24, 1864, from 2d Brig. 4th Division 5-Corps.

J. W. Hoffman	Col. 56th Penna. Infy	Aug. 24, 1864, to Sept. 14, 1864.
A. H. Grimshaw	Col. 4th Del. Infy	Sept. 14, 1864, to Nov. 1, 1864.
William Sergeant	Col. 210th Penna. Infy	Nov. 1, 1864, to Nov. 17, 1864.
A. H. Grimshaw	Col. 4th Del. Infy	Nov. 17, 1864, to Nov. 21, 1864.
James Gwyn	Bvt. Brig. General	Nov. 21, 1864, to Dec. 22, 1864.
William Sergeant	Col. 210th Penna. Infy	Dec. 22, 1864, to Feb. 2, 1865.
James Gwyn	Bvt. Brig. General	Feb. 2, 1865, to June 28, 1865.

5th N. Y. Infy	May, 1862	From Sykes Infy. Res. Potomac	No change to Muster Out	May, 1863
10th N. Y. Infy	May, 1862	From 1-Brig. 1-Div. Dept. Va	To 3-Brig. 3-Div. 2-Corps Pot	Oct., 1862
1st Conn. Heavy Arty	May, 1862	From Siege Arty. Potomac	To Siege Arty. Potomac	July, 1862
140th N. Y. Infy	Oct., 1862	From 2-Brig. 2-Div. 12-Corps Pot	To 4-Brig. 1-Div. 5-Corps Pot	Mch., 1864
146th N. Y. Infy	Oct., 1862	From Def. of Washington	To 4-Brig. 1-Div. 5-Corps Pot	Mch., 1864
91st Penna. Infy	May, 1863	From 1-Brig. 3-Div. 5-Corps Pot	To 4-Brig. 1-Div. 5-Corps Pot	Mch., 1864
155th Penna. Infy	May, 1863	From 2-Brig. 3-Div. 5-Corps Pot	To 4-Brig. 1-Div. 5-Corps Pot	Mch., 1864
1st Md Infy	Mch., 1864	From 2-Brig. 3-Div. 1-Corps Pot	To 2-Brig. 2-Div. 5-Corps Pot	June, 1864
4th Md. Infy	Mch., 1864	From 2-Brig. 3-Div. 1-Corps Pot	To 2-Brig. 2-Div. 5-Corps Pot	June, 1864
7th Md. Infy	Mch., 1864	From 2-Brig. 3-Div. 1-Corps Pot	To 2-Brig. 2-Div. 5-Corps Pot	June, 1864
8th Md. Infy	Mch., 1864	From 2-Brig. 3-Div. 1-Corps Pot	To 2-Brig. 2-Div. 5-Corps Pot	June, 1864
Purnell Md. Legion	May, 1864	From 1 Separate Brig. 8-Corps	To 2-Brig. 2-Div. 5-Corps Pot	July, 1864
6th N. Y. Heavy Arty	June, 1864	From Kitching's Indpt. Brig. 5-C	To Def. of Washington 22-Corps	Aug., 1864
15th N. Y. Heavy Arty	June, 1864	From Kitching's Indpt. Brig. 5-C	To 1-Brig. 2-Div. 5-Corps Pot	June, 1865
3d Del. Infy	Aug., 1864	From 2-Brig. 4-Div. 5-Corps Pot	No change to Muster Out	June, 1865
4th Del. Infy	Aug., 1864	From 2-Brig. 4-Div. 5-Corps Pot	No change to Muster Out	Sept., 1864
76th N. Y. Infy	Aug., 1864	From 2-Brig. 4-Div. 5-Corps Pot	To 3-Brig. 3-Div. 5-Corps Pot	Sept., 1864
95th N. Y. Infy	Aug., 1864	From 2-Brig. 4-Div. 5-Corps Pot	To 3-Brig. 3-Div. 5-Corps Pot	Sept., 1864
147th N. Y. Infy	Aug., 1864	From 2-Brig. 4-Div. 5-Corps Pot	To 3-Brig. 3-Div. 5-Corps Pot	Sept., 1864
56th Penna. Infy	Aug., 1864	From 2-Brig. 4-Div. 5-Corps Pot	Transferred to 191st Penna	Mch., 1865
157th Penna. Infy	Aug., 1864	From 1-Brig. 3-Div. 5-Corps Pot	No change to Muster Out	June, 1865
190th Penna. Infy	Sept., 1864	From 1-Brig. 3-Div. 5-Corps Pot	No change to Muster Out	June, 1865
191st Penna. Infy	Sept., 1864	From New Organization	No change to Muster Out	May, 1865
210th Penna. Infy	Sept., 1864	From New Organization	No change to Muster Out	June, 1865
8th Del. Infy	Mch., 1865	From Provost Guard Potomac	No change to Muster Out	June, 1865

ARTILERY, 2d DIVISION.—

Battys. L and M, 3d U. S. Arty	May, 1862	From Arty. Res. Potomac	To Arty. 1-Div. 9-Corps Potomac	Dec., 1862
Batty. I, 5th U. S. Arty	May, 1862	From Arty. Res. Potomac	To Arty. Brig. 5-Corps Potomac	May, 1863
Battys. E and G, 1st U. S. Arty	Aug., 1862	From 2-Brig. Arty. Res. 5-Corps P	To Arty. 3-Div. 5-Corps Potomac	Oct., 1862
Batty. K, 5th U. S. Arty	Aug., 1862	From 2-Brig. Arty. Res. 5-Corps P	To Arty. Res. Potomac	Oct., 1862
Batty. L, 1st Ohio Arty	Oct., 1862	From Arty. 3-Div. 5-Corps Pot	To Arty. Brig. 5-Corps Potomac	May, 1863

3d DIVISION.—   COMMANDERS.

Geo. A. McCall	Brigadier General	June 18, 1862, to June 30, 1862.
Truman Seymour	Brigadier General	June 30, 1862, to Aug. 26, 1862.

Division transferred to 3d Corps Army of Va. Aug. 26, 1862. Reorganized Sept. 12, 1862.

A. A. Humphreys	Brigadier General	Sept. 12, 1862, to Jan. 27, 1863.
E. M. Gregory	Col. 91st Penna. Infy	Jan. 27, 1863, to Feb. 12, 1863.
A. A. Humphreys	Brigadier General	Feb. 12, 1863, to May 25, 1863.

Division dissolved May 25, 1863. Reorganized June 28, 1863, From Penna. Reserve Division 22d Corps.

S. W. Crawford	Brigadier General	June 28, 1863, to Aug. 28, 1863.
W. McCandless	Col. 2d Penna. Res	Aug. 28, 1863, to Nov. 1, 1863.
S. W. Crawford	Brigadier General	Nov. 1, 1863, to Feb. 20, 1864.
W. McCandless	Col. 2d Penna. Res	Feb. 20, 1864, to May 1, 1864.
S. W. Crawford	Brigadier General	May 1, 1864, to Jan. 2, 1865.
F. Winthrop	Bvt. Brig. General	Jan. 2, 1865, to Jan. 27, 1865.
S. W. Crawford	Bvt. Major General	Jan. 27, 1865, to June 28, 1865.

1st BRIGADE, 3d DIVISION.—   COMMANDERS.

J. F. Reynolds	Brigadier General	June 18, 1862, to June 27, 1862.
S. G. Simmons	Col. 5th Penna. Res	June 27, 1862, to June 30, 1862.
R. B. Roberts	Col. 9th Penna. Res	June 30, 1862, to July 5, 1862.
Wm. Sinclair	Col. 6th Penna. Res	July 5, 1862, to Aug. 26, 1862.
E. B. Tyler	Brigadier General	Sept. 12, 1862, to Jan., 1863.
E. M. Gregory	Col. 91st Penna. Infy	Jan., 1863, to Jan. 27, 1863.
D. W. Rowe	Lt.-Col. 126th Penna. Infy	Jan. 27, 1863, to Feb. 12, 1863.
E. M. Gregory	Col. 91st Penna. Infy	Feb. 12, 1863, to March 28, 1863.
E. B. Tyler	Brigadier General	March 28, 1863, to May 25, 1863.
W. McCandless	Col. 2d Penna. Res	June 28, 1863, to Aug. 28, 1863.
W. O. Talley	Col. 1st Penna. Res	Aug. 28, 1863, to Nov. 1, 1863.
Wm. McCandless	Col. 2d Penna. Res	Nov. 1, 1863, to Feb. 20, 1864.
W. O. Talley	Col. 1st Penna. Res	Feb. 20, 1864, to May 1, 1864.
Wm. McCandless	Col. 2d Penna. Res	May 1, 1864, to May 8, 1864.
W. O. Talley	Col. 1st Penna. Res	May 8, 1864.
W. H. Ent	Col. 6th Penna. Res	May 8, 1864.
S. M. Jackson	Col. 11th Penna. Res	May 8, 1864, to May 18, 1864.
M. D. Hardin	Col. 12th Penna. Res	May 18, 1864, to May 25, 1864.

Brigade discontinued May 25, 1864. Reorganized June 6, 1864, from 1st Brig. 2d Div. 5th Corps.

Peter Lyle	Col. 90th Penna. Infy	June 6, 1864, to Aug. 27, 1864.
T. F. McCoy	Col. 107th Penna. Infy	Aug. 27, 1864, to Sept. 13, 1864.
E. S. Bragg	Brigadier General	Sept. 13, 1864, to Dec. 22, 1864.
H. A. Morrow	Col. 24th Mich. Infy	Dec. 22, 1864, to Jan. 18, 1865.
E. S. Bragg	Brigadier General	Jan. 18, 1865, to Feb. 14, 1865.
John A. Kellogg	Col. 6th Wis. Infy	Feb. 14, 1865, to April 28, 1865.
H. A. Morrow	Bvt. Brig. General	April 28, 1865, to June 28, 1865.

1st Penna. Res	June, 1862	From 1-Brig. 3-Div. Dept. Rapp	To 1-Brig. 3-Div. 3-Corps Army Va.	Aug., 1862
2d Penna. Res	June, 1862	From 1-Brig. 3-Div. Dept. Rapp	To 1-Brig. 3-Div. 3-Corps Army Va.	Aug., 1862
5th Penna. Res	June, 1862	From 1-Brig. 3-Div. Dept. Rapp	To 1-Brig. 3-Div. 3-Corps Army Va.	Aug., 1862

1st BRIGADE, 3d DIVISION.—Continued.

8th Penna. Res..........June, 1862	From 1-Brig. 3-Div. Dept. Rapp...	To 2-Brig. 3-Div. 3-Corps Army Va.	Aug.,	1862
91st Penna. Infy.........Sept., 1862	From Def. of Washington.........	To 3-Brig. 2-Div. 5-Corps Pot....	Mch.,	1863
126th Penna. Infy......Sept., 1862	From Def. of Washington.........	No change to Muster Out.........	May,	1863
129th Penna. Infy......Sept., 1862	From Def. of Washington.........	No change to Muster Out.........	May,	1863
134th Penna. Infy......Sept., 1862	From Def. of Washington.........	No change to Muster Out.........	May,	1863
1st Penna. Res..........June, 1863	From 1-Brig. Pa. Res. Div. 22-Corps	No change to Muster Out.........	May,	1864
2d Penna. Res..........June, 1863	From 1-Brig. Pa. Res. Div. 22-Corps	No change to Muster Out.........	May,	1864
6th Penna. Res..........June, 1863	From 1-Brig. Pa. Res. Div. 22-Corps	No change to Muster Out.........	May,	1864
13th Penna. Res..........June, 1863	From 1-Brig. Pa. Res. Div. 22-Corps	No change to Muster Out.........	May,	1864
11th Penna. Res..........Nov., 1863	From 3-Brig. 3-Div. 5-Corps Pot..	No change to Muster Out.........	May,	1864
7th Penna. Res..........Apr., 1864	From Dist. Alexandria 22-Corps..	No change to Muster Out.........	May,	1864
94th N. Y. Infy........June, 1864	From 1-Brig. 2-Div. 5-Corps Pot..	To 2-Brig. 3-Div. 5-Corps Pot....	June,	1864
104th N. Y. Infy........June, 1864	From 1-Brig. 2-Div. 5-Corps Pot..	To 2-Brig. 3-Div. 5-Corps Pot....	Sept.,	1864
16th Me. Infy..........June, 1864	From 1-Brig. 2-Div. 5-Corps Pot..	To 2-Brig. 3-Div. 5-Corps Pot....	Sept.,	1864
13th Mass. Infy........June, 1864	From 1-Brig. 2-Div. 5-Corps Pot..	No change to Muster Out.........	July,	1864
39th Mass. Infy........June, 1864	From 1-Brig. 2-Div. 5-Corps Pot..	To 2-Brig. 3-Div. 5-Corps Pot....	Sept.,	1864
90th Penna. Infy........June, 1864	From 1-Brig. 2-Div. 5-Corps Pot..	To 2-Brig. 3-Div. 5-Corps Pot....	Sept.,	1864
107th Penna. Infy......June, 1864	From 1-Brig. 2-Div. 5-Corps Pot..	To 2-Brig. 3-Div. 5-Corps Pot....	Sept.,	1864
190th Penna. Infy.......Aug., 1864	From 3-Brig. 3-Div. 5-Corps Pot....	To 3-Brig. 2-Div. 5-Corps Pot....	Sept.,	1864
191st Penna. Infy.......Aug., 1864	From 3-Brig. 3-Div. 5-Corps Pot....	To 3-Brig. 2-Div. 5-Corps Pot....	Sept.,	1864
24th Mich. Infy.......Sept., 1864	From 3-Brig. 3-Div. 5-Corps Pot....	To Springfield, Ill..............	Feb.,	1865
19th Ind. Infy........Sept., 1864	From 3-Brig. 3-Div. 5-Corps Pot....	To Consol. with 20th Ind........	Oct.,	1864
143d Penna. Infy......Sept., 1864	From 1-Brig. 1-Div. 5-Corps Pot..	To Hart's Island, N. Y..........	Feb.,	1865
149th Penna. Infy......Sept., 1864	From 1-Brig. 1-Div. 5-Corps Pot..	No change to Muster Out.........	June,	1865
150th Penna. Infy......Sept., 1864	From 1-Brig. 1-Div. 5-Corps Pot..	No change to Muster Out.........	June,	1865
1st Battn. N. Y. S. S....Sept., 1864	From 3-Brig. 3-Div. 5-Corps Pot..	No change to Muster Out.........	June,	1865
2d Wis. Infy..........Sept., 1864	From 3-Brig. 3-Div. 5-Corps Pot..	To Consol. with 6th Wis........	Nov.,	1864
6th Wis. Infy..........Sept., 1864	From 3-Brig. 3-Div. 5-Corps Pot..	No change to Muster Out.........	June,	1865
7th Wis. Infy..........Sept., 1864	From 3-Brig. 3-Div. 5-Corps Pot..	No change to Muster Out.........	June,	1865
91st Penna. Infy........Mch., 1865	From 3-Brig. 1-Div. 5-Corps Pot..	No change to Muster Out.........	June,	1865
91st N. Y. Infy........Mch., 1865	From Baltimore, Md., 8-Corps......	No change to Muster Out.........	June,	1865

2d BRIGADE, 3d DIVISION.—   COMMANDERS.

Geo. G. Meade.........	Brigadier General	June 18, 1862, to June 30, 1862.
A. L. Majilton.........	Col. 4th Penna. Res.............	June 30, 1862, to Aug. 26, 1862.
P. H. Allabach.........	Col. 131st Penna. Infy..........	Sept. 12, 1862, to Feby. 15, 1863.
J. B. Clark...........	Col. 123d Penna. Infy..........	Feb. 15, 1863, to Mch. 7, 1863.
P. H. Allabach.........	Col. 131st Penna. Infy..........	Mch. 7, 1863, to May 25, 1863.

Brigade discontinued May, 1863, by reason of Muster Out of Regiments. Reorganized June 6, 1864, from 2-Brig. 2-Div. 5-Corps.

James L. Bates........	Col. 12th Mass. Infy............	June 6, 1864, to June 25, 1864.
Henry Baxter	Brigadier General	June 25, 1864, to Aug. 15, 1864.
Rich'd Coulter	Col. 11th Penna. Infy...........	Aug. 15, 1864, to Aug. 18, 1864.
Chas. Wheelock	Col. 97th N. Y. Infy...........	Aug. 18, 1864, to Aug. 29, 1864.
Henry Baxter	Brigadier General	Aug. 29, 1864, to June 28, 1865.

3d Penna. Res..........June, 1862	From 2-Brig. 3-Div. Dept. Rappa...	To 1-Brig. 3-Div. 3-Corps Army Va..	Aug.,	1862
4th Penna. Res..........June, 1862	From 2-Brig. 3-Div. Dept. Rappa...	To 1-Brig. 3-Div. 3-Corps Army Va..	Aug.,	1862
7th Penna. Res..........June, 1862	From 2-Brig. 3-Div. Dept. Rapp....	To 2-Brig. 3-Div. 3-Corps Army Va..	Aug.,	1862
11th Penna. Res..........June, 1862	From 2-Brig. 3-Div. Dept. Rapp....	To 3-Brig. 3-Div. 3-Corps Army Va..	Aug.,	1862
123d Penna. Infy........Sept., 1862	New organization..............	No change to muster out.........	May,	1863
131st Penna. Infy........Sept., 1862	New organization..............	No change to muster out.........	May,	1863
133d Penna. Infy........Sept., 1862	New organization..............	No change to muster out.........	May,	1863
155th Penna. Infy........Sept., 1862	New organization..............	To 3 Brig. 2-Div. 5-Corps Pot..	May,	1863
12th Mass. Infy........May, 1864	From 2-Brig. 2-Div. 5-Corps Pot....	No change to muster out.........	July,	1864
83d N. Y. Infy........May, 1864	From 2-Brig. 2-Div. 5-Corps Pot....	No change to muster out.........	June,	1864
97th N. Y. Infy........May, 1864	From 2-Brig. 2-Div. 5-Corps Pot....	No change to muster out.........	July,	1865
11th Penna. Infy........May, 1864	From 2-Brig. 2-Div. 5-Corps Pot....	To 3-Brig. 3-Div. 5-Corps Pot....	Nov.,	1864
88th Penna. Infy........May, 1864	From 2-Brig. 2-Div. 5-Corps Pot....	To 3-Brig. 3-Div. 5-Corps Pot....	Mch.,	1865
94th N. Y. Infy........May, 1864	From 1-Brig. 2-Div. 5-Corps Pot....	To 3-Brig. 3-Div. 5-Corps Pot....	Nov.,	1864
16th Me. Infy..........Sept., 1864	From 1-Brig. 3-Div. 5-Corps Pot....	No change to muster out.........	June,	1865
39th Mass. Infy........Sept., 1864	From 1-Brig. 3-Div. 5-Corps Pot....	No change to muster out.........	June,	1865
104th N. Y. Infy........Sept., 1864	From 1-Brig. 3-Div. 5-Corps Pot....	To Provost Guard 5-Corps Pot....	Nov.,	1864
90th Penna. Infy........Sept., 1864	From 1-Brig. 3-Div. 5-Corps Pot....	Consol. with 11th Penna...........	Nov.,	1864
107th Penna. Infy........Sept., 1864	From 1-Brig. 3-Div. 5-Corps Pot....	To 3-Brig. 3-Div. 5-Corps Pot....	Feb.,	1865
104th N. Y. Infy........May, 1865	From Provost Guard 5-Corps.......	No change to muster out.........	July,	1865

3d BRIGADE, 3d DIVISION.—   COMMANDERS.

Truman Seymour	Brigadier General...............	June 18, 1862, to June 30, 1862.
C. F. Jackson..........	Col. 9th Penna. Reserves.........	June 30, 1862, to Aug. 26, 1862.

No 3-Brig. till June, 28, 1863, when reorganized from Res. Div. 22-Corps.

Jos. W. Fisher........	Col. 5th Penna. Reserves.........	June 28, 1863, to Sept. 18, 1863.
M. D. Hardin.........	Col 12th Penna. Reserves.........	Sept. 18, 1863, to Dec. 4, 1863.
Jos. W. Fisher........	Col. 5th Penna. Reserves.........	Dec. 4, 1863, to May 30, 1864.
W. R. Hartshorne......	Major 12th Penna. Reserves......	May 30, 1864, to June 6, 1864.
James Carle	Col. 191st Penna. Infy...........	June 6, 1864, to July 26, 1864.
W. R. Hartshorne......	Col. 12th Penna. Reserves.......	July 26, 1864, to Aug. 21, 1864.

Brigade discontinued Aug. 21, 1864. Consolidated with 1-Brig. 3-Div. 5-Corps. Reorganized from 1-Brig. 4-Div. 5-Corps Aug. 24, 1864.

E. S. Bragg...........	Brigadier General...............	Aug. 24, 1864, to Sept. 13, 1864.
J. W. Hoffman.........	Col. 56th Penna. Infy...........	Sept. 13, 1864, to Jan. 24, 1865.
H. A. Morrow.........	Col. 24th Mich. Infy...........	Jan. 24, 1865, to Feb. 10, 1865.
J. W. Hoffman.........	Col. 56th Penna. Infy...........	Feb. 10, 1865, to Feb. 15, 1865.
Richard Coulter.......	Col. 11th Penna. Infy...........	Feb. 15, 1865, to May 13, 1865.
A. R. Root...........	Col. 97th N. Y. Infy...........	May 13, 1865, to June 28, 1865.

8th Penna. Reserves......June, 1862	From 3-Brig. 2-Div. Dept. Rapp....	To 1-Brig. 3-Div. 3-Corps Army Va..	Aug.,	1862
9th Penna. Reserves......June, 1862	From 3-Brig. 2-Div. Dept. Rapp....	To 3-Brig 3-Div. 3-Corps Army Va..	Aug.,	1862
10th Penna. Reserves......June, 1862	From 3-Brig. 2-Div. Dept. Rapp....	To 3-Brig 3-Div. 3-Corps Army Va..	Aug.,	1862
12th Penna. Reserves......June, 1862	From 3-Brig. 2-Div. Dept. Rapp....	To 3-Brig 3-Div. 3-Corps Army Va..	Aug.,	1862
13th Penna. Reserves......June, 1862	From 3-Brig. 2-Div. Dept. Rapp....	To 2-Brig. 3-Div. 3-Corps Army Va..	Aug.,	1862
5th Penna. Reserves......June, 1863	From Res. Div. 22-Corps..........	No change to muster out.........	May,	1864
9th Penna. Reserves......June, 1863	From Res. Div. 22-Corps..........	No change to muster out.........	May,	1864
10th Penna. Reserves......June, 1863	From Res. Div. 22-Corps..........	No change to muster out.........	May,	1864
11th Penna. Reserves......June, 1863	From Res. Div. 22-Corps..........	To 1-Brig. 3-Div. 5-Corps Pot....	Nov.,	1863
12th Penna. Reserves......June, 1863	From Res. Div. 22-Corps..........	No change to muster out.........	May,	1864
8th Penna. Reserves......June, 1863	From Dist. Alexandria 22-Corps...	No change to muster out.........	May,	1864
190th Penna. Infy........May, 1864	From Veterans Penna. Res. Corps...	To 1-Brig. 3-Div. 5-Corps Pot....	Aug.,	1864
191st Penna. Infy........May, 1864	From Veterans Penna. Res. Corps...	To 1-Brig. 3-Div. 5-Corps Pot....	Aug.,	1864
7th Ind. Infy..........Aug., 1864	From 1-Brig. 4-Div. 5-Corps Pot....	No change to muster out.........	Sept.,	1864
19th Ind. Infy..........Aug., 1864	From 1-Brig. 4-Div. 5-Corps Pot....	To 1-Brig. 3-Div. 5-Corps Pot......	Sept.,	1864

3d BRIGADE, 3d DIVISION.—Continued.

24th Mich. Infy.........Aug., 1864	From 1-Brig. 4-Div. 5-Corps Pot....	To 1-Brig. 3-Div. 5-Corps Pot......	Sept., 1864
2d Wis. Infy............Aug., 1864	From 1-Brig. 4-Div. 5-Corps Pot....	To 1-Brig. 3-Div. 5-Corps Pot......	Sept., 1864
6th Wis. Infy...........Aug., 1864	From 1-Brig. 4-Div. 5-Corps Pot....	To 1-Brig. 3-Div. 5-Corps Pot......	Sept., 1864
7th Wis. Infy...........Aug., 1864	From 1-Brig. 4-Div. 5-Corps Pot....	To 1-Brig. 3-Div. 5-Corps Pot......	Sept., 1864
1st Battn. N. Y. S. S....Aug., 1864	From 1-Brig. 4-Div. 5-Corps Pot....	To 1-Brig. 3-Div. 5-Corps Pot......	Sept., 1864
94th N. Y. Infy.........Sept., 1864	From 2-Brig. 3-Div. 5-Corps Pot....	To 2-Brig. 3-Div. 5-Corps Pot......	Oct., 1864
95th N. Y. Infy.........Sept., 1864	From 3-Brig. 2-Div. 5-Corps Pot....	No change to muster out..........	July, 1865
147th N. Y. Infy........Sept., 1864	From 3-Brig. 2-Div. 5-Corps Pot....	No change to muster out..........	June, 1865
56th Penna. Infy........Sept., 1864	From 3-Brig. 2-Div. 5-Corps Pot....	No change to muster out..........	July, 1865
121st Penna. Infy.......Sept., 1864	From 3-Brig. 2-Div. 5-Corps Pot....	No change to muster out..........	June, 1865
142d Penna. Infy........Sept., 1864	From 1-Brig. 1-Div. 5-Corps Pot....	No change to muster out..........	May, 1865
76th N. Y. Infy.........Oct., 1864	From 3-Brig. 2-Div. 5-Corps Pot....	No change to muster out..........	Jan., 1865
94th N. Y. Infy.........Nov., 1864	From 2-Brig. 3-Div. 5-Corps Pot....	No change to muster out..........	July, 1865
107th Penna. Infy.......Feby., 1865	From 2-Brig. 3-Div. 5-Corps Pot....	No change to muster out..........	July, 1865
11th Penna. Infy........Mch., 1865	From 2-Brig. 3-Div. 5-Corps Pot....	No change to muster out..........	June, 1865
88th Penna. Infy........Mch., 1865	From 2-Brig. 3-Div. 5-Corps Pot....	No change to muster out..........	June, 1865

ARTILLERY, 3d DIVISION.—

Batty A, 1st Penna. Arty..June, 1862	From Arty. 2-Div. Dept. Rapp......	To Arty. 3-Div. 3-Corps Army Va...	Aug., 1862
Batty. B, 1st Penna. Arty..June, 1862	From Arty. 2-Div. Dept. Rapp......	To Arty. 3-Div. 3-Corps Army Va...	Aug., 1862
Batty. G, 1st Penna. Arty..June, 1862	From Arty. 2-Div. Dept. Rapp......	To Arty. 3-Div. 3-Corps Army Va...	Aug., 1862
Batty. C. 5th U. S. Arty....June, 1862	From Arty. 2-Div. Dept. Rapp......	To Arty. 3-Div. 3-Corps Army Va...	Aug., 1862
Batty. C, 1st N. Y. Arty..Sept., 1862	From Def. of Washington...........	To Arty. Brig. 5-Corps Pot........	May, 1863
Batty L. 1st Ohio Arty..Sept., 1862	From Def. of Washington...........	To Arty. 2-Div. 5-Corps. Pot.......	Oct., 1862
Battys. E and G, 1st U. S..Oct., 1862	From Arty. 2-Div. 5-Corps Pot.....	To 2-Regular Brig. Arty. Res. Pot..	May, 1863

4th DIVISION.—Organized Mch. 25, 1864. Discontinued Aug. 24, 1864.

COMMANDERS.

J. S. Wadsworth.......	Brigadier General..................	Mch. 25, 1864, to May 6, 1864.	Killed.
L. Cutler..............	Brigadier General..................	May 6, 1864, to Aug. 24, 1864.	

1st BRIGADE, 4th DIVISION.— COMMANDERS.

L. Cutler..............	Brigadier General..................	Mch. 25, 1864, to May 6, 1864.	
W. W. Robinson........	Col. 6th Wis. Infy.................	May 6, 1864, to June 7, 1864.	
E. S. Bragg...........	Brigadier General..................	June 7, 1864, to Aug. 24, 1864.	

19th Ind. Infy...........Mch., 1864	From 1-Brig. 1-Div. 1-Corps Pot....	To 3-Brig. 3-Div. 5-Corps Pot......	Aug., 1864
24th Mich. Infy.........Mch., 1864	From 1-Brig. 1-Div. 1-Corps Pot....	To 3-Brig. 3-Div. 5-Corps Pot......	Aug., 1864
2d Wis. Infy............Mch., 1864	From 1-Brig. 1-Div. 1-Corps Pot....	To 3-Brig. 3-Div. 5-Corps Pot......	Aug., 1864
6th Wis. Infy...........Mch., 1864	From 1-Brig. 1-Div. 1-Corps Pot....	To 3-Brig. 3-Div. 5-Corps Pot......	Aug., 1864
7th Wis. Infy...........Mch., 1864	From 1-Brig. 1-Div. 1-Corps Pot....	To 3-Brig. 3-Div. 5-Corps Pot......	Aug., 1864
1st N. Y. Battn. S. S......Mch., 1864	From 1-Brig. 1-Div. 1-Corps Pot....	To 3-Brig. 3-Div. 5-Corps Pot......	Aug., 1864
7th Ind. Infy...........Apr., 1864	From 2-Brig. 4-Div. 5-Corps Pot....	To 3-Brig. 3-Div. 5-Corps Pot......	Aug., 1864

2d BRIGADE, 4th DIVISION.— COMMANDERS.

J. C. Rice..............	Brigadier General..................	Mch. 25, 1864, to May 10, 1864.	Killed.
E. B. Fowler...........	Col. 84th N. Y. Infy...............	May 10, 1864, to May 22, 1864.	
J. W. Hoffman.........	Col. 56th Penna. Infy..............	May 22, 1864, to Aug. 24, 1864.	

7th Ind. Infy...........Mch., 1864	From 2-Brig. 1-Div. 1-Corps Pot....	To 1-Brig. 4-Div. 5-Corps Pot......	Apr., 1864
76th N. Y. Infy.........Mch., 1864	From 2-Brig. 1-Div. 1-Corps Pot....	To 3-Brig. 2-Div. 5-Corps Pot......	Aug., 1864
84th N. Y. Infy.........Mch., 1864	From 2-Brig. 1-Div. 1-Corps Pot....	No change to muster out..........	June, 1864
95th N. Y. Infy.........Mch., 1864	From 2-Brig. 1-Div. 1-Corps Pot....	To 3-Brig. 2-Div. 5-Corps Pot......	Aug., 1864
147th N. Y. Infy........Mch., 1864	From 2-Brig. 1-Div. 1-Corps Pot....	To 3-Brig. 2-Div. 5-Corps Pot......	Aug., 1864
56th Penna. Infy........Mch., 1864	From 2-Brig. 1-Div. 1-Corps Pot....	To 3-Brig. 2-Div. 5-Corps Pot......	Aug., 1864
46th N. Y. Infy.........May, 1864	From 2-Brig. 1-Div. 9-Corps Pot....	To 2-Brig. 3-Div. 9-Corps Pot......	June, 1864
3d Del. Infy............May, 1864	From 1 Separate Brig. 8-Corps Pot..	To 3-Brig. 2-Div. 5-Corps Pot......	Aug., 1864
157th Penna. Infy........June, 1864	From 1-Brig. Tyler's Div. 22-Corps..	To 3-Brig. 2-Div. 5-Corps Pot......	Aug., 1864
4th Del. Infy...........June, 1864	From 1-Brig. Tyler's Div. 22-Corps..	To 3-Brig. 2-Div. 5-Corps Pot......	Aug., 1864

3d BRIGADE, 4th DIVISION.— COMMANDERS.

Roy Stone.............	Col. 149th Penna. Infy.............	Mch., 25, 1864, to May 6, 1864.	
E. S. Bragg...........	Col. 6th Wis. Infy.................	May 6, 1864, to June 6, 1864.	

Brigade transferred to 1-Brig. 1-Div. 5-Corps, June 6, 1864.

121st Penna. Infy........Mch., 1864	From 1-Brig. 3-Div. 1-Corps Pot....	To 1-Brig. 1-Div. 5-Corps Pot......	June, 1864
142 Penna. Infy........Mch., 1864	From 1-Brig. 3-Div. 1-Corps Pot....	To 1-Brig. 1-Div. 5-Corps Pot......	June, 1864
143d Penna. Infy........Mch., 1864	From 3-Div. 1-Corps Pot....	To 1-Brig. 1-Div. 5-Corps Pot......	June, 1864
149th Penna. Infy........Mch., 1864	From 1-Brig. 3-Div. 1-Corps Pot....	To 1-Brig. 1-Div. 5-Corps Pot......	June, 1864
150th Penna. Infy........Mch., 1864	From 1-Brig. 3-Div. 1-Corps Pot....	To 1-Brig. 1-Div. 5-Corps Pot......	June, 1864

KITCHING'S INDPT. BRIGADE.— COMMANDER.

J. Howard Kitching....	Col. 6th N. Y. Heavy Arty.		

6th N. Y. Heavy Arty....May, 1864	From 1-Brig. Arty. Reserve Pot.....	To 3-Brig. 2-Div. 5-Corps Pot......	June, 1864
15th N. Y. Heavy Arty....May, 1864	From 1-Brig. Arty. Reserve Pot.....	To 1-Brig. 2-Div. 5-Corps Pot......	June, 1864

ARTILLERY RESERVE.—Attached to 5th Corps, May 18, 1862, to Sept., 1862.

1st BRIGADE HORSE ARTY.—

Batty A, 2d U. S. Arty....May, 1862	From Arty. Reserve Pot............	To Cav. Div. Army Pot.............	Sept., 1862
Battys. B and L, 2d U. S..May, 1862	From Arty. Reserve Pot............	To Cav. Div. Army Pot.............	Sept., 1862
Batty. M, 2d U. S. Arty....May, 1862	From Arty. Reserve Pot............	To Cav. Div. Army Pot.............	Sept., 1862
Battys. C and G, 3d U. S..May, 1862	From Arty. Reserve Pot............	To Cav. Div. Army Pot.............	Sept., 1862

2d BRIGADE.—

Batty. E, 1st U. S. Arty..May, 1862	From Arty. Reserve Pot............	To Arty. 2-Div. 5-Corps Pot........	Sept., 1862
Batty. G, 1st U. S. Arty..May, 1862	From Arty. Reserve Pot............	To Arty., 2-Div. 5-Corps Pot........	Sept., 1862
Batty. K, 1st U. S. Arty..May, 1862	From Arty. Reserve Pot............	To Arty. 1-Div. 3-Corps Pot........	Aug., 1862
Batty. G, 4th U. S. Arty..May, 1862	From Arty. Reserve Pot............	To Arty. Reserve 5th-Corps Pot.....	Sept., 1862
Batty. A, 5th U. S. Arty..May, 1862	From Arty. Reserve Pot............	To Arty. 3-Div. 9-Corps Pot........	Sept., 1862
Batty. K, 5th U. S. Arty..May, 1862	From Arty. Reserve Pot............	To Arty. 2-Div. 5-Corps Pot........	Sept., 1862

3d BRIGADE.—

1st Batt'n N. Y., Batty A..May, 1862	From Arty. Reserve Pot............	To Reserve Arty. 5-Corps Pot.......	Sept., 1862
1st Batt'n N. Y., Batty. B..May, 1862	From Arty. Reserve Pot............	To Reserve Arty. 5-Corps Pot.......	Sept., 1862
1st Batt'n N. Y., Batty. C..May, 1862	From Arty. Reserve Pot............	To Reserve Arty. 5-Corps Pot.......	Sept., 1862
1st Batt'n N. Y. Batty. D..May, 1862	From Arty. Reserve Pot............	To Reserve Arty. 5-Corps Pot.......	Sept., 1862

4th BRIGADE.—

Batty. A, Md. Arty.......May, 1862	From Middle Dept..................	To Arty. 1-Div. 6-Corps Pot........	Sept., 1862
Batty. B, Md. Arty.......May, 1862	From Middle Dept..................	To Arty 2-Div. 6-Corps Pot........	Sept., 1862

5th BRIGADE.—

Batty. E, 2d U. S. Arty....May, 1862	From Arty. Reserve Pot............	To Arty. 1-Div. 9-Corps Pot........	Sept., 1862
Battys. F and K, 3d U. S..May, 1862	From Arty. Reserve Pot............	To Arty. 1-Div. 3-Corps Pot........	Sept., 1862

KITCHING'S INDPT. BRIGADE.—Continued.

UNATTACHED.—

Batty. G, 1st N. Y. Arty.	May, 1862	From Arty. 1-Div. 2-Corps Pot	To Res. Arty. 2-Corps Pot	June, 1862
5th N. Y. Indpt. Batty.	May, 1862	From Arty. Reserve, Pot	To Res. Arty. 5-Corps Pot	Sept., 1862

SIEGE TRAIN.—

1st Conn. Heavy Arty.	May, 1862	From Arty. Reserve, Pot	To 3-Brig. 2-Div. 5-Corps Pot	May, 1862

RESERVE ARTILLERY, 5th CORPS.—

Batty. A, 1st N. Y. Batt'n.	Sept. 1862	From 3-Brig. Arty. Res. 5-Corps Pot.	To Arty. Reserve Pot	Nov., 1862
Batty B, 1st N. Y. Batt'n.	Sept. 1862	From 3-Brig. Arty. Res. 5-Corps Pot.	To Arty. Reserve Pot	Nov., 1862
Batty. C, 1st N. Y. Batt'n.	Sept. 1862	From 3-Brig. Arty. Res. 5-Corps Pot.	To Arty. Reserve Pot	Nov., 1862
Batty. D, 1st N. Y. Batt'n.	Sept. 1862	From 3-Brig. Arty. Res. 5-Corps Pot.	To Arty. Reserve Pot	Nov., 1862
5th N. Y. Indpt. Batty.	Sept. 1862	From Unatt. Arty. Res. 5-Corps Pot.	To Arty. Reserve Pot	Nov., 1862
Batty. K, 1st U. S. Arty.	Sept. 1862	From Arty. 1-Div. 3-Corps Pot	To Arty. Reserve Pot	Nov., 1862
Batty. G, 4th U. S. Arty.	Sept. 1862	From 2-Brig. Arty. Res. 5-Corps Pot.	To Arty. Reserve Pot	Nov., 1862

ARTILLERY BRIGADE, 5th CORPS.—

3d Mass. Indpt. Batty.	May, 1863	From Arty. 1-Div. 5-Corps Pot.	No change to muster out	Sept., 1864
Batty. L, 1st Ohio Arty.	May, 1863	From Arty. 3-Div. 5-Corps Pot.	To Camp Barry Wash'ton 22-Corps.	Apr., 1864
Batty. C, 1st N. Y. Arty.	May, 1863	From Arty. 3-Div. 5-Corps Pot.	To 3-Brig. Arty Res. Pot.	Mch., 1864
Batty. D, 5th U. S. Arty.	May, 1863	From Arty. 1-Div. 5-Corps Pot.	To Dept. Washington.	May, 1865
Batty. I, 5th U. S. Arty.	May, 1863	From Arty. 2-Div. 5-Corps Pot.	To Camp Barry Wash'ton 22-Corps.	July, 1863
5th Mass. Indpt. Batty.	July, 1863	From 1-Vol. Brig. Arty. Res. Pot.	No change to muster out	June, 1865
Battys. F and K, 3d U. S.	Nov., 1863	From 1-Reg. Brig. Arty. Res. Pot.	To Arty Reserve Pot	Mch., 1864
Batty. D, 5th U. S. Arty.	Mch., 1864	From Camp Barry Wash'n 22 Corps.	To Dept. Washington.	June, 1865
Batty. E, 1st N. Y. Arty.	Mch., 1864	From Arty. Brig. 1-Corps Pot.	To Arty. Reserve Pot	Mch., 1864
Batty. H, 1st N. Y. Arty.	Mch., 1864	From Arty. Brig. 1-Corps Pot.	No change to muster out	June, 1865
Batty. L, 1st N. Y. Arty.	Mch., 1864	From Arty. Brig. 1-Corps Pot.	To Arty. Reserve Pot	Mch., 1864
Batty. D, 1st N. Y. Arty.	Mch., 1864	From Arty. Brig. 3-Corps Pot.	No change to muster out	June, 1865
Batty. B, 1st Penna. Arty.	Mch., 1864	From Arty. Brig. 1-Corps Pot.	To Arty. Reserve Pot	Mch., 1864
Batty. B, 4th U. S. Arty.	Mch., 1864	From Arty. Brig. 1-Corps Pot.	To Dept. Washington.	June, 1865
4th N. Y. H'vy Arty, 2 B'n.	Mch., 1864	From 3-Brig. DeRussy's Div. 22 C'ps.	To 2-Brig. 3-Div. 2-Corps Pot	June, 1864
9th Mass. Indpt. Batty.	May, 1864	From 3-Brig. Arty. Res. Pot.	To Arty. Reserve Pot	Mch., 1865
Batty B, 1st N. Y. Arty.	May, 1864	From 2-Brig. Arty. Res. Pot.	No change to muster out	June, 1865
Batty. C, 1st N. Y. Arty.	May, 1864	From 3-Brig. Arty. Res. Pot.	To Arty. Reserve Pot	Mch., 1865
15th N. Y. Indpt. Batty.	May, 1864	From 2-Brig. Arty. Res. Pot.	To Dept. Washington 22-Corps	Dec., 1864
5th N. Y. Indpt. Batty.	May, 1864	From 2-Brig. Arty. Res. Pot.	To Def. Washington 22-Corps	May, 1864
15 N. Y. H'vy Arty., Co. M.	Jan., 1865	From 1-Brig. 2-Div. 5-Corps Pot.	To Arty. Reserve Pot.	Apr., 1865
Batty. C, 1st N. Y. Arty.	Apr., 1865	From Arty. Res. Pot.	No change to muster out	June, 1865
Batty. E, 1st N. Y. Arty.	Apr., 1865	From Arty. Res. Pot.	No change to muster out	June, 1865
Batty. L, 1st N. Y. Arty.	Apr., 1865	From Arty. Res. Pot.	No change to muster out	June, 1865

CAVALRY.—

4th Penna. Cavalry	June, 1862	From McCall's Div. Dept. Rapp.	To Averill's Cav. Brig. Pot.	Sept., 1862
8th Ill. Cavalry	June, 1862	From Stoneman's Cav. Command Pot.	To 2-Brig. Cav. Div. Pot.	Sept., 1862

Sixth Army Corps

Created and organized provisionally May 18, 1862. General Order No. 125, Army of the Potomac. Confirmed by War Department July 22, 1862. Transferred to Army of the Shenandoah, Middle Military Division, July, 1864. Rejoined Army of the Potomac Dec. 6, 1864. Discontinued June 28, 1865.

CORPS COMMANDERS.

Wm. B. Franklin	Major General	May 18, 1862, to Nov. 16, 1862.	
W. F. Smith	Major General	Nov. 16, 1862, to Feb. 4, 1863.	
John Sedgwick	Major General	Feb. 4, 1863, to Apr. 6, 1864.	
J. B. Ricketts	Brigadier General	Apr. 6, 1864, to Apr. 13, 1864.	
John Sedgwick	Major General	Apr. 13, 1864, to May 9, 1864.	
H. G. Wright	Major General	May 9, 1864, to July 8, 1864.	Killed.
	See Army Shenandoah to Dec., 1864.		
H. G. Wright	Major General	Dec. 6, 1864, to Jan. 16, 1865.	
Geo. W. Getty	Bvt. Major General	Jan. 16, 1865, to Feb. 11, 1865.	
H. G. Wright	Major General	Feb. 11, 1865, to June 28, 1865.	

1st DIVISION.— COMMANDERS.

H. W. Slocum	Brigadier General	May 18, 1862, to Oct. 15, 1862.
John Newton	Brigadier General	Oct. 15, 1862, to Oct. 18, 1862.
W. T. H. Brooks	Brigadier General	Oct. 18, 1862, to May 23, 1863.
H. G. Wright	Brigadier General	May 23, 1862, to Dec. 16, 1863.
D. A. Russell	Brigadier General	Dec. 16, 1863, to May 25, 1864.
A. T. A. Torbert	Brigadier General	Mch. 25, 1864, to Apr. 23, 1864.
H. G. Wright	Major General	Apr. 23, 1864, to May 9, 1864.
D. A. Russell	Brigadier General	May 9, 1864, to July 8, 1864.
	See Army Shenandoah to Dec., 1864.	
Frank Wheaton	Brigadier General	Dec. 6, 1864, to June 28, 1865.

1st BRIGADE, 1st DIVISION.— COMMANDERS.

G. W. Taylor	Brigadier General	May 18, 1862, to Aug. 29, 1862.	Killed.
A. T. A. Torbert	Col. 1st N. J. Infy	Aug. 29, 1862, to Dec. 24, 1862.	
H. W. Brown	Col. 3d N. J. Infy	Dec. 24, 1862, to Feb. 8, 1863.	
A. T. A. Torbert	Brigadier General	Feb. 8, 1863, to Apr. 10, 1863.	
H. W. Brown	Col. 3d N. J. Infy	Apr. 10, 1863, to May 3, 1863.	
W. H. Penrose	Col. 15th N. J. Infy	May 3, 1863.	
S. L. Buck	Col. 2d N. J. Infy	May 3, 1863, to May 4, 1863.	
W. H. Penrose	Col. 15th N. J. Infy	May 4, 1863, to June 27, 1863.	
A. T. A. Torbert	Brigadier General	June 27, 1863, to Mch. 25, 1864.	
H. W. Brown	Col. 3d N. J. Infy	Mch. 25, 1864, to May 9, 1864.	
W. H. Penrose	Col. 15th N. J. Infy	May 9, 1864, to July 8, 1864.	
	See Army Shenandoah to Dec., 1864.		
B. Hufty	Capt. 4th N. J. Infy	Dec. 6, 1864, to Jan. 5, 1865.	
E. L. Campbell	Lt.-Col. 15th N. Y. Infy	Jan. 5, 1865, to Feb. 26, 1865.	
W. H. Penrose	Col. 15th N. J. Infy	Feb. 26, 1865, to June 28, 1865.	

1st BRIGADE, 1st DIVISION.—Continued.

1st N. J. Infy..........May, 1862	From 1-Brig. 1-Div. Dept. Rapp....	No change to Muster Out.........	June,	1864
2d N. J. Infy..........May, 1862	From 1-Brig. 1-Div. Dept. Rapp....	No change to Muster Out.........	June,	1864
3d N. J. Infy..........May, 1862	From 1-Brig. 1-Div. Dept. Rapp....	No change to Muster Out.........	June,	1864
4th N. J. Infy..........May, 1862	From 1-Brig. 1-Div. Dept. Rapp....	To 1-Brig. 1-Div. 6-Corps Shen....	July,	1864
15th N. J. Infy..........Oct., 1862	From Def. of Washington.........	To 1-Brig. 1-Div. 6-Corps Shen....	July,	1864
23d N. J. Infy..........Oct., 1862	New Organization...............	No change to Muster Out.........	June,	1863
10th N. J. Infy..........Apr., 1864	From Pennsylvania...............	To 1-Brig. 1-Div. 6-Corps Shen....	July,	1864
1st. Del. Cav. Dismt'd....May, 1864	From 1-Separate Brig. 8-Corps.....	To 1-Separate Brig. 8-Corps........	July,	1864
1st N. J. Vet'n. Infy......Dec., 1864	New Organization...............	No change to Muster Out.........	June,	1865
2d N. J. Vet'n. Infy......Dec., 1864	New Organization...............	No change to Muster Out.........	June,	1865
40th N. J. Infy..........Dec., 1864	New Organization...............	No change to Muster Out.........	June,	1865
4th N. J. Infy..........Dec., 1864	From 1-Brig. 1-Div. 6-Corps Shen..	No change to Muster Out.........	June,	1865
10th N. J. Infy..........Dec., 1864	From 1-Brig. 1-Div. 6-Corps Shen..	No change to Muster Out.........	June,	1865
15th N. J. Infy..........Dec., 1864	From 1-Brig. 1-Div. 6-Corps Shen..	No change to Muster Out.........	July,	1865
3d N. J. Vet'n. Infy......Dec., 1864	New Organization...............	No change to Muster Out.........	July,	1865

2d BRIGADE, 1st DIVISION.—   COMMANDERS.

J. J. Bartlett.........	Brigadier General.................	May 18, 1862, to Nov. .., 1862.
H. L. Cake............	Col. 96th Penna. Infy.............	Nov. .., 1862, to Dec. .., 1862.
J. J. Bartlett.........	Brigadier General.................	Dec. .., 1862, to July 1, 1863.
Emory Upton..........	Col. 121st N. Y. Infy.............	July 1, 1863, to July 2, 1863.
J. J. Bartlett.........	Brigadier General.................	July 2, 1863, to July 4, 1863.
Emory Upton..........	Col. 121st N. Y. Infy.............	July 4, 1863, to Aug. 5, 1863.
J. J. Bartlett.........	Brigadier General.................	Aug. 5, 1863, to Nov. 6, 1863.
Emory Upton..........	Col. 121st N. Y. Infy.............	Nov. 6, 1863, to July 8, 1864.
	See Army Shenandoah to Dec., 1864.	
R. S. Mackenzie.......	Col. 2d Conn. Heavy Arty.........	Dec. 6, 1864, to Jan. 23, 1865.
J. Hubbard...........	Col. 2d Conn. Heavy Arty.........	Jan. 23, 1865, to Feb. 6, 1865.
R. S. Mackenzie.......	Brigadier General.................	Feb. 6, 1865, to Mch. 17, 1865.
J. E. Hamblin.........	Col. 65th N. Y. Infy.............	Mch. 17, 1865, to June 28, 1865.

5th Me. Infy..........May, 1862	From 2-Brig. 1-Div. Dept. Rapp....	No change to Muster Out.........	June,	1864
16th N. Y. Infy..........May, 1862	From 2-Brig. 1-Div. Dept. Rapp....	No change to Muster Out.........	May,	1863
27th N. Y. Infy..........May, 1862	From 2-Brig. 1-Div. Dept. Rapp....	No change to Muster Out.........	May,	1863
96th Penna. Infy..........May, 1862	From 2-Brig. 1-Div. Dept. Rapp....	To 2-Brig. 1-Div. 6-Corps Shen....	July,	1864
121st N. Y. Infy..........Sept., 1862	New Organization...............	To 2-Brig. 1-Div. 6-Corps Shen....	July,	1864
95th Penna. Infy..........May, 1863	From 3-Brig. 1-Div. 6-Corps Pot....	To 2-Brig. 1-Div. 6-Corps Shen....	July,	1864
31st N. Y. Infy..........May, 1863	From Light Div. 6-Corps Pot......	No change to Muster Out.........	June,	1863
2d Conn. Heavy Arty....May, 1864	From Def. of Washington 22-C.....	To 2-Brig. 1-Div. 6-Corps Shen....	July,	1864
65th N. Y. Infy..........July, 1864	From 4-Brig. 1-Div. 6-Corps Pot....	To 2-Brig. 1-Div. 6-Corps Shen....	July,	1864
67th N. Y. Infy..........July, 1864	From 4-Brig. 1-Div. 6-Corps Pot....	To 2-Brig. 1-Div. 6-Corps Shen....	July,	1864
65th N. Y. Infy..........Dec., 1864	From 2-Brig. 1-Div. 6-Corps Shen...	No change to Muster Out.........	July,	1865
121st N. Y. Infy..........Dec., 1864	From 2-Brig. 1-Div. 6-Corps Shen...	No change to Muster Out.........	June,	1865
95th Penna. Infy..........Dec., 1864	From 2-Brig. 1-Div. 6-Corps Shen...	No change to Muster Out.........	June,	1865
2d Conn. Heavy Arty....Dec., 1864	From 2-Brig. 1-Div. 6-Corps Shen...	To 2-Brig. DeRussy's Div. 22-C....	June,	1865

3d BRIGADE, 1st DIVISION.—   COMMANDERS.

John Newton..........	Brigadier General.................	May 18, 1862, to Sept. 21, 1862.
R. Matthewson........	Col. 32d N. Y. Infy.............	Sept. 21, 1862, to Oct. .., 1862.
E. H. Stoughton.......	Col. 4th Vt. Infy...............	Oct. .., 1862, to Nov. .., 1862.
G. W. Town...........	Col. 95th Penna. Infy.............	Nov. .., 1862, to Dec. 10, 1862.
D. A. Russell.........	Brigadier General.................	Dec. 10, 1862, to Feb. 23, 1863.
G. W. Town...........	Col. 95th Penna. Infy.............	Feb. 23, 1863, to Mch. 15, 1863.
D. A. Russell.........	Brigadier General.................	Mch. 15, 1863, to Nov. 20, 1863.
P. E. Ellmaker........	Col. 119th Penna. Infy...........	Nov. 20, 1863, to Dec. 5, 1863.
D. A. Russell.........	Brigadier General.................	Dec. 5, 1863, to Dec. 16, 1863.
G. Clarke.............	Lt.-Col. 119th Penna. Infy........	Dec. 16, 1863, to Jan. .., 1864.
Thos. S. Allen........	Col. 5th Wis. Infy...............	Jan. .., 1864, to Feb. .., 1864.
H. Burnham...........	Col. 6th Me. Infy...............	Feb. .., 1864, to Apr. 5, 1864.
D. A. Russell.........	Brigadier General.................	Apr. 5, 1864, to May 9, 1864.
H. L. Eustis..........	Brigadier General.................	May 9, 1864, to June 12, 1864.
Gideon Clarke........	Lt.-Col. 119th Penna. Infy........	June 12, 1864, to July 8, 1864.
	See Army Shenandoah to Dec., 1864.	
I. C. Bassett..........	Col. 82d Penna. Infy.............	Dec. 6, 1864, to Dec. 21, 1864.
Theo. S. Allen........	Col. 5th Wis. Infy...............	Dec. 21, 1864, to Jan. 9, 1865.
I. C. Bassett..........	Col. 82d Penna. Infy.............	Jan. 9, 1864, to Jan. 31, 1865.
J. E. Hamblin........	Col. 65th N. Y. Infy.............	Jan. 31, 1865, to Mch. 17, 1865.
O. Edwards...........	Col. 37th Mass. Infy.............	Mch. 17, 1865, to June 21, 1865.
J. R. Miller..........	Lt.-Col. 82d Penna. Infy.........	June 21, 1865, to June 28, 1865.

18th N. Y. Infy..........May, 1862	From 3-Brig. 1-Div. Dept. Rapp....	No change to Muster Out.........	May,	1863
31st N. Y. Infy..........May, 1862	From 3-Brig. 1-Div. Dept. Rapp....	To Light Div. 6-Corps Pot........	Jan.,	1863
32d N. Y. Infy..........May, 1862	From 3-Brig. 1-Div. Dept. Rapp....	No change to Muster Out.........	June,	1863
95th Penna. Infy..........May, 1862	From 3-Brig. 1-Div. Dept. Rapp....	To 2-Brig. 1-Div. 6-Corps Pot....	May,	1863
49th Penna. Infy..........Feb., 1863	From 1-Brig. 2-Div. 6-Corps Pot....	To 3-Brig. 1-Div. 6-Corps Shen....	July,	1864
119th Penna. Infy..........Feb., 1863	From 1-Brig. 2-Div. 6-Corps Pot....	To 3-Brig. 1-Div. 6-Corps Shen....	July,	1864
5th Wis. Infy..........May, 1863	From Light Div. 6-Corps Pot......	To 3-Brig. 2-Div. 6-Corps Pot.....	Jan.,	1864
6th Me. Infy..........May, 1863	From Light Div. 6-Corps Pot......	To 3-Brig. 1-Div. 6-Corps Shen....	July,	1864
5th Wis. Infy..........Feb., 1864	From 3-Brig. 2-Div. 6-Corps Pot....	To 3-Brig. 1-Div. 6-Corps Shen....	July,	1864
2d R. I. Infy..........July, 1864	From 4-Brig. 2-Div. 6-Corps Pot....	To 3-Brig. 1-Div. 6-Corps Shen....	July,	1864
37th Mass. Infy..........July, 1864	From 4-Brig. 2-Div. 6-Corps Pot....	To 3-Brig. 1-Div. 6-Corps Shen....	July,	1864
23d Penna. Infy..........July, 1864	From 4-Brig. 1-Div. 6-Corps Pot....	To 3-Brig. 1-Div. 6-Corps Shen....	July,	1864
82d Penna. Infy..........July, 1864	From 4-Brig. 1-Div. 6-Corps Pot....	To 3-Brig. 1-Div. 6-Corps Shen....	July,	1864
37th Mass. Infy..........Dec., 1864	From 3-Brig. 1-Div. 6-Corps Shen...	No change to Muster Out.........	June	1865
2d R. I. Infy..........Dec., 1864	From 3-Brig. 1-Div. 6-Corps Shen...	No change to Muster Out.........	July,	1865
49th Penna. Infy..........Dec., 1864	From 3-Brig. 1-Div. 6-Corps Shen...	No change to Muster Out.........	July,	1865
82d Penna. Infy..........Dec., 1864	From 3-Brig. 1-Div. 6-Corps Shen...	No change to Muster Out.........	July,	1865
119th Penna. Infy..........Dec., 1864	From 3-Brig. 1-Div. 6-Corps Shen...	No change to Muster Out.........	July,	1865
5th Wis. Infy..........Dec., 1864	From 3-Brig. 1-Div. 6-Corps Shen...	No change to Muster Out.........	July,	1865

4th BRIGADE, 1st DIVISION.—Organized April 18, 1864.
COMMANDERS.

Alexander Shaler.......	Brigadier General.................	Apr. 18, 1864, to May 6, 1864.
Nelson Cross..........	Col. 67th N. Y. Infy.............	May 6, 1864, to June 20, 1864.
Jos. E. Hamblin.......	Col. 65th N. Y. Infy.............	June 20, 1864, to July 6, 1864.
	Brigade discontinued July 6, 1864.	

65th N. Y. Infy..........Apr., 1864	From Johnson's Island, Ohio......	To 2-Brig. 1-Div. 6-Corps Pot.....	July,	1864
67th N. Y. Infy..........Apr., 1864	From Johnson's Island, Ohio......	To 2-Brig. 1-Div. 6-Corps Pot.....	July,	1864
122d N. Y. Infy..........Apr., 1864	From Johnson's Island, Ohio......	To 3-Brig. 2-Div. 6-Corps Pot.....	July,	1864
23d Penna. Infy..........Apr., 1864	From Johnson's Island, Ohio......	To 3-Brig. 1-Div. 6-Corps Pot.....	July,	1864
82d Penna. Infy..........Apr., 1864	From Johnson's Island, Ohio......	To 3-Brig. 1-Div. 6-Corps Pot.....	July,	1864

ARTILLERY, 1st DIVISION.—

1st Mass Indpt. Batty....May, 1862	From Arty. 1-Div. Dept. Rapp.....	To Arty. Brig. 6-Corps Pot........	May, 1863
Batty. A, N. J. Arty......May, 1862	From Arty. 1-Div. Dept. Rapp.....	To Arty. Brig. 6-Corps Pot........	May, 1863
Batty. F, 1st N. Y. Arty..May, 1862	From Arty. 1-Div. Dept. Rapp.....	To Yorktown Va. 4-Corps Pot......	June, 1862
Batty. D, 2d U. S. Arty..May, 1862	From Arty. 1-Div. Dept. Rapp.....	To Arty. Brig. 6-Corps Pot........	May, 1863
Batty. A, Md. Arty......Sept., 1862	From 4-Brig. Arty. Res. 5-Corps Pot	To 4-Vol. Brig. Arty. Res. Pot.....	May, 1863

CAVALRY.—

1st N. Y. (Lincoln) Cav..May, 1862	From Cav. 1-Div. Dept. Rapp......	To 1-Brig. Cav. Div. Pot..........	July, 1862

2d DIVISION.—   COMMANDERS.

W. F. Smith..........	Brigadier General...................	May 18, 1862, to Nov. 16, 1862.
A. P. Howe...........	Brigadier General...................	Nov. 16, 1862, to Jan. 4, 1864.
Thos. H. Neill........	Brigadier General...................	Jan. 4, 1864, to Feb. 21, 1864.
H. L. Eustis..........	Brigadier General...................	Feb. 21, 1864, to Mch. 25, 1864.
G. W. Getty..........	Brigadier General...................	Mch. 25, 1864, to May 6, 1864.
Frank Wheaton........	Brigadier General...................	May 6, 1864, to May 7, 1864.
Thos. H. Neill........	Brigadier General...................	May 7, 1864, to June 21, 1864.
Frank Wheaton........	Brigadier General...................	June 21, 1864, to June 28, 1864.
Geo. W. Getty........	Brigadier General...................	June 28, 1864, to July 8, 1864.
See Army Shenandoah to Dec., 1864.		
Geo. W. Getty........	Brigadier General	Dec. 6, 1864, to Jan. 16, 1865.
L. A. Grant..........	Brigadier General...................	Jan. 16, 1865, to Feb. 11, 1865.
Geo. W. Getty........	Bvt. Major General..................	Feb. 11, 1865, to June 28, 1865.

1st BRIGADE, 2d DIVISION.—   COMMANDERS.

W. S. Hancock........	Brigadier General...................	May 18, 1862, to Sept. 17, 1862.
Amasa Cobb...........	Col. 5th Wis. Infy..................	Sept. 17, 1862, to Sept. 25, 1862.
C. E. Pratt..........	Brigadier General...................	Sept. 25, 1862, to Jan. 26, 1863.
R. F. Taylor.........	Col. 33d N. Y. Infy.................	Jan. 26, 1863, to Mch. 24, 1863.
Brigade discontinued March 24, 1863. Reorganized March 24, 1864.		
Frank Wheaton........	Brigadier General...................	Mch. 24, 1864, to May 6, 1864.
J. F. Ballier.........	Col. 98th Penna. Infy...............	May 6, 1864, to May 7, 1864.
Frank Wheaton........	Brigadier General...................	May 7, *1864, to June 21, 1864.
J. F. Ballier.........	Col. 98th Penna. Infy...............	June 21, 1864, to June 28, 1864.
Frank Wheaton........	Brigadier General...................	June 28, 1864, to July 8, 1864.
	See Army Shenandoah to Dec., 1864.	
J. M. Warner.........	Col. 1st Vt. Heavy Arty............	Dec. 6, 1864, to Apr. 22, 1865.
C. W. Eckman........	Col. 92d Penna. Infy...............	Apr. 22, 1865, to May 2, 1865.
J. M. Warner.........	Brigadier General...................	May 2, 1865, to June 28, 1865.

6th Me. Infy............May, 1862	From 1-Brig. 2-Div. 4-Corps Pot....	To Light Div. 6-Corps Pot........	Jan., 1863
5th Wis. Infy..........May, 1862	From 1-Brig. 2-Div. 4-Corps Pot....	To Light Div. 6-Corps Pot........	Jan., 1863
43d N. Y. Infy.........May, 1862	From 1-Brig. 2-Div. 4-Corps Pot....	To Light Div. 6-Corps Pot........	Jan., 1863
49th Penna. Infy........May, 1862	From 1-Brig. 2-Div. 4-Corps Pot....	To 3-Brig. 1-Div. 6-Corps Pot......	Jan., 1863
137th Penna. Infy......Sept., 1862	Def. of Washington.................	To Prov. Guard Army Pot.........	Dec., 1862
119th Penna. Infy........Oct., 1862	Def. of Washington.................	To 3-Brig. 1-Div. 6-Corps Pot.....	Mch., 1863
33d N. Y. Infy..........Jan., 1863	From 3-Brig. 6-Corps Pot....	To 3-Brig. 1-Div. 6-Corps Pot.....	Mch., 1863
62d N. Y. Infy.........Mch., 1864	From Wheaton's Brig. Dept. W. Va..	To 1-Brig. 2-Div. 6-Corps Shen....	July, 1864
93d Penna. Infy........Mch., 1864	From Wheaton's Brig. Dept. W. Va..	To 1-Brig. 2-Div. 6-Corps Shen....	July, 1864
98th Penna. Infy........Mch., 1864	From Wheaton's Brig. Dept. W. Va..	To 1-Brig. 2-Div. 6-Corps Shen....	July, 1864
102d Penna. Infy........Mch., 1864	From Wheaton's Brig. Dept. W. Va..	To 1-Brig. 2-Div. 6-Corps Shen....	July, 1864
139th Penna. Infy.......Mch., 1864	From Wheaton's Brig. Dept. W. Va..	To 1 Brig. 2-Div. 6-Corps Shen....	July, 1864
62d N. Y. Infy.........Dec., 1864	From 1-Brig. 2-Div. 6-Corps Shen..	To Fort Schuyler, N. Y...........	June, 1865
93d Penna. Infy........Dec., 1864	From 1-Brig. 2-Div. 6-Corps Shen..	No change to Muster Out.........	June, 1865
98th Penna. Infy........Dec., 1864	From 1-Brig. 2-Div. 6-Corps Shen..	No change to Muster Out.........	June, 1865
102d Penna. Infy........Dec., 1864	From 1-Brig. 2-Div. 6-Corps Shen..	No change to Muster Out.........	June, 1865
139th Penna. Infy.......Dec., 1864	From 1-Brig. 2-Div. 6-Corps Shen..	No change to Muster Out.........	June, 1865

2d BRIGADE, 2d DIVISION.—   COMMANDERS.

W. T. H. Brooks.......	Brigadier General...................	May 18, 1862, to Oct. 18, 1862.
H. Whiting...........	Col. 2d Vt. Infy....................	Oct. 18, 1862, to Feb. .., 1863.
L. A. Grant..........	Col. 5th Vt. Infy...................	Feb. .., 1863, to Dec. .., 1863.
T. O. Seaver.........	Col. 3d Vt. Infy....................	Dec. .., 1863, to Jan. .., 1864.
L. A. Grant..........	Col. 5th Vt. Infy...................	Jan. .., 1864, to July 8, 1864.
	See Army Shenandoah to Dec., 1864.	
L. A. Grant..........	Brigadier General...................	Dec. 6, 1864, to Dec. 26, 1864.
Chas. Hunsdon........	Lt.-Col. 4th Vt. Infy...............	Dec. 26, 1864, to Jan. 16, 1865.
G. P. Foster.........	Col. 4th Vt. Infy...................	Jan. 16, 1865, to Feb. 11, 1865.
L. A. Grant..........	Brigadier General...................	Feb. 11, 1865, to Feb. 20, 1865.
G. P. Foster.........	Col. 4th Vt. Infy...................	Feb. 20, 1865, to Mch. 7, 1865.
L. A. Grant..........	Brigadier General...................	Mch. 7, 1865, to Apr. 2, 1865.
A. S. Tracy..........	Lt.-Col. 2d Vt. Infy................	Apr. 2, 1865.
L. A. Grant..........	Bvt. Major General.................	Apr. 2, 1865, to June 28, 1865.

2d Vt. Infy............May, 1862	From 2-Brig. 2-Div. 4-Corps Pot....	To 2-Brig. 2-Div. 6-Corps Shen....	July, 1864
3d Vt. Infy............May, 1862	From 2-Brig. 2-Div. 4-Corps Pot....	To 2-Brig. 2-Div. 6-Corps Shen....	July, 1864
4th Vt. Infy...........May, 1862	From 2-Brig. 2-Div. 4-Corps Pot....	To 2-Brig. 2-Div. 6-Corps Shen....	July, 1864
5th Vt. Infy...........May, 1862	From 2-Brig. 2-Div. 4-Corps Pot....	To 2-Brig. 2-Div. 6-Corps Shen....	July, 1864
6th Vt. Infy...........May, 1862	From 2-Brig. 2-Div. 4-Corps Pot....	To 2-Brig. 2-Div. 6-Corps Shen....	July, 1864
26th N. J. Infy.........Sept., 1862	New Organization...................	No change to Muster Out.........	June, 1863
11th Vt. (1st Heav. Arty.) May, 1864	From 1-Brig. Haskin's Div. 22-C..	To 2-Brig. 2-Div. 6-Corps Shen...	July 1864
2d Vt. Infy............Dec., 1864	From 2-Brig. 2-Div. 6-Corps Shen...	No change to Muster Out.........	July, 1865
3d Vt. Infy............Dec., 1864	From 2-Brig. 2-Div. 6-Corps Shen...	No change to Muster Out.........	July, 1865
4th Vt. Infy...........Dec., 1864	From 2-Brig. 2-Div. 6-Córps Shen...	No change to Muster Out.........	July, 1865
5th Vt. Infy...........Dec., 1864	From 2-Brig. 2-Div. 6-Corps Shen...	No change to Muster Out.........	June, 1865
6th Vt. Infy...........Dec., 1864	From 2-Brig. 2-Div. 6-Corps Shen...	No change to Muster Out.........	June, 1865
11th 1st Vt. Heavy Arty..Dec., 1864	From 2-Brig. 2-Div. 6-Corps Shen...	To Middle Department............	June, 1865

3d BRIGADE, 2d DIVISION.—   COMMANDERS.

J. W. Davidson........	Brigadier General...................	May 18, 1862, to July .., 1862.
J. W. Corning........	Lt.-Col. 33d N. Y. Infy.............	July .., 1862, to Aug. .., 1862.
E. Von Vegersack.....	Col. 20th N. Y. Infy................	Aug. .., 1862, to Sept. 25, 1862.
F. L. Hinton.........	Brigadier General...................	Sept. 25, 1862, to Dec. 13, 1862.
Thos. H. Neill........	Brigadier General...................	Dec. 13, 1862, to May 28, 1863.
D. D. Bidwell........	Col. 49th N. Y. Infy................	May 28, 1863, to June 10, 1863.
Thos. H. Neill........	Brigadier General...................	June 10, 1863, to Jan. 4, 1864.
E. C. Mason..........	Col. 7th Me. Infy...................	Jan. 4, 1864, to Feb. .., 1864.
D. D. Bidwell........	Col. 49th N. Y. Infy................	Feb. .., 1864, to Mch. 25, 1864.
Thos. H. Neill........	Brigadier General...................	Mch. 25, 1864, to May 6, 1864.
D. D. Bidwell........	Col. 49th N. Y. Infy................	May 6, 1864, to July 8, 1864.
	See Army Shenandoah to Dec., 1864.	
T. W. Hyde...........	Col. 1st Me. Vet'n. Infy............	Dec. 6, 1864, to June 28, 1865.

3d BRIGADE, 2d DIVISION.—Continued.

7th Me. Infy	May, 1862	From 3-Brig. 2-Div. 4-Corps Pot....	To 3-Brig. 2-Div. 6-Corps Shen....	July, 1864
33d N. Y. Infy	May, 1862	From 3-Brig. 2-Div. 4-Corps Pot....	To 1-Brig. 2-Div. 6-Corps Pot.....	Jan., 1863
49th N. Y. Infy	May, 1862	From 3-Brig. 2-Div. 4-Corps Pot....	To 3-Brig. 2-Div. 6-Corps Shen....	July, 1864
77th N. Y. Infy	May, 1862	From 3-Brig. 2-Div. 4-Corps Pot....	To 3-Brig. 2-Div. 6-Corps Shen....	July, 1864
20th N. Y. Infy	June, 1862	From 2-Brig. 1-Div. Dept. Va......	No change to Muster Out..........	May, 1863
21st N. J. Infy	Sept., 1862	New Organization...................	No change to Muster Out...........	June, 1863
33d N. Y. Infy	Mch., 1863	From 1-Brig. 2-Div. 6-Corps Pot....	No change to Muster Out...........	June, 1863
61st Penna. Infy	May, 1863	From Light Div. 6-Corps Pot.......	To 3-Brig. 2-Div. 6-Corps Shen....	July, 1864
43d N. Y. Infy	May, 1863	From Light Div. 6-Corps Pot......	To 3-Brig. 2-Div. 6-Corps Shen....	July, 1864
22d N. Y. N. G.	July, 1863	From 4-Brig. 1-Div. Dept. Susq.....	No change to Muster Out...........	July, 1863
5th Wis. Infy	Jan., 1864	From 3-Brig. 1-Div. 6-Corps Pot....	To 3-Brig. 1-Div. 6-Corps Pot......	Feb., 1864
122d N. Y. Infy	July, 1864	From 4-Brig. 1-Div. 6-Corps Pot....	To 3-Brig. 2-Div. 6-Corps Shen....	July, 1864
1st Me. Vet'n Infy	Dec., 1864	From 3-Brig. 2-Div. 6-Corps Shen...	No change to muster out..........	June, 1865
43d N. Y. Infy	Dec., 1864	From 3-Brig. 2-Div. 6-Corps Shen...	No change to muster out..........	June, 1865
49th N. Y. Infy	Dec., 1864	From 3-Brig. 2-Div. 6-Corps Shen...	No change to muster out..........	June, 1865
77th N. Y. Infy	Dec., 1864	From 3-Brig. 2-Div. 6-Corps Shen...	No change to muster out..........	June, 1865
122d N. Y. Infy	Dec., 1864	From 3-Brig. 2-Div. 6-Corps Shen...	No change to muster out..........	June, 1865
61st Penna. Infy	Dec., 1864	From 3-Brig. 2-Div. 6-Corps Shen...	No change to muster out..........	June, 1865

4th BRIGADDE, 2d DIVISION.—Organized Jan. 29, 1864, by assignment of 2-Brig. 3-Div. 6-Corps. Permanently organized Mch. 24, 1864. Discontinued July 6, 1864.

COMMANDERS.

O. Edwards	Col. 37th Mass. Infy	Jan. 29, 1864, to Mch. 26, 1864.
H. L. Eustis	Brigadier General	Mch. 26, 1864, to May 9, 1864.
O. Edwards	Col. 37th Mass. Infy	May 9, 1864, to July 6, 1864.

7th Mass. Infy	Jan., 1864	From 2-Brig. 3-Div. 6-Corps Pot....	No change to muster out..........	July, 1864
10th Mass. Infy	Jan., 1864	From 2-Brig. 3-Div. 6-Corps Pot....	No change to muster out..........	July, 1864
37th Mass. Infy	Jan., 1864	From 2-Brig. 3-Div. 6-Corps Pot....	To 3-Brig. 1-Div. 6-Corps Pot......	July, 1864
2d R. I. Infy	Jan., 1864	From 2-Brig. 3-Div. 6-Corps Pot....	To 3-Brig. 1-Div. 6-Corps Pot......	July, 1864

ARTILLERY, 2d DIVISION.—

Batty. E, 1st N. Y. Arty	May, 1862	From Arty. 2-Div. 4-Corps Pot......	To Arty Brig. 1-Corps Pot........	May, 1863
1st N. Y. Indpt. Batty	May, 1862	From Arty. 2-Div. 4-Corps Pot......	To Arty. Brig. 6-Corps Pot.......	May, 1863
2d N. Y. Indpt. Batty	May, 1862	From Arty. 2-Div. 4-Corps Pot......	To Arty. 1-Div. 4-Corps, Pot......	Sept., 1862
Batty. F, 5th U. S. Arty	May, 1862	From Arty. 2-Div. 4-Corps Pot......	To Arty. Brig. 6-Corps Pot.......	May, 1863
Batty. B, Md. Arty	Sept., 1862	From 4-Brig. Arty. Res. 5-Corps Pot.	To Unatt. Arty. Res. Pot..........	May, 1863
3d N. Y. Indpt. Batty	Nov., 1862	From Arty. 3-Div. 6-Corps Pot......	To Light Div. 6-Corps Pot.........	Jan.,

2d DIVISION.—Joined Corps as 1st Division, 4-Corps, Sept. 13, 1862. Permanently attached as 3d Division, Sept. 26, 1862. Discontinued Jan. 10, 1864. Reorganized from 3d Division 3-Corps, Mch. 4, 1864.

COMMANDERS.

D. N. Couch	Major General	Sept. 26, 1862, to Oct. 18, 1862.
John Newton	Brigadier General	Oct. 18, 1862, to Dec., 1862.
Chas. Devens, Jr	Brigadier General	Dec., 1862, to Feb., 1863.
John Newton	Brigadier General	Feb., 1863, to July 1, 1863.
Frank Wheaton	Brigadier General	July 1, 1863, to July 4, 1863.
J. J. Bartlett	Brigadier General	July 4, 1863, to Aug. 4, 1863.
H. D. Terry	Brigadier General	Aug. 4, 1863, to Jan. 10, 1864.
Henry Prince	Brigadier General	Mch. 25, 1864, to Apr. 4, 1864.
J. B. Ricketts	Brigadier General	Apr. 4, 1864, to July 8, 1864.
Truman Seymour	Brigadier General	Dec. 6, 1864, to Apr. 16, 1865.
J. B. Ricketts	Brigadier General	Apr. 16, 1865, to June 28, 1865.

1st BRIGADE, 3d DIVISION.— COMMANDERS.

Chas. Devens, Jr	Brigadier General	Sept. 26, 1862, to Oct., 1862.
John Cochrane	Brigadier General	Oct., 1862, to Mch., 1863.
Alexander Shaler	Col. 65th N. Y. Infy	Mch., 1863, to May, 1863.
S. Titus	Col. 122d N. Y. Infy	May, 1863, to June, 1863.
Alexander Shaler	Brigadier General	June, 1863, to Dec. 30, 1863.
J. E. Hamblin	Col. 65th N. Y. Infy	Dec. 30, 1863, to Jan. 10, 1864.
W. H. Morris	Brigadier General	Mch. 25, 1864, to May 13, 1864.
John W. Schall	Col. 87th Penna. Infy	May 13, 1864, to May 14, 1864.
Wm. S. Truex	Col. 14th N. J. Infy	May 14, 1864, to June 1, 1864.
C. K. Hall	Lt.-Col. 14th N. J. Infy	June 1, 1864, to June 2, 1864.
John W. Schall	Col. 87th Penna. Infy	June 2, 1864, to June 3, 1864.
C. K. Hall	Lt.-Col. 14th N. J. Infy	June 3, 1864.
Wm. S. Truex	Col. 14th N. J. Infy	June 3, 1864, to July 8, 1864.
Wm. S. Truex	Col. 14th N. J. Infy	Dec. 6, 1864, to Apr. 17, 1865.
Truman Seymour	Brigadier General	Apr. 17, 1865, to June 28, 1865.

7th Mass. Infy	Sept., 1862	From 1-Brig. 1-Div. 4-Corps Pot....	To 2-Brig. 3-Div. 6-Corps Pot......	Oct., 1862
10th Mass. Infy	Sept., 1862	From 1-Brig. 1-Div. 4-Corps Pot....	To 2-Brig. 3-Div. 6-Corps Pot......	Oct., 1862
2d R. I. Infy	Sept., 1862	From 1-Brig. 1-Div. 4-Corps Pot....	To 2-Brig. 3-Div. 6-Corps Pot......	Oct., 1862
36th N. Y. Infy	Sept., 1862	From 1-Brig. 1-Div. 4-Corps Pot....	To 2-Brig. 3-Div. 6-Corps Pot......	Oct., 1862
37th Mass. Infy	Sept., 1862	From New Organization.............	To 2-Brig. 3-Div. 6-Corps Pot......	Oct., 1862
65th N. Y. Infy	Oct., 1862	From 3-Brig. 3-Div. 6-Corps Pot....	To Johnson's Island, O............	Jan., 1864
67th N. Y. Infy	Oct., 1862	From 3-Brig. 3-Div. 6-Corps Pot....	To Johnson's Island, O............	Jan., 1864
122d N. Y. Infy	Oct., 1862	From 3-Brig. 3-Div. 6-Corps Pot....	To Johnson's Island, O............	Jan., 1864
23d Penna. Infy	Oct., 1862	From 3-Brig. 3-Div. 6-Corps Pot....	To Johnson's Island, O............	Jan., 1864
61st Penna. Infy	Oct., 1862	From 3-Brig. 3-Div. 6-Corps Pot....	To Light Div. 6-Corps Pot........	Feb., 1863
82d Penna. Infy	Oct., 1862	From 3-Brig. 3-Div. 6-Corps Pot....	To Johnson's Island, O............	Jan., 1864
14th N. J. Infy	Mch., 1864	From 1-Brig. 3-Div. 3-Corps Pot....	To 1-Brig. 3-Div. 6-Corps Shen...	July, 1864
106th N. Y. Infy	Mch., 1864	From 1-Brig. 3-Div. 3-Corps Pot....	To 1-Brig. 3-Div. 6-Corps Shen...	July, 1864
151st N. Y. Infy	Mch., 1864	From 1-Brig. 3-Div. 3-Corps Pot....	To 1-Brig. 3-Div. 6-Corps Shen...	July, 1864
87th Penna. Infy	Mch., 1864	From 1-Brig. 3-Div. 3-Corps Pot....	To 1-Brig. 3-Div. 6-Corps Shen...	July, 1864
10th Vt. Infy	Mch., 1864	From 1-Brig. 3-Div. 3-Corps Pot....	To 1-Brig. 3-Div. 6-Corps Shen...	July, 1864
14th N. J. Infy	Dec., 1864	From 1-Brig. 3-Div. 6-Corps Shen...	No change to muster out..........	June, 1865
106th N. Y. Infy	Dec., 1864	From 1-Brig. 3-Div. 6-Corps Shen...	No change to muster out..........	June, 1865
151st N. Y. Infy	Dec., 1864	From 1-Brig. 3-Div. 6-Corps Shen...	No change to muster out..........	June, 1865
87th Penna. Infy	Dec., 1864	From 1-Brig. 3-Div. 6-Corps Shen...	No change to muster out..........	June, 1865
10th Vt. Infy	Dec., 1864	From 1-Brig. 3-Div. 6-Corps Shen...	No change to muster out..........	June, 1865

2d BRIGADE, 3d DIVISION.— COMMANDERS.

A. P. Howe	Brigadier General	Sept. 26, 1862, to Oct., 1862.
Chas. Devens, Jr	Brigadier General	Oct., 1862, to Dec., 1862.
H. L. Eustis	Col. 10th Mass. Infy	Dec., 1862, to Jan., 1863.
W. H. Browne	Col. 36th N. Y. Infy	Jan., 1863, to Feb., 1863.
Chas. Devens, Jr	Brigadier General	Feb., 1863, to Apr., 1863.

2d BRIGADE, 3d DIVISION.—Continued.   COMMANDERS.

W. H. Browne	Col. 36th N. Y. Infy	Apr., 1863, to May 3, 1863.
H. L. Eustis	Col. 10th Mass. Infy	May 3, 1863, to Jan. 29, 1864.

Brigade transferred to 4-Brig. 2-Div. 6-Corps, Jan., 1864. Reorganized Mch. 25 1864, from 3d Corps Army Potomac.

D. A. Russell	Brigadier General	Mch. 25, 1864, to Apr. 7, 1864.
B. F. Smith	Col. 126th Ohio Infy	Apr. 7, 1864, to May 5, 1864.
Truman Seymour	Brigadier General	May 5, 1864, to May 6, 1864.
B. F. Smith	Col. 126th Ohio Infy	May 6, 1864, to July 6, 1864.

See Army Shenandoah to Dec., 1864.

J. W. Keifer	Col. 110th Ohio Infy	Dec. 6, 1864, to Dec. 29, 1864.
B. F. Smith	Col. 126th Ohio Infy	Dec. 29, 1864, to Feb. 8, 1865.
J. W. Keifer	Col. 110th Ohio Infy	Feb. 8, 1865, to June 28, 1865.

62d N. Y. Infy .... Sept., 1862	From 3-Brig. 1-Div. 4-Corps Pot....	To 3-Brig. 3-Div. 6-Corps Pot......	Oct., 1862
93d Penna. Infy .... Sept., 1862	From 3-Brig. 1-Div. 4-Corps Pot....	To 3-Brig. 3-Div. 6-Corps Pot......	Oct., 1862
98th Penna. Infy ...... Sept., 1862	From 3-Brig. 1-Div. 4-Corps Pot....	To 3-Brig. 3-Div. 6-Corps Pot......	Oct., 1862
102d Penna. Infy ...... Sept., 1862	From 3-Brig. 1-Div. 4-Corps Pot....	To 3-Brig. 3-Div. 6-Corps Pot......	Oct., 1862
139th Penna. Infy ..... Sept., 1862	From 3-Brig. 1-Div. 4-Corps Pot....	To 3-Brig. 3-Div. 6-Corps Pot......	Oct., 1862
7th Mass. Infy .... Oct., 1862	From 1-Brig. 3-Div. 6-Corps Pot....	To 4-Brig. 2-Div. 6-Corps Pot......	Jan., 1864
10th Mass. Infy .... Oct., 1862	From 1-Brig. 3-Div. 6-Corps Pot....	To 4-Brig. 2-Div. 6-Corps Pot......	Jan., 1864
37th Mass. Infy .... Oct., 1862	From 1-Brig. 3-Div. 6-Corps Pot....	To 4-Brig. 2-Div. 6-Corps Pot......	Jan., 1864
2d R. I. Infy .... Oct., 1862	From 1-Brig. 3-Div. 6-Corps Pot....	To 4-Brig. 2-Div. 6-Corps Pot......	Jan., 1864
36th N. Y. Infy .... Oct., 1862	From 1-Brig. 3-Div. 6-Corps Pot....	No change to Muster Out..........	June, 1863
6th Md. Infy .... Mch., 1864	From 2-Brig. 3-Div. 3-Corps Pot....	To 2-Brig. 3-Div. 6-Corps Pot......	July, 1864
110th Ohio Infy .... Mch., 1864	From 2-Brig. 3-Div. 3-Corps Pot....	To 2-Brig. 3-Div. 6-Corps Pot......	July, 1864
122d Ohio Infy .... Mch., 1864	From 2-Brig. 3-Div. 3-Corps Pot....	To 2-Brig. 3-Div. 6-Corps Pot......	July, 1864
126th Ohio Infy .... Mch., 1864	From 2-Brig. 3-Div. 3-Corps Pot....	To 2-Brig. 3-Div. 6-Corps Pot......	July, 1864
67th Penna. Infy ...... Mch., 1864	From 2-Brig. 3-Div. 3-Corps Pot....	To 2-Brig. 3-Div. 6-Corps Pot......	July, 1864
138th Penna. Infy ..... Mch., 1864	From 2-Brig. 3-Div. 3-Corps Pot....	To 2-Brig. 3-Div. 6-Corps Pot......	July, 1864
6th Md. Infy .... Dec., 1864	From 2-Brig. 3-Div. 6-Corps Shen...	No change to Muster Out..........	June, 1865
110th Ohio Infy .... Dec., 1864	From 2-Brig. 3-Div. 6-Corps Shen...	No change to Muster Out..........	June, 1865
122d Ohio Infy .... Dec., 1864	From 2-Brig. 3-Div. 6-Corps Shen...	No change to Muster Out..........	June, 1865
126th Ohio Infy .... Dec., 1864	From 2-Brig. 3-Div. 6-Corps Shen...	No change to Muster Out..........	June, 1865
67th Penna. Infy ...... Dec., 1864	From 2-Brig. 3-Div. 6-Corps Shen...	No change to Muster Out..........	June, 1865
138th Penna. Infy ..... Dec., 1864	From 2-Brig. 3-Div. 6-Corps Shen...	No change to Muster Out..........	June, 1865
9th N. Y. Heavy Arty.. Dec., 1864	From 2-Brig. 3-Div. 6-Corps Shen...	Consol. with 2d N. Y. H. A........	June, 1865

3d BRIGADE, 3d DIVISION.—   COMMANDERS.

John Cochrane	Brigadier General	Sept. 26, 1862, to Oct. .., 1862.

Brigade transferred to 1-Brig. 3-Div. 6-Corps, Oct., 1862. Reorganized by transfer of 2-Brig. 3-Div. 6-Corps, Oct., 1862.

A. P. Howe	Brigadier General	Oct. .., 1862, to Nov. .., 1862.
Thos. A. Rowley	Col. 102d Penna. Infy	Nov. .., 1862, to Dec. 15, 1862.
Frank Wheaton	Brigadier General	Dec. 15, 1862, to Jan. .., 1863.
F. H. Collier	Col. 139th Penna. Infy	Jan. .., 1863, to Feb. .., 1863.
Frank Wheaton	Brigadier General	Feb. .., 1863, to July 1, 1863.
D. J. Nevin	Col. 62d N. Y. Infy	July 1, 1863, to July 4, 1863.
Frank Wheaton	Brigadier General	July 4, 1863, to Jan. .., 1864.
J. F. Ballier	Col. 98th Penna. Infy	Jan. .., 1864, to Jan. 29, 1864.

Brigade discontinued Jan., 1864.

65th N. Y. Infy .... Sept., 1862	From 3-Brig. 1-Div. 4-Corps Pot....	To 1-Brig. 3-Div. 6-Corps Pot......	Oct., 1862
67th N. Y. Infy .... Sept., 1862	From 3-Brig. 1-Div. 4-Corps Pot....	To 1-Brig. 3-Div. 6-Corps Pot......	Oct., 1862
122d N. Y. Infy .... Sept., 1862	From 3-Brig. 1-Div. 4-Corps Pot....	To 1-Brig. 3-Div. 6-Corps Pot......	Oct., 1862
23d Penna. Infy .... Sept., 1862	From 3-Brig. 1-Div. 4-Corps Pot....	To 1-Brig. 3-Div. 6-Corps Pot......	Oct., 1862
61st Penna. Infy ...... Sept., 1862	From 3-Brig. 1-Div. 4-Corps Pot....	To 1-Brig. 3-Div. 6-Corps Pot......	Oct., 1862
82d Penna. Infy .... Sept., 1862	From 3-Brig. 1-Div. 4-Corps Pot....	To 1-Brig. 3-Div. 6-Corps Pot......	Oct., 1862
62d N. Y. Infy .... Oct., 1862	From 2-Brig. 3-Div. 6-Corps Pot....	To Wheaton's Brig. Dept. W. Va....	Jan., 1864
93d Penna. Infy .... Oct., 1862	From 2-Brig. 3-Div. 6-Corps Pot....	To Wheaton's Brig. Dept. W. Va....	Jan., 1864
98th Penna. Infy ...... Oct., 1862	From 2-Brig. 3-Div. 6-Corps Pot....	To Wheaton's Brig. Dept. W. Va....	Jan., 1864
102d Penna. Infy ...... Oct., 1862	From 2-Brig. 3-Div. 6-Corps Pot....	To Wheaton's Brig. Dept. W. Va....	Jan., 1864
139th Penna. Infy ..... Oct., 1862	From 2-Brig. 3-Div. 6-Corps Pot....	To Wheaton's Brig. Dept. W. Va....	Jan., 1864
ARTILLERY, 3d DIVISION.—			
3d N. Y. Indpt. Batty.. Sept., 1862	From Arty. 1-Div. 4-Corps Pot.....	To Arty. 2-Div. 6-Corps Pot.......	Nov., 1862
Batty. C, 1st Penna. Arty. Sept., 1862	From Arty. 1-Div. 4-Corps Pot.....	To Arty. Brig. 6-Corps Pot........	May, 1863
Batty. D, 1st Penna. Arty. Sept., 1862	From Arty. 1-Div. 4-Corps Pot.....	To Arty. Brig. 6-Corps Pot........	May, 1863
Batty. G, 2d U. S. Arty... Sept., 1862	From Arty. 1-Div. 4-Corps Pot.....	To Arty. Brig. 6-Corps Pot........	May, 1863

LIGHT DIVISION.—   COMMANDERS.

C. A. Pratt	Brigadier General	Jan. 26, 1863, to Apr. 28, 1863.	
Geo. C. Spear	Col. 61st Penna. Infy	Apr. 28, 1863, to May 3, 1863.	Killed.
H. Burnham	Col. 6th Me. Infy	May 3, 1863, to May 11, 1863.	

Discontinued May 11, 1863.

6th Me. Infy .... Jan., 1863	From 1-Brig. 2-Div. 6-Corps Pot....	To 3-Brig. 1-Div. 6-Corps Pot......	May, 1863
31st N. Y. Infy .... Jan., 1863	From 3-Brig. 1-Div. 6-Corps Pot....	To 2-Brig. 1-Div. 6-Corps Pot......	May, 1863
43d N. Y. Infy .... Jan., 1863	From 1-Brig. 2-Div. 6-Corps Pot....	To 3-Brig. 2-Div. 6-Corps Pot......	May, 1863
61st Penna. Infy ...... Jan., 1863	From 1-Brig. 3-Div. 6-Corps Pot....	To 3-Brig. 2-Div. 6-Corps Pot......	May, 1863
5th Wis. Infy .... Jan., 1863	From 1-Brig. 2-Div. 6-Corps Pot....	To 3-Brig. 1-Div. 6-Corps Pot......	May, 1863
3d N. Y. Indpt. Batty.. Jan., 1863	From Arty. 2-Div 6-Corps Pot......	To Arty. Brig. 6-Corps Pot........	May, 1863
ARTILLERY BRIGADE.—			
1st Mass. Indpt. Batty.. May, 1863	From Arty. 1-Div. 6-Corps Pot.....	To Arty. 1-Div. 6-Corps Shen......	July, 1864
Batty. A, N. J. Arty..... May, 1863	From Arty. 1-Div. 6-Corps Pot.....	To 4th Vol. Brig. Arty. Res. Pot...	June, 1864
1st N. Y. Indpt. Batty.. May, 1863	From Arty. 2-Div. 6-Corps Pot.....	To Arty. 2-Div. 6-Corps Shen......	July, 1864
3d N. Y. Indpt. Batty.. May, 1863	From Arty. Light Div. 6-Corps Pot..	To Arty. Res. Pot...............	July, 1864
Batty. C, 1st Pa. Arty... May, 1863	From Arty. 3-Div. 6-Corps Pot.....	To Camp Barry Wash. 22-Corps....	June, 1863
Batty. D, 1st Pa. Arty... May, 1863	From Arty. 3-Div. 6-Corps Pot.....	To Unatt. Dept. West Va..........	Aug., 1863
Batty. D. 2d U. S. Arty.. May, 1863	From Arty. 1-Div. 6-Corps Pot.....	To 1-Brig. Horse Arty. Pot.......	July, 1864
Batty. G, 2d U. S. Arty... May, 1863	From Arty. 3-Div. 6-Corps Pot.....	To 2-Brig. Horse Arty. Pot.......	Aug., 1863
Batty. F, 5th U. S. Arty.. May, 1863	From Arty. 3-Div. 6-Corps Pot.....	To Camp Barry Wash. 22-Corps....	Dec., 1863
Batty. C, 1st R. I. Arty.. June, 1863	From 3-Vol. Brig. Arty Res. Pot....	To Arty. Brig. 6-Corps Shen......	July, 1864
Batty. G, 1st R. I. Arty.. June, 1863	From 4-Vol. Brig. Arty. Res. Pot...	To Arty. Brig. 6-Corps Shen......	July, 1864
Batty. M, 5th U. S. Arty.. July, 1863	From Res. Arty. 4-Corps Pot......	To Arty. 3-Div. 6-Corps Shen......	July, 1864
Batty. C, 4th U. S. Arty.. Nov., 1863	From 1-Reg. Brig. Arty. Res. Pot..	To Arty. Res. Potomac..........	Mch., 1864
4th Me. Indpt. Batty..... Mch., 1864	From Arty. Brig. 3-Corps Pot.....	To Arty. Res. Potomac..........	July, 1864
Batty. E, 1st R. I. Arty.. Mch., 1864	From Arty. Brig. 3-Corps Pot.....	To Arty. Res. Potomac..........	July, 1864
4th N. Y. H. A. 3d Battn. Mch., 1864	From Arty. DeRussy's Div. 22-C..	To Arty. Brig. 2-Corps Pot........	May, 1864
Batty. A, N. J. Arty..... May, 1864	From 2-Brig. Arty. Res. Pot.......	To Arty. Res. Potomac..........	July, 1864
Batty. E, 5th U. S. Arty.. May, 1864	From 3-Brig. Arty. Res. Pot.......	To Arty. Res. Potomac..........	July, 1864
5th Me. Indpt. Batty.... May, 1864	From 2-Brig. Arty. Res. Pot.......	To Arty. Brig. 6-Corps Shen......	July, 1864
Batty. H, 1st Ohio Arty.. May, 1864	From 3-Brig. Arty. Res. Pot.......	To Arty. Res. Pot...............	July, 1864

ARTILLERY BRIGADE—Continued

9th N. Y. H. Arty. 2d Bn..May, 1864	From. Def. Wash. 22-Corps.........	To 1-Brig. Haskin's Div. 22-Corps...	June, 1864
4th Me. Indpt. Batty....Dec., 1864	From Arty. Res. Pot...............	To Arty. Res. Pot...............	Mch., 1865
3d Vt. Indpt. Batty......Dec., 1864	From Arty. Res. Pot...............	To Arty. Res. Pot...............	Mch., 1865
1st N. Y. Indpt. Batty..Dec., 1864	From Arty. Brig. 6 Corps Shen.....	No change to Muster Out..........	June, 1865
14th Mass. Indpt. Batty..Dec., 1864	From Arty. Res. Pot...............	To Arty. Res. Pot...............	Mch., 1865
Batty. H, 1st R. I. Arty..Dec., 1864	From Arty. Res. Pot...............	No change to Muster Out..........	June, 1865
3d N. Y. Indpt. Batty....Dec., 1864	From Arty. Res. Pot...............	No change to Muster Out..........	June, 1865
Batty. A, N. J. Arty.....Dec., 1864	From Arty. Res. Pot...............	No change to Muster Out..........	June, 1865
Batty. H, 1st Ohio Arty.Dec., 1864	From Arty. Res. Pot...............	To Arty. Res. Pot...............	Mch., 1865
Batty. E, 1st R. I. Arty..Dec., 1864	From Arty. Res. Pot...............	To Arty. Res. Pot...............	Mch., 1865
Batty. E, 5th U. S. Arty.Dec., 1864	From Arty. Res. Pot...............	To Dept. Washington.............	June, 1865
Batty. G, 1st R. I. Arty...Dec., 1864	From Arty. Brig. 6-Corps Shen.....	No change to Muster Out..........	June, 1865
CAVALRY.—			
1st N. Y. (Lincoln) Cav...May, 1862	From Dept. Rappahannock.........	To 1-Brig. Stoneman's Cav. Pot....	July, 1862

Ninth Army Corps

Created July 22, 1862, and organized by transfer of troops from the Department of North Carolina and from the Department of the South. Corps transferred to the Department of the Ohio March 19, 1863. Rejoined Army of the Potomac April, 1864. Transferred to the Department of Washington June, 1865, and discontinued Aug. 1, 1865.

CORPS COMMANDERS.

A. E. Burnside.........	Major General	July 22, 1862, to Sept. 3, 1862.	
J. L. Reno.............	Major General	Sept. 3, 1862, to Sept. 14, 1862.	Killed.
J. D. Cox.............	Brigadier General...............	Sept. 14, 1862, to Oct. 8, 1862.	
O. D. Willcox.........	Brigadier General...............	Oct. 8, 1862, to Jan. 16, 1863.	
John Sedgwick........	Major General	Jan. 16, 1863, to Feb. 5, 1863.	
W. F. Smith..........	Major General	Feb. 5, 1863, to Mch. 17, 1863.	
A. E. Burnside........	Major General	Mch. 17, 1863, to Mch. 19, 1863.	
J. G. Parke...........	Major General	Mch. 19, 1863, to Apr. 4, 1863.	
	See Dept. Ohio to April, 1864.		
A. E. Burnside........	Major General	Apr. 13, 1864, to Aug. 14, 1864.	
J. G. Parke..........	Major General	Aug. 14, 1864, to Dec. 31, 1864.	
O. B. Willcox........	Brigadier General...............	Dec. 31, 1864, to Jan. 12, 1865.	
J. G. Parke..........	Major General	Jan. 12, 1865, to Jan. 24, 1865.	
O. B. Willcox........	Bvt. Major General...............	Jan. 24, 1865, to Feb. 2, 1865.	
J. G. Parke..........	Major General...............	Feb. 2, 1865, to June 17, 1865.	
O. B. Willcox........	Bvt. Major General...............	June 17, 1865, to July 2, 1865.	
J. G. Parke..........	Major General...............	July 2, 1865, to Aug. 1, 1865.	

1st DIVISION.—	COMMANDERS.		
I. I. Stevens.........	Brigadier General...............	July 22, 1862, to Sept. 1, 1862.	Killed.
B. C. Christ..........	Col. 50th Penna. Infy.............	Sept. 1, 1862, to Sept. 8, 1862.	
O. B. Willcox........	Brigadier General...............	Sept. 8, 1862, to Oct. 8, 1862.	
Wm. M. Fenton.......	Col. 8th Mich. Infy...............	Oct. 8, 1862, to Oct. 26, 1862.	
Daniel Leasure........	Col. 100th Penna. Infy............	Oct. 26, 1862, to Nov. 2, 1862.	
W. W. Burns.........	Brigadier General...............	Nov. 2, 1862, to Feb. 7, 1863.	
O. B. Willcox........	Brigadier General...............	Feb. 7, 1863, to Apr. 4, 1863.	
	See Dept. Ohio to April, 1864.		
E. Ferrero............	Brigadier General...............	Mch. 14, 1864, to Apr. 19, 1864.	
T. G. Stevenson......	Brigadier General...............	Apr. 19, 1864, to May 10, 1864.	Killed.
Daniel Leasure.......	Col. 100th Penna. Infy............	May 10, 1864, to May 12, 1864.	
T. L. Crittenden......	Major General...................	May 12, 1864, to June 9, 1864.	
J. H. Ledlie.........	Brigadier General...............	June 9, 1864, to Aug. 6, 1864.	
Julius White.........	Brigadier General...............	Aug. 6, 1864, to Aug. 28, 1864.	
J. F. Hartranft......	Brigadier General...............	Aug. 28, 1864, to Sept. 1, 1864.	
Division discontinued Sept. 1, 1864. Reorganized from 3d Division 9-Corps Sept. 13, 1864.			
O. B. Willcox........	Brigadier General...............	Sept. 13, 1864, to Dec. 30, 1864.	
N. B. McLaughlin.....	Col. 57th Mass. Infy.............	Dec. 30, 1864, to Feb. 2, 1865.	
O. B. Willcox........	Brigadier General...............	Feb. 2, 1865, to Feb. 25, 1865.	
N. B. McLaughlin.....	Col. 57th Mass. Infy.............	Feb. 25, 1865, to March 7, 1865.	
O. B. Willcox........	Brigadier General...............	March 7, 1865, to June 17, 1865.	
W. F. Bartlett........	Brigadier General...............	June 17, 1865, to July 15, 1865.	
N. B. McLaughlin.....	Col. 57th Mass. Infy.............	July 15, 1865, to Aug. 1, 1865.	

1st BRIGADE, 1st DIVISION.—	COMMANDERS.		
W. M. Fenton.........	Col. 8th Mich. Infy...............	July 25, 1862, to Aug. 3, 1862.	
B. C. Christ..........	Col. 50th Penna. Infy.............	Aug. 3, 1862, to Sept. 1, 1862.	
W. M. Fenton........	Col. 8th Mich. Infy...............	Sept. 1, 1862, to Sept. 8, 1862.	
B. C. Christ..........	Col. 50th Penna. Infy.............	Sept. 8, 1862, to Sept. 24, 1862.	
David Morrison.......	Col. 79th N. Y. Infy.............	Sept. 24, 1862, to Oct. 26, 1862.	
W. H. Withington.....	Col. 17th Mich. Infy.............	Oct. 26, 1862, to Nov. 15, 1862.	
O. M. Poe...........	Col. 2d Mich. Infy...............	Nov. 15, 1862, to Dec. 15, 1862.	
W. M. Fenton........	Col. 8th Mich. Infy...............	Dec. 15, 1862, to Feb. 11, 1863.	
O. M. Poe...........	Col. 2d Mich. Infy...............	Feb. 11, 1863, to April 11, 1863.	
	See Dept. Ohio to April, 1864.		
David Morrison.......	Col. 79th N. Y. Infy.............	March 14, 1864, to April 25, 1864.	
S. Carruth..........	Col. 35th Mass. Infy.............	April 25, 1864, to May 6, 1864.	
J. P. Gould..........	Col. 59th Mass. Infy.............	May 6, 1864, to May 8, 1864.	
S. M. Weld..........	Lt.-Col. 56th Mass. Infy.........	May 8, 1864, to May 12, 1864.	
J. H. Ledlie.........	Brigadier General...............	May 12, 1864, to June 9, 1864.	
J. P. Gould..........	Col. 59th Mass. Infy.............	June 9, 1864, to July 23, 1864.	
W. F. Bartlett.......	Brigadier General...............	July 23, 1864, to July 30, 1864.	
J. H. Barnes........	Lt.-Col. 29th Mass. Infy.........	July 30, 1864, to Sept. 1, 1864.	
Brigade discontinued Sept. 1, 1864. Reorganized Sept. 13, 1864, from 1-Brig. 3-Div. 9-Corps.			
B. C. Christ..........	Col. 50th Penna. Infy............	Sept. 13, 1864, to Sept. 30, 1864.	
S. Harriman..........	Col. 37th Wis. Infy.............	Sept. 30, 1864, to Oct. 24, 1864.	
J. I. Curtin.........	Col. 45th Penna. Infy............	Oct. 24, 1864, to Oct. 25, 1864.	
J. F. Hartranft......	Brigadier General...............	Oct. 25, 1864, to Nov. 28, 1864.	
James Bintliff........	Col. 38th Wis. Infy.............	Nov. 28, 1864, to Dec. 17, 1864.	
S. Harriman..........	Col. 37th Wis. Infy.............	Dec. 17, 1864, to July 17, 1865.	
John Green..........	Lt.-Col. 37th Wis. Infy.........	July 17, 1865, to July 27, 1865.	

1st BRIGADE, 1st DIVISION.—Continued.   COMMANDERS.

50th Penna. Infy........July, 1862	From Dist. Beaufort, S. C., D. S...	To 2-Brig. 1-Div. 9-Corps Pot....	Sept., 1862
8th Mich. Infy........July, 1862	From 1-Brig. 2-Div. Dept. South..	To 2-Brig. 1-Div. 9-Corps Pot....	Sept., 1862
28th Mass. Infy........July, 1862	From 1-Brig. 2-Div. Dept. South..	To 2-Brig. 1-Div. 2-Corps Potomac.	Dec., 1862
79th N. Y. Infy........Sept., 1862	From 2-Brig. 1-Div. 9-Corps Pot..	To 1-Brig. 1-Div. 9-Corps Ohio...	Apr., 1863
17th Mich. Infy........Sept., 1862	From New Organization...........	To 1-Brig. 1-Div. 9-Corps Ohio...	Apr., 1863
20th Mich. Infy........Sept., 1862	From New Organization...........	To 1-Brig. 1-Div. 9-Corps Ohio...	Apr., 1863
2d Mich. Infy........Nov., 1862	From 3-Brig. 1-Div. 3-Corps Pot..	To 1-Brig. 1-Div. 9-Corps Ohio...	Apr., 1863
8th Mich. Infy........Dec., 1862	From 2-Brig. 1-Div. 9-Corps Pot..	To 1-Brig. 1-Div. 9-Corps Ohio...	Apr., 1863
35th Mass. Infy........Apr., 1864	From 2-Brig. 2-Div. 9-Corps Ohio	To Act. Eng. 1-Div. 9-Corps Pot...	May, 1864
56th Mass. Infy........Apr., 1864	From New Organization...........	To 2-Brig. 2-Div. 9-Corps Pot...	Sept., 1864
57th Mass. Infy........Apr., 1864	From New Organization...........	To 3-Brig. 1-Div. 9-Corps Pot...	Sept., 1864
59th Mass. Infy........May, 1864	From New Organization...........	To 3-Brig. 1-Div. 9-Corps Pot...	Sept., 1864
4th United States Infy..May, 1864	From Dept. East.................	To Grant's Hd'qrs. City Point, Va.	June, 1864
10th United States Infy..May, 1864	From Dept. East.................	To 1-Brig. 2-Div. 9-Corps Pot....	June, 1864
29th Mass. Infy........June, 1864	From 3-Brig. 1-Div. 5-Corps Pot..	To 2-Brig. 1-Div. 9-Corps Pot....	June, 1864
3d Md. Infy........June, 1864	From 2-Brig. 1-Div. 9-Corps Pot..	To 2-Brig. 1-Div. 9-Corps Pot....	July, 1864
100th Penna. Infy........June, 1864	From 2-Brig. 1-Div. 9-Corps Pot..	To 3-Brig. 1-Div. 9-Corps Pot....	Sept., 1864
21st Mass. Infy........June, 1864	From 2-Brig. 1-Div. 9-Corps Pot..	To 1-Brig. 1-Div. 9-Corps Pot....	Sept., 1864
179th N. Y. Infy........June, 1864	From 2-Brig. 1-Div. 9-Corps Pot..	To 2-Brig. 2-Div. 9-Corps Pot....	July, 1864
35th Mass. Infy........July, 1864	From Act. Eng. 1-Div. 9-Corps P..	To 1-Brig. 2-Div. 9-Corps Pot....	Sept., 1864
29th Mass. Infy........July, 1864	From 2-Brig. 1-Div. 9-Corps Pot..	To 3-Brig. 1-Div. 9-Corps Pot....	Sept., 1864
8th Mich. Infy........Sept., 1864	From 1-Brig. 3-Div. 9-Corps Pot..	To 2-Brig. 1-Div. 9-Corps Pot....	Apr., 1865
79th N. Y. Infy........Sept., 1864	From 2-Brig. 3-Div. 9-Corps Pot..	To Provost Guard 9-Corps........	Oct., 1864
27th Mich. Infy........Sept., 1864	From 1-Brig. 3-Div. 9-Corps Pot..	No change to Muster Out........	July, 1865
109th N. Y. Infy........Sept., 1864	From 1-Brig. 3-Div. 9-Corps Pot..	No change to Muster Out........	July, 1865
51st Penna. Infy........Sept., 1864	From 1-Brig. 3-Div. 9-Corps Pot..	No change to Muster Out........	July, 1865
37th Wis. Infy........Sept., 1864	From 1-Brig. 3-Div. 9-Corps Pot..	No change to Muster Out........	July, 1865
38th Wis. Infy........Sept., 1864	From 1-Brig. 3-Div. 9-Corps Pot..	No change to Muster Out........	July, 1865
13th Ohio Cav. Dism'td..Sept., 1864	From 1-Brig. 3-Div. 9-Corps Pot..	To 3-Brig. 2-Div. Cav. Corps Pot..	Dec., 1864
17th Mich. Infy........Apr., 1865	From Act. Eng. 1-Div. 9-Corps....	No change to Muster Out........	July, 1865

2d BRIGADE, 1st DIVISION.—   COMMANDERS.

Daniel Leasure........	Col. 100th Penna. Infy............	July 22, 1862, to Aug. 3, 1862.
Thos. Welch...........	Col. 45th Penna. Infy.............	Aug. 3, 1862, to Sept. 24, 1862.
B. C. Christ..........	Col. 50th Penna. Infy.............	Sept. 24, 1862, to Sept. 30, 1862.
W. M. Fenton.........	Col. 8th Mich. Infy..............	Sept. 30, 1862, to Oct. 8, 1862.
B. C. Christ..........	Col. 50th Penna. Infy.............	Oct. 8, 1862, to Oct. 26, 1862.
W. M. Fenton.........	Col. 8th Mich. Infy..............	Oct. 25, 1862, to Dec. 15, 1862.
B. C. Christ..........	Col. 50th Penna. Infy.............	Dec. 15, 1862, to Jan., 1863.
G. W. Mindil.........	Col. 27th N. J. Infy.............	Jan., 1863, to Feb., 1863.
B. C. Christ..........	Col. 50th Penna. Infy.............	Feb., 1863, to March 19, 1863.
	See Dept. Ohio to April, 1864.	
Jos. H. Barnes........	Lt.-Col. 29th Mass. Infy.........	March 19, 1864, to April, 1864.
Daniel Leasure........	Col. 100th Penna. Infy............	April, 1864, to May 10, 1864.
G. P. Robinson........	Lt.-Col. 3d Md. Infy.............	May 10, 1864, to May 12, 1864.
Daniel Leasure........	Col. 100th Penna. Infy............	May 12, 1864, to May 14, 1864.
G. P. Robinson........	Lt.-Col. 3d Md. Infy.............	May 14, 1864, to May 31, 1864.
J. M. Sudsburg........	Col. 3d Md. Infy................	May 31, 1864, to June 4, 1864.
E. W. Pierce..........	Col. 29th Mass. Infy.............	June 4, 1864, to June 17, 1864.
Jos. H. Barnes........	Lt.-Col. 29th Mass. Infy.........	June 17, 1864, to July 21, 1864.
E. G. Marshall........	Col. 14th N. Y. Heavy Arty.......	July 21, 1864, to July 30, 1864.
G. P. Robinson........	Lt.-Col. 3d Md. Infy.............	July 30, 1864, to Sept. 1, 1864.
Wm. Humphreys........	Col. 2d Mich. Infy...............	Sept. 1, 1864, to Sept. 30, 1864.
J. F. Hartranft.......	Brigadier General................	Sept. 30, 1864, to Oct. 9, 1864.
W. C. Newberry........	Lt.-Col. 24th N. Y. Cav..........	Oct. 9, 1864, to Oct. 16, 1864.
B. M. Cutcheon........	Col. 20th Mich. Infy.............	Oct. 16, 1864, to March 10, 1865.
R. Ely................	Col. 8th Mich. Infy.............	March 10, 1865, to June 11, 1865.
W. H. Telford.........	Col. 50th Penna. Infy............	June 11, 1865, to July 1, 1865.
S. R. Schwenck........	Lt.-Col. 50th Penna. Infy........	July 1, 1865, to July 30, 1865.

46th N. Y. Infy........July, 1862	From 2-Brig. 2-Div. Dept. South..	To 1-Brig. 1-Div. 9-Corps Ohio...	Mch., 1863
79th N. Y. Infy........July, 1862	From 2-Brig. 2-Div. Dept. South..	To 1-Brig. 1-Div. 9-Corps Pot....	Sept., 1862
100th Penna. Infy........July, 1862	From 2-Brig. 2-Div. Dept. South..	To 3-Brig. 1-Div. 9-Corps Pot....	Sept., 1862
45th Penna. Infy........Aug., 1862	From 2-Brig. 1-Div. Dept. South..	To 3-Brig. 1-Div. 9-Corps Pot....	Sept., 1862
8th Mich. Infy........Sept., 1862	From 1-Brig. 1-Div. 9-Corps Pot..	To 1-Brig. 1-Div. 9-Corps Pot....	Dec., 1862
50th Penna. Infy........Sept., 1862	From 1-Brig. 1-Div. 9-Corps Pot..	To 2-Brig. 1-Div. 9-Corps Ohio...	Mch., 1863
29th Mass. Infy........Dec., 1862	From 2-Brig. 1-Div. 2-Corps Pot..	To 2-Brig. 1-Div. 9-Corps Ohio...	Mch., 1863
27th N. J. Infy........Dec., 1862	From 2-Brig. Casey's Div. Wash...	To 1-Brig. 1-Div. 9-Corps Ohio...	Mch., 1863
3d Md. Infy........Apr., 1864	From 1-Brig. 1-D. 12-Corps Cum'd	To 1-Brig. 1-Div. 9-Corps Pot....	June, 1864
100th Penna. Infy........Apr., 1864	From 2-Brig. 1-Div. 9-Corps Ohio..	To 1-Brig. 1-Div. 9-Corps Pot....	June, 1864
21st Mass. Infy........Apr., 1864	From 1-Brig. 2-Div. 9-Corps Ohio..	To 1-Brig. 1-Div. 9-Corps Pot....	June, 1864
24th N. Y. Cav. Dismt'd.June, 1864	From Prov'l. Brig. 1-Div. 9-Corps.	To 2-Brig. 3-Div. 9-Corps Pot....	June, 1864
179th N. Y. Infy........June, 1864	From Def. of Washington.........	To 1-Brig. 1-Div. 9-Corps Pot....	June, 1864
29th Mass. Infy........June, 1864	From 1-Brig. 1-Div. 9-Corps Pot..	To 1-Brig. 1-Div. 9-Corps Pot....	July, 1864
2d Penna. Prov'l. H. A...June, 1864	From 3-Brig. 1-Div. 9-Corps Pot..	Consol. with 2d Penna. H. A....	Aug., 1864
14th N. Y. Heavy Arty...June, 1864	From 3-Brig. 1-Div. 9-Corps Pot..	To 3-Brig. 1-Div. 9-Corps Pot....	Sept., 1864
3d Md. Infy........July, 1864	From 1-Brig. 1-Div. 9-Corps Pot..	To 3-Brig. 1-Div. 9-Corps Pot....	Sept., 1864
179th N. Y. Infy........July, 1864	From 1-Brig. 1-Div. 9-Corps Pot..	To 2-Brig. 2-Div. 9-Corps Pot....	Sept., 1864
1st Mich. S. S........Sept., 1864	From 2-Brig. 3-Div. 9-Corps Pot..	No change to Muster Out........	July, 1865
2d Mich. Infy........Sept., 1864	From 2-Brig. 3-Div. 9-Corps Pot..	No change to Muster Out........	July, 1865
20th Mich. Infy........Sept., 1864	From 2-Brig. 3-Div. 9-Corps Pot..	No change to Muster Out........	May, 1865
46th N. Y. Infy........Sept., 1864	From 2-Brig. 3-Div. 9-Corps Pot..	No change to Muster Out........	July, 1865
24th N. Y. Cav. Dismt'd..Sept., 1864	From 2-Brig. 3-Div. 9-Corps Pot..	To 1-Brig. 2-Div. Cav. Corps Pot..	Oct., 1864
50th Penna. Infy........Sept., 1864	From 2-Brig. 3-Div. 9-Corps Pot..	No change to Muster Out........	July, 1865
60th Ohio Infy........Sept., 1864	From 2-Brig. 3-Div. 9-Corps Pot..	No change to Muster Out........	July, 1865
8th Mich. Infy........Apr., 1865	From 1-Brig. 1-Div. 9-Corps Pot..	No change to Muster Out........	July, 1865

3d BRIGADE, 1st DIVISION.—   COMMANDERS.

Thomas Welch........	Col. 45th Penna. Infy............	Sept. 26, 1862, to Oct. 22, 1862.
Daniel Leasure........	Col. 100th Penna. Infy...........	Oct. 22, 1862, to Oct. 26, 1862.
Henry Bowman........	Col. 36th Mass. Infy.............	Oct. 26, 1862, to Nov. 2, 1862.
Daniel Leasure........	Col. 100th Penna. Infy...........	Nov. 2, 1862, to Jan. 27, 1863.
Thomas Welch........	Col. 45th Penna. Infy............	Jan. 27, 1863, to Feb. 7, 1863.
Daniel Leasure........	Col. 100th Penna. Infy...........	Feb. 7, 1863, to March 18, 1863.

See Dept. Ohio to Jan., 1864. Brigade reorganized June 11, 1864, from Prov'l. Brig. 1-Div. 9-Corps.

E. G. Marshall........	Col. 14th N. Y. Heavy Arty......	June 11, 1864, to June 17, 1864.
B. G. Barney.........	Lt.-Col. 2d Penna. Prov'l. H. A..	June 17, 1864, to June 18, 1864.

Brigade discontinued June 18, 1864. Reorganized Sept. 13, 1864,

J. H. Barnes.........	Lt.-Col. 29th Mass. Infy.........	Sept. 13, 1864, to Sept. 15, 1864.
N. B. McLaughlin.....	Col. 57th Mass. Infy............	Sept. 15, 1864, to Dec. 30, 1864.
G. P. Robinson........	Lt.-Col. 3d Md. Infy............	Dec. 30, 1864, to Feb. 2, 1865.

3d BRIGADE, 1st DIVISION.—Continued. COMMANDERS.

N. B. McLaughlin	Col. 57th Mass. Infy	Feb. 2, 1865, to Feb. 25, 1865.
G. P. Robinson	Lt.-Col. 3d Md. Infy	Feb. 25, 1865, to March 7, 1865.
N. B. McLaughlin	Col. 57th Mass. Infy	March 7, 1865, to March 25, 1865.
G. P. Robinson	Lt.-Col. 3d Md. Infy	March 25, 1865, to April 2, 1865.
J. Bintliff	Col. 37th Wis. Infy	April 2, 1865, to April 24, 1865.
E. C. Marshall	Col. 14th N. Y. Heaevy Arty	April 24, 1865, to May 11, 1865.
N. B. McLaughlin	Col. 57th Mass. Infy	May 11, 1865, to Aug. 1, 1865.

36th Mass. Infy........Sept., 1862	From New Organization	To 3-Brig. 1-Div. 9-Corps Ohio	Mch., 1863
45th Penna. Infy........Sept., 1862	From 2-Brig. 1-Div. 9-Corps Pot.	To 3-Brig. 1-Div. 9-Corps Ohio	Mch., 1863
100th Penna. Infy........Sept., 1862	From 2-Brig. 1-Div. 9-Corps Pot.	To 3-Brig. 1-Div. 9-Corps Ohio	Mch., 1863
2d N. Y. Mt'd. Rifles....June, 1864	From Prov'l. Brig. 1-Div. 9-Corps.	To 1-Brig. 2-Div. 9-Corps Pot	June, 1864
14th N. Y. Heavy Arty...June, 1864	From Prov'l. Brig. 1-Div. 9-Corps.	To 2-Brig. 1-Div. 9-Corps Pot	June, 1864
24th N. Y. Cav. Dismt'd..June, 1864	From Prov'l. Brig. 1-Div. 9-Corps.	To 2-Brig. 1-Div. 9-Corps Pot	June, 1864
2d Penna. Prov'l H. A...June, 1864	From Prov'l. Brig. 1-Div. 9-Corps.	To 2-Brig. 1-Div. 9-Corps Pot	June, 1864
3d Md. Infy........Sept., 1864	From 2-Brig. 1-Div. 9-Corps Pot.	No change to Muster Out	July, 1865
29th Mass. Infy........Sept., 1864	From 1-Brig. 1-Div. 9-Corps Pot.	No change to Muster Out	July, 1865
57th Mass. Infy........Sept., 1864	From 1-Brig. 1-Div. 9-Corps Pot.	No change to Muster Out	July, 1865
59th Mass. Infy........Sept., 1864	From 1-Brig. 1-Div. 9-Corps Pot.	No change to Muster Out	July, 1865
100th Penna. Infy........Sept., 1864	From 1-Brig. 1-Div. 9-Corps Pot.	No change to Muster Out	July, 1865
14th N. Y. Heavy Arty..Sept., 1864	From 2-Brig. 1-Div. 9-Corps Pot.	To Hardin's Div. 22-Corps	June, 1865

PROVISIONAL BRIGADE, 1st DIVISION—Organized May, 1864, transferred to 3d Brig. 1-Div. 9-Corps June 11, 1864.

COMMANDER.

E. G. Marshall	Col. 14th N. Y. Heavy Arty	May 12, 1864, to June 11, 1864.

2d N. Y. Mtd. Rifles.....May, 1864	From New Organization	To 2-Brig. 1-Div. 9-Corps Pot	June, 1864
14th N. Y. Heavy Arty...May, 1864	From N. Y. Harbor	To 3-Brig. 1-Div. 9-Corps Pot	June, 1864
24th N. Y. Cav. Dism'd..May, 1864	From New Organization	To 3-Brig. 1-Div. 9-Corps Pot	June, 1864
2d Penna. Prov'l H. A...May, 1864	From 2d Penna. Heavy Arty	To 3-Brig. 1-Div. 9-Corps Pot	June, 1864

ARTILLERY, 1st DIVISION.—

Batty. L. 2d N. Y. Arty..Sept., 1862	From 3-Brig. 2-Div. 1-Corps A. Va.	To Arty. 2-Div. 9-Corps Pot	Oct., 1862
8th Mass. Indpt. Batty..Sept., 1864	From Sturgis Brig. Dist. Wash..	No change to Muster Out	Nov., 1864
Batty. E, 2d U. S. Arty..Sept., 1862	From 5-Brig. Arty. Res. 5-Corps P.	To Arty. 3-Div. 9-Corps Potomac.	Dec., 1862
Batty. D. 1st N. Y. Arty..Sept., 1862	From Res. Arty. 3-Corps Pot	To Arty. 3-Corps Potomac	Feb., 1863
Battys. L and M. 3d U. S.Dec., 1862	From Arty. 2-Div. 5-Corps Pot	To Arty. 1-Div. 9-Corps Ohio	Mch., 1863
2d Maine Indpt. Batty...Apr., 1864	From Camp Barry Wash. 22-Corps.	To Arty. Brig. 9-Corps Potomac.	July, 1864
14th Mass. Indpt. Batty..Apr., 1864	From Camp Barry Wash. 22-Corps.	To Arty. Brig. 9-Corps Potomac.	July, 1864
27th N. Y. Indpt. Batty..June, 1864	From Res. Arty. 9-Corps Pot	To Arty. Brig. 9-Corps Potomac.	July, 1864

ENGINEERS, 1st DIVISION.—

35th Mass. Infy........May, 1864	From 1-Brig. 1-Div. 9-Corps Pot..	To 1-Brig. 1-Div. 9-Corps Potomac.	July, 1864
17th Mich. Infy........Sept., 1864	From. Act. Eng. 3-Div. 9-Corps P..	To 1-Brig. 1-Div. 9-Corps Potomac.	Apr., 1865

2d DIVISION.— COMMANDERS.

J. L. Reno	Major General	July 22, 1862, to Sept. 3, 1862.
S. D. Sturgis	Brigadier General	Sept. 3, 1862, to Feb. 7, 1863.
E. Ferrero	Brigadier General	Feb. 7, 1863, to Mch. 6, 1863.
S. D. Sturgis	Brigadier General	Mch. 6, 1863, to Mch. 19, 1863.
See Dept. Ohio to Mch., 1864.		
Z. R. Bliss	Col. 7th Rhode Island Infy	Mch. 16, 1864, to Apr. 2, 1864.
S. G. Griffin	Col. 6th New Hampshire Infy	Apr. 2, 1864, to May 1, 1864.
R. B. Potter	Brigadier General	May 1, 1864, to Dec. 22, 1864.
S. G. Griffin	Brigadier General	Dec. 22, 1864, to Jan., 1865.
R. B. Potter	Brigadier General	Jan., 1865, to Apr. 2, 1865.
S. G. Griffin	Brigadier General	Apr. 2, 1865, to Apr. 22, 1865.
J. J. Bartlett	Brigadier General	Apr. 22, 1865, to May 3, 1865.
S. G. Griffin	Brigadier General	May 3, 1865, to Aug. 1, 1865.

1st BRIGADE, 2d DIVISION.— COMMANDERS.

James Nagle	Brigadier General	July 22, 1862, to Feb., 1863.
S. G. Griffin	Col. 6th New Hampshire Infy	Feb., 1863, to Mch., 1863.
James Nagle	Brigadier General	Mch., 1863, to Mch. 19, 1863.
See Dept. Ohio to Mch., 1864.		
H. B. Titus	Col. 9th New Hampshire Infy	Mch., 1864, to Apr., 1864.
J. K. Sigfried	Col. 48th Penna. Infy	Apr., 1864, to May 6, 1864.
Z. R. Bliss	Col. 7th R. I. Infy	May 6, 1864.
J. I. Curtin	Col. 45th Penna. Infy	May 6, 1864, to June 18, 1864.
H. Pleasants	Lt.-Col. 45th Penna. Infy	June 18, 1864, to July 25, 1864.
Z. R. Bliss	Col. 7th Rhode Island Infy	July 25, 1864, to Aug. 21, 1864.
J. I. Curtin	Col. 45th Penna. Infy	Aug. 21, 1864, to Jan. 23, 1865.
S. Carruth	Col. 35th Mass. Infy	Jan. 23, 1865, to Feb. 11, 1865.
J. I. Curtin	Col. 45th Penna. Infy	Feb. 11, 1865, to May 4, 1865.
S. Carruth	Col. 35th Mass. Infy	May 4, 1865, to June 9, 1865.
J. F. Brannon	Col. 48th Penna. Infy	June 9, 1865, to July 8, 1865.
J. I. Curtin	Bvt. Brig. General	July 8, 1865, to Aug. 1, 1865.

2d Maryland Infy........July, 1862	From 1-Brig. 2-Div. Dept. N. C.	To 1-Brig. 2-Div. 9-Corps Ohio	Mch., 1863
6th New Hampshire Infy.July, 1862	From 4-Brig. 3-Div. Dept. N. C.	To 1-Brig. 2-Div. 9-Corps Ohio	Mch., 1863
48th Penna. Infy........July, 1862	From 1-Brig. 2-Div. Dept. N. C.	To 1-Brig. 2-Div. 9-Corps Ohio	Mch., 1863
9th New Hampshire Infy.Sept., 1862	From New Organization	To 1-Brig. 2-Div. 9-Corps Ohio	Mch., 1863
7th Rhode Island Infy...Oct., 1862	From New Organization	To 1-Brig. 2-Div. 9-Corps Ohio	Mch., 1863
12th Rhode Island Infy...Oct., 1862	From New Organization	To 1-Brig. 2-Div. 9-Corps Ohio	Mch., 1863
36th Mass. Infy........Apr., 1864	From 1-Brig. 2-Div. 9-Corps Ohio	No change to Muster Out	June, 1865
51st New York Infy......Apr., 1864	From 2-Brig. 2-Div. 9-Corps Ohio.	To Actg. Engrs. 2-Div. 9-Corps Pot.	May, 1864
45th Penna. Infy........Apr., 1864	From 2-Brig. 2-Div. 9-Corps Ohio.	No change to Muster Out	July, 1865
48th Penna. Infy........Apr., 1864	From 2-Brig. 2-Div. 9-Corps Ohio.	No change to Muster Out	July, 1865
7th Rhode Island Infy....Apr., 1864	From 2-Brig. 2-Div. 9-Corps Ohio.	To Actg. Engrs. 2-Div. 9-Corps Pot.	July, 1864
58th Mass. Infy........May, 1864	From New Organization	No change to Muster Out	July, 1865
2d N. Y. Mtd. Rifles......June, 1864	From 3-Brig. 1-Div. 9-Corps Potom.	To 2-Brig. 2-Div. 9-Corps Potomac.	Sept., 1864
4th Rhode Island Infy...July, 1864	From Dist. St. Mary's 22-Corps.	No change to Muster Out	Oct., 1864
51st New York Infy......July, 1864	From Actg. Engrs. 2-Div. 9-Corps..	No change to Muster Out	July, 1865
21st Mass. Infy........Sept., 1864	From 1-Brig. 1-Div. 9-Corps Potom.	Consolidated with 36th Mass	Oct., 1864
35th Mass. Infy........Sept., 1864	From 1-Brig. 1-Div. 9-Corps Potom.	No change to Muster Out	June, 1865
39th New Jersey........Oct., 1864	From Benham's Engr. Brig.	No change to Muster Out	June, 1865
7th Rhode Island Infy....Jan., 1865	From Actg. Engrs. 2-Div. 9-Corps..	No change to Muster Out	June, 1865

2d BRIGADE, 2d DIVISION.—

COMMANDERS.

E. Ferrero	Brigadier General	July 22, 1862, to Feb., 1863.
J. F. Hartranft	Col. 51st Penna. Infy	Feb., 1863, to Mch., 1863.
E. Ferrero	Brigadier General	Mch., 1863, to Mch. 19, 1863.
See Dept. Ohio to Mch., 1864.		
S. Carruth	Col. 35th Mass. Infy	Mch., 1864, to Apr., 1864.
H. B. Titus	Col. 9th New Hampshire Infy	Apr., 1864, to May 1, 1864.
S. G. Griffin	Col. 6th New Hampshire Infy	May 1. 1864, to Dec. 22, 1864.
H. B. Titus	Col. 9th New Hampshire Infy	Dec. 22, 1864, to Feb. 25, 1865.
S. G. Griffin	Brigadier General	Feb. 25, 1865, to Apr. 2, 1865.
W. Harriman	Col. 11th New Hampshire Infy	Apr. 2, 1865, to Apr. 22, 1865.
S. G. Griffin	Brigadier General	Apr. 22, 1865, to May 3, 1865.
H. B. Titus	Col. 9th N. H. Infy	May 3, 1865, to June 11, 1865.
S. M. Weld	Col. 56th Mass. Infy	June 11, 1865, to July 12, 1865.

21st Mass. Infy	July, 1862	From 2-Brig. 2-Div. Dept. N. C.	To 2-Brig. 2-Div. 9-Corps Ohio	Mch., 1863
51st N. Y. Infy	July, 1862	From 2-Brig. 2-Div. Dept. N. C.	To 2-Brig. 2-Div. 9-Corps Ohio	Mch., 1863
51st Penna. Infy	July, 1862	From 2-Brig. 2-Div. Dept. N. C.	To 2-Brig. 2-Div. 9-Corps Ohio	Mch., 1863
35th Mass. Infy	Sept., 1862	From New Organization	To 2-Brig. 2-Div. 9-Corps Ohio	Mch., 1863
11th N. H. Infy	Sept., 1862	From Casey's Brig. Dist. Wash.	To 2-Brig. 2-Div. 9-Corps Ohio	Mch., 1863
31st Me. Infy	Apr., 1864	From New Organization	No change to Muster Out	July, 1865
32d Me. Infy	Apr., 1864	From New Organization	Consol. with 31st Me.	Dec., 1864
6th N. H. Infy	Apr., 1864	From 1-Brig. 2-Div. 9-Corps Ohio	No change to Muster Out	July, 1865
9th N. H. Infy	Apr., 1864	From 1-Brig. 2-Div. 9-Corps Ohio	No change to Muster Out	June, 1865
11th N. H. Infy	Apr., 1864	From 1-Brig. 2-Div. 9-Corps Ohio	No change to Muster Out	June, 1865
17th Vt. Infy	Apr., 1864	From New Organization	No change to Muster Out	July, 1865
2d Md. Infy	June, 1864	From 2-Brig. 3-Div. 9-Corps Pot.	No change to Muster Out	July, 1865
2d N. Y. Mtd. Rifles	Sept., 1864	From 1-Brig. 2-Div. 9-Corps Pot.	To 3-Brig. 2-Div. Cav. Corps Pot.	Nov., 1864
56th Mass. Infy	Sept., 1864	From 1-Brig. 1-Div. 9-Corps Pot.	No change to Muster Out	July, 1865
179th N. Y. Infy	Sept., 1864	From 2-Brig. 1-Div. 9-Corps Pot.	No change to Muster Out	June, 1865
186th N. Y. Infy	Sept., 1864	From New Organization	No change to Muster Out	June, 1865

ARTILLERY, 2d DIVISION.—

Indpt. Batty. D, Penna.	Sept., 1862	From Arty. 1-Div. 3-Corps Army Va.	To Arty. 2-Div. 9-Corps Ohio	Mch., 1863
Batty. E, 4th U. S. Arty.	Sept., 1862	From Unatt. Arty. 3-Corps Army Va.	To Arty. Res. Cav. Corps Pot.	Feb., 1863
Batty. L, 2d N. Y. Arty	Oct., 1862	From Arty. 1-Div. 9-Corps Pot.	To Arty. 3-Div. 9-Corps Pot.	Jan., 1863
Batty. D, 1st R. I. Arty.	Oct., 1862	From Arty. 1-Div. 1-Corps Pot.	To Arty. 2-Div. 9-Corps Ohio	Mch., 1863
11th Mass. Indpt. Batty.	Apr., 1864	From Camp Barry Wash. 22-Corps.	To Arty. Brig. 9-Corps Pot.	July, 1864
19th N. Y. Indpt. Batty.	Apr., 1864	From Camp Barry Wash. 22-Corps.	To Arty. Brig. 9-Corps Pot.	July, 1864

ACTING ENGINEERS.—

51st N. Y. Infy	May, 1864	From 1-Brig. 2-Div. 9-Corps Pot.	To 1-Brig. 2-Div. 9-Corps Pot.	July, 1864
7th R. I. Infy	July, 1864	From 1-Brig. 2-Div. 9-Corps Pot.	To 1-Brig. 2-Div. 9-Corps Pot.	Jan., 1865

3d DIVISION.—

COMMANDERS.

J. G. Parke	Major General	July 22, 1862, to Sept. 3, 1862.	
I. P. Rodman	Brigadier General	Sept. 3, 1862, to Sept. 17, 1862.	Mort. Wnd.
J. G. Parke	Major General	Sept. 17, 1862, to Oct. 4, 1862.	
Geo. W. Getty	Brigadier General	Oct. 4, 1862, to Mch. 2, 1863.	
Transferred to Dept. of Virginia March 2, 1863. Reorganized April, 1864.			
O. B. Willcox	Brigadier General	Apr. 19, 1864, to Sept. 2, 1864.	
J. F. Hartranft	Brigadier General	Sept. 2, 1864, to Sept. 13, 1864.	
E. Ferrero	Brigadier General	Sept. 13, 1864, to Oct. 9, 1864.	
J. F. Hartranft	Brigadier General	Oct. 9, 1864, to Oct. 25, 1864.	
E. Ferrero	Brigadier General	Oct. 25, 1864, to Dec. 15, 1864.	
J. F. Hartranft	Brigadier General	Dec. 15, 1864, to May 3, 1865.	
J. I. Curtin	Col. 45th Penna. Infy	May 3, 1865, to July 8, 1865.	

1st BRIGADE, 3d DIVISION.—

COMMANDERS.

R. C. Hawkins	Col. 9th N. Y. Infy	July 22, 1862, to Aug. 3, 1862.
H. S. Fairchilds	Col. 89th N. Y. Infy	Aug. 3, 1862, to Dec. .., 1862.
R. C. Hawkins	Col. 9th N. Y. Infy	Dec. .., 1862, to Jan. .., 1863.
H. S. Fairchilds	Col. 89th N. Y. Infy	Jan. .., 1863, to Feb. .., 1863.
R. C. Hawkins	Col. 9th N. Y. Infy	Feb. .., 1863, to Mch. 2, 1863.
J. F. Hartranft	Col. 51st Penna. Infy	Apr. 20, 1864, to Aug. 28, 1864.
B. C. Christ	Col. 50th Penna. Infy	Aug. 28, 1864, to Sept. 13, 1864.
O. P. Stearns	Col. 39th U. S. C. T.	Sept. 13, 1864, to Oct. .., 1864.
Delavan Bates	Col. 30th U. S. C. T.	Oct. .., 1864, to Nov. 26, 1864.
J. A. Matthews	Col. 205th Penna. Infy	Nov. 26, 1864, to Dec. 15, 1864.
C. W. Diven	Col. 200th Penna. Infy	Dec. 15, 1864, to Feb. 11, 1865.
A. B. McCalmont	Col. 208th Penna. Infy	Feb. 11, 1865, to Feb. 25, 1865.
W. H. H. McCall	Lt.-Col. 200th Penna. Infy	Feb. 25, 1865, to Mch. 7, 1865.
C. W. Diven	Col. 200th Penna. Infy	Mch. 7, 1865, to Apr. 3, 1865.
A. B. McCalmont	Col. 208th Penna. Infy	Apr. 3, 1865, to June 1, 1865.

9th N. Y. Infy	July, 1862	From 4-Brig. 3-Div. Dept. N. C.	To 1-Brig. Getty's Div. Dept. Va.	Mch., 1863
39th N. Y. Infy	July, 1862	From 4-Brig. 3-Div. Dept. N. C.	To 1-Brig. Getty's Div. Dept. Va.	Mch., 1863
103d N. Y. Infy	July, 1862	From 1-Brig. 2-Div. Dept. N. C.	To 1-Brig. Getty's Div. Dept. Va.	Mch., 1863
10th N. H. Infy	Oct., 1862	From New Organization	To 1-Brig. Getty's Div. Dept. Va.	Mch., 1863
13th N. H. Infy	Dec., 1862	From 1-Brig. Casey's D. Dist. Wash.	To 3-Brig. 3-Div. 9-Corps Pot.	Jan., 1863
25th N. J. Infy	Dec., 1862	From 1-Brig. Casey's D. Dist. Wash.	To 3-Brig. 3-Div. 9-Corps Pot.	Jan., 1863
2d Mich. Infy	Apr., 1864	From 2-Brig. 1-Div. 9-Corps Ohio	To 2-Brig. 3-Div. 9-Corps Pot.	June, 1864
8th Mich. Infy	Apr., 1864	From 1-Brig. 1-Div. 9-Corps Ohio	To 1-Brig. 1-Div. 9-Corps Pot.	Sept., 1864
17th Mich. Infy	Apr., 1864	From 2-Brig. 1-Div. 9-Corps Ohio	Acting Engrs. 3-Div. 9-Corps Pot.	May, 1864
27th Mich. Infy	Apr., 1864	From 2-Brig. 1-Div. 9-Corps Ohio	To 1-Brig. 1-Div. 9-Corps Pot.	Sept., 1864
51st Penna. Infy	Apr., 1864	From 2-Brig. 2-Div. 9-Corps Ohio	To 1-Brig. 1-Div. 9-Corps Pot.	Sept., 1864
109th N. Y. Infy	Apr., 1864	From R. R. Guard Dist. Wash., 22-C.	To 1-Brig. 1-Div. 9-Corps Pot.	Sept., 1864
37th Wis. Infy	June, 1864	From Casey's Prov'l Brig. 22-Corps.	To 1-Brig. 1-Div. 9-Corps Pot.	Sept., 1864
38th Wis. Infy	June, 1864	From Casey's Prov'l Brig. 22-Corps.	To 1-Brig. 1-Div. 9-Corps Pot.	Sept., 1864
13th Ohio Cav. Dismtd.	June, 1864	From Casey's Prov'l Brig. 22-Corps.	To 1-Brig. 1-Div. 9-Corps Pot.	Sept., 1864
27th U. S. C. T.	Sept., 1864	From 1-Brig. 4-Div. 9-Corps Pot.	To 1-Brig. 1-Div. 25-Corps Pot.	Dec., 1864
30th U. S. C. T.	Sept., 1864	From 1-Brig. 4-Div. 9-Corps Pot.	To 1-Brig. 1-Div. 25-Corps Pot.	Dec., 1864
39th U. S. C. T.	Sept., 1864	From 1-Brig. 4-Div. 9-Corps Pot.	To 2-Brig. 1-Div. 25-Corps Pot.	Dec., 1864
43d U. S. C. T.	Sept., 1864	From 1-Brig. 4-Div. 9-Corps Pot.	To 3-Brig. 3-Div. 25-Corps Pot.	Dec., 1864
200th Penna. Infy	Dec., 1864	From Prov'l Brig. 9-Corps Pot.	No change to Muster Out	May, 1865
208th Penna. Infy	Dec., 1864	From Prov'l Brig. 9-Corps Pot.	No change to Muster Out	June, 1865
209th Penna. Infy	Dec., 1864	From Prov'l Brig. 9-Corps Pot.	No change to Muster Out	May, 1865

2d BRIGADE, 3d DIVISION.—

COMMANDERS.

E. Harland	Col. 8th Conn. Infy	July 22, 1862, to Mch. 2, 1863.
B. C. Christ	Col. 50th Penna. Infy	Apr. 20, 1864, to May 12, 1864.
Wm. Humphreys	Col. 2d Mich. Infy	May 12, 1864, to May 30, 1864.

2d BRIGADE, 3d DIVISION.—Continued. COMMANDERS.

B. C. Christ............	Col 50th Penna. Infy..............	May 30, 1864, to June 17, 1864.
Geo. W. Travers........	Lt.-Col. 46th N. Y. Infy..........	June 17, 1864, to June 18, 1864.
W. C. Newberry........	Lt.-Col. 24th N. Y. Cav..........	June 18, 1864, to June 19, 1864.
W. C. Raulston........	Lt.-Col. 24th N. Y. Cav..........	June 19, 1864.
Wm. Humphreys	Col. 2d Mich. Infy..............	June 19, 1864, to Sept. 13, 1864.
C. S. Russell..........	Col. 28th U. S. C. T.............	Sept. 13, 1864, to Oct. .., 1864.
H. G. Thomas........	Col. 19th U. S. C. T.............	Oct. .., 1864, to Nov. 26, 1864.
J. A. Matthews........	Col. 205th Penna. Infy..........	Dec. 15, 1864, to Feb. 1, 1865.
R. C. Cox.............	Col. 207th Penna. Infy..........	Feb. 1, 1865, to Feb. 21, 1865.
J. A. Matthews........	Col. 205th Penna. Infy..........	Feb. 21, 1865, to June 2, 1865.

8th Conn. Infy.........	July, 1862	From 1-Brig. 3-Div. Dept. N. C......	To 2-Brig. Getty's Div. Dept. Va.....	Mch., 1863
11th Conn. Infy........	July, 1862	From 1-Brig. 3-Div. Dept. N. C......	To 2-Brig. Getty's Div. Dept. Va.....	Mch., 1863
4th R. I. Infy.........	July, 1862	From 1-Brig. 3-Div. Dept. N. C......	To 3-Brig. 3-Div. 9-Corps Pot.....	Jan., 1863
16th Conn. Infy........	Sept., 1862	From New Organization............	To 2-Brig. Getty's Div. Dept. Va.....	Mch., 1863
21st Conn. Infy........	Sept., 1862	From New Organization............	To 3-Brig. 3-Div. 9-Corps Pot.....	Jan., 1863
15th Conn. Infy........	Dec., 1862	From 1-Brig. Casey's D. Dist. Wash..	To 2-Brig. Getty's Div. Dept. Va.....	Mch., 1863
1st Mich. S. S.........	Apr., 1864	From Camp Douglass, Ill..........	To 2-Brig. 1-Div. 9-Corps Pot.....	Sept., 1864
20th Mich. Infy........	Apr., 1864	From 1-Brig. 2-Div. 9-Corps Ohio....	To 2-Brig. 1-Div. 9-Corps Pot.....	Sept., 1864
79th N. Y. Infy........	Apr., 1864	From 1-Brig. 1-Div. 9-Corps Ohio....	To 1-Brig. 1-Div. 9-Corps Pot.....	Sept., 1864
60th Ohio Infy.........	Apr., 1864	From New Organization............	To 2-Brig. 1-Div. 9-Corps Pot.....	Sept., 1864
50th Penna. Infy.......	Apr., 1864	From 2-Brig. 1-Div. 9-Corps Ohio....	To 2-Brig. 1-Div. 9-Corps Pot.....	Sept., 1864
2d Md. Infy...........	Apr., 1864	From 2-Brig. 1-Div. 9-Corps Ohio....	To 2-Brig. 1-Div. 9-Corps Pot.....	Sept., 1864
46th N. Y. Infy........	June, 1864	From 2-Brig. 4-Div. 5-Corps Pot....	To 2-Brig. 1-Div. 9-Corps Pot.....	Sept., 1864
24th N. Y. Cav. Dismtd.	June, 1864	From 2-Brig. 1-Div. 9-Corps Pot....	To 2-Brig. 1-Div. 9-Corps Pot.....	Sept., 1864
2d Mich. Infy..........	June, 1864	From 1-Brig. 3-Div. 9-Corps Pot....	To 2-Brig. 1-Div. 9-Corps Pot.....	Sept., 1864
19th U. S. C. T........	Sept., 1864	From 2-Brig. 4-Div. 9-Corps Pot....	To 3-Brig. 3-Div. 25-Corps Pot....	Dec., 1864
23d U. S. C. T.........	Sept., 1864	From 2-Brig. 4-Div. 9-Corps Pot....	To 3-Brig. 3-Div. 25-Corps Pot....	Dec., 1864
28th U. S. C. T........	Sept., 1864	From 2-Brig. 4-Div. 9-Corps Pot....	To 3-Brig. 2-Div. 25-Corps Pot....	Dec., 1864
29th U. S. C. T........	Sept., 1862	From 2-Brig. 4-Div. 9-Corps Pot....	To 3-Brig. 2-Div. 25-Corps Pot....	Dec., 1864
31st U. S. C. T........	Sept., 1864	From 2-Brig. 4-Div. 9-Corps Pot....	To 3-Brig. 2-Div. 25-Corps Pot....	Dec., 1864
205th Penna. Infy......	Dec., 1864	From Prov'l Brig. 9-Corps Pot......	No change to Muster Out.........	June, 1865
207th Penna. Infy......	Dec., 1864	From Prov'l Brig. 9-Corps Pot......	No change to Muster Out.........	June, 1865
211th Penna. Infy......	Dec., 1864	From Prov'l Brig. 9-Corps Pot......	No change to Muster Out.........	June, 1865

3d BRIGADE, 3d DIVISION.— COMMANDERS.

A. F. Stevens..........	Col. 13th N. H. Infy..............	Jan. .., 1863, to Feb. .., 1863.
A. H. Dutton..........	Col. 21st Conn. Infy..............	Feb. .., 1862, to Mch. .., 1862.

13th N. H. Infy........	Jan., 1863	From 1-Brig. 3-Div. 9-Corps Pot....	To 3-Brig. Getty's Div. Dept. Va.....	Mch., 1863
4th R. I. Infy.........	Jan., 1863	From 2-Brig. 3-Div. 9-Corps Pot....	To 3-Brig. Getty's Div. Dept. Va.....	Mch., 1863
21st Conn. Infy........	Jan., 1863	From 2-Brig. 3-Div. 9-Corps Pot....	To 3-Brig. Getty's Div. Dept. Va.....	Mch., 1863
25th N. J. Infy........	Jan., 1863	From 1-Brig. 3-Div. 9-Corps Pot....	To 3-Brig. Getty's Div. Dept. Va.....	Mch., 1863

ARTILLERY, 3d DIVISION.—

Batty. A, 5th U. S. Arty.	Sept., 1862	From 2-Brig. Arty. Res. 5-Corps Pot.	To Arty. Getty's Div. Dept. Va......	Mch., 1863
Batty. E, 2d U. S. Arty.	Sept., 1862	From 5-Brig. Arty. Res. 5-Corps Pot.	To Arty. 1-Div. 9-Corps Ohio........	Mch., 1863
Batty. L, 2d N. Y. Arty.	Dec., 1862	From Arty. 2-Div. 9-Corps Pot......	To Arty. 2-Div. 9-Corps Pot........	Jan., 1863
Batty. A, 1st Pa. Arty.	Feb., 1863	From Arty. 3-Div. 1-Corps Pot......	To Arty. Getty's Div. Dept. Va......	Mch., 1863
7th Me. Indpt. Batty....	Apr., 1864	From Camp Barry, Wash., 22-Corps.	To Arty. Brig. 9-Corps Pot........	July, 1864
34th N. Y. Indpt. Batty.	Apr., 1864	From Arty. 1-Div. 9-Corps Ohio....	To Arty. Brig. 9-Corps Pot........	July, 1864

ACTING ENGINEERS.—

17th Mich. Infy.........	May, 1864	From 1-Brig. 3-Div. 9-Corps Pot....	To Acting Engrs. 1-Div. 9-Corps Pot.	Sept., 1864

4th DIVISION.— COMMANDERS.

E. Ferrero	Brigadier General	Apr. 18, 1864, to July 21, 1864.
Julius White	Brigadier General	July 21, 1864, to July 29, 1864.
E. Ferrero	Brigadier General	July 29, 1864, to Sept. 13, 1864.

1st BRIGADE, 4th DIVISION.— COMMANDER.

J. K. Sigfried..........	Col. 48th Penna. Infy..............	Apr. 18, 1864, to Sept. 13, 1864.

27th U. S. C. T........	Apr., 1864	From New Organization............	To 1-Brig. 3-Div. 9-Corps Pot......	Sept., 1864
30th U. S. C. T........	Apr., 1864	From New Organization............	To 1-Brig. 3-Div. 9-Corps Pot......	Sept., 1864
39th U. S. C. T........	Apr., 1864	From New Organization............	To 1-Brig. 3-Div. 9-Corps Pot......	Sept., 1864
43d U. S. C. T.........	Apr., 1864	From New Organization............	To 1-Brig. 3-Div. 9-Corps Pot......	Sept., 1864

2d BRIGADE, 4th DIVISION.— COMMANDERS.

H. G. Thomas..........	Col. 19th U. S. C. T..............	May 4, 1864, to Sept. 7, 1864.
C. S. Russell..........	Col. 28th U. S. C. T..............	Sept. 7, 1864, to Sept. 13, 1864.

30th Conn. Colored Infy.	Apr., 1864	From New Organization............	Consol. with 29th Conn. Col'd.......	May, 1864
19th U. S. C. T........	Apr., 1864	From New Organization............	To 2-Brig. 3-Div. 9-Corps Pot......	Sept., 1864
23d U. S. C. T.........	Apr., 1864	From New Organization............	To 2-Brig. 3-Div. 9-Corps Pot......	Sept., 1864
31st U. S. C. T........	May, 1864	From New Organization............	To 2-Brig. 3-Div. 9-Corps Pot......	Sept., 1864
28th U. S. C. T........	July, 1864	From Def. Washington 22-Corps....	To 2-Brig. 3-Div. 9-Corps Pot......	Sept., 1864
29th U. S. C. T........	July, 1864	From Def. Washington 22-Corps....	To 2-Brig. 3-Div. 9-Corps Pot......	Sept., 1864

ARTILLERY, 4th DIVISION.—

Indpt. Batty. D, Penna..	Apr., 1864	From Covington, Ky., Dept. Ohio....	To Arty. Brig. 9-Corps Pot........	July, 1864
3d Vt. Indpt. Batty.....	Apr., 1864	From Camp Barry, Wash., 22-Corps.	To Arty. Brig. 9-Corps Pot........	July, 1864

KANAWHA DIVISION.—Attached to Corps Sept. to Oct., 1862.

COMMANDER.

J. D. Cox.............	Brigadier General	

1st BRIGADE.—

12th Ohio Infy.........	Sept., 1862	From 1-Brig. Kanawha Div. W. Va..	To 1-Brig. Kanawha Div. W. Va..	Oct., 1862
23d Ohio Infy.........	Sept., 1862	From 1-Brig. Kanawha Div. W. Va..	To 1-Brig. Kanawha Div. W. Va..	Oct., 1862
30th Ohio Infy.........	Sept., 1862	From 1-Brig. Kanawha Div. W. Va..	To 1-Brig. Kanawha Div. W. Va..	Oct., 1862
1st Ohio Indpt. Batty...	Sept., 1862	From 1-Brig. Kanawha Div. W. Va..	To 1-Brig. Kanawha Div. W. Va..	Oct., 1862
Gilmore's W. Va. Cav. Co.	Sept., 1862	From 1-Brig. Kanawha Div. W. Va..	To 1-Brig. Kanawha Div. W. Va..	Oct., 1862
Harrison's W. Va. Cav. Co.	Sept., 1862	From 1-Brig. Kanawha Div. W. Va..	To 1-Brig. Kanawha Div. W. Va..	Oct., 1862

2d BRIGADE, KANAWHA DIVISION.—

11th Ohio Infy.........	Sept., 1862	From 2-Brig. Kanawha Div. W. Va..	To 2-Brig. Kanawha Div. W. Va..	Oct., 1862
28th Ohio Infy.........	Sept., 1862	From 2-Brig. Kanawha Div. W. Va..	To 2-Brig. Kanawha Div. W. Va..	Oct., 1862
36th Ohio Infy.........	Sept., 1862	From 2-Brig. Kanawha Div. W. Va..	To 2-Brig. Kanawha Div. W. Va..	Oct., 1862
Simmond's Ky. Batty. Ar.	Sept., 1862	From 2-Brig. Kanawha Div. W. Va..	To 2-Brig. Kanawha Div. W. Va..	Oct., 1862
Schambeck's Ill. Cav....	Sept., 1862	From 2-Brig. Kanawha Div. W. Va..	To 2-Brig. Kanawha Div. W. Va..	Oct., 1862
3d Indpt. Co. Ohio Cav..	Sept., 1862	From 2-Brig. Kanawha Div. W. Va..	To 2-Brig. Kanawha Div. W. Va..	Oct., 1862

KANAWHA DIVISION.—Continued.

RESERVE ARTILLERY, 9th CORPS.—

Batty. D, 1st R. I. Arty...Apr., 1864	From Arty. 1-Div. 9-Corps Ohio....	To 1-Brig. Haskin's Div. 22-Corps..	May,	1864
Batty. H, 1st R. I. Arty...Apr., 1864	From Camp Barry, Wash., 22-Corps..	To 2-Brig. DeRussy's Div. 22-Corps.	May,	1864
27th N. Y. Indpt. Batty...Apr., 1864	From Arty. 1-Div. 9-Corps Ohio....	To Arty. 1-Div. 9-Corps Pot.......	May,	1864
Batty. E, 2d U. S. Arty...Apr., 1864	From Arty. 1-Div. 9-Corps Ohio....	To Camp Barry, Wash., 22-Corps....	May,	1864
Batty. G, 2d U. S. Arty...Apr., 1864	From Reorganization	To 3-Brig. Haskin's Div. 22-Corps..	May,	1864
Battys. L & M, 3d U. S...Apr.,1864	From Arty. 1-Div. 9-Corps Ohio....	To Camp Barry, Wash., 22-Corps....	May,	1864

CAVALRY.—

3d N. J. Cav...........Apr., 1864	From New Organization...........	To 1-Brig. 3-Div. Cav. Corps Pot....	May,	1864
13th Penna. Cav.........Apr., 1864	From 2-Brig. 2-Div. Cav. Corps Pot..	To 2-Brig. 2-Div. Cav. Corps Pot....	May,	1864
22d N. Y. Cav..........Apr., 1864	From New Organization...........	To 2-Brig. 3-Div. Cav. Corps Pot....	May,	1864
2d Ohio Cav...........Apr., 1864	From Ohio	To 1-Brig. 3-Div. Cav. Corps Pot....	May,	1864

PROVOST GUARD.—

8th U. S. Infy..........Apr., 1864	From Dept. of the East..........	To 1-Brig. 2-Div. 5-Corps Pot......	Oct.,	1864
79th N. Y. Infy........Oct., 1864	From 1-Brig. 1-Div. 9-Corps Pot....	No change to Muster Out..........	June,	1865

ARTILLERY BRIGADE.—

2d Me. Indpt. Batty....July, 1864	From Arty. 1-Div. 9-Corps Pot.....	To Arty. Res. Pot.................	Aug.,	1864
3d Me. Indpt. Batty....July, 1864	From Camp Barry, Wash., 22-Corps..	To Arty. Res. Pot.................	Aug.,	1864
7th Me. Indpt. Batty....July, 1864	From Arty. 3-Div. 9-Corps Pot.....	No change to Muster Out..........	June,	1865
11th Mass. Indpt. Batty...July, 1864	From Arty. 2-Div. 9-Corps Pot.....	No change to Muster Out..........	June,	1865
14th Mass. Indpt. Batty...July, 1864	From Arty. 1-Div. 9-Corps Pot.....	To Arty. Res. Pot.................	Aug.,	1864
19th N. Y. Batty.......July, 1864	From Arty. 2-Div. 9-Corps Pot.....	No change to Muster Out..........	June,	1865
27th N. Y. Indpt. Batty...July, 1864	From Arty. 1-Div. 9-Corps Pot.....	No change to Muster Out..........	June,	1865
34th N. Y. Indpt. Batty...July, 1864	From Arty. 3-Div. 9-Corps Pot.....	No change to Muster Out..........	June,	1865
Indpt. Batty. D, Penna...July, 1864	From Arty. 4-Div. 9-Corps Pot.....	No change to Muster Out..........	June,	1865
3d Vt. Indpt. Batty.....July, 1864	From Arty. 4-Div. 9-Corps Pot.....	To Res. Arty. 2-Corps Pot........	Aug.,	1864

HARTRANFT'S PROVISIONAL BRIGADE.—Organized Nov. 28, 1864. Discontinued Dec. 15, 1864, and designated 3-Div. 9-Corps.

COMMANDER.

J. F. Hartranft...........	Brigadier General			

200th Penna. Infy.......Nov., 1864	From Engr. Brig. Army James.....	To 1-Brig. 3-Div. 9-Corps Pot......	Dec.,	1864
205th Penna. Infy.......Nov., 1864	From Engr. Brig. Army James.....	To 2-Brig. 3-Div. 9-Corps Pot......	Dec.,	1864
207th Penna. Infy.......Nov., 1864	From Engr. Brig. Army James.....	To 1-Brig. 3-Div. 9-Corps Pot......	Dec.,	1864
208th Penna. Infy.......Nov., 1864	From Engr. Brig. Army James.....	To 1-Brig. 3-Div. 9-Corps Pot......	Dec.,	1864
209th Penna. Infy.......Nov., 1864	From Engr. Brig. Army James.....	To 1-Brig. 3-Div. 9-Corps Pot......	Dec.,	1864
211th Penna. Infy.......Nov., 1864	From Engr. Brig. Army James.....	To 2-Brig. 3-Div. 9-Corps Pot......	Dec.,	1864

INDEPENDENT BRIGADE.—Organized Apr., 1865.

COMMANDER.

C. H. T. Collis..........	Bvt. Brig. General...............			

1st Mass. Cav..........Apr., 1865	From Provost Guard Pot..........	To Headqrs. Army Pot............	Apr.,	1865
61st Mass. Infy........Apr., 1865	From Engr. Brig. Army James.....	To 1-Brig. 2-Div. 5-Corps Pot......	Apr.,	1865
80th N. Y. Infy........Apr., 1865	From Provost Guard Pot..........	To Dept. of Va..................	Apr.,	1865
68th Penna. Infy........Apr., 1865	From Provost Guard Pot..........	To Hart's Island, N. Y..........	Apr.,	1865
114th Penna. Infy........Apr., 1865	From Provost Guard Pot..........	To 1-Brig. 2-Div. 5-Corps Pot......	Apr.,	1865

Eleventh Army Corps

Created Sept. 12, 1862, General Order No. 129, A. G. O., from 1st Corps, Army of Virginia. Transferred to Department of the Cumberland Sept. 25, 1863.

CORPS COMMANDERS.

Franz Sigel...........	Major General....................	Sept. 12, 1862, to Jan. 10, 1863.	
J. H. Stahel..........	Brigadier General................	Jan. 10, 1863, to Jan. 19, 1863.	
Carl Schurz..........	Major General....................	Jan. 19, 1863, to Feb. 5, 1863.	
Franz Sigel...........	Major General....................	Feb. 5, 1863, to Feb. 22, 1863.	
A. Von Steinwehr......	Brigadier General................	Feb. 22, 1863, to Mch. 5, 1863.	
Carl Schurz..........	Major General....................	Mch. 5, 1863, to Apr. 2, 1863.	
O. O. Howard..........	Major General....................	Apr. 2, 1863, to Sept. 25, 1863.	
Carl Schurz..........	Major General....................	Temporarily on July 1, 1863.	

1st DIVISION.—	COMMANDERS.		
J. H. Stahel..........	Brigadier General................	Sept. 12, 1862, to Jan. 10, 1863.	
N. C. McLean.........	Brigadier General................	Jan. 10, 1863, to Feb. 5, 1863.	
J. H. Stahel..........	Brigadier General................	Feb. 5, 1863, to Mch. 10, 1863.	
N. C. McLean.........	Brigadier Reorganization.........	Mch. 10, 1863, to Apr. 20, 1863.	
C. Devens, Jr........	Brigadier General................	Apr. 20, 1863, to May 2, 1863.	
N. C. McLean.........	Brigadier General................	May 2, 1863, to May 24, 1863.	
F. C. Barlow.........	Brigadier General................	May 24, 1863, to July 1, 1863.	
A. Ames.............	Brigadier General................	July 1, 1863, to July 14, 1863.	
A. Schimmelfenning....	Brigadier General................	July 14, 1863, to July 17, 1863.	
Geo. H. Gordon.......	Brigadier General................	July 17, 1863, to Aug. 5, 1863.	

Division discontinued Aug., 1863, and transferred to the Dept. of the South.

1st BRIGADE, 1st DIVISION.—	COMMANDERS.		
L. Von Gilsa...........	Col. 41st New York Infy..........	Sept. 12, 1862, to Jan. 12, 1863.	
G. Van Arnsburg......	Col. 45th New York Infy..........	Jan. 12, 1863, to Feb. 2, 1863.	
L. Von Gilsa...........	Col. 41st New York Infy..........	Feb. 2, 1863, to May 25, 1863.	
G. Bourry............	Col. 68th New York Infy..........	May 25, 1863, to June 5, 1863.	
L. Von Gilsa...........	Col. 41st New York Infy..........	June 5, 1863, to July 17, 1863.	
A. Schimmelfenning...	Brigadier General................	July 17, 1863, to Aug. 6, 1863.	

8th New York Infy.....Sept., 1862	From 1-B. 1-Div. 1-Corps Army Va.	No change to Muster Out..........	Apr.,	1863
41st New York Infy.....Sept., 1862	From 1-B. 1-Div. 1-Corps Army Va.	To 1-Brig. Gordon's Div. 10-Corps.	Aug.,	1863
45th New York Infy.....Sept., 1862	From 1-B. 1-Div. 1-Corps Army Va.	To 1-Brig. 3-Div. 11-Corps Potomac	May,	1863
27th Penna. Infy........Sept., 1862	From 1-B. 1-Div. 1-Corps Army Va.	To 1-Brig. 2-Div. 11-Corps Potomac.	Oct.,	1862
54th New York Infy......Oct., 1862	From 2-Brig. 3-Div. 11-Corps Pot..	To 1-Brig. Gordon's Div. 10-Corps..	Aug.,	1863
153d Penna. Infy........Nov., 1862	From New Organization...........	No change to Muster Out..........	July,	1863

1st BRIGADE, 1st DIVISION.—Continued.

68th New York Infy.....June, 1863	From 1-Brig. 3-Div. 11-Corps Pot..	To 2-Brig. 3-Div. 11-Corps Potomac	July,	1863
127th New York Infy....July, 1863	From 1-B. 2-Div. 4-Corps Dept. Va.	To 1-Brig. Gordon's Div. 10-Corps..	Aug.,	1863
142d New York Infy......July, 1863	From 1-B. 2-Div. 4-Corps Dept. Va.	To 1-Brig. Gordon's Div. 10-Corps..	Aug.,	1863
74th Penna. Infy......July, 1863	From 1-Brig. 3-Div. 11-Corps Pot..	To 1-Brig. Gordon's Div. 10-Corps..	Aug.,	1863
107th Ohio Infy.........July, 1863	From 2-Brig. 1-Div. 11-Corps Pot..	To 1-Brig. Gordon's Div. 10-Corps..	Aug.,	1863

2d BRIGADE, 1st DIVISION.—   COMMANDERS.

N. C. McLean..........	Col. 75th Ohio Infy...............	Sept. 12, 1862, to Jan. 10, 1863.
J. C. Lee.............	Col. 55th Ohio Infy...............	Jan. 10, 1863, to Feb. 5, 1863.
N. C. McLean..........	Brigadier General.................	Feb. 5, 1863, to Mch. 10, 1863.
J. C. Lee.............	Col. 55th Ohio Infy...............	Mch. 10, 1863, to Apr. 20, 1863.
N. C. McLean..........	Brigadier General.................	Apr. 20, 1863, to May 2, 1863.
J. C. Lee.............	Col. 55th Ohio Infy...............	May 2, 1863, to May 24, 1863.
A. Ames..............	Brigadier General.................	May 24, 1863, to July 1, 1863.
A. L. Harris..........	Col. 75th Ohio Infy...............	July 1, 1863, to July 4, 1863.
W. H. Noble..........	Col. 17th Conn. Infy..............	July 4, 1863, to July 14, 1863.
P. P. Brown..........	Col. 157th New York Infy.........	July 14, 1863, to July 17, 1863.
A. Ames..............	Brigadier General.................	July 17, 1863, to Aug. 6, 1863.

25th Ohio Infy.........Sept., 1862	From 2-B. 1-Div. 1-Corps Army Va.	To 2-Brig. Gordon's Div. 10-Corps.	Aug.,	1863
55th Ohio Infy.........Sept., 1862	From 2-B. 1-Div. 1-Corps Army Va.	To 2-Brig. 2-Div. 11-Corps Potomac.	May,	1863
73d Ohio Infy.........Sept., 1862	From 2-B. 1-Div. 1-Corps Army Va.	To 2-Brig. 2-Div. 11-Corps Potomac.	Oct.,	1862
75th Ohio Infy.........Sept., 1862	From 2-B. 1-Div. 1-Corps Army Va.	To 2-Brig. Gordon's Div. 10-Corps.	Aug.,	1863
82d Ohio Infy.............Oct., 1862	From Headqrs. 11th Corps Potomac	To Headqrs. 11-Corps Potomac......	Oct.,	1862
17th Conn. Infy.........Oct., 1862	From New Organization...........	To 2-Brig. Gordon's Div. 10-Corps.	Aug.,	1863
107th Ohio Infy.........Dec., 1862	From 2-Div. 3-Div. 11-Corps Potom.	To 1-Brig. 1-Div. 11-Corps Potomac.	July,	1863
40th Mass. Infy.......July, 1863	From 2-B. 2-Div. 4-Corps Dept. Va.	To 2-Brig. Gordon's Div. 10-Corps.	Aug.,	1863
144th New York Infy.....July, 1863	From 1-B. 2-Div. 4-Corps Dept. Va.	To 2-Brig. Gordon's Div. 10-Corps.	Aug.,	1863
157th New York Infy.....July, 1863	From 1-Brig. 3-Div. 11-Corps Potom.	To 2-Brig. Gordon's Div. 10-Corps.	Aug.,	1863

ARTILLERY, 1st DIVISION.—

2d N. Y. Indpt. Batty...Sept., 1862	From Arty. 1-Div. 1-Corps A. Va.	To Reserve Arty. 11-Corps Potomac	Mch.,	1863
Batty. K, 1st Ohio Arty...Sept., 1862	From Arty. 1-Div. 1-Corps A. Va.	To Reserve Arty. 11-Corps Potomac	Mch.,	1863
13th N. Y. Indpt. Batty. Sept., 1862	From Arty. 2-Div. 1-Corps. A. Va.	To Arty Brigade 11-Corps Potomac.	May,	1863

CAVALRY BRIGADE ATTACHED.—

1st Conn. Cav......Sept., 1862	From Cav. Brig. 1-Corps Army Va.	To Defences Baltimore 8-Corps.....	Dec.,	1862
4th New York Cav.....Sept., 1862	From Cav. Brig. 1-Corps Army Va.	To 1-Brig. 2-Div. Cav. Corps Pot..	Feb.,	1863
9th New York Cav.....Sept., 1862	From Cav. Brig. 1-Corps Army Va.	To 1-Brig. 1-Div. Cav. Corps Pot..	Feb.,	1863
6th Ohio Cav.........Sept., 1862	From Cav. Brig. 1-Corps Army Va.	To 1-Brig. 2-Div. Cav. Corps Pot..	Feb.,	1863
1st Maryland Cav......Sept., 1862	From Cav. Brig. 1-Corps Army Va.	To 2-Brig. 3-Div. Cav. Corps Pot..	Feb.,	1863
17th Penna. Cav.........Dec., 1862	From New Organization...........	To 2-Brig. 2-Div. Cav. Corps Pot..	Feb.,	1863

2d DIVISION.—   COMMANDERS.

A. Von Steinwehr......	Brigadier General.................	Sept. 12, 1862, to Feb. 22, 1863.
A. Buschbeck..........	Col. 27th Penna. Infy.............	Feb. 22, 1863, to Mch. 5, 1863.
A. Von Steinwehr......	Brigadier General.................	Mch. 5, 1863, to Mch. 28, 1863.
A. Buschbeck..........	Col. 27th Penna. Infy.............	Mch. 28, 1863, to Apr. 12, 1863.
A. Von Steinwehr......	Brigadier General.................	Apr. 12, 1863, to Sept. 25, 1863.

1st BRIGADE, 2d DIVISION.—   COMMANDERS.

G. A. Muhleck........	Col. 73d Penna. Infy.............	Sept. 12, 1862, to Oct. 27, 1862.
A. Buschbeck..........	Col. 27th Penna. Infy.............	Oct. 27, 1862, to Nov. 27, 1862.
G. A. Muhleck........	Col. 73d Penna. Infy.............	Nov. 27, 1862, to Dec., 1862.
A. Buschbeck..........	Col. 27th Penna. Infy.............	Dec., 1862, to Feb. 22, 1863.
C. Soest.............	Col. 29th New York Infy.........	Feb. 22, 1863, to Mch. 5, 1863.
A. Buschbeck..........	Col. 27th Penna. Infy.............	Mch. 5, 1863, to Mch. 28, 1863.
C. Soest.............	Col. 29th New York Infy.........	Mch. 28, 1863, to Apr. 12, 1863.
A. Buschbeck..........	Col. 27th Penna. Infy.............	Apr. 12, 1863, to June 10, 1863.
C. R. Coster..........	Col. 134th New York Infy.........	June 10, 1863, to July, 1863.
A. Buschbeck..........	Col. 27th Penna. Infy.............	July, 1863, to Sept. 25, 1863.

73d Penna. Infy.........Sept., 1862	From 1-Brig. 2-Div. 1-Corps A. Va.	To 1-Brig. 2-Div. 11-Corps Cumb'd	Sept.,	1863
29th New York Infy......Sept., 1862	From 1-Brig. 2-Div. 1-Corps A. Va.	No change to Muster Out...........	June,	1863
68th New York Infy.....Sept., 1862	From 1-Brig. 2-Div. 1-Corps A. Va.	To 1-Brig. 3-Div. 11-Corps Potom.	Oct.,	1862
154th New York Infy.....Oct., 1862	From New Organization...........	To 1-Brig. 2-Div. 11-Corps Cumb'd	Sept.,	1863
27th Penna. Infy.........Oct., 1862	From 1-Brig. 1-Div. 11-Corps Potom.	To 1-Brig. 2-Div. 11-Corps Cumb'd	Sept.,	1863
134th New York Infy....May, 1863	From 2-Brig. 2-Div. 11-Corps Potom.	To 1-Brig. 2-Div. 11-Corps Cumb'd	Sept.,	1863
173d Penna. Infy.......July, 1863	From 7-Corps Dept. Va...........	No change to Muster Out...........	Aug.,	1863
33d New Jersey Infy.....Sept., 1863	From New Organization...........	To 1-Brig. 2-Div. 11-Corps Cumb'd	Sept.,	1863

2d BRIGADE, 2d DIVISION.—Organized Oct. 25, 1862.

COMMANDERS.

Orland Smith..........	Col. 73d Ohio Infy................	Oct. 25, 1862, to Apr. 17, 1863.
F. C. Barlow..........	Brigadier General.................	Apr. 17, 1863, to May 24, 1863.
Orland Smith..........	Col. 73d Ohio Infy................	May 24, 1863, to Sept. 25, 1863.

33d Mass. Infy........Oct., 1862	From New Organization...........	To 2-Brig. 2-Div. 11-Corps Cumb'd	Sept.,	1863
134th New York Infy.....Oct., 1862	From New Organization...........	To 1-Brig. 2-Div. 11-Corps Potom.	May,	1863
61st Ohio Infy.........Oct., 1862	From 1-Brig. 3-Div. 11-Corps Potom.	To 1-Brig. 3-Div. 11-Corps Potom.	Nov.,	1862
73d Ohio Infy.........Oct., 1862	From 2-Brig. 1-Div. 11-Corps Potom.	To 2-Brig. 2-Div. 11-Corps Cumb'd	Sept.,	1863
136th New York Infy....Nov., 1862	From 1-Brig. 3-Div. 11-Corps Potom.	To 2-Brig. 2-Div. 11-Corps Cumb'd	Sept.,	1863
55th Ohio Infy.........May, 1863	From 2-Brig. 1-Div. 11-Corps Potom.	To 2-Brig. 2-Div. 11-Corps Cumb'd	Sept.,	1863
168th New York Infy.....July, 1863	From 3-B. 1-Div. 4-Corps Dept. Va.	To 2-Brig. 2-Div. 11-Corps Cumb'd	Sept.,	1863

ARTILLERY, 2d DIVISION.—

Batty. I, 1st N. Y. Arty..Sept., 1862	From 2-Div. 1-Corps Army Va.....	To Arty. Brigade 11-Corps Potom.	May,	1863
12th Ohio Indpt. Batty...Sept., 1862	From Milroy's Indpt. B. 1-Corps Va.	To Defences Washington...........	Dec.,	1862

3d DIVISION.—   COMMANDERS.

Carl Schurz..........	Brigadier General.................	Sept. 12, 1862, to Jan. 19, 1863.
A. Schimmelfenning....	Brigadier General.................	Jan. 19, 1863, to Feb. 5, 1863.
Carl Schurz..........	Brigadier General.................	Feb. 5, 1863, to Mch. 5, 1863.
A. Schimmelfenning....	Brigadier General.................	Mch. 5, 1863, to Apr. 2, 1863.
Carl Schurz..........	Major General....................	Apr. 2, 1863, to Sept. 25, 1863.
A. Schimmelfenning....	Brigadier General.................	Temporarily July 1, 1863.

1st BRIGADE, 3d DIVISION.—   COMMANDERS.

A. Schimmelfenning....	Brigadier General.................	Sept. 12, 1862, to Jan. 19, 1863.
G. Bourry............	Col. 68th New York Infy..........	Jan. 19, 1863, to Feb. 5, 1863.
A. Schimmelfenning....	Brigadier General.................	Feb. 5, 1863, to Mch. 5, 1863.
G. Von Arnsburg......	Col. 45th New York Infy..........	Mch. 5, 1863, to Apr. 2, 1863.

1st BRIGADE, 3d DIVISION.—Continued.   COMMANDERS.

A. Schimmelfenning....	Brigadier General..................	Apr. 2, 1863, to July 1, 1863.		
G. Von Arnsburg......	Col. 45th New York Infy..........	July 1, 1863, temporarily.		
A. Schimmelfenning....	Brigadier General..................	July 1, 1863, to July 13, 1863.		
Hector Tyndale........	Brigadier General..................	July 13, 1863, to Sept. 19, 1963.		
F. Hecker.............	Col. 82d Illinois Infy..............	Sept. 19, 1863, to Sept. 25, 1863.		
61st Ohio Infy...........Sept., 1862	From 1-Brig. 3-Div. 1-Corps A. Va.	To 2-Brig. 2-Div. 11-Corps Potomac	Oct.,	1862
74th Penna. Infy......Sept., 1862	From 1-Brig. 3-Div. 1-Corps A. Va.	To 1-Brig. 1-Div. 11-Corps Potomac	July,	1863
8th West Va. Infy.......Sept., 1862	From 1-Brig. 3-Div. 1-Corps A. Va.	To Dist. Kanawha, West Va........	Sept.,	1862
68th New York Infy.....Oct., 1862	From 1-Brig. 3-Div. 11-Corps Pot..	To 1-Brig. 1-Div. 11-Corps Potomac	June,	1863
136th New York Infy.....Oct., 1862	From New Organization..........	To 2-Brig. 2-Div. 11-Corps Potomac	Nov.,	1862
157th New York Infy.....Oct., 1862	From New Organization..........	To 2-Brig. 2-Div. 11-Corps Potomac	July,	1863
82d Illinois Infy........Oct., 1862	From New Organization..........	To 1-Brig. 3-Div. 11-Corps Cumb'd.	Sept.	1863
61st Ohio Infy...........Nov., 1862	From 2-Brig. 2-Div. 11-Corps Pot..	To 1-Brig. 3-Div. 11-Corps Cumb'd.	Sept.	1863
45th New York Infy.....May, 1863	From 1-Brig. 1-Div. 11-Corps Pot..	To 1-Brig. 3-Div. 11-Corps Cumb'd.	Sept.	1863
82d Ohio Infy.........July, 1863	From 2-Brig. 2-Div. 11-Corps Pot..	To 1-Brig. 3-Div. 11-Corps Cumb'd.	Sept.	1863
143d New York Infy......July, 1863	From 2-B. 3-Div. 4-Corps Dept. Va.	To 1-Brig. 3-Div. 11-Corps Cumb'd.	Sept.	1863
169th Penna. Infy......July, 1863	From 1-B. 1-Div. 4-Corps Dept. Va.	No change to Muster Out..........	July,	1863
172d Penna. Infy......July, 1863	From 3-B. 1-Div. 4-Corps Dept. Va.	No change to Muster Out..........	July,	1863

2d BRIGADE, 3d DIVISION.—   COMMANDER.

W. Krzyzonowski......	Col. 58th New York Infy..........	Sept. 12, 1862, to Sept. 25, 1863.		
54th New York Infy.....Sept., 1862	From 2-Brig. 3-Div. 1-Corps A. Va.	To 1-Brig. 1-Div. 11-Corps Potomac	Oct.,	1862
58th New York Infy.....Sept., 1862	From 2-Brig. 3-Div. 1-Corps A. Va.	To 2-Brig. 3-Div. 11-Corps Cumb'd.	Sept.,	1863
68th N. Y. Infy.........Sept., 1862	From 2-Brig. 3-Div. 1-Corps A. Va.	To 1-Brig. 1-Div. 11-Corps Pot...	Oct.,	1862
75th Penna. Infy.........Sept., 1862	From 2-Brig. 3-Div. 1-Corps A. Va.	To 2-Brig. 3-Div. 11-Corps Cumb'd.	Sept.,	1863
107th Ohio Infy.........Oct., 1862	From Def. Cincinnati, Ohio........	To 2-Brig. 1-Div. 11-Corps Pot...	Dec.,	1862
119th N. Y. Infy........Oct., 1862	From New Organization..........	To 2-Brig. 3-Div. 11-Corps Cumb'd.	Sept.,	1863
26th Wis. Infy..........Oct., 1862	From New Organization..........	To 2-Brig. 3-Div. 11-Corps Cumb'd.	Sept.,	1863
82d Ohio Infy.........May, 1863	From Hdq'rts. 11-Corps Potomac..	To 1-Brig. 3-Div. 11-Corps Pot...	July,	1863
68th N. Y. Infy.........July, 1863	From 1-Brig. 1-Div. 11-Corps Pot..	To 2-Brig. 3-Div. 11-Corps Cumb'd.	Sept.,	1863
141st N. Y. Infy........July, 1863	From 2-Brig. 2-Div. 4-Corps Va...	To 2-Brig. 3-Div. 11-Corps Cumb'd.	Sept.,	1863
ARTILLERY, 3d DIVISION.—				
Batty. I, 1st Ohio Arty..Sept., 1862	From Arty. 3-D. 1-Corps Army Va.	To Arty. Brig. 11-Corps Potomac.	May,	1863
Batty. I, 1st N. Y........Sept., 1862	From Arty 2-. 1-Corps Army Va..	To Arty. 2-Div. 11-Corps Potomac.	Oct.,	1862
Batty. C, W. Va. Arty....Sept., 1862	From Arty 2-. 1-Corps Army Va..	To Res. Arty. 11-Corps Potomac...	Mch.,	1863
RESERVE ARTILERY.—				
2d N. Y. Indpt. Batty...Mch., 1863	From Arty. 1-Div. 11-Corps Pot...	To Arty. Brig. 11-Corps Potomac..	May,	1863
Batty. K, 1st Ohio Arty..Mch., 1863	From Arty. 1-Div. 11-Corps Pot...	To Arty. Brig. 11-Corps Potomac..	May,	1863
Batty. C, W. Va. Arty...Mch., 1863	From Arty. 1-Div. 11-Corps Pot...	To 3-Vol. Brig. Arty. Res. Potomac.	May,	1863
ARTILERY BRIGADE.—				
Batty. I, 1st N. Y. Arty...May, 1863	From Arty. 3-Div. 11-Corps Pot...	To Arty. Brig. 11-Corps Cumb'd..	Sept.,	1863
2d N. Y. Indpt. Batty....May, 1863	From Arty. 1-Div. 11-Corps Pot...	No change to Muster Out.........	June,	1863
13th N. Y. Indpt. Batty..May, 1863	From Arty. 1-Div. 11-Corps Pot...	To Arty. Brig. 11-Corps Cumb'd..	Sept.,	1863
Batty. K, 1st Ohio Arty..May, 1863	From Arty. 1-Div. 11-Corps Pot...	To Arty. Brig. 11-Corps Cumb'd..	Sept.,	1863
Batty. I, 1st Ohio Arty..May, 1863	From Arty. 1-Div. 11-Corps Pot...	To Arty. Brig. 11-Corps Cumb'd..	Sept.,	1863
Batty. G, 4th U. S. Arty.July, 1863	From 1-Reg. Brig. Arty. Res. Pot..	To Arty. Brig. 11-Corps Cumb'd..	Sept.,	1863
12th Ohio Indpt. Batty...Sept., 1863	From Def. Washington 22-Corps..	To Arty. Brig. 11-Corps Cumb'd..	Sept.,	1863

Twelfth Army Corps

Created Sept. 12, 1862, by General Order No. 129, A. G. O., from the 2d Corps, Army of Virginia. Transferred to the Department of the Cumberland Sept. 25, 1863.

COMMANDERS.

J. F. K. Mansfieled.....	Major General.....................	Sept. 12, 1862, to Sept. 17, 1862.	Killed.
A. S. Williams........	Brigadier General.................	Sept. 17, 1862, to Oct. 20, 1862.	
H. W. Slocum........	Major General.....................	Oct. 20, 1862, to July 1, 1863.	
A. S. Williams........	Brigadier General.................	July 1, 1863, to July 4, 1863.	
H. W. Slocum........	Major General.....................	July 4, 1863, to Aug. 31, 1863.	
A. S. Williams........	Brigadier General.................	Aug. 31, 1863, to Sept. 13, 1863.	
H. W. Slocum..........	Major General.....................	Sept. 13, 1863, to Sept. 25, 1863.	

1st DIVISION.—   COMMANDERS.

A. S. Williams........	Brigadier General........	Sept. 12, 1862, to Sept. 17, 1862.
S. W. Crawford........	Brigadier General........	Sept. 17, 1862.
Geo. H. Gordon.......	Brigadier General........	Sept. 17, 1862, to Oct. 20, 1862.
A. S. Williams........	Brigadier General........	Oct. 20, 1862, to July 1, 1863.
Thos. H. Ruger........	Brigadier General........	July 1, 1863, to July 4, 1863.
A. S. Williams........	Brigadier General........	July 4, 1863, to Aug. 31, 1863.
J. F. Knipe...........	Brigadier General........	Aug. 31, 1863, ta Sept. 13, 1863.
A. S. Williams........	Brigadier General........	Sept. 13, 1863, to Sept. 25, 1863.

1st BRIGADE, 1st DIVISION.—   COMMANDERS.

S. W. Crawford.......	Brigadier General........	Sept. 12, 1862, to Sept. 17, 1862.		
J. F. Knipe...........	Col. 46th Penna. Infy.......	Sept. 17, 1862, to May 18, 1863.		
A. L. McDougall......	Col. 123d N. Y. Infy........	May 18, 1863, to July 26, 1863.		
J. F. Knipe...........	Brigadier General........	July 26, 1863, to Aug. 31, 1863.		
S. Ross...............	Col. 20th Conn. Infy........	Aug. 31, 1863, to Sept. 13, 1863.		
J. F. Knipe...........	Brigadier General........	Sept. 13, 1863, to Sept. 25, 1863.		
5th Conn. Infy.........Sept., 1862	From 1-Brig. 1-Div. 2-Corps A. Va.	To 1-Brig. 1-Div. 12-Corps Cumb'd.	Sept.	1863
10th Maine Infy........Sept., 1862	From 1-Brig. 1-Div. 2-Corps A. Va.	To Provost Guard 12-Corps Pot....	June,	1863
28th N. Y. Infy.........Sept., 1862	From 1-Brig. 1-Div. 2-Corps A. Va.	No change to Muster Out.........	May,	1863
46th Penna. Infy.......Sept., 1862	From 1-Brig. 1-Div. 2-Corps A. Va.	To 1-Brig. 1-Div. 12-Corps Cumb'd.	Sept.	1863
124th Penna. Infy.......Sept., 1862	From Def. of Washington........	To 2-Brig. 1-Div. 12-Corps Pot....	Oct.,	1862
125th Penna. Infy.......Sept., 1862	From Def. of Washington........	To 2-Brig. 1-Div. 12-Corps Pot....	Oct.,	1862
128th Penna. Infy.......Sept., 1862	From Def. of Washington........	No change to Muster Out.........	May,	1863
20th Conn. Infy........May, 1863	From 2-Brig. 1-Div. 12-Corps Pot..	To 1-Brig. 1-Div. 12-Corps Cumb'd.	Sept.,	1863
3d Md. Infy...........May, 1863	From 2-Brig. 1-Div. 12-Corps Pot..	To 1-Brig. 1-Div. 12-Corps Cumb'd.	Sept.,	1863
123d N. Y. Infy........May, 1863	From 2-Brig. 1-Div. 12-Corps Pot..	To 1-Brig. 1-Div. 12-Corps Cumb'd.	Sept.,	1863
145th N. Y. Infy........May, 1863	From 2-Brig. 1-Div. 12-Corps Pot..	To 1-Brig. 1-Div. 12-Corps Cumb'd.	Sept.,	1863

2d BRIGADE, 1st DIVISION.—Organized Oct. 3, 1862.

COMMANDERS.

Geo. L. Andrews.......	Col. 2d Mass. Infy................	Oct. 3, 1862, to Oct. 6, 1862.
T. L. Kane............	Brigadier General	Oct. 6, 1862, to Mch. 21, 1863.
N. J. Jackson.........	Brigadier General	Mch. 21, 1863, to Mch. 29, 1863.
S. Ross	Col. 20th Conn. Infy.............	Mch. 29, 1863, to May 28, 1863.
Brigade discontinued May 28, 1863, and merged into 1-Brig. 1-Div. 12-Corps. Reorganized July 1, 1863.		
B. H. Lockwood.......	Brigadier General	July 1, 1863, to July 15, 1863.
Discontinued July 15, 1863.		

20th Conn. Infy..........Oct., 1862	From New Organization...........	To 1-Brig. 1-Div. 12-Corps Pot.....	May, 1863
123d N. Y. Infy..........Oct., 1862	From New Organization...........	To 1-Brig. 1-Div. 12-Corps Pot.....	May, 1863
127th N. Y. Infy..........Oct., 1862	From New Organization...........	To 4-Brig. 1-Div. 12-Corps Pot.....	Oct., 1862
137th N. Y. Infy..........Oct., 1862	From New Organization...........	To 4-Brig. 1-Div. 12-Corps Pot.....	Oct., 1862
138th N. Y. Infy..........Oct., 1862	From New Organization...........	To 4-Brig. 1-Div. 12-Corps Pot......	Oct., 1862
140th N. Y. Infy..........Oct., 1862	From New Organization...........	To 2-Brig. 2-Div. 12-Corps Pot......	Oct., 1862
145th N. Y. Infy..........Oct., 1862	From New Organization...........	To 2-Brig. 1-Div. 12-Corps Pot.....	Oct., 1862
149th N. Y. Infy..........Oct., 1862	From New Organization...........	To 4-Brig. 1-Div. 12-Corps Pot.....	Oct., 1862
124th Penna. Infy..........Oct., 1862	From 1-Brig. 1-Div. 12-Corps Pot...	To 2-Brig. 1-Div. 12-Corps Pot.....	Jan., 1863
125th Penna. Infy..........Oct., 1862	From 1-Brig. 1-Div. 12-Corps Pot...	To 2-Brig. 1-Div. 12-Corps Pot.....	Jan., 1863
3d Md. Infy..........Jan., 1863	From 2-Brig. 2-Div. 12-Corps Pot...	To 1-Brig. 1-Div. 12-Corps Pot.....	May, 1863
145th N. Y. Infy..........May, 1863	From 2-Brig. 2-Div. 12-Corps Pot...	To 1-Brig. 1-Div. 12-Corps Pot.....	May, 1863
1st Md. Eastern Shore....July, 1863	From Lockwood's Brig. 8-Corps.....	To 2-Brig. Md. Hts. Div. W. Va....	July, 1863
2d Md. Eastern Shore....July, 1863	From Lockwood's Brig. 8-Corps.....	To 2-Brig. Md. Hts. Div. W. Va....	July, 1863
1st Md. Pot. Home Brig...July, 1863	From Lockwood's Brig. 8-Corps.....	To 2-Brig. Md. Hts. Div. W. Va....	July, 1863
150th N. Y. Infy..........July, 1863	From 3-Separate Brig. 8-Corps.....	To 3-Brig. 1-Div. 12-Corps Pot.....	July, 1863

3d BRIGADE, 1st DIVISION.—

COMMANDERS.

Geo. H. Gordon........	Brigadier General..................	Sept. 12, 1862, to Sept. 17, 1862.
T. H. Ruger..........	Col. 3d Wis. Infy................	Sept. 17, 1862, to Oct. 20, 1862.
Geo. H. Gordon........	Brigadier General..................	Oct. 20, 1862, to Oct. 26, 1862.
Brigade discontinued Oct. 26, 1862. Reorganized Dec. 9, 1862.		
J. K. Murphy..........	Col. 29th Penna. Infy.............	Dec. 9, 1862, to Feb. .., 1863.
T. H. Ruger..........	Col. 3d Wis. Infy................	Feb. .., 1863, to July 1, 1863.
Silas Cosgrove..........	Col. 27th Ind. Infy..............	July 1, 1863, to July 4, 1863.
T. H. Ruger..........	Brigadier General................	July 4, 1863, to Aug. 16, 1863.
E. A. Carmen..........	Col. 13th N. J. Infy..............	Aug. 16, 1863, to Sept. 16, 1863.
T. H. Ruger..........	Brigadier General................	Sept. 16, 1863, to Sept. 25, 1863.

2d Mass. Infy..........Sept., 1862	From 3-Brig. 1-Div. 2-Corps Army Va	To 3-Brig. 1-Div. 12-Corps, Cumb'd..	Sept., 1863
3d Wis. Infy..........Sept., 1862	From 3-Brig. 1-Div. 2-Corps Army Va	To 3-Brig. 1-Div. 12-Corps, Cumb'd..	Sept., 1863
107th N. Y. Infy..........Sept., 1862	From Whipple's Command Wash....	To 3-Brig. 1-Div. 12-Corps, Cumb'd..	Sept., 1863
Pa. Zouaves de Afrique...Sept., 1862	From 3-Brig. 1-Div. 2-Corps Army Va	Transferred to 114th Penna........	Sept., 1862
27th Ind. Infy..........Sept., 1862	From 3-Brig. 1-Div. 2-Corps Army Va	To 2-Brig. 2-Div. 12-Corps Cumb'd..	Sept., 1863
29th Penna. Infy..........Sept., 1862	From 3-Brig. 2-Div. 2-Corps Army Va	To 2-Brig. 2-Div. 12-Corps Pot......	Mch., 1863
13th N. J. Infy..........Sept., 1862	From 3-Brig. 2-Div. 2-Corps Army Va	To 3-Brig. 1-Div. 12-Corps Cumb'd..	Sept., 1863
150th N. Y. Infy..........July, 1863	From 2-Brig. 1-Div. 12-Corps Pot...	To 3-Brig. 1-Div. 12-Corps Cumb'd..	Sept., 1863

4th BRIGADE, 1st DIVISION.—Organized Oct. 6, 1862. Discontinued Oct. 26, 1862.

COMMANDER.

Geo. L. Andrews........	Col. 2d Mass. Infy................	Oct. 6, 1862, to Oct. 26, 1862.

127th N. Y. Infy..........Oct., 1862	From 2-Brig. 1-Div. 12-Corps Pot...	To 3-Brig. Abercromb's Div. Def. W.	Oct., 1862
137th N. Y. Infy..........Oct., 1862	From 2-Brig. 1-Div. 12-Corps Pot...	To 3-Brig. 2-Div. 12-Corps Pot......	Oct., 1862
138th N. Y. Infy..........Oct., 1862	From 2-Brig. 1-Div. 12-Corps Pot...	To 2-Brig. Haskin's Div. Def. Wash.	Oct., 1862
149th N. Y. Infy..........Oct., 1862	From 2-Brig. 1-Div. 12-Corps Pot...	To 3-Brig. 2-Div. 12-Corps Pot......	Oct., 1862
ARTILLERY, 1st DIVISION.—			
Batty. K, 1st N. Y. Arty..Sept., 1862	From Arty. 1-Div. 2-Corps Army Va.	To 4-Vol. Brig. Arty. Res. Pot.....	May, 1863
Batty. M, 1st N. Y. Arty..Sept., 1862	From Arty. 1-Div. 2-Corps Army Va.	To Arty. Brig. 12-Corps Pot........	May, 1863
10th N. Y. Indpt. Batty..Sept., 1862	From Arty. 1-Div. 2-Corps Army Va.	To Arty. Brig. 12-Corps Pot........	May, 1863
Batty. F, 4th U. S. Arty..Sept., 1862	From Arty. 1-Div. 2-Corps Army Va.	To Arty. 3-Div. 3-Corps Pot........	Sept., 1862

2d DIVISION.—

COMMANDERS.

Geo. S. Greene.........	Brigadier General.................	Sept. 12, 1862, to Oct. 15, 1862.
John W. Geary.........	Brigadier General.................	Oct. 15, 1862, to Sept. 25, 1863.

1st BRIGADE, 2d DIVISION.—

COMMANDERS.

Chas. Candy...........	Col. 66th Ohio Infy...............	Sept. 12, 1862, to Sept. 17, 1862.
Hector Tyndale........	Lt.-Col. 28 Penna. Infy...........	Sept. 17, 1862.
O. J. Crane...........	Major 7th Ohio Infy..............	Sept. 17, 1862, to Sept. 18, 1862.
Chas. Candy...........	Col. 66th Ohio Infy...............	Sept. 18, 1862, to Oct. 26, 1862.
T. H. Ruger..........	Col. 3d Wis. Infy................	Oct. 26, 1862, to Dec. 30, 1862.
Chas. Candy...........	Col. 66th Ohio Infy...............	Dec. 30, 1862, to Feb. .., 1863.
W. R. Creighton........	Col. 7th Ohio Infy................	Feb. .., 1863, to Mch. .., 1863.
Chas. Candy...........	Col. 66th Ohio Infy...............	Mch. .., 1863, to Aug. 6, 1863.
A. Pardee.............	Lt.-Col. 147th Penna. Infy........	Aug. 6, 1863, to Sept. 6, 1863.
Chas. Candy...........	Col. 66th Ohio Infy...............	Sept. 6, 1863, to Sept. 25, 1863.

5th Ohio Infy..........Sept., 1862	From 1-Brig. 2-Div. 2-Corps Army Va	To 1-Brig. 2-Div. 12-Corps Cumb'd..	Sept., 1863
7th Ohio Infy..........Sept., 1862	From 1-Brig. 2-Div. 2-Corps Army Va	To 1-Brig. 2-Div. 12-Corps Cumb'd..	Sept., 1863
29th Ohio Infy..........Sept., 1862	From 1-Brig. 2-Div. 2-Corps Army Va	To 1-Brig. 2-Div. 12-Corps Cumb'd..	Sept., 1863
66th Ohio Infy..........Sept., 1862	From 1-Brig. 2-Div. 2-Corps Army Va	To 1-Brig. 2-Div. 12-Corps Cumb'd..	Sept., 1863
28th Penna. Infy..........Sept., 1862	From 1-Brig. 2-Div. 2-Corps Army Va	To 1-Brig. 2-Div. 12-Corps Cumb'd..	Sept., 1863
147th Penna. Infy..........Oct., 1862	From New Organization............	To 1-Brig. 2-Div. 12-Corps Cumb'd..	Sept., 1863

2d BRIGADE, 2d DIVISION.—

COMMANDERS.

T. B. Van Buren......	Col. 102d N. Y. Infy..............	Sept. 12, 1862, to Sept. 15, 1862.
H. J. Steinrock........	Col. 109th Penna. Infy...........	Sept. 15, 1862, to Sept. 17, 1862.
J. C. Lane............	Lt.-Col. 102d N. Y. Infy..........	Sept. 17, 1862, to Oct. 28, 1862.
N. J. Jackson.........	Brigadier General................	Oct. 28, 1862, to Dec. 22, 1862.
J. M. Sudsburg........	Col. 3d Md. Infy................	Dec. 13, 1862, Temporarily.
H. J. Steinrock........	Col. 109th Penna. Infy...........	Dec. 22, 1862, to Jan. 3, 1863.
N. J. Jackson.........	Brigadier General................	Jan. 3, 1863, to Mch. 21, 1863.
Thos. L. Kane........	Brigadier General................	Mch. 21, 1863, to May 7, 1863.
Geo. A. Cobham, Jr.....	Col. 111th Penna. Infy...........	May 7, 1863, to July 2, 1863.
Thos. L. Kane........	Brigadier General................	July 2, 1863.
Geo. A. Cobham, Jr....	Col. 111th Penna. Infy...........	July 2, 1863, to Sept. 25, 1863.

3d Md. Infy..........Sept., 1862	From 2-Brig. 2-Div. 2-Corps Army Va	To 2-Brig. 1-Div. 12-Corps Pot......	Jan., 1863
102d N. Y. Infy..........Sept., 1862	From 2-Brig. 2-Div. 2-Corps Army Va	To 3-Brig. 2-Div. 12-Corps Pot......	Oct., 1862
109th Penna. Infy........Sept., 1862	From 2-Brig. 2-Div. 2-Corps Army Va	To 3-Brig. 2-Div. 12-Corps Pot......	Oct., 1862

2d BRIGADE, 2d DIVISION.—Continued.

111th Penna. Infy	Sept., 1862	From 2-Brig. 2-Div. 2-Corps Army Va.	To 3-Brig. 2-Div. 12-Corps Pot	Oct.,	1862
60th N. Y. Infy	Oct., 1862	From 3-Brig. 2-Div. 12-Corps Pot	To 3-Brig. 2-Div. 12-Corps Pot	May,	1863
3d Del. Infy	Oct., 1862	From 3-Brig. 2-Div. 12-Corps Pot	To Frederick, Md. 8-Corps	Dec.,	1862
Purnell Md. Legion	Oct., 1862	From 3-Brig. 2-Div. 12-Corps Pot	To Middle Dept. 8-Corps	Dec.,	1862
140th N. Y. Infy	Oct., 1862	From 2-Brig. 1-Div. 12-Corps Pot	To 3-Brig. 2-Div. 5-Corps Pot	Nov.,	1862
145th N. Y. Infy	Oct., 1862	From 2-Brig. 1-Div. 12-Corps Pot	To 2-Brig. 1-Div. 12-Corps Pot	May,	1863
109th Penna. Infy	Jan., 1863	From 3-Brig. 2-Div.. 12-Corps Pot	To 2-Brig. 2-Div. 12-Corps Cumb'd.	Sept.,	1863
111th Penna. Infy	Jan., 1863	From 3-Brig. 2-Div.. 12-Corps Pot	To 2-Brig. 2-Div. 12-Corps Cumb'a.	Sept.,	1863
124th Penna. Infy	Jan., 1863	From 2-Brig. 1-Div. 12-Corps Pot	No change to Muster Out	May,	1863
125th Penna. Infy	Jan., 1863	From 2-Brig. 1-Div. 12-Corps Pot	No change to Muster Out	May,	1863
29th Penna. Infy	Mch., 1863	From 3-Brig. 1-Div. 12-Corps Pot	To 2-Brig. 2-Div. 12-Corps Cumb'd.	Sept.,	1863
177th Penna. Infy	July, 1863	From Norfolk, Dept. Va	No change to Muster Out	Aug.,	1863

3d BRIGADE, 2d DIVISION.—   **COMMANDERS.**

Commander	Rank/Unit	Dates
W. B. Goodrich	Col. 60th N. Y. Infy	Sept. 12, 1862, to Sept. 17, 1862. Killed.
J. Austin	Lt.-Col. 78th N. Y. Infy	Sept. 17, 1862, to Sept. 18, 1862.
Geo. S. Greene	Brigadier General	Sept. 18, 1862, to Sept. 25, 1863.

1st Dist. Columbia Infy	Sept., 1862	From 3-Brig. 2-Div. 2-Corps Army Va.	To Dist. Alex. Def. Wash	Oct.,	1862
3d Del. Infy	Sept., 1862	From 3-Brig. 2-Div. 2-Corps Army Va.	To 2-Brig. 2-Div. 12-Corps Pot	Oct.,	1862
Purnell Md. Legion	Sept., 1862	From 3-Brig. 2-Div. 2-Corps Army Va.	To 2-Brig. 2-Div. 12-Corps Pot	Oct.,	1862
60th N. Y. Infy	Sept., 1862	From 3-Brig. 2-Div. 2-Corps Army Va.	To 2-Brig. 2-Div. 12-Corps Pot	Oct.,	1862
78th N. Y. Infy	Sept., 1862	From 3-Brig. 2-Div. 2-Corps Army Va.	To 3-Brig. 2-Div. 12-Corps Cumb'd.	Sept.,	1863
102d N. Y. Infy	Oct., 1862	From 2-Brig. 2-Div. 12-Corps Pot	To 3-Brig. 2-Div. 12-Corps Cumb'd.	Sept.,	1863
137th N. Y. Infy	Oct., 1862	From 4-Brig. 1-Div. 12-Corps Pot	To 3-Brig. 2-Div. 12-Corps Cumb'd.	Sept.,	1863
149th N. Y. Infy	Oct., 1862	From 4-Brig. 1-Div. 12-Corps Pot	To 3-Brig. 2-Div. 12-Corps Cumb'd.	Sept.,	1863
109th Penna. Infy	Oct., 1862	From 2-Brig. 2-Div. 12-Corps Pot	To 2-Brig. 2-Div. 12-Corps Pot	Jan.,	1863
111th Penna. Infy	Oct., 1862	From 2-Brig. 2-Div. 12-Corps Pot	To, 2-Brig. 2-Div. 12-Corps Pot	Jan.,	1863
60th N. Y. Infy	May, 1863	From 2-Brig. 2-Div. 12-Corps Pot	To 3-Brig. 2-Div. 12-Corps Cumb'd.	Sept.,	1863
ARTILLERY, 2d DIVISION.—					
6th Me. Indpt. Batty	Sept., 1862	From Arty. 1-Div. 3-Corps Army Va.	To 4-Vol. Brig. Arty. Res. Pot	May,	1863
Indpt. Batty. E, Penna	Sept., 1862	From Arty. 2-Div. 2-Corps Army Va.	To Arty. Brig. 12-Corps Pot	May,	1863
Indpt. Batty. F, Penna	Sept., 1862	From Arty. 2-Div. 2-Corps Army Va.	To 4-Vol. Brig. Arty. Res. Pot	May,	1863
4th Me. Indpt. Batty	Sept., 1862	From Arty. 2-Div. 2-Corps Army Va.	To Arty. Def. Upper Pot, 8-Corps	Dec.,	1862
ARTILLERY BRIGADE.—					
Batty. M, 1st N. Y.	May, 1863	From Arty. 1-Div. 12-Corps Pot	To Arty. Brig. 12-Corps Cumb'd	Sept.,	1863
Indpt. Batty. E, Penna	May, 1863	From Arty. 2-Div. 12-Corps Pot	To Arty. Brig. 12-Corps Cumb'd	Sept.,	1863
Batty. F, 4th U. S. Arty	May, 1863	From Arty. 1-Div. 12-Corps Pot	To Arty. Brig. 12-Corps Cumb'd	Sept.,	1863
Batty. K, 5th U. S. Arty	May, 1863	From Arty. Res. Pot	To Arty. Brig. 12-Corps Cumb'd	Sept.,	1863
PROVOST GUARD.—					
10th Me. Infy	May, 1863	From 1-Brig. 1-Div. 12-Corps Pot	To Headqrs. 12-Corps Cumb'd	Sept.,	1863

Cavalry Division, Army of the Potomac

As organized July, 1862.

COMMANDER.

Commander	Rank		
George Stoneman	Brigadier General		

1st BRIGADE.—   **COMMANDER.**

Commander	Rank		
W. W. Averill	Col. 3d Penna. Cav		

1st N. Y. (Lincoln) Cav	July, 1862	From Cav. 6-Corps Pot	To 4-Brig. Pleasanton's Cav. Div. Pot	Sept.,	1862
3d Penna. Cav	July, 1862	From Cav. 3-Corps Pot	To 5-Brig. Pleasanton's Cav. Div. Pot	Sept.,	1862
4th Penna. Cav	July, 1862	From Cav. 5-Corps Pot	To 3-Brig. Pleasanton's Cav. Div. Pot	Sept.,	1862
5th U. S. Cav	July, 1862	From 1-Brig. Cav. Res. Pot	To 1-Brig. Pleasanton's Cav. Div. Pot	Sept.,	1862

2d BRIGADE.—

Commander	Rank	Dates
D. McM. Gregg	Col. 8th Penna. Cav	July 7, 1862, to July 16, 1862.
A. Pleasanton	Col. U. S. A	July 16, 1862, to Sept. .., 1862.

6th Penna. Cav	July, 1862	From 1-Brig. Cav. Res. Pot	To 3-Brig. Pleasanton's Cav. Div. Pot	Sept.,	1862
8th Penna. Cav	July, 1862	From 2-Brig. Cav. Res. Pot	To 2-Brig. Pleasanton's Cav. Div. Pot	Sept.,	1862
8th Ill. Cav	July, 1862	From Cav. 5-Corps Pot	To 2-Brig. Pleasanton's Cav. Div. Pot	Sept.,	1862
1st U. S. Cav	July, 1862	From Headqrs. Army Pot	To Headqrs. Army Pot	Sept.,	1862
6th U. S. Cav	July, 1862	From 1-Brig. Cav. Res. Pot	To 1-Brig. Pleasanton's Cav. Div. Pot	Sept.,	1862
UNATTACHED.—					
Barker's Ill. Squad. Cav	July, 1862	From Unatt. Army Pot	To Headqrs. Army Pot	Sept.,	1862
5th Penna Cav	July, 1862	From Cav. 4-Corps Pot	To 4-Corps Dept. of Va	Sept.,	1862

PLEASANTON'S CAVALRY DIVISION, SEPT., 1862.—

COMMANDER.

Commander	Rank	Dates	
A. Pleasanton	Brigadier General	Sept. .., 1862, to Feb. .., 1863.	

1st BRIGADE.—   **COMMANDERS.**

Commander	Rank	Dates
Chas. J. Whiting	Major U. S. A	Sept. .., 1862, to Nov. .., 1862.
J. F. Farnsworth	Col. 8th Ill. Cav	Nov. .., 1862, to Jan. .., 1863.
William Gamble	Col. 8th Ill. Cav	Jan. .., 1863, to Feb. .., 1863.

5th U. S. Cav	Sept., 1862	From 1-Brig. Stoneman's Div	To Averill's Cav. Brig. Pot	Nov.,	1862
6th U. S. Cav	Sept., 1862	From 2-Brig. Stoneman's Cav. Div.	To 2-Brig. Pleasanton's Cav. Div.	Nov.,	1862
8th Ill. Cav	Nov., 1862	From 2-Brig. Pleasanton's Cav. Div.	To 1-Brig. 1-Div. Cav. Corps Pot	Feb.,	1863
3d Ind. Cav	Nov., 1862	From 2-Brig. Pleasanton's Cav. Div.	To 1-Brig. 1-Div. Cav. Corps Pot	Feb.,	1863
8th N. Y. Cav	Nov., 1862	From 5-Brig. Pleasanton's Cav. Div.	To 1-Brig. 1-Div. Cav. Corps Pot	Feb.,	1863

2d BRIGADE.—   **COMMANDERS.**

Commander	Rank	Dates
J. F. Farnsworth	Col. 8th Ill. Cav	Sept. .., 1862, to Nov. .., 1862.
D. McM. Gregg	Col. 8th Penna. Cav	Nov. .., 1862, to Dec. 13, 1862.
T. C. Devens	Col. 6th N. Y. Cav	Dec. 13, 1862, to Feb. .., 1863.

8th Ill. Cav	Sept., 1862	From 2-Brig. Stoneman's Cav. Div.	To 1-Brig. Pleasanton's Cav. Div.	Nov.,	1862
3d Ind. Cav	Sept., 1862	From Cav. Brig. 3-Corps Army Va.	To 1-Brig. Pleasanton's Cav. Div.	Nov.,	1862
1st Mass. Cav	Sept., 1862	From Dept. of the South	To Averill's Cav. Brig. Pot	Nov.,	1862
8th Penna. Cav	Sept., 1862	From 2-Brig. Stoneman's Cav. Div.	To 2-Brig. 1-Div. Cav. Corps Pot	Feb.,	1863
6th N. Y. Cav	Nov., 1862	From Cav. 9-Corps Pot	To 2-Brig. 1-Div. Cav. Corps Pot	Feb.,	1863
6th U. S. Cav	Nov., 1862	From 1-Brig. Pleasanton's Cav. Div.	To Res. Brig. Cav. Corps Pot	Feb.,	1863

3d BRIGADE.— COMMANDER.

Richard H. Rush	Col. 6th Penna. Cav	Sept. .., 1862, to Nov. .., 1862.	
4th Penna. Cav..........Sept., 1862	From 1-Brig. Stoneman's Cav. Div..	To Averill's Cav. Brig. Pot.........	Nov., 1862
6th Penna. Cav..........Sept., 1862	From 2-Brig. Stoneman's Cav. Div..	To Headqrs. Left Grand Div. Pot...	Nov., 1862
9th N. Y. Cav...........Sept., 1862	From Cav. Brig. 11-Corps Pot......	To Cav. Brig. 11 Corps.............	Nov., 1862

4th BRIGADE.— COMMANDER.

A. T. McReynolds	Col. 1st N. Y. (Lincoln) Cav........	Sept. .., 1862, to Oct. .., 1862.	
1st N. Y. (Lincoln) Cav..Sept., 1862	From 1-Brig. Stoneman's Cav. Div..	To Def. Upper Pot.................	Oct., 1862
12th Penna. Cav........Sept., 1862	From Mil. Dist. Washington, D. C..	To Def. Upper Pot.................	Oct., 1862

5th BRIGADE.— COMMANDER.

B. F. Davis	Col. 8th N. Y. Cav................	Sept. .., 1862, to Nov. .., 1862.	
8th N. Y. Cav..........Sept., 1862	From R. R. Brig. 8-Corps Mid. Dept.	To 1-Brig. Pleasanton's Cav. Div...	Nov., 1862
3d Penna. Cav..........Sept., 1862	From 1-Brig. Stoneman's Cav. Div..	To Averill's Cav. Brig. Pot.........	Nov., 1862
ARTILLERY.—			
Batty. A, 2d U. S. Arty...Sept., 1862	From 1-Brig. Horse Arty. Res. 5-C..	To 2-Div. Cav. Corps Pot..........	Feb., 1863
Bat. B. & L. 2d U. S. Arty.Sept., 1862	From 1-Brig. Horse Arty. Res. 5-C..	To Averill's Cav. Brig. Pot.........	Nov., 1862
Batty. M, 2d U. S. Arty..Sept., 1862	From 1-Brig. Horse Arty. Res. 5-C..	To 1-Div. Cav. Corps Pot..........	Feb., 1863
Bat. C. & G, 3d U. S. Arty.Sept., 1862	From 1-Brig. Horse Arty. Res. 5-C..	To Bayard's Cav. Brig. Pot.........	Nov., 1862

BAYARD'S CAVALRY BRIGADE.— COMMANDERS.

Geo. D. Bayard	Brigadier General...................	Sept. .., 1862, to Dec. 13, 1862.	Mort. Wnd.
D. McM. Gregg	Brigadier General...................	Dec. 13, 1862, to Feb. 12, 1863.	
1st Me. Cav............Sept., 1862	From Bayard's Cav. Brig. 3-Corps Va	To 1-Brig. 3-Div. Cav. Corps Pot....	Feb., 1863
1st N. J. Cav..........Sept., 1862	From Bayard's Cav. Brig. 3-Corps Va	To 1-Brig. 3-Div. Cav. Corps Pot....	Feb., 1863
2d N. Y. Cav...........Sept., 1862	From Bayard's Cav. Brig. 3-Corps Va	To 1-Brig. 3-Div. Cav. Corps Pot....	Feb., 1863
10th N. Y. Cav.........Sept., 1862	From Bayard's Cav. Brig. 3-Corps Va	To 1-Brig. 3-Div. Cav. Corps Pot....	Feb., 1863
1st Penna. Cav.........Sept., 1862	From Bayard's Cav. Brig. 3-Corps Va	To 2-Brig. 3-Div. Cav. Corps Pot....	Feb., 1863
Orton's D. C. Co. Cav....Sept., 1862	From Bayard's Cav. Brig. 3-Corps Va	To 2-Brig. 3-Div. Cav. Corps Pot....	Feb., 1863
Batty. C, 3d U. S. Arty...Nov., 1862	From Arty. Pleasanton's Cav. Div..	To Arty. 3-Div Cav. Corps Pot......	Feb., 1863

AVERILL'S CAVALRY BRIGADE.— COMMANDERS.

W. W. Averill	Brigadier General...................	Nov. .., 1862, to Jan. .., 1863.	
J. K. Kerr	Col. 4th Penna. Cav...............	Jan. .., 1863, to Feb. .., 1863.	
1st Mass. Cav..........Nov., 1862	From 2-Brig. Pleasanton's Cav. Div..	To 2-Brig. 2-Div. Cav. Corps Pot....	Feb., 1863
3d Penna. Cav..........Nov., 1862	From 5-Brig. Pleasanton's Cav. Div..	To 2-Brig. 2-Div. Cav. Corps Pot....	Feb., 1863
4th Penna. Cav.........Nov., 1862	From 3-Brig. Pleasanton's Cav. Div..	To 2-Brig. 2-Div. Cav. Corps Pot....	Feb., 1863
5th U. S. Cav..........Nov., 1862	From 1-Brig. Pleasanton's Cav. Div..	To Reserve Brig. Cav. Corps Pot....	Feb., 1863
1st R. I. Cav...........Dec., 1862	From Stoneman's Corps Observation.	To 1-Brig. 2-Div. Cav. Corps Pot....	Feb., 1863
16th Penna. Cav........Jan., 1863	From Def. of Washington..........	To 2-Brig. 2-Div. Cav. Corps Pot....	Feb., 1863
Bat. B. & L, 2d U. S. Arty.Nov., 1862	From Pleasanton's Cav. Div........	To Arty. 1-Div. Cav. Corps Pot.....	Feb., 1863

Cavalry Corps

Created and organized Feb., 1863. Broken up May, 1865.

CORPS COMMANDERS.

Geo. Stoneman	Major General...................	Feb. 12, 1863, to May 22, 1863.	
A. Pleasanton	Brigadier General................	May 22, 1863, to Jan. 22, 1864.	
D. McM. Gregg	Brigadier General................	Jan. 22, 1864, to Feb. 12, 1864.	
A. Pleasanton	Brigadier General................	Feb. 12, 1864, to Mch. 25, 1864.	
D. McM. Gregg	Brigadier General................	Mch. 25, 1864, to Apr. 4, 1864.	
P. H. Sheridan	Major General...................	Apr. 4, 1864, to Aug. 2, 1864.	
D. McM. Gregg	Brigadier General................	Aug. 2, 1864, to Aug. 6, 1864.	
A. T. A. Torbert	Brigadier General................	Aug. 6, 1864, to June 1, 1865.	
William Wells	Bvt. Brig. General................	June 1, 1865, to June 24, 1865.	

1st and 3d Divisions transferred to Army of the Shenandoah, Middle Military Division, Aug. 6, 1864.
Rejoined Army of the Potomac March 25, 1865.

Wesley Merritt	Major General...................	Mch. 25, 1865, to May 22, 1865.	
Geo. Crook	Major General...................	May 22, 1865, to June 27, 1865.	

1st DIVISION.— COMMANDERS.

A. Pleasanton	Brigadier General................	Feb. 12, 1863, to May 22, 17863.	
John Buford	Brigadier General................	May 22, 1863, to May 27, 1863.	
B. F. Davis	Col. 8th N. Y. Cav................	May 27, 1863, to June 6, 1863.	
Thos. C. Devin	Col. 6th N. Y. Cav................	June 6, 1863, to June 9, 1863.	
John Buford	Brigadier General................	June 9, 1863, to Aug. 15, 1863.	
Wesley Merritt	Brigadier General................	Aug. 15, 1863, to Sept. 15, 1863.	
John Buford	Brigadier General................	Sept. 15, 1863, to Nov. 21, 1863.	
Wesley Merritt	Brigadier General................	Nov. 21, 1863, to Apr. 10, 1864.	
A. T. A. Torbert	Brigadier General................	Apr. 10, 1864, to May 7, 1864.	
Wesley Merritt	Brigadier General................	May 7, 1864, to May 25, 1864.	
A. T. A. Torbert	Brigadier General................	May 25, 1864, to Aug. 6, 1864.	
	See Army Shenandoah to Mch. 25, 1865.		
T. C. Devin	Brigadier General................	Mch. 25, 1865, to May 28, 1865.	

1st BRIGADE, 1st DIVISION.— COMMANDERS.

B. F. Davis	Col. 8th N. Y. Cav................	Feb. 16, 1863, to May 27, 1863.	
William Gamble	Col. 8th Ill. Cav................	May 27, 1863, to June 6, 1863.	
B. F. Davis	Col. 8th N. Y. Cav................	June 6, 1863, to June 9, 1863.	
William Gamble	Col. 8th Ill. Cav................	June 9, 1863, to Sept. 2, 1863.	
Geo. H. Chapman	Col. 3d Ind. Cav................	Sept. 2, 1863, to Nov. 12, 1863.	
William Gamble	Col. 8th Ill. Cav................	Nov. 12, 1863, to Dec. 21, 1863.	
Geo. H. Chapman	Col. 3d Ind. Cav................	Dec. 21, 1863, to Mch. 25, 1864.	
Geo. A. Custer	Brigadier General................	Mch. 25, 1864, to Aug. 6, 1864.	
	See Army Shenandoah to Mch. 25, 1865.		
Peter Stagg	Col. 1st Mich. Cav................	Mch. 25, 1865, to June 1, 1865.	

1st BRIGADE, 1st DIVISION.—Continued.

8th N. Y. Cav..........Feb., 1863	From 1-Brig. Pleasanton's C. D. Pot.	To 2-Brig. 3-Div. Cav. Corps Pot...	Mch., 1864
9th N. Y. Cav..........Feb., 1863	From Cav. Brig. 11-Corps Potomac.	To 2-Brig. 1-Div. Cav. Corps Pot...	June, 1863
3d Ind. Cav..........Feb., 1863	From 1-Brig. Pleasanton's C. D. Pot.	To 2-Brig. 3-Div. Cav. Corps Pot...	Mch., 1864
8th Ill. Cav..........Feb., 1863	From 2-Brig. 3-Div. Cav. Corps Pot.	To 2-Brig. 3-Div. Cav. Corps Pot...	Mch., 1864
12th Ill. Cav..........June, 1863	From 2-Brig. 3-Div. Cav. Corps Pot.	To Chicago, Ill....................	Nov., 1863
1st Mich. Cav..........Mch., 1864	From 2-Brig. 3-Div. Cav. Corps Pot.	To 1-B. 1-Div. Cav. Corps M. M. D.	Aug., 1864
5th Mich. Cav..........Mch., 1864	From 2-Brig. 3-Div. Cav. Corps Pot.	To 1-B. 1-Div. Cav. Corps M. M. D.	Aug., 1864
6th Mich. Cav..........Mch., 1864	From 2-Brig. 3-Div. Cav. Corps Pot.	To 1-B. 1-Div. Cav. Corps M. M. D.	Aug., 1864
7th Mich. Cav..........Mch., 1864	From 2-Brig. 3-Div. Cav. Corps Pot.	To 1-B. 1-Div. Cav. Corps M. M. D.	Aug., 1864
1st Mich. Cav..........Mch., 1865	From 1-B. 1-Div. Cav. Corps M. M. D.	To Dept. Mo.......................	May, 1865
5th Mich. Cav..........Mch., 1865	From 1-B. 1-Div. Cav. Corps M. M. D.	To Dept. Mo.......................	May, 1865
6th Mich. Cav..........Mch., 1865	From 1-B. 1-Div. Cav. Corps M. M. D.	To Dept. Mo.......................	May, 1865
7th Mich. Cav..........Mch., 1865	From 1-B. 1-Div. Cav. Corps M. M. D.	To Dept. Mo.......................	May, 1865

2d BRIGADE, 1st DIVISION.— COMMANDERS.

Thos. C. Devin.........	Col. 6th N. Y. Cav..............	Feb. 16, 1863, to June 6, 1863.
J. H. Kellogg.........	Col. 17th Penna. Cav...........	June 6, 1863, to June 9, 1863.
Thos. C. Devin.........	Col. 6th N. Y. Cav..............	June 9, 1863, to Jan. 3, 1864.
Geo. S. Nichols.........	Lt.-Col. 9th N. Y. Cav.........	Jan. 3, 1864, to Jan. 10, 1864.
J. H. Kellogg.........	Col. 17th Penna. Cav...........	Jan. 10, 1864, to Jan. 25, 1864.
Thos. C. Devin.........	Col. 6th N. Y. Cav..............	Jan. 25, 1864, to Aug. 6, 1864.
	See Army Shenandoah to Mch. 25, 1865.	
C. L. Fitzhugh.........	Col. 6th N. Y. Cav..............	Mch. 25, 1865, to May 29, 1865.

6th N. Y. Cav..........Feb., 1863	From 2-Brig. Pleasanton's Cav. Div.	To 2-B. 1-Div. Cav. Corps M. M. D.	Aug., 1864
8th Penna. Cav..........Feb., 1863	From 2-Brig. Pleasanton's Cav. Div.	To 2-Brig. 2-Div. Cav. Corps Pot.	June, 1863
17th Penna. Cav..........Feb., 1863	From Cav. Brig. 11-Corps Potomac.	To 2-B. 1-Div. Cav. Corps M. M. D.	Aug., 1864
3d W. Va. Cav., Cos. A, C.June, 1863	From 3-Brig. Cav. Div. 22-Corps.	To Dept. W. Va....................	Nov., 1863
9th N. Y. Cav..........June, 1863	From 1-Brig. 1-Div. Cav. Corps Pot.	To 2-Brig. 1-Div. Cav. C. M. M. D.	Aug., 1864
4th N. Y. Cav..........Aug., 1863	From 2-Brig. 2-Div. Cav. Corps Pot.	To 2-Brig. 1-Div. Cav. C. M. M. D.	Aug., 1864
19th N. Y. Cav..........Mch., 1865	From 2-B. 1-Div. C. Corps M. M. D.	No change to Muster Out..........	June, 1865
6th N. Y. Cav..........Mch., 1865	From 2-B. 1-Div. C. Corps M. M. D.	No change to Muster Out..........	June, 1865
17th Penna. Cav..........Mch., 1865	From 2-B. 1-Div. C. Corps M. M. D.	Consol. with 1st and 6th Pa......	June, 1865
20th Penna. Cav..........Mch., 1865	From 2-B. 1-Div. C. Corps M. M. D.	Consol. with 2d Penna............	June, 1865
ARTILLERY.—			
6th N. Y. Indpt. Batty..Feb., 1863	From Arty. Res. Potomac..........	To 1-Brig. Horse Arty Potomac...	May, 1863

RESERVE BRIGADE—Attached to 1st Division June 6, 1863. COMMANDERS.

John Buford..........	Brigadier General................	Feb. 12, 1863, to May 22, 1863.
Chas. Whiting.........	Major, U. S. A...................	May 22, 1863, to June 9, 1863.
S. H. Starr..........	Major, U. S. A...................	June 9, 1863, to June 28, 1863.
Wesley Merritt.........	Brigadier General................	June 28, 1863, to Aug. 12, 1863.
A. Gibbs.........	Col. 19th N. Y. Cav..............	Aug. 12, 1863, to Sept. 12, 1863.
Wesley Merritt.........	Brigadier General................	Sept. 12, 1863, to Nov. 21, 1863.
A. Gibbs.........	Col. 19th N. Y. Cav..............	Nov. 21, 1863, to Apr. 10, 1864.
Wesley Merritt.........	Brigadier General................	Apr. 10, 1864, to May 7, 1864.
A. Gibbs.........	Col. 19th N. Y. Cav..............	May 7, 1864, to May 25, 1864.
Wesley Merritt.........	Brigadier General................	May 25, 1864, to Aug. 6, 1864.
	See Army Shenandoah to Mch. 25, 1865.	
A. Gibbs..............	Brigadier General................	Mch. 25, 1865, to May 25, 1865.

1st United States Cav...Feb., 1863	From Headqrs. Army Potomac......	To Res. Brig. 1-Div. Cav. C. M. M. D.	Aug., 1864
2d United States Cav...Feb., 1863	Fryom Provost Guard Potomac....	To Res. Brig. 1-Div. Cav. C. M. M. D.	Aug., 1864
5th United States Cav...Feb., 1863	From Averill's Cav. Brig. Potomac.	To Res. Brig. 1-Div. Cav. C. M. M. D.	Aug., 1864
6th United States Cav...Feb., 1863	From 2-Brig. Pleasanton's Cav. Div.	To Res. Brig. 1-Div. Cav. C. M. M. D.	Aug., 1864
6th Penna. Cav..........Feb., 1863	From Pleasanton's Cav. Div. Pot...	To Res. Brig. 1-Div. Cav. C. M. M. D.	Aug., 1864
19th N. Y. Cav..........Oct., 1863	From Unatt. Cav. Corps Potomac..	To Res. Brig. 1-Div. Cav. C. M. M. D.	Aug., 1864
	See Army Shenandoah to Mch. 25, 1865.		
2d Mass. Cav..........Mch., 1865	From Res. B, 1-Div. Cav. C. M. M. D.	No change to Muster Out..........	June, 1865
6th Penna. Cav..........Mch., 1865	From Res. B, 1-Div. Cav. C. M. M. D.	To 2d Penna. Prov'l. Cav.........	June, 1865
1st United States Cav...Mch., 1865	From Res. B, 1-Div. Cav. C. M. M. D.	To Dept. Washington..............	June, 1865
5th United States Cav...Mch., 1865	From Res. B, 1-Div. Cav. C. M. M. D.	To Dept. Washington..............	June, 1865
6th United States Cav...Mch., 1865	From Res. B, 1-Div. Cav. C. M. M. D.	To Dept. Washington..............	June, 1865

ARTILLERY RESERVE BRIGADE.

Battys. B and L, 2d U. S.Feb., 1863	From Averill's Cav. Brig. Potomac.	To 1-Brig Horse Arty. Potomac...	May, 1863
Batty. M, 2d U. S. Arty.Feb., 1863	From Pleasanton's Cav. Div. Pot...	To 1-Brig Horse Arty. Potomac...	May, 1863
Batty. E, 4th U. S. Arty.Feb., 1863	From Arty. 2-Div. 9-Corps Potomac.	To 1-Brig Horse Arty. Potomac...	May, 1863

2d DIVISION.— COMMANDERS

W. W. Averill.........	Brigadier General................	Feb. 12, 1863, to May 16, 1863.
A. N. Duffie.........	Col. 1st R. I. Cav..............	May 16, 1863, to June 11, 1863.
D. McM. Gregg.........	Brigadier General................	June 11, 1863, to Aug. 24, 1863.
John I. Gregg.........	Col. 16th Penna. Cav...........	Aug. 24, 1863, to Sept. 4, 1863.
D. McM. Gregg.........	Brigadier General................	Sept. 4, 1863, to Dec. 25, 1863.
John P. Taylor.........	Col. 1st Penna. Cav............	Dec. 25, 1863, to Jan. 5, 1864.
D. McM. Gregg.........	Brigadier General................	Jan. 5, 1864, to Jan. 22, 1864.
John P. Taylor.........	Col. 1st Penna. Cav............	Jan. 22, 1864, to Feb. 10, 1864.
C. H. Smith.........	Col. 1st Me. Cav...............	Feb. 10, 1864, to Feb. 12, 1864.
D. McM. Gregg.........	Brigadier General................	Feb. 12, 1864, to Mch. 25, 1864.
John I. Gregg.........	Col. 16th Penna. Cav...........	Mch. 25, 1864, to Apr. 4, 1864.
D. McM. Gregg.........	Brigadier General................	Apr. 4, 1864, to Aug. 2, 1864
John I. Gregg.........	Col.. 16th Penna. Cav..........	Aug. 2, 1864, to Aug. 6, 1864.
D. McM. Gregg.........	Brigadier General................	Aug. 6, 1864, to Sept. 15, 1864.
Henry E. Davies.........	Brigadier General................	Sept. 15, 1864, to Sept. 25, 1864.
D. McM. Gregg.........	Brigadier General................	Sept. 25, 1864, to Dec. 22, 1864.
Henry E. Davies.........	Brigadier General................	Dec. 22, 1864, to Jan. 19, 1865.
D. McM. Gregg.........	Bvt. Major General.............	Jan. 19, 1865, to Feb. 9, 1865.
John I. Gregg.........	Brigadier General................	Feb. 9, 1865, to Mch. 14, 1865.
Henry E. Davies.........	Bvt. Major General.............	Mch. 14, 1865, to Mch. 27, 1865.
George Crook.........	Major General...................	Mch. 27, 1865, to May 22, 1865.

1st BRIGADE, 2d DIVISION.— COMMANDERS.

A. N. Duffie.........	Col. 1st R. I. Cav..............	Feb. 16, 1863, to Feb. 26, 1863.
H. B. Sergeant.........	Col. 1st Mass. Cav.............	Feb. 26, 1863, to May 20, 1863.
L. P. DiCesnola.........	Col. 4th N. Y. Cav.............	May 20, 1863, to June 11, 1863.
J. B. McIntosh.........	Col. 3d Penna. Cav.............	June 11, 1863, to Oct. 1, 1863.
John P. Taylor.........	Col. 1st Penna. Cav............	Oct. 1, 1863, to Dec. 25, 1863.

1st BRIGADE, 2d DIVISION.—Continued.

COMMANDERS.

David Gardner	Lt.-Col. 1st Penna. Cav	Dec. 25, 1863, to Jan. 5, 1864.
John P. Taylor	Col. 1st Penna. Cav	Jan. 5, 1864, to Feb. 3, 1864.
William Stedman	Lt.-Col. 6th Ohio Cav	Feb. 3, 1864, to Feb. 12, 1864.
David Gardner	Col. 1st Penna. Cav	Feb. 12, 1864, to Apr. 17, 1864.
Henry E. Davies	Brigadier General	Apr. 17, 1864, to July 30, 1864.
William Stedman	Col. 6th Ohio Cav	July 30, 1864, to Sept. 13, 1864.
Henry E. Davies	Brigadier General	Sept. 13, 1864, to Sept. 15, 1864.
William Stedman	Col. 6th Ohio Cav	Sept. 15, 1864, to Sept. 25, 1864.
Henry E. Davies	Brigadier General	Sept. 25, 1864, to Dec. 22, 1864.
H. H. Janeway	Col. 1st N. J. Cav	Dec. 22, 1864, to Jan. 12, 1865.
Henry E. Davies	Brigadier General	Jan. 12, 1865, to Jan. 19, 1865.
W. C. Newberry	Lt.-Col. 24th N. Y. Cav	Jan. 19, 1865, to Jan. 25, 1865.
H. H. Janeway	Col. 1st N. J. Cav	Jan. 25, 1865, to Mch. 27, 1865.
Henry E. Davies	Brigadier General	Mch. 27, 1865, to May 22, 1865.

1st Mass. Cav. .....Feb., 1863	From Averill's Cav. Brig. Potomac.	To Provost Guard Army Potomac.	Mch., 1865
4th N. Y. Cav. .....Feb., 1863	From Cav. Brig. 11-Corps Potomac.	To 2-Brig. 2-Div. Cav. Corps Pot.	June, 1863
6th Ohio Cav. .....Feb., 1863	From Cav. Brig. 11-Corps Potomac.	To 2-Brig. 2-Div. Cav. Corps Pot.	June, 1863
1st R. I. Cav. .....Feb., 1863	From Averill's Cav. Brig. Potomac.	To 2-Brig. 2-Div. Cav. Corps Pot.	June, 1863
1st Md. Cav. .....June, 1863	From 2-Brig. 3-Div. Cav. Corps Pot.	To Provost Guard Potomac.	Oct., 1863
1st Penna. Cav. .....June, 1863	From 2-Brig. 3-Div. Cav. Corps Pot.	Transferred to 2d Penna Prov'l.	June, 1865
3d Penna. Cav. .....June, 1863	From 2-Brig. 3-Div. Cav. Corps Pot.	To Provost Guard Army Potomac.	Mch., 1864
1st N. J. Cav. .....June, 1863	From 2-Brig. 3-Div. Cav. Corps Pot.	To Dept. Washington	May, 1865
Co. A, Purnell Md. Legion.July, 1863	From 8-Corps Middle Dept.	To 8-Corps Middle Dept.	July, 1863
6th Ohio Cav. .....Aug., 1863	From 2-Brig. 2-Div. Cav. Corps Pot.	To 3-Div. Cav. Corps Pot.	Oct., 1864
1st R. I. Cav. .....Aug., 1863	From 2-Brig. 2-Div. Cav. Corps Pot.	To Def. of Washington 22-Corps.	Mch., 1864
10th N. Y. Cav. .....June, 1864	From 2-Brig. 2-Div. Cav. Corps Pot.	No change to Muster Out.	June, 1865
24th N. Y. Cav. .....Oct., 1864	From 2-Brig. 1-Div. 9-Corps Pot.	Consol. with 10th N. Y.	June, 1865
Batty. A, 2d U. S. Arty..Dec., 1864	From 2-Brig. Horse Arty. Potomac.	To Dept. Washington 22-Corps.	May, 1865

2d BRIGADE, 2d DIVISION.—

COMMANDERS.

J. B. McIntosh	Col. 3d Penna. Cav	Feb. 17, 1863, to May 13, 1863.
John I. Gregg	Col. 16th Penna. Cav	May 13, 1863, to June 14, 1863.
J. Kilpatrick	Col. 2d N. Y. Cav	June 14, 1863, to June 28, 1863.
P. Huey	Col. 8th Penna. Cav	June 28, 1863, to Aug. 12, 1863.
John I. Gregg	Col. 16th Penna. Cav	Aug. 12, 1863, to Aug. 24, 1863.
C. H. Smith	Col. 1st Me. Cav	Aug. 24, 1863, to Sept. 4, 1863.
John I. Gregg	Col. 16th Penna. Cav	Sept. 4, 1863, to Aug. 2, 1864.
M. Kerwin	Col. 13th Penna. Cav.	Aug. 2, 1864, to Aug. 6, 1864.
John I. Gregg	Col. 16th Penna. Cav	Aug. 6, 1864, to Aug. 16, 1864.
M. Kerwin	Col. 13th Penna. Cav	Aug. 16, 1864, to Aug. 27, 1864.
C. H. Smith	Col. 1st Me. Cav	Aug. 27, 1864, to Oct. 11, 1864.
M. Kerwin	Col. 13th Penna. Cav.	Oct. 11, 1864, to Nov. 10, 1864.
John I. Gregg	Col. 16th Penna. Cav	Nov. 10, 1864, to Feb. 9, 1865.
M. Kerwin	Col. 13th Penna. Cav	Feb. 9, 1865, to Feb. 17, 1865.
John I. Gregg	Brigadier General	Feb. 17, 1865, to Apr. 7, 1865.
S. B. M. Young	Col. 4th Penna. Cav.	Apr. 7, 1865, to May 28, 1865.

3d Penna. Cav. .....Feb., 1863	From Averill's Cav. Brig. Potomac.	To 1-Brig. 2-Div. Cav. Corps Pot.	June, 1863
4th Penna. Cav. .....Feb., 1863	From Averill's Cav. Brig. Potomac.	To 3-Brig. 2-Div. Cav. Corps Pot.	June, 1863
16th Penna. Cav. .....Feb., 1863	From Averill's Cav. Brig. Potomac.	To 3-Brig. 2-Div. Cav. Corps Pot.	June, 1863
2d N. Y. Cav. .....June, 1863	From 1-Brig. 3-Div. Cav. Corps Pot.	To 1-Brig. 3-Div. Cav. Corps Pot.	Aug., 1863
4th N. Y. Cav. .....June, 1863	From 1-Brig. 2-Div. Cav. Corps Pot.	To 2-Brig. 1-Div. Cav. Corps Pot.	Aug., 1863
6th Ohio Cav. .....June, 1863	From 2-Brig. 1-Div. Cav. Corps Pot.	To 1-Brig. 2-Div. Cav. Corps Pot.	Aug., 1863
8th Penna. Cav. .....June, 1863	From 2-Brig. 1-Div. Cav. Corps Pot.	To Dept. of Va.	May, 1865
1st R. I. Cav. .....July, 1863	From Camp Stoneman 22-Corps.	To 1-Brig. 2-Div. Cav. Corps Pot.	Aug., 1863
Orton's D. C. Cav. Co. .....Aug., 1863	From 3-Brig. 2-Div. Cav. Corps Pot.	To Middle Dept. 8-Corps Pot.	Dec., 1863
1st Me. Cav. .....Aug., 1863	From 3-Brig. 2-Div. Cav. Corps Pot.	To 3-Brig. 2-Div. Cav. Corps Pot.	Oct., 1864
10th N. Y. Cav. .....Aug., 1863	From 3-Brig. 2-Div. Cav. Corps Pot.	To 1-Brig. 2-Div. Cav. Corps Pot.	June, 1864
4th Penna. Cav. .....Aug., 1863	From 3-Brig. 2-Div. Cav. Corps Pot.	No change to Muster Out.	June, 1865
13th Penna. Cav. .....Aug., 1863	From 3-Brig. 2-Div. Cav. Corps Pot.	To Cav. 9-Corps Potomac.	Mch., 1864
16th Penna. Cav. .....Aug., 1863	From 3-Brig. 2-Div. Cav. Corps Pot.	No change to Muster Out.	June, 1865
2d Penna. Cav. .....Dec., 1863	From Provost Guard Army Pot.	To Provost Guard Army Potomac.	Mch., 1865
13th Penna. Cav. .....May, 1864	From Cav. 9-Corps Potomac.	To Dept. N. C.	Feb., 1865
21st Penna. Cav. .....Mch., 1865	From 3-Brig. 2-Div. Cav. Corps Pot.	To Dept. of Va.	May, 1865
ARTILLERY.—			
Battys. H and I, 1st U. S..Dec., 1864	From 2-Brig. Horse Arty. Potomac.	To Dept. of Washington.	May, 1865

3d BRIGADE, 2d DIVISION.—Organized June 14, 1863.

COMMANDERS.

John I. Gregg	Col. 16th Penna. Cav	June 14, 1863, to Aug. 17, 1863.
Discontinued Aug. 17, 1863. Reorganized Oct. 11, 1864.		
C. H. Smith	Col. 1st Me. Cav	Oct. 11, 1864, to Jan. 16, 1865.
O. B. Knowles	Col. 21st Penna. Cav	Jan. 16, 1865, to Feb. 6, 1865.
C. H. Smith	Col. 1st Me. Cav	Feb. 6, 1865, to May 12, 1865.

1st Me. Cav. .....June, 1863	From 1-Brig. 3-Div. Cav. Corps Pot.	To 2-Brig. 2-Div. Cav. Corps Pot.	Aug., 1863
10th N. Y. Cav. .....June, 1863	From 1-Brig. 3-Div. Cav. Corps Pot	To 2-Brig. 2-Div. Cav. Corps Pot.	Aug., 1863
4th Penna. Cav. .....June, 1863	From 1-Brig. 3-Div. Cav. Corps Pot.	To 2-Brig. 2-Div. Cav. Corps Pot.	Aug., 1863
16th Penna. Cav. .....June, 1863	From 1-Brig. 3-Div. Cav. Corps Pot.	To 2-Brig. 2-Div. Cav. Corps Pot.	Aug., 1863
Orton's D. C. Cav. Co. .....July, 1863	From Elliott's Command 8-Corps.	To 2-Brig. 2-Div. Cav. Corps Pot.	Aug., 1863
13th Penna. Cav. .....Oct., 1864	From 2-Brig. 2-Div. Cav. Corps Pot.	To Dept. of Va.	May, 1865
1st Me. Cav. .....Oct., 1864	From 2-Brig. 2-Div. Cav. Corps Pot.	To Dept. of Va.	May, 1865
6th Ohio Cav. .....Oct., 1864	From 2-Brig. 2-Div. Cav. Corps Pot.	To 2-Brig. 2-Div. Cav. Corps Pot.	Mch., 1865
21st Penna. Cav. .....Oct., 1864	From 1-Brig. 1-Div. 5-Corps Pot.	To Dept. of Va.	May, 1865
2d N. Y. Mtd. Rifles..Nov., 1864	From 2-Brig. 2-Div. 9-Corps Pot.	To Dept. of Va.	May, 1865
13th Ohio Cav. .....Dec., 1864	From 1-Brig. 1-Div. 9-Corps Pot.		
ARTILLERY, 2d DIVISION.—			
Batty. A, 2d U. S. Arty...Feb., 1863	From Pleasanton's Cav. Div. Pot.	To 2-Brig. Horse Arty. Potomac.	May, 1863

3d DIVISION.—

COMMANDERS.

D. McM. Gregg	Brigadier General	Feb. 12, 1863, to June 11, 1863.
Merged into 2d Division June 11, 1863. Reorganized June 28, 1863, from Cavalry Division 22-Corps.		
J. Kilpatrick	Brigadier General	June 28, 1863, to July 15, 1863.
Geo. A. Custer	Brigadier General	July 15, 1863, to Aug. 4, 1863.
J. Kilpatrick	Brigadier General	Aug. 4, 1863, to Nov. 25, 1863.
Geo. A. Custer	Brigadier General	Nov. 25, 1863, to Dec. 20, 1863.
J. Kilpatrick	Brigadier General	Dec. 20, 1863, to Apr. 13, 1864.
James H. Wilson	Brigadier General	Apr. 13, 1864, to Aug. 6, 1864.
	See Army Shenandoah to Mch. 25, 1865.	
Geo. A. Custer	Brigadier General	Mch. 25, 1865, to May 22, 1865.
Wells William		May 22, 1865, to June 1, 1865.

1st BRIGADE, 3d DIVISION.—

J. Kilpatrick	Col. 2d N. Y. Cav	Feb. 16, 1863, to May 13, 1863.	
C. Douty	Col. 1st Me. Cav	May 13, 1863, to June 7, 1863.	
J. Kilpatrick	Col. 2d N. Y. Cav	June 7, 1863, to June 14, 1863.	
E. J. Farnsworth	Brigadier General	June 28, 1863, to July 4, 1863.	Killed.
N. P. Richmond	Col. 1st W. Va. Cav	July 4, 1863, to July 9, 1863.	
O. D. Forest	Col. 5th N. Y. Cav	July 9, 1863, to July 15, 1863.	
H. E. Davies, Jr	Col. 2d N. Y. Cav	July 15, 1863, to July 25, 1863.	
E. B. Sawyer	Col. 1st Vt. Cav	July 25, 1863, to Aug. 22, 1863.	
H. E. Davies, Jr	Col. 2d N. Y. Cav	Aug. 22, 1863, to Feb. 12, 1864.	
T. M. Bryan, Jr	Col. 18th Penna. Cav	Feb. 12, 1864, to Apr. 12, 1864.	
H. E. Davies, Jr	Col. 2d N. Y. Cav	Apr. 12, 1864, to Apr. 30, 1864.	
T. M. Bryan, Jr	Col. 18th Penna. Cav	Apr. 30, 1864, to May 5, 1864.	
John B. McIntosh	Col. 3d Penna. Cav	May 5, 1864, to Aug. 6, 1864.	
	See Army Shenandoah to Mch. 25, 1865.		
A. C. M. Pennington	Col. 3d N. J. Cav	Mch. 25, 1865, to May 29, 1865.	

1st Me. Cav	Feb., 1863	From Gregg's Cav. Brig. Potomac..	To 3-Brig. 2-Div. Cav. Corps Pot....	June, 1863
2d N. Y. Cav	Feb., 1863	From Gregg's Cav. Brig. Potomac..	To 2-Brig. 2-Div. Cav. Corps Pot..	June, 1863
10th N. Y. Cav	Feb., 1863	From Gregg's Cav. Brig. Potomac..	To 3-Brig. 2-Div. Cav. Corps Pot..	June, 1863
Orton's D. C. Cav. Co	Feb., 1863	From Gregg's Cav. Brig. Potomac..	To 3-Brig. 2-Div. Cav. Corps Pot..	June, 1863
5th N. Y. Cav	June, 1863	From 3-Brig. Stahel's Cav. Div. 22-C.	To 1-Brig. 3-Div. Cav. Corps M. M. D.	Aug., 1864
18th Penna. Cav	June, 1863	From 2-Brig. Stahel's Cav. Div. 22-C.	To 1-B. 3-Div. Cav. Corps M. M. D.	Aug., 1864
1st Vermont Cav	June, 1863	From 3-Brig. Stahel's Cav. Div. 22-C.	To 2-Brig. 3-Div. Cav. Corps Pot..	Aug., 1862
1st W. Va. Cav	June, 1863	From 3-Brig. Stahel's Cav. Div. 22-C.	To Dept. W. Va.	Dec., 1863
2d N. Y. Cav	Aug., 1863	From 2-Div. Cav. Corps Pot.	To 1-Brig. 3-Div. Cav. Corps M. M. D.	Aug., 1864
1st Conn. Cav	Mch., 1864	From Cav. Res. 8-Corps	To 1-Brig. 3-Div. Cav. Corps M. M. D.	Aug., 1864
3d N. J. Cav	May, 1864	From Cav. 9-Corps Pot.	To 1-Brig. 3-Div. Cav. Corps M. M. D.	Aug., 1864
2d Ohio Cav	May, 1864	From Cav. 9-Corps Pot.	To 1-Brig. 3-Div. Cav. Corps M. M. D.	Aug., 1864
1st Conn. Cav	Mch., 1865	From 1-Brig. 3-Div. Cav. C. M. M. D.	To Cav. Brig. Dept. Wash.	June, 1865
3d N. J. Cav	Mch., 1865	From 1-Brig. 3-Div. Cav. C. M. M. D.	No change to Muster Out	June, 1865
2d N. Y. Cav	Mch., 1865	From 1-Brig. 3-Div. Cav. C. M. M. D.	No change to Muster Out	June, 1865
2d Ohio Cav	Mch., 1865	From 1-Brig. 3-Div. Cav. C. M. M. D.	To Dept. of Missouri	June, 1865

2d BRIGADE, 3d Division.— COMMANDERS.

E. Kielmansiegge	Col. 1st Md. Cav	Feb. 12, 1863, to Feb. 16, 1863.	
Percy Wyndham	Col. 1st N. J. Cav	Feb. 16, 1863, to June 9, 1863.	
J. P. Taylor	Col. 1st Penna. Cav	June 9, 1863, to June 28, 1863.	
Geo. A. Custer	Brigadier General	June 28, 1863, to July 15, 1863.	
C. H. Town	Col. 1st Mich. Cav	July 15, 1863, to Aug. 4, 1863.	
Geo. A. Custer	Brigadier General	Aug. 4, 1863, to Nov. 25, 1863.	
C. H. Town	Col. 1st Mich. Cav	Nov. 25, 1863, to Dec. 15, 1863.	
E. B. Sawyer	Col. 1st Vt. Cav	Dec. 15, 1863, to Dec. 20, 1863.	
Geo. A. Custer	Brigadier General	Dec. 20, 1863, to Jan. 7, 1864.	
R. A. Alger	Col. 5th Mich. Cav	Jan. 7, 1864, to Feb. 27, 1864.	
A. W. Preston	Lt.-Col. 1st Vt. Cav	Feb. 27, 1864, to Apr. 17, 1864.	
T. M. Bryant	Col. 18th Penna. Cav	Apr. 17, 1864, to Apr. 20, 1864	
Geo. H. Chapman	Col. 3d Ind. Cav	Apr. 20, 1864, to Aug. 7, 1864.	
	See Army of the Shenandoah, Middle Military Division, to March 25, 1865.		
William Wells	Col. 1st Vt. Cav	Mch. 25, 1865, to May 22, 1865.	

1st N. J. Cav	Feb., 1863	From Gregg's Cav. Brig. Pot.	To 1-Brig. 2-Div. Cav. Corps Pot....	June, 1863
1st Penna. Cav	Feb., 1863	From Gregg's Cav. Brig. Pot.	To 1-Brig. 2-Div. Cav. Corps Pot....	June, 1863
1st Md. Cav	Feb., 1863	From Cav. Brig. 11-Corps Pot.	To 1-Brig. 2-Div. Cav. Corps Pot....	June, 1863
12th Ill. Cav	Feb., 1863	From Def. Upper Pot.	To 1-Brig. 1-Div. Cav. Corps Pot....	June, 1863
1st Mich. Cav	June, 1863	From 1-Brig. Stahel's Cav. Div. 22-C	To 1-Brig. 1-Div. Cav. Corps Pot..	Mch., 1864
5th Mich. Cav	June, 1863	From 1-Brig. Stahel's Cav. Div. 22-C	To 1-Brig. 1-Div. Cav. Corps Pot..	Mch., 1864
6th Mich. Cav	June, 1863	From 1-Brig. Stahel's Cav. Div. 22-C	To 1-Brig. 1-Div. Cav. Corps Pot..	Mch., 1864
7th Mich. Cav	June, 1863	From 1-Brig. Stahel's Cav. Div. 22-C	To 1-Brig. 1-Div. Cav. Corps Pot..	Mch., 1864
1st Vt. Cav	Aug., 1863	From 1-Brig. 3-Div. Cav. Corps Pot..	To 2-Brig. 3-Div. Cav. C. M. M. D.	Aug., 1864
8th Ill. Cav	Mch., 1864	From 1-Brig. 1-Div. Cav. Corps Pot..	To Def. Wash. 22-Corps	May, 1864
3d Ind. Cav	Mch., 1864	From 1-Brig. 1-Div. Cav. Corps Pot..	To 2-Brig. 3-Div. Cav. C. M. M. D.	Aug., 1864
8th N. Y. Cav	Mch., 1864	From 1-Brig. 1-Div. Cav. Corps Pot..	To 2-Brig. 3-Div. Cav. C. M. M. D.	Aug., 1864
1st N. H. Cav	May, 1864	From Def. of Wash. 22-Corps.	To 2-Brig. 3-Div. Cav. C. M. M. D.	Aug., 1864
22d N. Y. Cav	May, 1864	From Cav. 9-Corps Pot.	To 2-Brig. 3-Div. Cav. C. M. M. D.	Aug., 1864
8th N. Y. Cav	Mch., 1865	From 2-Br. 3-Div. Cav. Corps M. M. D.	No change to Muster Out	June, 1865
15th N. Y. Cav	Mch., 1865	From 2-Br. 3-Div. Cav. Corps M. M. D.	To 2d N. Y. Prov'l Cav.	June, 1865
1st Vt. Cav	Mch., 1865	From 2-Br. 3-Div. Cav. Corps M. M. D.	No change to Muster Out	June, 1865
3d Ind. Cav	Mch., 1865	From 2-Br. 3-Div. Cav. Corps M. M. D.	No change to Muster Out	June, 1865

3d BRIGADE, 3d DIVISION.— COMMANDER.

Henry Capehart	Bvt. Brig. General	Mch. 25, 1865, to May 29, 1865.	

1st N. Y. (Lincoln) Cav	Mch., 1865	From 3-Brig. 3-Div. Cav. C. M. M. D.	No change to Muster Out	June, 1865
1st West Va. Cav	Mch., 1865	From 3-Brig. 3-Div. Cav. C. M. M. D.	No change to Muster Out	June, 1865
2d West Va. Cav	Mch., 1865	From 3-Brig. 3-Div. Cav. C. M. M. D.	No change to Muster Out	June, 1865
3d West Va. Cav	Mch., 1865	From 3-Brig. 3-Div. Cav. C. M. M. D.	No change to Muster Out	June, 1865

AT DIVISION HEADQUARTERS.—

1st Ohio Cav. Co's. A, C	June, 1863	From 2-Brig. Stahel's Cav. Div. 22-C	To Def. Wash. 22-Corps	Dec., 1863

Military District of Washington

Merged into the 22d Army Corps. February, 1863.
COMMANDERS.

J. S. Wadsworth	Brigadier General	Mch. 12, 1862, to Sept. 7, 1862.	
N. P. Banks	Major General	Sept. 7, 1862, to Oct. 27, 1862.	
S. P. Heintzelman	Major General	Oct. 27, 1862, to Feb. 1, 1863.	

INFANTRY.—

26th N. Y. Infy	Mch., 1862	From Unatt. Def. Washington	To 1-Brig. Ord's 2-Div. Dept. Rapp.	May, 1862
37th N. Y. Infy. I.H.I.	Mch., 1862	From Garrison Fort Washington	To 3-Brig. 3-Div. 3-Corps Pot.	Apr., 1862
59th N. Y. Infy	Mch., 1862	From 2-Brig. Casey's Div. Pot.	To Sturgis' Brig. Def. Wash.	May, 1862
76th N. Y. Infy	Mch., 1862	From 3-Brig. Casey's Div. Pot.	To Doubleday's Sep. Brig. Dept. Rapp	May, 1862
86th N. Y. Infy	Mch., 1862	From 2-Brig. Casey's Div. Pot.	To Piatt's Brig. Whipple's Div.	Aug., 1862
94th N. Y. Infy	Mch., 1862	From New Organization	To 1-Brig. Ord's Div. Dept. Rapp.	May, 1862
95th N. Y. Infy	Mch., 1862	From New Organization	To Doubleday's Sep. Brig. Dept. Rapp	May, 1862
97th N. Y. Infy	Mch., 1862	From New Organization	To 2-Brig. Ord's Div. Dept. Rapp.	May, 1862
101st N. Y. Infy	Mch., 1862	From New Organization	To Whipple's Brig. Def. Wash.	May, 1862
104th N. Y. Infy	Mch., 1862	From New Organization	To 2-Brig. Ord's Div. Dept. Rapp.	May, 1862
105th N. Y. Infy	Mch., 1862	From New Organization	To 2-Brig. Ord's Div. Dept. Rapp.	May, 1862
11th Penna. Infy	Mch., 1862	From Def. Washington	To 3-Brig. 2-Div. Dept. Rapp.	May, 1862
26th Penna. Infy. Co. B.	Mch., 1862	From 1-Brig. Hooker's Div. Pot.	To Dist. Wash. 22-Corps.	Feb., 1863
54th Penna. Infy	Mch., 1862	From New Organization	To R. R. Brig. Middle Dept.	Mch., 1862
56th Penna. Infy	Mch., 1862	From New Organization	To Doubleday's Sep. Brig. Dept. Rapp	May, 1862

MILITARY DISTRICT OF WASHINGTON.—Continued.

88th Penna. Infy.	Mch., 1862	From Unatt. Def. of Washington...	To 1-Brig. Ord's Div. Dept. Rapp....	May,	1862
90th Penna. Infy.	Mch., 1862	From Unatt. Def. of Washington...	To 1-Brig. Ord's Div. Dept. Rapp....	May,	1862
91st Penna. Infy.	Mch., 1862	From Unatt. Def. of Washington...	To 1-Brig. 3-Div. 5-Corps Pot......	Aug.,	1862
99th Penna. Infy.	Mch., 1862	From Jameson's Brig. Heintzel'ns C.	To 3-Brig. 3-Div. 3-Corps Pot......	June,	1862
107th Penna. Infy.	Mch., 1862	From New Organization	To 2-Brig. Ord's Div. Dept. Rapp..	May,	1862
10th N. J. Infy.	Mch., 1862	From Unatt. Def. Washington	To Dist. Wash. 22-Corps...........	Feb.,	1863
2d Dist. Columbia Infy.	Mch., 1862	From New Organization	To Dist. Wash. 22-Corps...........	Feb.,	1863
32d Mass. Infy.	May, 1862	From New Organization	To 1-Brig. 1-Div. 5-Corps Pot......	June,	1862
69th N. Y. Infy.	May, 1862	From New Organization	No change to Muster Out..........	Sept.,	1862
27th Penna. Co. F.	Aug., 1862	From 1-Brig. 1-Div. 1-C. Army Va.	To Dist. Wash. 22-Corps...........	Feb.,	1863
135th Penna. Infy.	Aug., 1862	From New Organization	To 1-Brig. 3-Div. 1-Corps Pot......	Feb.,	1863
136th Penna. Infy.	Aug., 1862	From New Organization	To 2-Brig. 2-Div. 1-Corps Pot......	Nov.,	1862
143d Penna. Infy.	Aug., 1862	From New Organization	To 2-Brig. 3-Div. 1-Corps Pot......	Feb.,	1863
149th Penna. Infy.	Aug., 1862	From New Organization	To 2-Brig. 3-Div. 1-Corps Pot......	Feb.,	1863
150th Penna. Infy.	Aug., 1862	From New Organization	To 2-Brig. 3-Div. 1-Corps Pot......	Feb.,	1863
19th Me. Infy.	Aug., 1862	From New Organization	To 1-Brig. 2-Div. 2-Corps Pot......	Oct.,	1862
151st Penna. Infy.	Aug., 1862	From New Organization	To 1-Brig. 3-Div. 1-Corps Pot......	Feb.,	1863
34th Mass. Infy.	Sept., 1862	From New Organization	To Dist. Alexandria...............	Dec.,	1862
22d N. J. Infy.	Sept., 1862	From New Organization	To Prov'l Br. Casey's Div. Dis. Wash.	Oct.,	1862
24th N. J. Infy.	Sept., 1862	From New Organization	To Prov'l Br. Casey's Div. Dis. Wash.	Oct.,	1862
25th N. J. Infy.	Sept., 1862	From New Organization	To 1-Brig. Casey's Div..........	Oct.,	1862
27th N. J. Infy.	Sept., 1862	From New Organization	To 1-Brig. Casey's Div..........	Oct.,	1862
28th N. J. Infy.	Sept., 1862	From New Organization	To Prov'l Brig. Casey's Div......	Oct.,	1862
29th N. J. Infy.	Sept., 1862	From New Organization	To Prov'l Brig. Casey's Div......	Oct.,	1862
30th N. J. Infy.	Sept., 1862	From New Organization	To Prov'l Brig. Casey's Div......	Oct.,	1862
31st N. J. Infy.	Sept., 1862	From New Organization	To Prov'l Brig. Casey's Div......	Oct.,	1862
11th R. I. Infy.	Oct., 1862	From New Organization	To Dist. Alexandria...............	Dec.,	1862
109th N. Y. Infy.	Oct., 1862	From Def. Balto. 8-Corps..........	To Unass'd R. R. Gd. Annapolis Jn.	Oct.,	1862
147th N. Y. Infy.	Oct., 1862	From New Organization	To Provost Guard Pot..............	Dec.,	1862

ARTILLERY.—

2d N. Y. Heavy Arty.	Mch., 1862	From Def. Washington.	To Whipple's Brig. Dist. Wash.....	May,	1862
4th N. Y. Heavy Arty.	Mch., 1862	From Def. Washington.	To Whipple's Brig. Dist. Wash.....	May,	1862
3d Battn. N. Y. H. Arty.	Mch., 1862	From Def. Washington.	To Whipple's Brig. Dist. Wash.....	May,	1862
N. Y. Rocket Battn.	Mch., 1862	From Def. Washington.	To Dept. North Carolina...........	Apr.,	1862
Batty. C, 1st N. Y. Arty.	Mch., 1862	From Def. Washington.	To Arty. 3-Div. 5-Corps Pot.......	Sept.,	1862
Batty. K, 1st N. Y. Arty.	Mch., 1862	From Def. Washington.	To R. R. Brig. Middle Dept.......	Apr.,	1862
Indpt. Batty. C, Pa. Arty.	Mch., 1862	From Def. Washington.	To Arty. 2-Div. Dept. Rapp........	May,	1862
9th N. Y. Indpt. Batty.	Mch., 1862	From Def. Washington.	To 2-Brig. Def. North Pot.. 22-Corps.	Feb.,	1863
11th N. Y. Indpt. Batty.	Mch., 1862	From Def. Washington.	To Whipple's Brig. Dist. Wash.....	May,	1862
12th N. Y. Indpt. Batty.	Mch., 1862	From Def. Washington.	To Light Arty. Camp 22-Corps.....	Feb.,	1863
16th N. Y. Indpt. Batty.	Mch., 1862	From New Organization	To Sturgis' Brig. Dist. Wash......	May,	1862
Batty. L, 2d N. Y. Arty.	Mch., 1862	From Def. Washington.	To Whipple's Brig. Dist. Wash.....	May,	1862
14th Mass. 1st H. A.	Mch., 1862	From Def. Washington.	To Whipple's Brig. Dist. Wash.....	May,	1862
1st Wis. H. A. Co. A.	Mch., 1862	From Def. Washington.	To Whipple's Brig. Dist. Wash.....	May,	1862
2d Penna. Heavy Arty.	Mch., 1862	From New Organization	To Def. North Potomac, Dist. Wash	Aug.,	1862
10th R. I. Batty. Arty.	Mch., 1862	From New Organization	No change to Muster Out..........	Aug.,	1862
10th N. Y. Indpt. Batty.	Apr., 1862	From New Organization	To Arty. 2-Corps Army Va.........	June,	1862
4th Me. Indpt. Batty.	Apr., 1862	From New Organization	To Arty. 2-Corps Army Va.........	June,	1862
5th Me. Indpt. Batty.	Apr., 1862	From New Organization	To Arty. 2-Div. Dept. Rapp........	May,	1862
6th Me. Indpt. Batty.	Apr., 1862	From New Organization	To Arty. 2-Corps Army Va.........	June,	1862
16th Ind. Batty.	May, 1862	From New Organization	To Arty. 2-Corps Army Va.........	June,	1862
Batty. A, 1st W. Va. Arty.	June, 1862	From Shields' Div. Dept. Rapp.....	To Light Arty. Camp 22-Corps.....	Feb.,	1863
Batty. B, 1st W. Va. Arty.	June, 1862	From Shields' Div. Dept. Rapp.....	To R. R. Dist. Dept. W. Va.......	Sept.,	1862
Batty. H, 1st Ohio Infy.	June, 1862	From Shields' Div. Dept. Rapp....;	To Whipple's Div. Dist. Wash......	Sept.,	1862
17th N. Y. Indpt. Batty.	Aug., 1862	From New Organization	To Abercrombie's Div. Dist. Wash..	Oct.,	1862
19th Conn. 2d H. Arty.	Aug., 1862	From New Organization	To Def. Alexandria...............	Dec.,	1862
1st Conn. Heavy Arty.	Aug., 1862	From Siege Arty. Army Pot........	To Def. Alexandria...............	Dec.,	1862
19th N. Y. Batty.	Oct., 1862	From New Organization	To Light Arty Camp 22 Corps.....	Feb.,	1863
22d N. Y. Indpt. Batty.	Oct., 1862	From New Organization	To 2-Brig. Def. North Pot. Wash....	Dec.,	1862
27th N. Y. Indpt. Batty.	Oct., 1862	From New Organization	To Light Arty. Camp 22 Corps.....	Feb.,	1863

CAVALRY.—

6th N. Y. Cav.	Mch., 1862	From Def. Washington.............	To Cav. 9-Corps Pot..............	Aug.,	1862
10th N. Y. Cav.	Mch., 1862	From Balto. Md. Middle Dept......	To Bayard's Cav. Brig. 3-Corps Va..	Aug.,	1862
11th N. Y. Cav.	Mch., 1862	From New Organization	To Dist. Wash. 22-Corps..........	Feb.,	1863
4th Penna. Cav.	Mch., 1862	From Def. Washington.............	To. Cav. Ord's Div. Dept. Rapp....	May,	1862
1st N. J. Cav.	Mch., 1862	From Def. Washington.............	To Bayard's Cav. Brig. Dept. Rapp.	May,	1862
2d Penna. Cav.	Apr., 1862	From Balto. Md. Middle Dept......	To Buford's Cav. Brig. 2-Corps Va..	Aug.,	1862
12th Penna. Cav.	Apr., 1862	From New Organization	To 4-Brig. Pleasanton's Cav. Div. Pot	Sept.,	1862
5th U. S. Cav. Det.	Apr., 1862	From Cav. Res. Pot...............	To 1-Brig. Pleasanton's Cav. Div. Pot	Sept.,	1862
6th U. S. Cav. Co. L.	Apr., 1862	From Cav. Res. Pot...............	To 1-Brig. Pleasanton's Cav. Div. Pot	Sept.,	1862
1st Mich. Cav. 6-Co's.	May, 1862	From Hatch's Cav. Brig. Dept. Shen.	To Hatch's Cav. Brig. 2-Corps Va..	June,	1862
9th N. Y. Cav.	May, 1862	From Arty. Res. Pot..............	To Cav. Brig. 1-Corps Army Va.....	June,	1862

CASEY'S PROV'L BRIGADE.—   **COMMANDER.**

Silas Casey		Major General			
15th Conn. Infy.	Aug., 1862	From New Organization	To 1-Brig. Casey's Div. Dist. Wash.	Oct.,	1862
Keystone Pa. Batty.	Aug., 1862	From New Organization	To Arty. Casey's Div. Dist. Wash..	Oct.,	1862
11th N. H. Infy.	Sept., 1862	From New Organization	To 2-Brig. 2-Div. 9-Corps Pot......	Oct.,	1862

GROVER'S BRIGADE.—   **COMMANDERS.**

C. Grover		Brigadier General	Oct. .., 1862, to Nov. .., 1862.		
A. B. Jewett		Col. 10th Vt. Infy	Nov. .., 1862, to Feb. .., 1863.		
22d Me. Infy.	Oct., 1862	From New Organization	To Dept. of the Gulf..............	Feb.,	1863
23d Me. Infy.	Oct., 1862	From New Organization	To Jewett's Brig. 22-Corps........	Feb.,	1863
14th N. H. Infy.	Oct., 1862	From New Organization	To Jewett's Brig. 22-Corps........	Feb.,	1863
10th Vt. Infy.	Oct., 1862	From New Organization	To Jewett's Brig. 22-Corps........	Feb.,	1863
39th Mass. Infy.	Oct., 1862	From New Organization	To Jewett's Brig. 22-Corps........	Feb.,	1863
10th Mass. Indpt. Batty.	Oct., 1862	From New Organization	To Jewett's Brig. 22-Corps........	Feb.,	1863

ARTILLERY CAMP.—   **COMMANDER.**

W. F. Barry		Brigadier General			
1st Del. Batty.	Oct., 1862	From New Organization	To Light Arty. Camp 22-Corps.....	Feb.,	1863
Batty. I, 1st Mich. Arty.	Oct., 1862	From New Organization	To Arty. Cav. Brig. 22-Corps......	Feb.,	1863
12th N. Y. Indpt. Batty.	Oct., 1862	From Mil. Dist. Washington.......	To Arty. Camp 22-Corps..........	Feb.,	1863
16th N. Y. Indpt. Batty.	Oct., 1862	From Mil. Dist. Washington.......	To Arty. Camp 22-Corps..........	Feb.,	1863
19th N. Y. Indpt. Batty.	Oct., 1862	From Mil. Dist. Washington.......	To Arty. Camp 22-Corps..........	Feb.,	1863
27th N. Y. Indpt. Batty.	Oct., 1862	From New Organization	To Arty. Camp 22-Corps..........	Feb.,	1863
Batty. H, 1st Pa. Arty.	Oct., 1862	From New Organization	To Arty. Camp 22-Corps..........	Feb.,	1863
Batty. A, 1st W. Va. Arty.	Oct., 1862	From Mil. Dist. Washington.......	To Arty. Camp 22-Corps..........	Feb.,	1863

R. R. GUARD.—

109th N. Y. Infy.	Oct., 1862	From Def. Washington.............	To R. R. Guard 22-Corps..........	Feb.,	1863

WHIPPLE'S COMMAND.—   COMMANDER.

A. W. Whipple	Brigadier General		
101st N. Y. Infy......May, 1862	From Mil. Dist. Washington......	To 2-Brig. 3-Div. 3-Corps Pot.....	June, 1862
16th Me. Infy......Aug., 1862	From New Organization..........	To 2-Brig. 2-Div. 1-Corps Pot.....	Sept., 1862
9th N. H. Infy......Aug., 1862	From New Organization..........	To 1-Brig. 2-Div. 9-Corps Pot.....	Sept., 1862
35th Mass. Infy......Aug., 1862	From New Organization..........	To 2-Brig. 2-Div. 9-Corps Pot.....	Sept., 1862
14th Conn. Infy......Aug., 1862	From New Organization..........	To 2-Brig. 3-Div. 2-Corps Pot.....	Sept., 1862
107th N. Y. Infy......Aug., 1862	From New Organization..........	To 3-Brig. 1-Div. 12-Corps Pot.....	Sept., 1862
108th N. Y. Infy......Aug., 1862	From New Organization..........	To 1-Brig. 2-Div. 3-Corps Pot.....	Sept., 1862
120th N. Y. Infy......Aug., 1862	From New Organization..........	To 1-Brig. 2-Div. 3-Corps Pot.....	Oct., 1862
124th Penna. Infy......Aug., 1862	From New Organization..........	To 1-Brig. 1-Div. 12-Corps Pot.....	Sept., 1862
125th Penna. Infy......Aug., 1862	From New Organization..........	To 1-Brig. 1-Div. 12-Corps Pot.....	Sept., 1862
127th Penna. Infy......Aug., 1862	From New Organization..........	To 3-Brig. 2-Div. 2-Corps Pot.......	Dec., 1862
128th Penna. Infy......Aug., 1862	From New Organization..........	To 1-Brig. 1-Div. 12-Corps Pot.....	Sept., 1862
129th Penna. Infy......Aug., 1862	From New Organization..........	To 1-Brig. 3-Div. 5-Corps Pot.....	Sept., 1862
130th Penna. Infy......Aug., 1862	From New Organization..........	To 2-Brig. 3-Div. 2-Corps Pot.....	Sept., 1862
131st Penna. Infy......Aug., 1862	From New Organization..........	To 2-Brig. 3-Div. 5-Corps Pot.....	Sept., 1862
132d Penna. Infy......Aug., 1862	From New Organization..........	To 1-Brig. 3-Div. 2-Corps Pot.....	Sept., 1862
11th N. J. Infy......Aug., 1862	From New Organization..........	To 1-Brig. 2-Div. 3-Corps Pot.....	Sept., 1862
ARTILLERY.—			
1st Mass. Heavy Arty....May, 1862	From Mil. Dist. Wash............	To Arty Def. Alexandria..........	Jan., 1863
6th Me. Indpt. Batty.....May, 1862	From Mil. Dist. Wash............	To Arty. 2-Corps Army Va......	June, 1862
2d N. Y. Heavy Arty....May, 1862	From Mil. Dist. Wash............	To Arty. Def. Alexandria........	Jan., 1863
4th N. Y. Heavy Arty....May, 1862	From Mil. Dist. Wash............	To Arty. Abercrombie's Div. Wash.	Oct., 1862
11th N. Y. Indpt. Batty.....May, 1862	From Mil. Dist. Wash............	To Arty. 3-Div. 3-Corps Pot.....	Nov., 1862
12th N. Y. Indpt. Batty.....May, 1862	From Mil. Dist. Wash............	To Camp Barry Wash..........	Jan., 1863
3d N. Y. Battn. L. A....May, 1862	From Mil. Dist. Wash............	To Arty. Def. Alexandria........	Jan., 1863
1st Wis. H. Arty. Co. A...May, 1862	From Mil. Dist. Wash............	To Arty. Def. Alexandria........	Jan., 1863
CAVALRY.—			
10th N. Y. Cav........Aug., 1862	From Mil. Dist. Wash............	To Bayard's Cav. Brig. Pot......	Oct., 1862
ENGINEERS.—			
Wrigley's Pa. Co. Engrs..Aug., 1862	From New Organization..........	To Def. Upper Pot..............	Oct., 1862

STURGIS' BRIGADE.—   COMMANDER.

S. D. Sturgis	Brigadier General		
9th R. I. Infy......May, 1862	From New Organization..........	No change to Muster Out..........	Aug., 1862
10th R. I. Infy......May, 1862	From New Organization..........	No change to Muster Out..........	Aug., 1862
59th N. Y. Infy......May, 1862	From Mil. Dist. Washington......	To 3-Brig. 2-Div. 2-Corps Pot.....	July, 1862
71st N. Y. S. M......May, 1862	From New Organization..........	No change to Muster Out..........	Sept., 1862
63d Ind. Infy......May, 1862	From New Organization..........	Piatt's Brig. Whipple's Div........	Aug., 1862
17th U. S. Infy. Batt......May, 1862	From Dept. of the East..........	To 2-Brig. 2-Div. 5-Corps Pot.....	Oct., 1862
19th U. S. Infy. Batt......May, 1862	From Dept. of the East..........	To 2-Brig. 2-Div. 5-Corps Pot.....	Oct., 1862
Batty. L. 2d N. Y. Arty...May, 1862	From Mil. Dist. Washington......	To Arty. 2-Corps Army Va........	June, 1862
8th Mass. Indpt. Batty...June, 1862	From New Organization..........	To Arty. 1-Div. 9-Corps Pot.......	Aug., 1862

DEFENCES NORTH OF THE POTOMAC.—   COMMANDER.

J. A. Haskins	Lieutenant-Colonel	Aug. .., 1862, to Feby. ..., 1863.	
18th Me., 1st H. A......Aug., 1862	From New Organization..........	To 3-Brig. 1-Div. 3-Corps Pot.....	Oct., 1862
19th Me. Infy......Aug., 1862	From New Organization..........	To 1-Brig. 2-Div. 2-Corps Pot.....	Oct., 1862
17th Mich. Infy......Aug., 1862	From New Organization..........	To 1-Brig. 1-Div. 9-Corps Pot.....	Sept., 1862
117th N. Y. Infy......Aug., 1862	From New Organization..........	To 2 and 3-Brig. Def. North Pot....	Oct., 1862
136th Penna. Infy......Aug., 1862	From New Organization..........	To 2-Brig. 2-Div. 1-Corps Pot.....	Sept., 1862
137th Penna. Infy......Aug., 1862	From New Organization..........	To 1-Brig. 2-Div. 6-Corps Pot.....	Sept., 1862
ARTILLERY.—			
18th Me., 1st H. A......Aug., 1862	From New Organization..........	To 2-Brig. Def. North Pot.....	Oct., 1862
2d Penna. Heavy Arty..Aug., 1862	From Mil. Dist. Washington......	To 1-Brig. Def. North Pot.....	Oct., 1862
113th N. Y., 7th H. A....Aug., 1862	From New Organization..........	To 2-Brig. Def. North Pot.....	Oct., 1862
138th N. Y., 9th H. A....Aug., 1862	From New Organization..........	To 2-Brig. Def. North Pot.....	Oct., 1862
5th Battn. N. Y. H. A....Aug., 1862	From New Organization..........	To 3-Brig. Def. North Pot.....	Oct., 1862
6th Battn. N. Y. H. A....Aug., 1862	From New Organization..........	To 3-Brig. Def. North Pot.....	Oct., 1862
7th Battn. N. Y. H. A....Aug., 1862	From New Organization..........	To 3-Brig. Def. North Pot.....	Oct., 1862
11th Vt., 1st H. A......Sept., 1862	From New Organization..........	To 1-Brig. Def. North Pot.....	Oct., 1862

1st BRIGADE.—   COMMANDER.

A. A. Gibson	Col. 2d Penna. Heavy Arty.........	Oct. .., 1862, to Feb. .., 1863.	
3d Me. Batty. Arty......Oct., 1862	From Pontooneers 3-Corps Army Va.	To 1-Brig. Def. North Pot. 22-Corps.	Feb., 1863
2d Penna. H. A......Oct., 1862	From Def. North Potomac..........	To 1-Brig. Def. North Pot. 22-Corps.	Feb., 1863
11th Vt., 1st H. A......Oct., 1862	From Def. North Potomac..........	To 1-Brig. Def. North Pot. 22-Corps.	Feb., 1863
143d Penna. Infy......Oct., 1862	From New Organization..........	To 2-Brig. 3-Div. 1-Corps Potomac.	Jan., 1863

2d BRIGADE.—   COMMANDER.

L. O. Morris	Col. 7th N. Y. Heavy Arty.........	Oct., 1862, to Feb., 1863.	
16th Ind. Batty......Oct., 1862	From Arty. 2-Div. 12Corps Potomac.	To Ft. Washington Def. Wash. 22-C.	Feb., 1863
1st Me. Heavy Arty......Oct., 1862	From Def. North Potomac........	To 2-Brig. Def. North Pot. 22-Corps.	Feb., 1863
7th N. Y. Heavy Arty...Oct., 1862	From Def. North Potomac........	To 2-Brig. Def. North Pot. 22-Corps.	Feb., 1863
9th N. Y. Heavy Arty...Oct., 1862	From Def. North Potomac........	To 2-Brig. Def. North Pot. 22-Corps.	Feb., 1863
22d N. Y. Indpt. Batty...Dec., 1862	From Mil. Dist. Washington......	To Co. M, 9th N. Y. Heavy Arty...	Feb., 1863
117th N. Y. Infy. 2d Bn...Oct., 1862	From Def. North Potomac........	To 2-Brig. Def. North Pot. 22-C....	Feb., 1863

3d BRIGADE.—   COMMANDER.

W. R. Pease	Col. 117th N. Y. Infy..............	Oct., 1862, to Feb., 1863.	
5th Batt'n. N. Y. H. Arty.Oct., 1862	From Def. North Potomac........	To 3-Brig. Def. North Pot. 22-Corps.	Feb., 1863
6th Batt'n. N. Y. H. Arty.Oct., 1862	From Def. North Potomac........	To 3-Brig. Def. North Pot. 22-Corps.	Feb., 1863
7th Batt'n. N. Y. H. Arty.Oct., 1862	From Def. North Potomac........	To 3-Brig. Def. North Pot. 22-Corps.	Feb., 1863
117th N. Y. Infy 1st Batt'n.Oct., 1862	From Def. North Potomac........	To 3-Brig. Def. North Pot. 22-Corps.	Feb., 1863

WHIPPLE'S DIVISION.—   COMMANDER.

A. W. Whipple	Brigadier General...............		

PIATT'S BRIGADE.—   COMMANDER.

A. S. Piatt	Brigadier General...............		
86th N. Y. Infy......Aug., 1862	From Mil. Dist. Washington......	To 1-Brig. 3-Div. 3-Corps Potomac.	Nov., 1862
124th N. Y. Infy......Aug., 1862	From New Organization..........	To 1-Brig. 3-Div. 3-Corps Potomac.	Nov., 1862
122d Penna. Infy......Aug., 1862	From New Organization..........	To 1-Brig. 3-Div. 3-Corps Potomac.	Nov., 1862
63d Ind. Infy......Aug., 1862	From Sturgis' Brig. Dist. Wash.....	To Indianapolis, Ind..............	Oct., 1862

2d BRIGADE.— COMMANDER.

S. S. Carroll	Col. 4th Ohio Infy	

1st W. Va. Infy	Sept., 1862	From 4-Brig. 2-Div. 3-Corps Va...	To Dept. W. Va.	Nov., 1862
84th Penna. Infy	Sept., 1862	From 4-Brig. 2-Div. 3-Corps Va...	To 2-Brig. 3-Div. 3-Corps Potomac.	Nov., 1862
110th Penna. Infy	Sept., 1862	From 4-Brig. 2-Div. 3-Corps Va...	To 2-Brig. 3-Div. 3-Corps Potomac.	Nov., 1862
163d N. Y. Infy	Oct., 1862	From New Organization	To 2-Brig. 3-Div. 3-Corps Potomac.	Nov., 1862

UNATTACHED.—

12th N. H. Infy	Sept. 1862	From New Organization	To 2-Brig. 3-Div. 3-Corps Potomac.	Nov., 1862
Batty. H, 1st Ohio Arty.	Sept., 1862	From Mil. Dist. Washington	To Arty. 3-Div. 3-Corps Potomac...	Nov., 1862

CASEY'S DIVISION.— COMMANDER.

Silas Casey	Major General	Oct., 1862, to Feb., 1863.

1st BRIGADE.— COMMANDERS.

Dexter Wright	Col. 15th Conn. Infy	Oct., 1862, to Dec., 1862.
F. Fessenden	Col. 25th Me. Infy	Dec., 1862, to Feb., 1863.

15th Conn. Infy	Oct., 1862	From Casey's Prov'l. Brig. Wash.	To 2-Brig. 3-Div. 9-Corps Potomac.	Dec., 1862
13th N. H. Infy	Oct., 1862	From New Organization	To 1-Brig. 3-Div. 9-Corps Potomac.	Dec., 1862
12th R. I. Infy	Oct., 1862	From New Organization	To 1-Brig. 2-Div. 9-Corps Potomac.	Dec., 1862
25th N. J. Infy	Oct., 1862	From Dist. Washington	To 1-Brig. 3-Div. 9-Corps Potomac.	Dec., 1862
27th N. J. Infy	Oct., 1862	From Dist. Washington	To 2-Brig. 1-Div. 9-Corps Potomac.	Dec., 1862
25th Me. Infy	Dec., 1862	From 3-Brig. Casey's Div	To 1-Brig. Casey's Div. 22-Corps.	Feb., 1863
27th Me. Infy	Dec., 1862	From 3-Brig. Casey's Div	To 1-Brig. Casey's Div. 22-Corps.	Feb., 1863

2d BRIGADE.— COMMANDERS.

A. P. Blount	Col. 12th Vt. Infy	Oct., 1862, to Nov. 5, 1862.
E. H. Stoughton	Brigadier General	Nov. 5, 1862, to Feb., 1863.

12th Vt. Infy	Oct., 1862	From New Organization	To 2-Brig. Casey's Div. 22-Corps.	Feb., 1863
13th Vt. Infy	Oct., 1862	From New Organization	To 2-Brig. Casey's Div. 22-Corps.	Feb., 1863
14th Vt. Infy	Oct., 1862	From New Organization	To 2-Brig. Casey's Div. 22-Corps.	Feb., 1863
15th Vt. Infy	Oct., 1862	From New Organization	To 2-Brig. Casey's Div. 22-Corps.	Feb., 1863
16th Vt. Infy	Oct., 1862	From New Organization	To 2-Brig. Casey's Div. 22-Corps.	Feb., 1863
2d Conn. Indpt. Batty.	Oct., 1862	From New Organization	To Arty. Casey's Div. 22-Corps.	Feb., 1863
Batty. H, 1st R. I. Arty.	Oct., 1862	From New Organization	To Arty. Casey's Div. 22-Corps.	Feb., 1863

3d BRIGADE.— COMMANDERS.

Frank Fessenden	Col. 25th Me. Infy	Oct., 1862, to Dec., 1862.
Alex. Hays	Brigadier General	Dec., 1862, to Feb., 1863.

22d Me. Infy	Oct., 1862	From New Organization	To Dept. of the Gulf	Dec., 1862
25th Me. Infy	Oct., 1862	From New Organization	To 1-Brig. Casey's Div	Dec., 1862
26th Me. Infy	Oct., 1862	From New Organization	To Dept. of the Gulf	Dec., 1862
27th Me. Infy	Oct., 1862	From New Organization	To 1-Brig. Casey's Div	Dec., 1862
11th Mass. Indpt. Batty.	Oct., 1862	From New Organization	To Arty. Casey's Div. 22-Corps.	Feb., 1863
Keystone Pa. Batty	Oct., 1862	From Casey's Prov'l. Brig	To Arty. Casey's Div. 22-Corps.	Feb., 1863
39th N. Y. Infy	Dec., 1862	From Camp Douglass, Ill	To 3-Brig. Casey's Div. 22-Corps.	Feb., 1863
111th N. Y. Infy	Dec., 1862	From Camp Douglass, Ill	To 3-Brig. Casey's Div. 22-Corps.	Feb., 1863
115th N. Y. Infy	Dec., 1862	From Camp Douglass, Ill	To Busteed's Indpt. Brig. 7-C. Va.	Dec., 1862
125th N. Y. Infy	Dec., 1862	From Camp Douglass, Ill	To 3-Brig. Casey's Div. 22-Corps.	Feb., 1863
126th N. Y. Infy	Dec., 1862	From Camp Douglass, Ill	To 3-Brig. Casey's Div. 22-Corps.	Feb., 1863
151st Penna. Infy	Dec., 1862	From New Organization	To 1-Brig. 3-Div. 1-Corps Potomac.	Feb., 1863

PROV'L. BRIG. CASEY'S DIVISION.

22d N. J. Infy	Oct., 1862	From Dist. of Washington	To Provost Guard Army Potomac.	Dec., 1862
29th N. J. Infy	Oct., 1862	From Dist. of Washington	To Provost Guard Army Potomac.	Dec., 1862
30th N. J. Infy	Oct., 1862	From Dist. of Washington	To Provost Guard Army Potomac.	Dec., 1862
31st N. J. Infy	Oct., 1862	From Dist. of Washington	To Provost Guard Army Potomac.	Dec., 1862
24th N. J. Infy	Oct., 1862	From Dist. of Washington	To 1-Brig. 3-Div. 2-Corps Potomac.	Dec., 1862
28th N. J. Infy	Oct., 1862	From Dist. of Washington	To 1-Brig. 3-Div. 2-Corps Potomac.	Dec., 1862

PROV'L. CAVALRY BRIGADE.— COMMANDER.

J. T. Copeland	Colonel 5th Mich. Cav.	

5th Mich. Cav.	Dec., 1862	From New Organization	To 1-Brig. Cav. Div. 22-Corps.	Feb., 1862
6th Mich. Cav.	Dec., 1862	From New Organization	To 1-Brig. Cav. Div. 22-Corps.	Feb., 1862

ABERCROMBIE'S DIVISION.— COMMANDER.

J. J. Abercrombie	Brigadier General	

2d BRIGADE.— COMMANDER.

R. Cowden	Brigadier General	Oct., 1862, to Feb., 1863.

22d Conn. Infy	Oct., 1862	From New Organization	To 2-Brig. Abercrombie's Div. 22-C.	Feb., 1863
40th Mass. Infy	Oct., 1862	From New Organization	To 2-Brig. Abercrombie's Div. 22-C.	Feb., 1863
16th W. Va. Infy	Oct., 1862	From New Organization	To 2-Brig. Abercrombie's Div. 22-C.	Feb., 1863
141st N. Y. Infy	Oct., 1862	From New Organization	To 2-Brig. Abercrombie's Div. 22-C.	Feb., 1863

3d BRIGADE.— COMMANDER.

William Gurney	Col. 127th N. Y. Infy	Oct., 1862, to Feb., 1863.

127th N. Y. Infy	Oct., 1862	From New Organization	To 3-Brig. Abercrombie's Div. 22-C.	Feb., 1863
142d N. Y. Infy	Oct., 1862	From New Organization	To 3-Brig. Abercrombie's Div. 22-C.	Feb., 1863
143d N. Y. Infy	Oct., 1862	From New Organization	To 3-Brig. Abercrombie's Div. 22-C.	Feb., 1863
144th N. Y. Infy	Oct., 1862	From New Organization	To 3-Brig. Abercrombie's Div. 22-C.	Feb., 1863

PROV'L. BRIGADE.— COMMANDER.

Clarence Buell	Col. 169th N. Y. Infy	Oct., 1862, to Feb., 1863.

119th N. Y. Infy	Oct., 1862	From New Organization	To Dist. Washington 22-Corps.	Feb., 1863
152d N. Y. Infy	Oct., 1862	From New Organization	To Dist. Washington 22-Corps.	Feb., 1863
153 New York Infy	Oct., 1862	From New Organization	To Dist. Alexandria 22-Corps.	Feb., 1863
169th New York Infy	Oct., 1862	From New Organization	To Dist. Alexandria 22-Corps.	Feb., 1863

ARTILLERY.—

9th Mass. Indpt. Batty.	Oct., 1862	From New Organization	To Arty. Abercrombie's D. 22-Corps	Feb., 1863
17th N. Y. Indpt. Batty.	Oct., 1862	From Dist. Washington	To Arty. Abercrombie's D. 22-Corps	Feb., 1863
4th N. Y. Heavy Arty.	Oct., 1862	From Whipple's Command	To Arty. Abercrombie's D. 22-Corps	Feb., 1863

DISTRICT ALEXANDRIA.— COMMANDER.

John P. Slough	Brigadier General	Oct., 1862, to Feb., 1863.	
1st Dist. Columbia Infy...Oct., 1862	From 3-Brig. 2-Div. 12-Corps Pot.	To Dist. Alexandria 22-Corps	Feb., 1863
26th Michigan Infy......Oct., 1862	From New Organization	To Dist. Alexandria 22-Corps	Feb., 1863
153d New York Infy......Oct., 1862	From Prov'l Brig. Abercrombie's D.	To Dist. Alexandria 22-Corps	Feb., 1863
11th Rhode Island Infy...Oct., 186.	From Dist. Washington	To Dist. Alexandria 22-Corps	Feb., 1863

ARTILLERY, DISTRICT ALEXANDRIA.— COMMANDER.

R. O. Tyler	Brigadier General.		
1st Conn Heavy Arty....Oct., 1862	From Dist. Washington	To Arty. Def. Alexandria 22-Corps.	Feb., 1865
19th Conn., 2d H. A.....Oct., 1862	From Dist. Washington	To Arty. Def. Alexandria 22-Corps.	Feb., 1863
14th Mass, 1st H. A.....Oct., 1862	From Whipple's Command So. Pot.	To Arty. Def. Alexandria 22-Corps.	Feb., 1863
2d New York Heavy A...Oct., 1862	From Whipple's Command So. Pot.	To Arty. Def. Alexandria 22-Corps.	Feb., 1863
3d Battn. N. Y. Heavy A...Oct., 1862	From Whipple's Command So. Pot.	To Arty. Def. Alexandria 22-Corps.	Feb., 1863
1st Wis. Heavy A. Co. A..Oct., 1862	From Whipple's Command So. Pot.	To Arty. Def. Alexandria 22-Corps.	Feb., 1863
34th Mass. Infy.........Oct., 1862	From Dist. Washington	To Arty. Def. Alexandria 22-Corps.	Feb., 1863

CAVALRY BRIGADE.— COMMANDER.

R. Butler Price	Col. 2d Penna. Cav.		
1st Michigan Cav.......Sept., 1862	From Cav. Brig. 2-Corps Army Va.	To 2-Brig. Cav. Div. 22-Corps	Feb., 1863
1st New Jer. Cav. Det...Sept., 1862	From Bayard's Cav. B. 3-Corps Va.	To Bayard's Cav. Brig. Potomac..	Sept., 1862
5th New York Cav......Sept., 1862	From Cav. Brig. 2-Corps Army Va.	To 3-Brig. Cav. Div. 22-Corps	Mch., 1863
1st Ohio Cav. Cos. A, C..Sept., 1862	From Headqrs. 2-Corps Army Va...	To 2-Brig. Cav. Div. 22-Corps	Mch., 1863
2d Penna. Cav.........Sept., 1862	From Cav. Brig. 2-Corps Army Va.	To 2-Brig. Cav. Div. 22-Corps	Mch., 1863
18th Penna. Cav.......Sept., 1862	From New Organization	To 3-Brig. Cav. Div. 22-Corps	Mch., 1863
1st Vermont Cav......Sept., 1862	From Cav. Brig. 2-Corps Army Va.	To 3-Brig. Cav. Div. 22-Corps	Mch., 1863
1st West Va. Cav......Sept., 1862	From Cav. Brig. 2-Corps Army Va.	To 3-Brig. Cav. Div. 22-Corps	Mch., 1863

Department of Virginia

Created May, 1861. Troops of the Department organized into the 7th Army Corps July 22, 1862. Department merged into Department of Virginia and North Carolina July 15, 1863. Department recreated Jany. 31, 1865.

COMMANDERS.

B. F. Butler	Major General	May 22, 1861, to Aug. 17, 1861.	
John E. Wool	Major General	Aug. 17, 1861, to June 2, 1862.	
John A. Dix	Major General	June 2, 1862, to July 15, 1863.	
George W. Getty	Brigadier General	July 15, 1863, to July 20, 1863.	
E. O. O. Ord	Major General	Jan. 31, 1865, to Apr. 16, 1865.	
H. W. Halleck	Major General	Apr. 16, 1865, to June 28, 1865.	

Department also known as Army of the James from Jan. 31, 1865.

FORTRESS MONROE AND CAMP HAMILTON.—

3d Mass. Infy..........Apr., 1861	From New Organization	No change to Muster Out	July, 1861
4th Mass. Infy..........Apr., 1861	From New Organization	To Newport News, Va.	May, 1861
1st Vermont Infy.......May, 1861	From New Organization	To Newport News, Va.	May, 1861
1st New York Infy......May, 1861	From New Organization	To Newport News, Va.	May, 1861
2d New York Infy......May, 1861	From New Organization	To Newport News, Va.	May, 1861
99th New York Infy.....May, 1861	From New Organization	To Robinson's Brig. Dept. Va.	May, 1862
3d New York Infy.......June, 1861	From New Organization	To Baltimore, Md.	July, 1861
10th New York Infy......June, 1861	From New Organization	To Viele's Brig. Dept. Va.	May, 1862
20th New York Infy......June, 1861	From New Organization	To Weber's Brig. Dept. Va.	May, 1862
1st Battn. Mass. Infy....June, 1861	From Indpt. Cos. at'ch'd to 3d & 4th	To Newport News, Va.	July, 1861
16th Mass. Infy.........Aug., 1861	From New Organization	To Viele's Brig. Dept. Va.	May, 1862
20th Indiana Infy.......Sept., 1861	From New Organization	To Robinson's Brig. Dept. Va.	May, 1862
1st Delaware Infy.......Oct., 1861	From New Organization	To Weber's Brig. Dept. Va.	May, 1862
1st Michigan Infy.......Mch., 1862	From R. R. Brigade Army Potomac	To Robinson's Brig. Dept. Va.	May, 1862
5th Maryland Infy.......Mch., 1862	From Dix's Div. Baltimore, Md....	To Weber's Brig. Div. at Suffolk.	July, 1862
58th Penna. Infy........Mch., 1862	From New Organization	To Weber's Brig. Dept. Va.	May, 1862
99th New York Infy.....May, 1862	From Robinson's Brig. Dept. Va...	To Viele's Command Norfolk	July, 1862

ARTILLERY.—

Batty. D, 4th U. S. Arty..Apr., 1861	From Regular Army	To Viele's Command Norfolk, Va...	July, 1862
Batty. L, 4th U. S. Arty..Apr., 1861	From Regular Army	To Division at Suffolk, 7-Corps....	July, 1862
7th Mass. Indpt. Batty...May, 1861	From New Organization	To Newport News, Va.	May, 1861
2d Wisconsin Batty.....Jan., 1862	From New Organization	To Fortress Monroe 7-Corps.	July, 1862
4th Wisconsin Batty.....Jan., 1862	From New Organization	To Fortress Monroe 7-Corps.	July, 1862

CAVALRY.—

1st N. Y. Mounted Rifles..July, 1861	From New Organization	To Div. at Suffolk 7-Corps.	July, 1862
11th Penna. Cav.........Nov., 1861	From New Organization	To Div. at Suffolk 7-Corps.	July, 1862

NEWPORT NEWS, VA.—

4th Mass. Infy..........May, 1861	From Camp Hamilton, Va.	No change to Muster Out.	July, 1861
1st Vermont Infy.......May, 1861	From Camp Hamilton, Va.	No change to Muster Out.	July, 1861
7th New York Infy......June, 1861	From New Organization	To 1-Brig. 1-Div. 2-Corps Potomac	May, 1862
1st New York Infy......June, 1861	From Camp Hamilton, Va.	To Viele's Brig. Dept. Va.	May, 1862
4th New York Infy......June, 1861	From Camp Hamilton, Va.	To Baltimore, Md.	July, 1861
5th New York Infy......June, 1861	From New Organization	To Baltimore, Md.	July, 1861
9th New York Infy......June, 1861	From New Organization	To 3-Brig Burnside's Expedition...	Jan., 1862
2d New York Infy......July, 1861	From Camp Hamilton, Va.	To Viele's Brig. Dept. Va.	May, 1862
1st Mass. Battn. Infy....Aug., 1861	From Camp Hamilton, Va.	Transferred to 29th Mass.	Dec., 1861
11th New York Infy.....Oct., 1861	From New York	To New York.	May, 1862
29th Mass. Infy.........Dec., 1861	From New Organization	To Viele's Brig. Dept. Va.	May, 1862
3d New York Infy.......June, 1862	From Dix's Div., Baltimore, Md....	To Weber's Brig. Div. at Suffolk..	July, 1862
4th New York Infy......June, 1862	From Dix's Div., Baltimore, Md....	To Weber's Brig. Div. at Suffolk..	July, 1862

ARTILLERY.—

7th Mass. Indpt. Batty...May, 1861	From Camp Hamilton, Va.	To Yorktown, Va.	July, 1862

VIELE'S BRIGADE.— COMMANDER.

Egbert L. Viele	Brigadier General	May 8, 1862, to June 1, 1862.	
1st New York Infy......May, 1862	From Newport News, Va.	To 3-Brig. 1-Div. 3-Corps Potomac	June, 1862
2d New York Infy......May, 1862	From Newport News, Va.	To 3-Brig. 2-Div. 3-Corps Potomac	June, 1862
10th New York Infy.....May, 1862	From Camp Hamilton, Va.	To 3-Brig. 2-Div. 5-Corps Potomac	June, 1862
16th Mass. Infy.........May, 1862	From Fortress Monroe, Va.	To 1-Brig. 2-Div. 3-Corps Potomac	June, 1862
29th Mass. Infy.........May, 1862	From Newport News, Va.	To 2-Brig. 1-Div. 2-Corps Potomac	June, 1862

WEBER'S BRIGADE.—

COMMANDER.

Max Weber	Brigadier General	May 8, 1862, to July 22, 1862.

1st Delaware Infy	May, 1862	From Camp Hamilton, Va	To Weber's Brig. Div. at Suffolk.. July, 1862
20th New York Infy	May, 1862	From Camp Hamilton, Va	To 3-Brig. 6-Div. 6-Corps Potomac June, 1862
58th Penna. Infy	May, 1862	From Camp Hamilton, Va	To Viele's Comm'd Norfolk 7-Corps July, 1862

ROBINSON'S BRIGADE.—

COMMANDER.

J. C. Robinson	Brigadier General	May 8, 1862, to May 28, 1862.

1st Michigan Infy	May, 1862	From Camp Hamilton, Va	To 1-Brig. 1-Div. 5-Corps Potomac May, 1862
20th Indiana Infy	May, 1862	From Newport News, Va	To 1-Brig. 3-Div. 3-Corps Potomac May, 1862
99th New York Infy	May, 1862	From Camp Hamilton, Va	To Camp Hamilton, Va May, 1862

UNATTACHED.—

Batty. D, 4th U. S. Arty	May, 1862	From Fortress Monroe, Va	To Arty. Div. at Suffolk 7-Corps.. July, 1862
Batty. L, 4th U. S. Arty	May, 1862	From Fortress Monroe, Va	To Arty. Div. at Suffolk 7-Corps.. July, 1862
7th Mass. Indpt. Batty	May, 1862	From Newport News, Va	To Arty. Yorktown, Va July, 1862
1st N. Y. Mounted Rifles	May, 1862	From Camp Hamilton, Va	To Unatt. Div. at Suffolk, 7-Corps.. July, 1862
11th Penna. Cav	May, 1862	From Camp Hamilton, Va	To Unatt. Div. at Suffolk, 7-Corps.. July, 1862

Seventh Army Corps

Organized July 22, 1862, from troops at Fortress Monroe, Camp Hamilton, Norfolk, Suffolk, Portsmouth, and Yorktown, Va., Department of Virginia. Discontinued Aug. 1, 1863, and troops merged into the Department of Virginia and North Carolina.

COMMANDERS.

John A. Dix	Major General	July 22, 1862, to July 16, 1863.
H. M. Naglee	Brigadier General	July 16, 1863, to July 20, 1863.
G. W. Getty	Brigadier General	July 20, 1863, to Aug. 1, 1863.

FORTRESS MONROE.—

2d Wis. Indpt. Batty	July, 1862	From Fortress Monroe, Dept. Va..	To Camp Hamilton, Va. 7-Corps.. Sept., 1862
4th Wis. Indpt. Batty	July, 1862	From Fortress Monroe, Dept. Va..	To Camp Hamilton, Va. 7-Corps.... Sept., 1862
3d New York Infy	Sept., 1862	From Div. at Suffolk 7-Corps	To Camp Hamilton, Va. 7-Corps.... Apr., 1863

CAMP HAMILTON, VA.—

5th Maryland Infy	July, 1862	From Fort. Monroe, Va. Dept. Va.	To Weber's Br. Div. at Suffolk 7-C. Sept., 1862
99th New York Infy	July, 1862	From Robinson's Brig. Dept. Va...	To Viele's Comnd. Norfolk 7-Corps July, 1862
7th New York Batty	July, 1862	From Arty. 2-Div. 4-Corps Potomac	To Viele's Comnd. Norfolk 7-Corps Sept., 1862
2d Wis. Indpt. Batty	Sept., 1862	From Fort. Monroe, Va., 7-Corps..	To Div. at Suffolk 7-Corps Jan., 1863
4th Wis. Indpt. Batty	Sept., 1862	From Fort. Monroe, Va., 7-Corps..	To Div. at Suffolk 7-Corps Jan., 1863
139th New York Infy	Sept., 1862	From New Organization	To Busteed's Indpt. Brig. 7-Corps.. Dec., 1862
3d Penna. Heavy Arty	Sept., 1862	From New Organization	To Ft. Monroe, Va., D. Va. & N. C. Aug., 1862

NORFOLK, VA.—

COMMANDER.

Egbert L. Viele	Brigadier General	July 22, 1862, to Aug. 1, 1863.

58th Penna. Infy	July, 1862	From Weber's Brig. Dept. Va	To Foster's Prov'l Brig. Div. Suffolk Oct., 1862
99th New York Infy	July, 1862	From Camp Hamilton, Va	To Terry's Brig. Div. Suffolk 7-C. Feb., 1863
19th Wisconsin Infy	July, 1862	From New Organization	To Reserve Brig. 7-Corps Apr., 1863
Batty. D, 4th U. S. Arty	July, 1862	From Fortress Monroe, Va	To Unatt. Arty. 7-Corps Apr., 1863
7th N. Y. Indpt. Batty	Sept., 1862	From Camp Hamilton, Va., 7-Corps	To U. S. Forces N'rf'k, D. Va. & N. C. July, 1863
148th New York Infy	Sept., 1862	From New Organization	To U. S. Forces N'rf'k, D. Va. & N. C. July, 1863
158th New York Infy	Nov., 1862	From New Organization	To Spinola's Brig. Div. Suffolk 7-C. Nov., 1862
173d Penna. Infy	Dec., 1862	From New Organization	To 1-Brig. 2-Div. 11-Corps Potomac July, 1863
177th Penna. Infy	Mch., 1863	From Terry's Brig. Div. Suffolk 7-C.	To 2-Brig. 2-Div. 12-Corps Potomac July, 1863

DIVISION AT SUFFOLK.—

COMMANDERS.

J. K. F. Mansfield	Brigadier General	July 22, 1862, to Sept. 8, 1862.
John J. Peck	Major General	Sept. 8, 1862, to Sept. 30, 1862.
M. Corcoran	Brigadier General	Sept. 30, 1862, to Jan. 2, 1863.
John J. Peck	Major General	Jan. 2, 1863, to Apr. 6, 1863.
E. D. Keyes	Major General	Apr. 6, 1863, to Apr. 14, 1863.
John J. Peck	Major General	Apr. 14, 1863, to Aug. 1, 1863.

WEBER'S BRIGADE.—

Max Weber	Brigadier General	July 22, 1862, to Sept. 8, 1862.

1st Del. Infy	July, 1862	From Weber's Brig. Dept. Va	To 3-Brig. 3-Div. 2-Corps Potomac Sept., 1862
2d N. Y. Infy	July, 1862	From Newport News, Va	To Fort Monroe, Va., 7-Corps Sept., 1862
4th N. Y. Infy	July, 1862	From Newport News, Va	To 3-Brig. 3-Div. 2-Corps Potomac Sept., 1862
5th Md. Infy	Sept., 1862	From Camp Hamilton, Va., 7-Corps.	To 3-Brig. 3-Div. 2-Corps Potomac Sept., 1862
13th N. Y. S. M. Infy	Sept., 1862	From Dix's Div. Balto., Md	No change to Muster Out Sept., 1862
25th N. Y. S. M. Infy	Sept., 1862	From Camp Hamilton, Va., 7-Corps.	No change to Muster Out Sept., 1862

WESSELL'S BRIGADE.—

COMMANDER.

H. W. Wessels	Brigadier General	Sept. 26, 1862, to Dec. 24, 1862.

Brigade transferred to Dept. North Carolina, Dec., 1862.

85th N. Y. Infy	Sept., 1862	From 2-Brig. 2-Div. 4-Corps Pot....	To 1-Brig. 1-Div. Dept. N. C Dec., 1862
92d N. Y. Infy	Sept., 1862	From 2-Brig. 2-Div. 4-Corps Pot....	To 1-Brig. 1-Div. Dept. N. C Dec., 1862
96th N. Y. Infy	Sept., 1862	From 2-Brig. 2-Div. 4-Corps Pot....	To 1-Brig. 1-Div. Dept. N. C Dec., 1862
85th Penna. Infy	Sept., 1862	From 2-Brig. 2-Div. 4-Corps Pot....	To 1-Brig. 1-Div. Dept. N. C Dec., 1862
101st Penna. Infy	Sept., 1862	From 2-Brig. 2-Div. 4-Corps Pot....	To 1-Brig. 1-Div. Dept. N. C Dec., 1862
103d Penna. Infy	Sept., 1862	From 2-Brig. 2-Div. 4-Corps Pot....	To 1-Brig. 1-Div. Dept. N. C Dec., 1862

FERRY'S BRIGADE.—

COMMANDER.

O. S. Ferry	Brigadier General	Sept. 23, 1862, to Dec. 26, 1862.

Brigade transferred to Dept. North Carolina, Dec., 1862.

13th Ind. Infy	Sept., 1862	From 3-Brig. 2-Div. 4-Corps Pot....	To Foster's Prov'l Brig. 7-Corps... Sept., 1862
39th Ill. Infy	Sept., 1862	From 3-Brig. 2-Div. 4-Corps Pot....	To 1-B. 3-Div. 18-Corps Dept. N. C. Jan., 1863
62d Ohio Infy	Sept., 1862	From 3-Brig. 2-Div. 4-Corps Pot....	To 1-B. 3-Div. 18-Corps Dept. N. C. Jan., 1863
67th Ohio Infy	Sept., 1862	From 3-Brig. 2-Div. 4-Corps Pot....	To 1-B. 3-Div. 18-Corps Dept. N. C. Jan., 1863
174th Penna. Infy	Dec., 1862	From New Organization	To 2-B. 3-Div. 18-Corps Dept. N. C. Jan., 1863
176th Penna. Infy	Dec., 1862	From Foster's Prov'l Brig. 7-Corps	To 1-B. 3-Div. 18-Corps Dept. N. C. Jan., 1863

FOSTER'S PROV'L BRIGADE.— COMMANDER.

R. S. Foster	Col. 13th Indiana Infy	Sept. 23, 1862, to April 9, 1863.	

13th Indiana Infy	Sept., 1862	From Ferry's B. Div. Suffolk 7-C.	To 2-Brig. 1-Div. 7-Corps Va	Apr., 1863
6th Mass. Infy	Sept., 1862	From New Organization	To 2-Brig. 1-Div. 7-Corps Va	Apr., 1863
112th New York Infy	Sept., 1862	From New Organization	To Gibbs' Prov'l Brig. Div. Suffolk	Dec., 1862
130th New York Infy	Sept., 1862	From New Organization	To Gibbs' Prov'l Brig. Div. Suffolk	Dec., 1862
58th Penna. Infy	Oct., 1862	From Norfolk, Va., 7-Corps	To Gibbs' Prov'l Brig. Div. Suffolk	Dec., 1862
165th Penna. Infy	Dec., 1862	From New Organization	To 2-Brig. 1-Div. 7-Corps Va	Apr., 1863
166th Penna. Infy	Dec., 1862	From New Organization	To 2-Brig. 1-Div. 7-Corps Va	Apr., 1863
167th Penna. Infy	Dec., 1862	From New Organization	To 1-Brig. 1-Div. 7-Corps Va	Apr., 1863
176th Penna. Infy	Dec., 1862	From New Organization	To Ferry's B. Div. at Suffolk 7-C.	Dec., 1862

EMPIRE BRIGADE.— COMMANDER.

F. B. Spinola	Brigadier General	Oct. 1, 1862, to Dec. 28, 1863.	

132d New York Infy	Oct., 1862	From New Organization	To 1-B. 5-Div. 18-Corps Dept. N. C.	Jan., 1863
158th Penna. Infy	Oct., 1862	From New Organization	To 1-B. 5-Div. 18-Corps Dept. N. C.	Jan., 1863
168th Penna. Infy	Oct., 1862	From New Organization	To 2-B. 5-Div. 18-Corps Dept. N. C.	Jan., 1863
171st Penna. Infy	Oct., 1862	From New Organization	To 1-B. 5-Div. 18-Corps Dept. N. C.	Jan., 1863
158th New York Infy	Dec., 1862	From Viele's Command Norfolk 7-C.	To 2-B. 5-Div. 18-Corps Dept. N. C.	Jan., 1863
175th Penna. Infy	Dec., 1862	From Gibbs' Prov'l B. D. at Suffolk.	To 1-B. 5-Div. 18-Corps Dept. N. C.	Jan., 1863

CORCORAN'S BRIGADE.— COMMANDER.

M. Corcoran	Brigadier General	Nov., 1862, to April 9, 1863.	

155th New York Infy	Nov., 1862	From New Organization	To 3-Brig. 1-Div. 7-Corps Va	Apr., 1863
164th New York Infy	Nov., 1862	From New Organization	To 3-Brig. 1-Div. 7-Corps Va	Apr., 1863
170th New York Infy	Nov., 1862	From New Organization	To 3-Brig. 1-Div. 7-Corps Va	Apr., 1863
182d (69-N. G. Art.) N. Y.	Nov., 1862	From New Organization	To 3-Brig. 1-Div. 7-Corps Va	Apr., 1863

GIBBS' 2d PROV'L BRIGADE.— COMMANDERS.

Alfred Gibbs	Col. 130th New York Infy	Dec. 5, 1862, to Jan. 21, 1863.	
H. D. Terry	Brigadier General	Jan. 21, 1863, to Apr. 9, 1863.	

112th New York Infy	Dec., 1862	From Foster's Brig. Div. Suffolk	To 2-Brig. 1-Div. 7-Corps Va	Apr., 1863
130th New York Infy	Dec., 1862	From Foster's Brig. Div. Suffolk	To 1-Brig. 1-Div. 7-Corps	Apr., 1863
58th Penna. Infy	Dec., 1862	From Foster's Brig. Div. Suffolk	To 2-B. 3-Div. 18-Corps Dept. N. C.	Jan., 1863
175th Penna. Infy	Dec., 1862	From New Organization	To Spinola's Brig. Div. Suffolk	Dec., 1862
177th Penna. Infy	Dec., 1862	From New Organization	To Viele's Command Norfolk, Va.	Mch., 1863
1st Battn. N. Y. Shrpshtrs.	Feb., 1863	From New Organization	To 1-Brig. 1-Div. 7-Corps Va	Apr., 1863
99th New York Infy	Feb., 1863	From Viele's Command Norfolk, Va.	To Reserve Brig. 7-Corps Va	Apr., 1863

1st DIVISION.—Organized April 9, 1863. COMMANDER.

M. Corcoran	Brigadier General	Apr. 9, 1863, to July 11, 1863.	

1st BRIGADE.— COMMANDER.

H. D. Terry	Brigadier General	Apr. 9, 1863, to July 11, 1863.	

130th New York Infy	Apr., 1863	From Terry's Prvl. B. D. Suffolk, Va.	To Def. Washington 22-Corps	July, 1863
152d New York Infy	Apr., 1863	From Defences of Washington	To New York Dept. East	July, 1863
1st Battn. New York S. S.	Apr., 1863	From Terry's Prvl. B. D. Suffolk, Va.	To 1-Brig. 1-Div. 1-Corps Potomac	July, 1863
167th Penna. Infy	Apr., 1863	From Terry's Prvl. B. D. Suffolk, Va.	To 1-Brig. 1-Div. 1-Corps Potomac	July, 1863
11th Rhode Island Infy	Apr., 1863	From Dist. Alexandria 22-Corps	To 2-Brig. 1-Div. 4-Corps Va	June, 1863
26th Michigan Infy	Apr., 1863	From Dist. Alexandria 22-Corps	To New York Dept. East	July, 1863

2d BRIGADE.— COMMANDER.

R. S. Foster	Brigadier General	April 9, 1863, to July 7, 1863.	

13th Indiana Infy	Apr., 1863	From Foster's Brig. Div. Suffolk	To Folly Island, S. C., 10-Corps So.	July, 1863
6th Mass. Infy	Apr., 1863	From Foster's Brig. Div. Suffolk	No change to Muster Out	July, 1863
165th Penna. Infy	Apr., 1863	From Foster's Brig. Div. Suffolk	No change to Muster Out	July, 1863
166th Penna. Infy	Apr., 1863	From Foster's Brig. Div. Suffolk	No change to Muster Out	July, 1863
112th New York Infy	Apr., 1863	From Gibbs' Brig. Div. at Suffolk	To Folly Island, S. C., 10-Corps So.	July, 1863
169th New York Infy	Apr., 1863	From Dist. Washington 22-Corps	To Folly Island, S. C., 10-Corps So.	July, 1863
7th Mass. Indpt. Batty.	June, 1863	From Unatt. Arty. 7-Corps	To Camp Barry 22-Corps	July, 1863

3d BRIGADE, 1st DIVISION.— COMMANDER.

M. Murphey	Col. 182d New York Infy	April 9, 1863, to July 11, 1863.	

10th New Jersey Infy	Apr., 1863	From Dist. Washington 22-Corps	To Phila., Penna	July, 1863
155th New York Infy	Apr., 1863	From Corcoran's Brig. Div. Suffolk	To Corcoran's Brig. King's D. 22-C.	July, 1863
164th New York Infy	Apr., 1863	From Corcoran's Brig. Div. Suffolk	To Corcoran's Brig. King's D. 22-C.	July, 1863
170th New York Infy	Apr., 1863	From Corcoran's Brig. Div. Suffolk	To Corcoran's Brig. King's D. 22-C.	July, 1863
182d New York Infy	Apr., 1863	From Corcoran's Brig. Div. Suffolk	To Corcoran's Brig. King's D. 22-C.	July, 1863
ARTILLERY.—				
2d Wisconsin Batty	May, 1863	From Unatt. Arty. 7-Corps	To 2-Brig. 1-Div. 4-Corps Dept. Va.	June, 1863
4th Wisconsin Batty	May, 1863	From Unatt. Arty. 7-Corps	To Arty. 2-Div. 4-Corps Dept. Va.	June, 1863
1st Delaware Batty	June, 1863	From Unatt. Arty. 7-Corps	To Def. Washington 22-Corps	July, 1863
19th N. Y. Indpt. Batty.	June, 1863	From Unatt. Arty. 7-Corps	To Def. Washington 22-Corps	July, 1863
Batty. D, 4th U. S. Arty.	June, 1863	From Unatt. Arty. 7-Corps	To U. S. Forces Nrflk. D. Va. & N. C.	July, 1863
Batty. L, 4th U. S. Arty.	June, 1863	From Unatt. Arty. 7-Corps	To U. S. Forces Nrflk. D. Va. & N. C.	July, 1863

2d DIVISION.— COMMANDER.

Geo. W. Getty	Brigadier General	Mch. 21, 1863, to Aug. 1, 1863.	

1st BRIGADE.— COMMANDERS.

H. S. Fairchilds	Col. 89th New York Infy	Mch. 21, 1863, to Apr. 9, 1863.	
R. C. Hawkins	Col. 9th New York Infy	Apr. 9, 1863, to May 8, 1863.	
W. R. Pease	Col. 117th New York Infy	May 8, 1863, to June 17, 1863.	
S. M. Alford	Col. 3d New York Infy	June 17, 1863, to July 7, 1863.	

3d New York Infy	Apr., 1863	From Camp Hamilton, Va., 7-Corps	To 1-Brig. Getty's Div. Va. & N. C.	July, 1863
9th New York Infy	Apr., 1863	From 1-Brig. 3-Div. 9-Corps Pot	No change to Muster Out	May, 1863
89th New York Infy	Apr., 1863	From 1-Brig. 3-Div. 9-Corps Pot	To 1-Brig. Getty's Div. Va. & N. C.	July, 1863
103d New York Infy	Apr., 1863	From 1-Brig. 3-Div. 9-Corps Pot	To 1-Brig. Getty's Div. Va. & N. C.	July, 1863
117th New York Infy	Apr., 1863	From Defences of Washington 22-C.	To 1-Brig. Getty's Div. Va. & N. C.	July, 1863
10th New Hamp. Infy	Apr., 1863	From 1-Brig. 3-Div. 9-Corps Pot	To 2-Brig. Getty's Div. Va. & N. C.	July, 1863

2d BRIGADE.—

COMMANDER.

E. Harland............	Col. 8th Conn. Infy................	Mch. 21, 1863, to July 31, 1863.

8th Conn. Infy........Apr., 1863	From 2-Brig. 3-Div. 9-Corps Pot...	To 2-Brig. Getty's Div. Va. & N. C.	July, 1863
11th Conn. Infy.......Apr., 1863	From 2-Brig. 3-Div. 9-Corps Pot...	To 2-Brig. Getty's Div. Va. & N. C.	July, 1863
15th Conn. Infy.......Apr., 1863	From 2-Brig. 3-Div. 9-Corps Pot...	To 2-Brig. Getty's Div. Va. & N. C.	July, 1863
16th Conn. Infy.......Apr., 1863	From 2-Brig. 3-Div. 9-Corps Pot...	To 2-Brig. Getty's Div. Va. & N. C.	July, 1863

3d BRIGADE.—

COMMANDERS.

A. H. Dutton.........	Col. 21st Conn. Infy...............	Mch. 21, 1863, to July 29, 1863.
W. H. P. Steare.......	Col. 4th Rhode Island Infy......	July 29, 1863, to Aug. 1, 1863.

13th New Hamp. Infy....Apr., 1863	From 3-Brig. 3-Div. 9-Corps Pot...	To 3-Brig. Getty's Div. Va. & N. C.	July, 1863
4th Rhode Island Infy....Apr., 1863	From 3-Brig. 3-Div. 9-Corps Pot...	To 3-Brig. Getty's Div. Va. & N. C.	July, 1863
21st Conn. Infy.......Apr., 1863	From 3-Brig. 3-Div. 9-Corps Pot...	To 3-Brig. Getty's Div. Va. & N. C.	July, 1863
25th New Jersey Infy....Apr., 1863	From 3-Brig. 3-Div. 9-Corps Pot...	No change to Muster Out.........	June, 1863
ARTILLERY.—			
Batty. A, 1st Penna. A..Apr., 1863	From Arty. 3-Div. 9-Corps Potomac	To Getty's Div. Dept. Va. & N. C.	July, 1863
Batty. A, 5th U. S. Arty..Apr., 1863	From Arty. 3-Div. 9-Corps Potomac	To Getty's Div. Dept. Va. & N. C.	July, 1863

GURNEY'S DIVISION.—Joined Corps from Department of Washington 22d Corps April, 1863.

COMMANDER.

William Gurney........	Col. 127th New York Infy..........	Apr. 17, 1863, to May 4, 1863.

Division transferred to 4th Corps May, 1863.

PORTER'S BRIGADE.—

COMMANDER.

Burr Porter..........	Col. 40th Mass. Infy..............	Apr. 17, 1863, to May 4, 1863.

40th Mass. Infy.........Apr., 1863	From 2-B. Abercrombie's Div. 22-C.	To 2-Brig. 2-Div. 4-Corps Va......	May, 1863
22d Conn. Infy........Apr., 1863	From 2-B. Abercrombie's Div. 22-C.	To 2-Brig. 2-Div. 4-Corps Va......	May, 1863
141st New York Infy.....Apr., 1863	From 2-B. Abercrombie's Div. 22-C.	To 2-Brig. 2-Div. 4-Corps Va......	May, 1863

HUGHSTON'S BRIGADE.—

COMMANDER.

R. S. Hughston........	Col. 144th New York Infy..........	Apr. 17, 1863, to May 4, 1863.

127th New York Infy....Apr., 1863	From 3-B. Abercrombie's Div. 22-C.	To 1-Brig. 2-Div. 4-Corps Va......	May, 1863
142d New York Infy.....Apr., 1863	From 3-B. Abercrombie's Div. 22-C.	To 1-Brig. 2-Div. 4-Corps Va......	May, 1863
143d New York Infy.....Apr., 1863	From 3-B. Abercrombie's Div. 22-C.	To 1-Brig. 2-Div. 4-Corps Va......	May, 1863
144th New York Infy.....Apr., 1863	From 3-B. Abercrombie's Div. 22-C.	To 1-Brig. 2-Div. 4-Corps Va......	May, 1863

RESERVE BRIGADE.—Organized April 24, 1863. COMMANDERS.

D. W. Wardrop........	Col. 99th New York Infy..........	April 24, 1863, to May 13, 1863.
I. J. Wistar..........	Brigadier General................	May 13, 1863, to June, 1863.

9th Vermont Infy......Apr., 1862?	From Camp Douglass, Ill......	To Wistar's Indpt. Brig. 7-Corps..	June, 1863
99th New York Infy....Apr., 1862?	From Terry's Brig. Div. Suffolk....	To Wardrop's Indpt. Brig. 7-Corps	June, 1863
118th New York Infy....Apr., 1863	From Dist. Washington 22-Corps..	To Wardrop's Indpt. Brig. 7-Corps	June, 1863
19th Wisconsin Infy.....Apr., 1863	From Viele's Command Norfolk....	To Wistar's Indpt. Brig. 7-Corps..	June, 1863
UNATTACHED ARTILLERY.—			
7th Mass. Indpt. Batty...Apr., 1863	From Arty. Div. at Suffolk, 7-Corps	To 2-Brig. 1-Div. 7-Corps........	June, 1863
16th N. Y. Indpt. Batty..Apr., 1863	From Arty. Camp Washington 22-C	To Wistar's Indpt. Brig. 7-Corps..	June, 1863
19th N. Y. Indpt. Batty..Apr., 1863	From Arty. Camp Washington 22-C	To Arty. 1-Div. 7-Corps........	June, 1863
3d Penna. Heavy Arty...Apr., 1863	From Fort Monroe. Va., 7-Corps...	To Fort. Monroe Dept. Va. & N. C.	July, 1863
1st Delaware Batty......Apr., 1863	From Arty. Camp Washington 22-C.	To Arty. 1-Div. 7-Corps........	June, 1863
2d Wisconsin Batty.....Apr., 1863	From Arty. Div. at Suffolk, 7-Corps	To Arty. 1-Div. 7-Corps........	May, 1863
4th Wisconsin Batty.....Apr., 1863	From Arty. Div. at Suffolk, 7-Corps	To Arty. 1-Div. 7-Corps........	May, 1863
Batty. D, 4th U. S. Arty..Apr., 1863	From Viele's Command Norfolk, Va.	To Arty. 1-Div. 7-Corps........	June, 1863
Batty. L, 4th U. S. Arty..Apr., 1863	From Arty. Div. at Suffolk, 7-Corps	To Arty. 1-Div. 7-Corps........	June, 1863
CAVALRY.—			
1st N. Y. Mounted Rifles..Apr., 1863	From Cav. Div. at Suffolk 7-Corps	To Portsmouth, Va., D. Va. & N. C.	July, 1863
11th Penna. Cav........Apr., 1863	From Cav. Div. at Suffolk 7-Corps	To Portsmouth, Va., D. Va. & N. C.	July, 1863

SPINOLA'S INDPT. BRIGADE.—

COMMANDER.

F. B. Spinola........	Brigadier General................	June, 1863, to July, 1863.

158th Penna. Infy......June, 1863	From Dist. Pamlico, Dept. N. C....	No change to Muster Out.........	Aug., 1863
168th Penna. Infy......June, 1863	From Dist. Pamlico, Dept. N. C....	No change to Muster Out.........	July, 1863
171st Penna. Infy......June, 1863	From Dist. Pamlico, Dept. N. C....	No change to Muster Out.........	Aug., 1863

WARDROP'S INDPT. BRIGADE.—

COMMANDER.

D. W. Wardrop......	Col. 99th New York Infy..........	June, 1863, to July, 1863.

99th New York Infy....June, 1863	From Reserve Brigade 7-Corps....	To Yorktown, Va., D. Va. & N. C.	July, 1863
118th New York Infy....June, 1863	From Reserve Brigade 7-Corps....	To Yorktown, Va., D. Va. & N. C.	July, 1863

WISTAR'S INDPT. BRIGADE.—

COMMANDER.

I. J. Wistar..........	Brigadier General................	June, 1863, to July, 1863.

9th Vermont Infy......June, 1863	From Reserve Brigade 7-Corps....	To Yorktown, Va., D. Va. & N. C.	July, 1863
19th Wisconsin Infy.....June, 1863	From Reserve Brigade 7-Corps....	To Yorktown, Va., D. Va. & N. C.	July, 1863
16th N. Y. Indpt. Batty..June, 1863	From Reserve Brigade 7-Corps....	To Yorktown, Va., D. Va. & N. C.	July, 1863

YORKTOWN, VA.—

COMMANDER.

E. D. Keyes..........	Major General.

BUSTEED'S INDPT. BRIGADE—Organized Dec., 1862.

COMMANDERS.

R. Busteed..........	Brigadier General................	Dec. 15, 1862, to Apr. 1, 1863.
Rufus King..........	Brigadier General................	Apr. 1, 1863, to June, 1863.

169th Penna. Infy......Dec., 1862	From New Organization..........	To King's Brig. 4-Corps Va........	May, 1863
178th Penna. Infy......Dec., 1862	From New Organization..........	To West's Advance Brig. 7-Corps..	Apr., 1863
179th Penna. Infy......Dec., 1862	From New Organization..........	To King's Brig. 4-Corps Va........	May, 1863
4th Delaware Infy......Dec., 1862	From Unatt. 8-Corps..........	To West's Advance Brig. 7-Corps..	Apr., 1863
139th New York Infy....Dec., 1862	From Camp Hamilton, Va., 7-Corps	To King's Brig. 4-Corps Va........	May, 1863
168th New York Infy....Dec., 1862	From New Organization..........	To King's Brig. 4-Corps Va........	May, 1863
115th New York Infy....Dec., 1862	From Defences Washington 22-C.	To Dist. Hilton Head Dept. South..	Jan., 1863

WEST'S ADVANCE BRIGADE.—Organized April 12, 1863. Transferr ed to 4th Corps Va. May 4, 1863.

COMMANDER.

R. M. West	Col. 1st Penna. Light Arty	Apr. 12, 1863 to May 4, 1863.	
139th New York Infy....Apr., 1863	From King's Indpt. Brig. Yorktown	To Advance Brig. 4-Corps Va......	May, 1863
172d Penna. Infy........Apr., 1863	From Unatt. Yorktown, Va........	To Advance Brig. 4-Corps Va......	May, 1863
178th Penna. Infy.......Apr., 1863	From King's Indpt. Brig. Yorktown	To Advance Brig. 4-Corps Va......	May, 1863
5th Penna. Cav..........Apr., 1863	From Unatt. Yorktown, Va........	To Advance Brig. 4-Corps Va......	May, 1863
UNATTACHED.—			
172d Penna. Infy........Dec., 1862	From New Organization............	To West's Advance B. 7-Corps Va.	Apr., 1863
ARTILLERY.—			
Batty. F, 1st N. Y. Arty..Dec., 1862	From Res. Arty. 4-Corps Potomac.	To Unatt. Arty. 4-Corps Va.......	May, 1863
Batty. H, 1st N. Y. Arty..Dec., 1862	From Res. Arty. 4-Corps Potomac.	To Unatt. Arty. 4-Corps Va.......	May, 1863
8th N. Y. Indpt. Batty....Dec., 1862	From Res. Arty. 4-Corps Potomac.	To Unatt. Arty. 4-Corps Va.......	May, 1863
Batty. E, 1st Penna. A...Dec., 1862	From Res. Arty. 4-Corps Potomac.	To Unatt. Arty. 4-Corps Va.......	May, 1863
Batty. H, 1st Penna. A...Dec., 1862	From Res. Arty. 4-Corps Potomac.	To Unatt. Arty. 4-Corps Va.......	May, 1863
Batty. M, 5th U. S. Arty..Dec., 1862	From Res. Arty. 4-Corps Potomac.	To Unatt. Arty. 4-Corps Va.......	May, 1863
CAVALRY.—			
5th Penna. Cav..........Dec., 1862	From Unatt. Cav. Yorkt'n 4-Corps	To Advance Brigade 7-Corps......	Apr., 1863
6th New York Cav. 2 Cos..Dec., 1862	From Unatt. Cav. Yorkt'n 4-Corps	To Unatt. Cav. 4-Corps Va........	May, 1863
2d Mass. Cav. 1st Battn..Feb., 1863	From New Organization............	To Unatt. Cav. 4-Corps Va........	May, 1863

Army of Occupation---West Virginia---Department of the Ohio

Designated Department of Western Virginia Oct. 11, 1861. Merged into Mountain Department March 11, 1862.

COMMANDERS.

Geo. B. McClellan.......	Major General...................	May 13, 1861, to July 23, 1861.	
W. S. Rosecrans........	Brigadier General	July 23, 1861, to Oct. 11, 1861.	

KELLY'S COMMAND.—

COMMANDER.

B. F. Kelly.............	Col. 1st W. Va. Infy..............	May to Aug., 1861.	
1st W. Va. Infy........May, 1861	From New Organization...........	No change to Muster Out..........	Aug., 1861
14th Ohio Infy.........May, 1861	From New Organization...........	No change to Muster Out..........	Aug., 1861
16th Ohio Infy.........May, 1861	From New Organization...........	To Hills' Brig...................	July, 1861
20th Ohio Infy.........May, 1861	From New Organization...........	No change to Muster Out..........	Aug., 1861
6th Ind. Infy..........May, 1861	From New Organization...........	To Morris' Ind. Brig.............	July, 1861
7th Ind. Infy..........May, 1861	From New Organization...........	To Morris' Ind. Brig.............	July, 1861
9th Ind. Infy..........May, 1861	From New Organization...........	To Morris' Ind. Brig.............	July, 1861
Barnett's Ohio Batty......May, 1861	From New Organization...........	To Morris' Ind. Brig.............	July, 1861

ROSECRANS' BRIGADE.—

COMMANDER.

W. S. Rosecrans........	Brigadier General	May to July, 1861.	
10th Ohio Infy.........June, 1861	From New Organization...........	To 2-Brig. Army of Occupation......	July, 1861
17th Ohio Infy.........June, 1861	From New Organization...........	To 2-Brig. Army of Occupation......	July, 1861
19th Ohio Infy.........June, 1861	From New Organization...........	No change to Muster Out..........	Aug., 1861
8th Ind. Infy..........June, 1861	From New Organization...........	No change to Muster Out..........	Aug., 1861
10th Ind. Infy.........June, 1861	From New Organization...........	No change to Muster Out..........	Aug., 1861
13th Ind. Infy.........June, 1861	From New Organization...........	To 1-Brig. Army of Occupation......	Aug., 1861
Burdsall's Ohio Cav.....June, 1861	From New Organization...........	To 1-Brig. Army of Occupation......	Aug., 1861

MORRRIS' INDIANA BRIGADE.—

COMMANDER.

T. A. Morris...........	Brigadier General		
6th Ind. Infy..........July, 1861	From Kelly's Command............	No change to Muster Out..........	Aug., 1861
7th Ind. Infy..........July, 1861	From Kelly's Command............	No change to Muster Out..........	Aug., 1861
9th Ind. Infy..........July, 1861	From Kelly's Command............	No change to Muster Out..........	Aug., 1861
14th Ohio Infy.........July, 1861	From Kelly's Command............	No change to Muster Out..........	Aug., 1861
Barnett's Ohio Batty.....July, 1861	From Kelly's Command............	No change to Muster Out..........	Aug., 1861

HILLS' BRIGADE.—

COMMANDER.

C. W. Hills............	Brigadier General		
8th Ohio Infy..........July, 1861	From New Organization...........	To 3-Brig. Army of Occupation.....	July, 1861
15th Ohio Infy.........July, 1861	From New Organization...........	No change to Muster Out..........	July, 1861
16th Ohio Infy.........July, 1861	From Kelly's Command............	No change to Muster Out..........	July, 1861

M'COOK'S ADVANCE BRIGADE.—

COMMANDER.

R. L. McCook...........	Col. 9th Ohio Infy................		
4th Ohio Infy..........July, 1861	From New Organization...........	To 3-Brig. Army of Occupation.....	July, 1861
9th Ohio Infy..........July, 1861	From New Organization...........	To 3-Brig. Army of Occupation.....	July, 1861
Batty. A, 1st Mich. Arty..July, 1861	From New Organization...........	To 1-Brig. Army of Occupation.....	July, 1861

1st BRIGADE.—

3d Ohio Infy...........July, 1861	From New Organization...........	To Reynolds' Command Cheat Mt...	Sept., 1861
6th Ohio Infy..........July, 1861	From New Organization...........	To Reynolds' Command Cheat Mt...	Sept., 1861
13th Ind. Infy.........July, 1861	From Rosecrans' Brig............	To Reynolds' Command Cheat Mt...	Sept., 1861
14th Ind. Infy.........July, 1861	From New Organization...........	To Reynolds' Command Cheat Mt...	Sept., 1861
15th Ind. Infy.........July, 1861	From New Organization...........	To Reynolds' Command Cheat Mt...	Sept., 1861
1st W. Va. Infy.........July, 1861	From Kelly's Command............	No change to Muster Out..........	Aug., 1861
2d W. Va. Infy.........July, 1861	From New Organization...........	To Reynolds' Command Cheat Mt...	Sept., 1861
Batty. A, 1st Mich. Arty..July, 1861	From McCook's Advance Brig.......	To Reynolds' Command Cheat Mt...	Sept., 1861
Bracken's Ind. Cav......July, 1861	From New Organization...........	To Reynolds' Command Cheat Mt...	Sept., 1861
Burdsall's Ohio Cav.....July, 1861	From Rosecrans' Brig............	No change to Muster Out..........	Aug., 1861

2d BRIGADE.—

10th Ohio Infy.........July, 1861	From Rosecrans' Brig.............	To Benham's Brig. Dist. Kanawha..	Sept., 1861
13th Ohio Infy.........July, 1861	From New Organization...........	To Benham's Brig. Dist. Kanawha..	Sept., 1861
17th Ohio Infy.........July, 1861	From Rosecrans' Brig.............	No change to Muster Out..........	Aug., 1861
28th Ohio Infy.........July, 1861	From New Organization...........	To McCook's Brig. Dist. Kanawha..	Sept., 1861
Schambeck's Ill. Cav......July, 1861	From New Organization...........	To McCook's Brig. Dist. Kanawha..	Sept., 1861
Batty. E, 4th U. S. Arty..July, 1861	From New Organization...........	To Scammon's Brig. Dist. Kanawha.	Sept., 1861

3d BRIGADE.—

4th Ohio Infy..........July, 1861	From McCook's Brig..............	To Kelly's R. R. Dist............	Sept., 1861
8th Ohio Infy..........July, 1861	From New Organization...........	To Kelly's R. R. Dist............	Sept., 1861
9th Ohio Infy..........July, 1861	From McCook's Brig..............	To McCook's Brig. Dist. Kanawha..	Sept., 1861
Batty. G, 4th U. S. Arty..July, 1861	From New Organization...........	To Milroy's Command Cheat Mt....	Sept., 1861

KANAWHA BRIGADE.— COMMANDER.

J. D. Cox.............. |Brigadier General ....

1st Ky. Infy	July, 1861	From New Organization	To Dist. Kanawha Dept. W. Va	Oct.,	1861
2d Ky. Infy	July, 1861	From New Organization	To Dist. Kanawha Dept. W. Va	Oct.,	1861
11th Ohio Infy	July, 1861	From New Organization	To Dist. Kanawha Dept. W. Va	Oct.,	1861
12th Ohio Infy	July, 1861	From New Organization	To Benham's Brig. Dist. Kanawha	Sept.,	1861
18th Ohio Infy	July, 1861	From New Organization	No change to Muster Out	Aug.,	1861
19th Ohio Infy	July, 1861	From New Organization	No change to Muster Out	Aug.,	1861
22d Ohio Infy	July, 1861	From New Organization	No change to Muster Out	Aug.,	1861
23d Ohio Infy	July, 1861	From New Organization	To Scammon's Brig. Dist. Kanawha	Sept.,	1861
Cotter's Ohio Batty	July, 1861	From New Organization	No change to Muster Out	Aug.,	1861
3d Indpt. Co. Ohio Cav	July, 1861	From New Organization	To Dist. Kanawha Dept. W. Va	Oct.,	1861
1st Ohio Indpt. Batty	Aug., 1861	From New Organization	To Benham's Brig. Dist. Kanawha	Sept.,	1861
26th Ohio Infy	Aug., 1861	From New Organization	To Dist. Kanawha Dept. W. Va	Oct.,	1861
30th Ohio Infy	Sept., 1861	From New Organization	To Scammon's Brig. Dist. Kanawha	Sept.,	1861
34th Ohio Infy	Sept., 1861	From New Organization	To Dist. Kanawha Dept. W. Va	Oct.,	1861
36th Ohio Infy	Sept., 1861	From New Organization	To Dist. Kanawha Dept. W. Va	Oct.,	1861
Schambeck's Ill. Cav	Sept., 1861	From 2-Brig. Army Occupation	To McCook's Brig. Dist. Kanawha	Sept.,	1861

BENHAM'S BRIGADE.— COMMANDER.

H. W. Benham......... |Brigadier General ....

10th Ohio Infy	Sept., 1861	From 2-Brig. Army Occupation	To 1-Brig. Dist. Kana. Dept. W. Va	Oct.,	1861
12th Ohio Infy	Sept., 1861	From Cox's Kanawha Brig	To 1-Brig. Dist. Kana. Dept. W. Va	Oct.,	1861
13th Ohio Infy	Sept., 1861	From 2-Brig. Army Occupation	To 1-Brig. Dist. Kana. Dept. W. Va	Oct.,	1861
37th Ohio Infy	Oct., 1861	From New Organization	To 1-Brig. Dist. Kana. Dept. W. Va	Oct.,	1861
44th Ohio Infy	Oct., 1861	From New Organization	To 1-Brig. Dist. Kana. Dept. W. Va	Oct.,	1861
1st Ohio Indpt. Batty	Sept., 1861	From Cox's Kanawha Brig	To 1-Brig. Dist. Kana. Dept. W. Va	Oct.,	1861

M'COOK'S BRIGADE.— COMMANDER.

R. L. McCook.......... |Col. 9th Ohio Infy ....

9th Ohio Infy	Sept., 1861	From 3-Brig. Army Occupation	To 2-Brig. Dist. Kana. Dept. W. Va	Oct.,	1861
28th Ohio Infy	Sept., 1861	From 2-Brig. Army Occupation	To 2-Brig. Dist. Kana. Dept. W. Va	Oct.,	1861
47th Ohio Infy	Sept., 1861	From New Organization	To 2-Brig. Dist. Kana. Dept. W. Va	Oct.,	1861
Schambeck's Ill. Cav	Sept., 1861	From 2-Brig. Army Occupation	To 2-Brig. Dist. Kana. Dept. W. Va	Oct.,	1861

SCAMMON'S BRIGADE.—

23d Ohio Infy	Sept., 1861	From Cox's Kanawha Brig	To 3-Brig. Dist. Kana. Dept. W. Va	Oct.,	1861
30th Ohio Infy	Sept., 1861	From Cox's Kanawha Brig	To 3-Brig. Dist. Kana. Dept. W. Va	Oct.,	1861
Batty. E, 4th U. S. Arty	Sept., 1861	From 2-Brig. Army Occupation	To Kelly's R. R. Dist. Dept. W. Va	Oct.,	1861

UNATTACHED INFANTRY.—

5th Ohio Infy	July, 1861	From New Organization	To Kelly's R. R. Dist. Dept. W. Va	Oct.,	1861
7th Ohio Infy	July, 1861	From New Organization	To Kelly's R. R. Dist. Dept. W. Va	Oct.,	1861
17th Ind. Infy	July, 1861	From New Organization	To Reynolds' Command Cheat Mt	Sept.,	1861

UNATTACHED ARTILLERY.—

Wilder's Ind. Batty	July, 1861	From New Organization	To Reynolds' Command Cheat Mt	Sept.,	1861
Batty. A, 1st W. Va. Arty	July, 1861	From New Organization	To Reynolds' Command Cheat Mt	Sept.,	1861
Batty. I, 4th U. S. Arty	July, 1861	From New Organization	To 3-Brig. Dist. Kanawha	Sept.,	1861

UNATTACHED CAVALRY.—

George's Ohio Cav. Co	July, 1861	From New Organization	No change to Muster Out	Sept.,	1861
Stewart's Ind. Cav	July, 1861	From New Organization	To Headqrs. Dept. W. Va	Oct.,	1861
1st Ohio Cav. (Co.'s A, C)	July, 1861	From New Organization	To Cheat Mt. Dist. Dept. W. Va	Oct.,	1861
Ringgold Penna. Cav	July, 1861	From New Organization	To Cheat Mt. Dist. Dept. W. Va	Oct.,	1861

REYNOLDS' CHEAT MOUNTAIN DISTRICT.— COMMANDER.

J. J. Reynolds......... |Brigadier General ....

3d Ohio Infy	Sept., 1861	From 1-Brig. Army Occupation	To Cheat Mt. Dist. Dept. W. Va	Oct.,	1861
6th Ohio Infy	Sept., 1861	From 1-Brig. Army Occupation	To Cheat Mt. Dist. Dept. W. Va	Oct.,	1861
24th Ohio Infy	Sept., 1861	From New Organization	To Cheat Mt. Dist. Dept. W. Va	Oct.,	1861
25th Ohio Infy	Sept., 1861	From New Organization	To Cheat Mt. Dist. Dept. W. Va	Oct.,	1861
32d Ohio Infy	Sept., 1861	From New Organization	To Cheat Mt. Dist. Dept. W. Va	Oct.,	1861
7th Ind. Infy	Sept., 1861	From New Organization	To Cheat Mt. Dist. Dept. W. Va	Oct.,	1861
9th Ind. Infy	Sept., 1861	From New Organization	To Cheat Mt. Dist. Dept. W. Va	Oct.,	1861
13th Ind. Infy	Sept., 1861	From 1-Brig. Army Occupation	To Cheat Mt. Dist. Dept. W. Va	Oct.,	1861
14th Ind. Infy	Sept., 1861	From 1-Brig. Army Occupation	To Cheat Mt. Dist. Dept. W. Va	Oct.,	1861
15th Ind. Infy	Sept., 1861	From 1-Brig. Army Occupation	To Cheat Mt. Dist. Dept. W. Va	Oct.,	1861
17th Ind. Infy	Sept., 1861	From Unatt. Army Occupation	To Cheat Mt. Dist. Dept. W. Va	Oct.,	1861
2d W. Va. Infy	Sept., 1861	From 1-Brig. Army Occupation	To Cheat Mt. Dist. Dept. W. Va	Oct.,	1861
3d W. Va. Infy	Sept., 1861	From New Organization	To Cheat Mt. Dist. Dept. W. Va	Oct.,	1861
12th Ohio Indpt. Batty	Sept., 1861	From Co. D, 25th Ohio Infy	To Cheat Mt. Dist. Dept. W. Va	Oct.,	1861
Rigby's Ind. Batty	Sept., 1861	From Co. A, 17th Ind. Infy	To Cheat Mt. Dist. Dept. W. Va	Oct.,	1861
Batty. A, 1st Mich. Arty	Sept., 1861	From 1-Brig. Army Occupation	To Cheat Mt. Dist. Dept. W. Va	Oct.,	1861
Batty. G, 4th U. S. Arty	Sept., 1861	From 3-Brig. Army Occupation	To Cheat Mt. Dist. Dept. W. Va	Oct.,	1861
1st Ohio Cav. (Co.'s A, C)	Sept., 1861	From Unatt. Army Occupation	To Cheat Mt. Dist. Dept. W. Va	Oct.,	1861
Bracken's Ind. Cav	Sept., 1861	From 1-Brig. Army Occupation	To Cheat Mt. Dist. Dept. W. Va	Oct.,	1861
Batty. A. 1st W. Va. Arty	Sept., 1861	From Unatt. Army Occupation	To Cheat Mt. Dist. Dept. W. Va	Oct.,	1861

Department of Western Virginia

Organized Oct. 11, 1861, from the Dept. of the Ohio. Merged into the Mountain Department March 11, 1862.

COMMANDER.

W. S. Rosecrans....... |Brigadier General .... |Oct. 11, 1861, to Mch. 11, 1862.

CHEAT MOUNTAIN DISTRICT.— COMMANDER.

R. H. Milroy........... |Brigadier General .... |Oct. 11, 1861, to Mch. 11, 1862.

3d Ohio Infy	Oct., 1861	From Reynolds' Command Cheat Mt	To 17-Brig. Army Ohio	Nov.,	1861
6th Ohio Infy	Oct., 1861	From Reynolds' Command Cheat Mt	To 17-Brig. Army Ohio	Nov.,	1861
24th Ohio Infy	Oct., 1861	From Reynolds' Command Cheat Mt	To 10-Brig. Army Ohio	Nov.,	1861
25th Ohio Infy	Oct., 1861	From Reynolds' Command Cheat Mt	To Milroy's Brig. Mt. Dept	Mch.,	1862
32d Ohio Infy	Oct., 1861	From Reynolds' Command Cheat Mt	To Milroy's Brig. Mt. Dept	Mch.,	1862
7th Ind. Infy	Oct., 1861	From Reynolds' Command Cheat Mt	To 3-Brig. Lander's Div. Dept. W. Va	Jan.,	1862
9th Ind. Infy	Oct., 1861	From Reynolds' Command Cheat Mt	To 19-Brig. 4-Div. Army Ohio	Feb.,	1862
13th Ind. Infy	Oct., 1861	From Reynolds' Command Cheat Mt	To 2-Brig. Lander's Div. Dept. W. Va	Jan.,	1862

GREAT MOUNTAIN DISTRICT.—Continued.

14th Ind. Infy.............Oct., 1861	From Reynolds' Command Cheat Mt..	To 1-Brig. Lander's Div. Dept. W. Va	Jan., 1862
15th Ind. Infy.............Oct., 1861	From Reynolds' Command Cheat Mt..	To 15-Brig. Army Ohio............	Nov., 1861
17th Ind. Infy.............Oct., 1861	From Reynolds' Command Cheat Mt..	To 15-Brig. Army Ohio............	Nov., 1861
2d W. Va. Infy.........Oct., 1861	From Reynolds' Command Cheat Mt..	To Milroy's Brig. Mt. Dept.........	Mch., 1862
3d W. Va. Infy.........Oct., 1861	From Reynolds' Command Cheat Mt..	To Milroy's Brig. Mt. Dept.........	Mch., 1862
73d Ohio Infy.........Jan., 1862	From New Organization............	To Schenck's Brig. Mt. Dept.......	Mch., 1862
75th Ohio Infy.........Feb., 1862	From New Organization............	To Schenck's Brig. Mt. Dept.......	Mch., 1862
10th W. Va. Infy.........Mch., 1862	From New Organization............	To R. R. Dist. Mt. Dept..........	Mch., 1862

ARTILLERY, CHEAT MOUNTAIN DISTRICT.—

12th Ohio Indpt. Batty....Oct., 1861	From Reynolds' Command Cheat Mt.	To Milroy's Brig. Mt. Dept.........	Mch., 1862
26th Ohio Indpt. Batty....Oct., 1861	From Co. F. 32d Ohio Infy.........	To Milroy's Brig. Mt. Dept.........	Mch., 1862
Batty. A, 1st Mich. Arty...Oct., 1861	From Reynolds' Cheat Mt. Dist......	To Arty. 3-Div. Army Ohio........	Dec., 1861
Wilder's Ind. Batty......Oct., 1861	From Reynolds' Cheat Mt. Dist......	To Milroy's Brig. Mt. Dept.........	Mch., 1862
Batty. A, 1st W. Va. Arty..Oct., 1861	From Reynolds' Cheat Mt. Dist......	To Lander's Div. W. Va............	Jan., 1862
Batty. B, 1st W. Va. Arty..Oct., 1861	From New Organization............	To Lander's Div. W. Va............	Jan., 1862
Batty. G. 4th U. S. Arty...Oct., 1861	From Reynolds' Command Cheat Mt..	To Arty. Res. Washington...........	Nov., 1861

CAVALRY, CHEAT MOUNTAIN DISTRICT.—

1st Ohio Cav. (Co.'s A, C).Oct., 1861	From Reynolds' Command Cheat Mt..	To Lander's Div. W. Va............	Jan., 1862
1st W. Va. Cav.........Oct., 1861	From New Organization............	To Lander's Div. W. Va............	Jan., 1862
Ringgold Penna. Cav......Oct., 1861	From Reynolds' Command Cheat Mt..	To Lander's Div. W. Va............	Jan., 1862

RAILROAD DISTRICT.—   COMMANDER.

B. F. Kelly.............	Brigadier General	Oct. 11. 1861. to Mch. 11, 1862.	
4th Ohio Infy...........Oct., 1861	From 3-Brig. Army Occupation......	To 1-Brig. Lander's Div. W. Va....	Jan., 1862
5th Ohio Infy...........Oct., 1861	From Unatt. Army Occupation.......	To 2-Brig. Lander's Div. W. Va....	Jan., 1862
7th Ohio Infy...........Oct., 1861	From Unatt. Army Occupation.......	To 3-Brig. Lander's Div. W. Va....	Jan., 1862
8th Ohio Infy...........Oct., 1861	From 3-Brig. Army Occupation......	To 1-Brig. Lander's Div. W. Va....	Jan., 1862
1st W. Va. Infy.........Oct., 1861	From New Organization............	To 3-Brig. Lander's Div. W. Va....	Jan., 1862
6th W. Va. Infy.........Oct., 1861	From New Organization............	To R. R. Dist. Mt. Dist. W. Va.....	Mch., 1862
7th W. Va. Infy.........Oct., 1861	From New Organization............	To 1-Brig. Lander's Div. W. Va....	Jan., 1862
11th W. Va. Infy.........Oct., 1861	From New Organization............	To R. R. Dist. Mt. Dept..........	Mch., 1862
39th Ill. Infy...........Oct., 1861	From New Organization............	To 1-Brig. Lander's Div. W. Va....	Jan., 1862
2d. Md. Pot. Home Brig...Oct., 1861	From New Organization............	To R. R. Dist. Mt. Dept..........	Mch., 1862
3d Md. Pot. Home Brig...Oct., 1861	From New Organization............	To Lander's Div. W. Va............	Jan., 1862
55th Ohio Infy.........Feb., 1862	From New Organization............	To R. R. Dist. Mt. Dept..........	Mch., 1862
Batty. E. 4th U. S. Arty...Oct., 1861	From Scammon's Brig. Army Occ...	To R. R. Dist. Mt. Dept..........	Jan., 1862

DISTRICT OF THE KANAWHA.—   COMMANDER.

J. D. Cox.............	Brigadier General	Oct. 11. 1861. to Mch. 11, 1862.

1st BRIGADE.—   COMMANDER.

R. C. Schenck.........	Brigadier General		
10th Ohio Infy...........Oct., 1861	From Benham's Brig. Dist. Kanawha.	To 17-Brig. Army Ohio............	Nov., 1861
12th Ohio Infy...........Oct., 1861	From Benham's Brig. Dist. Kanawha.	To 1-Brig. Dist. Kanawha Mt. Dept.	Mch., 1862
13th Ohio Infy...........Oct., 1861	From Benham's Brig. Dist. Kanawha.	To 17-Brig. Army Ohio............	Nov., 1861
37th Ohio Infy...........Oct., 1861	From Benham's Brig. Dist. Kanawha.	To 2-Brig. Dist. Kanawha Mt. Dept.	Mch., 1862
44th Ohio Infy...........Oct., 1861	From Benham's Brig. Dist. Kanawha.	To 3-Brig. Dist. Kanawha Mt. Dept.	Mch., 1862
1st Ohio Indpt. Batty....Oct., 1861	From Benham's Brig. Dist. Kanawha.	To 1-Brig. Dist. Kanawha Mt. Dept.	Mch., 1862

2d BRIGADE.—   COMMANDERS.

R. L. McCook..........	Col. 9th Ohio Infy..............	Oct., 1861, to Nov., 1861.	
A. Moor	Col. 28th Ohio Infy..............	Nov., 1861, to Mch., 1862.	
9th Ohio Infy...........Oct., 1861	From McCook's Brig. Dist. Kanawha.	To 3-Brig. Army Ohio............	Nov., 1861
11th Ohio Infy...........Oct., 1861	From Cox's Kanawha Brig.........	To 3-Brig. Dist. Kanawha Mt. Dept.	Mch., 1862
28th Ohio Infy...........Oct., 1861	From McCook's Brig. Dist. Kanawha.	To 2-Brig. Dist. Kanawha Mt. Dept.	Mch., 1862
47th Ohio Infy...........Oct., 1861	From McCook's Brig. Dist. Kanawha.	To 2-Brig. Dist. Kanawha Mt. Dept.	Mch., 1862
Schambeck's Ill. Cav......Oct., 1861	From McCook's Brig. Dist. Kanawha.	To 4-Brig. Dist. Kanawha Mt. Dept.	Mch., 1862

3d BRIGADE.—   COMMANDER.

E. P. Scammon..........	Col. 23d Ohio Infy...............		
23d Ohio Infy...........Oct., 1861	From Scammon's Brig. Dist. Kana...	To 1-Brig. Dist. Kanawha Mt. Dept.	Mch., 1862
30th Ohio Infy...........Oct., 1861	From Scammon's Brig. Dist. Kana...	To 1-Brig. Dist. Kanawha Mt. Dept.	Mch., 1862
Batty. I, 4th U. S. Arty...Oct., 1861	From Unatt. Arty. Dist. Kanawha..	To Arty. 1-Div. Army Ohio........	Dec., 1861

UNATTACHED.—

1st Ky. Infy...........Oct., 1861	From Cox's Kanawha Brig.........	To Dept. Ohio...................	Jan., 1862
2d Ky. Infy...........Oct., 1861	From Cox's Kanawha Brig.........	To Dept. Ohio...................	Jan., 1862
26th Ohio Infy...........Oct., 1861	From Cox's Kanawha Brig.........	To 15-Brig. 6-Div. Army Ohio.....	Jan., 1862
34th Ohio Infy...........Oct., 1861	From Cox's Kanawha Brig.........	To 2-Brig. Dist. Kanawha Mt. Dept.	Mch., 1862
36th Ohio Infy...........Oct., 1861	From Cox's Kanawha Brig.........	To 3-Brig. Dist. Kanawha Mt. Dept.	Mch., 1862
4th W. Va. Infy.........Oct., 1861	From New Organization............	To 4-Brig. Dist. Kanawha Mt. Dept.	Mch., 1862
5th W. Va. Infy.........Oct., 1861	From New Organization............	To Dist. Cumb'd Mt. Dept.........	Mch., 1862
8th W. Va. Infy.........Nov., 1861	From New Organization............	To Unatt. Kanawha Dist. Mt. Dept.	Mch., 1862
9th W. Va. Infy.........Dec., 1861	From New Organization............	To 4-Brig. Dist. Kanawha Mt. Dept.	Mch., 1862

CAVALRY.—

3d Indpt. Co. Ohio Cav...Oct., 1861	From Dist. Kanawha..............	To Unatt. Dist. Kanawha Mt. Dept.	Mch., 1862
2d W. Va. Cav...........Oct., 1861	From New Organization............	To Unatt. Dist. Kanawha Mt. Dept.	Mch., 1862

ARTILLERY.—

Simmonds' Ky. Batty......Oct., 1861	From Co. E, 1st Ky. Infy..........	To 2-Brig. Dist. Kanawha Mt. Dept.	Mch., 1862

LANDERS' DIVISION.—   COMMANDERS.

F. W. Landers.........	Brigadier General	Jan. 5. 1862, to Mch. 3, 1862.
Nathan Kimball	Col. 14th Ind. Infy..............	Mch. 3, 1862. to Mch. 6, 1862.
James Shields	Brigadier General	Mch. 6, 1862. to Mch. 13, 1862.

1st BRIGADE.—   COMMANDER.

Nathan Kimball	Col. 14th Ind. Infy..............	Jan., 1862, to Mch., 1862.	
4th Ohio Infy...........Jan., 1862	From R. R. Dist. Dept. W. Va......	To 1-Brig. 2-Div. Banks' 5-C. Pot...	Mch., 1862
8th Ohio Infy...........Jan., 1862	From R. R. Dist. Dept. W. Va......	To 1-Brig. 2-Div. Banks' 5-C. Pot...	Mch., 1862
67th Ohio Infy...........Jan., 1862	From New Organization............	To 1-Brig. 2-Div. Banks' 5-C. Pot...	Mch., 1862
14th Ind. Infy...........Jan., 1862	From Cheat Mt. Dist. Dept. W. Va.	To 1-Brig. 2-Div. Banks' 5-C. Pot...	Mch., 1862
7th W. Va. Infy.........Jan., 1862	From R. R. Dist. Dept. W. Va......	To 1-Brig. 2-Div. Banks' 5-C. Pot...	Mch., 1862
84th Penna. Infy.........Jan., 1862	From New Organization............	To 1-Brig. 2-Div. Banks' 5-C. Pot...	Mch., 1862

2d BRIGADE.—

	COMMANDER.	
J. C. Sullivan..........|Col. 13th Ind. Infy.............|Jan., 1862, to Mch., 1862.	

5th Ohio Infy...........Jan., 1862	From R. R. Dist. Dept. W. Va......	To 2-Brig. 2-Div. Banks' 5-Corps Pot.	Mch., 1862
62d Ohio Infy...........Jan., 1862	From New Organization...........	To 2-Brig. 2-Div. Banks' 5-Corps Pot.	Mch., 1862
66th Ohio Infy...........Jan., 1862	From New Organization...........	To 2-Brig. 2-Div. Banks' 5-Corps Pot.	Mch., 1862
13th Ind. Infy...........Jan., 1862	From Cheat Mt. Dist. Dept. W. Va..	To 2-Brig. 2-Div. Banks' 5-Corps Pot.	Mch., 1862
39th Ill. Infy...........Jan., 1862	From R. R. Dist. Dept. W. Va......	To 2-Brig. 2-Div. Banks' 5-Corps Pot.	Mch., 1862

3d BRIGADE.—

	COMMANDER.	
E. B. Tyler...........|Col. 7th Ohio Infy.............|Jan., 1862, to Mch., 1862.	

7th Ohio Infy...........Jan., 1862	From R. R. Dist. Dept. W. Va......	To 3-Brig. 2-Div. Banks' 5-Corps Pot.	Mch., 1862
29th Ohio Infy...........Jan., 1862	From New Organization...........	To 3-Brig. 2-Div. Banks' 5-Corps Pot.	Mch., 1862
1st W. Va. Infy...........Jan., 1862	From R. R. Dist. Dept. W. Va......	To 3-Brig. 2-Div. Banks' 5-Corps Pot.	Mch., 1862
7th Ind. Infy...........Jan., 1862	From Cheat Mt. Dist. Dept. W. Va..	To 3-Brig. 2-Div. Banks' 5-Corps Pot.	Mch., 1862
110th Penna. Infy...........Jan., 1862	From New Organization...........	To 3-Brig. 2-Div. Banks' 5-Corps Pot.	Mch., 1862
Andrews' Mass. S. S......Jan., 1862	From New Organization...........	To 1-Brig. 2-Div. 2-Corps Pot.......	Mch., 1862
ARTILLERY.—			
Batty. H, 1st Ohio Arty...Jan., 1862	From New Organization...........	To Arty. 2-Div. Banks' 5-Corps Pot..	Mch., 1862
Batty. L, 1st Ohio Arty...Jan., 1862	From New Organization...........	To Arty. 2-Div. Banks' 5-Corps Pot..	Mch., 1862
Batty. A, 1st W. Va. Arty.Jan., 1862	From Cheat Mt. Dist. Dept. W. Va..	To Arty. 2-Div. Banks' 5-Corps Pot..	Mch., 1862
Batty. B, 1st W. Va. Arty.Jan., 1862	From Cheat Mt. Dist. Dept. W. Va..	To Arty. 2-Div. Banks' 5-Corps Pot..	Mch., 1862
Batty. E, 4th U. S. Arty...Jan., 1862	From R. R. Dist. Dept. W. Va......	To Arty. 2-Div. Banks' 5-Corps Pot..	Mch., 1862
CAVALRY.—			
1st W. Va. Cav. Sqdn.....Jan., 1862	From Cheat Mt. Dist. Dept. W. Va..	To Hatch's Cav. Brig. Banks' 5-C...	Mch., 1862
1st Md. Pot. H. Brig. Cav.Jan., 1862	From Cheat Mt. Dist. Dept. W. Va..	To Hatch's Cav. Brig. Banks' 5-C...	Mch., 1862
Ringgold Pa. Cav. Battn...Jan., 1862	From Unatt. Dept. W. Va.........	To Hatch's Cav. Brig. Banks' 5-C...	Mch., 1862
1st Ohio Cav. (Co's A, C).Jan., 1862	From Cheat Mt. Dist. Dept. W. Va..	To Hatch's Cav. Brig. Banks' 5-C...	Mch., 1862
UNATTACHED.—			
3d Md. Pot. Home Brig...Jan., 1862	From R. R. Dist. Dept. W. Va......	To R. R. Dist. Mt. Dept...........	Mch., 1862

Mountain Department

Created March 11, 1862, from Department of Western Virginia. Merged into 1st Corps, Army of Virginia, June 26, 1862

COMMANDERS.

W. S. Rosecrans.......	Brigadier General	Mch. 11, 1862, to Mch. 29, 1862.
John C. Fremont.......	Major General	Mch. 29, 1862, to June 26, 1862.

DISTRICT OF CUMBERLAND.—

	COMMANDER.	
R. C. Schenck..........	Brigadier General	

5th W. Va. Infy........Mch., 1862	From Unatt. Dist. Kana. Dept. W. Va.	To Milroy's Brig. Dept. Mt.........	Apr., 1862
82d Ohio Infy..........Mch., 1862	From New Organization...........	To Schenck's Brig. Dept. Mt.......	Apr., 1862
2d Md. Pot. Home Brig..Mch., 1862	From R. R. Dist. Dept. W. Va......	To R. R. Dist. Mt. Dept...........	Apr., 1862

CHEAT MOUNTAIN DISTRICT.—

	COMMANDERS.	
R. H. Milroy..........	Brigadier General	Mch. 11, 1862, to Apr. 19, 1862.
T. M. Harris..........	Col. 10th W. Va. Infy.........	Temporarily.

2d W. Va. Infy.........Mch., 1862	From Cheat Mt. Dist. Dept. W. Va..	To Milroy's Brig. Mt. Dept.......	Apr., 1862
3d W. Va. Infy.........Mch., 1862	From Cheat Mt. Dist. Dept. W. Va..	To Milroy's Brig. Mt. Dept.......	Apr., 1862
10th W. Va. Infy.........Mch., 1862	From Cheat Mt. Dist. Dept. W. Va..	To R. R. Dist. Mt. Dept.........	Apr., 1862
25th Ohio Infy.........Mch., 1862	From Cheat Mt. Dist. Dept. W. Va..	To Milroy's Brig. Mt. Dept.......	Apr., 1862
32d Ohio Infy.........Mch., 1862	From Cheat Mt. Dist. Dept. W. Va..	To Schenck's Brig. Mt. Dept......	Apr., 1862
73d Ohio Infy.........Mch., 1862	From Cheat Mt. Dist. Dept. W. Va..	To Schenck's Brig. Mt. Dept......	Apr., 1862
75th Ohio Infy.........Mch., 1862	From Cheat Mt. Dist. Dept. W. Va..	To Milroy's Brig. Mt. Dept.......	Apr., 1862
12th Ohio Indpt. Batty...Mch., 1862	From Cheat Mt. Dist. Dept. W. Va..	To Milroy's Brig. Mt. Dept.......	Apr., 1862
Rigby's Ind. Batty......Mch., 1862	From Cheat Mt. Dist. Dept. W. Va..	To Milroy's Brig. Mt. Dept.......	Apr., 1862
Batty. I, 1st Ohio Arty..Mch., 1862	From Cheat Mt. Dist. Dept. W. Va..	To Milroy's Brig. Mt. Dept.......	Apr., 1862
Batty. K, 1st Ohio Arty..Mch., 1862	From Cheat Mt. Dist. Dept. W. Va..	To Schenck's Brig. Dept. Mt......	Apr., 1862
1st W. Va. Cav.........Mch., 1862	From Cheat Mt. Dist. Dept. W. Va..	To Milroy's Brig. Mt. Dept.......	Apr., 1862

RAILROAD DISTRICT.—

	COMMANDER.	
B. F. Kelly...........	Brigadier General	Mch. 11, 1862, to June 26, 1862.

6th W. Va. Infy........Mch., 1862	From R. R. Dist. Dept. W. Va.....	To R. R. Dist. 8-Corps Middle Dept..	July, 1862
11th W. Va. Infy.......Mch., 1862	From R. R. Dist. Dept. W. Va.....	To R. R. Dist. 8-Corps Middle Dept..	July, 1862
55th Ohio Infy.........Mch., 1862	From R. R. Dist. Dept. W. Va.....	To Schenck's Brig. Mt. Dept.......	Apr., 1862
2d Md. Pot. Home Brig..Mch., 1862	From Dist. Cumb'd Dept. W. Va....	To R. R. Dist. 8-Corps Middle Dept..	Apr., 1862
3d Md. Pot. Home Brig..Mch., 1862	From Unatt. Landers' D. Dpt. W. Va.	To R. R. Dist. 8-Corps Middle Dept..	July, 1862
10th W. Va. Infy........Apr., 1862	From Cheat Mt. Dist. Mt. Dept....	To R. R. Dist. 8-Corps Middle Dept..	July, 1862
84th Ohio Infy.........June, 1862	From New Organization..........	To R. R. Dist. 8-Corps Middle Dept..	July, 1862
86th Ohio Infy.........June, 1862	From New Organization..........	To R. R. Dist. 8-Corps Middle Dept..	July, 1862
23d Ill. Infy...........June, 1862	From Camp Douglass, Ill.........	To R. R. Dist. 8-Corps Middle Dept..	July, 1862
65th Ill. Infy...........June, 1862	From New Organization..........	To R. R. Dist. 8-Corps Middle Dept..	July, 1862
CAVALRY.—			
1st Conn. Cav.........Mch., 1862	From Unatt. Dept. W. Va.........	To Schenck's Brig. Mt. Dept.......	Apr., 1862
Stewart's Ind. Cav......Mch., 1862	From R. R. Dist. Dept. W. Va.....	To Headqrs. Mt. Dept.............	Mch., 1862
Bracken's Ind. Cav......Mch., 1862	From R. R. Dist. Dept. W. Va.....	To Headqrs. Mt. Dept.............	Mch., 1862
Ringgold Penna. Cav.....Apr., 1862	From Hatch's Cav. Brig. Banks' 5-C.	To R. R. Dist. 8-Corps Middle Dept..	July, 1862
Washington Co. Cav. Co..Apr., 1862	From Hatch's Cav. Brig. Banks' 5-C.	To R. R. Dist. 8-Corps Middle Dept..	July, 1862
ARTILLERY.—			
Batty. C, 1st W. Va. Arty..Apr., 1862	From New Organization...........	To 1-Brig. Blenker's Div. Mt. Dept..	May, 1862
Batty. G, 1st W. Va. Arty..Apr., 1862	From New Organization...........	To R. R. Dist. 8-Corps Middle Dept..	July, 1862
Batty. L, 1st Ill. Arty...Apr., 1862	From Milroy's Brig. Mt. Dept.....	To R. R. Dist. 8-Corps Middle Dept..	July, 1862

SCHENCK'S INDEPENDENT BRIGADE.—

	COMMANDER.	
R. C. Schenck.........	Brigadier General	Apr. 1862, to June 26, 1862.

32d Ohio Infy..........Apr., 1862	From Cheat Mt. Dist. Mt. Dept.....	To Piatt's Brig. 1-Corps Army Va..	June, 1862
55th Ohio Infy..........Apr., 1862	From R. R. Dist. Mt. Dept.......	To 2-Brig. 1-Div. 1-Corps Army Va..	June, 1862
73d Ohio Infy..........Apr., 1862	From Cheat Mt. Dist. Mt. Dept.....	To 2-Brig. 1-Div. 1-Corps Army Va..	June, 1862
75th Ohio Infy..........Apr., 1862	From Cheat Mt. Dist. Mt. Dept.....	To 2-Brig. 1-Div. 1-Corps Army Va..	June, 1862
82d Ohio Infy..........Apr., 1862	From Dist. Cumb'd Mt. Dept......	To Milroy's Indpt. Brig. 1-Corps Va.	June, 1862
Batty. K, 1st Ohio Arty..Apr., 1862	From Cheat Mt. Dist. Mt. Dept.....	To 2-Brig. 1-Div. 1-Corps Army Va..	June, 1862
Rigby's Ind. Batty.......Apr., 1862	From Cheat Mt. Dist. Mt. Dept.....	To Piatt's Brig. 1-Corps Army Va.,	June, 1862
1st Conn. Cav..........Apr., 1862	From R. R. Dist. Mt. Dept........	To Cav. Brig. 1-Corps Army Va.....	June, 1862

MILROY'S INDEPENDENT BRIGADE.—   COMMANDER.

R. H. Milroy	Brigadier General	Apr. 19, 1862, to June 26, 1862.

2d W. Va. Infy.........Apr., 1862	From Cheat Mt. Dist. Mt. Dept.....	To Milroy's Indpt. Brig. 1-Corps Va.	June, 1862
3d W. Va. Infy.........Apr., 1862	From Cheat Mt. Dist. Mt. Dept.....	To Milroy's Indpt. Brig. 1-Corps Va.	June, 1862
5th W. Va. Infy.........Apr., 1862	From Dist. Cumb'd Mt. Dept.....	To Milroy's Indpt. Brig. 1-Corps Va.	June, 1862
25th Ohio Infy.........Apr., 1862	From Cheat Mt. Dist. Mt. Dept.....	To 2-Brig. 1-Div. 1-Corps Army Va..	June, 1862
Batty. I, 1st Ohio Arty....Apr., 1862	From Cheat Mt. Dist. Mt. Dept.....	To Unatt. 3-Div. 1-Corps Army Va..	June, 1862
12th Ohio Indpt. Batty...Apr., 1862	From Cheat Mt. Dist. Mt. Dept.....	To Milroy's Indpt. Brig. 1-Corps Va.	June, 1862
Batty. G, 1st W. Va. Arty.Apr., 1862	From Cheat Mt. Dist. Mt. Dept.....	To R. R. Dist. Mt. Dept............	Apr., 1862
1st W. Va. Cav. Co......Apr., 1862	From Cheat Mt. Dist. Mt. Dept.....	To Milroy's Indpt. Brig. 1-Corps Va.	June, 1862
(Co's C, E, L.)			

DISTRICT OF THE KANAWHA.—   COMMANDERS.

J. D. Cox	Brigadier General	Mch. 11, 1862, to Aug. 15, 1862.
J. A. J. Lightburn	Col. 4th W. Va. Infy	Aug. 15, 1862, to Sept., 1862.

1st BRIGADE.—   COMMANDER.

E. P. Scammon	Col. 23d Ohio Infy	

12th Ohio Infy.........Mch., 1862	From 1-Br. Dist. Kana. Dept. W. Va.	To 1-Brig. Kanawha Div. 9-C. Pot..	Sept., 1862
23d Ohio Infy.........Mch., 1862	From 3-Br. Dist. Kana. Dept. W. Va.	To 1-Brig. Kanawha Div. 9-C. Pot..	Sept., 1862
30th Ohio Infy.........Mch., 1862	From 3-Br. Dist. Kana. Dept. W. Va.	To 1-Brig. Kanawha Div. 9-C. Pot..	Sept., 1862
1st Ohio Indpt. Batty....Mch., 1862	From Arty. Dist. Kana. Dept. W. Va.	To 1-Brig. Kanawha Div. 9-C. Pot..	Sept., 1862

2d BRIGADE.—   COMMANDER.

A. Moor	Col. 28th Ohio Infy	

28th Ohio Infy.........Mch., 1862	From 2-Br. Dist. Kana. Dept. W. Va.	To 2-Brig. Kanawha Div. 9-C. Pot..	Sept., 1862
34th Ohio Infy.........Mch., 1862	From Unat. Dist. Kana. Dept. W. Va.	To Unatt. Dist. Kanawha Dept. Ohio.	Sept., 1862
37th Ohio Infy.........Mch., 1862	From 1-Br. Dist. Kana. Dept. W. Va.	To Unatt. Dist. Kanawha Dept. Ohio.	Sept., 1862
47th Ohio Infy.........Mch., 1862	From 2-Br. Dist. Kana. Dept. W. Va.	To 3-Brig. Kanawha Div. Mt. Dept..	May, 1862
Simmond's Ky. Batty....Mch., 1862	From Arty. Dist. Kana. Dept. W. Va.	To 2-Brig. Kanawha Div. 9-C. Pot..	Sept., 1862

3d BRIGADE.—   COMMANDER.

George Crook	Col. 36th Ohio Infy	

11th Ohio Infy.........Mch., 1862	From 2-Br. Dist. Kana. Dept. W. Va.	To 2-Brig. Kanawha Div. 9-C. Pot..	Sept., 1862
36th Ohio Infy.........Mch., 1862	From Unat. Dist. Kana. Dept. W. Va.	To 2-Brig. Kanawha Div. 9-C. Pot..	Sept., 1862
44th Ohio Infy.........Mch., 1862	From 1-Br. Dist. Kana. Dept. W. Va.	To Unatt. Dist. Kanawha Dept. Ohio.	Sept., 1862
47th Ohio Infy.........May, 1862	From 2-Brig. Kana. Div. Mt. Dept...	To Unatt. Dist. Kanawha Dept. Ohio.	Sept., 1862

4th BRIGADE.—   COMMANDER.

J. A. J. Lightburn	Col. 4th W. Va. Infy	

4th W. Va. Infy.........Mch., 1862	From Unatt. Dist. Kanawha, W. Va.	To Dist. Kanawha Dept. Ohio......	Sept., 1862
9th W. Va. Infy.........Mch., 1862	From Unatt. Dist. Kanawha, W. Va.	To Dist. Kanawha Dept. Ohio......	Sept., 1862
1st W. Va. Cav. Det.....Mch., 1862	From Unatt. Dist. Kanawha, W. Va.	To R. R. Dist. W. Va. Dept Ohio...	Sept., 1862
Schambeck's Ill. Cav.....Mch., 1862	From 2-Br. Dist. Kana. Dept. W. Va.	To 2-Brig. Kanawha Div. 9-C. Pot..	Sept., 1862
UNATTACHED.—			
8th W. Va. Infy.........Mch., 1862	From Unat. Dist. Kana. Dept. W. Va.	To Cluserett's Adv. Brig. Mt. Dept..	May, 1862
60th Ohio Infy.........Mch., 1862	From New Organization..........	To Cluserett's Adv. Brig. Mt. Dept..	May, 1862
2d W. Va. Cav.........Mch., 1862	From Unat. Dist. Kana. Dept. W. Va.	To Unatt. Dist. Kanawha Dept. Ohio.	Sept., 1862
3d. Indpt. Co. Ohio Cav..Mch., 1862	From Unat. Dist. Kana. Dept. W. Va.	To Kanawha Div. 9-Corps Pot.....	Sept., 1862

BLENKER'S DIVISION.—   COMMANDER.

Louis Blenker	Brigadier General	Apr. 1, 1862, to June 26, 1862.

1st BRIGADE.—   COMMANDER.

J. H. Stahel	Brigadier General	Apr. 1, 1862, to June 26, 1862.

8th N. Y. Infy.........Apr., 1862	From 1-Brig. Blenker's Div. 2-Corps.	To 1-Brig. 1-Div. 1-Corps Army Va.	June, 1862
39th N. Y. Infy.........Apr., 1862	From 1-Brig. Blenker's Div. 2-Corps.	To Winchester, Va., 1-Corps A'y Va.	June, 1862
41st N. Y. Infy.........Apr., 1862	From 1-Brig. Blenker's Div. 2-Corps.	To 1-Brig. 1-Div. 1-Corps Army Va.	June, 1862
45th N. Y. Infy.........Apr., 1862	From 1-Brig. Blenker's Div. 2-Corps.	To 1-Brig. 1-Div. 1-Corps Army Va.	June, 1862
27th Penna. Infy.........Apr., 1862	From 1-Brig. Blenker's Div. 2-Corps.	To 1-Brig. 1-Div. 1-Corps Army Va.	June, 1862
2d N. Y. Indpt. Batty....Apr., 1862	From 1-Brig. Blenker's Div. 2-Corps.	To 1-Brig. 1-Div. 1-Corps Army Va.	June, 1862
Batty. C, 1st W. Va. Arty.May, 1862	From R. R. Dist. Mt. Dept.........	To Res. Arty. 1-Corps Army Va....	June, 1862

2d BRIGADE.—   COMMANDER.

A. Von Steinwehr	Brigadier General	Apr. 1, 1862, to June 26, 1862.

29th N. Y. Infy.........Apr., 1862	From 2-Brig. Blenker's Div. 2-Corps.	To 1-Brig. 2-Div. 1-Corps Army Va.	June, 1862
54th N. Y. Infy.........Apr., 1862	From 2-Brig. Blenker's Div. 2-Corps.	To 3-Brig. Blenker's Div. Mt. Dept..	Apr., 1862
68th N. Y. Infy.........Apr., 1862	From 2-Brig. Blenker's Div. 2-Corps.	To 1-Brig. 2-Div. 1-Corps Army Va.	June, 1862
73d Penna. Infy.........Apr., 1862	From 2-Brig. Blenker's Div. 2-Corps.	To 1-Brig. 2-Div. 1-Corps Army Va.	June, 1862
13th N. Y. Indpt. Batty...Apr., 1862	From Arty. Blenker's Div. 2-Corps..	To Res. Arty. 1-Corps Army Va....	June, 1862

3d BRIGADE.—   COMMANDER.

Henry Bohlen	Brigadier General	To June 26, 1862.

54th N. Y. Infy.........Apr., 1862	From 2-Brig. Blenker's Div. Mt. Dept.	To 2-Brig. 3-Div. 1-Corps Army Va.	June, 1862
58th N. Y. Infy.........Apr., 1862	From 3-Brig. Blenker's Div. 2-Corps.	To 2-Brig. 3-Div. 1-Corps Army Va.	June, 1862
74th Penna. Infy.........Apr., 1862	From 3-Brig. Blenker's Div. 2-Corps.	To 1-Brig. 3-Div. 1-Corps Army Va.	June, 1862
75th Penna. Infy.........Apr., 1862	From 3-Brig. Blenker's Div. 2-Corps.	To 2-Brig. 3-Div. 1-Corps Army Va.	June, 1862
Batty. I, 1st N. Y. Arty..Apr., 1862	From 3-Brig. Blenker's Div. 2-Corps.	To Res. Arty. 1-Corps Army Va....	June, 1862

ADVANCE BRIGADE.—   COMMANDER.

A. Cluserett	Colonel	To June 26, 1862.

8th W. Va. Infy.........May, 1862	From Unatt. Dist. Kana. Mt. Dept...	To 1-Brig. 3-Div. 1-Corps Army Va.	June, 1862
60th Ohio Infy.........May, 1862	From Unatt. Dist. Kana. Mt. Dept...	To Winchester, Va., 1-Corps A'y Va.	June, 1862
4th N. Y. Cav.........May, 1862	From Blenker's Div. 2-Corps Pot....	To Cav. Brig. 1-Corps Army Va....	June, 1862
UNATTACHED.—			
3d W. Va. Cav.........May, 1862	From R. R. Dist. Mt. Dept.........	To 2-Brig. 2-Div. 1-Corps Army Va.	June, 1862
6th Ohio Cav.........May, 1862	From New Organization...........	To 2-Brig. 2-Div. 1-Corps Army Va.	June, 1862

CAVALRY BRIGADE.—   COMMANDER.

Geo. D. Bayard	Brigadier General	

1st N. J. Cav.........June, 1862	From Bayard's Cav. Brig. Dept. Rap.	To Bayard's Cav. Brig. 3-Corps Va..	June, 1862
1st Penna. Cav.........June, 1862	From Bayard's Cav. Brig. Dept. Rap.	To Bayard's Cav. Brig. 3-Corps Va..	June, 1862
13th Penna. Res.........June, 1862	From Bayard's Cav. Brig. Dept. Rap.	To Unatt. Dept. Rappahannock......	June, 1862
(1st Rifles.)			
2d Me. Indpt. Batty.....June, 1862	From Bayard's Cav. Brig. Dept. Rap.	To Unatt. Dept. Rappahannock......	June, 1862

Middle Department

Created March 22, 1862, to consist of New Jersey, Pennsylvania, Delaware and Eastern Shore of Maryland and Virginia, and the Counties of Cecil, Harford, Baltimore and Ann Arundel, Maryland. Designated 8th Army Corps July 22, 1862.

COMMANDERS.

John A. Dix............	Major General	Mch. 22, 1862, to June 9, 1862.
John E. Wool.........	Major General	June 9, 1862, to July 22, 1862.

3d N. Y. Infy.........Mch., 1862	From Dix's Div. Army Pot.........	To Newport News, Va., Dept. Va....	June,	1862
4th N. Y. Infy.........Mch., 1862	From Dix's Div. Army Pot.........	To Newport News, Va., Dept. Va...	June,	1862
11th Penna. Infy........Mch., 1862	From Dix's Div. Army Pot.........	To Wadsworth's Command Wash....	Apr.,	1862
87th Penna. Infy........Mch., 1862	From Dix's Div. Army Pot.........	To R. R. Dist. 8-Corps Middle Dept..	July,	1862
111th Penna. Infy.......Mch., 1862	From New Organization............	To 1-Brig. Sigel's Div. Dept. Shen..	May,	1862
2d Del. Infy............Mch., 1862	From Dix's Div. Balto. Pot........	To 3-Brig. 1-Div. 2-Corps Pot......	June,	1862
2d Md. Infy............Mch., 1862	From Dix's Div. Balto. Pot........	To 1-Brig. 2-Div. Dept. N. C......	Apr.,	1862
3d Md. Infy............Mch., 1862	From Dix's Div. Balto. Pot........	To 1-Brig. Sigel's Div. Dept. Shen.	May,	1862
Balto., Md., Light Infy..Mch., 1862	From Dix's Div. Balto. Pot........	Consol. with 3d Md. Infy..........	May,	1862
67th Penna. Infy........Apr., 1862	From New Organization............	To Annapolis 8-Corps Middle Dept..	July,	1862
7th N. Y. State Militia..May, 1862	From New Organization............	To Balto., Md., 8 Corps Middle Dept.	July,	1862
13th N. Y. State Militia..May, 1862	From New Organization............	To Balto., Md., 8 Corps Middle Dept.	July,	1862
22d N. Y. State Militia..May, 1862	From New Organization............	To Balto., Md., 8 Corps Middle Dept.	July,	1862
37th N. Y. State Militia..May, 1862	From New Organization............	To Balto., Md., 8 Corps Middle Dept.	July,	1862
47th N. Y. State Militia..May, 1862	From New Organization............	To Balto., Md., 8 Corps Middle Dept.	July,	1862
19th N. Y. State Militia..June, 1862	From New Organization............	To Balto., Md., 8 Corps Middle Dept.	July,	1862
1st Md. Infy...........June, 1862	From 1-Brig. 1-Div. Dept. Shenan...	To Md. Brig. Balto., Md., 8-Corps.	July,	1862
ARTILLERY.—				
Batty. I, 2d U. S. Arty....Mch., 1862	From Dix's Command Balto. Md....	To Def. Balto. 8-Corps Middle Dept.	July,	1862
Batty. A, Md. Arty......Mch., 1862	From Dix's Command Balto. Md....	To 4-Brig. Arty. Res. 5-Corps Pot..	May,	1862
Batty. B, Md. Arty......Mch., 1862	From Dix's Command Balto. Md....	To 4-Brig. Arty. Res. 5-Corps Pot..	May,	1862
Batty. L, 1st N. Y. Arty..Mch., 1862	From Dix's Command Balto. Md....	To 1-Brig. Sigel's Div. Dept. Shen..	May,	1862
5th N. Y. Heavy Arty....May, 1862	From New Organization............	To Balto. Md. 8-Corps Middle Dept.	July,	1862
CAVALRY.—				
10th N. Y. Cav.........Mch., 1862	From Dix's Command Balto. Md....	To Mil. Dist. Washington D. C.....	Apr.,	1862
1st Md. Cav............Mch., 1862	From Dix's Command Balto. Md....	To Hatch's Cav. Brig. Dept. Shen..	Apr.,	1862
Purnell Legion Md. Cav..Mch., 1862	From Dix's Command Balto. Md....	To Balto. Md. 8-Corps Middle Dept.	July,	1862
2d Penna. Cav..........Apr., 1862	From New Organization............	To Mil. Dist. Washington D. C......	Apr.,	1862
13th Penna. Cav........Apr., 1862	From New Organization............	To Balto. Md-8-Corps Mid. Dept....	July,	1862
8th N. Y. Cav.........June, 1862	From Cav. Brig. 2-Corps Army Va..	To R. R. Brig. 8 Corps Mid. Dept..	July,	1862

RAILROAD BRIGADE.—   COMMANDER.

D. S. Miles...........	Col. 2d U. S. Infy.................	Mch. 22, 1862, to July 22, 1862.

10th Me. Infy.........Mch., 1862	From Dix's Div. Balto. Md.........	To 1-Brig. 1-Div. Dept. Shen.......	May,	1862
60th N. Y. Infy.........Mch., 1862	From Dix's Div. Balto. Md.........	To 2-Brig. Sigel's Div. Dept. Shen..	May,	1862
54th Penna. Infy........Mch., 1862	From Def. of Washington..........	To R. R. Dist. 8-Corps Mid. Dept..	July,	1862
1st Md. Pot. Home Brig..Mch., 1862	From Banks' Command Dept. Shen..	To R. R. Dist. 8-Corps Mid. Dept..	July,	1862
4th Md. Pot. Home Brig..Mch., 1862	From Banks' Command Dept. Shen..	To R. R. Brig. 8-Corps Mid. Dept..	July,	1862
Patapsco Md. Guard......Mch., 1862	From Dix's Div. Balto. Md.........	To R. R. Brig. 8-Corps Mid. Dept..	July,	1862
1st Md. Pot. Home Br. Cav.Apr., 1862	From Hatch's Cav. Brig. Dept. Shen.	To R. R. Brig. 8-Corps Mid. Dept..	July,	1862
Batty. K, 1st N. Y. Arty..Apr., 1862	From Mil. Dist. Washington D. C..	To 2-Brig. Sigel's Div. Dept. Shen..	May,	1862
12th N. Y. State Militia..May, 1862	From New Organization............	To R. R. Brig. 8-Corps Mid. Dept..	July,	1862
8th N. Y. Cav.........May, 1862	From Hatch's Cav. Brig. Dept. Shen.	To R. R. Brig. 8-Corps Mid. Dept..	July,	1862
DISTRICT OF EASTERN SHORE.—				
1st Md. Eastern Shore....Mch., 1862	From Dix's Div. Balto. Md.........	To Dist. East. Shore 8-Corps.......	July,	1862
2d Md. Eastern Shore....Mch., 1862	From Dix's Div. Balto. Md.........	To Dist. East. Shore 8-Corps.......	July,	1862
Purnell Md. Legion.......Mch., 1862	From Dix's Div. Balto. Md.........	To 2-Brig. Sigel's Div. Dept. Shen..	May,	1862
Purnell Md. Leg. Cav "A".July, 1862	From Balto. Md. Middle Dept......	To Dist. East. Shore 8-Corps.......	July,	1862

Eighth Army Corps---Middle Department

Created July 22, 1862, from Troops in the Middle Department. Discontinued Aug. 1, 1865.

CORPS COMMANDERS.

John E. Wool.........	Major General......................	July 22, 1862, to Dec. 22, 1862.
Robert C. Schenck.....	Major General......................	Dec. 22, 1862, to Mch. 12, 1863.
W. W. Morris.........	Bvt. Brig. General.................	Mch. 12, 1863, to Mch. 22, 1863.
Robert C. Schenck.....	Major General......................	Mch. 22, 1863, to Aug. 10, 1863.
W. W. Morris.........	Bvt. Brig. General.................	Aug. 10, 1863, to Aug. 31, 1863.
Robert C. Schenck.....	Major General......................	Aug. 31, 1863, to Sept. 22, 1863.
W. W. Morris.........	Bvt. Brig. General.................	Sept. 22, 1863, to Sept. 28, 1863.
E. B. Tyler...........	Brigadier General..................	Sept. 28, 1863, to Oct. 10, 1863.
Robert C. Schenck.....	Major General......................	Oct. 10, 1863, to Dec. 5, 1863.
H. H. Lockwood.......	Brigadier General..................	Dec. 5, 1863, to Mch. 22, 1864.
Lew Wallace..........	Major General......................	Mch. 22, 1864, to Feb. 1, 1865.
W. W. Morris.........	Bvt. Brig. General.................	Feb. 1, 1865, to Apr. 19, 1865.
Lew Wallace..........	Major General......................	Apr. 19, 1865, to Aug. 1, 1865.

RAILROAD DISTRICT.—   COMMANDER.

B. F. Kelly...........	Brigadier General..................	July 22, 1862, to Sept. 20, 1862.

Dist. Transferred to West Va., Dept. Ohio.

6th West Va. Infy......July, 1862	From R. R. Dist. Mountain Dept..	To R. R. Dist. Dist. W. Va. Dept. O.	Sept.,	1862
10th West Va. Infy......July, 1862	From R. R. Dist. Mountain Dept..	To R. R. Dist. Dist. W. Va. Dept. O.	Sept.,	1862
11th West Va. Infy......July, 1862	From R. R. Dist. Mountain Dept..	To R. R. Dist. Dist. W. Va. Dept. O.	Sept.,	1862
1st Md. Pot. Home Brig..July, 1862	From R. R. Brig. Middle Dept.....	To Annapolis, Md., 8-C. Middle Dept.	Sept.,	1862
2d Md. Pot. Home Brig...July, 1862	From R. R. Dist. Mountain Dept..	To R. R. Dist. Dist. W. Va. Dept. O.	Sept.,	1862
Loudoun, Va., Rangers...July, 1862	From New Organization...........	To R. R. Dist. Dist. W. Va. Dept. O.	Sept.,	1862
87th Penna. Infy........July, 1862	From Balto., Md., Middle Dept....	To R. R. Dist. Dist. W. Va. Dept. O.	Sept.,	1862
54th Penna. Infy........July, 1862	From R. R. Brig. Middle Dept....	To R. R. Dist. Dist. W. Va. Dept. O.	Sept.,	1862
84th Ohio Infy.........July, 1862	From R. R. Dist. Mountain Dept..	No change to Muster Out..........	Sept.,	1862
86th Ohio Infy.........July, 1862	From R. R. Dist. Mountain Dept..	No change to Muster Out..........	Sept.,	1862
23d Illinois Infy........July, 1862	From R. R. Dist. Mountain Dept..	To R. R. Dist. Dist. W. Va. Dept. O.	Sept.,	1862
12th West Va. Infy......Aug., 1862	From New Organization...........	To R. R. Dist. Dist. W. Va. Dept. O.	Sept.,	1862
106th New York Infy....Aug., 1862	From New Organization...........	To R. R. Dist. Dist. W. Va. Dept. O.	Sept.,	1862

RAILROAD DISTRICT.—Continued.

65th Illinois Infy......July, 1862	From R. R. Dist. Mountain Dept..	Captured at Harper's Ferry, Va...	Sept., 1862
Ringgold, Pa., Cav......July, 1862	From R. R. Dist. Mountain Dept..	To R. R. Dist. Dist. W. Va. Dept. O.	Sept., 1862
Wash. Co., Pa., Cav......July, 1862	From R. R. Dist. Mountain Dept..	To R. R. Dist. Dist. W. Va. Dept. O.	Sept., 1862
Batty. L, 1st Illinois A...July, 1862	From R. R. Dist. Mountain Dept..	To R. R. Dist. Dist. W. Va. Dept. O.	Sept., 1862
Batty. G, 1st West Va. A..July, 1862	From R. R. Dist. Mountain Dept..	To R. R. Dist. Dist. W. Va. Dept. O.	Sept., 1862
Batty. F, 1st West Va. A..July, 1862	From R. R. Dist. Mountain Dept..	To R. R. Dist. Dist. W. Va. Dept. O.	Sept., 1862

RAILROAD BRIGADE.— COMMANDER.

D. S. Miles.............	Col. 2d U. S. Infy.................	July 22, 1862, to Sept. 14, 1862.	
12th N. Y. State Militia..July, 1862	From R. R. Brig. Middle Dept.....	Captured at Harper's Ferry, Va...	Aug., 1862
4th Md. Pot. Home Brig...July, 1862	From R. R. Brig. Middle Dept.....	Consolidated with 3d Md. P. H. B..	Sept., 1862
Patapsco, Md., Guards....July, 1862	From R. R. Brig. Middle Dept.....	To Def. Baltimore 8-Corps........	Sept., 1862
1st Md. P. Home B. Cav..July, 1862	From R. R. Brig. Middle Dept.....	To Cav. 12-Corps Potomac........	Sept., 1862
8th New York Cav.......July, 1862	From R. R. Brig. Middle Dept.....	To 5-Brig. Pleasanton's Cav. D. Pot.	Sept., 1862
87th Ohio Infy........July, 1862	From New Organization............	Captured at Harper's Ferry, Va...	Sept., 1862
3d Md. Pot. Home Brig...July, 1862	From R. R. Dist. Mountain Dept..	Captured at Harper's Ferry, Va...	Sept., 1862
5th N. Y. H. A. Cos. A, F.July, 1862	From Balto, Md., Middle Dept......	Captured at Harper's Ferry, Va...	Sept., 1862
1st Md. Pot. Home Brig..Sept., 1862	From R. R. Dist. 8-Corps.........	Captured at Harper's Ferry, Va...	Sept., 1862
111th New York Infy....Sept., 1862	From New Organization............	Captured at Harper's Ferry, Va...	Sept., 1862
115th New York Infy....Sept., 1862	From New Organization............	Captured at Harper's Ferry, Va...	Sept., 1862
125th New York Infy....Sept., 1862	From New Organization............	Captured at Harper's Ferry, Va...	Sept., 1862
126th New York Infy....Sept., 1862	From New Organization............	Captured at Harper's Ferry, Va...	Sept., 1862
39th New York Infy.....Sept., 1862	From White's Brig. Army Va.......	Captured at Harper's Ferry, Va...	Sept., 1862
32d Ohio Infy...........July, 1862	From Piatt's Brig. Army Va.......	Captured at Harper's Ferry, Va...	Sept., 1862
60th Ohio Infy..........July, 1862	From Piatt's Brig. Army Va.......	Captured at Harper's Ferry, Va...	Sept., 1862
9th Vermont Infy.......Sept., 1862	From Piatt's Brig. Army Va.......	Captured at Harper's Ferry, Va...	Sept., 1862
ARTILLERY.—			
Batty. M, 2d Ills. Arty...July, 1862	From New Organization............	Captured at Harper's Ferry, Va...	Sept., 1862
15th Indiana Batty......Sept., 1862	From White's Brig. Army of Va....	Captured at Harper's Ferry, Va...	Sept., 1862
Wilder's Ind. Batty......Sept., 1862	From Piatt's Brig. Army of Va....	Captured at Harper's Ferry, Va...	Sept., 1862
26th Ohio Batty........Sept., 1862	From White's Brig. Army of Va...	Captured at Harper's Ferry, Va...	Sept., 1862
CAVALRY.—			
12th Illinois Cav.......Sept., 1862	From White's Brig. Army Va......	To Defences Upper Potomac 8-Corps	Sept., 1862

DISTRICT EASTERN SHORE.—Designated 1st Separate Brigade Jan. 5, 1863. Recreated Dec. 13, 1864. Consolidated with District of Delaware as District Delaware and Eastern Shore Feb., 1865.

COMMANDERS.

H. H. Lockwood........	Brigadier General.................	July 22, 1862, to Jan. 5, 1863.	
John R. Kenly.........	Brigadier General.................	Dec. 13, 1864, to June 1, 1865.	
J. M. Wilson.........	Col. 155th Indiana Infy........	June 1, 1865, to July, 1865.	
1st Md. Eastern Shore...July, 1862	From Dist. Eastern Shore Middle D.	To 1-Separate Brig. 8-Corps........	Jan., 1863
2d Md. Eastern Shore...July, 1862	From Dist. Eastern Shore Middle D.	To 1-Separate Brig. 8-Corps........	Jan., 1863
Purnell, Md., Cav. Co. A..July, 1862	From Dist. Eastern Shore Middle D.	To 1-Separate Brig. 8-Corps........	Jan., 1863
Smith's Co., Md., Cav.....Oct., 1862	From New Organization............	To 1-Separate Brig. 8-Corps........	Jan., 1863

DEFENCES OF BALTIMORE.—Designated 2d Separate Brigade Jan. 5, 1863. Recreated June 29, 1863. Discontinued Oct., 1863, and designated 3d Separate Brigade.

COMMANDERS.

W. W. Morris..........	Bvt. Brig. General.................	July 22, 1862, to Jan. 5, 1863.	
E. B. Tyler.............	Brigadier General.................	June 29, 1863, to Oct., 1863.	
7th New York S. M. Infy.July, 1862	From Balto, Md., Middle Dept.....	No change to Muster Out.........	Sept., 1862
13th N. Y. S. M. Infy....July, 1862	From Balto, Md., Middle Dept.....	No change to Muster Out.........	Sept., 1862
19th N. Y. S. M. Infy....July, 1862	From Balto, Md., Middle Dept.....	No change to Muster Out.........	Sept., 1862
22d N. Y. S. M. Infy....July, 1862	From Balto, Md., Middle Dept.....	No change to Muster Out.........	Sept., 1862
37th N. Y. S. M. Infy....July, 1862	From Balto, Md., Middle Dept.....	No change to Muster Out.........	Sept., 1862
47th N. Y. S. M. Infy....July, 1862	From Balto, Md., Middle Dept.....	No change to Muster Out.........	Sept., 1862
18th Conn. Infy........Aug., 1862	From New Organization............	To 2-Separate Brig. 8-Corps......	Jan., 1863
106th New York Infy....Aug., 1862	From New Organization............	To R. R. Dist. 8-Corps..........	Aug., 1862
109th New York Infy....Aug., 1862	From New Organization............	To Def. of Washington..........	Oct., 1862
110th New York Infy....Aug., 1862	From New Organization............	To New Orleans Dept. Gulf......	Nov., 1862
138th Penna. Infy.......Aug., 1862	From New Organization............	To 3-Separate Brig. 8-Corps......	Feb., 1863
114th New York Infy....Sept., 1862	From New Organization............	To New Orleans Dept. Gulf......	Nov., 1862
116th New York Infy....Sept., 1862	From New Organization............	To New Orleans Dept. Gulf......	Nov., 1862
14th New Jersey Infy....Sept., 1862	From New Organization............	To 3-Separate Brig. 8-Corps......	Feb., 1863
Patapsco, Md., Guard....Sept., 1862	From R. R. Brig. 8-Corps.........	To 2-Separate Brig. 8-Corps......	Jan., 1863
1st Maryland Infy.......Sept., 1862	From Reorganization..............	To Md. Brig. Def. Upper Pot. 8-C.	Sept., 1862
4th Maryland Infy.......Sept., 1862	From New Organization............	To Md. Brig. Def. Upper Pot. 8-C.	Sept., 1862
6th Maryland Infy.......Sept., 1862	From New Organization............	To Md. Brig. Def. Upper Pot. 8-C.	Sept., 1862
7th Maryland Infy.......Sept., 1862	From New Organization............	To Md. Brig. Def. Upper Pot. 8-C.	Sept., 1862
8th Maryland Infy.......Sept., 1862	From New Organization............	To Md. Brig. Def. Upper Pot. 8-C.	Sept., 1862
128th New York Infy....Sept., 1862	From New Organization............	To New Orleans, La. Dept. Gulf....	Nov., 1862
38th Mass. Infy..........Oct., 1862	From New Organization............	To New Orleans, La. Dept. Gulf....	Nov., 1862
150th New York Infy....Oct., 1862	From New Organization............	To 2-Separate Brig. 8-Corps......	Jan., 1863
151st New York Infy....Oct., 1862	From New Organization............	To 2-Separate Brig. 8-Corps......	Jan., 1863
Purnell Md. Legion.....Dec., 1862	From 2-Brig. 2-Div. 12-Corps Pot.	To 3-Separate Brig. 8-Corps......	Feb., 1863
3d Delaware Infy.......Dec., 1862	From 2-Brig. 2-Div. 12-Corps Pot.	To 3-Separate Brig. 8-Corps......	Feb., 1863
179th Penna. (2 Cos.)....Dec., 1862	From New Organization............	To 2-Separate Brig. 8-Corps......	Jan., 1863
84th New York S. M. Infy.July, 1863	From New Organization............	No change to Muster Out.........	Aug., 1863
CAVALRY.—			
13th Penna. Cav.......July, 1862	From Baltimore, Md. Middle Dept...	To R. R. Dist. West Va..........	Oct., 1862
Purnell Md. Cav. Co. C...Sept., 1862	From New Organization............	To 2-Separate Brig. 8-Corps......	Jan., 1863
Smith's Co. Md. Cav.....Sept., 1862	From New Organization............	To Dist. East. Shore 8-Corps......	Oct., 1862
1st Conn. Cav...........Jan., 1863	From Cav. 11-Corps Potomac......	To 2-Separate Brig. 8-Corps......	Jan., 1863
1st Delaware Cav.......June, 1863	From 1-Separate Brig. 8-Corps....	To 3-Separate Brig. 8-Corps......	Oct., 1863
Purnell Md. Cav. Co. B...June, 1863	From Annapolis, Md. 8-Corps......	To Annapolis, Md. 8-Corps......	Oct., 1863
1st Delaware Cav.......Dec., 1863	From 3-Separate Brig. 5-Corps....	To 1-Separate Brig. 8-Corps......	Jan., 1864
ARTILLERY.—			
5th N. Y. Heavy Arty....July, 1862	From Baltimore, Md. Middle Dept..	To 2-Separate Brig. 8-Corps......	Jan., 1863
Batty. I, 2d U. S. Arty....July, 1862	From Baltimore, Md. Middle Dept..	To 2-Separate Brig. 8-Corps......	Jan., 1863
17th Indiana Batty.......July, 1862	From New Organization............	To Def. Upper Potomac 8-Corps...	Jan., 1863
8th N. Y. Heavy Arty....Aug., 1862	From New Organization............	To 2-Separate Brig. 8-Corps......	Jan., 1863
Baltimore, Md. Batty....Aug., 1862	From New Organization............	To Md. Brig. Def. Upper Pot. 8-Corps	Sept., 1862
6th N. Y. Heavy Arty....Sept., 1862	From New Organization............	To Def. Upper Potomac 8-Corps...	Dec., 1862
15th N. Y. Indpt. Batty....Oct., 1862	From Arty. Res. Pot. B, 1st N. Y. Bn.	To Arty. Res. Potomac..........	Jan., 1863
Batty. L, 5th U. S. Arty...Oct., 1862	From New Organization............	To 2-Separate Brig. 8-Corps......	Jan., 1863
Baltimore, Md. Batty....July, 1863	From Arty. French's Div. 8-Corps..	To 3-Separate Brig. 8-Corps......	Oct., 1863
5th N. Y. H. A., Co's B. C..July, 1863	From 2-Separate Brig. 8-Corps....	To 3-Separate Brig. 8-Corps......	Oct., 1863

DEFENCES OF BALTIMORE.—Continued.

3d Penna. H. A. Co. H...July, 1863	From 3-Separate Brig. 8-Corps...	To 3-Separate Brig. 8-Corps	Oct.,	1863
Batty. A, Md. Jr. Batty..July, 1863	From New Organization	To 3-Separate Brig. 8-Corps	Oct.,	1863
Batty. B, Md. Jr. Batty..July, 1863	From New Organization	To 3-Separate Brig. 8-Corps	Oct.,	1863

ANNAPOLIS.—

Purnell Md. Cav. Co. B...July, 1862	From Baltimore, Md. Middle Dept...	To Def. Balto., Md. 8-Corps	June,	1863
67th Penna. Infy....July, 1862	From Baltimore, Md. Middle Dept...	To Def. Upper Potomac 8-Corps...	Jan.,	1863
131st New York Infy....Sept., 1862	From New Organization	To New Orleans, La., Dept. Gulf..	Nov.,	1862
3d Md. Pot. Home Brig...Sept., 1862	From Prisoners of War	To 1-Separate Brig. 8-Corps	June,	1863
1st Md. Pot. Home Brig...Jan. 1863	From Prisoners of War	To 1-Separate Brig. 8-Corps	Feb.,	1863
2d Md. Cav., 5 Co's...July, 1863	From New Organization	No change to Muster Out	Feb.,	1864
Purnell Md. Cav. Co. B...Jan. 1864	From 1-Separate Brig. 8-Corps	To 2-Brig. 2-Div. 5-Corps Potomac..	May,	1864

WILLIAMSPORT, MD., MARYLAND BRIGADE.—   COMMANDER.

J. R. Kenly	Brigadier General	Sept. 17, 1862, to Jan. 5, 1863.		
1st Maryland Infy......Sept., 1862	From Def. of Balto. Md. 8-Corps...	To Md. Brig. Def. Upper Potomac..	Jan.,	1863
4th Maryland Infy......Sept., 1862	From Def. of Balto. Md. 8-Corps...	To Md. Brig. Def. Upper Potomac..	Jan.,	1863
6th Maryland Infy......Sept., 1862	From Def. of Balto. Md. 8-Corps...	To Md. Brig. Def. Upper Potomac..	Jan.,	1863
7th Maryland Infy......Sept., 1862	From Def. of Balto. Md. 8-Corps...	To Md. Brig. Def. Upper Potomac..	Jan.,	1863
8th Maryland Infy......Sept., 1862	From Def. of Balto. Md. 8-Corps...	To Md. Brig. Def. Upper Potomac..	Jan.,	1863
Baltimore, Md., Batty....Sept., 1862	From Def. of Balto. Md. 8-Corps...	To Md. Brig. Def. Upper Potomac..	Jan.,	1863

UNATTACHED.—

12th New Jersey Infy....Sept., 1862	From New Organization	To Def. of Washington	Dec.,	1862
4th Delaware Infy......Sept., 1862	From New Organization	To Busteed's Indpt. Brig. 7-Corps..	Dec.,	1862
109th New York Infy....Sept., 1862	From New Organization	To Def. of Washington	Oct.,	1862
141st New York Infy....Sept., 1862	From New Organization	To 2-Brig. Abercrombie's Div. Wash.	Oct.,	1862
140th Penna. Infy......Sept., 1862	From New Organization	To 3-Brig. 1-Div. 2-Corps Potomac.	Dec.,	1862
148th Penna. Infy......Sept., 1862	From New Organization	To 1-Brig. 1-Div. 2-Corps Potomac.	Dec.,	1862
Patapsco, Md. Guard.....Sept., 1862	From R. R. Brig. 8-Corps	To 2-Separate Brig. 8-Corps	Jan.,	1863

DEFENSES UPPER POTOMAC—Organized Jan. 5, 1863. Discontinued Feb., 1863.

COMMANDER.

B. F. Kelly	Brigadier General	Jan. 5, 1863, to Feb., 1863.	

HARPER'S FERRY, MARYLAND BRIGADE.—   COMMANDER.

J. R. Kenly	Brigadier General	Jan. 5, 1863, to Feb., 1863.		
1st Maryland Infy......Jan. 1863	From Md. Brig. Williamsport, Md...	To 1-Brig. 1-Div. 8-Corps	Mch.,	1863
4th Maryland Infy......Jan. 1863	From Md. Brig. Williamsport, Md...	To 1-Brig. 1-Div. 8-Corps	Mch.,	1863
6th Maryland Infy......Jan. 1863	From Md. B. Williamsport, Md. 8-C.	To 3-Brig. 2-Div. 8-Corps	Mch.,	1863
7th Maryland Infy......Jan., 1863	From Md. B. Williamsport, Md. 8-C.	To 1-Brig. 1-Div. 8-Corps	Mch.,	1863
8th Maryland Infy......Jan., 1863	From Md. B. Williamsport, Md. 8-C.	To 1-Brig. 1-Div. 8-Corps	Mch.,	1863

ARTILLERY.—

6th N. Y. Heavy Arty....Jan. 1863	From Def. Balto., Md. 8-Corps	To 2-Brig. 1-Div. 8-Corps	Mch.,	1863
4th Mass. Heavy Arty....Jan., 1863 (Cos. B, C, H, I.)	From Whipple's Div. Def. Wash....	To 2-Brig. 1-Div. 8-Corps	Mch.,	1863
Baltimore, Md. Batty....Jan., 1863	From Md. B. Williamsport, Md. 8-C.	To 3-Brig. 2-Div. 8-Corps	Mch.,	1863
17th Indiana Batty......Jan., 1863	From Def. Balto. 8-Corps	To 1-Brig. 1-Div. 8-Corps	Mch.,	1863
4th Maine Indpt. Batty...Jan., 1863	From Arty. 2-Div. 12-Corps Pot...	To 2-Brig. 1-Div. 8-Corps	Mch.,	1863

CAVALRY.—

14th Penna. Cav......Jan., 1863	From R. R. Dist. West Va	To 1-Brig. 1-Div. 8-Corps	Mch.,	1863
1st Maryland Cav. (H. I.).Jan., 1863	From R. R. Dist. West Va	To 2-Brig. 3-Div. Cav. Corps Pot...	Mch.,	1863

NEW CREEK, VA.—

23d Illinois Infy......Jan., 1863	From R. R. Dist. West Va	To 5-Brig. 1-Div. 8-Corps	Mch.,	1863
14th West Va. Infy......Jan., 1863	From R. R. Dist. West Va	To 5-Brig. 1-Div. 8-Corps	Mch.,	1863
Batty. L, 1st Ill. Arty....Jan., 1863	From R. R. Dist. West Va	To 5-Brig. 1-Div. 8-Corps	Mch.,	1863

NORTH MOUNTAIN.—

54th Penna. Infy......Jan., 1863	From R. R. Dist. West Va	To 4-Brigg. 1-Div. 8-Corps	Mch.,	1863
1st West Va. Infy......Jan., 1863	From R. R. Dist. West Va	To 4-Brigg. 1-Div. 8-Corps	Mch.,	1863

ROMNEY.—

116th Ohio Infy......Jan., 1863	From R. R. Dist. West Va	To 1-Brig. 2-Div. 8-Corps	Mch.,	1863
123d Ohio Infy......Jan., 1863	From R. R. Dist. West Va	To 1-Brig. 2-Div. 8-Corps	Mch.,	1863
Ringgold Pa. Cav......Jan., 1863	From R. R. Dist. West Va	To 4-Brig. 1-Div. 8-Corps	Mch.,	1863
Batty. E, 1st West Va. A.Jan., 1863	From R. R. Dist. West Va	To 1-Brig. 1-Div. 8-Corps	Mch.,	1863
Batty. D, 1st West Va. A.Jan., 1863	From R. R. Dist. West Va	To 1-Brig. 2-Div. 8-Corps	Mch.,	1863
Batty. G, 1st West Va. A.Jan., 1863	From R. R. Dist. West Va	To 4-Separate Brig. 8-Corps	Mch.,	1863

CLARKSBURG.—

6th West Va. Infy......Jan., 1863	From R. R. Dist. West Va	To 6-Brig. 1-Div. 8-Corps	Mch.,	1863

CUMBERLAND, MD.—

2d Md. Pot. Home Brig..Jan., 1863	From R. R. Dist. West Va	To 5-Brig. 1-Div. 8-Corps	Mch.,	1863

KEARNYSVILLE.—

12th Penna. Cav........Jan., 1863	From R. R. Dist. West Va	To 1-Brig. 2-Div. 8-Corps	Mch.,	1863

PARKERSBURG, W. VA.—

11th West Va. Infy......Jan., 1863	From R. R. Dist. West Va	To 6-Brig. 1-Div. 8-Corps	Mch.,	1863

POINT OF ROCKS.—

5th Maryland Infy......Jan., 1863	From 3-Brig. 3-Div. 2-Corps Pot...	To 2-Brig. 1-Div. 8-Corps	Mch.,	1863
Loudoun Va. Rangers....Jan., 1863	From R. R. Dist. West Va	To Unattached 8-Corps	Mch.,	1863

SIR JOHN'S RUN.—

15th West Va. Infy......Jan., 1863	From R. R. Dist. West Va	To 3-Brig. 1-Div. 8-Corps	Mch.,	1863

SPRINGFIELD.—

Wash. Co. Pa. Cav. Co....Jan., 1863	From R. R. Dist. West Va	To 4-Brig. 1-Div. 8-Corps	Mch.,	1863

MARTINSBURG, WEST VA.—   COMMANDER.

A. T. McReynolds	Col. 1st N. Y. Lincoln Cav			
106th New York Infy....Jan., 1863	From R. R. Dist. West Va	To 3-Brig. 1-Div. 8-Corps	Mch.,	1863
126th Ohio Infy........Jan., 1863	From R. R. Dist. West Va	To 3-Brig. 1-Div. 8-Corps	Mch.,	1863
2d Md. P. H. B. Cav. Cs. B, F.Jan., 1863	From R. R. Dist. West Va	To 3-Brig. 1-Div. 8-Corps	Mch.,	1863
6th West Va. Infy. Co. F.Jan., 1863	From R. R. Dist. West Va	To 6-Brig. 1-Div. 8-Corps	Mch.,	1863

MILROY'S DIVISION WINCHESTER, VA.—Organized Jan., 1863. Designated 2-Div. 8-Corps Feb., 1863.

COMMANDER.

R. H. Milroy	Brigadier General	Jan., 1863, to Feb., 1863.		
87th Penna. Infy......Jan., 1863	From R. R. Dist. West Va	To 2-Brig. 2-Div. 8-Corps	Feb.,	1863
9th West Va. Infy......Jan., 1863	From Point Pleasant Dist. Kanawha	To 2-Brig. 2-Div. 8-Corps	Feb.,	1863
10th West Va. Infy......Jan., 1863	From R. R. Dist. West Va	To 2-Brig. 2-Div. 8-Corps	Feb.,	1863
12th West Va. Infy......Jan., 1863	From R. R. Dist. West Va	To 2-Brig. 2-Div. 8-Corps	Feb.,	1863
110th Ohio Infy........Jan., 1863	From R. R. Dist. West Va	To 1-Brig. 2-Div. 8-Corps	Feb.,	1863
122d Ohio Infy........Jan., 1863	From R. R. Dist. West Va	To 1-Brig. 2-Div. 8-Corps	Feb.,	1863

MILROY'S DIVISION, WINCHESTER, VA.—Continued.

CAVALRY.—

1st N. Y. Lincoln Cav.....Jan., 1863	From Def. Upper Potomac.........	To 3-Brig. 2-Div. 8-Corps.........	Feb.,	1863
12th Penna. Cav..........Jan., 1863	From Def. Upper Potomac.........	To 1-Brig. 2-Div. 8-Corps.........	Feb.,	1863
13th Penna. Cav..........Jan., 1863	From Def. Upper Potomac.........	To 1-Brig. 2-Div. 8-Corps.........	Feb.,	1863
1st West Va. Cav. Co. K..Jan., 1863	From Def. Upper Potomac.........	To 2-Brig. 2-Div. 8-Corps.........	Feb.,	1863
3d West Va. Cav. Co. D...Jan., 1863	From Def. Upper Potomac.........	To 2-Brig. 2-Div. 8-Corps.........	Feb.,	1863

ARTILLERY MILROY'S DIVISION.—

Batty. B, 1st W. Va. Arty.Jan., 1863	From R. R. Dist. West Va..........	To 4th Separate Brig. 8-Corps......	Feb.,	1863
Batty. D, 1st W. Va. Arty..Jan., 1862	From R. R. Dist. West Va..........	To 1-Brig. 2-Div. 8-Corps.........	Feb.,	1863

1st SEPARATE BRIGADE.—Organized Jan. 5, 1863. Transferred to the Army of the Potomac, June, 1863. Reorganized Oct., 1863. Discontinued July 31, 1865.

COMMANDERS.

H. H. Lockwood........	Brigadier General..............	Jan. 5, 1863, to Feb. 4, 1863.
S. A. Graham..........	Col. Purnell Md. Legion............	Feb. 4, 1863, to Feb. 14, 1863.
H. H. Lockwood........	Brigadier General..............	Feb. 14, 1863, to June 26, 1863.
H. H. Lockwood........	Brigadier General..............	Oct. 28, 1863, to Dec. 18, 1863.
E. B. Tyler............	Brigadier General..............	Dec. 18, 1863, to Mch. 12, 1864.
H. H. Lockwood........	Brigadier General..............	Mch. 12, 1864, to Mch. 24, 1864.
E. B. Tyler............	Brigadier General..............	Mch. 24, 1864, to Nov. 18, 1864.
J. R. Kenly..........	Brigadier General..............	Nov. 18, 1864, to Dec. 20, 1864.
E. B. Tyler............	Brigadier General..............	Dec. 20, 1864, to June 5, 1865.
J. R. Kenly..........	Brigadier General..............	June 5, 1865, to July 31, 1865.

1st Md. Eastern Shore....Jan., 1863	From Dist. East. Shore 8-Corps....	To Lockwood's Brig. 8-Corps........	June,	1863
2d Md. Eastern Shore....Jan., 1863	From Dist. East. Shore 8-Corps....	To Lockwood's Brig. 8-Corps........	June,	1863
Smith's Md. Co. Cav......Jan., 1863	From Dist. East. Shore 8-Corps....	To Unatt. Eastern Shore 8-Corps...	June,	1863
Purnell Md. Cav. Co. A...Jan., 1863	From Dist. East. Shore 8-Corps....	To Lockwood's Brig. 8-Corps........	June,	1863
1st Md. Pot. Home Brig...Feb., 1863	From Annapolis Md. 8-Corps........	To Lockwood's Brig. 8-Corps........	June,	1863
1st Del. Cav. 4-Co's......Feb., 1863	From New Organization.............	To Def. Balto. Md. 8-Corps........	June,	1863
Purnell Md. Cav. Co. C...Feb., 1863	From 2-Separate Brig. 8-Corps.....	To 3-Separate Brig. 8-Corps........	June,	1863
11th N. Y. Cav. 3-Co's...Feb., 1863	From Def. of Wash. 22-Corps......	To Def. Washington 22-Corps.......	June,	1863
3d Del. Infy.............Oct., 1863	From 3 Separate Brig. 8-Corps.....	To 2-Brig. 4-Div. 5-Corps Pot......	May,	1864
3d Md. Pot. Home Brig...Oct., 1863	From Monocacy Junction 8-Corps...	To Kenly's Indpt. Brig. 6-Corps.....	July,	1864
Purnell Md. Legion.......Oct., 1863	From Fort Del. Dist. Del. 8-Corps..	To 3-Brig. 2-Div. 5-Corps Pot......	May,	1864
1st Md. E. S. Infy........Oct., 1863	From 2-Br. Md. Hts. Div. West Va.	To 3-Separate Brig. 8-Corps........	Mch.,	1864
Purnell Md. Cav. Co. B....Dec., 1863	From 3-Separate Brig. 8-Corps.....	To Annapolis Md. 8-Corps..........	Jan.,	1864
9th Md. Infy............Jan., 1864	From 1-Brig. Md. Hts. Div. West Va.	No change to Muster Out..........	Feb.,	1864
1st Del. Cav. 1st Bn.....Jan., 1864	From Cav. Res. Def. Balto. 8 Corps.	To 1-Brig. 1-Div. 6-Corps Pot......	May,	1864
5th N. Y. H. Arty. Co. F..Jan., 1864	From 2-Separate Brig. 8-Corps.....	To 2-Separate Brig. 8-Corps........	Mch.,	1864
8th N. Y. H. Arty. Co. F..Mch., 1864	From 2-Separate Brig. 8-Corps.....	To Def. Balto. 8-Corps...........	May,	1864
1st Md. Eastern Shore....June, 1864	From 3-Separate Brig. 8-Corps.....	To Res. Div. West Va.............	Sept.,	1864
144th Ohio Infy.........May, 1864	From New Organization.............	To Kenly's Indpt. Brig. 6-Corps Shen.	July,	1864
157th Ohio Infy.........May, 1864	From New Organization.............	No change to Muster Out..........	Aug.,	1864
1st Md. Cav. Co's C, F...May, 1864	From 3-Separate Brig. 8-Corps.....	To 3-Br. 1-Div. 10-C. Dept. Va.&N.C.	June,	1864
149th Ohio Infy.........July, 1864	From 3-Separate Brig. 8-Corps.....	To Kenly's Indpt. Brig. 6-Corps Shen.	July,	1864
1st Del. Cav.............July, 1864	From 1-Brig. 1-Div. 6-Corps Pot....	No change to Muster Out..........	July,	1865
1st N. J. Militia.........July, 1864	From New Organization.............	No change to Muster Out..........	Aug.,	1864
93d N. Y. Militia........July, 1864	From New Organization.............	No change to Muster Out..........	Nov.,	1864
11th Md. Infy...........July, 1864	From New Organization.............	No change to Muster Out..........	June,	1865
195th Penna. Infy.......July, 1864	From New Organization.............	To Res. Div. West Va.............	Oct.,	1864
8th Ill. Cav. Det........July, 1864	From Def. Washington 22-Corps....	To Def. Washington 22-Corps.......	Oct.,	1864
1st N. Y. Cav. Det......July, 1864	From Dept. West Va..............	To 2-Brig. 2-Cav. Div. West Va....	Oct.,	1864
21st N. Y. Cav. Det......July, 1864	From Dept. West Va..............	To Res. Div. West Va.............	Oct.,	1864
8th Ohio Cav. Det.......July, 1864	From Dept. West Va..............	To 1-Brig. 2-Div. Cav. West Va....	Oct.,	1864
8th N. Y. Heavy Arty. Det.July, 1864	From 2-Brig. 2-Div. 2-Corps Pot....	No change to Muster Out..........	June,	1865
9th N. Y. Heavy Arty. Det.July, 1864	From 2-Brig. 3-Div. 6-Corps Pot....	To Def. Washington..............	June,	1865
3d Penna. H. Arty. Co. H..July, 1864	From 3-Separate Brig. 8-Corps.....	No change to Muster Out..........	July,	1865
12th Md. Infy...........Aug., 1864	From New Organization.............	To Res. Div. West Va.............	Sept.,	1864
Smith's Co. Md. Cav......Oct., 1864	From 3-Separate Brig. 8-Corps.....	No change to Muster Out..........	June,	1865

2d SEPARATE BRIGADE—Organized Jan. 5, 1863. Discontinued July 29, 1865.

COMMANDERS.

W. W. Morris..........	Bvt. Brig. General..............	Jan. 5, 1863, to Jan. 20, 1864.
P. A. Porter............	Col. 8th N. Y. Heavy Arty.........	Jan. 20, 1864, to May 10, 1864.
W. W. Morris..........	Bvt. Brig. General..............	May 10, 1864, to Jan. 31, 1865.
D. Macauley...........	Col. 11th Ind. Infy.............	Jan. 31, 1865, to Apr. 19, 1865.
W. W. Morris..........	Bvt. Brig. General..............	Apr. 19, 1865, to July 29, 1865.

1st Conn. Cav. Battn.....Jan., 1863	From Def. Balto. 8-Corps.......	To Cav. Res. Balto. Md. 8-Corps....	Dec.,	1863
18th Conn. Infy.........Jan., 1863	From Def. Balto. 8-Corps.......	To 2-Brig. 2-Div. 8-Corps........	Feb.,	1863
5th N. Y. Heavy Arty.....Jan., 1863	From Def. Balto. 8-Corps.......	To Res. Div. Harper's Ferry W. Va.	Apr.,	1864
8th N. Y. Heavy Arty.....Jan., 1863	From Def. Balto. 8-Corps.......	To Tyler's H. Div. Div. 22-Corps.	May,	1864
150th N. Y. Infy.........Jan., 1863	From Def. Balto. 8-Corps.......	To 3-Separate Brig. 8-Corps......	Feb.,	1863
151st N. Y. Infy.........Jan., 1863	From Def. Balto. 8-Corps.......	To 3-Separate Brig. 8-Corps......	Feb.,	1863
179th Penna. Infy. 2-Co's..Jan., 1863	From Def. Balto. 8-Corps.......	No change to Muster Out.........	July,	1863
Batty. I, 2d U. S. Arty....Jan., 1863	From Def. Balto. 8-Corps.......	To 2-Brig. Haskin's Div. 22-Corps.	May,	1864
Batty. L, 5th U. S. Arty...Jan., 1863	From Def. Balto. 8-Corps.......	To 3-Separate Brig. 8-Corps......	Feb.,	1863
Purnell Md. Leg. Cv. Co. C.Jan., 1863	From Def. Balto. 8-Corps.......	To 1-Separate Brig. 8-Corps......	Feb.,	1863
Patapsco Md. Guards......Jan., 1863	From Def. Balto. 8-Corps.......	To York, Pa., Dept. Susquehanna...	June,	1863
3d Penna. H. Arty. Co. H..Mch., 1863	From Fort Delaware 8-Corps......	To 3-Separate Brig. 8-Corps......	June,	1863
5th Del. Infy............June, 1863	From Unatt. Delaware 8-Corps.....	To Fort Delaware 8-Corps........	June,	1863
7th N. Y. S. M...........June, 1863	From New Organization...........	To New York..................	July,	1863
17th N. Y. S. M...........July, 1863	From New Organization...........	No change to Muster Out.........	Aug.,	1863
18th N. Y. S. M...........July, 1863	From New Organization...........	No change to Muster Out.........	Aug.,	1863
22d N. Y. S. M...........July, 1863	From New Organization...........	No change to Muster Out.........	Aug.,	1863
55th N. Y. S. M...........July, 1863	From New Organization...........	No change to Muster Out.........	Aug.,	1863
69th N. Y. S. M...........July, 1863	From New Organization...........	No change to Muster Out.........	Aug.,	1863
10th Md. Infy...........Dec., 1863	From 1-Brig. Md. Hts. Div. W. Va.	No change to Muster Out.........	Jan.,	1864
131st Ohio Infy..........May, 1864	From New Organization...........	No change to Muster Out.........	Aug.,	1864
137th Ohio Infy..........May, 1864	From New Organization...........	No change to Muster Out.........	Aug.,	1864
192d Penna. Infy........July, 1864	From New Organization...........	To Dept. Ohio................	Aug.,	1864
5th Mass. Infy..........Aug., 1864	From New Organization...........	No change to Muster Out.........	Nov.,	1864
Battys. H & K, 2d U. S....Aug., 1864	From Dist. Fla. Dept. Gulf.......	No change to end of war........	Aug.,	1865
91st N. Y. Infy.........Oct., 1864	From Veteran Furlough...........	To 1-Brig. 3-Div. 5-Corps Pot......	Feb.,	1865
11th Ind. Infy...........Jan., 1865	From 2-Br. 2-Div. 19-Corps M. M. D.	No change to Muster Out.........	July,	1865
7th N. Y. Heavy Arty....Feb., 1865	From 2-Brig. 1-Div. 2-Corps Pot....	No change to Muster Out.........	Aug.,	1865

3d SEPARATE BRIGADE.—Organized Feb. 14, 1863. Discontinued June 26, 1863. Reorganized July 12, 1863. Discontinued Aug. 10, 1863. Reorganized Oct. 1, 1863, from Defences of Baltimore. Discontinued Dec. 18, 1863. Reorganized March 24, 1864. Discontinued July 31, 1865.

COMMANDERS.

H. S. Briggs	Brigadier General	Feb. 14, 1863, to June 25, 1863.
S. A. Graham	Col. Purnell Md. Legion	July 12, 1863, to Aug. 10, 1863.
E. B. Tyler	Brigadier General	Oct. 1, 1863, to Dec. 18, 1863.
H. H. Lockwood	Brigadier General	Mch. 24, 1864, to May 16, 1864.
J. R. Kenly	Brigadier General	May 16, 1864, to July 20, 1864.
H. H. Lockwood	Brigadier General	July 20, 1864, to July 31, 1865.

3d Del. Infy	Feb., 1863	From Frederick Md. 8-Corps	To Lockwood's Command 8-Corps	June, 1863
Purnell Md. Legion	Feb., 1863	From Frederick Md. 8-Corps	To Lockwood's Command 8-Corps	June, 1863
14th N. J. Infy	Feb., 1863	From Frederick Md. 8-Corps	To 3-Prov'l Brig. French's Div. 8-C.	June, 1863
150th N. Y. Infy	Feb., 1863	From Def. of Balto. 8-Corps	To 2-Brig. 1-Div. 12-Corps Pot	July, 1863
151st N. Y. Infy	Feb., 1863	From Def. of Balto. 8-Corps	To 3-Prov'l Brig. French's Div. 8-C.	June, 1863
138th Penna. Infy	Feb., 1863	From Relay House 8-Corps	To Elliott's Command 8-Corps	June, 1863
Batty. L, 5th U. S. Arty	Feb., 1863	From 2-Separate Brig. 8-Corps	To 2-Brig. 2-Div. 8-Corps	Mch., 1863
Loudoun Va. Rangers	May, 1863	From Pt. of Rocks, Def. Upper Pot.	To Lockwood's Command 8-Corps	June, 1863
3d Penna. H. Arty. Co. H.	May, 1863	From 2-Separate Brig. 8-Corps	To Def. Balto. 8-Corps	June, 1863
3d Del. Infy	July, 1863	From Lockwood's Command 8-Corps	To 1-Separate Brig. 8-Corps	Oct., 1863
3d Md. Pot. Home Brig	July, 1863	From Annapolis Md. 8-Corps	To Monocacy Junction 8-Corps	Aug., 1863
Purnell Md. Legion	July, 1863	From Lockwood's Command 8-Corps	To Fort Delaware 8-Corps	Aug., 1863
Loudoun Va. Rangers	July, 1863	From Lockwood's Command 8-Corps	To 2-Brig. Md. Heights Div. W. Va.	Aug., 1863
Batty. L, 5th U. S. Arty	July, 1863	From 1-Brig. 2-Div. 8-Corps	To Camp Barry Wash. 22-Corps	Aug., 1863
Balto. Md. Batty	Oct., 1863	From Def. Balto. 8-Corps	To Arty. Res. 8-Corps	Dec., 1863
3d Pa. H. Arty. Co. H	Oct., 1863	From Def. Balto. 8-Corps	To Arty. Res. 8-Corps	Dec., 1863
Batty. A, Jr. Md. Arty	Oct., 1863	From Def. Balto. 8-Corps	To Arty. Res. 8-Corps	Dec., 1863
Batty. B, Jr. Md. Arty	Oct., 1863	From Def. Balto. 8-Corps	To Arty. Res. 8-Corps	Dec., 1863
5th N. Y. H. Arty. B. C.	Oct., 1863	From Def. Balto. 8-Corps	To 2-Separate Brig. 8-Corps	Dec., 1863
1st Conn. Cav	Oct., 1863	From Def. Balto. 8-Corps	To Cav. Res. 8-Corps	Dec., 1863
1st Del. Cav	Oct., 1863	From Def. Balto. 8-Corps	To Cav. Res. 8-Corps	Dec., 1863
Purnell Md. Cav. Co. B	Oct., 1863	From Def. Balto. 8-Corps	To 1-Separate Brig. 8-Corps	Dec., 1863
1st Md. Eastern Shore	Mch., 1864	From 1-Separate Brig. 8-Corps	To 1-Separate Brig. 8-Corps	June, 1863
1st Del. Cav. Co. E	Mch., 1864	From 1-Separate Brig. 8-Corps	To 1-Brig. 1-Div. 6-Corps Pot	May, 1864
1st Md. Cav	Mch., 1864	From Provost Guard Army Pot	To 3-Brig. 1-Div. 10-Corps Va. & N. C.	June, 1864
Smith's Md. Cav. Co	Mch., 1864	From Unatt. Dist. Eastern Shore	To 1-Separate Brig. 8-Corps	Oct., 1864
Balto. Md. Batty	Mch., 1864	From Arty. Res. Balto. Md. 8 Corps.	To Dist. Harper's Ferry West Va.	July, 1864
Batty. D, Md. Arty	Mch., 1864	From New Organization	To 3-Brig. DeRussy's Div. 22-Corps.	June, 1864
3d Pa. Heavy Arty Co. H.	Mch., 1864	From Arty. Res. Balto. 8-Corps	To 1st Separate Brig. 8-Corps	July, 1864
149th Ohio Infy	May, 1864	From New Organization	To 1st Separate Brig. 8-Corps	July, 1864
159th Ohio Infy	May, 1864	From New Organization	No change to Muster Out	Aug., 1864
5th Md. Infy. Det	May, 1864	From Dist. Del. 8-Corps	To 3-Brig. 2-Div. 18-C. Va. & N. C.	June, 1864
144th Ohio Infy. Co. G	May, 1864	From 1-Separate Brig. 8-Corps	No change to Muster Out	Aug., 1864
11th Md. Infy	June, 1864	From New Organization	To 1-Separate Brig. 8-Corps	July, 1864
7th Del. Infy	July, 1864	From New Organization	No change to Muster Out	Aug., 1864
5th Mass. Infy	July, 1864	From New Organization	To 2-Separate Brig. 8-Corps	Aug., 1864
8th Mass. Infy	July, 1864	From New Organization	No change to Muster Out	Nov., 1864
193d Penna. Infy	July, 1864	From New Organization	No change to Muster Out	Nov., 1864
194th Penna. Infy	July, 1864	From New Organization	No change to Muster Out	Nov., 1864
196th Penna. Infy	July, 1864	From New Organization	To Camp Douglass, Chicago, Ill	Aug., 1864
197th Penna. Infy	July, 1864	From New Organization	To Rock Island, Ill	Aug., 1864
2d Del. Cav. Co. A	July, 1864	From New Organization	No change to Muster Out	Aug., 1864
97th Penna. Infy. 1-Co	Dec., 1864	From 2-Brig. 2-Div. 10-C. Va. & N. C.	No change to Muster Out	Aug., 1865
8th U. S. Infy	Dec., 1864	From Provost Guard 9-Corps Pot	To Regular Establishment	Aug., 1865
1st Md. East. Shore Det	Dec., 1864	From 1-Separate Brig. 8-Corps	To Consol. with 11th Md	Feb., 1865
91st N. Y. Infy. Det	Dec., 1864	From 2-Separate Brig. 8-Corps	To 1-Brig. 3-Div. 5-Corps Pot	Feb., 1865
1st Del. Cav	Dec., 1864	From 1-Separate Brig. 8-Corps	No change to Muster Out	June, 1865

4th SEPARATE BRIGADE.—Organized March 11, 1863. Transferred to Department of West Virginia, June 26, 1863.

COMMANDERS.

B. S. Roberts	Brigadier General	Mch. 11, 1863, to May 23, 1863.
W. W. Averill	Brigadier General	May 23, 1863, to June 26, 1863.

28th Ohio Infy	Mch., 1863	From Dist. Kanawha W. Va. Dept. O.	To 4-Separate Brig. Dept. W. Va.	June, 1863
2d West Va. Infy	Mch., 1863	From Dist. Kanawha W. Va. Dept. O.	To 4-Separate Brig. Dept. W. Va.	June, 1863
3d West Va. Infy	Mch., 1863	From Dist. Kanawha W. Va. Dept. O.	To 4-Separate Brig. Dept. W. Va.	June, 1863
8th West Va. Infy	Mch., 1863	From Dist. Kanawha W. Va. Dept. O.	To 4-Separate Brig. Dept. W. Va.	June, 1863
10th West Va. Infy	Mch., 1863	From 2-Brig. 2-Div. 8-Corps	To 4-Separate Brig. Dept. West Va.	June, 1863
Batty. E, 1st W. Va. Arty	Mch., 1863	From 2-Brig. 2-Div. 8-Corps	To 4-Separate Brig. Dept. West Va.	June, 1863
Batty. G, 1st W. Va. Arty	Mch., 1863	From R. R. Dist. West Va.	To 4-Separate Brig. Dept. West Va.	June, 1863
1st West Va. Cav. Co. A	Mch., 1863	From R. R. Dist. West Va.	To 4-Separate Brig. Dept. West Va.	June, 1863
3d W. Va. Cav. Cos E, H, I.	Mch., 1863	From Kanawha Div. Dist. W. Va.	To 4-Separate Brig. Dept. West Va.	June, 1863
16th Ill. Cav. Co	Mch., 1863	From Kanawha Div. Dist. W. Va.	To 4-Separate Brig. Dept. West Va.	June, 1863
3d Indpt. Co. Ohio Cav	Mch., 1863	From Kanawha Div. Dist. W. Va.	To 4-Separate Brig. Dept. West Va.	June, 1863
14th Penna. Cav	Mch., 1863	From Def. Upper Pot	To 4-Separate Brig. Dept. West Va.	June, 1863

1st DIVISION.—Organized March, 1863.   COMMANDERS.

B. F. Kelly	Brigadier General	Mch. 27, 1863, to June 26, 1863.

1st BRIGADE, 1st DIVISION.—   COMMANDER.

J. R. Kenly	Brigadier General	Mch. 27, 1863, to June 26, 1863.

1st Md. Infy	Mch., 1863	From Md. Brig. Def. Upper Pot	To Md. Brig. French's Div. 8-Corps.	June, 1863
4th Md. Infy	Mch., 1863	From Md. Brig. Def. Upper Pot	To Md. Brig. French's Div. 8-Corps.	June, 1863
7th Md. Infy	Mch., 1863	From Md. Brig. Def. Upper Pot	To Md. Brig. French's Div. 8-Corps.	June, 1863
8th Md. Infy	Mch., 1863	From Md. Brig. Def. Upper Pot	To Md. Brig. French's Div. 8-Corps.	June, 1863
14th Penna. Cav	Mch., 1863	From Md. Brig. Def. Upper Pot	To 4-Separate Brig. 8-Corps	Mch., 1863
17th Ind. Batty. Arty	Mch., 1863	From Md. Brig. Def. Upper Pot	To Md. Brig. French's Div. 8-Corps.	June, 1863

2d BRIGADE, 1st DIVISION.—   COMMANDER.

W. H. Morris	Brigadier General	Mch. 27, 1863, to June 26, 1863.

5th Md. Infy	Mch., 1863	From Def. Upper Pot. 8-Corps	To Def. Balto. Md. 8-Corps	June, 1863
1st Mass. Heavy Arty (Co's B, C, H, I.)	Mch., 1863	From Def. Upper Pot. 8-Corps	To Md. Brig. French's Div. 8-Corps.	June, 1863
6th N. Y. Heavy Arty	Mch., 1863	From Def. Upper Pot. 8-Corps	To 3-Prov'l Brig. French's Div.	June, 1863
50th N. Y. Engrs. Co. G	Mch., 1863	From Def. Upper Pot. 8-Corps	To Engineer Brig. Pot	June, 1863
Gaskell's Pa. Engr. Co	Mch., 1863	From Def. South Pot	To Unatt. Dept. West Va	June, 1863
4th Me. Batty	Mch., 1863	From Def. Upper Pot. 8-Corps	To French's Div. 8-Corps	June, 1863

3d BRIGADE, 1st DIVISION.—

COMMANDER.		
B. F. Smith............Col. 126th Ohio Infy...............	Mch. 27, 1863, to June 26, 1863.	

126th Ohio Infy.........Mch., 1863	From Martinsburg W. Va. 8-Corps..	To 3-Brig. French's Div. 8-Corps...	June, 1863
106th N. Y. Infy......Mch., 1863	From Martinsburg .W. Va. 8-Corps..	To 3-Brig. French's Div. 8-Corps...	June, 1863
15th West Va. Infy......Mch., 1863	From Sir John's Run 8-Corps.......	To New Creek W. Va..............	June, 1863
1st Md. Pot. Home Br. Cav.Mch., 1863	From Def. Upper Pot.............	To Md. Heights Div. Dept. W. Va..	July, 1863
2d Md. Pot. Home Br. Cav.Mch., 1863	From Martinsburg W. Va. 8-Corps..	To Md. Heights Div. Dept. W. Va..	July, 1863
Batty. F, 1st W. Va. Arty..Mch., 1863	From Martinsburg W. Va. 8-Corps..	To Arty. French's Div. 8-Corps.....	June, 1863

4th BRIGADE, 1st DIVISION.—

COMMANDER.		
J. M. Campbell.........Col. 54th Penna. Infy.............	Mch. 27, 1863, to June 26, 1863.	

54th Penna. Infy.........Mch., 1863	From North Mt. Def. Upper Pot....	To Campbell's Brig. Scammon's Div.	June, 1863
1st West Va. Infy......Mch., 1863	From North Mt. Def. Upper Pot.....	To Campbell's Brig. Scammon's Div.	June, 1863
Lafayette Pa. Co. Cav...Mch., 1863	From Romney Def. Upper Pot......	To Campbell's Brig. Scammon's Div.	June, 1863
Wash. Co. Pa. Co. Cav....Mch., 1863	From Springfield Def. Upper Pot...	To Campbell's Brig. Scammon's Div.	June, 1863
Ringgold Pa. Cav.......Mch., 1863	From Romney W. Va. Def. Upper P.	To Campbell's Brig. Scammon's Div.	June, 1863
Batty. E, 1st W. Va. Arty.Mch., 1863	From Romney W. Va. Def. Upper P.	To Campbell's Brig. Scammon's Div.	June, 1863

5th BRIGADE, 1st DIVISION.—

COMMANDER.		
Jas. A. Mulligan.........Col. 23d Ill. Infy.................	Mch. 27, 1863, to June 26, 1863.	

2d Md. P. H. B...........Mch., 1863	From Cumb'd Md. Def. Upper Pot..	To Mulligan's Brig. Scammon's Div.	June, 1863
23d Ill. Infy.............Mch., 1863	From New Creek W. Va. Def. Up. P.	To Mulligan's Brig. Scammon's Div.	June, 1863
14th West Va. Infy......Mch., 1863	From New Creek W. Va. Def. Up. P.	To Mulligan's Brig. Scammon's Div.	June, 1863
Batty. L, 1st Ill. Arty....Mch., 1863	From New Creek W. Va. Def. Up. P.	To Mulligan's Brig. Scammon's Div.	June, 1863

6th BRIGADE, 1st DIVISION.—

COMMANDER.		
N. Wilkinson.........Col. 6th West Va. Infy............	Mch. 27, 1863, to June 26, 1863.	

6th West Va. Infy........Mch., 1863	From Clarksburg W. Va. Upper Pot.	To Wilkinson's Brig. Scammon's Div.	June, 1863
11th West Va. Infy........Mch., 1863	From Parkersburg W. Va. Upper Pt.	To Wilkinson's Brig. Scammon's Div.	June, 1863

2d DIVISION.—Organized Feb. 1863, from Milroy's Division, Def. Upper Potomac, 8-Corps.

COMMANDER.	
R. H. Milroy..........Brigadier General..................	Feb. .., 1863, to June 26, 1863.

1st BRIGADE, 2d DIVISION.—

COMMANDER.	
W. L. Elliott...........Brigadier General..................	Feb. .., 1863, to June 26, 1863.

110th Ohio Infy.........Feb., 1863	From Milroy's Com. Winchester, Va.	To Elliott's Command 8-Corps......	June, 1863
116th Ohio Infy.........Feb., 1863	From Romney W. Va. Def. Up. Pot.	To Elliott's Command 8-Corps......	June, 1863
122d Ohio Infy.........Feb., 1863	From Milroy's Com. Winchester, Va.	To Elliott's Command 8-Corps......	June, 1863
123d Ohio Infy.........Feb., 1863	From Romney W. Va. Def. Up. Pot.	To Elliott's Command 8-Corps......	June, 1863
1st N. Y. Lincoln Cav...Feb., 1863	From Milroy's Com. Winchester, Va.	To 3-Brig. 2-Div. 8-Corps..........	Mch., 1863
12th Penna. Cav.........Feb., 1863	From Kearnysville Def. Upper Pot..	To McReynolds Com. Susquehanna.	July, 1863
13th Penna. Cav.........Feb., 1863	From Milroy's Com. Winchester, Va.	To 2-Brig. 2-Div. Cav. Corps Pot..	July, 1863
Batty. D, 1st W. Va. Arty.Feb., 1863	From Milroy's Com. Winchester, Va.	To 2-Brig. 2-Div. 8-Corps..........	June, 1863
Batty. L, 5th U. S. Arty..June, 1863	From 2-Brig. 2-Div. 8-Corps........	To 3-Separate Brig. 8-Corps........	July, 1863

2d BRIGADE, 2d DIVISION.—

COMMANDERS.		
A. Cluseret............Brigadier General..................	Feb. 5, 1863, to Feb. 12, 1863.	
Geo. Hays..............Col. 87th Penna. Infy...............	Feb. 12, 1863, to May 25, 1863.	
Wm. G. Ely............Col. 18th Conn. Infy...............	May 25, 1863, to June 26, 1863.	

87th Penna. Infy.........Feb., 1863	From Milroy's Com. Winchester, Va.	To Bloody Run Dept. Susquehanna.	June, 1863
9th W. Va. Infy.........Feb., 1863	From Milroy's Com. Winchester, Va.	To 1-Brig. Scammon's Div. W. Va..	June, 1863
10th W. Va. Infy.........Feb., 1863	From Milroy's Com. Winchester, Va.	To 4-Separate Brig. 8-Corps.......	May, 1863
12th W. Va. Infy.........Feb., 1863	From Milroy's Com. Winchester, Va.	To McReynold's Com. Dept. Susq...	June, 1863
1st W. Va. Cav. Co. K...Feb., 1863	From Milroy's Com. Winchester, Va.	To Bloody Run Dept. Susquehanna.	June, 1863
3d W. Va. Cav. Cos. D, E.Feb., 1863	From Milroy's Com. Winchester, Va.	To Bloody Run Dept. Susquehanna.	June, 1863
Batty. B, 1st W. Va. Arty.Feb., 1863	From Milroy's Com. Winchester, Va.	To 4th Separate Brig. 8-Corps......	May, 1863
Batty. L, 5th U. S. Arty..Feb., 1863	From Milroy's Com. Winchester, Va.	To 1-Brig. 2-Div. 8-Corps..........	June, 1863
18th Conn. Infy.........May, 1863	From 2-Separate Brig. 8-Corps......	To Dept. Susquehanna..............	June, 1863
Batty. D, 1st W. Va. Arty.June, 1863	From 1-Brig. 2-Div. 8-Corps........	To Bloody Run Dept. Susquehanna.	June, 1863

3d BRIGADE, 2d DIVISION.—

COMMANDERS.		
John F. Staunton......Col. 67th Penna. Infy..............	Feb., 1863 to Mch., 1863.	
A. T. McReynolds......Col. 1st N. Y. Lincoln Cav..........	Mch., 1863, to June, 1863.	

6th Maryland Infy.......Feb., 1863	From Md. Brig. Def. Upper Potomac.	To Elliott's Command 8-Corps......	June, 1863
67th Penna. Infy.........Feb., 1863	From Annapolis, Md. 8-Corps......	To Elliott's Command 8-Corps......	June, 1863
1st N. Y. Lincoln Cav....Feb., 1863	From 1-Brig. 2-Div. 8-Corps........	To McReynold's Command D. Sus..	June, 1863
Baltimore, Md. Batty.....Feb., 1863	From Md. Brig. Def. Upper Potomac.	To French's Div. 8-Corps..........	June, 1863

3d DIVISION—Organized March, 1863, from Kanawha Div. W. Va. Transferred to Dept. W. Va. June, 1863.

COMMANDERS.		
B. S. Roberts..........Brigadier General..................	Mch. 11, 1863, to Mch. 16, 1863.	
B. F. Kelly............Brigadier General..................	Mch. 16, 1863, to Mch. 27, 1963.	
E. P. Scammon.........Brigadier General..................	Mch. 27, 1863, to June 26, 1863.	

1st BRIGADE, 3d DIVISION.—

COMMANDER.		
R. B. Hayes...........Col. 23d Ohio Infy..............	Mch. 17, 1863, to June 26, 1863.	

23d Ohio Infy...........Mch., 1863	From Kanawha Div. W. Va. D. Ohio.	To 1-Brig. Scammon's D. D. W. Va.	June, 1863
5th West Va. Infy.......Mch., 1863	From Kanawha Div. W. Va. D. Ohio.	To 1-Brig. Scammon's D. D. W. Va.	June, 1863
13th West Va. Infy......Mch., 1863	From Kanawha Div. W. Va. D. Ohio.	To 1-Brig. Scammon's D. D. W. Va.	June, 1863
1st W. Va. Cav. 2-Cos...Mch., 1863	From Kanawha Div. W. Va. D. Ohio.	To 1-Brig. Scammon's D. D. W. Va.	June, 1863
3d W. Va. Cav. Co. G....Mch., 1863	From Kanawha Div. W. Va. D. Ohio.	To 1-Brig. Scammon's D. D. W. Va.	June, 1863
Simmond's Ky. Batty. A.Mch., 1863	From Kanawha Div. W. Va. D. Ohio.	To 1-Brig. Scammon's D. D. W. Va.	June, 1863

2d BRIGADE, 3d DIVISION.—

COMMANDER.		
Carr B. White..........Col. 12th Ohio Infy.............	Mch. 5, 1863, to June 26, 1863.	

12th Ohio Infy..........Mch., 1863	From Kanawha Div. W. Va. D. Ohio.	To 2-Brig. Scammon's D. D. W. Va.	June, 1863
34th Ohio Infy..........Mch., 1863	From Kanawha Div. W. Va. D. Ohio.	To 2-Brig. Scammon's D. D. W. Va.	June, 1863
91st Ohio Infy..........Mch., 1863	From Kanawha Div. W. Va. D. Ohio.	To 2-Brig. Scammon's D. D. W. Va.	June, 1863
2d W. Va. Cav. Cos. G, K.Mch., 1863	From Kanawha Div. W. Va. D. Ohio.	To 2-Brig. Scammon's D. D. W. Va.	June, 1863
1st Ohio Indpt. Batty...Mch., 1863	From Kanawha Div. W. Va. D. Ohio.	To 2-Brig. Scammon's D. D. W. Va.	June, 1863
UNATTACHED.—			
2d West Va. Cav........Mch., 1863	From Kanawha Div. W. Va. D. Ohio.	To Scammon's Div. Dept. W. Va...	June, 1863

ELLIOTT'S COMMAND.—

	COMMANDER.		
W. L. Elliott.........	Brigadier General.................		
6th Maryland Infy.......June, 1863	From 3-Brig. 2-Div. 8-Corps.......	To 3-Brig. 3-Div. 3-Corps Potomac.	July, 1863
110th Ohio Infy........June, 1863	From 1-Brig. 2-Div. 8-Corps.......	To 2-Brig. 3-Div. 3-Corps Pottomac.	July, 1863
116th Ohio Infy........June, 1863	From 1-Brig. 2-Div. 8-Corps.......	To Bloody Run Dept. Susquehanna.	June, 1863
122d Ohio Infy.........June, 1863	From 1-Brig. 2-Div. 8-Corps.......	To 2-Brig. 3-Div. 3-Corps Potomac.	July, 1863
123d Ohio Infy.........June, 1863	From 1-Brig. 2-Div. 8-Corps.......	To Bloody Run Dept. Susquehanna.	June, 1863
126th Ohio Infy........June, 1863	From 1-Brig. 1-Div. 8-Corps.......	To 3-Brig. 3-Div. 3-Corps Potomac.	July, 1863
67th Penna. Infy.......June, 1863	From 3-Brig. 2-Div. 8-Corps.......	To 3-Brig. 3-Div. 3-Corps Potomac.	July, 1863
87th Penna. Infy.......June, 1863	From 3-Brig. 2-Div. 8-Corps.......	To 3-Brig. 3-Div. 3-Corps Potomac.	July, 1863
138th Penna. Infy......June, 1863	From 3-Separate Brig. 8-Corps.....	To 2-Brig. 3-Div. 3-Corps Potomac.	July, 1863
106th N. Y. Infy.......June, 1863	From 3-Brig. 1-Div. 8-Corps.......	To 3-Brig. 3-Div. 3-Corps Potomac.	July, 1863

FRENCH'S COMMAND.—

	COMMANDER.		
W. H. French.........	Major General..................		

MARYLAND BRIGADE.—

1st Maryland Infy.......June, 1863	From 1-Brig. 1-Div. 8-Corps.......	To 3-Brig. 3-Div. 1-Corps Potomac.	July, 1863
4th Maryland Infy......June, 1863	From 1-Brig. 1-Div. 8-Corps.......	To 3-Brig. 3-Div. 1-Corps Potomac.	July, 1863
7th Maryland Infy......June, 1863	From 1-Brig. 1-Div. 8-Corps.......	To 3-Brig. 3-Div. 1-Corps Potomac.	July, 1863
8th Maryland Infy......June, 1863	From 1-Brig. 1-Div. 8-Corps.......	To 3-Brig. 3-Div. 1-Corps Potomac.	July, 1863
1st Mass. H. A. (B.C.H.I.) June, 1863	From 2-Brig. 1-Div. 8-Corps.......	To Arty. Res. Potomac.............	July, 1863
17th Ind. Batty. Arty....June, 1863	From 1-Brig. 1-Div. 8-Corps.......	To 2-Brig. Md. Heights Div. W. Va.	July, 1863

3d PROV'L. BRIGADE, FRENCH'S COMMAND.—

14th N. J. Infy........June, 1863	From 3-Separate Brig. 8-Corps.....	To 1-Brig. 3-Div. 3-Corps Potomac.	July, 1863
6th N. Y. Heavy Arty....June, 1863	From 2-Brig. 1-Div. 8-Corps.......	To 1-Brig. 3-Div. 3-Corps Potomac.	July, 1863
151st N. Y. Infy.......June, 1863	From 3-Separate Brig. 8-Corps.....	To 1-Brig. 3-Div. 3-Corps Potomac.	July, 1863
10th Vt. Infy..........June, 1863	From Jewett's Command 22-Corps..	To 1-Brig. 3-Div. 3-Corps Potomac.	July, 1863

ARTILLERY, FRENCH'S DIVISION.—

4th Maine Batty. Arty....June, 1863	From 2-Brig. 1-Div. 8-Corps.......	To Arty. Brig. 3-Corps Potomac...	July, 1863
10th Mass. Indpt. Batty..June, 1863	From Jewett's Command 22-Corps..	To Arty. Brig. 3-Corps Potomac...	July, 1863
Baltimore, Md. Batty.....June, 1863	From 3-Brig. 2-Div. 8-Corps.......	To Def. Baltimore 8-Corps........	July, 1863
Batty. F, 1st W. Va......June, 1863	From 3-Brig. 1-Div. 8-Corps.......	To Camp Barry Wash. 22-Corps....	July, 1863

DISTRICT OF DELAWARE.—

	COMMANDERS.		
D. Tyler...............	Brigadier General.................	July 3, 1863, to Jan. 19, 1864.	
H. B. Judd.............	Major U. S. A...................	Jan. 19, 1864, to Apr. 2, 1864.	
J. R. Kenly...........	Brigadier General.................	Apr. 2, 1864, to May 5, 1864.	
Discontinued May 5, 1864. Reorganized Aug. 20, 1864.			
S. M. Bowman........	Col. 84th Penna. Infy.............	Aug. 20, 1864, to Mch. 24, 1865.	
Consolidated with Dist. East. Shore, Md., Mch. 24, 1865.			
J. R. Kenly...........	Brigadier General.................	Mch. 24, 1865, to June 5, 1865.	
J. M. Wilson..........	Col. 155th Indiana Infy...........	June 5, 1865, to Aug. 1, 1865.	
3d Pa. Heavy Arty Co. M.July, 1863	From New Organization...........	To Dept. Va. and N. C.	Aug., 1863
Indpt. Batty. A, Pa. Arty.July, 1863	From Fort Delaware.............	No change to Muster Out........	June, 1865
Indpt. Batty. G, Pa. Arty.July, 1863	From Fort Delaware.............	No change to Muster Out........	June, 1865
5th Del. Infy..........July, 1863	From 2-Separate Brig. 8-Corps.....	No change to Muster Out........	Aug., 1863
Ahl's Del. H. A. Co......Aug., 1863	From New Organization...........	No change to Muster Out........	July, 1865
Purnell Md. Cav. Co. C...Aug., 1863	From 3-Separate Brig. 8-Corps.....	No change to Muster Out........	Oct., 1864
1st Del. Cav. D. E......Jan., 1864	From Cav. Res. 8-Corps...........	To 1-Separate Brig. 8-Corps......	May, 1864
1st Md. East. Shore Co. H.Apr., 1864	From Dist. East. Shore 8-Corps...	To Dist. East. Shore 8-Corps.....	May, 1864
8th Del. Infy..........Oct., 1864	From New Organization...........	No change to Muster Out........	June, 1865

ARTILLERY RESERVE.—

Batty. A, Jr. Md. Arty...Dec.,1863	From 3-Separate Brig. 8-Corps.....	No change to Muster Out........	Jan., 1864
Batty. B, Jr. Md. Arty....Dec., 1863	From 3-Separate Brig. 8-Corps.....	No change to Muster Out........	Jan., 1864
Baltimore, Md. Batty....Dec., 1863	From 3-Separate Brig. 8-Corps.....	To 3-Separate Brig. 8-Corps......	Mch., 1864
3d Pa. Heavy Arty. Co. H.Dec., 1863	From 3-Separate Brig. 8-Corps.....	To 3-Separate Brig. 8-Corps......	Mch., 1864

CAVALRY RESERVE.—

1st Conn. Cav.........Dec., 1863	From 3-Separate Brig. 8-Corps.....	To 1-Brig. 3-Div. Cav. Corps Pot....	Apr., 1864
1st Del. Cav..........Dec., 1863	From 3-Separate Brig. 8-Corps.....	To 1-Separate Brig. 8-Corps......	Jan., 1864
3d Md. Cav............Dec., 1863	From New Organization...........	To Dept. of the Gulf.............	Jan., 1864

BENEDICT, MD.—

7th U. S. C. T.........Jan., 1864	From New Organization...........	To Dist. Fla. Dept. South.........	Apr., 1864
9th U. S. C. T.........Jan., 1864	From New Organization...........	To Dist. Hilton Head Dept. South...	Apr., 1864
19th U. S. C. T.........Jan., 1864	From New Organization...........	To 2-Brig. 4-Div. 9-Corps Potomac.	Apr., 1864

Department of the Shenandoah

Recreated and organized April 4, 1862, from Banks' 5th Army Corps, Potomac. Merged into Pope's Army of Virginia as the 2d Army Corps June 26, 1862.

	COMMANDER.		
N. P. Banks............	Major General...................	Apr. 4, 1862, to June 26, 1862.	

1st DIVISION.—

	COMMANDER.		
A. S. Williams........	Brigadier General.................	Apr. 4, 1862, to June 26, 1862.	

1st BRIGADE.—

	COMMANDERS.		
D. Donnelly...........	Col. 28th N. Y. Infy..........	Apr. 4, 1862 to May 27, 1862.	
S. W. Crawford........	Brigadier General.................	May 27, 1862, to June 26, 1862.	
5th Conn. Infy.........Apr., 1862	From 1-Brig. 1-Div. Banks' 5-Corps.	To 1-Brig. 1-Div. 2-Corps Army Va.	June, 1862
28th N. Y. Infy........Apr., 1862	From 1-Brig. 1-Div. Banks' 5-Corps.	To 1-Brig. 1-Div. 2-Corps Army Va.	June, 1862
28th Penna. Infy.......Apr., 1862	From 1-Brig. 1-Div. Banks' 5-Corps.	To Geary's Indpt. Brig. Dept. Shen.	Apr., 1862
47th Penna. Infy.......Apr., 1862	From 1-Brig. 1-Div. Banks' 5-Corps.	To 1-Brig. 1-Div. 2-Corps Army Va.	June, 1862
1st Md. Infy..........Apr., 1862	From 1-Brig. 1-Div. Banks' 5-Corps.	To Baltimore, Md.	May, 1862
10th Maine Infy........May, 1862	To Unatt. Dept. Shenandoah......	To 1-Brig. 1-Div. 2-Corps Army Va.	June, 1862

2d BRIGADE.—   COMMANDERS.

J. J. Abercrombie......	Brigadier General...................	Apr. 4, 1862, to Apr. 30, 1862.
Geo. L. Hartsuff.......	Brigadier General...................	Apr. 30, 1862, to May 10, 1862.

Brigade transferred to Dept. of Rappahannock.

12th Mass. Infy.........Apr., 1862	From 2-Brig. 1-Div. Banks' 5-Corps.	To 3-Brig. 2-Div. Dept. Rappahn'k..	May,	1862
13th Mass. Infy.........Apr., 1862	From 2-Brig. 1-Div. Banks' 5-Corps.	To 3-Brig. 2-Div. Dept. Rappahn'k..	May,	1862
83d (9-S. M.) N. Y. Infy..Apr., 1862	From 2-Brig. 1-Div. Banks' 5-Corps.	To 3-Brig. 2-Div. Dept. Rappahn'k..	May,	1862
12th Indiana Infy.......Apr., 1862	From 2-Brig. 1-Div. Banks' 5-Corps.	No change to Muster Out..........	May,	1862
16th Indiana Infy.......Apr., 1862	From 2-Brig. 1-Div. Banks' 5-Corps.	No change to Muster Out..........	May,	1862

3d BRIGADE.—   COMMANDERS.

Geo. H. Gordon.........	Col. 2d Mass. Infy..............	Apr. 4, 1862, to May 27, 1862.
Geo. S. Greene.........	Brigadier General..............	May 27, 1862, to June 18, 1862.
Geo. H. Gordon.........	Brigadier General..............	June 18, 1862, to June 26, 1862.

27th Indiana Infy.......Apr., 1862	From 3-Brig. 1-Div. Banks' 5-Corps.	To 3-Brig. 1-Div. 2-Corps Army Va.	June,	1862
2d Mass. Infy..........Apr., 1862	From 3-Brig. 1-Div. Banks' 5-Corps.	To 3-Brig. 1-Div. 2-Corps Army Va.	June,	1862
29th Penna. Infy........Apr., 1862	From 3-Brig. 1-Div. Banks' 5-Corps.	To 3-Brig. 1-Div. 2-Corps Army Va.	June,	1862
3d Wis. Infy..........Apr., 1862	From 3-Brig. 1-Div. Banks' 5-Corps.	To 3-Brig. 1-Div. 2-Corps Army Va.	June,	1862
Collis' Penna. Zouaves....Apr., 1862	From Geary's Indpt. Brig.	To Unattt. 2-Corps Army Va......	June,	1862
ARTILLERY.—				
Batty. M, 1st N. Y. Arty..Apr., 1862	From Arty. 1-Div. Banks' 5-Corps.	To Arty. 2-Corps Army Va.........	June,	1862
Indpt. Batty. E, Pa. Arty..Apr., 1862	From Arty. 1-Div. Banks' 5-Corps.	To Arty. 2-Corps Army Va.........	June,	1862
Indpt. Batty. F, Pa. Arty..Apr., 1862	From Arty. 1-Div. Banks' 5-Corps.	To Arty. 2-Corps Army Va.........	June,	1862
Batty. F, 1st Penna. Arty..Apr., 1862	From Arty. 1-Div. Banks' 5-Corps.	To Arty. 2-Corps Army Va.........	June,	1862
Batty. F, 4th U. S. Arty..Apr., 1862	From Arty. 1-Div. Banks' 5-Corps.	To Arty. 2-Corps Army Va.........	June,	1862

2d DIVISION.—   COMMANDERS.

James Shields.........	Brigadier General...................	Apr. 4, 1862, to May 10, 1862.

Division transferred to the Dept. of the Rappahannock.

1st BRIGADE.—   COMMANDER.

Nathan Kimball........	Col. 14th Indiana Infy............	Apr. 4, 1862, to May 10, 1862.

4th Ohio Infy..........Apr., 1862	From 1-Brig. 2-Div. Banks' 5-Corps.	To 1-Brig. Shields' Div. Dept. Rapp.	May,	1862
8th Ohio Infy..........Apr., 1862	From 1-Brig. 2-Div. Banks' 5-Corps.	To 1-Brig. Shields' Div. Dept. Rapp.	May,	1862
67th Ohio Infy.........Apr., 1862	From 1-Brig. 2-Div. Banks' 5-Corps.	To 1-Brig. Shields' Div. Dept. Rapp.	May,	1862
14th Indiana Infy.......Apr., 1862	From 1-Brig. 2-Div. Banks' 5-Corps.	To 2-Brig. Shields' Div. Dept. Rapp.	**May, 1862**
84th Penna. Infy........Apr., 1862	From 1-Brig. 2-Div. Banks' 5-Corps.	To 4-Brig. Shields' Div. Dept. Rapp.	May,	1862
7th West Va. Infy.......Apr., 1862	From 1-Brig. 2-Div. Banks' 5-Corps.	To 1-Brig. Shields' Div. Dept. Rapp.	May,	1862

2d BRIGADE.—   COMMANDERS.

J. C. Sullivan..........	Col. 13th Indiana Infy.............	Apr. 4, 1862, to May 1, 1862.
O. S. Ferry...........	Brigadier General...................	May 1, 1862, to May 10, 1862.

5th Ohio Infy..........Apr., 1862	From 2-Brig. 2-Div. Banks' 5-Corps.	To 3-Brig. Shields' Div. Dept. Rapp.	May,	1862
62d Ohio Infy..........Apr., 1862	From 2-Brig. 2-Div. Banks' 5-Corps.	To 2-Brig. Shields' Div. Dept. Rapp.	May,	1862
66th Ohio Infy.........Apr., 1862	From 2-Brig. 2-Div. Banks' 5-Corps.	To 2-Brig. Shields' Div. Dept. Rapp.	May,	1832
13th Indiana Infy.......Apr., 1862	From 2-Brig. 2-Div. Banks' 5-Corps.	To 2-Brig. Shields' Div. Dept. Rapp.	May,	1862
39th Illinois Infy.......Apr., 1862	From 2-Brig. 2-Div. Banks' 5-Corps.	To 2-Brig. Shields' Div. Dept. Rapp.	May,	1862

3d BRIGADE.—   COMMANDER.

E. B. Tyler...........	Brigadier General...................	Apr. 4, 1862, to May 10, 1862.

1st West Va. Infy.......Apr., 1862	From 3-Brig. 2-Div. Banks' 5-Corps.	To 4-Brig. Shields' Div. Dept. Rapp.	May,	1862
110th Penna. Infy.......Apr., 1862	From 3-Brig. 2-Div. Banks' 5-Corps.	To 4-Brig. Shields' Div. Dept. Rapp.	May,	1862
7th Ohio Infy..........Apr., 1862	From 3-Brig. 2-Div. Banks' 5-Corps.	To 3-Brig. Shields' Div. Dept. Rapp.	May,	1862
29th Ohio Infy.........Apr., 1862	From 3-Brig. 2-Div. Banks' 5-Corps.	To 3-Brig. Shields' Div. Dept. Rapp.	May,	1862
7th Indiana Infy........Apr., 1862	From 3-Brig. 2-Div. Banks' 5-Corps.	To 4-Brig. Shields' Div. Dept. Rapp.	May,	1862
ARTILLERY.—				
Batty. A, 1st W. Va. Arty..Apr., 1862	From Arty. 2-Div. Banks' 5-Corps.	To Arty. Shields' Div. Dept. Rapp.	May,	1862
Batty. B, 1st W. Va. Arty..Apr., 1862	From Arty. 2-Div. Banks' 5-Corps.	To Arty. Shields' Div. Dept. Rapp.	May,	1862
Batty. H, 1st Ohio Arty..Apr., 1862	From Arty. 2-Div. Banks' 5-Corps.	To Arty. Shields' Div. Dept. Rapp.	May,	1862
Batty. L, 1st Ohio Arty..Apr., 1862	From Arty. 2-Div. Banks' 5-Corps.	To Arty. Shields' Div. Dept. Rapp.	May,	1862
Batty. E, 4th U. S. Arty..Apr., 1862	From Arty. 2-Div. Banks' 5-Corps.	To Arty. Shields' Div. Dept. Rapp.	May,	1862

SIGEL'S DIVISION.—   COMMANDER.

Franz Sigel............	Major General........................	June 4, 1862, to June 26, 1862.

1st BRIGADE.—   COMMANDER.

James Cooper..........	Brigadier General..................	June 4, 1862, to June 26, 1862.

3d Maryland Infy.......June, 1862	From Def. Baltimore Middle Dept...	To 1-Brig. 2-Div. 2-Corps Army Va.	June,	1862
102d N. Y. Infy........June, 1862	From Def. of Washington..........	To 1-Brig. 2-Div. 2-Corps Army Va.	June,	1862
109th Penna. Infy.......June, 1862	From Def. of Washington..........	To 1-Brig. 2-Div. 2-Corps Army Va.	June,	1862
111th Penna. Infy.......June, 1862	From Def. of Washington..........	To 1-Brig. 2-Div. 2-Corps Army Va.	June,	1862
8th & 12th U. S. Infy. Bn.June, 1862	From Def. of Washington..........	To 1-Brig. 2-Div. 2-Corps Army Va.	June,	1862
Batty. L, 1st N. Y. Arty.June, 1862	From Def. Baltimore Middle Dept...	To Arty. 2-Div. 2-Corps Army Va..	June,	1862

2d BRIGADE.—   COMANDER.

J. P. Slough...........	Brigadier General..................	June 4, 1862, to June 26, 1862.

3d Del. Infy...........June, 1862	From New Organization...........	To 2-Brig. 2-Div. 2-Corps Army Va.	June,	1862
1st Dist. Columbia Infy..June, 1862	From Def. of Washington..........	To 2-Brig. 2-Div. 2-Corps Army Va.	June,	1862
60th N. Y. Infy........June, 1862	From R. R. Brig. Middle Dept......	To 2-Brig. 2-Div. 2-Corps Army Va.	June,	1862
78th N. Y. Infy........June, 1862	From R. R. Brig. Middle Dent......	To 2-Brig. 2-Div. 2-Corps Army Va.	June,	1862
Purnell Md. Legion Infy..June, 1862	From Lockwood's Brig. Middle Dept.	To 2-Brig. 2-Div. 2-Corps Army Va.	June,	1862
11th N. Y. S. M. Infy..June, 1862	From New Organization...........	To Harper's Ferry, Va.............	June,	1862
Batty. K, 1st N. Y. Arty.June, 1862	From R. R. Brig. Middle Dept......	To Arty. 2-Corps Army Va........	June,	1862

CAVALRY COMMAND.—   COMMANDER.

J. P. Hatch............	Brigadier General..................	Apr. 4, 1862, to June 26, 1862.

1st Maine Cav. 7 Cos.....Apr., 1862	From Cav. Banks' 5-Corps...	To Bayard's Cav. Brig. 3-Corps Va.	June,	1862
1st Vermont Cav........Apr., 1862	From Cav. Banks' 5-Corps...	To Hatch's Cav. Brig. 2-Corps Va..	June,	1862
5th N. Y. Cav..........Apr., 1862	From Cav. Banks' 5-Corps...	To Hatch's Cav. Brig. 2-Corps Va..	June,	1862
8th N. Y. Cav..........Apr., 1862	From Cav. Banks' 5-Corps...	To R. R. Brig. Middle Dept.......	June,	1862
1st Mich. Cav..........Apr., 1862	From Cav. Banks' 5-Corps...	To Hatch's Cav. Brig. 2-Corps Va..	June,	1862
1st R. I. Cav..........Apr., 1862	From Cav. Banks' 5-Corps...	To Ord's Div. Dept. Rappahannock..	May,	1862
1st Md. Cav...........Apr., 1862	From Dix's Div. Balto. Mid. Dept...	To Cav. Brig. 1-Corps Army Va.....	June,	1862
1st Md. Pot. Home Br. Cav.Apr., 1862	From Cav. Banks' 5-Corps...	To R. R. Brig. Middle Dept.......	June,	1862
1st West Va. Cav. Sqdn..Apr., 1862	From Cav. Banks' 5-Corps...	To Hatch's Cav. Brig. 2-Corps Va..	June,	1862
1st Ohio Cav. Co's A. C...Apr., 1862	From Cav. Banks' 5-Corps...	To Cav. Shields' Div. Dept. Rapp...	May,	1862

Department of the Rappahannock

Constituted April 4, 1862, from original 1st Army Corps, Army of the Potomac. Department to consist of that portion of Virginia east of the Blue Ridge and west of the Potomac River, the Fredericksburg and Richmond R. R., including the District of Columbia and the country between the Potomac and Petuxent Rivers. Merged into Pope's Army of Va. June 26, 1862, as 3d Corps.

COMMANDER.

Irvin McDowell........|Major General.....................|Apr. 4, 1862, to June 26, 1862. |

1st DIVISION.—   **COMMANDER.**

W. B. Franklin........|Brigadier General....................|Apr. 4, 1862, to May 18, 1862. |
Division transferred to 6th Army Corps. Army Potomac, May 18, 1862.

1st BRIGADE.—   **COMMANDER.**

Philip Kearny.........|Brigadier General....................|Apr. 4, 1862, to May 18, 1862. |

1st N. J. Infy	Apr., 1862	From 1-Brig. 1-Div. 1-Corps Pot	To 1-Brig. 1-Div. 6-Corps Pot	May, 1862
2d N. J. Infy	Apr., 1862	From 1-Brig. 1-Div. 1-Corps Pot	To 1-Brig. 1-Div. 6-Corps Pot	May, 1862
3d N. J. Infy	Apr., 1862	From 1-Brig. 1-Div. 1-Corps Pot	To 1-Brig. 1-Div. 6-Corps Pot	May, 1862
4th N. J. Infy	Apr., 1862	From 1-Brig. 1-Div. 1-Corps Pot	To 1-Brig. 1-Div. 6-Corps Pot	May, 1862

2d BRIGADE.—   **COMMANDER.**

H. W. Slocum.........|Brigadier General....................|Apr. 4, 1862, to May 18, 1862. |

5th Me. Infy	Apr., 1862	From 2-Brig. 1-Div. 1-Corps Pot	To 2-Brig. 1-Div. 6-Corps Pot	May, 1862
16th N. Y. Infy	Apr., 1862	From 2-Brig. 1-Div. 1-Corps Pot	To 2-Brig. 1-Div. 6-Corps Pot	May, 1862
27th N. Y. Infy	Apr., 1862	From 2-Brig. 1-Div. 1-Corps Pot	To 2-Brig. 1-Div. 6-Corps Pot	May, 1862
96th Penna. Infy	Apr., 1862	From 2-Brig. 1-Div. 1-Corps Pot	To 2-Brig. 1-Div. 6-Corps Pot	May, 1862

3d BRIGADE.—   **COMMANDER.**

John Newton..........|Brigadier General....................|Apr. 4, 1862, to May 18, 1862. |

18th N. Y. Infy	Apr., 1862	From 3-Brig. 1-Div. 1-Corps Pot	To 3-Brig. 1-Div. 6-Corps Pot	May, 1862
31st N. Y. Infy	Apr., 1862	From 3-Brig. 1-Div. 1-Corps Pot	To 3-Brig. 1-Div. 6-Corps Pot	May, 1862
32d N. Y. Infy	Apr., 1862	From 3-Brig. 1-Div. 1-Corps Pot	To 3-Brig. 1-Div. 6-Corps Pot	May, 1862
95th Penna. Infy	Apr., 1862	From 3-Brig. 1-Div. 1-Corps Pot	To 3-Brig. 1-Div. 6-Corps Pot	May, 1862

ARTILLERY.—

1st Mass. Indpt. Batty	Apr., 1862	From Arty. 1-Div. 1-Corps Pot	To Arty. 1-Div. 6-Corps Pot	May, 1862
Batty. F, 1st N. Y. Arty	Apr., 1862	From Arty. 1-Div. 1-Corps Pot	To Arty. 1-Div. 6-Corps Pot	May, 1862
Batty. A, N. J. Arty	Apr., 1862	From Arty. 1-Div. 1-Corps Pot	To Arty. 1-Div. 6-Corps Pot	May, 1862
Batty. D, 2d U. S. Arty	Apr., 1862	From Arty. 1-Div. 1-Corps Pot	To Arty. 1-Div. 6-Corps Pot	May, 1862

CAVALRY.—

| 1st N. Y. (Lincoln) Cav | Apr., 1862 | From Cav. 1-Div. 1-Corps Pot | To Cav. 1-Div. 6-Corps Pot | May, 1862 |

SHIELDS' DIVISION.—   **COMMANDER.**

James Shields.........|Brigadier General....................|May 10, 1862, to June 26, 1862. |

1st BRIGADE.—   **COMMANDER.**

Nathan Kimball.......|Brigadier General....................|May 10, 1862, to June 26, 1862. |

4th Ohio Infy	May, 1862	From 1-Brig. 2-Div. Dept. Shen	To Kimball's Indpt. Brig. 2 Corps P.	July, 1862
8th Ohio Infy	May, 1862	From 1-Brig. 2-Div. Dept. Shen	To Kimball's Indpt. Brig. 2 Corps P.	July, 1862
67th Ohio Infy	May, 1862	From 1-Brig. 2-Div. Dept. Shen	To 2-Brig. Shields' Div. Dept. Rapp.	May, 1862
14th Ind. Infy	May, 1862	From 1-Brig. 2-Div. Dept. Shen	To Kimball's Indpt. Brig. 2 Corps P.	July, 1862
7th West Va. Infy	May, 1862	From 1-Brig. 2-Div. Dept. Shen	To Kimball's Indpt. Brig. 2 Corps P.	July, 1862

2d BRIGADE.—   **COMMANDER.**

O. S. Ferry...........|Brigadier General....................|May 10, 1862, to June 26, 1862. |

62d Ohio Infy	May, 1862	From 2-Brig. 2-Div. Dept. Shen	To 3-Brig. 2-Div. 4-Corps Pot	July, 1862
66th Ohio Infy	May, 1862	From 2-Brig. 2-Div. Dept. Shen	To 3-Brig. Shields' Div. Dept. Rapp.	June, 1862
13th Ind. Infy	May, 1862	From 2-Brig. 2-Div. Dept. Shen	To 3-Brig. 2-Div. 4-Corps Pot	July, 1862
39th Ill. Infy	May, 1862	From 2-Brig. 2-Div. Dept. Shen	To 3-Brig. 2-Div. 4-Corps Pot	July, 1862
67th Ohio Infy	May, 1862	From 1-Brig. Shields' Div. Dept. R..	To 3-Brig. 2-Div. 4-Corps Pot	July, 1862

3d BRIGADE.—   **COMMANDER.**

E. B. Tyler...........|Brigadier General....................|May 10, 1862, to June 26, 1862. |

5th Ohio Infy	May, 1862	From 2-Brig. 2-Div. Dept. Shen	To 2-Brig. 1-Div. 2-Corps Army Va..	June, 1862
7th Ohio Infy	May, 1862	From 3-Brig. 2-Div. Dept. Shen	To 2-Brig. 1-Div. 2-Corps Army Va..	June, 1862
29th Ohio Infy	May, 1862	From 3-Brig. 2-Div. Dept. Shen	To 2-Brig. 1-Div. 2-Corps Army Va..	June, 1862
66th Ohio Infy	June, 1862	From 2-Brig. Shields' Div. Dept. R..	To 2-Brig. 1-Div. 2-Corps Army Va..	June, 1862

4th BRIGADE.—   **COMMANDER.**

S. S. Carroll..........|Col. 4th Ohio Infy...........|May 10, 1862, to June 26, 1862. |

1st West Va.	May, 1862	From 3-Brig. 2-Div. Dept. Shen	To 4-Brig. 2-Div. 3-Corps Army Va..	June, 1862
7th Ind. Infy	May, 1862	From 3-Brig. 2-Div. Dept. Shen	To 4-Brig. 2-Div. 3-Corps Army Va..	June, 1862
84th Penna. Infy	May, 1862	From 3-Brig. 2-Div. Dept. Shen	To 4-Brig. 2-Div. 3-Corps Army Va..	June, 1862
110th Penna. Infy	May, 1862	From 3-Brig. 2-Div. Dept. Shen	To 4-Brig. 2-Div. 3-Corps Army Va..	June, 1862

ARTILLERY.—

Batty. A, 1st W. Va. Arty	May, 1862	From Arty. 2-Div. Dept. Shen	To Def. Washington	June, 1862
Batty. B, 1st W. Va. Arty	May, 1862	From Arty. 2-Div. Dept. Shen	To Def. Washington	June, 1862
Batty. H, 1st Ohio Arty	May, 1862	From Arty. 2-Div. Dept. Shen	To Def. Washington	June, 1862
Batty. L, 1st Ohio Arty	May, 1862	From Arty. 2-Div. Dept. Shen	To Def. Washington	June, 1862
Batty. E, 4th U. S. Arty	May, 1862	From Arty. 2-Div. Dept. Shen	To Unatt. 3-Corps Army Va	June, 1862

CAVALRY.—

| 1st Penna. Cav | May, 1862 | From McCall's Div. Dept. Rappa | To Bayard's Cav. Brig. 3-Corps Va.. | June, 1862 |
| 1st Ohio Cav. (Co.'s A, C) | May, 1862 | From Shields' 2-Div. Dept. Shen | To Headqrs. 2-Corps Army Va | June, 1862 |

2d DIVISION.—   **COMMANDER.**

Geo. A. McCall.......|Brigadier General ....|Apr. 4, 1862, to June 12, 1862. |
Division transferred to 5th Army Corps Army Potomac, June 12, 1862.

1st BRIGADE.—   **COMMANDER.**

J. F. Reynolds........|Brigadier General ....|Apr. 4, 1862, to June 12, 1862. |

1st Penna. Res	Apr., 1862	From 1-Brig. 2-Div. 1-Corps Pot	To 1-Brig. 3-Div. 5-Corps Pot	June, 1862
2d Penna. Res	Apr., 1862	From 1-Brig. 2-Div. 1-Corps Pot	To 1-Brig. 3-Div. 5-Corps Pot	June, 1862
5th Penna. Res	Apr., 1862	From 1-Brig. 2-Div. 1-Corps Pot	To 1-Brig. 3-Div. 5-Corps Pot	June, 1862
8th Penna. Res	Apr., 1862	From 1-Brig. 2-Div. 1-Corps Pot	To 1-Brig. 3-Div. 5-Corps Pot	June, 1862

2d BRIGADE.—   COMMANDER.

Geo. G. Meade	Brigadier General	Apr. 4. 1862, to June 12, 1862.	

3d Penna. Res.	Apr., 1862	From 2-Brig. 2-Div. 1-Corps Pot.	To 2-Brig. 3-Div. 5-Corps Pot.	June, 1862
4th Penna. Res.	Apr., 1862	From 2-Brig. 2-Div. 1-Corps Pot.	To 2-Brig. 3-Div. 5-Corps Pot.	June, 1862
7th Penna. Res.	Apr., 1862	From 2-Brig. 2-Div. 1-Corps Pot.	To 2-Brig. 3-Div. 5-Corps Pot.	June, 1862
11th Penna. Res.	Apr., 1862	From 2-Brig. 2-Div. 1-Corps Pot.	To 2-Brig. 3-Div. 5-Corps Pot.	June, 1862

3d BRIGADE.—   COMMANDERS.

E. O. C. Ord	Brigadier General	Apr. 4. 1862, to May 16, 1862.	
Truman Seymour	Brigadier General	May 16, 1862, to June 12, 1862.	

6th Penna. Res.	Apr., 1862	From 3-Brig. 2-Div. 1-Corps Pot.	To 3-Brig. 3-Div. 5-Corps Pot.	June, 1862
9th Penna. Res.	Apr., 1862	From 3-Brig. 2-Div. 1-Corps Pot.	To 3-Brig. 3-Div. 5-Corps Pot.	June, 1862
10th Penna. Res.	Apr., 1862	From 3-Brig. 2-Div. 1-Corps Pot.	To 3-Brig. 3-Div. 5-Corps Pot.	June, 1862
12th Penna. Res.	Apr., 1862	From 3-Brig. 2-Div. 1-Corps Pot.	To 3-Brig. 3-Div. 5-Corps Pot.	June, 1862
13th Pa. Res. (1st Rifles)	Apr., 1862	From 3-Brig. 2-Div. 1-Corps Pot.	To 3-Brig. 3-Div. 5-Corps Pot.	June, 1862
ARTILLERY.—				
Batty. A, 1st Pa. Arty.	Apr., 1862	From Arty. 2-Div. 1-Corps Pot.	To Arty. 3-Div. 5-Corps Pot.	June, 1862
Batty. B, 1st Pa. Arty.	Apr., 1862	From Arty. 2-Div. 1-Corps Pot.	To Arty. 3-Div. 5-Corps Pot.	June, 1862
Batty. G, 1st Pa. Arty.	Apr., 1862	From Arty. 2-Div. 1-Corps Pot.	To Arty. 3-Div. 5-Corps Pot.	June, 1862
Batty. C, 5th U. S. Arty.	Apr., 1862	From Arty. 2-Div. 1-Corps Pot.	To Arty. 3-Div. 5-Corps Pot.	June, 1862
CAVALRY.—				
1st Penna. Cav.	Apr., 1862	From 2-Div. 1-Corps Pot.	To Shields' Div. Dept. Rappa.	May, 1862
4th Penna. Cav.	May. 1862	From Def. of Washington.	To 3-Div. 5-Corps Pot.	June, 1862

ORD'S DIVISION.—   COMMANDERS.

E. O. C. Ord	Brigadier General	May 16, 1862, to June 10, 1862.	
J. B. Ricketts	Brigadier General	June 10. 1862. to June 26, 1862.	

1st BRIGADE.—   COMMANDERS.

J. B. Ricketts	Brigadier General	May 16, 1862, to June 10, 1862.	
A. Duryea	Brigadier General	June 10, 1862, to June 26, 1862.	

26th N. Y. Infy.	May, 1862	From Def. of Washington.	To 2-Brig. 2-Div. 3-Corps Army Va.	June, 1862
94th N. Y. Infy.	May, 1862	From Def. of Washington.	To 2-Brig. 2-Div. 3-Corps Army Va.	June, 1862
88th Penna. Infy.	May, 1862	From Def. of Washington.	To 2-Brig. 2-Div. 3-Corps Army Va.	June, 1862
90th N. Y. Infy.	May, 1862	From Def. of Washington.	To 2-Brig. 2-Div. 3-Corps Army Va.	June, 1862

2d BRIGADE.—   COMMANDERS.

A. Duryea	Brigadier General	May 16, 1862, to June 10, 1862.	
Z. B. Tower	Brigadier General	June 10, 1862, to June 26, 1862.	

97th N. Y. Infy.	May, 1862	From Def. of Washington.	To 1-Brig. 2-Div. 3-Corps Army Va.	June, 1862
104th N. Y. Infy.	May, 1862	From Def. of Washington.	To 1-Brig. 2-Div. 3-Corps Army Va.	June, 1862
105th N. Y. Infy.	May, 1862	From Def. of Washington.	To 1-Brig. 2-Div. 3-Corps Army Va.	June, 1862
107th Penna. Infy.	May, 1862	From Def. of Washington.	To 1-Brig. 2-Div. 3-Corps Army Va.	June, 1862

3d BRIGADE.—   COMMANDER.

G. L. Hartsuff	Brigadier General	To 3-Brig. 2-Div. 3-Corps Army Va.	

12th Mass. Infy.	May, 1862	From 2-Brig. 1-Div. Dept. Shenan.	To 3-Brig. 2-Div. 3-Corps Army Va.	June, 1862
13th Mass. Infy.	May, 1862	From 2-Brig. 1-Div. Dept. Shenan.	To 3-Brig. 2-Div. 3-Corps Army Va.	June, 1862
11th Penna. Infy.	May, 1862	From Mil. Dist. Washington.	To 3-Brig. 2-Div. 3-Corps Army Va.	June, 1862
83d (9-S. M.) N. Y. Infy.	May, 1862	From 2-Brig. 1-Div. Dept. Shenan.	May 16, 1862, to June 26, 1862.	June, 1862
ARTILLERY.—				
2d Me. Indpt. Batty.	May, 1862	From Portland. Me.	To Unatt. Pontooneers 3-Corps Va.	June, 1862
5th Me. Indpt. Batty.	May, 1862	From Def. of Washington.	To Arty. 2-Div. 3-Corps Army Va.	June, 1862
Indpt. Batty. C. Pa. Arty.	May, 1862	From Def. of Washington.	To Arty. 2-Div. 3-Corps Army Va.	June, 1862
Batty. F. 1st Pa. Arty.	May, 1862	From Arty. 1-Div. Dept. Shenan.	To Arty. 2-Div. 3-Corps Army Va.	June, 1862
CAVALRY.—				
1st Me. Cav. A, B, E, H, M.	May, 1862	From Hartsuff's Brig. Dept. Shen.	To Bayard's Cav. Brig. 3-Corps Va.	June, 1862
1st R. I. Cav.	May, 1862	From Cav. Brig. Dept. Shen.	To Bayard's Cav. Brig. 3-Corps Va.	June, 1862

KING'S 3d DIVISION.—   COMMANDER.

Rufus King	Brigadier General	Apr. 4. 1862. to June 26, 1862.	

1st BRIGADE.—   COMMANDER.

C. C. Augur	Brigadier General	Apr. 4. 1862, to June 26, 1862.	

22d N. Y. Infy.	Apr., 1862	From 1-Brig. 3-Div. 1-Corps Pot.	To 1-Brig. 1-Div. 3-Corps Army Va.	June, 1862
24th N. Y. Infy.	Apr., 1862	From 1-Brig. 3-Div. 1-Corps Pot.	To 1-Brig. 1-Div. 3-Corps Army Va.	June, 1862
30th N. Y. Infy.	Apr., 1862	From 1-Brig. 3-Div. 1-Corps Pot.	To 1-Brig. 1-Div. 3-Corps Army Va.	June, 1862
84th (14 Bkln.) N. Y. Infy.	Apr., 1862	From 1-Brig. 3-Div. 1-Corps Pot.	To 1-Brig. 1-Div. 3-Corps Army Va.	June, 1862
2d U. S. Sharpshooters.	Apr., 1862	From 1-Brig. 3-Div. 1-Corps Pot.	To 1-Brig. 1-Div. 3-Corps Army Va.	June, 1862

2d BRIGADE.—   COMMANDER.

M. R. Patrick	Brigadier General	Apr. 4. 1862, to June 26. 1862.	

21st N. Y. Infy.	Apr., 1862	From 2-Brig. 3-Div. 1-Corps Pot.	To 3-Brig. 1-Div. 3-Corps Army Va.	June, 1862
23d N. Y. Infy.	Apr., 1862	From 2-Brig. 3-Div. 1-Corps Pot.	To 3-Brig. 1-Div. 3-Corps Army Va.	June, 1862
35th N. Y. Infy.	Apr., 1862	From 2-Brig. 3-Div. 1-Corps Pot.	To 3-Brig. 1-Div. 3-Corps Army Va.	June, 1862
80th (20-S. M.) N. Y. Infy.	Apr., 1862	From 2-Brig. 3-Div. 1-Corps Pot.	To 3-Brig. 1-Div. 3-Corps Army Va.	June, 1862

3d BRIGADE.—   COMMANDERS.

L. Cutler	Col. 6th Wis. Infy.	Apr. 4. 1862, to May 7, 1862.	
John Gibbon	Brigadier General	May 7. 1862, to June 26, 1862.	

2d Wis. Infy.	Apr., 1862	From 3-Brig. 3-Div. 1-Corps Pot.	To 4-Brig. 1-Div. 3-Corps Army Va.	June, 1862
6th Wis. Infy.	Apr., 1862	From 3-Brig. 3-Div. 1-Corps Pot.	To 4-Brig. 1-Div. 3-Corps Army Va.	June, 1862
7th Wis. Infy.	Apr., 1862	From 3-Brig. 3-Div. 1-Corps Pot.	To 4-Brig. 1-Div. 3-Corps Army Va.	June, 1862
19th Ind. Infy.	Apr., 1862	From 3-Brig. 3-Div. 1-Corps Pot.	To 4-Brig. 1-Div. 3-Corps Army Va.	June, 1862
ARTILLERY.—				
Batty. A, N. H. Arty.	Apr., 1862	From Arty. 3-Div. 1-Corps Pot.	To Arty. 1-Div. 3-Corps Army Va.	June, 1862
Batty. D, 1st R. I. Arty.	Apr., 1862	From Arty. 3-Div. 1-Corps Pot.	To Arty. 1-Div. 3-Corps Army Va.	June, 1862
Indpt. Batty. D, Pa. Arty.	Apr., 1862	From Arty. 3-Div. 1-Corps Pot.	To Arty. 1-Div. 3-Corps Army Va.	June, 1862
Batty. B. 4th U. S. Arty.	Apr., 1862	From Arty. 3-Div. 1-Corps Pot.	To Arty. 1-Div. 3-Corps Army Va.	June, 1862
CAVALRY.—				
2d N. Y. Cav.	Apr., 1862	From 3-Div. 1-Corps Pot.	To Bayard's Cav. Brig. 3-Corps Va.	June, 1862

BAYARD'S CAVALRY BRIGADE.— COMMANDER.

Geo. D. Bayard	Brigadier General		Apr. 4, 1862, to June 26, 1862.		
1st Me. Cav (7 Co's)	May, 1862	From Cav. Brig. Dept. Shenan	To Bayard's Cav. Brig. 3-Corps Va	June, 1862
1st Penna. Cav.	May, 1862	From Shields' Div. Dept. Rappa	To Bayard's Cav. Brig. Dept. Mt	June, 1862
1st N. J. Cav.	May, 1862	From Def. of Washington	To Bayard's Cav. Brig. Dept. Mt	June, 1862
1st Penna. Rifles Battn	May, 1862	From McCall's Div. Dept. Rappa	To Bayard's Cav. Brig. Dept. Mt	June, 1862

DOUBLEDAY'S SEPARATE BRIGADE.— COMMANDER.

Abner Doubleday	Brigadier General		May and June, 1862.		
76th N. Y. Infy	May, 1862	From Mil. Dist. Washington	To 2-Brig. 1-Div. 3-Corps Army Va	June, 1862
95th N. Y. Infy	May, 1862	From Mil. Dist. Washington	To 2-Brig. 1-Div. 3-Corps Army Va	June, 1862
56th Penna. Infy	May, 1862	From Mil. Dist. Washington	To 2-Brig. 1-Div. 3-Corps Army Va	June, 1862
B, 2d N. Y. Lt. Art. Battn	May, 1862	From Mil. Dist. Washington	To Def. of Washington	June, 1862

GEARY'S SEPARATE BRIGADE.— COMMANDER.

John W. Geary	Brigadier General				
28th Penna. Infy	May, 1862	From Geary's Command Dept. Shen	To 2-Brig. 1-Div. 2-Corps Army Va	June, 1862
3d Ind. Cav.	May, 1862	From Eastern Shore Middle Dept	To Unatt. 3-Corps Army Va	June, 1862
1st W. Va. Cav.	May, 1862	From Cav. Brig. Dept. Shen	To Cav. Brig. 2-Corps Army Va	June, 1862
Indpt. Batty E, Pa. Arty	May, 1862	From Geary's Command Dept. Shen	To Arty. 2-Corps Army Va	June, 1862

Army of Virginia

Organized June 26, 1862, by consolidation of the Mountain Department, the Department of the Shenandoah, and the Department of the Rappahannock. Discontinued Sept. 12, 1862, and merged into the Army of the Potomac.

COMMANDER.

John Pope	Major General		June 26, 1862, to Sept. 12, 1862.

First Army Corps

Organized June 26, 1862, from Mountain Department. Merged into Department of the Potomac as the ELEVENTH ARMY CORPS Sept. 12, 1862.

COMMANDERS.

J. C. Fremont	Major General		June 26, 1862, to June 28, 1862.
R. C. Schenck	Brigadier General		June 28, 1862, to June 30, 1862.
Franz Sigel	Major General		June 30, 1862, to July 7, 1862.
R. C. Schenck	Brigadier General		July 7, 1862, to July 12, 1862.
Franz Sigel	Major General		July 12, 1862, to Sept. 12, 1862.

1st DIVISION.— COMMANDERS.

R. C. Schenck	Brigadier General		June 26, 1862, to Aug. 30, 1862.
J. H. Stahel	Brigadier General		Aug. 30, 1862, to Sept. 12, 1862.

1st BRIGADE.— COMMANDERS.

J. H. Stahel	Brigadier General		June 26, 1862, to Aug. 30, 1862.		
A. Bushbeck	Col. 27th Penna. Infy		Aug. 30, 1862, to Sept. 12, 1862.		
8th N. Y. Infy	June, 1862	From 1-Br. Blenker's Div. Mt. Dept.	To 1-Brig. 1-Div. 11-Corps Pot	Sept., 1862
41st N. Y. Infy	June, 1862	From 1-Br. Blenker's Div. Mt. Dept.	To 1-Brig. 1-Div. 11-Corps Pot	Sept., 1862
45th N. Y. Infy	June, 1862	From 1-Br. Blenker's Div. Mt. Dept.	To 1-Brig. 1-Div. 11-Corps Pot	Sept., 1862
27th Penna. Infy	June, 1862	From 1-Br. Blenker's Div. Mt. Dept.	To 1-Brig. 1-Div. 11-Corps Pot	Sept., 1862
2d N. Y. Indpt. Batty	June, 1862	From 1-Br. Blenker's Div. Mt. Dept.	To Arty. 1-Div. 11-Corps Pot	Sept., 1862

2d BRIGADE.— COMMANDER.

N. C. McLean	Col. 75th Ohio Infy		June 26, 1862, to Sept. 12, 1862.		
25th Ohio Infy	June, 1862	From Milroy's Brig. Mt. Dept.	To 2-Brig. 1-Div. 11-Corps Pot	Sept., 1862
32d Ohio Infy	June, 1862	From Schenck's Brig. Mt. Dept.	To Piatt's Brig. Winchester, Va	July, 1862
55th Ohio Infy	June, 1862	From Schenck's Brig. Mt. Dept.	To 2-Brig. 1-Div. 11-Corps Pot	Sept., 1862
73d Ohio Infy	June, 1862	From Schenck's Brig. Mt. Dept.	To 2-Brig. 1-Div. 11-Corps Pot	Sept., 1862
75th Ohio Infy	June, 1862	From Schenck's Brig. Mt. Dept.	To 2-Brig. 1-Div. 11-Corps Pot	Sept., 1862
Batty. K, 1st Ohio Arty	June, 1862	From Schenck's Brig. Mt. Dept.	To Arty. 1-Div. 11-Corps Pot	Sept., 1862

2d DIVISION.— COMMANDER.

A. Von Steinwehr	Brigadier General		June 26, 1862, to Sept. 12, 1862.

1st BRIGADE.— COMMANDERS.

John A. Koltes	Col. 73d Penna. Infy		June 26, 1862, to Aug. 30, 1862.	Killed.	
G. A. Muhleck	Lt.-Col. 73d Penna. Infy		Aug. 30, 1862, to Sept. 12, 1862.		
29th N. Y. Infy	June, 1862	From 2-Br. Blenker's Div. Mt. Dept.	To 1-Brig. 2-Div. 11-Corps Pot	Sept., 1862
68th N. Y. Infy	June, 1862	From 2-Br. Blenker's Div. Mt. Dept.	To 1-Brig. 2-Div. 11-Corps Pot	Sept., 1862
73d Penna. Infy	June, 1862	From 2-Br. Blenker's Div. Mt. Dept.	To 1-Brig. 2-Div. 11-Corps Pot	Sept., 1862

2d BRIGADE.—

3d W. Va. Cav.	June, 1862	From Unatt. Mt. Dept.	To Dept. W. Va.	Sept., 1862
6th Ohio Cav.	June, 1862	From Unatt. Mt. Dept.	To Cav. Brig. 11-Corps Pot	Sept., 1862
Batty. I, 1st N. Y. Arty	June, 1862	From 3-Br. Blenker's Div. Mt. Dept.	To Arty. 3-Div. 11-Corps Pot	Sept., 1862
13th N. Y. Indpt. Batty	June, 1862	From 2-Br. Blenker's Div. Mt. Dept.	To Arty. 1-Div. 11-Corps Pot	Sept., 1862
Batty. C, 1st W. Va. Arty	June, 1862	From 1-Br. Blenker's Div. Mt. Dept.	To Arty. 3-Div. 11-Corps Pot	Sept., 1862

3d DIVISION.— COMMANDER.

Carl Schurz	Brigadier General		June 26, 1862, to Sept. 12, 1862.

1st BRIGADE.— COMMANDERS.

Henry Bohlen	Brigadier General		June 26, 1862, to Aug. 22, 1862.	Killed.	
A. Schimmelfenning	Col. 74th Penna. Infy		Aug. 22, 1862, to Sept. 12, 1862.		
61st Ohio Infy	June, 1862	From New Organization	To 1-Brig. 3-Div. 11-Corps Pot	Sept., 1862
74th Penna. Infy	June, 1862	From 3-Br. Blenkers' Div. Mt. Dept.	To 1-Brig. 3-Div. 11-Corps Pot	Sept., 1862
8th W. Va. Infy	June, 1862	From Cluseret's Advance Brig	To 1-Brig. 3-Div. 11-Corps Pot	Sept., 1862
Indpt. Batty. F, Pa. Arty	Aug., 1862	From Arty. 2-Corps Army Va	To Arty. 2-Div. 12-Corps Pot	Sept., 1862

2d BRIGADE.—   COMMANDER.

W. Krzanowski	Col. 58th N. Y. Infy	June 26, 1862, to Sept. 12, 1862.	
54th N. Y. Infy........June, 1862	From 3-Br. Blenkers' Div. Mt. Dept.	To 2-Brig. 3-Div. 11-Corps Pot....	Sept., 1862
58th N. Y. Infy........June, 1862	From 3-Br. Blenkers' Div. Mt. Dept.	To 2-Brig. 3-Div. 11-Corps Pot....	Sept., 1862
75th Penna. Infy......June, 1862	From 3-Br. Blenkers' Div. Mt. Dept.	To 2-Brig. 3-Div. 11-Corps Pot....	Sept., 1862
Batty. L, 2d N. Y. Arty...Aug., 1862	From Arty. 2-Corps Army Va......	To Arty. 1-Div. 9-Corps Pot......	Sept., 1862
UNATT. THIRD DIVISION.—			
Batty. I, 1st Ohio Arty..June, 1862	From Milroy's Brig. Mt. Dept......	To Arty. 3-Div. 11-Corps Potomac..	Sept., 1862

MILROY'S INDPT. BRIGADE.—   COMMANDER.

R. H. Milroy	Brigadier General	June 26, 1862, to Sept. 12, 1862.	
2d West Va. Infy......June, 1862	From Milroy's Brig. Mt. Dept......	To Dept. West Va.................	Sept., 1862
3d West Va. Infy......June, 1862	From Milroy's Brig. Mt. Dept......	To Dept. West Va.................	Sept., 1862
5th West Va. Infy.....June, 1862	From Milroy's Brig. Mt. Dept......	To Dist. Kanawha West Va........	Sept., 1862
82d Ohio Infy.........June, 1862	From Schenck's Brig. Mt. Dept....	To Headq'rs 11-Corps Potomac.....	Sept., 1862
1st W. Va. C. Cs. C, E, L..June, 1862	From Milroy's Brig. Mt. Dept......	To Cav. Brig. Dept. Washington...	Sept., 1862
12th Ohio Indpt. Batty...June, 1862	From Milroy's Brig. Mt. Dept......	To Arty. 2-Div. 11-Corps Potomac.	Sept., 1862
Rigby's Indiana Batty...June, 1862	From Milroy's Brig. Mt. Dept......	To Piatt's Brig. Winchester, Va...	July, 1862

CAVALRY BRIGADE.—   COMMANDER.

John Beardsley	Col. 9th N. Y. Cav		
1st Conn. Cav. Batt'n....June, 1862	From Schenck's Brig. Mt. Dept.....	To Cav. Brig. 11-Corps Potomac...	Sept., 1862
1st Maryland Cav......June, 1862	From Dept. Shenandoah...........	To Cav. Brig. 11-Corps Potomac...	Sept., 1862
4th New York Cav.....June, 1862	From Blenker's Div. Mt. Dept......	To Cav. Brig. 11-Corps Potomac...	Sept., 1862
9th New York Cav.....June, 1862	From Def. of Washington.........	To Cav. Brig. 11-Corps Potomac...	Sept., 1862

Second Army Corps---Army of Virginia

Organized June 26, 1862, from the Department of the Shenandoah. Discontinued Sept. 12, 1862, and merged into TWELFTH ARMY CORPS, Army Potomac.

COMMANDERS.

N. P. Banks.............	Major General...................	June 26, 1862, to Sept. 4, 1862.	
A. S. Williams.........	Brigadier General.................	Sept. 4, 1862, to Sept. 12, 1862.	

1st DIVISION.—   COMMANDERS.

A. S. Williams.........	Brigadier General.................	June 26, 1862, to Sept. 4, 1862.	
S. W. Crawford........	Brigadier General.................	Sept. 4, 1862, to Sept. 12, 1862.	

1st BRIGADE.—   COMMANDERS.

S. W. Crawford........	Brigadier General.................	June 26, 1862, to Sept. 4, 1862.	
J. F. Knipe.............	Col. 46th Penna. Infy...........	Sept. 4, 1862, to Sept. 12, 1862.	
5th Conn. Infy........June, 1862	From 1-Brig. 1-Div. Dept. Shen....	To 1-Brig. 1-Div. 12-Corps Pot....	Sept., 1862
10th Maine Infy.......June, 1862	From 1-Brig. 1-Div. Dept. Shen....	To 1-Brig. 1-Div. 12-Corps Pot....	Sept., 1862
28th New York Infy....June, 1862	From 1-Brig. 1-Div. Dept. Shen....	To 1-Brig. 1-Div. 12-Corps Pot....	Sept., 1862
46th Penna. Infy......June, 1862	From 1-Brig. 1-Div. Dept. Shen....	To 1-Brig. 1-Div. 12-Corps Pot....	Sept., 1862

2d BRIGADE.—Discontinued Aug., 1862.   COMMANDERS.

John W. Geary.........	Brigadier General.................	June 26, 1862, to July 16, 1862.	
Charles Candy.........	Col. 66th Ohio Infy..............	July 16, 1862, to Aug. 9, 1862.	
5th Ohio Infy..........June, 1862	From 3-B. Shield's Div. Dept. Rapp.	To 1-Brig. 2-Div. 2-Corps Army Va.	Aug., 1862
7th Ohio Infy..........June, 1862	From 3-B. Shield's Div. Dept. Rapp.	To 1-Brig. 2-Div. 2-Corps Army Va.	Aug., 1862
29th Ohio Infy.........June, 1862	From 3-B. Shield's Div. Dept. Rapp.	To 1-Brig. 2-Div. 2-Corps Army Va.	Aug., 1862
66th Ohio Infy.........June, 1862	From 3-B. Shield's Div. Dept. Rapp.	To 1-Brig. 2-Div. 2-Corps Army Va.	Aug., 1862
28th Penna. Infy......June, 1862	From Geary's Indpt. Brig. D. Rapp.	To 1-Brig. 2-Div. 2-Corps Army Va.	Aug., 1862

3d BRIGADE.—   COMMANDERS.

Geo. H. Gordon........	Brigadier General.................	June 26, 1862, to Sept. 12, 1862.	
2d Mass. Infy.........June, 1862	From 3-Brig. 1-Div. Dept. Shen....	To 3-Brig. 1-Div. 12-Corps Potomac.	Sept., 1862
27th Indiana Infy......June, 1862	From 3-Brig. 1-Div. Dept. Shen....	To 3-Brig. 1-Div. 12-Corps Potomac.	Sept., 1862
3d Wisconsin Infy......June, 1862	From 3-Brig. 1-Div. Dept. Shen....	To 3-Brig. 1-Div. 12-Corps Potomac.	Sept., 1862
29th Penna. Infy......June, 1862	From 3-Brig. 1-Div. Dept. Shen....	To 3-Brig. 1-Div. 12-Corps Potomac.	Sept., 1862
Collis Penna. Zouaves...June, 1862	From 3-Brig. 1-Div. Dept. Shen....	To 3-Brig. 1-Div. 12-Corps Potomac.	Sept., 1862

2d DIVISION.—   COMMANDERS.

James Cooper..........	Brigadier General.................	June 26, 1862, to July 7, 1862.	
C. C. Augur...........	Brigadier General.................	July 7, 1862, to Aug. 9, 1862.	
Henry Prince..........	Brigadier General.................	Aug. 9, 1862.	
Geo. S. Greene.........	Brigadier General.................	Aug. 9, 1862, to Sept. 12, 1862.	

1st BRIGADE.—   COMMANDERS.

James Cooper..........	Brigadier General.................	June 26, 1862, to July 16, 1862.	
John W. Geary.........	Brigadier General.................	July 16, 1862, to Aug. 9, 1862.	
Charles Candy.........	Col. 66th Ohio Infy..............	Aug. 9, 1862, to Sept. 12, 1862.	
3d Maryland Infy.......June, 1862	From 1-Brig. Sigel's D. Dept. Shen.	To 2-Brig. 2-Div. 2-Corps Army Va.	Aug., 1862
102d N. Y. Infy........June, 1862	From 1-Brig. Sigel's D. Dept. Shen.	To 2-Brig. 2-Div. 2-Corps Army Va.	Aug., 1862
109th Penna. Infy......June, 1862	From 1-Brig. Sigel's D. Dept. Shen.	To 2-Brig. 2-Div. 2-Corps Army Va.	Aug., 1862
111th Penna. Infy......June, 1862	From 1-Brig. Sigel's D. Dept. Shen.	To 2-Brig. 2-Div. 2-Corps Army Va.	Aug., 1862
8th and 12th U. S. Infy..June, 1862	From 1-Brig. Sigel's D. Dept. Shen.	To 2-Brig. 2-Div. 2-Corps Army Va.	Aug., 1862
5th Ohio Infy..........Aug., 1862	From 2-B. 1-Div. 2-Corps Army Va.	To 1-Brig. 2-Div. 12-Corps Potomac	Sept., 1862
7th Ohio Infy..........Aug., 1862	From 2-B. 1-Div. 2-Corps Army Va.	To 1-Brig. 2-Div. 12-Corps Potomac	Sept., 1862
29th Ohio Infy.........Aug., 1862	From 2-B. 1-Div. 2-Corps Army Va.	To 1-Brig. 2-Div. 12-Corps Potomac	Sept., 1862
66th Ohio Infy.........Aug., 1862	From 2-B. 1-Div. 2-Corps Army Va.	To 1-Brig. 2-Div. 12-Corps Potomac	Sept., 1862
28th Penna. Infy......Aug., 1862	From 2-B. 1-Div. 2-Corps Army Va.	To 1-Brig. 2-Div. 12-Corps Potomac	Sept., 1862

2d BRIGADE.—   COMMANDERS.

J. P. Slough..........	Brigadier General................	June 26, 1862, to July 1, 1862.	
James A. Tate........	Col. 1st Dist. Columbia Infy......	July 1, 1862, to July 10, 1862.	
Daniel Ullman........	Col. 10th New York Infy..........	July 10, 1862, to July 16, 1862.	
Henry Prince.........	Brigadier General................	July 16, 1862, to Aug. 9, 1862.	
D. P. DeWitt..........	Col. 3d Maryland Infy............	Aug. 9, 1862, to Aug. 12, 1862.	
M. Schlandecker.......	Col. 111th Penna. Infy...........	Aug. 12, 1862, to Aug. 30, 1862.	
T. P. Van Buren.......	Col. 102d New York Infy..........	Aug. 30, 1862, to Sept. 12, 1862.	

2d BRIGADE.—Continued.

3d Delaware Infy......June, 1862	From 2-B. Sigel's Div. Dept. Shen.	To 3-Brig. 2-Div. 2-Corps Army Va.	Aug., 1862
1st Dist. Columbia Infy..June, 1862	From 2-B. Sigel's Div. Dept. Shen.	To 3-Brig. 2-Div. 2-Corps Army Va.	Aug., 1862
60th New York Infy.....June, 1862	From 2-B. Sigel's Div. Dept. Shen.	To 3-Brig. 2-Div. 2-Corps Army Va.	Aug., 1862
78th New York Infy.....June, 1862	From 2-B. Sigel's Div. Dept. Shen.	To 3-Brig. 2-Div. 2-Corps Army Va.	Aug., 1862
Purnell, Md., Leg'n Infy..June, 1862	From 2-B. Sigel's Div. Dept. Shen.	To 3-Brig. 2-Div. 2-Corps Army Va.	Aug., 1862
3d Maryland Infy........Aug., 1862	From 1-B. 2-Div. 2-Corps Army Va.	To 2-Brig. 2-Div. 12-Corps Potomac	Sept., 1862
102d New York Infy......Aug., 1862	From 1-B. 2-Div. 2-Corps Army Va.	To 2-Brig. 2-Div. 12-Corps Potomac	Sept., 1862
109th Penna. Infy.......Aug., 1862	From 1-B. 2-Div. 2-Corps Army Va.	To 2-Brig. 2-Div. 12-Corps Potomac	Sept., 1862
111th Penna. Infy.......Aug., 1862	From 1-B. 2-Div. 2-Corps Army Va.	To 2-Brig. 2-Div. 12-Corps Potomac	Sept., 1862
8th & 12th U. S. Infy....Aug., 1862	From 1-B. 2-Div. 2-Corps Army Va.	To Headqrs. Army Potomac........	Sept., 1862

3d BRIGADE.—

COMMANDERS.		
Geo. S. Greene........	Brigadier General................	Aug. 1, 1862, to Aug. 9, 1862.
J. A. Tate.............	Col. 1st Dist. Columbia Infy......	Aug. 9, 1862, to Sept. 12, 1862.

3d Delaware Infy......Aug., 1862	From 2-B. 2-Div. 2-Corps Army Va.	To 3-Brig. 2-Div. 12-Corps Potomac	Sept., 1862
Purnell, Md. Leg'n Infy..Aug., 1862	From 2-B. 2-Div. 2-Corps Army Va.	To 3-Brig. 2-Div. 12-Corps Potomac	Sept., 1862
60th New York Infy.....Aug., 1862	From 2-B. 2-Div. 2-Corps Army Va.	To 3-Brig. 2-Div. 12-Corps Potomac	Sept., 1862
78th New York Infy.....Aug., 1862	From 2-B. 2-Div. 2-Corps Army Va.	To 3-Brig. 2-Div. 12-Corps Potomac	Sept., 1862
1st Dist. Columbia Infy..Aug., 1862	From 2-B. 2-Div. 2-Corps Army Va.	To 3-Brig. 2-Div. 12-Corps Potomac	Sept., 1862
13th New Jersey Infy....Aug., 1862	From New Organization..........	To 3-Brig. 2-Div. 12-Corps Potomac	Sept., 1862

ARTILLERY.—

4th Maine Indpt. Batty..June, 1862	From Defences Washington........	To Arty. 2-Div. 12-Corps Potomac..	Sept., 1862
6th Maine Indpt. Batty..June, 1862	From Defences Washington........	To Arty. 2-Div. 12-Corps Potomac..	Sept., 1862
Batty. K, 1st N. Y. Arty..June, 1862	From Sigel's Div. Dept. Shen.....	To Arty. 1-Div. 12-Corps Potomac..	Sept., 1862
Batty. L, 1st N. Y. Arty..June, 1862	From Sigel's Div. Dept. Shen.....	To Arty. 1-Div. 3-Corps Army Va..	June, 1862
Batty. M, 1st N. Y. Arty..June, 1862	From 1-Div. Dept. Shenandoah....	To Arty. 1-Div. 12-Corps Potomac..	Sept., 1862
Batty. L, 2d N. Y. Arty..June, 1862	From Sturgis' Div. Def. Washington	To 2-Brig. 3-Div. 1-Corps Army Va.	Aug., 1862
10th N. Y. Indpt. Batty..June, 1862	From Sturgis' Div. Def. Washington	To Arty. 1-Div. 12-Corps Potomac..	Sept., 1862
Indpt. Batty. E, Pa. A..June, 1862	From 1-Div. Dept. Shenandoah....	To Arty. 1-Div. 12-Corps Potomac..	Sept., 1862
Indpt. Batty. F, Pa. A..June, 1862	From 1-Div. Dept. Shenandoah....	To Arty. 2-Div. 12-Corps Potomac..	Sept., 1862
Batty. F, 4th U. S. Arty..June, 1862	From 1-Div. Dept. Shenandoah....	To Arty. 1-Div. 12-Corps Potomac..	Sept., 1862
16th Indiana Batty.....June, 1862	From Defences Washington........	To Def. Washington North Potomac	Sept., 1862

CAVALRY BRIGADE.—

COMMANDERS.		
John P. Hatch........	Brigadier General................	June 26, 1862, to July 27, 1862.
John Bulford.........	Brigadier General................	July 27, 1862, to Sept. 12, 1862.

1st Michigan Cav.......June, 1862	From Hatch's Cav. Brig. Dept. Shen.	To Cav. Brig. Def. Washington.....	Sept., 1862
5th New York Cav......June, 1862	From Hatch's Cav. Brig. Dept. Shen.	To Cav. Brig. Def. Washington.....	Sept., 1862
1st West Va. Cav......June, 1862	From Hatch's Cav. Brig. Dept. Shen.	To Cav. Brig. Def. Washington.....	Sept., 1862
1st Vermont Cav.......June, 1862	From Hatch's Cav. Brig. Dept. Shen.	To Cav. Brig. Def. Washington.....	Sept., 1862
2d Penna. Cav.........Aug., 1862	From Mil. Dist. Washington.......	To Cav. Brig. Def. Washington.....	Sept., 1862

CORPS HEADQRS.—

1st Ohio Cav. Cos. A, C...June, 1862	From Shield's Div. Dept. Shenand'h	To Cav. Brig. Def. Washington	Sept., 1862

Third Army Corps---Army of Virginia

• Organized June 26, 1862, from Department of the Rappahannock. Discontinued Sept. 12, 1862, and troops merged into Army Potomac as Reorganized First Army Corps.

COMMANDERS.		
Irvin McDowell.......	Major General.....................	June 26, 1862, to Sept. 5, 1862.
J. B. Ricketts........	Brigadier General................	Sept. 5, 1862, to Sept. 6, 1862.
Joseph, Hooker.......	Major General...................	Sept. 6, 1862, to Sept. 12, 1862.

1st DIVISION.—

COMMANDERS.		
Rufus King..........	Brigadier General................	June 26, 1862, to Aug. 28, 1862.
J. F. Hatch...........	Brigadier General................	Aug. 28, 1862, to Aug. 30, 1862.
A. Doubleday.........	Brigadier General................	Aug. 30, 1862, to Sept. 12, 1862.

1st BRIGADE.—

COMMANDERS.		
C. C. Augur..........	Brigadier General................	June 26, 1862, to July 7, 1862.
T. Sullivan...........	Col. 24th New York Infy..........	July 7, 1862, to July 27, 1862.
J. P. Hatch...........	Brigadier General................	July 27, 1862, to Aug. 28, 1862.
T. Sullivan...........	Col. 24th New York Infy..........	Aug. 28, 1862, to Sept. 12, 1862.

22d New York Infy......June, 1862	From 1-B. 3-D. Dept. Rappahannock	To 1-Brig. 1-Div. 1-Corps Potomac	Sept., 1862
24th New York Infy.....June, 1862	From 1-B. 3-D. Dept. Rappahannock	To 1-Brig. 1-Div. 1-Corps Potomac	Sept., 1862
30th New York Infy.....June, 1862	From 1-B. 3-D. Dept. Rappahannock	To 1-Brig. 1-Div. 1-Corps Potomac	Sept., 1862
84th (14-Bklyn.) N. Y. I..June, 1862	From 1-B. 3-D. Dept. Rappahannock	To 1-Brig. 1-Div. 1-Corps Potomac	Sept., 1862
2d U. S. Sharpshooters...June, 1862	From 1-B. 3-D. Dept. Rappahannock	To 1-Brig. 1-Div. 1-Corps Potomac	Sept., 1862

2d BRIGADE.—

COMMANDERS.		
A. Doubleday.........	Brigadier General................	June 26, 1862, to Aug. 30, 1862.
J. W. Hoffman........	Col. 56th Penna. Infy............	Aug. 30, 1862, to Sept. 12, 1862.

76th New York Infy.....June, 1862	From Doubleday's Sep. Brig. Rapp.	To 2-Brig. 1-Div. 1-Corps Potomac	Sept., 1862
95th New York Infy.....June, 1862	From Doubleday's Sep. Brig. Rapp.	To 2-Brig. 1-Div. 1-Corps Potomac	Sept., 1862
56th Penna. Infy.......June, 1862	From Doubleday's Sep. Brig. Rapp.	To 2-Brig. 1-Div. 1-Corps Potomac	Sept., 1862
7th Indiana Infy........Sept., 1862	From 4-Brig. 2-Div. 3-Corps Va....	To 2-Brig. 1-Div. 1-Corps Potomac	Sept., 1862

3d BRIGADE.—

COMMANDER.		
M. R. Patrick........	Brigadier General................	June 26, 1862, to Sept. 12, 1862.

21st New York Infy.....June, 1862	From 2-Brig. 3-Div. Dept. Rapp...	To 3-Brig. 1-Div. 1-Corps Potomac	Sept., 1862
23d New York Infy......June, 1862	From 2-Brig. 3-Div. Dept. Rapp...	To 3-Brig. 1-Div. 1-Corps Potomac	Sept., 1862
35th New York Infy.....June, 1862	From 2-Brig. 3-Div. Dept. Rapp...	To 3-Brig. 1-Div. 1-Corps Potomac	Sept., 1862
80th (20-S. M.) N. Y. I..June, 1862	From 2-Brig. 3-Div. Dept. Rapp...	To 3-Brig. 1-Div. 1-Corps Potomac	Sept., 1862

4th BRIGADE.—

COMMANDER.		
John Gibbon..........	Brigadier General................	June 26, 1862, to Sept. 12, 1862.

2d Wisconsin Infy......June, 1862	From 3-Brig. 3-Div. Dept. Rapp.	To 4-Brig. 1-Div. 1-Corps Potomac	Sept., 1862
6th Wisconsin Infy......June, 1862	From 3-Brig. 3-Div. Dept. Rapp.	To 4-Brig. 1-Div. 1-Corps Potomac	Sept., 1862
7th Wisconsin Infy......June, 1862	From 3-Brig. 3-Div. Dept. Rapp.	To 4-Brig. 1-Div. 1-Corps Potomac	Sept., 1862
19th Indiana Infy.......June, 1862	From 3-Brig. 3-Div. Dept. Rapp.	To 4-Brig. 1-Div. 1-Corps Potomac	Sept., 1862

ARTILLERY.—

1st New Hamp. Batty...June, 1862	From Arty. 3-Div. Dept. Rapp.....	To Arty. 1-Div. 1-Corps Potomac..	Sept., 1862
Batty. D, 1st R. I. Arty..June, 1862	From Arty. 3-Div. Dept. Rapp.....	To Arty. 1-Div. 1-Corps Potomac..	Sept., 1862
Batty. L, 1st N. Y. Arty..June, 1862	From Arty. 2-Corps Army Va......	To Arty. 1-Div. 1-Corps Potomac..	Sept., 1862
Indpt. Batty. D, Pa. A...June, 1862	From Arty. 3-Div. Dept. Rapp.....	To Arty. 2-Div. 9-Corps Potomac..	Sept., 1862
Batty. B, 4th U. S. Arty..June, 1862	From Arty. 3-Div. Dept. Rapp.....	To Arty. 1-Div. 1-Corps Potomac..	Sept., 1862

2d DIVISION.— COMMANDER.

J. B. Ricketts........	Brigadier General.................	June 26, 1862, to Sept. 12, 1862.

1st BRIGADE.— COMMANDER.

A. Duryea.............	Brigadier General.................	June 26, 1862, to Sept. 12, 1862.

97th New York Infy....June, 1862	From 2-Brig. Ord's Div. Dept. Rapp.	To 1-Brig. 2-Div. 1-Corps Potomac	Sept., 1862
104th New York Infy....June, 1862	From 2-Brig. Ord's Div. Dept. Rapp.	To 1-Brig. 2-Div. 1-Corps Potomac	Sept., 1862
105th New York Infy....June, 1862	From 2-Brig. Ord's Div. Dept. Rapp.	To 1-Brig. 2-Div. 1-Corps Potomac	Sept., 1862
107th Penna. Infy.......June, 1862	From 2-Brig. Ord's Div. Dept. Rapp.	To 1-Brig. 2-Div. 1-Corps Potomac	Sept., 1862

2d BRIGADE.— COMMANDERS.

Z. B. Tower..........	Brigadier General.................	June 26, 1862, to Aug. 30, 1862.
W. H. Christian........	Col. 26th New York Infy...........	Aug. 30, 1862, to Sept. 12, 1862.

26th New York Infy.....June, 1862	From 1-Brig. Ord's Div. Dept. Rapp.	To 2-Brig. 2-Div. 1-Corps Potomac	Sept., 1862
94th New York Infy.....June, 1862	From 1-Brig. Ord's Div. Dept. Rapp.	To 2-Brig. 2-Div. 1-Corps Potomac	Sept., 1862
88th Penna. Infy.....June, 1862	From 1-Brig. Ord's Div. Dept. Rapp.	To 2-Brig. 2-Div. 1-Corps Potomac	Sept., 1862
90th Penna. Infy.....June, 1862	From 1-Brig. Ord's Div. Dept. Rapp.	To 2-Brig. 2-Div. 1-Corps Potomac	Sept., 1862

3d BRIGADE.— COMMANDERS.

Geo. L. Hartsuff.......	Brigadier General.................	June 26, 1862, to Aug. 29, 1862.
J. W. Stiles...........	Col. 83d New York Infy...........	Aug. 29, 1862, to Sept. 2, 1862.
Geo. L. Hartsuff.......	Brigadier General.................	Sept. 2, 1862, to Sept. 12, 1862.

12th Mass. Infy.........June, 1862	From 3-Brig. Ord's Div. Dept. Rapp.	To 3-Brig. 2-Div. 1-Corps Potomac	Sept., 1862
13th Mass. Infy........June, 1862	From 3-Brig. Ord's Div. Dept. Rapp.	To 3-Brig. 2-Div. 1-Corps Potomac	Sept., 1862
11th Penna. Infy........June, 1862	From 3-Brig. Ord's Div. Dept. Rapp.	To 3-Brig. 2-Div. 1-Corps Potomac	Sept., 1862
83d (9-S. M.) N. Y. Infy..June, 1862	From 3-Brig. Ord's Div. Dept. Rapp.	To 3-Brig. 2-Div. 1-Corps Potomac	Sept., 1862

4th BRIGADE.— COMMANDERS.

S. S. Carroll...........	Col. 4th Ohio Infy................	June 26, 1862, to Aug. 24, 1862.
Jos. Thoburn..........	Col. 1st West Va. Infy.............	Aug. 24, 1862, to Sept. 12, 1862.

84th Penna. Infy.......June, 1862	From 4-B. Shield's Div. Dept. Rapp.	To Whipple's Div. Def. Washington	Sept., 1862
110th Penna. Infy.......June, 1862	From 4-B. Shield's Div. Dept. Rapp.	To Whipple's Div. Def. Washington	Sept., 1862
1st West Va. Infy.......June, 1862	From 4-B. Shield's Div. Dept. Rapp.	To Whipple's Div. Def. Washington	Sept., 1862
7th Indiana Infy.......June, 1862	From 4-B. Shield's Div. Dept. Rapp.	To 2-Brig. 1-Div. 3-Corps Army Va.	Sept., 1862

ARTILLERY, 2d DIVISION.—

2d Maine Indpt. Batty...June, 1862	From Arty. 2-Div. Dept. Rapp.....	To Unatt. Pontooneers 3-Corps Va..	June, 1862
5th Maine Indpt. Batty...June, 1862	From Arty. 2-Div. Dept. Rapp.....	To Arty. 2-Div. 1-Corps Potomac..	Sept., 1862
Indpt. Batty. C, Pa. A...June, 1862	From Arty. 2-Div. Dept. Rapp.....	To Arty. 2-Div. 1-Corps Potomac..	Sept., 1862
Batty. F, 1st Pa. Arty...June, 1862	From Arty. 2-Div. Dept. Rapp.....	To Arty. 2-Div. 1-Corps Potomac..	Sept., 1862

3d DIVISION.—Joined from 5th Corps Potomac.

COMMANDER.

J. F. Reynolds........	Brigadier General.................	Aug. 26, 1862, to Sept. 12, 1862.

1st BRIGADE.— COMMANDER.

Truman Seymour......	Brigadier General.................	Aug. 26, 1862, to Sept. 12, 1862.

1st Penna. Reserve......Aug., 1862	From 1-Brig. 3-Div. 5-Corps Potom.	To 1-Brig. 3-Div. 1-Corps Potomac	Sept., 1862
2d Penna. Reserve.....Aug., 1862	From 1-Brig. 3-Div. 5-Corps Potom.	To 1-Brig. 3-Div. 1-Corps Potomac	Sept., 1862
5th Penna. Reserves....Aug., 1862	From 1-Brig. 3-Div. 5-Corps Potom.	To 1-Brig. 3-Div. 1-Corps Potomac	Sept., 1862
6th Penna. Reserves....Aug., 1862	From 3-Brig. 3-Div. 5-Corps Potom.	To 1-Brig. 3-Div. 1-Corps Potomac	Sept., 1862

2d BRIGADE, 3d DIVISION.— COMMANDER.

Geo. G. Meade........	Brigadier General.................	Aug. 26, 1862, to Sept. 12, 1862.

3d Penna. Reserves.....Aug., 1862	From 2-Brig. 3-Div. 5-Corps Potom.	To 2-Brig. 3-Div. 1-Corps Potomac.	Sept., 1862
4th Penna. Reserves.....Aug., 1862	From 2-Brig. 3-Div. 5-Corps Potom.	To 2-Brig. 3-Div. 1-Corps Potomac.	Sept., 1862
7th Penna. Reserves.....Aug., 1862	From 2-Brig. 3-Div. 5-Corps Potom.	To 2-Brig. 3-Div. 1-Corps Potomac.	Sept., 1862
8th Penna. Reserves.....Aug., 1862	From 1-Brig. 3-Div. 5-Corps Potom.	To 2-Brig. 3-Div. 1-Corps Potomac.	Sept., 1862
13th Penna. Reserves.....Aug., 1862	From 3-Brig. 3-Div. 5-Corps Potom.	To 1-Brig. 3-Div. 1-Corps Potomac.	Sept., 1862

3d BRIGADE.— COMMANDERS.

C. F. Jackson.........	Brigadier General.................	Aug. 26, 1862, to Aug. 30, 1862.
Robt. Anderson........	Lt.-Col. 9th Pa. Reserves..........	Aug. 30, 1862, to Sept. 1, 1862.
T. F. Gallagher.......	Col. 11th Penna. Reserves.........	Sept. 1, 1862, to Sept. 12, 1862.

9th Penna. Reserves....Aug., 1862	From 3-Brig. 3-Div. 5-Corps Potom.	To 3-Brig. 3-Div. 1-Corps Potomac.	Sept., 1862
10th Penna. Reserves....Aug., 1862	From 3-Brig. 3-Div. 5-Corps Potom.	To 3-Brig. 3-Div. 1-Corps Potomac.	Sept., 1862
11th Penna. Reserves....Aug., 1862	From 2-Brig. 3-Div. 5-Corps Potom.	To 3-Brig. 3-Div. 1-Corps Potomac.	Sept., 1862
12th Penna. Reserves....Aug., 1862	From 3-Brig. 3-Div. 5-Corps Potom.	To 3-Brig. 3-Div. 1-Corps Potomac.	Sept., 1862

ARTILLERY.—

Batty. A, 1st Pa. Arty..Aug., 1862	From Arty. 3-Div. 5-Corps Potomac	To Arty. 3-Div. 1-Corps Potomac..	Sept., 1862
Batty. B, 1st Pa. Arty..Aug., 1862	From Arty. 3-Div. 5-Corps Potomac	To Arty. 3-Div. 1-Corps Potomac..	Sept., 1862
Batty. G, 1st Pa. Arty..Aug., 1862	From Arty. 3-Div. 5-Corps Potomac	To Arty. 3-Div. 1-Corps Potomac..	Sept., 1862
Batty. C, 5th U. S. Arty..Aug., 1862	From Arty. 3-Div. 5-Corps Potomac	To Arty. 3-Div. 1-Corps Potomac..	Sept., 1862

BAYARD'S CAVALRY BRIGADE.— COMMANDER.

Geo. D. Bayard........	Brigadier General.................	June 26, 1862, to Sept. 12, 1862.

1st Maine Cav..........June, 1862	From Cav. B. Dept. Rappahannock	To Bayard's Cav. Brig. Potomac...	Sept., 1862
1st R. I. Cav...........June, 1862	From Cav. B. Dept. Rappahannock	To Bayard's Cav. Brig. Potomac...	Sept., 1862
2d New York Cav......June, 1862	From Cav. B. Dept. Rappahannock	To Bayard's Cav. Brig. Potomac...	Sept., 1862
1st New Jersey Cav......June, 1862	From Cav. B. Dept. Rappahannock	To Bayard's Cav. Brig. Potomac...	Sept., 1862
1st Penna. Cav..........June, 1862	From Cav. B. Dept. Rappahannock	To Bayard's Cav. Brig. Potomac...	Sept., 1862
10th New York Cav......June, 1862	From Mil. Dist. Washington.......	To Bayard's Cav. Brig. Potomac...	Sept., 1862
3d Ind. Cav............June, 1862	From Geary's Sep. Brig. Dept. Rapp.	To 2-Brig. Cav. Div. Pot..........	Sept., 1862
13th Pa. Res., C. G. H. I...June, 1862	From Dept. Rappahannock.........	To 1-Brig. 3-Div. 1-Corps Pot......	Sept., 1862
2d Me. Indpt. Batty.....June, 1862	From Arty. 2-Div. Dept. Rapp......	To 1-Brig. Haskin's Div. Wash.....	Sept., 1862
Batty. E. 4th U. S. Arty..June, 1862	From Arty. Shields' Div. Dept. Rapp.	To Arty. 2-Div. 9-Corps Pot.......	Aug., 1862

PONTOONEERS.—

3d Me. Batty. Arty.......June, 1862	From Pontooneers Dept. Rapp......	To 1-Brig. Haskin's Div. Wash......	Sept., 1862

Burnside's Expeditionary Corps

Organized Dec., 1861. Merged into Department of North Carolina, April, 1862.

COMMANDER.

Ambrose E. Burnside,.	Major General.....................	

FOSTER'S BRIGADE.— COMMANDER.

J. G. Foster...........	Brigadier General..................		
23d Mass. Infy..........Dec., 1861	From New Organization............	To 1-Brig. 1-Div. Dept. N. C.......	Apr., 1862
24th Mass. Infy..........Dec., 1861	From New Organization............	To 2-Brig. 1-Div. Dept. N. C......	Apr., 1862
25th Mass. Infy..........Dec., 1861	From New Organization............	To 1-Brig. 1-Div. Dept. N. C......	Apr., 1862
27th Mass. Infy..........Dec., 1861	From New Organization............	To 2-Brig. 1-Div. Dept. N. C......	Apr., 1862
10th Conn. Infy..........Dec., 1861	From New Organization............	To 2-Brig. 1-Div. Dept. N. C......	Apr., 1862
17th Mass. Infy.........Mch., 1862	From Dix's Div. Baltimore, Md.....	To 1-Brig. 1-Div. Dept. N. C......	Apr., 1862

RENO'S BRIGADE.— COMMANDER.

J. L. Reno............	Brigadier General..................		
21st Mass. Infy..........Dec., 1861	From New Organization............	To. 2-Brig. 2-Div. Dept. N. C......	Apr., 1862
51st N. Y. Infy..........Dec., 1861	From New Organization............	To. 2-Brig. 2-Div. Dept. N. C......	Apr., 1862
51st Penna. Infy..........Dec., 1861	From New Organization............	To. 2-Brig. 2-Div. Dept. N. C......	Apr., 1862
9th N. J. Infy..........Dec., 1861	From New Organization............	To. 2-Brig. 2-Div. Dept. N. C......	Apr., 1862

PARKE'S BRIGADE.— COMMANDER.

J. G. Parke...........	Brigadier General..................		
4th R. I. Infy..........Dec., 1861	From New Organization............	To 1-Brig. 3-Div. Dept. N. C......	Apr., 1862
5th R. I. Infy..........Dec., 1861	From New Organization............	To 1-Brig. 3-Div. Dept. N. C......	Apr., 1862
8th Conn. Infy..........Dec., 1861	From New Organization............	To 1-Brig. 3-Div. Dept. N. C......	Apr., 1862
9th N. Y. Infy..........Dec., 1861	From Dept. of Va.................	To 4-Brig. Dept. N. C.............	Apr., 1862

WILLIAMS' BRIGADE.— COMMANDER.

Thos. Williams.........	Brigadier General..................		
6th N. H. Infy..........Dec., 1861	From New Organization............	To 4-Brig. Dept. N. C.............	Apr., 1862
11th Conn. Infy..........Dec., 1861	From New Organization............	To 2-Brig. 2-Div. Dept. N. C......	Apr., 1862
89th N. Y. Infy..........Dec., 1861	From New Organization............	To 4-Brig. Dept. N. C.............	Apr., 1862
48th Penna Infy..........Dec., 1861	From New Organization............	To 4-Brig. Dept. N. C.............	Apr., 1862
UNATTACHED.—			
Batty. F, 1st R. I. Arty...Dec., 1861	From New Organization............	To Unatt. Dept. N. C.............	Apr., 1862
Batty. C, 1st U. S. Arty...Dec., 1861	From Fortress Monroe, Va........	To Unatt. Dept. N. C.............	Apr., 1862
99th N. Y. Infy Co. B...Dec., 1861	From New Organization............	To Dept. Va......................	Apr., 1862

Department of North Carolina

Created Jany. 7, 1862, to consist of the State of North Carolina. Merged into the Department of Virginia and North Carolina July 15, 1863. Recreated Jany. 31, 1865.

COMMANDERS.

A. E. Burnside........	Major General.....................	Jan. 13, 1862, to July 6, 1862.
J. G. Foster...........	Major General.....................	July 6, 1862, to July 15, 1863.

1st DIVISION.— COMMANDERS.

J. G. Foster...........	Brigadier General..................	Apr. 2, 1862, to July 6, 1862.
T. J. C. Amory........	Col. 17th Mass. Infy..............	July 6, 1862, to Sept., 1862.
	Division reorganized Dec. 28, 1862.	
H. W. Wessells........	Brigadier General..................	Dec. 28, 1862, to Jan. 2, 1863.

1st BRIGADE.— COMMANDERS.

T. J. C. Amory........	Col. 17th Mass. Infy..............	Apr. 2, 1862, to Dec. 10, 1862.	
L. C. Hunt...........	Brigadier General..................	Dec. 28, 1862, to Jan. 2, 1863.	
17th Mass. Infy..........Apr., 1862	From 1-Brig. Burnside Exp........	To Amory's Unatt. Brig. Dept. N. C.	Dec., 1862
23d Mass. Infy..........Apr., 1862	From 1-Brig. Burnside Exp........	To Heckman's Un. Brig. Dept. N. C.	Dec., 1862
25th Mass. Infy..........Apr., 1862	From 1-Brig. Burnside Exp........	To Lee's Unatt. Brig. Dept. N. C...	Dec., 1862
27th Mass. Infy..........Aug., 1862	From 2-Brig. 1-Div. 9-Corps Pot....	To Lee's Unatt. Brig. Dept. N. C...	Dec., 1862
43d Mass. Infy..........Nov., 1862	From New Organization............	To Amory's Unatt. Brig. Dept. N. C.	Dec., 1862
45th Mas. Infy..........Nov., 1862	From New Organization............	To Amory's Unatt. Brig. Dept. N. C.	Dec., 1862
51st Mass. Infy..........Nov., 1862	From New Organization............	To Amory's Unatt. Brig. Dept. N. C.	Dec., 1862
85th N. Y. Infy..........Dec., 1862	From Wessell's Brig. Div. Suf. 7-C.	To 1-Br. 4-Div. 18-Corps. Dept. N. C.	Jan., 1863
92d N. Y. Infy..........Dec., 1862	From Wessell's Brig. Div. Suf. 7-C.	To 1-Br. 4-Div. 18-Corps. Dept. N. C.	Jan., 1863
96th N. Y. Infy..........Dec., 1862	From Wessell's Brig. Div. Suf. 7-C.	To 1-Br. 4-Div. 18-Corps. Dept. N. C.	Jan., 1863
85th Penna. Infy..........Dec., 1862	From Wessell's Brig. Div. Suf. 7-C.	To 2-Br. 3-Div. 18-Corps. Dept. N. C.	Jan., 1863
101st Penna. Infy..........Dec., 1862	From Wessell's Brig. Div. Suf. 7-C.	To 1-Br. 4-Div. 18-Corps. Dept. N. C.	Jan., 1863
103d Penna. Infy..........Dec., 1862	From Wessell's Brig. Div. Suf. 7-C.	To 1-Br. 4-Div. 18-Corps. Dept. N. C.	Jan., 1863

2d BRIGADE.— COMMANDER.

T. J. Stevenson........	Col. 24th Mass. Infy..............	Apr. 2, 1862, to Jan. 2, 1863.	
10th Conn. Infy..........Apr., 1862	From 1-Brig. Burnside Exp........	To 2-Br. 4-Div. 18-Corps Dept. N. C.	Jan., 1863
24th Mass. Infy..........Apr., 1862	From 1-Brig. Burnside Exp........	To 2-Br. 4-Div. 18-Corps Dept. N. C.	Jan., 1863
27th Mass. Infy..........Apr., 1862	From 1-Brig. Burnside Exp........	To 2-Brig. 1-Div. 9-Corps Pot....	July, 1862
9th N. J. Infy..........July, 1862	From 1-Brig. 3-Div. Dept. N. C....	To 3-Brig. 1-Div. 9-Corps Pot.......	Nov., 1862
5th R. I. Infy..........July, 1862	From 1-Brig. 3-Div. Dept. N. C.....	To 2-Br. 4-Div. 18-Corps Dept. N. C.	Jan., 1863
8th Mass. Infy..........Nov., 1862	From New Organization............	To Heckman's Unatt. Br. Dept. N. C.	Dec., 1862
44th Mass. Infy..........Nov., 1862	From New Organization............	To 2-Br. 4-Div. 18-Corps Dept. N. C.	Jan., 1863

3d BRIGADE.— COMMANDER.

Horace C. Lee..........	Col. 27th Mass. Infy..............	Nov., 1862, to Dec. 10, 1862.	
3d Mass. Infy..........Nov., 1862	From New Organization............	To Heckman's Unatt. Br. Dept. N. C.	Dec., 1862
5th Mass. Infy..........Nov., 1862	From New Organization............	To Lee's Unatt. Brig. Dept. N. C.	Dec., 1862
27th Mass. Infy..........Nov., 1862	From 1-Brig. 1-Div. Dept. N. C....	To Lee's Unatt. Brig. Dept. N. C.	Dec., 1862
46th Mass. Infy..........Nov., 1862	From New Organization............	To Lee's Unatt. Brig. Dept. N. C.	Dec., 1862
9th N. J. Infy..........Nov., 1862	From 2-Brig. 1-Div. Dept. N. C.....	To Heckman's Unatt. Br. Dept. N. C.	Dec., 1862

2d DIVISION.— COMMANDER.

J. L. Reno.............	Brigadier General.................	Apr. 2, 1862, to July 6, 1862.

1st BRIGADE.— COMMANDER.

James Nagle..........	Col. 48th Penna. Infy..............	Apr. 2, 1862, to July 6, 1862.	
2d Maryland Infy........Apr., 1862	From Dix's Div. Baltimore, Md.....	To 1-Brig. 2-Div. 9-Corps Pot......	July, 1862
103d N. Y. Infy.........Apr., 1862	From Norfolk, Va.................	To 1-Brig. 3-Div. 9-Corps Pot......	July, 1862
48th Penna. Infy........Apr., 1862	From 4-Brig. Burnside Exp........	To 1-Brig. 2-Div. 9-Corps Pot......	July, 1862

2d BRIGADE.— COMMANDER.

E. Ferrero..............	Col. 51st N. Y. Infy..............	Apr. 2, 1862, to July 6, 1862.	
11th Conn. Infy.........Apr., 1862	From 4-Brig. Burnside Exp........	To 2-Brig. 3-Div. 9-Corps Pot......	July, 1862
21st Mass. Infy.........Apr., 1862	From 2-Brig. Burnside Exp........	To 2-Brig. 2-Div. 9-Corps Pot......	July, 1862
51st N. Y. Infy.........Apr., 1862	From 2-Brig. Burnside Exp........	To 2-Brig. 2-Div. 9-Corps Pot......	July, 1862
51st Penna. Infy........Apr., 1862	From 2-Brig. Burnside Exp........	To 2-Brig. 2-Div. 9-Corps Pot.....	July, 1862

3d DIVISION.— COMMANDER.

J. G. Parke............	Brigadier General.................	Apr. 2, 1862, to July 6, 1862.

1st BRIGADE.— COMMANDER.

C. A. Heckman........	Col. 9th N. J. Infy................	Apr. 2, 1862, to July 6, 1862.	
4th R. I. Infy.........Apr., 1862	From 3-Brig. Burnside Exp.........	To 2-Brig. 3-Div. 9-Corps Pot......	July, 1862
5th R. I. Infy.........Apr., 1862	From 3-Brig. Burnside Exp.........	To 2-Brig. 1-Div. Dept. N. C......	July, 1862
8th Conn. Infy.........Apr., 1862	From 3-Brig. Burnside Exp.........	To 2-Brig. 3-Div. 9-Corps Pot......	July, 1862
9th N. J. Infy.........Apr., 1862	From 2-Brig. Burnside Exp.........	To 2-Brig. 1-Div. Dept. N. C.......	July, 1862

4th BRIGADE.— COMMANDER.

R. C. Hawkins..........	Col. 9th N. Y. Infy..............	Apr. 2, 1862, to July 6, 1862.	
9th N. Y. Infy.........Apr., 1862	From 3-Brig. Burnside Exp.........	To 1-Brig. 3-Div. 9-Corps Pot......	July, 1862
89th N. Y. Infy.........Apr., 1862	From 4-Brig. Burnside Exp.........	To 1-Brig. 3-Div. 9-Corps Pot......	July, 1862
6th N. H. Infy.........Apr., 1862	From 4-Brig. Burnside Exp.........	To 1-Brig. 2-Div. 9-Corps Pot......	July, 1862

AMORY'S UNATT. BRIGADE.— COMMANDER.

T. J. C. Amory........	Col. 17th Mass. Infy..............	Dec. 10, 1862, to Jan. 2, 1863.	
17th Mass. Infy........Dec., 1862	From 1-Brig. 1-Div. Dept. N. C....	To 1-Br. 1-Div. 18-Corps Dept. N. C.	Jan., 1863
43d Mass. Infy.........Dec., 1862	From 1-Brig. 1-Div. Dept. N. C....	To 1-Br. 1-Div. 18-Corps Dept. N. C.	Jan., 1863
45th Mass. Infy.........Dec., 1862	From 1-Brig. 1-Div. Dept. N. C....	To 1-Br. 1-Div. 18-Corps Dept. N. C.	Jan., 1863
51st Mass. Infy.........Dec., 1862	From 1-Brig. 1-Div. Dept. N. C....	To 1-Br. 1-Div. 18-Corps Dept. N. C.	Jan., 1863

LEE'S UNATT. BRIGADE.— COMMANDER.

Horace C. Lee........	Col. 27th Mass. Infy..............	Dec. 10, 1862, to Jan. 2, 1863.	
5th Mass. Infy.........Dec., 1862	From 3-Brig. 1-Div. Dept. N. C....	To 2-Br. 1-Div. 18-Corps Dept. N. C.	Jan., 1863
25th Mass. Infy.........Dec., 1862	From 1-Brig. 1-Div. Dept. N. C....	To 2-Br. 1-Div. 18-Corps Dept. N. C.	Jan., 1863
27th Mass. Infy.........Dec., 1862	From 3-Brig. 1-Div. Dept. N. C....	To 2-Br. 1-Div. 18-Corps Dept. N. C.	Jan., 1863
46th Mass. Infy.........Dec., 1862	From 3-Brig. 1-Div. Dept. N. C....	To 2-Br. 1-Div. 18-Corps Dept. N. C.	Jan., 1863

HECKMAN'S UNATT. BRIGADE.— COMMANDER.

C. A. Heckman........	Col. 9th N. J. Infy..............	Dec. 10, 1862, to Jan. 2, 1863.	
3d Mass. Infy.........Dec., 1862	From 3-Brig. 1-Div. Dept. N. C....	To 2-Br. 5-Div. 18-Corps Dept. N. C.	Jan., 1863
8th Mass. Infy.........Dec., 1862	From 3-Brig. 1-Div. Dept. N. C....	To 2-Br. 5-Div. 18-Corps Dept. N. C.	Jan., 1863
23d Mass Infy.........Dec., 1862	From 1-Brig. 1-Div. Dept. N. C....	To 1-Br. 2- Div. 18-Corps Dept. N. C.	Jan., 1863
9th N. J. Infy.........Dec., 1862	From 2-Brig. 1-Div. Dept. N. C....	To 1-Br. 2- Div. 18-Corps Dept. N. C.	Jan., 1863

NAGLEE'S BRIGADE.— COMMANDER.

H. M. Naglee..........	Brigadier General.................	Dec., 1862, to Jan. 2, 1863.	
11th Me. Infy.........Dec., 1862	From 1-Brig. 2-Div. 4-Corps Pot....	To 2-Br. 2-Div. 18-Corps Dept. N. C.	Jan., 1863
56th N. Y. Infy.........Dec., 1862	From 1-Brig. 2-Div. 4-Corps Pot....	To 2-Br. 3-Div. 18-Corps Dept. N. C.	Jan., 1863
81st N. Y. Infy.........Dec., 1862	From 1-Brig. 2-Div. 4-Corps Pot....	To 1-Br. 2-Div. 18-Corps Dept. N. C.	Jan., 1863
98th N. Y. Infy.........Dec., 1862	From 1-Brig. 2-Div. 4-Corps Pot....	To 1-Br. 2-Div. 18-Corps Dept. N. C.	Jan., 1863
100th N. Y. Infy.........Dec., 1862	From 1-Brig. 2-Div. 4-Corps Pot....	To 2-Br. 2-Div. 18-Corps Dept. N. C.	Jan., 1863
Indpt. N. Y. Battn. Infy..Dec., 1862	From 1-Brig. 2-Div. 4-Corps Pot....	To 2-Br. 2-Div. 18-Corps Dept. N. C.	Jan., 1863
52d Penna. Infy.........Dec., 1862	From 1-Brig. 2-Div. 4-Corps Pot....	To 2-Br. 2-Div. 18-Corps Dept. N. C.	Jan., 1863
104th Penna. Infy.........Dec., 1862	From 1-Brig. 2-Div. 4-Corps Pot....	To 2-Br. 2-Div. 18-Corps Dept. N. C.	Jan., 1863

UNATTACHED ARTILLERY.—

Batty. F. 1st R. I. Arty...Apr., 1862	From Unatt. Burnside Exp.........	To Arty Brig. Dept. N. C..........	Dec., 1862
Batty. C. 1st U. S. Arty...Apr., 1862	From Unatt. Burnside Exp.........	To Arty Brig. Dept. N. C..........	Dec., 1862
1st N. Y. Marine Arty.....Apr., 1862	From New Organization............	To Arty Brig. Dept. N. C..........	Dec., 1862
N. Y. Rocket Battn......Apr., 1862	From Def. Wash..................	To 23d and 24th N. Y. Indpt. Battys.	Nov., 1862
23d N. Y. Indpt. Batty...Nov., 1862	From N. Y. Rocket Battalion......	To Arty. Brig. Dept. N. C..........	Dec., 1862
24th N. Y. Indpt. Batty...Nov., 1862	From N. Y. Rocket Battalion.......	To Arty. Brig. Dept. N. C..........	Dec., 1862

ARTILLERY BRIGADE.— COMMANDER.

J. H. Ledlie..........	Col. 3d N. Y. Arty..............	Dec. 4, 1862, to Jan. 2, 1863.	
3d N. Y. Arty.........Dec., 1862	From Unatt. Dept. N. C..........	To Arty. Brig. 18-Corps Dept. N. C.	Jan., 1863
Batty. C. 1st U. S. Arty...Dec., 1862	From Unatt. Dept. N. C..........	To Arty. Brig. 18-Corps Dept. N. C.	Jan., 1863
Batty. F. 1st R. I. Arty...Dec., 1862	From Unatt. Dept. N. C..........	To Arty. Brig. 18-Corps Dept. N. C.	Jan., 1863
23d N. Y. Indpt. Batty...Dec., 1862	From Unatt. Dept. N. C..........	To Arty. Brig. 18-Corps Dept. N. C.	Jan., 1863
24th N. Y. Indpt. Batty...Dec., 1862	From Unatt. Dept. N. C..........	To Arty. Brig. 18-Corps Dept. N. C.	Jan., 1863

CAVALRY.—

3d N. Y. Cav.............Apr., 1862	From Def. of Washington.........	To Unatt. Cav. 18-Corps Dept. N. C.	Jan., 1863

Eighteenth Army Corps---Department of North Carolina

Created Dec. 24, 1862, from Troops in the Department of North Carolina. Transferred to the Department of Virginia and North Carolina July 15, 1863.

COMMANDER.

J. G. Foster	Major General	Dec. 24, 1862, to July 18, 1863.

1st DIVISION.— COMMANDERS.

I. N. Palmer	Brigadier General	Jan. 30, 1863, to May 23, 1863.
T. J. C. Amory	Col. 17th Mass. Infy	May 23, 1863, to July 15, 1863.

Division discontinued July, 15, 1863.

1st BRIGADE.— COMMANDERS.

T. J. C. Amory	Col. 17th Mass. Infy	Jan. 2, 1863, to May 23, 1863.
C. L. Holbrook	Col. 43d Mass. Infy	May 23, 1863, to June 24, 1863.
L. Day	Capt. 17th Mass Infy	June 24, 1863, to July 15, 1863.

17th Mass. Infy	Jan., 1863	From Amory's Unatt. Br. Dept. N. C.	To Def. Newberne 18-Cps. Va. & N.C. July, 1863
43d Mass. Infy	Jan., 1863	From Amory's Unatt. Br. Dept. N. C.	To 1-Brig. Md. Heights Div. 8-Corps June, 1863
45th Mass. Infy	Jan., 1863	From Amory's Unatt. Br. Dept. N. C.	No change to Muster Out. June, 1863
51st Mass. Infy	Jan., 1863	From Amory's Unatt. Br. Dept. N. C.	To 8-Corps Middle Dept. June, 1863

2d BRIGADE.— COMMANDERS.

H. C. Lee	Col. 27th Mass. Infy	Jan. 2, 1863, to May, 12, 1863.
G. N. Pierson	Col. 5th Mass. Infy	May 12, 1863, to June 7, 1863.
H. C. Lee	Col. 27th Mass. Infy	June 7, 1863, to July 15, 1863.

5th Mass. Infy	Jan., 1863	From Lee's Unatt. Brig. Dept. N. C.	No change to Muster Out. June, 1863
25th Mass. Infy	Jan., 1863	From Lee's Unatt. Brig. Dept. N. C.	To Def. Newberne 18-Cps. Va. & N.C. July, 1863
27th Mass. Infy	Jan., 1863	From Lee's Unatt. Brig. Dept. N. C.	To Def. Newberne 18-Cps. Va. & N.C. July, 1863
46th Mass Infy	Jan., 1863	From Lee's Unatt. Brig. Dept. N. C.	To 8-Corps Middle Dept. June, 1863

2d DIVISION.— COMMANDERS.

H. M. Naglee	Brigadier General	Jan. 2, 1863, to Mch. 6, 1863.
C. A. Heckman	Brigadier General	Mch. 6, 1863, to Apr. 16, 1863.
H. M. Naglee	Brigadier General	Apr. 16, 1863, to May 10, 1863.

Designation of Division changed to District of Beaufort May, 1863.

1st BRIGADE.— COMMANDERS.

C. A. Heckman	Brigadier General	Jan. 2, 1863, to Mch. 6, 1863.
T. J. Stevenson	Brigadier General	Mch. 6, 1863, to April 16, 1863.
C. A. Heckman	Brigadier General	Apr. 16, 1863, to May 10, 1863.

23d Mass. Infy	Jan., 1863	From Heckman's Un. Br. Dept. N. C.	To 1-Brig. 1-Div. 18-Corps Dept. S. Feb., 1863
81st N. Y. Infy	Jan., 1863	From Naglee's Brig. Dept. N. C.	To 1-Brig. 1-Div. 18-Corps Dept. S. Feb., 1863
98th N. Y. Infy	Jan., 1863	From Naglee's Brig. Dept. N. C.	To 1-Brig. 1-Div. 18-Corps Dept. S. Feb., 1863
9th N. J. Infy	Jan., 1863	From Heckman's Un. Br. Dept. N. C.	To 1-Brig. 1-Div. 18-Corps Dept. S. Feb., 1863

2d BRIGADE.— COMMANDER.

W. W. H. Davis	Col. 104th Penna. Infy	Jan. 2, 1863, to Feb. 5, 1863.

11th Me. Infy	Jan., 1863	From Naglee's Brig. Dept. N. C.	To 1-Brig. 2-Div. 18-Corps Dept. S. Feb., 1863
100th N. Y. Infy	Jan., 1863	From Naglee's Brig. Dept. N. C.	To 1-Brig. 2-Div. 18-Corps Dept. S. Feb., 1863
Indpt. Battn. N. Y. Infy	Jan., 1863	From Naglee's Brig. Dept. N. C.	To 1-Brig. 2-Div. 18-Corps Dept. S. Feb., 1863
52d Penna. Infy	Jan., 1863	From Naglee's Brig. Dept. N. C.	To 2-Brig. 1-Div. 18-Corps Dept S. Feb., 1863
104th Penna. Infy	Jan., 1863	From Naglee's Brig. Dept. N. C.	To 2-Brig. 1-Div. 18-Corps Dept S. Feb., 1863

3d DIVISION.— COMMANDER.

O. S. Ferry	Brigadier General	Jan. 6, 1863, to Feb., 1863.

1st BRIGADE.— COMMANDER.

Thos. O. Osborn	Col. 39th Ill. Infy	Jan. 6, 1863, to Feb., 1863.

39th Ill. Infy	Jan., 1863	From Ferry's Brig. Div. Suffolk 7-C.	To 3-Brig. 2-Div. 18-Corps Dept. S. Feb., 1863
62d Ohio Infy	Jan., 1863	From Ferry's Brig. Div. Suffolk 7-C.	To 3-Brig. 2-Div. 18-Corps Dept. S. Feb., 1863
67th Ohio Infy	Jan., 1863	From Ferry's Brig. Div. Suffolk 7-C.	To 3-Brig. 2-Div. 18-Corps Dept. S. Feb., 1863
176th Penna. Infy	Jan., 1863	From Ferry's Brig. Div. Suffolk 7-C.	To 3-Brig. 2-Div. 18-Corps Dept. S. Feb., 1863

2d BRIGADE.— COMMANDER.

J. B. Howell	Col. 85th Penna. Infy	Jan. 6, 1863, to Feb., 1863.

56th N. Y. Infy	Jan., 1863	From Naglee's Brig. Dept. N. C.	To 2-Brig. 2-Div. 18-Corps Dept. S. Feb., 1863
58th Penna. Infy	Jan., 1863	From Gibb's Prov'l Brig. Suffolk 7-C.	To J'rdan's Br. Def. Newberne, 18-C. Apr., 1863
85th Penna. Infy	Jan., 1863	From 1-Brig. 1-Div. Dept. N. C.	To 2-Brig. 2-Div. 18-Corps Dept. S. Feb., 1863
174th Penna. Infy	Jan., 1863	From Ferry's Brig. Suffolk 7-Corps	To 2-Brig. 2-Div. 18-Corps Dept. S. Feb., 1863

4th DIVISION.— COMMANDERS.

H. W. Wessells	Brigadier General	Jan. 2, 1863, to Mch. 14, 1863.
T. F. Lehman	Col. 103d Penna. Infy	Mch. 14, 1863, to Apr. 14, 1863.
H. W. Wessells	Brigadier General	Apr. 14, 1863, to May 3, 1863.

Division termed District of the Albemarle 18-Corps, May 3, 1863.

1st BRIGADE.— COMMANDERS.

L. C. Hunt	Brigadier General	Jan. 2, 1863, to Mch. 12, 1863.
J. S. Belknap	Col. 85th N. Y. Infy	Mch. 12, 1863, to Apr. 13, 1863.
L. C. Hunt	Brigadier General	Apr. 13, 1863, to May 3, 1863.

85th N. Y. Infy	Jan., 1863	From 1-Brig. 1-Div. Dept. N. C.	To Dist. Albemarle, 18-C. Dept. N. C. May, 1863
92d N. Y. Infy	Jan., 1863	From 1-Brig. 1-Div. Dept. N. C.	To Lee's Brig. Def. Newberne 18-C. May, 1863
96th N. Y. Infy	Jan., 1863	From 1-Brig. 1-Div. Dept. N. C.	To Dist. Albemarle, 18-C. Dept. N. C. May, 1863
98th N. Y. Infy	Jan., 1863	From 1-Brig. 1-Div. Dept. N. C.	To Dist. Albemarle, 18-C. Dept. N. C. May, 1863
101st Penna. Infy	Jan., 1863	From 1-Brig. 1-Div. Dept. N. C.	To Dist. Albemarle, 18-C. Dept. N. C. May, 1863
103d Penna. Infy	Jan., 1863	From 1-Brig. 1-Div. Dept. N. C.	To Dist. Albemarle, 18-C. Dept. N. C. May, 1863

2d BRIGADE.—

COMMANDER.

T. G. Stevenson......	Brigadier General	Jan. 2, 1863, to Feb., 1863.

10th Conn. Infy.........Jan., 1863	From 2-Brig. 1-Div. Dept. N. C.....	To 2-Brig. 1-Div. 18-C. Dept. South..	Feb., 1863
24th Mass. Infy.........Jan., 1863	From 2-Brig. 1-Div. Dept. N. C.....	To 2-Brig. 1-Div. 18-C. Dept. South..	Feb., 1863
44th Mass. Infy.........Jan., 1863	From 2-Brig. 1-Div. Dept. N. C.....	To Lee's Brig. Def. Newberne 18-C.	May, 1863
5th R. I. Infy.........Jan., 1863	From 2-Brig. 1-Div. Dept. N. C.....	To Lee's Brig. Def. Newberne 18-C.	May, 1863

5th DIVISION.—

COMMANDER.

Henry Prince	Brigadier General	Jan. 11, 1863, to Apr. 22, 1863.

Division termed District of the Pamlico, Apr. 22, 1863.

1st BRIGADE.—

COMMANDER.

F. B. Spinola........	Brigadier General	Jan. 11, 1863, to Apr. 22, 1863.

132d N. Y. Infy.......Jan., 1863	From Spinola's Br. Div. Suffolk 7-C.	To 2-Brig. 5-Div. 18-C. Dept. N. C..	Mch., 1863
158th Penna. Infy......Jan., 1863	From Spinola's Br. Div. Suffolk 7-C.	To Dist. Pamlico 18 C. Dept. N. C..	Mch., 1863
171st Penna. Infy......Jan., 1863	From Spinola's Br. Div. Suffolk 7-C.	To Dist. Pamlico 18 C. Dept. N. C..	Mch., 1863
175th Penna. Infy......Jan., 1863	From Spinola's Br. Div. Suffolk 7-C.	To Dist. Pamlico 18 C. Dept. N. C..	Mch., 1863

2d BRIGADE.—

COMMANDER.

James Jourdan	Col. 158th N. Y. Infy..............	Jan. 11, 1863, to Apr. 22, 1863.

3d Mass. Infy.........Jan., 1863	From Heckman's Brig. Dept. N. C..	To Jourdan's In. Br. Def. Newberne.	Apr., 1863
8th Mass. Infy.........Jan., 1863	From Heckman's Brig. Dept. N. C..	To Jourdan's In. Br. Def. Newberne.	Apr., 1863
158th N. Y. Infy.......Jan., 1863	From Spinola's Br. Div. Suffolk 7-C.	To Jourdan's In. Br. Def. Newberne.	Apr., 1863
168th Penna. Infy......Jan., 1863	From Spinola's Br. Div. Suffolk 7-C.	To Dist. Pamlico 18-C. Dept. N. C..	Apr., 1863
132d N. Y. Infy.........Mch., 1863	From 1-Brig. 5-Div. 18-Corps......	To Unatt. Def. Newberne 18 Corps..	Apr., 1863

ARTILLERY BRIGADE.—

COMMANDER.

J. H. Ledlie...........	Brigadier General	Jan., 1863, to May, 1863.

3d N. Y. Lt. Arty....Jan., 1863	From Arty. Brig. Dept. N. C.......	To Def. Newberne 18-C. Dept. N. C.	May, 1863
23d N. Y. Indpt. Batty....Jan., 1863	From Arty. Brig. Dept. N. C.......	To Dist. Pamlico 18-C. Dept. N. C..	May, 1863
24th N. Y. Batty.......Jan., 1863	From Arty. Brig. Dept. N. C.......	To Dist. Albemarle, 18-C. Dept. N. C.	May, 1863
Batty. F, 1st R. I. Arty..Jan., 1863	From Arty. Brig. Dept. N. C.......	To Def. Newberne 18-C. Dept. N. C.	May, 1863
Batty. C, 1st U. S. Arty....Jan.,1863	From Arty. Brig. Dept. N. C.......	To Dist. Beaufort 18-C. Dept. N. C.	May, 1863

CAVALRY BRIGADE.—Organized May, 1863.

COMMANDER.

S. H. Mix.............	Col. 3d N. Y. Cav................	

2d N. Y. Cav.........May, 1863	From Unatt. 18-Corps Dept. N. C...	To Def. Newberne Dist. N.C.Va.&N.C.	July, 1863
12th N. Y. Cav.........May, 1863	From New Organization...........	To Def. Newberne Dist. N.C.Va.&N.C.	July, 1863
23d N. Y. Cav.........May, 1863	From New Organization...........	To Def. Newberne Dist. N.C.Va.&N.C.	July, 1863

UNATTACHED.—

3d N. Y. Cav.........Dec., 1862	From Unatt. Cav. Dept. N. C.......	To Cav. Brig. 18-Corps Dept. N. C..	May, 1863
1st N. C. Infy.........Dec., 1862	From Dept. N. C................	To Dist. Pamlico..........	May, 1863

DISTRICT OF THE PAMLICO.—Organized April 22, 1863, from 5th Division 18th Corps. Designated Sub-District of the Pamlico, District North Carolina, 18-Corps, Department of Virginia and North Carolina, July 26, 1863.

COMMANDERS.

Henry Prince	Brigadier General	Apr. 22, 1863, to June 20, 1863.
J. M. McChesney.......	Lt.-Col. 1st N. C. Infy.............	June 20, 1863, to July 26, 1863.

KEYSTONE BRIGADE.—

COMMANDERS.

F. B. Spinola........	Brigadier General	Apr. 22, 1863, to May 9, 1863.
D. B. McKibben........	Col. 158th Penna. Infy.............	May 9, 1863, to May 29, 1863.
F. B. Spinola........	Brigadier General	May 29, 1863, to June 26, 1863.

Brigade transferred to 7th Corps Dept. of Va., June, 1863.

158th Penna. Infy......Apr., 1863	From 1-Brig. 5-Div. 18-C. Dept. N. C.	To Spinola's Brig. 7-Corps Dept. Va.	June, 1863
168th Penna. Infy......Apr., 1863	From 2-Brig. 5-Div. 18-C. Dept. N. C.	To Spinola's Brig. 7-Corps Dept. Va.	June, 1863
171st Penna. Infy......Apr., 1863	From 1-Brig. 5-Div. 18-C. Dept. N. C.	To Spinola's Brig. 7-Corps Dept. Va.	June, 1863
175th Penna. Infy......Apr., 1863	From 1-Brig. 5-Div. 18-C. Dept. N. C.	To Unatt. 8-Corps Middle Dept......	June, 1863
1st N. C. Infy.........Apr., 1863	From Unatt. 18-Corps Dept. N. C..	To Sub-Dist. Pamlico Dept. Va.&N.C.	July, 1863
58th Penna. Infy......Apr., 1863	From Jourdan's Brig. Def. Newberne 18-C.	To Sub-Dist. Pamlico Dept. Va.&N.C.	July, 1863
23d N. Y. Indpt. Batty....Apr., 1863	From Arty. Brig. 18-Corps.........	To Sub-Dist. Pamlico Dept. Va.&N.C.	July, 1863
3d New Cav. (2 Co's)...Apr., 1863	From Cav. Brig. 18-Corps..........	To Cav. Brig. Def. Newberne 18-C.	June, 1863

DISTRICT OF THE ALBEMARLE.—Organized May 3, 1863, from 4-Division, 18th Corps. Designated Sub-District of the Albemarle Dist. of North Carolina, Department of Virginia and North Carolina, July 26, 1863.

COMMANDER.

H. W. Wessells........	Brigadier General	May 3, 1863, to Aug. 1, 1863.

LEAHMAN'S BRIGADE.—

COMMANDER.

T. F. Leahman........	Col. 103d Penna. Infy.............	May 3, 1863, to Aug. 1, 1863.

85th N. Y. Infy........May, 1863	From 1-Brig. 4-Div. 18-Corps.......	To Sub-Dist. Albemarle Va. & N. C.	July, 1863
96th N. Y. Infy........May, 1863	From 1-Brig. 4-Div. 18-Corps.......	To Sub-Dist. Albemarle Va. & N. C.	July, 1863
101st Penna. Infy........May, 1863	From 1-Brig. 4-Div. 18-Corps.......	To Sub-Dist. Albemarle Va. & N. C.	July, 1863
103d Penna. Infy........May, 1863	From 1-Brig. 4-Div. 18-Corps.......	To Sub-Dist. Albemarle Va. & N. C.	July, 1863
8th Mass. Infy (3 Co's)..May, 1863	From Jourdan's Brig. Def. Newberne.	To Jourdan's Brig. Def. Newberne..	June, 1863
24th N. Y. Indpt. Batty...May, 1863	From Arty. Brig. 18-Corps..........	To Sub-Dist. Albemarle Va. & N. C.	July, 1863
12th N. Y. Cav. (Co. E)..June, 1863	From Cav. Brig. 18-Corps..........	To Sub-Dist. Albemarle Va. & N. C.	July, 1863
3d N. Y. Cav. (Co. D)..May, 1863	From Cav. Brig. 18-Corps..........	To Cav. Brig. Def. Newberne.......	June, 1863

DISTRICT OF BEAUFORT.—Organized May 2, 1863, from 2d Division 18th Corps. Designated Sub-District of Beaufort, District of North Carolina, Dept. of Virginia and North Carolina, July, 1863.

COMMANDERS.

C. A. Heckman........	Brigadier General	May 2, 1863, to May 25, 1863.
F. B. Spinola........	Brigadier General	May 25, 1863, to May 29, 1863.
C. A. Heckman........	Brigadier General	May 29, 1863, to July 21, 1863.
T. J. C. Amory........	Col. 17th Mass. Infy...............	July 21, 1863, to Aug. 1, 1863.

23d Mass. Infy.........May, 1863	From 1-Brig. 1-Div. 18-C. Dept. South	To Def. Newberne 18 Corps.........	July, 1863
9th N. J. Infy.........May, 1863	From 1-Brig. 1-Div. 18-C. Dept. South	To Jourdan's Brig. Def. Newberne..	June, 1863
81st N. Y. Infy........May, 1863	From 1-Brig. 1-Div. 18-C. Dept. South	To Sub-Dist. Beaufort Dept. Va.&N.C.	Aug., 1863
98th N. Y. Infy........May, 1863	From 1-Brig. 1-Div. 18-C. Dept. South	To Sub-Dist. Beaufort Dept. Va.&N.C.	Aug., 1863
Batty. C, 1st U. S. Arty..May, 1863	From Arty. Brig. 18-Corps.........	To Sub-Dist. Beaufort Dept. Va.&N.C.	Aug., 1863
3d N. Y. Cav. (Co's B, C).May, 1863	From Cav. Brig. 18-Corps..........	To Cav. Brig. Def. Newberne.......	June, 1863

NEWBERNE.—
JOURDAN'S INDPT. BRIGADE.—Organized April 22, 1863, from 2d Brig., 5th Div., 18th Corps. Transferred to the Defences of Newberne, 18th Corps, July 21, 1863.

COMMANDER.

James Jourdan	Col. 158th N. Y. Infy	Apr. 22, 1863, to July 21, 1863.	

3d Mass. Infy	Apr., 1863	From 2-Brig. 5-Div. 18-Corps	No change to Muster Out	June, 1863
8th Mass. Infy	Apr., 1863	From 2-Brig. 5-Div. 18-Corps	To 8-Corps Middle Dept	June, 1863
158th N. Y. Infy	Apr., 1863	From 2-Brig. 5-Div. 18-Corps	To Def. Newberne 18-Corps	July, 1863
58th Penna. Infy	Apr., 1863	From 2-Brig. 3-Div. 18-Corps	To Dist. Pamlico 18-Corps	June, 1863
9th N. J. Infy	June, 1863	From Dist. Beaufort 18-Corps	To Sub-Dist. Beaufort Dept.Va.&N.C.	July, 1863

LEE'S INDEPENDENT BRIGADE.—Organized May, 1863. Discontinued June, 1863.

COMMANDER.

F. L. Lee	Col. 44th Mass. Infy	May, 1863, to June, 1863.	

44th Mass. Infy	May, 1863	From 2-Brig. 4-Div. 18-Corps	No change to Muster Out	June, 1863
5th R. I. Infy	May, 1863	From 2-Brig. 4-Div. 18-Corps	To Unatt. Def. Newberne 18-Corps	June, 1863
92d N. Y. Infy	May, 1863	From 1-Brig. 4-Div. 18-Corps	To Unatt. Def. Newberne 18-Corps	June, 1863

UNATTACHED.—

132d N. Y. Infy	Apr., 1863	From 2-Brig. 5-Div. 18-Corps	To Def. Newberne 18-Corps	July, 1863
92d N. Y. Infy	June, 1863	From Lee's Indpt. Brig	To Sub-Dist. Albemarle Dept.Va.&N.C.	July, 1863
5th R. I. Infy	June, 1863	From Lee's Indpt. Brig	To Def. Newberne 18-Corps	July, 1863
1st N. C. Colored	June, 1863	From New Organization	To Sub-Dist. Pamlico Dept. Va.&N.C.	July, 1863

ARTILLERY, NEWBERNE.—

3d N. Y. Arty	May, 1863	From Arty. Brig. 18-Corps	To Def. Newberne Dept. Va. & N. C.	July, 1863
Batty. F, 1st R. I. Arty	May, 1863	From Arty. Brig. 18-Corps	To Def. Newberne Dept. Va. & N. C.	July, 1863

DEFENCES OF NEWBERNE.—Organized July, 1863. Designated Defences of Newberne, District of North Carolina, Department of Virginia and North Carolina, Aug. 1, 1863.

COMMANDER.

C. A. Heckman	Brigadier General	July 21, 1863, to Aug. 1, 1863.	

17th Mass. Infy	July, 1863	From 1-Brig. 1-Div. 18-Corps	To Def. Newberne Dept. Va. & N. C.	Aug., 1863
23d Mass. Infy	July, 1863	From Dist. Beaufort 18-Corps	To Def. Newberne Dept. Va. & N. C.	Aug., 1863
25th Mass. Infy	July, 1863	From 2-Brig. 1-Div. 18-Corps	To Def. Newberne Dept. Va. & N. C.	Aug., 1863
27th Mass. Infy	July, 1863	From 2-Brig. 1-Div. 18-Corps	To Def. Newberne Dept. Va. & N. C.	Aug., 1863
92d N. Y. Infy	July, 1863	From Unatt. Newberne 18-Corps	To Def. Newberne Dept. Va. & N. C.	Aug., 1863
132d N. Y. Infy	July, 1863	From Unatt. Newberne 18-Corps	To Def. Newberne Dept. Va. & N. C.	Aug., 1863
158th N. Y. Infy	July, 1863	From Jourdan's Indpt. Brig	To Def. Newberne Dept. Va. & N. C.	Aug., 1863
5th R. I. Infy	July, 1863	From Unatt. Newberne 18-Corps	To Def. Newberne Dept. Va. & N. C.	Aug., 1863
1st N. C. Colored	July, 1863	From Unatt. Newberne 18-Corps	To 3-African Br. Folly Isl. 10-Corps	Aug., 1863

ARTILLERY.—

3d N. Y. Arty	July, 1863	From Arty. Def. Newberne 18-Corps	To Def. Newberne Dept. Va. & N. C.	Aug., 1863
Batty. F. 1st R. I. Arty	July, 1863	From Arty. Def. Newberne 18-Corps	To Def. Newberne Dept. Va. & N. C.	Aug., 1863

CAVALRY.—

3d N. Y. Cav	July, 1863	From Cav. Brig. Def. Newberne	To Def. Newberne Dept. Va. & N. C.	Aug., 1863
12th N. Y. Cav	July, 1863	From Cav. Brig. Def. Newberne	To Def. Newberne Dept. Va. & N. C.	Aug., 1863
23d N. Y. Cav	July, 1863	From Cav. Brig. Def. Newberne	To Def. Newberne Dept. Va. & N. C.	Aug., 1863

DEPARTMENT OF NORTH CAROLINA.—As reorganized Jan. 31, 1865.

COMMANDERS.

I. N. Palmer	Brigadier General	Jan. 31, 1865, to Feb. 9, 1865.	
J. M. Schofield	Major General	Feb. 9, 1865, to June 17, 1865.	
J. D. Cox	Major General	June 17, 1865, to June 27, 1865.	
T. H. Ruger	Bvt. Major General	June 27, 1865, to July 17, 1865.	
J. M. Schofield	Major General	July 17, 1865.	

SUB-DISTRICT OF NEWBERNE.— COMMANDERS.

Edward Harland	Brigadier General	Jan. 31, 1865, to Feb. 9, 1865.	
I. N. Palmer	Brigadier General	Feb. 9, 1865, to June 27, 1865.	

15th Conn. Infy	Jan., 1865	From Def. Newberne Dept. Va.&N.C.	To 2-Br. 2-Div. Dist. Beaufort, N. C.	Mch., 1865
23d Mass. Infy	Jan., 1865	From Def. Newberne Dept. Va.&N.C.	To 1-Br. 1-Div. Dist. Beaufort, N. C.	Mch., 1865
25th Mass. Infy	Jan., 1865	From Def. Newberne Dept. Va.&N.C.	To 3-Br. 2-Div. Dist. Beaufort, N. C.	Mch., 1865
27th Mass. Infy	Jan., 1865	From Sub-Dist. B'Fort Dept.Va.&N.C.	To 3-Br. 2-Div. Dist. Beaufort, N. C.	Mch., 1865
99th N. Y. Infy. (3 Co's)	Jan., 1865	From Def. Newberne Dept. Va.&N.C.	No change to Muster Out	July, 1865
132d N. Y. Infy	Jan., 1865	From Def. Newberne Dept. Va.&N.C.	To 2-Br. 1-Div. Dist. Beaufort, N. C.	Mch., 1865
1st N. C. Infy	Jan., 1865	From Sub-Dist. B'fort Dept.Va.&N.C.	No change to Muster Out	June, 1865
2d N. C. Infy	Jan., 1865	From Sub-Dist. B'fort Dept.Va.&N.C.	Consol. with 1st N. C.	Feb., 1865
27th Mass. Infy	Mch., 1865	From 2-Brig. 2-Div. Dist. Beaufort	No change to Muster Out	June, 1865
23d Mass. Infy	Mch., 1865	From Unatt. Kinston, N. C.	No change to Muster Out	June, 1865
15th Conn. Infy	Mch., 1865	From Unatt. Kinston, N. C.	No change to Muster Out	June, 1865

CAVALRY.—

12th N. Y. Cav	Jan., 1865	From Def. Newberne Dept. Va.&N.C.	To Dist. Beaufort Dept. N. C.	Mch., 1865
23d N. Y. Cav	Jan., 1865	From Def. Newberne Dept. Va.&N.C.	To Dist. Beaufort Dept. N. C.	Mch., 1865

ARTILLERY.—

2d Mass. Heavy Arty	Jan., 1865	From Def. Newberne Dept. Va.&N.C.	To 1-Brig. 1-Div. Dist. Beaufort	Mch., 1865
3d N. Y. Light Arty	Jan., 1865	From Def. Newberne Dept. Va.&N.C.	To Arty. Dist. Beaufort	Mch., 1865
5th R. I. Heavy Arty	Jan., 1865	From Def. Newberne Dept. Va.&N.C.	No change to Muster Out	June, 1865
23d N. Y. Batty	Jan., 1865	From Def. Newberne Dept. Va.&N.C.	To 3-Cav. Div. Army Ga.	Apr., 1865
Batty. F, 1st Mich. Arty	Apr., 1865	From Arty. 1-Div. 23-C. Dept. N. C.	No change to Muster Out	June, 1865
3d N. Y. Light Arty	Apr., 1865	From Arty. Dist. B'fort Dept. N. C.	No change to Muster Out	July, 1865

ROANOKE ISLAND.— COMMANDER.

T. F. Leahman	Col. 103d Penna. Infy		

16th Conn. Infy	Jan., 1865	From Sub-Dist. Albemarle Va.&N.C.	No change to Muster Out	June, 1865
101st Penna. Infy	Jan., 1865	From Sub-Dist. Albemarle Va.&N.C.	No change to Muster Out	June, 1865
103d Penna. Infy	Jan., 1865	From Sub-Dist. Albemarle Va.&N.C.	No change to Muster Out	June, 1865
5th R. I. H. A. (Co's D, K)	Jan., 1865	From Sub-Dist. Albemarle Va.&N.C.	To Dist. Newberne Dept. N. C.	June, 1865
24th N. Y. Indpt. Batty	Jan., 1865	From Sub-Dist. Albemarle Va.&N.C.	To Dist. Newberne Dept. N. C.	June, 1865

SUB-DISTRICT BEAUFORT.— COMMANDERS.

James Stewart, Jr.	Col. 9th N. J. Infy	Jan. 7, 1865, to Feb. 25, 1865.	
I. N. Palmer	Brigadier General	Feb. 25, 1865, to Mch. 1, 1865.	

17th Mass. Infy	Jan., 1865	From Sub-Dist. Beaufort Va. & N. C.	To 3-Brig. 2-Div. Dist. Beaufort	Mch., 1865
9th N. J. Infy	Jan., 1865	From Sub-Dist. Beaufort Va. & N. C.	To 1-Brig. 1-Div. Dist. Beaufort	Mch., 1865
14th U. S. Col'd H. A.	Jan., 1865	From Sub-Dist. Beaufort Va. & N. C.	No change to Muster Out	Dec., 1865
Batty. C, 3d N. Y. Arty	Jan., 1865	From Sub-Dist. Beaufort Va. & N. C.	To Arty. 1-Div. Dist. Beaufort	Mch., 1865

PROVISIONAL CORPS—DEPARTMENT OF NORTH CAROLINA.—

COMMANDER.

J. D. Cox	Major General	Feb. 25, 1865, to Mch. 31, 1865.

1st DIVISION, 23d CORPS.— COMMANDER.

T. H. Ruger	Brigadier General	Feb. 25, 1865, to Mch. 18, 1865.

1st BRIGADE.— COMMANDERS.

J. M. Orr	Col. 124th Ind. Infy.	Feb. 25, 1865, to Mch. 14, 1865.
I. N. Stiles	Bvt. Brig. General	Mch. 14, 1865, to Mch. 18, 1865.

120th Ind. Infy..........Feb., 1865	From 1-Brig. 1-Div. 23-Corps Ohio..	To 1-Br. 1-Div. 23-Corps Dept. N. C.	Mch., 1865
124th Ind. Infy..........Feb., 1865	From 1-Brig. 1-Div. 23-Corps Ohio..	To 1-Br. 1-Div. 23-Corps Dept. N. C.	Mch., 1865
128th Ind. Infy..........Feb., 1865	From 1-Brig. 1-Div. 23-Corps Ohio..	To 1-Br. 1-Div. 23-Corps Dept. N. C.	Mch., 1865
180th Ohio Infy..........Feb., 1865	From 1-Brig. 1-Div. 23-Corps Ohio..	To 1-Br. 1-Div. 23-Corps Dept. N. C.	Mch., 1865

2d BRIGADE.— COMMANDER.

J. C. McQuiston	Col. 123d Ind. Infy.	Feb. 25, 1865, to Mch. 18, 1865.

123d Ind. Infy..........Feb., 1865	From 2-Brig. 1-Div. 23-Corps Ohio..	To 2-Br. 1-Div. 23-Corps Dept. N. C.	Mch., 1865
129th Ind. Infy..........Feb., 1865	From 2-Brig. 1-Div. 23-Corps Ohio..	To 2-Br. 1-Div. 23-Corps Dept. N. C.	Mch., 1865
130th Ind. Infy..........Feb., 1865	From 2-Brig. 1-Div. 23-Corps Ohio..	To 2-Br. 1-Div. 23-Corps Dept. N. C.	Mch., 1865
28th Mich. Infy..........Feb., 1865	From 2-Brig. 1-Div. 23-Corps Ohio..	To 2-Br. 1-Div. 23-Corps Dept. N. C.	Mch., 1865

3d BRIGADE.— COMMANDER.

M. T. Thomas	Bvt. Brig. General	Feb. 25, 1865, to Mch. 18, 1865.

8th Minn. Infy..........Feb., 1865	From 3-Brig. 1-Div. 23-Corps Ohio..	To 3-Br. 1-Div. 23-Corps Dept. N. C.	Mch., 1865
174th Ohio Infy..........Feb., 1865	From 3-Brig. 1-Div. 23-Corps Ohio..	To 3-Br. 1-Div. 23-Corps Dept. N. C.	Mch., 1865
178th Ohio Infy..........Feb., 1865	From 3-Brig. 1-Div. 23-Corps Ohio..	To 3-Br. 1-Div. 23-Corps Dept. N. C.	Mch., 1865

ARTILLERY, 1st DIVISION.—

22d Ind. Batty..........Feb., 1865	From Arty. 1-Div. 23-Corps Ohio....	To Arty. 1-Div. 23-Corps Dept. N. C.	Mch., 1865
Batty. F, 1st Mich. Arty..Feb., 1865	From Arty. 1-Div. 23-Corps Ohio....	To Arty. 1-Div. 23-Corps Dept. N. C.	Mch., 1865
Elgin, Ill., Batty..........Feb., 1865	From Arty. 1-Div. 23-Corps Ohio....	To Arty. 1-Div. 23-Corps Dept. N. C.	Mch., 1865

Terry's Provisional Corps---Department of North Carolina

Organized for Fort Fisher Expedition Jan. 6, 1865. Merged into the Reorganized 10th Army Corps, Dept. N. C., March 27, 1865.

COMMANDER.

Alfred H. Terry	Major General	Jan. 6, 1865, to Mch. 27, 1865.

2d BRIGADE, 1st DIVISION, 24th CORPS.— COMMANDER.

J. C. Abbott	Col. 7th N. H. Infy.	Jan. 6, 1865, to Mch. 27, 1865.

3d N. H. Infy..........Jan., 1865	From 2-Br. 1-Div. 24-C. Army James.	To 2-Br. 1-Div. 10-Corps Dept. N. C.	Mch., 1865
7th N. H. Infy..........Jan., 1865	From 2-Br. 1-Div. 24-C. Army James.	To 2-Br. 1-Div. 10-Corps Dept. N. C.	Mch., 1865
6th Conn. Infy..........Jan., 1865	From 2-Br. 1-Div. 24-C. Army James.	To 2-Br. 1-Div. 10-Corps Dept. N. C.	Mch., 1865
7th Conn. Infy..........Jan., 1865	From 2-Br. 1-Div. 24-C. Army James.	To 2-Br. 1-Div. 10-Corps Dept. N. C.	Mch., 1865
16th N. Y. H. A. (6 Co's).Jan., 1865	From 2-Br. 1-Div. 24-C. Army James.	To 2-Br. 1-Div. 10-Corps Dept. N. C.	Mch., 1865

2d DIVISION, 24th CORPS.— COMMANDER.

Adelbert Ames	Brigadier General	Jan. 6, 1865, to Mch. 27, 1865.

1st BRIGADE.— COMMANDERS.

N. M. Curtis	Bvt. Brig. General	Jan. 6, 1865, to Jan. 15, 1865.
Ezra L. Walrath	Major 112th N. Y. Infy	Jan. 15, 1865.
Rufus Daggett	Col. 117th N. Y. Infy.	Jan. 15, 1865, to Mch. 27, 1865.

3d N. Y. Infy..........Jan., 1865	From 1-Br. 2-Div. 24-C. Army James.	To 1-Br. 2-Div. 10-Corps Dept. N. C.	Mch., 1865
112th N. Y. Infy..........Jan., 1865	From 1-Br. 2-Div. 24-C. Army James.	To 1-Br. 2-Div. 10-Corps Dept. N. C.	Mch., 1865
117th N. Y. Infy..........Jan., 1865	From 1-Br. 2-Div. 24-C. Army James.	To 1-Br. 2-Div. 10-Corps Dept. N. C.	Mch., 1865
142d N. Y. Infy..........Jan., 1865	From 1-Br. 2-Div. 24-C. Army James.	To 1-Br. 2-Div. 10-Corps Dept. N. C.	Mch., 1865

2d BRIGADE.— COMMANDERS.

G. Pennypacker	Col. 97th Penna. Infy.	Jan. 6, 1865, to Jan. 15, 1865.
C. P. Harding	Major 203d Penna. Infy	Jan. 15, 1865, to Feb. 14, 1865.
J. A. Colvin	Lt.-Col. 169th N. Y. Infy	Feb. 14, 1865, to Mch. 16, 1865.
William B. Coan	Col. 48th N. Y. Infy	Mch. 16, 1865, to Mch. 28, 1865.

47th N. Y. Infy..........Jan., 1865	From 2-Br. 2-Div. 24-C. Army James.	To 2-Br. 2-Div. 10-Corps Dept. N.	Mch., 1865
48th N. Y. Infy..........Jan., 1865	From 2-Br. 2-Div. 24-C. Army James.	To 2-Br. 2-Div. 10-Corps Dept. N. C.	Mch., 1865
76th Penna. Infy..........Jan., 1865	From 2-Br. 2-Div. 24-C. Army James.	To 2-Br. 2-Div. 10-Corps Dept. N. C.	Mch., 1865
97th Penna. Infy..........Jan., 1865	From 2-Br. 2-Div. 24-C. Army James.	To 2-Br. 2-Div. 10-Corps Dept. N. C.	Mch., 1865
203d Penna. Infy..........Jan., 1865	From 2-Br. 2-Div. 24-C. Army James.	To 2-Br. 2-Div. 10-Corps Dept. N. C.	Mch., 1865

3d BRIGADE, 2d DIVISION, 24th CORPS.— COMMANDERS.

Louis Bell	Col. 4th N. H. Infy	Jan. 6, 1865, to Jan. 15, 1865.	Killed.
Alonzo Alden	Col. 169th N. Y. Infy.	Jan. 15, 1865.	
N. J. Johnson	Lt.-Col. 115th N. Y. Infy.	Jan. 15, 1865, to Feb. 14, 1865.	
G. F. Granger	Col. 9th Me. Infy.	Feb. 14, 1865, to Mch. 27, 1865.	

9th Me. Infy..........Jan., 1865	From 3-Brig. 2-Div. 24-Corps A. Jas.	To 3-Br. 2-Div. 10-Corps Dept. N. C.	Mch., 1865
4th N. H. Infy..........Jan., 1865	From 3-Brig. 2-Div. 24-Corps A. Jas.	To 3-Br. 2-Div. 10-Corps Dept. N. C.	Mch., 1865
115th N. Y. Infy..........Jan., 1865	From 3-Brig. 2-Div. 24-Corps A. Jas.	To 3-Br. 2-Div. 10-Corps Dept. N. C.	Mch., 1865
169th N. Y. Infy..........Jan., 1865	From 3-Brig. 2-Div. 24-Corps A. Jas.	To 3-Br. 2-Div. 10-Corps Dept. N. C.	Mch., 1865
13th Ind. Infy..........Jan., 1865	From 3-Brig. 2-Div. 24-Corps A. Jas.	To 3-Br. 2-Div. 10-Corps Dept. N. C.	Mch., 1865

3d DIVISION, 25th CORPS.— COMMANDER.

Charles J. Paine	Brigadier General	Jan. 6, 1865, to Mch. 27, 1865.

1st BRIGADE.— COMMANDER.

Delevan Bates	Bvt. Brig. General	Jan. 6, 1865, to Mch. 27, 1865.

1st U. S. Colored Infy...Jan., 1865	From 1-Brig. 3-Div. 25-Corps A. Jas.	To 3-Brig. 3-Div. 25-Corps N. C....	Feb., 1865
30th U. S. Colored Infy...Jan., 1865	From 1-Brig. 3-Div. 25-Corps A. Jas.	To 2-Brig. 3-Div. 25-Corps N. C....	Feb., 1865
107th U. S. Colored Infy...Jan., 1865	From 1-Brig. 3-Div. 25-Corps A. Jas.	To 1-Br. 3-Div. 10-Corps Dept. N. C.	Mch., 1865

2d BRIGADE.— COMMANDERS.

J. W. Ames............	Col. 6th U. S. C. T............	Jan. 6, 1865, to Feb. 27, 1865.
S. A. Duncan..........	Bvt. Brig. General............	Feb. 27, 1865, to Mch. 27, 1865.

4th U. S. Colored Infy...Jan., 1865	From 2-Brig. 3-Div. 25-Corps A. Jas.	To 2-Br. 3-Div. 10-Corps Dept. N. C.	Mch., 1865
6th U. S. Colored Infy...Jan., 1865	From 2-Brig. 3-Div. 25-Corps A. Jas.	To 3-Br. 3-Div. 10-Corps Dept. N. C.	Mch., 1865
39th U. S. Colored Infy...Jan., 1865	From 2-Brig. 3-Div. 25-Corps A. Jas.	To 2-Br. 3-Div. 10-Corus Dept. N. C.	Mch., 1865
30th U. S. Colored Infy...Feb., 1865	From 1-Brig. 3-Div. 25-Corps N. C..	To 1-Br. 3-Div. 10-Corps Dept. N. C.	Mch., 1865

3d BRIGADE.— COMMANDERS.

E. Wright................	Col. 10th U. S. C. T.........	Jan. 6, 1863, to Feb. 20, 1865.
J. H. Holman............	Col. 1st U. S. Colored Infy.........	Feb. 20, 1865, to Mch. 27, 1865.

5th U. S. Colored Infy...Jan., 1865	From 3-Brig. 3-Div. 25-Corps A. Jas.	To 2-Br. 3-Div. 10-Corps Dept. N. C.	Mch., 1865
27th U. S. Colored Infy...Jan., 1865	From 3-Brig. 3-Div. 25-Corps A. Jas.	To 3-Br. 3-Div. 10-Corps Dept. N. C.	Mch., 1865
37th U. S. Colored Infy...Jan., 1865	From 3-Brig. 3-Div. 25-Corps A. Jas.	To 3-Br. 3-Div. 10-Corps Dept. N. C.	Mch., 1865
1st U. S. Colored Infy...Jan., 1865	From 1-Brig. 3-Div. 25-Corps N. C.	To 1-Br. 3-Div. 10-Corps Dept. N. C.	Mch., 1865
ARTILLERY.—			
Batty. E. 3d U. S. Arty..Jan., 1865	From Arty Brig. 25-Corps A. Jas.	To Arty. 3-Div. 10-Corps Dept. N. C.	Mch., 1865
16th N. Y. Indpt. Batty..Jan., 1865	From Arty. Brig. 24th Corps A. Jas.	To Arty. 2-Div. 10-Corps Dept. N. C.	Mch., 1865
1st Ct. H. A., Cos. B, C, L.Jan., 1865	From Siege Arty. Army James......	To Unatt. 10-Corps Dept. N. C.....	Mch., 1865
2d Penna. H. A. Co. A....Jan., 1865	From Siege Arty. Army James......	To Unatt. 10-Corps Dept. N. C.....	Mch., 1865
CAVALRY.—			
13th Penna. Cav.........Feb., 1865	From 2-Brig. 2-Div. Cav. Corps Pot.	To 3-Br. Kilpatrick's Cav. Div A. Ga.	Apr., 1865

1st DIVISION, DISTRICT OF BEAUFORT.—Organized Mch. 1, 1865. Discontinued Mch. 18, 1865.

COMMANDER.

I. N. Palmer..........	Brigadier General..........	Mch. 1, 1865, to Mch., 18, 1865.

1st BRIGADE.— COMMANDERS.

Edward Harland.......	Brigadier General..........	Mch. 1, 1865, to Mch., 18, 1865.

9th N. J. Infy.........Mch., 1865	From Sub. Dist. Beaufort.........	To 2-Br. Div. Dist. B'ufort Dept.N.C.	Mch., 1865
23d Mass. Infy.........Mch., 1865	From Sub Dist. Newberne.........	To Post Kinston Dept. N. C.......	Mch., 1865
2d Mass. Heavy Arty...Mch., 1865	From Sub Dist. Newberne.........	To Post Kinston Dept. N. C.......	Mch., 1865
15th Conn. Infy.......Mch., 1865	From 2-Brig. 2-Div. Dist. Beaufort.	To Post Kinston Dept. N. C.......	Mch., 1865
Batty. A, 3d N. Y. Arty...Mch., 1865	From Arty. 2-Div. Dist. Beaufort..	To Dist. Newberne N. C..........	Mch., 1865

2d BRIGADE.— COMMANDER.

P. J. Classon........Mch., 1865	Col. 132d N. Y. Infy........	Mch. 1, 1865, to Mch. 18, 1865.

132d N. Y. Infy.......Mch., 1865	From Sub Dist. Newberne.........	To 1-Brig. Div. Dist. Beaufort.....	Mch., 1865
Battn. Prov'l Troops.....Mch., 1865	From Prov'l Div. Army Tenn......	To Respective Commands..........	Mch., 1865

3d BRIGADE.— COMMANDER.

Horace Boughton......	Col. 143d N. Y. Infy............	Mch. 1, 1865, to Mch. 18, 1865.

143d N. Y. Infy. Vets...Mch., 1865	From Prov'l Div. Army Tenn......	To Respective Commands..........	Mch., 1865
18th Wis. Infy.......Mch., 1865	From Prov'l Div. Army Tenn......	To Respective Commands..........	Mch., 1865
Battn. Prov'l Troops....Mch., 1865	From Prov'l Div. Army Tenn......	To Respective Commands..........	Mch., 1865
ARTILLERY, 1st DIVISION.—			
Batty. C, 3d N. Y. Arty....Mch., 1865	From Sub Dist. Beaufort..........	To Arty. Div. Dist. Beaufort.......	Mch., 1865
Batty. D, 3d N. Y. Arty...Mch., 1865	From Sub Dist. Newberne.........	To Arty. Div. Dist. Beaufort.......	Mch., 1865

2d DIVISION, DISTRICT OF BEAUFORT.—

COMMANDER.

S. P. Carter..........	Brigadier General..........	Mch. 1, 1865, to Mch. 18, 1865.

Discontinued March 18, 1865.

1st BRIGADE.— COMMANDER.

A. G. Malloy..........	Col. 17th Wis. Infy........	Mch. 1, 1865, to Mch. 18, 1865.

85th N. Y. Infy.........Mch., 1865	From Reorganization.............	To 2-Brig. Div. Dist. Beaufort......	Mch., 1865
2d Battn. Prov'l Troops..Mch., 1865	From Prov'l Div. Army Tenn......	To Respective Commands..........	Mch., 1865

2d BRIGADE, 2d DIVISION.— COMMANDER.

C. L. Upham..........	Col. 15th Conn. Infy........	Mch. 1, 1865, to Mch. 18, 1865.

15th Conn. Infy.......Mch., 1865	From Sub Dist. Newberne.........	To 1-Brig. 1-Div. Dist. Beaufort....	Mch., 1865
27th Mass Infy.........Mch., 1865	From Sub Dist. Newberne.........	To Dist. Newberne...............	Mch., 1865

3d BRIGADE.— COMMANDER.

H. Splaine...................	Col. 17th. Mass. Infy........	Mch. 1, 1865, to Mch. 18, 1865.

17th Mass. Infy.......Mch., 1865	From Sub Dist. Beaufort..........	To 1-Brig. Div. Dist. Beaufort......	Mch., 1865
25th Mass Infy.........Mch., 1865	From Sub Dist. Newberne.........	To 2-Brig. Div. Dist. Beaufort......	Mch., 1865
ARTILLERY.—			
Batty. A, 3d N. Y. Arty..Mch., 1865	From Sub Dist. Newberne.........	To 1-Brig. 1-Div. Dist. Beaufort....	Mch., 1865
Batty. G, 3d N. Y. Arty..Mch., 1865	From Sub Dist. Newberne.........	To Arty. Div. Dist. Beaufort.......	Mch., 1865
Batty. I, 3d N. Y. Arty..Mch., 1865	From Sub Dist. Newberne.........	To Arty. Div. Dist. Beaufort.......	Mch., 1865
CAVALRY.—			
12th N. Y. Cav.........Mch., 1865	From Sub Dist. Newberne.........	To Cav. Div. Dist. Beaufort.......	Mch., 1865

DIVISION DISTRICT OF BEAUFORT.—

COMMANDER.

S. P. Carter..........	Brigadier General..........	Mch. 18, 1865, to Apr. 2, 1865.

Discontinued April 2, 1865.

1st BRIGADE.— COMMANDER.

P. J. Classon..........	Col. 132d N. Y. Infy........	Mch. 18, 1865, to Apr. 2, 1865.

17th Mass. Infy.........Mch., 1865	From 3-Brig. 2-Div. Dist. Beaufort..	To 3-Br. 3-Div. 23-C. Dept. N. C..	Apr., 1865
132d N. Y. Infy.........Mch., 1865	From 2-Brig. 1-Div. Dist. Beaufort..	To 1-Br. 2-Div. 23-C. Dept. N. C..	Apr., 1865

2d BRIGADE.— COMMANDER.

James Stewart, Jr.....	Col. 9th N. J. Infy..........	Mch. 18, 1865, to Apr. 2, 1865.

25th Mass. Infy.........Mch., 1865	From 3-Brig. 2-Div. Dist. Beaufort..	To 3-Br. 1-Div. 23-C. Dept. N. C...	Apr., 1865
9th N. J. Infy.........Mch., 1865	From 1-Brig. 1-Div. Dist. Beaufort..	To 2-Br. 3-Div. 23-C. Dept. N. C..	Apr., 1865
85th N. Y. Infy.........Mch., 1865	From 1-Brig. 2-Div. Dist. Beaufort..	To Unatt. 23-Corps Dept. N. C.....	Apr., 1865
RESERVE ARTILLERY.—			
3d N. Y. Arty. C, D, G, I..Mch., 1865	From Arty. 1st & 2d Divs. D. Beauf't.	To Dist. Newberne...............	Apr., 1865
CAVALRY.—			
12th N. Y. Cav..........Mch., 1865	From Cav. 2-Div. Dist. Beaufort...	To Kilpatrick's 3-Cav. Div. Ga.....	Apr., 1865

Twenty-Third Army Corps---Department of North Carolina

Transferred from Army and Department of the Ohio Feb., 1865.   Discontinued Aug. 1, 1865.

CORPS COMMANDERS.

J. M. Schofield........	Major General..................	Feb. 9, 1865, to Mch. 31, 1865.
J. D. Cox.............	Major General..................	Mch. 31, 1865, to June 17, 1865.
T. H. Ruger..........	Bvt. Major General.............	June 17, 1865, to June 27, 1865.
S. P. Carter..........	Brigadier General..............	June 27, 1865, to Aug. 1, 1865.

1st DIVISION.—Joined from Provisional Corps, Dept. N. C., March 18, 1865.

COMMANDERS.

Thos. H. Ruger.......	Brigadier General..............	Mch. 18, 1865, to June 17, 1865.
M. T. Thomas........	Bvt. Brig. General.............	June 17, 1865, to July 10, 1865.
G. W. Schofield......	Bvt. Brig. General.............	July 10. 1865, to Aug. 1, 1865.

1st BRIGADE.—   COMMANDERS.

I. N. Stiles...........	Bvt. Brig. General.............	Mch. 18, 1865, to May 18, 1865.
J. M. Orr............	Col. 124th Ind. Infy...........	May 18, 1865, to June 27, 1865.
A. W. Prather........	Col. 120th Ind. Infy...........	June 27, 1865, to Aug. 1, 1865.

120th Ind. Infy........Mch.,	1865	From 1-Brig. 1-Div. Prov'l C. N. C..	To Dept. N. C..................	Aug., 1865
124th Ind. Infy........Mch.,	1865	From 1-Brig. 1-Div. Prov'l C. N. C..	No change to Muster Out........	Aug., 1865
128th Ind. Infy........Mch.,	1865	From 1-Brig. 1-Div. Prov'l C. N. C..	To Dept. N. C..................	Aug., 1865
180th Ohio Infy........Mch.,	1865	From 1-Brig. 1-Div. Prov'l C. N. C..	No change to Muster Out........	Aug.. 1865

2d BRIGADE.—   COMMANDER.

J. C. McQuiston........	Col. 123d Ind. Infy............	Mch. 18, 1865, to Aug. 1, 1865.

123d Ind. Infy.........Mch.,	1865	From 2-Brig. 1-Div. Prov'l C. N. C..	No change to Muster Out........	Aug., 1865
129th Ind. Infy........Mch.,	1865	From 2-Brig. 1-Div. Prov'l C. N. C..	No change to Muster Out........	Aug., 1865
130th Ind. Infy........Mch.,	1865	From 2-Brig. 1-Div. Prov'l C. N. C..	To Dept. N. C..................	Aug., 1865
28th Mich. Infy........Mch.,	1865	From 2-Brig. 1-Div. Prov'l C. N. C..	To Dept. N. C..................	Aug., 1865

3d BRIGADE, 1st DIVISION.—   COMMANDERS.

M. T. Thomas........	Col. 8th Minn. Infy............	Mch. 18, 1865, to June 17, 1865.
James Tucker.........	Lt.-Col. 25th Mass. Infy.......	June 17, 1865, to July 13, 1865.

8th Minn. Infy..........Mch.,	1865	From 3-Brig. 1-Div. Prov'l C. N. C..	No change to Muster Out........	July, 1865
174th Ohio Infy.........Mch.,	1865	From 3-Brig. 1-Div. Prov'l C. N. C..	No change to Muster Out........	June, 1865
178th Ohio Infy.........Mch.,	1865	From 3-Brig. 1-Div. Prov'l C. N. C..	No change to Muster Out........	June, 1865
25th Mass. Infy.........Apr.,	1865	From 2-Br. Div. Dist. Beauf't N. C..	No change to Muster Out........	June, 1865
ARTILLERY, 1st DIVISION.—				
Batty. F. 1st Mich Arty..Mch.,	1865	From Arty. 1-Div. Prov'l C. N. C...	To Dist. Newberne, N. C........	Apr., 1865
Elgin Ill. Batty.........Mch.,	1865	From Arty. 1-Div. Prov'l C. N. C...	No change to Muster Out........	July, 1865
22d Ind. Batty..........Mch.,	1865	From Arty. 1-Div. Prov'l C. N. C...	To Arty. 1-Div. 10-Corps Dept. N. C.	Apr., 1865

2d DIVISION.—   COMMANDERS.

D. N. Couch..........	Major General..................	Feb. 9, 1865, to Feb. 28, 1865.
N. C. McLean........	Brigadier General..............	Feb. 28, 1865, to Apr. 4, 1865.
O. H. Moore..........	Col. 25th Mich. Infy...........	Apr. 4, 1865, to Apr. 8, 1865.
D. N. Couch..........	Major General..................	Apr. 8. 1865, to Apr. 20, 1865.
J. A. Cooper.........	Brigadier General..............	Apr. 20, 1865, to Apr. 26, 1865.
D. N. Couch..........	Major General..................	Apr. 26, 1865, to Apr. 30, 1865.
J. A. Cooper.........	Brigadier General..............	Apr. 30, 1865, to June 12, 1865.
G. W. Schofield......	Bvt. Brig. General.............	June 12, 1865, to July 4, 1865.

1st BRIGADE.—   COMMANDERS.

J. A. Cooper..........	Brigadier General..............	Feb. 9, 1865, to Mch. 6, 1865.
O. H. Moore..........	Col. 25th Mich. Infy...........	Mch. 6, 1865, to Apr. 4, 1865.
J. A. Cooper..........	Brigadier General..............	Apr. 4, 1865, to Apr. 20, 1865.
O. H. Moore..........	Col. 25th Mich. Infy...........	Apr. 20, 1865, to Apr. 26, 1865.
J. A. Cooper..........	Brigadier General..............	Apr. 26, 1865, to Apr. 30, 1865.
O. H. Moore..........	Col. 25th Mich. Infy...........	Apr. 30, 1865, to June 24, 1865.
J. B. Conyningham....	Col. 52d Penna. Infy...........	June 24, 1865, to July 4, 1865.

6th Tenn. Infy.........Feb.,	1865	From 1-Brig. 2-Div. 23-C. Army O..	No change to Muster Out........	Mch., 1865
26th Ky. Infy..........Feb.,	1865	From 1-Brig. 2-Div. 23-C. Army O..	No change to Muster Out........	July, 1865
25th Mich. Infy........Feb.,	1865	From 1-Brig. 2-Div. 23-C. Army O..	No change to Muster Out........	June, 1865
52d Penna. Infy........Apr.,	1865	From 1-Sep. Brig. Dept. South..	No change to Muster Out........	July, 1865
132d N. Y. Infy........Apr.,	1865	From 1-Brig. Div. Dist. Beauf't N. C.	No change to Muster Out........	June, 1865

2d BRIGADE.—   COMMANDERS.

O. H. Moore..........	Col. 25th Mich. Infy...........	Feb. 9, 1865, to Feb. 27, 1865.
J. Mehringer.........	Col. 91st Ind. Infy............	Feb. 27, 1865, to June 9, 1865.
O. L. Spaulding......	Col. 23d Mich. Infy............	June 9, 1865, to June 28, 1865.

23d Mich. Infy.........Feb.,	1865	From 2-Brig. 2-Div. 23-C. Ohio.....	No change to Muster Out........	June, 1865
111th Ohio Infy........Feb.,	1865	From 2-Brig. 2-Div. 23-C. Ohio.....	No change to Muster Out........	June, 1865
118th Ohio Infy........Feb.,	1865	From 2-Brig. 2-Div. 23-C. Ohio.....	No change to Muster Out........	June, 1865
80th Ind. Infy.........Feb.,	1865	From 2-Brig. 2-Div. 23-C. Ohio.....	No change to Muster Out........	June, 1865
107th Ill. Infy........Feb.,	1865	From 2-Brig. 2-Div. 23-C. Ohio.....	No change to Muster Out........	June, 1865
103d Ohio.............May,	1865	From 2-Brig. 3-Div. 23-C. N. C.....	No change to Muster Out........	June, 1865

3d BRIGADE.—   COMMANDERS.

N. C. McLean.........	Brigadier General..............	Feb. 9, 1865, to Feb. 28, 1865.
S. A. Strickland......	Col. 50th Ohio Infy............	Feb. 28, 1865, to June 9, 1865.
J. Mehringer.........	Col. 91st Ind. Infy............	June 9, 1865, to June 27, 1865.
G. W. Hoge..........	Col. 183d Ohio Infy............	June 27, 1865, to July 4, 1865.

50th Ohio Infy.........Feb.,	1865	From 3-Brig. 2-Div. 23-C. Ohio.....	No change to Muster Out........	July, 1865
181st Ohio Infy........Feb.,	1865	From 3-Brig. 2-Div. 23-C. Ohio.....	No change to Muster Out........	June, 1865
183d Ohio Infy.........Feb.,	1865	From 3-Brig. 2-Div. 23-C. Ohio.....	No change to Muster Out........	July, 1865
91st Ind. Infy.........Feb.,	1865	From 3-Brig. 2-Div. 23-C. Ohio.....	No change to Muster Out........	June, 1865
ARTILLERY, 2d DIVISION.—				
15th Ind. Infy.........Feb.,	1865	From Arty. 2-Div. 23-C. Ohio......	No change to Muster Out........	July, 1865
19th Ohio Infy.........Feb.,	1865	From Arty. 2-Div. 23-C. Ohio......	No change to Muster Out........	June, 1865

3d DIVISION.—

	COMMANDERS.	
J. D. Cox	Major General	Feb. 9, 1865, to Feb. 25, 1865.
J. W. Reilly	Brigadier General	Feb. 25, 1865, to Apr. 7, 1865.
S. P. Carter	Brigadier General	Apr. 7, 1865, to June 27, 1865.
James Stewart, Jr.	Col. 9th N. J. Infy.	June 27, 1865, to July 1, 1865.

1st BRIGADE.—

	COMMANDERS.		
O. W. Sterl	Col. 104th Ohio Infy.	Feb. 9, 1865, to June 27, 1865.	
W. S. Stewart Jr.	Col. 65th Ill. Infy.	June 27, 1865, to June 28, 1865.	
100th Ohio Infy. ...... Feb., 1865	From 1-Brig. 3-Div. 23-C. Ohio	No change to Muster Out	June, 1865
104th Ohio Infy. ...... Feb., 1865	From 1-Brig. 3-Div. 23-C. Ohio	No change to Muster Out	June, 1865
12th Ky. Infy. ...... Feb., 1865	From 1-Brig. 3-Div. 23-C. Ohio	No change to Muster Out	July, 1865
16th Ky. Infy. ...... Feb., 1865	From 1-Brig. 3-Div. 23-C. Ohio	No change to Muster Out	July, 1865
8th Tenn. Infy. ...... Feb., 1865	From 1-Brig. 3-Div. 23-C. Ohio	No change to Muster Out	June, 1865

2d BRIGADE.—

	COMMANDERS.		
J. S. Casement	Col. 103d Ohio Infy.	Feb. 9, 1865, to Feb. 25, 1865.	
A. T. Willcox	Col. 177th Ohio Infy.	Feb. 25, 1865, to Mch. 6, 1865.	
J. S. Casement	Col. 103d Ohio Infy.	Mch. 6, 1865, to May 1, 1865.	
C. M. Schofield	Bvt. Brig. General	May 1, 1865, to June 12, 1865.	
L. H. Rousseau	Lt.-Col. 12th Ky. Infy.	June 12, 1865, to June 28, 1865.	
103d Ohio Infy. ...... Feb., 1865	From 2-Brig. 3-Div. 23-C. Ohio	No change to Muster Out	May, 1865
177th Ohio Infy. ...... Feb., 1865	From 2-Brig. 3-Div. 23-C. Ohio	No change to Muster Out	June, 1865
65th Ill. Infy. ...... Feb., 1865	From 2-Brig. 3-Div. 23-C. Ohio	No change to Muster Out	June, 1865
65th Ind. Infy. ...... Feb., 1865	From 2-Brig. 3-Div. 23-C. Ohio	No change to Muster Out	June, 1865
9th N. J. Infy. ...... Apr., 1865	From 1-Brig. Div. Dist. Beauf't N. C.	No change to Muster Out	June, 1865

3d BRIGADE.—

	COMMANDER.		
T. J. Henderson	Bvt. Brig. General	Feb. 9, 1865, to June 28, 1865.	
112th Illinois Infy. ...... Feb., 1865	From 3-Brig. 3-Div. 23-Corps Ohio	No change to Muster Out	June, 1865
63d Indiana Infy. ...... Feb., 1865	From 3-Brig. 3-Div. 23-Corps Ohio	No change to Muster Out	June, 1865
140th Indiana Infy. ...... Feb., 1865	From 3-Brig. 3-Div. 23-Corps Ohio	No change to Muster Out	July, 1865
17th Mass. Infy. ...... Apr., 1865	From 1-B. Div. Dist. Beaufort, N. C.	No change to Muster Out	July, 1865
ARTILLERY, 3d DIVISION.—			
Batty. D, 1st Ohio Arty. .. Feb., 1865	From Arty. 3-Div. 23-Corps A. Ohio	No change to Muster Out	July, 1865
23d Indiana Batty. ...... Feb., 1865	From Arty. 3-Div. 23-Corps A. Ohio	No change to Muster Out	July, 1865

Tenth Army Corps---Department of North Carolina

Reorganized from Terry's Provisional Corps, Dept. of North Carolina, March 27, 1865. Discontinued Aug. 1, 1865.

CORPS COMMANDERS.

Alfred H. Terry	Major General	Mch. 27, 1865, to May 13, 1865.
Adelbert Ames	Bvt. Major General	May 13, 1865, to Aug. 1, 1865.

1st DIVISION.—

	COMMANDER.	
Henry W. Birge	Bvt. Major General	Mch. 27, 1865, to July 4, 1865.

Discontinued July 4, 1865.

1st BRIGADE.—

	COMMANDER.		
H. Graham	Col. 22d Iowa Infy.	Mch. 27, 1865, to July 4, 1865.	Apr., 1865
13th Conn. Infy. ...... Mch., 1865	From Dist. Savannah Dept. South	To Dist. Savannah Dept. South	Apr., 1865
131st New York Infy. .... Mch., 1865	From Dist. Savannah Dept. South	To Dist. Savannah Dept. South	Apr., 1865
159th New York Infy. .... Mch., 1865	From Dist. Savannah Dept. South	To Dist. Savannah Dept. South	Apr., 1865
22d Iowa Infy. ...... Mch., 1865	From Dist. Savannah Dept. South	To Dist. Savannah Dept. South	Apr., 1865
28th Iowa Infy. ...... Mch., 1865	From Dist. Savannah Dept. South	To Dist. Savannah Dept. South	Apr., 1865

2d BRIGADE, 1st DIVISION.—

	COMMANDER.		
Jos. C. Abbott	Bvt. Brig. General	Mch. 27, 1865, to Apr. 1, 1865.	
3d New Hampshire Infy. .. Mch., 1865	From Abbott's B. Prov'l Corps N. C.	To Abbott's Det. Brig. Wilmington	Apr., 1865
7th New Hamp. Infy. .... Mch., 1865	From Abbott's B. Prov'l Corps N. C.	To Abbott's Det. Brig. Wilmington	Apr., 1865
6th Conn. Infy. ...... Mch., 1865	From Abbott's B. Prov'l Corps N. C.	To Abbott's Det. Brig. Wilmington	Apr., 1865
7th Conn. Infy. ...... Mch., 1865	From Abbott's B. Prov'l Corps N. C.	To Abbott's Det. Brig. Wilmington	Apr., 1865
16th N. Y. H. A. 6 Cos. .. Mch., 1865	From Abbott's B. Prov'l Corps N. C.	To Abbott's Det. Brig. Wilmington	Apr., 1865

3d BRIGADE.—

	COMMANDER.		
N. W. Day	Col. 131st New York Infy.	Mch. 27, 1865, to July 4, 1865.	
38th Mass. Infy. ...... Mch., 1865	From Dist. Savannah Dept. South	To Dist. Savannah Dept. South	Apr., 1865
128th New York Infy. .... Mch., 1865	From Dist. Savannah Dept. South	To Dist. Savannah Dept. South	Apr., 1865
156th New York Infy. .... Mch., 1865	From Dist. Savannah Dept. South	To Dist. Savannah Dept. South	Apr., 1865
175th New York Infy. .... Mch., 1865	From Dist. Savannah Dept. South	To Dist. Savannah Dept. South	Apr., 1865
176th New York Infy. .... Mch., 1865	From Dist. Savannah Dept. South	To Dist. Savannah Dept. South	Apr., 1865
ARTILLERY.—			
2d Indiana Batty. ...... Apr., 1865	From Arty. 1-Div. 23-C. Dept. N. C.	No change to Muster Out	June, 1865

2d DIVISION.—

	COMMANDERS.	
Adelbert Ames	Bvt. Major General	Mch. 27, 1865, to May 13, 1865.
R. Daggett	Col. 117th New York Infy.	May 13, 1865, to June 8, 1865.
J. S. Littell	Col. 76th Penna. Infy.	June 8, 1865, to July 18, 1865.
W. B. Coan	Col. 48th New York Infy.	July 18, 1865, to Aug. 1, 1865.

1st BRIGADE, 2d DIVISION.—

	COMMANDERS.	
R. Daggett	Col. 117th N. Y. Infy.	Mch. 27, 1865, to May 13, 1865.
A. M. Barney	Col. 142d N. Y. Infy.	May 13, 1865, to June 7, 1865.

Discontinued June, 1865. Reorganized July, 1865, from 3d Brig. 2d. Div.

	COMMANDER.		
F. W. Parker	Col. 4th N. H. Infy.	July 20, 1865, to Aug. 1, 1865.	
3d N. Y. Infy. ...... Mch., 1865	From 1-Brig. 2-Div. Prov'l C. N. C.	No change to Muster Out	Aug., 1865
112th N. Y. Infy. ...... Mch., 1865	From 1-Brig. 2-Div. Prov'l C. N. C.	No change to Muster Out	June, 1865
117th N. Y. Infy. ...... Mch., 1865	From 1-Brig. 2-Div. Prov'l C. N. C.	No change to Muster Out	June, 1865
142d N. Y. Infy. ...... Mch., 1865	From 1-Brig. 2-Div. Prov'l C. N. C.	No change to Muster Out	June, 1865
4th N. H. Infy. ...... July, 1865	From 3-Br. 2-Div. 10-C. Dept. N. C.	No change to Muster Out	Aug., 1865
13th Ind. Infy. ...... July, 1865	From 3-Br. 2-Div. 10-C. Dept. N. C.	No change to Muster Out	Aug., 1865

2d BRIGADE.— COMMANDERS.

W. B. Coan.............	Col. 48th N. Y. Infy................	Mch. 27, 1865, to Apr. 5, 1865.
J. S. Littell.............	Col. 76th Penna. Infy.................	Apr. 5, 1865, to June 9, 1865.
W. B. Coan.........	Col. 48th N. Y. Infy.................	June 9, 1865, to July 18, 1865.
C. R. McDonald.........	Col. 47th N. Y. Infy................	July 18, 1865, to Aug. 1, 1865.

47th N. Y. Infy........	Mch., 1865	From 2-Brig. 2-Div. Prov'l C. N. C..	No change to Muster Out.........	Aug.,	1865
48th N. Y. Infy........	Mch., 1865	From 2-Brig. 2-Div. Prov'l C. N. C..	No change to Muster Out.........	Aug.,	1865
76th Penna. Infy.......	Mch., 1865	From 2-Brig. 2-Div. Prov'l C. N. C..	No change to Muster Out.........	July,	1865
97th Penna. Infy.......	Mch., 1865	From 2-Brig. 2-Div. Prov'l C. N. C..	No change to Muster Out.........	Aug.,	1865
203d Penna. Infy.......	Mch., 1865	From 2-Brig. 2-Div. Prov'l C. N. C..	No change to Muster Out.........	June,	1865

3d BRIGADE.— COMMANDERS.

G. F. Granger..........	Col. 9th Me. Infy....................	Mch. 27, 1865, to June 12, 1865.
A. Alden..............	Col. 169th N. Y. Infy...............	June 12, 1865, to July 18, 1865.
Transferred to 1st Brigade, 2d Division, July, 1865.		

4th N. H. Infy..........	Mch., 1865	From 3-Brig. 2-Div. Prov'l C. N. C.	To 1-Brig. 2-Div. 10-Corps N. C....	July,	1865
13th Ind. Infy........	Mch., 1865	From 3-Brig. 2-Div. Prov'l C. N. C.	To 1-Brig. 2-Div. 10-C. N. C.....	July,	1865
9th Me. Infy..........	Mch., 1865	From 3-Brig. 2-Div. Prov'l C. N. C.	No change to Muster Out.........	July,	1865
115th N. Y. Infy......	Mch., 1865	From 3-Brig. 2-Div. Prov'l C. N. C.	No change to Muster Out.........	July,	1865
169th N. Y. Infy......	Mch., 1865	From 3-Brig. 2-Div. Prov'l C. N. C.	No change to Muster Out.........	July,	1865
ARTILLERY.—					
16th N. Y. Batty........	Mch., 1865	From Arty. Terry's Prov'l C. N. C..	No change to Muster Out.........	July,	1865

3d DIVISION.— COMMANDERS.

C. J. Paine............	Brigadier General...................	Mch. 27, 1865, to July 6, 1865.
D. Bates..............	Col. 30th U. S. Col. Infy..........	July 6, 1865, to Aug. 1, 1865.

1st BRIGADE.— COMMANDERS.

D. Bates......	Col. 30th U. S. Col. Infy..........	Mch. 27, 1865, to July 6, 1865.
W. H. Revere, Jr.....	Col. 107th U. S. Col. Infy.........	July 6, 1865, to Aug. 1, 1865.

1st U. S. Col. Infy.....	Mch., 1865	From 3-Brig. 3-Div. Prov'l C. N. C.	To Dept. Va......................	Aug.,	1865
30th U. S. Col. Infy.....	Mch., 1865	From 2-Brig. 3-Div. Prov'l C. N. C.	To Dept. Va......................	Aug.,	1865
107th U. S. Col. Infy.....	Mch., 1865	From 1-Brig. 3-Div. Prov'l C. N. C.	To Dept. Va......................	Aug.,	1865

2d BRIGADE.— COMMANDERS.

S. A. Duncan..........	Col. 4th U. S. Col. Infy..........	Mch. 27, 1865, to June 14, 1865.
O. P. Stearns..........	Col. 39th U. S. Col. Infy.........	June 14, 1865, to Aug. 1, 1865.

4th U. S. Col. Infy......	Mch., 1865	From 2-Brig. 3-Div. Prov'l C. N. C.	To Dept. N. C...................	Aug.,	1865
5th U. S. Col. Infy......	Mch., 1865	From 3-Brig. 3-Div. Prov'l C. N. C.	To Dept. N. C...................	Aug.,	1865
39th U. S. Col. Infy.....	Mch., 1865	From 2-Brig. 3-Div. Prov'l C. N. C.	To Dept. N. C...................	Aug.,	1865

3d BRIGADE, 3d DIVISION.— COMMANDERS.

J. H. Holman..........	Col. 1st U. S. Col. Infy..........	Mch. 27, 1865, to Apr. 22, 1865.
A. M. Blackman.......	Col. 27th U. S. Col. Infy........	Apr. 22, 1865, to May 12, 1865.
Nathan Goff, Jr.......	Col. 37th U. S. Col. Infy........	May 12, 1865, to June 9, 1865.
A. G. Chamberlin......	Lt.-Col. 37th U. S. Col. Infy........	June 9, 1865, to July 1, 1865.
Nathan Goff, Jr.......	Col. 37th U. S. Col. Infy........	July 1, 1865, to Aug. 1, 1865.

6th U. S. Col. Infy.....	Mch., 1865	From 2-Brig. 3-Div. Prov'l C. N. C.	To Dept. North Carolina..........	Aug.,	1865
27th U. S. Col. Infy.....	Mch., 1865	From 3-Brig. 3-Div. Prov'l C. N. C.	To Dept. North Carolina..........	Aug.,	1865
37th U. S. Col. Infy.....	Mch., 1865	From 3-Brig. 3-Div. Prov'l C. N. C.	To Dept. North Carolina..........	Aug.,	1865

DISTRICT OF WILMINGTON.—Organized March 1, 1865.

COMMANDERS.

J. R. Hawley..........	Brigadier General...................	Mch. 1, 1865, to June 23, 1865.
J. W. Ames...........	Bvt. Brig. General..................	June 23, 1865, to Sept. 20, 1865.

ABBOTT'S DETACHED BRIGADE.— COMMANDER.

J. C. Abbott...........	Bvt. Brig. General.................	Apr. 1, 1865, to July 1, 1865.

3d N. H. Infy..........	Mch., 1865	From 2-Brig. 1-Div. 10-C. N. C.....	No change to Muster Out.........	July,	1865
7th N. H. Infy..........	Mch., 1865	From 2-Brig. 1-Div. 10-C. N. C.....	No change to Muster Out.........	July,	1865
6th Conn. Infy..........	Mch., 1865	From 2-Brig. 1-Div. 10-C. N. C.....	No change to Muster Out.........	July,	1865
7th Conn. Infy..........	Mch., 1865	From 2-Brig. 1-Div. 10-C. N. C.....	No change to Muster Out.........	July,	1865
16th N. Y. H. Arty. 6-Co's.	Mch., 1865	From 2-Brig. 1-Div. 10-C. N. C.....	To Dept. Washington, D. C........	July,	1865

South Carolina Expeditional Corps

Organized Sept. and Oct., 1861. Termed Department of the South, March 15, 1862.

COMMANDER.

T. W. Sherman........	Brigadier General...................	Sept. 19, 1861, to Mch. 15, 1862.

1st BRIGADE.— COMMANDER.

E. L. Viele............	Brigadier General...................	

8th Me. Infy...........	Oct., 1861	From New Organization..........	To 1-Brig. 1-Div. Dept. South......	Apr.,	1862
3d N. H. Infy..........	Oct., 1861	From New Organization..........	To 3-Brig. 1-Div. Dept. South......	Apr.,	1862
46th N. Y. Infy.........	Oct., 1861	From New Organization...........	To 2-Brig. 2-Div. Dept. South......	Apr.,	1862
47th N. Y. Infy.........	Oct., 1861	From New Organization..........	To 1-Brig. 1-Div. Dept. South......	Apr.,	1862
48th N. Y. Infy.........	Oct., 1861	From New Organization..........	To Ft. Pulaski, Ga., Dept. South....	Apr.,	1862
55th Penna. Infy.......	Jan., 1862	From Unass'd S. C. Exp. Corps.....	To Edisto Island, S. C.............	Feb.,	1862

2d BRIGADE.— COMMANDER.

I. I. Stevens..........	Brigadier General..................	

8th Mich. Infy..........	Oct., 1861	From New Organization...........	To 1-Brig. 2-Div. Dept. South......	Apr.,	1862
79th N. Y. Infy.........	Oct., 1861	From Stevens' Brig. Smith's Div. P.	To 2-Brig. 2-Div. Dept. South......	Apr.,	1862
50th Penna. Infy........	Oct., 1861	From New Organization...........	To Dist. Beaufort, Dept. South.....	Apr.,	1862
100th Penna. Infy.......	Oct., 1861	From New Organization...........	To 2-Brig. 2-Div. Dept. South......	Apr.,	1862

3d BRIGADE.— COMMANDER.

H. G. Wright	Brigadier General			
9th Me. Infy............Oct., 1861	From New Organization............	To Fernandina, Fla., Dept. South..	Feb.,	1862
4th N. H. Infy...........Oct., 1861	From New Organization............	To St. Augustine, Fla., Dept. South.	Feb.,	1862
6th Conn. Infy...........Oct., 1861	From New Organization............	To 1-Brig. 1-Div. Dept. South......	Apr.,	1862
7th Conn. Infy...........Oct., 1861	From New Organization............	To 1-Brig. 2-Div. Dept. South......	Apr.,	1862
76th Penna. Infy.........Oct., 1861	From New Organization............	To 2-Brig. 1-Div. Dept. South......	Apr.,	1862
97th Penna. Infy.........Dec., 1861	From New Organization............	To 2-Brig. 1-Div. Dept. South......	Apr.,	1862
UNATTACHED.—				
1st N. Y. Engr...........Oct., 1861	From New Organization............	To Dist. Hilton Head, Dept. South..	Apr.,	1862
3d R. I. Heavy Arty......Oct., 1861	From New Organization............	To 3-Brig. 1-Div. Dept. South......	Apr.,	1862
Batty. E, 3d U. S. Arty....Oct., 1861	From Porter's Div. Pot............	To 2-Brig. 1-Div. Dept. South......	Apr.,	1862
45th Penna. Infy.........Dec., 1861	From New Organization............	To 2-Brig. 1-Div. Dept. South......	Apr.,	1862
55th Penna. Infy.........Dec., 1861	From New Organization............	To 1-Brig. S. C. Exp. Corps.......	Jan.,	1862
1st Conn. Batty..........Jan., 1862	From New Organization............	To 3-Brig. 2-Div. Dept. South......	Apr.,	1862
1st Mass. Cav............Jan., 1862	From New Organization............	To 3-Brig. 2-Div. Dept. South......	Apr.,	1862
28th Mass. Infy.........Feb., 1862	From New Organization............	To 1-Brig. 2-Div. Dept. South......	Apr.,	1862

Department of the South

Constituted March 15, 1862, and to consist of the States of South Carolina, Georgia and Florida. Department of Key West added March 15, 1862. District of West Florida detached Aug. 8, 1862. and annexed to the Dept. of the Gulf.

COMMANDERS.

T. W. Sherman........	Brigadier General............	Mch. 15, 1862, to Mch. 31, 1862.	
David Hunter.........	Major General............	Mch. 31, 1862, to Aug. 22, 1862.	
John M. Brennan......	Brigadier General............	Aug. 22, 1862, to Sept. 17, 1862.	
O. M. Mitchell.......	Major General............	Sept. 17, 1862, to Oct. 27, 1862.	
John M. Brennan......	Brigadier General............	Oct. 27, 1862, to Jan. 20, 1863.	
David Hunter.........	Major General............	Jan. 20, 1863, to June 12, 1863.	
Q. A. Gillmore........	Brigadier General............	June 12, 1863, to May 1, 1864.	
J. P. Hatch..........	Brigadier General............	May 1, 1864, to May 26, 1864.	
J. G. Foster..........	Major General............	May 26, 1864, to Feb. 9, 1865.	
Q. A. Gillmore........	Major General............	Feb. 9, 1865, to June 26, 1865.	

1st DIVISION.—Organized April, 1862. COMMANDER.

H. G. Wright..........	Brigadier General............	Apr. .., 1862, to July .., 1862.	

1st BRIGADE.— COMMANDER.

J. L. Chatfield..........	Col. 6th Conn. Infy............	Apr. .., 1862, to July .., 1862.		
6th Conn. Infy..........Apr., 1862	From 3-Brig. S. C. Exp. Corps......	To Dist. Beaufort S. C. Dept. South.	July,	1862
47th N. Y. Infy..........Apr., 1862	From 1-Brig. S. C. Exp. Corps......	To Dist. Hilton H'd S. C. Dept. So.	July,	1862
97th Penna. Infy.........Apr., 1862	From 3-Brig. S. C. Exp. Corps......	To Dist. Hilton H'd S. C. Dept. So..	July,	1862

2d BRIGADE.— COMMANDER.

Thos. Welsh..........	Col. 45th Penna. Infy............	Apr. .., 1862, to July .., 1862.		
45th Penna. Infy.........Apr., 1862	From Unatt. S. C. Exp. Corps......	To 2-Brig. 1-Div. 9-Corps Pot.....	July,	1862
76th Penna. Infy.........Apr., 1862	From 3-Brig. S. C. Exp. Corps......	To Dist. Hilton Head S. C.........	July,	1862
Batty. E, 3d U. S, Arty....Apr., 1862	From Unatt. S. C. Exp. Corps......	To Dist. Hilton Head S. C.........	July,	1862

2d DIVISION.— COMMANDER.

I. I. Stevens............	Brigadier General............	Apr. .., 1862, to July .., 1862.	

1st BRIGADE.— COMMANDER.

William Fenton........	Col. 8th Mich. Infy............	Apr. .., 1862, to July .., 1862.		
28th Mass. Infy.........Apr., 1862	From Unatt. S. C. Exp. Corps......	To 1-Brig. 1-Div. 9-Corps Pot......	July,	1862
7th Conn. Infy..........Apr., 1862	From 3-Brig. S. C. Exp. Corps......	To Dist. Hilton H'd S. C. Dept. So.	July,	1862
8th Mich. Infy..........Apr., 1862	From 2-Brig. S. C. Exp. Corps......	To 1-Brig. 1-Div. 9-Corps Pot......	July,	1862

2d BRIGADE.— COMMANDER.

A. Farnsworth..........	Col. 79th N. Y. Infy............	Apr. .., 1862, to July .., 1862.		
46th N. Y. Infy..........Apr., 1862	From 1-Brig. S. C. Exp. Corps......	To 2-Brig. 1-Div. 9-Corps Pot......	July,	1862
79th N. Y. Infy..........Apr., 1862	From 2-Brig. S. C. Exp. Corps......	To 2-Brig. 1-Div. 9-Corps Pot......	July,	1862
100th Penna. Infy........Apr., 1862	From 2-Brig. S. C. Exp. Corps......	To 2-Brig. 1-Div. 9-Corps Pot......	July,	1862

3d BRIGADE, 2d DIVISION.— COMMANDER.

Robert Williams	Col. 1st Mass. Cav............	Apr., 1862, to July, 1862.		
3d N. H. Infy...........Apr., 1862	From 1-Brig. S. C. Exp. Corps.....	To Dist. Hilton Head, S. C.........	July,	1862
1st N. Y. Engrs.........Apr., 1862	From Unatt. S. C. Exp. Corps.....	To Dist. Hilton Head, S. C.........	July,	1862
1st Conn. Batty.........Apr., 1862	From Unatt. S. C. Exp. Corps.....	To Dist. Beaufort, S. C...........	July,	1862
3d R. I. Heavy Arty......Apr., 1862	From Unatt. S. C. Exp. Corps.....	To Hilton Head, S. C............	July,	1862
1st Mass. Cav..........Apr., 1862	From Unatt. S. C. Exp. Corps.....	To Army Pot. (8 Co's)............	July,	1862
EDISTO ISLAND, S. C.—				
55th Penna. Infy.........Apr., 1862	From Edisto Island S. C. Exp. Corps.	To Dist. Beaufort, S. C...........	July,	1862

DISTRICT OF BEAUFORT, S. C.—Designated District of Beaufort 10-Corps, Sept. 3, 1862.

COMMANDERS.

John M. Brannan......	Brigadier General	June, 1862, to Aug. 22, 1862.		
T. H. Good............	Col. 47th Penna. Infy............	Aug. 22, 1862, to Sept. 3, 1862.		
8th Me. Infy............Apr., 1862	From 1-Brig. S. C. Exp. Corps......	To U. S. Forces Beaufort 10-Corps..	Sept.,	1862
50th Penna. Infy.........Apr., 1862	From 2-Brig. S. C. Exp. Corps......	To 1-Brig. 1-Div. 9-Corps Pot......	July,	1862
7th N. H. Infy..........June, 1862	From Dist. Fla..................	To St. Augustine, Fla............	Aug.,	1862
47th Penna. Infy.........June, 1862	From Dist. Fla..................	To U. S. Forces Beaufort 10-Corps..	Sept.,	1862
4th N. H. Infy..........June, 1862	From St. Augustine, Fla...........	To U. S. Forces Beaufort 10-Corps..	Sept.,	1862
(Co's B, H, K.)				
Batty. B, 1st U. S. Arty..June, 1862	From Dist. Key West, Fla.........	To U. S. Forces Beaufort 10-Corps..	Sept.,	1862
Batty. D, 1st U. S. Arty..June, 1862	From Fort Taylor, Fla............	To U. S. Forces Beaufort 10-Corps..	Sept.,	1862
Batty. M, 1st U. S. Arty..June, 1862	From Fort Jefferson, Fla..........	To U. S. Forces Beaufort 10-Corps..	Sept.,	1862
6th Conn. Infy..........July, 1862	From 1-Brig. 1-Div. Dept South....	To U. S. Forces Beaufort 10-Corps..	Sept.,	1862
55th Penna. Infy.........July, 1862	From Edisto Island, S. C..........	To U. S. Forces Beaufort 10-Corps..	Sept.,	1862
1st Conn. Batty..........July, 1862	From 3-Brig. 2-Div. Dept. South....	To U. S. Forces Beaufort 10-Corps..	Sept.,	1862
1st Mass. Cav. I, K, L, M..July, 1862	From Dist. Hilton Head, S. C.......	To U. S. Forces Beaufort 10-Corps..	Sept.,	1862

DISTRICT OF HILTON HEAD, S. C.—Designated U. S. Forces Hilton Head, S. C., 10-Corps, Sept. 3, 1862.

COMMANDERS.

Robt. Williams	Col. 1st Mass. Cav................	July, 1862, to Aug., 1862.
A. H. Terry	Brigadier General	Aug., 1862, to Sept. 3, 1862.

3d N. H. Infy..........July, 1862	From 3-Brig. 2-Div. Dept. South....	To U. S. Forces Hilton Hd. 10-Corps.	Sept., 1862
7th Conn. Infy..........July, 1862	From 1-Brig. 1-Div. Dept. South....	To U. S. Forces Hilton Hd. 10-Corps.	Sept., 1862
47th N. Y. Infy..........July, 1862	From 1-Brig. 1-Div. Dept. South....	To U. S. Forces Hilton Head 10-C..	Sept., 1862
76th Penna. Infy..........July, 1862	From 2-Brig. 1-Div. Dept. South....	To U. S. Forces Hilton Head 10-C..	Sept., 1862
97th Penna. Infy..........July, 1862	From 1-Brig. 1-Div. Dept. South....	To U. S. Forces Hilton Head 10-C..	Sept., 1862
3d R. I. Heavy Arty......July, 1862	From 3-Brig. 2-Div. Dept. South....	To U. S. Forces Hilton Head 10-C..	Sept., 1862
1st N. Y. Engineers......July, 1862	From 3-Brig. 2-Div. Dept. South....	To U. S. Forces Hilton Head 10-C..	Sept., 1862
Batty. E, 3d U. S. Arty....July, 1862	From 3-Brig. 2-Div. Dept. South....	To U. S. Forces Hilton Head 10-C..	Sept., 1862

FORT PICKENS AND PENSACOLA, FLA.—Transferred to Dept. Gulf, Sept., 1862.

COMMANDER.

L. G. Arnold..........	Brigadier General...................	Apr., 1862, to Sept., 1862.

6th N. Y. Infy..........Apr., 1862	From Dept. Fla................	To Dist. West Fla., Dept. Gulf......	Sept., 1862
75th N. Y. Infy..........Apr., 1862	From Dept. Fla................	To Dist. West Fla., Dept. Gulf......	Sept., 1862
91st N. Y. Infy..........Apr., 1862	From Dept. Fla................	To Dist. West Fla., Dept. Gulf......	Sept., 1862
Batty. A, 1st U. S. Arty....Apr., 1862	From Dept. Fla................	To Dist. West Fla., Dept. Gulf......	Sept., 1862
Batty. F, 1st U. S. Arty....Apr., 1862	From Dept. Fla................	To Dist. West Fla., Dept. Gulf......	Sept., 1862
Batty. L, 1st U. S. Arty....Apr., 1862	From Dept. Fla................	To Dist. West Fla., Dept. Gulf......	Sept., 1862
Battys. C, K, 2d U. S. Arty.Apr. 1862	From Dept. Fla................	To Dist. West Fla., Dept. Gulf......	Sept., 1862

KEY WEST, FLA.—   COMMANDER.

John M. Brannan........	Brigadier General...................	Mch., 1862, to June, 1862.

47th Penna. Infy..........Apr., 1862	From Dept. Fla................	To Dist. Beaufort Dept. South......	June, 18
90th N. Y. Infy..........Apr., 1862	From Dept. Fla................	To Key West Dist. Hilton Head 10-C.	Sept., 1862
FERNANDINA, FLA.—			
9th Me. Infy..........Mch., 1862	From 3-Brig. S. C. Exp. Corps......	To Fernandina, Fla. 10-Corps........	Sept., 1862
ST. AUGUSTINE, FLA.—			
4th N. H. Infy..........Apr., 1862	From 3-Brig. S. C. Exp. Corps......	To Dist. Beaufort 10-Corps........	Sept., 1862
FORT PULASKI, GA.—			
48th N. Y. Infy..........Apr., 1862	From 1-Brig. S. C. Exp. Corps......	To Ft. Pulaski Dist. Hilton Hd., 10-C.	Sept., 1862
3d R. I. Heavy Arty, Co. G.Apr., 1862	From 3-Brig. 2-Div. Dept. South....	To Ft. Pulaski Dist. Hilton Hd., 10-C.	Sept., 1862

Tenth Army Corps---Department of the South

Created Sept. 3, 1862, from Troops in the Dept. of the South. Mostly transferred to the Dept. of Va. and N. C., April, 1864, and Corps discontinued in the Dept. of the South.

CORPS COMMANDERS.

John M. Brannan.......	Brigadier General...................	Sept. 3, 1862, to Sept. 17, 1862.
O. M. Mitchell..........	Major General...................	Sept. 17, 1862, to Oct. 27, 1862.
John M. Brannan.......	Brigadier General...................	Oct. 27, 1862, to Jan. 20, 1863.
David Hunter..........	Major General...................	Jan. 20, 1863, to June 12, 1863.
Q. A. Gilmore..........	Major General...................	June 12, 1863, to Apr. 17, 1864.

U. S. FORCES BEAUFORT, S. C.—Designated U. S. Forces Port Royal Island, S. C., 10-Corps, Nov., 1862.
Command transferred to Reorganized Department of the South, April, 1864.

COMMANDERS.

T. H. Good............	Col. 47th Penna. Infy.............	Sept. 3, 1862, to Sept. 17, 1862.
John M. Brannan.......	Brigadier General.................	Sept. 17, 1862, to Oct. 1, 1862.
J. L. Chatfield.........	Col. 6th Conn. Infy.............	Oct. 1, 1862, to Oct. 27, 1862.
T. H. Good............	Col. 47th Penna. Infy.............	Oct. 27, 1862, to Dec. 26, 1862.
Truman Seymour......	Brigadier General.................	Dec. 26, 1862, to Feb. 9, 1863.
T. H. Good............	Col. 47th Penna. Infy.............	Feb. 9, 1862, to Feb. 19, 1863.
Rufus Saxton.........	Brigadier General.................	Feb. 19, 1863, to June 14, 1863.
W. W. H. Davis........	Col. 104th Penna. Infy.............	June 14, 1863, to July 6, 1863.
Rufus Saxton.........	Brigadier General.................	July 6, 1863, to Apr. 17, 1864.

8th Me. Infy..........Sept., 1862	From Dist. Beaufort Dept. South....	To U. S. Forces Hilton Head 10-C..	Apr., 1863
6th Conn. Infy..........Sept., 1862	From Dist. Beaufort Dept. South....	To Jacksonville, Fla..............	Mch., 1863
7th Conn. Infy..........Sept., 1862	From Dist. Beaufort Hilton Head Dept. South.	To Fernandina, Fla...............	Jan., 1863
4th N. H. Infy..........Sept., 1862	From St. Augustine, Fla...........	To U. S. Forces Folly Island 10-C..	Apr., 1863
47th Penna. Infy..........Sept., 1862	From Dist. Beaufort Dept. South....	To Key West, Fla................	Nov., 1862
55th Penna. Infy..........Sept., 1862	From Dist. Beaufort Dept. South....	To 1-Brig. 3-Div. 10-C'ps Va. & N. C.	Apr., 1864
Batty. B, 1st U. S. Arty....Sept., 1862	From Dist. Beaufort Dept. South....	To U. S. Forces Hilton Head 10-C..	May, 1863
Batty. D, 1st U. S. Arty....Sept., 1862	From Dist. Beaufort Dept. South....	To Arty. 2-Div. 10-Corps Va. & N. C.	Apr., 1864
Batty. M, 1st U. S. Arty....Sept., 1862	From Dist. Beaufort Dept. South....	To U. S. Forces Hilton Head 10-C..	Nov., 1863
1st Conn. Batty..........Sept., 1862	From Dist. Beaufort Dept. South....	To U. S. Forces Folly Island 10-C..	July, 1863
1st Mass. Cav. I. K. L. M...Sep., 1862	From Dist. Beaufort Dept. South....	To Dist. of Fla. 10-Corps..........	Feb., 1864
90th N. Y. Infy..........Nov., 1862	From Key West, Fla...............	To Key West, Fla................	Mch., 1863
Batty. A, 3d R. I. H'y Arty.Jan., 1863	From U. S. Forces Hilton Head.....	To U. S. Forces Folly Island, S. C.	Oct., 1863
3d R. I. Heavy Arty, Co. C.Jan., 1863	From U. S. Forces Hilton Head.....	To St. Helena Island, S. C........	June, 1863
174th Penna. Infy........Feb., 1863	From 2-Brig. 2-Div. 18-Corps....	To Dist. Hilton Head, S. C........	June, 1863
176th Penna. Infy........Feb., 1863	From 3-Brig. 2-Div. 18-Corps....	To Dist. Hilton Head, S. C........	June, 1863
11th Me. Infy..........Apr., 1863	From 1-Brig. 2-Div. 18-Corps....	To Fernandina, Fla..............	June, 1863
Indpt. N. Y. Batt'n........Apr., 1863	From 1-Brig. 2-Div. 18-Corps....	To St. Helena Island, S. C........	June, 1863
52d Penna. Infy..........Apr., 1863	From 2-Brig. 1-Div. 18-Corps....	To 2-Brig. 1-Div. Morris Island.....	July, 1863
104th Penna. Infy........Apr., 1863	From 2-Brig. 1-Div. 18-Corps....	To 2-Brig. 1-Div. Morris Island.....	July, 1863
1st N. Y. Engineers, Co. K.May, 1863	From U. S. Forces Hilton Head, S. C.	To U. S. Forces Hilton Head, S. C.	Dec., 1863
115th N. Y. Infy........June, 1863	From U. S. Forces Hilton Head, S. C.	To U. S. Forces Hilton Head, S. C.	Dec., 1863
1st S. C. Col'd..........June, 1863	From New Organ. (33-U. S. C. T.).	To Dist. Beaufort, S. C., Dept. South.	Apr., 1864
56th N. Y. Infy..........Aug., 1863	From Davis Brig. Folly Island, S. C.	To Dist. Beaufort, S. C., Dept. South.	Apr., 1864
8th Me. Infy..........Nov., 1863	From U. S. Forces Hilton Head, S. C.	To 2-Brig. 3-Div. 10-C Va. & N. C.	Apr., 1864
4th N. H. Infy..........Jan., 1864	From 1-Brig. Morris Island, S. C....	To 1-Brig. Vodges' Div. Dist. Fla...	Feb., 1864

U. S. FORCES HILTON HEAD, S. C. Organized Sept., 1862. Designated Hilton Head District Jan., 1864, and transferred to Reorganized Department of the South April, 1864.

COMMANDERS.

N. W. Brown	Col. 3d R. I. Heavy Arty	Sept. 3, 1862, to Oct. 5, 1862.
J. L. Frazer	Col. 47th N. Y. Infy	Oct. 5, 1862, to Oct. 20, 1862.
A. H. Terry	Brigadier General	Oct. 20, 1862, to May 12, 1863.
J. L. Chatfield	Col. 6th Conn. Infy	May 12, 1863, to July 2, 1863.
E. Metcalf	Col. 3d R. I. Heavy Arty	July 2, 1863, to Aug. 6, 1863.
D. W. C. Strawbridge	Col. 76th Penna. Infy	Aug. 6, 1863, to Nov. 9, 1863.
William B. Barton	Col. 48th N. Y. Infy	Nov. 9, 1863, to Dec. 6, 1863.
Truman Seymour	Brigadier General	Dec. 6, 1863, to Feb. 5, 1864.
J. B. Howell	Col. 85th Penna. Infy	Feb. 5, 1864, to Apr. 26, 1864.

7th Conn. Infy	Sept., 1862	From Dist. Hilton Head Dept. South.	To U. S. Forces Beaufort, S. C.	Sept., 1862
3d N. H. Infy	Sept., 1862	From Dist. Hilton Head Dept. South.	To Guss' Brig. Seabrook Island, S. C.	Apr., 1863
47th N. Y. Infy	Sept., 1862	From Dist. Hilton Head Dept. South.	To Ossabaw Sound 10-Corps	Apr., 1863
76th Penna. Infy	Sept., 1862	From Dist. Hilton Head Dept. South.	To Guss' Brig. Seabrook Island, S. C.	Apr., 1863
97th Penna. Infy	Sept., 1862	From Dist. Hilton Head Dept. South.	To Stevenson's Brig., Seabrook Isl.	Apr., 1863
3d R. I. H'vy Arty., Co. A.	Sept., 1862	From Dist. Hilton Head Dept. South.	To U. S. Forces Beaufort, S. C.	Jan., 1863
3d R. I. H'vy Arty., Co. B.	Sept., 1862	From Dist. Hilton Head Dept. South.	To U. S. Forces Folly Island, S. C.	July, 1863
3d R. I. H'vy Arty., Co. C.	Sept., 1862	From Dist. Hilton Head Dept. South.	To U. S. Forces, Beaufort, S. C.	Jan., 1863
3d R. I. H'vy Arty., Co. D.	Sept., 1862	From Dist. Hilton Head Dept. South.	To U. S. Forces, Folly Island, S. C.	Apr., 1863
3d R. I. H'vy Arty., Co. E.	Sept., 1862	From Dist. Hilton Head Dept. South.	To U. S. Forces Morris Island, S. C.	Nov., 1863
3d R. I. H'vy Arty., Co. F.	Sept., 1862	From Dist. Hilton Head Dept. South.	To Fort Pulaski, Ga.	Dec., 1863
3d R. I. H'vy Arty., Co. G.	Sept., 1862	From Dist. Hilton Head Dept. South.	To U. S. Forces Morris Island, S. C.	July, 1863
3d R. I. H'vy Arty., Co. H.	Sept., 1862	From Dist. Hilton Head Dept. South.	To U. S. Forces Folly Island, S. C.	Apr., 1863
3d R. I. H'vy Arty., Co. I.	Sept., 1862	From Dist. Hilton Head Dept. South.	To Fort Pulaski, Ga.	Dec., 1863
3d R. I. H'vy Arty., Co. K.	Sept., 1862	From Dist. Hilton Head Dept. South.	To Fort Pulaski, Ga.	Dec., 1863
3d R. I. H'vy Arty., Co. L.	Sept., 1862	From Dist. Hilton Head Dept. South.	To U. S. Forces Morris Island, S. C.	July, 1863
3d R. I. H'vy Arty., Co. M.	Sept., 1862	From Dist. Hilton Head Dept. South.	To Dist. Hilton Head Dept. South.	Apr., 1864
1st N. Y. Engineers	Sept., 1862	From Dist. Hilton Head Dept. South.	Dept. Va. and N. C. Co's B, D, E, F, H, K, L, M.	
Batty. E, 3d U. S. Arty.	Sept., 1862	From Dist. Hilton Head Dept. South.	To U. S. Forces Folly Island, S. C.	June, 1863
1st Mass. Cav., Co. M.	Dec., 1862	From U. S. Forces Beaufort, S. C.	To Henry's B'g. Dist. Hilt'n H'd, S. C.	Jan., 1864
115th N. Y. Infy	Jan., 1863	From Busteed's Brig. 4-Corps, Va.	To U. S. Forces Beaufort, S. C.	June, 1863
9th Me. Infy	Jan., 1863	From Fernandina, Fla.	To U. S. Forces St. Helena Island	June, 1863
8th Me. Infy	Apr., 186"	From U. S. Forces Beaufort, S. C.	To U. S. Forces Beaufort, S. C.	Nov., 1863
7th Conn. Infy. A. B. I. K.	Apr., 1863	From Fernandina, Fla.	To St. Helena Island, S. C.	June, 1863
6th Conn. Infy.	Apr., 1863	From Jacksonville, Fla.	To U. S. Forces Folly Island, S. C.	Apr., 1863
Batty. C, 1st U. S. Arty.	Apr., 1863	From Arty. Brig. 18-Corps.	To U. S. Forces Folly Island, S. C.	Apr., 1863
Batty. B, 1st U. S. Arty.	May, 1863	From U. S. Forces Beaufort, S. C.	To U. S. Forces St. Helena Island	June, 1863
1st Mass. Cav., Co. I.	May, 1863	From U. S. Forces Beaufort, S. C.	To Henry's Brig. Dist. Hilton Head	Jan., 1864
76th Penna. Infy.	June, 1863	From Guss' Brig. Seabrook Island	To U. S. Forces St. Helena Island	June, 1863
174th Penna. Infy.	June, 1863	From U. S. Forces Beaufort, S. C.	No change to Muster Out	Aug., 1863
176th Penna. Infy.	June, 1863	From U. S. Forces Beaufort, S. C.	No change to Muster Out	Aug., 1863
2d S. C. Col'd Infy.	June, 1863	From New Organization	To 2-Brig. 1-Div. Morris Island, S. C.	July, 1863
3d S. C. Col'd Infy.	June, 1863	From New Organization	To Barton's Brig. Hilton Head, S. C.	Dec., 1863
6th Conn. Infy.	July, 1863	From 1-Brig. Morris Island, S. C.	To 3-Brig. 1-Div. 10-Corps Va. & N. C.	Apr., 1864
76th Penna. Infy.	Aug., 1863	From 1-Brig. Morris Island, S. C.	To Barton's Brig. Hilton Head, S. C.	Dec., 1863
47th N. Y. Infy.	Nov., 1863	From Davis Brig. Folly Island, S. C.	To Barton's Brig. Hilton Head, S. C.	Dec., 1863
48th N. Y. Infy.	Nov., 1863	From St. Augustine and Beaufort.	To Barton's Brig. Hilton Head, S. C.	Dec., 1863
Batty. M, 1st U. S. Arty.	Nov., 1863	From U. S. Forces Beaufort, S. C.	To Arty. Dist. Fla.	Feb., 1864
115th N. Y. Infy.	Dec., 1863	From U. S. Forces Beaufort, S. C.	To Barton's Brig. Hilton Head, S. C.	Dec., 1863
Indpt. Batt'n N. Y. Infy.	Dec., 1863	From 2-Brig. Morris Island, S. C.	To Consol. with 47th N. Y.	Jan., 1864
3d R. I. H'vy Arty., Co. C.	Dec., 1863	From Gordon's Div. Folly Isl., S. C.	To Arty. Dist. Fla.	Feb., 1864
4th S. C. Col'd Infy.	Dec., 1863	From New Organization	To Barton's Brig. Hilton Head, S. C.	Dec., 1863
25th Ohio Infy.	Jan., 1864	From 2-B. Gordon's D. S. E. Fol. I.	To Dist. Hilton Head Dept. South.	Apr., 1864
3d R. I. H'vy Arty., Co. A.	Feb., 1864	From Folly Island Northern Dist.	To Arty. Dist. Fla.	Feb., 1864
3d R. I. H'vy Arty., Co. B.	Mch., 1864	From Morris Island Northern Dist.	To Dist. Hilton Head Dept. South.	Apr., 1864
9th U. S. Col'd Infy.	Mch., 1864	From New Organization	To Dist. Beaufort Dept. South.	Apr., 1864
76th Penna. Infy.	Mch., 1864	From Barton's Brig. Hilton Head	To 2-Brig. 2-Div. 10-C'ps Va. & N. C.	Apr., 1864

BARTON'S BRIGADE.—Org. Dec. 28, 1863. Transferred to Dist. Fla., Feb. 6, 1864.

COMMANDER.

William B. Barton	Col. 48th N. Y. Infy	Dec., 1863, to Feb., 1864.

47th N. Y. Infy	Dec., 1863	From Unatt. Hilton Head, S. C.	To Barton's Brig. Dist. Fla.	Feb., 1864
48th N. Y. Infy	Dec., 1863	From Unatt. Hilton Head, S. C.	To Barton's Brig. Dist. Fla.	Feb., 1864
115th N. Y. Infy	Dec., 1863	From Unatt. Hilton Head, S. C.	To Barton's Brig. Dist. Fla.	Feb., 1864
3d S. C. Col'd Infy	Dec., 1863	From Unatt. Hilton Head, S. C.	To 3-Brig. Vodges Div. Dist. Fla.	Feb., 1864
4th S. C. Col'd Infy	Dec., 1863	From Unatt. Hilton Head, S. C.	To Consol. with 3d S. C.	Jan., 1864
76th Penna. Infy	Jan., 1864	From Unatt. Hilton Head, S. C.	To Dist. Hilton Head, S. C.	Feb., 1864

HOWELL'S BRIGADE.—Org. Dec., 1863.

COMMANDER.

J. B. Howell	Col. 85th Penna. Infy	Dec. 28, 1863, to Feb. 6, 1864.
R. Duryea	Col. 6th Penna. Infy	Feb. 6, 1864, to April 25, 1864.

85th Penna. Infy	Dec., 1863	From Howell's Brig. Morris Island.	To 1-Brig. 1-Div. 10-C'ps Va. & N. C.	Apr., 1864
62d Ohio Infy	Dec., 1863	From Howell's Brig. Morris Island.	To 1-Brig. 1-Div. 10-C'ps Va. & N. C.	Apr., 1864
67th Ohio Infy	Dec., 1863	From Howell's Brig. Morris Island.	To 1-Brig. 1-Div. 10-C'ps Va. & N. C.	Apr., 1864
39th Illinois	Dec., 1863	From Howell's Brig. Morris Island.	To 1-Brig. 1-Div. 10-C'ps Va. & N. C.	Apr., 1864
8th U. S. Col'd Infy	Jan., 1864	From New Organization	To Hawley's Brig. Dist Fla.	Feb., 1864

MONTGOMERY'S BRIGADE.—Organized Jan. 31, 1864. Transferred to Dist. Fla., Feb., 1864.

COMMANDER.

J. Montgomery	2d S. C. Col'd Infy	Jan. 31, 1864, to Feb. 6, 1864.

3d U. S. Col'd Infy	Jan., 1864	From 3-Brig. Morris Island, S. C.	To 2-Brig. Vodges Div. Dist. Fla.	Feb., 1864
2d S. C. Col'd Infy	Jan., 1864	From 3-Brig. Morris Island, S. C.	To 3-Brig. Vodges Div. Dist. Fla.	Feb., 1864
54th Mass. Col'd Infy	Jan., 1864	From 3-Brig. Morris Island, S. C.	To 3-Brig. Ames Div. Dist. Fla.	Feb., 1864

HENRY'S BRIGADE.—Organized Jan. 18, 1864. Transferred to Dist. of Fla., Feb., 1864.

COMMANDER.

Guy V. Henry	Col. 40th Mass. Infy	Jan. 18, 1864, to Feb. 6, 1864.

40th Mass. Infy	Jan., 1864	From 2-B. Gordon's D. S. E. Folly Is.	To Light Brig. Dist. Fla.	Feb., 1864
Indpt. Batt'n Mass. Cav.	Jan., 1864	From Unatt. Hilton Hd. and Beauf't.	To Light Brig. Dist. Fla.	Feb., 1864
Batty B, 1st U. S. Arty.	Jan., 1864	From Arty. Gordon's D. S. E. Fol. Is.	To Light Brig. Dist. Fla.	Feb., 1864

FORT PULASKI, GA.—

48th N. Y. Infy..........Sept., 1862	From Dist. Hilton Head, S. C.......	To St. Helena Island, S. C., 8 Co's..	June,	1863
3d R. I. H'vy Arty., Co. G.Sept., 1862	From Dist. Hilton Head, S. C.......	To Morris Island Northern Dist.....	Mch.,	1864
3d R. I. H'vy Arty., Co. F.Dec., 1863	From Dist. Hilton Head, S. C.......	To Ft. Pulaski Dist. Hilton Head....	Apr.,	1864
3d R. I. H'vy Arty., Co. K.Dec., 1863	From Dist. Hilton Head, S. C.......	To Ft. Pulaski Dist. Hilton Head....	Apr.,	1864
3d R. I. H'vy Arty., Co. L.Dec., 1863	From Dist. Hilton Head, S. C.......	To Ft. Pulaski Dist. Hilton Head....	Apr.,	1864
3d R. I. H'vy Arty., Co. D.Mch., 1864	From Dist. Hilton Head, S. C.......	To Ft. Pulaski Dist. Hilton Head....	Apr.,	1864

ST. AUGUSTINE, FLA.—

4th N. H. Infy..........Sept., 1862	From St. Augustine Fla. Dept. South.	To U. S. Forces Beaufort, S. C......	Sept.,	1862
7th N. H. Infy..........Sept., 1862	From U. S. Forces Beaufort, S. C....	To Fernandina, Fla.................	May,	1863
7th Conn. Infy, 6-Co's.....Apr., 1863	From Fernandina, Fla...............	To 3-Brig. Morris Island, S. C.....	Aug.,	1863
48th N. Y. Infy, 8 Co's.....Aug., 1863	From 2-Brig. 2-Div. Morris I., S. C.	To U. S. Forces Hilton Head, S. C...	Oct.,	1863
24th Mass. Infy..........Sept., 1863	From 3-Brig. Morris Island, S. C...	To Jacksonville, Fla...............	Feb.,	1864
10th Conn. Infy..........Oct., 1863	From 3-Brig. Morris Island, S. C...	To 2-Brig. 1-Div. 10-C'ps Va. & N. C.	Apr.,	1864

FERNANDINA, FLA.—

9th Me. Infy..........Sept., 1862	From Fernandina, Fla., Dept. South..	To U. S. Forces Hilton Head, S. C..	Jan.,	1863
7th Conn. Infy..........Jan., 1863	From. U. S. Forces Beaufort, S. C...	To St. August., Fla. C. D. E. F. G. H.	Apr.,	1863
		To St. Helena Isl. S. C. A. B. I. K..	Apr.,	1863
7th N. H. Infy..........May, 1863	From St. Augustine, Fla............	To U. S. Forces St. Helena Island...	June,	1863
11th Me. Infy..........June, 1863	From U. S. Forces Beaufort, S. C....	To 1-Brig. Morris Island, S. C.....	Oct.,	1863
4th S. C. Col'd Infy......Sept., 1863	From New Organization.............	To U. S. Forces Hilton Head, S. C..	Dec.,	1863
97th Penna. Infy..........Oct., 1863	From 1-Brig. Morris Island, S. C.....	To 1-Brig. 3-Div. 10-C'ps Va. & N. C.	Apr.,	1864

OSSABAW SOUND, GA.—

47th N. Y. Infy..........Apr., 1863	From U. S. Forces Hilton Head, S. C.	To U. S. Forces Folly Island, S. C..	July,	1863

KEY WEST, FLA.—

90th N. Y. Infy..........Sept., 1862	From Key West Dept. South.......	To U. S. Forces Beaufort, S. C.....	Nov.,	1862
47th Penna. Infy..........Nov., 1862	From U. S. Forces Beaufort, S. C...	To Dist. Key West Dept. Gulf......	Nov.,	1862
90th N. Y. Infy..........Mch., 1863	From U. S. Forces Beaufort, S. C...	To Dist. Key West Dept. Gulf......	Apr.,	1863

DETACHMENT 18th ARMY CORPS, ST. HELENA ISLAND.

COMMANDERS.

J. G. Foster.............	Major General.....................	Jan., 1863, to Feb., 1863.	
H. M. Naglee..........	Brigadier General.................	Temp'y in Feby.	

1st DIVISION.— COMMANDERS.

H. M. Naglee..........	Brigadier General.................	Jan., 1863, to Mch. 5, 1863.	
O. S. Ferry...........	Brigadier General................	Mch. 5, 1863, to Apr. 17, 1863.	

1st BRIGADE.— COMMANDERS.

C. A. Heckman..........	Brigadier General.................	Jan., 1863, to Mch. 6, 1863.	
T. G. Stevenson.........	Brigadier General.................	Mch. 6, 1863, to Apr. 17, 1863.	

23d Mass. Infy..........Jan., 1863	From 1-Bg. 2-Div. 18-C'ps Dept. N. C.	To Dist. Beaufort, S. C., 10-Corps....	Apr.,	1863
9th N. J. Infy..........Jan., 1863	From 1-Bg. 2-Div. 18-C'ps Dept. N. C.	To Dist. Beaufort, S. C., 10-Corps....	Apr.,	1863
81st N. Y. Infy..........Jan., 1863	From 1-Bg. 2-Div. 18-C'ps Dept. N. C.	To Dist. Beaufort, S. C., 10-Corps....	Apr.,	1863
98th N. Y. Infy..........Jan., 1863	From 1-Bg. 2-Div. 18-C'ps Dept. N. C.	To Dist. Beaufort, S. C., 10-Corps....	Apr.,	1863

2d BRIGADE.— COMMANDER.

W. W. H. Davis..........	Col. 104th Penna. Infy...........	Jan., 1863, to Apr., 1863.	

10th Conn. Infy..........Jan., 1863	From 2-Bg. 4-Div. 18-C'ps Dept. N. C.	To Stevenson's Brig. Seabrook Isl...	Apr.,	1863
24th Mass. Infy..........Jan., 1863	From 2-Bg. 4-Div. 18-C'ps Dept. N. C.	To Stevenson's Brig. Seabrook Isl...	Apr.,	1863
52d Penna. Infy..........Jan., 1863	From 2-Bg. 2-Div. 18-C'ps Dept. N. C.	To U. S. Forces Beaufort, S. C.....	Apr.,	1863
104th Penna. Infy..........Jan., 1863	From 2-Bg. 2-Div. 18-C'ps Dept. N. C.	To U. S. Forces Beaufort, S. C.....	Apr.,	1863

2d DIVISION.— COMMANDERS.

O. S. Ferry.............	Brigadier General.................	Jan., 1863, to Mch. 6, 1863.	
C. A. Heckman..........	Brigadier General.................	Mch. 5, 1863, to Apr. 16, 1863.	

1st BRIGADE.— COMMANDERS.

T. G. Stevenson.........	Brigadier General.................	Jan., 1863, to Mch. 6, 1863.	
J. J. De Forest...........	Col. 81st N. Y. Infy.............	Mch. 6, 1863, to Apr. 16, 1863.	

11th Me. Infy..........Jan., 1863	From 2-Bg. 2-Div. 18-C'ps, Dept. N. C.	To U. S. Forces Beaufort, S. C.....	Apr.,	1863
100th N. Y. Infy..........Jan., 1863	From 2-Bg. 2-Div. 18-C'ps, Dept. N. C.	To Stevenson's Brig. Seabrook I...	Apr.,	1863
Indpt. Batt'n N. Y. Infy..Jan., 1863	From 2-Bg. 2-Div. 18-C'ps, Dept. N. C.	To U. S. Forces Beaufort, S. C.....	Apr.,	1863

2d BRIGADE.— COMMANDER.

J. B. Howell............	Col. 85th Penna. Infy...........	Jan., 1863, to Apr., 1863.	

56th N. Y. Infy..........Jan., 1863	From 2-Brig. 3-Div. 18-C. Dept. N. C.	To Stevenson's Brig. Seabrook I...	Apr.,	1863
85th Penna. Infy..........Jan., 1863	From 2-Brig. 3-Div. 18-C. Dept. N. C.	To U. S. Forces Folly Island, S. C..	Apr.,	1863
174th Penna. Infy..........Jan., 1863	From 2-Brig. 3-Div. 18-C. Dept. N. C.	To U. S. Forces Beaufort, S. C.....	Apr.,	1863

3d BRIGADE.— COMMANDER.

T. O. Osborne..........	Col. 39th Ill. Infy.............	Jan., 1863, to Apr., 1863.	

39th Ill. Infy..........Jan., 1863	From 1-Brig. 3-Div. 18-C. Dept. N. C.	To U. S. Forces Folly Island, S. C..	Apr.,	1863
62d Ohio Infy..........Jan., 1863	From 1-Brig. 3-Div. 18-C. Dept. N. C.	To U. S. Forces Folly Island, S. C..	Apr.,	1863
67th Ohio Infy..........Jan., 1863	From 1-Brig. 3-Div. 18-C. Dept. N. C.	To U. S. Forces Folly Island, S. C..	Apr.,	1863
176 Penna. Infy..........Jan., 1863	From 1-Brig. 3-Div. 18-C. Dept. N. C.	To Hilton Head, S. C..............	Feb.,	1863

ARTILLERY.—

Batty. B, 3d N. Y. Arty....Jan., 1863	From Arty. Brig. 18-C. Dept. N. C.	To Seabrook Island, S. C...........	Apr.,	1863
Batty. C, 3d N. Y. Arty....Jan., 1863	From Arty. Brig. 18-C. Dept. N. C.	No change to Muster Out...........	May,	1863
Batty F. 3d N. Y. Arty....Jan., 1863	From Arty. Brig. 18-C. Dept. N. C.	To U. S. Forces Folly Island, S. C..	Apr.,	1863
N. Y. Marine Arty. Det....Jan., 1863	From Arty. Brig. 18-C. Dept. N. C.	Broken Up.......................	Mch.,	1863
Batty. C, 1st U. S. Arty....Jan., 1863	From Arty. Brig. 18-C. Dept. N. C.	To U. S. Forces Hilton Head, S. C..	Apr.,	1863

U. S. FORCES ST. HELENA ISLAND.—Organized June 10, 1863. Transferred to U. S. Forces Morris Island, S. C., July, 1863. Reorganized Dec., 1863. Transferred to District of Florida, Feb. 5, 1864.

COMMANDERS.

Geo. C. Strong........	Brigadier General.................	June 13, 1863, to July 5, 1863.	
J. R. Hawley...........	Col. 7th Conn. Infy...............	Dec., 1863, to Feb. 5, 1864.	

9th Me. Infy..........June, 1863	From U. S. Forces Hilton Head, S. C.	To 2-Brig. U. S. Forces Folly Island.	July,	1863
7th N. H. 5 Co's..........June, 1863	From U. S. Forces Hilton Head, S. C.	To 1-Brig. U. S. Forces Folly Island.	July,	1863
76th Penna. Infy..........June, 1863	From U. S. Forces Hilton Head, S. C.	To 2-Brig. U. S. Forces Folly Island.	July,	1863
7th Conn. In. Co's A, B, I, K June, '63	From U. S. Forces Hilton Head, S. C.	To 2-Brig. U. S. Forces Folly Island.	July,	1863
54th Mass. Col'd Infy.....June, 1863	From New Organization...........	To 3-Brig. 1-Div. Morris Island.....	July,	1863
3d N. H. Infy..........June, 1863	From U. S. Forces Seabrook Island..	To 2-Brig. U. S. Forces Folly Island.	July,	1863

U. S. FORCES ST. HELENA ISLAND.—Continued.

48th N. Y. Infy...........June, 1863	From Fort Pulaski, Ga............	To 2-Brig. U. S. Forces Folly Island.	July, 1863
Indpt. Batt'n N. Y. Infy..June, 1863	From Dist. Beaufort, S. C......	To 1 Brig. U. S. Forces Folly Island.	July, 1863
Batty. B, 1st U. S. Arty..June, 1863	From U. S. Forces Beaufort, S. C...	To Arty. 1-Div. Morris Island, S. C.	July, 1863
Batty. C, 3d R. I. H. A..June, 1863	From U. S. Forces Beaufort, S. C...	To 2-Brig. U. S. Forces Folly Island.	July, 1863
7th Conn. Infy...........Nov., 1863	From 3-Brig. U. S. Forces Morris I.	To Hawley's Brig. Dist. Fla.......	Feb., 1864
7th N. H. Infy Seabrook Isl..Dec., 1863	From 3-Brig. U. S. Forces Morris I.	To Hawley's Brig. Dist. Fla.......	Feb., 1864

U. S. FORCES SEABROOK ISLAND.—Organized April, 1863. Transferred to Morris Island, S. C., July, 1863.

COMMANDERS.

O. S. Ferry............	Brigadier General...............	Apr. 16, 1863, to May 11, 1863.
T. G. Stevenson........	Brigadier General...............	May 11, 1863, to July 6, 1863.

STEVENSON'S BRIGADE.—   COMMANDER.

T. G. Stevenson........	Brigadier General...............	

10th Conn. Infy.........Apr., 1863	From 2-Brig. 1-Div. Det. 18-Corps..	To 1-Brig. 1-Div. Morris Island, S. C.	July, 1863
24th Mass. Infy..........Apr., 1863	From 2-Brig. 1-Div. Det. 18-Corps..	To 1-Brig. 1-Div. Morris Island, S. C.	July, 1863
56th N. Y. Infy..........Apr., 1863	From 2-Brig. 2-Div. Det. 18-Corps..	To 2-Brig. 1-Div. Morris Island, S. C.	July, 1863
97th Penna. Infy.........Apr., 1863	From U. S. Forces Hilton Head, S. C.	To 1-Brig. 1-Div. Morris Island, S. C.	July, 1863
Batty. B, 3d N. Y. Arty....June, 1863	From Guss' Brig. Seabrook Island..	To Arty. 1-Div. Morris Island, S. C.	July, 1863

GUSS' BRIGADE.—   COMMANDER.

H. R. Guss.............	Col. 76th Penna. Infy............	Apr., 1863, to June, 1863.

3d N. H. Infy...........Apr., 1863	From U. S. Forces Hilton Head, S. C.	To U. S. Forces St. Helena Island...	June, 1863
76th Penna. Infy.........Apr., 1863	From U. S. Forces Hilton Head, S. C.	To U. S. Forces St. Helena Island...	June, 1863
Batty. B, 3d N. Y. Arty...Apr., 1863	From Arty. Brig. 18-Corps.........	To Stevenson's Brig. Seabrook I....	June, 1863

U. S. FORCES FOLLY ISLAND, S. C.—Organized Apr., 1863. Transferred to U. S. Forces Morris Island, S. C., July, 1863.

COMMANDERS.

Israel Vodges..........	Brigadier General...............	Apr. 8, 1863, to July 19, 1863.
W. W. H. Davis........	Col. 104th Penna. Infy...........	July 19, 1863, to July 28, 1863.

6th Conn. Infy..........Apr., 1863	From U. S. Forces Hilton Head, S. C.	To 2-Brig. Folly Island, S. C.......	June, 1863
39th Ill. Infy...........Apr., 1863	From 3-Brig. 2-Div. Det. 18-Corps...	To 2-Brig. Folly Island, S. C.......	June, 1863
62d Ohio Infy...........Apr., 1863	From 3-Brig. 2-Div. Det. 18-Corps...	To 1-Brig. Folly Island, S. C.......	June, 1863
67th Ohio Infy...........Apr., 1863	From 3-Brig. 2-Div. Det. 18-Corps...	To 1-Brig. Folly Island, S. C.......	June, 1863
100th N. Y. Infy..........Apr., 1863	From 1-Brig. 2-Div. Det. 18-Corps..	To 2-Brig. Folly Island, S. C.......	June, 1863
85th Penna. Infy.........Apr., 1863	From 2-Brig. 2-Div. Det. 18-Corps..	To 2-Brig. Folly Island, S. C.......	June, 1863
3d R. I. H'vy Arty., Co. D.Apr., 1863	From U. S. Forces Hilton Head, S. C.	To U. S. Forces Morris Island, S. C.	July, 1863
3d R. I. H'vy Arty., Co. I.Apr., 1863	From U. S. Forces Hilton Head, S. C.	To U. S. Forces Morris Island, S. C.	July, 1863
Batty. F, 3d N. Y. Arty..Apr., 1863	From U. S. Forces St. Helena Isl..	To U. S. Forces Morris Island, S. C.	July, 1863
Batty. C, 1st U. S. Arty..Apr., 1863	From U. S. Forces Hilton Head....	To U. S. Forces Morris Island, S. C.	July, 1863
1st Mass. Cav. Det.......Apr., 1863	From U. S. Forces Hilton Head....	To Unatt. Morris Island, S. C......	July, 1863
4th N. H. Infy...........Apr., 1863	From U. S. Forces Beaufort, S. C...	To 1-Br. U. S. Forces Folly Isl., S. C.	June, 1863
Batty. E, 3d U. S. Arty...June, 1863	From U. S. Forces Hilton Head, S. C	To U. S. Forces Morris Island, S. C.	July, 1863

1st BRIGADE.—Organized June, 1863. Discontinued July, 1863.

COMMANDER.

H. S. Putnam..........	Col. 7th N. H. Infy............	June, 1863, to July 18, 1863.	Killed.

4th N. H. Infy...........June, 1863	From U. S. Forces Folly Isl., S. C..	To 1-Brig. Terry's 1-Div. Morris Isl.	July, 1863
7th N. H. Infy...........June, 1863	From Fernandina, Fla............	To 1-Brig. 2-Div. Morris Island.....	July, 1863
62d Ohio Infy...........June, 1863	From U. S. Forces Folly Isl., S. C..	To 1-Brig. 2-Div. Morris Island.....	July, 1863
67th Ohio Infy...........June, 1863	From U. S. Forces Folly Isl., S. C..	To 1-Brig. 2-Div. Morris Island.....	July, 1863
39th Ill. Infy...........July, 1863	From 2-Br. U. S. Forces Folly I., S.C.	To 1-Brig. 2-Div. Morris Island.....	July, 1863
100th N. Y. Infy..........July, 1863	From 2-Br. U. S. Forces Folly I., S.C.	To 2-Brig. 1-Div. Morris Island.....	July, 1863
85th Penna. Infy.........July, 1863	From 2-Br. U. S. Forces Folly I., S.C.	To 1-Brig. 2-Div. Morris Island.....	July, 1863
Indpt. Battn. N. Y. Infy..July, 1863	From U. S. Forces St. Helena Isl...	To 1-Brig. 2-Div. Morris Island.....	July, 1863

2d BRIGADE.—   COMMANDER.

J. B. Howell..........	Col. 85th Penna. Infy............	June, 1863, to July, 1863.

6th Conn. Infy..........June, 1863	From U. S. Forces Folly Isl., S. C..	To 2-Brig. 2-Div. Morris Island.....	July, 1863
39th Ill. Infy...........June, 1863	From U. S. Forces Folly Isl., S. C..	To 1-Brig. Folly Island, S. C.......	July, 1863
100th N. Y. Infy..........June, 1863	From U. S. Forces Folly Isl., S. C..	To 1-Brig. Folly Island, S. C.......	July, 1863
85th Penna. Infy.........June, 1863	From U. S. Forces Folly Isl., S. C..	To 1-Brig. Folly Island, S. C.......	July, 1863
7th Conn. Infy..........July, 1863	From U. S. Forces St. Helena Isl...	To 2-Brig. 2-Div. Morris Island.....	July, 1863
(Co's A, B, I, K.)			
9th Me. Infy...........July, 1863	From U. S. Forces St. Helena Isl...	To 2-Brig. 2-Div. Morris Island.....	July, 1863
3d N. H. Infy...........July, 1863	From U. S. Forces St. Helena Isl...	To 2-Brig. 2-Div. Morris Island.....	July, 1863
48th N. Y. Infy..........July, 1863	From U. S. Forces St. Helena Isl...	To 2-Brig. 2-Div. Morris Island.....	July, 1863
76th Penna. Infy.........July, 1863	From U. S. Forces St. Helena Isl...	To 2-Brig. 2-Div. Morris Island.....	July, 1863
3d R. I. Heavy Art. Co. C.July, 1863	From U. S. Forces St. Helena Isl...	To U. S. Forces Morris Island......	July, 1863

DAVIS' BRIGADE.—   COMMANDER.

W. W. H. Davis........	Col. 104th Penna. Infy...........	July 19, 1863, to Aug. 30, 1863.

56th N. Y. Infy..........July, 1863	From 2-Brig. 1-Div. Morris Isl., S. C.	To U. S. Forces Beaufort, S. C.....	Aug., 1863
52d Penna. Infy.........July, 1863	From 2-Brig. 1-Div. Morris Isl., S. C.	To 5-Brig. U. S. Forces Morris Isl..	Aug., 1863
104th Penna. Infy........July, 1863	From 2-Brig. 1-Div. Morris Isl., S. C.	To 5-Brig. U. S. Forces Morris Isl..	Aug., 1863
MISCELLANEOUS.—			
47th N. Y. Infy..........July, 1863	From Ossabaw Sound, Ga.........	To 5-Brig. U. S. Forces Morris Isl..	Aug., 1863
Indpt. Battn. N. Y. Infy..July, 1863	From 1-Brig. 2-Div. Morris Isl., S. C.	To 5-Brig. U. S. Forces Morris Isl..	Aug., 1863
1st Conn. Batty.........July, 1863	From U. S. Forces Beaufort, S. C...	To Vodges' Div. N. E. Folly Isl., S. C.	Aug., 1863
Batty. B, 3d N. Y. Arty...July, 1863	From U. S. Forces Seabrook I., S. C.	To U. S. Forces Morris Island, S. C.	Aug., 1863

TERRY'S 1st DIVISION, 10th CORPS.—Organized July, 1863. Reorganized U. S. Forces Morris Island, S. C., July 19, 1863.

COMMANDER.

A. H. Terry............	Brigadier General................	July 6, 1863, to July 19, 1863.

1st BRIGADE.—   COMMANDER.

T. G. Stevenson........	Brigadier General................	July 6, 1863, to July 19, 1863.

10th Conn. Infy.........July, 1863	From U. S. Forces Seabrook I., S. C.	To 3-Brig. U. S. Forces Morris Isl..	July, 1863
97th Penna. Infy.........July, 1863	From U. S. Forces Seabrook I., S. C.	To 3-Brig. U. S. Forces Morris Isl..	July, 186.
4th N. H. Infy...........July, 1863	From 1-Brig. U. S. Forces Folly Isl.	To 1-Brig. U. S. Forces Morris Isl..	July, 1863
24th Mass. Infy..........July, 1863	From 1-Brig. U. S. Forces Seabrook I.	To 3-Brig. U. S. Forces Morris Isl..	July, 1863

2d BRIGADE.—

	COMMANDER.		
W. W. H. Davis........	Col. 104th Penna. Infy............	July 6, 1863. to July 19, 1863.	

56th N. Y. Infy.......July, 1863	From U. S. Forces Seabrook Island.	To Davis' Brig. Folly Island, S. C..	July, 1863
100th N. Y. Infy.......July, 1863	From 1-Brig. U. S. Forces Folly Isl.	To 3-Brig. U. S. Forces Morris Isl..	July, 1863
52d Penna. Infy.......July, 1863	From U. S. Forces Beaufort, S. C...	To Davis' Brig. Folly Island, S. C..	July, 1863
104th Penna. Infy.......July, 1863	From U. S. Forces Beaufort, S. C...	To Davis' Brig. Folly Island, S. C..	July, 1863

3d BRIGADE.—

	COMMANDER.		
James Montgomery	Col. 2d S. C. Col'd Infy............	July 6, 1863, to July 19, 1863.	

54th Mass. Col'd Infy.....July, 1863	From U. S. Forces St. Helena Island.	To 4-Brig. U. S. Forces Morris Isl..	July, 1863
2d S. C. Col'd Infy......July, 1863	From U. S. Forces Hilton Head, S. C.	To 4-Brig. U. S. Forces Morris Isl..	July, 1863

SEYMOUR'S 2d DIVISION.—Merged into U. S. Forces Morris Island, S. C., July 19, 1863.

	COMMANDER.		
Truman Seymour	Brigadier General	July 6. 1863, to July 19, 1863.	

1st BRIGADE.—

	COMMANDER.		
Israel Vodges	Brigadier General	July 6, 1863, to July 19, 1863.	

7th N. H. Infy.......July, 1863	From 1-Brig. U. S. Forces Folly Isl.	To 2-Brig. U. S. Forces Morris Isl..	July, 1863
Indpt. Battn. N. Y. Infy.July, 1863	From 1-Brig. U. S. Forces Folly Isl.	To 2-Brig. U. S. Forces Morris Isl..	July, 1863
85th Penna. Infy.......July, 1863	From 1-Brig. U. S. Forces Folly Isl.	To 2-Brig. U. S. Forces Morris Isl..	July, 1863
62d Ohio Infy..........July, 1863	From 1-Brig. U. S. Forces Folly Isl.	To 2-Brig. U. S. Forces Morris Isl..	July, 1863
67th Ohio Infy..........July, 1863	From 1-Brig. U. S. Forces Folly Isl.	To 2-Brig. U. S. Forces Morris Isl..	July, 1863
39th Ill. Infy..........July, 1863	From 1-Brig. U. S. Forces Folly Isl.	To 2-Brig. U. S. Forces Morris Isl..	July, 1863

2d BRIGADE.—

	COMMANDER.		
Geo. C. Strong........	Brigadier General	July 6, 1863. to July 18, 1863.	Mort. Wnd.

9th Me. Infy.......July, 1863	From 2-Brig. U. S. Forces Folly Isl.	To 1-Brig. U. S. Forces Morris Isl..	July, 1863
3d N. H. Infy.......July, 1863	From 2-Brig. U. S. Forces Folly Isl.	To 1-Brig. U. S. Forces Morris Isl..	July, 1863
6th Conn. Infy.......July, 1863	From 2-Brig. U. S. Forces Folly Isl.	To 1-Brig. U. S. Forces Morris Isl..	July, 1863
7th Conn. Infy.......July, 1863	From 2-Brig. U. S. Forces Folly Isl.	To 1-Brig. U. S. Forces Morris Isl..	July, 1863
(Co's A, B, I, K.)			
48th N. Y. Infy.......July, 1863	From 2-Brig. U. S. Forces Folly Isl.	To 1-Brig. U. S. Forces Morris Isl..	July, 1863
76th Penna. Infy.......July, 1863	From 2-Brig. U. S. Forces Folly Isl.	To 1-Brig. U. S. Forces Morris Isl..	July, 1863

U. S. FORCES MORRIS ISLAND, S. C.—Organized July 19, 1863. Transferred to Morris Island, Northern District, Jan. 15, 1864.

	COMMANDERS.		
A. H. Terry............	Brigadier General	July 19, 1863, to Oct. 18, 1863.	
Truman Seymour	Brigadier General	Oct. 18. 1863, to Nov. 10, 1863.	
A. H. Terry............	Brigadier General	Nov. 10. 1863, to Jan. 15. 1864.	

1st BRIGADE.—

	COMMANDER.		
Israel Vodges	Brigadier General	July 19, 1863, to Aug. 1, 1863.	
H. R. Guss............	Col. 97th Penna. Infy............	Aug. 1, 1863, to Oct. 11, 1863.	
H. M. Plaisted........	Col. 11th Me. Infy................	Oct. 11. 1863, to Nov. 23, 1863.	
T. G. Stevenson........	Brigadier General	Nov. 23, 1863, to Jan. 15, 1864.	

9th Me. Infy..........July, 1863	From 2-Brig. 2-Div. Morris Island..	To 1-Brig. Morris Isl., North. Dist..	Jan., 1864
3d N. H. Infy..........July, 1863	From 2-Brig. 2-Div. Morris Island..	To 1-Brig. Morris Isl., North. Dist..	Jan., 1864
4th N. H. Infy..........July, 1863	From 2-Brig. 1-Div. Morris Island..	To 1-Brig. Morris Isl., North. Dist..	Jan., 1864
6th Conn. Infy..........July, 1863	From 2-Brig. 2-Div. Morris Island..	To U. S. Forces Hilton Head, S. C..	July, 1863
7th Conn. Infy..........July, 1863	From 2-Brig. 2-Div. Morris Island..	To 3-Brig. U. S. Forces Morris Isl..	Aug., 1863
(Co's A, B, I, K.)			
48th N. Y. Infy..........July, 1863	From 2-Brig. 2-Div. Morris Island..	To St. Augustine, Fla............	July, 1863
76th Penna. Infy..........July, 1863	From 2-Brig. 2-Div. Morris Island..	To U. S. Forces Hilton Head, S. C..	Aug., 1863
11th Me. Infy..........Oct., 1863	From Fernandina, Fla............	To 1-Brig. Morris Isl., North. Dist..	Jan., 1864
7th N. H. Infy..........Nov., 1863	From 3-Brig. U. S. Forces Morris I.	To St. Helena Island, S. C.........	Dec.. 1863
7th Conn. Infy..........Nov., 1863	From St. Helena Island, S. C.......	To St. Helena Island, S. C.........	Dec.. 1863

2d BRIGADE.—Transferred to Gordon's Division, Folly Island, S. C., Oct., 1863. Reorganized Nov., 1863, from 5th Brigade U. S. Forces Morris Island, S. C.

	COMMANDERS.		
J. B. Howell...........	Col. 85th Penna. Infy............	July 19. 1863, to Sept. 19, 1863.	
T. O. Osborne........	Col. 39th Ill. Infy................	Sept. 19, 1863, to Oct. 12, 1863.	
W. W. H. Davis.......	Col. 104th Penna. Infy............	Nov. 23, 1863, to Dec. 5, 1863.	
G. B. Dandy........	Col. 100th N. Y. Infy............	Dec. 5. 1863, to Dec. 20, 1863.	
W. W. H. Davis........	Col. 104th Penna. Infy............	Dec. 20, 1863, to Jan. 15. 1864.	

85th Penna. Infy........July, 1863	From 1-Brig. 2-Div. Morris Island..	To 3-Br. Gordon's Div. S. E. Folly I.	Oct., 1863
Indpt. Battn. N. Y. Infy..July, 1863	From 1-Brig. 2-Div. Morris Island..	To Davis' Brig. Folly Island, S. C..	July, 1863
62d Ohio Infy........July, 1863	From 1-Brig. 2-Div. Morris Island..	To 3-Br. Gordon's Div. S. E. Folly I.	Oct., 1863
67th Ohio Infy........July, 1863	From 1-Brig. 2-Div. Morris Island..	To 3-Br. Gordon's Div. S. E. Folly I.	Oct., 1863
39th Ill. Infy........July, 1863	From 1-Brig. 2-Div. Morris Island..	To 3-Br. Gordon's Div. S. E. Folly I.	Oct., 1863
2d S. C. Col'd Infy......July, 1863	From 3-Brig. 1-Div. Morris Island..	To 4-Brig. U. S. Forces Morris Isl..	Aug., 1863
52d Penna. Infy......Nov., 1863	From 5-Brig. U. S. Forces Morris I.	To 2-Brig. Morris Isl., North. Dist..	Jan., 1864
104th Penna. Infy......Nov., 1863	From 5-Brig. U. S. Forces Morris I.	To 2-Brig. Morris Isl., North. Dist..	Jan., 1864
100th N. Y. Infy......Nov., 1863	From 3-Brig. U. S. Forces Morris I.	To 2-Brig. Morris Isl., North. Dist..	Jan., 1864
Indpt. Battn. N. Y. Infy..Nov., 1863	From 5-Brig. U. S. Forces Morris I.	To Dist. Hilton Head. S. C.........	Dec.. 1863

3d BRIGADE.—Discontinued Nov., 1863. Reorganized Nov. 23, 1863, from 4th Brigade U. S. Forces Mor ris Island. S. C. Transferred to Dist. Hilton Head, S. C., Jan. 15, 1864.

	COMMANDERS.		
T. G. Stevenson........	Brigadier General	July 19, 1863. to Sept. 19, 1863.	
J. R. Hawley..........	Col. 7th Conn. Infy...............	Sept. 19, 1863, to Oct. 19, 1863.	
T. G. Stevenson........	Brigadier General	Oct. 19. 1863, to Nov. 23, 1863.	
J. Montgomery	Col. 2d S. C. Col'd Infy............	Nov. 23, 1863, to Jan. 15. 1864.	

7th N. H. Infy..........July, 1863	From 1-Brig. 2-Div. Morris Island..	To 1-Brig. U. S. Forces Morris Isl..	Nov., 1863
24th Mass. Infy........July, 1863	From 1-Brig. 1-Div. Morris Island..	To St. Augustine. Fla............	Sept., 1863
54th Mass. Col'd Infy.....July, 1863	From 3-Brig. 1-Div. Morris Island..	To 4-Brig. U. S. Forces Morris Isl..	Aug., 1863
10th Conn. Infy........July, 1863	From 1-Brig. 1-Div. Morris Island..	To St. Augustine. Fla............	Oct., 1863
97th Penna. Infy........July, 1863	From 1-Brig. 1-Div. Morris Island..	To 1-Brig. U. S. Forces Morris Isl..	Nov., 1863
100th N. Y. Infy........July, 1863	From 1-Brig. 2-Div. Morris Island..	To 2-Brig. U. S. Forces Morris Isl..	Nov., 1863
7th Conn. Infy........Aug., 1863	From 1-Brig. U. S. Forces Morris I.	To St. Helena Island, S. C.........	Nov., 1863
54th Mass. Col'd Infy......Nov., 1863	From 4-Brig. U. S. Forces Morris I.	To Dist. Hilton Head. S. C.........	Jan., 1864
2d S. C. Col'd Infy......Nov., 1863	From 4-Brig. U. S. Forces Morris I.	To Dist. Hilton Head. S. C.........	Jan., 1864
3d U. S. Col'd Infy......Nov., 1863	From 4-Brig. U. S. Forces Morris I.	To Dist. Hilton Head. S. C.........	Jan., 1864

4th BRIGADE.—Organized Aug. 24, 1863. Discontinued Nov., 1863, and transferred to 3d Brigade, U. S. Forces. Morris Island.

COMMANDER.

J. Montgomery	Col. 2d S. C. Col'd Infy	Aug. 24, 1863, to Nov., 1863.		
54th Mass. Col'd Infy.....Aug., 1863	From 3-Brig. U. S. Forces Morris I.	To 3-Brig. U. S. Forces Morris Isl..	Nov.,	1863
2d S. C. Col'd Infy.......Aug., 1863	From 3-Brig. U. S. Forces Morris I.	To 3-Brig. U. S. Forces Morris Isl..	Nov.,	1863
3d U. S. Col'd Infy.......Aug., 1863	From New Organization	To 3-Brig. U. S. Forces Morris Isl..	Nov.,	1863

5th BRIGADE.—Organized Aug. 30, 1863, from Folly Island. S. C. Discontinued Nov., 1863. Transferred to 2d Brigade.

COMMANDER.

W. W. H. Davis	Col. 104th Penna. Infy	Aug. 30, 1863, to Nov. 23, 1863.		
47th N. Y. Infy.........Aug., 186?	From Unatt. Folly Island, S. C......	To U. S. Forces Hilton Head, S. C..	Nov.,	1863
Indpt. Battn. N. Y. Infy..Aug., 186?	From Unatt. Folly Island, S. C......	To 2-Brig. U. S. Forces Morris Isl.	Nov.,	1863
52d Penna. Infy..........Aug., 186?	From Davis' Brig. Folly Island, S. C	To 2-Brig. U. S. Forces Morris Isl.	Nov.,	1863
104th Penna. Infy........Aug., 1863	From Davis' Brig. Folly Island, S. C	To 2-Brig. U. S. Forces Morris Isl..	Nov.,	1863
ARTILLERY.—				
Batty. B, 3d N. Y. Arty...July, 1863	From St. Helena Island, S. C......	To Arty. Northern Dist............	Jan.,	1864
Batty. F, 3d N. Y. Arty...July, 1863	From U. S. Forces Folly Isl., S. C..	To Arty. Folly Island North. Dist..	Jan.,	1864
Batty. B, 1st U. S. Arty..July, 1863	From U. S. Forces Folly Isl., S. C..	To Gordon's Div. Folly Island, S. C.	Dec.,	1863
Batty. C, 1st U. S. Arty..July, 1863	From U. S. Forces Folly Isl., S. C..	To Sub-Dist. B'fort, N. C., Va.&N.C.	Aug.,	1863
Batty. E, 3d U. S. Arty..July, 1863	From U. S. Forces Folly Isl., S. C..	To Folly Island Northern Dist.....	Jan.,	1864
3d R. I. H. A., Co. C.....July, 1863	From U. S. Forces Folly Isl., S. C..	To Gordon's Div. Folly Island......	Oct.,	1863
3d R. I. H. A., Co. D.....July, 1863	From U. S. Forces Hilton Hd., S. C.	To Morris Island Northern Dist.....	Jan.,	1864
3d R. I. H. A., Co. H.....July, 1863	From U. S. Forces Hilton Hd., S. C.	To Morris Island Northern Dist.....	Jan.,	1864
3d R. I. H. A., Co. I.....July, 1863	From U. S. Forces Folly Isl., S. C..	To Morris Island Northern Dist.....	Jan.,	1864
3d R. I. H. A., Co. M.....July, 1863	From U. S. Forces Folly Isl., S. C..	To Morris Island Northern Dist.....	Jan.,	1864
3d R. I. H. A., Co. A.....Nov., 1863	From U. S. Forces Beaufort, S. C..	To Folly Island Northern Dist.....	Jan.,	1864
3d R. I. H. A., Co. B.....Nov., 1863	From U. S. Forces Folly Isl., S. C..	To Morris Island Northern Dist.....	Jan.,	1864
3d R. I. H. A., Co. E.....Nov., 1863	From U. S. Forces Hilton Hd., S. C.	To Morris Island Northern Dist.....	Jan.,	1864

U. S. FORCES NORTH END OF FOLLY ISLAND.—Organized Aug. 16, 1863. Designated U. S. Forces Folly Island, Northern District, Jan. 15, 1864.

COMMANDERS.

Israel Vodges	Brigadier General	Aug. 16, 1863, to Dec. 16, 1863.	
R. S. Foster	Brigadier General	Dec. 16, 1863, to Jan. 15, 1864.	

FOSTER'S 1st BRIGADE.—

COMMANDERS.

R. S. Foster	Brigadier General	Aug. 16, 1863, to Dec. 16, 1863.		
J. C. Drake	Col. 112th N. Y. Infy	Dec. 16, 1863, to Jan. 15, 1864.		
13th Ind. Infy...........Aug., 1863	From 2-Brig. 1-Div. 7-C. Dept. Va..	To 1-Br. Vodges' Div. North. Dist...	Jan.,	1864
112th N. Y. Infy.........Aug., 1863	From 2-Brig. 1-Div. 7-C. Dept. Va..	To 1-Br. Vodges' Div. North. Dist...	Jan.,	1864
169th N. Y. Infy.........Aug., 1863	From 2-Brig. 1-Div. 7-C. Dept. Va..	To 1-Br. Vodges' Div. North. Dist...	Jan.,	1864

ALFORD'S 2d BRIGADE.—

COMMANDERS.

S. M. Alford	Col. 3d N. Y. Infy	Aug. 16, 1863, to Oct. 16, 1863.		
H. S. Fairchild	Col. 89th N. Y. Infy	Oct. 16, 1863, to Nov. 17, 1863.		
S. M. Alford	Col. 3d N. Y. Infy	Nov. 17, 1863, to Jan. 15, 1864.		
3d N. Y. Infy............Aug., 1863	From 1-Brig. 2-Div. 7-C. Dept. Va..	To 1-Br. Vodges' Div. North. Dist...	Jan.,	1864
89th N. Y. Infy..........Aug., 1863	From 1-Brig. 2-Div. 7-C. Dept. Va..	To 1-Br. Vodges' Div. North. Dist...	Jan.,	1864
103d N. Y. Infy..........Aug., 1863	From 1-Brig. 2-Div. 7-C. Dept. Va..	To 1-Br. Vodges' Div. North. Dist...	Jan.,	1864
117th N. Y. Infy.........Aug., 1863	From 1-Brig. 2-Div. 7-C. Dept. Va..	To 1-Br. Vodges' Div. North. Dist...	Jan.,	1864

3d or AFRICAN BRIGADE.—

COMMANDERS.

E. A. Wild	Brigadier General	Aug. 16, 1863, to Oct. 2, 1863.		
James C. Beecher	Col. 1st N. C. Col'd Infy	Oct. 2, 1863, to Nov. 6, 1863.		
M. S. Littlefield	Col. 4th S. C. Col'd Infy	Nov. 6, 1863, to Dec. 14, 1863.		
James C. Beecher	Col. 1st N. C. Col'd Infy	Dec. 14, 1863, to Jan. 15, 1864.		
55th Mass. Col'd Infy.....Aug., 1863	From New Organization	To 3-Br. Vodges' Div. North. Dist...	Jan.,	1864
1st N. C. Col'd Infy.....Aug., 1863	From Dept. Va. & N. C.	To 3-Br. Vodges' Div. North. Dist...	Jan.,	1864
2d N. C. Col'd Infy.....Aug., 1863	From Dept. Va. & N. C.	To Norfolk, Va. Dept. Va. & N. C..	Dec.,	1863
3d N. C. Col'd Infy.....Aug., 1863	From Dept. Va. & N. C.	To Norfolk, Va. Dept. Va. & N. C..	Dec.,	1863

U. S. FORCES SOUTH END OF FOLLY ISLAND.—Discontinued Jan. 15, 1864, and termed U. S. Forces Folly Island, Northern District, Tenth Army Corps.

COMMANDERS.

Geo. H. Gordon	Brigadier General	Aug. 16, 1863, to Oct. 24, 1863.	
A. Schimmelfenning	Brigadier General	Oct. 24, 1863, to Nov. 28, 1863.	
Geo. H. Gordon	Brigadier General	Nov. 28, 1863, to Jan. 15, 1864.	

1st BRIGADE.—

COMMANDERS.

A. Schimmelfenning	Brigadier General	Aug. 16, 1863, to Oct. 24, 1863.		
L. Von Gilsa	Col. 41st N. Y. Infy	Oct. 24, 1863, to Nov. 28, 1863.		
William Gurney	Col. 127th N. Y. Infy	Nov. 28, 1863, to Jan. 13, 1864.		
L. Von Gilsa	Col. 41st N. Y. Infy	Jan. 13, 1864, to Jan. 15, 1864.		
41st N. Y. Infy..........Aug., 1863	From 1-Brig. 1-Div. 11-Corps Pot..	To 1-Brig. Folly Island North. Dist.	Jan.,	1864
54th N. Y. Infy..........Aug., 1863	From 1-Brig. 1-Div. 11-Corps Pot..	To 1-Brig. Folly Island North. Dist.	Jan.,	1864
127th N. Y. Infy.........Aug., 1863	From 1-Brig. 1-Div. 11-Corps Pot..	To 1-Brig. Folly Island North. Dist.	Jan.,	1864
142d N. Y. Infy..........Aug., 1863	From 1-Brig. 1-Div. 11-Corps Pot..	To 1-Brig. Folly Island North. Dist.	Jan.,	1864
74th Penna. Infy.........Aug., 1863	From 1-Brig. 1-Div. 11-Corps Pot..	To 1-Brig. Folly Island North. Dist.	Jan.,	1864
107th Ohio Infy..........Aug., 1863	From 1-Brig. 1-Div. 11-Corps Pot..	To 2-Brig. Folly Island North. Dist.	Jan.,	1864

2d BRIGADE.—

COMMANDERS.

Adelbert Ames	Brigadier General	Aug. 16, 1863, to Nov. 27, 1863.		
W. H. Noble	Col. 17th Conn. Infy	Nov. 27, 1863, to Jan. 15, 1864.		
17th Conn. Infy..........Aug., 186?	From 2-Brig. 1-Div. 11-Corps Pot..	To 2-Brig. Folly Island North. Dist.	Jan.,	1864
40th Mass. Infy..........Aug., 186?	From 2-Brig. 1-Div. 11-Corps Pot..	To 2-Brig. Folly Island North. Dist.	Jan.,	1864
144th N. Y. Infy.........Aug., 1863	From 2-Brig. 1-Div. 11-Corps Pot..	To 2-Brig. Folly Island North. Dist.	Jan.,	1864
157th N. Y. Infy.........Aug., 1863	From 2-Brig. 1-Div. 11-Corps Pot..	To 2-Brig. Folly Island North. Dist.	Jan.,	1864
25th Ohio Infy...........Aug., 1863	From 2-Brig. 1-Div. 11-Corps Pot..	To U. S. Forces Hilton Head S. C..	Jan.,	1864
75th Ohio Infy...........Aug., 1863	From 2-Brig. 1-Div. 11-Corps Pot..	To 2-Brig. Folly Island North. Dist.	Jan.,	1864

3d BRIGADE.—Joined from Morris Island, S. C., Oct., 1863. Transferred to District Hilton Head, S. C., Dec., 1863.

COMMANDER.

J. B. Howell..........Col. 85th Penna. Infy.............Oct. .., 1863, to Dec. .., 1863.		

85th Penna. Infy..........Oct., 1863	From 2-Brig. U. S. Forces Morris I.	To U. S. Forces Hilton Head S. C..	Dec., 1863
39th Ill. Infy..............Oct., 1863	From 2-Brig. U. S. Forces Morris I.	To U. S. Forces Hilton Head S. C..	Dec., 1863
62d Ohio Infy.............Oct., 1863	From 2-Brig. U. S. Forces Morris I.	To U. S. Forces Hilton Head S. C..	Dec., 1863
67th Ohio Infy.............Oct., 1863	From 2-Brig. U. S. Forces Morris I.	To U. S. Forces Hilton Head S. C..	Dec., 1863
ARTILLERY.—			
3d R. I. H. Arty., Co C...Oct., 1863	From U. S. Forces Morris Island..	To U. S. Forces Hilton Head S. C..	Dec., 1863
Batty. B, 1st U. S. Arty...Dec., 1863	From U. S. Forces Morris Island..	To U. S. Forces Hilton Head S. C..	Jan., 1864

NORTHERN DISTRICT.—Organized Jan. 1, 1864, from United States Forces Folly and Morris Islands. Transferred to Reorganized Department of the South, April 25, 1864.

COMMANDERS.

A. H. Terry............	Brigadier General...................	Jan. 17, 1864, to Feb. .., 1864.
A. Schimmelfenning....	Brigadier General...................	Feb. .., 1864, to Mch. .., 1864.
A. H. Terry............	Brigadier General...................	Mch. .., 1864, to Apr. .., 1864.
United States Forces Folly Island.		
Adelbert Ames.........	Brigadier General...................	Jan. 15, 1864, to Jan. 23, 1864.

GORDON'S DIVISION.—

COMMANDERS.

Geo. H. Gordon........	Brigadier General...................	Jan. 15, 1864, to Jan. 28, 1864.
Adelbert Ames.........	Brigadier General...................	Jan. 28, 1864, to Feb. 25, 1864.
A. Schimmelfenning....	Brigadier General...................	Feb. 25, 1864, to Apr. 25, 1864.

1st BRIGADE.—

COMMANDER.

L. Von Gilsa............Col. 41st N. Y. Infy...............Jan. 15, 1864, to Apr. 25, 1864.		

41st N. Y. Infy..........Jan., 1864	From 1-Brig. Gordon's Div. Folly I.	To Folly Island Northern Dist.....	Apr., 1864
54th N. Y. Infy..........Jan., 1864	From 1-Brig. Gordon's Div. Folly I.	To Folly Island Northern Dist.....	Apr., 1864
127th N. Y. Infy..........Jan., 1864	From 1-Brig. Gordon's Div. Folly I.	To Morris Island Northern Dist.....	Apr., 1864
142d N. Y. Infy..........Jan., 1864	From 1-Brig. Gordon's Div. Folly I.	To 1-Brig. 2-Div. 10-C. Va. & N. C..	Apr., 1864
74th Penna. Infy..........Jan., 1864	From 1-Brig. Gordon's Div. Folly I.	To Folly Island Northern Dist.....	Apr., 1864

2d BRIGADE.—Discontinued Feb., 1864, by transfer to Dist. of Florida. Reorganized Feb., 1864, by assignment of 2d Brigade Vodges' Division.

COMMANDERS.

William H. Noble......	Col. 17th Conn. Infy................	Jan. 15, 1864, to Jan. 23, 1864.
Adelbert Ames.........	Brigadier General...................	Jan. 23, 1864, to Jan. 28, 1864.
William H. Noble......	Col. 17th Conn. Infy................	Jan. 28, 1864, to Feb. .., 1864.
S. M. Alford...........	Col. 3d N. Y. Infy..................	Feb. .., 1864, to Mch. .., 1864.
William Heine.........	Col. 103d N. Y. Infy................	Mch. .., 1864, to Apr. 25, 1864.

17th Conn. Infy..........Jan., 1864	From 2-Brig. Gordon's Div. Folly I.	To 1-Brig. Ames' Div. Dist. Fla....	Feb., 1864
40th Mass. Infy..........Jan., 1864	From 2-Brig. Gordon's Div. Folly I.	To Dist. Hilton Head, S. C........	Jan., 1864
144th N. Y. Infy..........Jan., 1864	From 2-Brig. Gordon's Div. Folly I.	To 1-Brig. Ames' Div. Dist. Fla....	Feb., 1864
157th N. Y. Infy..........Jan., 1864	From 2-Brig. Gordon's Div. Folly I.	To 1-Brig. Ames' Div. Dist. Fla....	Feb., 1864
107th Ohio Infy..........Jan., 1864	From 2-Brig. Gordon's Div. Folly I.	To 1-Brig. Ames' Div. Dist. Fla....	Feb., 1864
3d N. Y. Infy............Feb., 1864	From 2-Brig. Vodges' Div. N. Dist..	To 1-Brig. 2-Div. 10-C. Va. & N. C.	Apr., 1864
89th N. Y. Infy...........Feb., 1864	From 2-Brig. Vodges' Div. N. Dist..	To 1-Brig. 2-Div. 10-C. Va. & N. C.	Apr., 1864
103d N. Y. Infy...........Feb., 1864	From 2-Brig. Vodges' Div. N. Dist..	To Folly Island Northern Dist.....	Apr., 1864
117th N. Y. Infy...........Feb., 1864	From 2-Brig. Vodges' Div. N. Dist..	To 1-Brig. 2-Div. 10-C. Va. & N. C.	Apr., 1864

VODGES' DIVISION NORTHERN DISTRICT.—Discontinued Feb., 1864, and transferred to Dist. of Florida.

COMMANDER.

R. S. Foster............Brigadier General...................Jan. 15, 1864, to Feb. 25, 1864.		

1st BRIGADE.—

COMMANDER.

J. C. Drake............Col. 112th N. Y. Infy...............Jan. 15, 1864, to Feb. 25, 1864.		

13th Ind. Infy..........Jan., 1864	From 1-Br. Vodges' Div. N. E. Fol. I.	To 1-Brig. Vodges' Div. Dist. Fla....	Feb., 1864
112th N. Y. Infy..........Jan., 1864	From 1-Br. Vodges' Div. N. E. Fol. I.	To 1-Brig. Vodges' Div. Dist. Fla....	Feb., 1864
169th N. Y. Infy..........Jan., 1864	From 1-Br. Vodges' Div. N. E. Fol. I.	To 1-Brig. Vodges' Div. Dist. Fla....	Feb., 1864

2d BRIGADE.—

COMMANDER.

S. M. Alford............Col. 3d N. Y. Infy.................Jan. 15, 1864, to Feb. 25, 1864.		

3d N. Y. Infy..........Jan., 1864	From 2-Br. Vodges' Div. N. E. Fol. I.	To 2-Brig. Gordon's Div. North Dist.	Feb., 1864
89th N. Y. Infy..........Jan., 1864	From 2-Br. Vodges' Div. N. E. Fol. I.	To 2-Brig. Gordon's Div. North Dist.	Feb., 1864
103d N. Y. Infy..........Jan., 1864	From 2-Br. Vodges' Div. N. E. Fol. I.	To 2-Brig. Gordon's Div. North Dist.	Feb., 1864
117th N. Y. Infy..........Jan., 1864	From 2-Br. Vodges' Div. N. E. Fol. I.	To 2-Brig. Gordon's Div. North Dist.	Feb., 1864

3d BRIGADE.—

COMMANDER.

James C. Beecher......Col. 1st N. C. Col'd Infy...........Jan. 15, 1864, to Feb. 25, 1864.		

55th Mass. Col'd Infy.....Jan., 1864	From 3-Br. Vodges' Div. N. E. Fol. I.	To 3-Brig. Ames' Div. Dist. Fla...	Feb., 1864
1st N. C. Col'd Infy......Jan., 1864	From 3-Br. Vodges' Div. N. E. Fol. I.	To 2-Brig. Vodges' Div. Dist. Fla...	Feb., 1864
ARTILLERY.—			
1st Conn. Batty..........Jan., 1864	From Vodges' Div. N. E. Folly Isl..	To Arty. 1-Div. 10-C. Va. & N. C....	Apr., 1864
Batty. F, 3d N. Y. Arty...Jan., 1864	From Vodges' Div. N. E. Folly Isl..	To Dist. Beaufort Dept. South......	Feb., 1864
Batty. E, 3d U. S. Arty....Jan., 1864	From Vodges' Div. N. E. Folly Isl..	To Ames' Div. Dist. Fla...........	Feb., 1864
3d R. I. Heavy Arty. Co. A.Jan., 1864	From Vodges' Div. N. E. Folly Isl..	To Dist. Hilton Head, S. C.........	Feb., 1864

MORRIS ISLAND, NORTHERN DISTRICT.—Organized Jan. 15, 1864. Transferred to Dept. of the South April, 1864.

COMMANDERS.

D. W. H. Davis.........	Col. 104th Penna. Infy..............	Jan. 17, 1864, to Apr. 18, 1864.
E. N. Hallowell........	Col. 54th Mass. Col'd Infy..........	Apr. 18, 1864, to Apr. 25, 1864.

1st BRIGADE.—

COMMANDERS.

H. M. Plaisted.........	Col. 11th Me. Infy..................	Jan. .., 1864, to Mch. .., 1864.
W. P. Spofford.........	Lt.-Col. 11th Me. Infy..............	Mch. .., 1864, to Apr. .., 1864.

9th Me. Infy.............Jan., 1864	From 1-Brig. U. S. Forces Morris I..	To 1-Brig. 3-Div. 10-C. Va. & N. C..	Apr., 1864
11th Me. Infy.............Jan., 1864	From 1-Brig. U. S. Forces Morris I..	To 2-Brig. 1-Div. 10-C. Va. & N. C..	Apr., 1864
3d N. H. Infy.............Jan., 1864	From 1-Brig. U. S. Forces Morris I..	To Light Brig. Dist. Fla..........	Apr., 1864
4th N. H. Infy.............Jan., 1864	From 1-Brig. U. S. Forces Morris I..	To Dist. Beaufort, Dept. South.....	Jan., 1864

2d BRIGADE.—

COMMANDERS.

H. M. Hoyt...........	Col. 52d Penna. Infy..............	Jan. 17, 1864, to Feb. 12, 1864.
T. D. Hart...........	Lt.-Col. 104th Penna. Infy.......	Feb. 12, 1864, to Apr. 25, 1864.

100th New York Infy...Jan., 1864	From 2-Brig. U. S. Forces Morris I.	To 2-B. 1-Div. 10-Corps Va. & N. C.	Apr., 1864
52d Penna. Infy.........Jan., 1864	From 2-Brig. U. S. Forces Morris I.	To Dist. Hilton Head. Dept. South..	Apr., 1864
104th Penna. Infy.......Jan., 1864	From 2-Brig. U. S. Forces Morris I.	To Dist. Hilton Head. Dept. South..	Apr., 1864

UNATTACHED.—

3d R. I. H'vy A., 3d Bn...Jan., 1864	From U. S. Forces Morris Island....	To Morris Island Northern Dist. So.	Apr., 1864
Batty. B, 3d N. Y. Arty...Jan., 1864	From U. S. Forces Morris Island....	To Morris Island Northern Dist. So.	Apr., 1864

DISTRICT OF FLORIDA.—Organized Feb. 16, 1864. Transferred to the Dept. of the South April 25, 1864.

COMMANDERS.

Truman Seymour......	Brigadier General.................	Feb. 16, 1864, to Mch. 24, 1864.
J. P. Hatch...........	Brigadier General.................	Mch. 24, 1864, to Apr. 25, 1864.

BARTON'S BRIGADE.—

COMMANDER.

W. B. Barton..........	Col. 48th New York Infy..........	Feb. 16, 1864, to Feb. 29, 1864.

47th New York Infy......Feb., 1864	From Barton's Brig. Hilton Head..	To Barton's B. Ames' Div. Dist. Fla.	Feb., 1864
48th New York Infy......Feb., 1864	From Barton's Brig. Hilton Head..	To Barton's B. Ames' Div. Dist. Fla.	Feb., 1864
115th New York Infy.....Feb., 1864	From Barton's Brig. Hilton Head..	To Barton's B. Ames' Div. Dist. Fla.	Feb., 1864

HAWLEY'S BRIGADE.—

COMMANDER.

J. R. Hawley..........	Col. 7th Conn. Infy..............	Feb. 16, 1864, to Feb. 29, 1864.

7th Conn. Infy........Feb., 1864	From St. Helena Island, S. C......	To 2-Brig. Ames' Div. Dist. Fla....	Feb., 1864
7th New Hampshire Infy..Feb., 1864	From St. Helena Island, S. C......	To 2-Brig. Ames' Div. Dist. Fla....	Feb., 1864
8th U. S. Col'd Infy......Feb., 1864	From New Organization...........	To 2-Brig. Ames' Div. Dist. Fla....	Feb., 1864

MONTGOMERY'S BRIGADE.—

COMMANDERS.

J. Montgomery........	Col. 2d S. C. Colored Infy.........	Feb. 6, 1864, to Feb. 15, 1864.
M. S. Littlefield........	Col. 21st U. S. Col'd Infy.........	Feb. 15, 1864, to Feb. 25, 1864.

54th Mass. Col'd Infy....Feb., 1864	From Montgomery's B. Hilton Head	To 3-Brig. Ames' Div. Dist. Fla....	Feb., 1864
1st N. C. (35th U. S. C. T.).Feb., 1864	From Folly Island, Northern Dist..	To 2-Brig. Vodges' Div. Dist. Fla...	Feb., 1864
3d U. S. Colored Infy....Feb., 1864	From Montgomery's B. Hilton Head.	To 2-Brig. Vodges' Div. Dist. Fla...	Feb., 1864

LIGHT BRIGADE.—

COMMANDER.

Guy V. Henry.........	Col. 40th Mass. Infy.............	Feb. 16, 1864, to Apr. 25, 1864.

Discontinued Apr. 25, 1864.

40th Mass. Infy.........Feb., 1864	From Dist. Hilton Head. S. C.......	To 1-B. 2-Div. 10-Corps Va. & N. C.	Apr., 1864
Indpt. Battn. Mass. Cav. (I, K, L, M, 4th Cav.)..Feb., 1864	From Dist. Hilton Head. S. C.......	To Unattached 10-Corps Va. & N. C.	Apr., 1864
Batty. B, 1st U. S. Arty..Feb., 1864	From Dist. Hilton Head. S. C.......	To Arty. 2-Div. 10-Corps Va. & N. C.	Apr., 1864
3d New Hampshire Infy..Apr., 1864	From 1-Brig. Morris I. North'n Dist.	To 3-Br. 1-Div. 10-Corps Va. & N. C.	Apr., 1864

AMES' 1st DIVISION.—

COMMANDER.

Adelbert Ames........	Brigadier General.................	Feb. 25, 1864, to Apr. 25, 1864.

1st BRIGADE.—

COMMANDER.

William H. Noble......	Col. 17th Conn. Infy.............	Feb. 25, 1864, to Apr. 25, 1864.

17th Conn. Infy........Feb., 1864	From 2-Brig. Gordon's Div. Folly I.	To Dist. Fla. Dept. South..........	Apr., 1864
144th New York Infy....Feb., 1864	From 2-Brig. Gordon's Div. Folly I.	To Dist. Fla. Dept. South..........	Apr., 1864
157th New York Infy....Feb., 1864	From 2-Brig. Gordon's Div. Folly I.	To Dist. Fla. Dept. South..........	Apr., 1864
75th Ohio Infy..........Feb., 1864	From 2-Brig. Gordon's Div. Folly I.	To Dist. Fla. Dept. South..........	Apr., 1864
107th Ohio Infy.........Feb., 1864	From 2-Brig. Gordon's Div. Folly I.	To Dist. Fla. Dept. South..........	Apr., 1864

2d BRIGADE.—

COMMANDER.

J. R. Hawley..........	Col. 7th Conn. Infy..............	Feb. 25, 1864, to Apr. 25, 1864.

7th New Hampshire Infy..Feb., 1864	From Hawley's Brig. Fla. Expeditn.	To 3-B. 1-Div. 10-Corps Va. & N. C.	Apr., 1864
7th Conn. Infy..........Feb., 1864	From Hawley's Brig. Fla. Expeditn.	To 3-B. 1-Div. 10-Corps Va. & N. C.	Apr., 1864
8th U. S. Col'd Infy......Feb., 1864	From Hawley's Brig. Fla. Expeditn.	To Dist. Fla. Dept. South..........	Apr., 1864

3d BRIGADE.—

COMMANDERS.

M. S. Littlefield........	Col. 21st U. S. Col'd Infy.........	Feb. 25, 1864, to Feb. 29, 1864.
E. N. Hallowell........	Col. 54th Mass. Col'd Infy........	Feb. 29, 1864, to Apr. 25, 1864.

54th Mass. Col'd Infy....Feb., 1864	From Montgomery's Brig. Fla. Exp.	To Morris Island, S. C., N'rth'n Dist.	Apr., 1864
55th Mass. Col'd Infy....Feb., 1864	From 3-Brig. Vodges' Div. Folly I.	To Folly Island, S. C., North'n Dist.	Apr., 1864

BARTON'S BRIGADE.—

COMMANDER.

W. B. Barton..........	Col. 48th New York Infy..........	Feb. 25, 1864, to Apr. 25, 1864.

47th New York Infy......Feb., 1864	From Barton's Brig. Fla. Expeditn.	To 2-B. 2-Div. 10-Corps Va. & N. C.	Apr., 1864
48th New York Infy......Feb., 1864	From Barton's Brig. Fla. Expeditn.	To 2-B. 2-Div. 10-Corps Va. & N. C.	Apr., 1864
115th New York Infy....Feb., 1864	From Barton's Brig. Fla. Expeditn.	To 2-B. 2-Div. 10-Corps Va. & N. C.	Apr., 1864

VODGES' 2d DIVISION.—

COMMANDERS.

Israel Vodges.........	Brigadier General.................	Feb. 25, 1864, to Feb. 28, 1864.
R. S. Foster..........	Brigadier General.................	Feb. 28, 1864, to Apr. 25, 1864.

1st BRIGADE.—

COMMANDERS.

R. S. Foster..........	Brigadier General.................	Feb. 25, 1864, to Feb. 28, 1864.
J. C. Drake...........	Col. 112th N. Y. Infy.............	Feb. 28, 1864, to Mch., 1864.
C. I. Dobbs..........	Col. 13th Indiana Infy............	Mch., 1864, to Apr., 1864.

4th New Hamp. Infy.....Feb., 1864	From Dist. Beaufort, S. C..........	To 3-B. 2-Div. 10-Corps Va. & N. C.	Apr., 1864
24th Mass. Infy.........Feb., 1864	From St. Augustine, Fla...........	To 2-B. 1-Div. 10-Corps Va. & N. C.	Apr., 1864
112th New York Infy....Feb., 1864	From 1-Brig. Vodges' Div. Folly I.	To 2-B. 3-Div. 10-Corps Va. & N. C.	Apr., 1864
169th New York Infy....Feb., 1864	From 1-Brig. Vodges' Div. Folly I.	To 2-B. 3-Div. 10-Corps Va. & N. C.	Apr., 1864
13th Indiana Infy........Feb., 1864	From 1-Brig. Vodges' Div. Folly I.	To 3-B. 2-Div. 10-Corps Va. & N. C.	Apr., 1864

2d BRIGADE.—

COMMANDER.

B. C. Tilghman........	Col. 3d U. S. Col'd Infy...........	Feb. 25, 1864, to Apr. 25, 1864.

1st N. C. (35th U. S. C. T.).Feb., 1864	From Montgomery's Brig. Fla. Exp.	To Dist. Fla. Dept. South..........	Apr., 1864
3d U. S. Colored Infy....Feb., 1864	From Montgomery's Brig. Fla. Exp.	To Dist. Fla. Dept. South..........	Apr., 1864

3d BRIGADE.—   **COMMANDER.**

James Montgomery....	Col. 2d S. C. Col'd Infy............	Feb. 25, 1864, to Apr. 25, 1864.		
2d S. C. Colored Infy...Feb., 1864	From Montgomery's Brig. Fla. Exp.	To Folly Island, Northern Dist....	Apr.,	1864
3d S. C. Colored Infy...Feb., 1864	From Dist. Hilton Head, S. C.	To Folly Island, Northern Dist....	Apr.,	1864
ARTILLERY.—				
Batty. M, 1st U. S. Arty...Feb., 1864	From Dist. Hilton Head, S. C......	To Arty. 1-Div. 10-Corps Va. & N. C.	Apr.,	1864
Batty. E, 3d U. S. Arty...Feb., 1864	From Folly Island, Northern Dist..	To Arty. 3-Div. 10-Corps Va. & N. C.	Apr.,	1864
3d R. I. H'vy A. Co. C...Feb., 1864	From Dist. Hilton Head, S. C......	To Arty. 3-Div. 10-Corps Va. & N. C.	Apr.,	1864
3d R. I. H'vy A. Co A....Apr., 1864	From Dist. Hilton Head, S. C......	To Dist. Fla. Dept. South.........	Apr.,	1864

Department of the South

As reorganized April 25, 1864, after transfer of the 10th Corps to Dept. of Virginia and North Carolina.

NORTHERN DISTRICT—FOLLY AND MORRIS ISLANDS.—Designated 1st Separate Brigade Dept. South Oct., 1864.

COMMANDERS.

A. Schemmelfenning....	Brigadier General..................	Apr. 25, 1864, to Sept. 1, 1864.	
Rufus Saxton..........	Brigadier General..................	Sept. 1, 1864, to Oct. 3, 1864.	
E. P. Scammon.........	Brigadier General..................	Oct. 3, 1864, to Oct. 26, 1864.	

FOLLY ISLAND, S. C.—   **COMMANDER.**

L. Von Gilsa...........	Col. 41st N. Y. Infy.	Apr. 25, 1864, to Oct. 26, 1864.		
41st N. Y. Infy........Apr., 1864	From 1-Brig. Gordon's Div. Folly I.	To Dist. Hilton Head, S. C........	June,	1864
54th N. Y. Infy........Apr., 1864	From 1-Brig. Gordon's Div. Folly I.	To 1st Sep. Brig. Northern Dist...	Oct.,	1864
103d N. Y. Infy........Apr., 1864	From 2-Brig. Gordon's Div. Folly I.	To 3-Brig. Def. South Pot. 22-C...	Aug.,	1864
74th Penna. Infy.......Apr., 1864	From 1-Brig. Gordon's Div. Folly I.	To 2-Brig. Def. South Pot. 22-C...	Aug.,	1864
55th Mass. Col. Infy...Apr., 1864	From 3-Brig. Ames' 1-Div. Dist. Fla.	To 1st Sep. Brig. Northern Dist...	Oct.,	1864
33d U. S. Col. Infy.....July, 1864	From Dist. Beaufort, S. C.	To 1st Sep. Brig. Northern Dist...	Oct.,	1864

MORRIS ISLAND, S. C.—   **COMMANDER.**

William Gurney........	Col. 127th N. Y. Infy.............	Apr. 25, 1864, to Oct. 26, 1864.		
127th N. Y. Infy.......Apr., 1864	From 1-Brig. Gordon's Div. Folly I.	To Dist. Beaufort, S. C.	Oct.,	1864
54th Mass. Col'd Infy..Apr., 1864	From 3-Brig. Ames 1-Div. Dist. Fla.	To 1st Separate Brig. Northern Dist.	Oct.,	1864
21st U. S. Col'd Infy....Apr., 1864	From 3-Br. Vodges' 2-Div. Dist. Fla.	To 1st Separate Brig. Northern Dist.	Oct.,	1864
34th U. S. Col'd Infy....Apr., 1864	From 3-Br. Vodges' 2-Div. Dist. Fla.	To Dist. Beaufort, S. C............	June,	1864
3d R. I. H'vy Arty. 5-Cos. Apr., 1864	From Morris Island Northern Dist.	To 1st Separate Brig. Northern Dist.	Oct.,	1864
Batty. B, 3d N. Y. Arty...Apr., 1864	From Morris Island Northern Dist.	To 1st Separate Brig. Northern Dist.	Oct.,	1864
52d Penna Infy........June, 1864	From Dist. Hilton Head, S. C......	To 1st Separate Brig. Northern Dist.	Oct.,	1864
32d U. S. Col'd Infy....June, 1864	From Dist. Hilton Head, S. C......	To 3d Separate Brig. Dept. South..	Oct.,	1864
56th N. Y. Infy........Aug., 1864	From Dist. Beaufort, S. C.........	To 1st Separate Brig. Northern Dist.	Oct.,	1864

DISTRICT OF BEAUFORT, S. C.—Organized April 25, 1864. Designated 2d Separate Brigade Oct., 1864.

COMMANDER.

Rufus Saxton..........	Brigadier General..................	Apr. 25, 1864, to Sept. 1, 1864.		
29th Conn. Col'd Infy....Apr., 1864	From Annapolis, Md...............	To 1-Brig. 3-Div. 10-Corps Va.&N.C.	Aug.,	1864
56th N. Y. Infy........Apr., 1864	From U. S. Forces Pt. Royal Island	To Morris Island Northern Dist....	Aug.,	1864
26th U. S. Col'd Infy....Apr., 1864	From New Organization...........	To 2d Separate Brig. Dept. South...	Oct.,	1864
33d U. S. Col'd Infy....Apr., 1864	From U. S. Forces Pt. Royal Island	To Folly Island Northern Dist.....	Aug.,	1864
9th U. S. Col'd Infy....Apr., 1864	From Dist. Hilton Head, S. C......	To 1-Brig. 3-Div. 10-Corps Va.&N.C.	Aug.,	1864
102d U. S. Col'd Infy...Apr., 1864	From New Organization...........	To Dist. Fla......................	Aug.,	1864
Batty. F, 3d N. Y. Arty...Apr., 1864	From Folly Island Northern Dist..	To Dist. Fla......................	Sept.,	1864
34th U. S. Col'd Infy....Aug., 1864	From Morris Island Northern Dist..	To Dist. Fla......................	Aug.,	1864
Batty. G, 2d U. S. C. Arty. Aug., 1864	From Dist. Hilton Head, S. C......	To 2-Separate Brig. Dist. Beaufort..	Oct.,	1864
3d R. I. Heavy Arty. Co. A Oct., 1864	From District of Fla..............	To 2-Separate Brig. Dist. Beaufort..	Oct.,	1864
127th N. Y. Infy.........Oct., 1864	From Morris Island Northern Dist..	To 2-Separate Brig. Dist. Beaufort..	Oct.,	1864

DISTRICT OF HILTON HEAD, S. C.—Organized April 25, 1864. Designated 3d Separate Brig. Dept. South Oct., 1864.

COMMANDERS.

W. H. H. Davis.........	Col. 104th Penna. Infy............	Apr. 26, 1864, to May 13, 1864.		
William Birney........	Brigadier General..................	May 13, 1864, to June 2, 1864.		
J. P. Hatch...........	Brigadier General..................	June 2, 1864, to Aug. 1, 1864.		
E. E. Potter...........	Brigadier General..................	Aug. 1, 1864, to Oct. 26, 1864.		
52d Penna. Infy.......Apr., 1864	From 2-Brig. Morris Island, S. C..	To Morris Island Northern Dist...	June,	1864
104th Penna. Infy......Apr., 1864	From 2-Brig. Morris Island, S. C..	To Morris Island Northern Dist...	June,	1864
9th U. S. Col'd Infy....Apr., 1864	From Camp Benedict. Md. 8-Corps..	To 1-Brig. 3-Div. 10-Corps Va.&N.C.	Aug.,	1864
32d U. S. Col'd Infy.....Apr., 1864	From New Organization...........	To Morris Island Northern Dist...	June,	1864
102d U. S. Col'd Infy...Apr., 1864	From New Organization...........	To Dist. Beaufort, S. C...........	Apr.,	1864
25th Ohio Infy........Apr., 1864	From U. S. Forces Hilton H., 10-C.	To 3d Separate Brig. Dept. South..	Oct.,	1864
3d R. I. Heavy Arty..				
(Cos. B, D, G, H, L.)..Apr., 1864	From Morris Island Northern Dist.	To Morris Island Northern Dist...	Oct.,	1864
1st N. Y. Engrs., A, C, G, I, Apr., 1864	From Unatt. 10th Corps Dept. South	To 3d Separate Brig. Dept. South..	Oct.,	1864
4th Mass. Cav. 2d Battn..Apr., 1864	From New Organization...........	To 3d Separate Brig. Dept. South..	Oct.,	1864
41st N. Y. Infy........June, 1864	From Folly Island Northern Dist..	To 1-Brig. Def. North Pot. 22-Corps	Aug.,	1864
144th N. Y. Infy.......June, 1864	From Dist. Fla. Dept. South......	To 3d Separate Brig. Dept. South...	Oct.,	1864
157th N. Y. Infy.......June, 1864	From Dist. Fla. Dept. South......	To 3d Separate Brig. Dept. South..	Oct.,	1864
2d U. S. Col'd Arty. Co. G June, 1864	From New Organization...........	To Dist. Beaufort Dept. South....	Oct.,	1864
32d U. S. Col'd Infy....Oct., 1864	From Morris Island Northern Dist.	To 3d Separate Brig. Dept. South..	Oct.,	1864

DISTRICT OF FLORIDA.—Organized Apr. 25, 1864. Designated 4th Separate Brigade Dept. South, Oct., 1864.

COMMANDERS.

William Birney........	Brigadier General..................	Apr. 25, 1864, to May 13, 1864.		
Geo. H. Gordon........	Brigadier General..................	May 13, 1864, to June 2, 1864.		
William Birney........	Brigadier General..................	June 2, 1864, to July 29, 1864.		
W. H. Noble..........	Col. 17th Conn. Infy..............	July 29, 1864, to Aug. 4, 1864.		
J. P. Hatch..........	Brigadier General..................	Aug. 4, 1864, to Oct. 26, 1864.		
75th Ohio Infy........Apr., 1864	From 1-Brig. Ames' Div. Dist. Fla.	To 4th Separate Brig. Dist. Fla....	Oct.,	1864
107th Ohio Infy........Apr., 1864	From 1-Brig. Ames' Div. Dist. Fla.	To 4th Separate Brig. Dist. Fla....	Oct.,	1864
17th Conn. Infy........Apr., 1864	From 1-Brig. Ames' Div. Dist. Fla.	To 4th Separate Brig. Dist. Fla....	Oct.,	1864
144th N. Y. Infy........Apr., 1864	From 1-Brig. Ames' Div. Dist. Fla.	To Dist. Hilton Head, S. C........	Oct..	1864

DISTRICT OF FLORIDA.—Continued.

157th N. Y. Infy..........Apr., 1864	From 1-Brig. Ames' Div. Dist. Fla.	To Dist. Hilton Head, S. C........	Oct.,	1864
3d U. S. Col'd Infy....Apr., 1864	From 2-Br. Vodges' 2-Div. Dist. Fla.	To 4th Separate Brig. Dist. Fla....	Oct.,	1864
7th U. S. Col'd Infy......Apr., 1864	From Camp Benedict, Md. 8-Corps.	To 1-Brig. 3-Div. 10-Corps Va.&N.C.	Aug.,	1864
8th U. S. Col'd Infy......Apr., 1864	From 2-Brig. Ames' 1-Div. Dist. Fla.	To 1-Brig. 3-Div. 10-Corps Va.&N.C.	Aug.,	1864
35th U. S. Col'd Infy....Apr., 1864	From 2-Br. Vodges' 2-Div. Dist. Fla.	To 4th Separate Brig. Dist. Fla....	Oct.,	1864
3d R. I. Heavy Arty. Co. A Apr., 1864	From Arty. Dist. Fla. 10-Corps...	To 2-Separate Brig. Dist. Beaufort.	Oct.,	1864
4th Mass. Cav., 2 Cos....June, 1864	From Dist. Beaufort Dept. South..	To 4th Separate Brig. Dist. Fla....	Oct.,	1864
104th Penna Infy.........Aug., 1864	From Morris Island Northern Dist..	To 3-Brig. Def. South Pot. 22-Corps	Aug.,	1864
102d U. S. Col'd Infy....Aug., 1864	From Dist. Beaufort Dept. South..	To 2d Separate Brig. Dist. Beaufort	Oct.,	1864
34th U. S. Col'd Infy....Aug., 1864	From Dist. Beaufort Dept. South..	To 4th Separate Brig. Dist. Fla....	Oct.,	1864

1st SEPARATE BRIGADE, MORRIS AND FOLLY ISLANDS.—Organized Oct., 1864.

COMMANDERS.

E. E. Potter...........	Brigadier General...............	Oct. 26, 1864, to Nov. 14, 1864.	
J. P. Hatch...........	Brigadier General...............	Nov. 14, 1864, to Nov. 28, 1864.	
A. Schimmelfenning....	Brigadier General...............	Nov. 28, 1864, to Jan. 23, 1865.	
J. P. Hatch...........	Brigadier General...............	Jan. 23, 1865, to Feb. 26, 1865.	
A. Schimmelfenning....	Brigadier General...............	Feb. 26, 1865, to Apr. 8, 1865.	

54th N. Y. Infy......Oct., 1864	From Folly Island Northern Dist..	To Dist. Wilmington Dept. N. C....	Mch.,	1865
56th N. Y. Infy........Oct., 1864	From Dist. Beaufort, S. C........	To 1-Brig. Coast Div. Dept. South..	Nov.,	1864
52d Penna. Infy......Oct., 1864	From Folly Island Northern Dist...	To Dist. Wilmington Dept. N. C....	Mch.,	1865
54th Mass. Col'd Infy....Oct., 1864	From Folly Island Northern Dist...	To 2-Brig. Coast Div. Dept. South..	Nov.,	1864
55th Mass. Col'd Infy....Oct., 1864	From Folly Island Northern Dist...	To 2-Brig. Coast Div. Dept. South..	Nov.,	1864
21st U. S. Col'd Infy.....Oct., 1864	From Morris Island Northern Dist..	To Garrison of Charleston, S. C....	Feb.,	1865
33d U. S. Col'd Infy......Oct., 1864	From Folly Island Northern Dist...	To Dist. Savannah, Ga.............	Mch.,	1865
3d R. I. H'vy Arty. 1-Bn. Oct., 1864	From Morris Island Northern Dist..	To Dept. S. C....................	June,	1865
Batty. B, 3d N. Y. Arty..Oct., 1864	From Morris Island Northern Dist..	To Arty. Brig. Coast Div.........	Nov.,	1864
56th N. Y. Infy......Feb., 1865	From 1-Brig. Coast Div. Dept. South	To Dist. Wilmington, N. C. Dept.N.C.	Mch.,	1865
54th Mass. Col'd Infy....Feb., 1865	From 2-Brig. Coast Div. Dept. South	To Dept. S. C....................	June,	186b
55th Mass. Col'd Infy....Feb., 1865	From 2-Brig. Coast Div. Dept. South	To Dept. S. C....................	June,	1865
26th U. S. Col'd Infy....Feb., 1865	From 2-Separate Brig. Dept. South	To 2d Separate Brig. Dept. South..	Feb.,	1865
Batty. B, 3d N. Y. Arty..Feb., 1865	From Arty. Brig. Coast Div	No change to Muster Out.........	July,	1865
127th N. Y. Infy........Mch., 1865	From Garrison of Charleston, S. C..	No change to Muster Out.........	June,	1865
157th N. Y. Infy........Mch., 1865	From 1-Brig. Coast Div. Dept. South	To Dept. S. C....................	June,	1865
25th Ohio Infy.........Mch., 1865	From 3d Separate Brig. Dept. South	To Dept. S. C....................	June,	1865
107th Ohio Infy.........Mch., 1865	From 1-Brig. Coast Div. Dept. South	To Dept. S. C....................	June,	1865
35th U. S. Col'd Infy.....Mch., 1865	From 2d Br. Coast Div. Dept. South	To Dept. S. C....................	June,	1865
102d U. S. Col'd Infy.....Mch., 1865	From 2d Separate Brig. Dept. South	To Dept. S. C....................	June,	186b
Batty. F, 3d N. Y. Arty..Mch., 1865	From Arty. Brig. Coast Div.......	No change to Muster Out.........	June,	1865

2d SEPARATE BRIGADE.—Organized Oct., 1864, from District of Beaufort, S. C. Consolidated with District of Hilton Head as District of Port Royal, S. C., May 13, 1865.

COMMANDERS.

Rufus Saxton.........	Brigadier General...............	Oct. 26, 1864, to Jan. 23, 1865.	
E. E. Potter.........	Brigadier General...............	Jan. 23, 1865, to May 13, 1865.	

127th N. Y. Infy........Oct., 1864	From Dist. Beaufort, S. C.........	To. 1-Brig. Coast Div. Dept. South	Nov.,	1864
26th U. S. Col'd Infy....Oct., 1864	From Dist. Fla.................	To 1st Separate Brig. Dept. South	Feb.,	1865
102d U. S. Col'd Infy....Oct., 1864	From Dist. Fla.................	To 2-Brig. Coast Div. Dept. South..	Nov.,	1864
Batty. A, 3 R. I. H'vy Arty. Oct., 1864	From Dist. Fla.................	To Arty. Brig. Coast Div.........	Nov.,	1864
G 2d U. S. Col'd Arty....Oct., 1864	From Dist. Fla.................	To Dept. S. C....................	June,	1865
32d U. S. Col'd Infy.....Dec., 1864	From 2-Brig. Coast Div. Dept. South	To Dept. S. C....................	June,	1865
26th U. S. Col'd Infy....Feb., 186b	From 1st Separate Brig. Dept. South	To Dept. S. C....................	June,	1865
102d U. S. Col'd Infy....Feb., 1865	From 2-Brig. Coast Div. Dept. South	To 1st Separate Brig. Dept. South..	Mch.,	1865

3d SEPARATE BRIGADE.—Organized from Dist. Hilton Head, S. C., Oct. , 1864. Merged into Dist. Port Royal, May 13, 1865.

COMMANDERS.

P. P. Brown...........	Col. 157th N. Y. Infy.............	Oct. 26, 1864, to Nov. 1, 1864.	
E. P. Scammon.......	Brigadier General...............	Nov. 1, 1864, to Nov. 14, 1864.	
E. E. Potter.........	Brigadier General...............	Nov. 14, 1864, to Nov. 28, 1864.	
M. S. Littlefield......	Bvt. Brig. General..............	Nov. 28, 1864, to May 13, 1865.	

144th N. Y. Infy........Oct., 1864	From Dist. Hilton Head, S. C......	To 1-Brig. Coast Div. Dept. South..	Nov.,	1864
157th N. Y. Infy........Oct., 1864	From Dist. Hilton Head, S. C......	To 1-Brig. Coast Div. Dept. South..	Nov.,	1864
25th Ohio Infy.........Oct., 1864	From Dist. Hilton Head, S. C......	To 1-Brig. Coast Div. Dept. South..	Nov.,	1864
32d U. S. Col'd Infy....Oct., 1864	From Dist. Hilton Head, S. C......	To 1-Brig. Coast Div. Dept. South..	Nov.,	1864
1st N. Y. Engrs. Battn...Oct., 1864	From Dist. Hilton Head, S. C......	To Dist. Savannah, Ga............	Mch.,	1865
4th Mass. Cav. 2 Cos...Oct., 1864	From Dist. Hilton Head, S. C......	To Cav. Coast Div. Dept. South....	Nov.,	1864
75th Ohio Infy.........Dec., 1864	From 4th Separate Brig. Dept. South	To 1-Brig. Coast Div. Dept. South..	Dec.,	1864
107th Ohio Infy.........Dec., 1864	From 4th Separate Brig. Dept. South	To 1-Brig. Coast Div. Dept. South..	Dec.,	1864
144th N. Y. Infy.........Dec., 1864	From 1-Brig. Coast Div. Dept. South	No change to Muster Out.........	June,	1865
25th Ohio Infy.........Feb., 1865	From 1-Brig. Coast Div. Dept. South	To 1-Separate Brig. Dept. South...	Mch.,	1865

4th SEPARATE BRIGADE.—Organi zed from Dist. Fla., Oct., 1864.

COMMANDERS.

J. P. Hatch...........	Brigadier General...............	Oct. 26, 1864, to Nov. 14, 1864.	
E. P. Scammon.......	Brigadier General...............	Nov. 14, 1864, to Apr. 7, 1865.	
B. C. Tilghman........	Col. 3d U. S. Col'd Infy.........	Apr. 7, 1865, to Apr. 19, 1865.	
I. Vodges.............	Brigadier General...............	Apr. 19, 1865, to July 10, 1865.	

17th Conn. Infy........Oct., 1864	From Dist. Fla.................	No change to Muster Out.........	July,	1865
75th Ohio Infy.........Oct., 1864	From Dist. Fla.................	To 1-Brig. Coast Div. Dept. South..	Dec.,	1864
10th Ohio Infy.........Oct., 1864	From Dist. Fla.................	To 1-Brig. Coast Div. Dept. South..	Dec.,	1864
3d U. S. Col'd Infy......Oct., 1864	From Dist. Fla.................	To Dept. Fla....................	July,	1865
34th U. S. Col'd Infy.....Oct., 1864	From Dist. Fla.................	To 2-Brig. Coast Div. Dept. South..	Nov.,	1864
35th U. S. Col'd Infy.....Oct., 1864	From Dist. Fla.................	To 2-Brig. Coast Div. Dept. South..	Nov.,	1864
4th Mass. Cav. 2 Cos...Oct., 1864	From Dist. Fla.................	To Cav. Brig. Coast Div..........	Nov.,	1864
1st East Fla. Cav.......Oct., 1864	From Dist. Fla.................	To Dept. Florida................	July,	1865
Batty. F, 3d N. Y. Arty....Oct., 1864	From Dist. Fla.................	To Arty. Brig. Coast Div.........	Nov.,	1864
75th Ohio Infy.........Jan., 1865	From 1-Brig. Coast Div. Dept. South	No change to Muster Out.........	July,	1865
34th U. S. Col'd Infy......Jan., 1865	From 2-Brig. Coast Div. Dept. South	To Dept. Fla....................	July,	1865

COAST DIVISION.—Organized Nov., 1864. Discontinued Mch., 1865.

COMMANDER.

J. P. Hatch..........	Brigadier General...............	Nov., 1864, to Mch., 1865.	

1st BRIGADE.— COMMANDERS.

E. E. Potter	Brigadier General	Nov. 28, 1864, to Jan. 23, 1865.	
C. H. Van Wyck	Col. 56th N. Y. Infy	Jan. 23, 1865, to Mch., 1865.	

56th N. Y. Infy	Nov., 1864	From 1st Separate Brig. Dept. South	To 1st Separate Brig. Dept. South	Dec., 1864
127th N. Y. Infy	Nov., 1864	From 2d Separate Brig. Dept. South	To Garrison Charleston, S. C	Feb., 1865
144th N. Y. Infy	Nov., 1864	From 3d Separate Brig. Dept. South	To 3d Separate Brig. Dept. South	Feb., 1865
157th N. Y. Infy	Nov., 1864	From 3d Separate Brig. Dept. South	To 3d Separate Brig. Dept. South	Feb., 1865
25th Ohio Infy	Nov., 1864	From 3d Separate Brig. Dept. South	To 3d Separate Brig. Dept. South	Feb., 1865
32d U. S. Col'd Infy	Nov., 1864	From 3d Separate Brig. Dept. South	To 3d Separate Brig. Dept. South	Feb., 1865
34th U. S. Col'd Infy	Dec., 1864	From 2-Brig. Coast Div. Dept. South	To 2-Brig. Coast Div. Dept. South	Dec., 1864
75th Ohio Infy	Dec., 1864	From 3d Separate Brig. Dept. South	To 4th Separate Brig. Dept. South	Jan., 1865
107th Ohio Infy	Dec., 1864	From 3d Separate Brig. Dept. South	To 1st Separate Brig. Dept. South	Feb., 1865

2d BRIGADE.—

54th Mass. Col'd Infy	Nov., 1864	From 1st Separate Brig. Dept. South	To 1st Separate Brig. Dept. South	Dec., 1864
55th Mass. Col'd Infy	Nov., 1864	From 1st Separate Brig. Dept. South	To 1st Separate Brig. Dept. South	Dec., 1864
32d U. S. Col'd Infy	Nov., 1864	From 3d Separate Brig. Dept. South	To 2d Separate Brig. Dept. South	Dec., 1864
34th U. S. Col'd Infy	Nov., 1864	From 4th Separate Brig. Dept. South	To 1-Brig. Coast Div. Dept. South	Dec., 1864
35th U. S. Col'd Infy	Nov., 1864	From 4th Separate Brig. Dept. South	To 4th Separate Brig. Dept. South	Mch., 1865
102d U. S. Col'd Infy	Dec., 1864	From 2d Separate Brig. Dept. South	To 2d Separate Brig. Dept. South	Feb., 1865
34th U. S. Col'd Infy	Dec., 1864	From 1-Brig. Coast Div. Dept. South	To 4th Separate Brig. Dept. South	Mch., 1865

ARTILLERY BRIGADE.—

3d R. I. H'vy Arty. Co. A.	Nov., 1864	From 2d Separate Brig. Dept. South	To 2d Separate Brig. Dept. South	Dec., 1864
Batty. B, 3d N. Y. Arty.	Nov., 1864	From 1st Separate Brig. Dept. South	To 1st Separate Brig. Dept. South	Dec., 1864
Batty. F, 3d N. Y. Arty.	Nov., 1864	From 4th Separate Brig. Dept. South	To 4th Separate Brig. Dept. South	Dec., 1864

CAVALRY.—

4th Mass. Cav. 2d Battn.	Nov., 1864	From 3d & 4th Separate Brigades	To 4th Separate Brig. Dept. South	Dec., 1864

DISTRICT OF SAVANNAH.— COMMANDERS.

Cuvier Grover	Bvt. Major General	Feb. 12, 1865, to June 5, 1865.	
H. W. Birge	Bvt. Major General	June 5, 1865, to June 26, 1865.	

GROVER'S DIVISION.— COMMANDERS.

Cuvier Grover	Bvt. Major General	Jan. 6, 1865, to Feb. 12, 1865.	
H. W. Birge	Bvt. Major General	Feb. 12, 1865, to Mch. 26, 1865.	

1st BRIGADE.— COMMANDERS.

H. W. Birge	Brigadier General	Jan. 6, 1865, to Feb. 12, 1865.	
H. D. Washburn	Col. 18th Infy	Feb. 12, 1865, to Mch. 27, 1865.	

12th Me. Infy	Jan., 1865	From 1-Brig. 2-Div. 19-C. Shenandoah	To Dept. S. C	June, 1865
14th Me. Infy	Jan., 1865	From 1-Brig. 2-Div. 19-C. Shenandoah	To Dept. S. C	June, 1865
14th N. H. Infy	Jan., 1865	From 1-Brig. 2-Div. 19-C. Shenandoah	To Dept. S. C	June, 1865
9th Conn. Infy	Jan., 1865	From 1-Brig. 2-Div. 19-C. Shenandoah	To Dept. S. C	June, 1865
75th N. Y. Infy	Jan., 1865	From 1-Brig. 2-Div. 19-C. Shenandoah	To Dept. S. C	June, 1865
8th Ind. Infy	Jan., 1865	From 1-Brig. 2-Div. 19-C. Shenandoah	To Dept. S. C	June, 1865
18th Ind. Infy	Jan., 1865	From 1-Brig. 2-Div. 19-C. Shenandoah	To Dept. S. C	June, 1865

2d BRIGADE.—Designated 1-Brig. 1-Div. 10-Corps Dept. N. C., Mch. 27, 1865.
COMMANDERS.

E. L. Molineux	Col. 159th N. Y. Infy	Jan. 6, 1865, to Feb. 17, 1865.	
N. W. Day	Col. 131st N. Y. Infy	Feb. 17, 1865, to Mch. 17, 1865.	
Harvey Graham	Col. 22d Iowa Infy	Mch. 17, 1865, to Mch. 27, 1865.	

13th Conn. Infy	Jan., 1865	From 2-Brig. 2-Div. 19-C. Shenandoah	To 1-Brig. 1-Div. 10-C. Dept. N. C.	Mch., 1865
131st N. Y. Infy	Jan., 1865	From 2-Brig. 2-Div. 19-C. Shenandoah	To 1-Brig. 1-Div. 10-C. Dept. N. C.	Mch., 1865
159th N. Y. Infy	Jan., 1865	From 2-Brig. 2-Div. 19-C. Shenandoah	To 1-Brig. 1-Div. 10-C. Dept. N. C.	Mch., 1865
22d Iowa Infy	Jan., 1865	From 2-Brig. 2-Div. 19-C. Shenandoah	To 1-Brig. 1-Div. 10-C. Dept. N. C.	Mch., 1865
28th Iowa Infy	Jan., 1865	From 2-Brig. 2-Div. 19-C. Shenandoah	To 1-Brig. 1-Div. 10-C. Dept. N. C.	Mch., 1865

3d BRIGADE.—Designated 3-Brig. 1-Div. 10-Corps Dept. N. C., Mch. 27, 1865.
COMMANDERS.

J. P. Richardson	Lt.-Col. 38th Mass. Infy	Jan. 6, 1865, to Mch. 4, 1865.	
H. D. Washburn	Col. 18th Ind. Infy	Mch. 4, 1865, to Mch. 27, 1865.	

38th Mass. Infy	Jan., 1865	From 3-Brig. 2-Div. 19-C. Shenandoah	To 3-Brig. 1-Div. 10-C. Dept. N. C.	Mch., 1865
24th Iowa Infy	Jan., 1865	From 3-Brig. 2-Div. 19-C. Shenandoah	To 3-Brig. 1-Div. 10-C. Dept. N. C.	Mch., 1865
128th N. Y. Infy	Jan., 1865	From 3-Brig. 2-Div. 19-C. Shenandoah	To 3-Brig. 1-Div. 10-C. Dept. N. C.	Mch., 1865
156th N. Y. Infy	Jan., 1865	From 3-Brig. 2-Div. 19-C. Shenandoah	To 3-Brig. 1-Div. 10-C. Dept. N. C.	Mch., 1865
175th N. Y. Infy	Jan., 1865	From 3-Brig. 2-Div. 19-C. Shenandoah	To 3-Brig. 1-Div. 10-C. Dept. N. C.	Mch., 1865
176th N. Y. Infy	Jan., 1865	From 3-Brig. 2-Div. 19-C. Shenandoah	To 3-Brig. 1-Div. 10-C. Dept. N. C.	Mch., 1865

UNATTACHED.—

33d U. S. Col'd Infy	Mch., 1865	From 1st Separate Brig. Dept. South	To Dept. S. C	June, 1865
103d U. S. Col'd Infy	Mch., 1865	From New Organization	To Dept. S. C	June, 1865
1st N. Y. Engrs. Battn.	Mch., 1865	From 3d Separate Brig. Dept. South	No change to Muster Out	June, 1865

Twenty-Second Army Corps---Department of Washington

Created Feb. 2, 1863, by General Order No. 26, A. G. O., and designated the 22d Army Corps. Discontinued June 11, 1866.

CORPS COMMANDERS.

S. P. Heintzelman	Major General	Feb. 2, 1863, to Oct. 13, 1863.	
C. C. Augur	Major General	Oct. 13, 1863, to June 7, 1865.	
J. G. Parke	Major General	June 7, 1865, to June 26, 1865.	
C. C. Augur	Major General	June 26, 1865, to June 11, 1866.	

ABERCROMBIE'S DIVISION.— COMMANDER.

J. J. Abercrombie	Brigadier General	Feb. 2, 1863, to June 26, 1863.	

Division transferred to Army Potomac June, 1863.

1st BRIGADE.—Organized April, 1863, from 1st Brigade Casey's Division.
COMMANDER.

Francis Fessenden	Col. 25th Maine Infy	Apr. 18, 1863, to June 28, 1863.	

25th Maine Infy	Apr., 1862	From 1-Brig. Casey's Div. 22-Corps	No change to Muster Out	July, 1863
27th Maine Infy	Apr., 1862	From 1-Brig. Casey's Div. 22-Corps	No change to Muster Out	July, 1863

2d BRIGADE.— COMMANDERS.

R. Cowdin	Brigadier General	Feb. 2, 1863, to Mch. 31, 1863.
B. Porter	Col. 40th Mass. Infy	Mch. 31, 1863, to Apr. 17, 1863.
Brigade transferred to Dept. Va. Apr., 1863. Reorganized from 2-Brig. Casey's Div. Apr., 1863.		
G. J. Stannard	Brigadier General	Apr. 17, 1863, to June 26, 1863.

22d Conn. Infy	Feb., 1863	From 2-Brig. Abercrombie's Div....	To 1-Brig. Gurney's Div. 7-Corps...	Apr., 1863
40th Mass. Infy	Feb., 1863	From 2-Brig. Abercrombie's Div....	To 1-Brig. Gurney's Div. 7-Corps...	Apr., 1863
141st New York Infy	Feb., 1863	From 2-Brig. Abercrombie's Div....	To 1-Brig. Gurney's Div. 7-Corps...	Apr., 1863
16th West Va. Infy	Feb., 1863	From 2-Brig. Abercrombie's Div....	To 2-Brig. Def. South Pot. 22-Corps	Apr., 1863
12th Vermont Infy	Feb., 1863	From 2-Brig. Casey's Div. 22-Corps	To 3-Brig. 3-Div. 1-Corps Potomac.	June, 1863
13th Vermont Infy	Apr., 1863	From 2-Brig. Casey's Div. 22-Corps	To 3-Brig. 3-Div. 1-Corps Potomac.	June, 1863
14th Vermont Infy	Apr., 1863	From 2-Brig. Casey's Div. 22-Corps	To 3-Brig. 3-Div. 1-Corps Potomac.	June, 1863
15th Vermont Infy	Apr., 1863	From 2-Brig. Casey's Div. 22-Corps	To 3-Brig. 3-Div. 1-Corps Potomac.	June, 1863
16th Vermont Infy	Apr., 1863	From 2-Brig. Casey's Div. 22-Corps	To 3-Brig. 3-Div. 1-Corps Potomac.	June, 1863

3d BRIGADE.— COMMANDER.

William Gurney	Col. 127th New York Infy	Feb. 2, 1863, to Apr. 17, 1863.
Brigade transferred to Dept. of Va. April, 1863. Reorganized April, 1863, from 3d Brigade Casey's Division.		
Alex. Hays	Brigadier General	Apr. 17, 1863, to Apr. 26, 1863.
G. L. Willard	Col. 125th New York Infy	Apr. 26, 1863, to May 6, 1863.
Alex. Hays	Brigadier General	May 6, 1863, to June 26, 1863.

127th New York Infy	Feb., 1863	From 3-Brig. Abercrombie's Div...	To 2-Brig. Gurney's Div. 7-Corps..	Apr., 1863
142d New York Infy	Feb., 1863	From 3-Brig. Abercrombie's Div...	To 2-Brig. Gurney's Div. 7-Corps..	Apr., 1863
143d New York Infy	Feb., 1863	From 3-Brig. Abercrombie's Div...	To 2-Brig. Gurney's Div. 7-Corps..	Apr., 1863
144th New York Infy	Feb., 1863	From 3-Brig. Abercrombie's Div...	To 2-Brig. Gurney's Div. 7-Corps..	Apr., 1863
39th New York Infy	Apr., 1863	From 3-Brig. Casey's Div. Wash...	To 3-Brig. 3-Div. 2-Corps Potomac.	June, 1863
111th New York Infy	Apr., 1863	From 3-Brig. Casey's Div. Wash...	To 3-Brig. 3-Div. 2-Corps Potomac.	June, 1863
125th New York Infy	Apr., 1863	From 3-Brig. Casey's Div. Wash...	To 3-Brig. 3-Div. 2-Corps Potomac.	June, 1863
126th New York Infy	Apr., 1863	From 3-Brig. Casey's Div. Wash...	To 3-Brig. 3-Div. 2-Corps Potomac.	June, 1863

UNASSIGNED.—

9th Mass. Indpt. Batty	Feb., 1863	From Abercrombie's Div. Wash....	To 1-Vol. Brig. Arty. Res. Potomac	June, 1863
4th N. Y. Heavy Arty	Feb., 1863	From Abercrombie's Div. Wash....	To 1-Brig. Def. South Pot. 22-Corps	Apr., 1863
17th N. Y. Indpt. Batty	Feb., 1863	From Abercrombie's Div. Wash....	To Camp Barry 22-Corps	June, 1863
2d Conn. Indpt. Batty	Apr., 1863	From Arty. Casey's Div. 22-Corps..	To 2-Vol. Brig. Arty. Res. Potomac.	June, 1863
11th Mass. Indpt. Batty	Apr., 1863	From Arty. Casey's Div. 22-Corps..	No change to Muster Out.	May, 1863
Batty. H, 1st R. I. Arty	Apr., 1863	From Arty. Casey's Div. 22-Corps..	To 3-Brig. Def. South Pot. 22-Corps	May, 1863
Keystone, Pa., Batty	Apr., 1863	From Arty. Casey's Div. 22-Corps..	To Camp Barry 22-Corps	June, 1863

CASEY'S DIVISION.—Discontinued April, 1863.

COMMANDER.

Silas Casey	Major General	Feb. 2, 1863, to Apr. 17, 1863.

1st BRIGADE.— COMMANDER.

Francis Fessenden	Col. 25th Maine Infy	Feb. 2, 1863, to Apr. 17, 1863.
Brigade transferred to Abercrombie's Division Apr., 1863.		

25th Maine Infy	Feb., 1863	From 1-Brig. Casey's Div. Wash...	To. 1-Brig. Abercrombie's Div. 22-C.	Apr., 1863
27th Maine Infy	Feb., 1863	From 1-Brig. Casey's Div. Wash...	To. 1-Brig. Abercrombie's Div. 22-C.	Apr., 1863

2d BRIGADE.— COMMANDERS.

E. H. Stoughton	Brigadier General	Feb. 2, 1863, to Mch. 9, 1863.
Asa P. Blount	Col. 12th Vermont Infy	Mch. 8, 1863, to Apr. 17, 1863.
Brigade transferred to Abercrombie's Division April, 1863.		

12th Vermont Infy	Feb., 1863	From 2-Brig. Casey's Div. Wash...	To 2-Brig. Abercrombie's Div. 22-C.	Apr., 1863
13th Vermont Infy	Feb., 1863	From 2-Brig. Casey's Div. Wash...	To 2-Brig. Abercrombie's Div. 22-C.	Apr., 1863
14th Vermont Infy	Feb., 1863	From 2-Brig. Casey's Div. Wash...	To 2-Brig. Abercrombie's Div. 22-C.	Apr., 1863
15th Vermont Infy	Feb., 1863	From 2-Brig. Casey's Div. Wash...	To 2-Brig. Abercrombie's Div. 22-C.	Apr., 1863
16th Vermont Infy	Feb., 1863	From 2-Brig. Casey's Div. Wash...	To 2-Brig. Abercrombie's Div. 22-C.	Apr., 1863

3d BRIGADE.— COMMANDER.

Alex. Hays	Brigadier General	Feb. 2, 1863, to Apr. 17, 1863.
Brigade transferred to Abercrombie's Division Apr., 1863.		

39th New York Infy	Feb., 1863	From 3-Brig. Casey's Div. Wash...	To 3-Brig. Abercrombie's Div. 22-C.	Apr., 1863
111th New York Infy	Feb., 1863	From 3-Brig. Casey's Div. Wash...	To 3-Brig. Abercrombie's Div. 22-C.	Apr., 1863
125th New York Infy	Feb., 1863	From 3-Brig. Casey's Div. Wash...	To 3-Brig. Abercrombie's Div. 22-C.	Apr., 1863
126th New York Infy	Feb., 1863	From 3-Brig. Casey's Div. Wash...	To 3-Brig. Abercrombie's Div. 22-C.	Apr., 1863

ARTILLERY.—

2d Conn. Indpt. Batty	Feb., 1863	From Casey's Div. Washington....	To Abercrombie's Div. 22-Corps....	Apr., 1863
11th Mass. Indpt. Batty	Feb., 1863	From Casey's Div. Washington....	To Abercrombie's Div. 22-Corps....	Apr., 1863
Batty. H, 1st R. I. Arty	Feb., 1863	From Casey's Div. Washington....	To Abercrombie's Div. 22-Corps....	Apr., 1863
Keystone, Pa., Batty	Feb., 1863	From Casey's Div. Washington....	To Abercrombie's Div. 22-Corps....	Apr., 1863

DISTRICT OF ALEXANDRIA.— COMMANDERS.

J. P. Slough	Brigadier General	Feb. 2, 1863, to Nov. 5, 1864.
H. H. Wells	Col. 26th Michigan Infy	Nov. 5, 1864, to Dec. 5, 1864.
J. P. Slough	Brigadier General	Dec. 5, 1864, to Apr. 26, 1865.
J. G. Parke	Major General	Apr. 26, 1865, to June 5, 1865.
J. P. Slough	Brigadier General	June 5, 1865, to July 20, 1865.
Discontinued July 20, 1865.		

1st Dist. Columbia Infy	Feb., 1863	From Dist. Alexandria Def. Wash..	Consolidated with 2d Dist. Columbia	Feb., 1865
26th Michigan Infy	Feb., 1863	From Dist. Alexandria Def. Wash..	To 1-Brig. 1-Div. 7-Corps Dept. Va.	Apr., 1863
153d New York Infy	Feb., 1863	From Dist. Alexandria Def. Wash..	To Dist. Washington 22-Corps.....	July, 1863
11th Rhode Island Infy	Feb., 1863	From Dist. Alexandria Def. Wash..	To 1-Brig. 1-Div. 7-Corps Dept. Va.	Apr., 1863
23d Maine Infy	Apr., 1863	From Jewett's Brigade 22-Corps...	No change to Muster Out	July, 1863
Indpt. Batty. H, Pa. Arty	Apr., 1863	From Artillery Camp 22-Corps.....	To Camp Barry 22-Corps	Nov., 1864
4th Delaware Infy	Dec., 1863	From King's Div. 22-Corps	To 1-Brig. Tyler's Div. 22-Corps...	Dec., 1863
5th New York Vet'n Infy	Dec., 1863	From New Organization	To 1-Brig. 1-Div. 5-Corps Potomac	May, 1864
2d Dist. Columbia Infy	May, 1864	From 1-Brig. Tyler's Div. 22-Corps.	No change to Muster Out	Sept., 1865
26th Mich. Infy. Co. F	July, 1864	From 1-Brig. 1-Div. 2-Corps Potom.	No change to Muster Out	June, 1865
201st Penna. Infy	Oct., 1864	From New Organization	To Fort Delaware	May, 1865
202d Penna. Infy	Oct., 1864	From New Organization	To 1-Separate Brig. 22-Corps	Nov., 1864
5th Penna. Heavy Arty	Oct., 1864	From New Organization	To 1-Separate Brig. 22-Corps	Nov., 1864
6th Penna. Heavy Arty	Oct., 1864	From New Organization	To 2-Brig. DeRussy's Div. 22-Corps.	Nov., 1864
Battys. L. & M. 3d U. S.	Feb., 1865	From Camp Barry 22-Corps	To Regular Establishment	Aug., 1865

2d BRIGADE, PENNA. RESERVE CORPS.— COMMANDERS.

H. G. Sickel	Col. 3d Penna. Reserves	April, 1863, to Sept., 1863.	*
H. C. Bollinger	Col. 7th Penna. Reserves	Sept., 1863, to Oct., 1863.	
H. G Sickel	Col. 3d Penna. Reserves	Oct., 1863, to Apr., 1864.	

3d Penna. Reserves	Apr., 1863	From 2-Brig. Pa. Reserve Div. 22-C.	To 3-Brig. 2-Infy. Div. Dept. W. Va.	Apr., 1864
4th Penna. Reserves	Apr., 1863	From 2-Brig. Pa. Reserve Div. 22-C.	To 3-Brig. 2-Infy. Div. Dept. W. Va.	Apr., 1864
7th Penna. Reserves	Apr., 1863	From 2-Brig. Pa. Reserve Div. 22-C.	To 1-Brig. 3-Div. 5-Corps Potomac.	Apr., 1864
8th Penna. Reserves	Apr., 1863	From 2-Brig. Pa. Reserve Div. 22-C.	To 3-Brig. 3-Div. 5-Corps Potomac.	Apr., 1864

ARTILLERY DEFENCES OF ALEXANDRIA.— COMMANDER.

R. O. Tyler	Brigadier General	Feb. 2, 1863, to Apr. 15, 1863.	

Designated 2d Brigade Defences South of the Potomac April 15, 1863.

1st Conn. Heavy Arty	Feb., 1863	From D. Alexandria, Mil. D. Wash.	To 2-Brig. Def. South Pot. 22-Corps	Apr., 1863
19th Conn. 2d H. A.	Feb., 1863	From D. Alexandria, Mil. D. Wash.	To 2-Brig. Def. South Pot. 22-Corps	Apr., 1863

ARTY. BRIGADE SOUTH OF THE POTOMAC.— COMMANDERS.

M. Cogswell	Col. 2d N. Y. Heavy Arty	Feb. 2, 1863, to Apr. 9, 1863.	
T. R. Tannatt	Col. 1st Mass. Heavy Arty	Apr. 9, 1863, to Apr. 15, 1863.	

1st Mass. Heavy Arty	Feb., 1863	From D. Alexandria, Mil. D. Wash.	To 1-Brig. Def. South Pot. 22-Corps	Apr., 1863
14th Mass. Infy	Feb., 1863	From D. Alexandria, Mil. D. Wash.	To 1-Brig. Def. South Pot. 22-Corps	Apr., 1863
2d N. Y. Heavy Arty	Feb., 1863	From D. Alexandria, Mil. D. Wash.	To 1-Brig. Def. South Pot. 22-Corps	Apr., 1863
3d Battn. N. Y. Heavy A.	Feb., 1863	From D. Alexandria, Mil. D. Wash.	To 1-Brig. Def. South Pot. 22-Corps	Apr., 1863
1st Wis. Heavy A. Co. A.	Feb., 1863	From D. Alexandria Mil. D. Wash.	To 1-Brig. Def. South Pot. 22-Corps	Apr., 1863

PENNA.—RESERVE DIVISION.— COMMANDER.

H. G. Sickel	Col. 3d Penna. Reserves	Feb. 6, 1863, to Apr. 12, 1863.	

1st BRIGADE.— COMMANDERS.

Wm. McCandless	Col. 2d Penna. Reserves	Feb. 6, 1863, to Mch. 29, 1863.	
W. Sinclair	Col. 6th Penna. Reserves	Mch. 29, 1863, to May 29, 1863.	
Wm. McCandless	Col. 2d Penna. Reserves	May 29, 1863, to June 26, 1863.	

Brigade transferred to Army Potomac June, 1863.

1st Penna. Reserves	Feb., 1863	From 1-Brig. 3-Div. 1-Corps Potom.	To 1-Brig. 3-Div. 5-Corps Potomac.	June, 1863
2d Penna. Reserves	Feb., 1863	From 1-Brig. 3-Div. 1-Corps Potom.	To 1-Brig. 3-Div. 5-Corps Potomac.	June, 1863
6th Penna. Reserves	Feb., 1863	From 1-Brig. 3-Div. 1-Corps Potom.	To 1-Brig. 3-Div. 5-Corps Potomac.	June, 1863
13th Penna. Reserves	Feb., 1863	From 1-Brig. 3-Div. 1-Corps Potom.	To 1-Brig. 3-Div. 5-Corps Potomac.	June, 1863

2d BRIGADE.— COMMANDERS.

H. C. Bollinger	Col. 7th Penna. Reserves	Feb. 6, 1863, to April 12, 1863.	
H. G. Sickel	Col. 3d Penna. Reserves	Apr. 12, 1863, to April 15, 1863.	

3d Penna. Reserves	Feb., 1863	From 2-Brig. 3-Div. 1-Corps Potom.	To Dist. Alexandria 22-Corps	Apr., 1863
4th Penna. Reserves	Feb., 1863	From 2-Brig. 3-Div. 1-Corps Potom.	To Dist. Alexandria 22-Corps	Apr., 1863
7th Penna. Reserves	Feb., 1863	From 2-Brig. 3-Div. 1-Corps Potom.	To Dist. Alexandria 22-Corps	Apr., 1863
8th Penna. Reserves	Feb., 1863	From 2-Brig. 3-Div. 1-Corps Potom.	To Dist. Alexandria 22-Corps	Apr., 1863

3d BRIGADE.— COMMANDER.

J. W. Fisher	Col. 5th Penna. Reserves	Feb. 6, 1863, to June 26, 1863.	

Brigade transferred to Army Potomac June, 1863.

5th Penna. Reserves	Feb., 1863	From 3-Brig. 3-Div. 1-Corps Potom.	To 3-Brig. 3-Div. 5-Corps Potomac.	June, 1863
9th Penna. Reserves	Feb., 1863	From 3-Brig. 3-Div. 1-Corps Potom.	To 3-Brig. 3-Div. 5-Corps Potomac.	June, 1863
10th Penna. Reserves	Feb., 1863	From 3-Brig. 3-Div. 1-Corps Potom.	To 3-Brig. 3-Div. 5-Corps Potomac.	June, 1863
11th Penna. Reserves	Feb., 1863	From 3-Brig. 3-Div. 1-Corps Potom.	To 3-Brig. 3-Div. 5-Corps Potomac.	June, 1863
12th Penna. Reserves	Feb., 1863	From 3-Brig. 3-Div. 1-Corps Potom.	To 3-Brig. 3-Div. 5-Corps Potomac.	June, 1863

DISTRICT OF WASHINGTON.—Discontinued Dec. 10, 1864. Reorganized April 25, 1865. Discontinued Aug. 2, 1865. COMMANDERS.

J. H. Martindale	Brigadier General	Feb. 2, 1863, to Sept. 16, 1863.	
J. P. Sherbourne	Major A. A. G. U. S. A.	Temporarily in Sept., 1863.	
M. N. Wisewell	Col. 6th V. R. C.	Sept. 16, 1863, to Oct. 1, 1863.	
J. H. Martindale	Brigadier General	Oct. 1, 1863, to May 2, 1864.	
M. N. Wisewell	Col. 6th V. R. C.	May 2, 1864, to Dec. 10, 1864.	
O. B. Willcox	Bvt. Major General	Apr. 25, 1865, to Aug. 2, 1865.	

2d Dist. Columbia Infy	Feb., 1863	From Mil. Dist. Washington	To 1-Brig. Tyler's Div. 22-Corps	Jan., 1864
10th New Jersey Infy	Feb., 1863	From Mil. Dist. Washington	To 3-Brig. 1-Div. 7-Corps Dept. Va.	Apr., 1863
118th New York Infy	Feb., 1863	From Prov'l Brig. Abercrombie's D.	To Reserve Brig. 7-Corps Dept. Va.	Apr., 1863
152d New York Infy	Feb., 1863	From Prov'l Brig. Abercrombie's D.	To 3-Brig. 1-Div. 7-Corps Dept. Va.	Apr., 1863
169th New York Infy	Feb., 1863	From Prov'l Brig. Abercrombie's D.	To 2-Brig. 1-Div. 7-Corps Dept. Va.	Apr., 1863
27th Penna. Infy., Co. F.	Feb., 1863	From Mil. Dist. Washington	No change to Muster Out	June, 1864
150th Pa. Infy., Co. K.	Feb., 1863	From Mil. Dist. Washington	No change to Muster Out	June, 1865
157th Pa. Infy. 4 Cos.	Feb., 1863	From New Organization	To 1-Brig. Tyler's Div. 22-Corps	Jan., 1864
34th Mass. Infy	May, 1863	From 1-Brig. Def. South Pot. 22-C.	To 1-B. Md. Heights Div. D. W. Va.	July, 1863
39th Mass. Infy	May, 1863	From Jewett's Brigade 22-Corps	To 1-Brig. 2-Div. 1-Corps Potomac.	July, 1863
14th New Hamp. Infy	May, 1863	From Jewett's Brigade 22-Corps	To New Orleans Dept. Gulf.	Feb., 1864
153d New York Infy	July, 1863	From Dist. Alexandria 22-Corps	To 1-B. 1-Div. 19-Corps Dept. Gulf.	Feb., 1864
178th New York Infy	July, 1863	From 3-Brig. Def. South Pot. 22-C.	To Dist. Col. 6-Div. 16-Corps Tenn.	Oct., 1863
1st Veteran Res. Corps	Oct., 1863	From New Organization	To 1-B. V. R. C. Dist. Wash. 22-C.	Mch., 1864
6th Veteran Res. Corps	Oct., 1863	From New Organization	To 1-B. V. R. C. Dist. Wash. 22-C.	Mch., 1864
9th Veteran Res. Corps	Oct., 1863	From New Organization	To 1-B. V. R. C. Dist. Wash. 22-C.	Mch., 1864

1st BRIGADE.—Organized Mch. 23, 1864. COMMANDERS.

R. H. Rush	Col. 1st V. R. C.	Mch. 23, 1864, to May 21, 1864.	
M. N. Wisewell	Col. 6th V. R. C.	May 21, 1864, to July 6, 1864.	
G. W. Gile	Col. 9th V. R. C.	July 6, 1864, to May, 1865.	

Brigade transferred to Garrison Washington.

1st Veteran Res. Corps	Mch., 1864	From Dist. Washington 22-Corps	To Garrison Washington 22-Corps.	May, 1865
6th Veteran Res. Corps	Mch., 1864	From Dist. Washington 22-Corps	To Garrison Washington 22-Corps.	May, 1865
9th Veteran Res. Corps	Mch., 1864	From Dist. Washington 22-Corps	To Garrison Washington 22-Corps.	May, 1865
19th Veteran R. Corps	Mch., 1864	From New Organization	To Garrison Washington 22-Corps.	May, 1865
22d Veteran Res. Corps	Mch., 1864	From New Organization	To Garrison Washington 22-Corps.	May, 1865
24th Veteran R. Corps	Mch., 1864	From New Organization	To 2-Brig. V. R. C. Dist. Wash.	May, 1864
18th Veteran R. Corps	Aug., 1864	From 2-Brig. Veteran Res. Corps	To Garrison Washington 22-Corps.	May, 1865
24th Veteran R. Corps	Aug., 1864	From 2-Brig. Veteran Res. Corps	To Garrison Washington 22-Corps.	May, 1865
3d Veteran Res. Corps	Oct., 1864	From 2-Brig. Hardin's Div. 22-Corps	To Garrison Washington 22-Corps.	May, 1865
7th Veteran Res. Corps	Oct., 1864	From 2-Brig. Hardin's Div. 22-Corps	To Garrison Washington 22-Corps.	May, 1865
10th Veteran Res. Corps	Oct., 1864	From 2-Brig. Hardin's Div. 22-Corps	To Garrison Washington 22-Corps.	May, 1865
21st Veteran Res. Corps	Oct., 1864	From 2-Brig. Hardin's Div. 22-Corps	To Garrison Washington 22-Corps.	May, 1865

2d BRIGADE.—Organized May 28, 1864.   COMMANDER.

W. H. Browne.........	Col. 24th Veteran Res. Corps......	May 28, 1864, to Aug. 1, 1864.	

Brigade discontinued Aug. 1, 1864.

18th Veteran R. Corps....May,1864	From New Organization...........	To 1-Brig. Veteran Res. Corps.....	Aug., 1864
24th Veteran R. Corps....May, 1864	From New Organization...........	To 1-Brig. Veteran Res. Corps.....	Aug., 1864

CAVALRY.—

11th New York Cav......Feb., 1863	From. Mil. Dist. Washington......	To Dist. LaFourche Dept. Gulf....	Mch., 1864
1st Dist. Columbia Cav....Dec., 1863	From New Organization...........	To Norfolk, Va., Dept. Va. & N. C.	Apr., 1864
8th Illinois Cav.........Apr., 1864	From Veteran Furlough...........	To Unatt. 22-Corps........	May, 1864
Union Light Guard Ohio..Apr., 1864	From New Organization...........	No change to Muster Out........	Sept., 1865

LIGHT ARTILLERY CAMP—CAMP BARRY.—   COMMANDERS.

William F. Barry......	Brigadier General..................	Feb. 2, 1863, to Mch. 3, 1863.
A. P. Howe...........	Brigadier General..................	Mch. 3, 1863, to July 9, 1864.
J. A. Hall...........	Major 1st Maine H. A.	July 9, 1864, to Aug. 9, 1864.
A. P. Howe...........	Brigadier General..................	Aug. 9, 1864, to Sept. 22, 1864.
J. A. Hall...........	Major 1st Maine H. A.	Sept. 22, 1864, to Oct. 12, 1864.
A. P. Howe...........	Brigadier General..................	Oct. 12, 1864, to Oct. 26, 1864.
J. A. Hall...........	Lt.-Col. 1st Maine H. A.	Oct. 26, 1864, to Nov. 1, 1864.
A. P. Howe...........	Brigadier General..................	Nov. 1, 1864, to Apr. 7, 1865.
J. A. Hall...........	Lt.-Col. 1st Maine H. A.	Apr. 7, 1865, to May 7, 1865.
A. P. Howe...........	Brigadier General..................	May 7, 1865, to July 20, 1865.

Batty. I. 1st Mich. Arty...Feb., 1863	From New Organization...........	To Cav. Div. 22-Corps...........	Mch., 1863
Batty. K, 1st Mich. Arty...Feb., 1863	From New Organization...........	To 1-Brig. Def. South Pot. 22-Corps	Apr., 1863
Batty. A, 1st N. Y. Arty...Feb., 1863	From New Organization...........	To Dept. Susquehanna.............	June, 1863
12th N. Y. Indpt. Batty...Feb., 1863	From Camp Barry Dist. Wash......	To Arty. Brig. 3-Corps Pot.......	July, 1863
16th N. Y. Indpt. Batty...Feb., 1863	From Camp Barry Dist. Wash......	To Unatt. Suffolk, Va. 7-C. Dept. Va.	Apr., 1863
Indpt. Batty H. Pa. Arty...Feb., 1863	From Camp Barry Dist. Wash......	To Dist. Alexandria 22-Corps......	Apr., 1863
19th N. Y. Indpt. Batty...Feb., 1863	From Camp Barry Dist. Wash......	To Unatt. Arty. 7-Corps Dept. Va.	Apr., 1863
27th N. Y. Indpt. Batty...Feb., 1863	From Camp Barry Dist. Wash......	To Phila., Pa. Dept. Susquehanna..	July, 1863
Batty. A, 1st W. Va. Arty...Feb., 1863	From Camp Barry Dist. Wash......	To Md. Heights Div. Dept. W. Va..	July, 1863
1st Del. Batty..........Feb., 1863	From Camp Barry Dist. Wash......	To Unatt. Arty. 7-C. Dept. Va......	Apr., 1863
Batty. B, Md. Arty.....June, 1863	From Unatt. Arty. Res. Pot........	To 2-Br. Md. H'ts Div. Dept. W. Va.	July, 1863
17th N. Y. Indpt. Batty..June, 1863	From Abercrombie's Div. 22-Corps..	To Arty. King's Div. 22-Corps.....	July, 1863
30th N. Y. Indpt. Batty..June, 1863	From 2-Vol. Brig. Arty. Res. Pot..	To 1-Div. Dept. Susquehanna......	July, 1863
32d N. Y. Indpt. Batty...June, 1863	From 2-Vol. Brig. Arty. Res. Pot..	To 2-Brig. Md. Heights Div. W. Va.:	July, 1863
12th Ohio Indpt. Batty..June, 1863	From Unatt. Arty. Res. Pot.......	To Arty. Brig. 11-Corps Pot.......	Sept., 1863
Batty. C, 1st Pa. Arty..June, 1863	From Arty. Brig. 6-Corps Pot......	To 1-Brig. Md. Heights Div. W. Va.	July, 1863
Indpt. Batty. D, Pa. Arty.June, 1863	From Arty. Brig. 6-Corps Pot......	To Unatt. Md. Heights Div. W. Va.	Aug., 1863
Keystone Penna. Batty..June, 1863	From Abercrombie's Div. 22-Corps..	To Unatt. Md. Heights Div. W. Va.	July, 1863
Batty. K, 1st Mich. Arty..June, 1863	From 1-Brig. Def. South Pot. 22-C..	To Arty. Brig. 11-Corps Pot.......	Sept., 1863
2d Conn. Indpt. Batty...July, 1863	From 2-Vol. Brig. Arty. Res. Pot..	To N. Y. City Dept. East.........	Aug., 1863
19th N. Y. Indpt. Batty..July, 1863	From Arty. 1-Div. 7-Corps Dept. Va.	To Arty. 2-Div. 19-C. Dept. Gulf..	Apr., 1864
1st Del. Batty.........July, 1863	From Arty. 1-Div. 7-Corps Dept. Va.	To N. Y. City Dept. East.........	Aug., 1863
10th N. Y. Indpt. Batty..July, 1863	From 1-Vol. Brig. Arty. Res. Pot..	To Transferred to 6th N. Y. Batty..	June, 1864
7th Mass. Indpt. Batty..July, 1863	From 2-Br. 1-Div. 7-Corps Dept. Va.	To Arty. 2-Div. 19-C. Dept. Gulf..	Jan., 1864
Batty. F, 1st N. Y. Arty..July, 1863	From Yorktown, Va. Res. Arty. 4-C.	To 2-Brig. Def. South Pot. 22-Corps	May, 1864
Batty. H. 1st N. Y. Arty..July, 1863	From Yorktown, Va. Res. Arty. 4-C.	To Arty. Brig. 1-Corps Pot.......	Oct., 1863
4th N. Y. Indpt. Batty..July, 1863	From 1-Vol. Brig. Arty. Res. Pot...	To 1-Vol. Brig. Arty. Res. Pot....	Sept., 1863
Batty. H. 1st Pa. Arty..July, 1863	From Arty. 4-Corps Dept. Va......	To 1-Brig. Def. South Pot. 22-C...	May, 1864
Batty. F. 1st W. Va. Arty..July, 1863	From French's Div. 8-Corps.......	To 3-Brig. 2-Div. Dept. W. Va....	Dec., 1863
Batty. I, 5th U. S. Arty..July, 1863	From Arty. Brig. 6-Corps Pot......	To Arty. Brig. 2-Corps Pot.......	Nov., 1863
Batty. L, 5th U. S. Arty..Aug., 1863	From 3-Separate Brig. 8-Corps.....	To Arty. 2-Cav. Div. Dept. W. Va..	July, 1864
2d Conn. Indpt. Batty...Oct., 1863	From Dept. of the East...........	To Dept. Gulf.............	Feb., 1864
1st Del. Batty.........Oct., 1863	From Dept. of the East...........	To Dept. of the Gulf.............	Feb., 1864
3d N. J. Batty.........Oct., 1863	From New Organization...........	To Abercrombie's Com. Belle Pl....	May, 1864
4th N. J. Batty.........Oct., 1863	From New Organization...........	To Arty. 2-Div. 10-C. Dept.Va.&N.C.	Apr., 1864
5th N. J. Batty.........Oct., 1863	From New Organization...........	To Arty. 1-Div. 10-C. Va. & N. C...	Apr., 1864
2d Me. Indpt. Batty.....Oct., 1863	From Arty. Brig. 1-Corps Pot......	To Arty. Brig. 1-Div. 9-Corps Pot..	Apr., 1864
33d N. Y. Indpt. Batty...Oct., 1863	From New Organization...........	To U. S. Forces Yorktown, Va.&N.C.	Feb., 1864
Batty. H. 1st R. I. Arty...Oct., 1863	From 3-Brig. Def. South Pot. 22-C..	To Arty. Res. 9-Corps Pot........	Apr., 1864
Batty. D. 5th U. S. Arty..Nov., 1863	From Arty. Brig. 5-Corps Pot......	To Arty. Brig. 5-Corps Pot........	Mch., 1864
Batty. F. 5th U. S. Arty..Dec., 1863	From Arty. Brig. 6-Corps Pot......	To Arty. Brig. 18-Corps Va. & N. C.	July, 1864
Indpt. Batty. I. Pa. Arty..Jan., 1864	From New Organization...........	To 2-Brig. Def. South Pot. 22-Corps	May, 1864
27th N. Y. Indpt. Batty..Jan., 1864	From Dept. Susquehanna.........	To Arty. 3-Div. 9-Corps Pot......	Apr., 1864
3d Vt. Batty...........Jan., 1864	From New Organization...........	To Arty. 4-Div. 9-Corps Pot......	Apr., 1864
3d Me. Indpt. Batty.....Feb., 1864	Reorganized from M. 1st Me. H. A.	To Arty. 3-Div. 9-Corps Pot......	July, 1864
7th Me. Indpt. Batty.....Feb., 1864	From New Organization...........	To Arty. 3-Div. 9-Corps Pot......	Apr., 1864
11th Mass. Indpt. Batty..Feb., 1864	From New Organization...........	To Arty. 2-Div. 9-Corps Pot......	Apr., 1864
13th Mich. Indpt. Batty..Feb., 1864	From New Organization...........	To 1-Brig. Def. North Pot 22-Corps	May, 1864
14th Mich. Indpt. Batty..Feb., 1864	From New Organization...........	To 1-Brig. Def. North Pot 22-Corps	May, 1864
1st Me. Indpt. Batty.....Mch., 1864	From Veteran furlough...........	To 1-Brig. Def. South Pot. 22-Corps	May, 1864
Batty. A. Md. Arty......Mch., 1864	From New Organization...........	To 2-Brig. Def. South Pot. 22-Corps	June, 1864
16th Mass. Indpt. Batty..Mch., 1864	From New Organization...........	To Arty. Brig. 18-Corps Va. & N. C.	July, 1864
17th N. Y. Indpt. Batty..Mch., 1864	From King's Div. 22-Corps........	To 2-Brig. Def. North Pot. 22-Corps	May, 1864
Batty. L. 1st Ohio Arty..Mch., 1864	From Arty. Brig. 5-Corps Pot......	To 2-Brig. Def. South Pot. 22-Corps	May, 1864
Batty. G. 1st Pa. Arty..Mch., 1864	From Arty. Brig. 5-Corps Pot......	No change to Muster Out........	June, 1865
Indpt. Batty. C. Pa. Arty..Mch., 1864	From Arty. Brig. 2-Corps Pot......	To 2-Brig. Def. South Pot. 22-Corps	May, 1864
Indpt. Batty. F. Pa. Arty..Mch., 1864	From Arty. Brig. 2-Corps Pot......	To 2-Brig. Def. South Pot. 22-Corps	May, 1864
Batty. C. 1st W. Va. Arty..Mch., 1864	From 1-Vol. Brig. Arty. Res. Pot..	To 2-Brig. Def. South Pot. 22-Corps	May, 1864
Batty. K. 1st N. Y. Arty..Mch., 1864	From 2-Vol. Brig. Arty. Res. Pot..	To 1-Brig. Def. South Pot. 22-Corps	May, 1864
Batty. A. 4th U. S. Arty..June, 1864	From 1-Brig. Horse Arty. Pot.....	To Regular Establishment.........	Aug., 1865
6th N. Y. Indpt. Batty..June, 1864	From 1-Brig. Horse Arty. Pot.....	To Horse Arty. Army Shenandoah..	Aug., 1864
Batty. K. 1st U. S. Arty..June, 1864	From 2-Brig. Horse Arty. Pot.....	To Horse Arty. Army Shenandoah..	Aug., 1864
Battys. C. & E. 2d U. S...July, 1864	From Arty. 2-Div. 19-C. Dept. Gulf	To Regular Establishment.........	Aug., 1865
16th Mass. Indpt. Batty..July, 1864	From 2-Brig. Def. South Pot. 22-C.	To 1-Separate Brig. 22-Corps......	Nov., 1864
Battys. L. & M. 3d U. S...July, 1864	From Res. Arty. 9-Corps Pot......	To Dist. Alexandria 22-Corps......	Feb., 1865
Battys. A. & F. 1st U. S...Aug., 1864	From Dept. of the Gulf..........	To 1-Brig. Def. South Pot. 22-C...	Dec., 1864
Indpt. Batty. H. Pa. Arty..Nov., 1864	From Dist. Alexandria, 22-Corps....	No change to Muster Out.........	June, 1865
Batty. I. 3d U. S. Arty..Nov., 1864	From Dept. East...............	To Regular Establishment.........	Aug., 1865
Batty. C. 1st R. I. Arty..Nov., 1864	From Arty. Brig. 6-Corps Pot......	Consol. with Batty. G. 1st R. I....	Dec., 1864
Batty. G. 1st R. I. Arty..Nov., 1864	From Arty. Brig. 6-Corps Pot......	To Arty. Brig. 6-Corps Pot.......	Dec., 1864
30th N. Y. Indpt. Batty..Jan., 1865	From Res. Div. Harper's F'y, W. Va.	No change to Muster Out........	June, 1865
Batty. E. 1st W. Va. Arty..Jan., 1865	From Res. Div. Harper's F'y, W. Va.	No change to Muster Out........	June, 1865
Batty. M. 5th U. S. Arty..Jan., 1865	From Res. Div. Harper's F'y, W. Va.	To Regular Establishment.........	Aug., 1865
Baltimore, Md. Batty......Jan., 1865	From Res. Div. Harper's F'y, W. Va.	No change to Muster Out........	June, 1865
Batty. G. 4th U. S. Arty..Feb., 1865	From Dept. Cumberland reorganized.	To Regular Establishment.........	Aug., 1865
Battys. F. & H. 4th U. S...Mch., 1865	From Reorganized..............	To Regular Establishment.........	Aug., 1865
Batty. G. 1st Pa. Arty...Apr., 1865	From Unatt. 3-Div. W. Va........	No change to Muster Out.........	June, 1865

JEWETT'S INDPT. BRIGADE.—

COMMANDER.

A. B. Jewett	Col. 10th Vt. Infy	Feb. 2, 1863 to June 26, 1863.

23d Me. Infy...........Feb., 1863	From Jewett's Brig. Dist. Wash....	To Dist. Alexandria 22-Corps.......	May, 1863
14th N. H. Infy.........Feb., 1863	From Jewett's Brig. Dist. Wash....	To Dist. Washington 22-Corps......	May, 1863
10th Vt. Infy...........Feb., 1863	From Jewett's Brig. Dist. Wash....	To French's Div. 8-Corps...........	June, 1863
39th Mass. Infy........Feb., 1863	From Jewett's Brig. Dist. Wash....	To Dist. Washington 22-Corps......	May, 1863
10th Mass. Indpt. Batty...Feb., 1863	From Jewett's Brig. Dist. Wash....	To French's Div. 8-Corps...........	June, 1863
11th N. Y. Cav. Cos E, F, I Feb., 1863	From Dist. of Wash...............	To Dist. Wash. 22-Corps...........	June, 1863

INDPT. CAVALRY BRIGADE.—

COMMANDERS.

R. Butler Price	Col. 2d Penna. Cav	Feb. 2, 1863, to Mch. 21, 1863.

Transferred to Cav. Div. 22-Corps, Mch. 21, 1863. Reorganized Aug. 1, 1863.

C. R. Lowell, Jr........	Col. 2d Mass. Cav...............	Aug. 1, 1863, to Feb., 1864.
H. M. Lazelle..........	Col. 16th N. Y. Cav.............	Feb., 1864, to Apr., 1864.
C. R. Lowell, Jr........	Col. 2d Mass. Cav...............	Apr., 1864, to July, 1864.
H. M. Lazelle..........	Col. 16th N. Y. Cav.............	July, 1864, to Oct., 1864.
H. S. Gansevoort......	Col. 13th N. Y. Cav.............	Oct., 1864, to Nov., 1864.

Brigade discontinued Nov., 1864.

1st Vt. Cav............Feb., 1863	From Indpt. Cav. Brig. Dist. Wash.	To 2-Brig. Cav. Div. 22-Corps.......	Mch., 1863
5th N. Y. Cav..........Feb., 1863	From Indpt. Cav. Brig. Dist. Wash.	To 3-Brig. Cav. Div. 22-Corps.......	Mch., 1863
2d Penna. Cav.........Feb., 1863	From Indpt. Cav. Brig. Dist. Wash.	To 2-Brig. Cav. Div. 22-Corps.......	Mch., 1863
18th Penna. Cav.......Feb., 1863	From Indpt. Cav. Brig. Dist. Wash.	To 3-Brig. Cav. Div. 22-Corps.......	Mch., 1863
1st Ohio Cav. Co's A, C...Feb., 1863	From Indpt. Cav. Brig. Dist. Wash.	To 2-Brig. Cav. Div. 22-Corps.......	Mch., 1863
1st West Va. Cav......Feb., 1863	From Indpt. Cav. Brig. Dist. Wash.	To 3-Brig. Cav. Div. 22-Corps.......	Mch., 1863
1st Mich. Cav.........Feb., 1863	From Indpt. Cav. Brig. Dist. Wash.	To 2-Brig. Cav. Div. 22-Corps.......	Mch., 1863
2d Mass. Cav..........Aug., 1863	From King's Div. 22-Corps.........	To Res. Br. 1-Div. Cav. C. M. D. M.	Aug., 1864
13th N. Y. Cav.........Aug., 1863	From New Organization...........	To 1-Sep. Brig. 22-Corps..........	Nov., 1864
16th N. Y. Cav.........Aug., 1863	From New Organization...........	To 1-Sep. Brig. 22-Corps..........	Nov., 1864

CAVALRY DIVISION.—Organized March 21, 1863.

COMMANDER.

J. H. Stahel...........	Major General..................	Mch. 2, 1863, to June 26, 1863.

Division Transferred to Army Potomac, June 26, 1863.

1st BRIGADE.—

COMMANDER.

J. T. Copeland.........	Brigadier General..............	Mch. 2, 1863, to June 26, 1863.

5th Mich. Cav...........Mch., 1863	From Prov'l Brig. Casey's Div. 22-C.	To 2-Brig. 3-Div. Cav. Corps Pot....	June, 1863
6th Mich. Cav...........Mch., 1863	From Prov'l Brig. Casey's Div. 22-C.	To 2-Brig. 3-Div. Cav. Corps Pot....	June, 1863
7th Mich. Cav...........Mch., 1863	From New Organization...........	To 2-Brig. 3-Div. Cav. Corps Pot....	June, 1863
1st Mich. Cav...........June, 1863	From 2-Brig. Cav. Div. 22-Corps....	To 2-Brig. 3-Div. Cav. Corps Pot....	June, 1863

2d BRIGADE.—

COMMANDER.

R. Butler Price........	Col. 2d Penna. Cav.............	Mch. 2, 1863, to June 26, 1863.

1st Mich. Cav...........Mch., 1863	From Indpt. Cav. Brig. 22-Corps....	To 1-Brig. Cav. Div. 22-Corps......	June, 1863
1st Ohio Cav. Co's A, C...Mch., 1863	From Indpt. Cav. Brig. 22-Corps....	To Headqrs. 3-Div. Cav. Corps Pot..	June, 1863
2d Penna. Cav..........Mch., 1863	From Indpt. Cav. Brig. 22-Corps....	To Provost Guard Army Pot.......	June, 1863
1st Vt. Cav............Mch., 1863	From Indpt. Cav. Brig. 22-Corps....	To 3-Brig. Cav. Div. 22-Corps......	May, 1863
18th Penna. Cav........May, 1863	From 3-Brig. Cav. Div. 22-Corps....	To 1-Brig. 3-Div. Cav. Corps Pot....	June, 1863

3d BRIGADE.—

COMMANDERS.

R. Johnston...........	Lt.-Col. 5th N. Y. Cav...........	Mch. 2, 1863, to Apr., 1863.
O. DeForest...........	Col. 5th N. Y. Cav..............	Apr. 9, 1863, to June 26, 1863.

5th N. Y. Cav..........Mch., 1863	From Indpt. Cav. Brig. 22-Corps....	To 1-Brig. 3-Div. Cav. Corps Pot....	June, 1863
18th Penna. Cav........Mch., 1863	From Indpt. Cav. Brig. 22-Corps....	To 2-Brig. Cav. Div. 22-Corps......	May, 1863
1st West Va. Cav.......Mch., 1863	From Indpt. Cav. Brig. 22-Corps....	To 1-Brig. 3-Div. Cav. Corps Pot....	June, 1863
1st Vt. Cav............June, 1863	From 2-Brig. Cav. Div. 22-Corps....	To 1-Brig. 3-Div. Cav. Corps Pot....	June, 1863

ARTILLERY.—

Batty. I, 1st Mich. Arty...Mch., 1863	From Arty. Camp 22-Corps.........	To 1-Brig. Horse Arty. Pot........	June, 1863

KING'S DIVISION.—Organized July 15, 1863.

COMMANDERS.

Rufus King............	Brigadier General..............	July 15, 1863, to Oct. .., 1863.
M. Corcoran..........	Brigadier General..............	Oct. .., 1863, to Dec. .., 1863.
C. M. Alexander.......	Col. 2d Dist. Columbia Infy......	Dec. .., 1863, to Jan. .., 1864.
R. O. Tyler...........	Brigadier General..............	Jan. .., 1864, to May .., 1864.

1st BRIGADE.—

COMMANDERS.

M. Corcoran..........	Brigadier General..............	July 15, 1863, to Oct. .., 1863.
M. Murphy............	Col. 182d N. Y. Infy............	Oct. .., 1863, to Dec. .., 1863.
J. P. McIvor..........	Col. 170th N. Y. Infy...........	Dec. .., 1863, to Jan. .., 1864.
A. H. Grimshaw.......	Col. 4th Del. Infy.............	Jan. .., 1864, to Mch. .., 1864.
C. M. Alexander.......	Col. 2d Dist. Columbia Infy......	Mch. .., 1864, to Apr. .., 1864.
A. H. Grimshaw.......	Col. 4th Del. Infy.............	Apr. .., 1864, to May .., 1864.

155th N. Y. Infy........July, 1863	From 3-Brig. 1-Div. 7-C. Dept. Va.	To 2-Brig. Tyler's Div. 22-Corps....	Jan., 1864
164th N. Y. Infy........July, 1863	From 3-Brig. 1-Div. 7-C. Dept. Va.	To 2-Brig. Tyler's Div. 22-Corps....	Jan., 1864
170th N. Y. Infy........July, 1863	From 3-Brig. 1-Div. 7-C. Dept. Va.	To 2-Brig. Tyler's Div. 22-Corps....	Jan., 1864
182d N. Y. Infy........July, 1863	From 3-Brig. 1-Div. 7-C. Dept. Va.	To 2-Brig. Tyler's Div. 22-Corps....	Jan., 1864
4th Del. Infy..........Jan., 1864	From Unatt. King's Div. 22-Corps.	To 2-Brig. 4-Div. 5-Corps Pot......	June, 1864
2d Dist. Columbia Infy...Jan., 1864	From Dist. Wash. 22-Corps........	To Dist. Alexandria 22-Corps......	May, 1864
157th Pa. Infy. A, B, C, D...Jan., 1864	From Unatt. King's Div. 22-Corps.	To 2-Brig. 4-Div. 5-Corps Pot......	June, 1864

2d BRIGADE.—Organized Jan., 1864.

COMMANDERS.

M. Murphy............	Col. 182d N. Y. Infy...........	Jan. .., 1864, to Mch. .., 1864.
J. P. McIvor..........	Col. 170th N. Y. Infy...........	Mch. .., 1864, to Apr. .., 1864.
M. Murphy............	Col. 182d N. Y. Infy...........	Apr. .., 1864, to May .., 1864.

155th N. Y. Infy........Jan., 1864	From 1-Brig. King's Div. 22-Corps..	To 4-Brig. 2-Div. 2-Corps Pot.......	May, 1864
164th N. Y. Infy........Jan., 1864	From 1-Brig. King's Div. 22-Corps..	To 4-Brig. 2-Div. 2-Corps Pot.......	May, 1864
170th N. Y. Infy........Jan., 1864	From 1-Brig. King's Div. 22-Corps..	To 4-Brig. 2-Div. 2-Corps Pot.......	May, 1864
182d N. Y. Infy........Jan., 1864	From 1-Brig. King's Div. 22-Corps..	To 4-Brig. 2-Div. 2-Corps Pot.......	May, 1864

ARTILLERY.—

17th N. Y. Indpt. Batty...July, 1863	From Camp Barry 22-Corps.......	To Camp Barry 22-Corps..........	Mch., 1864

NOT BRIGADED.—

4th Del. Infy..........July, 1863	From Unatt. 4-Corps Dept. Va.....	To 1-Brig. Tyler's Div. 22-Corps....	Jan., 1864
2d Mass. Cav..........July, 1863	From Prov'l Brig. 22-Corps & 4-C..	To Cav. Brig. 22-Corps..........	Aug., 1864
6th N. Y. Cav. 2 Cos...July, 1863	From Adv. Brig. 4-Corps Dept. Va.	To 2-Brig. 1-Div. Cav. Corps Pot...	Sept., 1863
157th Pa. Infy. A, B, C, D...Dec., 1863	From Dist. Washington 22-Corps....	To 1-Brig. Tyler's Div. 22-Corps....	Jan., 1864

ST. MARY'S DISTRICT.—Created by transfer from Dept. of Va. & N. C. June, 1864. Discontinued April 26, 1865.

COMMANDERS.

A. G. Draper	Col. 36th U. S. Col'd Troops	June .., 1864, to July 2, 1864.
James Barnes	Brigadier General	July 2, 1864, to Apr. 26, 1865.

139th Ohio Infy	June, 1864	From New Organization	No change to Muster Out	Aug., 1864
4th R. I. Infy	June, 1864	From Dist. St. Mary's D. Va. & N. C.	To 1-Brig. 2-Div. 9-Corps Pot	July, 1864
2d Wis. Batty	June, 1864	From Dist. St. Mary's D. Va. & N. C.	No change to Muster Out	July, 1865
5th Mass. Col'd Cav	July, 1864	From 1-Br. 3-Div. 18-C. Va. & N. C.	To Unatt. 25-Corps Army James	Mch., 1865
29th Conn. Col'd Infy	Apr., 1865	From 2-Br. 1-Div. 25-C. Army Jas	To Dept. Texas	May, 1865
10th U. S. Col'd Infy	Apr., 1865	From Att'd Brig. 1-Div. 25-Corps	To Dept. Texas	May, 1865
28th U. S. Col'd Infy	Apr., 1865	From Att'd Brig. 1-Div. 25-Corps	To Dept. Texas	May, 1865
11th and 20th U. S. Res. Corps				

1st SEPARATE BRIGADE.—Organized Nov., 1864.

COMMANDERS.

William Gamble	Col. 8th Ill. Cav	Nov. .., 1864, to June 22, 1865.
William Wells	Brigadier General	June 22, 1865, to July 7, 1865.

202d Penna. Infy	Nov., 1864	From Dist. Alexandria 22-Corps	No change to Muster Out	June, 1865
8th Ill. Cav	Nov., 1864	From Muddy Run, Md	No change to Muster Out	July, 1865
13th N. Y. Cav	Nov., 1864	From Cav. Brig. 22-Corps	To 3d N. Y. Prov'l Cav	June, 1865
16th N. Y. Cav	Nov., 1864	From Cav. Brig. 22-Corps	To 3d N. Y. Prov'l Cav	June, 1865
16th Mass. Indpt. Batty	Nov., 1864	From Camp Barry 22-Corps	No change to Muster Out	June, 1865
5th Penna. Heavy Arty	Nov., 1864	From Dist. Alexandria 22-Corps	No change to Muster Out	June, 1865

DWIGHT'S DIVISION.—From Army Shenandoah.   **COMMANDER.**

William Dwight	Brigadier General	

1st BRIGADE.—				
29th Me. Infy	Apr., 1865	From 1-Br. 1-Prov'l Div. Army Shen.	To Department of the South	May, 1865
30th Mass. Infy	Apr., 1865	From 1-Br. 1-Prov'l Div. Army Shen.	To Department of the South	May, 1865
90th N. Y. Infy	Apr., 1865	From 1-Br. 1-Prov'l Div. Army Shen.	To Department of the South	May, 1865
114th N. Y. Infy	Apr., 1865	From 1-Br. 1-Prov'l Div. Army Shen.	To Department of the South	May, 1865
116th N. Y. Infy	Apr., 1865	From 1-Br. 1-Prov'l Div. Army Shen.	To Department of the South	May, 1865
2d BRIGADE.—				
12th Conn. Infy	Apr., 1865	From 2-Br. 1-Prov'l Div. Army Shen	To Department of the South	May, 1865
15th Me. Infy	Apr., 1865	From 2-Br. 1-Prov'l Div. Army Shen	To Department of the South	May, 1865
8th Vt. Infy	Apr., 1865	From 2-Br. 1-Prov'l Div. Army Shen	To Department of the South	May, 1865
47th Penna. Infy	Apr., 1865	From 2-Br. 1-Prov'l Div. Army Shen	To Department of the South	May, 1865
153d N. Y. Infy	Apr., 1865	From 2-Br. 1-Prov'l Div. Army Shen	To Department of the South	May, 1865
3d BRIGADE.—				
30th Me. Infy	Apr., 1865	From 3-Br. 1-Prov'l Div. Army Shen	To Department of the South	May, 1865
133d N. Y. Infy	Apr., 1865	From 3-Br. 1-Prov'l Div. Army Shen	To Department of the South	May, 1865
160th N. Y. Infy	Apr., 1865	From 3-Br. 1-Prov'l Div. Army Shen	To Department of the South	May, 1865
162d N. Y. Infy	Apr., 1865	From 3-Br. 1-Prov'l Div. Army Shen	To Department of the South	May, 1865
165th N. Y. Infy	Apr., 1865	From 3-Br. 1-Prov'l Div. Army Shen	To Department of the South	May, 1865
173d N. Y. Infy	Apr., 1865	From 3-Br. 1-Prov'l Div. Army Shen	To Department of the South	May, 1865
HORSE ARTILLERY RESERVE.—				
6th N. Y. Indpt. Batty	Apr., 1865	From Horse Arty. Res. Army Shen	No change to Muster Out	June, 1865
Battys. B & L, 2d U. S	Apr., 1865	From Horse Arty. Res. Army Shen	To Regular Establishment	Aug., 1865
Batty. D, 2d U. S. Arty	Apr., 1865	From Horse Arty. Res. Army Shen	To Regular Establishment	Aug., 1865
Batty. M, 2d U. S. Arty	Apr., 1865	From Horse Arty. Res. Army Shen	To Regular Establishment	Aug., 1865
Batty. C, 3d U. S. Arty	Apr., 1865	From Horse Arty. Res. Army Shen	To Regular Establishment	Aug., 1865
Battys. C & E, 4th U. S	Apr., 1865	From Horse Arty. Res. Army Shen	To Regular Establishment	Aug., 1865

CAVALRY DIVISION, CAMP STONEMAN.—Organized Jan. 9, 1864. Discontinued Nov., 1864.

COMMANDERS.

J. B. McIntosh	Col. 3d Penna. Cav	Jan. 9, 1864, to May 2, 1864.
William Gamble	Col. 8th Ill. Cav	May 2, 1864, to Nov., 1864.

Detachments of 1-Div., 2-Div., 3-Div. and Reserve Brig. Cav. Corps Army of the Potomac.

1st N. Y. Vet. Cav	Jan., 1864	From New Organization	To 1-Brig. 1-Cav. Div. Dept. W. Va.	Feb., 1864
1st R. I. Cav	Jan., 1864	From 1-Brig. 2-Div. Cav. Corps Pot.	To Abercrombie's Command Pot	May, 1864
2d N. Y. Vet. Cav	Jan., 1864	From New Organization	To Dept. Gulf	May, 1864
1st N. H. Cav	Apr., 1864	From New Organization	To 2-Brig. 3-Div. Cav. Corps Pot	May, 1864
2d N. Y. Mtd. Rifles	Apr., 1864	From New Organization	To Prov'l Brig. 9-Corps Pot	May, 1864
24th N. Y. Cav	Apr., 1864	From New Organization	To Prov'l Brig. 9-Corps Pot	May, 1864
25th N. Y. Cav	Apr., 1864	From New Organization	To Provost Guard Army Pot	June, 1864
2d Ohio Cav	Apr., 1864	From Columbus, Ohio	To Cav. 9-Corps Pot	May, 1864
8th Ill. Cav	June, 1864	From Unatt. 22-Corps	Muddy Branch, Md	July, 1864

PROVISIONAL TROOPS.—Discontinued Mch. 24, 1865.

COMMANDER.

Silas Casey	Major General	Feb. 2, 1863, to Mch. 24, 1865.

2d N. H. Infy	May, 1863	From New Hampshire	To 3-Brig. 2-Div. 3-Corps Pot	June, 1863
1st U. S. Col'd Troops	June, 1863	From New Organization	To U. S. Forces Yorktown Va. & N. C.	Dec., 1863
2d U. S. Col'd Troops	July, 1863	From New Organization	To Dept. Gulf	Dec., 1863
23d U. S. Col'd Troops	Dec., 1863	From New Organization	To 2-Brig. 4-Div. 9-Corps Pot	Apr., 1864
75th N. Y. Infy (Vets.)	Apr., 1864	From Veteran Furlough	To Dept. Gulf	May, 1864
43d U. S. Col'd Troops	July, 1864	From Phila., Penna	To 1-Brig. 3-Div. 9-Corps Pot	Sept., 1864
45th U. S. C. T. Det	July, 1864	From Phila., Penna	To 2-Brig. 2-Div. 25-C. Army James	Mch., 1865
RAILROAD GUARD.—				
109th N. Y. Infy	Feb., 1863	From R. R. Guard Dist. Wash	To 1-Brig. 3-Div. 9-Corps Pot	Apr., 1864

DEFENCES NORTH OF THE POTOMAC.—   **COMMANDERS.**

J. A. Haskins	Lt.-Col. A. D. C.	Feb. 2, 1863, to July 8, 1864.
M. D. Hardin	Brigadier General	July 8, 1864, to Aug. 2, 1865.

1st BRIGADE.—   **COMMANDERS.**

A. A. Gibson	Col. 2d Penna. Heavy Arty	Feb. 2, 1863, to Mch. 26, 1864.
J. M. Warner	Col. 1st Vt. Heavy Arty	Mch. 26, 1864, to May 12, 1864.
W. H. Hayward	Col. 150th Ohio Infy	May 12, 1864, to July 6, 1864.
J. M. C. Marble	Col. 151st Ohio Infy	July 6, 1864, to Aug. 16, 1864.
J. H. Kitching	Col. 6th N. Y. Heavy Arty	Aug. 16, 1864, to Sept. 17, 1864.
T. Allcock	Lt.-Col. 4th N. Y. Heavy Arty	Sept. 17, 1864, to Oct. 1, 1864.
G. S. Worcester	Major 3d Mass. Heavy Arty	Oct. 1, 1864, to Nov. 10, 1864.
C. H. Long	Col. 1st Me. Heavy Arty	Nov. 10, 1864, to June 15, 1865.
E. G. Marshall	Col. 14th N. Y. Heavy Arty	June 15, 1865, to Aug. 2, 1865.

1st BRIGADE.—Continued.

3d Me. Indpt. Batty.	Feb., 1863	From 1-Br. Def. North Pot. Dist. W.	To 1st Me. Heavy Arty. as Co. M	Mch.,	1863
2d Penna. Heavy Arty.	Feb., 1863	From 1-Br. Def. North Pot. Dist. W.	To 1-Brig. Def. South Pot 22-Corps.	Mch.,	1864
1st Vt. Heavy Arty.	Feb., 1863	From 1-Br. Def. North Pot. Dist. W.	To 2-Brig. 2-Div. 6-Corps Pot	May,	1864
1st Me. H. A., Co. M	Mch., 1863	From 3d Me. Indpt. Batty.	To 2-Brig. Def. North Pot 22-Corps.	June,	1863
143d Ohio Infy.	May, 1864	From New Organization	To 1-Brig. 3-Div. 10-Corps Va. & N. C.	June,	1864
150th Ohio Infy.	May, 1864	From New Organization	To 2-Brig. Def. North Pot 22-Corps.	July,	1864
13th Mich. Indpt. Batty.	May, 1864	From Camp Barry 22-Corps	To Fort Foote Def. North Pot. 22-C.	July,	1864
14th Mich. Indpt. Batty.	May, 1864	From Camp Barry 22-Corps	To 2-Brig. Def. North Pot. 22-Corps.	Aug.,	1864
1st Penna. Arty. Battn.	June, 1864	From 3-Brig. Def. North Pot. 22-C.	No change to Muster Out	Sept.,	1864
Batty. D, 1st R. I. Arty.	June, 1864	From Res. Arty. 9-Corps Pot	To Res. Arty. 19-Corps M. M. D	July,	1864
Batty. A, 4th U. S. Arty.	June, 1864	From 1-Brig. Horse Arty. Pot	To Camp Barry 22-Corps	July,	1864
151st Ohio Infy.	July, 1864	From 2-Brig. Def. North Pot. 22-C.	No change to Muster Out	Aug.,	1864
1st Co. N. H. H. A.	July, 1864	From 2-Brig. Def. North Pot. 22-C.	To 2-Brig. Def. North Pot. 22-Corps.	Aug.,	1864
9th N. Y. H. A. (4 Co's)	July, 1864	From Arty. Brig. 6-Corps Pot	To 2-Brig. 3-Div. 6-Corps Shen	Sept.,	1864
Batty. I, 2d U. S. Arty.	July, 1864	From 2-Brig. Def. North Pot. 22-C.	To Fort Foote Def. North Pot. 22-C.	Nov.,	1864
Batty. G, 3d U. S. Arty.	July, 1864	From 3-Brig. Def. North Pot. 22-C.	To Fort Foote Def. North Pot. 22-C.	Nov.,	1864
6th N. Y. Heavy Arty.	Aug., 1864	From 3-Brig. 2-Div. 5-Corps Pot.	To 1-Brig. Kitching's Prov'l Div.	Sept.,	1864
41st N. Y. Infy.	Aug., 1864	From Dist. Hilton Head Dept. South.	To 2-Brig. Kitching's Prov'l Div.	Sept.,	1864
8th Co. Mass. H. A.	Oct., 1864	From 3-Brig. Def. North Pot. 22-C.	To 2-Brig. Def. North Pot. 22-Corps.	Dec.,	1864
11th Co. Mass. H. A.	Oct., 1864	From 3-Brig. Def. North Pot. 22-C.	To 2-Brig. Def. North Pot. 22-Corps.	Dec.,	1864
12th Co. Mass. H. A.	Oct., 1864	From 3-Brig. Def. North Pot. 22-C.	To 2-Brig. Def. North Pot. 22-Corps.	Dec.,	1864
13th Mich. Indpt. Batty.	Oct., 1864	From Fort Foote Def. North Pot.	No change to Muster Out	June,	1865
1st N. H. H. A.	Nov., 1864	From Portsmouth, N. H.	No change to Muster Out	Sept.,	1865

2d BRIGADE.— COMMANDERS.

L. O. Morris	Col. 7th N. Y. Heavy Arty.	Feb. 2, 1863, to May 16, 1864.
H. Miller	Col. 163d Ohio Infy.	May 16, 1864, to June, 1864.
J. M. C. Markle	Col. 151st Ohio Infy.	June, 1864, to July, 1864.
W. H. Hayward	Col. 150th Ohio Infy.	July, 1864, to Aug., 1864.
H. G. Thomas	Lt.-Col. 7th V. R. C.	Aug., 1864, to Nov., 1864.
J. A. P. Allen	Major 3d Mass. Heavy. Arty.	Nov., 1864, to Dec., 1864.
W. S. Abert	Col. 3d Mass. Heavy Arty.	Dec., 1864, to Aug., 1865.

1st Me. Heavy Arty.	Feb., 1863	From 2-Brig. Def. North Pot. Wash.	To Tyler's Heavy Arty. Div. 2-Corps.	May,	1864
7th N. Y. Heavy Arty.	Feb., 1863	From 2-Brig. Def. North Pot. Wash.	To Tyler's Heavy Arty. Div. 2-Corps.	May,	1864
9th N. Y. Heavy Arty.	Feb., 1863	From 2-Brig. Def. North Pot. Wash.	To 3-Brig. Def. North Pot. 22-Corps.	Apr.,	1864
9th N. Y. Indpt. Batty.	Feb., 1863	From 2-Brig. Def. North Pot. Wash.	To 3-Brig. Def. North Pot. 22-Corps.	Apr.,	1864
117th N. Y. Infy., 2d Battn.	Feb., 1863	From 2-Brig. Def. North Pot. Wash.	To 1-Brig. 2-Div. 7-Corps Dept. Va.	Apr.,	1863
151st Ohio Infy.	May, 1864	From New Organization	To 1-Brig. Def. North Pot. 22-Corps.	July,	1864
163d Ohio Infy.	May, 1864	From New Organization	To 1-Brig. 3-Div. 10-Corps Va.&N.C.	June,	1864
170th Ohio Infy.	May, 1864	From New Organization	To Res. Div. Dept. W. Va.	July,	1864
1st Co. N. H. H. A.	May, 1864	From New Hampshire	To 1-Brig. Def. North Pot. 22-Corps.	July,	1864
Batty. L, 1st Ohio Arty.	May, 1864	From Camp Barry 22-Corps	To Arty. 1-Div. 19-Corps M. M. D.	July,	1864
Batty. I, 2d U. S. Arty.	May, 1864	From 2d Separate Brig. 8-Corps	To 1-Brig. Def. North Pot. 22-Corps.	July,	1864
150th Ohio Infy.	July, 1864	From 1-Brig. Def. North Pot. 22-C.	No change to Muster Out	Aug.,	1864
7th Vet. Res. Corps.	July, 1864	From New Organization	To 1-Brig. V. R. C. Dist. Wash.	Oct.,	1864
21st Vet. Res. Corps.	July, 1864	From New Organization	To 1-Brig. V. R. C. Dist. Wash.	Oct.,	1864
4th Vet. Res. Corps.	Aug., 1864	From New Organization	To 1-Brig. V. R. C. Dist. Wash.	Oct.,	1864
10th Vet. Res. Corps.	Aug., 1864	From New Organization	To 1-Brig. V. R. C. Dist. Wash.	Oct.,	1864
14th Mich. Indpt. Batty.	Aug., 1864	From 1-Brig. Def. North Pot. 22-C.	To 3-Brig. Def. North Pot. 22-Corps.	Dec.,	1864
1st Co. N. H. H. A.	Aug., 1864	From 1-Brig. Def. North Pot. 22-C.	To Portsmouth, N. H.	Nov.,	1864
9th Co. Mass. H. A.	Oct., 1864	From 3-Brig. Def. North Pot. 22-C.	To Co. E, 3d Mass. Heavy Arty.	Dec.,	1864
11th Co. N. H. H. A.	Oct., 1864	From New Organization	To 1-Brig. Def. North Pot. 22-Corps.	Dec.,	1864
3d Mass. Heavy Arty.	Dec., 1864	From Unatt. Co's Mass. H. A.	No change to Muster Out	Sept.,	1865
Batty. G, 3d U. S. Arty.	Apr., 1865	From Fort Foote Def. North Pot.	To Regular Establishment	Aug.,	1865

3d BRIGADE.— COMMANDERS.

W. R. Pease	Col. 117th N. Y. Infy.	Feb. 2, 1863, to Apr. 14, 1863.
A. Piper	Col. 10th N. Y. Heavy Arty.	Apr. 14, 1863, to Mch. 26, 1864.
J. Welling	Col. 9th N. Y. Heavy Arty.	Mch. 26, 1864, to May 27, 1864.
J. H. Oberteuffer	Lt.-Col. 2d Penna. Heavy Arty.	May 27, 1864, to Jan. 3, 1865.
G. S. Worcester	Major 3d Mass. Heavy Arty.	Jan. 3, 1865, to June 5, 1865.
R. B. Shepherd	Col. 1st Me. Heavy Arty.	June 5, 1865, to Aug. 1, 1865.

5th N. Y. H. A., I,K,L,M.	Mch., 1863	From 3-Brig. Def. North Pot. Wash.	To 1-Brig. Def. South Pot 22-Corps	May,	1863
10th N. Y. Heavy Arty.	Mch., 1863	From 3-Brig. Def. North Pot. Wash.	To 1-Brig. Def. South Pot. 22-Corps.	Mch.,	1864
117th N. Y. Inf., 1st Battn.	Mch., 1863	From 3-Brig. Def. North Pot. Wash.	To 1-Brig. 2-Div. 7-Corps Dept. Va.	Apr.,	1863
9th N. Y. Heavy Arty.	Apr., 1864	From 2-Brig. Def. North Pot. 22-C.	To 2-Brig. 3-Div. 6-Corps Pot	May,	1864
9th N. Y. Indpt. Batty.	Apr., 1864	From 2-Brig. Def. North Pot. 22-C.	No change to Muster Out	June,	1864
6th Co. Mass. H. A.	May, 1864	From Boston Harbor	To Co. B, 3d Mass. H. A. (No change to Muster Out.)	Sept.,	1865
7th Co. Mass. H. A.	May, 1864	From Boston Harbor	To Co. C, 3d Mass. H. A. (No change to Muster Out.)	Sept.,	1865
8th Co. Mass. H. A.	May, 1864	From Boston Harbor	To 1-Brig. Def. North Pot. 22-Corps.	Oct.,	1864
9th Co. Mass. H. A.	May, 1864	From Boston Harbor	To Co. E, 3d Mass. H. A. (No change to Muster Out.)	Sept.,	1865
10th Co. Mass. H. A.	May, 1864	From Boston Harbor	To 2-Brig. Def. North Pot. 22-Corps.	Oct.,	1864
11th Co. Mass. H. A.	May, 1864	From Boston Harbor	To 1-Brig. Def. North Pot. 22-Corps.	Oct.,	1864
12th Co. Mass. H. A.	May, 1864	From Boston Harbor	To 1-Brig. Def. North Pot. 22-Corps.	Oct.,	1864
1st Penna. L. A. Battn.	May, 1864	From New Organization	To 1-Brig. Def. North Pot. 22-Corps.	Oct.,	1864
Batty. G, 3d U. S. Arty.	June, 1864	From Res. Arty. 9-Corps Pot	To 1-Brig. Def. North Pot. 22-Corps.	July,	1864
14th Co. Mass. H. A.	June, 1864	From Boston Harbor	To 2-Brig. Def. South Pot. 22-Corps.	Oct.,	1864
14th Mich. Indpt. Batty.	Dec., 1864	From 2-Brig. Def. North Pot.	No change to Muster Out	July,	1865
1st Ohio Indpt. Batty.	Apr., 1865	From 1-Brig. 3-Div. Dept. W. Va.	No change to Muster Out	June,	1865
Indpt. Batty. F, Pa. Arty.	Apr., 1865	From 1-Sep. Brig. 3-Div. W. Va.	No change to Muster Out	June,	1865
FORT FOOTE, NORTH POTOMAC.—					
2d Co. N. H. H. A.	May, 1864	From New Organization	To Portsmouth, N. H.	Feb.,	1865
13th Mich. Indpt. Batty.	July, 1864	From 1-Brig. Def. North Pot. 22-C.	To 1-Brig. Def. North Pot. 22-Corps.	Oct.,	1865
Co. B, Me. Coast Guard.	May, 1864	From New Organization	No change to Muster Out	June,	1865
Batty. I, 2d U. S. Arty.	Dec., 1864	From 1-Brig. Def. North Pot.	To Regular Establishment	Aug.,	1865
Batty. G, 3d U. S. Arty.	Dec., 1864	From 1-Brig. Def. North Pot.	To 2-Brig. Def. North Pot. 22-Corps.	Apr.,	1865
Batty. G, 1st Penna. Arty.	Apr., 1865	From Unatt. 3-Div. W. Va.	No change to Muster Out	June,	1865

DEFENCES SOUTH OF THE POTO MAC.—Organized Apr. 15, 1863, from the Artillery Defences of Alexandria.

COMMANDERS.

R. O. Tyler	Brigadier General	Apr. 15, 1863, to Apr. 26, 1863.
T. R. Tannatt	Col. 1st Mass. Heavy Arty.	Apr. 26, 1863, to May 25, 1863.
G. A. DeRussy	Brigadier General	May 25, 1863, to Aug. 20, 1865.

1st BRIGADE.— COMMANDERS.

T. R. Tannatt	Col. 1st Mass. Heavy Arty	Apr. 15, 1863, to Aug. 11, 1863.
J. N. G. Whistler	Col. 2d N. Y. Heavy Arty	Aug. 11, 1863, to Sept. 16, 1863.
T. R. Tannatt	Col. 1st Mass. Heavy Arty	Sept. 16, 1863, to Mch. 10, 1864.
A. A. Gibson	Col. 2d Penna. Heavy Arty	Mch. 10, 1864, to May 16, 1864.
J. C. Lee	Col. 164th Ohio Infy	May 16, 1864, to July 9, 1864.
J. N. G. Whistler	Col. 2d N. Y. Heavy Arty	July 9, 1864, to Aug. 20, 1865.

1st Mass. Heavy Arty	Apr., 1863	From Arty. Def. Alexandria 22-Corps.	To 2-Brig. Def. South Pot. 22-Corps.	Apr., 1864
2d N. Y. Heavy Arty	Apr., 1863	From Arty. Def. Alexandria 22-Corps.	To 2-Brig. Def. South Pot. 22-Corps.	Apr., 1864
3d Battn. N. Y. H. A.	Apr., 1863	From Arty. Def. Alexandria 22-Corps.	To 2-Brig. Def. South Pot. 22-Corps.	June, 1863
1st Wis. H. A., Co. A	Apr., 1863	From Arty. Def. Alexandria 22-Corps.	To 3-Brig. Def. South Pot. 22-Corps.	May, 1863
4th N. Y. Heavy Arty	Apr., 1863	From Abercrombie's Div. 22-Corps.	To 4-Brig. Def. South Pot. 22-Corps.	May, 1863
10th Mich. Batty	Apr., 1863	From Arty. Camp 22-Corps	To Arty. Camp 22-Corps	June, 1863
5th N. Y. H. A., I,K,L,M	May, 1863	From 3-Brig. Def. North Pot. 22-C.	To Arty. 1-Div. Dept. W. Va.	Nov., 1863
47th N. Y. S. M.	June, 1863	From New Organization	To 3-Brig. Def. South Pot. 22-Corps.	July, 1863
2d Penna. Heavy Arty	Mch., 1864	From 1-Brig. Def. North Pot. 22-C.	To 3-Brig. 2-Div. 18-Corps Va. & N. C.	June, 1864
138th Ohio Infy	May, 1864	From New Organization	To 2-Brig. 3-Div. 10-Corps Va. & N. C.	June, 1864
145th Ohio Infy	May, 1864	From New Organization	No change to Muster Out	Aug., 1864
147th Ohio Infy	May, 1864	From New Organization	To 2-Brig. Def. South Pot. 22-Corps.	July, 1864
164th Ohio Infy	May, 1864	From New Organization	No change to Muster Out	Aug., 1864
169th Ohio Infy	May, 1864	From New Organization	To 2-Brig. Def. South Pot. 22-Corps.	July, 1864
1st Me. Indpt. Batty	May, 1864	From Camp Barry 22-Corps	To Arty. 2-Div. 19-Corps Army Shen.	Aug., 1864
Batty. A, Md. Arty	May, 1864	From Camp Barry 22-Corps	To Arty. Res. Div. Dept. W. Va.	July, 1864
Batty. K, 1st N. Y. Arty	May, 1864	From Camp Barry 22-Corps	To 2-Brig. Def. South Pot. 22-Corps.	July, 1864
5th N. Y. Indpt. Batty	May, 1864	From Arty. Brig. 5-Corps Pot.	To Arty. Brig. 6-Corps Pot.	July, 1864
Batty. G, 1st Penna. Arty	May, 1864	From Camp Barry 22-Corps	To Arty. Res. Div. Dept. W. Va.	July, 1864
Batty. H, 1st Penna. Arty	May, 1864	From Camp Barry 22-Corps	No change to Muster Out	June, 1865
Batty. D, Md. Arty	June, 1864	From 3d Separate Brig. 8-Corps	To 4-Brig. Def. South Pot. 22-Corps.	Aug., 1864
Batty. G, 2d U. S. Arty	June, 1864	From 2-Brig. Horse Arty. Pot.	To Regular Establishment	Aug., 1865
6th Mass. S. M. Infy	July, 1864	From New Organization	To Fort Delaware	Aug., 1864
18th Mass. Co.	July, 1864	From New Organization	No change to Muster Out	Nov., 1864
84th N. Y. Infy. S. M.	July, 1864	From New Organization	To Winchester, Va., Dept. W. Va.	Aug., 1864
Penna. Battn., 2 Co's	July, 1864	From New Organization	No change to Muster Out	Nov., 1864
Batty. H, 1st R. I. Arty	July, 1864	From 2-Brig. Def. South Pot. 22-C.	To Def. City Pt., Va., Dept. Va.&N.C.	Oct., 1864
Batty. E, 1st U. S. Arty	July, 1864	From 2-Brig. Def. South Pot. 22-C.	To Regular Establishment	Aug., 1865
10th N. Y. Heavy Arty	Aug., 1864	From 1-Brig. 2-Div. 18-C. Va. & N. C.	To 2-Brig. Kitching's Prov'l Div.	Sept., 1864
3d Co. Mass. H. A.	Oct., 1864	From 3-Brig. Def. South Pot. 22-C.	To 2-Br. Def. N. Pot, C, 3d Mass.H.A.	Dec., 1864
15th Co. Mass. H. A.	Oct., 1864	From 3-Brig. Def. South Pot. 22-C.	To 2-Br. Def. N. Pot., L, 3d Mass.H.A.	Dec., 1864
16th Co. Mass. H. A.	Oct., 1864	From New Organization	To 2-Br. Def. N. Pot., M, 3d Mass.H.A.	Dec., 1864
17th Co. Mass. H. A.	Oct., 1864	From New Organization	To 3-Br. Def. S. Pot., 4th Mass. H. A.	Dec., 1864
19th Co. Mass. H. A.	Oct., 1864	From New Organization	To 3-Br. Def. S. Pot., 4th Mass. H. A.	Dec., 1864
20th Co. Mass. H. A.	Oct., 1864	From New Organization	To 3-Br. Def. S. Pot., 4th Mass. H. A.	Dec., 1864
21st Co. Mass. H. A.	Oct., 1864	From New Organization	To 3-Br. Def. S. Pot., 4th Mass. H. A.	Dec., 1864
24th Co. Mass. H. A.	Oct., 1864	From New Organization	To 3-Br. Def. S. Pot., 4th Mass. H. A.	Dec., 1864
26th Co. Mass. H. A.	Oct., 1864	From New Organization	To 3-Br. Def. S. Pot., 4th Mass. H. A.	Dec., 1864
27th Co. Mass. H. A.	Oct., 1864	From New Organization	To 3-Br. Def. S. Pot., 4th Mass. H. A.	Dec., 1864
29th Co. Mass. H. A.	Oct., 1864	From New Organization	To 3-Br. Def. S. Pot., 4th Mass. H. A.	Dec., 1864
30th Co. Mass. H. A.	Oct., 1864	From New Organization	To 3-Br. Def. S. Pot., 4th Mass. H. A.	Dec., 1864
Batty. K, 1st N. Y. Arty	Dec., 1864	From 2-Brig. Def. South Pot. 22-C.	No change to Muster Out	June, 1865
16th Ind. Batty	Dec., 1864	From 3-Brig. Def. South Pot. 22-C.	No change to Muster Out	June, 1865
Batty. D, Md. Arty	Dec., 1864	From 3-Brig. Def. South Pot. 22-C.	No change to Muster Out	June, 1865
Batty. F, 1st N. Y. Arty	Dec., 1864	From 3-Brig. Def. South Pot. 22-C.	No change to Muster Out	June, 1865
6th Pa. H. A., Co's E, H	Dec., 1864	From 3-Brig. Def. South Pot. 22-C.	No change to Muster Out	June, 1865
Indpt. Batty. I, Pa. Arty	Dec., 1864	From 3-Brig. Def. South Pot. 22-C.	No change to Muster Out	June, 1865
Batty. C, 1st W. Va. Arty	Dec., 1864	From 3-Brig. Def. South Pot. 22-C.	No change to Muster Out	June, 1865
Battys. A & F, 1st U. S.	Dec., 1864	From Camp Barry 22-Corps	To Regular Establishment	Aug., 1865

2d BRIGADE.—Organized from Artillery Defences South of the Potomac, April 15, 1863.

COMMANDERS.

G. D. Wells	Col. 34th Mass. Infy	Apr. 15, 1863, to May 3, 1863.
L. W. Wessells	Col. 19th Conn. Heavy Arty	May 3, 1863, to Sept. 20, 1863.
L. Schirmer	Col. 15th N. Y. Heavy Arty	Sept. 20, 1863, to Oct., 1863.
L. Schamberger	Major 15th N. Y. Heavy Arty	Oct., 1863, to Nov., 1863.
H. L. Abbot	Col. 1st Conn. Heavy Arty	Nov., 1863, to Mch., 1864.
T. R. Tannatt	Col. 1st Mass. Heavy Arty	Mch., 1864, to May 16, 1864.
W. S. Irwin	Col. 136th Ohio Infy	May 16, 1864, to July, 1864.
T. Wilhelmn	Col. 2d Pa. Prov'l H. A.	July, 1864, to Sept. 29, 1864.
James Brady	Lt.-Col. 1st Pa. Light Arty	Sept. 29, 1864, to Nov. 14, 1864.
Charles Barnes	Col. 6th Penna. Heavy Arty	Nov. 14, 1864, to June 26, 1865.
J. Hubbard	Col. 2d Conn. Heavy Arty	June 26, 1865, to Aug., 1865.

1st Conn. Heavy Arty	Apr., 1863	From Arty. Def. Alexandria 22-C.	To 3-Brig. Def. South Pot. 22-Corps	May, 1863
19th Conn. 2d H. A.	Apr., 1863	From Arty. Def. Alexandria 22-C.	To 4-Brig. Def. South Potomac	Feb., 1864
34th Mass. Infy	Apr., 1863	From Arty. Def. Alexandria 22-C.	To Dist. Washington 22-Corps	May, 1863
16th West Va. Infy	Apr., 1863	From 2-Brig. Abercrombie's D. 22-C.	No change to Muster Out	June, 1863
3d Battn. N. Y. H. Arty	May, 1863	From 1-Brig. Def. South Pot. 22-C.	To 4-B. Def. So. Pot. 15-N. Y. H. A.	Jan., 1864
1st Conn. Heavy Arty	Dec., 1863	From 3-Brig. Def. South Pot. 22-C.	To 4-Brig. Def. South Pot. 22-Corps	Mch., 1864
1st Mass. Heavy Arty	Apr., 1864	From 1-Brig. Def. South Pot. 22-C.	To Tyler's Heavy Arty. Div. 2-C.	May, 1864
2d N. Y. Heavy Arty	Apr., 1864	From 1-Brig. Def. South Pot. 22-C.	To Tyler's Heavy Arty. Div. 2-C.	May, 1864
136th Ohio Infy	May, 1864	From New Organization	To 3-Brig. Def. South Pot. 22-Corps	July, 1864
142d Ohio Infy	May, 1864	From New Organization	To 3-Brig. Def. South Pot. 22-Corps	July, 1864
166th Ohio Infy	May, 1864	From New Organization	To 3-Brig. Def. South Pot. 22-Corps	July, 1864
16th Ind. Batty	May, 1864	From Fort Washington 22-Corps	To 3-Brig. Def. South Pot. 22-Corps	July, 1864
3d Co. Mass. Heavy Arty	May, 1864	From Boston Harbor	To 3-Brig. Def. South Pot. 22-Corps	July, 1864
10th N. Y. H'vy A. Det.	May, 1864	From 3-Brig. Def. North Pot. 22-C.	To 4-Brig. Def. South Pot. 22-Corps	July, 1864
Batty. F, 1st N. Y. Arty	May, 1864	From Arty. Camp 22-Corps	To 3-Brig. Def. South Pot. 22-Corps	July, 1864
17th N. Y. Indpt. Batty	May, 1864	From Arty. King's Div. 22-Corps	To Arty. Brig. 18-Corps Va. & N. C.	July, 1864
Indpt. Batty. F, Pa. Arty	May, 1864	From Arty. Camp 22-Corps	To Arty. Res. Div. Dept. W. Va.	July, 1864
Indpt. Batty. I, Pa. Arty	May, 1864	From Arty. Camp 22-Corps	To 3-Brig. Def. South Pot. 22-Corps	July, 1864
Batty. C, 1st W. Va. A.	May, 1864	From Arty. Camp 22-Corps	To 4-Brig. Def. South Pot. 22-Corps	July, 1864
1st Wis. Heavy A. Co. A.	May, 1864	From 3-Brig. Def. South Pot. 22-C.	To Arty. Camp 22-Corps	July, 1864
16th Mass. Indpt. Batty.	June, 1864	From New Organization	To 3-Brig. Def. South Pot. 22-Corps	July, 1864
15th Co. Mass. H'vy A.	June, 1864	From Arty. Camp 22-Corps	To Arty. Camp 22-Corps	July, 1864
Indpt. Batty. C, Pa. A.	June, 1864	From Arty. Camp 22-Corps	To 1-Brig. Def. South Potomac 22-C.	July, 1864
Batty. H, 1st R. I. Arty	June, 1864	From Res. Arty. 9-Corps Potomac.	To 1-Brig. Def. South Potomac 22-C.	July, 1864
Batty. E, 1st U. S. Arty	June, 1864	From 2-Brig. Horse Arty. Potomac	To 1-Brig. Def. South Potomac 22-C.	July, 1864
147th Ohio Infy	July, 1864	From 1-Brig. Def. South Pot. 22-C.	No change to Muster Out	Aug., 1864
169th Ohio Infy	July, 1864	From 1-Brig. Def. South Pot. 22-C.	No change to Muster Out	Aug., 1864
Batty. K, 1st N. Y. Arty	July, 1864	From 1-Brig. Def. South Pot. 22-C.	To 1-Brig. Def. South Potomac 22-C.	Oct., 1864
74th Penna. Infy	Aug., 1864	From Folly Island, S. C., Dept. So.	To Res. Div. Dept. W. Va.	Oct., 1864
14th Co. Mass. Heavy A.	Oct., 1864	From 3-Brig. Def. North Pot. 22-C.	To 2-B. D. N. P. 22-C. 3d Mass. H. A.	Dec., 1864
18th Co. Mass. Heavy A.	Oct., 1864	From New Organization	To 3-B. D. S. P. 22-C. 4th Mass. H. A.	Dec., 1864

2d BRIGADE.—Continued.

22d Co. Mass. Heavy A...Oct., 1864	From New Organization.............	To 3-B. D. S. P. 22-C. 4th Mass. H. A.	Dec.,	1864
23d Co. Mass. Heavy A...Oct., 1864	From New Organization.............	To 3-B. D. S. P. 22-C. 4th Mass. H. A.	Dec.,	1864
25th Co. Mass. Heavy A..Oct., 1864	From New Organization.............	To 3-B. D. S. P. 22-C. 4th Mass. H. A.	Dec.,	1864
28th Co. Mass. Heavy A..Oct., 1864	From New Organization.............	To 3-B. D. S. P. 22-C. 4th Mass. H. A.	Dec.,	1864
6th Penna. Heavy Arty..Nov., 1864	From New Organization.............	No change to Muster Out...........	June,	1865

3d BRIGADE.—Organized May, 1863.   Discontinued May, 1864.   Reorganized July, 1864.

COMMANDERS.

H. L. Abbot............	Col. 1st Conn. Heavy Arty..........	May 12, 1863, to Nov 5, 1863.
J. C. Tidball..........	Col. 4th N. Y. Heavy Arty......	Nov. 5, 1863, to Mch. 26, 1864.
Alex. Piper...........	Col. 10th N. Y. Heavy Arty.......	Mch. 26, 1864, to May 14, 1864.
W. S. Irwin...........	Col. 136th Ohio Infy...........	July 10, 1864, to Aug. 22, 1864.
Wm. Heine............	Col. 103d New York Infy.........	Aug. 22, 1864, to Sept. 23, 1864.
W. H. H. Beadle.......	Major 1st Vet. Res. Corps.......	Sept. 23, 1864, to Oct. 20, 1864.
I. McL. Barron........	Lt.-Col. 1st N. H. Heavy Arty......	Oct. 20, 1864, to Nov. 12, 1864.
James Brady..........	Lt.-Col. 1st Pa. Light Arty......	Nov. 12, 1864, to Dec. 16, 1864.
W. S. King...........	Col. 4th Mass. Heavy Arty.......	Dec. 16, 1864, to Apr. 27, 1865.
S. C. Hart...........	Lt.-Col. 4th Mass. H. A........	Apr. 27, 1865, to June 15, 1865.
H. T. Lee............	Major 4th N. Y. Heavy Arty......	June 15, 1865, to June 30, 1865.
J. C. Tidball........	Col. 4th N. Y. Heavy Arty........	June 30, 1865, to Aug. 20, 1865.

1st Conn. Heavy Arty....May, 1863	From 2-Brig. Def. South Pot. 22-C.	To 2-Brig. Def. South Pot. 22-Corps	Jan.,	1864
178th New York Infy....May, 1863	From New Organization...........	To Dist. Washington 22-Corps.....	July,	1863
Batty. H, 1st R. I. Arty..May, 1863	From Abercrombie's Div. 22-Corps.	To Arty. Camp 22-Corps...........	Oct.,	1863
1st Wis. Heavy A. Co. A..May, 1863	From 1-Brig. Def. South Pot. 22-C.	To 4-Brig. Def. South Pot. 22-Corps	Dec.,	1863
47th New York S. M.....July, 1863	From 1-Brig. Def. South Pot. 22-C.	No change to Muster Out..........	July	1863
4th N. Y. Heavy Arty....Dec., 1863	From 4-Brig. Def. South Pot. 22-C.	To Arty. Brig. 2d, 5th & 6th Corps	Mch.,	1864
1st Wis. H'vy A. Co. A..Mch., 1864	From 4-Brig. Def. South Pot. 22-C.	To 2-Brig. Def. South Pot. 22-Corps	May,	1864
10th N. Y. Heavy Arty...Mch., 1864	From 3-Brig. Def. North Pot. 22-C.	To 1-B. 2-Div. 18-Corps Va. & N. C.	June,	1864
Batty. D, Maryland A....June, 1864	From 3d Separate Brig. 8-Corps....	To 4-Brig. Def. South Pot. 22-Corps	Aug.,	1864
136th Ohio Infy.........July, 1864	From 2-Brig. Def. South Pot. 22-C.	No change to Muster Out..........	Aug.,	1864
142d Ohio Infy..........July, 1864	From 2-Brig. Def. South Pot. 22-C.	No change to Muster Out..........	Aug.,	1864
166th Ohio Infy.........July, 1864	From 2-Brig. Def. South Pot. 22-C.	No change to Muster Out..........	Aug.,	1864
16th Indiana Batty......July, 1864	From 2-Brig. Def. South Pot. 22-C.	To 1-Brig. Def. South Pot. 22-Corps	Dec.,	1864
3d Co. Mass. Heavy A....July, 1864	From 2-Brig. Def. South Pot. 22-C.	To 1-Brig. Def. South Pot. 22-Corps	Aug.,	1864
15th Co. Mass. Heavy A..July, 1864	From 2-Brig. Def. South Pot. 22-C.	To 1-Brig. Def. South Pot. 22-Corps	Dec.,	1864
Batty. F, 1st N. Y. Arty.July, 1864	From 2-Brig. Def. South Pot. 22-C.	To 1-Brig. Def. South Pot. 22-Corps	Dec.,	1864
Indpt Batty. I, Pa. Arty..July, 1864	From 2-Brig. Def. South Pot. 22-C.	To 1-Brig. Def. South Pot. 22-Corps	Dec.,	1864
72d Penna. Infy. Det...July, 1864	From 3-Brig. 2-Div. 2-Corps Potom.	No change to Muster Out..........	Aug.,	1864
106th Penna. Infy. Det..July, 1864	From 3-Brig. 2-Div. 2-Corps Potom.	No change to Muster Out..........	Aug.,	1864
103d New York Infy.....Aug., 1864	From Morris Island, S. C., Dept. So.	To 1-Brig. Kitching's Prov'l Div...	Sept.,	1864
104th Penna. Infy.......Aug., 1864	From Morris Island, S. C., Dept. So.	To 1-Brig. Kitching's Prov'l. Div...	Sept.,	1864
3d Veteran Res. Corps...Aug., 1864	From Dist. Washington 22-Corps....	To 1-Brig. Vet. Res. Corps 22-Corps.	Oct.,	1864
Batty. D, Maryland Arty..Oct., 1864	From 4-Brig. Def. So. Pot. 22-Corps.	To 1-Brig. Def. So. Pot. 22-Corps.	Dec.,	1864
3d Co. N. H. H. A......Oct., 1864	From New Organization...........	To 1-B. Def. N. Pot. 1st N. H. H. A.	Dec.,	1864
4th Co. N. H. H. A......Oct., 1864	From New Organization...........	To 1-B. Def. N. Pot. 1st N. H. H. A.	Dec.,	1864
5th Co. N. H. H. A......Oct., 1864	From New Organization...........	To 1-B. Def. N. Pot. 1st N. H. H. A.	Dec.,	1864
6th Co. N. H. H. A......Oct., 1864	From New Organization...........	To 1-B. Def. N. Pot. 1st N. H. H. A.	Dec.,	1864
7th Co. N. H. H. A......Oct., 1864	From New Organization...........	To 1-B. Def. N. Pot. 1st N. H. H. A.	Dec.,	1864
8th Co. N. H. H. A......Oct., 1864	From New Organization...........	To 1-B. Def. N. Pot. 1st N. H. H. A.	Dec.,	1864
9th Co. N. H. H. A......Oct., 1864	From New Organization...........	To 1-B. Def. N. Pot. 1st N. H. H. A.	Dec.,	1864
2d Penna. H. Arty. Det..Oct., 1864	From 3-B. 2-D. 18-Corps Va. & N. C.	To Def. Bermuda Hundred, Va.....	Dec.,	1864
Batty. C, 1st W. Va. Arty.Oct., 1864	From 4-Brig. Def. So. Pot. 22-Corps.	To 1-Brig. Def. So. Pot. 22-Corps...	Dec.,	1864
1st Wis. H. Arty., Co. F..Oct., 1864	From New Organization...........	To 4-Brig. Def. So. Pot. 22-Corps	Dec.,	1864
6th Pa. H. A. Cos. C, M..Dec., 1864	From 2-B. Def. South Pot. 22-Corps.	No change to Muster Out..........	June,	1865
4th Mass. Heavy Arty...Dec., 1864	From Unass'd Cos. Mass. H. A.	No change to Muster Out..........	June,	1865

4th BRIGADE, DEFENCES SOUTH OF THE POTOMAC.—Organized July 2, 1863.   Discontinued May, 1864.   Reorganized July, 1864.

COMMANDERS.

H. H. Hall.............	Col. 4th N. Y. H. A..............	July 2, 1863, to Aug. 6, 1863.
T. Allcock.............	Lt.-Col. 4th N. Y. Heavy Arty......	Aug. 6, 1863, to Sept. 2, 1863.
J. C. Tidball..........	Col. 4th N. Y. Heavy Arty.........	Sept. 2, 1863, to Nov. 5, 1863.
L. Schirmer...........	Col. 15th N. Y. Heavy Arty.......	Nov. 5, 1863, to Jan. 12, 1864.
L. Schamberger........	Major 15th N. Y. Heavy Arty......	Jan. 12, 1864, to Feb. 12, 1864.
L. Schirmer...........	Col. 15th N. Y. Heavy Arty.......	Feb. 12, 1864, to Mch. 14, 1864.
H. L. Abbot...........	Col. 1st Conn. Heavy Arty........	Mch. 14, 1864, to Apr. 25, 1864.
C. C. Meservey........	Major 1st Wis. Heavy Arty.......	July 1, 1864, to Aug. 6, 1864.
A. Farnsworth.........	Col. 12th Vet. Res. Corps.......	Aug. 6, 1864, to Oct. 6, 1864.
C. C. Meservey........	Col. 1st Wis. Heavy Arty........	Oct. 6, 1864, to June 28, 1865.
J. Dieckmann..........	Major 15th N. Y. Heavy Arty......	June 28, 1865, to July 16, 1865.
H. L. Abbot...........	Bvt. Brig. General..............	July 16, 1865, to Aug. 2, 1865.

4th N. Y. Heavy Arty....July, 1863	From 1-Brig. Def. So. Pot. 22-Corps.	To 3-Brig. Def. So. Pot. 22-Corps...	Dec.,	1863
2d Mass. C. Cs. B, C, D, K.Aug., 1863	From King's Div. 22-Corps........	To Cav. Brig. 22-Corps............	Aug.,	1864
15th N. Y. Heavy Arty. :.Dec., 1863	From 2-Brig. Def. So. Pot. 22-Corps.	To 1-Vol. Brig. Arty. Res. Potomac.	Mch.,	1864
1st Wis. Heavy A, Co. A.Dec., 1863	From 3-Brig. Def. So. Pot. 22-Corps.	To 3-Brig. Def. So. Pot. 22-Corps...	Mch.,	1864
1st Conn. Heavy Arty....Mch., 1864	From 2-Brig. Def. So. Pot. 22-Corps.	To Dept. Va. and N. C.	May,	1864
2d Conn. Heavy Arty....Mch., 1864	From 2-Brig. Def. So. Pot. 22-Corps.	To 2-Brig. 1-Div. 6-Corps Potomac.	May,	1864
66th N. Y. Infy. Det......July, 1864	From 4-Brig. 1-Div. 2-Corps Pot...	To 4-Brig. 1-Div. 2-Corps Potomac.	Aug.,	1864
136th Ohio I, A, B, D, K.July, 1864	From 2-Brig. Def. So. Pot. 22-Corps.	No change to Muster Out..........	Aug.,	1864
10th N. Y. Heavy A. Det.July, 1864	From 2-Brig. Def. So. Pot. 22-Corps.	To 1-Brig. Def. So. Pot. 22-Corps...	Aug.,	1864
Batty. C, 1st W. Va. Arty.July, 1864	From 2-Brig. Def. So. Pot. 22-Corps.	To 3-Brig. Def. So. Pot. 22-Corps	Oct.,	1864
1st Wis. Heavy A. Co. A.July, 1864	From 2-Brig. Def. So. Pot. 22-Corps.	No change to Muster Out..........	June,	1865
Batty. D, Md. Arty.......Aug., 1864	From 3-Brig. Def. So. Pot. 22-Corps.	To 3-Brig. Def. So. Pot. 22-Corps	Oct.,	1864
12th Vet. Res. Corps.....Aug., 1864	From Dist. Washington 22-Corps...	To Dist. Alexandria 22-Corps......	Aug.,	1864
1st Wis. Heavy Arty......Oct., 1864	From New Organization...........	No change to Muster Out..........	June,	1865
10th N. Y. H. Arty. Det...Oct., 1864	From 1-Brig. Kitching's Div. Shen..	To 2-Brig. Prov'l. Div. Army James.	Dec.,	1864
FORT WASHINGTON.—				
16th Ind. Batty..........Feb., 1863	From Dist. Washington...........	To 2-Brig. Def. So. Pot. 22-Corps...	May,	1864
Co. A, Me. Coast Guard...Mch., 1864	From New Organization...........	No change to Muster Out..........	May,	1865

Department of West Virginia

As reorganized June 28, 1863, from Eight Corps Middle Dept.

COMMANDERS.

B. F. Kelly	Brigadier General	June 24, 1863, to Mch. 10, 1864.
Franz Sigel	Major General	Mch. 10, 1864, to May 21, 1864.
David Hunter	Major General	May 21, 1864, to Aug. 8, 1864.
Geo. Crook	Bvt. Major General	Aug. 8, 1864, to Feb. 22, 1865.
J. D. Stevenson	Brigadier General	Feb. 22, 1865, to Feb. 27, 1865.
S. S. Carroll	Bvt. Major General	Feb. 27, 1865, to Mch. 7, 1865.
W. S. Hancock	Major General	Mch. 7, 1865, to Mch. 20, 1865.
George Crook	Major General	Mch. 20, 1865, to Mch. 22, 1865.
W. S. Hancock	Major General	Mch. 22, 1865, to June 27, 1865.
W. H. Emory	Bvt. Major General	Temporarily in Apr., 1865.

SCAMMON'S DIVISION.—   COMMANDER.

E. P. Scammon	Brigadier General

1st BRIGADE.—   COMMANDER.

R. B. Hayes............Col. 23d Ohio Infy

23 Ohio Infy	June, 1863	From 1-Brig. 3-Div. 8-Corps	To 1-Brig. 3-Div. West Va. Dec., 1863
5th West Va. Infy	June, 1863	From 1-Brig. 3-Div. 8-Corps	To 1-Brig. 3-Div. West Va. Dec., 1863
9th West Va. Infy	June, 1863	From 2-Brig. 2-Div. 8-Corps	To 2-Brig. Scammon's Div. West Va. Aug., 1863
13th West Va. Infy	June, 1863	From 2-Div. 8-Corps	To 1-Brig. 3-Div. West Va. Dec., 1863
1st West Va. Cav. 2-Cos.	June, 1863	From 1-Brig. 3-Div. 8-Corps	To 1-Brig. 3-Div. West Va. Dec., 1863
2d West Va. Cav. Co. L.	June, 1863	From 1-Brig. 3-Div. 8-Corps	To 3-Brig. Scammon's Div. West Va. July, 1863
3d West Va. Cav. Co. G.	June, 1863	From 1-Brig. 3-Div. 8-Corps	To 1-Brig. 3-Div. West Va. Dec., 1863
Simmond's Ky. Batty	June, 1863	From 1-Brig. 3-Div. 8-Corps	To 3-Brig. 3-Div. West Va. Dec., 1863

2d BRIGADE.—   COMMANDER.

Carr B. White............Col. 12th Ohio Infy

12th Ohio Infy	June, 1863	From 2-Brig. 3-Div. 8-Corps	To 2-Brig. 3-Div. West Va. Dec., 1863
34th Ohio Infy	June, 1863	From 2-Brig. 3-Div. 8-Corps	To 3-Brig. Scammon's Div. West Va. July, 1863
91st Ohio Infy	June, 1863	From 2-Brig. 3-Div. 8-Corps	To 2-Brig. 3-Div. West Va. Dec., 1863
2d W. Va. Cav. 2-Cos.	June, 1863	From 2-Brig. 3-Div. 8-Corps	To 3-Brig. Scammon's Div. W. Va. July, 1862
1st Ohio Batty	June, 1863	From 2-Brig. 3-Div. 8-Corps	To 2-Brig. 3-Div. West Va. Dec., 1863
9th W. Va. Infy	Aug., 1863	From 1-Brig. Scammon's Div. W. Va.	To 2-Brig. 3-Div. West Va. Dec., 1863

3d BRIGADE.—Organized July 8, 1863.   COMMANDERS.

J. T. Tolland	Col. 34th Ohio Infy	July 8, 1863, to July 18, 1863.
F. E. Franklin	Col. 34th Ohio Infy	July 18, 1863, to Dec., 1863.

34th Ohio Infy	July, 1863	From 2-Brig. Scammon's Div. W. Va.	To 3-Brig. 3-Div. West Va. Dec., 1863
2d West Va. Cav.	July, 1863	From Unatt. Scammon's Div. W. Va.	To 3-Brig. 3-Div. West Va. Dec., 1863

CAMPBELL'S SEPARATE BRIGADE.—   COMMANDER.

J. M. Campbell............Col. 54th Penna. Infy

54th Penna. Infy	June, 1863	From 4-Brig. 1-Div. 8-Corps	To 1-Brig. 2-Div. West Va. Dec., 1863
1st West Va. Infy	June, 1863	From 4-Brig. 1-Div. 8-Corps	To 2-Brig. 2-Div. West Va. Dec., 1863
Lafayette Penna. Cav.	June, 1863	From 4-Brig. 1-Div. 8-Corps	To 2-Brig. 2-Div. West Va. Dec., 1863
Washington Pa. Cav.	June, 1863	From 4-Brig. 1-Div. 8-Corps	To 2-Brig. 2-Div. West Va. Dec., 1863
Ringgold Penna. Cav.	June, 1863	From 4-Brig. 1-Div. 8-Corps	To 1-Brig. 2-Div. West Va. Dec., 1863
Batty. E, 1st W. Va. Arty.	June, 1863	From 4-Brig. 1-Div. 8-Corps	To 2-Brig. 2-Div. West Va. Dec., 1863
15th West Va. Infy	July, 1863	From Unatt. New Creek, Va.	To 2-Brig. 2-Div. West Va. Dec., 1863
20th Penna. Cav.	July, 1863	From Cav. 1-Div. Dept. Susquehanna	To Cav. Brig. 1-Div. West Va. Dec., 1863

MULLIGAN'S SEPARATE BRIGADE.—   COMMANDER.

J. A. Mulligan............Col. 23d Ill. Infy

23d Illinois Infy	June, 1863	From 5-Brig. 1-Div. 8-Corps	To 2-Brig. 2-Div. West Va. Dec., 1863
2d Md. Pot. Home Brig.	June, 1863	From 5-Brig. 1-Div. 8-Corps	To 2-Brig. 2-Div. West Va. Dec., 1863
14th West Va. Infy	June, 1863	From 5-Brig. 1-Div. 8-Corps	To 2-Brig. 2-Div. West Va. Dec., 1863
Batty. L, 1st Ill. Arty.	June, 1863	From 5-Brig. 1-Div. 8-Corps	To 2-Brig. 2-Div. West Va. Dec., 1863
Tyler's Pa. Heavy A. Co.	Aug., 1863	From New Organization	To Arty. 1-Div. West Va. Dec., 1863
Batty. D, 1st West Va. A.	Aug., 1863	From Unatt. Dept. Susquehanna	To 2-Brig. 2-Div. W. Va. Dec., 1863

WILKINSON'S SEPARATE BRIGADE.—   COMMANDER.

N. Wilkinson............Col. 6th West Va. Infy

6th West Va. Infy	June, 1863	From 6-Brig. 1-Div. 8-Corps	To 3-Brig. 2-Div. West Va. Dec., 1863
11th West Va. Infy	June, 1863	From 6-Brig. 1-Div. 8-Corps	To 3-Brig. 2-Div. West Va. Dec., 1863
55th Penna. Militia	July, 1863	From New Organization	No change to Muster Out Aug., 1863
4th West Va. Cav.	Aug., 1863	From New Organization	To 3-Brig. 2-Div. West Va. Dec., 1863

AVERILL'S 4th SEPARATE BRIGADE.—   COMMANDER.

W. W. Averill............Brigadier General

28th Ohio Infy	June, 1863	From 4-Separate Brig. 8-Corps	To 1-Brig. 4-Div. West Va. Dec., 1863
2d West Va. Infy	June, 1863	From 4-Separate Brig. 8-Corps	To 3-Brig. 4-Div. West Va. Dec., 1863
3d West Va. Infy	June, 1863	From 4-Separate Brig. 8-Corps	To 3-Brig. 4-Div. West Va. Dec., 1863
8th West Va. Infy	June, 1863	From 4-Separate Brig. 8-Corps	To 3-Brig. 4-Div. West Va. Dec., 1863
10th West Va. Infy	June, 1863	From 4-Separate Brig. 8-Corps	To 1-Brig. 4-Div. West Va. Dec., 1863
16th Illinois Cav. Co. C.	June, 1863	From 4-Separate Brig. 8-Corps	To 2-Brig. 4-Div. West Va. Dec., 1863
3d Indpt. Co. Ohio Cav.	June, 1863	From 4-Separate Brig. 8-Corps	To 2-Brig. 4-Div. West Va. Dec., 1863
14th Penna. Cav.	June, 1863	From 4-Separate Brig. 8-Corps	To 2-Brig. 4-Div. West Va. Dec., 1863
1st West Va. Cav. Co. A.	June, 1863	From 4-Separate Brig. 8-Corps	To 2-Brig. 4-Div. West Va. Dec., 1863
3d W. Va. C. Cos. E, F, H.	June, 1863	From 4-Separate Brig. 8-Corps	To 2-Brig. 4-Div. West Va. Dec., 1863
Batty. B, 1st W. Va. Arty.	June, 1863	From 4-Separate Brig. 8-Corps	To 1-Brig. 4-Div. West Va. Dec., 1863
Batty. C, 1st W. Va. Arty.	June, 1863	From 4-Separate Brig. 8-Corps	To 3-Brig. 4-Div. West Va. Dec., 1863

UNATTACHED.—

15th W. Va. Infy	June, 1863	From 3-Brig. 1-Div. 8-Corps	To Campbell's Brigade W. Va. July, 1863
21st Penna. Cav.	July, 1863	From New Organization Dept. Susq.	To Cav. Brig. 1-Div. West Va. Dec., 1863
18th Conn. Infy	July, 1863	From Dept. Susquehanna	To 3-Brig. 2-Div. West Va. Dec., 1863
Batty. B, 5th U. S. Arty.	July, 1863	From Arty. 1-Div. Dept. Susq.	To 3-Brig. 2-Div. West Va. Dec., 1863
Batty. D, 1st Pa. Arty.	Aug., 1863	From Camp Barry Washington 22-C.	To 1-Brig. 1-Div. West Va. Dec., 1863
22d Penna. Cav.	Aug., 1863	From Dept. Susquehanna	To Cav. Brig. West Va. Dec., 1863
2d Penna. Batt'n. Infy.	Aug., 1863	From Dept. Susquehanna	To 1-Brig. 2-Div. West Va. Dec., 1863

MARYLAND HEIGHTS DIVISION.— COMMANDERS.

H. H. Lockwood........	Brigadier General..................	July 10, 1863, to Sept. 18, 1863.
J. C. Sullivan..........	Brigadier General..................	Sept. 18, 1863, to Dec., 1863.

1st BRIGADE.— COMMANDER.

George D. Wells.......	Co. 34th Mass. Infy..............	July, 1863, to Dec., 1863.	
9th Maryland Infy........July, 1863	From 2-B. Md. Heights Div. W. Va.	To 1-Brig. 1-Div. West Va..........	Dec., 1863
10th Maryland Infy.....July, 1863	From 2-B. Md. Heights Div. W. Va.	To 2-Separate Brig. 8-Corps......	Dec., 1863
34th Mass. Infy.......July, 1863	From Def. of Washington 22-Corps.	To 1-Brig. 1-Div. West Va........	Dec., 1863
1st Conn. C. Cos. A, B, E.July, 1863	From Def. Baltimore 8-Corps.......	To Cav. Brig. 1-Div. West Va.....	Dec., 1863
6th Mich. Cav. H. M....July, 1863	From 2-Brig. 3-Div. Cav. Corps Pot.	To Cav. Brig. 1-Div. West Va.....	Dec., 1863
2d Md. Pot. Home B. Cav.July, 1863	From 3-Brig. 3-Div. 8-Corps......	To Cav. Brig. 1-Div. West Va.....	Dec., 1863
17th Ind. Batty.......July, 1863	From French's Div. 8-Corps.......	To 1-Brig. 1-Div. West Va.......	Dec., 1863
Batty. C, 1st Penna. Arty.July, 1863	From Camp Barry Washington 22-C.	Consol. with Batty. D, 1-Pa......	Oct., 1863
43d Mass. Infy..........July, 1863	From Def. Baltimore 8-Corps.......	No change to Muster Out........	July, 1863
175th Penna. Infy.......July, 1863	From Def. Baltimore 8-Corps.......	No change to Muster Out........	July, 1863

2d BRIGADE.— COMMANDERS.

Peter A. Porter.........	Col. 8th N. Y. Heavy Arty..........	July 10, 1863, to Aug. 3, 1863.	
W. P. Maulsby..........	Col. 1st Md. P. H. B. Infy......	Aug. 3, 1863, to Dec., 1863.	
1st Md. Pot. Home Brig.July, 1863	From 2-Brig. 1-Div. 12-Corps Pot.	To 2-Brig. 1-Div. West Va........	Dec., 1863
1st Md. Eastern Shore...July, 1863	From 2-Brig. 1-Div. 12-Corps Pot.	To 1-Separate Brig. 8-Corps......	Oct., 1863
2d Md. Eastern Shore....July, 1863	From 2-Brig. 1-Div. 12-Corps Pot.	To 2-Brig. 1-Div. West Va........	Dec., 1863
1st Md. P. H. B. Cav....July, 1863	From 3-Brig. 1-Div. 8-Corps......	To Cav. Brig. 1-Div. West Va.....	Dec., 1863
Loudoun Va. Rangers....July, 1863	From 3-Separate Brig. 8-Corps....	To Unatt. 1-Div. West Va........	Dec., 1863
Batty. B, Md. Arty......July, 1863	From Camp Barry Washington 22-C.	To 2-Brig. 1-Div. West Va........	Dec., 1863
32d N. Y. Indpt. Batty..July, 1863	From Camp Barry Washington 22-C.	To 2-Brig. 1-Div. West Va........	Dec., 1863
9th Maryland Infy......July, 1863	From New Organization...........	To 1-B. Md. Heights Div. W. Va...	July, 1863
10th Maryland Infy.....July, 1863	From New Organization...........	To 1-B. Md. Heights Div. W. Va...	July, 1863
8th N. Y. Heavy Arty...July, 1863	From Def. Baltimore 8-Corps.......	To Def. Baltimore 8-Corps.......	Aug., 1863
UNATTACHED.—			
1st Mass. Heavy A. 4 Cos.July, 1863	From Arty. Res. Potomac..........	To Def. So. Pot. 22-Corps.......	Dec., 1863
Batty. A, 1st W. Va. Arty.July, 1863	From Camp Barry Washington 22-C.	To 1-Brig. 1-Div. West Va.......	Dec., 1863
Keystone Penna. Batty...July, 1863	From Camp Barry Washington 22-C.	No change to Muster Out..........	Aug., 1863

MARTINSBURG. W. VA.— COMMANDER.

A. T. McReynolds......	Col. 1st N. Y. Lincoln Cav......		
116th Ohio Infy........July, 1863	From 1-Brig. 1-Div. Dept. Susq....	To 3-Brig. 1-Div. West Va........	Dec., 1863
123d Ohio Infy........July, 1863	From 1-Brig. 1-Div. Dept. Susq....	To 3-Brig. 1-Div. West Va........	Dec., 1863
12th West Va. Infy.....July, 1863	From 1-Brig. 1-Div. Dept. Susq....	To 1-Brig. 1-Div. West Va.......	Dec., 1863
1st West Va. Cav. Co. K..July, 1863	From 1-Brig. 1-Div. Dept. Susq....	To 1-Brig. 3-Div. West Va.......	Dec., 1863
3d W. Va. Cav. Cos. D, E..July, 1863	From 1-Brig. 1-Div. Dept. Susq....	To 3-Brig. 3-Div. West Va.......	Dec., 1863
1st Md. P. H. B. C. Co. B.Aug., 1863	From 3-Brig. 1-Div. 8-Corps......	To Cav. Brig. 1-Div. West Va.....	Dec., 1863
1st N. Y. Lincoln Cav....Aug., 1863	From 1-Brig. 1-Div. Dept. Susq....	To Cav. Brig. 1-Div. West Va.....	Dec., 1863
12th Penna. Cav........Aug., 1863	From 1-Brig 1-Div. Dept. Susq....	To 3-Brig. 1-Div. West Va.......	Dec., 1863
30th N. Y. Indpt. Batty...Aug., 1863	From Arty. 1-Div. Dept. Susq......	To 2-Brig. 1-Div. West Va.......	Dec., 1863

1st DIVISION.— COMMANDER.

J. C. Sullivan..........	Brigadier General..................	

1st BRIGADE.— COMMANDER.

Geo. D. Wells..........	Col. 34th Mass. Infy..............		
9th Maryland Infy......Dec., 1863	From 1-B. Md. Heights Div. W. Va.	To 2-Separate Brig. 8-Corps.....	Jan., 1864
34th Mass. Infy........Dec., 1863	From 1-B. Md. Heights Div. W. Va.	To Unatt. 1-Div. West Va........	Jan., 1864
12th West Va. Infy.....Dec., 1863	From Martinsburg, W. Va.........	To 1-Brig. 2-Div. West Va.......	Jan., 1864
17th Ind. Batty........Dec., 1863	From 1-B. Md. Heights Div. W. Va.	To Arty. Wheaton's B. 1-Div. W. Va.	Jan., 1864
Batty. D, 1st Penna. Arty.Dec., 1863	From 1-B. Md. Heights Div. W. Va.	To Arty. Wheaton's B. 1-Div. W. Va.	Jan., 1864
Batty. A, 1st W. Va. Arty.Dec., 1863	From Unatt. West Va............	To Arty. Wheaton's B. 1-Div. W. Va.	Jan., 1864

2d BRIGADE.— COMMANDER.

W. P. Maulsby..........	Col. 1st Md. Pot. Home Brig. Infy..		
1st Md. P. H. B. Infy...Dec., 1863	From 2-B. Md. Heights Div. W. Va.	To Reserve Div. West Va........	Apr., 1864
2d Md. Eastern Shore...Dec., 1863	From 2-B. Md. Heights Div. W. Va.	To 1-Brig. 1-Infy. Div. West Va....	Apr., 1864
Batty. B, Maryland Arty.Dec., 1863	From 2-B. Md. Heights Div. W. Va.	To Arty. 1-Div. West Va.........	Jan., 1864
30th N. Y. Indpt. Batty..Dec., 1863	From Martinsburg, W. Va.........	To Arty. 1-Div. West Va.........	Jan., 1864
32d N. Y. Indpt. Batty...Dec., 1863	From 2-B. Md. Heights Div. W. Va.	To Arty. 1-Div. West Va.........	Jan., 1864

3d BRIGADE.— COMMANDER.

R. S. Rodgers..........	Col. 2d Md. Eastern Shore Infy....		
18th Conn. Infy.........Dec., 1863	From Unatt. Dept. West Va.......	To 1-Brig. 1-Infy. Div. West Va....	Apr., 1864
116th Ohio Infy........Dec., 1863	From Martinsburg, W. Va.........	To 1-Brig. 1-Infy. Div. West Va....	Apr., 1864
123d Ohio Infy.........Dec., 1863	From Martinsburg, W. Va.........	To 1-Brig. 1-Infy. Div. West Va....	Apr., 1864
12th Penna. Cav........Dec., 1863	From Martinsburg, W. Va.........	To Res. Div. Harper's Ferry, W. Va.	Apr., 1864
1st West Va. Cav. Co. K..Dec., 1863	From Martinsburg, W. Va.........	To 2-Brig. 2-Cav. Div. West Va...	Apr., 1864
Batty. B, 5th U. S. Arty..Dec., 1863	From Unatt. Arty. Dept. W. Va....	To Res. Div. Harper's Ferry, W. Va.	Apr., 1864

CAVALRY BRIGADE, 1st DIVISION.— COMMANDERS.

William H. Boyd......	Col. 21st Penna. Cav..............	Dec., 1863, to Feb., 1864.	
C. F. Fitzsimons........	Lt.-Col. 21st N. Y. Cav..........	Feb., 1864, to Apr., 1864.	Dec., 1864
1st Conn. Cav. Det......Dec., 1863	From 1-B. Md. Heights Div. W. Va.	To Baltimore, Md. 8-Corps......	Jan., 1864
20th Penna. Cav........Dec., 1863	From Campbell's Brig. West Va....	No change to Muster Out........	Jan., 1864
21st Penna. Cav........Dec., 1863	From Unatt. Dept. West Va.......	No change to Muster Out........	Feb., 1864
22d Penna. Cav........Dec., 1863	From Unatt. Dept. West Va.......	No change to Muster Out........	Feb., 1864
1st Md. P. H. B. Cav....Dec., 1863	From 2-B. Md. Heights Div. W. Va.	To 1-Brig. 1-Div. Cav. West Va....	Apr., 1864
1st N. Y. Lincoln Cav....Dec., 1863	From Martinsburg, W. Va.........	To 1-Brig. 1-Div. Cav. West Va....	Apr., 1864
15th N. Y. Cav.........Jan., 1864	From Def. Washington 22-Corps...	To 2-Brig. 1-Cav. Div. West Va....	Apr., 1864
1st N. Y. Vet. Cav......Feb., 1864	From Def. Washington 22-Corps...	To 1-Brig. 1-Cav. Div. West Va....	Apr., 1864
21st N. Y. Cav.........Feb., 1864	From Def. Washington 22-Corps...	To 1-Brig. 1-Cav. Div. West Va....	Apr., 1864
20th Penna. Cav........Feb., 1864	From Reorganization.............	To 2-Brig. 1-Cav. Div. West Va...	Apr., 1864
22d Penna. Cav........Feb., 1864	From Reorganization.............	To 2-Brig. 1-Cav. Div. West Va...	Apr., 1864
ARTILLERY, 1st DIVISION.—			
5th N. Y. H. A. I, K, L, M.Dec., 1863	From Def. Washington 22-Corps...	To 2-Brig. 1-Infy. Div. West Va....	Apr., 1864
Tyler's Penna. H. A. Co..Dec., 1863	From Mulligan's Brig. Dept. W. Va.	No change to Muster Out.........	Jan., 1864
Batty. H, 1st W. Va. Arty.Dec., 1863	From New Organization..........	To Kelly's Res. Div. West Va......	Apr., 1864
Batty. B, Md. Arty......Jan., 1864	From 2-Brig. 1-Div. West Va......	To Arty. Brig. West Va..........	Apr., 1864
30th N. Y. Indpt. Batty..Jan., 1864	From 2-Brig. 1-Div. West Va......	To Arty. Brig. West Va..........	Apr., 1864
32d N. Y. Indpt. Batty...Jan., 1864	From 2-Brig. 1-Div. West Va......	To Arty. Brig. West Va..........	Apr., 1864

UNATTACHED.—

Gaskill's Penna. Eng.....Dec., 1863	From Unatt. Md. Heights D. W. Va.	To Res. Div. Harper's Ferry, W. Va.	Apr.,	1864
Loudoun, Va. Rangers....Dec., 1863	From 2-Brig. Md. Heights D. W. Va.	To Res. Div. Harper's Ferry, W. Va.	Apr.,	1864
34th Mass. Infy..........Jan., 1864	From 1-Brig. 1-Div. West Va.......	To Res. Div. Harper's Ferry, W. Va.	Apr.,	1864

WHEATON'S BRIGADE.—   COMMANDER.

J. F. Ballier............	Col. 98th Penna. Infy..............	Jan., 1864, to Mch., 1864.		
62d N. Y. Infy..........Jan., 1864	From 2-Brig. 3-Div. 6-Corps Pot....	To 1-Brig. 2-Div. 6-Corps Pot......	Mch.,	1864
93d Penna. Infy.........Jan., 1864	From 2-Brig. 3-Div. 6-Corps Pot....	To 1-Brig. 2-Div. 6-Corps Pot......	Mch.,	1864
98th Penna. Infy........Jan., 1864	From 2-Brig. 3-Div. 6-Corps Pot....	To 1-Brig. 2-Div. 6-Corps Pot......	Mch.,	1864
102d Penna. Infy........Jan., 1864	From 2-Brig. 3-Div. 6-Corps Pot....	To 1-Brig. 2-Div. 6-Corps Pot......	Mch.,	1864
139th Penna. Infy.......Jan., 1864	From 2-Brig. 3-Div. 6-Corps Pot....	To 1-Brig. 2-Div. 6-Corps Pot......	Mch.,	1864
17th Ind. Batty........Jan., 1864	From 1-Brig. 1-Div. West Va.......	To Res. Div. Harper's Ferry, W. Va.	Mch.,	1864
Batty. D, 1st Penna. Arty.Jan., 1864	From 1-Brig. 1-Div. West Va.......	To Res. Div. Harper's Ferry, W. Va.	Mch.,	1864
Batty. A, 1st W. Va. Arty.Jan., 1864	From 1-Brig. 1-Div. West Va.......	To Res. Div. Harper's Ferry, W. Va.	Mch.,	1864

2d DIVISION.—   COMMANDER.

J. A. Mulligan.........	Col. 23d Ill. Infy..................	Dec., 1863, to Apr., 1864.

1st BRIGADE.—   COMMANDERS.

M. McCarlin..........	Col. 15th West Va. Infy..........	Dec., 1863, to Apr. 2, 1864.		
J. M. Campbell........	Col. 54th Penna. Infy...........	Apr. 2, 1864, to Apr. 14, 1864.		
54th Penna. Infy.......Dec., 1863	From Campbell's Brig. West Va....	To 2-Brig. 1-Infy. Div. West Va....	Apr.,	1864
15th W. Va. Infy.......Dec., 1863	From Campbell's Brig. West Va....	To 3-Brig. 2-Infy. Div. West Va....	Apr.,	1864
Batty. E, 1st W. Va. Arty.Dec., 1863	From Campbell's Brig. West Va....	To Res. Div. Harper's Ferry, W. Va.	Apr.,	1864
2d Penna. Batt'n........Dec., 1863	From Unatt. Dept. West Va........	No change to Muster Out..........	Jan.,	1864
12th W. Va. Infy.......Jan., 1864	From 1-Brig. 1-Div. West Va......	To 2-Brig. 1-Infy. Div. West Va....	Apr.,	1864
13th W. Va. Infy.......Jan., 1863	From 1-Brig. 3-Div. West Va......	To 1-Brig. 2-Infy. Div. West Va....	Apr.,	1864

2d BRIGADE.—   COMMANDER.

Joseph Thoburn........	Col. 1st West Va. Infy.............	Dec., 1863, to Apr., 1864.		
23d Ill. Infy...........Dec., 1863	From Mulligan's Brig. Dept. W. Va.	To 1-Brig. 2-Infy. Div. West Va..	Apr.,	1864
2d Md. Pot. Home Brig..Dec., 1863	From Mulligan's Brig. Dept. W. Va.	To Res. Div. Harper's Ferry, W. Va.	Apr.,	1864
1st W. Va. Infy.........Dec., 1863	From Campbell's Brig. Dept. W. Va.	To 2-Brig. 1-Infy. Div. West Va..	Apr.,	1864
14th W. Va. Infy.......Dec., 1863	From Mulligan's Brig. West Va....	To 2-Brig. 2-Infy. Div. West Va..	Apr.,	1864
Lafayette Pa. Cav......Dec., 1863	From Campbell's Brig. West Va...	To 22d Penna. Cav...............	Feb.,	1864
Washington Pa. Cav.....Dec., 1863	From Campbell's Brig. West Va...	To 22d Penna. Cav...............	Feb.,	1864
Ringgold Pa. Cav.......Dec., 1863	From Campbell's Brig. West Va...	To 22d Penna. Cav...............	Feb.,	1864
Batty. L, 1st Ill. Arty...Dec., 1863	From Mulligan's Brig. West Va....	To Res. Div. Harper's Ferry, W. Va.	Apr.,	1864
Batty. D, 1st W. Va. Arty.Dec., 1863	From Mulligan's Brig. West Va....	To Arty. 2d Infy. Div. West Va....	Apr.,	1864

3d BRIGADE.—   COMMANDER.

N. Wilkinson..........	Col. 6th West Va. Infy.............	Dec., 1863, to Apr., 1864.		
6th West Va. Infy.......Dec., 1863	From Wilkinson's Brig. West Va..	To Res. Div. Harper's Ferry, W. Va..	Apr.,	1864
11th West Va. Infy......Dec., 1863	From Wilkinson's Brig. West Va..	To 1-Brig. 3-Div. West Va........	Jan.,	1864
4th West Va. Cav.......Dec., 1863	From Wilkinson's Brig. West Va..	No change to Muster Out..........	Apr.,	1864
Batty. F, 1st W. Va. Infy.Dec., 1863	From Camp Barry 22-Corps........	To Res. Div. Harper's Ferry, W. Va.	Apr.,	1864

3d DIVISION.—   COMMANDERS.

E. P. Scammon........	Brigadier General................	Dec., 1863, to Feb. 11, 1864.
Geo. Crook.............	Brigadier General................	Feb. 11, 1864, to Apr., 1864.

1st BRIGADE.—   COMMANDER.

R. B. Hayes...........	Col. 23d Ohio Infy................	Dec., 1863, to Apr., 1864.		
23d Ohio Infy..........Dec., 1863	From 1-Brig. Scammon's D. W. Va.	To 1-Brig. 2-Infy. Div. West Va...	Apr.,	1864
5th West Va. Infy......Dec., 1863	From 1-Brig. Scammon's D. W. Va.	To 1-Brig. 2-Infy. Div. West Va...	Apr.,	1864
13th West Va. Infy......Dec., 1863	From 1-Brig. Scammon's D. W. Va.	To 1-Brig. 2-Infy. Div. West Va...	Apr.,	1864
1st West Va. Cav., A, G..Dec., 1863	From 1-Brig. Scammon's D. W. Va.	To 2-Brig. 2-Cav. Div. W. Va......	Apr.,	1864
3d West Va. Cav., Co. G..Dec., 1863	From 1-Brig. Scammon's D. W. Va.	To 3-Brig. 2-Cav. Div. West Va....	Apr.,	1864
11th West Va. Infy......Jan., 1863	From 3-Brig. 2-Div. West Va......	To 3-Brig. 2-Infy. Div. West Va...	Apr.,	1864

2d BRIGADE.—   COMMANDER.

Carr B. White..........	Col. 12th Ohio Infy...............	Dec., 1863, to Apr., 1864.		
12th Ohio Infy..........Dec., 1863	From 2-Brig. Scammon's D. W. Va.	To 2-Brig. 2-Infy. Div. West Va...	Apr.,	1864
91st Ohio Infy..........Dec., 1863	From 2-Brig. Scammon's D. W. Va.	To 2-Brig. 2-Infy. Div. West Va...	Apr.,	1864
9th West Va. Infy......Dec., 1863	From 2-Brig. Scammon's D. W. Va.	To 2-Brig. 2-Infy. Div. West Va...	Apr.,	1864
1st Ohio Batty.........Dec., 1863	From 2-Brig. Scammon's D. W. Va.	To Arty. 2-Infy. Div. West Va.....	Apr.,	1864

3d BRIGADE.—   COMMANDER.

A. N. Duffie...........	Brigadier General................	Dec., 1863, to Apr., 1864.		
34th Ohio Infy..........Dec., 1863	From 3-Brig. Scammon's D. W. Va..	To 1-Brig. 2-Cav. Div. West Va...	Apr.,	1864
2d West Va. Cav.......Dec., 1863	From 3-Brig. Scammon's D. W. Va.	To 1-Brig. 2-Cav. Div. West Va...	Apr.,	1864
3d West Va. Cav., 3 Cos..Dec., 1863	From 1-Brig. Scammon's D. W. Va.	To 3-Brig. 2-Cav. Div. West Va...	Apr.,	1864
Simmonds' Ky. Batty...Dec., 1863	From 1-Brig. Scammon's Div. W. Va.	To Arty. 2-Infy. Div. West Va.....	Apr.,	1864

4th DIVISION.—   COMMANDER.

W. W. Averill........	Brigadier General................	Dec., 1863, to Apr., 1864.

1st BRIGADE.—   COMMANDERS.

M. S. Hall.............	Lt.-Col. 10th West Va. Infy........	Dec., 1862, to Jan., 1864.		
A. Moor...............	Col. 28th Ohio Infy...............	Jan., 1864, to Apr., 1864.		
28th Ohio Infy..........Dec., 1863	From Averill's 4th Separate Brig....	To 1-Brig. 1-Infy. Div. West Va....	Apr.,	1864
10th West Va. Infy......Dec., 1863	From Averill's 4th Separate Brig....	To Res. Div. Harper's Ferry, W. Va.	Apr.,	1864
Batty. A, 1st West Va. A..Dec., 1863	From Averill's 4th Separate Brig....	To Arty. 1-Cav. Div. West Va......	Apr.,	1864

2d BRIGADE.—   COMMANDER.

J. M. Schoonmaker......	Col. 14th Penna. Cav..............	Dec., 1863, to Apr., 1864.		
16th Ill. Cav. Co. C......Dec., 1863	From Averill's 4th Separate Brig...	To Res. Div. Harper's Ferry, W. Va.	Apr.,	1864
3d Indpt. Co. Ohio Cav...Dec., 1863	From Averill's 4th Separate Brig...	To Res. Div. Harper's Ferry, W. Va.	Apr.,	1864
14th Penna. Cav........Dec., 1863	From Averill's 4th Separate Brig...	To Res. Div. Harper's Ferry, W. Va.	Apr.,	1864
1st West Va. Cav. Co. A..Dec., 1863	From Averill's 4th Separate Brig...	To Res. Div. Harper's Ferry, W. Va.	Apr.,	1864
3d W. Va. Cav. Cos. E, H, I.Dec., 1863	From Averill's 4th Separate Brig...	To Res. Div. Harper's Ferry, W. Va.	Apr.,	1864

3d BRIGADE.— COMMANDER.

J. H. Oley	Col. 7th West Va. Cav	Dec., 1863, to Apr., 1864.

5th W. Va. Cav. (2-Infy.).Dec., 1863	From Averill's 4th Separate Brig...	To 3-Brig. 2-Cav. Div. West Va...	Apr., 1862
6th W. Va. Cav. (3-Infy.).Dec., 1863	From Averill's 4th Separate Brig...	To Res. Div. Harper's Ferry, W. Va.	Apr., 1862
7th W. Va. Cav. (8-Infy.).Dec., 1863	From Averill's 4th Separate Brig...	To 3-Brig. 2-Cav. Div. West Va...	Apr., 1862
Batty. G, 1st W. Va. Arty.Dec., 1863	From Averill's 4th Separate Brig...	To Arty. 2-Cav. Div. West Va	Apr., 1862

1st INFANTRY DIVISION.— COMMANDERS.

J. C. Sullivan	Brigadier General	Apr., 1864, to July 3, 1864.	
George Crook	Brigadier General	July 3, 1864, to July 22, 1864.	
Jos. Thoburn	Brigadier General	July 22, 1864, to Oct. 19, 1864.	Killed.
I. M. Harris	Col. 10th West Va. Infy	Oct. 19, 1864, to Dec. 24, 1864.	
I. H. Duval	Col. 9th West Va. Infy	Jan., 1865, to Feb. 25, 1865.	
R. B. Hayes	Col. 23d Ohio Infy	Feb. 25, 1865, to Apr., 1865.	
James McMillen	Bvt. Major General	Apr., 1865, to May, 1865.	
F. Fessenden	Brigadier General		

1st BRIGADE.— COMMANDERS.

A. Moor	Col. 28th Ohio Infy	Apr., 1864, to June 8, 1864.	
Geo. D. Wells	Col. 34th Mass. Infy	June 8, 1864, to Oct. 19, 1864.	Killed.
I. F. Wildes	Lt.-Col. 116th Ohio Infy	Oct. 19, 1864, to Dec. 24, 1864.	
R. B. Hayes	Col 23d Ohio Infy	Jan., 1865, to Feb. 25, 1865.	

18th Conn. Infy........Apr., 1864	From 3-Brig. 1-Div. West Va	To 2-Brig. 1-Infy. Div. W. Va	July, 1864
2d Md. Eastern Shore....Apr., 1864	From 2-Brig. 1-Div. West Va	To 2-Brig. 1-Infy. Div. W. Va	July, 1864
28th Ohio Infy........Apr., 1864	From 1-Brig. 4-Div. West Va..:...	No change to Muster Out	June, 1864
116th Ohio Infy........Apr., 1864	From 3-Brig. 1-Div. West Va	To 1-Brig. Indpt. Div. 24-Corps...	Dec., 1864
123d Ohio Infy........Apr., 1864	From 3-Brig. 1-Div. West Va	To 1-Brig. Indpt. Div. 24-Corps...	Dec., 1864
34th Mass. Infy......June, 1864	From 2-Brig. 1-Infy. Div. W. Va...	To 1-Brig. Indpt. Div. 24-Corps...	Dec., 1864
5th N. Y. H. A, B, C, D.June, 1864	From 2-Brig. 1-Infy. Div. W. Va...	To Res. Div. Harper's Ferry, W. Va.	July, 1864
23d Ohio Infy........Jan., 1865	From 1-Brig. 2-Infy. Div. West Va.	To 1-Brig. 4-Prov'l. Div. W. Va...	Apr., 1865
36th Ohio Infy........Jan., 1865	From 1-Brig. 2-Infy. Div. West Va.	To 1-Brig. 4-Prov'l. Div. W. Va...	Apr., 1865
1st W. Va. Vet. Infy.....Jan., 1865	From 1-Brig. 2-Infy. Div. West Va.	To 1-Brig. 4-Prov'l. Div. W. Va...	Apr., 1865
13th W. Va. Infy........Jan., 1865	From 1-Brig. 2-Infy. Div. West Va.	To 1-Brig. 4-Prov'l. Div. W. Va...	Apr., 1865
3d Md. P. H. B.........Apr., 1865	From Res. Div. Harper's Ferry	No change to Muster Out	May, 1865
28th Ohio Infy........Apr., 1865	From Res. Div. Harper's Ferry	No change to Muster Out	July, 1865
74th Penna. Infy........Apr., 1865	From Res. Div. Harper's Ferry	To Clarksburg, W. Va	June, 1865
6th West Va. Infy......Apr., 1865	From Res. Div. Harper's Ferry	No change to Muster Out	June, 1865
17th West Va. Infy......Apr., 1865	From Res. Div. Harper's Ferry	No change to Muster Out	July, 1865
8th Ohio Cav........Apr., 1865	From Res. Div. Harper's Ferry	No change to Muster Out	July, 1865
1st W. Va. Cav. Co. A....Apr., 1865	From Res. Div. Harper's Ferry	No change to Muster Out	July, 1865
32d N. Y. Batty......Apr., 1865	From Res. Div. Harper's Ferry	No change to Muster Out	July, 1865
Batty. D, W. Va Arty.....Apr., 1865	From Res. Div. Harper's Ferry	No change to Muster Out	June, 1865

2d BRIGADE.— COMMANDERS.

Jos. Thoburn	Col. 1st W. Va. Infy	Apr., 1864, to July 22, 1864.	
Wm. G. Ely	Col. 18th Conn. Infy	July 22, 1864, to Sept. 18, 1864.	
R. S. Northcott	Lt.-Col. 12th W. Va. Infy	Sept. 18, 1864, to Oct., 1864.	
Wm. B. Curtis	Col. 12th West Va. Infy	Oct., 1864, to Dec., 1864.	
B. F. Coates	Col. 91st Ohio Infy	Jan., 1865, to Apr., 1865.	

34th Mass. Infy......Apr., 1864	From Unatt. 1-Div. West Va	To 1-Brig. 1-Infy. Div. W. Va	June, 1864
5th N. Y. H. A, A, B, C, D.Apr., 1864	From Res. Div. Harper's Ferry	To 1-Brig. 1-Infy. Div. W. Va	June, 1864
54th Penna. Infy......Apr., 1864	From 1-Brig. 2-Div. West Va	To 3-Brig. 1-Infy. Div. W. Va	June, 1864
1st West Va. Infy......Apr., 1864	From 2-Brig. 2-Div. West Va	To Res. Div. West Va	Sept., 1864
12th West Va. Infy......Apr., 1864	From 1-Brig. 2-Div. West Va	To 2-Brig. Indpt. Div. 24-Corps...	Dec., 1864
4th West Va. Infy......May, 1864	From Veteran Furlough	Transferred to 1st W. Va. Veteran.	Dec., 1864
18th Conn. Infy......June, 1864	From 1-Brig. 1-Infy. Div. West Va.	To New Haven, Conn. Dept. East..	Oct., 1864
2d Md. E. S. Infy......July, 1864	From 1-Brig. 1-Infy. Div. West Va.	To Res. Div. West Va	Jan., 1865
34th Ohio Infy........Jan., 1865	From 2-Brig. 2-Infy. Div. West Va.	Consolidated with 36th Ohio	Feb., 1865
91st Ohio Infy........Jan., 1865	From 2-Brig. 2-Infy. Div. West Va.	To 1-Brig. 4-Prov'l. Div. W. Va...	Apr., 1865
14th W. Va. Infy........Jan., 1865	From 2-Brig. 2-Infy. Div. West Va.	No change to Muster Out	June, 1865
2d Md. P. H. B.........Apr., 1865	From Res. Div. West Va	No change to Muster Out	May, 1865
2d West Va. Vet. Infy...Apr., 1865	From Res. Div. West Va	No change to Muster Out	July, 1865
3d Indpt. Co. Ohio Cav...Apr., 1865	From Res. Div. West Va	No change to Muster Out	May, 1865
22d Penna. Cav......Apr., 1865	From Res. Div. West Va	Consolidated with 18th Pa. Cav...	June, 1865
Simmons' Ky Batty......Apr., 1865	From Res. Div. West Va	No change to Muster Out	July, 1865
Batty. B, Md. Arty......Apr., 1865	From Res. Div. West Va	No change to Muster Out	July, 1865
Batty. H, 1st W. Va. Arty.Apr., 1865	From Res. Div. West Va	No change to Muster Out	July, 1865

3d BRIGADE.— COMMANDERS.

J. M. Campbell	Col. 54th Penna. Infy	July, 1864, to Aug., 1864.	
T. M. Harris	Col. 10th West Va. Infy	Aug., 1864, to Oct. 19, 1864.	
Milton Wells	Col. 15th West Va. Infy	Oct. 19, 1864, to Dec. 24, 1864.	

23d Ill. Infy........July, 1864	From 1-Brig. 3-Infy. Div. West Va.	To 2-Brig. Indpt. Div. 24-Corps...	Dec., 1864
54th Penna. Infy......July, 1864	From 2-Brig. 3-Infy. Div. West Va.	To 2-Brig. Indpt. Div. 24-Corps...	Dec., 1864
10th West Va. Infy....July, 1864	From 1-Brig. 3-Infy. Div. West Va.	To 3-Brig. Infy. Div. 24-Corps...	Dec., 1864
11th West Va. Infy....July, 1864	From 2-Brig. 3-Infy. Div. West Va.	To 3-Brig. Infy. Div. 24-Corps...	Dec., 1864
15th West Va. Infy....July, 1864	From 2-Brig. 3-Infy. Div. West Va.	To 3-Brig. Infy. Div. 24-Corps...	Dec., 1864
ARTILLERY.—			
Batty. B, Md. Arty....Apr., 1864	From Arty. 1-Div. West Va	To Arty. Brig. West Va	May, 1864
30th N. Y. Batty......Apr., 1864	From Arty. 1-Div. West Va	To Arty. Brig. West Va	May, 1864

2d INFANTRY DIVISION.— COMMANDERS.

Geo. Crook	Brigadier General	Apr., 1864, to July 22, 1864.	
I. H. Duval	Col. 9th West Va. Infy	July 22, 1864, to Oct. 19, 1864.	
R. B. Hayes	Col. 23d Ohio Infy	Oct. 19, 1864, to Dec. 24, 1864.	
I. H. Duval	Brigadier General	Dec. 24, 1864, to Jan. .., 1865.	
J. A. J. Lightburn	Brigadier General	Jan. .., 1865, to May .., 1865.	
W. P. Carlin	Bvt. Major General	May .., 1865.	

1st BRIGADE.— COMMANDERS.

R. B. Hayes	Col. 23d Ohio Infy	Apr. .., 1864, to Oct. 19, 1864.	
H. F. Devol	Col. 36th Ohio Infy	Oct. 19, 1864, to Dec. 24, 1864.	
R. B. Hayes	Col. 23d Ohio Infy	Dec. 24, 1864, to Jan. .., 1865.	
N. Wilkinson	Col. 6th West Va. Infy	Jan. .., 1865, to May .., 1865.	
F. Fessenden	Brigadier General	May .., 1865.	

1st BRIGADE.—Continued.

23d Ohio Infy............Apr., 1864	From 1-Brig. 3-Div. West Va......	To 1-Brig. 1-Infy. Div. West Va....	Jan., 1865
36th Ohio Infy...........Apr., 1864	From 1-Br. 3-Div. 14-C. Cumb'd.....	To 1-Brig. 1-Infy. Div. West Va....	Jan., 1865
5th West Va. Infy.......Apr., 1864	From 1-Brig. 3-Div. West Va.......	To Consol. with 9th West Va.......	Nov., 1864
13th West Va. Infy......Apr., 1864	From 1-Brig. 3-Div. West Va.......	To 1-Brig. 1-Infy. Div. West Va....	Jan., 1865
1st West Va. Vet. Infy..Nov., 1864	From Consol. of 5th and 9th W. Va.	To 1-Brig. 1-Infy. Div. West Va....	Jan., 1865
18th Conn. Infy.........Jan., 1865	From 1-Brig. 3-Infy. Div. West Va.	No change to Muster Out.........	June, 1865
13th Md. Infy...........Apr., 1865	From 1st Md. P. H. B...........	No change to Muster Out.........	May, 1865
1st Md. P. H. B. Cav....Apr., 1865	From 1-Brig. 3-Infy. Div. West Va.	No change to Muster Out.........	June, 1865
Batty. C, 1st Penna. Arty.Apr., 1865	From Arty. 3-Infy. Div. West Va....	No change to Muster Out.........	June, 1865
6th West Va. Infy.......Apr., 1865	From Res. Div. West Va........	No change to Muster Out.........	June, 1865

2d BRIGADE.— COMMANDERS.

Carr B. White..........	Col. 12th Ohio Infy...............	Apr., 1864, to July .., 1864.
D. D. Johnson..........	Col. 14th West Va. Infy...........	July .., 1864, to Sept. 19, 1864.
B. F. Coates............	Lt.-Col. 91st Ohio Infy...........	Sept. 19, 1864.
D. D. Johnson..........	Col. 14th West Va. Infy...........	Sept. 19, 1864, to Jan. .., 1865.
Jacob Weddle..........	Lt.-Col. 14th W. Va. Infy........	Jan. .., 1865.
S. Graham.............	Col. 5th N. Y. Heavy Arty........	Apr., 1865, to July .., 1865.

12th Ohio Infy.........Apr., 1864	From 2-Brig. 3-Div. West Va...	No change to Muster Out.........	July, 1864
91st Ohio Infy.........Apr., 1864	From 2-Brig. 3-Div. West Va...	To 2-Brig. 1-Infy. Div. West Va....	Jan., 1865
9th West Va. Infy......Apr., 1864	From 2-Brig. 3-Div. West Va...	To 1st West Va. Veteran Infy......	Nov., 1864
14th West Va. Infy......Apr., 1864	From 2-Brig. 2-Div. West Va...	To 2-Brig. 1-Infy. Div. West Va....	Jan., 1865
34th Ohio Infy..........July, 1864	From 2-Brig. 2-Cav. Div. West Va.	To 2-Brig. 1-Infy. Div. West Va....	Jan., 1865
5th N. Y. Heavy Arty.....Apr., 1865	From 2-Brig. 3-Div. West Va...	No change to Muster Out.........	July, 1865

3d BRIGADE.— COMMANDERS.

H. G. Sickel...........	Col. 3d Pa. Res. Corps............	Apr. .., 1864, to June 9, 1864.
J. M. Campbell.........	Col. 54th Penna. Infy............	June 9, 1864, to July .., 1864.

3d Penna. Res. Corps....Mch., 1864	From Dist. Alexandria 22-Corps....	No change to Muster Out.........	June, 1864
4th Penna. Res. Corps...Mch., 1864	From Dist. Alexandria 22-Corps....	No change to Muster Out.........	June, 1864
11th West Va. Infy......Mch., 1864	From 3-Brig. 2-Div. West Va...	To 2-Brig. 3-Infy. Div. West Va....	July, 1864
15th West Va. Infy......Mch., 1864	From 1-Brig. 2-Div. West Va...	To 2-Brig. 3-Infy. Div. West Va....	July, 1864
54th Penna. Infy........June, 1864	From 2-Brig. 1-Infy. Div. West Va.	To 2-Brig. 3-Infy. Div. West Va....	July, 1864
ARTILLERY 2d DIVISION.—			
1st Ohio Batty..........Apr., 1864	From 2-Brig. 3-Div. West Va...	To Res. Div. Harper's Ferry.......	July, 1864
Simmons' Ky. Batty......	From 2-Brig. 3-Div. West Va...	To Res. Div. Harper's Ferry.......	July, 1864
Batty. L, 1st Ohio Arty...Apr., 1865	From 1-Sep. Brig. 3-Div. West Va.	No change to Muster Out.........	July, 1865
Batty. B, 5th U. S. Arty..Apr., 1865	From 1-Sep. Brig. 3-Div. West Va.	To Washington, D. C., 22-Corps....	July, 1865
UNATTACHED 2d DIVISION.—			
25th N. Y. Cav..........Jan., 1865	From 1-Brig. 1-Div. Cav. C. Shen...	No change to Muster Out.........	June, 1865
Loudon Va. Rangers.....Jan., 1865	From 3-Brig. 3-Div. West Va...	No change to Muster Out.........	May, 1865
Batty. L, 1st Ill. Arty....Jan., 1865	From Unatt. 3-Div. West Va...	No change to Muster Out.........	July, 1865
Batty. D, 1st Pa. Arty....Jan., 1865	From 1-Sep. Brig. 3-Div. West Va.	No change to Muster Out.........	June, 1865

3d DIVISION.— COMMANDERS.

James A. Mulligan......	Col. 23d Ill. Infy...............	July, 1864, to July 24, 1864.	Killed.
J. D. Stevenson........	Brigadier General...............	Jan. .., 1865, to Apr. .., 1865.	

1st BRIGADE.— COMMANDERS.

Thos. M. Harris........	Col. 10th West Va. Infy...........	July, 1864.
W. H. Seward..........	Brigadier General...............	Jan. .., 1865, to Apr. .., 1865.

23d Ill. Infy............July, 1864	From Res. Div. Harper's Ferry......	To 3-Brig. 1-Infy. Div. West Va....	July, 1864
10th West Va. Infy......July, 1864	From Res. Div. Harper's Ferry......	To 3-Brig. 1-Infy. Div. West Va....	July, 1864
Reorganized Jan., 1865.			
18th Conn. Infy.........Jan., 1865	From Dist. Harper's Ferry, W. Va..	To 1-Brig. 2-Infy. Div. West Va....	Apr., 1865
195th Penna. Infy.......Jan., 1865	From Dist. Harper's Ferry, W. Va..	To 2-Brig. 3-Prov'l Div. Army Shen.	Apr., 1865
1st Md. P. H. B. Cav....Jan., 1865	From Dist. Harper's Ferry, W. Va..	To 1-Brig. 2-Infy. Div. W. Va......	Apr., 1865
1st Ohio Batty..........Jan., 1865	From Dist. Harper's Ferry, W. Va..	To 3-Brig. Hardin's Div. 22-Corps..	Apr., 1865

2d BRIGADE.— COMMANDERS.

J. P. Linton............	Lt.-Col. 11th W. Va. Infy..........	
Reorganized Jan., 1865.		
Sam'l Graham..........	Col. 5th N. Y. Heavy Arty........	

54th Penna. Infy........July, 1864	From 3-Brig. 2-Infy. Div. West Va..	To 3-Brig. 1-Infy. Div. West Va....	July, 1864
11th West Va. Infy......July, 1864	From 3-Brig. 2-Infy. Div. West Va..	To 3-Brig. 1-Infy. Div. West Va....	July, 1864
15th West Va. Infy......July, 1864	From 3-Brig. 2-Infy. Div. West Va..	To 3-Brig. 1-Infy. Div. West Va....	July, 1864
5th N. Y. Heavy Arty....Jan., 1865	From Dist. Harper's Ferry, W. Va..	To 2-Brig. 2-Div. West Va.........	Apr., 1865

3d BRIGADE.— COMMANDER.

R. E. Cook.............	Col. 13th Md. Infy. (1st P. H. B.)...	

1st Md. P. H. B. Infy....Jan., 1865	From Dist. Harper's Ferry, W. Va..	Transferred to 13th Md...........	Apr., 1865
Batty. A, Md. Arty......Jan., 1865	From Dist. Harper's Ferry, W. Va..	Consol. with Batty. B, Md.........	Mch., 1865
Loudon Va. Rangers.....Jan., 1865	From Dist. Harper's Ferry, W. Va..	To Unatt. 2d Div. West Va........	Jan., 1865
1st SEPARATE BRIGADE, 3D DIVISION.—			
Batty. L, 1st Ohio Arty....Jan., 1865	From Arty. Dist. Harper's F., W. Va.	To Arty. Brig. 2-Div. West Va.....	Apr., 1865
Batty. D, 1st Penna. Arty.Jan., 1865	From Arty. Dist. Harper's F., W. Va.	To Unatt. 2-Div. West Va.........	Jan., 1865
Indpt. Batty. F, Pa. Arty.Jan., 1865	From Arty. Dist. Harper's F., W. Va.	To Def. Washington 22-Corps......	Apr., 1865
Batty. B, 5th U. S. Arty..Jan., 1865	From Arty. Dist. Harper's F., W. Va.	To Arty. Brig. 2-Div. West Va.....	Apr., 1865

UNATTACHED 3d DIVISION.—

12th Penna. Cav........Jan., 1865	From Dist. Harper's Ferry, W. Va..	To Cav. Brig. Army Shenandoah....	Apr., 1865
Batty. L, 1st Ill. Arty....Jan., 1865	From Dist. Harper's Ferry, W. Va..	To Unatt. 2-Div. West Va.........	Jan., 1865
Batty. C, 1st Penna. Arty.Jan., 1865	From Dist. Harper's Ferry, W. Va..	To 1-Brig. 2-Div. West Va.........	Apr., 1865
Batty. G, 1st Penna. Arty.Jan., 1865	From Dist. Harper's Ferry, W. Va..	To Def. Washington, D. C.........	Apr., 1865

1st CAVALRY DIVISION.— COMMANDERS.

J. Stahel..............	Brigadier General................	Apr. .., 1864, to June 9, 1864.
A. N. Duffie...........	Brigadier General................	June 9, 1864, to Oct. 20, 1864.
J. E. Wynkoop.........	Col. 20th Penna. Cav.............	Temporary.

1st BRIGADE.—Discontinued Sept. 5, 1864. COMMANDERS.

W. B. Tibbets.........	Col. 21st N. Y. Cav.............	Apr. .., 1864, to June .., 1864.
R. F. Taylor..........	Col. 1st N. Y. Vet. Cav..........	June .., 1864, to July .., 1864.
W. B. Tibbets.........	Col. 21st N. Y. Cav.............	July .., 1864, to Aug. .., 1864.
R. F. Taylor..........	Col. 1st N. Y. Vet. Cav..........	Aug. .., 1864, to Sept. 5, 1864.

1st BRIGADE.—Continued.

1st Md. P. H. B. Cav.....Apr., 1864	From Cav. Brig. 1-Div. W. Va......	To 3-Brig. 1-Div. Cav. Corps Shen..	Aug., 1864
1st N. Y. Lincoln Cav.....Apr., 1864	From Cav. Brig. 1-Div. W. Va......	To 2-Brig. 1-Div. Cav. W. Va......	June, 1864
1st N. Y. Veteran Cav.....Apr., 1864	From Cav. Brig. 1-Div. W. Va......	To 2-Brig. 1-Div. Cav. W. Va......	July, 1864
21st N. Y. Cav.....Apr., 1864	From Cav. Brig. 1-Div. W. Va......	To 2-Brig. 1-Div. Cav. W. Va......	Aug., 1864
14th Penna. Cav. Det.....Apr., 1864	From 2-Brig. 4-Div. W. Va.........	To 2-Brig. 2-Cav. Div. W. Va......	Apr., 1864
15th N. Y. Cav.....June, 1864	From 2-Brig. 1-Cav. Div. W. Va....	To 2-Brig. 1-Cav. Div. W. Va......	July, 1864
1st N. Y. Lincoln Cav....July, 1864	From 2-Brig. 1-Cav. Div. W. Va....	To 2-Brig. 2-Cav. Div. W. Va......	Aug., 1864
12th Penna. Cav.....July, 1864	From Res. Div. Harper's F'y, W. Va.	To Res. Div. Harper's Ferry.......	Aug., 1864
22d Penna. Cav.....Aug., 1864	From 3-Brig. 1-Div. Cav. Corps Shen.	To 2-Brig. 1-Div. Cav. W. Va......	Aug., 1864
15th N. Y. Cav.....Aug., 1864	From 2-Brig. 1-Cav. Div. W. Va....	To 2-Brig. 3-Div. Cav. Corps Shen.	Sept., 1864
1st N. Y. Veteran Cav.....Aug., 1864	From 2-Brig. 1-Cav. Div. W. Va....	To 1st Separate Brig. Dist. Kanawha	Sept., 1864

2d BRIGADE.—   **COMMANDERS.**

J. E. Wynkoop.........	Col. 20th Penna. Cav............	Apr., 1864, to July, 1864.
J. Higgins.............	Col. 22nd Penna. Cav...........	July 22, 1864, to July 30, 1864.
A. J. Greenfield........	Col. 22nd Penna. Cav...........	July 30, 1864, to Aug. 15, 1864.
R. F. Taylor..........	Col. 1st N. Y. Veteran Cav......	Aug. 15, 1864, to Aug. 22, 1864.
Timothy Quinn.........	Major 1st N. Y. Lincoln Cav.....	Aug. 22, 1864, to Aug. 29, 1864.
J. E. Wynkoop.........	Col. 20th Penna. Cav...........	Aug. 29, 1864, to Sept. 15, 1864.
R. M. Richardson......	Col. 21st N. Y. Cav............	Sept. 15, 1864, to Oct. 14, 1864.
J. E. Wynkoop.........	Col. 20th Penna. Cav...........	Oct. 14, 1864, to Oct. 20, 1864.

15th N. Y. Cav.....Apr., 1864	From Cav. Brig. 1-Div. W. Va......	To 1-Brig. 1-Cav. Div. W. Va......	June, 1864
20th Penna. Cav.....Apr., 1864	From Cav. Brig. 1-Div. W. Va......	To 1-Brig. 1-Div. Cav. Corps Shen.	Aug., 1864
22d Penna. Cav.....Apr., 1864	From Res. Div. Harper's F'y, W. Va.	To 3-Brig. 1-Div. Cav. Corps Shen.	Aug., 1864
1st N. Y. Lincoln Cav...June, 1864	From 1-Brig. 1-Cav. Div. W. Va....	To 1-Brig. 1-Cav. Div. W. Va......	July, 1864
15th N. Y. Cav.....July, 1864	From 1-Brig. 1-Cav. Div. W. Va....	To 1-Brig. 1-Cav. Div. W. Va......	Aug., 1864
1st N. Y. Vet. Cav.....July, 1864	From 1-Brig. 1-Cav. Div. W. Va....	To 1-Brig. 1-Cav. Div. W. Va......	Sept., 1864
21st N. Y. Cav.....Aug., 1864	From 1-Brig. 1-Cav. Div. W. Va....	To 1-Brig. 2-Cav. Div. W. Va......	Nov., 1864
ARTILLERY.—			
Batty. B, W. Va. Arty..Apr., 1864	From 1-Brig. 4-Div. W. Va........	To Arty. Brig. W. Va............	July, 1864
Batty. E, W. Va. Arty..July, 1864	From Arty. Reserve Div. W. Va....	To Arty. Brig. W. Va............	July, 1864

2d CAVALRY DIVISION.—   **COMMANDERS.**

W. W. Averill.........	Brigadier General..................	Apr. 26, 1864, to Sept. 26, 1864.
Geo. A. Custer........	Brigadier General..................	Sept. 26, 1864, to Sept. 30, 1864.
W. H. Powell.........	Col. 2d W. Va. Cav..............	Sept. 30, 1864, to Jan. 13, 1865.
Geo. H. Chapman......	Brigadier General..................	Jan. 13, 1865, to Feb., 1865.
W. B. Tibbets.........	Bvt. Brig. General................	Feb., 1865, to Apr., 1865.

1st BRIGADE.—   **COMMANDERS.**

A. N. Duffie..........	Brigadier General................	Apr. 26, 1864, to June 6, 1864.
J. M. Schoonmaker.....	Col. 14th Penna. Cav...........	June 6, 1864, to June 9, 1864.
J. H. Oley...........	Col. 7th W. Va. Cav...........	June 9, 1864, to July, 1864.
J. M. Schoonmaker.....	Col. 14th Penna. Cav...........	July, 1864, to Oct., 1864.
A. S. Moore..........	Col. 8th Ohio Cav.............	Oct., 1864.
Thos. Gibson.........	Major 14th Pa. Cav............	Oct., 1864, to Nov. 10, 1864.
W. B. Tibbets........	Col. 21st N. Y. Cav...........	Nov. 10, 1864, to Feb., 1865.

2d W. Va. Cav...........Apr., 1864	From 3-Brig. 3-Div. W. Va........	To 3-Brig. 2-Cav. Div. W. Va......	May, 1864
34th Ohio Mtd. Infy.....Apr., 1864	From 3-Brig. 3-Div. W. Va........	To 3-Brig. 2-Cav. Div. W. Va......	May, 1864
8th Ohio Cav.....Apr., 1864	From New Organization...........	To Reserve Div. W. Va...........	Dec., 1864
14th Penna. Cav.....May, 1864	From 2-Brig. 2-Cav. Div. W. Va....	To 3-Brig. 1-Div. Cav. Corps Shen.	Aug., 1864
22d Penna. Cav.....Aug., 1864	From 1-Brig. 1-Cav. Div. W. Va....	To 2-Brig. 1-Cav. Div. W. Va......	Apr., 1865
14th Penna. Cav.....Aug., 1864	From 3-Brig. 1-Cav. Div. W. Va....	To 1st Sep. Br. DeRussy's Div. 22-C.	Apr., 1865
21st N. Y. Cav.....Nov., 1864	From 2-Brig. 1-Cav. Div. W. Va....	To Cav. Div. 22-Corps............	Apr., 1865

2d BRIGADE.—   **COMMANDERS.**

J. M. Schoonmaker.....	Col. 14th Penna. Cav............	Apr. 26, 1864, to June, 1864.
J. H. Oley...........	Col. 7th W. Va. Cav...........	June, 1864, to Aug., 1864.
W. H. Powell.........	Col. 2d W. Va. Cav...........	Aug., 1864, to Sept. 26, 1864.
Henry Capehart.......	Col. 1st W. Va. Cav...........	Sept. 26, 1864, to Dec. 28, 1864.
W. B. Tibbets........	Col. 21st N. Y. Cav...........	Dec. 28, 1864, to Jan. 13, 1865.
Henry Capehart.......	Col. 1st W. Va. Cav...........	Jan. 13, 1865, to Feb., 1865.

14th Penna. Cav.....Apr., 1864	From 1-Brig. 1-Cav. Div. W. Va....	To 1-Brig. 2-Cav. Div. W. Va......	May, 1864
1st W. Va. Cav.....Apr., 1864	From Unass'd W. Va.............	To 3-Brig. 3-Div. W. Va.........	May, 1864
3d W. Va. Cav.....May, 1864	From 1-Brig. 2-Cav. Div. W. Va....	To 3-Brig. 3-Div. Cav. Corps Shen.	Jan., 1865
5th W. Va. Cav.....May, 1864	From 3-Brig. 2-Cav. Div. W. Va....	To Reserve Div. W. Va...........	July, 1864
7th W. Va. Cav.....May, 1864	From 3-Brig. 2-Cav. Div. W. Va....	To 1st Sep. Brig. Dist. Kanawha....	July, 1864
34th Ohio Mtd. Infy.....July, 1864	From 3-Brig. 2-Cav. Div. W. Va....	To 2-Brig. 2-Infy. Div. W. Va......	Aug., 1864
1st W. Va. Cav.....July, 1864	From 3-Brig. 2-Cav. Div. W. Va....	To 3-Brig. 3-Div. Cav. Corps Shen.	Jan., 1865
2d W. Va. Cav.....July, 1864	From 3-Brig. 2-Cav. Div. W. Va....	To 3-Brig. 3-Div. Cav. Corps Shen.	Jan., 1865
1st N. Y. Lincoln Cav..Aug., 1864	From 1-Brig. 1-Cav. Div. W. Va....	To 3-Brig. 3-Div. Cav. Corps Shen.	Jan., 1865

3d BRIGADE.—   **COMMANDERS.**

J. H. Oley...........	Col. 7th W. Va. Cav...........	Apr., 1864, to June 10, 1864.
W. H. Powell.........	Col. 2d W. Va. Cav...........	June 10, 1864, to July, 1864.

3d W. Va. Cav.....Apr., 1864	From 3-Brig. 3-Div. W. Va........	To 2-Brig. 2-Cav. Div. W. Va......	May, 1864
5th W. Va. Cav.....Apr., 1864	From 3-Brig. 4-Div. W. Va........	To 2-Brig. 2-Cav. Div. W. Va......	May, 1864
7th W. Va. Cav.....Apr., 1864	From 3-Brig. 4-Div. W. Va........	To 2-Brig. 2-Cav. Div. W. Va......	May, 1864
1st W. Va. Cav.....May, 1864	From 2-Brig. 2-Cav. Div. W. Va....	To 2-Brig. 2-Cav. Div. W. Va......	July, 1864
34th Ohio Mtd. Infy.....May, 1864	From 2-Brig. 2-Cav. Div. W. Va....	To 2-Brig. 2-Cav. Div. W. Va......	July, 1864
2d W. Va. Cav.....May, 1864	From 1-Brig. 2-Cav. Div. W. Va....	To 2-Brig. 2-Cav. Div. W. Va......	July, 1864
ARTILLERY.—			
Batty. G, W. Va. Arty...Apr., 1864	From 3-Brig. 4-Div. W. Va........	No change to Muster Out.........	June, 1864
Batty. L, 5th U. S. Arty...July, 1864	From Camp Barry 22-Corps.......	To Res. Horse Arty. Cav: Corps Shen.	Nov., 1864
ARTILLERY BRIGADE.—			
Batty. B, Md. Arty.......May, 1864	From Arty 1-Infy. Div. W. Va......	To Res. Div. Harper's Ferry, W. Va.	July, 1864
30th N. Y. Batty.......May, 1864	From Arty 1-Infy. Div. W. Va......	To Res. Div. Harper's Ferry, W. Va.	July, 1864
Batty. D, 1st W. Va. Arty..May, 1864	From Arty. 2-Infy. Div. W. Va......	To Res. Div. Harper's Ferry, W. Va.	Aug., 1864
Batty. B, 5th U. S. Arty..May, 1864	From Arty 1-Infy. Div. W. Va......	To 1st Sep. Brig. 3-Div. W. Va......	Jan., 1865
Batty. G, 1st W. Va. Ar'y..June, 1864	From Res. Div. Harper's F'y, W. Va.	No change to Muster Out.........	June, 1864
1st Ohio Batty.......July, 1864	From Arty. 2-Infy. Div. W. Va......	To Res. Div. Harper's Ferry, W. Va.	Aug., 1864
Batty. B, 1st W. Va. Arty.July, 1864	From Arty. 1-Cav. Div. W. Va......	Consolidated with Batty. E........	Dec., 1864
Batty. E, 1st W. Va. Arty.July, 1864	From Arty. 1-Cav. Div. W. Va......	To Res. Div. Harper's Ferry, W. Va.	Oct., 1864
Batty. F, 1st W. Va. Arty.July, 1864	From Res. Div. W. Va...........	No change to Muster Out.........	Aug., 1864
Batty. D, 1st Penna. Arty. Aug., 1864	From Res. Div. W. Va...........	To 1st Sep. Brig. 3-Div. W. Va......	Jan., 1865
Batty. L, 1st Ohio Arty...Sept., 1864	From Res. Div. W. Va...........	To 1st Sep. Brig. 3-Div. W. Va......	Jan., 1865

RESERVE DIVISION.—	COMMANDER.		
B. F. Kelly	Brigadier General		

HARPER'S FERRY, W. VA.— COMMANDERS.

Franz Sigel	Major General	May 24, 1864, to July 8, 1864.	
A. P. Howe	Brigadier General	July 8, 1864, to Aug. 6, 1864.	
Max Weber	Brigadier General	Aug. 6, 1864, to Aug. 15, 1864.	
J. D. Stevenson	Brigadier General	Aug. 15, 1864, to Feb. 21, 1865.	
W. H. Seward	Brigadier General	Feb. 21, 1865, to Feb. 27, 1865.	
J. D. Stevenson	Brigadier General	Feb. 27, 1865 to	

MONOCACY TO SLEEPY HOLLOW. COMMANDER.

Max Weber	Brigadier General	Aug. 15, 1864, to Oct. 20, 1864.	
1st Maryland P. H. B....Apr., 1864	From 2-Brig. 1-Div. W. Va.	To 3-Brig. 3-Div. W. Va.	Jan., 1865
135th Ohio Infy....May, 1864	From New Organization	No change to Muster Out	Sept., 1864
148th Ohio Infy....May, 1864	From New Organization	To 1-Brig. 3-Div. 10-Corps	June, 1864
152d Ohio Infy....May, 1864	From New Organization	To Kelly's Com. Res. Div. W. Va.	July, 1864
155th Ohio Infy....May, 1864	From New Organization	To Norfolk, Va. Dept. Va. and N. C.	June, 1864
160th Ohio Infy....May, 1864	From New Organization	No change to Muster Out	Sept., 1864
161st Ohio Infy....May, 1864	From New Organization	No change to Muster Out	Sept., 1864
KENLY'S BRIGADE.—			
2d Maryland P. H. B..,Aug., 1864	From Kelly's Com'd Res. D. W. Va.	To Kelly's Com'd Res. Div. W. Va.	Oct., 1864
3d Maryland P. H. B....Aug., 1864	From Kenly's Indpt. B. 6-C. Shen.	To Kelly's Com'd Res. Div. W. Va.	Oct., 1864
49th Penna. Infy....Aug., 1864	From 3-Brig. 1-Div. 6-Corps	To 3-Brig. 1-Div. 6-Corps	Sept., 1864
1st Maryland E. S....Sept., 1864	From 1st Separate Brig. 8-Corps	To 3-Brig. 3-Div. West Va.	Jan., 1865
12th Maryland Infy....Sept., 1864	From 1st Separate Brig. 8-Corps	No change to Muster Out	Nov., 1864
195th Pa. Infy. 3 Cos....Sept., 1864	From 1st Separate Brig. 8-Corps	To 1-Brig. 3-Div. West Va.	Jan., 1865
13th Maine Infy....Sept., 1864	From 2-Brig. 1-Div. 19-Corps Shen.	No change to Muster Out	Dec., 1864
15th Maine Infy....Sept., 1864	From 2-Brig. 1-Div. 19-Corps Shen.	To 1-Brig. 1-Div. 19-Corps Shen.	Jan., 1865
2d Maryland E. S....Oct., 1864	From 2-Brig. 1-Div. West Va.	Consolidated with 1st Md. E. S.	Jan., 1865
18th Conn. Infy....Dec., 1864	From New Haven, Conn.	To 1-Brig. 3-Div. West Va.	Jan., 1865
CAVALRY.—			
1st N. Y. Lincoln C. Det..Apr., 1864	From Cav. Brig. 1-Div. West Va.	To 1-Brig. 1-Cav. Div. West Va.	June, 1864
12th Penna. Cav....Apr., 1864	From 3-Brig. 1-Div. West Va.	To Unatt. 3-Div. West Va.	Jan., 1865
14th Penna. Cav. Det....Apr., 1864	From 2-Brig. 4-Div. West Va.	To 1-Brig. 2-Cav. Div. West Va.	June, 1864
6th West Va. Cav....Apr., 1864	From 3-Brig. 4-Div. West Va.	To Kelly's Com'd Res. Div. W. Va.	June, 1864
Loudon, Va., Rangers....Apr., 1864	From Unatt. 1-Div. West Va.	To 3-Brig. 3-Div. West Va.	Jan., 1865
1st Md. P. H. B. Cav....Oct., 1864	From 3-Brig. 1-Div. Cav. C. Shen.	To 1-Brig. 3-Div. West Va.	Jan., 1865
ARTILLERY.—			
5th N. Y. H'vy A. 8 Cos..Apr., 1864	From Def. Harper's Ferry, W. Va.	To 2-Brig. 3-Div. West Va.	Jan., 1865
17th Indiana Batty....Apr., 1864	From Wheaton's Brig. 1-D. W. Va.	To Reserve Arty. 19-Corps Shen.	Aug., 1864
32d New York Batty....Apr., 1864	From Arty. 1-Div. West Va.	To 1-Brig. 1-Div. West Va.	Apr., 1865
Batty. D, 1st W. Va. A..Apr., 1864	From Wheaton's Brig. 1-D. W. Va.	To 1-Brig. 1-Div. West Va.	Apr., 1865
Batty. A, 1st W. Va. A..Apr., 1864	From Wheaton's Brig. 1-D. W. Va.	To 1st Separate B. Dist. Kanawha.	Oct., 1864
Batty. G, 1st W. Va. A..Apr., 1864	From 3-Brig. 4-Div. West Va.	To Arty. Brigade West Va.	June, 1864
Simmonds' Ky. Batty....July, 1864	From Arty. 2-Infy. Div. West Va.	To 2-Brig. 1-Infy. Div. W. Va.	Jan., 1865
Batty. A, Md. Arty....July, 1864	From 1-Brig. DeRussy's Div. 22-C.	To 3-Brig. 3-Infy. Div. W. Va.	Jan., 1865
Baltimore, Md., Batty....July, 1864	From 3d Separate Brig. 8-Corps	To Camp Barry 22-Corps	Jan., 1865
30th New York Batty....July, 1864	From Arty. Brig. West Va.	To Camp Barry 22-Corps	Jan., 1865
1st Ohio Batty....July, 1864	From Arty. 2-Infy. Div. West Va.	To 1-Brig. 3-Div. West Va.	Jan., 1865
Batty. L, 1st Ohio Arty..July, 1864	From Def. Washington 22-Corps	To Arty. Brigade West Va.	Aug., 1864
Indpt. Batty. F, Pa. Arty.July, 1864	From De Russy's Div. 22-Corps	To 1st Separate Brig. 3-Div. W. Va.	Jan., 1865
Batty. G, 1st Penna. Arty.July, 1864	From De Russy's Div. 22-Corps	To Unatt. 3-Div. West Va.	Jan., 1865
Batty. E, 1st West Va...Oct., 1864	From Arty. Brig. West Va.	To Camp Barry 22-Corps	Jan., 1865
Batty. C, 1st Penna. Arty.Dec., 1864	From New Organization	To Unatt. 3-Div. West Va.	Jan., 1865
Batty. B, 5th U. S. Arty..Dec., 1864	From Arty. Brig. 6-Corps Shen.	To 1st Separate Brig. 3-Div. W. Va.	Jan., 1865
Batty. M, 5th U. S. Arty..Dec., 1864	From Arty. Brig. West Va.	To Def. Washington 22-Corps	Jan., 1865
ENGINEERS.—			
Gaskill's Penna. Co....Apr., 1864	From Unatt. 1-Div. West Va.	No change to Muster Out	July, 1865

RESERVE DIVISION WEST OF SLEEPY HOLLOW.— COMMANDER.

B. F. Kelly	Bvt. Major General		
23d Illinois Infy....Apr., 1864	From 2-Brig. 2-Div. West Va.	To 3-Brig. 1-Infy. Div. West Va.	June, 1864
133d Ohio Infy....May, 1864	From New Organization	To 1-Brig. 3-Div. 10-Corps	June, 1864
134th Ohio Infy....May, 1864	From New Organization	To 2-Brig. 3-Div. 10-Corps	June, 1864
153d Ohio Infy....May, 1864	From New Organization	No change to Muster Out	Sept., 1864
154th Ohio Infy....May, 1864	From New Organization	No change to Muster Out	Sept., 1864
6th West Va. Infy....May, 1864	From 3-Brig. 2-Div. West Va.	To 1-Brig. 2-Infy. Div. West Va.	Jan., 1865
10th West Va. Infy....May, 1864	From 1-Brig. 4-Div. West Va.	To 3-Brig. 1-Infy. Div. West Va.	Jan., 1865
11th West Va. Infy....May, 1864	From 3-Brig. 4-Div. West Va.	To 3-Brig. 1-Infy. Div. West Va.	Jan., 1865
2d Md. P. H. B....June, 1864	From Unass'd 1-Infy. Div. West Va.	To Kenly's B. D. Harper's Ferry	Aug., 1864
152d Ohio Infy....July, 1864	From Weber's Com. Res. Div.	No change to Muster Out	Sept., 1864
156th Ohio Infy....July, 1864	From Cincinnati, Ohio	No change to Muster Out	Sept., 1864
176th Ohio Infy....July, 1864	From 2-Brig. Hardin's Div. 22-Corps	No change to Muster Out	Sept., 1864
3d Md. P. H. B....Oct., 1864	From Weber's Com. Res. Div. W. Va.	To 1-Brig. 1-Infy. Div. West Va.	Jan., 1865
28th Ohio Infy....Oct., 1864	From Reorganization	To 1-Brig. 1-Infy. Div. West Va.	Jan., 1865
74th Penna. Infy....Oct., 1864	From 2-Brig. DeRussy's Div. 22-C.	To 1-Brig. 1-Infy. Div. West Va.	Jan., 1865
1st West Va. Infy....Oct., 1864	From 2-Brig. 1-Infy. Div. West Va.	Consolidated with 4th W. Va.	Dec., 1864
17th West Va. Infy....Oct., 1864	From New Organization	To 1-Brig. 1-Infy. Div. West Va.	Jan., 1865
2d W. Va. Vet. Infy....Dec., 1864	From Consol. of 1st and 4th W. Va.	To 2-Brig. 1-Infy. West Va.	Jan., 1865
CAVALRY.—			
16th Ill. Cav. Co. C....Apr., 1864	From 2-Brig. 4-Div. West Va.	No change to Muster Out	July, 1864
21st N. Y. Cav. Det....Apr., 1864	From Cav. Brig. 1-Div. West Va.	To 1-Brig. 1-Cav. Div. West Va.	June, 1864
3d Ohio Indpt. Co. Cav..Apr., 1864	From 2-Brig. 4-Div. West Va.	To 2-Brig. 1-Infy. Div. West Va.	July, 1864
22d Penna. Cav. Det....Apr., 1864	From New Organization	To 2-Brig. 1-Cav. Div. West Va.	June, 1864
Batty. A, 1st West Va. A..Apr., 1864	From 2-Brig. 4-Div. West Va.	To 3-Brig. 3-Div. Cav. Corps Shen.	Jan., 1865
6th West Va. Cav....July, 1864	From Dist. Harper's Ferry	To Pleasant Valley, Md.	Jan., 1865
5th West Va. Cav....July, 1864	From 2-Brig. 2-Cav. Div. West Va.	Transferred to 6-W. Va. Cav.	Dec., 1864
2d Md. P. H. B. Co. F....July, 1864	From Kelly's Command Res. Div.	To 2-Brig. 1-Div. West Va.	Jan., 1865
8th Ohio Cav. Det....Aug., 1864	From 1-Brig. 2-Cav. Div. W. Va.	To 1-Brig. 1-Infy. Div. West Va.	Jan., 1865
ARTILLERY.—			
Batty. L, 1st Ill. Arty....Apr., 1864	From 2-Brig. 2-Div. West Va.	To Unatt. 3-Div. West Va.	Jan., 1865
Batty. E, 1st West Va. A..Apr., 1864	From 1-Brig. 2-Div. West Va.	To Arty. 1-Cav. Div. West Va.	July, 1864
Batty. F, 1st West Va....Apr., 1864	From 3-Brig. 2-Div. West Va.	Transferred to Batty. A, W. Va.	Sept., 1864
Batty. H, 1st W. Va. A..Apr., 1864	From Arty. 1-Div. West Va.	To 2-Brig. 1-Infy. Div. West Va.	Apr., 1865
Batty. B, Maryland Arty..July, 1864	From Arty. Brigade West Va.	To 2-Brig. 1-Infy. Div. West Va.	Apr., 1865
Batty. D, 1st W. Va. A..Aug., 1864	From Arty. Brigade West Va.	To 1-Brig. 1-Infy. Div. West Va.	Apr., 1865
15th New York Batty....Dec., 1864	From Def. Washington, D. C., 22-C.	Transferred to 32d N. Y. Batty.	Feb., 1865

1st SEPARATE BRIGADE, KANAWHA DISTRICT.—

COMMANDERS.

J. H. Oley	Col. 7th West Va. Cav.	July, 1864, to Aug. 6, 1864.
J. C. Sullivan	Brigadier General	Aug. 6, 1864, to Oct. 9, 1864.
J. H. Oley	Bvt. Brig. General	Oct. 9, 1864, to Aug. 1, 1865.

7th West Va. Cav.	July, 1864	From 2-Brig. 2-Cav. Div. West Va.	No change to Muster Out	Aug., 1865
140th Ohio Infy.	May, 1864	From New Organization	No change to Muster Out	Sept., 1864
141st Ohio Infy.	May, 1864	From New Organization	No change to Muster Out	Sept., 1864
146th Ohio Infy.	May, 1864	From New Organization	No change to Muster Out	Sept., 1864
167th Ohio Infy.	May, 1864	From New Organization	No change to Muster Out	Sept., 1864
1st N. Y. Veteran Cav.	Oct., 1864	From 1-Brig. 1-Cav. Div. West Va.	No change to Muster Out	July, 1865
Batty. A, 1st W. Va. A.	Oct., 1864	From Reserve Div. Harper's Ferry.	No change to Muster Out	July, 1865

Department of Virginia and North Carolina

Created July 15, 1863, by consolidation of the Departments of Virginia and North Carolina. Troops of old Fourth and Seventh Army Corps, Department of Virginia, merged into the 18th Army Corps Aug. 1, 1863, which Corps was reorganized in April, 1864, and with the Tenth Army Corps from Department of the South, was designated as the Army of the James. Departments separated Jan. 31, 1865, and resumed their respective names.

DEPARTMENT COMMANDERS.

J. G. Foster	Major General	July 18, 1863, to Nov. 11, 1863.
B. F. Butler	Major General	Nov. 11, 1863, to Aug. 27, 1864.
E. O. C. Ord	Major General	Aug. 27, 1864, to Sept. 5, 1864.
D. B. Birney	Major General	Sept. 5, 1864, to Sept. 7, 1864.
B. F. Butler	Major General	Sept. 7, 1864, to Dec. 14, 1864.
E. O. C. Ord	Major General	Dec. 14, 1864, to Dec. 24, 1864.
B. F. Butler	Major General	Dec. 24, 1864, to Jan. 8, 1865.
E. O. C. Ord	Major General	Jan. 8, 1865, to Jan. 31, 1865.

Eighteenth Army Corps

Discontinued Dec. 3, 1864, and merged into the 24th and 25th Corps, Army of the James.

CORPS COMMANDERS.

Innes N. Palmer	Brigadier General	July 18, 1863, to Aug. 18, 1863.
J. G. Foster	Major General	Aug. 18, 1863, to Nov. 11, 1863.
B. F. Butler	Major General	Nov. 11, 1863, to May 2, 1864.
W. F. Smith	Major General	May 2, 1864, to July 10, 1864.
J. H. Martindale	Brigadier General	July 10, 1864, to July 21, 1864.
E. O. C. Ord	Major General	July 21, 1864, to Sept. 4, 1864.
John Gibbon	Major General	Sept. 4, 1864, to Sept. 22, 1864.
E. O. C. Ord	Major General	Sept. 22, 1864, to Sept. 29, 1864.
C. A. Heckman	Brigadier General	Sept. 29, 1864, to Oct. 1, 1864.
Godfrey Weitzel	Bvt. Major General	Oct. 1, 1864, to Dec. 3, 1864.

Corps discontinued Dec. 3, 1864, and merged into the 24th and 25th Corps.

DISTRICT OF VIRGINIA.—Organized Aug. 12, 1863. Discontinued Sept. 23, 1863.

COMMANDER.

H. M. Naglee	Brigadier General	Aug. 12, 1863, to Sept. 23, 1863.

U. S. FORCES NORFOLK AND PORTSMOUTH, VA.—Organized Sept. 23, 1863. Discontinued April 28, 1864.

COMMANDERS.

E. E. Potter	Brigadier General	Sept. 23, 1863, to Oct. 1, 1863.
James Barnes	Brigadier General	Oct. 1, 1863, to Jan. 8, 1864.
E. A. Wild	Brigadier General	Jan. 8, 1864, to Apr. 28, 1864.

GETTY'S DIVISION.—

COMMANDERS.

Geo. W. Getty	Brigadier General	July 15, 1863, to Jan. 14, 1864.
C. A. Heckman	Brigadier General	Jan. 14, 1864, to Apr. 28, 1864.

1st BRIGADE.—

COMMANDERS.

S. M. Alford	Col. 3d New York Infy.	July 15, 1863, to Aug. 1, 1863.
Brigade transferred to Dept. of the South Aug., 1863. Reorganized March, 1864.		
S. H. Roberts	Col. 139th New York Infy.	Mch. 15, 1864, to Apr. 28, 1864.

3d New York Infy.	July, 1863	From 1-B. 2-Div. 7-Corps Dept. Va.	To 2-Brig. Vodges' Div. 10-C. South	Aug., 1863
89th New York Infy.	July, 1863	From 1-B. 2-Div. 7-Corps Dept. Va.	To 2-Brig. Vodges' Div. 10-C. South	Aug., 1863
103d New York Infy.	July, 1863	From 1-B. 2-Div. 7-Corps Dept. Va.	To 2-Brig. Vodges' Div. 10-C. South	Aug., 1863
117th New York Infy.	July, 1863	From 1-B. 2-Div. 7-Corps Dept. Va.	To 2-Brig. Vodges' Div. 10-C. South	Aug., 1863
81st New York Infy.	Mch., 1864	From D. Currituck, D. Va. & N. C.	To 1-Brig. 1-Div. 18-Corps A. Jas.	Apr., 1864
96th New York Infy.	Mch., 1864	From D. Currituck, D. Va. & N. C.	To 1-Brig. 1-Div. 18-Corps A. Jas.	Apr., 1864
98th New York Infy.	Mch., 1864	From D. Currituck, D. Va. & N. C.	To 1-Brig. 1-Div. 18-Corps A. Jas.	Apr., 1864
139th New York Infy.	Mch., 1864	From D. Currituck, D. Va. & N. C.	To 1-Brig. 1-Div. 18-Corps A. Jas.	Apr., 1864

2d BRIGADE.—

COMMANDERS.

Edward Harland	Brigadier General	July 15, 1863, to Dec. 29, 1863.
Francis Beech	Col. 16th Conn. Infy.	Dec. 29, 1863, to Jan. 25, 1864.
Brigade discontinued Jan. 25, 1864. Reorganized March 2, 1864.		
H. C. Lee	Col. 27th Mass. Infy.	Mch. 2, 1864, to Apr. 28, 1864.

8th Conn. Infy.	July, 1863	From 2-Brig. 2-Div. 7-C. Dept. Va.	To Sub-Dist. Albemarle Dist. N. C.	Jan., 1864
11th Conn. Infy.	July, 1863	From 2-Brig. 2-Div. 7-C. Dept. Va.	To Wistar's Com'd Yorktown, Va.	Oct., 1863
15th Conn. Infy.	July, 1863	From 2-Brig. 2-Div. 7-C. Dept. Va.	To Sub-Dist. Albemarle Dist. N. C.	Jan., 1864
16th Conn. Infy.	July, 1863	From 2-Brig. 2-Div. 7-C. Dept. Va.	To Sub-Dist. Albemarle Dist. N. C.	Jan., 1864
23d Mass. Infy.	Mch., 1864	From 3-Brig. Heckman's Div. Ports.	To 1-Brig. 2-Div. 18-Corps A. Jas.	Apr., 1864
25th Mass. Infy.	Mch., 1864	From U. S. Forces Norfolk & Ports.	To 1-Brig. 2-Div. 18-Corps A. Jas.	Apr., 1864
27th Mass. Infy.	Mch., 1864	From U. S. Forces Norfolk & Ports.	To 1-Brig. 2-Div. 18-Corps A. Jas.	Apr., 1864
9th New Jersey Infy.	Mch., 1864	From 3-Brig. Heckman's Div. Ports.	To 1-Brig. 2-Div. 18-Corps A. Jas.	Apr., 1864

3d BRIGADE.—   COMMANDER.

W. H. P. Steere........	Col. 4th Rhode Island Infy	July 15, 1863, to Apr. 28, 1864.

10th New Hamp. Infy..July,	1863	From 3-B. 2-Div. 7-Corps Dept. Va.	To 2-Brig. 1-Div. 18-Corps A. Jas.	Apr.,	1864
13th New Hamp. Infy..July,	1863	From 3-B. 2-Div. 7-Corps Dept. Va.	To 2-Brig. 1-Div. 18-Corps A. Jas.	Apr.,	1864
4th Rhode Island Infy...July,	1863	From 3-B. 2-Div. 7-Corps Dept. Va.	To Dist. of St. Mary's Va. & N. C.	Apr.,	1864
21st Conn. Infy........July,	1863	From 3-B. 2-Div. 7-Corps Dept. Va.	To Heckman's C'm'd Newport News	Nov.,	1863
23d Mass. Infy.........Jan.,	1864	From Heckman's B. Newport News	To 2-Brig. Heckman's Div. Ports.	Mch.,	1864
9th New Jersey Infy....Jan.,	186(	From Heckman's B. Newport News	To 2-Brig. Heckman's Div. Ports.	Mch.,	1864
ARTILLERY.—					
Batty. A, 1st Pa. Arty...July,	1863	From Arty. 2-Div. 7-C. Dept. Va.	To Arty. Brig. U. S. Forces Yorkt'n	Oct.,	1863
Batty. A, 5th U. S. Arty..July,	1863	From Arty. 2-Div. 7-C. Dept. Va.	To Arty. Brig. U. S. Forces Yorkt'n	Oct.,	1863
CAVALRY.—					
1st N. Y. Mounted Rifles..July,	1863	From Cav. 7-Corps Dept. Va.	To Wistar's Command Yorktown	Oct.,	1863
11th Penna. Cav........July,	1863	From Cav. 7-Corps Dept. Va.	To Cav. Brig. U. S. Forces Ports.	Dec.,	1863

CAVALRY BRIGADE PORTSMOUT H.—Organized Dec., 1863.

     COMMANDER.

N. B. Lord............	Col. 20th New York Cav.	

5th Penna. Cav........Dec.,	1863	From U. S. Forces Yorktown, Va.	To 2-Brig. Cav. Div. Army James.	Apr.,	1864
11th Penna. Cav.......Dec.,	1863	From U. S. Cav. Forces Portsmouth	To Cav. Brig. Yorktown, Va.	Jan.,	1864
20th New York Cav.....Dec.,	1863	From New Organization	To Norfolk & Ports. Dist. E. Va.	Apr.,	1864
ARTILLERY BRIGADE.—					
Batty. M, 3d N. Y. Arty..Dec.,	1863	From Heckman's C. Newport News	To Arty. 1-Div. 18-Corps Army Jas.	Apr.,	1864
Batty. A, 1st Penna. A..Dec.,	1863	From Unatt. Getty's D. Portsmouth	To Norfolk & Ports. Dist. E. Va.	Apr.,	1864
4th Wisconsin Batty...Dec.,	1863	From Un. U. S. Forces Yorkt'n, Va.	To Arty. 1-Div. 18-Corps Army Jas.	Apr.,	1864
Batty. D, 4th U. S. Arty..Dec.,	1863	From Unatt. Getty's D. Portsmouth	To Arty. 2-Div. 18-Corps Army Jas.	Apr.,	1864
Batty. A, 5th U. S. Arty..Dec.,	1863	From Unatt. Getty's D. Portsmouth	To Arty. 1-Div. 18-Corps Army Jas.	Apr.,	1864
13th N. Y. Heavy Arty....Dec.,	1863	From New Organization	To Norfolk & Ports. Dist. E. Va.	Apr.,	1864

AFRICAN BRIGADE.—Organized Nov. 2, 1863.   COMMANDERS.

E. A. Wild............	Brigadier General	Nov. 2, 1863, to Jan. 19, 1864.
J. H. Holman..........	Col. 1st U. S. Colored Infy	Jan. 19, 1864, to Feb. 5, 1864.
A. G. Chamberlain....	Lt.-Col. 37th U. S. Colored Troops..	Feb. 5, 1864, to Apr. 28, 1864.

55th Mass. Col'd I. Det..Nov.,	1863	From New Organization	To Dept. of the South	Jan.,	1864
1st N. C. Col'd Infy Det..Nov.,	1863	From New Organization	To Dept. of the South	Jan.,	1864
2d N. C. Colored Infy....Nov.,	1863	From 3-Brig. Vodges' Div. 10-Corps	To Dist. St. Mary's Va. & N. C.	Apr.,	1864
3d N. C. Colored Infy...Dec.,	1863	From Folly Island, S. C., Dept. So.	To Norfolk & Ports. Dist. E. Va.	Apr.,	1864
1st U. S. Colored Infy...Dec.,	1863	From Def. Washington 22-Corps.	To 1-Brig. Hinck's Div. 18-Corps.	Apr.,	1864
5th U. S. Colored Infy..Dec.,	1863	From New Organization	To 2-Brig. U. S. Forces Yorktown.	Jan.,	1864
10th U. S. Colored Infy..Dec.,	1863	From New Organization	To 1-Brig. Hinck's Div. 18-Corps.	Apr.,	1864
UNATTACHED.—					
3d Pa. H. A. Cos. F, G, M.July,	1863	From Camp Hamilton, Va.	To Fort Monroe, Va.	Apr.,	1864
Batty. D, 4th U. S. Arty..July,	1863	From Arty. 1-D. 7-Corps Dept. Va.	To Arty. Brig. U. S. Forces Ports.	Dec.,	1863
Batty. L, 4th U. S. Arty..July,	1863	From Arty. 1-D. 7-Corps Dept. Va.	To Arty. U. S. Forces Yorktown.	Dec.,	1863
7th N. Y. Indpt. Batty...July,	1863	From Norfolk, Va.. 7-C. Dept. Va.	To Arty. Yorktown, Va.	Mch.,	1864
27th Mass. Infy........Jan.,	1864	From Heckman's B. Newport News	To 1-Brig. 2-Div. 18-Corps A. Jas.	Apr.,	1864
2d Mass. H. A. Cos. G & H . Jan.,	1864	From New Organization	To Dist. Newberne Dist. N. C.	Feb.,	1864
FORTRESS MONROE.—					
3d Penna. H'vy Arty.....July,	1863	From Fort Monroe Dept. Va.	To Fort Monroe Dist. E. Va.	May,	1864
1st U. S. Colored Cav.....Dec.,	1863	From New Organization	To Unatt. Williamsburg, Va.	Apr.,	1864
2d U. S. Colored Cav.....Jan.,	1864	From New Organization	To Unatt. Williamsburg, Va.	Apr.,	1864
Batty. B, 2d U. S. A. Col..Feb.,	1864	From New Organization	To Arty. Hinck's Div. 18-Corps.	Apr.,	1864

U. S. FORCES YORKTOWN AND VICINITY.—Organized Aug. 1, 1863.

     COMMANDERS.

I. J. Wistar...........	Brigadier General	Aug. 1, 1863, to Dec. 22, 1863.
R. M. West............	Col. 1st Pa. Light Arty	Dec. 22, 1863, to Jan. 22, 1864.
I. J. Wistar...........	Brigadier General	Jan. 22, 1864, to Feb. 16, 1864.
R. M. West............	Col. 1st Pa. Light Arty	Feb. 16, 1864, to Mch. 8, 1864.
I. J. Wistar...........	Brigadier General	Mch. 8, 1864, to Apr. 28, 1864.

Discontinued April, 1864.

9th Vermont Infy.......Aug.,	1863	From Wistar's Indpt. Brig. 7-C. Va.	To Sub-Dist. Beaufort Dist. N. C.	Oct.,	1863
99th New York Infy....Aug.,	1863	From Wardrop's Indpt. B. 7-C. Va.	To Def. Newberne Dist. N. C.	Oct.,	1863
118th New York Infy....Aug.,	1863	From Wardrop's Indpt. B. 7-C. Va.	To Heckman's Com'd Newport News	Oct.,	1863
139th New York Infy....Aug.,	1863	From West's Indpt. Brig. 7-C. Va.	To 1-Brig. U. S. Forces Yorkt'n, Va.	Jan.,	1864
19th Wisconsin Infy.....Aug.,	1863	From Wistar's Indpt. Brig. 7-C. Va.	To Def. Newberne Dist. N. C.	Oct.,	1863
5th Penna. Cav.........Aug.,	1863	From Unatt. 4-Corps Dept. Va.	To Cav. Br. Norfolk & Portsmouth.	Dec.,	1863
11th Conn. Infy........Oct.,	1863	From 2-Brig. Getty's Div. P'tsmouth	To 2-Brig. 2-Div. 18-Corps A. James.	Apr.,	1864
148th N. Y. Infy........Oct.,	1863	From U. S. Forces Norfolk & Ports.	To 2-Brig. 2-Div. 18-Corps A. James.	Apr.,	1864
4th U. S. Col'd Infy.....Oct.,	1863	From New Organization Balto., Md.	To 2-Br. U. S. Forces Yorktown, Va.	Jan.,	1864
6th U. S. Col'd Infy.....Oct.,	1863	From New Organization, Phila., Pa.	To 2-Br. U. S. Forces Yorktown, Va.	Jan.,	1864
11th Conn. Infy. Det.....Feb.,	1864	From 1-Brig. U. S. Forces Yorktown	To 2-Brig. 2-Div. 18-Corps A. James.	Apr.,	1864
25th Mass. Infy. Det.....Feb.,	1864	From 1-Brig. U. S. Forces Yorktown	To 2-Br. U. S. Forces Portsmouth.	Mch.,	1864
118th N. Y. Infy........Feb.,	1864	From 1-Brig. U. S. Forces Yorktown	To 2-Brig. 1-Div. 18-Corps A. James.	Apr.,	1864
4th U. S. Col'd Infy.....Feb.,	1864	From 2-Brig. U. S. Forces Yorktown	To 2-Brig. Hinck's Div. 18-Corps.	Apr.,	1864
5th U. S. Col'd Infy.....Feb.,	1864	From 2-Brig. U. S. Forces Yorktown	To 2-Brig. Hinck's Div. 18-Corps.	Apr.,	1864
6th U. S. Col'd Infy.....Feb.,	1864	From 2-Brig. U. S. Forces Yorktown	To 2-Brig. Hinck's Div. 18-Corps.	Apr.,	1864

1st BRIGADE.—Organized Jan. 22, 1864.   COMMANDER.

R. M. West............	Col. 1st Penna. Light Arty	Jan. 22, 1864, to Feb. 16, 1864.

Discontinued April, 1864.

11th Conn. Infy. Det.....Jan.,	1864	From U. S. Forces Yorktown, Va.	To Unatt. U. S. Forces Yorkt'n, Va.	Feb.,	1864
25th Mass. Infy. Det.....Jan.,	1864	From Heckman's Com. Newp't News	To 2-Brig. U. S. Forces Portsmouth.	Feb.,	1864
118th N. Y. Infy........Jan.,	1864	From Heckman's Com. Newp't News	To Unatt. U. S. Forces Yorkt'n, Va.	Feb.,	1864
139th N. Y. Infy........Jan.,	1864	From U. S. Forces Yorktown, Va.	To Dist. Currituck, Va. & N. C.	Feb.,	1864

2d BRIGADE.—Organized Jan. 20, 1864. Discontinued Feb. 16, 1864.

     COMMANDER.

S. A. Duncan..........	Col. 4th U. S. Col'd Infy	Jan. 20, 1864, to Feb. 16, 1864.

4th U. S. Col'd Infy.....Jan.,	1864	From U. S. Forces Yorktown, Va.	To U. S. Forces Yorktown, Va.	Feb.,	1864
5th U. S. Col'd Infy.....Jan.,	1864	From U. S. Forces Portsmouth, Va.	To U. S. Forces Yorktown, Va.	Feb.,	1864
6th U. S. Col'd Infy.....Jan.,	1864	From U. S. Forces Yorktown, Va.	To U. S. Forces Yorktown, Va.	Feb.,	1864

CAVALRY BRIGADE.—Organized Jany. 25, 1864.

COMMANDER.

S. P. Spear............	Col. 11th Penna. Cav...............	Jan. 25, 1864, to Apr. 28, 1864.

1st Dist. Columbia Cav...Jan., 1864	From New Organization............	To 1-Brig. Cav. Div. Dept. Va.&N.C.	Apr.,	1864
1st N. Y. Mtd. Rifles.....Jan., 1864	From U. S. Forces Yorktown, Va..	To Def. Yorktown and Williamsburg	Apr.,	1864
11th Penna. Cav........Jan., 1864	From Cav. Br. U. S. Forces P'mouth	To 2-Brig. Cav. Div. Dept. Va.&N.C.	Apr.,	1864

ARTILLERY U. S. FORCES YORKTOWN.——

8th N. Y. Indpt. Batty...Aug., 1863	From 1-Br. 1-Div. 4-Corps Dept. Va.	To Norfolk & Portsmouth.........	Apr.,	1864
16th N. Y. Indpt. Batty..Aug., 1863	From Wistar's Indpt. Br. 7-C. Va..	To Heckman's Com. Newport News.	Oct.,	1863
Batty. E, 1st Penna. A'y..Aug., 1863	From 2-Brig. 1-Div. 4-Corps Dept. Va.	To Def. Yorktown & Williamsburg.	Apr.,	1864
2d Wisconsin Batty......Aug., 1863	From U. S. Forces Yorktown, Va...	To Dist. St. Mary's Dept. Va.&N.C.	Jan.,	1864
4th Wisconsin Batty......Aug., 1863	From Arty. 2-Div. 4-Corps Dept. Va.	To Arty. Brig. Norfolk & Ports....	Dec.,	1864
6th N. Y. H'y Arty. 5-Cos. Dec., 1863	From New Organization.........	To Unatt. 1-Div. 18-C. A. James....	Apr.,	1864
Batty. L, 4th U. S. Arty...Dec., 1863	From Un. Norfolk & P'tmouth, Va.	To Arty. 1-Div. 18-C. A. James....	Apr.,	1864
Batty. F, 1st R. I. Arty...Jan., 1864	From Dist. St. Mary's Dept.Va.&N.C.	To Arty. 2-Div. 18-C. A. James....	Apr.,	1864
7th N. Y. Indpt. Batty...Mch., 1864	From Un. Norfolk & P'tmouth, Va.	To Arty. 2-Div. 18-C. A. James....	Apr.,	1864

NEWPORT NEWS, VA.—Organized Oct. 18, 1863.

COMMANDERS.

C. A. Heckman......	Brigadier General............	Oct. 18, 1863, to Jan. 14, 1864.
A. H. Dutton........	Col. 21st Conn. Infy...........	Jan. 14, 1864, to Feb. 16, 1864.

21st Conn. Infy..........Oct., 1863	From 3-Brig. Getty's Div. Ports.....	To Def. Newberne Dist. N. C......	Feb.,	1864
23d Mass. Infy..........Oct., 1863	From Def. Newberne Dist. N. C....	To 3-Brig. Getty's Div. Ports. Va...	Jan.,	1864
25th Mass. Infy..........Oct., 1863	From Def. Newberne Dist. N. C....	To 1-Brig. 2-Div. 18-C. A. James...	Apr.,	1864
27th Mass. Infy..........Oct., 1863	From Def. Newberne Dist. N. C....	To Unatt. U. S. Forces Nor. & P.	Nov.,	1864
9th N. J. Infy...........Oct., 1863	From Sub Dist. Beaufort, N. C....	To 3-Brig. Norfolk & Portsmouth..	Jan.,	1864
81st N. Y. Infy..........Oct., 1863	From Sub Dist. Beaufort, N. C....	To Dist. Currituck, Va. & N. C....	Dec.,	1863
96th N. Y. Infy..........Oct., 1863	From Sub Dist. Albemarle, N. C....	To Dist. Currituck, Va. & N. C....	Dec.,	1863
98th N. Y. Infy..........Oct., 1863	From Dist. Beaufort, N. C.........	To Dist. Currituck, Va. & N. C....	Dec.,	1863
118th N. Y. Infy..........Oct., 1863	From U. S. Forces Yorktown, Va...	To 1-Brig. U. S. Forces Yorkt'n, Va.	Jan.,	1864
3d N. Y. Cav...........Oct., 1863	From Def. Newberne, N. C........	To 1-Brig. Cav. Div. Dept. Va.&N.C.	Apr.,	1864
Batty. H, 3d N. Y. Arty...Oct., 1863	From Def. Newberne, N. C........	To Arty. Norfolk & Portsmouth, Va.	Apr.,	1864
Batty. M, 3d N. Y. Arty...Oct., 1863	From Def. Newberne, N. C........	To U. S. Forces Nor. & Prtsmuth..	Jan.,	1864
16th N. Y. Indpt. Batty...Oct., 1863	From Arty. U. S. Forces Yorkt'n, Va.	To Arty. Brig. 18-C. Army James..	June,	1864

DISTRICT OF ST. MARYS.—Organized Dec. 1, 1863.

COMMANDERS.

Gilbert Marston........	Brigadier General............	Dec. 1, 1863, to Apr. 28, 1864.
A. G. Draper..........	Col. 36th U. S. Col'd Infy.........	Apr., 28, 1864, to July 2, 1864.
James Barnes..........	Brigadier General............	July 2, 1864, to July 7, 1864.
Discontinued, transferred to Defences of Washington, July 7, 1864.		

2d N. H. Infy..........Dec., 1863	From Marston's Brig. Point Lookout	To 2-Brig. 2-Div. 18-C. A. James...	Apr.,	1864
5th N. H. Infy..........Dec., 1863	From Marston's Brig. Point Lookout	To 1-Brig. 1-Div. 2-Corps Pot......	Apr.,	1864
12th N. H. Infy..........Dec., 1863	From Marston's Brig. Point Lookout	To 2-Brig. 2-Div. 18-C. A. James...	Apr.,	1864
Batty. F, 1st R. I. Arty..Dec., 1863	From Def. Newberne Dist. N. C....	To Arty. U. S. Forces Yorktown, Va.	Jan.,	1864
2d Wis. Batty..........Dec., 1863	From Arty. U. S. Forces Yorkt'n, Va.	To Dist. St. Mary's 22-Corps.......	July,	1864
4th R. I. Infy..........Apr., 1864	From 3-Brig. Getty's Div. Ports....	To 1-Brig. 2-Div. 9-Corps Pot......	July,	1864
36th U. S. Col'd Infy......Apr., 1864	From African Brig. Norfolk & Ports.	To Unatt. Army of the James......	July,	1864
139th Ohio Infy..........May, 1864	From New Organization.........	No change to Muster Out........	Aug.,	1864
5th Mass. Col'd Cav.....June, 1864	From 1-Brig. 3-Div. 18-Corps A, Jas.	To Dist. St. Mary's 22-Corps........	July,	1864

DISTRICT OF THE CURRITUCK.— Organized Dec. 11, 1863.

COMMANDERS.

James H. Ledlie......	Brigadier General...............	Dec. 11, 1863, to Feb. 16, 1864.
S. H. Roberts..........	Col. 139th N. Y. Infy...........	Feb. 16, 1864, to Mch. 15, 1864.
Discontinued and designated 1st Brigade Getty's Division, Mch., 15, 1864.		

81st N. Y. Infy..........Dec., 1863	From Heckman's Com. Newport News	To 1-Brig. Heckman's Div. Ports...	Mch.,	1864
96th N. Y. Infy..........Dec., 1863	From Heckman's Com. Newport News	To 1-Brig. Heckman's Div. Ports...	Mch.,	1864
98th N. Y. Infy..........Dec., 1863	From Heckman's Com. Newport News	To 1-Brig. Heckman's Div. Ports...	Mch.,	1864
3d N. Y. Cav. Cos. B, C..Dec., 1863	From Heckman's Com. Newport News	To Cav. Newport News, Va........	Mch.,	1864
5th Penna. Cav. Sqdn.....Dec., 1863	From U. S. Forces Yorktown, Va...	To Cav. Brig. U. S. Forces Ports...	Mch.,	1864
139th N. Y. Infy..........Dec., 1863	From 1-Brig. U. S. Forces Yorktown	To 1-Brig. Heckman's Div. Ports...	Mch.,	1864
20th N. Y. Cav. Cos. H. I..Feb., 1863	From Cav. Brig. U. S. Forces Ports.	To Cav. U. S. Forces Ports........	Mch.,	1864

HINCKS' DIVISION U. S. C. T.—Organized April 20, 1864.

COMMANDER.

E. W. Hincks..........	Brigadier General...............	Apr. 20, 1864, to June 19, 1864.
Division designated 3d Division, 18th Corps June 19, 1864.		

1st BRIGADE.——

COMMANDER.

E. A. Wild............	Brigadier General...............	Apr. 20, 1864, to June 19, 1864.

1st U. S. Col'd Infy.....Apr., 1864	From African Brig. Norfolk & Ports.	To 1-Brig. 3-Div. 18-Corps.........	June,	1864
10th U. S. Col'd Infy.....Apr., 1864	From Drummondsville, Va..........	To Unatt. Army James..........	June,	1864
22d U. S. Col'd Infy.....Apr., 1864	From U. S. Forces Yorktown, Va...	To 2-Brig. 3-Div. 18-Corps.........	June,	1864
37th U. S. Col'd Infy.....May, 1864	From Norfolk and Portsmouth......	To Unatt. Army James..........	June,	1864

2d BRIGADE, HINCKS' DIVISION.

S. A. Duncan..........	Col. 4th U. S. Col'd Infy.........	Apr. 20, 1864, to June 19, 1864

4th U. S. Col'd Infy.....Apr., 1864	From U. S. Forces Yorktown, Va...	To 2-Brig. 3-Div. 18-C. A. James...	June,	1864
5th U. S. Col'd Infy.....Apr., 1864	From U. S. Forces Yorktown, Va...	To 2-Brig. 3-Div. 18-C. A. James...	June,	1864
6th U. S. Col'd Infy.....Apr., 1864	From U. S. Forces Yorktown, Va...	To 2-Brig. 3-Div. 18-C. A. James...	June,	1864

ARTILLERY.——

Batty. B, 2d U. S. Col. A'y.Apr., 1864	From Fort Monroe, Va.............	To Rand's Prov'l Brig. 18-Corps...	June, 1864

DISTRICT OF NORTH CAROLINA.—Organized Aug. 1, 1863.

COMMANDERS.

John J. Peck..........	Major General...............	Aug. 14, 1863, to Jan. 4, 1864.
I. N. Palmer..........	Brigadier General...............	Jan. 4, 1864, to Feb. 5, 1864.
John J. Peck..........	Major General...............	Feb. 5, 1864, to Apr. 28, 1864.
I. N. Palmer..........	Brigadier General...............	Apr. 28, 1864, to Jan. 31, 1865.

SUB DISTRICT OF THE PALMICO.— COMMANDERS.

O. Moulton	Lt.-Col. 25th Mass. Infy	Aug. 1, 1863, to Sept. 8, 1863.
J. Pickett	Col. 25th Mass. Infy	Sept. 8, 1863, to Oct. 26, 1863.
J. M. McChesney	Col. 1st N. C.	Oct. 26, 1863, to Mch. 13, 1864.
Edw. Harland	Brigadier General	Mch. 13, 1864, to May 2, 1864.

Discontinued May 2, 1864.

25th Mass. Infy. 5-Cos.	Aug., 1863	From Def. Newberne 18-Corps	To Heckman's Com. Newport News.	Oct.,	1863
1st N. C. Infy	Aug., 1863	From New Organization	To Sub Dist. Beaufort Dist. N. C.	Apr.,	1864
58th Penna. Infy	Aug., 1863	From Dist. Pamlico Dept. N. C.	To 3-Brig. 1-Div. 18-C. A. James.	Apr.,	1864
23d N. Y. Indpt Batty	Aug., 1863	From Dist. Pamlico Dept. N. C.	To Sub Dist. Newberne Dist. N. C.	May,	1864
12th N. Y. Cav. Co. C.	Aug., 1863	From Cav. Brig. Def. Newberne 18-C.	To Sub Dist. Newberne Dist. N. C.	May,	1864
5th R. I. H'y Arty. C. G.	Aug., 1863	From Sub Dist. Newberne 18-C.	To Sub Dist. Newberne Dist. N. C.	May,	1864
21st Conn. Infy	Mch., 1864	From Sub Dist. Newberne 18-C.	To 3-Brig. 1-Div. 18-C. A. James.	May,	1864

SUB DISTRICT OF THE ALBEMARLE.— COMMANDER.

H. W. Wessells	Brigadier General	Aug. 1, 1863, to Apr., 1864.

85th N. Y. Infy	Aug., 1863	From Dist. Albemarle Dept. N. C.	To Captured Plymouth, N. C.	Apr.,	1864
92d N. Y. Infy	Aug., 1863	From Dist. Albemarle Dept. N. C.	To 3-Brig. 1-Div. 18-C. A. James.	Apr.,	1864
96th N. Y. Infy	Aug., 1863	From Dist. Albemarle Dept. N. C.	To Heckman's Com. Newport News.	Oct.,	1863
101st Penna. Infy	Aug., 1863	From Dist. Albemarle Dept. N. C.	To Roanoke Island Dept. N. C.	Jan.,	1865
103d Penna. Infy	Aug., 1863	From Dist. Albemarle Dept. N. C.	To Roanoke Island Dept. N. C.	Jan.,	1865
24th N. Y. Indpt Batty	Aug., 1863	From Dist. Albemarle Dept. N. C.	To Roanoke Island Dept. N. C.	Jan.,	1865
12th N. Y. Cav. Det.	Aug., 1863	From Cav. Br. Def. Newb'e Dept.N.C.	To Sub Dist. Newberne Dist. N. C.	Apr.,	1864
8th Conn. Infy	Jan., 1864	From Heckman's Div. Ports., Va.	To 2-Brig. 1-Div. 18-C. A. James.	Apr.,	1864
15th Conn. Infy	Jan., 1864	From Heckman's Div. Ports., Va.	To Sub Dist. Newberne Dist. N. C.	Apr.,	1864
16th Conn. Infy	Jan., 1864	From Heckman's Div. Ports., Va.	To Roanoke Island Dept. N. C.	Jan.,	186b
Batty. D, 5th R. I. H. A'y.	May., 1864	From Def. Newberne Dist. N. C.	To Roanoke Island Dept. N. C.	Jan.,	186b
Batty. I, 5th R. I. H. A'y.	May., 1864	From Def. Newberne Dist. N. C.	To Def. Newberne Dist. N. C.	June,	1864
Batty. K, 5th R. I. H. A'y.	May., 1864	From Def. Newberne Dist. N. C.	To Roanoke Island Dept. N. C.	Jan.,	186b

SUB DISTRICT OF BEAUFORT.— COMMANDERS.

T. J. C. Amory	Col. 17th Mass. Infy	Aug. 1, 1863, to Aug. 14, 1863.
C. A. Heckman	Brigadier General	Aug. 14, 1863, to Oct. 11, 1863.
James Jourdan	Col. 158th N. Y. Infy	Oct. 11, 1863, to June 27, 1864.
T. J. C. Amory	Col. 17th Mass. Infy	June 27, 1864, to Oct. 7, 1864.
James Stewart, Jr.	Col. 9th N. J. Infy	Oct. 7, 1864, to Jan. 31, 1865.

9th N. J. Infy	Aug., 1863	From Sub Dist. Beaufort Dept.N.C.	To Heckman's Com. Newport News.	Oct.,	1863
81st N. Y. Infy	Aug., 1863	From Sub Dist. Beaufort Dept.N.C.	To Heckman's Com. Newport News.	Oct.,	1863
98th N. Y. Infy	Aug., 1863	From Sub Dist. Beaufort Dept.N.C.	To Heckman's Com. Newport News.	Oct.,	1863
12th N. Y. Cav. Co. D.	Aug., 1863	From Cav. Brig. Def. Newberne.	To Def. Newberne Dist. N. C.	Oct.,	1863
Batty. C, 1st U. S. Arty.	Aug., 1863	From Arty. Morris I. S. C. South.	To Arty. Br. 10-C. Consol. with D.	July,	1864
2d Mass. H. A. (Cos. A, B, C, D)	Sept., 1863	From New Organization	To Def. Newberne Dist. N. C.	July,	1864
23d N. Y. Cav	Oct., 1863	From Cav. Def. Newberne Dist. N.C.	To Sub Dist. Newberne Dept. N. C.	Jan.,	1865
9th Vt. Infy	Oct., 1863	From U. S. Forces Portsmouth, Va.	To Def. Newberne Dist. N. C.	July,	1864
158th N. Y. Infy	Dec., 1863	From Def. Newberne Dist. N. C.	To 1-Brig. 2-Div. 18-C. A. James.	Aug.,	1864
Batty. A, 5th R. I. H'y A'y.	Dec., 1863	From Def. Newberne Dist. N. C.	To Def. Newberne Dist. N. C.	Jan.,	1864
2d N. C. Infy	Jan., 1864	From New Organization	To Sub Dist. Newberne Dept. N. C.	Jan.,	1865
1st N. C. Infy	Apr., 1864	From Sub Dist. Pamlico Dist. N. C.	To Sub Dist. Newberne Dept. N. C.	Jan.,	1865
12th N. Y. Cav. Co. E.	Apr., 1864	From Cav. Def. Newberne Dist. N. C.	To Def. Newberne Dist. N. C.	Aug.,	1864
Batty. C, 3d N. Y. Arty.	May	From Arty. Def. Newberne Dist. N.C.	To Sub. Dist. Beaufort Dept. N. C.	Jan.,	1865
17th Mass. Infy	July, 1864	From Def. Newberne Dist. N. C.	To Sub Dist. Beaufort Dept. N. C.	Jan.,	1865
27th Mass. Infy	Sept., 1864	From 1-Brig. 2-Div. 18-C. A. James.	To Sub Dist. Newberne Dept. N. C.	Jan.,	1865
9th N. J. Infy	Sept., 1864	From 1-Brig. 2-Div. 18-C. A. James.	To Sub. Dist. Beaufort Dept. N. C.	Jan.,	1865

DEFENCES OF NEWBERNE.— COMMANDERS.

C. A. Heckman	Brigadier General	Aug. 1, 1863, to Aug. 14, 1863.
I. N. Palmer	Brigadier General	Aug. 14, 1863, to Oct. 7, 1863.
T. J. C. Amory	Col. 17th Mass. Infy	Oct. 7, 1863, to Nov. 7, 1863.
I. N. Palmer	Brigadier General	Nov. 7, 1863, to Jan. 15, 1864.
T. J. C. Amory	Col. 17th Mass. Infy	Jan. 15, 1864, to July 27, 1864.
Edward Harland	Brigadier General	July 27, 1864, to Jan. 31, 1865.

17th Mass. Infy	Aug., 1863	From Def. Newberne Dept. N. C.	To Sub. Dist. Beaufort Dist. N. C.	July,	1864
23d Mass. Infy	Aug., 1863	From Def. Newberne Dept. N. C.	To Heckman's Com. Newport News.	Oct.,	1863
25th Mass. Infy	Aug., 1863	From Def. Newberne Dept. N. C.	To Heckman's Com. Newport News.	Oct.,	1863
27th Mass. Infy	Aug., 1863	From Def. Newberne Dept. N. C.	To Heckman's Com. Newport News.	Oct.,	1863
92d N. Y. Infy	Aug., 1863	From Def. Newberne Dept. N. C.	To 3-Brig. 1-Div. 18-C. A. James.	Apr.,	1864
132d N. Y. Infy	Aug., 1863	From Def. Newberne Dept. N. C.	To Sub Dist. Newberne Dept. N. C.	Jan.,	1865
158th N. Y. Infy	Aug., 1863	From Def. Newberne Dept. N. C.	To Sub Dist Beaufort Dist. N. C.	Dec.,	1863
3d N. Y. Cav.	Aug., 1863	From Def. Newberne Dept. N. C.	To Heckman's Com. Newport News.	Oct.,	1863
12th N. Y. Cav.	Aug., 1863	From Def. Newberne Dept. N. C.	To Sub Dist. Newberne Dept. N. C.	Jan.,	1865
23d N. Y. Cav.	Aug., 1863	From Def. Newberne Dept. N. C.	To Sub Dist. Beaufort Dist. N. C.	Oct.,	1863
3d N. Y. Lt. Arty. 9 Cos.	Aug., 1863	From Def. Newberne Dept. N. C.	To Sub Dist. Newberne Dept. N. C.	Jan.,	1865
Batty. F, 1st R. I. Arty.	Aug., 1863	From Def. Newberne Dept. N. C.	To Dist. St. Mary's	Nov.,	1863
5th R. I. Heavy Arty.	Aug., 1863	From Def. Newberne Dept. N. C.	To Sub Dist. Newberne Dept. N. C.	Jan.,	1865
99th N. Y. Infy	Oct., 1863	From U. S. Forces Yorktown, Va.	To Sub Dist. Newberne Dept. N. C.	Jan.,	1865
19th Wis. Infy	Oct., 1863	From U. S. Forces Yorktown, Va.	To 3-Brig. 1-Div. 18-C. A. James.	Apr.,	1864
2d Mass. Heavy Arty.	Oct., 1863	From New Organization	To Sub Dist. Newberne Dept. N. C.	Jan.,	1865
21st Conn. Infy	Feb., 1864	From Heckman's Div. Ports., Va.	To Dist. Pamlico Dist. N. C.	Mch.,	1864
15th Conn. Infy	Apr., 1864	From Sub. Dist. Albemarle Dist.N.C.	To Sub Dist. Newberne Dept. N. C.	Jan.,	1865
23d N. Y. Indpt. Batty.	Apr., 1864	From Sub. Dist. Albemarle Dist.N.C.	To Sub Dist. Newberne Dept. N. C.	Jan.,	1865
1st N. C. Col'd H'y. A't.	Apr., 1864	From New Organization	To Sub Dist. Beaufort Dept. N. C.	Jan.,	1865
9th Vt. Infy	Apr., 1864	From Sub Dist. Beaufort Dist. N. C.	To 2-Brig. 2-Div. 18-C. A. James.	Sept.,	1864
23d Mass. Infy	Sept., 1864	From 1-Brig. 2-Div. 18-Corps.	To Sub Dist. Newberne Dept. N. C.	Jan.,	1865
25th Mass. Infy	Sept., 1864	From 1-Brig. 2-Div. 18-Corps.	To Sub Dist. Newberne Dept. N. C.	Jan.,	1865

Tenth Army Corps---Army of the James

Organized Apr. 28, 1864, from the Department of the South. Discontinued Dec. 3, 1864, and merged into the 24th Corps, Army of the James.

COMMANDERS.

A. H. Terry	Brigadier General	Apr. 28, 1864, to May 4, 1864.
Q. A. Gillmore	Major General	May 4, 1864, to June 14, 1864.
A. H. Terry	Brigadier General	June 14, 1864, to June 21, 1864.
W. T. H. Brooks	Brigadier General	June 21, 1864, to July 18, 1864.
A. H. Terry	Brigadier General	July 18, 1864, to July 23, 1864.
D. B. Birney	Major General	July 23, 1864, to Oct. 10, 1864.
A. H. Terry	Brigadier General	Oct. 10, 1864, to Nov. 4, 1864.
Adelbert Ames	Brigadier General	Nov. 4, 1864, to Nov. 18, 1864.
A. H. Terry	Brigadier General	Nov. 18, 1864, to Dec. 3, 1864.

1st DIVISION.— COMMANDERS.

R. S. Foster	Brigadier General	Apr. 28, 1864, to May 4, 1864.
A. H. Terry	Brigadier General	May 4, 1864, to June 11, 1864.
J. B. Howell	Col. 85th Penna. Infy	June 11, 1864, to June 14, 1864.
R. S. Foster	Brigadier General	June 14, 1864, to June 21, 1864.
A. H. Terry	Brigadier General	June 21, 1864, to July 18, 1864.
R. S. Foster	Brigadier General	July 18, 1864, to July 23, 1864.
A. H. Terry	Brigadier General	July 23, 1864, to Oct. 10, 1864.
Adelbert Ames	Brigadier General	Oct. 10, 1864, to Nov. 4, 1864.
A. C. Voris	Col. 67th Ohio Infy	Nov. 4, 1864, to Nov. 18, 1864.
Adelbert Ames	Brigadier General	Nov. 18, 1864, to Dec. 3, 1864.

1st BRIGADE.— COMMANDERS.

F. B. Pond	Col. 62d Ohio Infy	Apr. 28, 1864, to May 2, 1864.
J. B. Howell	Col. 85th Penna. Infy	May 2, 1864, to June 11, 1864.
F. B. Pond	Col. 62d Ohio Infy	June 11, 1864, to June 14, 1864.
J. B. Howell	Col. 85th Penna. Infy	June 14, 1864, to July 28, 1864.
F. B. Pond	Col. 62d Ohio Infy	July 28, 1864, to Aug. 16, 1864.
A. C. Voris	Col. 67th Ohio Infy	Aug. 16, 1864, to Aug. 18, 1864.
J. B. Howell	Col. 85th Penna. Infy	Aug. 18, 1864, to Sept. 1, 1864.
F. B. Pond	Col. 62d Ohio Infy	Sept. 1, 1864, to Sept. 13, 1864.
A. C. Voris	Col. 67th Ohio Infy	Sept. 13, 1864, to Sept. 24, 1864.
F. B. Pond	Col. 62d Ohio Infy	Sept. 24, 1864, to Sept. 29, 1864.
A. C. Voris	Col. 67th Ohio Infy	Sept. 29, 1864, to Oct. 4, 1864.
F. B. Pond	Col. 62d Ohio Infy	Oct. 4, 1864, to Oct. 26, 1864.
A. C. Voris	Col. 67th Ohio Infy	Oct. 26, 1864, to Nov. 6, 1864.
J. C. Briscoe	Col. 199th Penna. Infy	Nov. 6, 1864, to Nov. 18, 1864.
A. C. Voris	Col. 67th Ohio Infy	Nov. 18, 1864, to Dec. 3, 1864.

85th Penna. Infy	Apr., 1864	From Dist. Hilton Head Dept. South.	To 1-Brig. 1-Div. 24-C. Army James.	Dec., 1864
62d Ohio Infy	Apr., 1864	From Dist. Hilton Head Dept. South.	To 1-Brig. 1-Div. 24-C. Army James.	Dec., 1864
67th Ohio Infy	Apr., 1864	From Dist. Hilton Head Dept. South.	To 1-Brig. 1-Div. 24-C. Army James.	Dec., 1864
39th Ill. Infy	Apr., 1864	From Dist. Hilton Head Dept. South.	To 1-Brig. 1-Div. 24-C. Army James.	Dec., 1864
199th Penna. Infy	Oct., 1864	From New Organization	To 1-Brig. 1-Div. 24-C. Army James.	Dec., 1864

2d BRIGADE.— COMMANDERS.

H. M. Plaisted	Col. 11th Me. Infy	Apr. 28, 1864, to May 2, 1864.
J. R. Hawley	Col. 7th Conn. Infy	May 2, 1864, to Sept. 12, 1864.
J. C. Abbott	Col. 7th N. H. Infy	Sept. 12, 1864, to Oct. 12, 1864.
J. R. Hawley	Brigadier General	Oct. 12, 1864, to Oct. 20, 1864.
J. C. Abbott	Col. 7th N. H. Infy	Oct. 20, 1864, to Oct. 29, 1864.
J. R. Hawley	Brigadier General	Oct. 29, 1864, to Nov. 4, 1864.
J. C. Abbott	Col. 7th N. H. Infy	Nov. 4, 1864, to Nov. 18, 1864.
J. R. Hawley	Brigadier General	Nov. 18, 1864, to Dec. 3, 1864.

11th Me. Infy	Apr., 1864	From 1-Brig. Morris Island 10-Corps.	To 3-Brig. 1-Div. 10-C. Army James.	May, 1864
24th Mass. Infy	Apr., 1864	From 1-Brig. Vodges' Div. Dist. Fla.	To 3-Brig. 1-Div. 10-C. Army James.	May, 1864
10th Conn. Infy	Apr., 1864	From St. Augustine, Fla., Dept. So.	To 3-Brig. 1-Div. 10-C. Army James.	May, 1864
100th N. Y. Infy	Apr., 1864	From 2-Brig. Morris Island 10-Corps.	To 3-Brig. 1-Div. 10-C. Army James.	May, 1864
3d N. H. Infy	May, 1864	From 3-Br. 1-Div. 10-C. Army James.	To 2-Brig. 1-Div. 24-C. Army James.	Dec., 1864
7th N. H. Infy	May, 1864	From 3-Br. 1-Div. 10-C. Army James.	To 2-Brig. 1-Div. 24-C. Army James.	Dec., 1864
6th Conn. Infy	May, 1864	From 3-Br. 1-Div. 10-C. Army James.	To 2-Brig. 1-Div. 24-C. Army James.	Dec., 1864
7th Conn. Infy	May, 1864	From 3-Br. 1-Div. 10-C. Army James.	To 2-Brig. 1-Div. 24-C. Army James.	Dec., 1864
16th N. Y. Heavy Arty.	July, 1864	From Def. Yorktown, Va.	To 2-Brig. 1-Div. 24-C. Army James.	Dec., 1864
(Co's A, B, C, F, G, K, M.)				

3d BRIGADE.— COMMANDERS.

J. R. Hawley	Col. 7th Conn. Infy	Apr. 28, 1864, to May 2, 1864.
H. M. Plaisted	Col. 11th Me. Infy	May 2, 1864, to June 23, 1864.
R. S. Foster	Brigadier General	June 23, 1864, to July 18, 1864.
H. M. Plaisted	Col. 11th Me. Infy	July 18, 1864, to July 23, 1864.
R. S. Foster	Brigadier General	July 23, 1864, to Aug. 23, 1864.
H. M. Plaisted	Col. 11th Me. Infy	Aug. 23, 1864, to Nov. 2, 1864.
G. B. Dandy	Col. 100th N. Y. Infy	Nov. 2, 1864, to Dec. 3, 1864.

3d N. H. Infy	Apr., 1864	From Lt. Br. Dist. Fla. Dept. South.	To 2-Brig. 1-Div. 10-C. Army James.	May, 1864
7th N. H. Infy	Apr., 1864	From 2-Brig. Ames' Div. Dist. Fla.	To 2-Brig. 1-Div. 10-C. Army James.	May, 1864
6th Conn. Infy	Apr., 1864	From Dist. Hilton Head Dept. South.	To 2-Brig. 1-Div. 10-C. Army James.	May, 1864
7th Conn. Infy	Apr., 1864	From 2-Brig. Ames' Div. Dist. Fla.	To 2-Brig. 1-Div. 10-C. Army James.	May, 1864
10th Conn. Infy	May, 1864	From 2-Br. 1-Div. 10-C. Army James.	To 3-Brig. 1-Div. 24-C. Army James.	Dec., 1864
11th Me. Infy	May, 1864	From 2-Br. 1-Div. 10-C. Army James.	To 3-Brig. 1-Div. 24-C. Army James.	Dec., 1864
24th Mass. Infy	May, 1864	From 2-Br. 1-Div. 10-C. Army James.	To 3-Brig. 1-Div. 24-C. Army James.	Dec., 1864
100th N. Y. Infy	May, 1864	From 2-Br. 1-Div. 10-C. Army James.	To 3-Brig. 1-Div. 24-C. Army James.	Dec., 1864
1st Md. Cav. Dismtd.	June, 1864	From 3-Separate Brig. 8-Corps.	To 3-Brig. Cav. Div. Dept. Va. & N. C.	Oct., 1864
206th Penna. Infy	Nov., 1864	From Engr. Brig. Army James.	To 3-Brig. 1-Div. 24-C. Army James.	Dec., 1864

ARTILLERY.—

1st Conn. Batty.	Apr., 1864	From Folly Isl., S. C., Dept. South.	To Arty. Brig. 10-Corps Army James.	Aug., 1864
5th N. J. Batty.	Apr., 1864	From Camp Barry, Wash., 22-Corps.	To Arty. Brig. 10-Corps Army James.	Aug., 1864
Batty. M, 1st U. S. Arty.	May, 1864	From Arty. Dist. Fla. Dept. South.	To Arty. 3-Div. 10-C. Army James.	May, 1864
Batty. E, 3d U. S. Arty.	May, 1864	From Arty. 3-Div. 10-C. Army James.	To Arty. 2-Div. 10-C. Army James.	June, 1864
Batty. C, 3d R. I. Arty.	June, 1864	From Unatt. Arty. 10-C. Army James.	To Arty. Brig. 10-Corps Army James.	Aug., 1864
Batty. E, 3d N. Y. Arty.	June, 1864	From Arty. Brig. 18-C. Army James.	To Arty. Brig. 10-Corps Army James.	Aug., 1864

2d DIVISION.— COMMANDERS.

S. M. Alford	Col. 3d N. Y. Infy	Apr. 28, 1864, to May 2, 1864.
J. W. Turner	Brigadier General	May 2, 1864, to May 28, 1864.

Division transferred to 18th Corps, May 28, 1864. Rejoined Corps, June 16, 1864.

Adelbert Ames	Brigadier General	June 16, 1864, to June 22, 1864.
J. W. Turner	Brigadier General	June 22, 1864, to Aug. 23, 1864.
R. S. Foster	Brigadier General	Aug. 23, 1864, to Dec. 3, 1864.

1st BRIGADE.— COMMANDERS.

Guy V. Henry	Col. 40th Mass. Infy	Apr. 28, 1864, to May 2, 1864.
S. M. Alford	Col. 3d N. Y. Infy	May 2, 1864, to May 28, 1864.

Brigade transferred to 18th Corps, May 28, 1864. Reorganized June 21, 1864.

N. M. Curtis	Col. 142d N. Y. Infy	June 21, 1864, to Sept. 17, 1864.
Rufus Daggett	Col. 117th N. Y. Infy	Sept. 17, 1864, to Sept. 29, 1864.
A. M. Barney	Lt.-Col. 142d N. Y. Infy	Sept. 29, 1864, to Oct. 4, 1864.
N. M. Curtis	Col. 142d N. Y. Infy	Oct. 4, 1864, to Oct. 29, 1864.
A. M. Barney	Lt.-Col. 142d N. Y. Infy	Oct. 29, 1864, to Nov. 14, 1864.
N. M. Curtis	Col. 142d N. Y. Infy	Nov. 14, 1864, to Dec. 3, 1864.

40th Mass. Infy	Apr., 1864	From Light Brig. Dist. Fla. South	To 3-Brig. 1-Div. 18-Corps	May, 1864
3d N. Y. Infy	Apr., 1864	From 2-Brig. Gordon's Div. South	To 1-Brig. 3-Div. 18-Corps	May, 1864
89th N. Y. Infy	Apr., 1864	From 2-Brig. Gordon's Div. South	To 1-Brig. 2-Div. 18-Corps	May, 1864
117th N. Y. Infy	Apr., 1864	From 2-Brig. Gordon's Div. South	To 3-Brig. 3-Div. 18-Corps	May, 1864
142d N. Y. Infy	Apr., 1864	From 2-Brig. Gordon's Div. South	To 3-Brig. 3-Div. 18-Corps	May, 1864
3d N. Y. Infy	June, 1864	From 3-Brig. 3-Div. 18-Corps	To 1-Brig. 2-Div. 24-C. Army James.	Dec., 1864
112th N. Y. Infy	June, 1864	From 2-Brig. 3-Div. 18-Corps	To 1-Brig. 2-Div. 24-C. Army James.	Dec., 1864
117th N. Y. Infy	June, 1864	From 3-Brig. 3-Div. 18-Corps	To 1-Brig. 2-Div. 24-C. Army James.	Dec., 1864
142d N. Y. Infy	June, 1864	From 3-Brig. 3-Div. 18-Corps	To 1-Brig. 2-Div. 24-C. Army James.	Dec., 1864

2d BRIGADE.— COMMANDERS.

W. B. Barton	Col. 48th N. Y. Infy	Apr. 28, 1864, to May 28, 1864.
Edward Eddy	Major 47th N. Y. Infy	June 16, 1864, to June 18, 1864.
W. B. Barton	Col. 48th N. Y. Infy	June 18, 1864, to July 2, 1864.
W. B. Coan	Lt.-Col. 48th N. Y. Infy	July 2, 1864, to Aug. 28, 1864.
W. B. Barton	Col. 48th N. Y. Infy	Aug. 28, 1864, to Sept. 14, 1864.
G. Pennypacker	Col. 97th Penna. Infy	Sept. 14, 1864, to Dec. 3, 1864.

47th N. Y. Infy	Apr., 1864	From Barton's Brig. Dist. Fla.	To 1-Brig. 3-Div. 18-C. Army James.	May, 1864
48th N. Y. Infy	Apr., 1864	From Barton's Brig. Dist. Fla.	To 1-Brig. 3-Div. 18-C. Army James.	May, 1864
115th N. Y. Infy	Apr., 1864	From Barton's Brig. Dist. Fla.	To 1-Brig. 3-Div. 18-C. Army James.	May, 1864
76th Penna. Infy	Apr., 1864	From Dist. Hilton Head, S. C., South.	To 1-Brig. 3-Div. 18-C. Army James.	May, 1864
47th N. Y. Infy	June, 1864	From 1-Brig. 3-Div. 18-Corps	To 2-Brig. 2-Div. 24-C. Army James.	Dec., 1864
48th N. Y. Infy	June, 1864	From 1-Brig. 3-Div. 18-Corps	To 2-Brig. 2-Div. 24-C. Army James.	Dec., 1864
115th N. Y. Infy	June, 1864	From 1-Brig. 3-Div. 18-Corps	To 3-Brig. 2-Div. 10-C. Army James.	July, 1864
76th Penna. Infy	June, 1864	From 1-Brig. 3-Div. 18-Corps	To 2-Brig. 2-Div. 24-C. Army James.	Dec., 1864
97th Penna. Infy	July, 1864	From 3-Brig. 2-Div. 10-Corps	To 2-Brig. 2-Div. 24-C. Army James.	Dec., 1864
203d Penna. Infy	Oct., 1864	From New Organization	To 2-Brig. 2-Div. 24-C. Army James.	Dec., 1864

3d BRIGADE.—Organized June 20, 1864. COMMANDERS.

Louis Bell	Col. 4th N. H. Infy	June 20, 1864, to Aug. 13, 1864.
F. A. Osborn	Col. 24th Mass. Infy	Aug. 13, 1864, to Aug. 16, 1864.
E. L. Walrath	Major 115th N. Y. Infy	Aug. 16, 1864.
Frank W. Parker	Capt. 4th N. H. Infy	Aug. 16, 1864.
Robt. J. Gray	Capt. 9th Me. Infy	Aug. 16, 1864, to Aug. 20, 1864.
F. A. Osborn	Col. 24th Mass. Infy	Aug. 20, 1864, to Sept. 23, 1864.
Louis Bell	Col. 4th N. H. Infy	Sept. 23, 1864, to Dec. 3, 1864.

13th Ind. Infy	June, 1864	From 2-Brig. 3-Div. 18-Corps	To 3-Brig. 2-Div. 24-C. Army James.	Dec., 1864
9th Me. Infy	June, 1864	From 2-Brig. 3-Div. 18-Corps	To 3-Brig. 2-Div. 24-C. Army James.	Dec., 1864
4th N. H. Infy	June, 1864	From 2-Brig. 3-Div. 18-Corps	To 3-Brig. 2-Div. 24-C. Army James.	Dec., 1864
169th N. Y. Infy	June, 1864	From 2-Brig. 3-Div. 18-Corps	To 3-Brig. 2-Div. 24-C. Army James.	Dec., 1864
97th Penna. Infy	June, 1864	From 3-Brig. 3-Div. 18-Corps	To 2-Brig. 2-Div. 10-Corps	July, 1864
115th N. Y. Infy	July, 1864	From 2-Brig. 2-Div. 10-Corps	To 3-Brig. 2-Div. 24-C. Army James.	Dec., 1864

ARTILLERY, 2d DIVISION.—

4th N. J. Batty.	Apr., 1864	From Camp Barry, Wash., 22-Corps.	To Unatt. Arty. 10-C. Army James.	May, 1864
Batty. B, 1st U. S. Arty.	Apr., 1864	From Light Brig. Dist. Fla. South	To Arty. 1-Div. 18-C. Army James.	May, 1864
Batty. D, 1st U. S. Arty.	Apr., 1864	From Dist. Beaufort, S. C., 10-Corps.	To Unatt. Arty. 10-C. Army James.	May, 1864
Batty. D, 4th U. S. Arty.	June, 1864	From Arty. 2-Div. 18-Corps	To Arty. Brig. 10-Corps Army James.	Aug., 1864
Batty. E, 3d U. S. Arty.	June, 1864	From Arty. 1-Div. 10-Corps	To Arty. Brig. 10-Corps Army James.	Aug., 1864
Batty. D, 1st U. S. Arty.	June, 1864	From Unatt. Arty. 10-Corps	To Arty. Brig. 10-Corps Army James.	Aug., 1864
4th N. J. Batty.	June, 1864	From Unatt. Arty. 10-Corps	To Arty. Brig. 10-Corps Army James.	Aug., 1864

3d DIVISION.—Discontinued May 28, 1864. Transferred to the 18th Corps. Reorganized from new Regiments, June, 1864. Discontinued Sept., 1864. Reorganized Oct. 5, 1864.

COMMANDERS.

Adelbert Ames	Brigadier General	Apr. 28, 1864, to May 28, 1864.
O. S. Ferry	Brigadier General	June 19, 1864, to Aug. 27, 1864.
William Birney	Brigadier General	Aug. 27, 1864, to Sept. 1, 1864.
J. B. Howell	Col. 85th Penna. Infy	Sept. 1, 1864, to Sept. 13, 1864.
F. B. Pond	Col. 62d Ohio Infy	Sept. 13, 1864, to Sept. 24, 1864.
William Birney	Brigadier General	Oct. 5, 1864, to Oct. 20, 1864.
J. R. Hawley	Brigadier General	Oct. 20, 1864, to Oct. 29, 1864.
William Birney	Brigadier General	Oct. 29, 1864, to Dec. 3, 1864.

1st BRIGADE.— COMMANDERS.

Richard White	Col. 55th Penna. Infy	Apr. 28, 1864, to May 16, 1864.
Louis Bell	Col. 4th N. H. Infy	May 16, 1864, to May 18, 1864.
H. R. Guss	Col. 97th Penna. Infy	May 18, 1864, to May 28, 1864.
Gilbert Marston	Brigadier General	June 19, 1864, to Aug. 27, 1864.
James Shaw, Jr.	Col. 7th U. S. Colored Infy	Aug. 27, 1864, to Sept. 1, 1864.
William Birney	Brigadier General	Sept. 1, 1864, to Oct. 5, 1864.
A. C. Voris	Col. 67th Ohio Infy	Oct. 5, 1864, to Oct. 26, 1864.
James Shaw, Jr.	Col. 7th U. S. Colored Infy	Oct. 26, 1864, to Dec. 3, 1864.

9th Me. Infy	Apr., 1864	From 1-Brig. Morris Island South	To 2-Brig. 3-Div. 10-C. Army James.	May, 1864
4th N. H. Infy	Apr., 1864	From 1-Brig. Vodges' Div. Dist. Fla.	To 3-Brig. 3-Div. 10-Corps	May, 1864
55th Penna. Infy	Apr., 1864	From Dist. B'fort, S. C., Dept. South.	To 1-Brig. 2-Div. 18-Corps	May, 1864
97th Penna. Infy	Apr., 1864	From Fernandina, Fla., Dept. South.	To 3-Brig. 3-Div. 18-Corps	May, 18
8th Me. Infy	May, 1864	From 2-Br. 3-Div. 10-C. Army James.	To 2-Brig. 2-Div. 18-Corps	May, 1864
133d Ohio Infy	June, 1864	From Dept. W. Va.	No change to Muster Out	Aug., 1864
143d Ohio Infy	June, 1864	From 1-Brig. Def. North Pot. 22-C.	No change to Muster Out	Aug., 1864
148th Ohio Infy	June, 1864	From Res. Div. W. Va.	No change to Muster Out	Aug., 1864

1st BRIGADE.—Continued.

163d Ohio Infy...........June, 1864	From Def. Washington 22-Corps.....	No change to Muster Out..........	Aug., 1864
16th N. Y. H. A., G, K....July, 1864	From Yorktown, Va., Dist E. Va....	To Sep. Brig. Dept. Va. & N. C.....	Aug., 1864
3d Penna. H. A. Det......July, 1864	From Fort Monroe, Va............	To Sep. Brig. Dept. Va. & N. C.....	Aug., 1864
29th Conn. Col'd Infy......Aug., 1864	From Dist. Beaufort Dept. South....	To 2-Brig. 3-Div. 25-C. Army James.	Oct., 1864
7th U. S. Col'd Infy.......Aug., 1864	From Dist. Fla. Dept. South......	To 1-Brig. 3-Div. 10-C. Army James.	Dec., 1864
8th U. S. Col'd Infy.......Aug., 1864	From Dist. Fla. Dept. South......	To 2-Brig. 3-Div. 10-C. Army James.	Sept., 1864
9th U. S. Col'd Infy.......Aug., 1864	From Dist. Beaufort Dept. South....	To 2-Brig. 3-Div. 25-C. Army James.	Dec., 1864
41st U. S. Col'd Infy......Oct., 1864	From New Organization..........	To 2-Brig. 3-Div. 10-C. Army James.	Nov., 1864
127th U. S. Col'd Infy......Oct., 1864	From New Organization..........	To 2-Brig. 3-Div. 10-C. Army James.	Nov., 1864
29th Conn. Col'd Infy.....Nov., 1864	From 2-Brig. 3-Div. 10-Corps.......	To 2-Brig. 3-Div. 25-C. Army James.	Dec., 1864

2d BRIGADE.— COMMANDERS.

J. D. Rust............	Col. 8th Me. Infy................	Apr. 28, 1864, to May 2, 1864.
J. C. Drake............	Col. 112th N. Y. Infy.............	May 2, 1864, to May 28, 1864.
J. B. Armstrong........	Col. 134th Ohio Infy.............	June 19, 1864, to Aug. 25, 1864.
S. C. Armstrong........	Lt.-Col. 9th U. S. Colored Infy......	Oct. 6, 1864, to Oct. 8, 1864.
U. Doubleday	Col. 45th U. S. Colored Infy.......	Oct. 8, 1864, to Oct. 29, 1864.
E. Wright	Col. 10th U. S. Colored Infy.......	Oct. 29, 1864, to Nov. 6, 1864.
U. Doubleday	Col. 45th U. S. Colored Infy.......	Nov. 6, 1864, to Dec. 3, 1864.

13th Ind. Infy...........Apr., 1864	From 1-Brig. Vodges' Div. Dist. Fla.	To 2-Brig. 3-Div. 18-C. Army James.	May, 1864
8th Me. Infy..............Apr., 1864	From Dist. Beaufort Dept. South....	To 1-Brig. 3-Div. 10-C. Army James.	May, 1864
112th N. Y. Infy..........Apr., 1864	From 1-Brig. Vodges' Div. Dist. Fla.	To 2-Brig. 3-Div. 18-C. Army James.	May, 1864
169th N. Y. Infy..........Apr., 1864	From 1-Brig. Vodges' Div. Dist. Fla.	To 2-Brig. 3-Div. 18-C. Army James.	May, 1864
9th Me. Infy.............May, 1864	From 1-Brig. 3-Div. 10-Corps.......	To 2-Brig. 3-Div. 18-C. Army James.	May, 1864
130th Ohio Infy..........June, 1864	From New Organization..........	No change to Muster Out..........	Aug., 1864
132d Ohio Infy..........June, 1864	From Def. Washington 22-Corps....	No change to Muster Out..........	Aug., 1864
134th Ohio Infy..........June, 1864	From Def. Washington 22-Corps....	No change to Muster Out..........	Aug., 1864
138th Ohio Infy..........June, 1864	From Def. Washington 22-Corps....	No change to Muster Out..........	Aug., 1864
142d Ohio Infy..........June, 1864	From Def. Washington 22-Corps....	No change to Muster Out..........	Aug., 1864
37th U. S. Col'd Infy......June, 1864	From 1-Brig. 3-Div. 18-Corps......	To Unatt. Army James.	July, 1864
1st U. S. Col'd Infy......Aug., 1864	From 1-Brig. 3-Div. 18-Corps......	To 1-Brig. 3-Div. 18-C. Army James.	Sept., 1864
22d U. S. Col'd Infy......Aug., 1864	From 1-Brig. 3-Div. 18-Corps......	To 1-Brig. 3-Div. 18-C. Army James.	Sept., 1864
29th Conn. Col'd Infy......Oct., 1864	From 1-Brig. 3-Div. 10-Corps......	To 1-Brig. 3-Div. 10-C. Army James.	Nov., 1864
8th U. S. Col'd Infy....Oct., 1864	From 1-Brig. 3-Div. 10-Corps......	To 2-Brig. 2-Div. 25-C. Army James.	Dec., 1864
45th U. S. Col'd Infy....Oct., 1864	From New Organization..........	To 2-Brig. 2-Div. 25-C. Army James.	Dec., 1864
41st U. S. Col'd Infy.....Nov., 1864	From 1-Brig. 3-Div. 10-Corps......	To 3-Brig. 2-Div. 25-C. Army James.	Dec., 1864
127th U. S. Col'd Infy.....Nov., 1864	From 1-Brig. 3-Div. 10-Corps......	To 2-Brig. 2-Div. 25-C. Army James.	Dec., 1864

ARTILLERY, 3d DIVISION.—

Batty. C, 3d R. I. Arty...Apr., 1864	From Arty. Dist. Fla. Dept. South.	To Unatt. Arty. 10-C. Army James.	May, 1864
33d N. Y. Indpt. Batty....Apr., 1864	From Def. Washington 22-Corps....	To Unatt. Arty. 10-C. Army James.	May, 1864
Batty. E, 3d U. S. Arty...Apr., 1864	From Arty. Dist. Fla. Dept. South.	To Arty. 1-Div. 10-C. Army James.	May, 1864
Batty. M, 1st U. S. Arty..May, 1864	From Arty. 1-Div. 10-Corps.......	To Arty. Brig. 10-C. Army James.	Aug., 1864
33d N. Y. Indpt. Batty....June, 1864	From Unatt. Arty. 10-Corps........	To Arty. Brig. 10-C. Army James.	Aug., 1864

ARTILLERY BRIGADE.—

1st Conn. Batty..........Aug., 1864	From Arty. 1-Div. 10-C. Army James.	To Arty. Brig. 25-C. Army James.	Dec., 1864
4th N. J. Batty...........Aug., 1864	From Arty. 2-Div. 10-C. Army James.	To Arty. Brig. 25-C. Army James.	Dec., 1864
5th N. J. Batty...........Aug., 1864	From Arty. 1-Div. 10-C. Army James.	To Arty. Brig. 25-C. Army James.	Dec., 1864
Batty. E, 3d N. Y. Arty...Aug., 1864	From Arty. 1-Div. 10-C. Army James.	To Arty. Brig. 18-C. Army James.	Oct., 1864
Batty. H, 3d N. Y. Arty...Aug., 1864	From Arty. Brig. 18-C. Army James.	To Arty. Brig. 18-Corps Army James.	Oct., 1864
16th N. Y. Indpt. Batty...Aug., 1864	From Arty. Brig. 18-C. Army James.	To Arty. Brig. 18-Corps Army James.	Oct., 1864
33d N. Y. Indpt. Batty...Aug., 1864	From Arty. 3-Div. 10-C. Army James.	To Separate Brig. Army James......	Dec., 1864
Batty. A, 1st Penna. Arty.Aug., 1864	From Unatt. Dept. Va. & N. C......	To Arty. Brig. 25-C. Army James.	Oct., 1864
Batty. E, 1st Penna. Arty.Aug., 1864	From Arty. Brig. 18-C. Army James.	To Arty. Brig. 25-C. Army James.	Dec., 1864
Batty. C, 3d R. I. Arty...Aug., 1864	From Arty. 1-Div. 10-C. Army James.	To Arty. Brig. 25-C. Army James.	Dec., 1864
Batty. D, 1st U. S. Arty...Aug., 1864	From Arty. 3-Div. 10-C. Army James.	To Arty. Brig. 25-C. Army James.	Dec., 1864
Batty. M, 1st U. S. Arty...Aug., 1864	From Arty. 2-Div. 10-C. Army James.	To Arty. Brig. 25-Corps Army James.	Dec., 1864
Batty. E, 3d U. S. Arty...Aug., 1864	From Arty. 1-Div. 10-C. Army James.	To Arty. Brig. 25-Corps Army James.	Dec., 1864
Batty. D, 4th U. S. Arty...Aug., 1864	From Arty. 2-Div. 10-C. Army James.	To Arty. Brig. 25-Corps Army James.	Dec., 1864
16th N. Y. H. A. Det......Oct., 1864	From 3-Div. 10-Corps Army James.	To Separate Brig. Army James......	Dec., 1864

UNATTACHED.—

4th Mass. Cav............Apr., 1864	From Light Brig. Dist. Fla. South..	To Rand's Prov'l Brig. 18-Corps.....	May, 1864
(Co's E, F, G, H)			
1st N. Y. Engrs., 8 Co's...Apr., 1864	From Dist. Hilton Head Dept. South.	To Engrs. Dept. Va. & N. C........	June, 1864
4th N. J. Batty...........May, 1864	From Arty. 2-Div. 10-C. Army James.	To Arty. 2-Div. 10-C. Army James.	June, 1864
33d N. Y. Indpt. Batty....May, 1864	From Arty. 2-Div. 10-C. Army James.	To Arty. 3-Div. 10-C. Army James.	June, 1864
Batty. C, 3d R. I. Arty...May, 1864	From Arty. 3-Div. 10-C. Army James.	To Arty. 1-Div. 10-C. Army James.	June, 1864
Batty. D, 1st U. S. Arty...May, 1864	From Arty. 2-Div. 10-C. Army James.	To Arty. 2-Div. 10-C. Army James.	June, 1864
37th U. S. Col'd Infy......June, 1864	From 1-Brig. Hincks' Div. 18-Corps.	To Unatt. Dept. Va. & N. C........	July, 1864
37th N. J. Infy..........June, 1864	From New Organization..........	To Unatt. Dept. Va. & N. C........	July, 1864
1st N. Y. Mtd. Rifles Det.June, 1864	From Unatt. Cav. Dept. Va. & N. C...	To Unatt. Dept. Va. & N. C........	July, 1864
116th U. S. Col'd Infy.....Oct., 1864	From New Organization...........	To 1-Brig. 2-Div. 25-C. Army James.	Dec., 1864

Eighteenth Army Corps

As reorganized Apr., 1864, from Troops in the Department of Virginia and North Carolina. Corps discontinued Dec. 3, 1864, and merged into the 24th and 25th Corps.

COMMANDERS.

W. F. Smith...........	Major General	May 2, 1864, to July 10, 1864.
J. H. Martindale.......	Brigadier General	July 10, 1864, to July 21, 1864.
E. O. C. Ord..........	Major General	July 21, 1864, to Sept. 4, 1864.
John Gibbon	Major General	Sept. 4, 1864, to Sept. 22, 1864.
E. O. C. Ord..........	Major General	Sept. 22, 1864, to Sept. 29, 1864.
C. A. Heckman.........	Brigadier General	Sept. 29, 1864, to Oct. 1, 1864.
Godfrey Weitzel	Major General	Oct. 1, 1864, to Dec. 3, 1864.

1st DIVISION.— COMMANDERS.

W. T. H. Brooks.......	Brigadier General	Apr. 28, 1864, to June 18, 1864.
Gilbert Marston	Brigadier General	June 18, 1864, to June 20, 1864.
Geo. J. Stannard	Brigadier General	June 20, 1864, to July 31, 1864.
H. Burnham	Brigadier General	July 31, 1864, to Aug. 3, 1864.
J. B. Carr............	Brigadier General	Aug. 3, 1864, to Sept. 3, 1864.
Gilbert Marston	Brigadier General	Sept. 3, 1864, to Sept. 15, 1864.
Geo. J. Stannard.......	Brigadier General	Sept. 15, 1864, to Sept. 29, 1864.
Gilbert Marston	Brigadier General	Sept. 29, 1864, to Oct. 29, 1864.
Chas. Devens, Jr.......	Brigadier General	Oct. 29, 1864, to Dec. 3, 1864.

1st BRIGADE.— COMMANDERS.

J. J. DeForest	Col. 81st N. Y. Infy	Apr. 28, 1864, to May 1, 1864.
Gilbert Marston	Brigadier General	May 1, 1864, to June 18, 1864.
E. M. Cullen	Col. 96th N. Y. Infy	June 18, 1864, to July 12, 1864.
A. F. Stevens	Col. 13th N. H. Infy	July 12, 1864, to Sept. 29, 1864.
Thos. Mulcahy	Lt.-Col. 139th N. Y. Infy	Sept. 29, 1864.
J. B. Raulston	Lt.-Col. 81st N. Y. Infy	Sept. 29, 1864, to Dec. 3, 1864.

81st N. Y. Infy	Apr., 1864	From 1-Brig. Heckman's Div. Ports.	To 1-Brig. 3-Div. 24-C. Army James.	Dec., 1864
96th N. Y. Infy	Apr., 1864	From 1-Brig. Heckman's Div. Ports.	To 2-Brig. 1-Div. 18-C. Army James.	July, 1864
98th N. Y. Infy	Apr., 186	From 1-Brig. Heckman's Div. Ports.	To 1-Brig. 3-Div. 24-C. Army James.	Dec., 1864
139th N. Y. Infy	Apr., 1864	From 1-Brig. Heckman's Div. Ports.	To 1-Brig. 3-Div. 24-C. Army James.	Dec., 1864
13th N. H. Infy	July, 1864	From 2-Br. 1-Div. 18-C. Army James.	To 1-Brig. 3-Div. 24-C. Army James.	Dec., 1864
2d N. H. Infy	Aug., 1864	From Provost Guard 18-Corps	To 1-Brig. 3-Div. 24-C. Army James.	Dec., 1864

2d BRIGADE.— COMMANDERS.

H. Burnham	Brigadier General	Apr. 28, 1864, to July 31, 1864.	
E. M. Cullen	Col. 96th New York Infy	July 31, 1864, to Sept. 27, 1864.	
H. Burnham	Brigadier General	Sept. 27, 1864, to Sept. 29, 1864.	Killed.
M. T. Donohoe	Col. 10th New Hampshire	Sept. 29, 1864.	
E. M. Cullen	Col. 96th New York Infy	Sept. 29, 1864, to Dec. 3, 1864.	

8th Conn. Infy	Apr., 1864	From Sub-Dist. Albemarle D. N. C.	To Povost Guard 18-Corps	Aug., 1864
10th New Hamp. Infy	Apr., 1864	From 3-Brig. Heckman's D. Ports.	To 2-Brig. 3-Div. 24-Corps A. Jas.	Dec., 1864
13th New Hamp. Infy	Apr., 1864	From 3-Brig. Heckman's D. Ports.	To 1-Brig. 1-Div. 18-Corps	July, 1864
118th New York Infy	Apr., 1864	From U. S. Forces Yorktown, Va.	To 2-Brig. 3-Div. 24-Corps A. Jas.	Dec., 1864
96th New York Infy	July, 1864	From 1-Brig. 1-Div. 18-Corps	To 2-Brig. 3-Div. 24-Corps A. Jas.	Dec., 1864
5th Maryland Infy	Aug., 1864	From 3-Brig. 2-Div. 18-Corps	To 2-Brig. 3-Div. 24-Corps A. Jas.	Dec., 1864
92d New York Infy	Oct., 1864	From 3-Brig. 2-Div. 18-Corps	Consolidated with 96th N. Y.	Dec., 1864

3d BRIGADE.— COMMANDERS.

H. T. Sanders	Col. 19th Wisconsin Infy	Apr. 28, 1864, to May 17, 1864.	
A. H. Dutton	Col. 21st Conn. Infy	May 17, 1864, to May 26, 1864. Mort.	Wnd.
Chas. Devens, Jr	Brigadier General	May 26, 1864, to May 30, 1864.	
Guy V. Henry	Col. 40th Mass. Infy	May 30, 1864, to Aug. 12, 1864.	
S. K. Bowen	Lt.-Col. 188th Penna. Infy	Aug. 12, 1864, to Aug. 20, 1864.	
S. H. Roberts	Col. 139th New York Infy	Aug. 20, 1864, to Oct. 14, 1864.	
J. N. Patterson	Lt.-Col. 2d New Hampshire	Oct. 14, 1864, to Oct. 20, 1864.	
S. H. Roberts	Col. 139th New York Infy	Oct. 20, 1864, to Oct. 29, 1864.	
E. M. Cullen	Col. 96th New York Infy	Oct. 29, 1864.	
J. N. Patterson	Lt.-Col. 2d New Hampshire	Oct. 29, 1864, to Oct. 30, 1864.	
Guy V. Henry	Col. 40th Mass. Infy	Oct. 30, 1864, to Dec. 3, 1864.	

19th Wisconsin Infy	Apr., 1864	From Def. Newberne Dist. N. C.	To 2-Brig. 2-Div. 18-Corps	June, 1864
92d New York Infy	Apr., 1864	From Dist. Albemarle Dist. N. C.	To 2-Brig. 1-Div. 18-Corps	Oct., 1864
188th Penna. Infy	Apr., 1864	From New Organization	To 3-Brig. 3-Div. 24-Corps A. Jas.	Dec., 1864
58th Penna. Infy	May, 1864	From Sub-Dist. Pamlico Dist. N. C.	To 3-Brig. 3-Div. 24-Corps A. Jas.	Dec., 1864
21st Conn. Infy	May, 1864	From Sub-Dist. Pamlico Dist. N. C.	To 3-Brig. 3-Div. 24-Corps A. Jas.	Dec., 1864
40th Mass. Infy	May, 1864	From 1-Brig. 2-D. 10-Corps A. Jas.	To 3-Brig. 3-Div. 24-Corps A. Jas.	Dec., 1864
2d New Hampshire Infy	Oct., 1864	From 1-Brig. 1-Div. 18-Corps	To 3-Brig. 3-Div. 24-Corps A. Jas.	Dec., 1864

ARTILLERY.—

4th Wisconsin Batty	Apr., 1864	From U. S. Forces Yorktown, Va.	To Arty. Brig. 18-Corps A. James.	June, 1864
Batty. L, 4th U. S. Arty.	Apr., 1864	From U. S. Forces Yorktown, Va.	To Arty. Brig. 18-Corps A. James.	June, 1864
Batty. A, 5th U. S. Arty.	Apr., 1864	From U. S. Forces Yorktown, Va.	To Arty. Brig. 18-Corps A. James.	June, 1864
Batty. K, 3d N. Y. Arty.	Apr., 1864	From Def. Newberne Dist. N. C.	To Arty. Hinck's Div. 18-Corps.	May, 1864
Batty. M, 3d N. Y. Arty.	Apr., 1864	From Arty. Heckman's D. Ports., Va.	To Arty. Hinck's Div. 18-Corps.	May, 1864
Batty. B, 1st U. S. Arty.	May, 1864	From Arty. 2-Div. 10-Corps A. Jas.	To Arty. Brig. 18-Corps	June, 1864

UNATTACHED.—

16th N. Y. Heavy Arty.	Apr., 1864	From U. S. Forces Yorktown, Va.	To U. S. Forces Yorktown, Va.	May, 1864

2d DIVISION.— COMMANDERS.

I. J. Wistar	Brigadier General	Apr. 22, 1864, to May 7, 1864.
Godfrey Weitzel	Brigadier General	May 7, 1864, to May 20, 1864.
J. H. Martindale	Brigadier General	May 20, 1864, to July 10, 1864.
Adelbert Ames	Brigadier General	July 10, 1864, to Sept. 17, 1864.
C. A. Heckman	Brigadier General	Sept. 17, 1864, to Dec. 3, 1864.

1st BRIGADE.— COMMANDERS.

C. A. Heckman	Brigadier General	Apr. 26, 1864, to May 16, 1864.
Geo. J. Stannard	Brigadier General	May 16, 1864, to June 20, 1864.
Alex. Piper	Col. 10th N. Y. Heavy Arty	June 20, 1864, to July 24, 1864.
James Stewart, Jr	Col. 9th New Jersey Infy	July 24, 1864, to Sept. 30, 1864.
G. M. Guion	Col. 148th New York Infy	Sept. 30, 1864, to Oct. 17, 1864.
W. H. McNary	Lt.-Col. 158th New York Infy	Oct. 17, 1864, to Nov. 2, 1864.
James Jourdan	Col. 158th New York Infy	Nov. 2, 1864, to Dec. 3, 1864.

23d Mass. Infy	Apr., 1864	From 2-B. Heckman's D. Ports., Va.	To Def. Newberne Dist. N. C.	Sept., 1864
25th Mass. Infy	Apr., 1864	From 2-B. Heckman's D. Ports., Va.	To Def. Newberne Dist. N. C.	Sept., 1864
27th Mass. Infy	Apr., 1864	From 2-B. Heckman's D. Ports., Va.	To Sub-Dist. Beaufort Dist. N. C.	Sept., 1864
9th New Jersey Infy	Apr., 1864	From 2-B. Heckman's D. Ports., Va.	To Sub-Dist. Beaufort Dist. N. C.	Sept., 1864
55th Penna. Infy	May, 1864	From 1-Brig. 3-Div. 10-C. A. Jas.	To 4-Brig. 1-Div. 24-Corps	Dec., 1864
89th New York Infy	May, 1864	From 1-Brig. 2-Div. 10-C. A. Jas.	To 3-Brig. 2-Div. 18-Corps	June, 1864
10th N. Y. Heavy Arty.	June, 1864	From 3-Brig. DeRussy's Div. 22-C.	To 1-Brig. DeRussy's Div. 22-Corps	Aug., 1864
158th New. York Infy	Aug., 1864	From Sub-Dist. Beaufort Dist. N. C.	To 4-Brig. 1-Div. 24-Corps	Dec., 1864
148th New York Infy	Sept., 1864	From 2-Brig. 2-Div. 18-Corps	To 4-Brig. 1-Div. 24-Corps	Dec., 1864

2d BRIGADE.— COMMANDERS.

G. A. Stedman, Jr	Col. 11th Conn. Infy	Apr. 23, 1864, to May 7, 1864.	
I. J. Wister	Brigadier General	May 7, 1864, to May 18, 1864.	
G. A. Stedman, Jr	Col. 11th Conn. Infy	May 18, 1864, to Aug. 26, 1864.	Killed.
G. M. Guion	Col. 148th New York Infy	Aug. 26, 1864, to Sept. 19, 1864.	
E. H. Ripley	Col. 9th Vermont Infy	Sept. 19, 1864, to Dec. 3, 1864.	

11th Conn. Infy	Apr., 1864	From U. S. Forces Yorktown, Va.	To Prov'l Div. Dept. Va. & N. C.	Oct., 1864
2d New Hampshire Infy	Apr., 1864	From Dist. St. Mary's	To Provost Guard 18-Corps	June, 1864
12th New Hamp. Infy	Apr., 1864	From Dist. St. Mary's	To Prov'l Div. Dept. Va. & N. C.	Oct., 1864
148th New York Infy	Apr., 1864	From U. S. Forces Yorktown, Va.	To 1-Brig. 2-Div. 18-Corps	Sept., 1864
8th Maine Infy	May, 1864	From 1-Brig. 3-Div. 10-Corps	To 4-Brig. 1-Div. 24-Corps	Dec., 1864
19th Wisconsin Infy	June, 1864	From 3-Brig. 1-Div. 18-Corps	To Norfolk, Va., Dept. Va. & N. C.	Aug., 1864
9th Vermont Infy	Sept., 1864	From Def. Newberne Dist. N. C.	To 2-Brig. 3-Div. 24-Corps	Dec., 1864

3d BRIGADE.—Organized June 18, 1864. COMMANDERS.

A. A. Gibson	Col. 2d Penna. Heavy Arty	June 18, 1864, to June 20, 1864.		
Adelbert Ames	Brigadier General	June 20, 1864, to July 10, 1864.		
H. S. Fairchilds	Col. 89th New York Infy	July 10, 1864, to Dec. 3, 1864.		
5th Maryland Infy......June, 1864	From 8-Corps Middle Dept	To 2-Brig. 1-Div. 18-Corps	Aug.,	1864
89th New York Infy......June, 1864	From 1-Brig. 2-Div. 18-Corps	To 4-Brig. 1-Div. 24-Corps	Dec.,	1864
2d Penna. Heavy Arty...June, 1864	From 1-Brig. South Pot. 22-Corps	To Prov'l B. Bermuda Hundred, Va.	Dec.,	1864
19th Wisconsin Infy......Oct., 1864	From Norfolk, Va., Dept. Va & N. C.	To 1-Brig. 3-Div. 24-Corps	Dec.,	1864
ARTILLERY.—				
7th N. Y. Indpt. Batty...Apr., 1864	From U. S. Forces Yorktown, Va.	To Arty. Brig. 18-Corps	June,	1864
Batty. E, 3d N. Y. Arty...Apr., 1864	From Def. Newberne Dist. N. C.	To Arty. Brig. 18-Corps	June,	1864
Batty. F, 1st R. I. Arty...Apr., 1864	From U. S. Forces Yorktown, Va.	To Arty. Brig. 18-Corps	June,	1864
Batty. D, 4th U. S. Arty...Apr., 1864	From U. S. Forces Norfolk & Ports.	To Arty. 2-Div. 10-Corps Army Jas.	June,	1864

3d DIVISION.—Organized temporarily May 30, 1864, from 2d and 3d Divisions 10th Army Corps. Permanently organized June 16, 1864, from Hincks' Colored Division.

COMMANDERS.

Chas. Devens, Jr.	Brigadier General	May 30, 1864, to June 4, 1864.
Adelbert Ames	Brigadier General	June 4, 1864, to June 16, 1864.
E. W. Hincks	Brigadier General	June 16, 1864, to July 1, 1864.
J. H. Holman	Col. 1st U. S. Colored Infy	July 1, 1864, to July 27, 1864.
S. A. Duncan	Col. 4th U. S. Colored Infy	July 27, 1864, to July 29, 1864.
J. B. Carr	Brigadier General	July 29, 1864, to Aug. 3, 1864.
Chas. J. Paine	Brigadier General	Aug. 3, 1864, to Oct. 14, 1864.
J. H. Holman	Col. 1st U. S. Colored Infy	Oct. 14, 1864, to Oct. 28, 1864.
A. G. Draper	Col. 36th U. S. Colored Infy	Oct. 28, 1864, to Nov. 3, 1864.
Chas. J. Paine	Brigadier General	Nov. 3, 1864, to Dec. 3, 1864.

1st BRIGADE.— COMMANDERS.

W. B. Barton	Col. 48th New York Infy	May 30, 1864, to June 19, 1864.		
E. A. Wild	Brigadier General	June 19, 1864, to June 23, 1864.		
J. H. Holman	Col. 1st U. S. Colored Infy	June 23, 1864, to July 1, 1864.		
J. Garrard	Col. 1st U. S. Colored Cav	July 1, 1864, to Aug. 3, 1864.		
J. H. Holman	Col. 1st U. S. Colored Infy	Aug. 3, 1864, to Oct. 14, 1864.		
A. G. Chamberlin	Lt.-Col. 37th U. S. Colored Infy	Oct. 14, 1864, to Nov. 6, 1864.		
E. Wright	Col. 10th U. S. Colored Infy	Nov. 6, 1864, to Dec. 3, 1864.		
47th New York Infy.....May, 1864	From 2-Brig. 2-D. 10-Corps A. Jas.	To 2-Brig. 2-Div. 10-Corps A. Jas.	June,	1864
48th New York Infy.....May, 1864	From 2-Brig. 2-D. 10-Corps A. Jas.	To 2-Brig. 2-Div. 10-Corps A. Jas.	June,	1864
115th New York Infy.....May, 1864	From 2-Brig. 2-D. 10-Corps A. Jas.	To 2-Brig. 2-Div. 10-Corps A. Jas.	June,	1864
76th Penna. Infy.......May, 1864	From 2-Brig. 2-D. 10-Corps A. Jas.	To 2-Brig. 2-Div. 10-Corps A. Jas.	June,	186
1st U. S. Colored Infy....June, 1864	From 1-Brig. Hincks' Div. 18-Corps	To 1-Brig. 1-Div. 25-Corps A. Jas.	Dec.,	1864
10th U. S. Colored Infy....June, 1864	From 1-Brig. Hincks' Div. 18-Corps	To Unattached Dept. Va. & N. C.	June,	1864
22d U. S. Colored Infy....June, 1864	From 1-Brig. Hincks' Div. 18-Corps	To 2-Brig. 3-Div. 18-Corps A. Jas.	June,	1864
37th U. S. Colored Infy....June, 1864	From 1-Brig. Hincks' Div. 18-Corps	To 2-Brig. 3-Div. 10-Corps A. Jas.	June,	1864
1st U. S. Colored Cav....June, 1864	From Unatt. Dept. Va. & N. C.	To Def. Portsmouth, Va.	Aug.,	1864
5th Mass. Colored Cav...June, 1864	From Prov'l Brig. Hincks' D. 18-C.	To Dist. St. Mary's	June,	1864
22d U. S. Colored Infy....Aug., 1864	From 2-Brig. 3-Div. 18-Corps	To 1-Brig. 3-Div. 18-Corps A. Jas.	Dec.,	1864
37th U. S. Colored Infy...Aug., 1864	From Unatt. Dept. Va. & N. C.	To 3-Brig. 1-Div. 25-Corps A. Jas.	Dec.,	1864

2d BRIGADE.— COMMANDERS.

J. C. Drake	Col. 112th New York Infy	May 30, 1864, to June 1, 1864.	Killed.	
Z. B. Robinson	Lt.-Col. 112th N. Y. Infy	June 1, 1864, to June 5, 1864.		
Alex. Piper	Col. 10th N. Y. Heavy Arty	June 5, 1864, to June 9, 1864.		
N. M. Curtis	Col. 142d New York Infy	June 9, 1864, to June 19, 1864.		
S. A. Duncan	Col. 4th U. S. Colored Infy	June 19, 1864, to Aug. 15, 1864.		
E. Wright	Col. 10th U. S. Colored Infy	Aug. 15, 1864, to Aug. 22, 1864.		
A. G. Draper	Col. 36th U. S. Colored Infy	Aug. 22, 1864, to Oct. 28, 1864.		
J. W. Ames	Col. 6th U. S. Colored Infy	Temporarily in Sept., 1864.		
D. E. Clapp	Lt.-Col. 38th U. S. Col'd Infy	Oct. 28, 1864.		
G. W. Shurtliff	Lt.-Col. 5th U. S. Col'd Infy	Oct. 28, 1864, to Nov. 3, 1864.		
A. G. Draper	Col. 36th U. S. Colored Infy	Nov. 3, 1864, to Dec. 3, 1864.		
13th Indiana Infy........May, 1864	From 2-Brig. 3-Div. 10-C. A. James	To 3-Brig. 2-Div. 10-Corps A. Jas.	June,	1864
9th Maine Infy.........May, 1864	From 2-Brig. 3-Div. 10-C. A. James	To 3-Brig. 2-Div. 10-Corps A. Jas.	June,	1864
112th New York Infy.....May, 1864	From 2-Brig. 3-Div. 10-C. A. James	To 3-Brig. 2-Div. 10-Corps A. Jas.	June,	1864
169th New York Infy.....May, 1864	From 2-Brig. 3-Div. 10-C. A. James	To 3-Brig. 2-Div. 10-Corps A. Jas.	June,	1864
10th N. Y. Heavy Arty...June, 1864	From 3-Brig. Def. South Pot. 22-C.	To 1-Brig. 2-Div. 18-Corps A. Jas.	June,	1864
4th U. S. Colored Infy...June, 1864	From 2-Brig. Hincks' Div. 18-Corps	To 3-Brig. 3-Div. 18-Corps A. Jas.	Aug.,	1864
5th U. S. Colored Infy...June, 1864	From 2-Brig. Hincks' Div. 18-Corps	To 3-Brig. 1-Div. 25-Corps A. Jas.	Dec.,	1864
6th U. S. Colored Infy...June, 1864	From 2-Brig. Hincks' Div. 18-Corps	To 3-Brig. 3-Div. 18-Corps A. Jas.	Aug.,	1864
22d U. S. Colored Infy...June, 1864	From 1-Brig. 3-Div. 18-Corps.	To 1-Brig. 3-Div. 18-Corps A. Jas.	Aug.,	1864
2d U. S. Colored Cav....June, 1864	From Unatt. Dept. Va. & N. C.	To Unatt. 3-Div. 18-Corps A. James	Aug.,	1864
36th U. S. Colored Infy...Aug., 1864	From Unatt. Dept. Va. & N. C.	To 1-Brig. 3-Div. 25-Corps A. Jas.	Dec.,	1864
38th U. S. Colored Infy...Aug., 1864	From Unatt. Dept. Va. & N. C.	To 1-Brig. 3-Div. 25-Corps A. Jas.	Dec.,	1864

3d BRIGADE.— COMMANDERS.

Adelbert Ames	Brigadier General	May 30, 1864, to June 4, 1864.		
H. R. Guss	Col. 97th Penna. Infy	June 4, 1864, to June 9, 1864.		
Louis Bell	Col. 4th New Hampshire Infy	June 9, 1864, to June 19, 1864.		
Brigade discontinued June 19, 1864. Reorganized Aug. 22, 1864.				
S. A. Duncan	Col. 4th U. S. Colored Infy	Aug. 22, 1864, to Sept. 29, 1864.		
J. W. Ames	Col. 6th U. S. Colored Infy	Sept. 29, 1864, to Dec. 3, 1864.		
4th New Hampshire Infy..May, 1864	From 1-Brig. 3-Div. 10-C. A. Jas.	To 3-Brig. 2-Div. 10-Corps A. Jas.	June,	1864
3d New York Infy......May, 1864	From 1-Brig. 2-Div. 10-C. A. Jas.	To 1-Brig. 2-Div. 10-Corps A. Jas.	June,	1864
117th New York Infy.....May, 1864	From 1-Brig. 2-Div. 10-C. A. Jas.	To 1-Brig. 2-Div. 10-Corps A. Jas.	June,	1864
142d New York Infy.....May, 1864	From 1-Brig. 2-Div. 10-C. A. Jas.	To 1-Brig. 2-Div. 10-Corps A. Jas.	June,	1864
97th Penna. Infy.......May, 1864	From 1-Brig. 3-Div. 10-C. A. Jas.	To 3-Brig. 2-Div. 10-Corps A. Jas.	June,	1864
4th U. S. Colored Infy...Aug., 1864	From 2-Brig. 3-Div. 10-C. A. Jas.	To 2-Brig. 1-Div. 25-Corps A. Jas.	Dec.,	1864
6th U. S. Colored Infy...Aug., 1864	From 2-Brig. 3-Div. 10-C. A. Jas.	To 2-Brig. 1-Div. 25-Corps A. Jas.	Dec.,	1864
10th U. S. Colored Infy...Aug., 1864	From Unatt. 3-Div. 18-Corps A. Jas.	To 3-Brig. 1-Div. 25-Corps A. Jas.	Dec.,	1864
ARTILLERY.—				
Batty. K, 3d N. Y. Arty...June, 1864	From Arty. 1-Div. 18-Corps A. Jas.	To Arty. Brig. 18-Corps Army Jas.	June,	1864
Batty. M, 3d N. Y. Arty...June, 1864	From Arty. 1-Div. 18-Corps A. Jas.	To Arty. Brig. 18-Corps Army Jas.	June,	1864
Batty. B, 2d U. S. Col'd A..June, 1864	From Hincks' Div. 18-Corps A. Jas.	To Arty. Brig. 18-Corps Army Jas.	June,	1864

PROVISIONAL BRIGADE.—Organized May 27, 1864. Discontinued June, 1864.

COMMANDER.

A. A. Rand............	Col. 4th Mass. Cav................	May 27, 1864, to June 19, 1864.

13th N. Y. Heavy Arty...May, 1864	From Norfolk and Portsmouth, Va.	To Norfolk & Portsmouth D. E. Va.	June, 1864
Batty. B, 2d U. S. Col'd A...May, 1864	From Hincks' Colored Div. 18-C..	To Arty. Brig. 18-Corps.........	June, 1864
4th Mass. Cav......May, 1864	From Dist. Fla. Dept. South......	To Unatt. 10-Corps Army James...	June, 1864
5th Mass. Col'd Cav......May, 1864	From Def. Washington 22-Corps...	To 1-Brig. 3-Div. 18-Corps A. Jas.	June, 1864

ARTILLERY BRIGADE.—

Batty. E, 3d N. Y. Arty...June, 1864	From Arty. 2-Div. 18-Corps A. Jas.	To Arty. 1-Div. 10-Corps A. James	June, 1864
Batty. K, 3d N. Y. Arty...June, 1864	From Arty. 3-Div. 18-Corps A. Jas.	To Arty. Brig. 24-Corps A. James.	Dec., 1864
Batty. M, 3d N. Y. Arty...June, 1864	From Arty. 3-Div. 18-Corps A. Jas.	To Arty. Brig. 24-Corps A. James.	Dec., 1864
7th N. Y. Indpt. Batty...June, 1864	From Arty. 2-Div. 18-Corps A. Jas.	To Arty. Brig. 10-Corps A. James.	Aug., 1864
16th N. Y. Indpt. Batty...June, 1864	From Arty. Newport News, Va....	To Arty. Brig. 24-Corps A. James.	Dec., 1864
Batty. F, 1st R. I. Arty...June, 1864	From Arty. 2-Div. 18-Corps A. Jas.	To Cav. Div. Dept. Va. & N. C....	June, 1864
4th Wisconsin Batty....June, 1864	From Arty. 1-Div. 18-Corps A. Jas.	To Cav. Div. Dept. Va. & N. C....	Oct., 1864
Batty. B, 1st U. S. Arty...June, 1864	From Arty. 1-Div. 18-Corps A. Jas.	To Arty. Brig. 24-Corps A. James.	Dec., 1864
Batty. L, 4th U. S. Arty...June, 1864	From Arty. 1-Div. 18-Corps A. Jas.	To Arty. Brig. 24-Corps A. James.	Dec., 1864
Batty. A, 5th U. S. Arty...June, 1864	From Arty. 1-Div. 18-Corps A. Jas.	To Arty. Brig. 24-Corps A. James.	Dec., 1864
Batty. B, 2d U. S. Col'd A...June, 1864	From Arty. 3-Div. 18-Corps A. Jas.	To Unatt. Arty. Dept. Va. & N. C.	June, 1864
Batty. H, 3d N. Y. Arty...July, 1864	From Norfolk & Portsmouth, E. Va.	To Arty. Brig. 10-Corps A. James.	Aug., 1864
17th N. Y. Indpt. Batty...July, 1864	From 2-Brig. Def. South Pot. 22-C.	To Arty. Brig. 24-Corps A. James.	Dec., 1864
Batty. E, 1st Pa. Arty...July, 1864	From Unatt. Dept. Va. & N. C....	To Arty. Brig. 10-Corps A. James.	Aug., 1864
Batty. F, 5th U. S. Arty...July, 1864	From Camp Barry Wash. 22-Corps	To Arty. Brig. 24-Corps A. James.	Dec., 1864
16th N. Y. Indpt. Batty...Oct., 1864	From Arty. Brig. 10-Corps A. Jas.	To Arty. Brig. 24-Corps A. James.	Dec., 1864
Batty. H, 3d N. Y. Arty...Oct., 1864	From Arty. Brig. 10-Corps A. Jas.	To Arty. Brig. 24-Corps A. James.	Dec., 1864
Batty. A, 1st Pa. Arty...Oct., 1864	From Arty. Brig. 10-Corps A. Jas.	To Arty. Brig. 24-Corps A. James.	Dec., 1864

PROVISIONAL BRIGADE, 3d DIVISION.—Organized Oct., 1864.

COMMANDER.

E. Martindale.........	Col. 81st U. S. Colored Infy.......	Oct., 1864, to Dec. 3, 1864.

107th U. S. Col'd Infy.....Oct., 1864	From New Organization..........	To 3-Brig. 1-Div. 25-Corps A. James	Dec., 1864
117th U. S. Col'd Infy.....Oct., 1864	From New Organization..........	To 1-Brig. 2-Div. 25-Corps A. James	Dec., 1864
118th U. S. Col'd Infy.....Oct., 1864	From New Organization..........	To 1-Brig. 2-Div. 25-Corps A. James	Dec., 1864

PROVOST GUARD.—

2d New Hampshire Infy..June, 1864	From 2-Brig. 2-Div. 18-Corps A. Jas.	To 1-Brig. 1-Div. 18-Corps A. James	Aug., 1864
8th Conn. Infy........Aug., 1864	From 2-Brig. 1-Div. 18-Corps A. Jas.	To Provost Guard 24-Corps A. Jas.	Dec., 1864

MISCELLANEOUS.—

CAVALRY DIVISION.—

COMMANDERS.

A. V. Kautz............	Brigadier General	Apr. 28, 1864, to Oct. 23, 1864.
R. M. West............	Col. 5th Penna. Cav..........	Oct. 23, 1864, to Nov. 5, 1864.
A. V. Kautz............	Brigadier General	Nov. 5, 1864, to Mch. 11, 1865.
R. M. West............	Col. 5th Penna. Cav..........	Mch. 11, 1865, to Mch. 20, 1865.
R. S. Mackenzie.......	Brigadier General	Mch. 20, 1865, to May 9, 1865.

1st BRIGADE.—

COMMANDERS.

S. H. Mix............	Col. 3d N. Y. Cav............	Apr. 28, 1864, to June 15, 1864.	Killed.
R. M. West............	Col. 5th Penna. Cav..........	June 15, 1864, to Oct. 23, 1864.	
Geo. W. Lewis........	Col. 3d N. Y. Cav............	Oct. 23, 1864, to Nov. 5, 1864.	
R. M. West............	Col. 5th Penna. Cav..........	Nov. 5, 1864, to Mch. 11, 1865.	
N. B. Lord...........	Col. 20th N. Y. Cav..........	Mch. 11, 1865, to Mch. 20, 1865.	
R. M. West............	Col. 5th Penna. Cav..........	Mch. 20, 1865, to May, 1865.	

1st Dist. Columbia Cav...Apr., 1864	From Cav. Brig. Yorktown, Va....	To 2-Brig. Cav. Div. Dept. Va. & N. C.	June, 1864
3d N. Y. Cav........Apr., 1864	From Newport News, Va.........	To Norfolk & Portsmouth Dist. E. Va.	Dec., 1864
5th Penna. Cav........June, 1864	From 2-Brig. Cav. Div. Va. & N. C.	To Dept. Va....................	May, 1865
20th N. Y. Cav........Dec., 1864	From Norfolk & Ports. Dist. E. Va.	To Dept. Va....................	May, 1865

2d BRIGADE.—

COMMANDER.

S. P. Spear............	Col. 11th Penna. Cav..........	Apr. 28, 1864, to May 9, 1865.

5th Penna. Cav........Apr., 1864	From Cav. Br. U. S. Frcs. Ports., Va.	To 1-Brig. Cav. Div. Dept. Va. & N. C.	June, 1864
11th Penna. Cav........Apr., 1864	From Cav. Brig. Yorktown......	To Dept. Va....................	May, 1865
1st Dist. Columbia Cav...June, 1864	From 1-Br. Cav. Div. Dept. Va.&N.C.	To Dept. Va....................	May, 1865
1st Md. Cav............Mch., 1865	From 3-Br. Cav. Div. Dept.Va.&N.C.	To Dept. Va....................	May, 1865

3d BRIGADE.—Organized Oct. 14, 1864. Discontinued Mch. 28, 1865.

COMMANDERS.

A. W. Evans..........	Col. 1st Md. Cav............	Oct. 14, 1864, to Feb. 5, 1865.
E. V. Sumner.........	Col. 1st N. Y. Mtd. Rifles.........	Feb. 5, 1865, to Mch. 28, 1865.

1st Md. Cav.........Oct., 1864	From 3-Brig. 1-Div. 10-Corps......	To 2-Brig. Cav. Div. Army James...	Mch., 1865
1st N. Y. Mtd. Rifles......Oct., 1864	From Unatt. Cav. Army James......	To Dist. Eastern Va..............	Mch., 1865

ARTILLERY, CAVALRY DIVISION.—

8th N. Y. Ind. Batty. Sec..Apr., 1864	From Forces Norfolk & Portsmouth.	To Forces Norfolk & Portsmouth...	June, 1864
4th Wis. Batty........June, 1864	From Arty. Brig. 18-Corps........	To Dept. Va...................	May, 1865
Batty. B, 1st U. S. Arty..Oct., 1864	From Arty. Brig. 18-Corps........	To Arty. Brig. 24-Corps.........	Apr., 1865

NAVAL BRIGADE.—

COMMANDER.

C. K. Graham.........	Brigadier General	Apr. 28, 1864, to Feb. 17, 1865.

13th N. Y. Heavy Arty...Apr., 1864	From Forces Norfolk & Portsmouth.	No change to Muster Out.........	June, 1865
(Co's I, K, L, M.)			
3d Penna. Heavy Arty...Apr., 1864	From Fort Monroe, Va..........	No change to Muster Out.........	July, 1865
(Co's A, B, F, G.)			

ENGINEERS.—

1st N. Y. Engineers......Apr., 1864	From Engineers Dept. South.......	To Dept. Va....................	May, 1865

SIEGE ARTILLERY.—

1st Conn. Heavy Arty....May, 1864	From Def. Washington 22-Corps....	To Siege Train Army Pot.........	Dec., 1864
3d Penna. H. A., Co. M...May, 1864	From Fort Monroe, Va..........	To Def. Bermuda Hundred Army Jas.	Dec., 1864
13th N. Y. H. A., A, H...June, 1864	From Prov'l Brig. 18-Corps.......	To Def. Bermuda Hundred Army Jas.	Dec., 1864
3d Conn. Batty.........Nov., 1864	From New Organization..........	To Siege Train Army Pot.........	Dec., 1864

PONTOONEERS.—

13th Co. Mass. H. A.....Apr., 1864	From New Organization..........	To Dept. Va....................	May, 1865
(Co. I, 3d Mass. H. A.)			

SEPARATE BRIGADE.—

38th N. J. Infy...........Oct., 1864	From New Organization............	No change to Muster Out..........	June, 1865
184th N. Y. Infy..........Oct., 1864	From New Organization............	No change to Muster Out..........	June, 1865
(Co's C, E, G, H, I, K.)			
4th Mass. Cav., Co. M....Oct., 1864	From Unatt. Cav. 10-Corps........	To Dept. Va......................	June, 1865
1st U. S. Col'd Cav., E. I..Oct., 1864	From Norfolk & Portsmouth.......	To Dept. Va......................	June, 1865
33d N. Y. Indpt. Batty....Oct., 1864	From Arty. Brig. 10-Corps........	To Infy. Div. Bermuda Hund. A. Jas.	Jan., 1865
16th N. Y. H. A., E. K....Oct., 1864	From 1-Brig. 3-Div. 10-Corps......	To Dept. Va......................	June, 1865
3d Penna. H. A. Det......Oct., 1864	From 1-Brig. 3-Div. 10-Corps......	To Dept. Va......................	June, 1865

PROVISIONAL DIVISION.—Organized Oct., 1864.

COMMANDER.

J. H. Potter............	Col. 12th N. H. Infy.............		

9th Vt. Infy., 1 Co......Oct., 1864	From 2-Brig. 3-Div. 18-Corps......	To 2-Brig. 3-Div. 24-C. Army James.	Dec., 1864
11th Conn. Infy.........Oct., 1864	From 2-Brig. 2-Div. 18-Corps......	To 1-Brig. 3-Div. 24-C. Army James.	Dec., 1864
12th N. H. Infy.........Oct., 1864	From 2-Brig. 2-Div. 18-Corps......	To 2-Brig. 3-Div. 24-C. Army James.	Dec., 1864
200th Penna. Infy.......Oct., 1864	From New Organization...........	To Hartranft's Prov'l Brig. 9-C. Pot.	Nov., 1864
205th Penna. Infy.......Oct., 1864	From New Organization...........	To Hartranft's Prov'l Brig. 9-C. Pot.	Nov., 1864
207th Penna. Infy.......Oct., 1864	From New Organization...........	To Hartranft's Prov'l Brig. 9-C. Pot.	Nov., 1864
208th Penna. Infy.......Oct., 1864	From New Organization...........	To Hartranft's Prov'l Brig. 9-C. Pot.	Nov., 1864
209th Penna. Infy.......Oct., 1864	From New Organization...........	To Hartranft's Prov'l Brig. 9-C. Pot.	Nov., 1864
211th Penna. Infy.......Oct., 1864	From New Organization...........	To Hartranft's Prov'l Brig. 9-C. Pot.	Nov., 1864

DEFENCES OF BERMUDA HUNDRED.—
INFANTRY DIVISION.— COMMANDERS.

E. Ferrero	Brigadier General	Dec. 4, 1864, to Feb. 17, 1865.
C. K. Graham...........	Brigadier General	Feb. 17, 1865, to Mch. 19, 1865.
Geo. L. Hartsuff........	Brigadier General	Mch. 19, 1865, to Apr. 16, 1865.

1st BRIGADE.— COMMANDERS.

William Heine	Col. 103d N. Y. Infy.............	Dec. 5, 1864, to Mch. 20, 1865.
G. H. McKibben........	Bvt. Brig. General...............	Mch., 20, 1865, to Apr. 16, 1865.

41st N. Y. Infy..........Dec., 1864	From 2-Brig. Kitching's Prov'l Div..	To Dept. Va......................	Apr., 1865
103d N. Y. Infy.........Dec., 1864	From 2-Brig. Kitching's Prov'l Div..	To Dept. Va......................	Apr., 1865
104th Penna. Infy.......Dec., 1864	From 1-Brig. Kitching's Prov'l Div..	To Norf. & Portsmouth Dist. E. Va.	Apr., 1865
2d Penna. Heavy Arty....Mch., 1865	From Prov'l Brig. Def. Berm. Hund.	To Dept. Va......................	Apr., 1865

2d BRIGADE.— COMMANDERS.

J. B. Campbell.........	Major 10th N. Y. Heavy Arty......	Dec. 5, 1864, to Mch. 20, 1865.
Geo. C. Kibbe..........	Col. 6th N. Y. Heavy Arty.........	Mch. 20, 1865, to Apr. 16, 1865.

6th N. Y. Heavy Arty....Dec., 1864	From 1-Brig. Kitching's Prov'l Div..	To Dept. Va......................	Apr., 1865
10th N. Y. Heavy Arty....Dec., 1864	From 2-Brig. Kitching's Prov'l Div..	To Dept. Va......................	Apr., 1865

PROVISIONAL BRIGADE.— COMMANDER.

W. M. McClure.........	Col. 2d Penna. Heavy Arty........	Dec. 3, 1864, to Mch. 20, 1865.

2d Penna. Heavy Arty....Dec., 1864	From 3-Brig. 2-Div. 18-Corps.......	To 1-Brig. Infy. Div. Bermuda Hund.	Mch., 1865

ARTILLERY DEFENSES OF BERMUDA HUNDRED.—

7th New York Batty......Mch., 1865	From Arty. Brig. 25-Corps........	To Arty. Brig. 24-Corps Army James.	Apr., 1865
33d N. Y. Indpt. Batty...Mch., 1865	From Separate Brig. Army James...	To Dept. Virginia................	Apr., 1865
13th N. Y. H. Arty. A. H.Mch., 1865	From Siege Arty. Army James......	To Dept. Virginia................	Apr., 1865
3d Penna. H. A. Det.....Mch., 1865	From Siege Arty. Army James......	To Dept. Virginia................	Apr., 1865

UNATTACHED.—

1st N. Y. Mounted Rifles.May, 1864	From Cav. Brig. Yorktown, Va......	To 3-Brig. Cav. Div. Army James...	Oct., 1864
1st U. S. Colored Cav....May, 1864	From Cav. Forces Yorktown, Va....	To 1-Brig. 3-Div. 18-Corps........	June, 1864
2d U. S. Colored Cav....May, 1864	From Cav. Forces Yorktown, Va....	To 2-Brig. 3-Div. 18-Corps........	June, 1864
13th Co. Mass. H. Arty..May, 1864	From Fort Monroe, Va.............	To Pontooneers Army James........	May, 1864
36th U. S. Colored Infy..June, 1864	From Dist. St. Marys.............	To 2-Brig. 3-Div. 18-Corps........	Aug., 1864
38th U. S. Colored Infy..June, 1864	From Forces Norfolk & Portsmouth.	To 2-Brig. 3-Div. 18-Corps........	Aug., 1864
Batty. B, 2d U. S. Col'd A.June, 1864	From Arty. Brig. 18-Corps.........	To Norfolk and Portsmouth........	Aug., 1864
37th New Jersey Infy....July, 1864	From Unatt. 10-Corps.............	No change to Muster Out..........	Oct., 1864
10th U. S. Colored Infy..July, 1864	From 1-Brig. 3-Div. 18-Corps......	To 3-Brig. 3-Div. 18-Corps........	Aug., 1864
37th U. S. Colored Infy..July, 1864	From 2-Brig. 3-Div. 10-Corps......	To 1-Brig. 3-Div. 18-Corps........	Aug., 1864
Batty. A, 1st Penna. Arty.July, 1864	From Norfolk and Portsmouth......	To Arty. Brig. 10-Corps..........	Aug., 1864
5th Mass. Colored Cav....Mch., 1865	From Point Lookout, Md..........	To Dept. Texas...................	June, 1864

DETACHMENT NINETEENTH CORPS.—
1st BRIGADE, 2d DIVISION.—

9th Conn. Infy..........July, 1864	From 1-Brig. 2-Div. 19-Corps Gulf..	To 1-Brig. 2-Div. 19-Corps Shen....	Aug., 1864
12th Maine Infy.........July, 1864	From 1-Brig. 2-Div. 19-Corps Gulf..	To 1-Brig. 2-Div. 19-Corps Shen....	Aug., 1864
14th Maine Infy.........July, 1864	From 1-Brig. 2-Div. 19-Corps Gulf..	To 1-Brig. 2-Div. 19-Corps Shen....	Aug., 1864
26th Mass. Infy.........July, 1864	From 1-Brig. 2-Div. 19-Corps Gulf..	To 1-Brig. 2-Div. 19-Corps Shen....	Aug., 1864
14th N. H. Infy.........July, 1864	From 1-Brig. 2-Div. 19-Corps Gulf..	To 1-Brig. 2-Div. 19-Corps Shen....	Aug., 1864
75th New York Infy.....July, 1864	From 1-Brig. 2-Div. 19-Corps Gulf..	To 1-Brig. 2-Div. 19-Corps Shen....	Aug., 1864

2d BRIGADE.—

131st New York Infy.....July, 1864	From 2-Brig. 2-Div. 19-Corps Gulf..	To 2-Brig. 2-Div. 19-Corps Shen....	Aug., 1864
159th New York Infy.....July, 1864	From 2-Brig. 2-Div. 19-Corps Gulf..	To 2-Brig. 2-Div. 19-Corps Shen....	Aug., 1864
22d Iowa Infy..........July, 1864	From 2-Brig. 2-Div. 19-Corps Gulf..	To 2-Brig. 2-Div. 19-Corps Shen....	Aug., 1864

DISTRICT OF EASTERN VIRGINIA.—
NORFOLK AND PORTSMOUTH.— COMMANDERS.

Geo. F. Shepley........	Brigadier General................		
Israel Vodges..........	Brigadier General................		

13th N. H. Infy. Det....Apr., 1864	From 3-Brig. Heckman's Div. Ports.	To 2-Brig. 1-Div. 18-Corps........	Apr., 1864
11th Penna. Cav. Det...Apr., 1864	From Cav. Brig. Def. Yorktown, Va.	To 2-B. Cav. Div. Dept. Va. & N. C.	Apr., 1864
2d Mass. Heavy A. 3d Bn.Apr., 1864	From New Organization...........	To Dept. North Carolina..........	Apr., 1865
Batty. H, 3d N. Y. Arty.Apr., 1864	From Newport News, Va...........	To Arty. Brig. 18-Corps..........	July, 1864
8th N. Y. Indpt. Batty...Apr., 1864	From Arty. Yorktown, Va.........	No change to Muster Out..........	June, 1865
13th N. Y. Heavy Arty...Apr., 1864	From Forces Norfolk & Portsmouth.	To Prov'l Brig. 18-Corps.........	May, 1864
Batty. A, 1st Penna. Arty.Apr., 1864	From Forces Norfolk & Portsmouth.	To Unatt. Dept. Va. and N. C......	July, 1864
1st U. S. Vols..........Apr., 1864	From New Organization...........	To Dept. Virginia................	June, 1865
37th U. S. Colored Infy..Apr., 1864	From New Organization...........	To 1-Brig. Hinck's Div. 18-Corps...	May, 1864
38th U. S. Colored Infy..Apr., 1864	From New Organization...........	To Unatt. Dept. Va. & N. C........	June, 1864

NORFOLK AND PORTSMOUTH.—Continued.

20th New York Cav......Apr., 1864	From Cav. Brig. Portsmouth, Va....	To 1-B. Cav. Div. Dept. Va. & N. C.	Dec.,	1864
155th Ohio Infy........Apr., 1864	From Reserve Div. West Va......	No change to Muster Out..........	Aug.,	1864
Batty. B, 2d U. S. Col. A.Aug., 1864	From Unatt. Arty. Dept. Va. & N. C.	To Dept. Texas.................	May,	1865
1st U. S. Colored Cav....Aug., 1864	From 1-Brig. 3-Div. 18-Corps.......	To Dept. Virginia.............	May,	1865
85th Penna. Infy Det...Oct., 1864	From 1-Brig. 1-Div. 10-Corps.......	Consolidated with 188th Penna......	Nov.,	1864
2d U. S. Vols.........Oct., 1864	From New Organization...........	To Dept. Virginia.............	May,	1865
4th U. S. Vols.........Nov., 1864	From New Organization...........	To Dept. Virginia.............	May,	1865
3d New York Cav.......Dec., 1864	From 1-B. Cav. Div. D. Va. & N. C.	To Dept. Virginia.............	May,	1865
104th Penna. Infy.......Apr., 1865	From 1-B. Def. Bermuda Hundred..	No change to Muster Out..........	Aug.,	1865

EASTERN SHORE.—

Purnell Legion Md. Cav..June, 1864	From Eastville, Md., Dept. Va.&N.C.	No change to Muster Out..........	July,	1865
1st Va. Loyal Co. A.....June, 1864	From New Organization...........	No change to Muster Out..........	Oct.,	1865
11th Pa. Cav., Co. L.....Aug., 1864	From 2-B. Cav. Div. D. Va. & N. C.	No change to Muster Out..........	Aug.,	1865
3d Penna. H. A. Det.....Aug., 1864	From Norfolk & Portsmouth E. Va.	To Dept. Virginia.............	June,	1865
20th N. Y. Cav., Co. E....Dec., 1864	From Norfolk & Portsmouth E. Va.	No change to Muster Out..........	June,	1865

DEFENSES YORKTOWN AND WILLIAMSBURG.—

1st N. Y. Mounted Rifles..Apr., 1864	From Cav. Brig. Yorktown.........	To Unatt. Dept. Va. & N. C......	May,	1864
Batty. E, 3d N. Y. Arty..Apr., 1864	From Arty. Brig. Yorktown.......	To Arty. 2-Div. 18-Corps......	May,	1864
Batty. E, 1st Penna. Arty.Apr., 1864	From Arty. Brig. Yorktown.......	To Unatt. Dept. Va. and N. C......	June,	1864
1st U. S. Colored Cav....Apr., 1864	From Fort Monroe..............	To 1-Brig. 3-Div. 18-Corps......	June,	1864
2d U. S. Colored Cav.....Apr., 1864	From Fort Monroe..............	To 2-Brig. 3-Div. 10-Corps......	June,	1864
16th N. Y. Heavy Arty....Apr., 1864	From Arty. U. S. Forces Yorktown..	To 1-Brig. 3-Div. 10-Corps, Cos. G. K.	July,	1864
		To 2-B. 1-D. 10-Corps,A,B,C,F,G,L,M.	July,	1864

Twenty-Fourth Army Corps

Created Dec. 3, 1864, General Order No. 297, A. G. O., and composed of the White Troops of the 10th and 18th Army Corps, Army of the James, Department of Virginia and North Carolina. Discontinued Aug. 1, 1865, by General Order No. 131, A. G. O.

CORPS COMMANDERS.

E. O. C. Ord..........	Major General.....................	Dec. 3, 1864, to Dec. 6, 1864.
A. H. Terry..........	Bvt. Major General...............	Dec. 6, 1864, to Jan. 2, 1865.
Charles Devens, Jr.....	Brigadier General.................	Jan. 2, 1865, to Jan. 15, 1865.
John Gibbon..........	Major General.....................	Jan. 15, 1865, to Apr. 27, 1865.
John W. Turner........	Bvt. Major General...............	Apr. 27, 1865, to May 17, 1865.
John Gibbon..........	Major General.....................	May 17, 1865, to July 8, 1865.
John W. Turner........	Bvt. Major General...............	July 8, 1865, to Aug. 1, 1865.

1st DIVISION.—   **COMMANDERS.**

A. H. Terry..........	Bvt. Major General...............	Dec. 3, 1864, to Dec. 6, 1864.
R. S. Foster..........	Brigadier General.................	Dec. 6, 1864, Jan. 1, 1865.
J. R. Hawley..........	Brigadier General.................	Jan. 1, 1865, to Feb. 2, 1865.
R. S. Foster..........	Brigadier General.................	Feb. 2, 1865, to May 2, 1865.
T. O. Osborne..........	Bvt. Brig. General................	May 2, 1865, to July 8, 1865.
R. S. Foster..........	Bvt. Major General...............	July 8, 1865, to Aug. 1, 1865.

1st BRIGADE.—   **COMMANDERS.**

A. C. Voris..........	Col. 67th Ohio Infy..............	Dec. 3, 1864, to Dec. 12, 1864.
T. O. Osborne..........	Col. 39th Illinois Infy...........	Dec. 12, 1864, to May 2, 1865.
J. C. Briscoe..........	Bvt. Brig. General...............	May 2, 1865, to June 28, 1865.
H. R. West..........	Lt.-Col. 62d Ohio Infy...........	June 28, 1865, to July 8, 1865.
T. O. Osborne..........	Bvt. Brig. General...............	July 8, 1865, to July 25, 1865.
H. S. Fairchild..........	Bvt. Brig. General...............	July 25, 1865, to Aug. 1, 1865.

85th Penna. Infy........Dec., 1864	From 1-Brig. 1-Div. 10-Corps......	Consolidated with 188th Penna......	Dec.,	1864
199th Penna. Infy........Dec., 1864	From 1-Brig. 1-Div. 10-Corps......	Consolidated with 188th Penna......	June,	1865
62d Ohio Infy...........Dec., 1864	From 1-Brig. 1-Div. 10-Corps......	To Dept. Virginia................	Aug.,	1865
67th Ohio Infy..........Dec., 1864	From 1-Brig. 1-Div. 10-Corps......	To Dept. Virginia................	Aug.,	1865
39th Illinois Infy........Dec., 1864	From 1-Brig. 1-Div. 10-Corps......	To Dept. Virginia................	Aug.,	1865

2d BRIGADE.—   **COMMANDERS.**

J. R. Hawley..........	Brigadier General.................	Dec. 3, 1864, to Jan. 1, 1865.
J. C. Abbott..........	Col. 7th N. H. Infy...............	Jan. 1, 1865, to Jan. 6, 1865.

Brigade transferred to Terry's Provisional Corps, North Carolina, Jan., 1865. Reorganized from 4th Brigade, 1st Division, May, 1865.

H. S. Fairchild..........	Col. 89th N. Y. Infy.............	May 20, 1865, to July 25, 1865.
G. B. Dandy..........	Bvt. Brig. General...............	July 25, 1865, to Aug. 1, 1865.

3d N. H. Infy..........Dec., 1864	From 2-Brig. 1-Div. 10-Corps......	To Terry's Prov'l. Corps N. C......	Jan.,	1865
7th N. H. Infy..........Dec., 1864	From 2-Brig. 1-Div. 10-Corps......	To Terry's Prov'l. Corps N. C......	Jan.,	1865
6th Conn. Infy..........Dec., 1864	From 2-Brig. 1-Div. 10-Corps......	To Terry's Prov'l. Corps N. C......	Jan.,	1865
7th Conn. Infy..........Dec., 1864	From 2-Brig. 1-Div. 10-Corps......	To Terry's Prov'l. Corps N. C......	Jan.,	1865
16th N. Y. Heavy Arty...Dec., 1864	From 2-Brig. 1-Div. 10-Corps......	To Terry's Prov'l. Corps N. C......	Jan.,	1865
(Cos. A, B, C, F, G, K, M.)				
8th Maine Infy.........May, 1865	From 4-Brig. 1-Div. 24-Corps......	To Dept. of Virginia...........	Aug.,	1865
89th N. Y. Infy.........May, 1865	From 4-Brig. 1-Div. 24-Corps......	No change to Muster Out..........	Aug.,	1865
148th N. Y. Infy.........May, 1865	From 4-Brig. 1-Div. 24-Corps......	No change to Muster Out..........	June,	1865
158th N. Y. Infy.........May, 1865	From 4-Brig. 1-Div. 24-Corps......	No change to Muster Out..........	Aug.,	1865
55th Penna. Infy........May, 1865	From 4-Brig. 1-Div. 24-Corps......	No change to Muster Out..........	Aug.,	1865
100th N. Y. Infy.........July, 1865	From 3-Brig. 1-Div. 24-Corps......	To Dept. of Virginia...........	Aug.,	1865
24th Mass. Infy.........July, 1865	From 3-Brig. 1-Div. 24-Corps......	To Dept. of Virginia...........	Aug.,	1865
10th Conn. Infy.........July, 1865	From 3-Brig. 1-Div. 24-Corps......	To Dept. of Virginia...........	Aug.,	1865
11th Maine Infy.........July, 1865	From 3-Brig. 1-Div. 24-Corps......	No change to Muster Out..........	Aug.,	1865

3d BRIGADE.—   **COMMANDERS.**

H. M. Plaisted..........	Col. 11th Maine Infy.............	Dec. 3, 1864, to Feb. 2, 1865.
G. B. Dandy..........	Col. 100th N. Y. Infy.............	Feb. 2, 1865, to May 12, 1865.
E. S. Greely..........	Col. 10th Conn. Infy.............	May 12, 1865, to June 12, 1865.
G. B. Dandy..........	Col. 100th N. Y. Infy.............	June 12, 1865, to July 25, 1865.

11th Maine Infy.........Dec., 1864	From 3-Brig. 1-Div. 10-Corps......	To 2-Brig. 1-Div. 24-Corps........	July,	1865
24th Mass. Infy.........Dec., 1864	From 3-Brig. 1-Div. 10-Corps......	To 2-Brig. 1-Div. 24-Corps........	July,	1865
10th Conn. Infy.........Dec., 1864	From 3-Brig. 1-Div. 10-Corps......	To 2-Brig. 1-Div. 24-Corps........	July,	1865
100th N. Y. Infy.........Dec., 1864	From 3-Brig. 1-Div. 10-Corps......	To 2-Brig. 1-Div. 24-Corps........	July,	1865
206th Penna. Infy.......Dec., 1864	From 3-Brig. 1-Div. 10-Corps......	No change to Muster Out..........	June,	1865

4th BRIGADE.— COMMANDERS.

James Jourdan	Bvt. Brig. General	Dec. 3, 1864, to Mch. 17, 1865.
H. S. Fairchild	Col. 89th New York Infy	Mch. 17, 1865, to May 20, 1865.

Brigade discontinued May, 1865, and transferred to 2d Brigade 1st Division.

8th Maine Infy....Dec., 1864	From 2-Brig. 2-Div. 18-Corps	To 2-Brig. 1-Div. 24-Corps	May, 1865
89th New York Infy....Dec., 1864	From 3-Brig. 2-Div. 18-Corps	To 2-Brig. 1-Div. 24-Corps	May, 1865
148th New York Infy....Dec., 1864	From 1-Brig. 2-Div. 18-Corps	To 2-Brig. 1-Div. 24-Corps	May, 1865
158th New York Infy....Dec., 1864	From 1-Brig. 2-Div. 18-Corps	To 2-Brig. 1-Div. 24-Corps	May, 1865
55th Penna. Infy....Dec., 1864	From 1-Brig. 2-Div. 18-Corps	To 2-Brig. 1-Div. 24-Corps	May, 1865

2d DIVISION.— COMMANDER.

Adelbert Ames	Brigadier General	Dec. 3, 1864, to Jan. 6, 1865.

Division transfered to Terry's Provisional Corps, North Carolina, Jan., 1865.

1st BRIGADE.— COMMANDER.

N. M. Curtis	Bvt. Brig. General	Dec. 3, 1864, to Jan. 6, 1865.

3d New York Infy....Dec., 1864	From 1-Brig. 2-Div. 10-Corps	To Terry's Prov'l Corps N. C.	Jan., 1865
112th New York Infy....Dec., 1864	From 1-Brig. 2-Div. 10-Corps	To Terry's Prov'l Corps N. C.	Jan., 1865
117th New York Infy....Dec., 1864	From 1-Brig. 2-Div. 10-Corps	To Terry's Prov'l Corps N. C.	Jan., 1865
142d New York Infy....Dec., 1864	From 1-Brig. 2-Div. 10-Corps	To Terry's Prov'l Corps N. C.	Jan., 1865

2d BRIGADE.— COMMANDER.

G. Pennypacker	Col. 97th Penna. Infy	Dec. 3, 1864, to Jan. 6, 1865.

47th New York Infy....Dec., 1864	From 2-Brig. 2-Div. 10-Corps	To Terry's Prov'l Corps N. C.	Jan., 1865
48th New York Infy....Dec., 1864	From 2-Brig. 2-Div. 10-Corps	To Terry's Prov'l Corps N. C.	Jan., 1865
76th Penna. Infy....Dec., 1864	From 2-Brig. 2-Div. 10-Corps	To Terry's Prov'l Corps N. C.	Jan., 1865
97th Penna. Infy....Dec., 1864	From 2-Brig. 2-Div. 10-Corps	To Terry's Prov'l Corps N. C.	Jan., 1865
203d Penna. Infy....Dec., 1864	From 2-Brig. 2-Div. 10-Corps	To Terry's Prov'l Corps N. C.	Jan., 1865

3d BRIGADE.— COMMANDER.

Louis Bell	Col. 4th New Hampshire Infy	Dec. 3, 1864, to Jan. 6, 1865.

13th Indiana Infy....Dec., 1864	From 3-Brig. 2-Div. 10-Corps	To Terry's Prov'l Corps N. C.	Jan., 1865
9th Maine Infy....Dec., 1864	From 3-Brig. 2-Div. 10-Corps	To Terry's Prov'l Corps N. C.	Jan., 1865
4th New Hampshire Infy....Dec., 1864	From 3-Brig. 2-Div. 10-Corps	To Terry's Prov'l Corps N. C.	Jan., 1865
115th New York Infy....Dec., 1864	From 3-Brig. 2-Div. 10-Corps	To Terry's Prov'l Corps N. C.	Jan., 1865
169th New York Infy....Dec., 1864	From 3-Brig. 2-Div. 10-Corps	To Terry's Prov'l Corps N. C.	

3d DIVISION.— COMMANDER.

Charles Devens, Jr.	Brigadier General	Dec. 3, 1864, to July 10, 1865.

Division discontinued July 10, 1865.

1st BRIGADE.— COMMANDERS.

J. B. Raulston	Lt.-Col. 81st New York Infy	Dec. 3, 1864, to Jan. 15, 1865.
William Kreutzer	Lt.-Col. 98th New York Infy	Jan. 15, 1865, to Jan. 16, 1865.
E. M. Cullen	Col. 96th New York Infy	Jan. 16, 1865, to Mch. 22, 1865.
E. H. Ripley	Col. 9th Vermont Infy	Mch. 22, 1865, to Apr. 16, 1865.
G. F. Nichols	Col. 118th New York Infy	Apr. 16, 1865, to May 5, 1865.
E. H. Ripley	Bvt. Brig. General	May 5, 1865, to June 13, 1865.
R. H. Rice	Col. 11th Conn. Infy	June 13, 1865, to July 10, 1865.

11th Conn. Infy....Dec., 1864	From 2-Brig. 2-Div. 18-Corps	To 1st Indpt. Brig. 24-Corps	July, 1865
13th New Hamp. Infy....Dec., 1864	From 1-Brig. 1-Div. 18-Corps	No change to Muster Out	June, 1865
81st New York Infy....Dec., 1864	From 1-Brig. 1-Div. 18-Corps	To 1st Indpt. Brig. 24-Corps	July, 1865
98th New York Infy....Dec., 1864	From 1-Brig. 1-Div. 18-Corps	To 2-Brig. 3-Div. 24-Corps	June, 1865
139th New York Infy....Dec., 1864	From 1-Brig. 1-Div. 18-Corps	No change to Muster Out	June, 1865
19th Wisconsin Infy....Dec., 1864	From 2-Brig. 1-Div. 18-Corps	To 1st Indpt. Brig. 25-Corps	July, 1865
96th New York Infy....June, 1865	From 2-Brig. 3-Div. 24-Corps	To 1st Indpt. Brig. 25-Corps	July, 1865

2d BRIGADE.— COMMANDERS.

J. H. Potter	Col. 12th N. H. Infy	Dec. 3, 1864, to Jan. 17, 1865.
V. G. Barney	Lt.-Col. 9th Vermont Infy	Jan. 17, 1865, to Feb. 6, 1865.
J. E. Ward	Col. 8th Conn. Infy	Feb. 6, 1865, to Mch. 27, 1865.
M. T. Donohoe	Col. 10th N. H. Infy	Mch. 27, 1865, to June 30, 1865.
J. N. Patterson	Col. 2d N. H. Infy	June 30, 1865, to July 10, 1865.

5th Maryland Infy....Dec., 1864	From 3-Brig. 2-Div. 18-Corps	To 2d Indpt. Brig. 24-Corps	July, 1865
10th N. H. Infy....Dec., 1864	From 2-Brig. 1-Div. 18-Corps	No change to Muster Out	June, 1865
12th N. H. Infy....Dec., 1864	From Prov'l. Div. Dept. Va. & N. C.	No change to Muster Out	June, 1865
9th Vermont Infy....Dec., 1864	From 2-Brig. 2-Div. 18-Corps	To 2d Indpt. Brig. 24-Corps	July, 1865
96th N. Y. Infy....Dec., 1864	From 2-Brig. 1-Div. 18-Corps	To 1-Brig. 3-Div. 24-Corps	June, 1865
118th N. Y. Infy....Dec., 1864	From 2-Brig. 1-Div. 18-Corps	No change to Muster Out	June, 1865
8th Conn. Infy....June, 1865	From Headquarters 24-Corps	To 2d Indpt. Brig. 24-Corps	July, 1865
98th N. Y. Infy....June, 1865	From 1-Brig. 3-Div. 24-Corps	To 2d Indpt. Brig. 24-Corps	July, 1865

3d BRIGADE.— COMMANDER.

Guy V. Henry	Bvt. Brig. General	Dec. 3, 1864, to Jan. 29, 1865.
S. H. Roberts	Col. 139th N. Y. Infy	Jan. 29, 1865, to June 30, 1865.

Brigade discontinued June, 1865.

21st Conn. Infy....Dec., 1864	From 3-Brig. 1-Div. 18-Corps	No change to Muster Out	June, 1865
40th Mass. Infy....Dec., 1864	From 3-Brig. 1-Div. 18-Corps	No change to Muster Out	June, 1865
2d N. H. Infy....Dec., 1864	From 3-Brig. 1-Div. 18-Corps	No change to Muster Out	June, 1865
58th Penna. Infy....Dec., 1864	From 3-Brig. 1-Div. 18-Corps	To 1st Indpt. Brig. 24-Corps	July, 1865
188th Penna. Infy....Dec., 1864	From 3-Brig. 1-Div. 18-Corps	To 2d Indpt. Brig. 24-Corps	July, 1865

INDEPENDENT DIVISION.—Joined Corps from West Virginia Dec. 24, 1864.
COMMANDERS.

T. M. Harris	Bvt. Brig. General	Dec. 24, 1864, to Mch. 25, 1865.
John W. Turner	Bvt. Major General	Mch. 25, 1865, to Apr. 27, 1865.
T. M. Harris	Bvt. Brig. General	Apr. 27, 1865, to July 10, 1865.

1st BRIGADE.— COMMANDERS.

I. F. Wildes	Lt.-Col. 116th Ohio Infy	Dec. 24, 1864, to Feb. 3, 1865.
Andrew Potter	Lt.-Col. 34th Mass. Infy	Feb. 3, 1865, to Apr. 27, 1865.
W. S. Lincoln	Col. 34th Mass. Infy	Apr. 27, 1865, to June, 1865.
S. A. Simonson	Lt.-Col. 23d Illinois Infy	June, 1865, to July 10, 1865.

1st BRIGADE.—Continued.

34th Mass. Infy	Dec., 1864	From 2-Brig. 1-Infy. Div. W. Va..	No change to Muster Out	June,	1865
116th Ohio Infy	Dec., 1864	From 1-Brig. 1-Infy. Div. W. Va..	No change to Muster Out	June,	1865
123d Ohio Infy	Dec., 1864	From 1-Brig. 1-Infy. Div. W. Va..	No change to Muster Out	June,	1865
23d Illinois Infy	June, 1864	From 2-Brig. Indpt. Div. 24-Corps..	No change to Muster Out	July,	1865
54th Penna. Infy	June, 1864	From 2-Brig. Indpt. Div. 24-Corps..	No change to Muster Out	July,	1865
10th West Va. Infy	June, 1864	From 3-Brig. Indpt. Div. 24-Corps..	No change to Muster Out	July,	1865

2d BRIGADE.—   **COMMANDER.**

William B. Curtis	Col. 12th West Va. Infy	Dec. 24, 1864, to June 1, 1865.			
23 Illinois Infy	Dec., 1864	From 3-Brig. 1-Infy. Div. W. Va..	To 1-Brig. Indpt. Div. 24-Corps.	June,	1865
54th Penna. Infy	Dec., 1864	From 3-Brig. 1-Infy. Div. W. Va..	To 1-Brig. Indpt. Div. 24-Corps.	June,	1865
12th West Va. Infy	Dec., 1864	From 2-Brig. 1-Infy. Div. W. Va..	No change to Muster Out	June,	1865

3d BRIGADE.—   **COMMANDERS.**

M. S. Hall	Lt.-Col. 10th West Va. Infy	Dec. 24, 1864, to Mch. 25, 1865.			
T. M. Harris	Bvt. Brigadier General	Mch. 25, 1865, to Apr. 27, 1865.			
J. W. Holliday	Lt.-Col. 15th West Va. Infy	Apr. 27, 1865, to June 1, 1865.			
10th West Va. Infy	Dec., 1864	From 3-Brig. 1-Infy. Div. W. Va..	To 1-Brig. Indpt. Div. 24-Corps.	June,	1865
11th West Va. Infy	Dec., 1864	From 3-Brig. 1-Infy. Div. W. Va..	No change to Muster Out	June,	1865
15th West Va. Infy	Dec., 1864	From 3-Brig. 1-Infy. Div. W. Va..	No change to Muster Out	June,	1865

1st INDEPENDENT BRIGADE.—Organized July 10, 1865, from 3d Division. T. M. Harris, Brigadier General.

11th Conn. Infy	July, 1865	From 1-Brig. 3-Div. 24-Corps	To Dept. Virginia	Aug.,	1865
81st N. Y. Infy	July, 1865	From 1-Brig. 3-Div. 24-Corps	To Dept. Virginia	Aug.,	1865
96th N. Y. Infy	July, 1865	From 1-Brig. 3-Div. 24-Corps	No change to Muster Out	Aug.,	1865
19th Wis. Infy	July, 1865	From 1-Brig. 3-Div. 24-Corps	No change to Muster Out	Aug.,	1865
58th Penna. Infy	July, 1865	From 3-Brig. 3-Div. 24-Corps	To Dept. Virginia	Aug.,	1865

2d INDEPENDENT BRIGADE.—Organized July 10, 1865, from 3d Division. J. C. Briscoe, Bvt. Brig. General.

9th Vermont Infy	July, 1865	From 2-Brig. 3-Div. 24-Corps	To Dept. Virginia	Aug.,	1865
8th Conn. Infy	July, 1865	From 2-Brig. 3-Div. 24-Corps	To Dept. Virginia	Aug.,	1865
98th N. Y. Infy	July, 1865	From 2-Brig. 3-Div. 24-Corps	No change to Muster Out	Aug.,	1865
5th Maryland Infy	July, 1865	From 2-Brig. 3-Div. 24-Corps	No change to Muster Out	Aug.,	1865
188th Penna. Infy	July, 1865	From 3-Brig. 3-Div. 24-Corps	To Dept. Virginia	Aug.,	1865

ARTILLERY BRIGADE.—

Batty. E, 3d N. Y. Arty	Dec., 1864	From Arty. Brig. 18-Corps	No change to Muster Out	June,	1865
Batty. H, 3d N. Y. Arty	Dec., 1864	From Arty. Brig. 18-Corps	No change to Muster Out	June,	1865
Batty. K, 3d N. Y. Arty	Dec., 1864	From Arty. Brig. 18-Corps	No change to Muster Out	June,	1865
Batty. M, 3d N. Y. Arty	Dec., 1864	From Arty. Brig. 18-Corps	No change to Muster Out	June,	1865
7th N. Y. Indpt. Batty	Dec., 1864	From Arty. Brig. 18-Corps	To Ferrero's Div. Bermuda Hundred.	Jan.,	1865
16th N. Y. Indpt. Batty	Dec., 1864	From Arty. Brig. 18-Corps	To Terry's Prov'l Corps N. C.	Jan.,	1865
17th N. Y. Indpt. Batty	Dec., 1864	From Arty. Brig. 18-Corps	No change to Muster Out	June,	1865
Batty. A, 1st Penna. Arty	Dec., 1864	From Arty. Brig. 10-Corps	No change to Muster Out	July,	1865
Batty. F, 1st R. I. Arty	Dec., 1864	From Arty. Brig. 18-Corps	No change to Muster Out	June,	1865
Batty. L, 4th U. S. Arty	Dec., 1864	From Arty. Brig. 18-Corps	To Dept. Virginia	Aug.,	1865
Batty. A, 5th U. S. Arty	Dec., 1864	From Arty. Brig. 18-Corps	To Dept. Virginia	Aug.,	1865
Batty. F, 5th U. S. Arty	Dec., 1864	From Arty. Brig. 18-Corps	To Dept. Virginia	Aug.,	1865
Batty. B, 1st U. S. Arty	Apr., 1865	From Arty. Brig. 18-Corps	To Dept. Virginia	Aug.,	1865
7th N. Y. Indpt. Batty	Apr., 1865	From Def. Bermuda Hundred	No change to Muster Out	July,	1865

UNATTACHED.—

8th Conn. Infy	Dec., 1864	From 2-Brig. 1-Div. 18-Corps	To 2-Brig. 3-Div. 24-Corps	June,	1865
4th Mass. Cav., F, K	Dec., 1864	From Unatt. 18-Corps	To Dept. Virginia	Aug.,	1865

Twenty-Fifth Army Corps

Created Dec. 3, 1865, General Order No. 297, A. G. O., and composed of the Colored Troops of the 10th and 18th Army Corps, Army of the James, Dept. Va. & N. C. Corps transferred to Texas, May, 1865, and discontinued Jan. 8, 1866.

CORPS COMMANDERS.

Godfrey Weitzel	Major General	Dec. 3, 1864, to Jan. 1, 1865.
C. A. Heckman	Brigadier General	Jan. 1, 1865, to Feb. 2, 1865.
Godfrey Weitzel	Major General	Feb. 2, 1865, to Jan. 8, 1866.

1st DIVISION.—   **COMMANDERS.**

Charles J. Paine	Brigadier General	Dec. 3, 1864, to Dec. 31, 1864.

Designation of Division changed to 3d Division Dec. 31, 1864. Reorganized from 3d Division Dec. 31, 1864.

E. A. Wild	Brigadier General	Dec. 31, 1864, to Mch. 27, 1865.
A. V. Kautz	Bvt. Major General	Mch. 27, 1865, to May 4, 1865.
A. G. Draper	Brigadier General	May 4, 1865, to May 29, 1865.
G. A. Smith	Brigadier General	May 29, 1865, to Dec. 28, 1865.
J. G. Perkins	Col. 19th U. S. Colored Infy	Dec. 28, 1865, to Jan. 8, 1866.

1st BRIGADE.—   **COMMANDERS.**

Delevan Bates	Bvt. Brig. General	Dec. 3, 1864, to Dec. 31, 1864.
A. G. Draper	Bvt. Brig. General	Dec. 31, 1864, to May 4, 1865.
J. C. Moon	Col. 118th U. S. Colored Infy	May 4, 1865, to June 3, 1865.
A. G. Draper	Bvt. Brig. General	June 3, 1865, to July 7, 1865.
J. C. Moon	Col. 118th U. S. Colored Infy	July 7, 1865, to Sept. 22, 1865.
R. M. Hall	Col. 38th U. S. Colored Infy	Sept. 22, 1865, to Oct. 5, 1865.
T. M. Bayley	Col. 9th U. S. Colored Infy	Oct. 5, 1865, to Dec. 28, 1865.
J. G. Perkins	Col. 19th U. S. Colored Infy	Dec. 28, 1865, to Jan. 2, 1866.
G. M. Dennett	Lt.-Col. 9th U. S. Colored Infy	Jan. 2, 1866, to Jan. 8, 1866.

1st U. S. Colored Infy	Dec., 1864	From 1-Brig. 3-Div. 18-Corps	To 1-Brig. 3-Div. 25-Corps	Dec.,	1864
27th U. S. Colored Infy	Dec., 1864	From 1-Brig. 3-Div. 9-Corps	To 3-Brig. 3-Div. 25-Corps	Dec.,	1864
30th U. S. Colored Infy	Dec., 1864	From 1-Brig. 3-Div. 9-Corps	To 1-Brig. 3-Div. 25-Corps	Dec.,	1864
22d U. S. Colored Infy	Dec., 1863	From 1-Brig. 3-Div. 25-Corps	To Dept. Texas	May,	1865
36th U. S. Colored Infy	Dec., 1864	From 1-Brig. 3-Div. 25-Corps	To Dept. Texas	May,	1865
38th U. S. Colored Infy	Dec., 1864	From 1-Brig. 3-Div. 25-Corps	To Dept. Texas	May,	1865
38th U. S. Colored Infy	Dec., 1864	From 1-Brig. 6-Div. 25-Corps	To Dept. Texas	May,	1865
118th U. S. Colored Infy	Dec., 1864	From 1-Brig. 3-Div. 25-Corps	To Dept. Texas	May,	1865

2d BRIGADE.— COMMANDERS.

S. A. Duncan	Bvt. Brig. General	Dec. 3, 1864, to Dec. 31, 1864.
J. W. Ames	Col. 6th U. S. Colored Infy	Dec. 31, 1864, to Jan. 20, 1865.
C. S. Russell	Bvt. Brig. General	Jan. 20, 1865, to Feb. 27, 1865.
T. M. Bayley	Col. 9th U. S. Colored Infy	Feb. 27, 1865, to Mch. 3, 1865.
T. D. Sedgwick	Col. 114th U. S. Colored Infy	Mch. 3, 1865, to Mch. 28, 1865.
E. A. Wild	Brigadier General	Mch. 28, 1865, to Apr. 18, 1865.
T. D. Sedgwick	Col. 114th U. S. Colored Infy	Apr. 18, 1865, to Sept. 22, 1865.
T. M. Bayley	Col. 9th U. S. Colored Infy	Sept. 22, 1865, to Oct. 5, 1865.
R. M. Hall	Col. 38th U. S. Colored Infy	Oct. 5, 1865, to Dec. 8, 1865.
J. C. Moon	Col. 118th U. S. Colored Infy	Dec. 8, 1865, to Jan. 2, 1866.
D. Branson	Lt.-Col. 62d U. S. Colored Infy	Jan. 2, 1866, to Jan. 8, 1866.

4th U. S. Colored Infy	Dec., 1864	From 3-Brig. 3-Div. 18-Corps	To 2-Brig. 3-Div. 25-Corps	Dec., 1864
6th U. S. Colored Infy	Dec., 1864	From 3-Brig. 3-Div. 18-Corps	To 2-Brig. 3-Div. 25-Corps	Dec., 1864
39th U. S. Colored Infy	Dec., 1864	From 1-Brig. 3-Div. 9-Corps	To 2-Brig. 3-Div. 25-Corps	Dec., 1864
29th Conn. Colored Infy	Dec., 1864	From 2-Brig. 3-Div. 25-Corps	To Dist. St. Mary's	Apr., 1865
9th U. S. Colored Infy	Dec., 1864	From 2-Brig. 3-Div. 25-Corps	To Dept. Texas	May, 1865
41st U. S. Colored Infy	Dec., 1864	From 2-Brig. 3-Div. 25-Corps	To 2-Brig. 2-Div. 25-Corps	Jan., 1865
117th U. S. Colored Infy	Jan., 1865	From 1-Brig. 2-Div. 25-Corps	To Dept. Texas	May, 1865
115th U. S. Colored Infy	Mch., 1865	From 1-Brig. 2-Div. 25-Corps	To Dept. Texas	May, 1865
114th U. S. Colored Infy	Apr., 1865	From 3-Brig. 1-Div. 25-Corps	To Dept. Texas	May, 1865

3d BRIGADE.— COMMANDERS.

E. Wright	Col. 10th U. S. Colored Infy	Dec. 3, 1864, to Dec. 31, 1864.
H. G. Thomas	Brigadier General	Dec. 31, 1864, to Apr. 27, 1865.
S. B. Yeoman	Col. 43d U. S. Colored Infy	Apr. 27, 1865, to July 27, 1865.
T. H. Barrett	Col. 62d U. S. Colored Infy	July 27, 1865, to Sept. 29, 1865.
J. G. Perkins	Lt.-Col. 9th U. S. Colored Infy	Sept. 29, 1865, to Oct 10, 1865.

Brigade discontinued Oct. 1865.

5th U. S. Colored Infy	Dec., 1864	From 2-Brig. 3-Div. 18-Corps	To 3-Brig. 3-Div. 25-Corps	Dec., 1864
10th U. S. Colored Infy	Dec., 1864	From 1-Brig. 3-Div. 18-Corps	To 3-Brig. 3-Div. 25-Corps	Dec., 1864
37th U. S. Colored Infy	Dec., 1864	From 1-Brig. 3-Div. 18-Corps	To 3-Brig. 3-Div. 25-Corps	Dec., 1864
107th U. S. Colored Infy	Dec., 1864	From rPov'l Brig. 3-Div. 18-Corps	To 3-Brig. 3-Div. 25-Corps	Dec., 1864
19th U. S. Col'd Infy	Dec., 1864	From 3-Brig. 3-Div. 25-Corps	To Dept. Texas	May, 1865
23d U. S. Col'd Infy	Dec., 1864	From 3-Brig. 3-Div. 25-Corps	To Dept. Texas	May, 1865
43d U. S. Col'd Infy	Dec., 1864	From 3-Brig. 3-Div. 25-Corps	To Dept. Texas	May, 1865
114th U. S. Col'd Infy	Jan., 1865	From Dept. Ky.	To 2-Brig. 1-Div. 25-Corps	Apr., 1865
10th U. S. Col'd Infy	Mch., 1865	From 3-Brig. 3-Div. 25-Corps	To Dist. St. Mary's 22-Corps	Apr., 1865
28th U. S. Col'd Infy	Mch., 1865	From 3-Brig. 2-Div. 25-Corps	To Dist. St. Mary's 22-Corps	Apr., 1865

2d DIVISION.— COMMANDERS.

William Birney	Brigadier General	Dec. 3, 1864, to Feb. 21, 1865.
J. Shaw, Jr.	Col. 7th U. S. Colored Infy	Feb. 21, 1865, to Mch. 27, 1865.
William Birney	Brigadier General	Mch. 27, 1865, to Apr. 10, 1865.
R. H. Jackson	Bvt. Brig. General	Apr. 10, 1865, to Nov. 4, 1865.
T. H. Barrett	Col. 62d U. S. Colored Infy	Nov. 4, 1865, to Jan. 8, 1866.

1st BRIGADE.— COMMANDERS.

J. Shaw, Jr.	Col. 7th U. S. Colored Infy	Dec. 3, 1864, to Dec. 8, 1864.
C. S. Russell	Col. 28th U. S. Colored Infy	Dec. 8, 1864, to Jan. 1, 1865.
J. Shaw, Jr.	Col. 7th U. S. Colored Infy	Jan. 1, 1865, to Feb. 21, 1865.
O. A. Bartholomew	Col. 109th U. S. Colored Infy	Feb. 21, 1865, to Mch. 27, 1865.
J. Shaw, Jr.	Col. 7th U. S. Colored Infy	Mch. 27, 1865, to June 20, 1865.
H. W. Barry	Col. 8th U. S. Colored Infy	June 20, 1865, to July 1, 1865.
J. Shaw, Jr.	Col. 7th U. S. Colored Infy	July 1, 1865, to Jan. 8, 1866.

7th U. S. Colored Infy	Dec., 1864	From 1-Brig. 3-Div. 10-Corps	To Dept. Texas	May, 1865
109th U. S. Colored Infy	Dec., 1864	From Dept. Kentucky	To Dept. Texas	May, 1865
116th U. S. Colored Infy	Dec., 1864	From Unatt. 10th Corps	To 3-Brig. 2-Div. 25-Corps	Apr., 1865
117th U. S. Colored Infy	Dec., 1864	From Prov'l Brig. 3-Div. 18-Corps	To Dept. Texas	May, 1865
115th U. S. Colored Infy	Jan., 1865	From Dept. Kentucky	To 2-Brig. 1-Div. 25-Corps	Mch., 1865
8th U. S. Colored Infy	Apr., 1865	From 2-Brig. 2-Div. 25-Corps	To Dept. Texas	May, 1865

2d BRIGADE.— COMMANDERS.

U. Doubleday	Bvt. Brig. General	Dec. 3, 1864, to May, 1865.
L. F. Haskell	Bvt. Brig. General	May, 1865, to June, 1865.
U. Doubleday	Bvt. Brig. General	June, 1865, to July, 1865.
L. F. Haskell	Bvt. Brig. General	July, 1865, to Sept., 1865.
S. C. Armstrong	Col. 8th U. S. Colored Infy	Sept., 1865, to Oct. 12, 1865.
T. H. Barrett	Col. 62d U. S. Colored Infy	Oct. 12, 1865, to Nov. 4, 1865.
L. G. Brown	Col. 117th U. S. Colored Infy	Nov. 4, 1865, to Jan. 8, 1866.

8th U. S. Colored Infy	Dec., 1864	From 2-Brig. 3-Div. 10-Corps	To 1-Brig. 2-Div. 25-Corps	Apr., 1865
45th U. S. Colored Infy	Dec., 1864	From 2-Brig. 3-Div. 10-Corps	To Dept. Texas	May, 1865
127th U. S. Colored Infy	Dec., 1864	From 2-Brig. 3-Div. 10-Corps	To Dept. Texas	May, 1865
41st U. S. Colored Infy	Jan., 1865	From 2-Brig. 1-Div. 25-Corps	To Dept. Texas	May, 1865

3d BRIGADE.— COMMANDERS.

C. S. Russell	Col. 28th U. S. Colored Infy	Dec. 3, 1864, to Dec. 8, 1864.
H. C. Ward	Col. 31st U. S. Colored Infy	Dec. 8, 1864, to Jan. 10, 1865.
E. Martindale	Col. 81st U. S. Colored Infy	Jan. 10, 1865, to Mch. 23, 1865.
W. W. Woodward	Col. 116th U. S. Colored Infy	Mch. 23, 1865, to Sept. 15, 1865.
H. C. Ward	Col. 31st U. S. Colored Infy	Sept. 15, 1865, to Oct. 22, 1865.

Brigade discontinued Oct., 1865.

28th U. S. Colored Infy	Dec., 1864	From 2-Brig. 3-Div. 9-Corps	To Attached Brig. 1-Div. 25-Corps	Apr., 1865
29th U. S. Colored Infy	Dec., 1864	From 2-Brig. 3-Div. 9-Corps	To Dept. Texas	May, 1865
31st U. S. Colored Infy	Dec., 1864	From 2-Brig. 3-Div. 9-Corps	To Dept. Texas	May, 1865
116th U. S. Colored Infy	Apr., 1865	From 1-Brig. 2-Div. 25-Corps	To Dept. Texas	May, 1865

3d DIVISION.— COMMANDERS.

C. A. Heckman	Brigadier General	Dec. 3, 1864, to Dec. 30, 1864.
E. A. Wild	Brigadier General	Dec. 30, 1864, to Dec. 31, 1864.

Designation changed to 1st Division Dec. 31, 1864. Reorganized from 1st Division Dec. 31, 1864.

Chas. J. Paine	Brigadier General	Dec. 31, 1864, to Jan. 6, 1865.

Division transferred to Terry's Provisional Corps, North Carolina.
Division reorganized in Texas July 6, 1865.

A. G. Draper	Bvt. Brig. General	July 6, 1865, to Aug. 1, 1865.
W. T. Clark	Brigadier General	Aug. 1, 1865, to Oct. 25, 1865.
G. W. Cole	Bvt. Brig. General	Oct. 25, 1865, to Dec. 20, 1865.
W. T. Clark	Brigadier General	Dec. 20, 1865, to Jan. 8, 1866.

1st BRIGADE.—

COMMANDERS.

A. G. Draper	Bvt. Brig. General	Dec. 3, 1864, to Dec. 31, 1864.
Delevan Bates	Bvt. Brigadier General	Dec. 31, 1864, to Jan. 6, 1865.
C. S. Russell	Bvt. Brig. General	July 6, 1865, to Oct. 25, 1865.
T. J. White	Lt.-Col. 2d U. S. Colored Infy	Oct. 25, 1865, to Jan. 8, 1866.

22d U. S. Colored Infy	Dec., 1864	From 1-Brig. 3-Div. 18-Corps	To 1-Brig. 1-Div. 25-Corps	Dec., 1864
36th U. S. Colored Infy	Dec., 1864	From 2-Brig. 3-Div. 18-Corps	To 1-Brig. 1-Div. 25-Corps	Dec., 1864
38th U. S. Colored Infy	Dec., 1864	From 2-Brig. 3-Div. 18-Corps	To 1-Brig. 1-Div. 25-Corps	Dec., 1864
118th U. S. Colored Infy	Dec., 1864	From Prov'l Brig. 3-Div. 18-Corps	To 1-Brig. 1-Div. 25-Corps	Dec., 1864
1st U. S. Colored Infy	Dec., 1864	From 1-Brig. 1-Div. 25-Corps	To 1-Brig. 3-Div. Terry's Prov'l C.	Jan., 1865
27th U. S. Colored Infy	Dec., 1864	From 1-Brig. 1-Div. 25-Corps	To 3-Brig. 3-Div. 25-Corps	Jan., 1865
30th U. S. Colored Infy	Dec., 1864	From 1-Brig. 1-Div. 25-Corps	To 1-Brig. 3-Div. Terry's Prov'l C.	Jan., 1865
107th U. S. Colored Infy	Jan., 1865	From 3-Brig. 3-Div. 25-Corps	To 1-Brig. 3-Div. Terry's Prov'l C.	Jan., 1865

2d BRIGADE.—

COMMANDERS.

E. Martindale	Col. 81st U. S. Colored Infy	Dec. 3, 1864, to Dec. 31, 1864.
J. W. Ames	Col. 6th U. S. Colored Infy	Dec. 31, 1864, to Jan. 6, 1865.
J. Given	Lt.-Col. 127th U. S. Colored Infy	July 20, 1865, to Oct. 12, 1865.
J. H. Davidson	Col. 122d U. S. Colored Infy	Oct. 12, 1865, to Nov. 5, 1865.
E. H. Powell	Lt.-Col. 10th U. S. Colored Infy	Nov. 5, 1865, to Jan. 8, 1866.

29th Conn. Colored Infy	Dec., 1864	From 1-Brig. 3-Div. 10-Corps	To 2-Brig. 1-Div. 25-Corps	Dec., 1864
9th U. S. Colored Infy	Dec., 1864	From 1-Brig. 3-Div. 10-Corps	To 2-Brig. 1-Div. 25-Corps	Dec., 1864
41st U. S. Colored Infy	Dec., 1864	From 2-Brig. 3-Div. 10-Corps	To 2-Brig. 1-Div. 25-Corps	Dec., 1864
4th U. S. Colored Infy	Dec., 1864	From 1-Brig. 1-Div. 25-Corps	To 2-Brig. 3-Div. Terry's Prov'l C.	Jan., 1865
6th U. S. Colored Infy	Dec., 1864	From 1-Brig. 1-Div. 25-Corps	To 2-Brig. 3-Div. Terry's Prov'l C.	Jan., 1865
39th U. S. Colored Infy	Dec., 1864	From 1-Brig. 1-Div. 25-Corps	To 2-Brig. 3-Div. Terry's Prov'l C.	Jan., 1865

3d BRIGADE.—

COMMANDERS.

H. G. Thomas	Brigadier General	Dec. 15, 1864, to Dec. 31, 1864.
E. Wright	Col. 10th U. S. Colored Infy	Dec. 31, 1864, to Jan. 6, 1865.
Reorganized from Cavalry Brigade July, 1865.		
G. W. Cole	Bvt. Brig. General	July, 1865, to Oct., 1865.
Brigade discontinued Oct., 1865.		

19th U. S. Colored Infy	Dec., 1864	From 2-Brig. 3-Div. 9-Corps	To 3-Brig. 1-Div. 25-Corps	Dec., 1864
23d U. S. Colored Infy	Dec., 1864	From 3-Div. 9-Corps	To 3-Brig. 1-Div. 25-Corps	Dec., 1864
43d U. S. Colored Infy	Dec., 1864	From 1-Brig. 3-Div. 9-Corps	To 3-Brig. 1-Div. 25-Corps	Dec., 1864
5th U. S. Colored Infy	Dec., 1864	From 3-Brig. 1-Div. 25-Corps	To 2-Brig. 3-Div. Terry's Prov'l C.	Jan., 1865
10th U. S. Colored Infy	Dec., 1864	From 3-Brig. 1-Div. 25-Corps	To Attached Brig. 1-Div. 25-Corps	Jan., 1865
37th U. S. Colored Infy	Dec., 1864	From 3-Brig. 1-Div. 25-Corps	To 3-Brig. 3-Div. Terry's Prov'l C.	Jan., 1865
107th U. S. Colored Infy	Dec., 1864	From 3-Brig. 1-Div. 25-Corps	To 1-Brig. 3-Div. 25-Corps	Jan., 1865
27th U. S. Colored Infy	Jan., 1865	From 1-Brig. 3-Div. 25-Corps	To 3-Brig. 3-Div. Terry's Prov'l C.	Jan., 1865

ARTILLERY BRIGADE.—

1st Conn. Batty	Dec., 1864	From Arty. Brig. 10-Corps	No change to Muster Out	June, 1865
4th New Jersey Batty	Dec., 1864	From Arty. Brig. 10-Corps	No change to Muster Out	June, 1865
5th New Jersey Batty	Dec., 1864	From Arty. Brig. 10-Corps	No change to Muster Out	June, 1865
16th N. Y. Heavy Arty Det.	Dec., 1864	From Arty. Brig. 10-Corps	To Dept. Washington 22-Corps	July, 1865
Batty. E, 1st Penna. Arty	Dec., 1864	From Arty. Brig. 10-Corps	No change to Muster Out	July, 1865
Batty. C, 3d R. I. Arty	Dec., 1864	From Arty. Brig. 10-Corps	No change to Muster Out	June, 1865
Batty. D, 1st U. S. Arty	Dec., 1864	From Arty. Brig. 10-Corps	To Dept. Texas	May, 1865
Batty. M, 1st U. S. Arty	Dec., 1864	From Arty. Brig. 10-Corps	To Dept. Texas	May, 1865
Batty. E, 3d U. S. Arty	Dec., 1864	From Arty. Brig. 10-Corps	To Arty. 3-Div. Terry's Prov'l C.	Jan., 1865
Batty. D, 4th U. S. Arty	Dec., 1864	From Arty. Brig. 10-Corps	To Dept. Texas	May, 1865

CAVALRY BRIGADE.—Organized May, 1865. Designated 3d Brigade, 3d Division, 25-Corps, July, 1865.

COMMANDER.

G. W. Cole	Bvt. Brig. General	May, 1865, to July, 1865.

1st U. S. Colored Cav	May, 1865	From Unatt. Dept. Va.	To Dept. Texas	May, 1865
2d U. S. Colored Cav	May, 1865	From Unatt. 25-Corps	To Dept. Texas	May, 1865
UNASSIGNED.—				
2d U. S. Colored Cav	Dec., 1864	From Unatt. 3-Div. 10-Corps	To Cav. Brig. 25-Corps	May, 1865
5th Mass. Cav. Colored	Mch., 1865	From Point Lookout, Md.	To Dept. Texas	May, 1865
122d U. S. Colored Infy	Apr., 1865	From Dept. Kentucky	To Dept. Texas	May, 1865

Middle Military Division---Department of the Shenandoah

Organized Aug., 1864, by transfer of the 6th Army Corps from Army of the Potomac, Detachment of the 19th Army Corps, Department of the Gulf, 1st and 3d Divisions Cavalry Corps Army of the Potomac and the Army of West Virginia.

COMMANDERS.

Philip H. Sheridan	Major General	Aug. 6, 1864, to Feb. 28, 1865.
A. T. A. Torbert	Major General	Feb. 28, 1865, to Mch. 7, 1865.
W. S. Hancock	Major General	Mch. 7, 1865, to June 27, 1865.

Army of the Shenandoah

COMMANDERS.

Philip H. Sheridan	Major General	Aug. 6, 1864, to Oct. 16, 1864.
H. G. Wright	Major General	Oct. 16, 1864, to Oct. 19, 1864.
Philip H. Sheridan	Major General	Oct. 19, 1864, to Feb. 28, 1865.
A. T. A. Torbert	Major General	Feb. 28, 1865, to June 27, 1865.

Sixth Army Corps

COMMANDERS.

H. G. Wright	Major General	Aug. 6, 1864, to Oct. 16, 1864.
J. B. Ricketts	Brigadier General	Oct. 16, 1864, to Oct. 19, 1864.
Geo. W. Getty	Bvt. Major General	Oct. 19, 1864.
H. G. Wright	Major General	Oct. 19, 1864, to Dec. 6, 1864.
Rejoined Army of the Potomac.		

1st DIVISION.— COMMANDERS.

D. A. Russell	Brigadier General	Aug. 6, 1864, to Sept. 19, 1864.	Killed.
Emory Upton	Brigadier General	Sept. 19, 1864.	
Oliver Edwards	Col. 37th Mass. Infy	Sept. 19, 1864, to Sept. 21, 1864.	
Frank Wheaton	Brigadier General	Sept. 21, 1864, to Dec. 6, 1864.	

1st BRIGADE.— COMMANDERS.

W. H. Penrose	Col. 15th N. J. Infy	Aug. 6, 1864, to Sept. 18, 1864.	
E. L. Campbell	Lt.-Col. 4th N. J. Infy	Sept. 18, 1864 to Sept. 20, 1864.	
W. H. Penrose	Col. 15th N. J. Infy	Sept. 20, 1864, to Oct. 19, 1864.	
E. L. Campbell	Lt.-Col. 4th N. J. Infy	Oct. 19, 1864.	
B. Hufty	Capt. 4th N. J. Infy	Oct. 19, 1864, to Dec. 6, 1864.	

4th N. J. Infy	Aug., 1864	From 1-Brig. 1-Div. 6-Corps Pot	To 1-Brig. 1-Div. 6-Corps Pot	Dec.,	1864
10th N. J. Infy	Aug., 1864	From 1-Brig. 1-Div. 6-Corps Pot	To 1-Brig. 1-Div. 6-Corps Pot	Dec.,	1864
15th N. J. Infy	Aug., 1864	From 1-Brig. 1-Div. 6-Corps Pot	To 1-Brig. 1-Div. 6-Corps Pot	Dec.,	1864

2d BRIGADE.— COMMANDERS.

Emory Upton	Brigadier General	Aug. 6, 1864, to Sept. 19, 1864.	
J. E. Hamblin	Col. 65th N. Y. Infy	Sept. 19, 1864, to Oct. 19, 1864.	
E. Olcott	Lt.-Col. 121st N. Y. Infy	Oct. 19, 1864, to Nov. 3, 1864.	
R. S. Mackenzie	Col. 2d Conn. Heavy Arty	Nov. 3, 1864, to Dec. 6, 1864.	

2d Conn. Heavy Arty	Aug., 1864	From 2-Brig. 1-Div. 6-Corps Pot	To 2-Brig. 1-Div. 6-Corps Pot	Dec.,	1864
65th N. Y. Infy	Aug., 1864	From 2-Brig. 1-Div. 6-Corps Pot	To 2-Brig. 1-Div. 6-Corps Pot	Dec.,	1864
67th N. Y. Infy	Aug., 1864	From 2-Brig. 1-Div. 6-Corps Pot	No change to Muster Out	Sept.,	1864
121st N. Y. Infy	Aug., 1864	From 2-Brig. 1-Div. 6-Corps Pot	To 2-Brig. 1-Div. 6-Corps Pot	Dec.,	1864
95th Penna. Infy	Aug., 1864	From 2-Brig. 1-Div. 6-Corps Pot	To 2-Brig. 1-Div. 6-Corps Pot	Dec.,	1864
96th Penna. Infy	Aug., 1864	From 2-Brig. 1-Div. 6-Corps Pot	No change to Muster Out	Oct.,	1864

3d BRIGADE.— COMMANDERS.

Oliver Edwards	Col. 37th Mass. Infy	Aug. 6, 1864, to Sept. 19, 1864.	
I. C. Bassett	Col. 82d Penna. Infy	Sept. 19, 1864, to Sept. 21, 1864.	
Oliver Edwards	Col. 37th Mass. Infy	Sept. 21, 1864, to Oct. 31, 1864.	
Theodore S. Allen	Col. 5th Wis. Infy	Oct. 31, 1864, to Nov. 30, 1864.	
I. C. Bassett	Col. 82d Penna. Infy	Nov. 30, 1864, to Dec. 6, 1864.	

6th Me. Infy	Aug., 1864	From 3-Brig. 1-Div. 6-Corps Pot	No change to Muster Out	Aug.,	1864
37th Mass. Infy	Aug., 1864	From 3-Brig. 1-Div. 6-Corps Pot	To 3-Brig. 1-Div. 6-Corps Pot	Dec.,	1864
2d R. I. Infy	Aug., 1864	From 3-Brig. 1-Div. 6-Corps Pot	To 3-Brig. 1-Div. 6-Corps Pot	Dec.,	1864
23d Penna. Infy	Aug., 1864	From 3-Brig. 1-Div. 6-Corps Pot	No change to Muster Out	Sept.,	1864
49th Penna. Infy	Aug., 1864	From 3-Brig. 1-Div. 6-Corps Pot	To 3-Brig. 1-Div. 6-Corps Pot	Dec.,	1864
82d Penna. Infy	Aug., 1864	From 3-Brig. 1-Div. 6-Corps Pot	To 3-Brig. 1-Div. 6-Corps Pot	Dec.,	1864
119th Penna. Infy	Aug., 1864	From 3-Brig. 1-Div. 6-Corps Pot	To 3-Brig. 1-Div. 6-Corps Pot	Dec.,	1864
5th Wis. Infy	Aug., 1864	From 3-Brig. 1-Div. 6-Corps Pot	To 3-Brig. 1-Div. 6-Corps Pot	Dec.,	1864

ARTILLERY.—

1st Mass. Indpt. Batty	Aug., 1864	From Arty. Brig. 6-Corps Pot	To Arty. Brig. 6-Corps Shenandoah	Sept.,	1864

2d DIVISION.— COMMANDERS.

George W. Getty	Brigadier General	Aug. 6, 1864, to Oct. 19, 1864.	
L. A. Grant	Brigadier General	Oct. 19, 1864.	
George W. Getty	Brigadier General	Oct. 19, 1864, to Dec. 6, 1864.	

1st BRIGADE.— COMMANDERS.

Frank Wheaton	Brigadier General	Aug. 6, 1864, to Sept. 21, 1864.	
J. M. Warner	Col. 11th Vt. (1st H. A.)	Sept. 21, 1864, to Dec. 6, 1864.	

62d N. Y. Infy	Aug., 1864	From 1-Brig. 2-Div. 6-Corps Pot	To 1-Brig. 2-Div. 6-Corps Pot	Dec.,	1864
93d Penna. Infy	Aug., 1864	From 1-Brig. 2-Div. 6-Corps Pot	To 1-Brig. 2-Div. 6-Corps Pot	Dec.,	1864
98th Penna. Infy	Aug., 1864	From 1-Brig. 2-Div. 6-Corps Pot	To 1-Brig. 2-Div. 6-Corps Pot	Dec.,	1864
102d Penna. Infy	Aug., 1864	From 1-Brig. 2-Div. 6-Corps Pot	To 1-Brig. 2-Div. 6-Corps Pot	Dec.,	1864
139th Penna. Infy	Aug., 1864	From 1-Brig. 2-Div. 6-Corps Pot	To 1-Brig. 2-Div. 6-Corps Pot	Dec.,	1864

2d BRIGADE.— COMMANDERS.

L. A. Grant	Brigadier General	Aug. 6, 1864, to Sept. 18, 1864.	
J. M. Warner	Col. 11th Vt. (1st H. A.)	Sept. 18, 1864, to Sept. 21, 1864.	
George P. Foster	Col. 4th Vt. Infy	Sept. 21, 1864, to Oct. 3, 1864.	
L. A. Grant	Brigadier General	Oct. 3, 1864, to Oct. 19, 1864.	
A. S. Tracy	Lt.-Col. 4th Vt. Infy	Oct. 19, 1864.	
L. A. Grant	Brigadier General	Oct. 19, 1864, to Dec. 6, 1864.	

2d Vt. Infy	Aug., 1864	From 2-Brig. 2-Div. 6-Corps Pot	To 2-Brig. 2-Div. 6-Corps Pot	Dec.,	1864
3d Vt. Infy	Aug., 1864	From 2-Brig. 2-Div. 6-Corps Pot	To 2-Brig. 2-Div. 6-Corps Pot	Dec.,	1864
4th Vt. Infy	Aug., 1864	From 2-Brig. 2-Div. 6-Corps Pot	To 2-Brig. 2-Div. 6-Corps Pot	Dec.,	1864
5th Vt. Infy	Aug., 1864	From 2-Brig. 2-Div. 6-Corps Pot	To 2-Brig. 2-Div. 6-Corps Pot	Dec.,	1864
6th Vt. Infy	Aug., 1864	From 2-Brig. 2-Div. 6-Corps Pot	To 2-Brig. 2-Div. 6-Corps Pot	Dec.,	1864
11th Vt. (1st H. A.)	Aug., 1864	From 2-Brig. 2-Div. 6-Corps Pot	To 2-Brig. 2-Div. 6-Corps Pot	Dec.,	1864

3d BRIGADE.— COMMANDERS.

D. D. Bidwell	Col. 49th N. Y. Infy	Aug. 6, 1864, to Oct. 19, 1864.	Killed.
W. B. French	Lt.-Col. 77th N. Y. Infy	Oct. 19, 1864, to Oct. 20, 1864.	
Thos. W. Hyde	Col. 1st Me. Veteran Infy	Oct. 20, 1864, to Dec. 6, 1864.	

7th Me. Infy	Aug., 1864	From 3-Brig. 2-Div. 6-Corps Pot	No change to Muster Out	Aug.,	1864
43d N. Y. Infy	Aug., 1864	From 3-Brig. 2-Div. 6-Corps Pot	To 3-Brig. 2-Div. 6-Corps Pot	Dec.,	1864
49th N. Y. Infy	Aug., 1864	From 3-Brig. 2-Div. 6-Corps Pot	To 3-Brig. 2-Div. 6-Corps Pot	Dec.,	1864
77th N. Y. Infy	Aug., 1864	From 3-Brig. 2-Div. 6-Corps Pot	To 3-Brig. 2-Div. 6-Corps Pot	Dec.,	1864
122d N. Y. Infy	Aug., 1864	From 3-Brig. 2-Div. 6-Corps Pot	To 3-Brig. 2-Div. 6-Corps Pot	Dec.,	1864
61st Penna. Infy	Aug., 1864	From 3-Brig. 2-Div. 6-Corps Pot	To 3-Brig. 2-Div. 6-Corps Pot	Dec.,	1864
1st Me. Veteran Infy	Aug., 1864	From Veterans 5th, 6th and 7th Me.	To 3-Brig. 2-Div. 6-Corps Pot	Dec.,	1864

ARTILLERY.—

1st N. Y. Indpt. Batty	Aug., 1864	From Arty. Brig. 6-Corps Pot	To Arty. Brig. 6-Corps Shen	Sept.,	1864

3d DIVISION.— COMMANDERS.

J. B. Ricketts	Brigadier General	Aug. 6, 1864, to Oct. 16, 1864.	
J. W. Keifer	Col. 110th Ohio Infy	Oct. 16, 1864, to Oct. 19, 1864.	
Truman Seymour	Brigadier General	Oct. 19, 1864, to Dec. 6, 1864.	

1st BRIGADE.—

COMMANDERS.

William Emmerson	Col. 151st N. Y. Infy..............	Aug. 6, 1864, to Nov., 1864.
W. S. Truex........	Col. 14th N. J. Infy..............	Nov., 1864, to Dec. 6, 1864.

10th Vt. Infy..........Aug., 1864	From 1-Brig. 3-Div. 6-Corps Pot....	To 1-Brig. 3-Div. 6-Corps Pot.....	Dec.,	1864
106th N. Y. Infy........Aug., 1864	From 1-Brig. 3-Div. 6-Corps Pot....	To 1-Brig. 3-Div. 6-Corps Pot.....	Dec.,	1864
151st N. Y. Infy........Aug., 1864	From 1-Brig. 3-Div. 6-Corps Pot....	To 1-Brig. 3-Div. 6-Corps Pot.....	Dec.,	1864
14th N. J. Infy........Aug., 1864	From 1-Brig. 3-Div. 6-Corps Pot....	To 1-Brig. 3-Div. 6-Corps Pot.....	Dec.,	1864
87th Penna. Infy........Aug., 1864	From 1-Brig. 3-Div. 6-Corps Pot....	To 1-Brig. 3-Div. 6-Corps Pot.....	Dec.,	1864
184th N. Y. Infy........Sept., 1864	From New Organization...........	To 1-Brig. 3-Div. 6-Corps Pot.....	Dec.,	1864

2d BRIGADE.—

COMMANDERS.

J. F. Stanton..........	Col. 67th Penna. Infy..............	Aug. 6, 1864, to Aug. 26, 1864.
J. W. Keifer..........	Col. 110th Ohio Infy..............	Aug. 26, 1864, to Oct. 16, 1864.
W. H. Ball..........	Col. 122d Ohio Infy..............	Oct. 16, 1864, to Oct. 19, 1864.
J. W. Keifer..........	Col. 110th Ohio Infy..............	Oct. 19, 1864 to Dec. 6, 1864.

9th N. Y. Heavy Arty....Aug., 1864	From 2-Brig. 3-Div. 6-Corps Pot....	To 2-Brig. 3-Div. 6-Corps Pot.....	Dec.,	1864
67th Penna. Infy........Aug., 1864	From 2-Brig. 3-Div. 6-Corps Pot....	To 2-Brig. 3-Div. 6-Corps Pot.....	Dec.,	1864
138th Penna. Infy........Aug., 1864	From 2-Brig. 3-Div. 6-Corps Pot....	To 2-Brig. 3-Div. 6-Corps Pot.....	Dec.,	1864
6th Md. Infy..........Aug., 1864	From 2-Brig. 3-Div. 6-Corps Pot....	To 2-Brig. 3-Div. 6-Corps Pot.....	Dec.,	1864
110th Ohio Infy........Aug., 1864	From 2-Brig. 3-Div. 6-Corps Pot....	To 2-Brig. 3-Div. 6-Corps Pot.....	Dec.,	1864
122d Ohio Infy........Aug., 1864	From 2-Brig. 3-Div. 6-Corps Pot....	To 2-Brig. 3-Div. 6-Corps Pot.....	Dec.,	1864
126th Ohio Infy........Aug., 1864	From 2-Brig. 3-Div. 6-Corps Pot....	To 2-Brig. 3-Div. 6-Corps Pot.....	Dec.,	1864
ARTILLERY.—				
Batty. M, 5th U. S. Arty..Aug., 1864	From Arty. Brig. 6-Corps Pot......	To Arty. Brig. 6-Corps Shen.......	Sept.,	1864
ARTILLERY BRIGADE.—				
5th Me. Indpt. Batty.....Aug., 1864	From Arty. Brig. 6-Corps Pot......	To Arty. Res. 19-Corps Shen.......	Dec.,	1864
Batty. C, 1st R. I. Arty..Aug., 1864	From Arty. Brig. 6-Corps Pot......	Consol. with Batty. G.............	Dec.,	1864
Batty. G, 1st R. I. Arty..Aug., 1864	From Arty. Brig. 6-Corps Pot......	To Arty. Brig. 6-Corps Pot.......	Dec.,	1864
5th N. Y. Indpt. Batty...Aug., 1864	From 1-Brig. Def. South Pot. 22-C..	To Arty. 1-Div. 19-Corps Shen.....	Aug.,	1864
1st Mass. Indpt. Batty...Sept., 1864	From Arty. 1-Div. 6-Corps Shen....	No change to Muster Out..........	Oct.,	1864
1st N. Y. Indpt. Batty...Sept., 1864	From Arty. 2-Div. 6-Corps Shen....	To Arty. Brig. 6-Corps Pot.......	Dec.,	1864
Batty. M, 5th U. S. Arty..Sept., 1864	From Arty. 3-Div. 6-Corps Shen....	To Dist. Harper's Ferry Dept. W. Va.	Dec.,	1864

Nineteenth Army Corps

Known as Detachment 19th Army Corps, consisting of the 1st and 2d Divisions of the Original 19th Army Corps, Department of the Gulf. Officially designated 19th Army Corps, Nov. 7, 1864. Discontinued Mch. 20, 1865, by General Order No. 4, A. G. O.

COMMANDERS.

William H. Emory.....	Brigadier General	Aug. 6, 1864, to Dec. 8, 1864.
Cuvier Grover	Brigadier General	Dec. 8, 1864, to Dec. 28, 1864.
William H. Emory.....	Bvt. Major General	Dec. 28, 1864, to Mch. 20, 1865.

1st DIVISION.—

COMMANDERS.

William Dwight	Brigadier General	Aug. 6, 1864 to Oct. 15, 1864.
James W. McMillan....	Brigadier General	Oct. 15, 1864, to Oct. 24, 1864.
William Dwight	Brigadier General	Oct. 24, 1864, to Jan. 25, 1865.
James W. McMillan....	Brigadier General	Jan. 25, 1865, to Mch. 1, 1865.
William Dwight	Brigadier General	Mch. 1, 1865, to Mch. 20, 1865.

1st BRIGADE.—

COMMANDERS.

Geo. L. Beale..........	Col. 29th Me. Infy..............	Aug. 6, 1864, to Oct. 13, 1864.
E. P. Davis............	Col. 153d N. Y. Infy..............	Oct. 13, 1864, to Oct. 30, 1864.
Geo. M. Love..........	Col. 116th N. Y. Infy..............	Oct. 30, 1864, to Nov. 1, 1864.
N. A. M. Dudley.......	Col. 30th Mass. Infy..............	Nov. 1, 1864, to Dec. 13, 1864.
Geo. L. Beale..........	Brigadier General	Dec. 13, 1864, to Mch. 20, 1865.

29th Me. Infy..........Aug., 1864	From 1-Brig. 1-Div. 19-Corps Gulf...	To 1-Brig. 1-Prov'l Div. Shen......	Mch.,	1864
30th Mass. Infy........Aug., 1864	From 1-Brig. 1-Div. 19-Corps Gulf...	To 1-Brig. 1-Prov'l Div. Shen......	Mch.,	1864
90th N. Y. Infy........Aug., 1864	From 2-Brig. 2-Div. 19-Corps Gulf...	To 1-Brig. 1-Prov'l Div. Shen......	Mch.,	1864
114th N. Y. Infy........Aug., 1864	From 1-Brig. 1-Div. 19-Corps Gulf...	To 1-Brig. 1-Prov'l Div. Shen......	Mch.,	1864
116th N. Y. Infy........Aug., 1864	From 1-Brig. 1-Div. 19-Corps Gulf...	To 1-Brig. 1-Prov'l Div. Shen......	Mch.,	1864
153d N. Y. Infy........Aug.,1864	From 1-Brig. 1-Div. 19-Corps Gulf...	To 2-Brig. 1-Div. 19-Corps Shen....	Jan.,	1865

2d BRIGADE.—

COMMANDERS.

James W. McMillan.....	Brigadier General	Aug. 6, 1864, to Oct. 15, 1864.
Samuel Thomas	Col. 8th Vt. Infy..............	Oct. 15, 1864, to Oct. 24, 1864.
James W. McMillan.....	Brigadier General	Oct. 24, 1864, to Oct. 26, 1864.
James D. Fessenden....	Brigadier General	Oct. 26, 1864, to Nov. 1, 1864.
Samuel Thomas	Col. 8th Vt. Infy..............	Nov. 1, 1864, to Dec. 3, 1864.
James W. McMillan.....	Brigadier General	Dec. 3, 1864, to Jan. 25, 1865.
E. P. Davis............	Col. 153d N. Y. Infy..............	Jan. 25, 1865, to Mch. 20, 1865.

13th Me. Infy..........Aug., 1864	From 2-Brig. 1-Div. 19-Corps Gulf..	No change to Muster Out.........	Jan.,	1865
15th Me. Infy..........Aug., 1864	From 2-Brig. 1-Div. 19-Corps Gulf..	To 2-Brig. 1-Prov'l Div. Shen......	Mch.,	1865
8th Vt. Infy..........Aug., 1864	From 2-Brig. 1-Div. 19-Corps Gulf..	To 2-Brig. 1-Prov'l Div. Shen......	Mch.,	1865
12th Conn. Infy........Aug., 1864	From 2-Brig. 1-Div. 19-Corps Gulf..	To 2-Brig. 1-Prov'l Div. Shen......	Mch.,	1865
47th Penna. Infy........Aug., 1864	From 2-Brig. 1-Div. 19-Corps Gulf..	To 2-Brig. 1-Prov'l Div. Shen.....	Mch.,	1865
26th Mass. Infy........Jan., 1865	From 1-Brig. 2-Div. 19-Corps Shen..	To 2-Brig. 1-Prov'l Div. Shen......	Mch.,	1865
153d N. Y. Infy........Jan., 1865	From 1-Brig. 1-Div. 19-Corps Shen..	To 2-Brig. 1-Prov'l Div. Shen......	Mch.,	1865

3d BRIGADE.—

COMMANDERS.

L. D. H. Currie.........	Col. 133d N. Y. Infy..............	Aug. 6, 1864, to Oct. 26, 1864.
N. A. M. Dudley.......	Col. 30th Mass. Infy..............	Oct. 26, 1864, to Nov. 1, 1864.
James D. Fessenden....	Brigadier General	Nov. 1, 1864, to Mch. 20, 1865.

30th Me. Infy..........Aug., 1864	From 3-Brig. 1-Div. 19-Corps Gulf..	To 3-Brig. 1-Prov'l Div. Shen......	Mch.,	1865
133d N. Y. Infy........Aug., 1864	From 3-Brig. 1-Div. 19-Corps Gulf..	To 3-Brig. 1-Prov'l Div. Shen......	Mch.,	1865
160th N. Y. Infy........Aug., 1864	From 3-Brig. 1-Div. 19-Corps Gulf..	To 3-Brig. 1-Prov'l Div. Shen......	Mch.,	1865
162d N. Y. Infy........Aug., 1864	From 3-Brig. 1-Div. 19-Corps Gulf..	To 3-Brig. 1-Prov'l Div. Shen......	Mch.,	1865
165th N. Y. Infy........Aug., 1864	From 3-Brig. 1-Div. 19-Corps Gulf..	To 3-Brig. 1-Prov'l Div. Shen......	Mch.,	1865
173d N. Y. Infy........Aug., 1864	From 3-Brig. 1-Div. 19-Corps Gulf..	To 3-Brig. 1-Prov'l Div. Shen......	Mch.,	1865
ARTILLERY.—				
5th N. Y. Batty.........Aug., 1864	From Arty. Brig. 6-Corps Shen.....	To Arty. Brig. 19-Corps Shen.......	Dec.,	1864

2d DIVISION.—

	COMMANDERS.	
Cuvier Grover	Brigadier General	Aug. 6, 1864, to Oct. 19, 1864.
H. W. Birge	Brigadier General	Oct. 19, 1864, to Nov. 10, 1864.
Cuvier Grover	Brigadier General	Nov. 10, 1864, to Dec. 8, 1864.
H. W. Birge	Brigadier General	Dec. 8, 1864, to Dec. 28, 1864.
Cuvier Grover	Brigadier General	Dec. 28, 1864, to Jan. 6, 1865.

Division transferred to District of Savannah, Dept. South.

1st BRIGADE.—

	COMMANDERS.	
H. W. Birge	Brigadier General	Aug. 6, 1864, to Oct. 19, 1864.
T. W. Porter	Col. 14th Me. Infy	Oct. 19, 1864, to Nov. 10, 1864.
H. W. Birge	Brigadier General	Nov. 10, 1864, to Dec. 8, 1864.
H. D. Washburn	Col. 18th Ind. Infy	Dec. 8, 1864, to Dec. 28, 1864.
H. W. Birge	Brigadier General	Dec. 28, 1864, to Jan. 6, 1865.

12th Me. Infy	Aug., 1864	From 1-Brig. 2-Div. 19-Corps Gulf..	To 1-Brig. Grover's Div. Dist. Savan.	Jan., 1865
14th Me. Infy	Aug., 1864	From 1-Brig. 2-Div. 19-Corps Gulf..	To 1-Brig. Grover's Div. Dist. Savan.	Jan., 1865
14th N. H. Infy	Aug., 1864	From 1-Brig. 2-Div. 19-Corps Gulf..	To 1-Brig. Grover's Div. Dist. Savan.	Jan., 1865
26th Mass. Infy	Aug., 1864	From 1-Brig. 2-Div. 19-Corps Gulf..	To 2-Brig. 1-Div. 19-Corps Shen....	Jan., 1865
9th Conn. Infy	Aug., 1864	From 1-Brig. 2-Div. 19-Corps Gulf..	To 1-Brig. Grover's Div. Dist. Savan.	Jan., 1865
75th N. Y. Infy	Aug., 1864	From 1-Brig. 2-Div. 19-Corps Gulf..	To 1-Brig. Grover's Div. Dist. Savan.	Jan., 1865
8th Ind. Infy	Dec., 1864	From 4-Brig. 2-Div. 19-Corps Shen..	To 1-Brig. Grover's Div. Dist. Savan.	Jan., 1865
18th Ind. Infy	Dec., 1864	From 4-Brig. 2-Div. 19-Corps Shen..	To 1-Brig. Grover's Div. Dist. Savan.	Jan., 1865

2d BRIGADE.—

	COMMANDERS.	
E. L. Molineux	Col. 159th N. Y. Infy	Aug. 6, 1864, to Nov. 1, 1864.
N. W. Day	Col. 131st N. Y. Infy	Nov. 1, 1864, to Dec. 9, 1864.
E. L. Molineux	Col. 159th N. Y. Infy	Dec. 9, 1864, to Jan. 6, 1865.

3d Mass. Cav. Dismtd	Aug., 1864	From 2-Brig. 2-Div. 19-Corps Gulf..	To Cav. Army Shen	Jan., 1865
13th Conn. Infy	Aug., 1864	From 2-Brig. 2-Div. 19-Corps Gulf..	To 2-Brig. Grover's Div. Dist. Savan.	Jan., 1865
90th N. Y. Infy	Aug., 1864	From 2-Brig. 2-Div. 19-Corps Gulf..	To 1-Brig. 1-Div. 19-Corps Shen....	Aug., 1864
131st N. Y. Infy	Aug., 1864	From 2-Brig. 2-Div. 19-Corps Gulf..	To 2-Brig. Grover's Div. Dist. Savan.	Jan., 1865
159th N. Y. Infy	Aug., 1864	From 2-Brig. 2-Div. 19-Corps Gulf..	To 2-Brig. Grover's Div. Dist. Savan.	Jan., 1865
11th Ind. Infy	Aug., 1864	From 2-Brig. 2-Div. 19-Corps Gulf..	To 2-Separate Brig. 8-Corps	Jan., 1865
22d Iowa Infy	Aug., 1864	From 2-Brig. 2-Div. 19-Corps Gulf..	To 2-Brig. Grover's Div. Dist. Savan.	Jan., 1865
28th Iowa Infy	Dec., 1864	From 4-Brig. 2-Div. 19-Corps Shen..	To 2-Brig. Grover's Div. Dist. Savan.	Jan., 1865

3d BRIGADE.—

	COMMANDERS.	
Jacob Sharpe	Col. 156th N. Y. Infy	Aug. 6, 1864, to Sept. 21, 1864.
D. Macauley	Col. 11th Ind. Infy	Sept. 21, 1864, to Oct. 19, 1864.
Alfred Neafie	Lt.-Col. 156th N. Y. Infy	Oct. 19, 1864, to Dec. 5, 1864.
J. P. Richardson	Lt.-Col. 8th Mass. Infy	Dec. 5, 1864, to Jan. 6, 1865.

38th Mass. Infy	Aug., 1864	From 3-Brig. 2-Div. 19-Corps Gulf..	To 3-Brig. Grover's Div. Dist. Savan.	Jan., 1865
128th N. Y. Infy	Aug., 1864	From 3-Brig. 2-Div. 19-Corps Gulf..	To 3-Brig. Grover's Div. Dist. Savan.	Jan., 1865
156th N. Y. Infy	Aug., 1864	From 3-Brig. 2-Div. 19-Corps Gulf..	To 3-Brig. Grover's Div. Dist. Savan.	Jan., 1865
175th N. Y. Infy	Aug., 1864	From 3-Brig. 2-Div. 19-Corps Gulf..	To 3-Brig. Grover's Div. Dist. Savan.	Jan., 1865
176th N. Y. Infy	Aug., 1864	From 3-Brig. 2-Div. 19-Corps Gulf..	To 3-Brig. Grover's Div. Dist. Savan.	Jan., 1865
8th Ind. Infy	Aug., 1864	From 3-Brig. 2-Div. 19-Corps Gulf..	To 4-Brig. 2-Div. 19-Corps Shen....	Aug., 1864
18th Ind. Infy	Aug., 1864	From 3-Brig. 2-Div. 19-Corps Gulf..	To 4-Brig. 2-Div. 19-Corps Shen....	Aug., 1864
24th Iowa Infy	Aug., 1864	From 3-Brig. 2-Div. 19-Corps Gulf..	To 4-Brig. 2-Div. 19-Corps Shen....	Aug., 1864
28th Iowa Infy	Aug., 1864	From 3-Brig. 2-Div. 19-Corps Gulf..	To 4-Brig. 2-Div. 19-Corps Shen....	Aug., 1864
24th Iowa Infy	Dec., 1864	From 4-Brig. 2-Div. 19-Corps Shen..	To 3-Brig. Grover's Div. Dist. Savan.	Jan., 1865

4th BRIGADE.—

	COMMANDERS.	
David Shunk	Col. 8th Ind. Infy	Aug., 1864, to Nov. 12, 1864.
H. D. Washburn	Col. 18th Ind. Infy	Nov. 12, 1864, to Dec. 31, 1864.

8th Ind. Infy	Aug., 1864	From 3-Brig. 2-Div. 19-Corps Shen..	To 1-Brig. 2-Div. 19-Corps Shen....	Dec., 1864
18th Ind. Infy	Aug., 1864	From 3-Brig. 2-Div. 19-Corps Shen..	To 1-Brig. 2-Div. 19-Corps Shen....	Dec., 1864
24th Iowa Infy	Aug., 1864	From 3-Brig. 2-Div. 19-Corps Shen..	To 3-Brig. 2-Div. 19-Corps Shen....	Dec., 1864
28th Iowa Infy	Aug., 1864	From 3-Brig. 2-Div. 19-Corps Shen..	To 2-Brig. 2-Div. 19-Corps Shen....	Dec., 1864

ARTILLERY.—

1st Me. Batty	Aug., 1864	From Camp Barry, Wash., 22-Corps.	To Arty. Brig. 19-Corps Shen	Dec., 1864

ARTILLERY BRIGADE.—

1st Me. Batty	Dec., 1864	From Arty. 2-Div. 19-Corps Shen....	To Arty. Res. Army Shen	Mch., 1865
5th Me. Batty	Dec., 1864	From Arty. Brig. 6-Corps Shen	To Arty. Res. Army Shen	Mch., 1865
5th N. Y. Indpt. Batty	Dec., 1864	From Arty. 1-Div. 19-Corps Shen....	To Arty. Res. Army Shen	Mch., 1865
Batty. D, 1st R. I. Arty	Dec., 1864	From Arty. Res. 19-Corps Shen....	To Arty. Res. Army Shen	Mch., 1865
17th Ind. Batty	Dec., 1864	From Arty. Res. 19-Corps Shen....	To Arty. Res. Army Shen	Mch., 1865

RESERVE ARTILLERY.—

Batty. D, 1st R. I. Arty	Aug., 1864	From 1-Brig. Def. N. Pot. 22-Corps.	To Arty. Brig. 19-Corps Shen	Dec., 1864
17th Ind. Batty	Aug., 1864	From Res. Div. W. Va	To Arty. Brig. 19-Corps Shen	Dec., 1864

Cavalry Corps

Formed Aug., 1864, from 1st and 3d Divisions, Cavalry Corps, Army Potomac. Rejoined Army Potomac, Mch. 25, 1865.

	COMMANDERS.	
A. T. A. Torbert	Brigadier General	Aug. 6, 1864, to Jan. 26, 1864.
Wesley Merritt	Brigadier General	Jan. 26, 1864, to Mch. 25, 1865.

1st DIVISION.—

	COMMANDERS.	
Wesley Merritt	Brigadier General	Aug. 6, 1864, to Nov. 13, 1864.
T. C. Devin	Brigadier General	Nov. 13, 1864, to Nov. 28, 1864.
Wesley Merritt	Brigadier General	Nov. 28, 1864, to Dec. 31, 1864.
T. C. Devin	Brigadier General	Dec. 31, 1864, to Jan. 15, 1865.
Wesley Merritt	Brigadier General	Jan. 15, 1865, to Jan. 26, 1865.
C. Crowninshield	Col. 2d Mass. Cav.	Jan. 26, 1865, to Jan. 31, 1865.
Peter Stagg	Col. 1st Mich. Cav.	Jan. 31, 1865, to Feb. 3, 1865.
A. Gibbs	Brigadier General	Feb. 3, 1865, to Feb. 10, 1865.
T. C. Devin	Brigadier General	Feb. 10, 1865, to Mch. 25, 1865.

1st BRIGADE.—

	COMMANDERS.	
Geo. A. Custer	Brigadier General	Aug. 6, 1864, to Sept. 26, 1864.
J. H. Kidd	Col. 6th Mich. Cav.	Sept. 26, 1864, to Oct. 26, 1864.
Peter Stagg	Col. 1st Mich. Cav.	Oct. 26, 1864, to Mch. 25, 1865.

1st Mich. Cav	Aug., 1864	From 1-Brig. 1-Div. Cav. Corps Pot.	To 1-Brig. 1-Div. Cav. Corps Pot....	Mch., 1865
5th Mich. Cav	Aug., 1864	From 1-Brig. 1-Div. Cav. Corps Pot.	To 1-Brig. 1-Div. Cav. Corps Pot....	Mch., 1865
6th Mich. Cav	Aug., 1864	From 1-Brig. 1-Div. Cav. Corps Pot.	To 1-Brig. 1-Div. Cav. Corps Pot....	Mch., 1865
7th Mich. Cav	Aug., 1864	From 1-Brig. 1-Div. Cav. Corps Pot.	To 1-Brig. 1-Div. Cav. Corps Pot....	Mch., 1865
25th N. Y. Cav	Sept., 1864	From 3-Brig. 1-Div. Cav. Corps Shen.	To Unatt. 2-Div. W. Va	Jan., 1865

2d BRIGADE.— COMMANDERS.

L. P. DiCesnola	Col. 4th N. Y. Cav	Aug. 6, 1864, to Aug. 30, 1864.
T. C. Devin	Brigadier General	Aug. 30, 1864, to Nov. 13, 1864.
A. Gibbs	Brigadier General	Nov. 13, 1864, to Nov. 28, 1864.
T. C. Devin	Brigadier General	Nov. 28, 1864, to Dec. 31, 1864.
Geo. S. Nichols	Lt.-Col. 9th N. Y. Cav	Dec. 31, 1864, to Jan. 15, 1865.
C. L. Fitzhugh	Col. 6th N. Y. Cav	Jan. 15, 1865, to Mch. 25, 1865.

4th N. Y. Cav	Aug., 1864	From 2-Brig. 1-Div. Cav. Corps Pot..	Consol. with 9th N. Y. Cav	Feb.,	1865
6th N. Y. Cav	Aug., 1864	From 2-Brig. 1-Div. Cav. Corps Pot..	To 2-Brig. 1-Div. Cav. Corps Pot..	Mch.,	1865
9th N. Y. Cav	Aug., 1864	From 2-Brig. 1-Div. Cav. Corps Pot..	To 2-Brig. 1-Div. Cav. Corps Pot..	Mch.,	1865
17th Penna. Cav	Aug., 1864	From 2-Brig. 1-Div. Cav. Corps Pot..	To 2-Brig. 1-Div. Cav. Corps Pot..	Mch.,	1865
19th N. Y. Cav	Sept., 1864	From Res. Brig. 1-Div. Cav. Corps..	To 2-Brig. 1-Div. Cav. Corps Pot..	Mch.,	1865
20th Penna. Cav	Nov., 1864	From 1-Brig. 1-Cav. Div. W. Va.....	To 2-Brig. 1-Div. Cav. Corps Pot..	Mch.,	1865

3d BRIGADE.—Organized Aug. 9, 1864. Discontinued Sept. 8, 1864.

COMMANDER.

C. R. Lowell, Jr	Col. 2d Mass. Cav	Aug. 9, 1864, to Sept. 8, 1864.

2d Mass. Cav	Aug., 1864	From Cav. Brig. Def. Wash. 22-C..	To Res. Brig. 1-Div. Cav. Corps Shen	Sept.,	1864
25th N. Y. Cav	Aug., 1864	From Cav. Brig. Def. Wash. 22-C..	To 1-Brig. 1-Div. Cav. Corps Shen..	Sept.,	1864
14th Penna. Cav	Aug., 1864	From 1-Brig. 2-Cav. Div. W. Va..	To 1-Brig. 2-Div. Cav. W. Va	Aug.,	1864
22d Penna. Cav	Aug., 1864	From 1-Brig. 1-Cav. Div. W. Va..	To 1-Brig. 2-Div. Cav. W. Va	Aug.,	1864
1st Md. P. H. B. Cav	Aug., 1864	From 1-Brig. 1-Cav. Div. W. Va...	To Res. Div. Harper's Ferry, W. Va.	Sept.,	1864

RESERVE BRIGADE.— COMMANDERS.

A. Gibbs	Brigadier General	Aug. 6, 1864, to Sept. 8, 1864.	
C. R. Lowell, Jr	Col. 2d Mass. Cav	Sept. 8, 1864, to Oct. 19, 1864.	Mort. Wnd.
C. Crowninshield	Lt.-Col. 2d Mass. Cav	Oct. 19, 1864, to Dec. 13, 1864.	
A. Gibbs	Brigadier General	Dec. 13, 1864, to Dec. 31, 1864.	
A. McKendrie	Major 2d Mass. Cav	Dec. 31, 1864, to Jan. 6, 1865.	
C. Crowninshield	Lt.-Col. 2d Mass. Cav	Jan. 6, 1865, to Jan. 15, 1865.	
A. Gibbs	Brigadier General	Jan. 15, 1865, to Jan. 18, 1865.	
C. Crowninshield	Lt.-Col. 2d Mass. Cav	Jan. 18, 1865, to Jan. 26 1865.	
W. M. Rumery	Capt. 2d Mass. Cav	Jan. 26, 1865, to Jan. 31, 1865.	
C. Crowninshield	Lt.-Col. 2d Mass. Cav	Jan. 31, 1865, to Feb. 10, 1865.	
A. Gibbs	Brigadier General	Feb. 10, 1865, to Mch. 25, 1865.	

19th N. Y. Cav	Aug., 1864	From Res. Br. 1-Div. Cav. Corps Pot.	To 2-Brig. 1-Div. Cav. Corps Shen..	Sept.,	1864
6th Penna. Cav	Aug., 1864	From Res. Br. 1-Div. Cav. Corps Pot.	To 3-Res. Br. 1-Div. Cav. Corps Pot.	Mch.,	1865
1st U. S. Cav	Aug., 1864	From Res. Br. 1-Div. Cav. Corps Pot.	To Headqrs. Cav. Corps Shen	Dec.,	1864
2d U. S. Cav	Aug., 1864	From Res. Br. 1-Div. Cav. Corps Pot.	To Cav. Brig. Army Shen	Mch.,	1865
5th U. S. Cav	Aug., 1864	From Res. Br. 1-Div. Cav. Corps Pot.	To 3-Res. Br. 1-Div. Cav. Corps Pot.	Mch.,	1865
6th U. S. Cav	Aug., 1864	From Res. Br. 1-Div. Cav. Corps Pot.	To Headqrs. Cav. Corps Shen	Oct.,	1864
2d Mass. Cav	Sept., 1864	From 3-Brig. 1-Div. Cav. Corps Shen.	To 3-Res. Br. 1-Div. Cav. Corps Pot.	Mch.,	1865
1st R. I. Cav	Oct., 1864	From Headqrs. Cav. Corps Shen	To Cav. Brig. Army Shen	Mch.,	1865
6th U. S. Cav	Dec., 1864	From Headqrs. Cav. Corps Shen	To 3-Res. Br. 1-Div. Cav. Corps Pot.	Mch.,	1865

ARTILLERY.—

Battys. K & L, 1st U. S.	Aug., 1864	From Horse Arty. Army Pot	To Res. Horse Arty. Shen	Oct.,	1864
Batty. D, 2d U. S. Arty	Aug., 1864	From Horse Arty. Army Pot	To Res. Horse Arty. Shen	Oct.,	1864
Battys. C & E. 2d U. S.	Dec., 1864	From Horse Arty. Army Pot	To 3-Res. Br. 1-Div. Cav. Corps Pot.	Mch.,	1865

2d DIVISION.—(See 2d Cav. Div. W. Va. Attached temporarily.)

3d DIVISION.— COMMANDERS.

James H. Wilson	Brigadier General	Aug. 6, 1864, to Sept. 30, 1864.
Geo. A. Custer	Brigadier General	Sept. 30, 1864, to Jan. 5, 1865.
Geo. H. Chapman	Brigadier General	Jan. 5, 1865, to Jan. 30, 1865.
Geo. A. Custer	Brigadier General	Jan. 30, 1865, to Mch. 25, 1865.

1st BRIGADE.— COMMANDERS.

J. B. McIntosh	Brigadier General	Aug. 6, 1864, to Sept. 19, 1864.
Geo. A. Purington	Lt.-Col. 2d Ohio Cav	Sept. 19, 1864, to Oct. 7, 1864.
A. C. M. Pennington	Col. 3d N. J. Cav	Oct. 7, 1864, to Nov. 10, 1864.
Geo. H. Chapman	Brigadier General	Nov. 10, 1864, to Jan. 5, 1865.
A. C. M. Pennington	Col. 3d N. J. Cav	Jan. 5, 1865, to Jan. 30, 1865.
Geo. H. Chapman	Brigadier General	Jan. 30, 1865, to Feb. 25, 1865.
A. C. M. Pennington	Col. 3d N. J. Cav	Feb. 25, 1865, to Mch. 25 1865.

1st Conn. Cav	Aug., 1864	From 1-Brig. 3-Div. Cav. Corps Pot.	To 1-Brig. 3-Div. Cav. Corps Pot...	Mch.,	1865
3d N. J. Cav	Aug., 1864	From 1-Brig. 3-Div. Cav. Corps Pot.	To 1-Brig. 3-Div. Cav. Corps Pot...	Mch.,	1865
2d N. Y. Cav	Aug., 1864	From 1-Brig. 3-Div. Cav. Corps Pot.	To 1-Brig. 3-Div. Cav. Corps Pot...	Mch.,	1865
5th N. Y. Cav	Aug., 1864	From 1-Brig. 3-Div. Cav. Corps Pot.	To Cav. Brig. Army Shen	Mch.,	1865
2d Ohio Cav	Aug., 1864	From 1-Brig. 3-Div. Cav. Corps Pot.	To 1-Brig. 3-Div. Cav. Corps Pot...	Mch.,	1865
18th Penna. Cav	Aug., 1864	From 1-Brig. 3-Div. Cav. Corps Pot.	To Cav. Brig. Army Shen	Mch.,	1865

2d BRIGADE.— COMMANDERS.

Geo. H. Chapman	Brigadier General	Aug. 6, 1864, to Sept. 19, 1864.
William Wells	Col. 1st Vt. Cav	Sept. 19, 1864, to Oct. 22, 1864.
John L. Thompson	Col. 1st N. H. Cav	Oct. 22, 1864, to Nov. 1, 1864.
Geo. H. Chapman	Brigadier General	Nov. 1, 1864, to Nov. 10, 1864.
John J. Coppinger	Col. 15th N. Y. Cav	Nov. 10, 1864, temporarily.
William Wells	Col. 1st Vt. Cav	Nov. 10, 1864, to Mch. 25, 1865.

3d Ind. Cav	Aug., 1864	From 2-Brig. 3-Div. Cav. Corps Pot.	To 2-Brig. 3-Div. Cav. Corps Pot...	Mch.,	1865
1st N. H. Cav	Aug., 1864	From 2-Brig. 3-Div. Cav. Corps Pot.	To Cav. Brig. Army Shen	Mch.,	1865
8th N. Y. Cav	Aug., 1864	From 2-Brig. 3-Div. Cav. Corps Pot.	To 2-Brig. 3-Div. Cav. Corps Pot...	Mch.,	1865
22d N. Y. Cav	Aug., 1864	From 2-Brig. 3-Div. Cav. Corps Pot.	To Cav. Brig. Army Shen	Mch.,	1865
1st Vt. Cav	Aug., 1864	From 2-Brig. 3-Div. Cav. Corps Pot.	To 2-Brig. 3-Div. Cav. Corps Pot...	Mch.,	1865
15th N. Y. Cav	Sept., 1864	From 1-Brig. 1-Cav. Div. W. Va..	To 2-Brig. 3-Div. Cav. Corps Pot...	Mch.,	1865

3d BRIGADE.—Organized Dec. 28, 1864. COMMANDER.

Henry Capehart	Col. 1st W. Va. Cav	Dec. 28, 1864, to Mch. 25, 1865.

1st N. Y. Lincoln Cav	Dec., 1864	From 2-Brig. 2-Cav. Div. W. Va..	To 3-Brig. 3-Div. Cav. Corps Pot....	Mch.,	1865
1st W. Va. Cav	Dec., 1864	From 2-Brig. 2-Cav. Div. W. Va..	To 3-Brig. 3-Div. Cav. Corps Pot....	Mch.,	1865
2d W. Va. Cav	Dec., 1864	From 2-Brig. 2-Cav. Div. W. Va..	To 3-Brig. 3-Div. Cav. Corps Pot....	Mch.,	1865
3d W. Va. Cav	Dec., 1864	From 2-Brig. 2-Cav. Div. W. Va..	To 3-Brig. 3-Div. Cav. Corps Pot....	Mch.,	1865

HORSE ARTILLERY.—

6th N. Y. Indpt. Batty	Aug., 1864	From Camp Barry 22-Corps	To Res. Horse Arty. Army Shen	Dec.,	1864
Battys. K & L, 1st U. S.	Aug., 1864	From Camp Barry 22-Corps	To Res. Horse Arty. Army Shen	Dec.,	1864
Battys. B & L, 2d U. S.	Aug., 1864	From 1-Brig. Horse Arty. Pot	To Res. Horse Arty. Army Shen	Dec.,	1864
Batty. D, 2d U. S. Arty	Aug., 1864	From 1-Brig. Horse Arty. Pot	To Res. Horse Arty. Army Shen	Dec.,	1864
Batty. M, 2d U. S. Arty	Aug., 1864	From 1-Brig. Horse Arty. Pot	To Res. Horse Arty. Army Shen	Dec.,	1864
Battys. C, F, & K, 3d U. S.	Aug., 1864	From 1-Brig. Horse Arty. Pot	To Res. Horse Arty. Army Shen	Dec.,	1864
Battys. C & E, 4th U. S.	Aug., 1864	From 1-Brig. Horse Arty. Pot	To 3-Res. Br. 1-Div. Cav. Corps Pot.	Dec.,	1864
Batty. L, 5th U. S. Arty	Nov., 1864	From Arty. 2-Cav. Div. W. Va....	To Res. Horse Arty. Army Shen	Dec.,	1864

KITCHING'S PROVISIONAL DIVISION.— COMMANDERS.

J. H. Kitching.........	Col. 6th N. Y. Heavy Arty.........	Sept. 27, 1864, to Oct. 19, 1864.	Killed.
William Heine	Col. 103d N. Y. Infy..............	Oct. 19, 1864, to Dec. 3, 1864.	

1st BRIGADE.— COMMANDERS.

William Heine	Col. 103d N. Y. Infy..............	Sept. 27, 1864, to Oct. 19, 1864.	
T. D. Hart..............	Lt.-Col. 104th Penna. Infy........	Oct. 19, 1864, to Dec. 3, 1864.	
6th N. Y. Heavy Arty....Sept., 1864	From 1-Brig. Def. N. Pot. 22-Corps.	To 2-Brig. Def. Bermuda Hund., Va.	Dec., 1864
103d N. Y. Infy.........Sept., 1864	From 3-Brig. DeRussy's Div. 22-C..	To 1-Brig. Def. Bermuda Hund., Va.	Dec., 1864
104th Penna. Infy........Sept., 1864	From 3-Brig. DeRussy's Div. 22-C..	To 1-Brig. Def. Bermuda Hund., Va.	Dec., 1864

2d BRIGADE.— COMMANDER.

G. DePeyster Arden....	Lt.-Col. 10th N. Y. Heavy Arty.....	Sept. 27, 1864, to Dec. 3, 1864.
41st N. Y. Infy.........Sept., 1864	From 1-Brig. Def. N. Pot. 22-Corps.	To 2-Brig. Def. Bermuda Hund., Va.	Dec., 1864
10th N. Y. Heavy Arty...Sept., 1864	From 1-Brig. Def. S. Pot. 22-Corps.	To 2-Brig. Def. Bermuda Hund., Va.	Dec., 1864

1st PROVISIONAL DIVISION.— COMMANDER.

James W. McMillan....	Bvt. Major General..........

1st BRIGADE.— COMMANDER.

Geo. L. Beale..........	Brigadier General ....
29th Me. Infy...........Mch., 1865	From 1-Brig. 1-Div. 19-Corps Shen..	To 1-Brig. Dwight's Div. Def. Wash.	Apr., 1865
30th Mass. Infy.........Mch., 1865	From 1-Brig. 1-Div. 19-Corps Shen..	To 1-Brig. Dwight's Div. Def. Wash.	Apr., 1865
90th N. Y. Infy.........Mch., 1865	From 1-Brig. 1-Div. 19-Corps Shen..	To 1-Brig. Dwight's Div. Def. Wash.	Apr., 1865
114th N. Y. Infy........Mch., 1865	From 1-Brig. 1-Div. 19-Corps Shen..	To 1-Brig. Dwight's Div. Def. Wash.	Apr., 1865
116th N. Y. Infy........Mch., 1865	From 1-Brig. 1-Div. 19-Corps Shen..	To 1-Brig. Dwight's Div. Def. Wash.	Apr., 1865

2d BRIGADE.— COMMANDER.

E. P. Davis............	Col. 153d N. Y. Infy..............
15th Me. Infy...........Mch., 1865	From 2-Brig. 1-Div. 19-Corps Shen..	To 2-Brig. Dwight's Div. Def. Wash.	Apr., 1865
8th Vt. Infy............Mch., 1865	From 2-Brig. 1-Div. 19-Corps Shen..	To 2-Brig. Dwight's Div. Def. Wash.	Apr., 1865
12th Conn. Infy.........Mch., 1865	From 2-Brig. 1-Div. 19-Corps Shen..	To 2-Brig. Dwight's Div. Def. Wash.	Apr., 1865
47th Penna. Infy........Mch., 1865	From 2-Brig. 1-Div. 19-Corps Shen..	To 2-Brig. Dwight's Div. Def. Wash.	Apr., 1865
153d N. Y. Infy.........Mch., 1865	From 2-Brig. 1-Div. 19-Corps Shen..	To 2-Brig. Dwight's Div. Def. Wash.	Apr., 1865

3d BRIGADE.— COMMANDER.

J. D. Fessenden........	Brigadier General ....
30th Me. Infy...........Mch., 1865	From 3-Brig. 1-Div. 19-Corps Shen..	To 3-Brig. Dwight's Div. Def. Wash.	Apr., 1865
133d N. Y. Infy.........Mch., 1865	From 3-Brig. 1-Div. 19-Corps Shen..	To 3-Brig. Dwight's Div. Def. Wash.	Apr., 1865
160th N. Y. Infy........Mch., 1865	From 3-Brig. 1-Div. 19-Corps Shen..	To 3-Brig. Dwight's Div. Def. Wash.	Apr., 1865
162d N. Y. Infy.........Mch., 1865	From 3-Brig. 1-Div. 19-Corps Shen..	To 3-Brig. Dwight's Div. Def. Wash.	Apr., 1865
165th N. Y. Infy........Mch., 1865	From 3-Brig. 1-Div. 19-Corps Shen..	To 3-Brig. Dwight's Div. Def. Wash.	Apr., 1865
173d N. Y. Infy........Mch., 1865	From 3-Brig. 1-Div. 19-Corps Shen..	To 3-Brig. Dwight's Div. Def. Wash.	Apr., 1865

2d PROVISIONAL DIVISION.— COMMANDER.

J. R. Brooke...........	Bvt. Major General..............

1st BRIGADE.—

144th Ind. Infy.........Apr., 1865	From New Organization............	No change to Muster Out....:.....	Aug., 1865
146th Ind. Infy.........Apr., 1865	From New Organization............	No change to Muster Out..........	Aug., 1865
150th Ind. Infy.........Apr., 1865	From New Organization............	No change to Muster Out..........	Aug., 1865

2d BRIGADE.—

191st Ohio Infy.........Apr., 1865	From New Organization............	No change to Muster Out..........	Aug., 1865
192d Ohio Infy..........Apr., 1865	From New Organization............	No change to Muster Out..........	Aug., 1865
193d Ohio Infy..........Apr., 1865	From New Organization............	No change to Muster Out..........	Aug., 1865
196th Ohio Infy.........Apr., 1865	From New Organization............	To Def. Baltimore 8-Corps.........	July, 1865

3d PROVISIONAL DIVISION.— COMMANDER.

T. W. Egan.............	Bvt. Major General..............

1st BRIGADE.—

147th Ind. Infy.........Apr., 1865	From New Organization............	To Def. Baltimore 8-Corps.........	July, 1865
152d Ind. Infy..........Apr., 1865	From New Organization............	To Def. Baltimore 8-Corps.........	July, 1865
194th Ohio Infy.........Apr., 1865	From New Organization............	To Def. Washington 22-Corps.......	Apr., 1865
195th Ohio Infy.........Apr., 1865	From New Organization............	To Def. Washington 22-Corps.......	Apr., 1865

2d BRIGADE.—

192d N. Y. Infy.........Apr., 1865	From Dept. Ohio..................	No change to Muster Out..........	Aug., 1865
192d Penna. Infy........Apr., 1865	From Dept. Ohio..................	No change to Muster Out..........	Aug., 1865
195th Penna. Infy.......Apr., 1865	From 1-Brig. 3-Div. W. Va.........	To Def. Washington 22-Corps.......	July, 1865
214th Penna. Infy.......Apr., 1865	From New Organization............	To Def. Washington 22-Corps.......	July, 1865

4th PROVISIONAL DIVISION.— COMMANDER.

S. S. Carroll..........	Bvt. Major General..............

1st BRIGADE.—

23d Ohio Infy...........Apr., 1865	From 1-Brig. 1-Infy. Div. W. Va....	No change to Muster Out..........	July, 1865
36th Ohio Infy..........Apr., 1865	From 1-Brig. 1-Infy. Div. W. Va....	No change to Muster Out..........	July, 1865
91st Ohio Infy..........Apr., 1865	From 2-Brig. 1-Infy. Div. W. Va....	No change to Muster Out..........	July, 1865
1st W. Va. Vet. Infy.....Apr., 1865	From 1-Brig. 1-Infy. Div. W. Va....	No change to Muster Out..........	July, 1865
13th W. Va. Infy........Apr., 1865	From 1-Brig. 1-Infy. Div. W. Va....	No change to Muster Out..........	June, 1865

2d BRIGADE.—

1st U. S. Veteran Infy....Apr., 1865	From Def. Washington 22-Corps....	To Middle Dept. 8-Corps...........	July, 1865
2d U. S. Veteran Infy....Apr., 1865	From Def. Washington 22-Corps....	To Dist. N. W. New York..........	June, 1865
3d U. S. Veteran Infy....Apr., 1865	From Def. Washington 22-Corps....	To Camp Butler, Ill..............	June, 1865

CAVALRY BRIGADE.—

3d Mass. Cav............Mch., 1865	From 2-Brig. 2-Div. 19-Corps Shen..	To Def. Washington 22-Corps.......	Apr., 1865
1st N. H. Cav...........Mch., 1865	From 2-Brig. 3-Div. Cav. Corps Shen.	To Cav. Def. Washington 22-Corps..	Apr., 1865
5th N. Y. Cav...........Mch., 1865	From 2-Br. 3-Div. Cav. Corps Shen..	No change to Muster Out..........	July, 1865
22d N. Y. Cav...........Mch., 1865	From 2-Br. 3-Div. Cav. Corps Shen..	No change to Muster Out..........	Aug., 1865
12th Penna. Cav.........Mch., 1865	From Unatt. 3-Div. W. Va..........	No change to Muster Out..........	July, 1865
18th Penna. Cav.........Mch., 1865	From 1-Br. 3-Div. Cav. Corps Shen..	Transferred to 3d Pa. Prov'l Cav..	June, 1865
1st R. I. Cav...........Mch., 1865	From Res. Br. 1-Div. Cav. C. Shen..	To Middle Dept. 8-Corps..........	June, 1865
2d U. S. Cav...........Mch., 1865	From Res. Br. 1-Div. Cav. C. Shen..	To Regular Establishment.........	Aug., 1865
Battys. K & L, 1st U. S..Mch., 1865	From Horse Arty. Res. Shen.......	To Regular Establishment.........	Aug., 1865

HORSE ARTILLERY RESERVE.—

6th N. Y. Batty...........Dec., 1864	From Horse Arty. Cav. Corps Shen..	To Horse Arty. Brig. 22-Corps......	Apr., 1865
Battys. B & L, 2d U. S...Dec., 1864	From Horse Arty. Cav. Corps Shen..	To Horse Arty. Brig. 22-Corps......	Apr., 1865
Batty. D, 2d U. S. Arty...Dec., 1864	From Horse Arty. Cav. Corps Shen..	To Horse Arty. Brig. 22-Corps......	Apr., 1865
Batty. M, 2d U. S. Arty...Dec., 1864	From Horse Arty. Cav. Corps Shen..	To Horse Arty. Brig. 22-Corps......	Apr., 1865
Batty. C, 3d U. S. Arty...Dec., 1864	From Horse Arty. Cav. Corps Shen..	To Horse Arty. Brig. 22-Corps......	Apr., 1865

ARTILLERY RESERVE.—

1st Me. Batty...........Mch., 1865	From Arty. Brig. 19-Corps Shen....	No change to Muster Out..........	July, 1865
5th Me. Batty...........Mch., 1865	From Arty. Brig. 19-Corps Shen....	No change to Muster Out..........	July, 1865
Batty. D, 1st R. I. Arty..Mch., 1865	From Arty. Brig. 19-Corps Shen....	No change to Muster Out..........	July, 1865
5th N. Y. Indpt. Batty...Mch., 1865	From Arty. Brig. 19-Corps Shen....	No change to Muster Out..........	July, 1865
17th Ind. Batty.........Mch., 1865	From Arty. Brig. 19-Corps Shen....	No change to Muster Out..........	July, 1865

Western Departments and Armies

Index to Western Departments and Armies

Western Departments and Armies

Department and Army of the Ohio and Cumberland

Was first started by a small body of Kentucky Volunteers, organized at Camp Joe Holt, near Louisville, Ky., by Colonel, afterwards Major General Lovell H. Rousseau, in the spring and early summer of 1861. The State of Kentucky lying within 100 miles of the Ohio River was constituted the Department of Kentucky May 28, 1861, but was merged into the Department of the Cumberland August 15, 1861, which Department consisted of the States of Kentucky and Tennessee. This Department was again changed to the Department of the Ohio, Nov. 9, 1861, embracing the States of Ohio, Michigan, Indiana, all of Kentucky lying east of the Cumberland River, and the State of Tennessee. The Department was merged into Halleck's Department of the Mississippi, March 11, 1862, but its army retained its original title and organization as Army of the Ohio until Oct. 24, 1862, when the Department of the Cumberland was again recreated, to consist of Tennessee, East of the Tennessee River, and such parts of Alabama and Georgia as may be taken possession of by United States Troops. The title being changed to Army of the Cumberland.

The several Commanders and Troops attached to this Department were as follows:

DEPARTMENT AND ARMY COMMANDERS.

Robert Anderson	Brigadier General	May 28, 1861, to Oct. 8, 1861.
W. T. Sherman	Brigadier General	Oct. 8, 1861, to Nov. 9, 1861.
D. C. Buell	Major General	Nov. 15, 1861, to Oct. 30, 1862.
W. S. Rosecrans	Major General	Oct. 30, 1862, to Oct. 20, 1863.
George H. Thomas	Major General	Oct. 20, 1863, to July, 1865.

THOMAS' COMMAND, CAMP DICK ROBINSON, ETC.—

COMMANDER.

Geo. H. Thomas	Brigadier General	

3d Ky. Infy	Oct., 1861	From New Organization	To 11-Brig. Army Ohio	Nov., 1861
4th Ky. Infy	Oct., 1861	From New Organization	To 2-Brig. Army Ohio	Nov., 1861
7th Ky. Infy	Oct., 1861	From New Organization	To Unass'd Camp Dick Robinson, Ky.	Nov., 1861
8th Ky. Infy	Oct., 1861	From New Organization	To Unass'd Camp Dick Robinson, Ky.	Nov., 1861
9th Ky. Infy	Oct., 1861	From New Organization	To 11-Brig. Army Ohio	Nov., 1861
1st Tenn. Infy	Oct., 1861	From New Organization	To 12-Brig. Army Ohio	Nov., 1861
2d Tenn. Infy	Oct., 1861	From New Organization	To 12-Brig. Army Ohio	Nov., 1861
14th Ohio Infy	Oct., 1861	From New Organization	To 2-Brig. Army Ohio	Nov., 1861
35th Ohio Infy	Oct., 1861	From New Organization	To 3-Brig. Army Ohio	Nov., 1861
Batty. A, 1st Ohio Arty	Oct., 1861	From New Organization	To McCook's Command Nolin	Nov., 1861
Batty. B, 1st Ohio Infy	Oct., 1861	From New Organization	To Arty. 1-Div. Army Ohio	Dec., 1861
Batty. C, 1st Ohio Arty	Oct., 1861	From New Organization	To Arty. 1-Div. Army Ohio	Dec., 1861
Batty. B, Ky. Arty	Oct., 1861	From New Organization	To Arty. 1-Div. Army Ohio	Dec., 1861
1st Ky. Cav	Oct., 1861	From New Organization	To Cav. 1-Div. Army Ohio	Dec., 1861
BARDSTOWN, KY.—				
10th Ind. Infy	Oct., 1861	From New Organization	To 2-Brig. Army Ohio	Nov., 1861
CRAB ORCHARD, KY.—				
33d Ind. Infy	Oct., 1861	From New Organization	To 1-Brig. Army Ohio	Nov., 1861
JEFFERSONVILLE, IND.—				
34th Ind. Infy	Oct., 1861	From New Organization	To 10-Brig. Army Ohio	Nov., 1861
36th Ind. Infy	Oct., 1861	From New Organization	To 10-Brig. Army Ohio	Nov., 1861
1st Wis. Infy	Oct., 1861	From New Organization	To 7-Brig. Army Ohio	Nov., 1861
MOUTH OF SALT RIVER.—				
37th Ind. Infy	Oct., 1861	From New Organization	To 16-Brig. Army Ohio	Nov., 1861
9th Mich. Infy	Oct., 1861	From New Organization	To 16-Brig. Army Ohio	Nov., 1861
LEBANON JUNCTION.—				
2d Minn. Infy	Oct., 1861	From New Organization	To 3-Brig. Army Ohio	Nov., 1861
OLYMPIAN SPRINGS.—				
2d Ohio Infy	Oct., 1861	From New Organization	To 9-Brig. Army Ohio	Nov., 1861
59th Ohio Infy	Oct., 1861	From New Organization	To 11-Brig. Army Ohio	Nov., 1861
NICHOLASVILLE.—				
21st Ohio Infy	Oct., 1861	From New Organization	To 9-Brig. Army Ohio	Nov., 1861
38th Ohio Infy	Oct., 1861	From New Organization	To 1-Brig. Army Ohio	Nov., 1861
BIG HILL.—				
17th Ohio Infy	Oct., 1861	From New Organization	To 1-Brig. Army Ohio	Nov., 1861
COLESBURG.—				
24th Ill. Infy	Oct., 1861	From New Organization	To 8-Brig. Army Ohio	Nov., 1861
ELIZABETHTOWN.—				
19th Ill. Infy	Oct., 1861	From New Organization	To 8-Brig. Army Ohio	Nov., 1861
OWENSBURG.—				
31st Ind. Infy	Oct., 1861	From New Organization	To 13-Brig. Army Ohio	Nov., 1861
CYNTHIANA.—				
35th Ohio Infy	Oct., 1861	From New Organization	To 3-Brig. Army Ohio	Nov., 1861

McCOOK'S COMMAND AT NOLIN.—   COMMANDER.

A. McD. McCook	Brigadier General	

ROUSSEAU'S 1st BRIGADE.—   COMMANDER.

L. H. Rousseau	Brigadier General			
5th Ky. Infy	Oct., 1861	From New Organization	To 4-Brig. Army Ohio	Nov., 1861
6th Ky. Infy	Oct., 1861	From New Organization	To 12-Brig. Army Ohio	Nov., 1861
15th U. S. Infy	Oct., 1861	From New Organization	To 4-Brig. Army Ohio	Nov., 1861
19th U. S. Infy	Oct., 1861	From New Organization	To 4-Brig. Army Ohio	Nov., 1861
6th Ind. Infy	Oct., 1861	From New Organization	To 4-Brig. Army Ohio	Nov., 1861
Batty. A, Ky. Arty	Oct., 1861	From New Organization	To Arty. 2-Div. Army Ohio	Dec., 1861
2d Ky. Cav	Oct., 1861	From New Organization	To Unatt. 2-Div. Army Ohio	Dec., 1861

WOOD'S 2d BRIGADE.—   COMMANDER.

Thos. J. Wood	Brigadier General			
29th Ind. Infy	Oct., 1861	From New Organization	To 5-Brig. Army Ohio	Nov., 1861
30th Ind. Infy	Oct., 1861	From New Organization	To 5-Brig. Army Ohio	Nov., 1861
38th Ind. Infy	Oct., 1861	From New Organization	To 7-Brig. Army Ohio	Nov., 1861
39th Ind. Infy	Oct., 1861	From New Organization	To 6-Brig. Army Ohio	Nov., 1861

JOHNSON'S 3d BRIGADE.—   COMMANDER.

R. W. Johnson	Brigadier General			
15th Ohio Infy	Oct., 1861	From New Organization	To 6-Brig. Army Ohio	Nov., 1861
49th Ohio Infy	Oct., 1861	From New Organization	To 6-Brig. Army Ohio	Nov., 1861
34th Ill. Infy	Oct., 1861	From New Organization	To 5-Brig. Army Ohio	Nov., 1861
32d Ind. Infy	Oct., 1861	From New Organization	To 6-Brig. Army Ohio	Nov., 1861

NEGLEY'S 4th BRIGADE.—   COMMANDER.

J. S. Negley	Brigadier General		
77th Penna. Infy........Oct., 1861	From New Organization............	To 5-Brig. Army Ohio............	Nov., 1861
78th Penna. Infy........Oct., 1861	From New Organization............	To 7-Brig. Army Ohio............	Nov., 1861
79th Penna. Infy........Oct., 1861	From New Organization............	To 7-Brig. Army Ohio............	Nov., 1861
Indpt. Batty. B, Pa. Arty..Oct., 1861	From New Organization............	To Arty. 2-Div. Army Ohio........	Nov., 1861
Batty. A, 1st Ohio Arty...Nov., 1861	From Thomas' Command...........	To Arty. 2-Div. Army Ohio.......	Nov., 1861

BRIGADES ORGANIZED Nov., 1861.—
1st BRIGADE.—   COMMANDER.

A. Schoepff	Brigadier General		
33d Ind. Infy........Nov., 1861	From Thomas' Com'd, Army Ohio...	To 1-Brig. 1-Div. Army Ohio.......	Dec., 1861
12th Ky. Infy........Nov., 1861	From Thomas' Com'd, Army Ohio...	To 1-Brig. 1-Div. Army Ohio.......	Dec., 1861
17th Ohio Infy........Nov., 1861	From Thomas' Com'd, Army Ohio...	To 1-Brig. 1-Div. Army Ohio.......	Dec., 1861
38th Ohio Infy........Nov., 1861	From Thomas' Com'd, Army Ohio...	To 1-Brig. 1-Div. Army Ohio.......	Dec., 1861

2d BRIGADE.—   COMMANDER.

M. D. Manson	Col. 10th Ind. Infy		
10th Ind. Infy........Nov., 1861	From Thomas' Com'd, Army Ohio...	To 2-Brig. 1-Div. Army Ohio.......	Dec:, 1861
4th Ky. Infy........Nov., 1861	From Thomas' Com'd, Army Ohio...	To 2-Brig. 1-Div. Army Ohio.......	Dec., 1861
10th Ky. Infy........Nov., 1861	From New Organization............	To 2-Brig. 1-Div. Army Ohio.......	Dec., 1861
14th Ohio Infy........Nov., 1861	From Thomas' Com'd, Army Ohio...	To 2-Brig. 1-Div. Army Ohio.......	Dec., 1861

3d BRIGADE.—   COMMANDER.

R. L. McCook	Col. 9th Ohio Infy		
2d Minn. Infy........Nov., 1861	From Thomas' Com'd, Army Ohio...	To 3-Brig. 1-Div. Army Ohio.......	Dec., 1861
9th Ohio Infy........Nov., 1861	From 2-Brig. Kanawha Div. W. Va.	To 3-Brig. 1-Div. Army Ohio.......	Dec., 1861
35th Ohio Infy........Nov., 1861	From Thomas' Com'd, Army Ohio...	To 3-Brig. 1-Div. Army Ohio.......	Dec., 1861
18th U. S. Infy........Nov., 1861	From New Organization............	To 3-Brig. 1-Div. Army Ohio.......	Dec., 1861

4th BRIGADE.—   COMMANDER.

L. H. Rousseau	Brigadier General		
6th Ind. Infy........Nov., 1861	From 1-Brig. McCook's Command...	To 4-Brig. 2-Div. Army Ohio.......	Dec., 1861
5th Ky. Infy........Nov., 1861	From 1-Brig. McCook's Command...	To 4-Brig. 2-Div. Army Ohio.......	Dec., 1861
15th U. S. Infy........Nov., 1861	From 1-Brig. McCook's Command...	To 4-Brig. 2-Div. Army Ohio.......	Dec., 1861
19th U. S. Infy........Nov., 1861	From 1-Brig. McCook's Command...	To 4-Brig. 2-Div. Army Ohio.......	Dec., 1861
1st Ohio Infy........Nov., 1861	From New Organization............	To 4-Brig. 2-Div. Army Ohio.......	Dec., 1861

5th BRIGADE.—   COMMANDER.

Thomas J. Wood	Brigadier General		
34th Ill. Infy........Nov., 1861	From 3-Brig. McCook's Command...	To 5-Brig. 2-Div. Army Ohio.......	Dec., 1861
29th Ind. Infy........Nov., 1861	From 2-Brig. McCook's Command...	To 5-Brig. 2-Div. Army Ohio.......	Dec., 1861
30th Ind. Infy........Nov., 1861	From 2-Brig. McCook's Command...	To 5-Brig. 2-Div. Army Ohio.......	Dec., 1861
77th Penna. Infy........Nov., 1861	From 4-Brig. McCook's Command...	To 5-Brig. 2-Div. Army Ohio.......	Dec., 1861

6th BRIGADE.—   COMMANDER.

R. W. Johnson	Brigadier General		
32d Ind. Infy........Nov., 1861	From 3-Brig. McCook's Command...	To 6-Brig. 2-Div. Army Ohio.......	Dec., 1861
39th Ind. Infy........Nov., 1861	From 2-Brig. McCook's Command...	To 6-Brig. 2-Div. Army Ohio.......	Dec., 1861
15th Ohio Infy........Nov., 1861	From 3-Brig. McCook's Command...	To 6-Brig. 2-Div. Army Ohio.......	Dec., 1861
49th Ohio Infy........Nov., 1861	From 3-Brig. McCook's Command...	To 6-Brig. 2-Div. Army Ohio.......	Dec., 1861

7th BRIGADE.—   COMMANDER.

James S. Negley	Brigadier General		
38th Ind. Infy........Nov., 1861	From 2-Brig. McCook's Command...	To 7-Brig. 2-Div. Army Ohio.......	Dec., 1861
78th Penna. Infy........Nov., 1861	From 4-Brig. McCook's Command...	To 7-Brig. 2-Div. Army Ohio.......	Dec., 1861
79th Penna. Infy........Nov., 1861	From 4-Brig. McCook's Command...	To 7-Brig. 2-Div. Army Ohio.......	Dec., 1861
1st Wis. Infy........Nov., 1861	From Thomas' Com'd, Army Ohio...	To 7-Brig. 2-Div. Army Ohio.......	Dec., 1861

8th BRIGADE.—   COMMANDER.

J. B. Turchin	Col. 19th Ill. Infy		
19th Ill. Infy........Nov., 1861	From Thomas' Com'd, Army Ohio...	To 8-Brig. 3-Div. Army Ohio...	Dec., 1861
24th Ill. Infy........Nov., 1861	From Thomas' Com'd, Army Ohio...	To 8-Brig. 3-Div. Army Ohio...	Dec., 1861
37th Ind. Infy........Nov., 1861	From Thomas' Com'd, Army Ohio...	To 8-Brig. 3-Div. Army Ohio...	Dec., 1861
18th Ohio Infy........Nov, 1861	From New Organization............	To 8-Brig. 3-Div. Army Ohio...	Dec., 1861

9th BRIGADE.—   COMMANDER.

J. W. Sill	Col. 33d Ohio Infy		
2d Ohio Infy........Nov., 1861	From Thomas' Com'd, Army Ohio...	To 9-Brig. 3-Div. Army Ohio...	Dec., 1861
21st Ohio Infy........Nov., 1861	From Thomas' Com'd, Army Ohio...	To 9-Brig. 3-Div. Army Ohio...	Dec., 1861
33d Ohio Infy........Nov., 1861	From Thomas' Com'd, Army Ohio...	To 9-Brig. 3-Div. Army Ohio...	Dec., 1861
10th Wis. Infy........Nov., 1861	From New Organization............	To 9-Brig. 3-Div. Army Ohio...	Dec., 1861

10th BRIGADE.—   COMMANDER.

Jacob Ammon	Col. 24th Ohio Infy		
34th Ind. Infy........Nov., 1861	From Thomas' Com'd, Army Ohio...	To 10-Brig. 4-Div. Army Ohio.......	Dec., 1861
36th Ind. Infy........Nov., 1861	From Thomas' Com'd, Army Ohio...	To 10-Brig. 4-Div. Army Ohio.......	Dec., 1861
6th Ohio Infy........Nov., 1861	From Cheat Mt. Dist. West Va....	To 10-Brig. 4-Div. Army Ohio.......	Dec., 1861
24th Ohio Infy........Nov., 1861	From Cheat Mt. Dist. West Va.....	To 10-Brig. 4-Div. Army Ohio.......	Dec., 1861

11th BRIGADE.—   COMMANDER.

J. T. Doyle	Brigadier General		
3d Ky. Infy........Nov., 1861	From Thomas' Com'd, Army Ohio...	To Unatt. Army Ohio............	Dec., 1861
9th Ky. Infy........Nov., 1861	From Thomas' Com'd, Army Ohio...	To 11-Brig. 1-Div. Army Ohio.......	Dec., 1861
19th Ohio Infy........Nov., 1861	From Thomas' Com'd, Army Ohio...	To 11-Brig. 1-Div. Army Ohio.......	Dec., 1861
59th Ohio Infy........Nov., 1861	From Thomas' Com'd, Army Ohio...	To 11-Brig. 1-Div. Army Ohio.......	Dec., 1861

12th BRIGADE.—   COMMANDER.

S. P. Carter	Brigadier General		
6th Ky. Infy........Nov., 1861	From 1-Brig. McCook's Command...	To 12-Brig. 1-Div. Army Ohio...	Dec., 1861
31st Ohio Infy........Nov., 1861	From Thomas' Com'd, Army Ohio...	To 12-Brig. 1-Div. Army Ohio...	Dec., 1861
1st Tenn. Infy........Nov., 1861	From Thomas' Com'd, Army Ohio...	To 12-Brig. 1-Div. Army Ohio...	Dec., 1861
2d Tenn. Infy........Nov., 1861	From Thomas' Com'd, Army Ohio...	To 12-Brig. 1-Div. Army Ohio...	Dec., 1861

13th BRIGADE.— COMMANDER.

Charles Cruft..........Col. 31st Ind. Infy..............				
31st Ind. Infy..........Nov., 1861	From New Organization............	To 13-Brig. 5-Div. Army Ohio.......	Dec.,	1861
44th Ind. Infy..........Nov., 1861	From New Organization............	To 13-Brig. 5-Div. Army Ohio.......	Dec.,	1861
17th Ky. Infy..........Nov., 1861	From New Organization............	To 13-Brig. 5-Div. Army Ohio.......	Dec.,	1861
25th Ky. Infy..........Nov., 1861	From New Organization............	To 13-Brig. 5-Div. Army Ohio.......	Dec.,	1861

14th BRIGADE.— COMMANDER.

J. G. Jones.............Col. 42d Ind. Infy..............				
42d Ind. Infy..........Nov., 1861	From New Organization............	To 14-Brig. 5-Div. Army Ohio.......	Dec.,	1861
43d Ind. Infy..........Nov., 1861	From New Organization............	To 14-Brig. 5-Div. Army Ohio.......	Dec.,	1861
11th Ky. Infy..........Nov., 1861	From New Organization............	To 14-Brig. 5-Div. Army Ohio.......	Dec.,	1861
26th Ky. Infy..........Nov., 1861	From New Organization............	To 14-Brig. 5-Div. Army Ohio.......	Dec.,	1861

15th BRIGADE.— COMMANDER.

M. S. Hascall..........Col. 17th Ind. Infy..............				
15th Ind. Infy..........Nov., 1861	From Cheat Mt. Dist. West Va.....	To 15-Brig. 4-Div. Army Ohio.......	Dec.,	1861
17th Ind. Infy..........Nov., 1861	From Cheat Mt. Dist. West Va.....	To 15-Brig. 4-Div. Army Ohio.......	Dec.,	1861
41st Ohio Infy..........Nov., 1861	From New Organization............	To 15-Brig. 4-Div. Army Ohio.......	Dec.,	1861
51st Ohio Infy..........Nov., 1861	From New Organization............	To 15-Brig. 4-Div. Army Ohio.......	Dec.,	1861

16th BRIGADE.— COMMANDER.

W. T. Ward.............Brigadier General..............				
13th Ky. Infy..........Nov., 1861	From New Organization............	To 11-Brig. Army Ohio............	Dec.,	1861
15th Ky. Infy..........Nov., 1861	From New Organization............	To 17-Brig. Army Ohio............	Dec.,	1861
9th Mich Infy..........Nov., 1861	From Thomas' Com'd, Army Ohio...	To 23d Indpt. Brig. Army Ohio.....	Mch.,	1862
3d Minn. Infy..........Nov., 1861	From New Organization............	To 23d Indpt. Brig. Army Ohio.....	Mch.,	1862
8th Ky. Infy..........Jan., 1862	From Thomas' Com'd, Army Ohio...	To 23d Indpt. Brig. Army Ohio.....	Mch.,	1862
28th Ky. Infy..........Jan., 1862	From New Organization............	To Unatt. Army Ohio..............	Mch.,	1862

17th BRIGADE.— COMMANDER.

E. Dumont.............Brigadier General..............				
15th Ky. Infy..........Dec., 1861	From 16-Brig. Army Ohio.........	To 17-Brig. 3-Div. Army Ohio.......	Dec.,	1861
3d Ohio Infy..........Dec., 1861	From Cheat Mt. Dist. West Va....	To 17-Brig. 3-Div. Army Ohio.......	Dec.,	1861
10th Ohio Infy..........Dec., 1861	From 1-Brig. Dist. Kanawha W. Va..	To 17-Brig. 3-Div. Army Ohio.......	Dec.,	1861
13th Ohio Infy..........Dec., 1861	From 1-Brig. Dist. Kanawha W. Va..	To 17-Brig. 3-Div. Army Ohio.......	Dec.,	1861

18th BRIGADE.—Organized Dec. 17, 1861.

COMMANDER.

James A. Garfield.......Col. 42d Ohio Infy..............				
40th Ohio Infy..........Dec., 1861	From New Organization............	To District of Eastern Ky..........	Mch.,	1862
42d Ohio Infy..........Dec., 1861	From New Organization............	To 26-Brig. 7-Div. Army Ohio......	Mch.,	1862
14th Ky. Infy..........Dec., 1861	From New Organization............	To 27-Brig. 7-Div. Army Ohio......	Mch.,	1862
22d Ky. Infy..........Dec., 1861	From New Organization............	To 26-Brig. 7-Div. Army Ohio......	Mch.,	1862
McLaughlin's O. Cav. Sqdn.Dec., 1861	From New Organization............	To Dist Eastern Ky..............	Mch.,	1862
6th Ky. Cav. (6 Co's)....Dec., 1861	From New Organization............	To Unatt. 7-Div. Army Ohio.......	Mch.,	1862
16th Ky. Infy..........Jan., 1862	From New Organization............	To Dist. Eastern Ky..............	Mch.,	1862

19th BRIGADE.—(Brigade organized Jan. 3, 1862.)

COMMANDER.

William B. Hazen.......Col. 41st Ohio Infy..............				
41st Ohio Infy..........Jan., 1862	From New Organization............	To 19-Brig. 4-Div. Army Ohio......	Jan.,	1862
46th Ind. Infy..........Jan., 1862	From New Organization............	To 19-Brig. 4-Div. Army Ohio......	Jan.,	1862
47th Ind. Infy..........Jan., 1862	From New Organization............	To 19-Brig. 4-Div. Army Ohio......	Jan.,	1862
6th Ky. Infy..........Jan., 1862	From 12-Brig. 1-Div. Army Ohio....	To 19-Brig. 4-Div. Army Ohio......	Jan.,	1862

20th BRIGADE.—Organized Jan. 8, 1862.

COMMANDER.

J. W. Forsythe.........Col. 64th Ohio Infy..............				
64th Ohio Infy..........Jan., 1862	From New Organization............	To 20-Brig. 6-Div. Army Ohio.......	Jan.,	1862
65th Ohio Infy..........Jan., 1862	From New Organization............	To 20-Brig. 6-Div. Army Ohio.......	Jan.,	1862
51st Ind. Infy..........Jan., 1862	From New Organization............	To 20-Brig. 6-Div. Army Ohio.......	Jan.,	1862
19th Ky. Infy..........Jan., 1862	From New Organization............	To 20-Brig. 6-Div. Army Ohio.......	Jan.,	1862

21st BRIGADE.—Organized Jan. 8, 1862.

COMMANDER.

H. M. Carr.............Col. 58th Ind. Infy..............				
40th Ind. Infy..........Jan., 1862	From New Organization............	To 21-Brig. 6-Div. Army Ohio.......	Jan.,	1862
57th Ind. Infy..........Jan., 1862	From New Organization............	To 21-Brig. 6-Div. Army Ohio.......	Jan.,	1862
58th Ind. Infy..........Jan., 1862	From New Organization............	To 21-Brig. 6-Div. Army Ohio.......	Jan.,	1862
24th Ky. Infy..........Jan., 1862	From New Organization............	To 21-Brig. 6-Div. Army Ohio.......	Jan.,	1862

22d BRIGADE.—Organized Jan. 18, 1862. (Assigned to 4-Div. Feb. 11, 1862.)

COMMANDER.

S. D. Bruce............Col. 20th Ky. Infy..............				
1st Ky. Infy..........Jan., 1862	From Dist. Kanawha, West Va.....	To 22-Brig. 4-Div. Army Ohio......	Feb.,	1862
2d Ky. Infy..........Jan., 1862	From Dist. Kanawha, West Va.....	To 22-Brig. 4-Div. Army Ohio......	Feb.,	1862
20th Ky. Infy..........Jan., 1862	From New Organization............	To 22-Brig. 4-Div. Army Ohio......	Feb.,	1862

BRIGADES ASSIGNED TO DIVISIONS Dec. 2, 1861, as follows:

1st DIVISION.— COMMANDER.

George H. Thomas.....Brigadier General..............	Dec. 2, 1861, to Sept. 29, 1862.	

1st BRIGADE.— COMMANDER.

A. Schoepff............Brigadier General..............	Dec. 2, 1862, to Sept. 29, 1862.			
12th Ky. Infy..........Dec., 1861	From 1-Brig. Army Ohio............	To 27-Brig. 7-Div. 3-C. Army Ohio...	Mch.,	1862
33d Ind. Infy..........Dec., 1861	From 1-Brig. Army Ohio............	To 1-Brig. 1-Div. 3-C. Army Ohio...	Sept.,	1862
17th Ohio Infy..........Dec., 1861	From 1-Brig. Army Ohio............	To 1-Brig. 1-Div. 3-C. Army Ohio...	Sept.,	1862
38th Ohio Infy..........Dec., 1861	From 1-Brig. Army Ohio............	To 1-Brig. 1-Div. 3-C. Army Ohio...	Sept.,	1862
31st Ohio Infy..........Jan., 1862	From 12-Brig. 1-Div. Army Ohio....	To 1-Brig. 1-Div. 3-C. Army Ohio...	Sept.,	1862
82d Ind. Infy..........Sept., 1862	From New Organization............	To 1-Brig. 1-Div. 3-C. Army Ohio...	Sept.,	1862

2d BRIGADE.—   COMMANDERS.

M. D. Manson..........	Col. 10th Ind. Infy.................	Dec. 2, 1861, to Mch. 22, 1862.
S. S. Fry.............	Brigadier General.................	Mch. 22, 1862, to Sept. 29, 1862.

Unit	Date	From	To	Date
10th Ind. Infy	Dec., 1861	From 2-Brig. Army Ohio...........	To 2-Brig. 1-Div. 3-C. Army Ohio...	Sept., 1862
4th Ky. Infy	Dec., 1861	From 2-Brig. Army Ohio...........	To 2-Brig. 1-Div. 3-C. Army Ohio...	Sept., 1862
10th Ky. Infy	Dec., 1861	From 2-Brig. Army Ohio...........	To 2-Brig. 1-Div. 3-C. Army Ohio...	Sept., 1862
14th Ohio Infy	Dec., 1862	From 2-Brig. Army Ohio...........	To 2-Brig. 1-Div. 3-C. Army Ohio...	Sept., 1862
74th Ind. Infy	Sept., 1862	From New Organization...........	To 2-Brig. 1-Div. 3-C. Army Ohio...	Sept., 1862

3d BRIGADE.—   COMMANDERS.

R. L. McCook..........	Col. 9th Ohio Infy.................	Dec. 2, 1861, to Aug. 6, 1862.*
F. Vanderveer	Col. 35th Ohio Infy................	Aug. 6, 1862, to Sept. 29, 1862.

*Shot by guerillas while lying sick in an ambulance.

Unit	Date	From	To	Date
2d Minn. Infy	Dec., 1861	From 3-Brig. Army Ohio........	To 3-Brig. 1-Div. 3-Corps Army Ohio.	Sept., 1862
9th Ohio Infy	Dec., 1861	From 3-Brig. Army Ohio........	To 3-Brig. 1-Div. 3-Corps Army Ohio.	Sept., 1862
35th Ohio Infy	Dec., 1861	From 3-Brig. Army Ohio........	To 3-Brig. 1-Div. 3-Corps Army Ohio.	Sept., 1862
18th U. S. Infy	Dec., 1861	From 3-Brig. Army Ohio........	To 8-Brig. 1-Div. 3-Corps Army Ohio.	Sept., 1862
87th Ind. Infy	Sept., 1862	From New Organization.........	To 3-Brig. 1-Div. 3-Corps Army Ohio.	Sept., 1862

11th BRIGADE.—Transferred to 5th Division, Mch. 9, 1862.

COMMANDER.

J. I. Boyle..............	Brigadier General	Dec. 5, 1861, to Mch. 9, 1862.

Unit	Date	From	To	Date
3d Ky. Infy	Dec., 1861	From 11-Brig. Army Ohio..........	To Unatt. Army Ohio..............	Jan., 1862
9th Ky. Infy	Dec., 1861	From 11-Brig. Army Ohio..........	To 11-Brig. 5-Div. Army Ohio......	Mch., 1862
19th Ohio Infy	Dec., 1861	From 11-Brig. Army Ohio..........	To 11-Brig. 5-Div. Army Ohio......	Mch., 1862
59th Ohio Infy	Dec., 1861	From 11-Brig. Army Ohio..........	To 11-Brig. 5-Div. Army Ohio......	Mch., 1862
13th Ky. Infy	Jan., 1862	From 16-Brig. Army Ohio..........	To 11-Brig. 5-Div. Army Ohio......	Mch., 1862
21st Ky. Infy	Jan., 1862	From New Organization...........	To 11-Brig. 5-Div. Army Ohio......	Mch., 1862

12th BRIGADE.—Detached from Division Dec. 5, 1861, to report to Headquarters Army Ohio direct.

COMMANDER.

S. P. Carter...........	Brigadier General	

Unit	Date	From	To	Date
31st Ohio Infy	Dec., 1861	From 12-Brig. Army Ohio..........	To 1-Brig. 1-Div. Army Ohio......	Jan., 1862
6th Ky. Infy	Dec., 1861	From 12-Brig. Army Ohio..........	To 19-Brig. 4-Div. Army Ohio......	Jan., 1862
2d Tenn. Infy	Dec., 1861	From 12-Brig. Army Ohio..........	To 24-Brig. 7-Div. Army Ohio......	Mch., 1862
16th Ohio Infy	Jan., 1862	From 12-Brig. Army Ohio..........	To 24-Brig. 7-Div. Army Ohio......	Mch., 1862
49th Ind. Infy	Jan., 1862	From New Organization...........	To 26-Brig. 7-Div. Army Ohio......	Mch., 1862
7th Ky. Infy	Jan., 1862	From New Organization...........	To 24-Brig. 7-Div. Army Ohio......	Mch., 1862
6th Ky. Cav	Jan., 1862	From Unas. Camp Dick Robinson, Ky.	To 24-Brig. 7-Div. Army Ohio......	Mch., 1862
9th Ohio Batty	Jan., 1862	From New Organization...........	To Cav. 7-Div. Army Ohio........	Mch., 1862
1st Tenn. Infy	Dec., 1861	From New Organization...........	To Arty. 7-Div. Army Ohio........	Mch., 1862

ARTILLERY, 1st DIVISION.—

Unit	Date	From	To	Date
Batty. B, 1st Ohio Arty	Dec., 1861	From Camp Dick Robinson, Ky.....	To Unatt. Army Ohio..............	June, 1862
Batty. C, 1st Ohio Arty	Dec., 1861	From Camp Dick Robinson, Ky.....	To Arty. 1-Div. 3-Corps Army Ohio.	Sept., 1862
Batty. B, Ky. Arty	Dec., 1861	From Camp Dick Robinson, Ky.....	To Unatt. Army Ohio........	Mch., 1862
Batty. D, 1st Mich. Arty	Jan., 1863	From New Organization...........	To Arty. 1-Div. 3-Corps Army Ohio.	Sept., 1862
Batty. I, 4th U. S. Arty	Jan., 1863	From Unatt. Army Ohio...........	To Arty. 1-Div. 3-Corps Army Ohio.	Sept., 1862
7th Ind. Batty	June, 1862	From Arty. 4-Div. Army Ohio......	To Arty. 5-Div. 2-Corps Army Ohio.	Sept., 1862

CAVALRY.—

Unit	Date	From	To	Date
1st Ky. Cav	Dec., 1861	From Camp Dick Robinson, Ky.....	To Unatt. Army Ohio..............	Mch., 1862
3d Ind. Cav., Co. G	Dec., 1861	From New Organization...........	To Cav. Brig. Army Ohio..........	June, 1862
1st Ohio Cav	Jan., 1862	From New Organization...........	To 1-Div. 3-Corps Army Ohio......	Sept., 1862

2d DIVISION.—   COMMANDER.

Alex. McD. McCook.........	Brigadier General	Dec. 2, 1861, to Sept. 29, 1862.

4th BRIGADE.—   COMMANDERS.

L. H. Rousseau..........	Brigadier General	Dec. 2, 1861, to July 11, 1862.
H. M. Buckley..........	Col. 5th Ky. Infy.................	July 11, 1862, to Aug. 10, 1862.
J. W. Sill..............	Brigadier General	Aug. 10, 1862, to Sept. 29, 1862.

Unit	Date	From	To	Date
6th Ind. Infy	Dec., 1861	From 4-Brig. Army Ohio...........	To 4-Brig. 2-Div. 1-Corps Army Ohio.	Sept., 1862
5th Ky. Infy	Dec., 1861	From 4-Brig. Army Ohio...........	To 4-Brig. 2-Div. 1-Corps Army Ohio.	Sept., 1862
1st Ohio Infy	Dec., 1861	From 4-Brig. Army Ohio...........	To 4-Brig. 2-Div. 1-Corps Army Ohio.	Sept., 1862
15th U. S. Infy	Dec., 1861	From 4-Brig. Army Ohio...........	To 4-Brig. 2-Div. 1-Corps Army Ohio.	Sept., 1862
16th U. S. Infy	Dec., 1861	From 4-Brig. Army Ohio...........	To 4-Brig. 2-Div. 1-Corps Army Ohio.	Sept., 1862
19th U. S. Infy	Dec., 1861	From 4-Brig. Army Ohio...........	To 4-Brig. 2-Div. 1-Corps Army Ohio.	Sept., 1862

5th BRIGADE.—   COMMANDERS.

Thos. J. Wood..........	Brigadier General	Dec. 2, 1861, to Jan. 8, 1862.
E. N. Kirk.............	Col. 34th Ill. Infy................	Jan. 8, 1862, to Apr. 7, 1862.
F. S. Stambaugh.......	Col. 77th Penna. Infy.............	Apr. 7, 1862, to June 20, 1862.
E. N. Kirk.............	Col. 34th Ill. Infy................	June 20, 1862, to Sept. 29, 1862.

Unit	Date	From	To	Date
34th Ill. Infy	Dec., 1861	From 5-Brig. Army Ohio...........	To 5-Brig. 2-Div. 1-Corps Army Ohio.	Sept., 1862
29th Ind. Infy	Dec., 1861	From 5-Brig. Army Ohio...........	To 5-Brig. 2-Div. 1-Corps Army Ohio.	Sept., 1862
30th Ind. Infy	Dec., 1861	From 5-Brig. Army Ohio...........	To 5-Brig. 2-Div. 1-Corps Army Ohio.	Sept., 1862
77th Penna. Infy	Dec., 1861	From 5-Brig. Army Ohio...........	To 5-Brig. 2-Div. 1-Corps Army Ohio.	Sept., 1862

6th BRIGADE.—   COMMANDERS.

R. W. Johnson..........	Brigadier General	Dec. 2, 1861, to July 24, 1862.
W. H. Gibson..........	Col. 49th Ohio Infy...............	July 24, 1862, to Aug. 10, 1862.
A. Willich	Brigadier General	Aug. 10, 1862, to Sept. 29, 1862.

Unit	Date	From	To	Date
32d Ind. Infy	Dec., 1861	From 6-Brig. Army Ohio...........	To 6-Brig. 2-Div. 1-Corps Army Ohio.	Sept., 186.
38th Ind. Infy	Dec., 1861	From 6-Brig. Army Ohio...........	To 6-Brig. 2-Div. 1-Corps Army Ohio.	Sept., 1862
15th Ohio Infy	Dec., 1861	From 6-Brig. Army Ohio...........	To 6-Brig. 2-Div. 1-Corps Army Ohio.	Sept., 1862
49th Ohio Infy	Dec., 1861	From 6-Brig. Army Ohio...........	To 6-Brig. 2-Div. 1-Corps Army Ohio.	Sept., 1862

7th BRIGADE.—Brigade detached from Division, Mch. 15, 1862, as an Independent Brigade.

COMMANDER.

James S. Negley.......	Brigadier General	

Unit	Date	From	To	Date
38th Ind. Infy	Dec., 1861	From 7-Brig. Army Ohio...........	To 7-Indpt. Brig. Army Ohio.......	Mch., 1862
78th Penna. Infy	Dec., 1861	From 7-Brig. Army Ohio...........	To 7-Indpt. Brig. Army Ohio.......	Mch., 1862
79th Penna. Infy	Dec., 1861	From 7-Brig. Army Ohio...........	To 7-Indpt. Brig. Army Ohio.......	Mch., 1862
1st Wis. Infy	Dec., 1861	From 7-Brig. Army Ohio...........	To 7-Indpt. Brig. Army Ohio.......	Mch., 1862

ARTILLERY, 2d DIVISION.—

Batty. A, 1st Ohio Arty..Dec., 1861	From McCook's Command Nolin....	To Arty. 2-Div. 1-Corps Army Ohio..	Sept., 1862
Batty. A, Ky. Arty........Dec., 1861	From McCook's Command Nolin....	To 28-Br. 3-Div. 1-Corps Army Ohio..	Sept., 1862
Indpt. Batty. B, Pa. Arty.Dec., 1861	From Negley's Brig. McCook's Com.	To Arty. 5-Div. Army Ohio.........	June, 1862
Batty. H, 5th U. S. Arty..Dec., 1861	From New Organization...........	To Arty. 2-Div. 1-Corps Army Ohio..	Sept., 1862
Batty. D, 1st Ohio Arty..Dec., 1861	From Nelson's Command Army Ohio.	To Arty. 4-Div. Army Ohio.........	Feb., 1862
Batty. E, 1st Ohio Arty..Sept., 1862	From Arty. 3-Div. Army Ohio......	To Arty. 2-Div. 1-Corps Army Ohio..	Sept., 1862
CAVALRY.			
2d Kentucky Cav........Dec.,1861	From Camp Nolin, Ky.............	To Unatt. Cav. 1-Corps Army Ohio.	Sept., 1862

3d DIVISION.—

O. M. Mitchell........	Brigadier General...............	Dec. 2, 1861, to July 2, 1862.	
W. S. Smith...........	Brigadier General...............	July 2, 1862, to July 11, 1862.	
L. H. Rousseau........	Brigadier General...............	July 11, 1862, to Sept. 29, 1862.	

8th BRIGADE.
Brigade discontinued July, 1862.   COMMANDER.

J. B. Turchin........	Col. 19th Illinois Infy.........	Dec. 2, 1861, to July 2, 1862.	
19th Illinois Infy........Dec.,1861	From 8-Brig. Army Ohio........	To Unatt. R. R. Guard Army Ohio..	July, 1862
24th Illinois Infy........Dec., 1861	From 8-Brig. Army Ohio........	To Unatt. R. R. Guard Army Ohio..	July, 1862
37th Indiana Infy........Dec., 1861	From 8-Brig. Army Ohio........	To Unatt. R. R. Guard Army Ohio..	July, 1862
18th Ohio Infy..........Dec., 1861	From 8-Brig. Army Ohio........	To Unatt. R. R. Guard Army Ohio..	July, 1862

9th BRIGADE.—   COMMANDERS.

J. W. Sill...........	Col. 33d Ohio Infy.............	Dec. 2, 1861, to Aug. 10, 1862.	
L. A. Harris.........	Col. 2d Ohio Infy..............	Aug. 10, 1862, to Sept. 29, 1862.	
2d Ohio Infy............Dec., 1861	From 9-Brig. Army Ohio........	To 9-Brig. 3-Div. 1-Corps Army Ohio.	Sept., 1862
21st Ohio Infy..........Dec., 1861	From 9-Brig. Army Ohio........	To 7th Indpt. Brig. Army Ohio.....	July, 1862
33d Ohio Infy..........Dec., 1861	From 9-Brig. Army Ohio........	To 9-Brig. 3-Div. 1-Corps Army Ohio.	Sept., 1862
10th Wisconsin Infy......Dec., 1861	From 9-Brig. Army Ohio........	To 9-Brig. 3-Div. 1-Corps Army Ohio.	Sept., 1862
38th Indiana Infy........July, 1862	From 7th Indpt. Brig. Army Ohio...	To 9-Brig. 3-Div. 1-Corps Army Ohio.	Sept., 1862
17th Kentucky Infy......July, 1862	From 10-Brig. 4-Div. Army Ohio..	To Clarksville, Tenn..............	Aug., 1862

17th BRIGADE.—   COMMANDERS.

W. H. Lytle..........	Col. 10th Ohio Infy.............	Dec. 2, 1861, to Dec. 22, 1861.	
E. Dumont...........	Brigadier General...............	Dec. 22, 1861, to Mch. 21, 1862.	
W. H. Lytle..........	Col. 10th Ohio Infy.............	Mch. 21, 1862, to Aug. 19, 1862.	
W. S. Smith..........	Brigadier General...............	Aug. 19, 1862, to Aug. 23, 1862.	
W. H. Lytle..........	Col. 10th Ohio Infy.............	Aug. 23, 1862, to Sept. 29, 1862.	
3d Ohio Infy............Dec., 1861	From 17-Brig. Army Ohio..........	To 17-B. 3-Div. 1-Corps Army Ohio.	Sept., 1862
10th Ohio Infy..........Dec., 1861	From 17-Brig. Army Ohio..........	To 17-B. 3-Div. 1-Corps Army Ohio.	Sept., 1862
13th Ohio Infy..........Dec., 1861	From 17-Brig. Army Ohio..........	To 14-Brig. 5-Div. Army Ohio......	Mch., 1862
15th Kentucky Infy......Dec., 1861	From 17-Brig. Army Ohio..........	To 17-B. 3-Div. 1-Corps Army Ohio.	Sept., 1862
42d Indiana Infy........Mch., 1862	From 14-Brig. 5-Div. Army Ohio...	To 17-B. 3-Div. 1-Corps Army Ohio.	Sept., 1862
88th Indiana Infy........Sept., 1862	From New Organization...........	To 17-B. 3-Div. 1-Corps Army Ohio.	Sept., 1862

28th BRIGADE.—Organized Aug., 1862.   Attached to 3-Div., Aug., 1862.
                                   COMMANDER.

J. C. Starkweather....	Col. 1st Wis. Infy.............		
24th Ill. Infy..........Aug., 1862	From Unatt. Army Ohio...........	To 28-Brig. 3-Div. 1-Corps Army O.	Sept., 1862
79th Penna. Infy........Aug., 1862	From Unatt. Army Ohio...........	To 28-Brig. 3-Div. 1-Corps Army O.	Sept., 1862
1st Wis. Infy..........Aug., 1862	From 7-Indpt. Brig. Army Ohio.....	To 28-Brig. 3-Div. 1-Corps Army O.	Sept., 1862
21st Wis. Infy..........Aug., 1862	From New Organization...........	To 28-Brig. 3-Div. 1-Corps Army O.	Sept., 1862
4th Ind. Batty........Aug., 1862	From Arty. Res., Army Ohio.......	To 28-Brig. 3-Div. 1-Corps Army O.	Sept., 1862
Batty. A, Ky. Arty......Aug., 1862	From Arty. 2-Div. Army Ohio......	To 28-Brig. 3-Div. 1-Corps Army O.	Sept., 1862
ARTILLERY, 3d DIVISION.—			
Batty. A, 1st Mich. Arty.Dec., 1861	From Cheat Mt. Dist. West Va.....	To Arty. 3-Div. 1-Corps Army Ohio.	Sept., 1862
5th Indiana Batty......Dec., 1861	From New Organization...........	To Arty. 3-Div. 1-Corps Army Ohio.	Sept., 1862
Batty. E, 1st Ohio Arty..Dec., 1861	From New Organization...........	To Arty. 2-Div. Army Ohio.........	Sept., 1862
CAVALRY.—			
4th Ohio Cav...........Dec., 1861	From New Organization...........	To 2-Brig. Cav. Div. Army Ohio....	Sept., 1862

4th DIVISION.—   COMMANDERS.

William Nelson........	Brigadier General...............	Dec. 2, 1861, to Aug. 16, 1862.	
Jacob Ammen..........	Brigadier General...............	Aug. 16, 1862, to Aug. 23, 1862.	
W. S. Smith..........	Brigadier General...............	Aug. 23, 1862, to Sept. 29, 1862.	

10th BRIGADE.—   COMMANDERS.

Jacob Ammen..........	Col. 24th Ohio Infy.............	Dec. 2, 1861, to Aug. 16, 1862.	
William Grose........	Col. 36th Indiana Infy.........	Aug. 16, 1862, to Sept. 29, 1862.	
34th Indiana Infy.......Dec., 1861	From 10-Brig. Army Ohio.........	To 1-Brig. 2-Div. Army Miss......	Feb., 1862
36th Indiana Infy.......Dec., 1861	From 10-Brig. Army Ohio.........	To 10-B. 4-Div. 2-Corps Army Ohio.	Sept., 1862
6th Ohio Infy..........Dec., 1861	From 10-Brig. Army Ohio.........	To 22-Brig. 4-Div. Army Ohio......	Mch., 1862
24th Ohio Infy.........Dec., 1861	From 10-Brig. Army Ohio.........	To 10-B. 4-Div. 2-Corps Army Ohio.	Sept., 1862
6th Ohio Infy..........Mch., 1862	From 22-Brig. 4-Div. Army Ohio...	To 10-B. 4-Div. 2-Corps Army Ohio.	Sept., 1862
17th Kentucky Infy......Apr., 1862	From 3-Brig. 4-Div. Army Tenn....	To 9-Brig. 3-Div. Army Ohio......	July, 1862
51st Ohio Infy.........June, 1862	From Unatt. Nashville, Tenn......	To 23d Indpt. Brig. Army Ohio....	July, 1862
23d Kentucky Infy.......July, 1862	From 23d Indpt. Brig. Army Ohio..	To 10-B. 4-Div. 2-Corps Army Ohio.	Sept., 1862

15th BRIGADE.—Transferred to 6th Div. Mch. 9, 1862.
                                   COMMANDER.

M. S. Hascall.........	Col. 17th Indiana Infy.........	Dec. 2, 1861, to Mch. 9, 1862.	
15th Indiana Infy.......Dec., 1861	From 15-Brig. Army Ohio.........	To 15-Brig. 6-Div. Army Ohio.....	Mch., 1862
17th Indiana Infy.......Dec., 1861	From 15-Brig. Army Ohio.........	To 15-Brig. 6-Div. Army Ohio.....	Mch., 1862
41st Ohio Infy.........Dec., 1861	From 15-Brig. Army Ohio.........	To 19-Brig. 4-Div. Army Ohio......	Jan., 1862
51st Ohio Infy.........Dec., 1861	From 15-Brig. Army Ohio.........	To Unatt. Nashville, Tenn........	Mch., 1862
50th Indiana Infy.......Jan., 1862	From New Organization...........	To Unatt. R. R. Guard Army Ohio..	Mch., 1862
26th Ohio Infy.........Jan., 1862	From Dist. Kanawha West Va......	To 15-Brig. 6-Div. Army Ohio.....	Mch., 1862
58th Indiana Infy.......Jan., 1862	From New Organization...........	To 15-Brig. 6-Div. Army Ohio.....	Mch., 1862
13th Michigan Infy......Jan., 1862	From New Organization...........	To 20-Brig. 6-Div. Army Ohio.....	Mch., 1862
3d Kentucky Infy........Mch., 1862	From Unatt. Army Ohio..........	To 15-Brig. 6-Div. Army Ohio.....	Mch., 1862

19th BRIGADE.— COMMANDERS.

William B. Hazen	Col. 41st Ohio Infy	Jan. 3, 1862, to June 2, 1862.	
William Grose	Col. 36th Indiana Infy	June 2, 1862, to July 10, 1862.	
William B. Hazen	Col. 41st Ohio Infy	July 10, 1862, to Sept. 29, 1862.	

41st Ohio Infy..........Jan., 1862	From 19-Brig. Army Ohio..........	To 19-B. 4-Div. 2-Corps Army Ohio.	Sept., 1862
46th Indiana Infy.......Jan., 1862	From 19-Brig. Army Ohio..........	To 1-Brig. 2-Div. Army Miss.......	Feb., 1862
47th Indiana Infy.......Jan., 1862	From 19-Brig. Army Ohio..........	To 1-Brig. 2-Div. Army Miss.......	Feb., 1862
6th Kentucky Infy.......Jan., 1862	From 19-Brig. Army Ohio..........	To 19-B. 4-Div. 2-Corps Army Ohio.	Sept., 1862
9th Indiana Infy........Mch., 1862	From Cheat Mt. Dist. West Va......	To 19-B. 4-Div. 2-Corps Army Ohio.	Sept., 1862
27th Kentucky Infy......Mch., 1862	From New Organization............	To 19-B. 4-Div. 2-Corps Army Ohio.	Sept., 1862

22d BRIGADE.—Assigned Feb. 11, 1862. COMMANDERS.

S. D. Bruce	Col. 20th Kentucky Infy	Feb. 11, 1862, to Apr. 13, 1862.	
T. D. Sedgwick	Col. 1st Kentucky Infy	Apr. 13, 1862, to May 30, 1862.	
M. D. Manson	Brigadier General	May 30, 1862, to Aug. 16, 1862.	
S. D. Bruce	Col. 20th Kentucky Infy	Aug. 16, 1862, to Sept. 29, 1862.	

1st Kentucky Infy.......Feb., 1862	From 22-Brig. Army Ohio..........	To 22-B. 4-Div. 2-Corps Army Ohio.	Sept., 1862
2d Kentucky Infy........Feb., 1862	From 22-Brig. Army Ohio..........	To 22-B. 4-Div. 2-Corps Army Ohio.	Sept., 1862
20th Kentucky Infy......Feb., 1862	From 22-Brig. Army Ohio..........	To 22-B. 4-Div. 2-Corps Army Ohio.	Sept., 1862
6th Ohio Infy...........Mch., 1862	From 10-Brig. 4-Div. Army Ohio...	To 10-Brig. 4-Div. Army Ohio......	Mch., 1862
31st Indiana Infy.......Apr., 1862	From 3-Brig. 4-Div. Army Tenn....	To 22-B. 4-Div. 2-Corps Army Ohio.	Sept., 1862
90th Ohio Infy.........Sept., 1862	From New Organization............	To 22-B. 4-Div. 2-Corps Army Ohio.	Sept., 1862

ARTILLERY, 4th DIVISION.—

Batty. F, 1st Ohio Arty.Dec., 1861	From New Organization............	To Arty. F. 4-Div. Army Ohio.......	Feb., 1862
7th Indiana Batty.......Jan., 1862	From New Organization............	To Arty. 5-Div. Army Ohio.........	June, 1862
8th Indiana Batty.......Jan., 1862	From New Organization............	To Arty. 6-Div. Army Ohio.........	Mch., 1862
10th Indiana Batty......Jan., 1862	From New Organization............	To Res. Arty. Army Ohio...........	June, 1862
Batty. D, 1st Ohio Arty.Feb., 1862	From Arty. 2-Div. Army Ohio......	Captured at Munfordsville........	Sept., 1862
By. H and M, 4th U. S. A.May, 1862	From Arty. 5-Div. Army Ohio......	To 10-B. 4-Div. 2-Corps Army Ohio.	Sept., 1862
Batty. B, 1st Ohio Arty.July, 1862	From 7th Indpt. Brig. Army Ohio..	To 22-B. 4-Div. 2-Corps Army Ohio.	Sept., 1862
Batty. F. 1st Ohio Arty..July, 1862	From Arty. 6-Div. Army Ohio......	To 19-B. 4-Div. 2-Corps Army Ohio.	Sept., 1862

CAVALRY.—

2d Indiana Cav..........Dec., 1861	From New Organization............	To Cav. Brig. Army Ohio..........	June, 1862
3d Indiana Cav., Co. K..Dec., 1861	From New Organization............	To Cav. Brig. Army Ohio..........	June, 1862

5th DIVISION.— COMMANDER.

T. L. Crittenden	Brigadier General	Dec. 2, 1861, to Sept. 29, 1862.	

13th BRIGADE.— COMMANDER.

Charles Crufts	Col. 31st Indiana Infy	Dec. 2, 1861, to Feb. 16, 1862.	

31st Indiana Infy.......Dec., 1861	From 13-Brig. Army Ohio..........	To 1-Brig. 3-Div. Army Tenn......	Feb., 1862
44th Indiana Infy.......Dec., 1861	From 13-Brig. Army Ohio..........	To 1-Brig. 3-Div. Army Tenn......	Feb., 1862
17th Kentucky Infy......Dec., 1861	From 13-Brig. Army Ohio..........	To 1-Brig. 3-Div. Army Tenn......	Feb., 1862
25th Kentucky Infy......Dec., 1861	From 13-Brig. Army Ohio..........	To 1-Brig. 3-Div. Army Tenn......	Feb., 1862

14th BRIGADE.— COMMANDERS.

W. S. Smith	Col. 13th Ohio Infy	Dec. 2, 1861, to July 2, 1862.	
H. P. Van Cleve	Brigadier General	July 2, 1862, to Sept. 29, 1862.	

42d Indiana Infy........Dec., 1861	From 14-Brig. Army Ohio..........	To 17-Brig. 3-Div. Army Ohio......	Mch., 1862
43d Indiana Infy........Dec., 1861	From 14-Brig. Army Ohio..........	To 1-Brig. 2-Div. Army Ohio.......	Feb., 1862
11th Kentucky Infy......Dec., 1861	From 14-Brig. Army Ohio..........	To 14-B. 5-Div. 2-Corps Army Ohio.	Sept., 1862
26th Kentucky Infy......Dec., 1861	From 14-Brig. Army Ohio..........	To 14-B. 5-Div. 2-Corps Army Ohio.	Sept., 1862
13th Ohio Infy..........Apr., 1862	From 17-Brig. 3-Div. Army Ohio...	To 14-B. 5-Div. 2-Corps Army Ohio.	Sept., 1862
44th Indiana Infy.......Apr., 1862	From 3-Brig. 4-Div. Army Tenn....	To 14-B. 5-Div. 2-Corps Army Ohio	Sept., 1862
86th Indiana Infy......Sept., 1862	From New Organization............	To 14-B. 5-Div. 2-Corps Army Ohio	Sept., 1862

11th BRIGADE.—Assigned Mch. 9, 1862. COMMANDERS.

J. T. Boyle	Brigadier General	Mch. 9, 1862, to May 27, 1862.	
Samuel Beatty	Col. 19th Ohio Infy	May 27, 1862, to Sept. 29, 1862.	

19th Ohio Infy..........Mch., 1862	From 11-Brig. 1-Div. Army Ohio...	To 11-B. 5-Div. 2-Corps Army Ohio.	Sept., 1862
59th Ohio Infy..........Mch., 1862	From 11-Brig. 1-Div. Army Ohio...	To 11-B. 5-Div. 2-Corps Army Ohio.	Sept., 1862
9th Kentucky Infy.......Mch., 1862	From 11-Brig. 1-Div. Army Ohio...	To 11-B. 5-Div. 2-Corps Army Ohio.	Sept., 1862
13th Kentucky Infy......Mch., 1861	From 11-Brig. 1-Div. Army Ohio...	To 11-B. 5-Div. 2-Corps Army Ohio.	Sept., 1862
21st Kentucky Infy......Mch., 1862	From 11-Brig. 1-Div. Army Ohio...	To 7th Indpt. Brig. Army Ohio......	June, 1862
79th Indiana Infy......Sept., 1862	From New Organization............	To 11-B. 5-Div. 2-Corps Army Ohio.	Sept., 1862

23d BRIGADE.—Attached to Division Aug., 1862. COMMANDER.

Stanley Matthews	Col. 51st Ohio Infy		

8th entucky Infy........Aug., 1862	From 23d Indpt. Brig. Army Ohio...	To 23-B. 5-Div. 2-Corps Army Ohio.	Sept., 1862
21st Kentucky Infy......Aug., 1862	From 23d Indpt. Brig. Army Ohio...	To 23-B. 5-Div. 2-Corps Army Ohio.	Sept., 1862
51st Ohio Infy..........Aug., 1862	From 23d Indpt. Brig. Army Ohio...	To 23-B. 5-Div. 2-Corps Army Ohio.	Sept., 1862
35th Indiana Infy.......Aug., 1862	From 23d Indpt. Brig. Army Ohio...	To 23-B. 5-Div. 2-Corps Army Ohio.	Sept., 1862
99th Ohio Infy.........Sept., 1862	From New Organization	To 23-B. 5-Div. 2-Corps Army Ohio.	Sept., 1862

ARTILLERY, 5th DIVISION.—

Batty. E, 1st Mich. Arty.Dec., 1861	From New Organization	To Arty Reserve Army Ohio.......	June, 1862
6th Indiana Batty.......Dec., 1861	From New Organization............	To Paducah, Ky....................	Mch., 1862
Batty. H & M, 4th U. S. A.Feb., 1862	From Unatt. Army Ohio..........	To Arty. 4-Div. Army Ohio........	June, 1862
Batty. G, 1st Ohio Arty..Feb., 1862	From New Organization............	To Arty. Res., Army Ohio.........	June, 1862
Indpt. Batty. B, Pa. Arty.June, 1862	From Arty. 2-Div. Army Ohio......	To Arty. 5-Div. 2-Corps Army Ohio.	Sept., 1862
6th Ohio Batty..........Jan., 1862	From New Organization............	To Arty. Res., Army Ohio.........	Mch., 1862
3d Wis. Batty..........Mch., 1862	From New Organization............	To Arty. 5-Div. 2-Corps Army Ohio.	Sept., 1862

CAVALRY.—

3d Ky. Cav.............Dec., 1861	From New Organization............	To Cav. Brig. Army Ohio..........	June, 1862
1st O. Cav., F, I, K, L, M.Aug., 1862	From 1-Div. Army Ohio............	To 5-Div. 2-Corps Army Ohio......	Sept., 1862

6th DIVISION.—Organized Feb. 11, 1862. COMMANDER.

Thomas J. Wood	Brigadier General	Feb. 11, 1862, to Sept. 29, 1862.	

20th BRIGADE.— COMMANDERS.

J. M. Forsythe	Col. 64th Ohio Infy	Feb. 11, 1862, to Apr. 5, 1862.	
J. A. Garfield	Brigadier General	Apr. 5, 1862, to July 10, 1862.	
C. G. Harker	Col. 65th Ohio Infy	July 10, 1862, to Sept. 29, 1862.	

64th Ohio Infy..........Feb., 1862	From 20-Brig. Army Ohio..........	To 20-Brig. 6-Div. 2-Corps Army O.	Sept., 1862
65th Ohio Infy..........Feb., 1862	From 20-Brig. Army Ohio..........	To 20-Brig. 6-Div. 2-Corps Army O.	Sept., 1862
19th Ky. Infy...........Feb., 1862	From 20-Brig. Army Ohio..........	To 27-Div. 7-Corps Army Ohio......	Mch., 1862
51st Ind. Infy..........Feb., 1862	From 20-Brig. Army Ohio..........	To 20-Brig. 6-Div. 2-Corps Army O.	Sept., 1862
13th Mich. Infy.........Mch., 1862	From 15-Brig. 4-Div. Army Ohio...	To 20-Brig. 6-Div. 2-Corps Army O.	Sept., 1862
3d Ky. Infy............Mch., 1862	From 15-Brig. 4-Div. Army Ohio...	To 15-Brig. 6-Div. Army Ohio.....	Mch., 1862
73d Ind. Infy..........Sept., 1862	From New Organization............	To 20-Brig. 6-Div. 2-Corps Army O.	Sept., 1862

21st BRIGADE.—

COMMANDER.

G. D. Wagner	Col. 15th Ind. Infy	Feb. 11, 1862, to Sept. 29, 1862.

40th Ind. Infy..........Feb., 1862	From 21-Brig. Army Ohio.........	To 21-Brig. 6-Div. 2-Corps Army O.	Sept., 1862
57th Ind. Infy..........Feb., 1862	From 21-Brig. Army Ohio.........	To 21-Brig. 6-Div. 2-Corps Army O.	Sept., 1862
58th Ind. Infy..........Feb., 1862	From 21-Brig. Army Ohio.........	To 15-Brig. 6-Div. Army Ohio.....	Mch., 1862
24th Ky. Infy..........Feb., 1862	From 21-Brig. Army Ohio.........	To 21-Brig. 6-Div. 2-Corps Army O.	Sept., 1862
15th Ind. Infy..........Mch., 1862	From 15-Brig. 6-Div. Army Ohio....	To 21-Brig. 6-Div. 2-Corps Army O.	Sept., 1862
97th Ohio Infy.........Sept., 1862	From New Organization...........	To 21-Brig. 6-Div. 2-Corps Army O.	Sept., 1862

15th BRIGADE.—Assigned March 9, 1862.

COMMANDER.

M. S. Hascall	Col. 17th Indiana Infy	Mch. 9, 1862, to Sept. 29, 1862.

15th Indiana Infy.......Mch., 1862	From 15-Brig. 4-Div. Army Ohio...	To 21-Brig. 6-Div. Army Ohio......	Mch., 1862
17th Indiana Infy.......Mch., 1862	From 15-Brig. 4-Div. Army Ohio...	To 15-Brig. 6-Div. 2-Corps Army O.	Sept., 1862
26th Ohio Infy.........Mch., 1862	From 15-Brig. 4-Div. Army Ohio...	To 15-Brig. 6-Div. 2-Corps Army O.	Sept., 1862
13th Michigan Infy......Mch., 1862	From 15-Brig. 4-Div. Army Ohio...	To 20-Brig. 6-Div. Army Ohio......	Mch., 1862
3d Kentucky Infy........Mch., 1862	From 15-Brig. 4-Div. Army Ohio...	To 15-Brig. 6-Div. 2-Corps Army O.	Sept., 1862
58th Indiana Infy.......Mch., 1862	From 21-Brig. 6-Div. Army Ohio...	To 15-Brig. 6-Div. 2-Corps Army O.	Sept., 1862
ARTILLERY, 6th DIVISION.—			
Batty. F, 1st Ohio Arty..Mch., 1862	From Arty. 4-Div. Army Ohio......	To Arty. 4-Div. Army Ohio........	July, 1862
8th Ind. Batty..........Mch., 1862	From Arty. 4-Div. Army Ohio......	To 15-Brig. 6-Div. 2-Corps Army O.	Sept., 1862
6th Ohio Batty.........June, 1862	From Arty. Res. Army Ohio........	To 20-Brig. 6-Div. 2-Corps Army O.	Sept., 1862
10th Ind. Batty.........July, 1862	From Arty. Res. Army Ohio........	To 21-Brig. 6-Div. 2-Corps Army O.	Sept., 1862
CAVALRY.—			
3d Ohio Cav............Mch., 1862	From Jeffersonville, Ind..........	To Cav. Brig. Army Ohio........	June, 1862

7th DIVISION.—Organized March 26, 1862.

COMMANDER.

Geo. W. Morgan	Brigadier General	Mch. 26, 1862, to Oct. 10, 1862.

24th BRIGADE.—

COMMANDER.

S. P. Carter	Brigadier General	Mch. 26, 1862, to Oct. 10, 1862.

49th Ind. Infy..........Mch., 1862	From 12-Brig. 1-Div. Army Ohio...	To 3-Brig. Cumb'd Div. Dist. W. Va.	Oct., 1862
7th Ky. Infy...........Mch., 1862	From 12-Brig. 1-Div. Army Ohio...	To 3-Brig. Cumb'd Div. Dist. W. Va.	Oct., 1862
1st Tenn. Infy.........Mch., 1862	From 12-Brig. 1-Div. Army Ohio...	To 3-Brig. Cumb'd Div. Dist. W. Va.	Oct., 1862
2d Tenn. Infy..........Mch., 1862	From 12-Brig. 1-Div. Army Ohio...	To 3-Brig. Cumb'd Div. Dist. W. Va.	Oct., 1862

25th BRIGADE.—

COMMANDER.

J. G. Spear	Brigadier General	Mch. 26, 1862, to Oct. 10, 1862.

3d Tenn. Infy..........Mch., 1862	From New Organization...........	To 1-Brig. Cumb'd Div. Dist. W. Va.	Oct., 1862
4th Tenn. Infy.........Mch., 1862	From New Organization...........	To 1-Brig. Cumb'd Div. Dist. W. Va.	Oct., 1862
5th Tenn. Infy.........Mch., 1862	From New Organization...........	To 1-Brig. Cumb'd Div. Dist. W. Va.	Oct., 1862
6th Tenn. Infy.........Mch., 1862	From New Organization...........	To 1-Brig. Cumb'd Div. Dist. W. Va.	Oct., 1862

26th BRIGADE.—

COMMANDER.

Geo. F. DeCourcy	Col. 16th Ohio Infy	Mch. 26, 1862, to Oct. 10, 1862.

22d Ky. Infy..........Mch., 1862	From 18-Brig. Army Ohio.........	To 4-Brig. Cumb'd Div. Dist. W. Va.	Oct., 1862
16th Ohio Infy.........Mch., 1862	From 12-Brig. 1-Div. Army Ohio...	To 4-Brig. Cumb'd Div. Dist. W. Va.	Oct., 1862
42d Ohio Infy..........Mch., 1862	From 18-Brig. Army Ohio.........	To 4-Brig. Cumb'd Div. Dist. W. Va.	Oct., 1862

27th BRIGADE.—

COMMANDERS.

John Coburn	Col. 33d Ind. Infy	Mch. 26, 1862, to Apr. 12, 1862.
A. Baird	Brigadier General	Apr. 12, 1862, to Oct. 10, 1862.

33d Ind. Infy..........Mch., 1862	From 1-Brig. 1-Div. Army Ohio...	To 1-Brig. 3-Div. Army Ky. Dept. O.	Oct., 1862
14th Ky. Infy..........Mch., 1862	From 18-Brig. Army Ohio.........	To 2-Brig. 3-Div. Army Ky. Dept. O.	Oct., 1862
19th Ky. Infy..........Mch., 1862	From New Organization...........	To 2-Brig. 1-Div. Army Ky. Dept. O.	Oct., 1862
ARTILLERY.—			
9th Ohio Batty.........Mch., 1862	From 12-Brig. 1-Div. Army Ohio...	To Unatt. Army Ky. Dept. Ohio...	Oct., 1862
Batty. G, 1st. Mich. Arty..Mch., 1862	From New Organization...........	To Arty. Cumb'd Div. Dist. W. Va..	Oct., 1862
1st Wis. Batty.........Mch., 1862	From New Organization...........	To Arty. Cumb'd Div. Dist. W. Va..	Oct., 1862
CAVALRY.—			
6 Ky. Cav. (Munday's B'n) Mch., '62	From 12-Brig. 1-Div. Army Ohio...	To Unatt. Louisville, Ky., Dept. O.	Oct., 1862
ENGINEERS.—			
Patterson's Ky. Co......Mch., 1862	From Unatt. Army Ohio.........	To 9-Div. R. W. 13-C'ps Army Tenn.	Oct., 1862

7th INDEPENDENT BRIGADE.—Detached from 2-Div., Mch. 15, 1862.

COMMANDERS.

James S. Negley	Brigadier General	
J. F. Miller	Col. 29th Ind. Infy	

35th Ind. Infy..........Mch., 1862	From New Organization...........	To 23d Indpt. Brig. Army Ohio....	July, 1862
38th Ind. Infy..........Mch., 1862	From 7-Brig. 2-Div. Army Ohio...	To 9-Brig. 3-Div. Army Ohio.....	July, 1862
78th Penna. Infy.......Mch., 1862	From 7-Brig. 2-Div. Army Ohio...	To Unatt. Army Ohio............	June, 1862
79th Penna. Infy.......Mch., 1862	From 7-Brig. 2-Div. Army Ohio...	To Unatt. Army Ohio............	July, 1862
1st Wis. Infy..........Mch., 1862	From 7-Brig. 2-Div. Army Ohio...	To 28-Brig. Army Ohio..........	Aug., 1862
21st Ky. Infy..........June, 1862	From 11-Brig. 5-Div. Army Ohio...	To 23d Indpt. Brig. Army Ohio.....	July, 1862
21st Ohio Infy.........July, 1862	From 9-Brig. Army Ohio.........	To 7-Brig. 8-Div. Army Ohio.....	Sept., 1862
Batty B, 1st Ohio Arty..Mch., 1862	From Unatt. Army Ohio.........	To Arty. 4-Div. Army Ohio.......	July, 1862
4th Ind. Batty.........July, 1862	From Arty. Res., Army Ohio.......	To 28-Brig. 3-Div. Army Ohio.....	Aug., 1862
7th Pa. Cav. A, D, H, I.Mch., 1862	From Unatt. Army Ohio........	To Cav. 8-Div. Army Ohio........	Sept., 1862

23d INDEPENDENT BRIGADE.—Organized Mch. 8, 1862.

COMMANDERS.

W. W. Duffield	Col. 9th Mich. Infy	Mch. 8, 1862, to May 14, 1862.
H. C. Lester	Col. 3d Minn. Infy	May 14, 1862, to July 10, 1862.
Stanley Matthews	Col. 51st Ohio Infy	July 17, 1862, to Aug., 1862.

8th Ky. Infy...........Mch., 1862	From Unatt. Army Ohio.........	To 23-Brig. 5-Div. Army Ohio......	Aug., 1862
23d Ky. Infy..........Mch., 1862	From New Organization.........	To 10-Brig. 4-Div. Army Ohio.....	July, 1862
9th Mich. Infy.........Mch., 1862	From 16-Brig. Army Ohio.........	To Unatt. Tullahoma, Tenn......	July, 1862
3d Minn. Infy..........Mch., 1862	From 16-Brig. Army Ohio.........	Captured at Murfreesboro, Tenn...	July, 1862
35th Ind. Infy.........July, 1862	From 7-Indpt. Brig. Army Ohio....	To 23-Brig. 5-Div. Army Ohio.....	Aug., 1862
51st Ohio Infy.........July, 1862	From Unatt. Army Ohio.........	To 23-Brig. 5-Div. Army Ohio.....	Aug., 1862
21st Ky. Infy..........July, 1862	From 7-Indpt. Brig. Army Ohio....	To 23-Brig. 5-Div. Army Ohio.....	Aug., 1862
Batty. B, Ky. Arty.....Mch., 1862	From Unatt. Army Ohio.........	To Arty 8-Div. Army Ohio........	Sept., 1862
7th Pa. Cav., B, G, L, M.Mch., 1862	From New Organization.........	To Headqrs. Army Ohio..........	Sept., 1862

8th DIVISION.—Organized Sept. 14, 1862.

	COMMANDER.			
Jas. S. Negley	Brigadier General			

7th BRIGADE.—

	COMMANDER.			
G. F. Miller	Col. 78th Penna. Infy			
37th Ind. Infy......Sept., 1862	From Unatt. R. R. Guard Army O..	To 3-Brig. 2-Div. Centre 14-C. C'b'd.	Nov.,	1862
21st Ohio Infy......Sept., 1862	From 7th Indpt. Brig. Army Ohio..	To 3-Brig. 2-Div. Centre 14-C. C'b'd.	Nov.,	1862
74th Ohio Infy......Sept., 1862	From Unatt. R. R. Guard Army O..	To 3-Brig. 2-Div. Centre 14-C. C'b'd.	Nov.,	1862
78th Penna. Infy......Sept., 1862	From Unatt. R. R. Guard Army O..	To 3-Brig. 2-Div. Centre 14-C. C'b'd.	Nov.,	1862

29th BRIGADE.—

	COMMANDER.			
T. R. Stanley	Col. 18th Ohio Infy			
19th Ill. Infy......Sept., 1862	From Unatt. R. R. Guard Army O..	To 2-Brig. 2-Div. Centre 14 C. C'b'd.	Nov.,	1862
11th Mich. Infy......Sept., 1862	From Unatt. R. R. Guard Army O..	To 2-Brig. 2-Div. Centre 14 C. C'b'd.	Nov.,	1862
18th Ohio Infy......Sept., 1862	From Unatt. R. R. Guard Army O..	To 2-Brig. 2-Div. Centre 14 C. C'b'd.	Nov.,	1862
69th Ohio Infy......Sept., 1862	From Unatt. R. R. Guard Army O..	To 2-Brig. 2-Div. Centre 14 C. C'b'd.	Nov.,	1862
ARTILLERY.—				
Batty. B, Ky. Arty......Sept., 1862	From 23d Indpt. Brig. Army Ohio..	To Arty. 2-Div. Centre 14 C. C'b'd..	Nov.,	1862
Batty. G, 1st Ohio Arty..Sept., 1862	From Arty. Res. Army Ohio........	To Arty. 2-Div. Centre 14 C. C'b'd..	Nov.,	1862
Batty. M, 1st Ohio Arty..Sept., 1862	From Arty. Res. Army Ohio........	To Arty. 2-Div. Centre 14 C. C'b'd..	Nov.,	1862
CAVALRY.—				
7th Pa. Cav. (1 and 2 B'n)..Sept., '62	From Unatt. Army Ohio..........	To 1-Brig. Cav. Div. Cumb'd........	Nov.,	1862

9th DIVISION.—Organized Sept., 1862, from 4-Div. Army Miss.

	COMMANDER.			
R. B. Mitchell	Brigadier General			

30th BRIGADE.—

	COMMANDER.			
Michael Gooding	Col. 22d Ind. Infy			
59th Ill. Infy......Sept., 1862	From 1-Brig. 4-Div. Army Miss....	To 30-Brig. 9-Div. 3-Corps Army O.	Sept.,	1862
74th Ill. Infy......Sept., 1862	From New Organization...........	To 30-Brig. 9-Div. 3-Corps Army O.	Sept.,	1862
75th Ill. Infy......Sept., 1862	From New Organization...........	To 30-Brig. 9-Div. 3-Corps Army O.	Sept.,	1862
22d Ind. Infy......Sept., 1862	From 1-Brig. 4-Div. Army Miss....	To 30-Brig. 9-Div. 3-Corps Army O.	Sept.,	1862
5th Wis. Batty......Sept., 1862	From Arty. 4-Div. Army Miss......	To 30-Brig. 9-Div. 3-Corps Army O.	Sept.,	1862

31st BRIGADE.—

	COMMANDER.			
William P. Carlin	Col. 38th Ill. Infy			
21st Ill. Infy......Sept., 1862	From 2-Brig. 4-Div. Army Miss....	To 31-Brig. 9-Div. 3-Corps Army O.	Sept.,	1862
38th Ill. Infy......Sept., 1862	From 2-Brig. 4-Div. Army Miss....	To 31-Brig. 9-Div. 3-Corps Army O.	Sept.,	1862
15th Wis. Infy......Sept., 1862	From 2-Brig. 4-Div. Army Miss....	To 31-Brig. 9-Div. 3-Corps Army O.	Sept.,	1862
101st Ohio Infy......Sept., 1862	From New Organization...........	To 31-Brig. 9-Div. 3-Corps Army O.	Sept.,	1862
2d Minn. Batty......Sept., 1862	From Arty. 4-Div. Army Miss......	To 31-Brig. 9-Div. 3-Corps Army O.	Sept.,	1862

32d BRIGADE.—

	COMMANDER.			
W. W. Caldwell	Col. 81st Ind. Infy			
25th Ill. Infy......Sept., 1862	From 3-Brig. 4-Div. Army Miss....	To 32-Brig. 9-Div. 3-Corps Army O.	Sept.,	1862
35th Ill. Infy......Sept., 1862	From 3-Brig. 4-Div. Army Miss....	To 32-Brig. 9-Div. 3-Corps Army O.	Sept.,	1862
8th Kan. Infy......Sept., 1862	From 3-Brig. 4-Div. Army Miss....	To 32-Brig. 9-Div. 3-Corps Army O.	Sept.,	1862
81st Ind. Infy......Sept., 1862	From New Organization...........	To 32-Brig. 9-Div. 3-Corps Army O.	Sept.,	1862
8th Wis. Batty......Sept., 1862	From Arty. 4-Div. Army Miss......	To 32-Brig. 9-Div. 3-Corps Army O.	Sept.,	1862
CAVALRY.—				
Co. B, 36th Ill. Infy....Sept., 1862	From 4-Div. Army Miss...........	To 9-Div. 3-Corps Army Ohio......	Sept.,	1862

10th DIVISION.—Organized Sept., 1862.

	COMMANDER.			
J. S. Jackson	Brigadier General			

33d BRIGADE.—

	COMMANDER.			
W. W. Terrell	Brigadier General			
80th Ill. Infy......Sept., 1862	From New Organization...........	To 33-Brig. 10-Div. 1-Corps Army O.	Sept.,	1862
123d Ill. Infy......Sept., 1862	From New Organization...........	To 33-Brig. 10-Div. 1-Corps Army O.	Sept.,	1862
101st Ind. Infy......Sept., 1862	From New Organization...........	To 33-Brig. 10-Div. 1-Corps Army O.	Sept.,	1862
105th Ohio Infy......Sept., 1862	From New Organization...........	To 33-Brig. 10-Div. 1-Corps Army O.	Sept.,	1862
Garrard's Det. (7th & 32d				
Ky. and 3d Tenn.)....Sept., 1862	From Unatt. Army Ohio..........	To 33-Brig. 10-Div. 1-Corps Army O.	Sept.,	1862
Parson's Batty......Sept., 1862	From Unatt. Army Ohio..........	To 33-Brig. 10-Div. 1-Corps Army O.	Sept.,	1862

34th BRIGADE.—

	COMMANDER.			
George Webster	Col. 98th Ohio Infy			
80th Ind. Infy......Sept., 1862	From New Organization...........	To 34-Brig. 10-Div. 1-Corps Army O.	Sept.,	1862
50th Ohio Infy......Sept., 1862	From New Organization...........	To 34-Brig. 10-Div. 1-Corps Army O.	Sept.,	1862
98th Ohio Infy......Sept., 1862	From New Organization...........	To 34-Brig. 10-Div. 1-Corps Army O.	Sept.,	1862
121st Ohio Infy......Sept., 1862	From New Organization...........	To 34-Brig. 10-Div. 1-Corps Army O.	Sept.,	1862
19th Ind. Batty......Sept., 1862	From New Organization...........	To 34-Brig. 10-Div. 1-Corps Army O.	Sept.,	1862

11th DIVISION.—Organized Sept., 1862, from 5-Div. Army Miss.

	COMMANDER.			
P. H. Sheridan	Brigadier General			

35th BRIGADE.—

	COMMANDER.			
B. Leiboldt	Lt.-Col. 2d Mo. Infy			
2d Mo. Infy......Sept., 1862	From 1-Brig. 5-Div. Army Miss....	To 35-Brig. 11-Div. 3-Corps Army O.	Sept.,	1862
15th Mo. Infy......Sept., 1862	From 1-Brig. 5-Div. Army Miss....	To 35-Brig. 11-Div. 3-Corps Army O.	Sept.,	1862
44th Ill. Infy......Sept., 1862	From 1-Brig. 5-Div. Army Miss....	To 35-Brig. 11-Div. 3-Corps Army O.	Sept.,	1862
73d Ill. Infy......Sept., 1862	From New Organization...........	To 35-Brig. 11-Div. 3-Corps Army O.	Sept.,	1862

36th BRIGADE.—

	COMMANDER.			
Daniel McCook	Col. 52d Ohio Infy			
85th Ill. Infy......Sept., 1862	From New Organization...........	To 36-Brig. 11-Div. 3-Corps Army O.	Sept.,	1862
86th Ill. Infy......Sept., 1862	From New Organization...........	To 36-Brig. 11-Div. 3-Corps Army O.	Sept.,	1862
125th Ill. Infy......Sept., 1862	From New Organization...........	To 36-Brig. 11-Div. 3-Corps Army O.	Sept.,	1862
52d Ohio Infy......Sept., 1862	From New Organization...........	To 36-Brig. 11-Div. 3-Corps Army O.	Sept.,	1862

37th BRIGADE.— COMMANDER.

N. Greusel	Col. 36th Ill. Infy		
36th Ill. Infy	Sept., 1862	From 1-Brig. 5-Div. Army Miss	To 37-Brig. 11-Div. 3-Corps Army O.	Sept., 1862
88th Ill. Infy	Sept., 1862	From New Organization	To 37-Brig. 11-Div. 3-Corps Army O.	Sept., 1862
21st Mich. Infy	Sept., 1862	From New Organization	To 37-Brig. 11-Div. 3-Corps Army O.	Sept., 1862
24th Wis. Infy	Sept., 1862	From New Organization	To 37-Brig. 11-Div. 3-Corps Army O.	Sept., 1862

ARTILLERY.—

Batty. I, 2d Ill. Arty	Sept., 1862	From Arty. Army Miss	To Arty. 11-Div. 3-Corps Army O.	Sept., 1862
Batty. G, 1st Mo. Arty	Sept., 1862	From Arty. Army Miss	To Arty. 11-Div. 3-Corps Army O.	Sept., 1862

12th DIVISION.—Organized Sept., 1862. COMMANDER.

E. Dumont	Brigadier General		

38th BRIGADE.— COMMANDER.

W. M. Chapin	Col. 23d Michigan Infy		
129th Illinois Infy	Sept., 1862	From New Organization	To Dist. West Ky. Dept. Ohio	Nov., 1862
23d Michigan Infy	Sept., 1862	From New Organization	To Dist. West Ky. Dept. Ohio	Nov., 1862
102d Ohio Infy	Sept., 1862	From New Organization	To Dist. West Ky. Dept. Ohio	Nov., 1862
111th Ohio Infy	Sept., 1862	From New Organization	To Dist. West Ky. Dept. Ohio	Nov., 1862

39th BRIGADE.— COMMANDER.

George T. Lunberg	Col. 108th Ohio Infy		
78th Illinois Infy	Sept., 1862	From New Organization	To Dist. West Ky. Dept. Ohio	Nov., 1862
104th Illinois Infy	Sept., 1862	From New Organization	To Dist. West Ky. Dept. Ohio	Nov., 1862
106th Ohio Infy	Sept., 1862	From New Organization	To Dist. West Ky. Dept. Ohio	Nov., 1862
108th Ohio Infy	Sept., 1862	From New Organization	To Dist. West Ky. Dept. Ohio	Nov., 1862

40th BRIGADE.— COMMANDER.

A. O. Miller	Col. 72d Indiana Infy		
98th Illinois Infy	Sept., 1862	From New Organization	To 2-Brig. 5-Div. Cen. 14-Corps	Nov., 1862
72d Indiana Infy	Sept., 1862	From New Organization	To 2-Brig. 5-Div. Cen. 14-Corps	Nov., 1862
75th Indiana Infy	Sept., 1862	From New Organization	To 2-Brig. 5-Div. Cen. 14-Corps	Nov., 1862

WARD'S BRIGADE.— COMMANDER.

W. T. Ward	Brigadier General		
102d Illinois Infy	Sept., 1862	From New Organization	To Ward's Brig. Gallatin, Tenn	Nov., 1862
105th Illinois Infy	Sept., 1862	From New Organization	To Ward's Brig. Gallatin, Tenn	Nov., 1862
79th Ohio Infy	Sept., 1862	From New Organization	To Ward's Brig. Gallatin, Tenn	Nov., 1862
93d Ohio Infy	Sept., 1862	From New Organization	To 4-Brig. 2-Div. 1-Corps Army Ohio	Sept., 1862
70th Indiana Infy	Sept., 1862	From New Organization	To Ward's Brig. Gallatin, Tenn	Nov., 1862

ARTILLERY.—

Board Trade Ill. Batty	Sept., 1862	From New Organization	To Pioneer Brig. Cumberland	Nov., 1862
13th Indiana Batty	Sept., 1862	From Army Ky. Dept. Ohio	To Ward's Brig. Gallatin, Tenn	Nov., 1862
18th Indiana Batty	Sept., 1862	From New Organization	To Arty. 5-Div. Centre 14-Corps	Nov., 1862

13th DIVISION.—Organized Sept., 1862, from 1-Division Army Miss. COMMANDER.

John M. Palmer	Brigadier General		

1st BRIGADE.— COMMANDER.

G. W. Roberts	Col. 42d Illinois Infy		
22d Illinois Infy	Sept., 1862	From 1-Brig. 1-Div. Army Miss	To 3-Brig. 3-Div. Right Wing 14-C.	Nov., 1862
27th Illinois Infy	Sept., 1862	From 1-Brig. 1-Div. Army Miss	To 3-Brig. 3-Div. Right Wing 14-C.	Nov., 1862
42d Illinois Infy	Sept., 1862	From 1-Brig. 1-Div. Army Miss	To 3-Brig. 3-Div. Right Wing 14-C.	Nov., 1862
51st Illinois Infy	Sept., 1862	From 1-Brig. 1-Div. Army Miss	To 3-Brig. 3-Div. Right Wing 14-C.	Nov., 1862
10th Wisconsin Batty	Sept., 1862	From Arty. 1-Div. Army Miss	To Arty. 2-Div. Centre 14-Corps	Nov., 1862

2d BRIGADE.— COMMANDER.

J. D. Morgan	Brigadier General		
10th Illinois Infy	Sept., 1862	From 2-Brig. 1-Div. Army Miss	To 1-Brig. 4-Div. Centre 14-Corps	Nov., 1862
16th Illinois Infy	Sept., 1862	From 2-Brig. 1-Div. Army Miss	To 1-Brig. 4-Div. Centre 14-Corps	Nov., 1862
60th Illinois Infy	Sept., 1862	From 2-Brig. 1-Div. Army Miss	To 1-Brig. 4-Div. Centre 14-Corps	Nov., 1862
10th Michigan Infy	Sept., 1862	From 2-Brig. 1-Div. Army Miss	To 1-Brig. 4-Div. Centre 14-Corps	Nov., 1862
14th Michigan Infy	Sept., 1862	From 2-Brig. 1-Div. Army Miss	To 1-Brig. 4-Div. Centre 14-Corps	Nov., 1862
Batty. C, 1st Ill. Arty	Sept., 1862	From Arty. 1-Div. Army Miss	To 3-Brig. 3-Div. Right Wing 14-C.	Nov., 1862

ARTILLERY RESERVE.—

4th Indiana Batty	June, 1862	From Unatt. Arty. Army Ohio	To 7th Indpt. Brig. Army Ohio	July, 1862
Batty. E, 1st Mich. Arty	June, 1862	From Arty. 5-Div. Army Ohio	To Garrison Nashville, Tenn	Sept., 1862
Batty. G, 1st Ohio Arty	June, 1862	From Arty. 5-Div. Army Ohio	To Arty. 8-Div. Army Ohio	Sept., 1862
Batty. M, 1st Ohio Arty	June, 1862	From Unatt. Arty. Army Ohio	To Arty. 6-Div. Army Ohio	July, 1862
10th Indiana Batty	June, 1862	From Arty. 4-Div. Army Ohio	To Garrison Nashville, Tenn	Sept., 1862
11th Indiana Batty	June, 1862	From Unatt. Arty. Army Ohio	To Garrison Nashville, Tenn	Sept., 1862
12th Indiana Batty	June, 1862	From Unatt. Arty. Army Ohio	To Garrison Nashville, Tenn	Sept., 1862

CAVALRY BRIGADE.—

2d Indiana Cav	June, 1862	From Cav. 4-Div. Army Ohio	To 1-Brig. Cav. Div. Army Ohio	Sept., 1862
3d Indiana Cav. 3 Cos	June, 1862	From Cav. 2d and 4th Divs. A. Ohio	To Cav. 2-Div. 1-Corps Army Ohio	Sept., 1862
3d Kentucky Cav	June, 1862	From Cav. 5-Div. Army Ohio	To 1-Brig. Cav. Div. Army Ohio	Sept., 1862
3d Ohio Cav	June, 1862	From Cav. 6-Div. Army Ohio	To 2-Brig. Cav. Div. Army Ohio	Sept., 1862

UNATTACHED ARMY OHIO.—

3d Kentucky Infy	Dec., 1861	From 11-Brig. Army Ohio	To 15-Brig. 4-Div. Army Ohio	Mch., 1862
18th Kentucky Infy	Mch., 1862	From New Organization	To Cruft's Brig. Army Ky. D. Ohio	Aug., 1862
50th Indiana Infy	Mch., 1862	From 15-Brig. 4-Div. Army Ohio	To Dist. Louisville, Ky., Dept. Ohio	Aug., 1862
16th Kentucky Infy	Mch., 1862	From 18-Brig. Army Ohio	From Unatt. Arty. Army Ohio	Aug., 1862
11th Michigan Infy	Mch., 1862	From Bardstown, Ky	To 29-Brig. 8-Div. Army Ohio	Sept., 1862
40th Ohio Infy	Mch., 1862	From 18-Brig. Army Ohio	To Dist. Eastern Ky. Dept. Ohio	Aug., 1862
51st Ohio Infy	Mch., 1862	From 10-Brig. 4-Div. Army Ohio	To 10-Brig. 4-Div. Army Ohio	July, 1862
69th Ohio Infy	Apr., 1862	From New Organization	To 29-Brig. 8-Div. Army Ohio	Sept., 1862
74th Ohio Infy	Apr., 1862	From New Organization	To 7-Brig. 8-Div. Army Ohio	Sept., 1862
78th Penna. Infy	June, 1862	From 7-Indpt. Brig. Army Ohio	To 7-Brig. 8-Div. Army Ohio	Aug., 1862
79th Penna. Infy	July, 1862	From 7-Indpt. Brig. Army Ohio	To 28-Brig. 3-Div. Army Ohio	Aug., 1862
18th Ohio Infy	July, 1862	From 8-Brig. 3-Div. Army Ohio	To 29-Brig. 8-Div. Army Ohio	Sept., 1862
37th Indiana Infy	July, 1862	From 8-Brig. 3-Div. Army Ohio	To 7-Brig. 8-Div. Army Ohio	Sept., 1862
19th Illinois Infy	July, 1862	From 8-Brig. 3-Div. Army Ohio	To 29-Brig. 8-Div. Army Ohio	Sept., 1862
24th Illinois Infy	July, 1862	From 8-Brig. 3-Div. Army Ohio	To 28-Brig. 3-Div. Army Ohio	Aug., 1862

ARTILLERY.—

4th Indiana Batty........Oct., 1861	From New Organization............	To Arty. Res. Army Ohio.........	June, 1862
11th Indiana Batty......Jan., 1862	From New Organization............	To Arty. Res. Garrison Nashville...	June, 1862
12th Indiana Batty......Jan., 1862	From New Organization............	To Arty. Res. Garrison Nashville...	June, 1862
6th Ohio Batty.........Mch., 1862	From Arty. 5-Div. Army Ohio.....	To Arty. 6-Div. Army Ohio.......	June, 1862
Batty. B, Ky. Arty........Mch., 1862	From Arty. 1-Div. Army Ohio.....	To 23d Indpt. Brig. Army Ohio....	Mch., 1862
Batty. B, 1st Ohio Arty..Mch., 1862	From Arty. 1-Div. Army Ohio.....	To 7-Indpt. Brig. Army Ohio.....	Mch., 1862
Batty. M, 1st Ohio Arty..Mch., 1862	From Unass'd Bacon Creek, Ky.....	To Arty Res. Army Ohio.........	June, 1862

CAVALRY.—

1st Kentucky Cav.......Mch., 1862	From 1-Div. Army Ohio...........	To 1-Brig. Cav. Div. Army Ohio.....	Sept., 1862
4th Kentucky Cav.......Mch., 1862	From New Organization...........	To 1-Brig. Cav. Div. Army Ohio.....	Sept., 1862
5th Kentucky Cav.......Mch., 1862	From New Organization...........	To 2-Brig. Cav. Div. Army Ohio.....	Sept., 1862
9th Penna. Cav.........Mch., 1862	From New Organization...........	To 3-Brig. Cav. Div. Army Ohio....	Sept., 1862
Anderson Penna. Troop...Mch., 1862	From New Organization...........	To Headquarters Army Ohio......	Sept., 1862
Fry's Kentucky Scouts...Mch., 1862	From New Organization...........	To Post Nashville, Tenn...........	July, 1862

ENGINEERS.—

1st Michigan Eng........Dec., 1861	From New Organization...........	To Unatt. Army Ohio..............	Sept., 1862

Army of the Ohio

As organized into Corps Sept. 29, 1862.

COMMANDERS.

D. C. Buell.............	Major General.....................
Geo. H. Thomas........	Major General, 2d in command......

GENERAL HEADQUARTERS.—

7th Pa. Cav., B, G, L, M.Sept., 1862	From 23d Indpt. Brig. Army Ohio...	To 1-Brig. Cav. Div. Army Ohio.....	Oct., 1862
4th U. S. Cav..........Sept., 1862	From Army Miss.................	To Headquarters Army Cumberland.	Nov., 1862
Anderson Penna. Troop..Sept., 1862	From Headquarters Army Ohio....	To Headquarters Army Cumberland.	Nov., 1862
1st Michigan Eng........Sept., 1862	From Unatt. Army Ohio...........	To Engineers Army Cumberland....	Nov., 1862

First Army Corps

COMMANDER.

A. McDowell McCook...	Major General.....................

2d DIVISION.— COMMANDER.

R. W. Johnson.........	Brigadier General.................

4th BRIGADE.— COMMANDER.

H. M. Buckley.........	Col. 5th Kentucky Infy............

6th Indiana Infy.......Sept., 1862	From 4-Brig. 2-Div. Army Ohio....	To 3-B. 2-Div. Right Wing 14-Corps.	Nov., 1862
5th Kentucky Infy......Sept., 1862	From 4-Brig. 2-Div. Army Ohio....	To 3-B. 2-Div. Right Wing 14-Corps.	Nov., 1862
1st Ohio Infy.........Sept., 1862	From 4-Brig. 2-Div. Army Ohio....	To 3-B. 2-Div. Right Wing 14-Corps.	Nov., 1862
93d Ohio Infy..........Sept., 1862	From Ward's B. 12-Div. Army Ohio.	To 3-B. 2-Div. Right Wing 14-Corps.	Nov., 1862
15th U. S. Infy.......Sept., 1862	From 4-Brig. 2-Div. Army Ohio....	To 3-B. 2-Div. Right Wing 14-Corps.	Nov., 1862
18th U. S. Infy.......Sept., 1862	From 4-Brig. 2-Div. Army Ohio....	To 3-B. 2-Div. Right Wing 14-Corps.	Nov., 1862
19th U. S. Infy........Sept., 1862	From 4-Brig. 2-Div. Army Ohio....	To 3-B. 2-Div. Right Wing 14-Corps.	Nov., 1862

5th BRIGADE.— COMMANDER.

E. N. Kirk.............	Col. 34th Illinois Infy............

34th Illinois Infy.......Sept., 1862	From 5-Brig. 2-Div. Army Ohio....	To 2-B. 2-Div. Right Wing 14-Corps.	Nov., 1862
29th Indiana Infy......Sept., 1862	From 5-Brig. 2-Div. Army Ohio....	To 2-B. 2-Div. Right Wing 14-Corps.	Nov., 1862
30th Indiana Infy......Sept., 1862	From 5-Brig. 2-Div. Army Ohio....	To 2-B. 2-Div. Right Wing 14-Corps.	Nov., 1862
77th Penna. Infy.......Sept., 1862	From 5-Brig. 2-Div. Army Ohio....	To 2-B. 2-Div. Right Wing 14-Corps.	Nov., 1862
79th Illinois Infy.......Sept., 1862	From New Organization...........	To 2-B 2-Div. Right Wing 14-Corps.	Nov., 1862

6th BRIGADE.— COMMANDER.

W. H. Gibson..........	Col. 49th Ohio Infy...............

32d Indiana Infy.......Sept., 1862	From 6-Brig. 2-Div. Army Ohio....	To 1-B. 2-Div. Right Wing 14-Corps.	Nov., 1862
39th Indiana Infy......Sept., 1862	From 6-Brig. 2-Div. Army Ohio....	To 1-B. 2-Div. Right Wing 14-Corps.	Nov., 1862
15th Ohio Infy.........Sept., 1862	From 6-Brig. 2-Div. Army Ohio....	To 1-B. 2-Div. Right Wing 14-Corps.	Nov., 1862
49th Ohio Infy.........Sept., 1862	From 6-Brig. 2-Div. Army Ohio....	To 1-B. 2-Div. Right Wing 14-Corps.	Nov., 1862
89th Illinois Infy......Sept., 1862	From New Organization...........	To 1-B. 2-Div. Right Wing 14-Corps.	Nov., 1862

ARTILLERY, 2d DIVISION.—

Batty. A, 1st Ohio Arty..Sept., 1862	From Arty. 2-Div. Army Ohio.....	To 1-B. 2-Div. Right Wing 14-Corps.	Nov., 1862
Batty. E, 1st Ohio Arty..Sept., 1862	From Arty. 2-Div. Army Ohio.....	To 2-B. 2-Div. Right Wing 14-Corps.	Nov., 1862
Batty. H, 5th U. S. Arty..Sept., 1862	From Arty. 2-Div. Army Ohio.....	To 3-B. 2-Div. Right Wing 14-Corps.	Nov., 1862

CAVALRY.—

3d Ind. Cav. G, H, I, K.Sept., 1862	From Cav. Brig. Army Ohio........	To Cav. Right Wing 14-Corps......	Nov., 1862

3d DIVISION.— COMMANDER.

L. H. Rousseau........	Brigadier General.................

9th BRIGADE.— COMMANDER.

L. A. Harris...........	Col. 2d Ohio Infy.................

38th Indiana Infy.......Sept., 1862	From 9-Brig. 3-Div. Army Ohio.....	To 1-Brig. 1-Div. Centre 14-Corps..	Nov., 1862
2d Ohio Infy..........Sept., 1862	From 9-Brig. 3-Div. Army Ohio.....	To 1-Brig. 1-Div. Centre 14-Corps..	Nov., 1862
33d Ohio Infy..........Sept., 1862	From 9-Brig. 3-Div. Army Ohio.....	To 1-Brig. 1-Div. Centre 14-Corps..	Nov., 1862
10th Wisconsin Infy.....Sept., 1862	From 9-Brig. 3-Div. Army Ohio.....	To 1-Brig. 1-Div. Centre 14-Corps..	Nov., 1862
94th Ohio Infy.........Sept., 1862	From New Organization...........	To 1-Brig. 1-Div. Centre 14-Corps..	Nov., 1862
5th Indiana Batty.......Sept., 1862	From Arty. 3-Div. Army Ohio.....	To 3-B. 2-Div. Right Wing 14-Corps.	Nov., 1862

17th BRIGADE.— COMMANDERS.

W. H. Lytle...........	Col. 10th Ohio Infy..............	To Oct. 18, 1862.
J. G. Jones...........	Col. 42d Infy...................	To Nov. 5, 1862.

42d Indiana Infy.......Sept., 1862	From 17-Brig. 3-Div. Army Ohio...	To 2-Brig. 1-Div. Centre 14-Corps..	Nov., 1862
88th Indiana Infy......Sept., 1862	From 17-Brig. 3-Div. Army Ohio...	To 2-Brig. 1-Div. Centre 14-Corps..	Nov., 1862
15th Kentucky Infy.....Sept., 1862	From 17-Brig. 3-Div. Army Ohio...	To 2-Brig. 1-Div. Centre 14-Corps..	Nov., 1862
3d Ohio Infy...........Sept., 1862	From 17-Brig. 3-Div. Army Ohio...	To 2-Brig. 1-Div. Centre 14-Corps..	Nov., 1862
10th Ohio Infy.........Sept., 1862	From 17-Brig. 3-Div. Army Ohio...	To Provost Guard Army Cumb'd...	Nov., 1862
Batty. A. 1st Mich. Arty..Sept., 1862	From Arty. 3-Div. Army Ohio.....	To Arty. 1-Div. Centre 14-Corps...	Nov., 1862

28th BRIGADE.—   COMMANDER.

J. C. Starkweather.....	Col. 1st Wisconsin Infy...........	
24th Illinois Infy.......Sept., 1862	From 28-Brig. 3-Div. Army Ohio...	To 3-Brig. 1-Div. Centre 14-Corps...	Nov., 1862
79th Penna. Infy.......Sept., 1862	From 28-Brig. 3-Div. Army Ohio...	To 3-Brig. 1-Div. Centre 14-Corps...	Nov., 1862
1st Wisconsin Infy......Sept., 1862	From 28-Brig. 3-Div. Army Ohio...	To 3-Brig. 1-Div. Centre 14-Corps...	Nov., 1862
21st Wisconsin Infy.....Sept., 1862	From 28-Brig. 3-Div. Army Ohio...	To 3-Brig. 1-Div. Centre 14-Corps...	Nov., 1862
4th Indiana Batty......Sept., 1862	From 28-Brig. 3-Div. Army Ohio....	To 1-B. 3-Div. Right Wing 14-Corps.	Nov., 1862
Batty. A, Kentucky Arty.Sept., 1862	From 28-Brig. 3-Div. Army Ohio....	To 1-B. 3-Div. Right Wing 14-Corps.	Nov., 1862
CAVALRY.—		
2d Kentucky Cav........Sept., 1862	From Unatt. 2-Div. Army Ohio......	To Cav. 1-Div. Centre 14-Corps.....	Nov., 1862

10th DIVISION.—   COMMANDERS.

J. S. Jackson..........	Brigadier General.................	To Oct. 8, 1862.
C. C. Gilbert..........	Brigadier General.................	To Nov. 5, 1862. Killed.

33d BRIGADE.—   COMMANDERS.

W. R. Terrill..........	Brigadier General.................	To Oct. 8, 1862. Killed.
A. S. Hall.............	Col. 105th Ohio Infy..............	To Nov. 5, 1862.
80th Illinois Infy.......Sept., 1862	From 33-Brig. 10-Div. Army Ohio..	To 1-Brig. 5-Div. Centre 14-Corps..	Nov., 1862
123d Illinois Infy......Sept., 1862	From 33-Brig. 10-Div. Army Ohio..	To 1-Brig. 5-Div. Centre 14-Corps..	Nov., 1862
101st Indiana Infy......Sept., 1862	From 33-Brig. 10-Div. Army Ohio..	To 1-Brig. 5-Div. Centre 14-Corps..	Nov., 1862
105th Ohio Infy........Sept., 18	From 33-Brig. 10-Div. Army Ohio..	To 1-Brig. 5-Div. Centre 14-Corps..	Nov., 1862
Garrard's Detch. (7th and		
32d Ky. and 3d Tenn)..Sept., 1862	From 33-Brig. 10-Div. Army Ohio..	To Dept. Ohio....................	Nov., 1862
Parson's Batty. (Batty. D,		
1st Ohio Arty. Sec)....Sept., 1862	From 33-Brig. 10-Div. Army Ohio..	To Minty's Cav. Brig. Army Cumb'd.	Nov., 1862

34th BRIGADE.—   COMMANDERS.

Geo. Webster..........	Col. 98th Ohio Infy..............	To Oct. 8, 1862. Killed.
S. A. Strickland........	Col. 50th Ohio Infy..............	To Nov. 5, 1862.
80th Indiana Infy......Sept., 1862	From 34th Brig. 10-Div. Army Ohio.	To Dist. West Ky. Dept. Ohio......	Nov., 1862
50th Ohio Infy.........Sept., 1862	From 34th Brig. 10-Div. Army Ohio.	To Dist. West Ky. Dept. Ohio......	Nov., 1862
98th Ohio Infy.........Sept., 1862	From 34th Brig. 10-Div. Army Ohio.	To Dist. West Ky. Dept. Ohio......	Nov., 1862
121st Ohio Infy........Sept., 1862	From 34th Brig. 10-Div. Army Ohio.	To Dist. West Ky. Dept. Ohio......	Nov., 1862
19th Indiana Batty......Sept., 1862	From 34th Brig. 10-Div. Army Ohio.	To Arty. 5-Div. Centre 14-Corps...	Nov., 1862

Second Army Corps

      COMMANDER.

T. L. Crittenden.......	Major General....................	

4th DIVISION.—   COMMANDER.

W. S. Smith..........	Brigadier General.................	

10th BRIGADE.—   COMMANDER.

William Grose.........	Col. 36th Indiana Infy...........	
36th Indiana Infy.......Sept., 1862	From 10-Brig. 4-Div. Army Ohio...	To 3-B. 2-Div. Left Wing 14-Corps.	Nov., 1862
23d Kentucky Infy......Sept., 1862	From 10-Brig. 4-Div. Army Ohio....	To 3-B. 2-Div. Left Wing 14-Corps.	Nov., 1862
6th Ohio Infy..........Sept., 1862	From 10-Brig. 4-Div. Army Ohio....	To 3-B. 2-Div. Left Wing 14-Corps.	Nov., 1862
24th Ohio Infy.........Sept., 1862	From 10-Brig. 4-Div. Army Ohio....	To 3-B. 2-Div. Left Wing 14-Corps.	Nov., 1862
84th Illinois Infy.......Sept., 1862	From New Organization...........	To 3-B. 2-Div. Left Wing 14-Corps.	Nov., 1862
Battys. H & M, 4th U.S.A.Sept., 1862	From 10-Brig. 4-Div. Army Ohio...	To Arty. 2-Div. Left Wing 14-Corps.	Nov., 1862

19th BRIGADE.—   COMMANDER.

W. B. Hazen..........	Col. 41st Ohio Infy..............	
9th Indiana Infy.......Sept., 1862	From 19-Brig. 4-Div. Army Ohio....	To 2-B. 2-Div. Left Wing 14-Corps.	Nov., 1862
6th Kentucky Infy......Sept., 1862	From 19-Brig. 4-Div. Army Ohio....	To 2-B. 2-Div. Left Wing 14-Corps.	Nov., 1862
27th Kentucky Infy.....Sept., 1862	From 19-Brig. 4-Div. Army Ohio....	To 2-B. 2-Div. Left Wing 14-Corps.	Nov., 1862
41st Ohio Infy.........Sept., 1862	From 19-Brig. 4-Div. Army Ohio....	To 2-B. 2-Div. Left Wing 14-Corps.	Nov., 1862
110th Illinois Infy......Sept., 1862	From New Organization...........	To 2-B. 2-Div. Left Wing 14-Corps.	Nov., 1862
Batty. F, 1st Ohio Arty...Sept., 1862	From Arty. 4-Div. Army Ohio......	To Arty. 2-Div. Left Wing 14-Corps.	Nov., 1862

22d BRIGADE.—   COMMANDER.

Charles Cruft.........	Brigadier General.................	
31st Indiana Infy.......Sept., 1862	From 22-Brig. 4-Div. Army Ohio...	To 1-B. 2-Div. Left Wing 14-Corps.	Nov., 1862
1st Kentucky Infy......Sept., 1862	From 22-Brig. 4-Div. Army Ohio...	To 1-B. 2-Div. Left Wing 14-Corps.	Nov., 1862
2d Kentucky Infy.......Sept., 1862	From 22-Brig. 4-Div. Army Ohio...	To 1-B. 2-Div. Left Wing 14-Corps.	Nov., 1862
20th Kentucky Infy.....Sept., 1862	From 22-Brig. 4-Div. Army Ohio...	To 1-B. 2-Div. Left Wing 14-Corps.	Nov., 1862
90th Ohio Infy.........Sept., 1862	From 22-Brig. 4-Div. Army Ohio...	To 1-B. 2-Div. Left Wing 14-Corps.	Nov., 1862
Batty. B, 1st Ohio Arty..Sept., 1862	From Arty. 4-Div. Army Ohio......	To Arty. 2-Div. Left Wing 14-Corps.	Nov., 1862

5th DIVISION.—   COMMANDER.

H. P. Van Cleve.......	Brigadier General...............	

11th BRIGADE.—   COMMANDER.

Samuel Beatty........	Col. 19th Ohio Infy..............	
9th Kentucky Infy......Sept., 1862	From 11-Brig. 5-Div. Army Ohio...	To 1-B. 3-Div. Left Wing 14-Corps.	Nov., 1862
13th Kentucky Infy.....Sept., 1862	From 11-Brig. 5-Div. Army Ohio...	To 1-B. 3-Div. Left Wing 14-Corps.	Nov., 1862
19th Ohio Infy.........Sept., 1862	From 11-Brig. 5-Div. Army Ohio...	To 1-B. 3-Div. Left Wing 14-Corps.	Nov., 1862
59th Ohio Infy.........Sept., 1862	From 11-Brig. 5-Div. Army Ohio...	To 1-B. 3-Div. Left Wing 14-Corps.	Nov., 1862
79th Indiana Infy.......Sept., 1862	From 11-Brig. 5-Div. Army Ohio...	To 1-B. 3-Div. Left Wing 14-Corps.	Nov., 1862

14th BRIGADE.—   COMMANDER.

P. B. Hawkins.........	Col. 11th Ky. Infy...............	
13th Ohio Infy.........Sept., 1862	From 14-Brig. 5-Div. Army Ohio....	To 2-Brig. 3-Div. Lf. Wing 14-C'ps.	Nov., 1862
11th Ky. Infy..........Sept., 1862	From 14-Brig. 5-Div. Army Ohio....	To 2-Brig. 3-Div. Lf. Wing 14-C'ps.	Nov., 1862
26th Ky. Infy..........Sept., 1862	From 14-Brig. 5-Div. Army Ohio....	To 2-Brig. 3-Div. Lf. Wing 14-C'ps.	Nov., 1862
44th Ind. Infy.........Sept., 1862	From 14-Brig. 5-Div. Army Ohio....	To 2-Brig. 3-Div. Lf. Wing 14-C'ps.	Nov., 1862
86th Ind. Infy.........Sept., 1862	From 14-Brig. 5-Div. Army Ohio....	To 2-Brig. 3-Div. Lf. Wing 14-C'ps.	Nov., 1862

23d BRIGADE.— COMMANDER.

Stanley Matthews......	Col. 51st Ohio Infy..............		

35th Ind. Infy.........Sept., 1862	From 23-Brig. 5-Div. Army Ohio....	To 3-Brig. 3-Div. Lf. Wing 14-C'ps.	Nov., 1862
8th Ky. Infy...........Sept., 1862	From 23-Brig. 5-Div. Army Ohio....	To 3-Brig. 3-Div. Lf. Wing 14-C'ps.	Nov., 1862
21st Ky. Infy..........Sept., 1862	From 23-Brig. 5-Div. Army Ohio....	To 3-Brig. 3-Div. Lf. Wing 14-C'ps.	Nov., 1862
51st Ohio Infy.........Sept., 1862	From 23-Brig. 5-Div. Army Ohio....	To 3-Brig. 3-Div. Lf. Wing 14-C'ps.	Nov., 1862
99th Ohio Infy.........Sept., 1862	From 23-Brig. 5-Div. Army Ohio....	To 3-Brig. 3-Div. Lf. Wing 14-C'ps.	Nov., 1862
ARTILLERY.—			
7th Ind. Batty.........Sept., 1862	From Arty. 1-Div. Army Ohio......	To Arty. 3-Div Left Wing 14-C'ps..	Nov., 1862
Indpt. Batty. B, Pa. Arty.Sept., 1862	From Arty. 5-Div. Army Ohio......	To Arty. 3-Div. Left Wing 14-C'ps..	Nov., 1862
3d Wis. Batty..........Sept., 1862	From Arty. 5-Div. Army Ohio......	To Arty. 3-Div. Left Wing 14-C'ps..	Nov., 1862

6th DIVISION.— COMMANDER.

T. J. Wood...........	Brigadier General................	

15th BRIGADE.— COMMANDER.

M. S. Hascall.........	Brigadier General................	

17th Ind. Infy.........Sept., 1862	From 15-Brig. 6-Div. Army Ohio....	To 1-Brig. 1-Div. Lf. Wing 14-C'ps.	Nov., 1862
58th Ind. Infy.........Sept., 1862	From 15-Brig. 6-Div. Army Ohio....	To 1-Brig. 1-Div. Lf. Wing 14-C'ps.	Nov., 1862
3rd Ky. Infy..........Sept., 1862	From 15-Brig. 6-Div. Army Ohio....	To 1-Brig. 1-Div. Lf. Wing 14-C'ps.	Nov., 1862
26th Ohio Infy.........Sept., 1862	From 15-Brig. 6-Div. Army Ohio....	To 1-Brig. 1-Div. Lf. Wing 14-C'ps.	Nov., 1862
100th Ind. Infy........Sept., 1862	From New Organization...........	To 1-Brig. 1-Div. Lf. Wing 14-C'ps.	Nov., 1862
8th Ind. Batty.........Sept., 1862	From Arty. 6-Div. Army Ohio......	To 1-Brig. 1-Div. Lf. Wing 14-C'ps.	Nov., 1862

20th BRIGADE.— COMMANDER.

C. G. Harker.........	Col. 65th Ohio Infy..............	

51st Ind. Infy.........Sept., 1862	From 20-Brig. 6-Div. Army Ohio....	To 3-Brig. 1-Div. Lf. Wing 14-C'ps.	Nov., 1862
73d Ind. Infy..........Sept., 1862	From 20-Brig. 6-Div. Army Ohio....	To 3-Brig. 1-Div. Lf. Wing 14-C'ps.	Nov., 1862
13th Mich. Infy........Sept., 1862	From 20-Brig. 6-Div. Army Ohio....	To 3-Brig. 1-Div. Lf. Wing 14-C'ps.	Nov., 1862
64th Ohio Infy.........Sept., 1862	From 20-Brig. 6-Div. Army Ohio....	To 3-Brig. 1-Div. Lf. Wing 14-C'ps.	Nov., 1862
65th Ohio Infy.........Sept., 1862	From 20-Brig. 6-Div. Army Ohio....	To 3-Brig. 1-Div. Lf. Wing 14-C'ps.	Nov., 1862
6th Ohio Batty.........Sept., 1862	From Arty. 6-Div. Army Ohio......	To 3-Brig. 1-Div. Lf. Wing 14-C'ps.	Nov., 1862

21st BRIGADE.— COMMANDER.

Geo. D. Wagner.......	Col. 15th Ind. Infy..............	

15th Ind. Infy.........Sept., 1862	From 21-Brig. 6-Div. Army Ohio....	To 2-Brig. 1-Div. Lf. Wing 14-C'ps.	Nov., 1862
40th Ind. Infy.........Sept., 1862	From 21-Brig. 6-Div. Army Ohio....	To 2-Brig. 1-Div. Lf. Wing 14-C'ps.	Nov., 1862
57th Ind. Infy.........Sept., 1862	From 21-Brig. 6-Div. Army Ohio....	To 2-Brig. 1-Div. Lf. Wing 14-C'ps.	Nov., 1862
24th Ky. Infy..........Sept., 1862	From 21-Brig. 6-Div. Army Ohio....	To 2-Brig. 1-Div. Lf. Wing 14-C'ps.	Nov., 1862
97th Ohio Infy.........Sept., 1862	From 21-Brig. 6-Div. Army Ohio....	To 2-Brig. 1-Div. Lf. Wing 14-C'ps.	Nov., 1862
10th Ind. Batty........Sept., 1862	From Arty. 6-Div. Army Ohio......	To 2-Brig. 1-Div. Lf. Wing 14-C'ps.	Nov., 1862
CAVALRY.—			
1st Ohio Cav., I, K, L, M.Sept., 1862	From Unatt. 5-Div. Army Ohio.....	To 2-Brig. Cav. Div. Army Ohio....	Oct., 1862

Third Army Corps

COMMANDER.

C. C. Gilbert.........	Major General...................	

1st DIVISION.— COMMANDER.

A. Schoepff...........	Brigadier General................	

1st BRIGADE.— COMMANDER.

M. B. Walker.........	Col. 31st Ohio Infy..............	

12th Ky. Infy..........Sept., 1862	From 1-Brig. 1-Div. Army Ohio....	To 1-Brig. 3-Div. Centre 14-Corps.	Nov., 1862
17th Ohio Infy.........Sept., 1862	From 1-Brig. 1-Div. Army Ohio....	To 1-Brig. 3-Div. Centre 14-Corps.	Nov., 1862
31st Ohio Infy.........Sept., 1862	From 1-Brig. 1-Div. Army Ohio....	To 1-Brig. 3-Div. Centre 14-Corps.	Nov., 1862
38th Ohio Infy.........Sept., 1862	From 1-Brig. 1-Div. Army Ohio....	To 1-Brig. 3-Div. Centre 14-Corps.	Nov., 1862
82d Ind. Infy..........Sept., 1862	From 1-Brig. 1-Div. Army Ohio....	To 1-Brig. 3-Div. Centre 14-Corps.	Nov., 1862

2d BRIGADE.— COMMANDERS.

S. S. Fry...........	Brigadier General................	To Oct. 18, 1862.	
John M. Harlan........	Col. 10th Ky. Infy...............	To Nov. 5, 1862.	

10th Ind. Infy.........Sept., 1862	From 2-Brig. 1-Div. Army Ohio....	To 2-Brig. 3-Div. Centre 14-Corps.	Nov., 1862
74th Ind. Infy.........Sept., 1862	From 2-Brig. 1-Div. Army Ohio....	To 2-Brig. 3-Div. Centre 14-Corps.	Nov., 1862
4th Ky. Infy..........Sept., 1862	From 2-Brig. 1-Div. Army Ohio....	To 2-Brig. 3-Div. Centre 14-Corps.	Nov., 1862
10th Ky. Infy..........Sept., 1862	From 2-Brig. 1-Div. Army Ohio....	To 2-Briᵍ. 3-Div. Centre 14-Corps.	Nov., 1862
14th Ohio Infy.........Sept., 1862	From 2-Brig. 1-Div. Army Ohio....	To 2-Brig. 3-Div. Centre 14-Corps.	Nov., 1862

3d BRIGADE.— COMMANDER.

J. B. Steedman........	Brigadier General................	

2d Minn. Infy..........Sept., 1862	From 3-Brig. 1-Div. Army Ohio....	To 3-Brig. 3-Div. Centre 14 Corps.	Nov., 1862
87th Ind. Infy.........Sept., 1862	From 3-Brig. 1-Div. Army Ohio....	To 3-Brig. 3-Div. Centre 14 Corps.	Nov., 1862
9th Ohio Infy..........Sept., 1862	From 3-Brig. 1-Div. Army Ohio....	To 3-Brig. 3-Div. Centre 14 Corps.	Nov., 1862
35th Ohio Infy.........Sept., 1862	From 3-Brig. 1-Div. Army Ohio....	To 3-Brig. 3-Div. Centre 14 Corps.	Nov., 1862
18th Ohio Infy.........Sept., 1862	From 3-Brig. 1-Div. Army Ohio....	To 3-Brig. 3-Div. Centre 14 Corps.	Nov., 1862
ARTILLERY.—			
Batty. D, 1st Mich. Arty.Sept., 1862	From Arty. 1-Div. Army Ohio......	To Arty. 3-Div. Centre 14-Corps..	Nov., 1862
Batty. C, 1st Ohio Arty..Sept., 1862	From Arty. 1-Div. Army Ohio......	To Arty. 3-Div. Centre 14-Corps..	Nov., 1862
Batty. I, 4th U. S. Arty..Sept., 1862	From Arty. 1-Div. Army Ohio......	To Arty. 3-Div. Centre 14-Corps..	Nov., 1862
CAVALRY.—			
1st O. Cav., A, B, D, G, H.Sept., 1862	From 1 Div. Army Ohio...........	To 2-Brig. Cav. Div. Army Ohio....	Oct., 1862

9th DIVISION.— COMMANDER.

R. B. Mitchell........	Brigadier General................	

30th BRIGADE.— COMMANDER.

M. Gooding...........	Col. 22d Ind. Infy..............	

59th Ill. Infy.........Sept., 1862	From 30-Brig. 9-Div. Army Ohio....	To 1-Brig. 1-Div. Rt. Wing 14-C'ps.	Nov., 1862
74th Ill. Infy.........Sept., 1862	From 30-Brig. 9-Div. Army Ohio....	To 1-Brig. 1-Div. Rt. Wing 14-C'ps.	Nov., 1862
75th Ill. Infy.........Sept., 1862	From 30-Brig. 9-Div. Army Ohio....	To 1-Brig. 1-Div. Rt. Wing 14-C'ps.	Nov., 1862
22d Ind. Infy..........Sept., 1862	From 30-Brig. 9-Div. Army Ohio....	To 1-Brig. 1-Div. Rt. Wing 14-C'ps.	Nov., 1862
5th Wis. Batty.........Sept., 1862	From 30-Brig. 9-Div. Army Ohio....	To 1-Brig. 1-Div. Rt. Wing 14-C'ps.	Nov., 1862

31st BRIGADE.— COMMANDER.

W. P. Carlin	Col. 38th Ill. Infy		
21st Ill. Infy.........Sept., 1862	From 31-Brig. 9-Div. Army Ohio....	To 2-Brig. 1-Div. Rt. Wing 14-C'ps.	Nov., 1862
38th Ill. Infy.........Sept., 1862	From 31-Brig. 9-Div. Army Ohio....	To 2-Brig. 1-Div. Rt. Wing 14-C'ps.	Nov., 1862
101st Ohio Infy........Sept., 1862	From 31-Brig. 9-Div. Army Ohio....	To 2-Brig. 1-Div. Rt. Wing 14-C'ps.	Nov., 1862
15th Wis. Infy.........Sept., 1862	From 31-Brig. 9-Div. Army Ohio....	To 2-Brig. 1-Div. Rt. Wing 14-C'ps.	Nov., 1862
2d Minn. Batty.........Sept., 1862	From 31-Brig. 9-Div. Army Ohio....	To 2-Brig. 1-Div. Rt. Wing 14-C'ps.	Nov., 1862

32d BRIGADE.— COMMANDERS.

W. W. Caldwell	Col. 81st Ind. Infy	To Oct. 8, 1862.	
J. S. McClelland	Lt.-Col. 25th Ill. Infy	To Nov. 5, 1862.	
25th Ill. Infy.........Sept., 1862	From 32-Brig. 9-Div. Army Ohio....	To 3-Brig. 1-Div. Rt. Wing 14-C'ps.	Nov., 1862
35th Ill. Infy.........Sept., 1862	From 32-Brig. 9-Div. Army Ohio....	To 3-Brig. 1-Div. Rt. Wing 14-C'ps.	Nov., 1862
81st Ind. Infy.........Sept., 1862	From 32-Brig. 9-Div. Army Ohio....	To 3-Brig. 1-Div. Rt. Wing 14-C'ps.	Nov., 1862
8th Kan. Infy.........Sept., 1862	From 32-Brig. 9-Div. Army Ohio....	To 3-Brig. 1-Div. Rt. Wing 14-C'ps.	Nov., 1862
8th Wis. Batty........Sept., 1862	From 32-Brig. 9-Div. Army Ohio....	To 3-Brig. 1-Div. Rt. Wing 14-C'ps.	Nov., 1862
CAVALRY.—			
Co. B, 36th Ill. Infy....Sept., 1862	From 9-Div. Army Ohio	To Headqrs. Right Wing 14-Corps..	Nov., 1862

11th DIVISION.— COMMANDER.

P. H. Sheridan	Brigadier General		

35th BRIGADE.— COMMANDERS.

B. Laiboldt	Lt.-Col. 2d Mo. Infy	To Oct. 8, 1862.	
Frederick Schaeffer	Col. General Staff	To Nov. 5, 1862.	
44th Ill. Infy.........Sept., 1862	From 35-Brig. 11-Div. Army Ohio..	To 2-Brig. 3-Div. Rt. Wing 14-C'ps.	Nov., 1862
73d Ill. Infy.........Sept., 1862	From 35-Brig. 11-Div. Army Ohio..	To 2-Brig. 3-Div. Rt. Wing 14-C'ps.	Nov., 1862
2d Mo. Infy.........Sept., 1862	From 35-Brig. 11-Div. Army Ohio..	To 2-Brig. 3-Div. Rt. Wing 14-C'ps.	Nov., 1862
15th Mo. Infy.........Sept., 1862	From 35-Brig. 11-Div. Army Ohio..	To 2-Brig. 3-Div. Rt. Wing 14-C'ps.	Nov., 1862

36th BRIGADE.— COMMANDER.

Daniel McCook	Col. 52d Ohio Infy		
85th Ill. Infy.........Sept., 1862	From 36-Brig. 11-Div. Army Ohio..	To 2-Brig. 4-Div. Centre 14-Corps..	Nov., 1862
86th Ill. Infy.........Sept., 1862	From 36-Brig. 11-Div. Army Ohio..	To 2-Brig. 4-Div. Centre 14-Corps..	Nov., 1862
125th Ill. Infy.........Sept., 1862	From 36-Brig. 11-Div. Army Ohio..	To 2-Brig. 4-Div. Centre 14-Corps..	Nov., 1862
52d Ohio Infy.........Sept., 1862	From 36-Brig. 11-Div. Army Ohio..	To 2-Brig. 4-Div. Centre 14-Corps..	Nov., 1862

37th BRIGADE.— COMMANDER.

N. Greusel	Col. 36th Illinois Infy.		
36th Illinois Infy......Sept., 1862	From 37-Brig. 11-Div. Army Ohio..	To 1-Brig. 3-Div. Right Wing 14-C.	Nov., 1862
88th Illinois Infy......Sept., 1862	From 37-Brig. 11-Div. Army Ohio..	To 1-Brig. 3-Div. Right Wing 14-C.	Nov., 1862
21st Michigan Infy......Sept., 1862	From 37-Brig. 11-Div. Army Ohio..	To 1-Brig. 3-Div. Right Wing 14-C.	Nov., 1862
24th Wisconsin Infy.....Sept., 1862	From 37-Brig. 11-Div. Army Ohio..	To 1-Brig. 3-Div. Right Wing 14-C.	Nov., 1862
ARTILLERY.—			
Batty. I, 2d Ill. Arty....Sept., 1862	From Arty. 11-Div. Army Ohio.....	To 2-Brig. 4-Div. Centre, 14-Corps.	Nov., 1862
Batty. G, 1st Mo. Arty..Sept., 1862	From Arty. 11-Div. Army Ohio.....	To 2-Brig. 3-Div. Right Wing, 14-C.	Nov., 1862

CAVALRY DIVISION.—Organized Sept. 5, 1862.

COMMANDER.

John Kennett	Col. 4th Ohio Cav.		

1st BRIGADE.— COMMANDER.

E. M. McCook	Col. 2d Indiana Cav.		
2d Indiana Cav.........Sept., 1862	From Cav. Brig. Army Ohio......	To 1-Brig. Cav. Div. Army Cumb'd	Nov., 1862
1st Kentucky Cav......Sept., 1862	From Unatt. Cav. Army Ohio......	To Post Gallatin, Tenn...........	Nov., 1862
3d Kentucky Cav......Sept., 1862	From Cav. Brig. Army Ohio......	To 1-Brig. Cav. Div. Army Cumb'd	Nov., 1862
4th Kentucky Cav......Sept., 1862	From Unatt. Cav. Army Ohio......	To Dist. West Ky. Dept. Ohio......	Nov., 1862
7th Penna. Cav. 1st Bn..Sept., 1862	From Unatt. Cav. Army Ohio......	To 1-Brig. Cav. Div. Army Cumb'd	Nov., 1862
4th Michigan Cav......Oct., 1862	From New Organization..........	To 1-Brig. Cav. Div. Army Cumb'd	Nov., 1862

2d BRIGADE.— COMMANDER.

Lewis Zahm	Col. 3d Ohio Cav.		
5th Kentucky Cav......Sept., 1862	From Unatt. Cav. Army Ohio......	To 4-Div. Centre, 14-Corps........	Nov., 1862
3d Ohio Cav.........Sept., 1862	From Cav. Brig. Army Ohio......	To 2-Brig. Cav. Div. Army Cumb'd	Nov., 1862
4th Ohio Cav.........Sept., 1862	From Cav. 3-Div. Army Ohio......	To 2-Brig. Cav. Div. Army Cumb'd	Nov., 1862
1st Ohio Cav.........Oct., 1862	From 2d and 3d Corps, Army Ohio.	To 2-Brig. Cav. Div. Army Cumb'd	Nov., 1862

3d BRIGADE.— COMMANDER.

Ebenezer Gay	Col. 9th Penna. Cav.		
9th Kentucky Cav. Det..Sept., 1862	From New Organization..........	To Dist. Louisville, Ky., Dept. Ohio	Nov., 1862
2d Michigan Cav.......Sept., 1862	From Cav. Div. Army Miss........	To Unass'd Army Ky. Dept. Ohio..	Nov., 1862
9th Penna. Cav.......Sept., 1862	From Unatt. Cav. Army Ohio......	To Dist. Louisville, Ky., Dept. Ohio	Nov., 1862

FORCES NASHVILLE, TENN.— COMMANDER.

James S. Negley	Brigadier General	Sept. 20, 1862.	
50th Indiana Infy. 3 Cos..Sept., 1862	From Unatt. Infy. Army Ohio......	To Dist. Louisville, Ky., Dept. Ohio	Nov., 1862
10th Tennessee Infy.....Sept., 1862	From New Organization..........	To Unatt. 4-Div. Centre, 14-Corps.	Nov., 1862
5th Tennessee Cav.....Sept., 1862	From New Organization..........	To Res've Cav. Cav. Div. A. Cumb'd	Nov., 1862
11th Indiana Batty......Sept., 1862	From Arty. Reserve Army Ohio....	To Reserve Arty. Centre, 14-Corps	Nov., 1862
12th Indiana Batty......Sept., 1862	From Arty. Reserve Army Ohio....	To Reserve Arty. Centre, 14-Corps	Nov., 1862
Batty. E, 1st Mich. Arty..Sept., 1862	From Arty. Reserve Army Ohio....	To Reserve Arty. Centre, 14-Corps	Nov., 1862
Batty. A, Tenn. Arty.....Sept., 1862	From Unatt. Arty. Army Ohio.....	To Post Clarksville, Tenn.........	Nov., 1862

1st DIVISION, ARMY MISS.—(See 13th Division, Army Ohio.)

8th DIVISION, ARMY OHIO.—(See 8th Division, Army Ohio.)

Army and Department of the Cumberland

Created Oct. 24, 1862, from Department of the Ohio, and designated Fourteenth Army Corps, by General Order No. 168, A. G. O., to consist of Tennessee east of the Tennessee River, and such parts of Alabama and Georgia as may be taken possession of by United States Troops. Organized into Right Wing, Centre, and Left Wing Nov., 1862, which designations were changed into 14th, 20th and 21st Army Corps Jan. 9, 1863.

COMMANDING ARMY AND DEPARTMENT.

W. S. Rosecrans......|Major General....................|Oct. 24, 1862, to Jan. 9, 1863.	

GENERAL HEADQUARTERS.—ESCORT.
Anderson Penna. Troop..Nov., 1862 From Headquarters Army Ohio....|To Headquarters Dept. Cumb'd....|Jan., 1863
PROVOST GUARD.—

10th Ohio Infy..........Nov., 1862	From 17-Brig. 3-Div. 1-Corps Ohio	To Headquarters Dept. Cumb'd....	Jan., 1863

Right Wing, Fourteenth Army Corps---Army of the Cumberland

COMMANDER.

A. McD. McCook......	Major General....................	Oct. 24, 1862, to Jan. 9, 1863.

ESCORT.—

Co. B, 36th Ill. Infy......Nov., 1862	From 9-Div. 3-Corps Ohio.........	To 15th Illinois Cav. Co. K.......	Dec., 1862

1st DIVISION (Formerly 9-Div. 3-Corps Ohio).— COMMANDERS.

R. B. Mitchell........|Brigadier General...................|Oct. 24, 1862, to Nov. 5, 1862.	
J. C. Davis............|Brigadier General...................|Nov. 5, 1862, to Jan. 9, 1863.	

1st BRIGADE (Formerly 30-Brig. 9-Div. 3-Corps Ohio).—

COMMANDER.

P. S. Post............|Col. 59th Illinois Infy.............|Nov. 5, 1862, to Jan. 9, 1863.	

59th Illinois Infy......Nov., 1862	From 30-Brig. 9-Div. 3-Corps Ohio	To 1-Brig. 1-Div. 20-Corps Cumb'd	Jan., 1863
74th Illinois Infy......Nov., 1862	From 30-Brig. 9-Div. 3-Corps Ohio	To 1-Brig. 1-Div. 20-Corps Cumb'd	Jan., 1863
75th Illinois Infy......Nov., 1862	From 30-Brig. 9-Div. 3-Corps Ohio	To 1-Brig. 1-Div. 20-Corps Cumb'd	Jan., 1863
22d Indiana Infy......Nov., 1862	From 30-Brig. 9-Div. 3-Corps Ohio	To 1-Brig. 1-Div. 20-Corps Cumb'd	Jan., 1863
5th Wisconsin Batty.....Nov., 1862	From 30-Brig. 9-Div. 3-Corps Ohio	To Arty. 1-Div. 20-Corps Cumb'd..	Jan., 1863

2d BRIGADE (Formerly 31-Brig. 9-Div. 3-Corps Ohio).—

COMMANDER.

William P. Carlin.....|Col. 38th Illinois Infy.............|Nov. 5, 1862, to Jan. 9, 1863.	

21st Illinois Infy......Nov., 1862	From 31-Brig. 9-Div. 3-Corps Ohio	To 2-Brig. 1-Div. 20-Corps Cumb'd	Jan., 1863
38th Illinois Infy......Nov., 1862	From 31-Brig. 9-Div. 3-Corps Ohio	To 2-Brig. 1-Div. 20-Corps Cumb'd	Jan., 1863
101st Ohio Infy........Nov., 1862	From 31-Brig. 9-Div. 3-Corps Ohio	To 2-Brig. 1-Div. 20-Corps Cumb'd	Jan., 1863
15th Wisconsin Infy.....Nov., 1862	From 31-Brig. 9-Div. 3-Corps Ohio	To 3-Brig. 1-Div. 20-Corps Cumb'd	Jan., 1863
2d Minnesota Batty......Nov., 1862	From 31-Brig. 9-Div. 3-Corps Ohio	To Arty. 1-Div. 20-Corps Cumb'd..	Jan., 1863

3d BRIGADE (Formerly 32-Brig. 9-Div. 3-Corps Ohio).—

COMMANDERS.

J. S. McClelland.......|Lt.-Col. 25th Illinois Infy..........|Nov. 5, 1862, to Dec. 24, 1862.	
William E. Woodruff..|Col. ....|Dec. 24, 1862, to Jan. 9, 1863.	

25th Illinois Infy......Nov., 1862	From 32-Brig. 9-Div. 3-Corps Ohio	To 3-Brig. 1-Div. 20-Corps Cumb'd	Jan., 1863
35th Illinois Infy......Nov., 1862	From 32-Brig. 9-Div. 3-Corps Ohio	To 3-Brig. 1-Div. 20-Corps Cumb'd	Jan., 1863
81st Indiana Infy......Nov., 1862	From 32-Brig. 9-Div. 3-Corps Ohio	To 2-Brig. 1-Div. 20-Corps Cumb'd	Jan., 1863
8th Kansas Infy........Nov., 1862	From 32-Brig. 9-Div. 3-Corps Ohio	To 3-Brig. 1-Div. 20-Corps Cumb'd	Jan., 1863
8th Wisconsin Batty.....Nov., 1862	From 32-Brig. 9-Div. 3-Corps Ohio	To Arty. 1-Div. 20-Corps Cumb'd..	Jan., 1863

2d DIVISION (Formerly 2-Div. 1-Corps Ohio).— COMMANDER.

R. W. Johnson........|Brigadier General...................|Nov. 5, 1862, to Jan. 9, 1863.	

1st BRIGADE (Formerly 6-Brig. 2-Div. 1-Corps Ohio).—

COMMANDERS.

A. Willich.............|Brigadier General...................|Nov. 5, 1862, to Dec. 31, 1862.	
William Wallace.......|Col. 15th Ohio Infy...............|Dec. 31, 1862.	
W. H. Gibson..........|Col. 49th Ohio Infy...............|Dec. 31, 1862, to Jan. 9, 1863.	

89th Illinois Infy......Nov., 1862	From 6-Brig. 2-Div. 1-Corps Ohio..	To 1-Brig. 2-Div. 20-Corps Cumb'd	Jan., 1863
32d Indiana Infy......Nov., 1862	From 6-Brig. 2-Div. 1-Corps Ohio..	To 1-Brig. 2-Div. 20-Corps Cumb'd	Jan., 1863
39th Indiana Infy......Nov., 1862	From 6-Brig. 2-Div. 1-Corps Ohio..	To 1-Brig. 2-Div. 20-Corps Cumb'd	Jan., 1863
15th Ohio Infy.........Nov., 1862	From 6-Brig. 2-Div. 1-Corps Ohio..	To 1-Brig. 2-Div. 20-Corps Cumb'd	Jan., 1863
49th Ohio Infy.........Nov., 1862	From 6-Brig. 2-Div. 1-Corps Ohio..	To 1-Brig. 2-Div. 20-Corps Cumb'd	Jan., 1863
Batty. A, 1st Ohio Arty..Nov., 1862	From Arty. 2-Div. 1-Corps Ohio...	To Arty. 2-Div. 20-Corps Cumb'd..	Jan., 1863

2d BRIGADE (Formerly 5-Brig. 2-Div. 1-Corps Ohio).—

COMMANDERS.

E. N. Kirk............|Brigadier General...................|Nov. 5, 1862, to Dec. 31, 1862.	
J. B. Dodge...........|Col. 30th Indiana Infy............|Dec. 31, 1862, to Jan. 9, 1863.	

34th Illinois Infy......Nov., 1862	From 5-Brig. 2-Div. 1-Corps Ohio..	To 2-Brig. 2-Div. 20-Corps Cumb'd	Jan., 1863
79th Illinois Infy......Nov., 1862	From 5-Brig. 2-Div. 1-Corps Ohio..	To 2-Brig. 2-Div. 20-Corps Cumb'd	Jan., 1863
29th Indiana Infy......Nov., 1862	From 5-Brig. 2-Div. 1-Corps Ohio..	To 2-Brig. 2-Div. 20-Corps Cumb'd	Jan., 1863
30th Indiana Infy......Nov., 1862	From 5-Brig. 2-Div. 1-Corps Ohio..	To 2-Brig. 2-Div. 20-Corps Cumb'd	Jan., 1863
77th Penna. Infy......Nov., 1862	From 5-Brig. 2-Div. 1-Corps Ohio..	To 2-Brig. 2-Div. 20-Corps Cumb'd	Jan., 1863
Batty. E, 1st Ohio Arty..Nov., 1862	From Arty. 2-Div. 1-Corps Ohio...	To Arty. 2-Div. 20-Corps Cumb'd..	Jan., 1863

3d BRIGADE, 2d DIVISION.—(Formerly 4-Brig. 2-Div. 1-Corps Ohio.)

COMMANDERS.

H. M. Buckley	Col. 5th Ky. Infy	Nov. 5, 1862, to Dec. 24, 1862.	
P. P. Baldwin	Col. 6th Ind. Infy	Dec. 24, 1862, to Jan. 9, 1863.	

6th Ind. Infy	Nov., 1862	From 4-Brig. 2-Div. 1-Corps Ohio	To 3-Brig. 2-Div. 20-Corps Cumb'd..	Jan., 1863
5th Ky. Infy	Nov., 1862	From 4-Brig. 2-Div. 1-Corps Ohio	To 3-Brig. 2-Div. 20-Corps Cumb'd..	Jan., 1863
1st Ohio Infy	Nov., 1862	From 4-Brig. 2-Div. 1-Corps Ohio	To 3-Brig. 2-Div. 20-Corps Cumb'd..	Jan., 1863
93d Ohio Infy	Nov., 1862	From 4-Brig. 2-Div. 1-Corps Ohio	To 3-Brig. 2-Div. 20-Corps Cumb'd..	Jan., 1863
15th U. S. Infy	Nov., 1862	From 4-Brig. 2-Div. 1-Corps Ohio	To 4-Brig. 1-Div. Centre 14-Corps..	Dec., 1862
16th U. S. Infy	Nov., 1862	From 4-Brig. 2-Div. 1-Corps Ohio	To 4-Brig. 1-Div. Centre 14-Corps..	Dec., 1862
19th U. S. Infy	Nov., 1862	From 4-Brig. 2-Div. 1-Corps Ohio	To 4-Brig. 1-Div. Centre 14-Corps..	Dec., 1862
Batty. H, 5th U. S. Arty	Nov., 1862	From Arty. 2-Div. 1-Corps Ohio	To 4-Brig. 1-Div. Centre 14-Corps...	Dec., 1863
5th Ind. Batty	Nov., 1862	From 9-Brig. 3-Div. 1-Corps Ohio	To Arty. 2-Div. 29-Corps Cumb'd...	Jan., 1863

3d DIVISION.—(Formerly 11-Div. 3-Corps Ohio.)

COMMANDER.

P. H. Sheridan	Brigadier General	Nov. 5, 1862, to Jan. 9, 1863.	

1st BRIGADE.—(Formerly 37-Brig. 11-Div. 3-Corps Ohio.)

COMMANDERS.

J. W. Sill	Brigadier General	Nov. 5, 1862, to Dec. 31, 1862.	Killed.
N. Greusel	Col. 36th Ill. Infy	Dec. 31, 1862, to Jan. 9, 1863.	

36th Ill. Infy	Nov., 1862	From 37-Brig. 11-Div. 3-Corps Ohio.	To 1-Brig. 3-Div. 20-Corps Cumb'd..	Jan., 1863
88th Ill. Infy	Nov., 1862	From 37-Brig. 11-Div. 3-Corps Ohio.	To 1-Brig. 3-Div. 20-Corps Cumb'd..	Jan., 1863
21st Mich. Infy	Nov., 1862	From 37-Brig. 11-Div. 3-Corps Ohio.	To 1-Brig. 3-Div. 20-Corps Cumb'd..	Jan., 1863
24th Wis. Infy	Nov., 1862	From 37-Brig. 11-Div. 3-Corps Ohio.	To 1-Brig. 3-Div. 20-Corps Cumb'd..	Jan., 1863
4th Ind. Batty	Nov., 1862	From 28-Brig. 3-Div. 1-Corps Ohio.	To Arty. 3-Div. 20-Corps Cumb'd....	Jan., 1863

2d BRIGADE.—(Formerly 35-Brig. 11-Div. 3-Corps Ohio.)

COMMANDERS.

Fdk. Schaeffer	Col. General Staff	Nov. 5, 1862, to Dec. 31, 1862.	Killed.
B. Laiboldt	Lt.-Col. 2d Mo. Infy	Dec. 31, 1862, to Jan. 9, 1863.	

44th Ill. Infy	Nov., 1862	From 35-Brig. 11-Div. 3-Corps Ohio.	To 2-Brig. 3-Div. 20-Corps Cumb'd..	Jan., 1863
73d Ill. Infy	Nov., 1862	From 35-Brig. 11-Div. 3-Corps Ohio.	To 2-Brig. 3-Div. 20-Corps Cumb'd..	Jan., 1863
2d Mo. Infy	Nov., 1862	From 35-Brig. 11-Div. 3-Corps Ohio.	To 2-Brig. 3-Div. 20-Corps Cumb'd..	Jan., 1863
15th Mo. Infy	Nov., 1862	From 35-Brig. 11-Div. 3-Corps Ohio.	To 2-Brig. 3-Div. 20-Corps Cumb'd..	Jan., 1863
Batty. G, 1st Mo. Arty	Nov., 1862	From Arty. 11-Div. 3-Corps Ohio...	To Arty. 3-Div. 20-Corps Cumb'd....	Jan., 1863

3d BRIGADE.—(Formerly 1-Brig. 13-Div. Army Ohio.)

COMMANDERS.

G. W. Roberts	Col. 42d Ill. Infy	Nov. 5, 1862, to Dec. 31, 1862.	Killed.
L. P. Bradley	Col. 51st Ill. Infy	Dec. 31, 1862, to Jan. 9, 1863.	

22d Ill. Infy	Nov., 1862	From 1-Brig. 13-Div. Army Ohio.	To 3-Brig. 3-Div. 20-Corps Cumb'd..	Jan., 1863
27th Ill. Infy	Nov., 1862	From 1-Brig. 13-Div. Army Ohio.	To 3-Brig. 3-Div. 20-Corps Cumb'd..	Jan., 1863
42d Ill. Infy	Nov., 1862	From 1-Brig. 13-Div. Army Ohio.	To 3-Brig. 3-Div. 20-Corps Cumb'd..	Jan., 1863
51st Ill. Infy	Nov., 1862	From 1-Brig. 13-Div. Army Ohio.	To 3-Brig. 3-Div. 20-Corps Cumb'd..	Jan., 1863
Batty. C, 1st Ill. Arty	Nov., 1862	From 2-Brig. 13-Div. Army Ohio.	To Arty. 3-Div. 20-Corps Cumb'd....	Jan., 1863
CAVALRY RIGHT WING.—				
3d Ind. Cav. E, H, I, K	Nov., 1862	From 2-Div. 1-Corps Ohio	To 1-Br. 1-Cav. Div. Army Cumb'd..	Jan., 1863

Centre, Fourteenth Army Corps---Army of the Cumberland

Designated 14th Army Corps Jan. 9, 1863.

COMMANDER.

George H. Thomas	Major General	Nov. 5, 1862, to Jan. 9, 1863.	

1st DIVISION.—(Formerly 3-Div. 1-Corps, Ohio.)

COMMANDER.

L. H. Rousseau	Major General	Nov. 5, 1862, to Jan. 9, 1863.	

1st BRIGADE.—(Formerly 9-Brig. 3-Div. 1-Corps Ohio.)

COMMANDER.

B. F. Scribner	Col. 38th Ind. Infy	Nov. 5, 1862, to Jan. 9, 1863.	

38th Ind. Infy	Nov., 1862	From 9-Brig. 3-Div. 1-Corps Ohio...	To 1-Brig. 1-Div. 14-Corps Cumb'd..	Jan., 1863
2d Ohio Infy	Nov., 1862	From 9-Brig. 3-Div. 1-Corps Ohio...	To 1-Brig. 1-Div. 14-Corps Cumb'd..	Jan., 1863
33d Ohio Infy	Nov., 1862	From 9-Brig. 3-Div. 1-Corps Ohio...	To 1-Brig. 1-Div. 14-Corps Cumb'd..	Jan., 1863
94th Ohio Infy	Nov., 1862	From 9-Brig. 3-Div. 1-Corps Ohio...	To 1-Brig. 1-Div. 14-Corps Cumb'd..	Jan., 1863
10th Wis. Infy	Nov., 1862	From 9-Brig. 3-Div. 1-Corps Ohio...	To 1-Brig. 1-Div. 14-Corps Cumb'd..	Jan., 1863

2d BRIGADE.—(Formerly 17-Brig. 3-Div. 1-Corps Ohio.)

COMMANDERS.

J. G. Jones	Col. 42d Ind. Infy	Nov. 5, 1862, to Dec. 26, 1862.	
John Beatty	Col. 3d Ohio Infy	Dec. 26, 1862, to Jan. 9, 1863.	

42d Ind. Infy	Nov., 1862	From 17-Brig. 3-Div. 1-Corps Ohio..	To 2-Brig. 1-Div. 14-Corps Cumb'd..	Jan., 1863
88th Ind. Infy	Nov., 1862	From 17-Brig. 3-Div. 1-Corps Ohio..	To 2-Brig. 1-Div. 14-Corps Cumb'd..	Jan., 1863
15th Ky. Infy	Nov., 1862	From 17-Brig. 3-Div. 1-Corps Ohio..	To 2-Brig. 1-Div. 14-Corps Cumb'd..	Jan., 1863
3d Ohio Infy	Nov., 1862	From 17-Brig. 3-Div. 1-Corps Ohio..	To 2-Brig. 1-Div. 14-Corps Cumb'd..	Jan., 1863
Batty. A, 1st Mich. Arty	Nov., 1862	From 17-Brig. 3-Div. 1-Corps Ohio..	To Arty. 1-Div. 14-Corps Cumb'd....	Jan., 1863

3d BRIGADE.—(Formerly 28-Brig. 3-Div. 1-Corps Ohio.)

COMMANDERS.

H. A. Hambright	Col. 79th Penna. Infy	Nov. 5, 1862, to Dec. 20, 1862.	
J. C. Starkweather	Col. 1st Wis. Infy	Dec. 20, 1862, to Jan. 9, 1863.	

24th Ill. Infy	Nov., 1862	From 28-Brig. 3-Div. 1-Corps Ohio..	To 3-Brig. 1-Div. 14-Corps Cumb'd..	Jan., 1863
79th Penna. Infy	Nov., 1862	From 28-Brig. 3-Div. 1-Corps Ohio..	To 3-Brig. 1-Div. 14-Corps Cumb'd..	Jan., 1863
1st Wis. Infy	Nov., 1862	From 28-Brig. 3-Div. 1-Corps Ohio..	To 3-Brig. 1-Div. 14-Corps Cumb'd..	Jan., 1863
21st Wis. Infy	Nov., 1862	From 28-Brig. 3-Div. 1-Corps Ohio..	To 3-Brig. 1-Div. 14-Corps Cumb'd..	Jan., 1863
Batty. A, Ky. Arty	Nov., 1862	From 28-Brig. 3-Div. 1-Corps Ohio..	To Arty. 1-Div. 14-Corps Cumb'd...	Jan., 1863

4th BRIGADE.—Organized Dec. 18, 1862.   COMMANDER.

O. L. Shepherd.........	Lt.-Col. 18th U. S. Infy.............	Dec. 18, 1862, to Jan. 9, 1863.	

15th U. S. Infy...........Dec., 1862	From 3-Brig. 2-Div. R. Wing 14-C..	To 4-Brig. 1-Div. 14-Corps Cumb'd..	Jan.,	1863
16th U. S. Infy...........Dec., 1862	From 3-Brig. 2-Div. R. Wing 14-C..	To 4-Brig. 1-Div. 14-Corps Cumb'd..	Jan.,	1863
18th U. S. Infy...........Dec., 1862	From 3-Brig. 3-Div. Centre 14-C....	To 4-Brig. 1-Div. 14-Corps Cumb'd..	Jan.,	1863
19th U. S. Infy...........Dec., 1862	From 3-Brig. 2-Div. R. Wing 14-C..	To 4-Brig. 1-Div. 14-Corps Cumb'd..	Jan.,	1863
Batty. H, 5th U. S. Arty.Dec., 1862	From 3-Brig. 2-Div. R. Wing 14-C..	To 4-Brig. 1-Div. 14-Corps Cumb'd..	Jan.,	1863
CAVALRY.—				
2d Ky. Cav...............Dec., 1862	From Unatt. 1-Corps Army Ohio....	To 2-Brig. 2-Cav. Div. Cumb'd.....	Jan.,	1863

2d DIVISION.—(Formerly 8th Division Army Ohio.)   COMMANDER.

J. S. Negley............	Brigadier General..................	Nov. 5, 1862, to Jan. 9, 1863.	

1st BRIGADE.—   COMMANDER.

J. G. Spear.............	Brigadier General..................	Nov. 12, 1862, to Jan. 9, 1863.	

1st Tenn. Infy...........Nov., 1862	From 3-Br. Cumb'd Div. Dt. W. Va..	To 1-Brig. 2-Div. 14-Corps Cumb'd..	Jan.,	1863
2d Tenn. Infy...........Nov., 1862	From 3-Br. Cumb'd Div. Dt. W. Va..	To 1-Brig. 2-Div. 14-Corps Cumb'd..	Jan.,	1863
3d Tenn. Infy...........Nov., 1862	From 3-Br. Cumb'd Div. Dt. W. Va..	To 1-Brig. 2-Div. 14-Corps Cumb'd..	Jan.,	1863
5th Tenn. Infy...........Nov., 1862	From 3-Br. Cumb'd Div. Dt. W. Va..	To 1-Brig. 2-Div. 14-Corps Cumb'd..	Jan.,	1863
6th Tenn. Infy...........Nov., 1862	From 3-Br. Cumb'd Div. Dt. W. Va..	To 1-Brig. 2-Div. 14-Corps Cumb'd..	Jan.,	1863

2d BRIGADE.—(Formerly 29-Brig. 8-Div. Army Ohio.)   COMMANDER.

T. R. Stanley........	Col. 18th Ohio Infy.............	Nov. 5, 1862, to Jan. 9, 1863.	

19th Ill. Infy............Nov., 1862	From 29-Brig. 8-Div. Army Ohio...	To 2-Brig. 2-Div. 14-Corps Cumb'd..	Jan.,	1863
11th Mich. Infy...........Nov., 1862	From 29-Brig. 8-Div. Army Ohio...	To 2-Brig. 2-Div. 14-Corps Cumb'd..	Jan.,	1863
18th Ohio Infy...........Nov., 1862	From 29-Brig. 8-Div. Army Ohio...	To 2-Brig. 2-Div. 14-Corps Cumb'd..	Jan.,	1863
69th Ohio Infy...........Nov., 1862	From 29-Brig. 8-Div. Army Ohio...	To 2-Brig. 2-Div. 14-Corps Cumb'd..	Jan.,	1863

3d BRIGADE.—(Formerly 7-Brig. 8-Div. Army Ohio.)   COMMANDER.

J. F. Miller............	Col. 29th Ind. Infy..............	Nov. 5, 1862, to Jan. 9, 1863.	

37th Ind. Infy..........Nov., 1862	From 7-Brig. 8-Div. Army Ohio....	To 3-Brig. 2-Div. 14-Corps Cumb'd..	Jan.,	1863
21st Ohio Infy...........Nov., 1862	From 7-Brig. 8-Div. Army Ohio....	To 3-Brig. 2-Div. 14-Corps Cumb'd..	Jan.,	1863
74th Ohio Infy...........Nov., 1862	From 7-Brig. 8-Div. Army Ohio....	To 3-Brig. 2-Div. 14-Corps Cumb'd..	Jan.,	1863
78th Penna. Infy........Nov., 1862	From 7-Brig. 8-Div. Army Ohio....	To 3-Brig. 2-Div. 14-Corps Cumb'd..	Jan.,	1863
ARTILLERY.—				
Batty. B, Ky. Arty.......Nov., 1862	From Arty. 8-Div. Army Ohio.......	To Arty. 2-Div. 14-Corps Cumb'd...	Jan.,	1863
Batty. G, 1st Ohio Arty...Nov., 1862	From Arty. 8-Div. Army Ohio.......	To Arty. 2-Div. 14-Corps Cumb'd...	Jan.,	1863
Batty. M, 1st Ohio Arty..Nov., 1862	From Arty. 8-Div. Army Ohio.......	To Arty. 2-Div. 14-Corps Cumb'd...	Jan.,	1863

3d DIVISION.—(Formerly 1-Div. 3-Corps Ohio.)   COMMANDER.

S. S. Fry..............	Brigadier General..................	Nov. 5, 1862, to Jan. 9, 1863.	

1st BRIGADE.—(Formerly 1-Brig. 1-Div. 3-Corps.)   COMMANDERS.

M. B. Walker..........	Col. 31st Ohio Infy................	Nov. 5, 1862, to Jan. 9, 1863.	
J. M. Connell.........	Col. 17th Ohio Infy................	Temp'y in Dec., 1862.	

82d Ind. Infy............Nov., 1862	From 1-Brig. 1-Div. 3-Corps Ohio...	To 1-Brig. 3-Div. 14-Corps Cumb'd..	Jan.,	1863
12th Ky. Infy............Nov., 1862	From 1-Brig. 1-Div. 3-Corps Ohio...	To 1-Brig. 3-Div. 14-Corps Cumb'd..	Jan.,	1863
17th Ohio Infy...........Nov., 1862	From 1-Brig. 1-Div. 3-Corps Ohio...	To 1-Brig. 3-Div. 14-Corps Cumb'd..	Jan.,	1863
31st Ohio Infy...........Nov., 1862	From 1-Brig. 1-Div. 3-Corps Ohio...	To 1-Brig. 3-Div. 14-Corps Cumb'd..	Jan.,	1863
38th Ohio Infy...........Nov., 1862	From 1-Brig. 1-Div. 3-Corps Ohio...	To 1-Brig. 3-Div. 14-Corps Cumb'd..	Jan.,	1863

2d BRIGADE.—   COMMANDER.

John M. Harlan........	Col. 12th Ky. Infy.................	Nov. 5, 1862, to Jan. 9, 1863.	

10th Ind. Infy...........Nov., 1862	From 2-Brig. 1-Div. 3-Corps Ohio...	To 2-Brig. 3-Div. 14-Corps Cumb'd..	Jan.,	1863
74th Ind. Infy...........Nov., 1862	From 2-Brig. 1-Div. 3-Corps Ohio...	To 2-Brig. 3-Div. 14-Corps Cumb'd..	Jan.,	1863
4th Ky. Infy............Nov., 1862	From 2-Brig. 1-Div. 3-Corps Ohio...	To 2-Brig. 3-Div. 14-Corps Cumb'd..	Jan.,	1863
10th Ky. Infy............Nov., 1862	From 2-Brig. 1-Div. 3-Corps Ohio...	To 2-Brig. 3-Div. 14-Corps Cumb'd..	Jan.,	1863
14th Ohio Infy...........Nov., 1862	From 2-Brig. 1-Div. 3-Corps Ohio...	To 2-Brig. 3-Div. 14-Corps Cumb'd..	Jan.,	1863

3d BRIGADE.—   COMMANDER.

J. B. Steedman.........	Brigadier General..................	Nov. 5, 1862, to Jan. 9, 1863.	

87th Ind. Infy...........Nov., 1862	From 3-Brig. 1-Div. 3-Corps, Ohio...	To 3-Brig. 3-Div. 14 Corps Cumb'd..	Jan.,	1863
2d Minn. Infy...........Nov., 1862	From 3-Brig. 1-Div. 3-Corps, Ohio...	To 3-Brig. 3-Div. 14 Corps Cumb'd..	Jan.,	1863
9th Ohio Infy...........Nov., 1862	From 3-Brig. 1-Div. 3-Corps, Ohio...	To 3-Brig. 3-Div. 14 Corps Cumb'd..	Jan.,	1863
35th Ohio Infy...........Nov., 1862	From 3-Brig. 1-Div. 3-Corps, Ohio...	To 3-Brig. 3-Div. 14 Corps Cumb'd..	Jan.,	1863
ARTILLERY.—				
Batty. D, 1st Mich. Arty..Nov., 1862	From Arty. 1-Div. 3-Corps Ohio....	To Arty. 3-Div. 14-Corps Cumb'd...	Jan.,	1863
Batty. C, 1st Ohio Arty...Nov., 1862	From Arty. 1-Div. 3-Corps Ohio....	To Arty. 3-Div. 14-Corps Cumb'd...	Jan.,	1863
Batty. I, 4th U. S. Arty...Nov., 1862	From Arty. 1-Div. 3-Corps Ohio....	To Arty. 3-Div. 14-Corps Cumb'd...	Jan.,	1863

4th DIVISION.—   COMMANDER.

R. B. Mitchell..........	Brigadier General..................	Nov. 5, 1862, to Jan. 9, 1863.	

1st BRIGADE.—   COMMANDER.

J. D. Morgan..........	Brigadier General..................	Nov. 5, 1862, to Jan. 9, 1863.	

10th Ill. Infy...........Nov., 1863	From 2-Brig. 13-Div. Army Ohio...	To 1-Brig. 4-Div. 14-Corps Cumb'd..	Jan.,	1863
16th Ill. Infy...........Nov., 1863	From 2-Brig. 13-Div. Army Ohio...	To 1-Brig. 4-Div. 14-Corps Cumb'd..	Jan.,	1863
60th Ill. Infy...........Nov., 1863	From 2-Brig. 13-Div. Army Ohio...	To 1-Brig. 4-Div. 14-Corps Cumb'd..	Jan.,	1863
10th Mich. Infy...........Nov., 1863	From 2-Brig. 13-Div. Army Ohio...	To 1-Brig. 4-Div. 14-Corps Cumb'd..	Jan.,	1863
14th Mich. Infy...........Nov., 1863	From 2-Brig. 13-Div. Army Ohio...	To 1-Brig. 4-Div. 14-Corps Cumb'd..	Jan.,	1863

2d BRIGADE.—(Formerly 36-Brig. 11-Div. 3-Corps Ohio.)   COMMANDER.

Daniel McCook.........	Col. 52d Ohio Infy................	Nov. 5, 1862, to Jan. 9, 1863.	

85th Ill. Infy............Nov., 1862	From 36-Brig. 11-Div. 3-Corps Ohio..	To 2-Brig. 4-Div. 14-Corps Cumb'd..	Jan.,	1863
86th Ill. Infy............Nov., 1862	From 36-Brig. 11-Div. 3-Corps Ohio..	To 2-Brig. 4-Div. 14-Corps Cumb d..	Jan.,	1863
125th Ill. Infy...........Nov., 1862	From 36-Brig. 11-Div. 3-Corps Ohio..	To 2-Brig. 4-Div. 14-Corps Cumb'd..	Jan.,	1863
52d Ohio Infy............Nov., 1862	From 36-Brig. 11-Div. 3-Corps Ohio..	To 2-Brig. 4-Div. 14-Corps Cumb'd..	Jan.,	1863

ARTILLERY.—

Batty. I, 2d Ill. Arty.	Nov., 1862	From Arty. 11-Div. 3-Corps Cumb'd..	To Arty. 4-Div. 14-Corps Cumb'd....	Jan., 1863
10th Wis. Batty.	Nov., 1862	From Arty. 13-Div. Army Ohio......	To Arty. 4-Div. 14-Corps Cumb'd....	Jan., 1863

CAVALRY.—

5th Ky. Cav.	Nov., 1862	From 2-Brig. Cav. Div. Army Ohio..	To 2-Brig. 1-Cav. Div. Cumb'd......	Jan., 1863
3d Tenn. Cav.	Nov., 1862	From New Organization............	To Unatt. Nashville, Tenn...........	Jan., 1863

ARTILLERY RESERVE.—

Batty. E, 1st Mich. Arty.	Nov., 1862	From Post Nashville, Tenn.........	To Garrison Arty. Nashville, Tenn..	Jan., 1863
11th Ind. Batty.	Nov., 1862	From Post Nashville, Tenn.........	To Garrison Arty. Nashville, Tenn..	Jan., 1863
12th Ind. Batty.	Nov., 1862	From Post Nashville, Tenn.........	To Garrison Arty. Nashville, Tenn..	Jan., 1863

UNATTACHED CENTRE.—

1st Middle Tenn. Infy.	Nov., 1862	From Post Nashville, Tenn.........	To Garrison Nashville, Tenn.......	Jan., 1863
10th Tenn. Infy.	Nov., 1862	From Post Nashville, Tenn.........	To Garrison Nashville, Tenn.......	Jan., 1863

5th DIVISION.—   COMMANDERS.

E. Dumont	Brigadier General	Nov. 5, 1862, to Dec. 11, 1862.
J. J. Reynolds	Major General	Dec. 11, 1862, to Jan. 9, 1863.

1st BRIGADE.—(Formerly 33-Brig. 10-Div. 1-Corps Ohio.)

COMMANDER.

A. S. Hall	Col. 105th Ohio Infy.	Nov. 5, 1862, to Jan. 9, 1863.

80th Illinois Infy.	Nov., 1862	From 33-Brig. 10-Div. 1-Corps Ohio.	To 1-Brig. 5-Div. 14-C. Cumberland.	Jan., 1863
123d Illinois Infy.	Nov., 1862	From 33-Brig. 10-Div. 1-Corps Ohio.	To 1-Brig. 5-Div. 14-C. Cumberland.	Jan., 1863
101st Indiana Infy.	Nov., 1862	From 33-Brig. 10-Div. 1-Corps Ohio.	To 1-Brig. 5-Div. 14-C. Cumberland.	Jan., 1863
105th Ohio Infy.	Nov., 1862	From 33-Brig. 10-Div. 1-Corps Ohio.	To 1-Brig. 5-Div. 14-C. Cumberland.	Jan., 1863

2d BRIGADE.—(Formerly 40-Brig. 12-Div. Army Ohio.)

COMMANDER.

A. O. Miller	Col. 72d Illinois Infy.	Nov. 5, 1862, to Jan. 9, 1863.

98th Illinois Infy.	Nov., 1862	From 40-Brig. 12-Div. Army Ohio..	To 2-Brig. 5-Div. 14-Corps Cumb'd..	Jan., 1863
17th Indiana Infy.	Nov., 1862	From 1-B. 1-Div. Left Wing 14-Corps	To 2-Brig. 5-Div. 14-Corps Cumb'd..	Jan., 1863
72d Indiana Infy.	Nov., 1862	From 40-Brig. 12-Div. Army Ohio...	To 2-Brig. 5-Div. 14-Corps Cumb'd..	Jan., 1863
75th Indiana Infy.	Nov., 1862	From 40-Brig. 12-Div. Army Ohio...	To 2-Brig. 5-Div. 14-Corps Cumb'd..	Jan., 1863

ARTILLERY.—

18th Indiana Batty.	Nov., 1862	From Arty. 12-Div. Army Ohio.....	To Arty 5-Div. 14-Corps Cumb'd....	Jan., 1863
19th Indiana Batty.	Nov., 1862	From 34-Brig. 10-Div. 1-Corps Ohio.	To Arty 5-Div. 14-Corps Cumb'd....	Jan., 1863

Left Wing, Fourteenth Army Corps---Army of the Cumberland

(Formerly 2d Corps Army Ohio. Designated 21st Army Corps Jan. 9, 1863.)

COMMANDER.

T. L. Crittenden	Major General	Nov. 5, 1862, to Jan. 9, 1863.

1st DIVISION.—(Formerly 6-Div. 2-Corps Ohio.)

COMMANDERS.

Thos. J. Wood	Brigadier General	Nov. 5, 1862, to Dec. 31, 1862.
M. S. Hascall	Brigadier General	Dec. 31, 1862, to Jan. 9, 1863.

1st BRIGADE—(Formerly 15-Brig. 6-Div. Army Ohio.)

COMMANDERS.

M. S. Hascall	Brigadier General	Nov. 5, 1862, to Dec. 31, 1862.
Geo. P. Buell	Col. 58th Indiana Infy.	Dec. 31, 1862, to Jan. 9, 1863.

100th Illinois Infy.	Nov., 1862	From 15-Brig. 6-Div. 2-Corps Ohio.	To 1-Brig. 1-Div. 21-Corps Cumb'd.	Jan., 1863
17th Indiana Infy.	Nov., 1862	From 15-Brig. 6-Div. 2-Corps Ohio.	To 2-Brig. 5-Div. Centre 14-Corps...	Nov., 1862
58th Indiana Infy.	Nov., 1862	From 15-Brig. 6-Div. 2-Corps Ohio.	To 1-Brig. 1-Div. 21-Corps Cumb'd.	Jan., 1863
3d Kentucky Infy.	Nov., 1862	From 15-Brig. 6-Div. 2-Corps Ohio.	To 1-Brig. 1-Div. 21-Corps Cumb'd.	Jan., 1863
26th Ohio Infy.	Nov., 1862	From 15-Brig. 6-Div. 2-Corps Ohio.	To 1-Brig. 1-Div. 21-Corps Cumb'd.	Jan., 1863
8th Indiana Batty.	Nov., 1862	From 15-Brig. 6-Div. 2-Corps Ohio.	To Arty. 1-Div. 21-Corps..........	Jan., 1863

2d BRIGADE.—(Formerly 21-Brig. 6-Div. Army Ohio.)

COMMANDER.

Geo. D. Wagner	Col. 15th Indiana Infy.	Nov. 5, 1862, to Jan. 9, 1863.

15th Indiana Infy.	Nov., 1862	From 21st Brig. 6-Div. 2-Corps Ohio.	To 2-Brig. 1-Div. 21-Corps Cumb'd.	Jan., 1863
40th Indiana Infy.	Nov., 1862	From 21st Brig. 6-Div. 2-Corps Ohio.	To 2-Brig. 1-Div. 21-Corps Cumb'd.	Jan., 1863
57th Indiana Infy.	Nov., 1862	From 21st Brig. 6-Div. 2-Corps Ohio.	To 2-Brig. 1-Div. 21-Corps Cumb'd.	Jan., 1863
97th Ohio Infy.	Nov., 1862	From 21st Brig. 6-Div. 2-Corps Ohio.	To 2-Brig. 1-Div. 21-Corps Cumb'd.	Jan., 1863
10th Indiana Batty.	Nov., 1862	From 21st Brig. 6-Div. 2-Corps Ohio.	To Arty. 1-Div. 21-Corps Cumb'd.	Jan., 1863

3d BRIGADE.—Formerly 20-Brig. 6-Div. Army Ohio.)

COMMANDER.

C. G. Harker	Col. 65th Ohio Infy.	Nov. 5, 1862, to Jan. 9, 1863.

13th Michigan Infy.	Nov., 1862	From 20-Brig. 6-Div. 2-Corps Ohio..	To 3-Brig. 1-Div. 21-Corps Cumb'd.	Jan., 1863
51st Indiana Infy.	Nov., 1862	From 20-Brig. 6-Div. 2-Corps Ohio..	To 3-Brig. 1-Div. 21-Corps Cumb'd.	Jan., 1863
73d Indiana Infy.	Nov., 1862	From 20-Brig. 6-Div. 2-Corps Ohio..	To 3-Brig. 1-Div. 21-Corps Cumb'd.	Jan., 1863
64th Ohio Infy.	Nov., 1862	From 20-Brig. 6-Div. 2-Corps Ohio..	To 3-Brig. 1-Div. 21-Corps Cumb'd.	Jan., 1863
65th Ohio Infy.	Nov., 1862	From 20-Brig. 6-Div. 2-Corps Ohio..	To 3-Brig. 1-Div. 21-Corps Cumb'd.	Jan., 1863
6th Ohio Batty.	Nov., 1862	From 20-Brig. 6-Div. 2-Corps Ohio..	To Arty. 1-Div. 21-Corps Cumb'd.	Jan., 1863

2d DIVISION.—(Formerly 4-Div. 2-Corps Ohio.)

COMMANDERS.

W. S. Smith	Brigadier General	Nov. 5, 1862, to Dec. 10, 1862.
John M. Palmer	Brigadier General	Dec. 10, 1862, to Jan. 9, 1863.

1st BRIGADE.—(Formerly 22-Brig. 4-Div. 2-Corps Ohio.)

COMMANDER.

C. Cruft	Brigadier General	Nov. 5, 1862, to Jan. 9, 1863.

31st Indiana Infy.	Nov., 1862	From 22-Brig. 4-Div. 2-Corps Ohio.	To 1-Brig. 2-Div. 21-Corps Cumb'd.	Jan., 1863
1st Kentucky Infy.	Nov., 1862	From 22-Brig. 4-Div. 2-Corps Ohio.	To 1-Brig. 2-Div. 21-Corps Cumb'd.	Jan., 1863
2d Kentucky Infy.	Nov., 1862	From 22-Brig. 4-Div. 2-Corps Ohio.	To 1-Brig. 2-Div. 21-Corps Cumb'd.	Jan., 1863
20th Kentucky Infy.	Nov., 1862	From 22-Brig. 4-Div. 2-Corps Ohio.	To Dept. Ohio....................	Dec., 1862
90th Ohio Infy.	Nov., 1862	From 22-Brig. 4-Div. 2-Corps Ohio.	To 1-Brig. 2-Div. 21-Corps Cumb'd.	Jan., 1863

2d BRIGADE.—(Formerly 19-Brig. 4-Div. Army Ohio.)

COMMANDER.

W. B. Hazen...........	Brigadier General..................	Nov. 5, 1862, to Jan. 9, 1863.

110th Illinois Infy.......	Nov., 1862	From 19-Brig. 4-Div. 2-Corps Ohio..	To 2-Brig. 2-Div. 21-Corps Cumb'd..	Jan., 1863
9th Indiana Infy.........	Nov., 1862	From 19-Brig. 4-Div. 2-Corps Ohio..	To 2-Brig. 2-Div. 21-Corps Cumb'd..	Jan., 1863
41st Ohio Infy...........	Nov., 1862	From 19-Brig. 4-Div. 2-Corps Ohio..	To 2-Brig. 2-Div. 21-Corps Cumb'd..	Jan., 1863
6th Kentucky Infy......	Nov., 1862	From 19-Brig. 4-Div. 2-Corps Ohio..	To 2-Brig. 2-Div. 21-Corps Cumb'd..	Jan., 1863
27th Kentucky Infy......	Nov., 1862	From 19-Brig. 4-Div. 2-Corps Ohio..	To Dept. Ohio....................	Dec., 1862

3d BRIGADE.—(Formerly 10-Brig. 4-Div. Army Ohio.)

COMMANDER.

William Grose.........	Col. 36th Indiana Infy..............	Nov. 5, 1862, to Jan. 9, 1863.

84th Illinois Infy.........	Nov., 1862	From 10-Brig. 4-Div. 2-Corps Ohio..	To 3-Brig. 2-Div. 21-Corps Cumb'd..	Jan., 1863
36th Indiana Infy.........	Nov., 1862	From 10-Brig. 4-Div. 2-Corps Ohio..	To 3-Brig. 2-Div. 21-Corps Cumb'd..	Jan., 1863
23d Kentucky Infy.......	Nov., 1862	From 10-Brig. 4-Div. 2-Corps Ohio..	To 3-Brig. 2-Div. 21-Corps Cumb'd..	Jan., 1863
6th Ohio Infy...........	Nov., 1862	From 10-Brig. 4-Div. 2-Corps Ohio..	To 3-Brig. 2-Div. 21-Corps Cumb'd..	Jan., 1863
24th Ohio Infy...........	Nov., 1862	From 10-Brig. 4-Div. 2-Corps Ohio..	To 3-Brig. 2-Div. 21-Corps Cumb'd..	Jan., 1863
ARTILLERY.—				
Batty. B, 1st Ohio Arty...	Nov., 1862	From Arty. 4-Div. 2-Corps Ohio....	To Arty. 2-Div. 21-Corps Cumb'd..	Jan., 1863
Batty. F, 1st Ohio Arty..	Nov., 1862	From Arty. 4-Div. 2-Corps Ohio....	To Arty. 2-Div. 21-Corps Cumb'd..	Jan., 1863
Batty. H & M, 4th U. S. A.	Nov., 1862	From Arty. 4-Div. 2-Corps Ohio....	To Arty. 2-Div. 21-Corps Cumb'd	Jan., 1863

3d DIVISION.—(Formerly 5-Div. 2-Corps Army Ohio.)

COMMANDERS.

H. P. Van Cleve........	Brigadier General..................	Nov. 5, 1862, to Dec. 31, 1862.
Samuel Beatty.........	Col. 19th Ohio Infy................	Dec. 31. 1862, to Jan. 9, 1863.

1st BRIGADE.—(Formerly 11-Brig. 5-Div. Army Ohio.)

COMMANDERS.

Samuel Beatty.........	Col. 19th Ohio Infy................	Nov. 5, 1862, to Dec. 31, 1862.
B. C. Crider............	Col. 9th Kentucky Infy............	Dec. 31. 1862, to Jan. 9, 1863.

79th Indiana Infy.......	Nov., 1862	From 11-Brig. 5-Div. 2-Corps Ohio..	To 1-Brig. 3-Div. 21-Corps Cumb'd..	Jan., 1863
19th Ohio Infy.........	Nov., 1862	From 11-Brig. 5-Div. 2-Corps Ohio..	To 1-Brig. 3-Div. 21-Corps Cumb'd..	Jan., 1863
9th Kentucky Infy.......	Nov., 1862	From 11-Brig. 5-Div. 2-Corps Ohio..	To 1-Brig. 3-Div. 21-Corps Cumb'd..	Jan., 1863
11th Kentucky Infy......	Nov., 1862	From 11-Brig. 5-Div. 2-Corps Ohio..	To Dept. Ohio....................	Jan., 1863
13th Kentucky Infy......	Nov., 1862	From 11-Brig. 5-Div. 2-Corps Ohio..	To Dept. Ohio....................	Nov., 1862

2d BRIGADE.—(Formerly 14-Brig. 5-Div. Army Ohio.)

COMMANDER.

James P. Fyffe.........	Col. 59th Ohio Infy................	Nov. 5, 1862, to Jan. 9, 1863.

44th Indiana Infy.........	Nov., 1862	From 14-Brig. 5-Div. 2-Corps Ohio..	To 2-Brig. 3-Div. 21-Corps Cumb'd..	Jan., 1863
86th Indiana Infy.........	Nov., 1862	From 14-Brig. 5-Div. 2-Corps Ohio..	To 2-Brig. 3-Div. 21-Corps Cumb'd..	Jan., 1863
13th Ohio Infy...........	Nov., 1862	From 14-Brig. 5-Div. 2-Corps Ohio..	To 2-Brig. 3-Div. 21-Corps Cumb'd..	Jan., 1863
59th Ohio Infy...........	Nov., 1862	From 11-Brig. 5-Div. 2-Corps Ohio..	To 2-Brig. 3-Div. 21-Corps Cumb'd..	Jan., 1863
26th Kentucky Infy......	Nov., 1862	From 14-Brig. 5-Div. 2-Corps Ohio..	To Dept. Ohio....................	Nov., 1862

3d BRIGADE.—(Formerly 23-Brig. 5-Div. Army Ohio.)

COMMANDERS.

Stanley Matthews......	Col. 51st Ohio Infy................	Nov. 5, 1862, to Dec. 31, 1862.
S. W. Price............	Col. 21st Kentucky Infy............	Dec. 31, 1862, to Jan. 9, 1863.

35th Indiana Infy.........	Nov., 1862	From 23-Brig. 5-Div. 2-Corps Ohio..	To 3-Brig. 3-Div. 21-Corps Cumb'd..	Jan., 1863
8th Kentucky Infy.......	Nov., 1862	From 23-Brig. 5-Div. 2-Corps Ohio..	To 3-Brig. 3-Div. 21-Corps Cumb'd..	Jan., 1863
21st Kentucky Infy......	Nov., 1862	From 23-Brig. 5-Div. 2-Corps Ohio..	To 3-Brig. 3-Div. 21-Corps Cumb'd..	Jan., 1863
51st Ohio Infy...........	Nov., 1862	From 23-Brig. 5-Div. 2-Corps Ohio..	To 3-Brig. 3-Div. 21-Corps Cumb'd.	Jan., 1863
99th Ohio Infy...........	Nov., 1862	From 23-Brig. 5-Div. 2-Corps Ohio..	To 3-Brig. 3-Div. 21-Corps Cumb'd.	Jan., 1863
ARTILLERY, 3d DIVISION.—				
7th Indiana Batty.......	Nov., 1862	From Arty. 5-Div. 2-Corps Ohio....	To Arty. 3-Div. 21-Corps Cumb'd...	Jan., 1863
Indpt. Batty. B, Penna. A.	Nov., 1862	From Arty. 5-Div. 2-Corps Ohio....	To Arty. 3-Div. 21-Corps Cumb'd...	Jan., 1863
3d Wisconsin Batty......	Nov., 1862	From Arty. 5-Div. 2-Corps Ohio....	To Arty. 3-Div. 21-Corps Cumb'd..	Jan., 1863

CAVALRY DIVISION.—

COMMANDER.

D. S. Stanley..........	Brigadier General..................	Nov. 5, 1862, to Jan. 9, 1863.

1st BRIGADE.—

COMMANDER.

R. H. G. Minty........	Col. 4th Michigan Cav.............	Nov. 5, 1862, to Jan. 9, 1863.

2d Indiana Cav.........	Nov., 1862	From 1-Brig. Cav. Div. Army Ohio..	To 1-Brig. 1-Cav. Div. Cumb'd....	Jan., 1863
3d Kentucky Cav.......	Nov., 1862	From 1-Brig. Cav. Div. Army Ohio..	To 1-Brig. 1-Cav. Div. Cumb'd....	Jan., 1863
4th Michigan Cav.......	Nov., 1862	From 1-Brig. Cav. Div. Army Ohio..	To 1-Brig. 1-Cav. Div. Cumb'd....	Jan., 1863
7th Penna. Cav.........	Nov., 1862	From 1-Brig. Cav. Div. Army Ohio..	To 1-Brig. 1-Cav. Div. Cumb'd....	Jan., 1863

2d BRIGADE.—

COMMANDER.

Lewis Zahm ...:......	Col. 3d Ohio Cav..................	Nov. 5, 1862, to Jan. 9, 1863.

1st Ohio Cav...........	Nov., 1862	From 2-Brig. Cav. Div. Army Ohio..	To 2-Brig. 1-Cav. Div. Cumb'd......	Jan., 1863
3d Ohio Cav...........	Nov., 1862	From 2-Brig. Cav. Div. Army Ohio..	To 2-Brig. 1-Cav. Div. Cumb'd......	Jan., 1863
4th Ohio Cav...........	Nov., 1862	From 2-Brig. Cav. Div. Army Ohio..	To 2-Brig. 1-Cav. Div. Cumb'd......	Jan., 1863
ARTILLERY.—				
Batty. D, 1st Ohio Ar. Sec.	Nov., 1862	From 33-Brig. 10-Div. 3-Corps Ohio..	To Arty. 1-Cav. Div. Cumb'd........	Jan., 1863
RESERVE CAVALRY.—				
15th Penna. Cav.........	Nov., 1862	From New Organization............	To Headqrs. Dept. Cumb'd.........	Jan., 1863
2d Tenn. Cav..........	Nov., 1862	From Dist. W. Va. Dept. Ohio......	To 2-Brig. 1-Cav. Div. Cumb'd.....	Jan., 1863
5th Tenn. Cav..........	Nov., 1862	From New Organization............	To 1-Brig. 2-Cav. Div. Cumb'd.....	Jan., 1863
(1st Middle.)				
UNATTACHED CAVALRY.—				
4th U. S. Cav..........	Nov., 1862	From Headqrs. Army Ohio.........	To 1-Brig. 2-Cav. Div. Cumb'd.....	Jan., 1863
ENGINEERS.—				
1st Mich. Engrs.........	Nov., 1862	From Unatt. Army Ohio...........	To Unatt. Army Cumb'd...........	Jan., 1863

PIONEER BRIGADE.—

COMMANDER.

St. Clair Morton......	Capt. U. S. A.....................	

1st Battalion	Dec., 1862	From Right Wing Army Cumb'd....	To Pioneer Brig. Dept. Cumb'd.....	Jan., 1863
2d Battalion	Dec., 1862	From Centre Army Cumb'd........	To Pioneer Brig. Dept. Cumb'd.....	Jan., 1863
3d Battalion	Dec., 1862	From Left Wing Army Cumb'd..:..	To Pioneer Brig. Dept. Cumb'd.....	Jan., 1863
Board of Trade Ill. Batty.	Dec., 1862	From New Organization............	To Pioneer Brig. Dept. Cumb'd.....	Jan., 1863
PROVOST GUARD.—				
9th Mich. Infy..........	Nov., 1862	From Unatt. Army Ohio...........	To Headqrs. 14-Corps Cumb'd.......	Jan., 1863

POST OF GALLATIN, TENN.— COMMANDER.

E. A. Paine	Brigadier General	Nov. 24, 1862, to May, 14, 1863.

WARD'S BRIGADE.—

102d Ill. Infy...........Nov., 1862	From Ward's Brig. 12-Div. A'y Ohio.	To 2-Brig. 3-Div. Res. Corps Cumb'd.	June, 1863
105th Ill. Infy...........Nov., 1862	From Ward's Brig. 12-Div. A'y Ohio.	To 2-Brig. 3-Div. Res. Corps Cumb'd.	June, 1863
70th Ind. Infy...........Nov., 1862	From Ward's Brig. 12-Div. A'y Ohio.	To 2-Brig. 3-Div. Res. Corps Cumb'd.	June, 1863
79th Ohio Infy...........Nov., 1862	From Ward's Brig. 12-Div. A'y Ohio.	To 2-Brig. 3-Div. Res. Corps Cumb'd.	June, 1863
13th Ind. Batty...........Nov., 1862	From Ward's Brig. 12-Div. A'y Ohio.	To Post Gallatin, Tenn., Res. Corps.	June, 1863
1st Ky. Cav.............Nov., 1862	From 1-Brig. Cav. Div. Army Ohio..	To 1-Brig. 1-Div. 23-Corps Ohio....	June, 1863
7th Ky. Cav.............Nov., 1862	From Unass'd Army Ky. Dept Ohio..	To 1-Brig. 1-Cav. Div. Cumb'd.....	June, 1863
11th Ky. Cav.............Nov., 1862	From New Organization............	To 2-Brig. 3-Div. 23-Corps Ohio....	June, 1863
129th Ill. Infy...........June, 1863	From Unatt. Dist. W. Ky. Dept Ohio.	To 2-Brig. 3-Div. Res. Corps Cumb'd.	June, 1863
106th Ohio Infy...........June, 1863	From Unatt. Dist. W. Ky. Dept Ohio.	To Post Gallatin, Tenn., Res. Corps.	June, 1863

Army and Department of the Cumberland

As organized into Corps Jan. 9, 1863, by General Order No. 9, A. G. O.

Fourteenth Army Corps

Organized Jan. 9, 1863, from Centre 14th Corps, Department of the Cumberland. Discontinued Aug. 1, 1865.

COMMANDERS.

George H. Thomas.....	Major General	Jan. 9, 1863, to Oct. 28, 1863.
John M. Palmer........	Major General	Oct. 28, 1863, to Aug. 7, 1864.
R. W. Johnson........	Brigadier General	Aug. 7, 1864, to Aug. 22, 1864.
Jeff C. Davis..........	Major General	Aug. 22, 1864, to Aug. 1, 1865.

1st DIVISION.— COMMANDERS.

L. H. Rousseau........	Major General	Jan. 9, 1863, to Jan. 17, 1863.
R. S. Granger.........	Brigadier General	Jan. 17, 1863, to Mch. 29, 1863.
L. H. Rousseau........	Major General	Mch. 29, 1863, to July 26, 1863.
J. H. King............	Brigadier General	July 26, 1863, to Aug. 23, 1863.
A. Baird..............	Brigadier General	Aug. 23, 1863, to Sept. 21, 1863.
L. H. Rousseau........	Major General	Sept. 21, 1863, to Nov. 17, 1863.
R. W. Johnson........	Brigadier General	Nov. 17, 1863, to May 29, 1864.
J. H. King............	Brigadier General	May 29, 1864, to June 6, 1864.
R. W. Johnson........	Brigadier General	June 6, 1864, to June 13, 1864.
J. H. King............	Brigadier General	June 13, 1864, to July 13, 1864.
R. W. Johnson........	Brigadier General	July 13, 1864, to Aug. 7, 1864.
J. H. King............	Brigadier General	Aug. 7, 1864, to Aug. 17, 1864.
W. P. Carlin..........	Brigadier General	Aug. 17, 1864, to Nov. 2, 1863.
R. W. Johnson........	Brigadier General	Nov. 2, 1864, to Nov. 8, 1864.
W. P. Carlin..........	Brigadier General	Nov. 8, 1864, to Mch. 28, 1865.
G. P. Buell...........	Bvt. Brig. General	Mch. 28, 1865, to Apr. 4, 1865.
C. C. Walcutt.........	Bvt. Major General	Apr. 4, 1865, to June 17, 1865.
G. P. Buell...........	Bvt. Brig. General	June 17, 1865, to June 27, 1865.
C. C. Walcutt.........	Bvt. Major General	June 27, 1865, to July 18, 1865.

1st BRIGADE.— COMMANDERS.

B. F. Scribner........	Col. 38th Ind. Infy................	Jan. 9, 1863, to Oct. 19, 1863.
W. P. Carlin..........	Brigadier General	Oct. 19, 1863, to Dec. 5, 1863.
B. F. Scribner........	Col. 38th Ind. Infy................	Dec. 5, 1863, to Jan. 5, 1864.
W. P. Carlin..........	Brigadier General	Jan. 5, 1864, to July 2, 1864.
A. G. McCook.........	Col. 2d Ohio Infy.................	July 2, 1864, to July 27, 1864.
M. C. Taylor..........	Col. 15th Ky. Infy................	July 27, 1864, to Aug. 3, 1864.
W. P. Carlin..........	Brigadier General.	Aug. 3, 1864, to Aug. 17, 1864.
M. C. Taylor..........	Col. 15th Ky. Infy................	Aug. 17, 1864, to Sept. 20, 1864.
D. Hapeman...........	Lt.-Col. 104th Ill.................	Sept. 20, 1864, to Nov. 5, 1864.
H. C. Hobart.........	Col. 21st Wis. Infy...............	Nov. 5, 1864, to June 8, 1865.
H. A. Hambright......	Col. 79th Penna. Infy.............	June 8, 1865, to July 18, 1865.

38th Ind. Infy.............Jan., 1863	From 1-Brig. 1-Div. Centre 14-C...	To 3-Brig. 1-Div. 14-Corps.........	Apr., 1864
2d Ohio Infy..............Jan., 1863	From 1-Brig. 1-Div. Centre 14-C...	To Headqrs. 14-Corps.............	June, 1864
33d Ohio Infy.............Jan., 1863	From 1-Brig. 1-Div. Centre 14-C...	No change to Muster Out..........	July, 1865
94th Ohio Infy.............Jan., 1863	From 1-Brig. 1-Div. Centre 14-C...	No change to Muster Out..........	June, 1865
10th Wis. Infy.............Jan., 1863	From 1-Brig. 1-Div. Centre 14-C...	No change to Muster Out..........	Oct., 1864
15th Ky. Infy.............Oct., 1863	From 1-Brig. 2-Div. 14-Corps.......	To Post Chattanooga, Tenn........	Nov., 1863
42d Ind. Infy.............Oct., 1863	From 1-Brig. 2-Div. 14-Corps.......	No change to Muster Out..........	June, 1865
88th Ind. Infy.............Oct., 1863	From 1-Brig. 2-Div. 14-Corps.......	No change to Muster Out..........	June, 1865
104th Ill. Infy.............Oct., 1863	From 1-Brig. 2-Div. 14-Corps.......	No change to Muster Out..........	June, 1865
15th Ky. Infy.............Apr., 1864	From Post Chattanooga, Tenn.......	No change to Muster Out..........	Jan., 1865
21st Wis. Infy.............Apr., 1864	From 3-Brig. 1-Div. 14-Corps.......	No change to Muster Out..........	June, 1865
21st Ohio Infy.............June, 1865	From 3-Brig. 1-Div. 14-Corps.......	No change to Muster Out..........	July, 1865
38th Ind. Infy.............June, 1865	From 3-Brig. 1-Div. 14-Corps.......	No change to Muster Out..........	July, 1865

2d BRIGADE.—Transferred to 2d Division April 17, 1863. Reorganized from 3-Brig. 1-Div. 14-Corps April 17, 1863. Transferred from Corps Sept., 1864. Reorganized Nov., 1864.

COMMANDERS.

John Beatty...........	Col. 3d Ohio Infy.................	Jan. 9, 1863, to Apr. 17, 1863.
H. A. Hambright......	Col. 79th Penna. Infy.............	Apr. 17, 1863, to Apr. 21, 1863.
J. C. Starkweather....	Col. 1st Wis. Infy................	Apr. 21, 1863, to June 15, 1863.
H. A. Hambright......	Col. 79th Penna. Infy.............	June 15, 1863, to July 30, 1863.
J. C. Starkweather.....	Brigadier General................	July 30, 1863, to Sept. 28, 1863.
H. A. Hambright......	Col. 79th Penna. Infy.............	Sept. 28, 1863, to Oct. 9, 1863.
J. H. King............	Brigadier General................	Oct. 9, 1863, to Oct. 13, 1863.
M. F. Moore..........	Col. 69th Ohio Infy...............	Oct. 13, 1863, to Nov. 15, 1863.
J. H. King............	Brigadier General................	Nov. 15, 1863, to June 13, 1864.
W. L. Stoughton......	Col. 11th Mich. Infy..............	June 13, 1864, to July 4, 1864.
M. F. Moore..........	Col. 69th Ohio Infy...............	July 4, 1864, to July 13, 1864.
J. H. King............	Brigadier General................	July 13, 1864, to Aug. 7, 1864.
J. R. Edie...........	Major 15th U. S. Infy.............	Aug. 7, 1864, to Sept. 12, 1864.
M. F. Moore..........	Col. 69th Ohio Infy...............	Sept. 12, 1864, to Sept. 30, 1864.
J. H. Brigham........	Lt.-Col. 69th Ohio Infy...........	Nov. 13, 1864, to Jan. 17, 1865.
G. P. Buell...........	Bvt. Brig. General................	Jan. 17, 1864, to Mch. 28, 1865.
M. H. Fitch..........	Lt.-Col. 21st Wis. Infy...........	Mch. 28, 1865, to Apr. 4, 1865.
G. P. Buell...........	Bvt. Brig. General................	Apr. 4, 1865, to July 18, 1865.

2d BRIGADE.—Continued.

42d Ind. Infy	Jan., 1863	From 2-Brig. 1-Div. Centre 14-C....	To 1-Brig. 2-Div. 14-Corps..........	Apr., 1863
88th Ind. Infy	Jan., 1863	From 2-Brig. 1-Div. Centre 14-C....	To 1-Brig. 2-Div. 14-Corps..........	Apr., 1863
15th Ky. Infy	Jan., 1863	From 2-Brig. 1-Div. Centre 14-C....	To 1-Brig. 2-Div. 14-Corps..........	Apr., 1863
3d Ohio Infy	Jan., 1863	From 2-Brig. 1-Div. Centre 14-C....	To Streight's Prov'l Brig. 14-Corps..	Apr., 1863
79th Penna. Infy	Apr., 1863	From 3-Brig. 1-Div. 14-Corps........	To 3-Brig. 1-Div. 14-Corps..........	Oct., 1863
24th Ill. Infy	Apr., 1863	From 3-Brig. 1-Div. 14-Corps........	To 3-Brig. 1-Div. 14-Corps..........	Oct., 1863
1st Wis. Infy	Apr., 1863	From 3-Brig. 1-Div. 14-Corps........	To 3-Brig. 1-Div. 14-Corps..........	Oct., 1863
21st Wis. Infy	Apr., 1863	From 3-Brig. 1-Div. 14-Corps........	To 3-Brig. 1-Div. 14-Corps..........	Oct., 1863
18th Ohio Infy	Oct., 1863	From 2-Brig. 2-Div. 14-Corps........	To Engr. Brig. Army Cumberland......	Nov., 1863
69th Ohio Infy	Oct., 1863	From 2-Brig. 2-Div. 14-Corps........	To 3-Brig. 1-Div. 14-Corps..........	Sept., 1864
11th Mich. Infy	Oct., 1863	From 2-Brig. 2-Div. 14-Corps........	No change to Muster Out.............	Sept., 1864
19th Ill. Infy	Oct., 1863	From 2-Brig. 2-Div. 14-Corps........	To 1-Brig. 3-Div. 14-Corps..........	Oct., 1863
15th U. S. Infy	Oct., 1863	From 3-Brig. 1-Div. 14-Corps........	To Post. Chattanooga Dept. Cumb'd..	Sept., 1864
16th U. S. Infy	Oct., 1863	From 3-Brig. 1-Div. 14-Corps........	To Post. Chattanooga Dept. Cumb'd..	Sept., 1864
18th U. S. Infy	Oct., 1863	From 3-Brig. 1-Div. 14-Corps........	To Post. Chattanooga Dept. Cumb'd..	Sept., 1864
19th U. S. Infy	Oct., 1863	From 3-Brig. 1-Div. 14-Corps........	To Post. Chattanooga Dept. Cumb'd..	Sept., 1864
69th Ohio Infy	Nov., 1864	From 3-Brig. 1-Div. 14-Corps........	No change to Muster Out.............	July, 1865
13th Mich. Infy	Nov., 1864	From Engineer Brig. Army Cumb'd..	No change to Muster Out.............	July, 1865
21st Mich. Infy	Nov., 1864	From Engineer Brig. Army Cumb'd..	No change to Muster Out.............	June, 1865
74th Ohio Infy	June, 1865	From 3-Brig. 1-Div. 14-Corps........	No change to Muster Out.............	July, 1865

3d BRIGADE, 1st DIVISION.—   COMMANDERS.

Commander	Rank/Regiment	Dates
J. C. Starkweather	Col. 1st Wis. Infy	Jan. 9, 1863, to Mch. 9, 1863,
H. A. Hambright	Col. 79th Penna. Infy	Mch. 9, 1863, to Apr. 17, 1863.

Brigade transferred to 2d Brig. 1st Div. April 17, 1863. Reorganized April 17, 1863, from 4th Brig. 1st Division.

R. S. Granger	Brigadier General	Apr. 17, 1863, to May 6, 1863.
J. H. King	Brigadier General	May 6, 1863, to July 26, 1863.
S. K. Dawson	Major 19th U. S. Infy	July 26, 1863, to Aug. 24, 1863.
J. H. King	Brigadier General	Aug. 24, 1863, to Oct. 10, 1863.
William Sirwell	Col. 78th Penna. Infy	Oct. 10, 1863, to Jan. 12, 1864.
H. A. Hambright	Col. 79th Penna. Infy	Jan. 12, 1864, to Mch. 23, 1864.
J. M. Neibling	Col. 21st Ohio Infy	Mch. 12, 1864, to May 3, 1864.
B. F. Scribner	Col. 38th Ind. Infy	May 3, 1864, to July 5, 1864.
Josiah Given	Col. 74th Ohio Infy	July 5, 1864, to July 15, 1864.
M. F. Moore	Col. 69th Ohio Infy	July 15, 1864, to Sept. 12, 1864.
H. A. Hambright	Col. 79th Penna. Infy	Sept. 12, 1864, to Nov. 18, 1864.
D. Miles	Lt.-Col. 79th Penna. Infy	Nov. 18, 1864, to Mch. 19, 1865.
A. McMahon	Lt.-Col. 21st Ohio Infy	Mch. 19, 1865, to Mch. 28, 1865.
H. A. Hambright	Col. 79th Penna. Infy	Mch. 28, 1865, to June 6, 1865.

Brigade discontinued June 6, 1865.

24th Ill. Infy	Jan., 1863	From 3-Brig. 1-Div. Center, 14-C....	To 2-Brig. 1-Div. 14-Corps..........	Apr., 1863
79th Penna. Infy	Jan., 1863	From 3-Brig. 1-Div. Center, 14-C....	To 2-Brig. 1-Div. 14-Corps..........	Apr., 1863
1st Wis. Infy	Jan., 1863	From 3-Brig. 1-Div. Center, 14-C....	To 2-Brig. 1-Div. 14-Corps..........	Apr., 1863
21st Wis. Infy	Jan., 1863	From 3-Brig. 1-Div. Center, 14-C....	To 2-Brig. 1-Div. 14-Corps..........	Apr., 1863
15th U. S. Infy	Apr., 1863	From 4-Brig. 1-Div. 14-Corps........	To 2-Brig. 1-Div. 14-Corps..........	Oct., 1863
16th U. S. Infy	Apr., 1863	From 4-Brig. 1-Div. 14-Corps........	To 2-Brig. 1-Div. 14-Corps..........	Oct., 1863
18th U. S. Infy	Apr., 1863	From 4-Brig. 1-Div. 14-Corps........	To 2-Brig. 1-Div. 14-Corps..........	Oct., 1863
19th U. S. Infy	Apr., 1863	From 4-Brig. 1-Div. 14-Corps........	To 2-Brig. 1-Div. 14-Corps..........	Oct., 1863
37th Ind. Infy	Oct., 1863	From 2-Div. 14-Corps........	To 3-Brig. 2-Div. 14-Corps..........	Oct., 1864
24th Ill. Infy	Oct., 1863	From 2-Brig. 1-Div. 14-Corps........	To 1-Brig. 3-Div. 14-Corps..........	May, 1864
21st Ohio Infy	Oct., 1863	From 2-Brig. 1-Div. 14-Corps........	To 1-Brig. 1-Div. 14-Corps..........	June, 1865
74th Ohio Infy	Oct., 1863	From 2-Brig. 1-Div. 14-Corps........	To 2-Brig. 1-Div. 14-Corps..........	June, 1865
78th Penna. Infy	Oct., 1863	From 2-Brig. 2-Div. 14-Corps........	To Unass'd 4-Div. 20-Corps..........	July, 1864
79th Penna. Infy	Oct., 1863	From 2-Brig. 1-Div. 14-Corps........	No change to Muster Out.............	July, 1865
1st Wis. Infy	Oct., 1863	From 2-Brig. 1-Div. 14-Corps........	No change to Muster Out.............	Oct., 1864
21st Wis. Infy	Oct., 1863	From 2-Brig. 1-Div. 14-Corps........	To 1-Brig. 1-Div. 14-Corps..........	Apr., 1864
38th Ind. Infy	Apr., 1864	From 1-Brig. 1-Div. 14-Corps........	To 1-Brig. 1-Div. 14-Corps..........	June, 1865
69th Ohio Infy	Sept., 1864	From 2-Brig. 1-Div. 14-Corps........	To 2-Brig. 1-Div. 14-Corps..........	Nov., 1864

4th BRIGADE.—Discontinued April 17, 1863. Transferred to 3d Brigade, 1st Division.
    COMMANDER.

Commander	Rank/Regiment	Dates
O. L. Shepherd	Lt.-Col. 18th U. S. Infy	Jan. 9, 1863, to Apr. 17, 1863.

15th U. S. Infy	Jan., 1863	From 4-Brig. 1-Div. Center 14-C....	To 3-Brig. 1-Div. 14-Corps..........	Apr., 1863
16th U. S. Infy	Jan., 1863	From 4-Brig. 1-Div. Center 14-C....	To 3-Brig. 1-Div. 14-Corps..........	Apr., 1863
18th U. S. Infy	Jan., 1863	From 4-Brig. 1-Div. Center 14-C....	To 3-Brig. 1-Div. 14-Corps..........	Apr., 1863
19th U. S. Infy	Jan., 1863	From 4-Brig. 1-Div. Center 14-C....	To 3-Brig. 1-Div. 14-Corps..........	Apr., 1863

ARTILLERY, 1st DIVISION.—

Batty. A, 1st Mich	Jan., 1863	From 2-Brig. 1-Div. Center 14-C....	To Garrison Arty. Chattanooga, Tenn.	Apr., 1864
Batty. A, 1st Ky. Arty	Jan., 1863	From 3-Brig. 1-Div. Center 14-C....	To Unass'd Dept. Cumberland........	Oct., 1863
Batty. H, 5th U. S. Arty	Jan., 1863	From 3-Brig. 1-Div. Center 14-C....	To Arty. 2-Div. 4-Corps.............	Nov., 1863
4th Ind. Batty	June, 1863	From 3-Div. 20-Corps Cumb'd......	To 2-Div. Arty. Res. Cumberland...	Oct., 1863
Batty. C, 1st Ill. Arty	Oct., 1863	From 3-Div. 20-Corps Cumb'd......	To Arty. Brig. 14-Corps.............	July, 1864
Batty. I, 1st Ohio Arty	Apr., 1864	From Garrison Arty. Chattanooga...	To Arty. Brig. 14-Corps.............	July, 1864

2d DIVISION.—   COMMANDERS.

Commander	Rank	Dates
James S. Negley	Major General	Jan. 9, 1863, to Oct. 10, 1863.
J. C. Davis	Brigadier General	Oct. 10, 1863, to Aug. 22, 1864.
J. D. Morgan	Brigadier General	Aug. 22, 1864, to June 23, 1865.
William Vandever	Brigadier General	June 23, 1865, to July 18, 1865.

1st BRIGADE, 2d DIVISION.—   COMMANDERS.

Commander	Rank/Regiment	Dates
J. G. Spear	Brigadier General	Jan. 9, 1863, to Apr. 17, 1863.

Brigade discontinued April 17, 1863. Reorganized April 17, 1863, from 2d Brigade, 1st Division.

John Beatty	Brigadier General	Apr. 17, 1863, to Oct. 10, 1863.
R. F. Smith	Col. 16th Ill. Infy	Oct. 10, 1863, to Nov. 12, 1863.
J. D. Morgan	Brigadier General	Nov. 12, 1863, to Aug. 22, 1864.
C. M. Lum	Col. 10th Mich. Infy	Aug. 22, 1864, to Oct. 15, 1864.
R. F. Smith	Col. 16th Ill. Infy	Oct. 15, 1864, to Jan. 18, 1865.
William Vandever	Brigadier General	Jan. 18, 1865, to June 23, 1865.
G. W. Grummond	Lt.-Col. 14th Mich. Infy	June 23, 1865, to July 18, 1865.

1st Tenn. Infy	Jan., 1863	From 1-Brig. 2-Div. Center 14-C....	To Dist. West Ky. Dept. Ohio......	Apr., 1863
2d Tenn. Infy	Jan., 1863	From 1-Brig. 2-Div. Center 14-C....	To Dist. West Ky. Dept. Ohio......	Apr., 1863
3d Tenn. Infy	Jan., 1863	From 1-Brig. 2-Div. Center 14-C....	To Dist. West Ky. Dept. Ohio......	Apr., 1863
5th Tenn. Infy	Jan., 1863	From 1-Brig. 2-Div. Center 14-C....	To Dist. West Ky. Dept. Ohio......	Apr., 1863
6th Tenn. Infy	Jan., 1863	From 1-Brig. 2-Div. Center 14-C....	To Dist. West Ky. Dept. Ohio......	Apr., 1863
42d Ind. Infy	Apr., 1863	From 2-Brig. 1-Div. 14-Corps........	To 1-Brig. 1-Div. 14-Corps..........	Oct., 1863

1st BRIGADE, 2d DIVISION.—Continued.

88th Ind. Infy............Apr., 1863	From 2-Brig. 1-Div. 14-Corps.......	To 1-Brig. 1-Div. 14-Corps..........	Oct., 1863
15th Ky. Infy............Apr., 1863	From 2-Brig. 1-Div. 14-Corps.......	To 1-Brig. 1-Div. 14-Corps..........	Oct., 1863
104th Ill. Infy...........June, 1863	From Prisoners of War..........	To 1-Brig. 1-Div. 14-Corps..........	Oct., 1863
10th Ill. Infy............Oct., 1863	From 1-Brig. 2-Div. Res. Corps......	To 3-Brig. 4-Div. 16-Corps Tenn....	Aug., 1864
16th Ill. Infy............Oct., 1863	From 1-Brig. 2-Div. Res. Corps......	No change to Muster Out...........	July, 1865
60th Ill. Infy............Oct., 1863	From 1-Brig. 2-Div. Res. Corps......	No change to Muster Out...........	July, 1865
10th Mich. Infy...........Oct., 1863	From 1-Brig. 2-Div. Res. Corps......	No change to Muster Out...........	July, 1865
14th Mich. Infy...........Oct., 1863	From 1-Brig. 2-Div. Res. Corps......	No change to Muster Out...........	July, 1865
17th N. Y. Vet. Infy.....Aug., 1864	From 3-Brig. 4-Div. 16-Corps Tenn.	No change to Muster Out...........	July, 1865

2d BRIGADE.—   **COMMANDERS.**

A. W. Raffen...........	Lt.-Col. 19th Ill. Infy..............	Jan. 9, 1863, to Feb. 5, 1863.
M. F. Moore...........	Col. 69th Ohio Infy...............	Feb. 5, 1863, to Mch. 5, 1863.
T. R. Stanley..........	Col. 18th Ohio Infy...............	Mch. 5, 1863, to June 23, 1863.
W. L. Stoughton.......	Col. 11th Mich. Infy.............	June 23, 1863, to July 23, 1863.
T. R. Stanley..........	Col. 18th Ohio Infy...............	July 23, 1863, to Sept. 20, 1863.
W. L. Stoughton.......	Col. 11th Mich. Infy.............	Sept. 20, 1863, to Oct. 10, 1863.
J. G. Mitchell..........	Col. 113th Ohio Infy..............	Oct. 10, 1863, to Nov. 10, 1863.
John Beatty...........	Brigadier General................	Nov. 10, 1863, to Feb. 1, 1864.
J. G. Mitchell..........	Col. 113th Ohio Infy..............	Feb. 1, 1864, to Sept. 26, 1864.
J. S. Pearce...........	Lt.-Col. 98th Ohio Infy...........	Sept. 26, 1864, to Feb. 7, 1865.
J. G. Mitchell..........	Brigadier General................	Feb. 7, 1865, to June 20, 1865.
Peter Ege.............	Col. 34th Ill. Infy...............	June 20, 1865, to July 18, 1865.

19th Ill. Infy............Jan., 1863	From 2-Brig. 2-Div. Center 14-C....	To 2-Brig. 1-Div. 14-Corps..........	Oct., 1863
11th Mich. Infy...........Jan., 1863	From 2-Brig. 2-Div. Center 14-C....	To 2-Brig. 1-Div. 14-Corps..........	Oct., 1863
18th Ohio Infy...........Jan., 1863	From 2-Brig. 2-Div. Center 14-C....	To 2-Brig. 1-Div. 14-Corps..........	Oct., 1863
69th Ohio Infy...........Jan., 1863	From 2-Brig. 2-Div. Center 14-C....	To 2-Brig. 1-Div. 14-Corps..........	Oct., 1863
78th Ill. Infy............Oct., 1863	From 2-Brig. 1-Div. Res. Corps......	No change to Muster Out...........	June, 1865
98th Ohio Infy...........Oct., 1863	From 2-Brig. 1-Div. Res. Corps......	No change to Muster Out...........	June, 1865
113th Ohio Infy..........Oct., 1863	From 2-Brig. 1-Div. Res. Corps......	No change to Muster Out...........	July, 1865
121st Ohio Infy..........Oct., 1863	From 2-Brig. 1-Div. Res. Corps......	No change to Muster Out...........	June, 1865
3d Tenn. Infy............Oct., 1863	From 3-Brig. 3-Div. Res. Corps......	To Spear's Brig. Chattanooga, Tenn.	Nov., 1863
5th Tenn. Infy............Oct., 1863	From 3-Brig. 3-Div. Res. Corps......	To Spear's Brig. Chattanooga, Tenn.	Nov., 1863
6th Tenn. Infy............Oct., 1863	From 3-Brig. 3-Div. Res. Corps......	To Spear's Brig. Chattanooga, Tenn.	Nov., 1863
3d Ohio Infy.............Nov., 1863	From Unass'd Dept. Cumberland....	To Garrison Chattanooga, Tenn.....	Apr., 1864
108th Ohio Infy..........Nov., 1863	From Unass'd Dept. Cumberland....	No change to Muster Out...........	June, 1865
34th Ill. Infy............Nov., 1863	From Unass'd Dept. Cumberland....	No change to Muster Out...........	July, 1865

3d BRIGADE.—   **COMMANDERS.**

J. F. Miller............	Col. 29th Ind. Infy................	Jan. 9, 1863, to June 9, 1863.	
William Sirwell........	Col. 78th Penna. Infy...........	June 9, 1863, to Oct. 10, 1863.	
Daniel McCook........	Col. 52d Ohio Infy.............	Oct. 10, 1863, to Dec. 16, 1863.	
O. F. Harmon.........	Col. 125th Ill. Infy............	Dec. 16, 1863, to Feb. 15, 1864.	
Daniel McCook........	Col. 52d Ohio Infy.............	Feb. 15, 1864, to June 27, 1864.	Mort. Wd.
O. F. Harmon.........	Col. 125th Ill. Infy............	June 27, 1864.	
C. J. Dilworth.........	Col. 85th Ill. Infy.............	June 27, 1864, to Sept. 1, 1864.	
J. W. Langley..........	Lt.-Col. 125th Ill. Infy.........	Sept. 1, 1864, to Jan. 10, 1865.	
B. D. Fearing.........	Col. 92d Ohio Infy.............	Jan. 10, 1865, to Mch. 19, 1865.	
J. W. Langley..........	Lt.-Col. 125th Ill. Infy.........	Mch. 19, 1865, to June 9, 1865.	

37th Ind. Infy...........Jan., 1863	From 3-Brig. 2-Div. Center 14-C....	To 3-Brig. 1-Div. 14-Corps..........	Oct., 1863
21st Ohio Infy...........Jan., 1863	From 3-Brig. 2-Div. Center 14-C....	To 3-Brig. 1-Div. 14-Corps..........	Oct., 1863
74th Ohio Infy...........Jan., 1863	From 3-Brig. 2-Div. Center 14-C....	To 3-Brig. 1-Div. 14-Corps..........	Oct., 1863
78th Penna. Infy.........Jan., 1863	From 3-Brig. 2-Div. Center 14-C....	To 3-Brig. 1-Div. 14-Corps..........	Oct., 1863
85th Ill. Infy............Oct., 1863	From 2-Br. 2-Div. Res. Corps Cumb'd.	No change to Muster Out...........	June, 1865
86th Ill. Infy............Oct., 1863	From 2-Br. 2-Div. Res. Corps Cumb'd.	No change to Muster Out...........	June, 1865
110th Ill. Infy...........Oct., 1863	From Unatt. 21-Corps Cumb'd.....	No change to Muster Out...........	June, 1865
125th Ill. Infy...........Oct., 1863	From 2-Br. 2-Div. Res. Corps Cumb'd.	No change to Muster Out...........	June, 1865
22d Mich. Infy...........Oct., 1863	From 2-Br. 2-Div. Res. Corps Cumb'd.	To Engineer Brig. Dept. Cumb'd....	Nov., 1863
52d Ohio Infy...........Oct., 1863	From 2-Br. 2-Div. Res. Corps Cumb'd.	No change to Muster Out...........	June, 1865
22d Ind. Infy............Apr., 1864	From 1-Br. 2-Div. 4-Corps Cumb'd.	No change to Muster Out...........	July, 1865
37th Ind. Infy...........Oct., 1864	From 3-Brig. 1-Div. 14-Corps.......	No change to Muster Out...........	July, 1865

ARTILLERY, 2d DIVISION.—

Batty. B, Ky. Arty.....Jan., 1863	From Arty. 2-Div. Center 14-C....	To Unass'd Dept. Cumberland......	Oct., 1863
Batty. G, 1st Ohio Arty...Jan., 1863	From Arty. 2-Div. Center 14-C....	To 1-Div. Arty. Res. Cumberland...	Oct., 1863
Batty. M, 1st Ohio Arty...Jan., 1863	From Arty. 2-Div. Center 14-C....	To 1-Div. Arty. Res. Cumberland...	Oct., 1863
Bridge's Ill. Batty.......Aug., 1863	From Pioneer Brig. Cumb'd........	To Arty. 3-Div. 4-Corps Cumb'd....	Oct., 1863
Batty. I, 2d Ill. Arty.....Oct., 1863	From Arty. Res. Corps Cumb'd.	To Arty. Brig. 14-Corps Cumb'd....	July, 1864
2d Minn. Batty........Oct., 1863	From Arty. 1-Div. 20-Corps Cumb'd.	To Garrison Arty. Chattanooga, Tenn.	July, 1864
5th Wis. Batty........Oct., 1863	From Arty. 1-Div. 20-Corps Cumb'd.	To Arty. Brig. 14-Corps............	July, 1864

3d DIVISION.—   **COMMANDERS.**

J. B. Steedman........	Brigadier General................	Jan. 9, 1863, to Apr. 17, 1863.
J. M. Schofield........	Brigadier General................	Apr. 17, 1863, to May 10, 1863.
J. M. Brannan.........	Brigadier General................	May 10, 1863, to Oct. 10, 1863.
A. Baird.............	Brigadier General................	Oct. 10, 1863, to Oct. 25, 1863.
G. P. Estes...........	Col. 14th Ohio Infy..............	Oct. 25, 1863, to Nov. 25, 1863.
A. Baird.............	Brigadier General................	Nov. 25, 1863, to July 20, 1865.

1st BRIGADE, 3d DIVISION.—   **COMMANDERS.**

M. B. Walker..........	Col. 31st Ohio Infy...............	Jan. 9, 1863, to July 27, 1863.
J. M. Connell..........	Col. 17th Ohio Infy...............	July 27, 1863, to Oct. 9, 1863.
J. B. Turchin..........	Brigadier General................	Oct. 9, 1863, to July 15, 1864.
M. B. Walker..........	Col. 31st Ohio Infy...............	July 15, 1864, to Sept. 13, 1864.
M. C. Hunter.........	Col. 82d Ind. Infy................	Sept. 13, 1864, to June 9, 1865.
H. K. Milward........	Lt.-Col. 18th Ky. Infy............	June 9, 1865, to July 18, 1865.

17th Ohio Infy...........Jan., 1863	From 1-Brig. 3-Div. Center 14-C....	No change to Muster Out...........	July, 1865
31st Ohio Infy...........Jan., 1863	From 1-Brig. 3-Div. Center 14-C....	No change to Muster Out...........	July, 1865
38th Ohio Infy...........Jan., 1863	From 1-Brig. 3-Div. Center 14-C....	To 3-Brig. 3-Div. 14-Corps..........	Oct., 1863
82d Ind. Infy............Jan., 1863	From 1-Brig. 3-Div. Center 14-C....	No change to Muster Out...........	June, 1865
12th Ky. Infy............Jan., 1863	From 1-Brig. 3-Div. Center 14-C....	To 1-Brig. 2-Div. 23-Corps Ohio....	June, 1865
11th Ohio Infy...........Oct., 1863	From 3-Brig. 4-Div. 14-Corps.......	No change to Muster Out...........	June, 1865
36th Ohio Infy...........Oct., 1863	From 3-Brig. 4-Div. 14-Corps.......	To 1-Brig. 2-Div. W. Va...........	Apr., 1864
89th Ohio Infy...........Oct., 1863	From 3-Brig. 4-Div. 14-Corps.......	No change to Muster Out...........	June, 1865
92d Ohio Infy...........Oct., 1863	From 3-Brig. 4-Div. 14-Corps.......	No change to Muster Out...........	June, 1865
19th Ill. Infy............Oct., 1863	From 3-Brig. 1-Div. 14-Corps.......	No change to Muster Out...........	June, 1864
24th Ill. Infy............May, 1864	From 3-Brig. 1-Div. 14-Corps.......	No change to Muster Out...........	June, 1864
23d Mo. Infy............May, 1864	From Unass'd 4-Div. 20-Corps......	No change to Muster Out...........	July, 1865
2d Minn. Infy...........June, 1865	From 2-Brig. 3-Div. 14-Corps.......	No change to Muster Out...........	July, 1865
101st Ind. Infy..........June, 1865	From 2-Brig. 3-Div. 14-Corps.......	No change to Muster Out...........	July, 1865
18th Ky. Infy............June, 1865	From 3-Brig. 3-Div. 14-Corps.......	No change to Muster Out...........	July, 1865

2d BRIGADE.— COMMANDERS.

J. M. Harlan............	Col. 10th Ky. Infy................	Jan. 9, 1863, to Mch. 6, 1863.
C. W. Chapman........	Col. 74th Ind. Infy.............	Mch. 6, 1863, to Apr. 27, 1863.
J. B. Steedman.........	Brigadier General	Apr. 27, 1863, to Aug. 15, 1863.
J. T. Croxton..........	Col. 4th Ky. Infy...............	Aug. 15, 1863, to Sept. 20, 1863.
William H. Hays.......	Col. 10th Ky. Infy..............	Sept. 20, 1863.
C. W. Chapman........	Col. 74th Ind. Infy.............	Sept. 20, 1863, to Oct. 10, 1863.
James George..........	Col. 2d Minn. Infy..............	Oct. 10, 1863, to Nov. 30, 1863.
F. Van Derveer........	Colo. 35th Ohio Infy...........	Nov. 30, 1863, to Jan. 14, 1864.
G. Kammerling........	Col. 9th Ohio Infy..............	Jan. 14, 1864, to Feb. 16, 1864.
F. Van Derveer........	Col. 35th Ohio Infy.............	Feb. 16, 1864, to June 27, 1864.
N. Gleason...........	Col. 87th Ind. Infy.............	June 27, 1864, to Jan. 21, 1865.
T. Doan	Lt.-Col. 101st Ind. Infy........	Jan. 21, 1865, to Apr. 3, 1865.
N. Gleason...........	Col. 87th Ind. Infy.............	Apr. 3, 1865, to June 9, 1865.
B. H. Shower.........	Lt.-Col. 17th Ohio Infy.........	June 9, 1865, to July 18, 1865.

10th Ind. Infy...........Jan., 1863	From 2-Brig. 3-Div. Centre 14-Corps.	To 3-Brig. 3-Div. 14-Corps.........	Oct.,	1863
74th Ind. Infy...........Jan., 1863	From 2-Brig. 3-Div. Centre 14-Corps.	To 3-Brig. 3-Div. 14-Corps.........	Oct.,	1863
14th Ohio Infy...........Jan., 1863	From 2-Brig. 3-Div. Centre 14-Corps.	To 3-Brig. 3-Div. 14-Corps.........	Oct.,	1863
4th Ky. Infy............Jan., 1863	From 2-Brig. 3-Div. Centre 14-Corps.	To 3-Brig. 3-Div. 14-Corps.........	Oct.,	1863
10th Ohio Infy...........Jan., 1863	From 2-Brig. 3-Div. Centre 14-Corps.	To 3-Brig. 3-Div. 14-Corps.........	Oct.,	1863
9th Ohio Infy...........Oct., 1863	From 3-Brig. 3-Div. 14-Corps.......	No change to Muster Out.........	May,	1864
35th Ohio Infy..........Oct., 1863	From 3-Brig. 3-Div. 14-Corps.......	No change to Muster Out.........	Aug.,	1864
105th Ohio Infy.........Oct., 1863	From 2-Brig. 4-Div. 14-Corps.......	No change to Muster Out.........	June,	1865
68th Ind. Infy..........Oct., 1863	From 2-Brig. 4-Div. 14-Corps.......	To 1-Brig. 3-Div. 4-Corps Cumb'd...	Oct.,	1863
75th Ind. Infy..........Oct., 1863	From 2-Brig. 4-Div. 14-Corps.......	No change to Muster Out.........	June,	1865
87th Ind. Infy..........Oct., 1863	From 2-Brig. 4-Div. 14-Corps.......	No change to Muster Out.........	June,	1865
101st Ind. Infy.........Oct., 1863	From 2-Brig. 4-Div. 14-Corps.......	To 1-Brig. 3-Div. 14-Corps.........	June,	1865
2d Minn. Infy..........Oct., 1863	From 3-Brig. 3-Div. 14-Corps.......	To 1-Brig. 3-Div. 14-Corps.........	June,	1865

3d BRIGADE.— COMMANDERS.

J. B. Steedman.........	Brigadier General	Jan. 9, 1863, to Jan. 28, 1863.
F. Van Derveer........	Col. 35th Ohio Infy..............	Jan. 28, 1863, to Oct. 10, 1863.
E. H. Phelps...........	Col. 38th Ohio Infy..............	Oct. 10, 1863, to Nov. 25, 1863.
W. H. Hays...........	Col. 10th Ky. Infy..............	Nov. 25, 1863, to Apr. 1, 1864.
G. P. Este............	Col. 14th Ohio Infy'.............	Apr. 1, 1864, to Oct. 25, 1864.
H. K. Milward.........	Lt.-Col. 18th Ky. Infy..........	Oct. 25, 1864, to Nov. 16, 1864.
G. P. Este............	Col. 14th Ohio Infy..............	Nov. 16, 1864, to Mch. 29, 1865.
H. K. Milward.........	Lt.-Col. 18th Ky. Infy..........	Mch. 29, 1865, to Apr. 9, 1865.
G. S. Greene..........	Bvt. Major General	Apr. 9, 1865, to June 6, 1865.

9th Ohio Infy...........Jan., 1863	From 3-Brig. 3-Div. Centre 14-Corps.	To 2-Brig. 3-Div. 14-Corps.........	Oct.,	1863
35th Ohio Infy..........Jan., 1863	From 3-Brig. 3-Div. Centre 14-Corps.	To 2-Brig. 3-Div. 14-Corps.........	Oct.,	1863
87th Ind. Infy..........Jan., 1863	From 3-Brig. 3-Div. Centre 14-Corps.	To 2-Brig. 3-Div. 14-Corps.........	Oct.,	1863
2d Minn. Infy..........Jan., 1863	From 3-Brig. 3-Div. Centre 14-Corps.	To 2-Brig. 3-Div. 14-Corps.........	Oct.,	1863
14th Ohio Infy..........Oct., 1863	From 2-Brig. 3-Div. 14-Corps.......	No change to Muster Out.........	July,	1865
10th Ind. Infy..........Oct., 1863	From 2-Brig. 3-Div. 14-Corps.......	To Garrison Chattanooga, Tenn.....	Dec.,	1863
74th Ind. Infy..........Oct., 1863	From 2-Brig. 3-Div. 14-Corps.......	No change to Muster Out.........	July,	1865
4th Ky. Infy...........Oct., 1863	From 2-Brig. 3-Div. 14-Corps.......	To 1-Brig. 1-Div. Cav. Corps Cumb'd..	Apr.,	1864
10th Ky. Infy..........Oct., 1863	From 3-Brig. 3-Div. 14-Corps.......	No change to Muster Out.........	Dec.,	1864
18th Ky. Infy..........Oct., 1863	From 3-Brig. 4-Div. 14-Corps.......	To 1-Brig. 3-Div. 14-Corps.........	June,	1865
38th Ohio Infy..........Oct., 1863	From 1-Brig. 3-Div. 14-Corps.......	No change to Muster Out.........	July,	1865
10th Ind. Infy..........Apr., 1864	From Garrison Chattanooga, Tenn..	No change to Muster Out.........	Sept.,	1864
ARTILLERY, 3d DIVISION.—				
Batty. D, 1st Mich. Arty..Jan., 1863	From Arty. 3-Div. Centre 14-Corps..	To 2-Div. Arty. Res. Dept. Cumb'd..	Oct.,	1863
Batty. C, 1st Ohio Arty...Jan., 1863	From Arty. 3-Div. Centre 14-Corps..	To 1-Div. Arty. Res. Dept. Cumb'd..	Oct.,	1863
Batty. I, 4th U. S. Arty..Jan., 1863	From Arty. 3-Div. Centre 14-Corps..	To Garrison Arty. Nashville, Tenn..	Apr.,	1864
7th Ind. Batty..........Oct., 1863	From 3-Div. 21-Corps Dept. Cumb'd.	To Arty. Brig. 14-Corps............	July,	1864
19th Ind. Batty..........Oct., 186..	From 4-Div. 14-Corps Dept. Cumb'd.	To Arty. Brig. 14-Corps............	July,	1864

4th DIVISION.— COMMANDERS.

J. D. Morgan...........	Brigadier General	Jan. 9, 1863, to May 5, 1863.
R. F. Smith............	Col. 16th Ill. Infy................	May 5, 1863, to June 8, 1863.

Division transferred to Reserve Corps, Dept. of the Cumb'd, June 8, 1863. Reorganized June 8, 1863, from 5th Division, 14th Corps. Discontinued Oct. 9, 1863.

J. J. Reynolds..........	Major General	June 8, 1863, to Oct. 9, 1863.

1st BRIGADE.— COMMANDERS.

R. F. Smith............	Col. 16th Ill. Infy................	Jan. 9, 1863, to May 5, 1863.
C. M. Lum............	Col. 10th Mich. Infy..............	May 5, 1863, to June 8, 1863.
J. T. Wilder...........	Col. 17th Ind. Infy...............	June 8, 1863, to July 10, 1863.
A. O. Miller...........	Col. 72d Ind. Infy................	July 10, 1863, to Aug. 10, 1863.
J. T. Wilder...........	Col. 17th Ind. Infy...............	Aug. 10, 1863, to Oct. 9, 1863.

10th Mich. Infy..........Jan., 1863	From 1-Brig. 4-Div. Centre 14-Corps.	To 1-Brig. 2-Div. Res. Corps Cumb'd.	June,	1863
14th Mich. Infy..........Jan., 1863	From 1-Brig. 4-Div. Centre 14-Corps.	To 1-Brig. 2-Div. Res. Corps Cumb'd.	June,	1863
10th Ill. Infy...........Jan., 1863	From 1-Brig. 4-Div. Centre 14-Corps.	To 1-Brig. 2-Div. Res. Corps Cumb'd.	June,	1863
16th Ill. Infy...........Jan., 1863	From 1-Brig. 4-Div. Centre 14-Corps.	To 1-Brig. 2-Div. Res. Corps Cumb'd.	June,	1863
60th Ill. Infy...........Jan., 1863	From 1-Brig. 4-Div. Centre 14-Corps.	To 1-Brig. 2-Div. Res. Corps Cumb'd.	June,	1863
17th Ind. Infy..........June, 1863	From 2-Brig. 5-Div. 14-Corps.......	To Wilder's Mtd. Infy. Brig........	Oct.,	1863
72d Ind. Infy..........June, 1863	From 2-Brig. 5-Div. 14-Corps.......	To Wilder's Mtd. Infy. Brig........	Oct.,	1863
98th Ill. Infy..........June, 1863	From 2-Brig. 5-Div. 14-Corps.......	To Wilder's Mtd. Infy. Brig........	Oct.,	1863
133d Ill. Infy..........June, 1863	From 1-Brig. 5-Div. 14-Corps.......	To Wilder's Mtd. Infy. Brig........	Oct.,	1863
92d Ill. Infy...........July, 1863	From 1-Brig. 1-Div. Res. C. Cumb'd.	To Wilder's Mtd. Infy. Brig........	Oct.,	1863

2d BRIGADE.— COMMANDERS.

Daniel McCook	Col. 52d Ohio Infy...............	Jan. 9, 1863, to June 8, 1863.	
A. S. Hall.............	Col. 105th Ohio Infy.............	June 8, 1863, to July 8, 1863.	
M. S. Robinson.........	Col. 75th Ind. Infy..............	July 8, 1863, to Aug. 2, 1863.	
Eli. King	Col. 68th Ohio Infy..............	Aug. 2, 1863, to Sept. 20, 1863.	Killed.
M. S. Robinson.........	Col. 75th Ind. Infy..............	Sept. 20, 1863, to Oct. 9, 1863.	

52d Ohio Infy...........Jan., 1863	From 2-Brig. 4-Div. Centre 14-Corps.	To 2-Brig. 2-Div. Res. Corps Cumb'd.	June,	1863
85th Ill. Infy...........Jan., 1863	From 2-Brig. 4-Div. Centre 14-Corps.	To 2-Brig. 2-Div. Res. Corps Cumb'd.	June,	1863
86th Ill. Infy...........Jan., 1863	From 2-Brig. 4-Div. Centre 14-Corps.	To 2-Brig. 2-Div. Res. Corps Cumb'd.	June,	1863
125th Ill. Infy..........Jan., 1863	From 2-Brig. 4-Div. Centre 14-Corps	To 2-Brig. 2-Div. Res. Corps Cumb'd.	June,	1863
105th Ohio Infy.........June, 1863	From 1-Brig. 5-Div. 14-Corps.......	To 2-Brig. 3-Div. 14-Corps.........	Oct.,	1863
68th Ind. Infy..........June, 1863	From Indianapolis, Ind...........	To 1-Brig. 3-Div. 4-Corps Cumb'd...	Oct.,	1863
75th Ind. Infy..........June, 1863	From 1-Brig. 5-Div. 14-Corps.......	To 2-Brig. 3-Div. 14-Corps.........	Oct.,	1863
101st Ind. Infy.........June, 1863	From 1-Brig. 5-Div. 14-Corps.......	To 2-Brig. 3-Div. 14-Corps.........	Oct.,	1863
80th Ill. Infy..........June, 1863	From Streight's Indpt. Brig.......	To 3-Brig. 3-Div. 11-Corps Cumb'd..	Sept.,	1863

3d BRIGADE.—   COMMANDERS.

George Crook	Brigadier General	June 8, 1863, to July 28, 1863.		
J. B. Turchin	Brigadier General	July 28, 1863, to Oct. 9, 1863.		
11th Ohio Infy..........June, 1863	From Crook's Br. A'y Ky. Dept. Cum.	To 1-Brig. 3-Div. 14-Corps	Oct.,	1863
36th Ohio Infy..........June, 1863	From Crook's Br. A'y Ky. Dept. Cum.	To 1-Brig. 3-Div. 14-Corps	Oct.,	1863
89th Ohio Infy..........June, 1863	From Crook's Br. A'y Ky. Dept. Cum.	To 1-Brig. 3-Div. 14-Corps	Oct.,	1863
92d Ohio Infy..........June, 1863	From Crook's Br. A'y Ky. Dept. Cum.	To 1-Brig. 3-Div. 14-Corps	Oct.,	1863
18th Ky. Infy..........June, 1863	From Crook's Br. A'y Ky. Dept. Cum.	To 3-Brig. 3-Div. 14-Corps	Oct.,	1863
ARTILLERY, 4th DIVISION.—				
Batty. I, 2d Ill. Arty.....Jan., 1863	From Arty. 4-Div. Centre 14-Corps...	To 2-Div. Res. Corps Cumb'd	June,	1863
10th Wis. Batty..........Jan., 1863	From Arty. 4-Div. Centre 14-Corps...	To 2-Div. Res. Corps Cumb'd	June,	1863
18th Ind. Batty..........June, 1863	From Arty. 5-Div. 14-Corps	To Wilder's Mtd. Infy. Brig	June,	1863
19th Ind. Batty..........June, 1863	From Arty. 5-Div. 14-Corps	To Arty. 3-Div. 14-Corps	Oct.,	1863
21st Ind. Batty..........June, 1863	From Crook's Brig. Baird's Div	To 2-Div. Arty. Res. Cumb'd	Oct.,	1863

5th DIVISION.—   COMMANDER.

J. J. Reynolds	Brigadier General	Jan. 9, 1863, to June 8, 1863.
Division discontinued June 8, 1863. Transferred to 4th Division.		

1st BRIGADE.—   COMMANDER.

J. T. Wilder	Col. 17th Ind. Infy	Jan. 9, 1863, to June 8, 1863.		
80th Ill. Infy..........Jan., 1863	From 1-Brig. 5-Div. Centre 14-Corps.	To Streight's Indpt. Brig. 14-Corps..	Apr.,	1863
123d Ill. Infy..........Jan., 1863	From 1-Brig. 5-Div. Centre 14-Corps.	To 1-Brig. 4-Div. 14-Corps	June,	1864
101st Ind. Infy..........Jan., 1863	From 1-Brig. 5-Div. Centre 14-Corps.	To 2-Brig. 4-Div. 14-Corps	June,	1864
105th Ohio Infy..........Jan., 1863	From 1-Brig. 5-Div. Centre 14-Corps.	To 2-Brig. 4-Div. 14-Corps	June,	1864

2d BRIGADE.—   COMMANDER.

A. S. Hall	Col. 105th Ohio Infy	Jan. 9, 1863, to June 8, 1863.		
98th Ill. Infy..........Jan., 1863	From 2-Brig. 5-Div. Centre 14-Corps.	To 1-Brig. 4-Div. 14-Corps	June,	1863
17th Ind. Infy..........Jan., 1863	From 2-Brig. 5-Div. Centre 14-Corps.	To 1-Brig. 4-Div. 14-Corps	June,	1863
72d Ind. Infy..........Jan., 1863	From 2-Brig. 5-Div. Centre 14-Corps.	To 1-Brig. 4-Div. 14-Corps	June,	1863
75th Ind. Infy..........Jan., 1863	From 2-Brig. 5-Div. Centre 14-Corps.	To 2-Brig. 4-Div. 14-Corps	June,	1863
ARTILLERY.—				
18th Ind. Batty..........Jan., 1863	From Arty. 5-Div. Centre 14-Corps..	To Arty. 4-Div. 14-Corps	June,	1863
19th Ind. Batty..........Jan., 1863	From Arty. 5-Div. Centre 14-Corps..	To Arty. 4-Div. 14-Corps	June,	1863
ARTILLERY BRIGADE.—				
Batty. C, 1st Ill. Arty....July, 1864	From Arty. 1-Div. 14-Corps	No change to Muster Out	June,	1865
Batty. I, 2d Ill. Arty....July, 1864	From Arty. 2-Div. 14-Corps	No change to Muster Out	June,	1865
7th Ind. Batty..........July, 1864	From Arty. 3-Div. 14-Corps	To Garr. Arty. Chattanooga, Tenn...	Oct.,	1864
19th Ind. Batty..........July, 1864	From Arty. 3-Div. 14-Corps	No change to Muster Out	June,	1865
Batty. I, 1st Ohio Arty...July, 1864	From Arty. 1-Div. 14-Corps	To Garr. Arty. Chattanooga, Tenn...	Sept.,	1864
5th Wis. Batty..........July, 1864	From Arty. 2-Div. 14-Corps	No change to Muster Out	June,	1865
20th Ind. Batty..........Aug., 1864	From Arty. 4-Div. 20-Corps	To Post Chattanooga. Tenn	Oct.,	1864

STREIGHT'S PROVISIONAL BRIGADE.—   COMMANDER.

A. D. Streight	Col. 51st Ind. Infy			
51st Ind. Infy..........Apr., 1863	From 3-Brig. 1-Div. 21-C. Cumb'd...	Captured. Prisoners of War	May,	1863
73d Ind. Infy..........Apr., 1863	From 3-Brig. 1-Div. 21-C. Cumb'd...	Captured. Prisoners of War	May,	1863
3d Ohio Infy..........Apr., 1863	From 2-Brig. 1-Div. 14-Corps	Captured. Prisoners of War	May,	1863
80th Ill. Infy..........Apr., 1863	From 1-Brig. 5-Div. 14-Corps	Captured. Prisoners of War	May,	1863

Twentieth Army Corps

Created Jan. 9, 1863, General Order No. 9, A. G. O., from Right Wing 14th Army Corps, Dept. of the Cumberland.
Discontinued Oct. 9, 1863, and consolidated with 21st Corps to form reorganized 4th Army Corps.

COMMANDER.

A. McD. McCook	Brigadier General	Jan. 9, 1863, to Oct. 9, 1863.

1st DIVISION.—   COMMANDER.

J. C. Davis	Brigadier General	Jan. 9, 1863, to Oct. 9, 1863.

1st BRIGADE.—   COMMANDER.

P. S. Post	Col. 59th Ill. Infy	Jan. 9, 1863, to Oct. 9, 1863.		
59th Ill. Infy..........Jan., 1863	From 1-Br. 1-Div. Right Wing 14-C.	To 2-Brig. 1-Div. 4-Corps Cumb'd...	Oct.,	1863
74th Ill. Infy..........Jan., 1863	From 1-Br. 1-Div. Right Wing 14-C.	To 2-Brig. 1-Div. 4-Corps Cumb'd...	Oct.,	1863
75th Ill. Infy..........Jan., 1863	From 1-Br. 1-Div. Right Wing 14-C.	To 2-Brig. 1-Div. 4-Corps Cumb'd...	Oct.,	1863
22d Ind. Infy..........Jan., 1863	From 1-Br. 1-Div. Right Wing 14-C.	To 2-Brig. 1-Div. 4-Corps Cumb'd...	Oct.,	1863

2d BRIGADE.—   COMMANDERS.

W. P. Carlin	Col. 38th Ill. Infy	Jan. 9, 1863, to Feb. 15, 1863.		
H. C. Heg	Col. 15th Wis. Infy	Feb. 15, 1863, to Mch. 16, 1863.		
W. P. Carlin	Brigadier General	Mch. 16, 1863, to Oct. 10, 1863.		
21st Ill. Infy..........Jan., 1863	From 2-Br. 1-Div. Right Wing 14-C.	To 1-Brig. 4-Corps Cumb'd...	Oct.,	1863
38th Ill. Infy..........Jan., 1863	From 2-Br. 1-Div. Right Wing 14-C.	To 1-Brig. 4-Corps Cumb'd...	Oct.,	1863
101st Ohio Infy..........Jan., 1863	From 2-Br. 1-Div. Right Wing 14-C.	To 1-Brig. 4-Corps Cumb'd...	Oct.,	1863
15th Wis. Infy..........Jan., 1863	From 2-Br. 1-Div. Right Wing 14-C.	To 3-Brig. 1-Div. 20-Corps Cumb'd..	Mch.,	1863
81st Ind. Infy..........Mch., 1863	From 3-Brig. 1-Div. 20-C. Cumb'd...	To 1-Brig. 4-Corps Cumb'd...	Oct.,	1863

3d BRIGADE.—   COMMANDERS.

W. W. Caldwell	Col. 81st Ind. Infy	Jan. 9, 1863, to Mch. 9, 1863.		
T. T. Crittenden	Brigadier General	Mch. 9, 1863, to Apr. 5, 1863.		
W. W. Caldwell	Col. 81st Ind. Infy	Apr. 5, 1863, to May 15, 1863.		
H. C. Heg	Col. 15th Wis. Infy	May 15, 1863, to Sept. 19, 1863.	Killed.	
J. A. Martin	Col. 8th Kansas Infy	Sept. 19, 1863, to Oct. 9, 1863.		
25th Ill. Infy..........Jan., 1863	From 3-Br. 1-Div. Right Wing 14-C.	To 1-Brig. 3-Div. 4-Corps Cumb'd...	Oct.,	1863
35th Ill. Infy..........Jan., 1863	From 3-Br. 1-Div. Right Wing 14-C.	To 1-Brig. 3-Div. 4-Corps Cumb'd...	Oct.,	1863
81st Ind. Infy..........Jan., 1863	From 3-Br. 1-Div. Right Wing 14-C.	To 2-Brig. 1-Div. 20-Corps Cumb'd..	Mch.,	1863
15th Wis. Infy..........Mch., 1863	From 2-Brig. 1-Div. 20-Corps	To 1-Brig. 3-Div. 4-Corps Cumb'd...	Oct.,	1863
8th Kansas Infy..........June, 1863	From Post of Nashville, Tenn	To 1-Brig. 3-Div. 4-Corps Cumb'd...	Oct.,	1863

ARTILLERY, 1st DIVISION.—

5th Wis. Batty..........Jan., 1863	From 1-Br. 1-Div. Right Wing 14-C.	To Arty., 2-Div. 14-Corps............	Oct.,	1863
8th Wis. Batty..........Jan., 1863	From 3-Br. 1-Div. Right Wing 14-C.	To 2-Div. Arty. Res. Cumb'd.......	Oct.,	1863
2d Minn. Infy...........Jan., 1863	From 2-Br. 1-Div. Right Wing 14-C.	To Arty. 2-Div. 14-Corps............	Oct.,	1863

2d DIVISION.—   COMMANDERS.

R. W. Johnson.........	Brigadier General	Jan. 9, 1863, to Jan. 19, 1863.
W. H. Gibson..........	Col. 46th Ohio Infy...............	Jan. 19, 1863, to Feb. 20, 1863.
R. W. Johnson.........	Brigadier General	Feb. 20, 1863, to Sept. 19, 1863.
A. Willich	Brigadier General	Sept. 19, 1863, to Oct. 9, 1863.

1st BRIGADE.—   COMMANDERS.

W. H. Gibson..........	Col. 46th Ohio Infy...............	Jan. 9, 1863, to Jan. 19, 1863.
F. A. Jones...........	Col. 39th Ind. Infy...............	Jan. 19, 1863, to Feb. 20, 1863.
W. Wallace	Col. 15th Ohio Infy...............	Feb. 20, 1863, to Mch. 5, 1863.
W. H. Gibson..........	Col. 46th Ohio Infy...............	Mch. 5, 1863, to May 28, 1863.
A. Willich	Brigadier General	May 28, 1863, to Sept. 19, 1863.
F. Erdelmeyer	Lt.-Col. 32d Ind. Infy............	Sept. 19, 1863, to Oct. 9, 1863.

89th Ill. Infy.........Jan., 1863	From 1-Br. 2-Div. Right Wing 14-C.	To 1-Brig. 3-Div. 4-Corps Cumb'd...	Oct.,	1863
32d Ind. Infy..........Jan., 1863	From 1-Br. 2-Div. Right Wing 14-C.	To 1-Brig. 3-Div. 4-Corps Cumb'd...	Oct.,	1863
39th Ind. Infy.........Jan., 1863	From 1-Br. 2-Div. Right Wing 14-C.	To Unass'd Cav. Corps Cumb'd......	Apr.,	1863
15th Ohio Infy.........Jan., 1863	From 1-Br. 2-Div. Right Wing 14-C.	To 1-Brig. 3-Div. 4-Corps Cumb'd...	Oct.,	1863
49th Ohio Infy.........Jan., 1863	From 1-Br. 2-Div. Right Wing 14-C.	To 1-Brig. 3-Div. 4-Corps Cumb'd...	Oct.,	1863

2d BRIGADE.—   COMMANDERS.

J. B. Dodge...........	Col. 30th Ind. Infy...............	Jan. 9, 1863, to May 18, 1863.
T. E. Rose............	Col. 77th Penna. Infy.............	May 18, 1863, to June 18, 1863.
J. B. Dodge...........	Col. 30th Ind. Infy...............	June 18, 1863, to Oct. 9, 1863.

29th Ind. Infy.........Jan., 1863	From 2-Br. 2-Div. Right Wing 14-C.	To 1-Brig. 1-Div. 4-Corps Cumb'd..	Oct.,	1863
30th Ind. Infy.........Jan., 1863	From 2-Br. 2-Div. Right Wing 14-C.	To 3-Brig. 1-Div. 4-Corps Cumb'd..	Oct.,	1863
34th Ill. Infy.........Jan., 1863	From 2-Br. 2-Div. Right Wing 14-C.	To Unatt. Dept. Cumb'd............	Oct.,	1863
79th Ill. Infy.........Jan., 1863	From 2-Br. 2-Div. Right Wing 14-C.	To 3-Brig. 2-Div. 4-Corps Cumb'd..	Oct.,	1863
77th Penna. Infy.......Jan., 1863	From 2-Br. 2-Div. Right Wing 14-C.	To 3-Brig. 2-Div. 4-Corps Cumb'd..	Oct.,	1863

3d BRIGADE.—   COMMANDERS.

P. P. Baldwin.........	Col. 6th Indiana Infy.............	Jan. 9, 1863, to Jan. 27, 1863.
E. A. Parrott.........	Col. 1st Ohio Infy................	Jan. 27, 1863, to Apr. 17, 1863.
P. P. Baldwin.........	Col. 6th Indiana Infy.............	Apr. 17, 1863, to Sept. 20, 1863. Killed.
W. W. Berry..........	Col. 5th Kentucky Infy............	Sept. 20, 1863, to Oct. 9, 1863.

1st Ohio Infy..........Jan., 1863	From 3-Brig. 2-Div. R. W. 14-Corps.	To 2-Brig. 3-Div. 4-Corps Cumb'd.	Oct.,	1863
93d Ohio Infy..........Jan., 1863	From 3-Brig. 2-Div. R. W. 14-Corps.	To 2-Brig. 3-Div. 4-Corps Cumb'd.	Oct.,	1863
6th Indiana Infy.......Jan., 1863	From 3-Brig. 2-Div. R. W. 14-Corps.	To 2-Brig. 3-Div. 4-Corps Cumb'd.	Oct.,	1863
5th Kentucky Infy......Jan., 1863	From 3-Brig. 2-Div. R. W. 14-Corps.	To 2-Brig. 3-Div. 4-Corps Cumb'd.	Oct.,	1863

ARTILLERY, 2d DIVISION.—

Batty. A, 1st Ohio Arty.Jan., 1863	From 1-Brig. 2-Div. R. W. 14-Corps.	To 1-Div. Arty. Res. Cumberland...	Oct.,	1863
Batty. E, 1st Ohio Arty.Jan., 1863	From 2-Brig. 2-Div. R. W. 14-Corps.	To Post Nashville, Tenn...........	Feb.,	1863
5th Indiana Batty......Jan., 1863	From 3-Brig. 2-Div. R. W. 14-Corps.	To Arty. 1-Div. 4-Corps Cumberland.	Oct.,	1863
20th Ohio Batty........Feb., 1863	From New Organization..........	To 1-Div. Arty. Res. Cumberland...	Oct.,	1863

1st BRIGADE.—   COMMANDER.

P. H. Sheridan........	Major General.....................	Jan. 9, 1863, to Oct. 9, 1863.

3d DIVISION.—   COMMANDERS.

N. Greusel............	Col. 36th Illinois Infy...........	Jan. 9, 1863, to Feb. 13, 1863.
F. T. Sherman........	Col. 88th Illinois Infy...........	Feb. 13, 1863, to Apr. 12, 1863.
W. H. Lytle..........	Brigadier General.................	Apr. 12, 1863, to Sept. 19, 1863. Killed.
Silas Miller..........	Col. 36th Illinois Infy...........	Sept. 19, 1863, to Sept. 28, 1863.
F. T. Sherman........	Col. 88th Illinois Infy...........	Sept. 28, 1863, to Oct. 9, 1863.

36th Illinois Infy.....Jan., 1863	From 1-Brig. 3-Div. R. W. 14-Corps	To 1-Brig. 2-Div. 4-Corps Cumb'd..	Oct.,	1863
88th Illinois Infy.....Jan., 1863	From 1-Brig. 3-Div. R. W. 14-Corps	To 1-Brig. 2-Div. 4-Corps Cumb'd..	Oct.,	1863
21st Michigan Infy.....Jan., 1863	From 1-Brig. 3-Div. R. W. 14-Corps	To 1-Brig. 2-Div. 4-Corps Cumb'd..	Oct.,	1863
24th Wisconsin Infy....Jan., 1863	From 1-Brig. 3-Div. R. W. 14-Corps	To 1-Brig. 2-Div. 4-Corps Cumb'd..	Oct.,	1863

2d BRIGADE.—   COMMANDERS.

B. Laiboldt...........	Col. 2d Missouri Infy.............	Jan. 9, 1863, to Feb. 2, 1863.
W. W. Barrett........	Col. 44th Illinois Infy...........	Feb. 2, 1863, to Mch. 3, 1863.
B. Laiboldt...........	Col. 2d Missouri Infy.............	Mch. 3, 1863, to Oct. 9, 1863.

44th Illinois Infy.....Jan., 1863	From 2-Brig. 3-Div. R. W. 14-Corps	To 1-Brig. 2-Div. 4-Corps Cumb'd..	Oct.,	1863
73d Illinois Infy......Jan., 1863	From 2-Brig. 3-Div. R. W. 14-Corps	To 1-Brig. 2-Div. 4-Corps Cumb'd..	Oct.,	1863
2d Missouri Infy.......Jan., 1863	From 2-Brig. 3-Div. R. W. 14-Corps	To 1-Brig. 2-Div. 4-Corps Cumb'd..	Oct.,	1863
15th Missouri Infy.....Jan., 1863	From 2-Brig. 3-Div. R. W. 14-Corps	To 1-Brig. 2-Div. 4-Corps Cumb'd..	Oct.,	1863

3d BRIGADE.—   COMMANDERS.

L. P. Bradley.........	Col. 51st Illinois Infy...........	Jan. 9, 1863, to Sept. 28, 1863.
N. H. Walworth........	Col. 42d Illinois Infy............	Sept. 28, 1863, to Oct. 9, 1863.

22d Illinois Infy......Jan., 1863	From 3-Brig. 3-Div. R. W. 14-Corps	To 3-Brig. 2-Div. 4-Corps Cumb'd..	Oct.,	1863
27th Illinois Infy.....Jan., 1863	From 3-Brig. 3-Div. R. W. 14-Corps	To 3-Brig. 2-Div. 4-Corps Cumb'd..	Oct.,	1863
42d Illinois Infy......Jan., 1863	From 3-Brig. 3-Div. R. W. 14-Corps	To 3-Brig. 2-Div. 4-Corps Cumb'd..	Oct.,	1863
51st Illinois Infy.....Jan., 1863	From 3-Brig. 3-Div. R. W. 14-Corps	To 3-Brig. 2-Div. 4-Corps Cumb'd..	Oct.,	1863

ARTILLERY.—

Batty. C, 1st Ill. Arty....Jan., 1863	From 3-Brig. 3-Div. R. W. 14-Corps	To Arty. 1-Div. 14-Corps..........	Oct.,	1863
4th Indiana Batty......Jan., 1863	From 1-Brig. 3-Div. R. W. 14-Corps	To Arty. 1-Div. 14-Corps..........	June,	1863
Batty. G, 1st Mo. Arty..Jan., 1863	From 2-Brig. 3-Div. R. W. 14-Corps	To Arty. 2-Div. 14-Corps..........	Oct.,	1863
11th Indiana Batty......June, 1863	From Post Nashville, Tenn........	To Arty. 2-Div. 4-Corps Cumb'd...	Oct.,	1863

Twenty-First Army Corps

Created Jan. 9, 1863, General Order No. 9, A. G. O., and organized from Left Wing 14th Corps, Army Cumberland. Discontinued Oct. 9, 1863, and merged into the reorganized 4th Corps, Dept. of the Cumberland.

COMMANDERS.

T. L. Crittenden	Major General	Jan. 9, 1863, to Feb. 19, 1863.
T. J. Wood	Brigadier General	Feb. 19, 1863, to Mch. 19, 1863.
T. L. Crittenden	Major General	Mch. 19, 1863, to July 15, 1863.
J. M. Palmer	Brigadier General	July 15, 1863, to Aug. 17, 1863.
T. L. Crittenden	Major General	Aug. 17, 1863, to Oct. 10, 1863.

1st DIVISION.— COMMANDERS.

M. S. Hascall	Brigadier General	Jan. 9, 1863, to Feb. 19, 1863.
G. D. Wagner	Col. 15th Indiana Infy	Feb. 19, 1863, to Apr. 13, 1863.
J. M. Brannan	Brigadier General	Apr. 13, 1863, to May 10, 1863.
T. J. Wood	Brigadier General	May 10, 1863, to Oct. 9, 1863.

1st BRIGADE.— COMMANDERS.

E. P. Fyffe	Col. 26th Ohio Infy	Jan. 9, 1863, to June 10, 1863.
G. P. Buell	Col. 58th Indiana Infy	June 10, 1863, to July 25, 1863.
F. A. Bartleson	Col. 100th Illinois Infy	July 25, 1863, to Aug. 3, 1863.
G. P. Buell	Col. 58th Indiana Infy	Aug. 3, 1863, to Oct. 9, 1863.

26th Ohio Infy	Jan., 1863	From 1-Brig. 1-Div. L. W. 14-Corps	To 2-Brig. 2-Div. 4-Corps Cumb'd.	Oct., 1863
58th Indiana Infy	Jan., 1863	From 1-Brig. 1-Div. L. W. 14-Corps	To 2-Brig. 2-Div. 4-Corps Cumb'd.	Oct., 1863
100th Illinois Infy	Jan., 1863	From 1-Brig. 1-Div. L. W. 14-Corps	To 2-Brig. 2-Div. 4-Corps Cumb'd.	Oct., 1863
3d Kentucky Infy	Jan., 1863	From 1-Brig. 1-Div. L. W. 14-Corps	To 3-Brig. 1-Div. 21-Corps	Apr., 1863
13th Michigan Infy	Apr., 1863	From 3-Brig. 1-Div. 21-Corps	To 2-Brig. 2-Div. 4-Corps Cumb'd.	Oct., 1863

2d BRIGADE.— COMMANDERS.

G. D. Wagner	Col. 15th Indiana Infy	Jan. 9, 1863, to Jan. 20, 1863.
M. Barnes	Lt.-Col. 97th Ohio Infy	Jan. 20, 1863, to Feb. 18, 1863.
G. A. Wood	Lt.-Col. 15th Indiana Infy	Feb. 18, 1863, to Apr. 13, 1863.
G. D. Wagner	Brigadier General	Apr. 13, 1863, to Oct. 9, 1863.

15th Indiana Infy	Jan., 1863	From 2-Brig. 1-Div. L. W. 14-Corps	To 2-Brig. 2-Div. 4-Corps Cumb'd.	Oct., 1863
40th Indiana Infy	Jan., 1863	From 2-Brig. 1-Div. L. W. 14-Corps	To 2-Brig. 2-Div. 4-Corps Cumb'd.	Oct., 1863
57th Indiana Infy	Jan., 1863	From 2-Brig. 1-Div. L. W. 14-Corps	To 2-Brig. 2-Div. 4-Corps Cumb'd.	Oct., 1863
97th Ohio Infy	Jan., 1863	From 2-Brig. 1-Div. L. W. 14-Corps	To 2-Brig. 2-Div. 4-Corps Cumb'd.	Oct., 1863

3d BRIGADE.— COMMANDERS.

C. G. Harker	Col. 65th Ohio Infy	Jan. 9, 1863, to Feb. 17, 1863.
M. Shoemaker	Col. 13th Michigan Infy	Feb. 17, 1863, to Mch. 17, 1863.
C. G. Harker	Col. 65th Ohio Infy	Mch. 17, 1863, to Oct. 9, 1863.

13th Michigan Infy	Jan., 1863	From 3-Brig. 1-Div. L. W. 14-Corps	To 1-Brig. 1-Div. 21-Corps	Apr., 1863
64th Ohio Infy	Jan., 1863	From 3-Brig. 1-Div. L. W. 14-Corps	To 3-Brig. 2-Div. 4-Corps Cumb'd	Oct., 1863
65th Ohio Infy	Jan., 1863	From 3-Brig. 1-Div. L. W. 14-Corps	To 3-Brig. 2-Div. 4-Corps Cumb'd	Oct., 1863
51st Indiana Infy	Jan., 1863	From 3-Brig. 1-Div. L. W. 14-Corps	To Streight's Prov'l Brig. 14-Corps	Apr., 1863
73d Indiana Infy	Jan., 1863	From 3-Brig. 1-Div. L. W. 14-Corps	To Streight's Prov'l Brig. 14-Corps	Apr., 1863
3d Kentucky Infy	Apr., 1863	From 1-Brig. 1-Div. 21-Corps	To 3-Brig. 2-Div. 4-Corps Cumb'd	Oct., 1863
125th Ohio Infy	June, 1863	From Franklin, Tenn., Army Ky.	To 3-Brig. 2-Div. 4-Corps Cumb'd	Oct., 1863
ARTILLERY.				
8th Indiana Batty	Jan., 1863	From 1-Brig. 1-Div. L. W. 14-Corps	To 2-Div. Arty. Reserve Cumb'd	Oct., 1863
10th Indiana Batty	Jan., 1863	From 2-Brig. 1-Div. L. W. 14-Corps	To Arty. 2-Div. 4-Corps Cumb'd	Oct., 1863
6th Ohio Batty	Jan., 1863	From 3-Brig. 1-Div. L. W. 14-Corps	To Arty. 3-Div. 4-Corps Cumb'd	Oct., 1863

2d DIVISION.— COMMANDERS.

J. M. Palmer	Major General	Jan. 9, 1863, to July 15, 1863.
Chas. Cruft	Brigadier General	July 15, 1863, to Aug. 17, 1863.
J. M. Palmer	Major General	Aug. 17, 1863, to Oct. 9, 1863.

1st BRIGADE.— COMMANDERS.

Chas. Cruft	Brigadier General	Jan. 9, 1863, to Mch. 21, 1863.
D. A. Enyart	Col. 1st Kentucky Infy	Mch. 21, 1863, to Apr. 21, 1863.
Chas. Cruft	Brigadier General	Apr. 21, 1863, to July 15, 1863.
T. D. Sedgwick	Col. 2d Kentucky Infy	July 15, 1863, to Aug. 17, 1863.
Chas. Cruft	Brigadier General	Aug. 17, 1863, to Oct. 9, 1863.

90th Ohio Infy	Jan., 1863	From 1-Brig. 2-Div. L. W. 14-Corps	To 1-Brig. 1-Div. 4-Corps Cumb'd.	Oct., 1863
31st Indiana Infy	Jan., 1863	From 1-Brig. 2-Div. L. W. 14-Corps	To 1-Brig. 1-Div. 4-Corps Cumb'd.	Oct., 1863
1st Kentucky Infy	Jan., 1863	From 1-Brig. 2-Div. L. W. 14-Corps	To 1-Brig. 1-Div. 4-Corps Cumb'd.	Oct., 1863
2d Kentucky Infy	Jan., 1863	From 1-Brig. 2-Div. L. W. 14-Corps	To 1-Brig. 1-Div. 4-Corps Cumb'd.	Oct., 1863

2d BRIGADE.— COMMANDERS.

W. B. Hazen	Brigadier General	Jan. 9, 1863, to Sept. 3, 1863.
O. H. Payne	Col. 124th Ohio Infy	Sept. 3, 1863, to Sept. 13, 1863.
W. B. Hazen	Brigadier General	Sept. 13, 1863, to Oct. 9, 1863.

41st Ohio Infy	Jan., 1863	From 2-Brig. 2-Div. L. W. 14-Corps	To 2-Brig. 3-Div. 4-Corps Cumb'd.	Oct., 1863
9th Indiana Infy	Jan., 1863	From 2-Brig. 2-Div. L. W. 14-Corps	To 3-Brig. 1-Div. 4-Corps Cumb'd.	Oct., 1863
110th Illinois Infy	Jan., 1863	From 2-Brig. 2-Div. L. W. 14-Corps	To Unattached 21-Corps	May, 1863
6th Kentucky Infy	Jan., 1863	From 2-Brig. 2-Div. L. W. 14-Corps	To 2-Brig. 3-Div. 4-Corps Cumb'd.	Oct., 1863
124th Ohio Infy	June, 1863	From Franklin, Tenn., Army Ky.	To 2-Brig. 3-Div. 4-Corps Cumb'd.	Oct., 1863

3d BRIGADE.— COMMANDERS.

William Grose	Col. 36th Indiana Infy	Jan. 9, 1863, to Mch. 12, 1863.
L. H. Waters	Col. 84th Illinois Infy	Mch. 12, 1863, to Apr. 14, 1863.
William Grose	Col. 36th Indiana Infy	Apr. 14, 1863, to Oct. 9, 1863.

6th Ohio Infy	Jan., 1863	From 3-Brig. 2-Div. L. W. 14-Corps	To 2-Brig. 3-Div. 4-Corps Cumb'd.	Oct., 1863
24th Ohio Infy	Jan., 1863	From 3-Brig. 2-Div. L. W. 14-Corps	To 3-Brig. 1-Div. 4-Corps Cumb'd.	Oct., 1863
36th Indiana Infy	Jan., 1863	From 3-Brig. 2-Div. L. W. 14-Corps	To 3-Brig. 1-Div. 4-Corps Cumb'd.	Oct., 1863
84th Illinois Infy	Jan., 1863	From 3-Brig. 2-Div. L. W. 14-Corps	To 3-Brig. 1-Div. 4-Corps Cumb'd.	Oct., 1863
23d Kentucky Infy	Jan., 1863	From 3-Brig. 2-Div. L. W. 14-Corps	To 2-Brig. 3-Div. 4-Corps Cumb'd.	Oct., 1863
ARTILLERY.—				
Batty. B, 1st Ohio Arty	Jan., 1863	From 2-Div. L. W. 14-Corps	To 1-Div. Arty. Reserve Cumb'd	Oct., 1863
Batty. F, 1st Ohio Arty	Jan., 1863	From 2-Div. L. W. 14-Corps	To 1-Div. Arty. Reserve Cumb'd	Oct., 1863
Batty. H, 4th U. S. Arty	Jan., 1863	From 2-Div. L. W. 14-Corps	To Arty. 1-Div. 4-Corps Cumb'd	Oct., 1863
Batty. M, 4th U. S. Arty	Jan., 1863	From 2-Div. L. W. 14-Corps	To Arty. 1-Div. 4-Corps Cumb'd	Oct., 1863

3d DIVISION.— COMMANDERS.

Samuel Beatty.........	Col. 19th Ohio Infy..............	Jan. 9, 1863, to Mch. 13, 1863.
H. P. Van Cleve.......	Brigadier General..................	Mch. 13, 1863, to Oct. 9, 1863.

1st BRIGADE.— COMMANDERS.

B. C. Grider...........	Col. 9th Kentucky Infy............	Jan. 9, 1863, to Feb. 12, 1863.
F. Kneffler............	Col. 79th Indiana Infy............	Feb. 12, 1863, to Apr. 11, 1863.
Samuel Beatty.........	Brigadier General.................	Apr. 11, 1863, to Oct. 9, 1863.

79th Indiana Infy........Jan., 1863	From 1-Brig. 3-Div. L. W. 14-Corps	To 3-Brig. 3-Div. 4-Corps Cumb'd..	Oct.	1863
9th Kentucky Infy......Jan., 1863	From 1-Brig. 3-Div. L. W. 14-Corps	To 3-Brig. 3-Div. 4-Corps Cumb'd..	Oct.,	1863
11th Kentucky Infy......Jan., 1863	From 1-Brig. 3-Div. L. W. 14-Corps	To Dist. West Ky. Dept. Ohio......	Apr.,	1863
19th Ohio Infy.........Jan., 1863	From 1-Brig. 3-Div. L. W. 14-Corps	To 3-Brig. 3-Div. 4-Corps Cumb'd..	Oct.,	1863
17th Kentucky Infy.....June, 1863	From Post Clarksville, Tenn.......	To 3-Brig. 3-Div. 4-Corps Cumb'd..	Oct.,	1863

2d BRIGADE.— COMMANDERS.

J. P. Fyffe............	Col. 59th Ohio Infy..............	Jan. 9, 1863, to Mch. 2, 1863.
G. F. Dick............	Col. 86th Indiana Infy............	Mch. 2, 1863, to Oct. 9, 1863.

13th Ohio Infy..........Jan., 1863	From 2-Brig. 3-Div. L. W. 14-Corps	To 3-Brig. 3-Div. 4-Corps Cumb'd..	Oct.,	1863
59th Ohio Infy..........Jan., 1863	From 2-Brig. 3-Div. L. W. 14-Corps	To 3-Brig. 3-Div. 4-Corps Cumb'd..	Oct.,	1863
44th Indiana Infy........Jan., 1863	From 2-Brig. 3-Div. L. W. 14-Corps	To 3-Brig. 3-Div. 4-Corps Cumb'd..	Oct.,	1863
86th Indiana Infy.......Jan., 1863	From 2-Brig. 3-Div. L. W. 14-Corps	To 3-Brig. 3-Div. 4-Corps Cumb'd..	Oct.,	1863

3d BRIGADE.— COMMANDERS.

Stanley Matthews.....	Col. 51st Ohio Infy..............	Jan. 9, 1863, to Apr. 14, 1863.
S. M. Barnes.........	Col. 8th Kentucky Infy...........	Apr. 14, 1863, to Oct. 9, 1863.

51st Ohio.............Jan., 1863	From 3-Brig. 3-Div. L. W. 14-Corps.	To 2-Brig. 1-Div. 4-Corps Cub'd....	Oct.,	1863
99th Ohio Infy..........Jan., 1863	From 3-Brig. 3-Div. L. W. 14-Corps.	To 2-Brig. 1-Div. 4-Corps Cub'd....	Oct.,	1863
35th Indiana Infy........Jan., 1863	From 3-Brig. 3-Div. L. W. 14-Corps.	To 2-Brig. 1-Div. 4-Corps Cub'd....	Oct.,	1863
8th Kentucky Infy......Jan., 1863	From 3-Brig. 3-Div. L. W. 14-Corps.	To 2-Brig. 1-Div. 4-Corps Cub'd....	Oct.,	1863
21st Kentucky Infy......Jan., 1863	From 3-Brig. 3-Div. L. W. 14-Corps.	To Unassigned Dept. Cumberland..	Oct.,	1863

ARTILLERY, 3d DIVISION.—

7th Indiana Batty......Jan., 1863	From Arty. 3-Div. L. W. Cub'd....	To Arty. 3-Div. 14-Corps..........	Oct.,	1863
Indpt. Batty. B, Pa. Arty.Jan., 1863	From Arty. 3-Div. L. W. Cub'd....	To Arty. 3-Div. 4-Corps Cumb'd...	Oct.,	1863
3d Wisconsin Batty......Jan., 1863	From Arty. 3-Div. L. W. Cub'd....	To 2-Div. Arty. Res. Cumberland..	Oct.,	1863

UNATTACHED.—

110th Illinois Infy.......May, 1863	From 2-Brig. 2-Div. 21-Corps.......	To 3-Brig. 2-Div. 14-Corps...........	Oct.,	1863

Army of Kentucky

Joined from Dept. Ohio Feb., 1863.

COMMANDER.

Gordon Granger.......	Major General.....................	

BAIRD'S DIVISION.— COMMANDER.

A. Baird................	Brigadier General.................	

1st BRIGADE.— COMMANDER.

John Coburn...........	Col. 33d Indiana Infy.............	

33d Indiana Infy........Feb., 1863	From 1-B. 3-Div. Army Ky. D. Ohio.	To 3-B. 1-Div. Res. Corps Cumb'd...	June,	1863
85th Indiana Infy.......Feb., 1863	From 1-B. 3-Div. Army Ky. D. Ohio.	To 3-B. 1-Div. Res. Corps Cumb'd...	June,	1863
19th Michigan Infy......Feb., 1863	From 1-B. 3-Div. Army Ky. D. Ohio.	To 3-B. 1-Div. Res. Corps Cumb'd...	June,	1863
22d Wisconsin Infy......Feb., 1863	From 1-B. 3-Div. Army Ky. D. Ohio.	To 3-B. 1-Div. Res. Corps Cumb'd...	June,	1863
9th Ohio Batty. Arty.....Feb., 1863	From Arty. 3-D. Army Ky. D. Ohio.	To Arty. 1-Div. Res. Corps Cumb'd	June,	1863

2d BRIGADE.— COMMANDER.

S. D. Atkins...........	Col. 92d Illinois Infy.............	

92d Illinois Infy.......Feb., 1863	From 2-B. 3-Div. Army Ky. D. Ohio.	To 1-B. 1-Div. Res. Corps Cumb'd...	June,	1863
96th Illinois Infy.......Feb., 1863	From 2-B. 3-Div. Army Ky. D. Ohio.	To 1-B. 1-Div. Res. Corps Cumb'd...	June,	1863
115th Illinois Infy.......Feb., 1863	From 2-B. 3-Div. Army Ky. D. Ohio.	To 1-B. 1-Div. Res. Corps Cumb'd...	June,	1863
84th Indiana Infy.......Feb., 1863	From Dist. E. Ky. Dept. Ohio......	To 1-B. 1-Div. Res. Corps Cumb'd...	June,	1863
40th Ohio Infy..........Feb., 1863	From Dist. E. Ky. Dept. Ohio......	To 1-B. 1-Div. Res. Corps Cumb'd...	June,	1863
18th Ohio Batty. Arty....Feb., 1863	From 2-Div. Army Ky. Dept. Ohio..	To Arty. 1-Div. Res. Corps Cumb'd	June,	1863

REED'S BRIGADE.— COMMANDER.

William P. Reed........	Col. 121st Ohio Infy.............	

78th Illinois Infy.......Feb., 1863	From Dist. West Ky. Dept. Ohio...	To 2-B. 1-Div. Res. Corps Cumb'd...	June,	1863
98th Ohio Infy..........Feb., 1863	From Dist. West Ky. Dept. Ohio...	To 2-B. 1-Div. Res. Corps Cumb'd...	June,	1863
113th Ohio Infy.........Feb., 1863	From Dist. West Ky. Dept. Ohio...	To 2-B. 1-Div. Res. Corps Cumb'd...	June,	1863
121st Ohio Infy.........Feb., 1863	From Dist. West Ky. Dept. Ohio...	To 2-R. 1-Div. Res. Corps Cumb'd...	June,	1863
Batty. M. 1st Ill. Arty...Feb., 1863	From Dist. West Ky. Dept. Ohio...	To 2-B. 1-Div. Res. Corps Cumb'd..	June,	1863

CROOK'S BRIGADE.— COMMANDER.

George Crook.........	Brigadier General.................	

11th Ohio Infy..........Feb., 1863	From 2-B. Kanawha D. Dist. W. Va.	To 3-Brig. 4-Div. 14-Corps.........	June,	1863
36th Ohio Infy..........Feb., 1863	From 2-B. Kanawha D. Dist. W. Va.	To 3-Brig. 4-Div. 14-Corps.........	June,	1863
89th Ohio Infy..........Feb., 1863	From 2-B. Kanawha D. Dist. W. Va.	To 3-Brig. 4-Div. 14-Corps.........	June,	1863
92d Ohio Infy..........Feb., 1863	From 2-B. Kanawha D. Dist. W. Va.	To 3-Brig. 4-Div. 14-Corps.........	June,	1863
18th Kentucky Infy......Feb., 1863	From 1-B. 2-Div. Army Ky. D. Ohio.	To 3-Brig. 4-Div. 14-Corps.........	June,	1863
21st Indiana Batty........Feb., 1863	From Arty. 3-D. Army Ky. D. Ohio.	To Arty. 4-Div. 14-Corps...........	June,	1863

UNATTACHED.—

124th Ohio Infy..........Feb., 1863	From Dist. W. Ky. Dept. Ohio......	To 2-Brig. 2-Div. 21-Corps..........	June,	1863
125th Ohio Infy..........Feb., 1863	From Dist. W. Ky. Dept. Ohio......	To 3-Brig. 1-Div. 21-Corps.........	June,	1863

Reserve Corps---Department of the Cumberland

Organized June 8, 1863. Discontinued Oct. 9, 1863, and merged into the reorganized 4th and 14th Corps, Cumberland.

COMMANDER.

Gordon Granger.......	Major General.....................	June 8, 1863, to Oct. 9. 1863.

1st DIVISION.—   COMMANDERS.

A. Baird...............	Brigadier General..................	June 8, 1863, to Aug. 11, 1863.
W. C. Whitaker........	Brigadier General..................	Aug. 11, 1863, to Aug. 15, 1863.
J. B. Steedman........	Brigadier General..................	Aug. 15, 1863, to Oct. 9, 1863.

1st BRIGADE.—   COMMANDERS.

S. D. Atkins...........	Col. 92d Ill. Infy..................	June 8, 1863, to July 15, 1863.	
T. E. Champion.........	Col. 96th Ill. Infy.................	July 15, 1863, to Aug. 15, 1863.	
W. C. Whitaker........	Brigadier General..................	Aug. 15, 1863, to Oct. 9, 1863.	
92d Ill. Infy............June, 1863	From 2-Brig. Baird's Div. Cumb'd...	To 1-Brig. 4-Div. 14-Corps Cumb'd...	July, 1863
96th Ill. Infy............June, 1863	From 2-Brig. Baird's Div. Cumb'd..:	To 3-Brig. 1-Div. 4-Corps Cumb'd...	Oct., 1863
115th Ill. Infy............June, 1863	From 2-Brig. Baird's Div. Cumb'd...	To 1-Brig. 2-Div. 4-Corps Cumb'd...	Oct., 1863
84th Ind. Infy.............June, 1863	From 2-Brig. Baird's Div. Cumb'd...	To 3-Brig. 1-Div. 4-Corps Cumb'd...	Oct., 1863
40th Ohio Infy...........June, 1863	From 2-Brig. Baird's Div. Cumb'd...	To 1-Brig. 2-Div. 4-Corps Cumb'd...	Oct., 1863
22d Mich. Infy............Sept., 1863	From 3-Brig. 2-Div. Res. Corps......	To 3-Brig. 3-Div. 14-Corps........	Oct., 1863
89th Ohio Infy...........Sept., 1863	From 3-Brig. 4-Div. 14-Corps.......	To 1-Brig. 3-Div. 14-Corps........	Oct., 1863

2d BRIGADE.—   COMMANDERS.

W. P. Reed............	Col. 121st Ohio Infy...............	June 8, 1863, to Sept. 9, 1863.	
John G. Mitchell........	Col. 113th Ohio Infy...............	Sept. 9, 1863, to Oct. 9, 1863.	
78th Ill. Infy............June, 1863	From Reed's Brig. Granger's A, Ky.	To 2-Brig. 2-Div. 14-Corps..........	Oct., 1863
98th Ohio Infy...........June, 1863	From Reed's Brig. Granger's A, Ky.	To 2-Brig. 2-Div. 14-Corps..........	Oct., 1863
113th Ohio Infy...........June, 1863	From Reed's Brig. Granger's A, Ky.	To 2-Brig. 2-Div. 14-Corps..........	Oct., 1863
121st Ohio Infy...........June, 1863	From Reed's Brig. Granger's A, Ky.	To 2-Brig. 2-Div. 14-Corps..........	Oct., 1863

3d BRIGADE.—   COMMANDERS.

W. L. Utley............	Col. 22d Wis. Infy.................	June 8, 1863, to June 24, 1863.	
H. C. Gilbert...........	Col. 19th Mich. Infy...............	June 24, 1863, to July 12, 1863.	
John Coburn............	Col. 33d Ind. Infy.................	July 12, 1863, to Oct. 10, 1863.	
33d Ind. Infy............June, 1863	From 1-Brig. Baird's Div. A, Ky....	To Unatt. Coburn's Br. Dept. Cumb'd.	Oct., 1863
85th Ind. Infy............June, 1863	From 1-Brig. Baird's Div. A, Ky....	To Unatt. Coburn's Br. Dept. Cumb'd.	Oct., 1863
19th Mich. Infy............June, 1863	From 1-Brig. Baird's Div. A, Ky....	To Unatt. Coburn's Br. Dept. Cumb'd.	Oct., 1863
22d Wis. Infy............June, 1863	From 1-Brig. Baird's Div. A, Ky....	To Unatt. Coburn's Br. Dept. Cumb'd.	Oct., 1863
ARTILLERY, 1st DIVISION.—			
Batty. M, 1st Ill. Arty....June, 1863	From Reed's Brig. Granger's A, Ky.	To Arty. 2-Div. 4 Corps Cumb'd....	Oct., 1863
9th Ohio Batty..........June, 1863	From 1-Brig. Baird's Div. Army Ky.	To Unatt. Coburn's Br. Dept. Cumb'd.	Oct., 1863
18th Ohio Batty..........June, 1863	From 2-Brig. Baird's Div. Army Ky.	To 1-Div. Arty. Res. Dept. Cumb'd...	Oct., 1863

2d DIVISION.—   COMMANDER.

J. D. Morgan..........	Brigadier General..................	June 8, 1863, to Oct. 8, 1863.

1st BRIGADE.—   COMMANDERS.

R. F. Smith............	Col. 16th Ill. Infy.................	June 8, 1863, to Aug. 3, 1863.	
John Tillson............	Col. 10th Ill. Infy.................	Aug. 3, 1863, to Oct. 10, 1863.	
10th Ill. Infy............June, 1863	From 1-Brig. 4-Div. 14-Corps......	To 1-Brig. 2-Div. 14-Corps..........	Oct., 1863
16th Ill. Infy............June, 1863	From 1-Brig. 4-Div. 14-Corps......	To 1-Brig. 2-Div. 14-Corps..........	Oct., 1863
60th Ill. Infy............June, 1863	From 1-Brig. 4-Div. 14-Corps......	To 1-Brig. 2-Div. 14-Corps..........	Oct., 1863
10th Mich. Infy............June, 1863	From 1-Brig. 4-Div. 14-Corps......	To 1-Brig. 2-Div. 14-Corps..........	Oct., 1863
14th Mich. Infy............June, 1863	From 1-Brig. 4-Div. 14-Corps......	To 1-Brig. 2-Div. 14-Corps..........	Oct., 1863

2d BRIGADE.—   COMMANDER.

Daniel McCook.........	Col. 52d Ohio Infy.................	June 8, 1863, to Oct. 9, 1863.	
85th Ill. Infy............June, 1863	From 2-Brig. 4-Div. 14-Corps........	To 3-Brig. 2-Div. 14-Corps........	Oct., 1863
86th Ill. Infy............June, 1863	From 2-Brig. 4-Div. 14-Corps........	To 3-Brig. 2-Div. 14-Corps........	Oct., 1863
125th Ill. Infy............June, 1863	From 2-Brig. 4-Div. 14-Corps........	To 3-Brig. 2-Div. 14-Corps........	Oct., 1863
52d Ohio Infy............June, 1863	From 2-Brig. 4-Div. 14-Corps........	To 3-Brig. 2-Div. 14-Corps........	Oct., 1863

3d BRIGADE.—   COMMANDERS.

C. C. Doolittle..........	Col. 19th Mich. Infy...............	June 8, 1863, to Aug. 10, 1863.	
H. LeFavour............	Col. 22d Mich. Infy................	Aug. 10, 1863, to Oct. 10, 1863.	
18th Mich. Infy..........June, 1863	From Post Nashville, Tenn.........	To Unatt. Dept. Cumb'd............	Oct., 1863
22d Mich. Infy..........June, 1863	From Post Nashville, Tenn.........	To 1-Brig. 1-Div. Res. Corps.......	Sept., 1863
106th Ohio Infy..........June, 1863	From Gallatin, Tenn..............	To Unatt. Gallatin, Dept. Cumb'd...	Oct., 1863
108th Ohio Infy..........June, 1863	From Dist. Ky. Dept. Ohio.........	To Unatt. Dept. Cumb'd............	Oct., 1863
1st Middle Tenn. Infy....June, 1863	From Post Nashville, Tenn.........	To Post Nashville, Tenn...........	Oct., 1863
ARTILLERY, 2d DIVISION.—			
Batty. E, 1st Ohio Arty...June, 1863	From Post Nashville, Tenn.........	To Unass'd Dept. Cumb'd...........	Oct., 1863
Batty. I, 2d Ill. Arty......June, 1863	From Arty. 4-Div. 14-Corps........	To Arty. 2-Div. 14-Corps..........	Oct., 1863
10th Wis. Batty..........June, 1863	From Arty. 4-Div. 14-Corps........	To Unass'd Dept. Cumb'd...........	Oct., 1863

3d DIVISION.—   COMMANDER.

R. S. Granger..........	Brigadier General..................	June 8, 1863, to Oct. 9, 1863.

1st BRIGADE.—   COMMANDERS.

W. P. Lyon............	Col. 13th Wis. Infy................	June 8, 1863, to July 10, 1863.	
S. D. Bruce............	Col. 20th Ky. Infy.................	July 10, 1863, to Oct. 9, 1863.	
71st Ohio Infy..........June, 1863	From Clarksville and Ft. Donelson.	To Gallatin, Tenn.................	Oct., 1863
102d Ohio Infy..........June, 1863	From Clarksville and Ft. Donelson.	To Unatt. Dept. Cumb'd............	Oct., 1863
83d Ill. Infy............June, 1863	From Clarksville and Ft. Donelson.	To Clarksville, Tenn..............	Oct., 1863
28th Ky. Infy...........June, 1863	From Clarksville and Ft. Donelson.	To Unass'd Dept. Cumb'd...........	Oct., 1863
Batty. C, 2d Ill. Arty.....June, 1863	From Clarksville and Ft. Donelson.	To Dist. Nashville Dept. Cumb'd....	Oct., 1863
Batty. H, 2d Ill. Arty.....June, 1863	From Clarksville and Ft. Donelson.	To Clarksville, Tenn..............	Oct., 1863
Batty. A, 1st Tenn. Arty..June, 1863	From 1-Brig. 1-Div. 23-Corps Ohio.	To 3-Brig. 3-Div. Res. Corps.......	Aug., 1863

2d BRIGADE.—

	COMMANDERS.	
W. T. Ward	Brigadier General	June 8, 1862, to Aug. 5, 1863.
Benj. Harrison	Col. 70th Ind. Infy	Aug. 5, 1863, to Oct. 9, 1863.

102d Ill. Infy	June, 1863	From Garrison Gallatin, Tenn	To Ward's Brig. Nashville, Tenn	Oct., 1863
105th Ill. Infy	June, 1863	From Garrison Gallatin, Tenn	To Ward's Brig. Nashville, Tenn	Oct., 1863
129th Ill. Infy	June, 1863	From Dist. West Ky. Dept. Ohio	To Ward's Brig. Nashville, Tenn	Oct., 1863
70th Ind. Infy	June, 1863	From Garrison Gallatin, Tenn	To Ward's Brig. Nashville, Tenn	Oct., 1863
79th Ohio Infy	June, 1863	From Garrison Gallatin, Tenn	To Ward's Brig. Nashville, Tenn	Oct., 1863
Batty. E, 1st Mich. Arty	June, 1863	From Arty. Nashville, Tenn	To Ward's Brig. Nashville, Tenn	Oct., 1863

3d BRIGADE.—

	COMMANDER.	
J. G. Spear	Brigadier General	Aug. 30, 1863, to Oct. 9, 1863.

3d Tenn. Infy	Aug., 1863	From 3-Brig. 3-Div. 23-Corps Ohio	To 2-Brig. 2-Div. 14-Corps	Oct., 1863
5th Tenn. Infy	Aug., 1863	From 3-Brig. 3-Div. 23-Corps Ohio	To 2-Brig. 2-Div. 14-Corps	Oct., 1863
6th Tenn. Infy	Aug., 1863	From 3-Brig. 3-Div. 23-Corps Ohio	To 2-Brig. 2-Div. 14-Corps	Oct., 1863
1st Tenn. Batty	Aug., 1863	From 1-Brig. 3-Div. Res. Corps	To 2-Div. Arty. Res. Cumb'd	Oct., 1863

NASHVILLE, TENN.—

	COMMANDER.	
R. S. Granger	Brigadier General	May 28, 1863.

17th Ky. Infy	June, 1863	From Post Nashville, Tenn	To 1-Brig. 3-Div. 21-Corps	
1st Middle Tenn. Infy	June, 1863	From Post Nashville, Tenn	To 1-Brig. 2-Div. Cav. C. Cumb'd	June, 1863
3d Tenn. Cav	June, 1863	From Post Nashville, Tenn	To 2-Brig. 1-Div. Cav. C. Cumb'd	June, 1863
4th Tenn. Cav	June, 1863	From Post Nashville, Tenn	To Dist. N. C. Ky. Dept. Ohio	Aug., 1863
12th Ind. Batty	June, 1863	From Post Nashville, Tenn	To Unatt. Post Nashville, Tenn	Oct., 1863
20th Ind. Batty	June, 1863	From Post Nashville, Tenn	To Unatt. Post Nashville, Tenn	Oct., 1863

GALLATIN, TENN.—

129th Ill. Infy	June, 1863	From Garrison Gallatin Cumb'd	To 2-Brig. 3-Div. Res. C. Cumb'd	June, 1863
106th Ohio Infy	June, 1863	From Dist. West Ky. Dept. Ohio	To Unass'd 4-Div. 20-Corps Cumb'd	Apr., 1864
13th Ind. Batty	June, 1863	From Ward's Brig. Gallatin, Tenn	To Unass'd 4-Div. 20-Corps Cumb'd	Apr., 1864
50th Ohio Infy	Sept., 1863	From Unatt. 2-Div. 23-Corps Ohio	To 3-Brig. 4-Div. 23-Corps Ohio	Apr., 1864
71st Ohio Infy	Sept., 1863	From 1-Brig. 3-Div. Res. Corps	To Unass'd 4-Div. 20-Corps Cumb'd	Apr., 1864

Fourth Army Corps---Army and Department of the Cumberland

Re-created Sept. 28, 1863, by General Order No. 322, A. G. O., and organized by consolidation of the 20th and 21st Army Corps, Dept. of the Cumberland. Discontinued Aug. 1, 1865.

	COMMANDERS.	
Gordon Granger	Major General	Oct. 10, 1863, to Apr. 10, 1864.
O. O. Howard	Major General	Apr. 10, 1864, to July 27, 1864.
D. S. Stanley	Major General	July 27, 1864, to Dec. 1, 1864.
T. J. Wood	Brigadier General	Dec. 1, 1864, to Jan. 31, 1865.
D. S. Stanley	Major General	Jan. 31, 1865, to Aug. 1, 1865.

1st DIVISION.—

	COMMANDERS.	
John M. Palmer	Major General	Oct. 10, 1863, to Oct. 27, 1863.
Charles Cruft	Brigadier General	Oct. 27, 1863, to Nov. 21, 1863.
D. S. Stanley	Major General	Nov. 21, 1863, to Feb. 13, 1864.
Charles Cruft	Brigadier General	Feb. 13, 1864, to Mch. 14, 1864.
D. S. Stanley	Major General	Mch. 14, 1864, to July 27, 1864.
William Grose	Col. 36th Ind. Infy	July 27, 1864, to Aug. 5, 1864.
Nathan Kimball	Brigadier General	Aug. 5, 1864, to Sept. 19, 1864.
W. C. Whittaker	Brigadier General	Sept. 19, 1864, to Nov. 28, 1864.
Nathan Kimball	Brigadier General	Nov. 28, 1864, to Feb. 16, 1865.
William Grose	Brigadier General	Feb. 16, 1865, to Mch. 16, 1865.
Nathan Kimball	Brigadier General	Mch. 16, 1865, to Aug. 1, 1865.

1st BRIGADE.—

	COMMANDERS.	
T. D. Sedgwick	Col. 2d Ky. Infy	Oct. 10, 1863, to Nov. 21, 1863.
D. A. Enyart	Col. 1st Ky. Infy	Nov. 21, 1863, to Jan. 15, 1864.
Charles Cruft	Brigadier General	Jan. 15, 1864, to Feb. 13, 1864.
D. A. Enyart	Col. 1st Ky. Infy	Feb. 13, 1864, to Mch. 14, 1864.
Charles Cruft	Brigadier General	Mch. 14, 1864, to June 10, 1864.
I. M. Kirby	Col. 101st Ohio Infy	June 10, 1864, to Sept. 20, 1864.
W. E. McMackin	Lt.-Col. 21st Ky. Infy	Sept. 20, 1864, to Oct. 21, 1864.
I. M. Kirby	Col. 101st Ohio Infy	Oct. 21, 1864, to June 12, 1865.
T. E. Rose	Col. 77th Penna. Infy	June 12, 1865, to Aug. 1, 1865.

21st Ill. Infy	Oct., 1863	From 2-Brig. 1-Div. 20-C. Cumb'd	To 2-Brig. 1-Div. 4-Corps Cumb'd	June, 1865
38th Ill. Infy	Oct., 1863	From 2-Brig. 1-Div. 20-C. Cumb'd	To 2-Brig. 1-Div. 4-Corps Cumb'd	June, 1865
29th Ind. Infy	Oct., 1863	From 2-Brig. 2-Div. 20-C. Cumb'd	To 1st Sep. Brig. Chattanooga	Apr., 1864
31st Ind. Infy	Oct., 1863	From 1-Brig. 2-Div. 21-C. Cumb'd	To Dept. Texas	Aug., 1865
81st Ind. Infy	Oct., 1863	From 2-Brig. 1-Div. 20-C. Cumb's.	No change to Muster Out	June, 1864
1st Ky. Infy	Oct., 1863	From 1-Brig. 2-Div. 21-C. Cumb'd	No change to Muster Out	June, 1864
2d Ky. Infy	Oct., 1863	From 1-Brig. 2-Div. 21-C. Cumb'd	No change to Muster Out	June, 1864
90th Ohio Infy	Oct., 1863	From 1-Brig. 2-Div. 21-C. Cumb'd	No change to Muster Out	June, 1865
101st Ohio Infy	Oct., 1863	From 2-Brig. 1-Div. 20-C. Cumb'd	No change to Muster Out	June, 1865
51st Ohio Infy	June, 1865	From 2-Brig. 1-Div. 4-Corps	To Dept. Texas	Aug., 1865
77th Penna. Infy	June, 1865	From 3-Brig. 1-Div. 4-Corps	To Dept. Texas	Aug., 1865
21st Ky. Infy	June, 1865	From 2-Brig. 1-Div. 4-Corps	To Dept. Texas	Aug., 1865
23d Ky. Infy	June, 1865	From 2-Brig. 1-Div. 4-Corps	To Dept. Texas	Aug., 1865

2d BRIGADE.—

	COMMANDERS.	
W. C. Whitaker	Brigadier General	Oct. 10, 1863, to Dec. 8, 1863.
S. M. Barnes	Col. 8th Ky. Infy	Dec. 8, 1863, to Jan. 15, 1864.
J. H. Moore	Col. 115th Ill. Infy	Jan. 15, 1864, to Mch. 15, 1864.
W. C. Whitaker	Brigadier General	Mch. 15, 1864, to June 30, 1864.
J. E. Taylor	Col. 40th Ohio Infy	June 30, 1864, to Sept. 21, 1864.
T. E. Champion	Col. 96th Ill. Infy	Sept. 21, 1864, to Oct. 30, 1864.
James C. Evans	Lt.-Col. 21st Ky. Infy	Oct. 30, 1864, to Nov. 28, 1864.
W. C. Whitaker	Brigadier General	Nov. 28, 1864, to Dec. 23, 1864.
J. H. Moore	Col. 115th Ill. Infy	Dec. 23, 1864, to June 7, 1865.
I. C. B. Suman	Col. 9th Ind. Infy	June 7, 1865, to Aug. 1, 1865.

2d BRIGADE.—Continued.

22d Ind. Infy	Oct., 1863	From 1-Brig. 1-Div. 20-C. Cumb'd	To 1-Brig. 2-Div. 4-Corps Cumb'd	Oct., 1864
35th Ind. Infy	Oct., 1863	From 3-Brig. 3-Div. 21-C. Cumb'd	No change to Muster Out	Aug., 1865
59th Ill. Infy	Oct., 1863	From 1-Brig. 1-Div. 20-C. Cumb'd	To 3-Brig. 1-Div. 4-Corps Cumb'd	Oct., 1864
74th Ill. Infy	Oct., 1863	From 1-Brig. 1-Div. 20-C. Cumb'd	To 1-Brig. 2-Div. 4-Corps Cumb'd	Oct., 1864
75th Ill. Infy	Oct., 1863	From 1-Brig. 1-Div. 20-C. Cumb'd	To 3-Brig. 1-Div. 4-Corps Cumb'd	Oct., 1864
8th Ky. Infy	Oct., 1863	From 3-Brig. 3-Div. 21-C. Cumb'd	To 1st Sep. Brig. Chattanooga	May, 1864
51st Ohio Infy	Oct., 1863	From 3-Brig. 3-Div. 21-C. Cumb'd	To 1-Brig. 1-Div. 4-Corps Cumb'd	June, 1865
99th Ohio Infy	Oct., 1863	From 3-Brig. 3-Div. 21-C. Cumb'd	To 2-Brig. 1-Div. 23-Corps Ohio	June, 1864
96th Ill. Infy	Oct., 1863	From 3-Brig. 1-Div. 4-Corps Cumb'd	No change to Muster Out	June, 1865
115th Ill. Infy	Oct., 1863	From 1-Brig. 2-Div. 4-Corps Cumb'd	No change to Muster Out	June, 1865
84th Ind. Infy	Oct., 1863	From 1-Brig. 1-Div. 4-Corps Cumb'd	To 3-Brig. 1-Div. 4-Corps Cumb'd	Aug., 1864
40th Ohio Infy	Oct., 1863	From 1-Brig. 2-Div. 4-Corps Cumb'd	No change to Muster Out	Nov., 1864
21st Ky. Infy	Jan., 1864	From Unass'd Dept. Cumb'd	To 1-Brig. 1-Div. 4-Corps Cumb'd	June, 1865
59th Ill. Infy	May, 1864	From 3-Brig. 1-Div. 4-Corps Cumb'd	To 3-Brig. 1-Div. 4-Corps Cumb'd	Aug., 1864
45th Ohio Infy	June, 1864	From 1-Brig. 2-Div. 23-Corps Ohio	No change to Muster Out	June, 1865
23d Ky. Infy	Aug., 1864	From 2-Brig. 3-Div. 4-Corps Cumb'd	To 1-Brig. 1-Div. 4-Corps Cumb'd	June, 1865
84th Ill. Infy	May, 1865	From 3-Brig. 1-Div. 4-Corps Cumb'd	No change to Muster Out	June, 1865
9th Ind. Infy	June, 1865	From 3-Brig. 1-Div. 4-Corps Cumb'd	To Dept. Texas	Aug., 1865
30th Ind. Infy	June, 1865	From 3-Brig. 1-Div. 4-Corps Cumb'd	To Dept. Texas	Aug., 1865
36th Ind. Infy	June, 1865	From 3-Brig. 1-Div. 4-Corps Cumb'd	No change to Muster Out	July, 1865
21st Ill. Infy	June, 1865	From 1-Brig. 1-Div. 4-Corps Cumb'd	To Dept. Teaxs	Aug., 1865
38th Ill. Infy	June, 1865	From 1-Brig. 1-Div. 4-Corps Cumb'd	To Dept. Texas	Aug., 1865

3d BRIGADE.— COMMANDERS.

Commander	Rank	Dates
William Grose	Col. 36th Ill. Infy	Oct. 10, 1863, to Dec. 31, 1863.
J. E. Bennett	Col. 75th Ill. Infy	Dec. 31, 1863, to Jan. 31, 1864.
William Grose	Col. 36th Ill. Infy	Jan. 31, 1864, to July 27, 1864.
P. S. Post	Col. 59th Ill. Infy	July 27, 1864, to Aug. 5, 1864.
William Grose	Brigadier General	Aug. 5, 1864, to Sept. 5, 1864.
J. E. Bennett	Col. 75th Ill. Infy	Sept. 5, 1864, to Oct. 21, 1864.
L. H. Waters	Col. 84th Ill. Infy	Oct. 21, 1864, to Nov. 29, 1864.
William Grose	Brigadier General	Nov. 29, 1864, to Feb. 16, 1865.
J. E. Bennett	Col. 75th Ill. Infy	Feb. 16, 1865, to Mch. 16, 1865.
William Grose	Brigadier General	Mch. 16, 1865, to Mch. 31, 1865.
J. E. Bennett	Col. 75th Ill. Infy	Mch. 31, 1865, to Apr. 9, 1865.
L. H. Waters	Col. 84th Ill. Infy	Apr. 9, 1865, to May 9, 1865.
William Grose	Brigadier General	May 9, 1865, to June 7, 1865.

Brigade discontinued June 7, 1865.

9th Ind. Infy	Oct., 1863	From 2-Brig. 2-Div. 21 C. Cumb'd	To 2-Brig. 1-Div. 4-Corps Cumb'd	June, 1865
30th Ind. Infy	Oct., 1863	From 2-Brig. 2-Div. 20-C. Cumb'd	To 2-Brig. 1-Div. 4-Corps Cumb'd	June, 1865
36th Ind. Infy	Oct., 1863	From 3-Brig. 2-Div. 21-C. Cumb'd	To 2-Brig. 1-Div. 4-Corps Cumb'd	Oct., 1863
84th Ind. Infy	Oct., 1863	From 1-Brig. 1-Div. Res. C. Cumb'd	To 2-Brig. 1-Div. 4-Corps Cumb'd	Oct., 1864
24th Ohio Infy	Oct., 1863	From 3-Brig. 2-Div. 21-C. Cumb'd	To 1st Sep. Brig. Chattanooga	May, 1864
77th Penna. Infy	Oct., 1863	From 2-Brig. 2-Div. 20-Corps Cumb'd	To 1-Brig. 1-Div. 4-Corps Cumb'd	June, 1865
84th Illinois Infy	Oct., 1863	From 3-Brig. 2-Div. 21-Corps Cumb'd	To 2-Brig. 1-Div. 4-Corps Cumb'd	May, 1865
96th Illinois Infy	Oct., 1863	From 1-Brig. 1-Div. Res. C. Cumb'd	To 2-Brig. 1-Div. 4-Corps Cumb'd	Oct., 1864
59th Illinois Infy	Oct., 1863	From 2-Brig. 1-Div. 4-Corps Cumb'd	To 2-Brig. 1-Div. 4-Corps Cumb'd	May, 1865
75th Illinois Infy	Oct., 1863	From 2-Brig. 1-Div. 4-Corps Cumb'd	No change to Muster Out	June, 1865
80th Illinois Infy	Dec., 1863	From 3-Brig. 3-Div. 11-Corps Cumb'd	No change to Muster Out	June, 1865
84th Indiana Infy	Aug., 1864	From 1-Brig. 1-Div. 4-Corps Cumb'd	No change to Muster Out	June, 1865
59th Illinois Infy	Aug., 1864	From 2-Brig. 1-Div. 4-Corps Cumb'd	To 2-Brig. 3-Div. 4-Corps Cumb'd	Aug., 1864

ARTILLERY, 1st DIVISION.—

5th Indiana Batty	Oct., 1863	From Arty. 2-Div. 20-Corps Cumb'd	To Arty. Brig. 4-Corps Cumb'd	July, 1864
Batty. H, 4th U. S. Arty.	Oct., 1863	From Arty. 2-Div. 21-Corps Cumb'd	To 1-Div. Arty. Res. Cumberland	Mch., 1864
Batty. M, 4th U. S. Arty.	Oct., 1863	From Arty. 2-Div. 21-Corps Cumb'd	To 1-Div. Arty. Res. Cumberland	Mch., 1864
Indpt. Batty. B, Pa. Arty.	Apr., 1864	From 3-Div. 4-Corps Cumberland	To Arty. Brig. 4-Corps Cumberland	July, 1864

2d DIVISION.— COMMANDERS.

Commander	Rank	Dates
P. H. Sheridan	Major General	Oct. 10, 1863, to Feb. 17, 1864.
G. D. Wagner	Brigadier General	Feb. 17, 1864, to Feb. 27, 1864.
P. H. Sheridan	Major General	Feb. 27, 1864, to Apr. 16, 1864.
John Newton	Brigadier General	Apr. 16, 1864, to Sept. 30, 1864.
D. G. Wagner	Brigadier General	Sept. 30, 1864, to Dec. 2, 1864.
W. L. Elliott	Brigadier General	Dec. 2, 1864, to June 24, 1865.
E. Opdycke	Col. 125th Ohio Infy	June 24, 1865, to July 11, 1865.
J. Conrad	Col. 15th Missouri Infy	July 11, 1865, to Aug. 2, 1865.

1st BRIGADE, 2d DIVISION.— COMMANDERS.

Commander	Rank	Dates
J. B. Steedman	Brigadier General	Oct. 10, 1863, to Oct. 18, 1863.
F. T. Sherman	Col. 88th Illinois Infy	Oct. 18, 1863, to Mch. 4, 1864.
J. F. Jaques	Col. 73d Illinois Infy	Mch. 4, 1864, to Apr. 6, 1864.
F. T. Sherman	Col. 88th Illinois Infy	Apr. 6, 1864, to May 22, 1864.
N. Kimball	Brigadier General	May 22, 1864, to Aug. 4, 1864.
E. Opdycke	Col. 125th Ohio Infy	Aug. 4, 1864, to Feb. 15, 1865.
John Russell	Lt.-Col. 44th Illinois Infy	Feb. 15, 1865, to Mch. 15, 1865.
E. Opdycke	Bvt. Brig. General	Mch. 15, 1865, to June 7, 1865.
John Russell	Lt.-Col. 44th Illinois Infy	June 7, 1865, to Aug. 1, 1865.

24th Wisconsin Infy	Oct., 1863	From 1-B. 3-Div. 20-Corps Cumb'd	No change to Muster Out	Nov., 1863
21st Michigan Infy	Oct., 1863	From 1-B. 3-Div. 20-Corps Cumb'd	To Eng. Brig. Dept. Cumberland	Aug., 1865
36th Illinois Infy	Oct., 1863	From 1-B. 3-Div. 20-Corps Cumb'd	To Dept. Texas	Aug., 1865
44th Illinois Infy	Oct., 1863	From 2-Brig. 3-Div. 20-Corps Cumb'd	To Dept. Texas	June, 1865
73d Illinois Infy	Oct., 1863	From 2-Brig. 3-Div. 20-Corps Cumb'd	No change to Muster Out	June, 1865
88th Illinois Infy	Oct., 1863	From 1-Brig. 3-Div. 20-Corps Cumb'd	No change to Muster Out	June, 1865
115th Illinois Infy	Oct., 1863	From 1-B. 1-Div. Res. Corps Cumb'd	To 2-Brig. 1-Div. 4-Corps	Oct., 1863
40th Ohio Infy	Oct., 1863	From 1-B. 1-Div. Res. Corps Cumb'd	To 2-Brig. 1-Div. 4-Corps	Oct., 1863
2d Missouri Infy	Oct., 1863	From 1-B. 3-Div. 20-Corps Cumb'd	To Dalton, Ga., Dept. Cumberland	May, 1864
15th Missouri Infy	Oct., 1863	From 2-Brig. 3-Div. 20-Corps Cumb'd	To 3-Brig. 2-Div. 4-Corps	Apr., 1864
22d Indiana Infy	Oct., 1863	From 2-Brig. 1-Div. 4-Corps Cumb'd	To 3-Brig. 2-Div. 14-Corps	Apr., 1864
74th Illinois Infy	Oct., 1863	From 2-Brig. 1-Div. 4-Corps Cumb'd	No change to Muster Out	June, 1865
28th Kentucky Infy	Apr., 1864	From Unassigned Dist. Nashville	To 2-Brig. 2-Div. 4-Corps	May, 1864
125th Ohio Infy	Oct., 1864	From 3-Brig. 2-Div. 4-Corps	To Dept. Texas	Aug., 1865
57th Indiana Infy	June, 1865	From 2-Brig. 2-Div. 4-Corps	To Dept. Texas	Aug., 1865
26th Ohio Infy	June, 1865	From 2-Brig. 2-Div. 4-Corps	To Dept. Texas	Aug., 1865
40th Indiana Infy	June, 1865	From 2-Brig. 2-Div. 4-Corps	To Dept. Texas	Aug., 1865

2d BRIGADE.— COMMANDERS.

G. D. Wagner.........	Brigadier General.................	Oct. 10, 1863, to Jan. 12, 1864.
J. Q. Lane............	Col. 97th Ohio Infy.............	Jan. 12, 1864, to Apr. 21, 1864.
G. D. Wagner.........	Brigadier General...............	Apr. 21, 1864, to July 10, 1864.
J. W. Blake..........	Col. 40th Indiana Infy.........	July 10, 1864, to July 25, 1864.
G. D. Wagner.........	Brigadier General...............	July 25, 1864, to Sept. 30, 1864.
J. W. Blake..........	Col. 40th Indiana Infy.........	Sept. 30, 1864, to Oct. 10, 1864.
William Grose........	Brigadier General...............	Oct. 10, 1864, to Nov. 29, 1864.
J. Q. Lane...........	Col. 97th Ohio Infy............	Nov. 29, 1864, to Feb. 8, 1865.
F. Van Derveer.......	Brigadier General...............	Feb. 8, 1865, to June 5, 1865.
L. P. Bradley........	Brigadier General...............	June 5, 1865, to June 16, 1865.
J. Conrad...........	Col. 15th Missouri............	June 16, 1865, to July 12, 1865.
E. D. Swain.........	Lt.-Col. 42d Illinois Infy.....	July 12, 1865, to Aug. 1, 1865.

100th Illinois Infy......Oct., 1863	From 1-Brig. 1-Div. 21-Corps Cumb'd	No change to Muster Out.......	June, 1865
13th Michigan Infy.......Oct., 1863	From 1-Brig. 1-Div. 21-Corps Cumb'd	To Eng. Brig. Dept. Cumberland....	Nov., 1863
26th Ohio Infy...........Oct., 1863	From 1-Brig. 1-Div. 21-Corps Cumb'd	To 1-Brig. 2-Div. 4-Corps.......	June, 1865
97th Ohio Infy...........Oct., 1863	From 2-Brig. 1-Div. 21-Corps Cumb'd	No change to Muster Out........	June, 1865
15th Indiana Infy........Oct., 1863	From 2-Brig. 1-Div. 21-Corps Cumb'd	To Garrison Chattanooga, Tenn.....	Apr., 1864
40th Indiana Infy........Oct., 1863	From 2-Brig. 1-Div. 21-Corps Cumb'd	To 1-Brig. 2-Div. 4-Corps.......	June, 1865
57th Indiana Infy........Oct., 1863	From 2-Brig. 1-Div. 21-Corps Cumb'd	To 1-Brig. 2-Div. 4-Corps.......	June, 1865
58th Indiana Infy........Oct., 1863	From 1-Brig. 1-Div. 21-Corps Cumb'd	To Pontoneers Dept. Cumberland...	Apr., 1864
28th Kentucky Infy.......May, 1864	From 1-Brig. 2-Div. 4-Corps Cumb'd	To Dept. Texas.............	Aug., 1865
51st Indiana Infy........Sept., 1864	From 1st Separate Brig. Chatt.....	To 1-Brig. 3-Div. 4-Corps......	Nov., 1864
64th Ohio Infy..........June, 1865	From 3-Brig. 2-Div. 4-Corps.....	To Dept. Texas.............	Aug., 1865
65th Ohio Infy..........June, 1865	From 3-Brig. 2-Div. 4-Corps.....	To Dept. Texas.............	Aug., 1865
42d Illinois Infy........June, 1865	From 3-Brig. 2-Div. 4-Corps.....	To Dept. Texas.............	Aug., 1865
51st Illinois Infy........June, 1865	From 3-Brig. 2-Div. 4-Corps.....	To Dept. Texas.............	Aug., 1865
15th Missouri Infy.......June, 1865	From 3-Brig. 2-Div. 4-Corps.....	To Dept. Texas.............	Aug., 1865

3d BRIGADE.— COMMANDERS.

C. G. Harker.........	Col. 65th Ohio Infy.............	Oct. 10, 1863, to June 27, 1864.	Killed.
L. P. Bradley........	Col. 51st Illinois Infy.........	June 27, 1864, to Dec. 16, 1864.
J. Conrad...........	Col. 15th Missouri Infy..........	Dec. 16, 1864, to May 25, 1865.
L. P. Bradley........	Brigadier General.................	May 25, 1865, to June 5, 1865.

Brigade discontinued June 7, 1865.

64th Ohio Infy..........Oct., 1863	From 2-B. 1-Div. 21-Corps Cumb'd.	To 2-Brig. 2-Div. 4-Corps.....	June, 1865
65th Ohio Infy..........Oct., 1863	From 2-B. 1-Div. 21-Corps Cumb'd.	To 2-Brig. 2-Div. 4-Corps.....	June, 1865
125th Ohio Infy..........Oct., 1863	From 2-B. 1-Div. 21-Corps Cumb'd.	To 1-Brig. 2-Div. 4-Corps.....	Oct., 1864
3d Kentucky Infy.........Oct., 1863	From 3-Brig. 1-Div. 21-Corps Cumb'd	No change to Muster Out.......	Jan., 1865
22d Illinois Infy.........Oct., 1863	From 3-Brig. 3-Div. 20-Corps Cumb'd	No change to Muster Out.......	June, 1864
27th Illinois Infy.........Oct., 1863	From 3-Brig. 3-Div. 20-Corps Cumb'd	No change to Muster Out.......	Aug., 1864
42d Illinois Infy.........Oct., 1863	From 3-Brig. 3-Div. 20-Corps Cumb'd	To 2-Brig. 2-Div. 4-Corps.....	June, 1865
51st Illinois Infy.........Oct., 1863	From 3-Brig. 3-Div. 20-Corps Cumb'd	To 2-Brig. 2-Div. 4-Corps.....	June, 1865
79th Illinois Infy.........Oct., 1863	From 2-Brig. 2-Div. 20-Corps Cumb'd	No change to Muster Out.......	June, 1865
15th Missouri Infy........Apr., 1864	From 1-Brig. 2-Div. 4-Corps.......	To 2-Brig. 2-Div. 4-Corps.....	June, 1865

ARTILLERY, 2d DIVISION.—

10th Indiana Batty.......Oct., 1863	From Arty. 1-Div. 21-Corps Cumb'd.	To Garrison Arty. Chattanooga....	Nov., 1863
11th Indiana Batty.......Oct., 1863	From Arty. 3-Div. 20-Corps Cumb'd	To 2-Div. Arty. Res. Cumberland....	Oct., 1863
Batty. G, 1st Mo. Arty...Oct., 1863	From Arty. 3-Div. 20-Corps Cumb'd	To Garrison Arty. Chattanooga.....	Nov. 1863
Batty. M, 1st Ill. Arty....Oct., 1863	From Arty. 1-Div. Res. Corps Cum'd	To Arty. Brig. 4-Corps.........	July, 1864
Batty. I, 1st Ohio Arty...Nov., 1863	From Arty. Brig. 11-Corps Cumb'd	To Garrison Arty. Chattanooga....	Dec., 1863
Batty. G, 4th U. S. Arty..Nov., 1863	From Arty. Brig. 11-Corps Cumb'd	To Arty. Brig. 11-Corps........	Dec., 1863
Batty. H, 5th U. S. Arty..Nov., 1863	From Arty. 1-Div. 14-Corps Cumb'd	To Arty. 1-Div. 14-Corps......	Dec., 1863
Batty. A, 1st Ohio Arty...Apr., 1864	From 2-Div. Arty. Reserve........	To Arty. Brig. 4-Corps.........	July, 1864

3d DIVISION.— COMMANDERS.

Thomas J. Wood......	Brigadier General.................	Oct. 10, 1863, to Jan. 8, 1864.
A. Willich...........	Brigadier General.................	Jan. 8, 1864, to Feb. 12, 1864.
Thomas J. Wood......	Brigadier General.................	Feb. 12, 1864, to Sept. 2, 1864.
P. S. Post...........	Col. 59th Illinois Infy.........	Sept. 2, 1864, to Sept. 6, 1864.
Thomas J. Wood......	Brigadier General.................	Sept. 6, 1864, to Dec. 2, 1864.
Samuel Beatty........	Brigadier General.................	Dec. 2, 1864, to Jan. 31, 1865.
Thomas J. Wood......	Major General	Jan. 31, 1865, to Feb. 7, 1865.
Samuel Beatty........	Brigadier General.................	Feb. 7, 1865, to Mch. 20, 1865.
Thomas J. Wood.....	Major General	Mch. 20, 1865, to Aug. 1, 1865.

1st BRIGADE.— COMMANDERS.

August Willich........	Brigadier General.................	Oct. 10, 1863, to Jan. 8, 1864.
R. H. Nodine.........	Col. 25th Illinois Infy.........	Jan. 8, 1864, to Mch. 11, 1864.
C. T. Hotchkiss.......	Col. 89th Illinois Infy.........	Mch. 11, 1864, to Apr. 20, 1864.
W. H. Gibson.........	Col. 49th Ohio Infy............	Apr. 20, 1864, to May 3, 1864.
August Willich........	Brigadier General.................	May 3, 1864, to May 15, 1864.
W. H. Gibson.........	Col. 49th Ohio Infy............	May 15, 1864, to June 21, 1864.
R. H. Nodine.........	Col. 25th Illinois Infy.........	June 21, 1864, to June 22, 1864.
W. H. Gibson.........	Col. 49th Ohio Infy............	June 22, 1864, to Aug. 25, 1864.
C. T. Hotchkiss.......	Col. 89th Illinois Infy.........	Aug. 25, 1864, to Sept. 15, 1864.
J. A. Martin.........	Col. 8th Kansas Infy............	Sept. 15, 1864, to Nov. 17, 1864.
A. D. Streight........	Col. 51st Indiana Infy..........	Nov. 17, 1864, to Mch. 15, 1865.
C. T. Hotchkiss.......	Col. 89th Illinois Infy.........	Mch. 15, 1865, to May 15, 1865.
C. C. Doolittle.......	Brigadier General.................	May 15, 1865, to June 2, 1865.
August Willich........	Brigadier General.................	June 2, 1865, to Aug. 1, 1865.

15th Ohio Infy..........Oct., 1863	From 1-Brig. 2-Div. 20-Corps Cumb'd	No change to Muster Out........	Aug., 1865
49th Ohio Infy..........Oct., 1863	From 1-Brig. 2-Div. 20-Corps Cumb'd	To Dept. Texas.............	Aug., 1865
32d Indiana Infy.........Oct., 1863	From 1-Brig. 2-Div. 20-Corps Cumb'd	To Post Chattanooga, Tenn.....	Oct., 1864
15th Wisconsin Infy......Oct., 1863	From 3-Brig. 1-Div. 20-Corps Cumb'd	To Post Chattanooga, Tenn.....	Oct., 1864
8th Kansas Infy.........Oct., 1863	From 3-Brig. 1-Div. 20-Corps Cumb'd	To Dept. Texas.............	Aug., 1865
25th Illinois Infy........Oct., 1863	From 3-Brig. 3-Div. 20-Corps Cumb'd	No change to Muster Out.......	Sept., 1864
35th Illinois Infy........Oct., 1863	From 3-Brig. 3-Div. 20-Corps Cumb'd	No change to Muster Out.......	Sept., 1864
89th Illinois Infy........Oct., 1863	From 1-Brig. 2-Div. 20-Corps Cumb'd	No change to Muster Out.......	June, 1865
68th Indiana............Oct., 1863	From 2-Brig. 4-Div. 14-Corps Cumb'd	To Garrison Chattanooga, Tenn..	Apr., 1864
51st Indiana Infy........Nov., 1864	From 2-Brig. 2-Div. 4-Corps Cumb'd	To Dept. Texas.............	Aug., 1865
32d Indiana Infy........June, 1865	From 2-B. 1-Sep. Div. D. Etowah C'd	To Dept. Texas.............	Aug., 1865
71st Ohio Infy..........June, 1865	From 2-Brig. 3-Div. 4-Corps........	To Dept. Texas.............	Aug., 1865

2d BRIGADE.— COMMANDERS.

W. B. Hazen	Brigadier General	Oct. 10, 1863, to Mch. 17, 1864.
N. L. Anderson	Col. 6th Ohio Infy	Mch. 17, 1864, to Apr. 17, 1864.
W. B. Hazen	Brigadier General	Apr. 17, 1864, to Aug. 17, 1864.
O. H. Payne	Col. 124th Ohio Infy	Aug. 17, 1864, to Aug. 19, 1864.
P. S. Post	Col. 59th Illinois Infy	Aug. 19, 1864, to Dec. 16, 1864.
R. L. Kimberly	Lt.-Col. 41st Ohio Infy	Dec. 16, 1864, to Dec. 26, 1864.
H. K. McConnell	Lt.-Col. 71st Ohio Infy	Dec. 26, 1864, to June 7, 1865.
Samuel Beatty	Brigadier General	June 7, 1865, to Aug. 1, 1865.

6th Indiana Infy	Oct., 1863	From 3-B. 2-Div. 20-Corps Cumb'd	No change to Muster Out	Sept., 1864
5th Kentucky Infy	Oct., 1863	From 3-B. 2-Div. 20-Corps Cumb'd	To Decatur, Ala., Dist North. Ala	July, 1864
6th Kentucky Infy	Oct., 1863	From 2-Brig. 2-Div. 21-Corps Cumb'd	To 3-Brig. Def. Nash. & Chat. R. R.	Aug., 1864
23d Kentucky Infy	Oct., 1863	From 3-Brig. 2-Div. 21-Corps Cmb'w	To 2-Brig. 1-Div. 4-Corps	Aug., 1864
1st Ohio Infy	Oct., 1863	From 3-Brig. 2-Div. 20-Corps Cumb'd	No change to Muster Out	Oct., 1864
6th Ohio Infy	Oct., 1863	From 3-Brig. 2-Div. 21-Corps Cmb'w	No change to Muster Out	June, 1864
41st Ohio Infy	Oct., 1863	From 2-Brig. 2-Div. 21-Corps Cumb'd	To Dept. Texas	Aug., 1865
93d Ohio Infy	Oct., 1863	From 3-Brig. 2-Div. 20-Corps Cumb'd	No change to Muster Out	June, 1865
124th Ohio Infy	Oct., 1863	From 2-Brig. 2-Div. 21-Corps Cumb'd	No change to Muster Out	June, 1865
59th Illinois Infy	Aug., 1864	From 3-Brig. 1-Div. 4-Corps Cumb'd	To Dept. Texas	Aug., 1865
71st Ohio Infy	Aug., 1864	From Unass'd 4-Div. 20-Corps	To 1-Brig. 3-Div. 4-Corps	June, 1865
3d Michigan Infy	June, 1865	From 3-Brig. 3-Div. 4-Corps	To Dept. Texas	Aug., 1865
4th Michigan Infy	June, 1865	From 3-Brig. 3-Div. 4-Corps	To Dept. Texas	Aug., 1865
13th Ohio Infy	June, 1865	From 3-Brig. 3-Div. 4-Corps	To Dept. Texas	Aug., 1865
19th Ohio Infy	June, 1865	From 3-Brig. 3-Div. 4-Corps	To Dept. Texas	Aug., 1865

3d BRIGADE.— COMMANDERS.

Samuel Beatty	Brigadier General	Oct. 10, 1863, to Feb. 7, 1864.
Alex. M. Stout	Col. 7th Kentucky Infy	Feb. 7, 1864, to Mch. 20, 1864.
Fred'k. Knefler	Col. 79th Indiana Infy	Mch. 20, 1864, to Apr. 16, 1864.
Samuel Beatty	Brigadier General	Apr. 16, 1864, to May 23, 1864.
Fred'k. Knefler	Col. 79th Indiana Infy	May 23, 1864, to Nov. 6, 1864.
Samuel Beatty	Brigadier General	Nov. 6, 1864, to Dec. 2, 1864.
Fred'k. Knefler	Col. 79th Indiana Infy	Dec. 2, 1864, to Feb. 21, 1865.
G. F. Dick	Col. 86th Indiana Infy	Feb. 21, 1865, to Mch. 20, 1865.
Samuel Beatty	Brigadier General	Mch. 20, 1865, to June 7, 1865.

Brigade discontinued June 7, 1865.

13th Ohio Infy	Oct., 1863	From 2-Brig. 3-Div. 21-Corps Cumb'd	To 2-Brig. 3-Div. 4-Corps	June, 1865
19th Ohio Infy	Oct., 1863	From 1-Brig. 3-Div. 21-Corps Cumb'd	To 2-Brig. 3-Div. 4-Corps	June, 1865
59th Ohio Infy	Oct., 1863	From 2-Brig. 3-Div. 21-Corps Cumb'd	To Unatt. 4-Div. 20-Corps	Sept., 1864
44th Indiana Infy	Oct., 1863	From 2-Brig. 3-Div. 21-Corps Cumb'd	To Post Chattanooga, Tenn.	Dec., 1863
79th Indiana Infy	Oct., 1863	From 1-Brig. 3-Div. 21-Corps Cumb'd	No change to Muster Out	June, 1865
86th Indiana Infy	Oct., 1863	From 1-Brig. 3-Div. 21-Corps Cumb'd	No change to Muster Out	June, 1865
9th Kentucky Infy	Oct., 1863	From 1-Brig. 3-Div. 21-Corps Cumb'd	No change to Muster Out	Dec., 1864
17th Kentucky Infy	Oct., 1863	From 1-Brig. 3-Div. 21-Corps Cumb'd	No change to Muster Out	Jan., 1865
40th Missouri Infy	Nov., 1864	From Dist. St. Louis Dept. Mo.	To 1-Brig. 3-Div. Det. Army Tenn.	Dec., 1864
3d Michigan Infy	Jan., 1865	From 1-B. Def. Nash. & Chatt. R. R.	To 2-Brig. 3-Div. 4-Corps	June, 1865
4th Michigan Infy	Jan., 1865	From 1-B. Def. Nash. & Chatt. R. R.	To 2-Brig. 3-Div. 4-Corps	June, 1865
13th Wisconsin Infy	Mch., 1865	From 1-Brig. 4-Div. 20-Corps Cumb'd	To 2-Brig. 3-Div. 4-Corps	June, 1865

ARTILLERY, 3d DIVISION.—

Bridge's Ill. Batty	Oct., 1863	From Arty. 2-Div. 14-Corps	To Arty. Brig. 4-Corps	July, 1864
6th Ohio Indpt. Batty	Oct., 1863	From Arty. 1-Div. 21-Corps	To Arty. Brig. 4-Corps	July, 1864
Indpt. Batty. B, Pa. Arty	Oct., 1863	From Arty. 3-Div. 21-Corps	To Arty. 1-Div. 4-Corps	Apr., 1864
20th Ohio Indpt. Batty	Nov., 1863	From 1-Div. Arty. Res. Cumb'd	To Garrison A. Chattanooga, Tenn.	Dec., 1863

ARTILLERY BRIGADE.— Organized July 26, 1864.

5th Indiana Batty	July, 1864	From Arty. 1-Div. 4-Corps	To Garrison A. Chattanooga, Tenn.	Sept., 1864
Indpt. Batty. B, Pa. Arty	July, 1864	From Arty. 1-Div. 4-Corps	To Dept. Texas	Aug., 1865
Batty. M, 1st Ill. Arty	July, 1864	From Arty. 2-Div. 4-Corps	To Garrison A. Chattanooga, Tenn.	Nov., 1864
Batty. A, 1st Ohio Arty	July, 1864	From Arty. 2-Div. 4-Corps	To Dist. Nashville, Tenn	Nov., 1864
6th Ohio Indpt. Batty	July, 1864	From Arty. 3-Div. 4-Corps	To Dept. Louisiana	June, 1865
Bridge's Ill. Batty	July, 1864	From Arty. 3-Div. 4-Corps	To Dist. Nashville, Tenn.	Dec., 1864
Batty. M, 1st Ohio Arty	July, 1864	From Arty. 2-Div. Arty. Res. Cumb'd	To Garrison A. Chattanooga, Tenn.	Oct., 1864
Batty. B, Kentucky Arty	Oct., 1864	From Unass'd Arty. Cumberland	No change to Muster Out	Nov., 1864
Batty. G, 1st Ohio Arty	Oct., 1864	From 2-Div. Arty. Res. Cumb'd	No change to Muster Out	Aug., 1865
Batty. A, Kentucky Arty	Nov., 1864	From 2-Div. Arty. Res. Cumb'd	To Dept. Texas	Aug., 1865
Batty. M, 4th U. S. Arty	Nov., 1864	From 1-Div. Arty. Res. Cumberland	To Garrison A. Bridgeport, Ala.	Feb., 1865
Batty. E, 1st Mich. Arty	Dec., 1864	From Garrison A. Nashville, Tenn.	To Unatt. Arty. Dept. Cumberland	Feb., 1865
25th Indiana Batty	Dec., 1864	From New Organization	To Unatt. Arty. Dept. Cumberland	Feb., 1865

Eleventh Army Corps---Army and Department of the Cumberland

Transferred from Army of the Potomac Sept. 25, 1863. Corps discontinued Apr. 14, 1864, and merged into the reorganized 20th Army Corps, Dept. of the Cumberland.

CORPS COMMANDERS.

O. O. Howard	Major General	Sept. 25, 1863, to Jan. 21, 1864.
Carl Schurz	Major General	Jan. 21, 1864, to Feb. 25, 1864.
O. O. Howard	Major General	Feb. 25, 1864, to Apr. 18, 1864.

1st DIVISION.— Organized Jan., 1864. COMMANDER.

W. T. Ward	Brigadier General	Jan. 12, 1864, to Apr. 16, 1864.

1st BRIGADE.— COMMANDER.

Benj. Harrison	Col. 70th Indiana Infy	Jan. 12, 1864, to Apr. 16, 1864.

70th Indiana Infy	Jan., 1864	From Ward's Brig. Nashville, Tenn.	To 1-Brig. 3-Div. 20-Corps	Apr., 1864
78th Ohio Infy	Jan., 1864	From Ward's Brig. Nashville, Tenn.	To 1-Brig. 3-Div. 20-Corps	Apr., 1864
102d Illinois Infy	Jan., 1864	From Ward's Brig. Nashville, Tenn.	To 1-Brig. 3-Div. 20-Corps	Apr., 1864
105th Illinois Infy	Jan., 1864	From Ward's Brig. Nashville, Tenn.	To 1-Brig. 3-Div. 20-Corps	Apr., 1864
129th Illinois Infy	Jan., 1864	From Ward's Brig. Nashville, Tenn.	To 1-Brig. 3-Div. 20-Corps	Apr., 1864

2d BRIGADE.— COMMANDERS.

John Coburn	Col. 33d Indiana Infy	Jan. 12, 1864, to Mch. 25, 1864.
J. P. Baird	Col. 85th Indiana Infy	Mch. 25, 1864, to Apr. 16, 1864.

33d Indiana Infy	Jan., 1864	From Coburn's Brig. Murfreesboro.	To 2-Brig. 3-Div. 20-Corps	Apr., 1864
85th Indiana Infy	Jan., 1864	From Coburn's Brig. Murfreesboro.	To 2-Brig. 3-Div. 20-Corps	Apr., 1864
22d Wisconsin Infy	Jan., 1864	From Coburn's Brig. Murfreesboro.	To 2-Brig. 3-Div. 20-Corps	Apr., 1864
19th Michigan Infy	Jan., 1864	From Coburn's Brig. Murfreesboro.	To 2-Brig. 3-Div. 20-Corps	Apr., 1864

ARTILLERY, 1st DIVISION.—

Batty. I, 2d Ills. Arty.....Jan., 1864	From Arty. 2-Div. 14-Corps........	To Arty. 2-Div. 14-Corps..........	Apr., 1864
20th Ind. Batty..........Jan., 1864	From Unass'd Dept. Cumb'd........	To Unatt. 4-Div. 20-Corps..........	Apr., 1864

2d DIVISION.—   COMMANDERS.

A. Von Steinwehr......	Brigadier General................	Sept. 25, 1863, to Nov. 28, 1863.
A. Bushbeck..........	Col. 27th Penna. Infy.............	Nov. 28, 1863, to Mch. 3, 1864.
A. Von Steinwehr......	Brigadier General................	Mch. 3, 1864, to Apr. 16, 1864.

1st BRIGADE.—   COMMANDERS.

A. Buschbeck..........	Col. 27th Penna. Infy.............	Sept. 25, 1863, to Nov. 28, 1863.
G. W. Mindel.........	Col. 33d N. J. Infy..............	Nov. 28, 1863, to Jan. 30, 1864.
P. H. Jones.........	Col. 154th N. Y. Infy...........	Jan. 30, 1864, to Feb. 25, 1864.
D. B. Allen.........	Lt.-Col. 154th N. Y. Infy.......	Feb. 25, 1864, to Mch. 3, 1864
A. Buschbeck..........	Col. 27th Penna. Infy.............	Mch. 3, 1864, to Apr. 16, 1864.

27th Penna. Infy.........Sept., 1863	From 1-Brig. 2-Div. 11-Corps Pot...	To 2-Brig. 2-Div. 20-Corps..........	Apr., 1864
73d Penna. Infy.........Sept., 1863	From 1-Brig. 2-Div. 11-Corps Pot...	To 2-Brig. 2-Div. 20-Corps..........	Apr., 1864
134th N. Y. Infy.........Sept., 1863	From 1-Brig. 2-Div. 11-Corps Pot...	To 2-Brig. 2-Div. 20-Corps..........	Apr., 1864
154th N. Y. Infy.........Sept., 1863	From 1-Brig. 2-Div. 11-Corps Pot...	To 2-Brig. 2-Div. 20-Corps..........	Apr., 1864
33d N. J. Infy.........Sept., 1863	From 1-Brig. 2-Div. 11-Corps Pot...	To 2-Brig. 2-Div. 20-Corps..........	Apr., 1864

2d BRIGADE.—   COMMANDERS.

Orland Smith..........	Col. 73d Ohio Infy...............	Sept. 25, 1863, to Jan. 3, 1864.
J. Wood................	Col. 136th N. Y. Infy............	Jan. 3, 1864, to Apr. 16, 1864.

33d Mass. Infy.........Sept., 1863	From 2-Brig. 2-Div. 11-Corps Pot...	To 3-Brig. 3-Div. 20-Corps..........	Apr., 1864
136th N. Y. Infy.........Sept., 1863	From 2-Brig. 2-Div. 11-Corps Pot...	To 3-Brig. 3-Div. 20-Corps..........	Apr., 1864
168th N. Y. Infy.........Sept., 1863	From 2-Brig. 2-Div. 11-Corps Pot...	No change to Muster Out............	Dec., 1863
55th Ohio Infy.........Sept., 1863	From 2-Brig. 2-Div. 11-Corps Pot...	To 3-Brig. 3-Div. 20-Corps..........	Apr., 1864
73d Ohio Infy.........Sept., 1863	From 2-Brig. 2-Div. 11-Corps Pot...	To 3-Brig. 3-Div. 20-Corps..........	Apr., 1864

ARTILLERY, 2d DIVISION.—

Batty. I, 1st N. Y. Arty...Mch., 1864	From Arty. Brig. 11-Corps..........	To Arty. 1-Div. 20-Corps..........	Apr., 1864
Batty. C, 1st Ohio Arty...Mch., 1864	From 1-Div. Army Res. Cumb'd......	To Arty. 3-Div. 20-Corps..........	Apr., 1864

3d DIVISION.—   COMMANDERS.

Carl Shurz............	Major General....................	Sept. 25, 1863, to Jan. 21, 1864.
S. J. McGroarty........	Col. 61st Ohio Infy..............	Jan. 21, 1864, to Feb. 15, 1864.
Hector Tyndale........	Brigadier General................	Feb. 15, 1864, to Apr. 16, 1864.

1st BRIGADE.—   COMMANDERS.

F. Hecker.............	Col. 82d Ill. Infy...............	Sept. 25, 1863, to Oct. 19, 1863.
S. J. McGroarty........	Col. 61st Ohio Infy..............	Oct. 19, 1863, to Jan. 21, 1864.
H. Boughton.........	Col. 143d N. Y. Infy.............	Jan. 21, 1864, to Feb. 15, 1864.
C. H. Fox.............	Col. 101st Ill. Infy..............	Feb. 15, 1864, to Mch. 13, 1864.
J. S. Robinson.........	Col. 82d Ohio Infy...............	Mch. 13, 1864, to Apr. 16, 1864.

45th N. Y. Infy..........Sept., 1863	From 1-Brig. 3-Div. 11-Corps Pot...	To 3-Brig. 1-Div. 20-Corps..........	Apr., 1864
143d N. Y. Infy.........Sept., 1863	From 1-Brig. 3-Div. 11-Corps Pot...	To 3-Brig. 1-Div. 20-Corps..........	Apr., 1864
82d Ill. Infy.........Sept., 1863	From 1-Brig. 3-Div. 11-Corps Pot...	To 3-Brig. 3-Div. 11-Corps Cumb'd..	Oct., 1863
61st Ohio Infy.........Sept., 1863	From 1-Brig. 3-Div. 11-Corps Pot...	To 3-Brig. 1-Div. 20-Corps..........	Apr., 1864
82d Ohio Infy.........Sept., 1863	From 1-Brig. 3-Div. 11-Corps Pot...	To 3-Brig. 1-Div. 20-Corps..........	Apr., 1864
101st Ill. Infy.........Oct., 1863	From Dist. Colum. 6-Div. 16-Corps..	To 3-Brig. 1-Div. 20-Corps..........	Apr., 1864

2d BRIGADE.—   COMMANDERS.

W. Krzyanowski.......	Col. 58th N. Y. Infy.............	Sept. 25, 1863, to Jan. 8, 1864.
J. T. Lockman.........	Col. 119th N. Y. Infy............	Jan. 8, 1864, to Mch. 7, 1864.
W. Krzyanowski.......	Col. 58th N. Y. Infy.............	Mch. 7, 1864, to Apr. 16, 1864.

58th N. Y. Infy..........Sept., 1863	From 2-Brig. 3-Div. 11-Corps Pot...	To Unatt. 4-Div. 20-Corps..........	Apr., 1864
68th N. Y. Infy.........Sept., 1863	From 2-Brig. 3-Div. 11-Corps Pot...	To 3-Brig. 3-Div. 11-Corps Cumb'd..	Oct., 1863
119th N. Y. Infy.........Sept., 1863	From 2-Brig. 3-Div. 11-Corps Pot...	To 2-Brig. 2-Div. 20-Corps..........	Apr., 1864
141st N. Y. Infy.........Sept., 1863	From 2-Brig. 3-Div. 11-Corps Pot...	To 1-Brig. 3-Div. 20-Corps..........	Apr., 1864
75th Penna. Infy.........Sept., 1863	From 2-Brig. 3-Div. 11-Corps Pot...	To 3-Brig. 3-Div. 11-Corps..........	Oct., 1863
26th Wis. Infy.........Sept., 1863	From 2-Brig. 3-Div. 11-Corps Pot...	To 3-Brig. 3-Div. 20-Corps..........	Apr., 1864

3d BRIGADE.—Organized Oct. 19, 1863. Discontinued March 24, 1864.
COMMANDERS.

F. Hecker.............	Col. 82d Ill. Infy...............	Oct. 19, 1863, to Feb. 15, 1864.
S. J. McGroarty........	Col. 61st Ohio Infy..............	Feb. 15, 1864, to Mch. 24, 1864.

68th N. Y. Infy..........Oct., 1863	From 2-Brig. 2-Div. 11-C. Cumb'd..	To Unatt. 4-Div. 20-Corps..........	Apr., 1864
75th Penna. Infy.........Oct., 1863	From 2-Brig. 3-Div. 11-C. Cumb'd..	To Unatt. 4-Div. 20-Corps..........	Apr., 1864
80th Ill. Infy.........Oct., 1863	From 1-Brig. 4-Div. 14-Corps......	To 3-Brig. 1-Div. 4-Corps..........	Dec., 1863
82d Ill. Infy.........Oct., 1863	From 1-Brig. 3-Div. 11-Corps......	To 3-Brig. 1-Div. 20-Corps..........	Apr., 1864

ARTILLERY, 3d DIVISION.—

13th N. Y. Indpt. Batty...Mch., 1864	From Arty. Brig. 11-Corps..........	To Arty. 2-Div. 20-Corps..........	Apr., 1864
Batty. I, 1st Mich. Arty..Mch., 1864	From Arty. Brig. 11-Corps..........	To Arty. 3-Div. 20-Corps..........	Apr., 1864

ARTILLERY BRIGADE.—

Batty. I, 1st N. Y. Arty..Sept., 1863	From Arty. Brig. 11-Corps Pot......	To Arty. 2-Div. 11-Corps Cumb'd...	Mch., 1864
13th N. Y. Indpt. Batty...Sept., 1863	From Arty. Brig. 11-Corps Pot......	To Arty. 3-Div. 11-Corps Cumb'd...	Mch., 1864
Batty. I, 1st Ohio Arty...Sept., 1863	From Arty. Brig. 11-Corps Pot......	To Arty. 2-Div. 4-Corps Cumb'd.....	Nov., 1863
Batty. K, 1st Ohio Arty...Sept., 1863	From Arty. Brig. 11-Corps Pot......	To Garrison Arty. Bridgeport, Ala..	Dec., 1863
Batty. G, 4th U. S. Arty...Sept., 1863	From Arty. Brig. 11-Corps Pot......	To 2-Div. 4-Corps Cumb'd.....	Nov., 1863
12th Ohio Indpt. Batty...Sept., 1863	From Arty. Brig. 11-Corps Pot......	To 2-Div. Arty. Res. Cumb'd......	Dec., 1863
Batty. I, 1st Mich. Arty..Sept., 1863	From Arty. Brig. 11-Corps Pot......	To Arty. 3-Div. 11-Corps Cumb'd...	Mch., 1864
Batty. K, 1st Mich. Arty..Sept., 1863	From Def. Washington 22-Corps....	To Garrison Arty. Chatta., Tenn....	Mch., 1864

Twelfth Army Corps

Transferred from the Army of the Potomac Sept. 25, 1863. Corps discontinued Apr. 14, 1864, and merged into the re-organized 20th Army Corps, Dept. of the Cumberland.

CORPS COMMANDER.

H. W. Slocum.........	Major General....................	Sept. 25, 1863, to Apr. 18, 1864.

1st DIVISION.—   COMMANDERS.

A. S. Williams..........	Brigadier General................	Sept. 25, 1863, to Dec. 22, 1863.
J. F. Knipe............	Brigadier General................	Dec. 22, 1863, to Jan. 30, 1864.
A. S. Williams..........	Brigadier General................	Jan. 30, 1864, to Apr. 14, 1864.

1st BRIGADE.— COMMANDERS.

J. F. Knipe	Brigadier General	Sept. 25, 1863, to Dec. 22, 1863.	
S. Ross	Col. 20th Conn. Infy	Dec. 22, 1863, to Jan. 30, 1864.	
J. F. Knipe	Brigadier General	Jan. 30, 1864, to Feb. 2, 1864.	
S. Ross	Col. 20th Conn. Infy	Feb. 2, 1864, to Mch. 5, 1864.	
J. F. Knipe	Brigadier General	Mch. 5, 1864, to Apr. 14, 1864.	

5th Conn. Infy	Sept., 1863	From 1-Brig. 1-Div. 12-Corps Pot	To 2-Brig. 3-Div. 20-Corps	Apr., 1864
20th Conn. Infy	Sept., 1863	From 1-Brig. 1-Div. 12-Corps Pot	To 1-Brig. 1-Div. 20-Corps	Apr., 1864
123d N. Y. Infy	Sept., 1863	From 1-Brig. 1-Div. 12-Corps Pot	To 1-Brig. 1-Div. 20-Corps	Apr., 1864
145th N. Y. Infy	Sept., 1863	From 1-Brig. 1-Div. 12-Corps Pot	Disbanded	Dec., 1863
46th Penna. Infy	Sept., 1863	From 1-Brig. 1-Div. 12-Corps Pot	To 1-Brig. 1-Div. 20-Corps	Apr., 1864
3d Md. Infy. Det	Sept., 1863	From 1-Brig. 1-Div. 12-Corps Pot	To 1-Brig. 1-Div. 20-Corps	Apr., 1864

3d BRIGADE.— COMMANDER.

T. H. Ruger	Brigadier General	Sept. 25, 1863, to Apr. 14, 1864.	

2d Mass. Infy	Sept., 1863	From 3-Brig. 1-Div. 12-Corps Pot	To 2-Brig. 1-Div. 20-Corps	Apr., 1864
107th N. Y. Infy	Sept., 1863	From 3-Brig. 1-Div. 12-Corps Pot	To 2-Brig. 1-Div. 20-Corps	Apr., 1864
150th N. Y. Infy	Sept., 1863	From 3-Brig. 1-Div. 12-Corps Pot	To 2-Brig. 1-Div. 20-Corps	Apr., 1864
33rd N. J. Infy	Sept., 1863	From 3-Brig. 1-Div. 12-Corps Pot	To 2-Brig. 1-Div. 20-Corps	Apr., 1864
27th Ind. Infy	Sept., 1863	From 3-Brig. 1-Div. 12-Corps Pot	To 2-Brig. 1-Div. 20-Corps	Apr., 1864
3d Wis. Infy	Sept., 1863	From 3-Brig. 1-Div. 12-Corps Pot	To 2-Brig. 1-Div. 20-Corps	Apr., 1864
ARTILLERY, 1st DIVISION.—				
Batty. M, 1st N. Y. Arty	Dec., 1863	From Arty. Brig. 12-C. Cumb'd	To 1-Div. 20-Corps	Apr., 1864
Batty. F, 4th U. S. Arty	Dec., 1863	From Arty. Brig. 12-C. Cumb'd	To 1-Div. Arty. Res. Cumb'd	Apr., 1864
Batty. B, Ky. Arty	Dec., 1863	From Unatt. Dept. Cumb'd	To Unass'd Arty. Dept. Cumb'd	Apr., 1864
9th Ohio Indpt. Batty	Dec., 1863	From Coburn's Brig. Dept. Cumb'd	To Unass'd 4-Div. 20-Corps	Apr., 1864

2d DIVISION.— COMMANDERS.

John W. Geary	Brigadier General	Sept. 25, 1863, to Jan. 27, 1864.	
D. Ireland	Col. 127th N. Y. Infy	Jan. 27, 1864, to Feb. 9, 1864.	
C. Candy	Col. 66th Ohio Infy	Feb. 9, 1864, to Feb. 18, 1864.	
John W. Geary	Brigadier General	Feb. 18, 1864, to Apr. 14, 1864.	

1st BRIGADE.— COMMANDERS.

C. Candy	Col. 66th Ohio Infy	Sept. 25, 1863, to Nov. 30, 1863.	
W. R. Creighton	Col. 7th Ohio Infy	Temporarily, Nov. 27, 1863.	
J. H. Patrick	Col. 5th Ohio Infy	Nov., 30, 1863, to Jan. 18, 1864.	Killed.
A. Pardee, Jr	Lt.-Col. 147th Pa. Infy	Jan. 18, 1864, to Feb. 18, 1864.	
C. Candy	Col. 66th Ohio Infy	Feb. 18, 1864, to Apr. 14, 1864.	

5th Ohio Infy	Sept., 1863	From 1-Brig. 2-Div. 12-Corps Pot	To 1-Brig. 2-Div. 20-Corps	Apr., 1864
7th Ohio Infy	Sept., 1863	From 1-Brig. 2-Div. 12-Corps Pot	To 1-Brig. 2-Div. 20-Corps	Apr., 1864
29th Ohio Infy	Sept., 1863	From 1-Brig. 2-Div. 12-Corps Pot	To 1-Brig. 2-Div. 20-Corps	Apr., 1864
66th Ohio Infy	Sept., 1863	From 1-Brig. 2-Div. 12-Corps Pot	To 1-Brig. 2-Div. 20-Corps	Apr., 1864
28th Penna. Infy	Sept., 1863	From 1-Brig. 2-Div. 12-Corps Pot	To 1-Brig. 2-Div. 20-Corps	Apr., 1864
147th Penna. Infy	Sept., 1863	From 1-Brig. 2-Div. 12-Corps Pot	To 1-Brig. 2-Div. 20-Corps	Apr., 1864

2d BRIGADE.— COMMANDERS.

C. A. Cobham, Jr	Lt.-Col. 111th Pa. Infy	Sept. 25, 1863, to Dec. 27, 1863.	
L. W. Ralston	Lt.-Col. 109th Pa. Infy	Dec. 27, 1863, to Jan. 24, 1864.	
B. Jelliff	Capt. 5th Ohio Infy	Jan. 24, 1864, to Feb. 4, 1864.	
W. F. Stevens	Capt. 29th Ohio Infy	Feb. 4, 1864, to Mch. 9, 1864.	
C. A. Cobham, Jr	Lt.-Col. 111th Pa. Infy	Mch. 9, 1864, to Apr. 14, 1864.	

29th Penna. Infy	Sept., 1863	From 2-Brig. 2-Div. 12-Corps Pot	To 3-Brig. 2-Div. 20-Corps	Apr., 1864
109th Penna. Infy	Sept., 1863	From 2-Brig. 2-Div. 12-Corps Pot	To 2-Brig. 2-Div. 20-Corps	Apr., 1864
111th Penna. Infy	Sept., 1863	From 2-Brig. 2-Div. 12-Corps Pot	To 3-Brig. 2-Div. 20-Corps	Apr., 1864

3d BRIGADE.— COMMANDERS.

George S. Greene	Brigadier General	Sept. 25, 1863, to Oct. 29, 1863.	
D. Ireland	Col. 137th N. Y. Infy	Oct. 29, 1863, to Jan. 27, 1864.	
K. S. Van Voorhees	Lt.-Col. 137th N. Y. Infy	Jan. 27, 1864, to Feb. 9, 1864.	
D. Ireland	Col. 137th N. Y. Infy	Feb. 9, 1864, to Apr. 14, 1864.	

60th N. Y. Infy	Sept., 1863	From 3-Brig. 2-Div. 12-Corps Pot	To 3-Brig. 2-Div. 20-Corps	Apr., 1864
78th N. Y. Infy	Sept., 1863	From 3-Brig. 2-Div. 12-Corps Pot	To 3-Brig. 2-Div. 20-Corps	Apr., 1864
102d N. Y. Infy	Sept., 1863	From 3-Brig. 2-Div. 12-Corps Pot	To 3-Brig. 2-Div. 20-Corps	Apr., 1864
137th N. Y. Infy	Sept., 1863	From 3-Brig. 2-Div. 12-Corps Pot	To 3-Brig. 2-Div. 20-Corps	Apr., 1864
149th N. Y. Infy	Sept., 1863	From 3-Brig. 2-Div. 12-Corps Pot	To 3-Brig. 2-Div. 20-Corps	Apr., 1864
ARTILLERY, 2d DIVISION.—				
Batty. K, 5th U. S. Arty	Sept., 1863	From Arty. Brig. 12-Corps Pot	To 1-Div. Arty. Res. Cumb'd	Mch., 1864
Indpt. Batty. E, Pa. Arty	Sept., 1863	From Arty. Brig. 12-Corps Pot	To Arty. 2-Div. 20-Corps	Apr., 1864
Batty. B, 1st Ohio Arty	Mch., 1864	From 1-Div. Arty. Res. Cumb'd	To Garrison Arty. Bridgeport, Ala	Apr., 1864

3d DIVISION.—Organized Jan. 2, 1864.— COMMANDER.

L. H. Rousseau	Major General	Jan. 2, 1864, to Apr. 14, 1864.	

1st BRIGADE.— COMMANDER.

R. S. Granger	Brigadier General	Jan. 2, 1864, to Apr. 14, 1864.	

18th Mich. Infy	Jan., 1864	From 1-Brig. Dist. Nashville, Tenn	To 1-Brig. 4-Div. 20-Corps	Apr., 1864
102d Ohio Infy	Jan., 1864	From 1-Brig. Dist. Nashville, Tenn	To 1-Brig. 4-Div. 20-Corps	Apr., 1864
73d Ind. Infy	Jan., 1864	From 1-Brig. Dist. Nashville, Tenn	To 1-Brig. 4-Div. 20-Corps	Apr., 1864
13th Wis. Infy	Jan., 1864	From 1-Brig. Dist. Nashville, Tenn	To 1-Brig. 4-Div. 20-Corps	Apr., 1864
10th Tenn. Infy	Jan., 1864	From 1-Brig. Dist. Nashville, Tenn	To 1-Brig. 4-Div. 20-Corps	Apr., 1864

2d BRIGADE.— COMMANDER.

H. P. Van Cleve	Brigadier General	Jan. 2, 1864, to Apr. 14, 1864.	

115th Ohio Infy	Jan., 1864	From Murfreesboro, Tenn	To Unass'd 4-Div. 20-Corps	Apr., 1864
31st Wis. Infy	Jan., 1864	From Murfreesboro, Tenn	To Unass'd 4-Div. 20-Corps	Apr., 1864
23d Mo. Infy	Jan., 1864	From Dist. Nashville, Tenn	To Unass'd 4-Div. 20-Corps	Apr., 1864
4th Tenn. Infy	Jan., 1864	From Dist. S. E. Ky. Dept. Ohio	To 3-Brig. 4-Div. 23-Corps Ohio	Apr., 1864

3d BRIGADE.— COMMANDERS.

J. G. Spear	Brigadier General	Jan. 2, 1864, to Feb. 6, 1864.	
William Cross	Col. 3d Tenn. Infy	Feb. 6, 1864, to Mch. 7, 1864.	
J. A. Cooper	Col. 6th Tenn. Infy	Mch. 7, 1864, to Apr. 14, 1864.	

3d Tenn. Infy	Jan., 1864	From Spear's Tenn. Br. 2-Div. 23-C.	To 1-Brig. 2-Div. 23-Corps Ohio	Apr., 1864
5th Tenn. Infy	Jan., 1864	From Spear's Tenn. Br. 2-Div. 23-C.	To 2-Brig. 3-Div. 23-Corps Ohio	Apr., 1864
6th Tenn. Infy	Jan., 1864	From Spear's Tenn. Br. 2-Div. 23-C.	To 1-Brig. 2-Div. 23-Corps Ohio	Apr., 1864

ARTILLERY BRIGADE.—

Batty. M, 1st N. Y. Arty.	Sept., 1863	From Arty. Brig. 12-Corps Pot	To Arty. 1-Div. 12-Corps Cumb'd	Dec.,	1863
Batty. F, 4th U. S. Arty.	Sept., 1863	From Arty. Brig. 12-Corps Pot	To Arty. 1-Div. 12-Corps Cumb'd	Dec.,	1863
Batty. E, Indpt. Pa. Arty.	Sept., 1863	From Arty. Brig. 12-Corps Pot	To Arty. 2-Div. 12-Corps Cumb'd	Dec.,	1863
Batty. K, 5th U. S. Arty.	Sept., 1863	From Arty. Brig. 12-Corps Pot	To Arty. 2-Div. 12-Corps Cumb'd	Dec.,	1863

UNATTACHED.—

10th Me. Infy. Battn	Sept., 1863	From Headqrs. 12-Corps Pot	Transferred to 29th Maine	Dec.,	1863

Twentieth Army Corps

As reorganized Apr., 1864, by consolidation of the 11th and 12th Army Corps, Dept. of the Cumberland. Discontinued June 1, 1865.

CORPS COMMANDERS.

Joseph Hooker	Major General	Apr. 14, 1864, to July 28, 1864.	
A. S. Williams	Brigadier General	July 28, 1864, to Aug. 27, 1864.	
H. W. Slocum	Major General	Aug. 27, 1864, to Nov. 11, 1864.	
A. S. Williams	Brigadier General	Nov. 11, 1864, to Apr. 2, 1865.	
J. A. Mower	Major General	Apr. 2, 1865, to June 9, 1865.	

1st DIVISION.— COMMANDERS.

A. S. Williams	Brigadier General	Apr. 14, 1864, to July 28, 1864.	
J. F. Knipe	Brigadier General	July 28, 1864, to Aug. 27, 1864.	
A. S. Williams	Brigadier General	Aug. 27, 1864, to Nov. 11, 1864.	
N. J. Jackson	Brigadier General	Nov. 11, 1864, to Apr. 2, 1865.	
A. S. Williams	Bvt. Major General	Apr. 2, 1865, to June 4, 1865.	

1st BRIGADE.— COMMANDERS.

J. F. Knipe	Brigadier General	Apr. 14, 1864, to July 3, 1864.	
W. W. Packer	Col. 5th Conn. Infy	July 3, 1864, to July 17, 1864.	
J. F. Knipe	Brigadier General	July 17, 1864, to July 28, 1864.	
W. W. Packer	Col. 5th Conn. Infy	July 28, 1864, to Aug. 28, 1864.	
J. F. Knipe	Brigadier General	Aug. 28, 1864, to Sept. 21, 1864.	
W. W. Packer	Col. 5th Conn. Infy	Sept. 21, 1864, to Oct. 20, 1864.	
J. L. Selfridge	Col. 46th Penna. Infy	Oct. 20, 1864, to June 1, 1865.	

5th Conn. Infy	Apr., 1864	From 2-Brig. 3-Div. 20-Corps	No change to Muster Out	July,	1865
20th Conn. Infy	Apr., 1864	From 1-Brig. 1-Div. 12-C. Cumb'd	To 2-Brig. 3-Div. 20-Corps	Apr.,	1864
3d Md. Infy. Detach	Apr., 1864	From 1-Brig. 1-Div. 12-C. Cumb'd	No change to Muster Out	Oct.,	1864
46th Penna. Infy	Apr., 1864	From 1-Brig. 1-Div. 12-C. Cumb'd	No change to Muster Out	June,	1865
123d N. Y. Infy	Apr., 1864	From 1-Brig. 1-Div. 12-C. Cumb'd	No change to Muster Out	June,	1865
141st N. Y. Infy	Apr., 1864	From 2-Brig. 3-Div. 11-C. Cumb'd	No change to Muster Out	June,	1865

2d BRIGADE.— COMMANDERS.

T. H. Ruger	Brigadier General	Apr. 14, 1864, to Sept. 17, 1864.	
E. A. Carman	Col. 13th N. J. Infy	Sept. 17, 1864, to Oct. 17, 1864.	
T. H. Ruger	Brigadier General	Oct. 17, 1864, to Nov. 5, 1864.	
E. A. Carman	Col. 13th N. J. Infy	Nov. 5, 1864, to Jan. 16, 1865.	
W. Hawley	Col. 3d Wis. Infy	Jan. 16, 1865, to June 1, 1865.	

2d Mass. Infy	Apr., 1864	From 3-Brig. 1-Div. 12-Corps Cumb'd	No change to Muster Out	July,	1865
3d Wisconsin Infy	Apr., 1864	From 3-Brig. 1-Div. 12-Corps Cumb'd	No change to Muster Out	July,	1865
13th New Jersey Infy	Apr., 1864	From 3-Brig. 1-Div. 12-Corps Cumb'd	No change to Muster Out	June,	1865
27th Indiana Infy	Apr., 1864	From 3-Brig. 1-Div. 12-Corps Cumb'd	No change to Muster Out	Nov.,	1864
107th New York Infy	Apr., 1864	From 3-Brig. 1-Div. 12-Corps Cumb'd	No change to Muster Out	June,	1865
150th New York Infy	Apr., 1864	From 3-Brig. 1-Div. 12-Corps Cumb'd	No change to Muster Out	June,	1865

3d BRIGADE.— COMMANDERS.

Hector Tyndale	Brigadier General	Apr. 14, 1864, to May 2, 1864.	
J. S. Robinson	Col. 82d Ohio Infy	May 2, 1864, to July 24, 1864.	
H. Boughton	Col. 143d New York Infy	July 24, 1864, to Sept. 27, 1864.	
J. S. Robinson	Col. 82d Ohio Infy	Sept. 27, 1864, to June 7, 1865.	

61st Ohio Infy	Apr., 1864	From 1-Brig. 3-Div. 11-Corps Cumb'd	Consolidated with 82d Ohio Infy	Mch.,	1865
82d Ohio Infy	Apr., 1864	From 1-Brig. 3-Div. 11-Corps Cumb'd	No change to Muster Out	July,	1865
45th New York Infy	Apr., 1864	From 1-Brig. 3-Div. 11-Corps Cumb'd	To 2-Brig. 4-Div. 20-Corps	July,	1864
143d New York Infy	Apr., 1864	From 1-Brig. 3-Div. 11-Corps Cumb'd	No change to Muster Out	July,	1865
82d Illinois Infy	Apr., 1864	From 3-Brig. 3-Div. 11-Corps Cumb'd	No change to Muster Out	June,	1865
101st Illinois Infy	Apr., 1864	From 1-Brig. 3-Div. 11-Corps Cumb'd	No change to Muster Out	June,	1865
31st Wisconsin Infy	July, 1864	From 2-Brig. 4-Div. 20-Corps Cumb'd	No change to Muster Out	June,	1865

ARTILLERY, 1st DIVISION.—

Batty. I, 1st N. Y. Arty	Apr., 1864	From Arty. 2-Div. 11-Corps Cumb'd	To Arty. Brig. 20-Corps	July,	1864
Batty. M, 1st N. Y. Arty	Apr., 1864	From Arty. 1-Div. 12-Corps Cumb'd	To Arty. Brig. 20-Corps	July,	1864

2d DIVISION.— COMMANDER.

John W. Geary	Brigadier General	Apr. 14, 1864, to June 1, 1865.	

1st BRIGADE.— COMMANDERS.

C. Candy	Col. 66th Ohio Infy	Apr. 14, 1864, to Aug. 4, 1864.	
A. Pardee, Jr	Col. 147th Penna. Infy	Aug. 4, 1864, to Sept. 27, 1864.	
J. Flynn	Col. 28th Penna. Infy	Sept. 27, 1864, to Oct. 28, 1864.	
A. Pardee, Jr	Col. 147th Penna. Infy	Oct. 28, 1864, to Apr. 11, 1865.	
G. W. Mindel	Col. 33d New Jersey Infy	Apr. 11, 1865, to May 10, 1865.	
A. Pardee, Jr	Col. 147th Penna. Infy	May 10, 1865, to June 1, 1865.	

5th Ohio Infy	Apr., 1864	From 1-Brig. 2-Div. 12-Corps Cumb'd	No change to Muster Out	July,	1865
7th Ohio Infy	Apr., 1864	From 1-Brig. 2-Div. 12-Corps Cumb'd	No change to Muster Out	June,	1864
29th Ohio Infy	Apr., 1864	From 1-Brig. 2-Div. 12-Corps Cumb'd	No change to Muster Out	July,	1865
66th Ohio Infy	Apr., 1864	From 1-Brig. 2-Div. 12-Corps Cumb'd	No change to Muster Out	July,	1865
28th Penna. Infy	Apr., 1864	From 1-Brig. 2-Div. 12-Corps Cumb'd	No change to Muster Out	July,	1865
147th Penna. Infy	Apr., 1864	From 1-Brig. 2-Div. 12-Corps Cumb'd	No change to Muster Out	July,	1865

2d BRIGADE.— COMMANDERS.

A. Buschbeck	Col. 27th Penna. Infy	Apr. 14, 1864, to May 22, 1864.
J. T. Lockman	Col. 119th New York Infy	May 22, 1864, to June 7, 1864.
P. H. Jones	Col. 154th New York Infy	June 7, 1864, to Aug. 8, 1864.
G. W. Mindel	Col. 33d New Jersey Infy	Aug. 8, 1864, to Sept. 17, 1864.
P. H. Jones	Col. 154th New York Infy	Sept. 17, 1864, to Jan. 19, 1865.
G. W. Mindel	Col. 33d New Jersey Infy	Jan. 19, 1865, to Mch. 30, 1865.
P. H. Jones	Col. 154th New York Infy	Mch. 30, 1865, to June 1, 1865.

27th Penna. Infy	Apr., 1864	From 1-Brig. 2-Div. 11-Corps Comb'd	No change to Muster Out	June, 1864
73d Penna. Infy	Apr., 1864	From 1-Brig. 2-Div. 11-Corps Comb'd	No change to Muster Out	July, 1865
109th Penna. Infy	Apr., 1864	From 2-Brig. 2-Div. 12-Corps Cumb'd	Consolidated with 111th Penna	Mch., 1865
33d New Jersey Infy	Apr., 1864	From 1-Brig. 2-Div. 11-Corps Cumb'd	No change to Muster Out	July, 1865
119th New York Infy	Apr., 1864	From 2-Brig. 3-Div. 11-Corps Cumb'd	No change to Muster Out	June, 1865
134th New York Infy	Apr., 1864	From 1-Brig. 2-Div. 11-Corps Cumb'd	No change to Muster Out	June, 1865
154th New York Infy	Apr., 1864	From 1-Brig. 2-Div. 11-Corps Cumb'd	No change to Muster Out	June, 1865

3d BRIGADE.— COMMANDERS.

D. Ireland	Col. 137th N. Y. Infy	Apr. 14, 1864, to May 15, 1864.
William Rickards, Jr.	Col. 29th Penna. Infy	May 15, 1864, to May 16, 1864.
G. A. Cobham, Jr.	Col. 111th Penna. Infy	May 16, 1864, to June 6, 1864.
D. Ireland	Col. 137th N. Y. Infy	June 6, 1864, to Sept. 9, 1864.
H. A. Barnum	Col. 149th N. Y. Infy	Sept. 9, 1864, to June 1, 1865.

60th New York Infy	Apr., 1864	From 3-Brig. 2-Div. 12-Corps Cumb'd	No change to Muster Out	July, 1865
78th New York Infy	Apr., 1864	From 3-Brig. 2-Div. 12-Corps Cumb'd	Consolidated with 102d N. Y.	July, 1864
102d New York Infy	Apr., 1864	From 3-Brig. 2-Div. 12-Corps Cumb'd	No change to Muster Out	July, 1865
137th New York Infy	Apr., 1864	From 3-Brig. 2-Div. 12-Corps Cumb'd	No change to Muster Out	June, 1865
149th New York Infy	Apr., 1864	From 3-Brig. 2-Div. 12-Corps Cumb'd	No change to Muster Out	June, 1865
29th Penna. Infy	Apr., 1864	6From 2-Brig. 2-Div. 12-Corps Cumb'd	No change to Muster Out	July, 1865
111th Penna. Infy	Apr., 1864	6From 2-Brig. 2-Div. 12-Corps Cumb'd	No change to Muster Out	July, 1865
ARTILLERY, 2d DIVISION.—				
13th N. Y. Indpt. Batty.	Apr., 1864	From Arty. 3-Div. 11-Corps Cumb'd.	To Arty. Brig. 20-Corps	July, 1864
Indpt. Batty. E, Pa. Arty.	Apr., 1864	From Arty. 2-Div. 12-Corps Cumb'd	To Arty. Brig. 20-Corps	July, 1864

3d DIVISION.— COMMANDERS.

D. Butterfield	Major General	Apr. 14, 1864, to June 29, 1864.
W. T. Ward	Brigadier General	June 29, 1864, to Sept. 23, 1864.
Daniel Dustin	Col. 105th Illinois Infy	Sept. 23, 1864, to Oct. 25, 1864.
W. T. Ward	Brigadier General	Oct. 25, 1864, to June 1, 1865.

1st BRIGADE.— COMMANDERS.

W. T. Ward	Brigadier General	Apr. 14, 1864, to May 15, 1864.
B. Harrison	Col. 70th Indiana Infy	May 15, 1864.
W. T. Ward	Brigadier General	May 15, 1864, to June 29, 1864.
Benj. Harrison	Col. 70th Indiana Infy	June 29, 1864, to Sept. 23, 1864.
F. C. Smith	Col. 102d Illinois Infy	Sept. 23, 1864, to Dec. 31, 1864.
H. Case	Col. 129th Illinois Infy	Dec. 31, 1864, to Apr. 19, 1865.
Benj. Harrison	Col. 70th Indiana Infy	Apr. 19, 1865, to June 1, 1865.

79th Ohio Infy	Apr., 1864	From 1-Brig. 1-Div. 11-Corps Cumb'd	No change to Muster Out	June, 1865
70th Indiana Infy	Apr., 1864	From 1-Brig. 1-Div. 11-Corps Cumb'd	No change to Muster Out	June, 1865
102d Illinois Infy	Apr., 1864	From 1-Brig. 1-Div. 11-Corps Cumb'd	No change to Muster Out	June, 1865
105th Illinois Infy	Apr., 1864	From 1-Brig. 1-Div. 11-Corps Cumb'd	No change to Muster Out	June, 1865
129th Illinois Infy	Apr., 1864	From 1-Brig. 1-Div. 11-Corps Cumb'd	No change to Muster Out	June, 1865

2d BRIGADE.— COMMANDERS.

S. Ross	Col. 20th Conn. Infy	Apr. 14, 1864, to May 9, 1864.
J. Coburn	Col. 33d Indiana Infy	May 9, 1864, to Sept. 22, 1864.
E. Bloodgood	Lt.-Col. 22d Wis. Infy	Sept. 22, 1864, to Oct. 30, 1864.
A. B. Crane	Col. 85th Indiana Infy	Oct. 30, 1864, to Nov. 11, 1864.
Daniel Dustin	Col. 105th Illinois Infy	Nov. 11, 1864, to June 1, 1865.

5th Conn. Infy	Apr., 1864	From 1-Brig. 1-Div. 12-Corps Cumb'd	To 1-Brig. 1-Div. 20-Corps	Apr., 186
33d Indiana Infy	Apr., 1864	From 2-Brig. 1-Div. 11-Corps Cumb'd	No change to Muster Out	July, 1865
85th Indiana Infy	Apr., 1864	From 2-Brig. 1-Div. 11-Corps Cumb'd	No change to Muster Out	June, 1865
19th Michigan Infy	Apr., 1864	From 2-Brig. 1-Div. 11-Corps Cumb'd	No change to Muster Out	June, 1865
22d Wisconsin Infy	Apr., 1864	From 2-Brig. 1-Div. 11-Corps Cumb'd	No change to Muster Out	June, 1865
20th Conn. Infy	Apr., 1864	From 1-Brig. 1-Div. 20-Corps	To 3-Brig. 3-Div. 20-Corps	May, 1864

3d BRIGADE.— COMMANDERS.

J. Wood, Jr.	Col. 136th N. Y. Infy	Apr. 14, 1864, to July 28, 1864.
L. B. Faulkner	Lt.-Col. 136th N. Y. Infy	July 28, 1864, to Aug. 5, 1864.
J. Wood, Jr.	Col. 136th N. Y. Infy	Aug. 5, 1864, to Sept. 23, 1864.
P. B. Buckingham	Lt.-Col. 20th Conn. Infy	Sept. 23, 1864, to Nov. 10, 1864.
S. Ross	Col. 20th Conn. Infy	Nov. 10, 1864, to Jan. 16, 1865.
William Cogswell	Col. 2d Mass. Infy	Jan. 16, 1865, to June 1, 1865.

33d Mass. Infy	Apr., 1864	From 2-Brig. 2-Div. 11-Corps Cumb'd	No change to Muster Out	June, 1865
136th New York Infy	Apr., 1864	From 2-Brig. 2-Div. 11-Corps Cumb'd	No change to Muster Out	June, 1865
55th Ohio Infy	Apr., 1864	From 2-Brig. 2-Div. 11-Corps Cumb'd	No change to Muster Out	July, 1865
73d Ohio Infy	Apr., 1864	From 2-Brig. 2-Div. 11-Corps Cumb'd	No change to Muster Out	July, 1865
26th Wisconsin Infy	Apr., 1864	From 2-Brig. 3-Div. 11-Corps Cumb'd	No change to Muster Out	June, 1865
20th Conn. Infy	May, 1864	From 2-Brig. 3-Div. 20-Corps	No change to Muster Out	June, 1865
ARTILLERY, 3d DIVISION.—				
Batty. I, 1st Mich. Arty.	Apr., 1864	From Arty. Res. Dept. Cumb'd	To Arty. Brig. 20-Corps	July, 1864
Batty. C, 1st Ohio Arty.	Apr., 1864	From Arty. 2-Div. 11-Corps Cumb'd.	To Arty. Brig. 20-Corps	July, 1864
ARTILLERY BRIGADE.—Organized July 27, 1864.				
Batty. I, 1st N. Y. Arty.	July, 1864	From Arty. 1-Div. 20-Corps	No change to Muster Out	June, 1865
Batty. M, 1st N. Y. Arty.	July, 1864	From Arty. 1-Div. 20-Corps	No change to Muster Out	June, 1865
13th N. Y. Indpt. Batty.	July, 1864	From Arty. 2-Div. 20-Corps	To Unatt. Dist. Tenn. Dept. Cumb'd.	Sept., 1864
Indpt. Batty. E, Pa. Arty.	July, 1864	From Arty. 2-Div. 20-Corps	No change to Muster Out	June, 1865
Batty. C, 1st Ohio Arty.	July, 1864	From Arty. 3-Div. 20-Corps	No change to Muster Out	June, 1865
Batty. I, 1st Mich. Arty.	July, 1864	From Arty. 3-Div. 20-Corps	To Res. Arty. Chattanooga, Tenn.	Oct., 1864
Batty. K, 5th U. S. Arty.	July, 1864	From 1-Div. Arty. Res. Comberland.	To Res. Arty. Chattanooga, Tenn.	Nov., 1864

4th DIVISION.— COMMANDER.

L. H. Rousseau	Major General	

1st BRIGADE.— COMMANDERS.

R. S. Granger	Brigadier General	Apr. 14, 1864, to June 2, 1864.
C. C. Doolittle	Col. 18th Michigan Infy	June 2, 1864, to Oct., 1864.
W. P. Lyon	Col. 13th Wisconsin Infy	Oct., 1864, to Mch., 1865.

1st BRIGADE.—Continued.

13th Wisconsin Infy	Apr., 1864	From 1-Brig. 3-Div. 12-Corps Cumb'd	To 3-Brig. 3-Div. 4-Corps	Mch.,	
18th Michigan Infy	Apr., 1864	From 1-Brig. 3-Div. 12-Corps Cumb'd	To 1-Brig. 1-Div. Dist. North Ala.	Mch.,	1865
10th Tennessee Infy	Apr., 1864	From 1-Brig. 3-Div. 12-Corps Cumb'd	To Governor's Guard Tenn		
73d Ind. Infy	Apr., 1864	From 1-Brig. 3-Div. 12-Corps Cumb'd.	To 1-Brig. 1-Div. Dist. N. Ala	Mch.,	1865
102d Ohio Infy	Apr., 1864	From 1-Brig. 3-Div. 12-Corps Cumb'd.	To 1-Brig. 1-Div. Dist. N. Ala	Mch.,	1865

2d BRIGADE.—Organized Nov. 25, 1864, from Garrison of Nashville, Tenn.

COMMANDER.

E. C. Mason	Col. 176th Ohio Infy	Nov., 1864, to Mch., 1865.

45th N. Y. Infy	Nov., 1864	From Unass'd 4-Div. 20-Corps	To 1-Brig. 1-Div. Dist. Middle Tenn.	Mch.,	1865
142d Ind. Infy	Nov., 1864	From New Organization	To 1-Brig. 1-Div. Dist. Middle Tenn.	Mch.,	1865
176th Ohio Infy	Nov., 1864	From Dist. Nashville, Tenn	To 1-Brig. 1-Div. Dist. Middle Tenn.	Mch.,	1865
179th Ohio Infy	Nov., 1864	From Dist. Nashville, Tenn	To 1-Brig. 1-Div. Dist. Middle Tenn.	Mch.,	1865
182d Ohio Infy	Nov., 1864	From Dist. Nashville, Tenn	To 1-Brig. 1-Div. Dist. Middle Tenn.	Mch.,	1865
45th Wis. Infy	Feb., 1865	From Dist. Nashville, Tenn	To 1-Brig. 1-Div. Dist. Middle Tenn.	Mch.,	1865

UNASSIGNED, 4th DIVISION.—

23d Mo. Infy	Apr., 1864	From 2-Brig. 3-Div. 12-Corps Cumb'd.	To 1-Brig. 3-Div. 14-Corps	July,	1864
75th Penna. Infy	Apr., 1864	From Veteran Furlough	To Def. Nashv. & N. W. R. R.	June,	1864
31st Wis. Infy	Apr., 1864	From 2-Brig. 3-Div. 12-Corps Cumb'd	To 3-Brig. 1-Div. 20-Corps	July,	1864
83d Ill. Infy	Apr., 1864	From Garrison Clarksville, Tenn	To 5th Sub.-Dist. Middle Tenn.	Mch.,	1865
58th N. Y. Infy	Apr., 1864	From 2-Brig. 3-Div. 11-Corps Cumb'd.	To 3-Brig. Def. Nashv. & Chatt. R. R.	July,	1864
68th N. Y. Infy	Apr., 1864	From 2-Brig. 3-Div. 11-Corps Cumb'd.	To 3-Brig. Def. Nashv. & Chatt. R. R.	July,	1864
71st Ohio Infy	Apr., 1864	From Post Gallatin, Tenn	To 2-Brig. 3-Div. 4-Corps	Aug.,	1864
106th Ohio Infy	Apr., 1864	From Post Gallatin, Tenn	To 3-Brig. Def. Nashv. & Chatt. R. R.	July,	1864
115th Ohio Infy	Apr., 1864	From 2-Brig. 3-Div. 12-Corps Cumb'd.	To 1-Brig. Def. Nashv. & Chatt. R. R.	July,	1864
20th Ind. Batty. Arty	Apr., 1864	From Dist. Nashville, Tenn	To Arty. Brig. 14-Corps	Aug.,	1864
9th Ohio Batty. Arty	Apr., 1864	From Arty. 1-Div. 12-Corps Cumb'd.	To 3-Brig. Def. Nashv. & Chatt. R. R.	July,	1864
45th N. Y. Infy	July, 1864	From 3-Brig. 1-Div. 20-Corps	To 2-Brig. 4-Div. 20-Corps	Nov.,	1864
75th Penna. Infy	Aug., 1864	From Def. Nashv. & N. W. R. R.	To 1-Brig. 1st Sub-Dist. Middle Tenn.	Mch.,	1865
78th Penna. Infy	July, 1864	From 3-Brig. 1-Div. 14-Corps	To Unatt. Nashville, Tenn	Nov.,	1864
5th Ky. Infy	July, 1864	From 2-Brig. 3-Div. 4-Corps	No change to Muster Out	Sept.,	1864
6th Ky. Infy	Sept., 1864	From 2-Brig. Def. Nashv. & Ch. R. R.	To 3-Brig. Def. Nashv. & Chatt. R. R.	Oct.,	1864
59th Ohio Infy	Sept., 1864	From 2-Brig. 3-Div. 4-Corps	To Def. Nashv. & Chatt. R. R.	Oct.,	1864
42d Mo. Infy	Jan., 1865	From Tullahoma, Tenn	To 2-Brig. Def. Nashv. & Chatt. R. R.	Mch.,	1865
61st Ill. Infy	Feb., 1865	From 1-Brig. Def. Nashv. & Ch. R. R.	To 2d Sub-Dist. Middle Tenn.	Mch.,	1865
29th Mich. Infy	Feb., 1865	From 3-Brig. Def. Nashv. & Ch. R. R.	To 3-Brig. 1st Sub-Dist. Mid. Tenn.	Mch.,	1865
175th Ohio Infy	Feb., 1865	From 3-Brig. 3-Div. 23-Corps	To 2d Sub-Dist. Middle Tenn.	Mch.,	1865
182d Ohio Infy	Feb., 1865	From 2-Brig. 4-Div. 20-Corps	To 1-Brig. 1-Div. Nashville, Tenn.	Mch.,	1865
115th Ohio Infy	Feb., 1865	From 1-Brig. Def. Nashv. & Ch. R. R.	To 1-Brig. 1-Div. Nashville, Tenn.	Mch.,	1865
58th N. Y. Infy	Feb., 1865	From 3-Brig. Def. Nashv. & Ch. R. R.	To Stevenson, Ala., Dist. N. Ala.	Mch.,	1865
106th Ohio Infy	Feb., 1865	From 3-Brig. Def. Nashv. & Ch. R. R.	To Stevenson, Ala., Dist. N. Ala.	Mch.,	1865

Cavalry Forces---Department of the Cumberland

COMMANDERS.

D. S. Stanley	Major General	Jan. 9, 1863, to Sept. 9, 1863.
R. B. Mitchell	Brigadier General	Sept. 9, 1863, to Nov. 9, 1863.
D. S. Stanley	Major General	Nov. 9, 1863, to Nov. 20, 1863.
W. L. Elliott	Brigadier General	Nov. 20, 1863, to Aug. 19, 1864.
R. W. Johnson	Brigadier General	Aug. 19, 1864, to Oct. 29, 1864.

1st DIVISION.— **COMMANDERS.**

D. S. Stanley	Major General	Jan. 9, 1863, to Mch., 1863.
R. B. Mitchell	Brigadier General	Mch., 1863, to Sept. 9, 1863.
E. M. McCook	Col. 2d Ind. Cav.	Sept. 9, 1863, to Oct. 12, 1863.
W. L. Elliott	Brigadier General	Oct. 12, 1863, to Nov. 20, 1863.
E. M. McCook	Col. 2d Ind. Cav.	Nov. 20, 1863, to Oct. 29, 1864.

1st BRIGADE.— **COMMANDERS.**

R. H. G. Minty	Col. 4th Mich. Cav.	Jan. 9, 1863, to Mch., 1863.
A. P. Campbell	Col. 9th Penna. Cav.	Mch., 1863, to Apr. 12, 1864.
J. B. Dorr	Col. 8th Iowa Cav.	Apr. 12, 1864, to July 20, 1864.
J. T. Croxton	Col. 4th Ky. Mtd. Infy	July 20, 1864, to July 30, 1864.
J. B. Dorr	Col. 8th Iowa Cav.	July 30, 1864.
J. P. Brownlow	Lt.-Col. 1st Tenn. Cav.	July 30, 1864, to Aug. 12, 1864.
J. T. Croxton	Brigadier General	Aug. 12, 1864, to Oct. 29, 1864.

2d Ind. Cav	Jan., 1863	From 1-Brig. Cav. Div. Dept Cumb'd	To 2-Brig. 1-Cav. Div. Cumb'd	Mch.,	1863
3d Ind. Cav	Jan., 1863	From Cav. Right Wing 14-Corps	To 1-Brig. 2-Cav. Div. Cumb'd	Mch.,	1863
4th Mich. Cav	Jan., 1863	From 1-Brig. Cav. Div. Dept Cumb'd	To 1-Brig. 2-Div. Cav. Cumb'd	Mch.,	1863
7th Penna. Cav	Jan., 1863	From 1-Brig. Cav. Div. Dept Cumb'd	To 1-Brig. 2-Div. Cav. Cumb'd	Mch.,	1863
3d Ky. Cav	Jan., 1863	From 1-Brig. Cav. Div. Dept Cumb'd	To Dist. West Ky. Dept. Ohio	Mch.,	1863
4th Ky. Cav	Mch., 1863	From Dist. West Ky. Dept. Ohio	To 3-Brig. 1-Cav. Div. Cumb'd	July,	1863
6th Ky. Cav	Mch., 1863	From Unatt. Army Ky. Dept. Ohio	To 3-Brig. 1-Cav. Div. Cumb'd	July,	1863
7th Ky. Cav	Mch., 1863	From Post Gallatin, Tenn	To 3-Brig. 1-Cav. Div. Cumb'd	July,	1863
2d Mich. Cav	Mch., 1863	From Dist. Central Ky., Dept. Ohio	To Dist. Nashville, Tenn	June,	1864
9th Penna. Cav	Mch., 1863	From Dist. Central Ky., Dept. Ohio	To Veteran Furlough	Apr.,	1864
1st Tenn. Cav	Mch., 1863	From Dist. Central Ky., Dept. Ohio	To 1-Br. 1-Div. Cav. Corps, M. D. M.	Oct.,	1864
8th Iowa Cav	Mch., 1864	From Def. Nashv. & N. W. R. R.	To 1-Br. 1-Div. Cav. Corps, M. D. M.	Oct.,	1864
4th Ky. Mtd. Infy	June, 1864	From 3-Brig. 3-Div. 14-Corps	To 1-Br. 1-Div. Cav. Corps, M. D. M.	Oct.,	1864
2d Mich. Cav	Oct., 1864	From Dist. Nashville, Tenn	To 1-Br. 1-Div. Cav. Corps, M. D. M.	Oct.,	1864

2d BRIGADE.— **COMMANDERS.**

E. M. McCook	Col. 2d Ind. Cav.	Jan. 9, 1863, to Sept. 9, 1863.
O. H. LaGrange	Col. 1st Wis. Cav.	Sept. 9, 1863, to Oct. 12, 1863.
E. M. McCook	Col. 2d Ind. Cav.	Oct. 12, 1863, to Nov. 20, 1863.
O. H. LaGrange	Col. 1st Wis. Cav.	Nov. 20, 1863, to Apr. 1, 1864.
D. M. Ray	Col. 2d Tenn. Cav.	Apr. 1, 1864, to Apr. 20, 1864.
O. H. LaGrange	Col. 1st Wis. Cav.	Apr. 20, 1864, to May 9, 1864.
J. W. Stewart	Lt.-Col. 2d Ind. Cav.	May 9, 1864, to May 26, 1864.
H. P. Lamson	Lt.-Col. 4th Ind. Cav.	May 26, 1864, to July 21, 1864.
W. H. Torrey	Lt.-Col. 1st Wis. Cav.	July 21, 1864, to July 30, 1864.
H. P. Lamson	Lt.-Col. 4th Ind. Cav.	July 30, 1864, to Oct. 29, 1864.

2d BRIGADE.—Continued.

1st Ohio Cav.	Jan., 1863	From 2-Brig. Cav. Div. Cumb'd	To 2-Brig. 2-Cav. Div. Cumb'd	Mch.,	1863
3d Ohio Cav.	Jan., 1863	From 2-Brig. Cav. Div. Cumb'd	To 2-Brig. 2-Cav. Div. Cumb'd	Mch.,	1863
4th Ohio Cav.	Jan., 1863	From 2-Brig. Cav. Div. Cumb'd	To 2-Brig. 2-Cav. Div. Cumb'd	Mch.,	1863
5th Ky. Cav.	Jan., 1863	From Cav. 4-Div. Centre 14-Corps	To 3-Brig. 1-Cav. Div. 16-C. Tenn.	July,	1863
2d Tenn. Cav.	Jan., 1863	From Reserve Cav. Cumb'd	To 3-Brig. 1-Cav. Div. 16-C. Tenn.	Jan.,	1864
2d Ind. Cav.	Mch., 1863	From 1-Brig. 1-Cav. Div. Cumb'd	To 2-Br. 1-Div. Cav. Corps M. D. M.	Oct.,	1864
4th Ind. Cav.	Mch., 1863	From Dist. West Ky. Dept. Ohio	To 2-Br. 1-Div. Cav. Corps M. D. M.	Oct.,	1864
1st Wis. Cav.	June, 1863	From Army S. E. Mo. Dept. Mo.	To 2-Br. 1-Div. Cav. Corps M. D. M.	Oct.,	1864
3d Tenn. Cav.	June, 1863	From Post Nashville, Tenn.	To 3-Brig. 1-Cav. Div. 16-C. Tenn.	Jan.,	1864

3d BRIGADE.—Organized July 8, 1863.— COMMANDERS.

L. D. Watkins	Col. 6th Ky. Cav.	July 8, 1863, to July 5, 1864.
J. K. Faulkner	Col. 7th Ky. Cav.	July 5, 1864, to Aug. 10, 1864.
L. D. Watkins	Col. 6th Ky. Cav.	Aug. 10, 1864, to Oct. 29, 1864.

4th Ky. Cav.	July, 1863	From 1-Brig. 1-Cav. Div. Cumb'd	To 2-Br. 1-Div. Cav. C. M. D. Miss.	Oct.,	1864
5th Ky. Cav.	July, 1863	From 2-Brig. 1-Cav. Div. Cumb'd	To 3-Br. 1-Cav. Div. 16-Corps, Tenn.	Jan.,	1864
6th Ky. Cav.	July, 1863	From 1-Brig. 1-Cav. Div. Cumb'd	To 1-Br. 1-Div. Cav. C. M. D. Miss.	Oct.,	1864
7th Ky. Cav.	July, 1863	From 1-Brig. 1-Cav. Div. Cumb'd	To 2-Br. 1-Div. Cav. C. M. D. Miss.	Oct.,	1864

ARTILLERY, 1st DIVISION.—

Batty. D, 1st O. Arty. Sec.	Jan., 1863	From Arty. Cav. Div. Cumb'd	To Arty. 2-Div. Cav. Div. Cumb'd	Mch.,	1863
18th Ind. Batty.	Jan., 1864	From Arty. 2-Cav. Div. Cumb'd	To Arty. 1-Div. Cav. Corps M. D. M.	Oct.,	1864

2d DIVISION.—Organized March, 1863.— COMMANDERS.

J. B. Turchin	Brigadier General	Mch. .., 1863, to July 28, 1863.
George Crook	Brigadier General	July 28, 1863, to Feb. 3, 1864.
Kennard Garrard	Brigadier General	Feb. 3, 1864, to Oct. 29, 1864

1st BRIGADE.— COMMANDERS.

R. H. G. Minty	Col. 4th Mich. Cav.	Mch. .., 1863, to Dec. .., 1863.
W. B. Sipes	Col. 7th Penna. Cav.	Dec. .., 1863, to Jan. 24, 1864.
W. W. Lowe	Col. 5th Iowa Cav.	Jan. 24, 1864, to Apr. 1, 1864.
R. H. G. Minty	Col. 4th Mich. Cav.	Apr. 1, 1864, to Sept. 29, 1864.
W. H. Jennings	Major 4th U. S. Cav.	Sept. 29, 1864, to Oct. 29, 1864.

3d Indiana Cav.	Mch., 1863	From 1-Brig. 1-Cav. Div. Cumb'd	To 1-Brig. 3-Cav. Div. Cumb'd	Apr.,	1864
4th Mich. Cav.	Mch., 1863	From 1-Brig. 1-Cav. Div. Cumb'd	To 2-Brig. 2-Cav. Div. Cumb'd	Nov.,	1863
7th Penna. Cav.	Mch., 1863	From 1-Brig. 1-Cav. Div. Cumb'd	To 2-Br. 2-Div. Cav. Corps M.D.Miss.	Oct.,	1864
5th Tenn. Cav.	Mch., 1863	From Reserve Cav. Cumb'd	To 3-Brig. 2-Cav. Div. Cumb'd	Aug.,	1863
4th U. S. Cav.	Mch., 1863	From Headqrs. Dept. Cumb'd	To Headqrs. Cav. Corps M. D. Miss.	Oct.,	1863
5th Iowa Cav.	June, 1863	From Fort Donelson, Tenn.	To 3-Brig. 2-Cav. Div. Cumb'd	Oct.,	1863
8th Ind. Cav.	Oct., 1863	From 39th Ind. Mtd. Infy.	To 2-Brig. 2-Cav. Div. Cumb'd	Apr.,	1864
5th Tenn. Cav.	Nov., 1863	From 3-Brig. 2-Cav. Div. Cumb'd	To 1-Brig. 3-Cav. Div. Cumb'd	Apr.,	1864
5th Iowa Cav.	Nov., 1863	From 3-Brig. 2-Cav. Div. Cumb'd	To 1-Brig. 3-Cav. Div. Cumb'd	Apr.,	1864
4th Mich. Cav.	Nov., 1863	From 2-Brig. 2-Cav. Div. Cumb'd	To 2-Br. 2-Div. Cav. Corps M.D.Miss.	Oct.,	1864

2d BRIGADE.— COMMANDERS.

Eli Long	Col. 4th Ohio Cav.	Mch., 1863, to Aug. 20, 1864.
B. B. Eggleston	Col. 1st Ohio Cav.	Aug. 20, 1864, to Oct. 29, 1864.

2d Ky. Cav.	Mch., 1863	From Cav. 1-Div. 14-Corps	To 2-Brig. 3-Cav. Div. Cumb'd	Apr.,	1864
1st Ohio Cav.	Mch., 1863	From 2-Brig. 1-Cav. Div. Cumb'd	To 2-Br. 2-Div. Cav. Corps M.D.Miss.	Oct.,	1864
3d Ohio Cav.	Mch., 1863	From 2-Brig. 1-Cav. Div. Cumb'd	To 2-Br. 2-Div. Cav. Corps M.D.Miss.	Oct.,	1864
4th Ohio Cav.	Mch., 1863	From 2-Brig. 1-Cav. Div. Cumb'd	To 2-Br. 2-Div. Cav. Corps M.D.Miss.	Oct.,	1864
10th Ohio Cav.	Mch., 1863	From New Organization	To 3-Brig. 2-Cav. Div. Cumb'd	Aug.,	1863
4th Mich Cav.	Nov., 1863	From 1-Brig. 2-Cav. Div. Cumb'd	To 1-Brig. 2-Cav. Div. Cumb'd	Nov.,	1863
10th Ohio Cav.	Nov., 1863	From 3-Brig. 2-Cav. Div. Cumb'd	To 1-Brig. 3-Cav. Div. Cumb'd	Apr.,	1864
17th Ind. Mtd. Infy.	Nov., 1863	From 3-Brig. 2-Cav. Div. Cumb'd	To 3-Brig. 2-Cav. Div. Cumb'd	Nov.,	1863
98th Ill. Mtd. Infy.	Nov., 1863	From 3-Brig. 2-Cav. Div. Cumb'd	To 3-Brig. 2-Cav. Div. Cumb'd	Nov.,	1863

3d BRIGADE.—Discontinued Nov. 8, 1863. Reorganized Nov. 8, 1863, by Assignment of Wilder's Mtd. Infy. Brigade.

COMMANDERS.

W. W. Lowe	Col. 5th Iowa Cav.	Aug. 5, 1863, to Nov. 8, 1863.
J. T. Wilder	Col. 17th Ind. Mtd. Infy.	Nov. 8, 1863, to Dec. 25, 1863.
A. O. Miller	Col. 72d Ind. Mtd. Infy.	Dec. 25, 1863, to Jan. 28, 1864.
S. D. Atkins	Col. 92d Ill. Mtd. Infy.	Jan. 28, 1864, to Feb. 20, 1864.
J. T. Wilder	Col. 17th Ind. Mtd. Infy.	Feb. 20, 1864, to June 14, 1864.
A. C. Miller	Col. 72d Ind. Mtd. Infy.	June 14, 1864, to Oct. 29, 1864.

5th Iowa Cav.	Aug., 1863	From 1-Brig. 2-Cav. Div. Cumb'd	To 1-Brig. 2-Cav. Div. Cumbd.	Nov.,	1863
10th Ohio Cav.	Aug., 1863	From 2-Brig. 2-Cav. Div. Cumb'd	To 2-Brig. 2-Cav. Div. Cumbd.	Nov.,	1863
5th Tenn. Cav.	Aug., 1863	From 1-Brig. 2-Cav. Div. Cumb'd	To 1-Brig. 2-Cav. Div. Cumbd.	Nov.,	1863
92d Ill. Mtd. Infy.	Nov., 1863	From Wilder's Mtd. Infy. Brig.	To 3-Brig. 2-Cav. Div. Cumb'd	Apr.,	1864
98th Ill. Mtd. Infy.	Nov., 1863	From Wilder's Mtd. Infy. Brig.	To 3-Brig. 2-Cav. Div. Cumb'd	Nov.,	1863
123d Ill. Mtd. Infy.	Nov., 1863	From Wilder's Mtd. Infy. Brig.	To 3-Br. 2-Div. Cav. Corps M.D.Miss.	Oct.,	1864
17th Ind. Mtd. Infy.	Nov., 1863	From Wilder's Mtd. Infy. Brig.	To 2-Brig. 2-Cav. Div. Cumb'd	Nov.,	1863
72d Ind. Mtd. Infy.	Nov., 1863	From Wilder's Mtd. Infy. Brig.	To 3-Br. 1-Cav. Div. 16-C. Tenn.	Jan.,	1864
18th Ind. Batty.	Nov., 1863	From Wilder's Mtd. Infy. Brig.	To Arty. 1-Cav. Div. Cumb'd	Jan.,	1864
17th Ind. Mtd. Infy.	Nov., 1863	From 2-Brig. 2-Cav. Div. Cumb'd	To 3-Br. 2-Div. Cav. Div. M. D. M.	Oct.,	1864
98th Ill. Mtd. Infy.	Nov., 1863	From 2-Brig. 2-Cav. Div. Cumb'd	To 3-Br. 2-Div. Cav. Div. M. D. M.	Oct.,	1864
72d Ind. Mtd. Infy.	Apr., 1864	From 3-Brig. 1-Cav. Div. 16-C. Tenn.	To 3-Br. 2-Div. Cav. Div. M. D. M.	Oct.,	1864

ARTILLERY, 2d DIVISION.—

Batty. D, 1st Ohio A'y Sec.	Mch., 1864	From Arty. 1-Div. Cav. Cumb'd	To Arty. 3-Div. 23-Corps Ohio	Dec.,	1863
Board Trade Ill. Batty.	Mch., 1864	From Pioneer Brig. Cumb'd	To Arty. 2-Div. Cav. Corps M. D. M.	Oct.,	1864

UNATTACHED.—

39th Ind. Mtd. Infy.	Apr., 1863	From 1-Brig. 2-Div. 20-Corps	To Unass'd as 8th Ind. Cav.	Oct.,	1863

3d DIVISION.—Organized April 2, 1864. COMMANDERS.

W. W. Lowe	Col. 5th Iowa Cav.	Apr. 2, 1864, to Apr. 17, 1864.
Eli H. Murray	Col. 3d Ky. Cav.	Apr. 17, 1864, to Apr. 26, 1864.
J. Kilpatrick	Brigadier General	Apr. 26, 1864, to May 13, 1864.
Eli H. Murray	Col. 3d Ky. Cav.	May 13, 1864, to May 21, 1864.
W. W. Lowe	Col. 5th Iowa Cav.	May 21, 1864, to July 23, 1864.
J. Kilpatrick	Brigadier General	July 23, 1864, to Oct. 29, 1864.

1st BRIGADE.—   COMMANDERS.

W. W. Lowe	Col. 5th Iowa Cav	Apr. 2, 1864, to May 21, 1864.
Robert Klein	Lt.-Col. 3d Ind. Cav	May 21, 1864, to Aug. 23, 1864.
M. T. Patrick	Col. 5th Iowa Cav	Aug. 23, 1864, to Aug. 26, 1864.
J. M. Young	Major 5th Iowa Cav	Aug. 26, 1864, to Sept. 5, 1864.
Thos. J. Jordan	Col. 9th Penna. Cav	Sept. 5, 1864, to Oct. 29, 1864.

3d Ind. Cav. 4 Cos.	Apr., 1864	From 1-Brig. 2-Cav. Div. Cumb'd	To 1-Br. 3-Div. Cav. Corps M. D. M.	Oct., 1864
5th Iowa Cav	Apr., 1864	From 1-Brig. 2-Cav. Div. Cumb'd	To 1-Br. 3-Div. Cav. Corps M. D. M.	Oct., 1864
9th Penna. Cav	Apr., 1864	From 1-Brig. 1-Div. Cav. Cumb'd	To 1-Br. 3-Div. Cav. Corps M. D. M.	Oct., 1864

2d BRIGADE.—   COMMANDERS.

C. C. Smith	Col. 10th Ohio Cav	Apr. 2, 1864, to July 27, 1864.
T. J. Harrison	Col. 8th Ind. Cav	July 27, 1864, to July 30, 1864.
C. C. Smith	Col. 10th Ohio Cav	July 30, 1864, to Aug. 6, 1864.
T. W. Sanderson	Major 10th Ohio Cav	Aug. 6, 1864, to Aug. 10, 1864.
F. A. Jones	Lt.-Col. 8th Ind. Cav	Aug. 10, 1864, to Sept. 26, 1864.
William Thayer	Major 10th Ohio Cav	Sept. 26, 1864, to Oct. 29, 1864.

8th Ind. Cav	Apr., 1864	From Dist. Nashville, Tenn	To 2-Br. 3-Div. Cav. Corps M. D. M.	Oct., 1864
2d Ky. Cav	Apr., 1864	From 2-Brig. 2-Cav. Div. Cumb'd	To 2-Br. 3-Div. Cav. Corps M. D. M.	Oct., 1864
10th Ohio Cav	Apr., 1864	From 2-Brig. 2-Cav. Div. Cumb'd	To 2-Br. 3-Div. Cav. Corps M. D. M.	Oct., 1864

3d BRIGADE.—   COMMANDERS.

Eli H. Murray	Col. 3d Ky. Cav	Apr. 2, 1864, to May 13, 1864.
S. D. Atkins	Col. 92d Ill. Mtd. Infy	May 13, 1864, to May 23, 1864.
Eli H. Murray	Col. 3d Ky. Cav	May 23, 1864, to Aug. 18, 1864.
R. H. King	Lt.-Col. 3d Ky. Cav	Aug. 18, 1864, to Aug. 22, 1864.
Eli H. Murray	Col. 3d Ky. Cav	Aug. 22, 1864, to Oct. 29, 1864.

92d Ill. Mtd. Infy	Apr., 1864	From 3-Brig. 2-Cav. Div. Cumb'd	To 3-Br. 3-Div. Cav. Corps M. D. M.	Oct., 1864
3d Ky. Cav	Apr., 1864	From 3-Brig. 2-Cav. Div. Cumb'd	To 3-Br. 3-Div. Cav. Corps M. D. M.	Oct., 1864
5th Ky. Cav	Apr., 1864	From 3-Brig. 1-Cav. Div. 16-C. Tenn.	To 3-Br. 3-Div. Cav. Corps M. D. M.	Oct., 1864

ARTILLERY, 3d DIVISION.—

10th Wis. Batty	Apr., 1864	From Unass'd Arty. Dept. Cumb'd	To Arty. 3-Div. Cav. Corps M. D. M.	Oct., 1864

UNATTACHED, 3d DIVISION.—

1st Ala. Cav	Sept., 1864	From Headqrs. 16-Corps Left Wing	To Un'as. 3-Div. Cav. Corps M. D. M.	Oct., 1864
9th Ill. Mtd. Infy	Sept., 1864	From 2-Brig. 2-Div. 16-C. Tenn.	To Un'as. 3-Div. Cav. Corps M. D. M.	Oct., 1864

4th DIVISION.—Organized April 1, 1864.   COMMANDERS.

A. C. Gillem	Brigadier General	Apr. 1, 1864, to Aug. 16, 1864.
George Spalding	Col. 12th Tenn. Cav	Aug. 16, 1864, to Oct. 29, 1864.

1st BRIGADE.—   COMMANDER.

D. G. Thornburg	Lt.-Col. 3d Tenn. Cav	Apr. 1, 1864, to Oct. 29, 1864.

2d Tenn. Cav	Apr., 1864	From 3-Brig. 1-Cav. Div. 16-C. Tenn.	To 1-Br. 4-Div. Cav. Corps M. D. M.	Oct., 1864
3d Tenn. Cav	Apr., 1864	From 3-Brig. 1-Cav. Div. 16-C. Tenn.	To 1-Br. 4-Div. Cav. Corps M. D. M.	Oct., 1864
4th Tenn. Cav	Apr., 1864	From 3-Brig. 1-Cav. Div. 16-C. Tenn.	To 1-Br. 4-Div. Cav. Corps M. D. M.	Oct., 1864
Batty. A, Tenn. Arty	Apr., 1864	From Decatur, Ala	To 1-Br. 4-Div. Cav. Corps M. D. M.	Oct., 1864

d BRIGADE.—   COMMANDERS.

Geo. Spalding	Lt.-Col. 12th Tenn. Cav	Apr. 1, 1864, to Aug. 16, 1864.
W. J. Clift	Lt.-Col. 5th Tenn. Cav	Aug. 16, 1864, to Oct. 29, 1864.

5th Tenn. Cav	Apr., 1864	From Dist. Nashville, Tenn	To 2-Br. 4-Div. Cav. Corps M. D. M.	Oct., 1864
10th Tenn. Cav	Apr., 1864	From Dist. Nashville, Tenn	To 2-Br. 4-Div. Cav. Corps M. D. M.	Oct., 1864
12th Tenn. Cav	Apr., 1864	From Def. Nash. & N. W. R. R.	To 2-Br. 4-Div. Cav. Corps M. D. M.	Oct., 1864
1st Kan. Batty	Apr., 1864	From Def. Nash. & N. W. R. R.	To Def. Nash. & N. W. R. R.	May, 1864

3d BRIGADE.—   COMMANDER.

J. K. Miller	Col. 13th Tenn. Cav	Apr. 1, 1864, to Oct. 19, 1864.

8th Tenn. Cav	Apr., 1864	From 2-Brig. 2-Div. Cav. Corps Ohio	To 3-Br. 4-Div. Cav. Corps M. D. M.	Oct., 1864
9th Tenn. Cav	Apr., 1864	From New Organization	To 3-Br. 4-Div. Cav. Corps M. D. M.	Oct., 1864
13th Tenn. Cav	Apr., 1864	From New Organization	To 3-Br. 4-Div. Cav. Corps M. D. M.	Oct., 1864

WILDER'S MOUNTED INFANTRY BRIGADE.—Assigned to Cav. Command Cumb'd from 4-Div. 14-Corps, Oct. 16, 1863. Assigned to 2-Cav. Division Nov. 8, 1863.

                                  COMMANDER.

J. T. Wilder	Col. 72d Ind. Mtd. Infy	Oct. 16, 1863, to Nov. 8, 1863.

92d Ill. Mtd. Infy	Oct., 1863	From 1-Brig. 4-Div. 14-Corps	To 3-Brig. 2-Div. Cav. Dept. Cumb'd.	Nov., 1863
98th Ill. Mtd. Infy	Oct., 1863	From 1-Brig. 4-Div. 14-Corps	To 3-Brig. 2-Div. Cav. Dept. Cumb'd.	Nov., 1863
123d Ill. Mtd. Infy	Oct., 1863	From 1-Brig. 4-Div. 14-Corps	To 3-Brig. 2-Div. Cav. Dept. Cumb'd.	Nov., 1863
17th Ind. Mtd. Infy	Oct., 1863	From 1-Brig. 4-Div. 14-Corps	To 3-Brig. 2-Div. Cav. Dept. Cumb'd.	Nov., 1863
72d Ind. Mtd. Infy	Oct., 1863	From 1-Brig. 4-Div. 14-Corps	To 3-Brig. 2-Div. Cav. Dept. Cumb'd.	Nov., 1863
18th Ind. Batty	Oct., 1863	To Arty. 4-Div. 14-Corps	To 3-Brig. 2-Div. Cav. Dept. Cumb'd.	Nov., 1863

Cavalry Corps---Military Division of the Mississippi

Organized Oct., 1864. Discontinued June 26, 1865.

                                  COMMANDER.

J. H. Wilson	Bvt. Major General	Oct. 29, 1864, to June 26, 1865.

1st DIVISION.—   COMMANDERS.

E. M. McCook	Brigadier General	Oct. 29, 1864, to June 26, 1865.
J. T. Croxton	Brigadier General	Temporarily in Feb., 1865.

1st BRIGADE.—   COMMANDER.

J. T. Croxton	Brigadier General	Oct. 29, 1864, to June 26, 1865.

8th Iowa Cav	Oct., 1864	From 1-Brig. 1-Cav. Div. Cumb'd	No change to Muster Out	Aug., 1865
4th Ky. Mtd. Infy	Oct., 1864	From 1-Brig. 1-Cav. Div. Cumb'd	No change to Muster Out	Aug., 1865
2d Mich. Cav	Oct., 1864	From 1-Brig. 1-Cav. Div. Cumb'd	No change to Muster Out	Aug., 1865
1st Tenn. Cav	Oct., 1864	From 1-Brig. 1-Cav. Div. Cumb'd	To Dist. Middle Tenn	Jan., 1865
6th Ky. Cav	Jan., 1865	From 3-Br. 1-Div. Cav. Corps M.D.M.	No change to Muster Out	Aug., 1865

2d BRIGADE.— COMMANDERS.

O. H. LaGrange.......	Col. 1st Wis. Cav...................	Oct. 29, 1864, to June 26, 1864.
H. P. Lamson..........	Lt.-Col. 4th Ind. Cav..............	Temporarily.

2d Ind. Cav.............Oct., 1864	From 2-Brig. 1-Cav. Div. Cumb'd...	No change to Muster Out.........	July,	1865
4th Ind. Cav.............Oct., 1864	From 2-Brig. 1-Cav. Div. Cumb'd...	No change to Muster Out.........	June,	1865
1st Wis. Cav.............Oct., 1864	From 2-Brig. 1-Cav. Div. Cumb'd...	No change to Muster Out.........	July,	1865
4th Ky. Cav.............Jan., 1865	From 3-Br. 1-Div. Cav. Corps M.D.M.	No change to Muster Out.........	Aug.,	1865
7th Ky. Cav.............Jan., 1865	From 3-Br. 1-Div. Cav. Corps M.D.M.	No change to Muster Out.........	July,	1865

3d BRIGADE.—Discontinued Jan. 23, 1865. COMMANDER.

L. D. Watkins.........	Bvt. Brig. General................	Oct. 29, 1864, to Jan. 23, 1865.

4th Ky. Cav.............Oct., 1864	From 3-Brig. 1-Cav. Div. Cumb'd...	To 2-Br. 1-Div. Cav. Corps M. D. M.	Jan.,	1865
6th Ky. Cav.............Oct., 1864	From 3-Brig. 1-Cav. Div. Cumb'd...	To 1-Br. 1-Div. Cav. Corps M. D. M.	Jan.,	1865
7th Ky. Cav.............Oct., 1864	From 3-Brig. 1-Cav. Div. Cumb'd...	To 2-Br. 1-Div. Cav. Corps M. D. M.	Jan.,	1865
ARTILLERY.—				
18th Ind. Batty..........Oct., 1864	From Arty. 1-Cav. Div. Cumb'd.....	No change to Muster Out..........	July,	1865

2d DIVISION.— COMMANDERS.

Kenner Garrard........	Brigadier General.................	Oct. 29, 1864, to Nov. 16, 1864.
Eli Long..............	Brigadier General.................	Nov. 16, 1864, to Apr. 2, 1865.
R. H. G. Minty........	Col. 4th Mich. Cav................	Apr. 2, 1865, to June 26, 1865.

1st BRIGADE.— COMMANDERS.

J. F. Andress..........	Major 7th Penna. Cav.............	Oct. 29, 1864, to Nov. 6, 1864.
A. O. Miller...........	Col. 72d Ind. Mtd. Infy...........	Nov. 6, 1864, to Apr. 2, 1865.
J. G. Vail.............	Col. 17th Ind. Mtd. Infy..........	Apr. 2, 1865, to Apr. 12, 1865.
Frank White...........	Lt.-Col. 17th Ind. Mtd. Infy......	Apr. 12, 1865, to June 26, 1865.

4th Mich. Cav........Oct., 1864	From 1-Brig. 2-Cav. Div. Cumb'd...	To 2-Br. 2-Div. Cav. Corps M. D. M.	Nov.,	1864
7th Penna. Cav........Oct., 1864	From 1-Brig. 2-Cav. Div. Cumb'd...	To 2-Br. 2-Div. Cav. Corps M. D. M.	Nov.,	1864
4th U. S. Cav.........Oct., 1864	From 1-Brig. 2-Cav. Div. Cumb'd...	To Headqrs. Cav. Corps M. D. M....	Oct.,	1864
17th Ind. Mtd. Infy.....Nov., 1864	To 3-Br. 2-Div. Cav. Corps M. D. M.	No change to Muster Out.........	June,	1865
72d Ind. Mtd. Infy......Nov., 1864	To 3-Br. 2-Div. Cav. Corps M. D. M.	No change to Muster Out.........	June,	1865
98th Ill. Mtd. Infy......Nov., 1864	To 3-Br. 2-Div. Cav. Corps M. D. M.	No change to Muster Out.........	Aug.,	1865
123d Ill. Mtd. Infy......Nov., 1864	To 3-Br. 2-Div. Cav. Corps M. D. M.	No change to Muster Out.........	June,	1865

2d BRIGADE.— COMMANDERS.

B. B. Eggleston.......	Col. 1st Ohio Cav................	Oct. 29, 1864, to Nov. 16, 1864.
R. H. G. Minty........	Col. 4th Michigan Cav............	Nov. 16, 1864, to Apr. 2, 1865.
H. N. Howland........	Col. 3d Ohio Cav................	Apr. 2, 1865, to June 26, 1865.

1st Ohio Cav............Oct., 1864	From 2-Brig. 2-Cav. Div. Cumb'd..	To 2-B. 4-Div. Cav. Corps M. D. M	Feb.,	1865
3d Ohio Cav............Oct., 1864	From 2-Brig. 2-Cav. Div. Cumb'd..	No change to Muster Out.........	Aug.,	1865
4th Ohio Cav............Oct., 1864	From 2-Brig. 2-Cav. Div. Cumb'd..	No change to Muster Out.........	July,	1865
4th Michigan Cav.......Nov., 1864	From 1-B. 2-D. Cav. Corps M. D. M.	No change to Muster Out.........	July,	1865
7th Penna. Cav.........Nov., 1864	From 1-B. 2-D. Cav. Corps M. D. M.	No change to Muster Out.........	Aug.,	1865

3d BRIGADE.—Transferred to 1st Brig. Nov., 1864.

COMMANDER.

A. O. Miller...........	Col. 72d Indiana Mtd. Infy........	Oct. 29, 1864, to Nov. 6, 1864.

17th Indiana Mtd. Infy...Oct., 1864	From 3-Brig. 2-Cav. Div. Cumb'd...	To 1-B. 2-Div. Cav. Corps M. D. M.	Nov.,	1864
72d Indiana Mtd. Infy....Oct., 1864	From 3-Brig. 2-Cav. Div. Cumb'd...	To 1-B. 2-Div. Cav. Corps M. D. M	Nov.,	1864
98th Illinois Mtd. Infy...Oct., 1864	From 3-Brig. 2-Cav. Div. Cumb'd...	To 1-B. 2-Div. Cav. Corps M. D. M.	Nov.,	1864
123d Illinois Mtd. Infy...Oct., 1864	From 3-Brig. 2-Cav. Div. Cumb'd...	To 1-B. 2-Div. Cav. Corps M. D. M.	Nov.,	1864
ARTILLERY.—				
Board Trade, Ill., Batty...Oct., 1864	From Arty. 2-Cav. Div. Cumb'd....	No change to Muster Out.........	July,	1865

3d DIVISION (With Sherman's Army).— COMMANDER.

Judson Kilpatrick......	Brigadier General.................	Oct. 29, 1864, to June 26, 1865.

1st BRIGADE.— COMMANDERS.

T. J. Jordan...........	Col. 9th Penna. Cav.............	Oct. 29, 1864, to Nov. 10, 1864.
Eli H. Murray..........	Col. 3d Kentucky Cav.............	Nov. 10, 1864, to Jan. 20, 1865.
T. J. Jordan...........	Col. 9th Penna. Cav.............	Jan. 20, 1865, to June 26, 1865.

3d Indiana Cav. Battn.....Oct., 1864	From 1-Brig. 3-Cav. Div. Cumb'd...	To 2-B. 3-Div. Cav. Corps M. D. M.	Nov.,	1864
5th Iowa Cav............Oct., 1864	From 1-Brig. 3-Cav. Div. Cumb'd..	To 2-B. 6-Div. Cav. Corps M. D. M.	Nov.,	1864
9th Penna. Cav..........Oct., 1864	From 1-Brig. 3-Cav. Div. Cumb'd..	To 3-B. 3-Div. Cav. Corps M. D. M	June,	1865
2d Kentucky Cav........Nov., 1864	From 2-B. 3-D. Cav. Corps M. D. M.	No change to Muster Out.........	July,	1865
3d Kentucky Cav........Nov., 1864	From 3-B. 3-D. Cav. Corps M. D. M.	No change to Muster Out.........	July,	1865
5th Kentucky Cav.......Nov., 1864	From 3-B. 3-D. Cav. Corps M. D. M.	To 3-B. 3-Div. Cav. Corps M. D. M.	Jan.,	1865
8th Indiana Cav.........Nov., 1864	From 2-B. 3-D. Cav. Corps M. D. M.	No change to Muster Out.........	July,	1865

2d BRIGADE.— COMMANDERS.

William Thayer........	Major 10th Ohio Cav.............	Oct. 29, 1864, to Nov. 5, 1864.
S. D. Atkins...........	Col. 92d Illinois Mtd. Infy..........	Nov. 5, 1864, to June 26, 1865.

8th Indiana Cav.........Oct., 1864	From 2-Brig. 3-Cav. Div. Cumb'd..	To 1-B. 3-Div. Cav. Corps M. D. M.	Nov.,	1864
2d Kentucky Cav........Oct., 1864	From 2-Brig. 3-Cav. Div. Cumb'd..	To 1-B. 3-Div. Cav. Corps M. D. M	Nov.,	1864
10th Ohio Cav...........Oct., 1864	From 2-Brig. 3-Cav. Div. Cumb'd..	No change to Muster Out.........	July,	1865
9th Michigan Cav.......Nov., 1864	From 1-Brig. Cav. Div. 23-Corps...	No change to Muster Out.........	July,	1865
5th Ohio Cav...........Nov., 1864	From Cav. 3-Div. 15-Corps Tenn..	To 3-B. 3-Div. Cav. Corps M. D. M	Jan.,	1865
9th Ohio Cav...........Nov., 1864	From Mtd. Brig. Cav. Div. 23-Corps	No change to Muster Out.........	June,	1865
McLaughlin's Ohio Sqdn..Nov., 1864	From 3-Brig. Cav. Div. 23-Corps..	No change to Muster Out.........	July,	1865
92d Illinois Mtd. Infy...Nov., 1864	From 3-B. 3-D. Cav. Corps M. D. M.	No change to Muster Out.........	June,	1865
3d Indiana Cav.........Nov., 1864	From 1-B. 3-Cav. Corps M. D. M.	Consolidated with 8th Ind. Cav....	Dec.,	1864

3d BRIGADE.—Discontinued Nov., 1864. Reorganized Jan., 1865.

COMMANDERS.

Eli H. Murray..........	Col. 3d Kentucky Cav.............	Oct. 29, 1864, to Nov. 10, 1864.
Geo. E. Spencer........	Col. 1st Alabama Cav.............	Jan., 1865, to Apr., 1865.
M. Kerwin.............	Col. 13th Penna. Cav.............	Apr., 1865, to Apr. 25, 1865.
T. T. Heath...........	Col. 5th Ohio Cav...............	Apr. 25, 1865, to June 26, 1865.

3d Kentucky Cav.......Oct., 1864	From 3-Brig. 3-Div. Div. Cumb'd..	To 1-B. 3-Div. Cav. Corps M. D. M.	Nov.,	1864
5th Kentucky Cav.......Oct., 1864	From 3-Brig. 3-Div. Div. Cumb'd..	To 1-B. 3-Div. Cav. Corps M. D. M.	Nov.,	1864
92d Illinois Mtd. Infy...Oct., 1864	From 3-Brig. 3-Div. Div. Cumb'd..	To 2-B. 3-Div. Cav. Corps M. D. M.	Nov.,	1864
1st Alabama Cav........Jan., 1865	From Unatt. 3-D. Cav. C'rps M. D. M.	To Dist. North Ala. Dept. Cumb'd..	June,	1865
5th Kentucky Cav.......Jan., 1865	From 1-B. 3-D. Cav. Corps M. D. M.	No change to Muster Out.........	May,	1865
5th Ohio Cav...........Jan., 1865	From 2-B. 3-D. Cav. Corps M. D. M.	To Dept. North Carolina..........	June,	1865
13th Penna. Cav........Apr., 1865	From Unatt. 10-Corps Dept. N. C...	No change to Muster Out.........	July,	1865
9th Penna. Cav.........June, 1865	From 1-B. 3-D. Cav. Corps M. D. M.	No change to Muster Out.........	July,	1865

ARTILLERY.—

10th Wisconsin Batty....Oct., 186	From Arty. 3-Cav. Div. Cumb'd....	No change to Muster Out.........	Apr.,	1865
23d N. Y. Indpt. Batty....Apr., 186?	From Dist. Beaufort Dept. N. C....	No change to Muster Out.........	July,	1865

UNASSIGNED.—

1st Alabama Cav........Oct., 1864	From Unatt. 3-Cav. Div. Cumb'd....	To 3-B. 3-Div. Cav. Corps M. D. M.	Jan.,	1865
9th Illinois Mtd. Infy.....Oct., 1864	From Unatt. 3-Cav. Div. Cumb'd...	No change to Muster Out.........	July,	1865

4th PROV'L BRIGADE.—Organized from dismounted men of the Division. W. B. May, Lt.-Col.
1st Regiment from 1st Brigade.
2d Regiment from 2d Brigade.
3d Regiment from 3d Brigade.
4th DIVISION.—   COMMANDERS.

Geo. Spalding.........	Col. 12th Tennessee Cav............	Oct. 29, 1864, to Nov. 9, 1864.	
B. H. Grierson........	Brigadier General.................	Nov. 9, 1864, to Dec. 13, 1864.	
Emory Upton..........	Bvt. Major General................	Dec. 13, 1864, to June 26, 1865.	

1st BRIGADE.—   COMMANDERS.

D. G. Thornburg.......	Lt.-Col. 3d Tennessee Cav........	Oct. 29, 1864, to Nov. 9, 1864.	
E. F. Winslow.........	Col. 4th Iowa Cav.................	Nov. 9, 1864, to June 26, 1865.	

2d Tennessee Cav........Oct., 1864	From 1-Brig. 4-Cav. Div. Cumb'd..	To 1-D. 7-Div. Cav. Corps M. D. M.	Nov.,	1864
3d Tennessee Cav........Oct., 1864	From 1-Brig. 4-Cav. Div. Cumb'd..	To 2-B. 6-Div. Cav. Corps M. D. M.	Nov.,	1864
4th Tennessee Cav.......Oct., 1864	From 1-Brig. 4-Cav. Div. Cumb'd..	To 1-B. 7-Div. Cav. Corps M. D. M.	Nov.,	1864
3d Iowa Cav............Nov., 1864	From 2-B. 2-D. Cav. Corps W. Tenn.	To 2-Brig. Cav. Div. Dist. W. Tenn.	Dec.,	1864
4th Iowa Cav...........Nov., 1864	From 2-B. 2-D. Cav. Corps W. Tenn.	To 2-Brig. Cav. Div. Dist. W. Tenn.	Dec.,	1864
10th Missouri Cav.......Nov., 1864	From 2-B. 2-D. Cav. Corps W. Tenn.	To 2-Brig. Cav. Div. Dist. W. Tenn.	Dec.,	1864
3d Iowa Cav............Feb., 1865	From 2-B. Cav. Div. Dist. W. Tenn.	No change to Muster Out.........	Aug.,	1865
4th Iowa Cav...........Feb., 1865	From 2-B. Cav. Div. Dist. W. Tenn.	No change to Muster Out.........	Aug.,	1865
10th Missouri Cav.......Feb., 1865	From 2-B. Cav. Div. Dist. W. Tenn.	To 2-B. 4-Div. Cav. Corps M. D. M.	May,	1865
1st Ohio Cav...........May, 1865	From 2-B. 4-D. Cav. Corps M. D. M.	To Dept. Georgia.................	July,	1865

2d BRIGADE.—   COMMANDERS.

W. J. Clift............	Lt.-Col. 5th Tennessee Cav........	Oct 29, 1864, to Nov. 9, 1864.	
Joseph Karge.........	Col. 2d New Jersey Cav............	Nov. 9, 1864, to Dec., 1864.	
I. Garrard...........	Col. 7th Ohio Cav................	Dec., 1864, to Feb. 10, 1865.	
J. I. Alexander........	Bvt. Brig. General................	Feb. 10, 1865, to June 26, 1865.	

5th Tennessee Cav.......Oct., 1864	From 2-Brig. 4-Cav. Div. Cumb'd..	To 3-B. 6-Div. Cav. Corps M. D. M.	Nov.,	1864
10th Tennessee Cav......Oct., 1864	From 2-Brig. 4-Cav. Div. Cumb'd..	To 1-B. 5-Div. Cav. Corps M. D. M.	Nov.,	1864
12th Tennessee Cav......Oct., 1864	From 2-Brig. 4-Cav. Div. Cumb'd..	To 2-B. 5-Div. Cav. Corps M. D. M.	Nov.,	1864
7th Indiana Cav........Nov., 1864	From 1-B. 2-D. Cav. Corps W. Tenn.	To 1-Brig. Cav. Div. Dist. W. Tenn.	Dec.,	1864
2d New Jersey Cav......Nov., 1864	From 1-B. 2-D. Cav. Corps W. Tenn.	To 1-Brig. Cav. Div. Dist. W. Tenn.	Dec.,	1864
19th Penna. Cav........Nov., 1864	From 1-B. 2-D. Cav. Corps W. Tenn.	To 1-B. 7-Div. Cav. Corps M. D. M.	Nov.,	1864
6th Tennessee Cav......Nov., 1864	From Unass'd Cav. Corps W. Tenn.	To 2-B. 7-Div. Cav. Corps M. D. M.	Nov.,	1864
1st Ohio Cav...........Feb., 1865	From 2-B. 2-D. Cav. Corps M. D. M.	To 1-B. 4-Div. Cav. Corps M. D. M.	May,	1865
7th Ohio Cav...........Feb., 1865	From 2-B. 6-Div. Cav. Corps M. D. M.	No change to Muster Out.........	July,	1865
5th Iowa Cav...........Feb., 1865	From 2-B. 6-Div. Cav. Corps M. D. M.	No change to Muster Out.........	Aug.,	1865
10th Missouri Cav.......May, 1865	From 1-B. 4-D. Cav. Corps M. D. M.	No change to Muster Out.........	July,	1865

3d BRIGADE.—   COMMANDER.

J. K. Miller...........	Col. 13th Tennessee Cav..........	Oct. 29, 1864, to Nov. 9, 1864.	

8th Tennessee Cav......Oct., 1864	From 3-Brig 4-Cav. Div. Cumb'd..	To Dist. East Tenn..............	Nov.,	1864
9th Tennessee Cav......Oct., 1864	From 3-Brig 4-Cav. Div. Cumb'd..	To Dist. East Tenn..............	Nov.,	1864
13th Tennessee Cav.....Oct., 1864	From 3-Brig 4-Cav. Div. Cumb'd..	To Dist. East Tenn..............	Nov.,	1864

ARTILLERY.—

Batty. A, Tenn. Arty.....Oct., 1864	From Arty. 4-Cav. Div. Cumberland	To Arty. 6-Div. Cav. Corps M. D. M.	Nov.,	1864
Batty. I, 4th U. S. Arty...Feb., 1865	From Arty. 6-D. Cav. Corps M. D. M.	To Regular Establishment.........	Aug.,	1865

5th DIVISION.—Organized Nov., 1864.   COMMANDERS.

E. W. Hatch..........	Brigadier General.	Nov. 9, 1864, to Jan. 18, 1865.	
R. R. Stewart..........	Col. 11th Indiana Cav............	Jan. 18, 1865, to May 28, 1865.	

1st BRIGADE.—   COMMANDERS.

R. R. Stewart..........	Col. 11th Indiana Cav............	Nov. 27, 1864, to Jan. 18, 1865.	
A. Shawa.............	Lt.-Col. 11th Indiana Cav.........	Jan. 18, 1865, to Feb. 3, 1865.	
R. H. Brown..........	Lt.-Col. 12th Missouri Cav........	Feb. 3, 1865, to Feb. 8, 1865.	
Oliver Wells..........	Col. 12th Missouri Cav...........	Feb. 8, 1865, to May 28, 1865.	

3d Illinois Cav..........Nov., 1864	From 1-B. 1-D. Cav. Corps W. Tenn.	To Dept. Northwest.............	May,	1865
7th Illinois Cav.........Nov., 1864	From 1-B. 1-D. Cav. Corps W. Tenn.	To 2-B. 5-Div. Cav. Corps M. D. M.	Nov.,	1864
12th Missouri Cav.......Nov., 1864	From 1-B. 1-D. Cav. Corps W. Tenn.	To Dept. Missouri..............	May,	1865
11th Indiana Cav........Nov., 1864	From Dist. North Ala............	To Dept. Missouri..............	May,	1865
10th Tennessee Cav......Nov., 1864	From 2-B. 4-D. Cav. Corps M. D. M.	To 1-B. 7-Div. Cav. Corps M. D. M.	Feb.,	1865
12th Tennessee Cav......Apr., 1865	From 2-B. 5-D. Cav. Corps M. D. M.	To Dept. Missouri..............	May,	1865

2d BRIGADE.—   COMMANDER.

D. E. Coon...........	Col. 2d Iowa Cav................	Nov. 27, 1864, to June, 1865.	

6th Illinois Cav.........Nov., 1864	From 2-B. 1-D. Cav. Corps W. Tenn.	To Dist. Alabama...............	July,	1865
7th Illinois Cav.........Nov., 1864	From 1-B. 5-D. Cav. Corps M. D. M.	To Dept. Miss.................	June,	1865
9th Illinois Cav.........Nov., 1864	From 2-B. 1-D. Cav. Corps W. Tenn.	To Dist. Alabama...............	July,	1865
2d Iowa Cav............Nov., 186?	From 2-B. 1-D. Cav. Corps W. Tenn.	To Dept. Miss.................	June,	1865
12th Tennessee Cav......Nov., 186?	From 2-B. 4-D. Cav. Corps M. D. M.	To 1-B. 5-Div. Cav. Corps M. D. M.	Apr.,	1865

ARTILLERY.—

Batty. I, 1st Ill. Arty....Nov., 1864	From Post Nashville, Tenn.........	No change to Muster Out.........	July,	1865

6th DIVISION.—Organized Nov. 17, 1864.   COMMANDER.

R. W. Johnson........	Brigadier General................	Nov. 17, 1864, to July, 1865.	

1st BRIGADE.—   COMMANDERS.

Horace Capron........	Col. 14th Illinois Cav............	Nov. 17, 1864, to Dec. 9, 1864.	
Thos. J. Harrison......	Col. 8th Indiana Cav.............	Dec. 9, 1864, to Feb. 17, 1865.	
T. H. Butler..........	Col. 5th Indiana Cav.............	Feb. 17, 1865, to June 27, 1865.	
E. Mix..............	Col. 8th Michigan Cav............	June 27, 1865, to July, 1865.	

14th Illinois Cav........Nov., 1864	From Dismtd. Brig. Cav. Div. 23-C.	To 2-B. 6-Div. Cav. Corps M. D. M.	Dec.,	1864
16th Illinois Cav........Nov., 1864	From Dismtd. Brig. Cav. Div. 23-C.	No change to Muster Out.........	Aug.,	1865
5th Indiana Cav.........Nov., 1864	From Dist. Louisville Dept. Ohio..	To 2-B. 6-Div. Cav. Corps M. D. M.	Dec.,	1864
8th Michigan Cav.......Nov., 1864	From 3-Brig. Cav. Div. 23-Corps..	To Dist. Middle Tenn...........	June,	1865
5th Iowa Cav...........Dec., 1864	From 2-B. 6-D. Cav. Corps M. D. M.	To 2-B. 6-Div. Cav. Corps M. D. M.	Dec.,	1864
7th Ohio Cav...........Dec., 1864	From 2-B. 6-D. Cav. Corps M. D. M.	To 2-B. 4-Div. Cav. Corps M. D. M.	Feb.,	1865
14th Illinois Cav........Dec., 1864	From 2-B. 6-D. Cav. Corps M. D. M.	To 2-B. 6-Div. Cav. Corps M. D. M.	June,	1865
6th Tennessee Cav......Feb., 1865	From 2-B. 7-Cav. D. C. C. M. D. M.	No change to Muster Out.......	July,	1865

2d BRIGADE.— COMMANDERS.

W. W. Lowe	Col. 5th Iowa Cav	Nov. 17, 1864, to Dec. 9, 1864.
James Biddle	Col. 6th Indiana Cav	Dec. 9, 1864, to Jan. 1, 1865.
W. W. Lowe	Col. 5th Iowa Cav	Jan. 1, 1865, to Feb., 1865.
James Biddle	Col. 6th Indiana Cav	Feb., 1865, to June 27, 1865.
F. M. Davidson	Col. 14th Illinois Cav	June 27, 1865.

6th Indiana Cav	Nov., 1864	From Dismtd. Brig. Cav. Div. 23-C.	To Dist. Middle Tenn	June, 1865
5th Iowa Cav	Nov., 1864	From Dist. Louisville Dept. Ohio.	To 1-B. 6-Div. Cav. Corps M. D. M.	Dec., 1864
7th Ohio Cav	Nov., 1864	From 2-Brig. Cav. Div. 23-Corps.	To 1-B. 6-Div. Cav. Corps M. D. M.	Dec., 1864
3d Tennessee Cav	Nov., 1864	From 1-B. 4-D. Cav. Corps M. D. M.	No change to Muster Out	Aug., 1865
14th Illinois Cav	Dec., 1864	From 1-B. 6-D. Cav. Corps M. D. M.	To 1-B. 6-Div. Cav. Corps M. D. M.	Dec., 1864
5th Indiana Cav	Dec., 1864	From 1-B. 6-D. Cav. Corps M. D. M.	No change to Muster Out	June, 1865
5th Iowa Cav	Dec., 1864	From 1-B. 6-D. Cav. Corps M. D. M.	To 2-B. 4-Div. Cav. Corps M. D. M.	Feb., 1865
14th Illinois Cav	June, 1865	From 1-B. 6-D. Cav. Corps M. D. M.	No change to Muster Out	July, 1865

3d BRIGADE.— COMMANDER.

W. J. Palmer	Col. 15th Penna. Cav	Nov., 1864, to Mch., 1865.

15th Penna. Cav	Nov., 1864	From Unatt. Dept. Cumb'd	To 1-B. Cav. Div. Dist. East Tenn.	Mch., 1865
5th Tennessee Cav	Nov., 1864	From 2-B. 4-D. Cav. Corps M. D. M.	To Dist. Middle Tenn	Mch., 1865
ARTILLERY.—				
Batty. A, Tenn. Arty	Nov., 1864	From Arty. 4-D. Cav. Corps M. D. M.	To Dist. Middle Tenn	Mch., 1865
Batty. I, 4th U. S. Arty	Nov., 1864	From 1-Div. Arty. Res. Cumb'd	To Arty. 4-Div. Cav. Corps M. D. M.	Feb., 1865

7th DIVISION.— COMMANDERS.

J. F. Knipe	Brigadier General	Nov. 16, 1864, to Jan. 3, 1865.
J. H. Hammond	Bvt. Brig. General	Jan. 3, 1865, to Feb. 3, 1865.
J. F. Knipe	Brigadier General	Feb. 3, 1865, to Feb. 19, 1865.

1st BRIGADE.— COMMANDERS.

J. H. Hammond	Bvt. Brig. General	Nov. 25, 1864, to Feb. 3, 1865.
Geo. W. Jackson	Col. 9th Indiana Cav	Feb. 3, 1865, to Mch. 18, 1865.

9th Indiana Cav	Nov., 1864	From Dist. North Ala	To Unatt. Cav. Dept. Miss	Mch., 1865
10th Indiana Cav	Nov., 1864	From Dist. North Ala	To 2-B. 1-Cav. Div. M. D. W. Miss.	Mch., 1865
19th Penna. Cav	Nov., 1864	From 2-B. 4-D. Cav. Corps M. D. M.	To 2-B. 7-Div. Cav. Corps M. D. M.	Feb., 1865
2d Tennessee Cav	Nov., 1864	From 1-B. 4-D. Cav. Corps M. D. M.	To Dept. Miss	Mch., 1865
4th Tennessee Cav	Nov., 1864	From 1-B. 4-D. Cav. Corps M. D. M.	To 2-B. 7-Div. Cav. Corps M. D. M.	Feb., 1865
10th Tennessee Cav	Feb., 1865	From 1-B. 5-D Cav. Corps M. D. M.	To 2-B. 7-Div. Cav. Corps M. D. M.	Feb., 1865

2d BRIGADE.— COMMANDER.

G. M. L. Johnson	Col. 13th Ind. Cav	Nov., 1864, to Mch., 1865.

12th Ind. Cav	Nov., 1864	From Dist. North Ala	To 1-Brig. 1-Cav. Div. M. D. W. M.	Mch., 1865
13th Ind. Cav	Nov., 1864	From Dist. North Ala	To 2-Brig. 1-Cav. Div. M. D. W. M.	Mch., 1865
6th Tenn. Cav	Nov., 1864	From 2-Div. 4-Div. Cav. Corps M. D. M.	To 1-Brig. 6-Div. Cav. C. M. D. M.	Feb., 1865
19th Penna. Cav	Feb., 1865	From 1-Br. 7-Div. Cav. Corps M. D. M.	To Cav. Brig. Dist. B'n Rouge Gulf.	Mch., 1865
4th Tenn. Cav	Feb., 1865	From 1-Br. 7-Div. Cav. Corps M. D. M.	To 2-Brig. 1-Cav. Div. M. D. W. M.	Mch., 1865
10th Tenn. Cav	Feb., 1865	From 1-Br. 7-Div. Cav. Corps M. D. M.	To Dept. Miss	Mch., 1865
ARTILLERY.—				
14th Ohio Batty	Nov., 1864	From Dist. Nashville, Tenn	To 1-Cav. Div. M. D. West. Miss	Mch., 1865
DEPARTMENT HEADQUARTERS.—				
10th Ohio Infy	Nov., 1862	From 17-Brig. 3-Div. 1-Corps Ohio	To Res. Brig. Cumb'd	May, 1864
Anderson Pa. Cav. (15th)	Nov., 1862	From Headqrs. Army Ohio	To Unass'd Cumb'd, 15th Pa. Cav.	Oct., 1863
4th U. S. Cav	Nov., 1862	From Headqrs. Army Ohio	To 1-Brig. 2-Cav. Div. Cumb'd	Mch., 1863
1st Battn. Ohio S. S.	Mch., 1863	From New Organization	No change to Muster Out	July, 1865
9th Mich. Infy	Feb., 1864	From Provost Guard 14-Corps	To Res. Brig. Cumb'd	May, 1864

PIONEER BRIGADE.— COMMANDERS.

St. Clair Morton	Brigadier General	Dec., 1862, to Jan., 1864.
Geo. P. Buell	Col. 58th Ind. Infy	Jan., 1864, to June, 1864.

1st Battalion	Dec., 1862	From Right Wing 14-Corps Cumb'd.	To 1st U. S. Vet. Vol. Engrs	June, 1864
2d Battalion	Dec., 1862	From Centre 14-Corps Cumb'd	To 1st U. S. Vet. Vol. Engrs	June, 1864
3d Battalion	Dec., 1862	From Left Wing 14-Corps Cumb'd	To 1st U. S. Vet. Vol. Engrs	June, 1864
Board of Trade Ill. Batty.	Dec., 1862	From Arty. 12-Div. Army Cumb'd	To 2-Brig. 2-Cav. Div. Cumb'd	Mch., 1863
Bridge's Ill. Batty.	Mch., 1863	From New Org. Co. G, 19th Ill. Infy.	To Arty. 3-Div. 4-Corps Cumb'd	Oct., 1863
4th Battalion	June, 1863	From Res. Corps Cumb'd	To 1st U. S. Vet. Vol. Engrs	June, 1864
ARTILLERY RESERVE.—Organized Oct. 15, 1863. Discontinued Nov. 13, 1864.				
1st DIVISION.—				
Batty. A, 1st Ohio Arty	Oct., 1863	From Arty. 2-Div. 20-Corps Cumb'd.	To 2-Div. Arty. Res. Cumb'd	Mch., 1864
Batty. B, 1st Ohio Arty	Oct., 1863	From Arty. 2-Div. 21-Corps Cumb'd.	To Arty. 2-Div. 12-Corps Cumb'd	Mch., 1864
Batty. C, 1st Ohio Arty	Oct., 1863	From Arty. 3-Div. 14-Corps Cumb'd.	To Arty. 2-Div. 11-Corps Cumb'd	Mch., 1864
Batty. F, 1st Ohio Arty	Oct., 1863	From Arty. 2-Div. 21-Corps Cumb'd.	To 2-Div. Arty. Res. Cumb'd	Mch., 1864
Batty. G, 1st Ohio Arty	Oct., 1863	From Arty. 2-Div. 14-Corps Cumb'd.	To 2-Div. Arty. Res. Cumb'd	Mch., 1864
Batty. M, 1st Ohio Arty	Oct., 1863	From Arty. 2-Div. 14-Corps Cumb'd.	To 2-Div. Arty. Res. Cumb'd	Mch., 1864
18th Ohio Indpt. Batty.	Oct., 1863	From Arty. 1-Div. Res. C. Cumb'd.	To 2-Div. Arty. Res. Cumb'd	Mch., 1864
20th Ohio Indpt. Batty.	Oct., 1863	From Arty. 2-Div. 20-Corps Cumb'd.	To Arty. 3-Div. 4-Corps Cumb'd	Nov., 1863
Batty. E, 1st Ohio Arty	Nov., 1863	From Unass'd Dept. Cumb'd	To Garrison at Bridgeport, Ala.	Dec., 1863
Batty. F, 4th U. S. Arty.	Mch., 1864	From Arty. Brig. 12-Corps Cumb'd.	To Arty. Res. Cumb'd	Nov., 1864
Batty. G, 4th U. S. Arty.	Mch., 1864	From Arty. 2-Div. 4-Corps Cumb'd.	Transferred to Batty. I, 4th Arty.	Oct., 1864
Batty. H, 4th U. S. Arty.	Mch., 1864	From Arty. 2-Div. 4-Corps Cumb'd.	Transferred to Batty. I, 4th Arty.	Oct., 1864
Batty. M, 4th U. S. Arty.	Mch., 1864	From Arty. 1-Div. 4-Corps Cumb'd.	To Arty. Brig. 4-Corps Cumb'd	Nov., 1864
Batty. H, 5th U. S. Arty.	Mch., 1864	From Arty. 2-Div. 4-Corps Cumb'd.	To Garrison Arty. Nashville, Tenn.	Aug., 1864
Batty. K, 5th U. S. Arty.	Mch., 1864	From Arty. 2-Div. 12-Corps Cumb'd.	To Arty. Brig. 20-Corps Cumb'd.	Nov., 1864
Batty. I, 4th U. S. Arty	Oct., 1864	From Post Nashville, Tenn	To 6-Div. Cav. Corps M. D. Miss.	Nov., 1864
2d DIVISION.—				
Batty. D, 1st Mich. Arty.	Oct., 1863	From Arty. 3-Div. 14-Corps Cumb'd.	To Garrison Arty. Murfreesboro.	Mch., 1864
Batty. A, Tenn. Arty	Oct., 1863	From Arty. 1-Brig. 3-Div. Res. Corps	To Garrison Arty. Decatur, Ala.	Mch., 1864
3d Wis. Batty.	Oct., 1863	From Arty. 3-Div. 21-Corps	To Garrison Arty. Chattanooga	Mch., 1864
8th Wis. Batty.	Oct., 1863	From Arty. 1-Div. 20-Corps	To Garrison Arty. Murfreesboro	Mch., 1864
4th Ind. Batty.	Oct., 1863	From Arty. 1-Div. 14-Corps	To Garrison Arty. Chattanooga	Mch., 1864
8th Ind. Batty.	Oct., 1863	From Arty. 1-Div. 21-Corps	To Garrison Arty. Chattanooga	Mch., 1864
11th Ind. Batty.	Oct., 1863	From Arty. 3-Div. 20-Corps	To Garrison Arty. Chattanooga	Mch., 1864
21st Ind. Batty.	Oct., 1864	From Arty. 4-Div. 14-Corps	To Garrison Arty. Columbia, Tenn.	Mch., 1864
10th Wis. Batty.	Oct., 1863	From Unass'd Dept. Cumb'd	To Arty. 3-Cav. Div. Cumb'd	Dec., 1863
Batty. C, 1st Wis. H. A.	Nov., 1863	From New Organization	To Garrison Arty. Chattanooga	Apr., 1864
12th Ohio Batty.	Dec., 1863	From Unass'd Dept. Cumb'd	To Garrison Arty. Murfreesboro	Nov., 1864
1st Ky. Batty.	Mch., 1864	From Garrison Arty. Murfreesboro.	To Arty. Brig. 4-Corps	Apr., 1864
Batty. A, 1st Ohio Arty	Mch., 1864	From 1-Div. Arty. Res	To Arty. 2-Div. 4-Corps	Apr., 1864
Batty. F, 1st Ohio Arty	Mch., 1864	From 1-Div. Arty. Res	To Garrison Arty. Decatur, Ala.	Mch., 1864
Batty. G, 1st Ohio Arty	Mch., 1864	From 1-Div. Arty. Res	To Arty. Brig. 4-Corps	Oct., 1864
Batty. M, 1st Ohio Arty	Mch., 1864	From 1-Div. Arty. Res	To Arty. Brig. 4-Corps	July, 1864
18th Ohio Batty.	Mch., 1864	From 1-Div. Arty. Res	To Prov'l Div. Dist. Etowah	Dec., 1864
Batty. E, 1st Ohio Arty	July, 1864	From Garrison Arty. Bridgeport	To Garrison Arty. Nashville, Tenn.	Nov., 1864

DISTRICT OF NASHVILLE.— COMMANDERS.

R. S. Granger..........	Brigadier General	June 2, 1863, to Nov. 10, 1863.
L. H. Rousseau.........	Major General	Nov. 10, 1863, to July 3, 1865.

POST OF NASHVILLE.— COMMANDERS.

R. S. Granger..........	Brigadier General	Nov., 1863, to June, 1864.
J. F. Miller............	Brigadier General	June, 1864, to July, 1865.

WARD'S BRIGADE.— COMMANDER.

W. T. Ward..........	Brigadier General	

79th Ohio Infy............	Oct., 1863	From 2-Brig. 3-Div. Res. Corps.....	To 1-Brig. 1-Div. 11-Corps Cumb'd..	Jan.,	1864
70th Ind. Infy...........	Oct., 1863	From 2-Brig. 3-Div. Res. Corps.....	To 1-Brig. 1-Div. 11-Corps Cumb'd..	Jan.,	1864
102d Ill. Infy...........	Oct., 1863	From 2-Brig. 3-Div. Res. Corps.....	To 1-Brig. 1-Div. 11-Corps Cumb'd..	Jan.,	1864
105th Ill. Infy...........	Oct., 1863	From 2-Brig. 3-Div. Res. Corps.....	To 1-Brig. 1-Div. 11-Corps Cumb'd..	Jan.,	1864
129th Ill. Infy...........	Oct., 1863	From 2-Brig. 3-Div. Res. Corps.....	To 1-Brig. 1-Div. 11-Corps Cumb'd..	Jan.,	1864
10th Tenn. Infy..........	Oct., 1863	From Post Nashville, Tenn.........	To Def. Nashv. & N. W. R. R......	Nov.,	1863
13th Wis. Infy...........	Oct., 1863	From 1-Brig. 3-Div. Res. Corps.....	To 1-Brig. Dist. Nashville, Tenn....	Jan.,	1864
18th Mich. Infy..........	Oct., 1863	From 3-Brig. 2-Div. Res. Corps.....	To 1-Brig. Dist. Nashville, Tenn....	Jan.,	1864
102d Ohio Infy...........	Nov., 1863	From Unass'd Dept. Cumb'd........	To 1-Brig. Dist. Nashville, Tenn....	Jan.,	1864
73d Ind. Infy............	Dec., 1863	From Prisoners of War...........	To 1-Brig. Dist. Nashville, Tenn....	Jan.,	1864

1st BRIGADE.—Organized Jan., 1864. COMMANDER.

R. S. Granger..........	Brigadier General	

102d Ohio Infy...........	Jan., 1864	From Unatt. Dist. Nashville........	To 1-Brig. 3-Div. 12-Corps Cumb'd..	Jan.,	1864
18th Mich. Infy..........	Jan., 1864	From Unatt. Dist. Nashville........	To 1-Brig. 3-Div. 12-Corps Cumb'd..	Jan.,	1864
13th Wis. Infy...........	Jan., 1864	From Unatt. Dist. Nashville........	To 1-Brig. 3-Div. 12-Corps Cumb'd..	Jan.,	1864
73d Ind. Infy............	Jan., 1864	From Unatt. Dist. Nashville........	To 1-Brig. 3-Div. 12-Corps Cumb'd..	Jan.,	1864
10th Tenn. Infy..........	Jan., 1864	From Nashv. & N. W. R. R.......	To 1-Brig. 3-Div. 12-Corps Cumb'd..	Jan.,	1864

2d BRIGADE.—Organized Jan., 1864. COMMANDER.

H. P. Van Cleve........	Brigadier General	

23d Mo. Infy............	Jan., 1864	From Unatt. Dist. Nashville........	To 2-Brig. 3-Div. 12-Corps Cumb'd..	Jan.,	1864
115th Ohio Infy..........	Jan., 1864	From Unatt. Dist. Nashville........	To 2-Brig. 3-Div. 12-Corps Cumb'd..	Jan.,	1864
4th Tenn. Infy..........	Jan., 1864	From Dist. N. C. Ky. Dept. Ohio....	To 2-Brig. 3-Div. 12-Corps Cumb'd..	Jan.,	1864
31st Wis. Infy...........	Jan., 1864	From Unatt. Dept. Cumb'd........	To 2-Brig. 3-Div. 12-Corps Cumb'd..	Jan.,	1864
13th U. S. Infy..........	Apr., 1864	From Headqrs. 15-Corps Tenn......	To St. Louis, Mo................	July,	1865
15th U. S. Col'd Infy.....	Apr., 1864	From Post Chattanooga, Tenn......	To Springfield, Tenn., Dist. Nashville.	Aug.,	1864
17th U. S. Col'd Infy.....	Apr., 1864	From Post Chattanooga, Tenn......	To 1-Col'd Brig. Dept. Cumb'd......	Dec.,	1864
176th Ohio Infy..........	Sept., 1864	From New Organization...........	To 2-Brig. 4-Div. 20-Corps.......	Nov.,	1864
173d Ohio Infy...........	Oct., 1864	From New Organization...........	To 3d Sub-Dist. Middle Tenn.......	Mch.,	1865
179th Ohio Infy..........	Oct., 1864	From New Organization...........	To 2-Brig. 4-Div. 20-Corps.......	Nov.,	1864
44th Wis. Infy...........	Nov., 1864	From New Organization...........	To Paducah, Ky., Dept. Ky.......	Mch.,	1865
45th Wis. Infy...........	Nov., 1864	From New Organization...........	To 2-Brig. 4-Div. 20-Corps.......	Nov.,	1864
28th Mich. Infy..........	Nov., 1864	From New Organization...........	To 2-Brig. 1-Div. 23-Corps Ohio....	Jan.,	1865
78th Penna. Infy.........	Nov., 1864	From Unatt. 4-Div. 20-Corps......	No change to Muster Out.........	Sept,	1865
182d Ohio Infy...........	Nov., 1864	From New Organization...........	To 2-Brig. 4-Div. 20-Corps.......	Dec.,	1864
5th Tenn. Infy...........	Jan., 1865	From 2-Brig. 3-Div. 23-Corps Ohio..	No change to Muster Out.........	June,	1865
17th U. S. Col'd Infy.....	Jan., 1865	From 1-Col'd Brig. Dept. Cumb'd...	To Dept. Tenn..................	July,	1865

1st BRIGADE, 1st DIVISION.— COMMANDER.

E. C. Mason..........	Col. 176th Ohio Infy...............	

45th N. Y. Infy..........	Mch., 1865	From 2-Brig. 4-Div. 20-Corps.......	No change to Muster Out.........	June,	1865
142d Ind. Infy...........	Mch., 1865	From 2-Brig. 4-Div. 20-Corps.......	No change to Muster Out.........	June,	1865
176th Ohio Infy..........	Mch., 1865	From 2-Brig. 4-Div. 20-Corps.......	No change to Muster Out.........	June,	1865
179th Ohio Infy..........	Mch., 1865	From 2-Brig. 4-Div. 20-Corps.......	No change to Muster Out.........	June,	1865
182d Ohio Infy...........	Mch., 1865	From Unatt. 4-Div. 20-Corps.......	No change to Muster Out.........	July,	1865
45th Wis. Infy...........	Mch., 1865	From 2-Brig. 4-Div. 20-Corps.......	No change to Muster Out.........	July,	1865
58th N. Y. Infy..........	July, 1865	From Stevenson, Ala., Dist. N. Ala.	No change to Muster Out.........	Oct.,	1865

ARTILLERY, DISTRICT OF NASHVILLE.—

12th Ind. Batty..........	Oct., 1863	From Garr. Arty. Nashville, Tenn....	No change to Muster Out.........	July,	1865
20th Ind. Batty..........	Oct., 1863	From Garr. Arty. Nashville, Tenn....	To Unatt. 4-Div. 20-Corps..........	Apr.,	1864
Batty. E, 1st Mich. Arty..	Oct., 1863	From 2-Brig. 3-Div. Res. Corps.....	To Arty. Brig. 4-Corps...........	Nov.,	1864
Batty. I, 4th U. S. Arty..	Oct., 1863	From Arty. 3-Div. 14-Corps......	To 1-Div. Arty. Res. Cumb'd.......	Oct.,	1864
Batty. C, Tenn. Arty.....	Mch., 1864	From New Organization...........	To 3d Sub-Dist. Middle Tenn.......	Mch.,	1865
Batty. D, Tenn. Arty.....	Mch., 1864	From New Organization...........	To 2-Brig. 4-Div. Dist. East. Tenn...	Mch.,	1865
Batty. M, 2d Ill. Arty....	Mch., 1864	From Dist. S. W. Ky. Dept. Ohio....	Disbanded	Apr.,	1864
Batty. I, 1st Ill. Arty....	Apr., 1864	From Arty. 1-Div. 15-Corps Tenn....	To Arty. 5-Div. Cav. Corps M. D. M.	Nov.,	1864
Batty. A, 2d U. S. Col'd..	Apr., 1864	From New Organization...........	To Dist. Middle Tenn.............	Mch.,	1865
Batty. E, Tenn. Arty.....	Apr., 1864	From Dist. N. C. Ky. Dept. Ohio....	To Cav. Div. Dist. East. Tenn.....	Mch.,	1865
Batty. I, 1st Mo. Arty....	May, 1864	From Arty. 2-Div. 16-Corps Tenn....	No change to Muster Out.........	June,	1864
2d Ind. Batty...........	Oct., 1864	From Reorganization	To Garrison Arty. Murfreesboro.....	Feb.,	1865
4th Ind. Batty...........	Oct., 1864	From Reorganization	To 1-Brig. 1st Sub-Dist. Middle Tenn.	Mch.,	1865
Batty. E, 1st Ohio Arty..	Nov., 1864	From 2-Div. Arty. Res. Cumb'd.....	No change to Muster Out.........	July,	1865
14th Ohio Batty..........	Nov., 1864	From Arty. 1-Div. 17-Corps Tenn....	To Arty. 7-Div. Cav. Corps M. D. M.	Nov.,	1864
Cogswell's Ill. Batty.....	Nov., 1864	From Arty. 3-Div. 15-Corps Tenn....	To 1-Brig. 1-Div. Det. Army Tenn...	Dec.,	1864
21st Ind. Batty..........	Nov., 1864	From Garrison Columbia, Tenn......	To 2d Sub-Dist. Middle Tenn.......	Mch.,	1865
22d Ind. Batty..........	Nov., 1864	From Arty. 2-Div. 23-Corps Ohio...	To Arty. 1-Div. 23-Corps Ohio.....	Dec.,	1864
24th Ind. Batty..........	Nov., 1864	From Arty. 2-Div. 23-Corps Ohio...	To Louisville, Ky................	Jan.,	1865
1st Kansas Batty.........	Nov., 1864	From Def. Nashv. & N. W. R. R...	To 1-Col'd Brig. Dist. Etowah......	Dec.,	1864
Batty. F, 1st Mich. Arty..	Nov., 1864	From Arty. 2-Div. 23-Corps Ohio...	To Arty. 1-Div. 23-Corps.........	Dec.,	1864
Batty. A, 1st Ohio Arty..	Nov., 1864	From Arty. Brig. 4-Corps.........	To 4th Sub-Dist. Middle Tenn......	Mch.,	1865
20th Ohio Batty..........	Nov., 1864	From Garrison Arty. Chattanooga....	To Garrison Arty. Chattanooga......	Feb.,	1865
Batty. A, 1st Ill. Arty....	Nov., 1864	From Arty. 2-Div. 15-Corps Tenn....	To Garrison Arty. Chattanooga......	Feb.,	1865
Batty. D, 1st Ill. Arty....	Nov., 1864	From Arty. 3-Div. 17-Corps Tenn....	To 5th Sub-Dist. Middle Tenn......	Mch.,	1865
Batty. F, 2d Ill. Arty....	Nov., 1864	From Arty. 4-Div. 17-Corps Tenn...	To 5th Sub-Dist. Middle Tenn......	Mch.,	1865
1st Iowa Batty..........	Nov., 1864	From Arty. 1-Div. 15-Corps Tenn....	No change to Muster Out.........	July,	1865
Batty. C, 1st Mo. Arty...	Nov., 1864	From Arty. 4-Div. 17-Corps Tenn....	No change to Muster Out.........	July,	1865
3d Ohio Batty...........	Nov., 1864	From Arty. 3-Div. 17-Corps Tenn....	To 5th Sub-Dist. Middle Tenn......	Mch.,	1865
4th Ohio Batty...........	Nov., 1864	From Arty. 1-Div. 15-Corps Tenn....	Consol. with 10th Ohio Batty......	Mch.,	1865
10th Ohio Batty..........	Nov., 1864	From Arty. 3-Div. 15-Corps Tenn....	To 2-Brig. 4-Div. Dist. East. Tenn..	Apr.,	1865
6th Wis. Batty...........	Nov., 1864	From Arty. 1-Div. 15-Corps Tenn....	To Garrison Arty. Chattanooga......	Feb.,	1865
Batty. F, 2d Mo. Arty...	Nov., 1864	From Arty. 1-Div. 15-Corps Tenn....	To 3d Sub-Dist. Middle Tenn.......	Mch.,	1865
Batty. F, 1st Ill. Arty....	Nov., 1864	From Arty. 4-Div. 15-Corps Tenn....	Discontinued	Feb.,	1865
Batty. H, 1st Mich. Arty..	Dec., 1864	From Garrison Arty. Chattanooga....	To Garrison Arty. Chattanooga......	Feb.,	1865
Bridge's Batty. B, 1st Ill.	Dec., 1864	From Arty. Brig. 4-Corps.........	No change to Muster Out.........	June,	1865
1st Kansas Batty.........	Jan., 1865	From 1-Col'd Brig. Dist. Etowah....	No change to Muster Out.........	July,	1865
Batty. F, 2d U. S. Col'd..	Feb., 1865	From Dist. West Tenn.?..........	To Dept. Tenn..................	July,	1865

CAVALRY, DISTRICT OF NASHVILLE.—

Regiment	Date	From	To	Date
4th Tenn. Cav.	Oct., 1863	From Post Nashville, Tenn.	To 3-Brig. Cav. Div. 16-Corp Tenn.	Jan., 1864
5th Tenn. Cav.	Nov., 1863	From 1-Brig. 2-Cav. Div. Cumb'd.	To 1-Brig. 4-Cav. Div. Cumb'd.	Apr., 1864
15th Penna. Cav.	May, 1864	From Unatt. Dept. Cumb'd.	To Unatt. Dept. Cumb'd.	Aug., 1864
9th Ind. Cav.	May, 1864	From New Organization.	To Decatur, Ala., Dist. N. Ala.	June, 1864
10th Ind. Cav.	May, 1864	From New Organization.	To Decatur, Ala., Dist. N. Ala.	June, 1864
11th Ind. Cav.	May, 1864	From New Organization.	To Decatur, Ala., Dist. N. Ala.	June, 1864
12th Ind. Cav.	May, 1864	From New Organization.	To Decatur, Ala., Dist. N. Ala.	June, 1864
13th Ind. Cav.	May, 1864	From New Organization.	To Decatur, Ala., Dist. N. Ala.	June, 1864
2d Mich. Cav.	June, 1864	From 1-Brig. 1-Cav. Div. Cumb'd.	To 1-Brig. 1-Div. Cav. Corps M. D. M.	Oct., 1864

POST CLARKSVILLE, TENN.—

83d Ill. Infy. Det.	Oct., 1863	From 1-Brig. 3-Div. Res. Corps.	To Unass'd 4-Div. 20-Corps.	Apr., 1864
Batty. H, 2d Ill. Arty.	Oct., 1863	From 1-Brig. 3-Div. Res. Corps.	To 5th Sub-Dist. Middle Tenn.	Mch., 1865

FORT DONELSON, TENN.—

83d Ill. Infy.	Oct., 1863	From 1-Brig. 3-Div. Res. Corps.	To Unass'd 4-Div. 20-Corps.	Apr., 1864
Batty. C, 2d Ill. Arty.	Oct., 1863	From 1-Brig. 3-Div. Res. Corps.	To 5th Sub-Dist. Middle Tenn.	Mch., 1865

POST OF GALLATIN, TENN.—

Regiment	Date	From	To	Date
50th Ohio Infy.	Oct., 1863	From Post Gallatin Res. Corps.	To 1-Brig. 3-Div. 23-Corps Ohio.	Feb., 1864
71st Ohio Infy.	Oct., 1863	From Post Gallatin Res. Corps.	To Unass'd 4-Div. 20-Corps.	Apr., 1864
106th Ohio Infy.	Oct., 1863	From Post Gallatin Res. Corps.	To Unass'd 4-Div. 20-Corps.	Apr., 1864
13th Ind. Batty.	Oct., 1863	From Post Gallatin Res. Corps.	To Post Chattanooga, Tenn.	Jan., 1865
14th U. S. Col'd Infy.	Dec., 1863	From New Organization.	To Unass'd Dept. Cumb'd.	Feb., 1864
11th Minn. Infy.	Oct., 1864	From New Organization.	To Def. Nashv. & Chatt. R. R.	Nov., 1864

POST OF MURFREESBORO.—

	COMMANDER.
H. P. Van Cleve	Brigadier General

COBURN'S BRIGADE.—

	COMMANDER.
John Coburn	Col. 33d Ind. Infy.

Regiment	Date	From	To	Date
33d Ind. Infy.	Dec., 1863	From Coburn's Unatt. Brig. Cumb'd.	To 2-Brig. 1-Div. 11-Corps Cumb'd.	Jan., 1864
85th Ind. Infy.	Dec., 1863	From Coburn's Unatt. Brig. Cumb'd.	To 2-Brig. 1-Div. 11-Corps Cumb'd.	Jan., 1864
19th Mich. Infy.	Dec., 1863	From Coburn's Unatt. Brig. Cumb'd.	To 2-Brig. 1-Div. 11-Corps Cumb'd.	Jan., 1864
22d Wis. Infy.	Dec., 1863	From Coburn's Unatt. Brig. Cumb'd.	To 2-Brig. 1-Div. 11-Corps Cumb'd.	Jan., 1864

UNATTACHED.—

Regiment	Date	From	To	Date
115th Ohio Infy.	Oct., 1863	From Cincinnati, Ohio.	To 2-Brig. Dist. Nashville.	Jan., 1864
31st Wis. Infy.	Oct., 1863	From Unass'd Dept. Cumb'd.	To 2-Brig. Dist. Nashville.	Jan., 1864
17th U. S. Col'd Infy.	Dec., 1863	From New Organization.	To Post Nashville.	Apr., 1864
1st Ky. Batty.	Dec., 1863	From Unass'd Arty. Cumb'd.	To 2-Div. Arty. Res. Cumb'd.	Mch., 1864
Batty. D, 1st Mich. Arty.	Apr., 1864	From 2-Div. Arty. Res. Cumb'd.	To 1-Brig. Def. Nash. & Chatt. R. R.	Aug., 1864
12th Ohio Batty.	Apr., 1864	From 2-Div. Arty. Res. Cumb'd.	To 1-Brig. Def. Nash. & Chatt. R. R.	Aug., 1864
8th Wis. Batty.	Apr., 1864	From 2-Div. Arty. Res. Cumb'd.	To 1-Brig. Def. Nash. & Chatt. R. R.	Aug., 1864
2d Ind. Batty.	Feb., 1865	From Dist. Nashville.	No change to Muster Out.	July, 1865

NASHVILLE & NORTHWESTERN R. R.—

12th U. S. Col'd Infy.	Nov., 1863	From New Organization.	To 2-Col'd Brig. Dist. Etowah.	Nov., 1864
13th U. S. Cold' Infy.	Nov., 1863	From New Organization.	To 2-Col'd Brig. Dist. Etowah.	Nov., 1864
10th Tenn. Infy.	Nov., 1863	From Post Nashville.	To 1-Brig. Dist. Nashville.	Jan., 1864
8th Iowa Cav.	Nov., 1863	From New Organization.	To 1-Brig. 1-Cav. Div. Cumb'd.	Mch., 1864
1st Kansas Batty.	Nov., 1863	From Dist. Columbus 6-Div. 16-C.	To 2-Col'd Brig. Dist. Etowah.	Nov., 1864
12th Tenn. Cav.	Jan., 1864	From Dist. N. C. Ky. Ohio.	To 2-Brig. 4-Cav. Div. Cumb'd.	Apr., 1864
1st Mo. Engrs.	Feb., 1864	From Reorganization.	To Engrs. Sherman's Army.	Apr., 1864
75th Penna. Infy.	June, 1864	From Unatt. 4-Div. 20-Corps.	To Unass'd 4-Div. 20-Corps.	Aug., 1864
40th U. S. Col'd Infy.	June, 1864	From Def. Louisville & Nashv. R. R.	To Def. Louisv. & Nashv. R. R.	Dec., 1864
100th U. S. Col'd Infy.	June, 1864	From New Organization.	To 2-Col'd Brig. Dist. Etowah.	Nov., 1864
43d Wis. Infy.	Oct., 1864	From New Organization.	To 3-Brig. Def. Nash. & Chatt. R. R.	Dec., 1864
12th U. S. Col'd Infy.	Jan., 1865	From 2-Col'd Brig. Dist. Etowah.	To 3d Sub-Dist. Middle Tenn.	Mch., 1865
13th U. S. Col'd Infy.	Jan., 1865	From 2-Col'd Brig. Dist. Etowah.	To 3d Sub-Dist. Middle Tenn.	Mch., 1865
110th U. S. Col'd Infy.	Feb., 1865	From Pulaski Dist. N. Ala.	To 3d Sub-Dist. Middle Tenn.	Mch., 1865
111th U. S. Col'd Infy.	Feb., 1865	From Pulaski Dist. N. Ala.	To 3d Sub-Dist. Middle Tenn.	Mch., 1865

COLUMBIA, TENN.—

14th Mich. Infy.	Dec., 1863	From 1-Brig. 2-Div. 14-Corps.	To 1-Brig. 2-Div. 14-Corps.	May, 1864
21st Ind. Batty.	Mch., 1864	From 2-Div. Arty. Res. Cumb'd.	To Post Nashville, Tenn.	Nov., 1864
175th Ohio Infy.	Oct., 1864	From New Organization.	To 3-Brig. 3-Div. 23-Corps Ohio.	Dec., 1864

BRIDGEPORT, ALA.—

Batty. E, 1st Ohio Arty.	Dec., 1863	From 1-Div. Arty. Res. Cumb'd.	To 2-Div. Arty. Res. Cumb'd.	July, 1864
Batty. K, 1st Ohio Arty.	Dec., 1863	From Arty. Brig. 11-Corps Cumb'd.	To Garrison Arty. Stevenson, Ala.	May, 1864
Batty. B, 1st Ohio Arty.	Apr., 1864	From Arty. 2-Div. 12-Corps Cumb'd.	No change to Muster Out.	July, 1865
133d Ind. Infy.	May, 1864	From New Organization.	No change to Muster Out.	Sept., 1864
9th Ohio Batty.	Dec., 1864	From 3-Br. Def. Nashv. & Ch. R. R.	No change to Muster Out.	July, 1865
Batty. M, 4th U. S. Arty.	Feb., 1865	From Arty. Brig. 4-Corps.	To Regular Establishment.	Aug., 1865
184th Ohio Infy.	Mch., 1865	From New Organization.	No change to Muster Out.	Sept., 1865
Batty. F, 2d U. S. Col'd.	Apr., 1865	From Arty. Res. Dist. West Tenn.	To Dept. Tenn.	July, 1865

STEVENSON, ALA.—

Regiment	Date	From	To	Date
Batty. K, 1st Ohio Arty.	May, 1864	From Garrison Arty. Bridgeport, Ala.	No change to Muster Out.	July, 1865

SPRINGFIELD.—

Regiment	Date	From	To	Date
15th U. S. Col'd Infy.	Aug., 1864	From Dist. Nashville, Tenn.	To 5th Sub-Dist. Middle Tenn.	Mch., 1865

LOUISVILLE AND NASHVILLE R. R.—

2d Tennessee Mtd. Infy.	Apr., 1864	From New Organization.	To 2-Brig. Dist. East Tenn.	Mch., 1865
40th U. S. Col'd Infy.	Apr., 1864	From New Organization.	To Def. Nash. & Northwestern R. R.	June, 1864
101st U. S. Col'd Infy.	Oct., 1864	From New Organization.	To Dept. Tenn.	July, 1865
11th Minnesota Infy.	Nov., 1864	From Post Gallatin, Tenn.	No change to Muster Out.	July, 1865
40th U. S. Col'd Infy.	Dec., 1864	From Def. Nash. & Northwest. R. R.	To 2-Brig. 4-Div. Dist. Tenn.	Apr., 1865

DEFENCES NASHVILLE & CHATTANOOGA R. R.—

	COMMANDER.
R. H. Milroy	Major General.

1st BRIGADE.—

COMMANDER.				
H. P. Van Cleve......	Brigadier General.			
115th Ohio Infy........July, 1864	From Unass'd 4-Div. 20-Corps......	To Unatt. 4-Div. 20-Corps..........	Feb.,	1865
12th Ohio Batty........July, 1864	From Garrison Arty. Murfreesboro.	No change to Muster Out..........	July,	1865
8th Wisconsin Batty....July, 1864	From Garrison Arty. Murfreesboro.	To 1-B. 1st Sub-Dist. Middle Tenn.	Mch.,	1865
Batty. D, 1st Mich. Arty..July, 1864	From Garrison Arty. Murfreesboro.	To 1-B. 1st Sub-Dist. Middle Tenn.	Mch.,	1865
174th Ohio Infy........Oct., 1864	From Dist. North Ala..............	To 3-Brig. 1-Div. 23-Corps Ohio...	Dec.,	1864
61st Illinois Infy........Nov., 1864	From Dept. Missouri Vet. furlough.	To Unatt. 4-Div. 20-Corps.........	Feb.,	1865
140th Indiana Infy......Nov., 1864	From New Organization...........	To 3-Brig. 3-Div. 23-Corps Ohio...	Jan.,	1865
3d Michigan Infy......Nov., 1864	From Dist. North Ala..............	To 3-Brig. 3-Div. 4-Corps.........	Jan.,	1865
4th Michigan Infy......Nov., 1864	From Dist. North Ala..............	To 3-Brig. 3-Div. 4-Corps.........	Jan.,	1865
29th Michigan Infy.....Nov., 1864	From Dist. North Ala..............	To 3-Brig. Def. Nash. & Chat. R. R.	Dec.,	1864
8th Minnesota Infy.....Nov., 1864	From Dept. Missouri..............	To 3-Brig. 1-Div. 23-Corps........	Jan.,	1865
181st Ohio Infy........Nov., 1864	From Decatur Dist. North Ala.....	To 3-Brig. 3-Div. 23-Corps........	Jan.,	1865
154th Illinois Infy......Mch., 1865	From New Organization...........	To 1-B. 1st Sub-Dist. Middle Tenn.	Apr.,	1865
143d Indiana Infy......Mch., 1865	From New Organization...........	To 1-B. 1st Sub-Dist. Middle Tenn.	Apr.,	1865
188th Ohio. Infy........Mch., 1865	From New Organization...........	To 1-B. 1st Sub-Dist. Middle Tenn.	Apr.,	1865

2d BRIGADE.—

COMMANDER.				
E. J. Robinson.........	Col. 137th Indiana Infy.			
137th Indiana Infy......Aug., 1864	From Unatt. R. R. Guard..........	No change to Muster Out..........	Sept.,	1864
138th Indiana Infy......Aug., 1864	From Unatt. R. R. Guard..........	No change to Muster Out..........	Sept.,	1864
6th Kentucky Infy......Aug., 1864	From 2-Brig. 3-Div. 4-Corps......	To Unass'd 4-Div. 20-Corps.......	Sept.,	1864
2d Kentucky Infy......Aug., 1864	From Unass'd Arty. Cumb'd.......	To Arty. Brig. 4-Corps...........	Oct.,	1864
42d Missouri Infy........Mch., 1865	From Unatt. 4-Div. 20-Corps......	To 2-B. 1st Sub-Dist. Middle Tenn.	Apr.,	1865
148th Illinois Infy......Mch., 1865	From New Organization...........	To 2-B. 1st Sub-Dist. Middle Tenn.	Apr.,	1865
152d Illinois Infy......Mch., 1865	From New Organization...........	To 2-B. 1st Sub-Dist. Middle Tenn.	Apr.,	1865
153d Illinois Infy......Mch., 1865	From New Organization...........	To 2-B. 1st Sub-Dist. Middle Tenn.	Apr.,	1865
155th Illinois Infy......Mch., 1865	From New Organization...........	To 2-B. 1st Sub-Dist. Middle Tenn.	Apr.,	1865
151st Indiana Infy......Mch., 1865	From New Organization...........	To 2-B. 1st Sub-Dist. Middle Tenn.	Apr.,	1865
47th Wisconsin Infy....Mch., 1865	From New Organization...........	To 2-B. 1st Sub-Dist. Middle Tenn.	Apr.,	1865

3d BRIGADE.—

COMMANDER.				
W. Krzyzanowski......	Col. 58th New York Infy.			
58th New York Infy.....July, 1864	From Unass'd 4-Div. 20-Corps.....	To Unatt. 4-Div. 20-Corps.........	Feb.,	1865
68th New York Infy.....July, 1864	From Unass'd 4-Div. 20-Corps.....	To Unass'd Dist. Etowah..........	Dec.,	1864
106th Ohio Infy.........July, 1864	From Unass'd 4-Div. 20-Corps.....	To Unatt. 4-Div. 20-Corps.........	Feb.,	1865
9th Ohio Batty.........July, 1864	From Unass'd 4-Div. 20-Corps.....	To Garrison Arty. Bridgeport, Ala.	Dec.,	1864
6th Kentucky Infy......Oct., 1864	From Unass'd 4-Div. 20-Corps.....	No change to Muster Out..........	Jan.,	1865
180th Ohio Infy.........Oct., 1864	From New Organization...........	To 1-Brig. 1-Div. 23-Corps Ohio..	Jan.,	1865
Batty. K, 1st Ohio Arty..Oct., 1864	From Stevenson, Ala., Dist. N. Ala.	To Stevenson, Ala., Dist. North Ala.	Feb.,	1865
29th Michigan Infy......Dec., 1864	From 1-B. Def. Nash. & Chat. R. R.	To Unatt. 4-Div. 20-Corps.........	Feb.,	1865
43d Wisconsin Infy......Dec., 1864	From Def. Nash. & Northwest. R. R.	To 3-B. 1st Sub-Dist. Middle Tenn.	Mch.,	1865
TULLAHOMA, TENN.—				
59th Ohio Infy.........Oct., 1864	From Unatt. 4-Div. 20-Corps......	To 2-B. 1st Sub-Dist. Middle Tenn.	Mch.,	1865
177th Ohio Infy.........Oct., 1864	From New Organization...........	To 2-Brig. 3-Div. 23-Corps Ohio...	Jan.,	1865
178th Ohio Infy.........Oct., 1864	From New Organization...........	To 3-Brig. 1-Div. 23-Corps Ohio...	Jan.,	1865
12th Indiana Cav.........Oct., 1864	From Dist. North Ala..............	To 2-B. 7th D. Cav. Corps M. D. M.	Nov.,	1864

ENGINEER BRIGADE, DEPT. CUMB'D.—Organized Nov., 1863.

COMMANDERS.				
T. R. Stanley..........	Col. 18th Ohio Infy...............	Nov., 1863, to Apr., 1864.		
W. B. McCreary.......	Col. 21st Mich. Infy..............	Apr., 1864, to Oct., 1864.		
1st Michigan Engineers..Nov., 1863	From Unatt. Dept. Cumberland.....	To Post Chattanooga, Tenn.......	Dec.,	1863
13th Michigan Infy......Nov., 1863	From 2-Brig. 2-Div. 4-Corps......	To 2-Brig. 1-Div. 14-Corps........	Oct.,	1864
21st Michigan Infy......Nov., 1863	From 1-Brig. 2-Div. 4-Corps......	To 2-Brig. 1-Div. 14-Corps........	Oct.,	1864
22d Michigan Infy......Nov., 1863	From 3-Brig. 2-Div. 14-Corps.....	To Reserve Brigade Cumb'd........	May,	1864
18th Ohio Infy.........Nov., 1863	From 2-Brig. 1-Div. 14-Corps......	No change to Muster Out.........	Oct.,	1864
1st U. S. Vet. Vol. Engrs.June, 1864	From New Organization...........	To Unatt. Engineers Dept. Cumb'd	Oct.,	1864
SIEGE ARTILLERY.—				
11th Indiana Batty.......May, 1864	From Garrison Arty. Chattanooga..	To Garrison Arty. Chattanooga....	Oct.,	1864

RESERVE BRIGADE.—Organized Apr., 1864.

COMMANDERS.				
J. W. Burke...........	Col. 10th Ohio Infy..............	Apr. 1864, to May 27, 1864.		
R. LeFavour...........	Col. 22d Michigan Infy..........	May 27, 1864, to Mch. 31, 1865.		
10th Ohio Infy..........Apr., 1864	From Headqrs. Dept. Cumb'd......	No change to Muster Out........	May,	1864
9th Michigan Infy.......Apr., 1864	From Headqrs. Dept. Cumb'd......	To Nashville Headqrs. Dept. Cumb'd	Mch.,	1865
22d Michigan Infy......Apr., 1864	From Engineer Brigade Cumb'd....	To 3-Brig. 2d Separate Div. Etowah	Mch.,	1865

UNASSIGNED DEPT. CUMB'D.—
COBURN'S BRIGADE.—

COMMANDER.				
John Coburn...........	Col. 33d Indiana Infy.			
33d Indiana Infy........Oct., 1863	From 3-B. 1-Div. Res. Corps Cumb'd	To Post Murfreesboro, Tenn.......	Dec.,	1863
85th Indiana Infy........Oct., 1863	From 3-B. 1-Div. Res. Corps Cumb'd	To Post Murfreesboro, Tenn.......	Dec.,	1863
19th Michigan Infy......Oct., 1863	From 3-B. 1-Div. Res. Corps Cumb'd	To Post Murfreesboro, Tenn.......	Dec.,	1863
22d Wisconsin Infy......Oct., 1863	From 3-B. 1-Div. Res. Corps Cumb'd	To Post Murfreesboro, Tenn.......	Dec.,	1863
9th Ohio Batty.........Oct., 1863	From 3-B. 1-Div. Res. Corps Cumb'd	To Post Murfreesboro, Tenn.......	Dec.,	1863
15th Penna. Cav........Oct., 1863	From Headqrs. Dept. Cumb'd......	To Dist. Nashville, Tenn.........	May,	1864
28th Kentucky Mtd. Infy..Oct., 1863	From 1-B. 3-Div. Res. Corps Cumb'd	To 1-Brig. 2-Div. 4-Corps........	Apr.,	1864
34th Illinois Infy.......Oct., 1863	From 2-B. 2-Div. 20-Corps Cumb'd	To 2-Brig. 2-Div. 14-Corps.......	Nov.,	1863
39th Indiana Mtd. Infy...Oct., 1863	From Unatt. Cav. Cumb'd.........	Designation changed to 8th Cav...	Oct.,	1863
21st Kentucky Infy......Oct., 1863	From 3-B. 3-Div. 21-Corps Cumb'd	To 2-Brig. 1-Div. 4-Corps........	Jan.,	1864
3d Ohio Infy...........Oct., 1863	From Prisoners of War...........	To 2-Brig. 2-Div. 14-Corps.......	Nov.,	1863
102d Ohio Infy.........Oct., 1863	From 1-B. 3-Div. Res. Corps Cumb'd	To Post Nashville, Tenn.........	Nov.,	1863
108th Ohio Infy........Oct., 1863	From 3-B. 2-Div. Res. Corps Cumb'd	To 2-Brig. 2-Div. 14-Corps.......	Nov.,	1863
31st Wisconsin Infy......Oct., 1863	From Dist. Columbus 6-Div. 16-C.	To 1-Brig. Dist. Nashville, Tenn..	Jan.,	1864
23d Missouri Infy.......Oct., 1863	From Dist. Rolla Dept. Missouri...	To 2-Brig. Dist. Nashville, Tenn..	Jan.,	1864
14th U. S. Col'd Infy....Feb., 1864	From Post Gallatin, Tenn.........	To Unass'd Dist. Etowah.........	Nov.,	1864
16th U. S. Col'd Infy....Feb., 1864	From New Organization...........	To Unass'd Dist. Etowah.........	Nov.,	1864
42d U. S. Col'd Infy....Apr., 1864	From New Organization...........	To Unass'd Dist. Etowah.........	Nov.,	1864
44th U. S. Col'd Infy....Apr., 1864	From New Organization...........	To Unass'd Dist. Etowah.........	Nov.,	1864
UNASSIGNED ARTILLERY.—				
10th Wisconsin Batty.....Oct., 1864	From Arty. 2-D. Res. Corps Cumb'd	To Arty. 3-Div. Cav. Cumb'd......	Apr.,	1864
1st Kentucky Batty......Oct., 1864	From Arty. 2-Div. 14-Corps......	To Post Murfreesboro, Tenn......	Nov.,	1863
2d Kentucky Batty......Oct., 1864	From Arty. 2-Div. 14-Corps......	To Arty. 1-Div. 12-Corps Cumb'd...	Dec.,	1863
Batty. E. 1st Ohio Arty..Oct. 1864	From Arty. 2-D. Res. Corps Cumb'd	To Garrison Arty. Bridgeport, Ala.	Nov.,	1863
10th Indiana Batty.......Apr., 1864	From Post Chattanooga, Tenn.....	To Decatur, Dist. North Ala.......	Aug.,	1864

UNASSIGNED ARTILLERY.—Continued.

2d Kentucky Batty......Apr., 1864	From Arty. 1-Div. 12-Corps Cumb'd	To 2-Brig. Def. Nash. & Chat. R. R.	Aug., 1864
Batty. K, 1st Ohio Arty..Apr., 1864	From Arty. Brig. 11-Corps Cumb'd	To Post Stevenson, Ala.	May, 1864
Batty. G, 1st Ohio Arty..Aug., 1864	From 2-Div. Arty. Reserve Cumb'd	To Arty. Brig. 4-Corps.	Oct., 1864
13th N. Y. Indpt. Batty..Sept., 1864	From Arty. Brig. 20-Corps.	To Tullahoma, Tenn., Dist. Nash.	Dec., 1864
Batty. M, 1st Ill. Arty....Oct., 1864	From Arty. Brig. 4-Corps.	To Gar's'n Arty. Chattanooga, Tenn.	Nov., 1864
Batty. I, 1st Mich. Arty..Oct., 1864	From Arty. Brig. 20-Corps.	To Gar's'n Arty. Chattanooga, Tenn.	Nov., 1864
25th Indiana Batty......Feb., 1865	From Arty. Brig. 4-Corps.	To Decatur, Dist. North Ala.	Mch., 1865
Batty. E, 1st Mich. Arty..Feb., 1865	From Arty. Brig. 4-Corps.	To Decatur, Dist. North Ala.	Mch., 1865

PONTONEERS.—

58th Indiana Infy......Apr., 1864	From 2-Brig. 2-Div. 4-Corps.	To Pontoneers' Army Ga.	Jan., 1865

POST OF CHATTANOOGA, TENN.—   COMMANDERS.

J. B. Steedman........	Major General.	Oct., 1863, to May, 1864.
T. R. Stanley.........	Col. 18th Ohio Infy.	May, 1864, to Oct. 17, 1864.
C. H. Carlton.........	Col. 89th Ohio Infy.	Oct. 17, 1864, to Nov. 12, 1864.

44th Indiana Infy......Nov., 1863	From 3-Brig. 3-Div. 4-Corps.	To 1st Separate Brig. Chattanooga.	Apr., 1864
15th Kentucky Infy......Nov., 1863	From 1-Brig. 1-Div. 14-Corps.	To 1-Brig. 1-Div. 14-Corps.	Apr., 1864

SPEAR'S BRIGADE.—   COMMANDER.

J. G. Spear...........	Brigadier General.	

3d Tennessee Infy......Nov., 1863	From 2-Brig. 2-Div. 14-Corps.	To Spear's Tenn. Brig. 23-Corps.	Dec., 1864
5th Tennessee Infy......Nov., 1863	From 2-Brig. 2-Div. 14-Corps.	To Spear's Tenn. Brig. 23-Corps.	Dec., 1864
6th Tennessee Infy......Nov., 1863	From 2-Brig. 2-Div. 14-Corps.	To Spear's Tenn. Brig. 23-Corps.	Dec., 1864
10th Indiana Infy......Dec., 1863	From 3-Brig. 3-Div. 14-Corps.	To 3-Brig. 3-Div. 14-Corps.	Jan., 1864
15th U. S. Col'd Infy....Jan., 1864	From New Organization.	To Dist. Nashville, Tenn.	Apr., 1864
51st Indiana Infy......Jan., 1864	From Prisoners of War.	To 1st Separate Brig. Chattanooga.	Apr., 1864
15th Indiana Infy......Feb., 1864	From 2-Brig. 2-Div. 4-Corps.	To 1st Separate Brig. Chattanooga.	Apr., 1864
29th Indiana Infy......Mch., 1864	From 1-Brig. 1-Div. 4-Corps.	To 1st Separate Brig. Chattanooga.	Apr., 1864
68th Indiana Infy......Apr., 1864	From 1-Brig. 3-Div. 4-Corps.	To 1st Separate Brig. Chattanooga.	Apr., 1864
3d Ohio Infy........Apr., 1864	From 2-Brig. 2-Div. 14-Corps.	To 1st Separate Brig. Chattanooga.	Apr., 1864

1st SEPARATE BRIGADE.—   COMMANDER.

T. R. Stanley.........	Col. 18th Ohio Infy.	Apr., 1864, to Nov., 1864.

15th Indiana Infy......Apr., 1864	From Post Chattanooga, Tenn.	No change to Muster Out.	June, 1864
29th Indiana Infy......Apr., 1864	From Post Chattanooga, Tenn.	To 2-Brig. 1-Sep. Div. Dist. Etowah.	Nov., 1864
44th Indiana Infy......Apr., 1864	From Post Chattanooga, Tenn.	To 2-Brig. 1-Sep. Div. Dist. Etowah.	Nov., 1864
51st Indiana Infy......Apr., 1864	From Post Chattanooga, Tenn.	To 2-Brig. 2-Div. 4-Corps.	Sept., 1864
68th Indiana Infy......Apr., 1864	From Post Chattanooga, Tenn.	To 2-Brig. 1-Sep. Div. Dist. Etowah.	Nov., 1864
8th Kentucky Infy......Apr., 1864	From 2-Brig. 1-Div. 4-Corps.	No change to Muster Out.	Nov., 1864
3d Ohio Infy........Apr., 1864	From Post Chattanooga, Tenn.	No change to Muster Out.	June, 1864
24th Ohio Infy........Apr., 1864	From 3-Brig. 1-Div. 4-Corps.	No change to Muster Out.	June, 1864

REGULAR BRIGADE.—   COMMANDER.

J. H. King...........	Brigadier General.	

15th U. S. Infy........Sept., 1864	From 2-Brig. 1-Div. 14-Corps.	To 1st Separate Brig. Chattanooga	Nov., 1864
16th U. S. Infy........Sept., 1864	From 2-Brig. 1-Div. 14-Corps.	To 1st Separate Brig. Chattanooga	Nov., 1864
18th U. S. Infy........Sept., 1864	From 2-Brig. 1-Div. 14-Corps.	To 1st Separate Brig. Chattanooga	Nov., 1864
19th U. S. Infy........Sept., 1864	From 2-Brig. 1-Div. 14-Corps.	To 1st Separate Brig. Chattanooga	Nov., 1864
32d Indiana Infy......Oct., 1864	From 1-Brig. 3-Div. 4-Corps.	To 2-Brig. 1-Sep. Div. Dist. Etowah.	Nov., 1864
15th Wisconsin Infy......Oct., 1864	From 1-Brig. 3-Div. 4-Corps.	To 2-Brig. 1-Sep. Div. Dist. Etowah.	Nov., 1864
11th Michigan Infy. Det..Oct., 1864	From 2-Brig. 1-Div. 14-Corps.	To 3-Brig. 2-Separate Div. Etowah.	Apr., 1865
16th U. S. Col'd Infy....Oct., 1864	From Unatt. Dept. Cumberland.	To Unass'd Dist. Etowah.	Nov., 1864
18th Ohio Infy........Oct., 1864	From Reorganization.	To 2-Brig. 1-Sep. Div. Dist. Etowah.	Nov., 1864
42d U. S. Col'd Infy....Oct., 1864	From New Organization.	To Unass'd Dist. Etowah.	Nov., 1864
44th U. S. Col'd Infy....Oct., 1864	From New Organization.	To Unass'd Dist. Etowah.	Nov., 1864

ARTILLERY CHATTANOOGA.—

4th Indiana Batty......Nov., 1863	From 2-Div. Arty. Res. Cumberland	No change to Muster Out.	Oct., 1864
8th Indiana Batty......Nov., 1863	From 2-Div. Arty. Res. Cumberland	Consolidated with 7th Batty.	Mch., 1865
11th Indiana Batty......Nov., 1863	From 2-Div. Arty. Res. Cumberland	To Siege Arty. Cumberland.	Apr., 1864
Batty. A, 1st Mich. Arty..Dec., 1863	From Arty. 1-Div. 14-Corps.	No change to Muster Out.	July, 1865
20th Ohio Batty......Dec., 1863	From Arty. 3-Div. 4-Corps.	To Garrison Arty. Nashville.	Nov., 1864
Batty. I, 1st Ohio Arty...Jan., 1864	From Arty. 2-Div. 4-Corps.	To Arty. 1-Div. 14-Corps.	Apr., 1864
3d Wisconsin Batty......Mch., 1864	From 2-Div. Arty. Res. Cumberland	To Garrison Arty. Murfreesboro.	Mch., 1865
10th Indiana Batty......Mch., 1864	From Arty. 2-Div. 4-Corps.	To Unatt. Arty. Cumberland.	Apr., 1864
Co. C, 1st Wis. H. Arty..Mch., 1864	From New Organization.	To 2-Brig. Dist. East Tenn.	Apr., 1865
Batty. K, 1st Mich. Arty..Mch., 1864	From Arty. Brig. 11-Corps.	To 2-Brig. 4-Div| Dist. East Tenn.	Mch., 1865
Batty. G, 1st Mo. Arty...Apr., 1864	From Arty 2-Div. 4-Corps.	To 1-Brig. 1st Sep. Div. Etowah.	Jan., 1865
2d Minn. Batty........July, 1864	From Arty 2-Div. 14-Corps.	To 2-Brig. 4-Div. Dist. East Tenn.	Mch., 1865
5th Ind. Batty........Sept., 1864	From Arty. Brig. 4-Corps.	No change to Muster Out.	Nov., 1864
Batty. I, 1st Ohio Arty..Sept., 1864	From Arty. Brig. 14-Corps.	To 1-Brig. 2d Sep. Div. Etowah.	Mch., 1865
Batty. G, 1st Ohio Arty..Oct., 1864	From 2-Div. Arty. Res. Cumb'd.	To Arty. Brig. 4-Corps.	Nov., 1864
11th Ind. Batty........Oct., 1864	From Siege Arty. Cumb'd.	Consolidated with 18th Batty.	Nov., 1864
1 Minn. H. Arty., A, B, C..Oct., 1864	From New Organization.	No change to Muster Out.	Sept., 1865
Batty. M, 1st Ohio Arty..Oct., 1864	From Arty. Brig. 4-Corps.	Consolidated with Batty I.	Apr., 1865
Batty. M, 1st Ill. Arty...Oct., 1864	From Arty. Brig. 4-Corps.	To Garrison Arty. Cleveland, Tenn.	Apr., 1865
Batty. H, 1st Mich. Arty..Oct., 1864	From Arty. 3-Div. 17-Corps, Tenn.	To Garrison Arty., Nashville, Tenn.	Nov., 1864
Batty. I, 1st Mich Arty..Oct., 1864	From Arty. Brig. 20-Corps.	No change to Muster Out.	July, 1865
7th Ind. Batty........Oct., 1864	From Arty. Brig. 14-Corps.	To Arty 4-Div. Dist. East Tenn.	Apr., 1865
20th Ind. Batty........Oct., 1864	From Arty. Brig. 14-Corps.	To Prov'l Div. Dist. Etowah.	Dec., 1864
Batty. K, 5th U. S. Arty..Oct., 1864	From Arty. Brig. 20-Corps.	To Regular Establishment.	Aug., 1865
18th Ohio Batty......Jan., 1865	From Art. Prov'l Div. Dist. Etowah.	No change to Muster Out.	June, 1865
20th Ind. Batty........Jan., 1865	From Art. Prov'l Div. Dist. Etowah.	No change to Muster Out.	July, 1865
13th Ind. Batty........Jan., 1865	From Garrison Arty. Post Gallatin.	No change to Muster Out.	July, 1865
20th Ohio Batty......Feb., 1865	From Garrison Arty. Nashville.	No change to Muster Out.	July, 1865
Batty. A, 1st Ill. Arty..Feb., 1865	From Garrison Arty. Nashville.	No change to Muster Out.	July, 1865
Batty. E, 1st Ill. Arty..Feb., 1865	From Arty. 1-Div. Det. Army Tenn.	No change to Muster Out.	July, 1865
Batty. H, 1st Mich. Arty..Feb., 1865	From Garrison Arty. Nashville.	No change to Muster Out.	July, 1865
6th Wis. Batty........Mch., 1865	From Arty. Nashville, Tenn.	No change to Muster Out.	July, 1865

DISTRICT NORTH ALABAMA.—   COMMANDER.

R. S. Granger........	Brigadier General.	June 2, 1864, to Sept. 10, 1865.

DECATUR, ALA., ETC.—

25th Ind. Infy........June, 1864	From Decatur, Ala., Dept. Tenn.	To 3-Brig. 4-Div. 16-Corps.	Aug., 1864
17th N. Y. Veteran Infy..June, 1864	From Decatur, Ala., Dept. Tenn.	To 3-Brig. 4-Div. 16-Corps.	Aug., 1864
32d Wis. Infy........June, 1864	From Decatur, Ala., Dept. Tenn.	To 3-Brig. 4-Div. 16-Corps.	Aug., 1864
Batty. D, 2d Ill. Arty....June, 1864	From Decatur, Ala., Dept. Tenn.	No change to Muster Out.	Nov., 1864
Batty. F, 1st Ohio Arty..June, 1864	From Decatur, Ala., Dept. Tenn.	No change to Muster Out.	July, 1865

DECATUR, ALA., ETC.—Continued.

9th Ohio Cav..........June, 1864	From Decatur, Ala., Dept. Tenn....	To Mounted Brig. Cav. Div. 23-C'ps.	Aug.,	1864
9th Ind. Cav..........June, 1864	From Dist. Nashville, Tenn........	To 1-B. 7-D. Cav. C'ps M. D. Miss.	Nov.,	1864
10th Ind. Cav..........June, 1864	From Dist. Nashville, Tenn........	To 1-B. 7-D. Cav. C'ps M. D. Miss.	Nov.,	1864
11th Ind. Cav..........June, 1864	From Dist. Nashville, Tenn........	To 1-B. 5-D. Cav. C'ps M. D. Miss.	Nov.,	1864
12th Ind. Cav..........June, 1864	From Dist. Nashville, Tenn........	To 2-B. 7-D. Cav. C'ps M. D. Miss.	Nov.,	1864
13th Ind. Cav..........June, 1864	From Dist. Nashville, Tenn........	To 2-B. 7-D. Cav. C'ps M. D. Miss.	Nov.,	1864
10th Ind. Batty..........Aug., 1864	From Unatt. Arty. Cumb'd........	No change to Muster Out..........	July,	1865
3d Mich Infy..........Oct., 1864	From New Organization...........	To 1-B. Def. Nash. & Chatta. R. R.	Nov.,	1864
4th Mich Infy...:......Oct., 1864	From New Organization...........	To 1-B. Def. Nash. & Chatta. R. R.	Nov.,	1864
29th Mich Infy..........Oct., 1864	From New Organization...........	To 1-B. Def. Nash. & Chatta. R. R.	Nov.,	1864
174th Ohio Infy..........Oct., 1864	From New Organization...........	To 1-B. Def. Nash. & Chatta. R. R.	Nov.,	1864
181st Ohio Infy..........Oct., 1864	From New Organization...........	To 1-B. Def. Nash. & Chatta. R. R.	Nov.,	1864
8th Minn. Infy..........Oct., 1864	From Minnesota...................	To 1-B. Def. Nash. & Chatta. R. R.	Nov.,	1864
149th Ind. Infy..........Feb., 1865	From New Organization...........	No change to Muster Out..........	Sept.,	1865
25th Ind. Batty..........Mch., 1865	From Unatt. Arty. Cumb'd........	No change to Muster Out..........	July,	1865
Batty. E, 1st Mich. Arty..Mch., 1865	From Unatt. Arty. Cumb'd........	No change to Muster Out..........	July,	1865
73d Ind. Infy..........Mch., 1865	From 1-Brig. 4-Div. 20-Corps.....	No change to Muster Out..........	July,	1865
18th Mich. Infy..........Mch., 1865	From 1-Brig. 4-Div. 20-Corps.....	No change to Muster Out..........	June,	1865
102d Ohio Infy..........Mch., 1865	From 1-Brig. 4-Div. 20-Corps.....	No change to Muster Out..........	June,	1865
189th Ohio Infy..........Mch., 1865	From New Organization...........	No change to Muster Out..........	Sept.,	1865
46th Mo. Infy..........Mch., 1865	From New Organization...........	No change to Muster Out..........	May,	1865
HUNTSVILLE, ALA.—				
Batty. D, 1st Mo. Arty..Sept., 1864	From Arty. 3-Div. 15-Corps., Tenn..	To Consol. with Batty. C, 1st Mo.	Apr.,	1865
STEVENSON, ALA.—				
Batty. K, 1st Ohio Arty..May, 1864	From Garrison Arty, Bridgep't, Ala.	No change to Muster Out..........	July,	1865
58th N. Y. Infy..........Mch., 1865	From Unatt. 4-Div. 20-Corps.....	To Dist. Nashville, Tenn..........	July,	1865
106th Ohio Infy..........Mch., 1865	From Unatt. 4-Div. 20-Corps.....	No change to Muster Out..........	July,	1865
Batty. I, 2d U. S. Arty..Apr., 1865	From Arty. Dist. West Tenn......	To Dept. Tenn...................	June,	1865

Detachment Army Tennessee---Department of the Cumberland

Formerly Right Wing 16th Army Corps, Army Tenn. Designated Detachment Army Tenn., Dec. 5, 1864. Transferred to reorganized 16th Army Corps, Military Div. West. Miss., Feb. 18, 1865.

COMMANDER.

A. J. Smith............	Major General		

1st DIVISION.— COMMANDER.

John McArthur	Brigadier General		

1st BRIGADE.— COMMANDERS.

W. L. McMillan........	Col. 95th Ohio Infy...............	Dec. 5, 1864, to Jan. 19, 1865.
C. G. Eaton.............	Lt.-Col. 72d Ohio Infy............	Jan. 19, 1865, to Feb. 6, 1865.
S. P. Jennison...........	Col. 10th Minn. Infy.............	Feb. 6, 1865, to Feb. 18, 1865.

114th Ill. Infy..........Dec., 1864	From 1-Brig. 1-Div. R. W. 16-Corps.	To Pontooneers 16-Corps Gulf......	Feb.,	1865
93d Ind. Infy..........Dec., 1864	From 1-Brig. 1-Div. R. W. 16-Corps.	To 1-Brig. 1-Div. 16-Corps Gulf....	Feb.,	1865
10th Minn. Infy..........Dec., 1864	From 1-Brig. 1-Div. R. W. 16-Corps.	To 1-Brig. 1-Div. 16-Corps Gulf....	Feb.,	1865
72d Ohio Infy..........Dec., 1864	From 1-Brig. 1-Div. R. W. 16-Corps.	To 1-Brig. 1-Div. 16-Corps Gulf....	Feb.,	1865
95th Ohio Infy..........Dec., 1864	From 1-Brig. 1-Div. R. W. 16-Corps.	To 1-Brig. 1-Div. 16-Corps Gulf....	Feb.,	1865
Cogswell's Ill. Batty.....Dec., 1864	From Arty. Res. Nashville, Tenn....	To Arty. Brig. 16-Corps Gulf......	Feb.,	1865

2d BRIGADE.— COMMANDER.

L. F. Hubbard.........	Col. 5th Minn. Infy................	Dec. 5, 1864, to Feb. 18, 1865.

5th Minn. Infy..........Dec., 1864	From 2-Brig. 1-Div. R. W. 16-Corps.	To 2-Brig. 1-Div. 16-Corps Gulf....	Feb.,	1865
9th Minn. Infy..........Dec., 1864	From 2-Brig. 1-Div. R. W. 16-Corps.	To 2-Brig. 1-Div. 16-Corps Gulf....	Feb.,	1865
11th Mo. Infy..........Dec., 1864	From 2-Brig. 1-Div. R. W. 16-Corps.	To 2-Brig. 1-Div. 16-Corps Gulf....	Feb.,	1865
8th Wis. Infy..........Dec., 1864	From 2-Brig. 1-Div. R. W. 16-Corps.	To 2-Brig. 1-Div. 16-Corps Gulf....	Feb.,	1865
2d Iowa Batty..........Dec., 1864	From 2-Brig. 1-Div. R. W. 16-Corps.	To Arty. 1-Div. 16-Corps Gulf......	Feb.,	1865
47th Ill. Infy..........Feb., 1865	From 2-Brig. 2-Div. Dist. Ky.......	To 2-Brig. 1-Div. 16-Corps Gulf....	Feb.,	1865

3d BRIGADE.— COMMANDERS.

S. G. Hill..........	Col. 35th Ill. Infy................	Dec. 5, 1864, to Dec. 15, 1864.
W. R. Marshall.........	Col. 7th Minn. Infy................	Dec. 15, 1864, to Feb. 4, 1865.
W. H. Heath..........	Lt.-Col. 33d Mo. Infy.............	Feb. 4, 1865, to Feb. 18, 1865.

12th Iowa Infy..........Dec., 1864	From 3-Brig. 1-Div. R. W. 16-Corps.	To 3-Brig. 1-Div. 16-Corps Gulf....	Feb.,	1865
35th Iowa Infy..........Dec., 1864	From 3-Brig. 1-Div. R. W. 16-Corps.	To 3-Brig. 1-Div. 16-Corps Gulf....	Feb.,	1865
7th Minn. Infy..........Dec., 1864	From 3-Brig. 1-Div. R. W. 16-Corps.	To 3-Brig. 1-Div. 16-Corps Gulf....	Feb.,	1865
33d Mo. Infy..........Dec., 1864	From 3-Brig. 1-Div. R. W. 16-Corps.	To 3-Brig. 1-Div. 16-Corps Gulf....	Feb.,	1865
Batty. I, 2d Mo. Arty.....Dec., 1864	From Dept. Mo....................	To Dist. Middle Tenn. Dept. Cumb'd.	Feb.,	1865
ARTILLERY, 1st DIVISION.—				
Batty. E, 1st Ill. Arty....Dec., 1864	From Arty. 1-Div. R. W. 16-Corps..	To Res. Arty. Chattanooga, Tenn....	Feb.,	1865

2d DIVISION.— COMMANDERS.

David Moore	Col. 21st Mo. Infy................	Dec. 5, 1864, to Dec. 7, 1864.
Kenner Garrard	Brigadier General	Dec. 7, 1864, to Feb. 18, 1865.

1st BRIGADE.— COMMANDERS.

T. J. Kinney...........	Col. 119th Ill. Infy...............	Dec. 5, 1864, to Dec. 7, 1864.
David Moore	Col. 21st Mo. Infy................	Dec. 7, 1864, to Feb. 11, 1865.
J. I. Rinaker...........	Col. 122d Ill. Infy................	Feb. 11, 1865, to Feb. 18, 1865.

119th Ill. Infy..........Dec., 1864	From 1-Brig. 3-Div. R. W. 16-Corps.	To 1-Brig. 2-Div. 16-Corps Gulf....	Feb.,	1865
122d Ill. Infy..........Dec., 1864	From 1-Brig. 3-Div. R. W. 16-Corps.	To 1-Brig. 2-Div. 16-Corps Gulf....	Feb.,	1865
89th Ind. Infy..........Dec., 1864	From 1-Brig. 3-Div. R. W. 16-Corps.	To 1-Brig. 2-Div. 16-Corps Gulf....	Feb.,	1865
21st Mo. Infy..........Dec., 1864	From 1-Brig. 3-Div. R. W. 16-Corps.	To 1-Brig. 2-Div. 16-Corps Gulf....	Feb.,	1865
9th Ind. Batty..........Dec., 1864	From Arty. 3-Div. R. W. 16-Corps..	To Indiana	Jan.,	1865

2d BRIGADE.— COMMANDER.

J. I. Gilbert...........	Col. 27th Iowa Infy...............	Dec. 5, 1864, to Feb. 18, 1865.

58th Ill. Infy..........Dec., 1864	From 1-Brig. 3-Div. R. W. 16-Corps.	To 2-Brig. 2-Div. 16-Corps Gulf....	Feb.,	1865
27th Iowa Infy..........Dec., 1864	From 2-Brig. 3-Div. R. W. 16-Corps.	To 2-Brig. 2-Div. 16-Corps Gulf....	Feb.,	1865
32d Iowa Infy..........Dec., 1864	From 2-Brig. 3-Div. R. W. 16-Corps.	To 2-Brig. 2-Div. 16-Corps Gulf....	Feb.,	1865
10th Kansas Infy..........Dec., 1864	From Unass'd 4-Corps Cumb'd......	To 2-Brig. 2-Div. 16-Corps Gulf....	Feb.,	1865
3d Ind. Batty..........Dec., 1864	From 2-Brig. 3-Div. R. W. 16-Corps.	To Arty. 1-Div. 16-Corps Gulf......	Feb.,	1865

3d BRIGADE.— COMMANDER.

E. H. Wolfe...........	Col. 52d Ind. Infy...................	Dec. 5, 1864, to Feb. 18, 1865.

49th Ill. Infy...........Dec., 1864	From 3-Brig. 3-Div. R. W. 16-Corps.	To Garrison Paducah, Ky., Dist. Ky.	Dec.,	1864
117th Ill. Infy...........Dec., 1864	From 3-Brig. 3-Div. R. W. 16-Corps.	To 3-Brig. 2-Div. 16-Corps Gulf....	Feb.,	1865
52d Ind. Infy.............Dec., 1864	From 3-Brig. 3-Div. R. W. 16-Corps.	To 3-Brig. 2-Div. 16-Corps Gulf....	Feb.,	1865
178th N. Y. Infy.........Dec., 1864	From 3-Brig. 3-Div. R. W. 16-Corps.	To 3-Brig. 2-Div. 16-Corps Gulf....	Feb.,	1865
Batty. G, 2d Ill. Arty....Dec., 1864	From 3-Brig. 3-Div. R. W. 16-Corps.	To Arty. 2-Div. 16-Corps Gulf......	Feb.,	1865
34th N. J. Infy..........Jan., 1865	From Paducah, Ky.	To 3-Brig. 2-Div. 16-Corps Gulf....	Feb.,	1865

3d DIVISION.— COMMANDERS.

J. B. Moore...........	Col. 33d Wis. Infy.................	Dec. 5, 1864, to Jan. 4, 1865.
T. K. Smith...........	Brigadier General	Jan. 4, 1865, to Jan. 17, 1865.
J. B. Moore...........	Col. 33d Mo. Infy..................	Jan. 17, 1865, to Feb. 18, 1865.

1st BRIGADE.— COMMANDERS.

L. M. Ward...........	Col. 14th Wis. Infy................	Dec. 5, 1864, to Jan. 4, 1865.
J. B. Moore...........	Col. 33d Wis. Infy................	Jan. 4, 1865, to Jan. 17, 1865.
L. M. Ward...........	Col. 14th Wis. Infy................	Jan. 17, 1865, to Feb. 18, 1865.

72d Ill. Infy.............Dec., 1864	From Unass'd 23-Corps............	To 1-Brig. 3-Div. 16-Corps Gulf....	Feb.,	1865
40th Mo. Infy............Dec., 1864	From 3-Brig. 3-Div. 4-Corps Cumb'd.	To 1-Brig. 3-Div. 16-Corps Gulf....	Feb.,	1865
14th Wis. Infy...........Dec., 1864	From 1-Brig. 3-Div. R. W. 16-Corps.	To 1-Brig. 3-Div. 16-Corps Gulf....	Feb.,	1865
33d Wis. Infy...........Dec., 1864	From 1-Brig. 3-Div. R. W. 16-Corps.	To 1-Brig. 3-Div. 16-Corps Gulf....	Feb.,	1865

2d BRIGADE.— COMMANDER.

L. Blandin	Col. 95th Ill Infy.................	Dec. 5, 1864, to Feb. 18, 1865.

81st Ill. Infy............Dec., 1864	From 2-Brig. Prov'l Div. 17-Corps..	To 2-Brig. 3-Div. 16-Corps Gulf....	Feb.,	1865
95th Ill. Infy...........Dec., 1864	From 2-Brig. Prov'l Div. 17-Corps..	To 2-Brig. 3-Div. 16-Corps Gulf....	Feb.,	1865
44th Mo. Infy...........Dec., 1864	From Unass'd 23-Corps Army Ohio..	To 2-Brig. 3-Div. 16-Corps Gulf....	Feb.,	1865
49th Mo. Infy...........Dec., 1864	From Unass'd 23-Corps Army Ohio..	To 2-Brig. 3-Div. 16-Corps Gulf....	Feb.,	1865
ARTILLERY.—				
14th Ind. Batty..........Dec., 1864	From Unass'd Dist. West. Tenn.....	To Arty. 3-Div. 16-Corps Gulf......	Feb.,	1865
Batty. A, 2nd Mo. Arty....Dec., 1864	From Dept. Mo.....................	To 3d Sub-Dist. Dist. Middle Tenn..	Feb.,	1865

DISTRICT OF THE ETOWAH.—Created Nov. 12, 1864.

COMMANDER.

J. B. Steedman........	Major General	To May, 1865.

1st SEPARATE DIVISION.—Created Jan. 14, 1865.

COMMANDER.

J. B. Steedman........	Major General	

1st BRIGADE.— COMMANDER.

J. H. King...........	Brigadier General	

15th U. S. Infy..........Nov., 1864	From Reg. Brig. Chattanooga, Tenn.	To Regular Establishment..........	Aug.,	1865
16th U. S. Infy..........Nov., 1864	From Reg. Brig. Chattanooga, Tenn.	To Regular Establishment..........	Aug.,	1865
18th U. S. Infy..........Nov., 1864	From Reg. Brig. Chattanooga, Tenn.	To Regular Establishment..........	Aug.,	1865
19th U. S. Infy..........Nov., 1864	From Reg. Brig. Chattanooga, Tenn.	To Regular Establishment..........	Aug.,	1865
Batty. G, 1st Mo. Arty...Jan., 1865	From Garr. Arty. Chattanooga, Tenn.	No change to Muster Out..........	July,	1865

2d BRIGADE.— COMMANDERS.

C. H. Carlton..........	Col. 89th Ohio Infy................	Nov., 1864, to Dec., 1864.
C. H. Grosvenor........	Col. 18th Ohio Infy................	Dec., 1864, to Mch. 7, 1865.
C. J. Dilworth.........	Col. 85th Ill. Infy................	Mch. 7, 1865, to June 1, 1865.
J. F. Curtis..........	Col. 44th Ind. Infy................	June, 1865.

29th Ind. Infy...........Nov., 1864	From 1-Sep. Brig. Post Chattanooga.	To 2-Brig. 2-Sep. Div. Dist. Etowah.	May,	1865
32d Ind. Infy...........Nov., 1864	From 1-Sep. Brig. Post Chattanooga.	To 1-Brig. 3-Div. 4-Corps Cumb'd...	June,	1865
44th Ind. Infy...........Nov., 1864	From 1-Sep. Brig. Post Chattanooga.	No change to Muster Out..........	Sept.,	1865
68th Ind. Infy...........Nov., 1864	From 1-Sep. Brig. Post Chattanooga.	No change to Muster Out..........	June,	1865
8th Ky. Infy.............Nov., 1864	From 1-Sep. Brig. Post Chattanooga.	No change to Muster Out..........	Feb.,	1865
18th Ohio Infy...........Nov., 1864	From Post Chattanooga, Tenn......	To Augusta, Ga...................	July,	1865
15th Wis. Infy...........Nov., 1864	From Post Chattanooga, Tenn......	No change to Muster Out..........	Feb.,	1865
186th Ohio Infy..........May, 1865	From 2-Br. 2-Sep. Div. Dist. Etowah.	No change to Muster Out..........	Sept.,	1865
UNASSIGNED.—				
14th U. S. C. T..........Nov., 1864	From Unass'd Dept. Cumb'd........	To 1-Col'd Brig. Dist. Etowah......	Dec.,	1864
16th U. S. C. T..........Nov., 1864	From Unass'd Dept. Cumb'd........	To 1-Col'd Brig. Dist. Etowah......	Dec.,	1864
42d U. S. C. T..........Nov., 1864	From Unass'd Dept. Cumb'd........	To 1-Col'd Brig. Dist. Etowah......	Dec.,	1864
44th U. S. C. T..........Nov., 1864	From Unass'd Dept. Cumb'd........	To 1-Col'd Brig. Dist. Etowah......	Dec.,	1864
18th U. S. C. T..........Dec., 1864	From Dept. Mo....................	To 1-Col'd Brig. Dist. Etowah......	Dec.,	1864
68th N. Y. Infy..........Dec., 1864	From 3-Brig. Def. Nashv. & Ch. R. R.	To 2-Brig. 2-Sep. Div. Dist. Etowah.	Mch.,	1865
14th U. S. C. T..........Jan., 1865	From 1-Col'd Brig. Dist. Etowah....	To 1-Col'd Brig. Dist. Etowah......	Mch.,	1865
16th U. S. C. T..........Jan., 1865	From 1-Col'd Brig. Dist. Etowah....	To 1-Col'd Brig. Dist. Etowah......	Mch.,	1865
18th U. S. C. T..........Jan., 1865	From 1-Col'd Brig. Dist. Etowah....	To 1-Col'd Brig. Dist. Etowah......	Mch.,	1865
42d U. S. C. T..........Jan., 1865	From 1-Col'd Brig. Dist. Etowah....	To 1-Col'd Brig. Dist. Etowah......	Mch.,	1865
44th U. S. C. T..........Jan., 1865	From 1-Col'd Brig. Dist. Etowah....	To 1-Col'd Brig. Dist. Etowah......	Mch.,	1865

1st COLORED BRIGADE.— COMMANDER.

Thomas J. Morgan.....	Col. 14th U. S. C. T..............	

14th U. S. C. T..........Dec., 1864	From Unass'd Dist. Etowah........	To Unass'd Dist. Etowah..........	Jan.,	1865
16th U. S. C. T..........Dec., 1864	From Unass'd Dist. Etowah........	To Unass'd Dist. Etowah..........	Jan.,	1865
17th U. S. C. T..........Dec., 1864	From Unass'd Post of Nashville....	To Post Nashville, Tenn..........	Jan.,	1865
18th U. S. C. T..........Dec., 1864	From Unass'd Dist. Etowah........	To Unass'd Dist. Etowah..........	Jan.,	1865
44th U. S. C. T..........Dec., 1864	From Unass'd Dist. Etowah........	To Unass'd Dist. Etowah..........	Jan.,	1865

Brigade discontinued Jan., 1865. Reorganized Mch. 1, 1865.

COMMANDERS.

Thomas J. Morgan.....	Col. 14th U. S. C. T..............	Mch., 1865, to Apr., 1865.
Lewis Johnson	Col. 44th U. S. C. T..............	Apr., 1865, to July, 1865.

14th U. S. C. T..........Mch., 1865	From Unatt. Dist. Etowah.........	To 1-Brig. 4-Div. Dist. East. Tenn..	July,	1865
16th U. S. C. T..........Mch., 1865	From Unatt. Dist. Etowah.........	To 2-Brig. 4-Div. Dist. East. Tenn..	July,	1865
18th U. S. C. T..........Mch., 1865	From Unatt. Dist. Etowah.........	To 2-Brig. 4-Div. Dist. East. Tenn..	July,	1865
42d U. S. C. T..........Mch., 1865	From Unatt. Dist. Etowah.........	To 2-Brig. 4-Div. Dist. East. Tenn..	July,	1865
44th U. S. C. T..........Mch., 1865	From Unatt. Dist. Etowah.........	To 2-Brig. 4-Div. Dist. East. Tenn..	July,	1865

2d COLORED BRIGADE.—

	COMMANDER.		
C. R. Thompson........	Col. 12th U. S. C. T.............		

12th U. S. C. T..........Dec., 1864	From Def. Nashv. & N. W. R. R....	To Def. Nashv. & N. W. R. R......	Jan.,	1865
13th U. S. C. T..........Dec., 1864	From Def. Nashv. & N. W. R. R....	To Def. Nashv. & N. W. R. R......	Jan.,	1865
100th U. S. C. T.........Dec., 1864	From Def. Nashv. & N. W. R. R....	To Def. Nashv. & N. W. R. R......	Jan.,	1865
1st Kansas Batty........Dec., 1864	From Def. Nashv. & N. W. R. R....	To Arty. Nashville, Tenn...........	Jan.,	1865

ARTILLERY.—

18th Ohio Batty.........Dec., 1864	From Arty. Post Chattanooga, Tenn.	To Garrison Arty. Chattanooga......	Jan.,	1865
20th Ind. Batty..........Dec., 1864	From Arty. Post Chattanooga, Tenn.	To Garrison Arty. Chattanooga......	Jan.,	1865

PROVISIONAL DIVISION.—Organized from Detachments belonging to 14th, 15th, 17th and 20th Army Corps unable to join their Commands.

	COMMANDER.		
Charles Crufts	Brigadier General		

1st BRIGADE.—

	COMMANDER.		
Benj. Harrison	Col. 70th Ind. Infy...............		

2d BRIGADE.—

	COMMANDER.		
J. G. Mitchell..........	Col. 113th Ohio Infy..............		

3d BRIGADE.—

	COMMANDER.		
C. H. Grosvenor.......	Lt.-Col. 18th Ohio Infy..........		

2d SEPARATE DIVISION.—Organized Mch., 1865.

	COMMANDERS.		
Charles Cruft	Bvt. Major General................		
H. M. Judah..........	Brigadier General		

1st BRIGADE.—Organized Mch. 15, 1865.

	COMMANDER.		
H. M. Judah..........	Brigadier General		

1st Ga. Battalion........Mch., 1865	From Unass'd Dist. Etowah........	No change to Muster Out..........	July,	1865
147th Ill. Infy..........Mch., 1865	From New Organization...........	To Dept. of Ga...................	July,	1865
151st Ill. Infy..........Mch., 1865	From New Organization...........	To Dept. of Ga...................	July,	1865
145th Ind. Infy.........Mch., 1865	From New Organization...........	To Dept. of Ga...................	July,	1865
187th Ohio Infy........Mch., 1865	From New Organization...........	No change to Muster Out..........	Sept.,	1865
6th Tenn. Mtd. Infy.....Mch., 1865	From Unatt. Dist. Etowah..........	No change to Muster Out..........	June,	1865
Batty. I, 1st Ohio Arty...Mch., 1865	From Arty. Chattanooga...........	No change to Muster Out..........	June,	1865

2d BRIGADE.—

	COMMANDERS.		
Felix Prince Salm......	Bvt. Brig. General................	Mch. 15, 1865, to June 20, 1865.	
J. F. Curtis..........	Col. 44th Ind. Infy...............		

149th Ill. Infy..........Mch., 1865	From New Organization...........	To Dept. of Ga...................	July,	1865
150th Ill. Infy..........Mch., 1865	From New Organization...........	To Dept. of Ga...................	July,	1865
68th N. Y. Infy.........Mch., 1865	From Def. Nashv. & Chatt. R. R....	To Dept. of Ga...................	July,	1865
186th Ohio Infy........Mch., 1865	From New Organization...........	To 2-Brig. 1-Sep. Div. Dist. Etowah.	May,	1865
29th Ind. Infy..........May, 1865	From 2-Brig. 1-Sept. Div. Etowah...	No change to Muster Out..........	Sept.,	1865

3d BRIGADE.—Organized Apr. 7, 1865.

	COMMANDERS.		
H. Le Favour..........	Col. 22d Michigan Infy..........	Apr. 7, 1865, to June 20, 1865.	
A. T. Smith..........	Col. 156th Illinois Infy..........		

11th Mich. Infy.........Apr., 1865	From New Organization...........	No change to Muster Out..........	Sept.	1865
22d Mich. Infy.........Apr., 1865	From Res. Brigade Dept. Cumberland	No change to Muster Out..........	June,	1865
156th Ill. Infy.........Apr., 1865	From New Organization...........	No change to Muster Out..........	Sept.,	1865

DISTRICT OF EAST TENNESSEE.—

	COMMANDERS.		
Davis Tillson	Brigadier General.................	Feb. 10, 1865, to Mch. 9, 1865.	
Geo. Stoneman	Major General..................	Mch. 9, 1865, to June 27, 1865.	

4th DIVISION.—

	COMMANDERS.		
Davis Tillson	Brigadier General.................	Feb. 10, 1865, to May 17, 1865.	
Charles Cruft	Bvt. Major General................	May 17, 1865, to June., 1865.	

1st BRIGADE.—

	COMMANDERS.		
W. C. Bartlett........	Col. 2d N. C. Mtd. Infy.............	Feb. 10, 1865 to Mch. 17, 1865	
C. G. Hawley.........	Col. 1st Ohio Heavy Arty..........	Mch. 17, 1865 to June, 1865	
Chas. Cruft	Bvt. Major General..............	June, 1865.	

34th Ky. Infy...........Feb., 1865	From 1-Brig. 4-Div. 23-Corps Ohio..	To 2-Brig. 4-Div. Dist. East Tenn...	Mch.,	1865
2d N. C. Mtd. Infy......Feb., 1865	From 1-Brig. 4-Div. 23-Corps Ohio..	No change to Muster Out..........	June,	1865
Batty. M, 1st Mich. Arty.Feb., 1865	From 1-Brig. 4-Div. 23-Corps Ohio..	To 2-Brig. 4-Div. Dist. East Tenn...	Mch.,	1865
Batty. B, 1st Tenn. Arty..Feb., 1865	From 1-Brig. 4-Div. 23-Corps Ohio..	To 2-Brig. 4-Div. Dist. East Tenn...	Mch.,	1865
3d N. C. Infy...........Mch., 1865	From 2-Brig. 4-Div. Dist. East Tenn.	No change to Muster Out..........	Aug.,	1865
4th Tenn. Infy..........Mch., 1865	From 2-Brig. 4-Div. Dist. East Tenn.	No change to Muster Out..........	Aug.,	1865
1st Ohio Heavy Arty....Mch., 1865	From Arty. 4-Div. Dist. East Tenn.	No change to Muster Out..........	July,	1865
1st U. S. C. Heavy Arty.Mch., 1865	From Arty. 4-Div. Dist. East Tenn.	To Dept. Tenn....................	July,	1865
Wilder's Ind. Batty......Mch., 1865	From Arty. 4-Div. Dist. East Tenn.	No change to Muster Out..........	July,	1865
10th Tenn. Infy.........Apr., 1865	From Governors' Guard Tenn......	No change to Muster Out..........	June,	1865
Batty. E, 1st Tenn. Arty..May, 1865	From Arty. Cav. Dist. East Tenn.	No change to Muster Out..........	July,	1865
14th U. S. C. T.........July, 1865	From 1st Colored Brig. Dist. Etowah	To Dept. Tenn....................	Aug.,	1865
40th U. S. C. T.........July, 1865	From 2-Brig. 4-Div. Dist. East Tenn.	To Dept. Tenn....................	Aug.,	1865
Batty. C, 1st Wis. H. A..July, 1865	From 3-Brig. 4-Div. Dist. East Tenn.	No change to Muster Out..........	Sept.,	1865

2d BRIGADE, 4th DIVISION.—

	COMMANDERS.		
H. G. Gibson..........	Col. 2d Ohio Heavy Arty..........	Feb. 10, 1865, to July, 1865.	
L. Johnson...........	Col. 44th U. S. C. T..............	July, 1865, to Aug., 1865.	

3d N. C. Mounted.......Feb., 1865	From 2-Brig. 4-Div. 23-Corps Ohio..	To 1-Brig. 4-Div. Dist. East Tenn..	Mch.	1865
1st Tennessee Infy.......Feb., 1865	From 2-Brig. 4-Div. 23-Corps Ohio..	No change to Muster Out..........	Aug.,	1865
2d Tennessee Infy.......Feb., 1865	From 2-Brig. 4-Div. 23-Corps Ohio..	No change to Muster Out..........	Aug.,	1865
4th Tennessee Infy.......Feb., 1865	From 2-Brig. 4-Div. 23-Corps Ohio..	To 1-Brig. 4-Div. Dist. East Tenn..	Mch.,	1865
10th Michigan Cav......Feb., 1865	From 2-Brig. 4-Div. 23-Corps Ohio..	To 1-Brig. Cav. Div. Dist. East Tenn.	Mch.,	1865
34th Kentucky Infy......Mch., 1865	From 1-Brig. 4-Div. Dist. East Tenn.	No change to Muster Out..........	June,	1865
7th Tenn. Mtd. Infy......Mch., 1865	From New Organization...........	No change to Muster Out..........	June,	1865

2d BRIGADE, 4th DIVISION.—Continued.

40th U. S. C. T.	Apr., 1865	From Def. Louisville and N. R. R..	To 1-Brig. 4-Div. Dist. East Tenn...	July,	1865
44th Indiana Infy	May, 1865	From 2-Brig. 1-Sep. Div. D.Etowah.	No change to Muster Out	Sept.,	1865
186th Ohio Infy	July, 1865	From 2-Brig. 1-Sep. Div. D.Etowah.	No change to Muster Out	Sept.,	1865
11th Michigan Infy	July, 1865	From 3-Brig. 2-Sep. Div. D. Etowah.	No change to Muster Out	Sept.,	1865
16th U. S. C. T.	July, 1865	From 1st Colored Brig. Dist. Etowah	To Dept. Tenn	Sept.,	1865
18th U. S. C. T.	July, 1865	From 1st Colored Brig. Dist. Etowah	To Dept. Tenn	Sept.,	1865
42d U. S. C. T.	July, 1865	From 1st Colored Brig. Dist. Etowah	To Dept. Tenn	Sept.,	186b
44th U. S. C. T.	July, 1865	From 1st Colored Brig. Dist. Etowah	To Dept. Tenn	Sept.,	1865
ARTILLERY.—					
Colvin's Ill. Batty	Feb., 1865	From 2-Brig. 4-Div. 23-Corps Ohio.	No change to Muster Out	July,	1865
Henshaw's Ill. Batty	Feb., 1865	From 3-Brig. 4-Div. 23-Corps Ohio.	No change to Muster Out	July,	1865
Elgin, Ill. Batty	Feb., 1865	From 2-Brig. 4-Div. 23-Corps Ohio..	To Arty. 1-Div. 23-Corps.	Apr.,	1865
Wilder's Indiana Batty	Feb., 186b	From 2-Brig. 4-Div. 23-Corps Ohio..	To 1-Brig. 4-Div. Dist. East Tenn.	Mch.,	1865
Batty. L, 1st Mich. Arty	Feb., 1865	From 2-Brig. 4-Div. 23-Corps Ohio..	No change to Muster Out	Aug.,	1865
21st Ohio Batty	Feb., 1865	From 2-Brig. 4-Div. 23-Corps Ohio..	No change to Muster Out	July,	1865
22d Ohio Batty	Feb., 1865	From 2-Brig. 4-Div. 23-Corps Ohiu..	No change to Muster Out	July,	1865
1st Ohio Heavy Arty	Feb., 1865	From 2-Brig. 4-Div. 23-Corps Ohio..	To 1-Brig. 4-Dic. Dist. East Tenn.	Mch.,	1865
2d Ohio Heavy Arty	Feb., 1865	From Unatt. 4-Div. 23-Corps Ohio..	No change to Muster Out	July,	1865
1st U. S. C. Heavy Arty	Feb., 1865	From 2-Brig. 4-Div. 23-Corps Ohio..	To 1-Brig. 4-Div. Dist. East Tenn.	Mch.,	1865
Batty. M, 1st Mich. Arty	Mch., 1865	From 1-Brig. 4-Div. Dist. East Tenn.	No change to Muster Out	Aug.,	1865
Batty. B, 1st Tenn. Arty	Mch., 1865	From 1-Brig. 4-Div. Dist. East Tenn.	No change to Muster Out	July,	1865
Batty. K, 1st Mich. Arty	Mch., 1865	From Arty. Chattanooga, Tenn	No change to Muster Out	July,	1865
7th Ind. Batty	Apr., 1865	From Arty. Chattanooga, Tenn	No change to Muster Out	July,	1865
2d Minn. Batty	Apr., 1865	From Arty. Chattanooga, Tenn	No change to Muster Out	July,	1865
10th Ohio Batty	Apr., 1865	From Arty. Nashville, Tenn	No change to Muster Out	July,	1865
Batty. D, 1st Tenn. Arty	Apr., 1865	From Arty. Nashville, Tenn	No change to Muster Out	July,	1865
Batty. C, 1st Wis. H. Arty	Apr., 1865	From Arty. Chattanooga, Tenn	To 1-Br. 4-Div. Dist. East Tenn.	July,	1865

GILLEM'S CAVALRY DIVISION.—Organized March 17, 1865. Discontinued July, 1865.

COMMANDER.

A. C. Gillem	Brigadier General		

1st BRIGADE.— **COMMANDERS.**

W. J. Palmer	Col. 15th Penna. Cav	Mch. 17, 1865, to June 17, 1865.
L. S. Trowbridge	Col. 10th Mich. Cav	June 17, 1865 to July .., 1865.

10th Mich. Cav	Mch., 1865	From 2-Br. 4-Div. Dist. East. Tenn.	To Cav. Brig. Dist. East Tenn.	July,	1865
12th Ohio Cav	Mch., 1865	From Mil. Dist. Ky.	To Cav. Brig. Dist. East Tenn.	July,	1865
15th Penna. Cav	Mch., 1865	From 3-Br. 6-Div. Cav. C. M. D. M.	No change to Muster Out	June,	1865
11th Mich. Cav	June, 1865	From 2-Br. Cav. Div. Dist. E. Tenn.	To Consol. with 8th Mich. Cav	July,	1865

2d BRIGADE.— **COMMANDER.**

S. B. Brown	Col. 11th Mich. Cav	

11th Ky. Cav	Mch., 1865	From Mil. Dist. Ky.	No change to Muster Out	July,	1865
12th Ky. Cav	Mch., 1865	From Mil. Dist. Ky.	To Cav. Brig. Dist. East Tenn.	July,	1865
11th Mich. Cav	Mch., 1865	From Mil. Dist. Ky.	To 1-Br. Cav. Div. Dist. E. Tenn.	June,	1865

3d BRIGADE.— **COMMANDER.**

John K. Miller	Col. 13th Tenn. Cav	

8th Tenn. Cav	Mch., 1865	From Dist. Tenn	To Cav. Brig. Dist. East Tenn.	July,	1865
9th Tenn. Cav	Mch., 1865	From Dist. Tenn	To Cav. Brig. Dist. East Tenn.	July,	1865
13th Tenn. Cav	Mch., 1865	From Dist. Tenn	To Cav. Brig. Dist. East Tenn.	July,	1865
ARTILLERY.—					
Batty. E, 1st Tenn. Arty	Mch., 1865	From Arty. Dist. Nashville, Tenn...	To 1-Brig 4-Div. Dist. East Tenn...	May,	1865

CAVALRY BRIGADE.— **COMMANDER.**

Emory Upton	Bvt. Major General	

12th Ky. Cav	July, 1865	From 2-Br. Cav. Div. Dist. E. Tenn.	No change to Muster Out	Aug.,	1865
10th Mich. Cav	July, 1865	From 1-Br. Cav. Div. Dist. E. Tenn.	No change to Muster Out	Nov.,	1865
12th Ohio Cav	July, 1865	From 1-Br. Cav. Div. Dist. E. Tenn.	No change to Muster Out	Nov.,	1865
8th Tenn. Cav	July, 1865	From 3-Br. Cav. Div. Dist. E. Tenn.	No change to Muster Out	Sept.,	1865
9th Tenn. Cav	July, 1865	From 3-Br. Cav. Div. Dist. E. Tenn.	No change to Muster Out	Sept.,	1865
13th Tenn. Cav	July, 1865	From 3-Br. Cav. Div. Dist. E. Tenn.	No change to Muster Out	Sept.,	1865

DISTRICT MIDDLE TENNESSEE.— **COMMANDER.**

L. H. Rousseau	Major General	

NASHVILLE, TENN. (See Post Nashville.)— **COMMANDER.**

J. F. Miller	Brigadier General	

1st SUB DISTRICT.— **COMMANDER.**

R. H. Milroy	Major General	

1st BRIGADE.— **COMMANDER.**

H. P. Van Cleve	Brigadier General	

154th Ill. Infy	Mch., 1865	From Def. Nash. and Chatta. R. R.	No change to Muster Out	Sept.,	1865
143d Ind. Infy	Mch., 1865	From New Organization	No change to Muster Out	Oct.,	1865
115th Ohio Infy	Mch., 1865	From Unatt. 4-Div. 20-Corps	No change to Muster Out	June,	1865
188th Ohio Infy	Mch., 1865	From New Organization	No change to Muster Out	Sept.,	1865
75th Penna. Infy	Mch., 1865	From Unass'd 4-Div. 20-Corps	No change to Muster Out	Sept.,	1865
1st Tenn. Mtd. Infy	Mch., 1865	From Dist. Mid. Tenn. Dept. Cumb'd.	No change to Muster Out	July,	1865
4th Ind. Batty	Mch., 1865	From Garrison Arty. Nash. Tenn...	No change to Muster Out	Aug.,	1865
Batty. D, 1st Mich. Arty	Mch., 1865	From 1-Br. Def. Nash. & Chat. R. R.	No change to Muster Out	Aug.,	1865
8th Wis. Batty	Mch., 1865	From 1-Br. Def. Nash. & Chat. R. R.	No change to Muster Out	July,	1865

2d BRIGADE.— **COMMANDER.**

N. A. M. Dudley	Bvt. Brigadier General	

148th Ill. Infy	Mch., 1865	From New Organization	To 3-Br. 1st Sub Dist. Mid. Tenn...	June,	1865
152d Ill. Infy	Mch., 1865	From New Organization	To 1st Infy. Brig. Dist. West Tenn.	July,	1865
153d Ill. Infy	Mch., 1865	From New Organization	To 1st Infy. Brig. Dist. West Tenn.	July,	1865
155th Ill. Infy	Mch., 1865	From New Organization	No change to Muster Out	Sept.,	1865
151st Ind. Infy	Mch., 1865	From New Organization	No change to Muster Out	Sept.,	1865
42d Mo. Infy	Mch., 1865	From Unatt. 4-Div. 20-Corps	No change to Muster Out	July,	1865
59th Ohio Infy	Mch., 1865	From Unatt. 4-Div. 20-Corps	No change to Muster Out	July,	1865
47th Wis. Infy	Mch., 1865	From 2-Br. Def. Nash. & Chat. R. R.	No change to Muster Out	Sept.,	1865
13th N. Y. Batty	Mch., 1865	From Tullahoma, Tenn	No change to Muster Out	July,	1865

3d BRIGADE.—Organized April 23, 1865.— COMMANDERS.

A. Cobb.............	Col. 43d Wis. Infy.................	To June 17, 1865.	
Thos. Saylor.........	Col. 29th Mich. Infy...............	To July .., 1865.	
29th Mich. Infy........Apr., 1865	From Unatt. 4-Div. 20-Corps.......	To Garrison Chattanooga, Tenn.....	July, 1865
43d Wis. Infy..........Apr., 1865	From Def. Nash. & Chatta. R. R....	No change to Muster Out..........	June, 1865
148th Ill. Infy..........June, 1865	From 2-Br. 1st Sub Dist. Mid. Tenn.	No change to Muster Out..........	Sept., 1865
156th Ill. Infy..........Apr., 1865	From New Organization............	No change to Muster Out..........	Sept., 1865

2d SUB DISTRICT.— COMMANDER.

R. W. Johnson.........	Brigadier General.................		
61st Ill. Infy..........Mch., 1865	From Unatt. 4-Div. 20-Corps........	No change to Muster Out..........	Sept., 1865
148th Ind. Infy.........Mch., 1865	From New Organization............	No change to Muster Out..........	Sept., 1865
175th Ohio Infy.........Mch., 1865	From Unatt. 4-Div. 20-Corps........	No change to Muster Out..........	June, 1865
21st Ind. Batty.........Mch., 1865	From Garrison Arty. Nash. Tenn....	No change to Muster Out..........	June, 1865

3d SUB DISTRICT.— COMMANDER.

C. R. Thompson........	Bvt. Brig. General.................		
173d Ohio Infy..........Mch., 1865	From Post Nashville..............	No change to Muster Out..........	July, 1865
12th U. S. C. T..........Mch., 1865	From Nash. & Northwestern R. R...	To Dept. Tenn....................	July, 1865
13th U. S. C. T..........Mch., 1865	From Nash. & Northwestern R. R...	To Dept. Tenn....................	July, 1865
110th U. S. C. T.........Mch., 1865	From Nash. & Northwestern R. R...	To Dept. Tenn....................	July, 1865
111th U. S. C. T.........Mch., 1865	From Nash. & Northwestern R. R...	To Dept. Tenn....................	July, 1865
Batty. A, 2d Mo. Arty...Mch., 1865	From Arty. 3-Div. Army Tenn.....	To St. Louis Mo..................	June, 1865
Batty. F, 2d Mo. Arty...Mch., 1865	From Arty. Nashville.............	To St. Louis Mo..................	June, 1865
Batty. I, 2d Mo. Arty....Mch., 1865	From 3-Brig. 1-Div. Det. Army Tenn.	To St. Louis Mo..................	June, 1865
Batty. C, 1st Tenn. Arty..Mch., 1865	From Garrison Arty. Nashville......	No change to Muster Out..........	July, 1865

4th SUB DISTRICT.— COMMANDER.

Jas. Gilfillan............	Col. 11th Minn. Infy..............		
11th Minn. Infy.........Mch., 1865	From Louisville & Nash. R. R.......	No change to Muster Out..........	July, 1865
8th Tenn. Mtd. Infy.....Mch., 1865	From New Organization............	No change to Muster Out..........	Aug., 1865
Batty. A, 1st Ohio Arty....Mch., 1865	From Garrison Arty. Nashville.....	No change to Muster Out..........	July, 1865

5th SUB DISTRICT.— COMMANDER.

A. A. Smith............	Col. 83d Ill. Infy.................		
83d Ill. Infy............Mch., 1865	From Unatt. 4-Div. 20-Corps.......	No change to Muster Out..........	June, 1865
15th U. S. C. T..........Mch., 1865	From Springfield, Tenn...........	To Dept. Tenn....................	Aug., 1865
Batty. D, 1st Ill. Arty....Mch., 1865	From Garrison Arty. Nashville......	No change to Muster Out..........	July, 1865
Batty. C, 2d Ill. Arty.....Mch., 1865	From Fort Donelson..............	No change to Muster Out..........	July, 1865
Batty. F, 2d Ill. Arty.....Mch., 1865	From Arty. Res. Army Tenn........	No change to Muster Out..........	July, 1865
Batty. H, 2d Ill. Arty.....Mch., 1865	From Garrison Clarksville, Tenn....	No change to Muster Out..........	July, 1865
3d Ohio Batty...........Mch., 1865	From Garrison Arty. Nash. Tenn...	No change to Muster Out..........	July, 1865

Army and Department of the Tennessee

Military District of Cairo. Cairo, Bird's Point, Cape Girardeau, Fort Holt, Mound City, Etc.

COMMANDERS.

U. S. Grant............	Brigadier General..................	Aug. 1, 1861, to Feb. 14, 1862.	
W. T. Sherman.........	Brigadier General..................	Feb. 14, 1862, to Mch. 8, 1862.	
7th Ill. Infy............Aug., 1861	From New Organization...........	To 4-Brig. Mil. Dist. Cairo........	Oct., 1861
8th Ill. Infy............Aug., 1861	From New Organization...........	To 4-Brig. Mil. Dist. Cairo........	Oct., 1861
9th Ill. Infy............Aug., 1861	From New Organization...........	To Dist. Paducah Ky..............	Sept., 1861
10th Ill. Infy...........Aug., 1861	From New Organization...........	To 1-Brig. Mil. Dist. Cairo........	Oct., 1861
11th Ill. Infy...........Aug., 1861	From New Organization...........	To 3-Brig. Mil. Dist. Cairo........	Oct., 1861
12th Ill. Infy...........Aug., 1861	From New Organization...........	To 3-Brig. Mil. Dist. Cairo........	Oct., 1861
17th Ill. Infy...........Aug., 1861	From New Organization...........	To 5-Brig. Mil. Dist. Cairo........	Oct., 1861
18th Ill. Infy...........Aug., 1861	From New Organization...........	To 1-Brig. Mil. Dist. Cairo........	Oct., 1861
20th Ill. Infy...........Aug., 1861	From New Organization...........	To Unatt. Bird's Point, Mo........	Oct., 1861
22d Ill. Infy............Aug., 1861	From New Organization...........	To 2-Brig. Mil. Dist. Cairo........	Oct., 1861
11th Mo. Infy...........Aug., 1861	From New Organization...........	To 5-Brig. Mil. Dist. Cairo........	Oct., 1861
27th Ill. Infy...........Sept., 1861	From New Organization...........	To Unatt. Cairo, Ill..............	Oct., 1861
28th Ill. Infy...........Sept., 1861	From New Organization...........	To 4-Brig. Mil. Dist. Cairo........	Oct., 1861
29th Ill. Infy...........Sept., 1861	From New Organization...........	To 1-Brig. Mil. Dist. Cairo........	Oct., 1861
30th Ill. Infy...........Sept., 1861	From New Organization...........	To 1-Brig. Mil. Dist. Cairo........	Oct., 1861
31st Ill. Infy...........Sept., 1861	From New Organization...........	To 1-Brig. Mil. Dist. Cairo........	Oct., 1861
41st Ill. Infy...........Sept., 1861	From New Organization...........	To Unatt. Dist. Cairo............	Oct., 1861
10th Iowa Infy..........Oct., 1861	From New Organization...........	To 5-Brig. Mil. Dist. Cairo........	Oct., 1861
48th Ill. Infy...........Nov., 1861	From New Organization...........	To 2-Brig. 1-Div. Mil. Dist. Cairo..	Feb., 1862
45th Ill. Infy...........Jan., 1862	From New Organization...........	To 2-Brig. 1-Div. Mil. Dist. Cairo..	Feb., 1862
Batty. A, 1st Ill. L. A....Aug., 1861	From New Organization...........	To 1-Brig. 1-Div. Dist. Cairo......	Feb., 1862
Batty. B, 1st Ill. L. A....Aug., 1861	From New Organization...........	To 3-Brig. Dist. Cairo............	Oct., 1861
Batty. E, 2d Ill. L. A.....Sept., 1861	From New Organization...........	To 1-Brig. Dist. Cairo............	Oct., 1861
Batty. C, 1st Ill. L. A....Oct., 1861	From New Organization...........	To 2-Brig. Dist. Cairo............	Oct., 1861
Batty. D, 1st Ill. L. A....Oct., 1861	From New Organization...........	To 4-Brig. Dist. Cairo............	Oct., 1861
Batty. G, 1st Ill. L. A....Oct., 1861	From New Organization...........	To Flotilla Brig. Army Miss........	Feb., 1862
Batty. D, 2d Ill. L. A.....Dec., 1861	From New Organization...........	To 1-Brig. 1-Div. Dist. West Tenn..	Feb., 1862
Batty. F, 2d Ill. L. A.....Dec., 1861	From New Organization...........	To Unatt. Arty. Army Tenn........	Mch., 1862
Carmichael's Ill. Cav....Sept., 1861	From New Organization...........	To 1-Brig. 1-Div. Mil. Dist. Cairo..	Feb., 1862
Dollins' Ill. Cav........Sept., 1861	From New Organization...........	To 1-Brig. 1-Div. Mil. Dist. Cairo...	Feb., 1862
O'Harnett's Ill. Cav.....Sept., 1861	From New Organization...........	To 1-Brig. 1-Div. Mil. Dist. Cairo...	Feb., 1862
Stewart's Ill. Cav.......Sept., 1861	From New Organization...........	To 1-Brig. 1-Div. Mil. Dist. Cairo...	Feb., 1862
2d Ill. Cav.............Oct., 1861	From New Organization...........	To 2-Brig. Mil. Dist. Cairo........	Oct., 1861
4th Ill. Cav............Nov., 1861	From New Organization...........	To 2-Brig. 1-Div. Mil. Dist. Cairo..	Feb., 1862
6th Ill. Cav............Nov., 1861	From New Organization...........	To Dist. Columbus, Ky............	Mch., 1862
7th Ill. Cav............Nov., 1861	From New Organization...........	To 4-Brig. 1-Div. Mil. Dist. Cairo....	Feb., 1862

1st BRIGADE.— COMMANDER.

John A. McClernand.... Brigadier General — Oct. 14, 1861, to Feb. 1, 1862.

Unit	Date	From	To	Date
10th Ill. Infy	Oct., 1861	From Military Dist. Cairo	To 4-Brig. 1-Div. Mil. Dist. Cairo	Feb., 1862
18th Ill. Infy	Oct., 1861	From Military Dist. Cairo	To 1-Brig. 1-Div. Mil. Dist. Cairo	Feb., 1862
29th Ill. Infy	Oct., 1861	From Military Dist. Cairo	To 1-Brig. 1-Div. Mil. Dist. Cairo	Feb., 1862
30th Ill. Infy	Oct., 1861	From Military Dist. Cairo	To 1-Brig. 1-Div. Mil. Dist. Cairo	Feb., 1862
31st Ill. Infy	Oct., 1861	From Military Dist. Cairo	To 1-Brig. 1-Div. Mil. Dist. Cairo	Feb., 1862
1st Ill. Cav.	Oct., 1861	From Military Dist. Cairo	To 4-Brig. 1-Div. Mil. Dist. Cairo	Feb., 1862
Batty. E, 2d Ill. L. A.	Oct., 1861	From Military Dist. Cairo	To 1-Brig. 1-Div. Mil. Dist. Cairo	Feb., 1862

2d BRIGADE.— COMMANDER.

R. J. Oglesby.... Col. 8th Ill. Infy — Oct. 14, 1861, to Feb. 1, 1862.

Unit	Date	From	To	Date
8th Ill. Infy	Oct., 1861	From Military Dist. Cairo	To 1-Brig. 1-Div. Mil. Dist. Cairo	Feb., 1862
22d Ill. Infy	Oct., 1861	From Military Dist. Cairo	To 4-Brig. 1-Div. Mil. Dist. Cairo	Feb., 1862
2d Ill. Cav.	Oct., 1861	From Military Dist. Cairo	To 1-Brig. 1-Div. Mil. Dist. Cairo	Feb., 1862
Batty. C, 1st Ill. L. A.	Oct., 1861	From Military Dist. Cairo	To 4-Brig. 1-Div. Mil. Dist. Cairo	Feb., 1862

3d BRIGADE.— COMMANDER.

W. H. L. Wallace.... Col. 11th Ill. Infy — Oct. 14, 1861, to Feb. 1, 1862.

Unit	Date	From	To	Date
11th Ill. Infy	Oct., 1861	From Military Dist. Cairo	To 2-Brig. 1-Div. Mil. Dist. Cairo	Feb., 1862
12th Ill. Infy	Oct., 1861	From Military Dist. Cairo	To Paducah, Ky.	Oct., 1861
2d Iowa Infy	Oct., 1861	From Military Dist. Cairo	To St. Louis, Mo.	Oct., 1861
Batty. B, 1st Ill. L. A.	Oct., 1861	From Military Dist. Cairo	To 2-Brig. 1-Div. Mil. Dist. Cairo	Feb., 1862

4th BRIGADE.— COMMANDER.

John Cook.... Col. 7th Ill. Infy — Oct. 14, 1861, to Feb. 1, 1862.

Unit	Date	From	To	Date
7th Ill. Infy	Oct., 1861	From Military Dist. Cairo	To 3-Brig. 2-Div. Dist. West Tenn.	Feb., 1862
28th Ill. Infy	Oct., 1861	From Military Dist. Cairo	To 1-Brig. 4-Div. Dist. West Tenn.	Feb., 1862
Batty. D, 1st Ill. L. A.	Oct., 1861	From Military Dist. Cairo	To 2-Brig. 1-Div. Mil. Dist. Cairo	Feb., 1862

5th BRIGADE.— COMMANDER.

J. B. Plummer.... Col. 11th Mo. Infy — Oct. 14, 1861, to Feb. 1, 1862.

Unit	Date	From	To	Date
17th Ill. Infy	Oct., 1861	From Military Dist. Cairo	To 3-Brig. 1-Div. Dist. West Tenn.	Feb., 1862
10th Iowa Infy	Oct., 1861	From Military Dist. Cairo	To 4-Brig. 1-Div. Dist. Cairo	Feb., 1862
11th Mo. Infy	Oct., 1861	From Military Dist. Cairo	To 2-Brig. 1-Div. Army Miss.	Feb., 1862

1st DIVISION.— COMMANDER.

John A. McClernand.... Brigadier General

1st BRIGADE.— COMMANDER.

R. J. Oglesby.... Col. 8th Ill. Infy — Feb. 1, 1862, to Feb. 21, 1862.

Unit	Date	From	To	Date
8th Ill. Infy	Feb., 1862	From 2-Brig. Mil. Dist. Cairo	To 1-Brig. 1-Div. Dist. West Tenn.	Feb., 1862
18th Ill. Infy	Feb., 1862	From 1-Brig. Mil. Dist. Cairo	To 2-Brig. 1-Div. Dist. West Tenn.	Feb., 1862
27th Ill. Infy	Feb., 1862	From Military Dist. Cairo	To Flotilla Brig. Army Miss.	Feb., 1862
29th Ill. Infy	Feb., 1862	From 1-Brig. Mil. Dist. Cairo	To 1-Brig. 1-Div. Dist. West Tenn.	Feb., 1862
30th Ill. Infy	Feb., 1862	From 1-Brig. Mil. Dist. Cairo	To 1-Brig. 1-Div. Dist. West Tenn.	Feb., 1862
31st Ill. Infy	Feb., 1862	From 1-Brig. Mil. Dist. Cairo	To 1-Brig. 1-Div. Dist. West Tenn.	Feb., 1862
Batty. E, 2d Ill. L. A.	Feb., 1862	From 1-Brig. Mil. Dist. Cairo	To 3-Brig. 1-Div. Dist. West Tenn.	Feb., 1862
Batty. A, 1st Ill. L. A.	Feb., 1862	From Military Dist. Cairo	To Arty. 3-Div. Dist. Cairo	Feb., 1862
Batty. D, 2d Ill. L. A.	Feb., 1862	From Military Dist. Cairo	To 1-Brig. 1-Div. Dist. West Tenn.	Feb., 1862
Carmichael's Ill. Cav.	Feb., 1862	From Military Dist. Cairo	To 1-Brig. 1-Div. Dist. West Tenn.	Feb., 1862
Dollin's Ill. Cav.	Feb., 1862	From Military Dist. Cairo	To 1-Brig. 1-Div. Dist. West Tenn.	Feb., 1862
O'Harnett's Ill. Cav.	Feb., 1862	From Military Dist. Cairo	To 1-Brig. 1-Div. Dist. West Tenn.	Feb., 1862
Stewart's Ill. Cav.	Feb., 1862	From Military Dist. Cairo	To 1-Brig. 1-Div. Dist. West Tenn.	Feb., 1862
2d Ill. Cav. (A. B.)	Feb., 1862	From Military Dist. Cairo	To 3-Brig. 2-Div. Dist. West Tenn.	Feb., 1862
2d U. S. Cav. (Co. C.)	Feb., 1862	From Military Dist. Cairo	To 2-Brig. 2-Div. Dist. West Tenn.	Feb., 1862
4th U. S. Cav. (Co. I.)	Feb., 1862	From Military Dist. Cairo	To 2-Brig. 2-Div. Dist. West Tenn.	Feb., 1862

2d BRIGADE.— COMMANDER.

W. H. L. Wallace.... Col. 11th Ill. Infy — Feb. 1, 1862, to Feb. 17, 1862.

Unit	Date	From	To	Date
11th Ill. Infy	Feb., 1862	From 3-Brig. Dist. Cairo	To 2-Brig. 1-Div. Dist. West Tenn.	Feb., 1862
20th Ill. Infy	Feb., 1862	From Dist. Cairo	To 2-Brig. 1-Div. Dist. West Tenn.	Feb., 1862
45th Ill. Infy	Feb., 1862	From Dist. Cairo	To 2-Brig. 1-Div. Dist. West Tenn.	Feb., 1862
48th Ill. Infy	Feb., 1862	From Dist. Cairo	To 2-Brig. 4-Div. Dist. West Tenn.	Feb., 1862
Batty. B, 1st Ill. L. A.	Feb., 1862	From 3-Brig. Dist. Cairo	To 2-Brig. 1-Div. Dist. West Tenn.	Feb., 1862
Batty. D, 1st Ill. L. A.	Feb., 1862	From 4-Brig. Dist. Cairo	To 1-Brig. 1-Div. Dist. West Tenn.	Feb., 1862
4th Ill. Cav. (1st Bn.)	Feb., 1862	From Dist. Cairo	To 2-Brig. 1-Div. Dist. West Tenn.	Feb., 1862
4th Ill. Cav. (2d Bn.)	Feb., 1862	From Dist. Cairo	To 1-Brig. 2-Div. Dist. West Tenn.	Feb., 1862
4th Ill. Cav. (3d Bn.)	Feb., 1862	From Dist. Cairo	To 3-Brig. 4-Div. Dist. West Tenn.	Feb., 1862

3d BRIGADE.— COMMANDERS.

Commander	Rank	Dates
E. A. Paine	Brigadier General	To Feb. 1, 1862.
W. R. Morrison	Col. 49th Ill. Infy	Feb. 1, 1862, to Feb. 15, 1862.
L. F. Ross	Col. 17th Ill. Infy	Feb. 15, 1862, to Feb. 17, 1862.

Unit	Date	From	To	Date
25th Ind. Infy	Feb., 1862	From Dept. Mo.	To 4-Brig. 2-Div. Dist. West Tenn.	Feb., 1862
17th Ill. Infy	Feb., 1862	From 5-Brig. Dist. Cairo	To 3-Brig. 1-Div. Dist. West Tenn.	Feb., 1862
43d Ill. Infy	Feb., 1862	From Dept. Mo.	To 3-Brig. 1-Div. Dist. West Tenn.	Feb., 1862
49th Ill. Infy	Feb., 1862	From New Organization	To 3-Brig. 1-Div. Dist. West Tenn.	Feb., 1862
8th Wis. Infy	Feb., 1862	From Dept. Mo.	To 1-Brig. 5-Div. Army Miss.	Feb., 1862

4th BRIGADE.— COMMANDER.

J. D. Morgan.... Col. 10th Ill. Infy — To Feb. 1, 1862.

Unit	Date	From	To	Date
10th Ill. Infy	Feb., 1862	From 1-Brig. Dist. Cairo	To 1-Brig. 4-Div. Army Miss.	Feb., 1862
16th Ill. Infy	Feb., 1862	From Dept. Mo.	To 1-Brig. 4-Div. Army Miss.	Feb., 1862
22d Ill. Infy	Feb., 1862	From 2-Brig. Dist. Cairo	To 2-Brig. 4-Div. Army Miss.	Feb., 1862
32d Ill. Infy	Feb., 1862	From New Organization	To 1-Brig. 4-Div. Dist. West Tenn.	Feb., 1862
10th Iowa Infy	Feb., 1862	From 5-Brig. Dist. Cairo	To 2-Brig. 2-Div. Army Miss.	Feb., 1862
Batty. C, 1st Ill. L. A.	Feb., 1862	From 2-Brig. Dist. Cairo	To Arty. Div. Army Miss.	Feb., 1862
1st Ill. Cav. (Co's H, I)	Feb., 1862	From 1-Brig. Dist. Cairo	To Cav. 4-Div. Army Miss.	Feb., 1862
7th Ill. Cav. (4 Co's)	Feb., 1862	From Dist. Cairo	To Cav. 3-Div. Army Miss.	Feb., 1862

2d DIVISION.— COMMANDER.

C. F. Smith.... Brigadier General — Feb. 1, 1862, to Feb. 17, 1862.

1st BRIGADE.— COMMANDERS.

John McArthur	Col. 12th Ill. Infy	Feb. 1, 1862, to Feb. 17, 1862.	

9th Ill. Infy	Feb., 1862	From Paducah, Ky., Dist. Cairo	To 2-Brig. 2-Div. Dist. West Tenn.	Feb., 1862
12th Ill. Infy	Feb., 1862	From Paducah, Ky., Dist. Cairo	To 2-Brig. 2-Div. Dist. West Tenn.	Feb., 1862
41st Ill. Infy	Feb., 1862	From Dist. Cairo	To 1-Brig. 4-Div. Dist. West Tenn.	Feb., 1862

3d BRIGADE.— COMMANDER.

John Cook	Col. 7th Ill. Infy	Feb. 1, 1862, to Feb. 17, 1862.	

7th Ill. Infy	Feb., 1862	From 4-Brig. Dist. Cairo	To 3-Brig. 2-Div. Dist. West Tenn.	Feb., 1862
50th Ill. Infy	Feb., 1862	From Dept. of Mo.	To 3-Brig. 2-Div. Dist. West Tenn.	Feb., 1862
52d Ill. Infy	Feb., 1862	From Dept. of Mo.	To 3-Brig. 1-Div. Dist. West Tenn.	Feb., 1862
12th Ia. Infy	Feb., 1862	From Dept. of Mo.	To 1-Brig. 2-Div. Dist. West Tenn.	Feb., 1862
13th Mo. Infy	Feb., 1862	From New Organization	To 2-Brig. 2-Div. Dist. West Tenn.	Feb., 1862
Batty. D, 1st Mo. L. A.	Feb., 1862	From New Organization	To Arty. 2-Div. Dist. West Tenn.	Feb., 1862
Batty. H, 1st Mo. L. A.	Feb., 1862	From New Organization	To Arty. 2-Div. Dist. West Tenn.	Feb., 1862
Batty. K, 1st Mo. L. A.	Feb., 1862	From New Organization	To Arty. 2-Div. Dist. West Tenn.	Feb., 1862

4th BRIGADE.— COMMANDER.

J. G. Lauman	Col. 7th Ia. Infy	Feb. 1, 1862, to Feb. 17, 1862.	

25th Ind. Infy	Feb., 1862	From Dept. of Mo.	To 2-Brig. 4-Div. Dist. West Tenn.	Feb., 1862
2d Ia. Infy	Feb., 1862	From St. Louis, Mo.	To 1-Brig. 2-Div. Dist. West Tenn.	Feb., 1862
7th Ia. Infy	Feb., 1862	From St. Louis, Mo.	To 1-Brig. 2-Div. Dist. West Tenn.	Feb., 1862
14th Ia. Infy	Feb., 1862	From St. Louis, Mo.	To 1-Brig. 2-Div. Dist. West Tenn.	Feb., 1862
Birge's Mo. S. S. 14th Infy	Feb., 1862	From Dept. of Mo.	To 2-Brig. 2-Div. Dist. West Tenn.	Feb., 1862

5th BRIGADE.— COMMANDER.

M. L. Smith	Col. 8th Mo. Infy	Feb. 1, 1862, to Feb. 17, 1862.	

11th Ind. Infy	Feb., 1862	From Paducah, Ky., Dist. Cairo	To 1-Brig. 3-Div. Dist. West Tenn.	Feb., 1862
8th Mo. Infy	Feb., 1862	From Paducah, Ky., Dist. Cairo	To 1-Brig. 3-Div. Dist. West Tenn.	Feb., 1862

3d DIVISION.— COMMANDER.

Lewis Wallace	Brigadier General	Feb. 1, 1862, to Feb. 17, 1862.	

1st BRIGADE.— COMMANDER.

Charles Cruft	Col. 31st Ind. Infy	Feb. 1, 1862, to Feb. 17, 1862.	

31st Ind. Infy	Feb., 1862	From 13-Brig. 5-Div. Army Ohio.	To 3-Brig. 4-Div. Dist. West Tenn.	Feb., 1862
44th Ind. Infy	Feb., 1862	From 13-Brig. 5-Div. Army Ohio.	To 3-Brig. 4-Div. Dist. West Tenn.	Feb., 1862
17th Ky. Infy	Feb., 1862	From 13-Brig. 5-Div. Army Ohio.	To 3-Brig. 4-Div. Dist. West Tenn.	Feb., 1862
25th Ky. Infy	Feb., 1862	From 13-Brig. 5-Div. Army Ohio.	To 3-Brig. 4-Div. Dist. West Tenn.	Feb., 1862

2d BRIGADE.—

46th Ill. Infy	Feb., 1862	From New Organization	To 2-Brig. 4-Div. Dist. West Tenn.	Feb., 1862
57th Ill. Infy	Feb., 1862	From New Organization	To 3-Brig. 2-Div. Dist. West Tenn.	Feb., 1862
58th Ill. Infy	Feb., 1862	From New Organization	To 3-Brig. 2-Div. Dist. West Tenn.	Feb., 1862

3d BRIGADE.— COMMANDER.

J. M. Thayer	Col. 1st Neb. Infy	Feb. 1, 1862, to Feb. 17, 1862.	

1st Neb. Infy	Feb., 1862	From Dept. of Mo.	To 2-Brig. 3-Div. Dist. West Tenn.	Feb., 1862
58th Ohio Infy	Feb., 1862	From New Organization	To 2-Brig. 3-Div. Dist. West Tenn.	Feb., 1862
68th Ohio Infy	Feb., 1862	From New Organization	To 2-Brig. 3-Div. Dist. West Tenn.	Feb., 1862
76th Ohio Infy	Feb., 1862	From New Organization	To 3-Brig. 3-Div. Dist. West Tenn.	Feb., 1862

ARTILLERY.—

Batty. A, 1st Ill. L. A.	Feb., 1862	From 1-Brig. 1-Div. Dist. Cairo	To 2-Brig. 2-Div. Dist. West Tenn.	Feb., 1862

CAVALRY.—

Co. A, 32d Ill.	Feb., 1862	From Dist. of Cairo	To 1-Brig. 4-Div. Dist. West Tenn.	Feb., 1862

Army of the Mississippi

Organized Feb. 23, 1862. Discontinued Oct. 26, 1862.

COMMANDERS.

John Pope	Major General	Feb. 23, 1862, to June 26, 1862.	
W. S. Rosecrans	Major General	June 26, 1862, to Oct. 24, 1862.	

1st DIVISION.— COMMANDERS.

S. Hamilton	Brigadier General	Feb. 23, 1862, to Mch. 4, 1862.	
D. S. Stanley	Brigadier General	Mch. 4, 1862, to Apr. 24, 1862.	
E. A. Paine	Brigadier General	Apr. 24, 1862, to July 15, 1862.	
J. D. Morgan	Brigadier General	July 15, 1862, to Aug. 15, 1862.	
E. A. Paine	Brigadier General	Aug. 15, 1862, to Aug. 30, 1862.	
J. D. Morgan	Brigadier General	Aug. 30, 1862, to Aug. 31, 1862.	
John M. Palmer	Brigadier General	Aug. 31, 1862, to Sept. 29, 1862.	

1st BRIGADE.— COMMANDERS.

John Groesbeck	Col. 39th Ohio Infy	Feb. 23, 1862, to Apr. 24, 1862.	
J. M. Palmer	Brigadier General	Apr. 24, 1862, to Aug. 10, 1862.	
G. W. Roberts	Col. 42d Ill. Infy	Aug. 10, 1862, to Sept. 29, 1862.	

27th Ohio Infy	Feb., 1862	From Dept. of Mo.	To 1-Brig. 2-Div. Army Miss.	Apr., 1862
39th Ohio Infy	Feb., 1862	From Dept. of Mo.	To 1-Brig. 2-Div. Army Miss.	Apr., 1862
43d Ohio Infy	Feb., 1862	From Dept. of Mo.	To 1-Brig. 2-Div. Army Miss.	Apr., 1862
22d Ill. Infy	Apr., 1862	From 2-Brig. 4-Div. Army Miss.	To 1-Brig. 13-Div. Army Ohio.	Sept., 1862
27th Ill. Infy	Apr., 1862	From Flotilla Brig. Army Miss.	To 1-Brig. 13-Div. Army Ohio.	Sept., 1862
42d Ill. Infy	Apr., 1862	From Flotilla Brig. Army Miss.	To 1-Brig. 13-Div. Army Ohio.	Sept., 1862
51st Ill. Infy	Apr., 1862	From 2-Brig. 4-Div. Army Miss.	To 1-Brig. 13-Div. Army Ohio.	Sept., 1862

2d BRIGADE.— COMMANDERS.

J. B. Plummer	Col. 11th Mo. Infy	Feb. 23, 1862, to Mch. 4, 1862.	
J. L. Kilby Smith	Col. 43d Ohio Infy	Mch. 4, 1862, to Apr. 24, 1862.	
J. D. Morgan	Col. 10th Ill. Infy	Apr. 24, 1862, to May 1, 1862.	
Daniel Tyler	Brigadier General	May 1, 1862, to June 27, 1862.	
J. D. Morgan	Col. 10th Ill. Infy	June 27, 1862, to July 17, 1862.	
R. F. Smith	Col. 16th Ill. Infy	July 17, 1862, to Aug. 15, 1862.	
J. D. Morgan	Brigadier General	Aug. 15, 1862, to Sept. 29, 1862.	

1st BRIGADE.—Continued.

Unit	Date	From	To	Date
26th Ill. Infy	Feb., 1862	From Dept. of Mo	To 2-Brig. 5-Div. Army Miss	Mch., 1862
11th Mo. Infy	Feb., 1862	From Dept. of Mo	To 2-Brig. 5-Div. Army Miss	Mch., 1862
63d Ohio Infy	Mch., 1862	From New Organization	To 1-Brig. 2-Div. Army Miss	Apr., 1862
43d Ohio Infy	Mch., 1862	From 1-Brig. 1-Div. Army Miss	To 1-Brig. 2-Div. Army Miss	Apr., 1862
10th Ill. Infy	Apr., 1862	From 1-Brig. 4-Div. Army Miss	To 2-Brig. 13-Div. Army Ohio	Sept., 1862
16th Ill. Infy	Apr., 1862	From 1-Brig. 4-Div. Army Miss	To 2-Brig. 13-Div. Army Ohio	Sept., 1862
64th Ill. Infy	Apr., 1862	From Unatt. Army Miss	To Unatt. Army Miss	May, 1862
10th Mich. Infy	Apr., 1862	From New Organization	To 2-Brig. 13-Div. Army Ohio	Sept., 1862
14th Mich. Infy	Apr., 1862	From New Organization	To 2-Brig. 13-Div. Army Ohio	Sept., 1862
60th Ill. Infy	May, 1862	From Cairo, Ill	To 2-Brig. 13-Div. Army Ohio	Sept., 1862
ARTILLERY.—				
Batty. C, 1st Ill. Arty	Apr., 1862	From Arty. Div. Army Miss	To Arty. 13-Div. Army Ohio	Sept., 1862
Batty. G, 1st Mo. Arty	Apr., 1862	From Arty. 3-Div. Army Miss	To Arty. 3-Div. Army Miss	July, 1862
Batty. M, 1st Mo. Arty	July, 1862	From Arty. Div. Army Miss	To Arty. 3-Div. Army Miss	Aug., 1862
10th Wis. Batty	July, 1862	From Arty. Div. Army Miss	To 32-Brig. 9-Div. Army Ohio	Sept., 1862

2d DIVISION.— COMMANDERS.

Commander	Rank	Dates
John M. Palmer	Brigadier General	Feb. 23, 1862, to Mch. 4, 1862.
S. Hamilton	Brigadier General	Mch. 4, 1862, to Apr. 24, 1862.
D. S. Stanley	Brigadier General	Apr. 24, 1862, to Oct. 26, 1862.

1st BRIGADE.— COMMANDERS.

Commander	Rank	Dates
J. R. Slack	Col. 47th Ind. Infy	Feb. 23, 1862, to Mch. 4, 1862.
W. H. Worthington	Col. 5th Ia. Infy	Mch. 4, 1862, to Apr. 24, 1862.
John Groesbeck	Col. 39th Ohio Infy	Apr. 24, 1862, to July 8, 1862.
J. L. Kilby Smith	Col. 43d Ohio Infy	July 8, 1862, to Sept. 10, 1862.
John W. Fuller	Col. 27th Ohio Infy	Sept. 10, 1862, to Oct. 26, 1862.

Unit	Date	From	To	Date
34th Ind. Infy	Feb., 1862	From 10-Brig. 4-Div. Army Ohio	To 1-Brig. 3-Div. Army Miss	Mch., 1862
43d Ind. Infy	Feb., 1862	From 14-Brig. 5-Div. Army Ohio	To 2-Brig. 3-Div. Army Miss	Mch., 1862
46th Ind. Infy	Feb., 1862	From 19-Brig. 4-Div. Army Ohio	To 2-Brig. 3-Div. Army Miss	Mch., 1862
47th Ind. Infy	Feb., 1862	From 19-Brig. 4-Div. Army Ohio	To 1-Brig. 3-Div. Army Miss	Mch., 1862
59th Ind. Infy	Feb., 1862	From New Organization	To 2-Brig. 3-Div. Army Miss	Apr., 1862
5th Iowa Infy	Mch., 1862	From Dept. of Mo	To 2-Brig. 3-Div. Army Miss	Apr., 1862
27th Ohio Infy	Apr., 1862	From 1-Brig. 1-Div. Army Miss	To 1-Brig. 8-Div. L. W. 13-Corps	Oct., 1862
39th Ohio Infy	Apr., 1862	From 1-Brig. 1-Div. Army Miss	To 1-Brig. 8-Div. L. W. 13-Corps	Oct., 1862
43d Ohio Infy	Apr., 1862	From 1-Brig. 1-Div. Army Miss	To 1-Brig. 8-Div. L. W. 13-Corps	Oct., 1862
63d Ohio Infy	Apr., 1862	From 1-Brig. 1-Div. Army Miss	To 1-Brig. 8-Div. L. W. 13-Corps	Oct., 1862
Jenks' Ill. Cav. Co	Oct., 1862	From Cav. Div. Army Miss	To Dist. Corinth 13-Corps	Oct., 1862

2d BRIGADE.— COMMANDERS.

Commander	Rank	Dates
W. H. Worthington	Col. 5th Iowa Infy	Feb. 23, 1862, to Mch. 4, 1862.
N. Perczel	Col. 10th Iowa Infy	Mch. 4, 1862, to Apr. 26, 1862.
J. B. Plummer	Brigadier General	Apr. 26, 1862, to May 29, 1862.
R. C. Murphy	Col. 8th Wis. Infy	May 29, 1862, to June 18, 1862.
J. B. Plummer	Brigadier General	June 18, 1862, to Aug. 9, 1862.
J. A. Mower	Col. 11th Mo. Infy	Aug. 9, 1862, to Oct. 26, 1862.

Unit	Date	From	To	Date
5th Iowa Infy	Feb., 1862	From Dept. of Mo	To 1-Brig. 2-Div. Army Miss	Mch., 1862
47th Ill. Infy	Feb., 1862	From Dept. of Mo	To 1-Brig. 5-Div. Army Miss	Mch., 1862
26th Mo. Infy	Feb., 1862	From Dept. of Mo	To 2-Brig. 3-Div. Army Miss	Apr., 1862
10th Iowa Infy	Mch., 1862	From Dept. of Mo	To 2-Brig. 3-Div. Army Miss	Apr., 1862
26th Ill. Infy	Apr., 1862	From 1-Brig. 3-Div. Army Miss	To 2-Brig. 8-Div. L. W. 13-Corps	Oct., 1862
47th Ill. Infy	Apr., 1862	From 1-Brig. 3-Div. Army Miss	To 2-Brig. 8-Div. L. W. 13-Corps	Oct., 1862
11th Mo. Infy	Apr., 1862	From 1-Brig. 3-Div. Army Miss	To 2-Brig. 8-Div. L. W. 13-Corps	Oct., 1862
8th Wis. Infy	Apr., 1862	From 1-Brig. 3-Div. Army Miss	To 2-Brig. 8-Div. L. W. 13-Corps	Oct., 1862
5th Minn.	May, 1862	From New Organization	To 2-Brig. 8-Div. L. W. 13-Corps	Oct., 1862
ARTILLERY, 2d DIVISION.—				
11th Ohio Batty	Mch., 1862	From Dept. Mo	To Arty. 3-Div. Army Miss	Apr., 1862
Batty. C, 1st Mich. Arty	Apr., 1862	From Arty. Div. Army Miss	To Arty. 6-Div. L. W. 13-C'ps, Tenn.	Oct., 1862
Batty. F, 2d U. S. Arty	Apr., 1862	From Arty. Div. Army Miss	To Arty. 8-Div. L. W. 13 C'ps Tenn.	Oct., 1862
2d Iowa Batty	Apr., 1862	From Arty. Div. Army Miss	To Arty. 8-Div. L. W. 13 C'ps Tenn.	Oct., 1862
8th Wis. Batty	Aug., 1862	From Arty. 4-Div. Army Miss	To 32-Brig. 9-Div. Army Ohio	Sept., 1862

3d DIVISION.— COMMANDERS.

Commander	Rank	Dates
John M. Palmer	Brigadier General	Mch. 4, 1862, to Apr. 24, 1862.
S. Hamilton	Brigadier General	Apr. 24, 1862, to May 29, 1862.
J. B. Plummer	Brigadier General	May 29, 1862, to June 18, 1862.
C. S. Hamilton	Brigadier General	June 18, 1862, to Oct. 26, 1862.
I. F. Quimby	Brigadier General	Oct. 26, 1862, to Nov. 2, 1862.

1st BRIGADE.— COMMANDERS.

Commander	Rank	Dates
J. R. Slack	Col. 47th Ind. Infy	Mch. 4, 1862, to Apr. 24, 1862.
J. B. Plummer	Brigadier General	Apr. 24, 1862, to Apr. 26, 1862.
N. B. Buford	Brigadier General	Apr. 26, 1862, to June 25, 1862.
J. B. Sanborn	Col. 4th Minn. Infy	June 25, 1862, to Sept. 20, 1862.
N. B. Buford	Brigadier General	Sept. 20, 1862, to Nov. 1, 1862.

Unit	Date	From	To	Date
34th Ind. Infy	Mch., 1862	From 1-Brig. 2-Div. Army Miss	To Garrison New Madrid	Apr., 1862
47th Ind. Infy	Mch., 1862	From 2-Brig. 5-Div. Army Miss	To Tiptonville, Mo	Apr., 1862
26th Ill. Infy	Apr., 1862	From 1-Brig. 5-Div. Army Miss	To 2-Brig. 2-Div. Army Miss	Apr., 1862
47th Ill. Infy	Apr., 1862	From 2-Brig. 5-Div. Army Miss	To 2-Brig. 2-Div. Army Miss	Apr., 1862
8th Wis. Infy	Apr., 1862	From 1-Brig. 5-Div. Army Miss	To 2-Brig. 2-Div. Army Miss	Apr., 1862
11th Mo. Infy	Apr., 1862	From 2-Brig. 5-Div. Army Miss	To 2-Brig. 2-Div. Army Miss	Apr., 1862
59th Ind. Infy	Apr., 1862	From 2-Brig. 3-Div. Army Miss	To 1-Brig. 7-Div. L. W. 13 C'ps Tenn.	Oct., 1862
5th Iowa Infy	Apr., 1862	From 2-Brig. 3-Div. Army Miss	To 2-Brig. 3-Div. Army Miss	May, 1862
10th Iowa Infy	Apr., 1862	From 2-Brig. 3-Div. Army Miss	To 1-Brig. 7-Div. L. W. 13 C'ps Tenn.	Oct., 1862
26th Mo. Infy	Apr., 1862	From 2-Brig. 3-Div. Army Miss	To 1-Brig. 7-Div. L. W. 13 C'ps Tenn.	Oct., 1862
48th Ind. Infy	May, 1862	From New Organization	To 1-Brig. 7-Div. L. W. 13 C'ps Tenn.	Oct., 1862
4th Minn. Infy	May, 1862			

2d BRIGADE.— COMMANDERS.

Commander	Rank	Dates
C. N. Fitch	Col. 46th Ind. Infy	Mch. 4, 1862, to Apr. 24, 1862.
N. B. Buford	Brigadier General	Apr. 24, 1862, to Apr. 26, 1862.
N. Perczel	Col. 10th Iowa Infy	Apr. 26, 1862, to June 20, 1862.
J. C. Sullivan	Brigadier General	June 20, 1862, to Oct. 3, 1862.
S. A. Holmes	Col. 10th Mo. Infy	Oct. 3, 1862, to Oct. 26, 1862.
E. R. Eckley	Col. 80th Ohio Infy	Oct. 26, 1862, to Nov. 1, 1862.

2d BRIGADE.—Continued.

43d Ind. Infy..........Mch., 1862	From 1-Brig. 2-Div. Army Miss....	To Fort Pillow, Tenn.............	Apr.,	1862
46th Ind. Infy..........Mch., 1862	From 1-Brig. 2-Div. Army Miss....	To Fort Pillow, Tenn.............	Apr.,	1862
5th Iowa Infy..........Apr., 1862	From 1-Brig. 2-Div. Army Miss....	To 1-Brig. 3-Div. Army Miss....	Apr.,	1862
10th Iowa Infy..........Apr., 1862	From 2-Brig. 2-Div. Army Miss....	To 1-Brig. 3-Div. Army Miss....	Apr.,	1862
59th Ind. Infy..........Apr., 1862	From 2-Brig. 2-Div. Army Miss....	To 1-Brig. 3-Div. Army Miss....	Apr.,	1862
26th Mo. Infy..........Apr., 1862	From 2-Brig. 2-Div. Army Miss....	To 1-Brig. 3-Div. Army Miss....	Apr.,	1862
48th Ind. Infy..........Apr., 1862	From Paducah, Ky..............	To 1-Brig. 3-Div. Army Miss....	Apr.,	1862
80th Ohio Infy..........Apr., 1862	From Paducah, Ky..............	To 2-B'g. 7-Div. L. W. 13-C'ps Tenn.	Oct.,	1862
10th Mo. Infy..........May, 1862	From Dept. of Mo.............	To 2-B'g. 7-Div. L. W. 13-C'ps Tenn.	Oct.,	1862
10th Iowa Infy..........May, 1862	From 1-Brig. 3-Div. Army Miss..	To 3-B'g. 7-Div. L. W. 13-C'ps Tenn.	Oct.,	1862
56th Ill. Infy..........May, 1862	From Paducah, Ky.............	To 2-B'g. 7-Div. L. W. 13-C'ps Tenn.	Oct.,	1862
17th Iowa Infy..........May, 1862	From New Organization........	To 2-B'g. 7-Div. L. W. 13-C'ps Tenn.	Oct.,	1862
24th Mo. Infy, Co. E..May, 1862	From Army Southwest Mo........	To 2-B'g. 7-Div. L. W. 13-C'ps Tenn.	Oct.,	1862

ARTILLERY, 3d DIVISION.—

Batty. G, 1st Mo. Arty..Mch., 1862	From Dept. of Mo.............	To Arty. 1-Div. Army Miss.......	Apr.,	1862
2d Iowa Batty............Apr., 1862	From Arty. Div. Army Miss......	To Arty. 2-Div. Army Miss......	Apr.,	1862
11th Ohio Batty..........Apr., 1862	From Arty. 2-Div. Army Miss......	To Arty. 7-Div. L. W. 13-C'ps Tenn.	Oct.,	1862
Batty I, 1st Mo. Arty....May, 1862	From Arty 2-Div. Army Tenn.....	To Arty. 2-Div. Army Tenn.......	Aug.,	1862
6th Wis. Batty..........Sept., 1862	From Arty. Div. Army Miss......	To Arty. 7-Div. L. W. 13-C'ps Tenn.	Oct.,	1862
12th Wis. Batty..........Sept., 1862	From Arty. Div. Army Miss......	To Arty. 7-Div. L. W. 13-C'ps Tenn.	Oct.,	1862
Batty. M, 1st Mo. Arty..Aug., 1862	From 1-Div. Army Miss.........	To Arty. 7-Div. L. W. 13-C'ps Tenn.	Oct.,	1862

CAVALRY.—

7th Ill. Cav..........Mch., 1862	From Dist. Cairo.............	To Cav. Div. Army Miss..........	Apr.,	1862

4th DIVISION.— COMMANDERS.

E. A. Paine............	Brigadier General...............	Mch. 4, 1862, to Apr. 24, 1862.
J. C. Davis............	Brigadier General...............	Apr. 24, 1862, to Aug. 12, 1862.
R. B. Mitchell.........	Brigadier General...............	Aug. 12, 1862, to Sept. 26, 1862.

1st BRIGADE.— COMMANDERS.

J. D. Morgan..........	Col. 10th Ill. Infy..............	Mch. 4, 1862, to Apr. 24, 1862.
R. B. Mitchell.........	Brigadier General...............	Apr. 24, 1862, to Aug. 12, 1862.
M. Gooding............	Col. 22d Ind. Infy..............	Aug. 12, 1862, to Sept. 26, 1862.

10th Illinois Infy......Mch., 1862	From Dept. of Missouri...........	To 2-Brig. 1-Div. Army Miss.......	Apr.,	1862
16th Illinois Infy......Mch., 1862	From Dept. of Missouri...........	To 2-Brig. 1-Div. Army Miss.......	Apr.,	1862
22d Indiana Infy......June, 1862	From 1-Brig. 3-Div. Army S. W. Mo.	To 30-Brig. 9-Div. Army Ohio......	Sept.,	1862
59th Illinois Infy......June, 1862	From 2-Brig. 1-Div. Army S. W. Mo.	To 30-Brig. 9-Div. Army Ohio......	Sept.,	1862
25th Illinois Infy......June, 1862	From 1-Brig. 1-Div. Army S. W. Mo.	To 32d Brig. 9-Div. Army Ohio....	Sept.,	1862
35th Illinois Infy......June, 1862	From 1-Brig. 4-Div. Army S. W. Mo.	To 32d Brig. 9-Div. Army Ohio....	Sept.,	1862
8th Kansas Infy (5 Cos.).July, 1862	From 2-Brig. 4-Div. Army Miss...	To 32d Brig. 9-Div. Army Ohio....	Sept.,	1862

2d BRIGADE.— COMMANDERS.

G. W. Cummings.......	Col. 51st Illinois Infy..............	Mch. 4, 1862, to Apr. 24, 1862.
W. P. Carlin..........	Col. 38th Illinois Infy..............	June 1, 1862, to Sept. 26, 1862.

22d Illinois Infy......Mch., 1862	From Dist. of Cairo..............	To 1-Brig. 1-Div. Army Miss.......	Apr.,	1862
51st Illinois Infy......Mch., 1862	From Dist. of Cairo..............	To 1-Brig. 1-Div. Army Miss.......	Apr.,	1862
21st Illinois Infy......June, 1862	From Steele's Div. S. E. Mo.......	To 31-Brig. 9-Div. Army Ohio......	Sept.,	1862
38th Illinois Infy......June, 1862	From Steele's Div. S. E. Mo.......	To 31-Brig. 9-Div. Army Ohio......	Sept.,	1862
15th Wisconsin Infy......July, 1862	From Garrison Island No. 10.......	To 31-Brig. 9-Div. Army Ohio......	Sept.,	1862
8th Kansas Infy (5 Cos.).June, 1862	From Dept. of Kansas...........	To 1-Brig. 4-Div. Army Miss.......	July,	1862

ARTILLERY, 4th DIVISION.—

2d Minnesota Batty....June, 1862	From New Organization........	To 31-Brig. 9-Div. Army Ohio......	Sept.,	1862
5th Wisconsin Batty....June, 1862	From Arty. Brig. Army Miss......	To 30-Brig. 9-Div. Army Ohio......	Sept.,	1862
8th Wisconsin Batty....June, 1862	From Dept. of Kansas...........	To Arty. 2-Div. Army Miss.........	Aug.,	1862

5th DIVISION.— COMMANDERS.

J. B. Plummer........	Brigadier General...................	Mch. 4, 1862, to Apr. 24, 1862.
A. Asboth............	Brigadier General...................	June 1, 1862, to July 30, 1862.
Gordon Granger.......	Brigadier General...................	July 30, 1862, to Sept. 4, 1862.

1st BRIGADE.— COMMANDERS.

John Bryner..........	Col. 47th Illinois Infy..............	Mch. 4, 1862, to Apr. 24, 1862.
N. Greusel..........	Col. 36th Ohio Infy.................	June 1, 1862, to Sept. 4, 1862.

47th Illinois Infy......Mch., 1862	From Dept. of Missouri...........	To 1-Brig. 3-Div. Army Miss.......	Apr.,	1862
8th Wisconsin Infy......Mch., 1862	From Dist. of Cairo..............	To 1-Brig. 3-Div. Army Miss.......	Apr.,	1862
36th Illinois Infy......June, 1862	From 2-Brig. 1-Div. Army S. W. Mo.	To 35-Brig. 11-Div. Army Ohio....	Sept.,	1862
44th Illinois Infy......June, 1862	From 1-Brig. 1-Div. Army S. W. Mo.	To 35-Brig. 11-Div. Army Ohio....	Sept.,	1862

2d BRIGADE.— COMMANDERS.

J. M. Loomis..........	Col. 26th Illinois Infy..............	Mch. 4, 1862, to Apr. 24, 1862.
B. Laibold............	Lt.-Col. 2d Missouri Infy.............	June 1, 1862, to Sept. 4, 1862.

26th Illinois Infy......Mch., 1862	From Dept. of Missouri...........	To 1-Brig. 3-Div. Army Miss.......	Apr.,	1862
11th Missouri Infy......Mch., 1862	From 2-Brig. 1-Div. Army Miss..	To 1-Brig. 3-Div. Army Miss.......	Apr.,	1862
2d Missouri Infy......June, 1862	From 1-Brig. 2-Div. Army S. W. Mo.	To 35-Brig. 11-Div. Army Ohio....	Sept.,	1862
15th Missouri Infy......June, 1862	From 1-Brig. 2-Div. Army S. W. Mo.	To 35-Brig. 11-Div. Army Ohio....	Sept.,	1862

ARTILLERY, 5th DIVISION.—

Batty. M, 1st Missouri A..Mch., 1862	From New Organization........	To Arty. Brig. Army Miss.........	Apr.,	1862
Batty. G, 1st Missouri A..July, 1862	From Arty. 1-Div. Army Miss......	To Arty. 11-Div. Army Ohio......	Sept.,	1862

FLOTILLA BRIGADE.— COMMANDER.

N. B. Buford..........	Brigadier General...................	Mch 4, 1862, to Apr. 24, 1862.

27th Illinois Infy......Feb., 1862	From Dist. of Cairo..............	To 1-Brig. 1-Div. Army Miss.......	Apr.,	1862
42d Illinois Infy......Feb., 1862	From Dist. of Cairo..............	To 1-Brig. 1-Div. Army Miss.......	Apr.,	1862
15th Wisconsin Infy......Feb., 1862	From Dist. of Cairo..............	To Garrison Island No. 10.........	Apr.,	1862
Batty. G, 1st Illinois Arty.Feb., 1862	From Dist. of Cairo..............	To Arty. Div. Army Miss.........	Apr.,	1862
Batty. I, 2d Illinois Arty.Feb., 1862	From Dist. of Cairo..............	To Arty. Div. Army Miss.........	Apr.,	1862

ARTILLERY DIVISION.—

2d Iowa Batty..........Feb., 1862	From Dept. Missouri...........	To Arty. 3-Div. Army Miss........	Apr.,	1862
5th Wisconsin Batty......Feb., 1862	From New Organization........	To Arty. 4-Div. Army Miss........	June,	1862
6th Wisconsin Batty......Feb., 1862	From New Organization........	To Arty. 3-Div. Army Miss........	Oct.,	1862
7th Wisconsin Batty......Feb., 1862	From New Organization........	To Dist. of Columbus, Ky.........	July,	1862
Batty. C, 1st Mich. Arty.Feb., 1862	From New Organization........	To Arty. 2-Div. Army Miss........	Apr.,	1862
Batty. H, 1st Mich. Arty.Feb., 1862	From New Organization........	To Dist. Columbus, Ky...........	July,	1862
Batty. C, 1st Illinois Arty.Feb., 1862	From Dist. of Cairo..............	To Arty. 1-Div. Army Miss........	Apr.,	1862
Batty. F, 2d U. S. Arty...Feb., 1862	From Dept. of Missouri...........	To Arty. 2-Div. Army Miss........	Apr.,	1862
Batty. G, 1st Illinois Arty.Apr., 1862	From Flotilla Brig. Army Miss....	To Arty. Dist. Corinth...........	July,	1862
Batty. I, 2d Illinois Arty.Feb., 1862	From Flotilla Brig. Army Miss....	To Arty. 11-Div. Army Ohio......	Sept.,	1862
Batty. M, 1st Missouri A..Apr., 1862	From Arty. 5-Div. Army Miss.....	To Arty. 1-Div. Army Miss........	July,	1862
10th Wisconsin Batty......Apr., 1862	From New Organization........	To Arty. 1-Div. Army Miss........	July,	1862
12th Wisconsin Batty......Apr., 1862	From New Organization........	To Arty. 3-Div. Army Miss........	Sept.,	1862

CAVALRY ARMY MISS.— COMMANDERS.

Gordon Granger........	Brigadier General...............	Mch. 4, 1862, to July 30, 1862.	
W. L. Elliott..........	Brigadier General...............	July 30, 1862, to Aug. 11, 1862.	
J. K. Mizner..........	Col. 3d Michigan Cav...........	Aug. 11, 1862, to Nov. 1, 1862.	
2d Michigan Cav....Mch., 1862	From New Organization..........	To 2-Brig. Cav. Div. Army Miss...	Apr., 1862
3d Michigan Cav......Mch., 1862	From New Organization..........	To 1st Brig. Cav. Div. Army Miss..	Apr., 1862
2d Iowa Cav..........Mch., 1862	From Dept. of Missouri..........	To 2-Brig. Cav. Div. Army Miss....	Sept., 1862

1st BRIGADE.— COMMANDERS.

W. P. Kellogg........	Col. 7th Illinois Cav...........	Apr. 24, 1862, to June 1, 1862.	
J. K. Mizner..........	Col. 3d Michigan Cav..........	June 1, 1862, to Aug. 11, 1862.	
Edward Hatch........	Col. 2d Iowa Cav..............	Aug. 11, 1862, to Nov. 1, 1862.	
3d Michigan Cav........Apr., 1862	From Cav. Army Miss...........	To 2d Brig. Cav. Div. Army Miss...	Sept., 1862
7th Illinois Cav........Apr., 1862	From 3-Div. Army Miss.........	To 2-Brig. Cav. Div. 13-Corps Tenn.	Nov., 1862
2d Iowa Cav..........Sept., 1862	From 2-Brig. Cav. Div. Army Miss.	To 2-Brig. Cav. Div. 13-Corps Tenn.	Nov., 1862

2d BRIGADE.— COMMANDERS.

W. L. Elliott..........	Col. 2d Iowa Cav..............	Apr. 24, 1862, to June 1, 1862.	
P. H. Sheridan........	Col. 2d Michigan Cav..........	June 1, 1862, to Sept. 4, 1862.	
A. L. Lee............	Col. 7th Kansas Cav...........	Sept. 4, 1862, to Nov. 1, 1862.	
2d Michigan Cav........Apr., 1862	From Cav. Army Miss...........	To 3-Brig. Cav. Div. Army Ohio....	Sept., 1862
2d Iowa Cav..........Apr., 1862	From Cav. Army Miss...........	To 1-Brig. Cav. Div. Army Miss....	Sept., 1862
7th Kansas Cav........June, 1862	From Dept. of Kansas..........	To 1-Brig. Cav. Div. 13-Corps Tenn.	Nov., 1862
3d Michigan Cav........Sept., 1862	From 1-Brig. Cav. Div. Army Miss..	To 3-Brig. Cav. Div. 13-Corps Tenn.	Nov., 1862
5th Ohio Cav.. E, H, I, K.Sept., 1862	From Dist. Jackson............	To 2-Brig. Cav. Div. 13-Corps Tenn.	Nov., 1862

UNATTACHED ARMY MISS.—

Eng. Regt. of the West..Mch., 1862	From Dept. of Missouri..........	To Dist. of Columbus..............	July, 1862
22d Missouri Infy......Mch., 1862	From New Organization..........	Disbanded	Apr., 1862
1st U. S. Infy., A,B,C,D,H,I.Mch., 1862	From Dept. of Missouri..........	To Post of Corinth................	Sept., 1862
2d Illinois Cav. (4 Cos.)..Mch., 1862	From Dist. Cairo................	To Dist. Columbus................	June, 1862
4th U. S. Cav., Cos. B, C, D.Mch., 1862	From Dept. Missouri............	To Unass'd Army Ohio............	Sept., 1862
64th Ill. Infy., Yates S. S..May, 1862	From 2-Brig. 1-Div. Army Miss.....	To Dist. of Corinth Dept. Tenn....	Nov., 1862
Jenks' Ill. Cav. Co........June, 1862	From Army of S. W. Mo..........	To 1-Brig. 2-Div. Army Miss.......	Oct., 1862

District and Army of West Tennessee

Organized Feb. 17, 1862. Merged into the Department of the Tennessee, Oct. 16, 1862.

COMMANDERS.

U. S. Grant...........	Major General..................	Feb. 21, 1862, to Oct. 16, 1862.	

1st DIVISION.— COMMANDERS.

J. A. McClernand......	Major General..................	Feb. 17, 1862, to May 3, 1862.	
H. M. Judah..........	Brigadier General...............	May 3, 1862, to May 14, 1862.	
L. F. Ross...........	Brigadier General...............	May 14, 1862, to June 2, 1862.	
T. A. Davies.........	Brigadier General...............	June 2, 1862, to June 10, 1862.	
J. A. McClernand......	Major General..................	June 10, 1862, to July, 1862.	

1st BRIGADE.—

R. J. Oglesby..........	Col. 8th Illinois Infy...........	Feb. 17, 1862, to Feb. 23, 1862.	
M. M. Crocker........	Col. 13th Iowa Infy............	Feb. 23, 1862, to Mch. 15, 1862.	
A. M. Hare..........	Col. 11th Iowa Infy............	Mch. 15, 1862, to Apr. 6, 1862.	
M. M. Crocker........	Col. 13th Iowa Infy............	Apr. 6, 1862.	
T. W. Sweeny........	Col. 52d Illinois Infy...........	Apr. 6, 1862, to Apr. 19, 1862.	
John A. Logan........	Brigadier General...............	Apr. 19, 1862, to July, 1862.	
8th Illinois Infy........Feb., 1862	From 1-Brig. 1-Div. Mil. Dist. Cairo.	To 1-Brig. 1-Div. Dist. Jackson.....	July, 1862
29th Illinois Infy.......Feb., 1862	From 1-Brig. 1-Div. Mil. Dist. Cairo.	To 3-Brig. 1-Div. Dist. West Tenn...	Mch., 1862
30th Illinois Infy.......Feb., 1862	From 1-Brig. 1-Div. Mil. Dist. Cairo.	To Garrison Fort Donelson, Tenn..	Feb., 1862
31st Illinois Infy.......Feb., 1862	From 1-Brig. 1-Div. Mil. Dist. Cairo.	To Garrison Fort Donelson, Tenn..	Feb., 1862
Batty. D, 2d Ill. L. A....Feb., 1862	From 1-Brig. 1-Div. Mil. Dist. Cairo.	To Arty. 1-Div. Dist. West Tenn...	Apr., 1862
Carmichael's Ill. Cav....Feb., 1862	From 1-Brig. 1-Div. Mil. Dist. Cairo.	To Stewart's Ill. Cav. Battalion...	Apr., 1862
Collins' Ill. Cav........Feb., 1862	From 1-Brig. 1-Div. Mil. Dist. Cairo.	To Stewart's Ill. Cav. Battalion...	Apr., 1862
O'Harnett's Ill. Cav.....Feb., 1862	From 1-Brig. 1-Div. Mil. Dist. Cairo.	To Stewart's Ill. Cav. Battalion...	Apr., 1862
Stewart's Ill. Cav.......Feb., 1862	From 1-Brig. 1-Div. Mil. Dist. Cairo.	To Stewart's Ill. Cav. Battalion...	Apr., 1862
13th Iowa Infy.........Feb., 1862	From Dept. of Missouri..........	To 3-Brig. 6-Div. Dist. West Tenn..	Apr., 1862
11th Iowa Infy.........Mch., 1862	From Dept. of Missouri..........	To 3-Brig. 6-Div. Dist. West Tenn..	Apr., 1862
18th Illinois Infy.......Mch., 1862	From 2-Brig.1-Div. Dist. West Tenn.	To 1-Brig. 1-Div. Dist. Jackson...	July, 1862
12th Michigan Infy......Apr., 1862	From 1-Brig. 6-Div. Dist. West Tenn.	To 1-Brig. 1-Div. Dist. Jackson...	July, 1862
30th Illinois Infy.......Apr., 1862	From Garrison Fort Donelson, Tenn.	To 1-Brig. 1-Div. Dist. Jackson...	July, 1862
31st Illinois Infy.......Apr., 1862	From Garrison Fort Donelson, Tenn.	To 1-Brig. 1-Div. Dist. Jackson...	July, 1862

2d BRIGADE.— COMMANDERS.

W. H. L. Wallace......	Col. 11th Illinois Infy...........	Feb. 17, 1862, to Mch. 29, 1862.	
C. C. Marsh..........	Col. 20th Illinois Infy...........	Mch. 29, 1862, to May 3, 1862.	
A. J. Babcock........	Col. 7th Illinois Infy...........	May 3, 1862, to July, 1862.	
11th Illinois Infy.......Feb., 1862	From 2-Brig. 1-Div. Dist. Cairo.....	To 2-Brig. 1-Div. Dist. Jackson......	July, 1862
18th Illinois Infy.......Feb., 1862	From 1-Brig. 1-Div. Dist. Cairo.....	To 1-Brig. 1-Div. Dist. West Tenn...	Mch., 1862
20th Illinois Infy.......Feb., 1862	From 2-Brig. 1-Div. Dist. Cairo.....	To 2-Brig. 1-Div. Dist. Jackson....	July, 1862
45th Illinois Infy.......Feb., 1862	From 2-Brig. 1-Div. Dist. Cairo.....	To 2-Brig. 1-Div. Dist. Jackson....	July, 1862
Batty. B, 1st Ill. L. A....Feb., 1862	From 2-Brig. 1-Div. Dist. Cairo.....	To Arty. 5-Div. Dist. West Tenn....	Apr., 1862
4th Ill. Cav. (1-Bat'n.)....Feb., 1862	From 2-Brig. 1-Div. Dist. Cairo.....	To Unatt. 1-Div. Dist. West Tenn...	Apr., 1862
48th Illinois Infy.......Mch., 1862	From 2-Brig. 4-Div. Dist. West Tenn.	To 2-Brig. 1-Div. Dist. Jackson....	July, 1862

3d BRIGADE.— COMMANDERS.

L. F. Ross...........	Col. 17th Illinois Infy...........	Feb. 17, 1862, to Apr. 1, 1862.	
J. S. Reardon........	Col. 29th Illinois Infy...........	Apr. 1, 1862, to Apr. 6, 1862.	
Julius Rath..........	Col. 43d Illinois Infy...........	Apr. 6, 1862.	Killed.
E. P. Wood..........	Lt.-Col. 17th Ill. Infy...........	Apr. 6, 1862, to Apr. 13, 1862.	
R. J. Oglesby.........	Brigadier General...............	Apr. 13, 1862, to Apr. 15, 1862.	
L. F. Ross...........	Brigadier General...............	Apr. 15, 1862, to July, 1862.	

3d BRIGADE.—Continued.

17th Illinois Infy	Feb., 1862	From 3-Brig. 1-Div. Dist. Cairo.....	To 3-Brig. 1-Div. Dist. Jackson....	July, 1862
43d Illinois Infy	Feb., 1862	From 3-Brig. 1-Div. Dist. Cairo.....	To 3-Brig. 1-Div. Dist. Jackson....	July, 1862
49th Illinois Infy	Feb., 1862	From 3-Brig. 1-Div. Dist. Cairo.....	To 3-Brig. 1-Div. Dist. Jackson....	July, 1862
52d Illinois Infy	Feb., 1862	From 3-Brig. 2-Div. Dist. Cairo....	To 2-Brig. 4-Div. Dist. West Tenn.	Mch., 1862
Batty. D, 1st Ill. L. A	Feb., 1862	From 3-Brig. 1-Div. Dist. Caro....	To Arty. 1-Div. Dist. Jackson......	July, 1862
Batty. E, 2d Ill. L. A	Feb., 1862	From 1-Brig. 1-Div. Dist. Cairo.....	To Arty. 1-Div. Dist. Jackson......	July, 1862
29th Illinois Infy	Mch., 1862	From 1-Brig. 1-Div. Dist. West Tenn.	To 3-Brig. 1-Div. Dist. Jackson....	July, 1862
UNASSIGNED, 1st DIVISION.—				
ARTILLERY.—				
Batty. D, 1st Illinois	Apr., 1862	From 1-Brig. 1-Div. Dist. West Tenn.	To Arty. 1-Div. Dist. Jackson.......	July, 1862
Batty. D, 2d Illinois	Apr., 1862	From 1-Brig. 1-Div. Dist. West Tenn.	To Arty. 1-Div. Dist. Jackson.......	
Batty. E, 2d Illinois	Apr., 1862	From 3-Brig. 1-Div. Dist. West Tenn.	To Arty. 1-Div. Dist. Jackson.......	July, 1862
14th Indiana Batty	Apr., 1862	From New Organization.............	To Arty. 1-Div. Dist. Jackson.......	July, 1862
14th Ohio Batty	Apr., 1862	From 1-Brig. 4-Div. Dist. West Tenn.	To Arty. 1-Div. Dist. Jackson.......	July, 1862
CAVALRY.—				
4th Illinois (1st Bat'n.)	Apr., 1862	From 2-Brig. 1-Div. Dist. West Tenn.	To Cav. 1-Div. Dist. Jackson.......	July, 1862
Stewart's Ill. Bat'n	Apr., 1862	From 1-Brig. 1-Div. Dist. West Tenn.	To Cav. 1-Div. Dist. Jackson..	July, 1862

2d DIVISION.— COMMANDERS.

C. F. Smith	Major General	Feb. 17, 1862, to Apr. 2, 1862.	
W. H. L. Wallace	Brigadier General	Apr. 2, 1862, to Apr. 6, 1862.	Mort. Wnd.
J. M. Tuttle	Col. 2d Iowa Infy	Apr. 6, 1862, to Apr. 9, 1862.	
John McArthur	Brigadier General	Apr. 9, 1862, to Apr. 14, 1862.	
T. A. Davies	Brigadier General	Apr. 14, 1862, to June 2, 1862.	
E. O. C. Ord	Major General	June 2, 1862, to Aug. 5, 1862.	

1st BRIGADE.— COMMANDERS.

J. G. Lauman	Col. 7th Iowa Infy	Feb. 17, 1862, to Apr. 5, 1862.
J. M. Tuttle	Col. 2d Iowa Infy	Apr. 5, 1862, to Apr. 6, 1862.
James Baker	Lt.-Col. 2d Iowa Infy	Apr. 6, 1862, to Apr. 9, 1862.
J. M. Tuttle	Col. 2d Iowa Infy	Apr. 9, 1862, to July, 1862.

2d Iowa Infy	Feb., 1862	From 4-Brig. 2-Div. Dist. Cairo.....	To 1-Brig. 2-Div. Dist. Corinth....	July, 1862
7th Iowa Infy	Feb., 1862	From 4-Brig. 2-Div. Dist. Cairo.....	To 1-Brig. 2-Div. Dist. Corinth....	July, 1862
12th Iowa Infy	Feb., 1862	From 3-Brig. 2-Div. Dist. Cairo.....	Captured at Shiloh, Tenn.	Apr., 1862
14th Iowa Infy	Feb., 1862	From 4-Brig. 2-Div. Dist. Cairo.....	To 1-Brig. 2-Div. Dist. Corinth......	July, 1862

2d BRIGADE.— COMMANDERS.

John McArthur	Col. 12th Illinois Infy	Feb. 17, 1862, to Apr. 9, 1862.
Thomas Morton	Col. 81st Ohio Infy	Apr. 9, 1862, to Apr. 15, 1862.
R. J. Oglesby	Brigadier General	Apr. 15, 1862, to July, 1862.

9th Illinois Infy	Feb., 1862	From 1-Brig. 2-Div. Dist. Cairo.....	To 2-Brig. 2-Div. Dist. Corinth......	July, 1862
12th Illinois Infy	Feb., 1862	From 1-Brig. 2-Div. Dist. Cairo.....	To 2-Brig. 2-Div. Dist. Corinth......	July, 1862
*13th Missouri Infy	Feb., 1862	From 3-Brig. 2-Div. Dist. Cairo.....	To 2-Brig. 2-Div. Dist. Corinth......	July, 1862
14th Mo. Infy., Birge's S.S.	Feb., 1862	From 4-Brig. 2-Div. Dist. Cairo.....	To 2-Brig. 2-Div. Dist. Corinth......	July, 1862
81st Ohio Infy	Mch., 1862	From Dept. of Missouri.............	To 2-Brig. 2-Div. Dist. Corinth......	July, 1862
Batty. A, 1st Ill. L. A	Mch., 1862	From Arty. 3-Div. Dist. Cairo.....	To Arty. 2-Div. Dist. Corinth........	July, 1862
2d U. S. Cav. (Co. C)	Mch., 1862	From 1-Brig. 1-Div. Dist. Cairo.....	To Cav. 2-Div. Dist. Corinth........	July, 1862
4th U. S. Cav. (Co. C)	Mch., 1862	From 1-Brig. 1-Div. Dist. Cairo.....	To Cav. 2-Div. Dist. Corinth........	July, 1862

*Designation changed to 22d Ohio Infy. May 29, 1862.

3d BRIGADE.— COMMANDERS.

John Cook	Col. 7th Illinois Infy	Feb. 17, 1862, to Mch. 29, 1862.
T. W. Sweeny	Col. 52d Illinois Infy	Mch. 29, 1862, to Apr. 7, 1862.
S. D. Baldwin	Col. 57th Illinois Infy	Apr. 7, 1862, to July, 1862.

7th Illinois Infy	Feb., 1862	From 3-Div. 2-Div. Dist. Cairo.....	To 3-Brig. 2-Div. Dist. Corinth.....	July, 1862
50th Illinois Infy	Feb., 1862	From 3-Brig. 2-Div. Dist. Cairo.....	To 3-Brig. 2-Div. Dist. Corinth.....	July, 1862
57th Illinois Infy	Feb., 1862	From 2-Brig. 3-Div. Dist. Cairo.....	To 3-Brig. 2-Div. Dist. Corinth.....	July, 1862
58th Illinois Infy	Feb., 1862	From 3-Brig. 2-Div. Dist. Cairo.....	To 1-Brig. 2-Div. Dist. West Tenn.	July, 1862
8th Iowa Infy	Feb., 1862	From Dept. of the Missouri.........	To 1-Brig. 2-Div. Dist. West Tenn.	Apr., 1862
Batty. D, 1st Mo. L. A	Feb., 1862	From 3-Brig. 2-Div. Dist. Cairo.....	To Arty. 2-Div. Dist. Corinth........	Apr., 1862
Batty. H, 1st Mo. L. A	Feb., 1862	From 3-Brig. 2-Div. Dist. Cairo.....	To Arty. 2-Div. Dist. Corinth........	July, 1862
Batty. K, 1st Mo. L. A	Feb., 1862	From 3-Brig. 2-Div. Dist. Cairo.....	To Arty. 2-Div. Dist. Corinth........	July, 1862
2d Ill. Cav. (Cos. A, B)	Feb., 1862	From 1-Brig. 1-Div. Dist. Cairo.....	To Cav. 2-Div. Dist. Corinth........	July, 1862
52d Illinois Infy	Mch., 1862	From 2-Brig. 4-Div. Dist. West Tenn.	To 3-Brig. 2-Div. Dist. Corinth.....	July, 1862
UNATTACHED 2d DIVISION.—				
ARTILLERY.—				
Buell's Batty. I, 1st Mo.	Apr., 1862	From Arty. 3-Div. Dist. West Tenn.	To Arty. 3-Div. Army Miss.........	July, 1862
CAVALRY.—				
5th Ohio Cav. (3d Bat'n.)	Apr., 1862	From 5-Div. Dist. West Tenn.......	To Unattached Dist. Corinth........	July, 1862

3d DIVISION.— COMMANDERS.

Lew Wallace	Major General	Feb. 17, 1862, to June, 1862.

1st BRIGADE.— COMMANDER.

M. L. Smith	Col. 8th Missouri Infy	Feb. 17, 1862, to June, 1862.

8th Missouri Infy	Feb., 1862	From 5-Brig. 2-Div. Dist. Cairo......	To 1-Brig. 5-Div. Dist. West Tenn..	May, 1862
11th Indiana Infy	Feb., 1862	From 5-Brig. 2-Div. Dist. Cairo.....	To Dist. Eastern Ark. Helena, Ark..	July, 1862
24th Indiana Infy	Feb., 1862	From Dept. of Missouri.............	To Dist. Eastern Ark. Helena, Ark..	July, 1862
52d Indiana Infy	Feb., 1862	From New Organization.............	To Garrison of Fort Henry, Tenn.	Mch., 1862
Buell's Mo. Batty. L. A	Feb., 1862	From Dept. of Missouri.............	To Arty. 3-Div. Dist. West Tenn....	Mch., 1862
61st Illinois Infy	Apr., 1862	From 2-Brig. 6-Div. Dist. West Tenn.	To 3-Brig. 1-Div. Dist. Jackson....	July, 1862

2d BRIGADE.— COMMANDER.

J. M. Thayer	Col. 1st Nebraska Infy	Feb. 17, 1862, to June, 1862.

1st Nebraska Infy	Feb., 1862	From 3-Brig. 3-Div. Dist. Cairo.....	To Dist. Eastern Ark. Helena, Ark.	July, 1862
58th Ohio Infy	Feb., 1862	From 3-Brig. 3-Div. Dist. Cairo.....	To Dist. Eastern Ark. Helena, Ark..	July, 1862
68th Ohio Infy	Feb., 1862	From 3-Brig. 3-Div. Dist. Cairo.....	To 3-Brig. 3-Div. Dist. West Tenn.	May, 1862
78th Ohio Infy	Feb., 1862	From New Organization.............	To 3-Brig. 3-Div. Dist. West Tenn..	Mch., 1862
23d Indiana Infy	Mch., 1862	From 3-Brig. 3-Div. Dist. West Tenn.	To Unattached Dist. Jackson.......	July, 1862
20th Ohio Infy	May, 1862	From 3-Brig. 3-Div. Dist. West Tenn.	To Unattached Dist. Jackson........	July, 1862

3d BRIGADE.— COMMANDER.

Chas. Whittlesey........	Col. 20th Ohio Infy...............	Feb. 17, 1862, to May, 1862.

20th Ohio Infy..........Feb., 1862	From Covington, Ky................	To 2-Brig. 3-Div. Dist. West Tenn..	May,	1862
56th Ohio Infy..........Feb., 1862	From Paducah, Ky..................	To Dist. Eastern Ark. Helena, Ark..	July,	1862
76th Ohio Infy..........Feb., 1862	From 3-Brig. 3-Div. Dist. Cairo....	To Dist. Eastern Ark. Helena, Ark..	July,	1862
23d Indiana Infy.........Feb., 1862	From Paducah, Ky..................	To 2-Brig. 3-Div. Dist. West Tenn..	Mch.,	1862
78th Ohio Infy..........Mch., 1862	From 2-Br. 3-Div. Dist. West Tenn..	To Unatt. Dist. Jackson............	July,	1862
68th Ohio Infy..........May, 1862	From 2-Br. 3-Div. Dist. West Tenn..	To Unatt. Dist. Jackson............	July,	1862

UNASSIGNED 3d DIVISION.—
ARTILLERY.—

9th Ind. Batty..........Apr., 1862	From New Organization............	To Arty. 1-Div. Dist. Jackson........	July,	1862
Batty. A, 1st Ill.........Apr., 1862	From Arty. 2d Div. Dist. West Tenn.	To Arty. 5-Div. Dist. Memphis.......	July,	1862
Batty. F, 1st Ill.........Apr., 1862	From Dept. Mo...................	To Arty. 5-Div. Dist. Memphis.......	July,	1862
Cogswell's Ill. Batty......Apr., 1862	From New Organization............	To Arty. 5-Div. Dist. Memphis.......	July,	1862
Buell's Batty. I, 1st Mo...Apr., 1862	From 1-Br. 3-Div. Dist. West Tenn..	To Arty. 2-Div. Dist. West Tenn....	Apr.,	1862
8th Ohio Batty..........Apr., 1862	From Arty. 5-Div. Dist. West Tenn.	To Arty. 5-Div. Dist. Memphis.......	July,	1862

CAVALRY.—

5th O. Cav. (1st & 2d Bn.)..Apr., 1862	From 5th Div. Dist. West Tenn.....	To 4-Div. Dist. West Tenn..........	Apr.,	1862
11th Ill. (3d Batt'n.)......Apr., 1862	From New Organization............	To Cav. Dist. Memphis.............	July,	1862

4th DIVISION.— COMMANDERS.

S. A. Hurlbut.........	Brigadier General.................	Feb. 17, 1862, to Apr. 6, 1862.
J. G. Lauman.........	Brigadier General.................	Apr. 6, 1862.
S. A. Hurlbut.........	Brigadier General.................	Apr. 6, 1862, to July .., 1862.

1st BRIGADE.— COMMANDERS.

Thos. J. Turner........	Col. 15th Ill. Infy...............	Feb. 17, 1862, to Mch. .., 1862.
N. G. Williams.........	Col. 3d Iowa Infy...............	Mch. .., 1862, to Apr. 6, 1862.
I. C. Pugh.............	Col. 41st Ill. Infy...............	Apr. 6, 1862.
J. G. Lauman.........	Brigadier General.................	Apr. 6, 1862, to July .., 1862.

15th Ill. Infy...........Feb., 1862	From Dept. Mo....................	To 2-Br. 4-Div. Dist. West Tenn....	Mch.,	1862
28th Ill. Infy...........Feb., 1862	From 4-Brig. Dist. Cairo...........	To 1-Brig. 4-Div. Dist. Memphis....	July,	1862
32d Ill. Infy...........Feb., 1862	From Dist. Cairo.................	To 1-Brig. 4-Div. Dist. Memphis....	July,	1862
41st Ill. Infy...........Feb., 1862	From Dist. Cairo.................	To 1-Brig. 4-Div. Dist. Memphis....	July,	1862
14th Ohio Batty.........Feb., 1862	From New Organization............	To Arty. 1-Div. Dist. West Tenn....	Apr.,	1862
3d Iowa Infy...........Mch., 1862	From Dept. Mo....................	To 1-Brig. 4-Div. Dist. Memphis....	July,	1862
52d Ill. Infy...........Apr., 1862	From Garrison Fort Henry, Tenn...	To 2-Brig. 4-Div. Dist. West Tenn..	May,	1862
53d Ill. Infy...........Apr., 1862	From New Organization............	To 1-Brig. 4-Div. Dist. Memphis....	July,	1862

2d BRIGADE.— COMMANDER.

J. C. Veatch..........	Col. 25th Ind. Infy...............	Feb. 17, 1862, to July .., 1862.

25th Ind. Infy..........Feb., 1862	From 4-Brig. 2-Div. Dist. Cairo.....	To 2-Brig. 4-Div. Dist. Memphis....	July,	1862
14th Ill. Infy...........Feb., 1862	From Dept. Mo...................	To 2-Brig. 4-Div. Dist. Memphis....	July,	1862
46th Ill. Infy...........Feb., 1862	From 2-Brig. 3-Div. Dist. Cairo....	To 2-Brig. 4-Div. Dist. Memphis....	July,	1862
48th Ill. Infy...........Feb., 1862	From 2-Brig. 1-Div. Dist. Cairo....	To 2-Brig. 1-Div. Dist. West Tenn..	Mch.,	1862
Mann's Mo. Batty........Feb., 1862	From New Organization............	To Arty. 4-Div. Dist. Memphis......	July,	1862
15th Ill. Infy...........Mch., 1862	From 1-Br. 4-Div. Dist. West Tenn.	To 2-Brig. 4-Div. Dist. Memphis....	July,	1862
52d Ill. Infy...........Mch., 1862	From 3-Br. 1-Div. Dist. West Tenn.	To 3-Brig. 2-Div. Dist. West Tenn..	Mch.,	1862
53d Ind. Infy...........Apr., 1862	From Indiana....................	To 2-Brig. 4-Div. Dist. Memphis....	July,	1862
52d Ind. Infy...........May, 1862	From 1-Br. 4-Div. Dist. West Tenn.	To 2-Brig. 4-Div. Dist. Memphis....	July,	1862

3d BRIGADE.— COMMANDERS.

Charles Crufts.........	Col. 31st Ind. Infy................	Feb. 17, 1862, to Apr. 5, 1862.
J. G. Lauman.........	Brigadier General.................	Apr. 5, 1862, to Apr. 6, 1862.
Charles Crufts.........	Col. 31st Ind. Infy................	Apr. .., 1862.

31st Ind. Infy..........Feb., 1862	From 1-Brig. 3-Div. Dist. Cairo....	To 22-Brig. 4-Div. Army Ohio......	Apr.,	1862
44th Ind. Infy..........Feb., 1862	From 1-Brig. 3-Div. Dist. Cairo....	To 14-Brig. 5-Div. Army Ohio......	Apr.,	1862
17th Ky. Infy...........Feb., 1862	From 1-Brig. 3-Div. Dist. Cairo....	To 10-Brig. 4-Div. Army Ohio......	Apr.,	1862
25th Ky. Infy...........Feb., 1862	From 1-Brig. 3-Div. Dist. Cairo....	Consolidated with 17th Ky.........	Mch.,	1862
4th Ill. Cav. (3d Batt'n.)..Feb., 1862	From 2-Brig. 1-Div. Dist. Cairo.....	To Unatt. 5-Div. Dist. West Tenn...	Apr.,	1862

UNATTACHED 4th DIVISION.—
ARTILLERY.—

Batty. B, 1st Mich.......Feb., 1862	From New Organization............	To Captured at Shiloh, Tenn........	Apr. 6,	'62
Mann's Mo. Batty.......Mch., 1862	From 2-Br. 4-Div. Dist. West Tenn.	To Arty. 4-Div. Dist. Memphis......	Apr.,	1862
13th Ohio Batty.........Mch., 1862	From New Organization............	Disbanded	Apr.,	1862
Batty. L, 2d Ill.........Apr., 1862	From New Organization............	To Arty. 4-Div. Dist. Memphis......	July,	1862
15th Ohio Batty.........Apr., 1862	From New Organization............	To Arty. 4-Div. Dist. Memphis......	July,	1862
Batty. B, 2d Ill.........May, 1862	From Unass'd Dist. West Tenn......	To Arty. 1-Div. Dist. Jackson.......	July,	1862
7th Ohio Batty..........July, 1862	From Arty. 5-Div. Dist. West Tenn.	To Arty. 4-Div. Dist. Memphis......	July,	1862

CAVALRY, 4th DIVISION.—

5th Ohio (1st & 2d Battn.).Apr., 1862	From 3-Div. Dist. West Tenn.......	To 4-Div. Dist. Memphis...........	July,	1862

5th DIVISION.— COMMANDER.

W. T. Sherman........	Brigadier General.................	Mch. 1, 1862, to July 21, 1862.

1st BRIGADE.— COMMANDERS.

S. G. Hicks...........	Col. 40th Ill. Infy...............	Mch. 1, 1862, to Mch. 20, 1862.
J. A. McDowell........	Col. 6th Iowa Infy...............	Mch. 20, 1862, to May 12, 1862.
M. L. Smith...........	Brigadier General.................	May 12, 1862, to July 21, 1862.

40th Ill. Infy...........Mch., 1862	From Paducah, Ky................	To 2-Brig. 5-Div. Dist. West Tenn..	May,	1862
6th Iowa Infy...........Mch., 1862	From Paducah, Ky................	To 2-Brig. 5-Div. Dist. West Tenn..	May,	1862
46th Ohio Infy..........Mch., 1862	From Paducah, Ky................	To 2-Brig. 5-Div. Dist. West Tenn..	May,	1862
55th Ill. Infy...........May, 1862	From 2-Br. 5-Div. Dist. West Tenn.	To 1-Brig. 5-Div. Dist. Memphis....	July,	1862
6th Mo. Infy...........May, 1862	From Dept. Mo...................	To 1-Brig. 5-Div. Dist. Memphis....	July,	1862
8th Mo. Infy...........May, 1862	From 1-Br. 3-Div. Dist. West Tenn.	To 1-Brig. 5-Div. Dist. Memphis....	July,	1862
54th Ohio Infy..........May, 1862	From 2-Div. 5-Div. Dist. West Tenn.	To 1-Brig. 5-Div. Dist. Memphis....	July,	1862
57th Ohio Infy..........May, 1862	From 3-Br. 5-Div. Dist. West Tenn.	To 1-Brig. 5-Div. Dist. Memphis....	July,	1862

2d BRIGADE.— COMMANDERS.

D. Stuart.............	Col. 55th Ill. Infy................	Mch. 1, 1862, to Apr. 6, 1862.
Oscar Malmsburg.......	Lt.-Col. 55th Ill. Infy.............	Apr. 6, 1862.
T. K. Smith...........	Col. 54th Ohio Infy...............	Apr. 6, 1862, to May 12, 1862.
J. A. McDowell........	Col. 6th Iowa Infy................	May 12, 1862, to July 21, 1862.

2d BRIGADE.—Continued.

55th Ill. Infy............Mch., 1862	From Paducah, Ky................	To 1-Brig. 5-Div. Dist. West Tenn..	May,	1862
54th Ohio Infy...........Mch., 1862	From Paducah, Ky................	To Garrison Fort Donelson, Tenn....	Apr.,	1862
71st Ohio Infy...........Mch., 1862	From Paducah, Ky................	To Garrison Fort Donelson, Tenn....	Apr.,	1862
40th Ill. Infy............May, 1862	From 1-Br. 5-Div. Dist. West Tenn..	To 2-Brig. 5-Div. Dist. Memphis..	July,	1862
6th Iowa Infy............May, 1862	From 1-Br. 5-Div. Dist. West Tenn..	To 2-Brig. 5-Div. Dist. Memphis..	July,	1862
46th Ohio Infy...........May, 1862	From 1-Br. 5-Div. Dist. West Tenn..	To 2-Brig. 5-Div. Dist. Memphis..	July,	1862
77th Ohio Infy...........May, 1862	From 3-Br. 5-Div. Dist. West Tenn..	To 2-Brig. 5-Div. Dist. Memphis..	July,	1862
14th Wis. Infy...........May, 1862	From Unatt. Dist. West Tenn......	To 2-Brig. 5-Div. Dist. Memphis..	July,	1862

3d BRIGADE.— COMMANDERS.

J. Hildebrand..........	Col. 77th Ohio Infy................	Mch. 1, 1862, to May 12, 1862.	
J. W. Denver...........	Brigadier General..................	May 12, 1862, to July 21, 1862.	
53d Ohio Infy...........Mch., 1862	From Paducah, Ky................	To 3-Brig. 5-Div. Dist. Memphis..	July, 1862
57th Ohio Infy...........Mch., 1862	From Paducah, Ky................	To 1-Brig. 5-Div. Dist. West Tenn..	May, 1862
77th Ohio Infy...........Mch., 1862	From Paducah, Ky................	To 2-Brig. 5-Div. Dist. West Tenn..	May, 1862
48th Ohio Infy...........May, 1862	From 4-Br. 5-Div. Dist. West Tenn..	To 3-Brig. 5-Div. Dist. Memphis..	July, 1862
70th Ohio Infy...........May, 1862	From 4-Br. 5-Div. Dist. West Tenn..	To 3-Brig. 5-Div. Dist. Memphis..	July, 1862
72d Ohio Infy...........May, 1862	From 4-Br. 5-Div. Dist. West Tenn..	To 3-Brig. 5-Div. Dist. Memphis..	July, 1862

4th BRIGADE.— COMMANDER.

R. P. Buckland.........	Col. 72d Ohio Infy................	Mch. 1, 1862, to May 15, 1862.	
48th Ohio Infy...........Mch., 1862	From Paducah, Ky................	To 3-Brig. 5-Div. Dist. West Tenn..	May, 1862
70th Ohio Infy...........Mch., 1862	From Paducah, Ky................	To 3-Brig. 5-Div. Dist. West Tenn..	May, 1862
72d Ohio Infy...........Mch., 1862	From Paducah, Ky................	To 3-Brig. 5-Div. Dist. West Tenn..	May, 1862

ARTILLERY, 5th DIVISION.—

6th Ind. Batty..........Mch., 1862	From Paducah, Ky................	To Arty. 5-Div. Dist. Memphis......	July, 1862
Batty. B, 1st Ill........Mch., 1862	From 2-Br. 1-Div. Dist. West Tenn..	To Arty. 5-Div. Dist. Memphis......	July, 1862
Batty. E, 1st Ill........Mch., 1862	From 3-Br. 5-Div. Dist. West Tenn..	To Arty. 5-Div. Dist. Memphis......	July, 1862
Batty. H, 1st Ill........Apr., 1862	From Unatt. Arty. Dist. West Tenn..	To Arty. 5-Div. Dist. Memphis......	July, 1862
Batty. I, 1st Ill.........Apr., 1862	From Unatt. Arty. Dist. West Tenn..	To Arty. 5-Div. Dist. Memphis......	July, 1862
7th Ohio Batty.........Apr., 1862	From New Organization............	To Arty. 5-Div. Dist. Memphis......	July, 1862
8th Ohio Batty.........Apr., 1862	From New Organization............	To Arty. 5-Div. Dist. Memphis......	July, 1862

CAVALRY, 5th DIVISION.—

Thielman's Illinois.......Mch., 1862	From Paducah, Ky................	To 5-Div. Dist. Memphis...........	July, 1862
5th Ohio Cav...........Mch., 1862	From Paducah, Ky................	To 2 and 4-Divs. Dist. West Tenn..	Apr., 1862
4th Ill. (1st & 2d Battn.)..Apr., 1862	From 4-Div. Dist. West Tenn......	To Cav. 4-Div. Dist. West Tenn.....	Apr., 1862

6th DIVISION.— COMMANDERS.

B. M. Prentiss.........	Brigadier General..................	Mch. 26, 1862, to Apr. 6, 1862.	
Francis Quinn..........	Col. 12th Mich. Infy...............	Apr. 6, 1862, to Apr. 10, 1862.	
Thos. J. McKean........	Brigadier General..................	Apr. 10, 1862, to Apr. 30, 1862.	
T. W. Sherman........	Brigadier General.................	Apr. 30, 1862, to June 10, 1862.	
T. J. McKean..........	Brigadier General.................	June 10, 1862, to June 15, 1862.	
J. B. S. Todd..........	Brigadier General.................	June 15, 1862, to July 16, 1862.	

1st BRIGADE.— COMMANDERS.

E. Peabody............	Col. 25th Mo. Infy.................	Mch. 26, 1862, to Apr. 6, 1862.	Killed.
J. J. Doran............	Col. 17th Wis. Infy................	Apr. 6, 1862, to May 23, 1862.	
J. M. Oliver...........	Col. 15th Mich. Infy...............	Apr. 1862, Temporarily.	
J. McArthur...........	Brigadier General..................	May 23, 1862, to July 24, 1862.	
21st Mo. Infy...........Mch., 1862	From New Organization...........	To 1-Brig. 6-Div. Dist. Corinth......	July, 1862
25th Mo. Infy...........Mch., 1862	From New Organization...........	To 1-Brig. 6-Div. Dist. Corinth......	July, 1862
16th Wis. Infy...........Mch., 1862	From New Organization...........	To 1-Brig. 6-Div. Dist. Corinth......	July, 1862
12th Mich. Infy..........Mch., 1862	From New Organization...........	To 1-Brig. 1-Div. Dist. West Tenn..	Apr., 1862
17th Wis. Infy...........Mch., 1862	From New Organization...........	To 1-Brig. 6-Div. Dist. Corinth....	July, 1862

2d BRIGADE.— COMMANDERS.

Madison Miller.........	Col. 18th Mo. Infy.................	Mch. 26, 1862, to Apr. 20, 1862.	
J. M. Oliver...........	Col. 15th Mich. Infy...............	Apr. 20, 1862, to July 24, 1862.	
61st Ill. Infy............Mch., 1862	From New Organization...........	To 1-Brig. 3-Div. Dist. West Tenn..	Apr., 1862
16th Iowa Infy..........Mch., 1862	From New Organization...........	To 3-Brig. 3-Div. Dist. West Tenn..	Apr., 1862
15th Mich. Infy..........Mch., 1862	From New Organization...........	To 2-Brig. 6-Div. Dist. Corinth.....	July, 1862
18th Mo. Infy...........Mch., 1862	From Dept. Mo..................	To 2-Brig. 6-Div. Dist. Corinth.....	July, 1862
18th Wis. Infy...........Mch., 1862	From New Organization...........	To 2-Brig. 6-Div. Dist. Corinth.....	July, 1862

3d BRIGADE.— COMMANDER.

M. M. Crocker..........	Col. 13th Iowa Infy...............	Apr. 8, 1862, to July 24, 1862.	
11th Iowa Infy..........Apr., 1862	From 1-Br. 1-Div. Dist. West Tenn..	To 3-Brig. 6-Div. Dist. Corinth.....	July, 1862
13th Iowa Infy..........Apr., 1862	From 1-Br. 1-Div. Dist. West Tenn..	To 3-Brig. 6-Div. Dist. Corinth.....	July, 1862
15th Iowa Infy..........Apr., 1862	From New Organization...........	To 3-Brig. 6-Div. Dist. Corinth.....	July, 1862
16th Iowa Infy..........Apr., 1862	From 2-Br. 6-Div. Dist. West Tenn..	To 3-Brig. 6-Div. Dist. Corinth.....	July, 1862

ARTILLERY, 6th DIVISION.—

Batty. F, 2d Ill..........Apr., 1862	From Unass'd Dist. West Tenn......	To Arty. 6-Div. Dist. Corinth......	July, 1862
1st Minn. Batty.........Apr., 1862	From New Organization...........	To Arty. 6-Div. Dist. Corinth......	July, 1862
3d Ohio Batty..........Apr., 1862	From New Organization...........	To Arty. 6-Div. Dist. Corinth......	July, 1862
5th Ohio Batty..........Apr., 1862	From Dept. Mo.................	To Arty. 6-Div. Dist. Corinth......	July, 1862
10th Ohio Batty.........Apr., 1862	From New Organization...........	To Arty. 6-Div. Dist. Corinth......	July, 1862

CAVALRY, 6th DIVISION.—

11th Ill. (1st & 2d Battns.).Apr., 1862	From New Organization...........	To Cav. 6-Div. Dist. Corinth........	July, 1862

UNATTACHED ARTILLERY, DIST. WEST TENN.—

Batty. H, 1st Ill........Apr., 1862	From New Organization...........	To Arty. 5-Div. Dist. West Tenn....	Apr., 1862
Batty. I, 1st Ill.........Apr., 1862	From New Organization...........	To Arty. 5-Div. Dist. West Tenn....	Apr., 1862
Batty. B, 2d Ill.........Apr., 1862	From New Organization...........	To Arty. 4-Div. Dist. West Tenn....	May, 1862
Batty. F, 2d Ill.........Apr., 1862	From New Organization...........	To Arty. 6-Div. Dist. West Tenn....	Apr., 1862
8th Ohio Batty.........Apr., 1862	From New Organization...........	To Arty. 5-Div. Dist. West Tenn....	May, 1862

DISTRICT OF JACKSON.—Designated 3d Division, District West Tenn., Sept. 24, 1862. Transferred to Dept. of the Tennessee as District of Jackson, 13th Army Corps, Oct. 26, 1863.

COMMANDERS.

John A. McClernand....	Major General....................	July .., 1862, to Sept. .., 1862.	
John A. Logan.........	Brigadier General..................	Sept. .., 1862.	
E. O. C. Ord..........	Major General....................	Sept. 24, 1862, to Oct. 5, 1862.	
S. A. Hurlbut..........	Major General....................	Oct. 5, 1862, to Oct. 26, 1862.	

POST OF JACKSON.— COMMANDER.

M. K. Lawler	Brigadier General	

1st DIVISION.—Designated 3d Division Sept. 24, 1862.

COMMANDER.

John A. McClernand	Major General	July .., 1862, to Sept. .., 1862.

1st BRIGADE.— COMMANDERS. (Not of record.)

John A. Logan	Brigadier General	July .., 1862, to Sept. .., 1862.

8th Ill. Infy	July, 1862	From 1-Br. 1-Div. Dist. West Tenn	To 4-Brig. Dist. Jackson	Sept., 1862
18th Ill. Infy	July, 1862	From 1-Br. 1-Div. Dist. West Tenn	To 2-Brig. Dist. Jackson	Sept., 1862
30th Ill. Infy	July, 1862	From 1-Br. 1-Div. Dist. West Tenn	To 3-Brig. Dist. Jackson	Sept., 1862
31st Ill. Infy	July, 1862	From 1-Br. 1-Div. Dist. West Tenn	To 2-Brig. Dist. Jackson	Sept., 1862
12th Mich. Infy	July, 1862	From 1-Br. 1-Div. Dist. West Tenn	To Unatt. Dist. Jackson	Sept., 1862

2d BRIGADE.— COMMANDERS. (Not of record.)

Lydorf Ozburn	Col.	

11th Ill. Infy	July, 1862	From 2-Br. 1-Div. Dist. West Tenn	To Cairo, Ill	Aug., 1862
20th Ill. Infy	July, 1862	From 2-Br. 1-Div. Dist. West Tenn	To 3-Brig. Dist. Jackson	Sept., 1862
45th Ill. Infy	July, 1862	From 2-Br. 1-Div. Dist. West Tenn	To 3-Brig. Dist. Jackson	Sept., 1862
48th Ill. Infy	July, 1862	From 2-Br. 1-Div. Dist. West Tenn	To Unatt. Dist. Jackson	Sept., 1862
18th Ill. Infy	Sept., 1862	From 1- Brig. 1-Div. Dist. Jackson	To Dist. Jackson 13th Army Corps	Nov., 1862
29th Ill. Infy	Sept., 1862	From 1- Brig. 1-Div. Dist. Jackson	To Dist. Jackson 13th Army Corps	Nov., 1862
31st Ill. Infy	Sept., 1862	From 1- Brig. 1-Div. Dist. Jackson	To 1-Br. 3-Div. Right Wing 13-C	Nov., 1862

3d BRIGADE.— COMMANDERS. (Not of record.)

C. C. Marsh	Col. 20th Ill. Infy	

17th Ill. Infy	July, 1862	From 3-Br. 1-Div. Dist. West Tenn	To Unatt. Dist. Jackson	Sept., 1862
29th Ill. Infy	July, 1862	From 3-Br. 1-Div. Dist. West Tenn	To 2-Brig. Dist. Jackson	Sept., 1862
43d Ill. Infy	July, 1862	From 3-Br. 1-Div. Dist. West Tenn	To Unatt. Dist. Jackson	Sept., 1862
49th Ill. Infy	July, 1862	From 3-Br. 1-Div. Dist. West Tenn	To Unatt. Dist. Jackson	Sept., 1862
61st Ill. Infy	July, 1862	From 3-Br. 1-Div. Dist. West Tenn	To Unatt. Dist. Jackson	Sept., 1862
20th Ill. Infy	Sept., 1862	From 2-Brig. 1-Div. Dist. Jackson	To 1-Brig. 3-Div. R. W. 13th Corps	Nov., 1862
30th Ill. Infy	Sept., 1862	From 1-Brig. 1-Div. Dist. Jackson	To 1-Brig. 3-Div. R. W. 13th Corps	Nov., 1862
45th Ill. Infy	Sept., 1862	From 2-Brig. 1-Div. Dist. Jackson	To 1-Brig. 3-Div. R. W. 13th Corps	Nov., 1862

4th BRIGADE.— COMMANDERS. (Not of record.)

F. L. Rhoads	Col.	

8th Ill. Infy	Sept., 1862	From 1-Brig. 1-Div. Dist. Jackson	To 4-Brig. 3-Div. R. W. 13th Corps	Nov., 1862
63d Ill. Infy	Sept., 1862	From Dist. Cairo	To 4-Brig. 3-Div. R. W. 13th Corps	Nov., 1862
7th Mo. Infy	Sept., 1862	From Unatt. Dist. Jackson	To 4-Brig. 3-Div. R. W. 13th Corps	Nov., 1862

4th DIVISION.— COMMANDERS.

S. A. Hurlbut	Major General	Sept. 24, 1862, to Oct. 5, 1862.
G. M. Dodge	Brigadier General	Oct. 5, 1862, to Oct. 30, 1862.

1st BRIGADE.— COMMANDER.

J. G. Lauman	Brigadier General	Sept. 24, 1862, to Oct. 26, 1862.

28th Ill. Infy	Sept., 1862	From 1-Brig. 4-Div. Dist. Memphis	To 3-Brig. 4-Div. R. W. 13th Corps	Nov., 1862
32d Ill. Infy	Sept., 1862	From 1-Brig. 4-Div. Dist. Memphis	To 3-Brig. 4-Div. R. W. 13th Corps	Nov., 1862
41st Ill. Infy	Sept., 1862	From 1-Brig. 4-Div. Dist. Memphis	To 1-Brig. 4-Div. R. W. 13th Corps	Nov., 1862
53d Ill. Infy	Sept., 1862	From 1-Brig. 4-Div. Dist. Memphis	To 1-Brig. 4-Div. R. W. 13th Corps	Nov., 1862
3d Iowa Infy	Sept., 1862	From 1-Brig. 4-Div. Dist. Memphis	To 1-Brig. 4-Div. R. W. 13th Corps	Nov., 1862

2d BRIGADE.— COMMANDER.

J. C. Veatch	Brigadier General	Sept. 24, 1862, to Oct. 26, 1862.

25th Ind. Infy	Sept., 1862	From 2-Brig. 4-Div. Dist. Memphis	To 3-Brig. 4-Div. R. W. 13th Corps	Nov., 1862
14th Ill. Infy	Sept., 1862	From 2-Brig. 4-Div. Dist. Memphis	To 2-Brig. 4-Div. R. W. 13th Corps	Nov., 1862
15th Ill. Infy	Sept., 1862	From 2-Brig. 4-Div. Dist Memphis	To 2-Brig. 4-Div. R. W. 13-Corps	Nov., 1862
46th Ill. Infy	Sept., 1862	From 2-Brig. 4-Div. Dist Memphis	To 2-Brig. 4-Div. R. W. 13-Corps	Nov., 1862
52d Ind. Infy	Sept., 1862	From 2-Brig. 4-Div. Dist Memphis	To Garrison Fort Pillow, Tenn	Oct., 1862
53d Ind. Infy	Sept., 1862	From 2-Brig. 4-Div. Dist Memphis	To 3-Brig. 4-Div. R. W. 13th Corps	Nov., 1862
76th Ill. Infy	Oct., 1862	From Dist. Columbus	To 2-Brig. 4-Div. R. W. 13-Corps	Nov., 1862
12th Wis. Infy	Oct., 1862	From Dist. Columbus	To 3-Brig. 4-Div. R. W. 13-Corps	Nov., 1862

ARTILLERY.—

Batty. L, 2d Ill	Sept., 1862	From Arty. 4-Div. Dist. Memphis	To Arty. 4-Div. R. W. 13-Corps	Nov., 1862
Batty. C, 1st Mo	Sept., 1862	From Arty. 4-Div. Dist. Memphis	To Arty. 4-Div. R. W. 13-Corps	Nov., 1862
3d Ohio Batty	Sept., 1862	From Arty. 6th Div. Dist Corinth	To Arty. 3-Div. R. W. 13-Corps	Nov., 1862
7th Ohio Batty	Sept., 1862	From Arty. 4-Div. Dist. Memphis	To Arty. 4-Div. R. W. 13-Corps	Nov., 1862
15th Ohio Batty	Sept., 1862	From Arty. 4-Div. Dist. Memphis	To Arty. Dist. Jackson 13-Corps	Nov., 1862

CAVALRY.—

2d Ill. Cav	Sept., 1862	From Dist. of Columbus	To Dist. Jackson 13-Corps	Nov., 1862
11th Ill. Cav	Sept., 1862	From 5-Div. Dist. Memphis	To Dist. Jackson 13-Corps	Nov., 1862
12th Ill. Cav., Co. H	Sept., 1862	From Dist. of Corinth	To Dist. Jackson 13-Corps	Nov., 1862
4th Ohio Indpt. Co	Sept., 1862	From Dept. Headqrs	To 4-Div. R. W. 13-Corps	Nov., 1862
5th O. (1 and 2 Batt'ns)	Sept., 1862	From Dist. of Memphis	To Dist. Jackson 13-Corps	Nov., 1862
7th Tenn. Cav	Sept., 1862	From New Organization	To Dist. Jackson 13-Corps	Nov., 1862

UNATTACHED INFANTRY, 1st DIVISION.—

23d Ind. Infy	July, 1862	From 2-B. 3-Div. Dist. West Tenn	To 2-Brig. 3-Div. R. W. 13-Corps	Nov., 1862
7th Mo. Infy	July, 1862	From Unatt. Pittsburg L'd'g, Tenn	To 4-Brig. Dist. Jackson	Sept., 1862
20th Ohio Infy	July, 1862	From 2-B. 3-Div. Dist. West Tenn	To 2-Brig. 3-Div. R. W. 13-Corps	Nov., 1862
68th Ohio Infy	July, 1862	From 3-B. 3-Div. Dist. West Tenn	To 2-Brig. 3-Div. R. W. 13-Corps	Nov., 1862
78th Ohio Infy	July, 1862	From 3-B. 3-Div. Dist. West Tenn	To 2-Brig. 3-Div. R. W. 13-Corps	Nov., 1862
12th Mich. Infy	Sept., 1862	From 1-Brig. 1-Div. Dist. Jackson	To Dist. Jackson R. W. 13-Corps	Nov., 1862
17th Ill. Infy	Sept., 1862	From 3-Brig. 1-Div. Dist. Jackson	To 4-Brig. 3-Div. R. W. 13-Corps	Nov., 1862
43d Ill. Infy	Sept., 1862	From 3-Brig. 1-Div. Dist. Jackson	To Dist. Jackson R. W. 13-Corps	Nov., 1862
48th Ill. Infy	Sept., 1862	From 2-Brig. 1-Div. Dist Jackson	To Dist. Jackson R. W. 13-Corps	Nov., 1862
49th Ill. Infy	Sept., 1862	From 3-Brig. 1-Div. Dist. Jackson	To Dist. Jackson R. W. 13-Corps	Nov., 1862
61st Ill. Infy	Sept., 1862	From 3-Brig. 1-Div. Dist. Jackson	To Dist. Jackson R. W. 13-Corps	Nov., 1862
62d Ill. Infy	Sept., 1862	From Dist. Columbus	To Dist. Jackson R. W. 13-Corps	Nov., 1862

UNATTACHED ARTILLERY.—

Batty. D, 1st Ill........July, 1862	From Arty. 1-Div. Dist. West Tenn.	To Arty. 3-Div. R. W. 13-Corps..	Nov.,	1862
Batty. B, 2d Ill........July, 1862	From Arty. 4-Div. Dist. West Tenn.	To Dist. Jackson 13-Corps........	Nov.,	1862
Batty. E, 2d Ill........July, 1862	From Arty. 1-Div. Dist. West Tenn.	To Arty. 3-Div. R. W. 13-Corps...	Nov.,	1862
9th Ind. Batty........July, 1862	From Arty. 3-Div. Dist. West Tenn.	To Arty 4-Div. 13-Corps........	Nov.,	1862
14th Ind. Batty........July, 1862	From Arty. 1-Div. Dist. West Tenn.	To Arty. Dist. Jackson 13-Corps....	Nov.,	1862
14th Ohio Batty........July, 1862	From Arty. 1-Div. Dist. West Tenn.	To Arty. Dist. Jackson 13-Corps....	Nov.,	1862

UNATTACHED CAVALRY.—

2d Ill., Co's A, B........July, 1862	From Cav. 1-Div. Dist. West Tenn.	To Dist. Jackson 13-Corps.........	Nov.,	1862
4th Ill., Co's A, B, C, D..July, 1862	From Cav. 1-Div. Dist. West Tenn.	To Dist. Jackson 13-Corps........	Nov.,	1862
Stewart's Ill. Batt'n......July, 1862	From Cav. 1-Div. Dist. West Tenn.	To Dist. Corinth 13-Corps.........	Nov.,	1862

DISTRICT OF CORINTH.—Designated 3d Division, District West Tennessee, Sept. 24, 1862. Transferred to Department of the Tennessee as District of Corinth, 13th Army Corps, Oct. 26, 1862.

COMMANDERS.

W. S. Rosecrans........	Major General.....................	July, 1862, to Oct. 20, 1862.
C. S. Hamilton..........	Brigadier General.................	Oct. 20, 1862, to Oct. 26, 1862.

2d DIVISION.— COMMANDERS.

E. O. C. Ord..........	Major General.....................	July, 1862, to Aug. 5, 1862.
T. A. Davies..........	Brigadier General.................	Aug. 5, 1862, to Oct. 24, 1862.
L. F. Ross..............	Brigadier General.................	Oct. 24, 1862, to Nov. 1, 1862.

1st BRIGADE.— COMMANDERS.

J. M. Tuttle..........	Brigadier General.................	July, 1862, to Aug. 12, 1862.
T. W. Sweeny..........	Col. 52d Illinois Infy.............	Aug. 12, 1862, to Sept. 1, 1862.
P. A. Hackleman.......	Brigadier General.................	Sept. 1, 1862, to Oct. 3, 1862.
T. W. Sweeny..........	Col. 52d Illinois Infy.............	Oct. 3, 1862, to Nov. 1, 1862.

2d Iowa Infy..........July, 1862	From 1-Brig. 2-Div. Dist. W. Tenn.	To 3-Brig. 2-Div. Dist. Corinth....	Sept.,	1862
7th Iowa Infy..........July, 1862	From 1-Brig. 2-Div. Dist. W. Tenn.	To 3-Brig. 2-Div. Dist. Corinth....	Sept.,	1862

UNION BRIGADE.—

8th Iowa Infy. Det....July, 1862	From 1-Brig. 2-Div. Dist. W. Tenn.	To 1-Brig. Dist. Corinth 13-Corps..	Nov.,	1862
12th Iowa Infy Det....July, 1862	From 1-Brig. 2-Div. Dist. W. Tenn.	To 1-Brig. Dist. Corinth 13-Corps..	Nov.,	1862
14th Iowa Infy. Det....July, 1862	From 1-Brig. 2-Div. Dist. W. Tenn.	To 1-Brig. Dist. Corinth 13-Corps..	Nov.,	1862
58th Illinois Infy. Det...July, 1862	From 1-Brig. 2-Div. Dist. W. Tenn.	To 1-Brig. Dist. Corinth 13-Corps..	Nov.,	1862
12th Illinois Infy......Sept., 1862	From 2-Brig. 2-Div. Dist. Corinth.	To 2-Brig. 2-Div. Dist Corinth....	Oct.,	1862
52d Illinois Infy......Sept., 1862	From 3-Brig. 2-Div. Dist. Corinth.	To 1-Brig. Dist. Corinth 13-Corps...	Nov.,	1862
22d Ohio Infy.........Sept., 1862	From 2-Brig. 2-Div. Dist. Corinth.	To 2-Brig. 2-Div. Dist Corinth....	Oct.,	1862
81st Ohio Infy........Sept., 1862	From 2-Brig. 2-Div. Dist. Corinth.	To 2-Brig. 2-Div. Dist Corinth....	Oct.,	1862
2d Iowa Infy..........Oct., 1862	From 3-Brig. 2-Div. Dist. Corinth.	To 1-Brig. Dist. Corinth 13-Corps...	Nov.,	1862
7th Iowa Infy..........Oct., 1862	From 3-Brig. 2-Div. Dist. Corinth.	To 1-Brig. Dist. Corinth 13-Corps..	Nov.,	1862

2d BRIGADE.— COMMANDERS.

R. J. Oglesby..........	Brigadier General.................	July, 1862, to Oct. 3, 1862.
Aug. Mersey...........	Col. 9th Illinois Infy.............	Oct. 3, 1862, to Nov. 1, 1862.

9th Illinois Infy......July, 1862	From 2-Brig. 2-Div. Dist. W. Tenn.	To 3-Brig. 2-Div. Dist. Corinth....	Sept.,	1862
12th Illinois Infy......July, 1862	From 2-Brig. 2-Div. Dist. W. Tenn.	To 1-Brig. 2-Div. Dist. Corinth....	Sept.,	1862
14th Missouri Infy......July, 1862	From 2-Brig. 2-Div. Dist. W. Tenn.	To 3-Brig. 2-Div. Dist. Corinth....	Sept.,	1862
22d Ohio Infy.........July, 1862	From 2-Brig. 2-Div. Dist. W. Tenn.	To 1-Brig. 2-Div. Dist. Corinth....	Sept.,	1862
81st Ohio Infy.........July, 1862	From 2-Brig. 2-Div. Dist. W. Tenn.	To 1-Brig. 2-Div. Dist. Corinth....	Sept.,	1862
9th Illinois Infy......Sept., 1862	From 3-Brig. 2-Div. Dist. Corinth.	To 2-Brig. Dist. Corinth 13-Corps..	Nov.,	1862
12th Illinois Infy......Sept., 1862	From 1-Brig. 2-Div. Dist. Corinth.	To 2-Brig. Dist. Corinth 13-Corps..	Nov.,	1862
22d Ohio Infy.........Sept., 1862	From 1-Brig. 2-Div. Dist. Corinth.	To 2-Brig. Dist. Corinth 13-Corps..	Nov.,	1862
81st Ohio Infy.........Sept., 1862	From 1-Brig. 2-Div. Dist. Corinth.	To 2-Brig. Dist. Corinth 13-Corps..	Nov.,	1862

3d BRIGADE.— COMMANDERS. (Not of Record.)

S. D. Baldwin..........	Col. 57th Illinois Infy.............	July, 1862, to Oct. 4, 1862.
J. V. DuBois..........	Col. 1st Mo. Light Arty...........	Oct. 4, 1862, to Oct. 14, 1862.

7th Illinois Infy......July, 1862	From 3-Brig. 2-Div. Dist. W. Tenn.	To 3-Brig. Dist. Corinth 13-Corps..	Nov.,	1862
50th Illinois Infy......July, 1862	From 3-Brig. 2-Div. Dist. W. Tenn.	To 3-Brig. Dist. Corinth 13-Corps..	Nov.,	1862
52d Illinois Infy......July, 1862	From 3-Brig. 2-Div. Dist. W. Tenn.	To 1-Brig. 2-Div. Dist. Corinth....	Sept.,	1862
57th Illinois Infy......July, 1862	From 3-Brig. 2-Div. Dist. W. Tenn.	To 3-Brig. Dist. Corinth 13-Corps..	Nov.,	1862
9th Illinois Infy......Sept., 1862	From 2-Brig. 2-Div. Dist. Corinth.	To 2-Brig. 2-Div. Dist. Corinth....	Oct.,	1862
2d Iowa Infy..........Sept., 1862	From 1-Brig. 2-Div. Dist. Corinth.	To 1-Brig. 2-Div. Dist. Corinth....	Oct.,	1862
7th Iowa Infy..........Sept., 1862	From 1-Brig. 2-Div. Dist. Corinth.	To 2-Brig. 2-Div. Dist. Corinth....	Oct.,	1862
14th Missouri Infy......Sept., 1862	From 2-Brig. 2-Div. Dist. Corinth.	To Unattached Dist. Corinth 13-C.	Nov.,	1862

ARTILLERY.—

Batty. D, 1st Missouri...July, 1862	From Arty. 2-Div. Dist. West Tenn.	To Arty. Dist. Corinth 13-Corps...	Nov.,	1862
Batty. H, 1st Missouri...July, 1862	From Arty. 2-Div. Dist. West Tenn.	To Arty. Dist. Corinth 13-Corps...	Nov.,	1862
Batty. I, 1st Missouri...July, 1862	From Arty. 2-Div. Dist. West Tenn.	To Arty. Dist. Corinth 13-Corps...	Nov.,	1862
Batty. K, 1st Missouri...July, 1862	From Arty. 2-Div. Dist. West Tenn.	To Arty. Dist. Corinth 13-Corps...	Nov.,	1862

CAVALRY.—

5th Ohio (3d Bat'n).....July, 1862	From Cav. 3-Div. Dist. West Tenn.	To Cav. Dist. Corinth 13-Corps....	Nov.,	1862

6th DIVISION.— COMMANDERS.

T. J. McKean..........	Brigadier General.................	July 24, 1862, to Sept. 21, 1862.
John McArthur........	Brigadier General.................	Sept. 21, 1862, to Oct. 3, 1862.
T. J. McKean..........	Brigadier General.................	Oct. 3, 1862, to Oct. 6, 1862.
John McArthur........	Brigadier General.................	Oct. 6, 1862, to Nov. 1, 1862.

1st BRIGADE.— COMMANDERS.

John McArthur........	Brigadier General.................	July 24, 1862, to Sept. 21, 1862.
John Allen............	Colonel	Sept. 21, 1862, to Oct. 3, 1862.
John McArthur........	Brigadier General.................	Oct. 3, 1862, to Oct. 6, 1862.
John Allen............	Colonel	Oct. 6, 1862, to Nov. 1, 1862.

21st Missouri Infy....July, 1862	From 1-Brig. 6-Div. Dist. W. Tenn.	To Dist. Columbus 13-Corps.......	Nov.,	1862
25th Missouri Infy......July, 1862	From 1-Brig. 6-Div. Dist. W. Tenn.	To Dept. Missouri................	Sept.,	1862
16th Wisconsin Infy....July, 1862	From 1-Brig. 6-Div. Dist. W. Tenn.	To 1-Brig. 6-Div. L. W. 13-Corps..	Nov.,	1862
17th Wisconsin Infy....July, 1862	From 1-Brig. 6-Div. Dist. W. Tenn.	To 2-Brig. 6-Div. L. W. 13-Corps..	Nov.,	1862
1st Kansas Infy........Sept., 1862	From Dist. Columbus..............	To 1-Brig. 6-Div. L. W. 13-Corps.	Nov.,	1862

2d BRIGADE.— COMMANDER.

John M. Oliver........	Col. 15th Michigan Infy...........	July 24, 1862, to Nov. 1, 1862.

15th Michigan Infy......July, 1862	From 2-Brig. 6-Div. Dist. W. Tenn.	To 2-Brig. 6-Div. L. W. 13-Corps..	Nov.,	1862
18th Missouri Infy......July, 1862	From 2-Brig. 6-Div. Dist. W. Tenn.	To 2-Brig. 6-Div. L. W. 13-Corps..	Nov.,	1862
18th Wisconsin Infy......July, 1862	From 2-Brig. 6-Div. Dist. W. Tenn.	To 2-Brig. 6-Div. L. W. 13-Corps..	Nov.,	1862
14th Wisconsin Infy.....Aug., 1862	From Unass'd Pittsburg Landing..	To 2-Brig. 6-Div. L. W. 13-Corps..	Nov.,	1862

3d BRIGADE.— COMMANDERS.

M. M. Crocker.........	Col. 13th Iowa Infy...............	July 24, 1862, to Nov. 1, 1862.	
H. T. Reed............	Colonel	Temporarily, in Oct.	

11th Iowa Infy.....July, 1862	From 3-Brig. 6-Div. Dist. W. Tenn.	To 3-Brig. 6-Div. L. W. 13-Corps..	Nov.,	1862
13th Iowa Infy.....July, 1862	From 3-Brig. 6-Div. Dist. W. Tenn.	To 3-Brig. 6-Div. L. W. 13-Corps..	Nov.,	1862
15th Iowa Infy.....July, 1862	From 3-Brig. 6-Div. Dist. W. Tenn.	To 3-Brig. 6-Div. L. W. 13-Corps..	Nov.,	1862
16th Iowa Infy.....July, 1862	From 3-Brig. 6-Div. Dist. W. Tenn.	To 3-Brig. 6-Div. L. W. 13-Corps..	Nov.,	1862

ARTILLERY.—

Batty. F, 2d Illinois.....July, 1862	From Arty. 6-Div. Dist. West Tenn.	To Arty. 6-Div. L. W. 13-Corps....	Nov.,	1862
1st Minnesota Batty.....July, 1862	From Arty. 6-Div. Dist. West Tenn.	To Arty. 6-Div. L. W. 13-Corps....	Nov.,	1862
3d Ohio Batty.........July, 1862	From Arty. 6-Div. Dist. West Tenn.	To Arty. 6-Div. R. W. 13-Corps....	Nov.,	1862
5th Ohio Batty.........July, 1862	From Arty. 6-Div. Dist. West Tenn.	To Arty. 6-Div. L. W. 13-Corps....	Nov.,	1862
10th Ohio Batty........July, 1862	From Arty. 6-Div. Dist. West Tenn.	To Arty. 6-Div. L. W. 13-Corps....	Nov.,	1862

CAVALRY.—

11th Illinois Cav.......July, 1862	From Cav. 6-Div. Dist. West Tenn.	To Cav. Dist. Jackson 13-Corps..	Nov.,	1862

UNATTACHED DISTRICT CORINTH.—

1st U. S. Infy...........July, 1862	From Unassigned Army Miss......	To Unatt. Dist. Corinth 13-Corps..	Nov.,	1862
64th Ill. (Yates' S. S.)...July, 1862	From Unassigned Army Miss......	To Unatt. Dist. Corinth 13-Corps..	Nov.,	1862
Lochbieller's Ky. Engrs...July, 1862	From Unassigned Army Miss......	To Unatt. Dist. Corinth 13-Corps..	Nov.,	1862
Jenk's Illinois Cavalry..Sept., 1862	From Unassigned Army Miss......	To Unatt. Dist. Corinth 13-Corps..	Nov.,	1862

DISTRICT OF MEMPHIS.—Designated 1st Division District of West Tennessee Sept. 24, 1862. Transferred to Dept. of Tennessee as District of Memphis, 13th Army Corps, Oct. 26, 1862.

COMMANDER.

W. T. Sherman........	Brigadier General.................	July 21, 1862, to Oct. 26, 1862.	

4th DIVISION.—Transferred to Dist. Jackson Sept., 1862.

COMMANDER.

S. A. Hurlbut.........	Major General....................	July, 1862, to Sept., 1862.	

1st BRIGADE.— COMMANDER.

J. G. Lauman.........	Brigadier General.................	July, 1862, to Sept., 1862.	

28th Illinois Infy......July, 1862	From 1-Brig. 4-Div. Dist. W. Tenn.	To 1-Brig. 4-Div. Dist. Jackson....	Sept.,	1862
32d Illinois Infy.......July, 1862	From 1-Brig. 4-Div. Dist. W. Tenn.	To 1-Brig. 4-Div. Dist. Jackson....	Sept.,	1862
41st Illinois Infy.......July, 1862	From 1-Brig. 4-Div. Dist. W. Tenn.	To 1-Brig. 4-Div. Dist. Jackson....	Sept.,	1862
53d Illinois Infy.......July, 1862	From 1-Brig. 4-Div. Dist. W. Tenn.	To 1-Brig. 4-Div. Dist. Jackson....	Sept.,	1862
3d Iowa Infy...........July, 1862	From 1-Brig. 4-Div. Dist. W. Tenn.	To 1-Brig. 4-Div. Dist. Jackson....	Sept.,	1862

2d BRIGADE.— COMMANDER.

Jas. C. Veatch.........	Brigadier General.................	July, 1862, to Sept., 1862.	

14th Illinois Infy......July, 1862	From 2-Brig. 4-Div. Dist. W. Tenn.	To 2-Brig. 4-Div. Dist. Jackson....	Sept.,	1862
15th Illinois Infy......July, 1862	From 2-Brig. 4-Div. Dist. W. Tenn.	To 2-Brig. 4-Div. Dist. Jackson....	Sept.,	1862
46th Illinois Infy......July, 1862	From 2-Brig. 4-Div. Dist. W. Tenn.	To 2-Brig. 4-Div. Dist. Jackson....	Sept.,	1862
25th Indiana Infy......July, 1862	From 2-Brig. 4-Div. Dist. W. Tenn.	To 2-Brig. 4-Div. Dist. Jackson....	Sept.,	1862
52d Indiana Infy......July, 1862	From 2-Brig. 4-Div. Dist. W. Tenn.	To 2-Brig. 4-Div. Dist. Jackson....	Sept.,	1862
53d Indiana Infy......July, 1862	From 2-Brig. 4-Div. Dist. W. Tenn.	To 2-Brig. 4-Div. Dist. Jackson....	Sept.,	1862

ARTILLERY.—

Batty. L, 2d Illinois.....July, 1862	From Arty. 4-Div. Dist. West Tenn.	To Arty. 4-Div. Dist. Jackson.....	Sept.,	1862
Batty. C, 1st Missouri...July, 1862	From Arty. 4-Div. Dist. West Tenn.	To Arty. 4-Div. Dist. Jackson.....	Sept.,	1862
7th Ohio Batty.........July, 1862	From Arty. 4-Div. Dist. West Tenn.	To Arty. 4-Div. Dist. Jackson.....	Sept.,	1862
15th Ohio Batty........July, 1862	From Arty. 4-Div. Dist. West Tenn.	To Arty. 4-Div. Dist. Jackson.....	Sept.,	1862

CAVALRY.—

5th Ohio, 1st & 2d Bat'ns.July, 1862	From Cav. 3-Div. Dist. West Tenn.	To Cav. 4-Div. Dist. Jackson......	Sept.,	1862

5th DIVISION.— COMMANDER.

W. T. Sherman........	Brigadier General.................	July 21, 1862, to Oct. 26, 1862.	

1st BRIGADE.— COMMANDER.

M. L. Smith...........	Brigadier General.................	July 21, 1862, to Oct. 26, 1862.	

55th Illinois Infy......July, 1862	From 1-Brig. 5-Div. Dist. W. Tenn.	To 1-B. Dist. Memphis R. W. 13-C.	Nov.,	1862
6th Missouri Infy......July, 1862	From 1-Brig. 5-Div. Dist. W. Tenn.	To 1-B. Dist. Memphis R. W. 13-C.	Nov.,	1862
8th Missouri Infy......July, 1862	From 1-Brig. 5-Div. Dist. W. Tenn.	To 1-B. Dist. Memphis R. W. 13-C.	Nov.,	1862
54th Ohio Infy.........July, 1862	From 1-Brig. 5-Div. Dist. W. Tenn.	To 1-B. Dist. Memphis R. W. 13-C.	Nov.,	1862
57th Ohio Infy.........July, 1862	From 1-Brig. 5-Div. Dist. W. Tenn.	To 1-B. Dist. Memphis R. W. 13-C.	Nov.,	1862

2d BRIGADE.— COMMANDER.

J. A. McDowell........	Col. 6th Iowa Infy...............	July 21, 1862, to Oct. 26, 1862.	

40th Illinois Infy......July, 1862	From 2-Brig. 5-Div. Dist. W. Tenn.	To 2-B. Dist. Memphis R. W. 13-C.	Nov.,	1862
6th Iowa Infy.........July, 1862	From 2-Brig. 5-Div. Dist. W. Tenn.	To 2-B. Dist. Memphis R. W. 13-C.	Nov.,	1862
46th Ohio Infy.........July, 1862	From 2-Brig. 5-Div. Dist. W. Tenn.	To 2-B. Dist. Memphis R. W. 13-C.	Nov.,	1862
77th Ohio Infy.........July, 1862	From 2-Brig. 5-Div. Dist. W. Tenn.	To Alton, Ill....................	Aug.,	1862

3d BRIGADE.— COMMANDER.

J. W. Denver..........	Brigadier General.................	July 21, 1862, to Oct. 26, 1862.	

48th Ohio Infy.........July, 1862	From 3-Brig. 5-Div. Dist. W. Tenn.	To 3-B. Dist. Memphis R. W. 13-C.	Nov.,	1862
53d Ohio Infy.........July, 1862	From 3-Brig. 5-Div. Dist. W. Tenn.	To 3-B. Dist. Memphis R. W. 13-C.	Nov.,	1862
70th Ohio Infy.........July, 1862	From 3-Brig. 5-Div. Dist. W. Tenn.	To 3-B. Dist. Memphis R. W. 13-C.	Nov.,	1862
72d Ohio Infy.........July, 1862	From 3-Brig. 5-Div. Dist. W. Tenn.	To 3-B. Dist. Memphis R. W. 13-C.	Nov.,	1862

CAVALRY.—

4th Illinois Cav.........July, 1862	From 5-Div. Dist. West Tenn......	To Dist. Columbus 13-Corps.......	Nov.,	1862
6th Illinois (5 Cos.)...July, 1862	From Dist. Columbus.............	To Dist. Memphis R. W. 13-Corps..	Nov.,	1862
11th Illinois (4 Cos.)...July, 1862	From 3-Div. Dist. West Tenn......	To Dist. Columbus 13-Corps.......	Nov.,	1862
Thielman's Illinois ......July, 1862	From 5-Div. Dist. West Tenn......	To Dist. Memphis R. W. 13-Corps..	Nov.,	1862

ARTILLERY.—

6th Indiana Batty.......July, 1862	From Arty. 5-Div. Dist. West Tenn.	To Dist. Memphis R. W. 13-Corps..	Nov.,	1862
Batty. A, 1st Illinois....July, 1862	From Arty. 3-Div. Dist. West Tenn.	To Dist. Memphis R. W. 13-Corps..	Nov.,	1862
Batty. B, 1st Illinois....July, 1862	From Arty. 5-Div. Dist. West Tenn.	To Dist. Memphis R. W. 13-Corps..	Nov.,	1862
Batty. E, 1st Illinois....July, 1862	From Arty. 5-Div. Dist. West Tenn.	To Dist. Memphis R. W. 13-Corps..	Nov.,	1862
Batty. F, 1st Illinois....July, 1862	From Arty. 5-Div. Dist. West Tenn.	To Dist. Memphis R. W. 13-Corps..	Nov.,	1862
Batty. H, 1st Illinois....July, 1862	From Arty. 5-Div. Dist. West Tenn.	To Dist. Memphis R. W. 13-Corps..	Nov.,	1862
Batty. I, 1st Illinois....July, 1862	From Arty. 5-Div. Dist. West Tenn.	To Dist. Memphis R. W. 13-Corps..	Nov.,	1862
Cogswell's Ill. Batty....July, 1862	From Arty. 3-Div. Dist. West Tenn.	To Dist. Memphis R. W. 13-Corps..	Nov.,	1862
8th Ohio Batty.........July, 1862	From Arty. 5-Div. Dist. West Tenn.	To Dist. Memphis R. W. 13-Corps..	Nov.,	1862

DISTRICT OF MISSISSIPPI.—Designated 4th Division, District of West Tennessee, Sept. 24, 1862. Transferred to Dept. of the Tennessee as District of Columbus, 13-Corps, Oct. 26, 1862.

COMMANDERS.

I. F. Quimby	Brigadier General	July 24, 1862, to Sept. 29, 1862.
G. M. Dodge	Brigadier General	Sept. 29, 1862, to Oct. 5, 1862.
T. A. Davies	Brigadier General	Oct. 5, 1862, to Oct. 30, 1862.

DISTRICT OF COLUMBUS.—

54th Illinois Infy	Apr., 1862	From Dist. of Cairo	To Jackson Dist. Columbus 13-Corps.	Nov.,	1862
62d Illinois Infy	Apr., 1862	From Dist. of Cairo	To Jackson Dist. Columbus 13-Corps.	Nov.,	1862
34th Indiana Infy	June, 1862	From 1-Brig. 3-Div. Army Miss.	To Dist. Eastern Ark	July,	1862
1st Kansas Infy	June, 1862	From Dept. of Kansas	To 1-Brig. 6-Div. Dist. Corinth	Sept.,	1862
5th Missouri Infy	June, 1862	From Dept. Missouri	To Dept. Missouri	Nov.,	1862
12th Missouri Infy	June, 1862	From Dept. Kansas	To 2-Brig. 4-Div. Dist. Jackson	Oct.,	1862
13th Wisconsin Infy	June, 1862	From Dept. Kansas	To Garrison Forts Henry & Donelson	Aug.,	1862
71st Illinois Infy	Aug., 1862	From Dist. Cairo	No change to Muster Out	Oct.,	1862
72d Illinois Infy	Sept., 1862	From New Organization	To 1-Brig. 7-Div. L. W. 13th Corps.	Nov.,	1862
76th Illinois Infy	Sept., 1862	From New Organization	To 2-Brig. 4-Div. Dist. Jackson	Oct.,	1862
81st Illinois Infy	Sept., 1862	From New Organization	To 1-Brig. 3-Div. R. W. 13-Corps.	Nov.,	1862
83d Illinois Infy	Sept., 1862	From New Organization	To Dist. Columbus 13-Corps	Nov.,	1862
2d Illinois Cav	July, 1862	From Dist. of Cairo	To 1-Brig. Cav. Div. 13-Corps	Nov.,	1862
6th Ill. Cav. (5 Cos.)	July, 1862	From Dist. of Cairo	To 3-Brig. Cav. Div. 13-Corps	Nov.,	1862
Hutchins' Ill. Cav	July, 1862	From New Organization	To Stewart's Ill. Cav. Dist. Jackson	July,	1862
Batty. K, 1st Ill. L. A.	Apr., 1862	From Dist. Cairo	To Dist. Columbus 13-Corps	Nov.,	1862
Batty. G, 2d Ill. L. A.	July, 1862	From Fort Holt, Ky.	To Dist. Columbus 13-Corps	Nov.,	1862
Batty. H, 2d Ill. L. A.	July, 1862	From Fort Holt, Ky.	To Dist. Columbus 13-Corps	Nov.,	1862
Batty. H, 1st Mich. L. A.	July, 1862	From Arty. Div. Army Miss.	To Arty. 3-Div. R. W. 13-Corps	Nov.,	1862
Batty. C, 2d Ill. L. A.	July, 1862	From Unassigned Dist. West Tenn.	To Dist. Columbus 13-Corps	Nov.,	1862
7th Wisconsin Batty.	July, 1862	From Arty. Div. Army Miss.	To Dist. Columbus 13-Corps	Nov.,	1862

DISTRICT OF CAIRO.—

COMMANDERS.

W. K. Stong	Brigadier General	July, 1862, to Aug. 12, 1862.
J. M. Tuttle	Brigadier General	Aug. 12, 1862, to Nov. 17, 1862.

63d Illinois Infy	July, 1862	From Henderson, Ky.	To 4-Brig. 1-Div. Dist. West Tenn.	Sept.,	1862
71st Illinois Infy	July, 1862	From New Organization	To Dist. Columbus Dist. West Tenn.	Sept.,	1862
71st Ohio Infy	July, 1862	From Garrison Fort Donelson	To Dist. Columbus 13-Corps	Nov.,	1862
Batty. K, 1st Ill. L. A.	July, 1862	From Unassigned Dist. West Tenn.	To Dist. Columbus 13-Corps	Nov.,	1862
Batty. C, 2d Ill. L. A.	July, 1862	From Unassigned Dist. West Tenn.	To Fort Donelson, Tenn.	Nov.,	1862
5th Iowa Cav	July, 1862	From Unassigned Ft. Donelson, Tenn.	To Dist. Columbus 13-Corps	Nov.,	1862
4th Ohio Indpt. Co. Cav	July, 1862	From Headquarters Dept. Miss.	To Dist. Jackson Dist. West Tenn.	Sept.,	1862
Ford's Ill. Co. Cav	July, 1862	From Dist. Columbus, Dist. W. Tenn.	To Dist. Corinth 13-Corps	Nov.,	1862

ENGINEER BRIGADE, DIST. WEST TENN.—

COMMANDER.

J. B. McPherson	Brigadier General	June 4, 1862, to Oct. 4, 1862.

1st Mich. Eng. and Mech.	June, 1862	From Unatt. Dist. West Tenn.	To Dept. of the Cumberland	Oct.,	1862
Engr. Regt. of the West.	June, 1862	From Unatt. Army Miss.	To Dist. of Columbus 13-Corps	Nov.,	1862

Department and Army of the Tennessee

Created Oct. 16, 1862, to include Cairo, Fort Henry, Fort Donelson, Northern Mississippi and portions of Kentucky and Tennessee west of the Tennessee river. The troops of this Department were designated as the 13th Army Corps, by G. O. 168, A. G. O., Oct., 24, 1862, but were reorganized on Dec. 18, 1862, into the 13th, 15th, 16th and 17th Army Corps.

COMMANDERS.

U. S. Grant	Major General	Oct. 16, 1862, to Oct. 24, 1863.	
W. T. Sherman	Major General	Oct. 24, 1863, to Mch. 26, 1864.	
Jas. B. McPherson	Major General	Mch. 26, 1864, to July 22, 1864.	Killed.
John A. Logan	Major General	July 22, 1864, to July 27, 1864.	
O. O. Howard	Major General	July 27, 1864, to May 19, 1865.	
John A. Logan	Major General	May 19, 1865, to Aug. 1, 1865.	

DISTRICT OF MEMPHIS, 13th ARMY CORPS.—

COMMANDERS.

W. T. Sherman	Major General	Oct. 24, 1862, to Nov. 25, 1862.
S. A. Hurlbut	Major General	Nov. 25, 1862, to Dec. 22, 1862.

1st BRIGADE.—

COMMANDER.

M. L. Smith	Brigadier General	Oct. 25, 1862, to Nov. 12, 1862.

113th Illinois Infy	Oct., 1862	From New Organization	To 1-Brig. 2-Div. Dist. Memphis	Nov.,	1862
120th Illinois Infy	Oct., 1862	From New Organization	To 1-Brig. 2-Div. Dist. Memphis	Nov.,	1862
6th Missouri Infy	Oct., 1862	From 1-Brig. 5-Div. Dist. Memphis.	To 1-Brig. 2-Div. Dist. Memphis	Nov.,	1862
8th Missouri Infy	Oct., 1862	From 1-Brig. 5-Div. Dist. Memphis.	To 1-Brig. 2-Div. Dist. Memphis	Nov.,	1862
54th Ohio Infy	Oct., 1862	From 1-Brig. 5-Div. Dist. Memphis.	To 1-Brig. 2-Div. Dist. Memphis	Nov.,	1862

2d BRIGADE.—

COMMANDER.

J. W. Denver	Brigadier General	Oct. 25, 1862, to Nov. 12, 1862.

40th Illinois Infy	Oct., 1862	From 2-Brig. 5-Div. Dist. Memphis.	To 1-Brig. 1-Div. Dist. Memphis	Nov.,	1862
12th Indiana Infy	Oct., 1862	Prisoners of War	To 1-Brig. 1-Div. Dist. Memphis	Nov.,	1862
100th Indiana Infy	Oct., 1862	From New Organization	To 1-Brig. 1-Div. Dist. Memphis	Nov.,	1862
6th Iowa Infy	Oct., 1862	From 2-Brig. 5-Div. Dist. Memphis.	To 1-Brig. 1-Div. Dist. Memphis	Nov.,	1862
46th Ohio Infy	Oct., 1862	From 2-Brig. 5-Div. Dist. Memphis.	To 1-Brig. 1-Div. Dist. Memphis	Nov.,	1862
13th U. S. Infy	Oct., 1862	From Alton, Ill.	To 1-Brig. 1-Div. Dist. Memphis	Nov.,	1862

3d BRIGADE.—

COMMANDER.

J. R. Cockerill	Col. 70th Ohio Infy	Oct. 26, 1862, to Nov. 12, 1862.

97th Indiana Infy	Oct., 1862	From Dist. Louisville, Ky., D. Ohio.	To 2-B. 1-Div. Dist. Memphis 13-C.	Nov.,	1862
99th Indiana Infy	Oct., 1862	From Dist. Louisville, Ky., D. Ohio.	To 2-B. 1-Div. Dist. Memphis 13-C.	Nov.,	1862
48th Ohio Infy	Oct., 1862	From 3-Brig. 5-Div. Dist. Memphis.	To 2-B. 1-Div. Dist. Memphis 13-C.	Nov.,	1862
53d Ohio Infy	Oct., 1862	From 3-Brig. 5-Div. Dist. Memphis.	To 2-B. 1-Div. Dist. Memphis 13-C.	Nov.,	1862
70th Ohio Inffy	Oct., 1862	From 3-Brig. 5-Div. Dist. Memphis.	To 2-B. 1-Div. Dist. Memphis 13-C.	Nov.,	1862

4th BRIGADE.— COMMANDER.

David Stuart	Col. 55th Illinois Infy	Oct. 26, 1862, to Nov. 12, 1862.	
55th Illinois Infy	Oct., 1862	From 1-Brig. 5-Div. Dist. Memphis..	To 2-B. 2-Div. Dist. Memphis 13-C.	Nov., 1862
116th Illinois Infy	Oct., 1862	From New Organization	To 2-B. 2-Div. Dist. Memphis 13-C.	Nov., 1862
127th Illinois Infy	Oct., 1862	From New Organization	To 2-B. 2-Div. Dist. Memphis 13-C.	Nov., 1862
83rd Indiana Infy	Oct., 1862	From New Organization	To 2-B. 2-Div. Dist. Memphis 13-C.	Nov., 1862
57th Ohio Infy	Oct., 1862	From 1-Brig. 5-Div. Dist. Memphis..	To 2-B. 2-Div. Dist. Memphis 13-C.	Nov., 1862

5th BRIGADE.— COMMANDER.

R. P. Buckland	Col. 72d Ohio Infy	Oct. 26, 1862, to Nov. 12, 1862.	
93d Illinois Infy	Oct., 1862	From New Organization	To 3-B. 1-Div. Dist. Memphis 13-C...	Nov., 1862
114th Illinois Infy	Oct., 1862	From New Organization	To 3-B. 1-Div. Dist. Memphis 13-C...	Nov., 1862
93d Indiana Infy	Oct., 1862	From New Organization	To 3-B. 1-Div. Dist. Memphis 13-C...	Nov., 1862
72d Ohio Infy	Oct., 1862	From 3-Brig. 5-Div. Dist. Memphis..	To 3-B. 1-Div. Dist. Memphis 13-C...	Nov., 1862
32d Wisconsin Infy	Oct., 1862	From New Organization	To 3-B. 1-Div. Dist. Memphis 13-C...	Nov., 1862

RESERVE (6th) BRIGADE.— COMMANDER.

J. G. Lauman	Brigadier General	Nov. 23, 1862, to Dec. 9, 1862.	
117th Illinois Infy	Nov., 1862	From New Organization	To Dist. Memphis 16-Corps	Dec., 1862
130th Illinois Infy	Nov., 1862	From New Organization	To Dist. Memphis 16-Corps	Dec., 1862
33d Wisconsin Infy	Nov., 1862	From New Organization	To 1-Brig. 4-Div. 17-Corps	Dec., 1862

ARTILLERY, DIST. OF MEMPHIS.—

Batty. A, 1st Illinois	Oct., 1862	From Arty. 5-Div. Dist. Memphis...	To Arty. 2-Div. Dist. Memphis 13-C.	Nov., 1862
Batty. B, 1st Illinois	Oct., 1862	From Arty. 5-Div. Dist. Memphis...	To Arty. 2-Div. Dist. Memphis 13-C.	Nov., 1862
Batty. E, 1st Illinois	Oct., 1862	From Arty. 5-Div. Dist. Memphis...	To 1-Div. Dist. Memphis 13-Corps..	Nov., 1862
Batty. F, 1st Illinois	Oct., 1862	From Arty. 5-Div. Dist. Memphis...	To 1-Div. Dist. Memphis 13-Corps..	Nov., 1862
Batty. H, 1st Illinois	Oct., 1862	From Arty. 5-Div. Dist. Memphis...	To 1-Div. Dist. Memphis 13-Corps..	Nov., 1862
Batty. I, 1st Illinois	Oct., 1862	From Arty. 5-Div. Dist. Memphis...	To 1-Div. Dist. Memphis 13-Corps..	Nov., 1862
Cogswell's Ill. Batty	Oct., 1862	From Arty. 5-Div. Dist. Memphis...	To 1-Div. Dist. Memphis 13-Corps..	Nov., 1862
Mercantile Ill. Batty	Oct., 1862	From New Organization	To 2-Div. Dist. Memphis 13-Corps..	Nov., 1862
6th Indiana Batty	Oct., 1862	From Arty. 5-Div. Dist. Memphis..	To 1-Div. Dist. Memphis 13-Corps...	Nov., 1862
8th Ohio Batty	Oct., 1862	From Arty. 5-Div. Dist. Memphis..	To 2-Div. Dist. Memphis 13-Corps...	Nov., 1862

CAVALRY.—

6th Illinois Cav	Oct., 1862	From Cav. 5-Div. Dist. Memphis....	To 3-Brig. Cav. Div. 13-Corps......	Nov., 1862
Thielman's Ill. Cav	Oct., 1862	From Cav. 5-Div. Dist. Memphis....	To 3-Brig. Cav. Div. 13-Corps......	Nov., 1862

1st DIVISION.—Organized Nov. 12, 1862. COMMANDER.

J. W. Denver	Brigadier General	Nov. 12, 1862, to Dec. 18, 1862.	

1st BRIGADE.— COMMANDER.

J. A. McDowell	Col. 6th Iowa Infy	Nov. 12, 1862, to Dec. 18, 1862.	
40th Illinois Infy	Nov., 1862	From 2-Brig. Dist. Memphis 13-C...	To 1-Brig. 1-Div. 17-Corps Tenn.....	Dec., 1862
12th Indiana Infy	Nov., 1862	From 2-Brig. Dist. Memphis 13-C...	To 1-Brig. 1-Div. 17-Corps Tenn.....	Dec., 1862
100th Indiana Infy	Nov., 1862	From 2-Brig. Dist. Memphis 13-C...	To 1-Brig. 1-Div. 17-Corps Tenn.....	Dec., 1862
6th Iowa Infy	Nov., 1862	From 2-Brig. Dist. Memphis 13-C...	To 1-Brig. 1-Div. 17-Corps Tenn.....	Dec., 1862
46th Ohio Infy	Nov., 1862	From 2-Brig. Dist. Memphis 13-C...	To 1-Brig. 1-Div. 17-Corps Tenn.....	Dec., 1862
13th U. S. Infy	Nov., 1862	From 2-Brig. Dist. Memphis 13-C...	To 1-B. 2-Div. Sherman's Yazoo Ex.	Dec., 1862

2d BRIGADE.— COMMANDER.

J. R. Cockerill	Col. 70th Ohio Infy	Nov. 12, 1862, to Dec. 18, 1862.	
97th Indiana Infy	Nov., 1862	From 1-Brig. Dist. Memphis 13-C...	To 2-Brig. 1-Div. 17-Corps Tenn....	Dec., 1862
99th Indiana Infy	Nov., 1862	From 3-Brig. Dist. Memphis 13-C...	To 2-Brig. 1-Div. 17-Corps Tenn....	Dec., 1862
48th Ohio Infy	Nov., 1862	From 3-Brig. Dist. Memphis 13-C...	To 2-B. 1-Div. Sherman's Yazoo Ex.	Dec., 1862
53d Ohio Infy	Nov., 1862	From 3-Brig. Dist. Memphis 13-C...	To 2-Brig. 1-Div. 17-Corps Tenn....	Dec., 1862
70th Ohio Infy	Nov., 1862	From 3-Brig. Dist. Memphis 13-C...	To 2-Brig. 1-Div. 17-Corps Tenn....	Dec., 1862

3d BRIGADE.— COMMANDER.

R. P. Buckland	Brigadier General	Nov. 12, 1862, to Dec. 18, 1862.	
93d Illinois Infy	Nov., 1862	From 5-Brig. Dist. Memphis 13-C...	To 3-Brig. 7-Div. 16-Corps Tenn....	Dec., 1862
114th Illinois Infy	Nov., 1862	From 5-Brig. Dist. Memphis 13-C...	To 3-Brig. 8-Div. 16-Corps Tenn....	Dec., 1862
93d Indiana Infy	Nov., 1862	From 5-Brig. Dist. Memphis 13-C...	To 3-Brig. 8-Div. 16-Corps Tenn....	Dec., 1862
72d Ohio Infy	Nov., 1862	From 5-Brig. Dist. Memphis 13-C...	To 3-Brig. 8-Div. 16-Corps Tenn....	Dec., 1862
32d Wisconsin Infy	Nov., 1862	From 5-Brig. Dist. Memphis 13-C...	To 3-Brig. 8-Div. 16-Corps Tenn....	Dec., 1862

ARTILLERY.—

Batty. E, 1st Illinois	Nov., 1862	From Arty. Dist. Memphis 13-Corps.	To 3-Brig. 8-Div. 16-Corps Tenn....	Dec., 1862
Batty. F, 1st Illinois	Nov., 1862	From Arty. Dist. Memphis 13-Corps.	To Arty. 1-Div. 17-Corps Tenn......	Dec., 1862
Batty. H, 1st Illinois	Nov., 1862	From Arty. Dist. Memphis 13-Corps.	To Arty. 1-Div. 17-Corps Tenn......	Dec., 1862
Batty. I, 1st Illinois	Nov., 1862	From Arty. Dist. Memphis 13-Corps.	To Arty. 1-Div. 17-Corps Tenn......	Dec., 1862
Cogswell's Ill. Batty	Nov., 1862	From Arty. Dist. Memphis 13-Corps.	To Arty. 1-Div. 17-Corps Tenn......	Dec., 1862
6th Indiana Batty	Nov., 1862	From Arty. Dist. Memphis 13-Corps.	To Arty. 1-Div. 17-Corps Tenn......	Dec., 1862

2d DIVISION.—Organized Nov. 12, 1862. COMMANDER.

M. L. Smith	Brigadier General	Nov. 12, 1862, to Dec. 18, 1862.	

1st BRIGADE.— COMMANDER.

Giles A. Smith	Brigadier General	Nov. 12, 1862, to Dec. 18, 1862.	
113th Illinois Infy	Nov., 1862	From 2-Brig. Dist. Memphis 13-Corps	To 2-B. 2-Div. Sherman's Yazoo Ex.	Dec., 1862
120th Illinois Infy	Nov., 1862	From 2-Brig. Dist. Memphis 13-Corps	To Dist. Memphis 16-Corps Tenn...	Dec., 1862
6th Missouri Infy	Nov., 1862	From 2-Brig. Dist. Memphis 13-Corps	To 1-B. 2-Div. Sherman's Yazoo Ex.	Dec., 1862
8th Missouri Infy	Nov., 1862	From 2-Brig. Dist. Memphis 13-Corps	To 1-B. 2-Div. Sherman's Yazoo Ex.	Dec., 1862
54th Ohio Infy	Nov., 1862	From 2-Brig. Dist. Memphis 13-Corps	To 2-B. 2-Div. Sherman's Yazoo Ex.	Dec., 1862

2d BRIGADE.— COMMANDER.

D. Stuart	Brigadier General	Nov. 12, 1862, to Dec. 18, 1862.	
55th Illinois Infy	Nov., 1862	From 4-Brig. Dist. Memphis 13-C...	To 2-B. 2-Div. Sherman's Yazoo Ex.	Dec., 1862
116th Illinois Infy	Nov., 1862	From 4-Brig. Dist. Memphis 13-C...	To 1-B. 2-Div. Sherman's Yazoo Ex.	Dec., 1862
127th Illinois Infy	Nov., 1862	From 4-Brig. Dist. Memphis 13-C...	To 2-B. 2-Div. Sherman's Yazoo Ex.	Dec., 1862
83d Indiana Infy	Nov., 1862	From 4-Brig. Dist. Memphis 13-C...	To 2-B. 2-Div. Sherman's Yazoo Ex.	Dec., 1862
57th Ohio Infy	Nov., 1862	From 4-Brig. Dist. Memphis 13-C...	To 2-B. 2-Div. Sherman's Yazoo Ex.	Dec., 1862

ARTILLERY.—

Batty. A, 1st Illinois	Nov., 1862	From Arty. Dist. Memphis 13-Corps.	To 2-Div. Sherman's Yazoo Exp....	Dec.,	1862
Batty. B, 1st Illinois	Nov., 1862	From Arty. Dist. Memphis 13-Corps.	To 2-Div. Sherman's Yazoo Exp....	Dec.,	1862
Mercantile Ill. Batty.	Nov., 1862	From Arty. Dist. Memphis 13-Corps.	To 1-Div. Sherman's Yazoo Exp....	Dec.,	1862
8th Ohio Batty.	Nov., 1862	From Arty. Dist. Memphis 13-Corps.	To 2-Div. Sherman's Yazoo Exp....	Dec.,	1862

DISTRICT OF CORINTH, 13th ARMY CORPS.—

COMMANDERS.

C. S. Hamilton	Brigadier General	Oct. 24, 1862, to Oct. 30, 1862.
I. F. Quimby	Brigadier General	Oct. 30, 1862, to Nov. 11, 1862.
G. M. Dodge	Brigadier General	Nov. 11, 1862, to Dec. 18, 1862.

1st BRIGADE.— COMMANDER.

T. W. Sweeny	Col. 52d Illinois Infy	Oct. 24, 1862, to Dec. 18, 1862.

2d Iowa Infy	Oct., 1862	From 1-Brig. 2-Div. Dist. Corinth...	To 1-Brig. Dist. Corinth 17-Corps..	Dec.,	1862
7th Iowa Infy	Oct., 1862	From 1-Brig. 2-Div. Dist. Corinth...	To 1-Brig. Dist. Corinth 17-Corps..	Dec.,	1862
52d Ill. Infy	Oct., 1862	From 1-Brig. 2-Div. Dist. Corinth...	To 1-Brig. Dist. Corinth 17-Corps..	Dec.,	1862
58th Illinois Infy. Det.	Oct., 1862	From 1-Brig. 2-Div. Dist. Corinth...	To Springfield, Ill.	Dec.,	1862
8th Iowa Infy. Det.	Oct., 1862	From 1-Brig. 2-Div. Dist. Corinth...	To Davenport, Iowa.	Dec.,	1862
12th Iowa Infy. Det.	Oct., 1862	From 1-Brig. 2-Div. Dist. Corinth...	To Davenport, Iowa.	Dec.,	1862
14th Iowa Infy. Det.	Oct., 1862	From 1-Brig. 2-Div. Dist. Corinth...	To Davenport, Iowa.	Dec.,	1862
66th Indiana Infy	Dec., 1862	From Indiana.	To 1-Brig. Dist. Corinth 17-Corps..	Dec.,	1862

2d BRIGADE.— COMMANDER.

A. Mersey	Col. 9th Illinois Infy	Oct. 24, 1862, to Dec. 18, 1862.

9th Illinois Infy	Oct., 1862	From 2-Brig. 2-Div. Dist. Corinth...	To 2-Brig. Dist. Corinth 17-Corps...	Dec.,	1862
12th Illinois Infy	Oct., 1862	From 2-Brig. 2-Div. Dist. Corinth...	To 2-Brig. Dist. Corinth 17-Corps...	Dec.,	1862
*22d Ohio Infy	Oct., 1862	From 2-Brig. 2-Div. Dist. Corinth...	To 2-Brig. Dist. Corinth 17-Corps...	Dec.,	1862
81st Ohio Infy	Oct., 1862	From 2-Brig. 2-Div. Dist. Corinth...	To 2-Brig. Dist. Corinth 17-Corps...	Dec.,	1862

*Designation changed from 14th Mo. Nov. 20, 1862.

3d BRIGADE.— COMMANDER.

M. M. Bane	Col. 50th Ill. Infy	Oct. 24, 1862, to Dec. 18, 1862.

7th Ill. Infy	Oct., 1862	From 3-Brig. 2-Div. Dist. Corinth...	To 3-Brig. Dist. Corinth 17-Corps..	Dec.,	1862
50th Ill. Infy	Oct., 1862	From 3-Brig. 2-Div. Dist. Corinth...	To 3-Brig. Dist. Corinth 17-Corps..	Dec.,	1862
57th Ill. Infy	Oct., 1862	From 3-Brig. 2-Div. Dist. Corinth...	To 3-Brig. Dist. Corinth 17-Corps..	Dec.,	1862

ARTILLERY.—

Batty. D, 1st Mo.	Oct., 1862	From Arty. 2-Div. Dist. Corinth....	To Arty. Dist. Corinth 17-Corps....	Dec.,	1862
Batty. H, 1st Mo.	Oct., 1862	From Arty. 2-Div. Dist. Corinth....	To Arty. Dist. Corinth 17-Corps....	Dec.,	1862
Batty. I, 1st Mo.	Oct., 1862	From Arty. 2-Div. Dist. Corinth....	To Arty. Dist. Corinth 17-Corps....	Dec.,	1862
Batty. K, 1st Mo.	Oct., 1862	From Arty. 2-Div. Dist. Corinth....	To Arty. Dist. Corinth 17-Corps....	Dec.,	1862

CAVALRY.—

Stewart's Ill. Battn.	Oct., 1862	From Cav. 2-Div. Dist. Corinth....	To Cav. Dist. Corinth 17-Corps.....	Dec.,	1862
Ford's Ill. Cav. Co.	Oct., 1862	From Cav. Dist. Columbus.	To 15th Ill. Cav. as Co. L.	Dec.,	1862
5th Ohio (3d Battn.)	Oct., 1862	From Cav. Dist. Corinth.	To Cav. Dist. Corinth 17-Corps....	Dec.,	1862

UNATTACHED.—

64th Ill. Infy	Oct., 1862	From Unatt. Dist. Corinth.	To Unatt. Dist. Corinth 17-Corps...	Dec.,	1862
66th Ill. Infy	Oct., 1862	From Unatt. Dist. Corinth.	To Unatt. Dist. Corinth 17-Corps...	Dec.,	1862
Jenks' Ill. Cav. Co.	Oct., 1862	From Unatt. Dist. Corinth.	To 15th Ill. Cav. as Co. I.	Dec.,	1862

DISTRICT OF JACKSON, 13th ARMY CORPS.—

COMMANDERS.

S. A. Hurlbut	Major General	Oct. 26, 1862, to Nov. 19, 1862.
J. C. Sullivan	Brigadier General	Nov. 19, 1862, to Dec. 22, 1862.

18th Ill. Infy	Oct., 1862	From 2-Br. Dist. Jackson Dist. W. T.	To 1-Brig. Dist. Jackson 16-Corps...	Dec.,	1862
29th Ill. Infy	Oct., 1862	From 3-Br. Dist. Jackson Dist. W. T.	To 1-Brig. Dist. Jackson 16-Corps...	Dec.,	1862
43d Ill. Infy	Oct., 1862	From 3-Br. Dist. Jackson Dist. W. T.	To Post Bethel Dist. Jackson 16-C..	Dec.,	1862
48th Ill. Infy	Oct., 1862	From 3-Br. Dist. Jackson Dist. W. T.	To Post Bethel Dist. Jackson 16-C..	Dec.,	1862
49th Ill. Infy	Oct., 1862	From 3-Br. Dist. Jackson Dist. W. T.	To Post Bethel Dist. Jackson 16-C..	Dec.,	1862
54th Ill. Infy	Oct., 1862	From Columbus Dist. Miss.	To 1-Brig. Dist. Jackson 16-Corps...	Dec.,	1862
61st Ill. Infy	Oct., 1862	From Unatt. Dist. J'ks'n Dist. W. T.	To Post Bolivar Dist. Jackson 16-C.	Dec.,	1862
62d Ill. Infy	Oct., 1862	From Unatt. Dist. J'ks'n Dist. W. T.	To 1-Brig. Dist. Jackson 16-Corps...	Dec.,	1862
106th Ill. Infy	Oct., 1862	From New Organization.	To 4-Brig. Dist. Jackson 16-Corps...	Dec.,	1862
109th Ill. Infy	Oct., 1862	From New Organization.	To Dist. Memphis 16-Corps.	Dec.,	1862
119th Ill. Infy	Oct., 1862	From New Organization.	To 3-Brig. Dist. Jackson 16-Corps...	Dec.,	1862
122d Ill. Infy	Oct., 1862	From New Organization.	To 4-Brig. Dist. Jackson 16-Corps...	Dec.,	1862
126th Ill. Infy	Oct., 1862	From New Organization.	To 3-Brig. Dist. Jackson 16-Corps...	Dec.,	1862
12th Mich. Infy	Oct., 1862	From Unatt. Dist. J'ks'n Dist. W. T.	To Post Bolivar Dist. Jackson 16-C.	Dec.,	1862
7th Tenn. Infy	Oct., 1862	From New Organization.	To 1-Brig. Dist. Jackson 16-Corps...	Dec.,	1862

ARTILLERY.—

Batty. D, 1st Ill.	Oct., 1862	From Arty. 1-D. Dist. Jackson W. T.	To 3-Div. R. W. 13-Corps.	Nov.,	1862
Batty. B, 2d Ill.	Oct., 1862	From Arty. Dist. Jackson Dist. W. T.	To Arty. Dist. Corinth 17-Corps....	Dec.,	1862
Batty. G, 2d Ill.	Oct., 1862	From Art. Columbus Dis. Miss. W. T.	To Arty. 3-Div. 17-Corps.	Dec.,	1862
Springfield (Ill.) Batty.	Oct., 1862	From New Organization.	To Post Bolivar Dist. Jackson 16-C.	Dec.,	1862
14th Ind. Batty.	Oct., 1862	From Arty. Dist. Jackson Dist. W. T.	To Arty. Dist. Jackson 16-Corps.	Dec.,	1862
14th Ohio Batty.	Oct., 1862	From Arty. Dist. Jackson Dist. W. T.	To Arty. Dist. Jackson 16-Corps.	Dec.,	1862
15th Ohio Batty.	Oct., 1862	From Arty. 4-D. Dist. Jackson W. T.	To Arty. 4-Div. R. W. 13-Corps.	Nov.,	1862
7th Wis. Batty.	Oct., 1862	From Art. Columbus Dis. Miss. W. T.	To Arty. Dist. Jackson 16-Corps.	Dec.,	1862

CAVALRY.—

2d Ill., Co. A	Oct., 1862	From Cav. Dist. Jackson Dist. W. T.	To Cav. Dist. Memphis 16-Corps.	Dec.,	1862
4th Ill. Cav.	Oct., 1862	From Cav. Dist. Jackson Dist. W. T.	To 1-Brig. Cav. Div. 13-Corps.	Nov.,	1862
11th Ill. Cav.	Oct., 1862	From Cav. Dist. Jackson Dist. W. T.	To Cav. Brig. Dist. Jackson 16-C...	Dec.,	1862
12th Ill., Co. H	Oct., 1862	From Cav. Dist. Jackson Dist. W. T.	To Cav. Brig. Dist. Jackson 16-C....	Dec.,	1862
4th Ohio Indpt. Cav. Co.	Oct., 1862	From Cav. Dist. Jackson Dist. W. T.	To Unatt. 4-Div. R. W. 13-Corps.	Nov.,	1862
5th Ohio (1 & 2 Battns.)	Oct., 1862	From Cav. Dist. Jackson Dist. W. T.	To 2-Brig. Cav. Div. 13-Corps.	Nov.,	1862
6th Tenn. Cav.	Oct., 1862	From Cav. Dist. Jackson Dist. W. T.	To Cav. Brig. Dist. Jackson 16-C...	Dec.,	1862
7th Tenn. Cav.	Oct., 1862	From Cav. Dist. Jackson Dist. W. T.	To Cav. Brig. Dist. Jackson 16-C...	Dec.,	1862

DISTRICT OF COLUMBUS.— COMMANDER.

T. A. Davies	Brigadier General	Nov. 1, 1862, to Dec. 22, 1862.

83d Ill. Infy	Nov., 1862	From Garrison Fort Donelson, Tenn.	To Dist. Columbus 16-Corps.	Dec.,	1862
111th Ill. Infy	Nov., 1862	From New Organization.	To Dist. Columbus 16-Corps.	Dec.,	1862
128th Ill. Infy	Nov., 1862	From New Organization.	To Dist. Columbus 16-Corps.	Dec.,	1862
52d Ind. Infy	Nov., 1862	From Dist. Miss. Dist. West Tenn.	To Dist. Columbus 16-Corps.	Dec.,	1862
35th Iowa Infy	Nov., 1862	From New Organization.	To Dist. Columbus 16-Corps.	Dec.,	1862
71st Ohio Infy	Nov., 1862	From Dist. of Cairo.	To Dist. Columbus 16-Corps.	Dec.,	1862
13th Wis. Infy	Nov., 1862	From Dist. Miss. Dist. West Tenn.	To Dist. Columbus 16-Corps.	Dec.,	1862

CAVALRY.—

5th Iowa Cav	Nov., 1862	From Dist. Miss. Dist. West Tenn..	To Dist. Columbus 16-Corps	Dec.,	1862
15th Ky. Cav	Nov., 1862	From Dist. Miss. Dist. West Tenn..	To Dist. Columbus 16-Corps	Dec.,	1862

ARTILLERY.—

Batty. K, 1st Ill	Nov., 1862	From Dist. Miss. Dist. West Tenn..	To Dist. Columbus 16-Corps	Dec.,	1862
Batty. C, 2d Ill	Nov., 1862	From Dist. Miss. Dist. West Tenn..	To Dist. Columbus 16-Corps	Dec.,	1862
Batty. H, 2d Ill	Nov., 1862	From Dist. Miss. Dist. West Tenn..	To Dist. Columbus 16-Corps	Dec.,	1862

RIGHT WING, 13th ARMY CORPS.—Discontinued Dec. 18, 1862.

COMMANDER.

J. B. McPherson	Brigadier General	Nov. 1, 1862, to Dec. 18, 1862.

3d DIVISION.—Organized Nov., 1862, from Troops in District of Jackson, District of West Tenn.

COMMANDER.

John A. Logan	Brigadier General	Nov. 1, 1862, to Dec. 18, 1862.

1st BRIGADE.— COMMANDERS.

C. C. Marsh	Col. 20th Ill. Infy	Nov., 1862, to Dec., 1862.
John E. Smith	Brigadier General	Dec., 1862, to Dec. 18, 1862.

20th Ill. Infy	Nov., 1862	From 3-Brig. Dist. Jackson W. Tenn.	To 1-Brig. 3-Div. 17-Corps	Dec.,	1862
30th Ill. Infy	Nov., 1862	From 3-Brig. Dist. Jackson W. Tenn.	To 2-Brig. 3-Div. 17-Corps	Dec.,	1862
31st Ill. Infy	Nov., 1862	From 2-Brig. Dist. Jackson W. Tenn.	To 1-Brig. 3-Div. 17-Corps	Dec.,	1862
45th Ill. Infy	Nov., 1862	From 3-Brig. Dist. Jackson W. Tenn.	To 1-Brig. 3-Div. 17-Corps	Dec.,	1862
81st Ill. Infy	Nov., 1862	From Dist. Columbus West Tenn...	To 3-Brig. 3-Div. 17-Corps	Dec.,	1862
124th Ill. Infy	Nov., 1862	From New Organization	To 1-Brig. 3-Div. 17-Corps	Dec.,	1862

2d BRIGADE.— COMMANDER.

M. D. Leggett	Col. 78th Ohio Infy	Nov. 1, 1862, to Dec. 18, 1862.

23d Ind. Infy	Nov., 1862	From Unatt. Dist. Jackson W. Tenn.	To 1-Brig. 3-Div. 17-Corps	Dec.,	1862
20th Ohio Infy	Nov., 1862	From Unatt. Dist. Jackson W. Tenn.	To 2-Brig. 3-Div. 17-Corps	Dec.,	1862
68th Ohio Infy	Nov., 1862	From Unatt. Dist. Jackson W. Tenn.	To 2-Brig. 3-Div. 17-Corps	Dec.,	1862
78th Ohio Infy	Nov., 1862	From Unatt. Dist. Jackson W. Tenn.	To 2-Brig. 3-Div. 17-Corps	Dec.,	1862

4th BRIGADE.— COMMANDER.

J. D. Stevenson	Col. 7th Mo. Infy	Nov. 1, 1862, to Dec. 18, 1862.

8th Ill. Infy	Nov., 1862	From 4-Brig. Dist. Jackson W. Tenn.	To 3-Brig. 3-Div. 17-Corps	Dec.,	1862
17th Ill. Infy	Nov., 1862	From 3-Brig. Dist. Jackson W. Tenn.	To 1-Brig. 6-Div. 16-Corps	Dec.,	1862
63d Ill. Infy	Nov., 1862	From 4-Brig. Dist. Jackson W. Tenn.	To 3-Brig. 3-Div. 17-Corps	Dec.,	1862
7th Mo. Infy	Nov., 1862	From 4-Brig. Dist. Jackson W. Tenn.	To 3-Brig. 3-Div. 17-Corps	Dec.,	1862

ARTILLERY.—

Batty. D, 1st Ill	Nov., 1862	From Arty. Dist. Jackson W. Tenn..	To Arty. 3-Div. 17-Corps	Dec.,	1862
Batty. E, 2d Ill	Nov., 1862	From Arty. Dist. Jackson W. Tenn..	To Arty. 4-Div. 17-Corps	Dec.,	1862
Batty. F, 2d Ill	Nov., 1862	From Arty. 6-Div. Dist. West Tenn.	To 1-Brig. 6-Div. 16-Corps	Dec.,	1862
Batty. H, 1st Mich	Nov., 1862	From Dist. Columbus West Tenn...	To Arty. 3-Div. 17-Corps	Dec.,	1862
3d Ohio Batty	Nov., 1862	From Arty. 6-Div. West Tenn	To Arty. 3-Div. 17-Corps	Dec.,	1862
14th Ohio Batty	Nov., 1862	From Arty. Dist. Jackson W. Tenn.	To Arty. Dist. Jackson 16-Corps	Dec.,	1862

4th DIVISION, 13th ARMY CORPS.— COMMANDERS.

G. M. Dodge	Brigadier General	Oct. 30, 1862, to Nov. 11, 1862.
T. J. McKean	Brigadier General	Nov. 11, 1862, to Dec. 9, 1862.
J. G. Lauman	Brigadier General	Dec. 9, 1862, to Dec. 18, 1862.

1st BRIGADE.— COMMANDER.

I. C. Pugh	Col. 41st Ill. Infy	Nov. 1, 1862, to Dec. 18, 1862.

41st Ill. Infy	Oct., 1862	From 1-Brig. 4-Div. Dist. Jackson.	To 1-Brig. 4-Div. 17-Corps	Dec.,	1862
53d Ill. Infy	Oct., 1862	From 1-Brig. 4-Div. Dist. Jackson.	To 1-Brig. 4-Div. 17-Corps	Dec.,	1862
3d Iowa Infy	Oct., 1862	From 1-Brig. 4-Div. Dist. Jackson.	To 1-Brig. 4-Div. 17-Corps	Dec.,	1862
33d Wis. Infy	Dec., 1862	From Res. Brig. Dist. Memphis....	To 1-Brig. 4-Div. 17-Corps	Dec.,	1862

2d BRIGADE.— COMMANDER.

Cyrus Hall	Col. 14th Ill. Infy	Nov. 1, 1862, to Dec. 18, 1862.

14th Ill. Infy	Nov., 1862	From 2-Brig. 4-Div. Dist. Jackson.	To 2-Brig. 4-Div. 17-Corps	Dec.,	1862
15th Ill. Infy	Nov., 1862	From 2-Brig. 4-Div. Dist. Jackson.	To 2-Brig. 4-Div. 17-Corps	Dec.,	1862
46th Ill. Infy	Nov., 1862	From 2-Brig. 4-Div. Dist. Jackson.	To 2-Brig. 4-Div. 17-Corps	Dec.,	1862
76th Ill. Infy	Nov., 1862	From 2-Brig. 4-Div. Dist. Jackson.	To 2-Brig. 4-Div. 17-Corps	Dec.,	1862
101st Ill. Infy	Nov., 1862	From New Organization	To 2-Brig. 4-Div. 17-Corps	Dec.,	1862

3d BRIGADE.— COMMANDER.

A. K. Johnson	Col. 28th Ill. Infy	Nov. 1, 1862, to Dec. 18, 1862.

28th Ill. Infy	Nov., 1862	From 1-Brig. 4-Div. Dist. Jackson.	To 3-Brig. 4-Div. 17-Corps	Dec.,	1862
32d Ill. Infy	Nov., 1862	From 1-Brig. 4-Div. Dist. Jackson.	To 3-Brig. 4-Div. 17-Corps	Dec.,	1862
25th Ind. Infy	Nov., 1862	From 2-Brig. 4-Div. Dist. Jackson.	To Dist. Memphis 16-Corps	Dec.,	1862
53d Ind. Infy	Nov., 1862	From 2-Brig. 4-Div. Dist. Jackson.	To 3-Brig. 4-Div. 17-Corps	Dec.,	1862
12th Wis. Infy	Nov., 1862	From 2-Brig. 4-Div. Dist. Jackson.	To 3-Brig. 4-Div. 17-Corps	Dec.,	1862

ARTILLERY.—

Batty. L, 2d Ill	Nov., 1862	From Arty. 4-Div. Dist. Jackson....	To Arty. 3-Div. 17-Corps	Dec.,	1862
9th Ind. Batty	Nov., 1862	From Arty. 4-Div. Dist. Jackson....	To Arty. 4-Div. 17-Corps	Dec.,	1862
Batty. C, 1st Mo	Nov., 1862	From Arty. 4-Div. Dist. Jackson....	To 2-Brig. 6-Div. 16-Corps	Dec.,	1862
7th Ohio Batty	Nov., 1862	From Arty. 4-Div. Dist. Jackson....	To Arty. 4-Div. 17-Corps	Dec.,	1862
15th Ohio Batty	Nov., 1862	From Arty. 4-Div. Dist. Jackson....	To Arty. 4-Div. 17-Corps	Dec.,	1862

CAVALRY.—

2d Ill. Cav	Nov., 1862	From Dist. Jackson West Tenn.....	To 1-Brig. Cav. Div. 13-Corps	Dec.,	1862
7th Ill. Cav	Nov., 1862	From Dist. Jackson West Tenn.....	To 2-Brig. Cav. Div. 13-Corps	Dec.,	1862
5th Ohio (1 & 2 Battns.)	Nov., 1862	From Dist. Jackson West Tenn.....	To 2-Brig. Cav. Div. 13-Corps	Dec.,	1862

UNATTACHED.—

4th Ohio Indpt. Cav. Co.	Nov., 1862	From Dist. Jackson West Tenn.....	To Unatt. 4-Div. 17-Corps	Dec.,	1862

LEFT WING, 13th ARMY CORPS.—Discontinued Dec. 18, 1862.

COMMANDER.

C. S. Hamilton	Brigadier General	Nov. 1, 1862, to Dec. 18, 1862.

6th DIVISION (M'ARTHUR'S), 13th ARMY CORPS.—

COMMANDER.

John McArthur	Brigadier General	Nov. 1, 1862, to Dec. 18, 1862.

1st BRIGADE.—   COMMANDER.

G. W. Deitzler............|Col. 1st Kansas Infy..............|Nov. 1, 1862, to Dec. 18, 1862.

17th Ill. Infy............Nov., 1862	From 4-Brig. Dist. Jackson.........	To 1-Brig. 6-Div. 16-Corps.........	Dec.,	1862
95th Ill. Infy............Nov., 1862	From New Organization...........	To 1-Brig. 6-Div. 16-Corps.........	Dec.,	1862
1st Kansas Infy.........Nov., 1862	From 1-Brig. 6-Div. Dist. Corinth...	To 1-Brig. 6-Div. 16-Corps.........	Dec.,	1862
21st Mo. Infy............Nov., 1862	From 1-Brig. 6-Div. Dist. Corinth...	To Dist. Columbus 16-Corps.........	Dec.,	1862
16th Wis. Infy...........Nov., 1862	From 1-Brig. 6-Div. Dist. Corinth...	To 1-Brig. 6-Div. 16-Corps.........	Dec.,	1862
17th Wis. Infy...........Nov., 1862	From 1-Brig. 6-Div. Dist. Corinth...	To 2-Brig. 6-Div. 16-Corps.........	Dec.,	1862

2d BRIGADE.—   COMMANDER.

G. Bouck ....|Col. 18th Wis. Infy..............|Nov. 1, 1862, to Dec. 18, 1862.

11th Ill. Infy............Nov., 1862	From Dist. Cairo Dist. West Tenn..	To 2-Brig. 6-Div. 16-Corps.........	Dec.,	1862
15th Mich. Infy..........Nov., 1862	From 2-Brig. 6-Div. Dist. Corinth...	To Unatt. 1-Div. 17-Corps.........	Dec.,	1862
18th Mo. Infy............Nov., 1862	From 2-Brig. 6-Div. Dist. Corinth...	To 3-Brig. Dist. Corinth 17-Corps...	Dec.,	1862
14th Wis. Infy...........Nov., 1862	From 2-Brig. 6-Div. Dist. Corinth...	To 2-Brig. 6-Div. 16-Corps.........	Dec.,	1862
18th Wis. Infy...........Nov., 1862	From 2-Brig. 6-Div. Dist. Corinth...	To 2-Brig. 6-Div. 16-Corps.........	Dec.,	1862

3d BRIGADE.—   COMMANDERS.

H. T. Reed............|Col. — Iowa Infy..............|Nov. 1, 1862, to Nov. 12, 1862.
M. M. Crocker..........|Col. 13th Iowa Infy..............|Nov. 12, 1862, to Dec. 18, 1862.

11th Iowa Infy...........Nov., 1862	From 3-Brig. 6-Div. Dist. Corinth...	To 3-Brig. 6-Div. 16-Corps.........	Dec.,	1862
13th Iowa Infy...........Nov., 1862	From 3-Brig. 6-Div. Dist. Corinth...	To 3-Brig. 6-Div. 16-Corps.........	Dec.,	1862
15th Iowa Infy...........Nov., 1862	From 3-Brig. 6-Div. Dist. Corinth...	To 3-Brig. 6-Div. 16-Corps.........	Dec.,	1862
16th Iowa Infy...........Nov., 1862	From 3-Brig. 6-Div. Dist. Corinth...	To 3-Brig. 6-Div. 16-Corps.........	Dec.,	1862
ARTILLERY.—				
Batty. F, 2d Ill.........Nov., 1862	From Arty. 6-Div. Dist. Corinth....	To 1-Brig. 6-Div. 16-Corps.........	Dec.,	1862
1st Minn. Batty.........Nov., 1862	From Arty. 6-Div. Dist. Corinth....	To 2-Brig. 6-Div. 16-Corps.........	Dec.,	1862
5th Ohio Batty..........Nov., 1862	From Arty. 6-Div. Dist. Corinth....	To Arty. 4-Div. 17-Corps.........	Dec.,	1862
10th Ohio Batty.........Nov., 1862	From Arty. 6-Div. Dist. Corinth....	To 3-Brig. 6-Div. 16-Corps.........	Dec.,	1862

7th DIVISION, 13th ARMY CORPS.—   COMMANDER.

I. F. Quimby..........|Brigadier General ....|Nov. 1, 1862, to Dec. 18, 1862.

1st BRIGADE.—   COMMANDER.

John B. Sanborn.......|Col. 4th Minn. Infy..............|Nov. 1, 1862, to Dec. 18, 1862.

72d Ill. Infy............Nov., 1862	From Dist. Columbus...........	To 1-Brig. 7-Div. 16-Corps.........	Dec.,	1862
48th Ind. Infy...........Nov., 1862	From 1-Brig. 3-Div. Army Miss.....	To 1-Brig. 7-Div. 16-Corps.........	Dec.,	1862
59th Ind. Infy...........Nov., 1862	From 1-Brig. 3-Div. Army Miss.....	To 1-Brig. 7-Div. 16-Corps.........	Dec.,	1862
4th Minn. Infy...........Nov., 1862	From 1-Brig. 3-Div. Army Miss.....	To 1-Brig. 7-Div. 16-Corps.........	Dec.,	1862

2d BRIGADE.—   COMMANDER.

E. R. Eckley...........|Col. 80th Ohio Infy..............|Nov. 1, 1862, to Dec. 18, 1862.

56th Ill. Infy............Nov., 1862	From 2-Brig. 3-Div. Army Miss....	To 2-Brig. 7-Div. 16-Corps.........	Dec.,	1862
17th Iowa Infy...........Nov., 1862	From 2-Brig. 3-Div. Army Miss..	To 2-Brig. 7-Div. 16-Corps.........	Dec.,	1862
10th Mo. Infy............Nov., 1862	From 2-Brig. 3-Div. Army Miss.....	To 2-Brig. 7-Div. 16-Corps.........	Dec.,	1862
24th Mo. Infy. (Co. E)...Nov., 1862	From 2-Brig. 3-Div. Army Miss.....	To 2-Brig. 7-Div. 16-Corps.........	Dec.,	1862
80th Ohio Infy...........Nov., 1862	From 2-Brig. 3-Div. Army Miss....	To 2-Brig. 7-Div. 16-Corps.........	Dec.,	1862

3d BRIGADE.—   COMMANDER.

G. B. Boomer..........|Col. 26th Mo. Infy..............|Nov. 1, 1862, to Dec. 18, 1862.

5th Iowa Infy...........Nov., 1862	From 1-Brig. 3-Div. Army Miss.....	To 3-Brig. 7-Div. 16-Corps.........	Dec.,	1862
10th Iowa Infy...........Nov., 1862	From 1-Brig. 3-Div. Army Miss.....	To 3-Brig. 7-Div. 16-Corps.........	Dec.,	1862
26th Mo. Infy............Nov., 1862	From 1-Brig. 3-Div. Army Miss.....	To 3-Brig. 7-Div. 16-Corps.........	Dec.,	1862
93d Ill. Infy............Nov., 1862	From New Organization...........	To 3-Brig. 7-Div. 16-Corps.........	Dec.,	1862
ARTILLERY.—				
Batty. M, 1st Mo........Nov., 1862	From 1-Brig. 3-Div. Army Miss.....	To Arty. 7-Div. 16-Corps.........	Dec.,	1862
11th Ohio Batty.........Nov., 1862	From 1-Brig. 3-Div. Army Miss.....	To Arty. 7-Div. 16-Corps.........	Dec.,	1862
6th Wis. Batty..........Nov., 1862	From 1-Brig. 3-Div. Army Miss.....	To Arty. 7-Div. 16-Corps.........	Dec.,	1862
12th Wis. Batty.........Nov., 1862	From 2-Brig. 3-Div. Army Miss.....	To Arty. 7-Div. 16-Corps.........	Dec.,	1862

8th DIVISION (STANLEY'S), 13th ARMY CORPS.—   COMMANDERS.

D. S. Stanley..........|Brigadier General ....|Nov. 1, 1862, to Nov. 11, 1862.
L. F. Ross.............|Brigadier General ....|Nov. 11, 1862, to Dec. 18, 1862.

1st BRIGADE.—   COMMANDER.

J. W. Fuller..........|Col. 27th Ohio Infy..............|Nov. 1, 1862, to Dec. 18, 1862.

27th Ohio Infy..........Nov., 1862	From 1-Brig. 2-Div. Army Miss.....	To 1-Brig. 8-Div. 16-Corps.........	Dec.,	1862
39th Ohio Infy..........Nov., 1862	From 1-Brig. 2-Div. Army Miss.....	To 1-Brig. 8-Div. 16-Corps.........	Dec.,	1862
43d Ohio Infy..........Nov., 1862	From 1-Brig. 2-Div. Army Miss.....	To 1-Brig. 8-Div. 16-Corps.........	Dec.,	1862
63d Ohio Infy..........Nov., 1862	From 1-Brig. 2-Div. Army Miss.....	To 1-Brig. 8-Div. 16-Corps.........	Dec.,	1862
Batty. C, 1st Mich. L. A..Nov., 1862	From 1-Brig. 2-Div. Army Miss.....	To 1-Brig. 8-Div. 16-Corps.........	Dec.,	1862

2d BRIGADE.—   COMMANDERS.

J. M. Loomis..........|Col. 26th Ill. Infy..............|Nov. 1, 1862, to Dec. 16, 1862.
Jos. A. Mower.........|Col. 11th Mo. Infy..............|Dec. 16, 1862, to Dec. 22, 1862.

26th Ill. Infy...........Nov., 1862	From 2-Brig. 2-Div. Army Miss....	To 2-Brig. 8-Div. 16-Corps.........	Dec.,	1862
47th Ill. Infy...........Nov., 1862	From 2-Brig. 2-Div. Army Miss.....	To 2-Brig. 8-Div. 16-Corps.........	Dec.,	1862
5th Minn. Infy...........Nov., 1862	From 2-Brig. 2-Div. Army Miss.....	To 2-Brig. 8-Div. 16-Corps.........	Dec.,	1862
11th Mo. Infy............Nov., 1862	From 2-Brig. 2-Div. Army Miss.....	To 2-Brig. 8-Div. 16-Corps.........	Dec.,	1862
8th Wis. Infy............Nov., 1862	From 2-Brig. 2-Div. Army Miss.....	To 2-Brig. 8-Div. 16-Corps.........	Dec.,	1862
2d Iowa Batty...........Nov., 1862	From 2-Brig. 2-Div. Army Miss.....	To 2-Brig. 8-Div. 16-Corps.........	Dec.,	1862
UNATTACHED ARTILLERY.—				
Batty. F, 2d U. S........Nov., 1862	From Arty. 2-Div. Army Miss......	To Arty. 8-Div. 16-Corps.........	Dec.,	1862

9th DIVISION, 13th ARMY CORPS.—   COMMANDER.

Geo. W. Morgan........|Brigadier General ....|

1st BRIGADE.—   COMMANDER.

L. A. Sheldon..........|Col. 42d Ohio Infy..............|

118th Ill. Infy..........Nov., 1862	From New Organization...........	To 1-Br. 3-Div. Sherman's Yazoo Ex.	Dec.,	1862
69th Ind. Infy...........Nov., 1862	From Indianapolis, Ind...........	To 1-Br. 3-Div. Sherman's Yazoo Ex.	Dec.,	1862
120th Ohio Infy.........Nov., 1862	From Unatt. Army Ky. Dept. Ohio.	To 1-Br. 3-Div. Sherman's Yazoo Ex.	Dec.,	1862

2d BRIGADE.— COMMANDER.

D. W. Lindsey	Col. 22d Ky. Infy.			
49th Ind. Infy.	Nov., 1862	From 3-Br. Cumb'd Div. Dept. Ohio.	To 2-Br. 3-Div. Sherman's Yazoo Ex.	Dec., 1862
7th Ky. Infy.	Nov., 1862	From 3-Br. Cumb'd Div. Dept. Ohio.	To 2-Br. 3-Div. Sherman's Yazoo Ex.	Dec., 1862
114th Ohio Infy.	Nov., 1862	From New Organization	To 2-Br. 3-Div. Sherman's Yazoo Ex.	Dec., 1862

3d BRIGADE.— COMMANDER.

J. F. DeCourcy	Col. 16th Ohio Infy.			
16th Ohio Infy.	Nov., 1862	From 4-Br. Cumb'd Div. Dept. Ohio.	To 3-Br. 3-Div. Sherman's Yazoo Ex.	Dec., 1862
42d Ohio Infy.	Nov., 1862	From 4-Br. Cumb'd Div. Dept. Ohio.	To 3-Br. 3-Div. Sherman's Yazoo Ex.	Dec., 1862
22d Ky. Infy.	Nov., 1862	From 4-Br. Cumb'd Div. Dept. Ohio.	To 3-Br. 3-Div. Sherman's Yazoo Ex.	Dec., 1862
54th Ind. Infy.	Nov., 1862	From New Organization	To 3-Br. 3-Div. Sherman's Yazoo Ex.	Dec., 1862
ARTILLERY.—				
Batty. G, 1st Mich. L. A.	Nov., 1862	From Arty. Cumb'd Div. Dept. Ohio.	To Arty. 3-Div. Sherman's Yazoo Ex.	Dec., 1862
1st Wis. Batty.	Nov., 1862	From Arty. Cumb'd Div. Dept. Ohio.	To Arty. 3-Div. Sherman's Yazoo Ex.	Dec., 1862

10th DIVISION, 13th ARMY CORPS.— COMMANDER.

A. J. Smith	Brigadier General			

1st BRIGADE.— COMMANDER.

S. G. Burbridge	Brigadier General			
16th Ind. Infy.	Nov., 1862	From Indianapolis, Ind.	To 1-Br. 1-Div. Sherman's Yazoo Ex.	Dec., 1862
60th Ind. Infy.	Nov., 1862	From Indianapolis, Ind.	To 1-Br. 1-Div. Sherman's Yazoo Ex.	Dec., 1862
67th Ind. Infy.	Nov., 1862	From Indianapolis, Ind.	To 1-Br. 1-Div. Sherman's Yazoo Ex.	Dec., 1862
83d Ohio Infy.	Nov., 1862	From 1-Brig. 1-Div. A'y Ky. Dept. O.	To 1-Br. 1-Div. Sherman's Yazoo Ex.	Dec., 1862
96th Ohio Infy.	Nov., 1862	From 1-Brig. 1-Div. A'y Ky. Dept. O.	To 1-Br. 1-Div. Sherman's Yazoo Ex.	Dec., 1862
23d Wis. Infy.	Nov., 1862	From 1-Brig. 1-Div. A'y Ky. Dept. O.	To 1-Br. 1-Div. Sherman's Yazoo Ex.	Dec., 1862

2d BRIGADE.— COMMANDER.

W. J. Landran	Col. 19th Ky. Infy.			
19th Ky. Infy.	Nov., 1862	From 2-Brig. 1-Div. A'y Ky. Dept. O.	To 2-Br. 1-Div. Sherman's Yazoo Ex.	Dec., 1862
77th Ill. Infy.	Nov., 1862	From 2-Brig. 1-Div. A'y Ky. Dept. O.	To 2-Br. 1-Div. Sherman's Yazoo Ex.	Dec., 1862
97th Ill. Infy.	Nov., 1862	From 2-Brig. 1-Div. A'y Ky. Dept. O.	To 2-Br. 1-Div. Sherman's Yazoo Ex.	Dec., 1862
108th Ill. Infy.	Nov., 1862	From 2-Brig. 1-Div. A'y Ky. Dept. O.	To 2-Br. 1-Div. Sherman's Yazoo Ex.	Dec., 1862
131st Ill. Infy.	Nov., 1862	From New Organization	To 2-Br. 1-Div. Sherman's Yazoo Ex.	Dec., 1862
ARTILLERY.—				
17th Ohio Batty.	Nov., 1862	From 1-Div. Army Ky. Dept. Ohio.	To Arty. 1-Div. Sherman's Yazoo Ex.	Dec., 1862
Mercantile Ill. Batty.	Nov., 1862	From 2-Div. Dist. Memphis 13-C.	To Arty. 1-Div. Sherman's Yazoo Ex.	Dec., 1862

11th DIVISION, 13th ARMY CORPS.—Organized from Steele's Division, District of Eastern Arkansas, Dec., 1862.

COMMANDER.

Frederick Steele	Major General			

1st BRIGADE.— COMMANDER.

Frank P. Blair, Jr.	Brigadier General			
29th Mo. Infy.	Dec., 1862	From Dept. of Mo.	To 1-Br. 4-Div. Sherman's Yazoo Ex.	Dec., 1862
30th Mo. Infy.	Dec., 1862	From Dept. of Mo.	To 1-Br. 4-Div. Sherman's Yazoo Ex.	Dec., 1862
31st Mo. Infy.	Dec., 1862	From Dept. of Mo.	To 1-Br. 4-Div. Sherman's Yazoo Ex.	Dec., 1862
32d Mo. Infy.	Dec., 1862	From Dept. of Mo.	To 1-Br. 4-Div. Sherman's Yazoo Ex.	Dec., 1862
13th Ill. Infy.	Dec., 1862	From 2-Brig. 2-Div. Dist. East. Ark.	To 1-Br. 4-Div. Sherman's Yazoo Ex.	Dec., 1862
58th Ohio Infy.	Dec., 1862	From 1-Brig. 1-Div. Dist. East. Ark.	To 1-Br. 4-Div. Sherman's Yazoo Ex.	Dec., 1862
4th Ohio Batty.	Dec., 1862	From Arty. Dist. East. Ark.	To 1-Br. 4-Div. Sherman's Yazoo Ex.	Dec., 1862

2d BRIGADE.— COMMANDER.

C. E. Hovey	Brigadier General			
25th Iowa Infy.	Dec., 1862	From 3-Brig. 1-Div. Dist. East. Ark.	To 2-Br. 4-Div. Sherman's Yazoo Ex.	Dec., 1862
31st Iowa Infy.	Dec., 1862	From 3-Brig. 1-Div. Dist. East. Ark.	To 2-Br. 4-Div. Sherman's Yazoo Ex.	Dec., 1862
3d Mo. Infy.	Dec., 1862	From 1-Brig. 1-Div. Dist. East. Ark.	To 2-Br. 4-Div. Sherman's Yazoo Ex.	Dec., 1862
12th Mo. Infy.	Dec., 1862	From 1-Brig. 1-Div. Dist. East. Ark.	To 2-Br. 4-Div. Sherman's Yazoo Ex.	Dec., 1862
17th Mo. Infy.	Dec., 1862	From 1-Brig. 1-Div. Dist. East. Ark.	To 2-Br. 4-Div. Sherman's Yazoo Ex.	Dec., 1862
76th Ohio Infy.	Dec., 1862	From 1-Brig. 1-Div. Dist. East. Ark.	To 2-Br. 4-Div. Sherman's Yazoo Ex.	Dec., 1862
Batty. F, 2d Mo. Arty.	Dec., 1862	From Arty. Dist. East. Ark.	To 2-Br. 4-Div. Sherman's Yazoo Ex.	Dec., 1862

3d BRIGADE.— COMMANDER.

John M. Thayer	Brigadier General			
4th Iowa Infy.	Dec., 1862	From 2-Brig. 2-Div. Dist. East. Ark.	To 3-Br. 4-Div. Sherman's Yazoo Ex.	Dec., 1862
9th Iowa Infy.	Dec., 1862	From 3-Brig. 1-Div. Dist. East. Ark.	To 3-Br. 4-Div. Sherman's Yazoo Ex.	Dec., 1862
26th Iowa Infy.	Dec., 1862	From 3-Brig. 1-Div. Dist. East. Ark.	To 3-Br. 4-Div. Sherman's Yazoo Ex.	Dec., 1862
30th Iowa Infy.	Dec., 1862	From 3-Brig. 1-Div. Dist. East. Ark.	To 3-Br. 4-Div. Sherman's Yazoo Ex.	Dec., 1862
34th Iowa Infy.	Dec., 1862	From 2-Brig. 1-Div. Dist. East. Ark.	To 3-Br. 4-Div. Sherman's Yazoo Ex.	Dec., 1862
1st Iowa Batty.	Dec., 1862	From Arty. Dist. East. Ark.	To 3-Br. 4-Div. Sherman's Yazoo Ex.	Dec., 1862

CAVALRY DIVISION, 13th ARMY CORPS.—Organized Nov. 26, 1862.

COMMANDER.

T. Lyle Dickey	Col. 4th Ill. Cav.	Nov. 26. 1862, to Dec. 18, 1862.	

1st BRIGADE.—Assigned to Left Wing. COMMANDER.

A. L. Lee	Col. 7th Kansas Cav.			
2d Ill. Cav.	Nov., 1862	From Cav. Dist. Jackson.	To Cav. Dist. Columbus 16-Corps.	Dec., 1862
4th Ill. Cav.	Nov., 1862	From Cav. Dist. Jackson.	To 2-Brig. Cav. Div. 16-Corps.	Dec., 1862
2d Iowa Cav. (2d Battn.)	Nov., 1862	From 1-Brig. Cav. Div. Army Miss.	To 1-Brig. Cav. Div. 16-Corps.	Dec., 1862
7th Kansas Cav.	Nov., 1862	From 2-Brig. Cav. Div. Army Miss.	To 2-Brig. Cav. Div. 16-Corps.	Dec., 1862

2d BRIGADE.—Assigned to Right Wing. COMMANDER.

E. W. Hatch	Col. 2d Iowa Cav.			
7th Ill. Cav.	Nov., 1862	From 4-Div. Dist. Jackson.	To 1-Brig. Cav. Div. 16-Corps.	Dec., 1862
2d Iowa Cav. (1st and 3d Battns.)	Nov., 1862	From 1-Brig. Cav. Div. Army Miss.	To 1-Brig. Cav. Div. 16-Corps.	Dec., 1862
5th Ohio Cav. (1st and 2d Battns.)	Nov., 1862	From Cav. Dist. Jackson.	To 2-Brig. Cav. Div. 16-Corps.	Dec., 1862

3d BRIGADE.—Assigned to Dist. of Memphis.

	COMMANDER.			
B. H. Grierson	Col. 6th Ill. Cav.			
3d Mich. Cav.............Nov., 1862	From 2-Brig. Cav. Div. Army Miss.	To Cav. Brig. Dist. Jackson 16-C...	Dec.,	1862
6th Ill. Cav.............Nov., 1862	From Cav. Dist. Memphis 13-Corps.	To 1-Brig. Cav. Div. 16-Corps......	Dec.,	1862
Thielman's Ill. Cav.......Nov., 1862	From Cav. Dist. Memphis 13-Corps..	To 2-Div. Sherman's Yazoo Exp.....	Dec.,	1862

W. T. Sherman's Yazoo Expedition

W. T. SHERMAN'S YAZOO EXPEDITION.—Organized Dec., 1862. (This Expeditionary Force was known as Major General John A. McClernand's Army of the Mississippi, Jan. 4 to Jan. 12, 1863, Steele's and Stuart's Divisions being designated as 1st and 2d Divisions, 15th Corps, under Major General W. T. Sherman; Smith's and Morgan's (Osterhaus') Divisions as 1st and 2d Divisions, 13th Corps, under Brigadier General Geo. W. Morgan, and participated in the Campaign against Arkansas Post, Ark.)

1st DIVISION.—

	COMMANDER.			
A. J. Smith	Brigadier General			

1st BRIGADE.—

	COMMANDER.			
S. G. Burbridge	Brigadier General			
16th Ind. Infy.............Dec., 1862	From 1-Brig. 10-Div. R. W. 13-Corps.	To 1-Brig. 10-Div. 13-Corps Tenn...	Jan.,	1863
60th Ind. Infy.............Dec., 1862	From 1-Brig. 10-Div. R. W. 13-Corps.	To 1-Brig. 10-Div. 13-Corps Tenn...	Jan.,	1863
67th Ind. Infy.............Dec., 1862	From 1-Brig. 10-Div. R. W. 13-Corps.	To 1-Brig. 10-Div. 13-Corps Tenn...	Jan.,	1863
83d Ohio Infy.............Dec., 1862	From 1-Brig. 10-Div. R. W. 13-Corps.	To 1-Brig. 10-Div. 13-Corps Tenn...	Jan.,	1863
96th Ohio Infy.............Dec., 1862	From 1-Brig. 10-Div. R. W. 13-Corps.	To 1-Brig. 10-Div. 13-Corps Tenn...	Jan.,	1863
23d Wis. Infy.............Dec., 1862	From 1-Brig. 10-Div. R. W. 13-Corps.	To 1-Brig. 10-Div. 13-Corps Tenn...	Jan.,	1863

2d BRIGADE.—

	COMMANDER.			
W. J. Landran	Col. 19th Ky. Infy.			
19th Ky. Infy.............Dec., 1862	From 2-Brig. 10-Div. R. W. 13-Corps.	To 2-Brig. 10-Div. 13-Corps Tenn...	Jan.,	1863
48th Ohio Infy.............Dec., 1862	From 1-Brig. Dist. Memphis 13-C...	To 2-Brig. 10-Div. 13-Corps Tenn...	Jan.,	1863
77th Ill. Infy.............Dec., 1862	From 2-Brig. 10-Div. R. W. 13-Corps.	To 2-Brig. 10-Div. 13-Corps Tenn...	Jan.,	1863
97th Ill. Infy.............Dec., 1862	From 2-Brig. 10-Div. R. W. 13-Corps.	To 2-Brig. 10-Div. 13-Corps Tenn...	Jan.,	1863
108th Ill. Infy.............Dec., 1862	From 2-Brig. 10-Div. R. W. 13-Corps.	To 2-Brig. 10-Div. 13-Corps Tenn...	Jan.,	1863
131st Ill. Infy.............Dec., 1862	From 2-Brig. 10-Div. R. W. 13-Corps.	To 2-Brig. 10-Div. 13-Corps Tenn...	Jan.,	1863
Mercantile Ill. Batty.....Dec. 1862	From Arty. 10-Div. R. W. 13-Corps.	To Arty. 10-Div. 13-Corps Tenn.....	Jan.,	1863
17th Ohio Batty..........Dec., 1862	From Arty. 10-Div. R. W. 13-Corps.	To Arty. 10-Div. 13-Corps Tenn.....	Jan.,	1863

2d DIVISION.—

	COMMANDERS.			
M. L. Smith	Brigadier General	To Dec. 28, 1862.		
D. Stuart	Brigadier General	To Jan. 4, 1863.		

1st BRIGADE.—

	COMMANDER.			
Giles A. Smith	Brigadier General			
6th Mo. Infy.............Dec., 1862	From 1-Brig. 2-Div. Dist. Mem. 13-C.	To 1-Brig. 2-Div. 15-Corps Tenn.....	Jan.,	1867
8th Mo. Infy.............Dec., 1862	From 1-Brig. 2-Div. Dist. Mem. 13-C.	To 1-Brig. 2-Div. 15-Corps Tenn.....	Jan.,	1865
113th Ill. Infy.............Dec., 1862	From 1-Brig. 2-Div. Dist. Mem. 13-C.	To 1-Brig. 2-Div. 15-Corps Tenn.....	Jan.,	1863
116th Ill. Infy.............Dec., 1862	From 1-Brig. 2-Div. Dist. Mem. 13-C.	To 1-Brig. 2-Div. 15-Corps Tenn.....	Jan.,	1867
13th U. S. Infy.............Dec., 1862	From 1-Brig. 2-Div. Dist. Mem. 13-C.	To 1-Brig. 2-Div. 15-Corps Tenn.....	Jan.,	1863

2d BRIGADE.—

	COMMANDERS.			
D. Stuart	Brigadier General	To Dec. 28, 1862.		
T. K. Smith	Col. 54th Ohio Infy.	To Jan. 4, 1863.		
54th Ohio Infy.............Dec., 1862	From 1-Brig. 2-Div. Dist. Mem. 13-C.	To 2-Brig. 2-Div. 15-Corps Tenn.....	Jan.,	1863
57th Ohio Infy.............Dec., 1862	From 2-Brig. 2-Div. Dist. Mem. 13-C.	To 2-Brig. 2-Div. 15-Corps Tenn.....	Jan.,	1863
83d Ind. Infy.............Dec., 1862	From 2-Brig. 2-Div. Dist. Mem. 13-C.	To 2-Brig. 2-Div. 15-Corps Tenn.....	Jan.,	1863
55th Ill. Infy.............Dec., 1862	From 2-Brig. 2-Div. Dist. Mem. 13-C.	To 2-Brig. 2-Div. 15-Corps Tenn.....	Jan.,	1863
127th Ill. Infy.............Dec., 1862	From 2-Brig. 2-Div. Dist. Mem. 13-C.	To 2-Brig. 2-Div. 15-Corps Tenn.....	Jan.,	1863
ARTILLERY.—				
Batty. A 1st Ill..........Dec., 1862	From Arty. 2-Div. Dist. Mem. 13-C..	To Arty. 2-Div. 15-Corps Tenn......	Jan.,	1863
Batty. B, 1st Ill..........Dec. 1862	From Arty. 2-Div. Dist. Mem. 13-C..	To Arty. 2-Div. 15-Corps Tenn......	Jan.,	1863
8th Ohio Batty..........Dec., 1862	From Arty. 2-Div. Dist. Mem. 13-C..	To Arty. 2-Div. 15-Corps Tenn......	Jan.,	1863
CAVALRY.—				
Thielman's Ill. Battn......Dec. 1862	From 3-Brig. Cav. Div. 13-Corps....	To Cav. 2-Div. 15-Corps Tenn......	Jan.,	1863

3d DIVISION.—

	COMMANDER.			
Geo. W. Morgan	Brigadier General			

1st BRIGADE.—

	COMMANDER.			
L. A. Sheldon	Col. 42d Ohio Infy.			
118th Ill. Infy.............Dec., 1862	From 1-Brig. 9-Div. R. W. 13-Corps.	To 1-Brig. 9-Div. 13-Corps Tenn.....	Jan.,	1863
69th Ind. Infy.............Dec., 1862	From 1-Brig. 9-Div. R. W. 13-Corps.	To 1-Brig. 9-Div. 13-Corps Tenn.....	Jan.,	1863
120th Ohio Infy.............Dec., 1862	From 1-Brig. 9-Div. R. W. 13-Corps.	To 1-Brig. 9-Div. 13-Corps Tenn.....	Jan.,	1863

2d BRIGADE.—

	COMMANDER.			
D. W. Lindsey	Col. 22d Ky. Infy.			
7th Ky. Infy.............Dec., 1862	From 2-Brig. 9-Div. R. W. 13-Corps.	To 2-Brig. 9-Div. 13-Corps Tenn.....	Jan.,	1863
49th Ind. Infy.............Dec., 1862	From 2-Brig. 9-Div. R. W. 13-Corps.	To 2-Brig. 9-Div. 13-Corps Tenn.....	Jan.,	1863
114th Ohio Infy.............Dec., 1862	From 2-Brig. 9-Div. R. W. 13-Corps.	To 2-Brig. 9-Div. 13-Corps Tenn.....	Jan.,	1863

3d BRIGADE.—

	COMMANDER.			
J. F. DeCourcy	Col. 16th Ohio Infy.			
16th Ohio Infy.............Dec., 1862	From 3-Brig. 9-Div. R. W. 13-Corps.	To 3-Brig. 9-Div. 13-Corps Tenn....	Jan.,	1863
42d Ohio Infy.............Dec., 1862	From 3-Brig. 9-Div. R. W. 13-Corps.	To 3-Brig. 9-Div. 13-Corps Tenn....	Jan.,	1863
54th Ind. Infy.............Dec., 1862	From 3-Brig. 9-Div. R. W. 13-Corps.	To 3-Brig. 9-Div. 13-Corps Tenn....	Jan.,	1863
22d Ky. Infy.............Dec., 1862	From 3-Brig. 9-Div. R. W. 13-Corps.	To 3-Brig. 9-Div. 13-Corps Tenn....	Jan.,	1863
ARTILLERY.—				
Batty. G, 1st Mich......Dec., 1862	From Arty. 9-Div. R. W. 13-Corps...	To Arty. 9-Div. 13-Corps Tenn......	Jan.,	1863
1st Wis. Batty..........Dec., 1862	From Arty. 9-Div. R. W. 13-Corps...	To Arty. 9-Div. 13-Corps Tenn......	Jan.,	1863

4th DIVISION.— COMMANDER.

Frederick Steele	Brigadier General			

1st BRIGADE.— COMMANDER.

Frank P. Blair, Jr.	Brigadier General			
29th Mo. Infy. .... Dec., 1862	From 1-Brig. 11-Div. R. W. 13-Corps.	To 1-Brig. 1-Div. 15-Corps Tenn....	Jan., 1863
30th Mo. Infy. .... Dec., 1862	From 1-Brig. 11-Div. R. W. 13-Corps.	To 1-Brig. 1-Div. 15-Corps Tenn....	Jan., 1863
31st Mo. Infy. .... Dec., 1862	From 1-Brig. 11-Div. R. W. 13-Corps.	To 1-Brig. 1-Div. 15-Corps Tenn....	Jan., 1863
32d Mo. Infy. .... Dec., 186	From 1-Brig. 11-Div. R. W. 13-Corps.	To 1-Brig. 1-Div. 15-Corps Tenn....	Jan., 1863
13th Ill. Infy. .... Dec., 1862	From 1-Brig. 11-Div. R. W. 13-Corps.	To 1-Brig. 1-Div. 15-Corps Tenn....	Jan., 1863
58th Ohio Infy. .... Dec., 1862	From 1-Brig. 11-Div. R. W. 13-Corps.	To 1-Brig. 1-Div. 15-Corps Tenn....	Jan., 1863
4th Ohio Batty. .... Dec., 1862	From 1-Brig. 11-Div. R. W. 13-Corps.	To Arty. 1-Div. 15-Corps Tenn......	Jan., 1863

2d BRIGADE.— COMMANDER.

C. E. Hovey	Brigadier General			
3d Mo. Infy. .... Dec., 1862	From 2-Brig. 11-Div. R. W. 13-Corps.	To 2-Brig. 1-Div. 15-Corps Tenn....	Jan., 1863
12th Mo. Infy. .... Dec., 1862	From 2-Brig. 11-Div. R. W. 13-Corps.	To 2-Brig. 1-Div. 15-Corps Tenn....	Jan., 1863
17th Mo. Infy. .... Dec., 1862	From 2-Brig. 11-Div. R. W. 13-Corps.	To 2-Brig. 1-Div. 15-Corps Tenn....	Jan., 1863
25th Iowa Infy. .... Dec., 1862	From 2-Brig. 11-Div. R. W. 13-Corps.	To 2-Brig. 1-Div. 15-Corps Tenn....	Jan., 1863
31st Iowa Infy. .... Dec., 1862	From 2-Brig. 11-Div. R. W. 13-Corps.	To 2-Brig. 1-Div. 15-Corps Tenn....	Jan., 1863
76th Ohio Infy. .... Dec., 1862	From 2-Brig. 11-Div. R. W. 13-Corps.	To 2-Brig. 1-Div. 15-Corps Tenn....	Jan., 1863
Batty. F, 2d Mo. Arty. ... Dec., 1862	From 2-Brig. 11-Div. R. W. 13-Corps.	To Arty. 2-Div. 15-Corps Tenn......	Jan., 1863

3d BRIGADE.— COMMANDER.

John M. Thayer	Brigadier General			
4th Iowa Infy. .... Dec., 1862	From 3-Brig. 11-Div. R. W. 13-Corps.	To 3-Brig. 1-Div. 15-Corps Tenn....	Jan., 1863
9th Iowa Infy. .... Dec., 1862	From 3-Brig. 11-Div. R. W. 13-Corps.	To 3-Brig. 1-Div. 15-Corps Tenn....	Jan., 1863
26th Iowa Infy. .... Dec., 1862	From 3-Brig. 11-Div. R. W. 13-Corps.	To 3-Brig. 1-Div. 15-Corps Tenn....	Jan., 1863
30th Iowa Infy. .... Dec., 1862	From 3-Brig. 11-Div. R. W. 13-Corps.	To 3-Brig. 1-Div. 15-Corps Tenn....	Jan., 1863
34th Iowa Infy. .... Dec., 1862	From 3-Brig. 11-Div. R. W. 13-Corps.	To 3-Brig. 1-Div. 15-Corps Tenn....	Jan., 1863
1st Iowa Batty. .... Dec., 1862	From 3-Brig. 11-Div. R. W. 13-Corps.	To Arty. 1-Div. 15-Corps Tenn......	Jan., 1863

Thirteenth Army Corps (New)---Department of the Tennessee

Reorganized from Old 13th Army Corps, Dept. Tennessee, by General Order No. 210, A. G. O., dated Dec. 18, 1862, to consist of the 9th and 10th Divisions, Dept. of the Tennessee, and all Troops operating on the Mississippi River below Memphis, Tenn., not included in the 15th Army Corps. (Known as 1st and 3d Divisions, Sherman's Expeditionary Corps, Dec. 18, 1862, to Jan. 4, 1863, and as 1st Corps, McClernand's Army Mississippi, Jan. 4 to 12, 1863.) Corps reorganized July 28, 1863, and transferred to Department of the Gulf Aug. 7, 1863.

COMMANDERS.

Geo. W. Morgan	Brigadier General	Jan. 4, 1863, to Jan. 31, 1863.	
J. A. McClernand	Major General	Jan. 31, 1863, to June 19, 1863.	
E. O. C. Ord	Major General	June 19, 1863, to July 28, 1863.	
C. C. Washburne	Major General	July 28, 1863, to Aug. 7, 1863.	

9th DIVISION.— COMMANDERS.

P. J. Osterhaus	Brigadier General	Jan. 4, 1863, to July 28, 1863.	
A. L. Lee	Brigadier General	Temporarily, May 17-19, 1863.	

(Division consolidated with 14th Division and designated 1st Division, July 28, 1863.)

1st BRIGADE.— COMMANDERS.

William Vandever	Brigadier General	Jan. 4, 1863, to Feb. 4, 1863.		
T. T. Garrard	Col. 7th Ky. Infy.	Feb. 4, 1863, to May 19, 1863.		
A. L. Lee	Brigadier General	May 19, 1863.		
J. Keigwin	Col. 49th Ind. Infy.	May 19, 1863, to July 28, 1863.		
69th Ind. Infy. .... Jan., 1863	From 1-Brig. 3-Div. Yazoo Exp....	To 3-Brig. 1-Div. 13-Corps Tenn....	July, 1863
120th Ohio Infy. .... Jan., 1863	From 1-Brig. 3-Div. Yazoo Exp....	To 3-Brig. 1-Div. 13-Corps Tenn....	July, 1863
118th Ill. Infy. .... Jan., 1863	From 1-Brig. 3-Div. Yazoo Exp....	To 3-Brig. 1-Div. 13-Corps Tenn....	July, 1863
49th Ind. Infy. .... Feb., 1863	From 2-Brig. 9-Div. 13-Corps......	To 3-Brig. 1-Div. 13-Corps Tenn....	July, 1863
7th Ky. Infy. .... Feb., 1863	From 2-Brig. 9-Div. 13-Corps......	To 3-Brig. 1-Div. 13-Corps Tenn....	July, 1863

2d BRIGADE.— COMMANDERS.

D. W. Lindsey	Col. 22d Ky. Infy.	Jan. 4, 1863, to Feb. 4, 1863.		
J. F. DeCourcy	Col. 16th Ohio Infy.	Feb. 4, 1863, to Feb. 9, 1863.		
L. A. Sheldon	Col. 42d Ohio Infy.	Feb. 9, 1863, to May 1, 1863.		
D. W. Lindsey	Col. 22d Ky. Infy.	May 1, 1863, to July 28, 1863.		
7th Ky. Infy. .... Jan., 1863	From 2-Brig. 3-Div. Yazoo Exp....	To 1-Brig. 9-Div. 13-Corps........	Jan., 1863
49th Ind. Infy. .... Jan., 1863	From 2-Brig. 3-Div. Yazoo Exp....	To 1-Brig. 9-Div. 13-Corps........	Jan., 1863
114th Ohio Infy. .... Jan., 1863	From 2-Brig. 3-Div. Yazoo Exp....	To 4-Brig. 1-Div. 13-Corps........	July, 1863
54th Ind. Infy. .... Feb., 1863	From 3-Brig. 9-Div. 13-Corps......	To 4-Brig. 1-Div. 13-Corps........	July, 1863
22d Ky. Infy. .... Feb., 1863	From 3-Brig. 9-Div. 13-Corps......	To 4-Brig. 1-Div. 13-Corps........	July, 1863
16th Ohio Infy. .... Feb., 1863	From 3-Brig. 9-Div. 13-Corps......	To 4-Brig. 1-Div. 13-Corps........	July, 1863
42d Ohio Infy. .... Feb., 1863	From 3-Brig. 9-Div. 13-Corps......	To 4-Brig. 1-Div. 13-Corps........	July, 1863

3d BRIGADE.—Discontinued Feb. 4, 1863. COMMANDER.

J. F. DeCourcy	Col. 16th Ohio Infy.	Jan. 4, 1863, to Feb. 4, 1863.		
54th Ind. Infy. .... Jan., 1863	From 3-Brig. 3-Div. Yazoo Exp....	To 2-Brig. 9-Div. 13-Corps........	Feb., 1863
22d Ky. Infy. .... Jan., 1863	From 3-Brig. 3-Div. Yazoo Exp....	To 2-Brig. 9-Div. 13-Corps........	Feb., 1863
16th Ohio Infy. .... Jan., 1863	From 3-Brig. 3-Div. Yazoo Exp....	To 2-Brig. 9-Div. 13-Corps........	Feb., 1863
42d Ohio Infy. .... Jan., 1863	From 3-Brig. 3-Div. Yazoo Exp....	To 2-Brig. 9-Div. 13-Corps........	Feb., 1863
ARTILLERY.—			
Batty. G, 1st Mich. ...... Jan., 1863	From 3-Div. Sherman's Yazoo Exp..	To Arty. 1-Div. 13-Corps..........	July, 1863
1st Wis. Batty. .... Jan., 1863	From 3-Div. Sherman's Yazoo Exp..	To Arty. 1-Div. 13-Corps..........	July, 1863
ENGINEERS.—			
Patterson's Ky. Co. ...... Jan., 1863	From Unatt. Dist. Corinth 13-Corps.	To Unatt. 13-Corps Gulf..........	Aug., 1863

10th DIVISION.—Designated 4th Division Aug. 7, 1863.

COMMANDER.

A. J. Smith	Brigadier General	Jan. 4, 1863, to Aug. 7, 1863.	

1st BRIGADE.—   COMMANDERS.

S. G. Burbridge	Brigadier General	Jan. 4, 1863, to July 28, 1863.
R. Owen	Col. 60th Ind. Infy	July 28, 1863, to Aug. 17, 1863.

16th Ind. Infy.........Jan., 1863	From 1-Brig. 1-Div. Yazoo Exp....	To 1-Brig. 4-Div. 13-Corps Gulf.....	Aug., 1863
60th Ind. Infy.........Jan., 1863	From 1-Brig. 1-Div. Yazoo Exp....	To 1-Brig. 4-Div. 13-Corps Gulf.....	Aug., 1863
67th Ind. Infy.........Jan., 1863	From 1-Brig. 1-Div. Yazoo Exp....	To 1-Brig. 4-Div. 13-Corps Gulf.....	Aug., 1863
83d Ohio Infy.........Jan., 1863	From 1-Brig. 1-Div. Yazoo Exp....	To 1-Brig. 4-Div. 13-Corps Gulf.....	Aug., 1863
96th Ohio Infy.........Jan., 1863	From 1-Brig. 1-Div. Yazoo Exp....	To 1-Brig. 4-Div. 13-Corps Gulf.....	Aug., 1863
23d Wis. Infy.........Jan., 1863	From 1-Brig. 1-Div. Yazoo Exp....	To 1-Brig. 4-Div. 13-Corps Gulf.....	Aug., 1863

2d BRIGADE.—   COMMANDERS.

W. J. Landran	Col. 19th Kentucky Infy	Jan. 4, 1863, to Feb. 9, 1863.
D. P. Grier	Col. 77th Illinois Infy	Feb. 9, 1863, to Mch. 9, 1863.
W. J. Landran	Col. 19th Kentucky Infy	Mch. 9, 1863, to Aug. 17, 1863.

19th Kentucky Infy.....Jan., 1863	From 2-Brig. 1-Div. Yazoo Exp....	To 2-Brig. 4-Div. 13-Corps Gulf...	Aug., 1863
48th Ohio Infy.........Jan., 1863	From 2-Brig. 1-Div. Yazoo Exp....	To 2-Brig. 4-Div. 13-Corps Gulf...	Aug., 1863
77th Illinois Infy......Jan., 1863	From 2-Brig. 1-Div. Yazoo Exp....	To 2-Brig. 4-Div. 13-Corps Gulf...	Aug., 1863
97th Illinois Infy......Jan., 1863	From 2-Brig. 1-Div. Yazoo Exp....	To 2-Brig. 4-Div. 13-Corps Gulf...	Aug., 1863
108th Illinois Infy.....Jan., 1863	From 2-Brig. 1-Div. Yazoo Exp....	To Detached Brig. Dist. N. E. La..	May, 1863
131st Illinois Infy.....Jan., 1863	From 2-Brig. 1-Div. Yazoo Exp....	To Dist. Memphis 16-Corps.....	Feb., 1863
130th Illinois Infy.....Mch., 1863	From Dist. Memphis 16-Corps.....	To 2-Brig. 4-Div. 13-Corps Gulf...	Aug., 1863
ARTILLERY.—			
Mercantile, Ill., Batty...Jan., 1863	From 1-Div. Sherman's Yazoo Exp.	To 2-Brig. 4-Div. 13-Corps Gulf...	Aug., 1863
17th Ohio Batty.........Jan., 1863	From 1-Div. Sherman's Yazoo Exp.	To 1-Brig. 4-Div. 13-Corps Gulf...	Aug., 1863

12th DIVISION.—Organized Jan. 22, 1863, from District of Eastern Arkansas. Designation changed to 3d Div. July 28, 1863.   COMMANDERS.

W. A. Gorman	Brigadier General	Jan. 22, 1863, to Feb. 8, 1863.
A. P. Hovey	Brigadier General	Feb. 8, 1863, to July 26, 1863.
A. L. Lee	Brigadier General	July 26, 1863, to July 28, 1863.

1st BRIGADE.—   COMMANDERS.

A. P. Hovey	Brigadier General	Jan. 22, 1863, to Feb. 8, 1863.
J. R. Slack	Col. 47th Indiana Infy	Feb. 8, 1863, to Feb. 20, 1863.
G. F. McGinnis	Brigadier General	Feb. 20, 1863, to July 14, 1863.
W. T. Spicely	Col. 24th Indiana Infy	July 14, 1863, to July 28, 1863.

43d Indiana Infy.........Jan., 1863	From 1-Brig. 2-Div. Dist. E. Ark.	To 1-Brig. 13-Div. 13-Corps.......	Feb., 1863
46th Indiana Infy.........Jan., 1863	From 1-Brig. 2-Div. Dist. E. Ark.	To 1-Brig. 13-Div. 13-Corps.......	Feb., 1863
47th Indiana Infy.........Jan., 1863	From 1-Brig. 2-Div. Dist. E. Ark.	To 1-Brig. 13-Div. 13-Corps.......	Feb., 1863
11th Indiana Infy.........Feb., 1863	From 3-Brig. 12-Div. 13-Corps....	To 1-Brig. 3-Div. 13-Corps.......	July, 1863
24th Indiana Infy.........Feb., 1863	From 3-Brig. 12-Div. 13-Corps....	To 1-Brig. 3-Div. 13-Corps.......	July, 1863
34th Indiana Infy.........Feb., 1863	From 3-Brig. 12-Div. 13-Corps....	To 1-Brig. 3-Div. 13-Corps.......	July, 1863
29th Wisconsin Infy.........Feb., 1863	From 3-Brig. 12-Div. 13-Corps....	To 1-Brig. 3-Div. 13-Corps.......	July, 1863
46th Indiana Infy.........Mch., 1863	From 1-Brig. 13-Div. 13-Corps....	To 1-Brig. 3-Div. 13-Corps.......	July, 1863

2d BRIGADE.—   COMMANDERS.

P. Kinney	Col. 56th Ohio Infy	Jan. 22, 1863, to Apr. 9, 1863.
J. R. Slack	Col. 47th Indiana Infy	Apr. 9, 1863, to July 28, 1863.

28th Iowa Infy.........Jan., 1863	From 2-Brig. 2-Div. Dist. E. Ark.	To 2-Brig. 3-Div. 13-Corps.......	July, 1863
35th Missouri Infy.........Jan., 1863	From 2-Brig. 2-Div. Dist. E. Ark.	To 2-Brig. 13-Div. 13-Corps.......	Feb., 1863
56th Ohio Infy.........Jan., 1863	From 2-Brig. 2-Div. Dist. E. Ark.	To 2-Brig. 3-Div. 13-Corps.......	July, 1863
24th Iowa Infy.........Feb., 1863	From 2-Brig. 13-Div. 13-Corps....	To 2-Brig. 3-Div. 13-Corps.......	July, 1863
47th Indiana Infy.........Mch., 1863	From 1-Brig. 13-Div. 13-Corps....	To 2-Brig. 3-Div. 13-Corps.......	July, 1863
87th Illinois Infy.........June, 1863	From 2-Brig. Dist. Memphis 16-C.	To 2-Brig. 3-Div. 13-Corps.......	July, 1863

3d BRIGADE.—Discontinued Feb., 1863.   COMMANDER.

G. F. McGinnis	Brigadier General	Jan. 22, 1863, to Feb., 1863.

11th Indiana Infy.........Jan., 1863	From 3-Brig. 2-Div. Dist. E. Ark..	To 1-Brig. 12-Div. 13-Corps.........	Feb., 1863
24th Indiana Infy.........Jan., 1863	From 3-Brig. 2-Div. Dist. E. Ark..	To 1-Brig. 12-Div. 13-Corps.........	Feb., 1863
34th Indiana Infy.........Jan., 1863	From 3-Brig. 2-Div. Dist. E. Ark..	To 1-Brig. 12-Div. 13-Corps.........	Feb., 1863
29th Wisconsin Infy.........Jan., 1863	From 3-Brig. 2-Div. Dist. E. Ark..	To 1-Brig. 12-Div. 13-Corps.........	Feb., 1863
ARTILLERY.—			
Batty. A, 2d Illinois.........Jan., 1863	From Arty. Dist. Eastern Ark.....	To Arty. 14-Div. 13-Corps.........	May, 1863
2d Ohio Batty.........Jan., 1863	From Arty. Dist. Eastern Ark.....	To 1-Brig. 3-Div. 13-Corps.......	July, 1863
16th Ohio Batty.........Jan., 1863	From Arty. Dist. Eastern Ark.....	To 1-Brig. 3-Div. 13-Corps.......	July, 1863
Batty. A, 1st Missouri...Mch., 1863	From Arty. 13-Div. 13-Corps......	To 2-Brig. 3-Div. 13-Corps.......	July, 1863
CAVALRY.—			
1st Indiana Cav. Co. C...Jan., 1863	From 1-B. 3-(Cav.)Div. Dist. E. Ark.	To Cav. Brig. 13-Corps Gulf.......	Aug., 1863

13th DIVISION.—Organized Jan. 22, 1863. Discontinued July 28, 1863, and transferred to the 16th Army Corps.   COMMANDERS.

Clinton B. Fisk	Brigadier General	Jan. 22, 1863, to Feb. 8, 1863.
L. F. Ross	Brigadier General	Feb. 8, 1863, to May 25, 1863.
F. Salomon	Brigadier General	May 25, 1863, to July 28, 1863.

1st BRIGADE.—   COMMANDERS.

C. W. Kittredge	Col. 36th Iowa Infy	Jan. 22, 1863, to Feb. 8, 1863.
F. Salomon	Brigadier General	Feb. 8, 1863, to May 25, 1863.
S. A. Foster	Col. 35th Missouri Infy	May 25, 1863, to June 12, 1863.
W. E. McLean	Col. 43d Indiana Infy	June 12, 1863, to July 28, 1863.

33d Iowa Infy.........Jan., 1863	From Dept. of Missouri..........	To 2-Brig. 13-Div. 13-Corps.......	Feb., 1863
36th Iowa Infy.........Jan., 1863	From Dept. of Missouri..........	To 2-Brig. 13-Div. 13-Corps.......	Feb., 1863
33d Missouri Infy.........Jan., 1863	From Dist. of St. Louis, Dept. Mo.	To 2-Brig. 13-Div. 13-Corps.......	Feb., 1863
43d Indiana Infy.........Feb., 1863	From 1-Brig. 12-Div. 13-Corps....	To 1-Brig. 13-Div. 16-Corps.......	July, 1863
46th Indiana Infy.........Feb., 1863	From 1-Brig. 12-Div. 13-Corps....	To 1-Brig. 12-Div. 13-Corps.......	Mch., 1863
47th Indiana Infy.........Feb., 1863	From 1-Brig. 12-Div. 13-Corps....	To 2-Brig. 13-Div. 13-Corps.......	Mch., 1863
28th Wisconsin Infy.........Mch., 1863	From 2-Brig. 13-Div. 13-Corps....	To 1-Brig. 13-Div. 16-Corps.......	July, 1863
35th Missouri Infy.........Mch., 1863	From 2-Brig. 13-Div. 13-Corps....	To 1-Brig. 13-Div. 16-Corps.......	July, 1863

2d BRIGADE.—   COMMANDERS.

James M. Lewis	Col. 28th Wisconsin Infy	Jan. 22, 1863, to Feb. 8, 1863.
Clinton B. Fisk	Brigadier General	Feb. 8, 1863, to June 10, 1863.
S. A. Rice	Col. 33d Iowa Infy	June 10, 1863, to July 28, 1863.

2d BRIGADE.—Continued.

24th Iowa Infy	Jan., 1863	From 2-Brig. 2-Div. Dist. E. Ark..	To 2-Brig. 12-Div. 13-Corps	Feb., 1863
29th Iowa Infy	Jan., 1863	From Dept. of Missouri	To 2-Brig. 13-Div. 16-Corps	July, 1863
28th Wisconsin Infy	Jan., 1863	From New Organization	To 1-Brig. 13-Div. 13-Corps	Mch., 1863
33d Iowa Infy	Feb., 1863	From 1-Brig. 13-Div. 13-Corps	To 2-Brig. 13-Div. 16-Corps	July, 1863
36th Iowa Infy	Feb., 1863	From 1-Brig. 13-Div. 13-Corps	To 2-Brig. 13-Div. 16-Corps	July, 1863
33d Missouri Infy	Feb., 1863	From 1-Brig. 13-Div. 13-Corps	To 2-Brig. 13-Div. 16-Corps	July, 1863
35th Missouri Infy	Feb., 1863	From New Organization	To 1-Brig. 13-Div. 13-Corps	Mch., 1863

ARTILLERY.—

Batty. A, 1st Missouri	Jan., 1863	From Arty. Dist. Eastern Ark....	To Arty. 12-Div. 13-Corps	Feb., 1863
3d Iowa Batty	Jan., 1863	From Arty. Dist. Eastern Ark....	To Arty. 13-Div. 16-Corps	July, 1863
Batty. K, 1st Missouri	June, 1863	From Arty. 1-Div. 16-Corps	To Arty. 13-Div. 16-Corps	July, 1863

14th DIVISION.—Organized March 26, 1863. Consolidated with 9th Division and designated 1st Division July 28, 1863.

COMMANDER.

Eugene A. Carr	Brigadier General	Mch. 28, 1863, to July 28, 1863.

1st BRIGADE.— COMMANDERS.

W. P. Benton	Brigadier General	Mch. 28, 1863, to May 31, 1863.
H. D. Washburn	Col. 18th Indiana Infy	May 31, 1863, to June 12, 1863.
D. Shunk	Col. 8th Indiana Infy	June 12, 1863, to July 28, 1863.

8th Indiana Infy	Mch., 1863	From 2-Brig. 1-Div. Army S. E. Mo.	To 1-Brig. 1-Div. 13-Corps	July, 1863
18th Indiana Infy	Mch., 1863	From 2-Brig. 1-Div. Army S. E. Mo.	To 1-Brig. 1-Div. 13-Corps	July, 1863
33d Illinois Infy	Mch., 1863	From 2-Brig. 1-Div. Army S. E. Mo.	To 1-Brig. 1-Div. 13-Corps	July, 1863
99th Illinois Infy	Mch., 1863	From 1-Brig. 1-Div. Army S. E. Mo.	To 1-Brig. 1-Div. 13-Corps	July, 1863
1st U. S. Infy	Mch., 1863	From Dist. Corinth 16-Corps	To Headquarters 13-Corps	July, 1863

2d BRIGADE.— COMMANDERS.

C. L. Harris	Col. 11th Wisconsin Infy	Mch. 28, 1863, to May 2, 1863.
M. K. Lawler	Brigadier General	May 2, 1863, to July 28, 1863.

21st Iowa Infy	Mch., 1863	From 2-Brig. 2-Div. Army S. E. Mo.	To 2-Brig. 1-Div. 13-Corps	July, 1863
22d Iowa Infy	Mch., 1863	From 2-Brig. 2-Div. Army S. E. Mo.	To 2-Brig. 1-Div. 13-Corps	July, 1863
23d Iowa Infy	Mch., 1863	From 2-Brig. 2-Div. Army S. E. Mo.	To 2-Brig. 1-Div. 13-Corps	July, 1863
11th Wisconsin Infy	Mch., 1863	From 1-Brig. 1-Div. Army S. E. Mo.	To 2-Brig. 1-Div. 13-Corps	July, 1863

ARTILLERY.—

Batty. A, 2d Illinois	May, 1863	From Arty. 12-Div. 13-Corps	To Arty. 1-Div. 13-Corps	July, 1863
1st Indiana Batty	Mch., 1863	From Arty. 1-Div. Army S. E. Mo.	To Arty. 1-Div. 13-Corps	July, 1863

2d CAVALRY DIVISION.—Organized Feb. 8, 1863.

COMMANDER.

C. C. Washburn	Brigadier General	Feb. 8, 1863, to Apr. 3, 1863.

1st BRIGADE.— COMMANDER.

Conrad Baker	Col. 5th Illinois Cav	Feb. 8, 1863, to Apr. 3, 1863.

5th Illinois Cav	Jan., 1863	From District of Eastern Ark	To 1-Brig. Cav. Div. Dist. E. Ark.	Apr., 1863
10th Ill. Cav. A, D, G, K.	Jan., 1863	From District of Eastern Ark	To 1-Brig. Cav. Div. Dist. E. Ark.	Apr., 1863
1st Indiana Cav	Jan., 1863	From District of Eastern Ark	To 1-Brig. Cav. Div. Dist. E. Ark.	Apr., 1863
6th Missouri Cav. 6 Cos.	Jan., 1863	From District of Eastern Ark	To Headquarters 13-Corps	Apr., 1863

2d BRIGADE.— COMMANDER.

Cyrus Bussey	Col. 3d Iowa Cav	Feb., 1863, to Apr., 1863.

2d Arkansas Cav. 4 Cos.	Jan., 1863	From District of Eastern Ark	To 2-Brig. Cav. Div. Dist. E. Ark.	Apr., 1863
9th Illinois Cav	Jan., 1863	From District of Eastern Ark	To 2-Brig. 1-Cav. Div. 16-Corps	Apr., 1863
3d Iowa Cav. (Cos. A, B, C, D, I, K)	Jan., 1863	From District of Eastern Ark	To 2-Brig. Cav. Div. Dist. E. Ark.	Apr., 1863
5th Kansas Cav	Jan., 1863	From District of Eastern Ark	To 2-Brig. Cav. Div. Dist. E. Ark.	Apr., 1863
2d Wisconsin Cav. 1 Co.	Jan., 1863	From District of Eastern Ark	To Dist. Memphis 5-Div. 16-Corps..	Apr., 1863

UNATTACHED CAVALRY.—

3d Illinois Cav	Jan., 1863	From Sherman's Yazoo Exp	To 2-Brig. 1-Cav. Div. 16-Corps Cos. B, C, D, H, I	Mch., 1863
			To Cav. B. 13-C. Gulf, A, E, G, K, L	Aug., 1863

GENERAL HEADQUARTERS.—

2d Illinois Cav. 6 Cos.	Jan., 1863	From Dist. Columbus 16-Corps....	To Cav. Brig. 13-Corps Gulf	Aug., 1863
6th Missouri Cav	Jan., 1863	From Sherman's Yazoo Exp	To Cav. Brig. 13-Corps Gulf	Aug., 1863

DISTRICT OF EASTERN ARKANSAS.— COMMANDERS.

Willis A. Gorman	Brigadier General	Dec. 22, 1862, to Feb. 8, 1863.
B. M. Prentiss	Brigadier General	Feb. 8, 1863, to Apr. 3, 1863.
C. C. Washburn	Brigadier General	Apr. 3, 1863, to June, 1863.
Fd'k. Salomon	Brigadier General	June, 1863 to July, 1863.

12th DIVISION.—(See 12-Div. 13-Corps.)
13th DIVISION.—(See 13-Div. 13-Corps.)

CAVALRY DIVISION.—Organized April, 1863. COMMANDERS.

Cyrus Bussey	Col. 3d Iowa Cav	To May, 1863.
C. C. Washburn	Brigadier General	To June, 1863.

1st BRIGADE.—

B. L. Wiley	Lt.-Col. 5th Ill. Cav	To May, 1863.

5th Illinois Cav	Apr., 1863	From 1-Brig. 2-Div. Cav. 13-Corps.	To Herron's Div. 13-Corps	June, 1863
1st Indiana Cav	Apr., 1863	From 1-Brig. 2-Div. Cav. 13-Corps.	To 2-Brig. Cav. Div. Dist. E. Ark..	May, 1863

2d BRIGADE.— COMMANDERS.

Powell Clayton	Col. 5th Kansas Cav	To May, 1863.
Cyrus Bussey	Col. 3d Iowa Cav	To June, 1863.

2d Arkansas Cav	Apr., 1863	From 2-Brig. 2d Cav. Div. 13-Corps	To Dept. of Missouri	May, 1863
3d Iowa Cav	Apr., 1863	From 2-Brig. 2d Cav. Div. 13-Corps	To Herron's Div. 13-Corps	June, 1863
5th Kansas Cav	Apr., 1863	From 2-Brig. 2d Cav. Div. 13-Corps	To Clayton's Indpt. Cav. Br. E. Ark.	June, 1863
1st Indiana Cav	May, 1863	From 1-Brig. Cav. Div. Dist. E. Ark.	To Clayton's Indpt. Cav. Br. E. Ark.	June, 1863

HERRON'S DIVISION.—Joined from Dept. Mo. June 11, 1863. **Designated** 2-Div. 13-Corps July 28, 1863.

COMMANDER.

F. J. Herron	Major General	June 11, 1863, to July 28, 1863.	

1st BRIGADE.—

COMMANDER.

Wm. Vandever	Brigadier General	June 11, 1863, to July 28, 1863.		
37th Illinois Infy	June, 1863	From 2-Brig. 2-Div. Army Frontier	To 1-Brig. 2-Div. 13-Corps	July, 1863
26th Indiana Infy	June, 1863	From 2-Brig. 2-Div. Army Frontier	To 1-Brig. 2-Div. 13-Corps	July, 1863
20th Iowa Infy	June, 1863	From 2-Brig. 2-Div. Army Frontier	To 1-Brig. 2-Div. 13-Corps	July, 1863
34th Iowa Infy	June, 1863	From Dist. St. Louis, Dept. Mo.	To 1-Brig. 2-Div. 13-Corps	July, 1863
38th Iowa Infy	June, 1863	From Dist. Columbus 6-Div. 16-C.	To 1-Brig. 2-Div. 13-Corps	July, 1863
Batty. E, 1st Mo. Arty	June, 1863	From 2-Brig. 3-Div. Army Frontier	To 1-Brig. 2-Div. 13-Corps	July, 1863
Batty. F, 1st Mo. Arty	June, 1863	From 2-Brig. 2-Div. Army Frontier	To 1-Brig. 2-Div. 13-Corps	July, 1863

2d BRIGADE.—

COMMANDER.

Wm. W. Orme	Brigadier General	June 11, 1863, to July 28, 1863.		
94th Illinois Infy	June, 1863	From 2-Brig. 3-Div. Army Frontier	To 2-Brig. 2-Div. 13-Corps	July, 1863
19th Iowa Infy	June, 1863	From 2-Brig. 3-Div. Army Frontier	To 2-Brig. 2-Div. 13-Corps	July, 1863
20th Wisconsin Infy	June, 1863	From 1-Brig. 3-Div. Army Frontier	To 2-Brig. 2-Div. 13-Corps	July, 1863
Batty. B, 1st Mo. Arty	June, 1863	From Dist. Southeast Mo.	To 2-Brig. 2-Div. 13-Corps	July, 1863
91st Illinois Infy	July, 1863	From Prisoners of War	To 2-Brig. 2-Div. 13-Corps	July, 1863

CAVALRY BRIGADE.—

COMMANDER.

Cyrus Bussey	Col. 3d Iowa Cav.			
5th Illinois Cav	June, 1863	From 1-B. Cav. Div. Dist. E. Ark.	To Cav. Brig. 3-Div. 15-Corps	Aug., 1863
3d Iowa Cav	June, 1863	From 2-B. Cav. Div. Dist. E. Ark.	To Res. Brig. 1-Cav. Div. Ark. Exp.	Aug., 1863
2d Wisconsin Cav	June, 1863	From 3-B. Dist. Memphis 5-D. 16-C.	To Cav. 1-Div. 17-Corps	Aug., 1863

Thirteenth Army Corps

As reorganized July 28, 1863. Transferred to Department of the Gulf Aug. 7, 1863.

COMMANDER.

C. C. Washburn	Major General	July 28, 1863, to Aug. 7, 1863.	

1st DIVISION.—Organized by consolidation of 9th and 14th Divisions.

COMMANDER.

W. P. Benton	Brigadier General	July 28, 1863, to Aug. 7, 1863.	

1st BRIGADE.—

COMMANDER.

W. P. Benton	Brigadier General	July 28, 1863, to Aug. 7, 1863.		
8th Indiana Infy	July, 1863	From 1-Brig. 14-Div. 13-Corps	To 1-Brig. 1-Div. 13-Corps Gulf	Aug., 1863
18th Indiana Infy	July, 1863	From 1-Brig. 14-Div. 13-Corps	To 1-Brig. 1-Div. 13-Corps Gulf	Aug., 1863
33d Illinois Infy	July, 1863	From 1-Brig. 14-Div. 13-Corps	To 1-Brig. 1-Div. 13-Corps Gulf	Aug., 1863
99th Illinois Infy	July, 1863	From 1-Brig. 14-Div. 13-Corps	To 1-Brig. 1-Div. 13-Corps Gulf	Aug., 1863
1st U. S. Infy	July, 1863	From 1-Brig. 14-Div. 13-Corps	To Headquarters 13-Corps Gulf	Aug., 1863

2d BRIGADE.—

COMMANDER.

W. M. Stone	Col. 22d Iowa Infy	July 28, 1863, to Aug. 7, 1863.		
21st Iowa Infy	July, 1863	From 2-Brig. 14-Div. 13-Corps	To 2-Brig. 1-Div. 13-Corps Gulf	Aug., 1863
22d Iowa Infy	July, 1863	From 2-Brig. 14-Div. 13-Corps	To 2-Brig. 1-Div. 13-Corps Gulf	Aug., 1863
23d Iowa Infy	July, 1863	From 2-Brig. 14-Div. 13-Corps	To 2-Brig. 1-Div. 13-Corps Gulf	Aug., 1863
11th Wisconsin Infy	July, 1863	From 2-Brig. 14-Div. 13-Corps	To 2-Brig. 1-Div. 13-Corps Gulf	Aug., 1863

3d BRIGADE.—

COMMANDER.

J. Keigwin	Col. 49th Indiana Infy	July 28, 1863, to Aug. 7, 1863.		
49th Indiana Infy	July, 1863	From 1-Brig. 9-Div. 13-Corps	To 3-Brig. 1-Div. 13-Corps Gulf	Aug., 1863
69th Indiana Infy	July, 1863	From 1-Brig. 9-Div. 13-Corps	To 3-Brig. 1-Div. 13-Corps Gulf	Aug., 1863
120th Ohio Infy	July, 1863	From 1-Brig. 9-Div. 13-Corps	To 3-Brig. 1-Div. 13-Corps Gulf	Aug., 1863
118th Illinois Infy	July, 1863	From 1-Brig. 9-Div. 13-Corps	To 3-Brig. 1-Div. 13-Corps Gulf	Aug., 1863
7th Kentucky Infy	July, 1863	From 1-Brig. 9-Div. 13-Corps	To 3-Brig. 1-Div. 13-Corps Gulf	Aug., 1863

4th BRIGADE.—

COMMANDER.

D. W. Lindsay	Col. 22d Ky. Infy	July 28, 1863, to Aug. 7, 1863.		
16th Ohio Infy	July, 1863	From 2-Brig. 9-Div. 13-Corps	To 4-Brig. 1-Div. 13-Corps Gulf	Aug., 1863
42d Ohio Infy	July, 1863	From 2-Brig. 9-Div. 13-Corps	To 4-Brig. 1-Div. 13-Corps Gulf	Aug., 1863
114th Ohio Infy	July, 1863	From 2-Brig. 9-Div. 13-Corps	To 4-Brig. 1-Div. 13-Corps Gulf	Aug., 1863
54th Ind. Infy	July, 1863	From 2-Brig. 9-Div. 13-Corps	To 4-Brig. 1-Div. 13-Corps Gulf	Aug., 1863
22d Ky. Infy	July, 1863	From 2-Brig. 9-Div. 13-Corps	To 4-Brig. 1-Div. 13-Corps Gulf	Aug., 1863

ARTILLERY.—

Batty. G, 1st Mich. Arty	July, 1863	From Arty. 9-Div. 13-Corps	To 3-Brig. 1-Div. 13-Corps Gulf	Aug., 1863
1st Wis. Batty	July, 1863	From Arty. 9-Div. 13-Corps	To 4-Brig. 1-Div. 13-Corps Gulf	Aug., 1863
Batty. A, 2d Ill. Arty	July, 1863	From Arty. 14-Div. 13-Corps	To 2-Brig. 1-Div. 13-Corps Gulf	Aug., 1863
1st Ind. Batty	July, 1863	From Arty. 14-Div. 13-Corps	To 1-Brig. 1-Div. 13-Corps Gulf	Aug., 1863

2d DIVISION.—Organized from Herron's Division 13th Army Corps.

COMMANDER.

F. J. Herron	Major General	July 28, 1863, to Aug. 7, 1863.	

1st BRIGADE.—

COMMANDER.

Wm. Vandever	Brigadier General	July 28, 1863, to Aug. 7, 1863.		
26th Ind. Infy	July, 1863	From 1-Brig. Herron's Div. 13-C.	To 1-Brig. 2-Div. 13-Corps Gulf	Aug., 1863
37th Ill. Infy	July, 1863	From 1-Brig. Herron's Div. 13-C.	To 1-Brig. 2-Div. 13-Corps Gulf	Aug., 1863
20th Iowa Infy	July, 1863	From 1-Brig. Herron's Div. 13-C.	To 1-Brig. 2-Div. 13-Corps Gulf	Aug., 1863
34th Iowa Infy	July, 1863	From 1-Brig. Herron's Div. 13-C.	To 1-Brig. 2-Div. 13-Corps Gulf	Aug., 1863
38th Iowa Infy	July, 1863	From 1-Brig. Herron's Div. 13-C.	To 1-Brig. 2-Div. 13-Corps Gulf	Aug., 1863

2d BRIGADE.— COMMANDER.

Wm. W. Orme	Brigadier General	July 28, 1863, to Aug. 7, 1863.	
91st Ill. Infy...........July, 1863	From 2-Brig. Herron's Div. 13-C....	To 2-Brig. 2-Div. 13-Corps Gulf....	Aug., 1863
94th Ill. Infy...........July, 1863	From 2-Brig. Herron's Div. 13-C....	To 2-Brig. 2-Div. 13-Corps Gulf....	Aug., 1863
19th Iowa Infy..........July, 1863	From 2-Brig. Herron's Div. 13-C....	To 2-Brig. 2-Div. 13-Corps Gulf....	Aug., 1863
20th Wis. Infy..........July, 1863	From 2-Brig. Herron's Div. 13-C....	To 2-Brig. 2-Div. 13-Corps Gulf....	Aug., 1863
ARTILLERY.—			
Batty. B, 1st Mo. Arty...July, 1863	From 2-Brig. Herron's Div. 13-C....	To 2-Brig. 2-Div. 13-Corps Gulf....	Aug., 1863
Batty. E, 1st Mo. Arty...July, 1863	From 1-Brig. Herron's Div. 13-C....	To 1-Brig. 2-Div. 13-Corps Gulf....	Aug., 1863
Batty. F, 1st Mo. Arty...July, 1863	From 1-Brig. Herron's Div. 13-C....	To 1-Brig. 2-Div. 13-Corps Gulf....	Aug., 1863
CAVALRY, 2d. DIVISION.—			
15th Ill. Cav. Co. F......July, 1863	From Herron's Div. 13-Corps.......	To Cav. Brig. 13-Corps Gulf........	Aug., 1863
15th Ill. Cav. Co. I......July, 1863	From Herron's Div. 13-Corps.......	To Cav. Brig. 13-Corps Gulf........	Aug., 1863
(Co. A, 36th)			

3d DIVISION.—Organized from 12th Division July 28, 1863.

COMMANDER.

A. L. Lee	Brigadier General	July 28, 1863, to Aug. 7, 1863.	

1st BRIGADE.— COMMANDER.

W. T. Spicely	Col. 24th Ind. Infy	July 28, 1863, to Aug. 7, 1863.	
11th Ind. Infy...........July, 1863	From 1-Brig. 12-Div. 13-Corps......	To 1-Brig. 3-Div. 13-Corps Gulf....	Aug., 1863
24th Ind. Infy...........July, 1863	From 1-Brig. 12-Div. 13-Corps......	To 1-Brig. 3-Div. 13-Corps Gulf....	Aug., 1863
34th Ind. Infy...........July, 1863	From 1-Brig. 12-Div. 13-Corps......	To 1-Brig. 3-Div. 13-Corps Gulf....	Aug., 1863
46th Ind. Infy...........July, 1863	From 1-Brig. 12-Div. 13-Corps......	To 1-Brig. 3-Div. 13-Corps Gulf....	Aug., 1863
29th Wis. Infy..........July, 1863	From 1-Brig. 12-Div. 13-Corps......	To 1-Brig. 3-Div. 13-Corps Gulf....	Aug., 1863

2d BRIGADE.— COMMANDER.

J. R. Slack	Col. 47th Ind. Infy	July 28, 1863, to Aug 7, 1863.	
56th Ohio Infy..........July, 1863	From 2-Brig. 12-Div. 13-Corps.....	To 2-Brig. 3-Div. 13-Corps Gulf....	Aug., 1863
47th Ind. Infy...........July, 1863	From 2-Brig. 12-Div. 13-Corps.....	To 2-Brig. 3-Div. 13-Corps Gulf....	Aug., 1863
87th Ill. Infy...........July, 1863	From 2-Brig. 12-Div. 13-Corps.....	To 2-Brig. 3-Div. 13-Corps Gulf....	Aug., 1863
24th Iowa Infy..........July, 1863	From 2-Brig. 12-Div. 13-Corps.....	To 2-Brig. 3-Div. 13-Corps Gulf....	Aug., 1863
28th Iowa Infy..........July, 1863	From 2-Brig. 12-Div. 13-Corps.....	To 2-Brig. 3-Div. 13-Corps Gulf....	Aug., 1863
ARTILLERY.—			
2d Ohio Batty..........July, 1863	From Arty. 12-Div. 13-Corps........	To 2-Brig. 3-Div. 13-Corps Gulf....	Aug., 1863
16th Ohio Batty.........July, 1863	From Arty. 12-Div. 13-Corps........	To 1-Brig. 3-Div. 13-Corps Gulf....	Aug., 1863
Batty. A, 1st Mo. Arty...July, 1863	From Arty. 12-Div. 13-Corps........	To 1-Brig. 3-Div. 13-Corps Gulf....	Aug., 1863
Batty. E, 2d Ill.........Aug., 1863	From Arty. 4-Div. 13-Corps.........	To 1-Brig. 3-Div. 13-Corps Gulf....	Aug., 1863

4th DIVISION.—Assigned from 16th Army Corps July 28, 1863. Transferred to 17th Army Corps, Aug, 17, 1863.

COMMANDER.

M. M. Crocker	Brigadier General	July 28, 1863, to Aug. 17, 1863.	

1st BRIGADE.— COMMANDER.

I. C. Pugh	Col. 41st Ill. Infy	July 28, 1863, to Aug. 17, 1863.	
41st Ill. Infy...........July, 1863	From 1-Brig. 4-Div. 16-Corps.......	To 1-Brig. 4-Div. 17-Corps..........	Aug., 1863
53d Ill. Infy............July, 1863	From 1-Brig. 4-Div. 16-Corps.......	To 1-Brig. 4-Div. 17-Corps..........	Aug., 1863
3d Iowa Infy............July, 1863	From 1-Brig. 4-Div. 16-Corps.......	To 1-Brig. 4-Div. 17-Corps..........	Aug., 1863
33d Wis. Infy...........July, 1863	From 1-Brig. 4-Div. 16-Corps.......	To 1-Brig. 4-Div. 17-Corps..........	Aug., 1863

2d BRIGADE.— COMMANDER.

Cyrus Hall	Col. 14th Ill. Infy	July 28, 1863, to Aug. 17, 1863.	
14th Ill. Infy...........July, 1863	From 2-Brig. 4-Div. 16-Corps.......	To 2-Brig. 4-Div. 17-Corps..........	Aug., 1863
15th Ill. Infy...........July, 1863	From 2-Brig. 4-Div. 16-Corps.......	To 2-Brig. 4-Div. 17-Corps..........	Aug., 1863
46th Ill. Infy...........July, 1863	From 2-Brig. 4-Div. 16-Corps.......	To 2-Brig. 4-Div. 17-Corps..........	Aug., 1863
76th Ill. Infy...........July, 1863	From 2-Brig. 4-Div. 16-Corps.......	To 2-Brig. 4-Div. 17-Corps..........	Aug., 1863

3d BRIGADE.— COMMANDER.

A. K. Johnson	Col. 28th Ill. Infy	July 28, 1863, to Aug. 17, 1863.	
28th Ill. Infy...........July, 1863	From 3-Brig. 4-Div. 16-Corps.......	To 3-Brig. 4-Div. 17-Corps..........	Aug., 1863
32d Ill. Infy............July, 1863	From 3-Brig. 4-Div. 16-Corps.......	To 3-Brig. 4-Div. 17-Corps..........	Aug., 1863
53d Ind. Infy...........July, 1863	From 3-Brig. 4-Div. 16-Corps.......	To 3-Brig. 4-Div. 17-Corps..........	Aug., 1863
12th Wis. Infy..........July, 1863	From 3-Brig. 4-Div. 16-Corps.......	To 3-Brig. 4-Div. 17-Corps..........	Aug., 1863
ARTILLERY.—			
Batty. E, 2d Ill.........July, 1863	From Arty. 4-Div. 16-Corps........	To Arty. 3-Div. 13-Corps...........	Aug., 1863
Batty. K, 2d Ill.........July, 1863	From Arty. 4-Div. 16-Corps........	To Arty. 4-Div. 17-Corps...........	Aug., 1863
7th Ohio Batty.........July, 1863	From Arty. 4-Div. 16-Corps........	To Arty. 4-Div. 17-Corps...........	Aug., 1863
15th Ohio Batty.........July, 1863	From Arty. 4-Div. 16-Corps........	To Arty. 4-Div. 17-Corps...........	Aug., 1863

Fifteenth Army Corps

Created Dec. 18, 1862, by General Order No. 210, A. G. O., to consist of the Old 5th Division and District of Memphis, Department of the Tennessee, and Steele's Division, from Helena, Ark. Known as 2d and 4th Divisions, Sherman's Yazoo Expedition, to Jan. 4, 1863, and as 2d Corps, Gen. McClernand's Army of the Mississippi, to Jan. 12, 1863.

COMMANDERS.

W. T. Sherman	Major General	Jan. 4, 1863, to Oct. 29, 1863.	
Frank P. Blair, Jr	Major General	Oct. 29, 1863, to Dec. 11, 1863.	
John A. Logan	Major General	Dec. 11, 1863, to July 22, 1864.	
M. L. Smith	Brigadier General	July 22, 1864, to July 27, 1864.	
John A. Logan	Major General	July 27, 1864, to Sept. 23, 1864.	
P. J. Osterhaus	Major General	Sept. 23, 1864, to Jan. 8, 1865.	
John A. Logan	Major General	Jan. 8, 1865, to May 23, 1865.	
W. B. Hazen	Major General	May 23, 1865, to Aug. 1, 1865.	

1st DIVISION.—

COMMANDERS.

Frederick Steele	Major General	Jan. 4, 1863, to July 27, 1863.
J. M. Thayer	Brigadier General	July 27, 1863, to July 28, 1863.
E. S. Dennis	Brigadier General	July 28, 1863, to Sept. 1, 1863.
P. J. Osterhaus	Brigadier General	Sept. 1, 1863, to Jan. 4, 1864.
Milo Smith	Col. 26th Iowa Infy	Jan. 4, 1864, to Jan. 13, 1864.
C. R. Woods	Brigadier General	Jan. 13, 1864, to Feb. 6, 1864.
P. J. Osterhaus	Brigadier General	Feb. 6, 1864, to July 15, 1864.
C. R. Woods	Brigadier General	July 15, 1864, to Aug. 19, 1864.
P. J. Osterhaus	Major General	Aug. 19, 1864, to Sept. 23, 1864.
C. R. Woods	Brigadier General	Sept. 23, 1864, to Apr. 2, 1865.
W. B. Woods	Bvt. Brig. General	Apr. 2, 1865, to Apr. 5, 1865.
C. R. Woods	Brigadier General	Apr. 5, 1865, to Aug. 1, 1865.

1st BRIGADE.—

COMMANDERS.

F. P. Blair, Jr.	Brigadier General	Jan. 4, 1863, to Apr. 1, 1863.
F. H. Manter	Col. 32d Mo. Infy	Apr. 1, 1863, to June 13, 1863.
B. G. Farrar	Col. 30th Mo. Infy	June 13, 1863, to July 28, 1863.
F. Fletcher	Col. 31st Mo. Infy	July 28, 1863, to Sept. 13, 1863.
C. R. Woods	Brigadier General	Sept. 13, 1863, to Dec. 14, 1863.
Milo Smith	Col. 26th Iowa Infy	Dec. 14, 1863, to Feb. 6, 1864.
C. R. Woods	Brigadier General	Feb. 6, 1864, to July 15, 1864.
Milo Smith	Col. 26th Iowa Infy	July 15, 1864, to Aug. 19, 1864.
C. R. Woods	Brigadier General	Aug. 19, 1864, to Aug. 22, 1864.
Milo Smith	Col. 26th Iowa Infy	Aug. 22, 1864, to Jan. 21, 1865.
William B. Woods	Bvt. Brig. General	Jan. 21, 1865, to June 16, 1865.
E. Briggs	Lt.-Col. 76th Ohio Infy	June 16, 1865, to July 15, 1865.

13th Ill. Infy	Jan., 1863	From 1-Brig. 4-Div. Yazoo Exp	To 2-Brig. 3-Div. 15-Corps	Apr., 1864
29th Mo. Infy	Jan., 1863	From 1-Brig. 4-Div. Yazoo Exp	To 2-Brig. 3-Div. 15-Corps	Dec., 1863
30th Mo. Infy	Jan., 1863	From 1-Brig. 4-Div. Yazoo Exp	To Dist. of Natchez	Aug., 1863
31st Mo. Infy	Jan., 1863	From 1-Brig. 4-Div. Yazoo Exp	To 2-Brig. 1-Div. 15-Corps	Dec., 1863
32d Mo. Infy	Jan., 1863	From 1-Brig. 4-Div. Yazoo Exp	To 3-Brig. 1-Div. 15-Corps	Dec., 1863
58th Ohio Infy	Jan., 1863	From 1-Brig. 4-Div. Yazoo Exp	To Iron Clads Miss. Squadron	Feb., 1863
27th Mo. Infy	Mch. 1863	From Dist. Rolla, Dept. Mo.	No change to Muster Out	June, 1865
3rd Mo. Infy	Sept., 1863	From 2-Brig. 1-Div. 15-Corps	To 3-Brig. 1-Div. 15-Corps	Dec., 1863
12th Mo. Infy	Sept., 1863	From 2-Brig. 1-Div. 15-Corps	To 3-Brig. 1-Div. 15-Corps	Dec., 1863
17th Mo. Infy	Sept., 1863	From 2-Brig. 1-Div. 15-Corps	To 3-Brig. 1-Div. 15-Corps	Dec., 1863
76th Ohio Infy	Sept., 1863	From 2-Brig. 1-Div. 15-Corps	No change to Muster Out	July, 1865
26th Iowa Infy	Dec., 1863	From 2-Brig. 1-Div. 15-Corps	To 3-Brig. 1-Div. 15-Corps	Apr., 1865
30th Iowa Infy	Dec., 1863	From 2-Brig. 1-Div. 15-Corps	To 3-Brig. 1-Div. 15-Corps	Sept., 1864
12th Ind. Infy	Sept., 1864	From 1-Brig. 4-Div. 15-Corps	No change to Muster Out	July, 1865
29th Mo. Infy	Sept., 1864	From 3-Brig. 1-Div. 15-Corps	To Unatt. 15-Corps Mounted	Nov., 1864
31st Mo. Infy	Sept., 1864	From 3-Brig. 1-Div. 15-Corps	No change to Muster Out	July, 1865
32d Mo. Infy	Sept., 1864	From 3-Brig. 1-Div. 15-Corps	No change to Muster Out	July, 1865
12th Ill. Infy	Apr., 1865	From 2-Brig. 4-Div. 15-Corps	No change to Muster Out	July, 1865
93d Ill. Infy	Apr., 1865	From 1-Brig. 3-Div. 15-Corps	No change to Muster Out	July, 1865
4th Minn. Infy	Apr., 1865	From 1-Brig. 3-Div. 15-Corps	No change to Muster Out	July, 1865

2d BRIGADE.—

COMMANDERS.

C. E. Hovey	Brigadier General	Jan. 3, 1863, to May 22, 1863.
C. R. Woods	Col. 76th Ohio Infy	May 22, 1863, to July 30, 1863.
Hugo Wangelin	Col. 12th Mo. Infy	July 30, 1863, to Aug. 24, 1863.
C. R. Woods	Brigadier General	Aug. 24, 1863, to Sept. 1, 1863.
J. A. Williamson	Col. 4th Iowa Infy	Sept. 1, 1863, to Dec. 28, 1863.
D. Carskadden	Col. 9th Iowa Infy	Dec. 28, 1863, to Jan. 29, 1864.
J. W. Jenkins	Lt.-Col. 31st Iowa Infy	Jan. 29, 1864, to Mch. 8, 1864.
G. A. Stone	Col. 25th Iowa Infy	Mch. 8, 1864, to Apr. 20, 1864.
D. Carskadden	Col. 9th Iowa Infy	Apr. 20, 1864, to May 5, 1864.
J. A. Williamson	Col. 4th Iowa Infy	May 5, 1864, to Sept. 25, 1864.
C. C. Walcutt	Brigadier General	Sept. 25, 1864, to Nov. 22, 1864.
R. F. Catterson	Col. 97th Ind. Infy	Nov. 22, 1864, to Mch. 28, 1865.
C. C. Walcutt	Brigadier General	Mch. 28, 1865, to Apr. 4, 1865.
R. F. Catterson	Col. 97th Ind. Infy	Apr. 4, 1865, to July 26, 1865.

25th Iowa Infy	Jan., 1863	From 2-Brig. 4-Div. Yazoo Exp	To 3-Brig. 1-Div. 15-Corps	Dec., 1863
31st Iowa Infy	Jan., 1863	From 2-Brig. 4-Div. Yazoo Exp	To 3-Brig. 1-Div. 15-Corps	Sept., 1864
3d Mo. Infy	Jan., 1863	From 2-Brig. 4-Div. Yazoo Exp	To 1-Brig. 1-Div. 15-Corps	Sept., 1863
12th Mo. Infy	Jan., 1863	From 2-Brig. 4-Div. Yazoo Exp	To 1-Brig. 1-Div. 15-Corps	Sept., 1863
17th Mo. Infy	Jan., 1863	From 2-Brig. 4-Div. Yazoo Exp	To 1-Brig. 1-Div. 15-Corps	Sept., 1863
76th Ohio Infy	Jan., 1863	From 2-Brig. 4-Div. Yazoo Exp	To 1-Brig. 1-Div. 15-Corps	Sept., 1863
4th Iowa Infy	Sept., 1863	From 3-Brig. 1-Div. 15-Corps	To 3-Brig. 1-Div. 15-Corps	Sept., 1864
9th Iowa Infy	Sept., 1863	From 3-Brig. 1-Div. 15-Corps	To 3-Brig. 1-Div. 15-Corps	Sept., 1864
26th Iowa Infy	Sept., 1863	From 3-Brig. 1-Div. 15-Corps	To 1-Brig. 1-Div. 15-Corps	Dec., 1863
30th Iowa Infy	Sept., 1863	From 3-Brig. 1-Div. 15-Corps	To 1-Brig. 1-Div. 15-Corps	Dec., 1863
29th Mo. Infy	Dec., 1863	From 1-Brig. 1-Div. 15-Corps	To 3-Brig. 1-Div. 15-Corps	Apr., 1864
31st Mo. Infy	Dec., 1863	From 1-Brig. 1-Div. 15-Corps	To 3-Brig. 1-Div. 15-Corps	Apr., 1864
25th Iowa Infy	Apr., 1864	From 3-Brig. 1-Div. 15-Corps	To 3-Brig. 1-Div. 15-Corps	Sept., 1864
97th Ind. Infy	Sept., 1864	From 2-Brig. 4-Div. 15-Corps	No change to Muster Out	June, 1865
100th Ind. Infy	Sept., 1864	From 2-Brig. 4-Div. 15-Corps	No change to Muster Out	June, 1865
26th Ill. Infy	Sept., 1864	From 2-Brig. 4-Div. 15-Corps	No change to Muster Out	July, 1865
40th Ill. Infy	Sept., 1864	From 2-Brig. 4-Div. 15-Corps	No change to Muster Out	July, 1865
103d Ill. Infy	Sept., 1864	From 2-Brig. 4-Div. 15-Corps	No change to Muster Out	June, 1865
6th Iowa Infy	Sept., 1864	From 2-Brig. 4-Div. 15-Corps	No change to Muster Out	July, 1865
46th Ohio Infy	Sept., 1864	From 2-Brig. 4-Div. 15-Corps	No change to Muster Out	July, 1865

3d BRIGADE.—Discontinued Sept., 1863. Reorganized Dec. 1, 1863.

COMMANDERS.

J. M. Thayer	Brigadier General	Jan. 3, 1863, to Aug. 1, 1863.
J. A. Williamson	Col. 4th Iowa Infy	Aug. 1, 1863, to Sept. 15, 1863.
G. A. Stone	Col. 25th Iowa Infy	Dec. 1, 1863, to Mch. 8, 1864.
H. Wangelin	Col. 12th Mo. Infy	Mch. 8, 1864, to Sept. 25, 1864.
William Smyth	Col. 31st Iowa Infy	Sept. 25, 1864, to Oct. 31, 1864.
G. A. Stone	Col. 25th Iowa Infy	Oct. 31, 1864, to Nov. 1, 1864.
J. A. Williamson	Col. 4th Iowa Infy	Nov. 1, 1864, to Dec. 28, 1864.
G. A. Stone	Col. 25th Iowa Infy	Dec. 28, 1864, to Dec. 31, 1864.
J. A. Williamson	Col. 4th Iowa Infy	Dec. 31, 1864, to Jan. 15, 1865.
G. A. Stone	Col. 25th Iowa Infy	Jan. 15, 1865, to June 6, 1865.

3d BRIGADE.—Continued.

4th Iowa Infy	Jan., 1863	From 3-Br. 4-Div. Sherman's Yazoo..	To 2-Brig. 1-Div. 15-Corps	Sept., 1863
9th Iowa Infy	Jan., 1863	From 3-Br. 4-Div. Sherman's Yazoo..	To 2-Brig. 1-Div. 15-Corps	Sept., 1863
26th Iowa Infy	Jan., 1863	From 3-Br. 4-Div. Sherman's Yazoo..	To 2-Brig. 1-Div. 15-Corps	Sept., 1863
30th Iowa Infy	Jan., 1863	From 3-Br. 4-Div. Sherman's Yazoo..	To 2-Brig. 1-Div. 15-Corps	Sept., 1863
34th Iowa Infy	Jan., 1863	From 3-Br. 4-Div. Sherman's Yazoo..	To Garrison Pilot Knob, Mo	Apr., 1863
25th Iowa Infy	Dec., 1863	From 2-Div. 7-Div. 15-Corps	To 2-Brig. 1-Div. 15-Corps	Apr., 1864
3d Mo. Infy	Dec., 1863	From 1-Brig. 1-Div. 15-Corps	No change to Muster Out	Sept., 1864
12th Mo. Infy	Dec., 1863	From 1-Brig. 1-Div. 15-Corps	No change to Muster Out	Aug., 1864
17th Mo. Infy	Dec., 1863	From 1-Brig. 1-Div. 15-Corps	No change to Muster Out	Sept., 1864
32d Mo. Infy	Dec., 1863	From 1-Brig. 1-Div. 15-Corps	To 1-Brig. 1-Div. 15-Corps	Sept., 1864
31st Mo. Infy	Apr., 1864	From 2-Brig. 1-Div. 15-Corps	To 1-Brig. 1-Div. 15-Corps	Sept., 1864
29th Mo. Infy	Apr., 1864	From 2-Brig. 1-Div. 15-Corps	To 1-Brig. 1-Div. 15-Corps	Sept., 1864
4th Iowa Infy	Sept., 1864	From 2-Brig. 1-Div. 15-Corps	No change to Muster Out	July, 1865
9th Iowa Infy	Sept., 1864	From 2-Brig. 1-Div. 15-Corps	No change to Muster Out	July, 1865
25th Iowa Infy	Sept., 1864	From 2-Brig. 1-Div. 15-Corps	No change to Muster Out	June, 1865
30th Iowa Infy	Sept., 1864	From 1-Brig. 1-Div. 15-Corps	No change to Muster Out	June, 1865
31st Iowa Infy	Sept., 1864	From 2-Brig. 1-Div. 15-Corps	No change to Muster Out	June, 1865
26th Iowa Infy	Apr., 1865	From 1-Brig. 1-Div. 15-Corps	No change to Muster Out	July, 1865
66th Ill. Infy	Apr., 1865	From 2-Brig. 4-Div. 15-Corps	No change to Muster Out	June, 1865

ARTILLERY.—

1st Iowa Batty	Jan., 1863	From 3-Br. 4-Div. Yazoo Exp	To Arty. 4-Div. 15-Corps	Apr., 1864
Mo. Flying Battery. (Batty. F, 2d Mo.)	Jan., 1863	From 2-Brig. 4-Div. Yazoo Exp....	To Arty. Res. Nashville	Nov., 1864
4th Ohio Batty	Jan., 1863	From 1-Brig. 4-Div. Yazoo Exp	No change to Muster Out	Aug., 1864
1st Iowa Batty	Sept., 1864	From Arty. 4-Div. 15-Corps	To Arty. Res. Nashville, Tenn	Nov., 1864

2d DIVISION.— COMMANDERS.

David Stuart	Brigadier General	Jan. 4, 1863, to Apr. 4, 1863.
F. P. Blair, Jr	Major General	Apr. 4, 1863, to July 26, 1863.
J. A. J. Lightburn	Brigadier General	July 26, 1863, to Sept. 10, 1863.
Giles A. Smith	Brigadier General	Sept. 10, 1863, to Oct. 6, 1863.
M. L. Smith	Brigadier General	Oct. 6, 1863, to July 22, 1864.
J. A. J. Lightburn	Brigadier General	July 22, 1864, to July 27, 1864.
M. L. Smith	Brigadier General	July 27, 1864, to Aug. 5, 1864.
J. A. J. Lightburn	Brigadier General	Aug. 5, 1864, to Aug. 17, 1864.
W. B. Hazen	Brigadier General	Aug. 17, 1864, to May 18, 1865.
J. M. Oliver	Brigadier General	May 18, 1865, to Aug. 1, 1865.

1st BRIGADE.— COMMANDERS.

Giles A. Smith	Col. 8th Mo. Infy	Jan. 4, 1863, to July 20, 1863.
J. H. Blood	Col. 6th Mo. Infy	July 20, 1863, to Sept. 10, 1863.
N. W. Tupper	Col. 116th Ill. Infy	Sept. 10, 1863, to Oct. 19, 1863.
Giles A. Smith	Brigadier General	Oct. 19, 1863, to Nov. 24, 1863.
N. W. Tupper	Col. 116th Ill. Infy	Nov. 24, 1863, to Jan. 1, 1864
D. C. Coleman	Lt.-Col. 8th Mo. Infy	Jan. 1, 1864, to Feb. 21, 1864.
Giles A. Smith	Brigadier General	Feb. 21, 1864, to July 20, 1864.
J. S. Martin	Col. 111th Ill. Infy	July 20, 1864, to Aug. 4, 1864.
Theodore Jones	Col. 30th Ohio Infy	Aug. 4, 1864, to June 20, 1865.
S. R. Mott	Lt.-Col. 57th Ohio Infy	June 20, 1865, to July 20, 1865.
Theodore Jones	Bvt. Brigadier General	July 20, 1865, to Aug. 1, 1865.

113th Ill. Infy	Jan., 1863	From 1-Brig. 2-Div. Yazoo Exp....	To 3-Brig. 2-Div. 16-Corps	Aug., 1863
116th Ill. Infy	Jan., 1863	From 1-Brig. 2-Div. Yazoo Exp....	No change to Muster Out	June, 1865
6th Mo. Infy	Jan., 1863	From 1-Brig. 2-Div. Yazoo Exp....	No change to Muster Out	Aug., 1865
8th Mo. Infy	Jan., 1863	From 1-Brig. 2-Div. Yazoo Exp....	No change to Muster Out	Aug., 1865
13th U. S. Infy	Jan., 1863	From 1-Brig. 2-Div. Yazoo Exp....	Headqrs. 15-Corps	Jan., 1863
55th Ill. Infy	Sept., 1863	From 2-Brig. 2-Div. 15-Corps	No change to Muster Out	Aug., 1865
127th Ill. Infy	Sept., 1863	From 2-Brig. 2-Div. 15-Corps	No change to Muster Out	June, 1865
57th Ohio Infy	Sept., 1863	From 2-Brig. 2-Div. 15-Corps	No change to Muster Out	Aug., 1865
13th U. S. Infy	Sept., 1863	From Headqrs. 15-Corps	Garrison at Nashville, Tenn	Dec., 1863
111th Ill. Infy	Mch., 1864	From 2-Brig. 2-Div. 16-Corps	To 2-Brig. 2-Div. 15-Corps	Aug., 1864
30th Ohio Infy	Aug., 1864	From 2-Brig. 2-Div. 15-Corps	No change to Muster Out	Aug., 1865
56th Ill. Infy	Apr., 1865	From 2-Brig. 3-Div. 15-Corps	No change to Muster Out	Aug., 1865
80th Ohio Infy	Apr., 1865	From 2-Brig. 3-Div. 15-Corps	No change to Muster Out	Aug., 1865

2d BRIGADE.— COMMANDERS.

T. K. Smith	Col. 54th Ohio Infy	Jan. 4, 1863, to May 23, 1863.
J. A. J. Lightburn	Brigadier General	May 23, 1863, to July 26, 1863.
B. J. Spooner	Col. 83d Ind. Infy	July 26, 1863, to Aug. 6, 1863.
A. Malmborg	Col. 55th Ill. Infy	Aug. 6, 1863, to Sept. 10, 1863.
B. J. Spooner	Col. 83d Ind. Infy	Sept. 10, 1863, to Oct. 19, 1863.
J. A. J. Lightburn	Brigadier General	Oct. 19, 1863, to Jan. 12, 1864.
Theodore Jones	Col. 30th Ohio Infy	Jan. 12, 1864, to Feb. 12, 1864.
J. A. J. Lightburn	Brigadier General	Feb. 12, 1864, to July 22, 1864.
Wells S. Jones	Col. 53d Ohio Infy	July 22, 1864, to July 27, 1864.
J. A. J. Lightburn	Brigadier General	July 27, 1864, to Aug. 5, 1864.
Wells S. Jones	Col. 53d Ohio Infy	Aug. 5, 1864, to Aug. 17, 1864.
J. A. J. Lightburn	Brigadier General	Aug. 17, 1864, to Aug. 24, 1864.
Wells S. Jones	Col. 53d Ohio Infy	Aug. 24, 1864, to Dec. 13, 1864.
J. S. Martin	Col. 111th Ill. Infy	Dec. 13, 1864, to Jan. 20, 1865.
Wells S. Jones	Col. 53d Ohio Infy	Jan. 20, 1865, to Aug. 1, 1865.

83d Ind. Infy	Jan., 1863	From 2-Brig. 2-Div. Yazoo Exp....	No change to Muster Out	June, 1865
55th Ill. Infy	Jan., 1863	From 2-Brig. 2-Div. Yazoo Exp....	To 1-Brig. 2-Div. 15-Corps	Sept., 1863
127th Ill. Infy	Jan., 1863	From 2-Brig. 2-Div. Yazoo Exp....	To 1-Brig. 2-Div. 15-Corps	Sept., 1863
54th Ohio Infy	Jan., 1863	From 2-Brig. 2-Div. Yazoo Exp....	No change to Muster Out	Aug., 1865
57th Ohio Infy	Jan., 1863	From 2-Brig. 2-Div. Yazoo Exp....	To 1-Brig. 2-Div. 15-Corps	Sept., 1863
30th Ohio Infy	Oct., 1863	From 3-Brig. 2-Div. 15-Corps	To 1-Brig. 2-Div. 15-Corps	Aug., 1864
37th Ohio Infy	Oct., 1863	From 3-Brig. 2-Div. 15-Corps	No change to Muster Out	Aug., 1865
47th Ohio Infy	Oct., 1863	From 3-Brig. 2-Div. 15-Corps	No change to Muster Out	Aug., 1865
4th W. Va. Infy	Oct., 1863	From 3-Brig. 2-Div. 15-Corps	To Dept. of W. Va	Apr., 1864
53d Ohio Infy	May, 1864	From 3-Brig. 4-Div. 15-Corps	No change to Muster Out	Aug., 1865
111th Ill. Infy	Aug., 1864	From 1-Brig. 2-Div. 15-Corps	No change to Muster Out	June, 1865

3d BRIGADE.—Discontinued Oct. 19, 1863. Reorganized Sept. 28, 1864.
COMMANDERS.

Hugh Ewing	Brigadier General	Jan. 9, 1863, to July 21, 1863.
E. Siber	Col. 37th Ohio Infy	July 21, 1863, to Oct. 19, 1863.
A. Fowler	Col. 99th Ind. Infy	Sept. 28, 1864, to Nov. 2, 1864.
J. M. Oliver	Col. 15th Mich. Infy	Nov. 2, 1864, to May 18, 1865.
F. S. Hutchinson	Col. 15th Mich. Infy	May 18, 1865, to June 23, 1865.
A. V. Rice	Brigadier General	June 23, 1865, to Aug. 1, 1865.

3d BRIGADE.—Continued.

30th Ohio Infy	Jan., 1863	From Dist. Kanawha Dept. Ohio....	To 2-Brig. 2-Div. 15-Corps	Oct.,	1863
37th Ohio Infy	Jan., 1863	From Dist. Kanawha Dept. Ohio....	To 2-Brig. 2-Div. 15-Corps	Oct.,	1863
47th Ohio Infy	Jan., 1863	From Dist. Kanawha Dept. Ohio....	To 2-Brig. 2-Div. 15-Corps	Oct.,	1863
4th W. Va. Infy	Jan., 1863	From Dist. Kanawha Dept. Ohio....	To 2-Brig. 2-Div. 15-Corps	Oct.,	1863
99th Ind. Infy	Sept., 1864	From 1-Brig. 4-Div. 15-Corps	No change to Muster Out	June,	1865
48th Ill. Infy	Sept., 1864	From 1-Brig. 4-Div. 15-Corps	No change to Muster Out	Aug.,	1865
90th Ill. Infy	Sept., 1864	From 1-Brig. 4-Div. 15-Corps	No change to Muster Out	June,	1865
15th Mich. Infy	Sept., 1864	From 1-Brig. 4-Div. 15-Corps	No change to Muster Out	Aug.,	1865
70th Ohio Infy	Sept., 1864	From 1-Brig. 4-Div. 15-Corps	No change to Muster Out	Aug.,	1865
10th Iowa Infy	Apr., 1865	From 2-Brig. 3-Div. 15-Corps	No change to Muster Out	Aug.,	1865
17th Iowa Infy	Apr., 1865	From 2-Brig. 3-Div. 15-Corps	No change to Muster Out	July,	1865
26th Mo. Infy	Apr., 1865	From 2-Brig. 3-Div. 15-Corps	No change to Muster Out	Aug.,	1865
ARTILLERY.—					
Batty. A, 1st Ill	Jan., 1863	From 2-Div. Sherman's Yazoo Exp..	To Garrison Arty. Nashville, Tenn.	Nov.,	1864
Batty. B, 1st Ill	Jan., 1863	From 2-Div. Sherman's Yazoo Exp..	No change to Muster Out	July,	1864
Batty. H, 1st Ill	Jan., 1863	From 2-Div. Sherman's Yazoo Exp..	To Arty. Brig. 15-Corps	Sept.,	1864
8th Ohio Batty. L. A	Jan., 1863	From 2-Div. Sherman's Yazoo Exp..	To Arty. 1-Div. 17-Corps	Sept.,	1863
CAVALRY.—					
Thielman's Ill. Battn	Jan., 1863	From 2-Div. Sherman's Yazoo Exp..	To Unatt. 15-Corps	May,	1863

3d DIVISION.—Joined Corps Apr., 1863. Transferred to 16th Corps Dec., 1863. Reorganized Dec. 20, 1863. Discontinued Apr. 26, 1865.

COMMANDERS.

J. M. Tuttle	Brigadier General	Apr. 3, 1863, to Aug. 9, 1863.
R. P. Buckland	Brigadier General	Aug. 9, 1863, to Sept. 11, 1863.
A. Asboth	Brigadier General	Sept. 11, 1863, to Sept. 21, 1863.
J. M. Tuttle	Brigadier General	Sept. 21, 1863, to Dec. 20, 1863.
J. E. Smith	Brigadier General	Dec. 20, 1863, to Apr. 26, 1865.

1st BRIGADE.—　　　　　　COMMANDERS.

R. P. Buckland	Brigadier General	Apr. 3, 1863, to June 22, 1863.
W. L. McMillan	Col. 95th Ohio Infy	June 22, 1863, to Aug. 3, 1863.
D. C. Thomas	Col. 93d Ind. Infy	Aug. 3, 1863, to Sept. 10, 1863.
R. P. Buckland	Brigadier General	Sept. 10, 1863, to Oct. 15, 1863.
W. L. McMillan	Col. 95th Ohio Infy	Oct. 15, 1863, to Nov. 15, 1863.
R. P. Buckland	Brigadier General	Nov. 15, 1863, to Dec. 20, 1863.
J. I. Alexander	Col. 59th Ind. Infy	Dec. 20, 1863, to Feb. 4, 1864.
G. Bouck	Col. 18th Wis. Infy	Feb. 4, 1864, to Mch. 12, 1864.
J. B. McCown	Col. 63d Ill. Infy	Mch. 12, 1864, to Apr. 2, 1864.
J. I. Alexander	Col. 59th Ind. Infy	Apr. 2, 1864, to Sept. 1, 1864.
J. B. McCown	Col. 63d Ill. Infy	Sept. 1, 1864, to Jan. 26, 1865.
W. T. Clark	Brigadier General	Jan. 26, 1865, to Apr. 26, 1865.

93d Ind. Infy	Apr., 1863	From 3-Brig. 8-Div. 16-Corps	To 1-Brig. 1-Div. 16-Corps	Dec.,	1863
114th Ill. Infy	Apr., 1863	From 3-Brig. 8-Div. 16-Corps	To 1-Brig. 1-Div. 16-Corps	Dec.,	1863
72d Ohio Infy	Apr., 1863	From 3-Brig. 8-Div. 16-Corps	To 1-Brig. 1-Div. 16-Corps	Dec.,	1863
95th Ohio Infy	Apr., 1863	From Dist. of Memphis 16-Corps	To 1-Brig. 1-Div. 16-Corps	Dec.,	1863
48th Ind. Infy	Dec., 1863	From 1-Brig. 2-Div. 17-Corps	To 2-Brig. 4-Div. 15-Corps	Apr.,	1865
59th Ind. Infy	Dec., 1863	From 1-Brig. 2-Div. 17-Corps	To 2-Brig. 4-Div. 15-Corps	Apr.,	1865
63d Ill. Infy	Dec., 1863	From 1-Brig. 2-Div. 17-Corps	To 2-Brig. 4-Div. 15-Corps	Apr.,	1865
4th Minn. Infy	Dec., 1863	From 1-Brig. 2-Div. 17-Corps	To 1-Brig. 1-Div. 15-Corps	Apr.,	1865
18th Wis. Infy	Dec., 1863	From 1-Brig. 2-Div. 17-Corps	To 2-Brig. 4-Div. 15-Corps	Apr.,	1865
93d Ill. Infy	Aug., 1864	From 3-Brig. 3-Div. 15-Corps	To 1-Brig. 1-Div. 15-Corps	Apr.,	1865

2d BRIGADE.—　　　　　　COMMANDERS.

J. A. Mower	Brigadier General	Apr. 3, 1863, to July 4, 1863.
L. F. Hubbard	Col. 5th Minn. Infy	July 4, 1863, to Sept. 15, 1863.
J. A. Mower	Brigadier General	Sept. 15, 1863, to Dec. 20, 1863.
C. R. Wever	Col. 17th Iowa Infy	Dec. 20, 1863, to Feb. 10, 1864.
G. B. Raum	Col. 56th Ill. Infy	Feb. 10, 1864, to Jan. 29, 1865.
C. R. Wever	Col. 17th Iowa Infy	Jan. 29, 1865, to Apr. 7, 1865.
J. E. Tourtelotte	Col. 4th Minn. Infy	Apr. 7, 1865, to Apr. 26, 1865.

47th Ill. Infy	Apr., 1863	From 2-Brig. 8-Div. 16-Corps	To 2-Brig. 1-Div. 16-Corps	Dec.,	1863
5th Minn. Infy	Apr., 1863	From 2-Brig. 8-Div. 16-Corps	To 2-Brig. 1-Div. 16-Corps	Dec.,	1863
11th Mo. Infy	Apr., 1863	From 2-Brig. 8-Div. 16-Corps	To 2-Brig. 1-Div. 16-Corps	Dec.,	1863
8th Wis. Infy	Apr., 1863	From 2-Brig. 8-Div. 16-Corps	To 2-Brig. 1-Div. 16-Corps	Dec.,	1863
56th Ill. Infy	Dec., 1863	From 2-Brig. 2-Div. 17-Corps	To 1-Brig. 2-Div. 15-Corps	Apr.,	1865
17th Iowa Infy	Dec., 1863	From 2-Brig. 2-Div. 17-Corps	Captured at Tilton, Ga	Oct.13,	'64
10th Mo. Infy	Dec., 1863	From 2-Brig. 2-Div. 17-Corps	No change to Muster Out	Oct.,	1864
24th Mo. Infy. (Co. E)	Dec., 1863	From 2-Brig. 2-Div. 17-Corps	No change to Muster Out	Oct.,	1864
80th Ohio Infy	Dec., 1863	From 2-Brig. 2-Div. 17-Corps	To 1-Brig. 2-Div. 15-Corps	Apr.,	1865
10th Iowa Infy	Aug., 1864	From 3-Brig. 3-Div. 15-Corps	To 3-Brig. 2-Div. 15-Corps	Apr.,	1865
26th Mo. Infy	Aug., 1864	From 3-Brig. 3-Div. 15-Corps	To 3-Brig. 2-Div. 15-Corps	Apr.,	1865
17th Iowa Infy	Jan., 1865	From Veteran Furlough	To 3-Brig. 2-Div. 15-Corps	Apr.,	1865

3d BRIGADE.—Discontinued Aug., 1864.　　　COMMANDERS.

J. J. Wood	Col. 12th Iowa Infy	Apr. 3, 1863, to May 2, 1863.
C. L. Mathies	Brigadier General	May 2, 1863, to June 1, 1863.
J. J. Wood	Col. 12th Iowa Infy	June 1, 1863, to Sept. 24, 1863.
J. L. Geddes	Col. 8th Iowa Infy	Sept. 24, 1863, to Dec. 20, 1863.
J. Banbury	Col. 5th Iowa Infy	Dec. 20, 1863, to Mch. 14, 1864.
C. L. Mathies	Brigadier General	Mch. 14, 1864, to May 15, 1864.
B. D. Dean	Col. 26th Mo. Infy	May 15, 1864, to May 31, 1864.
J. Banbury	Col. 5th Iowa Infy	May 31, 1864, to July 25, 1864.
B. D. Deen	Col. 26th Mo. Infy	July 25, 1864, to Aug. 6, 1864.

8th Iowa Infy	Apr., 1863	From Reorganization	To 3-Brig. 1-Div. 16-Corps	Dec.,	1863
12th Iowa Infy	Apr., 1863	From Reorganization	To 3-Brig. 1-Div. 16-Corps	Dec.,	1863
35th Iowa Infy	Apr., 1863	From Dist. Columbus 16-Corps	To 3-Brig. 1-Div. 16-Corps	Dec.,	1863
93d Ill. Infy	Dec., 1863	From 3-Brig. 2-Div. 17-Corps	To 1-Brig. 3-Div. 15-Corps	Aug.,	1864
5th Iowa Infy	Dec., 1863	From 3-Brig. 2-Div. 17-Corps	Transferred to 5th Iowa Cav	Sept.,	1864
10th Iowa Infy	Dec., 1863	From 3-Brig. 2-Div. 17-Corps	To 2-Brig. 3-Div. 15-Corps	Aug.,	1864
26th Mo. Infy	Dec., 1863	From 3-Brig. 2-Div. 17-Corps	To 2-Brig. 3-Div. 15-Corps	Aug.,	1864
ARTILLERY, 3d DIVISION.—					
Batty. E, 1st Illinois	Apr., 1863	From Arty. 8th Div. 16-Corps	To Arty. 1-Div. 16-Corps	Dec.,	1863
2d Iowa Batty	Apr., 1863	From Arty. 8th Div. 16-Corps	To Arty. 1-Div. 16-Corps	Dec.,	1863
6th Indiana Batty	Sept., 1863	From Arty. 4-Div. 15-Corps	To Arty. 1-Div. 16-Corps	Dec.,	1863
Cogswell's Ill. Batty	Dec., 1863	From Arty. 2-Div. 17-Corps	To Arty. Res. Nashville, Tenn	Apr.,	1864
6th Wisconsin Batty	Dec., 1863	From Arty. 2-Div. 17-Corps	To Arty. Res. Nashville, Tenn	Apr.,	1864
12th Wisconsin Batty	Dec., 1863	From Arty. 2-Div. 17-Corps	To Arty. Brig. 15-Corps	Sept.,	1864
Batty. D. 1st Missouri	May, 1864	From Arty. Res. Huntsville, Ala	To Arty. Res. Huntsville, Ala	Sept.,	1864

CAVALRY.—

5th Ohio Cav............Apr., 1864	From Unatt. 15-Corps.............	To 2-Brig. 3-(Kilpatrick's) Cav. Div.	Oct., 1863

UNASSIGNED.—

13th Illinois Infy........Apr., 1864	From 1-Brig. 1-Div. 15-Corps........	No change to Muster Out..........	June, 1864

4th DIVISION.—Joined Corps from 1-Div. 16-Corps, July 28, 1863. Discontinued Sept. 14, 1864. Reorganized Sept. 23, 1864, from 2-Div. 16-Corps.

COMMANDERS.

Hugh Ewing............	Brigadier General..................	July 28, 1863, to Sept. 1, 1863.
J. M. Corse.............	Brigadier General..................	Sept. 1, 1863, to Oct. 16, 1863.
Hugh Ewing............	Brigadier General..................	Oct. 16, 1863, to Feb. 8, 1864.
William Harrow........	Brigadier General..................	Feb. 8, 1864, to Sept. 14, 1864.
J. M. Corse.............	Brigadier General..................	Sept. 23, 1864, to July 24, 1865.

1st BRIGADE.

COMMANDERS.

J. M. Loomis............	Col. 26th Illinois Infy............	July 28, 1863, to Aug. 7, 1863.
R. Williams.............	Col. 12th Indiana Infy............	Aug. 7, 1863, to Sept. 8, 1863.
J. M. Loomis............	Col. 26th Illinois Infy............	Sept. 8, 1863, to Jan. 15, 1864.
R. Williams.............	Col. 12th Indiana Infy............	Jan. 15, 1864, to Mch. 12, 1864.
J. M. Loomis............	Col. 26th Illinois Infy............	Mch. 12, 1864, to Apr. 30, 1864.
R. Williams.............	Col. 12th Indiana Infy............	Apr. 30, 1864, to Aug. 4, 1864.
J. M. Oliver.............	Col. 15th Michigan Infy..........	Aug. 4, 1864, to Sept. 14, 1864.
R. Martin..............	Lt.-Col. 66th Ind. Infy............	Sept. 22, 1864, to Oct. 14, 1864.
E. W. Rice.............	Brigadier General..................	Oct. 14, 1864, to Aug. 1, 1865.

12th Indiana Infy.......July, 1863	From 1-Brig. 1-Div. 16-Corps....	To 1-Brig. 1-Div. 15-Corps........	Sept., 1864
100th Indiana Infy......July, 1863	From 1-Brig. 1-Div. 16-Corps....	To 2-Brig. 4-Div. 15-Corps........	Aug., 1864
26th Illinois Infy......July, 1863	From 1-Brig. 1-Div. 16-Corps....	To 2-Brig. 4-Div. 15-Corps........	Aug., 1864
90th Illinois Infy......July, 1863	From 1-Brig. 1-Div. 16-Corps....	To 3-Brig. 2-Div. 15-Corps........	Sept., 1864
99th Indiana Infy......Aug., 1864	From 3-Brig. 4-Div. 15-Corps....	To 3-Brig. 2-Div. 15-Corps........	Sept., 1864
48th Illinois Infy......Aug., 1864	From 3-Brig. 4-Div. 15-Corps....	To 3-Brig. 2-Div. 15-Corps........	Sept., 1864
15th Michigan Infy......Aug., 1864	From 3-Brig. 4-Div. 15-Corps....	To 3-Brig. 2-Div. 15-Corps........	Sept., 1864
70th Ohio Infy..........Aug., 1864	From 3-Brig. 4-Div. 15-Corps....	To 3-Brig. 2-Div. 15-Corps........	Sept., 1864
66th Indiana Infy......Sept., 1864	From 1-Brig. 2-Div. 16-Corps....	No change to Muster Out..........	June, 1865
52d Illinois Infy......Sept., 1864	From 1-Brig. 2-Div. 16-Corps....	No change to Muster Out..........	July, 1865
2d Iowa Infy...........Sept., 1864	From 1-Brig. 2-Div. 16-Corps....	No change to Muster Out..........	July, 1865
7th Iowa Infy..........Sept., 1864	From 1-Brig. 2-Div. 16-Corps....	No change to Muster Out..........	July, 1865

2d BRIGADE.—

COMMANDERS.

S. G. Hicks............	Col. 40th Illinois Infy............	July 28, 1863, to Aug. 5, 1863.
J. M. Oliver...........	Col. 15th Michigan Infy..........	Aug. 5, 1863, to Oct. 25, 1863.
J. M. Corse...........	Brigadier General..................	Oct. 25, 1863, to Nov. 25, 1863.
C. C. Walcutt.........	Col. 46th Ohio Infy..............	Nov. 25, 1863, to Mch. 12, 1864.
W. A. Dickerman.......	Col. 103d Illinois Infy............	Mch. 12, 1864, to Apr. 15, 1864.
C. C. Walcutt.........	Col. 46th Ohio Infy..............	Apr. 15, 1864, to Sept. 14, 1864.
W. S. Merriman........	Major 12th Ill. Infy..............	Sept. 14, 1864, to Oct. 5, 1864.
R. N. Adams...........	Col. 81st Ohio Infy..............	Oct. 5, 1864, to Apr. 26, 1865.
W. T. Clark...........	Brigadier General..................	Apr. 26, 1865, to May 1, 1865.
R. N. Adams...........	Col. 81st Ohio Infy..............	May 1, 1865, to July 13, 1865.

40th Illinois Infy........July, 1863	From 2-Brig. 1-Div. 16-Corps....	To 2-Brig. 1-Div. 15-Corps........	Sept., 1864
103d Illinois Infy........July, 1863	From 2-Brig. 1-Div. 16-Corps....	To 2-Brig. 1-Div. 15-Corps........	Sept., 1864
15th Michigan Infy........July, 1863	From 2-Brig. 1-Div. 16-Corps....	To Unassigned 4-Div. 15-Corps.....	Jan., 1864
46th Ohio Infy..........July, 1863	From 2-Brig. 1-Div. 16-Corps....	To 2-Brig. 1-Div. 15-Corps........	Sept., 1864
6th Iowa Infy...........Sept., 1863	From 4-Brig. 4-Div. 15-Corps....	To 2-Brig. 1-Div. 15-Corps........	Sept., 1864
97th Indiana Infy......Apr., 1864	From 3-Brig. 4-Div. 15-Corps....	To 2-Brig. 1-Div. 15-Corps........	Sept., 1864
26th Illinois Infy......Aug., 1864	From 1-Brig. 4-Div. 15-Corps....	To 2-Brig. 1-Div. 15-Corps........	Sept., 1864
100th Indiana Infy......Aug., 1864	From 1-Brig. 4-Div. 15-Corps....	To 2-Brig. 1-Div. 15-Corps........	Sept., 1864
12th Illinois Infy......Sept., 1864	From 2-Brig. 2-Div. 16-Corps....	To 2-Brig. 1-Div. 15-Corps........	Apr., 1865
66th Illinois Infy......Sept., 1864	From 2-Brig. 2-Div. 16-Corps....	To 3-Brig. 4-Div. 15-Corps........	Apr., 1865
81st Ohio Infy..........Sept., 1864	From 2-Brig. 2-Div. 16-Corps....	No change to Muster Out..........	July, 1865
48th Indiana Infy......Apr., 1865	From 1-Brig. 3-Div. 15-Corps....	No change to Muster Out..........	July, 1865
59th Indiana Infy......Apr., 1865	From 1-Brig. 3-Div. 15-Corps....	No change to Muster Out..........	July, 1865
63d Illinois Infy......Apr., 1865	From 1-Brig. 3-Div. 15-Corps....	No change to Muster Out..........	July, 1865
18th Wisconsin Infy......Apr., 1865	From 1-Brig. 3-Div. 15-Corps....	No change to Muster Out..........	July, 1865

3d BRIGADE.—Discontinued Aug. 4, 1864. Reorganized Sept. 23, 1864.

COMMANDERS.

J. R. Cockerill........	Col. 70th Ohio Infy..............	July 28, 1863, to Aug. 20, 1863.
A. Fowler.............	Col. 99th Indiana Infy............	Aug. 20, 1863, to Sept. 20, 1863.
J. R. Cockerill........	Col. 70th Ohio Infy..............	Sept. 20, 1863, to Jan. 27, 1864.
A. Fowler.............	Col. 99th Indiana Infy............	Jan. 27, 1864, to Mch. 12, 1864.
J. R. Cockerill........	Col. 70th Ohio Infy..............	Mch. 12, 1864, to Apr. 13, 1864.
Wells S. Jones........	Col. 53d Ohio Infy..............	Apr. 13, 1864, to May 6, 1864.
J. M. Oliver..........	Col. 15th Michigan Infy..........	May 6, 1864, to Aug. 4, 1864.
R. Rowett.............	Col. 7th Illinois Infy............	Sept. 23, 1864, to Oct. 20, 1864.
F. J. Hurlbut........	Lt.-Col. 57th Ill. Infy............	Oct. 20, 1864, to Apr. 22, 1865.
R. Rowett.............	Col. 7th Illinois Infy............	Apr. 22, 1865, to Apr. 26, 1865.
C. J. Stolbrand........	Brigadier General..................	Apr. 26, 1865, to July, 1865.

97th Indiana Infy.......July, 1863	From 3-Brig. 1-Div. 16-Corps....	To 2-Brig. 4-Div. 15-Corps........	Apr., 1864
99th Indiana Infy......July, 1863	From 3-Brig. 1-Div. 16-Corps....	To 1-Brig. 4-Div. 15-Corps........	Aug., 1864
53d Ohio Infy..........July, 1863	From 3-Brig. 1-Div. 16-Corps....	To 2-Brig. 2-Div. 15-Corps........	May, 1864
70th Ohio Infy..........July, 1863	From 3-Brig. 1-Div. 16-Corps....	To 1-Brig. 4-Div. 15-Corps........	Aug., 1864
48th Illinois Infy......Sept., 1863	From 4-Brig. 4-Div. 15-Corps....	To 1-Brig. 4-Div. 15-Corps........	Aug., 1864
15th Michigan Infy......Apr., 1864	From Unatt. 4-Div. 15-Corps....	To 1-Brig. 4-Div. 15-Corps........	Aug., 1864
7th Illinois Infy......Sept., 1864	From 3-Brig. 2-Div. 16-Corps....	No change to Muster Out..........	July, 1865
50th Illinois Infy......Sept., 1864	From 3-Brig. 2-Div. 16-Corps....	No change to Muster Out..........	July, 1865
57th Illinois Infy......Sept., 1864	From 3-Brig. 2-Div. 16-Corps....	No change to Muster Out..........	July, 1865
39th Iowa Infy..........Sept., 1864	From 3-Brig. 2-Div. 16-Corps....	No change to Muster Out..........	July, 1865

4th BRIGADE.—

COMMANDERS.

W. W. Sanford........	Col. 48th Illinois Infy............	July 28, 1863, to Aug. 27, 1863.
John M. Corse........	Brigadier General..................	Aug. 27, 1863, to Sept. 1, 1863.

6th Iowa Infy...........July, 1863	From 4-Brig. 1-Div. 16-Corps......	To 2-Brig. 4-Div. 15-Corps........	Sept., 1863
48th Illinois Infy......July, 1863	From 4-Brig. 1-Div. 16-Corps......	To 3-Brig. 4-Div. 15-Corps........	Sept., 1863

ARTILLERY.—

Batty. F, 1st Illinois....July, 1863	From Arty. 1-Div. 16-Corps........	To Arty. Res. Nashville, Tenn.....	Nov., 1864
Batty. I, 1st Illinois....July, 1863	From Arty. 1-Div. 16-Corps........	To Arty. Res. Nashville, Tenn.....	Apr., 1864
6th Indiana Batty.......July, 1863	From Arty. 1-Div. 16-Corps........	To Arty. 3-Div. 15-Corps..........	Sept., 1864
Cogswell's Ill. Batty....July, 1863	From Arty. 7-Div. 17-Corps........	To Arty. 2-Div. 17-Corps..........	Sept., 1864
Batty. D, 1st Missouri...Sept., 1863	From Arty. 2-D. Dist. Corinth 16-C.	To Arty. Res. Huntsville, Ala.....	Apr., 1864
1st Iowa Batty..........Apr., 1864	From Arty. 1-Div. 15-Corps........	To Arty. Res. Nashville, Tenn.....	Nov., 1864

ARTILLERY BRIGADE.—

Batty. H, 1st Illinois....Sept., 1864	From Arty. 2-Div. 15-Corps........	No change to Muster Out.........	June, 1865
Batty. B, 1st Michigan..Sept., 1864	From Arty. 2-Div. 16-Corps........	No change to Muster Out.........	June, 1865
Batty. H, 1st Missouri..Sept., 1864	From Arty. 2-Div. 16-Corps........	No change to Muster Out.........	June, 1865
12th Wisconsin Batty...Sept., 1864	From Arty. 3-Div. 15-Corps........	No change to Muster Out.........	June, 1865

CAVALRY BRIGADE.— COMMANDER.

E. F. Winslow........	Col. 4th Iowa Cav.................	Aug. 8, 1863, to Dec., 1863.	

4th Illinois Cav........Aug., 1863	From 1-Brig. 1-Cav. Div. 16-Corps	To Cavalry Brig. 17-Corps.........	Dec., 1863
5th Illinois Cav........Aug., 1863	From Cav. Herron's Div. 13-Corps	To Cavalry Brig. 17-Corps.........	Dec., 1863
11th Illinois Cav.......Aug., 1863	From 4-Brig. 1-Cav. Div. 16-Corps	To Cavalry Brig. 17-Corps.........	Dec., 1863
4th Iowa Cavalry.......Aug., 1863	From Unattached 15-Corps........	To Cavalry Brig. 17-Corps.........	Dec., 1863
10th Missouri Cav......Aug., 1863	From 3-Brig. Cav. Div. 16-Corps..	To Cavalry Brig. 17-Corps.........	Dec., 1863

UNATTACHED.—

Thielman's Ill. Cav.....May, 1863	From 2-Div. 15-Corps...........	To Left Wing Forces 23-Corps....	Dec., 1863
4th Iowa Cavalry.......May, 1863	From 2-Brig. 2-Cav. Div. 13-Corps	To Winslow's Cav. Brig. 15-Corps..	Aug., 1863
5th Ohio Cavalry........Oct., 1863	From 2-Brig. 1-Cav. Div. 16-Corps	To Cavalry 3-Div. 15-Corps........	Apr., 1864
15th Michigan Infy.....Jan., 1864	From 2-Brig. 4-Div. 15-Corps......	To 3-Brig. 4-Div. 15-Corps........	Apr., 1864
1st Alabama Cavalry....Sept., 1864	From 4-Div. 16-Corps...........	To Unattached 3-Cavalry Div.....	Oct., 1864
29th Missouri Infy. Mtd..Nov., 1864	From 1-Brig. 1-Div. 15-Corps.....	No change to Muster Out.........	June, 1865

Sixteenth Army Corps

Created Dec. 18, 1862, by General Order No. 210, A. G. O., to consist of the 6th, 7th and 8th Divisions, 13th Army Corps, Dept. of the Tennessee, and Districts of Memphis, Jackson and Columbus, 13th Army Corps, Dept. of the Tennessee. The 6th and 7th Divisions were transferred to 17th Army Corps Jan. 20, 1863, in exchange for the 1st and 4th Divisions of that Corps, and the District of Corinth was also transferred from the 17th Army Corps to this Corps Jan. 20, 1863.

COMMANDERS.

S. A. Hurlbut........	Major General.....................	Dec. 22, 1862, to Jan. 10, 1863.
C. S. Hamilton........	Brigadier General...................	Jan. 10, 1863, to Feb. 5, 1863.
S. A. Hurlbut........	Major General.....................	Feb. 5, 1863, to Apr. 17, 1864.
(No Commander from April 17, 1864, to Oct. 15, 1864.)		
N. J. T. Dana..........	Major General.....................	Oct. 15, 1863, to Nov. 7, 1864.

LEFT WING.—Organized Dec. 22, 1862. Discontinued Sept. 23, 1864.

COMMANDERS.

C. S. Hamilton........	Major General.....................	Dec. 22, 1862, to Apr. 1, 1863.
R. J. Oglesby.........	Major General.....................	Apr. 1, 1863, to July 7, 1863.
G. M. Dodge...........	Brigadier General...................	July 7, 1863, to Aug. 7, 1863.
A. Mersey.............	Col. 9th Ill. Infy.................	Aug. 7, 1863, to Sept. 3, 1863.
E. A. Carr.............	Brigadier General...................	Sept. 3, 1863, to Oct. 15, 1863.
G. M. Dodge...........	Brigadier General...................	Oct. 15, 1863, to Aug. 19, 1864.
T. E. G. Ransom......	Brigadier General...................	Aug. 19, 1864, to Sept. 23, 1864.

6th DIVISION.—Transferred to 17th Army Corps Jan. 20, 1863.

COMMANDER.

John McArthur........	Brigadier General...................	Dec. 22, 1862, to Jan. 20, 1863.

1st BRIGADE.— COMMANDER.

Geo. W. Deitzler.......	Brigadier General...................	Dec. 22, 1863, to Jan. 20, 1863.

17th Ill. Infy...........Dec., 1862	From 1-Brig. 6-Div. L. W. 13-Corps.	To 1-Brig. 6-Div. 17-Corps........	Jan., 1863
95th Ill. Infy...........Dec., 1862	From 1-Brig. 6-Div. L. W. 13-Corps.	To 1-Brig. 6-Div. 17-Corps........	Jan., 1863
1st Kan. Infy...........Dec., 1862	From 1-Brig. 6-Div. L. W. 13-Corps.	To 1-Brig. 6-Div. 17-Corps........	Jan., 1863
16th Wis. Infy..........Dec., 1862	From 1-Brig. 6-Div. L. W. 13-Corps.	To 1-Brig. 6-Div. 17-Corps........	Jan., 1863
Batty. F, 2d Ill. Arty....Dec., 1862	From 1-Brig. 6-Div. L. W. 13-Corps.	To 1-Brig. 6-Div. 17-Corps........	Jan., 1863

2d BRIGADE.— COMMANDER.

T. E. G. Ransom.....	Brigadier General...................	Dec. 22, 1862, to Jan. 20, 1863.

11th Ill. Infy...........Dec., 1862	From 2-Brig. 6-Div. L. W. 13-Corps.	To 2-Brig. 6-Div. 17-Corps........	Jan., 1863
14th Wis. Infy..........Dec., 1862	From 2-Brig. 6-Div. L. W. 13-Corps.	To 2-Brig. 6-Div. 17-Corps........	Jan., 1863
17th Wis. Infy..........Dec., 1862	From 2-Brig. 6-Div. L. W. 13-Corps.	To 2-Brig. 6-Div. 17-Corps........	Jan., 1863
18th Wis. Infy..........Dec., 1862	From 2-Brig. 6-Div. L. W. 13-Corps.	To 2-Brig. 6-Div. 17-Corps........	Jan., 1863
1st Minn. Batty.........Dec., 1862	From Unatt. 6-Div. L. W. 13-Corps.	To 2-Brig. 6-Div. 17-Corps........	Jan., 1863
Batty. C, 1st Mo. Arty....Dec., 1862	From Arty. 4-Div. R. W. 13-Corps.	To 2-Brig. 6-Div. 17-Corps........	Jan., 1863

3d BRIGADE.— COMMANDER.

M. M. Crocker.........	Brigadier General...................	Dec. 22, 1862, to Jan. 20, 1863.

11th Ia. Infy...........Dec., 1862	From 3-Brig. 6-Div. L. W. 13-Corps.	To 3-Brig. 6-Div. 17-Corps........	Jan., 1863
13th Ia. Infy...........Dec., 1862	From 3-Brig. 6-Div. L. W. 13-Corps.	To 3-Brig. 6-Div. 17-Corps........	Jan., 1863
15th Ia. Infy...........Dec., 1862	From 3-Brig. 6-Div. L. W. 13-Corps.	To 3-Brig. 6-Div. 17-Corps........	Jan., 1863
16th Ia. Infy...........Dec., 1862	From 3-Brig. 6-Div. L. W. 13-Corps.	To 3-Brig. 6-Div. 17-Corps........	Jan., 1863
10th Ohio Batty.........Dec., 1862	From 3-Brig. 6-Div. L. W. 13-Corps.	To 3-Brig. 6-Div. 17-Corps........	Jan., 1863

7th DIVISION.—Transferred to 17th Corps Jan. 20, 1863.

COMMANDER.

I. F. Quinby..........	Brigadier General...................	Dec. 22, 1862, to Jan. 20, 1863.

1st BRIGADE.— COMMANDERS.

J. I. Alexander........	Col. 59th Ind. Infy................	Dec. 22, 1862, to Jan. 1, 1863.
Norman Eddy.........	Col. 48th Ind. Infy................	Jan. 1, 1863, to Jan. 20, 1863.

72d Ill. Infy...........Dec., 1862	From 1-Brig. 7-Div. L. W. 13-Corps.	To 1-Brig. 7-Div. 17-Corps........	Jan., 1863
48th Ind. Infy..........Dec., 1862	From 1-Brig. 7-Div. L. W. 13-Corps.	To 1-Brig. 7-Div. 17-Corps........	Jan., 1863
59th Ind. Infy..........Dec., 1862	From 1-Brig. 7-Div. L. W. 13-Corps.	To 1-Brig. 7-Div. 17-Corps........	Jan., 1863
4th Minn. Infy..........Dec., 1862	From 1-Brig. 7-Div. L. W. 13-Corps.	To 1-Brig. 7-Div. 17-Corps........	Jan., 1863

2d BRIGADE.— COMMANDER.

E. R. Eckley	Col. 80th Ohio Infy	Dec. 22, 1862, to Jan. 20, 1863.		
80th Ohio Infy	Dec., 1863	From 2-Brig. 7-Div. L. W. 13-Corps.	To 2-Brig. 7-Div. 17-Corps	Jan., 1863
56th Ill. Infy	Dec., 1863	From 2-Brig. 7-Div. L. W. 13-Corps.	To 2-Brig. 7-Div. 17-Corps	Jan., 1863
17th Ia. Infy	Dec., 1863	From 2-Brig. 7-Div. L. W. 13-Corps.	To 2-Brig. 7-Div. 17-Corps	Jan., 1863
10th Mo. Infy	Dec., 1863	From 2-Brig. 7-Div. L. W. 13-Corps.	To 2-Brig. 7-Div. 17-Corps	Jan., 1863
24th Mo. Infy., Co. E	Dec., 1863	From 2-Brig. 7-Div. L. W. 13-Corps.	To 2-Brig. 7-Div. 17-Corps	Jan., 1863

3d BRIGADE.— COMMANDER.

C. L. Mathies	Brigadier General	Dec. 22, 1862, to Jan. 20, 1863.		
93d Ill. Infy	Dec., 1862	From 3-Brig. 7-Div. L. W. 13-Corps.	To 3-Brig. 7-Div. 17-Corps	Jan., 1863
5th Ia. Infy	Dec., 1862	From 3-Brig. 7-Div. L. W. 13-Corps.	To 3-Brig. 7-Div. 17-Corps	Jan., 1863
10th Ia. Infy	Dec., 1862	From 3-Brig. 7-Div. L. W. 13-Corps.	To 3-Brig. 7-Div. 17-Corps	Jan., 1863
26th Mo. Infy	Dec., 1862	From 3-Brig. 7-Div. L. W. 13-Corps.	To 3-Brig. 7-Div. 17-Corps	Jan., 1863
ARTILLERY.—				
Batty. M, 1st Mo. Arty	Dec., 1862	From Arty. 7-Div. L. W. 13-Corps..	To Arty. 7-Div. 17-Corps	Jan., 1863
11th Ohio Batty	Dec., 1862	From Arty. 7-Div. L. W. 13-Corps..	To Arty. 7-Div. 17-Corps	Jan., 1863
6th Wis. Batty	Dec., 1862	From Arty. 7-Div. L. W. 13-Corps..	To Arty. 7-Div. 17-Corps	Jan., 1863
12th Wis. Batty	Dec., 1862	From Arty. 7-Div. L. W. 13-Corps..	To Arty. 7-Div. 17-Corps	Jan., 1863

8th DIVISION.—Discontinued March, 1863.

COMMANDERS.

L. F. Ross	Brigadier General	Dec. 18, 1862, to Dec. 26, 1862.	
John E. Smith	Brigadier General	Dec. 26, 1862, to Apr. 3, 1863.	

1st BRIGADE.— COMMANDER.

J. W. Fuller	Col. 27th Ohio Infy	Dec. 18, 1862, to Apr. 3, 1863.		
27th Ohio Infy	Dec., 1862	From 1-Brig. 8-Div. L. W. 13-Corps.	To 4-Brig. 2-Div. 16-Corps	Mch., 1863
39th Ohio Infy	Dec., 1862	From 1-Brig. 8-Div. L. W. 13-Corps.	To 4-Brig. 2-Div. 16-Corps	Mch., 1863
43d Ohio Infy	Dec., 1862	From 1-Brig. 8-Div. L. W. 13-Corps.	To 4-Brig. 2-Div. 16-Corps	Mch., 1863
63d Ohio Infy	Dec., 1862	From 1-Brig. 8-Div. L. W. 13-Corps.	To 4-Brig. 2-Div. 16-Corps	Mch., 1863
Batty C, 1st Mich. Arty	Dec., 1862	From 1-Brig. 8-Div. L. W. 13-Corps.	To Arty. 2-Div. 16-Corps	Mch., 1863
Batty. F, 2d U. S. Arty	Dec., 1862	From Arty. 8-Div. L. W. 13-Corps.	To Arty. 2-Div. 16-Corps	Mch., 1863

2d BRIGADE.— COMMANDER.

J. A. Mower	Col. 11th Mo. Infy	Dec. 18, 1862, to Apr. 3, 1863.		
26th Ill. Infy	Dec., 1862	From 2-Brig. 8-Div. L. W. 13-Corps.	To 2-Brig. 1-Div. 17-Corps	Dec., 1862
47th Ill. Infy	Dec., 1862	From 2-Brig. 8-Div. L. W. 13-Corps.	To 2-Brig. 3-Div. 15-Corps	Mch., 1863
5th Minn. Infy	Dec., 1862	From 2-Brig. 8-Div. L. W. 13-Corps.	To 2-Brig. 3-Div. 15-Corps	Mch., 1863
11th Mo. Infy	Dec., 1862	From 2-Brig. 8-Div. L. W. 13-Corps.	To 2-Brig. 3-Div. 15-Corps	Mch., 1863
8th Wis. Infy	Dec., 1862	From 2-Brig. 8-Div. L. W. 13-Corps.	To 2-Brig. 3-Div. 15-Corps	Mch., 1863
2d Ia. Batty	Dec., 1862	From 2-Brig. 8-Div. L. W. 13-Corps.	To Arty. 3-Div. 15-Corps	Mch., 1863

3d BRIGADE.— COMMANDERS.

R. P. Buckland	Col. 72d Ohio Infy	Dec. 18, 1862, to Feb. 12, 1863.		
J. W. Judy	Col. 114th Ill. Infy	Feb. 12, 1863, to Apr. 3, 1863.		
72d Ohio Infy	Dec., 1862	From 3-Br. 1-Div. Dist. Mem. 13-C.	To 1-Brig. 3-Div. 15-Corps	Mch., 1863
114th Ill. Infy	Dec., 1862	From 3-Br. 1-Div. Dist. Mem. 13-C.	To 1-Brig. 3-Div. 15-Corps	Mch., 1863
93d Ind. Infy	Dec., 1862	From 3-Br. 1-Div. Dist. Mem. 13-C.	To 1-Brig. 3-Div. 15-Corps	Mch., 1863
32d Wis. Infy	Dec., 1862	From 3-Br. 1-Div. Dist. Mem. 13-C.	To 1-Brig. 3-Div. 15-Corps	Mch., 1863
Batty. E, 1st Ill. Arty	Dec., 1862	From Arty. 1-Div. Dist. Mem. 13-C.	To Arty. 3-Div. 15-Corps	Mch., 1863

CAVALRY DIVISION.— COMMANDER.

T. Lyle Dickey	Col. 4th Ill. Cav	Dec. 18, 1862, to Mch., 1863.	

1st BRIGADE.— COMMANDER.

B. H. Grierson	Col. 6th Ill. Cav	Dec. 18, 1862, to Mch., 1863.		
6th Ill. Cav	Dec., 1862	From 3-Brig. Cav. Div. 13-Corps	To 1-Brig. 1-Cav. Div. 16-Corps	Mch., 1863
7th Ill. Cav	Dec., 1862	From 1-Brig. Cav. Div. 13-Corps	To 1-Brig. 1-Cav. Div. 16-Corps	Mch., 1863
2d Ia. Cav	Dec., 1862	From 2-Brig. Cav. Div. 13-Corps	To 1-Brig. 1-Cav. Div. 16-Corps	Mch., 1863

2d BRIGADE.— COMMANDER.

A. L. Lee	Col. 7th Kan. Cav	Dec. 18, 1862, to Mch., 1863.		
2d Ill. Cav	Dec., 1862	From 1-Brig. Cav. Div. 13-Corps	To Headqrs. 13-Corps	Mch., 1863
4th Ill. Cav	Dec., 1862	From 1-Brig. Cav. Div. 13-Corps	To 2-Brig. 1-Cav. Div. 16-Corps	Mch., 1863
7th Kan. Cav	Dec., 1862	From 1-Brig. Cav. Div. 13-Corps	To 2-Brig. 2-Div. 16-Corps	Mch., 1863
5 O. Cav (1 and 2 Batt'ns)	Dec., 1862	From 2-Brig. Cav. Div. 13-Corps	To 3-B. Dist. Memphis 5-Div. 16-C.	Mch., 1863

DISTRICT OF MEMPHIS.—Known as 5th Division, 16th Army Corps, Mch. 31, 1863, to Jan. 25, 1864. Transferered to District of West Tennessee, June, 1864.

COMMANDERS.

S. A. Hurlbut	Major General	Dec. 18, 1862, to Jan. 5, 1863.	
J. C. Veatch	Brigadier General	Jan. 5, 1863, to Jan. 25, 1863.	
R. P. Buckland	Brigadier General	Jan. 25, 1863, to Mch. 31, 1863.	
J. C. Veatch	Brigadier General	Mch. 31, 1863, to Jan. 25, 1864.	
R. P. Buckland	Brigadier General	Jan. 25, 1864, to June, 1864.	
63d Ill. Infy	Dec., 1862	From 3-Brig. 3-Div. 17-Corps	To 4-Brig. 5-Div. 16-Corps	Mch., 1863
87th Ill. Infy	Dec., 1862	From New Organization	To 3-Brig. 5-Div. 16-Corps	Mch., 1863
101st Ill. Infy	Dec., 1862	From 2-Brig. 4-Div. 17-Corps	To Ram Fleet Miss. Squadron	Mch., 1863
109th Ill. Infy	Dec., 1862	From Dist. Jackson 16-Corps	To Consol. with 11th Ill	Mch., 1863
117th Ill. Infy	Dec., 1862	From Reserve Brig. Dist. Memphis	To 1-Brig. 5-Div. 16-Corps	Mch., 1863
120th Ill. Infy	Dec., 1862	From 1-B. 2-D. Dist Memphis 13-C.	To 2-Brig. 5-Div. 16-Corps	Mch., 1863
130th Ill. Infy	Dec., 1862	From Res. B'g. Dist. Memphis 13-C.	To 2-Brig. 10-Div. 13-Corps	Mch., 1863
25th Ind. Infy	Dec., 1862	From 3-Brig. 4-Div. 17-Corps	To 2-Brig. 5-Div. 16-Corps	Mch., 1863
89th Ind. Infy	Dec., 1862	From Prisoners of War	To 1-Brig. 5-Div. 16-Corps	Mch., 1863
95th Ohio Infy	Dec., 1862	From Prisoners of War	To 1-Brig. 3-Div. 15-Corps	Mch., 1863
2d Ia. Cav. (6 Co's)	Dec., 1862	From 1-Brig. Cav. Div. 16-Corps	To 1-Brig. 1-Cav. Div. 16-Corps	Mch., 1863
10th Mo. Cav	Dec., 1862	From Dist. St. Louis Dept. Mo.	To Cav. Brig. 2-Div. 16-Corps	Mch., 1863
3d U. S. Cav	Dec., 1862	From Dist. St. Louis Dept. Mo.	To Unatt. 5-Div. 16-Corps	Mch., 1863
1st Mo. Cav. (F, K, M)	Feb., 1863	From Dist. Eastern Ark	To 4-Brig. 5-Div. 16-Corps	Mch., 1863

1st BRIGADE.—   COMMANDER.

C. D. Murray..........	Col. 89th Ind. Infy...............	Mch. 31, 1863, to Jan. 25, 1864.

117th Ill. Infy...........Mch., 1863	From Unatt. Dist. Memphis 16-C..	To 3-Brig. 3-Div. 16-Corps........	Jan.,	1864
131st Ill. Infy...........Mch., 1863	From 2-Brig. 10-Div. 13-Corps.....	To Dist. Northeast, La............	May,	1863
89th Ind. Infy...........Mch., 1863	From Unatt. Dist. Memphis 16-C....	To 1-Brig. 3-Div. 16-Corps........	Jan.,	1864
1st Tenn. Col. H. Arty..June, 1863	From New Organization...........	To Garrison Ft. Pickering Memphis.	July,	1863

2d BRIGADE.—   COMMANDERS.

W. H. Morgan........	Col. 25th Ind. Infy..............	Mch. 31, 1863, to July 15, 1863.
J. H. Howe...........	Col. 32d Wis. Infy...............	July 15, 1863, to Aug. 15, 1863.
W. H. Morgan........	Col. 25th Ind. Infy..............	Aug. 15, 1863, to Nov., 1863.
Geo. B. Hoge........	Col. 113th Ill. Infy.............	Jan. 10, 1864, to June 1, 1864.

120th Ill. Infy...........Mch., 1863	From Unatt. Dist. Memphis 16-C...	To Dist. of Northeast La..........	May,	1863
25th Ind. Infy...........Mch., 1863	From Unatt. Dist. Memphis 16-C...	To 3-Brig. 1-Cav. Div. 16-Corps....	Nov.,	1863
32d Wis. Infy...........Mch., 1863	From 3-Brig. 8-Div. 16-Corps......	To 3-Brig. 1-Cav. Div. 16-Corps....	Nov.,	1863
3d U. S. Cav..........Mch., 1863	From Unatt. Dist. Memphis 16-C...	To Unatt. 15-Corps...............	Oct.,	1863
Batty. D, 2d Ill. Arty...May, 1863	From Arty. 1-Div. 16-Corps.......	To 3-Brig. 1-Cav. Div. 16-Corps....	Nov.,	1863
108th Ill. Infy...........Jan., 1864	From Post of Corinth, 2-Div. 16-C.	To 2-Brig. Sturgis' Expedition....	June,	1864
113th Ill. Infy...........Jan., 1864	From Post of Corinth, 2-Div. 16-C.	To 2-Brig. Sturgis' Expedition....	June,	1864
120th Ill. Infy...........Jan., 1864	From Post of Corinth, 2-Div. 16-C.	To 2-Brig. Sturgis' Expedition....	June,	1864

3d BRIGADE.—Transferred to 2-Div. 16-Corps, Nov., 1863.

COMMANDERS.

Thos. Stevens........	Col. 2d Wis. Cav................	Mch. 31, 1863, to May 1, 1863.
J. W. Fuller.........	Col. 27th Ohio Infy.............	May 1, 1863, to July 25, 1863.
J. W. Sprague........	Col. 63d Ohio Infy..............	July 25, 1863, to Aug. 25, 1863.
J. W. Fuller.........	Col. 27th Ohio Infy.............	Aug. 25, 1863, to Nov. 14, 1863.

87th Ill. Infy...........Mch., 1863	From Unatt. Dist. Memphis 16-C..	To 2-Brig. 12-Div. 13-Corps.......	May,	1863
5th O. Cav. (1, 2 Batt'ns).Mch., 1863	From 2-Brig. Cav. Div. 16-Corps...	To 4-Brig. 5-Div. 16-Corps.......	May,	1863
2d Wis. Cav..........Mch., 1863	From 2-Brig. 2-Cav. Div. 13-Corps.	To Cav. Herron's Div. 13-Corps....	June,	1863
27th Ohio Infy..........May, 1863	From 4-Brig. 2-Div. 16-Corps.....	To Fuller's Brig. 2-Div. 16-Corps..	Nov.,	1863
39th Ohio Infy..........May, 1863	From 4-Brig. 2-Div. 16-Corps.....	To Fuller's Brig. 2-Div. 16-Corps..	Nov.,	1863
43d Ohio Infy..........May, 1863	From 4-Brig. 2-Div. 16-Corps.....	To Fuller's Brig. 2-Div. 16-Corps..	Nov.,	1863
63d Ohio Infy..........May, 1863	From 4-Brig. 2-Div. 16-Corps.....	To Fuller's Brig. 2-Div. 16-Corps..	Nov.,	1863
Batty. C, 1st Mich. Arty..May, 1863	From 4-Brig. 2-Div. 16-Corps.....	To Fuller's Brig. 2-Div. 16-Corps..	Nov.,	1863
Batty. F, 2d U. S. Arty..May, 1863	From 4-Brig. 2-Div. 16-Corps.....	To Fuller's Brig. 2-Div. 16-Corps..	Nov.,	1863

4th BRIGADE.—   COMMANDERS.

J. F. Ritter..........	Col. 1st Mo. Cav................	Mch. 31, 1863, to May 16, 1863.
David Moore.........	Col. 21st Mo. Infy..............	May 16, 1863, to Aug. 6, 1863.
T. J. Kinney........	Col. 119th Ill. Infy.............	Aug. 6, 1863, to Sept. 6 1863.
David Moore.........	Col. 21st Mo. Infy..............	Sept. 6, 1863, to Jan. 25, 1864.

63d Ill. Infy...........Mch., 1863	From Unatt. Dist. Memphis 16-C..	To Dist. Northeastern La..........	May,	1863
1st Mo. Cav. (F, H, M)..Mch., 1863	From Unatt. Dist. Memphis 16-C..	To Dist. St. Louis Dept. Mo......	June,	1863
49th Ill. Infy..........May, 1863	From 4-Brig. 1-Div. 16-Corps.....	To 3-Brig. 3-Div. 16-Corps.......	July,	1863
119th Ill. Infy..........May, 1863	From 4-Brig. 1-Div. 16-Corps.....	To 1-Brig. 3-Div. 16-Corps.......	Jan.,	1864
21st Mo. Infy..........May, 1863	From Dist. Columbus, 6-Div. 16-C.	To 1-Brig. 3-Div. 16-Corps.......	Jan.,	1864
34th Wis. Infy. 6 Co's..May, 1863	From Dist. Colum. 6-Div. 16-Corps.	To Dist. Colum. 6-Div. 16-Corps..	Aug.,	1863
2d Ill. Cav...........May, 1863	From Dist. Colum. 6-Div. 16-Corps.	To Dist. Colum. 6-Div. 16-Corps..	Aug.,	1863
5th O. Cav. (1 & 2 Battn.).May, 1863	From 3-Brig. 5-Div. 16-Corps......	To 2-Brig. 1-Cav. Div. 16-Corps....	Aug.,	1863
7th Wis. Batty..........June, 1863	From Arty. 3-Div. 16-Corps.......	To Fort Pickering Dist. Memphis..	Jan.,	1864

GILBERT'S BRIGADE.—Assigned Nov. 22, 1863. Transferred to 3-Div. 16-Corps, Jan. 25, 1864.

COMMANDER.

John I. Gilbert.........	Col. 27th Iowa Infy.............	Nov. 22, 1863, to Jan. 25, 1864.

27th Iowa Infy...........Nov., 1863	From 1-Brig. 2-Div. Ark. Exp......	To 2-Brig. 3-Div. 16-Corps.........	Jan.,	1864
49th Ill. Infy...........Nov., 1863	From 1-Brig. 2-Div. Ark. Exp......	To 3-Brig. 3-Div. 16-Corps.........	Jan.,	1864

1st COLORED BRIGADE.—   COMMANDERS.

J. M. Alexander........	Col. 1st Ala. Col'd Infy...........	Jan. 30, 1864, to Mch. 14, 1864.
Edward Bouton.........	Col. 59th U. S. Col'd Infy........	Mch. 14, 1864, to June 28, 1864.

1st Ala. Infy. A. D				
(55th U. S. C. T.)......Jan., 1864	From Post Corinth 2-Div. 16-Corps..	To Fort Pickering Dist. Memphis....	May,	1864
1st Tenn. Infy. A. D.				
(59th U. S. C. T.)......Jan., 1864	From Post Corinth 2-Div. 16-Corps..	To 3-Brig. Sturgis' Exp............	June,	1864
2d Tenn. Infy. A. D.				
(61st U. S. C. T.)......Jan., 1864	From Post Corinth 2-Div. 16-Corps..	To 3-Brig. Sturgis' Exp............	June,	1864
Memphis Tenn. Batty.				
(Bat. F, 2d U. S. C. Ar.).Jan., 1864	From Post Pickering, Dist. Memphis.	To 3-Brig. Sturgis' Exp............	June,	1864
FORT PICKERING.—				
1st Tenn. Heavy Arty, A. D.				
(3d U. S. C. Heavy Art.).July, 1863	From 1-Brig. 5-Div. 16-Corps.......	To Fort Pickering Dist. West Tenn..	June,	1863
Memphis Tenn. Batty.				
(Bat. F, 2d U. S. C. Ar.).Nov., 1863	From New Organization...........	To 1st Col'd Brig. Dist. Memphis..	Jan.,	1864
Bat. C, 1 Tenn. Light Arty.Jan., 1864	From New Organization...........	To Def. Memphis Dist. West Tenn..	June,	1864
1st Ala. Col'd H. A.				
(7th U. S. C. Heavy Art.).Jan., 1864	From Post Corinth 2-Div. 16-Corps..	To Def. Memphis Dist. West Tenn..	June,	1864
Batty. G, 1st Ill. L. A....Jan., 1864	From Post Corinth 2-Div. 16-Corps..	To Def. Memphis Dist. West Tenn..	June,	1864
Batty. B, 2d Ill. L. A....Jan., 1864	From Post Corinth 2-Div. 16-Corps..	To 1-Brig. 1-Div. 16-Corps........	June,	1864
7th Wis. Batty.........Jan., 1864	From 4-Brig. 5-Div. 16-Corps......	To 2-Brig. Cav. Div. Sturgis' Exp...	June,	1864
55th U. S. C. T...........May, 1864	From 1st Col'd Brig. Dist. Memphis..	To 3-Brig. Sturgis' Exp............	June,	1864

DISTRICT OF JACKSON.—Designated 3d Division 16th Army Corps, March 18, 1863.

COMMANDER.

J. C. Sullivan.........	Brigadier General..................	Dec. 18, 1862, to Mch. 18, 1863.

1st BRIGADE.—   COMMANDER.

M. K. Lawler...........	Brigadier General..................	Dec. 18, 1862, to Mch. 18, 1863.

18th Ill. Infy...........Dec., 1862	From Dist. Jackson 13-Corps......	To 2-Brig. 3-Div. 16-Corps.........	Mch.,	1863
29th Ill. Infy. (Co's D-K.).Dec., 1862	From Dist. Jackson 13-Corps......	To Miss. Squadron................	Feb.,	1863
54th Ill. Infy...........Dec., 1862	From Dist. Jackson 13-Corps......	To 2-Brig. 3-Div. 16-Corps.........	Mch.,	1863
62d Ill. Infy...........Dec., 1862	From Dist. Jackson 13-Corps......	To 3-Brig. 3-Div. 16-Corps.........	Mch.,	1863
7th Tenn. Infy...........Dec., 1862	From Dist. Jackson 13-Corps......	To 3-Brig. 3-Div. 16-Corps.........	Mch.,	1863

2d BRIGADE.— COMMANDER.

C. L. Dunham..........Col. 50th Ind. Infy.................Dec. 18, 1862, to Mch. 18, 1863.		
50th Ind. Infy.............Dec., 1862	From Dist. Louisville Ky. Dept. O...	To 3-Brig. 3-Div. 16-Corps.........Mch., 1863
103d Ill. Infy.............Dec., 1862	From 1-Brig. 4-Div. L. W. 13-Corps..	To 2-Brig. 1-Div. 16-Corps.........Mch., 1863
27th Iowa Infy.............Dec., 1862	From Dept. Northwest..............	To 3-Brig. 3-Div. 16-Corps.........Mch., 1863

3d BRIGADE.— COMMANDER.

J. Richmond.........Col. 126th Ill. Infy.................Dec. 18, 1862, to Mch. 18, 1863.		
119th Ill. Infy.............Dec., 1862	From Dist. Jackson 13-Corps........	To 4-Brig. 1-Div. 16-Corps.........Mch., 1862
126th Ill. Infy.............Dec., 1862	From Dist. Jackson 13-Corps........	To 2-Brig. 3-Div. 16-Corps.........Mch., 1863

4th BRIGADE.— COMMANDER.

O. Wood...............Col. 22d Ohio Infy.................Dec. 18, 1862, to Mch. 18, 1863.		
106th Ill. Infy.............Dec., 1862	From Dist. Jackson 13-Corps........	To 1-Brig. 3-Div. 16-Corps.........Mch., 1863
122d Ill. Infy.............Dec., 1862	From Dist. Jackson 13-Corps........	To 2-Brig. Dist. Corinth 16-Corps.... Feb., 1863
22d Ohio Infy.............Dec., 1862	From 2-Brig. Dist. Corinth 13-Corps.	To 2-Brig. 3-Div. 16-Corps.........Mch., 1863

ARTILLERY.—

14th Ind. Batty.........Dec., 1862	From Dist. Jackson 13-Corps........	To Arty. 3-Div. 16-Corps.........Mch., 1863
14th Ohio Batty........Dec., 1862	From Dist. Jackson 13-Corps........	To Arty. 3-Div. 16-Corps.........Mch., 1863
Batty. K, 1st Mo. Arty....Jan., 1862	From Dist. Corinth 17-Corps........	To Arty. 1-Div. 16-Corps.........Mch., 1865
7th Wis. Batty............Dec., 1862	From Dist. Jackson 13-Corps........	To Arty. 3-Div. 16-Corps.........Mch., 1863

CAVALRY BRIGADE.— COMMANDER.

J. K. Mizner............Col. 3d Mich. Cav...............Dec. 18, 1862, to Mch. 18, 1863.		
4th Ill. Cav. 4 Co's.......Dec., 1862	From Cav. Dist. Jackson 13-Corps...	To 2-Brig. Cav. Div. 16-Corps........Dec., 1862
11th Ill. Cav.............Dec., 1862	From Cav. Dist. Jackson 13-Corps...	To Cav. Brig. 3-Div. 16-Corps.......Mch., 1863
3d Mich. Cav.............Dec., 1862	From 3-Brig. Cav. Div. 13-Corps....	To Cav. Brig. 3-Div. 16-Corps.......Mch., 1862
6th Tenn. Cav............Dec., 1862	From Cav. Dist. Jackson 13-Corps...	To Cav. Brig. 3-Div. 16-Corps.......Mch., 1862
7th Tenn. Cav............Dec., 1862	From Cav. Dist. Jackson 13-Corps...	To Cav. Brig. 3-Div. 16-Corps.......Mch., 1863

UNATTACHED GRAND JUNCTION.—

Batty. D, 2d Ill. Arty....Dec., 1862	From Dist. Jackson 13-Corps........	To Arty. 1-Div. 16-Corps.............Jan., 1862

POST OF BOLIVAR, TENN.—

43d Ill. Infy.............Dec., 1862	From Bolivar, Dist. Jackson 13-C...	To 1-Brig. 3-Div. 16-Corps.........Mch., 1863
61st Ill. Infy.............Dec., 1862	From Bolivar, Dist. Jackson 13-C...	To 1-Brig. 3-Div. 16-Corps.........Mch., 1863
12th Mich. Infy.............Dec., 1862	From Bolivar, Dist. Jackson 13-C...	To 1-Brig. 3-Div. 16-Corps.........Mch., 1865
Springfield, Ill. Batty......Dec., 1862	From Bolivar, Dist. Jackson 13-C...	To 1-Brig. 3-Div. 16-Corps.........Mch., 1863

POST BETHEL, TENN.—

48th Ill. Infy.............Dec., 1862	From Dist. Jackson 13-Corps........	To 4-Brig. 1-Div. 16-Corps.........Mch., 1863
49th Ill. Infy.............Dec., 1862	From Dist. Jackson 13-Corps........	To 4-Brig. 1-Div. 16-Corps.........Mch., 1865

DISTRICT OF COLUMBUS.—(Columbus, Ky., Cairo, Ill., Hickman, Ky., Fort, Pillow, Tenn., Island No. 10, Tenn., Fort Heiman, Tenn., Clinton, Ky., etc.). Designated 6th Division. 16th Army Corps, March 31, 1863. Discontinued as 6th Division Jan. 25, 1864, and redesignated District of Columbus. Transferred to Dept. of the Ohio Aug. 7, 1864.

COMMANDERS.

Thos. A. Davies........	Brigadier General...................	Dec. 18, 1862, to Jan. 11, 1863.
A. Asboth.............	Brigadier General...................	Jan. 11, 1863, to Aug. 5, 1863.
A. J. Smith............	Brigadier General...................	Aug. 5, 1863, to Jan. 25, 1864.
Henry Prince..........	Brigadier General...................	Jan. 25, 1864, to Aug. 7, 1864.
83d Ill. Infy.............Dec., 1862	From Dist. Columbus 13-Corps......	To 1-Brig. 3-Div. Res. C. Cumb'd....June, 1863
111th Ill. Infy.............Dec., 1862	From Dist. Columbus 13-Corps......	To 2-Brig. 2-Div. 16-Corps.........June, 1863
128th Ill. Infy.............Dec., 1862	From Dist. Columbus 13-Corps......	Disbanded.........................Apr., 1863
71st Ohio Infy.............Dec., 1862	From Dist. Columbus 13-Corps......	To 1-Brig. 3-Div. Res. C. Cumb'd....June, 1863
52d Ind. Infy.............Dec., 1862	From Dist. Columbus 13-Corps......	To 3-Brig. 3-Div. 16-Corps.........Jan., 1864
13th Wis. Infy.............Dec., 1862	From Dist. Columbus 13-Corps......	To 1-Brig. 3-Div. Res. C. Cumb'd....June, 1863
15th Wis. Infy, Co. I.....Dec., 1862	From Dist. Columbus 13-Corps......	To Regt. in Dept. Cumb'd..........Sept., 1863
21st Mo. Infy.............Dec., 1862	From 2-Brig. 6-Div. 13-Corps......	To 4-Brig. 5-Div. 16-Corps.........May, 1863
32d Iowa Infy.............Dec., 1862	From Dept. Mo.....................	To 1-Brig. 6-Div. 16-Corps.........July, 1863
35th Iowa Infy.............Dec., 1862	From Dist. Columbus 13-Corps......	To 3-Brig. 3-Div. 15-Corps.........Apr., 1863
38th Iowa Infy.............Dec., 1862	From New Organization.............	To New Madrid, Mo.................Jan., 1863
40th Iowa Infy.............Dec., 1862	From New Organization.............	To 3-Brig. Kimball's Prov'l D. 16-C..June, 1863
Batty. K, 1st Ill. Arty.....Dec., 1862	From Dist. Columbus 13-Corps......	To 3-Brig. 1st Cav. Div. 16-Corps...Oct., 1863
Batty. C, 2d Ill. Arty.....Dec., 1862	From Dist. Columbus 13-Corps......	To Arty. 3-Div. Res. Corps Cumb'd..June, 1862
Batty. H, 2d Ill. Arty.....Dec., 1862	From Dist. Columbus 13-Corps......	To Arty. 3-Div. Res. Corps Cumb'd..June, 1863
5th Iowa Cav.............Dec., 1862	From Dist. Columbus 13-Corps......	To 1-Brig. 2-Cav. Div. Cumb'd.....June, 1863
15th Ky. Cav.............Dec., 1862	From Dist. Columbus 13-Corps......	To Detach. Brig. 1-Cav. D. 16-Corps.Aug., 1863
3d Minn. Infy.............Feb., 1863	From Dept. Northwest..............	To 3-Brig. Kimball's Prov'l D. 16-C..June, 1863
14th Iowa Infy............Mch., 1863	From Reorganization...............	To 2-Brig. 3-Div. 16-Corps.........Jan., 1864
25th Wis. Infy............Mch., 1863	From Dept. Northwest..............	To 3-Brig. Kimball's Prov'l Div. 16-C..June, 1863
27th Wis. Infy............Mch., 1863	From New Organization.............	To 3-Br. Kimball's Prov'l Div. 16-C..Oct., 1863
31st Wis. Infy............Mch., 1863	From New Organization.............	To Unass'd Dept. Cumb'd...........Sept., 1863
34th Wis. Infy............Mch., 1863	From New Organization.............	No change to Muster Out............July, 1863
2d Ill. Cav...............Mch., 1863	From Dist. Columbus Cairo, Ill......	To 1-Brig. 6-Div. 16-Corps.........July, 1863
4th Mo. Cav.............Apr., 1863	From Cav. Br. Dist. St. L. Dept. Mo.	To 1-Brig. 6-Div. 16-Corps.........July, 1863
7th Tenn. Cav...........May, 1863	From Unass'd 1-Div. 16-Corps......	To 1-Brig. 6-Div. 16-Corps.........July, 1863
9th Ind. Batty..........Mch., 1863	From Arty. 4-Div. 16-Corps........	To 1-Brig. 6-Div. 16-Corps.........Jan., 1864
101st Ill. Infy...........June, 1863	From Reorganization...............	To 1-Brig. 3-Div. 16-Corps.........July, 1863
58th Ill. Infy............June, 1863	From Camp Butler, Ill..............	To 1-Brig. 6-Div. 16-Corps.........July, 1863
2d Tenn. Heavy Arty. A. D.June, 1863	From New Organization.............	To Consol. with Engr. Regt. of
24th Mo. Infy............June, 1863	From Dept. Mo....................	To 1-Brig. 6-Div. 16-Corps.........
25th Mo. Infy............June, 1863	From Dept. Mo....................	West to form 1st Mo. Engrs....Feb., 1864
1st Kan. Batty...........June, 1863	From Dist. Rolla, Dept. Mo........	To Def. N. & N. W. R. R. Dept. Cum.June, 1863
131st Ill. Infy............July, 1863	From Detached Brig. Dist. N. E. La.	To 1-Brig. 3-Div. 17-Corps.........Oct., 1863

1st BRIGADE.—Organized July 14, 1863. Transferred to Cavalry Division 16-Corps Dec. 31, 1863.

COMMANDERS.

Geo. E. Waring, Jr......	Col. 4th Mo. Cav..................	July 14, 1863, to Aug. 22, 1863.
C. H. Fox.............	Col. 101st Ill. Infy................	Aug. 22, 1863, to Sept. 3, 1863.
J. K. Mills............	Col. 24th Mo. Infy................	Sept. 3, 1863, to Oct. .., 1863.
Geo. E. Waring, Jr......	Col. 4th Mo. Cav..................	Oct. .., 1863, to Dec. 31, 1863.

1st BRIGADE.—Continued.

32d Wis. Infy	July, 1863	From Unass'd 6-Div. 16-Corps	To 2-Brig. 3-Div. 16-Corps	Jan.,	1864
101st Ill. Infy	July, 1863	From Unass'd 6-Div. 16-Corps	To 1-Br. 3-Div. 11-C. Dept. Cumb'd	Oct.,	1863
24th Mo. Infy	July, 1863	From Unass'd 6-Div. 16-Corps	To 2-Brig. 3-Div. 16-Corps	Jan.,	1864
2d Ill. Cav	July, 1863	From Unass'd 6-Div. 16-Corps	To Waring's Brig. 1-Cav. Div. 16-C.	Dec.,	1863
4th Mo. Cav	July, 1863	From Unass'd 6-Div. 16-Corps	To Waring's Brig. 1-Cav. Div. 16-C.	Dec.,	1863
7th Tenn. Cav	July, 1863	From Unass'd 6-Div. 16-Corps	To Det. Brig. 1-Cav. Div. 16-Corps	Aug.,	1863
9th Ind. Batty	July, 1863	From Unass'd 6-Div. 16-Corps	To Arty. 3-Div. 16-Corps	Jan.,	1864
2d Tenn. Heavy Arty. A. D.	July, 1863	From Unass'd 6-Div. 16-Corps	To Unass'd Dist. Colum. 16-Corps	Jan.,	1864
13th Tenn. Cav	Nov., 1863	From New Organization	To Dept. Cumb'd	Dec.,	1863
17th N. Y. Vet. Infy	Nov., 1863	From Def. Washington	To 2-Brig. 4-Div. 16-Corps	Jan.,	1864
178th N. Y. Infy	Nov., 1863	From Def. Washington	To 3-Brig. 3-Div. 16-Corps	Jan.,	1864
Batty. G, 2d Ill. Arty	Dec., 1863	From Arty. 3-Div. 17-Corps	To Arty. 3-Div. 16-Corps	Jan.,	1864
7th Ind. Cav	Dec., 1863	From New Organization	To Waring's Br. 1-Cav. Div. 16-C.	Dec.,	1863
19th Penna. Cav	Dec., 1863	From New Organization	To Waring's Br. 1-Cav. Div. 16-C.	Dec.,	1863
2d N. J. Cav	Dec., 1863	From Def. Washington	To Waring's Br. 1-Cav. Div. 16-C.	Dec.,	1863
34th N. J. Infy	Dec., 1863	From New Organization	To Dist. West Ky. Dept. Ohio	Aug.,	1864
35th N. J. Infy	Dec., 1863	From Def. Washington	To 1-Brig. 4-Div. 16-Corps	Jan.,	1864
122d Ill. Infy	Dec., 1863	From 2-Brig. 2-Div. 16-Corps	To 2-Brig. 3-Div. 16-Corps	June,	1864
2d Tenn. Heavy Arty. A. D.	Dec., 1863	From 1-Brig. 6-Div. 16-Corps	To Dist. West Ky. Dept. Ohio	Aug.,	1864
7th Minn. Infy	Apr., 1864	From Dept. Mo	To 3-Brig. 1-Div. 16-Corps	June,	1864
10th Minn. Infy	Apr., 1864	From Dept. Mo	To 1-Brig. 1-Div. 16-Corps	June,	1864
8th U. S. Col'd H. Arty	May, 1864	From New Organization	To Dist. West. Ky. Dept. Ohio	Aug.,	1864
132d Ind. Infy	June, 1864	From New Organization	To Dist. West. Ky. Dept. Ohio	Aug.,	1864
134th Ind. Infy	June, 1864	From New Organization	To Dist. West. Ky. Dept. Ohio	Aug.,	1864
136th Ind. Infy	June, 1864	From New Organization	To Dist. West. Ky. Dept. Ohio	Aug.,	1864
139th Ind. Infy	June, 1864	From New Organization	To Dist. West. Ky. Dept. Ohio	Aug.,	1864
141st Ind. Infy	June, 1864	From New Organization	To Dist. West. Ky. Dept. Ohio	Aug.,	1864

1st DIVISION.—Organized by transfer from 17th Corps, Jan. 20, 1863. Transferred to 15th Army Corps July 28, 1863. Reorganized Dec. 20, 1863, from 3d Division, 15th Army Corps.

COMMANDERS.

J. A. McDowell	Col. 6th Iowa Infy	Jan. 20, 1863, to Feb. 19, 1863.
J. W. Denver	Brigadier General	Feb. 19, 1863, to Mch. 22, 1863.
W. S. Smith	Brigadier General	Mch. 22, 1863, to July 20, 1863.
Hugh Ewing	Brigadier General	July 20, 1863, to July 28, 1863.
J. M. Tuttle	Brigadier General	Dec. 20, 1863, to Mch. 7, 1864.
J. A. Mower	Brigadier General	Mch. 7, 1864, to Oct. 11, 1864.
J. J. Woods	Col. 12th Iowa Infy	Oct. 11, 1864, to Nov. 3, 1864.
John McArthur	Brigadier General	Nov. 3, 1864, to Dec. 5, 1864.

1st BRIGADE.— **COMMANDERS.**

C. C. Walcutt	Col. 46th Ohio Infy	Jan. 20, 1863, to Mch. 22, 1863.
J. M. Loomis	Col. 26th Ill. Infy	Mch. 22, 1863, to July 28, 1863.
R. P. Buckland	Brigadier General	Dec. 20, 1863, to Jan. 26, 1864.
W. L. McMillan	Col. 95th Ohio Infy	Jan. 26, 1864, to Dec. 5, 1864.

40th Ill. Infy	Jan., 1863	From 1-Brig. 1-Div. 17-Corps	To 2-Brig. 1-Div. 16-Corps	Mch.,	1863
12th Ind. Infy	Jan., 1863	From 1-Brig. 1-Div. 17-Corps	To 1-Brig. 4-Div. 15-Corps	July,	1863
100th Ind. Infy	Jan., 1863	From 1-Brig. 1-Div. 17-Corps	To 1-Brig. 4-Div. 15-Corps	July,	1863
6th Iowa Infy	Jan., 1863	From 1-Brig. 1-Div. 17-Corps	To 2-Brig. 1-Div. 16-Corps	Mch.,	1863
46th Ohio Infy	Jan., 1863	From 1-Brig. 1-Div. 17-Corps	To 2-Brig. 1-Div. 16-Corps	Mch.,	1863
26th Ill. Infy	Mch., 1863	From 2-Brig. 1-Div. 17-Corps	To 1-Brig. 4-Div. 15-Corps	July,	1863
90th Ill. Infy	Mch., 1863	From 2-Brig. 1-Div. 17-Corps	To 1-Brig. 4-Div. 15-Corps	July,	1863
114th Ill. Infy	Dec., 1863	From 1-Brig. 3-Div. 15-Corps	To 1-Br. 1-D. Smith's Det. Army T'n.	Dec.,	1863
72d Ohio Infy	Dec., 1863	From 1-Brig. 3-Div. 15-Corps	To 1-Br. 1-D. Smith's Det. Army T'n.	Dec.,	1863
95th Ohio Infy	Dec., 1863	From 1-Brig. 3-Div. 15-Corps	To 1-Br. 1-D. Smith's Det. Army T'n.	Dec.,	1863
93d Ind. Infy	Dec., 1863	From 1-Brig. 3-Div. 15-Corps	To 1-Br. 1-D. Smith's Det. Army T'n.	Dec.,	1863
10th Minn. Infy	June, 1864	From Dist. Columbus	To 1-Br. 1-D. Smith's Det. Army T'n.	Dec.,	1863

2d BRIGADE.— **COMMANDERS.**

J. R. Cockrill	Col. 70th Ohio Infy	Jan. 20, 1863, to Mch. 22, 1863.
J. A. McDowell	Col. 6th Iowa Infy	Mch. .., 1863, Temporarily.
S. G. Hicks	Col. 40th Ill. Infy	Mch. .., 1863, to July 28, 1863.
Jos. A. Mower	Brigadier General	Dec. 20, 1863, to Mch. 7, 1864.
L. F. Hubbard	Col. 5th Minn. Infy	Mch. 7, 1864, to June 25, 1864.
Alex. Wilkins	Col. 9th Minn. Infy	June 25, 1864, to July 15, 1864.
J. D. McClure	Col. 47th Ill. Infy	July 15, 1864, to Aug. 18, 1864.
L. F. Hubbard	Col. 5th Minn. Infy	Aug. 18, 1864, to Dec. 5, 1864.

26th Ill. Infy	Jan., 1863	From 2-Brig. 1-Div. 17-Corps	To 1-Brig. 1-Div. 16-Corps	Mch.,	1863
90th Ill. Infy	Jan., 1863	From New Organization	To 1-Brig. 1-Div. 16-Corps	Mch.,	1863
97th Ind. Infy	Jan., 1863	From 2-Brig. 1-Div. 17-Corps	To 3-Brig. 1-Div. 16-Corps	Mch.,	1863
99th Ind. Infy	Jan., 1863	From 2-Brig. 1-Div. 17-Corps	To 3-Brig. 1-Div. 16-Corps	Mch.,	1863
53d Ohio Infy	Jan., 1863	From 2-Brig. 1-Div. 17-Corps	To 3-Brig. 1-Div. 16-Corps	Mch.,	1863
70th Ohio Infy	Jan., 1863	From 2-Brig. 1-Div. 17-Corps	To 3-Brig. 1-Div. 16-Corps	Mch.,	1863
6th Iowa Infy	Mch., 1863	From 1-Brig. 1-Div. 16-Corps	To 4-Brig. 1-Div. 16-Corps	May,	1863
40th Ill. Infy	Mch., 1863	From 1-Brig. 1-Div. 16-Corps	To 2-Brig. 4-Div. 15-Corps	July,	1863
103d Ill. Infy	Mch., 1863	From 2-Brig. Dist. Jackson 16-Corps.	To 2-Brig. 4-Div. 15-Corps	July,	1863
46th Ohio Infy	Mch., 1863	From 1-Brig. 1-Div. 16-Corps	To 2-Brig. 4-Div. 15-Corps	July,	1863
15th Mich. Infy	June, 1863	From Unass'd 1-Div. 16-Corps	To 2-Brig. 4-Div. 15-Corps	July,	1863
47th Ill. Infy	Dec., 1863	From 2-Brig. 3-Div. 15-Corps	To Chicago and Camp Butler Ill	Nov.,	1864
5th Minn. Infy	Dec., 1863	From 2-Brig. 3-Div. 15-Corps	To 2-Br. 1-Div. Smith's Det. Army T.	Dec.,	1864
11th Mo. Infy	Dec., 1863	From 2-Brig. 3-Div. 15-Corps	To 2-Br. 1-Div. Smith's Det. Army T.	Dec.,	1864
8th Wis. Infy	Dec., 1863	From 2-Brig. 3-Div. 15-Corps	To 2-Br. 1-Div. Smith's Det. Army T.	Dec.,	1864
9th Minn. Infy	May, 1861	From Dist. Rolla Dept. Mo	To 2-Br. 1-Div. Smith's Det. Army T.	Dec.,	1864

3d BRIGADE.—Organized March 22, 1863.— **COMMANDERS.**

J. R. Cockerill	Col. 70th Ohio Infy	Mch. 22, 1863, to July 28, 1863.
J. L. Geddes	Col. 8th Iowa Infy	Dec. 20, 1863, to Mch. 7, 1864.
S. G. Hill	Col. 35th Iowa Infy	Mch. 7, 1864, to June 10, 1864.
J. J. Woods	Col. 12th Iowa Infy	June 10, 1864, to Oct. 19, 1864.
S. G. Hill	Col. 35th Iowa Infy	Oct. 19, 1864, to Dec. 5, 1864.

97th Ind. Infy	Mch., 1863	From 2-Brig. 1-Div. 16-Corps	To 3-Brig. 4-Div. 15-Corps	July,	1863
99th Ind. Infy	Mch., 1863	From 2-Brig. 1-Div. 16-Corps	To 3-Brig. 4-Div. 15-Corps	July,	1863
53d Ohio Infy	Mch., 1863	From 2-Brig. 1-Div. 16-Corps	To 3-Brig. 4-Div. 15-Corps	July,	1863
70th Ohio Infy	Mch., 1863	From 2-Brig. 1-Div. 16-Corps	To 3-Brig. 4-Div. 15-Corps	July,	1863
8th Iowa Infy	Dec., 1863	From 3-Brig. 3-Div. 15-Corps	To Dist. Memphis Tenn	June,	1864
12th Iowa Infy	Dec., 1863	From 3-Brig. 3-Div. 15-Corps	To 3-Br. 1-Div. Smith's Det. A. Tenn.	Dec.,	1864
35th Iowa Infy	Dec., 1863	From 3-Brig. 3-Div. 15-Corps	To 3-Brig. 1-Div. Smith's Det. A. Tenn.	Dec.,	1864
33d Missouri Infy	Jan., 1864	From 1-Brig. 4-Div. 16-Corps	To 3-Brig. 1-Div. Smith's D. A. Tenn.	Dec.,	1864
7th Minnesota Infy	June, 1864	From Paducah, Ky	To 3-Brig. 1-Div. Smith's D. A. Tenn.	Dec.,	1864

4th BRIGADE.—Organized Mch. 22, 1863. Discontinued July 28, 1863. Reorganized June, 1864.

COMMANDERS.

W. W. Sanford.........	Col. 48th Illinois Infy.............	Mch. 22, 1863, to July 28, 1863.
J. B. Moore...........	Col. 33d Wisconsin Infy...........	June, 1864, to Dec. 5, 1864.

48th Illinois Infy........Mch., 1863	From Bethel D. of Jackson 16-Corps.	To 4-Brig. 4-Div. 15-Corps........	July, 1863
49th Illinois Infy........Mch., 1863	From Bethel D. of Jackson 16-Corps.	To 4-Brig. 5-Div. 16-Corps........	May, 1863
119th Illinois Infy.......Mch., 1863	From 3-Brig. Dist. Jackson........	To 4-Brig. 5-Div. 16-Corps........	May, 1863
6th Iowa Infy...........May, 1863	From 2-Brig. 1-Div. 16-Corps......	To 4-Brig. 5-Div. 16-Corps........	July, 1863
41st Illinois Infy.......June, 1864	From 1-Brig. Prov'l Div. 17-C. Gulf.	To 2-Brig. 1-Div. 17-Corps........	July, 1864
14th Wiscosin Infy.......June, 1864	From 1-Brig. Prov'l Div. 17-C. Gulf.	To 1-Brig. 3-Div. Smith's.........	Dec., 1864
33d Wisconsin Infy......June, 1864	From 1-Brig. Prov'l Div. 17-C. Gulf.	To 1-Brig. 3-Div. Smith's.........	Dec., 1864
81st Illinois Infy.......June, 1864	From 1-Brig. Prov'l Div. 17-C. Gulf.	To 1-Brig. 3-Div. Smith's.........	Dec., 1864
95th Illinois Infy.......June, 1864	From 1-Brig. Prov'l Div. 17-C. Gulf.	To 1-Br. 3-Div. Smith's Det. A. Tenn.	Dec., 1864
ARTILLERY, 4th BRIGADE.—			
Batty. B, 2d Ill. Arty....Apr., 1864	From Fort Pickering Memphis, Tenn.	To Post Memphis, Tenn., West Tenn.	June, 1864
UNATTACHED 1st DIVISION.—			
15th Michigan Infy......Jan., 1863	From Unatt. 17-Corps.............	To 2-Brig. 1-Div. 16-Corps........	June, 1863
ARTILLERY, 1st DIVISION.—			
Batty. F, 1st Ill. Arty...Jan., 1863	From Arty. 1-Div. 17-Corps........	To Arty. 4-Brig. 15-Corps........	July, 1863
Batty. I, 1st Ill. Arty...Jan., 1863	From Arty. 1-Div. 17-Corps........	To Arty. 4-Brig. 15-Corps........	July, 1863
Cogswell's Ill. Batty.....Jan., 1863	From Arty. 1-Div. 17-Corps........	To Arty. 7-Div. 17-Corps........	July, 1863
Batty. D, 2d Ill. Arty....Jan., 1863	From Arty. Dist. Jackson 16-Corps.	To 2-Brig. Dist. Memphis..........	May, 1863
6th Indiana Batty.......Jan., 1863	From Arty. 1-Div. 17-Corps........	To Arty. 3-Div. 15-Corps..........	July, 1863
Batty. K, 1st Mo. Arty...Mch., 1863	From Arty. Dist. Jackson 16-Corps..	To 13-Div. 13-Corps Dist..........	June, 1863
Batty. E, 1st Ill. Arty...Dec., 1863	From Arty. 3-Div. 15-Corps........	To 1-Div. Smith's Det. Army Tenn.	Dec., 1864
2d Iowa Batty..........Dec., 1863	From Arty. 3-Div. 15-Corps........	To 1-Div. Smith's Det. Army Tenn.	Dec., 1864
6th Indiana Batty.......Dec., 1863	From Arty. 3-Div. 15-Corps........	To Garrison at Memphis, Tenn.....	Nov., 1864
Batty. M, 1st Mo. Arty...June, 1864	From Prov'l. Div. 17-Corps Gulf...	To Unassigned Dist. West Tenn....	Sept., 1864

DISTRICT OF CORINTH, MISS.—Assigned from 17th Army Corps January 20, 1863. Designated 2d Div. Mch. 1863. Reorganized Dec., 1863. Discontinued Jan. 25, 1864.

COMMANDERS.

G. M. Dodge..........	Brigadier General.................	Jan. 20, 1863, to Mch. 18, 1863.
J. D. Stevenson.......	Brigadier General.................	Dec. 12, 1863, to Jan. 25, 1864.

1st BRIGADE.— COMMANDER.

T. W. Sweeney........	Brigadier General.................	Jan. 20, 1862, to Mch. 20, 1863.

2d Iowa Infy..........Jan., 1863	From 1-Brig. Dist. Corinth 17-Corps.	To 1-Brig. 2-Div. 16-Corps........	Mch., 1863
7th Iowa Infy.........Jan., 1863	From 1-Brig. Dist. Corinth 17-Corps.	To 1-Brig. 2-Div. 16-Corps........	Mch., 1863
66th Indiana Infy......Jan., 1863	From 1-Brig. Dist. Corinth 17-Corps.	To 1-Brig. 2-Div. 16-Corps........	Mch., 1863
56th Indiana Infy......Jan., 1863	From 1-Brig. Dist. Corinth 17-Corps.	To 1-Brig. 2-Div. 16-Corps........	Mch., 1863

2d BRIGADE.— COMMANDER.

A. Mersey............	Col. 9th Illinois Infy.............	Jan. 20, 1863, to Mch. 20, 1863.

9th Illinois Infy........Jan., 1863	From 2-Brig. Dist. Corinth 17-Corps.	To 2-Brig. 2-Div. 16-Corps........	Mch., 1863
12th Illinois Infy.......Jan., 1863	From 2-Brig. Dist. Corinth 17-Corps.	To 2-Brig. 2-Div. 16-Corps........	Mch., 1863
81st Ohio Infy.........Jan., 1863	From 2-Brig. Dist. Corinth 17-Corps.	To 2-Brig. 2-Div. 16-Corps........	Mch., 1863

3d BRIGADE.— COMMANDER.

M. M. Bane...........	Col. 50th Illinois Infy.............	Jan. 20, 1863, to Mch. 20, 1863.

7th Illinois Infy........Jan., 1863	From 3-Brig. Dist. Corinth 17-Corps.	To 3-Brig. 2-Div. 16-Corps........	Mch., 1863
50th Illinois Infy.......Jan., 1863	From 3-Brig. Dist. Corinth 17-Corps.	To 3-Brig. 2-Div. 16-Corps........	Mch., 1863
57th Illinois Infy.......Jan., 1863	From 3-Brig. Dist. Corinth 17-Corps.	To 3-Brig. 2-Div. 16-Corps........	Mch., 1863
18th Missouri Infy......Jan., 1863	From 3-Brig. Dist. Corinth 17-Corps.	To 3-Brig. 2-Div. 16-Corps........	Mch., 1863
39th Iowa Infy.........Jan., 1863	From 3-Brig. Dist. Corinth 17-Corps.	To 3-Brig. 2-Div. 16-Corps........	Mch., 1863
UNATTACHED.—			
64th Illinois Infy.......Jan., 1863	From Unatt. Dist. Corinth 17-Corps.	To Unatt. 2-Div. 16-Corps.........	Mch., 1863
66th Illinois Infy.:.....Jan., 1863	From Unatt. Dist. Corinth 17-Corps.	To Unatt. 2-Div. 16-Corps.........	Mch., 1863
1st U. S. Infy..........Jan., 1863	From Unatt. Dist. Corinth 17-Corps.	To 1-Brig. 14-Div. 13-Corps.......	Mch., 1863
ARTILLERY.—			
Batty. D, 1st Mo. Arty....Jan., 1863	From Dist. Corinth 17-Corps........	To Arty. 2-Div. 16-Corps..........	Mch., 1863
Batty. H, 1st Mo. Arty...Jan., 1863	From Dist. Corinth 17-Corps........	To Arty. 2-Div. 16-Corps..........	Mch., 1863
Batty. I, 1st Mo. Arty...Jan., 1863	From Dist. Corinth 17-Corps........	To Arty. 2-Div. 16-Corps..........	Mch., 1863
Batty. G, 1st Ill. Arty...Jan., 1863	From Dist. Corinth 17-Corps........	To Arty. 2-Div. 16-Corps..........	Mch., 1863
Batty. B, 2d Ill. Arty...Jan., 1863	From Dist. Jackson 16-Corps.......	To Arty. 2-Div. 16-Corps..........	Mch., 1863
Batty. B, 1st Mich. Arty..Jan., 1863	From Reorganization..............	To Afty. 2-Div. 16-Corps..........	Mch., 1863
CAVALRY DIST. OF CORINTH.—			
Stewart's Ill. Bat'n......Jan., 1863	From Dist. Corinth 17-Corps........	To Cav. Brig. 2-Div. 16-Corps.....	Mch., 1863
5th Ohio Cav., E,H,I,K...Jan., 1863	From Dist. Corinth 17-Corps........	To Cav. Brig. 2-Div. 16-Corps.....	Mch., 1863
1st Alabama Cav.......Jan., 1863	From New Organization...........	To Cav. Brig. 2-Div. 16-Corps.....	Mch., 1863
POST OF CORINTH.—			
1st Ala. Colored Infy.....			
(55th U. S. C. T.).....Nov., 1863	From Unatt. 2-Div. 16-Corps.......	To 1st Colored Brig. Dist. Memphis.	Jan., 1864
1st West Tenn. Colored			
(59th U. S. C. T.).....Nov., 1863	From Unatt. 2-Div. 16-Corps.......	To 1st Colored Brig. Dist. Memphis.	Jan., 1864
2d Tenn. Colored Infy			
(61st U. S. C. T.).....Nov., 1863	From 1-Brig. 2-Div. 16-Corps.......	To 1st Colored Brig. Dist. Memphis.	Jan., 1864
1st Ala. Siege Artillery			
7th U. S. C. H. A.)......Nov., 1863	From Unatt. 2-Div. 16-Corps.......	To Fort Pickering Memphis........	Jan., 1864
108th Illinois Infy......Nov., 1863	From 1-Brig. 2-Div. 16-Corps.......	To 2-Brig. Dist. Memphis..........	Jan., 1864
113th Illinois Infy......Nov., 1863	From 3-Brig. 2-Div. 16-Corps.......	To 2-Brig. Dist. Memphis..........	Jan., 1864
120th Illinois Infy......Nov., 1863	From 3-Brig. 2-Div. 16-Corps.......	To 2-Brig. Dist. Memphis..........	Jan., 1864
Batty. G, 1st Ill. Arty....Nov., 1863	From Arty. 2-Div. 16-Corps........	To Fort Pickering Memphis........	Jan., 1864
Batty. B, 2d Ill. Arty....Nov., 1863	From Arty. 2-Div. 16-Corps........	To Fort Pickering Memphis........	Jan., 1864
14th Indiana Batty......Nov., 1863	From Arty. 3-Div. 16-Corps........	To Fort Pickering Memphis........	Jan., 1864

2d DIVISION.—Organized Mch., 1863, from Dist. of Corinth 16th Army Corps. Transferred to 15th Army Corps as 4th Div. Sept. 23, 1864.

COMMANDERS.

G. M. Dodge..........	Brigadier General.................	Mch. 18, 1863, to Aug. 12, 1863.
A. Mersey............	Col. 9th Illinois Infy.............	Aug. 12, 1862, to Sept. 12, 1863.
T. W. Sweeney.......	Brigadier General.................	Sept. 12, 1863, to July 25, 1864.
E. W. Rice...........	Brigadier General.................	July 25, 1864, to July 26, 1864.
J. M. Corse..........	Brigadier General.................	July 26, 1864, to Sept. 23, 1864.

1st BRIGADE.—

COMMANDERS.

T. W. Sweeney	Brigadier General	Mch. 18, 1863, to July 20, 1863.
E. W. Rice	Col. 7th Iowa Infy	July 20, 1863, to Aug. 17, 1863.
D. C. Anthony	Col. 66th Indiana Infy	Aug. 17, 1863, to Sept. 7, 1863.
E. W. Rice	Col. 7th Iowa Infy	Sept. 7, 1863, to Dec. 15, 1863.
J. B. Weaver	Col. 2d Iowa Infy	Dec. 15, 1863, to Jan. 4, 1864.
D. C. Anthony	Col. 66th Indiana Infy	Jan. 4, 1864, to Mch. 1, 1864.
E. W. Rice	Brigadier General	Mch. 4, 1864, to Sept. 23, 1864.

2d Iowa Infy	Mch., 1863	From 2-Brig. Dist. Corinth 16-Corps.	To 1-Brig. 4-Div. 15-Corps	Sept., 1864
7th Iowa Infy	Mch., 1863	From 2-Brig. Dist. Corinth 16-Corps.	To 1-Brig. 4-Div. 15-Corps	Sept., 1864
52d Illinois Infy	Mch., 1863	From 2-Brig. Dist. Corinth 16-Corps.	To 1-Brig. 4-Div. 15-Corps	Sept., 1864
66th Indiana Infy	Mch., 1863	From 2-Brig. Dist. Corinth 16-Corps.	To 1-Brig. 4-Div. 15-Corps	Sept., 1864
108th Illinois Infy	Aug., 1863	From Det. Brig. Dist. N. E. La	To Post Corinth 16-Corps	Dec., 1863
2d Tenn. Colored Infy				
(61st U. S. C. T.)	Aug., 1863	From New Organization	To Post Corinth 16-Corps	Dec., 1863

2d BRIGADE.—

COMMANDERS.

A. Mersey	Col. 9th Illinois Infy	Mch. 18, 1863, to Aug. 12, 1863.	
J. I. Rinaker	Col. 122d Illinois Infy	Aug. 12, 1863, to Sept. 12, 1863.	
A. Mersey	Col. 9th Illinois Infy	Sept. 12, 1863, to Apr. 22, 1864.	
P. E. Burke	Col. 66th Illinois Infy	Apr. 22, 1864, to May 16, 1864.	Killed.
R. N. Adams	Lt.-Col. 81st Ohio Infy	May 16, 1864, to May 23, 1864.	
A. Mersey	Col. 9th Illinois Infy	May 23, 1864, to July 24, 1864.	
J. J. Phillips	Lt.-Col. 9th Illinois Infy	July 24, 1864, to Aug. 2, 1864.	
R. N. Adams	Lt.-Col. 81st Ohio Infy	Aug. 2, 1864, to Sept. 18, 1864.	
W. S. Merriman	Major	Sept. 18, 1864, to Sept. 23, 1864.	

9th Illinois Infy	Mch., 1863	From 2-Brig. Dist. Corinth 16-Corps.	To 2-Brig. 4-Div. 15-Corps	Sept., 1864
12th Illinois Infy	Mch., 1863	From 2-Brig. Dist. Corinth 16-Corps.	To 2-Brig. 4-Div. 15-Corps	Sept., 1864
122d Illinois Infy	Mch., 1863	From 2-Brig. Dist. Corinth 16-Corps.	To Dist. Columbus 6-Div	Dec., 1863
81st Ohio Infy	Mch., 1863	From 2-Brig. Dist. Corinth 16-Corps.	To 2-Brig. 4-Div. 15-Corps	Sept., 1864
111th Illinois Infy	Nov., 1863	From Dist. Columbus 6-Div. 16-Corps	To 1-Brig. 2-Div. 15-Corps	Mch., 1864
66th Illinois Infy	Nov., 1863	From Unatt. 2-Div. 16-Corps	To 1-Brig. 4-Div. 15-Corps	Sept., 1864

3d BRIGADE.—

COMMANDERS.

M. M. Bane	Col. 50th Illinois Infy	Mch. 18, 1863, to Aug. 25, 1863.
F. J. Hurlbut	Lt.-Col. 57th Illinois Infy	Aug. 25, 1863, to Sept. 25, 1863.
M. M. Bane	Col. 50th Illinois Infy	Sept. 25, 1863, to Jan. 18, 1864.
Madison Miller	Col. 18th Missouri Infy	Jan. 18, 1863, to Mch. 20, 1864.
M. M. Bane	Col. 50th Illinois Infy	Mch. 20, 1864, to June 20, 1864.
Wm. Vandever	Brigadier General	June 20, 1864, to Aug. 2, 1864.
H. J. B. Cummings	Col. 39th Iowa Infy	Aug. 2, 1864, to Aug. 15, 1864.
R. Rowett	Col. 7th Illinois Infy	Aug. 15, 1864, to Aug. 23, 1864.

7th Illinois Infy	Mch., 1863	From 3-Brig. Dist. Corinth 16-Corps.	To 3-Brig. 4-Div. 15-Corps	Sept., 1864
50th Illinois Infy	Mch., 1863	From 3-Brig. Dist. Corinth 16-Corps.	To 3-Brig. 4-Div. 15-Corps	Sept., 1864
57th Illinois Infy	Mch., 1863	From 3-Brig. Dist. Corinth 16-Corps.	To 3-Brig. 4-Div. 15-Corps	Sept., 1864
18th Missouri Infy	Mch., 1863	From 3-Brig. Dist. Corinth 16-Corps.	To 1-Brig. 4-Div. 16-Corps	Mch., 1864
39th Iowa Infy	Mch., 1863	From 3-Brig. Dist. Corinth 16-Corps.	To 3-Brig. 4-Div. 15-Corps	Sept., 1864
113th Illinois Infy	Aug., 1863	From 1-Brig. 2-Div. 15-Corps	To Post Corinth 16-Corps	Dec., 1863
120th Illinois Infy	Aug., 1863	To Det. Brig. Dist. N. E. La	To Post Corinth 16-Corps	Dec., 1863

4th BRIGADE.—Joined Division from 1st Brigade 8th Division 16th Army Corps March, 1863. Transferred Dist. Memphis 5-Div. 16th Corps May, 1863.

COMMANDER.

J. W. Fuller	Col. 27th Ohio Infy	Mch. 18, 1863, to May 2, 1863.

27th Ohio Infy	Mch., 1863	From 1-Brig. 8-Div. 16-Corps	To 3-B. 5-Div. Dist. Memphis 16-C.	May, 1863
39th Ohio Infy	Mch., 1863	From 1-Brig. 8-Div. 16-Corps	To 3-B. 5-Div. Dist. Memphis 16-C.	May, 1863
43d Ohio Infy	Mch., 1863	From 1-Brig. 8-Div. 16-Corps	To 3-B. 5-Div. Dist. Memphis 16-C.	May, 1863
63d Ohio Infy	Mch., 1863	From 1-Brig. 8-Div. 16-Corps	To 3-B. 5-Div. Dist. Memphis 16-C.	May, 1863
Batty. C, 1st Mich. Arty.	Mch., 1863	From 1-Brig. 8-Div. 16-Corps	To 3-B. 5-Div. Dist. Memphis 16-C.	May, 1863
Batty. F, 2d U. S. Arty.	Mch., 1863	From 1-Brig. 8-Div. 16-Corps	To 3-B. 5-Div. Dist. Memphis 16-C.	Nov., 1863
UNATTACHED.—				
64th Illinois Infy	Mch., 1863	From Unatt. Dist. Corinth 16-Corps.	To Fuller's Brig. 2-Div. 16-Corps	Nov., 1863
66th Illinois Infy	Mch., 1863	From Unatt. Dist. Corinth 16-Corps.	To 2-Brig. 2-Div. 16-Corps	Nov., 1863
1st Ala. Colored Infy	May, 1863	From New Organization	To Post Corinth 16-Corps	Nov., 1863
1st Ala. Colored H. A.	June, 1863	From New Organization	To Post Corinth 16-Corps	Nov., 1863
1st Tenn. Colored Infy	June, 1863	From New Organization	To Post Corinth 16-Corps	Nov., 1863

CAVALRY BRIGADE.—2d Division. Organized March, 1863. Discontinued July, 1863.

COMMANDER.

F. W. Cornyn	Col. 10th Missouri Cav	Mch., 1863, to June 9, 1863.

1st Alabama Cav	Mch., 1863	From New Organization	To 3-Brig. Cav. Div. 16-Corps	June, 1863
7th Kansas Cav	Mch., 1863	From 2-Brig. Cav. Div. 16-Corps	To 3-Brig. Cav. Div. 16-Corps	June, 1863
10th Missouri Cav	Mch., 1863	From Dist. Memphis 16-Corps	To 3-Brig. Cav. Div. 16-Corps	June, 1863
5th Ohio Cav. 3d Bn	Mch., 1863	From Dist. Corinth 16-Corps	To 3-Brig. Cav. Div. 16-Corps	June, 1863
15th Illinois Cav	Mch., 1863	From Dist. Corinth 16-Corps	To 3-Brig. Cav. Div. 16-Corps	June, 1863
ARTILLERY.—				
Batty. G, 1st Ill. Arty.	Mch., 1863	From Dist. Corinth 16-Corps	To Post Corinth 16-Corps	Dec., 1863
Batty. B, 2d Ill. Arty.	Mch., 1863	From Dist. Corinth 16-Corps	To Post Corinth 16-Corps	Dec., 1863
Batty. D, 1st Mo. Arty.	Mch., 1863	From Dist. Corinth 16-Corps	To Arty. 4-Div. 15-Corps	May, 1863
Batty. H, 1st Mo. Arty.	Mch., 1863	From Dist. Corinth 16-Corps	To Arty. Brig. 15-Div	Sept., 1864
Batty. I, 1st Mo. Arty.	Mch., 1863	From Dist. Corinth 16-Corps	No change to Muster Out	June, 1864
Batty B, 1st Mich.	Mch., 1863	From Dist. Corinth 16-Corps	To Arty. Brig. 15-Corps	Sept., 1864
14th Ohio Batty	June, 1863	From Arty. 3-Div. 16-Corps	To Arty. 4-Div. 16-Corps	Mch., 1864
14th Indiana Batty	June, 1863	From Arty. 2-Div. 16-Corps	To Post Corinth 16-Corps	Nov., 1863

FULLER'S BRIGADE, from 5th Division Dist. of Memphis Nov. 11, 1863. Designated 1st Brig. 4-Div. 16-Corps. Mch. 10, 1864.

COMMANDERS.

J. W. Fuller	Col. 27th Ohio Infy	Nov. 11, 1863, to Jan. 2, 1864.
Wm. Feeney	Capt. 27th Ohio Infy	Jan. 2, 1864, to Feb. 2, 1864.
J. W. Fuller	Col. 27th Ohio Infy	Feb. 2, 1864, to Mch. 10, 1864.

27th Ohio Infy	Nov., 1863	From Fuller's Brig. Dist. Memphis.	To 1-Brig. 4-Div. 16-Corps	Mch., 1864
39th Ohio Infy	Nov., 1863	From Fuller's Brig. Dist. Memphis.	To 1-Brig. 4-Div. 16-Corps	Mch., 1864
43d Ohio Infy	Nov., 1863	From Fuller's Brig. Dist. Memphis.	To 2-Brig. 4-Div. 16-Corps	Mch., 1864
63d Ohio Infy	Nov., 1863	From Fuller's Brig. Dist. Memphis.	To 2-Brig. 4-Div. 16-Corps	Mch., 1864
64th Illinois Infy	Nov., 1863	From Unatt. 2-Div. 16-Corps	To 1-Brig. 4-Div. 16-Corps	Mch., 1864
Batty. C, 1st Mich. Arty.	Nov., 1863	From Fuller's Brig. Dist. Memphis.	To Arty. 4-Div. 16-Corps	Mch., 1864
Batty. F, 2d U. S. Arty.	Nov., 1863	From Fuller's Brig. Dist. Memphis.	To Arty. 4-Div. 16-Corps	Mch., 1864
18th Missouri Infy	Nov., 1863	From 3-Brig. 2-Div. 16-Corps	To 3-Brig. 2-Div. 16-Corps	Jan., 1864

3d DIVISION, 16th ARMY CORPS.—(Or District of Jackson). Organized from District of Jackson March, 1863. Reorganized from District of Columbus, 6th Division 16th Army Corps, Jan. 24, 1864.

COMMANDERS.

Nathan Kimball........	Brigadier General.................	Mch., 1863, to May 28, 1863.
A. J. Smith............	Brigadier General.................	Jan. 24, 1864, to Mch. 7, 1864.
J. A. Mower...........	Brigadier General.................	Mch. 7, 1864, to
D. Moore..............	Col. 21st Missouri Infy.............	May 30, 1864, to July 31, 1864.
W. T. Shaw...........	Col. 14th Iowa Infy...............	July 31, 1864, to Oct. 29, 1864.
D. Moore..............	Col. 21st Missouri Infy.............	Oct. 29, 1864, to Dec. 5, 1864.

1st BRIGADE.— COMMANDERS.

M. Brayman...........	Brigadier General.................	Mch. 18, 1863, to May 28, 1863.
A. Engleman..........	Col. 43d Illinois Infy.............	May 28, 1864, to July 12, 1863.
Wm. R. Graves........	Col. 12th Mich. Infy.............	July 12, 1863, to Aug. 14, 1863.
D. Moore..............	Col. 21st Missouri Infy.............	Jan. 24, 1864, to Mch. 7, 1864.
W. F. Lynch..........	Col. 58th Illinois Infy.............	Mch. 7, 1864, to May 31, 1864.
C. D. Murray.........	Col. 89th Indiana Infy.............	May 31, 1864, to Sept. 14, 1864.
D. Moore..............	Col. 21st Missouri Infy.............	Sept. 14, 1864, to Oct. 29, 1864.
T. J. Kinney.........	Col. 119th Illinois Infy.............	Oct. 29, 1864, to Dec. 5, 1864.

43d Illinois Infy........	Mch., 1863	From Bolivar Dist. Jackson 16-Corps	To 1-Brig. Kimball's Prov'l. D. 16-C.	May, 1863
61st Illinois Infy.......	Mch., 1863	From Bolivar Dist. Jackson 16-Corps	To 1-Brig. Kimball's Prov'l. D. 16-C.	May, 1863
106th Illinois Infy.......	Mch., 1863	From 4-Brig. Dist. Jackson 16-Corps	To 1-Brig. Kimball's Prov'l. D. 16-C.	May, 1863
12th Michigan Infy......	Mch., 1863	From Bolivar Dist. Jackson 16-Corps	To 1-Brig. Kimball's Prov'l. D. 16-C.	May, 1863
Springfield, Ill. Batty...	Mch., 1863	From Bolivar Dist. Jackson 16-Corps	To 3-Brig. 3-Div. 16-Corps.........	May, 1863
58th Illinois Infy........	Jan., 1864	From Dist. Columbus 6-Div. 16-C...	To 2-Brig. 3-Div. 16-Corps........	Nov. 1864
119th Illinois Infy.......	Jan., 1864	From 4-Brig. Dist. Memphis 16-C..	To 1-Brig. 2-Div. Det. A. Tenn. Cm'd	Dec., 1864
89th Indiana Infy........	Jan., 1864	From 1-Brig. Dist. Memphis 16-C..	To 1-Brig. 2-Div. Det. A. Tenn. Cm'd	Dec., 1864
21st Missouri Infy.......	Jan., 1864	From 4-Brig. Dist. Memphis 16-C..	To 1-Brig. 2-Div. Det. A. Tenn. Cm'd	Dec., 1864
122d Illinois Infy........	Nov., 1864	From 2-Brig. 3-Div. 16-Corps.......	To 1-Brig. 2-Div. Det. A. Tenn. Cm'd	Dec., 1864

2d BRIGADE.— COMMANDERS.

M. K. Lawler.........	Col. 18th Illinois Infy.............	Mch. 18, 1862, to Apr. 22, 1863.
J. Richmond...........	Col. 126th Illinois Infy.............	Apr. 22, 1863, to May 28, 1863.
W. T. Shaw...........	Col. 14th Iowa Infy.............	Jan. 24, 1864, to June 11, 1864.
J. I. Gilbert..........	Col. 27th Iowa Infy.............	June 11, 1864, to Sept. 25, 1864.
Jas. K. Mills.........	Col. 24th Missouri Infy.............	Sept. 25, 1864, to Oct. 6, 1864.
J. F. Drish...........	Lt.-Col. 122d Ill. Infy.............	Oct. 6, 1864, to Oct. 15, 1864.
J. I. Gilbert..........	Col. 27th Iowa Infy.............	Oct. 15, 1864, to Dec. 5, 1864.

18th Illinois Infy........	Mch., 1863	From 1-Brig. Dist. Jackson 16-Corps.	To 2-Brig. Kimball's Prov'l Div....	May, 1863
54th Illinois Infy........	Mch., 1863	From 1-Brig. Dist. Jackson 16-Corps.	To 2-Brig. Kimball's Prov'l Div....	May, 1863
126th Illinois Infy.......	Mch., 1863	From 1-Brig. Dist. Jackson 16-Corps.	To 2-Brig. Kimball's Prov'l Div....	May, 1863
22d Ohio Infy...........	Mch., 1863	From 1-Brig. Dist. Jackson 16-Corps.	To 2-Brig. Kimball's Prov'l Div....	May, 1863
14th Iowa Infy..........	Jan., 1864	From Dist. Columbus 6-Div. 16-C...	To Springfield, Ill.................	Nov. 1864
27th Iowa Infy..........	Jan., 1864	From Gilbert's Brig. Dist. Memphis.	To 2-B. 2-Div. Det. Army Tenn. Cm'o	Dec., 1864
32d Iowa Infy...........	Jan., 1864	From Dist. Columbus 6-Div. 16-Corps	To 2-B. 2-Div. Det. Army Tenn. Cm'd	Dec., 1864
24th Missouri Infy.......	Jan., 1864	From Dist. Columbus 6-Div. 16-Corps	No change to Muster Out..........	Oct., 1864
122d Illinois Infy........	June, 1864	From Dist. Columbus 6-Div. 16-Corps	To 1-Brig. 3-Div. 16-Corps........	Nov., 1864
58th Illinois Infy........	Nov., 1864	From 1-Brig. 3-Div. 16-Corps........	To 1-Brig. 2-Div. Det. A. Tenn. Cm'd	Dec., 1864

3d BRIGADE.— COMMANDERS.

J. M. True............	Col. 62d Illinois Infy.............	Mch. 18, 1863, to July 19, 1863.
J. I. Gilbert..........	Col. 27th Iowa Infy.............	July 19, 1863, to Aug. 14, 1863.
E. H. Wolfe..........	Col. 52d Illinois Infy.............	Jan. 25, 1864, to Feb. 28, 1864.
R. M. Moon...........	Col. 117th Illinois Infy.............	Feb. 28, 1864, to May 21, 1864.
E. H. Wolfe..........	Col. 52d Illinois Infy.............	May 21, 1864, to Sept. 2, 1864.
Phineas Pease.........	Col. 46th Illinois Infy.............	Sept. 2, 1864, to Oct., 1864.
E. H. Wolfe..........	Col. 52d Illinois Infy.............	Oct., 1864, to Dec. 5, 1864.

62d Illinois Infy........	Mch., 1863	From 1-Brig. Dist. Jackson 16-Corps.	To True's Brig. Ark. Expedition....	Aug., 1863
50th Indiana Infy........	Mch., 1863	From 2-Brig. Dist. Jackson 16-Corps.	To True's Brig. Ark. Expedition....	Aug., 1863
27th Iowa Infy..........	Mch., 1863	From 2-Brig. Dist. Jackson 16-Corps.	To True's Brig. Ark. Expedition....	Aug., 1863
7th Tenn. Infy..........	Mch., 1863	From 1-Brig. Dist. Jackson 16-Corps.	No change to Muster Out..........	July, 1863
49th Illinois Infy........	July, 1863	From 4-Brig. Dist. Memphis 16-C...	To True's Brig. Ark. Expedition....	Aug., 1863
Springfield, Ill. Batty...	May, 1863	From 1-Brig. 3-Div. 16-Corps........	To True's Brig. Ark. Expedition....	Aug., 1863
49th Illinois Infy........	Jan., 1864	From Gilbert's Brig. Dist. Memphis.	To 3-Brig. 2-Div. Det. A. Tenn. Cm'd	Dec., 1864
117th Illinois Infy.......	Jan., 1864	From 1-Brig. Dist. Memphis 16-C...	To 3-Brig. 2-Div. Det. A. Tenn. Cm'd	Dec., 1864
52d Indiana Infy........	Jan., 1864	From Dist. Columbus 6-Div. 16-C...	To 3-Brig. 2-Div. Det. A. Tenn. Cm'd	Dec., 1864
178th New York Infy....	Jan., 1864	From Dist. Columbus 6-Div. 16-C...	To 3-Brig. 2-Div. Det. A. Tenn. Cm'o	Dec., 1864
ARTILLERY, 3d DIVISION.—				
14th Indiana Batty.......	Mch., 1863	From Dist. Jackson 16-Corps.......	To Dist. Corinth 2-Div. 16-Corps...	June, 1863
14th Ohio Batty.........	Mch., 1863	From Dist. Jackson 16-Corps.......	To Dist. Corinth 2-Div. 16-Corps...	June, 1863
7th Wisconsin Batty.....	Mch., 1863	From Dist. Jackson 16-Corps.......	To 4-Brig. Dist. Memphis 16-Corps..	July, 1863
3d Indiana Batty........	Jan., 1864	From St. Louis Dept. Mo...........	To 1-B. 2-Div. Det. A. Tenn. Cumb'd.	Dec., 1864
9th Indiana Batty........	Jan., 1864	From Dist. Columbus 6-Div. 16-C...	To 2-B. 2-Div. Det. A. Tenn. Cumb'd.	Dec., 1864
14th Indiana Batty.......	Jan., 1864	From Post Corinth 2-Div. 16-Corps.	To Unassigned Dist. West Tenn.....	June, 1864
Batty. G, 2d Ill. Arty....	June, 1864	From Dist. Columbus 6-Div. 16-C...	To 3-B. 2-Div. Det. A. Tenn. Cumb'd.	Dec., 1864

CAVALRY BRIGADE, 3d DIVISION.—Organized Mch., 1863. Transferred to 1st Cav. Div. 16-Corps.

COMMANDER.

J. K. Mizner..........	Col. 3d Michigan Cav.............	Mch., 1863, to June, 1863.

11th Illinois Cav........	Mch., 1863	From Cav. Brig. Dist. Jackson 16-C.	To 4-Brig. Cav. Div. 16-Corps......	June, 1863
3d Michigan Cav........	Mch., 1863	From Cav. Brig. Dist. Jackson 16-C.	To 2-Brig. 1-Cav. Div. 16-Corps....	June, 1863
6th Tenn. Cav..........	Mch., 1863	From Cav. Brig. Dist. Jackson 16-C.	To 2-Brig. 1-Cav. Div. 16-Corps....	June, 1863

4th DIVISION.—Assigned from 17th Army Corps Jan. 20, 1863. Transferred to 13th Army Corps July 28, 1863. Reorganized Jan. 24, 1864. Transferred to 17th Army Corps Sept. 23, 1864. Reorganized Oct. 1864. Discontinued Nov. 7, 1864.

COMMANDERS.

J. G. Lauman..........	Brigadier General.................	Jan. 20, 1863, to July 12, 1863.
A. P. Hovey..........	Brigadier General.................	July 12, 1863, to July 23, 1863.
M. M. Crocker........	Brigadier General.................	July 23, 1863, to July 28, 1863.
J. C. Veatch..........	Brigadier General.................	Jan. 24, 1864, to July 17, 1864.
J. W. Fuller..........	Brigadier General.................	July 17, 1864, to Aug. 4, 1864.
T. E. G. Ransom......	Brigadier General.................	Aug. 4, 1864, to Aug. 19, 1864.
J. W. Fuller..........	Brigadier General.................	Aug. 19, 1864, to Sept. 23, 1864.
J. P. Hawkins.........	Brigadier General.................	Oct. 11, 1864, to Nov. 7, 1864.

1st BRIGADE.— COMMANDERS.

I. C. Pugh	Col. 41st Illinois Infy	Jan. 20. 1863, to July 28, 1863.
M. Montgomery	Col. 25th Wisconsin Infy	Jan. 24, 1864, to Mch. 10, 1864.
J. W. Fuller	Col. 27th Ohio Infy	Mch. 10, 1864, to July 17, 1864.
John Morrill	Col. 64th Illinois Infy	July 17, 1864, to July 22, 1864.
H. T. McDowell	Lt.-Col. 39th Ohio Infy	July 22, 1864, to Aug. 4. 1864.
J. W. Fuller	Brigadier General	Aug. 4, 1864, to Aug. 19, 1864.
H. T. McDowell	Lt.-Col. 39th Ohio Infy	Aug. 19, 1864, to Sept. 23, 1864.
V. E. Young	Col. 49th U. S. C. T	Oct. 11, 1864, to Nov. 7, 1864.

41st Illinois Infy	Jan., 1863	From 1-Brig. 4-Div. 17-Corps	To 1-Brig. 4-Div. 13-Corps	July, 1863
53d Illinois Infy	Jan., 1863	From 1-Brig. 4-Div. 17-Corps	To 1-Brig. 4-Div. 13-Corps	July, 1863
3d Iowa Infy	Jan., 1863	From 1-Brig. 4-Div. 17-Corps	To 1-Brig. 4-Div. 13-Corps	July, 1863
33d Wisconsin Infy	Jan., 1863	From 1-Brig. 4-Div. 17-Corps	To 1-Brig. 4-Div. 13-Corps	July, 1863
33d Missouri Infy	Jan., 1864	From Helena, Ark	To 3-Brig. 1-Div. 16-Corps	Jan., 1864
35th New Jersey Infy	Jan., 1864	From Dist. Columbus 6-Div. 16-C.	To 2-Brig. 4-Div. 16-Corps	Mch., 1864
25th Wisconsin Infy	Jan., 1864	From 2-Brig. 2-Div. Ark. Exp.	To 2-Brig. 4-Div. 16-Corps	Mch., 1864
64th Illinois Infy	Mch., 1864	From 4-Brig. 2-Div. 16-Corps	To 1-Brig. 1-Div. 17-Corps	Sept., 1864
18th Missouri Infy	Mch., 1864	From 3-Brig. 2-Div. 16-Corps	To 1-Brig. 1-Div. 17-Corps	Sept., 1864
27th Ohio Infy	Mch., 1864	From 4-Brig. 2-Div. 16-Corps	To 1-Brig. 1-Div. 17-Corps	Sept., 1864
39th Ohio Infy	Mch., 1864	From 4-Brig. 2-Div. 16-Corps	To 1-Brig. 1-Div. 17-Corps	Sept., 1864
48th U. S. C. T.	Oct., 1864	From 1-Brig. 1-Div. U. S. C. T. Vicks.	To 1-B 1-Div. U. S. C. T. Dist Vicks	Nov., 1864
49th U. S. C. T.	Oct., 1864	From 1-Brig. 1-Div. U. S. C. T. Vicks.	To 1-B 1-Div. U. S. C. T. Dist Vicks	Nov., 1864
53d U. S. C. T.	Oct., 1864	From 1-Brig. 1-Div. U. S. C. T. Vicks.	To 1-B 1-Div. U. S. C. T. Dist Vicks	Nov., 1864

2d BRIGADE.— COMMANDERS.

Cyrus Hall	Col. 14th Illinois Infy	Jan. 20, 1863, to Mch. 22, 1863.
B. Dornblaser	Col. 46th Illinois Infy	Mch. 22, 1863, to Apr. 22, 1863.
Cyrus Hall	Col. 14th Illinois Infy	Apr. 22, 1863, to July 28, 1863.
J. H. Howe	Col. 32d Wisconsin Infy	Jan. 24, 1864, to Mch. 10, 1864.
J. W. Sprague	Col. 63d Ohio Infy	Mch. 10, 1864, to Sept. 18, 1864.
Wagar Swayne	Col. 43d Ohio Infy	Sept. 18, 1864, to Sept. 23, 1864.
Hiram Schofield	Col. 47th U. S. C. T.	Oct. 11, 1864, to Nov. 7, 1864.

14th Illinois Infy	Jan., 1863	From 2-Brig. 4-Div. 17-Corps	To 2-Brig. 4-Div. 13-Corps	July, 1863
15th Illinois Infy	Jan., 1863	From 2-Brig. 4-Div. 17-Corps	To 2-Brig. 4-Div. 13-Corps	July, 1863
46th Illinois Infy	Jan., 1863	From 2-Brig. 4-Div. 17-Corps	To 2-Brig. 4-Div. 13-Corps	July, 1863
76th Illinois Infy	Jan., 1863	From 2-Brig. 4-Div. 17-Corps	To 2-Brig. 4-Div. 13-Corps	July, 1863
101st Illinois Infy	Jan., 1863	From Holly Springs, Miss	To Dist. Memphis 16-Corps	Jan., 1863
25th Indiana Infy	Jan., 1864	From 3-Brig. 1-Cav. Div. 16-Corps	To 3-Brig. 4-Div. 16-Corps	Mch., 1864
17th N. Y. Veteran Infy	Jan., 1864	From Dist. Columbus 6-Div. 16-C.	To 3-Brig. 4-Div. 16-Corps	Mch., 1864
32d Wisconsin Infy	Jan., 1864	From 2-Brig. 5-Div. 16-Corps	To 3-Brig. 4-Div. 16-Corps	Mch., 1864
35th New Jersey Infy	Mch., 1864	From 1-Brig. 4-Div. 16-Corps	To 2-Brig. 1-Div. 17-Corps	Sept., 1864
43d Ohio Infy	Mch., 1864	From 4-Brig. 2-Div. 16-Corps	To 2-Brig. 1-Div. 17-Corps	Sept., 1864
63d Ohio Infy	Mch., 1864	From 4-Brig. 2-Div. 16-Corps	To 2-Brig. 1-Div. 17-Corps	Sept., 1864
25th Wisconsin Infy	Mch., 1864	From 1-Brig. 4-Div. 16-Corps	To 2-Brig. 1-Div. 17-Corps	Sept., 1864
47th U. S. C. T.	Oct., 1864	From 2-Brig. 1-Colored Div. Vicks.	To 2-Brig. 1st Colored Div. Vicks.	Nov., 1864
50th U. S. C. T.	Oct., 1864	From 2-Brig. 1-Colored Div. Vicks.	To 2-Brig. 1st Colored Div. Vicks.	Nov., 1864
52d U. S. C. T.	Oct., 1864	From 2-Brig. 1-Colored Div. Vicks.	To 2-Brig. 1st Colored Div. Vicks.	Nov., 1864

3d BRIGADE.— COMMANDERS.

A. K. Johnson	Col. 28th Illinois Infy	Jan. 20, 1863, to Feb. 3, 1863.
Geo. E. Bryant	Col. 12th Wisconsin Infy	Feb. 3, 1863, to June 9, 1863.
A. K. Johnson	Col. 28th Illinois Infy	June 9, 1863, to July 28, 1863.
J. H. Howe	Col. 32d Wisconsin Infy	Mch. 10, 1864, to July 21, 1864.
W. T. C. Grower	Col. 17th N. Y. Veteran Infy	July 21, 1864, to Aug. 20, 1864.
John Tillson	Col. 10th Illinois Infy	Aug. 20, 1864, to Sept. 23, 1864.

28th Illinois Infy	Jan., 1863	From 3-Brig. 4-Div. 17-Corps	To 3-Brig. 4-Div. 13-Corps	July, 1863
32d Illinois Infy	Jan., 1863	From 3-Brig. 4-Div. 17-Corps	To 3-Brig. 4-Div. 13-Corps	July, 1863
53d Indiana Infy	Jan., 1863	From 3-Brig. 4-Div. 17-Corps	To 3-Brig. 4-Div. 13-Corps	July, 1863
12th Wisconsin Infy	Jan., 1863	From 3-Brig. 4-Div. 17-Corps	To 3-Brig. 4-Div. 13-Corps	July, 1863
25th Indiana Infy	Mch., 1864	From 2-Brig. 4-Div. 16-Corps	To 3-Brig. 1-Div. 17-Corps	Sept., 1864
17th N. Y. Veteran Infy	Mch., 1864	From 2-Brig. 4-Div. 16-Corps	To 1-Brig. 2-Div. 14-Corps	Aug., 1864
32d Wisconsin Infy	Mch., 1864	From 2-Brig. 4-Div. 16-Corps	To 3-Brig. 1-Div. 17-Corps	Sept., 1864
10th Illinois Infy	Aug., 1864	From 2-Brig. 2-Div. 14-Corps	To 3-Brig. 1-Div. 17-Corps	Sept., 1864
ARTILLERY.—				
Batty. E, 2d Illinois Arty.	Jan., 1863	From Arty. 4-Div. 17-Corps	To Arty. 4-Div. 13-Corps	July, 1863
Batty. K, 2d Illinois Arty.	Jan., 1863	From Arty. 4-Div. 17-Corps	To Arty. 4-Div. 13-Corps	July, 1863
9th Indiana Batty	Jan., 1863	From Arty. 4-Div. 17-Corps	To Dist. Columbus 6-Div. 16-Corps.	Mch., 1863
5th Ohio Batty	Jan., 1863	From Arty. 4-Div. 17-Corps	To Arty. 13-Div. 16-Corps	July, 1863
7th Ohio Batty	Jan., 1863	From Arty. 4-Div. 17-Corps	To Arty. 4-Div. 13-Corps	July, 1863
15th Ohio Batty	Jan., 1863	From Arty. 4-Div. 17-Corps	To Arty. 4-Div. 13-Corps	July, 1863
Batty. D, 2d Ill. Arty.	Jan., 1864	From 3-Brig. 1-Cav. Div. 16-Corps.	To Decatur, Ala. Dist. North Ala.	Mch., 1864
Batty. C, 1st Mich. Arty.	Jan., 1864	From Fuller's Brig. 2-Div. 16-Corps.	To Arty. 1-Div. 17-Corps	Sept., 1864
14th Ohio Batty	Jan., 1864	From Arty. 2-Div. 16-Corps	To Arty. 1-Div. 17-Corps	Sept., 1864
Batty. F, 2d U. S. Arty.	Jan., 1864	From Fuller's Brig. 2-Div. 16-Corps.	To Arty. 1-Div. 17-Corps	Sept., 1864
CAVALRY.—				
1st Alabama Cav.	Apr., 1864	From 1-Brig. 1-Cav. Div. 16-Corps.	To Headquarters 16-Corps	May, 1864

1st CAVALRY DIVISION.—Organized Mch. 31, 1863. Transferred to Dist. of West. Tenn. June, 1864.

COMMANDERS.

C. C. Washburn	Major General	Mch. 31, 1863, to June 9, 1863.
J. K. Mizner	Col. 3d Michigan Cav	June 9, 1863, to July 24, 1863.
B. H. Grierson	Brigadier General	July 24, 1863, to Sept. 24, 1863.
Edward Hatch	Col. 2d Iowa Cav	Sept. 24, 1863, to Oct. 24, 1863.
B. H. Grierson	Brigadier General	Oct. 24, 1863, to Apr. 27, 1864.
George E. Waring, Jr.	Col. 4th Missouri Cav	Apr. 27, 1864, to May 11, 1864.
B. H. Grierson	Brigadier General	May 11. 1864, to June 20, 1864.

1st BRIGADE.— COMMANDERS.

B. H. Grierson	Col. 6th Illinois Cav	Mch. 31, 1863, to June 9, 1863.
L. F. McCrillis	Col. 3d Illinois Cav	June 9, 1863, to Aug. 20, 1863.
J. K. Mizner	Col. 3d Michigan Cav	Aug. 20, 1863, to Aug. 29, 1863.
T. P. Herrick	Col. 7th Kansas Cav	Aug. 29, 1863, to Sept. 17, 1863.
Thos. T. Heath	Col. 5th Ohio Cav	Sept. 17, 1863, to Oct. 12, 1863.
J. K. Mizner	Col. 3d Michigan Cav	Oct. 12, 1863, to Jan. 7, 1864.
Geo. E. Waring, Jr.	Col. 4th Missouri Cav	Jan. 7, 1864, to Apr. 27, 1864.
Joseph Karge	Col. 2d New Jersey Cav	Apr. 27, 1864, to May 11, 1864.
Geo. E. Waring, Jr.	Col. 4th Missouri Cav	May 11, 1864, to June 20, 1864.

1st BRIGADE.—Continued.

Unit	Date	From	To	Date
6th Illinois Cav.	Mch., 1863	From Grierson's Br. Cav. Div. 16-C..	To Cav. Brig. 19-Corps Gulf	May, 1863
7th Illinois Cav.	Mch., 1863	From Grierson's Br. Cav. Div. 16-C..	To Cav. Brig. 19-Corps Gulf	May, 1863
2d Iowa Cav.	Mch., 1863	From Grierson's Br. Cav. Div. 16-C..	To 2-Brig. 1-Cav. Div. 16-Corps	May, 1863
3d Illinois Cav.	June, 1863	From 2-Brig. 1-Cav. Div. 16-Corps...	To 2-Brig. 1-Cav. Div. 16-Corps	Aug., 1863
4th Illinois Cav.	June, 1863	From 2-Brig. 1-Cav. Div. 16-Corps...	To Winslow's Cav. Brig. Dist. Vicks.	Aug., 1863
9th Illinois Cav.	June, 1863	From 2-Brig. 1-Cav. Div. 16-Corps...	To 2-Brig. 1-Cav. Div. 16-Corps	Aug., 1863
1st Alabama Cav.	Aug., 1863	From 3-Brig. 1-Div. Cav. 16-Corps..	To Cav. 4-Div. 16-Corps	Feb., 1864
3d Michigan Cav.	Aug., 1863	From 2-Brig. 1-Cav. Div. 16-Corps..	To Veteran Furlough	Feb., 1864
7th Kansas Cav.	Aug., 1863	From 3-Brig. 1-Cav. Div. 16-Corps..	To Unatt. 1-Cav. Div. 16-Corps	Feb., 1864
10th Missouri Cav.	Aug., 1863	From 3-Brig. 1-Cav. Div. 16-Corps..	To Winslow's Cav. Br. Dist. Vicks.	Aug., 1863
5th Ohio Cav. 3d B'n	Aug., 1863	From 3-Brig. 1-Cav. Div. 16-Corps..	To Unatt. 15-Corps	Oct., 1863
5th Ohio C. (1st & 2d Bn.)	Aug., 1863	From 4-Brig. 5-Div. 16-Corps....	To Unatt. 15-Corps	Oct., 1863
6th Tennessee Cav.	Dec., 1863	From 2-Brig. 1-Cav. Div. 16-Corps..	To Unass'd. Dist. West Tenn.	June, 1864
3d Illinois Cav.	Dec., 1863	From 2-Brig. 1-Cav. Div. 16-Corps..	To 3-Brig. 1-Cav. Div. 16-Corps	Jan., 1864
2d Illinois Cav.	Jan., 1864	From Waring's B. 1-Cav. Div. 16-C.	To 2-Brig. Cav. Div. Dept. Gulf	June, 1864
7th Indiana Cav.	Jan., 1864	From Waring's B. 1-Cav. Div. 16-C.	To 1-B. 2-Cav. Div. Dist. W. Tenn.	June, 1864
4th Missouri Cav.	Jan., 1864	From Waring's B. 1-Cav. Div. 16-C.	To 1-B. 2-Cav. Div. Dist. W. Tenn.	June, 1864
2d New Jersey Cav.	Jan., 1864	From Waring's B. 1-Cav. Div. 16-C.	To 1-B. 2-Cav. Div. Dist. W. Tenn.	June, 1864
19th Penna. Cav.	Jan., 1864	From Waring's B. 1-Cav. Div. 16-C.	To 1-B. 2-Cav. Div. Dist. W. Tenn.	June, 1864

2d BRIGADE.—Discontinued Mch., 1864. Reorganized Apr., 1864.

COMMANDERS.

L. F. McCrillis	Col. 3d Ill. Cav.	Mch. 31, 1863, to June 9, 1863.
Edward Hatch	Col. 2d Iowa Cav.	June 9, 1863, to Aug. 20, 1863.
F. Hurst	Col. 6th Tenn. Cav.	Aug. 20, 1863, to Sept. 20, 1863.
L. F. McCrillis	Col. 3d Ill. Cav.	Sept. 20, 1863, to Nov. 17, 1863.
Edward Hatch	Col. 2d Iowa Cav.	Nov. 17, 1863, to Jan. 5, 1864.
A. G. Brackett	Col. 9th Ill. Cav.	Jan. 5, 1864, to Feb. 7, 1864.
W. P. Hepburn	Lt.-Col. 2d Iowa Cav.	Feb. 7, 1864, to Mch. 24, 1864.
E. F. Winslow	Col. 4th Iowa Cav.	Apr., 1864, to June 20, 1864.

Unit	Date	From	To	Date
4th Ill. Cav.	Mch., 1863	From 2-Brig. Cav. Div. 16-Corps....	To 1-Brig. 1-Cav. Div. 16-Corps	June, 1863
7th Kansas Cav.	Mch., 1863	From 2-Brig. Cav. Div. 16-Corps....	To 3-Brig. 1-Cav. Div. 16-Corps	June, 1863
5th Ohio Cav. (1st and 2d Battns.)	Mch., 1863	From 2-Brig. Cav. Div. 16-Corps....	To 3-Brig. 5-Div. 16-Corps	Mch., 1863
3d Ill. Cav. (5 Co's)	Apr., 1863	From Unatt. 13-Corps.	To 1-Brig. 1-Cav. Div. 16-Corps	June, 1863
9th Ill. Cav.	Apr., 1863	From 2-Br. 2-Cav. Div. Dist. E. Ark.	To 1-Brig. 1-Cav. Div. 16-Corps	June, 1863
2d Iowa Cav.	May, 1863	From 2-Br. 1-Cav. Div. 16-Corps..	To 3-Brig. 1-Cav. Div. 16-Corps	Aug., 1863
3d Mich. Cav.	June, 1863	From Cav. Brig. 3-Div. 16-Corps...	To 1-Brig. 1-Cav. Div. 16-Corps	Aug., 1863
6th Tenn. Cav.	June, 1863	From Cav. Brig. 3-Div. 16-Corps...	To 1-Brig. 1-Cav. Div. 16-Corps	Aug., 1863
3d Ill. Cav.	Aug., 1863	From 1-Brig. 1-Cav. Div. 16-Corps..	To 1-Brig. 1-Cav. Div. 16-Corps	Dec., 1863
9th Ill. Cav.	Aug., 1863	From 1-Brig. 1-Cav. Div. 16-Corps..	To 3-Brig. 1-Cav. Div. 16-Corps	Dec., 1863
6th Ill. Cav.	Nov., 1863	From 3-Brig. 1-Cav. Div. 16-Corps..	To 3-Brig. 1-Cav. Div. 16-Corps	Apr., 1864
7th Ill. Cav.	Nov., 1863	From 3-Brig. 1-Cav. Div. 16-Corps..	To 3-Brig. 1-Cav. Div. 16-Corps	Apr., 1864
2d Iowa Cav.	Nov., 1863	From 3-Brig. 1-Cav. Div. 16-Corps..	To 3-Brig. 1-Cav. Div. 16-Corps	Apr., 1864
Batty. K, 1st Ill. Arty.	Nov., 1863	From 3-Brig. 1-Cav. Div. 16-Corps..	To Dist. West Tenn.	June, 1864
3d Iowa Cav.	Apr., 1864	From 1-Brig. Cav. Div. 7-Corps Ark.	To 2-Br. 1-Cav. Div. Dist. W. Tenn.	June, 1864
4th Iowa Cav.	Apr., 1864	From Winslow's Cav. Brig. Vicks.	To 2-Br. 1-Cav. Div. Dist. W. Tenn.	June, 1864
10th Mo. Cav.	Apr., 1864	From Winslow's Cav. Brig. Vicks..	To 2-Br. 1-Cav. Div. Dist. W. Tenn.	June, 1864

3d BRIGADE.—Discontinued Nov., 1863. Reorganized Dec., 1863, from 2-Brig. 5-Div. 16-Corps. Discontinued March, 1864. Reorganized May, 1864.

COMMANDERS.

F. M. Cornyn	Col. 10th Mo. Cav.	June 9, 1863, to July 13, 1863.
Geo. A. Bacon	Col. 15th Ill. Cav.	July 13, 1863, to Aug. 20, 1863.
Edward Hatch	Col. 2d Iowa Cav.	Aug. 20, 1863, to Nov. 5, 1863.
W. H. Morgan	Col. 25th Ind. Infy.	Dec. 31, 1863, to Jan. 4, 1864.
L. F. McCrillis	Col. 3d Ill. Cav.	Jan. 4, 1864, to Mch. 14, 1864.
H. B. Burgh	Lt.-Col. 9th Ill. Cav.	May 4, 1864, to June 20, 1864.

Unit	Date	From	To	Date
10th Mo. Cav.	July, 1863	From Cav. Brig. 2-Div. 16-Corps....	To 1-Brig. 1-Cav. Div. 16-Corps	Aug., 1863
7th Kan. Cav.	July, 1863	From Cav. Brig. 2-Div. 16-Corps....	To 1-Brig. 1-Cav. Div. 16-Corps	Aug., 1863
5th Ohio Cav. 3d Battn.	July, 1863	From Cav. Brig. 2-Div. 16-Corps....	To 1-Brig. 1-Cav. Div. 16-Corps	Aug., 1863
15th Ill. Cav. (Stewart's Battn.)	July, 1863	From Cav. Brig. 2-Div. 16-Corps....	To Det. Brig. 1-Cav. Div. 16-Corps..	Aug., 1863
1st Ala. Cav.	July, 1863	From Cav. Brig. 2-Div. 16-Corps....	To 1-Brig. 1-Cav. Div. 16-Corps	Aug., 1863
6th Ill. Cav.	Aug., 1863	From Cav. Brig. Dept. Gulf	To 2-Brig. 1-Cav. Div. 16-Corps	Nov., 1863
7th Ill. Cav.	Aug., 1863	From Cav. Brig. Dept. Gulf	To 2-Brig. 1-Cav. Div. 16-Corps	Nov., 1863
2d Iowa Cav.	Aug., 1863	From 2-Brig. 1-Cav. Div. 16-Corps..	To 2-Brig. 1-Cav. Div. 16-Corps	Nov., 1863
Batty. K, 1st Ill. Arty.	Oct., 1863	From Dist. Colum. 6-Div. 16-Corps..	To 2-Brig. 1-Cav. Div. 16-Corps	Nov., 1863
25th Ind. Mtd. Infy.	Dec., 1863	From 2-Brig. 5-Div. 16-Corps	To 2-Brig. 4-Div. 16-Corps	Jan., 1864
32d Wis. Infy. Mtd.	Dec., 1863	From 2-Brig. 5-Div. 16-Corps	To 2-Brig. 4-Div. 16-Corps	Jan., 1864
Batty. D, 2d Ill. Arty.	Dec., 1863	From 2-Brig. 5-Div. 16-Corps	To Dist. Memphis 16-Corps	Jan., 1864
72d Ind. Mtd. Infy.	Jan., 1864	From 3-Brig. 2-Div. Cav. C. Cumb'd.	To 3-Brig. 2-Div. Cav. Corps Cumb'd.	Apr., 1864
5th Ky. Cav.	Jan., 1864	From 3-Br. 1-Div. Cav. C. Cumb'd.	To 3-Brig. 3-Div. Cav. Corps Cumb'd.	Apr., 1864
2d Tenn. Cav.	Jan., 1864	From 2-Br. 1-Div. Cav. C. Cumb'd.	To 1-Brig. 4-Div. Cav. Corps Cumb'd.	Apr., 1864
3d Tenn. Cav.	Jan., 1864	From 2-Br. 1-Div. Cav. C. Cumb'd.	To 1-Brig. 4-Div. Cav. Corps Cumb'd.	Apr., 1864
4th Tenn. Cav.	Jan., 1864	From Dist. Nashville, Tenn.	To 1-Brig. 4-Div. Cav. Corps Cumb'd.	Apr., 1864
3d Ill. Cav.	Jan., 1864	From 1-Brig. 1-Cav. Div. 16-Corps..	To 1-Br. 1-Div. Cav. Dist. W. Tenn.	June, 1864
6th Ill. Cav.	Apr., 1864	From 2-Brig. 1-Cav. Div. 16-Corps..	To 1-Br. 1-Cav. Div. Dist. W. Tenn.	June, 1864
7th Ill. Cav.	Apr., 1864	From 2-Brig. 1-Cav. Div. 16-Corps..	To 1-Br. 1-Cav. Div. Dist. W. Tenn.	June, 1864
9th Ill. Cav.	Apr., 1864	From 2-Brig. 1-Cav. Div. 16-Corps..	To 1-Br. 1-Cav. Div. Dist. W. Tenn.	June, 1864
2d Iowa Cav.	Apr., 1864	From 2-Brig. 1-Cav. Div. 16-Corps..	To 1-Br. 1-Cav. Div. Dist. W. Tenn.	June, 1864

4th BRIGADE.—Organized June, 1863. Discontinued Aug., 1863.

COMMANDER.

Name	Rank/Unit
B. D. Meek	Lt.-Col. 11th Ill. Cav.

Unit	Date	From	To	Date
6th Ill. Cav. Det.	June, 1863	From 1-Brig. 1-Cav. Div. 16-Corps..	To 3-Brig. 1-Cav. Div. 16-Corps	Aug., 1863
7th Ill. Cav. Det.	June, 1863	From 1-Brig. 1-Cav. Div. 16-Corps..	To 3-Brig. 1-Cav. Div. 16-Corps	Aug., 1863
11th Ill. Cav.	June, 1863	From Cav. Brig. 3-Div. 16-Corps...	To Winslow's Cav. Brig. Dist. Vicks.	Aug., 1863
7th Tenn. Cav.	June, 1863	From Unass'd 1-Div. 16-Corps	To Dist. Colum. 6-Div. 16-Corps	Aug., 1863
DETACHED BRIGADE.—				
15th Ill. Cav.	Aug., 1863	From 3-Brig. 1-Cav. Div. 16-Corps..	To Waring's Brig. 1-Cav. Div. 16-C.	Dec., 1863
15th Ky. Cav.	Aug., 1863	From Dist. Colum. 6-Div. 16-Corps..	No change to Muster Out	Oct., 1863
7th Tenn. Cav.	Aug., 1863	From Dist. Colum. 6-Div. 16-Corps..	To Waring's Brig. 1-Cav. Div. 16-C.	Dec., 1863

WARING'S BRIGADE.—Organized Dec., 1863, from 6-Div. 16-Corps. Discontinued Jan., 1864.

COMMANDER.

Geo. E. Waring, Jr	Col. 4th Mo. Cav			
2d Ill. Cav..............Dec., 1863	From 1-Brig. 6-Div. 16-Corps........	To 1-Brig. 1-Div. Cav. 16-Corps......	Jan.,	1864
15th Ill. Cav.............Dec., 1863	From Det. Brig. 1-Cav. Div. 16-C....	To Dist. Eastern Ark.............	Jan.,	1864
4th Mo. Cav..............Dec., 1863	From 1-Brig. 6-Div. 16-Corps........	To 1-Brig. 1-Cav. Div. 16-Corps......	Jan.,	1864
2d N. J. Cav.............Dec., 1863	From Cav. 6-Div. 16-Corps..........	To 1-Brig. 1-Cav. Div. 16-Corps......	Jan.,	1864
19th Penna. Cav..........Dec., 1863	From Cav. 6-Div. 16-Corps..........	To 1-Brig. 1-Cav. Div. 16-Corps......	Jan.,	1864
7th Tenn. Cav...........Dec., 1863	From Det. Brig. Cav. 16-Corps......	To Dist. Columbus 16-Corps.......	Jan.,	1864
7th Ind. Cav............Dec., 1863	From Cav. 6-Div. 16-Corps..........	To 1-Brig. 1-Cav. Div. 16-Corps......	Jan.,	1864

KIMBALL'S PROVISIONAL DIVISION.—Organized May 28, 1863. Transferred to Arkansas Expedition Aug. 10, 1863.

COMMANDER.

Nathan Kimball	Brigadier General	May 28, 1863, to Aug. 10, 1863.	

1st BRIGADE.—   COMMANDER.

A. Engleman	Col. 43d Ill. Infy	May 28, 1863, to Aug. 10, 1863.		
43d Ill. Infy..............May, 1863	From 1-Brig. 3-Div. 16-Corps.......	To 1-Br. Kimball's Div. Dist. E. Ark.	July,	1863
61st Ill. Infy.............May, 1863	From 1-Brig. 3-Div. 16-Corps.......	To 1-Br. Kimball's Div. Dist. E. Ark.	July,	1863
106th Ill. Infy............May, 1863	From 1-Brig. 3-Div. 16-Corps.......	To 1-Br. Kimball's Div. Dist. E. Ark.	July,	1863
12th Mich. Infy............May, 1863	From 1-Brig. 3-Div. 16-Corps.......	To 1-Br. Kimball's Div. Dist. E. Ark.	July,	1863

2d BRIGADE.—   COMMANDER.

J. Richmond	Col. 126th Ill. Infy	May 28, 1863, to Aug. 10, 1863.		
18th Ill. Infy.............May, 1863	From 2-Brig. 3-Div. 16-Corps.......	To 2-Br. Kimball's Div. Dist. E. Ark.	July,	1863
54th Ill. Infy.............May, 1863	From 2-Brig. 3-Div. 16-Corps.......	To 2-Br. Kimball's Div. Dist. E. Ark.	July,	1863
126th Ill. Infy............May, 1863	From 2-Brig. 3-Div. 16-Corps.......	To 2-Br. Kimball's Div. Dist. E. Ark.	July,	1863
22d Ohio Infy.............May, 1863	From 2-Brig. 3-Div. 16-Corps.......	To 2-Br. Kimball's Div. Dist. E. Ark.	July,	1863

3d BRIGADE.—   COMMANDER.

M. Montgomery	Col. 25th Wis. Infy	May 28, 1863, to Aug. 10, 1863.		
40th Iowa Infy............May, 1863	From Dist. Colum. 6-Div. 16-Corps..	To 3-Br. Kimball's Div. Dist. E. Ark.	July,	1863
3d Minn. Infy.............May, 1863	From Dist. Colum. 6-Div. 16-Corps..	To 3-Br. Kimball's Div. Dist. E. Ark.	July,	1863
25th Wis. Infy............May, 1863	From Dist. Colum. 6-Div. 16-Corps..	To 3-Br. Kimball's Div. Dist. E. Ark.	July,	1863
27th Wis. Infy............May, 1863	From Dist. Colum. 6-Div. 16-Corps..	To 3-Br. Kimball's Div. Dist. E. Ark.	July,	1863

DISTRICT OF EASTERN ARKANSAS.—Joined from 13th Army Corps July 29, 1863. Transferred to Dept. of Arkansas, 7th Corps, Jan. 6, 1864.

COMMANDERS.

B. M. Prentiss	Brigadier General	July 29, 1863, to Aug. 3, 1863.	
M. Montgomery	Col. 25th Wis. Infy	Aug. 3, 1863, to Sept. 19, 1863.	
N. B. Buford	Brigadier General	Sept. 19, 1863, to Jan. 6, 1864.	

KIMBALL'S DIVISION.—   COMMANDER.

Nathan Kimball	Brigadier General	July 29, 1863, to Aug. 4, 1863.	

1st BRIGADE.—   COMMANDER.

A. Engleman	Brigadier General	July 29, 1863, to Aug. 4, 1863.		
43d Ill. Infy.............July, 1863	From 1-Br. Kimball's Prov'l Div. 16C.	To 1-Brig. 2-Div. Ark. Exp..........	Aug.,	1863
61st Ill. Infy............July, 1863	From 1-Br. Kimball's Prov'l Div. 16C.	To 1-Brig. 2-Div. Ark. Exp..........	Aug.,	1863
106th Ill. Infy...........July, 1863	From 1-Br. Kimball's Prov'l Div. 16C.	To 1-Brig. 2-Div. Ark. Exp..........	Aug.,	1863
12th Mich. Infy...........July, 1863	From 1-Br. Kimball's Prov'l Div. 16C.	To 1-Brig. 2-Div. Ark. Exp..........	Aug.,	1863

2d BRIGADE.—   COMMANDER.

J. Richmond	Col. 126th Ill. Infy	July 29, 1863, to Aug. 6, 1863.		
18th Ill. Infy............July, 1863	From 2-Br. Kimball's Prov'l D. 16-C.	To 1-Brig. 2-Div. Ark. Exp..........	Aug.,	1863
54th Ill. Infy............July, 1863	From 2-Br. Kimball's Prov'l D. 16-C.	To 1-Brig. 2-Div. Ark. Exp..........	Aug.,	1863
126th Ill. Infy...........July, 1863	From 2-Br. Kimball's Prov'l D. 16-C.	To 2-Brig. 2-Div. Ark. Exp..........	Aug.,	1863
22d Ohio Infy............July, 1863	From 2-Br. Kimball's Prov'l D. 16-C.	To 2-Brig. 2-Div. Ark. Exp..........	Aug.,	1863

3d BRIGADE.—   COMMANDER.

M. Montgomery	Col. 25th Wis. Infy	July 29, 1863, to Aug. 6, 1863.		
40th Iowa Infy............July, 1863	From 3-Br. Kimball's Prov'l D. 16-C.	To 2-Brig. 2-Div. Ark. Exp..........	Aug.,	1863
3d Minn. Infy.............July, 1863	From 3-Br. Kimball's Prov'l D. 16-C.	To 2-Brig. 2-Div. Ark. Exp..........	Aug.,	1863
25th Wis. Infy............July, 1863	From 3-Br. Kimball's Prov'l D. 16-C.	To Garrison Helena, Ark..........	Aug.,	1863
27th Wis. Infy............July, 1863	From 3-Br. Kimball's Prov'l D. 16-C.	To 2-Brig. 2-Div. Ark. Exp..........	Aug.,	1863
ARTILLERY.—				
11th Ohio Batty..........July, 1863	From Arty. 7-Div. 17-Corps.........	To 2-Brig. 2-Div. Ark. Exp..........	Aug.,	1863

13th DIVISION.—Transferred from 13th Army Corps July 28, 1863, and to Arkansas Expedition Aug. 10, 1863.

COMMANDER.

Frederick Salomon	Brigadier General	July 28, 1863, to Aug. 10, 1863.	

1st BRIGADE.—   COMMANDERS.

Wm. E. McLean	Col. 43d Ind. Infy	July 28, 1863, to Aug. 7, 1863.		
C. W. Kittredge	Col. 36th Iowa Infy	Aug. 7, 1863, to Aug. 10, 1863.		
43d Ind. Infy.............July, 1863	From 1-Brig. 13-Div. 13-Corps.......	To 1-Brig. 3-Div. Ark. Exp..........	Aug.,	1863
35th Mo. Infy.............July, 1863	From 1-Brig. 13-Div. 13-Corps.......	To Garrison Helena, Ark............	Aug.,	1863
28th Wis. Infy............July, 1863	From 1-Brig. 13-Div. 13-Corps.......	To 2-Brig. 3-Div. Ark. Exp..........	Aug.,	1863
36th Iowa Infy............Aug., 1863	From 2-Brig. 13-Div. 16-Corps.......	To 1-Brig. 3-Div. Ark. Exp..........	Aug.,	1863

2d BRIGADE.—   COMMANDER.

S. A. Rice	Brigadier General	July 28. 1863, to Aug. 10, 1863.		
29th Iowa Infy............July, 1863	From 2-Brig. 13-Div. 13-Corps.......	To 2-Brig. 3-Div. Ark. Exp..........	Aug.,	1863
33d Iowa Infy.............July, 1863	From 2-Brig. 13-Div. 13-Corps.......	To 2-Brig. 3-Div. Ark. Exp..........	Aug.,	1863
36th Iowa Infy............July, 1863	From 2-Brig. 13-Div. 13-Corps.......	To 1-Brig. 13-Div. 16-Corps........	Aug.,	1863
33d Mo. Infy.............July, 1863	From 2-Brig. 13-Div. 13-Corps.......	To Garrison Helena, Ark............	Aug.,	1863
ARTILLERY.—				
Batty K, 1st Mo. Arty.....July, 1863	From Arty. 1-Div. 16-Corps..........	To Arty. 3-Div. Ark. Exp............	Aug.,	1863
3d Iowa Batty............July, 1863	From Arty. 13-Div. 13-Corps........	To Arty. 3-Div. Ark. Exp............	Aug.,	1863
5th Ohio Batty...........July, 1863	From Arty. 4-Div. 16-Corps.........	To Arty. 3-Div. Ark. Exp............	Aug.,	1863

CAVALRY BRIGADE.—   COMMANDER.

Powell Clayton	Col. 5th Kan. Cav.	July 28, 1863, to Aug. 10, 1863.	

1st Ind. Cav.	July, 1863	From 1-Brig. Cav. Div. 13-Corps	To Clayton's Cav. Brig. Ark. Exp.	Aug.,	1863
5th Kan. Cav.	July, 1863	From 1-Brig. Cav. Div. 13-Corps	To Clayton's Cav. Brig. Ark. Exp.	Aug.,	1863

Arkansas Expedition

Organized Aug. 10, 1863.   Transferred to Dept. Arkansas, 7th Corps, Jan. 6, 1864.

COMMANDER.

Frederick Steele	Major General	Aug. 10, 1863, to Jan. 6, 1864.	

HEADQUARTERS.—

Kane Co. Ill. Cav. Co.	Aug., 1863	From Dist. Eastern Ark.	To 10th Ill. Cav.	Jan., 1865

1st CAVALRY DIVISION.—   COMMANDERS.

J. W. Davidson	Brigadier General	Aug. 10, 1863, to Nov. 3, 1863.
Cyrus Bussey	Col. 3d Iowa Cav.	Nov. 3, 1863, to Dec. .., 1863.
J. W. Davidson	Brigadier General	Dec. .., 1863, to Jan 6, 1864.

1st BRIGADE.—   COMMANDERS.

Wm. F. Geiger	Col. 8th Mo. Cav.	Aug. .., 1863, to Oct. .., 1863.
Lewis Merrill	Col. 2d Mo. Cav.	Oct. .., 1863, to Dec. .., 1863.
Cyrus Bussey	Col. 3d Iowa Cav.	Dec. .., 1863, to Jan. 6, 1864.

2d Mo. Cav.	Aug., 1863	From 1-Br. Cav. Div. Dist. St. Louis.	To 2-Brig. 1-Cav. Div. Ark. Exp.	Dec.,	1863
7th Mo. Cav.	Aug., 1863	From 1-Br. Cav. Div. Dist. St. Louis.	To 1-Brig. 1-Cav. Div. Ark. Exp.	Dec.,	1863
8th Mo. Cav.	Aug., 1863	From 1-Br. Cav. Div. Dist. St. Louis.	To 2-Brig. 1-Cav. Div. Ark. Exp.	Dec.,	1863
3d Iowa Cav.	Dec., 1863	From Res. Cav. Brig. Ark. Exp.	To 1-Br. 1-Cav. Div. 7-Corps Ark.	Jan.,	1864
32d Iowa Infy.	Dec., 1863	From Res. Cav. Brig. Ark. Exp.	To 2-Brig. 3-Div. 16-Corps.	Jan.,	1864
1st Mo. Cav.	Dec., 1863	From Res. Cav. Brig. Ark. Exp.	To 1-Brig. 1-Cav. Div. 7-Corps Ark.	Jan.,	1864

2d BRIGADE.—   COMMANDERS.

J. M. Glover	Col. 3d Mo. Cav.	Aug. 10, 1863, to Dec. 2, 1863.
Lewis Merrill	Col. 2d Mo. Cav.	Dec. 2, 1863, to Jan. 6, 1864.

10th Ill. Cav.	Aug., 1863	From 2-Br. Cav. Div. Dist. St. Louis.	To 3-Brig. 1-Cav. Div. Ark. Exp.	Dec.,	1863
1st Iowa Cav.	Aug., 1863	From 2-Br. Cav. Div. Dist. St. Louis.	To 3-Brig. 1-Cav. Div. Ark. Exp.	Dec.,	1863
3d Mo. Cav.	Aug., 1863	From 2-Br. Cav. Div. Dist. St. Louis.	To 3-Brig. 1-Cav. Div. Ark. Exp.	Dec.,	1863
2d Mo. Cav.	Dec., 1863	From 1-Brig. 1-Cav. Div. Ark. Exp.	To 2-Brig. 1-Cav. Div. 7-Corps Ark.	Jan.,	1864
8th Mo. Cav.	Dec., 1863	From 1-Brig. 1-Cav. Div. Ark. Exp.	To 2-Brig. 1-Cav. Div. 7-Corps Ark.	Jan.,	1864

3d BRIGADE.—   COMMANDER.

Daniel Anderson	Col. 1st Iowa Cav.	Dec. .., 1863, to Jan. 6, 1864.

10th Ill. Cav.	Dec., 1863	From 2-Brig. 1-Cav. Div. Ark. Exp.	To 3-Brig. 1-Cav. Div. 7-Corps Ark.	Jan.,	1864
1st Iowa Cav.	Dec., 1863	From 2-Brig. 1-Cav. Div. Ark. Exp.	To 3-Brig. 1-Cav. Div. 7-Corps Ark.	Jan.,	1864
3d Mo. Cav.	Dec., 1863	From 2-Brig. 1-Cav. Div. Ark. Exp.	To 3-Brig. 1-Cav. Div. 7-Corps Ark.	Jan.,	1864

RESERVE BRIGADE.—   COMMANDER.

John F. Ritter	Col. 1st Mo. Cav.	Aug. 6, 1863, to Jan 6, 1864.

13th Ill. Cav.	Aug., 1863	From Res. Br. 1-C. D. Dist. St. Louis.	To Unatt. 1-Cav. Div. Ark. Exp.	Dec.,	1863
3d Iowa Cav.	Aug., 1863	From Res. Br. 1-C. D. Dist. St. Louis.	To 1-Brig. 1-Cav. Div. Ark. Exp.	Dec.,	1863
(Co.'s E, F, G, H, L, M.)					
32d Iowa Inf. Mtd.	Aug., 1863	From Res. Br. 1-C. D. Dist. St. Louis.	To 1-Brig. 1-Cav. Div. Ark. Exp.	Dec.,	1863
1st Mo. Cav.	Aug., 1863	From 1-Br. Cav. Dist. St. Louis.	To 1-Brig. 1-Cav. Div. Ark. Exp.	Dec.,	1863
UNATTACHED.—					
24th Mo. Infy., F, K.	Dec., 1863	From Res. Br. 1-Cav. Div. Ark. Exp.	To Unatt. 1-Cav. Div. 7-Corps Ark.	Jan.,	1864
13th Ill. Cav.	Dec., 1863	From Res. Br. 1-Cav. Div. Ark. Exp.	To 1-Brig. 1-Cav. Div. 7th Corps Ark.	Jan.,	1864
ARTILLERY.—					
Batty. K, 2d Mo. Arty.	Aug., 1863	From Res. Br. 1-Cav. Div. Dist. St. L.	Transferred to Batty. D, 2d Mo.	Sept.,	1863
Batty. M, 2d Mo. Arty.	Aug., 1863	From 1-Br. 1-Cav. Div. Dist. St. L.	Transferred to Batty. E, 2d Mo.	Sept.,	1863
25th Ohio Batty.	Aug., 1863	From 2-Br. 1-Cav. Div. Dist. St. L.	To Columbus, Ohio.	Jan.,	1864
Batty. D, 2d Mo. Arty.	Sept., 1863	From Consol. Mo. Battys.	To Arty. 1-Cav. Div. 7-Corps Ark.	Jan.,	1864
Batty. E, 2d Mo. Arty.	Sept., 1863	From Consol. Mo. Battys.	To Arty. 1-Cav. Div. 7-Corps Ark.	Jan.,	1864

2d DIVISION.—   COMMANDERS.

Wm. E. McLean	Col. 43d Ind. Infy.	Aug. 4, 1863, to Sept. 6, 1863.
A. Engleman	Brigadier General	Sept. 6, 1863, to Sept. 13, 1863.
Nathan Kimball	Brigadier General	Sept. 13, 1863, to Nov. 30, 1863.
E. A. Carr	Brigadier General	Nov. 30, 1863, to Jan. 6, 1864.

1st BRIGAGDE.—Discontinued Nov., 1863.   COMMANDER.

W. H. Graves	Col. 12th Mich. Infy.	Aug., 1863, to Nov., 1863.

18th Ill. Infy.	Aug., 1863	From 2-Brig. Kimball's Div. E. Ark.	To 3-Brig. 2-Div. Ark. Exp.	Nov.,	1863
43d Ill. Infy.	Aug., 1863	From 1-Brig. Kimball's Div. E. Ark.	To 2-Brig. 2-Div. Ark. Exp.	Nov.,	1863
54th Ill. Infy.	Aug., 1863	From 2-Brig. Kimball's Div. E. Ark.	To 3-Brig. 2-Div. Ark. Exp.	Nov.,	1863
61st Ill. Infy.	Aug., 1863	From 1-Brig. Kimball's Div. E. Ark.	To 3-Brig. 2-Div. Ark. Exp.	Nov.,	1863
106th Ill. Infy.	Aug., 1863	From 1-Brig. Kimball's Div. E. Ark.	To 3-Brig. 2-Div. Ark. Exp.	Nov.,	1863
12th Mich. Infy.	Aug., 1863	From 1-Brig. Kimball's Div. E. Ark.	To 3-Brig. 2-Div. Ark. Exp.	Nov.,	1863

2d BRIGADE.—   COMMANDERS.

Oliver Wood	Col. 22d Ohio Infy.	Aug. 6, 1863, to Sept. 13, 1863.
A. Engleman	Brigadier General	Sept. 13, 1863, to Jan. 6, 1864.

126th Ill. Infy.	Aug., 1863	From 2-Brig. Kimball's Div. E. Ark.	To 2-Brig. 2-Div. 7-Corps Ark.	Jan.,	1864
22d Ohio Infy.	Aug., 1863	From 2-Brig. Kimball's Div. E. Ark.	To 2-Brig. 2-Div. 7-Corps Ark.	Jan.,	1864
40th Iowa Infy.	Aug., 1863	From 3-Brig. Kimball's Div. E. Ark.	To 2-Brig. 2-Div. 7-Corps Ark.	Jan.,	1864
27th Wis. Infy.	Aug., 1863	From 3-Brig. Kimball's Div. E. Ark.	To 2-Brig. 2-Div. 7-Corps Ark.	Jan.,	1864
3d Minn. Infy.	Aug., 1863	From 3-Brig. Kimball's Div. E. Ark.	To 3-Brig. 2-Div. 7-Corps Ark.	Nov.,	1863
11th Ohio Batty.	Aug., 1863	From Kimball's Div. Eastern Ark.	To 2-Brig. 2-Div. 7-Corps Ark.	Jan.,	1864
43d Ill. Infy.	Nov., 1863	From 1-Brig. 2-Div. Ark. Exp.	To 2-Br. 2-Div. 7-Corps Ark.	Jan.,	1864

3d BRIGADE.—Organized Nov., 1863. COMMANDER.

Wm. H. Graves........	Col. 12th Mich. Infy................	Nov., 1863, to Jan. 6, 1864.

18th Ill. Infy..........Nov., 1863	From 1-Brig. 2-Div. Ark. Exp......	To 3-Brig. 2-Div. 7-Corps Ark.....	Jan., 1864
54th Ill. Infy..........Nov., 1863	From 1-Brig. 2-Div. Ark. Exp......	To 3-Brig. 2-Div. 7-Corps Ark.....	Jan., 1864
61st Ill. Infy..........Nov., 1863	From 1-Brig. 2-Div. Ark. Exp......	To 3-Brig. 2-Div. 7-Corps Ark.....	Jan., 1864
106th Ill. Infy..........Nov., 1863	From 1-Brig. 2-Div. Ark. Exp......	To 3-Brig. 2-Div. 7-Corps Ark.....	Jan., 1864
12th Mich. Infy..........Nov., 1863	From 1-Brig. 2-Div. Ark. Exp......	To 3-Brig. 2-Div. 7-Corps Ark.....	Jan., 1864
3d Minn. Infy..........Nov., 1863	From 2-Brig. 2-Div. Ark. Exp......	To 3-Brig. 2-Div. 7-Corps Ark.....	Jan., 1864
5th Ohio Batty..........Nov., 1863	From Arty. 3-Div. Ark. Exp......	To 3-Brig. 2-Div. 7-Corps Ark.....	Jan., 1864

3d DIVISION.— COMMANDERS.

Nathan Kimball........	Brigadier General................	Aug. 4, 1863, to Sept. 13, 1863.
S. A. Rice............	Brigadier General................	Sept. 13, 1863, to Oct. 8, 1863.
Frederick Salomon......	Brigadier General................	Oct. 8, 1863, to Jan. 6, 1864.

1st BRIGADE.— COMMANDERS.

C. W. Kittredge........	Col. 36th Iowa Infy................	Aug. 4, 1863, to Sept. 7, 1863.
W. E. McLean..........	Col. 43d Ind. Infy................	Sept. 7, 1863, to Jan. 6, 1864.

43d Ind. Infy..........Aug., 1863	From 1-Brig. 13-Div. 16-C. E. Ark.	To 1-Brig. 3-Div. 7-Corps Ark.....	Jan., 1864
36th Iowa Infy..........Aug., 1863	From 1-Brig. 13-Div. 16-C. E. Ark.	To 1-Brig. 3-Div. 7-Corps Ark.....	Jan., 1864
77th Ohio Infy..........Aug., 1863	From Alton, Ill................	To 1-Brig. 3-Div. 7-Corps Ark.....	Jan., 1864

2d BRIGADE.— COMMANDERS.

T. H. Benton..........	Col. 29th Iowa Infy................	Aug. 4, 1863, to Oct. 8, 1863.
S. A. Rice............	Brigadier General................	Oct. 8, 1863, to Nov. 12, 1863.
Jas. M. Lewis..........	Col. 28th Wis. Infy................	Nov. 12, 1863, to Jan. 6, 1864.

29th Iowa Infy..........Aug., 1863	From 2-Brig. 13-Div. 16-C. E. Ark.	To 2-Brig. 3-Div. 7-Corps Ark.....	Jan., 1864
33d Iowa Infy..........Aug., 1863	From 2-Brig. 13-Div. 16-C. E. Ark.	To 2-Brig. 3-Div. 7-Corps Ark.....	Jan., 1864
28th Wis. Infy..........Aug., 1863	From 1-Brig. 13-Div. 16-C. E. Ark.	To 2-Brig. 3-Div. 7-Corps Ark.....	Jan., 1864
9th Wis. Infy..........Aug., 1863	From Dist. St. Louis Dept. Mo......	To 2-Brig. 3-Div. 7-Corps Ark.....	Jan., 1864

ARTILLERY.—

Batty. K, 1st Mo......Aug., 1863	From Arty. 13-Div. 16-C. E. Ark....	To Arty. 1-Div. 7-Corps Ark.....	Jan., 1864
3d Iowa Batty..........Aug., 1863	From Arty. 13-Div. 16-C. E. Ark....	To Arty. 1-Div. 7-Corps Ark.....	Jan., 1864
5th Ohio Batty..........Aug., 1863	From Arty. 13-Div. 16-C. E. Ark....	To 3-Brig. 2-Div. Ark. Exp........	Nov., 1863

CLAYTON'S INDPT. CAVALRY BRIGADE.— COMMANDER.

Powell Clayton........	Col. 5th Kan. Cav................	Aug. 4, 1863, to Jan. 6, 1864.

1st Ind. Cav..........Aug., 1863	From Cav. Brig. Dist. E. Ark......	To Pine Bluff, Ark. 7-Corps Ark....	Jan., 1864
5th Kan. Cav..........Aug., 1863	From Cav. Brig. Dist. E. Ark......	To Pine Bluff, Ark., 7-Corps Ark....	Jan., 1864

TRUE'S BRIGADE.— COMMANDER.

J. M. True............	Col. 62d Ill. Infy................	

49th Ill. Infy..........Aug., 1863	From 3-Brig. 3-Div. 16-Corps......	To Gilbert's Brig. Dist. Memphis...	Nov., 1863
62d Ill. Infy..........Aug., 1863	From 3-Brig. 3-Div. 16-Corps......	To Unatt. 2-Div. 7-Corps Ark......	Jan., 1864
50th Ind. Infy..........Aug., 1863	From 3-Brig. 3-Div. 16-Corps......	To Unatt. 2-Div. 7-Corps Ark......	Jan., 1864
27th Iowa Infy..........Aug., 1863	From 3-Brig. 3-Div. 16-Corps......	To Gilbert's Brig. Dist. Memphis...	Nov., 1863
Springfield, Ill. Batty.....Aug., 1863	From 3-Brig. 3-Div. 16-Corps......	To Unatt. 2-Div. 7-Corps Ark......	Jan., 1864

LITTLE ROCK, ARK.—ARKANSAS EXPEDITION.—

2d Ark. Infy (A, D).....Dec., 1863	From New Organization..........	To Dist. Eastern Ark. 7-Corps Ark.	Jan., 1864
3d Ark. Cav..........Dec., 1863	From New Organization..........	To Dist. N. E. Ark., 7-Corps......	Jan., 1864
4th Ark. Cav..........Dec., 1863	From New Organization..........	To Dist. N. E. Ark., 7-Corps......	Jan., 1864

DISTRICT OF CAIRO.—Organized Jan., 1864. Transferred to Dist. of West Tenn., June, 1864.

COMMANDERS.

H. T. Reed............	Brigadier General................	Jan. 25, 1864, to Mch. 19, 1864.
M. Brayman............	Brigadier General................	Mch. 19, 1864, to Apr. 24, 1864.
H. Prince............	Brigadier General................	Apr. 24, 1864, to June, 1864.

DETACHED BRIGADE, 17th CORPS.—

81st Ill. Infy..........June, 1864	From 2-Brig. Sturgis' Expedition..	To 4-Brig. 1-Div. 16-Corps........	June, 1864
95th Ill. Infy..........June, 1864	From 2-Brig. Sturgis' Expedition..	To 4-Brig. 1-Div. 16-Corps........	June, 1864
14th Wis. Infy..........June, 1864	From 2-Brig. Prov. Div. 17-C. Gulf.	To 4-Brig. 1-Div. 16-Corps........	June, 1864
33d Wis. Infy..........June, 1864	From 2-Brig. Prov. Div. 17-C. Gulf.	To 4-Brig. 1-Div. 16-Corps........	June, 1864

Sturgis' Expedition

COMMANDER.

S. D. Sturgis..........	Brigadier General................	

1st BRIGADE.—

9th Minn. Infy..........June, 1864	From Dept. of Mo................	To 2-Brig. 1-Div. 16-Corps........	June, 1864
72d Ohio Infy..........June, 1864	From 1-Brig. 1-Div. 16-Corps......	To 1-Brig. 1-Div. 16-Corps........	June, 1864
95th Ohio Infy..........June, 1864	From 1-Brig. 1-Div. 16-Corps......	To 1-Brig. 1-Div. 16-Corps........	June, 1864
114th Ill. Infy..........June, 1864	From 1-Brig. 1-Div. 16-Corps......	To 1-Brig. 1-Div. 16-Corps........	June, 1864
93d Ind. Infy..........June, 1864	From 1-Brig. 1-Div. 16-Corps......	To 1-Brig. 1-Div. 16-Corps........	June, 1864
Batty E, 1st Ill. Arty....June, 1864	From Arty. 1-Div. 16-Corps........	To 1-Brig. 1-Div. 16-Corps........	June, 1864
6th Ind. Batty..........June, 1864	From Arty. 1-Div. 16-Corps........	To 1-B. Memphis Dist. West Tenn.	June, 1864

2d BRIGADE.—

81st Ill. Infy..........June, 1864	From 1-Brig. Prov. Div. 17-C. Gulf.	To 4-Brig. 1-Div. 16-Corps........	June, 1864
95th Ill. Infy..........June, 1864	From 1-Brig. Prov. Div. 17-C. Gulf.	To 4-Brig. 1-Div. 16-Corps........	June, 1864
108th Ill. Infy..........June, 1864	From 2-Brig. Dist. Memphis 16-C..	To 1-B. Memphis Dist. West Tenn.	June, 1864
113th Ill. Infy..........June, 1864	From 2-Brig. Dist. Memphis 16-C..	To 1-B. Memphis Dist. West Tenn.	June, 1864
120th Ill. Infy..........June, 1864	From 2-Brig. Dist. Memphis 16-C..	To 1-B. Memphis Dist. West Tenn.	June, 1864
Batty. B, 2d Ill. Arty....June, 1864	From Ft. Pickering Memphis 16-C.	To Ft. Pick'ng Mem. Dist. W. Tenn.	June, 1864

3d BRIGADE.—

55th U. S. C. T........June, 1864	From Ft. Pickering Memphis 16-C.	To 1-Col'd Brig. Dist. West Tenn..	June, 1864
59th U. S. C. T........June, 1864	From 1-Col'd Brig. Dist. Memphis..	To 1-Col'd Brig. Dist. West Tenn..	June, 1864
Batty. F, 2d U. S. C. Arty.June, 1864	From 1-Col'd Brig. Dist. Memphis..	To 1-Col'd Brig. Dist. West Tenn..	June, 1864

CAVALRY DIVISION, 1st BRIGADE.—

4th Mo. Cav............June, 1864	From 1-Brig. 1-Cav. Div. 16-Corps.	To 1-B. 2-Cav. Div. Dist. W. Tenn.	June, 1864
7th Ind. Cav...........June, 1864	From 1-Brig. 1-Cav. Div. 16-Corps.	To 1-B. 2-Cav. Div. Dist. W. Tenn.	June, 1864
2d N. J. Cav...........June, 1864	From 1-Brig. 1-Cav. Div. 16-Corps.	To 1-B. 2-Cav. Div. Dist. W. Tenn.	June, 1864
19th Penna. Cav........June, 1864	From 1-Brig. 1-Cav. Div. 16-Corps.	To 1-B. 2-Cav. Div. Dist. W. Tenn.	June, 1864
3d Ill. Cav...........June, 1864	From 3-Brig. 1-Cav. Div. 16-Corps.	To 1-B. 1-Cav. Div. Dist. W. Tenn.	June, 1864
9th Ill. Cav...........June, 1864	From 3-Brig. 1-Cav. Div. 16-Corps.	To 2-B. 1-Cav. Div. Dist. W. Tenn.	June, 1864

2d BRIGADE.—

3d Iowa Cav...........June, 1864	From 2-Brig. 1-Cav. Div. 16-Corps.	To 2-Br. 2-Cav. Div. Dist. W. Tenn.	June, 1864
4th Iowa Cav..........June, 1864	From 2-Brig. 1-Cav. Div. 16-Corps.	To 2-Br. 2-Cav. Div. Dist. W. Tenn.	June, 1864
10th Missouri Cav......June, 1864	From 2-Brig. 1-Cav. Div. 16-Corps.	To 2-Br. 2-Cav. Div. Dist. W. Tenn.	June, 1864
7th Wisconsin Batty....June, 1864	From 2-Brig. 1-Cav. Div. 16-Corps.	To 2-Brig. Memphis Dist. W. Tenn.	June, 1864

Right Wing, Sixteenth Army Corps

COMMANDER.

A. J. Smith...........	Major General...................	Mch. 7, 1864, to Dec. 5, 1864.	

DISTRICT OF WEST TENNESSEE. —   **COMMANDERS.**

C. C. Washburn.......	Major General..................	Apr. 17, 1864, to Feb. 3, 1865.	
B. S. Roberts.........	Brigadier General.............	Feb. 3, 1865, to Mch. 4, 1865.	
C. C. Washburn.......	Major General..................	Mch. 4, 1865, to May 29, 1865.	

DISTRICT OF MEMPHIS.—   **COMMANDERS.**

R. P. Buckland........	Brigadier General..............	June, 1864, to Jan., 1865.	
A. L. Chetlain........	Brigadier General.............	Jan. 26, 1865.	

1st BRIGADE.—   **COMMANDER.**

Geo. B. Hoge.........	Col. 113th Illinois Infy.		
108th Illinois Infy.....June, 1864	From 2-Brig. Sturgis' Exp........	To 3-Brig. 3-Div. 16-Corps Gulf..	Feb., 1865
113th Illinois Infy.....June, 1864	From 2-Brig. Sturgis' Exp........	To Unass'd Memphis Dist. W. Tenn.	Feb., 1865
120th Illinois Infy.....June, 1864	From 2-Brig. Sturgis' Exp........	To Unass'd Memphis Dist. W. Tenn.	Feb., 1865
7th Missouri Infy. Vet.June, 1864	From Post Vicksburg, Miss.......	Consolidated with 11th Mo. Infy..	July, 1864
Batty. G, 1st Ill. Arty.June, 1864	From Fort Pickering, Memphis...	To Arty. Reserve Dist. W. Tenn...	Dec., 1864
6th Indiana Batty......June, 1864	From 1-Brig. Sturgis' Exp........	To Arty. Reserve Dist. W. Tenn...	Dec., 1864
Batty. G, 2d Mo. Arty...Aug., 1864	From Dept. of Missouri..........	To Arty. Reserve Dist. W. Tenn...	Dec., 1864

2d BRIGADE.—   **COMMANDER.**

E. L. Buttrick.........	Col. 39th Wisconsin Infy.		
46th Iowa Infy........June, 1864	From New Organization..........	No change to Muster Out.........	Sept., 1864
39th Wisconsin Infy....June, 1864	From New Organization..........	No change to Muster Out.........	Sept., 1864
41st Wisconsin Infy....June, 1864	From New Organization..........	No change to Muster Out.........	Sept., 1864
7th Wisconsin Batty....June, 1864	From 2-Br. Cav. Div. Sturgis' Exp.	To Unatt. Memphis Dist. W. Tenn.	Sept., 1864

3d BRIGADE.—   **COMMANDER.**

John Wood............	Col. 137th Illinois Infy.		
137th Illinois Infy......June, 1864	From New Organization..........	No change to Muster Out.........	Sept., 1864
140th Illinois Infy......June, 1864	From New Organization..........	No change to Muster Out.........	Sept., 1864
142d Illinois Infy......June, 1864	From New Organization..........	No change to Muster Out.........	Sept., 1864
143d Illinois Infy......June, 1864	From New Organization..........	No change to Muster Out.........	Sept., 1864

1st BRIGADE, U. S. C. T.—   **COMMANDER.**

Edward Bouton.......	Col. 59th U. S. C. T.		
55th U. S. C. T.........June, 1864	From 3-Brig. Sturgis' Exp........	To 2-Brig. U. S. C. T. Morganza, La.	Feb., 1865
59th U. S. C. T.........June, 1864	From 3-Brig. Sturgis' Exp........	To Ft. Pickering Memphis W. Tenn.	Feb., 1865
61st U. S. C. T.........June, 1864	From Dist. Memphis 16-Corps.....	To 1-Brig. U. S. C. T. Morganza, La.	Feb., 1865
68th U. S. C. T.........June, 1864	From Dept. Missouri.............	To Ft. Pickering Memphis W. Tenn.	Dec., 1864
Batty. F, 2d U. S. C. A.June, 1864	From 3-Brig. Sturgis' Exp........	To Arty. Reserve Dist. W. Tenn..	Dec., 1864
Batty. I, 2d U. S. C. A.June, 1864	From Dist. Memphis..............	To Arty. Reserve Dist. W. Tenn..	Dec., 1864

FORT PICKERING, MEMPHIS, TENN.—

3d U. S. C. H'vy Arty...June, 1864	From Dist. Memphis..............	To Dist. West Tenn. Dept. Tenn..	June, 1865
7th U. S. C. H'vy Arty..June, 1864	From Dist. Memphis..............	To Dist. West Tenn. Dept. Tenn..	June, 1865
68th U. S. C. T.........Dec., 1864	From 1st Col'd Brig. Dist. W. Tenn.	To 3-Brig. 1-Div. U. S. C. T. Gulf..	Feb., 1865
11th U. S. C. T. (New)..Feb., 1865	From 7th U. S. C. Heavy Arty.....	To Dist. West Tenn. Dept. Tenn..	June, 1865
59th U. S. C. T.........Feb., 1865	From 1st Colored Brig. Memphis...	To Dist. West Tenn. Dept. Tenn..	June, 1865
88th U. S. C. T. (New)..Feb., 1865	From New Organization...........	To Dist. West Tenn. Dept. Tenn..	June, 1865

UNATTACHED.—

8th Iowa Infy.........June, 1864	From 3-Brig. 1-Div. 16-Corps......	To 3-Brig. 3-Div. 16-Corps........	Feb., 1865
6th Tennessee Cav.....June, 1864	From 1-Brig. 1-Cav. Div. 16-Corps	To 2-B. 4-D. Cav. C. Mil. D. Miss.	Nov., 1864
14th Indiana Batty......June, 1864	From Arty. 3-Div. 16-Corps.......	To Arty. 3-Div. Det. Army Tenn..	Dec., 1864
7th Wisconsin Batty....Sept., 1864	From 2-B. Memphis Dist. W. Tenn.	To Arty. Reserve Dist. W. Tenn..	Dec., 1864
113th Illinois Infy......Feb., 1865	From 1-B. Memphis Dist. W. Tenn.	No change to Muster Out.........	June, 1865
120th Illinois Infy......Feb., 1865	From 1-B. Memphis Dist. W. Tenn.	No change to Muster Out.........	Sept., 1865
69th U. S. C. T.........Feb., 1865	From New Organization..........	Discontinued	July, 1865

Cavalry Corps, District West Tennessee

COMMANDER.

B. H. Grierson........	Brigadier General.		

1st DIVISION.—   **COMMANDER.**

Edward Hatch.........	Brigadier General.		

1st BRIGADE.—   **COMMANDERS.**

T. P. Herrick.........	Col. 7th Kansas Cav...........	To Oct., 1864.	
Oliver Wells...........	Col. 12th Missouri Cav...........	To Nov., 1864.	
3d Illinois Cav........June, 1864	From 1-Brig. 1-Cav. Div. 16-Corps.	To 1-B. 5-D. Cav. C. Mil. D. Miss.	Nov., 1864
7th Illinois Cav........June, 1864	From 1-Brig. 1-Cav. Div. 16-Corps.	To 1-B. 5-D. Cav. C. Mil. D. Miss.	Nov., 1864
7th Kansas Cav........June, 1864	From Veteran Furlough..........	To Dist. St. Louis, Dept. Mo.....	Aug., 1864
12th Missouri Cav......June, 1864	From Dist. St. Louis, Dept. Mo....	To 1-B. 5-D. Cav. C. Mil. D. Miss.	Nov., 1864

2d BRIGADE.— COMMANDER.

D. E. Coon............Col. 2d Iowa Cav.

6th Illinois Cav........June, 1864	From 2-Brig. 1-Cav. Div. 16-Corps.	To 2-B. 5-D. Cav. C. Mil. D. Miss.	Nov.,	1864
9th Illinois Cav........June, 1864	From 2-Brig. 1-Cav. Div. 16-Corps.	To 2-B. 5-D. Cav. C. Mil. D. Miss.	Nov.,	1864
2d Iowa Cav............June, 1864	From 2-Brig. 1-Cav. Div. 16-Corps.	To 2-B. 5-D. Cav. C. Mil. D. Miss.	Nov.,	1864

2d DIVISION.— COMMANDERS.

E. F. Winslow........	Col. 4th Iowa Cav................	To Oct., 1864.	
F. W. Benteen.........	Lt.-Col. 10th Mo. Cav.............	To Nov., 1864.	

1st BRIGADE.— COMMANDER.

Jos. Karge............Col. 2d N. J. Cav.

7th Indiana Cav.......June, 1864	From 1-Brig. 1-Div. Cav. 16-Corps.	To 2-B. 4-D. Cav. C. Mil. D. Miss.	Nov.,	1864
1st Miss. Mtd. Rifles....June, 1864	From New Organization...........	To 2-B. 4-D. Cav. C. Mil. D. Miss.	Nov.,	1864
4th Missouri Cav......June, 1864	From 1-Brig. 1-Cav. Div. 16-Corps.	To 2-B. 4-D. Cav. C. Mil. D. Miss.	Nov.,	1864
2d New Jersey Cav.....June, 1864	From 1-Brig. 1-Cav. Div. 16-Corps.	To 2-B. 4-D. Cav. C. Mil. D. Miss.	Nov.,	1864
19th Penna. Cav.......June, 1864	From 1-Brig. 1-Cav. Div. 16-Corps.	To 2-B. 4-D. Cav. C. Mil. D. Miss.	Nov.,	1864

2d BRIGADE.— COMMANDER.

J. W. Noble............Col. 3d Iowa Cav.

3d Iowa Cav...........June, 1864	From 2-Brig. 1-Cav. Div. 16-Corps.	To 1-B. 4-D. Cav. C. Mil. D. Miss.	Nov.,	1864
4th Iowa Cav..........June, 1864	From 2-Brig. 1-Cav. Div. 16-Corps.	To 1-B. 4-D. Cav. C. Mil. D. Miss.	Nov.,	1864
10th Missouri Cav......June, 1864	From 2-Brig. 1-Cav. Div. 16-Corps.	To 1-B. 4-D. Cav. C. Mil. D. Miss.	Nov.,	1864

CAVALRY DIVISION.— West Tennessee. COMMANDERS.

B. H. Grierson.........	Brigadier General..................	Dec., 1864, to Mch., 1865.
S. O. Shorey.........	Lt.-Colonel	Temporarily in Feb., 1865.
E. D. Osband.........	Col. 3d U. S. Colored Cav.........	Mch., 1865, to May, 1865.
B. S. Roberts.........	Brigadier General.................	May 15, 1865, to July 14, 1865.
J. E. Phelps.........	Bvt. Brigadier General............	July 14, 1865.

1st BRIGADE.— COMMANDERS.

J. P. C. Shanks.........	Col. 7th Indiana Cav.............	Dec., 1864, to Feb., 1865.
S. O. Shorey.........	Lt.-Colonel	Feb., 1865, to Apr., 1865.
J. E. Phelps.........	Col. 2d Arkansas Cav.............	Apr., 1865, to June, 1865.
Otto Funke............	Col. 11th Illinois Cav............	June, 1865, to Sept., 1865.

7th Indiana Cav.........Dec., 1864	From 2-B. 4-D. Cav. C. Mil. D. Miss.	To Dept. of Texas................	June,	1865
1st Miss. Mtd. Rifles.....Dec., 1864	From 1-Brig. 2-Cav. Div. W. Tenn.	No change to Muster Out.........	June,	1865
4th Missouri Cav......Dec., 1864	From 1-Brig. 1-Cav. Div. 16-Corps.	To 2-Brig. 2-Cav. Div. Gulf......	May,	1865
2d New Jersey Cav.....Dec., 1864	From 2-B. 4-D. Cav. C. Mil. D. Miss.	To 1-Brig. 1-Cav. Div. West Miss.	Mch.,	1865
2d Arkansas Cav........Feb., 1865	From Unatt. Cav. Div. W. Tenn.	No change to Muster Out.........	June,	1865
5th Illinois Cav........Feb., 1865	From C. Br. Dist. Vicksburg, Miss.	To Dept. of Texas................	June,	1865
4th Illinois Cav........June, 1865	From 3-B. Cav. D. Dist. W. Tenn.	Consolidated with 12th Illinois..	June,	1865
11th Illinois Cav........June, 1865	From 3-B. Cav. D. Dist. W. Tenn.	No change to Muster Out.........	Sept.,	1865
3d U. S. Colored Cav.....June, 1865	From Unatt. Cav. D. Dist. W. Tenn.	To Dist. West Tenn.............	Sept.,	1865
11th New York Cav.....June, 1865	From 2-B. Cav. D. Dist. W. Tenn.	No change to Muster Out.........	Sept.,	1865

2d BRIGADE.— COMMANDERS.

E. F. Winslow.........	Col. 4th Iowa Cav...............	Dec., 1864, to Feb., 1865.
H. Davis............	Col. 12th Illinois Cav...........	Feb., 1865, to Apr., 1865.
Wm. Thompson.........	Col. 1st Iowa Cav...............	Apr., 1865, to June, 1865.
J. E. Phelps.........	Col. 2d Arkansas Cav...........	June 17, 1865, to July 14, 1865.

3d Iowa Cav..........Dec., 1864	From 1-B. 4-D. Cav. C. Mil. D. Miss.	To 1-Brig. 4-Div. Cav. Corps M. D. M.	Feb.,	1865
4th Iowa Cav..........Dec., 1864	From 1-B. 4-D. Cav. C. Mil. D. Miss.	To 1-Brig. 4-Div. Cav. Corps M. D. M.	Feb.,	1865
10th Missouri Cav......Dec., 1864	From 1-B. 4-D. Cav. C. Mil. D. Miss.	To 1-Brig. 4-Div. Cav. Corps M. D. M.	Feb.,	1865
12th Illinois Cav.......Feb., 1865	From 3-Brig. Cav. Div. Gulf......	To Dept. of Texas................	July,	1865
1st Iowa Cav..........Feb., 1865	From 1-Brig. Cav. Div. 7-C. Ark.	To Dept. of Texas................	July,	1865
2d Missouri Cav.......Feb., 1865	From 3-Brig. Cav. Div. 7-C. Ark.	No change to Muster Out.........	June,	1865
11th New York Cav......Feb., 1865	From 2-Brig. Cav. Div. Gulf......	To 1-Brig. Cav. Div. Dist. W. Tenn.	June,	1865

3d BRIGADE.— COMMANDERS.

Otto Funke............	Lt.-Col. 11th Illinois Cav..........	Dec., 1864, to Feb., 1865.
E. D. Osband..........	Col. 3d U. S. C. Cav.............	Feb., 1865, to Mch., 1865.
Otto Funke............	Lt.-Col. 11th Illinois Cav..........	Mch., 1865, to June, 1865.

4th Illinois Cav........Dec., 1864	From Dist. S. W. Mo. Dept. Mo...	To 1-Brig. Cav. Div. Dist. W. Tenn.	June,	1865
11th Illinois Cav........Dec., 1864	From C. Br. Dist. Vicksburg, Miss.	To 1-Brig. Cav. Div. Dist. W. Tenn.	June,	1865
3d U. S. C. Cav........Dec., 1864	From C. Br. Dist. Vicksburg, Miss.	To Unatt. Cav. Div. Dist. W. Tenn.	June,	1865
2d Wisconsin Cav.......Dec., 1864	From C. Br. Dist. Vicksburg, Miss.	To Dept. of Texas................	June,	1865
UNASSIGNED.—				
2d Arkansas Cav........Dec., 1864	From Dist. S. W. Mo. Dept. Mo...	To 1-Brig. Cav. Div. Dist. W. Tenn.	Feb.,	1865
Batty. K, 2d Ill. Arty....Dec., 1864	From P. Natchez, D. V'ksb'g, Miss.	To Unatt. Arty. Dist. West Tenn..	Feb.,	1865
3d U. S. C. Cav........June, 1865	From 3-B. Cav. Div. Dist. W. Tenn.	To 1-Brig. Cav. Div. Dist. W. Tenn.	June,	1865
ARTILLERY RESERVE.—				
Batty. G, 1st Ill. Arty....Dec., 1864	From 1-Brig. Dist. Memphis.......	No change to Muster Out.........	July,	1865
6th Indiana Batty......Dec., 1864	From 1-Brig. Dist. Memphis.......	No change to Muster Out.........	July,	1865
Batty. M, 1st Mo. Arty...Dec., 1864	From 4-Brig. 1-Div. 16-Corps......	No change to Muster Out.........	July,	1865
Batty. G. 1st Mo. Arty...Dec., 1864	From 1-Brig. Dist. Memphis.......	No change to Muster Out.........	Aug.,	1865
By. F, 2d U. S. C. Arty...Dec., 1864	From 1-Colored Brig. Memphis....	To Bridgeport, Ala..............	Apr.,	1865
By. I, 2d U. S. C. Arty...Dec., 1864	From 1-Colored Brig. Memphis....	To Dept. Tenn.................	July,	1865
7th Wisconsin Batty....Dec., 1864	From Unatt. Arty. Memphis.......	No change to Muster Out.........	July,	1865
Batty. K, 2d Ill. Arty....Feb., 1865	From Cav. Div. Dist. West Tenn..	No change to Muster Out.........	July,	1865

1st INFANTRY BRIGADE.— COMMANDER.

Geo. W. McKeag.......Col. 120th Illinois Infy.

120th Illinois Infy......July, 1865	From Unatt. Dist. West Tenn.....	No change to Muster Out.........	Sept.,	1865
152d Illinois Infy......July, 1865	From Unatt. Dist. West Tenn.....	No change to Muster Out.........	Sept.,	1865
153d Illinois Infy......July, 1865	From Unatt. Dist. West Tenn.....	No change to Muster Out.........	Sept.,	1865

2d INFANTRY BRIGADE.— COMMANDER.

I. G. Kappner.........Col. 3d U. S. C. Heavy Arty.

3d U. S. C. Heavy Arty..July, 1865	From Fort Pickering, Memphis....	To Dist. West Tenn.............	Sept.,	1865
11th U. S. C. T........July, 1865	From Fort Pickering, Memphis....	To Dist. West Tenn.............	Sept.,	1865
59th U. S. C. T........July, 1865	From Fort Pickering, Memphis....	To Dist. West Tenn.............	Sept.,	1865
88th U. S. C. T........July, 1865	From Fort Pickering, Memphis....	To Dist. West Tenn.............	Sept.,	1865
By. F, 2d U. S. C. Arty..July, 1865	From Arty. Reserve Dist. W. Tenn.	To Dist. West Tenn.............	Sept.,	1865
By. I. 2d U. S. C. Arty..July, 1865	From Arty. Reserve Dist. W. Tenn.	To Dist. West Tenn.............	Sept.,	1865

Seventeenth Army Corps

Created Dec. 18, 1862, by General Order No. 210, A. G. O., from 1st, 3d and 4th Divisions, Department of the Tennessee, 1st Cavalry Brigade, Dept. Tenn., and District of Corinth, Dept. Tenn. 1st and 4th Divisions exchanged for 6th and 7th Divisions, 16th Army Corps, Jan. 20, 1863, and District of Corinth transferred to 16th Army Corps Jan. 20, 1863. Corps discontinued Aug. 1, 1865.

COMMANDERS.

J. B. McPherson	Major General	Dec. 18, 1862, to Apr. 23, 1864.
F. P. Blair, Jr.	Major General	Apr. 23, 1864, to Sept. 22, 1864.
T. E. G. Ransom	Brigadier General	Sept. 22, 1864, to Oct. 10, 1864.
M. D. Leggett	Brigadier General	Oct. 10, 1864, to Oct. 24, 1864.
J. A. Mower	Major General	Oct. 24, 1864, to Oct. 31, 1864.
F. P. Blair, Jr.	Major General	Oct. 31, 1864, to July 19, 1865.
M. D. Leggett	Bvt. Major General	May 8, 1865. Temporarily.
W. W. Belknap	Brigadier General	July 19, 1865, to Aug. 1, 1865.

1st DIVISION.—   COMMANDERS.

J. W. Denver	Brigadier General	Dec. 18, 1862, to Jan. 19, 1863.
J. A. McDowell	Col. 6th Iowa Infy.	Jan. 19, 1863, to Jan. 20, 1863.

Division transferred to 16th Army Corps Jan. 20, 1863. Reorganized Sept. 14, 1863, from 6-Div. 17-Corps. Discontinued Sept. 22, 1864. Reorganized Sept. 22, 1864, from 4-Div. 16-Corps.

COMMANDERS.

A. Chambers	Brigadier General	Sept. 14, 1863, to Sept. 28, 1863.
John McArthur	Brigadier General	Sept. 28, 1863, to Oct. 23, 1863.
E. S. Dennis	Brigadier General	Oct. 23, 1863, to Sept. 22, 1864.
T. E. G. Ransom	Brigadier General	Sept. 22, 1864.
J. W. Fuller	Brigadier General	Sept. 22, 1864, to Oct. 23, 1864.
J. W. Sprague	Brigadier General	Oct. 23, 1864, to Oct. 31, 1864.
J. A. Mower	Major General	Oct. 31, 1864, to Apr. 5, 1865.
M. F. Force	Brigadier General	Apr. 5, 1865, to Aug. 1, 1865.

1st BRIGADE.—   COMMANDERS.

J. A. McDowell	Col. 6th Iowa Infy.	Dec. 18, 1862, to Jan. 19, 1863.
C. C. Walcutt	Col. 46th Ohio Infy.	Jan. 19, 1863, to Jan. 20, 1863.

Brigade reorganized Oct. 28, 1863.

F. A. Starring	Col. 72d Ill. Infy.	Oct. 28, 1863, to June 20, 1864.
E. P. Jackson	Col. 58th Ohio Infy.	June 29, 1864, to July 20, 1864.
F. A. Starring	Col. 72d Ill. Infy.	July 20, 1864, to Sept. 22, 1864.
H. T. McDowell	Col. 39th Ohio Infy.	Sept. 22, 1864, to Oct. 5, 1864.
C. S. Sheldon	Col. 18th Mo. Infy.	Oct. 5, 1864, to Nov. 7, 1864.
J. W. Fuller	Brigadier General	Nov. 7, 1864, to Dec. 24, 1864.
C. S. Sheldon	Col. 18th Mo. Infy.	Dec. 24, 1864, to Jan. 25, 1865.
J. W. Fuller	Brigadier General	Jan. 25, 1865, to June 24, 1865.
C. S. Sheldon	Col. 18th Mo. Infy.	June 24, 1865, to Aug. 1, 1865.

40th Ill. Infy.	Dec., 1862	From 1-Brig. 1-Div. Dist. Mem. 16-C.	To 1-Brig. 1-Div. 16-Corps	Jan., 1863
12th Ind. Infy.	Dec., 1862	From 1-Brig. 1-Div. Dist. Mem. 16-C.	To 1-Brig. 1-Div. 16-Corps	Jan., 1863
100th Ind. Infy.	Dec., 1862	From 1-Brig. 1-Div. Dist. Mem. 16-C.	To 1-Brig. 1-Div. 16-Corps	Jan., 1863
6th Iowa Infy.	Dec., 1862	From 1-Brig. 1-Div. Dist. Mem. 16-C.	To 1-Brig. 1-Div. 16-Corps	Jan., 1863
46th Ohio Infy.	Dec., 1862	From 1-Brig. 1-Div. Dist. Mem. 16-C.	To 1-Brig. 1-Div. 16-Corps	Jan., 1863
72d Ill. Infy.	Sept., 1863	From 2-Brig. 6-Div. 17-Corps	To Unass'd 23d Army Corps	Nov., 1864
58th Ohio Infy.	Sept., 1863	From Miss. Flotilla Navy	To Post of Vicksburg, Miss.	Sept., 1864
16th Wis. Infy.	Sept., 1863	From Dist. of Vicksburg, Miss.	To 1-Brig. 3-Div. 17-Corps	Apr., 1864
1st Kansas Infy.	Sept., 1863	From Dist. of Vicksburg, Miss.	To Unatt. 2-Div. 19-Corps Gulf	Aug., 1864
30th Mo. Infy.	Apr., 1864	From Vidalia Dist. Natchez, Miss.	To 1-Brig. 2-Div. 19-Corps Gulf	Aug., 1864
64th Ill. Infy.	Sept., 1864	From 1-Brig. 4-Div. 16-Corps	No change to Muster Out	July, 1865
18th Mo. Infy.	Sept., 1864	From 1-Brig. 4-Div. 16-Corps	No change to Muster Out	July, 1865
27th Ohio Infy.	Sept., 1864	From 1-Brig. 4-Div. 16-Corps	No change to Muster Out	July, 1865
39th Ohio Infy.	Sept., 1864	From 1-Brig. 4-Div. 16-Corps	No change to Muster Out	July, 1865

2d BRIGADE.—   COMMANDERS.

J. R. Cockerill	Col. 70th Ohio Infy.	Dec. 18, 1862, to Jan. 20, 1863.
T. K. Smith	Col. 95th Ohio Infy.	Sept. 14, 1863, to Oct. 29, 1863.
T. W. Humphrey	Col. 95th Ill. Infy.	Oct. 29, 1863, to Nov. 15, 1863.
A. G. Mallory	Col. 17th Wis. Infy.	Nov. 15, 1863, to Mch. 10, 1864.
J. H. Coates	Col. 11th Ill. Infy.	Mch. 10, 1864, to July 20, 1864.
B. Dornblaser	Col. 46th Ohio Infy.	July 20, 1864, to Sept. 22, 1864.
Wagar Swayne	Col. 43d Ohio Infy.	Sept. 22, 1864, to Nov. 1, 1864.
J. W. Sprague	Brigadier General	Nov. 1, 1864, to Jan. 29, 1865.
M. Montgomery	Col. 25th Wis. Infy.	Jan. 29, 1865, to Mch. 28, 1865.
J. W. Sprague	Brigadier General	Mch. 28, 1865, to May 20, 1865.
M. Montgomery	Col. 25th Wis. Infy.	May 20, 1865, to June 7, 1865.

53d Ohio Infy.	Dec., 1862	From 2-Brig. 1-Div. Dist. Mem. 16-C.	To 2-Brig. 1-Div. 16-Corps	Jan., 1863
70th Ohio Infy.	Dec., 1862	From 2-Brig. 1-Div. Dist. Mem. 16-C.	To 2-Brig. 1-Div. 16-Corps	Jan., 1863
97th Ind. Infy.	Dec., 1862	From 2-Brig. 1-Div. Dist. Mem. 16-C.	To 2-Brig. 1-Div. 16-Corps	Jan., 1863
99th Ind. Infy.	Dec., 1862	From 2-Brig. 1-Div. Dist. Mem. 16-C.	To 2-Brig. 1-Div. 16-Corps	Jan., 1863
26th Ill. Infy.	Dec., 1862	From 2-Brig. 8-Div. 16-Corps	To 2-Brig. 1-Div. 16-Corps	Jan., 1863
11th Ill. Infy.	Sept., 1863	From 2-Brig. 6-Div. 17-Corps	To 1-Brig. 2-Div. 19-Corps Gulf	Aug., 1864
95th Ill. Infy.	Sept., 1863	From 2-Brig. 6-Div. 17-Corps	To 2-Brig. Prov'l Div. 17-Corps	Mch., 1864
14th Wis. Infy.	Sept., 1863	From 2-Brig. 6-Div. 17-Corps	To 2-Brig. Prov'l Div. 17-Corps	Mch., 1864
17th Wis. Infy.	Sept., 1863	From 2-Brig. 6-Div. 17-Corps	To 3-Brig. 3-Div. 17-Corps	Mch., 1864
46th Ill. Infy.	Apr., 1864	From 2-Brig. 4-Div. 17-Corps	To 1-Brig. 2-Div. 19-Corps Gulf	Aug., 1864
76th Ill. Infy.	Apr., 1864	From 2-Brig. 4-Div. 17-Corps	To 1-Brig. 2-Div. 19-Corps Gulf	Aug., 1864
35th N. J. Infy.	Sept., 1864	From 2-Brig. 4-Div. 16-Corps	No change to Muster Out	July, 1865
43d Ohio Infy.	Sept., 1864	From 2-Brig. 4-Div. 16-Corps	No change to Muster Out	July, 1865
63d Ohio Infy.	Sept., 1864	From 2-Brig. 4-Div. 16-Corps	No change to Muster Out	July, 1865
25th Wis. Infy.	Sept., 1864	From 2-Brig. 4-Div. 16-Corps	No change to Muster Out	June, 1865

3d BRIGADE.—Discontinued Apr., 1864. Reorganized Sept., 1864.
COMMANDERS.

W. Hall	Col. 11th Iowa Infy.	Sept. 14, 1863, to Oct. 10, 1863.
A. Chambers	Brigadier General	Oct. 10, 1863, to Oct. 23, 1863.
J. Tillson	Col. 10th Ill. Infy.	Sept. 22, 1864, to Mch. 26, 1865.
C. H. DeGroat	Col. 32d Wis. Infy.	Mch. 26, 1865, to Apr. 10, 1865.
J. S. Wright	Lt.-Col. 25th. Ind. Infy.	Apr. 10, 1865, to Apr. 12, 1865.
J. Tillson	Col. 10th Ill. Infy.	Apr. 12, 1865, to July 4, 1865.

3d BRIGADE.—Continued.

11th Iowa Infy	Sept., 1863	From 3-Brig. 6-Div. 17-Corps	To 3-Brig. 4-Div. 17-Corps	Apr.,	1864
13th Iowa Infy	Sept., 1863	From 3-Brig. 6-Div. 17-Corps	To 3-Brig. 4-Div. 17-Corps	Apr.,	1864
15th Iowa Infy	Sept., 1863	From 3-Brig. 6-Div. 17-Corps	To 3-Brig. 4-Div. 17-Corps	Apr.,	1864
16th Iowa Infy	Sept., 1863	From 3-Brig. 6-Div. 17-Corps	To 3-Brig. 4-Div. 17-Corps	Apr.,	1864
10th Ill. Infy	Sept., 1864	From 3-Brig. 4-Div. 16-Corps	No change to Muster Out	July,	1865
25th Ind. Infy	Sept., 1863	From 3-Brig. 4-Div. 16-Corps	No change to Muster Out	July,	1865
32d Wis. Infy	Sept., 1863	From 3-Brig. 4-Div. 16-Corps	No change to Muster Out	July,	1865

UNATTACHED.—

15th Mich. Infy	Dec., 1862	From 2-Brig. 6-Div. L. W. 13-Corps	To Unatt. 1-Div. 16-Corps	Jan.,	1863

ARTILLERY.—

Batty. F, 1st Ill. Arty	Dec., 1863	From 1-Div. Dist. Memphis 13-Corps	To Arty. 1-Div. 16-Corps	Jan.,	1863
Batty. H, 1st Ill. Arty	Dec., 1863	From 1-Div. Dist. Memphis 13-Corps	To Arty. 2-Div. 15-Corps	Jan.,	1863
Batty. I, 1st Ill. Arty	Dec., 1863	From 1-Div. Dist. Memphis 13-Corps	To Arty. 1-Div. 16-Corps	Jan.,	1863
Cogswell's Ill. Batty	Dec., 1863	From 1-Div. Dist. Memphis 13-Corps	To Arty. 1-Div. 16-Corps	Jan.,	1863
6th Ind. Batty	Dec., 1863	From 1-Div. Dist. Memphis 13-Corps	To Arty. 1-Div. 16-Corps	Jan.,	1863
1st Minn. Batty	Sept., 1863	From Arty. 6-Div. 17-Corps	To Arty. 4-Div. 17-Corps	Jan.,	1864
Batty. C, 1st Mo. Arty	Sept., 1863	From Arty. 6-Div. 17-Corps	To Arty. 4-Div. 17-Corps	Apr.,	1864
Batty. M, 1st Mo. Arty	Sept., 1863	From Arty. 7-Div. 17-Corps	To Prov'l Div. 17-Corps Gulf	Mch.,	1864
8th Ohio Batty	Sept., 1863	From Arty. 2-Div. 15-Corps	To Maltby's Brig. Dist. Vicksburg	Apr.,	1864
10th Ohio Batty	Sept., 1863	From Arty. 6-Div. 17-Corps	To Arty. 4-Div. 17-Corps	Apr.,	1864
7th Ohio Batty	Sept., 1864	From Arty. 4-Div. 17-Corps	To Arty. Post Vicksburg, Miss	Sept.,	1864
Batty. L, 1st Ill. Arty	Sept., 1864	From Arty. 3-Div. 17-Corps	To Arty. Post Vicksburg, Miss	Sept.,	1864
Batty. C, 1st Mich. Arty	Sept., 1864	From Arty. 4-Div. 16-Corps	To Arty. Brig. 17-Corps	Nov.,	1864
14th Ohio Batty	Sept., 1864	From Arty. 4-Div. 16-Corps	To Arty. 7-Div. Cav. Corps M. D. M.	Nov.,	1864
Batty. F, 2d U. S. Arty	Sept., 1864	From Arty. 4-Div. 16-Corps	To Arty. Res. Nashville, Tenn	Nov.,	1864

CAVALRY.—

2d Wis. Cav	Sept., 1863	From Cav. Brig. 17-Corps	To Cav. Brig. Dist. Vicksburg, Miss	Apr.,	1864

3d DIVISION.— COMMANDERS.

John A. Logan	Major General	Dec. 18, 1862, to July 20, 1863.
J. E. Smith	Brigadier General	July 20, 1863, to July 22, 1863.
J. D. Stevenson	Brigadier General	July 22, 1863, to Sept., 1863.
John A. Logan	Major General	Sept., 1863, to Nov. 17, 1863.
M. D. Leggett	Brigadier General	Nov. 17, 1863, to Mch. 6, 1864.
J. A. Maltby	Brigadier General	Mch. 6, 1864, to Apr. 6, 1864.
M. D. Leggett	Brigadier General	Apr. 6, 1864, to Aug. 23, 1864.
C. R. Woods	Brigadier General	Aug. 23, 1864, to Sept. 22, 1864.
M. D. Leggett	Brigadier General	Sept. 22, 1864, to Jan. 15, 1865.
M. F. Force	Brigadier General	Jan. 15, 1865, to Apr. 3, 1865.
M. D. Leggett	Major General	Apr. 3, 1865, to Aug. 1, 1865.

1st BRIGADE.— COMMANDERS.

C. C. Marsh	Col. 20th Ill. Infy	Dec. 18, 1862, to Jan. 25, 1863.
I. N. Haynie	Brigadier General	Jan. 25, 1863, to Apr. 23, 1863.
J. E. Smith	Brigadier General	Apr. 23, 1863, to June 3, 1863.
M. D. Leggett	Brigadier General	June 3, 1863, to Nov. 17, 1863.
M. F. Force	Brigadier General	Nov. 17, 1863, to Mch. 6, 1864.
A. Mann	Major 124th Ill. Infy	Mch., 1864, to May 2, 1864.
M. F. Force	Brigadier General	May 2, 1864, to July 22, 1864.
G. E. Bryant	Col. 12th Wis. Infy	July 22, 1864, to Oct., 1864.
M. F. Force	Brigadier General	Oct., 1864, to Jan. 15, 1865.
C. Fairchilds	Col. 16th Wis. Infy	Jan. 15, 1865, to Apr. 3, 1865.
C. Ewing	Brigadier General	Apr. 3, 1865, to Aug. 1, 1865.

20th Ill. Infy	Dec., 1862	From 1-Brig. 3-Div. R. W. 13-Corps	To Provost Guard 3-Div. 17-Corps	July,	1864
31st Ill. Infy	Dec., 1862	From 1-Brig. 3-Div. R. W. 13-Corps	To 2-Brig. 4-Div. 17-Corps	Apr.,	1865
45th Ill. Infy	Dec., 1862	From 1-Brig. 3-Div. R. W. 13-Corps	No change to Muster Out	July,	1865
124th Ill. Infy	Dec., 1862	From 1-Brig. 3-Div. R. W. 13-Corps	To Maltby's Brig. Dist. Vicksburg	Apr.,	1864
23d Ind. Infy	Dec., 1862	From 2-Brig. 3-Div. R. W. 13-Corps	To 3-Brig. 4-Div. 17-Corps	Jan.,	1864
29th Ill. Infy	July, 1863	From St. Louis, Mo	To Post Natchez, Miss	Dec.,	1863
131st Ill. Infy	Oct., 1863	From Dist. Columbus 6-Div. 16-C	Consolidated with 29th Ill	Nov.,	1863
16th Wis. Infy	Mch., 1864	From 1-Brig. 1-Div. 17-Corps	No change to Muster Out	July,	1865
30th Ill. Infy	Apr., 1864	From 3-Brig. 3-Div. 17-Corps	No change to Muster Out	July,	1865
12th Wis. Infy	July, 1864	From 1-Brig. 4-Div. 17-Corps	No change to Muster Out	July,	1865
20th Ill. Infy	Apr., 1865	From Provost Guard 3 Div. 17-Corps	No change to Muster Out	July,	1865

2d BRIGADE.— COMMANDERS.

M. D. Leggett	Brigadier General	Dec. 18, 1862, to Apr. 13, 1863.
E. S. Dennis	Brigadier General	Apr. 13, 1863, to May 11, 1863.
M. D. Leggett	Brigadier General	May 11, 1863, to June 3, 1863.
M. F. Force	Col. 20th Ohio Infy	June 3, 1863, to Nov. 17, 1863.
B. F. Potts	Col. 32d Ohio Infy	Nov. 17, 1863, to Mch. 6, 1864.
R. K. Scott	Col. 68th Ohio Infy	Mch. 6, 1864, to July 22, 1864.
G. F. Wiles	Lt.-Col. 78th Ohio Infy	July 22, 1864, to Sept. 30, 1864.
R. K. Scott	Col. 68th Ohio Infy	Sept. 30, 1864, to Dec. 27, 1864.
G. F. Wiles	Lt.-Col. 78th Ohio Infy	Dec. 27, 1864, to Mch. 28, 1865.
R. K. Scott	Col. 68th Ohio Infy	Mch. 28, 1865, to Aug. 1, 1865.

30th Ill. Infy	Dec., 1862	From 1-Brig. 3-Div. R. W. 13-Corps	To 3-Brig. 3-Div. 17-Corps	Dec.,	1863
20th Ohio Infy	Dec., 1862	From 2-Brig. 3-Div. R. W. 13-Corps	No change to Muster Out	July,	1865
68th Ohio Infy	Dec., 1862	From 2-Brig. 3-Div. R. W. 13-Corps	No change to Muster Out	July,	1865
78th Ohio Infy	Dec., 1862	From 2-Brig. 3-Div. R. W. 13-Corps	No change to Muster Out	July,	1865
32d Ohio Infy	Dec., 1863	From 3-Brig. 3-Div. 17-Corps	To 1-Brig. 4-Div. 17-Corps	July,	1864
17th Wis. Infy	Nov., 1864	From 3-Brig. 3-Div. 17-Corps	No change to Muster Out	July,	1865

3d BRIGADE.—Discontinued Nov. 2, 1864. COMMANDERS.

J. D. Stevenson	Brigadier General	Dec. 18, 1862, to July 20, 1863.
F. Campbell	Col. 81st Ill. Infy	July 20, 1863, to Sept. 8, 1863.
J. A. Maltby	Brigadier General	Sept. 8, 1863, to May 1, 1864.
A. G. Mallory	Col. 17th Wis. Infy	May 1, 1864, to Sept. 22, 1864.
A. Worden	Major 14th Wis. Infy	Sept. 22, 1864, to Oct. 12, 1864.
D. D. Scott	Lt.-Col. 17th Wis. Infy	Oct. 12, 1864, to Nov. 2, 1864.

8th Ill. Infy	Dec., 1862	From 4-Brig. 3-Div. R. W. 13-Corps	To Maltby's Br. Dist. Vicksb'g, Miss	Apr.,	1864
63d Ill. Infy	Dec., 1862	From 4-Brig. 3-Div. R. W. 13-Corps	To Dist. Memphis 16-Corps	Jan.,	1863
81st Ill. Infy	Dec., 1862	From 1-Brig. 3-Div. R. W. 13-Corps	To 2-Brig. Prov'l Div. 17-Corps	Mch.,	1864
7th Mo. Infy	Dec., 1862	From 4-Brig. 3-Div. R. W. 13-Corps	To Maltby's Br. Dist. Vicksb'g, Miss	Apr.,	1864
32d Ohio Infy	Jan., 1863	From Prisoners of War	To 2-Brig. 3-Div. 17-Corps	Dec.,	1863
17th Ill. Infy	July, 1863	From 1-Brig. 6-Div. 17-Corps	To Maltby's Br. Dist. Vicksb'g, Miss	Apr.,	1864
30th Ill. Infy	Dec., 1863	From 2-Brig. 3-Div. 17-Corps	To 1-Brig. 3-Div. 17-Corps	Apr.,	1864
17th Wis. Infy	Apr., 1864	From 2-Brig. 1-Div. 17-Corps	To 2-Brig. 3-Div. 17-Corps	Nov.,	1864
81st Ill. Infy. Det.	Apr., 1864	From Veteran Furlough	To 2-Brig. 3-Div. Det. Army Tenn.	Dec.,	1864
95th Ill. Infy. Det.	Apr., 1864	From 2-Brig. 1-Div. 17-Corps	To 1-Brig. 3-Div. Det. Army Tenn.	Dec.,	1864
14th Wis. Infy. Det.	Apr., 1864	From 2-Brig. 1-Div. 17-Corps	To 2-Brig. 3-Div. Det. Army Tenn.	Dec.,	1864

ARTILLERY.—

Batty. D, 1st Ill. Arty....Dec., 1862	From Arty. 3-Div. R. W. 13-Corps...	To Arty. Res. Nashville, Tenn.....	Nov., 1864
Batty. G, 2d Ill. Arty....Dec., 1862	From Arty. 3-Div. R. W. 12-Corps...	To Dist. Columbus 6-Div. 16-Corps..	Dec., 1863
Batty. L, 2d Ill. Arty:...Dec., 1862	From Arty. 4-Div. R. W. 12-Corps...	To Arty. 1-Div. 17-Corps...........	Apr., 1864
Batty. H, 1st Mich. Arty..Dec., 1862	From Arty. 3-Div. R. W. 13-Corps..	To Post Chattanooga, Tenn.........	Oct., 1864
3d Ohio Batty..........Dec., 1862	From Arty. 3-Div. R. W. 1?-Corps..	To Arty. Res. Nashville, Tenn.....	Nov., 1864
32d Ohio Infy. (Co. F)...May, 1863	From 3-Brig. 3-Div. 17-Corps......	To 3-Brig. 3-Div. 17-Corps.......	Aug., 1863
26th Ohio Batty.........Dec., 1863	From Co. F, 32d Ohio.............	To Maltby's Brig. Dist. Vicksburg..	Apr., 1864
10th Ohio Batty.........Apr., 1864	From Arty. 4-Div. 17-Corps........	To Arty. 4-Div. 17-Corps...........	May, 1864

4th DIVISION.—Transferred to 16th Corps Jan. 20, 1863. Reorganized Aug. 7, 1863, from 4-Div. 13-Corps.

COMMANDERS.

J. G. Lauman.........	Brigadier General	Dec. 18,.1862, to Jan. 20, 1863.
M. M. Crocker........	Brigadier General	Aug. 7, 1863, to May 27, 1864.
W. Q. Gresham........	Brigadier General	May 27, 1864, to July 20, 1864.
William Hall.........	Col. 11th Iowa Infy.	July 20, 1864, to July 21, 1864.
Giles A. Smith.......	Brigadier General	July 21, 1864, to Sept. 20, 1864.
W. W. Belknap........	Brigadier General	Sept. 20, 1864, to Oct. 31, 1864.
Giles A. Smith.......	Brigadier General	Oct. 31, 1864, to June 1, 1865.
W. W. Belknap........	Brigadier General	June 1, 1865, to June 26, 1865.
B. F. Potts..........	Col. 32d Ohio Infy.	June 26, 1865, to July 9, 1865.
W. W. Belknap........	Brigadier General	July 9, 1865, to July 27, 1865.

1st BRIGADE.—Discontinued Feb., 1864. Transferred to Red River Expedition. Reorganized May, 1864.

COMMANDERS.

I. C. Pugh...........	Col. 41st Ill. Infy..........	Dec. 18, 1862, to Jan. 20, 1863.
I. C. Pugh...........	Col. 41st Ill. Infy...'......	Aug. 7, 1863, to Oct. 24, 1863.
T. K. Smith..........	Brigadier General	Oct. 24, 1863, to Feb. 28, 1864.
W. L. Sanderson......	Col. 23d Ind. Infy...........	May 26, 1864, to July 18, 1864.
B. F. Potts..........	Col. 32d Ohio Infy...........	July 18, 1864, to June 26, 1865.
J. J. Hibbetts.......	Col. 32d Ohio Infy...........	June 26, 1865, to July 9, 1865.
B. F. Potts..........	Brigadier General	July 9, 1865, to July 23, 1865.

41st Ill. Infy.............Dec., 1862	From 1-Brig. 4-Div. R. W. 13-Corps	To 1-Brig. 4-Div. 16-Corps..........	Jan., 1863
53d Ill. Infy.............Dec., 1862	From 1-Brig. 4-Div. R. W. 13-Corps	To 1-Brig. 4-Div. 16-Corps..........	Jan., 1863
3d Iowa Infy..............Dec., 1862	From 1-Brig. 4-Div. R. W. 13-Corps	To 1-Brig. 4-Div. 16-Corps..........	Jan., 1863
33d Wis. Infy.............Dec., 1862	From 1-Brig. 4-Div. R. W. 13-Corps	To 1-Brig. 4-Div. 16-Corps..........	Jan., 1863
41st Ill. Infy.............Aug., 1863	From 1-Brig. 4-Div. 13-Corps	To 1-Brig. Prov'l Div. 17-Corps...	Feb., 1864
53d Ill. Infy.............Aug., 1863	From 1-Brig. 4-Div. 13-Corps	To 2-Brig. 4-Div. 17-Corps.......	Apr., 1864
3d Iowa Infy..............Aug., 1863	From 1-Brig. 4-Div. 13-Corps	To 1-Brig. Prov'l Div. 17-Corps...	Feb., 1864
33d Wis. Infy.............Aug., 1863	From 1-Brig. 4-Div. 13-Corps	To 1-Brig. Prov'l Div. 17-Corps...	Feb., 1864
32d Ill. Infy.............Apr., 1864	From 3-Brig. 4-Div. 17-Corps	To 2-Brig. 4-Div. 17-Corps.......	July, 1864
23d Ind. Infy.............Apr., 1864	From 3-Brig. 4-Div. 17-Corps	No change to Muster Out..........	July, 1865
53d Ind. Infy.............Apr., 1864	From 3-Brig. 4-Div. 17-Corps	No change to Muster Out..........	July, 1865
12th Wis. Infy............Apr., 1864	From 3-Brig. 4-Div. 17-Corps	To 1-Brig. 3-Div. 17-Corps.......	July, 1864
3d Iowa Infy. Vets........Apr., 1864	From Veteran Furlough..........	Consolidated with 2d Iowa Infy..	Nov. 8, '64
32d Ohio Infy.............July, 1864	From 2-Brig. 3-Div. 17-Corps	To 2-Brig. 4-Div. 17-Corps.......	Apr., 1865
53d Ill. Infy.............July, 1864	From 2-Brig. 4-Div. 17-Corps	To 2-Brig. 4-Div. 17-Corps.......	Apr., 1865
14th Ill. Infy............Nov., 1864	From 2-Brig. 4-Div. 17-Corps	To 2-Brig. 4-Div. 17-Corps.......	Apr., 1865
15th Ill. Infy............Nov., 1864	From 2-Brig. 4-Div. 17-Corps	To 2-Brig. 4-Div. 17-Corps.......	Apr., 1865
41st Ill. Infy............Nov., 1864	From 2-Brig. 4-Div. 17-Corps	Consolidated with 53d Ill. Infy....	Dec.31, '64

2d BRIGADE.—Transferred to 16th Corps, Jan. 20, 1863. Reorganized Aug. 7, 1863, from 2-Brig. 4-Div. 13-Corps. Transferred to 2-Brig. 1-Div. 17-Corps, June 20, 1864. Reorganized June 20, 1864. Discontinued Nov. 6, 1864. Reorganized Apr. 28, 1865. Transferred from Corps, June 15, 1865.

COMMANDERS.

Cyrus Hall	Col. 14th Ill. Infy.	Dec. 18, 1862, to Jan. 20, 1863.
Cyrus Hall	Col. 14th Ill. Infy.	Aug. 7, 1863, to Mch. 16, 1864.
B. Dornblaser........	Col. 46th Ill. Infy.	Mch. 16, 1864, to June 20, 1864.
G. C. Rogers.........	Col. 15th Ill. Infy.	June 20, 1864, to July 5, 1864.
I. C. Pugh...........	Col. 41st Ill. Infy.	July 5, 1864, to July 19, 1864.
J. Logan.............	Col. 32d Ill. Infy.	July 19, 1864, to Oct. 1, 1864.
R. H. McFadden.......	Major 41st Ill. Infy.	Oct. 1, 1864, to Nov. 6, 1864.
C. J. Stolbrand......	Brigadier General	Apr. 28, 1865, to June 15, 1865.

14th Ill. Infy.............Dec., 1862	From 2-Brig. 4-Div. R. W. 13-C...	To 2-Brig. 4-Div. 16-Corps........	Jan., 1863
15th Ill. Infy.............Dec., 1862	From 2-Brig. 4-Div. R. W. 13-C...	To 2-Brig. 4-Div. 16-Corps........	Jan., 1863
46th Ill. Infy.............Dec., 1862	From 2-Brig. 4-Div. R. W. 13-C...	To 2-Brig. 4-Div. 16-Corps........	Jan., 1863
76th Ill. Infy.............Dec., 1862	From 2-Brig. 4-Div. R. W. 13-C...	To 2-Brig. 4-Div. 16-Corps........	Jan., 1863
101st Ill. Infy............Dec., 1862	From 2-Brig. 4-Div. R. W. 13-C...	To Dist. Memphis, Tenn. 16-Corps..	Jan., 1863
14th Ill. Infy.............Aug., 1863	From 2-Brig. 4-Div. 13-Corps	To 1-Brig. 4-Div. 17-Corps......	Nov., 1864
15th Ill. Infy.............Aug., 1863	From 2-Brig. 4-Div. 13-Corps	To 1-Brig. 4-Div. 17-Corps......	Nov., 1864
46th Ill. Infy.............Aug., 1863	From 2-Brig. 4-Div. 13-Corps	To 2-Brig. 1-Div. 17-Corps......	Apr., 1864
76th Ill. Infy.............Aug., 1863	From 2-Brig. 4-Div. 13-Corps	To 2-Brig. 1-Div. 17-Corps......	Apr., 1864
53d Ill. Infy.............Apr., 1864	From 1-Brig. 4-Div. 17-Corps	To 1-Brig. 4-Div. 17-Corps.......	July, 1864
41st Ill. Infy.............Apr., 1864	From Veteran Furlough	To 1-Brig. 4-Div. 17-Corps.......	Nov., 1864
32d Ill. Infy..............July, 1864	From 1-Brig. 4-Div. 17-Corps	To 3-Brig. 4-Div. 17-Corps.......	Nov., 1864
14th Ill. Infy.............Apr., 1865	From 1-Brig. 4-Div. 17-Corps	To Dept. of Mo................	June, 1865
15th Ill. Infy.............Apr., 1865	From 1-Brig. 4-Div. 17-Corps	To Dept. of Mo................	June, 1865
31st Ill. Infy.............Apr., 1865	From 1-Brig. 3-Div. 17-Corps	No change to Muster Out..........	July, 1865
32d Ill. Infy.............Apr., 1865	From 3-Brig. 4-Div. 17-Corps	No change to Muster Out..........	July, 1865
32d Ohio Infy.............Apr., 1865	From 1-Brig. 4-Div. 17-Corps	No change to Muster Out..........	July, 1865

3d BRIGADE.— COMMANDERS.

A. K. Johnson.........	Col. 28th Ill. Infy............	Dec. 18, 1862, to Jan. 20, 1863.
A. K. Johnson.........	Col. 28th Ill. Infy............	Aug. 7, 1863, to Aug. 26, 1863.
W. Q. Gresham........	Brigadier General	Aug. 26, 1863, to May 27, 1864.
William Hall..........	Col. 11th Iowa Infy.	May 27, 1864, to July 21, 1864.
John Shane..........	Col. 13th Iowa Infy.	July 21, 1864.
William Hall..........	Col. 11th Iowa Infy.	July 21, 1864, to July 31, 1864.
W. W. Belknap........	Brigadier General	July 31, 1864, to Sept. 21, 1864.
J. C. Abercrombie.....	Lt.-Col. 11th Iowa Infy.	Sept. 21, 1864, to Oct. 23, 1864.
G. Pomutz...........	Major 15th Iowa Infy.	Oct. 23, 1864, to Oct. 31, 1864.
W. W. Belknap........	Brigadier General	Oct. 31, 1864, to May 29, 1865.
B. Beach............	Lt.-Col. 11th Iowa Infy.	May 29, 1865, to June 16, 1865.
A. Hickenlooper......	Brigadier General................	June 16, 1865, to Aug. 1, 1865.

3d BRIGADE.—Continued.

28th Ill. Infy	Dec., 1862	From 3-Brig. 4-Div. R. W. 13-C	To 3-Brig. 4-Div. 16-Corps	Jan.,	1863
32d Ill. Infy	Dec., 1862	From 3-Brig. 4-Div. R. W. 13-C	To 3-Brig. 4-Div. 16-Corps	Jan.,	1863
25th Ill. Infy	Dec., 1862	From 3-Brig. 4-Div. R. W. 13-C	To 3-Brig. 4-Div. 16-Corps	Jan.,	1863
53d Ind. Infy	Dec., 1862	From 3-Brig. 4-Div. R. W. 13-C	To 3-Brig. 4-Div. 16-Corps	Jan.,	1863
12th Wis. Infy	Dec., 1862	From 3-Brig. 4-Div. R. W. 13-C	To 3-Brig. 4-Div. 16-Corps	Jan.,	1863
28th Ill. Infy	Aug., 1863	From 3-Brig. 4-Div. 13-Corps	To Post Natchez, Miss	Aug.,	1863
32d Ill. Infy	Aug., 1863	From 3-Brig. 4-Div. 13-Corps	To 1-Brig. 4-Div. 17-Corps	Apr.,	1864
53d Ind. Infy	Aug., 1863	From 3-Brig. 4-Div. 13-Corps	To 1-Brig. 4-Div. 17-Corps	Apr.,	1864
12th Wis. Infy	Aug., 1863	From 3-Brig. 4-Div. 13-Corps	To 1-Brig. 4-Div. 17-Corps	Apr.,	1864
23d Ind. Infy	Jan., 1864	From 1-Brig. 3-Div. 17-Corps	To 1-Brig. 4-Div. 17-Corps	Apr.,	1864
11th Iowa Infy	Apr., 1864	From 3-Brig. 1-Div. 17-Corps	No change to Muster Out	July,	1865
13th Iowa Infy	Apr., 1864	From 3-Brig. 1-Div. 17-Corps	No change to Muster Out	July,	1865
15th Iowa Infy	Apr., 1864	From 3-Brig. 1-Div. 17-Corps	No change to Muster Out	July,	1865
16th Iowa Infy	Apr., 1864	From 3-Brig. 1-Div. 17-Corps	No change to Muster Out	July,	1865
32d Ill. Infy	Nov., 1864	From 2-Brig. 4-Div. 17-Corps	To 2-Brig. 4-Div. 17-Corps	Apr.,	1865

ARTILLERY.—

Batty. E, 2d Ill. Arty	Dec., 1862	From Arty. 3-Div. R. W. 13-C	To Arty. 4-Div. 16-Corps	Jan.,	1863
Batty. K, 2d Ill. Arty	Dec., 1862	From Arty. 4-Div. R. W. 13-C	To Arty. 4-Div. 16-Corps	Jan.,	1863
9th Ind. Batty	Dec., 1862	From Arty. 4-Div. R. W. 13-C	To Arty. 4-Div. 16-Corps	Jan.,	1863
5th Ohio Batty	Dec., 1862	From Arty. 6-Div. L. W. 13-C	To Arty. 4-Div. 16-Corps	Jan.,	1863
7th Ohio Batty	Dec., 1862	From Arty 4-Div. R. W. 13-C	To Arty. 4-Div. 16-Corps	Jan.,	1863
15th Ohio Batty	Dec., 1862	From Arty. 4-Div R. W. 13-C	To Arty. 4-Div. 16-Corps	Jan.,	1863
Batty. K, 2d Ill. Infy	Aug., 1863	From Arty. 4-Div. 13-Corps	To Post Natchez, Miss	Aug.,	1863
7th Ohio Batty	Aug., 1863	From Arty. 4-Div. 13-Corps	To Arty. 1-Div. 17-Corps	Apr.,	1864
15th Ohio Batty	Aug., 1863	From Arty. 4-Div. 13-Corps	To Arty. Brig. 17-Corps	Nov.,	1864
Batty. F, 2d Ill. Arty	Aug., 1863	From Arty. 6-Div. 17-Corps	To Arty. Res. Dept. Cumb'd	Nov.,	1864
Batty. C, 1st Mo. Arty	Apr., 1864	From Arty. 1-Div. 17-Corps	To Arty. Res. Dept. Cumb'd	Nov.,	1864
1st Minn. Batty	Apr., 1864	From Arty. 1-Div. 17-Corps	To Arty. Brig. 17-Corps	Nov.,	1864
10th Ohio Batty	Apr., 1864	From Arty. 1-Div. 17-Corps	To Arty. Res. Nashville, Tenn	Nov.,	1864

DISTRICT OF CORINTH.—Transferred to 16th Army Corps Jan. 20, 1863.

COMMANDER.

G. M. Dodge	Brigadier General	Dec. 18, 1862, to Jan. 20, 1863.	

1st BRIGADE.— COMMANDER.

T. W. Sweeney	Col. 52d Ill. Infy	Dec. 18, 1862, to Jan. 20, 1863.	

2d Iowa Infy	Dec., 1862	From 1-Br. Dist. Corinth R. W. 13-C.	To 1-Brig. Dist. Corinth 16-Corps	Jan.,	1863
7th Iowa Infy	Dec., 1862	From 1-Br. Dist. Corinth R. W. 13-C.	To 1-Brig. Dist. Corinth 16-Corps	Jan.,	1863
66th Ind. Infy	Dec., 1862	From 1-Br. Dist. Corinth R. W. 13-C.	To 1-Brig. Dist. Corinth 16-Corps	Jan.,	1863
52d Ill. Infy	Dec., 1862	From 1-Br. Dist. Corinth R. W. 13-C.	To 1-Brig. Dist. Corinth 16-Corps	Jan.,	1863

2d BRIGADE.— COMMANDER.

A. Mersey	Col. 9th Ill. Infy	Dec. 18, 1862, to Jan. 20, 1863.	

9th Ill. Infy	Dec., 1862	From 2-Br. Dist. Corinth R. W .13-C.	To 2-Brig. Dist. Corinth 16-Corps	Jan.,	1863
12th Ill. Infy	Dec., 1862	From 2-Br. Dist. Corinth R. W .13-C.	To 2-Brig. Dist. Corinth 16-Corps	Jan.,	1863
22d Ohio Infy	Dec., 1862	From 2-Br. Dist. Corinth R. W .13-C.	To 4-Brig. Dist. Jackson 16-Corps	Dec.,	1863
81st Ohio Infy	Dec., 1862	From 2-Br. Dist. Corinth R. W .13-C.	To 2-Brig. Dist. Corinth 16-Corps	Jan.,	1863

3d BRIGADE.— COMMANDER.

M. M. Bane	Col. 50th Ill. Infy	Dec. 18, 1862, to Jan. 20, 1863.	

7th Ill. Infy	Dec., 1862	From 3-Br. Dist. Corinth R. W. 13-C.	To 3-Brig. Dist. Corinth 16-Corps	Jan.,	1863
50th Ill. Infy	Dec., 1862	From 3-Br. Dist. Corinth R. W. 13-C.	To 3-Brig. Dist. Corinth 16-Corps	Jan.,	1863
57th Ill. Infy	Dec., 1862	From 3-Br. Dist. Corinth R. W. 13-C.	To 3-Brig. Dist. Corinth 16-Corps	Jan.,	1863
19th Mo. Infy	Dec., 1862	From 3-Br. Dist. Corinth R. W. 13-C.	To 3-Brig. Dist. Corinth 16-Corps	Jan.,	1863
39th Iowa Infy	Dec., 1862	From 3-Br. Dist. Corinth R. W. 13-C.	To 3-Brig. Dist. Corinth 16-Corps	Jan.,	1863

UNATTACHED, DISTRICT OF CORINTH.—

64th Ill. Infy	Dec., 1862	From Un. Dist. Corinth R. W. 13-C.	To Unatt. Dist. Corinth 16-Corps	Jan.,	1863
66th Ill. Infy	Dec., 1862	From Un. Dist. Corinth R. W. 13-C.	To Unatt. Dist. Corinth 16-Corps	Jan.,	1863
1st U. S. Infy	Dec., 1862	From Un. Dist. Corinth R. W. 13-C.	To Unatt. Dist. Corinth 16-Corps	Jan.,	1863

ARTILLERY.—

Batty. D, 1st Mo. Arty	Dec., 1862	From Dist. Corinth R. W. 13-C.	To Dist. Corinth 16-Corps	Jan.,	1863
Batty. H, 1st Mo. Arty	Dec., 1862	From Dist. Corinth R. W. 13-C.	To Dist. Corinth 16-Corps	Jan.,	1863
Batty. I, 1st Mo. Arty	Dec., 1862	From Dist. Corinth R. W. 13-C.	To Dist. Corinth 16-Corps	Jan.,	1863
Batty. G, 1st Ill. Infy	Dec., 1862	From Dist. Corinth R. W. 13-C.	To Dist. Corinth 16-Corps	Jan.,	1863
Batty. K, 1st Mo. Arty	Dec., 1862	From Dist. Corinth R. W. 13-C.	To Dist. Corinth 16-Corps	Jan.,	1863

CAVALRY.—

5th Ohio Cav. 3d Battn.	Dec., 1862	From Dist. Corinth 13-Corps	To Dist. Corinth 16-Corps	Jan.,	1863
15th Ill. Cav. (Stewart's Batt'n.)	Dec., 1862	From Dist. Corinth 13-Corps	To Dist. Corinth 16-Corps	Jan.,	1863

6th DIVISION.—Organized by transfer from 16th Army Corps Jan. 20, 1863. Discontinued Sept. 14, 1863, and designated 1st Division 17th Army Corps.

COMMANDERS.

John McArthur	Brigadier General	Jan. 20, 1863, to July 30, 1863.	
A. Chambers	Col. 16th Iowa Infy	July 30, 1863, to Aug. 23, 1863.	
William Hall	Col. 11th Iowa Infy	Aug. 23, 1863, to Sept. 3, 1863.	
A. Chambers	Col. 16th Iowa Infy	Sept. 3, 1863, to Sept. 14, 1863.	

1st BRIGADE.— COMMANDERS.

G. W. Deitzler	Brigadier General	Jan. 20, 1863, to Apr. 22, 1863.	
H. T. Reid	Brigadier General	Apr. 22, 1863, to Aug. 1, 1863.	

17th Ill. Infy	Jan., 1863	From 1-Brig. 6-Div. 16-Corps	To 3-Brig. 3-Div. 17-Corps	May,	1863
95th Ill. Infy	Jan., 1863	From 1-Brig. 6-Div. 16-Corps	To 2-Brig. 6-Div. 17-Corps	May,	1863
16th Wis. Infy	Jan., 1863	From 1-Brig. 6-Div. 16-Corps	To Dist. of Vicksburg, Miss	Aug.,	1863
1st Kan. Infy	Jan., 1863	From 1-Brig. 6-Div. 16-Corps	To Dist. of Vicksburg, Miss	Aug.,	1863

2d BRIGADE.— COMMANDER.

T. E. G. Ransom	Brigadier General	Jan. 20, 1863, to Sept. 14, 1863.	

11th Ill. Infy	Jan., 1863	From 2-Brig. 6-Div. 16-Corps	To 2-Brig. 1-Div. 17-Corps	Sept.,	1863
14th Wis. Infy	Jan., 1863	From 2-Brig. 6-Div. 16-Corps	To 2-Brig. 1-Div. 17-Corps	Sept.,	1863
17th Wis. Infy	Jan., 1863	From 2-Brig. 6-Div. 16-Corps	To 2-Brig. 1-Div. 17-Corps	Sept.,	1863
18th Wis. Infy	Jan., 1863	From 2-Brig. 6-Div. 16-Corps	To 1-Brig. 7-Div. 17-Corps	May,	1863
72d Ill. Infy	Apr., 1863	From 1-Brig. 7-Div. 17-Corps	To 1-Brig. 1-Div. 17-Corps	Sept.,	1863
95th Ill. Infy	May, 1863	From 1-Brig. 6-Div. 17-Corps	To 1-Brig. 1-Div. 17-Corps	Sept.,	1863
63d Ill. Infy	June, 1863	From Detached Brig. Dist. N. E. La.	To 1-Brig. 7-Div. 17-Corps	July,	1863

3d BRIGADE.— COMMANDERS.

M. M. Crocker	Brigadier General	Jan. 20, 1863, to Apr. 30, 1863.
William Hall	Col. 11th Iowa Infy	Apr. 30, 1863, to June 6, 1863.
A. Chambers	Col. 16th Iowa Infy	June 6, 1863, to July 30, 1863.
William Hall	Col. 11th Iowa Infy	July 30, 1863, to Aug. 23, 1863.
A. Chambers	Col. 16th Iowa Infy	Aug. 23, 1863, to Sept. 14, 1863.

11th Iowa Infy..........Jan., 1863	From 3-Brig. 6-Div. 16-Corps......	To 3-Brig. 1-Div. 17-Corps........	Sept., 1863
13th Iowa Infy..........Jan., 1863	From 3-Brig. 6-Div. 16-Corps......	To 3-Brig. 1-Div. 17-Corps........	Sept., 1863
15th Iowa Infy..........Jan., 1863	From 3-Brig. 6-Div. 16-Corps......	To 3-Brig. 1-Div. 17-Corps........	Sept., 1863
16th Iowa Infy..........Jan., 1863	From 3-Brig. 6-Div. 16-Corps......	To 3-Brig. 1-Div. 17-Corps........	Sept., 1863

ARTILLERY.—

Batty. F, 2d Ill. Arty....Jan., 1863	From Arty. 6-Div. 16-Corps........	To Arty. 4-Div. 17-Corps..........	Aug., 1863
Batty. C, 1st Mo. Arty....Jan., 1863	From Arty. 6-Div. 16-Corps........	To Arty. 1-Div. 17-Corps..........	Sept., 1863
1st Minn. Batty.........Jan., 1863	From Arty. 6-Div. 16-Corps........	To Arty. 1-Div. 17-Corps..........	Sept., 1863
10th Ohio Batty.........Jan., 1863	From Arty. 6-Div. 16-Corps........	To Arty. 1-Div. 17-Corps..........	Sept., 1863

7th DIVISION.—Organized by transfer from 16th Army Corps Jan. 20, 1863. Discontinued Sept. 14, 1863, and designated 2d Division, 17th Army Corps.

COMMANDERS.

I. F. Quinby	Brigadier General	Jan. 20, 1863, to Apr. 14, 1863.
J. B. Sanborn	Col. 4th Minn. Infy	Apr. 14, 1863, to May 2, 1863.
M. M. Crocker	Brigadier General	May 2, 1863, to May 16, 1863.
I. F. Quinby	Brigadier General	May 16, 1863, to June 3, 1863.
J. E. Smith	Brigadier General	June 3, 1863, to Sept. 14, 1863.

1st BRIGADE.— COMMANDERS.

Norman Eddy	Col. 48th Ind. Infy	Jan. 20, 1863, to Feb. 5, 1863.
J. B. Sanborn	Col. 4th Minn. Infy	Feb. 5, 1863, to Apr. 12, 1863.
J. I. Alexander	Col. 59th Ind. Infy	Apr. 12, 1863, to May 2, 1863.
J. B. Sanborn	Col. 4th Minn. Infy	May 2, 1863, to Aug. 21, 1863.
J. Isaminger	Lt.-Col. 63d Ill. Infy	Aug. 21, 1863, to Sept. 14, 1863.

72d Ill. Infy..........Jan., 1863	From 1-Brig. 7-Div. 17-Corps......	To 2-Brig. 6-Div. 17-Corps........	May, 1863
48th Ind. Infy..........Jan., 1863	From 1-Brig. 7-Div. 17-Corps......	To 1-Brig. 2-Div. 17-Corps........	Sept., 1863
59th Ind. Infy..........Jan., 1863	From 1-Brig. 7-Div. 17-Corps......	To 1-Brig. 2-Div. 17-Corps........	Sept., 1863
4th Minn. Infy..........Jan., 1863	From 1-Brig. 7-Div. 17-Corps......	To 1-Brig. 2-Div. 17-Corps........	Sept., 1863
18th Wis. Infy..........May, 1863	From 2-Brig. 6-Div. 17-Corps......	To 1-Brig. 2-Div. 17-Corps........	Sept., 1863
63d Ill. Infy..........July, 1863	From 2-Brig. 6-Div. 17-Corps......	To 1-Brig. 2-Div. 17-Corps........	Sept., 1863

2d BRIGADE.— COMMANDERS.

E. R. Eckley	Col. 80th Ohio Infy	Jan. 20, 1863, to Feb. 12, 1863.
C. L. Mathies	Col. 5th Iowa Infy	Feb. 12, 1863, to Apr. 24, 1863.
S. A. Holmes	Col. 10th Mo. Infy	Apr. 24, 1863, to June 10, 1863.
G. B. Raum	Col. 56th Ill. Infy	June 10, 1863, to Aug. 12, 1863.
C. R. Wever	Col. 17th Iowa Infy	Aug. 12, 1863, to Sept. 14, 1863.

56th Ill. Infy..........Jan., 1863	From 2-Brig. 7-Div. 16-Corps......	To 2-Brig. 2-Div. 17-Corps........	Sept., 1863
17th Iowa Infy..........Jan., 1863	From 2-Brig. 7-Div. 16-Corps......	To 2-Brig. 2-Div. 17-Corps........	Sept., 1863
10th Mo. Infy..........Jan., 1863	From 2-Brig. 7-Div. 16-Corps......	To 2-Brig. 2-Div. 17-Corps........	Sept., 1863
24th Mo. Infy Co. E....Jan., 1863	From 2-Brig. 7-Div. 16-Corps......	To 2-Brig. 2-Div. 17-Corps........	Sept., 1863
80th Ohio Infy..........Jan., 1863	From 2-Brig. 7-Div. 16-Corps......	To 2-Brig. 2-Div. 17-Corps........	Sept., 1863

3d BRIGADE.— COMMANDERS.

C. L. Mathies	Col. 5th Iowa Infy	Jan. 20, 1863, to Feb. 12, 1863.	
G. B. Boomer	Col. 26th Mo. Infy	Feb. 12, 1863, to May 22, 1863.	Killed.
H. Putnam	Col. 93d Ill. Infy	May 22, 1863, to June 2, 1863.	
C. L. Mathies	Brigadier General	June 2, 1863, to July 27, 1863.	
B. D. Dean	Col. 26th Mo. Infy	July 27, 1863, to Aug. 28, 1863.	
C. L. Mathies	Brigadier General	Aug. 28, 1863, to Sept. 14, 1863.	

93d Ill. Infy..........Jan., 1863	From 3-Brig. 7-Div. 16-Corps......	To 3-Brig. 2-Div. 17-Corps........	Sept., 1863
5th Iowa Infy..........Jan., 1863	From 3-Brig. 7-Div. 16-Corps......	To 3-Brig. 2-Div. 17-Corps........	Sept., 1863
10th Iowa Infy..........Jan., 1863	From 3-Brig. 7-Div. 16-Corps......	To 3-Brig. 2-Div. 17-Corps........	Sept., 1863
26th Mo. Infy..........Jan., 1863	From 3-Brig. 7-Div. 16-Corps......	To 3-Brig. 2-Div. 17-Corps........	Sept., 1863

ARTILLERY.—

Batty. M, 1st Mo. Arty....Jan., 1863	From Arty. 7-Div. 16-Corps........	To Arty. 2-Div. 17-Corps..........	Sept., 1863
11th Ohio Batty.........Jan., 1863	From Arty. 7-Div. 16-Corps........	To Arty. Kimball's Div. Dist. E. Ark.	July, 1863
6th Wis. Batty.........Jan., 1863	From Arty. 7-Div. 16-Corps........	To Arty. 2-Div. 17-Corps..........	Sept., 1863
12th Wis. Batty.........Jan., 1863	From Arty. 7-Div. 16-Corps........	To Arty. 2-Div. 17-Corps..........	Sept., 1863
Cogswell's Ill. Batty.....July, 1863	From Arty. 1-Div. 16-Corps........	To Arty. 2-Div. 17-Corps..........	Sept., 1863

2d DIVISION.—Organized Sept. 14, 1863, from 7th Division 17th Corps. Transferred to 15th Corps Dec. 20, 1863.

COMMANDER.

John E. Smith	Brigadier General	Sept. 14, 1863, to Dec. 20, 1863.

1st BRIGADE.— COMMANDER.

J. I. Alexander	Col. 59th Ind. Infy	Sept. 14, 1863, to Dec. 20, 1863.

48th Ind. Infy..........Sept., 1863	From 1-Brig. 7-Div. 17-Corps......	To 1-Brig. 3-Div. 15-Corps........	Dec., 1863
59th Ind. Infy..........Sept., 1863	From 1-Brig. 7-Div. 17-Corps......	To 1-Brig. 3-Div. 15-Corps........	Dec., 1863
4th Minn. Infy..........Sept., 1863	From 1-Brig. 7-Div. 17-Corps......	To 1-Brig. 3-Div. 15-Corps........	Dec., 1863
18th Wis. Infy..........Sept., 1863	From 1-Brig. 7-Div. 17-Corps......	To 1-Brig. 3-Div. 15-Corps........	Dec., 1863
63d Ill. Infy..........Sept., 1863	From 1-Brig. 7-Div. 17-Corps......	To 1-Brig. 3-Div. 15-Corps........	Dec., 1863

2d BRIGADE.— COMMANDERS.

C. R. Wever	Col. 17th Iowa Infy	Sept. 14, 1863, to Oct. 2, 1863.
G. B. Raum	Col. 56th Illinois Infy	Oct. 2, 1863, to Nov. 25, 1863.
F. C. Deimling	Col. 10th Missouri Infy	Nov. 25, 1863.
C. R. Wever	Col. 17th Iowa Infy	Nov. 25, 1863, to Dec. 20, 1863.

56th Illinois Infy.......Sept., 1863	From 2-Brig. 7-Div. 17-Corps......	To 2-Brig. 3-Div. 15-Corps........	Dec., 1863
17th Iowa Infy.........Sept., 1863	From 2-Brig. 7-Div. 17-Corps......	To 2-Brig. 3-Div. 15-Corps........	Dec., 1863
10th Missouri Infy......Sept., 1863	From 2-Brig. 7-Div. 17-Corps......	To 2-Brig. 3-Div. 15-Corps........	Dec., 1863
24th Mo. Infy. Co. E....Sept., 1863	From 2-Brig. 7-Div. 17-Corps......	To 2-Brig. 3-Div. 15-Corps........	Dec., 1863
80th Ohio Infy.........Sept., 1863	From 2-Brig. 7-Div. 17-Corps......	To 2-Brig. 3-Div. 15-Corps........	Dec., 1863

3d BRIGADE.— COMMANDERS.

C. L. Mathies	Brigadier General	Sept. 14, 1863, to Nov. 25, 1863.
B. D. Dean	Col. 26th Missouri Infy	Nov. 25, 1863.
J. Banbury	Col. 5th Iowa Infy	Nov. 25, 1863, to Dec. 20, 1863.

3d BRIGADE.—Continued.

93d Illinois Infy.......Sept., 1863	From 3-Brig. 7-Div. 17-Corps......	To 3-Brig. 3-Div. 15-Corps........	Dec.,	1863
5th Iowa Infy.........Sept., 1863	From 3-Brig. 7-Div. 17-Corps......	To 3-Brig. 3-Div. 15-Corps........	Dec.,	1863
10th Iowa Infy........Sept., 1863	From 3-Brig. 7-Div. 17-Corps......	To 3-Brig. 3-Div. 15-Corps........	Dec.,	1863
26th Missouri Infy.....Sept., 1863	From 3-Brig. 7-Div. 17-Corps......	To 3-Brig. 3-Div. 15-Corps........	Dec.,	1863

ARTILLERY.—

Cogswell's Ill. Batty....Sept., 1863	From Arty. 7-Div. 17-Corps........	To Arty. 3-Div. 15-Corps.........	Dec.,	1863
6th Wisconsin Batty....Sept., 1863	From Arty. 7-Div. 17-Corps........	To Arty. 3-Div. 15-Corps.........	Dec.,	1863
12th Wisconsin Batty...Sept., 1863	From Arty. 7-Div. 17-Corps........	To Arty. 3-Div. 15-Corps.........	Dec.,	1863

ARTILLERY BRIGADE.—Organized Sept. 27, 1864.

Batty. C, 1st Mich. Arty..Sept., 1864	From Arty. 1-Div. 17-Corps........	No change to Muster Out.........	June,	1865
1st Minnesota Batty....Sept., 1864	From Arty. 4-Div. 17-Corps........	No change to Muster Out.........	July,	1865
15th Ohio Batty........Sept., 1864	From Arty. 4-Div. 17-Corps........	No change to Muster Out.........	June,	1865

CORPS HEADQUARTERS.—

4th Ohio Indpt. Cav. Co..Dec., 1862	From Dist. Jackson 13-Corps......	To Headquarters Army Tenn......	Apr.,	1864

CAVALRY BRIGADE.—   COMMANDER.

E. F. Winslow........	Col. 4th Iowa Cav................	Dec., 1863, to Apr., 1864.		
4th Illinois Cav.........Dec., 1863	From Cav. Brig. 3-Div. 15-Corps...	To Dist. Natchez, Miss........	Apr.,	1864
5th Illinois Cav.........Dec., 1863	From Cav. Brig. 3-Div. 15-Corps...	To Cav. Brig. Dist. Vicksburg, Miss.	Apr.,	1864
11th Illinois Cav........Dec., 1863	From Cav. Brig. 3-Div. 15-Corps...	To Cav. Brig. Dist. Vicksburg, Miss.	Apr.,	1864
4th Iowa Cav...........Dec., 1863	From Cav. Brig. 3-Div. 15-Corps...	To 2-Brig. 1-Cavalry Div. 16-Corps	Apr.,	1864
10th Missouri Cav.......Dec., 1863	From Cav. Brig. 3-Div. 15-Corps...	To 2-Brig. 1-Cavalry Div. 16-Corps	Apr.,	1864

DISTRICT OF NORTHEAST LOUISIANA.—   COMMANDERS.

E. S. Dennis..........	Brigadier General.................	May 11, 1863, to July 31, 1863.	
I. F. Shepard..........	Col. 1st Miss. Infy., A. D.........	July 31, 1863, to Aug., 1863.	
J. P. Hawkins........	Brigadier General.................	Aug. 1863, to Jan., 1864.	

DETACHED BRIGADE.—   COMMANDER.

Geo. W. Neely........	Col. 131st Illinois Infy.			
63d Illinois Infy........May, 1863	From 4-Brig. 5-Div. 16-Corps......	To 2-Brig. 6-Div. 17-Corps........	June,	1863
108th Illinois Infy......May, 1863	From 2-Brig. 10-Div. 13-Corps.....	To 1-Brig. 2-Div. 16-Corps........	Aug.,	1863
120th Illinois Infy......May, 1863	From 2-Brig. 5-Div. 16-Corps......	To 3-Brig. 2-Div. 16-Corps........	Aug.,	1863
131st Illinois Infy......May, 1863	From 1-Brig. 5-Div. 16-Corps......	To Paducah, Ky., 6-Div. 16-Corps.	Aug.,	1863
10th Ill. Cav., A, D, G, K..May, 1863	From 1-Brig. 2-Cav. Div. 13-Corps.	To Unass'd 13-Corps.............	June,	1863

AFRICAN BRIGADE.—   COMMANDER.

I. F. Shepard.........	Col. 1st Miss. Infy., A. D..........			
8th La. Infy., A. D......May, 1863 (47th U. S. C. T.)	From New Organization..........	To Post Vicksburg, Miss..........	July,	1863
9th La. Infy., A. D......May, 1863 (63d U. S. C. T.)	From New Organization..........	To Post Vicksburg, Miss..........	July,	1863
11th La. Infy., A. D......May, 1863 (49th U. S. C. T.)	From New Organization..........	To Post Goodrich Landing, La.....	July,	1863
12th La. Infy., A. D......May, 1863 (50th U. S. C. T.)	From New Organization..........	To Post Vicksburg, Miss..........	July,	1863
1st Miss. Infy., A. D......May, 1863 (51st U. S. C. T.)	From New Organization..........	To Post Vicksburg, Miss..........	July,	1863
3d Miss. Infy., A. D......May, 1863 (53d U. S. C. T.)	From New Organization..........	To Post Goodrich Landing........	July,	1863

POST GOODRICH LANDING.—

1st Ark. Infy., A. D......May, 1863 (46th U. S. C. T.)	From New Organization...........	To 1-Br. U. S. C. T. Vicksb'g, Miss.	Jan.,	1864
10th La. Infy., A. D......May, 1863 (48th U. S. C. T.)	From New Organization...........	To 1-Br. U. S. C. T. Vicksb'g, Miss.	Jan.,	1864
11th La. Infy., A. D......July, 1863 (49th U. S. C. T.)	From African Brig. Dist. N. E. La.	To 1-Br. U. S. C. T. Vicksb'g, Miss.	Jan.,	1864
3d Miss. Infy., A. D......July, 1863 (53d U. S. C. T.)	From African Brig. Dist. N. E. La.	To 1-Br. U. S. C. T. Vicksb'g, Miss.	Jan.,	1864
1st Miss. Cav. A. D......Dec., 1863 (3d U. S. C. Cav.)	From New Organization...........	To 1-Br. U. S. C. T. Vicksb'g, Miss.	Jan.,	1864
1st Miss. Infy., A. D.....Mch., 1864 (53d U. S. C. T.)	From Post Vicksburg, Miss........	To 1-Br. 1-D. U. S. C. T. Vicksb'g.	Dec.,	1864
4th Miss. Infy., A. D.....Mch., 1864 (66th U. S. C. T.)	From Post Vicksburg, Miss........	To Unatt. 2-D. 7-C. Little Rock, Ark.	Nov.,	1864
2d La. Batty., A. D.....Mch., 1864 (Batty. D, 2d U. S. C. Arty.)	From Post Vicksburg, Miss........	To Res. Arty. Dist. Vicksb'g, Miss.	Dec.,	1864
1st La. Batty., A. D.....Apr., 1864 (Batty. C, 2d U. S. C. Arty.)	From 1-Brig. U. S. C. T. Vicksburg	To Post Vicksburg................	May,	1864

NINTH ARMY CORPS.—Joined from Department of Ohio June 14-17, 1863.

COMMANDER.

J. G. Parke............	Major General....................	June 14, 1863, to Aug. 18, 1863.	

1st DIVISION.—   COMMANDER.

Thomas Welsh........	Brigadier General................	June 14, 1863, to Aug. 18, 1863.	

1st BRIGADE.—   COMMANDER.

Henry Bowman........	Col. 36th Mass. Infy..............	June 14, 1863, to Aug. 18, 1863.		
36th Mass. Infy........June, 1863	From 1-Brig. 1-Div. 9-Corps Ohio.	To 1-Brig. 1-Div. 9-Corps Ohio....	Aug.,	1863
17th Michigan Infy.....June, 1863	From 1-Brig. 1-Div. 9-Corps Ohio.	To 3-Brig. 1-Div. 9-Corps Ohio....	Aug.,	1863
27th Michigan Infy.....June, 1863	From 1-Brig. 1-Div. 9-Corps Ohio.	To 2-Brig. 1-Div. 9-Corps Ohio....	Aug.,	1863
45th Penna. Infy.......June, 1863	From 1-Brig. 1-Div. 9-Corps Ohio.	To 1-Brig. 1-Div. 9-Corps Ohio....	Aug.,	1863

3d BRIGADE.—   COMMANDER.

Daniel Leasure........	Col. 100th Penna. Infy............	June 14, 1863, to Aug. 18, 1863.		
2d Michigan Infy.......June, 1863	From 1-Brig. 1-Div. 9-Corps Ohio.	To 3-Brig. 1-Div. 9-Corps Ohio....	Aug.,	1863
8th Michigan Infy......June, 1863	From 1-Brig. 1-Div. 9-Corps Ohio.	To 3-Brig. 1-Div. 9-Corps Ohio....	Aug.,	1863
20th Michigan Infy.....June, 1863	From 1-Brig. 1-Div. 9-Corps Ohio.	To 3-Brig. 1-Div. 9-Corps Ohio....	Aug.,	1863
79th New York Infy.....June, 1863	From 1-Brig. 1-Div. 9-Corps Ohio.	To 3-Brig. 1-Div. 9-Corps Ohio....	Aug.,	1863
100th Penna. Infy.......June, 1863	From 3-Brig. 1-Div. 9-Corps Ohio.	To 3-Brig. 1-Div. 9-Corps Ohio....	Aug.,	1863

ARTILLERY.—

Batty. D, Penna. Arty...June, 1863	From Arty. 1-Div. 9-Corps Ohio...	To Arty. 2-Div. 9-Corps Ohio.....	Aug., 1863

2d DIVISION.— COMMANDER.

R. B. Potter.........	Brigadier General..................	June 14, 1863, to Aug. 18, 1863.	

1st BRIGADE.— COMMANDER.

S. G. Griffin..........	Col. 6th New Hampshire Infy.....	June 14, 1863, to Aug. 18, 1863.	
6th New Hamp. Infy....June, 1863	From 1-Brig. 2-Div. 9-Corps Ohio.	To 1-Brig. 2-Div. 9-Corps Ohio....	Aug., 1863
9th New Hamp. Infy....June, 1863	From 1-Brig. 2-Div. 9-Corps Ohio.	To 1-Brig. 2-Div. 9-Corps Ohio....	Aug., 1863
7th Rhode Island Infy..June, 1863	From 1-Brig. 2-Div. 9-Corps Ohio.	To 1-Brig. 2-Div. 9-Corps Ohio....	Aug., 1863

2d BRIGADE.— COMMANDER.

E. Ferrero............	Brigadier General..................	June 14, 1863, to Aug. 18, 1863.	
35th Mass. Infy........June, 1863	From 2-Brig. 2-Div. 9-Corps Ohio.	To 2-Brig. 2-Div. 9-Corps Ohio....	Aug., 1863
11th New Hamp. Infy....June, 1863	From 2-Brig. 2-Div. 9-Corps Ohio.	To 2-Brig. 2-Div. 9-Corps Ohio....	Aug., 1863
51st New York Infy.....June, 1863	From 2-Brig. 2-Div. 9-Corps Ohio.	To 2-Brig. 2-Div. 9-Corps Ohio....	Aug., 1863
51st Penna. Infy.......June, 1863	From 2-Brig. 2-Div. 9-Corps Ohio.	To 2-Brig. 2-Div. 9-Corps Ohio....	Aug., 1863

3d BRIGADE.— COMMANDER.

B. C. Christ..........	Col. 50th Penna. Infy..........	June 14, 1863, to Aug. 18, 1863.	
29th Mass. Infy.......June, 1863	From 2-Brig. 1-Div. 9-Corps Ohio.	To 2-Brig. 1-Div. 9-Corps Ohio....	Aug., 1863
46th New York Infy....June, 1863	From 2-Brig. 1-Div. 9-Corps Ohio.	To 2-Brig. 1-Div. 9-Corps Ohio....	Aug., 1863
50th Penna. Infy.......June, 1863	From 2-Brig. 1-Div. 9-Corps Ohio.	To 2-Brig. 1-Div. 9-Corps Ohio....	Aug., 1863

ARTILLERY.—

Batty. L, 2d N. Y. Arty.June, 1863	From Arty. 2-Div. 9-Corps Ohio...	To Arty. 2-Div. 9-Corps Ohio.....	Aug., 1863

ARTILLERY RESERVE.—

Batty. E, 2d U. S. Arty..June, 1863	From Arty. 1-Div. 9-Corps Ohio...	To Arty. 1-Div. 9-Corps Ohio.....	Aug., 1863

DISTRICT OF VICKSBURG.— COMMANDERS.

H. W. Slocum........	Major General...................	Apr. 20, 1864, to Aug. 14, 1864.	
N. J. T. Dana.........	Major General...................	Aug. 14, 1864, to May 14, 1865.	
District transferred to Dept. Miss. Nov. 28, 1864.			
G. K. Warren.........	Major General...................	May 14, 1865, to June 24, 1865.	
H. W. Slocum........	Major General...................	June 24, 1865, to	

POST OF VICKSBURG, MISS.— COMMANDERS.

John McArthur........	Brigadier General..................	Apr., 1864, to Sept. 27, 1864.	
M. L. Smith..........	Brigadier General..................	Sept. 27, 1864. to June 22, 1865.	
1st Miss. Infy., A. D.....July, 1863 (51st U. S. C. T.)	From African Brig. Dist. N. E. La.	To Post Goodrich Landing.........	Mch., 1864
2d Miss. Infy., A. D.....July, 1863 (52d U. S. C. T.)	From New Organization..........	To 2-Br. 1-Div. U. S. C. T. Vicksb.	Mch., 1864
8th La. Infy., A. D......July, 1863 (47th U. S. C. T.)	From African Brig. Dist. N. E. La.	To 2-Br. 1-Div. U. S. C. T. Vicksb.	Mch., 1864
9th La. Infy., A. D......July, 1863 (63d U. S. C. T.)	From African Brig. Dist. N. E. La.	To Dist. Memphis, Tenn., 5-D. 16-C.	Nov., 1863
12th La. Infy., A. D.....July, 1863 (50th U. S. C. T.)	From African Brig. Dist. N. E. La.	To 2-Br. 1-Div. U. S. C. T. Vicksb.	Mch., 1864
1st Miss. H. Arty., A. D..Aug., 1863 (5th U. S. C. Heavy Arty.)	From New Organization..........	To Unass'd 1-D. U. S. C. T. Vicksb.	Mch., 1864
7th La. Infy., A. D......Jan., 1864 (64th U. S. C. T.)	From New Organization..........	To Unass'd 1-D. U. S. C. T. Vicksb.	Mch., 1864
4th Miss. Infy., A. D....Jan., 1864 (66th U. S. C. T.)	From New Organization..........	To Post Goodrich Landing, La....	Mch., 1864
6th Miss. Infy., A. D....Jan., 1863 (58th U. S. C. T.)	From Post Natchez, Miss..........	To Post Natchez, Miss.............	Mch., 1864
2d Miss. H. Arty., A. D..Jan., 1864 (6th U. S. C. Heavy Arty.)	From Post Natchez, Miss..........	To Post Natchez, Miss.............	Mch., 1864
2d Louisiana Batty.......Jan., 1864 (Batty. D, 2d U. S. C. Arty.)	From New Organization..........	To Post Goodrich Landing.........	Mch., 1864
Batty. C, 2d U. S. C. A..May, 1864	From Post Goodrich Landing......	To Milliken's Bend, La.........	Sept., 1864
Miss. Marine Brigade...Sept., 1864	From Unatt. Dist. Vicksburg......	No change to Muster Out.........	Feb., 1865

MALTBY'S BRIGADE.— COMMANDER.

J. A. Maltby..........	Brigadier General.		
8th Illinois Infy........Apr., 1864	From 3-Brig. 3-Div. 17-Corps.....	To 1-Brig. 2-Div. 19-Corps Gulf...	Aug., 1864
17th Illinois Infy.......Apr., 1864	From 3-Brig. 3-Div. 17-Corps.....	No change to Muster Out..........	June, 1864
124th Illinois Infy......Apr., 1864	From 1-Brig. 3-Div. 17-Corps.....	To 1-Brig. 2-Div. 19-Corps Gulf...	Oct., 1864
7th Missouri Infy.......Apr., 1864	From 3-Brig. 3-Div. 17-Corps.....	No change to Muster Out..........	June, 1864
8th Ohio Batty.........Apr., 1864	From Arty. 1-Div. 17-Corps.......	To Reserve Arty. Dept. Miss.......	Nov., 1864
26th Ohio Batty........Apr., 1864	From 32d Ohio Infy., Co. F.......	To Post Natchez, Dept. Miss......	Nov., 1864
124th Illinois Infy......Oct., 1864	From 1-Brig. 2-Div. 19-Corps Gulf	To 3-Brig. 3-Div. 16-Corps Gulf...	Feb., 1865
58th Ohio Infy.........Sept., 1864	From 1-Brig. 1-Div. 17-Corps......	No change to Muster Out.........	Sept., 1865
Batty. L, 2d Ill. Arty...Sept., 1864	From Arty. 1-Div. 17-Corps.......	To Arty. Res. Vicksb'g, Dept. Miss.	Nov., 1864
7th Ohio Batty.........Sept., 1864	From Arty. 1-Div. 17-Corps.......	To Arty. Res. Vicksb'g, Dept. Miss.	Nov., 1864
Batty. C, Penna. Arty...Sept., 1864	From Miss. Marine Brigade......	Designated Batty. E, 1st Mo. Arty.	Sept., 1864
49th U. S. C. T.........Feb., 1865	From 1-B. 1-D. U. S. C. T. D'p't Miss.	To Unass'd Dept. Miss............	June, 1865
52d U. S. C. T.........Feb., 1865	From 1-B. 1-D. U. S. C. T. D'p't Miss.	To Unass'd Dept. Miss............	June, 1865

1st COLORED BRIGADE.—

46th U. S. C. T. (1-Ark.).Jan., 1864	From Post Goodrich Landing, La..	To Milliken's Bend, La..........	Apr., 1864
48th U. S. C. T. (10-La.).Jan., 1864	From Post Goodrich Landing, La..	To 1-Br. 1-Div. U. S. C. T. Vicksb'g	Apr., 1864
49th U. S. C. T. (11-La.).Jan., 1864	From Post Goodrich Landing, La..	To 1-Br. 1-Div. U. S. C. T. Vicksb'g	Apr., 1864
53d U. S. C. T. (3-Miss.).Jan., 1864	From Post Goodrich Landing, La..	To 1-Br. 1-Div. U. S. C. T. Vicksb'g	Apr., 1864
3d U. S. C. Cav. (1-Miss.).Jan., 1864	From Post Goodrich Landing, La..	To Cav. Brig. Dist. Vicksburg.....	Apr., 1864
Batty. C, 2d U. S. C. Arty.Jan., 1864	From New Organization..........	To Post Goodrich Landing, La.....	Apr., 1864

1st DIVISION, U. S. COLORED TROOPS.— COMMANDER.

J. P. Hawkins........	Brigadier General.		

1st BRIGADE.— COMMANDERS.

I. F. Shepard.........	Brigadier General.		
F. M. Crandall........	Col. 48th U. S. C. T.		
V. E. Young..........	Col. 49th U. S. C. T.		

1st BRIGADE.—Continued.

48th U. S. C. T. (10-La.).Mch.,	1864	From 1-B. U. S. C. T. Dist. Vicksb'g	To 3-B. 1-D. Steele's Com. W. Fla.	Feb.,	1865
49th U. S. C. T. (11-La.).Mch.,	1864	From 1-B. U. S. C. T. Dist. Vicksb'g	To Maltby's Brig. Dist. Vicksburg.	Feb.,	1865
53d U. S. C. T. (3-Miss.).Mch.,	1864	From 1-B. U. S. C. T. Dist. Vicksb'g	To Maltby's Brig. Dist. Vicksburg.	Feb.,	1865
51st U. S. C. T.........Dec.,	1864	From Post Goodrich Landing, La..	To 2-Br. 1-Div. U. S. C. T. W. Fla.	Feb.,	1865

2d BRIGADE.— COMMANDER.

Hiram Scofield........	Col. 47th U. S. C. T.				
47th U. S. C. T. (8-La.).Mch.,	1864	From Post Vicksburg............	To 2-Br. 1-Div. U. S. C. T. W. Fla.	Feb.,	1865
50th U. S. C. T. (12-La.).Mch.,	1864	From Post Vicksburg............	To 2-Br. 1-Div. U. S. C. T. W. Fla.	Feb.,	1865
52d U. S. C. T. (2-Miss.).Mch.,	1864	From Post Vicksburg............	To Unatt. Dept. Miss............	Feb.,	1865
46th U. S. C. T.........Dec.,	1864	From Post Milliken's Bend, La....	To Def. New Orleans, Dept. Gulf..	Feb.,	1865

UNATTACHED.—

64th U. S. C. T............Mch.,	1864	From Post Vicksburg............	To Post Natchez, Dist. Vicksburg.	May,	1864
5th U. S. C. Heavy A....Mch.,	1864	From Post Vicksburg............	To Post Vicksburg, Dept. Miss....	Nov.,	1864
64th U. S. C. T..........Dec.,	1864	From Post Davis' Bend...........	To Post Vicksburg, Dept. Miss....	Dec.,	1864

POST NATCHEZ, MISS.— COMMANDERS.

J. M. Tuttle...........	Brigadier General................	Aug., 1863, to July, 1864.		
M. Brayman...........	Brigadier General................	July 9, 1864, to Feb. 26, 1865.		
J. W. Davidson........	Brigadier General................	Feb. 26, 1865, to May, 1865.		

30th Missouri Infy......Aug.,	1863	From 1-Brig. 1-Div. 15-Corps......	To 1-Brig. 1-Div. 17-Corps........	Apr.,	1864
6th Miss. Infy., A. D....Aug.,	1863	From New Organization..........	To Dept. Miss...................	June,	1865
(58th U. S. C. T.)					
2d Miss. H. Arty., A. D...Aug.,	1863	From New Organization..........	To Dept. Miss...................	June,	1865
(6th U. S. C. Heavy Arty.)					
28th Illinois Infy......Aug.,	1863	From 3-Brig. 4-Div. 17-Corps......	To 3-Brig. 2-Div. 19-Corps Gulf...	Aug.,	1864
Batty. K, 2d Ill. Arty....Aug.,	1863	From Arty. 4-Div. 17-Corps.......	To Cav. Div. Dist. West Tenn.....	Dec.,	1864
29th Illinois Infy......Dec.,	1863	From 1-Brig. 3-Div. 17-Corps......	To 3-Brig. 2-Div. 19-Corps Gulf...	Aug.,	1864
4th Illinois Cav........Jan.,	1864	From Cav. Brig. 17-Corps........	To 3-Brig. Cav. Div. Dist. W. Tenn.	Dec.,	1864
63d U. S. C. T..........Mch.,	1864	From Dist. Memphis 16-Corps......	To Sub. Dist. Vidalia............	Feb.,	186b
64th U. S. C. T..........May,	1864	From Un. 1-Div. U. S. C. T. Vicksb'g	To Davis Bend, La...............	Sept.,	1864
70th U. S. C. T..........Apr.,	1864	From New Organization..........	To Dept. Miss...................	June,	1865
71st U. S. C. T..........Apr.,	1864	From New Organization..........	Consolidated with 70th U. S. C. T.	Nov.,	1864
8th N. H. Infy.........Sept.,	1864	From Def. of New Orleans, La.....	To Dist. Vidalia Dept. Miss.......	Jan.,	1865
83d Ohio Infy.........Dec.,	1864	From 3-Brig. 3-Div. 19-Corps......	To 3-Brig. Res. Corps Gulf.......	Jan.,	1865
5th Ill. Cav. 5 Cos......Dec.,	1864	From Cav. Brig. Dist. Vicksburg...	To 1-Brig. Cav. Div. Dist. W. Tenn.	Jan.,	1865
26th Ohio Batty.........Dec.,	1864	From Maltby's Brig. Vicksburg.....	To Dept. Texas..................	June,	1865

MILLIKEN'S BEND, LA.—

46th U. S. C. T..........Apr.,	1864	From 1-Brig. U. S. C. T. Vicksburg.	To 2-Br. 1-Div. U. S. C. T. Vicks....	Nov.,	1864
Batty. C, 2d U. S. C. Arty..Apr.,	1864	From Post Goodrich Landing......	To Res. Arty. Dept. Miss..........	Nov.,	1864

DAVIS BEND, LA.—

64th U. S. C. T.........Sept.,	1864	From Post Natchez, Miss..........	To Unass'd 1-Div. U. S. C. T........	Dec.,	1864

CAVALRY BRIGADE.— COMMANDERS.

H. P. Mumford.........	Major 5th Ill. Cav................			
J. H. Peters...........	Lieut. Col.......................			
E. D. Osband..........	Col. 3d U. S. C. Cav.............			
L. H. Kerr.............	Col. 11th Ill. Cav...............			

5th Ill. Cav............Apr.,	1864	From Cav. Brig. 17-Corps........	To 1-Br. Cav. Div. Dist. W. Tenn...	Feb.,	1865
11th Ill. Cav...........Apr.,	1864	From Cav. Brig. 17-Corps........	To 3-Br. Cav. Div. Dist. W. Tenn...	Dec.,	1864
2d Wis. Cav............Apr.,	1864	From Cav. 1-Div. 17-Corps.......	To 3-Br. Cav. Div. Dist. W. Tenn...	Dec.,	1864
3d U. S. Colored Cav....Apr.,	1864	From ¾-Colored Brig. Dist. Vicks..	To 3-Br. Cav. Div. Dist. W. Tenn...	Dec.,	1864

UNATTACHED CAVALRY.—

9th Ind. Cav...........Mch.,	1865	From 1-Br. 7-Div. Cav. C. M. Div. M.	No change to Muster Out.........	Nov.,	1865
4th Mo. Cav...........Mch.,	1865	From 1-Br. 7-Div. Cav. C. M. Div. M.	No change to Muster Out.........	Nov.,	1865
2d Tenn. Cav...........Mch.,	1865	From 1-Br. 7-Div. Cav. C. M. Div. M.	No change to Muster Out.........	July,	1865
10th Tenn. Cav.........Mch.,	1865	From 2-Br. 7-Div. Cav. C. M. Div. M.	No change to Muster Out.........	Aug.,	1865

ARTILLERY RESERVE, DEPT. OF MISSISSIPPI.—

7th Ohio Batty..........Nov.,	1864	From Arty. Post Vicksburg.......	No change to Muster Out.........	Aug.,	1865
8th Ohio Batty..........Nov.,	1864	From Maltby's Brig. Vicksburg.....	No change to Muster Out.........	Aug.,	1865
Batty. C, 2d U. S. C. Arty..Nov.,	1864	From Milliken's Bend, La.........	No change to Muster Out.........	Dec.,	1865
Batty. D, 2d U. S. C. Arty..Nov.,	1864	From Post Goodrich Landing......	No change to Muster Out.........	Dec.,	1865
Batty. L, 2d Ill. Arty.....Nov.,	1864	From Arty. Post Vicksburg.......	No change to Muster Out.........	Aug.,	1865
Batty. E, 1st Mo. Arty....Nov.,	1864	From Arty. Post Vicksburg.......	No change to Muster Out.........	Jan.,	1865

Army and Department of the Ohio

Recreated Aug. 19, 1862, to consist of the States of Ohio, Michigan, Indiana, Illinois, Wisconsin and Kentucky, East of the Tennessee River, including Cumberland Gap. Annexed to Department of the Cumberland Jan. 17, 1865.

COMMANDING DEPARTMENT.— COMMANDERS.

H. G. Wright........	Major General......................	Aug. 23, 1862, to Mch. 25, 1863.	
A. E. Burnside........	Major General......................	Mch. 25, 1863, to Dec. 9, 1863.	
J. G. Foster..........	Major General......................	Dec. 9, 1863, to Feb. 9, 1864.	
J. M. Schofield........	Major General......................	Feb. 9, 1864, to Nov. 8, 1864.	
George Stoneman.......	Major General......................	Nov. 8, 1864, to Jan. 17, 1865.	

ARMY OF KENTUCKY.—Created Aug. 25, 1862.

COMMANDERS.

William Nelson........	Brigadier General..................		
Gordon Granger........	Major General....................	Aug. 25, 1862, to Oct. 7, 1862.	

1st BRIGADE.— COMMANDER.

M. D. Manson..........	Brigadier General................	Oct. 7, 1862, to June 8, 1863.		
16th Ind. Infy..........Aug.,	1862	From New Organization............	Captured at Richmond, Ky.........	Aug., 1862
55th Ind. Infy..........Aug.,	1862	From Camp Morton, Ind..........	Captured at Richmond, Ky.........	Aug., 1862
69th Ind. Infy..........Aug.,	1862	From New Organization..........	Captured at Richmond, Ky.........	Aug., 1862
71st Ind. Infy..........Aug.,	1862	From New Organization..........	Captured at Richmond, Ky.........	Aug., 1862

2d BRIGADE.— COMMANDER.

Charles Cruft..........	Brigadier General..................		
12th Ind. Infy...........Aug., 1862	From New Organization...........	Captured at Richmond, Ky.........	Aug., 1862
66th Ind. Infy...........Aug., 1862	From New Organization...........	Captured at Richmond, Ky.........	Aug., 1862
18th Ky. Infy...........Aug., 1862	From Unatt. Army Ohio...........	Captured at Richmond, Ky.........	Aug., 1862
95th Ohio Infy...........Aug., 1862	From New Organization...........	Captured at Richmond, Ky.........	Aug., 1862
CAVALRY.—			
6th Ky. Cav.............Aug., 1862	From Cav. 7-Div. Army Ohio......	To Dist. Louisville, Ky. Army Ky..	Oct., 1862
7th Ky. Cav.............Aug., 1862	From New Organization...........	To Unatt. Army Ky..............	Oct., 1862
ARTILLERY.—			
Batty. F, 1st Mich. Arty..Aug., 1862	From West Point, Ky.............	To 2-Brig. 2-Div. Army Ky.....	Oct., 1862

1st DIVISION.— COMMANDERS.

S. G. Burbridge........	Brigadier General.................	To Oct., 1862.................	
A. J. Smith............	Brigadier General.................	To Nov. 13, 1862.................	

1st BRIGADE.— COMMANDER.

S. G. Burbridge........	Brigadier General.................	To Nov. 13, 1862.................	
83d Ohio Infy...........Oct., 1862	From 1-Brig. 2-Div. Army Ky......	To 1-Br. 10-Div. R. W. 13-C. Tenn.	Nov., 1862
96th Ohio Infy...........Oct., 1862	From 2-Brig. 2-Div. Army Ky......	To 1-Br. 10-Div. R. W. 13-C. Tenn.	Nov., 1862
23d Wis. Infy...........Oct., 1862	From 2-Brig. 2-Div. Army Ky......	To 1-Br. 10-Div. R. W. 13-C. Tenn.	Nov., 1862
118th Ohio Infy...........Oct., 1862	From 2-Brig. 2-Div. Army Ky......	To Unatt. Army Ky..............	Nov., 1862

2d BRIGADE.— COMMANDERS.

P. T. Swayne.........	Col. 99th Ohio Infy.............	To Oct., 1862.................	
W. J. Landran.........	Col. 19th Ky. Infy.............	To Nov. 13, 1862.................	
100th Ohio Infy...........Oct., 1862	From New Organization...........	To 2-Brig. 2-Div. Army Ky......	Oct., 1862
103d Ohio Infy...........Oct., 1862	From New Organization...........	To 2-Brig. 2-Div. Army Ky......	Oct., 1862
104th Ohio Infy...........Oct., 1862	From New Organization...........	To 2-Brig. 2-Div. Army Ky......	Oct., 1862
22d Wis. Infy...........Oct., 1862	From New Organization...........	To 1-Brig. 3-Div. Army Ky......	Oct., 1862
77th Ill. Infy...........Oct., 1862	From New Organization...........	To 2-Br. 10-Div. R. W. 13-C. Tenn.	Nov., 1862
97th Ill. Infy...........Oct., 1862	From New Organization...........	To 2-Br. 10-Div. R. W. 13-C. Tenn.	Nov., 1862
108th Ill. Infy...........Oct., 1862	From New Organization...........	To 2-Br. 10-Div. R. W. 13-C. Tenn.	Nov., 1862
19th Ky. Infy...........Oct., 1862	From New Organization...........	To 2-Br. 10-Div. R. W. 13-C. Tenn.	Nov., 1862

3d BRIGADE.— COMMANDER.

C. C. Doolittle..........	Col. 18th Mich. Infy.............		
18th Mich. Infy...........Oct., 1862	From New Organization...........	To 1-Brig. 2-Div. Army Ky........	Oct., 1862
22d Mich. Infy...........Oct., 1862	From New Organization...........	To 1-Brig. 2-Div. Army Ky........	Oct., 1862
17th Ohio Batty...........Oct., 1862	From New Organization...........	To Unatt. Lexington, Ky. Dept. Ohio	Oct., 1862
CAVALRY.—			
10th Ky. Cav...........Oct., 1862	From New Organization...........	To Unatt. Lexington, Ky. Dept. Ohio	Oct., 1862

2d DIVISION.— COMMANDERS.

Green Clay Smith......	Brigadier General.................	To Oct. 14, 1862.	
Q. A. Gillmore.........	Brigadier General.................	Oct. 14, 1862, to Jan. 25, 1863.	

1st BRIGADE.— COMMANDERS.

F. W. Moore...........	Col. 83d Ohio Infy.............	To Oct. 14, 1862.	
Green Clay Smith......	Brigadier General.................	Oct. 14, 1862, to Jan., 1863.	
85th Ind. Infy...........Oct., 1862	From New Organization...........	To 1-Brig. 3-Div. Army Ky........	Oct., 1862
83d Ohio Infy...........Oct., 1862	From New Organization...........	To 1-Brig. 1-Div. Army Ky........	Oct., 1862
18th Ky. Infy...........Oct., 1862	From Unatt. Army Ky.............	To Unatt. Army Ky..............	Oct., 1862
21st Ind. Batty...........Oct., 1862	From New Organization...........	To Unatt. Army Ky..............	Oct., 1862
112th Ill. Infy...........Oct., 1862	From New Organization...........	To 3-Brig. Dist. Central Ky........	Jan., 1863
18th Mich. Infy...........Oct., 1862	From 3-Brig. Army Ky......	To 3-Brig. Dist. Central Ky........	Jan., 1863
22d Mich. Infy...........Oct., 1862	From 3-Brig. 1-Div. Army Ky......	To 3-Brig. Dist. Central Ky........	Jan., 1863
45th Ohio Infy...........Oct., 1862	From New Organization...........	To 2-Brig. Dist. Central Ky........	Jan., 1863
18th Ky. Infy...........Oct., 1862	From Unatt. Army Ky.............	To Crook's Br. Baird's 3-Div. A. Ky.	Feb., 1863

2d BRIGADE.— COMMANDERS.

J. W. Vance...........	Col. 96th Ohio Infy.............	Oct., 1862.	
S. A. Gilbert.........	Col. 44th Ohio Infy.............	Oct., 1862, to Jan., 1863.	
96th Ohio Infy...........Oct., 1862	From New Organization...........	To 1-Brig. 1-Div. Army Ky........	Oct., 1862
118th Ohio Infy...........Oct., 1862	From New Organization...........	To 1-Brig. 1-Div. Army Ky........	Oct., 1862
23d Wis. Infy...........Oct., 1862	From New Organization...........	To 1-Brig. 1-Div. Army Ky........	Oct., 1862
Batty. F, 1st Mich. Arty..Oct., 1862	From Cruft's Brig. Army Ky......	To Dist. of Louisville, Ky........	Oct., 1862
44th Ohio Infy...........Oct., 1862	From 3-Brig. Kanawha Div. W. Va.	To 1-Brig. Dist. Central Ky........	Jan., 1863
100th Ohio Infy...........Oct., 1862	From 2-Brig. 1-Div. Army Ky......	To 1-Brig. Dist. Central Ky........	Jan., 1863
103d Ohio Infy...........Oct., 1862	From 2-Brig. 1-Div. Army Ky......	To 1-Brig. Dist. Central Ky........	Jan., 1863
104th Ohio Infy...........Oct., 1862	From 2-Brig. 1-Div. Army Ky......	To 1-Brig. Dist. Central Ky........	Jan., 1863
24th Ky. Infy...........Nov., 1862	From 2-Br. 1-Div. L. W. 14-Corps.	To 1-Brig. Dist. Central Ky........	Jan., 1863
ARTILLERY.—			
18th Ohio Batty...........Oct., 1862	From Unatt. Army Ky.............	To Reed's Br. Baird's 3-Div. A. Ky.	Feb., 1863
19th Ohio Batty...........Dec., 1862	From Unatt. Army Ky.............	To Dist. Central Ky.............	Jan., 1863

3d DIVISION.— COMMANDER.

Absalom Baird........	Brigadier General.................		

1st BRIGADE.— COMMANDER.

John Coburn..........	Col. 33d Ind. Infy.............		
33d Ind. Infy.............Oct., 1862	From 27-Brig. 7-Div. Army Ohio....	To Coburn's Br. Baird's Div. Cumb'd.	Feb., 1863
85th Ind. Infy...........Oct., 1862	From 1-Brig. 2-Div. Army Ky......	To Coburn's Br. Baird's Div. Cumb'd.	Feb., 1863
19th Mich. Infy...........Oct., 1862	From New Organization...........	To Coburn's Br. Baird's Div. Cumb'd.	Feb., 1863
22d Wis. Infy...........Oct., 1862	From 2-Brig. 1-Div. Army Ky......	To Coburn's Br. Baird's Div. Cumb'd.	Feb., 1863

2d BRIGADE.— COMMANDERS.

P. T. Swayne.........	Col. 99th Ohio Infy.............	Oct., 1862, to Nov., 1862.	
J. C. Cochran.........	Col. 14th Ky. Infy.............	Nov., 1862, to Feb., 1863.	
92d Ill. Infy.............Oct., 1862	From New Organization...........	To 2-Br. Baird's 3-Div. A'y Ky. Cbd.	Feb., 1863
96th Ill. Infy...........Oct., 1862	From New Organization...........	To 2-Br. Baird's 3-Div. A'y Ky. Cbd.	Feb., 1863
115th Ill. Infy...........Oct., 1862	From New Organization...........	To 2-Br. Baird's 3-Div. A'y Ky. Cbd.	Feb., 1863
14th Ky. Infy...........Oct., 1862	From 27-Brig. 7-Div. Army Ohio...	To Dist. Eastern Ky.............	Feb., 1863

ARTILLERY.—

19th Ohio Batty..........Oct., 1862	From New Organization............	To Unatt. Lexington, Ky...........	Oct.,	1862
21st Ind. Batty..........Dec., 1862	From Unatt. Army Ky.............	To Crook's Br. Baird's Div. A. Ky..	Feb.,	1863
9th Ohio Batty..........Dec., 1862	From Unatt. Army Ky.............	To Coburn's Br. Baird's Div. A. Ky.	Feb.,	1863

DISTRICT OF LOUISVILLE, KY.—Merged into Western District Ky. Nov. 17, 1862.

COMMANDER.

J. T. Boyle..........|Brigadier General.................|

50th Ind. Infy............Oct., 1862	From Unass'd Army Ohio...........	To 2-Brig. 1-Div. L. W. 14-Corps..	Nov., 1862
70th Ind. Infy............Oct., 1862	From New Organization............	To Ward's Br. Dumont's Div. Cum.	Nov., 1862
97th Ind. Infy............Oct., 1862	From New Organization............	To 3-Brig. Dist. Memphis 13-Corps.	Nov., 1862
99th Ind. Infy............Oct., 1862	From New Organization............	To 3-Brig. Dist. Memphis 13-Corps.	Nov., 1862
9th Mich. Infy, 4 Cos....Oct., 1862	From 23d Indpt. Brig. Army Ohio..	To Headquarters 14-Corps Cumb'd..	Nov., 1862
25th Mich. Infy...........Oct., 1862	From New Organization............	To Dist. Western Ky.............	Nov., 1862
28th Ky. Infy.............Oct., 1862	From Dumont's Indpt. Br. Army Ohio	To Dist. Western Ky.............	Nov., 1862
Batty. F, 1st Mich. Arty..Oct., 1862	From 2-Brig. 2-Div. Army Ky......	To Dist. Western Ky.............	Nov., 1862
Batty. M, 1st Ill. Arty....Oct., 1862	From New Organization............	To Dist. Western Ky.............	Nov., 1862
4th Ky. Cav.............Oct., 1862	From 1-Brig. Cav. Div. Army Ohio.	To Dist. Western Ky.............	Nov., 1862
6th Ky. Cav.............Oct., 1862	From Unatt. 7-Div. Army Ohio....	To Unatt. Army Ky.............	Nov., 1862
8th Ky. Cav.............Oct., 1862	From New Organization............	To Dist. Western Ky.............	Nov., 1862
9th Penna. Cav..........Oct., 1862	From 3-Brig. Cav. Div. Army Ohio.	To Dist. Central Ky.............	Nov., 1862

DISTRICT OF THE KANAWHA, W. VA.—Assigned Sept., 1862.

COMMANDER.

J. A. J. Lightburn......|Col. 4th W. Va. Infy.............|

34th Ohio Infy............Sept, 1862	From 2-Brig. Kanawha Div. W. Va.	To 2-Br. 3-Div. 8-C. Middle Dept..	Mch., 1863
37th Ohio Infy............Sept, 1862	From 2-Brig. Kanawha Div. W. Va.	To 2-Br. 3-Div. 8-C. Middle Dept..	Mch., 1863
44th Ohio Infy............Sept, 1862	From 3-Brig. Kanawha Div. W. Va.	To 2-Brig. 2-Div. Army Ky......	Sept., 1862
47th Ohio Infy............Sept, 1862	From 3-Brig. Kanawha Div. W. Va.	To 3-Brig. 2-Div. 15-Corps Tenn...	Jan., 1862
4th W. Va. Infy..........Sept, 1862	From 4-Brig. Kanawha Div. W. Va.	To 3-Brig. 2-Div. 15-Corps Tenn...	Jan., 1863
9th W. Va. Infy..........Sept, 1862	From 4-Brig. Kanawha Div. W. Va.	To Milroy's Com. Winchester, 8-C..	Jan., 1863
13th W. Va. Infy.........Sept, 1862	From New Organization............	To 1-Br. 3-Div. 8-C. Middle Dept...	Mch., 1863
2d W. Va. Cav..........Sept, 1862	From Unatt. Kanawha Div. W. Va..	To Un. 3-Div. 8-Corps Middle Dept.	Mch., 1863
5th W. Va. Infy.........Oct., 1862	From Milroy's Br. 1-Corps A. Va..	To 1-Br. 3-Div. 8-Corps Middle Dept.	Mch., 1863
8th W. Va. Infy.........Oct., 1862	From 1-Br. 3-Div. 11-Corps Pot...	To 4th Separate Brig. 8-Corps......	Jan., 1863
89th Ohio Infy...........Oct., 1862	From New Organization............	To Crook's Brig. Army Ky. Cumb'd..	Jan., 1863
91st Ohio Infy...........Oct., 1862	From New Organization............	To 2-Br. 3-Div. 8-C. Middle Dept..	Mch., 1863
92d Ohio Infy...........Oct., 1862	From New Organization............	To Crook's Brig. Army Ky. Cumb'd..	Jan., 1863
Simmond's Ky. Batty....Oct., 1862	From Kanawha Div. 9-Corps Pot....	To 1-Brig. 3-Div. 8-C. Middle Dept..	Mch., 1863

KANAWHA DIVISION.—

COMMANDERS.

George Crook.........|Brigadier General.................|
E. P. Scammon.........|Brigadier General.................|

1st BRIGADE.—

12th Ohio Infy............Oct., 1862	From 1-Br. Kanawha Div. 9-C. Pot.	To 2-Brig. 3-Div. 8-Corps..........	Mch., 1863
23d Ohio Infy............Oct., 1862	From 1-Br. Kanawha Div. 9-C. Pot.	To 1-Brig. 3-Div. 8-Corps..........	Mch., 1863
30th Ohio Infy............Oct., 1862	From 1-Br. Kanawha Div. 9-C. Pot.	To 3-Brig. 2-Div. 15-Corps Tenn....	Jan., 1863

2d BRIGADE.—   **COMMANDER.**

E. B. Andrews........|Col. 36th Ohio Infy.............|

11th Ohio Infy............Oct., 1862	From 2-Br. Kanawha Div. 9-C. Pot.	To Crook's Brig. Army Ky. Cumb'd..	Jan., 1863
28th Ohio................Oct., 1862	From 2-Br. Kanawha Div. 9-C. Pot.	To Clarksburg, W. Va. 8-Corps......	Jan., 1863
36th Ohio Infy............Oct., 1862	From 2-Br. Kanawha Div. 9-C. Pot.	To Crook's Brig. Army Ky. Cumb'd..	Jan., 1863

3d BRIGADE.—   **COMMANDER.**

J. Crainor.............|Col. 40th Ohio Infy.............|

84th Ind. Infy............Oct., 1862	From New Organization............	To Dist. Eastern Ky. Dept. Ohio...	Nov., 1862
40th Ohio Infy...........Oct., 1862	From Dist. Eastern Ky............	To Dist. Eastern Ky. Dept. Ohio...	Nov., 1862
1st Ohio Batty...........Oct., 1862	From 1-Br. Kanawha Div. 9-C. Pot.	To 2-Br. 3-Div. 8-Corps Middle Dept.	Mch., 1863

CAVALRY.—

Schambeck's Ill. Cav......Oct., 1862	From Kanawha Div. 9-Corps Pot...	To 4th Sep. Brig. 8-Corps..........	Mch., 1863
3d Indpt. Co. Ohio Cav...Oct., 1862	From Kanawha Div. 9-Corps Pot...	To 4th Sep. Brig. 8-Corps..........	Mch., 1863

RAILROAD DISTRICT, W. VA.—   **COMMANDER.**

B. F. Kelly............|Brigadier General.................|

6th W. Va. Infy..........Sept., 1862	From R. R. Dist. 8-Corps Mid. Dept.	To Clarksburg, W. Va. 8-Corps.....	Jan., 1863
10th W. Va. Infy.........Sept., 1862	From R. R. Dist. 8-Corps Mid. Dept.	To Milroy's Com. Winchester 8-C..	Jan., 1863
11th W. Va. Infy.........Sept., 1862	From R. R. Dist. 8-Corps Mid. Dept.	To Parkersburg, W. Va. 8-Corps....	Jan., 1863
12th W. Va. Infy.........Sept., 1862	From R. R. Dist. 8-Corps Mid. Dept.	To Milroy's Com. Winchester 8-C..	Jan., 1863
14th W. Va. Infy.........Sept., 1862	From New Organization............	To New Creek, W. Va. 8-Corps......	Jan., 1863
15th W. Va. Infy.........Sept., 1862	From New Organization............	To Sir John's Run 8-Corps........	Jan., 1863
106th N. Y. Infy..........Sept., 1862	From R. R. Dist. 8-Corps Mid. Dept.	To Martinsburg, W. Va. 8-Corps...	Jan., 1863
23d Ill. Infy.............Sept., 1862	From R. R. Dist. 8-Corps Mid. Dept.	To New Creek, W. Va. 8-Corps......	Jan., 1863
65th Ill. Infy.............Sept., 1862	From R. R. Dist. 8-Corps Mid. Dept.	To Miles' Com. Harper's Ferry....	Sept., 1862
54th Penna. Infy..........Sept., 1862	From R. R. Dist. 8-Corps Mid. Dept.	To North Mountain 8-Corps........	Jan., 1863
2d Md. P. H. B. Infy....Sept., 1862	From R. R. Dist. 8-Corps Mid. Dept.	To Cumberland, Md. 8-Corps........	Jan., 1863
87th Penna. Infy..........Sept., 1862	From R. R. Dist. 8-Corps Mid. Dept.	To Milroy's Com. Winchester 8-C..	Jan., 1863
110th Ohio Infy..........Oct., 1862	From New Organization............	To Milroy's Com. Winchester 8-C.	Jan., 1863
122d Ohio Infy..........Oct., 1862	From New Organization............	To Milroy's Com. Winchester 8-C.	Jan., 1863
126th Ohio Infy..........Oct., 1862	From New Organization............	To Martinsburg, W. Va............	Jan., 1863
116th Ohio Infy..........Nov., 1862	From New Organization............	To Romney, W. Va. 8-Corps.......	Jan., 1863
123d Ohio Infy..........Nov., 1862	From New Organization............	To Romney, W. Va. 8-Corps.......	Jan., 1863
1st W. Va. Infy.........Nov., 1862	From Unass'd Wheeling, W. Va.....	To North Mountain 8-Corps........	Jan., 1863

CAVALRY.—

Ringgold Pa. Cav.........Sept., 1862	From R. R. Dist. 8-Corps. Mid. Dept.	To Romney, W. Va. 8-Corps.......	Jan., 1863
Washington Pa. Cav......Sept., 1862	From R. R. Dist. 8-Corps. Mid. Dept.	To Springfield, W. Va. 8-Corps....	Jan., 1863
Loudoun Rangers........Sept., 1862	From R. R. Dist. 8-Corps. Mid. Dept.	To Point of Rocks, Md. 8-Corps....	Jan., 1863
1st W. Va. Cav. Det....Sept., 1862	From Def. of Washington, D. C....	To Milroy's Command Winchester...	Jan., 1863
14th Penna. Cav........Dec., 1862	From New Organization............	To Def. Upper Potomac 8-Corps....	Jan., 1863

ARTILLERY.—

Batty. B, 1st W. Va. Arty.Sept., 1862	From Def. Washington, D. C.......	To Milroy's Command Winchester..	Jan., 1863
Batty. D, 1st W. Va. Arty.Sept., 1862	From New Organization............	To Milroy's Command Winchester..	Jan., 1863
Batty. E, 1st W. Va. Arty.Sept., 1862	From New Organization............	To Romney, W. Va. 8-Corps........	Jan., 1863
Batty. F, 1st W. Va. Arty.Sept., 1862	From R. R. Dist. 8-Corps Mid. Dept.	To Martinsburg, W. Va. 8-Corps....	Jan., 1863
Batty. G, 1st W. Va. Arty.Sept., 1862	From R. R. Dist. 8-Corps Mid. Dept.	To Romney, W. Va. 8-Corps........	Jan., 1863
Batty. L, 1st Ill. Arty......Sept., 1862	From R. R. Dist. 8-Corps Mid. Dept.	To New Creek, W. Va. 8-Corps......	Jan., 1863

CUMBERLAND DIVISION.— COMMANDER.

George W. Morgan.....	Brigadier General	

1st BRIGADE.— COMMANDER.

J. G. Spear..........	Brigadier General			
3d Tenn. Infy..........Oct., 1862	From 25-Brig. 7-Div. Army Ohio....	To 1-Brig. 2-Div. Centre 14-Corps...	Nov.,	1862
4th Tenn. Infy..........Oct., 1862	From 25-Brig. 7-Div. Army Ohio....	To 1st Tenn. Cav....................	Nov.,	1862
5th Tenn. Infy..........Oct., 1862	From 25-Brig. 7-Div. Army Ohio....	To 1-Brig. 2-Div. Centre 14-Corps...	Nov.,	1862
6th Tenn. Infy..........Oct., 1862	From 25-Brig. 7-Div. Army Ohio....	To 1-Brig. 2-Div. Centre 14-Corps...	Nov.,	1862

3d BRIGADE.— COMMANDER.

D. W. Lindsey........	Col. 22d Ky. Infy................			
49th Ind. Infy..........Oct., 1862	From 24-Brig. 7-Div. Army Ohio....	To 2-Brig. 9-Div. R. W. 13-C. Tenn..	Nov.,	1862
7th Ky. Infy..........Oct., 1862	From 24-Brig. 7-Div. Army Ohio....	To 2-Brig. 9-Div. R. W. 13-C. Tenn..	Nov.,	1862
1st Tenn. Infy..........Oct., 1862	From 24-Brig. 7-Div. Army Ohio....	To 1-Brig. 2-Div. Centre 14-Corps...	Nov.,	1862
2d Tenn. Infy..........Oct., 1862	From 24-Brig. 7-Div. Army Ohio....	To 1-Brig. 2-Div. Centre 14-Corps...	Nov.,	1862

4th BRIGADE.— COMMANDER.

A. Baird	Brigadier General			
22d Ky. Infy..........Oct., 1862	From 26-Brig. 7-Div. Army Ohio....	To 3-Brig. 9-Div. R. W. 13-C. Tenn..	Nov.,	1862
16th Ohio Infy..........Oct., 1862	From 26-Brig. 7-Div. Army Ohio....	To 3-Brig. 9-Div. R. W. 13-C. Tenn..	Nov.,	1862
42d Ohio Infy..........Oct., 1862	From 26-Brig. 7-Div. Army Ohio....	To 3-Brig. 9-Div. R. W. 13-C. Tenn..	Nov.,	1862

ARTILLERY.—

Batty. G, 1st Mich. Arty..Oct., 1862	From Arty. 7-Div. Army Ohio......	To Arty. 9-Div. R. W. 13-C. Tenn...	Nov.,	1862
1st Wis. Batty..........Oct., 1862	From Arty. 7-Div. Army Ohio......	To Arty. 9-Div. R. W. 13-C. Tenn...	Nov.,	1862

CAVALRY.—

1st East Tenn. Cav......Oct., 1862	From 7-Div. Army Ohio...........	To Unatt. Cav. 14-Corps Cumb'd....	Nov.,	1862
2d East Tenn. Cav......Oct., 1862	From 7-Div. Army Ohio...........	To Unatt. Cav. 14-Corps Cumb'd....	Nov.,	1862

UNATTACHED, ARMY KENTUCKY.—

18th Ky. Infy..........Oct., 1862	From 1-Brig. 2-Div. Army Ky......	To 1-Brig. 2-Div. Army Ky........	Dec.,	1862
120th Ohio Infy..........Oct., 1862	From New Organization...........	To 1-Brig. 9-Div. R. W. 13-C. Tenn..	Nov.,	1862
4th Ind. Cav..........Oct., 1862	From New Organization...........	To Dist. Western Ky..............	Nov.,	1862
10th Ky. Cav..........Oct., 1862	From 1-Div. Army Ky............	To Dist. Central Ky..............	Dec.,	1862
21st Ind. Batty..........Oct., 1862	From 1-Brig. 2-Div. Army Ky......	To Arty. 3-Div. Army Ky........	Dec.,	1862
9th Ohio Batty..........Oct., 1862	From Arty. 7-Div. Army Ohio.....	To Arty. 3-Div. Army Ky........	Dec.,	1862
17th Ohio Batty..........Oct., 1862	From 3-Brig. 1-Div. Army Ky.....	To Arty. 10-Div. R. W. 13-C. Tenn...	Nov.,	1862
18th Ohio Batty..........Oct., 1862	From New Organization...........	To Arty. 2-Div. Army Ky........	Dec.,	1862
19th Ohio Batty..........Oct., 1862	From Arty. 3-Div. Army Ky......	To Arty. 2-Div. Army Ky........	Dec.,	1862
118th Ohio Infy..........Nov., 1862	From 1-Brig. 1-Div. Army Ky.....	To Dist. Central Ky..............	Nov.,	1862

RAILROAD GUARD, LOUISVILLE & NASHVILLE R. R.—

78th Ill. Infy..........Oct., 1862	From 39-Brig. 12-Div. Army Ohio...	To Dist. Western Ky..............	Nov.,	1862
91st Ill. Infy..........Oct., 1862	From New Organization...........	Prisoners of War.................	Dec.,	1862
107th Ill. Infy..........Oct., 1862	From New Organization...........	To Dist. Western Ky..............	Nov.,	1862

DISTRICT OF WESTERN KENTUCKY.—Constituted Nov. 17, 1862.

COMMANDERS.

J. T. Boyle.............	Brigadier General	Nov. 17, 1862, to Apr. 4, 1863.	
H. G. Wright.........	Major General	Nov. 17, 1862, to Apr. 4, 1863.	

34th BRIGADE.— COMMANDER.

S. A. Strickland........	Col. 50th Ohio Infy...........			
80th Ind. Infy..........Nov., 1862	From 34-Brig. 10-Div. 1-C. A'y Ohio.	To 2-Brig. 3-Div. 23-Corps Ohio.....	June,	1863
50th Ohio Infy..........Nov., 1862	From 34-Brig. 10-Div. 1-C. A'y Ohio.	To Unass'd 2-Div. 23-Corps Ohio....	June,	1863
98th Ohio Infy..........Nov., 1862	From 34-Brig. 10-Div. 1-C. A'y Ohio.	To Reed's Brig. Baird's Div. A'y Ky.	Feb.,	1863
121st Ohio Infy..........Nov., 1862	From 34-Brig. 10-Div. 1-C. A'y Ohio.	To Reed's Brig. Baird's Div. A'y Ky.	Feb.,	1863
Batty. M, 1st Ill. Arty..Nov., 1862	From Dist. Louisville, Ky..........	To Reed's Brig. Baird's Div. A'y Ky.	Feb.,	1863
78th Ill. Infy..........Nov., 1862	From Guard Louisv. & Nashv. R. R.	Prisoners of War..................	Dec.,	1862
104th Ill. Infy..........Nov., 1862	From 39-Brig. 12-Div. Army Ohio...	To 1-Brig. 3-Div. 23-Corps Ohio.....	June,	1863
107th Ill. Infy..........Nov., 1862	From Guard Louisv. & Nashv. R. R.	To 2-Brig. 3-Div. Res. Corps Cumb'd.	June,	1863
129th Ill. Infy..........Nov., 1862	From 38-Brig. 12-Div. Army Ohio...	To Clarksville, Tenn., Dept. Cumb'd.	Dec.,	1862
102d Ohio Infy..........Nov., 1862	From 38-Brig. 12-Div. Army Ohio...	Prisoners of War..................	Dec.,	1862
106th Ohio Infy..........Nov., 1862	From 39-Brig. 12-Div. Army Ohio...	Prisoners of War..................	Dec.,	1862
108th Ohio Infy..........Nov., 1862	From 39-Brig. 12-Div. Army Ohio...	To 1-Brig. 3-Div. 23-Corps Ohio.....	June,	1863
111th Ohio Infy..........Nov., 1862	From 38-Brig. 12-Div. Army Ohio...	To Reed's Brig. Baird's Div. A'y Ky.	Feb.,	1863
113th Ohio Infy..........Nov., 1862	From New Organization...........	To 2-Brig. 3-Div. 23-Corps Ohio.....	June,	1863
13th Ky. Infy..........Nov., 1862	From 11-Brig. 5-Div. 2-C. A'y Ohio.	To 1-Brig. 3-Div. 21Corps Cumb'd...	June,	1863
17th Ky. Infy..........Nov., 1862	From Dist. of Nashville, Tenn......	To Unass'd 2-Div. 23-Corps Ohio....	June,	1863
20th Ky. Infy..........Nov., 1862	From 22-Brig. 4-Div. 2-C. A'y Ohio.	To Unass'd 2-Div. 23-Corps Ohio....	June,	1863
26th Ky. Infy..........Nov., 1862	From 14-Brig. 5-Div. 2-C. A'y Ohio.	To Unass'd 2-Div. 23-Corps Ohio....	June,	1863
27th Ky. Infy..........Nov., 1862	From 19-Brig. 4-Div. 2-C. A'y Ohio.	To Post Clarksville, Tenn., Cumb'd..	Dec.,	1862
28th Ky. Infy..........Nov., 1862	From Dist. Louisville, Ky..........	To 2-Brig. Dist. Central Ky........	Apr.,	1863
32d Ky. Infy..........Nov., 1862	From New Organization...........	To Franklin, Tenn., A'y Ky. Cumb'd.	Feb.,	1863
124th Ohio Infy..........Dec., 1862	From New Organization...........	To Franklin, Tenn. A'y Ky. Cumb'd.	Feb.,	1863
125th Ohio Infy..........Dec., 1862	From New Organization...........	To 1-Brig. 3-Div. 23-Corps Ohio.....	June,	1863
12th Ky. Infy..........Dec., 1862	From 1-Brig. 3-Div. Centre 14-Corps.	To 2-Brig. 3-Div. 23-Corps Ohio.....	June,	1863
16th Ky. Infy..........Dec., 1862	From Unatt. Army Ohio..........	To Unass'd 2-Div. 23-Corps Ohio....	June,	1863
33d Ky. Infy..........Dec., 1862	From New Organization...........	To Unass'd 2-Div. 23-Corps Ohio....	June,	1863
34th Ky. Infy..........Dec., 1862	From New Organization...........	To 1-Brig. 3-Div. 23-Corps Ohio.....	June,	1863
23d Mich. Infy..........Dec., 1862	From 38-Brig. 12-Div. Army Ohio...	To Unatt. 2-Div. 23-Corps Ohio....	June,	1863
25th Mich. Infy..........Dec., 1862	From Dist. Louisville, Ky..........	To Unatt. 2-Div. 23-Corps Ohio....	June,	1863
63d Ind. Infy..........Dec., 1862	From New Organization...........	To 1-Brig. 2-Div. 23-Corps Ohio.....	June,	1863
65th Ind. Infy..........Dec., 1862	From New Organization...........	To Post Gal'tin, Tenn., Dept. Cumb'd.	June,	1863
91st Ind. Infy..........Dec., 1862	From Prisoners of War...........	To Post Gal'tin, Tenn., Dept. Cumb'd.	June,	1863
106th Ohio Infy..........Mch., 1863	From Prisoners of War...........	To 3-Brig. 3-Div. 23-Corps Ohio.....	June,	1863
11th Ky. Infy..........Apr., 1862	From 1-Brig. 3-Div. 21-C. Cumb'd...	To 3-Brig. 3-Div. 23-Corps Ohio.....	June,	1863

ARTILLERY.—

Elgin (Ill.) Batty........Nov., 1862	From New Organization...........	To 1-Brig. 3-Div. 23-Corps Ohio.....	June,	1863
1st Tenn. Batty..........Nov., 1862	From Post Nashville, Tenn., Cumb'd.	To Garrison Clarksville, Tenn......	Dec.,	1862
Batty. F, 1st Mich. Arty..Nov., 1862	From Dist. Louisville, Ky..........	To Unass'd 2-Div. 23-Corps Ohio....	June,	1863
Henshaw's Ill. Batty......Dec., 1862	From New Organization...........	To 1-Brig. 3-Div. 23-Corps Ohio.....	June,	1863
20th Ind. Batty..........Dec., 1862	From New Organization...........	To Post Nashville, Tenn., Cumb'd...	May,	1863
24th Ind. Batty..........Mch., 1863	From New Organization...........	To 2-Brig. 3-Div. 23-Corps.........	June,	1863

CAVALRY.—

4th Ind. Cav..........Nov., 1862	From Unatt. Army Ky.............	To 2-Brig. 1-Cav. Div. Cumb'd......	Mch., 1863
4th Ky. Cav..........Nov., 1862	From 1-Brig. Cav. Div. Army Ohio.	To 1-Brig. 1-Cav. Div. Cumb'd......	Mch., 1863
8th Ky. Cav..........Nov., 1862	From Dist. Louisville, Ky.........	To 1-Brig. 2-Div. 23-Corps Ohio..	June, 1863
9th Ky. Cav..........Nov., 1862	From 3-Brig. Cav. Div. Army Ohio.	To 1-Brig. 3-Div. 23-Corps Ohio..	June, 1863
11th Ky. Cav..........Nov., 1862	From New Organization............	To 2-Brig. 3-Div. 23-Corps Ohio..	June, 1863
12th Ky. Cav..........Nov., 1862	From New Organization............	To 2-Brig. 3-Div. 23-Corps Ohio..	June, 1863
5th Ind. Cav..........Mch., 1863	From New Organization............	To 1-Brig. 3-Div. 23-Corps Ohio..	June, 1863
14th Ill. Cav..........Mch., 1863	From New Organization............	To 1-Brig. 3-Div. 23-Corps Ohio..	June, 1863
3d Ky. Cav..........Mch., 1863	From 1-Brig. 1-Cav. Div. Cumb'd...	To 1-Brig. 2-Div. 23-Corps Ohio..	June, 1863

DISTRICT OF EASTERN KENTUCKY.—   COMMANDER.

J. Crainor..............	Col. 40th Ohio Infy..............		
40th Ohio Infy.........Nov., 1862	From 3-Br. Kanawha Div. Dist. W. V.	To 2-Br. Baird's 3-Div. A'y Ky. Cum.	Feb., 1863
117th Ohio Infy.........Nov., 1862	From New Organization............	Designation changed to 2d Ohio H. A.	May, 1863
84th Ind. Infy.........Nov., 1862	From 3-Br. Kanawha Div. Dist. W. V.	To 2-Br. Baird's 3-Div. A'y Ky. Cum.	Feb., 1863
McLaughlin's Ohio Cav...Nov., 1862	From Dist. Eastern Ky............	To 1-Brig. 4-Div. 23-Corps Ohio..	June, 1863
10th Ky. Cav. (2d Battn).Nov., 1862	From Unatt. Army Ky.............	To 1-Brig. 4-Div. 23-Corps Ohio..	June, 1863
14th Ky. Infy.........Feb., 1863	From 2-Brig. 3-Div. Army Ky......	To 1-Brig. 4-Div. 23-Corps Ohio..	June, 1863

DISTRICT OF CENTRAL KENTUCKY.—   COMMANDERS.

Gordon Granger	Brigadier General	Nov. 17, 1862, to Jan. 25, 1863.	
Q. A. Gillmore..........	Brigadier General	Jan. 25, 1863, to Apr. 10, 1863.	
O. B. Willcox..........	Brigadier General	Apr. 10, 1863, to June 4, 1863.	
S. D. Sturgis..........	Brigadier General	June 4, 1863, to June 24, 1863.	
118th Ohio Infy.........Nov., 1862	From Unatt. Army Ky.............	To 2-Brig. 4-Div. 23-Corps Ohio..	June, 1863
8th Tenn. Infy.........Nov., 1862	From New Organization............	To 2-Brig. 4-Div. 23-Corps Ohio..	June, 1863
6th Ky. Cav..........Nov., 1862	From Unatt. Louisville, Ky........	To 1-Brig. 1-Cav. Div. Cumb'd.....	Mch., 1863
7th Ky. Cav..........Nov., 1862	From New Organization Louisville..	To 1-Brig. 1-Cav. Div. Cumb'd.....	Mch., 1863
10th Ky. Cav..........Nov., 1862	From Unatt. Army Ky.............	To 2-Brig. 4-Div. 23-Corps Ohio..	June, 1863
14th Ky. Cav..........Nov., 1862	From New Organization............	To 2-Brig. 4-Div. 23-Corps Ohio..	June, 1863
2d Mich. Cav..........Nov., 1862	From 3-Brig. Cav. Div. Army Ohio..	To 1-Brig. 1-Cav. Div. Cumb'd.....	Jan., 1863
7th Ohio Cav..........Nov., 1862	From New Organization............	To 2-Brig. Dist. Central Ky......	Jan., 1863
9th Penna. Cav..........Dec., 1862	From Dist. Louisville, Ky.........	To 1-Brig. 1-Cav. Div. Cumb'd.....	Mch., 1863
19th Ohio Batty.........Jan., 1863	From Arty. 2-Div. Army Ky........	To 2-Brig. 4-Div. 23-Corps Ohio..	June, 1863
108th Ohio Infy.........Mch., 1863	From Prisoners of War............	To 3-Brig. 2-Div. Res. Corps Cumb'd.	June, 1863
1st Tenn. Infy.........Apr., 1863	From 1-Brig. 2-Div. 14-C. Cumb'd...	To 1-Brig. 1-Div. 23-Corps Ohio..	June, 1863
65th Ill. Infy.........Apr., 1863	From Reorganization	To 1-Brig. 1-Div. 23-Corps Ohio..	June, 1863
1st Ky. Cav..........Apr., 1863	From Post Gallatin, Tenn., Cumb'd..	To 1-Brig. 1-Div. 23-Corps Ohio..	June, 1863
5th Tenn. Cav. (4 Co's)..Apr., 1863	From New Organization............	To 2-Brig. 4-Div. 23-Corps Ohio..	June, 1863
9th Ohio Cav. (1st Batt.)..Apr., 1863	From New Organization............	To 2-Brig. 1-Div. 23-Corps Ohio..	June, 1863
Wilder's Ind. Batty.....Apr., 1863	From Reorganization	To 2-Brig. 1-Div. 23-Corps Ohio..	June, 1863
15th Ind. Batty.........Apr., 1863	From Prisoners of War............	To 2-Brig. 1-Div. 23-Corps Ohio..	June, 1863
Batty. E, 2d U. S. Arty...Apr., 1863	From Arty. 1-Div. 9-Corps Ohio....	To Arty. 1-Div. 9-Corps Ohio.....	June, 1863
1st Tenn. Batty.........Apr., 1863	From Clarksville, Tenn., Cumb'd....	To 1-Brig. 1-Div. 23-Corps Ohio..	June, 1863

EAST TENNESSEE BRIGADE.—   COMMANDER.

J. G. Spear............	Brigadier General		
3d Tenn. Infy.........Apr., 1863	From 1-Brig. 2-Div. 14-C. Cumb'd...	To 3-Brig. 3-Div. 23-Corps Ohio..	June, 1863
5th Tenn. Infy.........Apr., 1863	From 1-Brig. 2-Div. 14-C. Cumb'd...	To 3-Brig. 3-Div. 23-Corps Ohio..	June, 1863
6th Tenn. Infy.........Apr., 1863	From 1-Brig. 2-Div. 14-C. Cumb'd...	To 3-Brig. 3-Div. 23-Corps Ohio..	June, 1863

1st BRIGADE.—   COMMANDERS.

S. A. Gilbert..........	Col. 44th Ohio Infy..............	Jan. 25, 1863, to Mch. 18, 1863.	
S. P. Carter..........	Brigadier General	Mch. 18, 1863, to June 24, 1863.	
44th Ohio Infy.........Jan., 1863	From 2-Brig. 2-Div. Army Ky......	To 2-Brig. 1-Div. 23-Corps Ohio..	June, 1863
100th Ohio Infy.........Jan., 1863	From 2-Brig. 2-Div. Army Ky......	To 2-Brig. 1-Div. 23-Corps Ohio..	June, 1863
103d Ohio Infy.........Jan., 1863	From 2-Brig. 2-Div. Army Ky......	To 1-Brig. 1-Div. 23-Corps Ohio..	June, 1863
104th Ohio Infy.........Jan., 1863	From 2-Brig. 2-Div. Army Ky......	To 2-Brig. 1-Div. 23-Corps Ohio..	June, 1863
24th Ky. Infy.........Jan., 1863	From 2-Brig. 2-Div. Army Ky......	To 2-Brig. 1-Div. 23-Corps Ohio..	June, 1863

2d BRIGADE.—   COMMANDER.

B. P. Runkle...........	Col. 45th Ohio Infy..............	Jan. 25, 1863, to June 24, 1863.	
7th Ohio Cav..........Jan., 1863	From Unass'd Dist. Central Ky....	To 1-Cav. Brig. Dist. Central Ky....	Apr., 1863
10th Ky. Cav..........Jan., 1863	From Unass'd Dist. Central Ky....	To 2-Brig. 4-Div. 23-Corps Ohio..	June, 1863
45th Ohio Infy.........Jan., 1863	From 1-Brig. 2-Div. Army Ky......	To 2-Brig. 4-Div. 23-Corps Ohio..	June, 1863
112th Ill. Infy.........Apr., 1863	From 3-Brig. Dist. Central Ky.....	To 2-Brig. 4-Div. 23-Corps Ohio..	June, 1863
32d Ky. Infy.........Apr., 1863	From Dist. Western Ky...........	To 2-Brig. 4-Div. 23-Corps Ohio..	June, 1863
2d Tenn. Infy.........Apr., 1863	From 1-Brig. 2-Div. 14-C. Cumb'd..	To 1-Brig. 1-Div. 23-Corps Ohio..	June, 1863

3d BRIGADE.—   COMMANDER.

C. C. Doolittle.........	Col. 18th Mich. Infy.............		
18th Mich. Infy.........Jan., 1863	From 1-Brig. 2-Div. Army Ky......	To Nashville, Tenn., Cumb'd........	Apr., 1863
22d Mich. Infy.........Jan., 1863	From 1-Brig. 2-Div. Army Ky......	To Nashville, Tenn., Cumb'd........	Apr., 1863
112th Ill. Infy.........Jan., 1863	From 1-Brig. 2-Div. Army Ky......	To 2-Brig. Dist. Central Ky........	Apr., 1863

1st CAVALRY BRIGADE.—   COMMANDER.

A. V. Kautz...........	Col. 2d Ohio Cav...............		
2d Ohio Cav..........Apr., 1863	From Reorganization	To 3-Brig. 1-Div. 23-Corps Ohio..	June, 1863
7th Ohio Cav..........Apr., 1863	From 2-Brig. Dist. Central Ky......	To 3-Brig. 1-Div. 23-Corps Ohio..	June, 1863

Twenty-Third Army Corps

Created Apr. 27, 1863, from Troops in the Department of the Ohio, by General Order No. 103, A. G. O. Transferred to Department of North Carolina, Feb., 1865, except 4th and 5th Divisions, which were transferred to the Department of the Cumberland.   **COMMANDERS.**

G. L. Hartsuff.........	Major General	May 28, 1863, to Sept. 24, 1863.	
M. D. Manson..........	Brigadier General	Sept. 24, 1863, to Dec. 20, 1863.	
J. D. Cox..........	Brigadier General	Dec. 20, 1863, to Feb. 10, 1864.	
George Stoneman	Major General	Feb. 10, 1864, to Apr. 4, 1864.	
J. D. Cox..........	Brigadier General	Apr. 4, 1864, to Apr. 9, 1864.	
J. M. Schofield.........	Major General	Apr. 9, 1864, to May 26, 1864.	
J. D. Cox..........	Brigadier General	May 26, 1864, to May 27, 1864.	
J. M. Schofield.........	Major General	May 27, 1864, to Sept. 14, 1864.	
J. D. Cox..........	Brigadier General	Sept. 14, 1864, to Oct. 22, 1864.	
J. M. Schofield.........	Major General	Oct. 22, 1864, to Feb. 2, 1865.	

1st DIVISION.—Discontinued Jan., 1864. Reorganized Apr. 10, 1864. Served with 3d Division to Aug. 11, 1864. Reorganized Dec. 29, 1864.

COMMANDERS.

S. D. Sturgis	Brigadier General	June 24, 1863, to July 10, 1863.
S. P. Carter	Brigadier General	July 10, 1863, to July 15, 1863.
R. K. Byrd	Col. 1st Tenn. Infy	July 15, 1863, to Aug. 6, 1863.
J. T. Boyle	Brigadier General	Aug. 6, 1863, to Jan. 10, 1864.
A. P. Hovey	Brigadier General	Apr. 10, 1864, to June 9, 1864.
Thos. H. Ruger	Brigadier General	Dec. 29, 1864, to Feb. 2, 1865.

1st BRIGADE.—Discontinued Aug. 6, 1863. Reorganized Apr. 10, 1863. Served with 3d Division, June to Aug., 1864. Reorganized Dec. 29, 1864.

COMMANDERS.

S. P. Carter	Brigadier General	June 24, 1863, to July 10, 1863.
R. K. Byrd	Col. 1st Tenn. Infy	July 10, 1863, to July 15, 1863.
J. P. T. Carter	Col. 2d Tenn. Infy	July 15, 1863, to Aug. 6, 1863.
R. F. Barter	Col. 120th Ind. Infy	Apr. 10, 1864, to June 9, 1864.
J. M. Orr	Col. 124th Ind. Infy	Dec. 29, 1864, to Feb. 2, 1865.

32d Ky. Infy	June, 1863	From 2-Brig. Dist. Central Ky	No change to Muster Out	Aug., 1863
103d Ohio Infy	June, 1863	From 1-Brig. Dist. Central Ky	To 2-Brig. 3-Div. 23-Corps	Aug., 1863
12th R. I. Infy	June, 1863	From 1-Brig. 2-Div. 9-Corps	No change to Muster Out	July, 1863
1st Tenn. Infy	June, 1863	From Dist. Central Ky	To 1-Brig. 4-Div. 23-Corps	Aug., 1863
2d Tenn. Infy	June, 1863	From 2-Brig. Dist. Central Ky	To 3-Brig. 4-Div. 23-Corps	Aug., 1863
112th Ill. Infy	June, 1863	From 2-Brig. Dist. Central Ky	To 1-Brig. 4-Div. 23-Corps	Aug., 1863
1st Ky. Cav	June, 1863	From Dist. Central Ky	To Welford's Indpt. Cav. Brig	Aug., 1863
1st Tenn. Batty	June, 1863	From Dist. Central Ky	To 3-Brig. 3-Div. Res. Corps Cumb'd	Aug., 1863
120th Ind. Infy	Apr., 1864	From New Organization	To 4-Brig. 3-Div. 23-Corps	June, 1864
124th Ind. Infy	Apr., 1864	From New Organization	To 4-Brig. 3-Div. 23-Corps	June, 1864
128th Ind. Infy	Apr., 1864	From New Organization	To 4-Brig. 3-Div. 23-Corps	June, 1864
120th Ind. Infy	Dec., 1864	From 3-Brig. 3-Div. 23-Corps	To 1-Brig. 1-Div. 23-Corps Dept. N. C.	Feb., 1865
124th Ind. Infy	Dec., 1864	From 3-Brig. 3-Div. 23-Corps	To 1-Brig. 1-Div. 23-Corps Dept. N. C.	Feb., 1865
128th Ind. Infy	Dec., 1864	From 3-Brig. 3-Div. 23-Corps	To 1-Brig. 1-Div. 23-Corps Dept. N. C.	Feb., 1865
180th Ohio Infy	Jan., 1865	From 3-Brig. Def. Nashv. & Ch. R. R.	To 1-Brig. 1-Div. 23-Corps Dept. N. C.	Feb., 1865

2d BRIGADE.—Discontinued Aug. 6, 1863. Reorganized Apr. 10, 1864. Served with 2d Division, June to Aug., 1864. Discontinued Aug. 11, 1864. Reorganized Dec. 29, 1864.

COMMANDERS.

S. A. Gilbert	Col. 44th Ohio Infy	June 24, 1863, to June 30, 1863.
J. W. Reilly	Col. 104th Ohio Infy	June 30, 1863, to July 5, 1863.
S. A. Gilbert	Col. 44th Ohio Infy	July 5, 1863, to July 20, 1863.
S. R. Mott	Col. 118th Ohio Infy	July 20, 1863, to Aug. 6, 1863.
J. C. McQuiston	Col. 123d Ind. Infy	Apr. 10, 1864, to June 9, 1864.
J. C. McQuiston	Col. 123d Ind. Infy	Dec. 29, 1864, to Feb. 2, 1865.

24th Ky. Infy	June, 1863	From 1-Brig. Dist. Central Ky	To 2-Brig. 4-Div. 23-Corps	July, 1863
44th Ohio Infy	June, 1863	From 1-Brig. Dist. Central Ky	To 2-Brig. 4-Div. 23-Corps	July, 1863
45th Ohio Infy	June, 1863	From 2-Brig. Dist. Central Ky	To 2-Brig. 4-Div. 23-Corps	July, 1863
100th Ohio Infy	June, 1863	From 1-Brig. Dist. Central Ky	To 2-Brig. 4-Div. 23-Corps	July, 1863
104th Ohio Infy	June, 1863	From 1-Brig. Dist. Central Ky	To 2-Brig. 4-Div. 23-Corps	July, 1863
9th Ohio Cav	June, 1863	From New Organization	To 2-Brig. 4-Div. 23-Corps	July, 1863
Batty. D, 1st Ohio Arty	June, 1863	From Reorganization	To 2-Brig. 4-Div. 23-Corps	July, 1863
Wilder's Ind. Batty	June, 1863	From Dist. Central Ky	To 2-Brig. 4-Div. 23-Corps	July, 1863
118th Ohio Infy	July, 1863	From 2-Brig. 4-Div. 23-Corps	To 1-Brig. 2-Div. 23-Corps	Aug., 1863
8th Tenn. Infy	July, 1863	From 2-Brig. 4-Div. 23-Corps	To 2-Brig. 3-Div. 23-Corps	Aug., 1863
10th Ky. Cav	July, 1863	From 2-Brig. 4-Div. 23-Corps	To Dist. N. C. Ky. 1-Div. 23-Corps	Aug., 1863
14th Ky. Cav	July, 1863	From 2-Brig. 4-Div. 23-Corps	To Dist. N. C. Ky. 1-Div. 23-Corps	Aug., 1863
8th Mich. Cav	July, 1863	From 2-Brig. 4-Div. 23-Corps	To 1-Brig. 4-Div. 23-Corps	Aug., 1863
5th Tenn. Cav. (East.)	July, 1863	From 2-Brig. 4-Div. 23-Corps	To 2-Br. 4-Div. 23-C. (8th Tenn. C.)	Aug., 1863
15th Ind. Batty	July, 1863	From 2-Brig. 4-Div. 23-Corps	To 1-Brig. 4-Div. 23-Corps	Aug., 1863
19th Ohio Batty	July, 1863	From 2-Brig. 4-Div. 23-Corps	To Res. Arty. 23-Corps	Aug., 1863
123d Ind. Infy	Apr., 1864	From New Organization	To 4-Brig. 2-Div. 23-Corps	June, 1864
129th Ind. Infy	Apr., 1864	From New Organization	To 4-Brig. 2-Div. 23-Corps	June, 1864
130th Ind. Infy	Apr., 1864	From New Organization	To 4-Brig. 2-Div. 23-Corps	June, 1864
99th Ohio Infy	June, 1864	From 2-Brig. 1-Div. 4-Corps Cumb'd.	To 2-Brig. 1-Div. 23-Corps Dept. N. C.	Feb., 1865
123d Ind. Infy	Dec., 1864	From 3-Brig. 2-Div. 23-Corps	To 2-Brig. 1-Div. 23-Corps Dept. N. C.	Feb., 1865
129th Ind. Infy	Dec., 1864	From 2-Brig. 2-Div. 23-Corps	To 2-Brig. 1-Div. 23-Corps Dept. N. C.	Feb., 1865
130th Ind. Infy	Dec., 1864	From 1-Brig. 2-Div. 23-Corps	To 2-Brig. 1-Div. 23-Corps Dept. N. C.	Feb., 1865
28th Mich. Infy	Dec., 1864	From Post Nashville, Tenn	To 2-Brig. 1-Div. 23-Corps Dept. N. C.	Feb., 1865

3d BRIGADE.—Discontinued Aug. 6, 1863. Reorganized Dec. 30, 1864.

COMMANDERS.

A. V. Kautz	Col. 2d Ohio Cav	June 24, 1863, to Aug. 6, 1863.
M. T. Thomas	Col. 8th Minn. Infy	Dec. 30, 1864, to Feb. 2, 1865.

2d Ohio Cav	June, 1863	From 1-Cav. Brig. Dist. Central Ky.	To 3-Brig. 4-Div. 23-Corps	Aug., 1863
7th Ohio Cav	June, 1863	From 1-Cav. Brig. Dist. Central Ky.	To 3-Brig. 4-Div. 23-Corps	Aug., 1863
9th Mich. Cav	June, 1863	From New Organization	To 3-Brig. 4-Div. 23-Corps	Aug., 1863
8th Minn. Infy	Dec., 1864	From Dist. North Ala. Dept. Cumb'd.	To 3-Brig. 1-Div. 23-Corps Dept. N. C.	Feb., 1865
174th Ohio Infy	Dec., 1864	From Dist. North Ala. Dept. Cumb'd.	To 3-Brig. 1-Div. 23-Corps Dept. N. C.	Feb., 1865
178th Ohio Infy	Dec., 1864	From Def. Nashv. & Chatt. R. R.	To 3-Brig. 1-Div. 23-Corps Dept. N. C.	Feb., 1865

ARTILLERY.—

23d Ind. Batty	Apr., 1864	From Dist. Clinch Dept. Ohio	To Arty. 3-Div. 23-Corps	Aug., 1864
24th Ind. Batty	Apr., 1864	From Arty. Res. 23-Corps	To Arty. Cav. Div. 23-Corps	July, 1864
22d Ind. Batty	Dec., 1864	From Arty. 2-Div. 23-Corps	To Arty. 1-Div. 23-Corps Dept. N. C.	Feb., 1865
Batty. F, 1st Mich. Arty	Dec., 1864	From Arty. 2-Div. 23-Corps	To Arty. 1-Div. 23-Corps Dept. N. C.	Feb., 1865

UNASSIGNED.—

2d Maryland Infy	June, 1863	From 1-Brig. 2-Div. 9-Corps Ohio.	To Frankfort, Ky., 1-Div. 23-Corps	Oct., 1863
21st Mass. Infy	June, 1863	From 1-Brig. 2-Div. 9-Corps Ohio.	To Camp Nelson, Ky., 1-Div. 23-C.	Oct., 1863
48th Penna. Infy	June, 1863	From 1-Brig. 2-Div. 9-Corps Ohio.	To Lexington, Ky., 1-Div. 23-Corps	Oct., 1863
Batty. D, 1st R. I.	June, 1863	From 1-Brig. 2-Div. 9-Corps Ohio.	To Reserve Arty. 23-Corps	Aug., 1863

1st DIVISION as organized August, 1863, not Brigaded.—

BOWLING GREEN, KY.—

11th Kentucky Infy	Aug., 1863	From 3-Brig. 3-Div. 23-Corps	To 1-Brig. 4-Div. 23-Corps	Oct., 1863
26th Kentucky Infy	Aug., 1863	From Unatt. 2-Div. 23-Corps	To Dist. Southwest Ky. 1-Div. 23-C.	Oct., 1863
8th Kentucky Cav. 4 Cos.	Aug., 1863	From 1-Brig. 2-Div. 23-Corps	No change to Muster Out	Sept., 1863

MUNFORDSVILLE, KY.—

27th Kentucky Infy	Aug., 1863	From Unatt. 2-Div. 23-Corps	To 1-Brig. 4-Div. 23-Corps	Oct., 1863
33d Kentucky Infy	Aug., 1863	From Unatt. 2-Div. 23-Corps	To Dist. S. Central Ky. 1-Div. 23-C.	Oct., 1863
Batty. F, 1st Mich. Arty	Aug., 1863	From Unatt. 2-Div. 23-Corps	To Dist. S. Central Ky. 1-Div. 23-C.	Oct., 1863

LOUISA, KY., DISTRICT EASTERN KY.—

14th Kentucky Infy	Aug., 1863	From 1-Brig. 4-Div. 23-Corps	To Dist. East. Ky. 1-Div. 23-Corps	Oct., 1863
39th Kentucky Infy	Aug., 1863	From 1-Brig. 4-Div. 23-Corps	To Dist. East. Ky. 1-Div. 23-Corps	Oct., 1863

MOUNT STERLING, KY.—

10th Kentucky Cav	Aug., 1863	From 1-Brig. 4-Div. 23-Corps	No change to Muster Out	Sept., 1863
14th Ky. Cav. 4 Cos	Aug., 1863	From 2-Brig. 1-Div. 23-Corps	To Dist. N. Central Ky. 1-Div. 23-C.	Oct., 1863

CAMP NELSON, KY.—

21st Mass. Infy	Aug., 1863	From Unatt. 1-Div. 23-Corps	To 1-Brig. 2-Div. 9-Corps Ohio	Oct., 1863

FRANKFORT, KY.—

2d Maryland Infy	Aug., 1863	From Unatt. 1-Div. 23-Corps	To 1-Brig. 2-Div. 9-Corps Ohio	Oct., 1863

HOPKINSVILLE, KY.—

3d Kentucky Cav	Aug., 1863	From 1-Brig. 2-Div. 23-Corps	To Dist. S. Central Ky. 1-Div. 23-C.	Oct., 1863

NEW HAVEN, KY.—

63d Indiana Infy	Aug., 1863	From Unatt. 2-Div. 23-Corps	To Dist. S. Central Ky. 1-Div. 23-C.	Oct., 1863

LEXINGTON, KY.—

6th Indiana Cav. 4 Cos	Aug., 1863	From New Organization	To Dist. N. Central Ky. 1-Div. 23-C.	Sept., 1863
48th Penna. Infy	Aug., 1863	From Unatt. 1-Div. 23-Corps	To 1-Brig. 2-Div. 9-Corps Ohio	Oct., 1863

RUSSELLSVILLE, KY.—

91st Indiana Infy	Aug., 1863	From 1-Brig. 2-Div. 23-Corps	To Dist. Southwest Ky. 1-Div. 23-C.	Oct., 1863
3d Ky. Cav. 4 Cos	Aug., 1863	From 1-Brig. 2-Div. 23-Corps	To Dist. S. Central Ky. 1-Div. 23-C.	Oct., 1863
8th Ky. Cav. 4 Cos	Aug., 1863	From 1-Brig. 2-Div. 23-Corps	No change to Muster Out	Sept., 1863
22d Indiana Batty	Aug., 1863	From 1-Brig. 2-Div. 23-Corps	To Dist. Southwest Ky. 1-Div. 23-C.	Oct., 1863

LOUISVILLE, KY.—

20th Kentucky Infy	Aug., 1863	From Unass'd 2-Div. 23-Corps	To Dist. Southwest Ky. 1-Div. 23-C.	Oct., 1863
Batty. C, Ky. Arty	Sept., 1863	From New Organization	To Dist. Southwest Ky. 1-Div. 23-C.	Oct., 1863

EMMINENCE, KY.—

9th Kentucky Cav	Aug., 1863	From 2-Brig. 3-Div. 23-Corps	No change to Muster Out	Sept., 1863

GLASGOW, KY.—

34th Kentucky Infy	Aug., 1863	From Unatt. 2-Div. 23-Corps	To Dist. S. Central Ky. 1-Div. 23-C.	Oct., 1863

MULDRAUGH'S HILL, KY.—

50th Ohio Infy	Aug., 1863	From Unatt. 2-Div. 23-Corps	To Dist. S. Central Ky. 1-Div. 23-C.	Oct., 1863

1st DIVISION.—As organized Oct., 1863.

DISTRICT EASTERN KENTUCKY.—   **COMMANDER.**

G. W. Gallup	Col. 14th Kentucky Infy.			
14th Kentucky Infy	Aug., 1863	From 1-Brig. 4-Div. 23-Corps	To 1-B. 1-Div. Dist. Ky. 5-Div. 23-C.	Apr., 1864
39th Kentucky Infy	Aug., 1863	From 1-Brig. 4-Div. 23-Corps	To 1-B. 1-Div. Dist. Ky. 5-Div. 23-C.	Apr., 1864

DISTRICT NORTH CENTRAL KY.—   **COMMANDER.**

S. S. Fry	Brigadier General.			
6th New Hamp. Infy	Aug., 1863	From 1-Brig. 2-Div. 9-Corps Ohio	To 1-Brig. 2-Div. 9-Corps Ohio	Jan., 1864
9th New Hamp. Infy	Aug., 1863	From 1-Brig. 2-Div. 9-Corps Ohio	To 1-Brig. 2-Div. 9-Corps Ohio	Jan., 1864
7th Rhode Island Infy	Aug., 1863	From 1-Brig. 2-Div. 9-Corps Ohio	To 1-Brig. 2-Div. 9-Corps Ohio	Jan., 1864
40th Kentucky Infy	Aug., 1863	From New Organization	To Sub-Dist. S. W. Ky. 1-D. D. Ky.	Jan., 1864
47th Kentucky Infy	Aug., 1863	From New Organization	To Sub-Dist. S. W. Ky. 1-D. D. Ky.	Jan., 1864
51st New York Infy	Oct., 1863	From Dist. Somerset, Ky.	To 1-Brig. 2-Div. 9-Corps Ohio	Jan., 1864
45th Kentucky Infy	Nov., 1863	From New Organization	To Sub-Dist. S. W. Ky. 1-D. D. Ky.	Jan., 1864

CAVALRY.—

14th Kentucky Cav	Aug., 1863	From 2-Brig. 1-Div. 23-Corps	To Sub-Dist. S. W. Ky. 1-D. D. Ky.	Jan., 1864
10th Michigan Cav	Sept., 1863	From New Organization	To Unass'd 23-Corps	Jan., 1864
10th Tennessee Cav	Sept., 1863	From New Organization	To Dept. Cumberland	Jan., 1864
12th Tennessee Cav	Sept., 1863	From New Organization	To Dept. Cumberland	Jan., 1864
6th Indiana Cav. 4 Cos	Sept., 1863	From Lexington, Ky., 1-Div. 23-C.	To Left Wing Forces 23-Corps	Oct., 1863

ARTILLERY.—

Batty. E, 1st Ky. Arty	Oct., 1863	From New Organization	To Dist. S. W. Ky. 1-Div. Dist. Ky.	Jan., 1864
Batty. M, 2d Ill. Arty	Oct., 1863	From 2-Brig. 3-Div. 23-Corps	To Dist. S. W. Ky. 1-Div. Dist. Ky.	Jan., 1864
Batty. E, 1st Tenn. Arty	Oct., 1863	From New Organization	To Dist. Nashville, Tenn., Cumb'd	Jan., 1864
2d Ohio H. Arty. 2 Cos	Oct., 1863	From Dist. Eastern Ky	To Dist. S. W. Ky. 1-Div. Dist. Ky.	Jan., 1864
2d Ohio H. Arty. Co. L	Oct., 1863	From New Organization	To Dist. S. W. Ky. 1-Div. Dist. Ky.	Jan., 1864

DISTRICT OF SOMERSET, KY.—   **COMMANDER.**

T. T. Garrard	Brigadier General.			
49th Kentucky Infy	Aug., 1863	From New Organization	To Dist. S. W. Ky. 1-Div. Dist. Ky.	Jan., 1864
51st New York Infy	Aug., 1863	From 2-Brig. 2-Div. 9-Corps Ohio	To Dist. North Central Ky	Oct., 1863
91st Indiana Infy	Oct., 1863	From Dist. S. W. Ky	To Cumb'd Gap. Dist. Clinch	Jan., 1864
4th Kentucky Cav. 4 Cos	Oct., 1863	From New Organization	To 1-Br. 1-Div. Cav. Corps Cumb'd	Jan., 1864
14th Ky. Cav. 3 Cos	Dec., 1863	From Dist. North Central Ky	To Dist. S. W. Ky	Jan., 1864
7th Ohio Cav. Det	Dec., 1863	From 3-Brig. 4-Div. 23-Corps	To 1-Brig. 2-Div. Cav. Corps Ohio.	Jan., 1864
Batty. E, 1st Ky. Arty	Dec., 1863	From Dist. North Central Ky	To Dist. S. W. Ky	Jan., 1864

DISTRICT SOUTH CENTRAL KY.—   **COMMANDER.**

E. H. Hobson	Brigadier General.			
33d Ky. Infy., A, B, C, D	Oct., 1863	From Munfordsville, Ky., 1-D. 23-C.	To Dist. S. W. Ky	Jan., 1864
50th Ohio Infy. 6 Cos	Oct., 1863	From Muldraugh's Hill, Ky	To 3-Brig. 4-Div. 23-Corps	Apr., 1864
37th Ky. Infy. 7 Cos	Oct., 1863	From New Organization	To Dist. S. W. Ky	Jan., 1864
63d Indiana Infy. 6 Cos	Oct., 1863	From New Haven, Ky	To Dist. S. W. Ky	Jan., 1864
34th Ky. Infy. Co. G	Oct., 1863	From Glasgow, Ky	To Dist. Clinch, Dept. Ohio	Jan., 1864

CAVALRY.—

3d Kentucky Cav	Oct., 1863	From Hopkinsville 1-Div. 23-Corps	To Nashville, Tenn	Nov., 1863
13th Kentucky Cav	Oct., 1863	From New Organization	To Sub-Dist. S. W. Ky. Dist. Ky.	Jan., 1864
Batty. F, 1st Mich. Arty	Oct., 1863	From Munfordsville, Ky., 1-D. 23-C.	To Garrison Knoxville, Tenn	Jan., 1864
Batty. C, 1st Ky. Arty	Oct., 1863	From Louisville, Ky., 1-Div. 23-C.	To Sub-Dist. S. W. Ky. Dist. Ky.	Jan., 1864
2d Ohio H. Arty. 7 Cos	Oct., 1863	From New Organization	To Sub-Dist. S. W. Ky. Dist. Ky.	Jan., 1864
Batty. B, 1st Wis. H. A.	Oct., 1863	From Murfreesboro, Tenn	To Sub-Dist. S. W. Ky. Dist. Ky.	Jan., 1864

DISTRICT SOUTHWEST KENTUCKY.— COMMANDERS.

Cicero Maxwell	Col. 26th Kentucky Infy	To Jan., 1864.		
E. H. Hobson	Brigadier General	To Apr., 1864.		
26th Kentucky Infy......Oct., 1863	From Bowling Green, Ky	To 2-Brig. 2-Div. Dist. Ky	Apr.,	1864
35th Kentucky Infy......Oct., 1863	From New Organization	To 2-Brig. 2-Div. Dist. Ky	Apr.,	1864
91st Ind. Infy..........Oct., 1863	From Russellsville, Ky	To Dist. Somerset 1-Div. 23-Corps.	Oct.,	1863
48th Ky. Infy..........Dec., 1863	From New Organization	To 1-Brig. 2-Div. Dist. Ky	Apr.,	1864
2d Ohio Heavy Arty.				
(1st Battn.)........Dec., 1863	From Dist. South Central Ky	To 2-Brig. 2-Div. Dist. Ky	Apr.,	1864
22d Ind. Batty..........Dec., 1863	From Russellville, Ky	To Camp Burnside Dist. Ky	Apr.,	1864
20th Ky. Infy..........Jan., 1864	From Louisville, Ky	To 1-Brig. 2-Div. Dist. Ky	Apr.,	1864
33d Ky. Infy..........Jan., 1864	From Dist. South Central Ky	To Consol. with 26th Ky	Apr.,	1864
34th Ky. Infy. Co. G....Jan., 1864	From Dist. South Central Ky	To Dist. Clinch, Dept. Ohio	Jan.,	1864
37th Ky. Infy..........Jan., 1864	From New Organization	To 3-Brig. 1-Div. Dist. Ky	Apr.,	1864
40th Ky. Infy..........Jan., 1864	From Dist. North Central Ky	To 2-Brig. 1-Div. Dist. Ky	Apr.,	1864
45th Ky. Infy..........Jan., 1864	From Dist. North Central Ky	To 4-Brig. 1-Div. Dist. Ky	Apr.,	1864
47th Ky. Infy..........Jan., 1864	From Dist. North Central Ky	To 4-Brig. 1-Div. Dist. Ky	Apr.,	1864
48th Ky. Infy..........Jan., 1864	From New Organization	To 1-Brig. 2-Div. Dist. Ky	Apr.,	1864
49th Ky. Infy..........Jan., 1864	From Dist. Somerset	To 1-Brig. 2-Div. Dist. Ky	Apr.,	1864
7th R. I. Infy..........Jan., 1864	From Dist. North Central Ky	To 1-Brig. 2-Div. 9-Corps Ohio	Jan.,	1864
63d Ind. Infy..........Jan., 1864	From Dist. South Central Ky	To 2-Brig. 3-Div. 23-Corps	Apr.,	1864
13th Ky. Cav..........Jan., 1864	From Dist. South Central Ky	To 2-Brig. 1-Div. Dist. Ky	Apr.,	1864
14th Ky. Cav..........Jan., 1864	From Dist. North Central Ky	No change to Muster Out	Mch.,	1864
Batty. C, 1st Ky. Arty..Jan., 1864	From Dist. South Central Ky	To 3-Brig. 1-Div. Dist. Ky	Apr.,	1864
Batty. E, 1st Ky. Arty..Jan., 1864	From Dist. Somerset, Ky	To 4-Brig. 1-Div. Dist. Ky	Apr.,	1864
Batty. M, 2d Ill. Arty....Jan., 1864	From Dist. South Central Ky	Broken Up	Apr.,	1864

2d DIVISION.— COMMANDERS.

J. T. Boyle	Brigadier General	June 24, 1863, to Aug. 6, 1863.
M. D. Manson	Brigadier General	Aug. 6, 1863, to Aug. 21, 1863.
Julius White	Brigadier General	Aug. 21, 1863, to Dec. 24, 1863.
M. D. Manson	Brigadier General	Dec. 24, 1863, to Jan. 26, 1864.
H. M. Judah	Brigadier General	Jan. 26, 1864, to May 18, 1864.
M. S. Hascall	Brigadier General	May 18, 1864, to Oct. 11, 1864.
J. A. Cooper	Brigadier General	Oct. 11, 1864, to Nov. 11, 1864.
Thos. H. Ruger	Brigadier General	Nov. 11, 1864, to Dec. 8, 1864.
D. N. Couch	Major General	Dec. 8, 1864, to Jan. 14, 1865.
J. A. Cooper	Brigadier General	Jan. 14, 1865, to Feb. 2, 1865.

1st BRIGADE.— COMMANDERS.

J. M. Shackleford	Brigadier General	June 24, 1863, to Aug. 6, 1863.		
O. H. Moore	Col. 25th Mich. Infy	Aug. 6, 1863, to Oct. 20, 1863.		
S. R. Mott	Col. 118th Ohio Infy	Oct. 20, 1863, to Feb. 2, 1864.		
M. S. Hascall	Brigadier General	Feb. 2, 1864, to Apr. 16, 1864.		
W. E. Hobson	Col. 13th Ky. Infy	Apr. 16, 1864, to Apr. 25, 1864.		
J. A. Cooper	Brigadier General	Apr. 25, 1864, to May 3, 1864.		
N. C. McLean	Brigadier General	May 3, 1864, to June 4, 1864.		
J. A. Cooper	Brigadier General	June 4, 1864, to Oct. 11, 1864.		
G. W. Gallup	Col. 14th Ky. Infy	Oct. 11, 1864, to Nov. 11, 1864.		
J. A. Cooper	Brigadier General	Nov. 11, 1864, to Feb. 2, 1865.		
65th Ind. Infy..........June, 1863	From Unatt. Dist. Western Ky	To 2-Brig. 4-Div. 23-Corps	Aug.,	1863
91st Ind. Infy..........June, 1863	From Unatt. Dist. Western Ky	To Unatt. 1-Div. 23-C. Russellsv'e.	Aug.,	1863
12th Ky. Infy..........June, 1863	From Unatt. Dist. Western Ky	To 1-Brig. 3-Div. 23-Corps	Aug.,	1863
3d Ky. Cav..........June, 1863	From Unatt. Dist. Western Ky	To Unatt. 1-Div. 23-C. Hopkinsv'e.	Aug.,	1863
8th Ky. Cav..........June, 1863	From Unatt. Dist. Western Ky	To Unatt. 1-Div. 23-Corps	Aug.,	1863
15th Ky. Cav. Co. C....June, 1863	From Paducah Ky. 6-Div. 16-C. T..	To Unatt. 1-Div. 23-C. Smithl'd Ky.	Aug.,	1863
22d Ind. Batty..........June, 1863	From New Organization	To Unatt. 1-Div. 23-C. Russellsv'e.	Aug.,	1863
25th Mich. Infy..........Aug., 1863	From Lebanon Ky. 2-Div. 23-Corps.	To 2-Brig. 2-Div. 23-C. Dept. N. C.	Feb.,	1865
118th Ohio Infy..........Aug., 1863	From 2-Brig. 2-Div. 23-Corps	To 2-Brig. 2-Div. 23-Corps	Apr.,	1864
80th Ind. Infy..........Aug., 1863	From 2-Brig. 3-Div. 23-Corps	To 2-Brig. 2-Div. 23-Corps	June,	1864
16th Ky. Infy..........Aug., 1863	From 2-Brig. 3-Div. 23-Corps	To 1-Brig. 3-Div. 23-Corps	Apr.,	1864
Elgin, Ill. Batty..........Aug., 1863	From 1-Brig. 3-Div. 23-Corps	To 2-Brig. 4-Div. 23-Corps	Apr.,	1864
3d Tenn. Infy..........Apr., 1864	From 3-Brig. 1-Div. 12-C. Cumb'd..	To 2-Br. 2-Div. 23-Corps Dept. N. C.	Feb.,	1865
6th Tenn. Infy..........Apr., 1864	From 3-Brig. 1-Div. 12-C. Cumb'd..	To 2-Br. 2-Div. 23-Corps Dept. N. C.	Feb.,	1865
13th Ky. Infy..........June, 1864	From 2-Brig. 2-Div. 23-Corps	To 2-Brig. 2-Div. 23-Corps	June,	1864
45th Ohio Infy..........June, 1864	From 2-Brig. 2-Div. 23-Corps	To 2-Brig. 1-Div. 4-Corps Cumb'd.	June,	1864
91st Ind. Infy..........June, 1864	From 1-Brig. 4-Div. 23-Corps	To 3-Brig. 2-Div. 23-Corps	Aug.,	1864
99th Ohio Infy..........Aug., 1864	From 4-Brig. 2-Div. 23-Corps	To Consol. with 50th Ohio	Dec.,	1864
14th Ky. Infy..........Aug., 1864	From 3-Brig. 2-Div. 23-Corps	To Louisa Ky. Mil. Dist. Ky	Dec.,	1864
130th Ind. Infy..........Aug., 1864	From 4-Brig. 2-Div. 23-Corps	To 2-Brig. 1-Div. 23-Corps	Dec.,	1864
26th Ky. Infy..........Dec., 1864	From 2-Brig. 2-Div. Dist. Ky	To 1-Brig. 2-Div. 23-C. Dept. N. C.	Feb.,	1865

2d BRIGADE.—Organized Aug. 6, 1863.— COMMANDERS.

M. W. Chapin	Col. 23d Mich. Infy	Aug. 6, 1863, to Feb. 8, 1864.		
J. R. Bond	Col. 111th Ohio Infy	Feb. 8, 1864, to Apr. 16, 1864.		
M. S. Hascall	Brigadier General	Apr. 16, 1864, to May 16, 1864.		
J. R. Bond	Col. 111th Ohio Infy	May 16, 1864, to June 18, 1864.		
W. E. Hobson	Col. 13th Ky. Infy	June 18, 1864, to Aug. 11, 1864.		
J. R. Bond	Col. 111th Ohio Infy	Aug. 11, 1864, to Oct. 18, 1864.		
O. H. Moore	Col. 25th Mich. Infy	Oct. 18, 1864, to Feb. 2, 1865.		
23d Mich. Infy..........Aug., 1863	From 1-Brig. 3-Div. 23-Corps	To 2-Br. 2-Div. 23-Corps Dept. N. C.	Feb.,	1865
111th Ohio Infy..........Aug., 1863	From 1-Brig. 3-Div. 23-Corps	To 2-Br. 2-Div. 23-Corps Dept. N. C.	Feb.,	1865
107th Ill. Infy..........Aug., 1863	From 1-Brig. 3-Div. 23-Corps	To 2-Br. 2-Div. 23-Corps Dept. N. C.	Feb.,	1865
13th Ky. Infy..........Aug., 1863	From 2-Brig. 3-Div. 23-Corps	To 1-Brig. 2-Div. 23-Corps	Apr.,	1864
Henshaw's Ill. Batty....Aug., 1863	From 1-Brig. 3-Div. 23-Corps	To 3-Brig. 4-Div. 23-Corps	Apr.,	1864
45th Ohio Infy..........Apr., 1864	From 3-Brig. 1-Div. Cav. Corps O.	To 1-Brig. 2-Div. 23-Corps	June,	1864
118th Ohio Infy..........Apr., 1864	From 1-Brig. 2-Div. 23-Corps	To 2-Br. 2-Div. 23-Corps Dept. N. C.	Feb.,	1865
80th Ind. Infy..........June, 1864	From 1-Brig. 2-Div. 23-Corps	To 2-Br. 2-Div. 23-Corps Dept. N. C.	Feb.,	1865
13th Ky. Infy..........June, 1864	From 1-Brig. 2-Div. 23-Corps	No change to Muster Out	Jan.,	1865
129th Ind. Infy..........Aug., 1864	From 4-Brig. 2-Div. 23-Corps	To 2-Brig. 1-Div. 23-Corps	Dec.,	1864

3d BRIGADE.—Organized June, 1864.— COMMANDERS.

S. A. Strickland	Col. 50th Ohio Infy	June 19, 1864, to Sept. 23, 1864.
J. Mehringer	Col. 91st Ind. Infy	Sept. 23, 1864, to Oct. 24, 1864.
S. A. Strickland	Col. 50th Ohio Infy	Oct. 24, 1864, to Dec. 31, 1864.
John O'Dowd	Col. 181st Ohio Infy	Dec. 31, 1864, to Jan. 2, 1865.
N. C. McLean	Brigadier General	Jan. 2, 1865, to Jan. 8, 1865.
S. A. Strickland	Col. 50th Ohio Infy	Jan. 8, 1865, to Feb. 2, 1865.

3d BRIGADE.—Continued.

14th Ky. Infy............June, 1864	From 1-Brig. 1-Div. Dist. Ky......	To 1-Brig. 2-Div. 23-Corps.........	Aug., 1864
20th Ky. Infy............June, 1864	From 1-Brig. 2-Div. Dist. Ky......	To Mil. Dist. Ky...................	Dec., 1864
27th Ky. Infy............June, 1864	From 3-Brig. 4-Div. 23-Corps......	To Mil. Dist. Ky...................	Dec., 1864
50th Ohio Infy............June, 1864	From 3-Brig. 4-Div. 23-Corps......	To 3-Br. 2-Div. 23-Corps Dept. N. C.	Feb., 1865
91st Ind. Infy............Aug., 1864	From 1-Brig. 4-Div. 23-Corps......	To 3-Br. 2-Div. 23-Corps Dept. N. C.	Feb., 1865
123d Ind. Infy............Aug., 1864	From 4-Brig. 2-Div. 23-Corps......	To 2-Brig. 1-Div. 23-Corps........	Dec., 1864
183d Ohio Infy............Nov., 1864	From New Organization..........	To 3-Br. 2-Div. 23-Corps Dept. N. C.	Feb., 1865
181st Ohio Infy............Dec., 1864	From 1-Br. Def. Nash. & Chat. R. R.	To 3-Br. 2-Div. 23-Corps Dept. N. C.	Feb., 1865

4th BRIGADE.—Organized June 9, 1864. Broken up Aug. 11, 1864.

COMMANDERS.

J. C. McQuiston........	Col. 123d Ind. Infy...............	June 9, 1864, to June 11, 1864.
P. T. Swayne..........	Col. 99th Ohio Infy...............	June 11, 1864, to July 25, 1864.
C. S. Parrish..........	Col. 130th Ind. Infy..............	July 25, 1864, to Aug. 11, 1864.

123d Ind. Infy.........June, 1864	From 2-Brig. 1-Div. 23-Corps.....	To 3-Brig. 2-Div. 23-Corps........	Aug., 1864
129th Ind. Infy.........June, 1864	From 2-Brig. 1-Div. 23-Corps.....	To 2-Brig. 2-Div. 23-Corps........	Aug., 1864
130th Ind. Infy.........June, 1864	From 2-Brig. 1-Div. 23-Corps.....	To 1-Brig. 2-Div. 23-Corps........	Aug., 1864
99th Ohio Infy.........June, 1864	From 2-Brig. 1-Div. 23-Corps.....	To 1-Brig. 2-Div. 23-Corps........	Aug., 1864

UNATTACHED 2d DIVISION.—
1st EAST TENN. BRIGADE.— COMMANDER.

J. G. Spear............	Brigadier General...............	

3d Tenn. Infy...........Dec., 1863	From Post Chattanooga, Tenn.....	To 3-Brig. 1-Div. 12-Corps Cumb'd.	Jan., 1864
5th Tenn. Infy...........Dec., 1863	From Post Chattanooga, Tenn.....	To 3-Brig. 1-Div. 12-Corps Cumb'd.	Jan., 1864
6th Tenn. Infy...........Dec., 1863	From Post Chattanooga, Tenn.....	To 3-Brig. 1-Div. 12-Corps Cumb'd.	Jan., 1864

MUNFORDSVILLE, KY.—

27th Kentucky Infy......June, 1863	From Dist. West Ky..............	To Unatt. 1-Div. 23-Corps.........	Aug., 1863
33d Kentucky Infy......June, 1863	From Dist. West Ky..............	To Unatt. 1-Div. 23-Corps.........	Aug., 1863
Batty. F, 1st Mich. Arty.June, 1863	From Dist. West Ky..............	To Unatt. 1-Div. 23-Corps.........	Aug., 1863

BOWLING GREEN, KY.—

26th Kentucky Infy.......June, 1863	From Dist. West Ky..............	To Unatt. 1-Div. 23-Corps.........	Aug., 1863
34th Kentucky Infy.......June, 1863	From Dist. West Ky..............	To Unatt. 1-Div. 23-Corps.........	Aug., 1863

LEBANON, Ky., AND OTHER POINTS.—

63d Indiana Infy........June, 1863	From Dist. West Ky..............	To Unatt. 1-Div. 23-Corps.........	Aug., 1863
20th Kentucky Infy......June, 1863	From Dist. West Ky..............	To Unatt. 1-Div. 23-Corps.........	Aug., 1863
25th Michigan Infy......June, 1863	From Dist. West Ky..............	To 1-Brig. 2-Div. 23-Corps........	Aug., 1863
50th Ohio Infy..........June, 1863	From Dist. West Ky..............	To Unatt. 1-Div. 23-Corps.........	Aug., 1863

ARTILLERY, 2d DIVISION.—

19th Ohio Batty........Apr., 1864	From 1-Brig. 3-Div. 23-Corps.....	To Arty. 2-Div. 23-Corps Dept. N. C.	Feb., 1865
Batty. F, 1st Mich. Arty.Apr., 1864	From Garrison Knoxville, Tenn......	To Arty. 1-Div. 23-Corps...........	Dec., 1864
22d Indiana Batty.......June, 1864	From Camp Burnside..........	To Garrison Arty. Nashville, Tenn..	Nov., 1864
24th Indiana Batty......Aug., 1864	From Arty. Cav. Div. 23-Corps....	To Garrison Arty. Nashville, Tenn..	Oct., 1864
15th Indiana Batty.......Dec., 1864	From Arty. 3-Div. 23-Corps.......	To Arty. 2-Div. 23-Corps Dept. N. C.	Feb., 1865

3d DIVISION.— COMMANDERS.

H. M. Judah..........	Brigadier General..................	June 24, 1863, to Aug. 6, 1863.
M. S. Hascall..........	Brigadier General..................	Aug. 6, 1863, to Mch. 12, 1864.
J. W. Reilly..........	Col. 104th Ohio Infy.............	Mch. 12, 1864, to Apr. 3, 1864.
J. D. Cox............	Brigadier General..................	Apr. 3, 1864, to May 26, 1864.
J. W. Reilly..........	Col. 104th Ohio Infy.............	May 26, 1864, to May 27, 1864.
J. D. Cox............	Brigadier General..................	May 27, 1864, to Sept. 16, 1864.
J. W. Reilly..........	Col. 104th Ohio Infy.............	Sept. 16, 1864, to Oct. 21, 1864.
J. D. Cox............	Brigadier General..................	Oct. 21, 1864, to Jan. 13, 1865.
C. C. Doolittle........	Col. 18th Michigan Infy...........	Jan. 13, 1865, to Jan. 14, 1865.
J. D. Cox............	Brigadier General..................	Jan. 14, 1865, to Feb. 2, 1865.

1st BRIGADE.— COMMANDERS.

M. D. Manson..........	Brigadier General..................	June 24, 1863, to Aug. 6, 1863.
S. A. Gilbert..........	Col. 44th Ohio Infy..............	Aug. 6, 1863, to Oct. 21, 1863.
J. W. Reilly..........	Col. 104th Ohio Infy.............	Oct. 21, 1863, to Dec. 14, 1863.
S. A. Gilbert..........	Col. 44th Ohio Infy..............	Dec. 14, 1863, to Jan. 6, 1864.
J. W. Reilly..........	Col. 104th Ohio Infy.............	Jan. 6, 1864, to Jan. 16, 1864.
F. A. Reeve..........	Col. 8th Tenn. Infy..............	Jan. 16, 1864, to Apr. 3, 1864.
J. W. Reilly..........	Col. 104th Ohio Infy.............	Apr. 3, 1864, to May 26, 1864.
J. W. Gault..........	Col. 16th Kentucky Infy..........	May 26, 1864, to May 27, 1864.
J. W. Reilly..........	Col. 104th Ohio Infy.............	May 27, 1864, to Sept. 22, 1864.
S. P. Love............	Col. 11th Kentucky Infy..........	Sept. 22, 1864, to Oct. 22, 1864.
J. W. Reilly..........	Brigadier General..................	Oct. 22, 1864, to Dec. 14, 1864.
C. C. Doolittle........	Col. 18th Michigan Infy...........	Dec. 14, 1864, to Jan. 13, 1865.
C. W. Sterl..........	Col. 104th Ohio Infy.............	Jan. 13, 1864, to Feb. 2, 1865.

107th Illinois Infy........June, 1863	From Dist. West Kentucky........	To 2-Brig. 2-Div. 23-Corps.......	Aug., 1863
23d Michigan Infy.......June, 1863	From Dist. West Kentucky........	To 2-Brig. 2-Div. 23-Corps.......	Aug., 1863
111th Ohio Infy.........June, 1863	From Dist. West Kentucky........	To 2-Brig. 2-Div. 23-Corps.......	Aug., 1863
14th Illinois Cav.......June, 1863	From Dist. West Kentucky........	To 3-Brig. 4-Div. 23-Corps.......	Aug., 1863
5th Indiana Cav.........June, 1863	From Dist. West Kentucky........	To 2-Brig. 4-Div. 23-Corps.......	Aug., 1863
Elgin, Ill. Batty........June, 1863	From Dist. West Kentucky........	To 1-Brig. 2-Div. 23-Corps.......	Aug., 1863
Henshaw's Ill. Batty....June, 1863	From Dist. West Kentucky........	To 2-Brig. 2-Div. 23-Corps.......	Aug., 1863
44th Ohio Infy.........Aug., 1863	From 2-Brig. 4-Div. 23-Corps.....	Reorganized as 8th Ohio Cav.....	Jan., 1864
100th Ohio Infy.........Aug., 1863	From 2-Brig. 4-Div. 23-Corps.....	To 1-Brig. 3-Div. 23-Corps D. N. C.	Feb., 1865
104th Ohio Infy.........Aug., 1863	From 2-Brig. 4-Div. 23-Corps.....	To 1-Brig. 3-Div. 23-Corps D. N. C.	Feb., 1865
12th Kentucky Infy......Aug., 1863	From 1-Brig. 4-Div. 23-Corps.....	To Camp Burnside, Ky...........	Jan., 1864
Batty. D, 1st Ohio Arty..Aug., 1863	From 2-Brig. 4-Div. 23-Corps.....	To Arty. 3-Div. 23-Corps........	Jan., 1864
117th Indiana Infy......Dec., 1863	From 1-Brig. Left Wing Forces.....	To Dist. of the Clinch Dept. Ohio..	Jan., 1864
8th Tennessee Infy......Jan., 1864	From 1-Brig. Left Wing Forces.....	To 1-Brig. 3-Div. 23-Corps D. N. C.	Feb., 1865
19th Ohio Batty.........Jan., 1864	From Arty. Res. 23-Corps........	To Arty. 2-Div. 23-Corps........	Apr., 1864
63d Indiana Infy........Apr., 1864	From Sub-Dist. Southwest Ky.....	To 2-Brig. 3-Div. 23-Corps.......	Apr., 1864
16th Kentucky Infy......Apr., 1864	From 2-Brig. 2-Div. 23-Corps.....	To 1-Brig. 3-Div. 23-Corps D. N. C.	Feb., 1865
112th Illinois Infy.......May, 1864	From 2-Brig. 3-Div. 23-Corps.....	To 3-Brig. 3-Div. 23-Corps.......	Aug., 1864
11th Kentucky Infy......Aug., 1864	From 3-Brig. 3-Div. 23-Corps.....	No change to Muster Out.........	Dec., 1864
12th Kentucky Infy......Aug., 1864	From 3-Brig. 3-Div. 23-Corps.....	To 1-Brig. 3-Div. 23-Corps D. N. C...	Feb., 1865

2d BRIGADE.— COMMANDERS.

E. H. Robson	Brigadier General	June 24, 1863, to Aug. 6, 1863.
D. Cameron	Col. 65th Illinois Infy.	Aug. 6, 1863, to Feb. 14, 1864.
J. S. Casement	Col. 103d Ohio Infy.	Feb. 14, 1864, to Apr. 7, 1864.
M. D. Manson	Brigadier General	Apr. 7, 1864, to May 14, 1864.
J. S. Hurt	Col. 24th Kentucky Infy.	May 14, 1864, to May 16, 1864.
M. S. Hascall	Brigadier General	May 16, 1864, to May 18, 1864.
J. S. Hurt	Col. 24th Kentucky Infy.	May 18, 1864, to May 21, 1864.
J. S. Casement	Col. 103d Ohio Infy.	May 21, 1864, to June 4, 1864.
D. Cameron	Col. 65th Illinois Infy.	June 4, 1864, to July 31, 1864.
J. S. Casement	Col. 103d Ohio Infy.	July 31, 1864, to Feb. 2, 1865.

80th Indiana Infy	June, 1863	From Dist. Western Kentucky	To 1-Brig. 2-Div. 23-Corps	Aug.,	1863
13th Kentucky Infy	June, 1863	From Dist. Western Kentucky	To 2-Brig. 2-Div. 23-Corps	Aug.,	1863
16th Kentucky Infy	June, 1863	From Dist. Western Kentucky	To 1-Brig. 2-Div. 23-Corps	Aug.,	1863
9th Kentucky Cav	June, 1863	From Dist. Western Kentucky	To Unatt. 1-Div. 23-Corps	Aug.,	1863
11th Kentucky Cav	June, 1863	From Dist. Western Kentucky	To Indpt. Cav. Brig. 23-Corps	Aug.,	1863
12th Kentucky Cav	June, 1863	From Dist. Western Kentucky	To Indpt. Cav. Brig. 23-Corps	Aug.,	1863
24th Indiana Batty	June, 1863	From Dist. Western Kentucky	To 2-Brig. 4-Div. 23-Corps	Aug.,	1863
65th Illinois Infy	Aug., 1863	From 1-Brig. 4-Div. 23-Corps	To 2-Brig. 3-Div. 23-Corps D. N. C.	Feb.,	1865
103d Ohio Infy	Aug., 1863	From 1-Brig. 1-Div. 23-Corps	To 2-Brig. 3-Div. 23-Corps D. N. C.	Feb.,	1865
8th Tennessee Infy	Aug., 1863	From 2-Brig. 1-Div. 23-Corps	To 1-Brig. 3-Div. 23-Corps	Apr.,	1864
Batty. M, 2d Ill. Arty	Aug., 1863	From 1-Brig. 4-Div. 23-Corps	To Dist. N. C. Ky. 1-Div. 23-Corps	Sept.,	1863
24th Kentucky Infy	Aug., 1863	From 2-Brig. 4-Div. 23-Corps	To Louisa, Ky., Mil. Dist. Ky.	Dec.,	1864
Wilder's Indiana Batty	Aug., 1863	From 2-Brig. 4-Div. 23-Corps	To 2-Brig. 4-Div. 23-Corps	Apr.,	1864
63d Indiana Infy	Apr., 1864	From 3-Div. 23-Corps	To 3-Brig. 3-Div. 23-Corps	Aug.,	1864
5th Tennessee Infy	Apr., 1864	From 3-Brig. 3-Div. 12-Corps Cum'd.	To 3-Brig. 3-Div. 23-Corps	June,	1864
65th Indiana Infy	Apr., 1864	From 2-Brig. 2-Div. Cav. Corps Ohio	To 2-Brig. 3-Div. 23-Corps D. N. C.	Feb.,	1865
124th Indiana Infy	Aug., 1864	From 4-Brig. 3-Div. 23-Corps	To 1-Brig. 1-Div. 23-Corps	Dec.,	1864
5th Tennessee Infy	Dec., 1864	From 3-Brig. 3-Div. 23-Corps	To 2-Brig. 3-Div. 23-Corps D. N. C.	Feb.,	1865
177th Ohio Infy	Dec., 1864	To Def. Nash. and Chatt. R. R. Cm'd	To 2-Brig. 3-Div. 23-Corps D. N. C.	Feb.,	1865

3d BRIGADE.—Discontinued Aug. 6, 1863. Reorganized June 4, 1864.

COMMANDERS.

J. A. Cooper	Col. 6th Tennessee Infy.	June 1, 1863, to June 4, 1863.
N. C. McLean	Brigadier General	June 4, 1863, to June 17, 1863.
W. B. Stokes	Col. 5th Tennessee Cav.	June 17, 1863, to Aug. 6, 1863.
R. K. Byrd	Col. 1st Tennessee Infy.	June 4, 1864, to Aug. 9, 1864.
I. N. Stiles	Col. 63d Indiana Infy.	Aug. 9, 1864, to Sept. 17, 1864.
T. J. Henderson	Col. 112th Illinois Infy.	Sept. 17, 1864, to Dec. 15, 1864.
I. N. Stiles	Col. 63d Indiana Infy.	Dec. 15, 1864, to Jan. 29, 1865.
T. J. Henderson	Col. 112th Illinois Infy.	Jan. 29, 1865, to Feb. 2, 1865.

3d Tennessee Infy	June, 1863	From Dist. Central Kentucky	To 3-Brig. 3-Div. Res. Corps Cum'd.	Aug.,	1863
5th Tennessee Infy	June, 1863	From Dist. Central Kentucky	To 3-Brig. 3-Div. Res. Corps Cum'd.	Aug.,	1863
6th Tennessee Infy	June, 1863	From Dist. Central Kentucky	To 3-Brig. 3-Div. Res. Corps Cum'd.	Aug.,	1863
11th Kentucky Infy	June, 1863	From Dist. Western Kentucky	To Unatt. 1-Div. 23-Corps	Aug.,	1863
5th Tennessee Cav. 5 Cos.	July, 1863	From Dist. Central Kentucky	To 2-Brig. 4-Div. 23-Corps	Aug.,	1863
11th Kentucky Infy	June, 1864	From 3-Brig. 4-Div. 23-Corps	To 1-Brig. 3-Div. 23-Corps	Aug.,	1864
12th Kentucky Infy	June, 1864	From Camp Burnside Ky.	To 1-Brig. 3-Div. 23-Corps	Aug.,	1864
1st Tennessee Infy	June, 1864	From 3-Brig. 4-Div. 23-Corps	To 2-Brig. 4-Div. 23-Corps	Dec.,	1864
5th Tennessee Infy	June, 1864	From 2-Brig. 3-Div. 23-Corps	To 2-Brig. 3-Div. 23-Corps	Dec.,	1864
63d Indiana Infy	Aug., 1864	From 2-Brig. 3-Div. 23-Corps	To 3-Brig. 3-Div. 23-Corps D. N. C.	Feb.,	1865
120th Indiana Infy	Aug., 1864	From 4-Brig. 3-Div. 23-Corps	To 1-Brig. 1-Div. 23-Corps	Dec.,	1864
128th Indiana Infy	Aug., 1864	From 4-Brig. 3-Div. 23-Corps	To 1-Brig. 1-Div. 23-Corps	Dec.,	1864
112th Illinois Infy	Aug., 1864	From 1-Brig. 3-Div. 23-Corps	To 3-Brig. 3-Div. 23-Corps D. N. C.	Feb.,	1865
140th Indiana Infy	Dec., 1864	From Murfreesboro, Tenn.	To 3-Brig. 3-Div. 23-Corps D. N. C.	Feb.,	1865
175th Ohio Infy	Dec., 1864	From Columbia, Tenn.	To Unatt. 4-Div. 20-Corps Cumb'd.	Feb.,	1865

4th BRIGADE.— COMMANDER.

R. F. Barter	Col. 120th Indiana Infy.	June 9, 1864, to Aug. 11, 1864.

120th Indiana Infy	June, 1864	From 1-Brig. 1-Div. 23-Corps	To 3-Brig. 3-Div. 23-Corps	Aug.,	1864
124th Indiana Infy	June, 1864	From 1-Brig. 1-Div. 23-Corps	To 2-Brig. 3-Div. 23-Corps	Aug.,	1864
128th Indiana Infy	June, 1864	From 1-Brig. 1-Div. 23-Corps	To 3-Brig. 3-Div. 23-Corps	Aug.,	1864

DETACHED CAVALRY BRIGADE.—Attached to Division June 21, 1864. Transferred to Cavalry Division Aug. 22, 1864.

16th Illinois Cav	June, 1864	From 1-Brig. Cav. Div. Army Ohio	To 1-Brig. Cav. Div. Army Ohio	Aug.,	1864
12th Kentucky Cav	June, 1864	From 1-Brig. Cav. Div. Army Ohio	To 1-Brig. Cav. Div. Army Ohio	Aug.,	1864

ARTILLERY, 3d DIVISION.—

Batty. L, 1st Mich. Arty	June, 1863	From New Organization	To Cumberland Gap, L. W. Forces	Sept.,	1863
15th Indiana Batty	Apr., 1864	From Arty. 2-Div. 9-Corps Ohio	To Arty. 2-Div. 23-Corps	Dec.,	1864
Batty. D, 1st Ohio Arty	Apr., 1864	From 1-Brig. 3-Div. 23-Corps	To Arty. 3-Div. 23-Corps D. N. C.	Feb.,	1865
23d Indiana Batty	Aug., 1864	From Arty. 1-Div. 23-Corps	To Arty. 3-Div. 23-Corps D. N. C.	Feb.,	1865

4th DIVISION.—Discontinued and formed into a Cavalry Corps Nov. 3, 1863. Reorganized April 10, 1864. Transferred to Dept. Cumberland Feb. 10, 1865.

COMMANDERS.

Julius White	Brigadier General	June 24, 1863, to Aug. 6, 1863.
S. P. Carter	Brigadier General	Aug. 6, 1863, to Sept. 10, 1863.
J. M. Shackleford	Brigadier General	Sept. 10, 1863, to Nov. 3, 1863.
Jacob Ammen	Brigadier General	Apr. 10, 1864, to Jan. 14, 1865.
Davis Tillson	Brigadier General	Jan. 14, 1865, to Feb. 10, 1865.

1st BRIGADE.— COMMANDERS.

Daniel Cameron	Col. 65th Indiana Infy.	June 24, 1863, to Aug. 6, 1863.
Julius White	Brigadier General	Aug. 6, 1863, to Aug. 21, 1863.
Robt. K. Byrd	Col. 1st Tennessee Infy.	Aug. 21, 1863, to Oct. 10, 1863.
C. D. Pennypacker	Col. 27th Kentucky Infy.	Oct. 10, 1863, to Nov. 3, 1863.
John Mehringer	Col. 91st Indiana Infy.	Apr. 17, 1864, to May 17, 1864.
W. Y. Dillard	Col. 34th Kentucky Infy.	May 17, 1864, to Nov. 29, 1864.
W. C. Bartlett	Lt.-Col. 2d North Carolina	Nov. 29, 1864, to Feb. 10, 1865.

65th Illinois Infy	June, 1863	From Dist. Central Kentucky	To 2-Brig. 3-Div. 23-Corps	Aug.,	1863
14th Kentucky Infy	June, 1863	From Dist. Eastern Kentucky	To Dist. E. Ky. 1-Div. 23-Corps	Aug.,	1863
10th Kentucky Cav	June, 1863	From 2-Brig. Dist. Central Ky.	No change to Muster Out	Aug.,	1863
39th Kentucky Infy	June, 1863	From Dist. Eastern Kentucky	To Dist. E. Ky. 1-Div. 23-Corps	Aug.,	1863
McLaughlin's Ohio Cav	June, 1863	From Dist. Eastern Kentucky	To Headqu'rts 23-Corps Escort	Aug.,	1863
Batty. M, 2d Ill. Arty	June, 1863	From Reorganization	To 2-Brig. 3-Div. 23-Corps	Aug.,	1863
1st Tennessee Infy	Aug., 1863	From 1-Brig. 1-Div. 23-Corps	To 2-Brig. 4-Div. 23-Corps	Oct.,	1863

1st BRIGADE.—Continued.

Regiment	Date	From	To	Date
112th Illinois Infy	Aug., 1863	From 1-Brig. 1-Div. 23-Corps	To 2-Brig. 4-Div. 23-Corps	Oct., 1863
45th Ohio Infy	Aug., 1863	From 2-Brig. 4-Div. 23-Corps	To 2-Brig. 4-Div. 23-Corps	Oct., 1863
8th Michigan Cav	Aug., 1863	From 2-Brig. 1-Div. 23-Corps	To 2-Brig. 4-Div. 23-Corps	Oct., 1863
15th Indiana Batty	Aug., 1863	From 2-Brig. 1-Div. 23-Corps	To 2-Brig. 4-Div. 23-Corps	Oct., 1863
11th Ky. Mtd Infy	Oct., 1863	From Unass'd 1-Div. 23-Corps	To 3-Brig. 1-Cav. Div. 23-Corps	Nov., 1863
27th Ky. Mtd Infy	Oct., 1863	From Unass'd 1-Div. 23-Corps	To 3-Brig. 1-Cav. Div. 23-Corps	Nov., 1863
91st Indiana Infy	Apr., 1864	From Dist. Clinch Dept. Ohio	To 1-Brig. 2-Div. 23-Corps	June, 1864
34th Kentucky Infy	Apr., 1864	From Dist. South Central Ky	To 1-Brig. 4-Div. 23-Corps	Dec., 1864
2d North Carolina Mtd	Apr., 1864	From Dist. Clinch Dept. Ohio	To 1-Brig. 4-Div. Dist. E. Tenn C'md	Feb., 1865
11th Tennessee Cav	Apr., 1864	From Dist. Clinch Dept. Ohio	Consolidated with 9th Tenn. Cav	Jan., 1865
Batty. L, 1st Mich. Arty	Apr., 1864	From Dist. Clinch Dept. Ohio	To 2-Brig. 4-Div. 23-Corps	Aug., 1864
Batty. M, 1st Mich. Arty	Apr., 1864	From Dist. Clinch Dept. Ohio	To 1-Brig. 4-Div. Dist. E. Tenn. C'md	Feb., 1865
Batty. B, 1st Tenn. Arty	Apr., 1864	From Dist. Clinch Dept. Ohio	To 1-Brig. 4-Div. Dist. E. Tenn. C'md	Feb., 1865
22d Ohio Batty	Apr., 1864	From Dist. Clinch Dept. Ohio	To 2-Brig. 4-Div. 23-Corps	Aug., 1864
34th Kentucky Infy	Jan., 1865	From 2-Brig. 4-Div. 23-Corps	To 1-Brig. 4-Div. Dist. East Tenn	Feb., 1865

2d BRIGADE.—

COMMANDERS.

Commander	Rank/Unit	Dates
S. R. Mott	Col. 118th Ohio Infy	June 24, 1863, to July 8, 1863.
S. A. Gilbert	Col. 44th Ohio Infy	July 8, 1863, to Aug. 6, 1863.
E. H. Hobson	Brigadier General	Aug. 6, 1863, to Aug. 21, 1863.
F. W. Graham	Col. 5th Indiana Cav	Aug. 21, 1863, to Aug. 28, 1863.
J. W. Foster	Col. 65th Indiana Infy	Aug. 28, 1863, to Oct. 17, 1863.
E. S. Bond	Lt.-Col. 112th Ill. Infy	Oct. 17, 1863, to Nov. 3, 1863.
Davis Tillson	Brigadier General	Apr. 10, 1864, to Jan. 28, 1865.
H. G. Gibson	Col. 2d Ohio H. Arty	Jan. 28, 1864, to Feb. 10, 1865.

Regiment	Date	From	To	Date
118th Ohio Infy	June, 1863	From Dist. Central Ky	To 2-Brig. 1-Div. 23-Corps	July, 1863
8th Tennessee Infy	June, 1863	From Dist. Central Ky	To 2-Brig. 1-Div. 23-Corps	July, 1863
5th Middle Tenn. Cav	June, 1863	From Dist. Central Ky	To 2-Brig. 1-Div. 23-Corps	July, 1863
10th Kentucky Cav	June, 1863	From 2-Brig. Dist. Central Ky	To 2-Brig. 1-Div. 23-Corps	July, 1863
14th Kentucky Infy	June, 1863	From Dist. Central Ky	To 2-Brig. 1-Div. 23-Corps	July, 1863
8th Michigan Cav	June, 1863	From New Organization	To 2-Brig. 1-Div. 23-Corps	July, 1863
15th Indiana Batty	June, 1863	From Dist. Central Ky	To 2-Brig. 1-Div. 23-Corps	July, 1863
19th Ohio Batty	June, 1863	From Dist. Central Ky	To 2-Brig. 1-Div. 23-Corps	July, 1863
24th. Kentucky Infy	July, 1863	From 2-Brig. 1-Div. 23-Corps	To 2-Brig. 3-Div. 23-Corps	Aug., 1863
44th Ohio Infy	July, 1863	From 2-Brig. 1-Div. 23-Corps	To 1-Brig. 3-Div. 23-Corps	Aug., 1863
45th Ohio Infy	July, 1863	From 2-Brig. 1-Div. 23-Corps	To 1-Brig. 4-Div. 23-Corps	Aug., 1863
100th Ohio Infy	July, 1863	From 2-Brig. 1-Div. 23-Corps	To 1-Brig. 3-Div. 23-Corps	Aug., 1863
104th Ohio Infy	July, 1863	From 2-Brig. 1-Div. 23-Corps	To 1-Brig. 3-Div. 23-Corps	Aug., 1863
9th Ohio Cav	July, 1863	From 2-Brig. 1-Div. 23-Corps	To 4-Brig. 4-Div. 23-Corps	Oct., 1863
Batty. D, 1st Ohio Arty	July, 1863	From 2-Brig. 1-Div. 23-Corps	To 1-Brig. 3-Div. 23-Corps	Aug., 1863
Wilder's Indiana Batty	July, 1863	From 2-Brig. 1-Div. 23-Corps	To Res. Arty. 23-Corps	Aug., 1863
8th Tennessee Cav	Aug., 1863	From 2-Brig. 1-Div. 23-Corps	To 4-Brig. 4-Div. 23-Corps	Oct., 1863
65th Indiana Infy	Aug., 1863	From 1-Brig. 2-Div. 23-Corps	To 4-Brig. 4-Div. 23-Corps	Oct., 1863
24th Indiana Batty	Aug., 1863	From 2-Brig. 3-Div. 23-Corps	To Res. Arty. 23-Corps	Oct., 1863
14th Illinois Cav	Aug., 1863	From 1-Brig. 3-Div. 23-Corps	To 4-Brig. 4-Div. 23-Corps	Oct., 1863
5th Indiana Cav	Aug., 1863	From 1-Brig. 3-Div. 23-Corps	To 4-Brig. 4-Div. 23-Corps	Oct., 1863
Batty. M, 1st Illinois Arty	Aug., 1863	From 2-Brig. 3-Div. 23-Corps	To 4-Brig. 4-Div. 23-Corps	Oct., 1863
112th Illinois Infy	Oct., 1863	From 1-Brig. 4-Div. 23-Corps	To 2-Brig. 1-Div. Cav. Corps 23-C.	Nov., 1863
8th Michigan Cav	Oct., 1863	From 1-Brig. 4-Div. 23-Corps	To 2-Brig. 1-Div. Cav. Corps 23-C.	Nov., 1863
45th Ohio Infy	Oct., 1863	From 1-Brig. 4-Div. 23-Corps	To 2-Brig. 1-Div. Cav. Corps 23-C.	Nov., 1863
1st Tennessee Infy	Oct., 1863	From 1-Brig. 4-Div. 23-Corps	To 2-Brig. 1-Div. Cav. Corps 23-C.	Nov., 1863
15th Indiana Batty	Oct., 1863	From 1-Brig. 4-Div. 23-Corps	To 2-Brig. 1-Div. Cav. Corps 23-C.	Nov., 1863
10th Michigan Cav	Apr., 1864	From Dist. North Central Ky	To 2-Brig. 4-Div. Dist. E. Tenn. C'md	Feb., 1865
1st Ohio Heavy Arty	Apr., 1864	From Dist. North Central Ky	To Cleveland, Tenn	Oct., 1864
1st U. S. Colored H. A.	Apr., 1864	From New Organization	To 2-Brig. 4-Div. Dist. E. Tenn. C'md	Feb., 1865
Elgin Ill. Batty	Apr., 1864	From 1-Brig. 2-Div. 23-Corps	To Arty. 1-Div. 23-Corps	Jan., 1865
21st Ohio Batty	Apr., 1864	From Dist Clinch Dept. Ohio	To 2-Br. 4-D. Dist. E. Tenn. Cumb'd.	Feb., 1865
Wilder's Ind. Batty	Apr., 1864	From 2-Brig. 3-Div. 23-Corps	To 2-Br. 4-D. Dist. E. Tenn. Cumb'd.	Feb., 1865
Colvin's Ill. Batty	Apr., 1864	From 2-Br. 2-Div. Cav. C. Dept. O.	To 2-Br. 4-D. Dist. E. Tenn. Cumb'd.	Feb., 1865
2d Tenn. Infy	Apr., 1864	From 1-Br. 2-Div. Cav. C. Dept. O.	To 2-Br. 4-D. Dist. E. Tenn. Cumb'd.	Feb., 1865
3d North Carolina Mtd	July, 1864	From New Organization	To 2-Br. 4-D. Dist. E. Tenn. Cumb'd.	Feb., 1865
Batty. L, 1st Mich. Arty	Aug., 1864	From 1-Brig. 4-Div. 23-Corps	To 2-Br. 4-D. Dist. E. Tenn. Cumb'd.	Feb., 1865
22d Ohio Batty	Aug., 1864	From 1-Brig. 4-Div. 23-Corps	To 2-Br. 4-D. Dist. E. Tenn. Cumb'd.	Feb., 1865
2d Ohio Heavy Arty	Oct., 1864	From Cleveland, Tenn	To 2-Br. 4-D. Dist. E. Tenn. Cumb'd.	Feb., 1865
Henshaw's Ill. Batty	Oct., 1864	From 3-Brig. 4-Div. 23-Corps	To 2-Br. 4-D. Dist. E. Tenn. Cumb'd.	Feb., 1865
4th Tenn. Infy	Oct., 1864	From 3-Brig. 4-Div. 23-Corps	To 2-Br. 4-D. Dist. E. Tenn. Cumb'd.	Feb., 1865
12th Ky. Cav	Oct., 1864	From 1-Brig. Cav. Div. 23-Corps	To 2-Br. Cav. D. Dist. E. T. Cumb'd.	Feb., 1865
1st Tenn. Infy	Dec., 1864	From 3-Brig. 3-Div. 23-Corps	To 2-Br. 4-D. Dist. E. Tenn. Cumb'd.	Feb., 1865
34th Ky. Infy	Dec., 1864	From 1-Brig. 4-Div. 23-Corps	To 1-Brig. 4-Div. 23-Corps	Jan., 1865

3d BRIGADE.—Organized Aug. 6, 1863. Discontinued Nov. 3, 1863. Reorganized April 10, 1864. Discontinued Oct. 17, 1864.

COMMANDERS.

Commander	Rank/Unit	Dates
J. M. Shackleford	Brigadier General	Aug. 6, 1863, to Sept. 10, 1863.
J. P. T. Carter	Col. 2d Tenn. Infy	Sept. 10, 1863, to Nov. 3, 1863.
S. A. Strickland	Col. 50th Ohio Infy	Apr. 10, 1864, to May 1, 1864.
B. P. Runckle	Col. 45th Ohio Infy	May 1, 1864, to June 10, 1864.
M. L. Patterson	Lt.-Col. 4th Tenn. Infy	June 10, 1864, to Oct. 17, 1864.

Regiment	Date	From	To	Date
2d Tenn. Infy	Aug., 1863	From 1-Brig. 1-Div. 23-Corps	To 1-Br. 2-Div. Cav. Corps, Ohio	Nov., 1863
2d Ohio Cav	Aug., 1863	From 3-Brig. 1-Div. 23-Corps	To 1-Br. 2-Div. Cav. Corps, Ohio	Nov., 1863
7th Ohio Cav	Aug., 1863	From 3-Brig. 1-Div. 23-Corps	To 1-Br. 2-Div. Cav. Corps, Ohio	Nov., 1863
9th Mich. Cav	Aug., 1863	From 3-Brig. 1-Div. 23-Corps	To 1-Br. 2-Div. Cav. Corps, Ohio	Nov., 1863
1st Tenn. Batty	Aug., 1863	From 1-Brig. 1-Div. 23-Corps	To 2-Div. Arty. Res. Dept. Cumb'd.	Nov., 1863
27th Ky. Infy	Apr., 1864	From 3-Brig. 1-Div. Cav. C. Ohio.	To 3-Brig. 2-Div. 23-Corps	June, 1864
50th Ohio Infy	Apr., 1864	From Dist. South Central Ky	To 3-Brig. 2-Div. 23-Corps	June, 1864
1st Tenn. Infy	Apr., 1864	From 2-Brig. 1-Div. Cav. C. Ohio.	To 3-Brig. 2-Div. 23-Corps	June, 1864
4th Tenn. Infy	Apr., 1864	From Dist. North Central Ky	To 2-Brig. 4-Div. 23-Corps	Oct., 1864
14th Ill. Cav	Apr., 1864	From 2-Brig. 2-Div. Cav. C. Ohio.	To 3-Brig. Cav. Div. 23-Corps	June, 1864
Henshaw's Ill. Batty	Apr., 1864	From 2-Brig. 2-Div. Cav. C. Ohio.	To 2-Brig. 4-Div. 23-Corps	Oct., 1864
1st O. Heavy Arty. 3d Bn.	May, 1864	From Dist. North Central Ky	To Cleveland, Tenn	Oct., 1864
11th Ky. Mtd. Infy	Apr., 1864	From 3-Brig. 1-Div. Cav. C. Ohio.	To 3-Brig. 3-Div. 23-Corps	June, 1864

4th BRIGADE.—Organized Oct., 1863. Transferred to Cav. Corps Nov. 3, 1863.

COMMANDER.

Commander	Rank/Unit	
John W. Foster	Col. 65th Ind. Infy	

Regiment	Date	From	To	Date
14th Ill. Cav	Oct., 1863	From 2-Brig. 4-Div. 23-Corps	To 2-Brig. 2-Div. Cav. Corps Ohio	Nov., 1863
5th Ind. Cav	Oct., 1863	From 2-Brig. 4-Div. 23-Corps	To 2-Brig. 2-Div. Cav. Corps Ohio	Nov., 1863
65th Ind. Infy	Oct., 1863	From 2-Brig. 4-Div. 23-Corps	To 2-Brig. 2-Div. Cav. Corps Ohio	Nov., 1863
9th Ohio Cav	Oct., 1863	From 2-Brig. 4-Div. 23-Corps	To 2-Brig. 2-Div. Cav. Corps Ohio	Nov., 1863
8th Tenn. Cav	Oct., 1863	From 2-Brig. 4-Div. 23-Corps	To Dept. Cumb'd	Nov., 1863
Colvin's Ill. Batty	Oct., 1863	From New Organization	To 2-Brig. 2-Div. Cav. Corps Ohio	Nov., 1863

INDPT. CAVALRY BRIGADE.—Transferred to Cav. Corps Nov. 3, 1863.

COMMANDER.

F. Wolford	Col. 1st Ky. Cav.			
1st Ky. Cav. ....Aug., 1863	From 1-Brig. 1-Div. 23-Corps......	To 1-Brig. 1-Div. Cav. Corps Ohio.	Nov.,	1863
11th Ky. Cav. ....Aug., 1863	From 2-Brig. 3-Div. 23-Corps......	To 1-Brig. 1-Div. Cav. Corps Ohio.	Nov.,	1863
12th Ky. Cav. ....Aug., 1863	From 2-Brig. 3-Div. 23-Corps......	To 1-Brig. 1-Div. Cav. Corps Ohio.	Nov.,	1863

CAVALRY CORPS.—Organized Nov. 3, 1863, from 4th Division, 23d Corps.

COMMANDER.

S. D. Sturgis	Brigadier General	

1st DIVISION.—

COMMANDERS.

W. P. Sanders	Brigadier General	Nov. 3, 1863, to Nov. 16, 1863.	Killed.
Frank Wolford	Col. 1st Ky. Cav.	Nov. 16, 1863, to Apr. 8, 1864.	
C. D. Pennypacker	Col. 27th Ky. Infy.	Apr. 8, 1864, to Apr. 10, 1864.	

1st BRIGADE.—

COMMANDERS.

Frank Wolford	Col. 1st Ky. Cav.	Nov. 3, 1863, to Nov. 18, 1863.		
S. G. Adams	Lt.-Col. 1st Ky. Cav.	Nov. 18, 1863, to Apr. 8, 1864.		
Israel Garrard	Col. 7th Ohio Cav.	Apr. 8, 1864, to Apr. 10, 1864.		
1st Ky. Cav. ....Nov., 1863	From Indpt. Cav. Brig. 23-Corps..	To 3-Brig. Cav. Div. Dist. Ky.	Apr.,	1864
11th Ky. Cav. ....Nov., 1863	From Indpt. Cav. Brig. 23-Corps..	To 3-Brig. Cav. Div. Dist. Ky.	Apr.,	1864
12th Ky. Cav. ....Nov., 1863	From Indpt. Cav. Brig. 23-Corps..	To 1-Brig. 2-Div. Cav. Corps Ohio.	Apr.,	1864

2d BRIGADE.—

COMMANDERS.

E. S. Bond	Lt-Col. 112th Ill. Infy.	Nov. 3, 1863, to Jan. .., 1864.		
T. J. Henderson	Col. 112th Ill. Infy.	Jan. .., 1863, to Apr. .., 1864.		
112th Ill. Infy. ....Nov., 1863	From 2-Brig. 4-Div. 23-Corps......	To 1-Brig. 3-Div. 23-Corps......	Apr.,	1864
8th Mich. Cav. ....Nov., 1863	From 2-Brig. 4-Div. 23-Corps......	To 3-Brig. Cav. Div. Dist. Ky.	Apr.,	1864
45th Ohio Mtd. Infy. .....Nov., 1863	From 2-Brig. 4-Div. 23-Corps......	To 3-Brig. 1-Div. Cav. Corps Ohio.	Dec.,	1863
1st Tenn. Infy. ....Nov., 1863	From 2-Brig. 4-Div. 23-Corps......	To 3-Brig. 4-Div. 23-Corps......	Apr.,	1864
15th Ind. Batty. ....Nov., 1863	From 2-Brig. 4-Div. 23-Corps......	To Arty. 2-Div. 9-Corps Ohio......	Dec.,	1863
6th Ind. Cav. ....Apr., 1864	From Dist. Clinch Dept. Ohio.....	To 3-Brig. Cav. Div. Dist. Ky.	Apr.,	1864

3d BRIGADE.—

COMMANDERS.

C. D. Pennypacker	Col. 27th Ky. Infy.	Nov. .., 1863, to Jan. .., 1864.		
S. P. Love	Col. 11th Ky. Infy.	Jan. .., 1864, to Apr. .., 1864.		
11th Ky. Infy. ....Nov., 1863	From 1-Brig. 4-Div. 23-Corps......	To 3-Brig. 4-Div. 23-Corps......	Apr.,	1864
27th Ky. Infy. ....Nov., 1863	From 1-Brig. 4-Div. 23-Corps......	To 3-Brig. 4-Div. 23-Corps......	Apr.,	1864
45th Ohio Mtd. Infy. .....Dec., 1863	From 2-Brig. 1-Div. Cav. C. Ohio..	To 2-Brig. 2-Div. 23-Corps......	Apr.,	1864
16th Ill. Cav. ....Apr., 1864	From Dist. Clinch Dept. Ohio.....	To 3-Brig. Cav. Div. Dist. Ky.	Apr.,	1864

2d DIVISION.—

COMMANDERS.

J. W. Foster	Col. 65th Ind. Infy.	Nov. .., 1863, to Jan. .., 1864.	
Israel Garrard	Col. 7th Ohio Cav.	Jan. .., 1864, to Apr. .., 1864.	
Jas. Biddle	Col. 6th Ind. Cav.	Apr. .., 1864, to May .., 1864.	

1st BRIGADE.—

COMMANDERS.

Israel Garrard	Col. 7th Ohio Cav.	Nov. .., 1863, to Jan. .., 1864.		
Geo. G. Miner	Lt.-Col. 7th Ohio Cav.	Jan. .., 1864, to Apr. .., 1864.		
E. W. Crittenden	Col. 12th Ky. Cav.	Apr. .., 1864.		
2d Tenn. Mtd. ....Nov., 1863	From 3-Brig. 4-Div. 23-Corps......	To 2-Brig. 4-Div. 23-Corps......	Apr.,	1864
9th Mich. Cav. ....Nov., 1863	From 3-Brig. 4-Div. 23-Corps......	To 1-Brig. Cav. Div. Dist. Ky.	Apr.,	1864
2d Ohio Cav. ....Nov., 1863	From 3-Brig. 4-Div. 23-Corps......	To Columbus, Ohio.	Jan.,	1864
7th Ohio Cav. ....Nov., 1863	From 3-Brig. 4-Div. 23-Corps......	To 1-Brig. Cav. Div. Dist. Ky.	Apr.,	1864
12th Ky. Cav. ....Apr., 1864	From 1-Br. 1-Div. Cav. Corps Ohio..	To 3-Brig. Cav. Div. Dist. Ky.	Apr.,	1864

2d BRIGADE.—

COMMANDERS.

Horace Capron	Col. 14th Ill. Cav.	Nov. .., 1863, to Jan. .., 1864.		
T. H. Butler	Lt.-Col. 5th Ind. Cav.	Jan. .., 1864, to Feb. .., 1864.		
Horace Capron	Col. 14th Ill. Cav.	Feb. .., 1864, to Apr. ... 1864.		
14th Ill. Cav. ....Nov., 1863	From 4-Brig. 4-Div. 23-Corps......	To 3-Brig. Cav. Div. Dist. Ky.	Apr.,	1864
5th Ind. Cav. ....Nov., 1863	From 4-Brig. 4-Div. 23-Corps......	To 3-Brig. Cav. Div. Dist. Ky.	Apr.,	1864
65th Ind. Infy. ....Nov., 1863	From 4-Brig. 4-Div. 23-Corps......	To 2-Brig. 3-Div. 23-Corps......	Apr.,	1864
9th Ohio Cav. 4 Co's.....Nov., 1863	From 4-Brig. 4-Div. 23-Corps......	To Athens, Ala. Dist. N. Ala. Cumb'd.	Mch.,	1864
16th Ky. Cav. ....Nov., 1863	From New Organization...........	To 1-Brig. Cav. Div. Dist. Ky.	Apr.,	1864
8th Tenn. Cav. ....Nov., 1863	From 4-Brig. 4-Div. 23-Corps......	To 3-Br. 4-Div. Cav. Corps Cumb'd.	Apr.,	1864
ARTILLERY.—				
Colvin's Ill. Batty. ....Nov., 1863	From 4-Brig. 4-Div. 23-Corps......	To 2-Brig. 4-Div. 23-Corps......	Apr.,	1864

CAVALRY DIVISION.—Organized April 10, 1864.

COMMANDERS.

Geo. Stoneman	Major General	Apr. 10, 1864, to July 31, 1864.	
Horace Capron	Col. 14th Ill. Cav.	July 31, 1864, to Aug. 11, 1864.	
Israel Garrard	Col. 7th Ohio Cav.	Aug. 11, 1864, to Nov. 1, 1864.	

1st BRIGADE.—

COMMANDERS.

James Biddle	Col. 6th Ind. Cav.	May 1, 1864, to June 28, 1864.		
T. H. Butler	Col. 5th Ind. Cav.	June 28, 1864, to Aug. 11, 1864.		
Horace Capron	Col. 14th Ill. Cav.	Aug. 11, 1864, to Nov. 1, 1864.		
16th Ill. Cav. ....May, 1864	From 3-Brig. Cav. Div. Dist. Ky.	To Det. Cav. Brig. 3-Div. 23-Corps..	June,	1864
12th Ky. Cav. ....May, 1864	From 3-Brig. Cav. Div. Dist. Ky.	To Det. Cav. Brig. 3-Div. 23-Corps..	June,	1864
5th Ind. Cav. ....May, 1864	From 3-Brig. Cav. Div. Dist. Ky.	To 2-Brig. Cav. Div. 23-Corps......	July,	1864
6th Ind. Cav. ....May, 1864	From 3-Brig. Cav. Div. Dist. Ky.	To 2-Brig. Cav. Div. 23-Corps......	July,	1864
9th Mich. Cav. ....July, 1864	From 1-Brig. Cav. Div. Dist. Ky.	To Mtd. Brig. Cav. Div. 23-Corps..	Aug.,	1864
7th Ohio Cav. ....July, 1864	From 1-Brig. Cav. Div. Dist. Ky.	To Mtd. Brig. Cav. Div. 23-Corps..	Aug.,	1864
14th Ill. Cav. ....Sept., 1864	From Dism'd Brig. Cav. Div. 23-C..	To 1-Br. 6-Div. Wilson's Cav. Corps.	Nov.,	1864
16th Ill. Cav. ....Sept., 1864	From Dism'd Brig. Cav. Div. 23-C..	To 1-Br. 6-Div. Wilson's Cav. Corps.	Nov.,	1864
5th Ind. Cav. ....Sept., 1864	From Dism'd Brig. Cav. Div. 23-C..	To Louisville, Ky. Dist. Ky.	Sept.,	1864
6th Ind. Cav. ....Sept., 1864	From Dism'd Brig. Cav. Div. 23-C..	To 1-Br. 6-Div. Wilson's Cav. Corps.	Nov.,	1864
12th Ky. Cav. ....Sept., 1864	From Dism'd Brig. Cav. Div. 23-C..	To 2-Brig. 4-Div. 23-Corps......	Nov.,	1864

2d BRIGADE.—

COMMANDERS.

T. H. Butler	Col. 5th Ind. Cav.	July 31, 1864, to Aug. 11, 1864.	
Geo. S. Acker	Col. 9th Mich. Cav.	Sept. .., 1864, to Nov. .., 1864.	

5th Ind. Cav.	July, 1864	From 1-Brig. Cav. Div. 23-Corps...	To Dismt'd Brig. Cav. Div. 23-Corps.	Aug., 1864
6th Ind. Cav.	July, 1864	From 1-Brig. Cav. Div. 23-Corps...	To Dismt'd Brig. Cav. Div. 23-Corps.	Aug., 1864
9th Mich. Cav.	Sept., 1864	From Mtd. Brig. Cav. Div. 23-Corps.	To 2-Br. 3-Div. Cav. C. M. D. M.	Nov., 1864
7th Ohio Cav.	Sept., 1864	From Mtd. Brig. Cav. Div. 23-Corps.	To 1-Br. 6-Div. Cav. C. M. D. M.	Nov., 1864
9th Ohio Cav. Det.	Sept., 1864	From Mtd. Brig. Cav. Div. 23-Corps.	To 2-Br. 3-Div. Cav. C. M. D. M.	Nov., 1864
McLaughlin's Ohio Cav.	Sept., 1864	From Mtd. Brig. Cav. Div. 23-Corps.	To 2-Br. 3-Div. Cav. C. M. D. M.	Nov., 1864
22d Ind. Batty.	Sept., 1864	From Mtd. Brig. Cav. Div. 23-Corps.	To Garrison Arty. Nashville, T.	Nov., 1864

3d BRIGADE.—

COMMANDER.

Horace Capron	Col. 14th Ill. Cav.	June 28, 1864, to Aug. 11, 1864.	

14th Ill. Cav.	June, 1864	From 3-Brig. Cav. Div. Dist. Ky.	To Dismtd. Brig. Cav. Div. 23-C.	Aug., 1864
8th Mich. Cav.	June, 1864	From 3-Brig. Cav. Div. Dist. Ky.	To Prisoners of War.	Aug., 1864
McLaughlin's Ohio Cav.	June, 1864	From 3-Brig. Cav. Div. Dist. Ky.	To Mtd. Brig. Cav. Div. 23-Corps.	Aug., 1864
INDEPENDENT BRIGADE.—				
1st Ky. Cav.	June, 1864	From 3-Brig. Cav. Div. Dist. Ky.	To 4-Brig. 1-Div. Dist. Ky.	July, 1864
11th Ky. Cav.	June, 1864	From 3-Brig. Cav. Div. Dist. Ky.	To Mil. Dist. Ky.	July, 1864
ARTILLERY.—				
24th Ind. Batty.	July, 1864	From Arty. 1-Div. 23-Corps.	To Mtd. Brig. Cav. Div. 23-Corps.	Aug., 1864

MOUNTED BRIGADE.—Aug. and Sept., 1864.

COMMANDERS.

Geo. S. Acker	Col. 9th Mich. Cav.	Aug. 11, 1864, to Aug. 16, 1864.	
W. D. Hamilton	Col. 9th Ohio Cav.	Aug. 16, 1864, to Aug. 23, 1864.	
Geo. S. Acker	Col. 9th Mich. Cav.	Aug. 23, 1864, to Sept. .., 1864.	

9th Mich. Cav.	Aug., 1864	From 1-Brig. Cav. Div. 23-Corps.	To 2-Brig. Cav. Div. 23-Corps.	Sept., 1864
7th Ohio Cav.	Aug., 1864	From 1-Brig. Cav. Div. 23-Corps.	To 2-Brig. Cav. Div. 23-Corps.	Sept., 1864
9th Ohio Cav. Det.	Aug., 1864	From Cav. Dist. North Ala. Cumb'd.	To 2-Brig. Cav. Div. 23-Corps.	Sept., 1864
McLaughlin's Ohio Cav.	Aug., 1864	From 3-Brig. Cav. Div. 23-Corps.	To 2-Brig. Cav. Div. 23-Corps.	Sept., 1864

DISMOUNTED BRIGADE, CAVALRY DIVISION.—

COMMANDER.

Horace Capron	Col. 14th Ill. Cav.	Aug. 11, 1864, to Sept. 19, 1864.	

14th Ill. Cav.	Aug., 1864	From 3-Brig. Cav. Div. 23-Corps.	To 1-Brig. Cav. Div. 23-Corps.	Sept., 1864
16th Ill. Cav.	Aug., 1864	From Det. Brig. 3-Div. 23-Corps.	To 1-Brig. Cav. Div. 23-Corps.	Sept., 1864
5th Ind. Cav.	Aug., 1864	From 2-Brig. Cav. Div. 23-Corps.	To 1-Brig. Cav. Div. 23-Corps.	Sept., 1864
6th Ind. Cav.	Aug., 1864	From 2-Brig. Cav. Div. 23-Corps.	To 1-Brig. Cav. Div. 23-Corps.	Sept., 1864
12th Ky. Cav.	Aug., 1864	From Det. Brig. 3-Div. 23-Corps.	To 1-Brig. Cav. Div. 23-Corps.	Sept., 1864

5th DIVISION OR DISTRICT OF KENTUCKY.—Organized April 10, 1864. Transferred to Dept. of the Cumberland Jan. 17, 1865.

COMMANDERS.

E. H. Hobson	Brigadier General	Apr. 1, 1864, to Apr. 10, 1864.	
S. G. Burbridge	Brigadier General	Apr. 10, 1864, to Feb. 22, 1865.	

1st DIVISION.—

COMMANDERS.

E. H. Hobson	Brigadier General	Apr. 10, 1864, to July 6, 1864.	
N. C. McLean	Brigadier General	July 6, 1864, to Dec. 29, 1864.	
E. H. Hobson	Brigadier General	Dec. 29, 1864, to Jan. 17, 1865.	

1st BRIGADE.—

COMMANDERS.

G. W. Gallup	Col. 14th Ky. Infy.	Apr. 13, 1864, to May 8, 1864.	
S. B. Brown	Col. 11th Mich. Cav.	May 8, 1864, to July 6, 1864.	
E. H. Hobson	Brigadier General	July 6, 1864, to Oct. 15, 1864.	
C. J. True	Col. 40th Ky. Infy.	Oct. 15, 1864, to Jan. 17, 1865.	

14th Ky. Infy.	Apr., 1864	From Dist. Eastern Ky.	To 3-Brig. 2-Div. 23-Corps.	May, 1864
39th Ky. Infy.	Apr., 1864	From Dist. Eastern Ky.	To 3-Brig. 1-Div. Dist. Ky.	July, 1864
11th Mich. Cav.	Apr., 1864	From Lexington, Ky.	To 4-Brig. 1-Div. Dist. Ky.	July, 1864
35th Ky. Mtd. Infy.	July, 1864	From 2-Brig. 2-Div. Dist. Ky.	No change to Muster Out.	Dec., 1864
40th Ky. Mtd. Infy.	July, 1864	From 2-Brig. 1-Div. Dist. Ky.	No change to Muster Out.	Dec., 1864
13th Ky. Cav.	July, 1864	From 2-Brig. 1-Div. Dist. Ky.	No change to Muster Out.	Jan., 1865

2d BRIGADE.—

COMMANDERS.

C. J. True	Col. 40th Ky. Infy.	Apr. 10, 1864, to July 6, 1864.	
J. M. Brown	Col. 45th Ky. Infy.	July 6, 1864, to Sept. 2, 1864.	
F. N. Alexander	Col. 30th Ky. Infy.	Sept. 2, 1864, to Jan. 17, 1865.	

40th Ky. Infy.	Apr., 1864	From Dist. Southwest Ky.	To 1-Brig. 1-Div. Dist. Ky.	July, 1864
13th Ky. Cav.	Apr., 1864	From Dist. Southwest Ky.	To 1-Brig. 1-Div. Dist. Ky.	July, 1864
12th Ohio Cav.	Apr., 1864	From New Organization.	To 4-Brig. 1-Div. Dist. Ky.	July, 1864
30th Ky. Infy.	July, 1864	From 4-Brig. 1-Div. Dist. Ky.	To Louisa, Ky. Dist. Eastern Ky.	Jan., 1865
45th Ky. Infy.	July, 1864	From 4-Brig. 1-Div. Dist. Ky.	No change to Muster Out.	Jan., 1865

3d BRIGADE.—

COMMANDERS.

C. S. Hanson	Col. 37th Ky. Infy.	Apr. 13, 1864, to Oct. 7, 1864.	
B. J. Spaulding	Lt.-Col. 37th Ky. Infy.	Oct. 7, 1864, to Dec. 29, 1864.	

37th Ky. Infy.	Apr., 1864	From Dist. Southwest Ky.	No change to Muster Out.	Dec., 1864
52d Ky. Infy.	Apr., 1864	From New Organization.	To 2-Brig. 2-Div. Dept. Ky.	Feb., 1865
39th Ky. Infy.	July, 1864	From 1-Brig. 1-Div. Dist. Ky.	To Louisa, Dist. Eastern Ky.	Dec., 1864
109th U. S. C. T.	July, 1864	From New Organization.	To 1-Br. 2-Div. 25-C. Army James.	Dec., 1864
Batty. C, Ky. Arty.	July, 1864	From Dist. Southwest Ky.	To Mt. Sterling Ky. 1-Div. Dept. Ky.	Feb., 1865

4th BRIGADE.—

COMMANDERS.

J. M. Brown	Col. 45th Ky. Infy.	Apr. 10, 1864, to July 6, 1864.	
R. W. Ratliff	Col. 12th Ohio Cav.	July 6, 1864, to Jan. 17, 1865.	

30th Ky. Infy.	Apr., 1864	From New Organization.	To 2-Brig. 1-Div. Dist. Ky.	July, 1864
45th Ky. Infy.	Apr., 1864	From Dist. North Central Ky.	To 2-Brig. 1-Div. Dist. Ky.	July, 1864
47th Ky. Infy.	Apr., 1864	From Dist. Southwest Ky.	To Camp Nelson Dist. Ky.	Aug., 1864
49th Ky. Infy.	Apr., 1864	From Dist. Southwest Ky.	To Camp Nelson Dist. Ky.	Aug., 1864
1st Wis. H. A. Co. B.	Apr., 1864	From Dist. Southwest Ky.	To Lexington, Ky. Dist. Ky.	Dec., 1864
46th Ind. Infy.	July, 1864	From 1-Br. 3-Div. 13-C. Dept. Gulf.	To Lexington, Ky. Dist. Ky.	Dec., 1864
49th Ind. Infy.	July, 1864	From 2-Br. 1-Div. 13-C. Dept. Gulf.	To Lexington, Ky. Dist. Ky.	Dec., 1864
1st Ky. Cav.	July, 1864	From Indpt. Cav. Brig. 23-Corps.	To Camp Nelson, Ky. Dist. Ky.	Dec., 1864
11th Mich. Cav.	July, 1864	From 1-Brig. 1-Div. Dist. Ky.	To 2-Br. Cav. D. Dist. E. T. Cumb'd.	Feb., 1865
12th Ohio Cav.	July, 1864	From 2-Brig. 1-Div. Dist. Ky.	To 1-Br. Cav. D. Dist. E. T. Cumb'd.	Feb., 1865
Batty. E, Ky. Arty.	July, 1864	From Dist. Southwest Ky.	To Lexington, Ky. Dist. Ky.	Dec., 1864

2d DIVISION.— **COMMANDER.**

Hugh Ewing..........	Brigadier General..................	Apr. 7, 1864, to Jan. 17, 1865.

1st BRIGADE.— **COMMANDER.**

S. D. Bruce............	Col. 20th Ky. Infy.................	Apr. 10, 1864, to May 1, 1864.	
T. B. Farleigh........	Lt.-Col. 26th Ky. Infy............	May 1, 1864, to Sept. 8, 1864.	
J. H. Hammond........	Lt.-Col. A. A. G...................	Sept. 8, 1864, to Oct. 12, 1864.	
T. B. Farleigh........	Lt.-Col. 26th Ky. Infy............	Oct. 12, 1864, to Jan. 17, 1864.	

20th Kentucky Infy......Apr., 1864	From Dist. Southwest Ky..........	To 3-Brig. 2-Div. 23-Corps......	May,	1864
48th Kentucky Infy......Apr., 1864	From Dist. Southwest Ky..........	No change to Muster Out.........	Dec.,	1864
108th U. S. C. T.........July, 1864	From New Organization.............	To Mil. Dist. Ky...............	Jan.,	1865
139th Indiana Infy......July, 1864	From R. R. Guard Dept. Cumb'd....	No change to Muster Out..........	Sept.,	1864
52d Kentucky Infy......Oct., 1864	From 2-Brig. 2-Div. Dist. Ky......	No change to Muster Out.........	Jan.,	1865
12th U. S. C. Heavy Arty.Oct., 1864	From 2-Brig. 2-Div. Dist. Ky......	To Mil. Dist. Ky................	Jan.,	1865

2d BRIGADE.— **COMMANDERS.**

Cicero Maxwell........	Col. 26th Kentucky Infy..........	Apr. 10, 1864, to July 5, 1864.
J. H. Grider............	Col. 52d Kentucky Infy............	July 5, 1864, to Sept. 12, 1864.
Cicero Maxwell........	Col. 26th Kentucky Infy..........	Sept. 12, 1864, to Nov. 1, 1864.
S. P. Love.............	Col. 11th Kentucky Infy..........	Nov. 1, 1864, to Dec. 20, 1864.
D. J. Dill..............	Col. 30th Wisconsin Infy.........	Dec. 20, 1864, to Jan. 17, 1865.

26th Kentucky Infy......Apr., 1864	From Dist. Southwest Ky..........	To 1-Brig. 2-Div. 23-Corps......	Dec.,	1864
35th Kentucky Infy......Apr., 1864	From Dist. Southwest Ky..........	To 1-Brig. 1-Div. Dist. Ky......	July,	1864
2d Ohio Heavy Arty......Apr., 1864	From Dist. Southwest Ky..........	To Cleveland, Tenn.............	May,	1864
52d Kentucky Infy......July, 1864	From 3-Brig. 1-Div. Dist. Ky.....	To 1-Brig. 2-Div. Dist. Ky......	Oct.,	1864
12th U. S. C. H. Arty...Aug., 1864	From New Organization...........	To 1-Brig. 2-Div. Dist. Ky......	Oct.,	1864
47th Illinois Infy.......Dec., 1864	From Camp Butler, Ill...........	To 2-Brig. 1-Div. 16-Corps Gulf.....	Feb.,	1865
30th Wisconsin Infy.....Dec., 1864	From Dept. Missouri..............	To Louisville, Ky...............	Jan.,	1865
115th U. S. C. T..........Dec., 1864	From New Organization............	To 1-Brig. 2-Div. 25-Corps A. James.	Jan.,	

CAVALRY, DIST. KENTUCKY.— **COMMANDER.**

Israel Garrard........	Col. 7th Ohio Cav.................		

1st BRIGADE.—

16th Kentucky Cav.......Apr., 1864	From 2-Brig. 2-Div. Cav. Corps Ohio	Consolidated with 12th Ky. Cav.....	Oct.,	1864
9th Michigan Cav.......Apr., 1864	From 1-Brig. 2-Div. Cav. Corps Ohio	To 1-Brig. Cav. Div. 23-Corps.......	July,	1864
7th Ohio Cav.............Apr., 1864	From 1-Brig. 1-Div. Cav. Corps Ohio	To 1-Brig. Cav. Div. 23-Corps.......	July,	1864

3d BRIGADE.— **COMMANDER.**

Horace Capron.........	Col. 14th Illinois Cav.............		

14th Illinois Cav. Det.....Apr., 1864	From 2-Brig. 2-Div. Cav. Corps Ohio	To 3-Brig. Cav. Div. 23-Corps......	June,	1864
5th Indiana Cav.........Apr., 1864	From 2-Brig. 2-Div. Cav. Corps Ohio	To 1-Brig. Cav. Div. 23-Corps......	June,	1864
6th Indiana Cav.........Apr., 1864	From 2-Brig. 1-Div. Cav. Corps Ohio	To 1-Brig. Cav. Div. 23-Corps......	June,	1864
16th Illinois Cav.......Apr., 1864	From 3-Brig. 1-Div. Cav. Corps Ohio.	To 1-Brig. Cav. Div. 23-Corps......	June,	1864
1st Kentucky Cav.......Apr., 1864	From 1-Brig. 1-Div. Cav. Corps Ohio	To Indpt. Brig. Cav. Div. 23-Corps.	June,	1864
11th Kentucky Cav......Apr., 1864	From 1-Brig. 1-Div. Cav. Corps Ohio	To Indpt. Brig. Cav. Div. 23-Corps.	June,	1864
12th Kentucky Cav......Apr., 1864	From 1-Brig. 1-Div. Cav. Corps Ohio	To Detached Brig. 3-Div. 23-Corps..	June,	1864
8th Michigan Cav.......Apr., 1864	From 2-Brig. 1-Div. Cav. Corps Ohio.	To 3-Brig. Cav. Div. 23-Corps......	June,	1864
Laughlin's Ohio Cav.....Apr., 1864	From Headquarters 23-Corps.......	To 3-Brig. Cav. Div. 23-Corps......	June,	1864

CAMP NELSON, 1st DIVISION DIST., KY.—

47th Kentucky Infy......Aug., 1864	From 4-Brig. 1-Div. Dist. Ky......	No change to Muster Out........	Dec.,	1864
49th Kentucky Infy......Aug., 1864	From 4-Brig. 1-Div. Dist. Ky......	No change to Muster Out.........	Dec.,	1864
114th U. S. C. T ....Aug., 1864	From New Organization...........	To 3-B. 1-Div. 25-Corps Army James	Dec.,	1864
116th U. S. C. T.........Aug., 1864	From New Organization...........	To Unatt. 10-Corps Army James...	Nov.,	1864
5th U. S. C. Cav........Dec., 1864	From New Organization...........	To Dept. Kentucky..............	Feb.,	1865
6th U. S. C. Cav.........Dec., 1864	From New Organization...........	To Dept. Kentucky.............	Feb.,	1865
1st Kentucky Cav.......Dec., 1864	From 4-Brig. 1-Div. Dist. Ky......	To Dept. Kentucky.............	Feb.,	1865

CLEVELAND, TENN.—

2d Ohio Heavy Arty.......May, 1864	From Unass'd 23-Corps.............	To 2-Brig. 4-Div. 23-Corps.........	Oct.,	1864

RESERVE ARTILLERY 23 CORPS.—

Batty. D, 1st R. I........Aug., 1863	From Unass'd 1-Div. 23-Corps......	To Arty. 1-Div. 9-Corps...........	Oct.,	1863
19th Ohio Batty..........Aug., 1863	From 2-Brig. 4-Div. 23-Corps......	To 1-Brig. 3-Div. 23-Corps.......	Jan.,	1864
Wilder's Indiana Batty...Aug., 1863	From 2-Brig. 4-Div. 23-Corps......	To 1-Brig. 3-Div. 23-Corps.......	Oct.,	1863
24th Indiana Batty.......Aug., 1863	From 2-Brig. 4-Div. 23-Corps......	To Arty. 1-Div. 23-Corps.........	Apr.,	1864

Ninth Army Corps

Joined Dept. from Army Potomac Mch., 1863. Rejoined Army Potomac Mch., 1864.

COMMANDERS.

J. G. Parke...........	Major General......................	Mch. 19, 1863, to Apr. 11, 1863.	
O. B. Willcox.........	Brigadier General.................	Apr. 11, 1863, to June 5, 1863.	
J. G. Parke...........	Major General......................	June 5. 1863, to Aug. 25, 1863.	
R. B. Potter...........	Brigadier General.................	Aug. 25, 1863, to Jan. 17, 1864.	
O. B. Willcox.........	Brigadier General.................	Jan. 17, 1864, to Jan. 26, 1864.	
J. G. Parke...........	Major General......................	Jan. 26, 1864, to Mch. 16, 1864.	
O. B. Willcox.........	Brigadier General.................	Mch. 16, 1864, to Apr. 13, 1864.	

1st DIVISION.— **COMMANDERS.**

O. B. Willcox.........	Brigadier General.................	Mch. 19, 1863, to Apr. 13, 1863.	
Thos. Welsh..........	Brigadier General.................	Apr. 13, 1863, to Aug. 18, 1863.	.
E. Ferrero.............	Brigadier General.................	Aug. 18, 1863, to Apr. 19, 1864.	

1st BRIGADE.— **COMMANDERS.**

O. M. Poe.............	Col. 2d Michigan Infy.............	Mch. 19, 1863, to Apr. 11, 1863.
D. Morrison..........	Col. 79th New York Infy..........	Apr. 11, 1863, to June 4, 1863.
H. Bowman...........	Col. 36th Mass. Infy..............	June 4. 1863, to Aug. 18, 1863.
D. Morrison..........	Col. 79th New York Infy..........	Aug. 18. 1863. to Apr. 25, 1864.

1st BRIGADE.—Continued.

79th New York Infy......Mch., 1863	From 1-Brig. 1-Div. 9-Corps Pot....	To 3-Brig. 1-Div. 9-Corps Tenn....	June, 1863
2d Michigan Infy.......Mch., 1863	From 1-Brig. 1-Div. 9-Corps Pot...	To 3-Brig. 1-Div. 9-Corps Tenn...	June, 1863
8th Michigan Infy.......Mch., 1863	From 1-Brig. 1-Div. 9-Corps Pot...	To 3-Brig. 1-Div. 9-Corps Tenn...	June, 1863
17th Michigan Infy...Mch., 1863	From 1-Brig. 1-Div. 9-Corps Pot...	To 1-Brig. 1-Div. 9-Corps Tenn....	June, 1863
20th Michigan Infy......Mch., 1863	From 1-Brig. 1-Div. 9-Corps Pot...	To 1-Brig. 1-Div. 9-Corps Tenn...	June, 1863
36th Mass. Infy.........June, 1863	From 3-Brig. 1-Div. 9-Corps Ohio...	To 1-Brig. 1-Div. 9-Corps Tenn...	June, 1863
27th Michigan Infy......June, 1863	From 2-Brig. 1-Div. 9-Corps Ohio...	To 1-Brig. 1-Div. 9-Corps Tenn...	June, 1863
45th Penna. Infy........June, 1863	From 3-Brig. 1-Div. 9-Corps Ohio...	To 1-Brig. 1-Div. 9-Corps Tenn...	June, 1863
8th Michigan Infy......Aug., 1863	From 3-Brig. 1-Div. 9-Corps Tenn...	To 1-Brig. 3-Div. 9-Corps Potomac.	Apr., 1864
79th New York Infy.....Aug., 1863	From 3-Brig. 1-Div. 9-Corps Tenn...	To 2-Brig. 2-Div. 9-Corps Potomac.	Apr., 1864
36th Mass. Infy........Aug., 1863	From 3-Brig. 1-Div. 9-Corps Tenn...	To 2-Brig. 2-Div. 9-Corps Potomac.	Apr., 1864
45th Penna. Infy........Aug., 1864	From 1-Brig. 1-Div. 9-Corps Tenn...	To 1-Brig. 2-Div. 9-Corps Potomac.	Apr., 1864
20th Michigan Infy......Aug., 1863	From 3-Brig. 1-Div. 9-Corps Ohio...	To 2-Brig. 3-Div. 9-Corps Potomac..	Apr., 1864

2d BRIGADE.— COMMANDERS.

B. C. Christ............	Col. 50th Penna. Infy..............	Mch. 19, 1863, to Aug. 18, 1863.
E. W. Pierce............	Col. 29th Mass. Infy..............	Aug. 18, 1863, to Sept. 18, 1863.
B. C. Christ..........	Col. 50th Penna. Infy...............	Sept. 18, 1863, to Jan. 10, 1864.
E. W. Pierce........	Col. 29th Mass. Infy...............	Jan. 10, 1864, to Mch. 16, 1864.

46th New York Infy......Mch., 1863	From 2-Brig. 1-Div. 9-Corps Pot...	To 3-Brig. 2-Div. 9-Corps Tenn....	June, 1863
50th Penna. Infy........Mch., 1863	From 2-Brig. 1-Div. 9-Corps Pot...	To 3-Brig. 2-Div. 9-Corps Tenn...	June, 1863
29th Mass. Infy........Mch., 1863	From 2-Brig. 1-Div. 9-Corps Pot...	To 3-Brig. 2-Div. 9-Corps Tenn...	June, 1863
27th N. J. Infy...........Mch., 1863	From 2-Brig. 1-Div. 9-Corps Pot...	No change to Muster Out..........	June, 1863
27th Michigan Infy......Apr., 1863	From New Organization.............	To 1-Brig. 1-Div. 9-Corps Ohio...	June, 1863
29th Mass. Infy........Aug., 1863	From 3-Brig. 2-Div. 9-Corps Tenn...	To Veteran Furlough.............	Apr., 1864
46th New York Infy.....Aug., 1863	From 3-Brig. 2-Div. 9-Corps Tenn...	To 2-Brig. 1-Div. 9-Corps Potomac.	Apr., 1864
50th Penna. Infy........Aug., 1863	From 3-Brig. 2-Div. 9-Corps Tenn...	To 2-Brig. 1-Div. 9-Corps Potomac.	Apr., 1864
27th Michigan Infy......Aug., 1863	From 1-Brig. 1-Div. 9-Corps Tenn...	To 1-Brig. 3-Div. 9-Corps Potomac.	Apr., 1864
2d Michigan Infy.......Jan., 1864	From 3-Brig. 1-Div. 9-Corps Ohio...	To 1-Brig. 3-Div. 9-Corps Potomac.	Apr., 1864
100th Penna. Infy.......Jan., 1864	From 3-Brig. 1-Div. 9-Corps Ohio...	To 2-Brig. 3-Div. 9-Corps Potomac.	Apr., 1864
17th Michigan Infy......Jan., 1864	From 3-Brig. 1-Div. 9-Corps Ohio...	To 1-Brig. 3-Div. 9-Corps Potomac.	Apr., 1864

3d BRIGADE.— COMMANDERS.

Daniel Leasure........	Col. 100th Penna. Infy.............	Mch. 19, 1863, to Aug. 22, 1863.
C. Byington...........	Major 2d Mich. Infy.............	Aug. 22, 1863, to Sept. 22, 1863.
Daniel Leasure........	Col. 100th Penna. Infy............	Sept. 22, 1863, to Nov. 5, 1863.
Wm. Humphrey........	Col. 2d Michigan Infy.............	Nov. 5, 1863, to Jan. 25, 1864.

36th Mass. Infy.........Mch., 1862	From 3-Brig. 1-Div. 9-Corps Pot..	To 1-Brig. 1-Div. 9-Corps Tenn....	June, 1863
45th Penna. Infy.......Mch., 1862	From 3-Brig. 1-Div. 9-Corps Pot..	To 1-Brig. 1-Div. 9-Corps Tenn...	June, 1863
100th Penna. Infy.......Mch., 1862	From 3-Brig. 1-Div. 9-Corps Pot..	To 3-Brig. 1-Div. 9-Corps Tenn...	June, 1863
2d Michigan Infy........June, 186?	From 1-Brig. 1-Div. 9-Corps Ohio...	To 3-Brig. 1-Div. 9-Corps Tenn...	June, 1863
8th Michigan Infy.......June, 1862	From 1-Brig. 1-Div. 9-Corps Ohio...	To 3-Brig. 1-Div. 9-Corps Tenn...	June, 1863
20th Michigan Infy......June, 1863	From 1-Brig. 1-Div. 9-Corps Ohio...	To 3-Brig. 1-Div. 9-Corps Tenn...	June, 1863
79th New York Infy......June, 1862	From 1-Brig. 1-Div. 9-Corps Ohio...	To 3-Brig. 1-Div. 9-Corps Tenn...	June, 1863
2d Michigan Infy........Aug., 1862	From 3-Brig. 1-Div. 9-Corps Tenn...	To 2-Brig. 1-Div. 9-Corps Ohio.....	Jan., 1864
17th Michigan Infy......Aug., 1863	From 1-Brig. 1-Div. 9-Corps Tenn...	To 2-Brig. 1-Div. 9-Corps Ohio....	Jan., 1864
20th Michigan Infy......Aug., 1863	From 1-Brig. 1-Div. 9-Corps Tenn...	To 1-Brig. 1-Div. 9-Corps Ohio....	Jan., 1864
100th Penna. Infy.......Aug., 1863	From 3-Brig. 1-Div. 9-Corps Tenn...	To 2-Brig. 1-Div. 9-Corps Ohio....	Jan., 1864

ARTILLERY.—

Battys. L & M, 3d U. S..Mch., 1863	From Arty. 1-Div. 9-Corps Potomac..	To Arty. Res. 9-Corps Ohio........	June, 1862
Indpt. Batty. D, Penna A..June, 1863	From Arty. 2-Div. 9-Corps Ohio.....	To Arty. 1-Div. 9-Corps Tenn.....	June, 1863
Battys. L & M, 3d U. S..Aug., 1863	From Arty. Res. 9-Corps Ohio.....	To Arty. 2-Div. 9-Corps Ohio.......	Oct., 1863
Batty. L, 2d N. Y. Arty....Oct., 1863	From Arty. 2-Div. 9-Corps Ohio.....	To Arty. 3-Div. 9-Corps Potomac..	Apr., 1863
Batty. D, 1st R. I........Oct., 1863	From Arty Res. 23-Corps Ohio......	To Arty. Res. 9-Corps Potomac....	Apr., 1863
Battys. L and M, 3d U. S.Jan., 1864	From 2-Div. 9-Corps Ohio..........	To Arty. Res. 9-Corps Potomac....	Apr., 1863

2d DIVISION.— COMMANDERS.

S. D. Sturgis..........	Brigadier General..................	Mch. 19, 1863, to May 21, 1863.
J. F. Hartranft........	Col. 51st Penna. Infy.............	May 21, 1863, to June 5, 1863.
R. B. Potter..........	Brigadier General.................	June 5, 1863, to Aug. 25, 1863.
S. G. Griffin..........	Col. 6th New Hampshire...........	Aug. 25, 1863, to Oct., 1863.
J. K. Siegfried........	Col. 48th Penna. Infy.............	Oct., 1863, to Nov. 16, 1863.
J. F. Hartranft........	Col. 51st Penna. Infy..........	Nov. 16, 1863, to Jan. 26, 1864.
O. B. Willcox.........	Brigadier General.................	Jan. 26, 1864, to Mch. 16, 1864.
Z. R. Bliss...........	Col. 7th Rhode Island............	Mch. 16, 1864, to Apr. 2, 1864.
S. G. Griffin..........	Col. 6th New Hampshire........	Apr. 2, 1864, to May 1, 1864.

1st BRIGADE.— COMMANDERS.

James Nagle...........	Brigadier General..................	Mch. 19, 1863, to May 21, 1863.
S. G. Griffin..........	Col. 6th New Hampshire..........	May 21, 1863, to Aug. 30, 1863.
Z. R. Bliss...........	Col. 7th Rhode Island Infy.......	Aug. 30, 1863, to Sept. 30, 1863.
J. K. Siegfried........	Col. 48th Penna. Infy.............	Sept. 30, 1863, to Oct. 16, 1863.
T. B. Allard..........	Col. 2d Maryland Infy.............	Oct. 16, 1863, to Nov. 16, 1863.
J. K. Siegfried........	Col. 48th Penna. Infy.............	Nov. 16, 1863, to Mch. 16, 1864.

6th New Hampshire Infy.Mch., 1863	From 1-Brig. 2-Div. 9-Corps Pot....	To 1-Brig. 2-Div. 9-Corps Tenn....	June, 1863
9th New Hampshire Infy.Mch., 1863	From 1-Brig. 2-Div. 9-Corps Pot...	To 1-Brig. 2-Div. 9-Corps Tenn...	June, 1863
48th Penna. Infy.......Mch., 1863	From 1-Brig. 2-Div. 9-Corps Pot...	To Unass'd 1-Div. 23-Corps......	June, 1863
2d Maryland Infy.......Mch., 1863	From 1-Brig. 2-Div. 9-Corps Pot...	To Unass'd 1-Div. 23-Corps......	June, 1863
7th Rhode Island Infy....Mch., 1863	From 1-Brig. 2-Div. 9-Corps Pot...	To 1-Brig. 2-Div. 9-Corps Tenn....	June, 1863
12th Rhode Island Infy...Mch., 1863	From 1-Brig. 2-Div. 9-Corps Pot...	To 1-Brig. 1-Div. 23-Corps........	June, 1863
6th New Hampshire Infy.Aug., 1863	From 1-Brig. 2-Div. 9-Corps Tenn...	To Dist. N. Cen. Ky. 1-Div. 23-C..	Oct., 1863
9th New Hampshire Infy.Aug., 1863	From 1-Brig. 2-Div. 9-Corps Tenn...	To Dist. N. Cen. Ky. 1-Div. 23-C...	Oct., 1863
7th Rhode Island Infy...Aug., 1863	From 1-Brig. 2-Div. 9-Corps Tenn...	To Dist. N. Cen. Ky. 1-Div. 23-C...	Oct., 1863
2d Maryland Infy........Oct., 1863	From Unass'd 1-Div. 23-Corps......	To 2-Brig. 2-Div. 9-Corps Ohio...	Jan., 1864
21st Mass. Infy........Oct., 1863	From Unass'd 1-Div. 23-Corps......	To 2-Brig. 2-Div. 9-Corps Potomac.	Apr., 1864
48th Penna. Infy.......Oct., 1863	From Unass'd 1-Div. 23-Corps......	To 1-Brig. 2-Div. 9-Corps Potomac.	Apr., 1864
6th New Hampshire Infy.Feb., 1864	From Dist. N. Cen. Ky. 1-Div. 23-C.	To 2-Brig. 2-Div. 9-Corps Potomac.	Apr., 1864
9th New Hampshire Infy..Feb., 1864	From Dist. N. Cen. Ky. 1-Div. 23-C.	To 2-Brig. 2-Div. 9-Corps Potomac.	Apr., 1864
7th Rhode Island Infy...Feb., 1864	From Dist. N. Cen. Ky. 1-Div. 23-C.	To 1-Brig. 2-Div. 9-Corps Potomac.	Apr., 1864

2d BRIGADE.— COMMANDERS.

E. Ferrero.............	Brigadier General..................	Mch. 18, 1863, to Apr. 1863.
J. F. Hartranft........	Col. 51st Penna. Infy.............	Apr., 1863, to May, 1863.
Wm. Harriman.........	Col. 11th New Hampshire.........	May, 1863, to June 5, 1863.
E. Ferrero.............	Brigadier General.................	June 5, 1863, to Aug. 22, 1863.
Edw. Schall...........	Lt.-Col. 51st Penna. Infy.........	Aug. 22, 1863, to Dec. 12, 1863.
M. N. Collins..........	Col. 11th New Hampshire........	Dec. 12, 1863, to Feb. 20, 1864.
S. Carruth............	Col. 35th Mass. Infy..............	Feb. 20, 1864, to Apr. 18, 1864.

2d BRIGADE.—Continued.

21st Mass. Infy........Mch., 1863	From 2-Brig. 2-Div. 9-Corps Pot....	To Unatt. 1-Div. 23-Corps Ohio....	June, 1863
35th Mass. Infy........Mch., 1863	From 2-Brig. 2-Div. 9-Corps Pot....	To 2-Brig. 2-Div. 9-Corps Tenn....	June, 1863
51st Penna. Infy......Mch., 1863	From 2-Brig. 2-Div. 9-Corps Pot....	To 2-Brig. 2-Div. 9-Corps Tenn....	June, 1863
51st New York Infy....Mch., 1863	From 2-Brig. 2-Div. 9-Corps Pot....	To 2-Brig. 2-Div. 9-Corps Tenn....	June, 1863
11th New Hampshire Infy.Mch., 1863	From 2-Brig. 2-Div. 9-Corps Pot....	To 2-Brig. 2-Div. 9-Corps Tenn....	June, 1863
35th Mass. Infy........Aug., 1863	From 2-Brig. 2-Div. 9-Corps Tenn..	To 1-Brig. 1-Div. 9-Corps Potomac..	Apr., 1864
11th New Hampshire Infy.Aug., 1863	From 2-Brig. 2-Div. 9-Corps Tenn..	To 2-Brig. 2-Div. 9-Corps Potomac..	Apr., 1864
51st Penna. Infy......Aug., 1863	From 2-Brig. 2-Div. 9-Corps Tenn..	To 1-Brig. 3-Div. 9-Corps Potomac..	Apr., 1864
51st New York Infy....Aug., 1863	From 2-Brig. 2-Div. 9-Corps Tenn..	To Dist. N. Cen. Ky. 1-Div. 23-Corps.	Sept., 1863
2d Maryland Infy.......Jan., 1864	From 1-Brig. 2-Div. 9-Corps Ohio...	To 2-Brig. 3-Div. 9-Corps Potomac..	Apr., 1864
51st New York Infy.....Jan., 1864	From Dist. N. Cen. Ky. 1-Div. 23-C..	To 1-Brig. 2-Div. 9-Corps Potomac..	Apr., 1864

3d BRIGADE.—Organized June 5, 1863.   COMMANDERS.

B. C. Christ..........	Col. 50th Penna. Infy.............	June 5, 1863, to Aug. 22, 1863.	
Reorganized Oct., 1863.			
W. C. Lemert..........	Col. 86th Ohio Infy................	Oct. 12, 1863, to Jan. 25, 1864.	
Discontinued Jan. 25, 1864.			

29th Mass. Infy........June, 1863	From 2-Brig. 1-Div. 9-Corps Ohio...	To 3-Brig. 2-Div. 9-Corps Tenn.....	June, 1863
46th New York Infy.....June, 1863	From 2-Brig. 1-Div. 9-Corps Ohio...	To 3-Brig. 2-Div. 9-Corps Tenn.....	June, 1863
50th Penna. Infy......June, 1863	From 2-Brig. 1-Div. 9-Corps Ohio...	To 3-Brig. 2-Div. 9-Corps Tenn.....	June, 1863
86th Ohio Infy..........Oct., 1863	From Cumb'd Gap L. W. Forces....	To Dist. Clinch Dept. Ohio.........	Jan., 1864
129th Ohio Infy........Oct., 1863	From Cumb'd Gap L. W. Forces....	To Dist. Clinch Dept. Ohio.........	Jan., 1864
ARTILLERY, 2d DIVISION.—			
Indpt. Batty. D, Penna. A.Mch., 1863	From Arty. 2-Div. 9-Corps Potomac.	To Arty. 1-Div. 9-Corps Ohio......	June, 1863
Batty. D, 1st R. I......Mch., 1863	From Arty. 2-Div. 9-Corps Potomac.	To Unass'd 1-Div. 23-Corps........	June, 1863
Batty. L, 2d N. Y. Arty..Mch., 1863	From Arty. 2-Div. 9-Corps Potomac.	To Arty. 2-Div. 9-Corps Tenn......	June, 1863
Batty. E, 2d U. S. Arty..Mch., 1863	From Arty. 1-Div. 9-Corps Pot....	To Res. Arty. 9-Corps Tenn.......	June, 1863
Batty. L, 2d N. Y. Arty..Aug., 1863	From Arty. 2-Div. 9-Corps Tenn....	To Arty. 1-Div. 9-Corps Ohio......	Oct., 1863
Batty. E, 2d U. S. Arty..Aug., 1863	From Res. Arty. 9-Corps Tenn.....	To Res. Arty. 9-Corps Potomac....	Apr., 1864
Battys. L & M, 3d U. S. A.Oct., 1863	From Arty. 1-Div. 9-Corps Ohio....	To Arty. 2-Div. 9-Corps Ohio......	Jan., 1864
15th Indiana Batty.......Dec., 1863	From 2-Brig. 1-Div. Cav. Corps Ohio.	To Arty. 3-Div. 23-Corps..........	Apr., 1864

LEFT WING FORCES IN EAST TENNESSEE.—

COMMANDER.

O. B. Willcox..........	Brigadier General................	To Jan. 11, 1864.	

1st BRIGADE.—   COMMANDER.

J. R. Mahan...........	Col. 115th Indiana Infy...........	Sept., 1863, to Jan., 1864.	

115th Indiana Infy......Sept., 1863	From New Organization...........	No change to Muster Out.........	Jan., 1864
116th Indiana Infy......Sept., 1863	From New Organization...........	To 2-Brig. Left Wing Forces......	Oct., 1863
117th Indiana Infy......Sept., 1863	From New Organization...........	To 1-Brig. 3-Div. 23-Corps.......	Dec., 1863
118th Indiana Infy......Sept., 1863	From New Organization...........	To 2-Brig. Left Wing Forces......	Oct., 1863
2d North Carolina Mtd...Oct., 1863	From New Organization...........	To Dist. Clinch Dept. Ohio........	Jan., 1864
23d Indiana Batty.......Oct., 1863	From Arty. L. W. Forces..........	To Dist. Clinch Dept. Ohio........	Jan., 1864

2d BRIGADE.—   COMMANDER.

W. A. Haskins........	Col. 12th Kentucky Infy...........	Sept., 1863, to Dec., 1863.	

12th Kentucky Infy......Sept., 1863	From 1-Brig. 3-Div. 23-Corps......	To Camp Burnside Ky............	Jan., 1864
103d Ohio Infy..........Sept., 1863	From 2-Brig. 3-Div. 23-Corps......	To 2-Brig. 3-Div. 23-Corps.......	Jan., 1864
8th Tennessee Infy......Sept., 1863	From 2-Brig. 3-Div. 23-Corps......	To 1-Brig. 3-Div. 23-Corps.......	Jan., 1864
116th Indiana Infy......Oct., 1863	From 1-Brig. L. W. Forces........	To Dist. Clinch Dept. Ohio........	Jan., 1864
118th Indiana Infy......Oct., 1863	From 1-Brig. L. W. Forces........	To Dist. Clinch Dept. Ohio........	Jan., 1864
21st Ohio Batty.........Oct., 1863	From Arty. Left Wing Forces......	To Dist. Clinch Dept. Ohio........	Jan., 1864
ARTILLERY.—			
21st Ohio Batty.........Sept., 1863	From New Organization...........	To 2-Brig. Left Wing Forces.......	Oct., 1863
23d Indiana Batty.......Sept., 1863	From New Organization...........	To 1-Brig. Left Wing Forces.......	Oct., 1863
Batty. M, 1st Mich. Arty.Sept., 1863	From New Organization...........	To Dist. Clinch Dept. Ohio........	Jan., 1864
CUMBERLAND GAP.—			
86th Ohio Infy..........Sept., 1863	From New Organization...........	To 3-Brig. 2-Div. 9-Corps Ohio.....	Oct., 1862
129th Ohio Infy.........Sept., 1863	From New Organization...........	To 3-Brig. 2-Div. 9-Corps Ohio.....	Oct., 1862
16th Illinois Cav.......Sept., 1863	From New Organization...........	To Dist. Clinch Dept. Ohio........	Oct., 1862
4th Ohio Cav. B'n.......Sept., 1863	From New Organization...........	No change to Muster Out.........	Feb., 1864
11th Tennessee Cav......Sept., 1863	From New Organization...........	To Dist. Clinch Dept. Ohio........	Jan., 1864
Batty. L, 1st Mich. Arty..Sept., 1863	From Arty. 3-Div. 23-Corps.......	To Dist. Clinch Dept. Ohio........	Jan., 1864
22d Ohio Batty.........Sept., 1863	From New Organization...........	To Dist. Clinch Dept. Ohio........	Jan., 1864
Batty. B, 1st Tenn. Arty.Sept., 1863	From New Organization...........	To Dist. Clinch Dept. Ohio........	Jan., 1864
6th Indiana Cav........Oct., 1863	From Dist. North Central Ky......	To 1-Brig. 2-Div. Cav. Corps Cmb'd.	Dec., 1863
3d Indiana Cav. L. M....Oct., 1863	From New Organization...........	To Dist. Clinch Dept. Ohio........	Jan., 1864
34th Kentucky Infy......Oct., 1863	From Dist. South Central Ky......	To Dist. Clinch Dept. Ohio........	Jan., 1864

DISTRICT OF THE CLINCH.—   COMMANDER.

T. T. Garrard.........	Brigadier General................	Jan. .., 1864, to Apr. .., 1864.	

91st Ind. Infy..........Jan., 1864	From Somerset Ky. 1-Div. 23-Corps.	To 1-Brig. 4-Div. 23-Corps.........	Apr., 1864
116th Ind. Infy.........Jan., 1864	From 2-Brig. Left Wing Forces...	No change to Muster Out.........	Feb., 1864
117th Ind. Infy.........Jan., 1864	From 1-Brig. 3-Div. 23-Corps......	No change to Muster Out.........	Feb., 1864
118th Ind. Infy.........Jan., 1864	From 2-Brig. Left Wing Forces....	No change to Muster Out.........	Feb., 1864
34th Ky. Infy...........Jan., 1864	From Cumberland Gap...........	To 1-Brig. 4-Div. 23-Corps.........	Apr., 1864
2d N. C. Mtd...........Jan., 1864	From 1-Brig. Left Wing Forces....	To 1-Brig. 4-Div. 23-Corps.........	Apr., 1864
86th Ohio Infy..........Jan., 1864	From 3-Brig. 2-Div. 9-Corps Ohio..	No change to Muster Out.........	Feb., 1864
129th Ohio Infy.........Jan., 1864	From 3-Brig. 2-Div. 9-Corps Ohio..	No change to Muster Out.........	Feb., 1864
16th Ill. Cav...........Jan., 1864	From Cumberland Gap...........	To 3-Brig. 1-Div. Cav. C. Ohio....	Apr., 1864
6th Ind. Cav...........Jan., 1864	From Cumberland Gap...........	To 2-Brig. 1-Div. Cav. C. Ohio....	Apr., 1864
11th Tenn. Cav.........Jan., 1864	From Cumberland Gap...........	To 1-Brig. 4-Div. 23-Corps........	Apr., 1864
Batty. L, 1st Mich. Arty..Jan., 1864	From Cumberland Gap...........	To 1-Brig. 4-Div. 23-Corps........	Apr., 1864
Batty. M, 1st Mich. Arty..Jan., 1864	From Arty. Left Wing Forces.....	To 1-Brig. 4-Div. 23-Corps........	Apr., 1864
22d Ohio Batty.........Jan., 1864	From Cumberland Gap...........	To 1-Brig. 4-Div. 23-Corps........	Apr., 1864
Batty. B, 1st Tenn. Arty..Jan., 1864	From Cumberland Gap...........	To 1-Brig. 4-Div. 23-Corps........	Apr., 1864
23d Ind. Batty..........Jan., 1864	From 1-Brig. Left Wing Forces....	To Arty. 1-Div. 23-Corps..........	Apr., 1864
21st Ohio Batty.........Jan., 1864	From 2-Brig. Left Wing Forces....	To 2-Brig. 4-Div. 23-Corps........	Apr., 1864

DISTRICT OF WESTERN KENTUCKY.—   COMMANDERS.

E. A. Paine...........	Brigadier General................	Aug. 7, 1864, to Sept. 11, 1864.	
S. Meredith...........	Brigadier General................	Sept. 11, 1864, to May 21, 1865.	
C. H. Carlton.........	Col. 89th Ohio Infy...............	May 21, 1865.	

DISTRICT OF WESTERN KENTUCKY.—Continued.

132d Ill. Infy............Aug., 1864	From Dist. Columbus Dept. Tenn...	No change to Muster Out..........	Sept.,	1864
134th Ill. Infy...........Aug., 1864	From Dist. Columbus Dept. Tenn...	No change to Muster Out..........	Sept.,	1864
136th Ill. Infy...........Aug., 1864	From Dist. Columbus Dept. Tenn...	No change to Muster Out..........	Sept.,	1864
139th Ill. Infy...........Aug., 1864	From Dist. Columbus Dept. Tenn...	No change to Muster Out..........	Sept.,	1864
141st Ill. Infy...........Aug., 1864	From Dist. Columbus Dept. Tenn...	No change to Muster Out..........	Oct.,	1864
7th Tenn. Cav............Aug., 1864	From Dist. Columbus Dept. Tenn...	To Dist. West Ky. Dept. Ky......	Feb.,	1865
4th U. S. C. Heavy Arty..Aug., 1864	From Dist. Columbus Dept. Tenn...	To Dist. West Ky. Dept. Ky......	Feb.,	1865
8th U. S. C. Heavy Arty....Aug., 1864	From Dist. Columbus Dept. Tenn...	To Dist. West Ky. Dept. Ky......	Feb.,	1865
Batty. B, 2d Ill. Arty....Aug., 1864	From Dist. Columbus Dept. Tenn...	To Dist. West Ky. Dept. Ky......	Feb.,	1865
39th N. J. Infy...........Aug., 1864	From Dist. Columbus Dept. Tenn...	To 3-Brig. 2-Div. 16-Corps Gulf....	Feb.,	1865
161st N. Y. Infy..........Oct., 1864	From Dept. Gulf...................	To Dept. Gulf...................	Dec.,	1864
29th Ill. Infy.............Oct., 1864	From Post Natchez, Miss..........	To Memphis Dist. West Tenn......	Nov.,	1864
26th Ky. Infy.............Oct., 1864	From 2-Brig. 2-Div. Dist. Ky......	To 1-Brig. 2-Div. 23-Corps......	Dec.,	1864
1st La. Infy..............Oct., 1864	From Dept. Gulf...................	To Dept. Gulf...................	Dec.,	1864
30th Wis. Infy...........Oct., 1864	From Dept. Mo....................	To 2-Brig. 2-Div. Dist. Ky.......	Dec.,	1864

Department of Kentucky

Created February, 1865.

COMMANDER.

John M. Palmer........	Major General.....................	Feb. 10, 1865.

1st DIVISION.— COMMANDER.

E. H. Hobson..........	Brigadier General.................	

14th Ky. Infy............Feb., 1863	From Louisa, Ky. Dist. East. Ky...	No change to Muster Out..........	Sept.,	1865
24th Ky Infy...........Feb., 1863	From Louisa, Ky. Dist. East. Ky...	No change to Muster Out..........	Feb.,	1865
30th Ky. Infy...........Feb., 1863	From Louisa, Ky. Dist. East. Ky...	No change to Muster Out..........	Apr.,	1865
39th Ky. Infy............Feb., 1863	From Louisa, Ky. Dist. East. Ky...	No change to Muster Out..........	Sept.,	1865
53d Ky. Infy.............Feb., 1863	From Mil. Dist. Ky................	No change to Muster Out..........	Sept.,	1865
54th Ky. Infy.............Feb., 1863	From Mil. Dist. Ky................	No change to Muster Out..........	Sept.,	1865
55th Ky. Infy.............Feb., 1863	From Mil. Dist. Ky................	No change to Muster Out..........	Sept.,	1865
46th Ind. Infy............Feb., 1863	From Mil. Dist. Ky. Lexington, Ky.	No change to Muster Out..........	Sept.,	1865
49tn Ind. Infy............Feb., 1863	From Mil. Dist. Ky. Lexington, Ky.	No change to Muster Out..........	Sept.,	1865
1st Ky. Cav..............Feb., 1863	From 3-Brig. 1-Div. Dist. Ky......	No change to Muster Out..........	Sept.,	1865
5th U. S. C. Cav.........Feb., 1863	From Mil. Dist. Ky................	To Dept. Arkansas...............	July,	1865
1st Ohio Heavy Arty......Feb., 1863	From 2-Brig. 4-Div. Dist. Ky......	No change to Muster Out..........	July,	1865
Batty. B, 1st Wis. H. Arty.Feb., 1863	From Mil. Dist. Ky. Lexington, Ky.	No change to Muster Out..........	Aug.,	1865
Batty .C, 1st Ky. Arty...Feb., 1863	From 3-Brig. 1-Div. Dist. Ky......	No change to Muster Out..........	July,	1865
Batty. E, Ky Arty......Feb., 1863	From Mil. Dist. Ky. Lexington, Ky.	No change to Muster Out..........	Aug..	1865

2d DIVISION.— COMMANDER.

Hugh Ewing..........	Brigadier General.................	

27th Ky. Infy............Feb., 1865	From 3-Brig. 2-Div. 23-Corps......	No change to Muster Out..........	Mch.,	1865
52d Ky. Infy.............Feb., 1865	From Mil. Dist. Ky................	No change to Muster Out..........	Feb.,	1865
30th Wis. Infy...........Feb., 1865	From Dist. West Ky................	No change to Muster Out..........	Sept.,	1865
17th Ky. Cav............Feb., 1865	From New Organization............	No change to Muster Out..........	Sept.,	1865
24th Ind. Batty..........Feb., 1865	From Garrison Arty. Nashville, T..	No change to Muster Out..........	Aug.,	1865
12th U. S. C. H. Arty.....Feb., 1865	From New Organization............	No change to Muster Out..........	Apr.,	1866

DISTRICT WESTERN KENTUCKY.— COMMANDER.

Solomon Meredith......	Brigadier General.................	

49th Ill. Infy............Feb., 1865	From 3-Br. 2-Div. Det. Army Tenn.	No change to Muster Out..........	Sept.,	1865
7th Tenn. Cav...........Feb., 1865	From Dist. West Ky. Dept. Ohio....	No change to Muster Out..........	Aug.,	1865
4th U. S. C. H. Arty......Feb., 1865	From Dist. West Ky. Dept. Ohio....	No change to Muster Out..........	Feb.,	1866
8th U. S. C. H. Arty......Feb., 1865	From Dist. West Ky. Dept. Ohio....	No change to Muster Out..........	Feb.,	1866
13th U. S. C. H. Arty.....Feb., 1865	From Mil. Dist. Ky................	No change to Muster Out..........	Nov.,	1865
Batty. B, 2d Ill. Arty.....Feb., 1865	From Dist. West Ky................	No change to Muster Out..........	July,	1865

Department of Missouri

Created Nov. 9, 1861, to consist of Missouri, Iowa, Minnesota, Wisconsin, Arkansas, and that portion of Kentucky West of the Cumberland River. Merged into Dept. of the Mississippi, March 11, 1862. Erected into a Military District June 5, 1862, and divided into Divisions. Re-created as a Department Sept. 19, 1862, to consist of Missouri, Arkansas, Kansas and bordering Indian Territory. Colorado and Nebraska Territories added Oct. 11, 1862.

COMMANDERS.

Henry W. Halleck.....	Major General.....................	Nov. 19, 1861, to Mch. 11, 1862.	
J. M. Schofield.........	Brigadier General.................	June 5, 1862, to Sept. 24, 1862.	(Com'g Mil. Dist.)
S. R. Curtis............	Major General.....................	Sept. 24, 1862, to May 24, 1863.	
J. M. Schofield.........	Major General.....................	May 24, 1863, to Jan. 30, 1864.	
W. S. Rosecrans.......	Major General.....................	Jan. 30, 1864, to Dec. 9. 1864.	
G. M. Dodge...........	Major General.....................	Dec. 9, 1864, to July .., 1865.	

Army of Southwest Missouri

Created Dec., 1861. Merged into District of Eastern Arkansas. Dept. Tenn., Dec. 13, 1862.

COMMANDERS.

S. R. Curtis............	Brigadier General.................	Dec. 25, 1861, to Aug. 29, 1862.
Frederick Steele.......	Brigadier General.................	Aug. 29, 1862, to Oct. 7, 1862.
E. A. Carr.............	Brigadier General.................	Oct. 7, 1862, to Nov. 13, 1862.
Willis A. Gorman......	Brigadier General.................	Nov. 13, 1862, to Dec. 13, 1862.

1st BRIGADE.—

COMMANDER.

G. M. Dodge...........Col. 4th Iowa Infy................

35th Ill. Infy.	Jan., 1862	From Army of the West	To 1-Brig. 4-Div. Army S. W. Mo..	Feb.,	1862
4th Iowa Infy.	Jan., 1862	From Rolla, Mo. Dept. Mo.	To 1-Brig. 4-Div. Army S. W. Mo..	Feb.,	1862
24th Mo. Infy.	Jan., 1862	From New Organization	To Unass'd Army S. W. Mo.	Feb.,	1862
1st Iowa Batty.	Jan., 1862	From New Organization	To 1-Brig. 4-Div. Army S. W. Mo.	Feb.,	1862

2d BRIGADE.—

COMMANDER.

P. J. Osterhaus........Col. 12th Mo. Infy................

36th Ill. Infy.	Jan., 1862	From Unatt. Dept. Mo.	To 2-Brig. 1-Div. Army S. W. Mo..	Feb.,	1862
3d Mo. Infy.	Jan., 1862	From New Organization	To Unass'd Army S. W. Mo.	Feb.,	1862
12th Mo. Infy.	Jan., 1862	From New Organization	To 2-Brig. 1-Div. Army S. W. Mo.	Feb.,	1862
17th Mo. Infy.	Jan., 1862	From New Organization	To 2-Brig. 1-Div. Army S. W. Mo.	Feb.,	1862
Batty. A, 1st Mo. Arty.	Jan., 1862	From Dept. Mo.	To Steele's Command S. E. Mo.	Feb.,	1862
Batty. B, 1st Mo. Arty.	Jan., 1862	From Dept. Mo.	To Disbandment	Apr.,	1862

3d BRIGADE (Cavalry).—

COMMANDER.

E. A. Carr.............Col. 3d Ill. Cav................

3d Ill. Cav.	Jan., 1862	From Unatt. Dept. Mo.	To 2-Brig. 4-Div. Army W. Mo..	Feb.,	1862
1st Mo. Cav. (Bn.)	Jan., 1862	From Army West	To 2-Brig. 3-Div. Army S. W. Mo.	Feb.,	1862
4th Mo. Cav.	Jan., 1862	From New Organization	To Unass'd Army S. W. Mo.	Feb.,	1862

4th BRIGADE.—

COMMANDER.

Franz Sigel...........Brigadier General................

25th Ill. Infy.	Jan., 1862	From Unatt. Dept. Mo.	To 1-Brig. 1-Div. Army S. W. Mo..	Feb.,	1862
44th Ill. Infy.	Jan., 1862	From Unatt. Dept. Mo.	To 1-Brig. 1-Div. Army S. W. Mo..	Feb.,	1862

5th BRIGADE.—

COMMANDER.

A. Asboth.............Brigadier General................

2d Mo. Infy.	Feb., 1862	From Unatt. Dept. Mo.	To 1-Brig. 2-Div. Army S. W. Mo..	Feb.,	1862
15th Mo. Infy.	Feb., 1862	From Unatt. Dept. Mo.	To 1-Brig. 2-Div. Army S. W. Mo..	Feb.,	1862
Landgraeber's Mo. Batty.	Feb., 1862	From Unatt. Dept. Mo.	To Unatt. Army S. W. Mo.	Feb.,	1862
2d Ohio Batty.	Feb., 1862	From Dist. Rolla, Dept. Mo.	To Unatt. Army S. W. Mo.	Feb.,	1862

UNATTACHED.—

13th Ill. Infy.	Jan., 1862	From Dist. Rolla, Dept. Mo.	To 2-Div. Army S. W. Mo.	May,	1862
9th Iowa Infy.	Jan., 1862	From Unatt. Dept. Mo.	To 2-Brig. 4-Div. Army S. W. Mo.	May,	1862
4th Mo. Infy. Bn.	Jan., 1862	From New Organization	To Dist. Southwest Mo.	May,	1862
Bowen's Mo. Cav. Bn.	Jan., 1862	From Unatt. Dept. Mo.	To Unatt. Army S. W. Mo.	May,	1862
Phelps' Mo. Regt.	Jan., 1862	From Unatt. Dept. Mo.	To 2-Brig. 4-Div. Army S. W. Mo.	Feb.,	1862
3d Iowa Batty.	Jan., 1862	From New Organization	To 2-Brig. 4-Div. Army S. W. Mo.	Feb.,	1862
3d Iowa Cav.	Feb., 1862	From Benton Barracks, Mo.	To 1-Div. Army S. W. Mo.	May,	1862
3d Mo. Infy.	Feb., 1862	From 2-Brig. Army S. W. Mo.	To 3-Div. Army S. W. Mo.	May,	1862
24th Mo. Infy.	Feb., 1862	From 1-Brig. Army S. W. Mo.	To Unatt. Army S. W. Mo.	May,	1862
4th Iowa Cav.	Mch., 1862	From New Organization	To 2-Div. Army S. W. Mo.	May,	1862

1st DIVISION.—

COMMANDERS.

Franz Sigel	Brigadier General	Feb. .., 1862, to May 9, 1862.
Frederick Steele	Brigadier General	May 9, 1862, to Aug. 29, 1862.

1st BRIGADE.—

COMMANDER.

P. J. Osterhaus........Col. 12th Mo. Infy................

17th Mo. Infy.	Feb., 1862	From 2-Brig. Army S. W. Mo.	To 3-Div. Army S. W. Mo.	May,	1862
25th Ill. Infy.	Feb., 1862	From 4-Brig. Army S. W. Mo.	To 1-Brig. 4-Div. Army Miss.	June,	1862
44th Ill. Infy.	Feb., 1862	From 4-Brig. Army S. W. Mo.	To 1-Brig. 5-Div. Army Miss.	June,	1862

2d BRIGADE.—

COMMANDER.

N. Greusel.............Col. 36th Ill. Infy................

12th Mo. Infy.	Feb., 1862	From 2-Brig. Army S. W. Mo.	To 3-Div. Army S. W. Mo.	May,	1862
36th Ill. Infy.	Feb., 1862	From 2-Brig. Army S. W. Mo.	To 1-Brig. 5-Div. Army Miss.	June,	1862

ARTILLERY.—

Welfley's Mo. Batty.	Feb., 1862	From New Organization	To Arty. 3-Div. Army S. W. Mo.	May,	1862
4th Ohio Batty.	Feb., 1862	From Dist. Rolla, Dept. Mo.	To Arty. 3-Div. Army S. W. Mo.	May,	1862

2d DIVISION.—

COMMANDER.

A. Asboth.............Brigadier General................

1st BRIGADE.—

COMMANDER.

F. Schaeffer...........Col. Staff................

2d Mo. Infy.	Feb., 1862	From 5-Brig. Army S. W. Mo.	To 2-Brig. 5-Div. Army Miss.	June,	1862
15th Mo. Infy.	Feb., 1862	From 5-Brig. Army S. W. Mo.	To 2-Brig. 5-Div. Army Miss.	June,	1862

NOT BRIGADED.—

1st Mo. Flying Batty.	Feb., 1862	From 5-Brig. Army Southwest Mo.	To Arty. 2-Div. Army Southwest Mo.	May,	1862
2d Ohio Batty.	Feb., 1862	From 5-Brig. Army Southwest Mo.	To Arty. 3-D. Army Southwest Mo.	May,	1862
Benton's Mo. Hussars	Feb., 1862	From New Organization	To 5th Mo. Cav. Army S. W. Mo.	Feb.,	1862
Fremont's Mo. Hussars	Feb., 1862	From Unatt. Dept. Mo.	To 4th Mo. Cav. Army S. W. Mo.	Feb.,	1862

3d DIVISION.—

COMMANDER.

J. C. Davis............Col. 22d Indiana Infy.

1st BRIGADE.—

COMMANDER.

Thos. Patterson........Col. 18th Indiana Infy.

8th Indiana Infy.	Feb., 1862	From Army West Dept. Mo.	To 1-Div. Army Southwest Mo.	May,	1862
18th Indiana Infy.	Feb., 1862	From Army West Dept. Mo.	To 1-Div. Army Southwest Me.	May,	1862
22d Indiana Infy.	Feb., 1862	From Army West Dept. Mo.	To 1-Brig. 4-Div. Army Miss.	June,	1862
1st Indiana Batty.	Feb., 1862	From Army West Dept. Mo.	To 1-Div. Army Southwest Mo.	May,	1862

2d BRIGADE.—

COMMANDER.

Julius White...........Col. 37th Illinois Infy.

37th Illinois Infy.	Feb., 1862	From Army West Dept. Mo.	To Dist. Southwest Mo.	May,	1862
59th Ilinois Infy.	Feb., 1862	From Army West Dept. Mo.	To 1-Brig. 4-Div. Army Miss.	June,	1862
Batty. A, 2d Ill. Batty.	Feb., 1862	From Army West Dept. Mo.	To Arty. 3-D. Army Southwest Mo.	May,	1862
1st Missouri Cav. 3d Bn.	Feb., 1862	From Army West Dept. Mo.	To 2-Div., Army Southwest Mo.	May,	1862
1st Missouri Cav. 2d Bn.	Feb., 1862	From Army West Dept. Mo.	To Cassville Dept. Mo.	May,	1862

4th DIVISION.— COMMANDER.

E. A. Carr	Brigadier General.		

1st BRIGADE.— COMMANDER.

G. M. Dodge	Col. 4th Iowa Infy.		
4th Iowa Infy...........Feb., 1862	From 1-Brig. Army Southwest Mo....	To 2-Div.. Army Southwest Mo....	May, 1862
35th Illinois Infy.......Feb., 1862	From 1-Brig. Army Southwest Mo....	To 1-Brig. 4-Div. Army Miss.......	June, 1862
1st Iowa Batty..........Feb., 1862	From 1-Brig. Army Southwest Mo....	To 2-Div.. Army Southwest Mo....	May, 1862

2d BRIGADE.— COMMANDER.

Wm. Vandever	Col. 9th Iowa Infy.		
9th Iowa Infy............Feb., 1862	From Unatt. Army Southwest Mo..	To 2-Div. Army Southwest Mo....	May, 1862
Phelps' Missouri Regt....Feb., 1862	From Unatt. Army Southwest Mo..	No change to Muster Out..........	May, 1862
3d Illinois Cav.........Feb., 1862	From 3-Brig. Army Southwest Mo..	To 2-Div. Army Southwest Mo....	May, 1862
3d Iowa Batty..........Feb., 1862	From Unatt. Army Southwest Mo..	To 2-Div.. Army Southwest Mo....	May, 1862

ARMY SOUTHWEST MO.—May, 1862. Merged into District Eastern Arkansas Dec., 1862.

1st DIVISION.— COMMANDER.

Frederick Steele	Brigadier General.		
11th Wisconsin Infy......May, 1862	From Steele's Com'd Southeast Mo.	To 1-Brig. 1-Div. Dist. S. E. Mo..	Oct., 1862
8th Indiana Infy........May, 1862	From 1-Br. 3-Div. Army. S. W. Mo.	To 2-Brig. 1-Div. Dist. S. E. Mo..	Oct., 1862
18th Indiana Infy.......May, 1862	From 1-Br. 3-Div. Army. S. W. Mo.	To 2-Brig. 1-Div. Dist. S. E. Mo..	Oct., 1862
33d Illinois Infy........May, 1862	From Steele's Com'd Southeast Mo.	To 1-Brig. 1-Div. Dist. S. E. Mo..	Oct., 1862
Kane Co., Ill., Cav. Co..May, 1862	From Unatt. Dept. Mo............	To 1-Br. 3-(Cav.)Div. Dist. E. Ark.	Dec., 1862
1st Indiana Cav.........May, 1862	From Steele's Com'd Southeast Mo.	To 1-Br. 3-(Cav.)Div. Dist. E. Ark.	Dec., 1862
3d Iowa Cav. 6 Cos.....May, 1862	From Unatt. Army Southwest Mo..	To 2-Br. 3-(Cav.)Div. Dist. E. Ark.	Dec., 1862
1st Indiana Batty.......May, 1862	From 1-Br. 3-Div. Army. S. W. Mo.	To Arty. 1-Div. Army S. E. Mo....	Oct., 1862
16th Ohio Batty........May, 1862	From Steele's Com'd Southeast Mo.	To Arty. Dist. Eastern Ark.......	Dec., 1862
Batty. A, 1st Mo. Arty...May, 1862	From Steele's Com'd Southeast Mo.	To Arty. Dist. Eastern Ark.......	Dec., 1862

2d DIVISION.— COMMANDER.

E. A. Carr	Brigadier General.		
4th Iowa Infy............May, 1862	From 1-Br. 4-Div. Army S. W. Mo.	To 2-Br. 2-Div. Dist. Eastern Ark.	Dec., 1862
9th Iowa Infy...........May, 1862	From 2-Br. 4-Div. Army S. W. Mo.	To 3-Br. 1-Div. Dist. Eastern Ark.	Dec., 1862
13th Illinois Infy.......May, 1862	From Unatt. Army Southwest Mo..	To 2-Br. 2-Div. Dist. Eastern Ark.	Dec., 1862
4th Iowa Cav..........May, 1862	From Unatt. Army Southwest Mo..	To 2-Br. 3-(Cav.)Div. Dist. E. Ark.	Dec., 1862
3d Illinois Cav..........May, 1862	From 2-Br. 4-Div. Army S. W. Mo.	To 1-Br. 3-(Cav.)Div. Dist. E. Ark.	Dec., 1862
1st Mo. Cav. 3 Cos......May, 1862	From 2-Bd. 4-Div. Army S. W. Mo.	To 1-Br. 3-(Cav.)Div. Dist. E. Ark.	Dec., 1862
1st Iowa Batty.........May, 1862	From 1-Br. 4-Div. Army S. W. Mo.	To Arty. Dist. Eastern Ark.......	Dec., 1862
1st Mo. Flying Arty......May, 1862	From Unatt. 2-Div. Army S. W. Mo.	To Arty. Dist. Eastern Ark.......	Dec., 1862
3d Iowa Batty..........May, 1862	From Unatt. Army Southwest Mo..	To Arty. Dist. Eastern Ark.......	Dec., 1862

3d DIVISION.— COMMANDER.

P. J. Osterhaus	Brigadier General.		
3d Missouri Infy.........May, 1862	From Unatt. Army Southwest Mo.	To 1-Br. 1-Div. Dist. Eastern Ark.	Dec., 1862
12th Missouri Infy......May, 1862	From 2-Br. 1-Div. Army S. W. Mo.	To 1-Br. 1-Div. Dist. Eastern Ark.	Dec., 1862
17th Missouri Infy......May, 1862	From 1-Br. 1-Div. Army S. W. Mo.	To 1-Br. 1-Div. Dist. Eastern Ark.	Dec., 1862
4th Missouri Cav. 6 Cos..May, 1862	From Unatt. Army Southwest Mo.	To Cav. Brig. Dist. Southeast Mo..	Oct., 1862
5th Missouri Cav. 5 Cos..May, 1862	From 2-Div. Army Southwest Mo..	To Cav. Brig. Dist. Southeast Mo..	Oct., 1862
2d Ohio Batty...........May, 1862	From 2-Div. Army Southwest Mo..	To Arty. Dist. Eastern Ark.......	Dec., 1862
Peoria, Ill., Arty........May, 1862	From 2-Br. 3-Div. Army S. W. Mo..	To Arty. Dist. Eastern Ark.......	Dec., 1862
4th Ohio Batty..........May, 1862	From Arty. 1-Div. Army S. W. Mo.	To Arty. Dist. Eastern Ark.......	Dec., 1862
Welfley's Mo. Batty ......May, 1862	From Arty. 1-Div. Army S. W. Mo.	To Arty. Dist. Eastern Ark.......	Dec., 1862
UNATTACHED.—			
Bowen's Mo. Cav. Battn..May, 1862	From Unatt. Army Southwest Mo.	To 1-Brig. 3-Div. Army Frontier...	Oct., 1862
24th Missouri Infy......May, 1862	From Unatt. Army Southwest Mo.	To 2-Br. 2-Div. Dist. Southeast Mo.	Oct., 1862
1st Illinois Cav.........May, 1862	From Unatt. Army Southwest Mo.	To 2-Br. 2-Div. Dist. Southeast Mo.	Oct., 1862
5th Illinois Cav.........May, 1862	From Steele's Com'd Southeast Mo.	To 1-Br. 3-(Cav.)Div. Dist. E. Ark.	Dec., 1862
9th Illinois Cav.........May, 1862	From Steele's Com'd Southeast Mo.	To 2-Br. 3-(Cav.)Div. Dist. E. Ark.	Dec., 1862
13th Illinois Cav........May, 1862	From Steele's Com'd Southeast Mo.	To Cav. Brig. Dist. Southeast Mo..	Oct., 1862
5th Kansas Cav.........June, 1862	From Dept. Kansas...............	To 2-Br. 3-(Cav.)Div. Dist. E. Ark.	Dec., 1862
2d Wisconsin Cav.......June, 1862	From New Organization...........	To 2-Br. 3-(Cav.)Div. Dist. E. Ark.	Dec., 1862
1st Nebraska Infy.......July, 1862	From 2-Brig. 3-Div. Army Tenn...	To 2-Br. 2-Div. Dist. Southeast Mo.	Oct., 1862

DIST. OF SOUTHWEST MISSOURI.—Created June 5, 1862. Discontinued July 10, 1865.

COMMANDERS.

E. B. Brown	Brigadier General..................	June 5, 1862, to Sept. 24, 1862.
J. M. Schofield	Brigadier General..................	Sept. 24, 1862, to Nov. 10, 1862.
E. B. Brown	Brigadier General..................	Nov. 10, 1862, to Mch. 30, 1863.
J. M. Schofield	Major General.....................	Mch. 30, 1863, to May 24, 1863.
W. F. Cloud	Col. 2d Kansas Cav...............	May 24, 1863, to July 15, 1863.
John McNeil	Brigadier General..................	July 15, 1863, to Oct. 15, 1863.
J. B. Sanborn	Brigadier General..................	Oct. 15, 1863, to Dec. 9, 1864.
J. J. Gravely	Col. 8th Mo. S. M. Cav...........	Dec. 9, 1864, to Jan. 9, 1865.
J. B. Sanborn	Brigadier General..................	Jan. 9, 1865, to June 10, 1865.
J. D. Allen	Col. 15th Missouri Cav............	June 10, 1865, to June 19, 1865.
T. J. McKean	Brigadier General..................	June 19, 1865, to July 10, 1865.

4th Missouri Infy........June, 1862	From Unatt. Army Southwest Mo...	No change to Muster Out..........	Jan., 1863
37th Illinois Infy........June, 1862	From 2-Brig. 3-Div. Army S. W. Mo.	To 2-Brig. 2-Div. Army Frontier....	Oct., 1862
26th Indiana Infy.......June, 1862	From Sedalia, Mo................	To 1-Brig. 2-Div. Army Frontier...	Oct., 1862
1st Missouri Cav. 1st B'n.June, 1862	From Dept. Kansas...............	To 2-Brig. 2-Div. Army Frontier...	Oct., 1862
3d Missouri Cav. Det....June, 1862	From Dist. Rolla Dept. Mo........	To Dist. Rolla Dept. Mo...........	Sept., 1862
3d Missouri S. M. Cav....June, 1862	From New Organization...........	To Dist. Central Missouri.........	Dec., 1862
4th Missouri S. M. Cav...June, 1862	From New Organization...........	To Dist. Central Missouri.........	Dec., 1862
6th Missouri S. M. Cav...June, 1862	From Dist. Central Missouri.......	To Dist. Central Missouri.........	Dec., 1862
14th Missouri S. M. Cav..June, 1862	From New Organization...........	Disbanded	Mch., 1863
10th Illinois Cav........June, 1862	From Unatt. Army Southwest Mo...	To 1-Brig. 3-Div. Army Frontier...	Oct., 1862
1st Arkansas Cav........June, 1862	From New Organization...........	To 1-Brig. 3-Div. Army Frontier...	Oct., 1862
Batty. F, 1st Mo. Arty...June, 1862	From Unatt. Army Southwest Mo...	To 2-Brig. 2-Div. Army Frontier...	Oct., 1862
2d Arkansas Cav........July, 1862	From New Organization...........	To Helena, Ark..................	July, 1862
3d Iowa Cav. E, F, G, H..Aug., 1862	From Dist. North Mo.............	To Dist. Rolla Dept. Mo...........	Nov., 1862
18th Iowa Infy..........Sept., 1862	From New Organization...........	To 1-Brig. 2-Div. Army Frontier...	Oct., 1862
20th Iowa Infy..........Sept., 1862	From New Organization...........	To 2-Brig. 2-Div. Army Frontier...	Oct., 1862
7th Missouri S. M. Cav...Sept., 1862	From Unatt. Dept. Mo............	To Dist. Central Missouri.........	July, 1863
8th Missouri S. M. Cav...Sept., 1862	From Unatt. Dept. Mo............	No change to Muster Out..........	Apr., 1865

DIST. OF SOUTHWEST MISSOURI.—Continued.

Unit	Date	From	To	Date
13th Kansas Infy	Feb., 1863	From 2-Brig. 1-Div. Army Frontier..	To Dist. Frontier Dept. Mo.	June, 1863
2d Kansas Cav.	Feb., 1863	From 2-Brig. 1-Div. Army Frontier..	To Dist. Frontier Dept. Mo.	Dec., 1863
2d Indiana Batty.	Feb., 1863	From 3-Brig. 1-Div. Army Frontier.	To Dist. Frontier Dept. Mo.	June, 1863
3d Indiana Batty.	Feb., 1863	From Central Dist. Mo. Dept. Mo.	To Dist. Rolla Dept. Mo.	June, 1863
1st Kansas Batty.	Feb., 1863	From 1-Brig. 1-Div. Army Frontier.	To Dist. Rolla Dept. Mo.	June, 1863
2d Kansas Batty.	Feb., 1863	From 2-Brig. 1-Div. Army Frontier.	To Dist. Frontier Dept. Mo.	June, 1863
1st Arkansas Infy.	Mch., 1863	From New Organization	To 2-Brig. Dist. Frontier Dept. Mo.	Dec., 1863
2d Arkansas Cav.	May, 1863	From 2-Brig. Cav. Div. Dist. E. Ark.	To Unatt. Cav. Dist. West Tenn.	Dec., 1864
18th Iowa Infy.	June, 1863	From 1-Brig. 2-Div. Army Frontier	To Dist. Frontier Dept. Mo.	Oct., 1863
1st Ark. Cav.	June, 1863	From Unatt. Army Frontier	To 3-Brig. Frontier Div. 7-Corps Ark.	June, 1864
6th Mo. S. M. Cav.	July, 1863	From Dist. Central Mo. Dept. Mo.	To Dist. Northern Mo. Dept. Mo.	Oct., 1864
1st Ark. Batty.	Aug., 1863	From New Organization	To 2-Brig. Dist. Frontier 7-C. Ark.	Mch., 1864
6th Mo. E. M. 16th Cav.	Nov., 1863	From New Organization	To Dist. Northern Mo. Dept. Mo.	Apr., 1865
7th Mo. E. M. 15th Cav.	Nov., 1863	From New Organization	To Dist. Northern Mo. Dept. Mo.	Apr., 1865
Batty. L, 1st Mo. Arty.	Dec., 1863	From Dist. Rolla Dept. Mo.	To Dist. Northern Mo. Dept. Mo.	Apr., 1865
11th Mo. Cav.	Dec., 1863	From Dist. St. Louis, Mo., Dept. Mo.	To Dist. N. E. Ark.	Dec., 1863
Batty. M, 2d Mo. Arty.	Aug., 1864	From Dist. St. Louis, Mo., Dept. Mo.	To Arty. Res. Dist. St. Louis.	Dec., 1864
46th Mo. Infy.	Aug., 1864	From New Organization	To Dist. Central Mo.	Apr., 1865
6th Mo. S. M. Cav.	Feb., 1865	From Dist. North Mo.	No change to Muster Out	July, 1865

DISTRICT EASTERN ARKANSAS.—Transferred to Dept. Tenn., Dec., 1862.

COMMANDER.

Willis A. Gorman	Brigadier General

1st DIVISION.—

COMMANDER.

Fred'k Steele	Brigadier General

1st BRIGADE.—

COMMANDER.

P. J. Osterhaus	Brigadier General

Unit	Date	From	To	Date
3d Mo. Infy.	Dec., 1862	From 3-Div. Army S. W. Mo.	To 2-Brig. 11-Div. R. W. 13-C. Tenn.	Dec., 1862
12th Mo. Infy.	Dec., 1862	From 3-Div. Army S. W. Mo.	To 2-Brig. 11-Div. R. W. 13-C. Tenn.	Dec., 1862
17th Mo. Infy.	Dec., 1862	From 3-Div. Army S. W. Mo.	To 2-Brig. 11-Div. R. W. 13-C. Tenn.	Dec., 1862
58th Ohio Infy.	Dec., 1862	From Helena, Ark.	To 1-Brig. 11-Div. R. W. 13-C. Tenn.	Dec., 1862
76th Ohio Infy.	Dec., 1862	From Helena, Ark.	To 2-Brig. 11-Div. R. W. 13-C. Tenn.	Dec., 1862

2d BRIGADE.—

COMMANDER.

J. M. Thayer	Brigadier General

Unit	Date	From	To	Date
26th Iowa Infy.	Dec., 1862	From New Organization	To 3-Brig. 11-Div. R. W. 13-C. Tenn.	Dec., 1862
28th Iowa Infy.	Dec., 1862	From New Organization	To 2-Brig. 2-Div. Dist. East. Ark.	Dec., 1862
30th Iowa Infy.	Dec., 1862	From New Organization	To 3-Brig. 11-Div. R. W. 13-C. Tenn.	Dec., 1862
34th Iowa Infy.	Dec., 1862	From New Organization	To 3-Brig. 11-Div. R. W. 13-C. Tenn.	Dec., 1862

3d BRIGADE.—

Unit	Date	From	To	Date
9th Iowa Infy.	Dec., 1862	From 2-Div. Army S. W. Mo.	To 3-Brig. 11-Div. R. W. 13-C. Tenn.	Dec., 1862
24th Iowa Infy.	Dec., 1862	From New Organization	To 2-Brig. 2-Div. Dist. East. Ark.	Dec., 1862
25th Iowa Infy.	Dec., 1862	From New Organization	To 2-Brig. 11-Div. R. W. 13-C. Tenn.	Dec., 1862
31st Iowa Infy.	Dec., 1862	From New Organization	To 2-Brig. 11-Div. R. W. 13-C. Tenn.	Dec., 1862

2d DIVISION.—

COMMANDER.

A. P. Hovey	Brigadier General

1st BRIGADE.—

COMMANDER.

C. E. Hovey	Brigadier General

Unit	Date	From	To	Date
43d Ind. Infy.	Dec., 1862	From Helena, Ark.	To 1-Brig. 12-Div. 13-Corps Tenn.	Jan., 1863
46th Ind. Infy.	Dec., 1862	From Helena, Ark.	To 1-Brig. 12-Div. 13-Corps Tenn.	Jan., 1863
47th Ind. Infy.	Dec., 1862	From Helena, Ark.	To 1-Brig. 12-Div. 13-Corps Tenn.	Jan., 1863

2d BRIGADE.—

COMMANDER.

Peter Kinney	Col. 56th Ohio Infy.

Unit	Date	From	To	Date
13th Ill. Infy.	Dec., 1862	From 2-Div. Army S. W. Mo.	To 1-Brig. 11-Div. R. W. 13-C. Tenn.	Dec., 1862
4th Iowa Infy.	Dec., 1862	From 2-Div. Army S. W. Mo.	To 3-Brig. 11-Div. R. W. 13-C. Tenn.	Dec., 1862
56th Ohio Infy.	Dec., 1862	From Helena, Ark.	To 2-Brig. 12-Div. 13-Corps Tenn.	Jan., 1863
29th Wis. Infy.	Dec., 1862	From Helena, Ark.	To 3-Brig. 12-Div. 13-Corps Tenn.	Jan., 1863
28th Iowa Infy.	Dec., 1862	From 2-Brig. 1-Div. Dist. East. Ark.	To 2-Brig. 12-Div. 13-Corps Tenn.	Jan., 1863
24th Iowa Infy.	Dec., 1862	From 3-Brig. 1-Div. Dist. East. Ark.	To 2-Brig. 13-Div. 13-Corps Tenn.	Jan., 1863

3d BRIGADE.—

COMMANDER.

G. F. McGinnis	Brigadier General

Unit	Date	From	To	Date
11th Ind. Infy.	Dec., 1862	From Helena, Ark.	To 3-Brig. 12-Div. 13-Corps Tenn.	Jan., 1863
24th Ind. Infy.	Dec., 1862	From Helena, Ark.	To 3-Brig. 12-Div. 13-Corps Tenn.	Jan., 1863
34th Ind. Infy.	Dec., 1862	From Helena, Ark.	To 3-Brig. 12-Div. 13-Corps Tenn.	Jan., 1863

3d (CAVALRY) DIVISION.—

COMMANDER.

C. C. Washburn	Brigadier General

1st BRIGADE.—

COMMANDER.

Conrad Baker	Col. 1st Ind. Cav.

Unit	Date	From	To	Date
3d Ill. Cav.	Dec., 1862	From 2-Div. Army S. W. Mo.	To Sherman's Yazoo Exp.	Dec., 1862
5th Ill. Cav.	Dec., 1862	From Helena, Ark.	To 1-Brig. 2-Cav. Div. 13-C. Tenn.	Jan., 1863
10th Ill. Cav.	Dec., 1862	From Helena, Ark.	To 1-Brig. 2-Cav. Div. 13-C. Tenn.	Jan., 1863
Kane Co. (Ill.) Cav. Co.	Dec., 1862	From Helena, Ark.	To 15th Ill. Cav. as Co. H.	Dec., 1862
1st Ind. Cav.	Dec., 1862	From 1-Div. Army S. W. Mo.	To 1-Brig. 2-Cav. Div. 13-C. Tenn.	Jan., 1863
1st Mo. Cav., 3d Battn.	Dec., 1862	From 2-Div. Army S. W. Mo.	To Helena Dist. E. Ark. 13-C. Tenn	Jan., 1863
6th Mo. Cav., 6 Co's	Dec., 1862	From Helena, Ark.	To 1-Brig. 2-Cav. Div. 13-C. Tenn.	Jan., 1863

2d BRIGADE.—

COMMANDER.

Cyrus Bussey	Col. 3d Iowa Cav.

Unit	Date	From	To	Date
2d Ark. Cav.	Dec., 1862	From New Organization	To 2-Brig. 2-Cav. Div. 13-C. Tenn.	Jan., 1863
9th Ill. Cav.	Dec., 1862	From Helena, Ark.	To 2-Brig. 2-Cav. Div. 13-C. Tenn.	Jan., 1863
3d Iowa Cav., A,B,C,D,I,K.	Dec., 1862	From 1-Div. Army S. W. Mo.	To 2-Brig. 2-Cav. Div. 13-C. Tenn.	Jan., 1863
4th Iowa Cav.	Dec., 1862	From 2-Div. Army S. W. Mo.	To Helena Dist. E. Ark. 13-C. Tenn.	Jan., 1863
5th Kansas Cav.	Dec., 1862	From Helena, Ark.	To 2-Brig. 2-Cav. Div. 13-C. Tenn.	Jan., 1863
2d Wis. Cav.	Dec., 1862	From Helena, Ark.	To 2-Brig. 2-Cav. Div. 13-C. Tenn.	Jan., 1863

ARTILLERY, DISTRICT EASTERN ARKANSAS.—

1st Ind. Batty.	Dec., 1862	From Arty. 1-Div. Army S. W. Mo.	To Arty. 1-Div. Dist. S. E. Mo.	Oct., 1862
2d Ohio Batty.	Dec., 1862	From Arty. 3-Div. Army S. W. Mo.	To Arty. 12-Div. 13-Corps Tenn.	Jan., 1863
4th Ohio Batty.	Dec., 1862	From Arty. 3-Div. Army S. W. Mo.	To 1-Brig. 11-Div. R. W. 13-C. Tenn.	Dec., 1862
16th Ohio Batty.	Dec., 1862	From Arty. 3-Div. Army S. W. Mo.	To Arty. 12-Div. 13-Corps Tenn.	Jan., 1863
Batty. A, 1st Mo. Arty.	Dec., 1862	From Arty. 1-Div. Army S. W. Mo.	To Arty. 13-Div. Dist. S. E. Mo.	Jan., 1863
Welfley's Mo. Batty.	Dec., 1862	From Arty. 3-Div. Army S. W. Mo.	To Arty. 2-Div. Dist. S. E. Mo.	Oct., 1862
1st Mo. Flying Arty.	Dec., 1862	From Arty. 2-Div. Army S. W. Mo.	To 2-Brig. 11-Div. R. W. 13-C. Tenn.	Dec., 1862
1st Iowa Batty.	Dec., 1862	From Arty. 2-Div. Army S. W. Mo.	To 3-Brig. 11-Div. R. W. 13-C. Tenn.	Dec., 1862
3d Iowa Batty.	Dec., 1862	From Arty. 2-Div. Army S. W. Mo.	To Arty. 13-Div. 13-Corps Tenn.	Jan., 1863
Batty. A, 2d Ill. Arty.	Dec., 1862	From Arty. 3-Div. Army S. W. Mo.	To Arty. 12-Div. 13-Corps Tenn.	Jan., 1863

ARMY OF THE FRONTIER.—Organized Oct. 12, 1862, from forces in the field from Missouri and Kansas. Broken up June 5, 1863.

COMMANDERS.

J. M. Schofield	Major General	Oct. 12, 1862, to Mch. 30, 1863.
F. J. Herron	Major General	Mch. 30, 1863, to June 5, 1863.

1st DIVISION.— COMMANDERS.

J. G. Blunt	Brigadier General	Oct. 12, 1862, to Dec. 31, 1862.
William Weer	Col. 10th Kansas Infy.	Dec. 31, 1862, to Apr. 26, 1863.
Thos. Ewing, Jr.	Brigadier General	Apr. 26, 1863, to June 5, 1863.

1st BRIGADE.— COMMANDERS.

Fred'k Salomon	Brigadier General	
W. R. Judson	Col. 6th Kansas Cav.	

9th Wis. Infy.	Oct., 1862	From 1-Brig. Dept. Kansas.	To Dist. Rolla Dept. Mo.	June, 1863
11th Kansas Infy.	Oct., 1862	From New Organization.	To Dist. Rolla Dept. Mo.	Feb., 1863
9th Kansas Cav.	Oct., 1862	From 1-Brig. Dept. Kansas.	To Dist. Frontier Dept. Mo.	June, 1863
2d Ohio Cav.	Oct., 1862	From 1-Brig. Dept. Kansas.	To Columbus, Ohio.	Dec., 1862
3d Wis. Cav.	Oct., 1862	From Unatt. Dept. Kansas.	To Dist. Frontier Dept. Mo.	June, 1863
1st Kansas Batty.	Oct., 1862	From 2-Brig. Dept. Kansas.	To Dist. S. W. Mo. Dept. Mo.	Feb., 1863
6th Kansas Cav.	Feb., 1863	From 2-Brig. 1-Div. Army Frontier.	To Dist. Frontier Dept. Mo.	June, 1863
25th Ohio Batty.	Feb., 1863	From New Org. (3d Kansas Batty.).	To Arty. 1-Cav. Div. Dist. S. E. Mo.	June, 1863

2d BRIGADE.— COMMANDER.

William F. Cloud	Col. 2d Kansas Cav.	

10th Kansas Infy.	Oct., 1862	From 2-Brig. Dept. Kansas.	To Dist. Rolla Dept. Mo.	Feb., 1863
6th Kansas Cav.	Oct., 1862	From 2-Brig. Dept. Kansas.	To 1-Brig. 1-Div. Army Frontier.	Feb., 1863
13th Kansas Infy.	Oct., 1862	From New Organization.	To Dist. S. W. Mo.	Feb., 1863
2d Kansas Cav.	Oct., 1862	From 3-Brig. Dept. Kansas.	To Dist. S. W. Mo.	Feb., 1863
2d Kansas Batty.	Feb., 1863	From Fort Scott, Kansas.	To Dist. S. W. Mo.	Feb., 1863

3d BRIGADE.— COMMANDER.

William A. Phillips	Col. 3d Indian Home Guard.	

1st Indian Home Guard.	Oct., 1862	From 3-Brig. Dept. Kansas.	To Dist. N. W. Ark. Dept. Mo.	Feb., 1863
2d Indian Home Guard.	Oct., 1862	From 1-Brig. Dept. Kansas.	To Dist. N. W. Ark. Dept. Mo.	Feb., 18
3d Indian Home Guard.	Oct., 1862	From 2-Brig. Dept. Kansas.	To Dist. N. W. Ark. Dept. Mo.	Feb., 1863
2d Ind. Batty.	Oct., 1862	From 3-Brig. Dept. Kansas.	To Dist. S. W. Mo. Dept. Mo.	Feb., 1863
Hopkins' Kansas Batty.	Oct., 1862	From 3-Brig. Dept. Kansas.	To Dist. N. W. Ark. Dept. Mo.	Feb., 1863

2d DIVISION.— COMMANDERS.

James Totten	Brigadier General	Oct. 12, 1862, to Dec., 1862.
Daniel Huston, Jr.	Col. 7th Mo. Cav.	Dec., 1862, to Jan., 1863.
J. G. Clark	Col. 26th Ind. Infy.	Jan., 1863, to Mch., 1863.
D. Wickersham	Col. 10th Ill. Cav.	Mch., 1863, to May, 1863.
Wm. Vandever	Col. 9th Iowa Infy.	May 24, 1863, to June 5, 1863.

1st BRIGADE.— COMMANDERS.

D. Huston, Jr.	Col. 7th Mo. Cav.	Oct. 12, 1862, to Dec., 1862.
J. G. Clark.	Col. 26th Ind. Infy.	Dec., 1862, to Jan., 1863.
D. Huston, Jr.	Col. 7th Mo. Cav.	Jan., 1863, to June, 1863.

18th Iowa Infy.	Oct., 1862	From Dist. S. W. Mo. Dept. Mo.	To Dist. S. W. Mo. Dept. Mo.	June, 1863
26th Ind. Infy.	Oct., 1862	From Dist. S. W. Mo. Dept. Mo.	To 1-Brig. Herron's Div. 13-C. Tenn.	June, 1863
7th Mo. Cav.	Oct., 1862	From Dist. S. W. Mo. Dept. Mo.	To 1-Brig. 1-Cav. Div. Dist. S. E. Mo.	June, 1863
Batty. A, 2d Ill. Arty.	Oct., 1862	From Dist. S. W. Mo. Dept. Mo.	To Arty. 1-Cav. Div. Dist. S. E. Mo.	June, 1863
10th Ill. Cav.	Feb., 1863	From Unatt. Army Frontier.	To 2-Brig. 1-Cav. Div. Dist. S. E. Mo.	June, 1863

2d BRIGADE.— COMMANDER.

Wm. McE. Dye	Col. 20th Iowa Infy.	Oct. 12, 1862, to June 5, 1863.

37th Ill. Infy.	Oct., 1862	From Dist. S. W. Mo. Dept. Mo.	To 1-Brig. Herron's Div. 13-C. Tenn.	June, 1863
20th Iowa Infy.	Oct., 1862	From Dist. S. W. Mo. Dept. Mo.	To 1-Brig. Herron's Div. 13-C. Tenn.	June, 1863
3d Iowa Cav. Det.	Oct., 1862	From Dist. S. W. Mo. Dept. Mo.	To 2-Brig. 1-Cav. Div. Dist. S. E. Mo.	June, 1863
1st Mo. Cav., 1st Battn.	Oct., 1862	From Dist. S. W. Mo. Dept. Mo.	To 2-Brig. 3-Div. Army Frontier.	Feb., 1863
6th Mo. Cav., 2d Battn.	Oct., 1862	From Dist. S. W. Mo. Dept. Mo.	To Dist. S. E. Mo.	June, 1863
Batty. F, 1st Mo. Arty.	Oct., 1862	From Dist. S. W. Mo. Dept. Mo.	To 1-Brig. Herron's Div. 13-C. Tenn.	June, 1863

UNATTACHED, 2d DIVISION.—

1st Mo. Cav., 2d Battn.	Oct., 1862	From Cassville, Mo.	To 2-Brig. 3-Div. Army Frontier.	Feb., 1863

3d DIVISION.— COMMANDERS.

F. J. Herron	Brigadier General	Oct. 12, 1862, to Feb., 1863.
Jas. O. Gower	Col. 1st Iowa Cav.	Feb., 1863, to Mch. 30, 1863.
W. F. Geiger	Col. 8th Mo. Cav.	Mch. 30, 1863, to June 5, 1863.

1st BRIGADE.— COMMANDERS.

B. Pinckney	Col. 20th Wis. Infy.	Oct. 12, 1862, to Dec. 6, 1862.
Jas. O. Gower	Col. 1st Iowa Cav.	Dec. 6, 1862, to Feb., 1863.
Henry Bertram	Col. 20th Wis. Infy.	Feb., 1863, to June 5, 1863.

1st Ark. Cav.	Oct., 1862	From Dist. S. W. Mo.	To Unatt. Army Frontier.	Dec., 1862
20th Wis. Infy.	Oct., 1862	From New Organization.	To 2-Brig. Herron's Div. 13-C. Tenn.	June, 1863
10th Ill. Cav.	Oct., 1862	From Dist. S. W. Mo.	To Unatt. Army Frontier.	Dec., 1862
Bowen's Mo. Cav.	Oct., 1862	From Dist. S. W. Mo.	Transferred to 9th Mo. Cav.	Oct., 1862
2d Wis. Cav., A, D, G, K.	Oct., 1862	From Cassville, Mo., Dept. Mo.	To Dist. Rolla Dept. Mo.	June, 1863
Batty. L, 1st Mo. Arty.	Oct., 1862	From Dist. S. W. Mo.	To Dist. Rolla Dept. Mo.	June, 1863
1st Iowa Cav.	Nov., 1862	From 2-Brig. 3-Div. Army Frontier.	To 2-Brig. 1-Cav. Div. Dist. S. E. Mo.	June, 1863

2d BRIGADE.— COMMANDERS.

W. W. Orme............	Col. 94th Ill. Infy..................	Oct. 12, 1862, to Dec., 1862.
Benj. Crabb	Col. 19th Iowa Infy..............	Dec., 1862, to Mch. 30, 1863.
W. F. Geiger..........	Col. 8th Mo. Cav..............	Mch. 30, 1863, to Apr. 10, 1863.
W. W. Orme............	Brigadier General	Apr. 10, 1863, to June 5, 1863.

94th Ill. Infy......Oct., 1862	From New Organization............	To 2-Brig. Herron's Div. 13-C. Tenn.	June,	1863
19th Iowa Infy.........Oct., 1862	From New Organization............	To 2-Brig. Herron's Div. 13-C. Tenn.	June,	1863
8th Mo. Cav..........Oct., 1862	From New Organization............	To 1-Brig. 1-Cav. Div. Dist. S. E. Mo.	June,	1863
Batty. E, 1st Mo. Arty...Oct., 1862	From Dist. S. W. Mo..............	To 1-Brig. Herron's Div. 13-C. Tenn.	June,	1863
1st Iowa Batty.........Oct., 1862	From Dist. Central Mo............	To 1-Brig. 3-Div. Army Frontier....	Nov.,	1862
1st Mo. Cav., 8 Co's......Feb., 1863	From 2-Brig. 2-Div. Army Frontier..	To 1-Brig. 1-Cav. Div. Dist. S. E. Mo.	June,	1863
UNATTACHED.—				
1st Ark. Cav.........Dec., 1862	From 1-Brig. 2-Div. Army Frontier..	To Dist. S. W. Mo................	June,	1863
10th Ill. Cav.........Dec., 1862	From Dist. S. W. Mo..............	To 1-Brig. 2-Div. Army Frontier....	Feb.,	1863
7th Mo. S. M. Cav.......Dec., 1862	From Dist. S. W. Mo..............	To Central Dist. Mo..............	June,	1863

DISTRICT OF THE FRONTIER.—Constituted June 9, 1863. Transferred to Dept. Arkansas, Jan. 6, 1864.

COMMANDER.

Jas. G. Blunt.........	Major General	June 9, 1863, to Jan. 6, 1864.

1st Indian Home Guard...June, 1863	From 3-Brig. 1-Div. Army Frontier..	To 1-Brig. Dist. Frontier..........	Dec.,	1863
2d Indian Home Guard...June, 1863	From 3-Brig. 1-Div. Army Frontier..	To 1-Brig. Dist. Frontier..........	Dec.,	1863
3d Indian Home Guard...June, 1863	From 3-Brig. 1-Div. Army Frontier..	To 1-Brig. Dist. Frontier..........	Dec.,	1863
12th Kansas Infy.......June, 1863	From Unatt. Dept. Kansas..........	To Unatt. Dist. Front. 7-C. Dept. Ark.	Jan.,	1864
6th Kansas Cav.......June, 1863	From 1-Brig. 1-Div. Army Frontier..	To Unatt. Dist. Front. 7-C. Dept. Ark.	Jan.,	1864
9th Kansas Cav.......June, 1863	From 1-Brig. 1-Div. Army Frontier..	To Dist. Border Dept. Mo..........	July,	1863
1st Kansas Col'd Infy....June, 1863	From New Organization............	To Unatt. Dist. Frontier 7-C. Ark...	Jan.,	1864
4th Mo. S. M. Cav., I, M...June, 1863	From Dist. Central Mo............	To Dist. Border Dept. Mo..........	July,	1863
5th Mo. S. M. Cav.......June, 1863	From Dist. Rolla Dept. Mo.........	To Dist. Rolla Dept. Mo...........	Dec.,	1863
2d Colo. Infy., 6 Co's.....June, 1863	From Dist. S. E. Mo..............	To Dist. Border Dept. Mo..........	July,	1863
3d Wis. Cav.........June, 1863	From 1-Brig. 1-Div. Army Frontier..	To Dist. Frontier 7-Corps Dept. Ark.	Jan.,	1864
2d Kansas Batty.........June, 1863	From Dist. S. W. Mo..............	To Unass'd Dist. Frontier 7-C. Ark..	Jan.,	1864
3d Kansas Batty.........June, 1863	From Dist. N. W. Ark.............	To 3-Brig. Dist. Frontier Dept. Mo..	Dec.,	1863
9th Wis. Batty. Sec.....June, 1863	From Dist. Kansas...............	To Dist. Border Dept. Mo..........	Dec.,	1863
2d Ind. Batty.........June, 1863	From Dist. S. W. Mo..............	To 2-Brig. Dist. Frontier..........	Dec.,	1863
13th Kansas Infy.......June, 1863	From Dist. S. W. Mo..............	To 3-Brig. Dist. Frontier..........	Dec.,	1863
14th Kansas Cav.......June, 1863	From New Organization............	To Unatt. Dist. Frontier 7-C. Ark...	Jan.,	1864
2d Ark. Infy.........Oct., 1863	From New Organization............	To Unatt. Dist. Frontier 7-C. Ark...	Jan.,	1864
18th Iowa Infy.........Oct., 1863	From Dist. S. W. Mo..............	To 2-Brig. Dist. Frontier..........	Dec.,	1863
2d Kansas Col'd Infy......Oct., 1863	From New Organization............	To Unatt. Dist. Frontier 7-C. Ark...	Jan.,	1864

1st BRIGADE.— COMMANDER.

William A. Phillips.....	Col. 3d Indian Home Guard........	

1st Indian Home Guard...Dec., 1863	From Unatt. Dist. Frontier........	To 1-Brig. Dist. Frontier 7-C. Ark..	Jan.,	1864
2d Indian Home Guard...Dec., 1863	From Unatt. Dist. Frontier........	To 1-Brig. Dist. Frontier 7-C. Ark..	Jan.,	1864
3d Indian Home Guard...Dec., 1863	From Unatt. Dist. Frontier........	To 1-Brig. Dist. Frontier 7-C. Ark..	Jan.,	1864
14th Kansas Cav., Co. M.Dec., 1863	From Unatt. Dist. Frontier........	To 1-Brig. Dist. Frontier 7-C. Ark..	Jan.,	1864

2d BRIGADE.— COMMANDER.

John Edwards	Col 18th Iowa Infy..............	

1st Ark. Infy.............Dec., 1863	From Dist. S. W. Mo..............	To 2-Brig. Dist. Frontier 7-C. Ark..	Jan.,	1864
2d Kansas Cav...........Dec., 1863	From Dist. S. W. Mo..............	To 2-Brig. Dist. Frontier 7-C. Ark..	Jan.,	1864
2d Ind. Batty............Dec., 1863	From Dist. S. W. Mo..............	To 2-Brig. Dist. Frontier 7-C. Ark..	Jan.,	1864
18th Iowa Infy..........Dec., 1863	From Unatt. Dist. Frontier........	To 2-Brig. Dist. Frontier 7-C. Ark..	Jan.,	1864

3d BRIGADE.— COMMANDER.

Thomas M. Bowen......	Col. 13th Kansas Infy............	

13th Kansas Infy.......Dec., 1863	From Unatt. Dist. Frontier........	To 3-Brig. Dist. Frontier 7-C. Ark..	Jan.,	1864
3d Wis. Cav., 5 Co's.....Dec., 1863	From Unatt. Dist. Frontier........	To 3-Brig. Dist. Frontier 7-C. Ark..	Jan.,	1864
3d Kansas Batty.......Dec., 1863	From Unatt. Dist. Frontier........	To 3-Brig. Dist. Frontier 7-C. Ark..	Jan.,	1864

DISTRICT OF THE BORDER.—Constituted June 9, 1863. Discontinued Jan., 1864.

COMMANDER.

Thomas Ewing, Jr.....	Brigadier General	

9th Kansas Cav........July, 1863	From Dist. Frontier Dept. Mo......	To Dept. Kansas................	Jan.,	1864
11th Kansas Cav.......July, 1863	From Dist. Kansas Dept. Mo........	To Dept. Kansas................	Jan.,	1864
12th Kansas Infy.......July, 1863	From Dist. Frontier Dept. Mo......	To Unatt. Dist. Frontier 7-C. Ark..	Jan.,	1864
6th Kansas Cav., B, H...July, 1863	From Dist. Frontier Dept. Mo......	To Unatt. Dist. Frontier 7-C. Ark..	Jan.,	1864
1st Mo. S. M. Cav.......July, 1863	From Dist. Central Mo............	To Dist. Central Mo..............	Jan.,	1864
4th Mo. S. M. Cav.......July, 1863	From Dist. Central Mo............	To Dist. Central Mo..............	Jan.,	1864
2d Colo. Infy.........July, 1863	From Dist. Frontier.............	To Dist. St. Louis Dept. Mo.......	Jan.,	1864
9th Wis. Batty.........July, 1863	From Dist. Frontier.............	To Dept. Kansas................	Jan.,	1864
3d Wis. Cav., A, C, D, F..July, 1863	From Dist. Frontier.............	To 3-Brig. Dist. Frontier 7-C. Ark..	Dec.,	1863
15th Kansas Cav.......Oct., 1863	From New Organization............	To Dept. Kansas................	Jan.,	1864

DISTRICT OF SOUTHEAST MISSOURI.— COMMANDERS.

Frederick Steele	Brigadier General	Jan., 1862, to May 14, 1862.
J. W. Davidson.........	Brigadier General	Nov. 13, 1862, to Feb. 23, 1863.
C. B. Fisk........	Brigadier General	July 20, 1863, to Nov. 30, 1863.

11th Wis. Infy.......Mch., 1862	From Dept. Mo................	To 1-Div. Army S. W. Mo........	May,	1862
21st Ill. Infy..........Mch., 1862	From Dept. Mo................	To 2-Brig. 4-Div. Army Miss......	May,	1862
33d Ill. Infy..........Mch., 1862	From Dept. Mo................	To 1-Div. Army S. W. Mo........	May,	1862
38th Ill. Infy..........Mch., 1862	From Dept. Mo................	To 2-Brig. 4-Div. Army Miss......	May,	1862
5th Ill. Cav..........Mch., 1862	From Dept. Mo................	To Unatt. Army S. W. Mo........	May,	1862
9th Ill. Cav..........Mch., 1862	From Dept. Mo................	To Unatt. Army S. W. Mo........	May,	1862
13th Ill. Cav..........Mch., 1862	From Dept. Mo................	To Unatt. Army S. W. Mo........	May,	1862
1st Ind. Cav..........Mch., 1862	From Dept. Mo................	To 1-Div. Army S. W. Mo........	May,	1862
Batty. A, 1st Mo. Arty....Mch., 1862	From Dept. Mo................	To 1-Div. Army S. W. Mo........	May,	1862
16th Ohio Batty.......Mch., 1862	From Dept. Mo................	To 1-Div. Army S. W. Mo........	May,	1862
1st Wis. Cav.........May, 1862	From New Organization............	To Cav. Brig. Dist. S. E. Mo.......	Nov.,	1862

ARMY OF SOUTHEAST MISSOURI.—Organized Oct., 1862.

COMMANDER.

J. W. Davidson........	Brigadier General	

1st DIVISION.—   COMMANDER.

W. P. Benton	Brigadier General			

1st BRIGADE.—   COMMANDER.

Chas. L. Harris	Col. 11th Wis. Infy			
33d Ill. Infy............Oct., 1862	From 1-Div. Army S. W. Mo.......	To 1-Brig. 14-Div. 13-Corps Tenn...	Mch.,	1863
11th Wis. Infy...........Oct., 1862	From 1-Div. Army S. W. Mo.......	To 1-Brig. 14-Div. 13-Corps Tenn...	Mch.,	1863
99th Ill. Infy...........Oct., 1862	From Dist. Rolla Dept. Mo.......	To 1-Brig. 14-Div. 13-Corps Tenn...	Mch.,	1863

2d BRIGADE.—   COMMANDER.

David Shunk	Col. 8th Ind. Infy			
8th Ind. Infy...........Oct., 1862	From 1-Div. Army S. W. Mo........	To 1-Brig. 14-Div. 13-Corps Tenn...	Mch.,	1863
18th Ind. Infy..........Oct., 1862	From 1-Div. Army S. W. Mo........	To 1-Brig. 14-Div. 13-Corps Tenn...	Mch.,	1863

UNATTACHED.—

1st Ind. Batty...........Oct., 1862	From 1-Div. Army S. W. Mo........	To Arty. 14-Div. 13-Corps Tenn.....	Mch.,	1863

2d DIVISION.—   COMMANDERS.

S. H. Boyd	Col. 24th Mo. Infy	To Jan., 1863.		
Chester Harding	Col. 25th Mo. Infy	To Feb., 1863.		
E. A. Carr	Brigadier General	To Mch., 1863.		

1st BRIGADE.—   COMMANDER.

Chester Harding, Jr.	Col. 25th Mo. Infy			
23d Iowa Infy...........Oct., 1862	From New Organization............	To 2-Brig. 2-Div. Army S. E. Mo....	Feb.,	1863
25th Mo. Infy...........Oct., 1862	From 1-Brig. 6-Div. Army Tenn...	To Dist. S. E. Mo.................	Mch.,	1863
24th Mo. Infy...........Feb., 1863	From 2-Brig. 2-Div. Army S. E. Mo.	To Dist. S. E. Mo.................	Mch.,	1863
13th Ill. Cav...........Feb., 1863	From Cav. Brig. Army S. E. Mo....	To Dist. S. E. Mo.................	Mch.,	1863

2d BRIGADE.—   COMMANDERS.

R. R. Livingston	Col. 1st Neb. Infy	To Feb., 1863.		
Fitz Henry Warren	Brigadier General	To Mch., 1863.		
24th Mo. Infy...........Oct., 1862	From Unatt. Army S. W. Mo........	To 1-Brig. 2-Div. Army S. E. Mo...	Feb.,	1863
1st Neb. Infy...........Oct., 1862	From Unatt. Army S. W. Mo........	To Dist. S. E. Mo.................	Mch.,	1863
21st Iowa Infy..........Feb., 1863	From Dist. Rolla Dept. Mo.........	To 2-Brig. 14-Div. 13-Corps Tenn...	Mch.,	1863
22d Iowa Infy..........Feb., 1863	From Dist. Rolla Dept. Mo.........	To 2-Brig. 14-Div. 13-Corps Tenn...	Mch.,	1863
23d Iowa Infy..........Feb., 1863	From 1-Brig. 2-Div. Army S. E. Mo.	To 2-Brig. 14-Div. 13-Corps Tenn...	Mch.,	1863

ARTILLERY.—

Batty. B, 1st Mo. Arty....Oct., 1862	From Arty. 3-Div. Army S. W. Mo.	To Dist. S. E. Mo.................	Mch.,	1863
Batty. M, 2d Mo. Arty....Oct., 1862	From Dist. St. Louis, Mo., Dept. Mo.	To Dist. S. E. Mo.................	Mch.,	1863

CAVALRY BRIGADE.—   COMMANDER.

George E. Waring, Jr..	Col. 4th Mo. Cav			
13th Ill. Cav...........Oct., 1862	From Unatt. Army S. W. Mo........	To 1-Brig. 2-Div. Army S. E. Mo....	Feb.,	1863
4th Mo. Cav.............Oct., 1862	From 3-Div. Army S. W. Mo.......	To Cav. Dist. Columbus 6-Div. 16-C.	Apr.,	1863
5th Mo. Cav.............Oct., 1862	∟rom 3-Div. Army S. W. Mo.......	Consolidated with 4th Mo. Cav....	Nov.,	1862
1st Wis. Cav............Oct., 1862	From Dist. S. E. Mo..............	To 2-Brig. 1-Div. Cav. Corps Cumb'd.	June,	1863
3d Iowa Cav., E,F,G,H,L,M.Dec., 1862	From Dist. Rolla Dept. Mo.........	To 2-Brig. 1-Cav. Div. Dist. S. E. Mo.	June,	1863
3d Mo. Cav., 6 Co's......Feb., 1863	From Dist. Rolla Dept. Mo.........	To 2-Brig. 1-Cav. Div. Dist. S. E. Mo.	June,	1863

1st CAVALRY DIVISION.—   COMMANDER.

J. W. Davidson	Brigadier General	June 6 to Sept. 10, 1863.		

1st BRIGADE.—   COMMANDER.

Lewis Merrill	Col. 2d Mo. Cav	June 6 to Aug. 10, 1863.		
1st Mo. Cav.............June, 1863	From 2-Brig. 2-Div. Army Frontier.	To Res. Brig. 1-Cav. Div. Ark. Exp.	Aug.,	1863
2d Mo. Cav..............June, 1863	From Dist. N. E. Mo..............	To 1-Brig. 1-Cav. Div. Ark. Exp....	Aug.,	1863
7th Mo. Cav.............June, 1863	From 1-Brig. 2-Div. Army Frontier.	To 1-Brig. 1-Cav. Div. Ark. Exp.....	Aug.,	1863
8th Mo. Cav.............June, 1863	From 2-Brig. 3-Div. Army Frontier.	To 1-Brig. 1-Cav. Div. Ark. Exp....	Aug.,	1863

2d BRIGADE.—   COMMANDER.

J. M. Glover	Col. 3d Mo. Cav	June 6 to Aug. 10, 1863.		
10th Ill. Cav...........June, 1863	From 1-Brig. 2-Div. Army Frontier.	To 2-Brig. 1-Cav. Div. Ark. Exp....	Aug.,	1863
1st Iowa Cav............June, 1863	From 1-Brig. 3-Div. Army Frontier.	To 2-Brig. 1-Cav. Div. Ark. Exp....	Aug.,	1863
3d Iowa Cav., E,F,G,H,L,M.June, 1863	From Cav. Brig. Army S. E. Mo.....	To Res. Brig. 1-Cav. Div. Ark. Exp.	July,	1863
3d Mo. Cav.............June, 1863	From Cav. Brig. Army S. E. Mo.....	To 2-Brig. 1-Cav. Div. Ark. Exp....	Aug.,	1863

RESERVE CAVALRY BRIGADE.—   COMMANDER.

H. C. Caldwell	Lt.-Col. 3d Iowa Cav	July 6 to Aug. 10, 1863.		
3d Colo. Cav............July, 1863	From Dist. S. E. Mo..............	To Dist. S. E. Mo.................	July,	1863
32d Iowa Infy, A, D, F, G.July, 1863	From Dist. S. E. Mo..............	To Res. Brig. 1-Cav. Div. Ark. Exp.	Aug.,	1863
13th Ill. Cav...........July, 1863	From Cav. Brig. Dist. S. E. Mo.....	To Res. Brig. 1-Cav. Div. Ark. Exp.	Aug.,	1863
3d Iowa Cav.............July, 1863	From 2-Br. 1-Cav. Div. A'y S. E. Mo.	To Res. Brig. 1-Cav. Div. Ark. Exp.	Aug.,	1863
Batty. K, 2d Mo. Arty....July, 1863	From Arty. Dist. S. E. Mo.........	To Arty. 1-Cav. Div. Ark. Exp.....	Aug.,	1863
Batty. M, 2d Mo. Arty....July, 1863	From Arty. 1-Cav. Div. A'y S. E. Mo.	To Arty. 1-Cav. Div. Ark. Exp.....	Aug.,	1863

ARTILLERY.—

Peoria (Ill.) Batty. Sec...June, 1863	From 1-Brig. 2-Div. Army Frontier.	To Unatt. Dist. S. E. Mo...........	June,	1863
(Batty. A, 2d Arty.)				
Batty. K, 2d Mo. Arty....June, 1863	From Dist. St. Louis, Mo..........	To Arty. Res. Br. 1-Cav. Div. S.E.Mo.	July,	1863
25th Ohio Batty.........June, 1863	From 1-Brig. 1-Div. Army Frontier.	To Arty. 1-Cav. Div. Ark. Exp.....	Aug.,	1863
Batty. M, 2d Mo. Arty....June, 1863	From Arty. Dist. S. E. Mo.........	To Arty. Res. Br. 1-Cav. Div. S.E.Mo.	July,	1863

UNATTACHED, DISTRICT SOUTHEAST MISSOURI.—

32d Iowa Infy, A, D, F, G.Nov., 1862	From New Organization............	To Res. Cav. Br. 1-Cav. Div. S.E.Mo.	July,	1863
1st Neb. Infy...........Mch., 1863	From 2-Brig. 2-Div. Army S. E. Mo.	To Dist. N. E. Ark. Dept. Mo......	Oct.,	1863
3d Colo. Infy., 5 Co's.....Mch., 1863	From Dist. Colorado..............	Consolidated with 2d Colo. as 2d Cav.	Aug.,	1863
24th Mo. Infy...........Mch., 1863	From 1-Brig. 2-Div. Army S. E. Mo.	To Dist. Columbus 6-Div. 16-C. Tenn.	June,	1863
Batty. D, 2d Mo. Arty....Mch., 1863	From Dist. St. Louis, Mo..........	To Arty. Ark. Exp................	Aug.,	1863
101st Ill. Infy..........Mch., 1863	From Prisoners of War............	To Dist. Columbus 6-Div. 16-C. Tenn.	June,	1863
2d Mo. S. M. Cav........June, 1863	From Dist. St. Louis, Mo..........	To Dist. St. Louis, Mo............	July,	1863
3d Mo. S. M. Cav........June, 1863	From Dist. St. Louis, Mo..........	To Dist. St. Louis, Mo............	July,	1863
25th Mo. Infy...........June, 1863	From 1-Brig. 2-Div. Army S. E. Mo.	To Dist. Columbus 6-Div. 16-C. Tenn.	June,	1863
6th Mo. Cav., 5 Co's......June, 1863	From 2-Brig. 2-Div. Army Frontier.	To Dist. St. Louis, Mo............	Nov.,	1863
Peoria (Ill.) Batty. Sec...June, 1863	From Arty. 1-Cav. Div. A'y S. E. Mo.	To Dist. St. Louis, Mo............	Nov.,	1863

DISTRICT OF ST. LOUIS.— COMMANDERS.

J. M. Schofield	Brigadier General	Nov. 21, 1861, to Apr. 10, 1862.
Lewis Merrill	Col. 2d Mo. Cav.	Apr. 10, 1862, to Aug. 6, 1862.
J. W. Davidson	Brigadier General	Aug. 6, 1862, to Nov. 13, 1862.
E. A. Carr	Brigadier General	Nov. 13, 1862, to Feb. 23, 1863.
J. W. Davidson	Brigadier General	Feb. 23, 1863, to June 6, 1863.
W. K. Strong	Brigadier General	June 6, 1863, to Nov. 30, 1863.
C. B. Fisk	Brigadier General	Nov. 30, 1863, to Mch. 25, 1864.
Thos. Ewing, Jr.	Brigadier General	Mch. 25, 1864, to Nov. 21, 1864.
A. Pleasanton	Brigadier General	Nov. 21, 1864, to Dec. 9, 1864.
Thos. Ewing, Jr.	Brigadier General	Dec. 9, 1864, to Apr. 5, 1865.
J. L. Beveridge	Bvt. Brigadier General	Apr. 5, 1865, to Apr. 8, 1865.
Geo. D. Wagner	Brigadier General	Apr. 8, 1865, to June 20, 1865.
J. A. Williamson	Brigadier General	June 20, 1865, to July 21, 1865.

1st U. S. Res. Corps	Nov., 1861	From New Organization	No change to Muster Out	Sept., 1862
2d U. S. Res. Corps	Nov., 1861	From New Organization	No change to Muster Out	Sept., 1862
4th Mo. Infy	Jan., 1862	From New Organization	No change to Muster Out	Jan., 1863
5th Mo. Infy	Jan., 1862	From New Organization	To Dist. Columbus	Mch., 1862
1st Mo. S. M. Infy	Jan., 1862	From New Organization	To Dist. Columbus	May, 1862
2d Mo. Arty	Jan., 1862	From New Organization	To Dist. Plains	July, 1865
27th Mo. Infy	Sept., 1862	From New Organization	To Dist. Rolla Dept. Mo.	Jan., 1863
32d Mo. Infy	Oct., 1862	From New Organization	To 1-Brig. 11-Div. R. W. 13-C. Tenn.	Dec., 1862
37th Mo. Infy	Oct., 1862	From New Organization	Disbanded. Org. not completed.	
33d Mo. Infy	Oct., 1862	From New Organization	To 1-Brig. 13-Div. 13-Corps Tenn.	Jan., 1863
10th Mo. Cav.	Oct., 1862	From New Organization	To Dist. Memphis 16-Corps Tenn.	Jan., 1863
32d Iowa Infy	Dec., 1862	From New Organization	To Dist. Columbus 16-Corps Tenn.	Dec., 1862
8th Iowa Infy	Jan., 1863	From Reorganization	To 3-Brig. 3-Div. 15-Corps Tenn.	Apr., 1863
12th Iowa Infy	Jan., 1863	From Reorganization	To 3-Brig. 3-Div. 15-Corps Tenn.	Apr., 1863
14th Iowa Infy	Jan., 1863	From Reorganization	To 3-Brig. 3-Div. 15-Corps Tenn.	Apr., 1863
37th Iowa Infy	Jan., 1863	From New Organization	To Alton, Ill.	July, 1863
3d Mo. S. M. Cav.	Feb., 1863	From Reorganization	To Dist. S. E. Mo.	June, 1863
11th Mo. Cav.	Feb., 1863	From New Organization	To Dist. S. W. Mo.	Dec., 1863
91st Ill. Infy	Feb., 1863	From Prisoners of War	To 2-Brig. Herron's Div. 13-C. Tenn.	June, 1863
2d Mo. S. M. Cav.	Mch., 1863	From Dist. Northern Mo.	To Dist. S. E. Mo.	June, 1863
9th Wis. Infy	June, 1863	From Dist. Rolla Dept. Mo.	To 2-Brig. 3-Div. Ark. Exp.	Aug., 1863
10th Kansas Infy	June, 1863	From Dist. Rolla Dept. Mo.	To Dept. Kansas	Aug., 1863
1st Mo. Cav., H, I, L	June, 1863	From 2-Div. Army Frontier	To 1-Brig. 1-Div. Cav. A'y S. E. Mo.	June, 1863
Batty. L, 1st Mo. Arty	July, 1863	From Dist. Rolla Dept. Mo.	To Dist. S. W. Mo.	Dec., 1863
2d Mo. S. M. Cav.	July, 1863	From Dist. S. E. Mo.	No change to Muster Out	Apr., 1865
3d Mo. S. M. Cav.	July, 1863	From Dist. S. E. Mo.	No change to Muster Out	July, 1865
3d Ind. Batty.	July, 1863	From Dist. Rolla Dept. Mo.	To Arty. 3-Div. 16-Corps Tenn.	Jan., 1864
7th Minn. Infy	Oct., 1863	From Dept. Northwest	To Paducah, Ky.	Apr., 1864
10th Minn. Infy	Oct., 1863	From Dept. Northwest	To Dist. Columbus, Ky.	Apr., 1864
6th Mo. Cav., A, D, E, L	Dec., 1863	From Dist. S. E. Mo.	No change to Muster Out	Feb., 1865
1st Mo. Col'd Infy	Dec., 1863	From New Organization	To Prov'l Br. Dist. Morganza, La., G.	June, 1864
2d Mo. Col'd Infy	Dec., 1863	From New Organization	To Prov'l Br. Dist. Morganza, La., G.	June, 1864
9th Iowa Infy	Dec., 1863	From Dist. Border	To 3-Brig. 2-Div. 7-Corps Ark.	Apr., 1864
2d Colo. Cav.	Dec., 1863	From Dist. Central Mo.	To Dist. Central Mo.	Jan., 1864
12th Mo. Cav.	Mch., 1864	From New Organization	To 1-Brig. 1-Cav. Div. Dist. W. Tenn.	July, 1864
134th Ill. Infy	June, 1864	From New Organization	To Dist. Columbus Dept. Tenn.	June, 1864
144th Ill. Infy	June, 1864	From New Organization	No change to Muster Out	July, 1865
145th Ill. Infy	June, 1864	From New Organization	No change to Muster Out	Sept., 1865
17th Ill. Cav.	June, 1864	From Alton, Ill.	To Dist. Northern Mo.	Aug., 1865
47th Mo. Infy	June, 1864	From New Organization	No change to Muster Out	Mch., 1865
39th Mo. Infy	Aug., 1864	From New Organization	No change to Muster Out	July, 1865
10th Kansas Infy., 4 Co's	Aug., 1864	From Alton, Ill.	To Nashville, Tenn.	Nov., 1864
18th U. S. C. T.	Aug., 1864	From New Organization	To Dist. Etowah Dept. Cumb'd	Nov., 1864
2d Wis. Cav., 4 Co's	Aug., 1864	From Dist. Rolla Dept. Mo.	To Cav. Brig. Dist. Vicksburg	Sept., 1864
45th Mo. Infy	Aug., 1864	From New Organization	To Unatt. 4-Div. 23-Corps	Dec., 1864
40th Mo. Infy	Sept., 1864	From New Organization	To 3-Brig. 3-Div. 4-Corps Cumb'd	Nov., 1864
41st Mo. Infy	Sept., 1864	From New Organization	No change to Muster Out	July, 1865
7th Kansas Cav.	Sept., 1864	From 1-Br. 1-Cav. Div. Dist. W. T.	To Dept. Kansas	July, 1865
50th Mo. Infy	Oct., 1864	From New Organization	No change to Muster Out	Aug., 1865
14th Mo. Cav.	Nov., 1864	From New Organization	To Dist. Plains	June, 1865
6th Minn. Infy	Nov., 1864	From Dist. East. Ark. 7-Corps Ark.	To 2-Brig. 2-Div. 16-Corps (New)	Feb., 1865
51st Wis. Infy	Apr., 1865	From New Organization	To Dept. Kansas	June, 1865
52d Wis. Infy	Apr., 1865	From New Organization	To Dept. Kansas	June, 1865
53d Wis. Infy	Apr., 1865	From New Organization	To Dept. Kansas	June, 1865
17th Ill. Cav.	Apr., 1865	From Dist. Northern Mo.	To Dist. Plains	July, 1865

DISTRICT OF ROLLA.—Discontinued July 10, 1865.

COMMANDERS.

John M. Glover	Col. 3d Mo. Cav.	Mch. 11, 1862, to Mch. 13, 1863.
Wm. M. Stone	Col. 22d Iowa Infy	Temporarily in Dec., 1862.
T. A. Davies	Brigadier General	Mch. 13, 1863, to Mch. 25, 1864.
O. Guitar	Brigadier General	Mch. 25, 1864, to July 17, 1864.
Albert Sigel	Col. 5th Mo. S. M. Cav.	July 17, 1864, to July 19, 1864.
O. Guitar	Brigadier General	July 19, 1864, to Aug. 23, 1864.
John McNeil	Brigadier General	Aug. 23, 1864, to Sept. 5, 1864.
Albert Sigel	Col. 5th Mo. S. M. Cav.	Sept. 5, 1864, to Sept. 6, 1864.
J. Eppstein	Lt.-Col. 5th Mo. S. M. Cav.	Sept. 6, 1864, to Sept. 25, 1864.
O. Guitar	Brigadier General	Sept. 25, 1864, to Nov. 21, 1864.
Thos. Ewing, Jr.	Brigadier General	Nov. 21, 1864, to Dec. 9, 1864.
E. C. Catherwood	Lt.-Col. 13th Mo. Cav.	Dec. 9, 1864, to Dec. 31, 1864.
E. E. Brown	Brigadier General	Dec. 31, 1864, to Mch. 6, 1865.
E. C. Catherwood	Col. 13th Mo. Cav.	Mch. 6, 1865, to Mch. 17, 1865.
John Morrell	Brigadier General	Mch. 17, 1865, to July 10, 1865.

3d Mo. Cav.	Mch., 1862	From Unatt. Dept. Mo.	To Cav. Brig. Dist. S. E. Mo.	Feb., 1863
9th Mo. S. M. Cav.	May, 1862	From New Organization	To Dist. N. E. Mo.	Feb., 1863
13th Mo. S. M. Cav.	May, 1862	From Central Dist. Mo.	To Central Dist. Mo.	Feb., 1863
21st Iowa Infy	Sept., 1862	From New Organization	To 2-Brig. 2-Div. Army S. E. Mo.	Feb., 1863
22d Iowa Infy	Sept., 1862	From New Organization	To 2-Brig. 2-Div. Army S. E. Mo.	Feb., 1863
2d Mo. Cav., 4 Co's	Sept., 1862	From Dist. N. E. Mo.	To Dist. N. E. Mo.	Feb., 1863
99th Ill. Infy	Sept., 1862	From New Organization	To 1-Brig. 1-Div. Army S. E. Mo.	Feb., 1863
Batty. C, 2d Mo. Arty.	Sept., 1862	From Dist. St. Louis, Mo.	To Dist. St. Louis, Mo.	Feb., 1863
Batty. F, 2d Mo. Arty.	Sept., 1862	From Dist. St. Louis, Mo.	To Dist. St. Louis, Mo.	Feb., 1863
Batty. L, 2d Mo. Arty.	Sept., 1862	From Dist. St. Louis, Mo.	To Dist. St. Louis, Mo.	Feb., 1863
3d Ia. Cav., E,F,G,H,L,M	Nov., 1862	From Dist. S. W. Mo.	To Cav. Brig. Army S. E. Mo.	Dec., 1862
Batty. A, 2d Mo. Arty.	Nov., 1862	From Dist. St. Louis, Mo.	To Dist. St. Louis, Mo.	Feb., 1863
Batty. G, 2d Mo. Arty.	Nov., 1862	From Dist. St. Louis, Mo.	To Dist. St. Louis, Mo.	Feb., 1863
27th Mo. Infy	Jan., 1863	From Dist. St. Louis, Mo.	To 1-Brig. 1-Div. 15-Corps Tenn.	Mch., 1863

DISTRICT OF ROLLA.—Continued.

5th Mo. S. M. Cav.	Feb., 1863	From Central Dist. Mo.	To Central Dist. Mo.	Feb.,	1863
9th Wis. Infy.	June, 1863	From 1-Brig. 1-Div. Army Frontier.	To Dist. St. Louis, Mo.	July,	1863
1st Kansas Batty.	June, 1863	From Dist. S. W. Mo.	To Dist. Columbus 6-Div. 16-C. Tenn.	June,	1863
10th Kansas Infy.	June, 1863	From 2-Brig. 1-Div. Army Frontier.	To Dist. St. Louis, Mo.	June,	1863
11th Kansas Infy.	June, 1863	From 1-Brig. 1-Div. Army Frontier.	To Dist. Kansas Dept. Mo.	June,	1863
5th Mo. S. M. Cav.	June, 1863	From Central Dist. Mo.	No change to Muster Out.	June,	1863
2d Wis. Cav., A, D, G, K.	June, 1863	From 1-Brig. 3-Div. Army Frontier.	To Dist. North Mo.	Aug.,	1864
Batty. L, 1st Mo. Arty.	June, 1863	From 1-Brig. 3-Div. Army Frontier.	To Dist. S. W. Mo.	Dec.,	1863
3d Ind. Batty.	June, 1863	From 1-Brig. 3-Div. Army Frontier.	To Dist. St. Louis, Mo.	July,	1863
23d Mo. Infy.	July, 1863	From Dist. St. Louis, Mo.	To Unass'd Dist. Nashville, Tenn.	Dec.,	1863
9th Minn. Infy.	Oct., 1863	From Dept. Northwest.	To 2-Brig. 1-Div. 16-Corps Tenn.	May,	1864
145th Ill. Infy.	June, 1864	From New Organization.	No change to Muster Out.	Sept.,	1864
Batty. B, 2d Mo. Arty.	June, 1864	From Dist. St. Louis, Mo.	To Dist. St. Louis, Mo.	Oct.,	1864
13th Mo. Cav.	Oct., 1864	From New Organization.	To Dept. Mo.	July,	1865
40th Wis. Infy.	Mch., 1865	From New Organization.	To Dist. St. Louis, Mo.	July,	1865

DISTRICT CENTRAL MISSOURI.—Abolished July 10, 1865.

COMMANDERS.

James Totten	Brigadier General	Mch. 11, 1862, to Oct. 12, 1862.
Ben. Loan	Brigadier General	Oct. 12, 1862, to June 9, 1863.
E. B. Brown	Brigadier General	June 9, 1863, to July 24, 1864.
A. Pleasanton	Brigadier General	July 24, 1864, to Sept. 3, 1864.
E. E. Brown	Brigadier General	Sept. 3, 1864, to Nov. 3, 1864.
J. F. Phillips	Col. 7th Mo. S. M. Cav.	Nov. 3, 1864, to Feb. 27, 1865.
John McNeil	Brigadier General	Feb. 27, 1865, to Apr. 22, 1865.
Chester Harding	Col. 43d Mo. Infy.	Apr. 22, 1865, to June 25, 1865.
J. L. Beveridge	Bvt. Brigadier General	June 25, 1865, to July 10, 1865.

1st Iowa Cav.	Mch., 1862	From Unatt. Dept. Mo.	To 1-Brig. 3-Div. Army Frontier.	Dec.,	1862
3d Ind. Batty.	Mch., 1862	From Unatt. Jefferson Barracks, Mo.	To Dist. S. W. Mo.	Sept.,	1862
1st Mo. S. M. Cav.	Apr., 1862	From New Organization.	No change to Muster Out.	July,	1865
5th Mo. S. M. Cav.	Apr., 1862	From New Organization.	To Dist. Rolla.	Jan.,	1863
6th Mo. S. M. Cav.	Apr., 1862	From New Organization.	To Dist. S. W. Mo.	July,	1863
2d Battn. Mo. S. M. Cav.	May, 1862	From New Organization.	No change to Muster Out.	Mch.,	1863
1st Mo. S. M. Batty.	May, 1862	From New Organization.	Disbanded	Jan.,	1864
3d Mo. S. M. Cav.	Dec., 1862	From Dist. Southwest Mo.	Disbanded	Feb.,	1863
4th Mo. S. M. Cav.	Dec., 1862	From Dist. Southwest Mo.	No change to Muster Out.	July,	1865
6th Mo. S. M. Cav.	Dec., 1862	From Dist. Southwest Mo.	To Dist. Southwest Mo.	July,	1863
5th Mo. S. M. Cav.	Feb., 1863	From Dist. Rolla.	To Dist. Rolla.	June,	1863
7th Mo. S. M. Cav.	July, 1863	From Dist. Southwest Mo.	No change to Muster Out.	July,	1865
9th Minn. Infy. C, D, F, K.	Oct., 1863	From Dept. Northwest.	To 2-Brig. 1-Div. 16-Corps Tenn.	May,	1864
2d Colo. Cav.	Jan., 1864	From Dist. St. Louis, Mo.	To Dist. Upper Arkansas.	Dec.,	1864
Batty. L, 2d Mo. Arty.	Jan., 1864	From Dist. St. Louis, Mo.	To Dist. Plains.	July,	1865
135th Ill. Infy.	June, 1864	From New Organization.	No change to Muster Out.	Sept.,	1864
43d Mo. Infy.	Apr., 1865	From Dist. North Mo.	No change to Muster Out.	June,	1865
50th Wis. Infy.	Apr., 1865	From New Organization.	To Dept. Kansas.	June,	1865

DISTRICT NORTHERN MISSOURI, NORTHEASTERN MISSOURI.

COMMANDERS.

John McNeil	Brigadier General	June 5, 1862, to Jan. 29, 1863.
Thos. J. McKean	Brigadier General	Jan. 29, 1863, to June 4, 1863.
O. Guitar	Brigadier General	June 4, 1863, to June 10, 1864.
C. B. Fisk	Brigadier General	June 10, 1864, to May 24, 1865.
Geo. Spalding	Bvt. Brig. General	May 24, 1865, to July, 1865.

3d Iowa Cav. E,F,G,H,L,M.	Feb., 1862	From Army Southwest Mo.	To Dist. Southwest Mo.	Aug.,	1862
2d Mo. Cav.	Feb., 1862	From Northeast Mo.	To 1-Br. 1-Cav. Div. A. S. E. Mo.	June,	1863
2d Mo. S. M. Cav.	Feb., 1862	From Northeast Mo.	To Dist. St. Louis, Mo.	Mch.,	1863
9th Mo. S. M. Cav.	Feb., 1862	From Dist. Rolla.	No change to Muster Out.	July,	1865
17th Ill. Cav.	Aug., 1864	From Dist. St. Louis, Mo.	To Dist. St. Louis, Mo.	Apr.,	1865
Batty. C, 2d Mo. Arty.	Aug., 1864	From Dist. St. Louis, Mo.	To Dist. Plains.	July,	1865
3d Mo. S. M. Cav. 4 Cos.	Aug., 1864	From Dist. St. Louis, Mo.	No change to Muster Out.	July,	1865
6th Mo. S. M. Cav. 4 Cos.	Aug., 1864	From Dist. Southwest Mo.	To Dist. Southwest Mo.	Feb.,	1865
2d Wis. Cav. A, D, G, K.	Aug., 1864	From Dist. Rolla.	To Dist. Vicksburg, Miss.	Sept.,	1864
6th Mo. S. M. Cav. 8 Cos.	Oct., 1864	From Dist. Southwest Mo.	To Dist. Southwest Mo.	Feb.,	1865
43d Mo. Infy.	Oct., 1864	From New Organization.	To Dist. Central Mo.	Apr.,	1865
15th Mo. Cav.	Apr., 1865	From Dist. Southwest Mo.	No change to Muster Out.	July,	1865
16th Mo. Cav.	Apr., 1865	From Dist. Southwest Mo.	No change to Muster Out.	July,	1865

DISTRICT NORTHWEST MISSOURI (Missouri Enrolled Militia).—

COMMANDERS.

Ben. Loan	Brigadier General Mo. Militia	Mch. 12, 1862, to Aug. 25, 1862.
W. P. Hall	Brigadier General Mo. Militia	Aug. 25, 1862, to Apr. 10, 1863.
Chester Harding, Jr.	Col. Mo. Militia	Apr. 10, 1863, to June 23, 1863.

Army and Department of the Gulf

SHIP ISLAND EXPEDITION.—

COMMANDER.

John W. Phelps	Brigadier General	

12th Me. Infy.	Dec., 1861	From New Organization.	To 3-Brig. Dept. Gulf.	Mch.,	1862
26th Mass. Infy.	Dec., 1861	From New Organization.	To 2-Brig. Dept. Gulf.	Mch.,	1862
30th Mass. Infy.	Dec., 1861	From New Organization.	To 3-Brig. Dept. Gulf.	Mch.,	1862
9th Conn. Infy.	Dec., 1861	From New Organization.	To 1-Brig. Dept. Gulf.	Mch.,	1862
4th Mass. Batty.	Dec., 1861	From New Organization.	To 1-Brig. Dept. Gulf.	Mch.,	1862

Department of the Gulf

Constituted Feb. 23, 1862, to comprise all of the Coast of the Gulf of Mexico, West of Pensacola, Fla., and so much of the Gulf States as may be occupied by United States Troops. West Florida added Aug. 8, 1862. (Department embraced in Military Division West Miss. May 7, 1864, to May 17, 1865.)

COMMANDERS.

Benj. F. Butler	Major General	Mch. 20, 1862, to Dec. 17, 1862.
N. P. Banks	Major General	Dec. 17, 1862, to Sept. 23, 1864.
S. G. Hurlbut	Major General	Sept. 23, 1864, to Apr. 22, 1865.
N. P. Banks	Major General	Apr. 22, 1865, to June 3, 1865.
E. R. S. Canby	Major General	June 3, 1865.

BUTLER'S NEW ORLEANS EXPEDITIONARY CORPS.—

1st BRIGADE.— COMMANDER.

John W. Phelps........	Brigadier General.................		
9th Conn. Infy........Mch., 1862	From Ship Island Exp.............	To Def. New Orleans.............	Sept., 1862
12th Conn. Infy........Mch., 1862	From New Organization...........	To Weitzel's Res. Brigade........	Sept., 1862
13th Conn. Infy........Mch., 1862	From New Organization...........	To Weitzel's Res. Brigade........	Sept., 1862
8th N. H. Infy........Mch., 1862	From New Organization...........	To Indpt. Command Dept. Gulf.....	Sept., 1862
7th Vt. Infy........Mch., 1862	From New Organization...........	To Dist. West Florida............	Oct., 1862
8th Vt. Infy........Mch., 1862	From New Organization...........	To Indpt. Command Dept. Gulf.....	Sept., 1862
1st Vt. Batty........Mch., 1862	From New Organization...........	To Sherman's Div. Dept. Gulf.....	Sept., 1862
2d Vt. Batty........Mch., 1862	From New Organization...........	To Sherman's Div. Dept. Gulf.....	Sept., 1862
4th Mass. Batty........Mch., 1862	From Ship Island Exp.............	To Indpt. Com. Dept. Gulf........	Sept., 1862

2d BRIGADE.— COMMANDER.

Thomas Williams......	Brigadier General.................	Killed August 5, 1862.	
26th Mass. Infy........Mch., 1862	From Ship Island Exp.............	To Def. New Orleans.............	Sept., 1862
31st Mass. Infy........Mch., 1862	From New Organization...........	To Sherman's Div. Dept. Gulf......	Sept., 1862
6th Mich. Infy........Mch., 1862	From Dix's Com. Baltimore, Md....	To Sherman's Div. Dept. Gulf.....	Sept., 1862
21st Ind. Infy........Mch., 1862	From Dix's Com. Baltimore, Md....	To Indpt. Command Dept. Gulf.....	Sept., 1862
4th Wis. Infy........Mch., 1862	From Dix's Com. Baltimore, Md....	To Grover's Div. Dept. Gulf......	Dec., 1862
2d Mass. Batty........Mch., 1862	From Dix's Com. Baltimore, Md....	To Grover's Div. Dept. Gulf......	Dec., 1862
6th Mass. Batty........Mch., 1862	From New Organization...........	To Weitzel's Res. Brig...........	Sept., 1862

3d BRIGADE.— COMMANDER.

George F. Shepley......	Brigadier General.................		
12th Me. Infy........Mch., 1862	From Ship Island Expedition.......	To Grover's Div. Dept. Gulf......	Dec., 1862
13th Me. Infy........Mch., 1862	From New Organization...........	To Indpt. Command Dept. Gulf....	Sept., 1862
14th Me. Infy........Mch., 1862	From New Organization...........	To Sherman's Div. Dept. Gulf......	Sept., 1862
15th Me. Infy........Mch., 1862	From New Organization...........	To Dist. West Florida............	Sept., 1862
30th Mass. Infy........Mch., 1862	From New Organization...........	To Def. New Orleans.............	Sept., 1862
1st Me. Batty........Mch., 1862	From New Organization...........	To Weitzel's Res. Brig...........	Sept., 1862
UNATTACHED.—			
Indpt. Battn. Mass. Cav...Apr., 1862	From New Organization...........	To Def. New Orleans.............	Sept., 1862

PENSACOLA, FLA., DISTRICT WEST FLA.—Transferred from Dept. of the South Aug. 8, 1862.

COMMANDERS.

L. G. Arnold..........	Brigadier General..................	Aug. 8, 1862, to Sept. 22, 1862.
William Wilson........	Col. 6th N. Y. Infy...............	Sept. 22, 1862, to Oct. 2, 1862.
Neal Dow............	Brigadier General..................	Oct. 2, 1862, to Jan. 24, 1863.
Isaac Dyer............	Col. 15th Me. Infy...............	Jan. 24, 1863, to Apr. 21, 1863.
W. C. Holbrook........	Col. 7th Vt. Infy.................	Apr. 21, 1863, to May 21, 1863.
Isaac Dyer............	Col. 15th Me. Infy...............	May 21, 1863, to June 18, 1863.
W. C. Holbrook........	Col. 7th Vt. Infy.................	June 18, 1863, to Oct. 8, 1863.
A. Asboth............	Brigadier General..................	Oct. 8, 1863, to Oct. 20, 1864.
Jos. Bailey..........	Bvt. Brig. General.................	Oct. 20, 1864, to Nov. 25, 1864.
T. J. McKean..........	Brigadier General..................	Nov. 25, 1864, to Feb. 15, 1865.
A. Asboth............	Brigadier General..................	Feb. 15, 1865, to July, 1865.

6th N. Y. Infy........Aug., 1862	From Dist. Pensacola Dept. South..	To Grover's Div. Dept. Gulf......	Dec., 1862
75th N. Y. Infy........Aug., 1862	From Dist. Pensacola Dept. South..	To Weitzel's Res. Brig...........	Dec., 1862
91st N. Y. Infy........Aug., 1862	From Dist. Pensacola Dept. South..	To 3-Brig. 1-Div. 19-Corps Gulf..	Jan., 1863
Batty. A, 1st U. S. Arty..Aug., 1862	From Dist. Pensacola Dept. South...	To Def. New Orleans.............	Dec., 1862
Batty. F, 1st U. S. Arty..Aug., 1862	From Dist. Pensacola Dept. South...	To Def. New Orleans.............	Dec., 1862
Batty. L, 1st U. S. Arty..Aug., 1862	From Dist. Pensacola Dept. South...	To Grover's Div. Dept. Gulf......	Dec., 1862
Batty. C, 2d U. S. Arty..Aug., 1862	From Dist. Pensacola Dept. South...	To Grover's Div. Dept. Gulf......	Dec., 1862
Batty. H, 2d U. S. Arty..Aug., 1862	From Dist. Pensacola Dept. South...	To Dept. East..................	May, 1864
Batty. K, 2d U. S. Arty..Aug., 1862	From Dist. Pensacola Dept. South...	To Def. of Baltimore, Md. 8-Corps..	May, 1864
15th Me. Infy........Sept., 1862	From 3-Brig. Dept. Gulf.........	To Def. New Orleans.............	June, 1863
7th Vt. Infy........Oct., 1862	From 1-Brig. Dept. Gulf.........	To Def. New Orleans.............	Oct., 1864
28th Conn. Infy........Dec., 1862	From New Organization...........	To 1-Brig. 3-Div. 19-Corps......	May, 1863
14th Corps de Afrique.....Oct., 1863	From Def. New Orleans...........	To 1-Brig. 3-Div. U. S. C. T. Gulf..	Oct., 1864
(86th U. S. C. T.)			
14th N. Y. Cav. Co. M...Oct., 1863	From New Organization...........	To Dist. Morganza, La. Dept. Gulf..	Feb., 1865
82d U. S. C. T..........July, 1864	From 2-Br. 1-Div. Corps de Afrique	To 1-Brig. 3-Div. U. S. C. T. Gulf..	Oct., 1864
2d Me. Cav..........July, 1864	From Dist. La. Fourche, La.......	To 2-Brig. Dist. West Fla.......	Oct., 1864
25th U. S. C. T..........July, 1864	From New Organization...........	To 1-Brig. Dist. West Fla.......	Oct., 1864
19th Iowa Infy........Aug., 1864	From 2-Brig. U. S. Forces Texas...	To Dist. Southern Ala...........	Dec., 1864
1st Florida Cav........Aug., 1864	From New Organization...........	To 2-Brig. Dist. West Fla.......	Oct., 1864
25th U. S. C. T..........Mch., 1865	From 3-Brig. Dist. West Florida...	To Dept. of Florida.............	July, 1865
82d U. S. C. T..........May, 1865	From 1-Brig. 1-Div. U. S. C. T.....	To Dept. of Florida.............	July, 1865
86th U. S. C. T..........May, 1865	From 1-Brig. 1-Div. U. S. C. T.....	To Dept. of Florida.............	July, 1865
161st N. Y. Infy........May, 1865	From 3-Brig. 1-Div. 13-Corps Gulf..	No change to Muster Out.........	Nov., 1865

1st BRIGADE.—Organized Oct., 1864. COMMANDER.

L. L. Zulavski........	Col. 82d U. S. C. T.............		
25th U. S. C. T..........Oct., 1864	From 1-Brig. 3-Div. U. S. C. T. Gulf	To 3-Brig. Dist. West Fla.......	Jan., 1865
82d U. S. C. T..........Oct., 1864	From 1-Brig. 3-Div. U. S. C. T. Gulf	To 3-Brig. Dist. West Fla.......	Jan., 1865
86th U. S. C. T..........Oct., 1864	From 1-Brig. 3-Div. U. S. C. T. Gulf	To 3-Brig. Dist. West Fla.......	Jan., 1865
97th U. S. C. T..........Oct., 1864	From U. S. Forces Mobile Bay.....	To 3-Brig. Dist. West Fla.......	Jan., 1865

2d BRIGADE.—Organized Oct., 1864. COMMANDER.

E. W. Woodman........	Col. 2d Me. Cav.................		
1st Florida Cav..........Oct., 1864	From Dist. West Florida...........	To 3-Brig. Dist. West Fla.......	Jan., 1865
2d Me. Cav............Oct., 1864	From Dist. West Florida...........	To 3-Brig. Dist. West Fla.......	Jan., 1865

3d BRIGADE.—Organized Jan. 23, 1865. Discontinued March 17, 1865. COMMANDER.

E. W. Woodman........	Col. 2d Me. Cav.................		
25th U. S. C. T..........Jan., 1865	From 1-Brig. Dist. West Fla.......	To Unatt. Dist. West Fla........	Mch., 1865
82d U. S. C. T..........Jan., 1865	From 1-Brig. Dist. West Fla.......	To 1-Brig. 1-Div. U. S. C. T. Steele's	Mch., 1865
86th U. S. C. T..........Jan., 1865	From 1-Brig. Dist. West Fla.......	To 1-Brig. 1-Div. U. S. C. T. Steele's	Mch., 1865
97th U. S. C. T..........Jan., 1865	From 1-Brig. Dist. West Fla.......	To Engr. Brig. Mil. Div. W. Miss..	Mch., 1865
2d Me. Cav............Jan., 1865	From 2-Brig. Dist. West Fla.......	To 2-Br. Lucas' Cav. Div. M. D. W. M.	Mch., 1865
1st Fla. Cav............Jan., 1865	From 2-Brig. Dist. West Fla.......	To 2-Br. Lucas' Cav. Div. M. D. W. M.	Mch., 1865

DEFENCES OF NEW ORLEANS, LA.—Organized Dec. 16, 1862. Transferred to Dept. of the Gulf Aug. 25, 1863. Designated Southern District of Louisiana Feb. 9, 1865.

COMMANDERS.

George L. Andrews.....	Brigadier General...................	Sept. 22, 1862, to Dec. 16, 1862.
T. W. Cahill..........	Col. 9th Conn. Infy................	Dec. 16, 1862, to Jan. 9, 1863.
T. W. Sherman........	Brigadier General..................	Jan. 9, 1863, to May 21, 1863.
W. H. Emory.........	Brigadier General..................	May 21, 1863, to Aug. 25, 1863.
E. L. Beckwith........	Col.	Aug. 25, 1863, to Dec. 3, 1863.
J. J. Reynolds.........	Major General......................	Dec. 3, 1863, to June 18, 1864.
T. W. Sherman........	Brigadier General..................	June 18, 1864, to Feb. 9, 1865.

9th Conn. Infy..........Sept., 1862	From 1-Brig. Dept. Gulf............	To 1-Brig. 3-Div. 19-Corps.........	Feb., 1863
26th Mass. Infy........Sept., 1862	From 2-Brig. Dept. Gulf............	To 2-Brig. 2-Div. 19-Corps.........	Jan., 1863
30th Mass. Infy........Sept., 1862	From 3-Brig. Dept. Gulf............	To 3-Brig. 1-Div. 19-Corps.........	Jan., 1863
1st La. Native Guard...Sept., 1862	From New Organization.............	To Indpt. Command Dept. Gulf...	Dec., 1862
2d La. Native Guard...Sept., 1862	From New Organization.............	To Indpt. Command Dept. Gulf...	Dec., 1862
13th Me. Infy...........Dec., 1862	From Indpt. Command Dept. Gulf..	To 2-Brig. 4-Div. 19-Corps.........	Aug., 1863
2d La. Native Guard....Jan., 1863	From Indpt. Command Dept. Gulf..	To 1-Brig. 1-Div. Corps de Afrique..	Sept., 1863
23d Conn. Infy..........Jan., 1863	From Indpt. Command Dept. Gulf..	No change to Muster Out...........	Aug., 1863
176th N. Y. Infy........Jan., 1863	From New Organization.............	To 1-Brig. 3-Div. 19-Corps.........	Feb., 1864
24th Conn. Infy........July, 1863	From 2-Brig. 4-Div. 19-Corps......	No change to Muster Out...........	Sept., 1863
12th Me. Infy..........July, 1863	From 2-Brig. 4-Div. 19-Corps......	To 2-Brig. 4-Div. 19-Corps.........	Aug., 1863
15th Me. Infy..........July, 1863	From Pensacola Fl. Dist. West Fla..	To 2-Brig. 4-Div. 19-Corps.........	Aug., 1863
91st N. Y. Infy.........July, 1863	From 1-Brig. 4-Div. 19-Corps......	To Baltimore, Md. 8-Corps.........	Oct., 1864
1st Corps de Afrique Infy.July, 1863 (73d U. S. C. T.)	From Unatt. 1-Div. 19-Corps.......	From 1-Br. 1-Div. Corps de Afrique.	Sept., 1863
2d Corps de Afrique Infy.July, 1863 (74th U. S. C. T.)	From Unatt. 1-Div. 19-Corps.......	To 1-Brig. 1-Div. Corps de Afrique.	Sept., 1863
4th Corps de Afrique Infy.July, 1863 (76th U. S. C. T.)	From Unatt. 1-Div. 19-Corps.......	To 2-Brig. Corps de Afrique........	Sept., 1863
14th C. de Afrique Infy...July, 1863 (86th U. S. C. T.)	From New Organization.............	To 1-Brig. 2-Div. Corps de Afrique.	Sept., 1863
16th C. de Afrique Infy...July, 1863 (87th U. S. C. T.)	From New Organization.............	To 1-Brig. 2-Div. Corps de Afrique.	Sept., 1863
20th C. de Afrique Infy..Sept., 1863	From New Organization.............	To 2-Brig. 2-Div. Corps de Afrique.	Sept., 1863
1st U. S. Infy............Oct., 1863	From Headquarters 13-Corps........	To 2-Brig. 4-Div. 13-Corps.........	Feb., 1864
2d Corps de Afrique Infy..Oct., 1863	From 1-Brig. 1-Div. Corps de Afr...	To 3-Brig. 3-Div. U. S. C. T. Gulf..	Oct., 1864
133d N. Y. Infy.........Oct., 1863	From 2-Br. 3-Div. 19-Corps........	To 1-Brig. 2-Div. 19-Corps.........	Apr., 1864
2d New Orleans Infy....Dec., 1863	From New Organization.............	Transferred to 1st New Orleans....	Aug., 1864
5th Corps de Afrique Infy.Dec., 1863 (77th U. S. C. T.)	From New Organization.............	To 3-Brig. 3-Div. U. S. C. T. Gulf..	Oct., 1864
2d U. S. C. T..........Dec., 1863	From New Organization.............	To Dist. Key West, Fla.............	Feb., 1864
1st New Orleans Infy....Mch., 1864	From New Organization.............	To Dist. La Fourche, La............	Apr., 1865
1st U. S. Infy..........Mch., 1864	From 2-Brig. 4-Div. 13-Corps......	To Dist. La Fourche, La............	Apr., 1865
14th N. H. Infy........Mch., 1864	From Def. Wash. 22-Corps.........	To 1-Brig. 2-Div. 19-Corps.........	June, 1864
46th Ind. Infy Det.....May, 1864	From 1-Brig. 3-Div. 13-Corps......	To Dist. Ky. Dept. Ohio...........	Aug., 1864
77th Ill. Infy..........June, 1864	From 1-Brig. 4-Div. 13-Corps......	To 3-Brig. 3-Div. 19-Corps Gulf..	June, 1864
130th Ill. Infy.........June, 1864	From 2-Brig. 4-Div. 13-Corps......	To 3-Brig. 3-Div. 19-Corps Gulf..	June, 1864
34th Iowa Infy.........June, 1864	From 2-Brig. 4-Div. 13-Corps......	To 3-Brig. 3-Div. 19-Corps Gulf..	June, 1864
96th Ohio Infy.........June, 1864	From 1-Brig. 4-Div. 13-Corps......	To 3-Brig. 3-Div. 19-Corps Gulf..	June, 1864
67th Ind. Infy.........June, 1864	From 1-Brig. 4-Div. 13-Corps......	To 3-Brig. 3-Div. 19-Corps Gulf..	June, 1864
19th Ky. Infy..........June, 1864	From 1-Brig. 4-Div. 13-Corps......	To Dist. Baton Rouge, La..........	June, 1864
83d Ohio Infy..........June, 1864	From 1-Brig. 4-Div. 13-Corps......	To 3-Brig. 3-Div. 19-Corps.........	June, 1864
34th Ind. Infy.........June, 1864	From 1-Brig. 3-Div. 13-Corps......	To Brazos Santiago, Tex...........	Dec., 1864
79th U. S. C. T........June, 1864	From 2-Br. 2-Div. U. S. C. T. Gulf.	Disbanded	July, 1864
56th Ohio Infy.........June, 1864	From 2-Brig. 3-Div. 13-Corps......	No change to Muster Out...........	Apr., 1866
22d Iowa Infy..........June, 1864	From 1-Brig. 1-Div. 13-Corps......	To 2-Brig. 2-Div. 19-Corps.........	July, 1864
31st Mass. Infy........June, 1864	From 4-Brig. Cav. Div. Gulf......	To 1-Brig. Cav. Div. Gulf..........	Sept., 1864
24th Ind. Infy.........June, 1864	From 1-Brig. 3-Div. 13-Corps......	To Bailey's Engr. Brig. Gulf.......	July, 1864
49th Ind. Infy.........June, 1864	From 1-Brig. 1-Div. 13-Corps......	To Dist. Ky. Dept. Ohio...........	July, 1864
23d Wis. Infy..........June, 1864	From 1-Brig. 4-Div. 13-Corps......	To 3-Brig. 2-Div. 19-Corps.........	Aug., 1864
98th U. S. C. T........July, 1864	From Engineer Brigade, Gulf.......	To 2-Brig. 3-Div. U. S. C. T.......	Oct., 1864
77th U. S. C. T........Oct., 1864	From 3-Brig. 3-Div. U. S. C. T. Gulf	Consol. with 10th U. S. C. H. A...	Oct., 1865
20th U. S. C. T........July, 1864	From New Organization.............	To Dist. South Ala................	Dec., 1864
80th U. S. C. T........July, 1864	From 2-Brig. 1-Div. U. S. C. T......	To 3-Brig. 3-Div. U. S. C. T.......	Oct., 1864
31st Mass. Infy........Oct., 1864	From 1-Brig. Cav. Div. Gulf......	To 1-Brig. Cav. Div. Dist. W. Fla..	Feb., 1865
77th Ill. Infy..........Oct., 1864	From 3-Brig. 3-Div. 19-Corps......	To 1-Brig. 3-Div. 13-Corps.........	Feb., 1865
130th Ill. Infy.........Oct., 1864	From 3-Brig. 3-Div. 19-Corps......	To 1-Brig. 3-Div. 13-Corps.........	Feb., 1865
80th U. S. C. T........Oct., 1864	From 3-Brig. 3-Div. U. S. C. T. Gulf	To Northern Dist. La..............	Feb., 1865
7th Vt. Infy...........Oct., 1864	From Dist. West Fla...............	To 2-Brig. 3-Div. 13-Corps.........	Feb., 1865
74th U. S. C. T........Oct., 1864	From 3-Brig. 3-Div. U. S. C. T......	No change to Muster Out...........	Oct., 1865
48th Ohio Infy.........Nov., 1864	From Prisoners of War.............	To 3-Brig. Res. Corps. Gulf.......	Dec., 1864
91st Ill. Infy..........Dec., 1864	From Brazos, Santiago, Texas......	To 2-Brig. 3-Div. 13-Corps.........	Feb., 1865
20th U. S. C. T........Feb., 1865	From Dist. South Ala..............	To Dist. La Fourche. La...........	June, 1865
46th U. S. C. T........Feb., 1865	From 2-Brig. 1-Div. U. S. C. T. Miss.	To Southern Dist. La..............	June, 1865
CAVALRY.—			
In't Mass. B'n Cav. Co. C.Sept., 1862	From Unatt. Dept. Gulf............	To Cav. Brig. 19-Corps...........	May, 1863
2d R. I. Cav...........Dec., 1862	From New Organization.............	To Unatt. 1-Div. 19-Corps.........	Mch., 1863
1st Texas Cav..........Jan., 1863	From Indpt. Command Dept Gulf..	To Cav. Brig. 19-Corps...........	May, 1863
14th N. Y. Cav. Det......Mch., 1863	From New Organization.............	To Cav. Brig. 19-Corps...........	May, 1863
3d Mass. Cav..........July, 1863	From Cav. Brig. 19-Corps.........	To Cav. Port Hudson, La..........	Aug., 1863
1st La. Cav............July, 1863	From Cav. Brig. 19-Corps.........	To 1-Brig. Cav. Div. Gulf..........	Sept., 1863
14th N. Y. Cav.........July, 1863	From Cav. Brig. 19-Corps.........	To 1-Brig. Cav. Div. Gulf..........	Sept., 1863
1st Texas Cav..........Sept., 1863	From Cav. Brig. 19-Corps.........	To Unatt. 13-Corps Rio Grande Exp.	Oct., 1863
1st Corps De Afrique Cav.Sept., 1863 (4th U. S. C. Cav.)	From New Organization.............	To Dist. Port Hudson, La..........	Aug., 1864
36th Ill. Co. A Cav......Jan., 1864	From Unatt. Cav. Div. Gulf........	To Illinois	Feb., 1864
3d R. I. Cav...........Jan., 1864	From New Organization.............	To 5-Brig. Cav. Div. Gulf..........	Mch., 1864
15th Illinois Cav. Co. F..Jan., 1864	From Unatt. Cav. Div. Gulf........	To Regt. in Arkansas..............	Feb., 1864
3d Maryland Cav.......Jan., 1864	From Cav. Reserve 8-Corps........	To Dist. La Fourche Dept. Gulf....	Mch., 1864
1st Indiana Cav. Co. C...Jan., 1864	From Unatt. Cav. Div. Gulf........	To Dept. Arkansas 7-Corps........	July, 1864
3d Rhode Island Cav....June, 1864	From 5-Brig. Cav. Div. Gulf.......	To Dept. Arkansas 7-Corps........	Oct., 1864
2d Illinois Cav.........June, 1864	From Dist. Baton Rouge, La.......	To 2-Brig. Cav. Div. Gulf..........	Aug., 1864
2d New Hampshire Cav..July, 1864	From 4-Brig. Cav. Div. Gulf.......	To Natchez, Miss.................	Sept., 1864
14th New York Cav.....Apr., 1865	From D. Morganza, La., Dept. Gulf	To 1-Brig. 2-Cav. Div. West Miss..	May, 1865
ARTILLERY.—			
2d Vermont Batty......Sept., 1862	From 1-Brig. Dept. Gulf...........	To Arty. 3-Div. 19-Corps..........	Jan., 1863
Batty. A, 1st U. S. Arty..Dec., 1862	From Pensacola, Fla., Dist. W. Fla.	To Arty. 3-Div. 19-Corps..........	Jan., 1863
Batty. F, 1st U. S. Arty..Dec., 1862	From Pensacola, Fla., Dist. W. Fla.	To Arty. 3-Div. 19-Corps..........	Jan., 1863
Batty. L, 1st U. S. Arty..Dec., 1862	From Pensacola, Fla., Dist. W. Fla.	To Grover's Div. 19-Corps.........	Dec., 1862
1st La. Native Gd. H. A..Dec., 1862	From New Organization.............	Designated 1st C. de Afrique H. A.	Nov., 1863
13th Mass. Batty.......Jan., 1863	From New Organization.............	To Arty. 4-Div. 19-Corps..........	June, 1863
21st New York Batty....Jan., 1863	From New Organization.............	To Arty. 2-Div. 19-Corps..........	May, 1863

ARTILLERY.—Continued.

25th New York Batty.	Jan., 1862	From New Organization	To Arty. Reserve 19-Corps	July, 1863
26th New York Batty.	Jan., 1863	From New Organization	To Arty. Reserve 19-Corps	July, 1863
12th Mass. Batty.	Feb., 1863	From New Organization	To Arty. Reserve 19-Corps	July, 1863
15th Mass. Batty.	Apr., 1863	From New Organization	To Arty. Reserve 19-Corps	July, 1863
13th Mass. Batty.	Aug., 1863	From Arty. 4-Div. 19-Corps	Attached to 2d Mass. Batty.	Sept., 1863
12th Mass. Batty.	Aug., 1863	From Arty. Reserve 19-Corps	To Port Hudson, La.	Oct., 1863
15th Mass. Batty.	Aug., 1863	From Arty. Reserve 19-Corps	To Arty. Reserve Gulf	Aug., 1864
Batty. A, 1st U. S. Arty.	Aug., 1863	From Arty. 1-Div. 19-Corps	To Arty. 1-Div. 19-Corps	Feb., 1864
18th New York Batty.	Aug., 1863	From Arty. 1-Div. 19-Corps	To Dist. Baton Rouge, La.	Dec., 1863
14th R. I. H. A. 1st Bn.	Aug., 1863	From New Organization	To Unatt. 2-Div. 13-Corps Texas	Jan., 1864
1st Wisconsin Batty.	Aug., 1863	From Arty. 1-Div. 13-Corps	To Arty. 1-Div. 19-Corps	Jan., 1864
Batty. G, 5th U. S. Arty.	Aug., 1863	From Gar. Arty. Port Hudson, La.	To Arty. Cav. Div. Gulf	Feb., 1864
1st C. de Afrique H. A.	Nov., 1863	From 1st La. Native Guard H. A.	To 10th U. S. C. H. Arty. Def. N. O.	Apr., 1864
1st Wis. H. A. Co. D.	Feb., 1864	From New Organization	To Dist. La Fourche, La.	July, 1864
1st Delaware Batty.	Feb., 1864	From Camp Barry 22-Corps	To Arty. 1-Div 19-Corps Gulf	June, 1864
2d Conn. Batty.	Feb., 1864	From Def. of Wash., D. C., 22-Corps	To Arty. 4-Div. 13-Corps	Mch., 1864
14th R. I. H. A. 2d Bn.	Feb., 1864	From New Organization	Designated 11th U. S. C. Hvy. Arty.	May, 1864
14th R. I. H. A. 3d Bn.	Apr., 1864	From New Organization	Designated 11th U. S. C. Hvy. Arty.	May, 1864
4th Mass. Batty.	Apr., 1864	From Veteran Furlough	To Arty. 3-Div. 19-Corps Gulf	Aug., 1864
11th U. S. C. Hvy. Arty.	May, 1864	From 14th Rhode Island H. A.	No change to Muster Out.	Oct., 1865
25th New York Batty.	May, 1864	From Arty. 1-Div. 19-Corps	To Dist. La Fourche, La.	Aug., 1864
Batty. G, 1st Mich. Arty.	June, 1864	From Arty. 1-Div. 13-Corps	To Arty. Reserve Gulf	Aug., 1864
1st Indiana Batty.	June, 1864	From Arty. 1-Div. 13-Corps	To Arty. Reserve Gulf	Aug., 1864
Batty. F, 1st Mo. Arty.	June, 1864	From Arty. 4-Div. 13-Corps	To Arty. Reserve Gulf	Aug., 1864
16th Ohio Batty.	June, 1864	From Arty. 1-Div. 13-Corps	To Arty. Reserve Gulf	Aug., 1864
17th Ohio Batty.	June, 1864	From Arty. 4-Div. 13-Corps	To Unatt. 19-Corps Gulf	Aug., 1864
13th Mass. Batty.	June, 1864	From Reorganization	No change to Muster Out.	July, 1865
Batty. A, 1st Mo. Arty.	June, 1864	From Arty. 3-Div. 13-Corps	To Arty. Reserve Gulf	Aug., 1864
2d Conn. Batty.	June, 1864	From Arty. 4-Div. 13-Corps	To Unatt. 19-Corps Gulf	Aug., 1864
Batty. B, 1st Mo. Arty.	June, 1864	From U. S. Forces Texas	To Arty. Reserve Gulf	Aug., 1864
2d Ohio Batty.	June, 1864	From Arty. 3-Div. 13-Corps	To Arty. Reserve Gulf	Aug., 1864
Batty. A, 2d Ill. Arty.	June, 1864	From Arty. 1-Div. 13-Corps	To Dist. La Fourche, La.	Apr., 1865
Batty. E, 2d Ill. Arty.	June, 1864	From D. Baton Rouge, Plaquemine	No change to Muster Out.	Sept., 1864
4th Iowa Batty.	June, 1864	From Sully's Com. Dept. Northwest	To Dist. La Fourche, La.	June, 1864
6th Mass. Batty.	June, 1864	From Arty. 1-Div. 19-Corps	No change to Muster Out.	June, 1865
Mercantile Ill. Batty.	June, 1864	From Dist. Baton Rouge, La.	To Arty. Reserve Gulf	Aug., 1864
2d Conn. Batty.	Sept., 1864	From U. S. Forces Mobile Bay	To Arty. Reserve Corps Gulf	Dec., 1864
Mercantile Ill. Batty.	May, 1865	From Dist. Baton Rouge, La.	No change to Muster Out.	July, 1865

INDEPENDENT COMMANDS.—

13th Maine Infy.	Sept., 1862	From 3-Brig. Dept. Gulf	To Defences of New Orleans	Dec., 1862
8th New Hamp. Infy.	Sept., 1862	From 1-Brig. Dept. Gulf	To 2-Brig. 3-Div. 19-Corps	Jan., 1863
8th Vermont Infy.	Sept., 1862	From 1-Brig. Dept. Gulf	To Weitzel's Reserve Brigade	Dec., 1862
23d Conn. Infy.	Dec., 1862	From New Organization	To Defences of New Orleans	Jan., 1863
165th New York Infy.	Dec., 1862	From New Organization	To 3-Brig. 2-Div. 19-Corps	Jan., 1863
177th New York Infy.	Dec., 1862	From New Organization	To 3-Brig. 2-Div. 19-Corps	Jan., 1863
21st Indiana Infy.	Dec., 1862	From 2-Brig. Dept. Gulf	To Unatt. 1-Div. 19-Corps	Jan., 1863
1st La. Native Gd. Infy.	Dec., 1862	From Defences of New Orleans	To Unatt. 1-Div. 19-Corps	Jan., 1863
2d La. Native Gd. Infy.	Dec., 1862	From Defences of New Orleans	To Defences of New Orleans	Jan., 1863
3d La. Native Gd. Infy.	Dec., 1862	From New Organization	To Unatt. 1-Div. 19-Corps	Jan., 1863
1st Texas Cavalry	Dec., 1862	From New Organization	To Defences of New Orleans	Jan., 1863
4th Mass. Batty.	Dec., 1862	From 1-Brig. Dept. Gulf	To Arty. 3-Div. 19-Corps	Jan., 1863

WEITZEL'S RESERVE BRIGADE.—Organized Sept. 16, 1862. Transferred to 1st Division, 19-Corps, Jan. 3, 1863.

COMMANDER.

Godfrey Weitzel	Brigadier General		Sept. 22, 1862, to Jan. 3, 1863.	
12th Conn. Infy.	Sept., 1862	From 1-Brig. Dept. Gulf	To 2-Brig. 1-Div. 19-Corps	Jan., 1863
13th Conn. Infy.	Sept., 1862	From 1-Brig. Dept. Gulf	To Grover's Div. 19-Corps	Dec., 1862
1st Louisiana Infy.	Sept., 1862	From New Organization	To Grover's Div. 19-Corps	Jan., 1863
75th New York Infy.	Sept., 1862	From Dist. West Florida	To 2-Brig. 1-Div. 19-Corps	Jan., 1863
1st La. Cav., A, B.	Sept., 1862	From New Organization	To Unatt. 1-Div. 19-Corps	Jan., 1863
Co. B, Ind. Bn. Mass. C.	Sept., 1862	From Defences of New Orleans	To Unatt. 1-Div. 19-Corps	Jan., 1863
1st Maine Batty.	Sept., 1862	From 2-Brig. Dept. Gulf	To Arty. 1-Div. 19-Corps	Jan., 1863
6th Mass. Batty.	Sept., 1862	From 2-Brig. Dept. Gulf	To Arty. 1-Div. 19-Corps	Jan., 1863
8th Vermont Infy.	Dec., 1862	From Indpt. Command Gulf	To 2-Brig. 1-Div. 19-Corps	Jan., 1863

SHERMAN'S DIVISION.—U. S. Forces at Carrollton, La. Organized Sept. 18, 1862. Transferred to Defences of New Orleans Jan. 9, 1863.

COMMANDER.

T. W. Sherman	Brigadier General			
14th Maine Infy.	Sept., 1862	From 3-Brig. Dept. Gulf	To 3-Brig. 2-Div. 19-Corps	Jan., 1863
15th New Hamp. Infy.	Sept., 1862	From New Organization	To 1-Brig. 2-Div. 19-Corps	Jan., 1863
16th New Hamp. Infy.	Sept., 1862	From New Organization	To 1-Brig. 3-Div. 19-Corps	Jan., 1863
31st Mass. Infy.	Sept., 1862	From 2-Brig. Dept. Gulf	To 3-Brig. 3-Div. 19-Corps	Jan., 1863
42d Mass. Infy.	Dec., 1862	From New Organization	To 2-Brig. 2-Div. 19-Corps	Jan., 1863
26th Conn. Infy.	Dec., 1862	From New Organization	To 1-Brig. 2-Div. 19-Corps	Jan., 1863
110th New York Infy.	Dec., 1862	From Baltimore, Md.	To 3-Brig. 3-Div. 19-Corps	Jan., 1863
114th New York Infy.	Dec., 1862	From Baltimore, Md.	To 1-Brig. 2-Div. 19-Corps	Jan., 1863
116th New York Infy.	Dec., 1862	From Baltimore, Md.	To 1-Brig. 3-Div. 19-Corps	Jan., 1863
128th New York Infy.	Dec., 1862	From Baltimore, Md.	To 2-Brig. 2-Div. 19-Corps	Jan., 1863
156th New York Infy.	Dec., 1862	From New Organization	To 3-Brig. 3-Div. 19-Corps	Jan., 1863
160th New York Infy.	Dec., 1862	From New Organization	To 2-Brig. 1-Div. 19-Corps	Jan., 1863
162d New York Infy.	Dec., 1862	From Abercrombie's Div. Def. Wash.	To 3-Brig. 3-Div. 19-Corps	Jan., 1863
6th Michigan Infy.	Sept., 1862	From 2-Brig. Dept. Gulf	To 1-Brig. 2-Div. 19-Corps	Jan., 1863
1st Vermont Batty.	Sept., 1862	From 1-Brig. Dept. Gulf	To Arty. 2-Div. 19-Corps	Jan., 1863
18th New York Batty.	Dec., 1862	From New Organization	To Arty. 2-Div. 19-Corps	Jan., 1863
Co. A, Mass. Ind. Bn. C.	Sept., 1862	From Defences of New Orleans	To Cav. 2-Div. 19-Corps	Jan., 1863

GROVER'S DIVISION.—U. S. Forces Baton Rouge, La. Organized Dec. 16, 1862. Discontinued March, 1863.

COMMANDER.

Cuvier Grover	Brigadier General			
12th Maine Infy.	Dec., 1862	From 3-Brig. Dept. Gulf	To 2-Brig. 4-Div. 19-Corps	Mch., 1863
22d Maine Infy.	Dec., 1862	From DeRussy's Div. Def. Wash'n	To 1-Brig. 4-Div. 19-Corps	Mch., 1863
26th Maine Infy.	Dec., 1862	From Casey's Div. Def. Washington	To 3-Brig. 4-Div. 19-Corps	Mch., 1863
41st Mass. Infy.	Dec., 1862	From New Organization	To 2-Brig. 4-Div. 19-Corps	Mch., 1863
52d Mass. Infy.	Dec., 1862	From New Organization	To 2-Brig. 4-Div. 19-Corps	Mch., 1863
13th Conn. Infy.	Dec., 1862	From Weitzel's Reserve Brig.	To 3-Brig. 4-Div. 19-Corps	Mch., 1863
24th Conn. Infy.	Dec., 1862	From New Organization	To 2-Brig. 4-Div. 19-Corps	Mch., 1863

GROVER'S DIVISION.—Continued.

25th Conn. Infy..........Dec., 1862	From New Organization............	To 3-Brig. 4-Div. 19-Corps.........	Mch.,	1863
6th New York Infy......Dec., 1862	From Dist. West Florida..........	To 1-Brig. 4-Div. 19-Corps.......	Mch.,	1863
131st New York Infy....Dec., 1862	From Annapolis, Md..............	To 1-Brig. 4-Div. 19-Corps.......	Mch.,	1863
133d New York Infy......Dec., 1862	From Def. Washington, D. C......	To 2-Brig. 3-Div. 19-Corps.......	Jan.,	1863
159th New York Infy....Dec., 1862	From New Organization............	To 3-Brig. 4-Div. 19-Corps.......	Mch.,	1863
161st New York Infy....Dec., 1862	From New Organization............	To 3-Brig. 1-Div. 19-Corps.......	Jan.,	1863
173d New York Infy.....Dec., 1862	From New Organization............	To 2-Brig. 3-Div. 19-Corps.......	Jan.,	1863
174th New York Infy.....Dec., 1862	From New Organization............	To 2-Brig. 1-Div. 19-Corps.......	Jan.,	1863
4th Wisconsin Infy......Dec., 1862	From 2-Brig. Dept. Gulf.........	To 2-Brig. 3-Div. 19-Corps.......	Jan.,	1863
2d Louisiana Infy........Dec., 1862	From New Organization............	To 3-Brig. 1-Div. 19-Corps.......	Jan.,	1863
1st Louisiana Infy........Jan., 1863	From Weitzel's Reserve Brigade..	To 2-Brig. 1-Div. 19-Corps.......	Jan.,	1863
ARTILLERY.—				
2d Mass. Batty..........Dec., 1862	From 2-Brig. Dept. Gulf.........	To Arty. 4-Div. 19-Corps.........	Mch.,	1863
Batty. L, 1st U. S. Arty...Dec., 1862	From Defences New Orleans.......	To Arty. 4-Div. 19-Corps.........	Mch.,	1863
Batty. C, 2d U. S. Arty...Dec., 1862	From Defences New Orleans.......	To Arty. 4-Div. 19-Corps.........	Mch.,	1863
CAVALRY.—				
1st Louisiana Cav. Co. C..Dec., 1862	From New Organization............	To Unass'd 1-Div. 19-Corps........	Jan.,	1863
Co. B, Mass. Ind. Bn. Cav..Dec., 1862	From Defences New Orleans.......	To Unass'd 1-Div. 19-Corps........	Jan.,	1863

Nineteenth Army Corps

Organized Jan. 5, 1863, to date from Dec. 14, 1862, by General Order No. 5, A. G. O., from troops in the Department of the Gulf. Discontinued as a Corps in the Department of the Gulf Nov. 7, 1864.

COMMANDERS.

N. P. Banks..........	Major General.....................	Dec. 16, 1862, to Aug. 20, 1863.
William B. Franklin...	Major General.....................	Aug. 20, 1863, to May 2, 1864.
William H. Emory....,	Brigadier General.................	May 2, 1864, to July 2, 1864.
B. S. Roberts.........	Brigadier General.................	July 2, 1864, to July 6, 1864.
M. K. Lawler.........	Brigadier General.................	July 6, 1864, to July 7, 1864.
J. J. Reynolds........	Major General.....................	July 7, 1864 to Nov. 7, 1864.

1st DIVISION.—Organized Jan. 12, 1863.   COMMANDERS.

C. C. Augur...........	Major General.....................	Jan. 12, 1863, to July 15, 1863.
Godfrey Weitzel.......	Brigadier General.................	July 15. 1863, to July 28, 1863.
W. B. Franklin.......	Major General.....................	July 28, 1863, to Aug. 20, 1863.
Jacob Sharpe.........	Col. 156th New York Infy.........	Aug. 20, 1863, to Sept. 1, 1863.
Godfrey Weitzel.......	Brigadier General.................	Sept. 1, 1863, to Dec. 13, 1863.
W. H. Emory..........	Brigadier General.................	Dec. 13, 1863, to May 2, 1864.
J. W. McMillen........	Brigadier General.................	May 2, 1864, to June 25, 1864.
B. S. Roberts.........	Brigadier General.................	June 25, 1864, to July 1, 1864.
Wm. Dwight..........	Brigadier General.................	July 1, 1864, to July 5, 1864.

1st BRIGADE.—Organized Feb. 9, 1863.   COMMANDERS.

E. P. Chapin..........	Col. 116th New York Infy.........	Feb. 9, 1863, to May 27, 1863. Killed.
C. J. Paine...........	Col. 2d Louisiana Infy..........	May 27, 1863, to July 11, 1863.
N. A. M. Dudley.......	Col. 30th Mass. Infy............	July 11, 1863, to July 24, 1863.
Geo. M. Love.........	Col. 116th New York Infy........	July 24, 1863, to Feb. 20, 1864.
William Dwight.......	Brigadier General.................	Feb. 20, 1864, to Feb. 25, 1864.
Geo. M. Love.........	Col. 116th New York Infy........	Feb. 25, 1864, to Mch. 25, 1864.
William Dwight.......	Brigadier General.................	Mch. 25, 1864, to Apr. 18, 1864.
Geo. L. Beale.........	Col. 29th Maine Infy............	Apr. 18, 1864, to July 5, 1864.

21st Maine Infy.........Feb., 1863	From New Organization............	No change to Muster Out..........	July,	1863
48th Mass. Infy.........Feb., 1863	From New Organization............	No change to Muster Out..........	Aug.,	1863
49th Mass. Infy.........Feb., 1863	From New Organization............	No change to Muster Out..........	Aug.,	1863
116th New York Infy.....Feb., 1863	From 1-Brig. 3-Div. 19-Corps....	To 1-Brig. 1-Div. 19-Corps Shenan.	July,	1864
2d Louisiana Infy.......May, 1863	From 3-Brig. 1-Div. 19-Corps....	To 3-Brig. Cav. Div. Gulf........	Sept.,	1863
30th Mass. Infy........Aug., 1863	From 3-Brig. 1-Div. 19-Corps....	To 1-Brig. 1-Div. 19-Corps Shenan.	July,	1864
161st New York Infy....Aug., 1863	From 3-Brig. 1-Div. 19-Corps....	To Bailey's Engineer Brig. Gulf...	June,	1864
174th New York Infy....Aug., 1863	From 3-Brig. 1-Div. 19-Corps....	Consolidated with 162d N. Y......	Feb.,	1864
114th New York Infy....Feb., 1863	From 3-Brig. 1-Div. 19-Corps....	To 1-Brig. 1-Div. 19-Corps Shenan.	July,	1864
153d New York Infy.....Feb., 1864	From Garrison Washington, D. C..	To 1-Brig. 1-Div. 19-Corps Shenan.	July,	1864
29th Maine Infy.........Mch., 1864	From 2-Brig. 1-Div. 19-Corps....	To 1-Brig. 1-Div. 19-Corps Shenan.	July,	1864

2d BRIGADE.—   COMMANDERS.

Godfrey Weitzel.......	Brigadier General.................	Jan. 12, 1863, to May 14, 1863.
Stephen Thomas.......	Col. 8th Vermont Infy...........	May 14, 1863, to July 11, 1863.
O. P. Gooding.........	Col. 31st Mass. Infy............	July 11, 1863, to Aug. 15, 1863.
James Smith..........	Col. 128th New York Infy........	Aug. 15, 1863, to Sept. 12, 1863.
Jacob Sharpe.........	Col. 156th New York Infy........	Sept. 12, 1863, to Oct. 20, 1863.
O. P. Gooding.........	Col. 31st Mass. Infy............	Oct. 20, 1863, to Nov. 20, 1863.
Jacob Sharpe.........	Col. 156th New York Infy........	Nov. 20, 1863, to Feb. 15, 1864.
Geo. L. Beale.........	Col. 29th Maine Infy............	Feb. 15, 1864, to Mch. 24, 1864.
J. W. McMillan........	Brigadier General.................	Mch. 24, 1864, to May 29, 1864.
Henry Rust, Jr........	Col. 13th Maine Infy............	May 29, 1864, to June 20, 1864.
J. W. McMillan........	Brigadier General.................	June 20, 1864, to July 5, 1864.

75th New York Infy......Jan., 1863	From Weitzel's Reserve Brig......	To 3-Brig. 1-Div. 19-Corps.........	July,	1863
114th New York Infy.....Jan., 1863	From 1-Brig. 3-Div. 19-Corps....	To 3-Brig. 1-Div. 19-Corps.......	July,	1863
160th New York Infy....Jan., 1863	From Sherman's Div. Gulf........	To 3-Brig. 1-Div. 19-Corps.......	July,	1863
174th New York Infy....Jan., 1863	From Grover's Div. 19-Corps......	To 3-Brig. 1-Div. 19-Corps.......	July,	1863
1st Louisiana Infy.......Jan., 1863	From Weitzel's Reserve Brigade..	To 1-Brig. 4-Div. 19-Corps.......	Mch.,	1863
12th Conn. Infy........Jan., 1863	From Weitzel's Reserve Brigade..	To 3-Brig. 1-Div. 19-Corps.......	July,	1863
8th Vermont Infy.......Jan., 1863	From Weitzel's Reserve Brigade..	To 3-Brig. 1-Div. 19-Corps.......	July,	1863
31st Mass. Infy........July, 1863	From 3-Brig. 3-Div. 19-Corps....	To 4-Brig. Cav. Div. Gulf........	Dec.,	1863
38th Mass. Infy........July, 1863	From 3-Brig. 3-Div. 19-Corps....	To 3-Brig. 2-Div. 19-Corps.......	Feb.,	1864
53d Mass. Infy.........July, 1863	From 3-Brig. 3-Div. 19-Corps....	No change to Muster Out..........	Sept.,	1863
128th New York Infy....July, 1863	From 1-Brig. 3-Div. 19-Corps....	To 3-Brig. 2-Div. 19-Corps.......	Feb.,	1864
156th New York Infy....July, 1863	From 3-Brig. 3-Div. 19-Corps....	To 3-Brig. 2-Div. 19-Corps.......	Feb.,	1864
175th New York Infy....July, 1863	From 3-Brig. 3-Div. 19-Corps....	To 3-Brig. 2-Div. 19-Corps.......	Feb.,	1864
8th Vermont Infy.......Feb., 1864	From 3-Brig. 1-Div. 19-Corps....	To 2-Brig. 1-Div. 19-Corps Shenan.	July,	1864
12th Conn. Infy........Feb., 1864	From 3-Brig. 1-Div. 19-Corps....	To 2-Brig. 1-Div. 19-Corps Shenan.	July,	1864
13th Maine Infy........Feb., 1864	From 2-Brig. 4-Div. 13-Corps....	To 2-Brig. 1-Div. 19-Corps Shenan.	July,	1864
15th Maine Infy........Feb., 1864	From 2-Brig. 4-Div. 13-Corps....	To 2-Brig. 1-Div. 19-Corps Shenan.	July,	1864
29th Maine Infy........Feb., 1864	From New Organization............	To 1-Brig. 1-Div. 19-Corps.......	Mch.,	1864
169th New York Infy....Feb., 1864	From 3-Brig. 1-Div. 19-Corps....	To 3-Brig. 1-Div. 19-Corps.......	June,	1864
47th Penna. Infy........Feb., 1864	From Key West, Fla..............	To 2-Brig. 1-Div. 19-Corps Shenan.	July,	1864

3d BRIGADE.— COMMANDERS.

N. A. M. Dudley	Col. 30th Mass. Infy	Jan. 12, 1863, to July 10, 1863.	
R. B. Merritt	Col. 75th New York Infy	July 10, 1863, to Jan. 20, 1864.	
C. C. Dwight	Col. 160th N. Y. Infy	Jan. 20, 1864, to Feb. 15, 1864.	
F. Fessenden	Col. 30th Maine Infy	Feb. 15, 1864, to Mch. 29, 1864.	
Lewis Benedict	Col. 162d N. Y. Infy	Mch. 29, 1864, to Apr. 9, 1864.	Killed.
F. Fessenden	Col. 30th Maine Infy	Apr. 9, 1864, to Apr. 22, 1864.	
J. W. Blanchard	Lt.-Col. 162d N. Y. Infy	Apr. 22, 1864 to May 1, 1864.	
Geo. M. Love	Col. 116th N. Y. Infy	May 1, 1864, to June 25, 1864.	
L. D. H. Currie	Col. 133d N. Y. Infy	June 25, 1864, to July 5, 1864.	

30th Mass. Infy	Jan., 1863	From Defences of New Orleans	To 1-Brig. 1-Div. 19-Corps	Aug., 1863
50th Mass. Infy	Jan., 1863	From New Organization	No change to Muster Out	Aug., 1863
91st New York Infy	Jan., 1863	From Dist. W. Fla. Key West, Fla.	To 2-Brig. 4-Div. 19-Corps	Mch., 1863
161st New York Infy	Jan., 1863	From Grover's Division Gulf	To 1-Brig. 1-Div. 19-Corps	Aug., 1863
2d Louisiana Infy	Jan., 1863	From Grover's Division Gulf	To 1-Brig. 1-Div. 19-Corps	May, 1863
174th New York Infy	Feb., 1863	From 2-Brig. 1-Div. 19-Corps	To 1-Brig. 1-Div. 19-Corps	Aug., 1863
12th Conn. Infy	July, 1863	From 2-Brig. 1-Div. 19-Corps	To 2-Brig. 1-Div. 19-Corps	Feb., 1864
75th New York Infy	July, 1863	From 2-Brig. 1-Div. 19-Corps	To 1-Brig. Cav. Div. Gulf	Dec., 1863
114th New York Infy	July, 1863	From 2-Brig. 1-Div. 19-Corps	To 1-Brig. 1-Div. 19-Corps	Feb., 1864
160th New York Infy	July, 1863	From 2-Brig. 1-Div. 19-Corps	To 2-Brig. 1-Div. 19-Corps	Feb., 1864
174th N. Y. Infy	July, 1863	From 2-Brig. 1-Div. 19-Corps	To 1-Brig. 1-Div. 19-Corps	Aug., 1863
8th Vermont Infy	July, 1863	From 2-Brig. 1-Div. 19-Corps	To 2-Brig. 1-Div. 19-Corps	Feb., 1864
30th Me. Infy	Feb., 1864	From New Organization	To 3-Br. 1-Div. 19-Corps Shenandoah	July, 1864
162d N. Y. Infy	Feb., 1864	From 1-Brig. 3-Div. 19-Corps	To 3-Br. 1-Div. 19-Corps Shenandoah	July, 1864
165th N. Y. Infy	Feb., 1864	From 1-Brig. 3-Div. 19-Corps	To 3-Br. 1-Div. 19-Corps Shenandoah	July, 1864
173d N. Y. Infy	Feb., 1864	From 1-Brig. 3-Div. 19-Corps	To 3-Br. 1-Div. 19-Corps Shenandoah	July, 1864
133d N. Y. Infy	June, 1864	From 1-Brig. 3-Div. 19-Corps	To 3-Br. 1-Div. 19-Corps Shenandoah	July, 1864
160th N. Y. Infy	June, 1864	From 2-Brig. 1-Div. 19-Corps	To 3-Br. 1-Div. 19-Corps Shenandoah	July, 1864
ARTILLERY.—				
1st Me. Batty	Jan., 1863	From Weitzel's Res. Brigade	To Arty. 2-Div. 19-Corps	Jan., 1864
6th Mass. Batty	Jan., 1863	From Weitzel's Res. Brigade	To Arty. Reserve Gulf	Aug., 1863
Batty. A, 1st U. S. Arty	Jan., 1863	From Def. of New Orleans	To Arty. Reserve Gulf	Aug., 1863
1st Ind. Heavy Arty	Feb., 1863	From Indpt. Command Gulf	To Unatt. Dist. Baton Rouge, La.	July, 1863
12th Mass. Batty	Feb., 1863	From New Organization	To Arty. Reserve 19-Corps	July, 1864
18th N. Y. Batty	May, 1863	From Arty. 2-Div. 19-Corps	To Def. of New Orleans	Aug., 1863
Batty. G, 5th U. S. Arty	May, 1863	From Arty. 2-Div. 19-Corps	To Port Hudson, La.	July, 1863
6th Mass. Batty	Dec., 1863	From Arty Reserve Gulf	To Res. Arty. Def. New Orleans	June, 1864
Batty. L, 1st U. S. Arty	Jan., 1864	From Arty Reserve Gulf	To New York Dept. East	June, 1864
4th Mass. Batty	Feb., 1864	From Arty Reserve Gulf	To Def. New Orleans	Mch., 1864
25th N. Y. Batty	Feb., 1864	From Arty Reserve Gulf	To Def. New Orleans	May, 1864
Batty. A, 1st U. S. Arty	Feb., 1864	From Def. New Orleans	To Def. Washington, D. C. 22-Corps	July, 1864
1st Vt. Batty	Mch., 1864	From Dist. La. Fourche, La.	No change to Muster Out	July, 1864
13th Mass. Batty	Mch., 1864	From Arty. 4-Div. 19-Corps	To Def. New Orleans, La.	June, 1864
1st Del. Batty	June, 1864	From Def. New Orleans, La.	To Arty. 3-Div. 19-Corps Gulf	July, 1864
CAVALRY.—				
Co. B Mass. Indpt. Battn.	Jan., 1863	From Weitzel's Reserve Brigade	To 3d Mass. Cav.	June, 1863
2d R. I. Cav. Batn.	Jan., 1863	From New Organization	To 1st La. Cav.	Sept., 1863
1st La. Cav.	Jan., 1863	From Weitzel's Reserve Brigade	To Cav. Command 19-Corps	May, 1863
UNATTACHED.—				
1st La. Native Guard Infy.	Jan., 1863	From Indpt. Command Gulf	Designation changed to 1st C. de A.	June, 1863
3d La. Native Guard Infy.	Jan., 1863	From Indpt. Command Gulf	Designation changed to 3d C. de A.	June, 1863
4th La. Native Guard Infy.	Jan., 1863	From New Organization	Designation changed to 4th C. de A.	June, 1863
1st La. N. G. Engrs.	Jan., 1863	From New Organization	To Engr. Brig. Dept. Gulf	May, 1863

2d DIVISION.—Discontinued except 2d Brigade, July, 1863. Reorganized Feb. 15, 1864. Transferred to Army of the Shenandoah July, 1864. Reorganized in Dept. of the Gulf Aug. 18, 1864. Transferred to Reserve Corps, Mil. Div. West Miss., Nov. 7, 1864.

COMMANDERS.

T. W. Sherman	Brigadier General	Jan. 13, 1863, to May 27, 1863.	
Geo. L. Andrews	Brigadier General	May 27, 1863, to May 28, 1863.	
F. S. Nickerson	Col. 14th Me. Infy	May 28, 1863, to May 30, 1863.	
William Dwight	Brigadier General	May 30, 1863, to July 18, 1863.	
Cuvier Grover	Brigadier General	Feb. 15, 1864, to June 18, 1864.	
G. F. McGinnis	Brigadier General	June 18, 1864, to June 25, 1864.	
Cuvier Grover	Brigadier General	June 25, 1864, to July 5, 1864.	
E. S. Dennis	Brigadier General	Aug. 18, 1864, to Nov. 7, 1864.	

1st BRIGADE.— COMMANDERS.

T. S. Clark	Col. 6th Mich. Infy	Jan. 13, 1863, to Feb. 26, 1863.	
Neal Dow	Brigadier General	Feb. 26, 1863, to May 27, 1863.	
D. S. Cowles	Col. 128th N. Y. Infy	May 27, 1863.	Killed.
T. S. Clark	Col. 6th Mich. Infy	May 27, 1863, to July, 1863.	
F. S. Nickerson	Brigadier General	Feb. 15, 1864, to June 29, 1864.	
A. B. Farr	Col. 26th Mass. Infy	June 29, 1864, to July 2, 1864.	
H. W. Birge	Brigadier General	July 2, 1864, to July 5, 1864.	
B. Dornblaser	Col. 46th Ill. Infy	Aug. 18, 1864, to Nov. 7, 1864.	

15th N. H. Infy	Jan., 1863	From Sherman's Div. Gulf	To 2-Brig. 3-Div. 19-Corps	July, 1863
26th Conn. Infy	Jan., 1863	From Sherman's Div. Gulf	No change to Muster Out	Aug., 1863
128th N. Y. Infy	Jan., 1863	From Sherman's Div. Gulf	To 2-Brig. 1-Div. 19-Corps	July, 1863
6th Mich. Infy	Jan., 1863	From Sherman's Div. Gulf	To Dist. Port Hudson, La.	July, 1863
162d N. Y. Infy	May, 1863	From 1-Brig. 3-Div. 19-Corps	To 1-Brig. 3-Div. 19-Corps	July, 1863
16th N. H. Infy	May, 1863	From 1-Brig. 3-Div. 19-Corps	No change to Muster Out	Aug., 1863
12th Me. Infy	Feb., 1864	From 2-Brig. 4-Div. 19-Corps	To 1-Brig. 2-Div. 19-Corps Shen.	July, 1864
14th Me. Infy	Feb., 1864	From 2-Brig. 4-Div. 19-Corps	To 1-Brig. 2-Div. 19-Corps Shen.	July, 1864
9th Conn. Infy	Feb., 1864	From 2-Brig. 4-Div. 19-Corps	To Dept. of the East	Apr., 1864
176th N. Y. Infy	Feb., 1864	From Def. New Orleans	To 3-Brig. 2-Div. 19-Corps	Feb., 1864
133d N. Y. Infy	Apr., 1864	From Def. New Orleans	To 3-Brig. 1-Div. 19-Corps	June, 1864
14th N. H. Infy	June, 1864	From Def. New Orleans	To 1-Brig. 2-Div. 19-Corps Shen.	July, 1864
26th Mass. Infy	June, 1864	From 1-Brig. 2-Div. 19-Corps	To 1-Brig. 2-Div. 19-Corps Shen.	July, 1864
75th N. Y. Infy	June, 1864	From 1-Brig. Cav. Div. Gulf	To 1-Brig. 2-Div. 19-Corps Shen.	July, 1864
8th Ill. Infy	Aug., 1864	From Maltby's Brig. Dist. Vicksburg.	To 2-Brig. Res. Corps Gulf	Nov., 1864
11th Ill. Infy	Aug., 1864	From 2-Brig. 1-Div. 17-Corps Tenn.	To 2-Brig. Res. Corps Gulf	Nov., 1864
46th Ill. Infy	Aug., 1864	From 2-Brig. 1-Div. 17-Corps Tenn.	To 2-Brig. Res. Corps Gulf	Nov., 1864
76th Ill. Infy	Aug., 1864	From 2-Brig. 1-Div. 17-Corps Tenn.	To 2-Brig. Res. Corps Gulf	Nov., 1864
7th Mo. Infy	Aug., 1864	From Maltby's Brig. Dist. Vicksburg	Consolidated with 11th Mo.	Dec.17, '64
30th Mo. Infy	Aug., 1864	From 1-Brig. 1-Div. 17-Corps Tenn.	To 2-Brig. Res. Corps Gulf	Nov., 1864
124th Ill. Infy	Aug., 1864	From Maltby's Brig. Dist. Vicksburg.	To Maltby's Brig. Dist. Vicksburg.	Oct., 1864

2d BRIGADE.—Discontinued Aug. 15, 1863. Reorganized Feb. 15, 1864.

COMMANDERS.

A. B. Farr	Col. 26th Mass. Infy	Jan. 15, 1863, to May 12, 1863.
Thos. W. Cahill	Col. 9th Conn. Infy	May 12, 1863, to Aug. 15, 1863.
H. W. Birge	Brigadier General	Feb. 15, 1864, to Apr. 30, 1864.
E. L. Molineaux	Col. 159th N. Y. Infy	Apr. 30, 1864, to May 7, 1864.
H. W. Birge	Brigadier General	May 7, 1864, to June 27, 1864.
R. B. Merritt	Col. 75th N. Y. Infy	June 27, 1864, to July 2, 1864.
E. L. Molineaux	Col. 159th N. Y. Infy	July 2, 1864, to July 5, 1864.
J. R. Slack	Col. 47th Ind. Infy	Aug. 18, 1864, to Nov. 2, 1864.
Wm. A. Greene	Col. 29th Wis. Infy	Nov. 2, 1864, to Dec. 12, 1864.

28th Me. Infy	Jan., 1863	From New Organization	To 3-Brig. 2-Div. 19-Corps	May, 1863
26th Mass. Infy	Jan., 1863	From Def. New Orleans	To 2-Brig. 3-Div. 19-Corps	July, 1863
42d Mass. Infy	Jan., 1863	From Sherman's Div. Gulf	No change to Muster Out	Aug., 1863
47th Mass. Infy	Jan., 1863	From New Organization	No change to Muster Out	Aug., 1863
9th Conn. Infy	Mch., 1863	From 1-Brig. 3-Div. 19-Corps	To 2-Brig. 4-Div. 19-Corps	July, 1863
13th Conn. Infy	Feb., 1864	From 1-Brig. 4-Div. 19-Corps	To 2-Brig. 2-Div. 19-Corps Shen	July, 1864
1st La. Infy	Feb., 1864	From Dist. La Fourche, La	To Dist. La Fourche, La	June, 1864
90th N. Y. Infy	Feb., 1864	From 1-Brig. 4-Div. 19-Corps	To 1-Brig. 1-Div. 19-Corps	July, 1864
159th N. Y. Infy	Feb., 1864	From 1-Brig. 4-Div. 19-Corps	To 2-Brig. 2-Div. 19-Corps Shen	July, 1864
26th Mass. Infy	Feb., 1864	From 2-Brig. 3-Div. 19-Corps	To 1-Brig. 2-Div. 19-Corps	June, 1864
131st N. Y. Infy	Feb., 1864	From 1-Brig. 4-Div. 19-Corps	To 2-Brig. 2-Div. 19-Corps Shen	July, 1864
3d Mass. Cav	June, 1864	From 4-Brig. Cav. Div. Gulf	To 2-Brig. 2-Div. 19-Corps Shen	July, 1864
11th Ind. Infy	June, 1864	From 1-Brig. 3-Div. 13-Corps	To 2-Brig. 2-Div. 19-Corps Shen	July, 1864
22d Iowa Infy	June, 1864	From Def. New Orleans	To 2-Brig. 2-Div. 19-Corps Shen	July, 1864
47th Ind. Infy	Aug., 1864	From Dist. La Fourche, La	To 1-Brig. Res. Corps Gulf	Nov., 1864
99th Ill. Infy	Aug., 1864	From Dist. La Fourche, La	To 1-Brig. Res. Corps Gulf	Nov., 1864
21st Iowa Infy	Aug., 1864	From Dist. La Fourche, La	To 1-Brig. Res. Corps Gulf	Nov., 1864
29th Wis. Infy	Aug., 1864	From Dist. La Fourche, La	To 1-Brig. Res. Corps Gulf	Nov., 1864
120th Ohio Infy	Aug., 1864	From 2-Brig. 3-Div. 19-Corps	Consolidated with 114th Ohio	Nov.25, '64

3d BRIGADE.—Transferred to 3d Division Aug., 1863. Reorganized Feb., 1864.

COMMANDERS.

F. S. Nickerson	Col. 14th Me. Infy	Jan. 13, 1863, to Aug. 10, 1863.
Jacob Sharpe	Col. 156th N. Y. Infy	Feb. 15, 1864, to July 5, 1864.
J. G. Guppy	Col. 23d Wis. Infy	Aug. 18, 1864, to Oct. 27, 1864.
W. Slocum	Lieutenant-Colonel	Oct. 27, 1864, to Nov. 3, 1864.
Alex. Shaler	Brigadier General	Nov. 3, 1864, to Dec. 5, 1864.

14th Me. Infy	Jan., 1863	From Sherman's Div. Gulf	To 1-Brig. 3-Div. 19-Corps	July, 1863
24th Me. Infy	Jan., 1863	From New Organization	No change to Muster Out	Aug., 1863
165th N. Y. Infy	Jan., 1863	From Indpt. Command Gulf	To 1-Brig. 3-Div. 19-Corps	July, 1863
177th N. Y. Infy	Jan., 1863	From New Organization	To 1-Brig. 3-Div. 19-Corps	July, 1863
28th Me. Infy	May, 1863	From 2-Brig. 2-Div. 19-Corps	No change to Muster Out	Aug., 1863
175th N. Y. Infy	May, 1863	From 3-Brig. 3-Div. 19-Corps	To 2-Brig. 1-Div. 19-Corps	July, 1863
38th Mass. Infy	Feb., 1864	From 2-Brig. 1-Div. 19-Corps	To 3-Brig. 2-Div. 19-Corps Shen	July, 1864
128th N. Y. Infy	Feb., 1864	From 2-Brig. 1-Div. 19-Corps	To 3-Brig. 2-Div. 19-Corps Shen	July, 1864
156th N. Y. Infy	Feb., 1864	From 2-Brig. 1-Div. 19-Corps	To 3-Brig. 2-Div. 19-Corps Shen	July, 1864
175th N. Y. Infy	Feb., 1864	From 2-Brig. 1-Div. 19-Corps	To 3-Brig. 2-Div. 19-Corps Shen	July, 1864
176th N. Y. Infy	June, 1864	From 1-Brig. 2-Div. 19-Corps	To 3-Brig. 2-Div. 19-Corps Shen	July, 1864
161st N. Y. Infy	Aug., 1864	From Bailey's Engr. Brig. Gulf	To U. S. Forces White River Res. C.	Dec., 1864
23d Wis. Infy	Aug., 1864	From Def. New Orleans	To Guppy's Brig. Mobile Bay	Aug., 1864
1st La. Infy	Aug., 1864	From Dist. La Fourche, La	To Dist. La Fourche, La	Nov., 1864
28th Ill. Infy	Aug., 1864	From Dist. Natchez, Miss	To 1-Brig. Res. Corps Gulf	Dec., 1864
29th Ill. Infy	Aug., 1864	From Dist. Natchez, Miss	To 1-Brig. Res. Corps Gulf	Dec., 1864

ARTILLERY.—

1st Vt. Batty	Jan., 1863	From Sherman's Div. Gulf	To Arty. 3-Div. 19-Corps	July, 1863
18th N. Y. Batty	Jan., 1863	From Sherman's Div. Gulf	To Arty. 1-Div. 19-Corps	May, 1863
Batty. G, 5th U. S. Arty	Jan., 1863	From Def. New Orleans	To Arty. 1-Div. 19-Corps	May, 1863
21st N. Y. Batty	May, 1863	From Def. New Orleans	To Garrison Port Hudson, La	July, 1863
Batty. C, 2d U. S. Arty	Feb., 1864	From Arty. Dist. Baton Rouge, La	To Def. Washington, D. C., 22-Corps	July, 1864
26th N. Y. Batty	Feb., 1864	From Dist. La Fourche, La	To Dist. Morganza, La	July, 1864
1st Me. Batty	Feb., 1864	From Arty. 1-Div. 19-Corps	To Camp Barry, Washington, D. C.	July, 1864
1st Vt. Batty	Feb., 1864	From Dist. La Fourche, La	To Dist. Morganza, La	July, 1864
18th N. Y. Batty	Feb., 1864	From Dist. Baton Rouge, La	To Def. New Orleans, La	Mch., 1864
7th Mass. Batty	Mch., 1864	From Def. of Washington, D. C.	To Dist. Morganza, La	July, 1864
Batty. F, 2d U. S. Arty	Mch., 1864	From Arty. Cav. Div. Gulf	To Arty. Cav. Div. Gulf	Apr., 1864
7th Mass. Batty	Aug., 1864	From Dist. Morganza, La	To Arty. Res. Corps Gulf	Dec., 1864
26th N. Y. Batty	Aug., 1864	From Dist. Morganza, La	To Arty. Res. Corps Gulf	Dec., 1864

CAVALRY.—

Co. A, Mass. Indpt. Battn.	Jan., 1863	From Sherman's Div. Gulf	Consolidated with 3d Mass. Cav	June, 1863

UNATTACHED.—

1st Kansas Mtd. Infy	Aug., 1864	From 1-Brig. 1-Div. 17-Corps Tenn	To Dist. Eastern Ark. 7-Corps	Dec., 1864

3d DIVISION.—Discontinued Feb. 15, 1864. Reorganized June 27, 1864, from 13th Army Corps. Discontinued Nov. 7, 1864.

COMMANDERS.

Wm. H. Emory	Brigadier General	Jan. 3, 1863, to May 2, 1863.
H. E. Paine	Brigadier General	May 2, 1863, to June 14, 1863.
H. Fearing	Col. 8th N. H. Infy	June 14, 1863, to July 6, 1863.
William Dwight	Brigadier General	July 6, 1863, to Aug. 15, 1863.
F. S. Nickerson	Brigadier General	Aug. 15, 1863, to Aug. 29, 1863.
J. W. McMillan	Brigadier General	Aug. 29, 1863, to Sept. 4, 1863.
Wm. H. Emory	Brigadier General	Sept. 4, 1863, to Sept. 17, 1863.
J. W. McMillan	Brigadier General	Sept. 17, 1863, to Oct. 2, 1863.
Cuvier Grover	Brigadier General	Oct. 2, 1863, to Jan. 12, 1864.
J. W. McMillan	Brigadier General	Jan. 12, 1864, to Feb. 15, 1864.
M. K. Lawler	Brigadier General	June 27, 1864, to Aug. 25, 1864.
G. F. McGinnis	Brigadier General	Aug. 25, 1864, to Nov. 7, 1864.

1st BRIGADE.—

COMMANDERS.

Geo. L. Andrews	Brigadier General	Jan. 3, 1863, to Jan. 29, 1863.
T. Ingraham	Col. 38th Mass. Infy	Jan. 29, 1863, to Feb. 12, 1863.
Geo. L. Andrews	Brigadier General	Feb. 12, 1863, to Mch. 5, 1863.
T. Ingraham	Col. 38th Mass. Infy	Mch. 5, 1863, to June 14, 1863.
S. P. Ferris	Col. 28th Conn. Infy	June 14, 1863, to July 10, 1863.
F. S. Nickerson	Brigadier General	July 10, 1863, to Aug. 15, 1863.
T. W. Porter	Col. 14th Me. Infy	Aug. 15, 1863, to Aug. 29, 1863.
F. S. Nickerson	Brigadier General	Aug. 29, 1863, to Sept. 20, 1863.
Lewis Benedict	Col. 162d N. Y. Infy	Sept. 20, 1863, to Feb. 15, 1864.
A. L. Lee	Brigadier General	June 27, 1864, to Aug. 16, 1864.
L. A. Sheldon	Col. 42d Ohio Infy	Aug. 16, 1864, to Sept. 11, 1864.
W. McE. Dye	Col. 20th Iowa Infy	Sept. 11, 1864, to Nov. 1, 1864.
S. L. Glasgow	Col. 23d Iowa Infy	Nov. 1, 1864, to Nov. 7, 1864.

1st BRIGADE.—Continued.

Regiment	Date	From	To	Date
8th N. H. Infy	Jan., 1863	From Indpt. Command Gulf	To 2-Brig. 3-Div. 19-Corps	Jan., 1863
114th N. Y. Infy	Jan., 1863	From Sherman's Div. Gulf	To 2-Brig. 1-Div. 19-Corps	Jan., 1863
116th N. Y. Infy	Jan., 1863	From Sherman's Div. Gulf	To 1-Brig. 1-Div. 19-Corps	Jan., 1863
156th N. Y. Infy	Jan., 1863	From Sherman's Div. Gulf	To 3-Brig. 3-Div. 19-Corps	Jan., 1863
4th Mass. Infy	Feb., 1863	From New Organization	No change to Muster Out	Aug., 1863
110th N. Y. Infy	Feb., 1863	From 3-Brig. 3-Div. 19-Corps	To Key West, Fla.	Feb., 1864
162d N. Y. Infy	Feb., 1863	From 3-Brig. 3-Div. 19-Corps	To 1-Brig. 2-Div. 19-Corps	May, 1863
16th N. H. Infy	Feb., 1863	From 3-Brig. 3-Div. 19-Corps	To 1-Brig. 2-Div. 19-Corps	May, 1863
9th Conn. Infy	Feb., 1863	From Def. of New Orleans	To 2-Brig. 2-Div. 19-Corps	Mch., 1863
28th Conn. Infy	May, 1863	From Pensacola, Fla.	To 2-Brig. 3-Div. 19-Corps	July, 1863
14th Me. Infy	July, 1863	From 3-Brig. 2-Div. 19-Corps	To 2-Brig. 3-Div. 19-Corps	Sept., 1863
162d N. Y. Infy	July, 1863	From 1-Brig. 2-Div. 19-Corps	To 3-Brig. 1-Div. 19-Corps	Feb., 1864
165th N. Y. Infy	July, 1863	From 3-Brig. 2-Div. 19-Corps	To 3-Brig. 1-Div. 19-Corps	Feb., 1864
177th N. Y. Infy	July, 1863	From 3-Brig. 2-Div. 19-Corps	No change to Muster Out	Aug., 1863
173d N. Y. Infy	Sept., 1863	From 2-Brig. 3-Div. 19-Corps	To 3-Brig. 1-Div. 19-Corps	Feb., 1864
37th Ill. Infy	June, 1864	From 1-Brig. 2-Div. 13-Corps	To 4-Brig. Res. Corps Gulf	Dec., 1864
23d Iowa Infy	June, 1864	From 2-Brig. 1-Div. 13-Corps	To 4-Brig. Res. Corps Gulf	Dec., 1864
7th Ky. Infy	June, 1864	From 2-Brig. 1-Div. 13-Corps	To Dist. Baton Rouge, La.	Dec., 1864
42d Ohio Infy	June, 1864	From Plaquemine Dist. Baton Rouge.	No change to Muster Out	Dec., 1864
35th Wis. Infy	June, 1864	From Port Hudson, La.	To 4-Brig. Res. Corps Gulf	Dec., 1864
20th Iowa Infy	Sept., 1864	From U. S. Forces Mobile Bay	To 4-Brig. Res. Corps Gulf	Dec., 1864

2d BRIGADE.—   COMMANDERS.

H. E. Paine	Col. 4th Wis. Infy	Jan. 3, 1863, to June 14, 1863.
J. H. Alcot	Major 133d N. Y. Infy	June 14, 1863, to July 10, 1863.
H. Fearing	Col. 8th N. H. Infy	July 10, 1863, to Aug. 15, 1863.
J. W. McMillan	Brigadier General	Aug. 15, 1863, to Aug. 29, 1863.
A. B. Farr	Col. 26th Mass. Infy	Aug. 29, 1863, to Oct. 4, 1863.
J. W. McMillan	Brigadier General	Oct. 4, 1863, to Nov. 2, 1863.
A. B. Farr	Col. 26th Mass. Infy	Nov. 2, 1863, to Dec. 3, 1863.
J. W. McMillan	Brigadier General	Dec. 3, 1863, to Jan. 12, 1864.
J. A. Sawtell	Lt.-Col. 26th Mass. Infy	Jan. 12, 1864, to Feb. 15, 1864.
T. W. Bennett	Col. 69th Ind. Infy	June 27, 1864, to Aug. 18, 1864.
W. T. Spicely	Col. 24th Ind. Infy	Aug. 18, 1864, to Nov. 7, 1864.

Regiment	Date	From	To	Date
133d N. Y. Infy	Jan., 1863	From Grover's Div. Gulf	To Def. New Orleans	Oct., 1863
173d N. Y. Infy	Jan., 1863	From Grover's Div. Gulf	To 1-Brig. 3-Div. 19-Corps	Sept., 1863
174th N. Y. Infy	Jan., 1863	From Grover's Div. Gulf	To 3-Brig. 1-Div. 19-Corps	Feb., 1863
4th Wis. Infy	Jan., 1863	From Grover's Div. Gulf	To Cav. Command 19-Corps	July, 1863
8th N. H. Infy	Jan., 1863	From 1-Brig. 3-Div. 19-Corps	To 4-Brig. Cav. Div. Gulf	Dec., 1863
28th Conn. Infy	July, 1863	From 1-Brig. 3-Div. 19-Corps	No change to Muster Out	Aug., 1863
15th N. H. Infy	July, 1863	From 1-Brig. 2-Div. 19-Corps	No change to Muster Out	Aug., 1863
26th Mass. Infy	July, 1863	From 2-Brig. 2-Div. 19-Corps	To 2-Brig. 2-Div. 19-Corps	Feb., 1864
14th Me. Infy	Sept., 1863	From 1-Brig. 3-Div. 19-Corps	To 1-Brig. 2-Div. 19-Corps	Feb., 1864
69th Ind. Infy	June, 1863	From 3-Brig. 1-Div. 13-Corps	To Dist. Southern Ala.	Dec., 1864
22d Ky. Infy	June, 1864	From 2-Brig. 1-Div. 13-Corps	No change to Muster Out	Jan., 1865
16th Ohio Infy	June, 1864	From 2-Brig. 1-Div. 13-Corps	No change to Muster Out	Oct., 1864
114th Ohio Infy	June, 1864	From 2-Brig. 1-Div. 13-Corps	To 3-Brig. Res. Corps Gulf	Dec., 1864
120th Ohio Infy	June, 1864	From 2-Brig. 1-Div. 13-Corps	To 3-Brig. 2-Div. 19-Corps	Aug., 1864
97th Ill. Infy	June, 1864	From 2-Brig. 4-Div. 13-Corps	To 3-Brig. Res. Corps Gulf	Dec., 1864
24th Ind. Infy	Aug., 1864	From Bailey's Engr. Brig	To 3-Brig. Res. Corps Gulf	Dec., 1864

3d BRIGADE.—Transferred to 1st Division July 11, 1863. Reorganized July 5, 1864.

COMMANDERS.

O. P. Gooding	Col. 31st Mass. Infy	Jan. 24, 1863, to July 11, 1863.
F. W. Moore	Col. 83d Ohio Infy	July 5, 1864, to Oct. 1, 1864.
A. H. Brown	Lt.-Col. 96th Ohio Infy	Oct. 1, 1864, to Nov. 6, 1864.
G. F. McGinnis	Brigadier General	Nov. 6, 1864, to Dec. 5, 1864.

Regiment	Date	From	To	Date
13th Conn. Infy	Jan., 1863	From Sherman's Div. Gulf	To 2-Brig. 4-Div. 19-Corps	Jan., 1863
16th N. H. Infy	Jan., 1863	From Sherman's Div. Gulf	To 1-Brig. 3-Div. 19-Corps	Jan., 1863
110th N. Y. Infy	Jan., 1863	From Sherman's Div. Gulf	To 1-Brig. 3-Div. 19-Corps	Feb., 1863
162d N. Y. Infy	Jan., 1863	From Sherman's Div. Gulf	To 1-Brig. 3-Div. 19-Corps	Feb., 1863
31st Mass. Infy	Jan., 1863	From Def. New Orleans	To 2-Brig. 1-Div. 19-Corps	July, 1863
38th Mass. Infy	Jan., 1863	From Baltimore, Md., 8-Corps	To 2-Brig. 1-Div. 19-Corps	July, 1863
53d Mass. Infy	Jan., 1863	From New Organization	To 2-Brig. 1-Div. 19-Corps	July, 1863
156th N. Y. Infy	Jan., 1863	From 1-Brig. 3-Div. 19-Corps	To 2-Brig. 1-Div. 19-Corps	July, 1863
175th N. Y. Infy	Jan., 1863	From Suffolk, Va., Dept. Va. 7-C	To 3-Brig. 2-Div. 19-Corps	May, 1863
77th Ill. Infy	June, 1864	From Def. New Orleans	To Def. New Orleans	Oct., 1864
130th Ill. Infy	June, 1864	From Def. New Orleans	To Def. New Orleans	Oct., 1864
83d Ohio Infy	June, 1864	From 1-Brig. 4-Div. 13-Corps	To Post Natchez, Miss., Dept. Miss.	Dec., 1864
96th Ohio Infy	June, 1864	From 1-Brig. 4-Div. 13-Corps	To U. S. Forces White River	Dec., 1864
34th Iowa Infy	June, 1864	From 2-Brig. 4-Div. 13-Corps	To 3-Brig. Res. Corps Gulf	Dec., 1864
67th Ind. Infy	June, 1864	From 1-Brig. 4-Div. 13-Corps	To 3-Brig. Res. Corps Gulf	Dec., 1864
3d Md. Cav.	Aug., 1864	From Dist. La Fourche	To U. S. Forces Mobile Bay	Oct., 1864

ARTILLERY.—

Battery	Date	From	To	Date
2d Vt. Batty	Jan., 1863	From Def. New Orleans	To Garrison Arty. Port Hudson	July, 1863
4th Mass. Batty	Jan., 1863	From Indpt. Command Gulf	To Def. New Orleans	Apr., 1864
Batty. F, 1st U. S. Arty	Jan., 1863	From Def. New Orleans	To Arty. Cav. Div. Gulf	Nov., 1863
1st Vt. Batty	July, 1863	From Arty. 2-Div. 19-Corps	To Dist. La Fourche, La	Sept., 1863
1st Del. Batty	July, 1864	From Def. New Orleans Arty. Res	To Unatt. Arty. Res. Corps Gulf	Dec., 1864
4th Mass. Batty	July, 1864	From Def. New Orleans Arty. Res	To Unatt. Arty. Res. Corps Gulf	Dec., 1864

4th DIVISION.—Transferred to Defences New Orleans Aug., 1863. Discontinued Feb. 15, 1864.

COMMANDERS.

Cuvier Grover	Brigadier General	Jan. 3, 1863, to July 30, 1863.
Wm. H. Emory	Brigadier General	July 30, 1863, to Aug. 25, 1863.
E. G. Beckwith	Col. and A. D. C.	Aug. 25, 1863, to Jan. 25, 1864.
J. J. Reynolds	Major General	Jan. 25, 1864, to Feb. 15, 1864.

1st BRIGADE.—   COMMANDERS.

William Wilson	Col. 6th N. Y. Infy	Jan. 3, 1863, to Feb. 12, 1863.
William Dwight	Brigadier General	Feb. 12, 1863, to May 30, 1863.
J. S. Morgan	Col. 90th N. Y. Infy	May 30, 1863, to July 13, 1863.
J. Van Zant	Col. 91st N. Y. Infy	July 13, 1863, to Aug. 10, 1863.
H. W. Birge	Col. 13th Conn. Infy	Aug. 10, 1863, to Jan. 25, 1864.
E. L. Molineaux	Col. 159th N. Y. Infy	Jan. 25, 1864, to Feb. 15, 1864.

1st BRIGADE.—Continued.

1st La. Infy...............Jan., 1863	From 2-Brig. 1-Div. 19-Corps......	To 2-Brig. 4-Div. 19-Corps........	Aug., 1863
22d Me. Infy..............Jan., 1863	From Grover's Div. Gulf...........	No change to Muster Out.........	Aug., 1863
6th N. Y. Infy.............Jan., 1863	From Grover's Div. Gulf...........	No change to Muster Out.........	Aug., 1863
91st N. Y. Infy............Jan., 1863	From 2-Brig. 4-Div. 19-Corps......	To Garr. Fts. Jackson & St. Phillip.	July, 1863
131st N. Y. Infy...........Jan., 1863	From Grover's Div. Gulf...........	To 2-Brig. 2-Div. 19-Corps........	Feb., 1864
90th N. Y. Infy............May, 1863	From Dist. Key West, Fla..........	To 2-Brig. 2-Div. 19-Corps........	Feb., 1864
13th Conn. Infy...........Aug., 1863	From 3-Brig. 4-Div. 19-Corps......	To 2-Brig. 2-Div. 19-Corps........	Feb., 1864
159th N. Y. Infy...........Aug., 1863	From 3-Brig. 4-Div. 19-Corps......	To 2-Brig. 2-Div. 19-Corps........	Feb., 1864

2d BRIGADE.—   COMMANDERS.

J. Van Zant............	Col. 91st N. Y. Infy..........	Jan. 20, 1863, to Mch. 23, 1863.	
W. K. Kimball.........	Col. 12th Me. Infy...........	Mch. 23, 1863, to Aug. 15, 1863.	
Thos. W. Cahill.......	Col. 9th Conn. Infy..........	Aug. 15, 1863, to Feb. 15, 1864.	

91st New York Infy.....Jan., 1863	From 3-Brig. 1-Div. 19-Corps......	To 1-Brig. 4-Div. 19-Corps........	Jan., 1863
12th Maine Infy........Jan., 1863	From Grover's Div. Gulf...........	To 1-Brig. 2-Div. 19-Corps........	Feb., 1864
13th Conn. Infy........Jan., 1863	From 3-Brig. 3-Div. 19-Corps......	To 3-Brig. 3-Div. 19-Corps........	Jan., 1863
24th Conn. Infy........Jan., 1863	From Grover's Div. Gulf...........	To Def. New Orleans............	July, 1863
41st Mass. Infy........Jan., 1863	From Grover's Div. Gulf...........	Designation changed to 3d Cav.....	June, 1863
52d Mass. Infy........Jan., 1863	From Grover's Div. Gulf...........	No change to Muster Out.........	Aug., 1863
1st Louisiana Infy......Aug., 1863	From 1-Brig. 4-Div. 19-Corps......	To Dist. La Fourche, La.........	Oct., 1863
13th Maine Infy........Aug., 1863	From Def. of New Orleans........	To 2-Brig. 2-Div. 13-Corps........	Oct., 1863
15th Maine Infy........Aug., 1863	From Def. of New Orleans........	To 2-Brig. 2-Div. 13-Corps........	Oct., 1863
9th Conn. Infy.........Aug., 1863	From 2-Brig. 2-Div. 19-Corps......	To 1-Brig. 4-Div. 19-Corps........	Feb., 1864
97th Illinois Infy.......Dec., 1863	From 2-Brig. 4-Div. 13-Corps......	To 2-Brig. 4-Div. 13-Corps........	Feb., 1864

3d BRIGADE.—Discontinued Aug. 15, 1863.   COMMANDERS.

H. W. Birge............	Col. 13th Conn. Infy..............	Jan. 3, 1863, to July 10, 1863.	
E. L. Molineaux........	Col. 159th New York Infy.......	July 10, 1863, to Aug. 15, 1863.	

13th Conn. Infy........Jan., 1863	From Grover's Div. Gulf...........	To 1-Brig. 4-Div. 19-Corps........	Aug., 1863
25th Conn. Infy........Jan., 1863	From Grover's Div. Gulf...........	No change to Muster Out.........	Aug., 1863
26th Maine Infy........Jan., 1863	From Grover's Div. Gulf...........	No change to Muster Out.........	Aug., 1863
159th New York Infy....Jan., 1863	From Grover's Div. Gulf...........	To 1-Brig. 4-Div. 19-Corps........	Aug., 1863
ARTILLERY.—			
2d Mass. Batty.........Jan., 1863	From Grover's Div. Gulf...........	To Arty. Res. 19-Corps........	Aug., 1863
Batty. L, 1st U. S. Arty..Jan., 1863	From Grover's Div. Gulf...........	To Arty. Res. 19-Corps........	Aug., 1863
Batty. C, 2d U. S. Arty..Jan., 1863	From Grover's Div. Gulf...........	To Dist. Baton Rouge........	Nov., 1863
13th Mass. Batty.......June, 1863	From Def. New Orleans...........	To Def. New Orleans............	Aug., 1863
25th New York Batty....Aug., 1863	From Arty. Res. 19-Corps.......	To Arty. Res. 19-Corps........	Dec., 1863
26th New York Batty....Aug., 1863	From Arty. Res. 19-Corps.......	To Dist. La Fourche, La.........	Oct., 1863

DISTRICT KEY WEST AND TORTUGAS.—By transfer from Dept. South March, 1863.

COMMANDERS.

D. P. Woodbury........	Brigadier General................	Mch. 16, 1863, to Sept. 13, 1864.	
Chas. Hamilton.........	Col. 110th N. Y. Infy.............	Sept. 13, 1864, to Oct. 15, 1864.	
John Newton...........	Brigadier General................	Oct. 15, 1864, to July, 1865.	

90th New York Infy......Mch., 1863	From Key West, Fla. Dept. South..	To 1-Brig. 4-Div. 19-Corps........	Apr., 1863
47th Penna. Infy.........Mch., 1863	From Key West, Fla. Dept. South..	To 2-Brig. 1-Div. 19-Corps........	Feb., 1864
110th New York Infy.....Feb., 1864	From 1-Brig. 3-Div. 19-Corps......	No change to Muster Out.........	Aug., 1865
2d U. S. C. T............Mch., 864	From Def. New Orleans............	No change to Muster Out.........	Jan., 1866
2d Florida Cav..........July, 1864	From New Organization...........	No change to Muster Out.........	Nov., 1865
99th U. S. C. T..........Feb., 1865	From 2-Brig. 1-Div. U. S. C. T. Gulf.	No change to Muster Out.........	Apr., 1866

DISTRICT OF PORT HUDSON.—Organized July, 1863. Consolidated with District of Baton Rouge, La., Sept. 12, 1864, as District of Baton Rouge and Port Hudson, and designated Northern District of Louisiana Feb. 9, 1865.

COMMANDERS OF DISTRICT.

Geo. L. Andrews........	Brigadier General................	July 9, 1863, to Apr. 23, 1864.	
Daniel Ullman.........	Brigadier General................	Apr. 23, 1864, to June 9, 1864.	
John McNeil...........	Brigadier General................	June 9, 1864, to Aug. 6, 1864.	
F. J. Herron...........	Major General....................	Aug. 6, 1864, to Oct. 3, 1864.	
W. P. Benton...........	Brigadier General................	Oct. 3, 1864, to Dec. 26, 1864.	
Geo. L. Andrews........	Brigadier General................	Dec. 26, 1864, to Feb. 9, 1865.	
F. J. Herron...........	Major General....................	Feb. 9, 1865, to July, 1865.	

POST OF PORT HUDSON.—   COMMANDERS.

Geo. L. Andrews........	Brigadier General................	July 9, 1863, to Apr. 23, 1864.	
Daniel Ullman.........	Brigadier General................	Apr. 23, 1864, to June 9, 1864.	
John McNeil...........	Brigadier General................	June 9, 1864, to Aug. 6, 1864.	
Geo. L. Andrews........	Brigadier General................	Aug. 6, 1864, to Dec. 26, 1864.	
W. A. Pile.............	Brigadier General................	Dec. 26, 1864, to Feb. 13, 1865.	
Cyrus Hamlin..........	Brigadier General................	Feb. 13, 1865, to July, 1865.	

POST FORCES.—

1st Corps de Afrique (73d U. S. C. T.)............July, 1863	From Def. New Orleans............	To 1-Brig. 1-Div. Corps de Afrique.	Sept., 1863
3d Corps de Afrique (75th U. S. C. T.)............July, 1863	From Unatt. 1-Div. 19-Corps.......	To 1-Brig. 1-Div. Corps de Afrique.	Sept., 1863
6th Michigan Heavy Arty.July, 1863	From 1-Brig. 2-Div. 19-Corps......	To Bailey's Engineer Brig.........	June, 1864
21st New York Batty....July, 1863	From Arty. 1-Div. 19-Corps......	To Arty. Res. 19-Corps.........	July, 1864
Batty. G, 5th U. S. Arty..July, 1863	From Arty. 1-Div. 19-Corps......	To Def. New Orleans.............	Dec., 1863
2d Vermont Batty.......July, 1863	From Arty. 3-Div. 19-Corps......	To Arty. 2-Div. Corps de Afrique..	Sept., 1863
3d Mass. Cav..........July, 1863	From Cav. Brig. Gulf.............	To Unatt. Cav. Div. Gulf.........	Sept., 1863
12th Mass. Batty.......Oct., 1863	From Def. New Orleans..........	To Arty. 1-Div. Corps de Afrique..	Sept., 1863
80th U. S. C. T.........Mch., 1864	From 2-Brig. 1-Div. Corps de Afrique	To 2-Brig. 1-Div. U. S. C. T. Gulf.	June, 1864
12th Mass. Batty.......Mch., 1864	From Arty. 1-Div. Corps de Afrique	No change to Muster Out.........	July, 1865
2d Vermont Batty.......Mch., 1864	From Arty. 2-Div. Corps de Afrique	No change to Muster Out.........	July, 1865
35th Wisconsin Infy.....Apr., 1864	From New Organization...........	To 1-Brig. 3-Div. 19-Corps........	June, 1864
76th U. S. C. T.........July,1864	From 2-Brig. 2-Div. U. S. C. T. Gulf	To 2-Brig. 2-Div. U. S. C. T. Gulf.	Oct., 1864
78th U. S. C. T.........July, 1864	From 2-Brig. 2-Div. U. S. C. T. Gulf	To 2-Brig. 2-Div. U. S. C. T. Gulf.	Oct., 1864
81st U. S. C. T.........July, 1864	From 2-Brig. 2-Div. U. S. C. T. Gulf	To Eng. Brig. Gulf.............	July, 1864
2d La. Mtd. Infy.......Aug., 1864	From 1-Brig. Cav. Div. Gulf.......	To Dist Baton Rouge, La.........	Sept., 1864
4th U. S. C. Cav........Aug., 1864	From Def. New Orleans..........	To 1-Brig. 2-Div. U. S. C. T. Gulf.	Oct., 1864
62d U. S. C. T..........Sept., 1864	From 2-Brig. 1-Div. U. S. C. T. Gulf	To Brazos Santiago, Texas........	Sept., 1864
4th U. S. C. Cav........Dec., 1864	From 1-Brig. 2-Div. U. S. C. T. Gulf	To Dept. Miss................	July, 1865
81st U. S. C. T.........Feb., 1865	From 2-Brig. 2-Div. U. S. C. T. Gulf	To Dept. Gulf................	July, 1865
55th U. S. C. T.........Apr., 1865	From 1st Col'd Brig. Dist. W. Tenn.	To Dept. Gulf................	July, 1865

ULLMAN'S BRIGADE, CORPS DE AFRIQUE.—

6th Regt. 78th U. S. C. T.	July, 1863	From New Organization............	To 2-Brig. 2-Div. Corps de Afrique.	Sept., 1863
7th Regt. 79th U. S. C. T.	July, 1863	From New Organization............	To 2-Brig. 1-Div. Corps de Afrique.	Sept., 1863
8th Regt. 80th U. S. C. T.	July, 1863	From New Organization............	To 2-Brig. 1-Div. Corps de Afrique.	Sept., 1863
9th Regt. 81st U. S. C. T.	July, 1863	From New Organization............	To 2-Brig. 1-Div. Corps de Afrique.	Sept., 1863
10th Regt. 82d U. S. C. T.	July, 1863	From New Organization............	To 2-Brig. 1-Div. Corps de Afrique.	Sept., 1863

CORPS DE AFRIQUE.—Organized Sept. 22, 1863. Changed to U. S. C. T. April, 1864.

COMMANDERS.

Daniel Ullman.........	Brigadier General.................	Sept. 22, 1863, to Apr. 23, 1864.
Geo. L. Andrews.......	Brigadier General.................	Apr. 23, 1864, to June 9, 1864.

1st DIVISION.— COMMANDERS.

Daniel Ullman.........	Brigadier General.................	Sept. 22, 1863, to Apr. 23, 1864.
Cyrus Hamlin.........	Col. 80th U. S. C. T........	Apr. 23, 1864, to June 9, 1864.
Chas. W. Drew.......	Col. 76th U. S. C. T........	June 9, 1864, to July, 1864.
Daniel Ullman.........	Brigadier General.................	July, 1864, to Nov. 23, 1864.

1st BRIGADE.— COMMANDERS.

C. J. Bassett...........	Col. 74th U. S. C. T........	Sept. 22, 1863, to Jan., 1864.
W. H. Dickey..........	Col. 84th U. S. C. T........	Jan., 1864, to Aug., 1864.
H. N. Frisbie..........	Col. 92d U. S. C. T........	Aug., 1864, to Oct., 1864.
W. H. Dickey..........	Col. 84th U. S. C. T........	Oct., 1864, to Feb. 13, 1865.
W. A. Pile...........	Brigadier General.................	Feb. 13, 1865, to Apr., 1865.
L. L. Zulavski........	Col. 87th U. S. C. T........	Apr., 1865. to July, 1865.

1st Regt. 73d U. S. C. T.	Sept., 1863	From Unatt. Port Hudson, La.....	To 1-Br. 1-D. U.S.C.T. Morganza, La.	Aug., 1864
2d Regt. 74th U. S. C. T.	Sept., 1863	From Unatt. Port Hudson, La.....	To Def. New Orleans........	Oct., 1863
3d Regt. 75th U. S. C. T.	Sept., 1863	From Unatt. Port Hudson, La.....	To 1-Brig. 1-Div. Morganza, La.....	Aug., 1864
11th Regt. 83d U. S. C. T.	Sept., 1863	From New Organization...........	To Prov'l Brig. Dist. Morganza, La.	June, 1864
(Old.)				
12th Regt. 84th U. S. C. T.	Sept., 1863	From New Organization	To 1-Brig. 1-Div. Morganza, La....	Aug., 1864
22d Regt. 92d U. S. C. T.	Mch., 1864	From 2-Brig. 2-Div. Corps de Afrique	To 1-Brig. 1-Div. Morganza, La....	Aug., 1864
25th U. S. C. T........	Feb., 1865	From 1-Brig. Dist. West Fla......	To West Florida.............	Apr., 1865
82d U. S. C. T........	Feb., 1865	From 1-Brig. Dist. West Fla......	To Dept. Gulf.................	June, 1865
86th U. S. C. T........	Feb., 1865	From 1-Brig. Dist. West Fla......	To Dept. Gulf.................	June, 1865

2d BRIGADE.— COMMANDERS.

Cyrus Hamlin.........	Col. 10th C. de A........	Sept. 22, 1863, to Apr. 23, 1864.
J. F. Appleton........	Col. 81st U. S. C. T........	Apr. 23, 1864, to July, 1864.
A. J. Edgerton........	Col. 65th U. S. C. T........	July, 1864, to Aug., 1864.
Theo. H. Barrett......	Col. 62d U. S. C. T........	Aug., 1864, to Feb., 1865.
H. Scofield...........	Col. 47th U. S. C. T........	Feb., 1865, to June, 1865.

4th Regt. 76th U. S. C. T.	Sept., 1863	From Def. of New Orleans.........	To Post Port Hudson, La..........	July, 1864
7th Regt. 79th U. S. C. T.	Sept., 1863	From Ullman's B. Corps de Afrique.	To 2-Brig. 2-Div. U. S. C. T. Gulf.	June, 1864
8th Regt. 80th U. S. C. T.	Sept., 1863	From Ullman's B. Corps de Afrique.	To Post Port Hudson, La........	Mch., 1864
9th Regt. 81st U. S. C. T.	Sept., 1863	From Ullman's B. Corps de Afrique.	To Post Port Hudson, La........	July, 1864
10th Regt. 82d U. S. C. T.	Sept., 1863	From Ullman's B. Corps de Afrique.	To Pensacola, Fla.............	July, 1864
80th U. S. C. T........	June, 1864	From Post Port Hudson, La.	To Pensacola, Fla.............	July, 1864
78th U. S. C. T........	July, 1864	From 2-Brig. 2-Div. U. S. C. T. Gulf	To Post Port Hudson, La........	July, 1864
62d U. S. C. T. 1st Mo.	Aug., 1864	From Prov'l Brig. Dist. Morganza...	To Post Port Hudson, La........	Sept., 1864
65th U. S. C. T. 2d Mo.	Aug., 1864	From Prov'l Brig. Dist. Morganza..	To Dist. Morganza, La........	Feb., 1865
67th U. S. C. T. 3d Mo.	Aug., 1864	From Prov'l Brig. Dist. Morganza..	To Dist. Morganza, La........	Feb., 1865
99th U. S. C. T........	Oct., 1864	From Eng. Brig. Gulf.	To Dist. Key West, Fla........	Feb., 1865
47th U. S. C. T........	Feb., 1865	From 2-B. 1-Div. U. S. C. T. Vicks..	To Dept. Gulf.................	June, 1865
50th U. S. C. T........	Feb., 1865	From 2-B. 1-Div. U. S. C. T. Vicks..	To Dept. Gulf.................	June, 1865
51st U. S. C. T........	Feb., 1865	From 1-B. 1-Div. U. S. C. T. Vicks..	To Dept. Gulf.................	June, 1865

ARTILLERY.—

12th Mass. Batty.......	Dec., 1863	From Post Port Hudson...........	To Post Port Hudson...........	Mch., 1864

2d DIVISION.—Not of record. COMMANDER.

C. W. Drew............	Col. 76th U. S. C. T........	Oct. 18, 1864.

1st BRIGADE.—Broken up Dec., 1863. Reorganized Oct., 1864. Commanders not of record.

5th Regt. 77th U. S. C. T.	Sept., 1863	From Def. New Orleans, La.......	To Def. New Orleans, La........	Dec., 1863
13th Regt. 85th U. S. C. T.	Sept., 1863	From New Organization...........	To Unatt. 13-Corps Texas.......	Dec., 1863
14th Regt. 86th U. S. C. T.	Sept., 1863	From New Organization...........	To Dist. West Fla.............	Oct., 1863
15th Regt. 99th U. S. C. T.	Sept., 1863	From New Organization...........	To Eng. Brig. Gulf...........	Oct., 1863
16th R. 87st U. S. C. T.	O.Sept., 1863	From New Organization...........	To Unatt. 2-Div. 13-Corps Texas...	Oct., 1863
25th Regt. 93d U. S. C. T.	Dec., 1863	From New Organization...........	To Dist. La Fourche, La.........	Dec., 1863
62d U. S. C. T........	Oct., 1864	From Brazos Santiago, Texas......	To Brazos Santiago, Texas.......	Nov., 1864
76th U. S. C. T........	Oct., 1864	From Post Port Hudson, La.......	To 3-Br. 1-Div. U. S. C. Dist. W. Fla.	Feb., 1865
4th U. S. C. Cav........	Oct., 1864	From Post Port Hudson, La.......	To Dist. Port Hudson, La.......	Nov., 1864

2d BRIGADE.— COMMANDERS.

S. B. Jones...........	Col. 6th C. de A........	Sept. 22, 1863, to Jan., 1864.
L. Goodrich...........	Col. 17th C. de A........	Jan., 1864, to May 25, 1864.
J. C. Clark...........	Col. 79th U. S. C. T........	May 25, 1864, to July 28, 1864.
S. B. Jones...........	Col. 78th U. S. C. T........	Oct. 18, 1864, to Oct. 28, 1864.

6th Regt. 78th U. S. C. T.	Sept., 1863	From Ullman's B. Corps de Afrique.	To Post Port Hudson, La.......	July, 1864
17th Regt. 88th U. S. C. T.	Sept., 1863	From New Organization...........	Broken Up.................	July, 1864
18th Regt. 89th U. S. C. T.	Sept., 1863	From New Organization...........	Broken Up.................	July, 1864
19th Regt. 90th U. S. C. T.	Sept., 1863	From New Organization...........	Broken Up.................	July, 1864
20th Regt. 91st U. S. C. T.	Sept., 1863	From New Organization...........	Consolidated with 74th U. S. C. T.	July, 1864
22d Regt. 92d U. S. C. T.	Feb., 1864	From Dist. La Fourche...........	To 1-Brig. 1-Div. U. S. C. T. Gulf.	Mch., 1864
79th U. S. C. T........	June, 1864	From 2-Brig. 1-Div. U. S. C. T.....	To Def. New Orleans...........	June, 1864
78th U. S. C. T........	Oct., 1864	From Garrison Port Hudson......	To Dist. Morganza, La........	Oct., 1864
81st U. S. C. T........	Oct., 1864	From Eng. Brig. Gulf...........	To Port Hudson, La...........	Feb., 1865

ARTILLERY, 2d DIVISION.—

2d Vermont Batty.......	Sept., 1863	From Garrison Arty. Port Hudson..	To Garrison Arty. Port Hudson, La.	Mch., 1864

3d DIVISION, U. S. C. T.— COMMANDER.

Cyrus Hamlin.........	Brigadier General...............	

1st BRIGADE.— COMMANDER.

J. C. Cobb.............	Col. 96th U. S. C. T................		
25th U. S. C. T.........Oct., 1864	From Dist. West Florida...........	To 1-Brig. U. S. C. T. Dist. W. Fla.	Oct., 1864
82d U. S. C. T.........Oct., 1864	From Dist. West Florida...........	To 1-Brig. U. S. C. T. Dist. W. Fla.	Oct., 1864
86th U. S. C. T.........Oct., 1864	From Dist. West Florida...........	To 1-Brig. U. S. C. T. Dist. W. Fla.	Oct., 1864
96th U. S. C. T.........Oct., 1864	From U. S. Forces Mobile Bay......	To Unatt. U. S. Forces Mobile Bay.	Oct., 1864
97th U. S. C. T.........Oct., 1864	From U. S. Forces Mobile Bay......	To Unatt. U. S. Forces Mobile Bay.	Oct., 1864

2d BRIGADE.— COMMANDER.

Simon Jones...........	Col. 93d U. S. C. T................		
10th U. S. C. H. Arty.....Oct., 1864	From Def. New Orleans...........	To Def. New Orleans...............	Oct., 1864
93d U. S. C. T.........Oct., 1864	From Dist. La Fourche...........	To Dist. La Fourche...............	Oct., 1864
98th U. S. C. T.........Oct., 1864	From Def. New Orleans...........	To Dist. La Fourche...............	Oct., 1864

3d BRIGADE.— COMMANDER.

C. A. Hartwell........	Col. 77th U. S. C. T............		
74th U. S. C. T.........Oct., 1864	From Def. New Orleans...........	To Def. New Orleans...............	Oct., 1864
77th U. S. C. T.........Oct., 1864	From Def. New Orleans...........	To Def. New Orleans...............	Oct., 1864
80th U. S. C. T.........Oct., 1864	From Def. New Orleans...........	To Def. New Orleans...............	Oct., 1864

DISTRICT OF BATON ROUGE.—Organized July, 1863. Consolidated with District of Port Hudson as District of Baton Rouge and Port Hudson Sept. 14, 1864.

COMMANDERS.

P. St. G. Cooke........	Brigadier General...................	Oct. 8, 1863, to May 2, 1864.	
H. W. Birge...........	Brigadier General...................	May 2, 1864, to May 25, 1864.	
W. P. Benton..........	Brigadier General...................	May 25, 1864, to May 31, 1864.	
F. H. Warren..........	Brigadier General...................	May 31, 1864, to June 13, 1864.	
W. P. Benton..........	Brigadier General...................	June 13, 1864, to Dec. 3, 1864.	
Joseph Bailey.........	Brigadier General...................	Dec. 3, 1864, to Dec. 28, 1864.	
Geo. L. Andrews......	Brigadier General...................	Dec. 28, 1864, to Feb. 9, 1865.	
Jos. Bailey...........	Brigadier General...................	Feb. 9, 1865, to Mch. 11, 1865.	
E. J. Davis...........	Col. 1st Texas Cav................	Mch. 11, 1865, to Mch. 18, 1865.	
J. G. Fonda..........	Col. 118th Illinois Infy........	Mch. 18, 1865, to Mch. 23, 1865.	
M. K. Lawler.........	Brigadier General...................	Mch. 23, 1865, to May 30, 1865.	
J. G. Fonda..........	Col. 118th Illinois Infy........	May 30, 1865, to July, 1865.	
1st Indiana Heavy Arty..July, 1863	From Arty. 1-Div. 19-Corps........	To Unatt. Dept. Gulf..............	June, 1864
4th Wisconsin Cav......July, 1863	From Cav. Brig. 19-Corps........	To Unatt. Cav. Div. Gulf..........	Oct., 1863
2d Louisiana Infy......July, 1863	From 1-Brig. 1-Div. 19-Corps......	To Unatt. Cav. Div. Gulf..........	Sept., 1863
18th New York Batty....Dec., 1863	From Defences New Orleans.......	To Siege Arty. Mil. Div. W. Miss...	Feb., 1865
Batty. C, 2d U. S. Arty....Dec., 1863	From Arty. 4-Div. 19-Corps.......	To Arty. 2-Div. 19-Corps..........	Feb., 1864
4th Wisconsin Cav......Jan., 1864	From Unatt. Cav. Div. Gulf........	To 4-Brig. Cav. Div. Gulf..........	June, 1864
13th Wisconsin Batty....Mch., 1864	From New Organization...........	No change to Muster Out...........	July, 1865
19th Kentucky Infy......June, 1864	From 1-Brig. 4-Div. 13-Corps.......	No change to Muster Out...........	Jan., 1865
14th New York Cav......June, 1864	From 1-Brig. Cav. Div. Gulf........	To Sep. Cav. Brig. Baton Rouge, La.	Dec., 1864
2d Illinois Cav........June, 1864	From 4-Brig. Cav. Div. Gulf........	To Def. New Orleans...............	June, 1864
2d Louisiana Infy......Sept., 1864	From Dist. Port Hudson. La.......	To Prov'l Brig. Baton Rouge, La..	Apr., 1865
7th Kentucky Infy......Dec., 1864	From 1-Brig. 3-Div. 19-Corps Gulf..	To Prov'l Brig. Baton Rouge, La..	Apr., 1865
Mercantile Ill. Batty....Feb., 1865	From Cav. Div. Gulf..............	To Def. New Orleans, La...........	May, 1865
14th New York Cav......Feb., 1865	From Dist. West Florida...........	To Dist. Morganza, La.............	Feb., 1865
PLAQUEMINE, LA.—			
7th Kentucky Infy......Nov., 1863	From 3-Brig. 1-Div. 13-Corps.......	To 2-Brig. 1-Div. 13-Corps........	Mch., 1864
22d Kentucky Infy......Nov., 1863	From 3-Brig. 1-Div. 13-Corps.......	To 2-Brig. 1-Div. 13-Corps........	Mch., 1864
42d Ohio Infy.........Nov., 1863	From 3-Brig. 1-Div. 13-Corps.......	To 2-Brig. 1-Div. 13-Corps........	Mch., 1864
120th Ohio Infy........Nov., 1863	From 3-Brig. 1-Div. 13-Corps.......	To 2-Brig. 1-Div. 13-Corps........	Mch., 1864
Batty. E. 2d Ill. Arty....Nov., 1863	From Arty. 3-Div. 13-Corps........	To Def. New Orleans...............	June, 1864
2d Ohio Batty........Nov., 1863	From Arty. 3-Div. 13-Corps........	To Arty. 3-Div. 13-Corps..........	Mch., 1864

CAVALRY BRIGADE.—Organized Feb. 15, 1865. Discontinued May 30, 1865.

COMMANDERS.

E. J. Davis...........	Col. 1st Texas Cav................	Feb. 15, 1865, to Feb. 27, 1865.	
W. P. Moore..........	Lt.-Col........................	Feb. 27, 1865, to Mch. 18, 1865.	
John G. Fonda........	Col. 118th Illinois.............	Mch. 18, 1865, to May 30, 1865.	
118th Ill. Mtd Infy......Feb., 1865	From 1-Brig. Cav. Div. Gulf.......	To Dept. Texas..................	July, 1865
6th Missouri Cav........Feb., 1865	From 1-Brig. Cav. Div. Gulf.......	To Dept. Texas..................	July, 1865
1st Texas Cav..........Feb., 1865	From Cav. Brig. Res. Corps Gulf...	To Dept. Texas..................	July, 1865
4th Wisconsin Cav......Feb., 1865	From 2-Brig. Cav. Div. Gulf.......	To 1-Brig. 1-Cav. Div. W. Miss...	Mch., 1865
1st Wisconsin Batty......Feb., 1865	From Arty. Cav. Div. Gulf.........	No change to Muster Out..........	Mch., 1865
19th Penna. Cav........Mch., 1865	From 2-B. 7-Div. Cav. Corps M.D.M.	To Dept. Texas..................	July, 1865
PROVISIONAL BRIGADE.—			
7th Kentucky Infy......Apr., 1865	From Post Baton Rouge, La........	To Dept. Texas..................	July, 1865
2d Louisiana Infy......Apr., 1865	From Post Baton Rouge, La........	No change to Muster Out..........	Sept., 1865

SEPARATE CAVALRY BRIGADE.— COMMANDER.

Abraham Bassford.......	Col. 14th New York Cav............	Dec. 17, 1864.	
6th Missouri Cav........Dec., 1864	From Dist. Baton Rouge, La........	To Cav. Brig. Dist. Baton Rouge, La.	Feb., 1865
14th New York Cav......Dec., 1864	From 1-Brig. Cav. Div. Res. Corps..	To Dist. Morganza, La.............	Feb., 1865

Thirteenth Army Corps

Joined by transfer from Army Tennessee Aug., 1863. Discontinued June 11, 1864.

COMMANDERS.

C. C. Washburn........	Major General.....................	Aug. 7, 1863, to Sept. 15, 1863.	
E. O. C. Ord..........	Major General.....................	Sept. 15, 1863, to Oct. 19, 1863.	
C. C. Washburn........	Major General.....................	Oct. 19, 1863, to Oct. 25, 1863.	
N. J. T. Dana.........	Major General.....................	Oct. 25, 1863, to Jan. 9, 1864.	
E. O. C. Ord..........	Major General.....................	Jan. 9, 1864, to Feb. 20, 1864.	
J. A. McClermand......	Major General.....................	Feb. 20, 1864, to Mch. 15, 1864.	
T. E. G. Ransom.......	Brigadier General.................	Mch. 15, 1864, to Apr. 8, 1864.	
R. A. Cameron.........	Brigadier General.................	Apr. 8, 1864, to Apr. 27, 1864.	
M. K. Lawler.........	Brigadier General.................	Apr. 27, 1864, to May 9, 1864.	
W. P. Benton.........	Brigadier General.................	**May 9, 1864, to June 11, 1864.**	

1st DIVISION.— COMMANDERS.

W. P. Benton.........	Brigadier General..................	Aug. 7, 1863, to Sept. 15, 1863.
C. C. Washburn.......	Major General.....................	Sept. 15, 1863, to Oct. 19, 1863.
M. K. Lawler.........	Brigadier General..................	Oct. 19, 1863, to Oct. 26, 1863.
C. C. Washburn.......	Major General.....................	Oct. 26, 1863, to Nov. 25, 1863.
W. P. Benton.........	Brigadier General..................	Nov. 25, 1863, to Feb. 8, 1864.
F. H. Warren.........	Brigadier General..................	Feb. 8, 1864, to Mch. 11, 1864.
N. J. T. Dana........	Major General.....................	Mch. 11, 1864 to Apr. 3, 1864.
F. H. Warren.........	Brigadier General..................	Apr. 3, 1864, to May 23, 1864.
M. K. Lawler.........	Brigadier General..................	May 23, 1864, to June 11, 1864.

1st BRIGADE.— COMMANDERS.

D. Shunk.............	Col. 8th Indiana Infy.............	Aug. 7, 1863, to Oct. 12, 1863.
H. D. Washburn.......	Col. 18th Indiana Infy............	Oct. 12, 1863, to Nov. 25, 1863.
D. Shunk.............	Col. 8th Indiana Infy.............	Nov. 25, 1863, to Dec. 12, 1863.
F. H. Warren.........	Brigadier General..................	Dec. 12, 1863, to Jan. 28, 1864.
D. Shunk.............	Col. 8th Indiana Infy.............	Jan. 28, 1864, to Jan. 30, 1864.
F. H. Warren.........	Brigadier General..................	Jan. 30, 1864, to Feb. 8, 1864.
D. Shunk.............	Col. 8th Indiana Infy.............	Feb. 8, 1864, to Mch. 11, 1864.
F. H. Warren.........	Brigadier General..................	Mch. 11, 1864, to Apr. 3, 1864.
H. D. Washburn.......	Col. 18th Indiana Infy............	Apr. 3, 1864, to May 10, 1864.
G. W. K. Bailey......	Col. 99th Illinois Infy...........	May 10, 1864, to June 11, 1864.

8th Indiana Infy......	Aug., 1863	From 1-Brig. 1-Div. 13-Corps Tenn.	To Dist. La Fourche, La...........	June, 1864
18th Indiana Infy.....	Aug., 1863	From 1-Brig. 1-Div. 13-Corps Tenn.	To Dist. La Fourche, La...........	June, 1864
33d Illinois Infy.....	Aug., 1863	From 1-Brig. 1-Div. 13-Corps Tenn.	To Dist. La Fourche, La...........	June, 1864
99th Illinois Infy....	Aug., 1863	From 1-Brig. 1-Div. 13-Corps Tenn.	To Dist. La Fourche, La...........	June, 1864
21st Iowa Infy........	Mch., 1864	From 2-Brig. 1-Div. 13-Corps.......	To Dist. La Fourche, La...........	June, 1864
22d Iowa Infy.........	Mch., 1864	From 2-Brig. 1-Div. 13-Corps.......	To Dist. La Fourche, La...........	June, 1864
23d Iowa Infy.........	Mch., 1864	From 2-Brig. 1-Div. 13-Corps.......	To 1-Brig. 3-Div. 19-Corps Gulf....	June, 1864
11th Wisconsin Infy...	Mch., 1864	From 2-Brig. 1-Div. 13-Corps.......	To Dist. La Fourche, La...........	June, 1864

2d BRIGADE.— COMMANDERS.

W. M. Stone..........	Col. 22d Iowa Infy................	Aug. 7, 1863, to Aug. 15, 1863.
S. L. Glasgow........	Col. 23d Iowa Infy................	Aug. 15, 1863, to Sept. 16, 1863.
C. L. Harris.........	Col. 11th Wisconsin Infy..........	Sept. 16, 1863, to Feb. 11, 1864.
S. Merrill...........	Col. 21st Iowa Infy...............	Feb. 11, 1864, to Mch. 10, 1864.
M. K. Lawler.........	Brigadier General..................	Mch. 10, 1864, to Apr. 27, 1864.
L. A. Sheldon........	Col. 42d Ohio Infy................	Apr. 27, 1864, to May 9, 1864.
M. K. Lawler.........	Brigadier General..................	May 9, 1864, to May 23, 1864.
J. Keigwin...........	Col. 49th Indiana Infy............	May 23, 1864, to June 11, 1864.

21st Iowa Infy........	Aug., 1863	From 2-Brig. 1-Div. 13-Corps Tenn.	To 1-Brig. 1-Div. 13-Corps.........	Mch., 1864
22d Iowa Infy.........	Aug., 1863	From 2-Brig. 1-Div. 13-Corps Tenn.	To 1-Brig. 1-Div. 13-Corps.........	Mch., 1864
23d Iowa Infy.........	Aug., 1863	From 2-Brig. 1-Div. 13-Corps Tenn.	To 1-Brig. 1-Div. 13-Corps.........	Mch., 1864
11th Wisconsin Infy...	Aug., 1863	From 2-Brig. 1-Div. 13-Corps Tenn.	To 1-Brig. 1-Div. 13-Corps.........	Mch., 1864
16th Ohio Infy........	Mch., 1864	From 3-Brig. 1-Div. 13-Corps.......	To 2-Brig. 3-Div. 19-Corps Gulf....	June, 1864
42d Ohio Infy.........	Mch., 1864	From Plaquemine Dist. Baton Rouge	To 1-Brig. 3-Div. 19-Corps Gulf....	June, 1864
114th Ohio Infy.......	Mch., 1864	From 3-Brig. 1-Div. 13-Corps.......	To 2-Brig. 3-Div. 19-Corps Gulf....	June, 1864
120th Ohio Infy.......	Mch., 1864	From Plaquemine Dist. Baton Rouge	To 2-Brig. 3-Div. 19-Corps Gulf....	June, 1864
49th Indiana Infy.....	Mch., 1864	From 3-Brig. 1-Div. 13-Corps.......	To Def. New Orleans...............	June, 1864
34th Iowa Infy........	Mch., 1864	From 2-Brig. 4-Div. 13-Corps.......	To 2-Brig. 4-Div. 13-Corps.......	May, 1864
7th Kentucky Infy.....	Mch., 1864	From Plaquemine Dist. Baton Rouge	To 1-Brig. 3-Div. 19-Corps Gulf....	June, 1864
22d Kentucky Infy.....	Mch., 1864	From Plaquemine Dist. Baton Rouge	To 2-Brig. 3-Div. 19-Corps Gulf....	June, 1864
69th Indiana Infy.....	Mch., 1864	From 1-Brig. 1-Div. 13-Corps.......	To 2-Brig. 3-Div. 19-Corps Gulf....	June, 1864

3d BRIGADE.—Discontinued March 10, 1864. COMMANDERS.

J. Keigwin...........	Col. 49th Indiana Infy............	Aug. 7, 1863, to Aug. 15, 1863.
T. W. Bennett........	Col. 69th Indiana Infy............	Aug. 15, 1863, to Sept. 23, 1863.
M. K. Lawler.........	Brigadier General..................	Sept. 23, 1863, to Oct. 19, 1863.
L. A. Sheldon........	Col. 42d Ohio Infy................	Oct. 19, 1863, to Oct. 26, 1863.
M. K. Lawler.........	Brigadier General..................	Oct. 26, 1863, to Dec. 23, 1863.
J. Keigwin...........	Col. 49th Indiana Infy............	Dec. 23, 1863, to Feb. 28, 1864.
M. K. Lawler.........	Brigadier General..................	Feb. 28, 1864, to Mch. 10, 1864.

49th Indiana Infy......	Aug., 1863	From 3-Brig. 1-Div. 13-Corps Tenn.	To 2-Brig. 1-Div. 13-Corps.........	Mch., 1864
69th Indiana Infy......	Aug., 1863	From 3-Brig. 1-Div. 13-Corps Tenn.	To 2-Brig. 1-Div. 13-Corps.........	Mch., 1864
120th Ohio Infy.......	Aug., 1863	From 3-Brig. 1-Div. 13-Corps Tenn.	To Plaquemine, Dist. Baton Rouge.	Nov., 1863
118th Illinois Infy....	Aug., 1863	From 3-Brig. 1-Div. 13-Corps Tenn.	To 1-Brig. Cav. Div. Gulf.........	Sept., 1863
7th Kentucky Infy.....	Aug., 1863	From 3-Brig. 1-Div. 13-Corps Tenn.	To Plaquemine, Dist. Baton Rouge.	Nov., 1863
16th Ohio Infy........	Sept., 1863	From 4-Brig. 1-Div. 13-Corps.......	To 2-Brig. 1-Div. 13-Corps.........	Mch., 1864
42d Ohio Infy.........	Sept., 1863	From 4-Brig. 1-Div. 13-Corps.......	To Plaquemine, Dist. Baton Rouge.	Nov., 1863
114th Ohio Infy.......	Sept., 1863	From 4-Brig. 1-Div. 13-Corps.......	To 2-Brig. 1-Div. 13-Corps.........	Mch., 1864
22d Kentucky Infy.....	Sept., 1863	From 4-Brig. 1-Div. 13-Corps.......	To Plaquemine, Dist. Baton Rouge.	Nov., 1863
54th Indiana Infy.....	Sept., 1863	From 4-Brig. 1-Div. 13-Corps.......	No change to Muster Out..........	Dec., 1863

4th BRIGADE.—Discontinued Sept. 23, 1863. COMMANDER.

D. W. Lindsey........	Col. 22d Kentucky Infy............	

16th Ohio Infy........	Aug., 1863	From 4-Brig. 1-Div. 13-Corps Tenn..	To 3-Brig. 1-Div. 13-Corps.........	Sept., 1863
42d Ohio Infy.........	Aug., 1863	From 4-Brig. 1-Div. 13-Corps Tenn..	To 3-Brig. 1-Div. 13-Corps.........	Sept., 1863
114th Ohio Infy.......	Aug., 1863	From 4-Brig. 1-Div. 13-Corps Tenn..	To 3-Brig. 1-Div. 13-Corps.........	Sept., 1863
22d Kentucky Infy.....	Aug., 1863	From 4-Brig. 1-Div. 13-Corps Tenn..	To 3-Brig. 1-Div. 13-Corps.........	Sept., 1863
54th Indiana Infy.....	Aug., 1863	From 4-Brig. 1-Div. 13-Corps Tenn..	To 3-Brig. 1-Div. 13-Corps.........	Sept., 1863
ARTILLERY.—				
Batty. G, 1st Mich. Arty.	Aug. 1863	From Arty. 1-Div. 13-Corps Tenn.	To Def. New Orleans A. Res. Gulf.	June, 1864
1st Wis. Batty.......	Aug., 1863	From Arty. 1-Div. 13-Corps Tenn.	To Dist. Morganza, La...........	June, 1864
Batty. A, 2d Illinois Arty.	Aug., 1863	From Arty. 1-Div. 13-Corps Tenn.	To Def. New Orleans.............	June, 1864
1st Indiana Batty....	Aug., 1863	From Arty. 1-Div. 13-Corps Tenn.	To Arty. 4-Div. 13-Corps.........	Mch., 1864
16th Ohio Batty......	Jan., 1864	From Arty. 3-Div. 13-Corps.........	To Def. New Orleans, La..........	June, 1864
Mercantile Ill. Batty.	Mch., 1864	From Arty. 4-Div. 13-Corps.........	To Def. New Orleans, La..........	June, 1864

2d DIVISION.— COMMANDERS.

F. J. Herron.........	Major General.....................	Aug. 7, 1863, to Sept. 28, 1863.
N. J. T. Dana........	Major General.....................	Sept. 28, 1863, to Jan. 3, 1864.
F. J. Herron.........	Major General.....................	Jan. 3, 1864, to June 11, 1864.

1st BRIGADE.— COMMANDERS.

Wm. Vandever	Brigadier General	Aug. 7, 1863, to Aug. 25, 1863.
Wm. McE. Dye	Col. 20th Iowa Infy	Aug. 25, 1863, to Oct. 6, 1863.
Wm. Vandever	Brigadier General	Oct. 6, 1863, to Nov. 11, 1863.
J. C. Black	Col. 37th Illinois Infy	Nov. 11, 1863, to Feb. 11, 1864.
J. O. Hudnutt	Lt.-Col. 38th Iowa Infy	Feb. 11, 1864, to Apr. 8, 1864.
Wm. McE. Dye	Col. 20th Iowa Infy	Apr. 8, 1864, to June 11, 1864.

26th Indiana Infy	Aug., 1863	From 1-Brig. 2-Div. 13-Corps Tenn.	To Donaldsonville D.La Fourche, La.	June, 1864
20th Iowa Infy	Aug., 1863	From 1-Brig. 2-Div. 13-Corps Tenn.	To 2-Brig. 2-Div. 13-Corps	Oct., 1863
34th Iowa Infy	Aug., 1863	From 1-Brig. 2-Div. 13-Corps Tenn.	To 3-Brig. 2-Div. 13-Corps	Dec., 1863
38th Iowa Infy	Aug., 1863	From 1-Brig. 2-Div. 13-Corps Tenn.	To 1-Brig. U. S. Forces Texas	June, 1864
37th Illinois Infy	Aug., 1863	From 1-Brig. 2-Div. 13-Corps Tenn.	To 1-Brig. 3-Div. 19-Corps Gulf	June, 1864
91st Illinois Infy	Oct., 1863	From 2-Brig. 2-Div. 13-Corps.	To 1-Brig. U. S. Forces Texas	June, 1864

2d BRIGADE.— COMMANDERS.

W. W. Orme	Brigadier General	Aug. 7, 1863, to Aug. 25, 1863.
H. M. Day	Col. 91st Illinois Infy	Aug. 25, 1863, to Oct. 6, 1863.
Wm. McE. Dye	Col. 20th Iowa Infy	Oct. 6, 1863, to Jan. 10, 1864.
H. Bertram	Col. 20th Wisconsin Infy	Jan. 10, 1864, to Mch. 12, 1864.
J. McNulta	Col. 94th Illinois Infy	Mch. 12, 1864, to Apr. 17, 1864.
W. P. Benton	Brigadier General	Apr. 17, 1864, to May 9, 1864.
J. McNulta	Col. 94th Illinois Infy	May 9, 1864, to June 11, 1864.

91st Illinois Infy	Aug., 1863	From 2-Brig. 2-Div. 13-Corps Tenn.	To 1-Brig. 2-Div. 13-Corps	Oct., 1863
94th Illinois Infy	Aug., 1863	From 2-Brig. 2-Div. 13-Corps Tenn.	To 2-Brig. U. S. Forces Texas	June, 1864
19th Iowa Infy	Aug., 1863	From 2-Brig. 2-Div. 13-Corps Tenn.	To 2-Brig. U. S. Forces Texas	June, 1864
20th Wisconsin Infy	Aug., 1863	From 2-Brig. 2-Div. 13-Corps Tenn.	To 2-Brig. U. S. Forces Texas	June, 1864
20th Iowa Infy	Oct., 1863	From 1-Brig. 2-Div. 13-Corps.	To 2-Brig. 4-Div. 13-Corps	Jan., 1864
13th Maine Infy	Oct., 1863	From 2-Brig. 4-Div. 19-Corps.	To 3-Brig. 4-Div. 13-Corps	Dec., 1863
20th Iowa Infy	Feb., 1864	From 2-Brig. 4-Div. 13-Corps	To 1-Brig. U. S. Forces Texas	June, 1864

3d BRIGADE.—Organized Dec. 3, 1863. Discontinued Jan. 4, 1864.

COMMANDER.

T. E. G. Ransom	Brigadier General	

34th Iowa Infy	Dec., 1863	From 1-Brig. 2-Div. 13-Corps.	To 2-Brig. 4-Div. 13-Corps	Jan., 1864
13th Maine Infy	Dec., 1863	From 1-Brig. 2-Div. 13-Corps.	To 2-Brig. 4-Div. 13-Corps	Jan., 1864
15th Maine Infy	Dec., 1863	From 1-Brig. 2-Div. 13-Corps.	To 2-Brig. 4-Div. 13-Corps	Jan., 1864

ARTILLERY.—

Batty. B, 1st Mo. Arty	Aug., 1863	From Arty. 2-Div. 13-Corps Tenn.	To Arty. U. S. Forces Texas	June, 1864
Batty. E, 1st Mo. Arty	Aug., 1863	From Arty. 2-Div. 13-Corps Tenn.	No change to Muster Out	June, 1864
Batty. F, 1st Mo. Arty	Aug., 1863	From Arty. 2-Div. 13-Corps Tenn.	To Arty. 4-Div. 13-Corps	Feb., 1864

PROVISIONAL BRIGADE.— COMMANDER.

J. C. Cobb	Col. 96th U. S. C. T.	

96th U. S. C. T.	Mch., 1864	From Unatt. 13-Corps.	To Eng. Brig. Gulf	June, 1864
97th U. S. C. T.	Mch., 1864	From Unatt. 13-Corps.	To Eng. Brig. Gulf	June, 1864
13th Corps de Afrique	Mch., 1864	From Unatt. 13-Corps.	Broken Up	May, 1864
14th R. I. H. Arty. 1st B'n.	Mch., 1864	From Unatt. 13-Corps.	To Def. New Orleans, La.	May, 1864

UNATTACHED 2d DIVISION.—

15th Maine Infy	Oct., 1863	From 2-Brig. 4-Div. 19-Corps	To 3-Brig. 2-Div. 13-Corps	Dec., 1863
1st C. de Afrique Eng'rs. (95th U. S. C. T.)	Oct., 1863	From Eng. Brig. 19-Corps.	To Colored Brig. U. S. Forces Tex.	June, 1864
16th Corps de Afrique (87th U. S. C. T.)	Oct., 1863	From 1-Brig. 2-Div. Corps de Afrique	To Colored Brig. U. S. Forces Tex.	June, 1864
1st Texas Cav.	Oct., 1863	From Unatt. Cav. Div. Gulf.	To Cav. Brig. U. S. Forces Texas	June, 1864

3d DIVISION.— COMMANDERS.

A. L. Lee	Brigadier General	Aug. 7, 1863, to Sept. 13, 1863.
G. F. McGinnis	Brigadier General	Sept. 13, 1863, to Mch. 3, 1864.
R. A. Cameron	Brigadier General	Mch. 3, 1864, to Apr. 8, 1864.
W. H. Raynor	Col. 56th Ohio Infy	Apr. 8, 1864.
T. H. Brighurst	Col. 46th Indiana Infy	Apr. 9, 1864, to Apr. 27, 1864.
R. A. Cameron	Brigadier General	Apr. 27, 1864, to May 24, 1864.
G. F. McGinnis	Brigadier General	May 24, 1864, to June 11, 1864.

1st BRIGADE.— COMMANDERS.

G. F. McGinnis	Brigadier General	Aug. 7, 1863, to Sept. 13, 1863.
W. F. Spicely	Col. 24th Indiana Infy	Sept. 13, 1863, to Oct. 8, 1863.
R. A. Cameron	Brigadier General	Oct. 8, 1863, to Dec. 6, 1863.
D. Macauley	Col. 11th Indiana Infy	Dec. 6, 1863, to Feb. 5, 1864.
R. A. Cameron	Brigadier General	Feb. 5, 1864, to Mch. 3, 1864.
A. M. Flory	Lt.-Col. 46th Indiana Infy	Mch. 3, 1864, to Apr. 8, 1864.
B. Hancock	Major	Apr. 8, 1864, to Apr. 27, 1864.
T. H. Bringhurst	Col. 46th Indiana Infy	Apr. 27, 1864, to May 24, 1864.
R. A. Cameron	Brigadier General	May 24, 1864, to June 11, 1864.

11th Indiana Infy	Aug., 1863	From 1-Brig. 3-Div. 13-Corps Tenn.	To Dist. La Fourche, La.	June, 1864
24th Indiana Infy	Aug., 1863	From 1-Brig. 3-Div. 13-Corps Tenn.	To Unatt. Def. New Orleans	June, 1864
34th Indiana Infy	Aug., 1863	From 1-Brig. 3-Div. 13-Corps Tenn.	To Unatt. Def. New Orleans	June, 1864
46th Indiana Infy	Aug., 1863	From 1-Brig. 3-Div. 13-Corps Tenn.	To Dist. Ky. Dept. Ohio.	June, 1864
29th Wisconsin Infy	Aug., 1863	From 1-Brig. 3-Div. 13-Corps Tenn.	To Dist. La Fourche, La.	June, 1864

2d BRIGADE.— COMMANDERS.

J. R. Slack	Col. 47th Indiana Infy	Aug. 7, 1863, to Nov. 21, 1863.
W. H. Rayror	Col. 56th Ohio Infy	Nov. 21, 1863, to Apr. 8, 1864.
J. R. Slack	Col. 47th Indiana Infy	Apr. 8, 1864, to June 11, 1864.

56th Ohio Infy	Aug., 1863	From 2-Brig. 3-Div. 13-Corps Tenn.	To Def. New Orleans	June, 1864
47th Indiana Infy	Aug., 1863	From 2-Brig. 3-Div. 13-Corps Tenn.	To Dist. La Fourche	June, 1864
87th Illinois Infy	Aug., 1863	From 2-Brig. 3-Div. 13-Corps Tenn.	To Unatt. Cav. Div. Gulf.	Sept., 1863
24th Iowa Infy	Aug., 1863	From 2-Brig. 3-Div. 13-Corps Tenn.	To Dist. La Fourche, La.	June, 1864
28th Iowa Infy	Aug., 1863	From 2-Brig. 3-Div. 13-Corps Tenn.	To Dist. La Fourche, La.	June, 1864
83d Ohio Infy	Jan., 1864	From 1-Brig. 4-Div. 13-Cors.	To 2-Brig. 4-Div. 13-Corps	Mch., 1864

ARTILLERY.—

2d Ohio Batty	Aug., 1863	From Arty. 3-Div. 13-Corps Tenn.	To Plaquemine Dist. Baton Rouge	Nov., 1863
16th Ohio Batty	Aug., 1863	From Arty. 3-Div. 13-Corps Tenn.	To Arty. 1-Div. 13-Corps.	Jan., 1864
Batty. E, 2d Ill. Arty	Aug., 1863	From Arty. 3-Div. 13-Corps Tenn.	To Plaquemine Dist. Baton Rouge.	Nov., 1863
Batty. A, 1st Mo. Arty	Aug., 1863	From Arty. 3-Div. 13-Corps Tenn.	To Def. New Orleans, La.	June, 1864
2nd Ohio Batty	Mch., 1864	From Plaquemine Dist. Baton Rouge	To Def. New Orleans, La.	June, 1864

4th DIVISION.—From old 10th Division, 13th Army Corps, Tenn., Aug. 17, 1863.

COMMANDERS.

M. K. Lawler	Brigadier General	Aug. 17, 1863, to Sept. 20, 1863.
S. G. Burbridge	Brigadier General	Sept. 20, 1863, to Dec. 5, 1863.
W. J. Landran	Col. 19th Ky. Infy	Dec. 5, 1863, to Jan. 4, 1864.
T. E. G. Ransom	Brigadier General	Jan. 4, 1864, to Mch. 15, 1864.
W. J. Landran	Col. 19th Ky. Infy	Mch. 15, 1864, to May 29, 1864.
F. W. Moore	Col. 83d Ohio Infy	May 29, 1864, to June 11, 1864.

1st BRIGADE.— COMMANDERS.

S. G. Burbridge	Brigadier General	Aug. 17, 1863, to Sept. 20, 1863.
T. J. Lucas	Col. 16th Indiana Infy	Sept. 20, 1863, to Oct. 7, 1863.
R. Owen	Col. 60th Indiana Infy	Oct. 7, 1863, to Nov. 21, 1863.
W. J. Landran	Col. 19th Ky. Infy	Nov. 21, 1863, to Dec. 5, 1863.
J. Cowan	Lt.-Col. 19th Ky. Infy	Dec. 5, 1863, to Jan. 9, 1864.
W. J. Landran	Col. 19th Ky. Infy	Jan. 9, 1864, to Mch. 15, 1864.
J. Cowan	Lt.-Col. 19th Ky. Infy	Mch. 15, 1864, to Mch. 27, 1864.
F. Emerson	Col. 67th Indiana Infy	Mch. 27, 1864, to Apr. 8, 1864.
F. A. Sears	Major 67th Ind. Infy	Apr. 8, 1864, to Apr. 28, 1864.
F. W. Moore	Col. 83d Ohio Infy	Apr. 28, 1864, to May 30, 1864.
D. P. Greer	Col. 77th Ill. Infy	May 30, 1864, to June 11, 1864.

16th Indiana Infy	Aug., 1863	From 1-Brig. 10-Div. 13-Corps Tenn.	To Unatt. Cav. Div. Gulf	Sept., 1863
60th Indiana Infy	Aug., 1863	From 1-Brig. 10-Div. 13-Corps Tenn.	To Dist. La Fourche, La.	June, 1864
67th Indiana Infy	Aug., 1863	From 1-Brig. 10-Div. 13-Corps Tenn.	To 3-Brig. 3-Div. 19-Corps	June, 1864
83d Ohio Infy	Aug., 1863	From 1-Brig. 10-Div. 13-Corps Tenn.	To 2-Brig. 3-Div. 13-Corps	Jan., 1864
96th Ohio Infy	Aug., 1863	From 1-Brig. 10-Div. 13-Corps Tenn.	To Def. of New Orleans, La.	June, 1864
23d Wisconsin Infy	Aug., 1863	From 1-Brig. 10-Div. 13-Corps Tenn.	To Def. of New Orleans, La.	June, 1864
19th Kentucky Infy	Nov., 1863	From 2-Brig. 4-Div. 13-Corps	To Def. of New Orleans, La.	June, 1864
77th Illinois Infy	Jan., 1864	From 2-Brig. 4-Div. 13-Corps	To Def. of New Orleans, La.	June, 1864

2d BRIGADE.— COMMANDERS.

W. J. Landran	Col. 19th Ky. Infy	Aug. 17, 1863, to Aug. 24, 1863.
J. Cowan	Lt.-Col. 19th Ky Infy	Aug. 24, 1863, to Oct. 6, 1863.
W. J. Landran	Col. 19th Ky. Infy	Oct. 6, 1863, to Nov. 21, 1863.
D. P. Greer	Col. 77th Ill. Infy	Nov. 21, 1863, to Dec. 5, 1863.
M. V. Hotchkiss	Major 77th Ill. Infy	Dec. 5, 1863, to Jan. 27, 1864.
H. Rust, Jr.	Col. 13th Maine Infy	Jan. 27, 1864, to Mch. 14, 1864.
J. W. Vance	Col. 96th Ohio Infy	Mch. 14, 1864, to Apr. 9, 1864.
A. H. Brown	Lt.-Col. 96th Ohio Infy	Apr. 9, 1864, to Apr. 19, 1864.
J. R. Parker	Col. 46th Ohio Infy	Apr. 19, 1864, to May 11, 1864.
G. W. Clark	Col. 34th Iowa Infy	May 11, 1864, to June 11, 1864.

48th Ohio Infy	Aug., 1863	From 2-Brig. 10-Div. 13-Corps Tenn.	To Capture	Apr., 1864
19th Kentucky Infy	Aug., 1863	From 2-Brig. 10-Div. 13-Corps Tenn.	To 1-Brig. 4-Div. 13-Corps	Nov., 1863
77th Illinois Infy	Aug., 1863	From 2-Brig. 10-Div. 13-Corps Tenn.	To 1-Brig. 4-Div. 13-Corps	Feb., 1864
97th Illinois Infy	Aug., 1863	From 2-Brig. 10-Div. 13-Corps Tenn.	To 2-Brig. 4-Div. 19-Corps	Dec., 1863
130th Illinois Infy	Aug., 1863	From 2-Brig. 10-Div. 13-Corps Tenn.	To Def. of New Orleans, La.	June, 1864
34th Iowa Infy	Jan., 1864	From 3-Brig. 2-Div. 13-Corps	To 2-Brig. 1-Div. 13-Corps	Mch., 1864
13th Maine Infy	Jan., 1864	From 3-Brig. 2-Div. 13-Corps	To 2-Brig. 1-Div. 19-Corps	June, 1864
15th Maine Infy	Jan., 1864	From 3-Brig. 2-Div. 13-Corps	To 2-Brig. 1-Div. 19-Corps	June, 1864
20th Iowa Infy	Jan., 1864	From 2-Brig. 2-Div. 13-Corps	To 2-Brig. 2-Div. 13-Corps	Feb., 1864
1st U. S. Infy	Feb., 1864	From Def. New Orleans	To Def. New Orleans, La.	June, 1864
97th Illinois Infy	Feb., 1864	From 2-Brig. 4-Div. 19-Corps	To Def. New Orleans, La.	June, 1864
34th Iowa Infy	May, 1864	From 2-Brig. 1-Div. 13-Corps	To Def. New Orleans, La.	June, 1864

ARTILLERY.—

17th Ohio Batty	Aug., 1863	From Arty. 10-Div. 13-Corps Tenn.	To Def. New Orleans, La.	June, 1864
Mercantile Ill. Batty	Aug., 1863	From Arty. 10-Div. 13-Corps Tenn.	To Arty. 1-Div. 13-Corps	Mch., 1864
Batty. F, 1st Mo. Arty.	Feb., 1864	From Arty. 2-Div. 13-Corps	To Def. New Orleans, La.	June, 1864
1st Indiana Batty	Mch., 1864	From Arty. 1-Div. 13-Corps	To Def. New Orleans, La.	June, 1864
2d Conn. Batty	Mch., 1864	From Def. New Orleans, La.	To Def. New Orleans, La.	June, 1864

CAVALRY BRIGADE, 13th CORPS.—Organized Aug. 14, 1863. Transferred to Cavalry Division Gulf Sept. 14, 1863.

COMMANDER.

J. J. Mudd	Col. 2d Ill. Cav	

2d Illinois Cav	Aug., 1863	From Cav. 9-Div. 13-Corps Tenn.	To 2-Brig. Cav. Div. Gulf	Sept., 1864
3d Ill. Cav., A, E, G, K, L,	Aug., 1863	From Cav. 9-Div. 13-Corps Tenn.	To 2-Brig. Cav. Div. Gulf	Sept., 1864
15th Illinois Cav., Co. F.	Aug., 1863	From Cav. 13-Corps Tenn.	To 3-Brig. Cav. Div. Gulf	Sept., 1864
1st Indiana Cav., Co. C	Aug., 1863	From Cav. 12-Div. 13-Corps Tenn.	To 3-Brig. Cav. Div. Gulf	Sept., 1864
4th Indiana Cav., Co. C	Aug., 1863	From Cav. 10-Div. 13-Corps Tenn.	To 3-Brig. Cav. Div. Gulf	Sept., 1864
6th Missouri Cav	Aug., 1863	From Headquarters 13-Corps Tenn.	To 3-Brig. Cav. Div. Gulf	Sept., 1864
15th Illinois Cav., Co. I (Co. A, 36th Ill.)	Aug., 1863	From Cav. 13-Corps Tenn.	To 3-Brig. Cav. Div. Gulf	Sept., 1864

UNATTACHED 13TH CORPS.—

Patterson's Ky. Eng. Co.	Aug., 1863	From Unatt. 13-Corps Tenn.	To Unatt. Eng. 13-Corps Texas	Oct., 1863
1st U. S. Infy	Aug., 1863	From 1-Brig. 1-Div. 13-Corps	To Def. New Orleans	Oct., 1863
2d Corps de Afrique Eng. (96th U. S. C. T.)	Oct., 1863	From Eng. Brig. Gulf	To Prov'l Brig. 13-Corps	Mch., 1864
3d Corps de Afrique Eng.	Oct., 1863	From Eng. Brig. Gulf	To Prov'l Brig. 13-Corps	Mch., 1864
14th R. I. H. Arty. 1st Bn.	Oct., 1863	From Def. New Orleans, La.	To Prov'l Brig. 13-Corps	Mch., 1864
2d Texas Cav	Dec., 1863	From New Organization	To Cav. Brig. 13-Corps Texas	Dec., 1863
13th Corps de Afrique	Dec., 1863	From 1-Brig. 2-Div. Corps de Afrique	To Prov'l Brig. 13-Corps Texas	Mch., 1864

CAVALRY BRIGADE.—Organized May, 1863. COMMANDER.

B. H. Grierson	Col. 6th Ill. Cav	May, 1863, to July, 1863.

6th Illinois Cav	May, 1863	From Grierson's Brig. 1-C. D. 16-C.	To 3-B. 1-Cav. Div. 16-Corps Tenn.	July, 1863
7th Illinois Cav	May, 1863	From Grierson's Brig. 1-C. D. 16-C.	To 3-B. 1-Cav. Div. 16-Corps Tenn.	July, 1863
1st Louisiana Cav	May, 1863	From Unatt. 1st Div. 19-Corps	From Def. New Orleans, La.	July, 1863
Mass. Indpt. Btn. Cav.	May, 1863	From Unatt. 1st Div. 19-Corps	Consolidated with 3d Mass. Cav.	June, 1863
14th New York Cav	May, 1863	From Def. New Orleans	To Def. New Orleans	July, 1863
3d Mass. Cav	June, 1863	From 41st Mass. 2-B. 4-Div. 19-Corps	To Def. New Orleans	July, 1863
1st Texas Cav	July, 1863	From Def. New Orleans	To Def. New Orleans	July, 1863
4th Wisconsin Cav	July, 1863	From 2-Brig. 3-Div. 19-Corps	To Dist. Baton Rouge, La.	July, 1863
2d Rhode Island Cav	July, 1863	From Unatt. 1-Div. 19-Corps	Transferred to 2d La. Cav.	Aug., 1863

CAVALRY DIVISION.—Organized Sept. 14, 1863. Discontinued Feb. 9, 1865.

COMMANDERS.

A. L. Lee	Brigadier General	Sept. 14, 1863, to Apr. 18, 1864.
Richard Arnold	Brigadier General	Apr. 18, 1864, to June 25, 1864.
J. P. Sherbourne	Col. 11th New York Cav	June 25, 1864, to Aug. 18, 1864.
A. L. Lee	Brigadier General	Aug. 18, 1864, to Oct. 27, 1864.
O. P. Gooding	Col. 31st Mass. Mtd. Infy	Oct. 27, 1864, to Nov. 11, 1864.
B. S. Roberts	Brigadier General	Nov. 11, 1864, to Dec. 28, 1864.
Joseph Bailey	Brigadier General	Dec. 28, 1864, to Feb. 9, 1865.

1st BRIGADE.—

COMMANDERS.

John G. Fonda	Col. 118th Illinois Mtd. Infy	Sept. 14, 1863, to Nov. 3, 1863.
T. J. Lucas	Col. 16th Indiana Mtd. Infy	Nov. 3, 1863, to Apr. 9, 1864.
J. H. Redfield	Lt.-Col. 16th Ind. Mtd. Infy	Apr. 9, 1864, to May 25, 1864.
Chas. Everett	Col. 2d Louisiana Cav	May 25, 1864, to June 30, 1864.
N. A. M. Dudley	Col. 30th Mass. Infy	June 30, 1864, to July 3, 1864.
John G. Fonda	Col. 118th Ill. Mtd. Infy	July 3, 1864, to Sept. 24, 1864.
O. P. Gooding	Col. 31st Mass. Mtd. Infy	Sept. 24, 1864, to Oct. 27, 1864.

118th Ill. Mtd. Infy	Sept., 1863	From 3-Brig. 1-Div. 13-Corps	To 2-Brig. Cav. Div. Gulf — Nov., 1863
14th New York Cav	Sept., 1863	From Def. New Orleans	To 3-Brig. Cav. Div. Gulf — Nov., 1863
1st Louisiana Cav	Sept., 1863	From Def. New Orleans	To 3-Brig. Cav. Div. Gulf — Jan., 1864
6th Mo. Cav., 6 Cos	Sept., 1863	From Cav. Brig. 13-Corps	To 3-Brig. Cav. Div. Gulf — Nov., 1863
87th Illinois Mtd. Infy	Nov., 1863	From Unatt. Cav. Div. Gulf	To 3-Brig. Cav. Div. Gulf — Jan., 1864
16th Indiana Mtd. Infy	Nov., 1863	From Unatt. Cav. Div. Gulf	To 4-Brig. Cav. Div. Gulf — Aug., 1864
75th New York Mtd. Infy	Dec., 1863	From Unatt. Cav. Div. Gulf	To 1-Brig. 2-Div. 19-Corps — June, 1864
4th Ind. Cav., Co. C	Jan., 1864	From 3-Brig. Cav. Div. Gulf	To Unatt. Cav. Div. Gulf — June, 1864
2d La. Mtd. Infy	Jan., 1864	From 3-Brig. Cav. Div. Gulf	To Dist. Port Hudson — Aug., 1864
6th Mo. Cav	Jan., 1864	From 3-Brig. Cav. Div. Gulf	To Sep. Cav. Brig. Baton Rouge — Dec., 1864
14th N. Y. Cav	Jan., 1864	From 3-Brig. Cav. Div. Gulf	To Dist. Baton Rouge, La — July, 1864
12th Ill. Cav	Apr., 1864	From St. Louis, Mo	To Dist. La Fourche, La — July, 1864
118th Ill. Mtd. Infy	July, 1864	From 2-Brig. Cav. Div. Gulf	To 2-Brig. Cav. Div. Gulf — Sept., 1864
31st Mass. Mtd. Infy	Sept., 1864	From Def. New Orleans	To Def. New Orleans — Oct., 1864

2d BRIGADE.—

COMMANDERS.

John J. Mudd	Col. 2d Ill. Cav	Sept. 14, 1863, to Nov. 3, 1863.
John G. Fonda	Col. 118th Ill. Mtd. Infy	Nov. 3, 1863, to Aug. 18, 1864.
W. J. Landran	Col. 19th Ky. Infy	Aug. 18, 1864, to Sept. 24, 1864.
John G. Fonda	Col. 118th Ill. Mtd. Infy	Sept. 24, 1864, to Feb. 9, 1865.

2d Ill. Cav., 7 Co's	Sept., 1863	From Cav. Brig. 13-Corps	To 3-Brig. Cav. Div. Gulf — Dec., 1863
3d Ill. Cav., 5 Co's	Sept., 1863	From Cav. Brig. 13-Corps	To 1-Brig. 1-Cav. Div. 16-C. Tenn — Dec., 1863
15th Ill. Cav., Co. F	Sept., 1863	From Cav. Brig. 13-Corps	To 3-Brig. Cav. Div. Gulf — Oct., 1863
15th Ill. Cav., Co. I	Sept., 1863	From Cav. Brig. 13-Corps	To Unatt. Cav. Div. Gulf — Oct., 1863
1st Ind. Cav., Co. C	Sept., 1863	From Cav. Brig. 13-Corps	To 3-Brig. Cav. Div. Gulf — Oct., 1863
4th Ind. Cav., Co. C	Sept., 1863	From Cav. Brig. 13-Corps	To 3-Brig. Cav. Div. Gulf — Oct., 1863
118th Ill. Mtd. Infy	Nov., 1863	From 1-Brig. Cav. Div. Gulf	To 1-Brig. Cav. Div. Gulf — July, 1864
2d Ill. Cav	Aug., 1864	From Unatt. Dist. Baton Rouge, La.	To 3-Brig. Cav. Div. Gulf — Sept., 1864
11th N. Y. Cav	Aug., 1864	From Dist. La Fourche, La.	To 2-Brig. Cav. Div. Dist. W. Tenn. — Feb., 1865
4th Wis. Cav	Aug., 1864	From 4-Brig. Cav. Div. Gulf	To Cav. Brig. Dist. Baton Rouge — Feb., 1865
118th Ill. Mtd. Infy	Sept., 1864	From 1-Brig. Cav. Div. Gulf	To Cav. Brig. Dist. Baton Rouge — Feb., 1865

3d BRIGADE.—

COMMANDERS.

C. J. Paine	Col. 2d La. Mtd. Infy	Nov. 3, 1863, to Jan. 20, 1864.
H. Robinson	Col. 1st La. Cav	Jan. 20, 1864, to Apr. 8, 1864.
John M. Crebs	Lt.-Col. 87th Ill. Mtd. Infy	Apr. 8, 1864, to Aug. 24, 1864.

15th Ill. Cav., Co. F	Oct., 1863	From 2-Brig. Cav. Div. Gulf	To Unatt. Cav. Div. Gulf — Dec., 1863
1st Ind. Cav., Co. C	Oct., 1863	From 2-Brig. Cav. Div. Gulf	To Unatt. Cav. Div. Gulf — Dec., 1863
4th Ind. Cav., Co. C	Oct., 1863	From 2-Brig. Cav. Div. Gulf	To 1-Brig. Cav. Div. Gulf — Jan., 1864
2d La. Mtd. Infy	Oct., 1863	From Unatt. Cav. Div. Gulf	To 1-Brig. Cav. Div. Gulf — Jan., 1864
6th Mo. Cav., 7 Co's	Nov., 1863	From 1-Brig. Cav. Div. Gulf	To 1-Brig. Cav. Div. Gulf — Jan., 1864
14th N. Y. Cav., 6 Co's	Nov., 1863	From 1-Brig. Cav. Div. Gulf	To 1-Brig. Cav. Div. Gulf — Jan., 1864
2d Ill. Cav	Dec., 1863	From 2-Brig. Cav. Div. Gulf	To 4-Brig. Cav. Div. Gulf — Jan., 1864
87th Ill. Mtd. Infy	Jan., 1864	From 1-Brig. Cav. Div. Gulf	To Sep. Cav. Brig. Gulf — Aug., 1864
1st La. Cav	Jan., 1864	From 1-Brig. Cav. Div. Gulf	To Dist. Morganza, La — July, 1864
12th Ill. Cav	Sept., 1864	From 4-Brig. Cav. Div. Gulf	To 2-Brig. Cav. Div. Dist. W. Tenn. — Feb., 1865
2d Ill. Cav	Sept., 1864	From 2-Brig. Cav. Div. Gulf	To Sep. Cav. Brig. Dist. W. Fla. — Feb., 1865

4th BRIGADE.—Organized Dec., 1863. Broken up Sept. 22, 1864.

COMMANDERS.

N. A. M. Dudley	Col. 30th Mass. Infy	Dec., 1863, to Apr. 18, 1864.
E. J. Davis	Col. 1st Texas Cav	Apr. 18, 1864, to Aug. 6, 1864.
M. L. Chrysler	Col. 2d N. Y. Vet. Cav	Aug. 6, 1864, to Sept. 22, 1864.

8th N. H. Mtd. Infy	Dec., 1863	From 2-Brig. 3-Div. 19-Corps	To Def. New Orleans, La — July, 1864
31st Mass. Mtd. Infy	Dec., 1863	From 2-Brig. 1-Div. 19-Corps	To Def. New Orleans, La — July, 1864
2d Ill. Cav	Jan., 1864	From 3-Brig. Cav. Div. Gulf	To Unatt. Baton Rouge, La — June, 1864
3d Mass. Cav	Jan., 1864	From Unatt. Cav. Div. Gulf	To 2-Brig. 2-Div. 19-Corps — June, 1864
4th Wis. Infy	June, 1864	From Dist. Baton Rouge, La.	To 2-Brig. Cav. Div. Gulf — Aug., 1864
2d N. Y. Vet. Cav	June, 1864	From 5-Brig. Cav. Div. Gulf	To Sep. Cav. Brig. Gulf — Sept., 1864
12th Ill. Cav	Aug., 1864	From Dist. La Fourche, La.	To 3-Brig. Cav. Div. Gulf — Sept., 1864
16th Ind. Mtd. Infy	Aug., 1864	From 1-Brig. Cav. Div. Gulf	To Dist. La Fourche, La — Sept., 1864

5th BRIGADE.—

COMMANDER.

O. P. Gooding	Col. 31st Mass. Mtd. Infy

2d N. Y. Vet. Cav	Mch., 1864	From Def. Washington, D. C.	To 4-Brig. Cav. Div. Gulf — June, 1864
18th N. Y. Cav	Mch., 1864	From Def. Washington, D. C.	To Dist. La Fourche, La — June, 1864
3d R. I. Cav	Mch., 1864	From New Orleans, La	To Def. New Orleans — June, 1864
ARTILLERY.—			
2d Mass. Batty	Sept., 1863	From Arty. Res. Gulf	To Unatt. Arty. Gulf — Aug., 1864
Batty. F, 1st U. S. Arty	Nov., 1863	From Arty. 3-Div. 19-Corps	To Arty. 2-Div. 19-Corps — Mch., 1864
Batty. G, 5th U. S. Arty	Feb., 1864	From Def. New Orleans, La.	To Dist. La Fourche, La — June, 1864
Batty. F, 1st U. S. Arty	Apr., 1864	From Arty. 2-Div. 19-Corps	To Def. Washington, D. C. — July, 1864
1st Wis. Batty	Aug., 1864	From Dist. Morganza, La.	To Cav. Brig. Dist. Baton Rouge — Feb., 1865
Mercantile Ill. Batty	Nov., 1864	From Arty. Res. Def. New Orleans.	To Dist. Baton Rouge, La — Feb., 1865

UNATTACHED.—

87th Ill. Infy.	Sept., 1863	From 2-Brig. 3-Div. 13-Corps	To 1-Brig. Cav. Div. Gulf	Nov., 1863
16th Ind. Mtd. Infy.	Sept., 1863	From 1-Brig. 4-Div. 13-Corps	To 1-Brig. Cav. Div. Gulf	Nov., 1863
2d La. Mtd. Infy.	Sept., 1863	From 1-Brig. 1-Div. 13-Corps	To 3-Brig. Cav. Div. Gulf	Nov., 1863
15th Ill. Cav., Co. I	Oct., 1863	From 2-Brig. Cav. Div. Gulf	To Def. New Orleans	Jan., 1864
3d Mass. Cav.	Oct., 1863	From Dist. Port Hudson, La.	To 4-Brig. Cav. Div. Gulf	Jan., 1864
75th N. Y. Mtd. Infy.	Oct., 1863	From 3-Brig. 1-Div. 19-Corps	To 1-Brig. Cav. Div. Gulf	Dec., 1863
1st Texas Cav.	Oct., 1863	From Cav. Brig. 19-Corps	To Unatt. 2-Div. 13-Corps Texas	Oct., 1863
4th Wis. Cav.	Oct., 1863	From Dist. Baton Rouge, La.	To Dist. Baton Rouge, La.	Jan., 1864
15th Ill. Cav., Co. F	Dec., 1863	From 3-Brig. Cav. Div. Gulf	To Def. New Orleans	Jan., 1864
1st Ind. Cav., Co. C	Dec., 1863	From 3-Brig. Cav. Div. Gulf	To Def. New Orleans	Jan., 1864
3d Md. Cav.	Dec., 1863	From New Organization	To Def. New Orleans	Jan., 1864

SEPARATE CAVALRY BRIGADE.—Organized Aug. 24, 1864.

COMMANDERS.

J. M. Crebs	Lt.-Col. 87th Ill. Mtd. Infy	Aug. 24, 1864, to Oct., 1864.	
E. J. Davis	Col. 1st Texas Cav.	Oct., 1864, to Dec., 1864.	

1st Texas Cav.	Aug., 1864	From Dist. Morganza, La.	To 2-Sep. Cav. Brig. Gulf	Nov., 1864
2d Texas Cav.	Aug., 1864	From Dist. Morganza, La.	Consolidated with 1st Texas Cav.	Sept.10, '64
1st La. Cav.	Aug., 1864	From Dist. Morganza, La.	To 2-Sep. Cav. Brig. Gulf	Nov., 1864
2d N. Y. Vet. Cav.	Aug., 1864	From 4-Brig. Cav. Div. Gulf	To Cav. Brig. Res. Corps Gulf	Dec., 1864
87th Ill. Mtd. Infy.	Aug., 1864	From 3-Brig. Cav. Div. Gulf	To Cav. Brig. Res. Corps Gulf	Dec., 1864
2d Mass. Batty.	Aug., 1864	From Unatt. Arty. Gulf	To Cav. Brig. Res. Corps Gulf	Dec., 1864

2d SEPARATE CAVALRY BRIGADE.— **COMMANDER.**

Abraham Bassford	Col. 14th N. Y. Cav.	Nov. 23, 1864, to Dec. 17, 1864.	

1st La. Cav.	Nov., 1863	From 1-Sep. Brig. Gulf	To Sep. Cav. Brig. Res. Corps Gulf	Dec., 1864
1st Texas Cav.	Nov., 1863	From 1-Sep. Brig. Gulf	To Sep. Cav. Brig. Res. Corps Gulf	Dec., 1864

ENGINEER BRIGADE.—

1st Corps de Afr. Engrs. (95th U. S. C. T.)	Aug., 1863	From Unatt. 1-Div. 19-Corps	To Unatt. 2-Div. 13-Corps Texas	Oct., 1863
2d Corps de Afr. Engrs. (96th U. S. C. T.)	Aug., 1863	From New Organization	To Unatt. 13-Corps Texas	Dec., 1863
3d Corps de Afr. Engrs. (97th U. S. C. T.)	Aug., 1863	From New Organization	To Unatt. 13-Corps Texas	Dec., 1863
4th Corps de Afr. Engrs. (98th U. S. C. T.)	Sept., 1863	From New Organization	To Def. New Orleans, La.	July, 1864
15th C. de Afr., 5th Engrs.	Oct., 1863	From 1-Brig. 2-Div. Corps de Afr.	To 2-Brig. 1-Div. U. S. C. T. Gulf	Oct., 1864
81st U. S. C. T.	July, 1864	From Garrison Port Hudson, La.	To 2-Brig. 2-Div. U. S. C. T. Gulf	Oct., 1864
Patterson's Ky. Co. Engrs.	July, 1864	From Unatt. 13-Corps Texas	No change to Muster Out	Jan., 1865
96th U. S. C. T.	July, 1864	From Prov'l Brig. 13-Corps Texas	To 1-Brig. 3-Div. U. S. C. T. Gulf	Oct., 1864
97th U. S. C. T.	July, 1864	From Prov'l Brig. 13-Corps Texas	To 1-Brig. 3-Div. U. S. C. T. Gulf	Oct., 1864

BAILEY'S ENGINEER BRIGADE.—Organized June 10, 1864.

COMMANDER.

Joseph Bailey	Col. 4th Wis. Cav.	June 10 to Aug. 10, 1864.	

1st Mich. Heavy Arty.	June, 1864	From Dist. Port Hudson, La.	To U. S. Forces Mobile Bay	Aug., 1864
161st N. Y. Infy.	June, 1864	From 1-Brig. 1-Div. 19-Corps	To 3-Brig. 2-Div. 19-Corps Gulf	Aug., 1864
24th Ind. Infy.	June, 1864	From Def. New Orleans, La.	To 2-Brig. 3-Div. 19-Corps	Aug., 1864

ARTILLERY RESERVE.—

12th Mass. Batty.	July, 1863	From Def. New Orleans, La.	To Def. New Orleans, La.	Aug., 1863
15th Mass. Batty.	July, 1863	From Def. New Orleans, La.	To Def. New Orleans, La.	Aug., 1863
25th N. Y. Batty.	July, 1863	From Def. New Orleans, La.	To Arty. 4-Div. 19-Corps	Aug., 1863
26th N. Y. Batty.	July, 1863	From Def. New Orleans, La.	To Arty. 4-Div. 19-Corps	Aug., 1863
2d Mass. Batty.	Aug., 1863	From Arty. 4-Div. 19-Corps	To Unatt. Cav. Div. Gulf	Sept., 1863
6th Mass. Batty.	Aug., 1863	From Arty. 1-Div. 19-Corps	To Arty. 1-Div. 19-Corps	Dec., 1863
Batty. L, 1st U. S. Arty.	Aug., 1863	From Arty. 4-Div. 19-Corps	To Arty. 1-Div. 19-Corps	Jan., 1864
4th Mass. Batty.	Nov., 1863	From Arty. 3-Div. 19-Corps	To Arty. 1-Div. 19-Corps	Feb., 1864
25th N. Y. Batty.	Dec., 1863	From Arty. 4-Div. 19-Corps	To Arty. 1-Div. 19-Corps	Feb., 1864
1st Ind. Batty.	July, 1864	From Def. New Orleans	To Arty. 3-Div. 16-Corps (New)	Feb., 1865
21st N. Y. Batty.	July, 1864	From Def. Port Hudson, La.	To Arty. 3-Div. Res. Corps Gulf	Feb., 1865
Batty. A, 1st Mo. Arty.	July, 1864	From Def. New Orleans	No change to Muster Out	Aug., 1865
Batty. B, 1st Mo. Arty.	July, 1864	From Def. New Orleans	No change to Muster Out	Aug., 1865
Batty. F, 1st Mo. Arty.	July, 1864	From Def. New Orleans	To Dist. South Ala.	Dec., 1864
Batty. G, 1st Mich. Arty.	July, 1864	From Def. New Orleans	To U. S. Forces Mobile Bay	Oct., 1864
2d Ohio Batty.	July, 1864	From Def. New Orleans	No change to Muster Out	July, 1865
16th Ohio Batty.	July, 1864	From Def. New Orleans	No change to Muster Out	July, 1865
Mercantile Ill. Batty.	July, 1864	From Def. New Orleans	To Arty. Cav. Div. Gulf	Nov., 1864
15th Mass. Batty.	July, 1864	From Def. New Orleans	To Arty. 2-Div. Res. Corps Gulf	Feb., 1865
2d Conn. Batty.	July, 1864	From Def. New Orleans	To Unatt. Arty. 19-Corps	Aug., 1864

UNATTACHED ARTILLERY, GULF.—

2d Conn. Batty.	Aug., 1864	From Arty. Res. Gulf	To Arty. Res. Corps Gulf	Dec., 1864
2d Mass. Batty.	Aug., 1864	From Arty. Cav. Div. Gulf	To Arty. Res. Corps Gulf	Dec., 1864
17th Ohio Batty.	Aug., 1864	From Def. New Orleans, La.	To U. S. Forces Mobile Bay	Aug., 1864
17th Ohio Batty.	Sept., 1864	From U. S. Forces Mobile Bay	To Arty. Res. Corps Gulf	Dec., 1864

DISTRICT OF LA FOURCHE, LA.— **COMMANDERS.**

H. W. Birge	Brigadier General	Sept., 1863, to May 4, 1864.	
John McNeil	Brigadier General	May 4, 1864, to June 9, 1864.	
R. A. Cameron	Brigadier General	June 9, 1864, to July, 1865.	

1st La. Infy.	Sept., 1863	From 2-Brig. 4-Div. 19-Corps	To 2-Brig. 2-Div. 19-Corps	Feb., 1864
22d Corps de Afrique (92d U. S. C. T.)	Sept., 1863	From New Organization	To 2-Brig. 2-Div. Corps de Afrique	Feb., 1864
1st Ind. Batty.	Sept., 1863	From Arty. 1-Div. 13-Corps	To Arty. 1-Div. 13-Corps	Feb., 1864
26th N. Y. Batty.	Oct., 1863	From Arty. 4-Div. 19-Corps	To Arty. 2-Div. 19-Corps	Feb., 1864
1st Vt. Batty.	Oct., 1863	From Arty. 3-Div. 19-Corps	To Arty. 1-Div. 19-Corps	Feb., 1864
11th N. Y. Cav.	Mch., 1864	From Def. Washington, D. C.	To 2-Brig. Cav. Div. Gulf	Aug., 1864
93d U. S. C. T. (25th Corps de Afrique.)	Mch., 1864	From 1-Brig. 2-Div. Corps de Afr.	Broken up	June, 1865
3d Md. Cav.	Mch., 1864	From Def. New Orleans	To Dist. Morganza, La.	June, 1864
2d Me. Cav.	Apr., 1864	From New Organization	To Dist. West Fla.	July, 1864
33d Ill. Infy.	June, 1864	From 1-Brig. 1-Div. 13-Corps	To 1-Brig. 1-Div. 16-Corps (New)	Feb., 1865
11th Wis. Infy.	June, 1864	From 1-Brig. 1-Div. 13-Corps	To 3-Brig. 2-Div. 16-Corps (New)	Feb., 1865
25th N. Y. Batty.	June, 1864	From Def. New Orleans, La.	No change to Muster Out	July, 1865
4th Iowa Batty.	June, 1864	From Def. New Orleans	No change to Muster Out	July, 1865
Batty. G, 5th U. S. Arty.	June, 1864	From Arty. Cav. Div. Gulf	To U. S. Forces Mobile Bay	Aug., 1864

DISTRICT OF LA FOURCHE.—Continued.

11th Ind. Infy.	June, 1864	From 1-Brig. 1-Div. 13-Corps	To 2-Brig. 2-Div. 19-Corps Shen	Aug., 1864
60th Ind. Infy.	June, 1864	From 1-Brig. 4-Div. 13-Corps	To Dist. Southern Ala	Dec., 1864
18th N. Y. Cav.	June, 1864	From 5-Brig. Cav. Div. Gulf	To 1-Brig. 2-Cav. Div. West Miss	May, 1865
12th Ill. Cav.	June, 1864	From 1-Brig. Cav. Div. Gulf	To 4-Brig. Cav. Div. Gulf	Aug., 1864
47th Ind. Infy.	June, 1864	From 2-Brig. 3-Div. 13-Corps	To 2-Brig. 2-Div. 19-Corps Gulf	Aug., 1864
29th Wis. Infy.	June, 1864	From 1-Brig. 3-Div. 13-Corps	To 2-Brig. 2-Div. 19-Corps Gulf	Aug., 1864
24th Iowa Infy.	June, 1864	From 2-Brig. 3-Div. 13-Corps	To 3-Brig. 2-Div. 19-Corps Shen	Aug., 1864
28th Iowa Infy.	June, 1864	From 2-Brig. 3-Div. 13-Corps	To 3-Brig. 2-Div. 19-Corps Shen	Aug., 1864
99th Ill. Infy.	June, 1864	From 1-Brig. 1-Div. 13-Corps	To 2-Brig. 2-Div. 19-Corps Gulf	Aug., 1864
8th Ind. Infy.	June, 1864	From 1-Brig. 1-Div. 13-Corps	To 3-Brig. 2-Div. 19-Corps Shen	Aug., 1864
18th Ind. Infy.	June, 1864	From 1-Brig. 1-Div. 13-Corps	To 3-Brig. 2-Div. 19-Corps Shen	Aug., 1864
26th Ind. Infy.	June, 1864	From 1-Brig. 2-Div. 13-Corps	To 1-Brig. 1-Div. 16-Corps (New)	Feb., 1865
1st Vt. Batty.	June, 1864	From Arty. 1-Div. 19-Corps	No change to Muster Out	Aug., 1864
21st Iowa Infy.	June, 1864	From 1-Brig. 1-Div. 13-Corps	To 2-Brig. 2-Div. 19-Corps Gulf	Aug., 1864
1st La. Infy.	June, 1864	From 2-Brig. 2-Div. 13-Corps	To 2-Brig. 2-Div. 19-Corps Gulf	Aug., 1864
Batty. D, 1st Wis. H. A.	July, 1864	From Def. New Orleans	No change to Muster Out	July, 1865
16th Ind. Infy.	Aug., 1864	From 4-Brig. Cav. Div. Gulf	No change to Muster Out	June, 1865
38th Iowa Infy.	Oct., 1864	From U. S. Forces Mobile Bay	To 3-Brig. Res. Corps Gulf	Dec., 1864
98th U. S. C. T.	Oct., 1864	From 2-Brig. 3-Div. U. S. C. T.	Consolidated with 78th U. S. C. T.	Aug., 1865
3d R. I. Cav.	Oct., 1864	From Def. New Orleans, La.	No change to Muster Out	Aug., 1865
1st La. Infy.	Nov., 1864	From 2-Brig. 2-Div. 19-Corps Gulf	No change to Muster Out	Aug., 1865
75th U. S. C. T.	Feb., 1865	From Garrison Port Hudson, La.	To Dept. Gulf	Aug., 1865
78th U. S. C. T.	Feb., 1865	From Dist. Morganza, La.	To Dept. Gulf	Aug., 1865
Batty. A, 2d Ill. Arty.	Feb., 1865	From Def. New Orleans	No change to Muster Out	July, 1865

DETACHMENT ARMY TENNESSEE.—Joined from Army Tenn. for Red River Campaign March, 1864.

16th ARMY CORPS.—

COMMANDER.				
A. J. Smith	Major General			

1st DIVISION.—

COMMANDER.				
J. A. Mower	Brigadier General			

2d BRIGADE.—

COMMANDER.				
L. F. Hubbard	Col. 5th Minn. Infy.			
47th Ill. Infy.	Mch., 1864	From 2-Brig. 1-Div. 16-Corps Tenn.	To 2-Brig. 1-Div. R. W. 16-C. Tenn.	June, 1864
5th Minn. Infy.	Mch., 1864	From 2-Brig. 1-Div. 16-Corps Tenn.	To 2-Brig. 1-Div. R. W. 16-C. Tenn.	June, 1864
8th Wis. Infy.	Mch., 1864	From 2-Brig. 1-Div. 16-Corps Tenn.	To 2-Brig. 1-Div. R. W. 16-C. Tenn.	June, 1864

3d BRIGADE.—

COMMANDER.				
S. G. Hill	Col. 35th Iowa Infy.			
35th Iowa Infy.	Mch., 1864	From 3-Brig. 1-Div. 16-Corps Tenn.	To 3-Brig. 1-Div. R. W. 16-C. Tenn.	June, 1864
33d Mo. Infy.	Mch., 1864	From 3-Brig. 1-Div. 16-Corps Tenn.	To 3-Brig. 1-Div. R. W. 16-C. Tenn.	June, 1864

3d DIVISION.—

COMMANDER.				
J. A. Mower	Brigadier General			

1st BRIGADE.—

COMMANDER.				
W. F. Lynch	Col. 58th Ill. Infy.			
58th Ill. Infy.	Mch., 1864	From 1-Brig. 3-Div. 16-Corps Tenn.	To 1-Brig. 3-Div. R. W. 16-C. Tenn.	June, 1864
119th Ill. Infy.	Mch., 1864	From 1-Brig. 3-Div. 16-Corps Tenn.	To 1-Brig. 3-Div. R. W. 16-C. Tenn.	June, 1864
89th Ind. Infy.	Mch., 1864	From 1-Brig. 3-Div. 16-Corps Tenn.	To 1-Brig. 3-Div. R. W. 16-C. Tenn.	June, 1864

2d BRIGADE.—

COMMANDER.				
W. T. Shaw	Col. 14th Iowa Infy.			
14th Iowa Infy.	Mch., 1864	From 2-Brig. 3-Div. 16-Corps Tenn.	To 2-Brig. 3-Div. R. W. 16-C. Tenn.	June, 1864
27th Iowa Infy.	Mch., 1864	From 2-Brig. 3-Div. 16-Corps Tenn.	To 2-Brig. 3-Div. R. W. 16-C. Tenn.	June, 1864
32d Iowa Infy.	Mch., 1864	From 2-Brig. 3-Div. 16-Corps Tenn.	To 2-Brig. 3-Div. R. W. 16-C. Tenn.	June, 1864
24th Mo. Infy.	Mch., 1864	From 2-Brig. 3-Div. 16-Corps Tenn.	To 2-Brig. 3-Div. R. W. 16-C. Tenn.	June, 1864

3d BRIGADE.—

COMMANDER.				
R. M. Moore	Col. 117th Ill. Infy.			
49th Ill. Infy.	Mch., 1864	From 3-Brig. 3-Div. 16-Corps Tenn.	To 3-Brig. 3-Div. R. W. 16-C. Tenn.	June, 1864
117th Ill. Infy.	Mch., 1864	From 3-Brig. 3-Div. 16-Corps Tenn.	To 2-Brig. 3-Div. R. W. 16-C. Tenn.	June, 1864
178th N. Y. Infy.	Mch., 1864	From 3-Brig. 3-Div. 16-Corps Tenn.	To 3-Brig. 3-Div. R. W. 16-C. Tenn.	June, 1864
ARTILLERY.—				
3d Ind. Batty.	Mch., 1864	From Arty. 3-Div. 16-Corps Tenn.	To 2-Brig. 3-Div. R. W. 16-C. Tenn.	June, 1864
9th Ind. Batty.	Mch., 1864	From Arty. 3-Div. 16-Corps Tenn.	To 1-Brig. 3-Div. R. W. 16-C. Tenn.	June, 1864

PROVISIONAL DIVISION.—

COMMANDER.				
T. Kilby Smith	Brigadier General			

1st BRIGADE.—

COMMANDER.				
J. B. Moore	Col. 33d Wis. Infy.			
41st Ill. Infy.	Mch., 1864	From 1-Brig. 4-Div. 17-Corps Tenn.	To 4-Brig. 1-Div. R. W. 16-C. Tenn.	June, 1864
3d Ia. Infy. (Non-Vets.)	Mch., 1864	From 1-Brig. 4-Div. 17-Corps Tenn.	No change to Muster Out	June, 1864
33d Wis. Infy.	Mch., 1864	From 1-Brig. 4-Div. 17-Corps Tenn.	To 4-Brig. 1-Div. R. W. 16-C. Tenn.	June, 1864

2d BRIGADE.—

COMMANDER.				
L. M. Ward	Col. 14th Wis. Infy.			
81st Ill. Infy. (Non-Vets.)	Mch., 1864	From 3-Brig. 3-Div. 17-Corps Tenn.	To 2-Brig. Sturgis' Exp. Tenn.	June, 1864
95th Ill. Infy. (Non-Vets.)	Mch., 1864	From 2-Brig. 1-Div. 17-Corps Tenn.	To 2-Brig. Sturgis' Exp. Tenn.	June, 1864
14th Wis. Infy.	Mch., 1864	From 2-Brig. 1-Div. 17-Corps Tenn.	To 4-Brig. 1-Div. R. W. 16-C. Tenn.	June, 1864
ARTILLERY.—				
Batty. M, 1st Mo. Arty.	Mch., 1864	From Arty. 1-Div. 17-Corps	To 4-Brig. 1-Div. R. W. 16-C. Tenn.	June, 1864

MILITARY DIVISION OF WEST MISSISSIPPI.—Created May 7, 1864, to consist of the Departments of the Gulf and Arkansas. Abolished May 17, 1865.

COMMANDER.				
E. R. S. Canby	Major General			

U. S. FORCES, TEXAS.— COMMANDERS.

Francis J. Herron	Major General	May 1, 1864, to June 9, 1864.
F. H. Warren	Brigadier General	June 9, 1864, to Aug. 1, 1864.

1st BRIGADE.— COMMANDER.

Wm. McE. Dye	Col. 20th Iowa Infy			
91st Ill. Infy	June, 1864	From 1-Brig. 2-Div. 13-Corps	To Unatt. Brazos, Santiago, Texas	Aug., 1864
20th Iowa Infy	June, 1864	From 1-Brig. 2-Div. 13-Corps	To U. S. Forces Mobile Bay	Aug., 1864
38th Iowa Infy	June, 1864	From 1-Brig. 2-Div. 13-Corps	To U. S. Forces Mobile Bay	Aug., 1864

2d BRIGADE.— COMMANDERS.

John McNulta	Col. 94th Ill. Infy		To July 8, 1864.	
Henry Bertram	Col. 20th Wis. Infy		To Aug. 1, 1864.	
94th Ill. Infy	June, 1864	From 2-Brig. 2-Div. 13-Corps	To U. S. Forces Mobile Bay	Aug., 1864
19th Iowa Infy	June, 1864	From 2-Brig. 2-Div. 13-Corps	To Dist. West Fla	Aug., 1864
20th Wis. Infy	June, 1864	From 2-Brig. 2-Div. 13-Corps	To U. S. Forces Mobile Bay	Aug., 1864

COLORED BRIGADE.— COMMANDER.

Justin Hodge	Col. 95th U. S. C. T.			
87th U. S. C. T.	June, 1864	From Unatt. 2-Div. 13-Corps	To Unatt. U. S. Forces Texas	Aug., 1864
95th U. S. C. T.	June, 1864	From Unatt. 2-Div. 13-Corps	To Unatt. U. S. Forces Texas	Aug., 1864

CAVALRY BRIGADE.— COMMANDER.

Edward J. Noyes	Major 1st Texas Cav.			
1st Texas Cav	June, 1864	From Cav. Brig. 2-Div. 13-Corps	To U. S. Forces Morganza, La	Aug., 1864
2d Texas Cav	June, 1864	From Cav. Brig. 2-Div. 13-Corps	To U. S. Forces Morganza, La	Aug., 1864

ARTILLERY.—

Batty. B, 1st Mo. Arty	June, 1864	From Arty. 2-Div. 13-Corps	To Arty. Res. Gulf	July, 1864

UNATTACHED, TEXAS.—

91st Ill. Infy	Aug., 1864	From 1-Brig. U. S. Forces Texas	To Def. New Orleans, La	Dec., 1864
87th U. S. C. T.	Aug., 1864	From Cold' Brig. U. S. Forces Texas	To Dept. Texas	June, 1865
95th U. S. C. T.	Aug., 1864	From Cold' Brig. U. S. Forces Texas	Consolidated with 97th U. S. C. T.	Nov., 1864
67th U. S. C. T.	Sept., 1864	From Dist. Port Hudson	To Dept. Texas	June, 1865
81st U. S. C. T.	Sept., 1864	From Engr. Brig. Gulf	To Dept. Texas	June, 1865
34th Ind. Infy	Dec., 1864	From Def. New Orleans, La	To Dept. Texas	June, 1865

DISTRICT OF MORGANZA.—Organized June, 1864. Discontinued May 29, 1865.
COMMANDERS.

J. J. Reynolds	Major General	June 16, 1864, to July 5, 1864.
M. K. Lawler	Brigadier General	July 5, 1864, to Nov. 23, 1864.
Daniel Ullman	Brigadier General	Nov. 23, 1864, to Feb. 26, 1865.
H. W. Fuller	Col. 75th U. S. C. T.	Feb. 26, 1865, to Feb. 27, 1865.
E. J. Davis	Brigadier General	Feb. 27, 1865, to Mch. 3, 1865.
T. J. McKean	Brigadier General	Mch. 3, 1865, to Mch. 29, 1865.
W. H. Dickey	Col. 84th U. S. C. T.	Mch. 29, 1865, to May 29, 1865.

PROVISIONAL BRIGADE, U. S. C. T.— COMMANDER.

Theo. H. Barrett	Col. 62d U. S. C. T.		June to Aug., 1864.	
62d U. S. C. T.	June, 1864	From Dept. Mo	To 2-Brig. 1-Div. U. S. C. T. Gulf	Aug., 1864
65th U. S. C. T.	June, 1864	From Dept. Mo	To 2-Brig. 1-Div. U. S. C. T.	Aug., 1864
67th U. S. C. T.	June, 1864	From Dept. Mo	To 2-Brig. 1-Div. U. S. C. T.	Aug., 1864
83d U. S. C. T.	June, 1864	From 1-Brig. 1-Div. Corps de Afr	Broken up	July, 1864

1st BRIGADE (1-Brig. 1st Div. U. S. C. T.).— COMMANDERS.

H. N. Frisbie	Col. 92d U. S. C. T.		Aug., 1864, to Oct., 1864.	
W. H. Dickey	Col. 84th U. S. C. T.		Oct., 1864, to Feb., 1865.	
F. A. Kendrick	Col. 61st U. S. C. T.		Feb., 1865, to Mch., 1865.	
73d U. S. C. T.	Aug., 1864	From 1-Brig. 1-Div. Corps de Afr	To Dept. Gulf	May, 1865
75th U. S. C. T.	Aug., 1864	From 1-Brig. 1-Div. Corps de Afr	To Dist. La Fourche, La	Feb., 1865
84th U. S. C. T.	Aug., 1864	From 1-Brig. 1-Div. Corps de Afr	To 2-Brig. U. S. C. T. Morganza	Feb., 1865
92d U. S. C. T.	Aug., 1864	From 1-Brig. 1-Div. Corps de Afr	To 2-Brig. U. S. C. T. Morganza	Feb., 1865
61st U. S. C. T.	Feb., 1865	From 1-Col'd Brig. Dist. West Tenn	To 1-Br. 1-Div. U.S.C.T. Dist. W. Fla.	Apr., 1865
65th U. S. C. T.	Feb., 1865	From 2-Brig. 1-Div. U. S. C. T. Gulf	To Northern Dist. La	May, 1865
67th U. S. C. T.	Feb., 1865	From 2-Brig. 1-Div. U. S. C. T. Gulf	To Northern Dist. La	May, 1865

2d BRIGADE (2-Brig. 1st Div. U. S. C. T.).— COMMANDERS.

Theo. H. Barrett	Col. 62d U. S. C. T.		Aug., 1864, to Feb., 1865.	
W. H. Dickey	Col. 84th U. S. C. T.		Feb., 1865, to May, 1865.	
62d U. S. C. T.	Aug., 1864	From Prov'l Br. U. S. C. T. Morg'za	To Dist. Port Hudson, La	Sept., 1864
65th U. S. C. T.	Aug., 1864	From Prov'l Br. U. S. C. T. Morg'za	To 1-Brig. U. S. C. T. Morganza	Feb., 1865
67th U. S. C. T.	Aug., 1864	From Prov'l Br. U. S. C. T. Morg'za	To 1-Brig. U. S. C. T. Morganza	Feb., 1865
99th U. S. C. T.	Aug., 1864	From Engr. Brig. Gulf	To Dist. Key West, Fla	Feb., 1865
55th U. S. C. T.	Feb., 1865	From 1-Col'd Brig. Dist. West Tenn	To Dist. Port Hudson, La	Apr., 1865
84th U. S. C. T.	Feb., 1865	From 1-Brig. U. S. C. T. Morganza	To Northern Dist. La	May, 1865
92d U. S. C. T.	Feb., 1865	From 1-Brig. U. S. C. T. Morganza	To Northern Dist. La	May, 1865

UNATTACHED.—

90th U. S. C. T.	June, 1864	From New Organization	Broken up	July, 1864
97th U. S. C. T.	June, 1864	From Engr. Brig. Gulf	To 1-Brig. 3-Div. U. S. C. T. Gulf	Oct., 1864
1st Vt. Batty	June, 1864	From Arty. 2-Div. 19-Corps	No change to Muster Out	Aug., 1864
3d Md. Cav	June, 1864	From Dist. La Fourche, La	To 3-Brig. 3-Div. 19-Corps Gulf	Aug., 1864
1st Texas Cav	June, 1864	From Cav. Brig. U. S. Forces Texas	To Sep. Cav. Brig. 19-Corps	Aug., 1864
2d Texas Cav	June, 1864	From Cav. Brig. U. S. Forces Texas	Consolidated with 1st Texas Cav.	July, 1864
1st Wis. Batty	June, 1864	From Arty. 1-Div. 13-Corps	To Arty. Cav. Div. Gulf	Aug., 1864
1st La. Cav	July, 1864	From 3-Brig. Cav. Div. Gulf	To Sep. Cav. Brig. 19-Corps	Aug., 1864
14th N. Y. Cav	Feb., 1865	From Sep. Cav. Brig. Baton Rouge	To Def. New Orleans, La	Apr., 1865

U. S. FORCES MOBILE BAY.— COMMANDERS.

Geo. H. Gordon	Brigadier General	Aug. 1, 1864, to Aug. 31, 1864.
Henry Bertram	Col. 20th Wis. Infy	Aug. 31, 1864, to Oct., 1864.

BERTRAM'S BRIGADE.— COMMANDER.

Henry Bertram	Col. 20th Wis. Infy		Aug. 17, 1864, to Aug. 31, 1864.	
94th Ill. Infy	Aug., 1864	From 2-Brig. U. S. Forces Texas	To Unass'd Mobile Bay	Oct., 1864
20th Iowa Infy	Aug., 1864	From 1-Brig. U. S. Forces Texas	To 1-Brig. 3-Div. 19-Corps Gulf	Sept., 1864
38th Iowa Infy	Aug., 1864	From 1-Brig. U. S. Forces Texas	To Dist. La Fourche, La	Oct., 1864
20th Wis. Infy	Aug., 1864	From 1-Brig. U. S. Forces Texas	To Unass'd Mobile Bay	Oct., 1864

GUPPEY'S BRIGADE.—

COMMANDER.

J. A. Guppey	Col. 23d Wis. Infy	To Sept. 2, 1864.	
Wm. McE. Dye	Col. 20th Iowa Infy	To Oct., 1864.	

161st N. Y. Infy	Aug., 1864	From 3-Brig. 2-Div. 19-Corps Gulf..	To U. S. Forces Mouth White River..	Nov., 1864
23d Wis. Infy	Aug., 1864	From 3-Brig. 2-Div. 19-Corps Gulf..	To Dist. Eastern Ark. 7-Corps	Oct., 1864
2d Conn. Batty. Det	Aug., 1864	From Arty. Res. Gulf	To Def. New Orleans	Sept., 1864
17th Ohio Batty. Det	Aug., 1864	From Def. New Orleans	To Unatt. Arty. 19-Corps Gulf	Sept., 1864
UNASSIGNED.—				
94th Ill. Infy	Oct., 1864	From Bertram's Brig. U. S. Forces..	To Dist. South Ala	Dec., 1864
96th U. S. C. T.	Oct., 1864	From Engr. Brig. Gulf	To Dist. South Ala	Dec., 1864
97th U. S. C. T.	Oct., 1864	From Engr. Brig. Gulf	To Dist. South Ala	Dec., 1864
20th Wis. Infy	Oct., 1864	From Bertram's Brig. Mobile Bay...	To Dist. West Fla	Oct., 1864
Batty. G, 1st Mich. Arty	Oct., 1864	From Res. Arty. Gulf	To Dist. South Ala	Dec., 1864
6th Mich. Heavy Arty	Oct., 1864	From Bailey's Engr. Brig	To Dist. South Ala	Dec., 1864
3d Md. Cav	Oct., 1864	From 3-Brig. 3-Div. 19-Corps	To Dist. South Ala	Dec., 1864
96th U. S. C. T.	Oct., 1864	From 1-Brig. 3-Div. U. S. C. T. Gulf	To Dist. South Ala	Dec., 1864

DISTRICT SOUTH ALABAMA.—

COMMANDER.

Gordon Granger	Major General	To Feb., 1865.	

94th Ill. Infy	Dec., 1864	From U. S. Forces Mobile Bay...	To 1-Brig. 2-Div. Res. Corps Gulf..	Feb., 1865
97th Ill. Infy	Dec., 1864	From 2-Brig. 3-Div. 19-Corps...	To 3-Brig. Res. Corps Gulf	Dec., 1864
60th Ind. Infy	Dec., 1864	From Dist. La Fourche, La...	To 1-Brig. 2-Div. Res. Corps Gulf...	Feb., 1865
69th Ind. Infy	Dec., 1864	From 2-Brig. 3-Div. 19-Corps Gulf..	To 3-Brig. Res. Corps Gulf	Dec., 1864
19th Iowa Infy	Dec., 1864	From Dist. West Fla	To 1-Brig. 2-Div. Res. Corps Gulf..	Feb., 1865
20th Wis. Infy	Dec., 1864	From U. S. Forces Mobile Bay	To 1-Brig. 2-Div. Res. Corps Gulf..	Feb., 1865
20th U. S. C. T.	Dec., 1864	From Def. New Orleans	To Def. New Orleans, La	Feb., 1865
96th U. S. C. T.	Dec., 1864	From U. S. Forces Mobile Bay	To Engr. Brig. 13-Corps (New)	Feb., 1865
3d Md. Cav	Dec., 1864	From U. S. Forces Mobile Bay	To 1-Brig. 2-Div. Cav. West Miss..	May, 1865
6th Mo. Cav	Dec., 1864	From 1-Brig. Cav. Div. Gulf	To Cav. Brig. Dist. Baton Rouge, La.	Feb., 1865
Batty. G, 1st Mich. Arty	Dec., 1864	From U. S. Forces Mobile Bay	No change to Muster Out	July, 1865
6th Mich. Heavy Arty	Dec., 1864	From U. S. Forces Mobile Bay	No change to Muster Out	July, 1865
Batty. F, 1st Mo. Arty	Dec., 1864	From Res. Arty. Gulf	To 1-Brig. 2-Div. 13-Corps Gulf...	Feb., 1865

Reserve Corps

Organized Dec. 5, 1864, from troops formerly comprising 19th Corps, Dept. Gulf. Merged into reorganized 13th Army Corps Feb. 18, 1865.

COMMANDERS.

J. J. Reynolds	Major General	Dec. 5, 1864, to Jan. 12, 1865.	
Gordon Granger	Major General	Jan. 12, 1865, to Feb. 3, 1865.	

1st BRIGADE.—

COMMANDER.

M. K. Lawler	Brigadier General	

28th Ill. Infy	Dec., 1864	From 3-Brig. 2-Div. 19-Corps	To 1-Brig. 3-Div. Res. Corps	Feb., 1865
29th Ill. Infy	Dec., 1864	From 3-Brig. 2-Div. 19-Corps	To 3-Brig. 1-Div. Res. Corps	Feb., 1865
99th Ill. Infy	Dec., 1864	From 2-Brig. 2-Div. 19-Corps	To 1-Brig. 1-Div. Res. Corps	Feb., 1865
47th Ind. Infy	Dec., 1864	From 2-Brig. 2-Div. 19-Corps	To 1-Brig. 1-Div. Res. Corps	Feb., 1865
21st Iowa Infy	Dec., 1864	From 2-Brig. 2-Div. 19-Corps	To 1-Brig. 1-Div. Res. Corps	Feb., 1865
29th Wis. Infy	Dec., 1864	From 2-Brig. 2-Div. 19-Corps	To 1-Brig. 1-Div. Res. Corps	Feb., 1865

2d BRIGADE.—

COMMANDER.

E. S. Dennis	Brigadier General	

8th Illinois Infy	Dec., 1864	From 1-Brig. 2-Div. 19-Corps	To 2-Brig. 1-Div. Res. Corps	Feb., 1865
11th Illinois Infy	Dec., 1864	From 1-Brig. 2-Div. 19-Corps	To 2-Brig. 1-Div. Res. Corps	Feb., 1865
46th Illinois Infy	Dec., 1864	From 1-Brig. 2-Div. 19-Corps	To 2-Brig. 1-Div. Res. Corps	Feb., 1865
76th Illinois Infy	Dec., 1864	From 1-Brig. 2-Div. 19-Corps	To 2-Brig. 1-Div. Res. Corps	Feb., 1865
30th Missouri Infy	Dec., 1864	From 1-Brig. 2-Div. 19-Corps	To 3-Brig. 1-Div. Res. Corps	Feb., 1865

3d BRIGADE.—

COMMANDERS.

G. F. McGinnis	Brigadier General	Dec. 5, 1864, to Dec. 10, 1864,
C. C. Andrews	Brigadier General	Dec. 10, 1864, to Feb. 13, 1865.

24th Indiana Infy	Dec., 1864	From 2-Brig. 3-Div. 19-Corps	To 2-Brig. 2-Div. Res. Corps	Feb., 1865
67th Indiana Infy	Dec., 1864	From 3-Brig. 3-Div. 19-Corps	Consolidated with 24th Ind. Infy...	Dec., 1864
69th Indiana Infy	Dec., 1864	From Dist. South Ala	To 2-Brig. 2-Div. Res. Corps	Feb., 1865
97th Illinois Infy	Dec., 1864	From 2-Brig. 3-Div. 19-Corps	To 2-Brig. 2-Div. Res. Corps	Feb., 1865
34th Iowa Infy	Dec., 1864	From 3-Brig. 3-Div. 19-Corps	To 2-Brig. 2-Div. Res. Corps	Feb., 1865
38th Iowa Infy	Dec., 1864	From Dist. La Fourche, La	Consolidated with 34th Iowa	Dec., 1864
48th Ohio Infy	Dec., 1864	From Def. of New Orleans	Consolidated with 83d Ohio	Dec., 1864
83d Ohio Infy	Jan., 1865	From Post Natchez Dist. Vicksburg.		
114th Ohio Infy	Dec., 1864	From 2-Brig. 3-Div. 19-Corps	To 3-Brig. 2-Div. Res. Corps	Feb., 1865

4th BRIGADE.—

COMMANDER.

Wm. McE. Dye	Col. 20th Iowa Infy	

37th Illinois Infy	Dec., 1864	From 1-Brig. 3-Div. 19-Corps	To 3-Brig. 2-Div. Res. Corps	Feb., 1865
20th Iowa Infy	Dec., 1864	From 1-Brig. 3-Div. 19-Corps	To 3-Brig. 2-Div. Res. Corps	Feb., 1865
23d Iowa Infy	Dec., 1864	From 1-Brig. 3-Div. 19-Corps	To 1-Brig. 2-Div. Res. Corps	Feb., 1865
35th Wisconsin Infy	Dec., 1864	From 1-Brig. 3-Div. 19-Corps	To 1-Brig. 2-Div. Res. Corps	Feb., 1865

U. S. FORCES MOUTH WHITE RIVER.—

COMMANDER.

G. F. McGinnis	Brigadier General	To May 30, 1865.

161st New York Infy	Dec., 1864	From 3-Brig. 2-Div. 19-Corps	To 3-Brig. 1-Div. Res. Corps	Feb., 1865
96th Ohio Infy	Dec., 1864	From 3-Brig. 3-Div. 19-Corps	To 1-Brig. 3-Div. Res. Corps	Feb., 1865

SEPARATE CAVALRY BRIGADE.—

COMMANDER.

E. J. Davis	Col. 87th Illinois Infy	

87th Illinois Mtd. Infy	Dec., 1864	From Sep. Cav. Brig. 19-Corps Gulf.	To Dist. Eastern Ark. 7-Corps	Feb., 1865
1st Louisiana Cav	Dec., 1864	From Sep. Cav. Brig. 19-Corps Gulf.	To Sep. Cav. Brig. Dist. W. Fla	Feb., 1865
2d N. Y. Vet. Cav	Dec., 1864	From Sep. Cav. Brig. 19-Corps Gulf.	To Sep. Cav. Brig. Dist. W. Fla	Feb., 1865
1st Texas Cav	Dec., 1864	From 2d Sep. Cav. Brig. Gulf	To Cav. Brig. Dist. Baton Rouge, La.	Feb., 1865

ARTILLERY.—

2d Conn. Batty	Dec., 1864	From Unatt. Arty. Gulf	To Arty. 2-Div. Res. Corps	Feb.,	1865
1st Delaware Batty	Dec., 1864	From Arty. 3-Div. 19-Corps	To Arty. 2-Div. 7-Corps Dept. Ark.	Feb.,	1865
2d Mass. Batty	Dec., 1864	From Cav. Brig. 19-Corps	To Lucas Cav. Div. Dist. W. Fla.	Feb.,	1865
4th Mass. Batty	Dec., 1864	From Arty. 3-Div. 19-Corps	To Arty. 1-Div. Res. Corps	Feb.,	1865
7th Mass. Batty	Dec., 1864	From Arty. 2-Div. 19-Corps	To Arty. 1-Div. Res. Corps	Feb.,	1865
26th N. Y. Batty	Dec., 1864	From Arty. 2-Div. 19-Corps	To Arty. 3-Div. Res. Corps	Feb.,	1865
17th Ohio Batty	Dec., 1864	From Unatt. Arty. 19-Corps Gulf	To Arty. Brig. 16-Corps New	Feb.,	1865

Reserve Corps

As organized Feb. 3, 1865. Designated 13th Army Corps (New) Feb. 18, 1865.

COMMANDERS.

Gordon Granger	Major General	

1st DIVISION.— COMMANDERS.

Frederick Steele	Major General	To Feb. 8, 1865.
J. C. Veatch	Brigadier General	To Feb. 18, 1865.

1st BRIGADE.— COMMANDERS.

M. K. Lawler	Brigadier General	To Feb. 4, 1865.
J. A. McLaughlin	Lt.-Col. 47th Ind. Infy	To Feb. 18, 1865.

47th Ind. Inf	Feb., 1865	From 1-Brig. Res. Corps	To 1-Brig. 1-Div. 13-Corps New	Feb.,	1865
29th Wis. Infy	Feb., 1865	From 1-Brig. Res. Corps	To 1-Brig. 1-Div. 13-Corps New	Feb.,	1865
21st Iowa Infy	Feb., 1865	From 1-Brig. Res. Corps	To 1-Brig. 1-Div. 13-Corps New	Feb.,	1865
99th Ill. Infy	Feb., 1865	From 1-Brig. Res. Corps	To 1-Brig. 1-Div. 13-Corps New	Feb.,	1865

2d BRIGADE.— COMMANDER.

E. S. Dennis	Brigadier General	

8th Ill. Infy	Feb., 1865	From 2-Brig. Res. Corps	To 2-Brig. 1-Div. 13-Corps New	Feb.,	1865
11th Ill. Infy	Feb., 1865	From 2-Brig. Res. Corps	To 2-Brig. 1-Div. 13-Corps New	Feb.,	1865
46th Ill. Infy	Feb., 1865	From 2-Brig. Res. Corps	To 2-Brig. 1-Div. 13-Corps New	Feb.,	1865

3d BRIGADE.— COMMANDER.

L. Kent	Col. 29th Ill. Infy	

29th Ill. Infy	Feb., 1865	From 1-Brig. Res. Corps	To 3-Brig. 1-Div. 13-Corps New	Feb.,	1865
161st N. Y. Infy	Feb., 1865	From U. S. Forces Mouth White R.	To 3-Brig. 1-Div. 13-Corps New	Feb.,	1865
30th Mo. Infy	Feb., 1865	From 2-Brig. Res. Corps	To 3-Brig. 1-Div. 13-Corps New	Feb.,	1865
23d Wis. Infy	Feb., 1865	From Helena Ark. Dist. E. Ark. 7-C.	To 3-Brig. 1-Div. 13-Corps New	Feb.,	1865
ARTILLERY.—					
4th Mass. Batty	Feb., 1865	From Arty. Res. Corps	To Arty. 1-Div. 13-Corps New	Feb.,	1865
7th Mass. Batty	Feb., 1865	From Arty. Res. Corps	To Arty. 1-Div. 13-Corps New	Feb.,	1865

2d DIVISION.— COMMANDER.

C. C. Andrews	Brigadier General	

1st BRIGADE.— COMMANDER.

S. L. Glasgow	Col. 23d Iowa Infy	

20th Wis. Infy	Feb., 1865	From Dist. South Ala.	To 1-Brig. 2-Div. 13-Corps New	Feb.,	1865
19th Iowa Infy	Feb., 1865	From Dist. South Ala.	To 1-Brig. 2-Div. 13-Corps New	Feb.,	1865
23d Iowa Infy	Feb., 1865	From 4-Brig. Res. Corps	To 1-Brig. 2-Div. 13-Corps New	Feb.,	1865
60th Ind. Infy	Feb., 1865	From Dist. South Ala.	To 1-Brig. 2-Div. 13-Corps New	Feb.,	1865
94th Ill. Infy	Feb., 1865	From Dist. South Ala.	To 1-Brig. 2-Div. 13-Corps New	Feb.,	1865

2d BRIGADE.— COMMANDER.

W. T. Spicely	Col. 24th Ind. Infy	

76th Ill. Infy	Feb., 1865	From 2-Brig. Res. Corps	To 2-Brig. 2-Div. 13-Corps New	Feb.,	1865
97th Illinois Infy	Feb., 1865	From 3-Brig. Res. Corps	To 2-Brig. 2-Div. 13-Corps New	Feb.,	1865
24th Ind. Infy	Feb., 1865	From 3-Brig. Res. Corps	To 2-Brig. 2-Div. 13-Corps New	Feb.,	1865
69th Ind. Infy	Feb., 1865	From 3-Brig. Res. Corps	To 2-Brig. 2-Div. 13-Corps New	Feb.,	1865

3d BRIGADE.— COMMANDER.

J. C. Black	Col. 37th Ill. Infy	

37th Ill. Infy	Feb., 1865	From 4-Brig. Res. Corps	To 3-Brig. 2-Div. 13-Corps New	Feb.,	1865
83d Ohio Infy	Feb., 1865	From 3-Brig. Res. Corps	To 3-Brig. 2-Div. 13-Corps New	Feb.,	1865
114th Ohio Infy	Feb., 1865	From 3-Brig. Res. Corps	To 3-Brig. 2-Div. 13-Corps New	Feb.,	1865
20th Iowa Infy	Feb., 1865	From 4-Brig. Res. Corps	To 3-Brig. 2-Div. 13-Corps New	Feb.,	1865
34th Iowa Infy	Feb., 1865	From 3-Brig. Res. Corps	To 3-Brig. 2-Div. 13-Corps New	Feb.,	1865
ARTILLERY.—					
2d Conn. Batty	Feb., 1865	From Arty. Res. Corps	To Arty. 2-Div. 13-Corps New	Feb.,	1865
15th Mass. Batty	Feb., 1865	From Arty. Res. Gulf	To Arty. 2-Div. 13-Corps New	Feb.,	1865

3d DIVISION.— COMMANDER.

W. P. Benton	Brigadier General	

1st BRIGADE.— COMMANDER.

D. P. Greer	Col. 77th Ill. Infy	

28th Ill. Infy	Feb., 1865	From 1-Brig. Res. Corps	To 1-Brig. 3-Div. 13-Corps New	Feb.,	1865
77th Ill. Infy	Feb., 1865	From Def. New Orleans	To 1-Brig. 3-Div. 13-Corps New	Feb.,	1865
35th Wis. Infy	Feb., 1865	From 4-Brig. Res. Corps	To 1-Brig. 3-Div. 13-Corps New	Feb.,	1865
96th Ohio Infy	Feb., 1865	From U. S. Forces Mouth White R.	To 1-Brig. 3-Div. 13-Corps New	Feb.,	1865

2d BRIGADE, 3d DIVISION.— COMMANDER.

H. M. Day	Col. 91st Ill. Infy	

7th Vermont Infy	Feb., 1865	From Def. New Orleans	To 2-Brig. 3-Div. 13-Corps New	Feb.,	1865
29th Iowa Infy	Feb., 1865	From 2-Brig. 2-Div. 7-Corps Ark.	To 2-Brig. 3-Div. 13-Corps New	Feb.,	1865
91st Ill. Infy	Feb., 1865	From Def. New Orleans	To 2-Brig. 3-Div. 13-Corps New	Feb.,	1865
50th Ind. Infy	Feb., 1865	From 1-Brig. 1-Div. 7-Corps Ark.	To 2-Brig. 3-Div. 13-Corps New	Feb.,	1865

3d BRIGADE.—

	COMMANDER.	
C. Krez	Col. 27th Wis. Infy	

33d Iowa Infy	Feb., 1865	From 1-Brig. 1-Div. 7-Corps Ark	To 3-Brig. 3-Div. 13-Corps New	Feb., 1865
77th Ohio Infy	Feb., 1865	From 2-Brig. 1-Div. 7-Corps Ark	To 3-Brig. 3-Div. 13-Corps New	Feb., 1865
27th Wis. Infy	Feb., 1865	From 2-Brig. 1-Div. 7-Corps Ark	To 3-Brig. 3-Div. 13-Corps New	Feb., 1865
28th Wis. Infy	Feb., 1865	From 1-Brig. 1-Div. 7-Corps Ark	To 3-Brig. 3-Div. 13-Corps New	Feb., 1865
ARTILLERY.—				
21st N. Y. Batty	Feb., 1865	From Arty. Res. Gulf	To Arty. 3-Div. 13-Corps New	Feb., 1865
26th N. Y. Batty	Feb., 1865	From Arty. Res. Corps	To Arty. 3-Div. 13-Corps New	Feb., 1865

Thirteenth Army Corps

Reorganized Feb. 18, 1865, from Reserve Corps, Dept. of the Gulf. Discontinued July 20, 1865.

	COMMANDER.	
Gordon Granger	Major General	Feb. 18, 1865, to July 20, 1865.

1st DIVISION.—

	COMMANDERS.	
J. C. Veatch	Brigadier General	Feb. 18, 1865, to May 25, 1865.
E. S. Dennis	Brigadier General	May 25, 1865, to July 20, 1865.

1st BRIGADE.—

	COMMANDERS.	
J. A. McLaughlin	Lt.-Col. 47th Ind. Infy	Feb. 18, 1865, to Feb. 24, 1865.
J. R. Slack	Brigadier General	Feb. 24, 1865, to May 7, 1865.
J. A. McLaughlin	Lt.-Col. 47th Ind. Infy	May 7, 1865, to May 26, 1865.
J. R. Slack	Brigadier General	May 26, 1865, to July 20, 1865.

99th Ill. Infy	Feb., 1865	From 1-Brig. 1-Div. Res. Corps Gulf	No change to Muster Out	July, 1865
47th Ind. Infy	Feb., 1865	From 1-Brig. 1-Div. Res. Corps Gulf	To Dept. of Louisiana	May, 1865
21st Iowa Infy	Feb., 1865	From 1-Brig. 1-Div. Res. Corps Gulf	No change to Muster Out	July, 1865
29th Wis. Infy	Feb., 1865	From 1-Brig. 1-Div. Res. Corps Gulf	No change to Muster Out	June, 1865

2d BRIGADE.—

	COMMANDERS.	
E. S. Dennis	Brigadier General	Feb. 18, 1865, to May 25, 1865.
B. Dornblaser	Col. 46th Ill. Infy	May 25, 1865, to July 20, 1865.

8th Ill. Infy	Feb., 1865	From 2-Brig. 1-Div. Res. Corps Gulf	To Dept. of Louisiana	July, 1865
11th Ill. Infy	Feb., 1865	From 2-Brig. 1-Div. Res. Corps Gulf	To Dept. of Louisiana	July, 1865
46th Ill. Infy	Feb., 1865	From 2-Brig. 1-Div. Res. Corps Gulf	To Dept. of Louisiana	July, 1865

3d BRIGADE.—

	COMMANDERS.	
L. Kent	Col. 29th Ill. Infy	Feb. 18, 1865, to Mch. 15, 1865.
W. B. Kinsey	Lt.-Col. 161st N. Y. Infy	Mch. 15, 1865, to Apr. 15, 1865.
L. Kent	Col. 29th Ill. Infy	Apr. 15, 1865, to July 20, 1865.

29th Ill. Infy	Feb., 1865	From 3-Brig. 1-Div. Res. Corps Gulf	To Dept. Texas	July, 1865
30th Mo. Infy	Feb., 1865	From 3-Brig. 1-Div. Res. Corps Gulf	To Dept. Texas	July, 1865
161st N. Y. Infy	Feb., 1865	From 3-Brig. 1-Div. Res. Corps Gulf	To Dist. West Fla	May, 1865
23d Wis. Infy	Feb., 1865	From 3-Brig. 1-Div. Res. Corps Gulf	No change to Muster Out	July, 1865
ARTILLERY.—				
4th Mass. Batty	Feb., 1865	From Arty. 1-Div. Res. Corps Gulf	To Dept. Texas	July, 1865
7th Mass. Batty	Feb., 1865	From Arty. 1-Div. Res. Corps Gulf	To Dept. Texas	July, 1865

2d DIVISION.—

	COMMANDER.	
C. C. Andrews	Brigadier General	Feb. 18, 1865, to July 20, 1865.

1st BRIGADE.—

	COMMANDERS.	
S. L. Glasgow	Col. 23d Iowa Infy	Feb. 18, 1865, to Mch. 4, 1865.
Henry Bertram	Col. 20th Wis. Infy	Mch. 4, 1865, to May 8, 1865.
S. L. Glasgaw	Col. 23d Iowa Infy	May 8, 1865, to June 25, 1865.
J. McNulta	Col. 94th Ill. Infy	June 25, 1865, to July 20, 1865.

94th Ill. Infy	Feb., 1865	From 1-Brig. 2-Div. Res. Corps Gulf	No change to Muster Out	July, 1865
19th Iowa Infy	Feb., 1865	From 1-Brig. 2-Div. Res. Corps Gulf	No change to Muster Out	July, 1865
23d Iowa Infy	Feb., 1865	From 1-Brig. 2-Div. Res. Corps Gulf	No change to Muster Out	July, 1865
20th Wis. Infy	Feb., 1865	From 1-Brig. 2-Div. Res. Corps Gulf	No change to Muster Out	July, 1865
60th Ind. Infy	Feb., 1865	From 1-Brig. 2-Div. Res. Corps Gulf	No change to Muster Out	Mch., 1865
Batty. F, 1st Mo. Arty	Feb., 1865	From Dist. South Ala	No change to Muster Out	Aug., 1865

2d BRIGADE.—

	COMMANDER.	
W. T. Spicely	Col. 24th Ind. Infy	Feb. 18, 1865, to July 20, 1865.

76th Ill. Infy	Feb., 1865	From 2-Brig. 2-Div. Res. Corps Gulf	No change to Muster Out	July, 1865
97th Ill. Infy	Feb., 1865	From 2-Brig. 2-Div. Res. Corps Gulf	No change to Muster Out	July, 1865
24th Ind. Infy	Feb., 1865	From 2-Brig. 2-Div. Res. Corps Gulf	To Dept. Texas	July, 1865
69th Ind. Infy	Feb., 1865	From 2-Brig. 2-Div. Res. Corps Gulf	No change to Muster Out	July, 1865

3d BRIGADE.—

	COMMANDERS.	
J. C. Black	Col. 37th Ill. Infy	Feb. 18, 1865, to Mch. 5, 1865.
F. W. Moore	Col. 83d Ohio Infy	Mch. 5, 1865, to July 20, 1865.

37th Ill. Infy	Feb., 1865	From 3-Brig. 2-Div. Res. Corps Gulf	To Dept. Texas	July, 1865
20th Iowa Infy	Feb., 1865	From 3-Brig. 2-Div. Res. Corps Gulf	No change to Muster Out	July, 1865
34th Iowa Infy	Feb., 1865	From 3-Brig. 2-Div. Res. Corps Gulf	To Dept. Texas	July, 1865
83d Ohio Infy	Feb., 1865	From 3-Brig. 2-Div. Res. Corps Gulf	No change to Muster Out	July, 1865
114th Ohio Infy	Feb., 1865	From 3-Brig. 2-Div. Res. Corps Gulf	No change to Muster Out	July, 1865
ARTILLERY.—				
2d Conn. Batty	Feb., 1865	From Arty. 2-Div. Res. Corps Gulf	No change to Muster Out	July, 1865
15th Mass. Batty	Feb., 1865	From Arty. 2-Div. Res. Corps Gulf	No change to Muster Out	July, 1865

3d DIVISION.—

	COMMANDERS.	
W. P. Benton	Brigadier General	Feb. 18, 1865, to May 28, 1865.
D. P. Grier	Col. 77th Ill. Infy	May 28, 1865, to June 3, 1865.
W. P. Benton	Brigadier General	June 3, 1865, to July 20, 1865.

1st BRIGADE.— COMMANDERS.

D. P. Grier................	Col. 77th Ill. Infy................	Feb. 18, 1865, to May 28, 1865.	
H. Orff................	Col. 35th Wis. Infy................	May 28, 1865, to June 3, 1865.	
R. Ritter................	Col. 28th Ill. Infy................	June 3, 1865, to July 20, 1865.	

28th Ill. Infy............Feb., 1865	From 1-Brig. 3-Div. Res. Corps Gulf.	To Dept. Texas....................	July,	1865
77th Ill. Infy............Feb., 1865	From 1-Brig. 3-Div. Res. Corps Gulf.	No change to Muster Out.........	July,	1865
130th Ill. Infy............Feb., 1865	From Def. New Orleans...........	No change to Muster Out.........	Aug.,	1865
96th Ohio Infy............Feb., 1865	From 1-Brig. 3-Div. Res. Corps Gulf.	No change to Muster Out.........	July,	1865
35th Wis. Infy............Feb., 1865	From 1-Brig. 3-Div. Res. Corps Gulf.	No change to Muster Out.........	July,	1865

2d BRIGADE.— COMMANDER.

H. M. Day................	Col. 91st Ill. Infy................	Feb. 18, 1865, to July 20, 1865.	

91st Ill. Infy............Feb., 1865	From 2-Brig. 3-Div. Res. Corps Gulf.	No change to Muster Out.........	July,	1865
50th Ind. Infy............Feb., 1865	From 2-Brig. 3-Div. Res. Corps Gulf.	Consolidated with 52d Indiana......	May,	1865
29th Iowa Infy............Feb., 1865	From 2-Brig. 3-Div. Res. Corps Gulf.	To Dept. Texas....................	July,	1865
7th Vermont Infy............Feb., 1865	From 2-Brig. 3-Div. Res. Corps Gulf.	To Dept. Texas....................	July,	1865

3d BRIGADE.— COMMANDER.

C. Krez................	Col. 27th Wis. Infy................	Feb. 18, 1865, to July 20, 1865.	

33d Iowa Infy............Feb., 1865	From 3-Brig. 3-Div. Res. Corps Gulf.	No change to Muster Out.........	July,	1865
77th Ohio Infy............Feb., 1865	From 3-Brig. 3-Div. Res. Corps Gulf.	To Dept. Texas....................	July,	1865
27th Wis. Infy............Feb., 1865	From 3-Brig. 3-Div. Res. Corps Gulf.	To Dept. Texas....................	July,	1865
28th Wis. Infy............Feb., 1865	From 3-Brig. 3-Div. Res. Corps Gulf.	To Dept. Texas....................	July,	1865
ARTILLERY.—				
21st N. Y. Batty......Feb., 1865	From Arty. 3-Div. Res. Corps Gulf.	To Dept. Alabama..................	July,	1865
26th N. Y. Batty......Feb., 1865	From Arty. 3-Div. Res. Corps Gulf.	To Dept. Alabama..................	July,	1865

Sixteenth Army Corps

Reorganized from Detachment Army of the Tennessee, Dept. of the Cumberland, Feb. 18, 1865, by General Order No. 20, Military Division West Miss. Discontinued July 20, 1865.

CORPS COMMANDER.

A. J. Smith............	Major General....................	Feb. 18, 1865, to July 20, 1865.	

1st DIVISION.— COMMANDER.

John McArthur........	Brigadier General....................	Feb. 18, 1865, to July 20, 1865.	

1st BRIGADE.— COMMANDER.

W. L. McMillan........	Col. 95th Ohio Infy................	Feb. 18, 1865, to July 20, 1865.	

33d Ill. Infy............Feb., 1865	From Dist. La Fourche, La........	To Dept. Miss....................	July,	1865
26th Ind. Infy............Feb., 1865	From Dist. La Fourche, La........	To Dept. Miss....................	July,	1865
93d Indiana Infy............Feb., 1865	From 1-Brig. 1-Div. Det. Army Tenn.	To Dept. Miss....................	July,	1865
10th Minn. Infy............Feb., 1865	From 1-Brig. 1-Div. Det. Army Tenn.	To Dept. Miss....................	July,	1865
72d Ohio Infy............Feb., 1865	From 1-Brig. 1-Div. Det. Army Tenn.	To Dept. Miss....................	July,	1865
95th Ohio Infy............Feb., 1865	From 1-Brig. 1-Div. Det. Army Tenn.	To Dept. Miss....................	July,	1865

2d BRIGADE, 1st DIVISION.— COMMANDERS.

L. F. Hubbard........	Col. 5th Minn. Infy................	Feb. 18, 1865, to June 25, 1865.	
Alex. Wilkins........	Col. 9th Minn. Infy................	June 25, 1865, to July 15, 1865.	
J. D. McClure........	Col. 47th Ill. Infy................	July 15, 1865, to July 20, 1865.	

47th Ill. Infy............Feb., 1865	From 2-Brig. 1-Div. Det. Army Tenn.	To Dept. Alabama..................	July,	1865
8th Wis. Infy............Feb., 1865	From 2-Brig. 1-Div. Det. Army Tenn.	To Dept. Alabama..................	July,	1865
5th Minn. Infy............Feb., 1865	From 2-Brig. 1-Div. Det. Army Tenn.	To Dept. Alabama..................	July,	1865
9th Minn. Infy............Feb., 1865	From 2-Brig. 1-Div. Det. Army Tenn.	To Dept. Alabama..................	July,	1865
11th Mo. Infy............Feb., 1865	From 2-Brig. 1-Div. Det. Army Tenn.	To Dept. Alabama..................	July.	1865

3d BRIGADE.— COMMANDERS.

W. H. Heath........	Lt.-Col. 33d Mo. Infy................	Feb. 18, 1865, to Mch. 2, 1865.	
W. R. Marshall........	Col. 7th Minn. Infy................	Mch. 2, 1865, to July 20, 1865.	

12th Iowa Infy............Feb., 1865	From 3-Brig. 1-Div. Det. Army Tenn.	To Dept. Alabama..................	July,	1865
35th Iowa Infy............Feb., 1865	From 3-Brig. 1-Div. Det. Army Tenn.	To Dept. Alabama..................	July,	1865
7th Minn. Infy............Feb., 1865	From 3-Brig. 1-Div. Det. Army Tenn.	To Dept. Alabama..................	July,	1865
33d Mo. Infy............Feb., 1865	From 3-Brig. 1-Div. Det. Army Tenn.	To Dept. Alabama..................	July,	1865
ARTILLERY.—				
3d Indiana Batty........Feb., 1865	From 2-Brig. 2-Div. Det. Army Tenn.	To Arty. Brig. 16-Corps...........	Mch.,	1865
2d Iowa Batty..........Feb., 1865	From 2-Brig. 2-Div. Det. Army Tenn.	To Arty. Brig. 16-Corps...........	Mch.,	1865

2d DIVISION.— COMMANDER.

Kenner Garrard........	Brigadier General....................	Feb. 18, 1865, to July 20, 1865.	

1st BRIGADE.— COMMANDERS.

J. I. Rinaker........	Col. 122d Ill. Infy................	Feb. 18, 1865, to July 10, 1865.	
P. C. Smith........	Major 119th Ill. Infy................	July 10, 1865, to July 20, 1865.	

119th Ill. Infy............Feb., 1865	From 1-Brig. 2-Div. Det. Army Tenn.	No change to Muster Out.........	Aug.,	1865
122d Ill. Infy............Feb., 1865	From 1-Brig. 2-Div. Det. Army Tenn.	No change to Muster Out.........	Aug.,	1865
89th Ind. Infy............Feb., 1865	From 1-Brig. 2-Div. Det. Army Tenn.	No change to Muster Out.........	July,	1865
21st Mo. Infy............Feb., 1865	From 1-Brig. 2-Div. Det. Army Tenn.	No change to Muster Out.........	Aug.,	1865

2d BRIGADE.— COMMANDERS.

J. I. Gilbert........	Col. 27th Iowa Infy................	Feb. 18, 1865, to June 22, 1865.	
J. Merriam........	Lt.-Col. 117th Ill. Infy................	June 22, 1865, to July 20, 1865.	

27th Iowa Infy............Feb., 1865	From 2-Brig. 2-Div. Det. Army Tenn.	No change to Muster Out.........	Aug.,	1865
32d Iowa Infy............Feb., 1865	From 2-Brig. 2-Div. Det. Army Tenn.	No change to Muster Out.........	Aug.,	1865
10th Kansas Infy........Feb., 1865	From 3-Brig. 2-Div. Det. Army Tenn.	No change to Muster Out.........	Aug.,	1865
6th Minn. Infy............Feb., 1865	From Dist. St. Louis Dept. Mo...	No change to Muster Out.........	Aug.,	1865
58th Illinois Infy............Feb., 1865	From 2-Brig. 2-Div. Det. Army Tenn.	To 3-Brig. 2-Div. 16-Corps.........	Mch.,	1865
117th Ill. Infy............Mch., 1865	From 3-Brig. 2-Div. 16-Corps......	No change to Muster Out.........	Aug.,	1865

3d BRIGADE.—

	COMMANDERS.		
R. M. Moore..........	Col. 117th Ill. Infy...............	Feb. 18, 1865, to Mch. 5, 1865.	
C. L. Harris.............	Col. 11th Wis. Infy...............	Mch. 6, 1865, to July 20, 1865.	
117th Ill. Infy..........Feb., 1865	From 3-Brig. 2-Div. Det. Army Tenn.	To 2-Brig. 2-Div. 16-Corps.........	Mch., 1865
52d Ind. Infy...........Feb., 1865	From 3-Brig. 2-Div. Det. Army Tenn.	To Dept. Alabama..................	July, 1865
11th Wis. Infy..........Feb., 186	To Dist. La Fourche, La...........	To Dept. Alabama..................	July, 1865
34th N. J. Infy.........Feb., 1865	From 3-Brig. 2-Div. Det. Army Tenn.	To Dept. Alabama..................	July, 1865
178th N. Y. Infy........Feb., 1865	From 3-Brig. 2-Div. Det. Army Tenn.	To Dept. Alabama..................	July, 1865
58th Ill. Infy..........Mch., 1865	From 2-Brig. 2-Div. 16-Corps.......	To Dept. Alabama..................	July, 1865
ARTILLERY.—			
Batty. G, 2d Ill. Arty....Feb., 1865	From Arty. 2-Div. Det. Army Tenn.	To Arty. Brig. 16-Corps...........	Mch., 1865

3d DIVISION.—

	COMMANDERS.		
J. B. Moore.............	Col. 33d Wis. Infy................	Feb. 16, 1865, to Mch. 14, 1865.	
E. A. Carr..............	Brigadier General.................	Mch. 14, 1865, to July 20, 1865.	

1st BRIGADE.—

	COMMANDERS.		
L. M. Ward.............	Col. 14th Wis. Infy...............	Feb. 18, 1865, to Mch. 17, 1865.	
J. B. Moore.............	Col. 33d Wis. Infy...............	Mch. 17, 1865, to July 20, 1865.	
72d Ill. Infy...........Feb., 1865	From 1-Brig. 3-Div. Det. Army Tenn.	No change to Muster Out...........	Aug., 1865
40th Mo. Infy...........Feb., 1865	From 1-Brig. 3-Div. Det. Army Tenn.	To 2-Brig. 3-Div. 16-Corps........	Mch., 1865
14th Wis. Infy..........Feb., 1865	From 1-Brig. 3-Div. Det. Army Tenn.	To 2-Brig. 3-Div. 16-Corps........	Mch., 1865
33d Wis. Infy..........Feb., 1865	From 1-Brig. 3-Div. Det. Army Tenn.	No change to Muster Out...........	Aug., 1865
95th Ill. Infy..........Mch., 1865	From 2-Brig. 3-Div. 16-Corps.......	No change to Muster Out...........	Aug., 1865
44th Mo. Infy..........Mch., 1865	From 2-Brig. 3-Div. 16-Corps.......	No change to Muster Out...........	Aug., 1865

2d BRIGADE.—

	COMMANDERS.		
L. Blandin.............	Col. 95th Ill. Infy...............	Feb. 18, 1865, to Mch. 17, 1865.	
L. M. Ward.............	Col. 14th Wis. Infy...............	Mch. 17, 1865, to Apr. 29, 1865.	
S. A. Holmes...........	Col. 40th Mo. Infy...............	Apr. 29, 1865, to July 20, 1865.	
81st Ill. Infy..........Feb., 1865	From 2-Brig. 3-Div. Det. Army Tenn.	To 3-Brig. 3-Div. 16-Corps........	Mch., 1865
96th Ill. Infy..........Feb., 1865	From 2-Brig. 3-Div. Det. Army Tenn.	To 1-Brig. 3-Div. 16-Corps........	Mch., 1865
44th Mo. Infy...........Feb., 186	From 2-Brig. 3-Div. Det. Army Tenn.	To 1-Brig. 3-Div. 16-Corps........	Mch., 1865
49th Mo. Infy...........Feb., 1865	From 2-Brig. 3-Div. Det. Army Tenn.	To Dist. Alabama..................	July, 1865
14th Wis. Infy..........Mch., 1865	From 1-Brig. 3-Div. 16-Corps.......	To Dist. Alabama..................	July, 1865
40th Mo. Infy..........Mch., 1865	From 1-Brig. 3-Div. 16-Corps.......	No change to Muster Out...........	Aug., 1865

3d BRIGADE.—Organized March 6, 1865.

	COMMANDERS.		
C. Turner..............	Col. 108th Ill. Infy..............	Mch. 6, 1865, to Mch. 15, 1865.	
J. L. Geddes...........	Col. 8th Iowa Infy...............	Mch. 15, 1865, to June 30, 1865.	
C. Turner..............	Col. 108th Ill. Infy..............	June 30, 1865, to July 20, 1865.	
81st Ill. Infy..........Mch., 1865	From 2-Brig. 3-Div. 16-Corps.......	No change to Muster Out...........	Aug., 1865
108th Ill. Infy..........Mch., 1865	From Dist. Memphis, West Tenn..	No change to Muster Out...........	Aug., 1865
124th Ill. Infy..........Mch., 1865	From Maltby's Brig. Dist. Vicksburg	No change to Muster Out...........	Aug., 1865
8th Iowa Infy...........Mch., 1865	From Memphis, Tenn., D. W. Tenn..	To Dept. Alabama..................	Aug., 1865
ARTILLERY.—			
14th Ind. Batty..........Feb., 1865	From Arty. 3-Div. Det. Army Tenn..	To Arty. Brig. 16-Corps...........	Mch., 1865

ENGINEER BRIGADE.—

	COMMANDERS.		
Joseph Bailey..........	Brigadier General.................	Mch. 11, 1865, to May 2, 1865.	
J. C. Cobb.............	Col. 96th U. S. C. T.............	May 2, 1865, to July, 1865.	
96th U. S. C. T.........Feb., 1865	From Dist. South Ala.............	To Unassigned Dept. Gulf.........	July, 1865
97th U. S. C. T.........Feb., 1865	From Dist. West Fla..............	To Unassigned Dept. Gulf.........	July, 1865
PONTONEERS.—			
114th Ill. Infy..........Feb., 1865	From 1-Brig. 1-Div. Det. Army Tenn.	No change to Muster Out...........	Aug., 1865
ARTILLERY BRIGADE.—Organized Mch. 1865.			
Cogswell's Ill. Batty.....Mch., 1865	From Arty. 1-Div. Det. Army Tenn..	No change to Muster Out...........	Aug., 1865
Batty. G, 2d Ill. Arty...Mch., 1865	From Arty. 2-Div. 16-Corps.........	No change to Muster Out...........	July, 1865
1st Ind. Batty..........Mch., 1865	From Res. Arty. Gulf.............	No change to Muster Out...........	Aug., 1865
14th Ind. Batty.........Mch., 1865	From Arty. 3-Div. 16-Corps........	No change to Muster Out...........	Aug., 1865
17th Ohio Batty.........Mch., 1865	From Unatt. Arty. Res. Corps Gulf.	No change to Muster Out...........	Aug., 1865
2d Iowa Batty...........Mch., 1865	From Arty. 1-Div. 16-Corps........	No change to Muster Out...........	Aug., 1865
3d Ind. Batty...........Mch., 1865	From Arty. 1-Div. 16-Corps........	No change to Muster Out...........	Aug., 1865

Steele's Command, District West Florida

	COMMANDER.		
Frederick Steele.......	Major General.....................		

1st DIVISION U. S. C. T.—

	COMMANDER.		
J. P. Hawkins..........	Brigadier General.................		

1st BRIGADE.—

	COMMANDERS.		
Wm. A. Pile..........	Brigadier General.................	Feb. 19, 1865, to Apr. 25, 1865.	
L. L. Zulavski........	Col. 87th U. S. C. T.............	Apr. 25, 1865, to May 19, 1865.	
F. M. Crandall........	Col. 58th U. S. C. T.............	May 19, 1865, to June, 1865.	
73d U. S. C. T..........Mch., 1865	From 1-B. U. S. C. T. Morganza, La.	To 3-Brig. 1-Div. U. S. C. T.......	May, 1865
82d U. S. C. T..........Mch., 1865	From 1 Colored Brig. Dist. W. Fla.	To Dist. West Fla.................	May, 1865
86th U. S. C. T..........Mch., 1865	From 1 Colored Brig. Dist. W. Fla.	To Dist. West Fla.................	May, 1865
61st U. S. C. T..........Apr., 1865	From 1-Brig. U. S. C. T. Morganza.	To Dept. Miss....................	June, 1865
48th U. S. C. T..........May, 1865	From 3-Brig. 1-Div. U. S. C. T.....	To Dept. Miss....................	June, 1865
68th U. S. C. T..........May, 1865	From 3-Brig. 1-Div. U. S. C. T.....	To Dept. Miss....................	June, 1865
76th U. S. C. T..........May, 1865	From 3-Brig. 1-Div. U. S. C. T.....	To Dept. Miss....................	June, 1865

2d BRIGADE.—

	COMMANDER.		
Hiram Scofield........	Col. 47th U. S. C. T.............		
47th U. S. C. T..........Feb., 1865	From 2-B. 1-Div. U. S. C. T. Vicks.	To Dept. Gulf....................	July, 1865
50th U. S. C. T..........Feb., 1865	From 2-B. 1-Div. U. S. C. T. Vicks.	To Dept. Gulf....................	July, 1865
51st U. S. C. T..........Feb., 1865	From 1-Brig. 1-Div. U. S. C. T. Vicks.	To Dept. Gulf....................	July, 1865

3d BRIGADE.—

COMMANDERS.		
C. W. Drew	Col. 76th U. S. C. T.	Feb. 19, 1865, to Mch. 10, 1865.
L. L. Zulavski	Col. 87th U. S. C. T.	Mch. 10, 1865, to Apr. 25, 1865.

48th U. S. C. T.	Feb., 1865	From 1-B. 1-Div. U. S. C. T. Vicks.	To 1-Brig. 1-Div. U. S. C. T. W. Fla.	May,	1865
68th U. S. C. T.	Feb., 1865	From Memphis, Tenn., West Tenn...	To 1-Brig. 1-Div. U. S. C. T. W. Fla.	May,	1865
76th U. S. C. T.	Feb., 1865	From Port Hudson, La.	To 1-Brig. 1-Div. U. S. C. T. W. Fla.	May,	1865
73d U. S. C. T.	May, 1865	From 1-B. 1-D. U. S. C. T. D. W.Fla.	To Dept. Texas	July,	1865
ARTILLERY.—					
7th Mass. Batty.	Apr., 1865	From Arty. 1-Div. 13-Corps	To Dept. Texas	July,	1865

SEPARATE CAVALRY BRIGADE.—Organized Feb. 8, 1865.

COMMANDER.		
T. J. Lucas	Brigadier General	Feb. 8, 1865, to Mch. 28, 1865.

1st La. Cav.	Feb., 1865	From Sep. Cav. Brig. Res. C. Gulf.	To 1-Brig. Cav. Div. D. W. Fla.	Mch.,	1865
2d Ill. Cav.	Feb., 1865	From 3-Brig. Cav. Div. Gulf.	To 2-Brig. Cav. Div. Dist. W. Fla.	Mch.,	1865
2d N. Y. Vet. Cav.	Feb., 1865	From Sep. Cav. Brig. Res. Corps.	To 1-Brig. Cav. Div. Dist. W. Fla.	Mch.,	1865
31st Mass. Mtd. Infy.	Feb., 1865	From Def. New Orleans	To 1-Brig. Cav. Div. Dist. W. Fla.	Mch.,	1865

LUCAS' CAVALRY DIVISION.—Organized Mch. 28, 1865.

COMMANDER.		
Thomas J. Lucas	Brigadier General	

1st BRIGADE.—

COMMANDER.		
W. H. Chrysler	Col. 2d N. Y. Vet. Cav.	Mch. 28, 1865, to Apr. 14, 1865.

1st La. Cav.	Mch., 1865	From Sep. Cav. Brig. D. W. Fla.	To 3-B. 1-Div. Cav. Corps W. Miss.	Apr.,	1865
2d N. Y. Vet. Cav.	Mch., 1865	From Sep. Cav. Brig. D. W. Fla.	To 3-B. 1-Div. Cav. Corps W. Miss.	Apr.,	1865
31st Mass. Mtd. Infy.	Mch., 1865	From Sep. Cav. Brig. D. W. Fla.	To Dist. Mobile, Ala.	Apr.,	1865

2d BRIGADE.—

COMMANDER.		
A. B. Spurling	Col. 2d Maine Cav.	Mch. 28, 1865, to Apr. 14, 1865.

1st Florida Cav.	Mch., 1865	From 3-Brig. Dist. West Fla.	To Dist. West Fla.	Apr.,	1865
2d Ill. Cav.	Mch., 1865	From Sep. Cav. Brig. D. W. Fla.	To 3-B. 1-Div. Cav. Corps W. Miss.	Apr.,	1865
2d Maine Cav.	Mch., 1865	From 3-Brig. Dist. West Fla.	To Dist. West Fla.	Apr.,	1865
ARTILLERY.—					
2d Mass. Batty.	Feb., 1865	From Unatt. Arty. Res. Corps Gulf.	To 3-B. 1-Div. Cav. Corps W. Miss.	Apr.,	1865

Cavalry Corps, West Mississippi

COMMANDER.		
B. H. Grierson	Brigadier General	

1st DIVISION.—

COMMANDER.		
J. F. Knipe	Brigadier General	

1st BRIGADE.—

COMMANDERS.		
Jos. Karge	Col. 2d N. J. Cav.	Mch. 15, 1865, to Apr. 14, 1865.
J. R. West	Brigadier General	Apr. 14, 1865, to May 15, 1865.

2d N. J. Cav.	Mch., 1865	From 1-B. Cav. Div. Dist. W. Tenn.	To 2-B. 1-Div. Cav. Corps W. Miss.	Apr.,	1865
12th Ind. Cav.	Mch., 1865	From 2-B. 7-Div. Cav. Corps M. D. M.	To 2-B. 1-Div. Cav. Corps W. Miss.	Apr.,	1865
4th Wis. Cav.	Mch., 1865	From Cav. B. Dist. Baton Rouge, La.	To 2-B. 1-Div. Cav. Corps W. Miss.	Apr.,	1865
3d Mich. Cav.	Apr., 1865	From 1-Brig. Cav. Div. 7-Corps Ark.	To 2-B. 2-Div. Cav. Corps W. Miss.	May,	1865
10th Ill. Cav.	Apr., 1865	From 1-Brig. Cav. Div. 7-Corps Ark.	To 2-B. 2-Div. Cav. Corps W. Miss.	May,	1865

2d BRIGADE.—

COMMANDERS.		
G. M. L. Johnson	Col. 13th Ind. Cav.	Mch. 22, 1865, to Apr. 14, 1865.
J. F. Knipe	Brigadier General	Apr. 14, 1865, to Apr. 17, 1865.
Jos. Karge	Col. 2d N. J. Cav.	Apr. 17, 1865, to June 1, 1865.
G. M. L. Johnson	Col. 13th Ind. Cav.	June 1, 1865.

10th Ind. Cav.	Mch., 1865	From 1-B. 7-Div. Cav. Corps M. D. M.	To 3-B. 1-Div. Cav. Corps W. Miss.	May,	1865
13th Ind. Cav.	Mch., 1865	From 2-B. 7-Div. Cav. Corps M. D. M.	To Dept. Miss.	June,	1865
4th Tenn. Cav.	Mch., 1865	From 2-B. 7-Div. Cav. Corps M. D. M.	To 1-B. 2-Div. Cav. Corps W. Miss.	May,	1865
14th Ohio Batty.	Mch., 1865	From A. 7-Div. Cav. Corps M. D. M.	To Dept. Miss.	June,	1865
12th Ind. Cav.	Apr., 1865	From 1-B. 1-D. Cav. Corps W. Miss.	To Dept. Miss.	May,	1865
4th Wis. Cav.	Apr., 1865	From 1-B. 1-D. Cav. Corps W. Miss.	To 3-B. 1-Div. Cav. Corps W. Miss.	May,	1865
2d N. J. Cav.	Apr., 1865	From 1-B. 1-D. Cav. Corps W. Miss.	To Dept. Miss.	June,	1865

3d BRIGADE.—Organized Apr. 14, 1865.

COMMANDERS.		
Thos. J. Lucas	Brigadier General	Apr. 14, 1865, to Apr. 28, 1865.
M. H. Chrysler	Bvt. Brig. General	Apr. 28, 1865, to May 9, 1865.
Thomas J. Lucas	Brigadier General	May 9, 1865, to July, 1865.

2d Ill. Cav.	Apr., 1865	From 2-Brig. Cav. Div. D. W. Fla.	To Dept. Miss.	June,	1865
1st La. Cav.	Apr., 1865	From 1-Brig. Cav. Div. D. W. Fla.	To Dept. Louisiana	June,	1865
2d N. Y. Vet. Cav.	Apr., 1865	From 1-Brig. Cav. Div. D. W. Fla.	To Dept. Alabama	June,	1865
2d Mass. Batty.	Apr., 1865	From Arty. Cav. Div. Dist. W. Fla.	To Dept. Miss.	June,	1865
4th Wis. Cav.	May, 1865	From 1-B. 1-D. Cav. Corps W. Miss.	To Dept. Texas	July,	1865
10th Ind. Infy.	May, 1865	From 1-B. 1-D. Cav. Corps W. Miss.	To Dept. Miss.	June,	1865

2d DIVISION.—Organized May 15, 1865. Discontinued June 12, 1865.

COMMANDER.		
J. R. West	Brigadier General	

1st BRIGADE.—

COMMANDER.		
J. F. Knipe	Brigadier General	

4th Tenn. Cav.	May, 1865	From 2-B. 1-Div. Cav. Corps W. Miss.	No change to Muster Out	July,	1865
3d Md. Cav.	May, 1865	From Dist. South Alabama	To Dept. Miss.	June,	1865
14th N. Y. Cav.	May, 1865	From Dist. Morganza, La.	Consolidated with 18th N. Y. Cav.	June,	1865
18th N. Y. Cav.	May, 1865	From Dist. La Fourche, La.	To Dept. Louisiana	June,	1865

2d BRIGADE.—

COMMANDER.			
Jos. Bailey............	Brigadier General......................		

3d Mich. Cav............May, 1865	From 1-B. 1-Div. Cav. Corps W. Miss.	To Dept. Texas...................	July,	1865
4th Mo. Cav.............May, 1865	From 1-B. Cav. Div. Dist. W. Tenn.	To Dept. Texas...................	July,	1865
10th Ill. Cav...........May, 1865	From 1-B. 1-Div. Cav. Corps W. Miss.	To Dept. Texas...................	July,	1865

Department of Arkansas

Seventh Army Corps

Created Jan. 6, 1864, to consist of Arkansas, except Fort Smith. Fort Smith added April 17, 1864. Corps discontinued Aug. 1, 1865. (Department embraced in Military Division of West Mississippi May 7, 1864, to May, 1865. Major General E. R. S. Canby Commanding.)

COMMANDERS.

Frederick Steele........	Major General......................	Jan. 6, 1864, to Dec. 22, 1864.
J. J. Reynolds.........	Major General......................	Dec. 22, 1864, to Aug. 1, 1865.

COMMANDING DIST. LITTLE ROCK.

E. A. Carr............	Brigadier General...................	May 11, 1864, to Dec. 24, 1864.

1st (or CAVALRY) DIVISION.—Discontinued May 11, 1864. 1st Division reorganized May 11, 1864, by transfer of 3d Division, 7th Corps.

COMMANDERS.

J. W. Davidson........	Brigadier General...................	Jan. 6, 1864, to Feb. 13, 1864.
E. A. Carr...........	Brigadier General...................	Feb. 13, 1864, to May 11, 1864.
F'dk. Salomon.........	Brigadier General...................	May 11, 1864, to July 25, 1864.
Cyrus Bussey..........	Brigadier General...................	July 25, 1864, to Sept. 9, 1864.
A. Engleman..........	Col. 43d Ill. Infy...................	Sept. 9, 1864, to Sept. 25, 1864.
F'dk. Salomon.........	Brigadier General...................	Sept. 25, 1864, to Aug. 1, 1865.

1st BRIGADE.—

COMMANDERS.

J. F. Ritter............	Col. 1st Mo. Cav..................	Jan. 6, 1864, to May 11, 1864.
Chas. E. Salomon......	Col. 9th Wis. Infy................	May 11, 1864, to Nov. 25, 1864.
A. Jacobi............	Lt.-Col. 9th Wis. Infy............	Nov. 25, 1864, to Nov. 28, 1864.
C. H. Mackey.........	Col. 33d Iowa Infy...............	Nov. 28, 1864, to Jan. 7, 1865.
W. H. Graves.........	Col. 12th Mich. Infy..............	Jan. 7, 1865, to Feb. 1, 1865.
J. A. Garrett..........	Col. 40th Iowa Infy...............	Feb. 1, 1865, to Feb. 18, 1865.
A. Dengler...........	Lt.-Col. 43d Ill. Infy.............	Feb. 18, 1865, to Mch. 22, 1865.
T. M. Bowen..........	Col. 13th Kansas Infy.............	Mch. 22, 1865, to June 24, 1865.
A. Dengler...........	Lt.-Col. 43d Ill...................	June 24, 1865, to Aug. 1, 1865.

13th Ill. Cav. Det........Jan., 1864	From Res. Br. 1-Cav. Div. Ark. Exp.	To Clayton's Indpt. Cav. Brig. 7-C.	May,	1864
3d Iowa Cav. Det.......Jan., 1864	From Res. Br. 1-Cav. Div. Ark. Exp.	To 2-Brig. Cav. Div. 16-C. Tenn...	May,	1864
1st Mo. Cav. 8 Cos......Jan., 1864	From 1-Brig. 1-Cav. Div. Ark. Exp.	To 3-Brig. 1-Div. 7-Corps.........	May,	1864
7th Mo. Cav............Jan., 1864	From 1-Brig. 1-Cav. Div. Ark. Exp.	To Clayton's Indpt. Cav. Brig. 7-C.	May,	1864
3d Ark. Cav...........Apr., 1864	From New Organization............	To 3-Brig. 2-Div. 7-Corps.........	May,	1864
9th Wis. Infy..........May, 1864	From 1-Brig. 3-Div. 7-Corps.......	To Dept. Arkansas................	Aug.,	1865
28th Wis. Infy.........May, 1864	From Post Pine Bluff 7-Corps......	To 3-Brig. 3-Div. Res. Corps. Gulf.	Feb.,	1865
29th Iowa Infy.........May, 1864	From 1-Brig. 3-Div. 7-Corps.......	To 2-Brig. 2-Div. 7-Corps.........	Nov.,	1864
33d Iowa Infy..........May, 1864	From 1-Brig. 3-Div. 7-Corps.......	To 3-Brig. 3-Div. Res. Corps Gulf.	Feb.,	1865
50th Ind. Infy.........May, 1864	From 1-Brig. 3-Div. 7-Corps.......	To 2-Brig. 3-Div. Res. Corps Gulf.	Feb.,	1865
43d Ill. Infy..........Feb., 1865	From 2-Brig. 1-Div. 7-Corps.......	To Dept. Arkansas................	Aug.,	1865
36th Iowa Infy.........Feb., 1865	From 2-Brig. 1-Div. 7-Corps.......	To 1-Brig. 2-Div. 7-Corps.........	Mch.,	1865
40th Iowa Infy.........Feb., 1865	From 2-Brig. 1-Div. 7-Corps.......	To 1-Brig. 3-Div. 7-Corps.........	Feb.,	1865
12th Kansas Infy.......Feb., 1865	From 1-Brig. 3-Div. 7-Corps.......	No change to Muster Out..........	Aug.,	1865
2 Kansas Cav..........Feb., 1865	From 2-Brig. 3-Div. 7-Corps.......	No change to Muster Out..........	June,	1865
13th Kansas Infy.......Feb., 1865	From 1-Brig. 2-Div. 7-Corps.......	No change to Muster Out..........	June,	1865
35th Mo. Infy.........Feb., 1865	From Dist. Eastern Ark. 7-Corps..	No change to Muster Out..........	June,	1865
18th Ill. Infy..........May, 1865	From Pontooneers 7-Corps.........	To Dept. Ark....................	Aug.,	1865

2d BRIGADE.—

COMMANDERS.

W. F. Geiger..........	Col. 8th Mo. Cav.................	Jan. 6, 1864, to May 11, 1864.
A. Engleman.........	Col. 43d Ill. Infy................	May 11, 1864, to Nov. 10, 1864.
J. A. Garrett..........	Col. 40th Iowa Infy..............	Nov. 10, 1864, to Feb. 1, 1865.
J. M. Williams........	Col. 79th U. S. C. T.............	Feb. 1, 1865, to July 12, 1865.
J. G. Hudson.........	Col. 60th U. S. C. T.............	July 12, 1865, to Aug. 1, 1865.

2d Mo. Cav...........Jan., 1864	From 2-Brig. 1-Cav. Div. Ark. Exp.	To 3-Brig. 2-Div. 7-Corps.........	May,	1864
8th Mo. Cav...........Jan., 1864	From 2-Brig. 1-Cav. Div. Ark. Exp..	To 3-Brig. 2-Div. 7-Corps.........	May,	1864
43d Ind. Infy..........May, 1864	From 2-Brig. 3-Div. 7-Corps.......	To Camp Morton, Ind.............	June,	1864
36th Iowa Infy.........May, 1864	From 2-Brig. 3-Div. 7-Corps.......	To 1-Brig. 2-Div. 7-Corps.........	Apr.,	1865
40th Iowa Infy.........May, 1864	From 2-Brig. 3-Div. 7-Corps.......	To 1-Brig. 1-Div. 7-Corps.........	Feb.,	1865
77th Ohio Infy.........May, 1864	From 2-Brig. 3-Div. 7-Corps.......	To 3-Brig. 3-Div. Res. Corps Gulf.	Feb.,	1865
27th Wis. Infy.........May, 1864	From 2-Brig. 3-Div. 7-Corps.......	To 3-Brig. 3-Div. Res. Corps Gulf.	Feb.,	1865
43d Ill. Infy..........May, 1864	From 2-Brig. 3-Div. 7-Corps.......	To 1-Brig. 1-Div. 7-Corps.........	Feb.,	1865
112th U. S. C. T........Oct., 1864	From Unatt. 1-Div. 7-Corps.......	To Dept. Ark....................	Aug.,	1865
113th U. S. C. T........Oct., 1864	From Unatt. 1-Div. 7-Corps.......	To Dept. Ark....................	Aug.,	1865
11th U. S. C. T. (Old)..Feb., 1865	From 2-Brig. Frontier Div. 7-Corps.	Consol. with 112th and 113th......	Apr.,	1865
54th U. S. C. T........Feb., 1865	From 2-Brig. Frontier Div. 7-Corps.	To Dept. Ark....................	Aug.,	1865
57th U. S. C. T........Feb., 1865	From 1-Brig. 2-Div. 7-Corps.......	To Dept. Ark....................	Aug.,	1865
79th U. S. C. T........Feb., 1865	From 2-Brig. Dist. Frontier 7-Corps.	To Dept. Ark....................	Aug.,	1865
83d U. S. C. T........Feb., 1865	From 2-Brig. Dist. Frontier 7-Corps.	To Dept. Ark....................	Aug.,	1865
60th U. S. C. T........Apr., 1865	From Dist. Eastern Ark. 7-Corps...	To Dept. Ark....................	Aug.,	1865

3d BRIGADE.—

COMMANDERS.

Daniel Anderson	Col. 1st Iowa Cav................	Jan. 6, 1864, to May 11, 1864.
J. A. Leaman.........	Major 3d Mo. Cav................	May 11, 1864, to May 25, 1864.
Cyrus Bussey	Brigadier General	May 25, 1864, to July 25, 1864.
J. F. Ritter..........	Col. 1st Mo. Cav.................	July 25, 1864, to Sept. 15, 1864.
Brigade transferred to Cavalry Division Sept. 15, 1864.		

10th Ill. Cav. Det.......Jan., 1864	From 3-Brig. 1-Cav. Div. Ark. Exp.	To 3-Brig. 2-Div. 7-Corps.........	May,	1864
1st Iowa Cav..........Jan., 1864	From 3-Brig. 1-Cav. Div. Ark. Exp.	To 2-Brig. Cav. Div. 7-Corps......	Sept.,	1864
3d Mo. Cav...........Jan., 1864	From 3-Brig. 1-Cav. Div. Ark. Exp.	To 2-Brig. Cav. Div. 7-Corps......	Sept.,	1864
1st Mo. Cav...........May, 1864	From 1-Brig. 1-Cav. Div. 16-Corps.	To 2-Brig. Cav. Div. 7-Corps......	Sept.,	1864
4th Ark. Cav..........May, 1864	From New Organization...........	To 2-Brig. Cav. Div. 7-Corps......	Sept.,	1864
3d Iowa Cav. Det.......May, 1864	From 1-Brig. 1-Cav. Div. 7-Corps...	To 2-Brig. Cav. Div. 7-Corps......	Sept.,	1864

ARTILLERY.—

Batty. D, 2d Mo. Arty....Jan., 1864	From Arty. 1-Cav. Div. Ark. Exp...	To Arty. 2-Div. 7-Corps............	May,	1864
Batty. E, 2d Mo. Arty....Jan., 1864	From Arty. 1-Cav. Div. Ark. Exp...	To Arty. 3-Div. 7-Corps............	Apr.,	1864
Vaughan's Ill. Batty.....May, 1864	From Arty. 3-Div. 7-Corps.........	No change to Muster Out..........	June,	1865
Batty. E, 2d Mo. Arty....May, 1864	From Arty. 3-Div. 7-Corps.........	To Dept. Ark....................	Aug.,	1865
25th Ohio Batty.........May, 1864	From Arty. 3-Div. 7-Corps.........	To Arty. Cav. Div. 7-Corps......	Feb.,	1865
3d Iowa Batty...........May, 1864	From Arty. 3-Div. 7-Corps.........	To Dept. Ark....................	Aug.,	1865
5th Ohio Batty..........Oct., 1864	From Arty. 2-Div. 7-Corps.........	No change to Muster Out..........	July,	1865
Batty. K. 1st Mo. Arty....Feb., 1865	From Arty. 2-Div. 7-Corps.........	No change to Muster Out..........	July,	1865

UNATTACHED.—

24th Mo. Infy., F, K......Jan., 1864	From Unatt. 1-Div. Ark. Exp......	To 2-Brig. 3-Div. 16-Corps Tenn....	Feb.,	1864
5th Ark. Col'd...........June, 1864 (112th U. S. C. T.)	From New Organization...........	To 2-Brig. 1-Div. 7-Corps........	Oct.,	1864
6th Ark. Col'd...........June, 1864 (113th U. S. C. T.)	From New Organization...........	To 2-Brig. 1-Div. 7-Corps........	Oct.,	1864

2d DIVISION.— COMMANDERS.

E. A. Carr............	Brigadier General	Jan. 6, 1864, to Feb. 13, 1864.
Nathan Kimball	Brigadier General	Feb. 13, 1864, to Apr. 25, 1864.
J. R. West...........	Brigadier General	Apr. 25, 1864, to June 16, 1864.
C. C. Andrews........	Brigadier General	June 16, 1864, to Dec. 28, 1864.
A. Shaler	Brigadier General	Dec. 28, 1864, to Aug. 1, 1865.

1st BRIGADE.—Organized May 13, 1864. COMMANDERS.

W. H. Graves.........	Col. 12th Mich. Infy.............	May 13, 1864, to Sept. 10, 1864.
A. B. Morrison........	Col. 57th U. S. C. T............	Sept. 10, 1864, to Oct. 10, 1864.
H. Mattson	Col. 2d Minn. Infy..............	Oct. 10, 1864, to Feb. 6, 1865.
W. H. Graves.........	Col. 12th Mich. Infy.............	Feb. 6, 1865, to June 11, 1865.
F. M. Drake	Lt.-Col. 36th Iowa Infy.........	June 11, 1865, to Aug. 1, 1865.

3d Minn. Infy...........May, 1864	From 3-Brig. 2-Div. 7-Corps......	No change to Muster Out..........	Sept.,	1865
12th Mich. Infy.........May, 1864	From 3-Brig. 2-Div. 7-Corps......	To Dept. Ark....................	Aug.,	1865
18th Ill. Infy..........May, 1864	From Post Pine Bluff, Ark., 7-Corps.	To Pontooneers 7-Corps...........	Jan.,	1865
54th Ill. Infy..........May, 1864	From 3-Brig. 2-Div. 7-Corps......	To Dept. Ark....................	Aug.,	1865
61st Ill. Infy..........May, 1864	From 3-Brig. 2-Div. 7-Corps......	To Veteran Furlough.............	Aug.,	1864
57th U. S. C. T........May, 1864	From Dist. Eastern Ark. 7-Corps...	To 2-Brig. 1-Div. 7-Corps........	Feb.,	1865
6th Kansas Cav.........Feb., 1865	From 2-Brig. 3-Div. 7-Corps......	No change to Muster Out..........	July,	1865
13th Kansas Infy........Feb., 1865	From 1-Brig. 1-Div. 7-Corps......	To 1-Brig. 1-Div. 7-Corps........	Feb.,	1865
36th Iowa Infy..........Mch., 1865	From 1-Brig. 1-Div. 7-Corps......	No change to Muster Out..........	Aug.,	1865

2d BRIGADE.— COMMANDER.

A. Engleman	Col. 43d Ill. Infy................	Jan. 6, 1864, to Mch. 12, 1864.

Brigade discontinued Mch. 12, 1864. Reorganized May 19, 1864.
COMMANDERS.

C. C. Andrews........	Brigadier General	May 19, 1864, to June 16, 1864.
Oliver Wood	Col. 22d Ohio Infy..............	June 16, 1864, to Aug. 18, 1864.
Homer Thrall	Lt.-Col. 22d Ohio Infy...........	Aug. 18, 1864, to Sept. 25, 1864.
M. L. Stephenson......	Lt.-Col. 2d Ark. Infy...........	Sept. 25, 1864, to Nov. 16, 1864.
T. H. Benton, Jr......	Col. 29th Iowa Infy.............	Nov. 16, 1864, to Nov. 26, 1864.
Jas. M. True.........	Col. 62d Ill. Infy..............	Nov. 26, 1864, to Jan. 5, 1865.
T. H. Benton, Jr......	Col. 29th Iowa Infy.............	Jan. 5, 1865, to Jan. 15, 1865.
Jas. M. True.........	Col. 62d Ill. Infy..............	Jan. 15, 1865, to Apr. 30, 1865.
L. C. True...........	Lt.-Col. 62d Ill. Infy...........	Apr. 30, 1865, to May 7, 1865.
John Edwards	Brigadier General	May 7, 1865, to June 18, 1865.
L. W. Beal...........	Lt.-Col. 126th Ill. Infy.........	June 18, 1865, to July 26, 1865.
L. C. True...........	Lt.-Col. 62d Ill. Infy...........	July 26, 1865, to Aug. 1, 1865.

43d Ill. Infy...........Jan., 1864	From 2-Brig. 2-Div. Ark. Exp.....	To 3-Brig. 3-Div. 7-Corps........	Mch.,	1864
126th Ill. Infy.........Jan., 1864	From 2-Brig. 2-Div. Ark. Exp.....	To 3-Brig. 3-Div. 7-Corps........	Mch.,	1864
40th Iowa Infy..........Jan., 1864	From 2-Brig. 2-Div. Ark. Exp.....	To 3-Brig. 3-Div. 7-Corps........	Mch.,	1864
22d Ohio Infy...........Jan., 1864	From 2-Brig. 2-Div. Ark. Exp.....	To 3-Brig. 3-Div. 7-Corps........	Mch.,	1864
27th Wis. Infy..........Jan., 1864	From 2-Brig. 2-Div. Ark. Exp.....	To 3-Brig. 3-Div. 7-Corps........	Mch.,	1864
11th Ohio Batty.........Jan., 1864	From 2-Brig. 2-Div. Ark. Exp.....	To Arty. 2-Div. 7-Corps..........	May,	1864
62d Ill. Infy...........May, 1864	From Unass'd 2-Div. 7-Corps......	To Dept. Ark....................	Aug.,	1865
106th Ill. Infy.........May, 1864	From 3-Brig. 2-Div. 7-Corps......	No change to Muster Out..........	July,	1865
126th Ill. Infy.........May, 1864	From 3-Brig. 3-Div. 7-Corps......	To U. S. Forces Mouth White River.	Feb.,	1865
2d Ark. Infy...........May, 1864	From 1-Brig. Frontier Div. 7-Corps.	To 1-Brig. Dist. Frontier 7-Corps...	Dec.,	1864
22d Ohio Infy...........May, 1864	From 3-Brig. 3-Div. 7-Corps......	To 1-Brig. 3-Div. 7-Corps........	Feb.,	1865
29th Iowa Infy..........Nov., 1864	From 1-Brig. 1-Div. 7-Corps......	To 2-Brig. 3-Div. Res. Corps Gulf...	Feb.,	1865
11th Kansas Cav........Mch., 1865	From Dist. Upper Ark............	To Dist. Plains.................	Apr.,	1865

3d BRIGADE.—Transferred to Cav. Div. Sept. 15, 1864.
COMMANDERS.

G. M. Mitchell........	Col. 54th Ill. Infy..............	Jan. 6, 1864, to Feb. 12, 1864.
Henry Yates	Lt.-Col. 106th Ill. Infy.........	Feb. 12, 1864, to Apr. 9, 1864.
W. H. Graves.........	Col. 12th Mich. Infy.............	Apr. 9, 1864, to Apr. 16, 1864.
J. M. True...........	Col. 62d Ill. Infy..............	Apr. 16, 1864, to May 15, 1864.
W. F. Geiger.........	Col. 8th Mo. Cav...............	May 15, 1864, to Sept. 15, 1864.

18th Ill. Infy..........Jan., 1864	From 3-Brig. 2-Div. Ark. Exp.....	To 1-Brig. 2-Div. 7-Corps........	May,	1864
54th Ill. Infy..........Jan., 1864	From 3-Brig. 2-Div. Ark. Exp.....	To 1-Brig. 2-Div. 7-Corps........	May,	1864
61st Ill. Infy..........Jan., 1864	From 3-Brig. 2-Div. Ark. Exp.....	To 1-Brig. 2-Div. 7-Corps........	May,	1864
106th Ill. Infy.........Jan., 1864	From 3-Brig. 2-Div. Ark. Exp.....	To 2-Brig. 2-Div. 7-Corps........	May,	1864
3d Minn. Infy..........Jan., 1864	From 2-Brig. 2-Div. Ark. Exp.....	To 1-Brig. 2-Div. 7-Corps........	May,	1864
12th Mich. Infy.........Jan., 1864	From 3-Brig. 2-Div. Ark. Exp.....	To 1-Brig. 2-Div. 7-Corps........	May,	1864
5th Ohio Batty.........Jan., 1864	From 3-Brig. 2-Div. Ark. Exp.....	To Arty. 2-Div. 7-Corps..........	May,	1864
8th Mo. Cav...........May, 1864	From 2-Brig. 1-Cav. Div. 7-Corps..	To 3-Brig. Cav. Div. 7-Corps.....	Sept.,	1864
10th Ill. Cav..........May, 1864	From 3-Brig. 1-Cav. Div. 7-Corps..	To 3-Brig. Cav. Div. 7-Corps.....	Sept.,	1864
2d Mo. Cav...........May, 1864	From 2-Brig. 1-Cav. Div. 7-Corps..	To 3-Brig. Cav. Div. 7-Corps.....	Sept.,	1864
3d Ark. Cav...........May, 1864	From New Organization...........	To 4-Brig. Cav. Div. 7-Corps.....	Sept.,	1864
9th Iowa Cav..........June, 1864	From Dist. St. Louis, Mo.........	To 3-Brig. Cav. Div. 7-Corps.....	Sept.,	1864
3d. Mich. Cav..........June, 1864	From Dist. St. Louis, Mo.........	To 4-Brig. Cav. Div. 7-Corps.....	Sept.,	1864
11th Mo. Cav..........June, 1864	From Dist. Northeast Ark. 7-Corps.	To 3-Brig. Cav. Div. 7-Corps.....	Sept.,	1864
1st Neb. Cav., 3 Co's.....June, 1864	From Dist. Northeast Ark. 7-Corps.	To 4-Brig. Cav. Div. 7-Corps.....	Sept.,	1864

UNASSIGNED.—

62d Ill. Infy...........Jan., 1864	From True's Brig. Ark. Exp......	To 2-Brig. 2-Div. 7-Corps........	May,	1864
50th Ind. Infy..........Jan., 1864	From True's Brig. Ark. Exp......	To 1-Brig. 3-Div. 7-Corps........	Apr.,	1864
13th Ill. Cav., Co. C....Jan., 1864	From Unatt. 1-Cav. Div. Ark. Exp..	To Clayton's Indpt. Cav. Brig. 7-C..	Apr.,	1864
Vaughan's Ill. Batty.....Jan., 1864	From True's Brig. Ark. Exp......	To Arty. 3-Div. 7-Corps..........	Apr.,	1864
66th U. S. C. T........Feb., 1864	From Dist. Vicksburg, Miss.......	To Dist. Vicksburg, Miss.........	Feb.,	1865
4th Ark. Cav...........Feb., 1864	From 2-Brig. Cav. Div. 7-Corps....	No change to Muster Out..........	June,	1865
9th Kansas Cav.........Feb., 1864	From 4-Brig. Cav. Div. 7-Corps....	No change to Muster Out..........	July,	1865
3d Wis. Cav...........Apr., 1865	From Post Little Rock 7-Corps.....	To Dept. Ark....................	Aug.,	1865

ARTILLERY.—

Batty. D, 2d Mo. Arty.....May, 1864	From Arty. 1-Cav. Div. 7-Corps.....	To Mouth White River............	Feb., 1865
5th Ohio Batty..........May, 1864	From 3-Brig. 2-Div. 7-Corps........	To Arty. 1-Div. 7-Corps........	Feb., 1865
11th Ohio Batty..........May, 1864	From 2-Brig. 2-Div. 7-Corps........	No change to Muster Out........	Nov., 1864
Batty. K, 1st Mo. Arty.....May, 1864	From Arty. 3-Div. 7-Corps.........	To Arty. 1-Div. 7-Corps........	Feb., 1865
1st Del. Batty............Dec., 1864	From U. S. Forces White River.....	No change to Muster Out........	July, 1865

3d DIVISION.—Transferred to 1st Division May 11, 1864. Reorganized Feb. 6, 1865.

COMMANDERS.

Fred'k Salomon	Brigadier General	Jan. 6, 1864, to May 11, 1864.	
Cyrus Bussey	Brigadier General	Feb. 6, 1865, to Aug. 1, 1865.	

1st BRIGADE.—Transferred to 2-Brig. 3-Div. March 12, 1864. Reorganized from 2-Brig. 3-Div. March 12, 1864.

COMMANDERS.

W. E. McLean..........	Col. 43d Ind. Infy..........	Jan. 6, 1864, to Mch. 12, 1864.	
S. A. Rice..............	Brigadier General	Mch. 12, 1864, to Apr. 30, 1864.	Killed.
C. E. Salomon.........	Col. 9th Wis. Infy...........	Apr. 30, 1864, to May 11, 1864.	
John Edwards	Brigadier General	Feb. 16, 1865, to May 7, 1865.	
Jno. A. Garrett.........	Col. 40th Iowa Infy.......	May 7, 1865, to June 27, 1865.	
J. M. Johnson.........	Col. 1st Ark. Infy..........	June 27, 1865, to Aug. 1, 1865.	

43d Ind. Infy...........Jan., 1864	From 1-Brig. 3-Div. Ark. Exp.	To 2-Brig. 3-Div. 7-Corps........	Mch., 1864
36th Iowa Infy..........Jan., 1864	From 1-Brig. 3-Div. Ark. Exp.	To 2-Brig. 3-Div. 7-Corps..........	Mch., 1864
77th Ohio Infy..........Jan., 1864	From 1-Brig. 3-Div. Ark. Exp.	To 2-Brig. 3-Div. 7-Corps..........	Mch., 1864
29th Iowa Infy..........Mch., 1864	From 2-Brig. 3-Div. 7-Corps.	To 1-Brig. 1-Div. 7-Corps..........	May, 1864
33d Iowa Infy..........Mch., 1864	From 2-Brig. 3-Div. 7-Corps.	To 1-Brig. 1-Div. 7-Corps..........	May, 1864
9th Wis. Infy..........Mch., 1864	From 2-Brig. 3-Div. 7-Corps.	To 1-Brig. 1-Div. 7-Corps..........	May, 1864
50th Ind. Infy..........Apr., 1864	From Unatt. 2-Div. 7-Corps.	To 1-Brig. 1-Div. 7-Corps..........	May, 1864
1st Ark. Infy..........Feb., 1865	From 1-Brig. Dist. Frontier 7-Corps.	No change to Muster Out........	Aug., 1865
2d Ark. Infy..........Feb., 1865	From 1-Brig. Dist. Frontier 7-Corps.	No change to Muster Out........	Aug., 1865
18th Iowa Infy..........Feb., 1865	From 1-Brig. Dist. Frontier 7-Corps.	No change to Muster Out........	July, 1865
40th Iowa Infy..........Feb., 1865	From 1-Brig. 1-Div. 7-Corps.	No change to Muster Out........	Aug., 1865
22d Ohio Infy..........Feb., 1865	From 2-Brig. 2-Div. 7-Corps.	No change to Muster Out........	Aug., 1865
1st Ark. Cav..........Feb., 1865	From 2-Brig. 3-Div. 7-Corps.	No change to Muster Out........	Aug., 1865
1st Ark. Batty..........Feb., 1865	From 2-Brig. Frontier Div. 7-Corps.	No change to Muster Out........	Aug., 1865
12th Kansas Infy..........Feb., 1865	From 2-Brig. Frontier Div. 7-Corps.	To 1-Brig. 2-Div. 7-Corps..........	Feb., 1865
13th Kansas Infy..........Feb., 1865	From Fort Smith Dist. Frontier 7-C.	To 1-Brig. 2-Div. 7-Corps..........	Feb., 1865
2d Kansas Batty..........Feb., 1865	From 1-Brig. Frontier Div. 7-Corps.	No change to Muster Out........	Aug., 1865

2d BRIGADE.—Transferred to 1st Brigade March 12, 1864. Reorganized from 1st Brigade March 12, 1864. Transferred to 1st Division May 11, 1864.

COMMANDERS.

James M. Lewis.......	Col. 28th Wis. Infy.............	Jan. 6, 1864, to Feb. 1, 1864.	
S. A. Rice.............	Brigadier General	Feb. 1, 1864, to Mch. 12, 1864.	
W. F. McLean.........	Col. 43d Ind. Infy.............	Mch. 12, 1864, to May 11, 1864.	

29th Iowa Infy..........Jan., 1864	From 2-Brig. 3-Div. Ark. Exp.	To 1-Brig. 3-Div. 7-Corps..........	Mch., 1864
33d Iowa Infy..........Jan., 1864	From 2-Brig. 3-Div. Ark. Exp.	To 1-Brig. 3-Div. 7-Corps..........	Mch., 1864
9th Wis. Infy..........Jan., 1864	From 2-Brig. 3-Div. Ark. Exp.	To 1-Brig. 3-Div. 7-Corps..........	Mch., 1864
28th Wis. Infy..........Jan., 1864	From 2-Brig. 3-Div. Ark. Exp.	To Post Pine Bluff 7-Corps........	Mch., 1864
43d Ind. Infy..........Mch., 1864	From 1-Brig. 3-Div. 7-Corps.	To 1-Brig. 1-Div. 7-Corps..........	May, 1864
36th Iowa Infy..........Mch., 1864	From 1-Brig. 3-Div. 7-Corps.	To 2-Brig. 1-Div. 7-Corps..........	May, 1864
77th Ohio Infy..........Mch., 1864	From 1-Brig. 3-Div. 7-Corps.	To 2-Brig. 1-Div. 7-Corps..........	May, 1864
14th Kansas Cav..........Feb., 1865	From 3-Brig. Dist. Frontier 7-Corps.	To Unatt. Pine Bluff 7-Corps.......	Feb., 1865
2d Kansas Cav..........Feb., 1865	From 3-Brig. Dist. Frontier 7-Corps.	To Unatt. Lewisburg 7-Corps.......	Feb., 1865
6th Kansas Cav..........Feb., 1865	From 3-Brig. Dist. Frontier 7-Corps.	To 1-Brig. 2-Div. 7-Corps..........	Feb., 1865
1st Ark. Cav..........Feb., 1865	From 3-Brig. Dist. Frontier 7-Corps.	To 1-Brig. 3-Div. 7-Corps..........	Feb., 1865

3d BRIGADE.—Organized Mch. 12, 1864, from 2-Brig. 3-Div. 7-Corps. Transferred to 1st Division May 11, 1864. Reorganized Feb. 6, 1865, from Indian Brigade, Frontier Brigade, Frontier Division. Transferred to Dist. South Kansas May, 1865.

COMMANDERS.

A. Engleman .:........	Col. 43d Ill. Infy...............	Mch. 12, 1864, to May 11, 1864.	
Wm. A. Phillips........	Col. 3d Indian Home Guard........	Feb. 1, 1865, to May 10, 1865.	

22d Ohio Infy..........Mch., 1864	From 2-Brig. 2-Div. 7-Corps.	To 2-Brig. 1-Div. 7-Corps..........	May, 1864
43d Ill. Infy..........Mch., 1864	From 2-Brig. 2-Div. 7-Corps.	To 2-Brig. 1-Div. 7-Corps..........	May, 1864
126th Ill. Infy..........Mch., 1864	From 2-Brig. 2-Div. 7-Corps.	To 2-Brig. 1-Div. 7-Corps..........	May, 1864
40th Iowa Infy..........Mch., 1864	From 2-Brig. 2-Div. 7-Corps.	To 2-Brig. 1-Div. 7-Corps..........	May, 1864
27th Wis. Infy..........Mch., 1864	From 2-Brig. 2-Div. 7-Corps.	To 2-Brig. 1-Div. 7-Corps..........	May, 1864
1st Indian Home Guard...Feb., 1865	From Indian Brig. Frontier Div.	No change to Muster Out........	May, 1865
2d Indian Home Guard...Feb., 1865	From Indian Brig. Frontier Div....	No change to Muster Out........	May, 1865
3d Indian Home Guard...Feb., 1865	From Indian Brig. Frontier Div....	No change to Muster Out........	May, 1865
14th Kansas Cav., Co. M..Feb., 186?	From Indian Brig. Frontier Div....	No change to Muster Out........	May, 1865

ARTILLERY.—

3d Iowa Batty..........Jan., 1864	From Arty. 3-Div. Ark. Exp........	To Arty. 1-Div. 7-Corps..........	May, 1864
Batty K, 1st Mo. Arty...Jap., 1864	From Arty. 3-Div. Ark. Exp........	To Arty. 2-Div. 7-Corps..........	May, 1864
25th Ohio Batty..........Mch., 1864	From Veteran Furlough...........	To Arty. 1-Div. 7-Corps..........	May, 1864
Batty. E, 2d Mo. Arty....Apr., 1864	From 1-Cav. Div. 7-Corps.........	To Arty. 1-Div. 7-Corps..........	May, 1864
Vaughan's Ill. Batty......Apr., 1864	From Unatt. 2-Div. 7-Corps........	To Arty. 1-Div. 7-Corps..........	May, 1864
2d Kansas Batty..........Feb., 1865	From 1-Brig. Frontier Div. 7-Corps.	To 1-Brig. 3-Div. 7-Corps........	Feb., 1865
1st Ark. Batty..........Feb., 1865	From 2-Brig. Frontier Div. 7-Corps.	To 1-Brig. 3-Div. 7-Corps........	Feb., 1865

DISTRICT OF EASTERN ARKANSAS.— COMMANDERS.

N. B. Buford..........	Brigadier General	Jan. 6. 1864, to Aug. 6, 1864.	
William Crooks	Col. 6th Minn. Infy..............	Aug. 6, 1864, to Sept. 28, 1864.	
N. B. Buford..........	Brigadier General	Sept. 28, 1864, to Oct. 7, 1864.	
William Crooks..........	Col. 6th Minn. Infy..............	Oct. 7, 1864, to Oct. 10, 1864.	
N. B. Buford..........	Brigadier General	Oct. 10, 1864, to Mch. 9, 1865.	
A. McD. McCook.......	Major General	Mch. 9, 1865, to May 25, 1865.	
J. M. Thayer........	Brigadier General	May 25, 1865, to June 12, 1865.	
C. Bentzoni.........	Col. 56th U. S. C. T.............	June 12, 1865, to Aug. 1, 1865.	

2d Ark. Col'd Infy......Jan., 1864 (54th U. S. C. T.)	From Dist. Eastern Ark...........	To 2-Brig. Dist. Frontier 7-Corps...	Mch., 1864
3d Ark. Col'd Infy......Jan., 186? (56th U. S. C. T.)	From Dist. Eastern Ark...........	To Dept. Ark.....................	Aug., 1865
4th Ark. Col'd Infy......Jan., 1864 (57th U. S. C. T.)	From Dist. Eastern Ark...........	To 1-Brig. 2-Div. 7-Corps.........	May, 1864
1st Iowa Col'd Infy......Jan., 1864 (60th U. S. C. T.)	From New Organization............	To 2-Brig. 1-Div. 7-Corps.........	Apr., 1865
35th Mo. Infy...........Jan., 1864	From Garr. Helena, Ark., Dist. E. Ar.	To 1-Brig. 1-Div. 7-Corps.........	Feb., 1865

DISTRICT OF EASTERN ARKANSAS.—Continued.

25th Wis. Infy	Jan., 1864	From Garr. Helena, Ark., Dist. E. Ar.	To 1-Brig. 4-Div. 16-Corps Tenn....	Feb., 1864
15th Ill. Infy	Jan., 1864	From Waring's Det. Br. Cav. D. 16-C.	Consolidated with 10th Ill. Cav.....	Jan., 1865
3d La. Col'd Batty	Jan., 1864	From New Organization............	No change to Muster Out.........	Sept., 1865
(Batty. E, 2d U. S. C. Arty.)				
12th Iowa Infy	May, 1864	From 3-Brig. 1-Div. 16-Corps Tenn..	To 3-Brig. 1-Div. 16-Corps Tenn....	June, 1864
47th Iowa Infy	May, 1864	From New Organization............	No change to Muster Out.........	Sept., 1864
6th Minn. Infy	May, 1864	From Dept. Northwest..............	To Dist. St. Louis, Mo., Dept. Mo...	Nov., 1864
143d Ill. Infy	Aug., 1864	From New Organization............	No change to Muster Out.........	Sept., 1864
23d Wis. Infy	Oct., 1864	From Guppey's Brig. U. S. Forces Mobile Bay.	To 3-Brig. 1-Div. Res. Corps Gulf...	Feb., 1865
87th Ill. Mtd. Infy	Feb., 1865	From Sep. Cav. Brig. Res. C. Gulf.	No change to Muster Out.........	June, 1865

DISTRICT NORTHEAST ARKANSAS.—Designation changed to Indpt. Brig. May, 1864, and discontinued June, 1864.

COMMANDER.

L. L. Livingston.......	Col. 1st Neb. Cav..............			
4th Ark. Infy	Jan., 1864	From New Organization............	To Fort Smith, Ark., Dist. Frontier..	June, 1864
11th Mo. Cav	Jan., 1864	From Dist. N. E. Ark. Dept. Mo.....	To 3-Brig. 2-Div. 7-Corps.........	June, 1864
1st Neb. Cav	Jan., 1864	From Dist. N. E. Ark. Dept. Mo.....	To 3-Brig. 2-Div. 7-Corps.........	June, 1864
Batty. D, 2d Mo. Arty. Sec.	Jan., 1864		To Arty. 2-Div. 7-Corps...........	May, 1864

DISTRICT OF THE FRONTIER.—Designation changed to Frontier Division Dec. 3, 1864, and discontinued Feb. 1, 1865.

COMMANDERS.

W. R. Judson..........	Col. 6th Kansas Cav..............	Jan. 6, 1864, to Feb. 23, 1864.
John M. Thayer........	Brigadier General	Feb. 23, 1864, to Mch. 24, 1864.
W. R. Judson..........	Col. 6th Kansas Cav..............	Mch. 24, 1864, to May 19, 1864.
John M. Thayer........	Brigadier General	May 19, 1864, to Dec. 3, 1864.
John Edwards	Brigadier General	Dec. 3, 1864, to Jan. 5, 1865.
John M. Thayer.......	Brigadier General	Jan. 5, 1865, to Feb. 1, 1865.

1st BRIGADE.—Designated Indian Brigade, Dist. Frontier, Feb. 23, 1864. Reorganized Mch. 21, 1864, from 2d Brigade, District of the Frontier. Designated 1st Brigade, Frontier Division, Dec. 3, 1864. Transferred to 3-Division, 7-Corps, Feb., 1865.

COMMANDERS.

W. A. Phillips.........	Col. 3d Indian Home Guard.........	Jan. 6, 1864, to Feb. 23, 1864.
John Edwards	Col. 18th Iowa Infy...............	Mch. 21, 1864, to Dec. 3, 1864.
C. W. Adams..........	Brigadier General	Dec. 3, 1864, to Jan. 16, 1865.
John Edwards	Brigadier General	Jan. 16, 1865, to Feb. 1, 1865.

1st Indian Home Guard	Jan., 1864	From Dist. Frontier Dept. Mo......	To Indian Brig. Dist. Frontier......	Feb., 1864
2d Indian Home Guard	Jan., 1864	From Dist. Frontier Dept. Mo......	To Indian Brig. Dist. Frontier......	Feb., 1864
3d Indian Home Guard	Jan., 1864	From Dist. Frontier Dept. Mo......	To Indian Brig. Dist. Frontier......	Feb., 1864
14th Kansas Cav., Co. M.	Jan., 1864	From Dist. Frontier Dept. Mo......	To Indian Brig. Dist. Frontier......	Feb., 1864
1st Ark. Infy	Mch., 1864	From 2-Brig. Dist. Frontier 7-Corps.	To 1-Brig. 3-Div. 7-Corps.........	Feb., 1865
2d Ark. Infy	Mch., 1864	From 2-Brig. Dist. Frontier 7-Corps.	To 1-Brig. 3-Div. 7-Corps.........	Feb., 18
18th Iowa Infy	Mch., 1864	From 2-Brig. Dist. Frontier 7-Corps.	To 1-Brig. 3-Div. 7-Corps.........	Feb., 1865
2d Ind. Batty	Mch., 1864	From 2-Brig. Dist. Frontier 7-Corps.	To Indiana	Sept., 1864
2d Kansas Cav	Mch., 1864	From 2-Brig. Dist. Frontier 7-Corps.	To 3-Brig. Dist. Frontier 7-Corps...	Apr., 1864
12th Kansas Infy	May, 1864	From 2-Brig. Dist. Frontier 7-Corps.	To 1-Brig. 3-Div. 7-Corps.........	Feb., 1865
2d Kansas Batty	May, 1864	From Unass'd Dist. Frontier.......	To 1-Brig. 3-Div. 7-Corps.........	Feb., 1865
2d Ark. Infy	Dec., 1864	From 2-Brig. 2-Div. 7-Corps.......	To 1-Brig. 3-Div. 7-Corps.........	Feb., 1865

2d BRIGADE.—Transferred to 1st Brigade Mch. 21, 1864. Reorganized Mch. 21, 1864. Designated 2d Brigade, Frontier Division, Dec. 3, 1864. Discontinued Jan. 16, 1865. Reorganized from 3-Brig., Frontier Division, Jan. 16, 1865.

COMMANDERS.

John Edwards	Col. 18th Iowa Infy...............	Jan. 6, 1864, to Mch. 21, 1864.
C. W. Adams..........	Col. 12th Kansas Infy.............	Mch. 21, 1864, to May 7, 1864.
J. M. Williams.........	Col. 1st Kansas Col'd.............	May 7, 1864, to Jan. 16, 1865.
W. R. Judson.........	Col. 6th Kansas Cav.............	Jan. 16, 1865, to Feb. 1, 1865.

1st Ark. Infy	Jan., 1864	From 2-Brig. Dist. Frontier D. Mo.	To 1-Brig. Dist. Frontier 7-Corps...	Mch., 1864
2d Ark. Infy	Jan., 1864	From Unatt. Dist. Frontier D. Mo.	To 1-Brig. Dist. Frontier 7-Corps...	Mch., 1864
2d Kansas Cav	Jan., 1864	From 2-Brig. Dist. Frontier D. Mo.	To 1-Brig. Dist. Frontier 7-Corps...	Mch., 1864
18th Iowa Infy	Jan., 1864	From 2-Brig. Dist. Frontier D. Mo.	To 1-Brig. Dist. Frontier 7-Corps...	Mch., 1864
2d Ind. Batty	Jan., 1864	From 2-Brig. Dist. Frontier D. Mo.	To 2-Brig. 1-Div. 7-Corps.........	Feb., 1865
1st Kan. Colored Infy	Mch., 1864	From Unatt. Dist. Frontier 7-Corps.	To 2-Brig. 3-Div. 7-Corps.........	Feb., 1865
2d Kan. Colored Infy	Mch., 1864	From Unatt. Dist. Frontier 7-Corps.	To 2-Brig. Dist. Frontier 7-Corps..	May, 1864
12th Kansas Infy	Mch., 1864	From Dist. S. W. Mo. Dept. Mo.....	To 1-Brig. 3-Div. 7-Corps.........	Feb., 1865
1st Ark. Batty	Mch., 1864	From Dist. E. Ark. 7-Corps........	To 2-Brig. 1-Div. 7-Corps.........	Feb., 1865
11th U. S. C. T.	May, 1864	From New Organization............	To 2-Brig. 1-Div. 7-Corps.........	Feb., 1865
54th U. S. C. T.	May, 1864	From Dist. E. Ark. 7-Corps........	No change to Muster Out..........	Jan., 1865
3d Kan. Batty	May, 1864	From 3-Brig. Dist. Frontier 7-Corps.		

3d BRIGADE.—Discontinued Mch. 21, 1864. Reorganized April 18, 1864. Designation changed to 3-Brig., Frontier Division, Dec. 3, 1865, and to 2d Brig., Frontier Division, Jan. 16, 1865.

COMMANDERS.

T. M. Bowen..........	Col. 13th Kan. Infy...............	Jan. 6, 1864, to Mch. 21, 1864.
E. Lynde..............	Col. 9th Kan. Infy...............	Apr. 18, 1864, to July 2, 1864.
W. R. Judson.........	6th Kan. Cav....................	July 2, 1864, to Jan. 16, 1864.

13th Kan. Infy	Jan., 1864	From 3-B. Dist. Frontier Dept. Mo.	To Fort Smith Dist. Frontier 7-C...	Jan., 1864
3d Wis. Cav., A, C, D, F.	Jan., 1864	From 3-B. Dist. Frontier Dept. Mo.	To Fort Smith Dist. Frontier 7-C...	Jan., 1864
3d Kan. Batty	Jan., 1864	From 3-B. Dist. Frontier Dept. Mo.	To 2-Brig. Frontier Div. 7-Corps...	Mch., 1865
2d Kan. Cav	Mch., 1864	From 1-Brig. Dist. Frontier 7-Corps.	To 2-Brig. 3-Div. 7-Corps.........	Jan., 1865
6th Kan. Cav	Mch., 1864	From Unatt. Dist. Frontier 7-Corps.	To 2-Brig. 3-Div. 7-Corps.........	Jan., 1865
14th Kan. Cav	Mch., 1864	From Unatt. Dist. Frontier 7-Corps.	To 2-Brig. 3-Div. 7-Corps.........	Jan., 1865
9th Kan. Cav	May, 1864	From Dept. Kansas................	To 4-Brig. Cav. Div. 7-Corps......	Sept., 1864
1st Ark. Cav	June, 1864	From Dist. S. W. Mo. Dept. Mo.....	To 2-Brig. 3-Div. 7-Corps.........	Jan., 1865

INDIAN BRIGADE.—Organized Feb. 23, 1864, from 1-Brig., Dist. Frontier. Designated Indian Brigade, Frontier Division, Dec. 3, 1864. Transferred to 3-Div., 7-Corps, Feb. 1, 1865.

COMMANDERS.

William A. Phillips....	Col. 3d Indian Home Guard........	Feb. 23, 1864, to July 30, 1864.
S. H. Wattles.........	Col. 1st Indian Home Guard........	July 30, 1864, to Dec. 17, 1864.
Wm. A. Phillips........	Col. 3d Indian Home Guard........	Dec. 17, 1864, to Feb. 1, 1865.

1st Indian Home Guard	Feb., 1864	From 1-Brig. Dist. Frontier 7-Corps.	To 3-Brig. 3-Div. 7-Corps...........	Feb., 1865
2d Indian Home Guard	Feb., 1864	From 1-Brig. Dist. Frontier 7-Corps.	To 3-Brig. 3-Div. 7-Corps...........	Feb., 1865
3d Indian Home Guard	Feb., 1864	From 1-Brig. Dist. Frontier 7-Corps.	To 3-Brig. 3-Div. 7-Corps...........	Feb., 1865
14th Kan. Cav., Co. M	Feb., 1864	From 1-Brig. Dist. Frontier 7-Corps.	To 3-Brig. 3-Div. 7-Corps...........	Feb., 1865

UNATTACHED DISTRICT FRONTIER.—

2d Ark. Infy............Jan., 1864	From Unatt. Dist. Frontier D. Mo..	To 1-Brig. Dist. Frontier 7-Corps...	Mch., 1864
1st Kan. Colored Infy.....Jan., 1864	From Unatt. Dist. Frontier D. Mo..	To 2-Brig. Dist. Frontier 7-Corps...	Mch., 1864
12th Kan. Infy..........Jan., 1864	From Unatt. Dist. Frontier D. Mo..	To 2-Brig. Dist. Frontier 7-Corps...	Mch., 1864
6th Kan. Cav...........Jan., 1864	From Unatt. Dist. Frontier D. Mo..	To 3-Brig. Dist. Frontier 7-Corps...	Mch., 1864
2d Kan. Colored Infy.....Jan., 1864	From Unatt. Dist. Frontier D. Mo..	To 2-Brig. Dist. Frontier 7-Corps...	Mch., 1864
2d Kan. Batty..........Jan., 1864	From Unatt. Dist. Frontier D. Mo..	To 1-Brig. Dist. Frontier 7-Corps...	May, 1864
14th Kan. Cav..........Jan., 1864	From Unatt. Dist. Frontier D. Mo..	To 3-Brig. Dist. Frontier 7-Corps...	Mch., 1864

INDEPENDENT CAVALRY BRIGADE.—Discontinued Sept. 15, 1864.

COMMANDER.

Powell Clayton........	Col. 5th Kan. Cav..................	

1st Ind. Cav............Jan., 1864	From Clayton's I. Cav. B. Ark. Exp.	To 1-Brig. Cav. Div. 7-Corps........	Sept., 1864
5th Kan. Cav...........Jan., 1864	From Clayton's I. Cav. B. Ark. Exp.	To 1-Brig. Cav. Div. 7-Corps........	Sept., 1864
7th Mo. Cav...........Apr., 1864	From Dept. Mo....................	To 1-Brig. Cav. Div. 7-Corps........	Sept., 1864
13th Ill. Cav...........May, 1864	From 1-Brig. 1-Cav. Div. 7-Corps...	To 1-Brig. Cav. Div. 7-Corps........	Sept., 1864

CAVALRY DIVISION.—Organized Sept. 15, 1864. Discontinued March, 1865.

COMMANDER.

Joseph R. West........	Brigadier General.................	Sept. 15, 1864, to Mch. 18, 1865.

1st BRIGADE.—　　　　COMMANDERS.

Albert Erskine	Col. 13th Ill. Cav.................	Sept. 19, 1864, to Jan. 24, 1865.
M. H. Brawner........	Major 7th Mo. Cav.................	Jan. 24, 1865, to Feb. 1, 1865.
J. K. Mizner..........	Col. 3d Mich. Cav.................	Feb. 1, 1865, to Mch. 18, 1865.

13th Ill. Cav............Sept., 1864	From Clayton's Indpt. Brig. 7-Corps.	To Post Pine Bluff 7-Corps........	Feb., 1865
7th Mo. Cav...........Sept., 1864	From Clayton's Indpt. Brig. 7-Corps.	To 2-Brig. Cav. Div. 7-Corps.......	Feb., 1865
1st Ind. Cav...........Sept., 1864	From Clayton's Indpt. Brig. 7-Corps.	To Mouth White River...........	Feb., 1865
5th Kan. Cav...........Sept., 1864	From Clayton's Indpt. Brig. 7-Corps.	To Post St. Charles, Ark........	Feb., 1865
1st Iowa Cav...........Feb., 1865	From 2-Brig. Cav. Div. 7-Corps.....	To 2-Brig. Cav. Div. Dist. W. Tenn.	Feb., 1865
3d Mich. Cav...........Feb., 1865	From 4-Brig. Cav. Div. 7-Corps.....	To 1-B. 1-Div. Cav. Corps W. Miss..	Apr., 1865
10th Ill. Cav...........Feb., 1865	From 4-Brig. Cav. Div. 7-Corps.....	To 1-B. 1-Div. Cav. Corps W. Miss..	Apr., 1865

2d BRIGADE.—Designation changed to Dismounted Separate Cav. Brigade Mch. 18, 1865.

COMMANDERS.

J. F. Ritter............	Col. 1st Mo. Cav.................	Sept. 15, 1864, to Nov. 6, 1864.
Wm. Thompson.......	Col. 1st Iowa Cav.................	Nov. 6, 1864, to Dec. 1, 1864.
Cyrus Bussey........	Brigadier General.................	Dec. 1, 1864, to Feb. 1, 1865.
W. F. Geiger..........	Col. 8th Mo. Cav.................	Feb. 1, 1865, to Mch. 18, 1865.

1st Mo. Cav...........Sept., 1864	From 3-Brig. 1-Cav. Div. 7-Corps..	To 1st Sep. Cav. Brig. 7-Corps.....	Mch., 1865
3d Mo. Cav...........Sept., 1864	From 3-Brig. 1-Div. 7-Corps.......	To 1st Sep. Cav. Brig. 7-Corps.....	Mch., 1865
1st Iowa Cav...........Sept., 1864	From 3-Brig. 1-Div. 7-Corps.......	To 1-Brig. Cav. Div. 7-Corps......	Feb., 1865
4th Ark. Cav...........Sept., 1864	From 3-Brig. 1-Div. 7-Corps.......	To Cav. Brig. Little Rock, Ark......	Feb., 1865
3d U. S. Cav...........Sept., 1864	From Unatt. Cav. 7-Corps.........	To Cav. Brig. Little Rock, Ark......	Feb., 1865
7th Mo. Cav...........Feb., 1865	From 1-Brig. Cav. Div. 7-Corps....	Consolidated with 1st Mo. Cav.....	Feb., 1865
8th Mo. Cav...........Feb., 1865	From 3-Brig. Cav. Div. 7-Corps....	To 1st Sep. Cav. Brig. 7-Corps.....	Mch., 1865
11th Mo. Cav..........Feb., 1865	From 3-Brig. Cav. Div. 7-Corps....	To 1st Sep. Cav. Brig. 7-Corps.....	Mch., 1865

3d BRIGADE.—Discontinued Jan. 31, 1865.　　　　COMMANDER.

W. F. Geiger..........	Col. 8th Mo. Cav.................	Sept. 15, 1864, to Feb. 1, 1865.

2d Mo. Cav...........Sept., 1864	From 3-Brig. 2-Div. 7-Corps.......	To 2-Brig. Cav. Div. D. W. Tenn.	Feb., 1865
8th Mo. Cav...........Sept., 1864	From 3-Brig. 2-Div. 7-Corps.......	To 2-Brig. Cav. Div. 7-Corps.......	Feb., 1865
11th Mo. Cav..........Sept., 1864	From 3-Brig. 2-Div. 7-Corps.......	To 2-Brig. Cav. Div. 7-Corps.......	Feb., 1865
10th Ill. Cav...........Sept., 1864	From 3-Brig. 2-Div. 7-Corps.......	To 1-Brig. Cav. Div. 7-Corps.......	Feb., 1865
9th Iowa Cav...........Sept., 1864	From 3-Brig. 2-Div. 7-Corps.......	To Cav. Brig. Little Rock, Ark......	Feb., 1865

4th BRIGADE.—Organized Sept. 9, 1864. Discontinued Jan. 31, 1865.

COMMANDERS.

A. H. Ryan...........	Col. 3d Ark. Cav.................	Sept. 9, 1864, to Oct. 31, 1864.
J. K. Mizner..........	Col. 3d Mich. Cav.................	Oct. 31, 1864, to Feb. 1, 1865.

3d Mich. Cav...........Sept., 1864	From 3-Brig. 2-Div. 7-Corps.......	To 1-Brig. Cav. Div. 7-Corps.......	Feb., 1865
9th Kan. Cav...........Sept., 1864	From 3-Brig. Dist. Frontier 7-Corps.	To Unatt. Cav. 2-Div. 7-Corps.....	Feb., 1865
3d Ark. Cav...........Sept., 1864	From 3-Brig. 2-Div. 7-Corps.......	To Post Lewisburg, Ark.........	Feb., 1865
3d Wis. Cav...........Sept., 1864	From Unatt. Ft. Smith Dist. Front..	To Cav. Brig. Post Little Rock, Ark.	Feb., 1865
1st Neb. Cav...........Sept., 1864	From 3-Brig. 2-Div. 7-Corps.......	To Dist. Neb. Dept. Kansas.........	Oct., 1864

ARTILLERY, CAVALRY DIVISION.—

25th Ohio Batty.........Feb., 1865	From Arty. 1-Div. 7-Corps.........	To Dept. Arkansas.................	Aug., 1865

SEPARATE DISMOUNTED CAVALRY BRIGADE.—Organized March 18, 1865.

COMMANDERS.

W. F. Geiger..........	Col. 8th Mo. Cav.................	Mch. 18, 1865, to Apr. 30, 1865.
J. H. Reed............	Lt.-Col. 8th Mo. Cav.............	Apr. 30, 1865, to May 30, 1865.
Powell Clayton	Brigadier General.................	May 30, 1865, to June 10, 1865.
M. H. Brawner........	Lt.-Col. 1st Mo. Cav.............	June 10, 1865, to July 12, 1865.
Powell Clayton	Brigadier General.................	July 12, 1865, to Aug. 1, 1865.

1st Mo. Cav...........Mch., 1865	From 2-Brig. Cav. Div. 7-Corps.....	No change to Muster Out..........	Sept., 1865
3d Mo. Cav...........Mch., 1865	From 2-Brig. Cav. Div. 7-Corps.....	No change to Muster Out..........	June, 1865
8th Mo. Cav...........Mch., 1865	From 2-Brig. Cav. Div. 7-Corps.....	No change to Muster Out..........	July, 1865
11th Mo. Cav..........Mch., 1865	From 2-Brig. Cav. Div. 7-Corps.....	No change to Muster Out..........	July, 1865

CAVALRY BRIGADE, LITTLE ROCK.—Organized Feb. 1, 1865. Discontinued June, 1865.

COMMANDERS.

M. M. Trumbull.......	Col. 9th Iowa Cav.................	Feb. 1, 1865, to June 9, 1865.
L. Gregg..............	Col. 4th Ark. Cav.................	June 9, 1865, to June —, 1865.

4th Ark. Cav...........Feb., 1865	From Unatt. 2-Div. 7-Corps........	No change to Muster Out..........	June, 1865
9th Iowa Cav...........Feb., 1865	From 3-Brig. Cav. Div. 7-Corps.....	To Dept. Arkansas.................	Aug., 1865
3d U. S. Cav...........Feb., 1865	From 2-Brig. Cav. Div. 7-Corps.....	To Dept. Arkansas.................	Aug., 1865
3d Wis. Cav...........Feb., 1865	From 4-Brig. Cav. Div. 7-Corps.....	To Unassigned 1-Div. 7-Corps.....	Apr., 1865

COLORED BRIGADE.—Organized Jan. 16, 1865. Transferred to 2-Brig., 1-Div., 7-Corps, Feb. 6, 1865.

COMMANDER.

J. M. Williams	Col. 79th U. S. C. T.		
11th U. S. C. T......Jan., 1865	From 2-Brig. Dist. Frontier 7-Corps.	Consolidated with 112th and 113th..	Apr., 1865
54th U. S. C. T......Jan., 1865	From 2-Brig. Dist. Frontier 7-Corps.	To Dept. Arkansas................	Aug., 1865
57th U. S. C. T......Jan., 1865	From 1-Brig. 2-Div. 7-Corps......	To Dept. Arkansas................	Aug., 1865
79th U. S. C. T......Jan., 1865	From 2-Brig. Dist. Frontier 7-Corps.	To Dept. Arkansas................	Aug., 1865
83d U. S. C. T......Jan., 1865	From 2-Brig. Dist. Frontier 7-Corps.	To Dept. Arkansas................	Aug., 1865
112th U. S. C. T......Jan., 1865	From Unatt. 1-Div. 7-Corps......	Consol. with 11th and 113th U.S.C.T.	Apr., 1865
113th U. S. C. T......Jan., 1865	From Unatt. 1-Div. 7-Corps......	To Dept. Arkansas................	Aug., 1865

MOUTH OF WHITE RIVER.—From Reserve Corps, Dept. Gulf.

COMMANDER.

Geo. F. McGinnis	Brigadier General		
126th Ill. Infy......Feb., 1865	From 2-Brig. 2-Div. 7-Corps......	To Pine Bluff, Ark...............	June, 1865
1st Ind. Cav......Feb., 1865	From 1-Brig. Cav. Div. 7-Corps...	No change to Muster Out........	June, 1865
Batty. D, 2d Mo. Arty......Feb., 1865	From Arty. 1-Div. 7-Corps........	To Dept. Ark....................	Aug., 1865

POST PINE BLUFF, ARK.—

COMMANDER.

Powell Clayton	Col. 5th Kansas Cav.		
18th Ill. Infy......Apr., 1864	From 3-Brig. 2-Div. 7-Corps......	To 1-Brig. 2-Div. 7-Corps.......	May, 1864
28th Wis. Infy......Apr., 1864	From 2-Brig. 3-Div. 7-Corps......	To 1-Brig. 1-Div. 7-Corps.......	May, 1864
13th Ill. Cav......Jan., 1865	From 1-Brig. Cav. Div. 7-Corps...	No change to Muster Out........	Aug., 1865
14th Kan. Cav......Feb., 1865	From 2-Brig. 3-Div. 7-Corps......	No change to Muster Out........	June, 1865
DEPARTMENT HEADQUARTERS.—			
1st Kan. Mtd. Infy......Dec., 1864	From Unatt. 2-Div. 19-Corps......	No change to Muster Out........	Aug., 1865
18th Ill. Infy......Jan., 1865	From Post Pine Bluff, Ark........	To Dept. Ark....................	Aug., 1865

Department of Kansas

Created Nov. 9, 1861, to consist of the State of Kansas, the Indian Territory West of Arkansas, and the Territories of Nebraska, Colorado and Dakota. Merged into Department of the Mississippi March 11, 1862. Recreated May 2, 1862. Merged into Department of Missouri Sept. 19, 1862. Recreated Jan. 1, 1864. Merged into Department of Missouri Jan. 30, 1865.

COMMANDERS.

David Hunter	Major General	Nov. 20, 1861, to Mch. 11, 1862.	
James G. Blunt	Brigadier General	May 5, 1862, to Sept. 19, 1862.	
S. R. Curtis	Major General	Jan. 16, 1864, to Jan. 30, 1865.	
1st Mo. Cav., 1st Battn...Nov., 1861	From Army West Dept. Mo........	To Dist. Southwest Mo..........	May, 1862
1st Kansas Infy......Nov., 1861	From New Organization..........	To Dist. Columbus Dept. Tenn...	June, 1862
		To 2-Brig. 4-Div. Army Miss.... (B, E, H, I, K.)	June, 1862
8th Kansas Infy......Nov., 1861	From New Organization..........	To Dist. Nashville, Tenn........ (A, C, D, F, G.)	Feb., 1863
2d Kansas Cav......Nov., 1861	From New Organization..........	To 3-Brig. Dept. Kansas........	Aug., 1862
5th Kansas Cav......Nov., 1861	From New Organization..........	To Unatt. Army Southwest Mo....	June, 1862
6th Kansas Cav......Nov., 1861	From New Organization..........	To 2-Brig. Dept. Kansas........	Aug., 1862
7th Kansas Cav......Nov., 1861	From New Organization..........	To 5-Div. Army Miss............	June, 1862
9th Kansas Cav......Nov., 1861	From New Organization..........	To 1-Brig. Dept. Kansas........	Aug., 1862
1st Kansas Batty......Nov., 1861	From New Organization..........	To 2-Brig. Dept. Kansas........	Aug., 1862
2d Ind. Batty......Nov., 1861	From Dept. Mo.	To 3-Brig. Dept. Kansas........	Aug., 1862
1st U. S. Infy. Det......Nov., 1861	From Regular Establishment......	To Unatt. Dept. Kansas.........	Aug., 1862
2d U. S. Infy. Det......Nov., 1861	From Regular Establishment......	To Unatt. Dept. Kansas.........	Aug., 1862
10th U. S. Infy. Det...Nov., 1861	From Regular Establishment......	To Unatt. Dept. Kansas.........	Aug., 1862
2d U. S. Cav. Det......Nov., 1861	From Regular Establishment......	To Unatt. Dept. Kansas.........	Aug., 1862
4th U. S. Cav. Det......Nov., 1861	From Regular Establishment......	To Unatt. Dept. Kansas.........	Aug., 1862
6th U. S. Cav. Det......Nov., 1861	From Regular Establishment......	To 1-Brig. Dept. Kansas........	Aug., 1862
9th Wis. Infy......Jan., 1862	From New Organization..........	To Dist. Columbus Dept. Tenn...	June, 1862
12th Wis. Infy......Jan., 1862	From New Organization..........	To Dist. Columbus Dept. Tenn...	June, 1862
13th Wis. Infy......Jan., 1862	From New Organization..........	To 1-Brig. Dept. Kansas........	Aug., 1862
2d Ohio Cav......Jan., 1862	From New Organization..........	To Arty. 4-Div. Army Miss......	June, 1862
8th Wis. Batty......Apr., 1862	From St. Louis, Mo., Dept. Mo...	To 2-Brig. Dept. Kansas........	Aug., 1862
10th Kansas Infy......Apr., 1862	From New Organization..........	To 1-Brig. 1-Div. Army Frontier.	Oct., 1862
3d Wis. Cav......May, 1862	From Benton Barracks, Mo.......	To 3-Brig. Dept. Kansas........	Aug., 1862
1st Indian Home Guard...May, 1862	From New Organization..........	To 1-Brig. Dept. Kansas........	Aug., 1862
2d Indian Home Guard...July, 1862	From New Organization..........	To 1-Brig. Dept. Kansas........	Sept., 1862
Hopkins' Kansas Batty...Sept., 1862	From New Organization..........	To 2-Brig. Dept. Kansas........	Sept., 1862
3d Indian Home Guard...Sept., 1862	From New Organization..........	To Dist. Frontier Dept. Mo.....	June, 1863
12th Kansas Infy......Sept., 1862	From New Organization..........	To Dist. South Kansas..........	June, 1864
4th Wis. Batty......June, 1862	From 2d Ohio Cav.	To 1-Brig. Dept. Kansas........	Aug., 1862
25th Ohio Batty......June, 1862	From Dist. St. Louis, Mo.,, Dept. Mo.	To Alton, Ill...................	Jan., 1864
10th Kansas Infy......Aug., 1862	From Dist. St. Louis, Mo.,, Dept. Mo.	To Dist. Border Dept. Mo.......	July, 1863
11th Kansas Infy......June, 1863	From Dist. Rolla Dept. Mo.......	To 3-Brig. Dist. Frontier 7-C. Ark.	May, 1864
9th Kansas Cav......Jan., 1864	From Dist. Border Dept. Mo......	To Dist. South Kansas..........	June, 1864
11th Kansas Cav......Jan., 1864	From Dist. Border Dept. Mo......	To Dist. South Kansas..........	June, 1864
15th Kansas Cav......Jan., 1864	From New Organization..........	To Dist. North Kansas..........	June, 1864
16th Kansas Cav......Jan., 1864	From 3-Brig. Dist. Frontier......	To Dist. South Kansas..........	June, 1864
3d Wis. Cav., A, C, D, F..Jan., 1864			

1st BRIGADE.—

COMMANDER.

Frederick Salomon	Brigadier General	Aug. 24 to Oct. 12, 1862.	
9th Wis. Infy......Aug., 1862	From Unatt. Dept. Kansas......	To 1-Brig. 1-Div. Army Frontier....	Oct., 1862
2d Ohio Cav......Aug., 1862	From Unatt. Dept. Kansas......	To 1-Brig. 1-Div. Army Frontier....	Oct., 1862
9th Kansas Cav......Aug., 1862	From Unatt. Dept. Kansas......	To 1-Brig. 1-Div. Army Frontier....	Oct., 1862
2d Indian Home Guard...Aug., 1862	From Unatt. Dept. Kansas......	To 3-Brig. 1-Div. Army Frontier....	Oct., 1862
2d Kans. Batty., Hopkins'.Sept., 1862	From Unatt. Dept. Kansas......	To 1-Brig. 1-Div. Army Frontier....	Oct., 1862
25th Ohio Batty......Sept., 1862	From Unatt. Dept. Kansas......	To 1-Brig. 1-Div. Army Frontier....	Oct., 1862

2d BRIGADE.—

COMMANDER.

Wm. Weer	Col. 10th Kansas Infy.	Aug. 24 to Oct. 12, 1862.	
10th Kansas Infy......Aug., 1862	From Unatt. Dept. Kansas......	To 2-Brig. 1-Div. Army Frontier....	Oct., 1862
6th Kansas Cav......Aug., 1862	From Unatt. Dept. Kansas......	To 2-Brig. 1-Div. Army Frontier....	Oct., 1862
1st Kansas Batty......Aug., 1862	From Unatt. Dept. Kansas......	To 1-Brig. 1-Div. Army Frontier....	Oct., 1862
3d Indian Home Guard...Sept., 1862	From Unatt. Dept. Kansas......	To 3-Brig. 1-Div. Army Frontier....	Oct., 1862

3d BRIGADE.—

COMMANDER.

W. F. Cloud............	Col. 2d Kansas Cav...............	Aug. 24 to Oct. 12, 1862.	

2d Kansas Cav..........Aug., 1862	From Unatt. Dept. Kansas.........	To 2-Brig. 1-Div. Army Frontier....	Oct., 1862
1st Indian Home Guard...Aug., 1862	From Unatt. Dept. Kansas.........	To 3-Brig. 1-Div. Army Frontier....	Oct., 1862
2d Ind. Batty..........Aug., 1862	From Unatt. Dept. Kansas.........	To 3-Brig. 1-Div. Army Frontier....	Oct., 1862

DISTRICT OF NORTH KANSAS.—

COMMANDERS.

T. A. Davies...........	Brigadier General	June 25, 1864, to Apr. 4, 1865.
W. R. Davis...........	Col. 16th Kansas Cav...........	Apr. 4, 1865, to Apr. 11, 1865.
R. B. Mitchell..........	Brigadier General	Apr. 11, 1865, to June 28, 1865.

16th Kansas Cav........June, 1864	From Unatt. Dept. Kansas.........	To Dist. Plains................	Apr., 1865
138th Ill. Infy..........June, 1864	From New Organization...........	No change to Muster Out........	Oct., 1864
17th Kansas Infy., B, E...July, 1864	From New Organization...........	No change to Muster Out........	Nov., 1864
Indpt. Col'd Batty.......Jan., 1865	From New Organization...........	No change to Muster Out........	July, 1865
15th Kansas Cav........Apr., 1865	From Dist. South Kansas...........	No change to Muster Out........	Oct., 1865
McLean's Colo. Batty......Apr., 1865	From Dist. South Kansas...........	No change to Muster Out........	Aug., 1865
2d Kansas Batty........Apr., 1865	From Dist. South Kansas...........	No change to Muster Out........	Aug., 1865
3d Wis. Cav............Apr., 1865	From Dist. South Kansas...........	No change to Muster Out........	Sept., 1865

DISTRICT OF SOUTH KANSAS.—

COMMANDERS.

T. J. McKean.........	Brigadier General	June 25, 1864, to Sept. 1, 1864.
Geo. Sykes	Brigadier General	Sept. 1, 1864, to Oct. 10, 1864.
J. G. Blunt.............	Major General	Oct. 10, 1864, to June 28, 1865.
John A. Garrett........	Col. 40th Iowa Infy.............	June 28, 1865, to Aug. 1, 1865.

11th Kansas Cav........June, 1864	From Unatt. Dept. Kansas.........	To Dist. Upper Ark............	Feb., 1865
15th Kansas Cav........June, 1864	From Unatt. Dept. Kansas.........	To Dist. North Kansas.........	Apr., 1865
16th Kan. Cav., A,D,F,G,L.June, 1864	From Unatt. Dept. Kansas.........	To Dist. Upper Ark............	Feb., 1865
3d Wis. Cav., A,C,D,F,M..June, 1864	From Unatt. Dept. Kansas.........	To Dist. North Kansas.........	Apr., 1865
2d Kansas Batty. Sec....June 1864	From Unatt. Dept. Kansas.........	To Dist. North Kansas.........	Apr., 1865
17th Kansas Infy., Co. D.June, 1864	From New Organization...........	No change to Muster Out........	Nov., 1864
McLean's Colo. Batty.....Dec., 1864	From Dist. Upper Ark..........	To Dist. North Kansas.........	Apr., 1865
9th Wis. Batty..........Apr., 1865	From Dist. Upper Ark..........	No change to Muster Out........	Sept., 1865
3d Wis. Cav............June, 1865	From 7-Corps Dept. Ark..........	No change to Muster Out........	Sept., 1865

DISTRICT UPPER ARKANSAS.—Created July 25, 1864.

COMMANDERS.

J. G. Blunt.............	Major General	July 25, 1864, to Dec. 22, 1864.
J. H. Ford.............	Col. 2d Colo. Cav...................	Dec. 22, 1864, to July 1, 1865.
J. B. Sanborn...........	Brigadier General	July 1, 1865.

17th Kansas Infy........July, 1864	From New Organization...........	No change to Muster Out........	Nov., 1864
7th Iowa Cav., Co's G, H.July, 1864	From Dist. Nebraska.............	To Dist. Plains................	Apr., 1865
1st Colo. Cav..........July, 1864	From Colorado.................	To Dist. Plains................	Apr., 1865
McLean's Colo. Batty.....July, 1864	From Dist. South Kansas.........	To Dist. South Kansas.........	Dec., 1864
9th Wis. Batty..........July, 1864	From Dist. South Kansas.........	To Dist. South Kansas.........	Apr., 1865
2d Colo. Cav...........Dec., 1864	From Dist. Central Mo...........	No change to Muster Out........	Sept., 1865
11th Kansas Cav........Feb., 1865	From Dist. South Kansas.........	To 2-Brig. 2-Div. 7-Corps Ark......	Mch., 1865
16th Kansas Cav........Feb., 1865	From Dist. North Kansas.........	To Dist. Plains................	Apr., 1865

DISTRICT OF NEBRASKA.—

COMMANDERS.

James Craig	Brigadier General	June, 1862, to June 4, 1863.
T. J. McKean.........	Brigadier General	June 4, 1863, to Jan., 1864.
R. B. Mitchell.........	Brigadier General	Jan., 1864, to Apr. 11, 1865.

1st Ohio Ind. Battn. Cav..June, 1862	From New Organization...........	To Dist. Colorado.............	Dec., 1863
Detachments U. S. Regts.			
2d Neb. Cav..........Mch., 1863	From New Organization...........	No change to Muster Out........	Dec., 1863
7th Iowa Cav..........June, 1863	From New Organization...........	To Dist. Plains................	Apr., 1865
1st Neb. Cav..........Jan., 1864	From Dist. N. E. Ark. Dept. Mo....	To Dist. Plains................	Apr., 1865
1st Battn. Neb. Cav......Jan., 1864	From New Organization...........	To Dist. Plains................	Apr., 1865
11th Ohio Cav.........Feb., 1865	From Dist. Colorado.............	To Dist. Plains................	Apr., 1865

DISTRICT OF COLORADO.—

COMMANDERS.

J. M. Chivington.......	From 1st Colo. Cav.............	To Jan. 4, 1865.
Thos. Moonlight	Col. 11th Kansas Cav.............	Jan. 4, 1865.

1st Colo. Cav.		
2d Colo. Cav.		
3d Colo. Cav.		
1st Colo. Batty.		
9th Wis. Batty. Sec.		
11th Ohio Cav.